1,000,000 Books

are available to read at

www.ForgottenBooks.com

Read online
Download PDF
Purchase in print

ISBN 978-1-5278-6936-3
PIBN 10167779

1 MONTH OF
FREE
READING

at
www.ForgottenBooks.com

By purchasing this book you are eligible for one month membership to ForgottenBooks.com, giving you unlimited access to our entire collection of over 1,000,000 titles via our web site and mobile apps.

To claim your free month visit:
www.forgottenbooks.com/free167779

English
Français
Deutsche
Italiano
Español
Português

www.forgottenbooks.com

Mythology Photography **Fiction**
Fishing Christianity **Art** Cooking
Essays Buddhism Freemasonry
Medicine **Biology** Music **Ancient**
Egypt Evolution Carpentry Physics
Dance Geology **Mathematics** Fitness
Shakespeare **Folklore** Yoga Marketing
Confidence Immortality Biographies
Poetry **Psychology** Witchcraft
Electronics Chemistry History **Law**
Accounting **Philosophy** Anthropology
Alchemy Drama Quantum Mechanics
Atheism Sexual Health **Ancient History**
Entrepreneurship Languages Sport
Paleontology Needlework Islam
Metaphysics Investment Archaeology
Parenting Statistics Criminology
Motivational

PROCEEDINGS

IN

THE TRIAL OF ANDREW JOHNSON,

PRESIDENT OF THE UNITED STATES,

BEFORE

THE UNITED STATES SENATE,

ON

ARTICLES OF IMPEACHMENT·

EXHIBITED BY

THE HOUSE OF REPRESENTATIVES.

WITH AN APPENDIX.

WASHINGTON:
F. & J. RIVES & GEO. A. BAILEY,
REPORTERS AND PRINTERS OF THE DEBATES OF CONGRESS.
1868.

TRIAL

OF

ANDREW JOHNSON,

PRESIDENT OF THE UNITED STATES.

On Monday, February the 24th, 1868, the House of Representatives of the Congress of the United States resolved to impeach Andrew Johnson, President of the United States, of high crimes and misdemeanors, of which the Senate was apprised and arrangements were made for the trial. On Monday, the 2d of March, articles of impeachment were agreed upon by the House of Representatives, and on the 4th they were presented to the Senate by the managers on the part of the House, who were accompanied by the House, the grand inquest of the nation, as a Committee of the Whole on the state of the Union. Mr. BINGHAM, chairman of the managers, read the articles as follows:

Articles exhibited by the House of Representatives of the United States, in the name of themselves and all the people of the United States, against Andrew Johnson, President of the United States, in maintenance and support of their impeachment against him for high crimes and misdemeanors.

ARTICLE 1.

That said Andrew Johnson, President of the United States, on the 21st day of February, in the year of our Lord 1868, at Washington, in the District of Columbia, unmindful of the high duties of his office, of his oath of office, and of the requirement of the Constitution that he should take care that the laws be faithfully executed, did unlawfully and in violation of the Constitution and laws of the United States issue an order in writing for the removal of Edwin M. Stanton from the office of Secretary for the Department of War, said Edwin M. Stanton having been theretofore duly appointed and commissioned, by and with the advice and consent of the Senate of the United States, as such Secretary, and said Andrew Johnson, President of the United States, on the 12th day of August, in the year of our Lord 1867, and during the recess of said Senate, having suspended by his order Edwin M. Stanton from said office, and within twenty days after the first day of the next meeting of said Senate, that is to say, on the 12th day of December, in the year last aforesaid, having reported to said Senate such suspension, with the evidence and reasons for his action in the case and the name of the person designated to perform the duties of such office temporarily until the next meeting of the Senate, and said Senate thereafterward, on the 13th day of January, in the year of our Lord 1868, having duly considered the evidence and reasons reported by said Andrew Johnson for said suspension, and having refused to concur in said suspension, whereby and by force of the provisions of an act entitled "An act

regulating the tenure of certain civil offices," passed March 2, 1867, said Edwin M. Stanton did forthwith resume the functions of his office, whereof the said Andrew Johnson had then and there due notice, and said Edwin M. Stanton, by reason of the premises, on said 21st day of February, being lawfully entitled to hold said office of Secretary for the Department of War, which said order for the removal of said Edwin M. Stanton is in substance as follows, that is to say:

EXECUTIVE MANSION,
WASHINGTON, D. C., *February* 21, 1868.

SIR: By virtue of the power and authority vested in me as President by the Constitution and laws of the United States, you are hereby removed from office as Secretary for the Department of War, and your functions as such will terminate upon receipt of this communication.

You will transfer to Brevet Major General Lorenzo Thomas, Adjutant General of the Army, who has this day been authorized and empowered to act as Secretary of War *ad interim*, all records, books, papers, and other public property now in your custody and charge.

Respectfully yours, ANDREW JOHNSON.
Hon. EDWIN M. STANTON, *Washington, D. C.*

Which order was unlawfully issued with intent then and there to violate the act entitled "An act regulating the tenure of certain civil offices," passed March 2, 1867; and, with the further intent contrary to the provisions of said act, in violation thereof, and contrary to the provisions of the Constitution of the United States, and without the advice and consent of the Senate of the United States, the said Senate then and there being in session, to remove said Edwin M. Stanton from the office of Secretary for the Department of War, the said Edwin M. Stanton being then and there Secretary of War, and being then and there in the due and lawful execution and discharge of the duties of said office, whereby said Andrew Johnson, President of the United States, did then and there commit, and was guilty of a high misdemeanor in office.

ARTICLE II.

That on said 21st day of February, in the year of our Lord 1868, at Washington, in the District of Columbia, said Andrew Johnson, President of the United States, unmindful of the high duties of his office, of his oath of office, and in violation of the Constitution of the United States, and contrary to the provisions of an act entitled "An act regulating the tenure of certain civil offices," passed March 2, 1867, without the advice and consent of the Senate of the United States, said Senate then and there being in session, and without authority of law, did, with intent to violate the Constitution of the United States and the act aforesaid, issue and deliver to one Lorenzo Thomas a letter of authority in substance as follows, that is to say:

EXECUTIVE MANSION.
WASHINGTON, D. C., *February* 21, 1868.

SIR: Hon. Edwin M. Stanton having this day been removed from office as Secretary for the Department of War, you are hereby authorized and empowered to act as Secretary of War *ad interim*, and will immediately enter upon the discharge of the duties pertaining to that office.

Mr. Stanton has been instructed to transfer to you all the records, books, papers, and other public property now in his custody and charge.

Respectfully yours, ANDREW JOHNSON.

To Brevet Major General LORENZO THOMAS, *Adjutant General United States Army, Washington, D. C.*

then and there being no vacancy in said office of Secretary for the Department of War; whereby said Andrew Johnson, President of the United States, did then and there commit and was guilty of a high misdemeanor in office.

ARTICLE III.

That said Andrew Johnson, President of the United States, on the 21st day of February, in the year of our Lord 1868, at Washington, in the District of Columbia, did commit and was guilty of a high misdemeanor in office, in this, that, without authority of law, while the Senate of the United States was then and there in session, he did appoint one Lorenzo Thomas to be Secretary for the Department of War *ad interim*, without the advice and consent of the Senate, and with intent to violate the Constitution of the United States, no vacancy having happened in said office of Secretary for the Department of War during the recess of the Senate, and no vacancy existing in said office at the time, and which said appointment, so made by said Andrew Johnson, of said Lorenzo Thomas, is in substance as follows, that is to say:

EXECUTIVE MANSION,
WASHINGTON, D. C., *February* 21, 1868.

SIR: Hon. Edwin M. Stanton having been this day removed from office as Secretary for the Department of War, you are hereby authorized and empowered to act as Secretary of War *ad interim*, and will immediately enter upon the discharge of the duties pertaining to that office.

Mr. Stanton has been instructed to transfer to you all the records, books, papers, and other public property now in his custody and charge.

Respectfully yours, ANDREW JOHNSON.

To Brevet Major General LORENZO THOMAS, *Adjutant General United States Army, Washington, D. C.*

ARTICLE IV.

That said Andrew Johnson, President of the United States, unmindful of the high duties of his office and of his oath of office, in violation of the Constitution and laws of the United States, on the 21st day of February, in the year of our Lord 1868, at Washington, in the District of Columbia, did unlawfully conspire with one Lorenzo Thomas, and with other persons to the House of Representatives unknown, with intent by intimidation and threats unlawfully to hinder and prevent Edwin M. Stanton, then and there the Secretary for the Department of War, duly appointed under the laws of the United States, from holding said office of Secretary for the Department of War contrary to and in violation of the Constitution of the United States, and of the provisions of an act entitled "An act to define and punish certain conspiracies," approved July 31, 1861, whereby said Andrew Johnson, President of the United States, did then and there commit and was guilty of a high crime in office.

ARTICLE V.

That said Andrew Johnson, President of the United States, unmindful of the high duties of his office and of his oath of office, on the 21st day of February, in the year of our Lord 1868, and on divers other days and times in said year, before the 2d day of March, A. D. 1868, at Washington, in the District of Columbia, did unlawfully conspire with one Lorenzo Thomas, and with other persons to the House of Representatives unknown, to prevent and hinder the execution of an act entitled "An act regulating the tenure of certain civil offices," passed March 2, 1867, and in pursuance of said conspiracy did unlawfully attempt to prevent Edwin M. Stanton, then and there being Secretary for the Department of War, duly appointed and commissioned under the laws of the

United States, from holding said office, whereby the said Andrew Johnson, President of the United States, did then and there commit and was guilty of a high misdemeanor in office.

ARTICLE VI.

That said Andrew Johnson, President of the United States, unmindful of the high duties of his office and of his oath of office, on the 21st day of February, in the year of our Lord 1868, at Washington, in the District of Columbia, did unlawfully conspire with one Lorenzo Thomas by force to seize, take, and possess the property of the United States in the Department of War, and then and there in the custody and charge of Edwin M. Stanton, Secretary for said Department, contrary to the provisions of an act entitled "An act to define and punish certain conspiracies," approved July 31, 1861, and with intent to violate and disregard an act entitled "An act regulating the tenure of certain civil offices," passed March 2, 1867, whereby said Andrew Johnson, President of the United States, did then and there commit a high crime in office.

ARTICLE VII.

That said Andrew Johnson, President of the United States, unmindful of the high duties of his office and of his oath of office, on the 21st day of February, in the year of our Lord 1868, at Washington, in the District of Columbia, did unlawfully conspire with one Lorenzo Thomas with intent unlawfully to seize, take, and possess the property of the United States in the Department of War, in the custody and charge of Edwin M. Stanton, Secretary of said Department, with intent to violate and disregard the act entitled "An act regulating the tenure of certain civil offices," passed March 2, 1867, whereby said Andrew Johnson, President of the United States, did then and there commit a high misdemeanor in office.

ARTICLE VIII.

That said Andrew Johnson, President of the United States, unmindful of the high duties of his office and of his oath of office, with intent unlawfully to control the disbursements of the moneys appropriated for the military service and for the Department of War, on the 21st day of February, in the year of our Lord 1868, at Washington, in the District of Columbia, did unlawfully and contrary to the provisions of an act entitled "An act regulating the tenure of certain civil offices," passed March 2, 1867, and in violation of the Constitution of the United States, and without the advice and consent of the Senate of the United States, and while the Senate was then and there in session, there being no vacancy in the office of Secretary for the Department of War, with intent to violate and disregard the act aforesaid, then and there issue and deliver to one Lorenzo Thomas a letter of authority in writing, in substance as follows, that is to say:

EXECUTIVE MANSION,
WASHINGTON, D. C., *February* 21, 1868.

SIR: Hon. Edwin M. Stanton having been this day removed from office as Secretary for the Department of War, you are hereby authorized and empowered to act as Secretary of War *ad interim*, and will immediately enter upon the discharge of the duties pertaining to that office.

Mr. Stanton has been instructed to transfer to you all the records, books, papers, and other public property now in his custody and charge.

Respectfully yours, ANDREW JOHNSON.

To Brevet Major General LORENZO THOMAS, *Adjutant General United States Army, Washington, D. C.*

Whereby said Andrew Johnson, President of the United States, did then and there commit and was guilty of a high misdemeanor in office.

ARTICLE IX.

That said Andrew Johnson, President of the United States, on the 22d day of February, in the year of our Lord 1868, at Washington, in the District of Columbia, in disregard of the Constitution and the laws of the United States, duly enacted, as Commander-in-Chief of the Army of the United States, did bring before himself then and there William H. Emory, a major general by brevet in the Army of the United States, actually in command of the department of Washington and the military forces thereof, and did then and there, as such Commander-in-Chief, declare to and instruct said Emory that part of a law of the United States, passed March 2, 1867, entitled "An act making appropriations for the support of the Army for the year ending June 30, 1868, and for other purposes," especially the second section thereof, which provides, among other things, that "all orders and instructions relating to military operations issued by the President or Secretary of War shall be issued through the General of the Army, and, in case of his inability, through the next in rank," was unconstitutional, and in contravention of the commission of said Emory, and which said provision of law had been theretofore duly and legally promulgated by general order for the government and direction of the Army of the United States, as the said Andrew Johnson then and there well knew, with intent thereby to induce said Emory, in his official capacity as commander of the department of Washington, to violate the provisions of said act, and to take and receive, act upon, and obey such orders as he, the said Andrew Johnson, might make and give, and which should not be issued through the General of the Army of the United States, according to the provisions of said act, and with the further intent thereby to enable him, the said Andrew Johnson, to prevent the execution of an act entitled "An act regulating the tenure of certain civil offices," passed March 2, 1867, and to unlawfully prevent Edwin M. Stanton, then being Secretary for the Department of War, from holding said office and discharging the duties thereof, whereby said Andrew Johnson, President of the United States, did then and there commit and was guilty of a high misdemeanor in office.

ARTICLE X.

That said Andrew Johnson, President of the United States, unmindful of the high duties of his office and the dignity and proprieties thereof, and of the harmony and courtesies which ought to exist and be maintained between the executive and legislative branches of the Government of the United States, designing and intending to set aside the rightful authority and powers of Congress, did attempt to bring into disgrace, ridicule, hatred, contempt, and reproach the Congress of the United States and the several branches thereof, to impair and destroy the regard and respect of all the good people of the United States for the Congress and legislative power thereof, (which all officers of the Government ought inviolably to preserve and maintain,) and to excite the odium and resentment of all the good people of the United States against Congress and the laws by it duly and constitutionally enacted; and in pursuance of said design and intent, openly and publicly, and before divers assemblages of the citizens of the United States convened in divers parts thereof to meet and receive said Andrew Johnson as the Chief Magistrate of the United States, did, on the 18th day of August, in the year of our Lord 1866, and on divers other days and times, as well before as afterward, make and deliver with a loud voice certain intemperate, inflammatory, and scandalous harangues, and did therein utter loud threats and bitter menaces as well against Congress as the laws of the United States duly enacted thereby, amid the cries, jeers, and laughter of the multitudes then assembled and within hearing, which are set forth in the several specifications hereinafter written, in substance and effect, that is to say:

Specification First.—In this, that at Washington, in the District of Columbia, in the Executive Mansion, to a committee of citizens who called upon the President of the United States, speaking of and concerning the Congress of the United States, said Andrew Johnson, President of the United States, heretofore, to wit, on the 18th day of August, in the year of our Lord 1866, did, in a loud voice, declare in substance and effect, among other things, that is to say:

"So far as the executive department of the Government is concerned, the effort has been made to restore the Union, to heal the breach, to pour oil into the wounds which were consequent upon the struggle, and (to speak in common phrase) to prepare, as the learned and wise physician would, a plaster healing in character and coextensive with the wound. We

thought, and we think, that we had partially succeeded; but as the work progresses, as reconstruction seemed to be taking place, and the country was becoming reunited, we found a disturbing and marring element opposing us. In alluding to that element, I shall go no further than your convention and the distinguished gentleman who has delivered to me the report of its proceedings. I shall make no reference to it that I do not believe the time and the occasion justify.

"We have witnessed in one department of the Government every endeavor to prevent the restoration of peace, harmony, and Union. We have seen hanging upon the verge of the Government, as it were, a body called, or which assumes to be, the Congress of the United States, while in fact it is a Congress of only a part of the States. We have seen this Congress pretend to be for the Union, when its every step and act tended to perpetuate disunion and make a disruption of the States inevitable." * * * * "We have seen Congress gradually encroach step by step upon constitutional rights, and violate, day after day and month after month, fundamental principles of the Government. We have seen a Congress that seemed to forget that there was a limit to the sphere and scope of legislation. We have seen a Congress in a minority assume to exercise power which, allowed to be consummated, would result in despotism or monarchy itself."

Specification Second.—In this, that at Cleveland, in the State of Ohio, heretofore, to wit, on the 3d day of September, in the year of our Lord 1866, before a public assemblage of citizens and others, said Andrew Johnson, President of the United States, speaking of and concerning the Congress of the United States, did, in a loud voice, declare in substance and effect, among other things, that is to say:

"I will tell you what I did do. I called upon your Congress that is trying to break up the Government."

* * * * * * * *

"In conclusion, beside that, Congress had taken much pains to poison their constituents against him. But what had Congress done? Have they done anything to restore the union of these States? No; on the contrary, they had done everything to prevent it; and because he stood now where he did when the rebellion commenced he had been denounced as a traitor. Who had run greater risks or made greater sacrifices than himself? But Congress, factious and domineering, had undertaken to poison the minds of the American people."

Specification Third.—In this, that at St. Louis, in the State of Missouri, heretofore, to wit, on the 8th day of September, in the year of our Lord 1866, before a public assemblage of citizens and others, said Andrew Johnson, President of the United States, speaking of and concerning the Congress of the United States, did, in a loud voice, declare in substance and effect, among other things, that is to say:

"Go on. Perhaps if you had a word or two on the subject of New Orleans you might understand more about it than you do. And if you will go back—if you will go back and ascertain the cause of the riot at New Orleans, perhaps you will not be so prompt in calling out 'New Orleans.' If you will take up the riot at New Orleans and trace it back to its source or its immediate cause, you will find out who was responsible for the blood that was shed there. If you will take up the riot at New Orleans and trace it back to the Radical Congress you will find that the riot at New Orleans was substantially planned. If you will take up the proceedings in their caucuses you will understand that they there knew that a convention was to be called which was extinct by its power having expired; that it was said that the intention was that a new government was to be organized, and on the organization of that government the intention was to enfranchise one portion of the population, called the colored population, who had just been emancipated, and at the same time disfranchise white men. When you design to talk about New Orleans you ought to understand what you are talking about. When you read the speeches that were made, and take up the facts on the Friday and Saturday before that convention sat, you will there find that speeches were made incendiary in their character, exciting that portion of the population, the black population, to arm themselves and prepare for the shedding of blood.

You will also find that that convention did assemble in violation of law, and the intention of that convention was to supersede the reorganized authorities in the State government of Louisiana, which had been recognized by the Government of the United States; and every man engaged in that rebellion in that convention, with the intention of superseding and upturning the civil government which had been recognized by the Government of the United States, I say that he was a traitor to the Constitution of the United States, and hence you find that another rebellion was commenced having its origin in the Radical Congress."
* * * * * * * * * *

"So much for the New Orleans riot. And there was the cause and the origin of the blood that was shed; and every drop of blood that was shed is upon their skirts, and they are responsible for it. I could test this thing a little closer, but will not do it here to-night. But when you talk about the causes and consequences that resulted from proceedings of that kind, perhaps, as I have been introduced here, and you have provoked questions of this kind, though it does not provoke me, I will tell you a few wholesome things that have been done by this Radical Congress in connection with New Orleans and the extension of the elective franchise.

"I know that I have been traduced and abused. I know it has come in advance of me here, as elsewhere, that I have attempted to exercise an arbitrary power in resisting laws that were intended to be forced upon the Government; that I had exercised that power: that I had abandoned the party that elected me, and that I was a traitor, because I exercised the veto power in attempting and did arrest for a time a bill that was called a 'Freedman's Bureau' bill; yes, that I was a traitor. And I have been traduced, I have been slandered, I have been maligned, I have been called Judas Iscariot, and all that. Now, my countrymen here to-night, it is very easy to indulge in epithets; it is easy to call a man a Judas and cry out traitor; but when he is called upon to give arguments and facts he is very often found wanting. Judas Iscariot—Judas. There was a Judas and he was one of the twelve apostles. Oh! yes, the twelve apostles had a Christ. The twelve apostles had a Christ, and he never could have had a Judas unless he had had twelve apostles. If I have played the Judas, who has been my Christ that I have played the Judas with? Was it Thad. Stevens? Was it Wendell Phillips? Was it Charles Sumner? These are the men that stop and compare themselves with the Saviour; and everybody that differs with them in opinion, and to try and stay and arrest the diabolical and nefarious policy, is to be denounced as a Judas."
* * * * * * * * *

"Well, let me say to you, if you will stand by me in this action; if you will stand by me in trying to give the people a fair chance, soldiers and citizens, to participate in these offices, God being willing, I will kick them out. I will kick them out just as fast as I can.

"Let me say to you, in concluding, that what I have said I intended to say. I was not provoked into this, and I care not for their menaces, the taunts, and the jeers. I care not for threats. I do not intend to be bullied by my enemies nor overawed by my friends. But, God willing, with your help I will veto their measures whenever any of them come to me."

Which said utterances, declarations, threats, and harangues, highly censurable in any, are peculiarly indecent and unbecoming in the Chief Magistrate of the United States, by means whereof said Andrew Johnson has brought the high office of the President of the United States into contempt, ridicule, and disgrace, to the great scandal of all good citizens, whereby said Andrew Johnson, President of the United States, did commit, and was then and there guilty of, a high misdemeanor in office.

ARTICLE XI.

That said Andrew Johnson, President of the United States, unmindful of the high duties of his office and of his oath of office, and in disregard of the Constitution and laws of the United States, did heretofore, to wit: on the 18th day of August, 1866, at the city of Washington, in the District of Columbia, by public speech, declare and affirm in substance that the Thirty-Ninth Congress of the United States was not a Congress of the United States authorized by the Constitution to exercise legislative power under the same; but, on the contrary, was a Congress of only part of the States, thereby denying and intending to deny that the legislation of said Congress was valid or obligatory upon him, the said Andrew Johnson, except in so far as he saw fit to approve the same, and also thereby denying and intending to deny the power of the said Thirty-Ninth Congress to propose amendments to the Constitution of the United States; and, in pursuance of said declaration, the said Andrew Johnson, President of the United States, afterward, to wit: on the 21st day of February, 1868, at the city of Washington, in the District of Columbia, did unlawfully and in disregard of the requirements of the Constitution, that he should take care that the laws be faithfully executed, attempt to prevent the execution of an act entitled "An act regulating the tenure of certain civil offices," passed March 2, 1867, by unlawfully devising and contriving, and attempting to devise and contrive, means by which he should prevent Edwin M. Stanton from forthwith resuming the functions of the office of Secretary for the Department of War, notwithstanding the refusal of the Senate to concur in the suspension therefore made by said Andrew Johnson of said Edwin M. Stanton from said office of Secretary for the Department of War, and also by further unlawfully devising and contriving, and attempting to devise and contrive, means then and there to prevent the execution of an act entitled "An act making appropriations for the support of the Army for the fiscal year ending June 30, 1868, and for other purposes," approved March 2, 1867, and also to prevent the execution of an act entitled "An act to provide for the more efficient government of the rebel States," passed March 2, 1867; whereby the said Andrew Johnson, President of the United States, did then, to wit: on the 21st day of February, 1868, at the city of Washington, commit and was guilty of a high misdemeanor in office.

And the House of Representatives, by protestation, saving to themselves the liberty of exhibiting at any time hereafter any further articles or other accusation or impeachment against the said Andrew Johnson, President of the United States, and also of replying to his answers which he shall make unto the articles herein preferred against him, and of offering proof to the same and every part thereof, and to all and every other article, accusation, or impeachment which shall be exhibited by them, as the case shall require, do demand that the said Andrew Johnson may be put to answer the high crimes and misdemeanors in office herein charged against him, and that such proceedings, examinations, trials, and judgments may be thereupon had and given as may be agreeable to law and justice.

The Senate, in its preparation for so momentous an event, adopted rules of procedure and practice for the guidance of the court; and to accord with the conviction of the Chief Justice that the court should adopt its own rules, they were *pro forma* again adopted when the court met. They are as follows:

Rules of Procedure and Practice in the Senate when sitting on the Trial of Impeachments.

I. Whensoever the Senate shall receive notice from the House of Representatives that managers are appointed on their part to conduct an impeachment against any person, and are directed to carry articles of impeachment to the Senate, the Secretary of the Senate shall immediately inform the House of Representatives that the Senate is ready to receive the managers for the purpose of exhibiting such articles of impeachment agreeably to said notice.

II. When the managers of an impeachment shall be introduced at the bar of the Senate, and shall signify that they are ready to exhibit articles of impeachment against any person, the Presiding Officer of the Senate shall direct the Sergeant-at-Arms to make proclamation, who shall, after making proclamation, repeat the following words, viz: "All persons are commanded to keep silence, on pain of imprisonment, while the House of Representatives is exhibiting to the Senate of the United States articles of impeachment against ———;" after which the articles shall be exhibited, and then the Presiding Officer of the Senate shall inform the managers that the Senate will take proper order on the subject of the impeachment, of which due notice shall be given to the House of Representatives.

III. Upon such articles being presented to the Senate, the Senate shall, at one o'clock afternoon of the day (Sunday excepted) following such presentation, or sooner if so ordered by the Senate, proceed to the consideration of such articles, and shall continue in session from day to day, (Sundays excepted,) after the trial shall commence, (unless otherwise ordered by the Senate,) until final judgment shall be rendered, and so much longer as may, in its judgment, be needful. Before proceeding to the consideration of the articles of impeachment, the Presiding Officer shall administer the oath hereinafter provided to the members of the Senate then present, and to the other members of the Senate as they shall appear, whose duty it shall be to take the same.

IV. When the President of the United States, or the Vice President of the United States, upon whom the powers and duties of the office of President shall have devolved, shall be impeached, the Chief Justice of the Supreme Court of the United States shall preside; and in a case requiring the said Chief Justice to preside, notice shall be given to him by the Presiding Officer of the Senate, of the time and place fixed for the consideration of the articles of impeachment, as aforesaid, with a request to attend; and the said Chief Justice shall preside over the Senate during the consideration of said articles, and upon the trial of the person impeached therein.

V. The Presiding Officer shall have power to make and issue, by himself or by the Secretary of the Senate, all orders, mandates, writs, and precepts authorized by these rules, or by the Senate, and to make and enforce such other regulations and orders in the premises as the Senate may authorize or provide.

VI. The Senate shall have power to compel the attendance of witnesses, to enforce obedience to its orders, mandates, writs, precepts, and judgments, to preserve order, and to punish in a summary way contempts of and disobedience to its authority, orders, mandates, writs, precepts, or judgments, and to make all lawful orders, rules, and regulations, which it may deem essential or conducive to the ends of justice. And the Sergeant-at-Arms, under the direction of the Senate, may employ such aid and assistance as may be necessary to enforce, execute, and carry into effect the lawful orders, mandates, writs, and precepts of the Senate.

VII. The Presiding Officer of the Senate shall direct all necessary preparations in the Senate Chamber, and the presiding officer upon the trial shall direct all the forms of proceeding while the Senate are sitting for the purpose of trying an impeachment, and all forms during the trial not otherwise specially provided for. The presiding officer may, in the first instance, submit to the Senate, without a division, all questions of evidence and incidental questions; but the same shall, on the demand of one fifth of the members present, be decided by yeas and nays.

VIII. Upon the presentation of articles of impeachment and the organization of the Senate as hereinbefore provided, a writ of summons shall issue to the accused, reciting said articles and notifying him to appear before the Senate upon a day and at a place to be fixed by the Senate and named in such writ, and file his answer to said articles of impeachment, and to stand to and abide the orders and judgments of the Senate thereon; which writ shall be served by such officer or person as shall be named in the precept thereof such number of days prior to the day fixed for such appearance as shall be named in such precept, either by the delivery of an attested copy thereof to the person accused, or, if that cannot conveniently be done, by leaving such copy at the last known place of abode of such person or at his usual place of business, in some conspicuous place therein; or if such service shall be, in the judgment of the Senate, impracticable, notice to the accused to appear shall be given in such other manner, by publication or otherwise, as shall be deemed just; and if the writ aforesaid shall fail of service in the manner aforesaid the proceedings shall not thereby abate, but further service may be made in such manner as the Senate shall direct. If the accused, after service, shall fail to appear, either in person or by attorney, on the day so fixed therefor as aforesaid, or, appearing, shall fail to file his answer to such articles of impeachment, the trial shall proceed, nevertheless, as upon a plea of not guilty. If a plea of guilty shall be entered judgment may be entered thereon without further proceedings.

IX. At twelve o'clock and thirty minutes afternoon of the day appointed for the return of the summons against the person impeached, the legislative and executive business of the Senate shall be suspended, and the Secretary of the Senate shall administer an oath to the returning officer in the form following, viz: "I, ———, do solemnly swear that the return made by me upon the process issued on the —— day of ——, by the Senate of the United States, against ——— ———, is truly made, and that I have performed such service as therein described; so help me God." Which oath shall be entered at large on the records.

X. The person impeached shall then be called to appear and answer the articles of impeachment against him. If he appear, or any person for him, the appearance shall be recorded, stating particularly if by himself, or by agent, or attorney, naming the person appearing, and the capacity in which he appears. If he do not appear, either personally or by agent or attorney, the same shall be recorded.

XI. At twelve o'clock and thirty minutes afternoon of the day appointed for the trial of an impeachment, the legislative and executive business of the Senate shall be suspended, and the Secretary shall give notice to the House of Representatives that the Senate is ready to proceed upon the impeachment of ———, in the Senate Chamber, which Chamber is prepared with accommodations for the reception of the House of Representatives.

XII. The hour of the day at which the Senate shall sit upon the trial of an impeachment shall be (unless otherwise ordered) twelve o'clock m.; and when the hour for such sitting shall arrive, the Presiding Officer of the Senate shall so announce; and thereupon the presiding officer upon such trial shall cause proclamation to be made, and the business of the trial shall proceed. The adjournment of the Senate sitting in said trial shall not operate as an adjournment of the Senate; but on such adjournment the Senate shall resume the consideration of its legislative and executive business.

XIII. The Secretary of the Senate shall record the proceedings in cases of impeachment as in the case of legislative proceedings, and the same shall be reported in the same manner as the legislative proceedings of the Senate.

XIV. Counsel for the parties shall be admitted to appear and be heard upon an impeachment.

XV. All motions made by the parties or their counsel shall be addressed to the presiding officer, and if he, or any Senator, shall require it, they shall be committed to writing, and read at the Secretary's table.

XVI. Witnesses shall be examined by one person on behalf of the party producing them, and then cross-examined by one person on the other side.

XVII. If a Senator is called as a witness he shall be sworn and give his testimony standing in his place.

XVIII. If a Senator wishes a question to be put to a witness, or to offer a motion or order, (except a motion to adjourn,) it shall be reduced to writing, and put by the presiding officer.

XIX. At all times while the Senate is sitting upon the trial of an impeachment the doors of the Senate shall be kept open, unless the Senate shall direct the doors to be closed while deliberating upon its decisions.

XX. All preliminary or interlocutory questions, and all motions, shall be argued for not exceeding one hour on each side, unless the Senate shall, by order, extend the time.

XXI. The case, on each side, shall be opened by

one person. The final argument on the merits may be made by two persons on each side, (unless otherwise ordered by the Senate, upon application for that purpose,) and the argument shall be opened and closed on the part of the House of Representatives.

XXII. On the final question whether the impeachment is sustained, the yeas and nays shall be taken on each article of impeachment separately; and if the impeachment shall not, upon any of the articles presented, be sustained by the votes of two thirds of the members present, a judgment of acquittal shall be entered; but if the person accused in such articles of impeachment shall be convicted upon any of said articles by the votes of two thirds of the members present, the Senate shall proceed to pronounce judgment, and a certified copy of such judgment shall be deposited in the office of the Secretary of State.

XXIII. All the orders and decisions shall be made and had by yeas and nays, which shall be entered on the record, and without debate, except when the doors shall be closed for deliberation, and in that case no member shall speak more than once on one question, and for not more than ten minutes on an interlocutory question, and for not more than fifteen minutes on the final question, unless by consent of the Senate, to be had without debate; but a motion to adjourn may be decided without the yeas and nays, unless they be demanded by one fifth of the members present.

XXIV. Witnesses shall be sworn in the following form, namely: "You, ——, do swear (or affirm, as the case may be) that the evidence you shall give in the case now depending between the United States and —— shall be the truth, the whole truth, and nothing but the truth: so help you God." Which oath shall be administered by the Secretary or any other duly authorized person.

Form of subpœna to be issued on the application of the managers of the impeachment, or of the party impeached, or of his counsel:

To ——, greeting:

You and each of you are hereby commanded to appear before the Senate of the United States, on the —— day of ——, at the Senate Chamber, in the city of Washington, then and there to testify your knowledge in the cause which is before the Senate, in which the House of Representatives have impeached ——.

Fail not.

Witness ——, and Presiding Officer of the Senate, at the city of Washington, this —— day of ——, in the year of our Lord ——, and of the independence of the United States the ——.

Form of direction for the service of said subpœna:

The Senate of the United States to —— —— greeting:

You are hereby commanded to serve and return the within subpœna according to law.

Dated at Washington, this —— day of ——, in the year of our Lord ——, and of the independence of the United States the ——.

——————————
Secretary of the Senate.

Form of oath to be administered to the members of the Senate sitting in the trial of impeachments:

"I solemnly swear (or affirm, as the case may be) that in all things appertaining to the trial of the impeachment of ——, now pending, I will do impartial justice according to the Constitution and laws: so help me God."

Form of summons to be issued and served upon the person impeached:

THE UNITED STATES OF AMERICA, *ss:*

The Senate of the United States to —— —— greeting:

Whereas the House of Representatives of the United States of America did, on the —— day of ——, exhibit to the Senate articles of impeachment against you, the said —— ——, in the words following:

[Here insert the articles.]

And demand that you, the said —— ——, should be put to answer the accusations as set forth in said articles, and that such proceedings, examinations, trials, and judgments might be thereupon had as are agreeable to law and justice.

You, the said —— ——, are therefore hereby summoned to be and appear before the Senate of the United States of America, at their Chamber, in the city of Washington, on the —— day of —— at twelve o'clock and thirty minutes afternoon, then and there to answer to the said articles of impeachment, and then and there to abide by, obey, and perform such orders, directions, and judgments as the Senate of the United States shall make in the premises according to the Constitution and laws of the United States.

Hereof you are not to fail.

Witness ——, and Presiding Officer of the said Senate, at the city of Washington, this —— day of ——, in the year of our Lord ——, and of the independence of the United States the ——.

Form of precept to be indorsed on said writ of summons:

THE UNITED STATES OF AMERICA, *ss:*

The Senate of the United States, to —— ——, greeting:

You are hereby commanded to deliver to and leave with —— ——, if conveniently to be found, or, if not, to leave at his usual place of abode, or at his usual place of business, in some conspicuous place, a true and attested copy of the within writ of summons, together with a like copy of this precept; and in whichsoever way you perform the service let it be done at least —— days before the appearance day mentioned in said writ of summons.

Fail not, and make return of this writ of summons and precept, with your proceedings thereon indorsed, on or before the appearance day mentioned in the said writ of summons.

Witness ——, and Presiding Officer of the Senate, at the city of Washington, this —— day of ——, in the year of our Lord ——, and of the independence of the United States the ——.

All process shall be served by the Sergeant-at-Arms of the Senate, unless otherwise ordered by the court.

XXV. If the Senate shall at any time fail to sit for the consideration of articles of impeachment on the day or hour fixed therefor, the Senate may, by an order to be adopted without debate, fix a day and hour for resuming such consideration.

The court was organized on Thursday, the 5th of March, the oath being administered to the Chief Justice of the United States by Associate Justice NELSON, and by the Chief Justice to the Senators present, except Mr. WADE, whose right to sit on the trial was challenged. On Friday, the 6th, at the close of the debate on the point suggested, the objection was withdrawn and the oath was administered. On Friday, the 13th of March, the trial commenced, a detailed report of which follows. The preliminary proceedings are given in an Appendix at the end of this volume.

FRIDAY, *March* 13, 1868.

The Chief Justice entered the Senate Chamber and took the chair.

The CHIEF JUSTICE, (to the Sergeant-at-Arms.) Make proclamation.

The SERGEANT-AT-ARMS. Hear ye! hear ye! All persons are commanded to keep silence while the Senate of the United States is sitting for the trial of the articles of impeachment exhibited by the House of Representatives against Andrew Johnson, President of the United States.

Mr. HOWARD. Mr. President, I move for the order, which is usual in such cases, notifying the House of Representatives that the Senate is thus organized.

The CHIEF JUSTICE. The Journal of the last day's proceedings will first be read.

Mr. GRIMES. Mr. Chief Justice, there are several Senators to be sworn.

The CHIEF JUSTICE. The first business is to read the Journal of the last session of the court. The Senators will be sworn in afterwards.

The Secretary read the Journal of the proceedings of the Senate sitting for the trial of impeachment of Andrew Johnson, President of the United States, on Friday, March 6, 1868.

Mr. CONKLING. I move that the reading of the articles of impeachment *in extenso*, which I understand are entered on the Journal, be dispensed with. I understand that the other House is ready to be announced.

The CHIEF JUSTICE. That suggestion will be considered as agreed to if no objection be made.

The Secretary continued and concluded the reading of the Journal.

Mr. HOWARD. If it be now in order, to save time I ask that the order which I sent to the Chair be passed by the Senate, informing the House of Representatives that the Senate is organized for the trial of the impeachment.

The CHIEF JUSTICE. The Secretary will read the order submitted by the Senator from Michigan.

The Secretary read as follows:

Ordered, That the Secretary inform the House of Representatives that the Senate is in its Chamber, and ready to proceed with the trial of Andrew Johnson, President of the United States, and that seats are provided for the accommodation of the members.

The order was agreed to.

The CHIEF JUSTICE. The Sergeant-at-Arms will introduce the managers.

The managers on the part of the House of Representatives appeared at the bar, were announced by the Sergeant-at-Arms, and conducted to the position assigned them.

Managers—Hon. JOHN A. BINGHAM, of Ohio; GEORGE S. BOUTWELL, of Massachusetts; JAMES F. WILSON, of Iowa; JOHN A. LOGAN, of Illinois; THOMAS WILLIAMS, of Pennsylvania; BENJAMIN F. BUTLER, of Massachusetts; THADDEUS STEVENS, of Pennsylvania.

Mr. GRIMES. Mr. Chief Justice, there are several Senators who have not yet been sworn as members of this court. I therefore move that the oath be administered to them.

The CHIEF JUSTICE. The Secretary will call the names of Senators who have not yet been sworn.

The Secretary called the names of Senators who were not previously sworn.

Messrs. EDMUNDS, PATTERSON of New Hampshire, and VICKERS, severally, as their names were called, advanced to the desk, and the prescribed oath was administered to them by the Chief Justice.

The CHIEF JUSTICE. The Secretary of the Senate will read the return of the Sergeant-at-Arms to the summons directed to be issued by the Senate.

The Chief Clerk read the following return appended to the writ of summons:

The foregoing writ of summons, addressed to Andrew Johnson, President of the United States, and the foregoing precept, addressed to me, were this day duly served on the said Andrew Johnson, President of the United States, by delivering to and leaving with him true and attested copies of the same at the Executive Mansion, the usual place of abode of the said Andrew Johnson, on Saturday, the 7th day of March instant, at seven o'clock in the afternoon of that day. GEORGE T. BROWN, *Sergeant-at-Arms of the United States Senate.*

WASHINGTON, *March* 7, 1868.

The Chief Clerk administered to the Sergeant-at-Arms the following oath:

"I, George T. Brown, Sergeant-at-Arms of the Senate of the United States, do swear that the return made and subscribed by me upon the process issued on the 7th day of March, A. D. 1868, by the Senate of the United States against Andrew Johnson, President of the United States, is truly made, and that I have performed said service therein prescribed. So help me God."

The CHIEF JUSTICE. The Sergeant-at-Arms will call the accused.

The SERGEANT-AT-ARMS. Andrew Johnson, President of the United States, Andrew Johnson, President of the United States, appear and answer the articles of impeachment exhibited against you by the House of Representatives of the United States.

Mr. JOHNSON. I understand that the President has retained counsel, and that they are now in the President's room attached to this wing of the Capitol. They are not advised, I believe, of the court being organized. I move that the Sergeant-at-Arms inform them of that fact.

The CHIEF JUSTICE. If there be no objection the Sergeant-at-Arms will so inform the counsel of the President.

The Sergeant-at-Arms presently returned with Hon. Henry Stanbery, of Kentucky; Hon. Benjamin R. Curtis, of Massachusetts; and Hon. Thomas A. R. Nelson, of Tennessee; who were conducted to the seats assigned the counsel of the President.

Mr. CONKLING. To correct a clerical error in the rules or a mistake of the types which has introduced a repugnance into the rules, I offer the following resolution by direction of the committee which reported the rules:

Ordered, That the twenty-third rule, respecting proceedings on trial of impeachments, be amended by inserting after the word "debate" the words "subject, however, to the operation of rule seven."

If thus amended the rule will read:

All orders and decisions shall be made and had by yeas and nays, which shall be entered on the record and without debate, subject, however, to the operation of rule seven, except when the doors shall be closed, &c.

The whole object is to commit to the presiding officer the option to submit a question without the call of the yeas and nays, unless they be demanded. That was the intention originally, but the qualifying words were dropped out in the print.

The CHIEF JUSTICE. The question is on amending the rules in the manner proposed by the Senator from New York.

The amendment was agreed to.

The Sergeant-at-Arms announced the members of the House of Representatives, who entered the Senate Chamber preceded by the chairman of the Committee of the Whole House, (Mr. E. B. WASHBURNE, of Illinois,) into which that body had resolved itself to witness the trial, who was accompanied by the Speaker and Clerk.

The CHIEF JUSTICE, (to the counsel for the President.) Gentlemen, the Senate is now sitting for the trial of the President of the United States upon articles of impeachment exhibited by the House of Representatives. The court will now hear you.

Mr. STANBERY. Mr. Chief Justice, my brothers Curtis and Nelson and myself are here this morning as counsel for the President. I have his authority to enter his appearance, which, with your leave, I will proceed to read:

In the matter of the impeachment of Andrew Johnson, President of the United States.

Mr. CHIEF JUSTICE: I, Andrew Johnson, President of the United States, having been served with a summons to appear before this honorable court, sitting as a court of impeachment, to answer certain articles of impeachment found and presented against me by the honorable the House of Representatives of the United States, do hereby enter my appearance by my counsel, Henry Stanbery, Benjamin R. Curtis, Jeremiah S. Black, William M. Evarts, and Thomas A. R. Nelson, who have my warrant and authority therefor, and who are instructed by me to ask of this honorable court a reasonable time for the preparation of my answer to said articles.

After a careful examination of the articles of impeachment and consultation with my counsel, I am satisfied that at least forty days will be necessary for the preparation of my answer, and I respectfully ask that it be allowed.

ANDREW JOHNSON.

The CHIEF JUSTICE. The paper will be filed.

Mr. STANBERY. Mr. Chief Justice, I have also a professional statement in support of the application. Whether it is in order to offer it now or to wait until the appearance is entered your Honor will decide.

The CHIEF JUSTICE. The appearance will be considered as entered. You may proceed.

Mr. STANBERY. I will read the statement:

In the Matter of the Impeachment of Andrew Johnson, President of the United States.

Henry Stanbery, Benjamin R. Curtis, Jeremiah S. Black, William M. Evarts, and Thomas A. R. Nelson, of counsel for the respondent, move the court for the allowance of forty days for the preparation of the answer to the articles of impeachment, and in support of the motion make the following professional statement:

The articles are eleven in number, involving many questions of law and fact. We have, during the limited time and opportunity afforded us, considered as far as possible the field of investigation which must be explored in the preparation of the answer, and the conclusion at which we have arrived is that with the utmost diligence the time we have asked is reasonable and necessary.

The precedents as to time for answer upon impeachments before the Senate, to which we have had opportunity to refer, are those of Judge Chase and Judge Peck.

In the case of Judge Chase time was allowed from the 3d of January until the 4th of February next succeeding to put in his answer, a period of thirty-two days; but in this case there were only eight articles, and Judge Chase had been for a year cognizant of most of the articles, and had been himself engaged in preparing to meet them.

In the case of Judge Peck there was but a single article. Judge Peck asked for time from the 10th to the 25th of May to put in his answer, and it was granted. It appears that Judge Peck had been long cognizant of the ground laid for his impeachment; and had been present before the committee of the House upon the examination of the witnesses, and had been permitted by the House of Representatives to present to that body an elaborate answer to the charges.

It is apparent that the President is fairly entitled to more time than was allowed in either of the foregoing cases. It is proper to add that the respondents in these cases were lawyers, fully capable of preparing their own answers, and that no pressing official duties interfered with their attention to that business; whereas the President, not being a lawyer, must rely on his counsel. The charges involve his acts, declarations, and intentions, as to all which his counsel must be fully advised upon consultation with him, step by step, in the preparation of his defense. It is seldom that a case requires such constant communication between client and counsel as this, and yet such communication can only be had at such intervals as are allowed to the President from the usual hours that must be devoted to his high official duties.

We further beg leave to suggest for the consideration of this honorable court, that as counsel, careful as well of their own reputation as of the interests of their client in a case of such magnitude as this, so out of the ordinary range of professional experience, where so much responsibility is felt, they submit to the candid consideration of the court, that they have a right to ask for themselves such opportunity to discharge their duty as seems to them to be absolutely necessary.

HENRY STANBERY,
B. R. CURTIS,
JEREMIAH S. BLACK,
WILLIAM M. EVARTS, } per H. S.
THOMAS A. R. NELSON,
Of Counsel for the Respondent.
March 13, 1868.

Mr. Manager BINGHAM. Mr. President, I am instructed by my associate managers to suggest to the Senate that under the eighth rule adopted by the Senate for the government of this proceeding, after the appearance of the accused at its bar, until that rule be set aside by the action of the Senate a motion for continuance to answer is not allowed, the provision of the rule being that if he appear he shall answer; if he appear and fail to answer, the case shall proceed as upon the general issue; if he do not appear the case shall proceed as upon the general issue. The managers appeared at the bar of the Senate impressed with the belief that the rule meant precisely what it says; and that in default of an appearance the trial would proceed as upon the plea of not guilty; if upon appearance no answer should be filed, in the language of the rule the trial should still proceed as upon the plea of not guilty.

Mr. CURTIS. Mr. Chief Justice, if the construction which the honorable managers have placed upon this rule be the correct one, the counsel of the President have been entirely misled by its phraseology. They have construed the rule in the light of other similar rules existing in courts of justice. For instance, in a court of equity over which your Honor in another place presides, parties are by a subpœna required to appear on a certain day and answer the bill; but certainly it was never understood that they were to answer the bill on the day of the appearance. So it is in a variety of other legal proceedings; parties are summoned to appear on a certain day, but the day when they are to plead is either fixed by some general rule of the tribunal or there is to be a special order in the particular case. Here we find a rule by which the President is required to appear on this day and "answer" and "abide." Certainly that part of the rule which relates to abiding has reference to future proceedings and to the final result of the case. And so, as we have construed the rule, that part of it which relates to answering has reference to a future proceeding, which occurs in the ordinary course of justice, as I have stated, either under some general rule or by a special order of the court. We submit, therefore, as counsel for the President, that this interpretation of the rule which is placed upon it by the honorable managers is not the correct one.

Mr. Manager WILSON. Mr. President, I

desire to say on behalf of the managers that we do not see how it were possible for the eighth rule adopted by the Senate to mislead the respondent or counsel. That rule provides that—

"Upon the presentation of the articles of impeachment and the organization of the Senate as hereinbefore provided a writ of summons shall issue to the accused, reciting said articles, and notifying him to appear before the Senate on a day and at a place to be fixed by the Senate and named in such writ and file his answer to said articles of impeachment, and to stand to and abide the orders and judgments of the Senate thereon."

The rule further provides that—

"If the accused, after service, shall fail to appear, either in person or by attorney, on the day so fixed therefor, as aforesaid, or appearing shall fail to file his answer to such articles of impeachment, the trial shall proceed nevertheless as upon a plea of not guilty."

The learned counsel, in the professional statement submitted to the Senate, refer to the cases of Judge Chase and Judge Peck. I presume that in the examination of the records of those cases the attention of counsel was directed to the rules adopted by the Senate for the government of its action on the trial of those cases. By reference to the rules adopted by the Senate for the trial of the cases of Judge Chase and Judge Peck we find that a very material change has been made by the Senate in the adoption of the present rules. The third rule in the case of the trial of Judge Chase prescribed the form of summons, and required that on the day to be fixed the respondent should appear, and "then and there answer." The same rule was adopted in the Peck case. But the present rule adds to the rule of those cases the words to which I have called the attention of the Senate, that he shall appear "and file his answer to said articles of impeachment," and that if, on appearing, he "shall fail to file his answer to such articles of impeachment, the trial shall proceed nevertheless as upon a plea of not guilty."

I submit, therefore, Mr. President, that the change which has been made in the rules for the government of this case must have been made for some good reason. What that reason may have been may be a subject of discussion in this case hereafter; but the change meets us upon the presentation of this motion; and we therefore ask, on the part of the House of Representatives, which we are here representing, that the rule adopted by the Senate for the government of this case may be enforced. It is for the Senate to say whether the rule shall stand as a rule to govern the case, or whether it shall be changed; but, standing as a rule at this time, we ask for its enforcement.

Mr. STANBERY. Mr. Chief Justice, the objection taken by the honorable managers is so singular that in the whole course of my practice I have not met with an example like it. A case like this, Mr. Chief Justice, in which the President of the United States is arraigned upon an impeachment presented by the House of Representatives—a case of the greatest magnitude we have ever had—is, as to time, to be treated as if it were a case before a police court, to be put through with railroad speed on the first day the criminal appears! Where do my learned friends find a precedent for calling on the trial upon this day? It is in the language of their summons. They say, "We have notified you to appear here and answer on a given day." We are here; we enter our appearance; but they ask, "Where is your answer?" As my learned brother [Mr. Curtis] has said, you have used precisely the language that is used in a subpœna in chancery; but who ever heard that when the defendant in a chancery bill enters his appearance he must come with his answer, ready to go on with the case, and enter upon the trial? We were summoned to appear and answer; we have entered our appearance and stated that we propose to answer; we do not wish this case to go by default; we want a reasonable time; nothing more.

Consider, if you please, that it is but a few days since the President has been served with this summons; that, as yet, all his counsel are not present. Your Honor will observe that of the five counsel who have signed this professional statement two are not present and cannot be present to-day, and are not (at least, I am sure, one is not) in the city to-day. Not one of us, on looking at these rules, ever suspected that it was the intention to bring on the trial this day. And yet I understand the learned gentlemen who read these rules to so read them according to the letter that we must go on to-day. Now, let us see how it will do to read them all according to the letter. If the gentlemen are right, if we are here to answer to-day, and to go into the trial to-day, then this is the day fixed for the trial by your rules. Let us see whether it is.

Rule nine provides:

"At twelve o'clock and thirty minutes afternoon of the day appointed for the return of the summons against the person impeached,"

This is the return day; it is not the trial day. The letter answers the gentlemen. According to the letter of the eighth rule they say "this is the trial day; go on; not a moment's delay; file your answer and proceed to trial; or without your answer let a general plea of not guilty be entered, and proceed at once with the trial." The ninth rule says this is the return day, not the trial day. Then the tenth rule says:

"The person impeached shall then be called to appear and answer the articles of impeachment against him."

That is the call made on the return day. The accused is called to appear and answer. He is here; he appears; he states his willingness to answer; he only asks a reasonable time to prepare the answer. Then rule eleven speaks "of the day appointed for the trial." That is not this day. This day, the day which the gentlemen would make the first day of the

trial, is, in your own rules, put down for the return day, and you must have some other day for the trial day to suit the convenience of the parties; so that the letter of one rule answers the letter of another rule.

But, pray, Mr. Chief Justice, is it possible that under these circumstances we are to be caught in this trap of the letter? As yet there has not been time to prepare an answer to a single one of these articles. As yet the President has been engaged in procuring his counsel, and all the time occupied with so much consultation as was necessary to enable us to fix the shortest period which in our judgment is necessary for the due preparation of his answer.

Now, look back through the whole line of impeachments, even to the worst times, and where there was the greatest haste; go back to English precedents, and English fair play always gave fair time. This is the first instance to be found on record anywhere, in which, upon the appearance day, the defendant was required to put in his answer and immediately proceed to the trial. Why, sir, we have not a witness summoned; we hardly know what witnesses to summon until the pleadings are prepared. We are entirely at sea.

I submit, Mr. Chief Justice, to the honorable court that are to try this case, whether we are to be put through with this railroad speed? "Strike, but hear." Give us the opportunity that even in common civil cases is allowed to the defendant, hardly ever less than thirty days for his pleading and answer; more often sixty. Give us time; give us a reasonable time; and then, with a fair hearing, we shall be prepared for that sentence, whatever it may be, that you shall pronounce.

Mr. Manager BINGHAM. Mr. President, it was——

The CHIEF JUSTICE. Before counsel proceed, the Chief Justice desires to state to the Senate that he is somewhat embarrassed in the construction of the rule. The twenty-first rule provides that "the case on each side shall be opened by one person." He understands that as referring to the case made when the evidence is all in and the cause is ready for argument. The twentieth rule provides that—

"All preliminary or interlocutory questions and all motions shall be argued for not exceeding one hour on each side, unless the Senate shall by order extend the time."

Whether that limitation is intended to apply to the whole argument upon each side or to the argument of each counsel who may address the court is the question which the Chief Justice is at a loss to solve. On the pending motion he has allowed the argument to proceed without attempting to restrict the number of speakers, and, unless the Senate order otherwise, he will proceed in that course.

Mr. Manager BINGHAM. Mr. President, it was not my purpose when I raised the question, under the rule, to be decided by the Senate, to touch in any way upon the merits of any application that might hereafter be made, after issue joined, for an extension of time for preparation for the trial. The only object I had in view, Mr. President, was to see whether the Senate was disposed to abide by its own rules, and by raising the question to remind Senators of what they do know, that in this proceeding they are a rule and a law to themselves. Neither the common law nor the civil law furnishes any rule whatever for the conduct of this trial save, it may be, the rule which governs in matters of evidence.

There is nothing more clearly settled in this country, and in that country whence we derive our laws generally, than the proposition which I have just stated; and hence the necessity that the Senate should prescribe rules for the conduct of the trial; and, having prescribed rules, my associate managers and myself deemed it important to inquire whether those rules, upon the threshold of the proceeding, were to be disregarded and set aside.

I may be pardoned for saying that I am greatly surprised at the hasty word which dropped from the lips of my learned and accomplished friend who has just taken his seat, [Mr. Stanbery,] when he failed to discriminate between the objection made here and an objection that may hereafter be made to a motion for the continuance of the trial. When the learned gentleman spoke of the trial day, he seemed to forget that the trial day never comes until issue joined. Why, Mr. President, there is nothing clearer, nothing better known, I think, to my learned friend than this, that the making up of the issue before any tribunal of justice and the trial are very distinct transactions—perfectly distinct.

A very remarkable case in the twelfth volume of State Trials lies before me, wherein Lord Holt presided, on the trial of Sir Richard Grahme, Viscount Preston, and others, charged with high treason. In that case the accused appeared, as the accused by the learned gentlemen appears this morning, after the indictment presented in the court, and before plea asked for continuance. The answer that fell from the lips of the Lord Chief Justice was, we are not to consider the question of trial or the time of trial until plea be pleaded. Let me give his very words:

"L. C. HOLT. My lord, we debate the time of your trial too early; for you must put yourself upon your trial first by pleading."

And when Lord Preston presses him again on the point Lord Chief Justice Holt responds:

"My lord, we cannot dispute with you concerning your trial till you have pleaded. I know not what you will say to it; for aught I know there may be no occasion for a trial. I cannot tell what you will plead; your lordship must answer to the indictment before we can enter into the debate of this matter."—12 *State Trials*, 664.

The eighth rule of the Senate, last clause, provides that if the party appearing shall plead guilty there may be no further proceedings in the case, no trial about it; nothing remains to be done but to pronounce judgment under the Constitution. It is time enough for us to talk about a trial when we have an issue. The rule is a plain one, a simple one.

And I may be pardoned for saying that I fail to perceive anything in rules ten or eleven to which the learned counsel have referred that by any kind of construction can be supposed to limit the effect of the words in rule eight, to wit:

"If the accused, after service, shall fail to appear, either in person or by attorney, on the day so fixed therefor as aforesaid, or appearing shall fail to file his answer, [on the day on which he is summoned to appear,] the trial shall proceed nevertheless as upon a plea of not guilty."

When words are plain in a written law there is an end to all construction; they must be followed. The managers so thought when they appeared at this bar. All they ask is the enforcement of the rule, not a postponement of forty days, and at the end of that time to be met with a dilatory plea—a motion, if you please, to quash the articles, or a question raising the inquiry whether this is the Senate of the United States.

It seems to me, if I may be pardoned for making one further remark, that in prescribing by this rule that the summons, with a copy of the articles, should issue, to be returned on a day certain, giving, as in this case, six days in advance, it was intended thereby to require as well as to enable the party on the day fixed for his appearance, as the rule prescribes, to come to this bar prepared to make answer to the articles.

Permit me to say further—what is doubtless known to every one within the hearing of my voice—that technical rules do in no wise control or limit or fetter the action of this body; and under the plea of "not guilty," as provided in the rules, every conceivable defense that the party accused could make to the articles here preferred can be admitted. Why, then, this delay of forty days to draw up an answer of not guilty?

But what we desire to know on behalf of the House of Representatives, by whose order we appear here, is whether an answer is to be filed in accordance with the rule; and, if it be not filed, whether the rule itself is to be enforced by the Senate which made it, and a plea of not guilty be entered for the accused. That is our inquiry. It is not my purpose to enter into any discussion upon the question of postponing the day for the commencement of the trial. My desire is at present to see whether, under this rule, and by force of this rule, we can obtain an issue.

The CHIEF JUSTICE. Senators, the counsel for the President submit a motion that forty days be allowed for the preparation of his answer. The rule requires that this, as other questions, shall be taken without debate by Senators. You who are in favor of that motion will say "ay."

Mr. EDMUNDS. Upon that subject I submit the following order:

Ordered, That the respondent file his answer to the articles of impeachment on or before the 1st day of April next, and that the managers of the impeachment file their replication thereto within three days thereafter, and that the matter stand for trial on Monday, April 6, 1868.

Mr. MORTON. I move that the Senate retire to consult in regard to its determination.

Mr. Manager BINGHAM. I am instructed by the managers respectfully to ask that the Senate shall pass upon the motion to reject under the eighth rule of this Senate until that rule be set aside the application to defer the day of answer.

The CHIEF JUSTICE. The motion of the counsel for the President is in order. The Chair regards the motion submitted by the Senator from Vermont [Mr. EDMUNDS] as in the nature of an amendment; and the first question will be upon agreeing to the order submitted by him.

Mr. CONKLING. What becomes of the motion of the Senator from Indiana?

Mr. SUMNER. What was the motion of the Senator from Indiana?

Mr. MORTON. That the Senate retire to consult in regard to its determination.

Mr. SUMNER. That is the true motion.

The CHIEF JUSTICE. The question is on the motion of the Senator from Indiana, that the court now retire for consultation.

The motion was agreed to; and at three minutes before two o'clock the Senators, with the Chief Justice, repaired to the reception room of the Senate for consultation.

At eight minutes past four o'clock the Senators returned to the Senate Chamber, and the Chief Justice resumed the chair.

The CHIEF JUSTICE. The Chief Justice is instructed to state to the counsel for the accused that the motion made by them is overruled denied, and that the Senate has adopted an order, which will be read by the Secretary.

The Secretary read as follows:

Ordered, That the respondent file his answer to the articles of impeachment on or before Monday, the 23d day of March instant.

Mr. Manager BINGHAM. Mr. President, I am instructed by the managers to submit to the consideration of the Senate a motion which I send to the desk to be read.

The Secretary read as follows:

The managers ask the Senate respectfully to adopt the following order:

Ordered, That upon the filing of a replication by the managers on the part of the House of Representatives the trial of Andrew Johnson, President of the United States, upon the articles of impeachment exhibited by the House of Representatives shall proceed forthwith.

The CHIEF JUSTICE put the question upon the order asked by the managers and declared that it appeared to be refused.

Mr. SUMNER called for the yeas and nays, and they were ordered; and being taken, resulted—yeas 25, nays 26; as follows:

YEAS—Messrs. Cameron, Cattell, Chandler, Cole, Conkling, Conness, Corbett, Drake, Ferry, Harlan,

Howard, Morgan, Morton, Nye, Patterson of New Hampshire, Pomeroy, Ramsey, Ross, Stewart, Sumner, Thayer, Tipton, Williams, Wilson, and Yates—25.

NAYS—Messrs. Anthony, Bayard, Buckalew, Davis, Dixon, Edmunds, Fessenden, Fowler, Frelinghuysen, Grimes, Henderson, Hendricks, Howe, Johnson, McCreery, Morrill of Maine, Morrill of Vermont, Norton, Patterson of Tennessee, Saulsbury, Sherman, Sprague, Trumbull, Van Winkle, Vickers, and Willey—26.

ABSENT—Messrs. Cragin, Doolittle, and Wade—3.

The CHIEF JUSTICE. The order asked by the managers is denied.

Mr. SHERMAN. Mr. Chief Justice, I submit the following motion:

Ordered, That the trial of the articles of impeachment shall proceed on the 6th day of April next.

Mr. WILSON. I move to amend that order by striking out "the 6th day of April" and inserting "the 1st day of April."

Mr. Manager BUTLER. I should like to inquire of the President and the Senate if the managers in behalf of the House of Representatives have a right to be heard upon that motion?

Mr. SUMNER. Unquestionably.

The CHIEF JUSTICE. The Chair is of opinion that the managers have a right to be heard, and also the counsel for the accused.

Mr. Manager BUTLER. Mr. President, and gentlemen of the Senate, however ungracious it may seem on the part of the managers acting for the House of Representatives, and thereby representing the people of the United States, to press an early trial of the accused, yet your duty to those who sent us here, representing their wishes, speaking in their presence and by their command, the state of the country, the interests of the people, all seem to require that we should urge the speediest possible trial.

Among the reasons why the trial should be put off, which the learned gentlemen who appear for the accused have brought to the attention of the Senate, are precedents of delay in the trials of the earlier days of the Republic; and we were told that "railroad speed" ought not to be used in this trial. Sir, why not? Railroads have affected every other business in the civilized world; telegraphs have brought places together that were thousands of miles apart. It takes less time to send to California and get a witness—it takes infinitely less time, if I may use so strong an expression, to send a message for him—from California now than it took to send a witness from Philadelphia to Boston at the trial of Judge Chase. We must not shut our eyes to the fact that there are railroads and that there are telegraphs, as bearing upon this trial. They give the accused the privilege of calling his counsel together instantly, of getting answers from any witness that he may have instantly, of bringing him here in hours where it once, and not long ago, took months; and, therefore, I respectfully submit that it is not to be overlooked that railroads and telegraphs have changed the order of time. In every other business of life we recognize that change; and why should we not in this?

But passing from that, which is but an incident and a detail of the trial, will you allow me, further, to suggest that the ordinary course of justice, the ordinary delays in court, the ordinary time given in ordinary cases for men to answer when called before tribunals of justice, have no application to this case. The rules by which cases are heard and determined before the Supreme Court of the United States are not rules applicable to the case at bar; and for this reason, if for no other, when ordinary trials are had, when ordinary questions are examined at the bar of any court, there is no danger to the common weal in delay; the Republic may take no detriment if the trial is postponed; to give the accused time injures nobody; to grant him indulgence hurts no one, and may help one, and perhaps an innocent, man. But here the House of Representatives have presented at the bar of the Senate, in the most solemn form, the Chief Executive officer of the nation. They say (and they desire your judgment upon their accusation) that he has usurped power which does not belong to him; that he is at this very time breaking the laws solemnly enacted by you, the Senate, and those who present him here, the Congress of the United States, and that he still proposes so to do.

Sir, who is the criminal—I beg pardon for the word—the respondent at the bar? He is the Chief Executive of the nation; and when I have said that, I have taken out from all ordinary rules this trial, because I submit with deference that here and now, for the first time in the history of the world, has any nation brought its ruler to the bar of its highest tribunal in a constitutional method, under the rules and forms prescribed by its Constitution; and therefore all the rules, all the analogies, all the likeness to a common and ordinary trial of any cause, civil or criminal, cease at once, are silent, and ought not to weigh in judgment. Other nations have tried and condemned their kings and rulers, but the process has always been in violence and subversive of their Constitutions and framework of government, not in submission to and accordance with it.

When I name the respondent as the Chief Executive, I say he is the Commander-in-Chief of your armies; he specially claims that command, not by force and under the limitations of your laws, but as a prerogative of his office and subject to his arbitrary will. He controls, through his subordinates, your Treasury. He commands your Navy. Thus he has all elements of power. He controls your foreign relations. In any hour of passion, of prejudice, of revenge for fancied wrong in his own mind, he may complicate your peace with any nation of the earth, even while he is being arraigned as a respondent at your bar. And mark me, sir, may I respectfully submit that the very question here at issue this day and this hour is, whether he shall control beyond the reach of your laws, and outside of your laws, the Army of the United States. The one greatest of all questions here at issue is, whether he shall be able, against law—setting aside your laws, setting aside the decrees of the Senate, setting aside the laws enacted by Congress, overriding the legislative power of the country, claiming it as an attribute of executive power only, to control the great military arm of this Government, and control it if he chooses at his own good pleasure, its your ruin and the ruin of the country.

Indeed, sir, do we not know, may we not upon this motion assume, the fact upon common fame and the current history of events that the whole business of the War Department of this country pauses until this trial goes through? He will not recognize, as we all know, the Secretary of War, him whom this body has declared the legal Secretary of War, and whom Congress, under its power legitimately exercised, has determined shall be recognized as the legal Secretary of War. Do we not also know, that while he claims to have appointed a Secretary *ad interim*, he dare not recognize him; and thus the entire business of the War Department is stopped. The Senate of the United States have confirmed the appointment of many a gallant officer of the Army who, by law and by right, ought to have his duties and pay commence the day and the hour when his commission reaches him; yet those commissions have been delayed weeks, and the proposition on his part is that they shall be delayed at least forty days longer—as long as it took God to destroy the world by a flood—and for what? In order that five very respectable, highly intelligent, very learned, and able lawyers may write an answer to certain articles of impeachment. Having failed in that, now the proposition is to delay more and more, while there is at least one department of the Government thrown into confusion and disorganization, as we are thus delaying.

But, sir, this is the least of the mischiefs of delay. The great pulse of the nation beats perturbedly while even this strictly constitutional but highly and truly anomalous proceeding goes on. It pauses fitfully when we pause, and goes forward when we go forward; and the very question of national prosperity in this country arising out of the desire of men to have business interests settled, to have prosperity return, to have the spring open as auspiciously under our laws as it will under the laws of nature, depend upon our actions here and now. I say the very pulse of the country beats here, and, beating fitfully, requires us to still it by bringing this respondent to justice, from which God send him a good deliverance, if he so deserve, at the earliest possible hour, ay, the very earliest hour consistently with the preservation of his rights. Instead, therefore, of fixing a time now in advance when he shall be tried, (if you will allow me respectfully to say as much,) giving him time, which he may be supposed to want for preparation of his trial, fix the trial at an early day, and then, if his counsel choose to draw analogies from the trials of criminal law or the civil law, let him, when he comes here, under his oath and under the certificate of his counsel, say that he cannot get ready to meet a given article, and if he shows due diligence then give him all the time he ought to have to fairly put before you the exact form and feature of everything he has done.

But, I humbly submit, do not in advance presume that he cannot get ready until he comes and shows to the Senate some reason, upon his oath, why he may not be ready. Let every part of the case stand upon its own merits. If the respondent comes here and says to the Senate, after he puts in his answer, "I am not ready for trial, because I cannot get a given witness," let him, as his counsel claims we ought to do, follow the ordinary rule and say to the Senate, "If I could get that witness he would testify thus, and thus, and thus;" and the managers would answer, "We will either produce him here at the bar when you call him, or we will admit that he will testify thus, and thus, and thus, and you shall have the entire benefit of the testimony; for God forbid—and I speak with all reverence—that we shall deprive him of a single right or a single indulgence consistent with the public safety and speedy justice. Therefore, whenever any such motion is made, you, Senators, I respectfully submit, will be ready, able, and willing, desirous to meet it, and grant indulgence when a case is made out for indulgence.

Allow me one other word. We ask no more of the Senate as against this defendant than what we are willing to deal to ourselves. The great, perhaps the determining, act upon which the respondent is here brought to your bar was committed by him on the 21st of February. He knew it and all its consequences then as well and better than we could. The House of Representatives dealt with the action of the respondent on the 22d. On the 4th of March we brought before the Senate and to his notice what we claimed were the legal consequences of that act. We are now come here ready for trial of our accusation founded upon that act. We are here instant for trial, pressing for trial *de die in diem*. Make the days as long as the judges of England made them when they sat twenty-two hours out of the twenty-four in the trial of great criminals, and we, the managers on behalf of the House of Representatives, God giving us strength, will still attend here at your bar every hour and every moment, your humble servitors, for the purpose of justice. We have had only from the 22d of February to now to make ready for the trial of the accusation. He has had just as long. He knew at first more about this action of his than we could. He knows all about it now. He knows

exactly what he has done, and why and how he has done it. We can only partly guess at all he has done from the part we see yet. We are willing to go to trial on behalf of the people of the United States, say with only these fourteen days' preparation. You have granted him seven more, say twenty-one in all, and we ask, after you have given him one third more time, than we have had to prosecute, at least that he shall be held to meet us with the defense.

Sir, I trust you will pardon me a single further suggestion. I hope hereafter no man anywhere will say that the charges upon which we have arraigned Andrew Johnson at this bar are either frivolous, unsubstantial, or of none effect, because five gentlemen of the highest respectability, skill, and legal acumen as counsel—I know one of them would not for his life say what he did not believe—have told us that the articles of impeachment were so grave and so substantial that it would take them forty days even to write an answer to them. The charges are so grave, so momentous, so potent, that, with all their legal ability, forty days will be required to write an answer; and then, after they have had forty days in addition to ten already, giving them fifty days, they say they would need still further time for preparation to meet us on the trial of these charges. I may only humbly hope that I have made myself understood in this unprepared and hurried statement of some reasons which press on my associates and myself to urge forward this trial.

You will see their force and the arguments which should accompany them much better than I can state them. If I have brought your minds (perhaps a little swerved by pity and clemency for so great an accused,) again to their true poise of judgment upon the question of the necessity for this country that justice shall speedily be done upon the accused I have succeeded in all I could hope. If we are mistaken in all our accusations and the respondent is the great and good man he ought to be, and he shall go free, be it so; the country will have quiet then. If you come to the other determination which we present and demand you shall do if it be proved, then be that so, and the country will have quiet. But upon this so great trial, I pray, let us not belittle ourselves with the analogies of the common law courts or the equity courts or the criminal courts, because nothing is so dangerous to mislead us. Let us deal with this matter as one wherein the life of the nation hangs trembling in the scale; where the rights of the nation are put in the balance, and a trial is to be had upon the greatest question that ever yet engaged the attention of anybody, however learned or however wise, sitting in judgment.

Mr. NELSON. Mr. Chief Justice, and gentlemen of the Senate: I have entered this Chamber as one of the counsel of the President profoundly impressed with the idea that this is the most exalted judicial tribunal now upon earth. I have endeavored in coming here to divest my mind of the idea that we are to engage in political discussion, and to feel impressed with the thought that we appear before a tribunal the members of which are sworn as judges to try the great questions which have been submitted to their consideration; not as mere party questions, but as the grand tribunal of the nation, disposed to dispense justice equally between two of the greatest powers, if I may so express myself, in the land. I have come here under the impression that there is much force in the observation which the honorable manager made in regard to the forms of proceeding in this tribunal, that it is not to be governed by the iron and rigid rules of law, but that, seeking to attain justice, it is disposed to allow the largest liberty in the progress of the investigation, both to the honorable managers on the part of the House of Representatives and to the counsel in behalf of the President of the United States.

Impressed with the idea that this tribunal will discard in a great degree those forms and ceremonies which are known to the common law; that it does not stand upon demurrers; that it will not stand particularly upon the forms of evidence, or those technical rules which prevail in other courts, I have supposed that there was nothing improper in our making an appeal to this tribunal for time to answer the charges which have been preferred against the President of the United States; and that, instead of that being denied, much more liberality would be extended by the Senate of the nation sitting as a court of impeachment than we could even expect upon a trial in one of the courts of common law.

It is not my purpose, Mr. Chief Justice, to enter at this stage into a discussion of the charges which are preferred here, though it would seem to be invited by one or two of the observations which were made by the honorable manager, [Mr. Butler.] I do not propose at this stage of your proceedings to enter into any discussion of them. You are told, however, that it is right in a case of this kind to proceed with railroad speed; and that in consequence of the great improvements which have been made in the country we can proceed much more rapidly in the investigation of a case of this kind than such a case could be proceeded with a few years ago. Nevertheless, the charges which are made here are charges of the gravest importance. The questions which will have to be considered by this honorable body are questions of the deepest and profoundest interest. They are questions in which not only the Representatives of the people are concerned, but the people themselves have the deepest and most lasting interest in the result of this investigation. Questions are raised here in regard to differences of opinion between the Executive of the nation and the honorable House of Representatives

C. I.—2.

as to their constitutional powers and as to the rights which they respectively claim. These are questions of the utmost gravity, and questions which in the view we entertain of them should receive the most deliberate consideration on the part of the Senate.

I trust that I shall be pardoned by the Chief Justice and the Senators in making an allusion to a statute which has long been in force in the State from which I come. I only do it for the purpose of making a brief argument by analogy to you and the honorable body whom I am addressing. We have a statute in the State of Tennessee, which has long been in force, which provides that when a bill of indictment is found against an individual, and he thinks, owing to excitement or any other cause, he may not have a fair trial at the first term of the court, his case shall be continued until the next term. The mode of proceeding at law—and no man, I presume, in the United States is more familiar with it than the Chief Justice whom I have the honor of addressing on this occasion—is not the mode of railroad speed. If there is anything under the heavens that gives to judicial proceedings a claim to the consideration and the approbation of mankind it is the fact that judges and courts hasten slowly in the investigation of cases that are presented to them. Nothing is done or presumed to be done in a state of excitement. Every moment is allowed for calm and mature deliberation. The courts are in the habit of investigating cases slowly, carefully, cautiously, and when they form their judgments and pronounce their opinions, and those opinions are published to the world, they meet the sanction of judicial minds and legal minds everywhere, and they meet the approbation and the confidence of the people before whom they are promulgated. If this is and ever has been one of the proudest characteristics, if I may so express myself, of the forms of judicial proceedings in our courts, how much more in an exalted and honorable body like this; how much more in an assembly composed of some of the wisest and greatest men in the United States, Senators revered and honored by their countrymen, Senators who from their position are presumed to be free from reproach, who from their position are presumed to be calm in their deliberations and in their investigations—how much more in such a body as this ought we to proceed cautiously and ought every opportunity to be given for a fair investigation?

Mr. Chief Justice, I need not tell you, nor need I tell many of the honorable Senators whom I address on this occasion, many of whom are lawyers, many of whom have been clothed in times past with the judicial ermine, that in the courts of law the vilest criminal who ever was arraigned in the United States has been given time for preparation, time for hearing. The Constitution of the country secures to the vilest man in the land the right not only to be heard himself, but to be heard by counsel; and no matter how great his crime, no matter how deep may be the malignity of the offense with which he is charged, he is tried according to the forms of law; he is allowed to have counsel; continuances are granted to him; if he is unable to obtain justice time is given to him, and all manner of preparation is allowed him.

If this is so in courts of common law, that are fettered and bound by the iron rules to which I have adverted, how much more in a great tribunal like this, that does not follow the precedents of law, but that is aiming and seeking alone to attain justice, ought we to be allowed ample time for preparation in reference to charges of the nature which we have here? How much more, sir, should such time be given us?

We are told that the President acted in regard to one of the matters which is charged against him by the House of Representatives on the 21st of February, and that by the 4th of March—if I did not mistake the statement of the honorable manager—the House of Representatives had presented this accusation against the President of the United States; and that, therefore, the President, who knew what he was doing, should be prepared for his defense. Mr. Chief Justice, is it necessary for me to remind you and honorable Senators that you can upon a page of foolscap paper prepare a bill of indictment against an individual which may require weeks in the investigation? Is it necessary for me to remind this honorable body that it is an easy thing to make charges, but that it is often a laborious and difficult thing to make a defense against those accusations?

Reasoning from the analogy furnished by such proceedings at law, I earnestly maintain before this honorable body that suitable time should be given us to answer the charges which are made here. A large number of these charges—those of them connected with the President's action in reference to the Secretary of War—involve questions of the deepest importance. They involve an inquiry running back to the very foundation of the Government; they involve an examination of the precedents which have been set by different Administrations; they involve, in short, the most extensive range of inquiry. The two last charges that were presented by the House of Representatives, if I may be pardoned for using the expression in the view which I entertain of them, open Pandora's box, and will cause an investigation as to the great differences of opinion which have existed between the President and the House of Representatives, an inquiry which, so far as I can perceive, will be almost interminable in its character.

Now, what do we ask for the President of the United States? The honorable manager corrected himself in the expression that he was a criminal. What do we ask in behalf of the President of the United States, the highest officer in this land? Why, sir, we ask simply that he shall be allowed time for his defense. And upon whose judgment is he to rely in regard to that? He must, in great part, rely upon the judgment of his counsel, those to whom he has intrusted his defense. We, upon our professional responsibility, have asserted, in the presence of this Senate, in the face of the nation and of the whole world, that we believe it will require the number of days to prepare the President's answer which we stated to the Senate in the paper which we submitted to the Senate. Such is still our opinion. And when these grave charges are presented are they to be rushed through the Senate sitting as a judicial tribunal in hot haste and with railroad speed, without giving to the President of the United States the opportunity to answer them, that same opportunity which you would give to the meanest criminal that ever was arraigned before the bar of justice in any tribunal in this or in the country from which we borrowed our law?

I cannot believe, Mr. Chief Justice, that honorable Senators will hesitate for one moment in granting us all the time that may be necessary to prepare our defense, and that may be necessary to enable them to decide as judges carefully, deliberately, conscientiously, and with a view of their accountability, not only to their constituents, but their accountability to posterity who are to come after us, for the names of American Senators are dear not only to those who sent them here, but they are names which are to live after the scenes of to-day shall have passed away, I have no doubt that honorable Senators, in justice to themselves and in justice to the great land which they represent, will endeavor to conduct this investigation in a manner that will stamp the impress of honor and justice upon them and upon their proceedings not only now, but in all time to come, when they shall be cited after you and I and all of us shall have passed away from the stage of human action.

Mr. Chief Justice, this is an exalted tribunal. I say it in no spirit of compliment. I say it because I feel it. I feel that this is the most exalted tribunal that can be convened under the sun, a tribunal of Senators, honorable members, who are sent here to sit in judgment upon one of the gravest and greatest accusations that ever was made in the land. And I may say, in answer to an observation of the honorable manager on the other side, that I, for one, as an American citizen, feel proud that we are assembled here to-day and assembled under the circumstances which have brought us together. It is one of the first instances in the history of the world in which the ruler of a people has been presented by a portion of the Representatives of the people for trial before another branch of the law-making power sitting as a judicial tribunal. While that is so it is equally true that on the other hand the President, through his counsel, comes here and submits himself to the jurisdiction of this court, submits himself calmly, peaceably, and with a confident reliance on the justice of the honorable Senate who are to hear his cause.

Mr. Chief Justice, I sincerely hope that the resolution which has been offered will meet the approbation of the honorable Senate. I hope that time will be given us, and that this proceeding, which in all time to come will be quoted as a precedent for others, will be conducted with that gravity, that dignity, that decorum which are fit and becoming in the Representatives of a free and a great people.

Mr. CONKLING. I wish to submit an amendment to the proposition pending in the nature of a substitute:

Ordered, That, unless otherwise ordered by the Senate for cause shown, the trial of the pending impeachment shall proceed immediately after replication shall be filed.

The CHIEF JUSTICE. The amendment submitted by the Senator from New York does not appear to the Chair to be in order at present. The motion of the Senator from Ohio [Mr. SHERMAN] is that the Senate adopt the following order:

Ordered, That the trial of the articles of impeachment shall proceed on the 6th day of April next.

The Senator from Massachusetts [Mr. WILSON] moves to amend it by striking out the word "sixth" and inserting "first." That is the present motion.

Mr. WILSON. I propose to modify my amendment by saying Monday, the 30th of March.

Mr. CONKLING. Does the Chair decide that my proposition is not in order?

The CHIEF JUSTICE. The Chair does not conceive it to be in order at present.

Mr. CONKLING. Then I beg to modify in this way: I move to amend the amendment of the Senator from Massachusetts by striking out the date which he inserts, whatever that date may be, and inserting in lieu thereof the words "immediately after replication filed, unless otherwise ordered by the Senate."

The CHIEF JUSTICE. The Chair conceives that the amendment offered by the Senator from New York is not in order.

Mr. WILSON. For the purpose of bringing the motion made by the Senator from New York before the body I withdraw my amendment so that his amendment will be in order.

Mr. CONKLING. Then I offer my original proposition as a substitute for the proposition of the Senator from Ohio.

The CHIEF JUSTICE. The amendment of the Senator from New York will be read.

The CHIEF CLERK. The amendment is to strike out all after the word "ordered" in the proposition of Mr. SHERMAN and to insert in lieu thereof:

That, unless otherwise ordered by the Senate for cause shown, the trial of the pending impeachment shall proceed immediately after replication shall be filed.

Mr. Manager BINGHAM. Mr. President, I am instructed by the managers to say that the proposition just suggested by the honorable Senator from New York [Mr. CONKLING] is entirely satisfactory to the managers for the House, and to say further to the Senate that we believe it is in perfect accord with the precedents in this country. The Senate will doubtless remember that on the trial of Justice Chase, when a day was fixed for the answer, upon his own petition, verified by his affidavit, the Senate adopted an order which was substantially the order as suggested by the amendment of the honorable gentleman from New York. I beg leave to read that order in the hearing of the Senate:

"*Ordered,* That the 4th day of February next shall be the day for receiving the answer and proceeding with the trial of the impeachment against Samuel Chase."

If nothing further had been said touching the original proposition we would have been content and satisfied to leave this question without further remark to the decision of the Senate; but in view of what has been said by the counsel for the accused we beg leave to respond that we are chargeable with no indecent haste when we ask that no unnecessary delay shall interpose between the people and the trial of a man who is charged with having violated the greatest trusts ever committed to a single person; trusts that involve the highest interests of the whole people; trusts that involve the peace of the whole country; trusts that involve in some sense the success of this last great experiment of representative government upon the earth.

We may be pardoned, further, sir, for saying that it strikes us somewhat with surprise, without intending the slightest possible disrespect to any member of this body, that any proposition should be entertained for the continuance of a trial like this, when no formal application has been made by the accused himself. To be sure, a motion was interposed here to-day in the face of the written rule, order, and law of this body, for leave to file an answer at the end of forty days. The Senate has disposed of that motion, and in a manner, we venture to say, satisfactory to the whole country, as it is certainly satisfactory to the representatives of the people at this bar. Now, sir, that being disposed of, the Senate having determined the day on which answer shall be filed, we submit, with all respect to the Senate, that it is but just to the people of this country that we shall await the incoming of the answer and the replication thereto by the representatives of the people, and then see and know what colorable excuse can be offered, either by the accused President in his own person or through his representatives, why this trial should be delayed a single hour.

If he be innocent of the grave accusations prepared against him the truth will soon be ascertained by this enlightened body; and he has the right, if the fact so appear, to a speedy deliverance, and the country a right to a speedy determination of this important question. If, on the other hand, he be guilty of these grave and serious charges, what man is there within this body or outside of this body ready to say that he should one day or hour longer disgrace the high position which has been held hitherto by some of the noblest and most illustrious of the land?

We think that the executive power of this nation can only be reposed in the hands of men who are faithful to their great trust. The people so think. They have made that issue with the President of the United States at this bar; and while we demand that there shall be no indecent haste, we, too, demand in the name of all the people, most respectfully, that there shall be no unnecessary delay, and no delay at all until good cause is shown for delay in the mode and manner hitherto observed in proceedings of this sort.

Mr. JOHNSON. Mr. President, I ask that the resolution offered by the honorable member from Ohio shall be read. I did not hear it distinctly.

The CHIEF JUSTICE. It will be reported.

The CHIEF CLERK. The order, as submitted by the Senator from Ohio, is as follows:

Ordered. That the trial of the articles of impeachment shall proceed on the 6th day of April next.

The Senator from New York [Mr. CONKLING] moves to amend by striking out all after the word "ordered," and inserting:

That, unless otherwise ordered by the Senate for cause shown, the trial of the pending impeachment shall proceed immediately after replication shall be filed.

Mr. JOHNSON. Mr. President, I rise for information. Is there any period within which the replication is to be filed? There is nothing on the face of that order limiting the time within which the replication may be filed. If the managers propose to make that a part of the order to file the replication on the day the answer may come in, or on any specific day after the coming in of the answer, it would not, perhaps, be liable to objection; but the accused may well be in ignorance of the time when the trial will begin under the order as it stands.

Mr. Manager BINGHAM. Will the honorable Senator allow me to suggest to him that we can only file the replication with the consent and after consultation with the House of Representatives; and therefore the answer to his suggestion is that as soon as answer be made here according to the usage and practice in cases of this sort we will respectfully demand a copy of the answer that we may lay it before the House and report to this body as soon as the House will order us its replication. I have no doubt it will be done within one or two days after the answer is filed.

Mr. JOHNSON. What I meant——

Mr. CONKLING. I rise to a question of order. Reluctant as I am to make it, I ask

for the enforcement of the eighteenth and twenty-third rules.

The CHIEF JUSTICE. No debate can be had. The Chair understood the Senator from Maryland as simply asking for an explanation from the managers.

Mr. JOHNSON. What is the rule, Mr. President?

The CHIEF JUSTICE. The Secretary will read the rule.

Mr. JOHNSON. The honorable member from New York is mistaken in supposing that I rose to debate the question. I only rose for the purpose of inquiring what the question was. I suppose that is allowable.

The CHIEF JUSTICE. Is the Senate ready for the question on the substitute proposed by the Senator from New York?

Mr. DRAKE. On that question I ask for the yeas and nays.

The yeas and nays were ordered; and being taken resulted—yeas 40, nays 10; as follows:

YEAS—Messrs. Anthony, Cameron, Cattell, Chandler, Cole, Conkling, Conness, Corbett, Drake, Edmunds, Ferry, Fessenden, Fowler, Frelinghuysen, Grimes, Harlan, Henderson, Howard, Howe, Morgan, Morrill of Maine, Morrill of Vermont, Morton, Nye, Patterson of New Hampshire, Pomeroy, Ramsey, Ross, Sherman, Sprague, Stewart, Sumner, Thayer, Tipton, Trumbull, Van Winkle, Willey, Williams, Wilson and Yates—40.

NAYS—Messrs. Bayard, Buckalew, Davis, Dixon, Hendricks, Johnson, McCreery, Patterson of Tennessee, Saulsbury, and Vickers—10.

ABSENT—Messrs. Cragin, Doolittle, Norton, and Wade—4.

So the amendment was agreed to.

The CHIEF JUSTICE. The question recurs on the order as amended. The Clerk will report the order.

The Chief Clerk read it, as follows:

Ordered, That, unless otherwise ordered by the Senate for cause shown, the trial of the pending impeachment shall proceed immediately after replication shall be filed.

The order was agreed to.

Mr. HOWARD. If there be no motion for the court on behalf of the honorable managers of the House of Representatives, or on the part of the counsel for the accused, I move that the Senate sitting on the present impeachment adjourn to the 23d day of the present month, at one o'clock in the afternoon. I send an order to the Chair for that purpose. My motion is made subject to any action the managers may see fit to lay before us, or the counsel for the accused. I will not press it if they have anything to propose.

The CHIEF JUSTICE. Have the managers on the part of the House of Representatives anything to propose?

Mr. Manager BINGHAM. Nothing further at present.

The CHIEF JUSTICE. Have the counsel for the accused anything to propose?

Mr. CURTIS. Nothing.

The CHIEF JUSTICE. Senators, the motion is to adjourn the Senate sitting for the trial of this impeachment until the 23d of March.

The motion was agreed to.

MONDAY, *March* 23, 1868.

At one o'clock p. m. the Chief Justice of the United States entered the Senate Chamber, escorted by Mr. POMEROY, the chairman of the Senate committee heretofore appointed for that purpose, and took the chair.

The CHIEF JUSTICE. The Sergeant-at-Arms will open the court by proclamation.

The SERGEANT-AT-ARMS. Hear ye, hear ye, hear ye: all persons are commanded to keep silence while the Senate of the United States is sitting for the trial of the articles of impeachment exhibited by the House of Representatives against Andrew Johnson, President of the United States.

The managers of the impeachment on the part of the House of Representatives appeared at the door, and their presence was announced by the Sergeant-at-Arms.

The CHIEF JUSTICE. The Managers will take the seats assigned to them by the Senate.

The Managers accordingly took the seats provided for them in the area of the Senate to the left of the Presiding Officer.

The counsel for the President, Hon. Henry Stanbery, of Kentucky; Hon. B. R. Curtis, of Massachusetts; Hon. Thomas A. R. Nelson, of Tennessee; William M. Evarts, Esq., of New York, and Hon. William S. Groesbeck, of Ohio, appeared and took the seats assigned to them, on the right of the Chair.

The Sergeant-at-Arms announced the presence of the House of Representatives; and the Committee of the Whole House, headed by Mr. E. B. WASHBURNE, of Illinois, the chairman of the Committee of the Whole, and the Clerk of the House, entered the Chamber, and the members were conducted to the seats assigned them.

The Secretary called the name of Mr. DOOLITTLE, who had not heretofore been sworn, and the oath prescribed by the rules was administered to him by the Chief Justice.

The CHIEF JUSTICE. The Secretary will read the minutes of the proceedings of the last sitting.

The Secretary read the Journal of the proceedings of Friday, March 13, of the Senate sitting for the trial of the impeachment of Andrew Johnson, President of the United States, on articles of impeachment.

On the Journal of those proceedings occur the following entries as to the proceedings of the Senate on that occasion, when it had retired for deliberation:

"The Senate, with the Chief Justice, having retired to their conference chamber, proceeded to consider the motion submitted by Mr. EDMUNDS; and,

"After debate,

"On motion by Mr. DRAKE to amend the motion submitted by Mr. EDMUNDS, by striking out all after the word 'ordered,' and in lieu thereof inserting:

"'That the respondent file answer to the articles of impeachment on or before Friday, the 20th day of March instant,'

"It was determined in the affirmative—yeas 28, nays 20.

"On motion by Mr. DRAKE,

"The yeas and nays being desired by one fifth of the Senators present,

"Those who voted in the affirmative are—

"Messrs. Cameron, Cattell, Chandler, Cole, Conkling, Conness, Corbett, Drake, Ferry, Harlan, Howard, Howe, Morgan, Morrill of Vermont, Morton, Nye, Patterson of New Hampshire, Pomeroy, Ramsey, Sherman, Stewart, Sumner, Thayer, Trumbull, Willey, Williams, Wilson, and Yates.

"Those who voted in the negative are—

"Messrs. Anthony, Bayard, Buckalew, Davis, Dixon, Edmunds, Fessenden, Fowler, Frelinghuysen, Grimes, Henderson, Hendricks, Johnson, McCreery, Morrill of Maine, Norton, Patterson of Tennessee, Saulsbury, Van Winkle, and Vickers.

"So the amendment of Mr. DRAKE to the motion of Mr. EDMUNDS was agreed to.

"On the question to agree to the motion of Mr. EDMUNDS, as amended,

"After debate,

"On motion of Mr. TRUMBULL, that the Senate reconsider its vote agreeing to the amendment proposed by Mr. DRAKE to the motion of Mr. EDMUNDS,

"It was determined in the affirmative—yeas 27, nays 23.

"On motion of Mr. DRAKE,

"The yeas and nays being desired by one fifth of the Senators present,

"Those who voted in the affirmative are—

"Messrs. Anthony, Bayard, Buckalew, Cattell, Corbett, Davis, Dixon, Edmunds, Fessenden, Fowler, Frelinghuysen, Grimes, Henderson, Hendricks, Johnson, McCreery, Morrill of Vermont, Morton, Norton, Patterson of Tennessee, Saulsbury, Sherman, Sprague, Trumbull, Van Winkle, Vickers, and Willey.

"Those who voted in the negative are—

"Messrs. Cameron, Chandler, Cole, Conkling, Conness, Drake, Ferry, Harlan, Howard, Howe, Morgan, Morrill of Maine, Nye, Patterson of New Hampshire, Pomeroy, Ramsey, Stewart, Sumner, Thayer, Tipton, Williams, Wilson, and Yates.

"So the Senate reconsidered its vote agreeing to the amendment of Mr. DRAKE to the motion of Mr. EDMUNDS; and,

"The question recurring on the amendment of Mr. DRAKE,

"On motion of Mr. TRUMBULL to amend the amendment of Mr. DRAKE, by striking out the words 'Friday, the 20th,' and inserting the words 'Monday, the 23d,'

"It was determined in the affirmative; and,

"On the question to agree to the amendment, as amended on the motion of Mr. TRUMBULL,

"It was determined in the affirmative.

"The question again recurring on the motion of Mr. EDMUNDS, as amended on the motion of Mr. DRAKE, as amended by Mr. TRUMBULL, in the following words:

"'Ordered, That the respondent file answer to the articles of impeachment on or before Monday, the 23d day of March instant,'

"It was determined in the affirmative.

"Thereupon,

"The Senate returned to its Chamber."

Mr. DAVIS. Mr. Chief Justice, I rise to make the same question to the Court which I made in the Senate, and I think that now is the appropriate time before the court has decided to take up the case. I therefore submit to the Court a motion in writing.

The CHIEF JUSTICE. The Secretary will read the motion.

The Secretary read as follows:

Mr. DAVIS, a member of the Senate and of the Court of Impeachment, from the State of Kentucky, moves the court to make this order:

The Constitution having vested the Senate with the sole power to try the articles of impeachment of the President of the United States preferred by the House of Representatives, and having also declared that "the Senate of the United States shall be composed of two Senators from each State chosen by the Legislatures thereof;" and the States of Virginia, North Carolina, South Carolina, Georgia, Alabama, Mississippi, Arkansas, Louisiana, and Texas having, each by its Legislature, chosen two Senators who have been and continue to be excluded by the Senate from their seats, respectively, without any judgment by the Senate against them personally and individually on the points of their elections, returns, and qualifications, it is

Ordered, That a Court of Impeachment for the trial of the President cannot be legally and constitutionally formed while the Senators from the States aforesaid are thus excluded from the Senate; and this case is continued until the Senators from these States are permitted to take their seats in the Senate, subject to all constitutional exceptions to their elections, returns, and qualifications severally.

Mr. HOWARD. Mr. President——

The CHIEF JUSTICE. The rule does not admit of debate.

Mr. HOWARD. Mr. President, I object to the receiving of the paper as not in order.

Mr. CONNESS. Mr. President, I desire to submit a motion, which will cover the case, perhaps. I move that the paper be not received, upon which I call for the yeas and nays.

Mr. HOWE. Mr. President, I rise to submit a question of order.

The CHIEF JUSTICE. The Senator from Wisconsin.

Mr. HOWE. I submit if the motion offered by the Senator from Kentucky be in order.

The CHIEF JUSTICE. The motion comes before the Senate in the shape of an order submitted by a member of the Senate and of the Court of Impeachment. The twenty-third rule requires that "all the orders and decisions shall be made and had by yeas and nays, which shall be entered on the record, and without debate, subject, however, to the operation of rule seven." The seventh rule requires the Presiding Officer of the Senate to "submit to the Senate, without a division, all questions of evidence and incidental questions; but the same shall, on the demand of one fifth of the members present, be decided by yeas and nays." By amendment this rule has been applied to orders and decisions proposed by a member of the Senate under the twenty-third rule. The Chair rules, therefore, that the motion of the Senator from Kentucky is in order.

Mr. CONNESS. Mr. President——

The CHIEF JUSTICE. No debate is allowed.

Mr. CONNESS. Is the motion submitted by me in order in connection with it?

The CHIEF JUSTICE. The chair thinks not.

Several SENATORS. Let us have a square vote.

Other SENATORS. Let us have the yeas and nays on the order proposed.

The yeas and nays were ordered; and being taken, resulted—yeas 2, nays 49; as follows:

YEAS—Messrs. Davis and McCreery—2.
NAYS—Messrs. Anthony, Buckalew, Cameron, Cattell, Chandler, Cole, Conkling, Conness, Corbett, Cragin, Dixon, Doolittle, Drake, Edmunds, Ferry, Fessenden, Fowler, Frelinghuysen, Grimes, Harlan, Henderson, Hendricks, Howard, Howe, Johnson, Morgan, Morrill of Maine, Morrill of Vermont, Morton, Norton, Nye, Patterson of New Hampshire, Patterson of Tennessee, Pomeroy, Ramsey, Ross, Sherman, Sprague, Stewart, Sumner, Thayer, Tipton, Trumbull, Van Winkle, Vickers, Willey, Williams, Wilson, and Yates—49.
ABSENT—Messrs. Bayard, Saulsbury, and Wade—3.

The CHIEF JUSTICE. On the motion to adopt the order of the Senator from Kentucky, the yeas are 2, and the nays 49. The motion is lost.

Are the counsel for the President ready to file their answer.

Mr. STANBERY. Mr. Chief Justice, in obedience to the order of the honorable court, made at the last session, that the answer of the President should be filed to-day, we have it ready. The counsel, abandoning all other engagements, some of us quitting our courts, our cases, and our clients, have devoted every hour to the performance of this duty. The labor has been incessant and exhaustive. We have devoted, as I say, not only every hour ordinarily devoted to labor, but many required for necessary rest and recreation have been consumed in this work. It is a matter, Mr. Chief Justice, of profound regret to us that the honorable court did not allow us more time. Nevertheless we hope that the answer will be found in all respects sufficient within the law. Such as it is, we are now ready to read and file it.

The CHIEF JUSTICE. The counsel will read the answer of the President.

Mr. CURTIS proceeded to read the answer to the close of that portion relative to the first article of impeachment.

Mr. STANBERY read that portion of the answer beginning with the reply to the second article to the close of the response to the ninth article.

Mr. EVARTS read the residue of the answer.

The answer is as follows:

Senate of the United States, sitting as a Court of Impeachment for the trial of Andrew Johnson, President of the United States.

The answer of the said Andrew Johnson, President of the United States, to the articles of impeachment exhibited against him by the House of Representatives of the United States.

ANSWER TO ARTICLE I.

For answer to the first article he says: that Edwin M. Stanton was appointed Secretary for the Department of War on the 15th day of January, A. D. 1862, by Abraham Lincoln, then President of the United States, during the first term of his Presidency, and was commissioned, according to the Constitution and laws of the United States, to hold the said office during the pleasure of the President; that the office of Secretary for the Department of War was created by an act of the First Congress in its first session passed on the 7th day of August, A. D. 1789, and in and by that act it was provided and enacted that the said Secretary for the Department of War shall perform and execute such duties as shall from time to time be enjoined on and intrusted to him by the President of the United States, agreeably to the Constitution, relative to the subjects within the scope of the said Department; and furthermore, that the said Secretary shall conduct the business of the said Department in such a manner as the President of the United States shall, from time to time, order and instruct.

And this respondent, further answering, says that by force of the act aforesaid and by reason of his appointment aforesaid the said Stanton became the principal officer in one of the Executive Departments of the Government within the true intent and meaning of the second section of the second article of the Constitution of the United States, and according to the true intent and meaning of that provision of the Constitution of the United States; and, in accordance with the settled and uniform practice of each and every President of the United States, the said Stanton then became, and so long as he should continue to hold the said office of Secretary for the Department of War must continue to be, one of the advisers of the President of the United States, as well as the person intrusted to act for and represent the President in matters enjoined upon him or intrusted to him by the President touching the Department aforesaid, and for whose conduct in such capacity, subordinate to the President, the President is, by the Constitution and laws of the United States, made responsible. And this respondent, further answering, says he succeeded to the office of President of the United States upon, and by reason of, the death of Abraham Lincoln, then President of the United States, on the 15th day of April, 1865, and the said Stanton was then holding the said office of Secretary for the Department of War under and by reason of the appointment and commission aforesaid; and, not having been removed from the said office by this respondent, the said Stanton continued to hold the same under the appointment and commission aforesaid, at the pleasure of the President, until the time hereinafter particularly mentioned; and at no time received any appointment or commission save as above detailed.

And this respondent, further answering, says that on and prior to the 5th day of August, A. D. 1867, this respondent, the President of the United States—responsible for the conduct of the Secretary for the Department of War, and having the constitutional right to resort to and rely upon the person holding that office for advice concerning the great and difficult public duties enjoined on the President by the Constitution and laws of the United States—became satisfied that he could not allow the said Stanton to continue to hold the office of Secretary for the Department of War without hazard of the public interest; that the relations between the said Stanton and the President no longer permitted the President to resort to him for advice, or to be, in the judgment of the President, safely responsible for his conduct of the affairs of the Department of War, as by law required, in accordance with the orders and instructions of the President; and thereupon, by force of the Constitution and laws of the United States, which devolve on the President the power and the duty to control the conduct of the business of that executive department of the Government, and by reason of the constitutional duty of the President to take care that the laws be faithfully executed, this respondent did necessarily consider and did determine that the said Stanton ought no longer to hold the said office of Secretary for the Department of War. And this respondent, by virtue of the power and authority vested in him as President of the United States, by the Constitution and laws of the United States, to give effect to such his decision and determination, did, on the 5th day of August, A. D. 1867, address to the said Stanton a note, of which the following is a true copy:

"SIR: Public considerations of a high character constrain me to say that your resignation as Secretary of War will be accepted."

To which note the said Stanton made the following reply:

WAR DEPARTMENT,
WASHINGTON, *August* 5, 1867.

SIR: Your note of this day has been received, stating that "public considerations of a high character constrain you" to say "that my resignation as Secretary of War will be accepted."

In reply I have the honor to say that public considerations of a high character, which alone have induced me to continue at the head of this Department, constrain me not to resign the office of Secretary of War before the next meeting of Congress.

Very respectfully, yours,
EDWIN M. STANTON.

This respondent, as President of the United States, was thereon of opinion that, having regard to the necessary official relations and duties of the Secretary for the Department of War to the President of the United States, according to the Constitution and laws of the United States, and having regard to the responsibility of the President for the conduct of the said Secretary, and having regard to the permanent executive authority of the office which the respondent holds under the Constitution and laws of the United States, it was impossible, consistently with the public interests, to allow the said Stanton to continue to hold the said office of Secretary for the Department of War; and it then became the official duty of the respondent, as President of the United States, to consider and decide what act or acts should and might lawfully be done by him, as President of the United States, to cause the said Stanton to surrender the said office.

This respondent was informed and verily believed that it was practically settled by the First Congress of the United States, and had been so considered and, uniformly and in great numbers of instances, acted on by each Congress and President of the United States, in succession, from President Washington to, and including, President Lincoln, and from the First Congress to the Thirty-Ninth Congress, that the Constitution of the United States conferred on the President, as part of the executive power and as one of the necessary means and instruments of performing the executive duty expressly imposed on him by the Constitution of taking care that the laws be faithfully executed, the power at any and all times of removing from office all executive officers for cause to be judged of by the President alone. This respondent had, in pursuance of the Constitution, required the opinion of each principal officer of the Executive Departments upon this question of constitutional executive power and duty, and had been advised by each of them, including the said Stanton, Secretary for the Department of War, that under the Constitution of the United States this power was lodged by the Constitution in the President of the United States, and that, consequently, it could be lawfully exercised by him, and the Congress could not deprive him thereof; and this respondent, in his capacity of President of the United States, and because in that capacity he was both enabled and bound to use his best judgment upon this question, did, in good faith and with an earnest desire to arrive at the truth, come to the conclusion and opinion, and did make the same known to the honorable the Senate of the United States by a message dated on the 2d day of March, 1867, (a true copy whereof is hereunto annexed and marked A,) that the power last mentioned was conferred and the duty of exercising it, in fit cases, was imposed on the President by the Constitution of the United States, and that the President could not be deprived of this power or relieved of this duty, nor could the same be vested by law in the President and the Senate jointly, either in part or whole; and this has ever since remained and was the opinion of this respondent at the time when he was forced as aforesaid to consider and decide what act or acts should and might lawfully be done by this respondent, as President of the United States, to cause the said Stanton to surrender the said office.

This respondent was also then aware that by the first section of "an act regulating the tenure of certain civil offices," passed March 2, 1867, by a constitutional majority of both Houses of Congress, it was enacted as follows:

"That every person holding any civil office to which he has been appointed by and with the advice and consent of the Senate, and every person who shall hereafter be appointed to any such office, and shall become duly qualified to act therein, is and shall be entitled to hold such office until a successor shall have been in like manner appointed and duly qualified, except as herein otherwise provided: *Provided*, That the Secretaries of State, of the Treasury, of War, of the Navy, and of the Interior, the Postmaster General, and the Attorney General, shall hold their offices respectively for and during the term of the President by whom they may have been appointed, and one month thereafter, subject to removal by and with the advice and consent of the Senate."

This respondent was also aware that this act was understood and intended to be an expression of the opinion of the Congress by which that act was passed, that the power to remove executive officers for cause might, by law, be taken from the President and vested in him and the Senate jointly; and although this respondent had arrived at and still retained the opinion above expressed and verily believed, as he still believes, that the said first section of the last-mentioned act was and is wholly inoperative and void by reason of its conflict with the Constitution of the United States, yet, inasmuch as the same had been enacted by the constitutional majority in each of the two Houses of that Congress, this respondent considered it to be proper to examine and decide whether the particular case of the said Stanton, on which it was this respondent's duty to act, was within or without 'the terms of that first section of the act; or, if within it, whether the President had not the power, according to the terms of the act, to remove the said Stanton from the office of Secretary for the Department of War, and having, in his capacity of President of the United States, so examined and considered, did form the opinion that the case of the said Stanton and his tenure of office were not affected by the first section of the last-named act.

And this respondent further answering, says, that although a case thus existed which, in his judgment as President of the United States, called for the exercise of the executive power to remove the said Stanton from the office of Secretary for the Department of War, and although this respondent was of opinion, as is above shown, that under the Constitution of the United States the power to remove the said Stanton from the said office was vested in the President of the United States; and although this respondent was also of the opinion, as is above shown, that the case of the said Stanton was not affected by the first section of the last-named act; and although each of the said opinions had been formed by this respondent upon an actual case, requiring him, in his capacity of President of the United States, to come to some judgment and determination thereon, yet this respondent, as President of the United States, desired and determined to avoid, if possible, any question of the construction and effect of the said first section of the last-named act, and also the broader question of the executive power conferred on the President of the United States, by the Constitution of the United States, to remove one of the principal officers of one of the Executive Departments for cause seeming to him sufficient; and this respondent also desired and determined that, if from causes over which he could exert no control, it should become absolutely necessary to raise and have, in some way, determined either or both of the said last-named questions, it was in accordance with the Constitution of the United States and was required of the President thereby, that questions of so much gravity and importance, upon which the legislative and executive departments of the Government had disagreed, which involved powers considered by all branches of the Government, during its entire history down to the year 1867, to have been confided by the Constitution of the United States to the President, and to be necessary for the complete and proper execution of his constitutional duties, should be in some proper way submitted to that judicial department of the Government, intrusted by the Constitution with the power, and subjected by it to the duty, not only of determining finally the construction and effect of all acts of Congress, but of comparing them with the Constitution of the United States and pronouncing them inoperative when found in conflict with that fundamental law which the people have enacted for the government of all their servants. And to these ends, first, that through the action of the Senate of the United States, the absolute duty of the President to substitute some fit person in place of Mr. Stanton as one of his advisers, and as a principal subordinate officer whose official conduct he was responsible for and had lawful right to control, might, if possible, be accomplished without the necessity of raising any one of the questions aforesaid; and, second, if this duty could not be so performed, then that these questions, or such of them as might necessarily arise, should be judicially determined in manner aforesaid, and for no other end or purpose this respondent, as President of the United States, on the 12th day of August, 1867, seven days after the reception of the letter of the said Stanton of the 5th of August, hereinbefore stated, did issue to the said Stanton the order following, namely:

EXECUTIVE MANSION,
WASHINGTON, *August* 12, 1867.

SIR: By virtue of the power and authority vested in me as President by the Constitution and laws of the United States, you are hereby suspended from office as Secretary of War, and will cease to exercise any and all functions pertaining to the same.

You will at once transfer to General Ulysses S. Grant, who has this day been authorized and empowered to act as Secretary of War *ad interim*, all records, books, papers, and other public property now in your custody and charge.

Hon. EDWIN M. STANTON, *Secretary of War.*

To which said order the said Stanton made the following reply:

WAR DEPARTMENT,
WASHINGTON CITY, *August* 12, 1867.

"SIR: Your note of this date has been received, informing me that by virtue of the powers vested in you, as President, by the Constitution and laws of the United States, I am suspended from office as Secretary of War, and will cease to exercise any and all functions pertaining to the same; and also directing me at once to transfer to General Ulysses S. Grant, who has this day been authorized and empowered to act as Secretary of War *ad interim*, all records, books, papers, and other public property now in my custody and charge. Under a sense of public duty, I am compelled to deny your right, under the Constitution and laws of the United States, without the advice and consent of the Senate, and without legal cause, to suspend me from office as Secretary of War, or the exercise of any or all functions pertaining to the same, or without such advice and consent to compel me to transfer to any person the records, books, papers, and public property in my custody as Secretary. But inasmuch as the General commanding the armies of the United States has been appointed *ad interim*, and has notified me that he has accepted the appointment, I have no alternative but to submit, under protest, to superior force."

To the PRESIDENT.

And this respondent, further answering, says, that it is provided in and by the second section of "an act to regulate the tenure of certain civil offices," that the President may suspend an officer from the performance of the duties of the office held by him, for certain causes therein designated, until the next meeting of the Senate and until the case shall be acted on by the Senate; that this respondent, as President of the United States, was advised and he verily believed and still believes, that the executive power of removal from office confided to him by the Constitution as aforesaid, includes the power of suspension from office at the pleasure of the President and this respondent, by the order aforesaid, did suspend the said Stanton from office, not until the next meeting of the Senate, or until the Senate should have acted upon the case, but by force of the power and authority vested in him by the Constitution and laws of the United States, indefinitely and at the pleasure of the President, and the order, in form aforesaid, was made known to the Senate of the United States, on the 12th day of December, A. D. 1867, as will be more fully hereinafter stated.

And this respondent, further answering, says, that in and by the act of February 13, 1795, it was, among other things, provided and enacted that, in case of vacancy in the office of Secretary for the Department of War, it shall be lawful for the President, in case he shall think it necessary, to authorize any person to perform the duties of that office until a successor be appointed or such vacancy filled, but not exceeding the term of six months; and this respondent, being advised and believing that such law was in full force and not repealed, by an order dated August 12, 1867, did authorize and empower Ulysses S. Grant, General of the armies of the United States, to act as Secretary for the Department of War *ad interim*, in the form in which similar authority had theretofore been given, not until the next meeting of the Senate and until the Senate should act on the case, but at the pleasure of the President, subject only to the limitation of six months in the said last-mentioned act contained; and a copy of the last-named order was made known to the Senate of the United States on the 12th day of December, A. D. 1867, as will be hereinafter more fully stated; and in pursuance of the design and intention aforesaid, if it should become necessary, to submit the said questions to a judicial determination, this respondent, at or near the date of the last-mentioned order, did make known such his purpose to obtain a judicial decision of the said questions, or such of them as might be necessary.

And this respondent, further answering, says, that in further pursuance of his intention and design, if possible to perform what he judged to be his imperative duty, to prevent the said Stanton from longer holding the office of Secretary for the Department of War, and at the same time avoiding, if possible, any question respecting the extent of the power of removal from executive office confided to the President by the Constitution of the United States, and any question respecting the construction and effect of the first section of the said "act regulating the tenure of certain civil offices," while he should not, by any act of his, abandon and relinquish, either a power which he believed the Constitution had conferred on the President of the United States, to enable him to perform the duties of his office, or a power designedly left to him by the first section of the act of Congress last aforesaid, this respondent did, on the 12th day of December, 1867, transmit to the Senate of the United States, a message, a copy whereof is hereunto annexed and marked B, wherein he made known the orders aforesaid and the reasons which had induced the same, so far as this respondent then considered it material and necessary that the same should be set forth, and reiterated his views concerning the constitutional power of removal vested in the President, and also expressed his views concerning the construction of the said first section of the last mentioned act, as respected the power of the President to remove the said Stanton from the said office of Secretary for the Department of War, well hoping that this respondent could thus perform what he then believed, and still believes, to be his imperative duty in reference to the said Stanton, without derogating from the powers which this respondent believed were confided to the President, by the Constitution and laws, and without the necessity of raising, judicially, any questions respecting the same.

And this respondent, further answering, says, that this hope not having been realized, the President was compelled either to allow the said Stanton to resume the said office and remain therein contrary to the settled convictions of the President, formed as aforesaid, respecting the powers confided to him and the duties required of him by the Constitution of the United States, and contrary to the opinion formed as aforesaid, that the first section of the last-mentioned act did not affect the case of the said Stanton, and contrary to the fixed belief of the President that he could no longer advise with or trust or be responsible for the said Stanton, in the said office of Secretary for the Department of War, or else he was compelled to take such steps as might, in the judg-

ment of the President, be lawful and necessary to raise, for a judicial decision, the questions affecting the lawful right of the said Stanton to resume the said office, or the power of the said Stanton to persist in refusing to quit the said office if he should persist in actually refusing to quit the same; and to this end, and to this end only, this respondent did, on the 21st day of February, 1868, issue the order for the removal of the said Stanton, in the said first article mentioned and set forth, and the order authorizing the said Lorenzo F. Thomas to act as Secretary of War *ad interim*, in the said second article set forth.

And this respondent, proceeding to answer specifically each substantial allegation in the said first article, says: He denies that the said Stanton, on the 21st day of February, 1868, was lawfully in possession of the said office of Secretary for the Department of War. He denies that the said Stanton, on the day last mentioned, was lawfully entitled to hold the said office against the will of the President of the United States. He denies that the said order for the removal of the said Stanton was unlawfully issued. He denies that the said order was issued with intent to violate the act entitled "An act to regulate the tenure of certain civil offices." He denies that the said order was a violation of the last-mentioned act. He denies that the said order was a violation of the Constitution of the United States, or of any law thereof, or of his oath of office. He denies that the said order was issued with an intent to violate the Constitution of the United States or any law thereof, or this respondent's oath of office; and he respectfully, but earnestly, insists that not only was it issued by him in the performance of what he believed to be an imperative official duty, but in the performance of what this honorable court will consider was, in point of fact, an imperative official duty. And he denies that any and all substantive matters, in the said first article contained, in manner and form as the same are therein stated and set forth, do, by law, constitute a high misdemeanor in office, within the true intent and meaning of the Constitution of the United States.

ANSWER TO ARTICLE II.

And for answer to the second article this respondent says that he admits he did issue and deliver to said Lorenzo Thomas the said writing set forth in said second article, bearing date at Washington, District of Columbia, February 21, 1868, addressed to Brevet Major General Lorenzo Thomas, Adjutant General United States Army, Washington, District of Columbia, and he further admits that the same was so issued without the advice and consent of the Senate of the United States, then in session, but he denies that he thereby violated the Constitution of the United States, or any law thereof, or that he did thereby intend to violate the Constitution of the United States, or the provisions of any act of Congress; and this respondent refers to his answer to said first article for a full statement of the purposes and intentions with which said order was issued, and adopts the same as part of his answer to this article; and he further denies that there was then and there no vacancy in the said office of Secretary for the Department of War, or that he did then and there commit, or was guilty of a high misdemeanor in office, and this respondent maintains and will insist:

1. That at the date and delivery of said writing there was a vacancy existing in the office of Secretary for the Department of War.

2. That, notwithstanding the Senate of the United States was then in session, it was lawful and according to long and well established usage to empower and authorize the said Thomas to act as Secretary of War *ad interim*.

3. That, if the said act regulating the tenure of civil offices be held to be a valid law, no provision of the same was violated by the issuing of said order or by the designation of said Thomas to act as Secretary of War *ad interim*.

ANSWER TO ARTICLE III.

And for answer to said third article this respondent says that he abides by his answer to said first and second articles, in so far as the same are responsive to the allegations contained in the said third article, and, without here again repeating the same answer, prays the same be taken as an answer to this third article as fully as if here again set out at length; and as to the new allegation contained in said third article, that this respondent did appoint the said Thomas to be Secretary for the Department of War *ad interim*, this respondent denies that he gave any other authority to said Thomas than such as appears in said written authority set out in said article, by which he authorized and empowered said Thomas to act as Secretary for the Department of War *ad interim*; and he denies that the same amounts to an appointment and insists that it is only a designation of an officer of that Department to act temporarily as Secretary for the Department of War *ad interim* until an appointment should be made. But, whether the said written authority amounts to an appointment or to a temporary authority or designation, this respondent denies that in any sense he did thereby intend to violate the Constitution of the United States, or that he thereby intended to give the said order the character or effect of an appointment in the constitutional or legal sense of that term. He further denies that there was no vacancy in said office of Secretary for the Department of War existing at the date of said written authority.

ANSWER TO ARTICLE IV.

And for answer to said fourth article this respondent denies that on the said 21st day of February, 1868, at Washington aforesaid or at any other time or place, he did unlawfully conspire with the said Lorenzo Thomas, or with the said Thomas and any other person or persons, with intent by intimidations and threats unlawfully to hinder and prevent the said Stanton from holding said office of Secretary for the Department of War in violation of the Constitution of the United States or of the provisions of the said act of Congress in said article mentioned, or that he did then and there commit or was guilty of a high crime in office. On the contrary thereof, protesting that the said Stanton was not then and there lawfully the Secretary for the Department of War, this respondent states that his sole purpose in authorizing the said Thomas to act as Secretary for the Department of War *ad interim* was, as is fully stated in his answer to the said first article, to bring the question of the right of the said Stanton to hold said office, notwithstanding his said suspension and notwithstanding the said order of removal and notwithstanding the said authority of the said Thomas to act as Secretary of War *ad interim*, to the test of a final decision by the Supreme Court of the United States in the earliest practicable mode by which the question could be brought before that tribunal.

This respondent did not conspire or agree with the said Thomas or any other person or persons to use intimidation or threats to hinder or prevent the said Stanton from holding the said office of Secretary for the Department of War, nor did this respondent at any time command or advise the said Thomas or any other person or persons to resort to or use either threats or intimidation for that purpose. The only means in the contemplation or purpose of respondent to be used are set forth fully in the said orders of February 21, the first addressed to Mr. Stanton and the second to the said Thomas. By the first order the respondent notified Mr. Stanton that he was removed from the said office, and that his functions as Secretary for the Department of War were to terminate upon the receipt of that order, and he also thereby notified the said Stanton that the said Thomas had been authorized to act as Secretary for the Department of War *ad interim*, and ordered the said Stanton to transfer to him all the records, books, papers, and other public property in his custody and charge; and by the second order this respondent notified the said Thomas of the removal from office of the said Stanton, and authorized him to act as Secretary for the Department of War *ad interim*, and directed him to immediately enter upon the discharge of the duties pertaining to that office, and to receive the transfer of all the records, books, papers, and other public property from Mr. Stanton then in his custody and charge.

Respondent gave no instructions to the said Thomas to use intimidation or threats to enforce obedience to these orders. He gave him no authority to call in the aid of the military or any other force to enable him to obtain possession of the office, or of the books, papers, records, or property thereof. The only agency resorted to or intended to be resorted to was by means of the said executive orders requiring obedience. But the Secretary for the Department of War refused to obey these orders, and still holds undisturbed possession and custody of that Department, and of the records, books, papers, and other public property therein. Respondent further states that, in execution of the orders so by this respondent given to the said Thomas, he, the said Thomas, proceeded in a peaceful manner to demand of the said Stanton a surrender to him of the public property in the said Department, and to vacate the possession of the same, and to allow him, the said Thomas, peaceably to exercise the duties devolved upon him by authority of the President. That, as this respondent has been informed and believes, the said Stanton peremptorily refused obedience to the orders so issued. Upon such refusal no force or threat of force was used by the said Thomas, by authority of the President or otherwise, to enforce obedience, either then or at any subsequent time.

This respondent doth here except to the sufficiency of the allegations contained in said fourth article, and states for ground of exception that it is not stated that there was any agreement between this respondent and the said Thomas, or any other person or persons, to use intimidation and threats, nor is there any allegation as to the nature of said intimidation and threats, or that there was any agreement to carry them into execution, or that any step was taken or agreed to be taken to carry them into execution, and that the allegation in said article that the intent of said conspiracy was to use intimidation and threats is wholly insufficient, inasmuch as it is not alleged that the said intent formed the basis or became a part of any agreement between the said alleged conspirators, and, furthermore, that there is no allegation of any conspiracy or agreement to use intimidation or threats.

ANSWER TO ARTICLE V.

And for answer to the said fifth article this respondent denies that on the said 21st day of February, 1868, or at any other time or times in the same year before the said 2d day of March, 1868, or at any prior or subsequent time, at Washington aforesaid or at any other place, this respondent did unlawfully conspire with the said Thomas, or with any other person or persons, to prevent or hinder the execution of the said act entitled "An act regulating the tenure of certain civil offices," or that, in pursuance of said alleged conspiracy, he did unlawfully attempt to prevent the said Edwin M. Stanton from holding said office of Secretary for the Department of War, or that he did thereby commit, or that he was thereby guilty of, a high misdemeanor in office. Respondent, protesting that said Stanton was not then and there Secretary for the Department of War, begs leave to refer to his answer given to the fourth article and to his answer given to the first article as to his intent and purpose in issuing the orders for the removal of Mr. Stanton and the authority given to the said Thomas, and prays equal benefit therefrom as if the same were here again repeated and fully set forth.

And this respondent excepts to the sufficiency of the said fifth article, and states his ground for such exception, that it is not alleged by what means or by what agreement the said alleged conspiracy was formed or agreed to be carried out, or in what way the same was attempted to be carried out, or what were the acts done in pursuance thereof.

ANSWER TO ARTICLE VI.

And for answer to the said sixth article, this respondent denies that on the said 21st day of February, 1868, at Washington aforesaid, or at any other time or place, he did unlawfully conspire with the said Thomas by force to seize, take, or possess, the property of the United States in the Department of War, contrary to the provisions of the said acts referred to in the said article, or either of them, or with intent to violate either of them. Respondent, protesting that said Stanton was not then and there Secretary for the Department of War, not only denies the said conspiracy as charged, but also denies any unlawful intent in reference to the custody and charge of the property of the United States in the said Department of War, and again refers to his former answers for a full statement of his intent and purpose in the premises.

ANSWER TO ARTICLE VII.

And for answer to the said seventh article respondent denies that on the said 21st day of February, 1868, at Washington aforesaid, or at any other time and place, he did unlawfully conspire with the said Thomas with intent unlawfully to seize, take, or possess the property of the United States in the Department of War with intent to violate or disregard the said act in the said seventh article referred to, or that he did then and there commit a high misdemeanor in office. Respondent, protesting that the said Stanton was not then and there Secretary for the Department of War, again refers to his former answers, in so far as they are applicable, to show the intent with which he proceeded in the premises, and prays equal benefit therefrom, as if the same were here again fully repeated. Respondent further takes exception to the sufficiency of the allegations of this article as to the conspiracy alleged upon the same grounds as stated in the exception set forth in his answer to said article fourth.

ANSWER TO ARTICLE VIII.

And for answer to the said eighth article this respondent denies that on the 21st day of February, 1868, at Washington aforesaid, or at any other time and place, he did issue and deliver to the said Thomas the said letter of authority set forth in the said eighth article, with the intent unlawfully to control the disbursements of the money appropriated for the military service and for the Department of War. This respondent, protesting that there was a vacancy in the office of Secretary for the Department of War, admits that he did issue the said letter of authority, and he denies that the same was with any unlawful intent whatever, either to violate the Constitution of the United States or any act of Congress. On the contrary, this respondent again affirms that his sole intent was to vindicate his authority as President of the United States, and by peaceful means to bring the question of the right of the said Stanton to continue to hold the said office of Secretary of War to a final decision before the Supreme Court of the United States, as has been hereinbefore set forth; and he prays the same benefit from his answer in the premises as if the same were here again repeated at length.

ANSWER TO ARTICLE IX.

And for answer to the said ninth article the respondent states that on the said 22d day of February, 1868, the following note was addressed to the said Emory by the private secretary of respondent:

EXECUTIVE MANSION,
WASHINGTON, D. C., *February* 22, 1868.
GENERAL: The President directs me to say that he will be pleased to have you call upon him as early as practicable.
Respectfully and truly yours,
WILLIAM G. MOORE,
United States Army.

General Emory called at the Executive Mansion according to this request. The object of respondent was to be advised by General Emory, as commander of the department of Washington, what changes had been made in the military affairs of the department. Respondent had been informed that various changes had been made, which in nowise had been brought to his notice or reported to him from the Department of War or from any other quarter, and desired to ascertain the facts. After the said Emory had explained in detail the changes which had taken place, said Emory called the attention of respondent to a general order which he referred to and which this respondent then sent for, when it was produced. It is as follows:

[General Orders No. 17.]

WAR DEPARTMENT,
ADJUTANT GENERAL'S OFFICE,
WASHINGTON, *March* 14, 1867.
The following acts of Congress are published for the information and government of all concerned:

* * * * * * * * *

II—PUBLIC—No. 85.
An act making appropriations for the support of the Army for the year ending June 30, 1868, and for other purposes.

* * * * * * * *

SEC. 2. *And be it further enacted,* That the headquarters of the General of the Army of the United States shall be at the city of Washington, and all orders and instructions relating to military operations issued by the President or Secretary of War shall be issued through the General of the Army, and in case of his inability through the next in rank. The General of the Army shall not be removed, suspended, or relieved from command or assigned to duty elsewhere than at said headquarters, except at his own request, without the previous approval of the Senate; and any orders or instructions relating to military operations issued contrary to the requirements of this section shall be null and void; and any officer who shall issue orders or instructions contrary to the provisions of this section shall be deemed guilty of a misdemeanor in office; and any officer of the Army who shall transmit, convey, or obey any orders or instructions so issued contrary to the provisions of this section, knowing that such orders were so issued, shall be liable to imprisonment for not less than two nor more than twenty years, upon conviction thereof in any court of competent jurisdiction.

* * * * * * * * *

Approved March 2, 1867.

* * * * * * * * *

By order of the Secretary of War.
E. D. TOWNSEND,
Assistant Adjutant General.
Official:
————, *Assistant Adjutant General.*

General Emory not only called the attention of respondent to this order, but to the fact that it was in conformity with a section contained in an appropriation act passed by Congress. Respondent, after reading the order, observed, "This is not in accordance with the Constitution of the United States, which makes me Commander-in-Chief of the Army and Navy, or of the language of the commission which you hold." General Emory then stated that this order had met respondent's approval. Respondent then said in reply, in substance, "Am I to understand that the President of the United States cannot give an order but through the General-in-Chief, or General Grant?" General Emory again reiterated the statement that it had met respondent's approval, and that it was the opinion of some of the leading lawyers of the country that this order was constitutional. With some further conversation, respondent then inquired the names of the lawyers who had given the opinion, and he mentioned the names of two. Respondent then said that the object of the law was very evident, referring to the clause in the appropriation act upon which the order purported to be based. This, according to respondent's recollection was the substance of the conversation had with General Emory.

Respondent denies that any allegations in the said article of any instructions or declarations given to the said Emory then or at any other time contrary to or in addition to what is hereinbefore set forth are true. Respondent denies that, in said conversation with said Emory, he had any other intent than to express the opinions then given to the said Emory, nor did he then or at any time request or order the said Emory to disobey any law or any order issued in conformity with any law, or intend to offer any inducement to the said Emory to violate any law. What this respondent then said to General Emory was simply the expression of an opinion which he then fully believed to be sound and which he yet believes to be so, and that is, that by the express provisions of the Constitution this respondent, as President, is made the Commander-in-Chief of the Armies of the United States, and as such he is to be respected, and that his orders, whether issued through the War Department or through the General-in-Chief, or by any other channel of communication, are entitled to respect and obedience, and that such constitutional power cannot be taken from him by virtue of any act of Congress. Respondent doth therefore deny that by the expression of such opinion he did commit or was guilty of a high misdemeanor in office; and this respondent doth further say that the said article nine lays no foundation whatever for the conclusion stated in the said article, that the respondent, by reason of the allegations therein contained, was guilty of a high misdemeanor in office.

In reference to the statement made by General Emory that this respondent had approved of said act of Congress containing the section referred to, the respondent admits that his formal approval was given to said act, but accompanied the same by the following message, addressed and sent with the act to the House of Representatives, in which House the said act originated, and from which it came to respondent:

To the House of Representatives:

The act entitled "An act making appropriations for the support of the Army for the year ending June 30, 1868, and for other purposes," contains provisions to which I must call attention. These provisions are contained in the second section, which, in certain cases, virtually deprives the President of his constitutional functions as Commander-in-Chief of the Army, and in the sixth section, which denies to ten States of the Union their constitutional right to protect themselves, in any emergency, by means of their own militia. These provisions are out of place in an appropriation act, but I am compelled to defeat these necessary appropriations if I withhold my signature from the act. Pressed by these considerations, I feel constrained to return the bill with my signature, but to accompany it with my earnest protest against the sections which I have indicated.

WASHINGTON, D. C., *March 2, 1867.*

Respondent, therefore, did no more than to express to said Emory the same opinion which he had so expressed to the House of Representatives.

ANSWER TO ARTICLE X.

And in answer to the tenth article and specifications thereof the respondent says that on the 14th and 15th days of August, in the year 1866, a political convention of delegates from all or most of the States and Territories of the Union was held in the city of Philadelphia, under the name and style of the National Union Convention, for the purpose of maintaining and advancing certain political views and opinions before the people of the United States, and for their support and adoption in the exercise of the constitutional suffrage, in the elections of Representatives and Delegates in Congress, which were soon to occur in many of the States and Territories of the Union; which said convention, in the course of its proceedings, and in furtherance of the objects of the same, adopted a "declaration of principles" and "an address to the people of the United States," and appointed a committee of two of its members from each State and of one from each Territory and one from the District of Columbia to wait upon the President of the United States and present to him a copy of the proceedings of the convention; that on the 18th day of said month of August this committee waited upon the President of the United States at the Executive Mansion, and was received by him in one of the rooms thereof, and by their chairman, Hon. Reverdy Johnson, then and now a Senator of the United States, acting and speaking in their behalf, presented a copy of the proceedings of the convention, and addressed the President of the United States in a speech, of which a copy (according to a published report of the same, and as the respondent believes substantially a correct report,) is hereto annexed as a part of this answer, and marked Exhibit C.

That thereupon, and in reply to the address of said committee by their chairman, this respondent addressed the said committee so waiting upon him in one of the rooms of the Executive Mansion; and this respondent believes that this his address to said committee is the occasion referred to in the first specification of the tenth article; but this respondent does not admit that the passages therein set forth, as if extracts from a speech or address of this respondent upon said occasion, correctly or justly present his speech or address upon said occasion, but, on the contrary, this respondent demands and insists that if this honorable court shall deem the said article and the said first specification thereof to contain allegation of matter cognizable by this honorable court as a high misdemeanor in office, within the intent and meaning of the Constitution of the United States, and shall receive or allow proof in support of the same, that proof shall be required to be made of the actual speech and address of this respondent on said occasion, which this respondent denies that said article and specification contain or correctly or justly represent.

And this respondent, further answering the tenth article and the specifications thereof, says that at Cleveland, in the State of Ohio, and on the 3d day of September, in the year 1866, he was attended by a large assemblage of his fellow-citizens, and in deference and obedience to their call and demand he addressed them upon matters of public and political consideration; and this respondent believes that said occasion and address are referred to in the second specification of the tenth article; but this respondent does not admit that the passages therein set forth, as if extracts from a speech of this respondent on said occasion, correctly or justly present his speech or address upon said occasion; but, on the contrary, this respondent demands and insists that if this honorable court shall deem the said article and the said second specification thereof to contain allegation of matter cognizable by this honorable court as a high misdemeanor in office, within the intent and meaning of the Constitution of the United States, and shall receive or allow proof in support of the same, that proof shall be required to be made of the actual speech and address of this repondent on said occasion. which this respondent denies that said article and specification contain or correctly or justly represent.

And this respondent, further answering the tenth article and the specifications thereof, says that at St. Louis, in the State of Missouri, and on the 8th day of September, in the year 1866, he was attended by a numerous assemblage of his fellow-citizens, and in deference and obedience to their call and demand he addressed them upon matters of public and political consideration; and this respondent believes that said occasion and address are referred to in the third specification of the tenth article; but this respondent does not admit that the passages therein set forth, as if extracts from a speech of this respondent on said occasion, correctly or justly present his speech or address upon said occasion; but, on the contrary, this respondent demands and insists that if this honorable court shall deem the said article and the said third specification thereof to contain allegation of matter cognizable by this honorable court as a high misdemeanor in office, within the intent and meaning of the Constitution of the United States, and shall receive or allow proof in support of the same, that proof shall be required to be made of the actual speech and address of this respondent on said occasion, which this respondent denies that the said article and specification contain or correctly or justly represent.

And this respondent, further answering the tenth article, protesting that he has not been unmindful of the high duties of his office, or of the harmony or courtesies which ought to exist and be maintained between the executive and legislative branches of the Government of the United States, denies that he has ever intended or designed to set aside the rightful authority or powers of Congress, or attempted to bring into disgrace, ridicule, hatred, contempt, or reproach the Congress of the United States, or either branch thereof, or to impair or destroy the regard or respect of all or any of the good people of the United States for the Congress or the rightful legislative power thereof, or to excite the odium or resentment of all or any of the good people of the United States against Congress and the laws by it duly and constitutionally enacted. This respondent further says that at all times he has, in his official acts as President, recognized the authority of the several Congresses of the United States as constituted and organized during his administration of the office of President of the United States.

And this respondent, further answering, says that he has, from time to time, under his constitutional right and duty as President of the United States, communicated to Congress his views and opinions in regard to such acts or resolutions thereof as, being submitted to him as President of the United States in pursuance of the Constitution, seemed to this respondent to require such communications; and he has, from time to time, in the exercise of that freedom of speech which belongs to him as a citizen of the United States, and, in his political relations as President of the United States to the people of the United States, is upon fit occasions a duty of the highest obligation, expressed to his fellow-citizens his views and opinions respecting the measures and proceedings of Congress; and that in such addresses to his fellow-citizens and in such his communications to Congress he has expressed his views, opinions, and judgment of and concerning the actual constitution of the two Houses of Congress without representation therein of certain States of the Union, and of the effect that in wisdom and justice, in the opinion and judgment of this respondent, Congress, in its legislation and proceedings, should give to this political circumstance; and whatsoever he has thus communicated to Congress or addressed to his fellow-citizens or any assemblage thereof, this respondent says was and is within and according to his right and privilege as an American citizen and his right and duty as President of the United States.

And this respondent, not waiving or at all disparaging his right of freedom of opinion and of freedom of speech, as hereinbefore or hereinafter more particularly set forth, but claiming and insisting upon the same, further answering the said tenth article, says that the views and opinions expressed by this respondent in his said addresses to the assemblages of his fellow-citizens, as in said article or in this answer thereto mentioned, are not and were not intended to be other or different from those expressed by him in his communications to Congress—that the eleven States lately in insurrection never had ceased to be States of the Union, and that they were then entitled to representation in Congress by loyal Representatives and Senators as fully as the other States of the Union, and that, consequently, the Congress, as then constituted, was not, in fact, a Congress of all the States, but a Congress of only a part of the States. This respondent, always protesting against the unauthorized exclusion therefrom of the said eleven States, nevertheless gave his assent to all laws passed by said Congress which did not, in his opinion and judgment, violate the Constitution, exercising his constitutional authority of returning bills to said Congress with his objections when they appeared to him to be unconstitutional or inexpedient.

And, further, this respondent has also expressed the opinion, both in his communications to Congress and in his addresses to the people, that the policy adopted by Congress in reference to the States lately in insurrection did not tend to peace, harmony, and union, but, on the contrary, did tend to disunion and the permanent disruption of the States, and that, in following its said policy, laws had been passed by congress in violation of the fundamental principles of the Government, and which tended to consolidation and despotism; and, such being his deliberate opinions, he would have felt himself unmindful of the high duties of his office if he had failed to express them in his communications to Congress or in his addresses to the people when called upon by them to express his opinions on matters of public and political consideration.

And this respondent, further answering the tenth article, says that he has always claimed and insisted, and now claims and insists, that both in his personal and private capacity of a citizen of the United States, and in the political relations of the President of the United States to the people of the United States, whose servant, under the duties and reponsibilities of the Constitution of the United States, the President of 'the United States is and should always remain, this respondent had and has the full right, and in his office of President of the United States is held to the high duty, of forming, and on fit occasions expressing, opinions of and concerning the legislation of Congress, proposed or completed, in respect of its wisdom, expediency, justice, worthiness, objects, purposes, and public and political motives and tendencies; and within and as a part of such right and duty to form, and on fit occasions to express, opinions of and concerning the public character and conduct, views, purposes, objects, motives, and tendencies of all men engaged in the public service, as well in Congress as otherwise, and under no other rules or limits upon this right of freedom of opinion and of freedom of speech, or of responsibility and amenability for the actual exercise of such freedom of opinion and freedom of speech, than attend upon such rights and their exercise on the part of all other citizens of the United States, and on the part of all their public servants.

And this respondent, further answering said tenth article, says that the several occasions on which, as is alleged in the several specifications of said article, this respondent addressed his fellow-citizens on subjects of public and political considerations were not, nor was any one of them, sought or planned by this respondent; but, on the contrary, each of said occasions arose upon the exercise of a lawful and accustomed right of the people of the United States to call upon their public servants and express to them their opinions, wishes, and feelings upon matters of public and political consideration, and to invite from such, their public servants, an expression of their opinions, views, and feelings on matters of public and political consideration: and this respondent claims and insists before this honor-

able court, and before all the people of the United States, that of or concerning this his right of freedom of opinion and of freedom of speech, and this his exercise of such rights on all matters of public and political consideration, and in respect of all public servants or persons whatsoever engaged in or connected therewith, this respondent, as a citizen or as President of the United States, is not subject to question, inquisition, impeachment, or inculpation in any form or manner whatsoever.

And this respondent says that neither the said tenth article nor any specification thereof nor any allegation therein contained touches or relates to any official act or doing of this respondent in the office of President of the United States or in the discharge of any of its constitutional or legal duties or responsibilities; but said article and the specifications and allegations thereof, wholly and in every part thereof, question only the discretion or propriety of freedom of opinion or freedom of speech, as exercised by this respondent as a citizen of the United States in his personal right and capacity, and without allegation or imputation against this respondent of the violation of any law of the United States touching or relating to freedom of speech or its exercise by the citizens of the United States, or by this respondent as one of the said citizens or otherwise; and he denies that by reason of any matter in said article or its specifications alleged he has said or done anything indecent or unbecoming in the Chief Magistrate of the United States, or that he has brought the high office of the President of the United States into contempt, ridicule, or disgrace, or that he has committed or has been guilty of a high misdemeanor in office.

ANSWER TO ARTICLE XI.

And in answer to the eleventh article this respondent denies that on the 18th day of August, in the year 1866, at the city of Washington, in the District of Columbia, he did, by public speech or otherwise, declare or affirm, in substance or at all, that the Thirty-Ninth Congress of the United States was not a Congress of the United States authorized by the Constitution to exercise legislative power under the same, or that he did then and there declare or affirm that the said Thirty-Ninth Congress was a Congress of only part of the States in any sense or meaning other than that ten States of the Union were denied representation therein; or that he made any or either of the declarations or affirmations in this behalf, in the said article alleged, as denying or intending to deny that the legislation of said Thirty-Ninth Congress was valid or obligatory upon this respondent, except so far as this respondent saw fit to approve the same; and as to the allegation in said article, that he did thereby intend or mean to be understood that the said Congress had not power to propose amendments to the Constitution, this respondent says that in said address he said nothing in reference to the subject of amendments of the Constitution, nor was the question of the competency of the said Congress to propose such amendments, without the participation of said excluded States, at the time of said address, in any way mentioned or considered or referred to by this respondent, nor in what he did say had he any intent regarding the same, and he denies the allegation so made to the contrary thereof. But this respondent, in further answer to, and in respect of, the said allegations of the said eleventh article hereinbefore traversed and denied, claims and insists upon his personal and official right of freedom of opinion and freedom of speech, and his duty in his political relations as President of the United States to the people of the United States in the exercise of such freedom of opinion and freedom of speech, in the same manner, form, and effect as he has in this behalf stated the same in his answer to the said tenth article, and with the same effect as if he here repeated the same ; and he further claims and insists, as in said answer to said tenth article he has claimed and insisted, that he is not subject to question, inquisition, impeachment, or inculpation, in any form or manner, of or concerning such rights of freedom of opinion or freedom of speech or his said alleged exercise thereof.

And this respondent further denies that, on the 21st day of February, in the year 1868, or at any other time, at the city of Washington, in the District of Columbia, in pursuance of any such declaration as is in that behalf in said eleventh article alleged, or otherwise, he did unlawfully, and in disregard of the requirement of the Constitution that he should take care that the laws should be faithfully executed, attempt to prevent the execution of an act entitled "An act regulating the tenure of certain civil offices," passed March 2, 1867, by unlawfully devising or contriving, or attempting to devise or contrive, means by which he should prevent Edwin M. Stanton from forthwith resuming the functions of Secretary for the Department of War; or by unlawfully devising or contriving, or attempting to devise or contrive, means to prevent the execution of an act entitled "An act making appropriations for the support of the Army for the fiscal year ending June 30, 1868, and for other purposes," approved March 2, 1867, or to prevent the execution of an act entitled "An act to provide for the more efficient government of the rebel States," passed March 2, 1867.

And this respondent, further answering the said eleventh article, says that he has, in his answer to the first article, set forth in detail the acts, steps, and proceedings done and taken by this respondent to and toward or in the matter of the suspension or removal of the said Edwin M. Stanton in or from the office of Secretary for the Department of War, with the times, modes, circumstances, intents, views, purposes, and opinions of official obligation and duty under and with which such acts, steps,

C. I.—3.

and proceedings were done and taken ; and he makes answer to this eleventh article of the matters in his answer to the first article, pertaining to the suspension or removal of said Edwin M. Stanton, to the same intent and effect as if they were here repeated and set forth.

And this respondent, further answering the said eleventh article, denies that by means or reason of anything in said article alleged this respondent, as President of the United States, did, on the 21st day of February, 1868, or at any other day or time, commit, or that he was guilty of, a high misdemeanor in office.

And this respondent, further answering the said eleventh article, says that the same and the matters therein contained do not charge or allege the commission of any act whatever by this respondent, in his office of President of the United States, nor the omission by this respondent of any act of official obligation or duty in his office of President of the United States ; nor does the said article nor the matters therein contained name, designate, describe, or define any act or mode or form of attempt, device, contrivance, or means, or of attempt at device, contrivance, or means, whereby this respondent can know or understand what act or mode or form of attempt, device, contrivance, or means, or of attempt at device, contrivance, or means, are imputed to or charged against this respondent, in his office of President of the United States, or intended so to be, or whereby this respondent can more fully or definitely make answer unto the said article than he hereby does.

And this respondent, in submitting to this honorable court this his answer to the articles of impeachment exhibited against him, respectfully reserves leave to amend and add to the same from time to time, as may become necessary or proper, and when and as such necessity and propriety shall appear.

ANDREW JOHNSON.

HENRY STANBERY,
B. R. CURTIS,
THOMAS A. R. NELSON,
WILLIAM M. EVARTS,
W. S. GROESBECK,
Of Counsel.

EXHIBIT A.
Message, March 2, 1867.

To the Senate of the United States :

I have carefully examined the bill to regulate the tenure of certain civil offices. The material portion of the bill is contained in the first section, and is of the effect following, namely :

That every person holding any civil office to which he has been appointed by and with the advice and consent of the Senate, and every person who shall hereafter be appointed to any such office, and shall become duly qualified to act therein, is and shall be entitled to hold such office until a successor shall have been appointed by the President, with the advice and consent of the Senate, and duly qualified ; and that the Secretaries of State, of the Treasury, of War, of the Navy, and of the Interior, the Postmaster General, and the Attorney General, shall hold their offices respectively for and during the term of the President by whom they may have been appointed, and for one month thereafter, subject to removal by and with the advice and consent of the Senate.

These provisions are qualified by a reservation in the fourth section, "that nothing contained in the bill shall be construed to extend the term of any office the duration of which is limited by law." In effect the bill provides that the President shall not remove from their places any of the civil officers whose terms of service are not limited by law without the advice and consent of the Senate of the United States. The bill, in this respect, conflicts, in my judgment, with the Constitution of the United States. The question, as Congress is well aware, is by no means a new one. That the power of removal is constitutionally vested in the President of the United States is a principle which has been not more distinctly declared by judicial authority and judicial commentators than it has been uniformly practiced upon by the legislative and executive departments of the Government. The question arose in the House of Representatives so early as the 16th day of June, 1789, on the bill for establishing an executive Department, denominated "The Department of Foreign Affairs." The first clause of the bill, after recapitulating the functions of that officer and defining his duties, had these' words: "To be removable from office by the President of the United States." It was moved to strike out these words, and the motion was sustained with great ability and vigor. It was insisted that the President could not constitutionally exercise the power of removal exclusive of the Senate; that the Federalist so interpreted the Constitution when arguing for its adoption by the several States; that the Constitution had nowhere given the President power of removal, either expressly or by strong implication; but, on the contrary, had distinctly provided for removals from office by impeachment only. A construction which denied the power of removal by the President was further maintained by arguments drawn from the danger of the abuse of the power; from the supposed tendency of an exposure of public officers to capricious removal, to impair the efficiency of the civil service; from the alleged injustice and hardship of displacing incumbents, dependent upon their official stations, without sufficient consideration; from a supposed want of responsibilty on the part of the President, and from an imagined defect of guarantees against a vicious President, who might incline to abuse the power.

On the other hand, an exclusive power of removal by the President was defended as a true exposition of the text of the Constitution. It was maintained that there are certain causes for which persons ought to be removed from office without being guilty of treason, bribery, or malfeasance, and that the nature of things demands that it should be so. "Suppose," it was said, "a man becomes insane by the visitation of God, and is likely to ruin our affairs: are the hands of Government to be confined from warding off the evil? Suppose a person in office not possessing the talents he was judged to have at the time of the appointment: is the error not to be corrected? Suppose he acquire vicious habits and incurable indolence, or totally neglect the duties of his office, which shall work mischief to the public welfare: is there no way to arrest the threatened danger? Suppose he become odious and unpopular by reason of the measures he pursues, and this he may do without committing any positive offense against the law: must he preserve his office in despite of the popular will? Suppose him grasping for his own aggrandizement and the elevation of his connections by every means short of the treason defined by the Constitution, hurrying your affairs to the precipice of destruction, endangering your domestic tranquility, plundering you of the means of defense, alienating the affections of your allies, and promoting the spirit of discord: must the tardy, tedious, desultory road, by way of impeachment, be traveled to overtake the man who, barely confining himself within the letter of the law, is employed in "drawing off the vital principle of the Government?" The nature of things, the great objects of society, the express objects of the Constitution itself require that this thing should be otherwise. To unite the Senate with the President "in the exercise of the power," it was said, "would involve us" in the most serious difficulty. "Suppose a discovery of any of these events should take place when the Senate is not in session, how is the remedy to be applied? The evil could be avoided in no other way than by the Senate sitting always." In regard to the danger of the power being abused if exercised by one man, it was said "that the danger is as great with respect to the Senate, who are assembled from various parts of the continent, with different impressions and opinions;" that such a body is more likely to misuse the power of removal than the man whom the united voice of America calls to the presidential chair. As the nature of government requires the power of removal, it was maintained "that it should be exercised in this way by the hand capable of exerting itself with effect, and the power must be conferred on the President by the Constitution as the executive officer of the Government." Mr. Madison, whose adverse opinion in the Federalist had been relied upon by those who denied the exclusive power, now participated in the debate. He declared that he had reviewed his former opinions, and he summed up the whole case as follows:

"The Constitution affirms that the executive power is vested in the President. Are there exceptions to this proposition? Yes, there are. The Constitution says that in appointing to office the Senate shall be associated with the President, unless in the case of inferior officers, when the law shall otherwise direct. Have we (that is, Congress) a right to extend this exception? I believe not. If the Constitution has invested all executive power in the President, I return to assert that the Legislature has no right to diminish or modify his executive authority. The question now resolves itself into this: is there power of displacing an executive power? I conceive that if any power whatever is in the Executive it is in the power of appointing, overseeing, and controlling those who execute the laws. If the Constitution had not qualified the power of the President in appointing to office by associating the Senate with him in that business, would it not be clear that he would have the right by virtue of his executive power to make such appointment? Should we be authorized, in defiance of that clause in the Constitution—'the executive power shall be vested in the President'—to unite the Senate with the President in the appointment to office? I conceive not. It is admitted that we should not be authorized to do this. I think it may be disputed whether we have a right to associate them in removing persons from office, the one power being as much of an executive nature as the other; and the first is authorized by being excepted out of the general rule established by the Constitution in these words: 'The executive power shall be vested in the President.'"

The question thus ably and exhaustively argued was decided by the House of Representatives, by a vote of 34 to 20, in favor of the principle that the executive power of removal is vested by the Constitution in the Executive, and in the Senate by the casting vote of the Vice President. The question has often been raised in subsequent times of high excitement, and the practice of the Government has nevertheless conformed in all cases to the decision thus early made.

The question was revived during the administration of President Jackson, who made, as is well recollected, a very large number of removals, which were made an occasion of close and rigorous scrutiny and remonstrance. The subject was long and earnestly debated in the Senate, and the early construction of the Constitution was nevertheless freely accepted as binding and conclusive upon Congress.

The question came before the Supreme Court of the United States in January, 1839, *ex parte* Herren. It was declared by the court on that occasion that the power of removal from office was a subject much disputed, and upon which a great diversity of opinion was entertained in the early history of the Government. This related, however, to the power of the President to remove officers appointed with the concurrence of the Senate, and the great question was whether the removal was to be by the President alone or with the concurrence of the Senate, both constituting the appointing power. No one denied the power of the President and Senate jointly to remove where the tenure of the office was not fixed by the Constitution, which was a full recognition of the principle that the power of removal was incident to the power of appointment; but it was very early adopted as a practical construction of the Constitution that this power was vested in the President alone, and such would appear to have been the legislative construction of the Constitution, for in the organization of the three great Departments of State, War, and Treasury, in 1789, provision was made for the

appointment of a subordinate officer by the head of the Department, who should have charge of the records, books, and papers appertaining to the office when the head of the Department should be removed from office by the President of the United States. When the Navy Department was established, in the year 1798, provision was made for the charge and custody of the books, records, and documents of the Department in case of vacancy in the office of Secretary, by removal or otherwise. It is not here said "by removal of the President," as it is done with respect to the heads of the other Departments; yet there can be no doubt that he holds his office with the same tenure as the other Secretaries, and is removable by the President. The change of phraseology arose probably from its having become the settled and well-understood construction of the Constitution that the power of removal was vested in the President alone in such cases, although the appointment of the officer is by the President and Senate. (13 Peters, page 139.)

Our most distinguished and accepted commentators upon the Constitution concur in the construction thus early given by Congress, and thus sanctioned by the Supreme Court. After a full analysis of the congressional debate to which I have referred, Mr. Justice Story comes to this conclusion:

"After a most animated discussion, the vote finally taken in the House of Representatives was affirmative of the power of removal in the President without any coöperation of the Senate by the vote of 34 members against 20. In the Senate the clause in the bill affirming the power was carried by the casting vote of the Vice President. That the final decision of this question so made was greatly influenced by the exalted character of the President then in office was asserted at the time, and has always been believed; yet the doctrine was opposed as well as supported by the highest talent and patriotism of the country. The public have acquiesced in this decision, and it constitutes perhaps the most extraordinary case in the history of the Government of a power conferred by implication on the Executive by the assent of a bare majority of Congress which has not been questioned on many other occasions."

The commentator adds:

"Nor is this general acquiescence and silence without a satisfactory explanation."

Chancellor Kent's remarks on the subject are as follows: "On the first organization of the Government it was made a question whether the power of removal in case of officers appointed to hold at pleasure resided nowhere but in the body which appointed," and, of course, whether the consent of the Senate was not requisite to remove. This was the construction given to the Constitution while it was pending for ratification before the State conventions by the author of the Federalist. But the construction which was given to the Constitution by Congress after great consideration and discussion was different. The words of the act (establishing the Treasury Department) are, "and whenever the same shall be removed from office by the President of the United States, or in any case of vacancy in the office, the assistant shall act." This amounted to a legislative construction of the Constitution, and it has ever since been acquiesced in and acted upon as a decisive authority in the case.

It applies equally to every other officer of the Government appointed by the President whose term of duration is not specially declared. It is supported by the weighty reason that the subordinate officers in the executive department ought to hold at the pleasure of the head of the department, because he is invested generally with the executive authority, and the participation in that authority by the Senate was an exception to a general principle, and ought to be taken strictly. The President is the great responsible officer for the execution of the law, and the power of removal was incidental to that duty, and might often be requisite to fulfill it. Thus has the important question presented by this bill been settled, in the language of the late Daniel Webster, (who, while dissenting from it, admitted that it was settled,) by construction, settled by the practice of the Government, and settled by statute. The events of the last war furnished a practical confirmation of the wisdom of the Constitution as it has hitherto been maintained in many of its parts, including that which is now the subject of consideration. When the war broke out rebel enemies, traitors, abettors, and sympathisers were found in every department of the Government, as well in the civil service as in the land and naval military service. They were found in Congress and among the keepers of the Capitol, in foreign missions, in each and all of the Executive Departments, in the judicial service, in the Post Office, and among the agents for conducting Indian affairs, and upon probable suspicion they were promptly displaced by my predecessor, so far as they held their offices under executive authority, and their duties were confided to new and loyal successors. No complaints against that power or doubts of its wisdom were entertained in any quarter. I sincerely trust and believe that no such civil war is likely to occur again. I cannot doubt, however, that in whatever form and on whatever occasion sedition can rise, an effort to hinder or embarrass or defeat the legitimate action of this Government, whether by preventing the collection of revenue or disturbing the public peace, or separating the States, or betraying the country to a foreign enemy, the power of removal from office by the Executive, as it has heretofore existed and been practiced, will be found indispensable. Under these circumstances, as a depository of the executive authority of the nation, I do not feel at liberty to unite with Congress in reversing it by giving my approval of the bill.

At the early day when the question was settled, and, indeed, at the several periods when it has subsequently been agitated, the success of the Constitution of the United States as a new and peculiar system of free representative government was held doubtful in other countries, and was even a subject of patriotic apprehension among the American people themselves. A trial of nearly eighty years, through the vicissitudes of foreign conflicts and of civil war, is confidently regarded as having extinguished all such doubts and apprehensions for the future. During that eighty years the people of the United States have enjoyed a measure of security, peace, prosperity, and happiness never surpassed by any nation. It cannot be doubted that the triumphant success of the Constitution is due to the wonderful wisdom with which the functions of government were distributed between the three principal departments—the legislative, the executive, and the judicial—and to the fidelity with which each has confined itself or been confined by the general voice of the nation within its peculiar and proper sphere.

While a just, proper, and watchful jealousy of executive power constantly prevails, as it ought ever to prevail, yet it is equally true that an efficient Executive, capable, in the language of the oath prescribed to the President, of executing the laws within the sphere of executive action, of preserving, protecting, and defending the Constitution of the United States, is an indispensable security for tranquillity at home, and peace, honor, and safety abroad. Governments have been erected in many countries upon our model. If one or many of them have thus far failed in fully securing to their people the benefits which we have derived from our system, it may be confidently asserted that their misfortune has resulted from their unfortunate failure to maintain the integrity of each of the three great departments while preserving harmony among them all.

Having at an early period accepted the Constitution in regard to the executive office in the sense to which it was interpreted with the concurrence of its founders, I have found no sufficient grounds in the arguments now opposed to that construction or in any assumed necessity of the times for changing those opinions. For these reasons I return the bill to the Senate, in which House it originated, for the further consideration of Congress, which the Constitution prescribes. Insomuch as the several parts of the bill which I have not considered are matters chiefly of detail, and are based altogether upon the theory of the Constitution from which I am obliged to dissent, I have not thought it necessary to examine them with a view to make them an occasion of distinct and special objections. Experience, I think, has shown that it is the easiest, as it is also the most attractive, of studies to frame constitutions for the self-government of free States and nations.

But I think experience has equally shown that it is the most difficult of all political labors to preserve and maintain such free constitutions of self-government when once happily established. I know no other way in which they can be preserved and maintained except by a constant adherence to them through the various vicissitudes of national existence, with such adaptations as may become necessary, always to be effected, however, through the agencies and in the forms prescribed in the original constitutions themselves. Whenever administration fails or seems to fail in securing any of the great ends for which republican government is established, the proper course seems to be to renew the original spirit and forms of the Constitution itself.

ANDREW JOHNSON.
WASHINGTON, *March 2, 1867.*

EXHIBIT B.
Message to the Senate, December 12, 1867.
To the Senate of the United States:

On the 12th of August last I suspended Mr. Stanton from the exercise of the office of Secretary of War, and on the same day designated General Grant to act as Secretary of War *ad interim.*

The following are copies of the Executive orders:

EXECUTIVE MANSION,
WASHINGTON, *August 12, 1867.*

SIR: By virtue of the power and authority vested in me, as President, by the Constitution and the laws of the United States, you are hereby suspended from office as Secretary of War, and will cease to exercise any and all functions pertaining to the same.

You will at once transfer to General Ulysses S. Grant, who has this day been authorized and empowered to act as Secretary of War *ad interim,* all records, books, papers, and other public property now in your custody and charge.

Hon. EDWIN M. STANTON, *Secretary of War.*

EXECUTIVE MANSION,
WASHINGTON, D. C., *August 12, 1867.*

SIR: Hon. Edwin M. Stanton having been this day suspended as Secretary of War, you are hereby authorized and empowered to act as Secretary of War *ad interim,* and will at once enter upon the discharge of the duties of the office.

The Secretary of War has been instructed to transfer to you all the records, books, papers, and other public property now in his custody and charge.

General ULYSSES S. GRANT, *Washington, D. C.*

The following communication was received from Mr. Stanton:

WAR DEPARTMENT,
WASHINGTON CITY, *August 12, 1867.*

SIR: Your note of this date has been received informing me that by virtue of the powers and authority vested in you as President, by the Constitution and laws of the United States, I am suspended from office as Secretary of War, and will cease to exercise any and all functions pertaining to the same; and also directing me at once to transfer to General Ulysses S. Grant, who has this day been authorized and empowered to act as Secretary of War *ad interim,* all records, books, papers, and other public property now in my custody and charge.

Under a sense of public duty I am compelled to deny your right, under the Constitution and laws of the United States, without the advice and consent of the Senate, and without legal cause, to suspend me from office of Secretary of War, or the exercise of any or all functions pertaining to the same, or without such advice and consent to compel me to transfer to any person the records, books, papers, and public property in my custody as Secretary.

But, inasmuch as the General commanding the armies of the United States has been appointed *ad interim,* and has notified me that he has accepted the appointment, I have no alternative but to submit, under protest, to superior force.

To the PRESIDENT.

The suspension has not been revoked, and the business of the War Department is conducted by the Secretary *ad interim.* Prior to the date of this suspension I had come to the conclusion that the time had arrived when it was proper Mr. Stanton should retire from my Cabinet. The mutual confidence and general accord which should exist in such a relation had ceased. I supposed that Mr. Stanton was well advised that his continuance in the Cabinet was contrary to my wishes, for I had repeatedly given him so to understand by every mode short of an express request that he should resign. Having waited full time for the voluntary action of Mr. Stanton, and seeing no manifestation on his part of an intention to resign, I addressed him the following note on the 5th of August:

SIR: Public considerations of a high character constrain me to say that your resignation as Secretary of War will be accepted.

To this note I received the following reply:

WAR DEPARTMENT,
WASHINGTON, *August 5, 1867.*

SIR: Your note of this day has been received, stating that public considerations of a high character constrain you to say that my resignation as Secretary of War will be accepted.

In reply, I have the honor to say that public considerations of a high character, which alone have induced me to continue at the head of this Department, constrain me not to resign the office of Secretary of War before the next meeting of Congress.

EDWIN M. STANTON,
Secretary of War.

This reply of Mr. Stanton was not merely a declination of compliance with the request for his resignation; it was a defiance, and something more. Mr. Stanton does not content himself with assuming that public considerations bearing upon his continuance in office form as fully a rule of action for himself as for the President, and that upon so delicate a question as the fitness of an officer for continuance in his office, the officer is as competent and as impartial to decide as his superior who is responsible for his conduct; but he goes further and plainly intimates what he means by "public considerations of a high character;" and this is nothing less than his loss of confidence in his superior. He says that these public considerations have "alone induced me to continue at the head of this Department," and that they "constrain me not to resign the office of Secretary of War before the next meeting of Congress."

This language is very significant. Mr. Stanton holds the position unwillingly. He continues in office only under a sense of high public duty. He is ready to leave when it is safe to leave, and as the danger he apprehends from his removal then will not exist when Congress is here, he is constrained to remain during the *interim.* What, then, is that danger which can only be averted by the presence of Mr. Stanton or of Congress? Mr. Stanton does not say that "public considerations of a high character" constrain him to hold on to the office indefinitely. He does not say that no one other than himself can at any time be found to take his place and perform its duties. On the contrary, he expresses a desire to leave the office at the earliest moment consistent with these high public considerations. He says in effect that while Congress is away he must remain, but that when Congress is here he can go. In other words he has lost confidence in the President. He is unwilling to leave the War Department in his hands, or in the hands of any one the President may appoint or designate to perform its duties. If he resigns, the President may appoint a Secretary of War that Mr. Stanton does not approve. Therefore, he will not resign. But when Congress is in session the President cannot appoint a Secretary of War which the Senate does not approve. Consequently, when Congress meets Mr. Stanton is ready to resign.

Whatever cogency these "considerations" may have had upon Mr. Stanton, whatever right he may have had to entertain such considerations, whatever propriety there might be in the expression of them to others, one thing is certain—it was official misconduct, to say the least of it, to parade them before his superior officer. Upon the receipt of this extraordinary note I only delayed the order of suspension long enough to make the necessary arrangements to fill the office. If this were the only cause for his suspension it would be ample. Necessarily it must end our most important official relations, for I cannot imagine a degree of effrontery which would embolden the head of a Department to take his seat at the council table in the Executive Mansion after such an act. Nor can I imagine a President so forgetful of the proper respect and dignity which belong to his office as to submit to such intrusion. I will not do Mr. Stanton the wrong to suppose that he entertained any idea of offering to act as one of my constitutional advisers after that note was written. There was an interval of a week between that date and the order of suspension, during which two Cabinet meetings were held. Mr. Stanton did not present himself at either, nor was he expected. On the 12th of August Mr. Stanton was notified of his suspension and that General Grant had been authorized to take charge of the Department. In his answer to this notification, of the same date, Mr. Stanton expresses himself as follows:

"Under a sense of public duty I am compelled to deny your right, under the Constitution and laws of the United States, without the advice and consent of the Senate, to suspend me from office as Secretary of War or the exercise of any or all functions pertaining to the same, or without such advice and consent to compel me to transfer to any person the records, books, papers, and public property in my custody as Secretary. But inasmuch as the General commanding the armies of the United States has been appointed ad interim, and has notified me that he has accepted the appointment, I have no alternative but to submit, under protest, to superior force."

It will not escape attention that in his note of August 5 Mr. Stanton stated that he had been constrained to continue in the office, even before he was requested to resign, by considerations of a high public character. In this note of August 12 a new and different sense of public duty compels him to deny the President's right to suspend him from office without the consent of the Senate. This last is the public duty of resisting an act contrary to law, and he charges the President with violation of the law in ordering his suspension.

Mr. Stanton refers generally to the "Constitution and laws of the United States," and says that a sense of public duty "under" these compels him to deny the right of the President to suspend him from office. As to his sense of duty under the Constitution, that will be considered in the sequel. As to his sense of duty under "the laws of the United States," he certainly cannot refer to the law which creates the War Department, for that expressly confers upon the President the unlimited right to remove the head of the Department. The only other law bearing upon the question is the tenure-of-office act, passed by Congress over the presidential veto, March 2, 1867. This is the law which, under a sense of public duty, Mr. Stanton volunteers to defend. There is no provision in this law which compels any officer coming within its provisions to remain in office. It forbids removals, but not resignations. Mr. Stanton was perfectly free to resign at any moment, either upon his own motion, or in compliance with a request or an order. It was a matter of choice or of taste. There was nothing compulsory in the nature of legal obligation. Nor does he put his action upon that imperative ground. He says he acts under a "sense of public duty," not of legal obligation, compelling him to hold on, and leaving him no choice. The public duty which is upon him arises from the respect which he owes to the Constitution and the laws, violated in his own case. He is, therefore, compelled by this sense of public duty to vindicate violated law and to stand as its champion.

This was not the first occasion in which Mr. Stanton, in discharge of a public duty, was called upon to consider the provisions of that law. That tenure-of-office law did not pass without notice. Like other acts it was sent to the President for approval. As is my custom, I submitted its consideration to my Cabinet for their advice upon the question, whether I should approve it or not. It was a grave question of constitutional law, in which I would of course rely most upon the opinion of the Attorney General and of Mr. Stanton, who had once been Attorney General. Every member of my Cabinet advised me that the proposed law was unconstitutional. All spoke without doubt or reservation, but Mr. Stanton's condemnation of the law was the most elaborate and emphatic. He referred to the constitutional provisions, the debates in Congress—especially to the speech of Mr. Buchanan, when a Senator—to the decisions of the Supreme Court, and to the usage from the beginning of the Government through every successive Administration, all concurring to establish the right of removal, as vested by the Constitution in the President. To all these he added the weight of his own deliberate judgment, and advised me that it was my duty to defend the power of the President from usurpation and to veto the law.

I do not know when a sense of public duty is more imperative upon a head of Department than upon such an occasion as this. He acts then under the gravest obligations of law; for when he is called upon by the President for advice it is the Constitution which speaks to him. All his other duties are left by the Constitution to be regulated by statute; but this duty was deemed so momentous that it is imposed by the Constitution itself. After all this I was not prepared for the ground taken by Mr. Stanton in his note of August 12. I was not prepared to find him compelled, by a new and indefinite sense of public duty under "the Constitution," to assume the vindication of a law which, under the solemn obligations of public duty, imposed by the Constitution itself, he advised me was a violation of that Constitution. I make great allowance for a change of opinion, but such a change as this hardly falls within the limits of greatest indulgence. Where our opinions take the shape of advice and influence the action of others the utmost stretch of charity will scarcely justify us in repudiating them when they come to be applied to ourselves.

But to proceed with the narrative. I was so much struck with the full mastery of the question manifested by Mr. Stanton, and was at the time so fully occupied with the preparation of another veto upon the pending reconstruction act, that I requested him to prepare the veto upon this tenure-of-office bill. This he declined on the ground of physical disability to undergo, at the time, the labor of writing, but stated his readiness to furnish what aid might be required in the preparation of materials for the paper. At the time this subject was before the Cabinet it seemed to be taken for granted that as to those members of the Cabinet who had been appointed by Mr. Lincoln their tenure of office was not fixed by the provisions of the act. I do not remember that the point was distinctly decided; but I well recollect that it was suggested by one member of the Cabinet who was appointed by Mr. Lincoln, and that no dissent was expressed.

Whether the point was well taken or not did not seem to me of any consequence, for the unanimous expression of opinion against the constitutionality and policy of the act was so decided that I felt no concern, so far as the act had reference to the gentlemen then present, that I would be embarrassed in the future. The bill had not then become a law. The limitation upon the power of removal was not yet imposed, and there was yet time to make any changes. If any one of these gentlemen had then said to me that he would avail himself of the provisions of that bill in case it became a law, I should not have hesitated a moment as to his removal. No pledge was then expressly given or required. But there are circumstances when to give an express pledge is not necessary, and when to require it is an imputation of possible bad faith. I felt that if these gentlemen came within the purview of the bill it was, as to them, a dead letter, and that none of them would ever take refuge under its provisions. I now pass to another subject. When, on the 15th of April, 1865, the duties of the presidential office devolved upon me, I found a full Cabinet of seven members, all of them selected by Mr. Lincoln. I made no change. On the contrary, I shortly afterward ratified a change determined upon by Mr. Lincoln, but not perfected at his death, and admitted his appointee, Mr. Harlan, in the place of Mr. Usher, who was in office at the time.

The great duty of the time was to reëstablish government, law, and order in the insurrectionary States. Congress was then in recess, and the sudden overthrow of the rebellion required speedy action. This grave subject had engaged the attention of Mr. Lincoln in the last days of his life, and the plan according to which it was to be managed had been prepared and was ready for adoption. A leading feature of that plan was that it should be carried out by the executive authority, for, so far as I have been informed, neither Mr. Lincoln nor any member of his Cabinet doubted his authority to act or proposed to call an extra session of Congress to do the work. The first business transacted in Cabinet after I became President was this unfinished business of my predecessor. A plan or scheme of reconstruction was produced which had been prepared for Mr. Lincoln by Mr. Stanton, his Secretary of War. It was approved, and, at the earliest moment practicable, was applied in the form of a proclamation to the State of North Carolina, and afterward became the basis of action in turn for the other States.

Upon the examination of Mr. Stanton before the impeachment committee he was asked the following question:

"Did any one of the Cabinet express a doubt of the power of the executive branch of the Government to reorganize State governments which had been in rebellion without the aid of Congress?"

He answered:

"None whatever. I had myself entertained no doubt of the authority of the President to take measures for the organization of the rebel States on the plan proposed during the vacation of Congress, and agreed in the plan specified in the proclamation in the case of North Carolina."

There is, perhaps, no act of my administration for which I have been more denounced than this. It was not originated by me; but I shrink from no responsibility on that account, for the plan approved itself to my own judgment, and I did not hesitate to carry it into execution.

Thus far, and upon this vital policy, there was perfect accord between the Cabinet and myself, and I saw no necessity for a change. As time passed on there was developed an unfortunate difference of opinion and of policy between Congress and the President upon this same subject and upon the ultimate basis upon which the reconstruction of these States should proceed, especially upon the question of negro suffrage. Upon this point three members of the Cabinet found themselves to be in sympathy with Congress. They remained only long enough to see that the difference of policy could not be reconciled. They felt that they should remain no longer, and a high sense of duty and propriety constrained them to resign their positions. We parted with mutual respect for the sincerity of each other in opposite opinions, and mutual regret that the difference was on points so vital as to require a severance of official relations. This was in the summer of 1866. The subsequent sessions of Congress developed new complications when the suffrage bill for the District of Columbia and the reconstruction acts of March 2 and March 23, 1867, all passed over the veto. It was in Cabinet consultations upon these bills that a difference of opinion upon the most vital points was developed. Upon these questions there was perfect accord between all the members of the Cabinet and myself, except Mr. Stanton. He stood alone, and the difference of opinion could not be reconciled. That unity of opinion which upon great questions of public policy or administration is so essential to the Executive was gone.

I do not claim that the head of a Department should have no other opinions than those of the President. He has the same right, in the conscientious discharge of duty, to entertain and express his own opinions as has the President. What I do claim is that the President is the responsible head of the Administration, and when the opinions of a head of Department are irreconcilably opposed to those of the President in grave matters of policy and administration there is but one result which can solve the difficulty, and that is a severance of the official relation. This, in the past history of the Government, has always been the rule; and it is a wise one; for such differences of opinion among its members must impair the efficiency of any Administration.

I have now referred to the general grounds upon which the withdrawal of Mr. Stanton from my administration seemed to me to be proper and necessary; but I cannot omit to state a special ground which, if it stood alone, would vindicate my action.

The sanguinary riot which occurred in the city of New Orleans on the 30th of August, 1866, justly aroused public indignation and public inquiry, not only as to those who were engaged in it but as to those who, more or less remotely, might be held to responsibility for its occurrence. I need not remind the Senate

of the effort made to fix that responsibility on the President. The charge was openly made, and again and again reiterated through all the land, that the President was warned in time but refused to interfere.

By telegrams from the lieutenant governor and attorney general of Louisiana, dated the 27th and 28th of August, I was advised that a body of delegates, claiming to be a constitutional convention, were about to assemble in New Orleans; that the matter was before the grand jury, but that it would be impossible to execute civil process without a riot, and this question was asked: "Is the military to interfere to prevent process of court?" This question was asked at a time when the civil courts were in the full exercise of their authority, and the answer sent by telegraph, on the same 28th of August, was this:

"The military will be expected to sustain, and not to interfere with the proceedings of the courts."

On the same 28th of August the following telegram was sent to Mr. Stanton by Major General Baird, then (owing to the absence of General Sheridan) in command of the military at New Orleans:

Hon. EDWIN M. STANTON, *Secretary of War:*

A convention has been called with the sanction of Governor Wells, to meet here on Monday. The Lieutenant Governor and city authorities think it unlawful, and propose to break it up by arresting the delegates. I have given no orders on the subject, but have warned the parties that I could not countenance or permit such action without instructions to that effect from the President. Please instruct me at once by telegraph.

The 28th of August was on Saturday. The next morning, the 29th, this dispatch was received by Mr. Stanton at his residence in this city. He took no action upon it, and neither sent instructions to General Baird himself nor presented it to me for such instructions. On the next day (Monday) the riot occurred. I never saw this dispatch from General Baird until some ten days or two weeks after the riot, when, upon my call for all the dispatches, with a view to their publication, Mr. Stanton sent it to me. These facts all appear in the testimony of Mr. Stanton before the Judiciary Committee in the impeachment investigation. On the 30th, the day of the riot, and after it was suppressed, General Baird wrote to Mr. Stanton a long letter from which I make the following extracts:

"SIR: I have the honor to inform you that a very serious riot occurred here to-day. I had not been applied to by the convention for protection, but the Lieutenant Governor and the mayor had freely consulted with me, and I was so fully convinced that it was so strongly the intent of the city authorities to preserve the peace, in order to prevent military interference, that I did regard an outbreak as a thing to be apprehended. The Lieutenant Governor had assured me that even if a writ of arrest was issued by the court the sheriff would not attempt to serve it without my permission, and for to-day they designed to suspend it. I inclose herewith copies of my correspondence with the mayor and of a dispatch which the Lieutenant Governor claims to have received from the President. I regret that no reply to my dispatch to you of Saturday has yet reached me. General Sheridan is still absent in Texas."

The dispatch of General Baird of the 28th asks for immediate instructions, and his letter of the 30th, after detailing the terrible riot which had just happened, ends with the expression of regret that the instructions which he asked for were not sent. It is not the fault or the error or the omission of the President that this military commander was left without instructions; but for all omissions, for all errors, for all failures to instruct, when instruction might have averted this calamity, the President was openly and persistently held responsible. Instantly, without waiting for proof, the delinquency of the President was heralded in every form of utterance. Mr. Stanton knew then that the President was not responsible for this delinquency. The exculpation was in his power, but it was not given by him to the public, and only to the President in obedience to a requisition for all the dispatches.

No one regrets more than myself that General Baird's request was not brought to my notice. It is clear, from his dispatch and letter, that if the Secretary of War had given him proper instructions the riot which arose on the assembling of the convention would have been averted. There may be those ready to say that I would have given no instructions even if the dispatch had reached me in time; but all must admit that I ought to have had the opportunity.

The following is the testimony given by Mr. Stanton before the impeachment investigation committee as to the dispatch:

"*Question.* Referring to the dispatch of the 28th of July by General Baird, I ask you whether that dispatch, on its receipt, was communicated?

"*Answer.* I received that dispatch on Sunday forenoon; I examined it carefully and considered the question presented; I did not see that I could give any instructions different from the line of action which General Baird proposed, and made no answer to the dispatch.

"*Question.* I see it stated that this was received at ten o'clock and twenty minutes p. m. Was that the hour at which it was received by you?'

"*Answer.* That is the date of its reception in the telegraph office Saturday night. I received it on Sunday forenoon, at my residence; a copy of the dispatch was furnished to the President several days afterward, along with all the other dispatches and communications on that subject, but it was not furnished by me before that time; I suppose it may have been ten or fifteen days afterward.

"*Question.* The President himself being in correspondence with those parties upon the same subject, would it not have been proper to have advised him of the reception of that dispatch?

"*Answer.* I know nothing about his correspondence, and know nothing about any correspondence except this one dispatch. We had intelligence of the riot on Thursday morning. The riot had taken place on Monday."

It is a difficult matter to define all the relations which exist between the heads of Department and the President. The legal relations are well enough defined. The Constitution places these officers in the relation of his advisers when he calls upon them for advice. The acts of Congress go further. Take, for example, the act of 1789, creating the War Department. It provides that—

"There shall be a principal officer therein, to be called the Secretary for the Department of War, who shall perform and execute such duties as shall from time to time be enjoined on or intrusted to him by the President of the United States;" and furthermore,

"the said principal officer shall conduct the business of the said Department in such manner as the President of the United States shall from time to time order and instruct."

Provision is also made for the appointment of an inferior officer by the head of the Department, to be called the chief clerk, "who, whenever said principal officer shall be removed from office by the President of the United States," shall have the charge and custody of the books, records, and papers of the Department.

The legal relation is analogous to that of principal and agent. It is the President upon whom the Constitution devolves, as head of the executive department, the duty to see that the laws are faithfully executed; but as he cannot execute them in person he is allowed to select his agents, and is made responsible for their acts within just limits. So complete is this presumed delegation of authority in the relation of a head of Department to the President that the Supreme Court of the United States have decided that an order made by a head of Department is presumed to be made by the President himself.

The principal, upon whom such responsibility is placed for the acts of a subordinate, ought to be left as free as possible in the matter of selection and of dismissal. To hold him to responsibility for an officer beyond his control; to leave the question of the fitness of such an agent to be decided for him and not by him; to allow such a subordinate, when the President, moved by "public considerations of a high character," requests his resignation to assume for himself an equal right to act upon his own views of "public considerations," and to make his own conclusions paramount to those of the President—to allow all this is to reverse the just order of Administration, and to place the subordinate above the superior.

There are, however, other relations between the President and a head of Department beyond these defined legal relations which necessarily attend them, though not expressed. Chief among these is mutual confidence. This relation is so delicate that it is sometimes hard to say when or how it ceases. A single flagrant act may aid it at once, and then there is no difficulty. But confidence may be just as effectually destroyed by a series of causes too subtle for demonstration. As it is a plant of slow growth, so, too, it may be slow in decay. Such has been the process here. I will not pretend to say what acts or omissions have broken up this relation. They are hardly susceptible of statement, and still less of formal proof. Nevertheless no one can read the correspondence of the 5th of August without being convinced that this relation was effectually gone on both sides, and that, while the President was unwilling to allow Mr. Stanton to remain in his administration, Mr. Stanton was equally unwilling to allow the President to carry on his administration without his presence. In the great debate which took place in the House of Representatives in 1789, on the first organization of the principal Departments, Mr. Madison spoke as follows:

"It is evidently the intention of the Constitution that the First Magistrate should be responsible for the executive department. So far, therefore, as we do not make the officers who are to aid him in the duties of that department responsible to him, he is not responsible to the country. Again, is there no danger that an officer, when he is appointed by the concurrence of the Senate, and his friends in that body, may choose rather to risk his establishment on the favor of that branch than rest it upon the discharge of his duties to the satisfaction of the executive branch, which is constitutionally authorized to inspect and control his conduct? And if it should happen that the officers connect themselves with the Senate, they may mutually support each other, and for want of efficacy, reduce the power of the President to a mere vapor, in which case his responsibility would be annihilated, and the expectation of it is unjust. The high executive officers joined in cabal with the Senate would lay the foundation of discord, and end in an assumption of the executive power, only to be removed by a revolution of the Government."

Mr. Sedgwick, in the same debate, referring to the proposition that a head of Department should only be removed or suspended by the concurrence of the Senate, uses this language:

"But if proof be necessary, what is then the consequence? Why, in nine cases out of ten, where the case is very clear to the mind of the President that the man ought to be removed, the effect cannot be produced, because it is absolutely impossible to produce the necessary evidence. Are the Senate to proceed without evidence? Some gentlemen contend not. Then the object will be lost. Shall a man, under these circumstances, be saddled upon the President, who has been appointed for no other purpose but to aid the President in performing certain duties? Shall he be continued, I ask again, against the will of the President? If he is, where is the responsibility? Are you to look for it in the President, who has no control over the officer, no power to remove him if he acts unfeelingly or unfaithfully? Without you make him responsible, you weaken and destroy the strength and beauty of your system. What is to be done in cases which can only be known from a long acquaintance with the conduct of an officer?"

I had indulged the hope that upon the assembling of Congress Mr. Stanton would have ended this unpleasant complication according to the intimation given in his note of August 12. The duty which I have felt myself called upon to perform was by no means agreeable; but I feel that I am not responsible for the controversy, or for the consequences.

Unpleasant as this necessary change in my Cabinet has been to me, upon personal considerations, I have the consolation to be assured that, so far as the public interests are involved, there is no cause for regret. Salutary reforms have been introduced by the Secretary *ad interim*, and great reductions of expenses have been effected under his administration of its War Department, to the saving of millions to the Treasury.

ANDREW JOHNSON.

WASHINGTON, *December 12*, 1867.

EXHIBIT C.

Address to the President by Hon. Reverdy Johnson, August 18, 1866.

MR. PRESIDENT: We are before you as a committee of the National Union Convention. which met in Philadelphia, on Tuesday, the 14th instant, charged with the duty of presenting you with an authentic copy of its proceedings.

Before placing it in your hands, you will permit us to congratulate you that in the object for which the convention was called, in the enthusiasm with which in every State and Territory the call was responded to, in the unbroken harmony of its deliberations, in the unanimity with which the principles it has declared were adopted, and more especially in the patriotic and constitutional character of the principles themselves, we are confident that you and the country will find gratifying and cheering evidence that there exists among the people a public sentiment which renders an early and complete restoration of the Union as established by the Constitution certain and inevitable. Party faction, seeking the continuance of its misrule, may momentarily delay it, but the principles of political liberty, for which our fathers successfully contended, and to secure which they adopted the Constitution, are so glaringly inconsistent with the condition in which the country has been placed by such misrule, that it will not be permitted a much longer duration.

We wish, Mr. President, you could have witnessed the spirit of concord and brotherly affection which animated every member of the convention. Great as your confidence has ever been in the intelligence and patriotism of your fellow-citizens, in their deep devotion to the Union, and their present determination to reinstate and maintain it, that confidence would have become a positive conviction could you have seen and heard all that was done and said upon the occasion. Every heart was evidently full of joy, every eye beamed with patriotic animation; despondency gave place to the assurance that, our late dreadful civil strife ended, the blissful reign of peace, under the protection not of arms, but of the Constitution and laws, would have sway, and be in every part of our land cheerfully acknowledged and in perfect good faith obeyed. You would not have doubted that the recurrence of dangerous domestic insurrections in the future is not to be apprehended.

If you could have seen the men of Massachusetts and South Carolina coming into the convention on the first day of its meeting hand in hand, amid the rapturous applause of the whole body, awakened by heart-felt gratification at the event, filling the eyes of thousands with tears of joy, which they neither could nor desired to repress, you would have felt as every person present felt, that the time had arrived when all sectional or other perilous dissensions had ceased, and that nothing should be heard in the future but the voice of harmony proclaim-

had the same opportunites that the Managers on the part of the House of Representatives have had for preparation. They can and will have the same during the whole progress of this trial. It is not stated that any witness who will prove any material fact is not present, or whose presence cannot any day be procured. It is not stated that delay is necessary for the procurement of records, documents, persons, or papers material or immaterial in this case. Why, then, Mr. President, grant further time when no good cause under the rule is shown? The answer herein filed admits the order of removal of the Secretary of War and the order appointing a Secretary *ad interim*. The President knew what the law was when these orders were made, and knowing it violated it, for which violation we charge him with high misdemeanors in office. In the many trials we have reported in this and other countries this application has no precedent.

In the case of Judge Chase his application stated, in substance, that it was not in his power to obtain information respecting facts alleged against him to have taken place in Philadelphia and Richmond, in time to prepare and put in his answer and proceed to trial before the 5th day of March then next following; and further that he could not get his witnesses or counsel nor prepare his answer at the same time, disclaiming that this was done for delay. This application was sworn to by the respondent; he was given time, and the facts show that his answer was filed and his trial had, and he acquitted in five days' less time than he swore it would take him to prepare for trial.

In Judge Peck's case his application stated his difficulties in obtaining witnesses, the distance they lived from Washington, the time it would require them to travel from St. Louis to Washington, the necessity for copying and obtaining records; that four years had elapsed since the transpiring of the acts complained of against him. This application was also sworn to. If the learned counsel remember the trial of Queen Caroline before the Parliament of Great Britain, when time was granted for the procurement of evidence the learned attorney general then and there protested against this granting of time becoming a precedent for any future trial, this application being granted merely through courtesy to the queen, when witnesses were deemed absolutely necessary to protect, if possible, her reputation. This application differs in form and substance from any that our attention has been directed to, made by the counsel, signed by themselves, and sworn to by no one.

Mr. President, the rule in courts of law in applications for a continuance of the cause or the extension of time, is that reasons good and sufficient must be stated; if for want of a witness or witnesses you must give the name or names, the residence, and what you expect to prove by said witness or witnesses, and that you know of no other witnesses present by whom you can prove the same facts, and also that you have used due diligence to procure the evidence. This application certainly does not come under that rule. No evidence is stated that is expected to be produced. The name of no witness is given that is expected to be subpœnaed. No distance is mentioned that must be traveled. No residence is mentioned. It is not stated that any attempt has been made to obtain any evidence or to even have witnesses subpœnaed. But, sir, for what is this application made, and upon what is it based? It is based upon no urgent necessity for time, that justice may be done in the premises, but merely indicates to the Senate that time is desired to examine authorities, to prepare arguments, and for naught else can we discover that it is made.

Sirs, we insist, as Managers on the part of the House of Representatives and the people, that no more time shall be given in this case than is absolutely necessary to try it; there is no necessity for the extension for counsel to prepare on either side; none for the procurement of witnesses, as none has been asked on that ground. If time be now given on this application, perhaps when issue is joined and the time now extended elapses we may be met by an affidavit asking more time for the procurement of witnesses in some distant part of the country. In my judgment time should not be granted for the trial of the President of the United States on any different application from that required to give time for the trial of the poorest and humblest citizen in the land; he should be tried by the same rules and held amenable to the same laws that apply to any other citizen. Let it not be said that no harm may come to the country by postponement of this cause. If we are correct in our charges against him harm may come by a postponement.

We have charged him with intentionally violating the law; we have charged him with obstructing the law. Our charges are of such a character as show him to be a dangerous person to remain the Chief Magistrate of the nation, inasmuch as he, instead of administering, obstructs the law. It is said that time would be given to an ordinary criminal to prepare his defense. I may be pardoned for saying that we, as the Managers on the part of the House and the country, consider the President a criminal, but not an ordinary one. We charge him as a criminal, and are bound to so consider him until, by the verdict of his triers, he shall be acquitted of all the articles herein presented. The learned counsel for the respondent do not agree with us in this; nor do we ask the Senate to so adjudge until our charges are made good by competent testimony. The course in the case of ordinary criminals who commit crimes or misdemeanors is, or may be, different from the course in this case. But, sir, ordinary criminals are either arrested and put under bonds or imprisoned, that no further violations of law may be committed by them during the pendency of their trial. But, sir, in this case the President, who is charged with violating the law, has the same power to act to-day and still trample the laws and the Constitution under foot that he had the day we charged him with having committed these high crimes and misdemeanors; hence the reasons for not granting time in this case are stronger than could be urged in the case of an ordinary criminal.

In the one case you would give time where no danger might arise from doing so; but in this case danger to the people might arise, and hence the same reasoning does not operate in this that does in the case of an ordinary criminal; and we here enter our protest against any extension of time whatever in this case. What we desire is that the replication of the Managers may be filed to-morrow at one o'clock, and then we may be permitted to state our case to the Senate acting as a court of impeachment, and that we may follow it up with the evidence, and that the counsel for the respondent may then state their defense and produce their evidence, and that on the issue thus made the court may decide as to the guilt or innocence of the party accused.

This is what we ask, and this is what we have a right to expect. I presume no man will doubt that if an application of this kind were made to a court at law, the inquiry would be: "Have you issued your subpœnas; have you attempted to get your witnesses; have you attempted to make any preparation to try the cause?" And if the counsel would answer that they had made no preparation whatever; that they had issued no subpœnas; had made no attempt to procure witnesses or get ready for the trial of the cause, but merely desired time for thought and reflection, the application would certainly be denied. And against the granting of this, not made upon the oath of any person, not signed by the President, and merely intended for the benefit of counsel, we, the Managers, in the name of the House of Representatives and the whole people of this Republic, do most solemnly protest.

Mr. EVARTS. Mr. President, I may be allowed very briefly to call the attention of this honorable court to the attitude of the cause before them, as we conceive it to be. Other courts, except such as are called for a special trial upon a special and limited authority, have established regulations guarding the rights of defendants, either in civil or in criminal prosecutions, with established terms of court and well recognized and understood habits of the conduct of judicial business. In our estimate of the course of this proceeding before this honorable court we have not yet arrived at a time when it was the duty of counsel or was at the charge of the accused to know or consider what the issues were upon which he was to prepare on his side or expect on the other the production of proofs. Beyond that, we feel no occasion to present by affidavit to this honorable court a matter so completely within its cognizance that our time to plead was fixed so as to offer us but eight working days for that duty of counsel.

Obedient to the orders of the court, observant, as we propose at all times to be, of that public necessity and duty which require on the part of the President of the United States and his counsel, not less than on the part of the House of Representatives and its Managers, that diligence should be used, and that we his counsel should be withdrawn from all other professional or personal avocations, we yet cannot recognize in the presence of this court that that is an answer to an application for reasonable time to consider and prepare, to subpœna and produce, in all things to arrange and in all things to be ready, for the actual procedure of the trial. Nor, with great respect to the honorable Managers in this great procedure, do we esteem it a sufficient answer to our desire to be relieved from undue pressure of haste upon our part that equal pressure of haste may have been used on the other. We do not so understand the question of the just and orderly protection of public interests as that this compensation for haste required from the defendant may, be demanded by equal haste being necessary on the part of the prosecution.

But, beyond this, the honorable Managers give us more professional credit than we are entitled to when they assume to say that our standard of our duty and our means and our needs for properly performing it are necessarily to be measured by theirs. Nor do they sufficiently attend, as I say with great respect, to the position of the accused and his counsel in reference to the preparation of a defense with that which is occupied by the Managers and by the House of Representatives in reference to the explorations and the provision and the preparation of the accusation and of its evidence; for during a very considerable period, with the coercive power of summoning witnesses and calling for papers which rightfully belongs to the House of Representatives, all this matter upon the one side and the other, to a certain extent, may have been actually explored by them, and, as is known, to a very great extent, certainly has been.

Now, if this honorable court will give the counsel for the President of the United States due respect in regard to the position in which we present ourselves, due respect to our statement, it will understand that up to this time the consideration of the degree and measure, of the means and occasions, for proof has not yet possibly received our practical and responsible attention, and that within the limits of this accusation, unless it shall be narrowed more than we expect by the replication to be filed, there may be, there must be, a very considerable range of subjects and a very considerable variety of practical considerations that will need to come under the responsible judgment and for the responsible action of counsel.

It would seem to me that we are placed thus far in the attitude of a defendant in a civil or in a public prosecution who upon the issue joined desires time to prepare for trial. The ordinary course in such a case is that as matter of right, as matter of absolute and universal custom, one is not required or expected to give any cause of actual obstruction and difficulty in reference to a continuance to what is the term of the court, doubtless in most cases to occur within a brief period after the issue is joined. This court having no such arrangement and no such possible arrangement of its affairs in advance, we are obliged at each stage of regular proceeding to ask your attention as to what you will provide and consider in the particular case is, according to the general nature of the procedure and the understood attitude of both parties to it, a just and reasonable proposition to be made by us as to the time that should be allowed for the preparation in all respects for this trial after the issue shall have been joined. We do not ask any more time than in the interest of justice and duty under the actual circumstances of this case should be given to the poorest man in the country. The measure of justice and of duty has no respect whatever to poverty or station. The actual nature of the proceeding, the actual circumstances of the case are to furnish the rule for the exercise of whatever falls within the discretion of the court. If during the trial, on the part of the Managers, it should appear that, by accident or by any other just excuse, the attendance of a proper witness on their part was required, it would be the duty of this court, in the administration of justice, to allow proper time and delay for the production of the witness. And so, upon our part, if, foreseen or unforeseen, such an occasion should arise, it would be a necessary duty of the court to take it into consideration and provide for it as the occasion arose. The proposition that we now make to the court, and, unless there is to be a departure from the general habit of all courts in such a predicament of a procedure, what we expect their action according to and upon is this: that after issue joined we should have a reasonable time before we should be considered as bound to be in the condition of preparation for the proceeding in the cause.

Mr. Manager WILSON. Mr. President and Senators, the Managers on the part of the House of Representatives have determined, so far as may lie in their power, that this case shall not be taken out of the line of the precedents; therefore it is that we will resist all applications for unreasonable delay. The counsel for the respondent who has just taken his seat might well, in view of the remarks which he submitted, have waited until issue joined before presenting this motion; but it is here, and we are prepared here and now to take the motion as we find it, and deal with it as its form and merit of substance require.

It will be remembered that the first step taken by the counsel for the respondent on the 18th instant was in violation of the precedent established by the cases which have been tried by the Senate of the United States. Looking into the case of Judge Chase, we find that on the return day of the summons he appeared and made application for time to answer; but he did not stop at this; he coupled with his motion for time to answer a request for time to prepare for his trial. He supported his application by his solemn affidavit stating that he could not possibly prepare his case for trial before the 5th day of the succeeding March, and therefore he asked an allowance of time for preparation for trial until the commencement of the next session of Congress, as the then session would expire on the 4th day of that month.

In his application he disclosed the necessities inducing his request, among which were the distances lying between the capital and the places where he was to ascertain the facts and circumstances necessary for his defense and to find the witnesses to support it. After due consideration the Senate overruled his application and required him to answer on the 4th day of the succeeding February, thus allowing him, both for answer and preparation, thirty days instead of eleven months, as prayed for in his motion. And what was the result in that case? Why, that on the 1st day of March succeeding, four days before the time which he stated in his affidavit would be required for him to prepare for trial, the cause had been tried on such perfect preparation that it resulted in the acquittal of the respondent. The Senate judged better than he of the difficulties of his case and of the time required to overcome them. So in the case of Judge Peck, when he appeared on the return day of the writ, it having been served on him but three days prior to the return, he made his joint application for time to answer and time to prepare for trial, and supported it by his solemn affidavit. He was granted the time he desired to prepare his answer when, by an adjournment of Congress, his case went over for trial until the next session.

But we have had no such course pursued in this case. On the return day of the summons, notwithstanding the rule of the Senate required on that day and at that time the filing of the answer, we were met first with an application for forty days' leave in which to prepare an answer. The honorable Senate allowed ten days; and now, at the expiration of that time, we find a most elaborate answer presented by the counsel for the respondent; and in it is embodied the strongest argument against any delay in this case that has come from any source or is known to any person; and that is, that the respondent, by his answer, affirms as lying within his rightful powers under the Constitution, the right to do the very acts which we have charged against him at the bar of this Senate as criminal acts, and persists in his defiance of the laws and in the wickedness of the course which the Representatives of the people have challenged. That might not be a weighty consideration in an ordinary case. It might not weigh much if, instead of the present respondent, we had some other officer of the Government charged at the bar of the Senate with the offenses enumerated in the articles to which he has this day answered.

But in this case it is of weight, and should have due consideration. Why is it of weight? Because the respondent has devolved on him not only the duty which rests upon the citizen to obey the law, but also the higher duty to execute the law, and is clothed by the Constitution of the country with the whole executive power of the nation, that he may be enabled to discharge faithfully the duty thus imposed. He has not, in the judgment of the House of Representatives, discharged this duty as his oath of office requires, but has disregarded the law and defied its authority. For his failure to discharge it, for his acts of positive transgression of the laws of the land, he is arraigned at the bar of the Senate, and presenting answer, justifies the acts which make up his grave offenses, claims the right to repeat and extend them, and now asks for time that he may further imperil the nation while he endeavors to .make good his unlawful assumptions of power, in the meantime holding in his hands, under and by virtue of the Constitution, the executive power of the Republic. No provision having been made for its temporary surrender, he retains that power, disturbing the repose of the country and interfering with every interest of business and trade and commerce, by prolonging this unfortunate conflict between the two departments of the Government.

Mr. President and Senators, we feel it to be our most solemn duty to urge upon you, in the name of the Representatives of the people, and of the people themselves, that speedy progress toward a conclusion of this case which shall guard the rights and the interests of the people, their laws and their government, and at the same time observe with reasonable care the rights belonging to the respondent. The present application for delay is without precedent in the cases heretofore tried by the Senate; and were it not for the order adopted by this body on the 13th instant, which now must be regarded as a rule, this application could not be made, as that rule is the only thing which takes this case out of the line of precedents to which I have referred. It should have been coupled with the other motion made before the adoption of the rule, and the whole case so far as respects causes of delays in this proceeding disclosed at the threshold. The following order constitutes the rule to which I refer:

"*Ordered*, That unless otherwise ordered by the Senate for cause shown, the trial of the pending impeachment shall proceed immediately after replication shall be filed."

Now, I submit that the "cause shown" in this application is not such cause as will justify the Senate in the exercise of a sound discretion in granting the time which has been asked for by the respondent to enable him to prepare for trial. It does not show cause of substance, and presents mere questions of convenience.

Mr. HOWARD. Will the Manager please read that order again?

Mr. Manager WILSON. "*Ordered*, That unless otherwise ordered by the Senate for cause shown, the trial of the pending impeachment shall proceed immediately after replication shall be filed."

It will be observed—the interruption suggests it to my mind—that in view of this rule the Senate cannot, with due regard to its own action, grant this extension of time, because a sound discretion cannot be exercised under the rule and upon this application until issue be joined between the people and their Representatives and the respondent, though we waive this objection in the interest of the economy of time. But, as I have said, this application, considered now or at any other time, must be addressed to the sound discretion of the Senate, and it is for us to remember that a sound discretion acts not without rule to guide it. The discretion to which such motions are addressed must be directed by law—"it must be governed by rule, not by humor; it must not be arbitrary, vague, and fanciful, but legal and regular."

And I therefore deny that the application and the statements therein contained do or can convey to the mind of this Senate that view of this case which must be presented by the respondent in order to justify you in saying, upon the exercise of a sound discretion, that one hour's delay should be granted; for there is nothing of a substantive character affecting the merits of the case disclosed upon which it can act.

What is the application? . It is substantially that counsel have not had time to prepare and become familiar with the case, therefore they must be allowed opportunity to educate themselves in the particular matter committed to their charge. I apprehend that that is not good cause upon which this Senate may act and grant the prayer of this present application. More than that, it will be observed that the respondent has been carefully kept out of this case on these motions. In all other cases in this country of which I have any knowledge, the respondent has asked in his own name, supporting his request by his affidavit, for delay of proceedings; judges summoned from the bench and brought to this bar have presented their petitions in person, supported by their solemn affidavits, and asked upon the facts stated by them, covering and disclosing all of the features of their cases, and unfolding their line of defense, a reasonable time in which to prepare answer and to prepare for trial. But it is not so here; and we have to ask that while this case is thus kept out of the ordinary rule and uniform practice of former cases, the Senate will regard in some degree the voice of the Representatives as presented by the Managers, and put this respondent upon his speedy trial, to the end that peace may be restored to the country by the healing efficacy of a determination of this prosecution—the restoration of harmony between the two contending departments of the Government, and to the further end that all things may again move on in this land as they were accustomed in the times before this unfortunate conflict and its disturbing results occurred. Therefore, Senators, in the name of the House of Representatives, and of the people in whose names they have acted in this behalf, we ask that this application, as it is now presented and considered, may be denied by the Senate.

Mr. STANBERY. Mr. Chief Justice, on the 13th instant, when we entered our appearance, and when we supposed we had nothing to do but to enter our appearance and ask for time to answer, the honorable court made an order that we should have until the 23d, this day, to file our answer. They gave to the Managers leave to file replication, without limiting them at all as to time, but provided that upon the filing of the replication the case should proceed to trial unless reasonable cause should be shown for further delay. Then the honorable court meant us to have time to prepare for trial if we reasonably showed that it was necessary.

Now, what has happened, Mr. Chief Justice? What has been stated to this honorable court, composed in a great measure of members of the bar. by members of the bar that I hope have sufficient standing with this court to have some credit, at least, for professional statements made upon their honor? What have we stated? That since we had this leave every hour and every moment has been occupied with the pleadings; not an instant lost. not a counsel absent. We have refused all other occupation; we have devoted ourselves exclusively to this day and night, and I am sorry to be obliged to say two days sacred to other duty. There has been not a moment's delay. And how has this time been occupied, Mr. Chief Justice? Occupied, every instant of it, in the preparation of this answer. Allow me to say to the honorable court that it was not until fifteen minutes before we came here that our document was ready.

Certainly it was intended on the 13th to give us time not merely to prepare our answer, but to prepare for that still more material thing, the trial. And now I hope I shall obtain credit with the honorable court when I say that we have been so pressed with this duty of making up the issue and preparing the answer that we have not had an opportunity of asking the President "What witnesses will you have?" Nay, we have been so pressed that to the communications which we have received from the honorable Managers in regard to admissions and to facilitate proof we have been obliged to say, in reply, "We have not, gentlemen, as yet, a moment's time to consider your communications." All we know of this case is that it refers to transactions not only here, but at Cleveland and St. Louis, at distant points. They have sent us a list of witnesses who are to come from these various places as to matters in regard to which they expect to make proof against us as to what was said and done at those places, and as yet I do not know a single witness whom the President wants to call in his defense. I know that he wants to call witnesses, but I have not yet had an opportunity of knowing who those witnesses are. We have not subpœnaed one. We do not know the name of any one except those who happen to live here whom we shall want, nor which of them.

Now mark, all this time the advantage that the honorable Managers have had over us. As I understand it, and I suppose it will not be denied, almost every day since they have been engaged in the preparation for the trial. Their articles were framed long ago. While we were engaged in preparing our answer they have been, as I understand, most industriously engaged in preparing the witnesses. Day after day witnesses have been called before them and testimony taken. We have had no such power; we have had no such opportunity—not the slightest. We are here without any preparation in the way of witnesses, without having had a moment to consult with our client or among ourselves.

The gentlemen say that our anxiety is to prepare ourselves, whereas they are already prepared, completely prepared, so far as counsel need prepare themselves. I am very happy to hear that they are. I should be very far from saying that I am equally prepared. I have had no time to look to anything else except this necessary and all-absorbing duty which we have just completed. Now, if the Senate say we shall go on when this replication comes in, which, I am told, is to come in to-morrow, they will put me in a position that I have never been in before in all my practice anywhere, with a client and a case and a formidable array against me, and yet not a witness summoned; not a document prepared—all unarmed and defenseless.

I beg this honorable court to treat us with some leniency, to give us time. If you cannot give us all we ask give us, at least, some time within which, by the utmost diligence, we can make that preparation we deem to be useful, and without which we are unsafe and unprepared.

The gentlemen complain that we ought to have been ready on the 13th. They read against us a rule that that was the day fixed for not only the appearance but the filing of the answer. What! They read out of a rule that old formula that has come down to us for five hundred years, the order to "appear and answer" — the same language which was adopted at that early time when pleadings were *ore tenus* and by parol, when the defendant was called and answered immediately. But even our old independent and sturdy ancestors would not answer on that day, although they were to answer by word of mouth; and we know that always they demanded time and always had time, "leave to imparl" a day to answer.

We have preserved the same phraseology in our subsequent proceedings. The summons is still to a defendant "You are hereby summoned to appear on such a day and answer;" but whoever supposed he was then to file his answer? What lawyer that ever wrote a declaration does not recollect the beginning of it, "The defendant was summoned to appear and answer;" and yet every lawyer knows that the time for the defendant's answer has not yet come. Well, our answer has been presented. No day has yet peremptorily been fixed for trial. The Senate said to us, "You shall go to trial when the replication is filed, provided you do not show good cause." The cause we show is, may it please the honorable court, that we have not had one moment's time to prepare for trial.

Mr. HOWARD and Mr. Manager BINGHAM rose.

The CHIEF JUSTICE. The Senator from Michigan.

Mr. Manager BINGHAM. On the part of the Managers I beg to respond to what has just been said.

Mr. HOWARD. I beg to call the attention of the President to the rules that govern the body.

Mr. Manager BINGHAM. I will only say that we have used but thirty-five of the minutes of the time allowed us under the rule.

The CHIEF JUSTICE. The Chair announced at the last sitting that he would not undertake to restrict counsel as to number without the further order of the Senate, the rule not being very intelligible to him. He will state further that when counsel make a motion to the court the counsel who makes the motion has invariably the right to close the argument upon it.

Several SENATORS. Certainly.

Mr. Manager BINGHAM. Mr. President. with all respect touching the suggestion just made by the presiding officer of the Senate, I beg leave to remind the Senate that from time immemorial in proceedings of this kind the right of the Commons in England, and of the Representatives of the people in the United States, to close the debate has not been, by any rule, settled against them. On the contrary, in Lord Melville's case, if I may be allowed and pardoned for making reference to it, the last case, I believe, reported in England, Lord Erskine presiding, when the very question was made which has now been submitted by the presiding officer to the Senate, one of the managers of the House of Commons arose in his place and said that he owed it to the Commons to protest against the immemorial usage being denied to the Commons of England to be heard in reply to whatever might be said on behalf of the accused at the bar of the Peers. In that case the language of the manager, Mr. Giles, was:

" My lords, it was not my intention to trouble your lordships with any observations upon the arguments you have heard; and if I now do so, it is only for the sake of insisting upon and maintaining that right which the Commons contend is their acknowledged and undoubted privilege, the right of being heard after the counsel for the defendant has made his observations in reply. It has been invariably admitted when required."—*State Trials*, vol. 29, p. 762; 44 to 46 *George III.*

Lord Erskine " responded the right of the Commons to reply was never doubted or disputed."

Following the suggestion of the learned gentleman who has just taken his seat, I believe that when that utterance was made it had been the continued rule in England for nearly five hundred years.

In this tribunal, in the first case of impeachment that ever was tried before the Senate of the United States under the Constitution, (I refer to the case of Blount,) the Senate will see by a reference to it that although the accused had the affirmative of the issue, although he interposed a plea to the jurisdiction, the argument was closed in the case by the manager of the House, Mr. Harper. (Wharton's State Trials of the United States, pp. 314–15.)

When I rose, however, at the time the honorable Senator spoke, I rose for the purpose of making some response to the remarks last made for the accused; but as the presiding officer has interposed the suggestion to the Senate whether the Managers can further reply I do not deem it proper for me to proceed further until the Senate shall pass upon this question.

Mr. HOWARD. Mr. President, if the discussion is closed on the part of the Managers, and the counsel——

Mr. Manager BINGHAM. I desire to have the question submitted.

Mr. HOWARD. I was about to move that this motion be laid on the table.

Mr. Manager BINGHAM. I desire, if the Senator from Michigan will excuse me, to be heard in response to what has just fallen from the lips of the counsel for the accused, but deem it my duty not to proceed without the consent of the Senate, inasmuch as the presiding officer has already suggested to the Senate that the Managers could not be further heard; in other words, could not be permitted to make a final reply.

The CHIEF JUSTICE. The motion of the Senator from Michigan is that——

Mr. Manager BOUTWELL. Mr. President, will the Chair pardon me?

The CHIEF JUSTICE. Certainly.

Mr. Manager BOUTWELL. This seems to

the Managers, and to myself especially, a matter of so much moment as to whether the Managers are to be heard finally——

Mr. HOWARD. Excuse me a moment. It was not my intention to cut off debate or discussion on the part of the Managers or the counsel for the accused; and so I announced. If there is any desire on the part of either to proceed with the discussion, I withdraw my motion to lay the order on the table.

Mr. Manager BINGHAM. Now, Mr. President, if it be the pleasure of the Senate——

Mr. JOHNSON. I ask for the reading of the twentieth rule.

The CHIEF JUSTICE. The rule will be read.

The Secretary read rule twenty, as follows:

"20. All preliminary or interlocutory questions, and all motions, shall be argued for not exceeding one hour on each side, unless the Senate shall by order extend the time."

Mr. Manager BINGHAM. We have used but thirty-five minutes of our time.

Mr. GRIMES. What is the question?

The CHIEF JUSTICE. Do the managers desire to proceed?

Mr. Manager BINGHAM. Yes, sir; with the President's leave.

Mr. President and Senators: I deeply regret that the counsel for the accused have made any intimation here that question is made or intended to be made by the Managers touching the entire sincerity with which they act before this tribunal. I am sure that it was furthest from the purpose of my associates, as I know it was entirely foreign to any purpose of mine, to question for a moment their sincerity. The gentleman who took his seat spoke of their having presented this application upon their honor. No man questions their honor; no man who knows them will question their honor; but we may be pardoned for saying that it is unusual, altogether unusual, on questions of this sort to allow continuances to be obtained upon a mere point of honor! The rule of the Senate, which was adopted on the 13th instant, is a rule well understood, and is in the language of the ordinary rule which obtains in courts of law; that is to say, the trial shall proceed upon replication filed, except, for cause shown, further time be allowed.

I submit that a question of this magnitude has never been decided upon a mere presentation of a statement of counsel, in this country or in any country. To speak more plainly, a motion for continuance arising on a question of this sort, I venture to say, has never been decided affirmatively upon such an issue on a mere statement of counsel. If Andrew Johnson, the accused at this bar, has witnesses that were not within the process of this court up to this day, but whose attendance he can hope to procure if time be allowed him, he can make affidavit before this tribunal that they are material and set forth in his affidavit what he expects to prove by them. I concede that upon such a showing there would be something upon which the Senate might properly act.

But, sir, instead of that he throws himself back upon his counsel, and they make their statement here that they will require thirty days of time in which to prepare for trial. He sent these gentlemen to the bar of this tribunal on the 13th instant upon their honor to notify the Senate that it would require him forty days to prepare an answer. Now, he sends them back upon their honor to notify the Senate that it will require him thirty days to prepare for trial. I take it that the counsel for the accused have quite as much time for preparation if this trial shall proceed to-morrow as have the Managers on behalf of the House of Representatives, who are charged by the people with duties from day to day in the other end of the Capitol which they are not permitted to lay aside.

But, sir, I think upon the answer made here this day by the President of the United States, unless very good cause be shown, and that, too, under the obligation of his own oath at the bar of this Senate, not another hour's continuance should be allowed him after the case shall have been put at issue. We ask leave to suggest to the Senate that we hoped on to-morrow, by leave of the people's Representatives, to put this case at issue by filing a replication. That is all the delay we desire. The accused has had the opportunity for process ever since the 13th instant, at least. He is guilty of grave negligence in this behalf—I do not speak of the counsel; I speak of the accused. If he had witnesses to subpœna why was he not about it? And yet, sir, not a single summons has been required by him under the rule and order of the Senate to bring to its bar a single witness to testify in his behalf. He totally neglects the whole issue, and comes here with an attempt at a confession and avoidance of the matter presented by the House of Representatives, and tells this Senate and tells the country that he defies their power, trifling—I repeat it in the hearing of the Senate—trifling with the great power which the people for wise purposes have placed in the hands of their Representatives and their Senators in Congress assembled.

Why, sir, what is this power of impeachment worth if the President of the United States, holding the whole executive power of the nation, is permitted, when arraigned at the bar of the Senate in the name of all the people and charged with high crimes and misdemeanors, in that he has violated his oath, in that he has violated the Constitution of the country, in that he has violated the people's laws, and attempted by his violation of the laws to lay hands upon the people's Treasury; what is this great defensive power reposed by the people in their Representatives worth if the President, upon a mere statement of his counsel, is permitted to postpone the further inquiry for thirty days, until he prepares to do—what?

Until he prepares to make good his elaborate statement set forth in his answer, that the Constitution is but a cobweb in his hands, and that he defies your power to restrain him.

I remember very well, sir, it suggested itself to me when I heard this discussion going on, the weighty words of that great man (Chancellor Kent) whose luminous intellect shed luster upon the jurisprudence of his country in the State of New York for more than a third of a century, which he wrote down in his Commentaries upon the laws, and which will live as long as our language lives, that to prevent the abuse of the executive trust—

"The Constitution has rendered the President directly amenable, by law, for maladministration. The inviolability of any officer of Government is incompatible with the republican theory as well as with the principles of retributive justice." * * * * *
"If, then, neither the sense of duty, the force of public opinion, nor the transitory nature of the seat are sufficient to secure a faithful discharge of the executive trust, but the President will use the authority of his station to violate the Constitution or law of the land, the House of Representatives can arrest him in his career by resorting to the power of impeachment."—1 *Kent*, p. 313, sec. 289.

Faithful to the duty imposed upon us by our oaths as the Representatives of the people, we have interposed that remedy to arrest this man, and he comes to-day to answer, saying, "I defy your impeachment; by the executive power reposed in me under the Contitution"—and I believe I quote almost the words of the answer laid before us—"by the executive power reposed in me by the Constitution, I claim in the presence of the Senate, I claim in the presence of the country, the power, without challenge, let, or hinderance, to suspend every executive officer of this Government at my pleasure." I venture to say before the enlightened bar of public opinion in America, by these words incorporated in his answer, the President is as guilty of malfeasance and misdemeanor in office as ever man was guilty of malfeasance or misdemeanor in office since nations began to be upon the earth. What! That he will suspend all executive officers of this Government at his pleasure, not by force of the tenure-of-office act, to which he himself refers, and which he says is void and of no effect, but by force of the Constitution of the United States; and that, too, he adds, while the Senate of the United States is in session! What does he mean by it? Let the Senate answer when they come to vote on this proposition for the extension of time. Does he mean by it that he will vacate the executive offices and not fill them? Does he mean by it that your money appropriated by your laws for carrying on and administering the Government shall remain locked in the vaults of your Treasury, and shall not be applied as your law directs? Or does he mean by it that he will repeat what he has already done in the presence of the Senate, and in violation of the laws, that he will remove without the consent of the Senate, and he will appoint while the Senate is in session without its advice or consent, just such persons as will answer his own purposes? Is that what he means? If he does it is a very easy method of repealing the Constitution of the United States.

The appointing power is "by and with the advice and consent of the Senate." The power to fill vacancies under the Constitution is in the President only as to such vacancies as may happen during the recess of the Senate, and so the Constitution reads. But, according to the logic set out in this elaborate answer, to support which the President wishes thirty days of time for preparation, he is to vacate every executive office of the United States at his own pleasure, in the presence of the Senate, without its consent while they are in session, and fill it at his pleasure *ad interim* even while they are trying him. If this be permitted, and if his successors should follow his bad example, I ask the Senate to deliberate, to consider whether the time would not soon come, if that example were persisted in and followed, that not a single executive office in America would be filled by any man "by and with the advice and consent of the Senate;" but, on the contrary, every such office would be filled without the advice or consent of the Senate.

I admit, sir, it is a time-honored rule of the common law, the growth of centuries, the gathered wisdom of a thousand years, that the accused has the right to a speedy and impartial trial. I claim that the people also have a right to a speedy and impartial trial, and that the question pending here touches in some sort the right of the people. In their name we demand here a speedy and impartial trial. If the President is not guilty, we ask in behalf of the country that he shall be declared not guilty of the offenses with which he stands charged. If it be the judgment of the Senate that he has power thus to lay hands upon the Constitution of the country and rend it in tatters in the presence of its custodians, the sooner that judgment is pronounced the better.

In every view of this case, in the light of the answer to which we have listened, I feel myself justified in saying that the public interests demand that this trial shall proceed until, upon the solemn oath of the accused made at this bar, it shall appear that he cannot proceed on account of the absence of witnesses material to him, nor until he states what he expects to prove by them; because I venture to say that he can make no showing of that sort which we are not ready upon the spot to meet by saying we will admit that the witnesses will swear to his statement, and let him have the benefit of it. Nearly all the testimony involved in this issue is documentary. Much of it is official. Enough of it, I might say, is official in its character to justify the trial to proceed without further inquiry into the facts.

But be that as it may, although they did not request us to do so, although they had no right to demand it of us, we have taken pains to notify the counsel for the accused of the witnesses that we propose to call, the witnesses we have subpœnaed, so that they might prepare to meet them ; and it will occur to the Senate as this trial progresses that they have as much time for preparation by the end of that day when the case on the part of the Government of the United States shall be closed as we have. We make no boast of any superior preparation in this matter. We desire simply to discharge our duty as best we can. We assume no superiority to the counsel, as was intimated by the gentleman who last spoke, [Mr. Stanbery;] but we desire simply to discharge our duty here and to discharge it promptly and to discharge it faithfully, and we appeal to the Senate to grant us the opportunity of doing so, so that justice may be done between the people of the United States and the President, that the Constitution of the United States which he has violated may be vindicated, and that the wrongs which he has committed against an outraged and betrayed people may be speedily redressed.

Mr. HENDERSON. Mr. President, I propose an order which I send to the Chair.

The CHIEF JUSTICE. The Secretary will read the order.

The Chief Clerk read as follows :

Ordered, That the application of the counsel for the President to be allowed thirty days to prepare for the trial of the impeachment be postponed until after replication filed.

Mr. Manager BUTLER. Mr. President, I should like to call the attention of yourself and the Senate to the position in which that would place the Managers, and I beg to express the desire on the part of the Managers that this question of time shall be settled now. If a replication is needed at all, I think I can say for my associates that it will be the common and formal replication, the *sic similiter* of the profession, the simple joining issue upon this answer, and therefore for this purpose it may be considered as filed.

We shall have to be ready at all hazards to-morrow to go on with this case, with the uncertainty of having the court or the,Senate—I beg pardon for the word "court"—give thirty or more days' time in which the counsel may be prepared. In other words, we shall be obliged, under the high sense of duty which is pressing upon us, to get ready by day or by night, as the case may be, and then with entire uncertainty as to whether the Senate may or may not grant further time. I think I can say that upon this question we agree with the counsel for the defense that it is better for all that it be settled now. I know I speak for the Managers. I speak for the House of Representatives when I say it is better to have this point settled now. Our subpœnas are out; our witnesses are being summoned. We want to know when to bring them here. Fix a day; tell us when we can come here certain, and we will be here. That is all we desire, sir; and therefore I trust gentlemen will fix at this time the hour and the

day when this trial shall certainly proceed, the act of Providence preventing notwithstanding.

The CHIEF JUSTICE. The question is on the order moved by the Senator from Missouri, [Mr. HENDERSON.]

Mr. TRUMBULL. I ask for the yeas and nays.

The yeas and nays were ordered ; and being taken, resulted—yeas 25, nays 28 ; as follows :

YEAS—Messrs. Anthony, Buckalew, Cattell, Cole, Dixon, Doolittle, Edmunds, Fessenden, Fowler, Frelinghuysen, Grimes, Henderson, Hendricks, Johnson, McCreery, Morrill of Maine, Norton, Patterson of Tennessee, Ross, Saulsbury, Sherman, Sprague, Trumbull, Van Winkle, and Vickers—25.

NAYS—Messrs. Bayard, Cameron, Chandler, Conkling, Conness, Corbett, Cragin, Davis, Drake, Ferry, Harlan, Howard, Howe, Morgan, Morrill of Vermont, Morton, Nye, Patterson of New Hampshire, Pomeroy, Ramsey, Stewart, Sumner, Thayer, Tipton, Willey, Williams, Wilson, and Yates—28.

NOT VOTING—Mr. Wade—1.

So the order proposed by Mr. HENDERSON was not agreed to.

Mr. HOWARD. Mr. President, I now move that the motion of the counsel for the accused do lie on the table.

Mr. DRAKE. Mr. President, I rise to a question of order.

The CHIEF JUSTICE. The Senator will state his question of order.

Mr. DRAKE. That no motion to lay a proposition by the counsel for the defense, or one made by the Managers on the part of the prosecution, upon the table, can, under the rules of the Senate, be entertained, but that the Senate must come to a direct vote upon the proposition.

The CHIEF JUSTICE. The Chair is of opinion that the point of order is well taken, and that the motion of the Senator from Michigan, that the proposition of the counsel for the accused lie on the table, is not in order.

Several SENATORS. Question, question.

Mr. JOHNSON. Mr. Chief Justice, what is the question?

The CHIEF JUSTICE. The question is on the motion of the counsel for the accused, to be allowed thirty days for preparation.

Mr. DRAKE. On that question I ask for the yeas and nays.

The yeas and nays were ordered ; and being taken, resulted—yeas 12, nays 41 ; as follows :

YEAS—Messrs. Bayard, Buckalew, Davis, Dixon, Doolittle, Hendricks, Johnson, McCreery, Norton, Patterson of Tennessee, Saulsbury, and Vickers—12.

NAYS—Messrs. Anthony, Cameron, Cattell, Chandler, Cole, Conkling, Conness, Corbett, Cragin, Drake, Edmunds, Ferry, Fessenden, Fowler, Frelinghuysen, Grimes, Harlan, Henderson, Howard, Howe, Morgan, Morrill of Maine, Morrill of Vermont, Morton, Nye, Patterson of New Hampshire, Pomeroy, Ramsey, Ross, Sherman, Sprague, Stewart, Sumner, Thayer, Tipton, Trumbull, Van Winkle, Willey, Williams, Wilson, and Yates—41.

NOT VOTING—Mr. Wade—1.

The CHIEF JUSTICE. On this question the yeas are 12 and the nays are 41. So the application for thirty days for preparation is denied.

Mr. SHERMAN. I move that the Senate

sitting for this purpose adjourn until to-morrow at one o'clock.

Mr. EVARTS. Mr. President——

Mr. SHERMAN. Certainly. I withdraw the motion.

Mr. EVARTS. I now, Mr. Chief Justice and Senators, move, in behalf of the President and in the name of his counsel, that he be allowed (upon the application which we have made and in which we have named thirty days as a reasonable time) a reasonable time after the replication shall have been filed, to be now fixed by the Senate in their judgment.

Mr. JOHNSON. What time is that?

Mr. STANBERY. Such time as the Senate shall fix.

The CHIEF JUSTICE. The counsel will reduce his motion to writing.

Mr. EVARTS. I will state it. I move that on the application we have made, in which we have named thirty days as a reasonable time, there now be allowed to the President of the United States and his counsel such reasonable time for preparation for trial, after the replication shall have been filed, as shall now be fixed by the Senate.

The CHIEF JUSTICE. The counsel will reduce his motion to writing. Does the Senator from Ohio withdraw his motion to adjourn?

Mr. SHERMAN. Yes, sir; but after the motion is reduced to writing I will renew it.

Mr. JOHNSON. Mr. Chief Justice, is the motion proposed to be submitted by one of the counsel for the President of the United States before the Senate now?

The CHIEF JUSTICE. It is not before the Senate until it has been reduced to writing.

Mr. JOHNSON. I thought it had been so reduced.

The CHIEF JUSTICE. It has not.

Mr. EVARTS. It is now.

The CHIEF JUSTICE. The Clerk will report the order.

The Chief Clerk read as follows:

The counsel for the President now move that there be allowed for the preparation of the President of the United States for the trial, after the replication shall be filed and before the trial shall be required to proceed, such reasonable time as shall now be fixed by the Senate.

Mr. JOHNSON. Mr. Chief Justice, is it in order to amend that motion?

Several SENATORS. No, no.

The CHIEF JUSTICE. It is in order to propose an answer to it; not to amend it.

Mr. JOHNSON. I move, then, Mr. President, that ten days be allowed after filing the replication.

Mr. SHERMAN. I move that the Senate sitting as a Court of Impeachment adjourn until one o'clock to-morrow.

The motion was agreed to; and the Chief Justice declared the Senate sitting for the trial of the impeachment of Andrew Johnson adjourned until to-morrow at one o'clock.

TUESDAY, *March* 24, 1868.

The Chief Justice of the United States entered the Senate Chamber at one o'clock p. m., escorted by Mr. POMEROY, chairman of the committee heretofore appointed for the purpose, took the chair, and directed the Sergeant-at-Arms to open the court by proclamation.

The SERGEANT-AT-ARMS. Hear ye! hear ye! All persons are commanded to keep silence while the Senate of the United States is sitting for the trial of the articles of impeachment exhibited by the House of Representatives against Andrew Johnson, President of the United States.

The CHIEF JUSTICE. The Secretary will read the minutes.

The Secretary commenced to read the Journal of yesterday's proceedings.

Mr. JOHNSON. Mr. Chief Justice, I submit to the Chair whether it is not advisable to postpone the reading of the Journal until the Managers and the counsel for the accused are present?

The CHIEF JUSTICE. The Sergeant-at-Arms informs the Chief Justice that the Managers are at the door ; and he has directed the Secretary to suspend the reading of the minutes.

The counsel for the respondent, Messrs. Stanbery, Curtis, Evarts, Nelson, and Groesbeck entered the Chamber and took the seats assigned them.

At five minutes past one o'clock the presence of the Managers on the part of the House of Representatives was announced at the door of the Senate Chamber by the Sergeant-at-Arms.

The CHIEF JUSTICE. The Managers will please to take their seats within the bar.

The Managers were conducted to the seats provided for them.

The members of the House of Representatives appeared at the door, headed by Mr. E. B. WASHBURNE, chairman of the Committee of the Whole House, and accompanied by the Speaker and Clerk.

The CHIEF JUSTICE. The Secretary will now read the minutes.

The Secretary read the Journal of the proceedings of Monday, March 23, of the Senate sitting for the trial of the articles of impeachment exhibited by the House of Representatives against Andrew Johnson, President of the United States.

The CHIEF JUSTICE. The Chair will lay before the Senate a resolution which has been received from the House of Representatives.

The Secretary read as follows:

IN THE HOUSE OF REPRESENTATIVES, *March* 24, 1868.

Resolved, That a message be sent to the Senate by the Clerk of the House, informing the Senate that the House of Representatives has adopted a replication to the answer of the President of the United States, to the articles of impeachment exhibited against him, and that the same will be presented to the Senate by the Managers on the part of the House.

Attest: EDWARD McPHERSON,
                          Clerk of the House of Representatives.

The CHIEF JUSTICE. The Senate will receive the replication of the Managers.

Mr. Manager BOUTWELL. Mr. President and Senators, I am charged by the Managers with presenting the replication which has been adopted by the House of Representatives:

IN THE HOUSE OF REPRESENTATIVES,
            UNITED STATES, *March 24, 1868.*

Replication by the House of Representatives of the United States to the answer of Andrew Johnson, President of the United States, to the Articles of Impeachment exhibited against him by the House of Representatives.

The House of Representatives of the United States have considered the several answers of Andrew Johnson, President of the United States, to the several articles of impeachment against him by them exhibited in the name of themselves and of all the people of the United States, and reserving to themselves all advantage of exception to the insufficiency of his answer to each and all of the several articles of impeachment exhibited against said Andrew Johnson, President of the United States, do deny each and every averment in said several answers, or either of them, which denies or traverses the acts, intents, crimes, or misdemeanors charged against said Andrew Johnson in the said articles of impeachment, or either of them; and for replication to said answer do say that said Andrew Johnson, President of the United States, is guilty of the high crimes and misdemeanors mentioned in said articles, and that the House of Representatives are ready to prove the same.

                          SCHUYLER COLFAX,
            Speaker of the House of Representatives.
EDWARD McPHERSON,
            Clerk of the House of Representatives.

The CHIEF JUSTICE. The replication will be received by the Secretary and filed.

Mr. JOHNSON. Mr. Chief Justice, I move that an authenticated copy of the replication be furnished to the counsel of the President.

The motion was agreed to.

The CHIEF JUSTICE. When the Senate sitting as a court of impeachment adjourned yesterday evening, a motion was pending on the part of the counsel for the President that such time should be allowed for preparation as the Senate might please to determine, and thereupon the Senator from Maryland [Mr. JOHNSON] submitted an order which will be read by the Secretary.

The Secretary read as follows:

Ordered, That the Senate proceed to the trial of the President under the articles of impeachment exhibited against him at the expiration of ten days from this day, unless for causes shown to the contrary.

The CHIEF JUSTICE. The question is on agreeing to the order.

Mr. SUMNER. Mr. President, I send to the Chair an amendment, to come in immediately after the word "Ordered," being in the nature of a substitute.

The CHIEF JUSTICE. The Senator from Massachusetts moves to strike out all after the word "Ordered," and to substitute what will be read by the Secretary.

The Secretary read as follows:

Now that replication has been filed, the Senate, adhering to its rule already adopted, will proceed with the trial from day to day (Sundays excepted) unless otherwise ordered on reason shown.

The CHIEF JUSTICE. The question is on the amendment by way of substitute.

Mr. EDMUNDS. Mr. President, I move that the Senate retire to consider the pending question.

Mr. SUMNER and others. No; no.

The CHIEF JUSTICE. It is moved by the Senator from Vermont that the Senate retire to consider the question arising upon the order moved by the Senator from Maryland and the substitute proposed by the Senator from Massachusetts. [Having put the question.] The ayes appear to have it.

Mr. CONKLING and Mr. SUMNER called for the yeas and nays, and they were ordered; and being taken, resulted—yeas 29, nays 23; as follows:

YEAS—Messrs. Anthony, Bayard, Buckalew, Corbett, Davis, Dixon, Doolittle, Edmunds, Fessenden, Fowler, Frelinghuysen, Grimes, Henderson, Hendricks, Howe, Johnson, McCreery, Morrill of Maine, Morrill of Vermont, Morton, Norton, Patterson of New Hampshire, Patterson of Tennessee, Saulsbury, Sprague, Van Winkle, Vickers, Willey, and Williams—29.

NAYS—Messrs. Cameron, Cattell, Chandler, Cole, Conkling, Conness, Cragin, Drake, Ferry, Harlan, Howard, Morgan, Nye, Pomeroy, Ramsey, Ross, Sherman, Stewart, Sumner, Thayer, Tipton, Trumbull, and Wilson—23.

NOT VOTING—Messrs. Wade and Yates—2.

The CHIEF JUSTICE. On this question the yeas are 29 and the nays are 23. So the motion is agreed to, and the Senate will retire for consultation.

The Senate accordingly, at twenty-five minutes past one o'clock, retired, with the Chief Justice, to their conference chamber.

The Senate having been called to order in their conference chamber,

The CHIEF JUSTICE stated the question to be on the amendment proposed by Mr. SUMNER to the order submitted by Mr. JOHNSON.

Mr. JOHNSON modified the order submitted by him so as to read:

Ordered, That the Senate will commence the trial of the President upon the articles of impeachment exhibited against him on Thursday, the 2d of April.

Mr. WILLIAMS submitted the following order:

Ordered, That the further consideration of the respondent's application for time be postponed until the Managers have opened their case and submitted their evidence.

Mr. CONKLING moved to amend the order

proposed by Mr. JOHNSON, by striking out "Thursday, the 2d of April," and inserting "Monday, the 30th of March instant."

Mr. SUMNER called for the yeas and nays on this amendment, and they were ordered; and being taken, resulted—yeas 28, nays 24; as follows:

YEAS—Messrs. Cameron, Cattell, Chandler, Cole, Conkling, Conness, Cragin, Drake, Ferry, Harlan, Howard, Howe, Morgan, Morrill of Maine, Morrill of Vermont, Morton, Nye, Patterson of New Hampshire, Pomeroy, Ramsey, Ross, Stewart, Sumner, Thayer, Tipton, Willey, Williams, and Wilson—28.

NAYS—Messrs. Anthony, Bayard, Buckalew, Corbett, Davis, Dixon, Doolittle, Edmunds, Fessenden, Fowler, Frelinghuysen, Grimes, Henderson, Hendricks, Johnson, McCreery, Norton, Patterson of Tennessee, Saulsbury, Sherman, Sprague, Trumbull, Van Winkle, and Vickers—24.

NOT VOTING—Messrs. Wade and Yates—2.

So the amendment was agreed to.

The CHIEF JUSTICE stated the next question to be upon the adoption of the order proposed by Mr. WILLIAMS.

Mr. WILLIAMS called for the yeas and nays, and they were ordered; and being taken, resulted—yeas 9, nays 42; as follows:

YEAS—Messrs. Anthony, Chandler, Dixon, Grimes, Harlan, Howard, Morgan, Patterson of Tennessee, and Williams—9.

NAYS—Messrs. Bayard, Buckalew, Cameron, Cattell, Cole, Conkling, Conness, Cragin, Davis, Doolittle, Drake, Edmunds, Ferry, Fessenden, Fowler, Frelinghuysen, Henderson, Hendricks, Howe, Johnson, McCreery, Morrill of Maine, Morrill of Vermont, Morton, Norton, Nye, Patterson of New Hampshire, Pomeroy, Ramsey, Ross, Saulsbury, Sherman, Sprague, Stewart, Sumner, Thayer, Tipton, Trumbull, Van Winkle, Vickers, Willey, and Wilson—42.

NOT VOTING—Messrs. Corbett, Wade, and Yates—3.

So the order proposed by Mr. WILLIAMS was not agreed to.

The question recurring on the amendment proposed in the Senate Chamber by Mr. SUMNER to the order submitted by Mr. JOHNSON, Mr. SUMNER withdrew his amendment.

The CHIEF JUSTICE stated the question to be on the order proposed by Mr. JOHNSON, as amended, as follows:

Ordered, That the Senate will commence the trial of the President upon the articles of impeachment exhibited against him on Monday, the 30th of March instant.

Mr. HENDRICKS moved to amend the order by adding thereto the words, "and proceed therein with all convenient dispatch, under the rules of the Senate sitting upon the trial of an impeachment."

The amendment was adopted; and the order, as amended, was agreed to.

On motion of Mr. MORTON, the Senate agreed to return to the Senate Chamber.

The Senate returned to the Chamber, and the Chief Justice resumed the Chair at twenty-three minutes past three o'clock p. m.

The CHIEF JUSTICE. The Chief Justice is instructed to inform the counsel for the respondent that the Senate has agreed upon an order in response to their application, which will now be read.

The Chief Clerk read as follows:

Ordered, That the Senate will commence the trial of the President upon the articles of impeachment exhibited against him, on Monday, the 30th of March instant, and proceed therein with all convenient dispatch, under the rules of the Senate sitting upon the trial of an impeachment.

The CHIEF JUSTICE. Have the Managers on the part of the House anything further to propose?

Mr. Manager BINGHAM. Mr. President, we have nothing further to propose.

The CHIEF JUSTICE. Have the counsel for the respondent anything to propose?

[No response.]

Mr. Manager BUTLER. Will the President allow me to give notice to the witnesses on the part of the House of Representatives who are in attendance, that they must appear here at one o'clock on Monday, the 30th?

Mr. EDMUNDS. Half past twelve o'clock. The rules provide for half past twelve.

Mr. Manager BUTLER. Half past twelve o'clock on Monday, the 30th.

Mr. WILSON. I move that the Senate sitting for the trial of this impeachment adjourn until Monday next at half past twelve o'clock.

The motion was agreed to.

The CHIEF JUSTICE. The Senate sitting as a court of impeachment stands adjourned until half past twelve o'clock on Monday next, the 30th instant.

MONDAY, March 30, 1868.

At half past twelve o'clock p. m. the Chief Justice of the United States entered the Senate Chamber, escorted by Mr. POMEROY, chairman of the committee heretofore appointed for that purpose.

The CHIEF JUSTICE. The Sergeant-at-Arms will open the court by proclamation.

The SERGEANT-AT-ARMS. Hear ye! hear ye! hear ye! All persons are commanded to keep silence while the Senate of the United States is sitting for the trial of the articles of impeachment exhibited by the House of Representatives against Andrew Johnson, President of the United States.

The President's counsel, Messrs. Stanbery, Curtis, Evarts, Nelson, and Groesbeck entered the Chamber and took the seats assigned to them.

At twelve o'clock and thirty-five minutes p. m. the Sergeant-at-Arms announced the presence of the Managers of the Impeachment on the part of the House of Representatives, and they were conducted to the seats assigned to them.

Immediately afterward the presence of the members of the House of Representatives was announced, and the members of the Committee of the Whole House, headed by Mr. E. B. WASHBURNE, of Illinois, the chairman of that committee, and accompanied by the Speaker and Clerk of the House of Representatives, entered the Senate Chamber and took the seats prepared for them.

The CHIEF JUSTICE. The minutes of the last day's proceedings will now be read by the Secretary.

The Secretary read the proceedings of the Senate sitting on Tuesday, March 24, 1868, for the trial of Andrew Johnson, President of the United States.

The CHIEF JUSTICE. Gentlemen, Managers of the House of Representatives, you will now proceed in support of the articles of impeachment. Senators will please give their attention.

Opening Argument of Mr. BUTLER, *of Massachusetts, one of the Managers on the impeachment of the President.*

Mr. President and Gentlemen of the Senate:

The onerous duty has fallen to my fortune to present to you, imperfectly as I must, the several propositions of fact and law upon which the House of Representatives will endeavor to sustain the cause of the people against the President of the United States, now pending at your bar.

The high station of the accused, the novelty of the proceeding, the gravity of the business, the importance of the questions to be presented to your adjudication, the possible momentous result of the issues, each and all must plead for me to claim your attention for as long a time as your patience may endure.

Now, for the first time in the history of the world, has a nation brought before its highest tribunal its chief executive magistrate for trial and possible deposition from office upon charges of maladministration of the powers and duties of that office. In other times and in other lands it has been found that despotisms could only be tempered by assassination, and nations living under constitutional governments even have found no mode by which to rid themselves of a tyrannical, imbecile, or faithless ruler, save by overturning the very foundation and framework of the Government itself. And but recently, in one of the most civilized and powerful Governments of the world, from which our own institutions have been largely modeled, we have seen a nation submit for years to the rule of an insane king, because its constitution contained no method for his removal.

Our fathers, more wisely founding our Government, have provided for such and all similar exigencies a conservative, effectual, and practical remedy by the constitutional provision that the "President, Vice President, and all civil officers of the United States *shall* be removed from office on impeachment for and conviction of treason, bribery, or other high crimes and misdemeanors." The Constitution leaves nothing to implication, either as to the persons upon whom, or the body by whom, or the tribunal before which, or the offenses for which, or the manner in which this high power should be exercised; each and all are provided for by express words of imperative command.

The House of Representatives shall solely impeach; the Senate only shall try; and in case of conviction the judgment shall alone be removal from office and disqualification for office, one or both. These mandatory provisions became necessary to adapt a well-known procedure of the mother country to the institutions of the then infant Republic. But a single incident only of the business was left to construction, and that concerns the offenses or incapacities which are the groundwork of impeachment. This was wisely done, because human foresight is inadequate and human intelligence fails in the task of anticipating and providing for, by positive enactment, all the infinite gradations of human wrong and sin by which the liberties of a people and the safety of a nation may be endangered from the imbecility, corruption, and unhallowed ambition of its rulers.

It may not be uninstructive to observe that the framers of the Constitution, while engaged in their glorious and, I trust, ever-enduring work, had their attention aroused and their minds quickened most signally upon this very topic. In the previous year only Mr. Burke, from his place in the House of Commons in England, had preferred charges for impeachment against Warren Hastings, and three days before our convention sat he was impeached at the bar of the House of Lords for misbehavior in office as the ruler of a people whose numbers were counted by millions. The mails were then bringing across the Atlantic, week by week, the eloquent accusations of Burke, the gorgeous and burning denunciations of Sheridan, in behalf of the oppressed people of India, against one who had wielded over them more than regal power. May it not have been that the trial then in progress was the determining cause why the framers of the Constitution left the description of offenses because of which the conduct of an officer might be inquired of to be defined by the laws and usages of Parliament as found in the precedents of the mother country, with which our fathers were as familiar as we are with our own?

In the light, therefore, of these precedents, he question arises, *What are impeachable offenses* under the provisions of our Constitution?

To analyze, to compare, to reconcile these precedents is a work rather for the closet than the forum. In order, therefore, to spare your attention, I have preferred to state the result to which I have arrived, and that you may see the authorities and discussions, both in this country and in England, from which we deduce our propositions, so far as applicable to this case, I pray leave to lay before you, at the close of my argument, a brief of all the precedents and authorities upon this subject in both countries, for which I am indebted to the exhaustive and learned labors of my friend, Hon. WILLIAM LAWRENCE, of Ohio, member of the Judiciary Committee of the House of Representatives, in which I fully concur and which I adopt.

We define, therefore, an impeachable high crime or misdemeanor to be *one in its nature or consequences subversive of some fundamental or essential principle of government or highly prejudicial to the public interest, and this may consist of a violation of the Constitution, of law, of an official oath, or of duty, by an act committed or omitted, or, without violating a positive law, by the abuse of discretionary powers from improper motives, or for any improper purpose.*

The first criticism which will strike the mind on a cursory examination of this definition is that some of the enumerated acts are not within the common-law definition of crimes. It is but common learning that in the English precedents the words "high crimes and misdemeanors" are universally used; but any malversation in office highly prejudicial to the public interest, or subversive of some fundamental principle of government by which the safety of a people may be in danger, is a high crime against the nation, as the term is used in parliamentary law.

Hallam, in his Constitutional History of England, certainly deduces this doctrine from the precedents, and especially Lord Danby, case 14, State Trials, 600, of which he says:

"The Commons, in impeaching Lord Danby, went a great way toward establishing the principle that no minister can shelter himself behind the throne by pleading obedience to the orders of his sovereign. He is answerable for the *justice, the honesty, the utility of all measures emanating* from the crown, as well as for their *legality;* and thus the executive administration is, or ought to be, subordinate in all great matters of policy to the superintendence and virtual control of the two Houses of Parliament."

Mr. Christian, in his notes to the Commentaries of Blackstone, explains the collocation and use of the words "high crimes and misdemeanors" by saying:

"When the words 'high crimes and misdemeanors, are used in prosecutions by impeachment the words 'high crimes' have no definite signification, but are used merely to give greater solemnity to the charge."

A like interpretation must have been given by the framers of the Constitution, because a like definition to ours was in the mind of Mr. Madison, to whom more than to any other we are indebted for the phraseology of our Constitution, for, in the First Congress, when *discussing* the power to remove an officer by the President, which is one of the very material questions before the Senate at this moment, he uses the following words:

"The danger consists mainly in this: that the President can displace from office a man whose merits require he should be continued in it. In the first place, he will be impeachable by the House for such an act of maladministration, for I contend that the wanton removal of meritorious officers would subject him to impeachment and removal from his own high trust."

Strengthening this view, we find that within ten years afterward impeachment was applied by the very men who framed the Constitution to the acts of public officers which under no common-law definition could be justly called crimes or misdemeanors, either high or low. Leaving, however, the correctness of our proposition to be sustained by the authorities we furnish, we are naturally brought to the consideration of the method of the procedure and the nature of the proceedings in cases of impeachment, and the character and powers of the tribunal by which high crimes and misdemeanors are to be adjudged or determined.

One of the important questions which meets us at the outset is: is this proceeding a trial, as that term is understood so far as relates to the rights and duties of a court and jury upon an indictment for crime? Is it not rather more in the nature of an inquest of office?

The Constitution seems to have determined it to be the latter, because, under its provisions, the right to retain and hold office is the only subject that can be finally adjudicated; all preliminary inquiry being carried on solely to determine that question, and that alone.

All investigations of fact are, in some sense, trials, but not in the sense in which the word is used by courts.

Again, as a correlative question:

Is this body, now sitting to determine the accusation of the House of Representatives against the President of the United States, the Senate of the United States or a court?

I trust, Mr. President and Senators, I may be pardoned for making some suggestions upon these topics, because to us it seems these are questions not of forms, but of substance. If this body here is a court in any manner as contradistinguished from the Senate, then we agree that many, if not all, the analogies of the procedures of courts must obtain; that the common-law incidents of a trial in court must have place; that you may be bound in your proceedings and adjudication by the rules and precedents of the common or statute law; that the interest, bias, or preconceived opinions or affinities to the party of the judges may be open to inquiry, and even the rules of order and precedents in courts should have effect; that the Managers of the House of Representatives must conform to those rules as they would be applicable to public or private prosecutors of crime in courts, and that the accused may claim the benefit of the rule in criminal cases, that he may only be convicted when the evidence makes the fact clear beyond reasonable doubt, instead of by a preponderance of the evidence.

We claim, and respectfully insist, that this tribunal has none of the attributes of a judicial court as they are commonly received and understood. Of course this question must be largely determined by the express provisions of the Constitution, and in it there is no word, as is well known to you, Senators, which gives the slightest coloring to the idea that this is a court, save that in the trial of this particular respondent the Chief Justice of the Supreme Court must preside. But even this provision can have no determining effect upon the question, because is not this the same tribunal in all its powers, incidents, and duties, when other civil officers are brought to its bar for trial, when the Vice President (not a judicial officer) must preside? Can it be contended for a moment that this is the Senate of the United States when sitting on the trial of all other officers, and a court only when the President is at the bar, solely because in this case the Constitution has designated the Chief Justice as the presiding officer?

The fact that Senators are sitting for this purpose on oath or affirmation does not influence the argument, because it is well understood that that was but a substitute for the obligation of honor under which, by the theory of the British constitution, the peers of England were supposed to sit in like cases.

A peer of England makes answer in a court of chancery upon honor when a common person must answer upon oath. But our fathers, sweeping away all distinctions of caste, required every man alike, acting in a solemn proceeding like this, to take an oath. Our Constitution holds all good men alike honorable and entitled to honor.

The idea that this tribunal was a court seems to have crept in because of the analogy to similar proceedings in trials before the House of Lords.

Analogies have ever been found deceptive and illusory. Before such analogy is invoked we must not forget that the Houses of Parliament at first, and latterly the House of Lords, claimed and exercised jurisdiction over all crimes, even where the punishment extended to life and limb. By express provision of our Constitution all such jurisdiction is taken from the Senate and "the judicial power of the United States is vested in one Supreme Court and such inferior courts as from time to time Congress may ordain and establish."

We suggest, therefore, that we are in the presence of the Senate of the United States, convened as a constitutional tribunal, to inquire into and determine whether Andrew Johnson, because of malversation in office, is longer fit to retain the office of President of the United States, or hereafter to hold any office of honor or profit.

I respectfully submit that thus far your mode of proceeding has no analogy to that of a court. You issue a summons to give the respondent notice of the case pending against him. You do not sequester his person—you do not require his personal appearance even; you proceed against him and will *go on* to determine his cause in his absence, and make the final order therein. How different is each step from those of ordinary criminal procedure.

A constitutional tribunal solely, you are bound by no law, either statute or common, which may limit your constitutional prerogative. You consult no precedents save those of the law and custom of parliamentary bodies. You are a law unto yourselves, bound only by

the natural principles of equity and justice, and that *salus populi suprema est lex.*

Upon these principles and parliamentary law no judges can aid you, and, indeed, in late years the judges of England in the trial of impeachment, declined to speak to a question of parliamentary law, even at the request of the House of Peers, although they attended on them in their robes of office.

Nearly five hundred years ago, in 1388, the House of Lords resolved, in the case of Belknap and the other judges, "That these matters, when brought before them, shall be discussed and adjudged by the course of Parliament, and not by the civil law, nor by the common law of the land used in other inferior courts."

And that resolution, which was in contravention of the opinion of all the judges of England, and against the remonstrance of Richard II, remains the unquestioned law of England to this day.

Another determining quality of this tribunal, distinguishing it from a court and the analogies of ordinary legal proceedings, and showing that it is a Senate only, is, that there can be no right of challenge by either party to any of its members for favor or malice, affinity, or interest. This has been held from the earliest times in Parliament even when that was the high court of judicature of the realm sitting to punish all crimes against the peace.

In the case of the Duke of Somerset, (1 Howell's State Trials, page 521,) as early as 1551, it was held that the Duke of Northumberland and the Marquis of Northampton and the Earl of Pembroke, for an attempt upon whose lives Somerset was on trial, should sit in judgment upon him against the objection of the accused because "a peer of the realm might not be challenged."

Again, the Duke of Northumberland, (*ibid.,* 1 State Trials, p. 765,) Marquis of Northampton, and Earl of Warwick, being on trial for their lives, A. D. 1553, before the court of the Lord High Steward of England, one of the prisoners inquired whether any such persons as were equally culpable in that crime, and those by whose letters and commandments he was directed in all his doings, might be his judges, or pass upon his trial at his death. It was answered that, "If any were as deeply to be touched as himself in that case, yet as long as no attainder of record were against them, they were nevertheless persons able in the law to pass upon any trial, and not to be challenged therefor, but at the prince's pleasure."

Again, on the trial of Earls of Essex and Southampton (*ibid.,* 1 State Trials, p. 1335) for high treason. before all the justices of England, A. D. 1600, the Earl of Essex desired to know of my Lord Chief Justice whether he might challenge any of the peers or no. Whereunto the Lord Chief Justice answered "No."

Again, in Lord Audley's case (*ibid.,* 3 State Trials, p. 402, A. D., 1631) it was questioned whether a peer might challenge his peers, as in the case of common jurats. It was answered by all the judges, after consultation, "he might not." [This case is of more value because it was an indictment for being accessory to rape upon his own wife, and had no political influence in it whatever.] The same point was ruled in the Countess of Essex's case, on trial for treason. (Moore's Reports, 621.)

In the Earl of Portland's case, A. D. 1701, (*ibid.*, State Trials, p. 288,) the Commons objected that Lord Sommers, the Earl of Oxford, and Lord Halifax, who had been impeached by the Commons before the House of Lords for being concerned in the same acts for which Portland was being brought to trial, voted and acted with the House of Lords in the preliminary proceedings of said trial, and were upon a committee of conference in relation thereto. But the lords after discussion solemnly resolved "that no lord of Parliament, impeached of high crimes and misdemeanors, can be precluded from voting on any occasion, except on his own trial."

In the trial of Lord Viscount Melville, A. D. 1806, (*ibid.*, 29 State Trials, p. 1398,) some observations having been made as to the possible bias of some portion of the peers, (by the counsel for defendant,) Mr. Whitebread, one of the managers on the part of the Commons, answered as follows:

"My lords, as to your own court, something has been thrown out about the possibility of a challenge. Upon such a subject it will not be necessary to say more than this, which has been admitted: that an order was given by the House of Commons to prosecute Lord Melville in a court of law where he would have the *right* to challenge his jurors." * * * * "What did the noble viscount then do by the means of one of his friends?" * * * "From the mouth of that learned gentleman came at last the successful motion: 'that Henry, Viscount of Melville, be impeached of high crimes and misdemeanors.' I am justified, then, in saying that he is here by his own option." * * * * "But, my lords, a challenge to your lordships! Is not every individual peer the guardian of his own honor?"

In the trial of Warren Hastings the same point was ruled, or, more properly speaking, taken for granted, for of the more than one hundred and seventy peers who commenced the trial but twenty-nine sat and pronounced the verdict at the close, and some of those were peers created since the trial began, and had not heard either the opening or much of the evidence; and during the trial there had been by death, succession, and creation, more than one hundred and eighty changes in the House of Peers, who were his judges.

We have abundant authority also on this point in our own country.

In the case of Judge Pickering, who was tried in March, 1804, for drunkenness in office, although undefended in form, yet he had all his rights preserved.

This trial being postponed a session, three Senators—Samuel Smith of Maryland, Israel Smith of Vermont, and John Smith of New York—who had all been members of the House of Representatives, and there voted in favor of impeaching Judge Pickering, were Senators when his trial came off.

Mr. Smith, of New York, raised the question, by asking to be excused from voting. Mr. Smith, of Maryland, declared "he would not be influenced from his duty by any false delicacy; that he, for his part, felt no delicacy upon the subject; the vote he had given in the other House to impeach Judge Pickering would have no influence upon him in the court; his constituents had a right to his vote, and he would not by any act of his deprive, or consent to deprive, them of that right, but would claim and exercise it upon this as upon every other question that might be submitted to the Senate while he had the honor of a seat."

A vote being had upon the question, it was determined that these gentlemen should sit and vote on the trial. This passed in the affirmative by a vote of 19 to 7, and all the gentlemen sat and voted on every question during the trial.

On the trial of Samuel Chase before the Senate of the United States no challenge was attempted, although the case was decided by an almost strict party vote in high party times, and doubtless many of the Senators had formed and expressed opinions upon his conduct.

That arbitrary judge, but learned lawyer, knew too much to attempt any such futile movement as a challenge to a Senator. Certain it is that the proprieties of the occasion were not marred by the worse than anomalous proceeding of the challenge of one Senator to another, especially before the defendant had appeared.

Nor did the managers exercise the right of challenge, although Senators Smith and Mitchell, of New York, were members of the Senate on the trial and voted *not guilty* on every article, who had been members of the House when the articles were found, and had there voted steadily against the whole proceeding.

Judge Peck's case, which was tried in 1831, affords another instance in point.

The conduct of Judge Peck had been the subject of much animadversion and comment by the public, and had been for four years pending before the Congress of the United States before it finally came to trial. It was not possible but that many of the Senate had both formed and expressed opinions upon Peck's proceedings, and yet it never occurred to that good lawyer to make objection to his triers. Nor did the managers challenge, although Webster, of Massachusetts, was a member of the committee of the House of Representatives to whom the petition for impeachment was referred, and which, after examination, reported thereon "leave to withdraw," and Sprague, of Maine, voted against the proceedings of the House, while Livingston, of Louisiana, voted for them. All of these gentlemen sat upon the trial, and voted as they did in the House.

A very remarkable and instructive case was

that of Judge Addison, of Pennsylvania, in 1804: There, after the articles of impeachment were framed, the trial was postponed to another session of the Legislature. Meanwhile three members of the House of Representatives, who had voted for the articles of impeachment, were elected to the Senate and became the triers of the articles of impeachment of which they had solemnly voted the respondent to be guilty. To their sitting on the trial Judge Addison objected, but after an exhaustive argument his objection was overruled—17 to 6. Two of the minority were the gentlemen who had voted him guilty, and who themselves objected to sitting on the trial.

Thus stands the case upon authority. How does it stand upon principle?

In a conference held in 1691, between the Lords and Commons, on a proposition to limit the number of judges, the Lords made answer:

"That in the case of impeachments, which are the groans of the people, and for the highest crimes, and carry with them a greater supposition of guilt than any other accusation, there all the lords must judge."

There have been many instances in England where this necessity, that no peer be excused from sitting on such trials, has produced curious results. Brothers have sat upon the trials of brothers, fathers upon the trials of sons and daughters, uncles upon the trials of nephews and nieces; no excuse being admitted.

One, and a most peculiar and painful instance, will suffice upon this point to illustrate the strength of the rule. In the trial of Anne Bullen, the wife of one sovereign of England and the mother of another, her father, Lord Rochefort, and her uncle, the Duke of Norfolk, sat as judges and voted guilty, although one of the charges against the daughter and niece was a criminal intimacy with her brother, the son and nephew of the judges.

It would seem impossible that in a proceeding before such a tribunal so constituted there could be a challenge, because, as the number of triers is limited by law, and as there are not now, and never have been, any provisions, either in England or in this country, for substituting another for the challenged party, as a talesman is substituted in a jury, the accused might escape punishment altogether by challenging a sufficient number to prevent a quorum, or the accuser might oppress the respondent by challenging all persons favorable to him until the necessary unanimity for conviction was secured.

This proceeding being but an inquest of office, and, except in a few rare instances, always partaking, more or less, of political considerations, and requiring to be discussed, before presentation to the triers, by the coördinate branch of the Legislature, it is impossible that Senators should not have opinions and convictions upon the subject-matter more or less decidedly formed before the case reaches them. If, therefore, challenges could be allowed because of such opinions, as in the case of jurors, no trial could go forward, because every intelligent Senator could be objected to upon one side or the other.

I should have hardly dared to trouble the Senate with such minuteness of citation and argument upon this point, were it not that certain persons and papers outside of this body, by sophistries drawn from the analogies of the proceedings in courts before juries, have endeavored, in advance, to prejudice the public mind, but little instructed in this topic, because of the infrequency of impeachments, against the legal validity and propriety of the proceedings upon this trial.

I may be permitted, without offense, further to state that these and similar reasons have prevented the Managers from objecting by challenge or otherwise to the competency of one of the triers of near affinity to the accused.

We believe it is his right, nay, his duty to the State he represents, to sit upon the trial as he would upon any other matter which should come before the Senate. His seat and vote belong to his constituents, and not to himself, to be used according to his best judgment upon every grave matter that comes before the Senate.

Again, as political considerations are involved in this trial, raising questions of interest to the constituents of every Senator, it is his right and duty to express himself as fully and freely upon such questions as upon any other, even to express a belief in the guilt or innocence of the accused, or to say he will sustain him in the course he is taking, although he so says after accusation brought. Let me illustrate. Suppose that after this impeachment had been voted by the House of Representatives the constituents of any Senator had called a public meeting to sustain the President against what they were pleased to term the "tyrannical acts of Congress toward him in impeaching him," and should call upon their Senator to attend and take part in such meeting, I do not conceive that it would or ought to be legally objected against him as a disqualification to sit upon this trial, upon the principles I have stated, if he should attend the meeting or favor the object, or if his engagements in the Senate prevented his leaving. I have not been able to find any legal objection in the books to his writing a letter to such meeting, containing, among other things, statements like the following:

Senate Chamber, February 21, 1868.

Gentlemen: My public and professional engagements will be such on the 4th of March that I am reluctantly compelled to decline your invitation to be present and address the meeting to be held in our city on that day. * * * * * * * That the President of the United States has sincerely endeavored to preserve these (our free institutions) from violation I have no doubt, and I have, therefore, throughout the unfortunate difference of opinion between him and Congress, sustained him. And this I shall continue to do as long as he shall prove faithful to duty. With my best thanks for the honor you have done me by your invitation, and regretting that it is not in my power to accept it,

I remain, with regard, your obedient servant,
REVERDY JOHNSON.

We should have as much right to expect his vote on a clearly-proven case of guilty as had King Henry VIII to hope for the vote of her father against his wife. He got it.

King Henry knew the strength of his case, and we know the strength of ours against this respondent.

If it be said that this is an infelicity, it is a sufficient and decisive answer that it is the infelicity of a precise constitutional provision, which provides that the Senate shall have the sole power to try impeachments, and the only security against bias or prejudice on the part of any Senator is, that *two thirds* of the Senators present are necessary for conviction.

To this rule there is but one possible exception, founded on both reason and authority, that a Senator may not be a judge in his own case.

I have thought it necessary to determine the nature and attributes of the tribunal before we attend to the scope and meaning of the accusation before it.

The first eight articles set out in several distinct forms the acts of the respondent in removing Mr. Stanton from office, and appointing Mr. Thomas *ad interim*, differing in legal effect in the purposes for which and the intent with which either or both of the acts were done, and the legal duties and rights infringed and the acts of Congress violated in so doing.

All the articles allege these acts to be in contravention of his oath of office, and in disregard of the duties thereof.

If they are so, however, the President might have the *power* to do them under the law; still, being so done, they are acts of official misconduct, and, as we have seen, impeachable.

The President has the legal power to do many acts which, if done in disregard of his duty, or for improper purposes, then the exercise of that power is an official misdemeanor.

Ex. gr.: he has the power of pardon; if exercised in a given case for a corrupt motive, as for the payment of money, or wantonly pardoning all criminals, it would be a misdemeanor. Examples might be multiplied indefinitely.

Article first, stripped of legal verbiage, alleges that, having suspended Mr. Stanton and reported the same to the Senate, which refused to concur in the suspension, and Stanton having rightfully resumed the duties of his office, the respondent, with knowledge of the facts, issued an order which is recited for Stanton's removal, with intent to violate the act of March 2, 1867, to regulate the tenure of certain civil offices, and with the further intent to remove Stanton from the office of Secretary of War, then in the lawful discharge of its duties, in contravention of said act, without the advice and consent of the Senate, and against the Constitution of the United States.

Article two charges that the President, without authority of law, on the 21st of February, 1868, issued letter of authority to Lorenzo Thomas to act as Secretary of War *ad interim*,

the Senate being in session, in violation of the tenure-of-office act, and with intent to violate it and the Constitution, there being no vacancy in the office of Secretary of War.

Article three alleges the same act as done without authority of law, and alleges an intent to violate the Constitution.

Article four charges that the President conspired with Lorenzo Thomas and divers other persons, with intent, by *intimidation and threats*, to prevent Mr. Stanton from holding the office of Secretary of War, in violation of the Constitution and of the act of July 31, 1861.

Article five charges the same conspiracy with Thomas to prevent Mr. Stanton's holding his office, and thereby to prevent the execution of the civil-tenure act.

Article six charges that the President conspired with Thomas to seize and possess the property under the control of the War Department by *force*, in contravention of the act of July 31, 1861, and with intent to disregard the civil tenure-of-office act.

Article seven charges the same conspiracy, with intent only to violate the civil tenure-of-office act.

Articles three, four, five, six and seven, may all be considered together, as to the proof to support them.

It will be shown that, having removed Stanton and appointed Thomas, the President sent Thomas to the War Office to obtain possession; that having been met by Stanton with a denial of his rights, Thomas retired, and after consultation with the President Thomas asserted his purpose to take possession of the War Office by force, making his boast in several public places of his intentions so to do, but was prevented by being promptly arrested by process from the court.

This will be shown by the evidence of Hon. Mr. Van Horn, a member of the House, who was present when the demand for possession of the War Office was made by General Thomas, already made public.

By the testimony of Hon. Mr. Burleigh, who, after that, in the evening of the 21st of February, was told by Thomas that he intended to take possession of the War Office by force the following morning, and invited him up to see the performance. Mr. Burleigh attended, but the act did not come off, for Thomas had been arrested and held to bail.

By Thomas boasting at Willard's Hotel on the same evening that he should call on General Grant for military force to put him in possession of the office, and he did not see how Grant could refuse it.

Article eight charges that the appointment of Thomas was made for the purpose of getting control of the disbursement of moneys appropriated for the military service and Department of War.

In addition to the proof already adduced it will be shown that, after the appointment of Thomas, which must have been known to the members of his Cabinet, the President caused a formal notice to be served on the Secretary of the Treasury to the end that the Secretary might answer the requisitions for money of Thomas, and this was only prevented by the firmness with which Stanton retained possession of the books and papers of the War Office.

It will be seen that every fact charged in article one is admitted by the answer of the respondent; the intent is also admitted as charged; that is to say, to set aside the civil tenure-of-office act, and to remove Mr. Stanton from the office of the Secretary for the Department of War without the advice and consent of the Senate, and, if not justified, contrary to the provisions of the Constitution itself.

The only question remaining is, does the respondent justify himself by the Constitution and laws?

On this he avers, that by the Constitution there is "conferred on the President, as a part of the executive power, the power at any and all times of removing from office all executive officers for cause, to be judged of by the President alone, and that he verily believes that the executive power of removal from office confided to him by the Constitution, as aforesaid, includes the power of suspension from office indefinitely."

Now, these offices so vacated must be filled temporarily, at least, by his appointment, because government must go on; there can be no interregnum in the execution of the laws in an organized Government; he claims, therefore, of necessity, the right to fill their places with appointments of his choice, and that this power cannot be restrained or limited in any degree by any law of Congress, because, he avers, "that the power was conferred, and the duty of exercising it in fit cases was imposed on the President by the Constitution of the United States, and that the President could not be deprived of this power or relieved of this duty, nor could the same be vested by law in the President and the Senate jointly, either in part or whole."

This, then, is the plain and inevitable issue before the Senate and the American people:

Has the President, under the Constitution, the more than kingly prerogative at will to remove from office and suspend from office indefinitely, all executive officers of the United States, either civil, military, or naval, at any and all times, and fill the vacancies with creatures of his own appointment, for his own purposes, without any restraint whatever, or possibility of restraint by the Senate or by Congress through laws duly enacted?

The House of Representatives, in behalf of the people, join this issue by affirming that the exercise of such powers is a high misdemeanor in office.

If the affirmative is maintained by the respondent, then, so far as the first eight articles

are concerned—unless such corrupt purposes are shown as will of themselves make the exercise of a legal power a crime—the respondent must go, and ought to go quit and free.

Therefore, by these articles and the answers thereto, the momentous question, here and now, is raised whether the *presidential office itself* (*if it has the prerogatives and power claimed for it*) ought, *in fact, to exist as a part of the constitutional government of a free people*, while by the last three articles the simpler and less important inquiry is to be determined, whether Andrew Johnson has so conducted himself that he ought longer to hold any constitutional office whatever. The latter sinks to merited insignificance compared with the grandeur of the former.

If that is sustained, then a right and power hitherto unclaimed and unknown to the people of the country is ingrafted on the Constitution, most alarming in its extent, most corrupting in its influence, most dangerous in its tendencies, and most tyrannical in its exercise.

Whoever, therefore, votes ".not guilty" on these articles votes to enchain our free intitutions, and to prostrate them at the feet of any man who, being President, may choose to control them.

For this most stupendous and unlimited prerogative the respondent cites no line and adduces no word of constitutional enactment; indeed he could not, for the only mention of removal from office in the Constitution is as a part of the judgment in case of impeachment, and the only power of appointment is by nomination to the Senate of officers to be appointed by their advice and consent, save a qualified and limited power of appointment by the President when the Senate is not in session. Whence, then, does the respondent by his answer, claim to have derived this power? I give him the benefit of his own words, "that it was practically settled by the First Congress of the United States." Again, I give him the benefit of his own phrases as set forth in his messsage to the Senate of 2d of March, 1867, made a part of his answer: "the question was decided by the House of Representatives by a vote of 34 to 20, (in this, however, he is mistaken,) and in the Senate by the casting vote of the Vice President." In the same answer he admits that before he undertook the exercise of this most dangerous and stupendous power, after seventy-five years of study and examination of the Constitution by the people living under it, another Congress has decided that there was no such unlimited power; so that he admits that this tremendous power which he claims from the legislative construction of one Congress by a vote of 34 to 20 in the House and a tie vote in the Senate has been denied by another House of more than three times the number of members by a vote of 133 to 37, and by a Senate of more than double the number of Senators by a vote of 38 to 10, and this, too, after he had presented to them all the arguments in its favor that he could find to sustain his claim of power.

If he derives this power from the practical settlement of one Congress of a legislative construction of the constitutional provisions, why may not such construction be as practically settled more authoritatively by the greater unanimity of another Congress—yea, as we shall see, of many other Congresses?

The great question, however, still returns upon us, whence comes this power? How derived or conferred? Is it unlimited and unrestrained, illimitable and unrestrainable, as the President claims it to be?

In presenting this topic it will be my duty, and I shall attempt to do nothing more, to state the propositions of law and the authorities to support them, so far as they may come to my knowledge, leaving the argument and illustrations of the question to be extended in the close by abler and better hands.

If a power of removal in the Executive is found at all in the Constitution it is admitted to be an implied one, either from the power of appointment or because "the executive power is vested in the President."

Has the executive power granted by the Constitution by these words any limitations? Does the Constitution invest the President with all executive power, prerogatives, privileges, and immunities enjoyed by executive officers of other countries—kings and emperors—without limitation? If so, then the Constitution has been much more liberal in granting powers to the executive than to the legislative branch of the Government, as that has only "all legislative powers herein granted [which] shall be vested in the Congress of the United States;" not all uncontrollable legislative powers, as there are many limitations upon that power as exercised by the Parliament of England, for example. So there are many executive powers expressly limited in the Constitution, such as declaring war, making rules and regulations for the government of the Army and Navy, and coining money.

As some executive powers are limited by the Constitution itself, is it not clear that the words "the executive power is vested in the President" do not confer on him all executive powers, but must be construed with reference to other constitutional provisions granting or regulating specific powers? The executive power of appointment is clearly limited by the words:

"He shall nominate, and, by and with the advice and consent of the Senate, shall appoint, embassadors," * * * * "and all other officers of the United States whose appointments are not herein otherwise provided for, and which shall be established by law."

It is not, therefore, more in accordance with the theory of the Constitution to imply the power of removal from the power of appointment, restrained by like limitations, than to imply it

solely as a prerogative of executive power and, therefore, illimitable and uncontrollable? Have the people anywhere else in the Constitution granted illimitable and uncontrollable powers either to the executive or any other branch of the Government? Is not the whole frame of government one of checks, balances, and limitations? Is it to be believed that our fathers, just escaping from the oppressions of monarchical power, and so dreading it that they feared the very name of king, gave this more than kingly power to the Executive, illimitable and uncontrollable, and that, too, by implication merely?

Upon this point our proposition is, that the Senate being in session, and an office, not an inferior one, within the terms of the Constitution, being filled, the President has the implied power of inaugurating the removal *only* by nomination of a successor to the Senate, which, when consented to, works the full removal and supersedeas of the incumbent. Such has been, it is believed, the practice of the Government from the beginning down to the act about which we are inquiring. Certain it is that Mr. Webster, in the Senate in 1835, so asserted without contradiction, using the following language:

"If one man be Secretary of State and another be appointed, the first goes out by the mere force of the appointment of the other, without any previous act of removal whatever. And this is the practice of the Government, and has been from the first. In all the removals which have been made they have generally been effected simply by making other appointments. I cannot find a case to the contrary. There is no such thing as any distinct official act of removal. I have looked into the practice, and caused inquiries to be made in the Departments, and I do not learn that any such proceeding is known as an entry or record of the removal of an officer from office, and the President would only act in such cases by causing some proper record or entry to be made as proof of the fact of removal. I am aware that there have been some cases in which notice has been sent to persons in office that their services are or will be, after a given day, dispensed with. These are usually cases in which the object is, not to inform the incumbent that he is removed, but to tell him that a successor either is, or by a day named will be, appointed. If there be any instances in which such notice is given, without express reference to the appointment of a successor, they are few; and even in these such reference must be implied, because in no case is there any distinct official act of removal, as I can find, unconnected with the act of appointment."

This would seem to reconcile all the provisions of the Constitution, the right of removal being in the President, to be executed *sub modo*, as is the power of appointment, the appointment, when consummated, making the removal.

This power was elaborately debated in the First Congress upon the bills establishing a Department of Foreign Affairs and the War Department. The debate arose on the motion, in Committee of the Whole, to strike out, after the title of the officer, the words, "to be removable from office by the President of the United States." It was four days discussed in Committee of the Whole in the House, and the clause retained by a vote of 20 yeas to 34 nays, which seemed to establish the power of removal as either by a legislative grant or construction of the Constitution. But the triumph of its friends was short-lived, for, when the bill came up in the House, Mr. Benson moved to amend it by altering the second section of the bill, so as to *imply* only the power of removal to be in the President, by inserting that "whenever the principal officer shall be removed from office by the President of the United States, or in any other case of vacancy, the chief clerk shall, during such vacancy, have charge and custody of all records, books, and papers appertaining to the Department."

Mr. Benson "declared he would move to strike out the words in the first clause, to be removable by the President, which appeared somewhat like a grant. Now, the mode he took would evade that point and establish a legislative construction of the Constitution. He also hoped his amendment would succeed in reconciling both sides of the House to the decision and quieting the minds of the gentlemen."

After debate the amendment was carried, 30 to 18. Mr. Benson then moved to strike out the words "to be removable by the President of the United States," which was carried, 31 to 19; and so the bill was engrossed and sent to the Senate.

The debates of that body being in secret session, we have no record of the discussion which arose on the motion of Mr. Benson establishing the implied power of removal; but after very elaborate consideration on several successive days the words implying this power in the President were retained by the casting vote of the elder Adams, the Vice President. So this claimed "legislative settlement" was only established by the vote of the second executive officer of the Government. Alas! most of our woes in this Government have come from Vice Presidents. When the bill establishing the War Department came up the same words, "to be removable by the President," were struck out, on the motion of one of the opponents of the recognition of this power, by a vote of 24 to 22, a like amendment to that of the second section of the act establishing the Department of State being inserted. When, six years afterward, the Department of the Navy was established, no such recognition of the power of the President to remove was inserted; and as the measure passed by a strict party vote, 47 yeas to 41 nays, it may well be conceived that its advocates did not care to load it with this constitutional question when the executive power was about passing into other hands, for one cannot read the debates upon this question without being impressed with the belief that reverence for the character of Washington largely determined the argument in the First Congress. Neither party did or could have looked forward to such an executive administration as we have this day.

It has generally been conceded in subsequent discussions that here was a legislative determination of this question, but I humbly

C. I.—5.

submit that taking the whole action of Congress together it is very far from being determined. I should hardly have dared, in view of the eminent names of Holmes, Clay, Webster, and Calhoun, that have heretofore made the admission, to have ventured the assertion, were it not that in every case they, as do the President and his counsel, rely on the first vote in the Committee of the Whole, sustaining the words "to be removable by the President," and in no instance take any notice of the subsequent proceedings in the House by which those words were taken out of the bill. This may have happened because Eliot's Debates, which is the authority most frequently cited in these discussions, stops with the vote in committee, and takes no notice of the further discussion. But whatever may be the effect of this legislative construction the contemporaneous and subsequent practice of the Government shows that the President made no removals except by nominations to the Senate when in session, and superseding officers by a new commission to the confirmed nominee. Mr. Adams, in that remarkable letter to Mr. Pickering in which he desires his resignation, requests him to send it early in order that he may nominate to the Senate, then about to sit, and he in fact removes Mr. Pickering by a nomination. Certainly no such unlimited power has ever been claimed by any of the earlier Presidents, as has now been set up for the President by his most remarkable, ay, criminal answer.

It will not have escaped attention that no determination was made by that legislative construction as to *how* the removal, if in the President's power, should be made, which is now the question in dispute. *That* has been determined by the universal practice of the Government, with exceptions, if any, so rare as not to be worthy of consideration ; so tha we now claim the law to be what the practice has ever been. If, however, we concede the power of removal to be in the President as an implied power, yet we believe it cannot be successfully contended upon any authorities or constant practice of the Goverment that the execution of that power may not be regulated by the Congress of the United States under the clause in the Constitution which "vests in Congress the power to make all laws which shall be necessary and proper for carrying into execution" "all powers vested by this Constitution in the Government of the United States or in any department or officer thereof."

This power of regulation of the tenure of office, and the manner of removal, has always been exercised by Congress unquestioned until now.

On the 15th of May, 1820, (vol. 3 Statutes-at-Large, p. 582,) Congress provided for the term of office of certain officers therein named to be four years, but made them removable at pleasure. By the second section of the same act Congress removed from office all the officers therein commissioned, in providing a date when each commission should expire. Congress has thus asserted a legislative power of removal from office; sometimes by passing acts which appear to concede the power to the President to remove at pleasure, sometimes restricting that power in their acts by the most stringent provisions; sometimes conferring the power of removal, and sometimes that of appointment—the acts establishing the territorial officers being most conspicuous in this regard.

Upon the whole, no claim of exclusive right over removals or appointments seems to have been made either by the Executive or by Congress. No bill was ever vetoed on this account until now.

In 1818, Mr. Wirt, then Attorney General, giving the earliest official opinion on this question coming from that office, said that only where Congress had not undertaken to restrict the tenure of office, by the act creating it, would a commission issue to run during the pleasure of the President; but if the tenure was fixed by law, then commission must conform to the law. No constitutional scruples as to the power of Congress to limit the tenure of office seem to have disturbed the mind of that great lawyer. But this was before any attempt had been made by any President to arrogate to himself the official patronage for the purpose of party or personal aggrandizement, which gives the only value to this opinion as an authority. Since the Attorney General's office has become a political one, I shall not trouble the Senate with citing or examining the opinions of its occupants.

In 1826 a committee of the Senate, consisting of Mr. Benton of Missouri, chairman, Mr. Macon of North Carolina, Mr. Van Buren of New York, Mr. Dickerson of New Jersey, Mr. Johnson of Kentucky, Mr. White of Tennessee, Mr. Holmes of Maine, Mr. Hayne of South Carolina, and Mr. Findlay of Pennsylvania, was appointed to take into consideration the question of restraining the power of the President over removals from office, who made a report through their chairman, Mr. Benton, setting forth the extent of the evils arising from the power of appointment to, and removal from, office by the President, declaring that the Constitution had been changed in this regard, and that "construction and legislation have accomplished this change," and submitted two amendments to the Constitution, one providing a direct election of the President by the people, and another "that no Senator or Representative should be appointed to any place until the expiration of the presidential term in which such person shall have served as Senator or Representative," as remedies for some of the evils complained of; but .the committee say that, "not being able to reform the Constitution, in the election of President, they must go to work upon his powers, and trim down these by *statutory enactments* whenever it can be done by law and with a just regard to the proper

efficiency of government, and for this purpose reported six bills—one, to regulate the publication of the laws and public advertisements; another, *to secure in office* faithful collectors and disbursers of the revenues, and to displace defaulters—the first section of which vacated the commissions of "all officers, after a given date, charged with the collection and disbursement of the public moneys who had failed to account for such moneys on or before the 30th day of September preceding;" and the second section enacted that "at the same time a nomination is made to fill a vacancy occasioned by the exercise of the President's power to remove from office, the fact of the removal shall be stated to the Senate, with a report of the reasons for which such officers may have been removed; also a bill to regulate the appointment of postmasters; and a bill to prevent military and naval officers from being dismissed the service at the pleasure of the President, by inserting a clause in the commission of such officers that "it is to continue in force during good behavior," and "that no officer shall ever hereafter be dismissed the service except in pursuance of the sentence of a court-martial, or upon address to the President from the two Houses of Congress."

Is it not remarkable that exactly correlative measures to these have been passed by the Thirty-Ninth Congress, and are now the subject of controversy at this bar?

It does not seem to have occurred to this able committee that Congress had not the power to curb the Executive in this regard, because they asserted the practice of dismissing from office "to be a dangerous violation of the Constitution."

In 1830 Mr. Holmes introduced and discussed in the Senate a series of resolutions which contained, among other things, "the right of the Senate to inquire, and the duty of the President to inform them, when and for what causes any officer has been removed in the *recess*." In 1835 Mr. Calhoun, Mr. Southard, Mr. Bibb, Mr. Webster, Mr. Benton, and Mr. King of Georgia, of the Senate, were elected a committee to consider the subject of executive patronage, and the means of limiting it. That committee, with but one dissenting voice, (Mr. Benton,) reported a bill which provided in its third section "that in all nominations made by the President to the Senate, to fill vacancies occasioned by removal from office, the fact of the removal shall be stated to the Senate at the same time that the nomination is made, with a statement of the reasons for such removal."

It will be observed that this is the precise section reported by Mr. Benton in 1826, and passed to a second reading in the Senate. After much discussion, the bill passed the Senate, 31 yeas, 16 nays—an almost two-thirds vote. Thus it would seem that the ablest men of that day, of both political parties, subscribed to the power of Congress to limit and control the President in his removal from office.

One of the most marked instances of the assertion of this power in Congress will be found in the act of February 25, 1863, providing for a national currency and the office of Comptroller. (Statutes-at-Large, vol. 12, p. 665.) This controls both the appointment and the removal of that officer, enacting that he shall be appointed on the nomination of the Secretary of the Treasury, by and with the advice and consent of the Senate, and shall hold his office for the term of five years, unless sooner removed by the President, by and with the advice and consent of the Senate. This was substantially reënacted June 3, 1864, with the addition that "he shall be removed upon reasons to be communicated to the Senate."

Where were the vigilant gentlemen then, in both Houses, who now so denounce the power of Congress to regulate the appointment and removal of officers by the President as unconstitutional?

It will be observed that the Constitution makes no distinction between the officers of the Army and Navy and officers in the civil service, so far as their appointments and commissions, removals and dismissals, are concerned. Their commissions have ever run, "to hold office during the pleasure of the President;" yet Congress, by the act of 17th July, 1862, (Statutes-at-Large, vol. 12, p. 596,) enacted "that the President of the United States be, and hereby is, authorized and requested to dismiss and discharge from the military service, either in the Army, Navy, Marine corps, or volunteer force in the United States service, any officer for any cause which, in his judgment, either renders such officer unsuitable for, or whose dismission would promote, the public service."

Why was it necessary to authorize the President so to do if he had the constitutional power to dismiss a military officer at pleasure; and his powers, whatever they are, as is not doubted, are the same as in a civil office? The answer to this suggestion may be that this act was simply one of supererogation, only authorizing him to do what he was empowered already to do, and therefore not specially pertinent to this discussion.

But on the 13th day of July, 1866, Congress enacted "that no officer in the military or naval service *shall* in time of peace *be dismissed* from service except upon and in pursuance of the sentence of a court-martial to that effect." What becomes, then, of the respondent's objection that Congress cannot regulate his power of removal from office? In the snow-storm of his vetoes why did no flake light down on this provision? It concludes the whole question here at issue. It is approved; approval signed Andrew Johnson.

It will not be claimed, however, if the tenure-of-office act is constitutional, (and that question I shall not argue, except as has been

done incidentally, for reasons hereafter to be stated,) that he could remove Mr. Stanton provided the office of Secretary of War comes within its provisions, and one claim made here before you, by the answer, is that that office is excepted by the terms of the law. Of course I shall not argue to the Senate, composed mostly of those who passed the bill, what their wishes and intentions were. Upon that point I cannot aid them, but the construction of the act furnishes a few suggestions. First, let us determine the exact status of Mr. Stanton at the moment of its passage. The answer admits Mr. Stanton was appointed and commissioned and duly qualified as Secretary of War under Mr. Lincoln in pursuance of the act of 1789. In the absence of any other legislation or action of the President he legally held his office during the term of his natural life. This consideration is an answer to every suggestion as to the Secretary holding over from one presidential term to another.

On the 2d of March, 1867, the tenure-of-office act provided, in substance, that all civil officers duly qualified to act by appointment, with the advice and consent of the Senate, shall be entitled to hold such office until a successor shall have been in like manner appointed and duly qualified, except as herein otherwise provided, to wit : " provided that the Secretaries shall hold their office during the term of the President by whom they may have been appointed, and for one month thereafter, subject to removal by and with the advice and consent of the Senate."

By whom was Mr. Stanton appointed? By Mr. Lincoln. Whose presidential term was he holding under when the bullet of Booth became a proximate cause of this trial? Was not his appointment in full force at that hour? Had any act of the respondent up to the 12th day of August last vitiated or interfered with that appointment? Whose presidential term is the respondent now serving out? His own or Mr. Lincoln's? If his own, he is entitled to four years up to the anniversary of the murder, because each presidential term is four years by the Constitution, and the regular recurrence of those terms is fixed by the act of May 8, 1792. If he is serving out the remainder of Mr. Lincoln's term, then his term of office expires on the 4th of March, 1869, if it does not before.

Is not the statement of these propositions their sufficient argument? If Mr. Stanton's commission was vacated in any way by the "tenure-of-office act," then it must have ceased one month after the 4th of March, 1865, to wit, April 4, 1864. Or, if the "tenure-of-office act" had no retroactive effect, then his commission must have ceased if it had the effect to vacate his commission at all on the passage of the act, to wit, 2d March, 1867 ; and, in that case, from that date to the present he must have been exercising his office in contravention of the second section of the act, because he was not commissioned in accordance with its provisions. And the President, by "employing" him in so doing from the 2d March to 12th August, became guilty of a high misdemeanor under the provision of the sixth section of said act; so that if the President shall succeed in convincing the Senate that Mr. Stanton has been acting as Secretary of War against the provisions of the "tenure-of-office act," which *he will* do if he convince them that that act vacated in any way Mr. Stanton's commission, or·that he himself was not serving out the remainder of Mr. Lincoln's presidential term, then the House of Representatives have but to report another article for this misdemeanor to remove the President upon his own confession.

It has been said, however, that in the discussion at the time of the passage of this law observations were made by Senators tending to show that it did not apply to Mr. Stanton, because it was asserted that no member of the Cabinet of the President would wish to hold his place against the wishes of his chief, by whom he had been called into council; and these arguments have been made the groundwork of attack upon a meritorious officer, which may have so influenced the minds of Senators that it is my duty to observe upon them to meet arguments to the prejudice of my cause.

Without stopping to deny the correctness of the general proposition, there seems to be at least two patent answers to it.

The respondent *did not* call Mr. Stanton into his council. The blow of the assassin *did* call the respondent to preside over a Cabinet of which Mr. Stanton was then an honored member, beloved of its chief; and if the respondent deserted the principles under which he was elected, betrayed his trust, and sought to return rebels, whom the valor of our armies had subdued, again into power, are not those reasons not only why Mr. Stanton should not desert his post, but, as a true patriot, maintain it all the more firmly against this unlooked-for treachery?

Is it not known to you, Senators, and to the country, that Mr. Stanton retains this unpleasant and distasteful position, *not* of his own will alone, but at the behest of a majority of those who represent the people of this country in both Houses of its Legislature, and after the solemn decision of the Senate that any attempt to remove him without their concurrence is unconstitutional and unlawful?

To desert it now, therefore, would be to imitate the treachery of his accidental chief. But whatever may be the construction of the "tenure of civil office act" by others, or as regards others, Andrew Johnson, the respondent, is concluded upon it.

He permitted Mr. Stanton to exercise the duties of his office in spite of it, if that office were affected by it. He suspended him under its provisions; he reported that suspension to the Senate, with his reasons therefor in accordance with its provisions; and the Senate, acting under it, declined to concur with him, whereby Mr. Stanton was reinstated. In the well-known language of the law, is not the respondent *estopped* by his solemn official acts from denying the legality and constitutional propriety of Mr. Stanton's position?

Before proceeding further, I desire most earnestly to bring to the attention of the Senate the averments of the President in his answer, by which he justifies his action in attempting to remove Mr. Stanton, and the reasons which controlled him in so doing. He claims that on the 12th day of August last he had become fully of the opinion that he had the power to remove Mr. Stanton or any other executive officer, or suspend him from office and to appoint any other person to act instead "indefinitely and at his pleasure;" that he was fully advised and believed, as he still believes, that the tenure of civil office act was unconstitutional, inoperative, and void in all its provisions; and that he had then determined at all hazards, if Stanton could not be otherwise got rid of, to remove him from office in spite of the provisions of that act and the action of the Senate under it, if for no other purpose, in order to raise for a judicial decision the question affecting the lawful right of said Stanton to persist in refusing to quit the office.

Thus it appears that with full intent to resist the power of the Senate, to hold the tenure-of-office act void, and to exercise this illimitable power claimed by him, he did suspend Mr. Stanton, apparently in accordance with the provisions of the act; he did send the message to the Senate within the time prescribed by the act; he did give his reasons for the suspension to the Senate, and argued them at length, accompanied by what he claimed to be the evidence of the official misconduct of Mr. Stanton, and thus invoked the action of the Senate to assist him in displacing a high officer of the Government under the provisions of an act which he at that very moment believed to be unconstitutional, inoperative, and void, thereby showing that he was willing to make use of a void act and the Senate of the United States as his tools to do that which he believed neither had any constitutional power to do. Did not every member of the Senate, when that message came in announcing the suspension of Mr. Stanton, understand and believe that the President was acting in this case, as he had done in every other case, under the provisions of this act? Did not both sides discuss the question under its provisions? Would any Senator upon this floor, on either side, so demean himself as to consider the question one moment if he had known it was then within the intent and purpose of the President of the United States to treat the deliberations and action of the Senate as void and of none effect if its decision did not comport with his views and purposes; and yet, while acknowledging the intent was in his mind to hold as naught the judgment of the Senate if it did not concur with his own, and remove Mr. Stanton at all hazards, and as I charge it upon him here, as a fact no man can doubt, with the full knowledge also that the Senate understood that he was acting under the provisions of the tenure-of-office act, still thus deceiving them, when called to answer for a violation of that act, in his solemn answer, he makes the shameless avowal that he did transmit to the Senate of the United States a "message wherein he made known the orders aforesaid and the reasons which induced the same, so far as the respondent then considered it material and necessary that the same should be set forth." True it is, there is not one word, one letter, one implication in that message that the President was not acting in good faith under the tenure-of-office act and desiring the Senate to do the same. So the President of the United States, with a determination to assert at all hazards the tremendous power of removal of every officer, without the consent of the Senate, did not deem it "material or necessary" that the Senate should know that he had suspended Mr. Stanton indefinitely against the provisions of the tenure-of-office act, with full intent, at all hazards, to remove him, and that the solemn deliberations of the Senate, which the President of the United States was then calling upon them to make in a matter of the highest governmental concern, were only to be of use in case they suited his purposes; that it was not "material or necessary" for the Senate to know that its high decision was futile and useless; that the President was playing fast and loose with this branch of the Government—which was never before done save by himself.

If Andrew Johnson never committed any other offense—if we knew nothing of him save from this avowal—we should have a full picture of his mind and heart, painted in colors of living light, so that no man will ever mistake his mental and moral lineaments hereafter.

Instead of open and frank dealing as becomes the head of a great Government in every relation of life, and especially needful from the highest executive officer of the Government to the highest legislative branch thereof; instead of a manly, straightforward bearing, claiming openly and distinctly the rights which he believed pertained to his high office, and yielding to the other branches, fairly and justly, those which belong to them, we find him, upon his own written confession, keeping back his claims of power, concealing his motives, covering his purposes, attempting by indirection and subterfuge to do that as the ruler of a great nation which, if it be done at all, should have been done boldly, in the face of day; and upon this position he must stand before the Senate and the country if they believe his answer, which I

do not, that he had at that time these intents and purposes in his mind, and they are not the subterfuge and evasion and after-thought which a criminal brought to bay makes to escape the consequences of his acts.

Senators! he asked you for time in which to make his answer. You gave him ten days, and this is the answer he makes! If he could do this in ten days, what should we have had if you had given him forty? You show him a mercy in not extending the time for answer.

Passing from further consideration of the legality of the action of the respondent in removing Mr. Stanton from office in the manner and form and with the intent and purpose with which it has been done, let us now examine the appointment of Brevet Major General Lorenzo Thomas, of the United States Army, as Secretary of War *ad interim.*

I assume that it is not denied in any quarter that this *ad interim* appointment to this office is the mere creature of law, and if justified at all is to be so under some act of Congress. Indeed, the respondent in his answer says that in the appointment of General Grant *ad interim* he acted under the act of February 13, 1795, and subject to its limitations. By the act of August 7, 1789, creating the Department of War, (1 Statutes-at-Large, p. 49,) "in case of any vacancy" no provision is made for any appointment of an acting or *ad interim* Secretary. In that case the records and papers are to be turned over for safe keeping to the custody of the chief clerk. This apparent omission to provide for an executive emergency was attempted to be remedied by Congress by the act of May 8, 1792, (1 Statutes, 281,) which provides "that in case of the death, absence from the seat of Government, or sickness of the Secretary of State, Secretary of the Treasury, or of the Secretary of the War Department, or of any officer of either of the said Departments whose appointment is not in the head thereof, *whereby they cannot perform the duties of their respective offices,* it shall be lawful for the President of the United States, in case he shall think it necessary, to authorize any person or persons, at his discretion, to perform the duties of the said respective offices until a successor be appointed, or until such absence or inability by sickness shall cease."

It will be observed that this act provides for vacancies by death, absence, or sickness only, *whereby the head of a Department or any officer in it cannot perform his duty,* but makes no provision for vacancy by removal.

Two difficulties were found in that provision of law: first, that it provided only for certain enumerated vacancies; and also, it authorized the President to make an acting appointment of *any* person for *any length* of time. To meet these difficulties the act of 13th February, 1795, was passed, (1 Statutes-at-Large, 415) which provides "in case of vacancy, *whereby the Secretaries or any officer in any of the Departments cannot perform the duties of his office,* the President may appoint any person to perform the duties for a period *not exceeding six months.*"

Thus the law stood as to acting appointments in all of the Departments (except the Navy and Interior, which had no provision for any person to act in place of the Secretary) until the 19th of February, 1863, when, by the second section of an act approved at that date, (12 Statutes, 646,) it was "provided that no person acting or assuming to act as a civil, military, or naval officer shall have any money paid to him as salary in any office which is not authorized by some previously existing law." The state of the law upon this subject at that point of time is thus: in case of death, absence, or sickness, or of any vacancy *whereby* a Secretary or other officer of the State, War, or Treasury Department *could not perform the duties of the office,* any person could be authorized by the President to perform those duties for the space of six months.

For the Departments of the Interior and the Navy provision had been made for the appointment of an assistant Secretary, but *no* provision in case of vacancy in his office, and a restriction put upon any officers acting when not authorized by law, from receiving any salary whatever.

To meet those omissions and to meet the case of *resignation* of any officer of an executive Department, and also to meet what was found to be a defect in allowing the President to appoint *any* person to those high offices for the space of six months, whether such person had any acquaintance with the duties of the Department or not, an act was passed February 20, 1863, (12 Statutes, p. 656,) which provides, that in case of the death, *resignation,* absence from the seat of Government, or sickness of the head of an executive Department of the Government, or of any officer of either of the said Departments whose appointment is not in the head thereof, *whereby they cannot perform the duties of their respective offices,* it shall be lawful for the President of the United States, in case he shall think it necessary, to authorize the head of any other executive Department or other officer in either of said Departments whose appointment is vested in the President, at his discretion to perform the duties of the said respective offices until a successor be appointed, or until such absence or inability shall cease. Therefore, in case of the death, resignation, sickness, or absence of a head of an executive Department, whereby the incumbent could not perform the duties of his office, the President might authorize the head of another executive Department to perform the duties of the vacant office; and in case of like disability of any officer of an executive Department other than the head, the President might authorize an officer of the same Department to perform his duties for the space of six months.

It is remarkable that in all these statutes from 1789 down, no provision is made for the case of a removal, or that anybody is empowered to act for the removed officer, the chief clerk being empowered to take charge of the books and papers only.

Does not this series of acts conclusively demonstrate a legislative construction of the Constitution that there could be *no* removal of the chief of an executive Department by the act of the President save by the nomination and appointment of his successor, if the Senate were in session, or a qualified appointment till the end of the next session if the vacancy happened or was made in recess?

Let us now apply this state of the law to the appointment of Major General Thomas Secretary of War *ad interim* by executive order. Mr. Stanton had neither died nor resigned, was not sick nor absent. If he had been, under the act of March 3, 1863, which repeals all inconsistent acts, the President was authorized only to appoint the head of another executive Department to fill his place *ad interim.* Such was not General Thomas. He was simply an officer of the Army, the head of a bureau or department of the War Department, and not eligible under the law to be appointed. So that his appointment was an *illegal and void act.*

There have been two cases of *ad interim* appointments which illustrate and confirm this position; the one was the appointment of Lieutenant General Scott Secretary of War *ad interim,* and the other the appointment of General Grant *ad interim* upon the suspension of Mr. Stanton, in August last.

The appointment of General Scott was legal because that was done before the restraining act of March 2, 1863, which requires the detail of the head of another Department to act *ad interim.*

The appointment of General Grant to take the place of Mr. Stanton during his suspension would have been illegal under the acts I have cited, he being an officer of the Army and not the head of a department, if it had not been authorized by the second section of the "tenure-of-civil-office act," which provides that in case of suspension, and no other, the President may designate "some suitable person to perform temporarily the duties of such office until the next meeting of the Senate." Now, General Grant was such "suitable person," and was properly enough appointed under that provision.

This answers one ground of the defense which is taken by the President that he did *not* suspend Mr. Stanton under the "tenure-of-office act," but by his general power of suspension and removal of an officer. If the President did *not* suspend Stanton under the tenure-of-office act, because he deemed it unconstitutional and void, *then* there was no law authorizing him to appoint General Grant, and that appointment was unauthorized by law and a violation of his oath of office.

But the tenure-of-civil-office bill by its express terms forbids any employment, authorization, or appointment of any person in civil office where the appointment is by and with the advice and consent of the Senate, while the Senate is in session. If this act is constitutional, *i. e.*, if it is not so far in conflict with the paramount law of the land as to be inoperative and void, then the removal of Mr. Stanton and the appointment of General Thomas are both in direct violation of it, and are declared by it to be high misdemeanors.

The intent with which the President has done this is not doubtful, nor are we obliged to rely upon the principle of law that a man must be held to intend the legal consequences of all his acts.

The President admits that he intended to set aside the tenure-of-office act, and thus contravene the Constitution, if that law was unconstitutional.

Having shown that the President willfully violated an act of Congress, without justification, both in the removal of Stanton and the appointment of Thomas, for the purpose of obtaining wrongfully the possession of the War Office by force, if need be, and certainly by threats and intimidations, for the purpose of controlling its appropriations through its *ad interim* chief, who shall say that Andrew Johnson is not guilty of the high crime and misdemeanors charged against him in the first eight articles?

The respondent makes answer to this view, that the President, believing this civil tenure law to be unconstitutional, *had a right to violate it*, for the purpose of bringing the matter before the Supreme Court for its adjudication.

We are obliged. *in limine*, to ask the attention of the Senate to this consideration, that they may take it with them as our case goes forward.

We claim that the question of the constitutionality of any law of Congress is, upon this trial, a totally irrelevant one; because all the power or right in the President to judge upon any supposed conflict of an act of Congress with the paramount law of the Constitution is exhausted when he has examined a bill sent him and returned it with his objections. If then passed over his veto it becomes as valid as if in fact signed by him.

The Constitution has provided three methods, all equally potent, by which a bill brought into either House may become a law:

1. By passage by vote of both Houses, in due form, with the President's signature;

2. By passage by vote of both Houses, in due form, and the President's neglect to return it within ten days with his objections;

3. By passage by vote of both Houses, in due form, a veto by the President, a reconsideration by both Houses, and a passage by two-thirds votes.

The Constitution substitutes this reconsideration and passage as an equivalent to the President's signature. After that he and all other officers must execute the law, whether in fact constitutional or not.

For the President to refuse to execute a law duly passed because he thought it unconstitutional, after he had vetoed it for that reason, would, in effect, be for him to execute his veto and leave the law unexecuted.

It may be said that he may *do this at his peril.* True; but *that* peril is to be impeached for violating his oath of office, as is now being done.

If, indeed, laws duly passed by Congress affecting generally the welfare of any considerable portion of the people had been commonly, or, as a usage declared by the Supreme Court, unconstitutional, and therefore inoperative, there might seem to be some palliation if not justification to the Executive to refuse to execute a law in order to have its constitutionality tested by the court.

It is possible to conceive of so flagrant a case of unconstitutionality as to be such shadow of justification to the Executive, provided one at the same time conceives an equally flagrant case of stupidity, ignorance, and imbecility, or worse, in the Representatives of the people and in the Senate of the United States; but both conceptions are so rarely possible and absurd as not to furnish a ground of governmental action.

How stands the fact? Has the Supreme Court so frequently declared the laws of Congress in conflict with the Constitution as to afford the President just ground for belief, or hope even, that the court will do so in a given instance? I think I may safely assert as a legal fact that since the first decision of the Supreme Court till the day of this arraignment no law passed by Congress affecting the general welfare has ever, by the judgment of that court, been set aside or held for nought because of unconstitutionality as the groundwork of its decisions.

In three cases only has the judgment of that court been influenced by the supposed conflict between the law and the Constitution, and they were cases affecting the court itself and its own duties, and where the law seemed to interfere with its own prerogatives.

Touching privileges and prerogatives has been the shipwreck of many a wholesome law. It is the sore spot, the sensitive nerve of all tribunals, parliamentary or judicial.

The first case questioning the validity of a law of Congress is Hayburn's, (2 Dallas, 409,) where the court decided upon the unconstitutionality of the act of March 23, 1792, (Statutes-at-Large, vol. 1, p. 244,) which conferred upon the court the power to decide upon and grant certificates of invalid pensions. The court held that such power could not be conferred upon the court as an original jurisdiction, the court receiving all its original jurisdiction from the provisions of the Constitution. This decision would be nearly unintelligible were it not explained in a note to the case in United States *vs.* Ferreira, (13 Howard, p. 52,) reporting United States *vs.* Todd, decided February 17, 1794.

We learn, however, from both cases the cause of this unintelligibility of the decision in Hayburn's case. When the same question came up at the circuit court in New York the judges being of opinion that the law could not be executed by them as judges, because it was unconstitutional, yet determined to obey it until the case could be adjudicated by the whole court. They therefore, not to violate the law, *did execute it as commissioners* until it was repealed, which was done the next year.

The judges on the circuit in Pennsylvania all united in a letter to the Executive, most humbly apologizing, with great regret, that their convictions of duty did not permit them to execute the law according to its terms, and took special care that this letter should accompany their decision, so that they might not be misunderstood.

Both examples it would have been well for this respondent to have followed before he undertook to set himself to violate an act of Congress.

The next case where the court decided upon any conflict between the Constitution and the law is Gordon *vs.* United States, tried in April, 1865, seventy-one years afterward, two justices dissenting, without any opinion being delivered by the court.

The court here dismissed an appeal from the Court of Claims, alleging that, under the Constitution, no appellate jurisdiction could be exercised over the Court of Claims under an act of Congress which gave revisory power to the Secretary of the Treasury over a decision of the Court of Claims. This decision is little satisfactory, as it is wholly without argument or authority cited.

The next case is *ex parte* Garland, (4 Wallace, 333,) known as the Attorney's oath case, where the court decided, that an attorney was not an officer of the United States, and therefore might practice before that court without taking the test-oath.

The reasoning of the court in that case would throw doubt on the constitutionality of the law of Congress, but the decision of the invalidity of the law was not necessary to the decision of the case, which did not command a unanimity in the court, as it certainly did not the assent of the bar.

Yet in this case it will be observed that the court made a rule requiring the oath to be administered to the attorneys in obedience of the law until it came before them in a cause duly brought up for decision. *The Supreme Court obeyed the law up to the time* it was set aside. They did not violate it to make a test case.

Here is another example to this respondent, as to his duty in the case, which he will wish he had followed, I may venture to say, when he hears the judgment of the Senate upon the impeachment now pending.

There are several other cases wherein the validity of acts of Congress has been discussed before the Supreme Court, but none where the decision has turned on that point.

In Marbury *vs.* Madison (1 Cranch, 137) Chief Justice Marshall dismissed the case for want of jurisdiction, but took opportunity to deliver a chiding opinion against the administration of Jefferson before he did so.

In the Dred Scott case, so familiar to the public, the court decided it had no jurisdiction, but gave the Government and the people a lecture upon their political duties.

In the case of Fisher *vs.* Blight (2 Cranch, 358) the constitutionality of a law was very much discussed, but was held valid by the decision of the court.

In United States *vs.* Coombs, (12 Peters, 72,) although the power to declare a law of Congress in conflict with the Constitution was claimed in the opinion of the court *arguendo*, yet the law itself was sustained.

The case of Pollard *vs.* Hagan, (3 Howard, 212,) and the two cases, Goodtitle *vs.* Kibbe, (9 Howard, 271,) Hallett *vs.* Beebe, (13 Howard, 25,) growing out of the same controversy, have been thought to impugn the validity of two private acts of Congress; but a careful examination will show that it was the *operation* and not the *validity* of the acts which came in question and made the basis of the decision.

Thus it will be seen that the Supreme Court, in three instances only, have apparently, by its decision, impugned the validity of an act of Congress because of a conflict with the Constitution, and in each case a question of the rights and prerogatives of the court or its officers has been in controversy.

The cases where the constitutionality of an act of Congress has been doubted in the *obiter dicta* of the court, but were not the basis of decision, are open to other criticisms.

In Marbury *vs.* Madison Chief Justice Marshall had just been serving as Secretary of State in an opposing Administration to the one whose acts he was trying to overturn as Chief Justice.

In the Dred Scott case Chief Justice Taney —selected by General Jackson to remove the deposits because his bitter partisanship would carry him through where Duane halted and was removed—delivered the opinion of the court, whose *obiter dicta* fanned the flame of dissension which led to the civil war through which the people have just passed, and against that opinion the judgment of the country has long been recorded.

When *ex parte* Garland was decided the country was just emerging from a conflict of arms the passions and excitement of which had found their way upon the bench, and some of the judges, just coming from other service of the Government and from the bar, brought with them opinions. But I forbear. I am treading on dangerous ground. Time has not yet laid its softening and correcting hand long enough upon this decision to allow me further to comment upon it in this presence.

Mr. President and Senators, can it be said that the possible doubts thrown on three or four acts of Congress, as to their constitutionality, during a judicial experience of seventy-five years—hardly one to a generation—is a sufficient warrant to the President of the United States to set aside and violate any act of Congress whatever upon the plea that he believed the Supreme Court would hold it unconstitutional when a case involving the question should come before it, and especially one much discussed on its passage, to which the whole mind of the country was turned during the progress of the discussion, upon which he had argued with all his power his constitutional objections, and which, after careful reconsideration, had been passed over his veto ?

Indeed, will you hear an argument as a Senate of the United States, a majority of whom voted for that very bill, upon its constitutionality in the trial of an executive officer for willfully violating it before it had been doubted by any court?

Bearing upon this question, however, it may be said that the President removed Mr. Stanton for the very purpose of testing the constitutionality of this law before the courts, and the question is asked, Will you condemn him as for a crime for so doing? If this plea were a true one it ought not to avail; but it is a subterfuge. We shall show you that he has taken no step to submit the question to any court, although more than a year has elapsed since the passage of the act.

On the contrary, the President has recognized its validity and acted upon it in every department of the Government save in the War Department, and there except in regard to the head thereof solely. We shall show you he long ago caused all the forms of commissions and official bonds of all the civil officers of the Government to be altered to conform to its requirement. Indeed, the fact will not be denied—nay, in the very case of Mr. Stanton, he suspended him under its provisions, and asked this very Senate, before whom he is now being tried for its violation, to pass upon the sufficiency of his reasons for acting under it in so doing according to its terms; yet, rendered reckless and mad by the patience of Congress under his usurpation of other powers and his disregard of other laws, he boldly avows in his ·letter to the General of the Army that he intends to disregard its provisions, and summons the commander of the troops of this Department to seduce him from his duty so as to be able to command, in violation of another act of Congress, sufficient military power to enforce his unwarranted decrees.

The President knew, or ought to have known, his official adviser, who now appears as his counsel, could and did tell him, doubtless, that he alone, as Attorney General, could file, an information in the nature of a *quo warranto* to determine this question of the validity of the law.

Mr. Stanton, if ejected from office, was without remedy, because a series of decisions has settled the law to be that an ejected officer can not reinstate himself either by *quo warranto*, *mandamus* or other appropriate remedy in the courts.

If the President had really desired solely to test the constitutionality of the law or his legal right to remove Mr. Stanton, instead of his defiant message to the Senate of the 21st of February, informing them of the removal, but not suggesting this purpose, which is thus shown to be an afterthought, he would have said, in substance: "Gentlemen of the Senate, in order to test the constitutionality of the law entitled 'An act regulating the tenure of certain civil offices,' which I verily believe to be unconstitutional and void, I have issued an order of removal of E. M. Stanton from the office of Secretary of the Department of War. I felt myself constrained to make this removal lest Mr. Stanton should answer the information in the nature of a *quo warranto*, which I intend the Attorney General shall file at an early day, by saying that he holds the office of Secretary of War by the appointment and authority of Mr. Lincoln, which has never been revoked. Anxious that there shall be no collision or disagreement between the several departments of the Government and the Executive, I lay before the Senate this message, that the reasons for my action, as well as the action itself, for the purpose indicated, may meet your concurrence." Had the Senate received such a message the Representatives of the people might never have deemed it necessary to impeach the President for such an act to insure the safety of the country, even if they had denied the accuracy of his legal positions.

On the contrary, he issued a letter of removal, peremptory in form, intended to be so in effect, ordered an officer of the Army, Lorenzo Thomas, to take possession of the office and eject the incumbent, which he claimed he would do by force, even at the risk of inaugurating insurrection, civil commotion, and war.

Whatever may be the decision of the legal question involved, when the case comes before the final judicial tribunal who shall say that such conduct of the Executive under the circumstances, and in the light of the history of current events and his concomitant action, is not in Andrew Johnson a high crime and misdemeanor? Imagine, if it were possible, the consequence of a decision by the Senate in the negative—a verdict of not guilty upon this proposition.

A law is deliberately passed with all the form of legislative procedure, is presented to the

President for his signature, is returned by him to Congress with his objections, is thereupon reconsidered, and, by a yea and nay vote of three quarters of the Representatives of the people in the popular branch, and three fourths of the Senators representing the States in the higher branch, is passed again, notwithstanding the veto; is acquiesced in by the President, by all departments of the Government conforming thereto for quite a year, no court having doubted its validity. Now its provisions are willfully and designedly violated by the President with intent to usurp to himself the very powers which the law was designed to limit, for the purpose of displacing a meritorious officer whom the Senate just before had determined ought not and should not be removed; for which high-handed act the President is impeached in the name of all the people of the United States by three fourths of the House of Representatives, and presented at the bar of the Senate, and by the same Senate that passed the law, nay, more, by the very Senators who, when the proceeding came to their knowledge, after a redeliberation of many hours, solemnly declared the act unlawful and in violation of the Constitution; that act of usurpation is declared *not* to be a high misdemeanor in office by their solemn verdict of not guilty upon their oaths.

Would not such a judgment be a conscious self-abnegation of the intelligent capacity of the representatives of the people in Congress assembled to frame laws for their guidance in accordance with the principles and terms of their Constitution and frame of their Government?

Would it not be a notification—an invitation rather—standing to all time to any bold, bad, aspiring man to seize the liberties of the people, which they had shown themselves incapable of maintaining or defending, and playing the *rôle* of a Cæsar or Napoleon here to establish a despotism, while this the last and greatest experiment of freedom and equality of right in the people, following the long line of buried republics, sinks to its tomb under the blows of usurped power from which free representative Government shall arise to the light of a morn of resurrection *never more, never more forever!*

Article nine charges that Major General Emory, being in command of the military department of Washington, the President called him before him and instructed him that the act of March 2, 1867, which provides that all orders from the President shall be issued through the General of the Army, was unconstitutional and inconsistent with his commission, with intent to induce Emory to take orders directly from himself, and thus hinder the execution of the civil-tenure act and to prevent Mr. Stanton from holding his office of Secretary of War.

If the transaction set forth in this article stood alone we might well admit that doubts might arise as to the sufficiency of the proof. But the surroundings are so pointed and significant as to leave no doubt on the mind of an impartial man as to the intents and purposes of the President. No one would say that the President might not properly send to the commander of this department to make inquiry as to the disposition of his forces, but the question is, with what intent and purpose did the President send for General Emory at the time he did? Time, here, is an important element of the act.

Congress had passed an act in March, 1867, restraining the President from issuing military orders save through the General of the Army. The President had protested against that act. On the 12th of August he had attempted to get possession of the War Office by the removal of the incumbent, but could only do so by appointing the General of the Army thereto. Failing in his attempt to get full possession of the office through the Senate, he had determined, as he admits, to remove Stanton at all hazards, and endeavored to prevail on the General to aid him in so doing. He declines. For that the respondent quarrels with him, denounces him in the newspapers, and accuses him of bad faith and untruthfulness. Thereupon, asserting his prerogatives as Commander-in-Chief, he creates a new military department of the Atlantic. He attempts to bribe Lieutenant General Sherman to take command of it by promotion to the rank of general by brevet, trusting that his military services would compel the Senate to confirm him.

If the respondent can get a general by brevet appointed, he can then by simple order put him on duty according to his brevet rank and thus have a general of the Army in command at Washington, through whom he can transmit his orders and comply with the act which he did not dare transgress, as he had approved it, and get rid of the hated General Grant. Sherman spurned the bribe. The respondent, not discouraged, appointed Major General George H. Thomas to the same brevet rank, but Thomas declined.

What stimulated the ardor of the President just at that time, almost three years after the war closed, but just after the Senate had reinstated Stanton, to reward military service by the appointment of generals by brevet? Why did his zeal of promotion take that form and no other? There were many other meritorious officers of lower rank desirous of promotion. The purpose is evident to every thinking mind. He had determined to set aside Grant, with whom he had quarrelled, either by force or fraud, either in conformity with or in spite of the act of Congress, and control the military power of the country. On the 21st of February—for all these events cluster nearly about the same point of time—he appoints Lorenzo Thomas Secretary of War and orders Stanton out of the office. Stanton refuses to go; Thomas is about the streets declaring that he will put him out by force, "kick him out." He has caught his master's word.

On the evening of the 21st a resolution looking to impeachment is offered in the House.

The President, on the morning of the 22d, "as early as practicable," is seized with a sudden desire to know how many troops there were in Washington. What for, just then? Was that all he wanted to know? If so, his Adjutant General could have given him the official morning report, which would have shown the condition and station of every man. But that was not all. He directs the commander of the department to come as early as practicable. Why this haste to learn the number of troops? Observe, the order does not go through General Grant, as by law it ought to have done. General Emory, not knowing what is wanted, of course obeyed the order as soon as possible. The President asked him if he remembered the conversation which he had with him when he first took command of the department as to the strength of the garrison of Washington, and the general disposition of troops in the department. Emory replied that "he did distinctly;" that was last September. Then, after explaining to him fully as to all the changes, the President asked for recent changes of troops. Emory denied they could have been made without the order going through him, and then, with soldierly frankness, (as he evidently suspected what the President was after,) said by law no order could come to him, save through the General of the Army, and that had been approved by the President and promulgated in a General Order No. 17. The President wished to see it. It was produced. General Emory says: "Mr. President, I will take it as a great favor if you will permit me to call your attention to this order or act." Why a favor to Emory? Because he feared that he was to be called upon by the President to do something in contravention of that law. The President read it and said: "This is not in accordance with the Constitution of the United States, which makes me Commander-in-Chief of the Army and Navy, or with the language of your commission." Emory then said: "That is not a matter for the officers to determine. There was the order sent to us approved by him, and we were all governed by that order."

He said, "Am I to understand, then, that the President of the United States cannot give an order but through General Grant?" General Emory then made the President a short speech, telling him that the officers of the Army had been consulting lawyers on the subject, REVERDY JOHNSON and Robert J. Walker, and were advised that they were bound to obey that order. Said he, "I think it right to tell you the Army are a unit on this subject." After a short pause, "seeing there was nothing more to say," General Emory left. What made all the officers consult lawyers about obeying a law of the United States? What influence had been at work with them? The course of the President. In his message to Congress in December he had declared that the time might come when he would resist a law of Congress by force. How could General Emory tell that in the judgment of the President that time had not come, and hence was anxious to assure the President that he could not oppose the law?

In his answer to the first article he asserts that he had fully come to the conclusion to remove Mr. Stanton at all events, notwithstanding the law and the action of the Senate; in other words, he intended to make, and did make executive resistance to the law duly enacted. The consequences of such resistance he has told us in his message:

"Where an act has been passed according to the forms of the Constitution by the supreme legislative authority, and is regularly enrolled among the public statutes of the country, executive resistance to it, especially in times of high party excitement, would be likely to produce violent collision between the respective adherents of the two branches of the Government. This would be simply civil war, and civil war must be resorted to only as the last remedy for the worst evils." * * * * * * * *
"It is true that cases may occur in which the Executive would be compelled to stand on its rights, and maintain them, regardless of all consequences."

He admits, in substance, that he told Emory that the law was wholly unconstitutional, and, in effect, took away all his power as Commander-in-Chief. Was it not just such a law as he had declared he would resist? Do you not believe that if General Emory had yielded in the least to his suggestions the President would have offered him promotion to bind him to his purposes, as he did Sherman and Thomas?

Pray remember that this is not the case of one gentleman conversing with another on moot questions of law; but it is the President, the Commander-in-Chief, "the fountain of all honor and source of all power," in the eye of a military officer, teaching that officer to disobey a law which he himself has determined is void, with the power to promote the officer if he finds him an apt pupil.

Is it not a high misdemeanor for the President to assume to instruct the officers of the Army that the laws of Congress are not to be obeyed?

Article ten alleges that, intending to set aside the rightful authority and powers of Congress, and to bring into disgrace and contempt the Congress of the United States, and to destroy confidence in and to excite odium against Congress and its laws, he, Andrew Johnson, President of the United States, made divers speeches set out therein, whereby he brought the office of President into contempt, ridicule, and disgrace.

To sustain these charges there will be put in evidence the short-hand notes of reporters in each instance, who took these speeches or examined the sworn copies thereof, and one instance where the speech was examined and corrected by the Private Secretary of the President himself.

To the charges of this article the respondent

answers that a convention of delegates, of whom he does not say, sat in Philadelphia for certain political purposes mentioned, and appointed a committee to wait upon the respondent as President of the United States; that they were received, and by their chairman, Hon. REVERDY JOHNSON, then and now a Senator of the United States, addressed the respondent in a speech, a copy of which the respondent believes from a substantially correct report is made a part of the answer; that the respondent made a reply to the address of the committee. While, however, he gives us in his answer a copy of the speech made to him by Mr. REVERDY JOHNSON, taken from a newspaper, he wholly omits to give us an authorized version of his own speech, about which he may be supposed to know quite as much, and thus saved us some testimony. He does not admit that the extracts from his speech in the article are correct, nor does he deny that they are so.

In regard to the speech at Cleveland, he again does not admit that the extracts correctly or justly present his speech; but again he does not deny that they do so far as the same is set out.

As to the speech at St. Louis, he does not deny that he made it—says only that he does not admit it, and requires, in each case, that the whole speech shall be proved. In that, I beg leave to assure him and the Senate, his wishes shall be gratified to their fullest fruition. The Senate shall see the performance, so far as is in our power to photograph the scene by evidence, on each of these occasions, and shall hear every material word that he said. His defense, however, to the article is, that "he felt himself in duty bound to express opinions of and concerning the public character, conduct, views, purposes, motives, and tendencies of all men engaged in the public service, as well in Congress as otherwise," "and that for anything he may have said on either of these occasions he is justified under the constitutional right of freedom of opinion and freedom of speech, and is not subject to question, inquisition, impeachment, or inculpation in any manner or form whatsoever." He denies, however, that by reason of any matter in said article or its specifications alleged he has said or done anything indecent or unbecoming in the Chief Magistrate of the United States, or tending to bring his high office into contempt, ridicule, or disgrace.

The issue, then, finally, is this: that those utterances of his, in the manner and form in which they are alleged to have been made, and under the circumstances and at the time they were made, are decent and becoming the President of the United States, and do not tend to bring the office into ridicule and disgrace.

We accept the issues. They are two:

First. That he has the right to say what he did of Congress in the exercise of freedom of speech; and second, that what he did say in those speeches was a highly gentlemanlike and proper performance in a citizen, and still more becoming in a President of the United States.

Let us first consider the graver matter of the assertion of the right to cast contumely upon Congress; to denounce it as a "body hanging on the verge of the Government;" "pretending to be a Congress when, in fact, it was not a Congress;" "a Congress pretending to be for the Union when its every step and act tended to perpetuate disunion," "and make a disruption of the States inevitable;" "a Congress in a minority assuming to exercise power which, if allowed to be consummated, would result in despotism and monarchy itself;" "a Congress which had done everything to prevent the union of the States;" "a Congress factious and domineering;" "a Radical Congress which gave origin to another rebellion;" "a Congress upon whose skirts was every drop of blood that was shed in the New Orleans riots." You will find these denunciations had a deeper meaning than mere expressions of opinion. It may be taken as an axiom in the affairs of nations that no usurper has ever seized upon the Legislature of his country until he has familiarized the people with the possibility of so doing by vituperating and decrying it. Denunciatory attacks upon the Legislature have always preceded, slanderous abuse of the individuals composing it have always accompanied, a seizure by a despot of the legislative power of a country.

Two memorable examples in modern history will spring to the recollection of every man. Before Cromwell drove out by the bayonet the Parliament of England he and his partisans had denounced it, derided it, decried it, and defamed it, and thus brought it into ridicule and contempt. He villified it with the same name which—it is a significant fact—the partisans of Johnson, by a concerted cry, applied to the Congress of the United States when he commenced his memorable pilgrimage and crusade against it. It is a still more significant fact that the justification made by Cromwell and by Johnson for setting aside the authority of Parliament and Congress respectively was precisely the same, to wit: that they were elected by part of the people only. When Cromwell, by his soldiers, finally entered the hall of Parliament to disperse its members, he attempted to cover the enormity of his usurpation by denouncing this man personally as a libertine, that as a drunkard, another as a betrayer of the liberties of the people. Johnson started out on precisely the same course, but forgetting the parallel, too early he proclaims this patriot an assassin, that statesman a traitor; threatens to hang that man whom the people delight to honor, and breathes out "threatenings and slaughter" against this man whose services in the cause of human freedom have made his name a household word wherever the language is spoken. There is, however, an appreciable difference between Cromwell and Johnson, and there is a like difference in the results accomplished by each.

When Bonaparte extinguished the Legislature of France he waited until, through his press and his partisans and by his own denunciations, he brought its authority into disgrace and contempt; and when, finally, he drove the council of the nation from their chamber, like Cromwell, he justified himself by personal abuse of the individuals themselves as they passed by him.

That the attempt of Andrew Johnson to overthrow Congress has failed is because of the want of ability and power, not of malignity and will.

We are too apt to overlook the danger which may come from words: "We are inclined to say that is only *talk*—wait till some *act* is done, and then it will be time to move. But words may be, and sometimes are, things—living, burning things, that set a world on fire."

As a most notable instance of the power of words look at the inception of the rebellion through which we have just passed. For a quarter of a century the nation took no notice of the talk of disunion and secession which was heard in Congress and on the "stump" until in the South a generation was taught them by word, and the word suddenly burst forth into terrible, awful war. Does any one doubt that if Jackson had hanged Calhoun in 1832 for talking nullification and secession, which was embryo treason, the cannon of South Carolina against Fort Sumter would ever have been heard with all their fearful and deadly consequences? Nay, more; if the United States officers, Senators, and Representatives had been impeached or disqualified from office in 1832 for advocating secession on the "stump," as was done in 1862 by Congress, then our sons and brothers now dead in battle or starved in prison had been alive and happy; and a peaceful solution of the question of slavery had been found.

Does any one doubt that if the intentions of the respondent could have been carried out, and his denunciations had weakened the Congress in the affections of the people, so that those who had in the North sympathized with the rebellion could have elected such a minority even of the Representatives to Congress as, together with those sent up from the governments organized by Johnson in the rebellious States, should have formed a majority of both or either House of Congress, that the President would have recognized such body as the legitimate Congress, and attempted to carry out its decrees by the aid of the Army and Navy and the Treasury of the United States, over which he now claims such unheard-of and illimitable powers, and thus lighted the torch of civil war?

In all earnestness, Senators, I call each one of you upon his conscience to say whether he does not believe by a preponderance of evidence drawn from the acts of the respondent since he has been in office that if the people had not been, as they ever have been, true and loyal to their Congress and to themselves, such would not have been the result of these usurpations of power in the Executive?

Is it indeed to be seriously argued here that there is a constitutional right in the President of the United States, who during his official life can never lay aside his official character to denounce, malign, abuse, ridicule, and contemn, openly and publicly, the Congress of the United States—a coördinate branch of the Government?

It cannot fail to be observed that the President (shall I dare to say his counsel, or are they compelled by the exigencies of their defense,) has deceived himself as to the *gravamen* of the charge in this article. It does not raise the question of freedom of speech, but of propriety and decency of speech and conduct in a high officer of the Government.

Andrew Johnson, the private citizen, as I may reverently hope and trust he soon will be, has the full constitutional right to think and speak what he pleases, in the manner he pleases, and where he pleases, provided always he does not bring himself within the purview of the common law offenses of being a common railer and brawler or a common scold, which he may do, (if a male person is ever liable to commit that crime;) but the dignity of station, the proprieties of position, the courtesies of office, all of which are a part of the common law of the land, require the President of the United States to observe that gravity of deportment, that fitness of conduct, that appropriateness of demeanor, and those amenities of behavior which are a part of his high official functions. He stands before the youth of the country the exemplar of all that is of worth in ambition and all that is to be sought in aspiration; he stands before the men of the country as the grave magistrate who occupies, if he does not fill, the place once honored by Washington; nay, far higher and of greater consequence, he stands before the world as the representative of free institutions, as the type of man whom the suffrages of a free people have chosen as their chief. He should be the living evidence of how much better, higher, nobler, and more in the image of God is the elected ruler of a free people than a hereditary monarch, coming into power by the accident of birth; and when he disappoints all these hopes and all these expectations, and becomes the ribald, scurrilous blasphemer, bandying epithets and taunts with a jeering mob, shall he be heard to say that such conduct is not a high misdemeanor in office? Nay, disappointing the hopes; causing the cheek to burn with shame, exposing to the taunts and ridicule of every nation the good name and fame of the chosen institutions of thirty million people, is it not the highest possible crime and misdemeanor in office; and under the circumstances is the *gravamen* of the charges. The words are not alleged to be either false or defamatory, because it is not within the power of any man, however high his official position, in effect to slander the Congress of the United States, in the ordinary sense of that word, so as to call on Congress to answer as to the truth of the accusation. We do not go in, therefore, to any question of truth or falsity. We rest upon the scandal of the scene. We would as soon think, in the trial of an indictment against a termagant as a common scold, of summoning witnesses to prove that what she said was not true. It is the noise and disturbance in the neighborhood that is the offense, and not a question of the provocation or irritation which causes the outbreak.

At the risk of being almost offensive, but protesting that if so it is not my fault but that of the person whose acts I am describing, let me but faintly picture to you the scene at Cleveland and St. Louis.

It is evening; the President of the United States, on a journey to do homage at the tomb of an illustrious statesman, accompanied by the head of the Army and Navy and Secretary of State, has arrived in the great central city of the continent. He has been welcomed by the civic authorities. He has been escorted by a procession of the benevolent charitable societies and citizens and soldiers to his hotel. He has returned thanks in answer to address of the mayor to the citizens who has received him. The hospitality of the city has provided a banquet for him and his suite, when he is again expected to address the chosen guests of the city, where all things may be conducted in decency and order. While he was resting, as one would have supposed he would have wished to do from the fatigue of the day, a noisy crowd of men and boys, washed and unwashed, drunk and sober, black and white, assemble in the street, who make night hideous by their bawling; quitting the drawing-room, without the advice of his friends, the President of the United States rushes forth on to the balcony of the hotel to address what proves to have been a mob, and this he calls in his answer a "fit occasion on which he is held to the high duty of expressing opinions of and concerning the legislation of Congress, proposed or completed, in respect of its wisdom, expediency, justice, worthiness, objects, purposes, and public and political motives and tendencies."

Observe now, upon this "fit occasion," like in all respects to that at Cleveland, when the President is called upon by the constitutional requirements of his office to expound "the wisdom, expediency, justice, worthiness, objects, purposes, and tendencies of the acts of Congress," what he says, and the manner in which he says it. Does he speak with the gravity of a Marshall when expounding constitutional law? Does he use the polished sentences of a Wirt? Or, failing in these, which may be his misfortune, does he, in plain, homely words of truth and soberness, endeavor to instruct the men and youth before him in their duty to obey the laws and to reverence their rulers, and to prize their institutions of government? Although he may have been mistaken in the aptness of the occasion for such didactic instruction, still good teaching is never thrown away. He shows, however, by his language, as he had shown at Cleveland, that he meant to adapt himself to the occasion. He has hardly opened his mouth, as we shall show you, when some one in the crowd cries, "How about our British subjects?"

The Chief Executive, supported by his Secretary of State, so that all the foreign relations and diplomatic service were fully represented, with a dignity that not even his counsel can appreciate, and with an amenity which must have delighted Downing street, answers: "We will attend to John Bull after awhile, so far as that is concerned." The mob, ungrateful, receive this bit of "expression of opinion upon the justice, worthiness, objects, purposes, and public and political motives and tendencies" of our relations with the kingdom of Great Britain as they fell from the honored lips of the President of the United States with *laughter*, and the more unthinking *with cheers*.

Having thus disposed of our diplomatic relations with the first naval and commercial nation on earth, the President next proceeds to express his opinion in manner aforesaid and for the purposes aforesaid to this noisy mob on the subject of the riots, upon which his answer says "it is the constitutional duty of the President to express opinions for the purposes aforesaid." A voice calls out, "New Orleans! go on!" After a graceful exordium the President expresses his high opinion that a massacre, wherein his pardoned and unpardoned rebel associates and friends deliberately shot down and murdered unarmed Union men without provocation, even Horton, the minister of the living God, as his hands were raised to the Prince of Peace, praying, in the language of the great martyr, "Father, forgive them, for they know not what they do," was the result of the laws passed by the legislative department of your Government in the words following, that is to say:

"If you will take up the riot at New Orleans and trace it back to its source, or to its immediate cause, you will find out who was responsible for the blood that was shed there.

"If you take up the riot at New Orleans and trace it back to the radical Congress"—

This, as we might expect, was received by the mob, composed, doubtless, in large part of unrepentant rebels, with great cheers and cries of "bully." It was "bully"—if that means encouraging—for them to learn on the authority of the President of the United States that they might shoot down Union men and patriots, and lay the sin of murder upon the Congress of the United States; and this was another bit of "opinion" which the counsel say it was the high duty of the President to express upon the justice, the worthiness, objects, "purposes and public and political motives and tendencies of the legislation of your Congress."

After some further debate with the mob some one, it seems, had called out "traitor!" The President of the United States, on this fitting, constitutional occasion, immediately took this as personal, and replies to it:

"Now, my countrymen, it is very easy to indulge in epithets; it is very easy to call a man Judas, and cry out traitor, but when he is called upon to give arguments and facts he is very often found wanting."

What were the "facts that were found wanting," which, in the mind of the President, prevented him from being a Judas Iscariot? He shall state the "wanting" facts in his own language on this occasion when he is "exercising his high constitutional prerogative :"

"Judas Iscariot! Judas! There was a Judas once, one of the twelve apostles. Oh! yes, the twelve apostles had a Christ. [A voice, 'and a Moses, too;' great laughter.] The twelve apostles had a Christ, and he never could have had a Judas unless he had had the twelve apostles. If I have played the Judas, who has been my Christ that I have played the Judas with? Was it THAD. STEVENS? Was it Wendell Phillips? Was it CHARLES SUMNER?"

If it were not that the blasphemy shocks us we should gather from all this that it dwelt in the mind of the President of the United States that the only reason why he was not a Judas was that he had not been able to find a Christ toward whom to play the Judas.

It will appear that this bit of "opinion," given in pursuance of his constitutional obligation, was received with cheers and hisses. Whether the cheers were that certain patriotic persons named by him might be hanged, or the hissing was because of the inability of the President to play the part of Judas for the reason before stated, I am sorry to say the evidence will not inform us.

His answer makes the President say that it is his "duty to express opinions concerning the public characters, and the conduct, views, purposes, objects, motives, and tendencies of all men engaged in the public service."

Now, as "the character, motives, tendencies, purposes, objects, and views" of Judas alone had "opinions expressed" about them on this "fit occasion," (although he seemed to desire to have some others, whose names he mentioned, hanged,) I shall leave his counsel to inform you what were the public services of Judas Iscariot, to say nothing of Moses, which it was the constitutional duty and right of the President of the United States to discuss on this particularly fit occasion.

But I will not pursue this revolting exhibition any further.

I will only show you at Cleveland the crowd and the President of the United States, in the darkness of night, bandying epithets with each other, crying, "Mind your dignity, Andy;" "Don't get mad, Andy;" "Bully for you, Andy." I hardly dare shock, as I must, every sense of propriety by calling your attention to the President's allusion to the death of the

sainted martyr, Lincoln, as the means by which he attained his office, and if it can be justified in any man, public or private, I am entirely mistaken in the commonest proprieties of life. The President shall tell his own story:

"There was, two years ago, a ticket before you for the Presidency. I was placed upon that ticket with a distinguished citizen now no more. [Voices, 'Its a pity;' 'Too bad;' 'Unfortunate.'] Yes, I know there are some who say 'unfortunate.' Yes, unfortunate for some that God rules on high and deals in justice. [Cheers.] Yes, unfortunate. The ways of Providence are mysterious and incomprehensible, controlling all who exclaim 'unfortunate.'"

Is it wonderful at all that such a speech, which seems to have been unprovoked and coolly uttered, should have elicited the single response from the crowd, "Bully for you?"

I go no further. I might follow this *ad nauseam*. I grant the President of the United States further upon this disgraceful scene the mercy of my silence. Tell me now, who can read the accounts of this exhibition, and reflect that the result of our institutions of government has been to place such a man, so lost to decency and propriety of conduct, so unfit, in the high office of ruler of this nation, without blushing and hanging his head in shame as the finger of scorn and contempt for republican democracy is pointed at him by some advocate of monarchy in the Old World. What answer have you when an intelligent foreigner says, "Look! see! this is the culmination of the ballot unrestrained in the hands of a free people, in a country where any man may aspire to the office of President. Is not our Government of a hereditary king or emperor a better one, where at least our sovereign is born a gentleman, than to have such a *thing* as this for a ruler?"

Yes, we have an answer. We can say *this man* was not the choice of the people for the President of the United States. He was thrown to the surface by the whirlpool of civil war, and carelessly, we grant, elected to the second place in the Government, without thought that he might ever fill the first.

By murder most foul he succeeded to the Presidency, and is the elect of an assassin to that high office, and not of the people. "It was a grievous fault, and grievously have we answered it;" but let me tell you, O advocate of monarchy! that our frame of government gives us a remedy for such a misfortune, which yours, with its divine right of kings, does not. We can remove him—as we are about to do—from the office he has disgraced by the sure, safe, and constitutional method of impeachment; while your king, if he becomes a buffoon, or a jester, or a tyrant, can only be displaced through revolution, bloodshed, and civil war.

This, this, O monarchist! is the crowning glory of our institutions, because of which, if for no other reason, our form of government claims precedence over all other governments of the earth.

Article eleven charges that the President, having denied in a public speech on the 18th of

August, 1866, at Washington, that the Thirty-Ninth Congress was authorized to exercise legislative power, and denying that the legislation of said Congress was valid or obligatory upon him, or that it had power to propose certain amendments to the Constitution, did attempt to prevent the execution of the act entitled "An act regulating the tenure of certain civil offices," by unlawfully attempting to devise means by which to prevent Mr. Stanton from resuming the functions of the office of Secretary of the Department of War, notwithstanding the refusal of the Senate to concur in his suspension, and that he also contrived means to prevent the execution of an act of March 2, 1867, which provides that all military orders shall be issued through the General of the Army of the United States, and also another act of the same 2d of March, commonly known as the reconstruction act.

To sustain this charge proof will be given of his denial of the authority of Congress as charged; also his letter to the General of the Army, in which he admits that he endeavored to prevail on him by promises of pardon and indemnity to disobey the requirements of the tenure-of-office act, and to hold the office of Secretary of War against Mr. Stanton after he had been reinstated by the Senate; that he chided the General for not acceding to his request, and declared that had he known that he (Grant) would not have acceded to his wishes he would have taken other means to prevent Mr. Stanton from resuming his office; his admission in his answer that his purpose was from the first suspension of Mr. Stanton, August 12, 1867, to oust him from his office, notwithstanding the decision of the Senate under the act; his order to General Grant to refuse to recognize any order of Mr. Stanton purporting to come from himself after he was so reinstated, and his order to General Thomas as an officer of the Army of the United States to take possession of the War Office, not transmitted, as it should have been, through the General of the Army, and the declarations of General Thomas that as an officer of the Army of the United States he felt bound to obey the orders of the Commander-in-Chief.

To prove further the purpose and intent with which his declarations were made, and his denial of the power of Congress to propose amendments to the Constitution, and as one of the means employed by him to prevent the execution of the acts of Congress, we shall show he has opposed and hindered the pacification of the country and the return of the insurrectionary States to the Union, and has advised the Legislature of the State of Alabama not to adopt the constitutional amendment known as the fourteenth article, when appealed to to know if it was best for the Legislature so to do; and this, too, after that amendment had been adopted by a majority of the loyal State Legislatures, and after, in the election of 1866, it had been sustained by an overwhelming majority of the loyal people of the United States. I do not propose to comment further on this article, because, if the Senate shall have decided that all the acts charged in the preceding articles are justified by law, then so large a part of the intent and purposes with which the respondent is charged in this article would fail of proof that it would be difficult to say whether he might not, with equal impunity, violate the laws known as the reconstruction acts, which, in his message, he declares "as plainly unconstitutional as any that can be imagined." If that be so, why should he not violate them? If, therefore, the judgment of the Senate shall sustain us upon the other articles, we shall take judgment upon this by confession, as the respondent declares in the same message that he does not intend to execute them.

To the bar of this high tribunal, invested with all its great power and duties, the House of Representatives has brought the President of the United States by the most solemn form of accusation, charging him with high crimes and misdemeanors in office, as set forth in the several articles which I have thus feebly presented to your attention. Now, it seems necessary that I should briefly touch upon and bring freshly to your remembrance the history of some of the events of his administration of affairs in his high office, in order that the intents with which and the purposes for which the respondent committed the acts alleged against him may be fully understood.

Upon the first reading of the articles of impeachment the question might have arisen in the mind of some Senator, Why are these acts of the President only presented by the House when history informs us that others equally dangerous to the liberties of the people, if not more so, and others of equal usurpation of powers, if not greater, are passed by in silence?

To such possible inquiry we reply: that the acts set out in the first eight articles are but the culmination of a series of wrongs, malfeasances, and usurpations committed by the respondent, and therefore need to be examined in the light of his precedent and concomitant acts to grasp their scope and design. The last three articles presented show the perversity and malignity with which he acted, so that the man as he is known to us may be clearly spread upon record to be seen and known of all men hereafter.

What has been the respondent's course of administration? For the evidence we rely upon common fame and current history as sufficient proof. By the common law common fame, "si oriatur apud bonos et graves," was ground of indictment even; more than two hundred and forty years ago it was determined in Parliament "that common fame is a good ground for the proceeding of this House, either to inquire of here or to transmit the complaint, if the House find cause, to the king or lords."

Now, is it not well known to all good and

grave men "*bonos et graves*" that Andrew Johnson entered the office of President of the United States at the close of the armed rebellion making loud denunciation, frequently and everywhere, that traitors ought to be punished and treason should be made odious; that the loyal and true men of the South should be fostered and encouraged; and, if there were but few of them, to such only should be given in charge the reconstruction of the disorganized States?

Do not all men know that soon afterward he changed his course and only made treason odious, so far as he was concerned, by appointing traitors to office and by an indiscriminate pardon of all who "came in unto him?" Who does not know that Andrew Johnson initiated, of his own will, a course of reconstruction of the rebel States which at the time he claimed was provisional only, and until the meeting of Congress and its action thereon? Who does not know that when Congress met and undertook to legislate upon the very subject of reconstruction of which he had advised them in his message, which they alone had the constitutional power to do, Andrew Johnson last aforesaid again changed his course, and declared that Congress had no power to legislate upon that subject; that the two Houses had only the power *separately* to judge of the qualifications of the members who might be sent to each by rebellious constituencies, acting under State organizations which Andrew Johnson had called into existence by his late *fiat*, the electors of which were voting by his permission and under his limitations? Who does not know that when Congress, assuming its rightful power to propose amendments to the Constitution, had passed such an amendment, and had submitted it to the States as a measure of pacification, Andrew Johnson advised and counseled the Legislatures of the States lately in rebellion, as well as others, to reject the amendment, so that it might not operate as a law, and thus establish equality of suffrage in all the States and equality of right in the members of the Electoral College and in the number of the Representatives to the Congress of the United States?

Lest any one should doubt the correctness of this piece of history or the truth of this common fame we shall show you that while the Legislature of Alabama was deliberating upon the reconsideration of the vote whereby it had rejected the constitutional amendment, the fact being brought to the knowledge of Andrew Johnson and his advice asked, he, by a telegraphic message under his own hand, *here to be produced*, to show his intent and purposes, advised the Legislature against passing the amendment, and to remain firm in their opposition to Congress. We shall show like advice of Andrew Johnson, upon the same subject, to the Legislature of South Carolina, and this, too, in the winter of 1867, after the action of Congress in proposing the constitutional amend-

ment had been sustained in the previous election by an overwhelming majority. Thus we charge that Andrew Johnson, President of the United States, not only endeavors to thwart the constitutional action of Congress and bring it to naught, but also to hinder and oppose the execution of the will of the loyal people of the United States expressed, in the only mode by which it can be done, through the ballot-box, in the election of their Representatives. Who does not know that from the hour he began these his usurpations of power he everywhere denounced Congress, the legality and constitutionality of its action, and defied its legitimate powers, and, for that purpose, announced his intentions and carried out his purpose, as far as he was able, of removing every true man from office who sustained the Congress of the United States? And it is to carry out this plan of action that he claims the unlimited power of removal, for the illegal exercise of which he stands before you this day. Who does not know that, in pursuance of the same plan, he used his veto power indiscriminately to prevent the passage of wholesome laws enacted for the pacification of the country; and when laws were passed by the constitutional majority over his. vetoes he made the most determined opposition, both open and covert, to them, and, for the purpose of making that opposition effectual, he endeavored to array and did array all the people lately in rebellion to set themselves against Congress and against the true and loyal men, their neighbors, so that murders, assassinations, and massacres were rife all over the southern States, which he encouraged by his refusal to consent that a single murderer be punished, though thousands of good men have been slain; and, further, that he attempted by military orders to prevent the execution of acts of Congress by the military commanders who were charged therewith. These and his concurrent acts show conclusively that his attempt to get the control of the military force of the Government, by the seizing of the Department of War, was done in pursuance of his general design, if it were possible, to overthrow the Congress of the United States; and he now claims by his answer the right to control at his own will, for the execution of this very design, every officer of the Army, Navy, civil, and diplomatic service of the United States. He asks you here, Senators, by your solemn adjudication, to confirm him in that right, to invest him with that power, to be used with the intents and for the purposes which he has already shown.

The responsibility is with you; the safeguards of the Constitution against usurpation are in your hands; the interests and hopes of free institutions wait upon your verdict. The House of Representatives has done its duty. We have presented the facts in the constitutional manner; we have brought the criminal to your bar, and demand judgment at your hands for his so great crimes.

C. I.—6.

Never again, if Andrew Johnson go quit and free this day, can the people of this or any other country by constitutional checks or guards stay the usurpations of executive power.

I speak, therefore, not the language of exaggeration, but the words of truth and soberness, that the future political welfare and liberties of all men hang trembling on the decision of the hour.

A Brief of the Authorities upon the Law of Impeachable Crimes and Misdemeanors, prepared by Hon. WILLIAM LAWRENCE, *M. C., of Ohio; revised and presented by B. F.* BUTLER, *of Massachusetts, one of the Managers, as a part of his opening argument on the Impeachment of the President.*

In order to ascertain the impeachable character of an act done or omitted reference must be had to the Constitution, expounded as it is by history, by parliamentary and common law.

The provisions of the Constitution which relate to or illustrate the law of impeachment are these:

"The House of Representatives shall choose their Speaker and other officers, and shall have the sole power of impeachment." (Art. 1, sec. 2.)

"The Senate shall have the sole power to try all impeachments. When sitting for that purpose they shall be on oath or affirmation. When the President of the United States is tried the Chief Justice shall preside; and no person shall be convicted without the concurrence of two thirds of the members present.

"Judgment in cases of impeachment shall not extend further than to removal from office, and disqualification to hold and enjoy any office of honor, trust, or profit under the United States; but the party convicted shall nevertheless be liable and subject to indictment, trial, judgment, and punishment, according to law." (Art. 1, sec. 3.)

"In case of the removal of the President from office, or of his death, resignation, or inability to discharge the powers and duties of the said office, the same shall devolve on the Vice President, and the Congress may by law provide for the case of removal, death, resignation, or inability, both of the President and Vice President, declaring what officer shall then act as President, and such officer shall act accordingly, until the disability be removed or a President shall be elected." (Art. 2, sec 1.)

"The President shall be Commander-in-Chief of the Army and Navy of the United States, and of the militia of the several States when called into the actual service of the United States; he may require the opinion, in writing, of the principal officer in each of the Executive Departments, upon any subject relating to the duties of their respective offices; and he shall have power to grant reprieves and pardons for offenses against the United States, except in cases of impeachment." (Art. 2, sec. 2.*)

"The President, Vice President, and all civil officers of the United States shall be removed from office on impeachment for, and conviction of, treason, bribery, or other high crimes and misdemeanors." (Art. 2, sec. 4.)

"The trial of all crimes, except in cases of impeachment, shall be by jury; and such trial shall

* The clauses of the Constitution which declare that a party impeached shall be "liable to indictment;" that "the trial of all crimes, except incases of impeachment, shall be by jury;" that the President shall have power to grant "pardons for offenses against the United States, except in cases of impeachment," are all either parts of or modifications of the British constitution; they recognize statutory and common law crimes as a portion, but not all, of the impeachable offenses here as they were and are in England.

be held in the State where the said crimes shall have been committed; but when not committed within any State the trial shall be at such place or places as the Congress may by law have directed." (Art. 3, sec. 2.)

The convention which framed the Constitution on the subject of impeachment "proceeded in the same manner it is manifest they did in many other cases; they considered the *object* of their legislation as a *known thing*, having a previous definite existence. Thus existing, their work was solely to mold it into a suitable shape. They have given it to us, not as a thing of their *creation*, but merely of their *modification*."*

In England a majority of the lords impeach, though, by common law, twelve peers must be present and concur.† Here the concurrence of two thirds of the members [of the Senate] present is requisite.

In England the character and extent of the punishment are in the discretion of the lords. Here it cannot extend further than to removal from and disqualification to hold office.

In England "all the king's subjects are impeachable in Parliament."‡ Here, according to the received construction, "none are liable to impeachment except *officers* of the Government."‖

* Bayard on Blount's Trial, 264; and he added: "And therefore I shall insist that it remains as at common law, [parliamentary,] with the variance only of the positive provisions of the Constitution." (Wharton's State Trials, 264; Rawle on Constitution, 200.)

"The Constitution" * * * * "refers to" * * * * "impeachment without defining it. It assumes the existence" * * * * "and silently points us to English precedents for knowledge of details. We are reminded of the statement" * * * * "that 'the Constitution is an instrument of enumeration and not of definition.'" (Professor Dwight, 6 Am. Law Reg., N. S., 237.)

† 5 Comyn's Digest, 308, *Parliament* L.

‡ 2 Wooddeson's Lectures, 602.

‖ In Chase's Trial Mr. Rodney "utterly disclaimed the idea that" any but *officers* were liable to impeachment.

Wharton says, in reference to Blount's trial: "In a legal point of view all that this case decides is that a Senator of the United States who has been expelled from his seat is not, after such expulsion, subject to impeachment, and perhaps from this the broader proposition may be drawn that none are liable to impeachment except officers of the Government, in the technical sense, excluding thereby members of the national Legislature. Afterward, from the expulsion of Mr. Smith, a Senator from Ohio, for connection with Burr's conspiracy, instead of his impeachment, the same implication arises." (Wharton's State Trials, 317, note.)

In this case Mr. Bayard maintained "that all persons" * * * * "are liable to impeachment;" that the Constitution does not define the cases or describe the persons designed as the objects of impeachment. "We are designedly left to the regulations of the common [parliamentary] law." This view is confirmed by the fact that art. 2, sec. 4, *imperatively* requires "removal from office" in case of the President, Vice President, and officers, while art. 1, sec. 3, seems to admit of less punishment than this, and which must, therefore, apply to persons other than officers. (See Wickliffe's argument, Peck's Trial, 309.) The constitution of New York of 1777 is said to have been the model from which the impeachment clauses of the Constitution of the United States were copied. (6 Am. Law Reg., N. S., 277.) That

In England the lords are not sworn in trying an impeachment, but give their decision upon their honor. Here Senators act under the solemn sanction of an oath or affirmation. In England the crown is not impeachable. Here the President is.

In England, impeachment may, to some extent, be regarded as a mode of trial designed, *inter alia*, to punish crime, though not entirely so, since a judgment on an impeachment is no answer to an indictment in the king's bench.* Here impeachment is only designed to remove unfit persons from office; and the party convicted is subject to indictment, trial, and punishment in the proper courts.

It is absurd to say that impeachment is here a mode of procedure for *the punishment of crime*,† when the Constitution declares its object to be *removal from and disqualification to hold office*, and that "the party convicted shall nevertheless be liable and subject to indictment, trial, judgment, and punishment, according to law," for his "*crimes*."

Subject to these modifications, and adopting the recognized rule, that the Constitution should be construed so as to be equal to every occasion which might call for its exercise, and adequate to accomplish the purposes of its framers, impeachment remains here as it was recognized in England at and prior to the adoption of the Constitution.

These limitations were imposed in view of the abuses of the power of impeachment in English history.‡

These abuses were not guarded against in our Constitution by *limiting, defining*, or *reducing* impeachable *crimes*, since the same necessity existed here as in England for the remedy of impeachment, but by *other safeguards* thrown around in it that instrument. It will be observed that the "*sole power of impeachment*" is conferred on the House, and the sole power of *trial* on the Senate by article one, sections two and three. These are the only *jurisdictional* clauses, and they do not limit impeachment to crimes or misdemeanors. Nor is it elsewhere so limited. Section four of article two only makes it imperative when "the President, Vice President, and all civil officers" are convicted "of treason, bribery, or other high* crimes and misdemeanors," that they *shall* be removed from office.†

But, so far as the questions now before the country are concerned, it is not material whether the words "treason, bribery, or other high crimes and misdemeanors" confer or limit jurisdiction, or only prescribe an *imperative punishment* as to officers or a class of cases, since every act which by parliamentary usage is impeachable is defined a "high crime or misdemeanor;" and these are the words of the British constitution which describe impeachable conduct.‡ There may be cases appropriate for the exercise of the power of impeachment where no crime or misdemeanor has been committed.

---

of New York limits impeachments to officers in terms; that of the United States does not. There may be agents and others for whom impeachments would be salutary.

In England military and naval officers are impeachable. If a military or naval officer here should conspire with the President to overthrow Congress the impeachment of both would be a necessary protection, which it may be doubted if the Constitution intended to surrender. In such case a court-martial could not, against the President's will, remove from office; impeachment alone would be efficient. (Wharton's State Trials, 290.)

* *Fitzharris's Case*, 6 Am. Law Reg., N. S., 262.

† "Impeachment is a proceeding purely of a political nature. It is not so much designed to punish the offender as to secure the State. It touches neither his person nor his property, but simply divests him of his political capacity." (Bayard's Speech on Blount's Trial; Wharton's State Trials, 263.)

‡ The earliest recorded instance of impeachment by the Commons at the bar of the House of Lords was in the reign of Edward III, (1376.) Before that time the Lords appear to have tried both peers and commoners for great public offenses, but not upon complaints addressed to them by the Commons. During the next four reigns cases of regular impeachment were frequent; but no instances occurred in the reigns of Edward IV, Henry VII, Henry VIII, Edward VI, Queen Mary, and Queen Elizabeth.

"The institution had fallen into disuse," (says Mr. Hallam, 1 Const. Hist., 357,) "partly from the loss of that control which the Commons had obtained under Richard II and the Lancasterian kings, and partly from the preference the Tudor princes had given to bills of attainder or of pains and penalties, when they wished to turn the arm of Parliament against an obnoxious subject."

Prosecutions, also, in the Star Chamber, during that time, were perpetually resorted to by the Crown for the punishment of State offenders. In the reign of James I the practice of impeachment was revived, and was used with great energy by the Commons, both as an instrument of popular power and for the furtherance of public justice.

"Between the year 1620, when Sir Giles Mompesson and Lord Bacon were impeached, and the revolution in 1688, there were about forty cases of impeachment. In the reigns of William III, Queen Anne, and George I, there were fifteen; and in the reign of George II none but that of Lord Lovat, in 1746, for high treason. The last memorable cases are those of Warren Hastings in 1788, and Lord Melville in 1805." (May on Parliament, 49, 50; Ingersoll's speech on Blount's Trial, Wharton's State Trials, 285; 4 Hatsell, *passim*.)

* The word "high" applies as well to "misdemeanors" as to "crimes." (2 Chase's Trial, 383.)

† On Chase's trial Mr. Rodney so argued; and so Wickliffe on Peck's trial, 309. In Blount's trial Mr. Ingersoll insisted that art. 2, sec. 4, designates "the extent of the power of impeachment both as to the offenses and the persons liable." (Wharton's State Trials, 289; see p. 99 per Harper.)

‡ 4 Hatsell's Precedents, 73-76.

By the constitution of the State of Massachusetts the Senate is "to hear and determine all impeachments made by the House of Representatives against any officer or officers of the Commonwealth for misconduct and maladministration in office."

On the trial of Judge Prescott in 1821, Mr. Blake in defense, referring to the words *misconduct* and *maladministration*, said: "What, then, are the legal import and signification of these terms? We answer precisely the same as of *crimes and misdemeanors;* that they are in every respect equivalent to the more familiar terms that are employed by the constitution of Great Britain in its description of impeachable offences, subject only to the wholesome limitation which in this Commonwealth confines this extraordinary method of trial to the official misdemeanors of public functionaries." (Prescott's Trial, 117, 118.)

As these words are copied by our Constitution from the British constitutional and parliamentary law, they are, so far as applicable to our institutions and condition, to be interpreted not by English municipal law, but by the *lex parliamentaria.**

When, therefore, Blackstone† says that "an impeachment before the Lords by the Commons of Great Britain in Parliament is a prosecution of the already known and established law, and has been frequently put in practice," he must be understood to refer to the "established" *parliamentary*, not common municipal law, as administered in the ordinary courts, for it was the former that had been frequently put in practice.

Whatever "crimes and misdemeanors" were the subjects of impeachment in England prior to the adoption of our Constitution, and as understood by its framers, are, therefore, subjects of impeachment before the Senate of the United States, subject only to the limitations of the Constitution.

The framers of our Constitution, looking to the impeachment trials in England, and to the writers on parliamentary and common law, and to the constitutions and usages of our own States, saw that no act of Parliament or of any State Legislature ever undertook to define an impeachable crime. They saw that the whole system of crimes, as defined in acts of Parliament and as recognized at common law, was prescribed for and adapted to the ordinary courts. (2 Hale, Pl. Crown, ch. 20, p. 150; 6 Howell State Trials, 313, note.)

They saw that the High Court of Impeachment took jurisdiction of cases where no indictable crime had been committed, in many instances, and there were then, as there yet are, "two parallel modes of reaching" some, but not all offenders: one by impeachment, the other by indictment.

In such cases a party first indicted "may be impeached afterward, and the latter trial may proceed notwithstanding the indictment." *

On the other hand, the king's bench held in *Fitzharris's case* that an impeachment was no answer to an indictment in that court.†

The two systems are in no way connected, though each may adopt principles applicable to the other, and each may shine by the other's borrowed light.

With these landmarks to guide them, our fathers adopted a Constitution under which official malfeasance and nonfeasance, and, in some cases, misfeasance, may be the subject of impeachment, although not made criminal by act of Congress, or so recognized by the common law of England or of any State of the Union. They adopted impeachment as a means of removing men from office whose misconduct imperils the public safety and renders them unfit to occupy official position.

All this is supported by the elementary writers, both English and American, on parliamentary and common law; by the English and American usage in cases of impeachment; by the opinions of the framers of the Constitution; by contemporaneous construction, all uncontradicted by any author, authority, case, or jurist, for more than three quarters of a century after the adoption of the Constitution.

The authorities are abundant to show that the phrase "high crimes and misdemeanors," as used in the British and our Constitution, are not limited to crimes defined by statute or as recognized at common law.‡

Christian,* who may be supposed to have understood the British constitution when he wrote, says: "When the words high crimes and misdemeanors are used in prosecutions by impeachment, the words high crimes have no definite signification, but are used merely to give greater solemnity to the charge." ‖

Woodeson,§ whose lectures were read at Oxford in 1777, declared that impeachments extended to cases of which the ordinary courts had no jurisdiction. He says:

"Magistrates and officers" * * * * "may abuse their delegated powers to the extensive detriment of the community, and at the same time in a manner not *properly cognizable before the ordinary tribunals.*"

And he proceeds to say the remedy is by impeachment.

---

* *Pennock* vs. *Dialogue*, 2 Peters, 2-18. When foreign statutes are "adopted into our legislation the known and settled construction of those statutes by courts of law has been considered as silently incorporated into the acts." (*United States* vs. *Jones*, 3 Wash. C. C. R., 209; *Ex parte Hall*, 1 Pick., 261; Sedgwick on Stat. p. 262, 426; Story on Const., sec. 797; Rawle on Const., 200.) This author says in reference to impeachments, "We must have recourse to the common law of England for the definition of them;" that is, to the common parliamentary law. (3 Wheaton, 610; 1 Wood, and Minot, 448.)

The Constitution contains inherent evidence of this. By it "treason, bribery, and other high crimes and misdemeanors" are impeachable. "Treason" is defined in the Constitution; "bribery" is not; and it therefore means what the common law has defined it. As the Constitution thus itself resorts to the common and parliamentary law for the definition of its terms, the words "high crimes and misdemeanors" are to be interpreted by the same codes. They are as completely included as though every crime had been specifically named. Whatever by the common law was treason and which is not covered by the definition in the Constitution which defined it for the ordinary courts, is still impeachable crime so far as applicable to our institutions.

† 4 Blackstone's Com., 260, read in Oxford 1759. He says, also: "It may happen that a subject intrusted with the administration of public affairs may infringe the rights of the people and be guilty of such crimes as the ordinary magistrate either dares not *or cannot punish*," that is, cannot punish because not falling within his jurisdiction.

* *Stafford's Trial*, 7 Howard's State Trials, 1297.

† 6 Am. Law. Reg., N. S., 252.

‡ If an act to be impeachable must be indictable, then it might be urged that every act which is indictable must be impeachable. But this has never been pretended. As the Senate must, therefore, decide what acts are impeachable it cannot be governed by their indictable character.

‖ Note to 4 Blackstone, 5.

§ 2 Wooddeson's Lectures, 596.

English history presents many examples of this kind.*

* See Comyn's Digest, tit. *Parliament.* "In 1388 there are several proceedings before the Lords against the Archbishop of York and other great officers and against several of the judges, for having given extra-judicial opinions and misinterpreting the law;" 4 Hatsel, 76; and in a note it is said the Lords determined that such cases "*cannot be tried elsewhere than in Parliament,* nor by any other law than the law and course of Parliament." * * * *
It is elsewhere said, "such kind of misdeeds as peculiarly injure the Commonwealth by the abuse of high offices of trust are the most proper" * * * * "grounds for this kind of prosecutions. Thus" * * * * "if the judges mislead their sovereign by unconstitutional opinions, if any other magistrate attempt to subvert the fundamental laws or introduce arbitrary power," * * * * "So when a lord chancellor has been thought to put the seal to an ignominious treaty; a lord admiral to neglect the safeguard of the sea; an embassador to betray his trust; a privy counselor to propound or support pernicious and dishonorable measures, &c., &c." (2 Wooddeson's Lectures, 602; 1 Blackstone, 257.)
In the Virginia convention, Madison said, "If the President got up a treaty by surprise he would be impeached." (3 Eliot's Debates, 660, 516, 514, 496.)
In Ohio, before it was settled that the courts had power to declare legislative acts unconstitutional, one judge of the supreme court and one president judge of the common pleas were tried on impeachments for the exercise of this power, and each escaped conviction by only one vote. (20 Ohio Rep., Appendix, p. 3.)
The Duke of Suffolk was impeached for neglect of duty as an embassador; the Earl of Bristol that he gave counsel against a war with Spain, whose king had affronted the English nation; the Duke of Buckingham that he, being admiral, neglected the safeguard of the sea; Michael de la Pole that he, being chancellor, acted contrary to his duty; the Duke of Buckingham for having a plurality of office: and he whom the poet calls the 'greatest, wisest, meanest of mankind,' for bribery in his office of lord chancellor; the Lord Finch for unlawful methods of enlarging the forest, in his office of assistant to the justices on Eyre; the Earl of Oxford for selling goods to his own use captured by him as admiral without accounting for a tenth to others." (Ingersoll's Speech on Blount's Trial, Wharton's State Trials, 291.)
Dr. Sacheverel was impeached for preaching an improper sermon. (Harper's Speech, Blount's Trial, Wharton, 301.)
"Andrew Horne, in his Mirror of Justice, mentions many judges punished by King Alfred before the conquest for corrupt judgments." * * *
* "Our stories mention many punished in the time of Edward I; our Parliament rolls of Edward III's time, of Richard II's time *for the pernicious resolutions* given at Nottingham Castle, afford examples of this kind. In later times, the Parliament journals of 18 and 21 Jac., the judgment of the ship-money in the time of Charles I questioned, and the particular judges impeached." (Vaugh., 139; cited in Appendix to Addison's (Pennsylvania) Trial.)
Cases decided in England *since* the adoption of our Constitution cannot limit the powers it confers. But no case can be found in England which limits impeachment to crimes indictable by common law or act of Parliament. The power of impeachment for offenses against the State has been distinctly and continuously maintained.
The case of the *Earl of Clarendon* sustains this position. On the 10th July, 1663, the Earl of Bristol, without any action of the Commons, presented to the House of Lords "articles of high treason and other misdemeanors" against the Lord Chancellor. One was—
"That being in places of high trust, &c., he hath traitorously and maliciously endeavored to alienate the hearts of his majesty's subjects from him by words of his own." * * * * "That his majesty was inclined to popery, and had a design to alter the religion established in this kingdom."
The statute 13, Charles II, chapter 1, provides

that if any person shall maliciously affirm the king to be a heretic, a papist, or that he endeavors to introduce popery, every person shall be disabled to hold office, &c.
The Lords ordered the Chief Justice and judges to—
"Consider whether the said charge hath been brought in regularly and legally, and whether it may be proceeded in, and how, whether there be any treason in it or no."
The judges reported that they did not consider the question whether the impeachment could be proceeded in or not *if it came from the Commons,* but as the statute of 1 Henry IV, chapter fourteen, provides that "all appeals of things within the realm shall be tried and determined by the laws of the court," articles of impeachment could not be preferred "by the said earl or any private person," that appeals meant "accusation by single persons." The judges then say:
"That there was *no treason* in the charge, though the matters in it are alleged to be *traitorously* done. The great charge" * * * * "was that he did traitorously and maliciously to bring the king into contempt, and with an intent to alien the people's affections from him, say," &c. * * *
"And in like manner was most of the articles upon which the character of treason seemed to be fixed. I said that it is a *transcendent misprision or offense* to endeavor to bring the king into contempt, or to endeavor to alienate the people's affections from him, but yet it was *not treason.*" * * * *
"We did not meddle with anything concerning accusing him of *misdemeanor.*"
And so the Lords resolved, concurring in all these opinions. (6 Howard's State Trials, 318, 346.)
The Commons afterward presented articles of impeachment.
November 16, 1867, Sir R. Howard, in discussing the heads of charges in the Commons, said:
"Though common law has its proper sphere, it is not in this place—we are in a higher sphere."
November 11. The Commons resolved to impeach and notified the Lords, and demanded that Clarendon be sequestered from Parliament and committed. (6 Howell, 395.)
The Lords refused until the articles should be presented; and before the question was settled Clarendon escaped to the continent, and the statute 19 Charles II, chapter ten, of December 12, banished him.
The Lords therefore decided nothing.
Among the articles agreed on in the House were these:
IX. That he introduced an arbitrary government in his majesty's plantations, and hath caused such as complained therof before his majesty and counsel to be long imprisoned for so doing.
XI. That he advised and effected the sale of Dunkirk to the French king, being part of his majesty's dominions, together with ammunition, artillery, and all sorts of stores there, and for no greater value than the said ammunition, artillery, and stores were worth.
XVII. That he was a principal author of the fatal counsel of dividing the fleet about June, 1666.
The case of the Earl of Orrery proves nothing as to the law.
November 25, 1669, a petition was presented in the House of Commons charging the Earl with—
"Raising moneys by his own authority upon his majesty's subjects, defrauding the king's subjects of their estates. The money raised was for bribing hungry courtiers to come to his ends, and if the king would not he had fifty thousand swords to compel them."
The earl answered in person and denied the charges. Then—
"The question being propounded that a day be appointed for the accusers to produce witnesses to make good the charge," * * * * "it was negatived—121 to 118."
It was then resolved—
"That the accusation against the Earl of Orrery be left to be prosecuted at law."

sense. In the parliamentary sense, as applied to officers, it means "maladministration" or

It never was prosecuted. (6 Howell, State Trials, 915.)

Sir Adam Blair was impeached in 1690 by the Commons—

"For dispersing [distributing] a seditious and treasonable paper, printed and entitled 'A declaration of King James II.'"

On the question whether articles of impeachment should be preferred, Mr. Hawles said:

"I do not think this to be a plain case of treason by statute 25 Edward III. I do say no court can judge this offense to be treason; and *that statute did plainly not bind the superior court of Parliament* but the inferior only. The proper way is to judge this high treason; and therefore I am for proceeding by impeachment."

And it was resolved to impeach of high treason.

April 7, 1690, he was admitted to bail, and at the next session of Parliament he was discharged from bail.

Here was a case in which there was clearly no treason under the statute, and yet the Commons resolved that he should be impeached and so far decided that he was guilty of an *impeachable*, though not an *indictable* crime, and which they called treason; adopting the idea prevailing at the time as to constructive treason, but which might as well have been simply called an impeachable misdemeanor. (12 Howell, State Trials, 1213.)

Thomas, Earl of Macclesfield, Lord High Chancellor of England, was tried in May, 1725, before the House of Lords, on articles of impeachment, charging that he—

"In the office of chancellor did illegally and corruptly insist upon and take of divers persons great sums of money in order to and before their admission into their offices of master in chancery," to which he appointed them.

The answer was that the sums of money received were presents—

"Reckoned among the ancient and known perquisites" * * * * "and never before looked upon to be criminal;" * * * * "that the giving or receiving a present on such occasion is not *criminal in itself*, or by the *common law* of the realm, and that there is not any *act of Parliament* whatsoever by which the same is made criminal or subject to any punishment or judgment."

Replication that "the charge of high crimes and misdemeanors is true."

In the argument it was insisted by the managers that the acts complained of violated the statutes of 5 and 6 Edward VI, chapter 16, against selling offices, and violated the oath prescribed by statute 12 Richard II. (Moor, 781, Stockwith & Worth.)

But as a question of parliamentary law it was asserted, and not controverted, that acts may be *impeachable* which are not indictable by common law or act of Parliament.

Mr. Sergeant Pengelly, May 21, 1725, said:

"Your lordships are now exercising a power of judication reserved in the original frame of the English constitution for the punishment of offenses of a public nature which may affect the nation, as well in instances where the inferior courts *have no power* to *punish the crimes* committed by the ordinary rules of justice as in cases within the jurisdiction of the courts of Westminster Hall, where the person offending is by his degree raised above the apprehension of danger from a prosecution carried on in the more usual course of justice, and whose exalted station requires the united accusation of all the commons of Great Britain by their representatives in Parliament.

"This high jurisdiction may be exercised for the preservation of the rights of the Lords and Commons against the attempts of powerful evil ministers who depend upon the favor of the Crown; or it may be put in execution for the ease and relief of a good prince whose honor has been betrayed by a corrupt servant, and yet whose clemency makes him unwilling to punish; so that it becomes necessary for his faithful Commons to take into their care the protection of such an offender.

"Former reigns have supplied your journals with many examples of the first kind. The present reign produces an instance of the latter sort, wherein the Commons bring before your lordships in judgment a peer offending with the greatest ingratitude against a most just and most merciful sovereign." (6 State Trials, (Hargrave,) 733.)

And again it was said:

"My lords, if the *misdemeanors* of which the earl impeached stands accused were not *crimes* by the *ordinary rules of law* in *inferior courts*, as they have been made out to be, yet they would be *offenses* of a *public nature* against the *welfare* of the *subject* and the *common good* of the kingdom, committed by the highest officer of justice and attended with so great and immediate loss to a multitude of sufferers, and as such they would demand the exercise of the extraordinary jurisdiction vested in your *judication* for the *public safety* by virtue whereof your lordships can inflict that degree and kind of punishment which no other court can impose." (Page 746; 6 State Trials, (Hargrave,) 477, London, 1777. Same case, 16 Howell's State Trials, 823; and see 4 Campbell's Lord Chancellors, 536; 15 (sixth N. S.) American Law Register, 266.)

He was convicted.

Lord Melville was impeached before the Lords in 1806 for that, as treasurer of the navy, he had used the public money for purposes of private gain, prior to and since the statute of June, 1785. (25 George III, chapter 31.) It was conceded that he had properly accounted for all money; that he had properly paid all demands upon him as treasurer; that it had even been down to a certain period—

"Irreproachable to those who exercised that office to make use of the public money which passed through their hands." (Asperne's Report, 6.)

There was no complaint of any public act "against the welfare of the subject or the common good, or subversive of any fundamental principle of government.

He could not, therefore, be impeached unless he was indictable at common law or had violated a statute, to do which is by the common law indictable. The managers insisted that his conduct was an offense at common law, and since the statute of June, 1785, a violation of that act. (Asperne's Report, 138.)

He denied the charges. After hearing evidence questions were put to the judges:

1. Whether money issued from the exchequer to the credit of the treasurer of the navy in the Bank of England may be lawfully drawn therefrom by him for the purpose of paying bills actually drawn upon the treasurer, but not yet actually presented; and whether money so drawn may be deposited with a banker until the payment of such bills, and for the purpose of paying them; or whether such acts are in law a crime or offense.

Answer. The judges answered that such drawing and deposit of money were lawful and no crime.

2. Whether moneys issued from the exchequer to the credit of the treasurer of the navy in the Bank of England may be lawfully drawn therefrom by him to be ultimately applied to navy services, but in the meantime and until required for the purpose of being deposited with a private banker in the name and under the control of his (Melville's) private clerk.

Answer. The judges answered that if the object of drawing the money from the Bank of England was to deposit it with a private banker it was not lawful, although intended to be and in fact ultimately applied to naval service; but if so deposited *bona fide* as the means or supposed means of more conveniently applying the money to naval services the money may be lawfully drawn.

3. Whether it was lawful for the treasurer, before the statute 25 George III, chapter 31, (and especially as his salary had been augmented by the king's warrant in full satisfaction of all wages, fees, and profits,) to apply money impressed to him for naval services to any other use whatever, public or private, and whether such application would have been a misdemeanor punishable by information or indictment. The judges answered it was not unlawful, so as to

" misconduct," not necessarily indictable,* not only in England, but in the United States.† Demeanor is conduct, and he is guilty of misdemeanor who misdemeans or misconducts.

---

constitute a misdemeanor punishable by information or indictment.

The form of these questions implies that Melville had not used the public money for private purposes *since* the statute of 25 George III, chapter 31, and it was not at common law a misdemeanor to do so *prior* to the statute.

The case was one not calling for any decision of the general question whether an act to be impeachable must be indictable, nor was any such proposition discussed. The Lords decided he was *not guilty.*

The first charge against Judge Humphreys was for advocating secession in a public speech, December 29, 1860, which was no crime by common or statute law, and yet he was impeached and removed. There was no rebellion then and no "confederate" government. (4 Cranch, 75; 1 Dallas, 35; 2 Wallace, jr., 139; 2 Bishop, Criminal Law, 1183-1204; 23 Boston Law Reporter, 597, 705; 1 Bishop, 514; Burr's Trial, Coombe's edition, 322.

* " On the 16th of October, 1637, the House being informed that there have been some *innovations of late in trials of men for their lives and deaths,* and in some particular cases restraints have been put upon juries in the inquiries, this matter is referred to a committee. On the 18th of November this committee are empowered to receive information against the Lord Chief Justice Kelynge, for any other MISDEMEANORS besides those concerning juries; and on the 11th of December, 1637, this committee report several resolutions against the Lord Chief Justice Kelynge, *of illegal and arbitrary proceedings* in his office. The first of these resolutions is that the proceedings of the Lord Chief Justice in the cases now reported *are innovations in the trial of men for their lives* and liberties; and that he hath used an *arbitrary* and *illegal* power, which is of dangerous consequence to the lives and liberties of the people of England, and tends to the *introducing* of an arbitrary *Government.* The Lord Chief Justice hath *undervalued,* vilified, and contemned *Magna Charta,* the great preserver of our lives, freedom, and property." (4 Hatsel Prec., 113, cited 2 Chase's Trial, 461.)

One of the resolves against Chief Justice Scroggs was, " That the discharging the grand jury by the Court of King's Bench in Trinity term last before they had finished their presentments was illegal, arbitrary, and a *high misdemeanor.*" (4 Hatsel, 127; 7 State Trials, 479.)

" Misprisions which are merely positive are generally denominated contempts or high misdemeanors, of which—

" 1. The first and principal is the maladministration of such high offices as are in public trust and employment. This is usually punished by the method of parliamentary impeachment." (4 Blackstone, 121.)

† In Senate, July 8, 1797, it was " *Resolved,* That William Blount, esq., one of the Senators of the United States, having been guilty of a high *misdemeanor,* entirely inconsistent with his public trust and duty as a Senator, be, and he hereby is, expelled from the Senate of the United States." (Wharton's State Trials, 202.)

He was not guilty of an indictable crime. (Story on the Constitution, sec. 799, note.)

The offense charged, Judge Story remarks, "was not defined by any statute of the United States. It was an attempt to seduce a United States Indian interpreter from his duty, and to alienate the affections and conduct of the Indians from the public officers residing among them."

Blackstone says: " The fourth species of offense more immediately against the king and Government are entitled *misprisions* and *contempts.* Misprisions are, in the acceptation of our law, generally understood to be all such high offenses as are under the degree of capital, but nearly bordering thereon." * * * * * " Misprisions which are merely positive are generally denominated contempts or *high misdemeanors,* of which the first and principal is the *maladministration* of such high offices as are in

---

The power of impeachment, so far as the President is concerned, was inserted in the Constitution to secure "good behavior," to punish "misconduct," to defend "the community against the incapacity, negligence, or perfidy of the Chief Magistrate," to punish " abuse of power," "treachery," "corrupting his electors;" or, as Madison declared, " for any act which might be called a misdemeanor."* And

public trust and employment. This is usually punished by the method of *parliamentary impeachment.*" (Vol. 4, p. 121.)

(See Prescott's Trial, Massachusetts, 1821, pp. 79-80, 109, 117-20, 172-180, 191.)

On Chase's Trial the defense conceded that "to misbehave or to misdemean is precisely the same." (2 Chase's Trial, 145.)

* From 2 Madison's Papers, 1153, &c.

July 20, 1787.

The following clause, relative to the President, being under consideration:

"To be removable on impeachment and conviction for malpractice or neglect of duty.

"Mr. Pinckney moved to strike this out, and said, 'He ought not to be impeachable while in office.'

"Mr. Davee. If he be not impeachable while in office he will spare no efforts or means whatever to get himself reelected. He considered this as an essential security for the GOOD BEHAVIOR of the Executive.

"Mr. Wilson concurred.

"Mr. Gouverneur Morris. He can do no criminal act without coadjutors, who may be punished. In case he should be reelected that will be a sufficient proof of his innocence. Besides, who is to impeach? Is the impeachment to suspend his functions? If it is not the mischief will go on.

"Colonel Mason. No point is of more importance than that the right of impeachment should be continued. Shall any man be above justice? Above all, shall that man be above it who can commit the most extensive injustice?

"Dr. Franklin was for retaining the clause as favorable to the Executive. History furnishes one example only of a First Magistrate brought to public justice. Everybody cried out against this as unconstitutional. What was the practice before this in cases where the Chief Magistrate rendered himself obnoxious? Why, recourse was had to assassination, in which he was not only deprived of his life, but of the opportunity of vindicating his character. It would be the best way, therefore, to provide in the Constitution for the regular punishment of the Executive where his MISCONDUCT should deserve it, and for his honorable acquittal where he should be unjustly accused.

"G. Morris admits corruption and some few other offenses to be such as ought to be impeachable, but thought the cases ought to be enumerated and defined.

"Mr. Madison thought it indispensable that some provision should be made for defending the community against the *incapacity, negligence,* or *perfidy* of the Chief Magistrate. The limitation of the period of his service was not a sufficient security. He might lose his capacity after his appointment. He might pervert his administration into a scheme of peculation or oppression. He might betray his trust to foreign Powers. * * * In case of the Executive Magistrate, which was to be administered by a single man, loss of capacity or corruption was more within the compass of probable events, and either of them might be fatal to the Republic.

"Mr. Gerry urged the necessity of impeachments. A good magistrate will not fear them. A bad one ought to be kept in fear of them. He hoped the maxim would never be adopted here that the Chief Magistrate could do no wrong. * * * *

"Mr. Randolph. The propriety of impeachments was a favorite principle with him. Guilt, wherever found, ought to be punished. The Executive will have great opportunities of abusing his power, particularly in time of war.

"G. Morris. The Executive ought to be impeach-

Mr. Madison afterward maintained that "the wanton removal of meritorious officers would subject him (the President) to impeachment and removal from his own high trust."*

The Constitution declares that "the judges, both of the Supreme and inferior courts, shall hold their commissions during *good behavior*."†

able for treachery. Corrupting his electors and incapacity were other causes of impeachment. For the latter he should be punished not as a man, but as an officer, and punished only by degradation from his office.

"The proposition was agreed to by a vote of eight States to two."

September 8, 1787.

(From 3 Madison's Papers, 1528.)

"The clause referring to the Senate the trial of impeachment against the President for treason and bribery was taken up.

"Colonel Mason. Why is the provision restrained to treason and bribery? Treason, as defined in the Constitution, will not reach many great and dangerous offenses. Hastings is not guilty of treason. Attempts to subvert the Constitution may not be treason as above defined. As bills of attainder, which have saved the British constitution, are forbidden, it is the more necessary to extend the power of impeachments.

"He moved to add after 'bribery' or 'maladministration.'

"Mr. Madison. So vague a term will be equivalent to a tenure during the pleasure of the Senate.

"Colonel Mason withdrew 'maladministration' and substituted 'other high crimes and misdemeanors against the State.'

"Agreed to, eight States to three.

"Mr. Madison objected to the trial of the President by the Senate, especially as he was to be impeached by the other branch of the Legislature; and for any act which might be called a misdemeanor. The President, under these circumstances, was made improperly dependent. He would prefer the Supreme Court for the trial of impeachments." * * *

"Mr. Williamson thought there was more danger of too much lenity than of too much rigor."

The subject of impeachment will also be found referred to, under the following dates in 1787, to wit: May 28, June 2, June 18, July 18, August 6, August 20, August 22, September 4, and September 17. The propositions submitted declared officers impeachable "for mal and corrupt conduct," "for treason, bribery, or corruption," "for treason or bribery." But the Constitution finally rejected all these limitations, and gave the largest power of impeachment known to parliamentary law so far as it relates to misdemeanors.

* On the 16th June, 1789, on the bill to establish a Department of Foreign Affairs, Mr. Madison said in Congress: "Perhaps the great danger" * * * * "of abuse in the executive power lies in the improper continuance of bad men in office. But the power we contend for will not enable him to do this: for if an unworthy man be continued in office by an unworthy President, the House of Representatives can at any time impeach him, and the Senate can remove him whether the President chooses or not. The danger then consists merely in this: the President can displace from office a man whose merits require that he should be continued in it. What will be the motives which the President can feel for such abuse of his power and the restraints that operate to prevent it? In the first place, he will be impeachable by the House before the Senate for such an act of *maladministration*: for I contend that the wanton removal of meritorious officers would subject him to impeachment and removal from his own high trust." (4 Eliot's Debates, 380.)

†A statute of Henry VIII, providing for the appointment of a *custos rotulorum* and clerk of the peace for the several counties of England, provides that the *custos* shall hold his office until removed, and the clerk of the peace *durante se bene gesserit*. It recites that ignorant persons had got in by unfair means.

By a *public law* every judge is required to take an oath as follows:

"I do solemnly swear that I will administer justice without respect to persons, and do equal right to the poor and to the rich; and that I will faithfully and impartially discharge and perform all the duties incumbent on me as judge, &c., according to the best of my abilities and understanding, agreeably to the Constitution and laws of the United States. So help me God."▲

By another public law—the Constitution—the President is required to take an oath that he will "faithfully execute the office of President of the United States, and will to the best of his ability preserve, protect, and defend the Constitution of the United States."

These oaths are *public laws* defining duties, and a violation of them is an impeachable *misdemeanor*, for Judge Blackstone says:

" A crime or misdemeanor is an act committed or omitted in violation of a *public law*, either forbidding or commanding it."†

The Constitution contains inherent evidence,

And so is the tenure of judges in England by the Declaration of Right. The tenure *durante, &c.*, was introduced to enable a removal to be made for misbehavior.—(2 Chase's Trial, 337.) By act of 13 William 3, c. 2, s. 3, the commission of every judge runs "*quamdiu se bene gesserit*."—(2 Chase's Trial, 255, 336, 342, 386.) See p. 145 Peck's Trial, 427, where Buchanan said: "Judges hold during good behavior—official misbehavior is impeachable. What is misbehavior? We are bound to prove that the respondent has violated the Constitution or some known law of the land. This was the principle deduced from Chase's Trial in opposition to the principle" * * * "that in order to render an officer impeachable he must be indictable."

* Act of September 24, 1789, 1 Stat. 76; Chase's Trial, 402.

† " At common law an ordinary violation of a public statute, even by one not in office, though the statute in terms provides no punishment, is an indictable misdemeanor." (Bishop's MS. letter to a member of the Judiciary Committee, citing 1 Bishop Cr. Law, 3d ed., 187, 535.)

The term "*misdemeanor*" covers every act of "*misbehavior*," in the popular sense.

"Misdemeanor in office and misbehavior in office mean the same thing." (7 Dane's Abridgement, 365.)

Misbehavior, therefore, which is mere negation of "good behavior," is an express limitation of the office of a judge. (See North American Review for October, 1862.)

Alexander Hamilton, in discussing the judicial "tenure of good behavior," and the remedy in cases of "judiciary encroachments on the legislative authority" by pronouncing laws unconstitutional, says:

"It may, in the last place, be observed that the supposed danger of judiciary encroachments on the legislative authority, which has been upon many occasions reiterated, is, in reality, a phantom. Particular misconstructions and contraventions of the will of the Legislature may now and then happen, but they can never be so extensive as to amount to an inconvenience, or in any sensible degree to affect the order of the political system. This may be inferred with certainty, from the general nature of the judicial power; from the objects to which it relates; from the manner in which it is exercised; from its comparative weakness; and from its total incapacity to support its usurpations by force. And the inference is greatly fortified by the consideration of the important constitutional check which the power of instituting impeachments in one part of the legislative body, and of determining upon them in the other, would give to that body upon the members of the judicial department. This is alone a complete security. There never can be danger that the judges, by a series of deliberate usurpations on the authority of the Legislature, would hazard the united resentment

therefore, that as to judges they should be impeachable when their *behavior* is not *good*—and the Senate are made the exclusive judges of what is bad behavior.

The words "good behavior" are borrowed from the English laws and have been construed there in a way to enlarge the scope of impeachment to a wide range. They were first introduced into an English statute to procure the removal of officers who, on trial, might prove too *ignorant* to perform their duties.

These general views are sustained by the opinions of the framers of the Constitution, declared by themselves in convention, by Madson* in the Virginia convention of 1788, and by Alexander Hamilton† in the Federalist,

who says that "several of the State constitutions have followed the example" of Great Britain. And up to that time the State constitutions had adopted the British system with only some modifications, but none of them recognizing the idea that impeachment was limited to indictable acts, but all affirming "that the subjects of this jurisdiction were offenses of a political nature."* Some of

---

of the body intrusted with it, while this body was possessed of the power to punish them for their presumption by degrading them from their stations. While this ought to remove all apprehensions on the subject, it affords, at the same time, a cogent argument for constituting the Senate a court for the trial of impeachment." (Federalist, No. 81.)

Impeachment is not merely nor necessarily *punitive* only, but it may, and often must be, *protective*. The safety of the public may demand its exercise in cases where there has been no intentional wrong but only a mistake of judgment. The Republic cannot be suffered to perish or its great interests to be put in peril from any tender regard for individual feelings or errors,

And Thomas Jefferson evidently held that judges were impeachable for assumptions of power. (Letter to Mr. Jarvis, September 28, 1820; and see Jackson's veto message on the bank bill.)

* "Were the President to commit anything so atrocious as to summon only a few States (to consider a treaty) *he would be impeached and convicted, as a majority of the States would be affected by his misdemeanor.*"

And again:

"Mr. Madison, adverting to Mr. Mason's objection to the President's power of pardoning, said it would be extremely improper to vest it in the House of Representatives, and not much less so to place it in the Senate, because numerous bodies were actuated more or less by passion, and might, in the moment of vengeance, forget humanity. It was an established practice in Massachusetts for the Legislature to determine in such cases.

"It was found, says he, that two different sessions, before each of which the question came, with respect to pardoning the delinquents of the rebellion, were governed precisely by different sentiments—the one would execute with universal vengeance and the other would extend general mercy.

"There is one security in this case to which gentlemen may not have adverted: if the President be connected in any suspicious manner with any persons, and there be grounds to believe he will shelter himself, the House of Representatives can impeach him; they can remove him if found guilty; they can suspend him when suspected, and the power will devolve on the Vice President. Should he be suspected also he may, likewise, be suspended till he be impeached and removed, and the Legislature shall make a temporary appointment. This is a great security." (Debates of the Virginia Convention, printed at the Enquirer Press for Richey, Worsley & Augustine Davis, 1805, pp. 353-4; 11 Howell, statute seven, 733.)

† In the Federalist, No 65, he says:

"The subject of its jurisdiction are those offenses which proceed from the *misconduct* of *public* men, or, in other words, from the abuse or violation of some public trust. They are of a nature which may, with peculiar propriety, be denominated political, as they relate chiefly to injuries done immediately to the society itself."

"What," it may be asked, "is the true spirit of the institution itself? Is it not designed as a method of

national inquest into the conduct of public men? If this be the design of it who can so properly be the inquisitors for the nation as the representatives of the nation themselves? It is not disputed that the power of originating the inquiry, or, in other words, of preferring the impeachment, ought to be lodged in one branch of the legislative body; will not the reasons which indicate the propriety of this arrangement strongly plead for an admission of the other branch of that body to a share of the inquiry? The model from which the idea of this institution has been borrowed pointed out that course to the convention. In Great Britain it is the province of the House of Commons to prefer the impeachment and of the House of Lords to decide upon it. Several of the State constitutions have followed the example. As well the latter as the former seem to have regarded the practice of impeachments as a bridle in the hands of the legislative body upon the executive servants of the Government. Is not this the true light in which it is to be regarded."

To what extent this writer contemplated the exertion of this power is not left in doubt. In the succeeding number of the same commentary he observes:

"The convention might with propriety have meditated the punishment of the Executive for a deviation from the instructions of the Senate or a want of integrity in the conduct of the negotiations committed to him," clearly not statutory offenses.

* Thus, in that of Virginia, established in 1776, is seen this provision: "The Governor, when he is out of office, and others offending against the State, either by maladministration, corruption, or other means, shall be impeachable by the House of Delegates." In the same year, in the succeeding month, Delaware provided in her constitution that "the President when he is out of office, and eighteen months thereafter, and all others offending against the State, either by maladministration, corruption, or other means, by which the safety of the Commonwealth may be endangered, shall be impeachable by the House of Assembly." So North Carolina two months later provided in her constitution: "The Governor and other officers offending against the State by violating any part of this constitution, maladministration, or corruption may be prosecuted on the impeachment of the General Assembly, or presentment of the grand jury of any court of supreme jurisdiction in this State."

The constitution of Connecticut is stated to contain a provision "to call to account for any misdemeanor and maladministration." That of New York provides: "The power of impeaching all officers of the State for mal and corrupt conduct in their respective offices is vested in the representatives of the people in Assembly," and the trial is declared to be for "crimes and misdemeanors." So, in the elaborate constitution of Massachusetts, the eighth article declares: "The Senate shall be a court with full authority to hear and determine all impeachments made by the House of Representatives against any officer or officers of the Commonwealth for misconduct and maladministration in their offices." Hence, it will be remarked, that in all of the State constitutions to which we have had access, formed prior to that of the United States, the impeachable offenses are of a nature which may with peculiar propriety be denominated "political." In neither of them are the subjects of impeachment mere "statutory offenses." This minute recurrence to the constitutions of several States will not be deemed inappropriate when it is remembered that they are not only the most authentic evidence of the public sense of our country at an early period, but because, in the formation of the Federal Constitution, their provisions should have a con-

these constitutions limited impeachment to "mal and corrupt conduct in office," or, as in the New York constitution of 1777, to "venal and corrupt conduct in office," while the Constitution of the United States discarded all these limitations and gave the power in the broadest terms. It is said this provision in the Constitution of the United States was copied from that of New York.[*] If so, the change of phraseology is significant.

These general views are supported by the elementary writers, without exception, up to the last year.

Curtis, in his History of the Constitution,[†] says:

"Although an impeachment may involve an inquiry, whether a crime against any positive law has been committed, *yet it is not necessarily a trial for crime*, nor is there any necessity, in the case of crimes committed by public officers, for the institution of any special proceeding for the infliction of the punishment prescribed by the laws, since they, like all other persons, are amenable to the ordinary jurisdiction of the courts of justice, in respect of offenses against positive law. *The purposes of an impeachment lie wholly beyond the penalties of the statute or the customary law. The object of the proceeding is to ascertain whether cause exists for removing a public officer from office.* Such a cause may be found in the fact, that either in the discharge of his office, or aside from its functions, he has violated a law, or committed what is technically denominated a crime. But a cause for removal from office may exist where no offense against positive law has been committed, as where the individual has from *immorality*, or *imbecility*, *or maladministration become unfit to exercise the office*. The rules by which an impeachment is to be determined are therefore peculiar, and are not fully embraced by those principles or provisions of law which courts of ordinary jurisdiction are required to administer."

Selden says:

"Upon complaints and accusations of the Commons the Lords may proceed in judgment against the delinquent of what degree soever and what nature soever the offense be. For where the Commons complain the Lords do not assume to themselves *trial at common law*. Neither do the Lords, at the trial of a common impeachment by the Commons, *decedere de jure suo*, (depart from *their own law*.) For the Commons are there instead of a jury, and the parties answer, and examination of witnesses are to be in their presence, or they to have copies thereof; and judgment is not to be given but upon their demand, which is instead of a verdict, so the Lords do only judge, not try the delinquent." (Selden's Judicature in Parliaments, London, 1681, p. 6.)

Story says:[‡]

"Congress have unhesitatingly adopted the conclusion that no previous statute is necessary to authorize an impeachment for any official misconduct." * * * * "In the few cases of impeachment which have hitherto been tried no one of the

charges has rested upon any statutable misdemeanors." * * * * * * * * "The reasoning by which the power of the House of Representatives to punish for contempts (which are breaches of privilege and offenses not defined by any positive laws) has been upheld by the Supreme Court, stands upon similar grounds; for if the House had no jurisdiction to punish for contempts until the acts had been previously defined and ascertained by positive law, it is clear that the process of arrest would be illegal." (*Denn vs. Anderson*, 6 Wheat., 204.) "In examining the parliamentary history of impeachments, it will be found that many offenses not easily definable by law, and many of a purely political character, have been deemed high crimes and misdemeanors worthy of this extraordinary remedy."[*] "There are many offenses, purely political, which have been held to be within the reach of parliamentary impeachments, not one of which is, in the slightest manner, alluded to in our statute-books. And, indeed, political offenses are of so various and complex a character, so utterly incapable of being defined or classified, that the task of positive legislation would be impracticable, if it were not almost absurd to attempt it. What, for instance, could positive legislation do in cases of impeachment like the charges against Warren Hastings, in 1788? Resort then must be had either to parliamentary practice, and the common law, in order to ascertain what are high crimes and misdemeanors, or the whole subject must be left to the arbitrary discretion of the Senate for the time being. The latter is so incompatible with the genius of our institutions that no lawyer or statesman would be inclined to countenance so absolute a depotism of opinion and practice, which might make that a crime at one time or in one person, which would be deemed innocent at another time or in another person. The only safe guide in such cases must be the common law." * * * * "And however much it may fall in with the political theories of certain statesmen and jurists to deny the existence of a common law belonging to and applicable to the nation in ordinary cases, *no one has as yet been bold enough to assert* that the power of impeachment is limited to offenses positively defined in the statute-book of the Union, as impeachable high crimes and misdemeanors."[†]

Neither in Congress nor in any State has

* 1 Story on Const., sec. 800. He proceeds to cite numerous cases.

† 1 Story on Const., sec. 797.

Rawle, in his work on the Constitution, says: "The delegation of important trusts affecting the higher interests of society is always from various causes liable to abuse. The fondness frequently felt for the inordinate extension of power, the influence of party and of prejudice, the seductions of foreign States, or the baser appetite for illegitimate emoluments, are sometimes productions of what are not inaptly termed political offenses, (Federalist, No. 65,) which it would be difficult to take cognizance of in the ordinary course of judicial proceeding.

"The involutions and varieties of vice are too many and too artful to be anticipated by positive law." (Rawle on Const., 200.)

"In general, those offenses which may be committed equally by a private person as by a public officer are not the subjects of impeachment." (*Ib.*, 204.)

"We may perceive in this scheme one useful mode of removing from office those who is unworthy to fill it, in cases where the people and sometimes the President himself would be unable to accomplish that object." (*Ib.*, 208.)

Chancellor Kent, in discussing the subject of impeachment, says: "The Constitution has rendered him [the President] directly amenable by law for maladministration. The inviolability of any officer of the Government is incompatible with the republican theory as well as with the principles of retributive justice.

"If the President will use the authority of his station to violate the Constitution or law of the land, the House of Representatives can arrest him in his career by resorting to the power of impeachment." (1 Kent's Com., 289.)

trolling influence on the minds of their delegates to the general convention, seeking to commend it to their adoption by ingrafting into it parts of their own systems, and thus imparting to it the well-ascertained spirit and prudence of those who, if adopted, were to be its constituents." (From an able article by John C. Hamilton, Esq.)

* Vol. 6 Am. Law Reg. N. S. 277; Wharton's State Trials, 287.

† Curtis's Hist. of Const., 260-1; 5 Eliot, 507-529.

‡ 1 Story on Const., sec. 799. In a note he says: "It may be supposed that the first charge in the articles of impeachment against William Blount was a statutable offense; but on an accurate examination of the act of Congress of 1796, it will be found not to have been so."

any statute been proposed to define impeachable crimes : so uniform has been the opinion that none was necessary, even in those States, few in number, where common-law crimes do not exist.

The assertion, "that* unless the crime is specifically named in the Constitution, impeachments, like indictments, can only be instituted for crimes committed against the statutory law of the United States," is a view not yet a year old, which has not been held at any prior time, either in England or America.

It would certainly seem clear that impeachments are not necessarily limited to acts indictable by statute or common law, and that it would be impossible for human prescience or foresight to define in advance by statute the necessary subjects of impeachments. The Constitution contemplated no such absurd impossibility. It may be said there is danger in leaving to the Senate a power so undefined. It was because of this danger that the power has been limited as it is by the Constitution, and experience has shown that the limitations are more than sufficient.

The whole system of common-law crimes, as it exists in England, and in almost every State of the Union, is the result of a judicial power equally undefined.

The system of impeachment is to be governed by great general principles of right, and it is less probable that the Senate will depart from these, than that the whole Legislature would in the enactment of a law, or than courts in establishing the common law.†

* Vol. 6 Am. Law Reg., N. S., 269.

† The Constitution has made the Senate, like the House of Lords, sole judge of what the law is, assuming their wisdom to be equal to that of the common law courts. (2 Hale's P. C., 276; Barclay's Digest, 140; Constitution, article one, section three.) This is necessarily so; for though some statutory and common law crimes are impeachable, yet not all of them are, and the Senate decides which are and are not. It is said if the impeachable crimes are not defined by law the power of impeachment will be undefined and dangerous. The power to determine impeachable crimes by the Senate is no more undefined than the power of the common law courts to determine common-law crimes. Impeachment is regulated by principles as well defined and permanently settled as the fundamental and eternal doctrines of right, reason, and justice pervading the parliamentary jurisprudence of civilized nations, and, like the common law, it has emerged from primeval errors and adapted itself to an advanced civilization. The danger of imperiling the safety of nations in measuring parliamentary law by the rule which defines wrongs to individuals is infinitely greater than the evils which can flow from recognizing the law of impeachment as a parliamentary system resting upon its own solid foundations.

The rule which allows impeachments for indictable acts enables the legislative department or the Senate alone to declare trivial offenses impeachable while the parliamentary law limiting impeachable offenses to misdemeanors affecting the nation is less latitudinarian and attended with less danger of abuse. When impeachment is employed to remove officers for willful violation of the Constitution or laws, for exercising the powers of Congress, or the judiciary for performing acts affecting the nation unauthorized by law, for refusing to execute laws requiring that duty, for a perversion of lawful powers to accomplish unconstitutional objects—these are—

The Constitution contains *inherent evidence* that the *indictable* character of an act does not define its *impeachable* quality. It enumerates the classes of cases in which legislative power may be exercised, and it defines the class of persons and cases to which the judicial power extends; but there is no *such* enumeration of impeachable *cases*, though there is of *persons*.

In England and some of the States the power of removal of officers by the Executive, on the address or request of the Legislature,* exists, but the Constitution made no provision for this as to any officer, manifestly because the power of impeachment extended to *every proper case for removal*.

As to the President and Vice President there is this provision, that—

"Congress may by law provide for the case of *removal*, death, resignation, or *inability*," * * * "declaring what officer shall then act" * * "until the disability be removed or a President shall be elected." (Art. 2, sec. 1.)

It has already been shown that the framers of the Constitution regarded the power of impeachment as a means of defending "the community against the *incapacity*" of officers. This clause of the Constitution recognized the same view, article two, section one :

"Congress may by law provide for the case of" * * * "*inability*, both of the President and Vice President, declaring what officer shall then act as President, and such officer shall act accordingly, until the disability be removed or a President shall be elected."

"Offenses as tangible and as capable of being measured by fixed rules as any felony defined in criminal laws."

And this is as definite and no less latitudinarian than the common law itself, which is "the perfection of reason" as determined by courts. For even in England not all common-law offenses are impeachable, but only such of them (along with others not indictable) as by parliamentary usage or popular sense rise to the dignity of "high" misdemeanors, and of this the House of Lords are the sole judges. (Peck's Trial, 10 Selden, Judicature in Parliaments, 6; 2 Hale's P. C., 275; Barclay's Digest, 140.)

On the trial of Judge Prescott, in Massachusetts, in 1821, Mr. Shaw said : "The security of our rights depends rather upon the general tenor and character than upon particular provisions of our Constitution. The love of freedom and justice so deeply engraven upon the hearts of the people and interwoven in the whole texture of our social institutions, a thorough and intelligent acquaintance with their rights, and a firm determination to maintain them; in short, those moral and intellectual qualities without which social liberty cannot exist, and over which despotism can obtain no control, these stamp the character and give security to the rights of the free people of this Commonwealth." * * * * "But it has not been, and it cannot be, contended that, in its decisions and adjudications, this court is not governed by established laws. These may be positive and express, or they may depend upon reasoning and analogy. It would be idle to expect a rule applicable to every case in the text of the statute-book. Laws are founded on certain general principles and the relations of men in society. It is the province of this court, as of all other judicial tribunals, to search out and apply these principles to the particular cases in judgment before them." (See 4 Howard's State Trials, 47, per Selden; 6 Am. Law Reg., N. S., 264.)

* Removal on the address of *both* Houses of Parliament is provided for in the act of settlement, 3 Hallam, 262. In the convention which framed our national Constitution, June 2, 1787, Mr. John Dickin-

This and the power of impeachment are the only modes of getting rid of officers whose *inability* from *insanity* or otherwise renders them unfit to hold office, and whose every official act will necessarily be *misdemeanor*. As to the President and Vice President it was necessary to give Congress the power to designate a successor, and so do determine the disability. As to all other officers the Constitution or laws define the mode of designating a successor, and it is left to the impeaching power to remove in cases of insanity or misdemeanor arising from that or other cause. It cannot be supposed the whole nation must suffer without remedy if the whole Supreme Court or other officers should become utterly disabled from the performance of their duties. Such an occurrence is within the range of possibility, if not probability.

In our system it is utterly impossible to apply any test of common law or statutory criminality. The Supreme Court, without much consideration, has determined that the national courts have never been clothed with jurisdiction of common-law crimes.*

son, of Delaware, moved "That the Executive be made removable by the national Legislature on the request of a majority of the Legislatures of individual States." Delaware alone voted for this, and it was rejected. Impeachment was deemed sufficiently comprehensive to cover every proper case for removal.

* *The reason which denies jurisdiction of common-law crimes to the courts of the United States does not apply to impeachments.*
By the Constitution the trial for crimes must be had in the State and district where committed. (Article 6 Amendments.) By the judiciary act of September 24, 1789, the Supreme Court is restricted to holding sessions at Washington, (1 Statutes-at-Large, 73.) By the Constitution the judicial power of the United States is vested in the Supreme Court and such *inferior courts* as Congress may establish. (Article 3, section 1 ; article 1, section 10.)
It was held as early as 1812 that the circuit and district courts of the United States, being the "*inferior courts*" established by Congress, could exercise no common-law criminal jurisdiction. This doctrine was reaffirmed in 1816 by a divided court, and has never been authoritatively decided since. (United States *vs.* Hudson, 7 Cranch, 32; United States *vs.* Corlidge. 1 Wheaton, 415; 1 Galli's Reports, 488; United States *vs.* Lancaster, 2 McLean's Reports, 431; Washington Circuit Court Reports, 84; United States *vs.* Ravara, 2 Dallas, 297 ; United States *vs.* Worrall, 2 Dallas, 384 ; United States *vs.* Maurice, 2 Brock., 96 ; United States *vs.* New Bedford Bridge, 1 Woodbridge & Minot, 401 ; United States *vs.* Babcock, 4 McLean, 113-115.)
This ruling has been disapproved by the ablest commentators on constitutional and criminal law—by Story and Rawle and Bishop and Wharton, (1 Bishop's Criminal Law, third edition, 163, [20;] act of Congress of September 24, 1789, sections 9-11; Statutes 1842, chapter 188, section 3; Du Ponceau on Jurisdiction.)
The denial of common-law criminal jurisdiction in these inferior courts rests solely on the reasons that such tribunals being created *not by the Constitution*, but by *act of Congress*, they—
"Possess no jurisdiction but what is given them by the power that creates them;" and that—
"There exists no definite criterion of distribution [of jurisdiction] between the district and circuit courts of the same district."
And that common law—
"Jurisdiction has not been conferred by any legislative act."

When the Constitution was adopted all the States recognized common-law crimes. and those added since do so, with few exceptions. But there is something peculiar to each and different from all others in its common-law crimes, growing out of the rulings of judges or its condition, and in all statutes have made changes, so that no two States recognize the same crimes.

The Constitution authorizes Congress "to provide for the punishment of counterfeiting the securities and current coin of the United States ;" "to define and punish piracies and felonies committed on the high seas, and offenses against the law of nations ;" but nowhere declares they may define impeachable crimes, for the very good reason that common parliamentary law, subject, like the common law, to be molded to circumstances and adapted to times, had already sufficiently defined them. Congress cannot by any law abridge the right of the House to impeach or the Senate to try.

When the Constitution confers on the House the "sole power of impeachment," and on the Senate "the sole power of trial," these are independent powers, not to be controlled by the *joint* opinion of the two Houses previously incorporated into a law.* Suppose such a law passed. It cannot be repealed over a veto except by a two-thirds vote in each House. Yet a majority may impeach ; and, after the veto of a repealing law, can that majority be denied the constitutional privilege conferred on them ?

"Treason, bribery, and other high crimes and misdemeanors" are, of course, impeachable. Treason and bribery are specifically named. But "other high crimes and misdemeanors" are just as fully comprehended as though each was specified. The Senate is made the *sole judge* of what they are. There is no revising court. The Senate determines in the light of parliamentary law. Congress cannot define or limit by law that which the Constitution defines in two cases by enumera-

And it is said that the Supreme Court alone—
"Possesses jurisdiction derived immediately from the Constitution, and of which the legislative power cannot deprive it." (7 Cranch, 33.)
Where, therefore, a common-law jurisdiction is conferred by the Constitution on a court created by that instrument, it is one "of which the legislative power cannot deprive it." (7 Cranch, 33.)
And this is precisely what the Constitution has done as to impeachments; it has created the tribunal for their trial—the Senate; it has given that body jurisdiction of *all* "crimes and misdemeanors" impeachable by parliamentary usage, and no law can limit it. And this view has been sustained by Story and Rawle and Kent, *after* and *in view* of the decisions referred to. (6 American Law Register, 656.)
At the time the Constitution was adopted, and ever since in England and all the original States of the Union, what is known as the "*common law*" and "common-law crimes" existed, and yet exist, in addition to crimes defined by statute; and this is so in all the States except Ohio, and perhaps two or three others.

* "The Parliament cannot by any act restrain the power of a subsequent Parliament." (4 Inst., 42; 5 Com. Dig., 301.)

tion and in others by classification, and of which the Senate is sole judge.* It has never been pretended that treason and bribery would not be impeachable if not made criminal by statute or so recognized by national common law. They are impeachable because enumerated. Other high crimes and misdemeanors are equally designated by classification.

Suppose the Constitution had declared "that all persons committing 'treason, bribery, or other high crimes and misdemeanors' shall be punished by indictment in the courts of the United States," can it be doubted that every crime and misdemeanor recognized by the common law would be the subject of indictment? "This would be by force of the Constitution employing the words crimes and misdemeanors; for these are words known to the common law, and it is a universal principle of interpretation, acted on in all the courts, that a common-law term employed in conferring jurisdiction on courts is to bear its common-law meaning."

Now, when the Constitution says that all civil officers shall be removable on impeachment for high crimes and misdemeanors, and the Senate shall have the sole power of trial, the *jurisdiction* is *conferred*, and its scope is defined by common parliamentary law.†

The national courts do not take jurisdiction of common-law crimes, not because common-law crimes do not exist, but because their jurisdiction is only such as is expressly conferred on them, and no statute has conferred the jurisdiction. But in the District of Columbia, under national jurisdiction, common-law crimes and jurisdiction of them in the courts do exist.‡

In addition to this there are crimes exclusively of national jurisdiction and others exclusively of State cognizance. The murder of citizens in a State is not and cannot be made criminal by act of Congress where it is not perpetrated in the denial of a national right. The States alone provide for this and many other offenses. And in the States not recognizing common-law crimes they may omit to make homicide a penal offense as to Indians, negroes, or others, if the Legislature so determine, in the absence of a law of Congress similar to the "civil rights" act.*

If no act is impeachable which is not made criminal, then its criminality must depend—

1. On an act of Congress defining crimes; or,

2. On acts of State Legislatures defining crimes; or,

3. On the definition of common-law crimes in the States; or,

4. On the common-law crimes existing in England when the Constitution was adopted.

It is quite clear that national law in some form must control it, since "the United States have no concern with any but their own laws."†

The national Government is complete in itself, with powers which neither depend on nor can be abridged by State laws.‡

If, then, impeachment is limited to acts made criminal by a statute of Congress, an officer of the United States cannot be impeached, though he should go into the "Dominion of Canada" or the "republic of Mexico" and there stir up insurrection or be guilty of violating all the laws of the land; or if he should go into a

---

* "The *peers* are *judges of law* as well as of fact." (2 Hale's P. C., 275; Barclay's Digest, 140.) They, therefore, are not governed by the indictable character of an act. In fact, as the highest court, they make not only parliamentary law, but the law for the courts. (Regina *vs.* O'Connell.)

† Impeachable misdemeanors are determined by the Senate just as each House of Congress and the courts having the jurisdiction to punish for contempts determine what acts or neglect constitute them. (7 Cranch, 320.)

‡ "Common-law crimes do exist, they are indictable, and jurisdiction of them has existed in the courts of the United States for upward of a century in the District of Columbia." (1 Bishop on Criminal Law, section 167, [22;] Du Ponceau on Jurisdiction, 62-73; Kendall *vs.* United States, 12 Peters, 524-613; United Stats *vs.* Watkins, 3 Cranch, 441.)

The highest authority on criminal law in this country says:

"There must in reason and in legal principle be in those localities where State power is unknown common-law crimes against the United States. Especially this exception must in reason extend to all matters which concern our intercourse with foreign as well as to all local transactions beyond the territorial limits of the several States. The law of nations and the law of the admiralty concerning both civil and criminal things would seem, therefore, to have been made United States common law." * * * * "And so the United States tribunal would appear to have common law cognizance of offenses upon the high seas not defined by statutes, and of all other offenses within the proper cognizance of the criminal courts of a nation, committed beyond the jurisdiction of any particular State." (1 Bishop on Criminal Law, section 165, [21.])

The act of Congress of February 27, 1801, extended and continued in force over the District the common and statute law of Maryland, where common-law crimes existed, and organized a circuit court with the jurisdiction conferred on circuit courts of the United States by section eleven of the act of February 13, 1801. (2 United States Statutes-at-Large, 92; 2 Statutes, 103-105, sections 1-3.)

The criminal court organized by act of July 7, 1838, had the same criminal jurisdiction. (5 Statutes, 306.)

The supreme court of the District, organized by act of March 3, 1863, has the same jurisdiction of the prior courts thereby abolished. (12 Statutes, section 3.)

That jurisdiction is conferred in these words: "That," * * * "said courts" * * * "shall have cognizance of all crimes and offenses cognizable under the authority of the United States." (2 Statutes, 92, act February 13, 1801.)

* Act of April 9, 1866, 14 Stat., 27.

† "It was said by one of the counsel that the offense must be a breach either of the common law, a State law, or a law of the United States, and that no lawyer could speak of a misdemeanor but as an act violating some one of these laws. This doctrine surely is not warranted, for the Government of the United States have no concern with any but their own laws." * * * * "But as a member of the House of Representatives, and acting as a manager of an impeachment before the highest court in the nation, appointed to try the highest officers of the Government, when I speak of a misdemeanor I mean an act of official misconduct, a violation of official duty, whether it be a proceeding against a positive law or a proceeding unwarranted by law." (Per Nicholson *arguendo*, 2 Chase's Trial, 340; per Rodney, 387.)

‡ Weston *vs.* City Council of Charleston, 2 Peters, 449; McCulloch *vs.* Maryland, 4 Wheat., 316; Osborn *vs.* Bank of the United States, 9 Ib., 738.

State and violate all of its laws.* If so, a highway robber may be President, and he is exempt from impeachment!

It is not possible that a position so monstrous was intended by the framers of the Constitution. Nor can the criminal statutes or common law of the States limit or regulate national impeachable offenses. The fact that each State differs from all others in its laws renders this impossible. It never could have been designed to control the national power of impeachment by State laws, ever varying and conflicting as they are.†

If impeachments were limited in England to indictable offenses, as they never have been, it is manifest no such rule can be adopted here, for we have no uniform and single standard of the common law as there.

And as the Supreme Court has determined that the common-law crimes do not exist in our national system, it cannot be supposed they are more applicable to the Senate than to our ordinary courts. We can, therefore, safely adopt the remark of "the great Selden" on the impeachment of Ratcliffe:‡ "It were better‖ to examine this matter according to

the rules and foundations of this House ," that is, upon the great principles of parliamentary law adapted to our condition and circumstances, as modified by the Constitution, giving it a construction equal to every emergency which may call its powers into exercise, and giving in its interpretation full effect in constitutional forms to the maxim it was designed to make effectual—"that the safety of the Republic is the supreme law."*

If we adopt the test that an act to be impeachable must be indictable at common law, the Constitution will be practically nullified on this subject.

It is a rule of the common law "that judges of record are freed from all presentations whatever except in Parliament, where they may be punished for anything done by them in such courts as judges."†

Bishop declares that at common law "the doctrine appears to be sufficiently established that legislators, the judges of our highest courts, and of all courts of record acting judicially, jurors, and probably such of the high officers of each of the governments as are intrusted with responsible discretionary duties, are not liable to an ordinary criminal process, like an indictment, for their official doings, however corrupt." (1 Bishop's Crim. Law, 915 [362.])

"At common law an ordinary *violation of a public statute* by one not in office, though the statute in terms provides no punishment, is an indictable misdemeanor." (1 Bishop, 535 [187.])

And a similar violation by *inferior officers* was an indictable misdemeanor.

"If a public officer intrusted with definite powers, to be exercised for the benefit of the community, wickedly abuses or fraudulently exceeds them, he is punishable by indictment, though no injurious effects result to any individual from his misconduct." (Whart. Crim. Law, sec. 2514.)

"Whatever mischievously affects the person or property of another, or openly outrages de-

---

* Mr. Rodney, in the argument of Chase's trial, said: "When gentlemen talk of an indictment being a necessary substratum of an impeachment I should be glad to be informed in what court it must be supported. In the courts of the United States or in the State courts? If in the State courts, then in which of them; or provided it can be supported in any of them, will the act warrant an impeachment? If an indictment must lie in the courts of the United States, in the long catalogue of crimes there are a very few which an officer might not commit with impunity. He might be guilty of treason against an individual State; of murder, arson, forgery, and perjury in various forms, without being amenable to the Federal jurisdiction, and unless he could be indicted before them he could not be impeached." (2 Chase's Trial, 389.)

The doctrine that nothing is impeachable unless indictable by act of Congress is impracticable.

If only offences indictable by act of Congress are impeachable, the President and all civil officers will escape impeachment for many of the highest crimes. Murder, arson, robbery, and other crimes committed in a State are indictable by State laws, but cannot be made so by act of Congress.

† In the argument of Chase's trial Mr. Rodney said: "Are we then to resort to the erring *data* of the different States? In New Hampshire drunkenness may be an indictable offense, but not in another State. Shall a United States judge be impeached and removed for getting intoxicated in New Hampshire, when he may drink as he pleases in other States with impunity? In some States witchcraft is a heinous offense, which subjects the unfortunate person to indictment and punishment; in other States it is unknown as a crime. A great variety of cases might be put to expose the fallacy of the principle, and to prove how improper it would be for this court to be governed by the practice of the different States. The variation of such a compass is too great for it to be relied on. This honorable body must have a standard of their own, which will admit of no change or deviation." (2 Chase's Trial, 389.)

‡ Vol. 6 Am. Law Reg., N. S., 264; 4 Howard's State Trials, 47.

‖ A minister is answerable for the *justice*, the *honesty*, the *utility* of all measures emanating from the Crown, as well as for their *legality ;* and thus the executive administration is, or ought to be, subordinate, in all great matters of policy, to the superintendence and virtual control of the two houses of Parliament. (2 Hallam's Const. History, 550.)

* "It may be alleged that the power of impeachment belongs to the House of Representatives, and that with a view to the exercise of this power that House have the right to investigate the conduct of all public officers under the Government. This is cheerfully admitted. In such a case *the safety of the Republic would be the supreme law ;* and the power of the House in the pursuit of this object would penetrate into the most secret recesses of the executive department." (President Polk's Message, Jour. Ho. Rep., 29th Cong., 1st sess., 693.) "*Salus populi suprema lex ,*" Broom's Legal Maxims; *Blount's Trial,* Whart. State Trials 300, per Blount; Prescott's Trial, 181, per Shaw; *contra,* Blake, 116.

† 1 Hawkins, 192, ch. 73, sec. 6; 1 Salk., 306; 2 Woodeson, 596, 355; Jacob's Law Dic., tit. *Judges ;* 12 Coke, 25-6; Hammond *vs.* Howell, 2 Mod., 218; Floyd *vs.* Barker, 12 Co., 23-5. "The doctrine which holds a judge exempt from a civil suit or indictment for any act done or omitted to be done by him sitting as a judge has a deep root in the common law," per Kent: Yates *vs.* Lansing, 5 Johns., 291; 9 *Ib.,* 395; Cunningham *vs.* Bucklow, 8 Cow., 178; Peck's Trial, 492; 2 Chase's Trial, 389. But see the ruling of Chief Justice Shippen, referred to in Addison's (Pa.) Trial, 70; 1 Bishop on Crim. Law, 915 [362;] 4 Blackst., 121.

cency, or disturbs public order, or is injurious to public morals, or is a breach of official duty, when done corruptly, is the subject of indictment." (Whart., sec. 3.)

It may be said the immunity of a judge from indictment for his official acts at common law is placed on grounds of public policy, to secure his independence, and that it is the indictable character of the act, if done by a private individual, which gives jurisdiction by impeachment. But even this proves that personal liability to an indictment is no test of impeachability. And in the nature of things *official acts* cannot be done by private individuals, so that the indictable character of an act is no test of its impeachability; and no such test could have entered into the minds of the framers of the Constitution.

It is a rule of interpretation that a law or an instrument is not to be construed so as to make its "effects and consequences" absurd, if its language may be fairly understood otherwise.

To permit all acts to escape impeachment, unless indictable at common law,[*] would lead to consequences the most ruinous and absurd.[†]

If a judge should persistently hear the arguments of one party to causes privately and out of court the evil would become so intolerable in an officer holding for *good behavior* that he should be removed.

If the President should hold out promises of offices of honor and trust to the friends of Senators to influence their votes the consequences might be so pernicious and corrupting, especially in an hour of national peril, when a single vote might decide the life of the Government, that the safety of the Republic would demand impeachment. Such a President would violate his oath *faithfully* to execute his duties.

There are many breaches of trust not amounting to felonies, yet so monstrous as to render those guilty of them totally unfit for office.

Nor is it always necessary that an act to be impeachable must violate a positive law. There are many misdemeanors, in violation of official oaths and of duty alike shocking to the moral sense of mankind and repugnant to the pure administration of office, that may violate no positive law.[*]

---

[*] On the trial of Chase Mr. Nicholson said: "You, Mr. President, as Vice-President of the United States, together with the Secretary of the Treasury, the Chief Justice, and the Attorney General, as commissioners of the sinking fund, have annually at your disposal $8,000,000 for the purpose of paying the national debt. If, instead of applying it to this public use, you should divert it to another channel, or convert it to your own private uses, I ask if there is a man in the world who would hesitate to say that you ought to be impeached for this misconduct. And yet there is no court in this country in which you could be indicted for it. Nay, sir, it would amount to nothing more than a breach of trust, and would not be indictable under the favorite common law.

"If a judge should order a cause to be tried with eleven jurors only surely he might be impeached for it, and yet I believe there is no court in which he could be indicted." (2 Chase's Trial, 339.)

[†] On Chase's trial Mr. Rodney said: "I think I can put" * * * "striking cases of misconduct in a judge for which it must be admitted that an impeachment will lie, though no indictment [at common law] could be maintained." He puts the cases: if a judge at the time appointed for court "should appear and open the court, and, notwithstanding there was pressing business to be done, he should proceed knowingly and willfully to adjourn it until the next stated period." * * * "Suppose he proceeded in the dispatch of business, and from prejudice against one party or favor to his antagonist he ordered on the trial of a cause, though legal ground for postponement." "If when the jury returned to the bar to give the verdict he should knowingly receive the verdict of a majority."

"Were a judge to entertain the suitors with a farce or a comedy instead of hearing their causes, and turn a jester or buffoon on the bench, I presume he would subject himself to an impeachment." (2 Chase's Trial, 390.)

Mr. Harper, for the defense, practically abandoned the idea that an indictable offense was necessary. He said: "There are reasons which appear to me unanswerable in favor of the opinion that no offense is impeachable unless it be also the proper subject of an indictment." * * * * "I can suppose cases where a judge ought to be impeached for acts which I am not prepared to declare indictable [at common law.] Suppose, for instance, that a judge should constantly omit to hold court, or should habitually attend so short a time each day as to render it impossible to despatch the business." (2 Chase's Trial, 255.)

Mr. Randolph said: "The President of the United States has a qualified negative on all bills passed by the two Houses of Congress." * * * * "Let us suppose it exercised indiscriminately on every act presented for his acceptance. This surely would be an abuse of his constitutional power richly deserving impeachment; and yet no man will pretend to say it is an indictable offense." (2 Chase's Trial, 452; Wickliffe's argument on Peck's Trial, 311.)

On Peck's trial, Mr. Wickliffe put additional cases: "Suppose a judge under the influence of political feeling shall award to his favorite a new trial" * * * * "against known law, would this be an indictable offense?"

"Suppose a judge" * * * * "shall labor for two hours in abuse upon an unoffending citizen whom he has dragged before him." (Peck's Trial, 310.)

"If a head of a Department should divert his power and patronage for his personal or political aggrandizement." (Id., 310.)

On Peck's trial, Mr. Buchanan said: "The abuse of a power which has been given may be as criminal as the usurpation of a power which has not been granted. Suppose a man to be indicted for an assault and battery. He is tried and found guilty; and the judge, without any circumstances of peculiar aggravation having been shown, fines him $1,000, and commits him to prison for a year. Now, although the judge may possess the power to fine and imprison for this offense at his discretion, would not this punishment be such an abuse of judicial discretion, and afford such evidence of the tyrannical and arbitrary exercise of power as would justify the House of Representatives in voting an impeachment?" (Peck's Trial, 427.)

[*] "There are offenses for which an officer may be impeached, and against which there are no known positive laws. It is possible that the day may arrive when a President of the United States, having some great political object in view, may endeavor to influence Congress by holding out threats or inducements to them. A treaty may be made which the President, with some view, may be extremely anxious to have ratified. The hope of office may be held out to a Senator: and I think it cannot be doubted that for this the President would be liable to impeachment, although there is no positive law forbidding it. Again, sir, a member of the Senate or of the House of Representatives may have a very dear friend in office, and the President may tell him unless you vote for my measures your friend shall be dismissed. Where is the positive law forbidding this? Yet, where is the man who would be shameless enough to rise in

The indiscriminate veto of all bills by the President, his retaining in office men subject to his removal, knowing them to be utterly incapable of performing the duties of their office, and other misdemeanors, would manifestly be proper subjects of an impeachment, for otherwise a wicked, corrupt, or incompetent foreign minister might embroil the nation in a war imperiling our existence, to avoid which impeachment might be the only remedy.

The impeachment trials in the United States may be said to have conclusively settled these questions.*

The first case tried—that of William Blount, a Senator of the United States from Tennessee—simply decided that none but civil officers can be impeached, and that a Senator is not such civil officer. But the articles of impeachment —none of which charged a statutory crime, and some certainly no common-law offense—proceeded upon the idea that acts were impeachable† which were not indictable, so much so

the face of his country and defend such conduct, or be bold enough to contend that the President could not be impeached for it?" (Per Nicholson, 2 Chase's Trial, 339,341; see Peck's Trial, 309.)
"The abuse of a power given may be as criminal as the usurpation of a power not granted." (Per Buchanan on Peck's Trial, 427.)
He supposes the case of a judge having discretionary power to fine and imposing enormous and unnecessary punishment.
* Those before the Senate of the United States are the cases of—
1. William Blount, a Senator of the United States, July 1797, to January 1798. (Wharton's State Trials, 20.)
2. John Pickering, district judge, New Hampshire, 1803-04. (Annals of Congress; 2 Hildreth's History, 513.)
3. Samuel Chase, associate justice of the Supreme Court United States, 1804-05. (Trial of Chase, by Smith & Lloyd, 2 vols.)
4. James Peck, district judge, Missouri, 1826, 1831. (Peck's trial, by Stansbury, 1 vol.)
5. West W. Humphreys, district judge of Tennessee, 1862. (Congressional Globe, vols. 47, 48, 49, 2d session 37th Congress. See Report No. 44, 2d session 37th Congress, vol. 3, Reports of Committees.)
† There were five articles—
1. That in 1797 Spain, owning the Floridas and Louisiana, was at war with England, and Senator Blount "did conspire and contrive to create, promote, and set on foot"   *   *   *   "in the United States, and to conduct and carry on from thence a military hostile expedition against"   *   *   * "the Floridas and Louisiana"   *   *   * "for the purpose of wresting the same from" Spain, and of conquering the same for Great Britain, in violation of the obligations of neutrality of the United States.
2. That by the treaty of October 27, 1795, the United States and Spain agreed to restrain Indian hostilities in the country adjacent to the Floridas, yet Blount, in 1797, "did conspire and contrive to excite the Creek and Cherokee Indians" in the United States "to commence hostilities against the subjects and possessions in the Floridas and Louisiana, for the purpose of reducing the same to the dominion of"   *   *   * "Great Britain," in violation of the treaty, the obligations of neutrality and his duties as Senator.
3. That Blount, in April, 1797, to accomplish his designs aforesaid, did "conspire and contrive to alienate the confidence of said Indian tribes" from the United States Indian agent, "and to diminish, impair, and destroy" his influence "with the said Indian tribes, and their friendly intercourse and understanding with him."

that no objection was suggested on that account.

The next case is that of Judge Pickering,* who was convicted upon each of four several articles of impeachment before the Senate, and removed from office in March 1804.† This case

4. That Blount, in April, 1797, "did conspire and contrive to seduce" an Indian interpreter of the United States with the Indians under a treaty between them and the United States "from his duty, and to engage" him "to assist in the promotion and execution of his said criminal intentions and conspiracies."
5. That Blount, in April, 1797, "did conspire and contrive to diminish and impair the confidence of said Cherokee nation in the Government of the United States, and to create and foment discontents and disaffection among the said Indians toward the"   * *   *   *   "United States in relation to" ascertaining and marking the boundary line between the lands of the Indians and of the United States in pursuance of a treaty between them.
* The articles charged—
1. That the surveyor of the district of New Hampshire did, in the port of Portsmouth, seize the ship Eliza for unlading foreign goods contrary to law, and the marshal of the district, on the 16th of October, 1802, by order of Judge Pickering, did arrest and detain said ship for trial, and the act of Congress of March 2, 1789, provides that such ship may, by order of the judge, be delivered to the claimant on giving bond to the United States, and on producing a certificate from the collector of the district that the duties on the goods and tonnage duty of the ship had been paid; yet Judge Pickering, with intent to evade the act of Congress, ordered the ship to be restored to the claimant without producing the certificate of payment of duties and tonnage duty.
2. That at the district court of New Hampshire, in November, 1802, the collector having libeled said ship because of said unlawful unlading of goods and prayed her forfeiture to the United States, yet Judge Pickering, with intent to defeat the just claims of the United States, refused to hear the testimony of witnesses produced to sustain the claim of the United States, and without hearing them did order and decree said ship to be restored to the claimant, contrary to law.
3. That the act of 24th September, 1789, authorizes an appeal to the circuit court in such case, and the United States district attorney did claim an appeal from said decree, yet said judge, disregarding the law, intending to injure the revenues, refused to allow an appeal.
4. That Judge Pickering being a man of loose morals and intemperate habits, on 11th and 12th November, 1802, did appear on the bench of his court for the purpose of administering justice in a state of intoxication produced by inebriating liquors, and did then and there frequently and in a most profane and indecent manner invoke the name of the Supreme Being. (Annals of Congress of 1803-'4, page 319.)
† 1. This case was thus commented on during Peck's trial:
"I admit that if the charge against a judge be merely an illegal decision or a question of property in a civil cause his error ought to be gross and palpable indeed to justify the inference of a criminal intention and to convict him upon an impeachment. And yet one case of this character occurred in our history. Judge Pickering was tried and condemned upon all the four articles exhibited against him, although the first three contained no other charge than that of making decisions contrary to law in a cause involving a mere question of property, and then refusing to grant the party injured an appeal from his decision, to which he was entitled." (Per Buchanan, in Peck's Trial, 428.)
Mr. Nicholson arguendo, (2 Chase's Trial, 341,) in referring to Pickering's case, says he "was impeached for drunkenness and profane swearing on the bench, although there is no law of the United States forbidding them. Indeed, I do not know that there is any law punishing either in New Hampshire, where

proves that a *violation of law* of a particular character, and drunkenness and profanity on the bench, are each impeachable high crimes and misdemeanors. In this case the defense of insanity was made and supported by evidence. The case does not show the opinion of Senators on this evidence. But if the insanity was regarded as proved, this case shows that a criminal intent is not necessary to constitute an impeachable high crime and misdemeanor, but that the power of impeachment may be interposed to protect the public against the misconduct of an insane officer.

The next case is that of Samuel Chase,* an

---

the offense was committed. It was said by one of the counsel that these were indictable offenses. I, however, do not know where; certainly not in England. Drunkenness is punishable thereby the ecclesiastical authority; but the temporal magistrate never had any power over it until it was given by a statute of James I, and even then the power was not to be exercised by the courts, but only by a justice of the peace, as is now the case in Maryland, where a small fine may be imposed."

Mr. Harper had said: "Habitual drunkenness in a judge, and profane swearing in any person, are indictable offenses, [at common law.] And if they were not, still they are violations of the law. I do not mean to say that there is a statute against drunkenness and profane swearing. But they are offenses against good morals, and as such are forbidden by the common law. They are offenses in the sight of God and man." (2 Chase's Trial, 255, 400.)

* There were eight articles of impeachment:
1. That on the trial of Fries for treason in the circuit court of the United States for Pennsylvania, in April, 1800, he
(1.) Prepared and furnished counsel an opinion in writing on the questions of law in the case before trial or argument.
(2.) Restricted Fries's counsel from recurring to certain English authorities and statutes of the United States illustrative of positions for defense.
(3.) Denied counsel for defense the right to argue the law of the case to the jury, endeavoring to wrest from the jury the right to determine questions of law.
2. At the circuit court at Richmond, in May, 1800, Callender was arraigned for libel on John Adams, then President, and the judge, with intent to procure his conviction, overruled the objection of Basset, one of the jury, who wished to be excused because he had made up his mind, and required him to sit on the jury.
3. That with same intent the judge refused to permit the evidence of a witness to be given, on pretense that the witness could not prove the truth of the whole of one of the charges contained in an indictment embracing more than one fact.
4. Injustice and partiality in said case:
(1.) In compelling prisoner's counsel to reduce to writing all questions proposed to be put to that witness.
(2.) In refusing to postpone the trial on a sufficient affidavit filed.
(3.) Rude and contemptuous expressions to counsel.
(4.) Repeated and vexatious interruptions of counsel, inducing them to abandon their cause and client.
5. That the judge awarded a *capias* for the arrest of said Callender, when the statute of Virginia in such case only authorized a summons requiring the accused to answer.
6. The judge required Callender to submit to trial during the term at which he was indicted, in violation of the statute of Virginia, declaring that the accused shall not answer until the next succeeding term, the United States judiciary act of 24th September, 1789, recognizing the State laws as rules of decision.
7. At the circuit court in Delaware, in June, 1800, the judge refused to discharge the grand jury, although

C. I.—7.

---

associate justice of the Supreme Court of the United States. In this case it was insisted for the accused that "no judge can be impeached and removed from office for any act or offense for which he could not be indicted," either by statute or common law.* But this was denied with convincing argument,† and was practically abandoned by the defense.‡

In 1830, James H. Peck, judge of the United States district court for Missouri, was impeached by the House of Representatives for imprisoning and suspending from practice an attorney of his court.‖ The argument for the prosecution alluded to the proposition stated in Chase's trial, "that a judge cannot be impeached for any offense which is not indictable;"§ but the counsel for the accused repu-

---

entreated by several of the jury to do so, and after the jury had regularly declared through their foreman that they had found no bills of indictment, nor had any presentment to make, and instructed the jury that it was their duty to look after a certain seditious printer living in Wilmington. And the judge enjoined on the district attorney the necessity of procuring a file of a newspaper printed at Wilmington, to find some passage which might furnish the groundwork of a prosecution—all with intent to procure the prosecution of said printer.
8. That the judge at the circuit court at Baltimore, in May, 1803, perverted his official right and duty to address the grand jury, delivering to them an inflammatory political harangue, with intent to excite the people of Maryland against their State government and against the United States.
[His address was in part against universal suffrage.]

*1. Chase's Trial, 9-18, per Clark. Per Lee, 107, citing 2 Bacon, 97. Per Martin, 137. Per Harper, 254-9. Judge Chase in his answer declared that he was only liable for a misdemeanor, "consisting in some act done or omitted in violation of law forbidding or commanding it," and that he was not impeachable "except for some offense for which he may be indicted." (1 Chase's Trial, 47, 48; 1 Story on Const., sec. 796, note; 4 Eliot's Debates, 262.)

† 1 Chase's Trial, 353, per Campbell. Per Rodney, 378. 2 Chase's Trial, 335, 339-340, per Nicholson. 1 Chase's Trial, 335, 352; 2 Chase's Trial, 351. "It is sufficient to show that the accused has transgressed the line of his official duty in violation of the laws of his country, and that this conduct can only be accounted for on the ground of impure and corrupt motives." (1 Chase's Trial, 353, per Campbell.) "Violation of official duty, whether it be a proceeding against a positive law or a proceeding unwarranted by law." (2 Chase's Trial, 340, per Nicholson.)

‡ 3 Chase's Trial, 255, per Harper. On Peck's Trial, 427, Buchanan said: "The principle fairly to be deduced from all the arguments on the trial of Judge Chase, and from the votes of the Senate on the articles of impeachment against him," was to hold that a violation of the Constitution or law was impeachable, "in opposition to the principle," * * * * "that in order to render an offense impeachable it must be indictable."

‖ The charge was that, as judge of the district court for Missouri, he on the 21st April, 1826, imprisoned L. E. Lawless, an attorney, for twenty-four hours, and suspended him for eighteen months from practicing law, for an alleged contempt of court in publishing a newspaper article reviewing a published decision of said judge; that said judge, unmindful of the duties of his station, and that "he held the same by the Constitution *during good behavior* only, with intent wrongfully and unjustly to oppress, imprison, and injure said Lawless," &c. His answer conceded a liability to impeachment on facts which would not be indictable.

§ Peck's Trial, 308, per Wickliffe.

diated any such doctrine as a ground of defense.*

Mr. Wirt did not hazard his reputation by any such claim.† Peck was not convicted.

The case of West W. Humphreys, judge of the United States district court for the district of Tennessee, proceeded on the ground that an officer was impeachable without having committed a statutory or common-law offense.‡

* Mr. Meredith's propositions were (Peck's Trial, 327,) that the court had the power to punish contempts: that the case of Lawless was a contempt proper for its exercise; that the punishment was proper; and lastly, "that if the court had not the power, or if, having it, the case was not a case proper for its application, still the act did not proceed from the evil and malicious intention with which it is charged, and which it is absolutely necessary should have accompanied it to constitute the guilt of an impeachable offense.

Judge Peck, in the answer to his impeachment, said:

"In the digested report of the committee* of the House of Commons, which follows the report of the arguments of the managers who conducted that impeachment, (against Warren Hastings,) it will be seen, too, that in the estimation of that committee the proceedings of courts of law furnish no rule whatever for the proceedings in an impeachment, the latter being governed by no other law or custom than the *lex et consuetudo parliamenti,* which left the House at perfect liberty to pursue the great ends of justice untrammeled by any other rules than those which reason and public utility prescribe." (Peck's Trial, 10; see 2 Hale P. C., chapter 20, page 150; 6 Howell's State Trials, 313, 316, 346, note; note to Lord Capel's case, 4 Howell's State Trials, 12, 13; Case of Earl of Danby, A. D. 1678; 11 Howell's State Trials, 650; 4 Hatsel's Puc., 71.)

† He cites the opinion of Kent in a case in 5 Johns, Rep., 291, which was a civil action against Chancellor Lansing for punishing a contempt. Kent says: "There must be the *scienter* or *intentional violation of the statute,* and this can never be imputed to the judicial proceedings of a court. It would be an impeachable offense, which can never be averred or shown but under the process of impeachment." He conceded that an *intentional violation of the law was impeachable,* and cited Erskine's Speeches, vol. 1,374, (New York ed., 1813,) to show that impeachment should be used as an example "to corruption and willful abuse of authority by extra legal pains."

And, referring to *Hammond* vs. *Howell,* 1 Mod., 184, 2 Id., 218, and the remark that complaint should be made to the king to secure the removal of a judge who had unlawfully imprisoned a juror for contempt, said that course was proper "if the judge had acted *corruptly,*" * * * * "that is, with a wicked intention to oppress under color of law." (Peck's Trial, 493, 495.)

‡ The charges were:

1. For advocating secession *in a public speech* at Nashville, December 29, 1860.
2. For openly supporting and *advocating* the Tennessee ordinance of secession.
3. For aid in organizing armed rebellion.
4. For conspiring with Jefferson Davis and others to oppose by force the authority of the Government of the United States.
5. For neglecting and refusing to hold the district court of the United States.
6. For acting as a confederate judge, and, as such, sentencing men to be banished and imprisoned and their property to be confiscated for their loyalty, "and especially of property of one Andrew Johnson."
7. For the arrest and imprisonment of "one William G. Brownlow, exercising authority as judge of the district court of the confederate States."

He was convicted on all the articles *severally* by a

In fact the charge of advocating secession was a crime of which half the leading politicians of the south had been guilty for many years. In the seven articles of impeachment against him two may be said to charge treason; and it may be claimed that one good article will sustain a conviction, by way of analogy to the doctrine that one good count in an indictment, notwithstanding the presence of bad ones, will sustain a sentence. But even this is not law in England.* But there is no analogy. The Senate, by a *separate vote* on *each* article, specifically passed on the sufficiency of each article to constitute an impeachable offense, while a jury passes generally on all the counts of an indictment. And it is to be observed that the report of the Judiciary Committee recommending impeachment did not charge treason or other indictable crime, nor was there evidence of any;† and on the trial of the case no doubt was expressed as to the right to convict on each of the articles. The cases tried in the States fully sustain the same view, both before and since the adoption of our national Constitution.‡

vote on *each,* except that part of article six, which charges him with confiscating the property of Andrew Johnson. (49 Globe, 1861–62, pl. 4, p. 2950.)

* *Regina* vs. *O'Connell,* 11 Clark & Fin., 15; 9 Jurist, 30; Wharton's Crim. Law, sec. 3047.

† Report No. 44, 2d session 37th Congress, vol. 3 of House Reports.

‡ On the 12th July, 1788, three of the judges of the supreme court of Pennsylvania attached and fined Oswald ten pounds and imprisoned him one month for publishing a newspaper article having a tendency to prejudice the public with respect to the merits of a cause depending in court. (1 Dallas, 319.)

On 5th September, 1788, Oswald memorialized the General Assembly to determine "whether the judges did not infringe the Constitution in direct terms in the sentence they had pronounced, and whether, of course, they had not made themselves proper objects of impeachment."

The House, in Committee of the Whole, heard the evidence. Mr. Lewis, a member, maintained that the only grounds of impeachment were bribery, corruption, gross impartiality, or willful or arbitrary oppression, none of which being approved, the memorial ought to be dismissed.

Mr. Finley, then a member, said: "Though he deemed it his duty to pronounce that the decision of the supreme court was a deviation from the spirit and letter of the frame of government, yet he did not mean to assert that any ground had been shown for the impeachment of the judges; but, on the contrary, he agreed that bribery, corruption, or willful and arbitrary infraction of the law were the only true causes for instituting a prosecution of that nature." (See 1 Dallas, 335; Addison's Trial, 129.)

The House resolved, by 34 to 23, that the charges of arbitrary and oppressive proceedings in the judges of the supreme court are unsupported by the testimony introduced, and, consequently, that there is no just cause for impeaching the said justices. (See the report of this case in 1 Dallas, 3d ed., Phila., 1830, p. 353, [329].)

On the trial of Chase Mr. Rodney, referring to this case, said: "Three of the judges of the supreme court were accused of fining and imprisoning, without the intervention of a jury, a fellow-citizen for publishing a paper which they considered as a contempt of court. The judges were defended by two most able and eloquent counsel, who contended that the constitution, the laws, and the practice of Pennsylvania, by adopting the common-law doctrines on the subject, justified the proceeding, and that if there

Judge Addison* was impeached in Pennsylvania in 1802, and his defense was that he had committed no act indictable at common law; but the Senate almost unanimously convicted him, utterly repudiating that as a defense.

In Massachusetts,† the rule is well settled in conformity with what seems to be the recognized doctrine in the Senate of the United States.

Among the cases tried with great learning and ability there is that of James Prescott,* who was convicted before the Senate.

was no law to justify it their conduct flowed from an honest error in judgment. But, sir, they did not attempt to maintain the position contended for on this occasion, that to support an impeachment the conduct of a judge must be such as to subject him to an indictment." (See 2 Chase's Trial, 399.)

* Impeachment of Alexander Addison, president judge of the courts of common pleas of Westmoreland and other counties, 1802-3, convicted of 1. Directing a jury that the address of an associate judge to them "had nothing to do with the question before them;" and 2. Preventing an associate judge from addressing the grand jury concerning their duties, by denying the right, and by leaving the bench, and thus irregularly adjourning the court. (Addison's Trial, by Thomas Lloyd, 2d ed., Lancaster, 1803.) Mr. McKean, one of the managers, in opening the trial, said: "Offenses under color of office" * * * "have always been considered as the most proper, and of course the usual, ground of impeachment. They are such as the ordinary magistrates cannot or dare not punish." * * * * * "It often happens that officers may"and do abuse their power to the injury of the Commonwealth, and at the same time in such a manner as not to render their conduct congnizable before the ordinary tribunals of justice, so as to proceed by indictment or information." (See Addison's Trial, 31.) In Pennsylvania the courts entertain jurisdiction of common-law crimes. The attorney general filed a motion for a rule against Addison, to show cause in the supreme court why an information should not be filed against him. The court held that it was the right of the associate judge to address the grand jury; but the court, per Chief Justice Shippen, said: "The affidavit does not state malice. It would seem to be a mistake of right. Unless a crime is stated the court cannot take cognizance. There may be another remedy, [by impeachment.] It does not lie with us to say what that is. The proceeding was arbitrary, unbecoming, unhandsome, ungentlemanly, unmannerly, and improper; but there not being an imputation of willful misbehavior and malice, it is not indictable or the subject of an information." (Trial, 79.) Judge Addison, in his defense, said: "No impeachment will lie but for a misdemeanor in office, and every misdemeanor in office is indictable; the officer impeached still remains liable to indictment, trial, judgment, and punishment according to law. An impeachment lies only where an indictment lies. No officer can be convicted on an impeachment who ought not to be convicted on an indictment; and the punishment on impeachment is cumulative—not exclusive. The acts for which an officer may be impeached are precisely those for which he may be indicted as an officer; misdemeanors in office, offenses, or unlawful acts done with an evil intention in his official capacity." (Trial, 104.) "A mere unlawful act from a mistake or error in judgment cannot be alleged as a [impeachable] crime. Not only wrong, but wilful wrong, must be made out, or the offense is not complete." (Page 118.) "Though a judge acts unlawfully and unconstitutionally he cannot be convicted on an impeachment unless he has acted willfully so." (Page, 129; see 1 Dallas, 335.) But this position was denied, and Addison was found guilty by a vote of 20 to 4. (See this case referred to; Chase's Trial, 396.)

† The Massachusetts cases are— 1. Impeachment of William Greenleaf, sheriff of Worcester county, 1788. Convicted—(1.) Of detaining for his private use public moneys, when the Commonwealth has a right thereto; (2.) of exhibiting dishonest accounts of taxes collected; (3,) of detaining for two years public moneys from town of Petersham; (4,) of procuring from the treasurer of Commonwealth an execution for money previously collected by him; (5,) of false returns on executions; (6,) of procuring a warrant of distress for money previously paid him. 2. Impeachment of William Hunt, a justice of the peace of Watertown, 1794. Convicted of entering on his docket, on the trial day of causes, the personal appearance of plaintiffs who were absent, though defendants demanded their appearance. The Senate found Hunt guilty, but suspended judgment for a year. 3. Impeachment of John Vinal, a justice of the peace of Suffolk county, 1800. Convicted of extortion and bribery. 4. Impeachment of Moses Copeland, a justice of the peace for Lincoln county, 1807 and 1808. Acquitted on charges; first, that he bought a note indorsed in blank, and entertained suit in name of Samuel Kingsbury, and rendered judgment, though in fact the note was Copeland's; second, for defaulting a defendant, and entering judgment before the hour set for trial; third, bribery. 5. Impeachment of James Prescott, judge of probate for Middlesex, 1821. Convicted of exacting illegal fees, and of inserting by interlineation in a guardian's account, previously sworn to, an item due to and paid to himself, and then of settling the account as judge. See "Prescott's Trial, by Pickering and Gardner. Boston, 1821." In the appendix is an abstract of the preceding impeachments. On the trial of Prescott, it was said by Mr. Blake, argeundo, that "within the compass of forty long years three or four solitary instances of trial by impeachment have occurred in this Commonwealth. Of these, two, I believe, [three,] resulted in conviction; and I feel myself justified in stating that in neither of the instances alluded to was there any point of constitutional law involved in the inquiry." This case was conducted with great ability. And see report of the trial and acquittal of Edward Shippen, chief justice of Pennsylvania and others, before the Senate of that State, in 1865, by Wm. Hamilton. Trial of George W. Smith, county judge of Oneida county, before the Senate of New York, 1866. Trial of impeachment of Levi Hubbell, judge of the second circuit, by the Senate of Wisconsin, June, 1853. "An account of the impeachment and trial of the late Francis Hopkinson, Esq., judge of the court of admiralty for the Commonwealth of Pennsylvania; printed by Francis Bailey, Philadelphia, 1794." He was tried and acquitted in November and December, 1780. The same volume contains "An account of the Impeachment, trial, and acquittal of John Nicholson, Esq., comptroller general of Pennsylvania." He was acquitted April 7, 1794. * In 1821, Prescott, a judge of probate, was impeached before the Senate of Massachusetts. The 12th article charged that Ware was guardian of Birch, a non compos mentis; that Grout, one of the overseers of the poor, had some controversy with the guardian as to some property of the ward not involved in the account; that the judge, as attorney, advised the parties, and charged, and was paid five dollars by the guardian therefor; that the judge interlined this item in the account which had been previously sworn to, and settled the account allowing this item. (Prescott's Trial, 189.) The law did not prohibit judges from acting as attorneys in matters not coming before their court. It was objected by the defense that this was not an offense indictable, and so not impeachable; that especially was this so in Massachusetts, since the constitution authorized a removal upon the address of both Houses of the Legislature for any cause, and left impeachment against "officers for misconduct or maladministration in their offices."

Mr. Blake,* for the defense, insisted that impeachment is "a process which can only be resorted to for the punishment of some great offense against a known, settled law of the land." The prosecution maintained "that any willful violation of law or any willful and corrupt act of omission or commission in execution or under color of office" "is such an act of misconduct and maladministration in office as will render him liable to punishment by impeachment."†

Chief Justice Chase evidently holds that a failure to perform official duty is impeachable, without reference to its indictable character or the motives therefor. And further, that the Senate is so entirely the exclusive judge of what is official delinquency that the President cannot protect himself against ·impeachment for a failure to execute a law by the decree of a court enjoining him therefrom.

On the 15th April, 1867, in refusing the application of the so-called State of Mississippi for leave to file a bill to enjoin the execution of the "reconstruction acts" of Congress, he said:

"Suppose the bill filed and the injunction prayed for be allowed. If the President refuse obedience it is needless to observe that the court is without power to enforce its process. If, on the other hand, the President complies with the order of the court, and refuses to execute the act of Congress, is it not clear that a collision may occur between the executive and legislative departments of the Government? May not the House of Representatives impeach the President for such refusal? And in that case could this court interpose in behalf of the President, thus endangered by compliance with its mandate, and restrain by injunction the Senate of the United States from sitting as a court of impeachment? Would the strange spectacle be offered to the public wonder of an attempt by this court to arrest proceedings in that court? These questions answer themselves."

The question whether an act is impeachable which is not indictable at common law, when committed by officers who are answerable by indictment, is only important to determine how

But one of the managers said in substance: "We stand here on no statute, on no particular law of the Commonwealth; there is none for such a case. We stand here upon the broad principles of the common law—of common justice." * * * * "Such conduct is disgraceful and contrary to the usages of all civilized nations." * * * "We have shown the conduct of the respondent" * * * * "to have been grossly improper and mischievous in its tendency; this is quite enough; he has rendered himself unworthy of office, and therefore ought to be impeached and removed." (Prescott's Trial, 149. See Dutton's remarks, 193-4.)

And so the Senate decided by a vote of 19 to 6, and convicted Judge Prescott.

* Prescott's Trial, 114. He quoted 4 Blackstone, 259, that impeachment "is a prosecution of the already known and established law;" and 2 Wooddeson, 611; and part 1 of Dolby's Report of the trial of the Queen, p. 841, on a bill of pains and penalties for adultery, where it was said by the Earl of Liverpool, "he knew not how they could make that a subject of impeachment, which by the law of England was not a crime."

Mr. Webster for the defense said: "An impeachment is a prosecution for the violation of existing laws." (Prescott's Trial, 164.)

† Prescott's Trial, 182, per Shaw. See Dutton's speech, 194.

far the remedy by impeachment extends. But almost every conceivable act of official misdemeanor is at common law indictable, though, on grounds of public policy, the higher officers are not liable to prosecution in the ordinary courts for *official* misdemeanors.

But the question, as already shown, is put at rest by the practice in England, by the language of the Constitution, by the opinions of its framers, by contemporaneous exposition, by the uniform usage under it, and by the united opinion of all the elementary writers. The value of these it is unnecessary to discuss as they are understood by all lawyers.*

It has already been shown that the violation of a public statute, though the statute in terms provides no punishment, is at common law indictable.

But it may be urged that if an officer, charged by the Constitution and his oath with the duty of executing the laws, knowingly and intentionally suspends the operation of a particular statute, refuses to execute another, and violates a third, but does so with a *view to promote the public interest*, his *motives are good*, and he is not impeachable.†

This view, so plausible and insidious, is nevertheless so dangerous that its very monstrous character will show that it cannot be maintained. An example will illustrate it. Let it be supposed that with the initiatory steps of the rebellion the President had declared that the national Government had no constitutional power to suppress a rebellion by force of arms.‡

Now, whether such an utterance was extorted by fear, or might have been an honest, but perverted political theory, or the result of a treasonable purpose to aid traitors, would

*They are discussed in Sedgwick on Statutory and Constitutional Construction.

† But if an officer acts *without law*, or even in a mere ministerial capacity, *but having no discretion* under a law, and violates his duty so as to imperil the public safety, he is impeachable.

Bishop says: "When a man serves in a judicial or other capacity in which he is *called* (by law) *to exercise a judgment of his own*, he is not punishable for a mere error therein or for a mistake of the law. Here the act, to be cognizable criminally or even civilly, must be wilful and corrupt." (Criminal Law, 913.)

"When a statute [or the Constitution] forbids a thing affecting the public, but provides no penalty, the doing of it is indictable at common law." (535 [349] 187 [84.]) "Whenever the law, statutory or common, casts on one a duty of a public nature, any neglect of the duty or act done in violation of it is indictable." (Criminal Law, 537 [350,] 913.)

The same rule must exist when no law authorizes it. But it should be remembered that the rules which prevail in ordinary courts have no application in impeachment cases except as the reasons upon which they rest commend them to the consideration of and adoption by the Senate. The Senate is governed by the "*lex et consuetudo parliamenti.*"

‡ In the message of December 4, 1860, the President said: "The power to make war against a State is at variance with the whole spirit and intent of the Constitution." * * * "Our Union rests upon public opinion. If it cannot live in the affections of the people, it must one day perish. Congress possesses many means of preserving it by conciliation; but the sword was not placed in their hands to preserve it by force."

have been in its consequences to the nation all the same if it could have controlled the counsels of the nation. This sentiment, believed and acted on, would have witnessed the destruction of the Government. And must the nation perish because a President honestly believes in the fatal heresy that the Constitution and Congress are powerless for self-preservation? If so, the nation must die out of tender regard to the political idiosyncrasy of the President. The same fatal error of opinion and conduct will be impeachable in one President who knows the right and yet the wrong pursues, while another, who believes in a fallacy because he loves it, will escape unpunished, though the inherent wrong in principle and in effect is the same in both cases.

If the President would undertake to expel Congress as an illegal body, he could scarcely escape impeachment upon a plea of good motives. No tyrant ever yet reigned who did not plead good motives for his usurpations. But even these, if they could be so in fact, never sanctify criminal acts. As well might larceny be justified by a purpose to promote charitable objects, as violations of the Constitution by professions of securing the public interest. In both cases the *motive is illegal*, and no circumstances can justify a criminal act purposely committed. Congress may withhold punishment, or pass acts of indemnity, just as the President may pardon crime; but criminal purposes, studiously persisted in, present no case for clemency.

This subject, so far as it relates to ordinary courts, is well understood. Sedgwick, under the caption "Good faith no excuse for violation of statutes," says:

"We have already had occasion to notice the rule that ignorance of the law cannot be set up in defense. All are bound to know the law, and this holds good as well in regard to common as to statute law, as well in regard to criminal as to civil cases. In regard even to penal laws, it is strictly true that ignorance is no excuse for the violation of a statute.* So in regard to frequent attempts which have been made to exonerate individuals charged with disobedience to penal laws on the ground *of good faith or error of judgment*, it has been held that no *excuse of this kind will avail against the* peremptory words of a statute imposing a penalty. If the prohibited act has been done the penalty must be paid."†

* Smith *vs.* Brown, 1 *Wend.*, 231; Caswell *vs.* Allen, 7 *Johns,* 63.

† Sedgwick on Stat. and Const. Law, 100; *Calcraft vs. Gibbs,* 5 Term R., 19; *Morris* vs. *People,* 3 Denio, 381-402; *People* vs. *Brooks,* 1 Id., 457. On the trial of Warren Hastings, it was argued that he had exerted his "powers for the public good." But the Lord Chancellor said, "*however pure his intentions might have been,* if he violated every principle of morality and justice, he should *not think that any public exigency ought to be pleaded as a justification.*"

March 2, Lord Thurlow said: "The number of articles preferred were twenty, each containing a great number of allegations: of this number the Commons had given no evidence upon fourteen, and upon very inconsiderable parts of three more."

"The impeachment, however, might now be said to rest upon four points—breach of faith, oppression, and injustice, as in the two articles of Cheyt Sing and the Begum; corruption, as in the article of the presents; and a wanton waste of the public money for

And this but reiterates the law of impeachment as recognized in England and the United States.*

Judges have been impeached in England "for misinterpreting the laws," and the Earl of Bristol for advising "against a war with Spain." Yet these were doubtless honest, but were regarded by the impeaching power as mistaken and pernicious opinions.

Even Judge Humphreys, who was impeached before the Senate of the United States for making a secession speech, may have honestly believed what he said and might have supposed his motives good; but this consideration was so unimportant that it was never once mentioned on the trial.

The result is, that *an impeachable high crime or misdemeanor is one in its nature or consequences subversive of some fundamental or essential principle of government or highly prejudicial to the public interest, and this may consist of a violation of the Constitution, of law, of an official oath, or of duty, by an act committed or omitted, or, without violating a positive law, by the abuse of discretionary powers from improper motives or for an improper purpose.*

It should be understood, however, that while this is a proper definition, yet it by no means follows that the power of impeachment is limited to technical crimes or misdemeanors only. It may reach officers who, from incapacity or

private purposes, as in the contracts. In considering the first two points he conceived it would become their lordships to reflect on the situation in which Mr. Hastings was placed. Possessed of absolute power, the question would be, had he exerted that power for the public good, or had he on any occasion been actuated by base or malicious motives? If in the case of Cheyt Sing and the Begums, their lordships should be of opinion that he was neither malicious nor corrupt, the charges naturally fell to the ground.

"The Lord Chancellor concurred generally in what had fallen from the noble and learned lord, but could not go quite so far as to say that Mr. Hastings would be justified in any gross abuse of the arbitrary power which he possessed, even though it should be made clear that he was actuated neither by corrupt nor by malicious motives. Mr. Hastings had great power lodged in his hands undoubtedly. He was responsible to his country for a proper use of that power: and however *pure his intentions might have been,* if he violated every principle of morality and justice he should not think that any public exigency ought to be pleaded as a justification."

March 5. The Lord Chancellor said: "The conduct of the Governor General in relation to the transactions with Cheyt Sing in the year 1780, appeared to him to stand in a different point of view, and to call for other considerations. To say the least of that conduct on the part of Mr. Hastings, it merited a certain degree of blame: but how far it might rise up to a high crime and misdemeanor would depend on other and future proceedings of the Governor General that yet remained to be discussed."

* In the trial of Lord Melville it was insisted that his use of the public money was not impeachable unless the motive was guilty. "The question in the case," said the defense, "as in all cases, is the motive of the heart, *actio non est reus, nisi meus sit rea*—a person is not guilty if his heart is not guilty." (Aspernis Rep., 200.) But in the questions put to and decided by the judges, the *motive* was ignored, and only the *legality* of his conduct decided.

other cause, are absolutely unfit for the performance of their duties, when no other remedy exists, and where the public interests imperatively demand it.

When no other remedy can protect them, the interests of millions of people may not be imperiled from tender regard to official tenure which can only be held for their ruin.

Mr. BUTLER's speech occupied three hours in the delivery, with the exception of a recess of ten minutes, which was taken on the motion of Mr. Senator WILSON, when he had spoken about two hours. When he concluded—

Mr. Manager BINGHAM. Mr. President, I am instructed by my associates to say that we are ready to proceed with the evidence to make good the articles of impeachment exhibited by the House of Representatives against the President of the United States. My associate, Mr. WILSON, will present the testimony.

Mr. JOHNSON. We cannot hear, Mr. Chief Justice. I hope the honorable Manager will speak a little louder.

Mr. Manager BINGHAM. I repeat, for the information of the Senate, that the Managers on the part of the House of Representatives are ready to proceed with testimony to make good the articles of impeachment exhibited by the House of Representatives against the President of the United States, and that my associate, Mr. WILSON, will present the testimony.

The CHIEF JUSTICE. The Managers will proceed with their evidence.

Mr. Manager WILSON. I wish to state on behalf of the Managers that, notwithstanding many of the documents which we deem important to be presented in evidence have been set out in the exhibits accompanying the answers and also in some of the answers, we still are of opinion that it is proper for us to introduce the documents originally by way of guarding against any mishaps that might arise from imperfect copies being set out in the answer and in the exhibits.

I offer, first on behalf of the Managers, a certified copy of the oath of the President of the United States, which I will read:

I do solemnly swear that I will faithfully execute the office of the President of the United States, and will to the best of my ability preserve, protect, and defend the Constitution of the United States.
ANDREW JOHNSON.

To which is attached the following certificate:

I, Salmon P. Chase, Chief Justice of the Supreme Court of the United States, hereby certify that on this 15th day of April, 1865, at the city of Washington, in the District of Columbia, personally appeared Andrew Johnson, Vice President, upon whom, by the death of Abraham Lincoln, late President, the duties of the office of President of the United States have devolved, and took and subscribed the oath of office above set forth.
SALMON P. CHASE,
C. J. S. C. U. S.

The document is certified under the hand of the Acting Secretary of State, and attested by the seal of the Department, as follows:

UNITED STATES OF AMERICA,
DEPARTMENT OF STATE.
To all to whom these presents shall come, greeting:
I certify that the document hereto annexed is a correct copy of the original filed in this Department.
In testimony whereof I, Frederick W. Seward, Acting Secretary of State of the United States, have hereunto subscribed my name and caused the seal of the Department of State to be affixed.
Done at the city of Washington, this 12th day of March, A. D. 1868, and of the independence [L. S.] of the United States of America the ninety-second.
F. W. SEWARD.

I now offer the nomination of Mr. Stanton as Secretary of War by President Lincoln. It is as follows:

IN EXECUTIVE SESSION,
SENATE OF THE UNITED STATES,
January 13, 1862.
The following message was received from the President of the United States, by Mr. NICOLAY, his Secretary:
To the Senate of the United States:
I nominate Edwin M. Stanton, of Pennsylvania, to be Secretary of War, in place of SIMON CAMERON, nominated to be minister to Russia.
ABRAHAM LINCOLN.
EXECUTIVE MANSION, *January* 13, 1862.

I next offer, and will read, the action of the Senate, in executive session, upon said nomination:

IN EXECUTIVE SESSION,
SENATE OF THE UNITED STATES,
January 15, 1862.
Resolved, That the Senate advise and consent to the appointment of Edwin M. Stanton, of Pennsylvania, to be Secretary of War, agreeably to the nomination.

And this is certified by the Secretary of the Senate, as follows:

I, John W. Forney, Secretary of the Senate of the United States, do hereby certify that the foregoing are true extracts from the Journal of the Senate. These extracts are made and certified under the authority of the act approved 8th August, 1846, entitled "An act making copies of papers certified by the Secretary of the Senate and the Clerk of the House of Representatives legal evidence."
Given under my hand at Washington, this 11th day of March, 1868.
JOHN W. FORNEY,
Secretary of the Senate.

I next offer a copy of the communication made to the Senate December 12, 1867, by the President. As this document is somewhat lengthy I will not read it unless desired. It is the message of the President assigning his reasons for the suspension of the Secretary of War.

Mr. STANBERY. Read it, if you please.
Mr. Manager WILSON. It is as follows:

Communication from the President of the United States, relating to the suspension from the office of Secretary of War of Edwin M. Stanton.
To the Senate of the United States:
On the 12th of August last I suspended Mr. Stanton from the exercise of the office of Secretary of War, and on the same day designated General Grant to act as Secretary of War *ad interim.*
The following are copies of the executive orders:
EXECUTIVE MANSION,
WASHINGTON, *August* 12, 1867.
SIR: By virtue of the power and authority vested in me as President by the Constitution and laws of the United States, you are hereby suspended from

office as Secretary of War, and will cease to exercise any and all functions pertaining to the same.

You will at once transfer to General Ulysses S. Grant, who has this day been authorized and empowered to act as Secretary of War *ad interim*, all records, books, papers, and other public property now in your custody and charge.

Hon. EDWIN M. STANTON, *Secretary of War.*

EXECUTIVE MANSION,
WASHINGTON, D. C., *August* 12, 1867.

SIR: Hon. Edwin M. Stanton having been this day suspended as Secretary of War, you are hereby authorized and empowered to act as Secretary of War *ad interim*, and will at once enter upon the discharge of the duties of the office.

The Secretary of War has been instructed to transfer to you all the records, books, papers, and other public property now in his custody and charge.

General ULYSSES S. GRANT, *Washington, D. C.*

The following communication was received from Mr. Stanton:

WAR DEPARTMENT,
WASHINGTON CITY, *August* 12, 1867.

SIR: Your note of this date has been received, informing me that by virtue of the powers and authority vested in you as President by the Constitution and laws of the United States, I am suspended from office as Secretary of War, and will cease to exercise any and all functions pertaining to the same; and also directing me at once to transfer to General Ulysses S. Grant, who has this day been authorized and empowered to act as Secretary of War *ad interim*, all records, books, papers, and other public property now in my custody and charge.

Under a sense of public duty I am compelled to deny your right, under the Constitution and laws of the United States, without the advice and consent of the Senate, and without legal cause, to suspend me from office of Secretary of War, or the exercise of any or all functions pertaining to the same, or without such advice and consent to compel me to transfer to any person the records, books, papers, and public property in my custody as Secretary.

But, inasmuch as the General commanding the armies of the United States has been appointed *ad interim*, and has notified me that he has accepted the appointment, I have no alternative but to submit, under protest, to superior force.

To the PRESIDENT.

The suspension has not been revoked, and the business of the War Department is conducted by the Secretary *ad interim.*

Prior to the conclusion that the time had arrived when it was proper Mr. Stanton should retire from my Cabinet. The mutual confidence and general accord which should exist in such a relation had ceased. I supposed that Mr. Stanton was well advised that his continuance in the Cabinet was contrary to my wishes, for I had repeatedly given him so to understand by every mode short of an express request that he should resign. Having waited full time for the voluntary action of Mr. Stanton, and, seeing no manifestation on his part of an intention to resign, I addressed him the following note on the 5th of August:

"SIR: Public considerations of a high character constrain me to say that your resignation as Secretary of War will be accepted."

To this note I received the following reply:

WAR DEPARTMENT,
WASHINGTON, *August* 5, 1867.

SIR: Your note of this day has been received, stating that public considerations of a high character constrain you to say that my resignation as Secretary of War will be accepted.

In reply, I have the honor to say that public considerations of a high character, which alone have induced me to continue at the head of this Department, constrain me not to resign the office of Secretary of War before the next meeting of Congress.

EDWIN M. STANTON,
Secretary of War.

The reply of Mr. Stanton was not merely a declina-

tion of compliance with the request for his resignation; it was a defiance, and something more. Mr. Stanton does not content himself with assuming that public considerations bearing upon his continuance in office form as fully a rule of action for himself as for the President, and that upon so delicate a question as the fitness of an officer for continuance in his office the officer is as competent and as impartial to decide as his superior who is responsible for his conduct; but he goes further and plainly intimates what *he* means by "public considerations of a high character;" and this is nothing else than *his* loss of confidence in his superior. He says that these public considerations have "alone induced me to continue at the head of this Department," and that they "constrain me not to resign the office of Secretary of War before the next meeting of Congress."

This language is very significant. Mr. Stanton holds the position unwillingly. He continues in office only under a sense of high public duty. He is ready to leave when it is safe to leave, and as the danger he apprehends from his removal then will not exist when Congress is here he is constrained to remain during the interim. What, then, is that danger which can only be averted by the presence of Mr. Stanton or of Congress? Mr. Stanton does not say that "public considerations of a high character" constrain him to hold on to the office indefinitely. He does not say that no one other than himself can at any time be found to take his place and perform its duties. On the contrary, he expresses a desire to leave the office at the earliest moment consistent with these high public considerations. He says, in effect, that while Congress is away he must remain, but that when Congress is here he can go. In other words, he has lost confidence in the President. He is unwilling to leave the War Department in his hands or in the hands of any one the President may appoint or designate to perform its duties. If he resigns the President may appoint a Secretary of War that Mr. Stanton does not approve. Therefore he will not resign. But when Congress is in session the President cannot appoint a Secretary of War which the Senate does not approve. Consequently, when Congress meets Mr. Stanton is ready to resign.

Whatever cogency these "considerations" may have had upon Mr. Stanton, whatever right he may have had to entertain such considerations, whatever propriety there might be in the expression of them to others, one thing is certain, it was official misconduct, to say the least of it, to parade them before his superior officer.

Upon the receipt of this extraordinary note I only delayed the order of suspension long enough to make the necessary arrangements to fill the office. If this were the only cause for his suspension it would be ample. Necessarily it must end our most important official relations, for I cannot imagine a degree of effrontery which would embolden the head of a Department to take his seat at the council table in the Executive Mansion after such an act; nor can I imagine a President so forgetful of the proper respect and dignity which belong to his office as to submit to such intrusion. I will not do Mr. Stanton the wrong to suppose that he entertained any idea of offering to act as one of my constitutional advisers after that note was written. There was an interval of a week between that date and the order of suspension, during which two Cabinet meetings were held. Mr. Stanton did not present himself at either, nor was he expected.

On the 12th of August Mr. Stanton was notified of his suspension, and that General Grant had been authorized to take charge of the Department. In his answer to this notification, of the same date, Mr. Stanton expresses himself as follows: "Under a sense of public duty I am compelled to deny your right, under the Constitution and laws of the United States, without the advice and consent of the Senate, to suspend me from office as Secretary of War or the exercise of any or all functions pertaining to the same, or without such advice or consent to compel me to transfer to any person the records, books, papers, and public property in my custody as Secretary. But inasmuch as the General commanding the armies of the United States has been appointed *ad interim,* and has notified me that he has accepted the appointment, I have no alternative but to submit, under protest, to superior force."

It will not escape attention that in his note of August 5 Mr. Stanton stated that he had been constrained to continue in the office, even before he was requested to resign, by considerations of a high public character. In this note of August 12 a new and different sense of public duty compels him to deny the President's right to suspend him from office without the consent of the Senate. This last is the public duty of resisting an act contrary to law, and he charges the President with violation of the law in ordering his suspension.

Mr. Stanton refers generally to the "Constitution and laws of the United States," and says that a sense of public duty "under" these compels him to deny the right of the President to suspend him from office. As to his sense of duty under the Constitution, that will be considered in the sequel. As to his sense of duty under "the laws of the United States," he certainly cannot refer to the law which creates the War Department; for that expressly confers upon the President the unlimited right to remove the head of the Department. The only other law bearing upon the question is the tenure-of-office act passed by Congress, over the presidential veto, March 2, 1867. This is the law which, under a sense of public duty, Mr. Stanton volunteers to defend.

There is no provision in this law which compels any officer coming within its provisions to remain in office. It forbids removals, but not resignations. Mr. Stanton was perfectly free to resign at any moment, either upon his own motion, or in compliance with a request or an order. It was a matter of choice or of taste. There was nothing compulsory in the nature of legal obligation. Nor does he put his action upon that imperative ground. He says he acts under a "sense of public duty," not of legal obligation, compelling him to hold on, and leaving him no choice. The public duty which is upon him arises from the respect which he owes to the Constitution and the laws violated in his own case. He is, therefore, compelled by this sense of public duty to vindicate violated law, and to stand as its champion.

This was not the first occasion in which Mr. Stanton, in discharge of a public duty, was called upon to consider the provisions of that law. That tenure-of-office law did not pass without notice. Like other acts, it was sent to the President for approval. As is my custom, I submitted its consideration to my Cabinet for their advice upon the question whether I should approve it or not. It was a question of constitutional law, in which I would, of course, rely most upon the opinion of the Attorney General, and of Mr. Stanton, who had once been Attorney General. Every member of my Cabinet advised me that the proposed law was unconstitutional. All spoke without doubt or reservation; but Mr. Stanton's condemnation of the law was the most elaborate and emphatic. He referred to the constitutional provisions, the debates in Congress, especially to the speech of Mr. Buchanan when a Senator, to the decisions of the Supreme Court, and to the usage from the beginning of the Government through every successive Administration, all concurring to establish the right of removal as vested by the Constitution in the President. To all these he added the weight of his own deliberate judgment, and advised me that it was my duty to defend the power of the President from usurpation, and to veto the law.

I do not know when a sense of public duty is more imperative upon a head of Department than upon such an occasion as this. He acts, then, under the gravest obligations of law; for when he is called upon by the President for advice it is the Constitution which speaks to him. All his other duties are left by the Constitution to be regulated by statute; but this duty was deemed so momentous that it is imposed by the Constitution itself.

After all this I was not prepared for the ground taken by Mr. Stanton in his note of August 12. I was not prepared to find him compelled, by a new and indefinite sense of public duty under "the Constitution," to assume the vindication of a law which, under the solemn obligations of public duty imposed by the Constitution itself, he advised me was a violation of that Constitution. I make great allowance for a change of opinion, but such a change as this hardly falls

within the limits of greatest indulgence. Where our opinions take the shape of advice, and influence the action of others, the utmost stretch of charity will scarcely justify us in repudiating them when they come to be applied to ourselves.

But to proceed with the narrative. I was so much struck with the full mastery of the question manifested by Mr. Stanton, and was at the time so fully occupied with the preparation of another veto upon the pending reconstruction act, that I requested him to prepare the veto upon this tenure-of-office bill. This he declined on the ground of physical disability to undergo at the time the labor of writing, but stated his readiness to furnish what aid might be required in the preparation of materials for the paper.

At the time this subject was before the Cabinet it seemed to be taken for granted that as to those members of the Cabinet who had been appointed by Mr. Lincoln their tenure of office was not fixed by the provisions of the act. I do not remember that the point was distinctly decided, but I well recollect that it was suggested by one member of the Cabinet who was appointed by Mr. Lincoln, and that no dissent was expressed.

Whether the point was well taken or not did not seem to me of any consequence, for the unanimous expression of opinion against the constitutionality and policy of the act was so decided that I felt no concern, so far as the act had reference to the gentlemen then present, that I would be embarrassed in the future. The bill had not then become a law. The limitation upon the power of removal was not yet imposed, and there was yet time to make any changes. If any one of these gentlemen had then said to me that he would avail himself of the provisions of that bill in case it became a law, I should not have hesitated a moment as to his removal. No pledge was then expressly given or required. But there are circumstances when to give an express pledge is not necessary, and when to require it is an imputation of possible bad faith. I felt that if these gentlemen came within the purview of the bill it was as to them a dead letter, and that none of them would ever take refuge under its provisions.

I now pass to another subject. When, on the 15th of April, 1865, the duties of the presidential office devolved upon me, I found a full Cabinet of seven members, all of them selected by Mr. Lincoln. I made no change; on the contrary, I shortly afterward ratified a change determined upon by Mr. Lincoln, but not perfected at his death, and admitted his appointee, Mr. Harlan, in the place of Mr. Usher, who was in office at the time.

The great duty of the time was to reëstablish government, law, and order in the insurrectionary States. Congress was then in recess, and the sudden overthrow of the rebellion required speedy action. This grave subject had engaged the attention of Mr. Lincoln in the last days of his life, and the plan according to which it was to be managed had been prepared and was ready for adoption. A leading feature of that plan was that it should be carried out by the executive authority, for, so far as I have been informed, neither Mr. Lincoln nor any member of his Cabinet doubted his authority to act or proposed to call an extra session of Congress to do the work. The first business transacted in Cabinet after I became President was this unfinished business of my predecessor. A plan or scheme of reconstruction was produced which had been prepared for Mr. Lincoln by Mr. Stanton, his Secretary of War. It was approved, and, at the earliest moment practicable, was applied in the form of a proclamation to the State of North Carolina, and afterward became the basis of action in turn for the other States.

Upon the examination of Mr. Stanton before the Impeachment Committee he was asked the following question: "Did any one of the Cabinet express a doubt of the power of the executive branch of the Government to reorganize State governments which had been in rebellion without the aid of Congress?" He answered, "None whatever. I had myself entertained no doubt of the authority of the President to take measures for the organization of the rebel States on the plan proposed during the vacation of Congress, and agreed in the plan specified in the proclamation in the case of North Carolina."

There is, perhaps, no act of my administration for

which I have been more denounced than this. It was not originated by me; but I shrink from no responsibility on that account, for the plan approved itself to my own judgment, and I did not hesitate to carry it into execution.

Thus far and upon this vital policy there was perfect accord between the Cabinet and myself, and I saw no necessity for a change. As time passed on there was developed an unfortunate difference of opinion and of policy between Congress and the President upon this same subject, and upon the ultimate basis upon which the reconstruction of these States should proceed, especially upon the question of negro suffrage. Upon this point three members of the Cabinet found themselves to be in sympathy with Congress. They remained only long enough to see that the difference of policy could not be reconciled. They felt that they should remain no longer, and a high sense of duty and propriety constrained them to resign their positions. We parted with mutual respect for the sincerity of each other in opposite opinions, and mutual regret that the difference was on points so vital as to require a severance of official relations. This was in the summer of 1866. The subsequent sessions of Congress developed new complications when the suffrage bill for the District of Columbia and the reconstruction acts of March 2 and March 23, 1867, all passed over the veto. It was in Cabinet consultations upon these bills that a difference of opinion upon the most vital points was developed. Upon these questions there was perfect accord between all the members of the Cabinet and myself except Mr. Stanton. He stood alone, and the difference of opinion could not be reconciled. That unity of opinion which, upon great questions of public policy or administration, is so essential to the Executive was gone.

I do not claim that a head of Department should have no other opinions than those of the President. He has the same right, in the conscientious discharge of duty, to entertain and express his own opinions as has the President. What I do claim is that the President is the responsible head of the Administration, and when the opinions of a head of Department are irreconcilably opposed to those of the President in grave matters of policy and administration there is but one result which can solve the difficulty, and that is a severance of the official relation. This, in the past history of the Government, has always been the rule, and it is a wise one; for such differences of opinion among its members must impair the efficiency of any Administration.

I have now referred to the general grounds upon which the withdrawal of Mr. Stanton from my Administration seemed to me to be proper and necessary; but I cannot omit to state a special ground, which, if it stood alone, would vindicate my action.

The sanguinary riot which occurred in the city of New Orleans on the 30th of August, 1866, justly aroused public indignation and public inquiry, not only as to those who were engaged in it, but as to those who, more or less remotely, might be held to responsibility for its occurrence. I need not remind the Senate of the effort made to fix that responsibility on the President. The charge was openly made, and again and again reiterated through all the land, that the President was warned in time, but refused to interfere.

By telegrams from the Lieutenant Governor and attorney general of Louisiana, dated the 27th and 28th of August, I was advised that a body of delegates, claiming to be a constitutional convention, were about to assemble in New Orleans; that the matter was before the grand jury, but that it would be impossible to execute civil process without a riot, and this question was asked, "Is the military to interfere to prevent process of court?" This question was asked at a time when the civil courts were in the full exercise of their authority, and the answer sent by telegraph on the same 28th of August was this: "The military will be expected to sustain, and not to interfere with, the proceedings of the courts."

On the same 28th of August the following telegram was sent to Mr. Stanton by Major General Baird, then (owing to the absence of General Sheridan) in command of the military at New Orleans:

"Hon. EDWIN M. STANTON, *Secretary of War:*

"A convention has been called, with the sanction of Governor Wells, to meet here on Monday. The Lieutenant Governor and city authorities think it unlawful, and propose to break it up by arresting the delegates. I have given no orders on the subject, but have warned the parties that I could not countenance or permit such action without instructions to that effect from the President. Please instruct me at once by telegraph."

The 28th of August was on Saturday. The next morning, the 29th, this dispatch was received by Mr. Stanton at his residence in this city. He took no action upon it, and neither sent instructions to General Baird himself nor presented it to me for such instructions. On the next day (Monday) the riot occurred. I never saw this dispatch from General Baird until some ten days or two weeks after the riot, when upon my call for all the dispatches, with a view to their publication, Mr. Stanton sent it to me. These facts all appear in the testimony of Mr. Stanton before the Judiciary Committee in the impeachment investigation.

On the 30th, the day of the riot, and after it was suppressed, General Baird wrote to Mr. Stanton a long letter, from which I make the following extracts:

"SIR: I have the honor to inform you that a very serious riot has occurred here to-day. I had not been applied to by the convention for protection, but the Lieutenant Governor and the mayor had freely consulted with me, and I was so fully convinced that it was so strongly the intent of the city authorities to preserve the peace, in order to prevent military interference, that I did regard an outbreak as a thing to be apprehended. The Lieutenant Governor had assured me that, even if a writ of arrest was issued by the court, the sheriff would not attempt to serve it without my permission, and, for to-day, they designed to suspend it. I inclose herewith copies of my correspondence with the mayor, and of a dispatch which the Lieutenant Governor claims to have received from the President. I regret that no reply to my dispatch to you of Saturday has yet reached me. General Sheridan is still absent in Texas."

The dispatch of General Baird of the 28th asks for immediate instructions, and his letter of the 30th, after detailing the terrible riot which had just happened, ends with the expression of regret that the instructions which he asked for were not sent. It is not the fault or the error or the omission of the President that this military commander was left without instructions; but for all omissions, for all errors, for all failures to instruct when instruction might have averted this calamity, the President was openly and persistently held responsible. Instantly, without waiting for proof, the delinquency of the President was heralded in every form of utterance. Mr. Stanton knew then that the President was not responsible for *this delinquency.* The exculpation was in his power, but it was not given by him to the public, and only to the President in obedience to a requisition for all the dispatches.

No one regrets more than myself that General Baird's request was not brought to my notice. It is clear from his dispatch and letter, that if the Secretary of War had given him proper instructions, the riot which arose on the assembling of the convention would have been averted.

There may be those ready to say that I would have given no instructions even if the dispatch had reached me in time; but all must admit that I ought to have had the opportunity.

The following is the testimony given by Mr. Stanton before the Impeachment Investigation Committee as to this dispatch:

"*Question.* Referring to the dispatch of the 28th of July, by General Baird, I ask you whether that dispatch on its receipt was communicated?

"*Answer.* I received that dispatch on Sunday forenoon. I examined it carefully and considered the question presented. I did not see that I could give any instructions different from the line of action which General Baird proposed, and made no answer to the dispatch.

"*Question.* I see it stated that this was received at 10.20 p. m. Was that the hour at which it was received by you?

"*Answer.* That is the date of its reception in the telegraph office Saturday night. I received it on

Sunday forenoon at my residence. A copy of the dispatch was furnished to the President several days afterward, along with all the other dispatches and communications on that subject, but it was not furnished by me before that time. I suppose it may have been ten or fifteen days afterward.

"*Question.* The President himself being in correspondence with those parties upon the same subject, would it not have been proper to have advised him of the reception of that dispatch?

"*Answer.* I know nothing about his correspondence, and know nothing about any correspondence except this one dispatch. We had intelligence of the riot on Thursday morning. The riot had taken place on Monday."

It is a difficult matter to define all the relations which exist between the heads of Department and the President. The legal relations are well enough defined. The Constitution places these officers in the relation of his advisers when he calls upon them for advice. The acts of Congress go further: take, for example, the act of 1789, creating the War Department. It provides that "there shall be a principal officer therein, to be called the Secretary for the Department of War, who shall perform and execute such duties as shall from time to time be enjoined on or intrusted to him by the President of the United States;" "and furthermore, the said principal officer shall conduct the business of the said Department in such manner as the President of the United States shall, from time to time, order and instruct." Provision is also made for the appointment of an inferior officer by the head of the Department, to be called the chief clerk, "who, whenever said principal officer shall be removed from office by the President of the United States," shall have the charge and custody of the books, records, and papers of the Department.

The legal relation is analogous to that of principal and agent. It is the President upon whom the constitution devolves, as head of the executive department, the duty to see that the laws are faithfully executed; but, as he cannot execute them in person, he is allowed to select his agents, and is made responsible for their acts within just limits. So complete is this presumed delegation of authority in the relation of a head of Department to the President that the Supreme Court of the United States have decided that an order made by a head of Department is presumed to be made by the President himself.

The principal upon whom such a responsibility is placed for the acts of a subordinate ought to be left as free as possible in the matter of selection and of dismissal. To hold him to responsibility for an officer beyond his control, to leave the question of the fitness of such an agent to be decided *for* him and not *by* him, to allow such a subordinate, when the President, moved by "public considerations of a high character," requests his resignation, to assume for himself an equal right to act upon his own views of "public considerations," and to make his own conclusions paramount to those of the President—to allow all this, is to reverse the order of administration, and to place the subordinate above the superior.

There are, however, other relations between the President and a head of Department, beyond these defined legal relations, which necessarily attend them, though not expressed. Chief among these is mutual confidence. This relation is so delicate that it is sometimes hard to say when or how it ceases. A single flagrant act may end it at once, and then there is no difficulty. But confidence may be just as effectually destroyed by a series of causes too subtle for demonstration. As it is a plant of slow growth, so, too, it may be slow in decay. Such has been the process here. I will not pretend to say what acts or omissions have broken up this relation. They are hardly susceptible of statement, and still less of formal proof. Nevertheless, no one can read the correspondence of the 5th of August without being convinced that this relation was effectually gone on both sides, and that while the President was unwilling to allow Mr. Stanton to remain in his Administration, Mr. Stanton was equally unwilling to allow the President to carry on his Administration without his presence.

In the great debate which took place in the House of Representatives in 1789, in the first organization of the principal Departments, Mr. Madison spoke as follows:

"It is evidently the intention of the Constitution that the First Magistrate should be responsible for the executive department. So far, therefore, as we do not make the officers who are to aid *him* in the duties of that department responsible to him, he is not responsible to the country. Again, is there no danger that an officer, when he is appointed by the concurrence of the Senate, and has friends in that body, may choose rather to risk his establishment on the favor of that branch than rest it upon the discharge of his duties to the satisfaction of the executive branch, which is constitutionally authorized to inspect and control his conduct? And if it should happen that the officers connect themselves with the Senate, they may mutually support each other, and for want of efficacy reduce the power of the President to a mere vapor, in which case his responsibility would be annihilated, and the expectation of it is unjust. The high executive officers, joined in cabal with the Senate, would lay the foundation of discord and end in an assumption of the executive power only to be removed by a revolution of the Government."

Mr. Sedgwick in the same debate, referring to the proposition that a head of Department should only be removed or suspended by the concurrence of the Senate, uses this language:

"But if proof be necessary, what is, then, the consequence? Why, in nine cases out of ten, where the case is very clear to the mind of the President that the man ought to be removed, the effect cannot be produced, because it is absolutely impossible to produce the necessary evidence. Are the Senate to proceed without evidence? Some gentlemen contend not. Then the object will be lost. Shall a man, under these circumstances, be saddled upon the President, who has been appointed for no other purpose but to aid the President in performing certain duties? Shall he be continued, I ask again, against the will of the President? If he is, where is the responsibility? Are you to look for it in the President, who has no control over the officer, no power to remove him if he acts unfeelingly or unfaithfully? Without you make him responsible, you weaken and destroy the strength and beauty of your system. What is to be done in cases which can only be known from a long acquaintance with the conduct of an officer?"

I had indulged the hope that, upon the assembling of Congress, Mr. Stanton would have ended this unpleasant complication, according to the intimation given in his note of August 12. The duty which I have felt myself called upon to perform was by no means agreeable, but I feel that I am not responsible for the controversy or for the consequences.

Unpleasant as this necessary change in my Cabinet has been to me upon personal considerations, I have the consolation to be assured that, so far as the public interests are involved, there is no cause for regret. Salutary reforms have been introduced by the Secretary *ad interim,* and great reductions of expenses have been effected under his administration of the War Department, to the saving of millions to the Treasury.   ANDREW JOHNSON.

WASHINGTON, *December* 12, 1867.

Before the reading was completed—

Mr. SHERMAN. If the Manager will pause now, I desire to submit a motion to adjourn, that the Senate may transact some business of a legislative character.

Mr. SUMNER. I will suggest to my friend that the reading of this document was called for, and it has not yet been finished.

Mr. JOHNSON. We can consider it as read through.

Mr. SHERMAN. I understand that the counsel are willing to waive the further reading.

Mr. STANBERY. As far as we are concerned, we will dispense with its further reading if it is to be considered in evidence.

Mr. Manager WILSON. Then I will simply read the certificate.

Mr. STANBERY. That is unnecessary. We agree to it.

Mr. SHERMAN. I move that the Senate sitting as a court of impeachment adjourn until to-morrow at the usual hour.

Mr. SUMNER. I would suggest ten o'clock.

Mr. SHERMAN. The hour is fixed by the rule.

The CHIEF JUSTICE. The hour of meeting is fixed by the rule, and the motion of the Senator from Massachusetts is not in order. The Senator from Ohio moves to adjourn until to-morrow at half past twelve o'clock.

Several SENATORS. No; twelve o'clock; the rule fixes twelve.

The CHIEF JUSTICE. The Senator from Ohio moves an adjournment until to-morrow at twelve o'clock.

The question being put, the motion was agreed to; and the Chief Justice declared the Senate sitting as a court of impeachment adjourned until to-morrow at twelve o'clock.

TUESDAY, *March* 31, 1868.

At five minutes past twelve o'clock p. m. the Chief Justice of the United States entered the Senate Chamber and took the chair.

The CHIEF JUSTICE. The Sergeant-at-Arms will open the court by proclamation.

The SERGEANT-AT-ARMS. Hear ye, hear ye, hear ye: all persons are commanded to keep silence while the Senate of the United States is sitting for the trial of the articles of impeachment exhibited by the House of Representatives against Andrew Johnson, President of the United States.

The CHIEF JUSTICE. The Secretary will notify the House of Representatives.

The President's counsel, Messrs. Stanbery, Curtis, Evarts, Nelson, and Groesbeck, entered the Chamber and took the seats assigned to them.

At twelve o'clock and seven minutes p. m. the Sergeant-at-Arms announced the presence of the Managers of the Impeachment on the part of the House of Representatives, and they were conducted to the seats assigned to them.

Immediately afterward the presence of the members of the House of Representatives was announced, and the members of the Committee of the Whole House, headed by Mr. E. B. WASHBURNE, of Illinois, the chairman of that committee, and accompanied by the Speaker and Clerk of the House of Representatives, entered the Senate Chamber and took the seats prepared for them.

The CHIEF JUSTICE. Gentlemen Managers on the part of the House of Representatives, you will proceed with your evidence in support of the articles of impeachment. Senators will please to give their attention.

Mr. Manager WILSON. Mr. President and Senators, in continuation of the documentary evidence, I now offer the resolution passed by the Senate in executive session in response to the message of the President notifying the Senate of the suspension of Hon. Edwin M. Stanton as Secretary of War, as follows:

IN EXECUTIVE SESSION,
SENATE OF THE UNITED STATES,
January 13, 1868.

Resolved, That having considered the evidence and reasons given by the President in his report of the 12th of December, 1867, for the suspension from the office of Secretary of War of Edwin M. Stanton, the Senate do not concur in such suspension.

And following order:

IN EXECUTIVE SESSION,
SENATE OF THE UNITED STATES,
January 13, 1868.

Ordered, That the Secretary forthwith communicate an official and authenticated copy of the resolution of the Senate non-concurring in the suspension of Edwin M. Stanton as Secretary of War, this day adopted, to the President of the United States, to the said Edwin M. Stanton, and also to the said U. S. Grant, the Secretary of War *ad interim.*

And certified as follows:

I, John W. Forney, Secretary of the Senate of the United States, do hereby certify that the foregoing are true extracts from the Journal of the Senate.

These extracts are made and certified under the authority of the act approved 8th August, 1846, entitled "An act making copies of papers certified by the Secretary of the Senate and the Clerk of the House of Representatives legal evidence."

Given under my hand, at Washington, this 11th day of March, 1868.
[L. S.]
J. W. FORNEY,
Secretary of the Senate.

I next produce and offer as evidence the following extract from the Journal of the Senate:

IN EXECUTIVE SESSION,
SENATE OF THE UNITED STATES,
February 21, 1868.

The following message was received from the President of the United States, by Mr. MOORE, his Secretary:

WASHINGTON, D. C., *February* 21, 1868.

To the Senate of the United States:

On the 12th day of August, 1867, by virtue of the power and authority vested in the President by the Constitution and laws of the United States, I suspended Edwin M. Stanton from the office of Secretary of War. In further exercise of the power and authority so vested in the President I have this day removed Mr. Stanton from the office and designated the Adjutant General of the Army as Secretary of War *ad interim.*

Copies of the communications upon this subject, addressed to Mr. Stanton and the Adjutant General, are herewith transmitted for the information of the Senate.
ANDREW JOHNSON.

The copies attached are as follows:

EXECUTIVE MANSION,
WASHINGTON, D. C., *February* 21, 1868.

SIR: By virtue of the power and authority vested in me as President by the Constitution and laws of the United States, you are hereby removed from office as Secretary for the Department of War, and your functions as such will terminate upon the receipt of this communication.

You will transfer to Brevet Major General Lorenzo Thomas, Adjutant General of the Army, who has this day been authorized and empowered to act as Secretary of War *ad interim,* all records, books, papers, and other property now in your custody and charge.

Respectfully yours, ANDREW JOHNSON.
To Hon. EDWIN M. STANTON, *Washington, D. C.*

EXECUTIVE MANSION,
WASHINGTON, D. C., *February* 21, 1868.

SIR: Hon. Edwin M. Stanton having been this day

removed from office as Secretary for the Department of War, you are hereby authorized and empowered to act as Secretary of War *ad interim*, and will immediately enter upon the discharge of the duties pertaining to that office.

Mr. Stanton has been instructed to transfer to you all the records, books, papers, and other public property now in his custody and charge.

Respectfully yours, ANDREW JOHNSON.

To Brevet Major General LORENZO THOMAS, *Adjutant General United States Army, Washington, D. C.*

To these papers is appended this certificate :

I, John W. Forney, Secretary of the Senate of the United States, do hereby certify that the foregoing is an extract from the Journal of the Senate.

This extract is made and certified under the authority of the act approved 8th August 1846, entitled "An act making copies of papers certified by the Secretary of the Senate and the Clerk of the House of Representatives legal evidence."

Given under my hand, at Washington, this 11th day [L. S.] of March, 1868.

J. W. FORNEY,
Secretary of the Senate.

I now offer an extract from the Journal of the Senate showing the action taken by the Senate on the message notifying that body of the removal of the Secretary of War and the appointment of a Secretary of War *ad interim* :

IN EXECUTIVE SESSION,
SENATE OF THE UNITED STATES,
February 21, 1868.

Whereas the Senate have received and considered the communication of the President stating that he had removed Edwin M. Stanton, Secretary of War, and had designated the Adjutant General of the Army to act as Secretary of War *ad interim* : Therefore,

Resolved by the Senate of the United States, That under the Constitution and laws of the United States the President has no power to remove the Secretary of War and to designate any other officer to perform the duties of that office *ad interim.*

IN EXECUTIVE SESSION,
SENATE OF THE UNITED STATES,
February 21, 1868.

Resolved, That the Secretary of the Senate is hereby directed to communicate copies of the foregoing resolution to the President of the United States, to the Secretary of War, and to the Adjutant General of the Army of the United States.

To these papers this certificate is attached :

I, John W. Forney, Secretary of the Senate of the United States, do hereby certify that the foregoing are true extracts from the Journal of the Senate.

These extracts are made and certified under the authority of the act approved 8th August, 1846, entitled "An act making copies of papers certified by the Secretary of the Senate and the Clerk of the House of Representatives legal evidence."

Given under my hand at Washington, this 11th day [L. s.] of March, 1868.

J. W. FORNEY,
Secretary of the Senate,

I now offer an authenticated copy of the commission of Edwin M. Stanton as Secretary of War, and will here state that this is the only commission under which we claim that he has acted as Secretary of War :

ABRAHAM LINCOLN,
President of the United States of America :

To all who shall see these presents, greeting :

Know ye, that reposing special trust and confidence in the patriotism, integrity, and abilities of Edwin M. Stanton, I have nominated, and by and with the advice and consent of the Senate do appoint, him to be Secretary of War of the United States, and do authorize and empower him to execute and fulfill the duties of that office according to law, and to hold the said office with all the powers, privileges, and emoluments to the same of right appertaining, unto him, the said Edwin M. Stanton, during the pleasure of the President of the United States for the time being.

In testimony whereof I have caused these letters to be made patent and the seal of the United States to be hereunto affixed.

Given under my hand, at the city of Washington, the 15th day of January, in the year of our [L. s.] Lord 1862, and of the independence of the United States of America the eighty-sixth.

ABRAHAM LINCOLN.

By the President:

WILLIAM H. SEWARD,
Secretary of State.

UNITED STATES OF AMERICA,
DEPARTMENT OF STATE.

To all to whom these presents shall come, greeting :

I certify that the document hereunto annexed is a true copy from the records of this Department.

In testimony whereof I, William H. Seward, Secretary of State of the United States, have hereunto subscribed my name and caused the seal of the Department of State to be affixed.

Done at the city of Washington this 21st day of March, A. D. 1868, and of the independence of [L. s.] the United States of America the ninety-second. WILLIAM H. SEWARD,

Mr. Manager BUTLER. Mr. President, will the Senate allow me to call in a witness, William J. McDonald, of Washington. Mr. Sergeant-at-Arms, is he in attendance? I do not know but that the Managers will have to ask that the witnesses be allowed to come on the floor of the Senate, because there will otherwise be some delay in calling them. I believe the Sergeant-at-Arms has given them a room.

The CHIEF JUSTICE. Unless the Senate otherwise orders, the witnesses will remain in their room until they are called.

Mr. Manager BUTLER. I only spoke of the delay.

The CHIEF JUSTICE. Mr. McDonald is present. The witnesses will stand on the left of the Chair when examined.

Mr. Manager BUTLER. I move that this witness be sworn.

The Secretary of the Senate administered the following oath to Mr. McDonald, and to each of the other witnesses as sworn :

"You do swear that the evidence you shall give in the case now depending between the United States and Andrew Johnson shall be the truth, the whole truth, and nothing but the truth : so help you God."

WILLIAM J. McDONALD, being sworn, was examined as follows :

By Mr. Manager BUTLER :

Question. State your name and office?

Answer. William J. McDonald, Chief Clerk of the Senate.

Question. Will you look at that paper [exhibiting a paper] and read the certificate that appears to be signed by your name?

Answer. It is as follows :

OFFICE SECRETARY SENATE UNITED STATES,
WASHINGTON, *February 27, 1868.*

An attested copy of the foregoing resolution was left by me at the office of the President of the United States in the Executive Mansion, he not being present, about nine o'clock p. m. on the 13th of January, 1868.

W. J. McDONALD,
Chief Clerk Senate United States.

Question. Is that certificate a correct one of the acts done?

Answer. That is a correct certificate of the acts done.

Question. And the paper was left in accordance as that certificate states?

Answer. Yes, sir.

Mr. Manager BUTLER. I have nothing further to ask the witness.

The CHIEF JUSTICE. Are there any questions to be put on the part of the accused?

Mr. STANBERY and Mr. CURTIS. No, sir.

Mr. Manager BUTLER. I ask Mr. McDonald to take the stand again.

Question. Will you read that certificate? [handing a paper to the witness.]

Answer. It is—

OFFICE SECRETARY SENATE UNITED STATES,
WASHINGTON, *February 27, 1868.*

An attested copy of the foregoing resolution was delivered by me into the hands of the President of the United States at his office in the Executive Mansion about ten o'clock p. m. on the 21st of February, 1868.
W. J. McDONALD,
Chief Clerk Senate United States.

Question. Do you make the same statement as regards this service?

Answer. Yes, sir; the same statement in regard to that.

Mr. Manager BUTLER. We have nothing further to ask.

Mr. STANBERY. Nothing on our part.

Mr. Manager WILSON. The resolution to which the first certificate of Mr. McDonald refers is:

IN EXECUTIVE SESSION,
SENATE OF THE UNITED STATES,
January 13, 1868.

Resolved, That, having considered the evidence and reasons given by the President in his report of the 12th of December, 1868, for the suspension from the office of Secretary of War of Edwin M. Stanton, the Senate do not concur in such suspension.
Attested: J. W. FORNEY, *Secretary.*

The resolution as to the service of which the other certificate relates:

IN EXECUTIVE SESSION,
SENATE OF THE UNITED STATES,
February 21, 1868.

Whereas the Senate have received and considered the communication of the President stating that he has removed Edwin M. Stanton, Secretary of War, and designated the Adjutant General of the Army to act as Secretary of War *ad interim:* Therefore,

Resolved by the Senate of the United States, That, under the Constitution and laws of the United States, the President has no power to remove the Secretary of War and designate any other officer to perform the duties of that office *ad interim.*
Attest: J. W. FORNEY, *Secretary.*

Mr. Manager BUTLER. We now call J. W. Jones as a witness.

J. W. JONES sworn and examined.

By Mr. Manager BUTLER:

Question. Please state your name and position?

Answer. J. W. Jones, keeper of the stationery.

Question. An officer of the Senate?

Answer. Yes, sir.

Question. Do you know Major General Lorenzo Thomas, of the United States Army, Adjutant General?

Answer. I do, sir.

Question. How long have you known him?

Answer. I have known him about six or seven years.

Question. Were you employed by the Secretary of the Senate to serve a notice of the proceedings of the Senate upon him?

Answer. I was.

Question. Looking at that memorandum, [handing a paper to the witness,] what day did you attempt to make the service?

Answer. The 21st of February.

Question. What year?

Answer. The present year.

Question. Where did you find him?

Answer. I found him at Marini's Hall, at a masquerade ball.

Question. Was he masked?

Answer. He was.

Question. How did you know it was him?

Answer. I saw his shoulder-straps, and I asked him to unmask.

Question. Did he so do?

Answer. He did, sir.

Question. After ascertaining it was him, what did you do?

Answer. I handed him the resolution of the Senate.

Question. About what time of the day or night?

Answer. About eleven o'clock at night.

Question. Did you make the service then?

Answer. I did.

Question. Have you certified the fact on that paper?

Answer. Yes, sir.

Question. Is that certificate true?

Answer. It is.

Question. Will you read it?

Answer. Attached to this copy of the resolution is my certificate, in these words:

An attested copy of the foregoing resolution was placed in my hands by the Secretary of the Senate to be delivered to Brevet Major General Lorenzo Thomas, Adjutant General of the United States Army, and the same was by me delivered into the hands of General Thomas about the hour of eleven o'clock p. m. on the 21st day of February.
J. W. JONES.

Question. Is that certificate true?

Answer. It is, sir.

No cross-examination.

Mr. Manager WILSON. The document thus served is as follows:

IN EXECUTIVE SESSION,
SENATE OF THE UNITED STATES,
February 21, 1868.

Whereas the Senate have received and considered the communication of the President stating that he had removed Edwin M. Stanton, Secretary of War, and designated the Adjutant General of the Army to act as Secretary of War *ad interim:* Therefore,

Resolved by the Senate of the United States, That, under the Constitution and laws of the United States the President has no power to remove the Secretary of War and designate any other officer to perform the duties of that office *ad interim.*
Attest: J. W. FORNEY, *Secretary.*

Mr. Manager BUTLER. I desire to call C. E. Creecy, of the Treasury Department.

CHARLES E. CREECY sworn and examined.

By Mr. Manager BUTLER:

Question. What is your full name, and what is your official position, if any?

Answer. Charles Eaton Creecy; I am clerk in charge of the appointments in the Treasury Department.

Question. Will you look at the bundle of papers you have brought, in obedience to our subpœna, and give me the form of commission which was used in the Treasury Department before the passage of the act of March 2, 1867?

Answer. This is it; [producing a paper.]

Question. You produce this as such form?

Answer. Yes, sir; I do.

Question. Was that the ordinary form, or one used without exception?

Answer. It was the ordinary form for the permanent commission.

Mr. JOHNSON, and Mr. PATTERSON of Tennessee. We cannot hear one word.

Mr. HOWARD. The witness must speak louder.

Mr. JOHNSON. If his answer were repeated by the counsel it would be better.

Mr. Manager BUTLER. If it will not be considered improper, Mr. President, I will repeat the answer.

The CHIEF JUSTICE. The witness will speak for himself.

Mr. EVARTS. We prefer that the witness should speak so as to be heard.

Mr. Manager BUTLER. I have no desire to undertake the labor.

The CHIEF JUSTICE, (to the witness.) Mr. Creecy, you will raise your voice and speak as loud as possible.

The WITNESS. Yes, sir.

Mr. Manager BUTLER, (to the witness.) What is your answer, then? loud enough to be heard.

Mr. TRUMBULL. I think it would help us all to hear if the witness would stand further from the counsel. If he would stand on the other side of the Secretary's desk he would have to speak louder, and all could hear.

The CHIEF JUSTICE. That would be better. Mr. Creecy, you will go to the opposite side of the Secretary's desk.

The witness changed his position to the other side of the desk, and subsequent witnesses were examined, standing at the Secretary's desk, to the right of the presiding officer.

Mr. Manager BUTLER, (to the witness.) What is the answer to the question whether this is the ordinary form of commission used before March 2, 1867?

Answer. That is the ordinary form.

Question. For the class of appointments for which such commissions would be issued was there any other form used before that time?

Answer. I think that is the form for the permanent commission.

Question. Will you now give me the form which has been used since in the Treasury Department?

[The witness produced a paper and handed it to Mr. Manager BUTLER.]

Mr. STANBERY. Will the honorable Manager allow me to ask what is the object of this testimony?

Mr. Manager BUTLER. The object of this testimony is to show that prior to the passage of the act of March 2, 1867, known as the civil tenure-of-office bill, a certain form of commission had been used in the practice of the Government, and issued by the President of the United States; that after the passage of the civil tenure-of-office bill a new form was made conforming to the provisions of the tenure-of-office act, showing that the President acted in the Treasury Department under the tenure-of-office act as an actual and valid law. Is there any objection?

Mr. STANBERY. No, sir.

Mr. Manager BUTLER, (to the witness.) I return the first paper you handed me. I see there are certain interlineations; did you speak of the form before it was interlined, or subsequently, or both?

Answer. This is the commission. The alterations in this commission show the changes that have been made to conform to the tenure-of-office bill.

Question. There is a portion of that paper in print and a portion in writing. Do I understand you that the printed portion was the form used before?

Answer. Yes, sir.

Question. And the written portion shows the changes?

Answer. Yes, sir.

Question. Will you read with a loud voice so as to be heard the printed portion of the commission, the original commission, the whole commission?

Mr. CONNESS. I think if the reading should be done by the Clerk, who is in the habit of reading, it would be very much better for the whole Senate.

The CHIEF JUSTICE. The Secretary will read it.

The Secretary read as follows:

ANDREW JOHNSON,
President of the United States of America:
To all to whom these presents shall come, greeting:

Know ye, that reposing special trust and confidence in the integrity, diligence, and discretion of ——, I have nominated, and by and with the advice and consent of the Senate do appoint him —— and do authorize and empower him to execute and fulfill the duties of that office according to law, and to have and to hold the said office, with all the rights, privileges, and emoluments thereunto legally appertaining unto him the said —— during the pleasure of the President of the United States for the time being.

In testimony whereof I have caused these letters to be made patent and the seal of the Treasury Department of the United States to be hereunto affixed.

Given under my hand at the city of Washington the —— day of —— in the year of our Lord 18—, and of the independence of the United States of America the ——.

By the President:

—— ,
Secretary of the Treasury.

Question. Please state what was the alteration made of that printed form to conform to the provisions of the tenure-of-office act?

Answer. The words "during the pleasure of the President of the United States for the time being"——

Mr. JOHNSON. We cannot hear. The Clerk had better read those words.

The SECRETARY. The words written are as follows: "Until a successor shall have been appointed and duly qualified."

Mr. JOHNSON. What are the words stricken out?

The SECRETARY. The words stricken out are "during the pleasure of the President of the United States for the time being."

By Mr. Manager BUTLER:

Question. Since that act has any other form of commission been used than the one as altered for such permanent appointments?

Answer. No, sir.

Question. Have you now a form of official bond for officers as used prior to the civil tenure-of-office act?

Answer. Yes, sir; [producing a paper.]

Question. Has any change been made in that?

Answer. No, sir.

Question. Please give me, if you have it, a copy of the commissions issued for temporary appointments since the tenure-of-office act?

Mr. STANBERY. Is the bond put in?

Mr. Manager BUTLER. It is.

Mr. STANBERY. Will you have it read?

Mr. Manager BUTLER. No, unless you desire it. It is the common, ordinary form of bond.

Mr. STANBERY. Let me see it.

[The paper was handed to Mr. Stanbery, and read by him.]

Mr. Manager BUTLER, (to the witness.) State whether the printed part of this paper was the part in use prior to the tenure-of-office act?

Answer. It was.

Mr. CURTIS. What is the paper?

Mr. Manager BUTLER. The paper is the form of commission for temporary appointments. Will the Secretary read it?

The Secretary read as follows:

The President of the United States of America,
To all to whom these presents shall come, greeting:
Know ye, that reposing special trust and confidence in the integrity, diligence, and discretion of ——
——, I do appoint him —— —— and do authorize and empower him to execute and fulfill the duties of that office according to law, and to have and to hold the said office with all the rights, privileges, and emoluments thereunto legally appertaining, unto him the said ——, during the pleasure of the President of the United States for the time being, until the end of the next session of the Senate of the United States, and no longer.
In testimony whereof I have caused these letters to be made patent, and the seal of the Treasury Department of the United States to be hereunto affixed.
Given under my hand, at the city of Washington, this —— day of ——, in the year of our Lord 18—, and of the independence of the United States of America the ——.
By the President:

Secretary of the Treasury.

By Mr. Manager BUTLER:

Question. Was any change made in that commission?

Answer. The alteration shows the change.

Mr. Manager BUTLER. Read the alteration, Mr. Secretary.

The SECRETARY. Strike out "during the pleasure of the President of the United States for the time being," and insert "unless this commission be sooner revoked by the President of the United States for the time being."

By Mr. Manager BUTLER:

Question. Do you know whether before these changes were made the official opinion of the Solicitor of the Treasury was taken?

Answer. It was.

Question. Have you that opinion?

Answer. I have.

Mr. Manager BUTLER. I withdraw the question as to the opinion on consultation. [To the witness.] Do you know whether since the alteration of these forms any commissions have been issued signed by the President of the United States?

Answer. Yes, sir.

Question. As altered?

Answer. Yes, sir.

Question. It is suggested to me to ask you if the President had signed both forms—both the temporary and permanent forms as altered?

Answer. Yes, sir.

Question. Now look at the paper which I send you [handing a paper] and say what is that paper?

Answer. It is a commission issued to Mr. Cooper as Assistant Secretary of the Treasury.

Question. Under what date?

Answer. The 20th day of November, 1867.

Question. Who was Assistant Secretary of the Treasury at the time of the issuing of that commission?

Answer. Mr. W. E. Chandler was one.

Question. Do you happen to remember, as a matter of memory, whether the Senate was then in session?

Answer. I think it was not.

Question. State whether Mr. Cooper qualified and went into office under that first commission?

Answer. He did not qualify under the first commission at all.

Question. What is the paper I now send you? [Handing a paper.]

Answer. It is authority from the President to Edmund Cooper to act as Assistant Secretary of the Treasury.

Question. Read it.

Mr. EVARTS. Is the other considered as read, the one under which he did not qualify?

Mr. Manager BUTLER. Yes, sir; I meant so to consider it.

Mr. EVARTS. How are we ever to know the contents if they are not read when produced?

Mr. Manager BUTLER. It is exactly the same form as the other that has been read.

Mr. EVARTS. Then let it be so stated. We know nothing whatever about it.

Mr. Manager BUTLER. I will hand that first paper to the counsel.

[The paper was handed to the counsel for the President, examined by them, and returned.]

Mr. Manager BUTLER. Do the counsel for the President desire to have the paper read?

Mr. STANBERY. Certainly.

Mr. Manager BUTLER. Very well. Let the Secretary read it.

The Secretary read as follows:

ANDREW JOHNSON,
President of the United States of America:
To all who shall see these presents, greeting:

Know ye, that reposing special trust and confidence in the integrity and ability of Edmund Cooper, I do appoint him to be Assistant Secretary of the Treasury, and do authorize and empower him to execute and fulfill the duties of that office according to law, and to have and to hold the said office, with all the powers, privileges, and emoluments thereunto of right appertaining, unto him, the said Edmund Cooper, until the end of the next session of the Senate of the United States, and no longer, subject to the conditions prescribed by law.

In testimony whereof I have caused these letters to be made patent, and the seal of the United States to be hereunto affixed.

Given under my hand at the city of Washington, the 20th day of November, in the year of our [L. S.] Lord 1867, and of the independence of the United States of America the ninety-second.

ANDREW JOHNSON.

By the President:
WILLIAM H. SEWARD, Secretary of State.

Mr. Manager BUTLER, (to the witness.) Now, will you pass to the Secretary the letter of authority of which you have spoken, and let it be read?

The Secretary read as follows:

EXECUTIVE DEPARTMENT,
WASHINGTON, December 2, 1867.

Whereas a vacancy has occurred in the office of Assistant Secretary of the Treasury of the United States, in pursuance of the authority vested in me by the first section of the act of Congress approved February 13, 1795, entitled "An act to amend the act entitled 'An act making alterations in the Treasury and War Departments,'" Edmund Cooper is hereby authorized to perform the duties of Assistant Secretary of the Treasury until a successor be appointed or such vacancy be filled.

ANDREW JOHNSON.

By Mr. Manager BUTLER:

Question. How did Mr. Chandler get out of office?

Answer. He resigned.

Question. Have you a copy of his resignation?

Answer. I have not with me.

Question. Can you state from memory (if it is not objected to) at what time his resignation took effect?

Answer. I cannot. I think it was a day or two before this appointment or this authority was given to Mr. Cooper.

Question. Will you have the kindness to produce a copy of his resignation after you leave the stand?

Answer. I will try to do so.

Cross-examined by Mr. CURTIS:

Question. Can you fix the date when the change in the form of permanent appointments of which you have spoken first occurred?

Answer. I think it was about four days after the passage of the tenure-of-office act.

Question. With what confidence do you speak? Do you speak from any recollection?

Answer. We obtained an opinion from the Solicitor of the Treasury on the subject. It was given on the 6th, and from that day we followed his opinion.

Question. Then you would fix the date as the 6th of what month?

Answer. The 6th of March, 1867.

Hon. BURT VAN HORN sworn and examined.

By Mr. Manager BUTLER:

Question. Will you state whether you were present at the War Department when Major General Lorenzo Thomas, Adjutant General of the United States, was there to make demand for the office, property, books, and records?

Answer. I was.

Question. When was it?

Answer. It was on Saturday, the 22d of February, 1868, I believe.

Question. About what time in the day?

Answer. Perhaps a few minutes after eleven o'clock.

Question. Who were present?

Answer. General Charles H. Van Wyck, of New York; General G. M. Dodge, of Iowa; Hon. Freeman Clarke, of New York; Hon. J. K. Moorhead, of Pennsylvania; Hon. Columbus Delano, of Ohio; Hon. W. D. Kelley, of Pennsylvania; Hon. Thomas W. Ferry, of Michigan, and myself. The Secretary of War, Mr. Stanton, and his son were also present.

Question. Please state what took place.

Answer. The gentlemen mentioned and myself were in the office the Secretary of War usually occupies holding conversation; General Thomas came in; I saw him coming from the President's; he came into the building and came up stairs, and came into the Secretary's room first; he said, "Good morning, Mr. Secretary, and good morning gentlemen;" the Secretary replied, "Good morning," and I believe we all did; then began this conversation as follows: [Referring to a printed document.] "I am Secretary of War ad interim, and am ordered by the President of the United States to take charge of the office;" Mr. Stanton then replied, "I order you to repair to your room and exercise your functions as Adjutant General of the Army;" Mr. Thomas replied to this, "I am Secretary of War ad interim, and I shall not obey your orders; but I shall obey the orders of the President, who has ordered me to take charge of the War Office;" Mr. Stanton replied to this as follows, "As Secretary of War I order you to repair to your place as Adjutant General;" Mr. Thomas replied, "I shall not do so;" Mr. Stanton then said in reply, "Then you may stand there if you please," pointing to Mr. Thomas, "but you cannot act as Secretary of War; if you do, you do so at your peril;" Mr. Thomas replied to this, "I shall act as Secretary of War;" this was the conversation, I may say, in the Secretary's room.

Question. What happened then?

Answer. After that they went to the room of General Schriver, which is just across the hall, opposite the Secretary's room.

Question. Who went first?

Answer. I think, if I remember aright, that General Thomas went first, and was holding some conversation with General Schriver, which I did not hear. He was followed by Mr. Stanton, by General Moorhead, by General Ferry, and then by myself. Some little conversation was had there, which I did not hear; but after I got into the room, which was but a moment after they went in, however, Mr. Stanton addressed Mr. Thomas as follows, which I concluded was the summing up of the conversation had before——

Mr. CURTIS. No matter about that.

The WITNESS. Mr. Stanton then said, "Then you claim to be here as Secretary of War and refuse to obey my orders?" Mr. Thomas said, "I do, sir; I shall require the mails of the War Department to be delivered to me, and shall transact all the business of the War Department." That is the substance of the conversation which I heard, and, in fact, the conversation as I heard it entirely.

By Mr. Manager BUTLER:

Question. Did you make any memorandum of it afterward?

Answer. I made it at the time. I had my memorandum in my hand. When the conversation began I had paper and pencil and wrote it down as the conversation occurred, and after the conversation ended I drew it up from my pencil sketches in writing immediately in the office in the presence of the gentlemen who heard it.

Question. What was done after that? Where did Thomas go?

Answer. It was then after eleven o'clock, and my duties and the duties of the rest of us called us here to the House, and I left General Thomas in the room of General Schriver.

Cross-examined by Mr. STANBERY:

Question. Will you please state what was your business in the War Department on that morning?

Answer. Well, sir, I went there that morning, I suppose, as other gentlemen did; at least, I went there for the purpose of visiting the Secretary. I had no special public business.

Question. Was there no object in the visit, except merely to see him?

Answer. Yes, sir; I had an object. The times were rather exciting at that moment, and I went, as much as anything else, to talk with the Secretary, to confer with him about public affairs.

Question. Public affairs generally?

C. I.—8.

Answer. No, not public business particularly.

Question. What public affairs were the object of the conference?

Answer. Well, sir, the matter of the removal of Mr. Stanton. I felt an interest in that matter, and of course was talking with him upon that subject.

Question. Did you go with these other gentlemen whom you found there, or did you go there alone?

Answer. I think I did go in company with one or two of them.

Question. With whom did you go in company?

Answer. I think I went with Mr. Clarke, of New York, and General Van Wyck. I am not certain that any others were with me.

Question. When you arrived at his room what was the hour?

Answer. It was a little before eleven o'clock.

Question. Whom did you find there when you arrived? These other gentlemen whom you have mentioned?

Answer. Not all of them.

Question. Who were there when you arrived?

Answer. I think General Moorhead was there for one; I think Mr. Ferry was there; I think Mr. Delano was there. Two or three others came in after I got there.

Question. Do you know what their business was in the office that morning?

Answer. No, sir.

Question. Did they state any business?

Answer. No, sir; they stated no business to me.

Question. All being there, the next thing was that General Thomas came into the room?

Answer. After we had been there some moments.

Question. You say that when that conversation began between General Thomas and the Secretary you were ready to take notes?

Answer. I appeared to be ready. I had a large white envelope in my pocket, and I had a pencil also in my pocket; and when the conversation began it seemed to me that it might be well to note what was said.

Question. Are you in the habit, generally, in conversations of that kind, of making memoranda of what is said?

Answer. I do not know that I am, unless I deem it important to do so.

Question. Did any one request you take memoranda?

Answer. No, sir.

Question. It was on your own motion?

Answer. On my own responsibility, supposing I had a perfect right to do so.

Question. Undoubtedly. After the conversation was ended in the room with the Secretary, General Thomas, as I understand you, went out first?

Answer. I think he did; he went across the hall.

Question. Who went with the Secretary from his room across the hall to where General Thomas had gone?

Answer. I am not aware that any one went directly with him, but immediately after him, if not with him, General MOORHEAD and Mr. FERRY.

Question. How long after General Thomas had left the office was it that the Secretary of War followed him?

Answer. But a moment or two; perhaps two minutes.

Question. Did he state, when he left, what was his object?

Answer. I do not recollect that the Secretary stated anything. General Thomas was in the room talking.

Question. Did he request any gentleman to go along with him?

Answer. Not that I am aware of.

Question. Did you go upon your own motion, or by agreement?

Answer. I went upon my own motion.

Question. All that were there did not go?

Answer. I do not think they all went in. I think they did not all go in at that time. The two gentlemen named, I know, went in before me.

Question. How long after the Secretary went did you go?

Answer. Perhaps it was a minute. It was very soon. I followed the other two gentlemen very soon.

Question. What had taken place between the Secretary and General Thomas before you arrived in the room, or had anything?

Answer. I cannot say. They had some conversation; I cannot say what was said.

Question. As you have given the conversation in your notes, it would seem as if it then began after you first got in?

Answer. The conversation I have given began after I got in. As I said before, I heard some talking; but I do not know what was said.

Question. You mean you heard some talking before you got in there?

Answer. Certainly.

Question. Whose voices?

Answer. I heard General Thomas's voice and Mr. Stanton's voice. They had some conversation.

Question. But what that was you do not know?

Answer. I do not.

Question. Then the conversation followed which you have detailed?

Answer. Certainly. The first I heard when I went in was the question of Mr. Stanton, which I have stated, and the answer of General Thomas.

Question. Did you keep your notes with you and take your notes into that room?

Answer. I had my envelope in my hand when I went in.

Question. And your pencil?

Answer. And my pencil.

Question. Where is that envelope which you had at that time?

Answer. I cannot say. I presume it was destroyed. The envelope was a large, long, white envelope that I put in my pocket with letters. It was the only convenient thing I had at the time. I wrote on both sides of it, and then drew it off immediately on the Secretary's table.

Question. What did you do with that original memorandum—the envelope?

Answer. I presume it is torn up and destroyed; I do not know anything to the contrary.

Question. When did you destroy it?

Answer. That I cannot say; perhaps very soon after the conversation took place.

Question. Why did you destroy it?

Answer. I cannot say that it is destroyed; but I have no knowledge of it now. I cannot say that it is destroyed; perhaps it may be. I had no occasion to keep it. I supposed there was no occasion to keep it, because I had written the thing off, or rather, a young man wrote it off at the table as I read it, and that is the same thing, I suppose, and I compared what he wrote after it was written with the notes, because I wanted to be particular in regard to it.

Question. Is the document from which you have read here to-day a manuscript?

Answer. No, sir; it is my testimony before the committee, which is an exact copy of the notes I took.

Question. And those notes were written by some young man who was present?

Answer. At my suggestion he took the pen, and I read to him, and then compared it, and found it word for word.

Question. Where are those notes?

Answer. I do not know where they can be found. I did not suppose it important to keep the notes, because I had a copy of the notes before the committee and testified to it exactly.

Question. A copy of what notes do you mean?

Answer. I had the notes I took there.

Question. You mean the notes written by that young man?

Answer. Yes, sir; I had them there.

Question. What is his name? Who was he?

Answer. One of the clerks there. I do not recollect what the young man's name was. I do not know that I ever knew his name. I did not ask him his name. I would know him if I saw him.

Question. You preserved those notes until you testified?

Answer. Yes, sir.

Question. How long after you testified did you preserve them?

Answer. I cannot say that I kept them any length of time after that. I thought it was of no consequence.

Question. How you disposed of the envelope, or how you disposed of those notes, you have no recollection?

Answer. No, sir; I cannot say what became of the envelope; it may be in my papers somewhere.

Question. Have you made any search for them?

Answer. No, sir; my attention has not been called to that before.

Question. When you came back into the Secretary's room who suggested to you, or did you suggest the matter yourself, that the notes should be written out? How did that come to be?

Answer. It was upon my own motion.

Question. Did you ask for a clerk?

Answer. I had taken notes and proposed in the presence of the gentlemen who heard the conversation that they should see that I had them correct; and that was consented to by General MOORHEAD, Mr. KELLEY, and others who were present.

Question. Then you proposed to have them copied?

Answer. I proposed to have them drawn off. A young man was there ready to do it or willing to do it, and I asked him to write it out as I would read it to him from my notes.

Question. Now, did anything else take place in General Schriver's room besides this talk that you have testified to?

Answer. Not that I am aware of; only, as I have said, I heard some voices in there; but what was said I cannot say.

Question. After you went in, while you were there.

Answer. I think there was no conversation.

Question. I did not ask you simply for conversation, but what else took place?

Answer. Nothing took place that I am aware of.

Question. Who first left the room?

Answer. After this conversation?

Question. Yes, sir.

Answer. I cannot say whether I left it first or General MOORHEAD or Mr. FERRY. We were all there. I think we went out in a moment afterward.

Question. Did you leave Mr. Stanton there?

Answer. Mr. Stanton was there when I went out.

Question. Did you go into his room from there?

Answer. I did, sir.

Question. Did you leave Thomas there, also?

Answer. Yes, sir.

Question. How long did Mr. Stanton remain in Schriver's room?

Answer. I cannot say, because as soon as I had this copied I left for the House.

Question. Do you mean to say that he did not come in while you were engaged in having the copy taken?

Answer. At the moment of making the copy? I will not say that he came in while the copy was being taken or not. There was a short time consumed in taking it. He might have done so, but I will not say.

Question. Do you recollect whether you saw him at all in his office after you had left Schriver's room?

Answer. I cannot swear positively that I did. I saw him after I left the room. The doors were open. There are but a few feet from one room to the other. I saw him sitting in General Schriver's room. I will not swear positively that I saw him in his own office after I left that room.

Question. What took place between them afterward you do not know?

Answer. No, sir. I do not know because I left.

Question. Was there any friendly greeting or other circumstance took place at that time between the Secretary and General Thomas while you were in Schriver's room?

Answer. Well, sir, if there was, I did not see it. I do not know that there was while I was in. What happened before I cannot say.

Question. Was the memorandum that you made on that envelope complete or abbreviated?

Answer. The questions and answers as I have them were complete.

Question. Was the copy, then, an exact transcript of the memorandum?

Answer. It was merely questions and answers. The questions were short and the answers were short.

Question. Did it exhibit the whole conversation?

Answer. I cannot say. I will not say that it did every word. I think it did not. I recollect one expression, for instance, that General Thomas made that I did not put down; I did not think it material. I can state it if the court desire it. It occurs to me now. It is one expression that was used. I can state it if the gentleman wishes.

Question. All I want to know is whether it completely covered the conversation?

Answer. It covered all the conversation of any importance.

Question. That you thought important?

Answer. At least what I wrote. I wrote down just as the questions were given and answered. I took all the conversation in substance, and all of any account as it was had as the questions and answers were given.

Question. This conversation that you took down in that way, did you take it down in short hand?

Answer. No, sir; I did not.

Question. You wrote it out?

Answer. I wrote it out.

Question. Without abbreviation?

Answer. Without abbreviation.

Question. Were there pauses in their conversation? Did they pause to allow you to follow them?

Answer. The conversation, as I said before, was very slow and deliberate. There was sufficient time for me to write these questions and answers, as they were short, as counsel can see. General Thomas said but very little.

Question. Now, I will ask you if, in that conversation, Mr. Stanton asked him if he wished him to vacate immediately, or would give him time to arrange his private papers?

Answer. Mr. Stanton?

Question. Yes, sir; did Mr. Stanton ask Mr. Thomas whether he wished him to vacate immediately, or whether he would accord him (Stanton) time to arrange his private papers?

Answer. There was nothing said in that conversation in reference to that. There were other conversations, I understand, at other times, at which such remarks were made, as I saw in the papers; but there was nothing of that kind said at that time in that conversation. The question of giving time and changing papers did not come up in that conversation at all.

Reëxamined by Mr. Manager BUTLER:

Question. You said, if I understood you, that there was a single remark of Thomas that you did not write down, that now occurred to you, in answer to the counsel for the President; what was that remark?

Answer. I said that in answer to his question whether I had sworn to all that he did say. I recollect now General Thomas saying he did not wish any "*on*pleasantness." I did not think it necessary to put that in my record.

Question. Did he emphasize it in that "*on*pleasantness?"

Answer. The gentlemen heard it, and it was spoken of afterward, but I did not think it was anything pertaining to this question; and perhaps some other little words were said now and then that did not amount to anything.

Question. I must still ask you to give to the Senate with a little more distinctness whether it was the remark, saying, "I do not want any unpleasantness between us," or was it the use of what has almost become a technical term, that "there shall not be any *on*pleasantness?"

Answer. Well, sir, I can only state what General Thomas said.

Question. The emphasis is something.

Answer. "*On*pleasantness" was the expression used.

By Mr. STANBERY:

Question. This evidence is as to a word; I do not know its materiality; but did he speak the word in the ordinary way?

Answer. He spoke it in the way I have mentioned.

Question. Now give his expression?

Answer. He said as he came in, in connection with what I have said—I did not consider it material, and did not put it down—that he did not wish any "*on*pleasantness."

Question. In what part of the conversation did that come in?

Answer. Somewhere in the first part of the conversation; it was in the first part.

Question. Was it in the first part or after Stanton had ordered him to go to his room?

Answer. I think it was before that—in the forepart of his conversation.

Question. At the very beginning?

Answer. Yes, sir; near the beginning.

Question. Had you taken down anything before that was said?

Answer. Yes, sir; the first thing he said was, "Good morning, Mr. Secretary," and "Good morning, gentlemen."

Question. Did you take that down?

Answer. I did, sir.

Question. You thought that was material?

Answer. I took it down.

Question. Then next, after that, did he say he did not wish any unpleasantness?

Answer. I cannot say that the next words he said after that were those. It was in the forepart of the conversation.

Question. But that you thought immaterial?

Answer. I did not put it down; I thought, perhaps, it was immaterial. It occurs to me now, as I know it excited something of a smile at the time he spoke it.

Mr. Manager BINGHAM. As I understand it, the counsel are desiring to know of the witness what he thought of the importance that ought to be attached to the word. I suppose it is not for the witness to swear what he thought about it.

Mr. EVARTS. We are cross-examining as to the completeness or perfection of the witness's memorandum. It certainly is material to know why he omitted some parts and inserted others.

Mr. Manager BINGHAM. We will not press the objection.

Mr. STANBERY. We have nothing further to ask of this witness.

Hon. JAMES K. MOORHEAD sworn and examined.

By Mr. Manager BUTLER:

Question. I believe you are a member of the House of Representatives?

Answer. I am.

Question. We have learned from the testimony of the last witness that you were present at Mr. Secretary Stanton's office when General Thomas came in there to make some demand; will you state now in your own way, as well as you can, what took place there, assisting your memory, if you have any memorandum, as you please?

Answer. I will, sir. I was present at the War Department on Saturday morning, the 22d of February, I believe, and I understood that General Thomas was to be there to take possession of the Department that morning. I went from my boarding-house, which is Mrs. Carter's on the hill; I went to the War Department in company with Dr. BURLEIGH, who boarded there, a friend of Mr. Johnson's, who told me he had had a conversation with General Thomas the night before——

Mr. CURTIS. That is not material.

The WITNESS. I was giving the reason why

I went there. I was there, and General Thomas came in. The testimony of Mr. VAN HORN is correct as to what passed. I did not take any memorandum of the early part of the conversation; but I would corroborate his statement——

Mr. CURTIS. That we object to.

Mr. STANBERY. That will not do.

The WITNESS, (continuing.) Until the point at which he said General Thomas went across to General Schriver's room. He did go there; he was followed by Mr. Stanton, and Mr. Stanton asked me to go over there. After they got there Mr. Stanton put a direct question to General Thomas, and asked me to remember it. He said, "General MOORHEAD, I want you to take notice of this and of the answer;" and that induced me to make a memorandum of it, which I think I have among my papers now. [The witness proceeded to search his papers.] It is very brief, and was made roughly, but so I thought I could understand and know what it meant myself, and I can explain it to any person. [Reading.] Mr. Stanton said, "General Thomas, you claim to be here as Secretary of War, and refuse to obey my orders?" General Thomas replied, "I do, sir." After that had passed I walked to the door leading into the hall and I was called back, or from what I heard my attention was attracted so that I returned. Mr. Stanton then said, "General Thomas requires the mails of the Department to be delivered to him." General Thomas said: "I require the mails of the Department to be delivered to me, and I will transact the business of the office." I had not heard General Thomas say this entirely and clearly, but Mr. Stanton repeated it in this way, and said: "General Thomas says 'I require the mails of the Department to be delivered to me, and I will transact the business of the office.'" I asked General Thomas if he had made use of those words. I asked him if he had stated this; and he assented, and added: "You may make it as full as you please."

That is all the memorandum I made, and I made that at the time and place.

Cross-examined by Mr. STANBERY:

Question. When you arrived at Mr. Stanton's office whom did you find there?

Answer. I did not make a memorandum of that, and I cannot tell exactly. There were a number of members of Congress. When Mr. VAN HORN was reciting the names, I recognized them as having been there, and I remember Judge KELLEY in addition to the names mentioned.

[Mr. VAN HORN sitting in the Chamber said, "I mentioned him."]

Question. How long had you been at the office before General Thomas came in?

Answer. I think about half an hour.

Question. Did you see him coming?

Answer. Yes, sir; I saw him coming. The windows opened out toward the White House,

and it was announced by some person near the window that General Thomas was coming; and I, with some others, got up and looked out of the window and saw him coming along the walk, and we expected somewhat of a scene then.

Question. When he came in, did he come in attended, or was he alone?

Answer. He was alone.

Question. Was he armed in any way?

Answer. I did not notice any arms.

Question. Side arms or others?

Answer. I did not notice anything except what the Almighty had given him.

Question. Now, state just what took place and what was said after he came in, according to your own recollection?

Answer. I think I have stated it about as well as I can. When he came in he passed the compliments, "Good morning, Mr. Secretary;" and "Good morning, gentlemen;" and I think Mr. Stanton asked him if he had any business with him.

Question. Did Mr. Stanton return his salute?

Answer. Yes, sir; I think so.

Question. Was Mr. Stanton sitting or standing?

Answer. During the time I was there he was doing both; I cannot tell exactly what he was doing at the time General Thomas spoke to him, but he was down and up and walking around, sometimes sitting, sometimes standing.

Question. Did he ask the General to take a seat?

Answer. I think not, sir.

Question. Did he take a seat?

Answer. No, sir; he did not; he did not in that room. I think he took a seat when he went into General Schriver's room.

Question. But he neither took a seat nor, as you recollect, was asked to take a seat?

Answer. Not that I recollect.

Question. After these good mornings passed what was the next thing?

Answer. General Thomas said that he was there as Secretary of War *ad interim;* he was appointed by the President, and came to take possession.

Question. Was there nothing said before that?

Answer. Not to my recollection. I took no memorandum of anything before that, and before what I have stated already.

Question. Did I not understand you to say that Mr. Stanton, when he came in and the salutes were passed, asked him what business he had with him?

Answer. Yes, sir; and in reply to that he said what I have stated. I did not know you wished me to repeat what I had stated. I stated that.

Question. In reply to that question of Mr. Stanton, what did Mr. Thomas say?

Answer. He said he was there as Secretary of War *ad interim,* to take possession of the office. Mr. Stanton told him: "General Thomas, I am Secretary of War; you are the

Adjutant General; I order you to your room, sir."

Question. He ordered him to his room?

Answer. Yes, sir.

Question. What was the reply?

Answer. The reply was that he would not obey the order; that he (Thomas) was Secretary of War *ad interim.*

Question. What followed that?

Answer. I do not know that there was anything further. Very soon after that General Thomas retired over to General Schriver's room; Mr. Stanton followed him and asked me to go over, and I have given you what occurred there.

Question. After General Thomas left, did Mr. Stanton tell you why he wanted you to accompany him?

Answer. No.

Question. But he asked you to go with him?

Answer. Yes, sir.

Question. Did you know where he was going?

Answer. I knew he was going over to that room.

Question. Did you know he was going to have a further conversation with General Thomas?

Answer. I expected so; but he did not say so.

Question. Did he ask any one else besides yourself to go?

Answer. I expect not.

Question. Did any one else go besides yourself?

Answer. Mr. Van Horn and some other gentleman followed.

Question. Did you get into the room as soon as Mr. Stanton?

Answer. Immediately after him.

Question. Did you get there before any conversation began?

Answer. I think about the time. I followed immediately, and there was no conversation of any marked significance until that which I have mentioned.

Question. What was the conversation, significant or not, that took place between Mr. Stanton and General Thomas after you got into that room?

Answer. I cannot recite it, because, as I told you, I did not take a memorandum of it, and it was not important enough to be impressed on my mind. I do not recollect.

Question. But you have an impression that there was some?

Answer. I think there was some—perhaps joking or something of that kind. They appeared to be in pretty good humor with each other.

Question. That is, the parties did not seem to be in any passion at all?

Answer. Not hostile.

Question. But in good humor?

Answer. Yes, sir.

Question. Joking?

Answer. Yes, sir.

Question. Do you recollect any of the jokes that passed?

Answer. No, sir.

Question. Then who first commenced the serious conversation in Schriver's room?

Answer. Mr. Stanton, I think, asked this question.

Question. When the question was answered, as I understand, Mr. Stanton desired you to remember it?

Answer. Yes, sir.

Question. And then immediately you left the room?

Answer. Very shortly after.

Question. Do you recollect anything said between them except that before you left the room?

Answer. No, sir; I do not.

Question. Did you get back to Mr. Stanton's room, or only into the ante-chamber or hall, and then return?

Answer. I had got back to Mr. Stanton's room, I think, or to the door.

Question. What then induced you to return to General Schriver's room?

Answer. I found there was some question asked there then that I thought was important, and I paid some attention to that, and I then went to hear what that was; and then Mr. Stanton told me that he wanted me to take notice of that.

Question. That was as to the mails of the Department?

Answer. Yes, sir.

Question. Anything further?

Answer. Yes, sir; what I read. There was, in addition to the mails of the Department, a statement that he was there as Secretary of War.

Question. After that did you remain any longer in Schriver's room?

Answer. No, sir; I think not.

Question. Who came out first, Mr. Stanton or yourself?

Answer. I came out first and left Mr. Stanton there.

Question. How long did Mr. Stanton remain there after you left?

Answer. I think a very short time, for I left about that time to go to the Capitol. It was then getting on toward twelve o'clock; and I left, and I know I did not get to the Capitol till after twelve o'clock.

Question. Did all the company then leave?

Answer. Most of them left. I think the members of the House all left.

Question. Who stayed?

Answer. I do not remember who stayed. There were a number of gentlemen there, though.

Question. Who do you recollect was there, besides members of the House?

Answer. I cannot call to mind now or give the name of a gentleman that was there, but I know there were others.

Question. Were any other gentlemen there except the regular clerks of the Department at that time?

Answer. Yes, sir; others than clerks of the Department.

Question. Were they military men or civilians?

Answer. During some part of the morning there was a military man there. I believe during the time I was there I saw General Grant there.

Question. At what time was he there?

Answer. I think it was during that morning; but I am not certain. I have been there a good many times, and I have seen him there at different times.

Question. Was he there during either of these conversations that you have mentioned?

Answer. No, sir; he was not present at the conversations.

Question. Was it before or after the conversations that General Grant came in?

Answer. I have stated that I was not distinct about the time, nor certain whether it was that morning or at another, but I rather think he was there during that morning.

Question. Do you recollect any observation on the part of General Thomas to the effect that he wished no unpleasantness?

Answer. I do not think I recollect his using that term.

Question. Anything like it?

Answer. No, sir; I do not.

Question. Did there appear to be any unpleasantness?

Answer. There did not; General Thomas wanted to get in, I thought, and Mr. Stanton did not want to go out.

Question. But there was nothing offensive on either side?

Answer. There was nothing very belligerent on either side.

Question. Was there any joking in Mr. Stanton's room as well as in Schriver's room?

Answer. No, sir.

Question. Any occasion for a laugh?

Answer. It was more stern in Mr. Stanton's room, as he once or twice ordered General Thomas to go to his room as a subordinate.

Question. That was the only thing that looked like sternness?

Answer. That was rather stern, I thought.

Reëxamined by Mr. Manager BUTLER:

Question. The counsel for the President asked you if General Thomas was armed on that occasion: will you allow me to ask if on that occasion he was masked?

Answer. He was not, sir.

Hon. WALTER A. BURLEIGH sworn and examined.

By Mr. Manager BUTLER:

Question. What is your name and position?

Answer. My name is WALTER A. BURLEIGH. At present I am a Delegate from Dakota Territory in the lower House of Congress.

Question. Do you know Lorenzo Thomas, Adjutant General of the Army?

Answer. I do, sir.

Question. How long have you known him?

Answer. For several years; I cannot say how many.

Question. Have you been on terms of intimacy with him?

Answer. I have been.

Question. He visiting your house, and you his?

Answer. Yes, sir.

Question. Do you remember an occasion when you had some conversation with Mr. MOORHEAD about visiting Mr. Stanton's office? Do you remember that you had such a conversation?

Answer. I recollect going to the Secretary of War with Mr. MOORHEAD on the morning of the 22d of February last, I think.

Question. Had you on the evening before seen General Thomas?

Answer. I had.

Question. Where?

Answer. At his house.

Question. What time in the evening?

Answer. In the early part of the evening; I cannot name precisely the hour.

Question. Had you a conversation with him?

Answer. Yes, sir.

Mr. STANBERY. Wait a moment, if you please. What is the relevancy of that to this inquiry? I understand this is about a conversation of this witness with General Thomas.

Mr. Manager BUTLER. The object is to show the intent and purpose with which General Thomas went to the War Department on the morning of the 22d of February; that he went with the intent and purpose of taking possession by force; that he alleged that intent and purpose; that in consequence of that allegation Mr. BURLEIGH invited General MOORHEAD and went up to the War Office. The conversation which I expect to prove is this: after the President of the United States had appointed General Thomas and given him directions to take the War Office, and after he had made a quiet visit there on the 21st, on the evening of the 21st he told Mr. BURLEIGH that the next day he was going to take possession by force. Mr. BURLEIGH said to him——

Mr. STANBERY. No matter about that. We object to that testimony.

Mr. Manager BUTLER. You do not know what you object to if you do not hear what I offer.

Mr. STANBERY. We object to it.

Mr. CURTIS. We know sufficiently for the purpose of the objection.

The CHIEF JUSTICE. The Chief Justice thinks the testimony is competent, and it will be heard unless the Senate think otherwise.

Mr. DRAKE. I suppose, sir, that the question of the competency of evidence in this court is a matter to be determined by the Senate and not by the presiding officer of the court. The question should be submitted, I think, sir, to the Senate. I take exception to the presiding officer of the court undertaking to decide a point of that kind.

The CHIEF JUSTICE. The Chief Justice is of opinion that it is his duty to decide preliminarily upon objections to evidence. If he is incorrect in that opinion it will be for the Senate to correct him.

Mr. DRAKE. I appeal, sir, from the decision of the Chair, and demand a vote of the Senate upon the question.

Mr. FOWLER. Mr. Chief Justice, I beg to know what your decision is?

The CHIEF JUSTICE. The Chief Justice states to the Senate that in his judgment it is his duty to decide upon questions of evidence in the first instance, and that if any Senator desires that the question shall then be submitted to the Senate it is his duty to submit it. So far as he is aware, that has been the usual course of practice in trials of persons impeached in the House of Lords and in the Senate of the United States.

Mr. DRAKE. My position, Mr. President, is that there is nothing in the rules of this Senate sitting upon the trial of an impeachment which gives that authority to the Chief Justice presiding over the body.

Mr. FESSENDEN. The Senator is out of order.

Mr. JOHNSON. I call the honorable member from Missouri [Mr. DRAKE] to order. The question is not debatable in the Senate.

Mr. DRAKE. I am not debating it; I am stating my point of order.

The CHIEF JUSTICE. The Senator will come to order.

Mr. Manager BUTLER. If the President please, is not this question debatable?

The CHIEF JUSTICE. It is debatable by the Managers and counsel for the defendant; not by Senators.

Mr. Manager BUTLER. We have the honor, Mr. President and gentlemen of the Senate, to object to the ruling just attempted to be made by the presiding officer of the Senate; and, with the utmost submission, but with an equal degree of firmness, we must insist upon our objection, because, otherwise, it would always put the Managers in the condition, when the ruling was against them, of appealing to the Senate as a parliamentary body against the ruling of the Chair. We have been too long in parliamentary and other bodies not to know how much disadvantage it is to be put in that position—the position, whether real or apparent, of appealing from the ruling of the presiding officer of the Senate. We are very glad that this question has come up upon a ruling of the presiding officer which is in our favor, so that we do not appear to be invidious in making the objection. Although it has fallen from the presiding officer that he understands that all the precedents are in the direction of his intimation of opinion, yet, if we understand the position taken, the precedents are not in support of that position. Lest I should have the misfortune to misstate the position of the presiding

officer of the Senate, I will state it as I understand it, subject to his correction.

I understand the position to be that primarily, as a judge in court would have the right to do, the presiding officer of the Senate claims the right to rule a question of law, and then if any member of the court chooses to object, it must be done in the nature of an appeal, as taken by one Senator just now. If I am incorrect in my statement of the position of the presiding officer I beg to be corrected.

The CHIEF JUSTICE. The Chief Justice will state the rule which he conceives to be applicable, once more. In this body he is the presiding officer; he is so in virtue of his high office under the Constitution. He is Chief Justice of the United States, and therefore, when the President of the United States is tried by the Senate, it is his duty to preside in that body; and, as he understands, he is therefore the President of the Senate sitting as a court of impeachment. The rule of the Senate which applies to this question is the seventh rule, which declares that "the presiding officer may, in the first instance, submit to the Senate, without a division, all questions of evidence and incidental questions." He is not required by that rule so to submit those questions in the first instance; but for the dispatch of business, as is usual in the Supreme Court, he expresses his opinion in the first instance. If the Senate who constitute the court, or any member of it, desires the opinion of the Senate to be taken, it is his duty then to ask for the opinion of the court.

Mr. Manager BUTLER. May I respectfully inquire whether that would extend to a Manager; whether a Manager would have the right to ask that a question of law should be submitted to the Senate?

The CHIEF JUSTICE. The Chief Justice thinks not. It must be by the action of the court or a member of it.

Mr. Manager BUTLER. Then this matter becomes of very important and momentous substance, because the presiding officer, who is not a member of the court, who has no vote in the court, as we understand it, except possibly upon a question of equal division, gives a decision on a question of law, it may be of the first importance, which, if made, precludes the House of Representatives from asking even that the Senate, who are the triers, shall pass upon it. Therefore if this is to be adopted as a rule our hands are tied; and it was in order to get the exact rule that I have asked the presiding officer of the Senate to state, as he has kindly and fully stated, his exact position.

The CHIEF JUSTICE. Mr. Manager, the Chief Justice has no doubt of the right of the honorable Managers to propose any question they see fit to the Senate, but it is for the Senate itself to determine how a question shall be taken.

Mr. Manager BUTLER. I understand the

distinction. It is a plain one. The Managers may propose a question to the Senate, and the Chief Justice decides it, and we then cannot get the question we propose before the Senate unless through the courtesy of some Senator. I think I state the position with accuracy; and it is the one to which we object, I again say, respectfully as we ought, but firmly, as we must.

Now, how are the precedents upon this question? Sorry I am to be obliged to deny the position taken by the presiding officer of the Senate, that the precedents in this country and England are with him. I understand that this question, as a question of precedents in England, has been settled many, many years, hundreds of years. Not expecting that it would arise here, I have not at hand at this moment all the books to which I could refer, but I can give a leading case where this question arose. If I am not mistaken, it arose in the trial of Lord Strafford, in the thirty-second year of the reign of Charles II. The House of Lords had a rule prior to the trial of Strafford, by which the Commons were bound to address the lord high steward as his grace or "my lord," precisely as the counsel for the respondent seem to think themselves obliged to address the presiding officer of this body as "Mr. Chief Justice." When the preliminaries of the trial of Strafford and the other popish lords were settled, the Commons objected that, as a part of the Parliament of Great Britain, they ought not to be called upon through their managers to address any individual whatever, and that their address should be made to the Lords in Parliament. A committee of conference between the Commons and Peers was thereupon had, and the rule previously adopted in the House of Lords was, after much consideration, rescinded, and a rule was reported and adopted in that trial, and it has obtained ever since in all other trials. The result of the conference is stated in this way:

"On the 29th of November, 1680, it is agreed at the joint committee, upon the objection made by the Commons to one of the rules laid down by the Lords, viz: 'That when the Commons should ask any questions at the trial they should apply themselves to the lord steward, that the managers should speak to the Lords as a House, and say 'my lords,' and not to the lord high steward, and say 'my lord' or 'your grace.'"

A reason being given that the lord high steward was not a necessary part of the court, but only as Speaker of the House of Lords, and the Lords themselves were the only body of triers. When Lord Strafford came to the bar the Lords, conformably to this doctrine, on the 29th of November, 1680, order—

"That the Lord Strafford shall be directed to apply himself to the Lords, and not to the lord high steward, as often as he shall have occasion to speak at his trial."

And from that day to the latest trial in Parliament, which is the Earl of Cardigan case in 1841, the rule has been followed. Earl Cardigan being tried in the House of Lords, Lord Chief Justice Denman presided upon that trial, and in that case, as in all the others, the body was universally addressed by counsel on all sides, by prisoner, by managers, by everybody, as "my lords," so that there should be no recognition of any superior right in the presiding officer over any other member of the assembly. Nor need I upon this matter of precedents stop here. In more than these cases this question has arisen. In Lord Macclesfield's case in 1724, if I remember aright, the point arose whether the presiding officer should decide an incidental question on the trial; but in every case Lord Chief Justice King referred all questions wholly to the Lords, saying to the Lords "You may decide as you please."

Again, when Lord Erskine presided on the trial of Lord Melville, which was a trial early in the century, conducted with as much care, regard, forms, and with the utmost preservation of decency and order of the proceedings, the question was put to him whether he ruled points of law, and he expressly disclaimed that power; saying in substance, on every ruling of an incidental question, "Unless any noble lord should think that this matter should be further considered in the Chamber of Parliament, I will give my opinion," thereby always submitting the question to the lords in the first instance.

Again, in Lord Cardigan's case, to which I have just referred, when a question of evidence arose as to whether a card on which the name of Harvey Garnett Tuckett was placed should be given in evidence, the question being whether the man's name was Harvey Garnett Phipps Tuckett or only Harvey Garnett Tuckett, but a question on which the whole trial finally turned when afterward the whole evidence was in, Lord Denman, instead of deciding the question, submitted it to the Lords, as follows:

"The inconvenience of clearing the House is so great that I should rather venture to propose that the decision of this question, if your lordships should be called upon to decide it, had better be postponed."

The question was not at that time pressed.

And when the Attorney General of England made his argument upon the evidence Lord Denman arose and apologized to the House of Lords for having allowed him to argue, and said in substance he hoped this would not be drawn into a precedent in criminal trials, but that he did not think it quite right for him to interfere and stop him. And when, finally, the Lords deliberated with closed doors upon the point taken, and Lord Denman gave an opinion to the Lords upon whether the proof sustained the indictments his lordship said:

"If, my lords, the present were an ordinary case, tried before one of the inferior courts, and the same objection had been taken in this stage to the proof of identity, the judge would consult his notes, and explain how far he thought the objection well founded, and I apprehend that the jury would at once return a verdict of acquittal.
"Your lordships sitting in this High Court of Parliament, unite the functions of both. I have stated my own views, as an individual member of the court,

of the question by you to be considered, discussed, and decided. Though I have commenced the debate, it cannot be necessary for me to disclaim the purpose of dictating my own opinion, which is respectfully laid before you with the hope of eliciting those of the House at large. If any other duty is cast upon me, or if there is any more convenient course to be pursued, I shall be greatly indebted to any of your lordships who will be so kind as to instruct me in it. In the absence of any other suggestion, I venture to declare my own judgment, grounded on the reasons briefly submitted, that the Earl of Cardigan is entitled to be declared not guilty."

Now, then, in the light of authority, in the light of the precedents to which the presiding officer has appealed, in the light of reason, and in the light of principle, we are bound to object to this claim of power on the part of the Chief Justice. I say again it is not a mere question of form, for all mere forms we would waive; but it is a question of substance. It is a question whether the House of Representatives can bring, by their own motion, to the Senate a question of law, if the Chief Justice who is presiding chooses to stand between the Senate and the House and its prosecution. That is a question of vital importance, upon which, for the benefit of the people for all time hereafter, if it did not make any difference in this case, I would not yield one hair, because no jot or tittle of the rights of the people or of the House of Representatives, so far as I understand them, shall ever fall to the ground by any inattention or inadvertence or yielding of mine.

Allow me to state again the proposition declared by the learned presiding officer, because to me it seems an invasion of the privileges of the House of Representatives. It is this: that when the House of Representatives proposes a question of law to the Senate of the United States on the trial by impeachment of the President of the United States, the Chief Justice presiding in this as a court can stand between the House of Representatives and the Senate and decide the question; and then, unless by the courtesy of some Senator who may be induced to make a motion for them, the House of Representatives, through its Managers, cannot get that question of law decided by the Senate.

I should be inclined to deem it my duty, and I believe my associate Managers will agree with me if we are put in that position, to ask leave to withdraw and take instruction from the House before we lay the rights of the House, bound hand and foot, at the feet of any one man, however high or good or just he may be; for, as I respectfully bring to your attention, it is a question of most momentous consequence, although not so great, not of so much consequence now, when we have a learned, able, honest, candid, patriotic Chief Justice in the chair, as it may be hereafter. Let us look forward to the time which may come in the history of this nation when we get a Jeffries as lord high steward or Chief Justice. I want, then, that the precedent set in this good time, by good men, when everything is quiet, when

the country is not disturbed, to be such as to hold any future Jeffries as did the precedents of old; for this brings to my mind Jeffries' conduct on an exactly similar question, when he was held bound by the precedents of the House of Lords. In the trial of Lord Delamere, Chief Justice Jeffries, being lord high steward, presiding, said to the earl as he came to plead—I give substance now, not words—"My lord, you had better confess and throw yourself on the mercy of the king, your master; he is the fountain of all mercy, and it will be better for you so to do." The accused earl replied to him: "Are you, my lord, one of my judges, that give me such advice here on my trial for my death?" Jeffries, quailing before the indignant eye of the man whose rights he was interfering with, said: "No, I am not one of your judges; I only advise you as a friend." I desire the precedents fixed now in good time, as strong as they were before Jeffries's time, so that hereafter, when we get a Jeffries, if we ever have that misfortune, he shall be bound by them. We have had a Johnson in the presidential chair; and we cannot tell who may get into the chair of the Chief Justice in the far future; but, if we do ever get a Jeffries in that chair, I want the precedent upon this point so settled now that it cannot be in any way disturbed, so as to hold him to the true rule as with hooks of steel.

The CHIEF JUSTICE. The Chair will state the question for the consideration of the Senate. The honorable Manager put a question to the witness. It was objected to on the part of the counsel for the President. The Chief Justice is of opinion that it is his duty to express his judgment upon that question, subject to having the question put upon the requisition of any Senator to the Senate. Are you ready for the question?

Mr. GRIMES. The question is, whether the judgment of the Chief Justice shall stand as the judgment of the Senate?

The CHIEF JUSTICE. Yes, sir.

Mr. DRAKE. No, sir. I raise the question that the presiding officer of the Senate had no right to make a decision of that question.

The CHIEF JUSTICE. The Senator is not in order.

Mr. DRAKE. I wish that question put to the Senate, sir.

The CHIEF JUSTICE. The Senator will come to order.

Mr. CONKLING. Mr. President, I rise for information from the Chair. I beg to inquire whether the question upon which the Senate is about to vote is whether the proposed testimony be competent or not, or whether the presiding officer be competent to decide that question or not?

The CHIEF JUSTICE. It is the last question, whether the Chair in the first instance may state his judgment upon such a question. That is the question for the consideration of the Senate. The yeas and nays will be called.

Mr. CONKLING. Before the yeas and nays are called, I beg that the whole of the latter clause of the seventh rule may be read for the information of the Senate.

The CHIEF JUSTICE, (to the Secretary.) Read the rule.

Mr. HOWARD. Read the whole of the rule.

The Secretary read as follows:

"VII. The Presiding Officer of the Senate shall direct all necessary preparations in the Senate Chamber, and the presiding officer, upon the trial shall direct all the forms of proceeding while the Senate are sitting for the purpose of trying an impeachment, and all forms during the trial not otherwise specially provided for. The presiding officer may, in the first instance, submit to the Senate, without a division, all questions of evidence and incidental questions; but the same shall, on the demand of one fifth of the members present, be decided by yeas and nays."

Mr. Manager BINGHAM. Mr. President, after consultation with my associate Managers, I ask leave to make some additional remarks to the Senate before this vote be taken and to call the attention of Senators especially to rule seven to which the President made reference. We think ourselves justified in asking the Senate to consider that rule seven does not contemplate any departure from the long-established usage governing proceedings of this character; in other words, that rule seven simply does provide that, "The presiding officer may, in the first instance, submit to the Senate, without a division, all questions of evidence and incidental questions; but the same shall, on the demand of one fifth of the members present, be decided by yeas and nays." We respectfully submit to the Senate, with all respect to the presiding officer, that his rule means no more than this: that if no question be raised by the Senators and one fifth do not demand the yeas and nays, it authorizes the presiding officer simply to take the sense of the Senate upon all such questions without a division, and there it ends.

I beg leave further to say to the Senators, in connection with what has fallen already from my associate, that I look upon this question now involved in the decision of the presiding officer as settled by the very terms of the Constitution itself. The Constitution of the United States, as the Senators will remember, provides that the Senate shall have the sole power to try all impeachments. The expression, "the sole power," as the Senate will doubtless agree, necessarily means the only power. It includes everything pertaining to the trial. Every judgment that must be made is a part of the trial, whether it be upon a preliminary question or a final question. It seems to me that the words were incorporated in the Constitution touching this procedure in impeachment in the very light of the long continued usage and practice in Parliament. It is settled, I beg leave to remind Senators, in the very elaborate and exhaustive report of the Commons of England upon the Lords' Journals that the peers alone decide all questions of law and fact arising in such a trial.

It is settled, in other words, that the peers alone are the judges in every case of the law and the fact; that the lord chancellor presiding is but a ministerial officer to keep order; to present for the decision of the peers the various questions as they arise; to take their judgment upon them; and there his authority stops.

And this doctrine is considered so well settled, I may be permitted to say further, (here speaking from recollection of that which I have, however, carefully examined,) that it is carried into the great text-books of the law and finds a place in the fourth Institute of Coke, wherein he declares that the peers are the judges of the law and fact, and conduct the whole proceedings according to the law and usage of Parliament.

As I understand this question as it is presented here, I agree with my associate that it is of very great importance, not only as touching the admissibility of evidence—for we certainly have no ground of complaint of the presiding officer for the ruling he made touching the admissibility of the evidence which we offer through this witness—but as touching every other question that can arise; for example, questions that may involve the validity, legality, if you please, of any of the charges preferred in these articles. If such a ruling were asked here of the presiding officer, we submit that it is not competent for him to pronounce any judgment on the subject, that it is alone for the Senate to determine; and they determine it simply for the reason, as I said before, that they have the sole power to try all questions involved in the case.

We stand, then, upon what we believe has been the uniform practice touching this question in England, and we consider that the President presiding now in the Senate has no more power over this question before the Senate than has the lord chancellor, when he presides over the deliberations of the peers, to decide any question. Being himself a peer, he has but his own vote. I do not think a case can be found wherein it was consented by the peers that the lord chancellor should give a decision in any case which is to stand as the judgment of the court without consulting the peers. That is the position that we assume, and we ask it to be understood and considered by the Senate. We understand that the question upon which the vote of the Senate is to be had is, whether the Senate shall decide that the presiding officer, himself not being a member of that body which is invested with the sole power to try impeachments, and therefore to decide all questions in the trial, can himself make a decision, which decision is to stand as the judgment of this tribunal unless reversed by a subsequent action of the Senate. That we understand to be the question that is submitted, and upon which the Senate is about to vote.

Mr. Manager BUTLER. And that the Managers cannot raise the question.

Mr. Manager BINGHAM. It is also suggested by my associate that there is also involved in the question the further proposition that the Managers, in the event of such decision being made by the presiding officer, cannot call even for a review of that decision by the Senate.

Mr. WILSON. I move that the Senate retire for the purpose of consultation.

Several SENATORS. No, no.

Mr. SHERMAN. Before that is done I desire to submit a question to the Managers in accordance with the rule.

The CHIEF JUSTICE. Does the Senator from Massachusetts withdraw his motion?

Mr. WILSON. I withdraw it for a moment.

Mr. SHERMAN. I send to the Chair a question.

The CHIEF JUSTICE. The Secretary will read the question.

The Secretary read the question of Mr. SHERMAN, as follows:

I ask the Managers what are the precedents in the cases of impeachment in the United States upon this point? Did the Vice President, as Presiding Officer, decide preliminary questions, or did he submit them in the first instance to the Senate?

Mr. Manager BOUTWELL. Mr. President and gentlemen of the Senate, I am very much indisposed to ask the attention of the Senate further. As a question concerning the rights of the House in this proceeding, it seems to me of the gravest character; and yet I can very well foresee that the practical assertion on all questions arising in a protracted trial of the principle which the Managers assert here in behalf of the House is calculated to delay the proceeding, and very likely at times to involve us in temporary difficulties. In what I say I speak with the highest personal respect for the Chief Justice who presides, being fully assured that in the rulings he might make upon questions of law and the admissibility of testimony he would always be guided by that conscientious regard for the right for which he is eminently distinguished.

But I also foresee that if the Managers acting for the House in the case now before the Senate and before the country, and acting, I may say, in behalf of other generations and of other men who unfortunately may be similarly situated in future times, should admit that the Chief Justice of the Supreme Court of the United States, sitting here as the presiding officer of this body for a specified purpose, and for a specified purpose only, has a right to decide, even as preliminary to the final judgment of the Senate, questions of law and evidence which in the end may be vital in the decision of this tribunal upon the question of the guilt or the innocence of the person arraigned, they would make a surrender, in substance, of the constitutional rights of the House and the constitutional rights of the Senate sitting as the tribunal to try impeachments presented by the House of Representatives. With all def

ence I maintain that the language of the Constitution, in these words :

"When the President of the United States is tried the Chief Justice shall preside"—

is conclusive without argument. He presides here not as a member of this body ; for if that were assumed the claim would be in derogation, nay, in violation, of another provision of the Constitution which confides to the Senate the sole power of trying all impeachments. I know of no language which could be used more specific in its character, more inclusive and exclusive in its terms. The language includes, as has here been maintained by Mr. Manager BUTLER in the opening argument, all the members of the Senate, all the men chosen under the Constitution and representing the several States of the Union, whatever may be their qualities, whatever may be their capacities, whatever may be their interests, whatever may be their affiliation with or to the person accused. The Senate sits in its constitutional capacity to decide under the Constitution the question of the guilt of the accused, with all the felicities and with all the infelicities which belong to the tribunal organized under and by virtue of the Constitution. We must accept it as it is, with no power to change it in any particular.

So, also, the words of the Constitution are exclusive. With all deference I am forced to assert and maintain that these words exclude every other man, whatever his station, rank, position elsewhere, whatever his relations to this body under or by the Constitution. The Senate by the Constitution has the sole power to try all impeachments, and no person not of the Senate, and exercising the functions of a Senator in legislative and executive affairs, can in any way interfere to control or affect their decision or their judgment in the slightest degree. Therefore, Mr. President, it must follow as a constitutional duty that the Senate, without advice, as a matter of right, must decide every incidental question which by any possibility can control the ultimate judgment of the Senate upon the great question of the guilt or innocence of the party accused. If under any circumstances the testimony of a witness proffered may be denied or may be admitted upon the judgment of any person or by any authority, except upon the judgment and authority of the tribunal before which we here stand, then a party accused and impeached by the House of Representatives may be acquitted or he may be convicted upon any authority or opinion which is not in fact the judgment of the Senate itself. Upon this point I think there can finally be no difference of opinion.

But, Mr. President, as one of the Managers, and without having had an opportunity to consult my associates on the point, and speaking, therefore, with deference to what may be their judgment or what might be the judgment of the House, I should be willing to proceed in the conduct of this case upon the understanding that the right is here and now solemnly asserted by the Senate for themselves and as a precedent for all their successors that every question of law is to be decided by the Senate without consultation with the presiding officer. I hold that the judgment must be exclusively with the Senate. Still I am willing that in all these proceedings the presiding officer of the Senate shall give his opinion or his ruling, if you please to call it a ruling, upon questions incidental of law and evidence as they arise, unless some member of the Senate or the Managers or the counsel for the respondent should first desire the judgment of the Senate.

I happen to have an extract from the record in the case referred to by my associate, and I will read it in the presence of the Senate.

In the trial of Lord Melville, which is reported in the twenty-ninth volume of the State Trials, Lord Chancellor Erskine evidently acted upon this idea. Upon a question of the admissibility of testimony, it having been argued by the managers on one side and the counsel for the respondent on the other, Lord Erskine said:

"If any noble lord is desirous that this subject should be a matter of further consideration in the Chamber of Parliament, it will be proper that he should now move to adjourn; if not, I have formed an opinion, and shall express it."

To that theory of the administration of the duties of the Chair with reference to the rights of the House of Representatives and to the rights of the respondent, for myself, I should not object; but I cannot conscientiously, even in this presence, consent to the doctrine as a matter of right that the presiding officer of the Senate is to decide interlocutory questions, and especially to decide them under such circumstances that it will not be in the power of the Managers to take the judgment of the Senate upon the wisdom and justice of the decision.

Mr. Manager BINGHAM. By leave of the Senate I desire to read in their hearing an abstract which I have made touching this question from the authorities to which I referred, and which I believe is accurate. I read first in the hearing of the Senate the abstract which was made from the report of the Commons of England upon the Lords Journals:

"*Relation of Judges, &c., to the Court of Parliament.*

"Upon examining into the course of proceeding in the House of Lords, and into the relation which exists between the peers on the one hand, and their attendants and assistants, the judges of the realm, barons of the exchequer of the coif, the king's learned counsel, and the civilians masters of the chancery on the other, it appears to your committee that these judges and other persons learned in the common and civil laws are no integrant and necessary part of that court. Their writs of summons are essentially different; and it does not appear that they or any of them have, or of right ought to have, a deliberative voice, either actually or virtually, in the judgments given in that court is solely ministerial; and their answers to questions put to them are not to be regarded as declaratory of the law of Parliament, but as merely consultory responses, in order to furnish such matter (to be submitted to the judgment of the peers) as may be useful in reasoning by analogy, so far as the nature of the rules in the respective courts of the learned persons consulted shall appear to the peers to be applicable to the nature and circumstances of the case before them, and not otherwise."—8 *Burke* p. 42; Report on the Lords Journal; Trial of Warren Hastings.

In the volume of Burke here quoted the report is set out at length. I read further from the same report:

"*Jurisdiction of the Lords.*

"Your committee finds that in all impeachments of the Commons of Great Britain for high crimes and misdemeanors, before the peers in the high court of Parliament, the peers are not triers or jurors only, but by the ancient laws and constitution of this kingdom known by constant usage are judges both of law and fact; and we conceive that the Lords are bound not to act in such a manner as to give rise to an opinion that they have virtually submitted to a division of their legal powers, or that, putting themselves into the situation of mere triers or jurors, they may suffer the evidence in the cause to be produced or not produced before them, according to the discretion of the judges of the inferior courts"—8 *Burke*, p. 42; Report on the Lords Journals; Trial of Warren Hastings.

I read, also, the extract from fourth Institute to which I before referred:

"It is by the laws and customs of Parliament that all weighty matters in Parliament moved concerning the peers of the realm, &c., ought to be determined, adjudged, and discussed by the course of the Parliament, and not by the civil law, and yet by the common law of this realm used by the more inferior courts; for this reason the judges ought not to give any opinion in a matter of Parliament."—*Fourth Institute*, page 15.

Mr. Manager BUTLER. Mr. President, there was a question asked by one member of the Senate as to the precedents. I have sent for the trial of Judge Chase, which I read from the third volume of Benton's Abridgment of the Debates of Congress. The rule in that case was in the following words:

"All motions made by the parties or their counsel shall be addressed to the President of the Senate, and, if he shall require it shall be committed to writing, and read at the Secretary's table; and all decisions shall be had by yeas and nays, and without debate, which shall be entered on the records."

In the course of the trial there arose this question: whether a Mr. Hay, a witness in the case, should use a certain paper to refresh his memory.

"Mr. Harper here interrupted Mr. Hay, and said: 'The witness may refer to anything done by himself at the time the occurrence happened which he relates. But I submit it to the court how correct it is to refer to what was not done by him, or done at the time.'

"The President asked Mr. Hay whether the notes were taken by him.

"Mr. Hay. The statement was made by different persons. Some parts were made by myself, perhaps the greater part; the rest by Mr. Nicholas and Mr. Wirt. I believe I shall be able to state from it every material occurrence which took place at the time.

"The President. Have you the parts made by yourself separate?

"Mr. Hay said he had not.

"The President then put the question, whether the witness should be permitted to use the paper; and the question being taken by yeas and nays, passed in the negative—yeas 16, nays 18."

There, upon the question whether Mr. Hay should refresh his memory on the stand by notes which were not made by himself, which was certainly an incidental question of law, the President, instead of undertaking to decide it in Chase's case, directly put the question to the court and had it decided in the first instance by yea or nay, not expressing any opinion whatever upon that question.

We have nothing further to add.

Mr. EVARTS. I rise, Mr. Chief Justice and Senators, to make but a single observation in reference to a position or an argument pressed by one of the honorable Managers to aid the judgment of the Senate upon the question submitted to it. That question we understand to be whether, according to the rules of this body, the Chief Justice presiding shall determine, preliminarily, interlocutory questions of evidence and of law as they arise, subject to the decision of the Senate upon presentation by any Senator of the question to them. The honorable Manager, Mr. BOUTWELL, recognizing the great inconvenience that would arise in the retarding of the trial from this appeal to so numerous a body upon every interlocutory question, while he insists upon the magnitude and importance of the right determination, yet intimates that the Managers will allow the Chief Justice to decide, unless they see reason to object. On the part of the counsel for the President, I have only this to say: that we shall take from this court the rule as to whether the first preliminary decision is to be made by the Chief Justice or is to be made by the whole body, and we shall not submit to the choice of the Managers as to how far that rule shall be departed from. Whatever the rule is we shall abide by it. But if the court determines that in the first instance the proper appeal is to the whole body on every interlocutory question, we shall claim as a matter of right and as a matter of course that that proceeding shall be had.

Mr. Manager BOUTWELL. That is conceded, Mr. President. We do not debate that point.

Mr. WILSON. I renew my motion that the Senate retire for consultation.

Mr. THAYER. On that motion I call for the yeas and nays.

Mr. CAMERON. I hope we shall not retire.

Several SENATORS. Debate is out of order.

The CHIEF JUSTICE. The Senator is out of order.

Mr. CAMERON. Well, I only say that.

The question being taken by yeas and nays, resulted—yeas 25, nays 25; as follows:

YEAS—Messrs. Anthony, Buckalew, Cole, Conness, Corbett, Davis, Dixon, Edmunds, Fowler, Grimes, Hendricks, Howe, Johnson, McCreery, Morrill of Maine, Morrill of Vermont, Morton, Norton, Patterson of New Hampshire, Patterson of Tennessee, Pomeroy, Ross, Vickers, Williams, and Wilson—25.

NAYS—Messrs. Cameron, Cattell, Chandler, Conkling, Cragin, Doolittle, Drake, Ferry, Fessenden, Frelinghuysen, Henderson, Howard, Morgan, Nye, Ramsey, Saulsbury, Sherman, Sprague, Stewart, Sumner, Thayer, Tipton, Trumbull, Van Winkle, and Willey—25.

NOT VOTING—Messrs. Bayard, Harlan, Wade, and Yates—4.

The CHIEF JUSTICE. On this question the yeas are 25 and the nays are 25. The Chief Justice votes in the affirmative. The Senate will retire for conference.

The Senate, with the Chief Justice, thereupon (at seven minutes before three o'clock) retired to their conference room for consultation.

The Senate having retired,

Mr. SHERMAN submitted the following order:

Ordered, That under the rules, and in accordance with the precedents in the United States in cases of impeachment, all questions other than those of order should be submitted to the Senate.

After debate,

Mr. HENDERSON moved to postpone the present question for the purpose of taking up for consideration the seventh rule, that he might propose an amendment thereto.

Mr. CONNESS called for the yeas and nays on this motion, and they were ordered; and being taken resulted—yeas 32, nays 18; as follows:

YEAS—Messrs. Anthony, Bayard, Buckalew, Cameron, Cattell, Cole, Corbett, Cragin, Davis, Dixon, Doolittle, Edmunds, Fessenden, Fowler, Frelinghuysen, Henderson, Hendricks, Johnson, McCreery, Morrill of Vermont, Norton, Patterson of New Hampshire, Patterson of Tennessee, Pomeroy, Ross, Saulsbury, Sprague, Trumbull, Van Winkle, Vickers, Wiley, and Williams—32.

NAYS—Messrs. Chandler, Conkling, Conness, Drake, Ferry, Howard, Howe, Morgan, Morrill of Maine, Morton, Nye, Ramsey, Sherman, Stewart, Sumner, Thayer, Tipton, and Wilson—18.

NOT VOTING—Messrs. Grimes, Harlan, Wade, and Yates—4.

So the motion to postpone was agreed to.

Mr. HENDERSON submitted the following resolution:

Resolved, That Rule 7 be amended by substituting therefor the following:

The Presiding Officer of the Senate shall direct all necessary preparations in the Senate Chamber, and the presiding officer on the trial shall direct all the forms of proceeding while the Senate are sitting for the purpose of trying an impeachment, and all forms during the trial not otherwise specially provided for. And the presiding officer on the trial may rule all questions of evidence and incidental questions, which ruling shall stand as the judgment of the Senate, unless some member of the Senate shall ask that a formal vote be taken thereon, in which case it shall be submitted to the Senate for decision; or he may, at his option, in the first instance submit any such question to a vote of the members of the Senate.

Mr. MORRILL, of Maine, moved to amend the proposed rule by striking out the words "which ruling shall stand as the judgment of the Senate."

After debate,

The amendment was rejected.

Mr. SUMNER moved to amend the resolution by adding thereto:

That the Chief Justice of the United States, presiding in the Senate on the trial of the President of the United States, is not a member of the Senate, and has no authority, under the Constitution, to vote on any question during the trial, and he can pronounce decision only as the organ of the Senate, with its assent.

After debate,

Mr. SUMNER called for the yeas and nays

on his amendment, and they were ordered; and being taken, resulted—yeas 22, nays 26; as follows:

YEAS—Messrs. Cameron, Cattell, Chandler, Conkling, Conness, Corbett, Cragin, Drake, Howard, Morgan, Morrill of Maine, Morton, Nye, Pomeroy, Ramsey, Stewart, Sumner, Thayer, Tipton, Trumbull, Williams, and Wilson—22.

NAYS—Messrs. Bayard, Buckalew, Cole, Davis, Dixon, Doolittle, Edmunds, Ferry, Fessenden, Fowler, Frelinghuysen, Henderson, Hendricks, Howe, Johnson, McCreery, Morrill of Vermont, Norton, Patterson of New Hampshire, Patterson of Tennessee, Ross, Sherman, Sprague, Van Winkle, Vickers, and Willey—26.

NOT VOTING—Messrs. Anthony, Grimes, Harlan, Saulsbury, Wade, and Yates—6.

So the amendment of Mr. SUMNER was rejected.

Mr. DRAKE moved to amend the resolution by striking out all after the word "that" and inserting:

It is the judgment of the Senate that under the Constitution the Chief Justice presiding over the Senate in the pending trial has no privilege of ruling questions of law arising thereon, but that all such questions should be submitted to a decision by the Senate alone.

After debate,

Mr. DRAKE called for the yeas and nays, and they were ordered; and being taken, resulted—yeas 20, nays 30; as follows:

YEAS—Messrs. Cameron, Cattell, Chandler, Cole, Conkling, Conness, Drake, Ferry, Howard, Howe, Morgan, Morrill of Maine, Morton, Nye, Ramsey, Stewart, Sumner, Thayer, Tipton, and Wilson—20.

NAYS—Messrs. Anthony, Bayard, Buckalew, Corbett, Cragin, Davis, Dixon, Doolittle, Edmunds, Fessenden, Fowler, Frelinghuysen, Henderson, Hendricks, Johnson, McCreery, Morrill of Vermont, Norton, Patterson of New Hampshire, Patterson of Tennessee, Pomeroy, Ross, Saulsbury, Sherman, Sprague, Trumbull, Van Winkle, Vickers, Willey, and Williams—30.

NOT VOTING—Messrs. Grimes, Harlan, Wade, and Yates—4.

So the amendment was rejected.

The question recurring on the rule proposed by Mr. HENDERSON, after debate,

Mr. FERRY called for the yeas and nays, and they were ordered; and being taken, resulted in—yeas 31, nays 19; as follows:

YEAS—Messrs. Anthony, Bayard, Buckalew, Cameron, Corbett, Cragin, Davis, Dixon, Doolittle, Edmunds, Fessenden, Fowler, Frelinghuysen, Henderson, Hendricks, Johnson, McCreery, Morrill of Vermont, Norton, Patterson of New Hampshire, Patterson of Tennessee, Pomeroy, Ross, Saulsbury, Sherman, Sprague, Trumbull, Van Winkle, Vickers, Willey, and Williams—31.

NAYS—Messrs. Cattell, Chandler, Cole, Conkling, Conness, Drake, Ferry, Howard, Howe, Morgan, Morrill of Maine, Morton, Nye, Ramsey, Stewart, Sumner, Thayer, Tipton, and Wilson—19.

NOT VOTING—Messrs. Grimes, Harlan, Wade, and Yates—4.

So the resolution submitted by Mr. HENDERSON was agreed to.

Mr. SUMNER submitted the following resolution:

Resolved, That the Chief Justice of the United States presiding in the Senate on the trial of the President of the United States is not a member of the Senate, and has no authority under the Constitution to vote on any question during the trial.

Mr. HENDRICKS objected to the reception of the proposition, as it did not relate to the matter on which the Senate had retired to confer; and he moved that the Senate return to the Senate Chamber; which motion was agreed to.

The Senate returned to its Chamber at eighteen minutes past six o'clock p. m.

The CHIEF JUSTICE. The Senate has had under consideration the question before it when it retired; and has directed me to report the rule adopted, which will be read by the Secretary.

The SECRETARY. The seventh rule, as now amended, reads:

The Presiding Officer of the Senate shall direct all necessary preparations in the Senate Chamber, and the presiding officer on the trial shall direct all the forms of proceeding while the Senate are sitting for the purpose of trying an impeachment, and all forms during the trial not otherwise specially provided for. And the presiding officer on the trial may rule all questions of evidence and incidental questions, which ruling shall stand as the judgment of the Senate, unless some member of the Senate shall ask that a formal vote be taken thereon; in which case it shall be submitted to the Senate for decision, or he may, at his option, in the first instance submit any such question to a vote of the members of the Senate.

The CHIEF JUSTICE. Gentlemen Managers on the part of the House of Representatives, you will please state your question.

Mr. Manager BUTLER. Will you spare us a moment for consultation? The chairman of the Managers is out.

Mr. TRUMBULL. Mr. President, unless the Managers desire that we should continue now in session to take immediate action, I would propose that the Senate adjourn until half past twelve o'clock to-morrow.

Mr. FERRY and others. The rules fix twelve o'clock.

Mr. TRUMBULL. Very well; until twelve o'clock. If the Managers desire to submit any particular action at this moment I will withdraw the motion; if not, I insist upon it.

Mr. WILLIAMS. I move, first, that the rules, as amended, be printed for the use of the Senate.

The CHIEF JUSTICE. The Senator from Oregon moves that the rules, as amended, be printed for the use of the Senate.

The question being put, the motion was agreed to.

Mr. TRUMBULL. I now renew my motion that the Senate, sitting as a court of impeachment, adjourn.

Mr. Manager BUTLER. We have nothing to oppose to the motion.

The CHIEF JUSTICE. Have the counsel for the President anything to propose?

Messrs. STANBERY and EVARTS indicated that they had not.

The CHIEF JUSTICE. It is moved that the Senate, sitting as a court of impeachment, adjourn until to-morrow at twelve o'clock.

The motion was agreed to; and the Chief Justice declared the Senate, sitting as a court of impeachment, adjourned until to-morrow at twelve o'clock.

WEDNESDAY, *April* 1, 1868.

The Chief Justice of the United States entered the Senate Chamber at five minutes past twelve o'clock and took the chair.

The usual proclamation having been made by the Sergeant-at-Arms,

The Managers of the impeachment on the part of the House of Representatives appeared and took the seats assigned them.

The counsel for the respondent also appeared and took their seats.

The presence of the House of Representatives was next announced, and the members of the House, as in Committee of the Whole, headed by Mr. E. B. WASHBURNE, the chairman of the committee, accompanied by the Speaker and Clerk, entered the Chamber, and were conducted to the seats provided for them.

The CHIEF JUSTICE. The Secretary will read the minutes of the last day's proceedings.

The Secretary read the Journal of the proceedings of the Senate yesterday sitting for the trial of the impeachment.

Mr. SUMNER. Mr. President, I send to the Chair an order which is in the nature of a correction of the Journal.

The CHIEF JUSTICE. The Secretary will read the order proposed.

The Secretary read as follows:

It appearing from the reading of the Journal of yesterday that on a question where the Senate were equally divided the Chief Justice, presiding on the trial of the President, gave a casting vote, it is hereby declared that, in the judgment of the Senate, such vote was without authority under the Constitution of the United States.

Mr. SUMNER. On that question I ask for the yeas and nays.

The yeas and nays were ordered; and being taken, resulted—yeas 21, nays 27; as follows:

yEAS—Messrs. Cameron, Chandler, Cole, Conkling, Conness, Cragin, Drake, Howard, Howe, Morgan, Morrill of Maine, Morton, Pomeroy, Ramsey, Stewart, Sumner, Thayer, Tipton, Trumbull, Williams, and Wilson—21.

NAYS—Messrs. Anthony, Bayard, Buckalew, Corbett, Davis, Dixon, Doolittle, Edmunds, Ferry, Fessenden, Fowler, Frelinghuysen, Grimes, Henderson, Hendricks, Johnson, McCreery, Morrill of Vermont, Norton, Patterson of New Hampshire, Patterson of Tennessee, Ross, Sherman, Sprague, Van Winkle, Vickers, and Willey—27.

NOT VOTING—Messrs. Cattell, Harlan, Nye, Saulsbury, Wade, and Yates—6.

So the proposed order was rejected.

The CHIEF JUSTICE. Senators, during the proceedings yesterday a question was submitted by the Managers on the part of the impeachment in relation to evidence, and that question was objected to by the counsel for the President. The Managers will now please to submit that question in writing.

Mr. Manager BUTLER presented the question in writing at the Secretary's desk:

The CHIEF JUSTICE. The Secretary will read the question.

The Secretary read the following question proposed to be put to the witness, WALTER A. BURLEIGH:

"You said yesterday, in answer to my question, that you had a conversation with General Lorenzo Thomas on the evening of the 21st of February last. State if he said anything as to the means by which he intended to obtain, or was directed by the President to obtain, possession of the War Department? If so, state all he said as nearly as you can."

Mr. STANBERY. We object, Mr. Chief Justice.

The CHIEF JUSTICE. Do you desire to make any observations to the court?

Mr. STANBERY. We do, sir.

The CHIEF JUSTICE. The question will be submitted to the Senate.

Mr. HOWARD. What is the question?

The CHIEF JUSTICE. The Secretary will read the question again.

The Secretary again read the question.

Mr. FRELINGHUYSEN. Mr. President, I desire to submit a question.

The CHIEF JUSTICE. The Secretary will read the question submitted by the Senator from New Jersey [Mr. FRELINGHUYSEN] to the Managers.

The Secretary read as follows: ·

Do the Managers intend to connect the conversation between the witness and General Thomas with the respondent?

The CHIEF JUSTICE. Are the Managers prepared to reply to the question?

Mr. Manager BUTLER. Mr. President, if the point is to be argued, with the leave of the Senate we will endeavor to answer that question in the argument.

The CHIEF JUSTICE. It is to be argued. The honorable Manager will proceed, if he desires.

Mr. STANBERY. We do not hear the answer.

Mr. Manager BUTLER. The answer is, Mr. President, if you will allow me to repeat it, that, as I understand, the point raised is to be argued on the one side and the other, we will endeavor to answer the question submitted by the Senator from New Jersey in the course of our argument.

Mr. TRUMBULL. Mr. President, I should like to hear the question read again, as I think the answer to the inquiry of the Senator from New Jersey is in the question propounded by the Managers, as I heard it.

The CHIEF JUSTICE. The Secretary will read the question again. Senators will please give their attention.

The Secretary again read the question of Mr. Manager BUTLER.

The CHIEF JUSTICE. Do the Managers propose to answer the question of the Senator from New Jersey?

Mr. Manager BUTLER. If there is to be no argument, Mr. President, I will answer the question proposed. If there is to be an argument on the part of the counsel for the President, we propose, as a more convenient method, to answer the question in the course of our argument, because otherwise we might have to make an argument now. I can say that we do propose to connect the respondent with this testimony.

The CHIEF JUSTICE. Senators——

Mr. STANBERY. Is it in order now, Mr. Chief Justice, for us to argue the question?

The CHIEF JUSTICE. If the counsel desire to submit any observations to the Senate, they may do so.

Mr. STANBERY. Mr. Chief Justice and Senators, we have at length reached the domain of law; we are no longer to argue questions of mere form or modes of procedure, but have come at last to a distinct legal question, proper to be argued by lawyers and to be considered by lawyers.

The question now, Mr. Chief Justice and Senators, is, whether any foundation is laid, either in the articles or in any testimony yet given, why the declarations of General Thomas should be used in evidence against the President. General Thomas is not on trial; it is the President, the President alone, and the testimony to be offered must be testimony that is binding upon him or admissible against him.

It is agreed that the President was not present on the evening of the 21st of February, when General Thomas made these declarations. They were made in his absence. He had no opportunity of hearing them or contradicting them. If they are to be used against him, it is because they were uttered by some one speaking for him, who was authorized by him to make these declarations of his intentions and his purposes.

Now, first of all, what foundation is laid why the declarations of General Thomas as to what he intended to do, or what the President had authorized him to do, should be given in evidence against the President? It will be seen that by the first article the offense charged against the President is that he issued a certain order to Mr. Stanton for his removal; ordering his removal, and adding that General Thomas was authorized to receive from him a transfer of the books, papers, records, and property in the Department. Now, the offense laid in that article is not as to anything that was done under it, but simply that in itself the mere issuing of that order is the *gravamen* of the offense charged. So much for the first article.

What is the second? That on the same day, the 21st of February, 1868, the President issued a letter of authority to General Thomas, and the *gravamen* there is the issuing of that letter of authority, not anything done under it.

What next? The third article goes upon the same letter of authority, and charges the issuing of it to be an offense with intention to violate a certain statute.

Then we come to the fourth article, which charges a conspiracy. Senators will observe that in the three first articles the evidence charged is issuing certain orders, nothing beyond, as in violation either of the Constitution or of the act called the tenure-of-office act. But by the fourth article the Managers proceed

C. I.—9.

to charge us with an entirely new offense against a totally different statute, and that is a conspiracy between General Thomas and the President and other persons unknown, by "force" in one article, "by intimidation and threats" in another, to hinder and prevent Mr. Stanton from holding the office of Secretary of War, and that in pursuance of that conspiracy certain acts were done which are not named, with intent to violate the conspiracy act of July, 1861.

These are the only charges that have any relevancy to the question which is now put. I need not refer to the other articles, in which offenses are charged against the President arising out of his declarations to General Emory, the speeches made, one at the Executive Mansion in August, 1866, another at Cleveland on the 3d day of September, 1866, and another at St. Louis on the 8th of September, 1866. For the present they are out of the way.

Now, what proof has yet been made under the first eight articles? The proof is simply, so far as this question is concerned, the production in evidence of the orders themselves. There they are to speak for themselves. As yet we have not had one particle of proof of what was said by the President, either before or after he gave those orders or at the time that he gave those orders—not one word. The only foundation now laid for the introduction of this testimony is the production of the orders themselves. The attempt made here is, by the declarations of General Thomas, to show with what intent the President issued those orders; not by producing him here to testify what the President told him, but without having him sworn at all, to bind the President by his declarations not made under oath; made without the possibility of cross-examination or contradiction by the President himself; made as though they are made by the authority of the President.

Now, Senators, what foundation is laid to show such authority, given by the President to General Thomas, to speak for him as to his intent, or even as to General Thomas's intent, which is quite another question. You must find the foundation in the orders themselves, for as yet you have no other place to look for it. Now, what are these orders? That issued to General Thomas is the most material one; but, that I may take the whole, I will read also that issued and directed to Mr. Stanton himself. He says to Mr. Stanton, by his order of February 21, 1868:

"SIR: By virtue of the power and authority vested in me as President by the Constitution and laws of the United States you are hereby removed from office as Secretary for the Department of War, and your functions as such will terminate upon receipt of this communication.

"You will transfer to Brevet Major General Lorenzo Thomas, Adjutant General of the Army, who has this day been authorized and empowered to act as Secretary of War *ad interim*, all records, books, papers, and other public property now in your custody and charge."

So much for that. Then the order to General Thomas of the same day is:

Sir: Hon. Edwin M. Stanton having been this day removed from office as Secretary for the Department of War, you are hereby authorized and empowered to act as Secretary of War *ad interim*, and will immediately enter upon the discharge of the duties pertaining to that office.

Mr. Stanton has been instructed to transfer to you all the records, books, papers, and other public property now in his custody and charge.

Respectfully, yours, ANDREW JOHNSON.

To Brevet Major General LORENZO THOMAS, *Adjutant General United States Army, Washington, D. C.*

There they are; they speak for themselves, orders made by the President to two of his subordinates; an order directing one of them to vacate his office and to transfer the books and public property in his possession to another party, and the order to that other party to take possession of the office, receive a transfer of the books, and act as Secretary of War *ad interim*. Gentlemen, does that make them conspirators? Is that proof of a conspiracy or tending to have a conspiracy? Does that make General Thomas an agent of the President in such a sense as that the President is to be bound by everything he says and everything he does even within the scope of his agency? If it makes him his agent, does this letter of authority, this written authority, authorize him to do anything but that which he is commanded to do—go there and demand possession, go there and receive a transfer from the person? Does it authorize him to use force? Does it authorize him to go beyond the letter and the meaning of the authority which is given him? Not at all.

Now, in the first place, it must be either on the footing of a conspiracy between General Thomas and the President or upon the footing of a direct agency, in which the President is the principal and General Thomas is the agent, that the declarations of General Thomas, either as coconspirator or as agent of a principal, acting within his authority, are to be admitted in evidence. I do not know any other ground upon which the learned Managers can place the admissibility of this hearsay declaration, not under oath, by a party not on the record.

I agree that when a proper foundation is laid by proof of a conspiracy in which A, B, and C are concerned then the declarations of any one of the conspirators, made while the conspiracy is in process, made, too, in furtherance of the conspiracy, not outside of it, not in reference to any other unlawful act, but in reference to the very unlawful act agreed upon, may be admitted. ' I concede that, under these circumstances, the declaration of any one conspirator binds all his fellows, although made in their absense. So, too, I agree, Senators, that when an agency is established, either by parol proof or by writing—and when established by writing that is the measure of the agency, and you cannot extend it by parol proof—when an agency is constituted either by parol proof or by writing to do a certain thing, the

acts, and, under certain circumstances, the declarations of the agent, made in performance of that authority, not outside of it, but in performance of it, bind the principal.

Now, I ask this honorable court where is there any evidence yet establishing anything like a conspiracy between the President and General Thomas? Where is there any proof yet establishing any agency between General Thomas and the President, in which the President was principal and General Thomas the agent, save this letter of authority? I do not admit that this letter of authority constitutes the relation of principal and agent at all. I do not admit that the President is to be bound by any declarations made by General Thomas on the footing that he is agent of the President; but if he were, if this were a case strictly of principal and agent, then I say this letter of authority gives no authority to General Thomas to bind his principal beyond the express authority so given.

The object of this proof, as we are told by the learned Manager, is to show that General Thomas declared that it was his intention and the intention of the President, in executing that authority, to use force, intimidation, and threats. Does the authority authorize anything of that sort, even if it were a case of principal and agent? Suppose a principal gives authority to his agent to go and take possession of a house of his in the occupation of a tenant, and to receive from that tenant the delivery of the house; does it authorize the agent to go there *manu forti* to commit an assault and battery upon the tenant, to drive him out *vi et armis*, or even scarcely to use the *molliter manus?* I submit not. Is the principal to be made a criminal by the act of his agent acting simply under an authority which purports only to give a right of peaceable possession and of surrender by the consent of the party in possession? Is the principal to be bound by any excess of authority used by his agent in executing it; or is he, when the authority is in writing and does not authorize force to be bound by the declarations of the agent that force will be used? Which of us would ever be safe in giving any authority to an agent if we are to be submitted to consequences like these?

But, Senators, this is not a question of principal and agent. What, I pray you, has the President done that he is held to be a conspirator or as a principal giving unlawful authority to an agent? Does the President appoint General Thomas his agent in any individual capacity to take possession of an office that belonged to him or of books and papers that were his property? Not at all. What is the nature of this order? It is, according to the accustomed formula, the designation of an officer, an officer already known to the law, to do what? To exercise a public duty, to perform the duties of a public office. Is the person thus appointed by the President his agent? When he accepts his appointment does he act only under the instructions of the principal, and is he the agent of the principal to carry out a private purpose or to perform a private duty? Certainly not. He at once becomes an officer of the law, with liabilities himself as a public officer, liable to removal, liable to impeachment, liable to indictment and prosecution for anything which he may do in violation of his duties as a public officer.

Are all the officers of the United States who have been appointed just in this way the agents of the President? When the President gives a commission, either a permanent one or a temporary one, to fill a vacancy or to fill an office during a disability, are the persons so designated and appointed his agents, and is he bound by everything they do? If they take a bribe, is it a bribe to him? If they commit an assault and battery, is it an assault and battery committed by him? If they exceed their authority, does he become liable? Not at all. If third persons are injured by them in the exercise of the power which he has given, may those third persons go back upon the President as the responsible party under the principle *respondeat superior?*

There is no idea of principal and agent here; it is the case of one public officer giving orders to another public officer. He clothes him, not with his authority, but with the authority of the law, and the public officer so appointed stands under an obligation of oath, not to the principal, not to the President, but to the law itself; and if he does any act which injures a third person, or which violates any law, it is he that is responsible, not the President who has appointed him.

Senators, it seems to us that these conclusions are inevitable. I shall scarcely trouble this honorable court, made up so largely of lawyers of the greatest eminence, with the citation of authorities upon a point so clear as this. I understand the learned Managers to say that they expect hereafter to connect the President with these declarations of General Thomas.

Mr. Manager BUTLER. I believe I did not use the word "hereafter."

Mr. STANBERY. Does the learned Manager say that he has heretofore done it?

Mr. Manager BUTLER. I only say now that I did not say "hereafter."

Mr. STANBERY. You expect to do it, not that you have done it? I do not want to criticise the language of the gentleman nor to have mine criticised. What I understood the gentleman to say, in answer to the question put by a Senator, was that he did expect to show a connection. If he did not mean that he meant nothing; or he meant one thing and said another. It was to meet the objection that as yet you have laid no foundation that the question was put to the learned Manager "do you expect to lay a foundation;" and the answer was in the affirmative. Drawn out after one or two repetitions of the question, the honorable Manager tells us they expect to lay the foundation. Is that enough for the introduction of evidence which *prima facie* is inadmissible? Is that enough? It is not enough.

I agree that there are exceptions in cases of conspiracy, and, perhaps, of agency, to the necessity of the introduction of preliminary proof, laying the foundation before witnesses are called to state the declarations of a co-conspirator or of an agent. They are extreme cases and so put in the books, but no such extreme case is shown here. But we have heard no reason why we must in this case reverse the order of testimony and go into that which is *prima facie* inadmissible under the assurance that a foundation is hereafter to be laid.

What prevents the gentlemen from laying that foundation? What prevents them from showing a conspiracy in the first place? What prevents them from showing instructions outside of this letter of authority to use force, intimidation, or threats? What reason is there? None whatever is stated. Is it a matter merely at the option of counsel in the introduction of testimony to begin at the wrong end, to introduce what is clearly inadmissible without a foundation, and to say "We will give you the superstructure first and the foundation last?" Does that lie merely in the option of counsel? Was such a thing as that ever heard? None have ever heard it; and I say, and such are the authorities, that it must be an extreme case, founded upon direct assurance upon the professional honor of counsel, before a court will allow testimony *prima facie* inadmissible to be admitted under the statement that hereafter a proper foundation will be laid.

Mr. Manager BUTLER. Mr. President, I must ask that the usual rule shall be enforced here; that if any authorities are to be cited by the counsel for the President they must be cited in their opening, so that we can have opportunity to reply to them, and not after I have replied have authorities cited. If there are none I will go on.

The CHIEF JUSTICE. Such is the undoubted rule.

Mr. STANBERY. I think, Mr. Chief Justice, I will allow this question to stand without the production of authorities.

Mr. Manager BUTLER. Mr. President and Senators, the gravity of the question presented, being more than the mere decision of a given interrogatory, has induced the President's counsel to argue it at length, they seeing that largely upon this question and the testimony adduced under it upon one of the articles of this impeachment the fate of their client may depend. It is a grave question, and therefore I must ask the attention of the Senate and the presiding officer, as well as I may, to some considerations which determine it in my mind.

But before I do so I pray leave to sketch the exact status of the case up to the point at which the question is produced; and I may say—I trust without offense—that the learned counsel

132

for the President has entirely ignored that status. I take for the evidence of it the propositions put forward in the answer of the President, the papers that have been already adduced, and the testimony, so far. as we have gone. It appears, then, that on or about the 12th day of August last past, possibly before the President conceived the idea of removing Edwin M. Stanton from office at all hazards, claiming the power and right to do so against the provisions of the act known as the tenure of civil office act, he undertook to suspend him under that act. Therefore the decision of this question, in one of its aspects, will decide the great question here at issue this hour. Is that act, up to this time, to be treated as a law of the land, as an act of Congress valid and not to be infringed by any executive officer whatever? Because, if it is a law, then the President admits that he undertook to remove Mr. Stanton in violation of that law, and that he issued the order to General Thomas for that purpose, and only to violate it; and his palliation is that he meant to make a case for judicial decision, but to do so he intended to issue the order to Mr. Thomas, and Thomas was, under it, to act in violation of the provisions of that act. Am I not right upon this proposition?

That being so, then we have him on his part intending to violate the law; we have him, then, issuing an order in violation of the law; we have him then calling to his aid, to carry out the violation of that law, an officer of the Army.

Now, in the light of that position, what is the next thing we find? We find that he issues an order to Lorenzo Thomas to take possession of the War Department. The learned counsel for the President says that that is an order in the usual form. . I take issue with him. There are certain ear-marks about that order which show that it was not in the usual form. It has in it words of imperative command. It is not simply, "you are authorized and empowered to take possession of the War Department;" but it is "you will immediately"—all other things being laid aside, at once, whatever may oppose—"you will immediately enter upon the discharge of the duties of that office."

Now, we must take another thing which appears in this case beyond all possibility of cavil, and that is, that the President knew at that time that Mr. Stanton from the first, to wit, on the 12th of August last, claimed the right not to be put out of that office, and when he went out he notified the President solemnly that he only went out in obedience to superior force. To get him out, the President authorized to take possession the General of the Army of the United States; and that, for all legal purposes and for all actual purposes, was equivalent to using the force of the whole Army of the United States to take possession of that office, because if the General of the Army thought that the order was legal, he, obeying the orders of his superior, when he was ordered

to take possession by force, had a right to use the whole Army of the United States to enforce the President's order. Therefore, the President was notified that Mr. Stanton only yielded his office at first to superior force; and so he did wisely and patriotically, because if he had not yielded, a collision might have been brought which would have raised a civil war, which in the language of the late rebels and General Thomas, is an "onpleasantness" between loyal and rebel men.

The President knew that Mr. Stanton at first said, "I will only yield this office to superior force." Then Mr. Stanton having thus yielded it, the General of the Army took possession, and on the action of the Senate the General vacated it in obedience to the high behest of the Senate, and Mr. Stanton was reinstated in it in obedience to the high behest of the Senate, and being there he was still more fortified in his position than at first. If he would not yield it except to superior force on the 12th of August, 1867, do you believe, Senators, is any man so besotted as to believe that the President did not know that Mr. Stanton, so reinstated, so fortified, meant to hold the office against everything but force? The President had been notified that Stanton yielded only to the General of the Army; wielding superior force he had seen Stanton put back by the high authority of the Senate; he had seen Stanton sustained by a vote of the Senate, declaring that the attempt to remove him was illegal and unconstitutional; and then, for the purpose of bringing this to an issue, the President of the United States issued his order to General Thomas, another officer of the Army, "You will immediately enter upon the discharge of the duties of the War Office." What then? He had come to the conclusion to violate the law and take possession of the War Office; he had come to the conclusion to do that against the law and in violation of the law; he had sent for Thomas, and Thomas had agreed with him to do that by some means if the President would give him the order, and thus we have the agreement between two minds to do an unlawful act; and that, I believe, is the definition, of a conspiracy all over the world.

Let me restate this. You have the determination on the part of the President to do what had been declared to be, and is, an unlawful act; you have Thomas consenting; and you have therefore an agreement of two minds to do an unlawful act; and that makes a conspiracy, so far as I understand the law of conspiracy. So that upon that conspiracy we should rest this evidence under article seven, which alleges that—

"Andrew Johnson" * * * * "did unlawfully conspire with one Lorenzo Thomas, with intent unlawfully to seize, take, and possess the property of the United States in the Department of War in the custody and charge of Edwin M. Stanton."

And also under article five, which alleges a

like unlawful conspiracy not alleging that intent.

Then there is another ground upon which this evidence is admissible, and that is upon the ground of principal and agent. Let us, if you please, examine that ground for a few moments. The President claims by his answer here that every Secretary, every Attorney General, every executive officer of this Government exists by his will, upon his breath only; that they are all his servants only, and are responsible to him alone, not to the Senate or Congress or either branch of Congress; and he may remove them for such cause as he chooses; he appoints them for such cause as he chooses; and he claims this right to be illimitable and uncontrollable, and he says in his message to you of December 12, 1867, that if any one of his Secretaries had said to him that he would not agree with him upon the unconstitutionality of the act of March 2, 1867, he would have turned him out at once. All this had passed into history, and Mr. Thomas knew that as well as anybody else. Now, then, what is the position and duties of a Secretary of War, whether *ad interim* or permanent? It is that he—

"Shall perform and execute such duties as shall from time to time be enjoined on or intrusted to him by the President of the United States agreeably to the Constitution"—

Intrusted to him agreeably to the Constitution.

"Relative to military commissions, or to the land or naval forces, ships, or warlike stores of the United States, or such other matters respecting military or naval affairs as the President of the United States shall assign to the said Department," * * * * "and that the said principal officer shall conduct the business of the said Department in such manner as the President of the United States shall from time to time order or instruct."

Therefore, his commission is to do precisely as the President desires him to do about anything that pertains to the War Office, and he stands, then, as the agent of the principal—to do what? He was authorized by the President to obtain possession of the War Office. Was he authorized to do anything else that we hear of up to that time? No. He was to obtain possession of the office. Now, what do we propose to show by this evidence? Having shown that Thomas was authorized to obtain possession of the office; having shown that he had agreed with the President to obtain it; having put in testimony that the two stood together in the pursuit of one common object, the President wanting Thomas to get in, and Thomas wanting to get in, and both agreeing and concerting means together to get in, the question is whether, under every rule of law, we are not permitted to show the acts and declarations, however naked these declarations may be, of either of these two parties about the common object? And the very question presupposes that we are only to ask the declarations of Thomas about the common object. But the case does not quite stop here, because

we shall show that Thomas was then talking about to execute the common purpose. We asked Mr. BURLEIGH if he was a friend to General Thomas; he said yes; if they were intimate? yes; accustomed to visit backward and forward? yes. Governor MOORHEAD has already told you that Mr. BURLEIGH was a friend of the President. There needed somebody to aid in this enterprise; some moral support was wanted in this enterprise; and we propose to show that General Thomas was endeavoring to get one of the members of the House of Representatives to support him in the enterprise, and was laying out the plan, and that he asked him to go with him the next morning and aid him in the enterprise, and be there aiding and abetting in the enterprise. Such is the testimony we propose to show, and that is one way in which we propose to connect the President with the joint enterprise. Such is the exact condition of things.

Now, having shown a common object, whether a lawful or unlawful one would make no difference as to this point; but, as I contend, a common, unlawful object, and having shown the two parties agreeing upon one thing, having shown the authority of one to the other to do an act, can we not put in the declarations of both parties in regard to that act? Do not the acts of one become the acts of the other? Take the testimony we put in yesterday. Why did not my learned friends object to what Thomas said to Mr. Stanton when he demanded the War Office? The President was not there. To use the arguments of the learned counsel for the President, Thomas was not upon oath; he was acting in the President's absence. Why should we put in the act of Thomas there yesterday? It was because he was doing in relation to the thing itself.

Mr. STANBERY. That was within the authority.

Mr. Manager BUTLER. Ah! that was within the authority. How was it within the authority? It was within the authority because the President had commanded him to take possession. Now, then, I want to show the means by which he was to take possession. How was that to be done? Why, they say (and only the gravity of the occasion prevents me from believing it a stupendous joke) we should show what he said by calling Thomas. On the trial of one conspirator call the other to show the conspiracy! Was that ever done in any court upon any question whatever, except one conspirator turns State's evidence or king's evidence, as it is called? and Thomas, I believe, is not quite bad enough to do that yet. It was never done by intelligent counsel.

These, then, are the foundations on which we stand. Now, what are the authorities for receiving these declarations? I hold in my hand Roscoe's Criminal Evidence, and I propose to cite it upon this point: that we are not bound to put in all our evidence at once, and tha$t$, by the very acts and declarations of the conspirators themselves, we may prove the conspiracy:

I read from page 390:

"The rule, says Mr. Starkie, that one man is not to be affected by the acts and declarations of a stranger, rests on the principles of the purest justice"—

"Acts and declarations of a stranger," you will observe—

"and although the courts, in cases of conspiracy, have, out of convenience, and on account of the difficulty in otherwise proving the guilt of the parties, admitted the acts and declarations of strangers to be given in evidence, in order to establish the fact of a conspiracy, it is to be remembered that this is an inversion of the usual order, for the sake of convenience, and that such evidence is, in the result, material so far only as the assent of the accused to what has been done by others is proved."—2 *Stark. Ev.,* 235, second edition.

"It has since been held that.the prosecutor may either prove the conspiracy which renders the acts of the conspirators admissible in evidence, or he may prove the acts of the different persons, and thus prove the conspiracy."

And we have attempted to prove the conspiracy in the same way.

Again, the authority says:

"Where, therefore, a party met, which was joined by the prisoner the next day, it was held, that directions given by one of the party on the day of their meeting, as to where they were to go, and for what purpose, were admissible, and the case ,was said to fall within Rex *vs.* Hunt, 3 B., and Ald., 566, where evidence of drilling at a different place two days before, and hissing 'an obnoxious person, was held receivable."

The answer of the learned counsel to the authority would be to say, "those were acts." I agree; but declarations simply may be proof of such conspiracy. Now, then, if the Senate believe that we have shown any common purpose, which is all that is necessary, between the President and Thomas, then this authority which we find on page 393 is in point:

"The cases in which after the existence of a conspiracy is established, and the particular defendants have been proved to have been parties to it, the acts or declarations of other conspirators may be given in evidence against them, have already been considered (*vide ante,* pp. 76-80.) It seems to make no difference as to the admissibility of this evidence, whether the other conspirators be indicted or not, or tried or not; for the making of them codefendants would give no additional strength to their declarations as against others."

That authority answers the argument of the learned counsel for the defendant when he says Thomas is not here ou trial. No; but his conspirator is, his master is, his principal is, and the fact that he is not present makes no difference on the question of evidence. The evidence is admissible because of the mutual agreement.

To show that this doctrine stands upon the same ground, as well in civil cases as in criminal, I refer next to 2 Carrington and Payne, p. 232. This was an action of false imprisonment against three certain defendants:

"The plaintiff's counsel wished to give in evidence, that several weeks after all the defendants had locked the plaintiff up in the cage, the defendant, Court, said, 'I will take care that neither of the Wrights shall have a bed to lie on before the end of six months.' At the time this was said the other defendants were not present."

These three men had engaged in locking a man up in jail, and weeks afterward one of the defendants made a declaration as to his purpose, and that was to oppress the party injured by keeping him locked up and putting him to bodily inconvenience.

"Jervis, for the defendants, objected that this declaration of the defendant, Court, ought not to be received in evidence, because it was made in the absence of the other defendants."

* * * * * * * * * *

"GARROW, B.—I am of opinion that this declaration of the defendant, Court, is evidence. It is necessary that the plaintiff should connect all the defendants as joint trespassers in the fact of imprisonment; and, having done so, I must receive in evidence anything that either of the defendants said relative to the trespass, though in the absence of the others. So much as to the law. On the hardship of the case I need only say that if the law were not so, a man going to do another an injury might proclaim his malice in the market-place and yet shut out evidence of such malice from the consideration of the jury by only associating himself in the transaction with other persons a shade less guilty than himself; and persons may always avoid the declarations of the malice of their codefendants operating against them by taking care not to be concerned in the doing of things which they cannot afterward justify."

Is not this case precisely in point with ours, only a hundred times stronger? But I may be answered that that is an English case. Well, I have here a United States case, the case of the United States *vs.* Gooding, 12 Wheaton; I shall read from pages 469 and 470. Let me state the case. One Gooding had fitted out at Baltimore a slaver called the General Winder— and I may say, in passing, a very proper name for it—and having fitted her out he sent her to the West Indies, and there being at the West Indies, before she started on her voyage to Africa, the captain undertook to tell a witness on what voyage she was going, where she was bound; the evidence offered being:

"That he, Captain Coit, was at St. Thomas while the General Winder was at that island, in September, 1824, and was frequently on board the vessel at that time; that Captain Hill, the master of the vessel, then and there proposed to the witness to engage on board the General Winder as mate for the voyage then in progress, and described the same to be a voyage to the coast of Africa for slaves, and thence back to Trinidad de Cuba; that he offered to the witness seventy dollars per month, and five dollars per head for every prime slave which should be brought to Cuba; that on the witness inquiring who would see the crew paid in the event of a disaster attending the voyage, Captain Hill replied, 'Uncle John,' meaning (as the witness understood) John Gooding, the defendant."

The defendant being in Baltimore at that time. The first point taken in this case was that the act of hiring a man to be a mate was in the scope of his authority; and the second point was that telling who would pay him was a declaration of one of the principals, of one of the conspirators, if you please, of one party engaged in a joint transaction with the other. Upon that the court say:

"Those declarations and explanations are as much within the scope of the authority as the act of hiring itself. Our opinion of the admissibility of this evidence proceeds upon the ground that these were not the naked declarations of the master, unaccompanied with his acts in that capacity, but declarations coupled with proceedings for the objects of the voyage, and while it was in progress. We give no opinion upon the point whether mere declarations under other circumstances would have been admissible."

Now, let us see the condition of General Thomas. He had been on the 21st of February ordered to take possession "immediately," at once. He had gone to a friend of his, Mr. BURLEIGH, and wanted him to aid him in this object. He was hiring a mate, if you please, on that voyage, precisely within the case of Gooding. He was wanting somebody to aid him; and he thereupon describes to BURLEIGH the voyage; that it was to be a slaver's voyage; what he was to pay; how it was to be received; how he was to seize the slave; or, in other words, how he is to seize the War Department; and we offer to put these things in evidence by his declarations.

I have but one authority more, and I will cease troubling the Senate upon this point. I read from 3 Greenleaf on Evidence, section ninety-three:

"The evidence in proof of a conspiracy will generally, from the nature of the case, be 'circumstantial.' Though the common design is the essence of the charge, it is not necessary to prove that the defendants came together and actually agreed in terms to have that design and to pursue it by common means. If it be proved that the defendants pursued by their acts the same object, often by the same means, one performing one part and another another part of the same, so as to complete it with a view to the attainment of that same object, the jury will be justified in the conclusion that they were engaged in a conspiracy to effect that object."

Almost in the language of this authority the object was to get the War Department at all hazards. That is agreed; that is in the President's answer. It is there said to be a high constitutional prerogative to do it! They had been notified that Stanton would hold it by force, as, thank God, up to this hour, he has held it against these conspirators; and being notified that he would not deliver it except to force, they then started out to devise ways and means, and we shall show you, and by these very conversations with this very person, Thomas declared that if he had not been arrested he would have used the intervention of the courts he would have used force on the morning when he was there, as has been shown.

Now, are we, upon the trial of this issue, to be told that the President of the United States can employ men to go to do this, that, and the other, which is illegal, admitted to be illegal, unless the law is unconstitutional, and then turn back upon us and say, "Oh, you cannot put in what my agents said while they were pursuing this thing, while they were getting together means to execute my will." Let me illustrate for a moment. This is only to BURLEIGH. Suppose Thomas had gone to get the commander of this department, General Emory, with his forces. Suppose he had said to him, "I want you to come to-morrow to aid me and see me take this Department by force," could we not put that in? Is this objected to because he only asked Mr. BURLEIGH? If he

kept asking men enough to go with him he would have had enough, as he thought he had, until the hand of the law was laid upon him. Therefore I respectfully answer the question put by the learned Senator that we have connected and do expect to connect the President with this by a series of acts, a series of declarations, a series of operations which will leave no doubt on the mind of any Senator what this purpose was. But we claim, further, that there is no doubt upon any man's mind what the purpose was at that hour.

I desire, in closing, simply to call your attention to the opening address of the Attorney General—I beg pardon, the learned counsel for the defendant; he will pardon me, but I have been so accustomed to meet him in other relations that I sometimes forget. He says that we have now got to a question of law fit to be argued by lawyers to lawyers, implying that all other questions which have been argued before this high court, as he insists upon calling it, have not been fit to be argued either by lawyers or to lawyers. It is for you to defend yourselves from that sort of imputation. I had supposed the great questions we had been arguing were not only fit to be argued by lawyers to lawyers, but by statesmen to statesmen, by the Representatives of the people to the Senators of the United States. And I insist that this question is not one to be narrowed down to the attorney's office, but is to be viewed in the light of the law and enlightened jurisprudence as it will be administered by the Senate of the United States.

The question for you to determine is, will this evidence aid you, for you are both court and jury; this is not a case where the court rule one way and the jury may go another; but you are both court and jury—will this evidence enlighten you if you hear from this Secretary *ad interim* as to what he was doing and intending to do in this matter, joint enterprise of himself and the President. Will it enlighten you upon the judgment you are to render? If it will not, then you will say so, and vote that it shall not be heard, and the people's case will not be brought before the Senate. If, on the contrary, it will enlighten you, then I respectfully and earnestly urge that it may be received. And in this we are fortunate in being sustained by the high authority of the presiding officer. I had supposed this question was ruled and settled yesterday, and hardly expected to debate it this morning. All I can say is, as the decision is made, however much I might have objected to the mode in which it was made, I respectfully submit *stare decisus* let the decision stand, in the language of the rule, as the judgment of the Senate.

Mr. CURTIS. Mr. Chief Justice, I ask to have the question propounded by the honorable Managers read. It is long, and consists of different parts, and I desire it to be distinctly understood before I speak to it.

The CHIEF JUSTICE. The Secretary will read the question propounded by Mr. Manager BUTLER to the witness.

The Secretary read as follows:

"You said yesterday, in answer to my question, that you had a conversation with General Lorenzo Thomas on the evening of the 21st of February last. State if he said anything as to the means by which he intended to obtain, or was directed by the President to obtain, possession of the War Department. If so, state what he said as nearly as you can."

Mr. CURTIS. Mr. Chief Justice and Senators, you will observe that this question contains two distinct branches. The first inquires of the witness for declarations of General Thomas respecting his own intent. The second inquires of the witness for declarations of General Thomas respecting directions given to him by the President. In reference to the first branch, that is, the separate and independent intent of General Thomas himself, I am not aware that its subject-matter is anywhere put in issue by the articles. General Thomas is not on trial. It is the President who is on trial. It is his intentions or directions, the means, the unlawful means, which he is charged with having adopted and endeavored to carry into effect, which constitute criminality in those articles which relate at all to this subject; and therefore it seems to me that it is a sufficient objection to the first part of this question that it relates to a subject-matter wholly immaterial, and which, if proved by legitimate evidence, ought in no manner to affect the case of the President. The President is not charged here with any ill intentions or illegal intentions of General Thomas; he is charged here with his own illegal intentions; with them alone can he be charged; and therefore I respectfully submit to Senators that that branch of the question which seeks to draw into this case evidence of the intentions of General Thomas, aside from instructions given to him or views communicated to him by the President himself, is utterly immaterial, and ought not to be allowed to be proved by any evidence, whether competent or incompetent.

In the next place, I submit that the evidence which is offered to prove the intention of General Thomas, if that fact were in issue here, and could, when proved, have any effect upon the President's case, is not of an admissible character. The intent of a party, as every lawyer knows, is a fact, and it is a fact to be proved by legal and admissible evidence, just as much as any other fact. It is natural for a person not a lawyer to say that the true way to ascertain a man's intent is to take what he says is his intent; because intent is a state of mind, and when that is expressed that expression is fit evidence of it. All that is true; but inasmuch as it is not sworn evidence of it, inasmuch as it is not given by the man when on the stand in the presence of the accused and with opportunity for cross-examination, it is no evidence at all, unless you can bring the

case within one of the exceptions which exist in the law; one of these exceptions, as has been said by my associate counsel, being the case of principal and agent; the other the case of coconspirators.

I do not propose to go over the argument which was so clearly and forcibly put, as it seems to me, by my associate, who opened it. I think Senators must have understood perfectly well the grounds upon which it is our intention to rest this objection to the declarations of General Thomas so far as regards his own intent, that he was not the agent of the President, that he received from a superior officer an order to do a certain thing, and in no sense thereby became an agent of that superior officer, nor did that superior officer become accountable for the manner in which he might carry out that order; and that this is specially true when the nature of the order is nothing but the designation of one public officer to notify another public officer that he has been designated to discharge the duties of the office from which the latter has been removed; in which case whatever this designated person may do he does on his own account and by force of his own views of how the authority is to be carried out unless he has received some special instructions in regard to the mode of carrying them out.

We submit, then, in the first place, that the intentions of General Thomas are immaterial, and the President cannot be affected by them; and secondly, if they be material, they must be proved by sworn evidence, and not by hearsay statements.

The other part, Senators, of the question appears to me to admit of even less doubt; and that part is attempting to inquire of the witness what was said by General Thomas respecting directions or instructions given to him by the President, which presents the naked case of an attempt to prove an authority of an agent by the agent's own declarations. The question is whether the President gave instructions to General Thomas in regard to the particular manner or means by which this order was to be carried out. Upon its face the order is intelligible. We understand it to be in the usual form. There is no allusion made to the exercise of force, threats, or intimidation of any kind. Now they propose to superadd to this written order, by means of the declarations of the agent himself, that he had an authority to use threats, intimidation, or force; and no lawyer will say that that can be done unless there is first laid the foundation for it by showing that the two parties were connected together as coconspirators. I agree that if they could show a conspiracy between the President and General Thomas to which these declarations relate, then the declarations of one of them in reference to the subject-matter of that conspiracy would be evidence against the other. Now, what is the case as it stands here before you, and as is asserted by the honorable Manager himself? He starts out with the proposition that the President in his answer has admitted his intention to remove Mr. Stanton from office. That, he says, was an illegal intention. That, he says, was an intention to be carried out by means of the order given to General Thomas; and when the President, he says, gave that order to General Thomas, and General Thomas accepted it and undertook to execute it, there was an agreement between them to do an illegal act. What was the illegal act which thus far we have got what he calls a conspiracy to do? It was to remove Mr. Stanton; and, if that be contrary to the tenure-of-office act, that, when accomplished, may be an illegal act. But is that the illegal act which they are now undertaking to prove? Is that the extent of the conspiracy which they are now undertaking to show? Not at all. They are passing altogether beyond that. They now undertake to say, "We will show that he conspired with General Thomas to remove Mr. Stanton by force, threats, or intimidation, and thus to commit a totally distinct crime under the conspiracy act." That is the conspiracy which they propose to show. Having shown only an agreement to remove Mr. Stanton, and starting with that agreement, which of course makes the entire limits of the conspiracy, as they call it, of which they have given evidence, all circumscribed within this intention merely to remove Mr. Stanton, they now graft on to that by a pure and mere assumption a conspiracy to remove him by force; and so, having proved a conspiracy to remove him without force, we will now give in evidence the declarations of these coconspirators to show a conspiracy to remove him with force. I respectfully submit they have then traveled out of the limits of the conspiracy which they themselves pretend they have given any evidence of; and as soon as they get out of the limits of that conspiracy which they allege and say they have given some proof of, and advance to another and totally different conspiracy, namely, the conspiracy to turn out Mr. Stanton by force, then they must give some evidence of that other conspiracy before they can use the declarations of either of the parties to it as evidence against the President. .

But, Senators, I do not think this thing should be left here. It is an entire misconception of the relations of these two parties, the Commander-in-Chief and a subordinate officer, one receiving an order from the other, under any circumstances which appear here, or which there is any evidence here tending to prove, to call it a conspiracy. The learned Manager has said: "If I show an agreement between two persons to do an unlawful act that is a conspiracy, is it not?" It may be; but when the Commander-in-Chief gives an order to a subordinate officer to do an act, and the subordinate officer goes to do it, is that done by agreement between them? Does it derive its force

and character and operation from any agreement between them, any concurrence of their minds by which the two parties assent and agree together so as to accomplish something which without that assent and agreement could not be done? Is it not as plain as day that military obedience is not conspiracy and cannot be conspiracy? Is it not as plain as day that it is the duty of the subordinate officer when he receives an order from his commander to execute that order?

My associate [Mr. Evarts] suggests to me that, as is a well-known fact, and will, no doubt, appear in the course of the proceedings, when General Grant received an order from the President to take this same place, he put it upon the ground of military obedience. Was that a conspiracy? Senators, there can be no such thing as a conspiracy between the Commander-in-Chief and a subordinate officer, arising simply from the fact that the Commander-in-Chief issues an order and the subordinate officer obeys it. Therefore I respectfully submit that the honorable Managers have not only proved not even the conspiracy to remove Mr. Stanton without force, but they have offered no evidence here tending to prove any conspiracy at all. It rests exactly where the written orders place it; an order from a superior officer to an inferior officer and an assent by him to execute that order.

It has been said by the learned Manager in the course of his argument that we ought to have objected, if we took this view of the case, to the declarations made by General Thomas when he went to the War Department on Saturday, the 22d of February. We could not make any objection to what he then said. It was competent evidence. He was there in pursuance of the order given to him by the President. He was doing what the President authorized him to do, namely, delivering one order to Mr. Stanton, he being for that purpose merely the messenger of the President; and, having executed that, to take possession under the other order. Of course he authorized him to demand possession, and he did demand it; but that demand was as much an act and as capable of proof and proper to be proved as any other act. Therefore we could have taken no such exception; it could not have come at all within the range of any of the objections which we now take.

The learned Manager relies, also, on certain authorities which he has produced from the books. The first is a case stated in Roscoe's Criminal Evidence; page 390, I think, he read from, showing that under some circumstances the acts of coconspirators, even before the person on trial had joined the conspiracy, may be proved. I see no difficulty in that. The first thing is to prove a conspiracy, which is a separate and independent fact, or may be wholly separate and independent from the evidence by which you prove the other step, namely, that a particular person joined in it.

In that case the Government undertook to show, in the first place, that there was a conspiracy. They proved it by the assembling together of a body of men for the purpose of military training, &c. Having proved that there was a conspiracy, they then took the necessary step to show that the accused on a subsequent day joined himself in that conspiracy. That was all regular and proper.

If they will take the first step here and in support of their articles undertake to show by evidence a conspiracy between the President and General Thomas, when they have done that they may go on and give evidence of the declarations of one or both of them to charge the other; but until they do I submit that they cannot give such evidence.

The case from 2 Carrington and Payne was a case of a joint act of three persons falsely imprisoning a fourth. There was the conspiracy; there was the false imprisonment, the illegal act, done in pursuance of the conspiracy; and the court decided that a declaration made subsequent to the imprisonment as to what the intentions of the parties were and how they intended to carry it out would be admissible against the others, all of which falls easily within the same rule.

The case from 12 Wheaton was one where the owner of a ship having authorized the master to fit out a vessel, the declarations of the master were given in evidence to show the object and intentions of the voyage. Unquestionably, if he had made him his agent to carry on a slaving voyage he made him his agent to do all acts necessary to carry it out. What was the act that was given in evidence? It was an attempt to engage a person to go on a slave-trading voyage in a subordinate capacity. In the course of that attempt he stated to him what the character and purposes of the voyage were; but it was an act which he was engaged in, an act within the scope of his authority to carry on the voyage and to engage persons to assist him in doing so. This, also, falls easily within the scope of the principles upon which we rely.

We submit, then, to the Senate that neither of these questions should be allowed to be put to this witness. I ought to say, and I am reminded by one of my associates to say, that the statement by the honorable Manager that the answer of the President admits his intention to remove Mr. Stanton from office illegally and at all hazards is not true. The honorable Manager is mistaken if he has so read the answer. The answer distinctly says, in the first place, that the President believed, after the greatest consideration, that Mr. Stanton's case was not within the tenure-of-office act; and the answer further says that he never authorized General Thomas to employ threats, force, or intimidation, and if the honorable Manager refers to the answer as his evidence for one purpose he must take it as it stands.

Mr. Manager BINGHAM. Mr. President and Senators, I had occasion to remark yesterday, upon the ruling of the presiding officer of the Senate, that the Managers on the part of the House had no cause of complaint touching that ruling, which had relation to the introduction of this testimony. I said it, Senators, because I was assured when I did say it that the ruling of the presiding officer stands upon all the authorities, English and American, and upon that point I challenge to-day any authority to call in question the ruling that the testimony this morning objected to, and ruled as admissible yesterday by the presiding officer, is not admissible.

I have listened with due attention to the learned gentlemen who have argued in support of this objection. Admitting their premises, it might be but just to them to say that their conclusions follow; but, Senators, I deny their premises. There is nothing in the record that justifies that they shall assume here, for the purposes of this question, that we are restricted, as was intimated by the learned counsel for the President, to the article which alleges that this conspiracy was to be executed by force. There is nothing in this case, as it stands before the Senate, that justifies the assumption that the Senate is to be restricted in the decision of this question to the other article which alleges that this conspiracy was to be exercised by threats and intimidation. There is nothing in the question propounded by my associate to the witness which justifies the assumption made here that the witness is to testify that any force was to be employed at all, although, if he were so to testify, I claim upon the authorities, and upon all the authorities, that the testimony is admissible.

The Senate will notice that in article five there is no averment of force, there is no averment of threat or intimidation. There is simply an averment in article five of an unlawful conspiracy entered into between the accused and Lorenzo Thomas to violate the tenure-of-office act. My associate was right upon all authority, and it is conceded, that if two or more agree together to violate a law of the land it is a conspiracy. That is the point we make here. In article five there is no averment of force, nor is any needed; there is no averment of threat or intimidation, nor is any needed; but there is simply an averment of a conspiracy entered into between the accused and Lorenzo Thomas, and other persons unknown to the House of Representatives to prevent the execution of the tenure-of-office act. That act declares that a removal, appointment, or employment, made or had, contrary to the act, or an interference, if you please, with the provisions of the act and contrary to its requirements, shall be a misdemeanor on the part of any man. Of course, if a combination be entered into between two or more to prevent its execution, that combination itself amounts to a conspiracy.

The counsel have succeeded most admirably

in diverting the attention of Senators from the question which underlies the admissibility of this evidence, and which controls it. I refer now specifically to article five, upon which, among other articles, we claim this question arises which was not referred to by the counsel for the accused.

"That said Andrew Johnson, President of the United States, unmindful of the high duties of his office and of his oath of office, on the 21st day of February, in the year of our Lord 1868, and on divers other days and times in said year, before the 25th day of March, in the year of our Lord 1868, at Washington, in the District of Columbia, did unlawfully conspire with one Lorenzo Thomas, and with other persons to the House of Representatives unknown, to prevent and hinder the execution of an act entitled "An act regulating the tenure of certain civil offices," passed March 2, 1867, and in pursuance of said conspiracy, did unlawfully attempt to prevent Edwin M. Stanton, then and there being Secretary for the Department of War, duly appointed and commissioned under the laws of the United States, from holding said office, whereby the said Andrew Johnson, President of the United States, did then and there commit and was guilty of a high misdemeanor in office."

Now, the tenure-of-office act, which is recited in this article, provides expressly that the person holding any civil office at the time of its enactment, who has theretofore been appointed by and with the advice and consent of the Senate—

"And every person who shall hereafter be appointed to any such office, and shall become duly qualified to act therein, is and shall be entitled to hold such office until a successor shall have been in like manner appointed and duly qualified."

That is to say, all such officers shall hold their office until a successor be appointed by and with the advice and consent of the Senate. The act then provides that the President of the United States shall, during the recess of the Senate, not at any other time than during the recess of the Senate, in case he is satisfied that any officer is

"Guilty of misconduct in office or crime, or for any reason shall become incapable or legally disqualified to perform its duties, in such case, and in no other, the President may suspend such officer and designate some suitable person to perform temporarily the duties of such office until the next meeting of the Senate, and until the case shall be acted upon by the Senate; and such person so designated shall take the oaths and give the bonds required by law to be taken and given by the person duly appointed to fill such office; and in such case it shall be the duty of the President, within twenty days after the first day of such next meeting of the Senate, to report to the Senate such suspension, with the evidence and reasons for his action in the case, and the name of the person so designated to perform the duties of such office; and if the Senate shall concur in such suspension and advise and consent to the removal of such officer, they shall so certify to the President, who may thereupon remove such officer, and, by and with the advice and consent of the Senate, appoint another person to such office. But if the Senate shall refuse to concur in such suspension, such officer, so suspended, shall forthwith resume the functions of his office."

The sixth section of the same act provides:

"That every removal, appointment, or employment, made, had, or exercised contrary to the provisions of this act, and the making, signing, sealing, countersigning, or issuing of any commission or letter of authority for or in respect to any such appointment or employment, shall be deemed, and are hereby declared to be high misdemeanors."

The conspiracy entered into here between these two parties was to prevent the execution of this law, which is so plain that no man can mistake it; nor can the President, in the presence of this tribunal, or Lorenzo Thomas either, shelter himself by the intimation that it was a military order to a subordinate. Are we to be told in the presence of the Senate that it is competent for the President of the United States either to shelter himself or any of his subordinates, by issuing to-morrow a military order, either to Adjutant General Thomas or to any other officer of the Army of the United States, to disperse the Congress of the nation? This is an afterthought, gentlemen of the Senate. It is no military order; it is a letter of authority within the express words of the statute and in violation of it. The evidence is that Lorenzo Thomas accepted it and acted upon it. The evidence of his action upon it was given yesterday, and received by the Senate without objection. It is too late to raise the question of the competency of this testimony after there is evidence here tending to show a conspiracy to violate the plain letter of this law.

It is perfectly justifiable, I take it, in this tribunal for me to say further, and say it upon my own honor as one of the Managers on the part of the House, that we rely, not simply upon the declarations of Lorenzo Thomas to show this purpose of the accused at your bar to disregard this statute, to violate its plain provisions, that the officer thus affirmed by the Senate upon suspension shall forthwith enter upon the duties of his office, but we expect by the written confession of the accused himself to show to this Senate this day, or as soon thereafter as we can be heard, that it was his declared, fixed purpose, in any event, to defy the authority of the Senate and prevent Stanton from resuming the functions of the office. There was no reference then made to the intervention of courts. The accused grasped the power in his own hands of repealing the law of the nation, or challenging the power of the nation to bring him to its bar to answer; and now, when we attempt to progress with the trial according to the known and established rules of evidence in all courts of justice, we are met with the plausible and ingenious—more plausible and more ingenious than sound—remark of the learned counsel for the accused who has just taken his seat, that the declaration of one coconspirator cannot be given in evidence against another as to his mode of executing it. I state it, perhaps a little more strongly than the counsel stated it, but that was exactly the significance of his remark. I should like to know whence he derives any such authority.

A declaration of a coconspirator made in the prosecution of the conspiracy, I venture to say here upon all authority, is admissible, even as to the mode in which he would execute and carry out the common design—admissible not simply against himself, but admissible against his coconspirator, admissible against them, not to establish the original conspiracy, but, to prove the intent and purpose of the party to execute the conspiracy. The conspiracy is complete upon all authority whenever the agreement is entered into to violate the law, no matter whether an overt act is ever committed afterward in pursuance of it or not; but the overt acts that are committed afterward by any one of the conspirators in pursuance of the conspiracy are evidence against him, and against his coconspirators. That is precisely the ground upon which the ruling was made yesterday by the presiding officer of the court. That is the ground upon which we stand to-day.

I quite agree with the learned counsel for the accused that the declaration of a purpose to do some act independent of the original design of the conspiracy, to commit some substantive, independent crime, is evidence against nobody but the party who makes it; but how can the Senate judge that such was the declaration of Thomas, when not one word has dropped from the lips of the witness as to how he intended to carry into effect this conspiracy, which was to prevent the execution of this law, and which, in the language of the accused, as we hope to show it here to the Senate, was determined upon by himself, in which Lorenzo Thomas was in perfect accord with him, having voluntarily entered upon this duty? He did not act that day, Senators, as Adjutant General of the United States. He acted as Secretary of War *ad interim*; so denominated himself in presence of the Secretary; and claimed that he was Secretary of War by virtue of a letter of authority which he carried upon his person.

Now we are to be told that because he is not on trial before this tribunal his declarations cannot be admitted in evidence, while the counsel themselves read the text going to show that if they were joined in the record, as he may be hereafter, in the event of a certain decision by this tribunal, his declarations would be clearly admissible.

The Senate have it in their power, (and there is authority for saying that,) sitting as a high court of impeachment, to apply the reason of the rule, although by the order of the proceeding at the common law a different condition of things might obtain in which alone it would apply. We cannot impeach Lorenzo Thomas at all, for the reason that he is not a civil officer of the Government. So we understand it. The power of the House of Representatives does not extend beyond the President, Vice President, and other civil officers. To be sure he claims to be a civil officer; and he is one, if the President of the United States has power, by this combination with him, to repeal your statute and to repeal the Constitution of the country.

I have thus spoken on this question, Senators, for the purpose of exposing the significance and importance which I know the counsel for the accused attach to it. It is not simply that they desire (I say it with all respect) that this testimony shall be ruled out; but they desire in some sort, in some questionable shape, a judgment now, on the part of the Senate, upon the main question, whether Andrew Johnson is guilty of a crime, even though it be proved hereafter as charged. As I have intimated, it was his purpose to defy the final judgment of the Senate itself and the authority of the law which declares, if he does so defy it, his act shall be a high misdemeanor. That is what is to be signified by this decision of the Senate. It is not simply the incompetency of this evidence that is looked for, but the insufficiency of the charge in the fifth article against the accused which is hoped for by your decision.

I understand it was intimated by one of the counsel that, if this was a conspiracy, the acceptance by General Grant of the appointment of Secretary of War *ad interim* was also a conspiracy. The Senate will see very clearly from my reading of the statute, or from my reminding them, rather, of that which they do know, that this does not follow, and cannot be at all. It involves a very different question, for the reason that the statute expressly authorizes the President, for reasons of course satisfactory to himself, during the recess of the Senate, to suspend the Secretary of War, and to appoint a Secretary *ad interim*, upon the condition, nevertheless, that he shall, within twenty days after the next session of the Senate, report his action together with the evidence, and have the decision of the Senate upon it. He did so act. There was no conspiracy in it, and there is none alleged here. He did so act. He did recognize the obligation of the law. He did avail himself of the authority with which it invested him. He did suspend the Secretary of War and appoint a Secretary *ad interim*. He did within twenty days thereafter report the fact to the Senate together with his reasons. The Senate, in pursuance of the act, did pronounce judgment upon the sufficiency of the causes of suspension, and reversed, in accordance with the act, the action of the President. The Senate notified him of it. In the meantime he enters into his combinations, his conspiracies, to defeat the action of the Senate and to overturn the majesty of the law; and now, when we bring him to the bar of the Senate and produce his written letter of authority issued to his coconspirator in direct violation of the law, while the Senate was in session, and after its action upon this very question, and prove Thomas's act, in pursuance of the conspiracy, at the War Department asserting the authority to control that Department, declaring that he would take possession of its mails, declaring that he would not obey the orders of the Secretary of War, Edwin M. Stanton, who is declared such by the solemn action of the Senate and by the express letter of the law; and while we attempt to pursue it further by showing his declarations, coupled with an attempt, as I assert now in the presence of the Senate, to get additional aid in the execution of this conspiracy, we are told that it is not competent.

I desire to see the authority anywhere recognized as respectable in a court of justice that, when there is evidence tending to show a conspiracy for the accomplishment of a given purpose between two or more persons, it is not competent upon the trial of any one of the conspirators to prove the declarations and acts of any of his coconspirators, whether living or dead, whether on trial or not, made in the prosecution of the common design, no matter what means he intended to employ.

Now, I beg leave to say that I believe it will turn out—as I said before, the Senate will be the judge of that when they hear the evidence, and they cannot judge of it before—that there will be in this conversation between BURLEIGH and Thomas enough to indicate to the satisfaction of Senators that he did not simply desire to acquaint him of how this agreement and conspiracy between himself and Johnson was to be executed in the morning, but relying upon his personal friendship he desired his presence there on that occasion. If that be so, he was seeking for aid by which to carry into effect the original conspiracy and execute it, and what was that? To defeat the action of the Senate, to defeat the requirement of the law that the Secretary of War should forthwith resume the duties of the office and to control it himself.

I think that I have said all that it is needful for me to say. I leave the question for the decision of the Senate, perfectly assured that they will hear first and decide afterward. It is certainly very competent for the Senate, as it is competent for any court of justice in the trial of cases where questions of doubt arise, to hear the evidence, and, where they themselves are the judges both of the law and the fact, to dismiss so much of it as they may find incompetent, if there be any of it incompetent. I insist upon it that there is no word of this testimony which upon any just rule of evidence can for a moment be questioned or challenged by anybody.

Mr. JOHNSON. Mr. Chief Justice, I desire the honorable Managers to answer two questions which I send to the Chair.

The CHIEF JUSTICE. The Secretary will read the questions propounded by the Senator from Maryland.

The Secretary read as follows:

The honorable Managers are requested to say whether evidence hereafter will be produced to show—

First. That the President, before the time when the declarations of Thomas which they propose to prove were made, authorized him to obtain possession of the office by force or threats, or intimidation, if necessary; or,

Secondly, If not, that the President had knowledge that such declarations had been made and approved of them.

Mr. Manager BINGHAM. I am instructed by my associates to say—and I am in accord in judgment with them, Mr. President—that we do not deem it our duty to make answer to so general a question as that; and it will certainly occur to the Senate why we should not make answer to it.

Mr. EVARTS. Mr. Chief Justice, as we claim on the part of the counsel——

Mr. Manager BINGHAM. I rise to a question here. I understand that we speak here under a rule of the Senate, as yet at least, that requires us to be restricted to an hour on each side.

Mr. STANBERY. And one counsel, if you go according to the rule.

Mr. Manager BINGHAM. No; I do not understand that. I understand, on the contrary, that the practice heretofore thus far in the progress of this trial has been to allow the counsel to divide their time as they pleased, within but one hour on each side. The point to which I rise now, however, is this: that we understand that in a proceeding of this sort the Managers have always claimed and asserted where the point was raised at all, the right to conclude upon all questions that were raised in the progress of the trial. The hour has been well nigh expended in this instance on each side, as I am told, though I have not taken any special note of the time. But we raise the question; and I state that the fact that our time has been exhausted, as I am advised, is the only reason why I raise it now; and thus we are cut off from any further reply. Our only object in raising the question is that we shall not be deemed to have waived it, because we are advised that it was settled years ago in Melville's case by the lord chancellor presiding and by the peers that the Managers might waive their privilege by their silence.

Mr. Manager BUTLER. We have the affirmative.

Mr. STANBERY. On this question? Oh, no.

Mr. Manager BINGHAM. We have made the proposition to introduce the proof, but the objection to its admissibility comes from the other side.

The CHIEF JUSTICE. Do the Managers object to the counsel for the President proceeding?

Mr. Manager BINGHAM. We only raise the question to save our right of being heard in reply; and, as I stated before, the only reason we object now is that we understand, without notice given to us, that our hour has been exhausted. Therefore we object.

Mr. EVARTS. Mr. Chief Justice and Senators——

The CHIEF JUSTICE. Before the counsel proceeds the Chair desires to state to the Senate, and obtain their judgment upon the construction of this rule. In the present case, with the consent of the Senate, the Chief Justice will not apply the rule, but pursue the course which has been heretofore pursued, of allowing each counsel an hour and not limiting the number of persons speaking, but for future guidance the Chief Justice would like to take the sense of the Senate, and will as soon as this discussion is closed; or he will take it now if any Senator desires it.

Mr. Manager BUTLER. Will the presiding officer allow me a single observation here?

The CHIEF JUSTICE. Certainly.

Mr. Manager BUTLER. It is this: that I limited myself expressly, and divided my time with my brother Manager, in the argument, and left out many things that I should have endeavored to address to the Senate, upon the understanding of the rule that we could only have an hour on a side. The rule said so, and I supposed it meant what it said. Now, if the presiding officer and the Senate shall allow the gentlemen on the other side to have an hour each, there will have been an administration of the rule which is exceedingly onerous upon us, and which we ought to have been notified of before; and we should like to know whether we can ever have a conclusion on one of these questions, which is our right and the right of the people of the United States.

Mr. CONNESS. Mr. President, I ask for the application of the rule.

The CHIEF JUSTICE. Senators, the Chair will state the question to the Senate. The twentieth rule provides that—

"All preliminary or interlocutory questions and all motions shall be argued for not exceeding one hour on each side, unless the Senate shall, by order, extend the time."

The twenty-first rule provides:

"The case on each side shall be opened by one person. The final argument on the merits may be made by two persons on each side, (unless otherwise ordered by the Senate upon application for that purpose,) and the argument shall be opened and closed on the part of the House of Representatives."

On looking at these two rules together, the Chief Justice was under the impression that it was intended by the twentieth rule to limit the time, and not limit the persons; whereas, by the twenty-first rule, it was intended to limit the number of persons and leave the time unlimited; and he has acted upon that construction. He will now, with the leave of the Senate, submit to them the question: Does the twentieth rule limit the time without respect to the number of persons? Upon that question the Chair will take the sense of the Senate.

Mr. DRAKE. The yeas and nays are required, I suggest, Mr. President.

The CHIEF JUSTICE. They have not been required as yet.

Mr. DRAKE. I suggest now this point of order: that all orders and decisions must, since the change made in the seventh rule yesterday, be taken by yeas and nays; that there is no provision now existing in the rules for putting a division to the Senate without a division; that that is struck out; and that the twenty-third rule requires that "all the orders and decisions shall be made and had by yeas and nays.".

The CHIEF JUSTICE. The Chair sees nothing in the seventh rule which requires this question to be taken by yeas and nays unless they are demanded in the usual mode by one fifth of the Senators present. Senators, you who are of opinion that the limitation in the twentieth rule applies to the whole number of persons to argue will please say ay, and the contrary opinion no.

The question being put, it was decided in the affirmative *nem. con.*

The CHIEF JUSTICE. The Senate decides that the limitation of one hour has reference to the whole number of persons to speak on each side, and not to each person severally; and will apply the rule as thus construed.

Mr. CONKLING. Mr. President, I move that the counsel for the President, having been under misapprehension as to the application of this rule, owing to the suggestion of the Chair, have permission in this instance to submit any additional remarks which they may wish to submit.

Mr. TRUMBULL. Mr. President, before that motion is put I desire to inquire whether the counsel for the President have exhausted their hour.

The CHIEF JUSTICE. They have.

Mr. THAYER. Mr. President, I hope the Senator from New York——

The CHIEF JUSTICE. Debate is not in order.

Mr. THAYER. I desire to submit an amendment to the motion of the Senator from New York.

The CHIEF JUSTICE. The Senator will send his amendment to the Chair in writing.

Mr. EVARTS. Mr. Chief Justice, perhaps I may be allowed to say that we do not understand that as yet on our side we have transcended the twentieth rule. We have not occupied an hour in debate on our side of the question.

The CHIEF JUSTICE. The Chief Justice thinks that the counsel for the defendant have occupied one hour.

Mr. EVARTS. Subject, of course, to the computation of the Chair. If the hour has expired I was not aware of it. I do not desire, nor do my associates desire, that we should transcend the rule. We supposed we had some moments of the hour unoccupied. I rose with the intention, however, of claiming, on the part of the counsel for the President, the right of closing as well as opening according to the ordinary rules of interlocutory discussion.

The CHIEF JUSTICE. That question is not at present before the Senate.

Mr. CONKLING. After the suggestion of the counsel I withdraw my motion.

The CHIEF JUSTICE. The Secretary will read the question proposed by Mr. Manager BUTLER.

The Secretary read as follows:

You said yesterday, in answer to my question,

that you had a conversation with General Lorenzo Thomas on the evening of the 21st of February last. State if he said anything as to the means by which he intended to obtain, or was directed by the President to obtain, possession of the War Department? If so, state all he said as nearly as you can.

Mr. JOHNSON. I ask now that the question I sent to the Chair be read.

The CHIEF JUSTICE. The question before the Senate now is, Shall the question propounded by Mr. Manager BUTLER be put to the witness?

Mr. DRAKE. On that question the yeas and nays must be taken under the rules, I submit.

Mr. EDMUNDS and others. No, no.

Mr. DRAKE. It is so, sir.

Mr. EDMUNDS. It is not so.

The CHIEF JUSTICE. Upon the question of order raised by the Senator from Missouri, the Chair is of opinion that he may submit this question to the Senate without having the yeas and nays taken, unless the yeas and nays are demanded by one fifth of the members present.

Mr. TRUMBULL. I should like to hear the seventh rule read as amended.

The CHIEF JUSTICE. The Secretary will read the rule.

The Secretary read as follows:

"VII. The Presiding Officer of the Senate shall direct all necessary preparations in the Senate Chamber, and the presiding officer on the trial shall direct all the forms of proceeding while the Senate are sitting for the purpose of trying an impeachment, and all forms during the trial not otherwise specially provided for. And the presiding officer on the trial may rule all questions of evidence and incidental questions, which ruling shall stand as the judgment of the Senate, unless some member of the Senate shall ask that a formal vote be taken thereon, in which case it shall be submitted to the Senate for decision; or he may, at his option, in the first instance, submit any such question to a vote of the members of the Senate."

Mr. JOHNSON. The questions that I submitted——

The CHIEF JUSTICE. Debate is not in order.

Mr. JOHNSON. I am not about to debate. The questions that I submitted were not, as I think, heard by all the members of the Senate. I mean the questions which the honorable Managers thought it their duty to decline to answer. I ask that they be again read before the vote is taken.

The CHIEF JUSTICE. The questions submitted by the Senator from Maryland will be again read.

Mr. Manager BOUTWELL. May the Managers be allowed to suggest that the Managers heard the questions and respectfully declined to answer them? It seems to the Managers, also, somewhat in the nature of an argument upon the questions involved.

Mr. JOHNSON. Read the question.

The CHIEF JUSTICE. The Secretary will read the question.

The Secretary read as follows:

The honorable Managers are requested to say whether evidence hereafter will be produced to show—

1. That the President before the time when the declarations of Thomas which they propose to prove were made authorized him to obtain possession of the office by force, or threats, or intimidation, if necessary; or,

2. If not, that the President had knowledge that such declarations had been made and approved of them.

Several SENATORS. Question! Question!

The CHIEF JUSTICE. Senators——

Mr. DRAKE. I call for the yeas and nays, and let us see if the Senate will not order them.

The yeas and nays were ordered; and being taken, resulted—yeas 39, nays 11; as follows:

YEAS—Messrs. Anthony, Cameron, Cattell, Chandler, Cole, Conkling, Conness, Corbett, Cragin, Drake, Edmunds, Ferry, Fessenden, Fowler, Frelinghuysen, Grimes, Henderson, Howard, Howe, Morgan, Morrill of Maine, Morrill of Vermont, Morton, Nye, Patterson of New Hampshire, Pomeroy, Ramsey, Ross, Sherman, Sprague, Stewart, Sumner, Thayer, Tipton, Trumbull, Van Winkle, Willey, Williams, and Wilson—39.

NAYS—Messrs. Bayard, Buckalew, Davis, Dixon, Doolittle, Hendricks, Johnson, McCreery, Norton, Patterson of Tennessee, and Vickers—11.

NOT VOTING—Messrs. Harlan, Saulsbury, Wade, and Yates—4.

The CHIEF JUSTICE. On this question the yeas are 39, and the nays 11. So the Senate decides that the question proposed by Mr. Manager BUTLER shall be put to the witness.

Hon. WALTER A. BURLEIGH resumed the stand, and his examination was continued.

By Mr. Manager BUTLER:

Question. You said yesterday, in answer to my question, that you had a conversation with General Lorenzo Thomas on the evening of the 21st of February last. State if he said anything as to the means by which he intended to obtain or was directed by the President to obtain possession of the War Department? If so, state all he said, as nearly as you can?

Answer. On the evening of the 21st of February last, I learned that General Thomas had been appointed Secretary of War ad interim, I think while at the Metropolitan Hotel. I invited Mr. Leonard Smith, of Leavenworth, Kansas, to go with me up to his house and see him. We took a carriage and went up. I found the General there getting ready to go out with his daughters to spend the evening at some place of amusement. I told him I would not detain him if he was going out; but he insisted on my sitting down, and I sat down for a few moments. I told him that I had learned he had been appointed Secretary of War. He said he had; that he had been appointed that day, I think; that after receiving his appointment from the President he went to the War Office to show his authority or his appointment to Secretary Stanton, and also his order to take possession of the office; that the Secretary remarked to him that he supposed he would give him time to remove his personal effects or his private papers, something to that effect; and reply was "certainly." He said that in a short time the Secretary asked him if he would give him a copy of his order, and he replied "certainly," and gave it to him. He said that it was no more than right to give him time to take out his personal effects. I asked him when he was going to assume the duties of the office. He remarked that he should take possession the next morning at ten o'clock, which would be the 22d; and I think in that connection he stated that he had issued some order in regard to the observance of the day; but of that I am not quite sure. I remarked to him that I should be up at that end of the avenue the next day, and he asked me to come in and see him. I asked him where I would find him, and he said in the Secretary's room up-stairs. I told him I would be there. Said he, "Be there punctual at ten o'clock." Said I, "You are going to take possession to-morrow?" "Yes." Said I, "Suppose Stanton objects to it, resists." "Well," said he, "I expect to meet force by force" or "use force."

Mr. CONKLING. Repeat that.

The WITNESS. I asked him what he would do if Stanton objected or resisted. He said he would use force or resort to force. Said I, "Suppose he bars the doors?" His reply was, "I will break them down." I think that was about all the conversation that we had there at that time in that connection.

By Mr. Manager BUTLER:

Question. Did he say anything to you about being there at the time?

Answer. He told me to be there at ten o'clock, if I came.

Question. Was there anything said further in the conversation that you remember, by you to him, as to what purpose you would be there for?

Answer. Well, to witness the performance; to see him take possession of the office; nothing more than that.

Question. Were you up there at the office at any time before he assumed the duties of Secretary *ad interim* after he assumed the duties of Adjutant General?

The WITNESS. At the Secretary's office?

Mr. Manager BUTLER. At the Adjutant General's office?

Answer. Yes, sir. I have frequently been there.

Mr. CURTIS, (to Mr. Manager BUTLER.) Will you repeat the question?

Mr. Manager BUTLER. The question is whether you were at the Adjutant General's office after General Thomas assumed the duties of Adjutant General and before he attempted to assume the duties of Secretary *ad interim*. You say you were.

Answer. Yes, sir; I was there several times; I do not recollect how many; but two or three times.

Question. Did you hear him saying anything to the officers and clerks of the Department there as to what his intention was when he came in command?

Mr. EVARTS. That we object to. What date do you fix that inquiry as applying to, Mr. BUTLER?

Mr. Manager BUTLER. I believe he was restored by the President to the Adjutant General's office about a week, if I remember aright—you will correct me if I am wrong—before he was made Secretary *ad interim*; and it was within that week that he made these declarations which I now offer.

Mr. EVARTS. Your inquiry, then, is for declarations made antecedent to the action of the President of which you have given evidence?

Mr. Manager BUTLER. My inquiry is not for declarations. My inquiry is for attempts on his part to seduce the officers of the War Department to his allegiance by telling them what he would do for them when he came in over them, precisely as Absalom sat at the gate of Israel and attempted to seduce the people from their allegiance to David, the king, by telling them what he would do for them when he got to be king. [Laughter.]

Mr. EVARTS. Do you propose that in your question, about Absalom?

Mr. Manager BUTLER. No, sir; I put that in my illustration. [Laughter.]

The CHIEF JUSTICE. Do the counsel for the President object to the question?

Mr. EVARTS. We object.

Mr. Manager BUTLER. Shall I reduce it to writing?

The CHIEF JUSTICE. Yes, sir.

Mr. EDMUNDS, (at three o'clock p. m.) I move that the Senate sitting on this trial take a recess for fifteen minutes.

The motion was agreed to.

The CHIEF JUSTICE resumed the chair at three o'clock and fifteen minutes, and called the Senate to order.

Hon. WALTER A. BURLEIGH'S examination resumed:

Mr. Manager BUTLER. With the President's leave, I will withdraw the question I put for a moment, in order to put another which I think will not be objected to. [To the witness.] I observe, Mr. BURLEIGH—I did not observe at the moment, but I have observed since—that you did not answer one part of my first question to day, which was, whether anything was said by Thomas at that conversation as to what orders he had received from the President?

Mr. EVARTS. That is covered by our previous objection.

Mr. Manager BUTLER. Certainly; it is the same thing; part of the same question. [To the witness.] Will you answer?

Answer. During the conversation General Thomas, after stating, in reply to my inquiry, that he would use force if necessary, stated that he had been required or ordered by the President to take charge of the War Department, and he was bound to obey the President as his superior or superior officer.

Question. Did that come in before or after he spoke of force in the conversation?

Answer. It was in connection with the force, and it was repeated, also, in connection with the breaking of the door to which I have alluded. I thought I mentioned it; but perhaps I did not.

Mr. Manager BUTLER. I now offer the question which was objected to.

The CHIEF JUSTICE. The Secretary will read the question.

The Secretary read as follows:

Question. Shortly before this conversation about which you have testified, and after the President restored Major General Thomas to the office of Adjutant General, if you know the fact that he was so restored, were you present in the War Department and did you hear Thomas make any statements to the officers and clerks, or either of them, belonging to the War Office as to the rules and orders of Mr. Stanton or of the office which he, Thomas, would revoke, relax, or rescind in favor of such officers and employés when he had control of the affairs therein? If so, state when, as near as you can, it was such conversation occurred, and state all he said as nearly as you can?

Mr. EVARTS. The counsel for the President object to that question as irrelevant and immaterial to any issue in this cause, and as not to be brought in evidence against the President by any support given by the testimony already in, which would, under any ruling of this court, or on any principle of law, permit these declarations or statements of General Thomas made to the clerks of the War Department antecedent to the time of the issue of the orders by the President, which are in evidence, as to what he, Thomas, would do when he, Thomas, if at all, should become Secretary of War.

Mr. Manager BUTLER. Mr. President, I do not desire to argue this question, for the reason that I think it falls within the question last discussed. If Thomas, as was the ground we put the last question upon, was a coconspirator with the President, how can either my learned friends on the other or the Senate know when that conspiracy commenced? You will observe the question carries with it this state of facts: Thomas had been removed from the office of Adjutant General for many years under President Lincoln under the administration of Mr. Stanton of the War Office. That is a fact known to all men who know the history of the war. Just before he made him Secretary of War *ad interim* the President restored Thomas to the War Office as the Adjutant General of the Army. That was the first step to get him in condition to make a Secretary of War of him. That was the first performance of the President, the first act in the drama. He had to take a disgraced officer, and take away his disgrace, and put him into the Adjutant General's office, from which he had been by the action of President Lincoln and Mr. Stanton suspended for years, in order to get a fit instrument on which to operate; get him in condition. That was part of the training for the next stage. Having got him in that condition, he being sufficiently virulent toward Mr. Stanton for having suspended him from the office of Adjutant General, the President then is ready to appoint him Secretary *ad interim,* which he does within two or three days thereafter.

We charge that the whole procedure shows the conspiracy. Here is the taking up of this disgraced officer and restoring him to a position in the War Office when he was a known enemy of Mr. Stanton's, feeling aggrieved, undoubtedly, that Mr. Stanton had deposed him, and putting him in there so that he might have some official station; and then, after having done that, Mr. Thomas goes to seducing clerks to get them ready to receive him when he should be brought into the War Office itself as its head. Now, I propose to show his acts, the acts of one of these coconspirators, clustering about the point of time just before the period when he was going to break down the doors of this office with crowbars and axes and force, as has been testified as he said he was, that he was trying to seduce the clerks and employés from their allegiance. We insist it is all a part of one transaction, and entirely comes within the ruling which has just been made. I believe I have stated the matter as the Managers desired I should.

Mr. EVARTS. The question which led to the introduction of this witness' statements of General Thomas's statements to him, of his intentions, and of the President's instructions to him, General Thomas, was based upon the claim that the order of the President of the 21st of February, upon Mr. Stanton for removal, and upon General Thomas to take possession of the office, created and proved a conspiracy; and that thereafter, upon that proof, declarations and intentions were to be given in evidence. That step has been gained, and, in the judgment of this honorable court, in conformity with the rules of law and of evidence. That being gained, it is similarly argued that if, on a conspiracy proved, you can introduce declarations made thereafter, by the same rule you can introduce declarations made theretofore; and that is the only argument which is presented to the court for the admission of this evidence.

So far as the statements of the learned Manager relate to the office, the position, the character, and the conduct of General Thomas, it is sufficient for me to say that not one particle of evidence has been given in this cause bearing upon any one of those topics. If General Thomas has been a disgraced officer; if these aspersions, these revilings are just, they are not justified by any evidence before this court. And if, as matter of fact, applicable to the situation upon which this proof is sought to be introduced, the former employments of General Thomas and the recent restoration of him to the active duties of Adjutant General are pertinent, let them be proved; and then we shall have at least the basis of fact of General Thomas's previous relations to the War

C. I.—10.

Department, to Mr. Stanton, and to the office of Adjutant General.

And, now, having pointed out to this honorable court that the declarations sought to be given in evidence of General Thomas to affect the President with his intentions, are confessedly of a period antecedent to the date to which any evidence whatever before this court brings the President and General Thomas in connection, I might leave it safely there. But what is there in the nature of the general proof sought to be introduced that should affect the President of the United States with any responsibility for these general and vague statements of an officer of what he might or could or would do, if thereafter he should come into the possession of power over the Department?

Mr. Manager BINGHAM. I desire to say a word or two in reply. I am willing to concede that any question beyond what may have been said by one who is shown to have entered into a conspiracy before the transaction is not admissible. I concede it, however, subject to this exception: that the Senate being the triers of the fact as well as of the law, will remember that the rule of evidence has been so extended on very similar occasions in courts of justice as to allow of declarations of this sort so shortly anterior to the time in which the conspiracy is shown to have been actually entered into to go to the jury and allow them to determine what weight ought to be attached to them. That is the principle upon which the question is put. It is qualified by the words "shortly before." Suppose it were within two or three days, and the act done on the part of the coconspirator was an act tending to bring about the result sought to be accomplished by that which was afterward mutually agreed upon between them; is there any one here to doubt that it is evidence tending to show that beyond the facts, so far as they have been traced, some understanding, some arrangement was entered into, and, if you please, a voluntary one, on the part of the man who afterward became by solemn agreement a party to the conspiracy—a voluntary act committed on his part in order to commend him to the chief in the conspiracy itself. The general rule as stated in the book, would admit, I am satisfied, of that latitude of construction. I read from Roscoe's Criminal Evidence, p. 88:

"The evidence in conspiracy is wider than, perhaps, in any other case, other principles as well as that under discussion tending to give greater latitude in proving this offense. Taken by themselves the acts of a conspiracy are rarely of an unequivocally guilty character, and they can only be properly estimated when connected with all the surrounding circumstances.

"Not only, as in the cases before mentioned, may the acts and declarations of the prisoner himself on former occasions be admitted when referable to the point in issue, but also the acts and declarations of other persons"—

Meaning, of course, on former occasions, supplying the ellipsis—

"with whom he has conspired, may, if referable to the issue, be given in evidence against him."

That is the general rule: and yet I admit if it were so framed as not in probability to connect itself with the transaction, it ought not to be received; but the question is so restricted—and we do not stand here to claim it unless it falls out on the evidence that it is nearly connected in point of time with the operations of these parties—and the testimony itself manifestly, as is explained by the Manager on the part of the House who has put the question, indicates a desire and purpose on the part of Thomas to make his arrangements with the employés of the War Department.

The CHIEF JUSTICE. The Chief Justice is of opinion that no sufficient foundation has been laid for the introduction of this testimony. He will submit the question to the Senate with great pleasure, if any Senator desires it. The question is ruled to be inadmissible.

Mr. HOWARD. Mr. President——

Mr. Manager BUTLER. I respectfully——

The CHIEF JUSTICE. The Senator from Michigan. Does the Senator desire the question to be taken by the Senate?

Mr. HOWARD. Yes, Mr. President.

Mr. Manager BUTLER. I was about rising to ask the Senate if they would not relax the rule, and when the Managers on the part of the House of Representatives and of the people have a question which they deem of consequence to their case allow that to be put to the Senate upon the motion of the House of Representatives.

The CHIEF JUSTICE. The Secretary will read the question.

The Secretary read as follows:

Question. Shortly before this conversation about which you have testified, and after the President restored Major General Thomas to the office of Adjutant General, if you know the fact that he was so restored, were you present in the War Department, and did you hear Thomas make any statements to the officers and clerks, or either of them, belonging to the War Office, as to the rules and orders of Mr. Stanton or of the office which he, Thomas, would revoke, relax, or rescind in favor of such officers and employés when he had control of the affairs therein? If so, state as near as you can when it was such conversation occurred, and state all he said as nearly as you can.

The CHIEF JUSTICE. The question is, Shall the question proposed by Mr. Manager BUTLER be put to the witness?

Mr. HOWARD. On that question I ask for the yeas and nays.

The yeas and nays were ordered; and being taken, resulted—yeas 28, nays 22; as follows:

YEAS—Messrs. Anthony, Cameron, Cattell, Chandler, Cole, Conkling, Conness, Corbett, Cragin, Drake, Henderson, Howard, Howe, Morgan, Morrill of Vermont, Morton, Nye, Patterson of New Hampshire, Pomeroy, Ramsey, Ross, Sprague, Stewart, Sumner, Thayer, Tipton, Trumbull, and Wilson—28.

NAYS—Messrs. Bayard, Buckalew, Davis, Dixon, Doolittle, Edmunds, Ferry, Fessenden, Fowler, Frelinghuysen, Grimes, Hendricks, Johnson, McCreery, Morrill of Maine, Norton, Patterson of Tennessee, Sherman, Van Winkle, Vickers, Willey, and Williams—22.

NOT VOTING—Messrs. Harlan, Saulsbury, Wade, and Yates—4.

The CHIEF JUSTICE. On this question the yeas are 28 and the nays 22. So the Senate decides that the question shall be put to the witness.

Mr. Manager BUTLER. With the leave of the President, I will put this question by portions. [To the witness.] Shortly before the conversation about which you have testified, and after the President restored Major General Thomas to the office of Adjutant General, if you know the fact that he was so restored, were you present in the War Department?

Answer. Yes, sir; I was.

By the CHIEF JUSTICE:

Question. Did you know the fact that he was so restored?

Answer. He told me so. He was acting in the office.

By Mr. Manager BUTLER:

Question. Did you hear Thomas make any statement to the officers and clerks, or either of them, belonging to the War Office, as to the rules and orders of Mr. Stanton, or of the office, which he, Thomas, would revoke, relax, or rescind in favor of such officers and employés when he had control therein? If so, state when this conversation was as near as you can.

Answer. Soon after General Thomas was restored to his position as Adjutant General I had occasion to go to his office to transact some business with him; and after transacting the business I invited him to take a short walk with me. The general remarked that he had made an arrangement——

Mr. EVARTS. Mr. BUTLER, your question was "when?"

Mr. Manager BUTLER, (to the witness.) When was this?

Answer. Soon after General Thomas's restoration to office as Adjutant General.

Question. How long before the time when he was appointed Secretary of War?

Answer. I should think not more than a week or ten days. I have no definite means of knowing now.

Question. Go on.

Answer. He remarked to me——

Mr. EVARTS. Wait a moment, Mr. Witness. I understood your question, Mr. BUTLER, allowed by the Senate, to refer to statements made by General Thomas at the War Office, as heard by ‚this witness, to clerks there of the Department. The witness is now proceeding to state what took place in a walk between him and General Thomas.

The WITNESS. No, sir; we had not taken the walk. I am not in the habit of testifying before courts, and you will pardon me for a little latitude.

Mr. Manager BUTLER. He had not said that they took the walk.

Mr. EVARTS. This, I understand, is only inducement, Mr. BUTLER.

Mr. Manager BUTLER. The inducement to the conversation.

The WITNESS. The General remarked to me that he had made an arrangement to have

all of the heads or officers in charge of the different departments of the office come in with their clerks that morning, and he wanted to address them. He stated that the rules which had been adopted for the government of the clerks by his predecessor were of a very arbitrary character, and he proposed to relax them. I suggested to him that perhaps I had better go. Said he, "No; not at all; remain;" and I sat down, and he had some three or four officers—four or five perhaps—come in, and each one brought in a room-full of clerks, and he made an address to each company as they came in, stating to them that he did not propose to hold them strictly to the letter of the instructions; but when they wanted to go out they could go out, and when they wanted to come in they could come in; that he regarded them all as gentlemen, and supposed they would do their duty, and he should require them to do their duty; but so far as their little indulgences were concerned—I suppose such as going out across the street or something of that kind—he did not propose to interfere with them; all he expected was that they would do their duty. I waited until he concluded, and we took the walk, and I came away. I remarked to the General he would make a very fine politician.

Question. Did he say anything as to the character of the orders that existed before?

Answer. He said that they were very harsh and arbitrary—nothing more than that, that I know of—and he proposed to relax them.

Question. You have told us that you had known General Thomas for some time. Had he been off duty as Adjutant General of the Army for some time before this?

Answer. Yes, sir.

Question. How long?

Answer. I am not able to tell you; some two or three years, I should think.

Mr. STANBERY. Mr. Chief Justice, we object to this mode of proving orders for removal.

Mr. Manager BUTLER. I will not press it a hair. I will get the order.

Mr. STANBERY. Especially do we object when it is said to disgrace an officer. We would rather see the proof than hear the assertion.

Mr. Manager BUTLER. Does the gentleman, when he makes the gesture accompanying those words mean my assertion, for I am going to prove it upon the oath of a witness.

Mr. STANBERY. Is the gentleman speaking to me? What was the question?

Mr. Manager BUTLER. Whether you mean my assertion or the assertion of the witness?

The CHIEF JUSTICE. This controversy does not appear to have any proper relation to the case on trial.

Mr. Manager BUTLER, (to the witness.) Had he been away from the city, and not in the Adjutant General's office for a considerable period of time?

Answer. Yes, sir; he had been sent South.

Mr. STANBERY. That will not do.

Mr. *Manager BUTLER, (to the witness.)* How lately had he returned to the office when he made this speech?

Answer. I am not able to say; but a very few days.

Question. Since you had the conversation about breaking down the doors of the War Office by force have you seen General Thomas?

Answer. Yes, sir; I have.

Question. Were you called upon by the Managers to give your testimony in their room?

Answer. I was.

Question. Did you do so?

Answer. I did.

Question. Was it taken down in short-hand?

Answer. I am not able to say how it was taken down. I did not see it.

Question. After it was taken down after you gave it was General Thomas called in?

Answer. He told me he was to be called in. I did not see him go in. I saw him on the floor of the House, and he told me he had been summoned, and was going up as soon as some one came for him.

Question. Did you see him after he had been up?

Answer. I did.

Question. What did he tell you as to your testimony?

Mr. EVARTS. That we object to.

The CHIEF JUSTICE, (to the Managers.) The honorable Managers will reduce the question to writing.

Mr. Manager BUTLER. I have heard the objection. I propose to show, if I am allowed, that Mr. BURLEIGH's testimony before the Managers, which I propose to put in his hand and identify in a moment, was read to General Thomas, containing exactly what he has testified here, and General Thomas said it was all true and never informed Mr. BURLEIGH that it was not true. I do this by way of settling the question that there can be no mistake about it——

Mr. STANBERY. For what purpose?

The CHIEF JUSTICE. The Manager will reduce his question to writing, it being objected to.

Mr. Manager BUTLER. Well, I will not press it to take time by an argument. [To the witness.] Have you had any conversation since with him as to this conversation about which you have testified?

Answer. I have.

Question. What has he said about it?

Mr. STANBERY, Mr. EVARTS, and Mr. CURTIS. That we object to.

Mr. Manager BUTLER. I propose to put in subsequent declarations confirming exactly the declarations which have been allowed to be put in. I suppose I can put in the same declarations twice.

The CHIEF JUSTICE. The question will be reduced to writing if objected to.

Mr. Manager BUTLER. I will ask a single question before that, so as to fix the date. [To *the witness.*] When did *you* see him as near as you can recollect?

Answer. I have seen him nearly every day since then.

Question. At any time did you have any conversation with him about this conversation as to which you have testified?

Answer. I have had.

Mr. EVARTS. You mean the conversation with the clerks?

Mr. Manager BUTLER. No, sir; I mean the conversation about breaking down the doors of the War Office by force.

The WITNESS. I have, sir.

Mr. Manager BUTLER. Do you still object, gentlemen?

Mr. STANBERY. Let us see your question.

Mr. Manager BUTLER. I will put the question. The question is, at the time when you have seen him since has he restated to you any portion or all of that conversation about breaking down the doors of the War Office?

Mr. EVARTS. That we object to as leading, among other things.

Mr. STANBERY. It is clearly a leading question.

Mr. Manager BUTLER. I will put it in this form: Since the first conversation has he restated any portion of that conversation; and, if so, what portion?

Mr. STANBERY. We object to that as leading.

Mr. EVARTS. We object, if the court please, that the question should be what subsequent conversations he has had, if they are to be given in evidence.

Mr. Manager BUTLER. Very well; to save all objection, then, I will ask this question: What did he state to you, if anything, as to the conversation which he had previously had with you about breaking down the War Office?

Mr. EVARTS. That we object to. Ask what conversations the witness has had with him since, if you wish to give them in evidence.

Mr. Manager BUTLER. I am content with that, if that is not objected to. [To the witness.] What conversations have you had with him on that subject since?

Mr. EVARTS. That we object to as not admissible evidence.

Mr. Manager BUTLER. *Timeo Danaos et dona ferentes.* I shall not alter my question again.

The CHIEF JUSTICE. The question, being objected to, will be reduced to writing.

Mr. Manager BUTLER reduced his question to writing, and read it, as follows:

Question. Have you had any conversation since the first one and since his appointment as Secretary of War *ad interim* with Thomas when he said anything about using force in getting into the War Office or in any way or manner reasserting his former conversation, and, if so, state what he said?

The CHIEF JUSTICE. Do the counsel object to that question?

Mr. EVARTS. We object to the question, if the court please.

The CHIEF JUSTICE. Do you desire to be heard in support of the objection?

Mr. EVARTS. Very briefly. The acts of the President and the acts of General Thomas, in pursuance of any authority from the President or otherwise, have been given in evidence. That testimony is very limited. What occurred between General Thomas and Mr. Stanton at the War Office is the only measure and extent of evidence bearing upon the actual conduct either of the President, through his agent, or of the agent. It was allowed to give evidence of this appointee's declarations as to what he intended to do, and that evidence has been given. Now, statements after the action was complete as to what his intentions were before cannot be at all material, for intentions not executed in the subsequent action certainly are not material. But this is still more objectionable as being but an alleged repetition, after the transaction was complete, of what his intentions had been before or rather relative to what he said about what his intentions had been before. It is enough to prove what his intentions had been before under the latitude which has been allowed by the court to introduce that evidence, to wit, the declarations made to this witness; but General Thomas's statements afterward as to what previously he, General Thomas, had stated as to what his intentions were is not admissible within any rules of evidence.

Mr. Manager BUTLER. Mr. Chief Justice, I understand the Senate by solemn decision have decided that Adjutant General Thomas, being Secretary of War ad interim, under the circumstances, was so far in conspiracy or in agreement with the President, was so far his servant or agent, that in the course of the proceeding in which he was engaged his acts might be, and his declarations were, evidence. That decision, of course, covers all acts and all declarations. We have shown that on the night of the 21st of February General Thomas said: "I am going up to-morrow morning with axes and force, bills and bows, to go into the office, break open the door; I am going in by force; I am going to obey my orders; I am going to obey the orders of the President; I am going in with force, and I am going to break down the doors if they are not opened to me." Then it is also in evidence that Mr. Thomas went up the next morning, not at ten o'clock, but about half past eleven, in a much more mild and quiet manner than he had threatened over night to do.

The argument will be raised by the counsel for the President, "This was mere talk of Mr. Thomas, because if he meant anything by it, or if the President had so ordered him, if it was serious really, why did he not the next morning go up there with force, either with the Maryland militia, or the Virginia militia, or some other proper force with which Mr.

Thomas should deal, or with a portion of the regular Army of the United States?" That is the argument; and as he did not, these declarations meant nothing. I want to show that afterwards Mr. BURLEIGH asked him, "General Thomas, I went up there to see the performance, and it did not come off according to contract; what is the meaning of this? you did not go and break in; I wanted to see that go on; I was going to stand by you," or words to that effect: "I went there to give you my countenance," or something like that; and thereupon Mr. Thomas said: "Well, the reason I did not was that I was arrested by the courts and held to bail, and I could not; I concluded it was not best to use force; I did not dare do it." Is not that perfectly competent to meet this argument of the counsel, and to show what prevented the outbreak of a civil war; that it was not the President; it was not his coconspirator; it was not their malignity nor want of it; it was not their will or want of it; but it was the fortunate intervention of the tribunal of justice. That is the point upon which we propose to put in this question.

The CHIEF JUSTICE. The Secretary will read the question.

The Secretary read the question, as follows:

Question. Have you had any conversation since the first one and since his appointment as Secretary of War *ad interim*—with Thomas—where he has said anything about using force in getting into the War Office, or in any way or manner reasserting the former conversation; and if so, state what he said?

The CHIEF JUSTICE. Senators, the Chief Justice is of opinion that within the spirit of the decision just made by the Senate, this question is admissible. Does any Senator desire that the question shall be submitted to the Senate? If not, the question will be put.

Mr. Manager BUTLER, (to the witness.) Will you now state? Mr. BURLEIGH, you say you have had many conversations. I want to call your attention to one special conversation——

Mr. CURTIS. I suppose the question should be put to him.

Mr. Manager BUTLER, (to the witness.) Have you had any conversation since the first one and since his appointment as Secretary of War *ad interim*—with Thomas—wherein he said anything about using force in getting into the War Office, or in any way or manner reasserting the former conversation; and if so, state what he said?

Answer. Some time in the fore part of last week I met General Thomas and we were talking over this question; it had become noised about; and he told me that the only thing that prevented his taking possession of the War Department that morning was his arrest by the United States marshal, who called on him at a very unusual hour, I think about the time he was getting out of bed.

Question. You have stated what he said. Now say what you stated to him? Give us the whole conversation as well as you can on that occasion?

The WITNESS. This last occasion?

Mr. EVARTS. That is not within your question.

Mr. STANBERY. You are now asking for declarations of Mr. BURLEIGH.

Mr. Manager BUTLER. I am asking for both parts of the conversation, which I never yet heard objected to in a court of justice.

Mr. STANBERY. You ask for declarations of this witness.

Mr. Manager BUTLER, (to the witness.) What you said to Thomas and he said to you, part of which you have just given us.

The WITNESS. I do not now recollect the precise language which I used to him. It was, however, in connection with my having gone up there, and that the feast to which I was invited or the performance did not come off; and he gave me as a reason for it that he was arrested by the United States marshal and taken down before Judge Cartter's court, otherwise he should have gone in and taken possession of the office, as he told me he would.

Question. When was this last conversation, as near as you can tell?

Answer. I think it was about the first of last week.

Cross-examined by Mr. STANBERY:

Question. Referring to the interview you had with General Thomas in the Adjutant General's office prior to his appointment as Secretary of War, had you business there with him, as Adjutant General?

Answer. I had business with the Adjutant General. I can state what it was, if you desire to know.

Question. No. I do not care about that; but you went there to see the Adjutant General on business?

Answer. Yes, sir.

Question. And you say you had heard before that that General Thomas was restored to his office?

Answer. I think I had heard it the day before, and I think I heard it from himself.

Question. While you were there he sent for the heads of bureaus and their clerks, did he?

Answer. Yes, sir.

Question. Whom first did he send for?

Answer. I cannot name them now. In fact, I am not sufficiently familiar with their names to tell.

Question. Who first came in?

Answer. I am not able to say. General Williams was present. I do not know but that he came in first, and I do not know as he did.

Question. Did he make an address to each head of bureau and his clerks or did he talk to them all together?

Answer. Each one.

Question. In succession?

Answer. Yes, sir.

Question. How many addresses, then, did he make to separate assemblies?

Answer. I think he made four or five. I did not count them, and it was a matter that did not impress itself on my mind very much.

Question. Did he make the same address to all of them?

Answer. Very nearly the same.

Question. Now, please to state what his address was to each of them that he made on that occasion?

Answer. I can only give it to you in a very vague manner. It was a matter that did not concern me very much. It was to state to them that he had come back and assumed the duties of the office; that he was glad to see them; that he proposed to relax somewhat the arbitrary rules; perhaps he did not denominate them arbitrary rules; he had to me before that; that he did not wish to hold them up to so strict accountability in being there precisely at nine o'clock, and in not leaving without a written leave as he said had been the case before. He stated to them that he should expect them to discharge their duty, and if they did that it was all he cared about.

Question. When he said he had returned to his office what office did you understand him as returning to?

Answer. Adjutant General.

Question. When he gave these orders to these heads of bureaus and their clerks did you understand him to be giving orders as Adjutant General?

Answer. I did not understand him to be giving orders at all, but it was a mere address.

Question. Was he delivering an address then as Adjutant General?

Answer. Certainly.

Question. In reference to how he expected to carry on that office?

Answer. What he expected of them.

Question. You do not mean that he sent for all the employés in the War Department, do you?

Answer. I think he told me that he directed the head of every department connected with the Adjutant General's office to come.

Question. But not those connected with the other offices—those of the Commissary General, the Quartermaster General, &c.

Answer. No; only those that were under him.

Question. When these heads of bureau received these orders, did they object that he had no right to give them such orders, or did they thank him for them?

Answer. I heard no objection. They congratulated him, a great many of them.

Question. Was anything said about his giving them any other orders, or giving them to any other than his own officers, those under him as Adjutant General?

Answer. I did not understand it in any other way.

Question. Then did you hear or see anything

improper at that time, and if you did let us know what it was?

Answer. I do not know that I am the judge of what is proper or not proper in the Adjutant General's office. Nothing occurred that was very offensive to me.

Question. Did anything occur that was at all offensive?

Answer. No, sir.

SAMUEL WILKESON sworn and examined.

By Mr. Manager BUTLER:

Question. Do you know Lorenzo Thomas, Adjutant General of the United States Army?

Answer. I do.

Question. How long have you known him?

Answer. Between six and seven years.

Question. Have you had any conversation with him relative to the change in the War Department? If so, state as near as you can when it was and what it was in relation to that change.

Answer. I had a conversation with him respecting that change on the 21st day of February.

Question. What time in the day?

Answer. Between one and two o'clock in the afternoon.

Question. Where?

Answer. At the War Department, in his office.

Question. State what took place at that interview?

Mr. EVARTS. Do you propose this as covered by the former ruling?

Mr. Manager BUTLER. Entirely so, after he had his order.

The WITNESS. I asked him to tell me what had occurred that morning between him and the Secretary of War in his endeavor to take possession of the War Department. He hesitated to do so till I told him that the town was filled with rumors of the change that had been made, of the removal of Mr. Stanton and the appointment of himself. He then said that since the affair had become public he felt relieved to speak to me with freedom about it. He drew from his pocket a copy, or rather the original, of the order of the President of the United States, directing him to take possession of the War Department immediately. He told me that he had taken as a witness of his action General Williams, and had gone up into the War Department and had shown to Edwin M. Stanton the order of the President, and had demanded by virtue of that order the possession of the War Department and its books and papers. He told me that Edwin M. Stanton, after reading the order, had asked him if he would allow to him sufficient time for him to gather together his books, papers, and other personal property and take them away with him; that he told him that he would allow to him all necessary time to do so, and had then withdrawn from Mr. Stanton's room. He further told me, that day being Friday,

that the next day would be what he called a *dies non*, being the holiday of the anniversary of Washington's birthday, when he had directed that the War Department should be closed, that the day thereafter would be Sunday, and that on Monday morning he should demand possession of the War Department and of its property, and if that demand was refused or resisted he should apply to the General-in-Chief of the Army for a force sufficient to enable him to take possession of the War Department; and he added that he did not see how the General of the Army could refuse to obey his demand for that force. He then added that under the order that the President had given to him he had no election to pursue any other course than the one that he indicated; that he was a subordinate officer directed by an order from a superior officer, and that he must pursue that course.

Question. Did you see him afterward and have conversation with him on the subject?

Answer. I did.

Question. When was that?

Answer. That evening.

Question. Where?

Answer. At Willard's Hotel.

Question. What did he say there?

Answer. He then said that he should the next day demand possession of the War Department, and that if the demand was refused or resisted he should apply to General Grant for force to enable him to take possession, and he also repeated his declaration that he could not see how General Grant could refuse to obey that demand for force.

Question. State whether these were earnest conversations or otherwise?

Answer. Earnest conversations!

Question. Yes, sir, on his part.

Answer. If you mean by earnestness that he meant what he said——

Question. Yes.

Answer. They were in that sense earnest.

Cross-examined by Mr. EVARTS:

Question. Are you connected with the press?

Answer. I am a journalist by profession.

Question. And have been for a great number of years?

Answer. A great number of years.

Question. Living in Washington during the session of Congress for the most part?

Answer. I have for the last seven years lived in Washington in the winter.

Question. You say that General Thomas told you that, under the order of the President, he did not see how he could do otherwise than he had stated.

Mr. Manager BUTLER. Are you repeating the testimony of the witness?

Mr. EVARTS. Yes.

Mr. Manager BUTLER. I understood him to say "under the orders of the President."

Mr. EVARTS. I understood him to say "under the order."

Mr. Manager BUTLER. That I wanted certain.

The WITNESS. "Under the order," referring to the original?

Mr. EVARTS. Paper?

The WITNESS. The original paper.

Question. Nothing else?

Answer. Nothing else.

Mr. EVARTS, (to Mr. Manager BUTLER.) Now you are answered.

Mr. Manager BUTLER. Entirely.

Mr. EVARTS, (to the witness.) So all the difference between the conversation on Friday night and Friday forenoon was that at night he proposed to do what he did propose to do on Saturday, and in the forenoon conversation he proposed to do it on Monday?

Answer. On Monday.

Question. Did you say anything further regarding the expected holiday, Saturday, except that that would be a *dies non?*

Answer. Nothing, sir.

Question. No orders to that effect were referred to?

Answer. Pardon me; he told me that he had issued an order to close the War Department on Saturday.

Question. That he had himself?

Answer. That he had himself issued an order to close the War Department on Saturday.

Question. As Adjutant General?

Answer. He did not say whether he had done that as Adjutant General or as Secretary of War.

Question. You did not understand anything about that?

Answer. He simply told me he had issued an order to close the War Department on Saturday.

Question. This was in the morning conversation?

Answer. It was in the afternoon conversation of Friday.

Question. The one o'clock conversation?

Answer. Yes, sir.

Question. Did he tell you when that order had been issued?

Answer. No, sir.

Question. Did you know, from anything said in that conversation, when it had been issued?

Answer. No, sir.

Question. Did you know, from anything said in that conversation, by whom it had been issued other than that it was by him, General Thomas, in some capacity?

Answer. No, sir. He told me that it had been issued, and he told me that on Friday.

Question. So far as you know, or then understood, it might have been issued by him as Adjutant General?

Answer. I know nothing about that.

Reëxamined by Mr. Manager BUTLER:

Question. In either of these conversations, in connection with what he said, did he say whether he was Secretary of War, or did he claim to be?

Answer. Yes, sir; he claimed to be Secretary of War.

GEORGE W. KARSNER sworn and examined.

By Mr. Manager BUTLER:

Question. What is your full name?

Answer. George Washington Karsner.

Question. Of what place are you a citizen?

Answer. Delaware.

Question. What county?

Answer. New Castle county.

Question. Do you know Major General Lorenzo Thomas?

Answer. Yes, sir.

Question. How long have you known him?

Answer. I have known him a great while; I think I have known him since a short time after his graduation from West Point.

Question. Was he originally from the same county with you?

Answer. Yes, sir.

Question. Did you see him in Washington somewhere about the 1st of March of this year?

Answer. I think it was about the 9th of March I first recollect seeing him here.

Question. When had you seen him prior to that time?

Answer. Not for several years. I cannot remember exactly when I last saw him before that.

Question. Where did you see him in Washington?

Answer. I saw him in the President's House; in the East Room of the President's House.

Question. What time in the day or evening?

Answer. It was, perhaps, a quarter past ten o'clock in the evening.

Question. The evening of what day in the week; do you remember?

Answer. I think it was on a Monday evening.

Question. Was the President holding a levee that evening?

Answer. Yes, sir.

Question. Did you have any conversation with him?

Answer. Yes, sir.

Question. Please state how the conversation began; what was said?

Mr. EVARTS. With General Thomas?

Mr. Manager BUTLER. With General Thomas.

Answer. Well, it commenced by my approaching him and mentioning that I was a Delawarean, and I supposed he would recognize me, which I think he did, but could not remember my name. I then gave him my name, and told him I knew him a great many years ago, and knew his father and brother and all the family. I gave him my hand, and he talked. He said he was a Delaware boy, which I very well knew; and he asked me what we were doing in Delaware. I do not remember the answer I gave to him, but said I to him, "General, the eyes of Delaware are on you." [Laughter.]

The CHIEF JUSTICE. Order!

The WITNESS. I gave my advice to him. I told him I thought Delaware would require him to stand firm. "Stand firm, General," said I. He said he would, he was standing firm, and he would not disappoint his friends; and in two days, or two or three days, or a short time, he would kick that fellow out. [Laughter.]

Question. Was anything further said?

Answer. Yes; there was something further said. I will try to recollect it. [A pause.] I repeated again to him what the desire, I presumed, of Delaware would be, and he said I need not give myself any concern about that, he was going to remain firm, and kick that fellow out without fail.

Question. When he said he would "kick that fellow out" did he in any way indicate to you to whom he referred?

Answer. He did not mention any name.

Question. The question was whether he indicated to whom he referred?

Answer. Well, I think he referred to the Secretary of War. I did not have any doubt on my mind——

Mr. EVARTS. That was not the question.

Mr. Manager BUTLER. It answers all I desire. The witness is yours, gentlemen.

Cross-examined by Mr. STANBERY:

Question. You said you had known General Thomas many years before?

Answer. Yes, sir.

Question. Please to state as near as you can recollect when you had seen General Thomas before this interview in the East Room. How many years was it since you had seen him before?

Answer. I was in this city during the war, and perhaps I might have seen him then, but I am not certain.

Question. What is the time that you are certain that you last saw him?

Answer. It was a good many years; I cannot remember how long it was. I cannot remember the time.

Question. Where? In Delaware or here?

Answer. I think I saw him in New Castle at one time.

Question. Before or after he went to West Point?

Answer. Long since he left West Point; long since he was in the Army.

Question. On what occasion was it at New Castle that you think you recollect seeing him?

Answer. I saw him in the street. I do not recollect that I had any conversation with him at New Castle. His father lived there, and his brother.

Question. In which of the streets of New Castle did you see him?

Answer. Well, there are not many streets in New Castle. [Laughter.] I saw him in the main street, I think.

Question. What part of the street?

Answer. It was not in the middle of it; it was on the pavement, and I was standing by the court-house, to the best of my recollection.

Question. You were standing by the court-house, and he was on the pavement?

Answer. I think so.

Question. Was he walking past or standing there?

Answer. I cannot recollect.

Question. But you do recollect that one day being before the court-house you saw Thomas standing on the pavement?

Answer. I was standing by the court-house.

Question. How near?

Answer. Within half the space of this room.

Question. How far was he from you?

Answer. I think he was on the opposite side of the street.

Question. On the other pavement?

Answer. Yes; I think so. As regards the time and whether I spoke to him or not I cannot tell. I saw him there.

Question. That is what you recollect; seeing him there that day. Was he standing or walking?

Answer. I presume he was walking. I do not recollect.

Question. But you recollect seeing him there?

Answer. Yes.

Question. Can you not tell us whether he was standing or walking?

Answer. Sometimes it is a little difficult for a person's memory to run that well. That has been several years ago, many years before the war.

Question. When did you ever see him to speak with him?

Answer. I used to speak to him a great many years ago when he would be at New Castle visiting his people. He married his wife in New Castle.

Question. How many years and when? That is the question.

Answer. It is very difficult for me to answer how many years or when; but I saw him there and I saw him in the city of Washington.

Question. You now recollect that you saw him in the city of Washington; a little while ago you could not recollect that?

Answer. I think now I do recollect seeing him, but not to speak to him. He was an officer, I was a citizen.

Question. Whereabouts in Washington did you see him before this time?

Answer. I cannot tell that; but I have seen him in Washington. I know him when I see him.

Question. When, then, did you ever speak to him before this time? Name a time.

Answer. Every time I would come within speaking distance of him I have spoken to him; but to name a time I cannot.

Question. You cannot answer when it was or where you ever spoke to him before?

Answer. No, sir; not particularly.

Question. On this occasion did you come from Delaware to see General Thomas?

Answer. No, sir; I had other business in Washington.

Question. Did you expect to see him or intend to see him?

Answer. Well, I wished to see the President of the United States, and I wished to see the Cabinet. I saw them all except General Thomas in the reception room. I then walked into the East Room and I saw him there; I went to him in the East Room and spoke to him.

Question. You wanted to see him as well as the rest of the Cabinet?

Answer. Well, he was acting, the papers stated, as a member of the Cabinet.

Question. Whereabouts in the East Room did you encounter him?

Answer. On the west side, I think, of the East Room.

Question. Was it near the door of exit?

Answer. No, sir.

Question. Near the center of the room?

Answer. I think it was. It was not the center of the room exactly, but somewhere in the center of the distance between that and the place of going out.

Question. At that time was General Thomas apparently going out?

Answer. No, sir. When I first saw him there he was very much engaged, speaking with a gentleman very earnestly, and I waited until he had leisure and then I approached him.

Question. Did you know the gentleman he was speaking with?

Answer. No, sir.

Question. But you had something to say to him. What did you intend to say to him when you found out that he was there? You say you went over to see him; what did you intend to say to him?

Answer. Well, his being a Delawarean and I from the same State, I wanted to pass the compliments with him. I was glad to see him. I had no particular desire to see him on any business; but I just said to him what I have already stated.

Question. You did not go there especially to say to him that thing, then, but only to see him?

Answer. I was drawn there for the purpose of seeing Mr. Johnson, President of the United States; I had never seen him.

Question. After you had seen Mr. Johnson, and the other members of the Cabinet, I understand you to say you then wanted to see General Thomas?

Answer. I asked a friend with me where General Thomas was; said I, "I do not see him."

Question. Who was that friend that was with you?

Answer. It was John B. Tanner.

Question. Where was he from?

Answer. Washington.

Question. Does he live here?

Answer. Yes, sir.

Question. Did you go with Tanner to that levee?

Answer. Yes, sir.

Question. And after you had seen the President and Cabinet, you then asked him where you would find Thomas?

Answer. No; that was not the manner.

Question. What was it?

Answer. Said I, "I see them all but General Thomas." I did not know the members of the Cabinet personally, but they were pointed out to me—Mr. Browning and all the Cabinet except Mr. Thomas. I think they were all present in the reception room.

Question. And all were pointed out to you?

Answer. Yes, sir; they were pointed out to me.

Question. Having seen the President and having seen all the members of the Cabinet, then you asked where you could find General Thomas?

Answer. No, sir.

Question. What then?

Answer. I did not ask where I could find him. Said I, "I miss General Thomas here; he is not in this room." My friend said no, he was not in that room; and when we left the reception room and came into the East Room I saw him there.

Question. Did you go with your friend Tanner from the reception room to the East Room?

Answer. Yes, sir.

Question. Did he point out Thomas to you?

Answer. No, sir; I pointed him out myself.

Question. What was the first thing you said to Thomas after he was through with his conversation with the gentleman he was speaking to; how did you first address him?

Answer. I have already stated that.

Question. State it again.

Answer. I addressed him as a Delawarean, knowing him to be so. I told him I was from Delaware. He said he was a Delaware boy himself. I knew that very well, and knew his family.

Question. Did you shake hands with him?

Answer. Yes, sir.

Question. What followed when you told him that you were from Delaware?

Answer. As I before stated, he asked me how things were coming on in Delaware, how we were all getting along or how we were coming on; that was about the amount he asked me.

Question. What was your answer?

Answer. I do not recollect the answer I gave.

Question. What was said next, if you do not recollect that answer?

Answer. The next was, as I before stated, that I told him the eyes of Delaware were on him, and to stand firm: that was the language I addressed to him.

Question. Was that all you said?

Answer. Well, no; I repeated, perhaps, some

part of that or pretty much all. I repeated a portion of it, at any rate.

Question. When you asked him to stand firm what was his reply?

Answer. He said he was standing firm.

Question. What did you next say?

Answer. I told him the people of Delaware would expect it of him. He said they should not be disappointed.

Question. What next?

Answer. That he would stand firm; and he then remarked that he would kick that fellow out in two or three days, or in a short time, or in a few days; I cannot remember what his exact expression was.

Question. Now, I ask you, Mr. Karsner, if this idea of kicking out did not first come from you; whether you did not suggest it?

Answer. No, sir.

Question. You did not?

Answer. No, sir.

Question. You are sure of that?

Answer. I have taken an oath here.

Question. I ask you if you are sure of that?

Answer. I am sure of that.

Question. When he said he would kick him out did you reply?

Answer. I do not know what I did reply just to that, for it was a pretty severe expression.

Question. What did you reply, severe or not; what did you say to him?

Answer. I do not think I told him it would be all right even; I do not think I did.

Question. What did you tell him?

Answer. I said "I think Delaware will expect something from you." [Great laughter.]

Question. Was that what you meant by the severe remark you made to him?

The WITNESS. What do you mean?

Mr. STANBERY. Was that the severe remark, "that Delaware expected he would do something?"

The WITNESS. Delaware, I told him, would expect him to stand firm, and his conduct would be viewed by Delaware, or something to that effect.

Question. Was that the severe remark which you have said you made?

Answer. I did not make any severe remark.

Mr. Manager BUTLER. I think you misunderstood the witness, Mr. Stanbery. He said simply that it was a severe remark that General Thomas made.

The WITNESS. Yes, sir; that is what I intended to convey.

Mr. STANBERY, (to the witness.) Did the conversation stop there?

Answer. It was not a very long one. There might have been some few words said after that. Just before I left I renewed the desires of Delaware. [Laughter.]

The CHIEF JUSTICE. Order! order!

By Mr. STANBERY:

Question. How did you renew the desires of Delaware? Did you feel yourself authorized to speak for Delaware?

Answer. Oh, well, you know, when we get away from home we think a good deal of home, and are inclined to speak in behalf of our own State.

Question. At that time were you in sympathy with the wishes of Delaware that he should do something in regard to the War Office?

Mr. Manager BUTLER. I object.

Mr. STANBERY. What is the ground of the objection?

Mr. Manager BUTLER. I do not think this is the proper mode of proving the sympathies of Delaware on this occasion; and, if it is, the sympathies of Delaware are a matter wholly immaterial to this issue.

Mr. STANBERY. We agree to that. The question was as to the sympathies of the witness. I will put the question in this form. [To the witness.] Was the line of conduct he spoke of taking that which suited you?

Answer. I do not know whether it would or no.

Question. Did you in that conversation give him any advice beyond standing firm what he should do?

Answer. No, sir; not any advice further than I have stated.

Question. After you parted there to whom did you first communicate this conversation that you had had there with General Thomas?

Answer. Well, I communicated it—if the question is right for me to answer——

Mr. STANBERY. Yes, sir; you will answer it.

Answer. I communicated it to Mr. Tanner.

Question. Your friend?

Answer. Yes, sir; that night.

Question. Whereabouts did you communicate that to Mr. Tanner?

Answer. Going along the street.

Question. Going away from there that night?

Answer. Yes, sir; if my memory serves me aright, I think I did that night.

Question. To whom next?

Answer. I cannot tell the next one exactly.

Question. Do you mean to say you have no recollection now of telling anybody else but Tanner?

Answer. Yes; I told several that same thing. I did not charge my memory with the persons I told it to.

Question. You told several that night, the next day, or when?

Answer. The next day.

Question. In Washington?

Answer. Yes, sir.

Question. What did you tell, and whom to?

Answer. I say I cannot recollect precisely the persons I told it to. I told it to several.

Question. Do you recollect any one besides Tanner?

Answer. Yes, I recollect a gentleman from Delaware.

Question. What was his name?

Answer. His name was Smith. [Laughter.]

Question. What was the first name of that Mr. Smith?

Answer. It was not John. [Great laughter.]

Question. What was it, if you say you recollect it was not John?

Answer. I think it was William.

Question. Whereabouts did you see William Smith?

Answer. In Washington.

Question. Whereabouts?

Answer. I saw him on the street.

Question. Near the court-house?

Answer. No, sir.

Question. Whereabouts, then?

Answer. I do not know where your court-house is here.

Question. Whereabouts in Washington did you see Smith?

Answer. I think it was on Pennsylvania avenue.

Question. That is a pretty long avenue. Whereabouts on the avenue?

Answer. Not far from the National Hotel.

Question. On the street?

Answer. Yes, sir.

Question. What did you tell William Smith?

Answer. I told William Smith just what I have told you. [Laughter.] Yes, sir, I told him just what I have sworn to here.

Question. What part of Delaware was William Smith from?

Answer. He is from the banks of the Brandywine. [Great laughter.]

Question. Which bank of the Brandywine does he live on?

Answer. I think he is on the east bank of the Brandywine, or northeast.

Question. Does he live in town or country?

Answer. He lives in the country. He is a farmer.

The CHIEF JUSTICE. The Chief Justice thinks that this examination is irrelevant, and should not be protracted.

By Mr. STANBERY:

Question. Mr. Karsner, when were you summoned before any committee in this matter?

Answer. I do not recollect the day. It was about the 13th, I think.

Question. Did you remain in Washington from the 9th till the 13th?

Answer. Yes, sir. I was engaged in trying to get a mail route in Delaware to facilitate post office matters, and I was detained here. I had engaged our Representative, Mr. NICHOLSON, and his father was very ill at the time, and he was some time out of the House, which protracted my stay.

Question. Have you remained here ever since.

Answer. No, sir.

Question. Do you know at whose instance you were summoned?

Answer. No ; I cannot tell that exactly, at whose instance, what particular person had me summoned. I was summoned before the Managers of the House of Representatives, and ordered at a certain time to be at the judiciary apartment up stairs over the House of Representatives.

Reëxamined by Mr. Manager BUTLER:

Question. You have been asked if you were summoned before the Managers. Did you testify there?

Answer. I did.

Question. After you had testified there, was General Thomas called in?

Answer. Yes, sir.

Question. Was your testimony, as you have given it here, read over before him?

Mr. GROESBECK. We object to that.

The WITNESS. Yes, sir.

Mr. Manager BUTLER. Now, I propose to ask whether General Thomas was asked if that was true, and if he admitted upon his oath that it was true, all you have stated.

Mr. CURTIS. We object to that, Mr. Chief Justice.

Mr. Manager BUTLER. I think it is competent.

Mr. CURTIS. We do not think they can support their witness by showing what a third person, General Thomas, said.

The CHIEF JUSTICE, (to the Managers.) Do you press the question?

Mr. Manager BUTLER. I do press the question, Mr. Chief Justice, for this reason : upon an innocent and unoffending man there has been a very severe cross-examination within the duties of the counsel, undoubtedly— he did not mean to do more than his duty— attempting to discredit him here by that cross-examination as to a conversation. If that cross-examination meant anything, that is what it meant. Now, I propose to show that the co-conspirator here, Thomas, admitted the correctness of this man's statements. This man was heard as a witness by the House of Representatives ; the Managers of the House of Representatives, having taken his testimony, not willing to do any injustice to General Thomas, brought General Thomas in and sat him down and on his oath put the question to him, is what this man says true? being the same then as he swears here, and General Thomas admitted it word for word. I think it is competent and do press it.

Mr. CURTIS. Our view of it is, Mr. Chief Justice, that, having called this witness and put him on the stand, they cannot show that he has, on a different occasion, told the same story. That is a plain matter, and I do not understand that that is the ground which they take.

Mr. Manager BUTLER. We do not propose that.

Mr. CURTIS. Then they offer the declarations of General Thomas, not in reference to any conspiracy, not in reference to any agreement between himself and the President as to doing anything, not in reference to any act done pursuant to that conspiracy, but simply the declarations of General Thomas as to something which General Thomas had said to this witness to support the credit of the witness. We object to that as incompetent.

Mr. Manager BUTLER. Mr. President, having made the offer, and it being objected to, and it being clearly competent, if General Thomas is ever brought here to contradict it I will waive it.

Mr. CURTIS. Very well.

Mr. Manager BUTLER. Then we are through with the witness; but we must request him to remain in attendance until discharged.

Mr. DOOLITTLE. Now, Mr. Chief Justice, I move that the court adjourn until to-morrow at twelve o'clock.

The CHIEF JUSTICE. It is moved by the Senator from Wisconsin that the Senate, sitting as a court of impeachment, adjourn until to-morrow at twelve o'clock.

The motion was agreed to; and the Senate, sitting for the trial of the impeachment, adjourned until to-morrow at twelve o'clock.

THURSDAY, *April* 2, 1868.

The Chief Justice of the United States entered the Senate Chamber at five minutes past twelve o'clock and took the chair.

The usual proclamation having been made by the Sergeant-at-Arms,

The Managers of the impeachment on the part of the House of Representatives appeared and took the seats assigned them.

The counsel for the respondent also appeared and took their seats.

The presence of the House of Representatives was next announced, and the members of the House, as in Committee of the Whole, headed by Mr. E. B. WASHBURNE, the chairman of that committee, and accompanied by the Speaker and Clerk, entered the Senate Chamber, and were conducted to the seats provided for them.

The CHIEF JUSTICE. The Secretary will read the minutes of the last day's proceedings.

The Secretary read the Journal of the proceedings of the Senate yesterday sitting for the trial of the impeachment.

Mr. DRAKE. I send to the Chair and offer for adoption an amendment to the rules.

The CHIEF JUSTICE. The Secretary will read the amendment.

The Secretary read as follows:

Amend rule seven by adding the following:
Upon all such questions the votes hall be without a division, unless the yeas and nays be demanded by one fifth of the members present or requested by the presiding officer, when the same shall be taken.

Mr. DRAKE. Please read the rule as it would be if amended.

The Secretary read as follows:

VII. The Presiding Officer of the Senate shall direct all necessary preparations in the Senate Chamber, and the presiding officer on the trial shall direct all the forms of proceeding while the Senate are sitting for the purpose of trying an impeachment, and all forms during the trial not otherwise specially provided for. And the presiding officer on the trial may rule all questions of evidence and incidental

questions, which ruling shall stand as the judgment of the Senate, unless some member of the Senate shall ask that a formal vote be taken thereon, in which case it shall be submitted to the Senate, for decision; or he may, at his option, in the first instance, submit any such question to a vote of the members of the Senate. Upon all such questions the vote shall be without a division, unless the yeas and nays be demanded by one fifth of the members present or requested by the presiding officer, when the same shall be taken.

Mr. HENDRICKS. I suppose that, being a change of a rule, stands over for one day.

The CHIEF JUSTICE. If any Senator objects.

Mr. HENDRICKS. Yes, sir; I do object.

The CHIEF JUSTICE. It will lie over for one day.

The Managers on the part of the House of Representatives will proceed with their evidence. Senators will please to give their attention.

Mr. Manager BUTLER. We propose now to call General Emory.

Mr. STANBERY. Before the Managers proceed with another witness we wish to recall for a moment Mr. Karsner, the last witness.

Mr. Manager BUTLER. Mr. President, I submit that if Mr. Karsner is to be recalled, the examination and cross-examination having been finished on both sides, he must be recalled as the witness of the respondent, and the proper time to recall him will be when they put in their case.

Mr. STANBERY. We wish to recall him but a moment to ask a question which, perhaps, would have been put if it had not been stopped yesterday.

The CHIEF JUSTICE. Is there any objection to recalling the witness for the purpose of putting a single question to him?

Mr. Manager BUTLER. Not if it shall not be drawn into a precedent.

GEORGE W. KARSNER recalled.

By Mr. STANBERY:

Question. Mr. Karsner, where did you stay that night of the 9th of March after you had the conversation with General Thomas?

Answer. I stayed at the house of my friend, Mr. Tanner, in Georgetown.

Question. What is the employment of Mr. Tanner?

Answer. I believe he is engaged in one of the Departments here in Washington.

Question. In which one?

Answer. I think the War Department.

Question. Do you recollect whether on the next morning you accompanied Mr. Tanner to the War Department?

Answer. I do not.

Question. You do not recollect that?

Answer. I do not recollect whether I accompanied him or not. Sometimes I did and sometimes I did not. I had other business, and sometimes I was engaged in that and did not accompany him, and at other times I did accompany him.

Question. At any time did you go with him to the War Department and see Mr. Stanton in regard to your testimony?

The WITNESS. I appeal to the court.

The CHIEF JUSTICE. Answer the question.

Answer. I saw Mr. Stanton.

Several SENATORS. Louder; we cannot hear.

The CHIEF JUSTICE. Raise your voice so that you can be heard in the Chamber.

By Mr. STANBERY:

Question. You say you saw Mr. Stanton?

Answer. Yes, sir; I saw Mr. Stanton.

Question. What did you see him about?

Answer. Nothing particular about; only I was introduced to him.

Question. Whom by?

Answer. By Mr. Tanner.

Question. What was your object in seeing him?

Answer. Well, I had seen all the great men in Washington, and I wished to see him.

Question. That is your answer?

Answer. Yes, sir.

Question. In that conversation with Mr. Stanton was any reference made to your conversation with General Thomas?

Answer. I think there was.

Question. Did you receive a note from Mr. Stanton at that time, a memorandum?

Answer. No, sir.

Question. Did he give you any directions where to go?

Answer. No, sir.

Question. Did he speak about your being examined as a witness before the committee or that you should be?

Answer. There was something said to that effect.

Mr. STANBERY. That is all, sir.

Mr. Manager BUTLER. That is all, Mr. Karsner.

Hon. THOMAS W. FERRY sworn and examined.

By Mr. Manager BUTLER:

Question. Were you present at the War Office on the morning of the 22d of February when General Thomas came there?

Answer. I was.

Question. At the time when some demand was made?

Answer. I was.

Question. Will you state whether you paid attention to what was going on there, and whether you made any memorandum of it?

Answer. I did·pay attention, and I believe I made a memorandum of the occurrences as far as I observed them.

Question. Have you that memorandum?

Answer. Yes, sir, [producing a paper.]

Question. Will you please state, assisting your memory by that memorandum, what took place there, in the order as well as you can, and as distinctly as you can?

Answer. I believe. if my recollection serves

me, that the memorandum covers it perhaps as distinctly as I could possibly state it. I wrote it immediately after the occurrence of the appearance of General Thomas, and perhaps it will state substantially and more perfectly than I could state from memory now what occurred.

Question. Unless objected to you may read it.

Mr. STANBERY. We shall make no objection.

The witness read as follows:

WAR DEPARTMENT,
WASHINGTON CITY, *February* 22, 1868.

In the presence of Secretary Stanton, Judge KELLEY, MOORHEAD, DODGE, VAN WYCK, VAN HORN, DELANO, and Freeman Clarke, at twenty-five minutes past twelve m., General Thomas, Adjutant General, came into this Secretary of War Office, saying, "Good morning," the Secretary replying, "Good morning, sir." Thomas looked around and said, "I do not wish to disturb these gentlemen and will wait." Stanton said, "Nothing private here; what do you want, sir?"

Thomas demanded of Secretary Stanton the surrender of the Secretary of War Office. Stanton denied it to him, and ordered him back to his own office as Adjutant General. Thomas refused to go. "I claim the office of Secretary of War, and demand it by order of the President."

STANTON. "I deny your authority to act, and order you back to your own office."

THOMAS. "I will stand here. I want no unpleasantness in the presence of these gentlemen."

STANTON. "You can stand there if you please, but you cannot act as Secretary of War. I am Secretary of War. I order you out of this office and to your own."

THOMAS. "I refuse to go, and will stand here."

STANTON. "How are you to get possession; do you mean to use force?"

THOMAS. "I do not care to use force, but my mind is made up as to what I shall do. I want no unpleasantness, though. I shall stay here and act as Secretary of War."

STANTON. "You shall not, and I order you as your superior back to your own office."

THOMAS. "I will not obey you, but will stand here and remain here."

STANTON. "You can stand there, as you please. I order you out of this office to your own. I am Secretary of War, and your superior."

Thomas then went into opposite room across hall (General Schriver's) and commenced ordering General Schriver and General E. D. Townsend. Stanton entered, followed by MOORHEAD and FERRY, and ordered those generals not to obey or pay attention to General Thomas's orders; that he denied his assumed authority as Secretary of War *ad interim*, and forbade their obedience of his directions. "I am Secretary of War, and I now order you, General Thomas, out of this office to your own quarters."

THOMAS. "I will not go. I shall discharge the functions of Secretary of War."

STANTON. "You will not."

THOMAS. "I shall require the mails of the War Department to be delivered to me, and shall transact the business of the office."

STANTON. "You shall not have them, and I order you to your own office."

Mr. Manager BUTLER, (to the counsel for the respondent.) The witness is yours, gentlemen.

Cross-examined by Mr. STANBERY:

Question. Did the conversation stop there?

Answer. So far as I heard.

Question. You then left the office?

Answer. I left in about fifteen or twenty minutes after that. I left General Thomas in General Schriver's room, and returned into the Secretary of War's room.

Question. Did the Secretary return with you, or did he remain?

Answer. He remained a few moments in General Schriver's room, and then returned to his own room. When I left, he was in his own room.

Question. How early in the morning of the 22d did you get to the office of the Secretary of War?

Answer. My impression is it was about a quarter past eleven in the morning. It was a little after eleven, at any rate.

Question. Had you been there at all the night before?

Answer. I had not.

Question. Did you hear the orders given by General Thomas in Schriver's room?

Answer. Yes, sir.

Question. Were you in Schriver's room at the time those orders were given?

Answer. I was at the threshold; I had reached the threshold. I believe I was the first that followed Secretary Stanton. I believe I was the first and Mr. MOORHEAD second.

WILLIAM H. EMORY sworn and examined.

By Mr. Manager BUTLER:

Question. State your full name?

Answer. William Helmsley Emory.

Question. What is your rank and command in the Army?

Answer. I am colonel of the fifth cavalry, and brevet major general in the Army. My command is the department of Washington.

Question. How long have you been in command of that department?

Answer. Since the 1st of September, 1867.

Question. Soon after you went into command of the department did you have any conversation with the President of the United States as to the troops in the department or their station?

Answer. Yes.

Question. Before proceeding to give that conversation, will you state to the Senate the extent of the department of Washington, to what it extends, its territorial limits, I mean?

Answer. The department of Washington consists of the District of Columbia, Maryland, and Delaware, excluding Fort Delaware.

Question. State as well as you can; if you cannot give it all, give the substance of that conversation which you had with the President when you first entered upon command?

Answer. It is impossible for me to give anything like that conversation. I can only give the substance of it. It occurred long ago. He asked me about the location of the troops, and I told him the strength of each post, and as near as I can recollect the commanding officer of the post.

Question. Go on, sir; if that is not all.

Answer. That was the substance and important part of the conversation. There was some conversation as to whether more troops should be sent here or not. I recommended that there should be troops here, and called the President's attention to a report of General Canby, my predecessor, recommending that there should always be at the seat of Government at least a brigade of infantry, a battery of artillery, and a squadron of cavalry: and some conversation, mostly of my own, was had in reference to the formation of a military force in Maryland that was then going on.

Question. What military force?

Answer. A force organized by the State of Maryland.

Question. Please state as well as you can what you stated to the President, in substance, relative to the formation of that military force.

Answer. I merely stated that I did not see the object of it, as near as I can recollect, and that I did not like the organization; I saw no necessity for it.

Question. Did you state what your objections were to the organization?

Answer. I think it is likely I did; but I cannot recollect exactly at this time what they were. I think it likely that I stated that they were clothed in uniform that was offensive to our people, some portions of them; and that they were officered by gentlemen who had been in the southern army.

Question. By the offensive uniform do you mean the gray?

Answer. Yes, sir.

Question. Do you remember anything else at that time?

Answer. Nothing.

Question. Did you call upon the President upon your own thought or were you sent for at that time?

Answer. I was sent for.

Question. When again did he send for you for any such purpose?

Answer. I think it was about the 22d of February.

Question. In what manner did you receive the message?

Answer. I received a note from Colonel Moore.

Question. Who is Colonel Moore?

Answer. He is the Secretary of the President and an officer of the Army.

Question. Have you that note?

Answer. I have not. It may be in my desk at the office.

Question. Did you produce that note before the committee of the House of Representatives?

Answer. I read from it.

Question. Have you since seen that note as copied in their proceedings?

Answer. I have.

Question. Is that a correct copy?

Answer. That is a correct copy.

Mr. Manager BUTLER, (to the counsel for the respondent.) Shall I use it, gentlemen?

Mr. CURTIS. Certainly.

Mr. EVARTS. Use it, subject to the production of the original.

Mr. Manager BUTLER. If desired. I suppose it will not be insisted on. [Handing a printed paper to the witness.] Will you read it? The witness read as follows:

EXECUTIVE MANSION,
WASHINGTON, D. C., *February* 22, 1868.

GENERAL: The President directs me to say that he will be pleased to have you call on him as early as practicable.

Very respectfully and truly, yours,
WILLIAM G. MOORE,
United States Army.

Question. How early did you call?
Answer. I called immediately.
Question. How early in the day?
Answer. I think it was about midday.
Question. Whom did you find with the President, if anybody?
Answer. I found the President alone when I first went in.
Question. Will you have the kindness to state as nearly as you can what took place there?
Answer. I will try and state the substance of it, but the words I cannot undertake to state exactly. The President asked me if I recollected a conversation he had had with me when I first took command of the department? I told him that I recollected the fact of the conversation distinctly. He then asked me what changes had been made. I told him no material changes, but such as had been made I could state at once. I went on to state that in the fall six companies of the twenty-ninth infantry had been brought to this city to winter; but as an offset to that four companies of the twelfth infantry had been detached to South Carolina on the request of the commander of that district; that two companies of artillery that had been detached by my predecessor, one of them for the purpose of aiding in putting down the Fenian difficulties, had been returned to the command; that although the number of companies had been increased the numerical strength of the command was very much the same, growing out of an order reducing the artillery and infantry companies from the maximum of the war establishment to the minimum of the peace establishment. The President said, "I do not refer to those changes." I replied that if he would state what changes he referred to, or who made the report of the changes, perhaps I could be more explicit. He said, "I refer to recent changes, within a day or two," or something to that effect. I told him I thought I could assure him that no changes had been made; that under a recent order issued for the government of the armies of the United States, founded upon a law of Congress, all orders had to be transmitted through General Grant to the Army, and in like manner all orders coming from General Grant to any of his subordinate officers must necessarily come, if in my department, through me; that if by chance an order had been given to any junior officer of mine it was his duty at once to report the fact. The President asked

me, "What order do you refer to?" I replied, "To Order No. 17 of the series of 1867." He said, "I would like to see the order," and a messenger was dispatched for it. At this time a gentleman came in who I supposed had business in no way connected with the business that I had in hand, and I withdrew to the further end of the room, and while there the messenger came with the book of orders and handed it to me. As soon as the gentleman had withdrawn I returned to the President with the book in my hand, and said I would take it as a favor if he would permit me to call his attention to that order; that it had been passed in an appropriation bill, and I thought it not unlikely had escaped his attention. He took the order and read it, and observed, "This is not in conformity with the Constitution of the United States, that makes me Commander-in-Chief, or with the terms of your commission."

Mr. HOWARD. Repeat his language, if you please.

The WITNESS. I cannot repeat it any nearer than I am now doing.

Mr. CONKLING. Repeat your last answer louder, so that we may hear.

Mr. JOHNSON. What he said.

The WITNESS. What who said, the President or me?

Mr. HOWARD. The President.

The WITNESS. He said, "This is not in conformity with the Constitution of the United States, which makes me Commander-in-Chief, or with the terms of your commission." I replied, "That is the order which you have approved and issued to the Army for our government," or something to that effect. I cannot recollect the exact words, nor do I intend to quote the exact words, of the President. He said, "Am I to understand that the President of the United States cannot give an order except through the General of the Army," or "General Grant?" I said, in reply, that that was my impression, that that was the opinion that the Army entertained, and I thought upon that subject they were a unit. I also said, "I think it is fair, Mr. President, to say to you that when this order came out there was considerable discussion on the subject as to what were the obligations of an officer under that order, and some eminent lawyers were consulted—I myself consulted one—and the opinion was given to me decidedly and unequivocally that we were bound by the order, constitutional or not constitutional." The President observed that the object of the law was evident.

Mr. Manager BUTLER. Before you pass from that, did you state to him who the lawyers were who had been consulted?

Answer. Yes.

Question. What did you state on that subject?

Answer. Perhaps, in reference to that, a part of my statement was not altogether correct. In regard to myself, I consulted Mr. Robert J. Walker.

Question. State what you said to him, whether correct or otherwise?

Answer. I will state it. I stated that I had consulted Mr, Robert J. Walker, in reply to his question as to whom it was I had consulted; and I understood other officers had consulted Mr. REVERDY JOHNSON.

Question. Did you say to him what opinion had been reported from those consultations?

Answer. I stated before that the lawyer that I consulted stated to me that we were bound by it undoubtedly; and I understood from some officers, who I supposed had consulted Mr. JOHNSON, that he was of the same opinion.

Question. What did the President reply to that?

Answer. The President said "the object of the law is evident." There the conversation ended by my thanking him for the courtesy with which he had allowed me to express my own opinion.

Question. Did you then withdraw?

Answer. I then withdrew.

Question. Did you see General Thomas that morning?

Answer. I did not, that I recollect. I have no recollection of it.

Question. (Handing a paper to the witness.) State whether that is an official copy of the order to which you referred?

Answer. No, sir. It is only a part of the order. The order which I had in my hand, and which I have in my office, has the appropriation bill in front of it. That is, perhaps, another form issued from the Adjutant General's office; but it is the substance of one part of the order.

Question. Is it so far as it concerns this matter?

Answer. So far as concerns this matter it is the same order; but it is not the same copy, or, more properly, the same edition. There are two editions of the order, one published with the appropriation bill, and this is a section of the appropriation bill, and probably has been published as a detached section.

Question. Is that an official copy?

Answer. Yes, sir; that is an official copy.

Question. This, I observe, is headed "Order No. 15." I observed you said "No. 17." Do you refer to the same or different orders?

Answer. I refer to the same order, and I think Order No. 17 is the one containing the appropriation bill, the one I referred to, and the one I had in my hand, and, I think, the one that is on file in my office. That made the confusion in the first place. I may have said Order 15 or 17, but Order No. 17 embraces, I think, all the appropriation bill, and is the full order.

Question. This is No. 15, and covers the second and third sections of that act?

Answer. The sections are the same.

Mr. Manager BUTLER, (to the counsel for the respondent.) I propose to put this paper in evidence, if you do not object.

Mr. EVARTS. Allow us to look at it.

[The paper was handed to the counsel and examined.]

Mr. STANBERY. We have no objection.

Mr. EVARTS. We will treat that as equivalent to Order No. 17, unless some difference should appear.

Mr. Manager BUTLER. There is no difference, I believe, and it is the same as is set out in the answer. Do you desire to have it read?

Mr. JOHNSON. The Manager will read it, if he pleases.

Mr. Manager BUTLER read as follows:

[General Orders, No. 15.]

WAR DEPARTMENT,
ADJUTANT GENERAL'S OFFICE,
WASHINGTON, *March* 12, 1868.

The following extract of an act of Congress is published for the information and government of all concerned:

[PUBLIC—No. 85.]

"An act making appropriations for the support of the Army for the year ending June 30, 1868, and for other purposes."

* * * * * * * *

"SEC. 2. *And be it further enacted,* That the headquarters of the General of the Army of the United States shall be at the city of Washington, and all orders and instructions relating to military operations issued by the President or Secretary of War shall be issued through the General of the Army, and, in case of his inability, through the next in rank. The General of the Army shall not be removed, suspended, or relieved from command, or assigned to duty elsewhere than at said headquarters, except at his own request, without the previous approval of the Senate; and any orders or instructions relating to military operations issued contrary to the requirements of this section shall be null and void; and any officer who shall issue orders or instructions contrary to the provisions of this section shall be deemed guilty of a misdemeanor in office; and any officer of the Army who shall transmit, convey, or obey any orders or instructions so issued contrary to the provisions of this section, knowing that such orders were so issued, shall be liable to imprisonment for not less than two nor more than twenty years, upon conviction thereof in any court of competent jurisdiction.

"SEC. 3. *And be it further enacted,* That section three of the joint resolution relative to appointments to the Military Academy, approved June 16, 1866, be, and the same is hereby, repealed."

* * * * * * * *

"SEC. 5. *And be it further enacted,* That it shall be the duty of the officers of the Army and Navy and of the Freedmen's Bureau to prohibit and prevent whipping or maiming of the person as a punishment for any crime, misdemeanor, or offense, by any pretended civil or military authority in any State lately in rebellion until the civil government of such State shall have been restored, and shall have been recognized by the Congress of the United States.

"SEC. 6. *And be it further enacted,* That all military forces now organized or in service in either of the States of Virginia, North Carolina, South Carolina, Georgia, Florida, Alabama, Louisiana, Mississippi, and Texas, be forthwith disbanded, and that the further organization, arming, or calling into service of the said militia forces, or any part thereof, is hereby prohibited, under any circumstances whatever, until the same shall be authorized by Congress."

* * * * * * * *

"Approved March 2, 1867."

By order of the Secretary of War:

E. D. TOWNSEND,
Assistant Adjutant General.

Official:

E. D. TOWNSEND,
Assistant Adjutant General.

Question. You are still in command of the department, as I understand?

Answer. Yes, sir.

Cross-examined by Mr. STANBERY:

Question. The paper which you had and which was read by the President on that day was marked " Orders No. 17," was it?

Answer. Fifteen or seventeen.

Question. This is fifteen, is the other seventeen?

Answer. I think it was, but I will not be sure.

Question. In that paper marked No. 17 was the whole appropriation act printed and set out, and was it in other respects like this?

Answer. In other respects like that. There is one thing I wish to state. The copy on file in my office contains the appropriation bill, and I may have confounded them. It is numbered seventeen.

Question. And it is your impression that the paper read by you at the President's was the same you had?

Answer. That is my impression, although it may have been that now before you. I cannot say.

Question. As I understand you, when the document No. 17 was sent to the officers of the Army there was a discussion among them, you said?

Answer. Yes.

Question. I see this document contains no construction of that act, but simply gives the act for their information; is that so?

Answer. Yes, sir.

Question. Upon reading the act, then, a discussion arose among the officers of the Army?

Answer. Yes.

Question. As to its meaning, or what?

Answer. A discussion with a view of ascertaining what an officer's obligations were under that act.

Question. You had received no instructions from the War Department or elsewhere except what are contained in that document itself?

Answer. None whatever.

Question. It left you, then, to construe the act?

Answer. Yes, sir.

Question. Upon that you say that to settle your doubts you applied to an eminent lawyer?

Answer. I had no doubt myself, but to satisfy the doubts of others.

Question. You applied to an eminent lawyer?

Answer. Yes, sir.

Question. And that gentleman whom you applied to was Mr. Robert J. Walker?

Answer. Yes, sir.

Question. Was it he that advised you that you were bound to obey only orders coming through General Grant, whether it was constitutional or unconstitutional to send orders in that way?

Answer. The question of constitution was not raised; it was only a question of whether we were bound by that order.

Question. I understood you to say that the answer was "constitutional or not constitutional," in your response to General BUTLER.

' *Answer.* I made a mistake, then. The question was whether we were bound by it, and I should like to correct it.

Mr. Manager BUTLER. You may do so.

Mr. STANBERY. Certainly. [To the witness.] You said in your former answer that the advice was that you were bound to obey it whether it was constitutional or not.

Answer. Until it was decided. We had no right to judge of the Constitution—the officers had not.

Question. That was the advice you got?

Answer. Yes, sir.

Question. Until it was decided—decided by whom and where?

Answer. By the Supreme Court; and not only that, after the decision is made it must be promulgated to us in orders as null and void, and no longer operating.

Question. When you said to the President that he had approved something, did you speak in reference to that Order No. 17 which contained the whole of the act?

Answer. I did.

Question. What did you mean to say—that he had approved the order, or had approved the act?

Answer. As far as we are concerned, the order and the act are the same thing; and if you will observe, it is marked "approved." That means by the President.

Question. What is marked "approved," the order or the act?

Answer. The act is marked "approved." The order contains nothing but the act, not a word besides.

Question. Then the approval that you referred to was to the act?

Answer. I consider the act and the order the same.

Question. But the word "approved" you speak of was to the act?

Answer. Of course; but as far as we are concerned in the Army the act and the order are the same thing.

Mr. Manager WILSON. Mr. President, we now offer a duly authenticated copy of General Emory's commission:

The President of the United States:
    To all who shall see these presents, greeting ,

Know ye, that I do hereby confer on William H. Emory, of the Army of the United States, by and with the advice and consent of the Senate, the rank of major general by brevet in said Army, to rank as such from the 13th day of March, in the year of our Lord 1865, for gallant and meritorious services at the battle of Cedar creek, Virginia; and I do strictly charge and require all officers and soldiers to obey and respect him accordingly; and he is to observe and follow such orders and directions from time to time as he shall receive from me or the future President of the United States of America, and other officers set over him according to law, and the rules and discipline of war. This commission to continue in force during the pleasure of the President of the United States for the time being,

Given under my hand at the city of Washington,

this 17th day of July, in the year of our Lord 1866, and of the ninety-first year of the independence of the United States. ANDREW JOHNSON.
[Seal of the War Department.]
By the President:
 EDWIN M. STANTON,
   Secretary of War.

This is duly certified from the Department, the certificate being as follows:

   WAR DEPARTMENT,
  ADJUTANT GENERAL'S OFFICE,
    March 24, 1868.

It appears from the records of this office that the annexed document is a true copy of the original commission issued to Brevet Major General W. H. Emory, United States Army, from this office.
   E. D. TOWNSEND,
   Assistant Adjutant General.

Be it known that E. D. Townsend, who has signed the foregoing certificate, is an assistant adjutant general of the Army of the United States, and that to his attestation as such full faith and credit are and ought to be given.

In testimony whereof I, E. M. Stanton, Secretary of War, have hereunto set my hand, and [L. S.] caused the seal of the Department of War of the United States of America to be affixed on this 24th day of March, 1868.
   E. M. STANTON,
   Secretary of War.

We also offer the order assigning General Emory to the command of the department of Washington:

[Special Orders, No. 426.]
HEADQUARTERS ARMY OF THE UNITED STATES,
 ADJUTANT GENERAL'S OFFICE,
  WASHINGTON, *August* 27, 1867.

[Extract.]

25. Brevet Major General W. H. Emory will forthwith relieve Brevet Major General Canby, in command of the department of Washington, and by direction of the President is assigned to duty according to his brevet of major general while exercising such command.
By command of General Grant:
   E. D. TOWNSEND,
   Assistant Adjutant General.
Official:
 E. D. TOWNSEND,
  Assistant Adjutant General.

We now offer the order of the President, under which General Thomas resumed his duties as Adjutant General of the Army of the United States:

   EXECUTIVE MANSION,
 WASHINGTON, D. C., *February* 13, 1868.

GENERAL: I desire that Brevet Major General Lorenzo Thomas resume his duties as Adjutant General of the Army of the United States.
Respectfully, yours, ANDREW JOHNSON.
General U. S. GRANT, *commanding Army of the United States, Washington, D. C.*

It is the original order.

I now offer the original letter of General Grant requesting the President to put in writing a verbal order which he had given him prior to the date of this letter. Both the letter and the indorsement by the President are original.

Mr. STANBERY. Allow us to look at it.

Mr. Manager WILSON. Certainly.

[The letter was handed to counsel, and after examination returned to the Managers.]

Mr. Manager WILSON. I will read it:

HEADQUARTERS ARMY OF THE UNITED STATES,
  WASHINGTON, D. C., *January* 24, 1868.

SIR: I have the honor very respectfully to request to have in writing the order which the President gave me verbally on Sunday, the 19th instant, to disregard the orders of Hon. E. M. Stanton as Secretary of War until I knew from the President himself that they were his orders.

I have the honor to be, very respectfully, your obedient servant, U. S. GRANT, *General.*

His Excellency A. JOHNSON,
  President of the United States.

Upon which letter is the following indorsement:

   EXECUTIVE MANSION,
 WASHINGTON, D. C., *January* 29, 1868.

ANDREW JOHNSON, *President of the United States.*

In reply to request of General Grant of the 24th January, 1868, the President does so, as follows:

As requested in this communication, General Grant is instructed in writing not to obey any order from the War Department assumed to be issued by the direction of the President, unless such order is known by the General commanding the armies of the United States to have been authorized by the Executive.
   ANDREW JOHNSON.

Mr. CAMERON. I should be glad to have that read by the Clerk.

The CHIEF JUSTICE. The Secretary will read the order.

The Secretary read the letter of General Grant and the indorsement last read by Mr. Manager WILSON.

Mr. Manager WILSON. The next document which we produce is a letter written by the President of the United States to General Grant of date of February 10, 1868. It is the original letter, and I send it to counsel that they may examine it.

[The letter was handed to the counsel for the President, and examined by them.]

Mr. STANBERY. Mr. Chief Justice, it appears that this is a letter purporting to be a part of a correspondence between General Grant and the President. I ask the honorable Managers whether it is their intention to produce the entire correspondence?

Mr. Manager WILSON. It is not our intention to produce anything beyond this letter which we now offer.

Mr. STANBERY. No other part of the correspondence but this letter?

Mr. Manager WILSON. That is all we propose now to offer.

[The letter was returned to the Managers.]

Mr. STANBERY. We wish the honorable Managers to state what is the purpose of introducing this letter? What is the object? What is the relevancy? What does it relate to?

Mr. Manager WILSON. I may state that the special object we have in view in the introduction of this letter is to show the President's own declaration of his intent to prevent the Secretary of War, Mr. Stanton, resuming the duties of the office of Secretary of War, notwithstanding the action of the Senate on his case, and the requirement of the tenure-of-office bill. Do you desire it read?

Mr. STANBERY. Certainly, if it is to come in.

Mr. Manager WILSON. I ask the Secretary to read it.

The CHIEF JUSTICE. The Secretary will read it.

The Secretary read the letter, as follows:

EXECUTIVE MANSION, *February* 10, 1868.

GENERAL: The extraordinary character of your letter of the 3d instant would seem to preclude any reply on my part; but the manner in which publicity has been given to the correspondence of which that letter forms a part, and the grave questions which are involved, induce me to take this mode of giving, as a proper sequel to the communications which have passed between us, the statements of the five members of the Cabinet who were present on the occasion of our conversation on the 14th ultimo. Copies of the letters which they have addressed to me upon the subject are accordingly herewith inclosed.

You speak of my letter of the 31st ultimo as a reiteration of the "many and gross misrepresentations" contained in certain newspaper articles, and reassert the correctness of the statements contained in your communication of the 28th ultimo: adding—and here I give your own words—"anything in yours in reply to it to the contrary notwithstanding."

When a controversy upon matters of fact reaches the point to which this has been brought, further assertion or denial between the immediate parties should cease, especially where, upon either side, it loses the character of the respectful discussion which is required by the relations in which the parties stand to each other, and degenerates in tone and temper. In such a case, if there is nothing to rely upon but the opposing statements, conclusions must be drawn from those statements alone, and from whatever intrinsic probabilities they afford in favor of or against either of the parties. I should not shrink from this test in this controversy; but, fortunately, it is not left to this test alone. There were five Cabinet officers present at the conversation, the detail of which, in my letter of the 28th ultimo, you allow yourself to say, contains "many and gross misrepresentations." These gentlemen heard that conversation and have read my statement. They speak for themselves, and I leave the proof without a word of comment.

I deem it proper, before concluding this communication, to notice some of the statements contained in your letter.

You say that a performance of the promises alleged to have been made by you to the President "would have involved a resistance to law, and an inconsistency with the whole history of my connection with the suspension of Mr. Stanton." You then state that you had fears the President would, on the removal of Mr. Stanton, appoint some one in his place who would embarrass the Army in carrying out the reconstruction acts, and add:

"It was to prevent such an appointment that I accepted the office of Secretary of War *ad interim*, and not for the purpose of enabling you to get rid of Mr. Stanton by my withholding it from him in opposition to law, or, not doing so myself, surrendering it to one who would, as the statements and assumptions in your communication plainly indicate was sought."

First of all, you here admit that from the very beginning of what you term "the whole history" of your connection with Mr. Stanton's suspension, you intended to circumvent the President. It was to carry out that intent that you accepted the appointment. This was in your mind at the time of your acceptance. It was not, then, in obedience to the order of your superior, as has heretofore been supposed, that you assumed the duties of the office. You knew it was the President's purpose to prevent Mr. Stanton from resuming the office of Secretary of War; and you intended to defeat that purpose. You accepted the office, not in the interest of the President, but of Mr. Stanton. If this purpose, so entertained by you, had been confined to yourself; if, when accepting the office, you had done so with a mental reservation to frustrate the President, it would have been a tacit deception. In the ethics of some persons such a course is allowable. But you cannot stand even upon that questionable ground. The "history" of your connection with this transaction, as written by yourself,

places you in a different predicament, and shows that you not only concealed your design from the President, but induced him to suppose that you would carry out his purpose to keep Mr. Stanton out of office, by retaining it yourself after an attempted restoration by the Senate, so as to require Mr. Stanton to establish his right by judicial decision.

I now give that part of this "history," as written by yourself in your letter of the 28th ultimo:

"Some time after I assumed the duties of Secretary of War *ad interim*, the President asked me my views as to the course Mr. Stanton would have to pursue, in case the Senate should not concur in his suspension, to obtain possession of his office. My reply was, in substance, that Mr. Stanton would have to appeal to the courts to reinstate him, illustrating my position by citing the ground I had taken in the case of the Baltimore police commissioners."

Now, at that time, as you admit in your letter of the 3d instant, you held the office for the very object of defeating an appeal to the courts. In that letter you say that in accepting the office one motive was to prevent the President from appointing some other person who would retain possession, and thus make judicial proceedings necessary. You knew the President was unwilling to trust the office with any one who would not, by holding it, compel Mr. Stanton to resort to the courts. You perfectly understood that in this interview, "some time" after you accepted the office, the President, not content with your silence, desired an expression of your views, and you answered him that Mr. Stanton "would have to appeal to the courts."

If the President had reposed confidence before he knew your views, and that confidence had been violated, it might have been said he made a mistake; but a violation of confidence reposed after that conversation was no mistake of his, nor of yours. It is the fact only that needs be stated, that at the date of this conversation you did not intend to hold the office with the purpose of forcing Mr. Stanton into court, but did hold it then, and had accepted it, to prevent that course from being carried out. In other words, you said to the President, "that is the proper course," and you said to yourself, "I have accepted this office and now hold it to defeat that course." The excuse you make in a subsequent paragraph of that letter of the 28th ultimo, that afterward, you changed your views as to what would be a proper course, has nothing to do with the point now under consideration. The point is that before you changed your views you had secretly determined to do the very thing which at last you did—surrender the office to Mr. Stanton. You may have changed your views as to the law, but you certainly did not change your views as to the course you had marked out for yourself from the beginning.

I will only notice one more statement in your letter of the 3d instant—that the performance of the promises which it is alleged were made by you would have involved you in the resistance of law. I know of no statute that would have been violated had you, carrying out your promises in good faith, tendered your resignation when you concluded not to be made a party in any legal proceedings. You add:

"I am in a measure confirmed in this conclusion by your recent orders directing me to disobey orders from the Secretary of War, my superior, and your subordinate, without having countermanded his authority to issue the orders I am to disobey."

On the 24th ultimo you addressed a note to the President requesting in writing an order given to you verbally five days before to disregard orders from Mr. Stanton as Secretary of War until you "knew from the President himself that they were his orders."

On the 29th, in compliance with your request, I did give you instructions in writing "not to obey any order from the War Department, assumed to be issued by the direction of the President, unless such order is known by the General commanding the armies of the United States to have been authorized by the Executive."

There are some orders which a Secretary of War may issue without the authority of the President; there are others which he issues simply as the agent of the President, and which purport to be "by direction" of the President. For such orders the President is responsible, and he should therefore know and understand what they are before giving such "direction." Mr. Stanton states, in his letter of the 4th instant, which accompanies the published correspondence, that he "has had no correspondence with the President since the 12th of August last;" and he further says that since he resumed the duties of the office he has continued to discharge them "without any personal or written communication with the President;" and he adds, "no orders have been issued from this Department in the name of the President with my knowledge, and I have received no orders from him."

It thus seems that Mr. Stanton now discharges the duties of the War Department without any reference to the President, and without using his name.

My order to you had only reference to orders "assumed to be issued by the direction of the President." It would appear from Mr. Stanton's letter that you have received no such orders from him. However, in your note to the President of the 30th ultimo, in which you acknowledge the receipt of the written order of the 29th, you say that you have been informed by Mr. Stanton that he has not received any order limiting his authority to issue orders to the Army, according to the practice of the Department, and state that "while this authority to the War Department is not countermanded, it will be satisfactory evidence to me that any orders issued from the War Department by direction of the President are authorized by the Executive."

The President issues an order to you to obey no order from the War Department, purporting to be made "by the direction of the President," until you have referred it to him for his approval. You reply that you have received the President's order and will not obey it; but will obey an order purporting to be given by his direction, *if it comes from the War Department.* You will not obey the direct order of the President, but will obey his indirect order. If, as you say, there has been a practice in the War Department to issue orders in the name of the President without his direction, does not the precise order you have requested and have received change the practice as to the General of the Army? Could not the President countermand any such order issued to you from the War Department? If you should receive an order from that Department, issued in the name of the President, to do a special act, and an order directly from the President himself not to do the act, is there a doubt which you are to obey? You answer the question when you say to the President, in your letter of the 3d instant, the Secretary of War is "my superior and your subordinate," and yet you refuse obedience to the superior out of a deference to the subordinate.

Without further comment upon the insubordinate attitude which you have assumed, I am at loss to know how you can relieve yourself from obedience to the orders of the President, who is made by the Constitution the Commander-in-Chief of the Army and Navy, and is therefore the official superior as well of the General of the Army as of the Secretary of War.

Respectfully, yours,   ANDREW JOHNSON.

General U. S. GRANT, *Commanding Armies of the United States, Washington, D. C.*

[Several Senators had gone out during the reading of the letter.]

Mr. Manager WILSON. We now——

The CHIEF JUSTICE. Before the honorable Manager proceeds, he will wait until the seats of the Senators are filled. The Sergeant-at-Arms will inform Senators that their presence is wanted.

Several Senators having returned to the Chamber,

The CHIEF JUSTICE. The honorable Manager may proceed.

Mr. STANBERY. I ask the honorable Manager if he is done reading all that belongs to that letter. In that letter certain documents

are referred to as explanatory of it. Do you propose to read those papers?

Mr. Manager WILSON. All has been read which we propose to offer.

Mr. STANBERY. You do not, therefore, propose to offer the papers, copies of which accompany that letter and which are referred to in it?

Mr. Manager WILSON. I have stated to the counsel that we offered a letter of the President of the United States. It has been read. We proposed to offer the letter; we have offered it; and it is in evidence.

Mr. STANBERY. You do not now propose to offer——

Mr. Manager WILSON. The entire letter has been read.

Mr. STANBERY. We do not understand that. We ask that the documents referred to be read with that letter. They accompany it, and are referred to in it and explain it.

Mr. Manager WILSON. We offer nothing, sir, but the letter.

Mr. STANBERY. Then we object to it.

Mr. Manager WILSON. If the counsel have anything to offer when they come to present their case we will then consider it.

Mr. STANBERY. We ask it as a part of the letter. Suppose there were a postscript there, would you not read it?

Mr. Manager WILSON. There is no postscript. That settles it.

Mr. STANBERY. But there is matter added to it.

Mr. Manager WILSON. There is no matter added to it. The letter is there as written by the President.

Mr. STANBERY. Mr. Chief Justice, we will take a ruling upon that point. On the first page of the letter the matter is referred to, which I will read:

"GENERAL: The extraordinary character of your letter of the 3d instant would seem to preclude any reply on my part; but the manner in which publicity has been given to the correspondence of which that letter forms a part and the grave questions which are involved induce me to take this mode of giving, as a proper sequel to the communications which have passed between us, the statements of the five members of the Cabinet who were present on the occasion of our conversation on the 14th ultimo. Copies of the letters which they have addressed to me upon the subject are accordingly herewith inclosed."

Again, he says:

"There were five Cabinet officers present at the conversation, the detail of which, in my letter of the 28th ultimo, you allow yourself to say, contains 'many and gross misrepresentations.' These gentlemen heard that conversation and have read my statement. They speak for themselves, and I leave the proof without a word of comment."

That is an answer to the statement referred to and made a part of the letter.

Mr. Manager WILSON. I suppose the counsel does not claim that this is not the letter complete. We propose to offer nothing beyond that, and this letter is in evidence.

Mr. STANBERY. We wish to make the point, Mr. Chief Justice, that the gentlemen are now bound to produce those communications as a part of that letter.

The CHIEF JUSTICE. Do the counsel object to the introduction of the letter without the accompanying papers?

Mr. STANBERY. Certainly.

Mr. Manager WILSON. I submit, Mr. President, that the objection comes too late, even if it would have been of force if made at the proper time. The letter has been submitted and read, and is in evidence now.

Mr. STANBERY. We assumed that you were going to read the whole of it.

Mr. Manager WILSON. The whole of the letter has been read.

The CHIEF JUSTICE. The Chief Justice is of opinion that the objection may now be taken. [To the counsel for the respondent.] Do you object to the introduction of the letter without the accompanying papers?

Mr. STANBERY. We do, sir.

Mr. EVARTS. Our point is that these inclosures form a part of the communication made by the President to General Grant; and we assumed that they would be read as a part of it when the letter was offered.

Mr. Manager BINGHAM. We desire to state, Mr. President, that we claim that we are under no obligation by any rule of evidence whatever, in introducing a written statement of the accused, to give in evidence the statements of third persons referred to generally by him in that written statement. In the first place, their statements, we say, would not be evidence against the President at all. They would be hearsay. They would not be the best evidence of what the parties affirmed. The matter contained in the letter of the President shows that the papers, without producing them here, have relation to a question of fact between himself and General Grant, which question of fact, so far as the President is concerned, is affirmed in this letter by himself and for himself, and concludes him; and we insist that if forty members of his Cabinet were to write otherwise it could not affect this question. It concludes him; it is his own declaration; and the matter of dispute between himself and General Grant, although it is referred to in this letter, is no part of the matter upon which we rely in this accusation against the President.

Mr. STANBERY and Mr. CURTIS. We rely upon it.

Mr. Manager BINGHAM. Of course the gentlemen rely on it; but they ask us to introduce matter which we say by no rule of evidence is admissible at all, and for the reason which I have stated already; it is not the highest evidence of the fact. If we are to have the testimony of the members of this Cabinet about a matter of fact, and, as I said before, this letter discloses that it is a matter of fact, I claim that the highest evidence, so far as they are concerned, is not their unsworn letter, but is their sworn testimony; and that by no rule

of evidence is the letter admissible. I admit that if the letters, according to the statement here, showed a statement adopted by the President himself in regard to the matter with which we charge him, it would be a somewhat different question, although it would not take it then entirely out of the rule of evidence; but anybody can see by this reference that it is not the point at all. I venture to say that in these letters, when the gentlemen come to offer them in evidence here and we come to consider them, there is not a single statement of any Cabinet officer whatever that will in any manner qualify the confession of the President written upon the paper now read that his purpose was to prevent the execution of the tenure-of-office act and prevent the Secretary of War, after being confirmed by the Senate, and his suspension being non-concurred in, from entering upon forthwith and resuming, as that law requires, the duties of his office. That is the point of this matter. We introduce it for the purpose of showing the President's confession of his intent, and we say that in every point of light we can view it, for the reasons I have already stated, the letters referred to of the Cabinet ministers are foreign to the case, and we are under no obligation to introduce them, and in our judgment have no right to introduce them at all, being wholly irrelevant.

Mr. EVARTS. Mr. President——

The CHIEF JUSTICE. Before you proceed the counsel for the President will please to state their objection in writing.

The objection was reduced to writing and sent to the desk.

The CHIEF JUSTICE. The Secretary will read the objection made by the counsel for the President.

The Secretary read as follows:

The counsel for the President object that the letter is not in evidence in the case unless the honorable Managers shall also read the inclosures therein referred to and by the letter made part of the same.

Mr. STANBERY. Mr. Chief Justice, is the question now before your Honor or before the court?

The CHIEF JUSTICE. Before the body.

Mr. STANBERY. Before the body?

The CHIEF JUSTICE. Before the court.

Mr. STANBERY. The Managers read a letter from the President to use against him certain statements that are made in it, and perhaps the whole; we do not know the whole. They say the object is to prove a certain intent with regard to the exclusion of Mr. Stanton from office. In the letter the President refers to certain documents which are inclosed in it as throwing light upon the question and explaining his own views. Now, I put it to honorable Senators: suppose he had copied these letters in the body of his letter, and had said just as he says here, "I refer you to these; these are part of my communication," could any one doubt that these copies, although they come from other persons, would be admissible? He makes them his own. He chooses to use them as explanatory of his letter. He is not willing to let that letter go alone; he sends along with it certain explanatory matter. Now, you must admit, if he had taken the trouble to copy them himself in the body of his letter, they must be read. Suppose he attaches them, makes them a part, calls them "exhibits," affixes them, attaches them to the letter itself by tape or seal or otherwise, must they not be read as part of the communication, as the very matter which he has introduced as explanatory, without which he is not willing to send that letter? Undoubtedly. Does the form of the thing alter it? Is he not careful to send the documents not in a separate package, not in another communication, but enclosed in the letter itself, so that when the letter is read the documents must be read? It seems to me there cannot be a question but that they must read the whole and not merely the letter; for it was the whole that the President sent to be read to give his views, and not merely the letter unconnected with these documents.

Mr. Manager WILSON. Mr. President, the Managers do not care to protract this discussion. We have received from the files of the proper Department a letter complete in itself, a letter written by the President and signed by the President, in which, it is true, he refers to certain statements made by members of the Cabinet touching a question of veracity pending between the President and General Grant. Now, we insist that that question has nothing to do with this case. Everything contained in the letter which can by any possibility be considered as relevant to the case is tendered by offering the letter itself; and the statement of the President referring to the alleged inclosures shows that those inclosures relate exclusively to that question of veracity pending between himself and the General, and are in no wise connected with the issue pending between the President and the representatives of the people in this case. We are willing to submit this point without further discussion.

The CHIEF JUSTICE. Does the honorable Manager consider himself entitled to read an extract from the letter containing so much of it as would bear upon his immediate object without reading the whole letter?

Mr. Manager WILSON. We read all there is of the letter.

The CHIEF JUSTICE. That is not the question. Would the honorable Manager consider himself entitled to read so much of the letter as bore upon his immediate object without reading the whole?

Mr. Manager WILSON. I will state, in reply to the question propounded by the President, that we, of course, expect to use the letter for any proper purpose connected with the issues of the case.

The CHIEF JUSTICE. The Chief Justice will submit the objection to the consideration of the Senate. The Secretary will read the objection.

The Secretary read as follows:

The counsel for the President object that the letter is not evidence in the case unless the honorable Managers shall also read the inclosures therein referred to and by the letter made part of the same.

Mr. CONKLING. Mr. President, may I ask a question? I call for the reading of the words in the letter relied upon now for this purpose. I send my question to the Chair in writing.

The CHIEF JUSTICE. The Secretary will read the question proposed by the Senator from New York.

The Secretary read as follows:

The counsel for the respondent will please read the words in the letter relied upon touching inclosures.

Mr. STANBERY read as follows:

"GENERAL: The extraordinary character of your letter of the 3d instant would seem to preclude any reply on my part: but the manner in which publicity has been given to the correspondence of which that letter forms a part, and the grave questions which are involved, induce me to take this mode of giving, as a proper sequel to the communications which have passed between us, the statements of the five members of the Cabinet who were present on the occasion of our conversation on the 14th ultimo. Copies of the letters which they have addressed to me upon the subject are accordingly herewith inclosed."

The CHIEF JUSTICE. Senators, you who are of opinion that the objection of the counsel for the President be sustained will say "ay"——

Mr. CONNESS. I call for the yeas and nays.

The yeas and nays were ordered.

The CHIEF JUSTICE. Senators, you who are of opinion that the objection of the counsel for the President be sustained will answer "yea" as your names are called; those of the contrary opinion will answer "nay."

Mr. DRAKE. I ask for information, whether, if this objection is sustained, it has the effect of ruling out the letter as evidence altogether?

The CHIEF JUSTICE. It has.

Mr. ANTHONY. Mr. President, I would desire, if it is proper, that the question should be put in a different form; that it should be an affirmative vote.

The CHIEF JUSTICE. This is an affirmative form.

Mr. CONNESS. I wish the Chair would state the question.

The CHIEF JUSTICE. Senators, you who are of opinion that the objection of the counsel for the President be sustained will, as your names are called, answer "yea;" those of the contrary opinion, "nay." If the yeas carry it the effect will be to exclude the evidence. If the nays carry it the effect will be to admit it.

Mr. EVARTS. To exclude it, unless the inclosures are also offered, if our objection prevail.

Mr. ANTHONY. Mr. President, perhaps I am rather dull, but I do not precisely understand the effect of the decision of this question. A negative vote admits the evidence I understand.

The CHIEF JUSTICE. It does.

Mr. ANTHONY. And an affirmative vote excludes it.

The CHIEF JUSTICE. Unless the inclosures are produced and read.

Mr. HENDERSON. Mr. President, listening to the question asked by the Senator from Rhode Island, I presume he desires to know whether the letter with the inclosures can afterward be read as evidence, even if the objection be sustained.

The CHIEF JUSTICE. Undoubtedly it excludes the evidence only in the case that the inclosures be not read.

Mr. HENDERSON. So I understand.

The CHIEF JUSTICE, (to the Secretary.) Call the roll.

The Secretary called the roll down to the name of Mr. CAMERON.

Mr. JOHNSON. Mr. Chief Justice, I do not think the question is understood.

The CHIEF JUSTICE. The roll is being called.

Mr. JOHNSON. The question is not understood evidently.

The CHIEF JUSTICE, (to the Secretary.) Proceed with the call. The call of the roll cannot be interrupted.

The Secretary concluded the calling of roll, and the result was—yeas 20, nays 29; as follows:

YEAS—Messrs. Bayard, Conkling, Davis, Dixon, Joolittle, Fowler, Grimes, Henderson, Hendricks, ohnson, McCreery, Morrill of Vermont, Norton, Patterson of Tennessee, Ross, Sprague, Trumbull, Van Winkle, Vickers, and Willey—20.

NAYS—Messrs. Anthony, Buckalew, Cameron, Cattell, Chandler, Cole, Conness, Corbett, Cragin, Drake, Edmunds, Ferry, Fessenden, Frelinghuysen, Howard, Howe, Morgan, Morrill of Maine, Nye, Patterson of New Hampshire, Pomeroy, Ramsey, Sherman, Stewart, Sumner, Thayer, Tipton, Williams, and Wilson—29.

NOT VOTING—Messrs. Harlan, Morton, Saulsbury, Wade, and Yates—5.

The CHIEF JUSTICE. On this question the yeas are 20 and the nays 29. So the objection is not sustained.

Mr. Manager WILSON. I now offer the letter in evidence, it having already been read. I now offer a copy of the letter of appointment of the President appointing Lorenzo Thomas Secretary of War *ad interim*, as certified to by General Thomas. I will, however, in the first place, submit it to the counsel for examination, [submitting the paper to the counsel for the respondent.] I call the attention of counsel to one thing in connection with that letter, and that is, we offer it for the purpose of showing that General Thomas attempted to act as Secretary of War *ad interim*, and that his signature as such is attached to that copy. If we are not called upon to prove his signature, of course we shall not introduce any testimony for that purpose.

Mr. CURTIS. Stop one moment, if you please. Let us look at this paper further.

[The counsel for the respondent having examined the paper returned it to the Managers.]

Mr. STANBERY. We see that this is the copy Mr. Stanton requested. Read the indorsement if you please.

Mr. Manager WILSON. Have you any objection to its being read?

Mr. STANBERY. No; we want it read.

Mr. Manager WILSON. It is as follows:

EXECUTIVE MANSION,
WASHINGTON, D. C., *February* 21, 1868.

SIR: Hon. Edwin M. Stanton having been this day removed from office as Secretary for the Department of War, you are hereby authorized and empowered to act as Secretary of War *ad interim*, and will immediately enter upon the discharge of the duties pertaining to that office.

Mr. Stanton has been instructed to transfer to you all the records, books, papers, and other public property now in his custody and charge.

Respectfully, yours, ANDREW JOHNSON.

To Brevet Major General LORENZO THOMAS, *Adjutant General United States Army, Washington, D. C.*

Official copy:
Respectfully furnished to Hon. Edwin M. Stanton.
L. THOMAS,
Secretary of War ad interim.

Mr. CURTIS. We want the indorsement read.

Mr. Manager WILSON. The indorsement is, "Received 2.10 p. m., February 21, 1868; present General Grant."

Mr. EVARTS. That indorsement is whose?

Mr. STANBERY. It is in the handwriting of Mr. Stanton.

Mr. Manager WILSON. I do not know.

Mr. STANBERY. Is that fact admitted?

Mr. Manager BUTLER. It is in the handwriting of Mr. Stanton.

Mr. Manager WILSON. We next offer copies of the order removing Mr. Stanton and the letter of authority appointing General Thomas, with certain indorsements thereon, forwarded by the President to the Secretary of the Treasury for his information. [The document was handed to the counsel for the respondent, and afterward returned by them to the Managers.] Have the counsel for the respondent any objection to the introduction of that document? If not, I ask that it may be read by the Secretary.

The CHIEF JUSTICE. The Secretary will read the paper.

The Chief Clerk read as follows:

[Copy.]

EXECUTIVE MANSION,
WASHINGTON, D. C., *February* 21, 1868.

SIR: By virtue of the power and authority vested in me as President by the Constitution and laws of the United States, you are hereby removed from office as Secretary for the Department of War, and your functions as such will terminate upon receipt of this communication.

You will transfer to Brevet Major General Lorenzo Thomas, Adjutant General of the Army, who has this day been authorized and empowered to act as Secretary of War *ad interim*, all records, books, papers, and other public property now in your custody and charge.

Respectfully, yours, ANDREW JOHNSON.

To Hon. E. M. STANTON, *Washington, D. C.*

Official:
W. G. MOORE, *United States Army.*

[Copy.]

EXECUTIVE MANSION,
WASHINGTON, D. C., *February* 21, 1868.

SIR: Hon. Edwin M. Stanton having been this day removed from office as Secretary for the Department of War, you are hereby authorized and empowered to act as Secretary of War *ad interim*, and will immediately enter upon the discharge of the duties pertaining to that office.

Mr. Stanton has been instructed to transfer to you all the records, books, papers, and other public property now in his custody and charge.

Respectfully, yours, ANDREW JOHNSON.
To Brevet Major General LORENZO THOMAS, *Adjutant General United States Army, Washington, D. C.*
Official:

W. G. MOORE, *United States Army.*

February 21, 1868.
Respectfully referred to the honorable the Secretary of the Treasury, for his information.
By order of the President:
W. G. MOORE, *United States Army.*

TREASURY DEPARTMENT, *February* 29, 1868.
I certify the within to be true copies of the copies of orders of the President on file in this Department for the removal of Edwin M. Stanton from the office of Secretary for the Department of War and the appointment of Lorenzo Thomas to be Secretary *ad interim.*

H. McCULLOCH,
Secretary of the Treasury.

Mr. Manager BUTLER. Mr. President, we have here now an official copy of General Orders No. 17, of which General Emory spoke, and we now offer it, so that there may be no mistake that this document and the one shown to him are the same so far as regards the point at issue. [The document was handed to the counsel for the respondent, and presently returned to the Managers.] Do you want it read?

Mr. STANBERY. Oh, no.

Mr. Manager BUTLER. Then we offer it without reading it.

The document is as follows:

[General Orders, No. 17.]

WAR DEPARTMENT,
ADJUTANT GENERAL'S OFFICE,
WASHINGTON, *March* 14, 1867.

The following acts of Congress are published for the information and government of all concerned:

I. An act making appropriations for the support of the Military Academy for the year ending June 30, 1868.

II. An act making appropriations for the support of the Army for the year ending June 30, 1868.

III. An act making appropriations for fortifications for the year ending June 30, 1868.

I.—[PUBLIC—No. 54.]

An act making appropriations for the support of the Military Academy for the fiscal year ending June 30, 1868, and for other purposes.

Be it enacted by the Senate and House of Representatives of the United States of America in Congress assembled, That the following sums be, and the same are hereby, appropriated, out of any money in the Treasury not otherwise appropriated, for the support of the Military Academy for the year ending the 30th of June, 1868:

For pay of officers, instructors, cadets, and musicians, $154,840.

For commutation of subsistence, $5,050.

For pay in lieu of clothing for officers' servants, $156.

For current and ordinary expenses, $66,467.

For increase and expense of library, $3,000.

For expenses of Board of Visitors, $5,000.

For forage for artillery and cavalry horses, $9,000.

For horses for artillery and cavalry practice, $1,000.

For repairs of officers' quarters, $5,000.

For targets and batteries for artillery practice, $500.

For furniture of cadets' hospital, $200.

For gas pipes, gasometers, and retorts, $600.

For materials for quarters for subaltern officers, $5,000.

For ventilating and heating the barracks and other academic buildings; improving the apparatus for cooking for the cadets; repairing the hospital buildings, including the introduction of baths for the sick, the construction of water closets in the library building, and new furniture for the recitation-rooms, $40,000.

For purchase of fuel for cadets' mess-hall, $3,000.

For the removal and enlargement of the gas-works, $20,000.

For additional appropriations, for which estimates were not made last year:

For enlarging cadet laundry, $5,000.

For furniture for soldiers' hospital, $100.

For increasing the supply of water, replacing mains, &c., $15,000.

For ice-house and additional store and servants' rooms, $7,500.

For fire-proof building for public offices, $15,000.

For breast-high wall of water battery, $5,000.

For permanent derrick on the wharf, $2,500.

SEC. 2. *And be it further enacted,* That the cadets of the Military Academy be entitled to the ration now received by the acting midshipmen at the Naval Academy, commencing at the date of the approval of the law authorizing the same.

SEC. 3. *And be it further enacted,* That hereafter the assistant professor of Spanish shall receive the same pay and emoluments allowed to other assistant professors of the academy.

SEC. 4. *And be it further enacted,* That no part of the moneys appropriated by this or any other act shall be applied to the pay or subsistence of any cadet from any State declared to be in rebellion against the Government of the United States, appointed after the 1st day of January, 1867, until such State shall have been restored to its original relations to the Union.

Approved February 28, 1867.

II.—[PUBLIC—No. 85.]

An act making appropriations for the support of the Army for the year ending June 30, 1868, and for other purposes.

Be it enacted by the Senate and House of Representatives of the United States of America in Congress assembled, That the following sums be, and the same are hereby, appropriated, out of any money in the Treasury not otherwise appropriated, for the support of the Army for the year ending the 30th of June, 1868:

For expenses of recruiting, transportation of recruits, and compensation to citizen surgeons for medical attendance, $300,000.

For pay of the Army, $14,757,952.

For commutation of officers' subsistence, $2,228,982.

For commutation of forage for officers' horses, $104,600.

For payments in lieu of clothing for officers' servants, $276,978.

For payments to discharged soldiers for clothing not drawn, $200,000.

For contingencies of the Army, $100,000.

For artificial limbs for soldiers and seamen, $70,000.

For Army medical museum, $10,000.

For medical works for library of Surgeon General's office, $10,000.

For expenses of Commanding General's office, $10,000.

For repairs and improvements of armories and arsenals:

For arsenal and armory at Rock Island, Illinois, $686,500.

For the erection of a bridge at Rock Island, Illinois, as recommended by the chief of ordnance, $200,000: *Provided,* That the ownership of said bridge shall be and remain in the United States, and the Rock Island and Pacific Railroad Company shall have the right of way over said bridge for all purposes of transit across the island and river, upon the condition that the said company shall, before any money is expended by the Government, agree to pay and shall secure to the United States, first, half the cost of said bridge, and second, half the expenses of keeping said bridge in repair; and upon guarantying said conditions to the satisfaction of the Secretary of War, by contract or otherwise, the said company shall have the free use of said bridge for purposes of transit, but without any claim to ownership thereof.

For Watervliet arsenal, West Troy, New York, $38,200.

For current expenses of the ordnance service, $300,000.

For Alleghany arsenal, Pittsburg, Pennsylvania, $34 000.

For Champlain arsenal, at Vergennes, Vermont, $800.

For Columbus arsenal, Columbus, Ohio, $139,625.

For Fort Monroe arsenal, Old Point Comfort, Virginia, $6,000.

For ort Union arsenal, Fort Union, New Mexico, $10,000.

For Frankford arsenal, Bridesburg, Pennsylvania, $30,000.

For Kennebec arsenal, Augusta, Maine, $1,525.

For Indianapolis arsenal, Indianapolis, Indiana, $169,625.

For Leavenworth arsenal, Leavenworth, Kansas, $15,000.

For New York arsenal, Governor's Island, New York, $1,200.

For Pikesville arsenal, Pikesville, Maryland, $800.

For St. Louis arsenal, St. Louis, Missouri, $65,000.

For Washington arsenal, Washington, District of Columbia, $50,000.

For Watertown arsenal, Watertown, Massachusetts, $21,667.

For the purchase of the Willard Sears estate, adjoining the Watertown arsenal grounds, $49,700, or so much thereof as may be necessary; and the Secretary of War is hereby authorized to sell at public auction a lot of land belonging to the United States, situated in South Boston, if, in his opinion, the same is not needed for the public service, and pay the proceeds thereof into the Treasury.

Bureau of Refugees, Freedmen, and Abandoned Lands:

For salaries of assistant commissioners, sub-assistant commissioners, and agents, $147,500.

For salaries of clerks, $82,800.

For stationery and printing, $63,000.

For quarters and fuel, $200,000.

For commissary stores, $1,500,000.

For medical department, $500,000.

For transportation, $800,000.

For school superintendents, $25,000.

For buildings for schools and asylums, including construction, rental, and repairs, $500,000.

For telegraphing and postage, $18,000: Provided, That the Commissioner be hereby authorized to apply any balance on hand, at this date, of the refugees and freedmen's fund, accounted for in his last annual report, to aid educational institutions actually incorporated for loyal refugees and freedmen: And provided further, That no agent or clerk not heretofore authorized by law shall receive a monthly allowance exceeding the sum of $200.

SEC. 2. And be it further enacted, That the headquarters of the General of the Army of the United States shall be at the city of Washington, and all orders and instructions relating to military operations issued by the President or Secretary of War shall be issued through the General of the Army, and, in case of his inability, through the next in rank. The General of the Army shall not be removed, suspended, or relieved from command, or assigned to duty elsewhere than at said headquarters, except at his own request, without the previous approval of the Senate; and any orders or instructions relating to military operations issued contrary to the requirements of this section shall be null and void; and any officer who shall issue orders or instructions contrary to the provisions of this section shall be deemed guilty of a misdemeanor in office; and any officer of the Army who shall transmit, convey, or obey any orders or instructions so issued contrary to the provisions of this section, knowing that such orders were so issued, shall be liable to imprisonment for not less than two nor more than twenty years, upon conviction thereof in any court of competent jurisdiction.

SEC. 3. And be it further enacted, That section three of the joint resolution relative to appointments to the Military Academy, approved June 16, 1866, be, and the same is hereby, repealed.

SEC. 4. And be it further enacted, That the sum of $150,000 be, and the same is hereby, appropriated out of any moneys in the Treasury not otherwise appropriated, to be disbursed by the Secretary of War, in the erection of fire-proof buildings at or near the city of Jeffersonville, in the State of Indiana, to be used as storehouses for Government property.

SEC. 5. And be it further enacted, That it shall be the duty of the officers of the Army and Navy and of the Freedmen's Bureau to prohibit and prevent whipping or maiming of the person, as a punishment for any crime, misdemeanor, or offense, by any pretended civil or military authority in any State lately in rebellion until the civil government of such State shall have been restored and shall have been recognized by the Congress of the United States.

SEC. 6. And be it further enacted, That all militia forces now organized or in service in either of the States of Virginia, North Carolina, South Carolina, Georgia, Florida, Alabama, Louisiana, Mississippi, and Texas be forthwith disbanded, and that the further organization, arming, or calling into service of the said militia forces, or any part thereof, is hereby prohibited, under any circumstances whatever, until the same shall be authorized by Congress.

SEC. 7. And be it further enacted, That the paymaster general be authorized to pay, under such regulations as the Secretary of War shall prescribe, in addition to the amount received by them, for the traveling expenses of such California and Nevada volunteers as were discharged in New Mexico, Arizona, or Utah, and at points distant from the place or places of enlistment such proportionate sum according to the distance traveled as have been paid to the troops of other States similarly situated; and such amount as shall be necessary to pay the same is hereby appropriated out of any moneys in the Treasury not otherwise appropriated.

Approved March 2, 1867.

III.—[PUBLIC—No. 86.]

An act making appropriations for the construction, preservation, and repairs of certain fortifications and other works of defense for the fiscal year ending June 30, 1868.

Be it enacted by the Senate and House of Representatives of the United States of America in Congress assembled, That the following sums be, and they are hereby, appropriated out of any money in the Treasury not otherwise appropriated for the construction, preservation, and repair of certain fortifications and other works of defense for the year ending the 30th of June, 1868:

For Fort Scammel, Portland, Maine, $50,000.

For Fort Georges, on Hog Island ledge, Portland, Maine, $50,000.

For Fort Winthrop, Boston, Massachusetts, $50,000.

For Fort Warren, Boston, Massachusetts, $50,000.

For fort at entrance of New Bedford harbor, Massachusetts, $30,000.

For Fort Schuyler, East river, New York, $50,000.

For Fort at Willett's Point, opposite Fort Schuyler, New York, $50,000.

For fort on site of Fort Tompkins, Staten Island, New York, $50,000.

For fort at Sandy Hook, New Jersey, $50,000.

For repairs of Fort Washington, on the Potomac river, $25,000.

For Fort Monroe, Hampton Roads, Virginia, $50,000.

For Fort Taylor, Key West, Florida, $50,000.

For Fort Jefferson, Garden Key, Tortugas, $50,000.

For Fort Clinch, Amelia Island, Florida, $25,000.

For fort at Fort Point, San Francisco Bay, California, $50,000.

For fort at Lime Point, California, $50,000.

For fort at Alcatraz Island, San Francisco Bay, California, $10,000.

For Fort Preble, Portland harbor, Maine, $50,000.

For Fort McClary, Portsmouth harbor, New Hampshire, $50,000.

For Fort Independence, Boston harbor, Massachusetts, $50,000.

For survey of northern and northwestern lakes, $150,000.

For Fort Montgomery, at the outlet of Lake Champlain, $25,000.

For purchase and repair of instruments, $10,000.

For purchase of sites now occupied and lands proposed to be occupied for permanent sea-coast defenses: *Provided*, That no such purchase shall be made except upon the approval of its expediency by the Secretary of War and of the validity of the title by the Attorney General, $50,000.

For purchase of sites now occupied by temporary sea-coast defenses: *Provided*, That no such purchase shall be made except upon the approval of its expediency by the Secretary of War and of the validity of the title by the Attorney General, $25,000.

For construction and repair of barracks and quarters for engineer troops at the depot of engineer supplies near St. Louis, Missouri, $20,000.

For construction and repair of barracks and quarters for engineer troops at the depot of engineer supplies at Willett's Point, New York, $25,000.

SEC. 2. *And be it further enacted*, That there shall not be over fifty per cent. of the foregoing appropriations expended during the fiscal year ending 30th June, 1868, and the residue thereof shall not be expended till otherwise ordered.

SEC. 3. *And be it further enacted*, That, in order to determine the relative powers of resistance of the turret and the broadside systems of iron-clad vessels of war, and whether or not our present heaviest guns are adequate to the rapid destruction of the heaviest plated ships now built, or deemed practicable on either system, and whether or not our best stone forts will resist our heaviest guns, and, if not, what increase in strength, by adding either stone or iron or variation in form, is necessary to that end, the Secretary of War and the Secretary of the Navy are hereby authorized to detail a joint board of not less than six competent officers, three from the Army and three from the Navy, whose duty it shall be to construct and test, by firing upon them, such targets as they may deem necessary for the purposes above named. And the Secretary of War and the Secretary of the Navy are hereby authorized and directed to supply the board with such facilities for this purpose as they may require: *Provided*, It can be done from the unexpended funds and materials now at their disposal, the expenses to be borne equally by the War and Navy Departments, and from such funds at their disposal as the Secretary of War and the Secretary of the Navy may designate respectively.

Approved March 2, 1867.

By order of the Secretary of War.

E. D. TOWNSEND,
Assistant Adjutant General.

Official:

E. D. TOWNSEND,
Assistant Adjutant General.

GEORGE W. WALLACE sworn and examined.

By Mr. Manager BUTLER:

Question. What is your name and rank in the Army of the United States, if you have any?

Answer. George W. Wallace, lieutenant colonel of the twelfth infantry, commanding the garrison of Washington.

Question. How long have you been in command of the garrison of Washington?

Answer. Since August last.

Question. What time in August?

Answer. The latter part of the month. The exact date I do not recollect.

Question. State if at any time you were sent for to go to the Executive Mansion about the 23d of February last.

Answer. On the 22d of February I received a note from Colonel Moore desiring to see me the following morning at the Executive Mansion.

Question. Who is Colonel Moore?

Answer. He is on the staff of the President; an officer of the Army.

Question. Does he act as Secretary to the President?

Answer. I believe he does.

Question. You received that note on the night of the 22d; about what time at night?

Answer. About seven o'clock in the evening.

Question. Was any time designated when you should go?

Answer. Merely in the morning.

Question. Sunday morning! Did you go?

Answer. I did.

Question. At what time in the morning?

Answer. About ten o'clock.

Question. Did you meet Colonel Moore there?

Answer. I did.

Question. What was the business?

Answer. He desired to see me in reference to a matter directly concerning myself.

Question. How concerning yourself?

Answer. Some time in December my name had been submitted to the Senate for brevets. Those papers had been returned to the Executive Mansion, and on looking over them he was under the impression that my name had been set aside, and his object was to notify me of that fact in order that I might make use of influence, if I desired it, to have the matter rectified.

Question. After that did he say anything about your seeing the President?

Answer. I asked him how the President was. He replied " Very well; do you desire to see him," to which I replied " Certainly;" and in the course of a few moments I was admitted into the presence of the Executive.

Question. Was a messenger sent in to know if he would see you?

Answer. I am unable to answer. I had a conversation with Colonel Moore at the time. He notified him.

Question. Did Colonel Moore leave the room where you were conversing with him until you went in to see the President?

Answer. He left the room to bring out this package of papers. No other object that I am aware of.

Question. Did he go into the office of the President where the President was for that purpose?

Answer. Yes, sir; he passed in the same door I did.

Question. And came out and brought a package and explained to you that your name appeared to be rejected and then you went in to see the President?

Answer. I did. I went in at my own request.

Question. After you had passed the usual

salutations what was the first thing he said to you?

Answer. The President asked me if any changes had been made in the garrison within a short time; any movement of troops.

Question. The garrison of Washington?

Answer. The garrison of Washington.

Question. What did you tell him?

Answer. I replied that four companies of the twelfth infantry had been sent to the second military district on the 7th of January, and beyond that no other changes had been made. In doing so I omitted to mention another company that I have since thought of.

Question. Had he ever sent to you on such an errand before?

Mr. CURTIS and Mr. EVARTS. He did not send this time.

Mr. Manager BUTLER. Is that quite certain?

Mr. CURTIS. Yes; it is proved.

Mr. Manager BUTLER. Perhaps we shall see differently when we get through. [To the witness.] Did he ever get you into his room, directly or indirectly, in order to put such a question as that before?

Mr. EVARTS. That we object to. It assumes that he was got in then.

Mr. Manager BUTLER. If he was not got in, how was he there?

Mr. EVARTS. This witness has said that upon his inquiry how the President was the Private Secretary said "Would you like to see him?" and the witness said "Certainly," and went into his room. If that is being got into his room, directly or indirectly, I am very much mistaken.

Mr. Manager BUTLER. I assume one theory, Mr. President, and the counsel assume another.

Mr. EVARTS. No; I follow the testimony. I assume nothing.

Mr. Manager BUTLER. I again say that I assume another theory upon the testimony, and I think the testimony was that he came there by the procurement of the President. I should so argue to the Senate if it become my opportunity to argue; but, without pausing for that, I will ask this question. [To the witness.] Were you ever in that like position with regard to the President before you got there then?

Answer. Never.

Question. Did he say to you anything upon this subject: "I asked the same question of your commander, General Emory, yesterday, and he told me the same as you do?"

Answer. I do not understand the question.

Question. Did he say to you that he had asked the same question the day before of General Emory, and got the same answer?

Answer. No, sir.

Question. Did he speak of it as a thing that he desired to know or a thing that he did know already?

Mr. EVARTS. What he did say is the question?

Mr. STANBERY. We object, Mr. Chief Justice, to that mode of examination-in-chief. That way of examining a witness is altogether new to us.

Mr. Manager BUTLER. I will not press it, sir. I always desire to waive whenever I can. [To the witness.] Was there anything more said?

Answer. Nothing more said on that subject.

Question. On your part or his?

Answer. Neither.

Question. Did you find out next day that you had not been rejected by the Senate?

Mr. STANBERY. What has that got to do with it?

Mr. EVARTS. It is wholly immaterial.

Mr. Manager BUTLER. Not at all. The President sends for an officer of the Army through his Secretary, and informs him that the Senate has rejected him, and then having got him into his presence begins to inquire about the movement of troops when it was not true that he had been rejected.

The WITNESS. If I used the word "rejected" in my testimony I was not aware of it. I do not know that that was the expression; and when I come to reflect I think the language was that my name had been "set aside."

Mr. Manager BUTLER. What made you change it?

Mr. STANBERY. He did not change it. He said "set aside" before.

Mr. Manager BUTLER, (to the witness.) Do you say now that you did not understand that you were rejected?

Answer. That my name was set aside. My own view of the matter was that I had been rejected.

Question. If that was your view why did you change the language just now from "rejected" to "set aside?"

Mr. EVARTS. He did not change it. He said "set aside" before. It was you that changed it.

Mr. Manager BUTLER. I understand what he says, perfectly.

Mr. EVARTS and Mr. STANBERY. So do we.

Mr. Manager BUTLER, (to the witness.) Why did you interrupt, sir, and say, "Well, I do not know that I did say 'rejected?'"

The WITNESS. I have a perfect right, sir, I presume, to make use of such language as I think proper in my replies.

Mr. Manager BUTLER. Undoubtedly. I also have a right to ask why do you use it? I do not object to the right. I only want to know the reason.

The WITNESS. My reason was to correct any misapprehension in regard to the expression of Colonel Moore. My own view was that it amounted to a rejection; but he said "set aside;" he used that language, I believe.

Question. Did he make any difference between "set aside" and "rejected" that you know of at that time?

Answer. That is a question I never thought of.

Question. You did not think of it at that time?

Answer. No, sir.

Question. Did he advise you to use influence with Senators to get yourself confirmed?

· Mr. STANBERY. What has that to do with the question—what Colonel Moore advised him?

Mr. Manager BUTLER. In order to show whether he understood that he was rejected, because there was no occasion to use influence with Senators if he did not understand that he was rejected. [To the counsel for the respondent.] Do you continue your objection?

Mr. STANBERY. Certainly; but there is no use to continue it; you keep on asking the question in that way. [A pause.] Are you through with the witness, Mr. Manager?

Mr. Manager BUTLER. I will let you know when I am, sir. [A pause.] I am now through with the witness.

Mr. STANBERY. So are we.

Mr. DRAKE. Mr. President, I move that the Senate take a recess for ten minutes.

The motion was agreed to; and the Senate resumed its session at two o'clock and forty-five minutes p. m.

The CHIEF JUSTICE. The honorable Managers will proceed with their evidence.

Mr. Manager WILSON. We now, offer a certified copy of the order restoring General Thomas to the duties of the Adjutant General's office.

The CHIEF JUSTICE. Is there any objection to the order?

Mr. STANBERY. Has not that been put in before?

Mr. Manager WILSON. No, sir; this is the order of the General of the Army, issued in pursuance of the President's request, which we put in before.

The CHIEF JUSTICE. The Secretary will read the order.

The Secretary read as follows:

HEADQUARTERS ARMY OF THE UNITED STATES,
WASHINGTON, D. C., *February* 14, 1868.

SIR: General Grant directs me to say that the President of the United States desires you to resume your duties as Adjutant General of the Army.

Very respectfully, yours,

C. B. COMSTOCK,

Brevet Brigadier General, A. A. G. D. C.

General L. THOMAS, *Adjutant General.*

Official copy for Hon. E. M. Stanton, Secretary of War. L. THOMAS,

Adjutant General.

ADJUTANT GENERAL'S OFFICE, *February* 14, 1868.

WILLIAM E. CHANDLER sworn and examined.

By Mr. Manager BUTLER:

Question. Mr. Chandler, I believe you were once Assistant Secretary of the Treasury?

Answer. I was, sir.

Question. From what time to what time?

Answer. From June, 1865, until the 30th of November, 1867.

Question. While in the discharge of the duties of your office, did you learn the office routine of practice by which money was drawn from the Treasury for the use of the War Department?

Answer. I did, sir.

Question. Will you state the steps by which money could be drawn from the Treasury for the use of the War Department?

Answer. By requisition of the Secretary of War upon the Secretary of the Treasury, which requisition passes through the accounting offices of the Department, and is then honored by the issue of a warrant signed by the Secretary of the Treasury, upon which the money is paid by the Treasurer of the United States.

Question. Please name the accounting officers through whose offices it will pass.

Answer. The Second Comptroller of the Treasury has the control of the War and Navy accounts. Several of the auditing officers pass upon war requisitions—the Second Auditor and the Third Auditor, and possibly others.

Question. Please trace and give the offices, if you can, through which a requisition from the War Department for money would go, from one office to the other, until the money would get back to the War Office?

Answer. My attention has not been called to that subject until now, and I am not sure that I can state accurately the process in any given case. My impression, however, is that a requisition from the Secretary of War would come to the Secretary of the Treasury, and pass from the Secretary's office to the office of the Second Comptroller of the Treasury for the purpose of ascertaining whether or not the appropriation upon which the draft was to be made had, or had not, been overdrawn. The requisition would pass from the office of the Comptroller through the office of the Auditor, and thence back to the Secretary of the Treasury. Thereupon, in the warrant room of the Secretary of the Treasury, a warrant for the payment of the money would be issued, which would also pass through the office of the Comptroller, being countersigned by him. Then it would pass into the office of the Register of the Treasury to be there registered, and thence to the Treasurer of the United States, who, upon this requisition, would issue his draft for the payment of the money. This is substantially the process, although I am not sure that I have stated the different steps accurately.

Question. Ought it not to go to the Second Auditor first?

Answer. Quite possibly the requisition would first go to the Auditor.

Question. The Second Auditor and then the Comptroller?

Answer. The Second or Third Auditor, and then to the Comptroller.

Question. Is there any method known to you by which the President of the United States or any other person can get money from the Treasury of the United States for the use of the War Department except through a requisition of the Secretary of War?

Answer. There is not.

Question. I now desire to ask you what is the course of issuing a commission to an officer, say who has been confirmed by the Senate? What is the official routine in the Treasury Department? I suppose it is the same for all?

Answer. A commission is prepared in the Department and signed by the Secretary. It is forwarded to the President and signed by him. It is then returned to the Treasury Department, where, in the case of a bonded officer, it is held until his oath and bond have been filed and approved; in the case of an officer not required by law to give bond the commission is held until he qualifies by taking the oath. It is my impression that this is the usual form. There are some officers in the Treasury Department whose commissions are countersigned by the Secretary of State instead of by the Secretary of the Treasury. The Assistant Secretaries, for instance, have commissions which are countersigned by the Secretary of State and not by the Secretary of the Treasury.

Question. As I suppose the Secretary of the Treasury's own commission is?

Answer. It issues from the office of the Secretary of State, I suppose.

Question. On the 20th of November, 1867, was there any vacancy in the office of Assistant Secretary of the Treasury?

Answer. There was not, sir.

Question. Was there any vacancy up to the 30th of November?

Answer. There was not.

Question. Do you know Edmund Cooper?

Mr. STANBERY. Will the honorable Manager allow me to ask what is the object of this testimony about Mr. Cooper? What is the purpose?

Mr. Manager BUTLER. The object is to show that one of the ways and means described in the eleventh article by which the President proposed to get control of the moneys of the United States appropriated for the use of the War Department was, against law and without right, to appoint his Private Secretary Assistant Secretary of the Treasury.

Mr. CURTIS. Is that all the answer?

Mr. Manager BUTLER. I have answered so far. If you have any other question I shall be very glad to answer it.

Mr. CURTIS. Is that the only answer you make to the question?

Mr. Manager BUTLER. It is a sufficient answer, in my judgment, for the time.

Mr. EVARTS. What part of the eleventh article is this applicable to?

Mr. Manager BUTLER. Both the eighth and the eleventh articles. The eleventh article charges him with—

"Unlawfully devising and contriving, and attempting to devise and contrive, means by which he should prevent Edwin M. Stanton from forthwith resuming

the functions of the office of Secretary for the Department of War, notwithstanding the refusal of the Senate to concur, &c.; and, also, by further unlawfully devising and contriving, and attempting to devise and contrive, means, then and there, to prevent the execution of an act entitled 'An act making appropriations for the support of the Army for the fiscal year ending June 30, 1868, and for other purposes,' approved March 2, 1867; and also to prevent the execution of an act entitled 'An act to provide for the more efficient government of the rebel States,' passed," &c.

And in order to get the means of doing that, he wanted to control the purse as well as the sword, and he wanted his man, his Secretary, if in no warmer and closer relations to him, to be in the office of Assistant Secretary of the Treasury, the Assistant Secretary of the Treasury now by law being allowed to sign warrants.

Mr. Manager BINGHAM and Mr. Manager WILSON. Then the eighth article.

Mr. Manager BUTLER. Then, as my associates call to my attention, the eighth article charges that—

"With intent unlawfully to control the disbursement of the moneys appropriated for the military service and for the Department of War, on the 21st day of February, in the year of our Lord 1868"—

He—

"did, unlawfully and contrary to the provisions of an act," &c.—

Do these acts.

Mr. EVARTS. No; appointed Thomas. You now propose to prove under that that he appointed Cooper, or tried to do so.

Mr. Manager BUTLER. This is the means: "with intent unlawfully to control."

Mr. EVARTS and Mr. STANBERY. Did what?

Mr. Manager BUTLER.

"Did unlawfully and contrary to the provisions of an act entitled 'An act regulating the tenure of certain civil offices,' passed March 2, 1868, and in violation of the Constitution of the United States"—

And while the Senate was in session, not to go on with the verbiage, appoint Lorenzo Thomas.

Mr. EVARTS. The allegation is that with this intent which you have stated, the President did—

"There being no vacancy in the office of Secretary for the Department of War, and with intent to violate and disregard the act aforesaid"—

Which is the tenure-of-office act—

"Then and there issue and deliver to one Lorenzo Thomas a letter of authority in writing, in substance as follows; that is to say."

Now, you propose to prove under that, that there being no vacancy in the office of Assistant Secretary of the Treasury, he proposed to appoint his Private Secretary, Edmund Cooper, Assistant Secretary of the Treasury. That is the idea, is it under the eighth article? We object to this as not admissible under the eighth article. As by reference to it will be perceived, it charges nothing but an intent to violate the civil tenure act, and no mode of violating that except in the want of a vacancy in the War Department, the appointment of General Thomas contrary to that act.

As for the eleventh article the honorable court will remember that in our answer we stated that there was in that article no such description, designation of ways or means, or attempts at ways or means, whereby we could answer definitely; and the only allegations there are, that in pursuance of a speech that the President made on the 18th of August, 1866, he—

"Afterward, to wit, on the 21st day of February, A. D. 1868, at the city of Washington, in the District of Columbia, did, unlawfully, and in disregard of the requirement of the Constitution that he should take care that the laws be faithfully executed, attempt to prevent the execution of an act entitled 'An act regulating the tenure of certain civil offices,' passed March 2, 1867, by unlawfully devising and contriving, and attempting to devise and contrive means by which he should prevent Edwin M. Stanton from forthwith resuming the functions of the office of Secretary for the Department of War, notwithstanding the refusal of the Senate to concur in the suspension theretofore made by said Andrew Johnson of said Edwin M. Stanton from said office of Secretary for the Department of War; and also, by further unlawfully devising and contriving, and attempting to devise and contrive means, then and there, to prevent the execution of an act entitled 'An act making appropriations for the support of the Army for the fiscal year ending June 30, 1868, and for other purposes,' approved March 2, 1867; and, also, to prevent the execution of an act entitled 'An act to provide for the more efficient government of the rebel States,' passed March 2, 1867, whereby," &c.

The only allegation here as to time and principal action, in reference to which all these unnamed and undescribed ways and means were used, is, that on the 21st of February, 1868, at the city of Washington, he did unlawfully, and in disregard of the Constitution, attempt to prevent the execution of the civil tenure-of-office act, by unlawfully devising and contriving and attempting to devise and contrive means by which he should prevent Edwin M. Stanton from resuming his place in the War Department. And now proof is offered here, substantially, of efforts in November, 1867, to appoint, in the want of a vacancy in the office of Assistant Secretary of the Treasury, Mr. Edmund Cooper. We object to that evidence.

Mr. Manager BUTLER. The objection, Mr. President and Senators, is twofold: first, that the evidence is not competent; second, that the pleading is not sufficient. I do not propose now to discuss the question of pleading. It is said that the pleading is too general. If we were trying an indictment at common law for a conspiracy, or for any acts in the nature of a conspiracy, and we made the allegation too general, the only objection to that would be that it did not sufficiently inform the defendant under it what acts might be given in evidence; and the remedy for a defendant in that case would be to move for a specification or for a bill of particulars; and if he neglects to move for that, the court take care in the course of the case, if any surprise is upon him, because of evidence that he could not have known of, or could not have expected to allow him to come in and meet that new evidence. Therefore indictments for conspiracies are generally drawn as was the indictment in the Martha Washington case, which I now have in my mind, it having been drawn by an exceedingly good pleader, as tradition says, giving one general count, and then several specific counts, or setting out specific acts in the nature of specifications; so that, if the pleader fail in setting out his specific acts, he still may hold under the general count, and the count setting out specifications is instead of a bill of particulars. Now, then, I say we need not discuss the question of pleading.

The only question is, is this competent, if we can show it was one of the ways and means? The difficulty that rests in the minds of my learned friends on the other side is that they cluster everything about the 21st of February, 1868. They seem to forget that the act of the 21st of February, 1868, was only the culmination of a purpose formed long before, as in the President's answer he sets forth, to wit: as early as the 12th of August, 1867, that he was determined then to get out Mr. Stanton, at any rate—I would use the words "at all hazards;" but perhaps they might be subject to criticism until we get through our case—certainly by the use of force, as the evidence now in shows. He formed his purpose.

To carry it out there are various things to do. He must get control of the War Office; but what good does that do if he cannot get somebody who shall be his servant, his slave, dependent on his breath, to answer the requisitions of his pseudo officer whom he may appoint; and therefore he began when? Stanton was suspended, and as early as the 12th of December he had got to put that suspension and the reasons for it before the Senate, and he knew it would not live there one moment after it got fairly considered. Now he begins. What is the first thing he does? "To get somebody in the Treasury Department that will mind me precisely as Thomas will, if I can get him in the War Department." That is the first thing; and thereupon, without any vacancy, he must make an appointment. The difficulty that we find is that we are obliged to argue our case step by step upon a single point of evidence. It is one of the infelicities always of putting in a case that sharp, keen, ingenious counsel can insist at all steps on impaling you upon a point of evidence; and therefore I have got to proceed a little further.

Now, our evidence, if you allow it to come in is, first, that he made this appointment; that this failing, he sent it to the Senate, and Cooper was rejected. Still determined to have Cooper in, he appointed him *ad interim*, precisely as this *ad interim* Thomas was appointed, without law and against right. We put it as a part of the whole machinery by which to get hold, to get, if he could, his hand into the Treasury of the United States, although Mr. Chandler has just stated there was no way to get it except by a requisition through the War Department; and at the same moment, to show that this was part of the same illegal means we show you that although Mr. McCulloch, the Secretary of the Treasury, must have known that Thomas was appointed, yet the President took pains—we have put in the paper—to serve on Mr. McCulloch an attested copy of the appointment of Thomas *ad interim*, in order that he and Cooper might recognize his warrants.

Did I not answer my friends that this was a sufficient ground? More than that, I have yet to learn in a somewhat extended practice of the law, (not extending, however, so long as that of most of the gentlemen on the other side,) that it was ever objected anywhere, when I was tracing a man's motives, when I was tracing this course, that I had not a right to put in every act that he did, *valeat quantum*. Everything that comes out of his mouth, every act that he does, I have a right to put in.

Let us see if that is not sustained by authorities. The question arose in the trial of James Watson for high treason in the year 1817 before one of the best lawyers of England, Lord Ellenborough, assisted by Mr. Justice Holroyd, Mr. Justice Bayly, and Mr. Justice Abbott. The objection there was precisely the one the learned counsel raise here. It was alleged that certain speeches had been made which were treasonable speeches. That was all that was said about them; they were not set out any further. I got this book (32 State Trials) for an entirely different purpose; but it contains an authority directly in point. Certain speeches were alleged; the indictment charged that certain speeches were made without setting them out; and it was claimed that they could not be proved as overt acts; and the question was whether certain other speeches could be put in as tending to show the *animus* with which the first set of speeches had been spoken. Lord Ellenborough closed the discussion by saying:

"*Lord Ellenborough.* If there had been no particular overt act under which this evidence was receivable, it is an universal rule of evidence that what a party himself says may be given in evidence against him, to explain any part of his conduct to which it bears reference.

"*Mr. Wetherell,* (the counsel for the defendant.) We do not object that it is not evidence, but that it is not proof of the overt act.

"*Lord Ellenborough.* There cannot be a doubt that whatever proceeds from the mouth of man may be given in evidence against him; it shows the intention with which he acts."—32 *State Trials*, page 91.

"Whatever proceeds from his mouth." *A fortiori*, Senators, when it is under his hand like the seal of a commission, if his declarations can be given, may not his acts? I would not have troubled the presiding officer, I would not have troubled Senators so long upon this matter had it not been that there may be other acts all clustering around this grand conspiracy which we propose, if we are permitted, to put in.

The CHIEF JUSTICE. The Manager will reduce his question to writing.

Mr. Manager BUTLER. The simple question was, who was Edmund Cooper. I suppose my friends do not mean to object to that alone. The question was, do you know him and who is he?

Mr. STANBERY. We asked what you intended to prove in reference to Edmund Cooper?

Mr. Manager BUTLER. I have stated that at very considerable length. I propose to prove that Mr. Edmund Cooper took possession in the Treasury Department before the 30th of November, and that he had this commission, showing that the President gave a commission illegally in violation of the tenure-of-office act to which I wish to call your attention. The tenure-of-office act provides that "in such case and in no other," to wit, where an officer has been guilty of misconduct or crime, or for any reason becomes incapable or legally disqualified to perform the duties of his office, the President may suspend him; and then the sixth section provides that—

"The making, signing, sealing, countersigning, or issuing of any commission or letter of authority for or in respect to any such appointment or employment, shall be deemed, and are hereby declared to be, high misdemeanors."

Therefore the very signing and issuing of this commission—the signing it, if he did not issue it; the issuing of it, if he did not sign it—there being no vacancy which is contemplated by the act, is a crime, and another crime in and part of the great conspiracy. Therefore the question will be whether we shall be allowed to go into the condition of Mr. Cooper. I cannot put the whole of my offer in one question, because I cannot prove it all by one witness.

The CHIEF JUSTICE. It will be necessary to reduce the question to writing, in order that it may be submitted to the Senate.

Mr. Manager BUTLER. I will put it rather in the form of an offer to prove. I will write it as an offer to prove in a moment.

Mr. STANBERY. It is not a question so much, Mr. Chief Justice, as to who Edmund Cooper is, but what Edmund Cooper has got to do with this case; what the illegal appointment of Edmund Cooper to be Assistant Secretary of the Treasury *ad interim*, or otherwise, has to do with this case; or what the appointment of Edmund Cooper for the purpose of controlling the moneys in the Treasury Department has to do with this case. That is the material inquiry.

Now, I understand the learned Manager to say that the proof he intends to make in regard to Mr. Cooper is, in the first place, that there was an illegal appointment of Mr. Cooper, and in that the President violated the Constitution of the United States, and violated the tenure-of-office act. Well, Mr. Chief Justice, have they given us notice to come here to defend any such delinquency as that, if it be a delinquency? Have the House of Representatives impeached the President for anything done in the removal of Mr. Chandler, if he was removed, or in the appointment of Mr. Cooper, if he was appointed in his place? They selected one instance of what they claim to be a violation of the Constitution and of the tenure-of-office act in regard to a temporary appointment made during the session of the Senate; and that was the case of General Thomas, and of General Thomas alone. As to that, of course, we have no objection to their going into evidence, because we have had notice of it, and are here ready to meet it; but as to any high crime and misdemeanor in reference to the appointment of Mr. Cooper, certainly the gentlemen have no authority to make such a charge, because they come here with a delegated authority; they come here only to make the charges found good by the House of Representatives, and not the charges that they choose to manufacture here. The Managers have no right to amend these articles. They must go to the House even for that. If they choose to go to the House and get a new article founded upon an illegal act in the appointment of Mr. Cooper, let them go, and let us have time to answer it and to meet it.

So much for the admissibility of the testimony as to the illegal appointment of Mr. Cooper. It is a matter not charged. That is enough. It is a matter they are not authorized to charge; they have no such delegated authority here.

What is the next ground, Mr. Chief Justice, upon which they ask to prove anything in relation to Mr. Cooper? They say they expect to prove that Mr. Cooper was put into that place of Assistant Secretary of the Treasury by the President in order to control the disbursement of the moneys in that Department. That I understand to be the next ground. Now, let us see what they have charged about that. Here they have got an article charging an illegal act of the President in reference to the disbursement of the public money—article eight. Let us see what Mr. Cooper has to do with that.

"That said Andrew Johnson, President of the United States, unmindful of the high duties of his office and of his oath of office, with intent unlawfully to control the disbursements of the moneys appropriated for the military service and for the Department of War, on the 21st day of February"—

Did a certain thing. What was it? Appoint Mr. Cooper? Give him authority to act in any office? No. He appointed Thomas; and that appointment is the only appointment set out as the means to control those disbursements. If it was necessary to frame an article founded upon the appointment of Thomas as a means used by the President to get control of these public moneys, was it not equally necessary to have an article founded upon the same line of conduct in reference to Mr. Cooper? Unquestionably.

Then, in the eleventh article, what is there that authorizes the introduction of this testimony? That he made certain speeches. What then?

"Afterward, to wit, on the 21st day of February,

C. I.—12.

A. D. 1868, at the city of Washington, in the District of Columbia, did, unlawfully and in disregard of the requirement of the Constitution that he should take care that the laws be faithfully executed, attempt to prevent the execution of an act entitled 'An act regulating the tenure of certain civil offices.'"

That is the unlawful thing; and how?

"By unlawfully devising and contriving, and attempting to devise and contrive, means by which he should prevent Edwin M. Stanton from forthwith resuming the functions of the office of Secretary for the Department of War, notwithstanding the refusal of the Senate to concur in the suspension theretofore made by said Andrew Johnson of said Edwin M. Stanton from said office of Secretary of the Department of War; and, also, by furthur unlawfully devising and contriving, and attempting to devise and contrive, means, then and there, to prevent the execution of an act entitled 'An act making appropriations for the support of the Army for the fiscal year ending June 30, 1868, and for other purposes.'"

That is the act which contains the section requiring the orders for military operations to go through General Grant. That is the means he contrived there to get Stanton out. So that has nothing to do with this. What further?

"And, also, to prevent the execution of an act entitled 'An act to provide for the more efficient government of the rebel States.'"

Now, what relevancy has the appointment of Cooper with the government of the rebel States, or with the execution of the reconstruction acts, or, in fact, with any offense charged in any one of the eleven articles?

Mr. Manager BINGHAM. Mr. President, we consider the law to be well settled and accepted everywhere in this country and England to-day, that where an intent is the subject-matter of inquiry in a criminal prosecution, other and independent acts of the accused, looking to the same result, are admissible in evidence for the purpose of establishing that fact. And we go further than that. We undertake to say, upon very high and commanding authority, not to be challenged here or elsewhere, that it is settled that such other and independent acts, showing the purpose to bring about the same general result, although at the time of the inquiry the subject-matter of a separate indictment, are, nevertheless, admissible. I doubt not that it will occur to the recollection of honorable Senators that among other cases illustrative of the rule which I have just cited it has been stated in the books—the cases have been ruled first and then incorporated into books of standard authorities—that where a party, for example, was charged with shooting with intent to kill a person named, it was competent, in order to show the malice, the malicious intent of the act, to show that at another time and place he laid poison. A party is charged with passing a counterfeit note; it is competent, in order to prove the *scienter*, to show that he was in possession of other counterfeit notes of a different denomination; and the rule, as stated in the books, is, that what is competent to prove the *scienter*, as a general principle, is competent to prove the intent.

Now, what is the allegation in the eleventh article? That this procedure was taken on the part of the President for the purpose of setting aside and defeating the operation of that law. That law stands with the other legislation of this country.

Mr. STANBERY. What law?

Mr. Manager BINGHAM. The tenure-of-office act. That law stands with the other legislation of this country; and I undertake to say, without stopping to cite the statutes, that by the existing law of the United States the appropriations made for the support of the Department of War and for the support of the Army can only be reached in the Treasury of the nation through the requisitions drawn by the Secretary of War. Here is an independent act done by the accused, as is well said by my associate, for the purpose of aiding this result. How? By appointing an Assistant Secretary of the Treasury, who, under the law and regulations, is authorized to act upon the warrants that may be drawn upon the Treasury through that Department or any other Department; by appointing a person, in other words, to discharge the very duty which he desires him to discharge in aid of his design; and what is that? That the money appropriated by Congress, and not to be drawn from the Treasury except in pursuance of law, to-wit, through the Secretary of War, duly constituted such by the appointment of the President with the advice and consent of the Senate, may, nevertheless, be drawn out of the Treasury by a person acting as an officer, without the advice and consent of the Senate, through the requisitions made on the Treasury by his Secretary of War *ad interim*, appointed in the presence of the Senate, in defiance of the Senate, and in violation of the law.

If the appointment of such an officer throws no light on this subject, of course it has nothing to do with the matter; if it does, it has a great deal to do with it. If the question stops with the inquiry who Edmund Cooper is, of course it throws no light upon this subject; but if the testimony discloses such relations with the President and his appointment under such circumstances as indicates a purpose on the part of Cooper to coöperate with the President in this general design, I apprehend it will throw a great deal of light upon this subject. And, in the event of the removal of the head of the Department, (and if this rule is to be established that might happen any hour, without regard to the opinions of the Senate to the contrary or to the requirements of the law,) this Assistant Secretary of the Treasury would have the control of the whole question. I am free to say, so far as I am concerned in this matter, if nothing further be shown than the mere inquiry of the appointment of Cooper, it may not throw any light upon the subject; but I do not so understand the matter. There is more than that in it.

Mr. Manager BUTLER. In order that there may be a distinct proposition before the Senate we offer to prove that, there being no vacancy in the office of Assistant Secretary of the Treasury, the President unlawfully appointed his friend and theretofore Private Secretary, Edmund Cooper, to that position, as one of the means by which he intended to defeat the tenure of civil office act and other laws of Congress.

Mr. EVARTS. Will you be so good as to insert the date in your offer.

Mr. Manager BUTLER. I will, sir. [After a pause.] I have inserted a date satisfactory to myself, and I hope it will be to the counsel for the President.

Mr. EVARTS. I have no doubt it is correct.

Mr. Manager BUTLER. We offer to prove that after the President had determined on the removal of Mr. Stanton, Secretary of War, in spite of the action of the Senate, there being no vacancy in the office of Assistant Secretary of the Treasury, the President unlawfully appointed his friend and theretofore Private Secretary, Edmund Cooper, to that position, as one of the means by which he intended to defeat the tenure of civil office act and other laws of Congress.

Mr. EVARTS. I do not understand that to be a date. I ask you to be good enough to put in the 20th of November.

Mr. Manager BUTLER. I want to have it appear in relation to that.

Mr. EVARTS. Put in what you have also, if you please.

Mr. Manager BUTLER. If the learned counsel will allow me, I will make my offer as I like.

Mr. EVARTS. Undoubtedly. I only asked you to name the date. You can do as you please about it.

The CHIEF JUSTICE. The Secretary will read the proposition.

The Secretary read as follows:

We offer to prove that, after the President had determined on the removal of Mr. Stanton, Secretary of War, in spite of the action of the Senate, there being no vacancy in the office of Assistant Secretary of the Treasury, the President unlawfully appointed his friend and theretofore Private Secretary, Edmund Cooper, to that position, as one of the means by which he intended to defeat the tenure of civil office act and other laws of Congress.

Mr. EVARTS. The action of the Senate, I think, was in December, 1867.

Mr. STANBERY. February 13.

Mr. Manager BUTLER. January 13.

Mr. STANBERY. Yes; that is it.

Mr. EVARTS. January 13, 1868; so that what you now offer was after that.

Mr. Manager BUTLER. Oh, no. The President formed the purpose, as he tells us in the letter to General Grant and as he tells us in his answer, on the 12th of August, 1867, when he suspended Mr. Stanton, to suspend him indefinitely; to try to see if the Senate would not agree to that; if they would not, then to keep him suspended indefinitely, and remove him as soon as ever he could get anybody to aid him. That is our proposition of what the evidence and the claims of the President show; he meant to do that in spite of what happened; and we say after that intent was formed he made the appointment of Cooper.

Mr. EVARTS. After the 12th of August, 1867, then. We want to get at the date; that is all.

The CHIEF JUSTICE. Do the counsel for the President desire to be heard further?

Mr. EVARTS. No, sir; but we object to it. It is not within any article of impeachment.

The CHIEF JUSTICE. The Chief Justice will submit the question to the Senate. The question is, whether the evidence proposed by the honorable Managers shall be admitted?

Mr. SHERMAN. I should like to have the Managers answer a question before the vote is taken.

The CHIEF JUSTICE. The Secretary will read the question proposed by the Senator from Ohio.

The Secretary read as follows:

Will the Managers read the particular clauses of the eighth and eleventh articles to prove which this testimony is offered?

Mr. Manager BUTLER. As I understand it, it is to prove the intent alleged in the eighth article in these words:

"With intent unlawfully to control the disbursements of the moneys appropriated for the military service and for the Department of War."

He did a certain act with that intent. Now, to prove that intent, we show he did a certain other act which would enable him to control the moneys.

The CHIEF JUSTICE. The eighth article seems to say nothing about money.

Mr. Manager BUTLER. The eighth article reads:

"That said Andrew Johnson, President of the United States, unmindful of the high duties of his office, and of his oath of office, with intent unlawfully to control the disbursements of moneys appropriated."

The CHIEF JUSTICE. What act is charged?

Mr. Manager BUTLER. The act charged is, that with that intent, he appointed Thomas. Now, to prove the intent with which he appointed Thomas, we prove that he also prepared a man who, in the office of Assistant Secretary of the Treasury, would answer Thomas's requisitions.

Now, as to the other point, I will read, in answer to the question of the Senator, from the eleventh article:

"By unlawfully devising and contriving, and attempting to devise and contrive, means by which he should prevent Edwin M. Stanton from forthwith resuming the functions of the office of Secretary for the Department of War, notwithstanding the refusal of the Senate to concur in the suspension theretofore made by said Andrew Johnson of said Edwin M. Stanton from said office of Secretary for the Department of War; and also, by further unlawfully devising and contriving, and attempting to devise and contrive, means, then and there, to prevent the exe-

cution of an act entitled 'An act making appropriations for the support of the Army for the fiscal year ending June 30, 1868, and for other purposes,' approved March 2, and, also, to prevent the execution of an act entitled 'An act to provide for the more efficient government of the rebel States,' passed March 2, 1867."

He had done what he has been charged to have done. And now, in that connection, we claim that this was a part of the machinery to carry out this thing; because, suppose, looking forward to have happened exactly what did happen, to wit, that Mr. Stanton would not give up the War Department, then the question was, would Mr. McCulloch answer the requisitions of Thomas or of anybody else he should put in, if Stanton should hold on? It is clear that the President knew he would not, because, although he served a notice upon McCulloch to do it, McCulloch will not to-day, and he has not been able to get one through Thomas. Now, then, he gets Thomas in; he must put in somebody in the Treasury Department who will obey Thomas. Thereupon he puts Cooper in; and with a single stroke of his pen he claims to have the right to remove McCulloch; and he also claims, and has put it in his answer, that McCulloch, as one of his Cabinet, has agreed to go at a stroke of his pen; so that he has got the whole Army and Treasury of the United States within his control. It was with intent to do that that he made the appointment of Cooper; and to show that it was with that intent, we show, so anxious was he to do it, that he did not make the appointment lawfully; that he first made it when the Senate was not in session, by issuing a full commission; then he sent it to the Senate, and the Senate rejected Cooper; but still, so bent was he on having Cooper not Private Secretary, but Assistant Secretary of the Treasury, where he could control the moneys of the United States, that he first appointed him ad interim, showing that he got him under the same designation as Thomas; and the designation shows something.

The CHIEF JUSTICE. Are Senators ready for the question?

Mr. JOHNSON. I request the Managers to answer a question which I have sent to the Chair.

The CHIEF JUSTICE. The Secretary will read the question propounded by the Senator from Maryland.

The Secretary read as follows:

The Managers are requested to say whether they propose to show that Cooper was appointed by the President in November, 1867, as a means to obtain the unlawful possession of the public money, other than by the fact of the appointment itself?

Mr. Manager BUTLER. We certainly do —is that an answer?—more than by the appointment. That we may not be misunderstood hereafter, we propose to show that he appointed him, and thereupon Mr. Cooper went into the exercise of the duties of the office before his appointment could by any possibility be legal; and that he has been—we hope and believe we shall show that he has been—controlling other public moneys since.

The CHIEF JUSTICE having put the question on the admissibility of the evidence and declared that the negative appeared to prevail.

Mr. HOWARD and Mr. SUMNER called for the yeas and nays; and they were ordered.

Mr. HENDERSON. Before the vote is taken, I desire that some testimony shall be read. I send my request to the Chair.

The Secretary read Mr. HENDERSON's request, as follows:

It is requested that the testimony of the witness, Chandler, in regard to the mode and manner of obtaining money on a requisition of the Secretary of War be read.

The CHIEF JUSTICE. It can only be read from the notes of the short-hand reporter; but the witness can restate it.

Mr. HENDERSON. I will inquire if the witness will be permitted to restate it?

The CHIEF JUSTICE. Certainly.

Mr. HENDERSON. My object is to know whether money can be obtained upon the requisition of the Assistant Secretary, and not of the Secretary himself, just to that point.

Mr. EVARTS. Let him answer to that very point.

Mr. Manager BUTLER. Let him answer.

The CHIEF JUSTICE, (to the witness.) Answer the question proposed by the Senator from Missouri. Will the Senator state the question to the witness?

Mr. HENDERSON. I prefer that the Managers should do so.

Mr. Manager BUTLER, (to the witness.) Will you state now whether the Assistant Secretary can sign warrants?

Mr. CURTIS and Mr. EVARTS. That is not the question.

Mr. Manager BUTLER. For the payment of money?

Mr. CURTIS. The question is, whether on requisitions of the War Department——

Mr. Manager BUTLER. Whether, upon the requisition of any Department of the Government, the Assistant Secretary of the Treasury can sign warrants on the Treasury for the payment of money?

The WITNESS. Until the passage of a late statute, whenever the Secretary of the Treasury was present and acting, money could not be drawn from the Treasury upon the signature of the Assistant Secretary of the Treasury. An act has been passed within a year allowing the Assistant Secretary to sign covering-in warrants and warrants for the payment of money upon accounts stated; but the practice still continues of signing all customary warrants by the signature of the Secretary of the Treasury. The warrants are prepared and the initials of the Assistant Secretary in charge of the warrants placed upon them, and then they are signed by the Secretary of the Treasury when he is present.

Mr. FESSENDEN. I ask that that law may be read. I should like to know what it is exactly.

Mr. Manager BUTLER, (to the witness.) Do you remember the date of it?

The WITNESS. It is within a year. I can find it if you give me the statutes for the last year.

The CHIEF JUSTICE. The Chief Justice will put a question to the witness: whether before the passage of the act to which he refers any warrant could be drawn by the Assistant Secretary, unless he was acting Secretary in the absence of the Secretary?

Answer. There could not. Prior to the passage of this act no money could be drawn from the Treasury upon the signature of an Assistant Secretary, unless when acting Secretary under an appointment for that purpose.

By Mr. Manager BUTLER:

Question. When the Assistant Secretary acts for the Secretary, does he sign all warrants for the payment of money?

Answer. When acting Secretary, of course he signs all warrants for the payment of money.

Mr. CAMERON. I desire to ask a question.

The CHIEF JUSTICE. The Senator will reduce his question to writing and send it to the Chair.

Mr. CAMERON. I did not understand that. I desire to ask a question merely as to the practice. I can do it in less time than by writing it.

The CHIEF JUSTICE. The rule requires it to be reduced to writing.

Mr. Manager BUTLER. I will read the law to which reference has been made:

"An act supplemental to an act to establish the Treasury Department," approved the 2d of September, 1789.

"Be it enacted by the Senate and House of Representatives of the United States of America in Congress assembled, That the Secretary of the Treasury shall have power, by an appointment under his hand and official seal, to delegate to one of the Assistant Secretaries of the Treasury authority to sign in his stead all warrants for the payment of money into the public Treasury and all warrants for the disbursement from the public Treasury of money certified by the proper accounting officers of the Treasury to be due upon accounts duly audited and settled by them; and such warrants so signed shall be in all cases of the same validity as if they had been signed by the Secretary of the Treasury himself."

Mr. CONKLING and others. What is the date of that?

Mr. Manager BUTLER. The date is March 2, 1867, the same date as the tenure-of-office act.

A single other question, which, perhaps, is rather a conclusion of law than of fact. [To the witness.] In case of the removal or absence of Mr. McCulloch or the Secretary of the Treasury, as I understand, the Assistant Secretary performs all the acts of the Secretary?

Mr. EVARTS. That is a question of law.

Mr. Manager BUTLER. I said I doubted as to that. I was only asking for the practice. [To the witness.] Is that the practice?

Answer. I am not certain that it is, without an appointment as acting Secretary for the Assistant Secretary, signed by the President.

Mr. CAMERON. I desired to put a question, and I think it is contrary to the practice to require me to put it in writing; but I have reduced it to writing, and I ask that it be read.

The CHIEF JUSTICE. The Secretary will read the question proposed by the Senator from Pennsylvania.

The Secretary read as follows:

Can the Assistant Secretary of the Treasury, under the law, draw warrants for the payment of moneys by the Treasurer without the direction of the Secretary of the Treasury?

The WITNESS. Since the passage of the act, I understand, the Assistant Secretary can sign a warrant for the payment of money in the cases specified.

By Mr. EVARTS:

Question. Is not that by deputation?

Answer. Which is presumed rather to be with the assent and approval of the Secretary of the Treasury.

Mr. CAMERON. I will ask another question without reducing it to writing.

The CHIEF JUSTICE. If there be no objection, the Senator from Pennsylvania will be allowed to put a question without reducing it to writing.

Mr. WILLIAMS. Mr. President, I object.

The CHIEF JUSTICE. The Senator from Oregon objects.

Mr. CAMERON. The question I intended to ask was, has it been the practice——

The CHIEF JUSTICE. The Senator is not in order.

Mr. Manager BUTLER, (to the witness.) Has it been the practice for him to sign warrants?

Answer. Since the passage of the act in question it has.

The CHIEF JUSTICE. Senators, the question is: Shall the evidence proposed by the Managers be received?

Mr. FESSENDEN. I should like to put a question as soon as I have an opportunity to write it. [After writing.] There are two questions which I wish to put.

The CHIEF JUSTICE. The Secretary will read the questions proposed by the Senator from Maine.

The Secretary read as follows:

Question. Has it been the practice since the passage of the law for an Assistant Secretary to sign warrants unless specially appointed and authorized by the Secretary of the Treasury?

Question. Has any Assistant Secretary been authorized to sign any warrants except such as are specified in the act?

The WITNESS. It has not been the practice for an Assistant Secretary since the passage of the act to sign warrants except upon an appointment by the Secretary for that purpose in accordance with the provisions of the act. Immediately upon the passage of the act the Secretary authorized one of his Assistant Secretaries to sign warrants of the character described in the act, and they have been custom-

arily signed by that Assistant Secretary in all cases since that time.

Mr. FESSENDEN. Now, let the second question be read.

The Secretary read the second question, as follows:

Has any Assistant Secretary been authorized to sign any warrants except such as are specified by the act?

The WITNESS. No Assistant Secretary has been authorized to sign warrants except such as are specified in this act, unless when acting Secretary.

The CHIEF JUSTICE. Senators, you who are of opinion that the evidence offered on the part of the Managers should be admitted will, as your names are called, answer " yea;" those who are of the contrary opinion will say " nay." The Secretary will call the roll.

The question being taken, the result was announced—yeas 23, nays 26.

Mr. CONNESS. I desire to know how my name is recorded?

The CHIEF JUSTICE. The Senator is recorded among the yeas.

Mr. CONNESS. That is a mistake. I voted in the negative, and I wish myself recorded correctly.

The change being made, the result was announced—yeas 22, nays 27 ; as follows:

YEAS—Messrs. Anthony, Cameron, Cattell, Chandler, Cole, Conkling, Corbett, Cragin, Drake, Howard, Howe, Morgan, Morrill of Vermont, Nye, Pomeroy, Ramsey, Ross, Sprague, Sumner, Thayer, Tipton, and Wilson—22.

NAYS—Messrs. Bayard, Buckalew, Conness, Davis, Dixon, Doolittle, Edmunds, Ferry, Fessenden, Fowler, Frelinghuysen, Grimes, Henderson, Hendricks, Johnson, McCreery, Morrill of Maine, Norton, Patterson of New Hampshire, Patterson of Tennessee, Sherman, Stewart, Trumbull, Van Winkle, Vickers, Willey, and Williams—27.

NOT VOTING—Messrs. Harlan, Morton, Saulsbury, Wade, and Yates—5.

The CHIEF JUSTICE. The yeas are 22, the nays are 27. So the evidence is not received.

Mr. Manager BUTLER. Then I have nothing further to ask this witness at present. We may wish to call him again, however, at another part of the case, when we get along further, so that we can offer this in another view.

Mr. EVARTS. We shall reserve our questions till then.

CHARLES A. TINKER sworn and examined.

By Mr. Manager BUTLER:

Question. What is your full name?

Answer. Charles A. Tinker.

Question. What is your business?

Answer. I am a telegraph operator.

Question. Are you in charge of any office?

Answer. I am in charge of the Western Union Telegraph office in this city.

Question. Were you at any time in charge of the military telegraph office of the War Department?

Answer. I was.

Question. From what time to what time?

Answer. I can hardly tell from what time. I was in charge of the military telegraph office of the War Department up to August, 1867. I think I was personally in charge something like a year; I was connected with the office for something like five years.

Question. While in charge of that office state whether a dispatch from Lewis E. Parsons, of Montgomery, Alabama, came to Andrew Johnson, President of the United States, and if so at what date?

Answer. I think while in that office I saw a great many such dispatches.

Question. What paper have you in your hand?

Answer. I have what professes to be a copy of a telegram from Lewis E. Parsons, Montgomery, Alabama, addressed to "His Excellency Andrew Johnson, President."

Question. Do you know whether that telegram came through the office?

Answer. I recognize this as being the character of dispatch which passed through or was received at the military telegraph office.

Mr. CURTIS. That we must object to.

Mr. Manager BUTLER, (to the witness.) Were there duplicate originals of telegrams received kept at the military telegraph office?

Answer. What is called a press copy was taken of each dispatch before being delivered from the office.

Question. Was such a press copy taken of each dispatch before it was sent?

Answer. Not before being sent.

Question. The original was kept, then?

Answer. The original was kept on file in the office.

Question. State whether at my request you examined those press copies?

Answer. I did.

Question. Did you find such a dispatch as I have described among those press copies?

Answer. I did.

Question. Did you copy it?

Answer. I made a copy.

Question. Have you got that in your hand?

Answer. No, sir; I have not.

Question. Can you give an explanation as to that copy you now have in your hand?

Answer. I made a copy of the dispatch and answered the summons of the Managers, and I placed the copy in your hands, and I heard you order your clerk to make a copy of that, and after a short time the clerk returned with that copy and read the copy which he had made, and you returned to me the copy I had made.

Question. Have you that copy?

Answer. I have.

Question. Very well; produce the original dispatch and the copy both?

Mr. EVARTS. I ask what is meant by the "original dispatch." I understood this was a dispatch received here.

Mr. Manager BUTLER. The original press copy is meant.

The WITNESS. I mean to say that I have the original press copy.

[Producing a bound letter-book, the pages of which were press copies of dispatches.]

Question. Have you that original press copy?

Answer. I have it.

Mr. Manager BUTLER. Read from it, please?

Mr. STANBERY. Oh, no.

Mr. EVARTS. Let us see what it is.

[The book was handed to the counsel for the respondent.]

Mr. STANBERY. I wish to ask a preliminary question. [To the witness.] Did you make this press copy yourself?

Answer. The press copy is made by the clerk. The telegram is written by one of the operators.

Mr. EVARTS. By you?

The WITNESS. Not by me personally.

Mr. CURTIS. We object.

Mr. EVARTS. This book does not prove itself.

Mr. Manager BUTLER. I do not understand the objection, if there is any.

Mr. EVARTS. We do not understand that a telegraph company's books prove themselves like a record. You bring no living witness that verifies anything here.

Mr. Manager BUTLER. I will pass from this for a moment. [To the witness.] Do you remember, as an act of memory, whether such a telegram as that passed through the office?

Answer. I do not remember this dispatch having passed through the office; I cannot take my oath that I remember the particular dispatch.

Question. Will you state whether you have an original dispatch of the same date signed "Andrew Johnson?"

Answer. I have.

Question. Produce it?

Answer. I have a book in which the dispatch is filed.

[Producing a bound letter-book on the pages of which were pasted dispatches.]

Question. Are you so familiar with the signature of Andrew Johnson as to know whether that is his name signed to it?

Answer. I believe that to be his signature; I am very familiar with it.

Question. Have you any doubt in your own mind as to that?

Answer. None whatever.

Question. Is this book which I hold in my hand and you have just produced, the record book of the United States military telegraph, of the executive office wherein original dispatches are put on record?

Answer. It is the book in which the original dispatches were filed.

Question. Do you know whether this dispatch passed through the office to Lewis E. Parsons?

Answer. I do know from the marks it contains.

Mr. CURTIS. That is an inference.

The WITNESS. I can answer that. I saw the dispatch in the office.

By Mr. Manager BUTLER:

Question. And it bears the marks of having been sent?

Answer. Yes, sir.

Mr. STANBERY. Now, let us see the dispatch. [The book was handed to the counsel for the respondent and examined by them.] This is very good reading; but will you tell us what is the object of this testimony? We like the document; but what is the object of it here?

Mr. Manager BUTLER. Do you object to this document whatever the object is?

Mr. STANBERY. We object until we know the purpose.

Mr. Manager BUTLER. The question that I put now is simply whether you object to the vehicle of proof?

Mr. EVARTS. No.

Mr. Manager BUTLER. If it is proper to read it at all the question is whether it is proved.

Mr. EVARTS. It proceeded from the President, and therefore it is proved.

Mr. JOHNSON. What is the date?

Mr. Manager BUTLER. January 17, 1867; the same date with Parsons' dispatch.

Mr. STANBERY. Now, the object?

Mr. Manager BUTLER. Not yet, sir. [To the witness.] On the same day that this is dated do you find in the records of the Department a press copy of a dispatch from Lewis E Parsons to which this is in answer?

Answer. I find in the press copy book a copy of a dispatch which that is in answer to.

Mr. EVARTS. How does that appear?

Mr. Manager BUTLER. It appears because the witness has sworn to it.

Mr. EVARTS. If it is an answer, it speaks for itself.

Mr. Manager BUTLER. Again I must reply, if the question is put to me how it appears, he has sworn that it is an answer. [To the witness.] Now, what was this telegraph office? The heading of the dispatch is "United States Military Telegraph." Was this telegraph under the control of the War Department?

Answer. At that time it was not under the control of the War Department.

Question. Where were the books kept?

The WITNESS. Do I understand you to mean the lines?

Mr. Manager BUTLER. I do not mean the lines. I mean the office.

Answer. It was.

Question. Was it in the War Department building?

Answer. It was.

Question. And were the officers employés of the War Department?

Answer. They were.

Question. Were the records of its doings at that office kept in the War Department?

Answer. They were.

Question. And are these books and these papers produced from the War Department?

Answer. No, sir; they are not.

Question. Where do they come from now?

Answer. They come from the War Department through the telegraph office; it has the original dispatches of the War Department.

Question. They came to the telegraph office from the War Department?

Answer. Yes, sir.

Question. They came originally as records from the War Department?

Answer. From the War Department to the telegraph office, and I bring them here.

Mr. Manager BUTLER. I submit now to the Senate that I propose to use in evidence, if it is otherwise competent, the dispatch of Lewis E. Parsons to which Andrew Johnson made reply. Having proved what I have proved, is there any objection, I mean now as to the vehicle of evidence simply, not as to the competency of the contents?

Mr. EVARTS. On that point in this present case, although we regard the proof of Mr. Parsons' dispatch as incompetent and insufficient, we shall waive any objection of that kind, and the question may now stand upon the competency of the proof.

Mr. Manager BUTLER. On the question of relevancy, I suppose?

Mr. EVARTS. Yes, and competency; its admissibility in any way.

Mr. Manager BUTLER. Admissibility of the proof of the contents?

Mr. EVARTS. Yes. We have had no notice to produce the original, but we care nothing about that.

Mr. Manager BUTLER. To that I answer we have the original here.

Mr. EVARTS. No; but the original of Mr. Parsons' dispatch delivered to the President. We have had no notice to produce that; we know nothing about it; but we waive that. Now, we inquire in what view and under what article these dispatches dated prior to the civil tenure act are introduced?

Mr. Manager BUTLER. In order that the Senate acting both as court and jury may understand whether these papers are admissible in evidence, it becomes necessary, with the leave of the president and the Senate, to read them *de bene,* in order that we may show how they become competent.

Mr. CURTIS. We do not object to your reading them *de bene esse.*

Mr. Manager BUTLER. The dispatch of Mr. Parsons is:

MONTGOMERY, ALABAMA,
January 17, 1867.

Legislature in session. Efforts making to reconsider vote on constitutional amendment. Report from Washington says it is probable an enabling act will pass. We do not know what to believe. I find nothing here.   LEWIS E. PARSONS,
Exchange Hotel.

His Excellency ANDREW JOHNSON, *President.*

The response is:

UNITED STATES MILITARY TELEGRAPH,
EXECUTIVE OFFICE, WASHINGTON, D. C.,
January 17, 1867.

What possible good can be obtained by reconsidering the constitutional amendment? I know of none in the present posture of affairs; and I do not believe the people of the whole country will sustain any set of individuals in attempts to change the whole character of our Government by enabling acts or otherwise. I believe, on the contrary, that they will eventually uphold all who have patriotism and courage to stand by the Constitution and who place their confidence in the people. There should be no faltering on the part of those who are honest in their determination to sustain the several coördinate departments of the Government in accordance with its original design. ANDREW JOHNSON.

Hon. LEWIS E. PARSONS, *Montgomery, Alabama.*

I have no further call, after having read these dispatches, so that they may be seen of the Senate, to argue the question whether this is competent evidence upon articles charging Andrew Johnson with attempting to overthrow the acts of Congress, to oppose their validity, and to bring its legislation into contempt. It is either under the tenth or the eleventh article quite competent.

Mr. EVARTS. The tenth is confined to the President's speeches. It alludes to nothing else.

Mr. CURTIS. Speeches, not telegrams.

Mr. Manager BUTLER. I am reminded by the learned counsel that that article refers to speeches and not telegrams. I know it; but with what intent were those speeches made? For what purpose were they made? They were made for the purpose of arraying the country against the Congress of the United States and its lawful acts, and to bring it into ridicule and contempt. Now, I am upon the point where the attempt is made to array the people against the lawful acts of Congress and to " destroy the regard and respect of all the good people of the United States for the Congress and legislative power thereof," and " to excite the odium and resentment of all the good people of the United States against Congress and the laws by it duly and constitutionally enacted."

We must go back a moment, if the Senate please, and I shall take but a moment, because I think this is too clear for argument. The President had gone forward in August and September, 1866, declaring everywhere that Congress had no power to do what it was proposing to do. Congress had proposed the constitutional amendment to the people of the States, and for the purpose of preventing that constitutional amendment from being accepted, every possible contumely was thrown upon Congress and every possible step taken to prevent its acceptance, and this is one of the steps.

I will not argue further under that proposition. Then the eleventh article charges that, "intending to deny the power of the Thirty-Ninth Congress to propose amendments to the Constitution of the United States," he did declare so and so. We find with that intent that when Congress had passed an act for the pacification of the southern States and for the settlement of the difficulty, in the shape of a proposed amendment to the Constitution, and when that was being considered by the south-

ern States, the President of the United States, from his high position, was absolutely telegraphing to the Legislature, in answer to a question of those States when they were asking for advice, urging them not to accept the amendment to the Constitution. I do not care to argue this any further.

Mr. EVARTS. If we understand the honorable Managers aright, this evidence is supposed to be relevant and competent only in reference to the crimes charged in the tenth and eleventh articles. Is that so? Was that your proposition, Mr. BUTLER?

Mr. Manager BUTLER. My proposition is that it is relevant under those. I have made no proposition as to the rest——

Mr. EVARTS. You did not name any others.

Mr. Manager BUTLER. I did not think it necessary.

Mr. EVARTS. Very well; I shall not think it necessary to consider any others.

Mr. Manager BUTLER. Very well; we are agreed on that.

Mr. EVARTS. Now, if the Chief Justice and Senators will give their attention to the tenth article there is that the President—

"Designing and intending to set aside the rightful authority and powers of Congress, did attempt to bring into disgrace, ridicule, hatred, contempt, and reproach the Congress of the United States and the several branches thereof, to impair and destroy the regard and respect of all the good people of the United States for the Congress and legislative power thereof, (which all officers of the Government ought inviolably to preserve and maintain,) and to excite the odium and resentment of all the good people of the United States against Congress and the laws by it duly and constitutionally enacted."

That is the entire purview of the intent. Now, the only acts charged as done with this intent are the delivery of a speech at the Executive Mansion in August, 1866, and two speeches, one at St. Louis and the other at Cleveland, in September, 1866. The article concludes that by means of these utterances—

"Said Andrew Johnson has brought the high office of the President of the United States into contempt, ridicule, and disgrace, to the great scandal of all good citizens, whereby said Andrew Johnson, President of the United States, did commit, and was then and there guilty of, a high misdemeanor in office."

That is the *gravamen* of the crime; that he brought the presidential office into scandal by these speeches made with this intent. Senators will judge from the reading of this telegram, dated in January, 1867, whether that supports the principal charge or intent of his derogating from the credit of Congress or bringing the presidential office into discredit.

The eleventh article has for its substantive charge nothing but the making of the speech of the 18th of August, 1866, saying that by that speech he declared and affirmed—

"In substance, that the Thirty-Ninth Congress of the United States was not a Congress of the United States authorized by the Constitution to exercise legislative power under the same, but, on the contrary, was a Congress of only part of the States, thereby denying, and intending to deny, that the legislation of said Congress was valid or obligatory upon him, the said Andrew Johnson, except in so far as he saw fit to approve the same, and, also, thereby denying, and intending to deny, the power of the said Thirty-Ninth Congress to propose amendments to the Constitution of the United States; and in pursuance of said declaration"—

That is, in pursuance of the speech made at the Executive Mansion on the 18th of August, 1866—

"The said Andrew Johnson, President of the United States, afterward, to wit, on the 21st day of February, A. D. 1868, at the city of Washington, in the District of Columbia, did, unlawfully, and in disregard of the requirement of the Constitution that he should take care that the laws be faithfully executed, attempt to prevent the execution of an act entitled 'An act regulating the tenure of certain civil offices,' passed March 2, 1867"—

Which was after the date of this dispatch—

"By unlawfully devising and contriving, and attempting to devise and contrive, means by which he should prevent Edwin M. Stanton from forthwith resuming the functions of the office of Secretary for the Department of War."

The court will consider whether this dispatch touches that subject.

"And also by further unlawfully devising and contriving, and attempting to devise and contrive, means, then and there, to prevent the execution of an act entitled 'An act making appropriations for the support of the Army for the fiscal year ending June 30, 1868, and for other purposes,' approved March 2, 1867; and also to prevent the execution of an act entitled 'An act to provide for the more efficient government of the rebel States,' passed March 2, 1867."

Also, after the date of this dispatch. It is under one or the other of these two articles that this dispatch is, in its date and in its substance, supposed to be relevant. I will read it:

WASHINGTON, D. C., January 17, 1867.

What possible good can be obtained by reconsidering the constitutional amendment? I know of none in the present posture of affairs; and I do not believe that the people of the whole country will sustain any set of individuals in attempts to change the whole character of our Government by enabling acts or otherwise. I believe, on the contrary, that they will eventually uphold all who have patriotism and courage to stand by the Constitution, and who place their confidence in the people. There should be no faltering on the part of those who are honest in their determination to sustain the several coördinate departments of the Government in accordance with its original design. ANDREW JOHNSON.

Hon. LEWIS E. PARSONS, Montgomery, Alabama.

There is nothing here pertinent in depreciation of Congress, nothing that tends to the scandal of the presidential office, nothing that has relation to the defeat of laws not then passed, and not possible to be the subject of crime or misdemeanor on the part of the President in resisting or opposing; and we find nothing whatever in these transactions—if introduced undoubtedly leading into a wide field of inquiry — that touches any crime or any intent or any purpose mentioned in these articles.

Mr. Manager BOUTWELL. Mr. President and Senators, if this evidence is admissible under either of the articles—and I have no doubt it is admissible under both the tenth and eleventh—it is sufficient for our purpose. It is enough that we show it to be admissible

under one; and therefore I treat the proposition to introduce this evidence under the eleventh article only—from which I think it must appear to Senators that there can be no doubt upon this point. If attention be given to the eleventh article it will be seen that we charge that the President did—

"On the 18th day of August, A. D. 1866, at the city of Washington, and in the District of Columbia, by public speech, declare and affirm, in substance, that the Thirty-Ninth Congress of the United States was not a Congress of the United States authorized by the Constitution to exercise legislative power under the same, but, on the contrary, was a Congress of only part of the States, thereby denying and intending to deny that the legislation of said Congress was valid or obligatory upon him, and also thereby denying and intending to deny the power of the Thirty-Ninth Congress to propose amendments to the Constitution of the United States"—

The very subject of these telegraphic dispatches—

"And, in pursuance of said declaration, the said Andrew Johnson, President of the United States, afterward to wit, on the 21st day of February, A. D. 1868"—

Which we understand to include all these dates between the time when the declaration which is the basis of this article, to wit, August 18, 1866, up to and including the 21st of February, 1868, so that all that period is open to us for the introduction of testimony showing the transactions of the President on this point—

"On the 21st day of February, A. D. 1868, at the city of Washington, in the District of Columbia, did, unlawfully, and in disregard of the requirement of the Constitution that he should take care that the laws be faithfully executed, attempt to prevent the execution of an act entitled 'An act regulating the tenure of certain civil offices,' passed March 2, 1867, by unlawfully devising and contriving, and attempting to devise and contrive, means by which he should prevent Edwin M. Stanton from forthwith resuming the functions of the office of Secretary for the Department of War, notwithstanding the refusal of the Senate to concur in the suspension theretofore made by said Andrew Johnson of said Edwin M. Stanton from said office of Secretary for the Department of War; and, also, by further unlawfully devising and contriving, and attempting to devise and contrive means, then and there, to prevent the execution of an act entitled 'An act making appropriations for the support of the Army for the fiscal year ending June 30, 1868, and for other purposes,' approved March 2, 1867; and, also, to prevent the execution of an act entitled 'An act to provide for the more efficient government of the rebel States,' passed March 2, 1867,"

Herein we see the nature and extent of the influence of the conduct of the President in sending out this telegram. Here was Mr. Parsons, who is known upon public fame to have been the provisional Governor of the State of Alabama in the year 1865 and 1866, a man of influence in that part of the country, who asks the President's opinion upon the very matter of the reconstruction of the rebel States. He says:

"Legislature in session. Efforts making to reconsider vote on constitutional amendment. Report from Washington says it is probable an enabling act will pass."

Which, undoubtedly, related to those acts which have come to be called acts for the government of the rebel States, enabling acts; measures of Congress by and through which these States were to be restored to the Union. He asks the opinion of the President as to what they shall do. He says:

"We do not know what to believe."

Now, what does the President say?

"What possible good can be attained by reconsidering the constitutional amendment?"

Which had been rejected.

"I know of none in the present posture of affairs; and I do not believe the people of the whole country will sustain any set of individuals"—

Here is the gist of the offense of this particular telegraphic dispatch, and showing, also, wherein it applies under the charge contained in the eleventh article. We set forth in the eleventh article that in August, 1866, he had charged that Congress was not a constitutional body representing all the States of the Union. In this dispatch he speaks of Congress, because he can refer to no other set of men, as a "set of individuals." He says:

"I do not believe the people of the whole country will sustain any set of individuals"—

Thus characterizing Congress as a set of individuals, which is seen in what he says in regard to them—

"in attempts to change the whole character of our Government by enabling acts or otherwise."

And we say that herein we have evidence of the intent of the President to defeat the will of Congress in regard to the enforcement of the reconstruction laws, which is precisely the offense charged against him in the eleventh article preferred by the House of Representatives. I am reminded, too, that the original reconstruction act provides for the adoption of the constitutional amendment as one of the conditions-precedent to or coincident with the right of a State organized under the reconstruction laws to be admitted to representation in Congress.

The CHIEF JUSTICE. Do the counsel for the respondent desire to say anything further?

Mr. EVARTS and Mr. CURTIS. Nothing further.

Mr. Manager BUTLER. I wish, if the presiding officer will allow me, to call attention to the fifth section of the act of March 2, 1867, known as the reconstruction act, which is the act described in the eleventh article, which provides:

"And when such constitution shall be ratified by a majority of the persons voting on the question of ratification who are qualified as electors for delegates, and when such constitution shall have been submitted to Congress for examination and approval, and Congress shall have approved the same, and when said State, by a vote of its Legislature elected under said constitution, shall have adopted the amendment to the Constitution of the United States proposed by the Thirty-Ninth Congress, and known as article fourteen, and when said article shall have become a part of the Constitution of the United States, said State shall be entitled to representation in Congress, and Senators and Representatives shall be admitted therefrom on their taking the oaths prescribed by law."

So that the adoption of the fourteenth article is a part of the reconstruction acts.

The CHIEF JUSTICE. Do the counsel for the respondent desire to be heard further?

Mr. STANBERY. No, sir.

Mr. HOWARD. I offer a question to the Managers.

The CHIEF JUSTICE. The question offered by the Senator from Michigan will be read.

The Secretary read as follows:

What amendment of the Constitution is referred to in Mr. Parson's dispatch?

Mr. Manager BUTLER. I can answer. There was but one amendment at that time pending before the country, and that was known as the fourteenth article, the one concerning which I have just read, and which is required to be adopted by every State Legislature before the State can be admitted to representation in Congress.

The CHIEF JUSTICE. Senators, the Managers offer in support of the accusations of the House of Representatives two telegraphic messages, one signed by Lewis E. Parsons, and one signed by Andrew Johnson. The question is, is the evidence proposed on the part of the Managers admissible?

Mr. DRAKE. I ask for the yeas and nays.

The yeas and nays were ordered; and being taken, resulted—yeas 27, nays 17; as follows:

YEAS—Messrs. Anthony, Cameron, Cattell, Chandler, Cole, Conkling, Conness, Corbett, Cragin, Drake, Henderson, Howard, Morgan, Morrill of Vermont, Nye, Patterson of New Hampshire, Pomeroy, Ramsey, Ross, Sherman, Sprague, Stewart, Sumner, Thayer, Tipton, Willey, and Wilson—27.

NAYS—Messrs. Buckalew, Davis, Dixon, Doolittle, Edmunds, Ferry, Fessenden, Fowler, Frelinghuysen, McCreery, Morrill of Maine, Norton, Patterson of Tennessee, Trumbull, Van Winkle, Vickers, and Williams—17.

NOT VOTING—Messrs. Bayard, Grimes, Harlan, Hendricks, Howe, Johnson, Morton, Saulsbury, Wade, and Yates—10.

So the evidence was admitted.

Mr. Manager BUTLER. I suppose that the dispatches need not be read again; they have been read once or twice.

Mr. CURTIS. No; we waive the further reading.

Mr. DOOLITTLE. Mr. Chief Justice, the hour of five having arrived, I move that the court adjourn until to-morrow at twelve o'clock.

The CHIEF JUSTICE. It is moved that the Senate sitting as a court of impeachment now adjourn until to-morrow at twelve o'clock.

The question being put, it was declared that the motion was not agreed to.

Mr. FOWLER. I call for a division.

The CHIEF JUSTICE. The result has been announced. It is too late to call for a division.

Mr. RAMSEY. The question was not understood, I think.

The CHIEF JUSTICE. If that be the case, the question will be put again.

The question being put again, the Chief Justice declared that the motion appeared to be agreed to.

Mr. CONNESS and Mr. SUMNER called for the yeas and nays, and they were ordered; and being taken, resulted—yeas 22, nays 22; as follows:

YEAS—Messrs. Anthony, Buckalew, Cameron, Corbett, Cragin, Davis, Dixon, Doolittle, Fowler, Frelinghuysen, Henderson, McCreery, Morrill of Vermont, Norton, Patterson of Tennessee, Ramsey, Sprague, Tipton, Trumbull, Van Winkle, Vickers, and Willey—22.

NAYS—Messrs. Cattell, Chandler, Cole, Conkling, Conness, Drake, Edmunds, Fessenden, Howard, Howe, Morgan, Morrill of Maine, Nye, Patterson of New Hampshire, Pomeroy, Ross, Sherman, Stewart, Sumner, Thayer, Williams, and Wilson—22.

NOT VOTING—Messrs. Bayard, Ferry, Grimes, Harlan, Hendricks, Johnson, Morton, Saulsbury, Wade, and Yates—10.

The CHIEF JUSTICE. On this question the yeas are 22, and the nays are 22. The Chief Justice votes in the affirmative. The Senate, sitting as a court of impeachment, stands adjourned until to-morrow at twelve o'clock.

FRIDAY, *April 3,* 1868.

The Chief Justice of the United States entered the Senate Chamber at five minutes past twelve o'clock and took the chair.

The usual proclamation having been made by the Sergeant-at-Arms,

The Managers of the impeachment on the part of the House of Representatives appeared and took the seats assigned them.

The counsel for the respondent also appeared and took their seats.

The presence of the House of Representatives was next announced, and the members of the House, as in Committee of the Whole, headed by Mr. E. B. WASHBURNE, the chairman of that committee, and accompanied by the Speaker and Clerk, entered the Senate Chamber, and were conducted to the seats provided for them.

The CHIEF JUSTICE. The Secretary will read the minutes of the last day's proceedings.

The Secretary read the Journal of the proceedings of the Senate yesterday sitting for the trial of the impeachment.

Mr. DRAKE. Mr. President, I move that the Senate take up the proposition which I offered yesterday, to amend the seventh rule, and have a vote upon it.

The CHIEF JUSTICE. The amendment will be considered as before the Senate unless objected to.

Mr. EDMUNDS. Let it be read.

The CHIEF JUSTICE. The Secretary will read the amendment.

The Secretary read as follows:

Amend the seventh rule by adding the following: Upon all such questions the vote shall be without a division, unless the yeas and nays be demanded by one fifth of the members present or requested by the presiding officer, when the same shall be taken.

Mr. EDMUNDS. Mr. President, I move to strike out that part of it relating to the yeas and nays being taken upon the request of the presiding officer.

Mr. CONKLING. Not having heard the motion of the Senator from Vermont, I ask for the reading of the seventh rule as it is now, which is not before us, and which we have no means of knowing anything about.

The CHIEF JUSTICE. The Secretary will read the seventh rule.

The SECRETARY. The seventh rule is as follows:

"VII. The Presiding Officer of the Senate shall direct all necessary preparations in the Senate Chamber, and the presiding officer on the trial shall direct all the forms of proceeding while the Senate are sitting for the purpose of trying an impeachment, and all forms during the trial not otherwise specially provided for. And the presiding officer on the trial may rule all questions of evidence and incidental questions, which ruling shall stand as the judgment of the Senate, unless some member of the Senate shall ask that a formal vote be taken thereon, in which case it shall be submitted to the Senate for decision; or he may, at his option, in the first instance, submit any such question to a vote of the members of the Senate."

It is proposed to add the following to the rule:

Upon all such questions the vote shall be without a division, unless the yeas and nays be demanded by one fifth of the members present or requested by the presiding officer, when the same shall be taken.

Mr. DRAKE. I have no objection to the amendment proposed by the honorable Senator from Vermont.

The CHIEF JUSTICE. The amendment to the rule will be so modified if there be no objection. [To the Chief Clerk.] Read the amendment as modified.

The Chief Clerk read the amendment as modified, as follows:

At the end of rule seven insert: Upon all such questions the vote shall be without a division, unless the yeas and nays be demanded by one fifth of the members present, when the same shall be taken.

The amendment to the rules, as modified, was agreed to.

Mr. DRAKE. I move that the rules, as now amended, be printed for the use of the Senate.

The motion was agreed to.

The CHIEF JUSTICE. The Managers on the part of the House of Representatives will proceed with their evidence.

Mr. Manager BUTLER. Before putting any question to Mr. Tinker, the witness under examination at the adjournment, I will put in a single paper with the leave of the court. The paper is a "message of the President of the United States, communicating to the Senate a report of the Secretary of State, showing the proceedings under the concurrent resolution of the two Houses of Congress of the 13th instant, requesting the President to submit to the Legislatures of the States an additional article to the Constitution of the United States."

Mr. STANBERY. What article is that? What date?

Mr. Manager BUTLER. The fourteenth article. The document is dated June 22, 1866. It is the same article to which the dispatch related. We offer it in order to show to what the dispatch referred.

[The document was handed to the counsel for the respondent.]

Mr. STANBERY, (returning it.) Mr. Chief Justice, we do not see the particular relevancy of this message to any article which we are called upon to answer. However, we have no objection to the gentleman reading it.

Mr. Manager BUTLER. Mr. Clerk, will you read the message?

The Chief Clerk read as follows:

Message from the President of the United States, communicating to the Senate a report of the Secretary of State, showing the proceedings under concurrent resolutions of the two Houses of Congress of the 13th instant, requesting the President to submit to the Legislature of the States an additional article to the Constitution of the United States.

To the Senate and House of Representatives:

I submit to Congress a report of the Secretary of State, to whom was referred the concurrent resolution of the 18th instant, respecting a submission to the Legislatures of the States of an additional article to the Constitution of the United States. It will be seen from this report that the Secretary of State had, on the 16th instant, transmitted to the Governors of the several States certified copies of the joint resolution passed on the 13th instant, proposing an amendment to the Constitution.

Even in ordinary times any question of amending the Constitution must be justly regarded as of paramount importance. This importance is at the present time enhanced by the fact that the joint resolution was not submitted by the two Houses for the approval of the President, and that of the thirty-six States which constitute the Union eleven are excluded from representation in either House of Congress, although, with the single exception of Texas, they have been entirely restored to all their functions as States, in conformity with the organic law of the land, and have appeared at the national capital by Senators and Representatives who have applied for and have been refused admission to the vacant seats. Nor have the sovereign people of the nation been afforded an opportunity of expressing their views upon the important questions which the amendment involves. Grave doubts, therefore, may naturally and justly arise as to whether the action of Congress is in harmony with the sentiments of the people, and whether State Legislatures, elected without reference to such an issue, should be called upon by Congress to decide respecting the ratification of the proposed amendment.

Waiving the question as to the constitutional validity of the proceedings of Congress upon the joint resolution proposing the amendment, or as to the merits of the article which it submits, through the executive department, to the Legislatures of the States, I deem it proper to state that the steps taken by the Secretary of State, as detailed in the accompanying report, are to be considered as purely ministerial, and in no sense whatever committing the Executive to an approval or a recommendation of the amendment to the State Legislatures or to the people. On the contrary, a proper appreciation of the letter and spirit of the Constitution, as well as of the interests of national order, harmony, and union, and a due deference for an enlightened public judgment, may at this time well suggest a doubt whether any amendment to the Constitution ought to be proposed by Congress, and pressed upon the Legislatures of the several States for final decision, until after the admission of such loyal Senators and Representatives of the now unrepresented States as have been or as may hereafter be chosen in conformity with the Constitution and laws of the United States. ANDREW JOHNSON.

WASHINGTON, D. C., *June 22, 1866.*

DEPARTMENT OF STATE,
WASHINGTON, *June 20, 1866.*

The Secretary of State, to whom was referred the concurrent resolution of the two Houses of Congress of the 18th instant in the following words: "That the President of the United States be requested to transmit forthwith to the executives of the several States of the United States copies of the article of amendment proposed by Congress to the State Legislatures, to amend the Constitution of the United States, passed June 13, 1866, respecting citizenship, the basis of representation, disqualification for office, and validity of the public debt of the United States, &c., to the end that the said States may proceed to act upon the said article of amendment, and that he request the executive of each State that may ratify said amendment to transmit to the Secretary of State a certified copy of such ratification," has the honor to submit the following report, namely: that on the 16th instant Hon. AMASA COBB, of the Committee of the House of Representatives on Enrolled Bills, brought to this Department and deposited therein an enrolled resolution of the two Houses of Congress, which was thereupon received by the Secretary of State and deposited among the rolls of the Department, a copy of which is hereunto annexed. Thereupon the Secretary of State, on the 16th instant, in conformity with the proceeding which was adopted by him in 1865 in regard to the then proposed and afterward adopted congressional amendment of the Constitution of the United States concerning the prohibition of slavery, transmitted certified copies of the annexed resolution to the Governors of the several States, together with a certificate and circular letter. A copy of both of these communications is hereunto annexed.

Respectfully submitted:
WILLIAM H. SEWARD.

The PRESIDENT.

[Circular.]

DEPARTMENT OF STATE,
WASHINGTON, *June 16, 1866.*

SIR: I have the honor to transmit an attested copy of a resolution of Congress, proposing to the Legislatures of the several States a fourteenth article to the Constitution of the United States. The decisions of the several Legislatures upon the subject are required by law to be communicated to this Department.

An acknowledgment of the receipt of this communication is requested by your excellency's most obedient servant, WILLIAM H. SEWARD.

His Excellency the Governor of the State of ——.

UNITED STATES OF AMERICA,
DEPARTMENT OF STATE.

To all to whom these presents shall come, greeting:

I certify that annexed is a true copy of a concurrent resolution of Congress, entitled, "Joint resolution proposing an amendment to the Constitution of the United States," the original of which resolution, received to-day, is on file in this Department.

In testimony whereof, I, William H. Seward, Secretary of State of the United States, have hereunto subscribed my name and caused the seal of the Department of State to be affixed.

Done at the city of Washington, this 16th day [L. S.] of June, A. D. 1866, and of the independence of the United States of America the ninetieth.

WILLIAM H. SEWARD.

[Concurrent resolution, received at Department of State January 16, 1866.]

Joint resolution proposing an amendment to the Constitution of the United States.

Resolved by the Senate and House of Representatives of the United States of America in Congress assembled, (two thirds of both Houses concurring,) That the following article be proposed to the Legislatures of the several States as an amendment to the Constitution of the United States, which when ratified by three fourths of said Legislatures shall be valid as part of the Constitution, namely:

ARTICLE XIV.

SECTION 1. All persons born or naturalized in the

United States and subject to the jurisdiction thereof are citizens of the United States and of the State wherein they reside. No State shall make or enforce any law which shall abridge the privileges or immunities of citizens of the United States; nor shall any State deprive any person of life, liberty, or property without due process of law, nor deny any person within its jurisdiction the equal protection of the laws.

Sec. 2. Representatives shall be apportioned among the several States according to their respective numbers, counting the whole number of persons in each State, excluding Indians not taxed. But when the right to vote at any election for the choice of electors for President and Vice President of the United States, Representatives in Congress, the executive and judicial officers of a State, or the members of the Legislature thereof, is denied to any of the male inhabitants of such State being twenty-one years of age and citizens of the United States, or in any way abridged, except for participation in rebellion or other crime, the basis of representation therein shall be reduced in the proportion which the number of such male citizens shall bear to the whole number of male citizens twenty-one years of age in such State.

Sec. 3. No person shall be a Senator or Representative in Congress, or elector of President and Vice President, or hold any office, civil or military, under the United States, or under any State, who, having previously taken an oath as a member of Congress, or as an officer of the United States, or as a member of any State Legislature, or as an executive or judicial officer of any State, to support the Constitution of the United States, shall have engaged in insurrection or rebellion against the same, or given aid or comfort to the enemies thereof. But Congress may, by a vote of two thirds of each House, remove such disability.

Sec. 4. The validity of the public debt of the United States, authorized by law, including debts incurred for payment of pensions and bounties for services in suppressing insurrection or rebellion, shall not be questioned. But neither the United States nor any State shall assume or pay any debt or obligation incurred in aid of insurrection or rebellion against the United States, or any claim for the loss or emancipation of any slave; but all such debts, obligations, and claims shall be held illegal and void.

Sec. 5. The Congress shall have power to enforce, by appropriate legislation, the provisions of this article.

SCHUYLER COLFAX,
Speaker of the House of Representatives.
LA FAYETTE S. FOSTER,
President of the Senate pro tempore.

Attest:
EDWARD McPHERSON,
Clerk of the House of Representatives.
J. W. FORNEY,
Secretary of the Senate.

[To which is appended the certificate of J. W. Forney, Secretary of the Senate, dated April 2, 1868, that the foregoing are true extracts from the records of the Senate.]

CHARLES A. TINKER's examination resumed.
By Mr. Manager BUTLER:

Question. You told us yesterday you were manager of the Western Union Telegraph office. Have you from that office what purports to be a copy of a speech which was telegraphed to the country or any portion of the country, as made by Andrew Johnson on the 18th of August, 1866; if so, produce it?

Mr. DRAKE. I will state that we have not heard the question put by the honorable Manager.

The CHIEF JUSTICE. The Manager will be good enough to repeat the question.

Mr. Manager BUTLER. It is whether, being agent of the Western Union Telegraph Company, you have what purports to be a copy of a speech which was telegraphed over that line, made by Andrew Johnson on the 18th day of August, 1866; if so, produce it?

Answer. I have the files of the Associated Press dispatches sent on that day, containing what purports to be a copy of the speech delivered by the President. [Producing a roll of manuscript.]

Question. From the course of business of the office are you enabled to state whether this was sent?

Answer. It has the "sent" marks put upon all dispatches sent over the line.

Question. And this is the original manuscript?

Answer. That is the original manuscript telegraphed.

Question. By what association was this speech telegraphed?

Answer. By the Associated Press, by their agent in the city of Washington.

Mr. CURTIS. We must object to this, General BUTLER. He says it has a mark on it. He does not say he put the mark on it, or that he knows that anything was done, thus far.

Mr. Manager BUTLER, (to the witness.) Can you tell me, sir, to what extent over the country the telegraphic messages sent by the Associated Press go?

Answer. I suppose they go to all parts of the country; I cannot state positively. They are telegraphed direct from Washington to New York, Philadelphia, and Baltimore, there addressed to the agents of the Associated Press, and from New York they are distributed through the country.

Mr. Manager BUTLER, (to the counsel for the respondent.) The witness is yours, gentlemen.

Mr. CURTIS. We will not detain you, Mr. Tinker.

Mr. Manager BUTLER. You can step down for the present, Mr. Tinker; but do not leave.

JAMES B. SHERIDAN sworn and examined.
By Mr. Manager BUTLER:

Question. Your whole name, Mr. Sheridan.

Answer. James Bernard Sheridan.

Question. What is your business?

Answer. I am a stenographer.

Question. Where employed?

Answer. At present in New York city.

Question. What was your business on the 18th of August, 1866?

Answer. I was a stenographer.

Question. State whether you reported a speech of the President on the 18th of August, 1866, in the East Room of the President's Mansion.

Answer. I did.

Question. Have you the notes taken at the time of that speech?

Answer. I have; [producing a note-book containing short-hand notes.]

Question. Did you take down that speech correctly as it was given?

Answer. I did, to the best of my ability.

Question. How long experience have you had as a reporter?

Answer. Some fourteen years now.

Question. Did you write out that speech at the time?

Answer. I wrote out a part of it.

Question. Where?

Answer. At the Presidential Mansion.

Question. Who was present?

Answer. There were several reporters present, Mr. Clephane, Mr. Smith.

Question. What Clephane? Do you remember his first name?

Answer. James, I think, is his first name?

Question. What Mr. Smith?

Answer. Francis H., I believe, is his name.

Question. The official reporter of the House?

Answer. At that time, I believe, he was connected with the House.

Question. Who else?

Answer. I think Colonel Moore was in the room part of the time; I do not know that he was in all the time.

Question. What Colonel Moore?

Answer. The President's Private Secretary, William G.

Question. After it was written out, what, if anything, was done with it?

Mr. CURTIS. He says he wrote a part.

Mr. Manager BUTLER. The part that you wrote out?

Answer. I do not know. I think Mr. Moore took it. I was very sick at the time, and did not pay much attention to what was going on.

Question. You think Mr. Moore took it?

Answer. I think either he or Mr. Smith took it, as I wrote out my share of it. We divided it among us; Mr. Clephane, Mr. Smith, and I wrote out the speech, I think.

Question. Look at that manuscript, [handing to the witness the manuscript produced by C. A. Tinker,] and see whether you recognize your hand-writing.

The WITNESS, (having examined the manuscript.) No, sir; I do not recognize any of the writing here as mine.

Question. Have you since written out from your notes any portion of the speech as you reported it?

Answer. I wrote out a couple of extracts from it.

Question, (handing a paper to the witness.) Is that your writing?

Answer. Yes, sir.

Question. State whether what you hold in your hand is a correct transcript of that speech made from your notes?

Answer. It is.

Question. When was that written?

Answer. It was written when I appeared before the Board of Managers.

Question. Will you have the kindness to put your initials upon it?

[The witness marked it "J. B. S."]

Mr. Manager BUTLER, (to the counsel for the respondent.) The witness is yours, gentlemen.

Mr. STANBERY. Have you got through with this witness?

Mr. Manager BUTLER. I said the witness was yours, gentlemen.

Mr. STANBERY. Is this all you expect of this witness?

Mr. Manager BUTLER. All at present, and we may never recall him.

Cross-examined by Mr. EVARTS:

Question. You have produced a note-book of original stenographic report of a speech of the President?

Answer. Yes, sir.

Question. Is it of the whole speech?

Answer. Of the whole speech.

Question. Was it wholly made by you?

Answer. By me; yes, sir.

Question. How long did the speech occupy in the delivery?

Answer. Well, I suppose some twenty or twenty-five minutes.

Question. By what method of stenographic reporting did you proceed on that occasion?

Answer. Pitman's system of phonography.

Question. Which is, as I understand, reporting by sound, and not by sense?

Answer. We report the sense by the sound.

Question. I understand you report by sound wholly?

Answer. Signs.

Question. And not by memory of or attention to sense?

Answer. No good reporter can report unless he always pays attention and understands the sense of what he is reporting.

Question. That is the very point I wish to arrive at, whether you are attending to the sound and setting it down in your notation, or whether you are attending to the sense and setting it down from your memory or attention to the sense?

Answer. Both.

Question. Both at the same time?

Answer. Yes, sir.

Question. Your characters are arbitrary, are they not? That is, they are peculiar to your art?

Answer. Yes, sir.

Question. They are not letters?

Answer. No, sir.

Question. Nor words?

Answer. We have word signs.

Question. But generally sound signs?

Answer. We have signs for sounds, just as the letters of the alphabet represent sounds.

Question. But not the same?

Answer. No, sir.

Question. This transcript that you made of a portion of your report for the use of the committee was made recently, I suppose?

Answer. Yes, sir; a few weeks ago.

Question. Now, sir, what in the practice of your art is the experience as to the accuracy of transcribing from these stenographic notes after the lapse of a considerable period of time?

Answer. Perhaps I can illustrate better by the present case—this report which I made here—the extract I gave when I was called before the Managers, as I had accompanied the President on his tour. I did not know what they wanted me for; and when they told me to turn to this speech I did not even know that I had the notes of it with me; but I turned to the speech, and found it there in the book, and I read off, as they requested I should, the extracts which the Managers for the prosecution handed me, which I identified.

Question. You read, then, from your stenographic notes?

Answer. Yes, sir.

Question. And it was taken down?

Answer. The reporter of the Managers, I believe, took it down; but I afterward wrote it out for them.

Question. You do not make a sign for every word?

Answer. Almost every word. "Of the" we generally drop, and indicate that by putting the two words closer together. Of course we have rules governing us in writing.

Question. That is, you have signs which belong to every word excepting when you drop the particles?

Answer. Yes, sir.

Question. But not, as a matter of course, a sign that is the representative of a whole word?

Answer. Yes, sir; we have signs representing words.

Question. Some signs?

Answer. Yes, sir.

Question. For instance, for the word "jurisprudence," you have no one sign that represents it?

Answer. No, sir; I should write that "j-r-s-p."

Question. And that is an illustration of your course of proceeding, is it not?

Answer. Yes, sir.

Question. Are these letters that you thus use, or only signs that represent letters?

Answer. Yes, sir.

Mr. EVARTS, (to the witness.) That is all.

Mr. Manager BUTLER. That is all for the present; remain within call.

JAMES O. CLEPHANE sworn and examined.

By Mr. Manager BUTLER:

Question. What is your business?

Answer. I am at present deputy clerk of the supreme court of the District of Columbia.

Question. What was your employment on the 18th of August, 1866?

Answer. I was then secretary to Governor Seward, Secretary of State.

Question. Are you a phonographic reporter?

Answer. I am.

Question. How considerable has been your experience?

Answer. Some eight or nine years.

Question. Were you employed on the 18th of August, 1866, to make a report of the President's speech in reply to Mr. JOHNSON?

Answer. I was. I was engaged in connection with Mr. Smith for the Associated Press, and also for the Daily Chronicle at Washington.

Question. Did you make a report?

Answer. I did.

Question. Where was this speech made?

Answer. In the East Room of the White House.

Question. You say it was in reply to Mr. JOHNSON?

Answer. It was in reply to Hon. REVERDY JOHNSON.

Question. State partially who were present?

Answer. There were a great many persons present—the committee of the convention. I noticed among the prominent personages General Grant, who stood beside the President during the delivery of the speech. Several reporters were present—Mr. Murphy, Mr. Sheridan, Mr. Smith, and some others.

Question. Were any of the Cabinet officers present?

Answer. I do not recollect whether any of them were present or not.

Question. Did you report that speech?

Answer. I did.

Question. What was done with that report? State all the circumstances.

Answer. With regard to the Associated Press report I will state that Colonel Moore, the President's Private Secretary, desired the privilege of revising it before publication; and, in order to expedite matters, Mr. Sheridan, Mr. Smith, and myself united in the labor of transcribing it; Mr. Sheridan transcribed one portion, Mr. Smith another, and I a third. After it was revised by Colonel Moore it was then taken and handed to the agent of the Associated Press, who telegraphed it throughout the country.

Question. Look at that roll of manuscript lying before you and see if that is the speech that you transcribed and Moore corrected?

Answer., (having examined the manuscript produced by C. A. Tinker.) I will state here that I do not recognize any of my writing. It is possible I may have dictated to a long-hand writer on that occasion my portion, though I am not positive in regard to that.

Question. Who was present at the time of the writing out?

Answer. Mr. Smith, Mr. Sheridan, and Colonel Moore, as far as I recollect.

Question. Do you know Colonel Moore's handwriting?

Answer. I do not.

Question. Did you send your report to the Chronicle?

Answer. I would state that Mr. McFarland, who had engaged me to report for the Chronicle, was unwilling to take the revised report of the President's speech as made by Colonel Moore. He desired to have the speech as it was delivered, as he stated, with all its imperfections, and, as he insisted upon my rewriting the speech, I did so, and it was published in the Sunday Morning Chronicle of the 19th.

Question. Have you a copy of that paper?

Answer. I have not.

Question. After that report was published in the Chronicle of Sunday morning, the 19th, did you see the report?

Answer. I did, sir, and examined it very carefully, because I had a little curiosity to see how it would read under the circumstances, being a literal report, with the exception of a word, perhaps, changed here and there.

Question. You say with the exception of a word changed here and there; how?

Answer. Where the sentence was very awkward, and where the meaning was obscure, doubtless in that case I made a change. I recollect doing it in one or two instances, though I may not be able to point them out just now. If I had my original notes I could do so.

Question. With what certainty can you speak as to the Chronicle's report being an accurate one?

Answer. I think I can speak with certainty as to its being accurate, a literal report, with the exception that I have named, perhaps, a word or two here and there changed in order to make the meaning more intelligible, or to make the sentence a little more round.

Question. Will you give us an illustration of that change?

Mr. EVARTS. Some instance.

Mr. Manager BUTLER. Yes, some instance.

Mr. STANBERY. He said he could not recollect.

The WITNESS. I will state that my attention was called to a particular instance; I think it was a day or two after. Some correspondent, learning that the Chronicle had published a *verbatim* report, had carefully scrutinized it—some correspondent who had listened to the delivery of the speech; and he wrote to the Chronicle a complaint of its not being so, as, in one instance, there was an expression of "you and I has saw," or something of that sort, and that sentence, of course, was corrected in the report published in the Chronicle. It appeared in the notes "you and I has saw," as this correspondent stated.

By Mr. Manager BUTLER:

Question. How was it corrected in the Chronicle?

Answer. "You and myself have seen," or something to that effect; I do not now remember.

Mr. Manager BUTLER. I am informed, Mr. President, there being two manuscripts, that Mr. Tinker has given me the one which was written out at length as a duplicate, and not the original, as I had supposed, and I shall have to ask to bring him on again. I have sent for him for that purpose. He will be here in a moment. This witness is yours, gentlemen, [to the counsel for the respondent.]

Cross-examined by Mr. EVARTS.

Question. You acted upon the employment of the Associated Press?

Answer. Yes, sir; in connection with Mr. Smith.

Question. You were jointly to make a report, were you?

Answer. We were to take notes of the entire speech, each of us, and then we were to divide the labor of transcribing.

Question. Now, did you take phonographic notes of the whole speech?

Answer. I did.

Question. Where are your phonographic notes?

Answer. I have searched for them, but cannot find them.

Question. Now, sir, at any time after you had completed the phonographic notes did you translate or write them out?

Answer. I did.

Question. The whole?

Answer. The whole speech.

Question. Where is that translation or written transcript?

Answer. I do not know, sir. The manuscript, of course, was left in the Chronicle office. I wrote it out for the Chronicle.

Question. You have never seen it since, have you?

Answer. I have not.

Question. Have you made any search for it?

Answer. I have not.

Question. And these two acts of yours, the phonographic report and the translation or writing out, are all that you had to do with the speech, are they?

Answer. Yes, sir.

Question. Now, you say that subsequently you read a printed newspaper copy of the speech in the Washington Chronicle?

Answer. Yes, sir.

Question. When was it that you read that newspaper copy?

Answer. On the morning of the publication, August 19, Sunday morning.

Question. Where were you when you read it?

Answer. I presume I was at my room. I generally saw the Chronicle there.

Question. And you there read it?

Answer. Yes, sir.

Question. From this curiosity that you had?

Answer. Yes. I read it more carefully because of that reason.

Question. Had you before you your phonographic notes, or your written transcript from them?

Answer. I had not.

Question. And had not seen and have never seen them in comparison with the newspaper copy before you?

Answer. No, sir.

Reëxamined by Mr. Manager BUTLER:

Question, (handing to the witness a bound volume of the Washington Daily Chronicle.) Have you before you a copy of the Sunday Morning Chronicle of the 19th of August, 1866?

Answer. I have.

Question. Look upon the page before you and see if you can find the speech as you reported it?

Answer. I find it here, sir.

Question. Look at that speech, look at it a little carefully, and tell me whether you have any doubt that that is a correct report, a *verbatim* report of the speech of Andrew Johnson on that occasion; and if so, what ground have you for doubt?

Mr. EVARTS. Mr. Chief Justice, we object to that as a mode of proving the speech. It is apparent that there is a report of this speech, and that it has been written out, and that is the best and most trustworthy evidence of the actual speech as made. In all legal proceedings we are entitled to that degree of accuracy and trustworthiness which the nature of the case admits; and whenever evidence of that degree of authenticity is presented, then for the first time will arise the consideration of whether the evidence itself is competent and should be received. Now, it is impossible to contend, upon the testimony of this witness, as it stands at present, that he remembers the speech of the President so that he can produce it by recital, or so that he can say upon any memorandum of his own shown him (for none is shown) that from memory he can say it is the speech. What is offered? The same kind of evidence, and that alone, which would grow out of some person who heard the President deliver the speech, and subsequently read in the Chronicle the report of it, that he thinks that report was a true statement of the speech; for this witness has told us distinctly that reading this speech from curiosity to see how it would appear when reproduced, without the ordinary guarantees of accuracy he had neither his original notes nor his written transcript, and he read the newspaper as others would read it, but with more care, from this degree of curiosity which he had. If the true character of a production of this kind, as imputed to its author, is to be regarded as important, we insist that this kind of evidence concerning a newspaper report of it is not admissible.

Mr. Manager BUTLER. Mr. President, if I understand there is no question of degree of evidence. We must take the business of the world as we find it, and must not burrow ourselves and insist that we have awoken up a hundred years ago. The art of stenography and stenographic writing and phonography has progressed to a point which makes us rely upon it in all the business of life. There is not a gentleman of this Senate who does not rely upon it every day. There is not more than

C. I.--13.

one member of the Senate who in this trial is taking notes of the evidence. Why? Because you rely upon the busy fingers of the reporter who sits by my side to give you a transcript of it, upon which you must judge. Therefore, in every business of life, ay, in the very business of this court, we rely upon stenography.

Now, this gentleman says that he made a stenographic report of that speech; that that was jointly made up by himself, Mr. Sheridan, and Mr. Smith; that his employer, not being satisfied with that joint report, which was the President's utterance distilled through the alembic of Colonel Moore's critical discrimination, he drew out with care an exact literal transcript under the chiding of his employer, and for a given purpose; and that the next day, having curiosity to see what would be the difference, and how the President of the United States would appear if put to paper literally, he examined that speech in the Chronicle, and then with the matter fresh in his mind, only a few hours intervening, with his attention freshly called to it, he said then he knew that that was a correct copy; that that was the correct speech.

Now, the learned counsel say the manuscript is the better evidence. If there was any evidence that that manuscript had been preserved perhaps we might be called upon to produce it in some technicality of criticism of law as administered in a very technical manner. But who does not know the ordinary course of business, and, if that is to be disputed, I will ask the witness; but who does not know that the ordinary course of business in a newspaper office, after such manuscripts are got through with, is to throw them into the waste-paper basket; they are not preserved. Therefore I act upon that usual and ordinary and common understanding of the business of life as all courts must act upon it.

Then this is a question for the witness, and he testifies. The question that was objected to, the one we are discussing, is, looking at that report, from your knowledge of the report, having twice written it out, portions of it certainly, and from having seen it the next morning, with your curiosity awakened, can you tell the Senate whether that is a correct report? Thereupon the learned counsel for the President gets up and says he cannot. How does the learned counsel for the President know that? How does he know that Mr. Clephane is not one of those gentlemen who, in his profession, having once read a speech can repeat it the next day?

The difficulty is that I do not see how the objection arises. The question I put to the witness is a plain one. "Sir, there is what I say is a copy of that speech, is a transcript of that speech; from your knowledge, having heard it, having written it down in short-hand, having written it once for correction by the President's Private Secretary, and then having rewritten it again from your notes for publica-

194

tion in the Chronicle, and then having examined it immediately after publication—from all these sources of knowledge can you say that that is a correct copy?" Thereupon the counsel for the President says you cannot? How does he know that the witness cannot repeat every word of it?

The difficulty is the objection does not apply; and I should have contented myself with this statement except that, once for all, I propose to put before the Senate, so as not ever to have to argue it again in the course of putting in this class of testimony, the argument as to stenographic reporting. Now, allow me to state, once for all, two authorities upon this point, because I am not going to take the time of the Senate with arguing these questions hereafter, for by doing so, I should play into the hands of this delay which has been so often attempted here. In O'Connell's case, to prove his speeches on that great trial, the newspapers were introduced; and no trial was ever fought with more sharpness or bitterness—newspapers were introduced containing Mr. O'Connell's speeches, or what purported to be his speeches, and the only proof adduced was that they had been properly stamped and issued from the office, and the court held that Mr. O'Connell, allowing those speeches to go out without contradiction for months, must be held to be responsible for them to the public.

In the trial of James Watson, for high treason, reported in 32 State Trials, this question arose, and the question was whether a copy might be used, that copy made even of partially obliterated short-hand notes:

"*Mr. Attorney General*, (to Mr. Dowling.) You state that you took in short-hand the address of Mr. Watson to the people?
"I did."
"Have you your short-hand notes here?"
"I have."
"Be so good as to read to my lords and the jury what it was he said?"
"*Mr. Wetherell.* Pray, Mr. Short-hand Writer, when did you take that note?"
"I took it on the 2d of December, in Spafields."
"When did you copy it out?"
"I copied it out the same evening."
"Is that the copy you made that evening?"
"No; it is not. This is the short-hand note I took, and this is a literal copy; the short-hand note I took with a pencil, and in the crowd, and, perhaps, having been taken six months' back, it may be somewhat defaced: but I can read the short-hand note with a little difficulty, though certainly I could read the transcript with more ease; I will read the short-hand note if it is wished."
"*Mr. Justice Abbott.* You made that transcript the same evening?"
"I made this transcript yesterday; I made another transcript the same evening."

And he was allowed to read his transcript. While this authority is not exactly to the point of difference raised here, I say I put it in once for all upon the question, because I have heard a cross-examination as to the merits of Pitman's system of short-hand writing as if we were to have it put in controversy here, that the whole system of stenography was an unavailable means of furnishing information. Therefore my present proposition is the right to put

this question: Mr. Witness, looking at that, can you tell me whether that is a correct transcript of the speech made by the President?

Mr. EVARTS. The learned Manager is quite correct in saying that I do not know but that this witness can repeat from memory the President's speech; and whenever he offers him as a witness so to do I will not object. It is entirely competent for a person who has heard a speech to repeat it under oath, he asserting that he remembers it and can do so, and whenever Mr. Clephane undertakes that feat it is within the competency of evidence. What success he will have in it we shall determine when that experiment has been tried. That method of evidence from this witness is not attempted, but another form of trustworthy evidence is sought to be made competent; that is, that by his notes, and through his transcript of those notes, he is able to present, under his present oath and belief in his accuracy and competency as a reporter, this form of evidence. Whenever that is attempted we shall make no objection to that as trustworthy.

But when the Managers seek to avoid responsibility and accuracy through the oath of the witness applied in either form, and seek to put it, neither upon present memory nor upon his own memoranda, but upon the accuracy with which he has followed or detected inaccuracies in a newspaper report made the subsequent day, and thereupon to give credit and authenticity to the newspaper report upon his wholesale and general approval of it, then we must contend that the sacred right of freedom of speech is sought to be invaded by overthrowing certainly one of the responsible and important protections of it; and that the rule requiring the oath of somebody who heard and can remember, or, according to the rules of evidence, preserved the aids and assistances by which he presently in the court of justice may speak, should be adhered to. And we are not to be told that it is technical to maintain in defense of what has been regarded as one of the commonest and surest rights in any free country—freedom of speech, that whenever it is drawn in question it shall be drawn in question upon the surest and most faithful evidences.

The learned Manager has said that you are familiar, as a part of the daily routine of your congressional duties, with the habit of stenographic reporting and reproduction in the newspapers, and that you rely on it habitually; and I may add rely on it habitually to be habitually misled. Correction is the first demand of every public speaker—correction and revision, in order that this apparatus, depending upon the ear and the sudden strokes of the ready-writer, may not be the firm judgment against him of what was said by him. Now, when sedulously this newspaper has undertaken that no such considerations of accuracy shall be afforded to the President of the United States in respect of this speech to be spread before the country, but that express orders shall be given that it shall be reported with all its imperfections——

Mr. Manager BUTLER. I pray correction, sir. I have not sedulously done that; but offer it that the speech of the President's Private Secretary should not go before the country.

Mr. EVARTS. The instructions of the editor were that it should be reported "with all its imperfections" as caught by the shorthand writer, without the opportunity of that revision which every public speaker at the hustings or in the halls of debate demands as a primary and important right. Whenever, therefore, Mr. Clephane shall rise and speak from memory the speech of the President here, swearing to its accuracy, or whenever he shall produce his notes and their transcript as in Watson's case, some foundation for the proof of the speech will have been laid.

Mr. Manager BUTLER. Stand down, Mr. Clephane, for a moment. I will offer this directly. Now I will call Mr. Tinker.

CHARLES A. TINKER recalled.

The CHIEF JUSTICE. The witness states that he desires to make an explanation. He will make it.

THE WITNESS. Yesterday when called upon the stand I was attending to my duties in charge of the telegraph office in the gallery; I had not a moment's notice that I was to be called. I then telegraphed to my office for the documents contained in packages that were there, which I had been previously examined about before the Managers. These documents were brought to me by a boy from the office, and I put them upon the stand. Last night when taken from the stand I deposited them in the office of the Sergeant-at-Arms, and this morning brought one of these packages upon the stand, and I opened it here, supposing it to be the one on which I was to be examined. As I saw that the reporters were in trouble about it, I thought I had made a mistake, and I consequently went to my office after Mr. Clephane came upon the stand, and I have now the speech of the President telegraphed by the agent of the Associated Press on the 18th of August, 1866.

Mr. STANBERY. Mr. Tinker, what document was that General BUTLER handed you?

Answer. This is one of the documents.

Mr. STANBERY. Is that the speech of the 18th of August at all?

Answer. This is not the speech of the 18th of August.

Mr. Manager BUTLER. That is the 22d of February speech, is it? [Laughter.]

Mr. STANBERY. No matter what it is.

The WITNESS. I have not looked to see what this is.

Mr. Manager BUTLER. You will find out what that document is in good time.

Mr. STANBERY. You had better put it in "in good time."

Mr. Manager BUTLER. It was simply a mistake. [To the witness.] Now give me the document I asked for?

The WITNESS. Yes, sir. [Producing a roll of manuscript.]

By Mr. Manager BUTLER:

Question. Is this the document you supposed you were testifying about before?

Answer. This is.

Question. Do you give the same testimony about that that you did——

Mr. CURTIS and Mr. STANBERY. That will not do. Let us have his testimony about this.

Mr. Manager BUTLER. Well, sir, we will give all the delay possible. [To the witness.] Now, sir, will you tell us whether that was sent through the Associated Press?

Answer. It bears the marks of having been sent, and is filed with their dispatches of that date.

Question. From the course of business of your office, have you any doubt that it was so sent?

Answer. None whatever.

Mr. CURTIS. We object to that. If the witness can say it was sent from any knowledge he has, of course he will say so. He cannot reason on facts.

Mr. Manager BUTLER, (to the witness.) After that speech was sent, if it was, did you see it published in the Associated Press reports?

Answer. I cannot state positively; I think I did.

Question. Was that brought to your office for the purpose of being transmitted, whether it was or not?

Answer. I did not personally receive it; but it is in the dispatches of the Associated Press sent on that day.

Mr. Manager BUTLER. That is all at present. Now we will recall Mr. Sheridan.

JAMES B. SHERIDAN recalled.

By Mr. Manager BUTLER:

Question, (handing to the witness the manuscript last produced by Mr. Tinker.) Now, examine that manuscript and see whether you find any of your handwriting in it?

Answer, (having examined the manuscript.) I see my writing here.

Question. What is it you have there?

Answer. I have a report of the speech made by the President on the 18th of August.

Question. In what year?

Answer. Eighteen hundred and sixty-six.

Question. Have you ever seen Mr. Moore write?

Answer. A good many years ago, when he was reporter for the Intelligencer and I reported for the Washington Union, and we had seats together.

Question. He was a reporter for the Intelligencer, was he?

Answer. Yes, sir.

Question. Are there any corrections made in that report?

Answer. Yes, sir.

Question. Do you see any corrections there?

Answer. Yes, sir.

Question. Is that the manuscript which was prepared in the President's office?

Answer. I think it is; I am pretty certain it is.

Question. Have you any doubt in your mind?

Answer. Not the least.

Question. Was the President there to correct it?

Answer. No, sir.

Question. Then he did not exercise that great right of revision there, did he, to your knowledge.

Answer. I did not see the President after he left the East Room.

Question. Do you know whether Colonel Moore took any memoranda of that speech?

Answer. I do not. There was quite a crowd there. I had no opportunity of observing.

Question. Will you pick out and lay aside the portions that are in your handwriting?

[The witness proceeded to do so.]

Mr. Manager BUTLER. I will give you time to do that in a moment. [To the counsel for the respondent.] Anything further with this witness?

No response.

Question. Do you think you have now all that are in your handwriting?

Answer. Yes, sir.

[Selecting certain sheets and handing them to Mr. Manager BUTLER.]

Mr. EVARTS. We will now put a few questions.

Cross-examined by Mr. EVARTS:

Question. You have selected the pages that are in your handwriting and have them before you. How large a proportion do they make of the whole manuscript?

Answer. I can hardly tell. I have not examined the rest.

Question. Well, no matter; was this whole manuscript made as a transcript from your notes?

Answer. This part that I wrote out.

Question. Was the whole?

Answer. No, sir.

Question. The whole was not made from your notes?

Answer. No, sir; Mr. Clephane wrote his part from his notes, and Mr. Smith from his.

Question. Then it is only the part that you now hold in your hands that was produced from the original stenographic notes that you have brought in evidence here?

Answer. That is all.

Question. Did you write it out yourself from your stenographic notes, following the latter with your eye, or were your notes read to you by another person?

Answer. I wrote out from my own notes, reading my notes as I wrote.

Question. Have you made any subsequent comparison of the manuscript now in your hands with your stenographic notes?

Answer. I have not.

Question. When was this completed on your part?

Answer. A very few minutes after the speech was delivered.

Question. And what did you do with the manuscript after you had completed it?

Answer. I hardly know. I sat at the table there writing it out, and I think Mr. Smith took it as I wrote out; I am not certain about that.

Question. That ended your connection with it?

Answer. That ended my connection with it. I left for New York the same night.

Question. I desire that you should leave your original stenographic notes as part of the case subject to our disposal?

Answer. Certainly.

Mr. Manager BUTLER. Put your initials upon these papers.

The WITNESS. I will do so.

[The notes were marked "J. B. S."]

Mr. Manager BUTLER. One of my associates desires me to put this question, which I suppose you have answered before: whether that manuscript which you have produced in your handwriting was a true transcript of your notes of that speech?

Answer. It was. I will not say it was written out exactly as it was spoken.

Question. What is the change, if any?

Answer. I do not know that there were any changes, but frequently in writing out we exercise a little judgment. We do not always write out a speech just as it is delivered.

Question. Is that substantially a true version of what the President said?

Answer. It is undoubtedly.

FRANCIS H. SMITH sworn and examined.

By Mr. Manager BUTLER:

Question. Are you the official reporter of the House of Representatives?

Answer. I am, sir.

Question. How long have you been so engaged?

Answer. In the position I now hold since the 5th of January, 1865.

Question. How long have you been in the business of reporting?

Answer. For something over eighteen years.

Question. Were you employed, and if so by whom, to make a report of the President's speech in August, 1866?

Answer. I was employed at the instance of one of the agents of the Associated Press at Washington.

Question. Who aided in that report?

Answer. Mr. James O. Clephane and Mr. James B. Sheridan.

Question. Did you make such report?

Answer. I did.

Question. Have you got your short-hand notes?

Answer. I have.

Question. Here?

Answer. Yes, sir.

Question. Produce them?

Answer. I will do so, [producing a note-book.]

Question. After you had made your short-hand report, what did you do then?

Answer. In company with Mr. Clephane and Mr. Sheridan I retired to one of the offices in the Executive Mansion, and wrote out a portion of my notes.

Question. What did the others do?

Answer. The others wrote other portions of the same speech.

Question. What was done with the portion that you wrote?

Answer. It was delivered to Colonel Moore, Private Secretary of the President, sheet by sheet as written by me, for revision.

Question. How came you to deliver it to Colonel Moore?

Answer. I did it at his request.

Question. What did he do with it?

Answer. He read it over and made certain alterations.

Question. Was the President present while that was being done?

Answer. He was not.

Question. Had Colonel Moore taken any memoranda of the speech, to your knowledge?

Answer. I am not aware whether he had or not.

Question. Did Colonel Moore show you any means by which he knew what the President meant to say, so that he could correct the speech?

Answer. He did not. He stated to me prior to the delivery of the speech that he desired permission to revise the manuscript, simply to correct the phraseology, not to make any change in any substantial matter.

Question. (Handing to the witness the manuscript last produced by C. A. Tinker.) Will you look and see whether you can find any portion of the manuscript that you wrote out there?

Answer. I recognize some portion of it.

Question. Separate it as quickly as you can. [The witness separated the sheets written by him.]

Answer. I find what I wrote in two different portions of the speech.

Question. Have you now got the portions, occurring, you say, in two different portions of the speech, which you wrote out?

Answer. I have.

Question. Are there any corrections on that manuscript?

Answer. There are quite a number.

Question. In whose handwriting, if you know?

Answer. In the handwriting of Colonel Moore, so far as I see.

Question. Have you written out from your notes since the speech?

Answer. I have.

Question. (handing a manuscript to the witness.) Is that it?

Answer. It is.

Question. Is that speech as written out by you a correct transcript of your notes?

Answer, (having examined the manuscript.) It is, with the exception of two important corrections, which I handed to the committee a day or two afterward. I do not see them here.

Question. Do you remember what they were?

Answer. In the sentence "I could express more by remaining silent and letting silence speak what I should and what I ought to say," I think the correction was "and letting silence speak and you infer," the words "you infer" having been accidentally omitted. The other I do not see; it is the insertion of the word "overruling" before the words "unerring Providence."

Cross-examined by Mr. EVARTS :

Question. Is the last paper that has been shown you a transcript of the whole speech?

Answer. Of the entire speech.

Question. And from your notes exclusively?

Answer. From my notes exclusively.

Question. Have you any doubt that the transcript that you made at the Executive Mansion from your notes was correctly made?

Answer. I have no doubt the transcript I made from my notes at the Executive Mansion was substantially correctly made. I remember that, having learned that the manuscript was to be revised, I took the liberty of making certain revision myself as I went along, correcting ungrammatical expressions and changing the order of words in sentences in certain instances, corrections of that sort.

Question. Those two liberties, then, you took in writing out your own notes?

Answer. Yes, sir.

Question. Have you ever made any examination to see what changes you thus made?

Answer. I have not.

Question. And you cannot now point them out?

Answer. I cannot now point them out.

Question. You have made a more recent transcript from your notes?

Answer. Yes, sir.

Question. Did you allow yourself the same liberties in that?

Answer. I did not.

Question. That, then, you consider as the notes as they are?

Answer. A literal transcript of the notes as they are, and as they were taken.

Question. Do you report by the same system of sound, phonography, as it is called, that was spoken of by Mr. Sheridan?

Answer. I hardly know what system I do report by. I studied short-hand when I was a boy going to school, a system of phonography as then published by Andrews & Boyle, which

I have used for my own purposes since then, and made various changes from year to year.

Question. Can you phonographic reporters write out from one another's notes?

Answer. I do not think any one could write out my notes except myself.

Question. Can you write out anybody else's?

Answer. Probably not, unless written with a very great degree of accuracy and care.

JAMES O. CLEPHANE recalled.

By Mr. Manager BUTLER:

Question, (handing to the witness a part of the manuscript last produced by C. A. Tinker.) You have already told us that you took the speech and wrote it out. Is what I now hand you the manuscript of your writing out?

Answer. It is.

Question. Has it any corrections upon it?

Answer. It has quite a number.

Question. Who made those?

Answer. I presume they were made by Colonel Moore. He took the manuscript as I wrote it. I cannot testify positively as regards his handwriting. I am not sufficiently familiar with it.

Question. Was that manuscript as you wrote it a correct copy of the speech as made?

Answer. I cannot say that I adhered as closely to the notes in preparing this report as I did in regard to the Chronicle.

Question. Was it substantially accurate?

Answer. It was.

Question. Did you in any case change the sense?

Answer. Not at all, sir; merely the form of expression.

Question. And the form of expression, why?

Answer. Oftentimes it tended to obscure the meaning, and for that reason it was changed; or the sentence, perhaps, was an awkward one, and it was changed to make it more readable.

Cross-examined by Mr. EVARTS:

Question. What rules of change did you prescribe to yourself in the deviations you made from your phonographic notes?

Answer. As I have said, I merely changed the form of expression in order perhaps to make the meaning more intelligible or the sentence less awkward.

Question. That is to say, when the meaning did not present itself to you as it should, you made it clearer, did you?

Answer. I will state, sir, Mr. Johnson is in the habit of using quite often——

Question. I do not ask you about Mr. Johnson. What I asked you was this: When the meaning did not present itself to you as it should, you made it clearer?

Answer. I do not know that I in any case altered the meaning.

Question. But you made the meaning clearer?

Answer. I endeavored to do so.

Question. And you did, did you not?

Answer. I cannot say whether I succeeded or not.

Question. That was one rule; what other rule of change did you allow yourself?

Answer. No other.

Question. No grammatical improvement?

Answer. Yes, sir; I may say, if you will allow me, that very often the singular verb was used where perhaps the plural ought to be.

Question. You corrected, then, the grammar?

Answer. Yes, sir; in some instances.

Question. Can you suggest any other rule of change?

Answer. I cannot at the present time.

WILLIAM G. MOORE sworn and examined.

By Mr. Manager BUTLER:

Question. What is your rank?

Answer. I am a paymaster in the Army with the rank of major.

Question. When were you appointed?

Answer. On the 14th day of November, 1866.

Question. Did you every pay anybody.

Answer. No, sir; not with Government funds. [Laughter.]

Question. What has been your duty?

Answer. I have been on duty at the Executive Mansion.

Question. What kind of duty?

Answer. I have been acting in the capacity of Secretary to the President.

Question. Were you so acting before you were appointed?

Answer. I was.

Question. How long had you acted as Secretary before you were appointed major?

Answer. I was directed to report to the President in person in the month of November, 1865.

Question. Had you been in the Army prior to that time?

Answer. I had been a major and assistant adjutant general.

Question. In the War Department?

Answer. Yes, sir.

Question. Did you hear the President's speech of the 18th of August, 1866?

Answer. I did.

Question. Did you take any notes of it?

Answer. I did not.

Question, (placing the manuscript last produced by Mr. C. A. Tinker before the witness.) Look at the manuscript which lies before you and see whether you corrected it. [The witness proceeded to examine the manuscript.] I do not care whether you corrected it all; did you correct any portion of it?

Answer. Yes, sir.

Question. Where were the corrections made?

Answer. In an apartment in the Executive Mansion.

Question. Who was in the apartment when you made the corrections?

Answer. Messrs. Francis H. Smith, James

B. Sheridan, James O. Clephane, and, I think, Mr. Holland, of the Associated Press.

Question. Had you any memorandum from the President by which to correct it?

Answer. None, sir.

Question. Do you claim to have the power of remembering, on hearing a speech, what a man says?

Answer. I do not, sir.

Question. Do you not know that the President, on that occasion, had been exercising his great constitutional right of freedom of speech?

The WITNESS. Will you repeat that question, if you please?

Question. Did you not know that on that occasion the President had been exercising his great constitutional right of freedom of speech?

Mr. CURTIS. That puts a question of law to the witness, and I do not think it is admissible?

Mr. Manager BUTLER. I am not asking a question of law, but a question of fact. [To the witness.] Did you not so understand it?

Answer. I so understood it, sir.

Mr. STANBERY. Then we are to understand the fact that it was constitutional to exercise freedom of speech?

Mr. Manager BUTLER. In the idea of the President and this witness, he thinks it is constitutional to exercise it in this way. It may be constitutional, but I think not decent.

Mr. STANBERY. That is a matter of taste.

By Mr. Manager BUTLER:

Question. Now, then, sir, how dare you correct the President's great constitutional right of freedom of speech without any memorandum to do it by?

Answer. It was an authority I assumed.

Question. How came you to assume the authority to exercise this great constitutional right for the President?

Answer. Well, that is a difficult question to answer.

Mr. EVARTS. It ought to be a difficult one to ask.

By Mr. Manager BUTLER:

Question. Why should you assume the authority to correct his speech?

Answer. My object was, as the speech was an extemporaneous one, simply to change the language, and not to change the substance.

Question. Did you change the substance anywhere?

Answer. Not that I am aware of.

Question. Are there not pages there where your corrections are the most of it?

Answer. I am not aware of that fact.

Question. Look and see if there is not a larger number of corrections on some pages?

Answer, (after examining the manuscript.) In the hasty examination that I have made I find no one page—perhaps there may be a single exception—where my writing predominates.

There is a page in which several lines are erased: but whether or not I erased them I cannot say.

Question. Do you know of anybody else that had anything to do with revising it?

Answer. No, sir.

Question. Did you do that revision by the direction of the President?

Answer. I did not, sir, so far as I can recollect.

Question. He did not direct you?

Answer. No, sir.

Question. Did you say to Mr. Smith then and there that you did it by the direction of the President?

Answer. Not that I remember.

Question. Do you mean to say that you made these alterations and corrections upon this very solemn occasion of this speech without any authority whatever?

Answer. That is my impression.

Question. After you made the revision did you show it to the President?

Answer. No, sir.

Question. Did you ever tell him that you had taken that liberty with his constitutional rights?

Answer. I cannot recall the fact that I did.

Question. What did you do with the manuscript?

Answer. The manuscript, as it was revised, was handed, I think, to the agent of the Associated Press, who dispatched it from the office in order that it might be published in the afternoon papers.

Question. Was it published in the papers?

Answer. I think it was.

Question. Have you any doubt of that?

Answer. I cannot say positively, as I have not examined the papers. That was the object.

Question. Was the speech—whether correctly or not I do not ask—but was that speech, purporting to come from the President, published in the Associated Press dispatches?

Answer. I do not know. I refer more to the city papers than to those to which the Associated Press furnished information.

Question. Was the same speech published in the Intelligencer?

Answer. The speech was published in the Intelligencer.

Question. Is that newspaper taken at the Executive Mansion?

Answer. It is.

Question. Was it at that time?

Answer. It was at that time.

Question. Seen by the President?

Answer. Yes, sir; I presume it was.

Question. Did he ever chide you, or say anything to you that you had done wrong in the correction, or had misrepresented him in this speech at all?

Answer. He did not.

Question. Even down to this day?

Answer. He has never chided or rebuked me for the correction of a speech.

Question. Has he ever said there was anything wrong about it?

Answer. I have never heard him say so.

No cross-examination.

Mr. Manager BUTLER. I now propose, with your Honor's leave and the Senate's, to read the speech as corrected by Colonel Moore, unless that is objected to. If that is objected to, I propose to put in evidence the report of Mr. Smith, the Associated Press report, and the report of the Chronicle, reading one only. You are aware, sir, that the President complains in his answer that we do not give the whole speech. We have now brought all the versions that we can conveniently of his whole speech, and if not objected to we will put them all in. Otherwise, I will only put in the extracts.

Mr. EVARTS. What version do you now offer?

Mr. Manager BUTLER. All, hoping to get the truth out of the whole of them.

Mr. EVARTS. The speech as proved now by the witnesses, in the version which passed under Colonel Moore's eye?

Mr. Manager BUTLER. I think I must ask that the objection, if any is to be taken to my offer, shall be put in writing.

Mr. EVARTS. Before it is made?

Mr. Manager BUTLER. No, sir; as it is made.

Mr. EVARTS. Well, the speech as proved in Mr. Smith's and Mr. Sheridan's copy we regard as in the shape of evidence, the accuracy of the report to be judged of, there being competent evidence on the subject. The speech in the Chronicle we do not understand to be supported by any such evidence, and we shall object to that as not authentically proved. The speech in the Intelligencer, which seems to have been supported in the intent of the honorable Managers by proof of that newspaper being taken at the Executive Mansion, has not been produced, and has not been offered, as I understand.

Mr. Manager BUTLER. No.

Mr. EVARTS. Therefore we dismiss that. The Chronicle speech, then, we consider not proved by authentic evidence submitted to the court. The stenographic reports in the two forms indicated we suppose have proof to support them, which is competent, and enable the court under competent evidence to judge of their accuracy, their accuracy to be the subject of remark, of course, as the cause proceeds, and without desiring here to anticipate the discussion as to whether any evidence concerning them (as we have excepted and objected in our answer to the tenth and eleventh articles) is admissible. Saving that for the purpose of discussion in the body of the case, we make no other objection to the reading of the speeches.

Mr. Manager BUTLER. Do you want the whole of them read? We are content with one, the others being subject to be used by either party.

Mr. EVARTS. Whichever version you put in evidence we wish read.

Mr. Manager BUTLER. We put all versions in evidence, and we will read one.

Mr. EVARTS. We should like to have the one read that you rely on.

Mr. TIPTON. Mr. Chief Justice, I move that we now take a recess of fifteen minutes.

Mr. TRUMBULL. Before that motion is put I wish to put it in the form of an adjournment until three o'clock, that we may do some legislative business. ["No, no."] There is a rule that ought to be altered, and if the Senator from Nebraska will allow me I will move that the court adjourn until three o'clock.

The CHIEF JUSTICE. The Senator from Illinois proposes that the court adjourn until three o'clock.

Mr. JOHNSON. What for?

The CHIEF JUSTICE. The Senator from Illinois will state the object of the adjournment.

Mr. JOHNSON. I think the honorable member did state the purpose, but I did not hear him.

The CHIEF JUSTICE. The Senator from Illinois states that he desires an adjournment for the purpose of taking up a rule in legislative session. You who are, in favor of adjourning until three o'clock will say "ay," the contrary opinion "no."

The motion was not agreed to.

The CHIEF JUSTICE. The question now is on the motion of the Senator from Nebraska, [Mr. TIPTON.]

Mr. DRAKE. I suggest an amendment to the motion of the Senator from Nebraska, that we take a recess for twenty minutes.

The CHIEF JUSTICE. The Chair will put the question on the longest time first. The motion is to take a recess for twenty minutes.

The motion was not agreed to.

The CHIEF JUSTICE. The question now recurs on the motion of the Senator from Nebraska, to take a recess for fifteen minutes.

The motion was agreed to; and at the expiration of fifteen minutes the Chief Justice resumed the chair, and called the Senate to order at two o'clock, and forty-five minutes p. m.

Mr. GRIMES. I move that this court stand adjourned until Monday at twelve o'clock.

Mr. CONNESS. I hope not.

Mr. DRAKE. I ask for the yeas and nays upon that motion.

The CHIEF JUSTICE. It is moved that the Senate adjourn until Monday at twelve o'clock, and on this question the yeas and nays are demanded.

The yeas and nays were not ordered.

Mr. DRAKE. The rule requires us to sit every day.

Mr. JOHNSON. No; it does not. It is "unless otherwise ordered."

The CHIEF JUSTICE. The question is on the motion to adjourn.

Mr. SUMNER. The yeas and nays have been called for.

The CHIEF JUSTICE. There was not a

sufficient number rising to demand the yeas and nays, and they were not ordered.

Mr. SUMNER. Then there was a misapprehension, if the Chair will pardon me.

The CHIEF JUSTICE. The Chief Justice will put the question again on ordering the yeas and nays.

The yeas and nays were ordered; and being taken, resulted—yeas 19, nays 28; as follows:

YEAS—Messrs. Buckalew, Corbett, Davis, Dixon, Fessenden. Fowler, Grimes, Henderson, Hendricks, Johnson, McCreery, Norton, Patterson of Tennessee, Ramsey, Saulsbury, Trumbull, Van Winkle, Vickers, and Wilson—19.

NAYS—Messrs Anthony, Cameron, Cattell, Chandler, Cole, Conkling, Conness, Cragin, Drake, Edmunds, Ferry, Frelinghuysen, Howard, Howe, Morgan, Morrill of Maine, Morrill of Vermont, Nye, Patterson of New Hampshire, Pomeroy, Ross, Sprague, Stewart, Sumner, Thayer, Tipton, Willey, and Williams—28.

NOT VOTING—Messrs. Bayard, Doolittle, Harlan, Morton, Sherman, Wade. and Yates—7.

So the motion was not agreed to.

Mr. Manager BUTLER. I now offer the version of the speech sworn to by Mr. Smith:

Speech of the President of the United States, August 18, 1866.

The President said:

Mr. Chairman, and gentlemen of the committee:—Language is inadequate to express the emotions and feelings of this occasion; and perhaps I could express more by remaining silent and letting silence speak, what I would and what I ought to say. I confess, though having had some experience in public life, having been before many public audiences—I confess the present occasion and audience is well calculated, and not only well calculated, but has in fact, partially overwhelmed me. I have not language to express, or to convey, as I have said, in an adequate manner, the feelings and emotions produced by the present occasion. In listening to the address that your distinguished and eloquent chairman has just delivered, the proceedings of the convention, as they transpired, recur to my mind, and seemingly, that I partook here of the enthusiasm which seemed to prevail there. And upon the reception of the dispatch, sent by two distinguished members of that convention, conveying in terms the scenes that have just been described, of South Carolina and Massachusetts arm in arm, marching into that convention giving evidence that the two extremes could come together, that they could peril in future, for the preservation of the Union, as they had in the past, when the accompanying statement in that vast assembly of distinguished, eloquent, and intellectual persons that were there, every face was suffused with tears—when I undertook to read the dispatch to one associated with me in office, I could not give utterance to the feelings it produced. (Applause.)

I think we may justly, conclude we are moving under proper inspirations; I think I cannot be mistaken that an unerring Providence is in this matter. The nation is imperilled; it has just passed through a mighty, bloody and momentous ordeal; and while we have passed through that we do not find ourselves free from difficulties and dangers that surround us. While our brave men have performed their duties in the field—officers and men—while they have won laurels that are imperishable, there are still greater and more important duties yet to perform; and while we have had their coöperation in the field we want their support out of the field when we are trying to bring about peace.

Every effort has been made, so far as the executive department of the Government was concerned to restore the Union; to heal the breach, to pour oil into the wound which had been inflicted, and—to speak in common phrase, to prepare, as the learned and wise physician would, a plaster that was co-extensive with the wound and that was healing in its character. (Applause.)

We think, or thought, we had partially succeeded; but as the work progressed, as reconciliation seemed to be restored and the country become united, we found a disturbing and marring element of opposition thrown in; and in making any allusion to that, I shall make no more allusion than has been in the convention and by the distinguished gentleman who has placed the proceedings of the convention before me,—I shall make no more allusion than I think the times justify. We have witnessed in one Department of the Government every effort, as it were, to prevent the restoration of peace, harmony and union; we have seen, as it were, hanging upon the verge of the Government, as it were, a body, calling or assuming to be the Congress of the United States, when it was but a Congress of a part of the States; we have seen Congress assuming to be for the Union when every step they took was to perpetuate dissolution, and make disruption permanent. We have seen every step that has been taken, instead of bringing about reconciliation and harmony, has been legislation that took the character of penalties, retaliation and revenge. This has been the course; this has been the policy of one department of your Government. The humble individual who has been addressed here to-day, and now stands here before you, has been occupying another department of the Government. The manner of his getting there I shall not allude to now—suffice it to say, I was there by the Constitution of my country (applause,) and being there by the Constitution of my country, I placed my foot upon the Constitution as the great rampart of civil and religious liberty (applause,) having been taught in early life, and having practiced it through my whole career to venerate, respect, and make the Constitution of my fathers, my guide through my public life. (Applause.)

I know it has been said, and I must be permitted to indulge in this line, that the executive department of the Government, has been despotic and tyrannical. Why, let me ask this audience here to-day, and the distinguished gentlemen who stand around me; where is the vote I evergave,—where is the speech I ever made,—where is a single act of my whole public life but what has been arrayed against tyranny and against despotism? (Applause.) What position have I ever occupied, what ground have I ever stood upon, when I failed to advocate the amelioration and elevation of the great mass of my countrymen? (Applause.)

So far as charges of that kind is concerned, it is simply intended to deceive and delude the public mind, that there is some one in power who is seeking to trample upon and pervert the principles of the Constitution by endeavoring to cover and delude the people so far as their own public acts are concerned. I have felt it my duty, in vindication of the principles of the Constitution of my country, to call their attention to these proceedings; but when we go forward and examine who has been playing tyrant, and where has been the tyranny and despotism exercised, the elements of my nature, and the pursuits of my life, has not made me in my practice aggressive, nor in my feelings; but, my nature, rather on the contrary, is defensive; and having placed my feet, or taken my stand upon the broad principles of liberty and the Constitution, there is not enough power on earth to drive me from it. [Great Applause.]

Upon that broad platform I have taken my stand. I have not been awed, or dismayed, or intimidated by their words or encroachments; but I have stood there, in conjunction with patriotic spirits, sounding the tocsin of alarm that the citadel of liberty was encroached upon. [Applause.]

I said on one occasion before, and I repeat now, that all that was necessary in this great struggle was here, in the contest with tyranny and despotism, was for the struggle to be sufficiently audible that the great mass of the American people could hear the struggle that was going on, and when they understood and heard the struggle going on, and came up, and looked in, and saw who the contestants were, and understood about what that contest was, they would settle that question upon the side of the Constitution and principle. ["Good."]

It has been said here to-day, my faith is abiding in the great mass of the people. It is, and in the darkest moment of the struggle, when the clouds seemed to be the most lowering, my faith instead of giving way, loomed up as from the gloom of the cloud, through which I saw that all would be safe in the end.

But tyranny, and despotism! We all know that tyranny and despotism even, in the language of Thomas Jefferson, can be exercised, and exercised more effectually, by many than one. We have seen Congress organized; we have seen Congress in its advance, step by step, has gradually been encroaching upon constitutional rights and violating the fundamental principles of the Government, day after day, and month after month. We have seen a Congress that seemed to forget that there was a Constitution of the Constitution of the United States, that there was limits, that there was boundaries to the sphere or scope of legislation. We have seen Congress in a a minority, assume to exercise, and have exercised powers, if carried out and consummated, will result in despotism or monarchy itself. This is truth, and because I and others have seen proper to appeal to the country, to the patriotism and republican feeling of the country, I have been denounced; slander after slander, vituperation after vituperation of the most virulent character, has made its way through the press. What then has been my sin? What has been your sin? What has been the cause of your offending? Because you dare stand by the Constitution of our fathers. [Applause.]

I look upon the proceedings of this convention as being more important than any convention that ever sat in the United States. [Applause.] When I look at that collection of citizens coming together voluntarily, and sitting in council, with ideas, with principles and views, commensurate with all the States and coextensive with the whole people; and when I contrast it with a collection of gentlemen who were trying to destroy the country, I look upon it as more important than any convention that has sat, at least, since 1787; and I think I may say here too that in the declarations that it has made, which are equally important with the Declaration of Independence itself; and I here, to-day, pronounce it a second declaration of independence. [Great applause.]

In this connection, I may remark, when you talk about declarations of independence, there are a great many people in the United States, who want to be free, that cannot claim exactly, and in fact, that they are free at this time. I may say that your address and the declarations made, are nothing more nor less than a reaffirmation of the Constitution of the United States. [Great applause.] Yes, I will go further, and say that the declarations that you have there made, and the principles enunciated in that address, is a second proclamation of emancipation to the people of the United States [applause;] for in the promulgation, in the proclamation reaffirming these great truths, you have laid down a platform, a constitutional platform, upon which all can make common cause, and stand, rallying for the restoration of the States, and the restoration of the Union without reference to whether they belong to this association, or this party or that party; but the theory is, my country rises above party. Upon this common ground they can stand. [Applause.]

How many are there in the United States, that now require to be free? They have got shackles upon their limbs and are bound, as tight as though they were in fact in slavery. Then, I repeat, it is a second proclamation of emancipation to the people of the United States, and fixes a common ground upon which all may stand.

I have said more now, Mr. Chairman, and gentlemen of the committee, than I intended to have said; but, in this connection, and in conclusion, let me ask this intelligent audience, and committee here to-day, what have I or you to do, other than the promotion or advancement of the common weal? I am opposed to egotism—as much so as any one, but here, in a conversational manner and in the reception of the proceedings of this convention, I must add, what have I to gain, consulting human ambition, more than I have gained, excepting one thing? My race is run. I have been placed here by the Constitution of the country; and I may say here, from the lowest to the highest position in the Government, I have occupied. I passed through every single position from

alderman in a village, to the Presidency of the United States; and now, in standing before you, don't you think that all reasonable ambition should be gratified? If I wanted power, if I wanted to perpetuate my own power, and that of those who are around me, how easy would it have been for me to have held the power placed in my hands.

With the bill called the Freedmen's Bureau, and the Army placed at my discretion, [laughter and applause] I could have remained at the capital with fifty or sixty millions of appropriations, with the machinery to be worked by own hands, with my satraps and dependants in every township and civil district in the United States, where it might be necessary, with the Civil Rights bill coming along as an auxiliary [laughter] and all the other patronage of the Government, I could have proclaimed myself dictator. ["That's a fact."] My pride and my power is, if I have any, to occupy that position which retains the power in the hands of the people. ["Good" and applause.] It is upon them I have always relied; it is upon them I now rely. ["And they will not desert you either"—applause.] And I repeat, neither the taunts nor jeers of Congress, nor of a subsidized and culminating press can drive me from my purpose. [Applause.]

I acknowledge no superior but two,—my God,—the author of my existence, and the people of the United States. [Applause.] The one, I try to obey all His commands as best I can, compatible with mortal man; the other, in a political and representative sense, the high behest of the people has always been in strict respect, has always been obeyed by me. [Applause.]

Mr. Chairman, I have said more than I intended to say. For the kind allusions made in the address and in the resolutions or propositions adopted by your convention, I want to say to you that in this crisis, in this period of my public life, I prize that last resolution, more than all that has come to me. To have the endorsement of a convention, constituted as that was, emanating spontaneously, from the great mass of the people, I prize it above consideration, and I trust and hope my future conduct will not cause the convention that adopted that to have regretted the assurance they have given, ["Very sure of it."]

Before separating, and leaving you, gentlemen one and all, committee and strangers, please accept my thanks for this kind manifestation of regard and respect that you have manifested, on this occasion, and to one that feels so little entitled to it, except upon the simple consideration of having performed his duty.

I repeat again, as I have said in substance, that I have, and shall always continue to be guided by a conscientious conviction. That always gives me courage. The Constitution I have made my guide. Then, accept my sincere thanks for this manifestation of your approbation and regard.

Mr. Manager BUTLER, having concluded the reading, continued: I do not propose, gentlemen, to read any more of these versions, but to leave them here for any correction that may be desired.

Mr. ANTHONY. I offered an order in legislative session, and I do not know that it is proper to call it up at this time. If not, I should like to repeat it.

The CHIEF JUSTICE. The Chief Justice thinks it is not in order to call up any business transacted in legislative session.

Mr. CONKLING, (to Mr. ANTHONY.) Offer it originally now.

Mr. ANTHONY. Then I move that the presiding officer be authorized to assign a place upon the floor to the reporter of the Associated Press.

Mr. CONKLING. A single reporter.

The CHIEF JUSTICE. The Chief Justice thinks it is not in order to interrupt the business of the trial with such a motion.

Mr. EVARTS. General BUTLER, will you allow us to ask what copies or versions of the speech of August 18, 1866, you consider included in the testimony received? One has been read.

Mr. Manager BUTLER. I consider the two copies, one that Mr. Smith made, which has been read, and the corrected version, as the substantial copies.

Mr. EVARTS. And no others?

Mr. Manager BUTLER. I do not offer the Chronicle, not because it is not evidence, but because I have the same thing in Mr. Smith's report.

Mr. EVARTS. Then it is only those two, and they will both be printed as part of the evidence in the case?

Mr. Manager BUTLER. For aught I care.

The other report offered in evidence—the one revised by Colonel Moore and published—is as follows:

MR. CHAIRMAN AND GENTLEMEN OF THE COMMITTEE: Language is inadequate to express the emotions and feelings produced by this occasion. Perhaps I could express more by permitting silence to speak and you to infer what I ought to say. I confess that, notwithstanding the experience I have had in public life, and the audiences I have addressed, this occasion, and this assemblage are well calculated to, and do overwhelm me. As I have said, I have not language to convey adequately my present feelings and emotions. In listening to the address which your eloquent and distinguished chairman has just delivered, the proceedings of the Convention, as they transpired, recurred to my mind. Seemingly I partook of the inspiration that prevailed in the Convention when I received a despatch sent by two of its distinguished members, conveying in terms the scene which has just been described of South Carolina and Massachusetts, arm in arm, marching into that vast assemblage, and thus giving evidence that the two extremes had come together again, and that for the future they were united as they had been in the past, for the preservation of the Union. When the despatch informed me that in that vast body of men, distinguished for intellect and wisdom, every eye was suffused with tears on beholding the scene, I could not finish reading the despatch to one associated with me in the office, for my own feelings overcame me. [Applause.]

I think we may justly conclude that we are moving under a proper inspiration, and that we need not be mistaken that the finger of an Overruling and Unerring Providence is in this matter. The nation is in peril. We have just passed through a mighty, a bloody, a momentous ordeal, yet do not find ourselves free from the difficulties and dangers that at first surrounded us. While our brave men have performed their duties, both officers and men (turning to General Grant, who stood at his right,) while they have won laurels imperishable, there are still greater and more important duties to perform; and while we have had their co-operation in the field, we now need their support in our efforts to perpetuate peace, [Applause.] So far as the Executive Department of the government is concerned, the effort has been made to restore the Union, to heal the breach, to pour oil into the wounds which were consequent upon the struggle, and, to speak in common phrase, to prepare as the learned and wise physician would, a plaster, healing in character and co-extensive with the wound. [Applause.] We thought, and yet think, that we had partially succeeded, but as the work progressed, as reconciliation seemed to be taking place, and the country becoming united, we found a disturbing and marring element opposing us.

In alluding to that element I shall go no further than did your Convention and the distinguished gentleman who has delivered to me the report of its proceedings. I shall make no reference to it that I do not believe the time and the occasion justify. We have witnessed in one department of the government every effort, as it were, to prevent the restoration of peace and harmony in the Union. We have seen hanging upon the verge of the government, as it were, a body called, or which assumes to be, the Congress of the United States—but, in fact, a Congress of only part of the States. We have seen this Congress assume and pretend to be for the Union, when its every step and act tended to perpetuate disunion and make a disruption of the States inevitable. Instead of promoting reconciliation and harmony, its legislation has partaken of the character of penalties, retaliation, and revenge. This has been the course and the policy of one department of your government. The humble individual who is now addressing you stands the representative of another department of the government. The manner in which he was called upon to occupy that position I shall not allude to on this occasion; suffice it to say that he is here under the Constitution of the country, and being here by virtue of its provisions, he takes his stand upon that charter of our liberties as the great rampart of civil and religious liberty. [Prolonged cheering.] Having been taught in my early life to hold it sacred, and having practiced upon it during my whole public career, I shall ever continue to reverence the Constitution of my Fathers and to make it my guide. [Hearty applause.] I know it has been said, and I must be permitted to indulge in this remark that the Executive Department of the government has been despotic and tyrannical. Let me ask this audience of distinguished gentlemen around me here to-day to point to a vote I ever gave, to a speech I ever made, to a single act of my whole public life, that has not been against tyranny and despotism. What position have I ever occupied, what ground have I ever assumed, where it can be truthfully charged that I failed to advocate the amelioration and elevation of the great masses of my countrymen? [Cries of "Never," and great applause.]

So far as charges of that kind are concerned, I will say that they are simply intended to deceive and delude the public mind into the belief that there is some one in power who is usurping and trampling upon the rights and perverting the principles of the Constitution. It is done by those who make such charges for the purpose of covering their own acts. ["That's so," and applause.] I have felt it my duty, in vindication of principle and the Constitution of my country, to call the attention of my countrymen to these proceedings. When we come to examine who has been playing the tyrant, by whom do we find that despotism has been exercised? As to myself, the elements of my nature, the pursuits of my life, have not made me, either in my feelings or in my practice, aggressive. My nature, on the contrary, is rather defensive in its character; but I will say that, having taken my stand upon the broad principles of liberty and the Constitution, there is not power enough on earth to drive me from it. [Loud and prolonged applause.] Having placed myself upon that broad platform, I have not been awed, dismayed, or intimidated by either threats or encroachments, but have stood there, in conjunction with patriotic spirits, sounding the tocsin of alarm when I deemed the citadel of liberty in danger. [Great applause.] I said on a previous occasion, and repeat now, that all that was necessary in this great struggle against tyranny and despotism was, that the struggle should be sufficiently audible for the American people to hear and properly understand. They did hear, and looking on and seeing who the contestants were and what that struggle was about, they determined that they would settle this question on the side of the Constitution and of principle. [Cries of "That's so," and applause.]

I proclaim here to-day, as I have on other occasions, that my faith is abiding in the great mass of the people. In the darkest moment of this struggle, when the clouds seemed to be most lowering, my faith, instead of giving way, loomed up through the dark cloud far beyond—I saw that all would be safe in the end. My countrymen, we all know that, in the language of Thomas Jefferson, "tyranny and despotism even can be exercised and exerted more effectually by the many than the one." We have seen a Congress gradually encroach, step by step, upon constitutional rights, and violate, day after day, and month after month, the fundamental principles of the Government. (Cries of "That's so!" and applause.) We have seen a Congress that seemed to forget that there was a Constitution of the United States, and that there was a limit to the sphere and scope of legislation. We have seen a Congress in a minority assume to exercise powers which, if allowed to be carried out, would result in despotism or monarchy itself. (Enthusiastic applause.) This is truth; and because others as well as myself have seen proper to appeal to the patriotism and republican feeling of the country we have been denounced in the severest terms. Slander upon slander, vituperation upon vituperation, of the most villanous character, has made its way through the press.

What, gentlemen, has been your and my sin? What has been the cause of our offending? I will tell you—daring to stand by the Constitution of our fathers.

[Approaching Senator JOHNSON.] I consider the proceedings of this convention, sir, as more important than those of any convention that ever assembled in the United States. (Great applause.) When I look with my mind's eye upon that collection of citizens, coming together voluntarily, and sitting in council with ideas, with principles and views commensurate with all the States, and coextensive with the whole people, and contrast it with the collection of gentlemen who are trying to destroy the country, I regard it as more important than any convention that has sat at least since 1787. (Renewed applause.) I think I may say also that the declarations that were there made are equal with the Declaration of Independence itself, and I here to-day pronounce it a second Declaration of Independence. (Cries of "Glorious," and most enthusiastic and prolonged applause.) Your address and declarations are nothing more nor less than a reaffirmation of the Constitution of the United States. (Cries of "Good!" and applause.) Yes, I will go further, and say that the declarations you have made, that the principles you have enunciated in your address, are a second proclamation of emancipation to the people of the United States—(renewed applause)—for in proclaiming and reproclaiming these great truths you have laid down a constitutional platform upon which all can make common cause, and stand united together for the restoration of the States and the preservation of the Government without reference to party. The query only is the salvation of the country, for our country rises above all party considerations or influences. (Cries of "Good!" and applause.) How many are there in the United States that now require to be free?—they have the shackles upon their limbs, and are bound as rigidly as though they were in fact in slavery? I repeat, then, that your declaration is the second proclamation of emancipation to the people of the United States, and offers a common ground upon which all patriots can stand. (Applause.)

Mr. Chairman and gentlemen: Let me, in this connection, ask you what have I to gain more than the advancement of the public welfare? I am as much opposed to the indulgence of egotism as any one, but here, in a conversational manner, while formally receiving the proceedings of this convention, I may be permitted again to ask, what have I to gain, consulting human ambition, more than I have gained, except in one thing? My race is nearly run. I have been placed in the high office which I occupy under the Constitution of the country, and I may say that I have held, from lowest to highest, almost every position to which a man may attain in our Government. I have passed through every position, from an alderman of a village to the Presidency of the United States; and surely, gentlemen, this should be enough to gratify a reasonable ambition. If I wanted authority, or if I wished to perpetuate my power, how easy would it have been to hold and wield that which was placed in my hands by the measure called the "Freedmen's Bureau bill." (Laughter and applause.) With an army which it placed at my discretion I could have remained at the capital of the nation, and with fifty or sixty millions of appropriations at my disposal, with the machinery to be worked by my own hands, with my satraps and dependants in every town and village, and then with the "Civil Rights bill" following as an auxiliary—(laughter)—in connection with all the other appliances of the Government, I could

have proclaimed myself Dictator! ("That's true," and applause.)

But, gentlemen, my pride and ambition have been to occupy that position which retains all power in the hands of the people. (Great cheering.) It is upon that I have always relied; it is upon that I rely now, (A voice—"And the people will not disappoint you.") And I repeat, that neither the taunts nor jeers of Congress, nor of a subsidized, calumniating press, can drive me from my purpose. (Great applause.) I acknowledge no superior except my God, the author of my existence, and the people of the United States. (Prolonged and enthusiastic cheering.) For the one, I try to obey all His commands as best I can compatible with my poor humanity; for the other, in a political and representative sense, the high behests of the people have always been respected and obeyed by me. (Applause.) Mr. Chairman, I have said more than I intended to say. For the kind allusions to myself contained in your address and in the resolutions adopted by the convention, let me remark that, in this crisis, and at this period of my public life, I hold above all price, and shall ever recur with feelings of profound gratification to the last resolution containing the indorsement of a convention emanating spontaneously from the great mass of the people. I trust and hope that my future action may be such that you and the convention that you represent may not regret the assurance of confidence you have expressed. ("We are sure of it.") Before separating, my friends, one and all, committee and strangers, please accept my sincere thanks for the kind manifestations of regard and respect you have exhibited on this occasion. I repeat that I shall always continue to be guided by a conscientious conviction of duty, and that always gives me courage, under the Constitution, which I have made my guide.

WILLIAM N. HUDSON sworn and examined.

By Mr. Manager BUTLER:

Question. What is your business?

Answer. I am a journalist by occupation.

Question. Where is your home?

Answer. In Cleveland, Ohio.

Question. What paper do you have charge of?

Answer. The Cleveland Leader.

Question. Where were you about the 3d or 4th of September, 1866?

Answer. I was in Cleveland.

Question. What was your business then?

Answer. I was then one of the editors of the Leader.

Question. Did you hear the speech that President Johnson made there from the balcony of a hotel?

Answer. I did.

Question. Did you report it?

Answer. I did, with the assistance of another reporter.

Question. Who is he?

Answer. His name is Johnson.

Question. Was your report published in the paper the next day?

Answer. It was.

Question. Have you a copy?

Answer. I have.

Question. Will you produce it?

[The witness produced a copy of the Cleveland Leader of September 4, 1866.]

Question. Have you your original notes?

Answer. I have not.

Question. Where are they?

Answer. I cannot tell. They are probably destroyed.

Question. Have you the report in the paper of which you are the editor, which was published the next day?

Answer. I have the report which I have submitted.

Question. What can you say as to the accuracy of that report?

Answer. It is not a *verbatim* report, except in portions. There are parts of it which are *verbatim*, and parts are synopsis.

Question. Does the report distinguish the parts which are not *verbatim* from those which are?

Answer. It does.

Question. Is all put in that Mr. Johnson did say?

Mr. EVARTS. He says not.

By Mr. Manager BUTLER:

Question. Is anything left out which Johnson said?

Answer. Yes.

Mr. EVARTS. Do you mean the President or reporter Johnson?

Mr. STANBERY. Whom do you mean by Johnson?

Mr. EVARTS. There was another Johnson mentioned.

Mr. Manager BUTLER. Not on this occasion.

Mr. EVARTS. Yes, reporter Johnson.

Mr. Manager BUTLER. I mean Andrew Johnson "last aforesaid."

Answer. The report leaves out some portions of Mr. Johnson's speech; states them in synoptical form.

. *Question.* Is there anything put in there that he did not say?

Answer. There are words used which he did not use, in stating the substance of what he said. There is nothing substantially stated that he did not state.

·*Question.* When was that report prepared by yourself?

Answer. It was prepared on the evening of the delivery of the speech.

Question. Did you see it after it was printed?

Answer. I did.

Question. Did you examine it?

Answer. I did.

Question. Now, sir, what can you say as to the accuracy of the report wherever the words are professed to be given?

Answer. To the best of my remembrance it is accurate.

· *Question.* You now believe it to be accurate?

Answer. I do.

Question. How far do you say it is accurate where substance is professed to be given?

Answer. It gives the substance—the sense without the words.

Question. Taking the synoptical part and the *verbatim* part, does the whole give the substance of what he said on that occasion?

Answer. It does.

Question. By way of illustration of what I mean, take this part: "Haven't you got the court? Haven't you got the Attorney General? Who is your Chief Justice?" Is that the synoptical part or is that the *verbatim* part?

Answer. That is part of the *verbatim* report.

Mr. Manager BUTLER, (to the counsel for the respondent.) I propose now, gentlemen, to put this in evidence.

Mr. EVARTS. We will cross-examine him before you put the paper in evidence.

Mr. Manager BUTLER. Yes, sir.

Cross-examined by Mr. EVARTS:

Question. Mr. Hudson, was this newspaper that you edited and for which you reported of the politics of the President or of the opposite opinion?

Answer. It was Republican in politics.

Question. Opposite to the views of the President, as you understood them?

Answer. It was.

Question. At what time was this speech made?

Answer. On the 3d of September, 1866.

Question. At what hour of the day?

Answer. About nine in the evening.

Question. It commenced then?

Answer. It commenced.

Question. When did it conclude?

Answer. I think about a quarter before ten.

Question. And was there a large crowd there?

Answer. There was.

Question. Of the people of Cleveland?

Answer. Of the people of Cleveland and surrounding towns.

Question. Was this balcony from which the President spoke also crowded?

Answer. Yes.

Question. And where were you?

Answer. I was upon the balcony.

Question. What convenience or arrangement had you for taking notes?

Answer. I took my notes upon my knee as I sat.

Question. Where did you get light from?

Answer. From the gas above.

Question. At what time that evening did you begin to write out your notes?

Answer. To the best of my remembrance about eleven o'clock.

Question. And when did you finish?

Answer. Between twelve and one.

Question. And when did it go to press?

Answer. About three o'clock in the morning —between three and four.

Question. Did you write the synoptical parts from your notes, or from your recollection of the drift of the speech?

Answer. From my notes.

Question. You added nothing, you think, to the notes?

Answer. Nothing.

Question. But you did not produce all that was in the notes? Is that it?

Answer. I did not.

Question. You omitted wholly some parts that were in your notes, did you not ?

Answer. I endeavored to give the substance of all the President said.

Question. You mean the meaning, do you not ?

Answer. The meaning.

Question. As you understood it?

Answer. As I understood it.

Question. That is the drift of it ?

Answer. Exactly.

Question. That is what you mean exactly. You think you meant to give the drift of the whole that you did not report *verbatim ?*

Answer. Yes.

Question. Did you not leave out any of " the drift ?"

Answer. Not intentionally.

Question. But actually ?

Answer. Not to my remembrance.

Question. Have you ever looked to see?

Answer. I have not compared the speech with any full report of it.

Question. Nor with your notes ?

Answer. I did subsequently compare the speech with my notes.

Question. Do you mean this drift part?

Answer. I mean to say that I compared the speech as reported here with my notes.

Question. I mean the part that is synoptical ; did you compare that with your notes ?

Answer. I did.

Question. When?

Answer. On the next day, and I have had occasion to refer to it several times since.

Question. When did your notes disappear ?

Answer. In the course of a few weeks. They were not preserved at all.

Question. Are you sure, then, that you ever compared it with your notes after the immediately following day ?

Answer. I am.

Question. Did you destroy your notes intentionally ?

Answer. I did not.

Question. Where are they ?

Answer. I cannot tell.

Question. In regard to the part of the speech which you say you reported *verbatim,* did you at any time, after writing it out that night, compare the transcript with the notes ?

Answer. I did.

Question. For the purpose of seeing that it was accurate ?

Answer. I did.

Question. When was that ?

Answer. That was on the next day.

Question. With whose assistance ?

Answer. I think without assistance, to the best of my remembrance.

Question. Did you find any changes necessary ?

Answer. There were typographical errors in the reading of the proof. There were no material errors.

Question. But were there no errors in your transcript from the notes ?

Answer. I may have misapprehended the question. I did not compare my manuscript transcript ; I compared the speech as printed.

Question. With what ?

Answer. With my notes.

Question. That was not my question ; but you say you did compare the speech as printed with your notes, and not with your transcript ?

Answer. Not with the transcript.

Question. Did you find that there were no errors in the print as compared with the original notes ?

Answer. There were some typographical errors.

Question. No others ?

Answer. No others to the best of my remembrance.

Question. Not a word ?

Answer. I remember no others.

Question. Were there any others ?

Answer. Not that I remember.

Question. Are you prepared to say that you observed in comparing your printed paper of that morning with your phonographic notes that the printed paper was absolutely accurate?

Answer. My notes were not phonographic.

Question. What are they?

Answer. They were made in writing.

Question. Written out in long-hand?

Answer. Yes.

Question. Do you mean to say, sir, that you can write out in long-hand, word for word, a speech as it comes from the mouth of a speaker?

Answer. I mean to say that in this instance I did parts of the speech.

Question. Then you did not even have notes that were *verbatim* except for part of the speech ?

Answer. That was all.

Question. And then you made your synopsis or drift as it went along?

Answer. Yes.

Question. How and upon what rule did you select the parts that you should report accurately and those of which you should give "the drift?"

Answer. Whenever it was possible to report accurately and fully, I did so. When I was unable to keep up with the speaker I gave the substance as I could give it. There were times during the speech when, owing to the slowness with which the speaker spoke and the interruptions, a reporter was able to keep up writing in long-hand with the remarks of the President.

Question. Then that is your report of his speech ?

Answer. It is.

Question. Not by the aid of phonography or short-hand?

Answer. No.

Question. Did you abbreviate or write in full the words that you did write?

Answer. I abbreviated in many instances.

Question. Do you remember that?

Answer. I do.

Question. Can you give us an instance of one of your abbreviations that is now written out here in full?

Answer. I cannot.

Question. You cannot recall one?

Answer. I cannot.

Question. Now, sir, without any printed paper before you, how much of President Johnson's speech, as made at Cleveland on the 3d of September, can you repeat?

Answer. I can repeat none of it.

Question. None whatever?

Answer. *Verbatim*, none.

Question. Do you think you could give "the drift" of some of it?

Answer. I think I might.

Question. As you understand it and remember it?

Answer. Yes, sir.

Question. Do you mean to be understood that you wrote down one single sentence of the President's speech, word for word, as it came from his mouth?

Answer. I do.

Question. Will you point out anywhere any such sentence?

Answer. The sentences which were read by the Manager were written out word for word.

Question. Those three questions which he read? Now, do you mean to say that any ten consecutive lines of the printed report of your newspaper you wrote down in long-hand, word for word, as they came from the President's mouth?

Answer. I cannot tell how much of it I wrote down at this distance of time. It is my impression, however, that there were as much as that, and more.

Question. Can you say anything more than this, that you intended to report as nearly as you could and as well, under the circumstances, without the aid of short-hand faculty, what the President said?

Answer. I can say, in addition to that, that there are parts of this speech which were reported as he said them.

Question. From present memory?

Answer. From memory of the method in which those notes were taken.

Question. What parts can you so state? As to all that purports to be *verbatim* are you ready so to swear?

Answer. I cannot swear that it is the absolute language in all cases. I can swear that it is an accurate report.

Question. What do you mean by an accurate report, and not an absolute report?

Answer. I mean to say a report which gives the general form of each sentence as it was uttered, perhaps varying in one or two words occasionally.

Question. I asked you just now if you could say any more than that you intended to report as well as you could under the circumstances in which you were placed and without the aid of short-hand faculty?

Answer. I can say in addition to that, that there are portions of this which are reported *verbatim*.

Question. Now, I want you to tell me whether all that purports to be *verbatim* is, in your memory and knowledge, accurately reported?

Answer. It is accurately reported; I should not say with absolute accuracy.

Question. The whole?

Answer. Yes, sir.

Question. Now, in regard to the portion of the speech that you did not profess to report *verbatim*, what assurance have you that you did not omit some part of the speech?

Answer. There are portions which are not given with entire fullness; but the substance and meaning in all cases I intended to give.

Question. What assurance have you that some portions of the speech are not omitted entirely from your synoptical view?

Answer. I was able to take notes of nearly every sentence uttered by the President, and I am confident that I did not fail to take notes of at least any paragraph of the report.

Question. Any paragraph of the speech! That is to say, you are confident that nothing that would have been a paragraph after it was printed was left out by you?

Answer. Yes, sir.

Question. He did not speak in paragraphs, did he?

Answer. Of course not.

Question. You are sure you did not leave out what would be the whole of a paragraph; did you leave out what would be half of a paragraph?

Answer. I endeavored to state the substance of the President's remarks on each subject which he took up.

Question. That is the result; that you intended to state the substance of his remarks on each subject that he took up?

Answer. Yes, sir.

Question. And you supposed that you did so?

Answer. Yes, sir.

Question. Now, was this synoptical report that you wrote out anything but your original notes that you wrote out that night?

Answer. Condensed from them.

Question. Condensed from your original notes?

Answer. Yes, sir.

Question. That is to say, your original synoptical view, as written down, was again reduced in a shorter compend by you that night?

Answer. The part of the speech so reported.

Question. And still you think that in this last analysis you had the whole of the President's speech?

Answer. I endeavored to state his meaning.

Question. Now, can you pretend to say, sir, that in respect to any of that portion of your report it is presented in a shape in which any man should be judged as coming from his own mouth?

Mr. Manager BUTLER. Stop a moment. I object to the question.

Mr. EVARTS. It is as a test of his accuracy.

Mr. Manager BUTLER.' You may ask him how accurate; I do not object to that; but whether he thinks the man should be judged upon it is not a proper question.

Mr. EVARTS. I ask him if he professes to state in this synoptical portion of the printed speech made by him it is so produced as to be properly judged as having come from the mouth of the speaker?

The WITNESS. I can only say that it gives, to the best of my belief, a fair report of what was seen.

Question. In your estimate?

Answer. In my estimate.

Question. And view?

Answer. And belief.

Question. You spoke of a reporter Johnson, who took part as I understand you, in this business; what part did he take?

Answer. He also took notes of the speech.

Question. But independently from you?

Answer. Independently of me.

Question. But the speech as printed in your paper was made from your notes, not from his?

Answer. From mine with the assistance of his?

Question. Then you brought his in also?

Answer. Yes, sir.

Question. You condensed and mingled the reporter Johnson's report and your own, and produced this printed result?

Answer. I did.

Question. What plan did Johnson proceed with in giving the drift or effect of the President's speech? Do you know?

Answer. Johnson took as full notes as possible.

Question. As possible for him?

Answer. As full notes as possible for him of the President's speech.

Question. How much of this report, or how much of this analysis or estimate of what the President said was made out of your notes and how much out of Johnson's?

Answer. The substance of the report was made from my notes, the main portion of it.

Question. What as to the rest?

Answer. Wherever Mr. Johnson's notes were fuller than mine I used them to correct mine.

Question. Was that so in many instances?

Answer. That was not so in a majority of instances.

Question. But in a minority?

Answer. In a minority.

Question. A considerable minority?

Answer. Considerable.

Question. Did Johnson write long-hand, too?

Answer. Yes.'

Question. What connection had Johnson with you or the paper?

Answer. He was the reporter of the paper.

Question. Was there no phonographic reporter to take down this speech?

Answer. There was none for our paper. There were reporters present, I believe, for other papers, but I cannot swear to that of my own knowledge.

Mr. EVARTS. We submit upon this, Mr. Chief Justice——

Mr. Manager BUTLER. Wait for a moment. I have not yet got through with the witness.

Mr. EVARTS. Go on, sir.

Reëxamined by Mr. Manager BUTLER:

Question. You have been asked, Mr. Hudson, about the crowd and the manner in which you took the speech; were there considerable interruptions?

Answer. There were.

Question. Were there considerable pauses by the President from step to step in his speech?

Answer. There were; and necessary pauses.

Question. Why " necessary?"

Answer. Because of the interruptions of the crowd.

Question. Was the crowd a noisy one?

Answer. It was.

Question. Were they bandying back and forth epithets with the President?

Mr. EVARTS. We object to that. The question is what was said.

Mr. Manager BUTLER. I do not adopt that question. I will repeat my question whether epithets were thrown back and forward between the President and the crowd.

Mr. EVARTS and Mr. CURTIS. We object to the question. The proper question is what was said.

Mr. Manager BUTLER. That is your question.

Mr. EVARTS. The question as put is leading and assuming a state of facts. It is asking if they bandied epithets. Nobody knows what "bandying" is, or what "epithets" are.

Mr. Manager BUTLER, (to the witness.) Do you know what bandying means, Mr. Witness? Do you not know the meaning of the word?

Mr. CURTIS. I suppose our objection is first to be disposed of, Mr. Chief Justice.

Mr. Manager BUTLER. I wanted to see whether, in the first place, I had got an intelligible English word. However, I withdraw the question. [A pause.] My proposition is this, sir; it is not to give language——

Mr. EVARTS. There is no objection if you have withdrawn your question.

Mr. Manager BUTLER. I have not. I have only withdrawn the question as to the meaning of a word which one of the counsel for the President did not understand. I was about, sir, stating the question. In Lord George Gordon's case, when he was upon trial, as your honor will remember, the cries of the crowd were allowed to be put in evidence as cries, though it was objected that they could not be put in evidence. But that question precisely is not raised here because I am now upon the point, not of showing what was said, not repeating language, but of showing what was said and done by way of interruption. I am following the line of cross-examination which was opened to me. It was asked what interruptions there were; whether there was a crowd there; how far he was interrupted; how far he was disturbed. If the President stopped in the midst of a speech to put back an epithet which was thrown to him from the crowd, and if the crowd was answering back and he replying, if they were answering backward and forward, a man could very well write down in long-hand what he had just said.

Mr. EVARTS. The witness stated that there were interruptions.

Mr. Manager BUTLER. And I am following that up.

Mr. EVARTS. That is the only point of your inquiry.

Mr. Manager BUTLER. I asked the nature of them to know whether they would be likely to disturb a speaker and make him pause.

Mr. EVARTS. The question to which we objected was, "Was there a bandying of epithets backward and forward between the President and the crowd?"

The CHIEF JUSTICE. The honorable Manager will be good enough to reduce his question to writing.

Mr. Manager BUTLER. I will not stop to do it in that form; but I will put it in another shape. [To the witness.] What was said by the crowd to the President, and what was said by the President to the crowd?

Answer. The President was frequently interrupted by cheers, by hisses, and by cries apparently from those opposed to him in the crowd.

Mr. Manager BUTLER, (to the witness.) You have the right to refresh your memory by any memorandum which you have, or copy of memorandum made at the time.

Mr. EVARTS. Not a copy.

Mr. Manager BUTLER. Yes, sir, any copy of a memorandum which you know is a copy made at the time; and state, if you please, what kind of epithets passed.

[The witness, placing a newspaper before him, was about to read therefrom.]

Mr. EVARTS. We do not regard the newspaper as a memorandum made at the time.

Mr. Manager BUTLER. He may refer to it.

Mr. EVARTS. Our objection is that it is not a memorandum.

Mr. Manager BUTLER. We may as well have that settled at once, if it is to be done. When a man says, "I wrote down the best I could, and put it in type within four hours of that time, and I know it was correct, for I examined it," I insist that on every rule of law in every court where any man ever practiced that is a

C. I.—14.

memorandum by which the witness may refresh his recollection.

The CHIEF JUSTICE. Do the counsel for the President object to the proof of the loss of the original notes?

Mr. EVARTS. We do not on this question. This witness is to speak by his recollection if he can; if he cannot he is allowed to refresh it by the presence of a memorandum which he made at the time.

Mr. Manager BUTLER. We deny that to be the rule of law. It may be by any memorandum which was correct at the time to his knowledge. On this point I am not without authority. In Starkie on Evidence is a reference to a case in 2 Adolphus and Ellis, 210, where it was said:

"In many cases, such as where an agent has been employed to make a plan or map and has lost the items of actual admeasurement, all he can state is that the plan or map is correct, and has been constructed from materials which he knew at the time to be true."

He has then a right to use the map or plan which he made afterward, having lost his field-notes, to refresh his memory, saying he knew them to be true. If the witness puts down these cries at the time and these interruptions and these epithets, and he is willing to state that he knows them to be true, because he copied them off from his original notes, which he has not now, he has a right to refresh his memory by that copy. I read again from Starkie:

"If the witness be correct in that which he positively states from present recollection, namely, that at a prior time he had a perfect recollection, and having that recollection, truly stated it in the document produced in writing, though its contents are thus but mediately proved, must be true."

Mr. EVARTS. If he presently recollects.

Mr. Manager BUTLER. The question now is upon his using that memorandum to refresh that recollection. We cannot be drawn from the point.

The CHIEF JUSTICE. The honorable Manager will please reduce his question to writing.

Mr. Manager BUTLER, having reduced the question to writing, read it as follows:

Question. I desire to refresh your recollection from any memorandum made by you at or near the time which you have, which you know to be correct, and from that state what was said by the crowd to the President and what he said to the crowd?

Mr. EVARTS. That question I do not object to.

Mr. Manager BUTLER, (to the witness.) Look at the memorandum and go on.

Mr. EVARTS. That is not a memorandum; it is a newspaper.

The CHIEF JUSTICE, (to the witness.) Is that a memorandum made by you at the time?

The WITNESS. This is a copy of a memorandum made by me at the time.

The CHIEF JUSTICE. Are the notes from which you made that memorandum lost?

The WITNESS. They are.

The CHIEF JUSTICE. You may look at it unless there is some objection on the part of some Senator.

Mr. JOHNSON. Mr. Chief Justice, I do not understand the question asked by the Manager.

Mr. Manager BUTLER. I do not understand the counsel for the President as objecting.

Mr. JOHNSON. I am not objecting at all; I only want to know what the question is.

The CHIEF JUSTICE. It is inquired on the part of the Managers what interruptions there were, and the witness is requested to look at a memorandum made at the time in order to refresh his memory. Of that memorandum he has no copy, but he made one at the time, and it is lost. The Chief Justice rules that he is entitled to look at a paper which he knows to be a true copy of that memorandum. If there is any objection to that ruling, the question will be put to the Senate.

Mr. Manager BUTLER, (to the witness.) Go on now, sir, beginning at the beginning.

The WITNESS, (with a newspaper before him.) The first interruption of the President by the crowd occurred on his referring to——

Mr. EVARTS. Mr. Chief Justice, we understand the ruling of the court, to which of course we submit, that the witness is allowed to refresh himself by looking at a memorandum made at the time, which this is considered equivalent to, and thereupon, state from his memory, thus refreshed, what occurred. He must swear from memory refreshed by the memorandum, and not by reading the memorandum.

Mr. Manager BUTLER. He may read the memorandum to refresh his memory and then testify.

Mr. EVARTS. Yes, sir; but not to read it aloud to us.

The CHIEF JUSTICE, (to the witness.) Look at the memorandum and then testify.

Mr. Manager BUTLER. You may read it if you please.

The WITNESS. The first interruption of the President occurred when he referred to the name of General Grant. He said that a large number in the crowd desired to see General Grant, and to hear what he had to say, whereupon there were three cheers given for General Grant. The President went on, and the next interruption occurred when he spoke of his visit, and alluded to the name of Stephen A. Douglas, at which there were cheers. The next serious interruption occurred at the time that the President used this language: "I was placed upon that ticket," the ticket for the Presidency, "with a distinguished citizen now no more;" whereupon there were cries, "It's a pity;" "Too bad;" "Unfortunate." The President proceeded to say, "Yes, I know there are some who say 'unfortunate.'"

Mr. EVARTS and Mr. CURTIS. That will not do.

Mr. Manager BUTLER. What was then done by the crowd?

The WITNESS, (consulting the newspaper.) The President went on to say that it was unfortunate for some that God rules on high and deals in justice, and there were then cheers.

Mr. EVARTS. Mr. Chief Justice, the point made by the learned Manager was this, that in following his examination of this witness, in order to prove that he had times and chances to write out in long-hand what the President had said, he could show that there were interruptions of space. That is the whole matter as I understand it, and now he is reading the President's speech, which is not yet in evidence. nor permitted to be given in evidence, as a part of the question whether there were interruptions or not to allow him to write it out.

Mr. Manager BUTLER. He is, I understand, not giving the President's speech, but he is giving such portions only as show where the interruptions come in, because he has skipped long passages. Now, when we compare these interruptions with that which he took accurately, we shall see how he had time to take *verbatim* certain portions of the speech. We go on unless stopped.

The CHIEF JUSTICE, (to the witness.) The witness will look at the memorandum, and then testify as well as he can from his present recollection.

Mr. Manager BUTLER, (to the witness.) Go on, sir, from where you left off.

The WITNESS. The next interruption occurred where the President remarked that if his predecessor had lived——

Mr. EVARTS. The question is of the interruption and its duration and form, not of its being when the President said this or that, or what he said.

Mr. Manager BUTLER. I beg your pardon. I put the question, and it was expressly said there was no objection to it, "What did the President say to the crowd and what did the crowd say to the President?" That was not objected to, but it was said, "That is what we want." I put it in writing, and the writing is on the desk, that I want what the crowd said to the President and what the President said to the crowd. That was not objected to. [To the witness.] Go on, sir.

The WITNESS. When this remark was made the crowd responded "Never," "Never," and gave three cheers for the Congress of the United States. The President went on: "I came here as I was passing along, and having been called upon for the purpose of exchanging views and ascertaining if we could "——

The CHIEF JUSTICE. Mr. Manager, do we understand that this witness is to read the speech?

Mr. Manager BUTLER. No, sir; he is not reading the speech; he is skipping whole paragraphs, whole pages of it almost; it is only where the interruptions come in. [To the witness.] Now just read the last words before the interruptions come in, if you please, which will bring out all we want, and that will save all trouble.

The WITNESS. When the President remarked that he came here for the purpose of ascertaining, if he could, who was wrong and responsible, the crowd said: "You are," and there were long continued cries. The President inquired, later in the speech, who could place his finger upon any act of the President's deviating from right, whereupon there were cheers and counter-cries of "New Orleans" long continued; and that cry was repeated, frequently breaking the sentences of the President into clauses, and at the close of each sentence it was of some length. At the same time there were cries, "Why don't you hang Jeff. Davis?" The President responded, "Hang Jeff. Davis!" Then there were shouts and cries of "Down with him," and there were other cries of "Hang Wendell Phillips." The President asked, "Why don't you hang him?" There were answers given, "Give us an opportunity?" The President went on to ask: "Haven't you got the court? Haven't you got the Attorney General? Who is your Chief Justice, who has refused to sit on his trial?" He was then interrupted by "groans and cheers." He went on to speak of calling upon Congress, "that is trying to break up the Government"——

Mr. STANBERY. Stop.

Mr. Manager BUTLER, (to the witness.) Well, sir, state what took place then?

The WITNESS. When he said, "I called upon your Congress, that is trying to break up the Government" there were cries of "A lie" from the crowd, hisses, and voices cried "Don't get mad," and the President responded "I am not mad." There were then hisses. After a sentence or two there were three more cheers given for Congress. Then after another sentence voices cried "How about Moses?"

Question. What next?

Answer. The next interruption I find noted here——

Mr. EVARTS. That is not what you are to testify to; not what you find there, but what you remember.

Mr. Manager BUTLER. The question is whether after seeing it you can remember it to tell it to us?

Answer. The next interruption, I remember, was a cry of "Yes," when the President inquired "Will you hear me." These cries were taken up and were repeated sometimes for several minutes. There was all this time great confusion, cheers by the friends of the President, and counter-cries by those apparently opposed to him. The President repeated his question asking if the people would hear him for his cause and for the Constitution of his country, and there were again cries "Yes, yes," "Go on." He proceeded in the next sentence to inquire whether in any circumstances he ever violated the Constitution of the country, to which there were cries in response of "Never, never," and

counter cries. The interruptions continued. When Mr. Seward's name was mentioned there was a voice "God bless him," and cheers for Mr. Seward. He said that he would bring Mr. Seward before the people, show them his gaping wounds and bloody garments and ask who was the traitor. There were cries of "Thad. Stevens," when the President asked "Why don't you hang Thad. Stevens and Wendell Phillips?" and there were cheers and hisses. The President proceeded to say that, having fought traitors at the South, he would fight them at the North, when there were cheers and hisses, and there were also cries. when the President said that he would do this with the help of the people, "We won't give it." The interruptions continued in the shape of cheers and hisses and cries of the same sort throughout the speech.

Question. Were those cries and cheers and hisses continued so as to make the interruption go on for some time?

Answer. Frequently for several minutes.

Question. In that time would you be enabled to get up with him and get your report out?

Answer. I was able to make during most of these a *verbatim* report of what the President said.

Re-cross-examined by Mr. EVARTS:

Question. You made a memorandum at the time of these interruptions?

Answer. I did.

Question. Of these cries and hisses?

Answer. I did.

Question. And while you were doing that you could catch up with reporting the President's speech, could you?

Answer. Yes, sir.

Question. Now, sir, have you not in every statement that you have made of these interruptions read from that newspaper before you?

Answer. I have read from the newspaper some. I think that every one was in the newspaper.

Question. Are you not quite sure of it?

Answer. I will not be positive.

Question. Not positive but that you remember some that are not in the newspaper?

Answer. Possibly.

Question. Have you forgotten any that were in the newspaper?

Answer. No. I have not given all that occurred in the newspaper.

Question. Without that newspaper, do you recollect any of those interruptions?

Answer. I do.

Question. All of them?

Answer. I should not be able to give all of them without the aid of the memorandum.

Question. Did you not make a full report of these interruptions on your notes?

Answer. I did.

Question. Of all that the crowd said?

Answer. Not of all that they said.

Question. Why not of all that they said?
Answer. Of all that I was able to catch.
Question. All that you could put down?
Answer. Yes.
Question. You got all that you could put down, and you left out some of what they said because you had not time to put it down; and yet you were catching up with the President?
Answer. I gave my first attention to reporting the President. Whatever time I had for putting down cries besides that I did so.

By Mr. Senator GRIMES:

Question. I desire the witness to specify the particular part of the report, as published, which was supplied by the reporter Johnson?
Answer. It is impossible for me to do that at this time.

Mr. Manager BUTLER. If the Senator will allow me, I will ask the witness whether any special part of the report itself was supplied by Johnson or whether it was only corrected by Johnson's notes?

The WITNESS. The report was made out from my notes, corrected by Mr. Johnson's notes. I cannot say whether there were entire sentences from Mr. Johnson's notes or not.

By Mr. Manager BUTLER:

Question. I will ask you whether there can be such practice in reporting as to enable a person by long-hand to make out a substantially accurate report?

Mr. EVARTS. To that we object. You can ask whether this witness by his practice can do it, not whether other people can do it.

Mr. Manager BUTLER, (to the witness.) Have you had such practice?
Answer. I have had considerable practice in reporting in this way, and can make out a substantially accurate report.

[The witness, at the request of the honorable Manager, put his initials on the newspaper to which he had referred, the Cleveland Leader of September 4, 1866.]

DANIEL C. McEWEN sworn and examined.

By Mr. Manager BUTLER:

Question. What is your profession?
Answer. Short-hand writer.
Question. How long has that been your profession?
Answer. For about four or five years, I should judge.
Question. Were you employed in September, 1866, in reporting for any paper?
Answer. I was.
Question. What paper?
Answer. The New York World.
Question. Did you accompany Mr. Johnson and the presidential party when they went to lay the corner-stone of a monument in honor of Mr. Douglas?
Answer. I did.
Question. Where did you join the party?
Answer. I joined the party at West Point, New York.

Question. How long did you continue with the party?
Answer. I continued with them till they arrived at Cincinnati, on their return.
Question. Did you go professionally as a reporter?
Answer. I did.
Question. Had you accommodation in the train as such?
Answer. I had.
Question. The *entrée* of the President's car?
Answer. I had.
Question. Were you at Cleveland?
Answer. I was.
Question. Did you make a report of his speech at Cleveland from the balcony?
Answer. I did.
Question. How, phonographically or stenographically?
Answer. Stenographically.
Question. Have you your notes?
Answer. I have.
Question. Here?
Answer. Yes, sir.
Question. Produce them. [The witness produced a memorandum-book.] Have you, at my request, copied out those notes since you have been here?
Answer. I have.
Question, (exhibiting a manuscript to the witness.) Is that the copy of them?
Answer. It appears to be.
Question. Is that an accurate copy of your notes?
Answer. It is.
Question. How accurate a report of the speech is your notes?
Answer. My notes are, I consider, very accurate so far as I took them. Some few sentences in the speech were interrupted by confusion in the crowd, which I have indicated in making the transcript, and the parts about which I am uncertain I inclose in brackets.
Question. Where you have not inclosed in brackets, how is the transcript?
Answer. Correct.
Question. Was your report published?
Answer. I cannot say. I took notes of the speech, but owing to the lateness of the hour—it was eleven o'clock or after—it was impossible for me to write out a report of the speech and send it to the paper which I represented. Therefore I went to the telegraph office after the speech was given and dictated some of my notes to other reporters and correspondents, and we made a report which we gave to the agent of the Associated Press, Mr. Gobright.
Question. Did the agent of the Associated Press accompany the presidential party for a purpose?
Answer. Yes, sir.
Question. Was it his business and duty to forward reports of speeches?
Answer. I supposed it to be.
Question. Did you so deal with him?
Answer. I did.

Question. Have you put down the cheers and interruptions of the crowd or any portion of them?

Answer. I have put down a portion of them. It was impossible to take them all.

Question. State whether there was a good deal of confusion and noise there?

Answer. There was a great deal of it.

Question. Exhibition of ill-feeling and temper?

Answer. I thought there was.

Question. On the part of the crowd?

Answer. On the part of the crowd.

Question. How on the part of the President?

Answer. He seemed a little excited.

Question. Do you remember anything said there to him by the crowd about keeping his dignity?

Answer. I have not it in my notes.

Question. Do you remember it?

Answer. I do not remember it from hearing.

Question. Was anything said about not getting mad?

Answer. Yes, sir.

Question. Did the crowd caution him not to get mad?

Answer. The words used were, "Don't get mad, Andy."

Question. Was he then speaking in considerable excitement or otherwise? Did he appear considerably excited at that moment when they told him not to get mad?

Mr. EVARTS. That is not any part of the present inquiry, which is to verify these notes, to see whether they shall be in evidence or not.

Mr. Manager BUTLER. I understand; but I want to get as much as I can from memory and as much as I can from notes, and both together will make a perfect transcript of the scene.

Mr. EVARTS. But the present inquiry, I understand, is a verification of notes. Whenever that is abandoned and you go by memory let us know it.

Mr. Manager BUTLER. The allegation is that it was a scandalous and disgraceful scene. The difference between us is that the counsel for the President claim the freedom of speech and we claim the decency of speech. We are now trying to show the indecency of the occasion. That is the point between us, and the surroundings are as much part of the occasion as what was said.

Mr. EVARTS. I understand you regard the freedom of speech in this country to be limited to the right of speaking properly and discreetly.

Mr. Manager BUTLER. Oh, no. I regard freedom of speech in this country the freedom to say anything by a private citizen in a decent manner.

Mr. EVARTS. That is the same thing.

Mr. Manager BUTLER. Oh no.

Mr. EVARTS. And who is the judge of the decency?

Mr. Manager BUTLER. The court before whom the man is tried for breaking the laws of decency.

Mr. EVARTS. Did you ever hear of a man being tried for freedom of speech in this country?

Mr. Manager BUTLER. No; but I have seen two or three women tried; I never heard of a man being tried for it before. [Laughter.] [To the witness.] I was asking you whether there was considerable excitement in the manner of the President at the time he was cautioned by the crowd not to get mad?

Answer. I was not standing where I could see the President. I did not notice his manner; I only heard his tone of voice.

Question. Judging from what you saw and heard?

Answer. I did not see the President.

Question. What you heard?

Answer. He seemed excited; I do not know what his manner is from personal acquaintance when he is angry.

Mr. Manager BUTLER, (to the counsel for the respondent.) The witness is yours, gentlemen.

Mr. EVARTS. Do you propose to offer this report of the speech?

Mr. Manager BUTLER. I do.

Mr. EVARTS. Very well; then I will cross-examine the witness.

Cross-examined by Mr. EVARTS:

Question. Did you report the whole of the President's speech?

Answer. No, sir. The hour was late and I left shortly before the close; I do not know how long before he closed his speech.

Question. So your report does not profess to be of the whole of the speech?

Answer. No, sir.

Question. From the time that he commenced till the point at which you left off did you report the whole of his speech?

Answer. No, sir. Certain sentences were broken off by the interruptions of the crowd, as I before stated.

Question. But aside from the interruptions, did you continue through the whole tenor of the speech till the point at which you left?

Answer. I did.

Question. Did you make a report of it word for word as you supposed?

Answer. Yes, sir; as I understood the speech.

Question. And did you attempt to include, word for word, the interruptions of the assemblage?

Answer. I did. I took what appeared to be the principal exclamations of the crowd; I could not hear all of them.

Question. When did you make the copy or transcript that you produce here?

Answer. I made that about two weeks since, after I was summoned before the Managers of the impeachment, and gave evidence concerning the speech there.

Question. Can you be as accurate or as confident in a transcript made after a lapse of two years as if it had been made presently, when the speech was fresh?

Answer. I generally find that when a speech is fresh in my mind I read the notes with more readiness than when they become old; but as to the accuracy of the report I think I can make as accurate a transcript of the notes now as at that time.

Question. When you transcribe after the lapse of time you have nothing to help you except the figures that are before you in your notes?

Answer. That is all, with me.

Question. Are you not aware that in phonographic reporting there is frequent obscurity in the haste and brevity of the notation?

Answer. There sometimes is.

By Mr. Manager BUTLER:

Question. I observe that the counsel on the other side asked for the politics of the Leader. May I ask you for the politics of the World?

Answer. I have understood them to be Democratic.

EVERETT D. STARK sworn and examined.

By Mr. Manager BUTLER:

Question. What is your profession?

Answer. I practice law now.

Question. What was your profession in September, 1866?

Answer. I practiced law then.

Question. Where?

Answer. In Cleveland. I may say I was formerly a short-hand reporter, and do more or less of it now in law business.

Question. Did you report the speech of Andrew Johnson, President of the United States, from the balcony of the Cleveland Hotel on the night of the 3d of September, 1866?

Answer. Yes, sir.

Question. For what paper?

Answer. For the Cleveland Herald.

Question. Did you take it in short-hand?

Answer. I did.

Question. Was it written out by you and published?

Answer. It was.

Question. Was it published as written out by you?

Answer. Yes, sir.

Question. Have you your short-hand notes?

Answer. I have not.

Question. Are they in existence?

Answer. I suppose not. I paid no attention to them. I suppose they were thrown into the chip-basket.

Question. Did you ever compare the printed speech in the Herald with your notes for any purpose, or with the manuscript?

Answer. I did with the manuscript that night. That is, I compared the slips of proofs that were furnished with the copy as I took it from the original notes.

Question. How did it compare?

Answer. It was the same.

Question. Were the slips of proofs the same as the paper published the next day?

Answer. Just the same with such typographical corrections as were made there.

Question. Have you a copy of the paper?

Answer. I have.

Question. Will you produce it? [The witness produced a copy of the Cleveland Herald of September 4, 1866.] Can you now state whether this is a substantially accurate report in this paper of what Andrew Johnson said the night before?

Answer. Yes, sir; it is generally. There are some portions there that were cut down, and I can point out just where those places are.

Question. By being "cut down" do you mean the substance given instead of the words?

Answer. Yes, sir.

Question. Does it appear in the report which are substantial and which are the *verbatim* parts?

Answer. Not to any other person than myself, as I can tell from my recollection.

Question. Can you point out that which is substantial, and that which is accurate in the report?

The WITNESS. Do you wish me to go over the whole speech for that purpose?

Mr. Manager BUTLER. I will for the present confine myself to such portions as are in the articles. If my learned friends want you to go over the rest they will ask you.

The WITNESS. Commencing a little before where the specification in the articles of impeachment begins, I can read just what Mr. Johnson said at that point.

Question. Do so.

Answer, (reading.) "Where is the man living, or the woman, in the community, that I have wronged, or where is the person that can place their finger upon one single hair-breadth of deviation from one single pledge I have made, or one single violation of the Constitution of the country? What tongue does he speak? What religion does he profess? Let him come forward and place his finger upon one pledge I have violated." There there was some interruption by the crowd, and various remarks were made, of which I have noted one, because only one did Mr. Johnson pay any attention to, and that was a voice that cried "Hang Jeff. Davis." The President said, "Hang Jeff. Davis? Hang Jeff. Davis? Why don't you?" There was then some applause and interruption, and he repeated "Why don't you?" and there was again applause and interruption; and the President went on, "Have not you got the court? Have not you got the court," repeating it twice. "Have not you got the Attorney General? Who is your Chief Justice—and that refused to sit upon the trial?" There was then interruption and applause, and he went on to say: "I am not the prosecuting attorney; I am not the jury; but I will tell you what I did do: I called upon your Congress that is trying to break up the Government"—— At that point there was interruption and confusion, and there may have been words there uttered by the President that I did not hear, but I think not. "Yes, did your Congress order hanging Jeff. Davis?" and then there was confusion and applause. And then the President went on to say, "But let prejudices pass," and so on.

Question. Will you now come toward the conclusion of the other point mentioned in the specifications, and state whether you reported that accurately?

Answer. Commencing a little before where the specification is of the speech he said: "In bidding you farewell here to-night, I would ask you with all the pains Congress has taken to calumniate and malign me, what has Congress done? Has it done anything to restore the Union of the States? But, on the contrary, has it not done everything to prevent it? And because I stand now as I did when the rebellion commenced I have been denounced as a traitor. My countrymen, here to-night, who has suffered more than I? Who has run greater risk? Who has borne more than I? But Congress, factious, domineering, tyrannical Congress, has undertaken to poison the minds of the American people and create a feeling against me"—so far Mr. Johnson's words, and I concluded the sentence here in this fashion—"in consequence of the manner in which I have distributed the public patronage." These were not Mr. Johnson's words, but contained in a summary way the reasons that he gave just at that point for his action.

Mr. EVARTS, (to the Managers.) Do you propose to offer this report of the Cleveland speech also?

Mr. Manager BUTLER. I propose to read one and offer all, so that the President may have the privilege of collating them in order to have no injustice done him as to what he said.

Mr. EVARTS. We do not claim any privileges of that kind; on the contrary, we propose to object to all of them that they are not properly proved.

Mr. Manager BUTLER. Certainly. I observed that the President objected in his answer that we did not put in all he said, and I mean to do the best I can in that regard now.

Mr. EVARTS. That is exactly what we desire, if anything is to come in. Now, I will proceed with the witness.

Cross-examined by Mr. EVARTS:

Question. You have a newspaper report here?

Answer. I have.

Question. And that is all you have?

Answer. That is all the memorandum I have.

Question. The only memorandum is the newspaper report?

Answer. The newspaper report.

Question. What is the date of the newspaper?

Answer. September 4, 1866.

Question. Did you make a stenographic report of the whole of the President's speech?

Answer. I did with one exception.

Question. What exception is that?

Answer. It was a part of what he said about the Freedmen's Bureau. Somewhere about the commencement of, I should say, the latter half of his speech by time, he went somewhat into details and figures which I omitted to take down.

Question. Did you write out your notes in full?

Answer. No, sir.

Question. You never did that?

Answer. I never did that.

Question. And you have not now either the notes or any transcript of them?

Answer. Only this.

Question. You have got a newspaper; I understand that. Now, did you prepare for the newspaper the report that is there contained?

Answer. I did.

Question. And you prepared it on the plan of some part *verbatim* and some part condensed?

Answer. Yes, sir.

Question. What was your rule of condensation and the motive of it.

Answer. I had no definite rule that I can give. The reason why I left out a part of what he said of the Freedmen's Bureau was——

Question. That was not condensed at all, was it?

Answer. That part was not taken. That I did take was somewhat condensed.

Question. I am only asking about what you did take, not what you did not take. What was your rule in respect to what you put *verbatim* into your report and what you condensed? How did you determine which parts you would treat in one way or the other?

Answer. Well, sir, perhaps I was influenced somewhat by what I considered would be a little more spicy or entertaining to the reader.

Question. In which interest, that of the President or his opponents?

Answer. Well, I do not know that.

Question. Which side were you on?

Answer. I was opposed to the President.

Question. But you do not know which you thought the interest was you selected the spicy part for?

Answer. I was very careful of those parts that occasioned considerable excitement or interest in the crowd, in his hearers, to take them down carefully, as he said them.

Question. The parts that the crowd were most interested in you thought you would take down carefully?

Answer. With more particularity.

Question. And the parts that they were interested in, as you observed, were those that they made the most outcry about? Was it not so?

Answer. Yes, sir; partially so.

Question. That was your judgment and guide?

Answer. Considerably.

Question. Now, in regard to the condensed part of your report, are you able to say that there is a single expression in that portion of your report which was used by the President, so that the words as they came from his mouth were there set down?

Answer. No, sir; I think it is not the case in those particular points that I condensed. I did so by the use, in some part, of my own words.

Question. And for compression of space, did you not?

Answer. Yes, sir; primarily.

Question. Was not your rule for condensation partly when you had got tired of writing out?

Answer. No, sir.

Question. Not at all?

Answer. One reason was it was getting on between three and four o'clock, and I was directed to cut down toward the last, and I did so more toward the last than I did in the earlier parts of the speech.

Question. In order to be ready for the press?

Answer. In order to be ready for the morning press.

Mr. EVARTS. We object to this report as a report of the President's speech.

Mr. Manager BUTLER, (to the witness.) Mark it with your initials and leave it on the table. [The witness marked with his initials "E. D. S." the copy of the Cleveland Herald referred to by him.] I forgot to ask you what are the politics of the Herald.

The WITNESS. It was at that time what we called "Johnson Republican." Some called it "Post Office Republican." The editor of the Herald had the post office at that time.

Mr. Manager BUTLER. I propose now, sir, to offer as the foundation, as the one upon which I rely, the Leader's report as sworn to by Mr. Hudson, the first witness as to this speech.

Mr. EVARTS. That we object to; and the grounds of objection, made manifest doubtless to the observation of the Chief Justice and the Senators, are greatly enhanced when I find that the managers are in possession of the original minutes of a short-hand reporter of the whole speech and his transcript made therefrom and sworn to by him. We submit that to substitute for this evidence of the whole speech, upon this mode of authentication, the statement of Mr. Hudson upon the plan and theory as testified to by him, is contrary to the first principles of justice in evidence. He has not said how much is his and how much is the reporter Johnson's, and it is in considerable part condensed, a statement of "drift," determined by circumstances, not of the President's utter-

ance. The same objection will be made if this second or Cleveland Herald report is presented.

Mr. Manager BUTLER. I do not propose to argue the question. Suppose we were trying any other case for substantive words, would not this be a sufficient proof? I do not propose to withdraw the other report of Mr. McEwen. I propose to put it in, subject to comment, to be read if these gentlemen desire it read, and the other report, so that we may have all three reports: the Post office report, the Republican report, and the Democratic report. A natural leaning makes me lean to this particular report as the one which I mean shall be the standard report, because it is sworn to expressly by the party as having been written down by himself, published by himself, and corrected by himself, and I am only surprised that there should be objection to it.

Mr. EVARTS. Nothing can better manifest, Mr. Chief Justice, the soundness of our objection than the statement of the Manager. He selects by preference a report made by and through the agency of political hostility, and on the plan of condensation, and on the method of condensing another man's notes, the amount and quality relatively not being discerned, instead of a sworn report by a phonographer who took every word and brings his original notes transcribed and brings his transcription and swears to their accuracy; and here deliberately, in the face of this testimony as to what was said, thus authentically taken and authentically preserved and brought into court to be verified, the honorable Manager proposes to present, as of the speech in its production, the notes framed and published in the motive, and with the feeling and under the influence and in the method, that has been stated. We object to it as evidence of the words spoken.

Mr. Manager BUTLER. If, Mr. President and Senators, I had not lived too long in this world to be astonished at anything, I should have been surprised at the tone in which this proposition is argued. Do I keep back from these gentlemen anybody's report? Do I not give them all reports—everything I can lay my hand on? Am I obliged to go into the enemy's camp? Shall I not use the report of my friends and not of my enemies, and then give them an opportunity of having the reports of my enemies to correct that of my friends? Is all virtue, all propriety in the Democratic report? Can that never be wrong? At one time I think President Johnson, if I remember, would not like to have had me put in the "World's" report of him; and when they changed exactly I do not know. I have offered this report—why? Because this is the fullest complete report. The reason why I did not rely upon Mr. McEwen's report is that he testified on the stand that he got tired and went away and did not report the whole speech; but this is a report of the whole speech, and the only report which purports to be a report of the whole speech. Mr. Stark's report, as he says, left out a portion. Mr. McEwen expressly swear she left out a portion. Hence I cannot put them in, or if I offered to do so I should be met with the objection, "You do not put in the whole speech." I do choose the report which the witness swears is a complete report of the speech except so far as he synopsized; and then, so far as the other two reports go, I bring them in here to correct it, so that the President shall take no detriment. Oh, how he stickles now for exactness! The President was willing that Mr. Moore should make a speech for him on the 18th of August, and that went out. Now, then, here are three reports, representing the three unfortunate divisions of opinion on this question; and we offer them all to the counsel. We say which we prefer, and then he almost berates us, as much as his courtesy will allow him to do, because we choose our friends, and I am glad to say not his. The question is not of competency but of weight of evidence, and has simply been argued so. [Mr. EVARTS rose.] I ask that there may be a decision. I think I have the close sometimes, sir.

Mr. EVARTS. Not on our objection.

Mr. Manager BUTLER. I beg your pardon; it is on my offer.

Mr. EVARTS. Our objection.

Mr. Manager BUTLER. No; my offer.

The CHIEF JUSTICE. Do the counsel desire to be heard further?

Mr. Manager BUTLER. Does not the presiding officer think we have the close?

The CHIEF JUSTICE. The counsel for the respondent have not exhausted their hour.

Mr. Manager BUTLER. Have we got to keep on in order to get the close until we occupy our whole hour?

The CHIEF JUSTICE. The rule of the Senate is that each side shall have an hour.

Mr. Manager BUTLER. Be it so. I can even get on with that rule.

Mr. EVARTS. Discredit is now thrown upon the most authentic report, first by an observation that it omits a part of the speech, and secondly by a suggestion that it has but Democratic responsibility. There you have it fairly and squarely, that it is not on the accuracy of phonography nor on the honesty of transcription, but on the color of the mind through which the President's speech is to be run, and by double condensation reproduced to the tone and the temper of a party print. There is precisely that condensation in the first original notes of Mr. Hudson, and condensation then from those notes into the space that the newspaper takes, and is offered confessedly on the principle of selection by the learned Managers have adopted of preferring what they consider a friendly report. Mr. Chief Justice and Senators, I have read neither of them. I did not know before that the question of whether the authenticity of stenography was reliable depended upon the political opinions of the stenographer. We submit that there is no proper evidence; there is no living witness that by memory can produce the President's speech, and there is no such authentication of notes in any case but Mr. McEwen's that makes the published speeches evidence.

Mr. Manager BUTLER. I shall not debate the matter further. I rise simply to say that I have made no such proposition. I think this is an accurate report so far as we have put it into the articles. It is an accurate report, a sworn accurate report, and by a man whom we can trust and do trust. The others, we think, are just as accurate perhaps; that we do not go into; we simply put them forward, so that if there is any change the President may have the benefit of it. He comes in here in his answer and says that we will not give him the full benefit of all he said; and then, when we take great pains here to bring everybody that made a report that we can hear of in this case and we offer them all, he says we must take a given one. To that we answer we take the one that has the whole speech. And now I will test the question: if the gentlemen will agree not to object to McEwen's report, because it is not a report of the whole speech, I will take that.

Mr. EVARTS. We will not make that objection.

Mr. Manager BUTLER. Very good; put it in then.

The CHIEF JUSTICE. The honorable Manager then withdraws his proposition to read the Cleveland Leader?

Mr. Manager BUTLER. No, sir; I am going to read this and put in both the others as evidence, with your leave. I will take this as the standard copy.

Mr. HOWARD. Mr. President, if the Managers have no objection to it, I desire to move that the trial be postponed until to-morrow at the usual hour, for the purpose of enabling the Senate to transact some business.

Mr. CONKLING and others. Let us finish this matter.

Mr. HOWARD. I withdraw my motion for the present.

Mr. Manager BUTLER. Mr. Clerk, will you have the kindness to read this? [handing to the Chief Clerk the Cleveland Leader of September 4, 1866.]

Mr. EVARTS. The honorable Managers will correct us if we are in error in supposing that when I had made manifest our objections to the imperfect reports, as matter of lawful right on our part to object, the Managers said that if we would not object to McEwen's for incompleteness they would put that in as the report of the speech. Now, it seems, they propose to put the others in also.

Mr. Manager BUTLER. We want to be fully understood, so that we shall have no mistake. We put this in as the standard. We put in the other two, so that if the President comes in here with witnesses to say it is not true, (because all things are possible,) then we shall have the additional authentication of the other two reports.

Mr. EVARTS. The learned Manager is familiar enough with the course of trials to know that it will be time enough for him to bring forth these additional copies to contradict this movement of ours when we make it.

Mr. Manager BUTLER. I never knew that was the way. Will you allow this to be read, or do you still make any objection? I claim that they shall all go in.

Mr. EVARTS. We object to the two copies from newspapers.

Mr. Manager BUTLER. Very good. I ask that that question be decided, then. We say they all go in.

The CHIEF JUSTICE, (to the Managers.) You offer the Cleveland Leader first?

Mr. Manager BUTLER. I offer the whole three at once.

The CHIEF JUSTICE. The Chief Justice will not put the question upon all three at once unless so directed by the Senate.

Mr. Manager BUTLER. Under the direction of the presiding officer, I will offer first the Leader, and ask a vote on that.

The CHIEF JUSTICE. The Managers offer a report made in the Leader newspaper of Cleveland, as evidence in the cause. It appears from the statement of the witness, Hudson, that the report was not made by him wholly from his own notes, but from his own notes and the notes of another person whose notes are not produced, nor is that person himself produced for examination. Under these circumstances the Chief Justice thinks that that paper is inadmissible. Does any Senator desire a vote of the Senate on the question?

Mr. DRAKE. I ask for a vote on the question, sir.

Mr. Manager BUTLER. I supposed this question was to be decided without debate.

The CHIEF JUSTICE. It is. Senators, you who are of opinion that the Leader newspaper is admissible in evidence——

Mr. CONNESS and Mr. SUMNER called for the yeas and nays; and they were ordered.

The CHIEF JUSTICE. Senators, you who are of opinion that the Leader newspaper is admissible in evidence will, as your names are called, answer "yea;" those of the contrary opinion, "nay."

The question being taken by yeas and nays, resulted—yeas 35, nays 11; as follows:

YEAS—Messrs. Anthony, Cameron, Cattell, Chandler, Cole, Conkling, Conness, Corbett, Cragin, Drake, Edmunds, Ferry, Fessenden, Frelinghuysen, Henderson, Howard, Johnson, Morgan, Morrill of Maine, Morrill of Vermont, Norton, Nye, Patterson of New Hampshire, Pomeroy, Ramsey, Ross, Sherman, Sprague, Stewart, Sumner, Thayer, Tipton, Van Winkle, Willey, and Williams—35.

NAYS—Messrs. Buckalew, Davis, Dixon, Doolittle, Fowler, Hendricks, Howe, McCreery, Patterson of Tennessee, Trumbull, and Vickers—11.

NOT VOTING—Messrs. Bayard, Grimes, Harlan, Morton, Saulsbury, Wade, Wilson, and Yates—8.

The CHIEF JUSTICE. On this question the yeas are 35, and the nays are 11. So the report of the Leader is admitted in evidence.

Mr. Manager BUTLER. I now offer also the report of Mr. McEwen. Is that objected to?

Mr. EVARTS. Our former objection. We make no additional objection.

Mr. Manager BUTLER. Then I understand that is in evidence. I now offer the report of Mr. Stark in the Cleveland Herald. Is there any objection to that?

Mr. EVARTS. The same, I suppose.

Mr. Manager BUTLER. Now I will read the report in the Leader, as it is a short one.

Mr. HOWARD. I understand that the honorable Managers are about to read these speeches from the reports.

Mr. Manager BUTLER. Unless the reading may be dispensed with and they be put in print.

Mr. JOHNSON. Let them be considered as read.

Mr. STANBERY. We do not want them read.

Mr. Manager BUTLER. Very well, then, I do not want the reading. They will be taken as read, and printed. ["Agreed."]

The reports thus put in evidence are as follows:

[From the Cleveland Leader.]
President Johnson's Speech.

FELLOW CITIZENS:—It is not for the purpose of making a speech that I now appear before you. I am aware of the great curiosity which prevails to see strangers who have notoriety and distinction in the country. I know a large number of you desire to see General Grant, and to hear what he has to say. [A voice: "Three cheers for Grant."] But you cannot see him to-night. He is extremely ill. I repeat I am not before you now to make a speech, but simply to make your acquaintance—to say how are you and to bid you good-bye. We are on our way to Chicago, to participate in or witness the laying of the corner-stone of a monument to the memory of a distinguished fellow-citizen who is now no more. It is not necessary for me to mention the name of Stephen A. Douglas to the people of Ohio. (Applause.) I am free to say I am flattered by the demonstrations I have witnessed, and being flattered, I don't mean to think it personal, but as an evidence of what is pervading the public mind, and this demonstration is nothing more nor less than an indication of the latent sentiment or feeling of the great masses of the people with regard to this great question.

I come before you as an American citizen simply, and not as the Chief Magistrate clothed in the insignia and paraphernalia of state; being an inhabitant of a State of this Union. I know it has been said that I was an alien; (Laughter,) and that I did not reside in one of the States of the Union and therefore I could not be the Chief Magistrate, though the Constitution declares that I must be a citizen to occupy that office. Therefore all that was necessary to depose its occupant was to declare the office vacant, or under a pretext to prefer articles of impeachment. And thus the individual who occupies the Chief Magistracy was to be disposed of and driven from power.

There was, two years ago, a ticket before you for the Presidency. I was placed upon that ticket with a distinguished citizen, now no more. [Voices—"It's a pity;" "Too bad;" "Unfortunate."] Yes, I know there are some who say, "Unfortunate." Yes, unfortunate for some that God rules on high and deals in justice. (Cheers.) Yes, unfortunate! The ways of Providence are mysterious and incomprehensible, controlling all those who exclaim, "Unfortunate." ["Bully for you."] I was going to say, my countrymen, a short time since I was elected and placed upon the ticket. There was a platform proclaimed and adopted by those who placed me upon it. Notwithstanding a mendacious press; notwithanding a subsidized gang of hirelings who have not ceased to traduce me, I have discharged all my official duties, and fulfilled my pledges. And I say here to-night that if my predecessor had lived, the vials of wrath would have poured out upon him. (Cries, "Never!" "Never!" and three cheers for the Congress of the United States.) I came here as I was passing along, and having been called upon for the purpose of exchanging views, and ascertaining, if we could, who was wrong. [Cries, "You are!"] That was my object in appearing before you to-night. I want to say that I have lived among the American people, and have represented them in some public capacity for the last twenty-five years. Where is the man or the woman who can place his finger upon one single act of mine, deviating from any pledges of mine or in violation of the constitution of the country. [Cheers and cries of "New Orleans!"]

Who is he—what language does he speak?—what religion does he profess—that can come and place his finger upon one pledge I ever violated, or one principle I ever proved false to? [Voice "New Orleans!" Another, "Why don't you hang Jeff. Davis?"] Hang Jeff. Davis? [Shouts and cries of "Down with him!" Hang Jeff. Davis? [Voice "Hang Wendell Phillips!"] Why don't you hang him? [Cries of "Give us an opportunity!"] Haven't you got the court? Have n't you got the Attorney General? Who is your Chief Justice, who has refused to sit on his trial? [Groans and cheers.] I am not the Chief Justice! I am not the Attorney General! I am no jury! But I'll tell you what I did do. I called upon your Congress, that is trying to break up the Government. [Hisses and cries of "A lie!" Great confusion. Voice "Don't get mad!"] I am not mad. [Hisses.] I will tell you who is mad. "Whom the gods want to destroy they first make mad." Did your Congress order any of them to be tried? [Three cheers for Congress.] Then, fellow-citizens, we might as well allay our passion and permit reason to resume her empire and prevail. In presenting the few remarks that I designed to make, my intention was to address myself to your common sense, your judgment, your better feelings, not to the passion and malignancy of your hearts. [Voice, "How about Moses?"] This was my object in presenting myself on this occasion, and to say "how dye" and "good-bye." In the assembly here to-night the remark has been made "traitor!" Traitor, my countrymen! Will you hear me? (Cries, "Yes!") And will you hear me for my cause and for the constitution of my country? ["Yes! Yes! Go on!"]

I want to know when or where or under what circumstances Andrew Johnson, not as Executive, but in any capacity, ever deserted any principle, or violated the constitution of this country. [Never! never!] Let me ask this large and intelligent audience if your Secretary of State, who served four years under Mr. Lincoln, and who was placed upon the butcher's block as it were and hacked and gashed all to pieces, scarred by the assassin's knife—when he turned traitor? [Cries of "never!"] If I were disposed to play the orator and deal in declamation, even to-night I would imitate one of the ancient tragedies, and would take Mr. Seward, bring him before you, and point you to the hacks and scars upon his person. ["Voice, God bless him!"] I would exhibit the bloody garments saturated with gore from his gaping wounds. Then I would ask you, who is the traitor? [Voice, "Thad. Stevens!"] Why don't you hang Thad. Stevens and Wendell Phillips? [Cheers.] I have been fighting traitors in the South. They have been whipped and crushed. They knowledge their defeat and accept the terms of the constitution. And now, as I go round the circle, having fought traitors at the South, I am prepared to fight them at the North [Cheers,] God being willing with your help. [Cries, "we won't give it."] They will be crushed North and this glorious Union of ours will be preserved,]Cheers.] I do not come here as the Chief Magistrate of twenty-five States out of thirty-six. [Cheers.]

I come here to-night with the flag of my country and the constellation of thirty-six stars untarnished. Are you for dividing this country? [Cries "No."]

Then I am President, and President of the whole United States. [Cheers.] I will tell you another thing. I understand the discordant notes in this crowd to-night. He who is opposed to the restoration of the Government and the Union of the States is a greater traitor than Jeff. Davis or Wendell Phillips. [Loud cheers] I am against both of them. [Cries, "Give it to them."] Some of you talk about traitors in the South, who have not courage to go away from your homes to fight them. [Laughter and cheers] The courageous men, Grant, Sherman, Farragut, and the long list of the distinguished sons of the Union, were in the field, and led on their gallant hosts to conquest and to victory, while you remained cowardly at home. [Applause, Bully.] Now when these brave men have returned home many of whom have left an arm or a leg or their blood upon many a battle-field, they found you at home speculating and committing frauds upon the Government. [Laughter and cheers,] You pretend now, to have great respect and sympathy for the poor, brave fellow who has left an arm on the battlefield. [Cries, "Is this dignified?"] I understand you. You may talk about the dignity of the President. [Cries, "How was it about his making a speech on the 22d of February?"] I have been with you on the battle-fields of this country, and I can tell you furthermore to-night, who have to pay these brave men who shed their blood. You speculated and now the great mass of the people have got to work it out. [Cheers.]

It is time that the great mass of the American people should understand what your designs are. [A voice, "What did General Butler say?"] What did General Butler say? (Hisses.) What did Grant say? (cheers) and what does General Grant say about General Butler? (Laughter and cheers.) What does General Sherman say? [A voice, "What does Sheridan say? New Orleans! New Orleans!"] General Sheridan says that he is for the restoration of the government that General Sheridan fought for. (Bully.) But fellow citizens, let this all pass. I care not for my dignity. There is a certain portion of our countrymen will respect a citizen wherever he is entitled to respect. [A voice: "That's so."] There is another class that have no respect for themselves, and consequently they cannot respect any one else. [Laughter and cheers.] I know a man and a gentleman whenever I meet him. I have only to look in his face, and if I was to see yours by the light of day I do not doubt but that I should see cowardice and treachery written upon it. [Laughter and cheers.] Come out here where I can see you. [Cheers.] If you ever shoot a man you will do it in the dark, and pull the trigger when no one is by to see. [Cheers.] I understand traitors. I have been fighting them at the southern end of the line, and we are now fighting them in the other direction. [Laughter and cheers.] I came here neither to criminate or recriminate, but when attacked, my plan is to defend myself. [Cheers.]

When encroached upon, I care not from what quarter it comes, it will meet with resistance. As Chief Magistrate I felt, after taking the oath to support the Constitution, and when I saw encroachments upon your constitutional rights, I dared to sound the tocsin of alarm. (Three cheers for Andrew Johnson.) Then if this be right, the head and front of my offending is in telling when the Constitution of our country was trampled upon. Let me say to those who thirst for more blood, who are still willing to sacrifice human life, if you want a victim, and the country requires it, erect your altar and lay me upon it to pour the last libation to human freedom. [Loud applause.] I love my country. Every public act of my life testifies that it is so. Where is the man that can put his finger upon any one act of mine that goes to prove to the contrary. And what is my offending? (Voice, "Because you are not a radical," and cries of "veto.") Somebody says "veto." Veto of what? ——is called the Freedmen's Bureau bill? I can tell you what it is. Before the rebellion commenced there were four millions of slaves and about 340,000 white people living in the South. These latter paid expenses, bought the lands and cultivated them, and after the crops were gathered, pocketed the profits. That's the way the thing stood up to the rebellion. The rebellion commenced, the slaves were liberated, and then came up the Freedmen's Bureau bill. This provides for the appointment of agents and sub-agents in all States, counties, and school districts, who have power to make contracts for the freedmen and to hire them out, and to use the military power to carry them into execution. The cost of this to the people was twelve million dollars at the beginning. The further expense would be greater, and you are to be taxed for it, That is why I vetoed it. I might refer to the Civil Rights bill, which is even more atrocious. I tell you, my countrymen, that though the powers of hell and Thad. Stevens and his gang were by, they could not turn me from my purpose. There is no power that could turn me, except you and the God who spoke me into existence.

In conclusion, he said that Congress had taken much pains to poison their constituents against him. But what had Congress done? Have they done anything to restore the Union of these States? No, on the contrary, they had done everything to prevent it; and, because he stood now where he did when the rebellion commenced, he had been denounced as a traitor. Who had run greater risks or made greater sacrifices than himself? But Congress, factious and domineering, had taken to poisoning the minds of the American people. It was with them a question of power. Every friend of theirs who holds an office as assessor, collector, or postmaster, [A voice—"Turn Benedict out!"] wanted to retain his place. Rotation in office used to be thought a good doctrine by Washington, Jefferson, and Adams; and Andrew Jackson, God bless him, thought so. [Applause.] This gang of office-holders—these blood-suckers and cormorants—had got fat on the country. You have got them over your district. Hence you see a system of legislation proposed that these men shall not be turned out; and the President, the only channel through which they can be reached, is called a tyrant. He thought the time had come when those who had enjoyed fat offices for four years should give way for those who had fought for the country. Hence it was seen why he was assailed and denounced. He had stood by them in the field and God willing he would continue to stand by them. He had turned aside from the thread of his remarks to notice the insult sought to be given him. When an insult offered he would resent it in a proper manner. But he was free to say he had no revengeful or resentful feelings. All he wanted when the war was over and peace had come was for patriotic and Christian men to rally round the flag of the country in a fraternal hug, and resolved that all shall perish rather than that the Union shall not be restored. While referring to the question of suffrage, some one in the crowd asked him, "How about Louisiana?" To which he responded, "Let the negroes vote in Ohio before you talk about their voting in Louisiana." [Laughter and cries of "Good!"] Take the beam out of your own eye before you see the mote in your brother's." [Renewed laughter.] In conclusion, after some further remarks, he invoked God's best blessings on his hearers. [Applause.]

[D. C. McEwen's report of the Cleveland Speech.]

FELLOW CITIZENS OF THE CITY OF CLEVELAND: In being presented here to-night, not for the purpose of making a speech, I am well aware of the great curiosity that exists on the part of strangers in reference to seeing individuals who are here amongst them who have notoriety and distinction in the country. Most of the persons here to-night—[A voice "Louder!"] Well, you must remember there are a good many people here to-night, and it requires a pretty strong voice to reach the utmost verge of this audience to-night, and especially one who, from speaking for the last two or three days, has to some extent marred or destroyed what little voice he had. But for the time I consume, if you will bear with me, I will try and make myself heard, notwithstanding the hoarseness under which I labor. What I was going to say, though, is, I know that a large number are here who would desire to see Gen. Grant and to hear what he might say. [A voice—"That's so"]. But the fact is that Gen. Grant is extremely ill. His health will not permit of his appearing before this audience here to-night. It would be much more pleasure to me to hear him here before you, and to hear what he might have to say, than to give a speech of my own, or to

give the reasons of his absence on this occasion. So then it will not be expected he will be here. He will not address you to-night. You cannot see him to-night, so far as that goes, on account of his extreme indisposition.—

Fellow citizens, in being before you to-night, it is not for the purpose of making a speech, but simply to make your acquaintance, and while I am telling you "How do you do,"—at the very same time to tell you "Good bye." We are here to-day on our tour to a visit for the purpose of participating in or witnessing the laying of the chief corner stone to a monument to be erected to one of our distinguished fellow citizens who is no more. It is not necessary for me to mention the name of Stephen A. Douglas to the people of Ohio. [Cheers.] It is a name familiar to all; and, being on a tour to participate in the ceremonies, passing through this city, and section of country, and witnessing the demonstration or manifestations of regard and respect which have been made, I am free to say to you that so far as I am concerned,—and I think I may speak for all those who accompany me,—that we feel extremely flattered and gratified at the demonstrations that have been made by the people of the country through which we have passed. And in being flattered I want at the same time to state that I don't consider that entirely personal, but, as an evidence of what is pervading the public mind, that there is a great issue before the country that is not yet settled, and these demonstrations are nothing more nor less than an indication of a latent sentiment of the feeling of the great mass of the people which is being developed in reference to the proper settlement of those great questions, [Cheers.]

And in coming before you to-night, I come before you an American citizen. Not simply as the Chief Magistrate receiving, and going along as an officer with the insignia and paraphernalia of State, but appear before you as a fellow citizen, being an individual of one of the States of this Union. I know that it has been said and contended for on the part of some that I was an alien;—[laughter and cries of "shame"]—that I did not reside in one of the States of the Union, and therefore I could not be Chief Magistrate, though the Constitution declared that I was. And all that was necessary was simply to introduce a resolution declaring the office vacant or deposing the occupant or under pretext to prefer articles of impeachment, and state that the individual who occupied the Chief Magistracy was to be disposed of and driven from power [Cries of "Never."] But, fellow citizens, but a short time since you had a ticket before you for the Presidency and Vice Presidency. I was placed upon that ticket with a distinguished fellow citizen who is now no more, Yes, I know there are some that will complain. Unfortunate! Yes unfortunate for some that God rules on high and deals in right. Yes, unfortunate that the ways of Providence are mysterious and incomprehensible, controlling all those who exclaim "unfortunate." [Voices "Bully for you."] I was going to say, my countrymen, but a short time since I was selected and placed upon the ticket; and there was a platform proclaimed and adopted by those who placed me upon it.

And now, notwithstanding [?] a subsidized gang of hirelings (Cheers) [and traducers] I [have discharged all my official duties]. And I say here, if my predecessor had lived, the vials of wrath would have been poured out upon him. (Cheers. Cries of "Never;" three cheers for the Congress of the United States.) I came here to-night in passing along and being called upon for the purpose of exchanging, to the extent that the time would permit, of opinions and views, and to ascertain, if we could, who was in the wrong. [Laughter and cries of "Oh, oh."] That was object in appearing before you to-night, and I want to say this, that I have lived with and been among the American people and have represented them in some capacity for the last 25 years; and where is the man living, or the woman, in the community where I have lived and had the confidence of the people, that can place his finger upon one single [(?)] deviating from any pledge I ever made,—in violation of the laws of my country? (Cheers. A voice "How about New Orleans?") Where is he? What language does he speak, what religion does he profess that can come forward and place his finger upon óne pledge I have violated or one principle I (ever) [?] [A voice "New Orleans."] New Orleans. (Hang Jeff. Davis.) Just upon that subject—Hang Jeff. Davis? [Voices "No" and "Down with him."] [Hang Wendell Phillips."] Hang Jeff. Davis? ["No"] ["Yes"] Why don't you? Why don't you? [A voice, "Give us the opportunity." Haven't you got the court? Haven't you got the Attorney General? [A voice "No, he is removed."] Who is your Chief Justice and has refused to sit upon the trial? [Cheers.] I am not the Chief Justice; I am not the prosecuting Attorney. ["Good" and cheers.] I am not the Jury.

But I will tell you what I did do. I called up our Congress that is trying to break up the Government [A voice, "You lie," and cheers, "Not so." Hisses. "Don't get mad, Andy."]. Well, I will tell you who is mad, "Whom the Gods intend to destroy, they first make mad." Yes, Did your Congress order any of them to be tried? [Three cheers for Gen. Grant and Congress.] Then fellow citizens, we might as well allay our feelings and let passion subside and reason resume her empire and prevail [Cheers] In presenting myself in the few remarks that I intended to make, my intention was to address myself to your common sense, to your judgment, to the better feeling, not the passion and the malignancy of your hearts. (Cheers) This was my object in presenting myself on this occasion, and to merely tell you "How do you do," and at the same time to bid you "Good bye." In this crowd here to-night, the remark has been made "Traitor," "Traitor"? My countrymen will you hear me? [Voices "Yes"] And will you hear me for my cause and for the Constitution of my country? [Cries of "Yes"] I want to know from or where or under what circumstances Andrew Johnson—not as Chief Executive but acting in any other capacity—ever deserted any principle or violated the Constitution of his country [Cries of "Never" and "You abandoned your party."]

Let me ask this large and intelligent audience here to-night if your Secretary of State, who served four years under Mr. Lincoln, and who was placed upon the butcher's block, as it were, and chopped in pieces, hacked, and scarred all over by the assassin's knife, when he turned traitor? ("Cries of "Never.") But if I were disposed to play the orator and deal in declamation here to-night, I would imitate one of the ancient tragedies that we have such a graphic account of—yes, I would take William H. Seward, and I would bring him before you, and would point out to the hacks and scars upon his person (A voice, "God bless him") Yes, I would exhibit his bloody garments, caused by blood from wounds inflicted by the assassin's knife. (Three cheers for Seward.) Yes, I would unfold his bloody garments before you to-night, and ask who had committed treason. (A voice Thad. Stevens.) Yes, I would ask you why Jeff. Davis was not hanged? [And I would give the reason and hang Thad. Stevens and Wendell Phillips.]

I tell you, my countrymen, I have been fighting the South. They have been whipped, they have been crushed; and they are very willing to acknowledge their error and accept the terms of the Constitution; and now, as I go around the circle, having fought traitors at the South, I am prepared to fight traitors at the North. (Cheers.) God being willing with your help (Cries "We will do it," and "We won't do it,") they will be crushed North and South, and this glorious Union of ours will be preserved, and in coming here to-night [it] was not coming as the Chief Magistrate of twenty-five States. No. I came here to-night as the Executive of 36 States. [Cheers.] I come here to-night with the flag of my country in my hand, a constellation of 36, not twenty-five stars. [Cheers]. I come here to night with the constellation of my country intact—[noise and confusion]—determined to defend the Constitution of my country let the consequences be what they may. I come here to-night with the Union, the entire circle of the States [not a segment of a circle.] (A voice "How many States make you President?") How many States made me President? Wa'n't you against secession? [' Yes."] Were you for dissolving the Union? ["No."] Were you for dividing this Government? ["No."] Then I am President, and I am President of the whole United States. [Cheers,]

And I will tell you another thing. I will tell you another thing. I understand the discordant notes in this crowd here to-night. And I will tell you furthermore; he that is opposed to the restoration of the Government and the re-union of the States is as great a traitor as Jeff. Davis or Wendell Phillips [Loud Cheers] I am against both of them (A voice "Give it to them") I am against both of them.

I fought the traitors of the South, and I will now fight them in the North. And I will tell you another thing, I have been with them down there, and when [?] men were sleeping on their arms; [I knew who was with them and about them.] When some of you talk about traitor in the South you hadn't courage to get out of your [closets] but persuaded [somebody else] to go. [Laughter and applause.] The courageous men—while Grant, Sherman, Farragut,—the long list of the distinguished sons of the United States—were in the field of battle, leading on their gallant hosts to conquest and victory, you were cowardly at home. [Cheers.] [Cries of "Bully."] And now when these brave men have returned home, many of them leaving an arm or a leg or his blood in or upon some battle-field, you were at home speculating and committing frauds upon your government. [Laughter and cheers.] You pretend now as great respect and sympathy for the poor brave fellow that left his arm on the battle-field [voices and confusion] I understand you. And you may talk about the dignity of the President [if he does not make a speech on the 22d of July or the 22d of February.]

I have been with you (A voice "That was whisky") I have been with you in the battle of this country. And I can tell you furthermore I know who has to pay for it. These brave men shed their blood; you speculated and got the money, and now the great mass of people must work it out (cheers) [and all this hanging.] I care not for your prejudice; it is time for the great mass of the American people to understand what your designs are. [A voice, "That's so,"] and in addition to this, the South, in proposing to come to terms, even proposed to come forward and pay their part (A voice—"Let them come.") I say then let them come. (A voice—"That's right") and these brave men that conquered them, and after having prostrated them, [?] (while) these gentlemen with the heel of power upon their necks, what do they say? They do not say anything about it.—A voice—" What did General Butler say?"] Gen. Butler? [Hisses] What does General Grant say? [Cheers, And what does General Grant say about General Butler? [Laughter and applause] What does Gen. Sherman say? (A voice—"What did General Sheridan say?") General Sheridan says he is for a restoration of the Government. General Sheridan fought for it. [Cries of "Bully."]

But fellow citizens, let this all pass. I care not for my dignity. There is a certain portion of our countrymen that will respect their fellow citizen whenever he is entitled to respect, [A voice "that's so,"—and cheers.] There is another portion of them that have no respect for themselves, and consequently they cannot respect anybody else [cries of Bully, and cheers, and other exclamations in the audience.] I know a gentleman and a man whenever I can see him. And furthermore, I know [when I look a man in the face and can see him]—[The President was here understood to express a wish that he could see some one in the crowd] I will bet now if there can be a light that cowardice and treachery can be seen it. [Laughter & cheers] Come out here where we can see you. (Cheers) And if ever you shoot a man you will shoot in the dark and pull your trigger when no one is by. [Cheers] I understand traitors. I have been fighting them for five years. We (fought) it out on the Southern end of the line, and now we are going to go the other direction. And this man, such a one as insulted me to-night, when you [?] you will see that he has ceased to be a man. But in ceasing to be a man he shrank into the dimensions of a reptile [Cheers]. And having so shrank, as an honest man I will tread upon him. I came here to-night neither to criminate nor to recriminate; but when provoked, my nature is not to (advance), but it is to defend [Cheers]. And when encroached upon, I care not from what quarter it comes, it is entitled to resistance—[as resistance to oppression.]

As your Chief Magistrate [have I felt for taking

the oath to support the Constitution of my country, after I saw the encroachments of the enemy upon your constitutional rights.] I saw the citadel of liberty encroached upon, and as an honest man, and being placed there as your sentinel, I have dared to sound the tocsin of alarm, (A voice "God bless Andrew Johnson.") Should I have ears and not hear? Should I have a tongue and not speak? (Voices "No, no") Then if this be right, the head and front of my offending is in [saying] when the Constitution of my country was trampled upon. [A voice "Bully." And let me say to-night, though my [head] has been threatened, though it has been said that my blood is to be shed.—[A voice—"I can't see it."] Let me say to those that thirst for my blood—(A voice—"There is better blood than yours shed.")—Let me say to those who are still willing to sacrifice human life, let me say to those, if you want a victim, and my country requires it, erect your altar (A voice "Bully for you.") [The confusion prevented the reporter from hearing the remainder of the sentence save the words " and the individual who addresses you to-night."] Erect your altar if you still thirst for blood (Cries of "Never.") And if you want it, take out the individual who addresses you, lay him upon your altar, and the blood that now warms and animates his existence shall be poured out as the last libation to human freedom, (Loud applause.) I love my country [over popularity] and all my life testifies that it is so (A voice "That is so.") Where is the man that [used to be] toiling for a home and abiding place for his children that can look Andrew Johnson in the face and say that he was not his friend? Where is the man that has participated in any and all our wars, since our war with Mexico down to the present time, that can put his finger upon any one act that goes to prove [but what he stood at all times for the country?] (A voice "That is so."] Then what is my offending? (A voice—"Because you are not a Radical.") (Cries of "Veto.") Somebody says "Veto." (A voice—"Bully for the veto,"—cheers.) Veto of what? What is called the Freedmen's Bureau Bill. And I can tell you what it is. (A voice—"Tell us.") Before the Rebellion commenced there were four million of persons, that were called colored persons, that were held as slaves by about 340,000 people living in the South. These 340,000 slaveholders paid the expenses [worked the negroes] as they are commonly called, and at the expiration of the year, [when] the rice, tobacco, and cotton were sold, after paying all the expenses, the slaveholders put the money in their pockets. Your attention, they put the profits, if there was any, in their pockets. In many instances there were no profits, [thus he that bought the land and the slaves came out (?)] Well that is the way the thing stood before the rebellion. The rebellion commenced, the slaves were turned loose, and then we come up to the Freedmen's Bureau Bill. What did the Freedmen's Bureau propose? It is to appoint agents and sub-agents, in all the States, counties, school districts, and parishes, with power to make contracts for all the slaves, with power to control, power to hire them out and to dispose of them; and in addition to that the whole military power of the Government to aid the execution of the Freedmen's Bureau Bill (A voice—"Bully.") I never fear clamor (A voice—"Good for you.") I never [have] been afraid of the people, for it is in them I relied, and upon them I always relied. Then when I got the truth, the argument and the fact and reason on my side, neither clamor nor frowns nor menaces can drive me from my purpose. [Cries of "Bully," and cheers.] And now to the Freedmen's Bureau Bill. What was it? Four millions of slaves were emancipated, given an equal chance, a fair start to make their own support; to work, produce, and having worked and produced, to appropriate the product of their own labor to their own sustenance and support. But the Freedmen's Bureau comes along and says that we must take charge of four million of slaves. (Cries of "No," never.) The Freedmen's Bureau comes along and proposes to appropriate a fraction less than $12,000,000 to sustain this Freedmen's Bureau. I want to give some facts; I want to put the nail in, and having put it in, to clinch it on the other side. [Cheers] Then we come along and propose at the beginning, as an initiative, to appropriate $12,000,000

to defray the expense of emancipating four million of slaves. In the first instance it has cost you three thousand million of dollars. Three million of dollars you have expended; and after having given a full and fair opportunity to enjoy the products of his own labor, then these gentlemen that are such great philanthropists, that are such great friends to humanity—the great masses of the people who toil and labor six days in the week, and some of them not even resting on the 7th, must be taxed to pay $12,000,-000 to sustain that Freedmen's Bureau [The system so kept on the country would run up to fifty millions of dollars]. In the days of John Quincy Adams $12,000,000 was looked upon as an enormous expense [to the existence of the Government] but here are $12,000,000 for the Freedmen's Bureau. Your attention my countrymen. I have not got to the point yet. (Cheers)

Your attention, I would rather speak to five hundred men who would give me attention than to ten thousand who are not willing to hear me. How does the matter stand? The whole proposition stands to transfer 4,000,000 of slaves from the original owners—as I have just told you—in the South to their new taskmasters; [yes,] a worse system of slavery than ever existed before [was to transfer four million of slaves to a new set of task-masters who were to work them, to control them, to make their contracts; and in the end if there were any profits made, they would put them into their own pockets instead of—[the remainder of the sentence was broken by cheers and voices "True" " True"]. But on the other hand, if the system turned out to be unprofitable and was losing business, you the people had to foot up the bill and the Government pay the expense. That is the Freedmen's Bureau Bill.

Now when they talk about power and usurpation, I stand to-night where I have always stood. (See this measure before you.] Before this Congress came up or this rebellion commenced; and because I opposed it, exercising one of the most conservative powers in the Constitutions of the country. What could I do by the veto power [A voice "Send it over your head"] Can you [present anything?] No. But all that the Executive can do, who was the representative of the people, the people's tribune, is to say when a measure is unconstitutional, is to say when it is extravagant and improvident and [?] let the people consider of it (Cheers) Was there any tyranny in stopping the measure until you can get the people to consider it? [A voice "No."] Then as your tribune, as your representative, I said when this bill was [passed]—and a bill, too, if I had been disposed and with plenty of power, I could have taken it into my hands, with thousands of satraps and from 12 to 50 millions of expenditure, I could have declared my self dictator,—I said no, that the power is where the Constitution placed it, in the hands of the people. (Cheers) So much for the Freedmen's Bureau Bill.

And if I was disposed to [come] along, in connection with this [and] call your attention to the Civil Rights Bill, it is only more enormous than the other. [Confused voices mingled with cheers.] And let me say to you, all the threats and menaces emanating from what is called the extreme men, your STEVENSES, your SUMNERS, and your Phillipses, and from all that class, I care not; as they have once talked about forming a league with hell and a covenant with the devil. [Laughter and cries of "bully."] I tell you, my countrymen here to-night, that though the powers of hell and THAD. STEVENS and his gang [were by,] they could not turn me from my purpose. There is no power to control me save you and the God who spoke me into existence. ["Three cheers"]

In bidding you farewell, [I would be willing] that this Congress which has been in session and which has taken so much pains to poison the minds of their constituents against me—what has this Congress done? [A voice, "Nothing."] Has it done anything to restore the Union of these States? [A voice—"No."] But on the contrary, they have done everything in their power to prevent it. [A voice—"That is so."] But because I stand now where I did when this rebellion commenced, I have been denounced as a traitor and recreant to the cause of my country. [Cries of "Never."] My countrymen here to-night, who has suffered more than I? [Cries of "No one."] Who has run greater risks,—who has done more than

I that address you here to-night? [Cries of "No one," and "God bless you, old man."] But this factious, domineering tyrannical party in Congress has undertaken to poison the minds of the American people. (Voices—"That's so;" and cheers.) It is just a question of power; and the attempt has been [?] every man that held a place in their districts. The President cannot control it—oh no; [my] Congressmen control it. [Laughter.] Yes, your assessors and collectors and postmasters—(A Voice—"Hit 'em again.")—Why they used to have an axiom in old times that rotation in office was a good thing. Washington used to think so, Jefferson thought so, Monroe thought so; Jackson—God bless him!—thought so. [Cheers, a Voice, "Here's a second Jackson."] But now when we talk about—[The sentence was interrupted by confusion in the assembly.] Your attention. I would rather have your attention [than to listen to you.]

Now how does the matter stand? Why, this gang, this gang of cormorants and bloodsuckers, that have lived at home and fattened upon the country the last four or five years, never going into the field,—oh, they are great patriots and everybody [wants to turn them out(?)] Look at them [?.] Everybody are traitors that are against us. Hence you hear a system of legislation proposed, to do what? [Why that these men shall not be turned out. "We have got our particular friends in power in the districts(?)] and the President, the tribune of the people, the only channel through which you can reach and vacate these places and bring honest men in, is denounced as a tyrant because he stands [in vindication of the people. (Cheers.) All it wants is for the country to [understand.] I think the time has come when those who have stayed at home and enjoyed all the fat offices four or five years, got rich,—I think it is nothing more than right that a few of those who have fought the battles of the country [as well as] others who have staid at home [should join in] the benefits of the victory. [How it is with Tennessee? Why, it is that [I mean to say that I stood up with these men at home] and in the field, and God being willing, I intend to stand by them again. [Cries of "Good," "Bully," and cheers.]

Then, my countrymen,—I have been drawn into this. I intended simply to make my acknowledgements for the cordial welcome that you have given me. But even in going along, passing the civilities of life, if I am insulted while the civilities are going on I will resent it in a proper manner. [Cries of "Good" & cheers.] Then in parting with you here to-night, if I know the feelings of my own heart, there is no anger. I have no revengeful feelings to gratify. (A voice "Everybody loves you") All that I want is—now that peace has come, now when the war is over—is for all patriotic and Christian men to rally round the standard of their country, and unite in one [eternal, patriotic oath,] and swear by the altar and their God that all shall sink together but what this Union shall be restored. (Cheers.) Then in parting with you here to-night, I hand over to you this flag, not with 25 but with 36 stars; I hand over to you the Constitution of my country unimpaired, though breaches have been made upon it, with the confident hope that you will repair the breaches and preserve the Constitution intact. I hand it over to you, in whom I have always trusted, and upon whom I have always relied, and so far I have never deserted. And I feel confident, though speaking here to-night for heart that responds to heart—men that agree in principle, men that agree in some great doctrine [that compare ideas or notions, when they come to the hour of acting in harmony and concert.] Then in parting with you to-night, I hand over the flag, the Constitution and the Union into hands that I know will preserve it, and at the proper time will render the proper[?].

Then farewell; and the little ill-feeling that has been [stricken out]:—if some man who has been morose and felt malignant under the influence of some party leader and that don't feel that he is free, let me say just in conclusion, and in this connection I tell you there are a good many white men in this country need emancipating. And let the work of emancipating go on. Strike the shackles from the white man's limbs and let him stand erect. You free your folks at home before you go to the negroes. You let the negroes vote in Ohio before you talk about negroes voting in Louisiana. [A voice "Never."] Take the beam out of your own eye before you see the mote that is in your neighbor's. You are very much disturbed about New Orleans, but you won't let a negro [go] to the ballot box to vote in Ohio. [Then my countrymen this is my claim] We understand these questions.

Then in parting with you—[The speech is not concluded in my notes—D. C. McEwen.]

[Cleveland Herald report.]

Prest. Johnson then stepped forward and spoke as follows:

PREST. JOHNSON'S SPEECH.

Fellow Citizens of Cleveland:—It is not for the purpose of making a speech I came here to-night. I am aware of the great curiosity that exists on the part of strangers in reference to seeing individuals who are here amongst us. [Louder.] You must remember there are a good many people here to-night, and it requires a great voice to reach the utmost verge of this vast audience. I have used my voice so constantly for some days past that I do know as I shall be able to make you all hear, but I will do my best to make myself heard.

What I am going to say is: There is a large number here who would like to see General Grant, and hear him speak, and hear what he would have to say; but the fact is General Grant is not here. He is extremely ill. His health will not permit of his appearing before this audience to-night. It would be a greater pleasure to me to see him here and have him speak than to make a speech of my own. So then it will not be expected that he will be here to-night, & you cannot see him on account of his extreme indisposition.

Fellow Citizens: In being before you to-night it is not for the purpose of making a speech, but simply to make your acquaintance, and while I am telling you how to do, and at the same time tell you good-bye. We are here to-night on our tour towards a sister State for the purpose of participating in and witnessing the laying of the chief corner stone over a monument to one of our fellow citizens who is no more. It is not necessary for me to mention the name of Stephen A. Douglas to the citizens of Ohio. It is a name familiar to you all, and being on a tour to participate in the ceremonies, and passing through your State and section of country and witnessing the demonstration and manifestation of regard & respect which has been paid me, I am free to say to you that so far as I am concerned, and I think I am speaking for all the company, when I say we feel extremely gratified and flattered at the demonstration made by the country through which we have passed, and in being flattered, I want to state at the same time that I don't consider that entirely personal, but as evidence of what is pervading the public mind, that there is a great issue before the country, and that this demonstration of feeling, is more than anything else, an indication of a deep interest among the great mass of the people in regard to all these great questions that agitate the public mind. In coming before you to-night, I come before you as an American citizen, and not simply as your Chief Magistrate. I claim to be a citizen of the Southern States, and an inhabitant of one of the States of this Union. I know that it has been said, and contended for on the part of some, that I was an alien, for I did not reside in any one of the States of the Union, and therefore I could not be Chief Magistrate, though the States declared I was.

But all that was necessary was simply to introduce a resolution declaring the office vacant or depose the occupant, or under some pretext to prefer articles of impeachment, & the individual who occupies the Chief Magistracy would be deposed and deprived of power.

But, fellow-citizens, a short time since you had a ticket before you for the Presidency and Vice Presidency; I was placed upon that ticket, in conjunction with a distinguished fellow citizen who is now no more. (Voice, "a great misfortune too"). I know there are some who will exclaim, "unfortunate." I admit the ways of Providence are mysterious and unfortunate but uncontrolable by those who would exclaim unfortunate. I was going to say my countrymen, but a short time since, I was selected and placed upon a ticket. There was a platform prepared and adopted by those who placed me upon it, and now, notwithstanding all kinds of misrepresentation; notwithstanding since after the sluice of misrepresentation has been poured out, notwithstanding a subsidised gang of hirelings have traduced me and maligned me ever since I have entered upon the discharge of my official duties, yet I will say had my predecessor have lived, the vials of wrath would have been poured out on him (cries of never, never, never.) I come here to-night in passing along, and being called upon, for the purpose of exchanging opinions and views as time would permit, and to ascertain if we could who was in the wrong.

I appear before you to-night and I want to to say this: that I have lived and been among all American people, and have represented them in some capacity for the last twenty-five years. And where is the man living, or the woman in the community, that I have wronged, or where is the person that can place their finger upon one single hair breadth of deviation from one single pledge I have made, or one single violation of the Constitution of the country. What tongue does he speak? What religion does he profess? Let him come forward and place his finger upon one pledge I have violated. (A voice. "Hang Jeff Davis"): (Mr. President resumes.) Hang Jeff Davis? Hang Jeff, Davis? Why don't you? (Applause.) Why don't you? (Applause.) Have you not got the Court? Have you not got the Court? Have not you got the Attorney General? Who is your Chief Justice—and that refused to sit upon the trial? (Applause.) I am not the Prosecuting Attorney. I am not the jury. But I will tell you what I did do; I called upon your Congress, that is trying to break up the Government, (immense applause,) Yes, did your Congress order hanging Jeff Davis? (Prolonged applause, mingled with hisses.)

But, fellow citizens, we had as well let feelings and prejudices pass; let passion subside; let reason resume her empire. In presenting myself to you in the few remarks I intended to make, my intention was to address myself to your judgment and to your good sense, and not to your anger or the malignity of your hearts. This was my object in presenting myself on this occasion, and at the same time to tell you good-bye. I have heard the remark made in this crowd to-night, "Traitor, traitor!" (Prolonged confusion.) My countrymen, will you hear me for my cause? For the Constitution of my country? I want to know when, where and under what circumstances Andrew Johnson, either as Chief Executive, or in any other capacity ever violated the Constitution of his country. Let me ask this large and intelligent audience here to-night, if your Secretary of State, who served four years under Mr. Lincoln, who was placed under the butcher's blow and exposed to the assassin's knife, when he turned traitor. If I were disposed to play orator, and deal in declamation, here to-night, I would imitate one of the ancient tragedies we have such account of—I would take William H Seward and open to view the scars he has received. I would exhibit his bloody garment and show the rent caused by the assassin's knife. [Three cheers for Seward.] Yes, I would unfold his bloody garments here to-night and ask who had committed treason. I would ask why Jeff Davis was not hung? Why don't you hang Thad Stevens and Wendell Phillips? I can tell you, my countrymen I have been fighting traitors in the South, [prolonged applause,] and they have been whipped, and say they were wrong, acknowledge their error and accept the terms of the Constitution.

And now as I pass around the circle, having fought traitors at the South, I am prepared to fight traitors at the North, God being willing with your help ["You can't have it," and prolonged confusion,] they would be crushed worse than the traitors of the South, and this glorious Union of ours will be preserved. In coming here to-night, it was not coming as Chief Magistrate of twenty-five States, but I come here as the Chief Magistrate of thirty-six States. I came here to-night with the flag of my country in my hand, with a constellation of thirty-six and not twenty-five stars. I came here to-night with the Constitution of my country intact, determined to defend the Constitution, let the consequences be what they may. I came here to-night for the Union; the entire circle of these States. [A Voice. "How many States made you President?"] How many States made me "President? Was you against secession? Do you want to dissolve the Union? [A voice, No.] Then I am President of the whole United States, and I will tell you one thing. I understand the discordant notes in this audience here to-night. And I will tell you furthermore, that he that is opposed to the restoration of the Government and the union of the States, is as great a traitor as Jeff Davis, and I am against both of them. I fought traitors at the South, now I fight them at the North. (Immense applause.)

I will tell you another thing; I know all about those boys that have fought for their country. I have been with them down there when cities were besieged. I know who was with them when some of you, that talk about traitors, had not courage to come out of your closets, but persuaded somebody else to go. Very courageous men! While Grant, Sherman, Farragut, and a long host of the distinguished sons of the United States were in the field of battle you were cowards at home; and, now when these brave men have returned, many of them having left an arm or leg on some battle-field while you were at home speculating and committing frauds upon your government, you pretend now to have great respect and sympathy for the poor fellow who left his arm on the battle-field. I understand you, who talk about the duty of the President and object to his speech of the 22d of July, (Voice, "22d of February")—22d of February. I know who have fought the battles of the country, and I know who is to pay for it. Those brave men shed their blood and your speculated, got money, and now the great mass of the people must work it out. (Applause and confusion.) I care not for your prejudices. It is time for the great mass of the American people to understand what your designs are in not admitting the Southern States when they have come to terms and even proposed to pay their part of the national debt. I say, Let them come; and those brave men, having conquered them and having prostrated them in the dust with the heel of power upon them, What do they say? (Voice, "What does General BUTLER say?") General BUTLER! What does General Grant say? And what does General Grant say of General BUTLER? What does General Sherman say? He says he is for restoration of the Government; and General Sherman fought for it.

But fellow citizens let this all pass. I care not for malignity. There is a certain portion of our countrymen that will respect their fellow citizen whenever he is entitled to respect, and there is another portion that have no respect for themselves, and consequently have none for anybody else. I know a gentleman when I see him, And furthermore, I know when I look a man in the face—[Voice,—"Which you can't do."] I wish I could see you, I will bet now, if there could be a light reflected upon your face that cowardice and treachery could be seen in it. Show yourself. Come out here where we can see you. If ever you shoot a man, you will stand in the dark and pull your trigger. I understand traitors, I have been fighting them for five years. We fought it out on the Southern end of the line, now we are fighting in the other direction. And those men—such a one as insulted me to-night—you may say, has ceased to be a man, and in ceasing to a man shrunk into the denomination of a reptile, and having so shrunken, as an honest man, I tread upon him. I came here to-night not to criminate or recriminate, but when provoked my nature is, not to advance, but to defend, and when encroached upon, I care not from what quarter it comes, it will find resistance, and resistance at the threshold. As your Chief Magistrate I have felt, after taking an oath to support the Constitution of my country, that I saw the encroachments of the enemy upon your sovereign rights. I saw the citadel of liberty intrenched upon and, as an honest man, being placed there as a sentinel, I have dared to sound the tocsin of alarm. Should I have ears and not hear; have a tongue and not speak when the enemy approaches?

And let me say to-night that my head has been threatened. It has been said that my blood was to be shed. Let me say to those who are still willing to sacrifice my life [derisive laughter and cheers,] if you want a victim and my country requires it, erect your altar and the individual who addresses you to-night, while here a visitor, [No, No," and laughter] erect your altar if you still thirst for blood, and if you want it, take out the individual who now addresses you and lay him upon your altar, and the blood that now courses his veins and warms his existence, shall be poured out as a last libation to Freedom. I love my country, and I defy any man to put his finger upon anything to the contrary. Then what is my offense? |Voices, "You ain't a Radical," "New Orleans," "Veto"] Somebody says "Veto." Veto of what? What is called the Freedmen's Bureau Bill, and in fine, not to go into any argument here to-night, if you do not understand what the Freedmen's Bureau Bill is, I can tell you. [Voice—"Tell us"] Before the rebellion there were 4,000,000 called colored persons held as slaves by about 340,000 people living in the South. That is 340,000 slave owners paid expenses, bought land and worked the negroes, and at the expiration of the year when cotton, tobacco, and rice was gathered and sold, after all paying expenses, these slave owners put the money in their pocket—(slight interruption)—your attention—they put the property in their pocket. In many instances there was no profit and many come out in debt. Well, that is the way things stood before the rebellion. The rebellion commenced and the slaves were turned loose. Then we come to the Freedmen's Bureau Bill. And what did the bill propose? It proposed to appoint agents and sub-agents in all the cities, counties, school districts and parishes, with power to make contracts for all the slaves, power to control and power to hire them out—dispose of them, and in addition to that, the whole military power of the Government applied to carry it into execution.

Now [clamor and confusion] I never feared clamor. I have never been afraid of the people, for by them I have always been sustained. And when I have all the truth, argument, fact and reason on my side, clamor nor affront, nor animosities can drive me from my purpose.

Now to the Freedman's Bureau. What was it? Four million slaves were emancipated and given an equal chance and fair start to make their own support—to work and produce; and having worked and produced, to have their own property and apply it to their own support. But the Freedmen's Bureau comes and says we must take charge of these 4,000,000 slaves. The Bureau comes along and proposes, at an expense of a fraction less than $12,000,000 a year to take charge of these slaves. You had already expended three thousand million dollars to set them free and give them a fair opportunity to take care of themselves—then these gentlemen, who are such great friends of the people, tell us they must be taxed twelve million dollars to sustain the Freedman's Bureau. [Great confusion.] I would rather speak to five hundred men who would give me their attention than to one hundred thousand that would not, [With all this mass of patronage he said he could have declared himself dictator.]

The Civil Rights bill was more enormous than the other. I have exercised the veto power, they say. Let me say to you of the threats from your Stevenses, Sumners, Phillipses and all that class, I care not for them. As they once talked about forming a "league with Hell and a covenant with the devil." I tell you, my countrymen here to-night, through the power of Hell, death and Stevens with all his powers combined, there is no power than can control me save you the people and the God that spoke me into existence. In bidding you farewell here to-night, I would ask you with all the pains Congress has taken to calumniate and malign me, what has Congress done? Has it done anything to restore the Union of the States? But, on the contrary, has it not done everything to prevent it?

And remember I stand now as I did when the rebellion commenced, I have been denounced as a traitor. My countrymen here to-night, who has suffered more than I? Who has run greater risk? Who has borne more than I? But Congress, factious, domineering, tyrannical—Congress has undertaken to poison the minds of the American people, and create a feeling against me in consequence of the manner in which I have distributed the public patronage.

While this gang—this common gang of cormorants and bloodsuckers, have been fattening upon the country for the past four or five years—men never going into the field, who growl at being removed from their fat offices, they are great patriots! Look at them all over your district! Everybody is a traitor that is against them. I think the time has come, when those who stayed at home and enjoyed offices for the last four or five years—I think it would be no more than right for them to give way and let others participate in the benefits of office. Hence you can see why it is that I am traduced and assaulted. I stood up by these men who were in the field, and I stand by them now.

I have been drawn into this long speech, while I intended simply to make acknowledgments for the cordial welcome; but if I am insulted while civilities are going on I will resent it in a proper manner, and in parting here to-night, I have no anger nor revengeful feelings to gratify. All I want now—peace has come and war is over—is for all patriotic men to rally round the standard of their country and swear by their altars and their God, that all shall sink together but what this Union shall be supported. Then in parting with you to-night, I hang over you this flag—not of 25 but of 36 stars—I hand over to you the Constitution of my country—though imprisoned, though breaches have been made upon it—with confidence hoping you will repair the breaches, I hand it over to you, in whom I have always trusted and relied, and, so far, I have never deserted—and I feel confident, while speaking here to-night, for heart responds to heart of man, that you agree to the same great doctrine.

Then farewell! The little ill feelings aroused here to-night, for some men have felt a little ill; let us not cherish them. Let me say, in this connection, there are many white people in this country that need emancipation. Let the work of emancipation go on. Let white men stand erect and free. [A voice, "What about New Orleans"]. You complain of the disfranchisement of the negroes in the Southern States, while you would not give them the right of suffrage in Ohio to-day. Let your negroes vote in Ohio before you talk about negroes voting. Take the beam out of your own eye before you see the mote in your neighbours eye. You are very much disturbed about New Orleans—but you will not allow the negro to vote in Ohio.

This is all plain, we understand this all and in parting with you to-night let me invoke the blessing of God upon you, expressing my sincere thanks for the cordial manner in which you have received me.

Mr. EDMUNDS. I move that the Senate sitting for this trial stand adjourned until to-morrow at twelve o'clock.

Mr. FESSENDEN. I wish to make a motion that takes precedence of that, that when the court adjourns it adjourn to meet on Monday next.

Mr. DRAKE. That has been decided against,

Mr. FESSENDEN. It can be considered again, because other business has been done in the meantime.

Mr. EDMUNDS. I rise to a point of order, that under the rules the motion to adjourn takes precedence.

The CHIEF JUSTICE. The Chair is of opinion that the motion to adjourn takes precedence of every other motion if it is not withdrawn.

Mr. EDMUNDS. I will withdraw it at the request of the Senator from Maine.

Mr. FESSENDEN. I can afterward renew the motion to adjourn.

The CHIEF JUSTICE. The Senator from

C. I.—15.

Maine moves that when the Senate sitting as a court of impeachment adjourns it adjourn to meet at twelve o'clock on Monday.

Mr. FERRY called for the yeas and nays, and they were ordered; and being taken, resulted—yeas 16, nays 29; as follows:

YEAS—Messrs. Buckalew, Corbett, Davis, Dixon, Doolittle, Fessenden, Fowler, Henderson, Johnson, McCreery, Norton, Nye, Patterson of Tennessee, Trumbull, Van Winkle, and Vickers—16.

NAYS—Messrs. Anthony, Cameron, Cattell, Chandler, Cole, Conkling, Conness, Cragin, Drake, Edmunds, Ferry, Frelinghuysen, Hendricks, Howard, Howe, Morgan, Morrill of Maine, Morrill of Vermont, Patterson of New Hampshire, Pomeroy, Ross, Sherman, Sprague, Stewart, Sumner, Thayer, Willey, and Williams—29.

NOT VOTING—Messrs. Bayard, Grimes, Harlan, Morton, Ramsey, Saulsbury, Tipton, Wade, and Yates—9.

So the motion was not agreed to.

Mr. EDMUNDS. I move that the Senate sitting for this trial adjourn.

The CHIEF JUSTICE. The Senator from Vermont moves that the Senate sitting as a court of impeachment adjourn until to-morrow at twelve o'clock.

The motion was agreed to.

SATURDAY, *April* 4, 1868.

The Chief Justice of the United States entered the Senate Chamber at twelve o'clock and took the chair.

The usual proclamation having been made by the Sergeant-at-Arms,

The Managers of the impeachment on the part of the House of Representatives appeared and took the seats assigned them.

The counsel for the respondent also appeared and took their seats.

The presence of the House of Representatives was next announced, and the members of the House, as in Committee of the Whole, headed by Mr. E. B. WASHBURNE, the chairman of that committee, and accompanied by the Speaker and Clerk, entered the Senate Chamber, and were conducted to the seats provided for them.

The CHIEF JUSTICE. The Secretary will read the minutes of the last day's proceedings.

The Secretary read the Journal of the proceedings of the Senate yesterday sitting for the trial of the impeachment.

The CHIEF JUSTICE. Gentlemen Managers, you will please to proceed with your evidence. The Senators will please to give their attention.

L. L. WALBRIDGE sworn and examined.

By Mr. Manager BUTLER:

Question. What is your business?
Answer. Short-hand writer.
Question. How long have you been engaged in that business?
Answer. Nearly ten years.
Question. Have you had during that time any considerable experience; and if so, how much in that business?

Answer. Yes, sir; I have had experience during the whole of that time in connection with newspaper reporting and outside.
Question. Reporting for courts?
Answer. Yes, sir.
Question. With what papers have you been lately connected?
Answer. More recently with the Missouri Democrat; previous to that time with the Missouri Republican.
Question. Do the names of those papers indicate their party proclivities, or are they reversed?
Answer. They are the reverse.
Question. The Democrat means Republican, and the Republican means Democrat?
Answer. Exactly.
Question. To what paper were you attached on or about the 8th of September, 1866?
Answer. The Missouri Democrat.
Question. Did you report a speech delivered from the balcony of the Southern Hotel in St. Louis by Andrew Johnson?
Answer. I did.
Question. What time in the day was that speech delivered?
Answer. Between eight and nine o'clock in the evening.
Question. Was there a crowd in the streets?
Answer. Yes, sir, there was, and on the balcony also.
Question. Where were you?
Answer. I was on the balcony, within two or three feet of the President while he was speaking.
Question. Where were the rest of the presidential party?
Answer. I cannot tell you.
Question. Were they there?
Answer. I have no recollection of seeing any of the party on the balcony.
Question. Did the President come out to answer a call from the crowd in the street apparently?
Answer. Yes, sir, I judge so; I know there was a very large crowd in the street in front of the hotel, and there were continuous cries for the President, and in response to those cries I supposed he came forward.
Question. Had he been received in the city by a procession of the various charitable societies?
Answer. He had during the afternoon been received by the municipal authorities.
Question. Had the mayor made him an address of welcome?
Answer. He had.
Question. Had he answered that address?
Answer. He had.
Question. Did you take a report of that speech?
Answer. I did.
Question. How fully?
Answer. I took every word.
Question. After it was taken, how soon was it written out?

Answer. Immediately.

Question. How was it written out?

Answer. At my dictation.

Question. By whom?

Answer. The first part of the speech previous to the banquet was written out in one of the rooms of the Southern Hotel. That occupied about half an hour, I think. We then attended the banquet, at which other speeches were made. Immediately after the conclusion of the banquet we went to the Republican office, and there I dictated the speech to Mr. Monahan and Mr. McHenry, two attachés of the Republican.

Question. You have spoken of a banquet; was there a banquet given to the President and his suite by the city?

Answer. There was at the Southern Hotel, immediately after the speech on the balcony.

Question. At that banquet did the President speak?

Answer. He made a very short address.

Question. And there was other speaking there, I presume.

Answer. Yes, sir.

Question. After that speech was written out was it published?

Answer. It was.

Question. When?

Answer. On the very next morning, in the Sunday Republican.

Question. After it was published did you revise the publication by your notes?

Answer. I did.

Question. How soon?

Answer. Immediately after the speech was printed in the Sunday morning Republican I went to the Democrat office in company with my associate, Mr. Edmund T. Allen, and we very carefully revised the speech for the Monday morning Democrat.

Question. Then it was on the same Sunday that you made the revision?

Answer. Yes, sir; the Sunday after the speech.

Question. When you made the revision had you your notes?

Answer. I had.

Question. State whether you compared the speech as printed with those notes?

Answer. Yes, sir; I did at that time, and since.

Question. When you compared it did you make any corrections that were needed, if any were needed?

Answer. My recollection is that there were one or two simple corrections, errors either in transcribing or on the part of the printer. That is all that I remember in the way of corrections of the speech.

Question. Did you afterward have occasion to revise that speech with your notes?

Answer. I had.

Question. When was that?

Answer. I think that was little over a year ago.

Question. What occasion called you to revise it with your notes a little over a year ago?

Answer. I was summoned here by the Committee on the New Orleans Riots, and immediately after receiving the summons I hunted up my notes and again made a comparison with them of the printed speech.

Question. How far did that second comparison assure you of corrections?

Answer. It was perfectly correct.

Question. Now, in regard to particularity of reporting; were you enabled to report so correctly as to give inaccuracies of pronunciation even?

Answer. Yes, sir. I did so in that instance.

Question. Where are your original notes now?

Answer. I cannot tell you, sir. I searched for them immediately after I was summoned here, but failed to find them.

Question. You had them up to the time you were examined before the committee on the New Orleans riot?

Answer. I had, and brought them with me here, but I have no recollection of them since that time.

Question. Have you a copy of that paper?

Answer. I have.

Question. Will you produce it?

[The witness produced a newspaper, being the Missouri Democrat of Monday, September 10, 1866.]

Question. Is this it?

Answer. It is.

Question. From your knowledge of the manner in which you took the speech, and from your knowledge of the manner in which you corrected it, state whether you are now enabled to say that this paper which I hold in my hand contains an accurate report of the speech of the President delivered on that occasion?

Answer. Yes, sir; I am enabled to say it is an accurate report.

Mr. Manager BUTLER. I propose, if there is no objection, to offer this in evidence, and also if there is objection.

Mr. EVARTS. Before that is done let us cross-examine this witness.

Mr. Manager BUTLER. Certainly.

Cross-examined by Mr. EVARTS:

Question. I understand that you took down, as from the President's mouth, the entire speech, word for word, as he delivered it?

Answer. Yes, sir.

Question. In the transcript from your notes and in this publication did you preserve that form and degree of accuracy and completeness? Is it all the speech?

Answer. It is the whole speech.

Question. No part of it is condensed or paraphrased?

Answer. No, sir; the whole speech is there in complete form.

Question. You say that, beside the revision of the speech which you made on the Sunday following its delivery, you made a revision a year ago?

Answer. Yes, sir.

Question. For what reason and upon what occasion?

Answer. As I said, it was owing to my having been summoned before the Committee on the New Orleans Riot.

Question. A committee of Congress?

Answer. Yes, sir.

Question. At Washington?

Answer. Yes, sir.

Question. When was that?'

Answer. I should say a little over a year ago. I cannot fix the date precisely.

Question. Were you then inquired of in regard to that speech?

Answer. I was.

Question. And did you produce it then to that committee?

Answer. I did.

Question. Were you examined before any other committee than that?

Answer. No, sir.

Question. Was your testimony reduced to writing?

Answer. I believe so.

Question. And signed by you?

Answer. No, sir; not signed.

Mr. EVARTS. We suppose, if the court please, that this report is within the competency of proof.

Mr. Manager BUTLER, (to the witness.) Was your testimony published?

The WITNESS. The testimony I gave last winter?

Mr. Manager BUTLER. Yes, sir; before the New Orleans riot committee.

Answer. I am not aware whether it was or not.

Mr. Manager BUTLER. Will the Secretary have the kindness to read this speech?

The Chief Clerk read as follows, from the Missouri Democrat of Monday, September 10, 1866:

Speech of President Johnson.

Being set down at the Southern, a large crowd collected in Walnut street, and called loudly for the President. He answered their summons by the following address:

Fellow Citizens of St. Louis: In being introduced to you to-night it is not for the purpose of making a speech. It is true I am proud to meet so many of my fellow citizens here on this occasion, and under the favorable circumstances that I do. [Cry, "how about British subjects?"] We will attend to John Bull after a while so far as that is concerned. [Laughter and loud cheers.] I have just stated that I was not here for the purpose of making a speech, but after being introduced simply to tender my cordial thanks for the welcome you have given me in your midst. [A voice: "Ten thousand welcomes;" hurrahs and cheers.] Thank you, sir. I wish it was in my power to address you under favorable circumstances upon some of the questions that agitate and distract the public mind at this time. Questions that have grown out of a fiery ordeal we have just passed through and which I think as important as those we have just passed by. The time has come when it seems to me that all ought to be prepared for peace— the rebellion being suppressed, and the shedding of blood being stopped, the sacrifice of life being suspended and stayed, it seems that the time has arrived when we should have peace; when the bleeding arteries should be tied up [A voice: "New Orleans;" "Go on."]

Perhaps if you had a word or two on the subject of New Orleans, you might understand more about it than you do. [Laughter and cheers.] And if you will go back [Cries for Seward]—if you will go back and ascertain the cause of the riot at New Orleans, perhaps you would not be so prompt in calling out New Orleans. If you will take up the riot at New Orleans, and trace it back to its source, or to its immediate cause, you will find out who was responsible for the blood that was shed there.

If you will take up the riot at New Orleans, and trace it back to the Radical Congress [great cheering, and cries of "bully,"] you will find that the riot at New Orleans was substantially planned—if you will take up the proceedings in their caucuses you will understand that they there knew [cheers] that a convention was to be called which was extinct, by its powers having expired; that it was said, and the intention was that a new government was to be organized; and in the organization of that government the intention was to enfranchise one portion of the population called the colored population, who had just been emancipated, and at the same time disfranchise white men. [Great Cheering.] When you begin to talk about New Orleans [confusion] you ought to understand what you are talking about.

When you read the speeches that were made or take up the facts—on Friday and Saturday before that Convention sat—you will there find that speeches were made incendiary in their character, exciting that portion of the population, the black population, to arm themselves and prepare for the shedding of blood. [A Voice: "Thats so!" and cheers]. You will also find that that Convention did assemble in violation of law, and the intent of that Convention was to supersede the recognized authorities in the State government of Louisiana, which had been recognized by the Government of the United States, and every man engaged in that rebellion—in that Convention, with the intention of superseding and up turning the Civil Government which had been recognized by the Government of the United States—I say that he was a traitor to the Constitution of the United States, [cheers,] and hence you find that another rebellion was commenced, having its origin in the Radical Congress. Those men were to go there; a government was to be organized, and the one in existence in Louisiana was to be superseded, set aside and overthrown. You talk to me about New Orleans! And then the question was to *come up, when they had established their government*—a question of political power—which of the two governments was to be recognized—a new government inaugurated under this defunct Convention—set up in violation of law and without the consent of the people. And then when they had established their government, and extended universal or impartial franchise as they called it to this colored population, then this Radical Congress was to determine that a government established on negro votes was to be the government of Louisiana. [Voices—"Never," and cheers and "Hurrah for Andy."]

So much for the New Orleans riot—and there was the cause and the origin of the blood that was shed, and every drop of blood that was shed is upon their skirts, and they are responsible for it. [Cheers]. I could trace this thing a little closer but I will not do it here to-night. But when you talk about New Orleans, and talk about the causes and consequences that resulted from proceedings of that kind, perhaps, as I have been introduced here, and you have provoked questions of this kind, though it don't provoke me, I will tell you a few wholesome things that *has* been done by this Radical Congress. [Cheers].

In connection with New Orleans and the extension of the Elective franchise, I know that I have been traduced and abused. I know it has come in advance of me here, as it has elsewhere, and that I have attempted to exercise an arbitrary power in resisting laws that *was* intended to be enforced on the Government. [Cheers and cries of "hear"].

Yes, that I had exercised the veto power, ["bully for you,"] that I had abandoned the power that elected me, and that I was a t-r-ai-tor [cheers] because I exercised the veto power in attempting to, and did arrest for a time, a bill that was called a freedmen's bureau bill. [Cheers.] Yes that I was a t-r-ai-t-o-r! And I have been traduced, I have been slandered, I have been maligned, I have been called Judas,—Judas Iscariot, and all that. Now, my countrymen here to-night, it is very easy to indulge in epithets, it is very easy to call a man Judas, and cry out t-r-ai-tor, but when he is called upon to give arguments & facts, he is very often found wanting.

Judaas, Judas Iscariot, Judaas! There was a Judas once, one of the twelve apostles. Oh! yes, and these twelve apostles had a Christ. [a voice, "And a Moses, too." Great laughter.] The twelve apostles had a Christ, and he could not have had a Judas unless he had had twelve apostles. If I have played the Judas, who has been my Christ that I have played the Judas with? Was it Thad. Stevens? Was it Wendell Phillips? Was it Charles Sumner? [Hisses and cheers.] Are these the men that set up and compare themselves with the Saviour of men, and everybody that differs with them in opinion, and try to stay & arrest their diabolical and nefarious policy is to be denounced as a Judas. ["Hurrah for Andy," and cheers.]

In the days when there were twelve apostles, and when there were a Christ, while there were Judases, there were unbelievers, too. Y-a-s; while there were Judases there were unbelievers. [Voices—"hear." "Three groans for Fletcher."] Yes, oh! yes! unbelievers in Christ: men who persecuted and slandered and brought him before Pontius Pilate and preferred charges and condemned and put him to death on the cross, to satisfy unbelievers. And this same persecuting, diabolical and nefarious clan to-day would persecute and shed the blood of innocent men to carry out their purposes. [Cheers.] But let me tell you—let me give you a few words here to-night—and but a short time since I heard some one say in the crowd that we had a Moses. [Laughter and cheers.] Yes, there was a Moses. And I know sometimes it has been said that have said that I would be the Moses of the colored man. ["Never," and cheers.] Why, I have labored as much in the cause of emancipation as any other mortal man living. But while I have strived to emancipate the colored man, I have felt, and now feel, that we have a great many white men that want emancipation. [Laughter and cheers.] There is a set amongst you that have got shackles on their limbs, and are as much under the heel and control of their masters as the colored man that was emancipated. [Cheers]

I call upon you here to-night as freemen—as men who favor the emancipation of the white man as well as the colored ones. I have been in favor of emancipation, I have nothing to disguise about that—I have tried to do as much, and have done as much, and when they talk about Moses and the colored man being led into the promised land, where is the land that this clan proposes to lead them? [Cheers] When we talk about taking them out from among the white population and sending them to other climes, what is it they propose? Why, it is to give us a Freedmen's Bureau. And after giving us a freedmen's bureau, what then? Why, here in the South it is not necessary for me to talk to you, where I have lived and you have lived, and understand the whole system, and how it operates; we know how the slaves have been worked heretofore. Their original owners bought the land and raised the negroes, or purchased them, as the case might be; paid all the expenses of carrying on the farm, and, in the end, after producing tobacco, cotton, hemp and flax, and all the various products of the South, bringing them into the market without any profit to them, while these owners put it all into their own pockets. This was their condition before the emancipation. This was their condition before we added their "Moses." [Cheers and laughter]

Now what is the plan? I ask your attention. Come, as we have got to talking on this subject, give me your attention for a few minutes. I am addressing myself to your brains, and not to your prejudices; to your reason and not to your passions. And when reason and argument again resume their empire, this mist, this prejudice that has been incrusted upon the public mind must give way and reason become triumphant. [Cheers] Now, my countrymen, let me call your attention to a single fact, the Freedmen's Bureau. [Laughter and hisses] Yes; slavery was an accursed institution till emancipation took place. It was an accursed institution while one set of men worked them and got the profits. But after emancipation took place they gave us the Freedmen's Bureau. They gave us these agents to go into every county, every township, and into every school-district throughout the United States, and especially the Southern States. They gave us commissioners. They gave us $12,000,000 and placed the power in the hands of the Executive, who was to work this machinery, with the army brought to its aid, and to sustain it. Then let us run it, on the $12,000,000 as a beginning, and, in the end, receive $50,000,000 or $60,000,000, as the case may be, and let us work the 4,000,000 of slaves. In fine, the Freedmen's Bureau was a simple proposition to transfer 4,000,000 of slaves in the United States from their original owners to a new set of taskmasters. [voice; "Never," and cheers.] I have been laboring four years to emancipate them; and then I was opposed to seeing them transferred to a new set of taskmasters, to be worked with more rigor than they had been heretofore. [Cheers] Yes, under this new system they would work the slaves, and call on the Government to bear all the expense, and if there was any profits left, why they would pocket them, [laughter and cheers,] while you, the people, must pay the expense of running the machine out of your pockets, while they got the profits of it. So much for this question.

I simply intended to-night to tender you my sincere thanks. But as I go along, as we are talking about this Congress and these respected gentlemen, who contend that the President is wrong, because he vetoed the Freedmen's Bureau bill, and all this; because he chose to exercise the veto power, he committed a high offense, and therefore ought to be impeached. [voice, "never."] Y-a-s, y-a-s, they are ready to impeach him. [voice, "let them try it."] And if they were satisfied they had the next Congress, by as decided a majority as this, upon some pretext or other—violating the Constitution, neglect of duty, or omitting to enforce some act of law, upon some pretext or other, they would vacate the Executive Department of the United States. [A voice, "too bad they don't impeach him."] *Wha-t?* As we talk about this Congress, let me call the soldiers' attention to this immaculate Congress. Let me call your attention. Oh! this Congress, that could make war upon the Executive because he stands upon the Constitution and vindicates the rights of the people, exercising the veto power in their behalf—because he dared to do this, they can clamor, and talk about impeachment. And by way of elevating themselves and increasing confidence with the soldiers, throughout the country, they talk about impeachments.

So far as the Fenians are concerned; upon this subject of Fenians, let me ask you very plainly here to-night, to go back into my history of legislation, and even when Governor of a State—let me ask if there is a man here to-night, who, in the dark days of Know-nothingism, stood and sacrificed more for their rights? [Voice, "good," and cheers.]

It has been my peculiar misfortune always to have fierce opposition, because I have always struck my blows direct, and fought with right and the Constitution on my side. [Cheers.] Yes, I will come back to the soldiers again in a moment. Yes, here was a neutrality law. I was sworn to support the Constitution and see that that law was faithfully executed. And because it was executed, then they raised a clamor & tried to make an appeal to the foreigners; and especially the Fenians. And what did they do? They introduced a bill to tickle and play with the fancy, pretending to repeal the law, and at the same time making it worse and then left the law just where it is. [Voice—"That's so.]—They knew that whenever a law was presented to me, proper in its provisions, ameliorating and softening the rigors of the present law that it would meet my hearty approbation; but as they were pretty well broken down and losing public confidence, at the heels of the session they found they must do something. And hence, what did they do? They pretended to do something for the soldiers. Who has done more for the soldiers than I have? Who has periled more in this struggle than I have? [Cheers] But then, to make them their peculiar friends and favorites of the soldiers, they came forward with a proposition to do what? Why, we will give the soldier $50 bounty—$50 bounty—your attention to this—if he has served two years; and $100 if he has served three years.

Now, mark you, the colored man that served 2 years can get his $100 bounty. But the white man must serve *three* before he can get his. [Cheers]. But that is not the point. While they were tickling and attempting to please the soldiers, by giving them $50 bounty for two years' service, they took it into their heads to vote somebody else a bounty, [laughter] and they voted themselves not $50 for 2 years service; your attention—I want to make a lodgement in your minds of the facts because I want to put the nail in, and having put it in, I want to clinch it on the other side. [Cheers]. The brave boys, the patriotic young men who followed his gallant officers, slept in the tented field, and periled his life, and shed his blood, and left his limbs behind him and came home mangled and maimed, can get $50 bounty, if he has served 2 years. But the members of Congress, who never smelt gunpowder, can get $4,000 extra pay. [Loud cheering]

This is a faint picture, my countrymen, of what has transpired. [A Voice, "Stick to that question."] Fellow citizens you are all familiar with the work of restoration. You know that since the rebellion collapsed, since the armies were suppressed on the field, that everything that could be done has been done by the executive department of the Government for the restoration of the Government. Everything has been done with the exception of one thing, and that is the admission of members from the eleven States that went into the rebellion. And after having accepted the terms of the Government, having abolished slavery, having repudiated their debt, and sent loyal representatives, everything has been done, excepting the admission of Representatives which all the States are constitutionally entitled to [Cheers] When you turn and examine the Constitution of the United States, you can find that you cannot even amend that Constitution so as to deprive any State of its equal suffrage in the Senate. [A voice, "They have never been out."] It is said before me, "they have never been out." I say so, too and they cannot go out. [Cheers] That being the fact, under the Constitution they are entitled to equal suffrage in the Senate of the United States, and no power has the right to deprive them of it, without violating the Constitution. [Cheers]. And the same argument applies to the House of Representatives.

How, then does the matter stand? It used to be one of the arguments, that if the States withdrew their Representatives and Senators, that that was secession—a peaceable breaking up of the Government. Now, the Radical power in this Government turn around and assume that the States are out of the Union, that they are not entitled to representation in Congress. [Cheers.] That is to say, they are dissolutionists, and their position now is to perpetuate a disruption of the Government, and that, too, while they are denying the States the right of representation, they impose taxation upon them, a principle upon which, in the revolution, you resisted the power of Great Britain. We deny the right of taxation without representation. That is one of our great principles. Let the Government be restored. I have labored for it. Now I deny this doctrine of secession, come from what quarter it may, whether from the North or from the South. I am opposed to it. I am for the Union of the States [Voices, "that's right," and cheers.] I am for thirty-six States, remaining where they are, under the Constitution, as your fathers made it, and handed it down to you. And if it is altered, or amended, let it be done in the mode and manner pointed by that instrument itself, and in no other. [Cheers.]

I am for the restoration of peace. Let me ask this people here to-night if we have not shed enough blood: Let me ask, are you prepared to go into another civil war. Let we ask this people here to-night are they prepared to set man upon man, and, in the name of God, lift his hand against the throat of his fellow. [Voice "Never"] Are you prepared to see

our fields laid waste again, our business and commerce suspended and all trade stopped. Are you prepared to see this land again drenched in our brothers' blood? Heaven avert it, is my prayer. [Cheers.] I am one of those who believe that man does sin, and having sinned, I believe he must repent. And, sometimes, having sinned and having repented makes him a better man than he was before. [Cheers.] I know it has been said that I have exercised the pardoning power. Y-a-s, I have, [Cheers and "What about Drake's constitution?"] Y-a-s, I have, and don't you think it is to prevail? I reckon I have pardoned more men, turned more men loose and set them at liberty that were imprisoned, I imagine, than any other living man on God's habitable globe [Voice, "bully for you," and cheers.] Yes, I turned forty-seven thousand of our men who engaged in this struggle, with the arms they captured with them, and who were then in prison, I turned them loose. [Voice, "bully for you, old fellow," and laughter.]

Large numbers have applied for pardon, and I have granted them pardon. Yet there are some who condemn and hold me responsible for so doing wrong. Yes, there are some who stayed at home, who did not go into the field on the other side, that can talk about others being traitors and being treacherous. There are some who can talk about blood, and vengeance, and crime, and everything to "make treason odious," and all that, who never smelt gunpowder on either side. [Cheers] Yes, they can condemn others and recommend hanging and torture, and all that. If I have erred, I have erred on the side of mercy. Some of these croakers have dared to assume that they are better than was the Saviour of men himself—a kind of over righteousness—better than everybody else, and always wanting to do Deity's work, thinking he cannot do it as well as they can. [Laughter and cheers] Yes, the Saviour of man came on the earth and found the human race condemned and sentenced under the law. But when they repented and believed, he said, "Let them live." Instead of executing and putting the world to death, he went upon the cross and there was painfully nailed by these unbelievers that I have spoken of here to-night and there shed his blood that you and I might live. [Cheers] Think of it! To execute and hang, and put to death eight millions of people. [Voices, "never"] It is an absurdity, and such a thing is impracticable even if it were right. But it is the violation of all law, human and divine. [Voice, "hang Jeff. Davis."] You call on Judge Chase to hang Jeff. Davis, will you? [Great cheering] I am not the Court, I am not the jury, nor the judge. [Voice, "nor the Moses."] Before the case comes to me, and all other cases, it would have to come on application as a case for pardon. That is the only way the case can get to me. Why don't Judge Chase—Judge Chase, the Chief Justice of the United States, in whose district he is—why don't he try him? [Loud cheers.] But, perhaps, I could answer the question; as sometimes persons want to be facetious and indulge in repartee, I might ask you a question, why don't you hang Thad. Stevens and Wendell Phillips? [Great cheering.] A traitor at one end of the line is as bad as a traitor at the other.

I know that there are some who have got their little pieces and sayings to repeat on public occasions, like parrots, that have been placed in their mouths by their superiors, who have not the courage and the manhood to come forward and tell them themselves, but have their understrappers to do their work for them. [Cheers] I know there is some that talk about this universal elective franchise upon which they wanted to upturn the government of Louisiana and institute another; who contended that we must send men there to control, govern, and manage their slave population, because they are incompetent to do it themselves. And yet they turn round when they get there and say they are competent to go to Congress and manage the affairs of State [Cheers.] Before you commence throwing your stones, you ought to be sure you don't live in a glass house. Then, why all this clamor! Don't you see, my countrymen it is a question of power; and being in power as they are, their object is to perpetuate their power? Hence, when you talk about turning any of them out of office, oh, they talk about "bread and butter." [Laughter.] Yes, these men are the most perfect and complete "bread and butter party" that has over appeared in this government. [Great cheering.] When you make an effort, or struggle to take the nipple out of their mouths, how they clamor! They have staid at home here five or six years, held the offices, grown fat, and enjoyed all the emoluments of position; and now, when you talk about turning one of them out, "Oh, it is proscription;" and hence they come forward and propose in Congress to do what? To pass laws to prevent the Executive from turning anybody out. [Voice, "Put 'em out."] Hence, don't you see what the policy was to be? I believe in the good old doctrine advocated by Washington, Jefferson, and Madison, of rotation in office.

These people who have been enjoying these offices seem to have lost sight of this doctrine. I believe that when one set of men have enjoyed the emoluments of office long enough, they should let another portion of the people have a chance. [Cheers.] How are these men to be got out— [Voice, "Kick 'em out." Cheers and laughter] unless your Executive can put them, unless you can reach them through the President? Congress says he shall not turn them out, and they are trying to pass laws to prevent it being done. Well, let me say to you if you will stand by me in this action [Cheers,] if you will stand by me in trying to give the people a fair chance, soldiers, and citizens, to participate in those offices, God being willing, I *will* "kick them out" just as fast as I can. [Great cheering.] Let me say to you in concluding, what I have said, and I intended to say but little, but was provoked into this rather than otherwise, I care not for the menaces, the taunts and jeers, I care not for the threats; I do not intend to be bullied by my enemies nor overawed by my friends [cheers]; but, God willing with your help, I will veto their measures whenever they come to me. [Cheers.] I place myself upon the ramparts of the Constitution, and when I see the enemy approaching, so long as I have eyes to see, or ears to hear, or a tongue to sound the alarm, so help me God, I will do it and call upon the people to be my judges. [Cheers.] I tell you here to-night that the Constitution of the country is being enchroached upon, I tell you here to-night that the citadel of liberty is being endangered. [A voice—"Go it, Andy."]

I say to you then, go to work; take the constitution as your palladium of civil religious liberty; take it as our chief ark of safety. Just let me ask you here to-night to cling to the Constitution in this great struggle for freedom, and for its preservation, as the ship-wrecked mariner clings to the mast when the midnight tempest closes around him. [Cheers] So far as my public life has been advanced, the people of Missouri, as well as of other States, know that my efforts have been devoted in that direction which would ameliorate and elevate the interests of the great mass of the people. [Voice: "That's so"] Why, where's the speech, where's the vote to be got of mine, but what has always had a tendency to elevate the great working classes of the people? [Cheers] When they talk about tyranny and despotism, where's one act of Andrew Johnson's that ever encroached upon the rights of a freeman in this land? But because I have stood as a faithful sentinel upon the watch tower of freedom to sound the alarm, hence all this traduction and detraction that has been heaped upon me. ["Bully for Andy Johnson"]

I now, then, in conclusion, my countrymen, hand over to you the flag of your country with thirty-six stars upon it. I hand over to you your constitution with the charge and responsibility of preserving it intact. I hand over to you to-night the Union of these States, the great magic circle which embraces them all. I hand them all over to you, the people, in whom I have always trusted in all great emergencies—questions which are of such vital interest—I hand them over to you as men who can rise above party, who can stand around the altar of a common country with their faces upturned to heaven, swearing by Him that lives forever and ever that the altar and all shall sink in the dust, but that the constitution and the Union shall be preserved. Let us stand by the union of these States, let us fight enemies of the Government, come from what quarter they may. My stand has been taken. You understand what my position is, and in parting with you now, leave the Government in your hands, with the confidence I have always had that the people will ultimately redress all wrongs and set the Government right. Then, gentlemen, in conclusion, for the cordial welcome you have given me in this great city of the Northwest, whose destiny no one can foretell. Now, [Voice: "Three cheers for Johnson,"] then, in bidding you good night, I leave all in your charge, and thank you for the cordial welcome you have given me in this spontaneous outpouring of the people of your city."

JOSEPH A. DEAR sworn and examined.

By Mr. Manager BUTLER:

Question. What is your business?

Answer. Journalist.

Question. How long has that been your business?

Answer. Five years.

Question. Can you report speeches made?

Answer. I am a short-hand writer as well.

Question. Did you join the presidential party when it went to St. Louis, via Cleveland?

Answer. I did at Chicago on the 6th of September, 1866, I believe.

Question. Were you with the presidential party at St. Louis?

Answer. I was.

Question. Did you take a report of any of the speeches made there?

Answer. I reported all the speeches made there.

Question. For what paper were you reporting?

Answer. I was with the party as the correspondent of the Chicago Republican. I made the reports for the St. Louis Times.

Question. Have you your notes of that report?

Answer. I have part of them.

Question. Was there speaking on the steamboat?

Answer. There was.

Question. Did you report that speech?

Answer. I did; part of it. Yes, I reported that speech on the steamboat.

Question. Was that in answer to an address of welcome by the mayor?

Answer. I think that was a speech in answer to an address of welcome by Captain Eads.

Question. Who was he? Whom did he represent?

Answer. I believe he represented a committee of citizens which met the party at Alton.

Question. How did you make this report?

Answer. By short-hand writing.

Question. How soon did you write it out?

Answer. That evening.

Question. How accurate is it where it purports to be accurate?

Answer. It was a report made for the St. Louis Times; and, as a matter of course, reporting for a paper of strong Democratic politics, I corrected inaccuracies of grammar. That is all.

Question. Have you since written that out from your notes, so far as you have the notes?

Answer. I have.

Question, (handing a manuscript to the witness.) Look there and see if that is your writing out from your notes?

Answer, (examining the manuscript.) This is.

Question. An exact transcript?

Answer. An exact transcript.

Question. So far as it goes, is it an accurate report of the speech as delivered by Andrew Johnson?

Answer. With the exception I have mentioned.

Question. With the exception of inaccuracies of grammar——

Mr. STANBERY. Is that the speech at the steamboat or the hotel?

Mr. Manager BUTLER. At the Southern Hotel, on the balcony. They are both here; but I am now asking for the one at the balcony.

The WITNESS. The first is the speech at the Lindell Hotel. ·

Question. The other, the one we are inquiring about, was at the Southern Hotel?

Answer. At the Southern Hotel.

Mr. Manager BUTLER. I mistook. I saw the memorandum "steamboat" there. [To the witness.] Now take the speech at the Southern Hotel. So far as your report goes, as I understand, it is an accurate report of the speech?

Answer. It is.

Question. Why is it not all there?

Answer. I have lost part of my notes.

Question. Whereabouts does it commence?

Answer. The speech in my notes commences abruptly in the middle of a sentence, "Who have got the shackles upon their limbs, and which are as much under control and will of the master as the colored men who were emancipated."

Mr. HOWARD. Where was this speech made?

Mr. Manager BUTLER. At the Southern Hotel, St. Louis. It is the same speech that has been read. [To the witness.] Will you read, sir, where your report begins?

Answer, (reading.) "Who have got the shackles upon their limbs, and which are as much under control and will of the master as the colored men who were emancipated. [Hisses and cheers.] And I call upon you as freemen to advocate the freedom"——

Question. That will do for the present. Does the speech then go through?

Answer. It goes through to the end.

Mr. Manager BUTLER, (to the counsel for the respondent.) Gentlemen, you will see that this report begins at about the top of the first full column of the previous report after the speech commences. [To the witness.] Have you ever compared that with this paper?

Answer. I do not know what "this paper" is.

Question. This paper is the St. Louis Democrat.

Answer. No, sir; I never have.

Mr. Manager BUTLER. We offer this paper now in evidence; I do not care to read it. The variations are not remarkable.

Mr. STANBERY. We will first cross-examine the witness.

Mr. Manager BUTLER. Certainly.

Cross-examined by Mr. STANBERY:

Question. Was this copy of yours published anywhere?

Answer. Yes.

Question. In what paper?

Answer. In the St. Louis Times.

Question. What date?

Answer. The Sunday following; I think the 9th.

Question. State how much time it requires a short-hand writer to write out his notes in what is called long-hand, compared with that which is required in taking down the notation.

Answer. We generally reckon the difference between the rates of speed in writing long-hand and short-hand as about one sixth or one seventh.

Question. That is, it takes six or seven times as long to write out the speech as it does to take the notes?

Answer. No, sir.

Question. How then?

Answer. There are frequently interruptions in the course of a speech; there are frequent pauses of a speaker, and a great many things.

Question. But suppose there are no pauses, but you are merely taking down the speech?

Answer. If a man talks steadily for two or three minutes together, it will take from twelve to twenty minutes to write out what he may say in three minutes time ordinarily.

Question. That is, four times as long?

Answer. Yes.

Question. Suppose he speaks rapidly and excitedly?

Answer. If he is a very fluent speaker it may take longer.

Question. Of course there is a difference between speakers as to that?

Answer. A very great deal of difference.

Question. In a rapid speaker what is the proportion of time?

Answer. My last answer covers it; I cannot say more precisely than that.

Question. Does the standard you give of four times as long apply to those who speak deliberately?

Answer. Yes; I think that would. A man could easily write out the remarks of a deliberate speaker in four times the length of time.

Question. What, then, is the proportion of time in the case of a rapid speaker?

Answer. Some men speak about as high as two hundred and thirty words a minute. A long-hand writer can write out about twenty-eight or thirty words a minute steadily if he is a rapid penman and has no difficulty in reading his notes.

Question. Then it ought to be from eight to ten times as long for a rapid speaker?

Answer. About seven times as long.

Question. Twenty-eight to two hundred?

Answer. That is about seven times.

Question. Then the long-hand writer who is reporting will get, in case of a rapid speaker, one word in seven?

Answer. If he attempts to write out in full.

Reëxamined by Mr. Manager BUTLER:

Question. Do I understand you that the whole of your report of the speech was published in the Times from all your notes?

Answer. Not the whole of it.

Question. Was it condensed for that publication?

Answer. It was considerably condensed.

Question. Was Andrew Johnson a rapid speaker in the manner that he spoke?

Answer. Mr. Johnson is a very fluent speaker and a very incoherent one.

Question. Repeating frequently his words?

Answer. Very frequently; very tautological, very verbose.

Question. Does that enable him to be taken with more ease?

Answer. It enables him to be taken with more ease.

Question. Is it not within your experience that there are men who by practice in long-hand by abbreviations can follow very accurately or quite accurately a speaker who spoke as Andrew Johnson spoke?

Answer. I think they could give the sense of his speech without doing him any injustice.

Question. How was it, taking into consideration the interruptions, supposing such a writer had been taking him from the balcony?

Answer. He would have to indicate the interruptions; he could not write them out.

Question. But could he get the sense of what the speaker was saying?

Answer. Of the speaker, or the interruptions?

Question. Of the speaker.

Answer. Yes, he could.

By Mr. STANBERY:

Question. A long hand-writer may take the sense and substance of a speech; that is, he may take the sense and substance as to his ideas of what are the sense and substance?

Answer. Undoubtedly; he must rely on his own view of what was intended to be said.

By Mr. Manager BUTLER:

Question. By dictating a report from the notes, with another person to write out, it can be much more rapidly written out, can it not?

Answer. Yes, sir; at least one fourth.

Mr. Manager BUTLER. I put this report in evidence. I do not propose to read it.

Mr. STANBERY. Let it be printed.

Mr. Manager BUTLER. Certainly.

The report made by the witness, Joseph A. Dear, is as follows:

Speech from balcony of Southern Hotel.

After a few words of thanks Mr. Johnson was interrupted with inquiries "about New Orleans" and in reply he charged the responsibility of that riot on Congress, saying it was certainly planned and that every drop of blood shed in it rested on the skirts of the Radical Congress, defended himself from the charge of having been a traitor, asked had he played "Judas," to Thaddeus Stevens Wendell Phillips or Charles Sumner, spoke of the majority in Congress as "this same persecuting nefarious and diabolical clan" and referring to an interruption about "Moses" said that there were other men in the country who claimed their sympathy besides colored men.

(*Transcript of notes resumed.*) * * * * who have got the shackles upon their limbs and which are as much under control and will of the master as the colored men who were emancipated (hisses and cheers) and I call upon you as freemen to advocate the freedom of the white man as well as the colored man. I have nothing to complain about emancipation. I tried to do as much and have done as much as—and when they talk about Moses and the promised land—where is the promised land that these people propose to lead them to when they talk about taking them out of America and sending them to other climes what is it they propose? Why it is to give them a Freedman's Bureau and then what? Why here in the South it is not necessary for me to talk to you about the system and how it operates. We know slaves have been worked here before. Their original owners bought the land and bought the negroes, paid all the expenses of carrying on the farm and in the end after bringing the products to the market, if there was any profit on them these men put it into their pocket.

I am not addressing myself to your passions, and when reason and argument again resume their sway on the public mind this prejudice must give way and reason and argument become triumphant. Now let me call your attention to a single fact, the Bureau. This slavery was an \accursed institution but after emancipation took place the Congress here gave us our commissioners, gave us twelve millions of dollars, placed the power in the hands of the President or the Executive, who was to work this machinery with the army to sustain it, and let us work the four millions of slaves. In fine the freedmen's Bureau was a simple proposition to transfer the four million of slaves in the United States from their original owners to a new set of taskmasters. I had been laboring for years to try and get them freed and I was opposed to seeing them transferred to a new set of taskmasters to be worked with more rigor than before. Yes, under this new system they would work the slaves, the government was to bear all the expense and if there was any profits left they would pocket them. So much for this question. I merely intended to tender you here tonight my thanks tonight as we go along and not to talk about this Congress that says the President is wrong because he vetoed the freedmen's Bureau Bill, and because the President exercised the veto power, he has committed a high offence and therefore he ought to be impeached. (No) Yes they are ready to impeach him and if they were satisfied of having as large a majority in the next Congress as this, they would upon some pretext of violating some law or some provision of the constitution they would vacate the Executive of the United States. As they talking about the soldiers let me call the attention of the soldiers to this immaculate Congress, this Congress which can make war upon

upon the) the President because he stands by the } constitution and exercises the veto power in behalf of the people they dared to talk about impeachment

By way of immortalizing themselves and increasing the confidence of the soldiers, throughout this country at one time they talked about impeachment. (How about the Fenians?) (Laughter) So far as the Fenians are concerned let me ask any Fenians, if there are any here to-night, to go back to my history and say who in the dark days of Know-nothing-ism, stood and made more sacrifice for their rights. It has been my peculiar misfortune always to have fierce opposition because I have always struck my blows direct and fought with the right, and Constitution on my side. Yes here was the law of neutrality and I was sworn to support the Constitution and see that law faithfully executed ("Why didn't you do it?") The law was executed, and because it was executed they raised a clamor and made an appeal to the Fenians and they pretended to repeal the law, but left it just as it was. They knew that whenever a law was presented to me proper in its character and softening the provisions of the present law it would meet my hearty approbation. But, to return to the soldier, as they were pretty well broken down and losing confidence at the end of secession, they thought they must do something for the soldier. What did they do? Who has done more for the soldier than I have? who has sacrificed more for the soldier than I have? But they to make them the friends of the soldier they come forward with a proposition—to do what? To give to the soldier fifty dollars ($50) bounty if he has served two (2) years, one hundred dollars ($100) if he has served three (3) years. Now mark this. The colored man that served two years can get his one hundred ($100) dollars bounty, but the white man must serve three for his.

But that is not the point. While they were tickling and attempting to please the soldier by giving him fifty ($50) dollars for two (2) years services they took it into their head to give somebody else a bounty, not of fifty ($50) dollars for two years services—now, attention! as I want to make an impression on your minds of the facts—When, the brave boy who has followed his gallant Officer, who slept on the tented field, who perilled his life, shed his blood and left his limbs behind him, he can get fifty ($50) dollars bounty if he has served two years, but the Member of Congress who never smelt gunpowder can get four thousand dollars ($4,000) extra pay (Loud Cheers) That is a true picture my countrymen of what has transpired in the past. Fellow citizens you are all familiar with the work of restoration; you know that ever since the rebellion collapsed everything has been done that could be done by the Executive department of the Government—in fact, all has been done except the admission of the members of the eleven States that went into rebellion, but having laid down their arms, abolished slavery, repudiated their debts and sent loyal representatives, everything has been done except the admission of the representatives which all the States are constitutionally entitled to. When you examine the Constitution of the United states you will find that you cannot refuse to any state its suffrage in the Senate (They have never been out) That's so! and I have always said they could not go out (cheers) and that being so they are entitled to their equal suffrage in the United States Senate, and no power has the right or can deprive them of it without violating the Constitution of the United States. And the same argument applies to the Representatives in the House. It used to be said that when the states refused to send their representatives that that was secession, a breaking up of the Union.

Now the Radical party have turned round and say that the States are not entitled to representation in Congress. That is to say they are dissolutionists and their position now is to perpetuate the dissolution of the Union and that too while they deny the right of representation they impose on them taxation—a principle upon which in the revolution your fathers resisted the power of Great Britain. We deny the right of taxation without representation—this is one of the great principles of our government. (Cheers.) Let the government be restored, let peace be restored. Many years I have labored for and I am for it now. I deny this doctrine of secession come from whatever quarter it may, whether from the North or South. I am opposed to it. I am for the Union of these states for the thirty six stars representing thirty six states remaining where they are. I am for the Constitution as our fathers have made it and handed it down to us and if it is altered or amended let it be done in the mode appointed for it by that instrument itself and in no other. I am for the restoration of peace. Let me ask this people here tonight if we have not shed enough blood. Let me ask this people here to-night, are you prepared to go into, to go into, another civil war? (No.) Let me ask this people here to-night: are they prepared to set Man upon man and in the name of God lift up his hand against the throat of his brother? Are you prepared to see our fields again laid waste our commerce and business suspended and all trade stopped? Are we prepared to see this land that gave a brother birth, drenched in a brothers blood? I am one of those who believe that a man May sin and that a man May repent and sometimes that having sinned & having repented it makes him a better man than before, (Cheers.)

I know it has been said that I have exercised the pardoning power; Yes, I have (cheers) And I reckon I have pardoned more men than any other man living on the habitable globe. Yes, I turned forty-seven thousand of our men, who were engaged in this struggle, who were in prison with the arms we captured—I turned them loose. Large numbers have applied for pardons and thus I have granted pardons to some, But by some I am attempted to be held responsible for doing wrong. Yes, there are some who stayed at home and did not go into the field who call out about blood and punishment and making treason odious and all that (Laughter) who never smelled gunpowder on the other side. Yes they would condemn and they would hang and torture and all that and they that make the comparison—but if I have erred I have erred on mercys side and some of these croakers assume to set up that they are better than the Saviour of mankind, himself—a kind of over righteousness—thinking they are better than anybody-else and are always wanting to do the Deity's work, thinking they can do better than he can. Yes, the Saviour came and found man sentenced and under the law but when they repented he said "let them live." Instead of putting them to death he went upon and was there painfully nailed by those unbelievers that I have spoken of and there shed his blood and died that you and I might live. Will you execute and put to death eight million of people? It is an absurdity and is impracticable even if it were right, but it is a violation of all law human and divine. (Hang Jeff Davis.)

You call on Judge Chase to hang Jeff. Davis; will you? (Laughter.) I am not the court, I am not the Jury nor the Judge. Before the case comes to me, and all other cases, it would have to come as a case or application for pardon. That is the only way cases can come before me. Why don't Judge Chase, Chief Justice of the United States—in whose district he is—why don't he try him? But perhaps I can answer the question, and as sometimes people will be facetious and indulge in repartee, I might ask you a question—why dont you hang Thad Stevens and Wendell Phillips? [Hisses, Laughter, and Cheers.] I say that a traitor at one end of the line is as bad as a traitor at the other. I know men on some occasions who repeat sayings that have been placed in their mouths by their superiors. who have not the courage to come forward and say themselves, but have their understrappers come forward. I know there are some who talk about the elective franchise for which they wanted to overturn the Government of Louisiana, who say, "We must make contracts and send men to these colored people and manage their affairs for them, and yet say they are competent to go to Congress and and manage affairs of state. Before you commence throwing your stones you ought to be able to say that you dont live in glass houses. Then why all this clamor? Dont you see, my countrymen, it is a question of power and being in power it is their object to perpetuate their power. Hence when you turn any of them out of Office they talk about "bread and butter." Yes, it is the most perfect and complete bread and butter party that has ever appeared in this government, and hence when you make an offer to take a single piece out of their mouths how they clamor. The man who has stayed at home four or five or six years and grown fat and indulged in all the emoluments of office and grown rich, when you talk about turning one of them out it is "proscription,"·and hence it is one of the objects of the Congress of the United States to pass a law preventing the Executive from turning any one out. (Turn them all out.) Hence, dont you see what the policy was to be.

How were the people to get hold of the offices. The idea of rotation in office of the days of Madison and Jefferson seems to be lost sight of; but my belief is that when one set of men have been in long enough it is time somebody else should have a turn, How are these men to be turned out? (Kick them out) How is this to be done unless you can reach them through the Executive. Congress proposes to pass laws to keep them in. How is this to be done unless it is by the President of the United States. Well let me say to you, if you will stand by me in vindication of the constitution of the United States in trying to give the soldiers and people a chance, I will kick them out as fast as I can (Loud cheers). I care not for the menaces, for the taunts, the jeers, the threats. I don't intend to be bullied by my enemies or even overawed by my friends but God being willing with your help I will veto every measure of theirs whenever they come before me. I place myself on the ramparts of the constitution and when I see the enemy approaching so long as I have eyes to see or ears to hear or a tongue to sound the alarm so help me God I will do it and call for you to the rescue (Loud cheers). I tell you here to-night that the constitution of the country has been encroached upon, the citadel of liberty is being endangered (Go in Andy!) Come up to the work and protect your constitution as the palladium of our civil and religious liberty for it is the ark of our safety. Yes let me ask you to cling to the constitution in this great struggle for freedom as the shipwrecked mariner clings to the plank in the night when the tempest flows around him. So far as my public life is concerned the people of Missouri know that my efforts have been in that direction which would elevate the great masses of the people. Where is the speech or vote of mine but what has always had a tendency to elevate the great masses of the people and when they talk about tyranny or despotism where is one act of Andrew Johnson's that has encroached upon the rights of a freeman.

But because I have stood upon the outworks of freedom and have sounded an alarm hence all this detraction that has been heaped upon me. Then in conclusion here to-night I hand over the flag of your country with thirty-six stars upon it. I hand over the constitution of your country with the charge and responsibility of preserving it intact. I hand over to you to-night the great circle of these states. I hand them over to you, the people; I must I have always trusted the people. The great questions which pertain to your interest I hand them over to you with the charge to preserve them as men who can rise above party & come around the altar of a common country & with faces upturned to heaven swear by him and all shall sink into the dust but that the constitution shall be preserved. Let us stand up for the Union of these States, let us fight the enemies of the government come from whatever quarter they may. You understand what my position is—no tyranny—and with you to-night, I leave the Union in your hands with the confidence I have always had that the people will redress all wrongs and set the government right. Then gentlemen of this great city of the Western States in bidding you farewell I leave all in your charge and thank you greatly for the cordial welcome you have given me to your city (Loud cheers).   JOSEPH A. DEAR.

ROBERT S. CHEW sworn and examined.

By Mr. Manager BUTLER:

Question. You are employed in the State Department?

Answer. I am.

Question. In what capacity?

Answer. Chief clerk.

Question. Is it part of your duty to supervise and know the commissions issued?

Answer. The duty devolves particularly upon the commission clerk of the Department to prepare all commissions. The commission is first made out by a clerk who is called the commission clerk of the Department. It is brought to me, and by me sent to the President. When returned with the President's signature it is submitted by me to the Secretary of State, who countersigns it. It then goes to the commission clerk for the seal to be affixed.

Question. Then, when it does not belong to your Department, where does it go—when it is not a commission of an officer in your Department?

Answer. To the Treasury.

Question. That is to say, if I understand, the commissions of officers in the Treasury are prepared at your Department?

Answer. Yes, sir; of a portion of the officers of the Treasury.

Question. Such as whom?

Answer. Such as Comptrollers, Auditors, Treasurers, Assistant Treasurers, officers of the Mint, Commissioner of the Revenue.

Question. Secretary and Assistant Secretary?

Answer. Yes, sir.

Question. Then, after being prepared, they are sent to the Treasury?

Answer. Yes, sir.

Question. Those that belong there?

Answer. Yes, sir.

Question. Those belonging to your office are issued from your office?

Answer. From the Department of State.

Question. Now, will you have the kindness to tell us whether, after the passage of the civil tenure act, any change was made in the commissions of the officers of your Department to conform to that act?

Answer. There was.

Question. What was that change? Tell us how the commission ran in that regard before and how it has been since?

Answer. (referring to forms.) The form of the old commission was "during the pleasure of the President of the United States for the time being." Those words have been stricken out, and the words "subject to the conditions prescribed by law" inserted.

Question. Does that apply to all commissions?

Answer. That applies to all commissions.

Question. When was that done?

Answer. Shortly after the passage of the tenure-of-office act.

Question. About how soon, if you can tell us, one month or ten days?

Answer. I cannot say exactly, but when the first case came up, making it necessary for the commission clerk to prepare a commission, he applied for instructions under that act.

Question. Was the subject then examined in the Department?

Answer. It was.

Question. Was this change made after that examination or before?

Answer. After the examination.

Question. Was it made by the direction of the Secretary or not?

Answer. The case was submitted by the Secretary to the legal examiner, and upon his opinion the change was made.

Question. By order of the Secretary?

Answer. I think so.

Question. You print the form of your commissions on parchment by copper-plate, do you not?

Answer. Yes, sir.

Question. Was the copper-plate then changed to make all forms?

Answer. It was.

Question. For the various kind of commissions?

Answer. Yes, sir.

Question. Have you blank forms of the various kinds of commissions issued by your Department?

Answer. I have. [Producing a number of blank forms.]

Question. Prior to the passage of the act of the 2d of March, 1867, being the tenure of civil-office act, were all the commissions issued to hold office "during the pleasure of the President for the time being?" Were they all issued in that form?

Answer. They were all issued in that form.

Question. Since this change have all commissions been issued in the changed form?

Answer. They have been.

Question. Have such changed commissions been signed by the President?

Answer. They have been.

Question. Has there been, down to to-day, any other change than the one you have stated?

Answer. None at all, that I am aware of.

Question. Has any commission whatever for any officer been sent out from your Department since the passage of the act, except in this changed form?

Answer. I am not aware of any.

Question. Could there have been, except by accident, without your knowing it?

Answer. Not unless by accident.

Mr. Manager BUTLER, (to the counsel for the respondent.) I now propose, gentlemen, to offer these forms in evidence, but I will not read them unless you desire.

Mr. STANBERY. You will allow us to ask some questions first, I suppose.

Mr. Manager BUTLER. Certainly.

Cross-examined by Mr. STANBERY:

Question. Mr. Chew, as I understand you, the old form contained this clause, "said officer to hold and exercise the office during the pleasure of the. President of the United States for the time being." That was the old form?

Answer. Yes, sir.

Question. And I understand you that the words "during the pleasure of the President of the United States for the time being" are now left out, and the words "subject to the conditions prescribed by law" are inserted?

Answer. Yes, sir.

Question. Have you ever changed one of your plates or forms so as to introduce in place of what was there before these words, "to hold until removed by the President, with the consent of the Senate?"

Answer. No, sir.

Question. You never have?

Answer. We never have.

Question. Let me ask you if any commission has been issued to a head of Department different from those that you issued before the tenure-of-office act? Has any commission since

that act been issued to a head of Department?

Answer. I am not aware of any. I brought no forms of commission to a head of Department, and did not examine that question.

Question. Have you a separate plate for the commission of a head of Department?

Answer. I cannot answer that question.

Question. But you recollect no instance in which any change has been made there?

Answer. I do not.

By Mr. Manager BUTLER:

Question. Has there been any commission issued to a head of Department since March 2, 1867?

Answer. I do not recollect at this moment.

Mr. Manager BUTLER. Then, of course, there is no change.

Mr. STANBERY. Of course not; that is what we have proved.

Mr. Manager BUTLER, (to the witness.) Hand to the Clerk all the forms you have brought with you. We offer them in evidence.

The forms offered in evidence are as follows:

Temporary Commission of Deputy Postmaster—Old Form. In the form now used, the words in brackets are omitted, and the words "subject to the conditions prescribed by law" inserted.

President of the United States of America:

To all who shall see these presents, greeting:

Know ye, that, reposing special trust and confidence in the integrity, ability, and punctuality of ——, I do appoint —— deputy postmaster ——, and do authorize and empower him to execute and fulfill the duties of that office according to law; and to have and to hold the said office, with all the powers, privileges, and emoluments to the same of right appertaining unto him the said ——— [during the pleasure of the President of the United States for the time being, and] until the end of the next session of the Senate of the United States, and no longer.

In testimony whereof I have caused these letters to be made patent, and the seal of the United States to be hereunto affixed.

Given under my hand, at the city of Washington, the — day of ——, in the year of our Lord [L. S.] one thousand eight hundred and ——, and of the independence of the United States of America the ——.

——— ———.

By the President:

——— ———

Secretary of State.

New Form Permanent Postmaster—No Form of old Commission in the Department.

——— ———

President of the United States of America:

To all who shall see these presents, greeting:

Know ye, that, reposing special trust and confidence in the integrity, ability, and punctuality of ——, I have nominated, and by and with the advice and consent of the Senate do appoint, deputy postmaster ——, and do authorize and empower him to execute and fulfill the duties of that office according to law; and to have and to hold the said office, with all the powers, privileges, and emoluments to the same of right appertaining unto him, the said ———, for the term of ——, subject to the conditions prescribed by law.

In testimony whereof I have caused these letters

to be made patent, and the seal of the United States hereunto affixed.

Given under my hand, at the city of Washington, the — day of —, in the year of our Lord [L. S.] one thousand eight hundred and —, and of the independence of the United States of America the —.

By the President:

——————
Secretary of State.

[Postmasters are appointed for four years. The words "unless the President of the United States for the time being should be pleased sooner to revoke and determine this commission," are now omitted, and the words "subject to the conditions prescribed by law" inserted.]

New Form Temporary Commission of Marshal and Attorney. In Commissions of Marshal "diligence" is used instead of "learning."

President of the United States of America:
To all who shall see these presents, greeting:

Know ye, that reposing special trust and confidence in the integrity, ability, and learning of ——————, I do appoint him to be Attorney of the United States for the ——, and do authorize and empower him to execute and fulfill the duties of that office according to law; and to have and to hold the said office, with all the powers, privileges, and emoluments thereunto legally appertaining unto him, the said —————— [until the end of the next session of the Senate of the United States, and no longer;] subject to the conditions prescribed by law.

In testimony whereof I have caused these letters to be made patent, and the seal of the United States to be hereunto affixed.

Given under my hand, at the city of Washington, the — day of —, in the year of our Lord [L. S.] one thousand eight hundred and —, and of the independence of the United States of America the —.

By the President:

——————
Secretary of State.

[*Old form:* "During the pleasure of the President of the United States for the time being, and until the end of the next session of the Senate of the United States and no longer," instead of the words in brackets in the above form.]

New Form—Permanent Marshals and Attorneys.

——————,
President of the United States of America:
To all who shall see these presents, greeting:

Know ye, that, reposing special trust and confidence in the integrity, ability, and ——————, I have nominated, and, by and with the advice and consent of the Senate, do appoint him —————— of the United States in and for the ——————, and do authorize and empower him to execute and fulfill the duties of that office according to law; and to have and to hold the said office, with all the powers, privileges, and emoluments to the same, of right appertaining unto him, the said —————— for the term of —————— , subject to the conditions prescribed by law.

In testimony whereof I have caused these letters to be made patent, and the seal of the United States to be hereunto affixed.

Given under my hand, at the city of Washington, the — day of —, in the year of our Lord [L. S.] one thousand eight hundred and —, and of the independence of the United States of America the —.

By the President:

——————
Secretary of State.

[This commission is used for attorneys and marshals. The term of service is four years. The words "unless the President of the United States for the time being should be pleased to revoke and determine this commission" are now stricken out, and the words "subject to the conditions prescribed by law" are inserted.]

Form of Commission for Judges. Answers for permanent or temporary.

——————
President of the United States of America:
To all who shall see these presents, greeting:

Know ye, that reposing special trust and confidence in the wisdom, uprightness, and learning of ——————, I do authorize and empower him to execute and fulfill the duties of that office according to the Constitution and laws of the United States, and to have and to hold the said office with all the powers, privileges, and emoluments to the same of right appertaining unto him the said ——————

In testimony whereof I have caused these letters to be made patent, and the seal of the United States to be hereunto affixed.

Given under my hand, at the city of Washington, the — day of —, in the year of our Lord [L. S.] —, and of the independence of the United States of America the —.

By the President:

——————
Secretary of State.

[In case of judges of Territories the words "subject to the conditions prescribed by law," are inserted. This commission is used for judges of the Supreme Court of the United States, judges of district courts and Territories, and is temporary or permanent, as the case may be.]

Form of New Commission of Secretaries of Legation used either in the recess or session of the Senate.

——————
President of the United States of America:
To ——————, greeting:

Reposing special trust and confidence in your integrity, prudence, and ability, I do appoint (or nominate) —————— secretary of the legation of the United States of America ——————, authorizing you, hereby, to do and perform all such matters and things as to the said place or office doth appertain, or as may be duly given you in charge hereafter, and the same to hold and exercise, subject to the conditions prescribed by law.

In testimony whereof I have caused the seal of the United States to be hereunto affixed.

Given under my hand, at the city of Washington, the — day of —, in the year of our Lord one [L. S.] thousand eight hundred and —, and of the independence of the United States of America the —.

By the President:

——————
Secretary of State.

[The "words during the pleasure of the President of the United States for the time being" were formerly used.]

Old Temporary Consular Commission.
The President of the United States of America:
To all who shall see these presents, greeting:

Know ye, that reposing special trust and confidence in the abilities and integrity of —————— ——, I do appoint him consul of the United States of America —————— and such other parts as shall be nearer thereto than to the residence of any other consul or vice consul of the United States, within the same allegiance; and do authorize and empower him to have and to hold the said office, and to exercise and enjoy all the rights, preëminences, privileges, and authorities to the same of right appertaining, [during the pleasure of the President of the United States for the time being, and] until the end of the next session of the Senate of the United States, and no longer, he demanding and receiving no fees or perquisites of office whatever which shall not be expressly established by some law of the United States. And I do hereby enjoin all captains, masters, and commanders of ships and other vessels, armed or unarmed, sailing under the flag of the said States, as well as all other of their citizens, to acknowledge and consider him, the said ——, accordingly. And I do hereby pray and request ——, governors and officers, to permit the said ———— fully and peaceably to enjoy and exercise the said office without giving, or suffering to be given unto him, any molestation or trouble; but, on the contrary, to afford him all proper countenance and assistance; I offering to do the same for all those who shall, in like manner, be recommended to me by ——.

In testimony whereof I have caused these letters to be made patent, and the seal of the United States to be hereunto affixed.

Given under my hand, at the city of Washington,
[L. S.] the — day of ——, in the year of our Lord one thousand eight hundred and ——, and of the independence of the United States of America the ——.

————.

By the President:

————

Secretary of State.

[The words in brackets have been omitted since the passage of the tenure-of-office acts.]

New Permanent Consular Commissions.

The President of the United States of America:
To all who shall see these presents, greeting:

Know ye, that reposing special trust and confidence in the abilities and integrity of ——. I have nominated, and by and with the advice and consent of the Senate do appoint him, ——, of the United States of America —— and such other parts as shall be nearer thereto than to the residence of any other consul or vice consul of the United States within the same allegiance; and do authorize and empower him to have and to hold the said office, and to exercise and enjoy all the rights, preeminences, privileges, and authorities to the same of right appertaining, subject to the conditions prescribed by law; the said —— demanding and receiving no fees or perquisites of office whatever which shall not be expressly established by some law of the United States. And I do hereby enjoin all captains, masters, and commanders of ships and other vessels, armed or unarmed, sailing under the flag of the said States, as well as all other of their citizens, to acknowledge and consider him the said —— accordingly. And I do hereby pray and request ——, governors and officers, to permit the said —— fully and peaceably to enjoin and exercise the said office without giving, or suffering to be given unto him, any molestation or trouble; but, on the contrary, to afford him all proper countenance and assistance; I offering to do the same for all those who shall in like manner be recommended to me by ——.

In testimony whereof I have caused these letters to be made patent, and the seal of the United States to be hereunto affixed.

Given under my hand, at the city of Washington,
[L. S.] the —day of ——, in the year of our Lord one thousand eight hundred and ——, and of the independence of the United States of America the ——.

————.

By the President:

————

Secretary of State.

[Heretofore this commission read "during the pleasure of the President of the United States for the time being."]

Form of Commissions used for Governors, Secretaries of Territories, and officers under the supervision of other Departments, &c., either permanent or temporary, as the case may be.

President of the United States of America:
To all who shall see these presents, greeting:

Know ye, that reposing special trust and confidence in the integrity and ability of ———— I do appoint him ——, and do authorize and empower him to execute and fulfill the duties of that office according to law, and to have and to hold the said office, with all the powers, privileges, and emoluments thereunto of right appertaining, unto him, the said ——

In testimony whereof I have caused these letters to be made patent, and the seal of the United States to be hereunto affixed.

Given under my hand, at the city of Washington,
[L. S.] the — day of ——, in the year of our Lord one thousand eight hundred and ——, and of the independence of the United States of America the ——.

————.

By the President:

————

Secretary of State.

Form of Old Commission of Permanent Ministers Plenipotentiary issued as far back as 1790.

President of the United States of America:
To ———— , greeting:

Reposing special trust and confidence in your integrity, prudence, and ability, I have nominated, and by and with the advice and consent of the Senate do appoint, envoy extraordinary and minister plenipotentiary of the United States of America ——, authorizing you hereby to do and perform all such matters and things as to the said place or office doth appertain, or as may be duly given in charge hereafter, and the said office to hold and exercise during the pleasure of the President of the United States for the time being.

In testimony whereof I have caused the seal of the United States to be hereunto affixed.

Given under my hand, at the city of Washington,
[L. S.] the — day of ——, in the year of our Lord one thousand eight hundred and ——, and of the independence of the United States of America the ——.

————.

By the President:

————

Secretary of State.

[The words "during the pleasure of the President of the United States for the time being" are now stricken out and the words "subject to the conditions prescribed by law" inserted. The same with commissions for ministers resident and secretaries of legation]

Form of Old Commission of Ministers Resident, permanent or temporary, and is used for temporary commissions of Envoys Extraordinary and Ministers Plenipotentiary.

President of the United States of America:
To ———— , greeting:

Reposing special trust and confidence in your integrity, prudence, and ability, I, ————, of the United States of America, ————, authorizing you hereby to do and perform all such matters and things as to the said place or office doth appertain or as may be given you in charge hereafter, and the said office to hold and exercise [during the pleasure of the President of the United States for the time being.]

In testimony whereof I have caused the seal of the United States to be hereunto affixed.

Given under my hand at the city of Washington the — day of ——, in the year of our Lord one [L. S.] thousand eight hundred and ——, and of the independence of the United States of America the ——.

By the President: —— ——.

Secretary of State.

[If used as a temporary commission, the words used in place of those in brackets are "until the end of the next session of the Senate of the United States, and no longer."]

Examination of ROBERT S. CHEW resumed.

By Mr. STANBERY:

Question. Mr. Chew, how long have you been Chief Clerk?

Answer. Since July, 1866.

Question. How long have you been in the Department of State?

Answer. Since July, 1834.

Question. That is, you have been there thirty-four years?

Answer. Yes, sir.

Question. In all that time before this change did commissions run in this way "during the pleasure of the President?"

Answer. They did.

By Mr. Manager BUTLER:

Question. (handing a written paper to the witness.) I suppose you know Mr. Seward's handwriting?

Answer. I do.

Question. Is the letter I have just shown you signed by him?

Answer. It is.

Mr. Manager BUTLER, (to the counsel for the respondent.) I offer now, gentlemen, a list prepared by the Secretary of State, Mr. Seward, and sent to the Managers, of all the appointments and removals as they appear in the State Department of officers from the beginning of the Government.

Mr. STANBERY and Mr. CURTIS. Of all officers?

Mr. Manager BUTLER. Of heads of Departments. It is accompanied with a letter simply describing the list which I will read, as mere inducement.

Mr. CURTIS. We have no objection.

Mr. Manager BUTLER. I will read it:

DEPARTMENT OF STATE,
WASHINGTON, *March* 26, 1868.

SIR: In reply to the note which you addressed to me on the 23d instant, in behalf of the House of Representatives in the matter of the impeachment of the President, I have the honor to submit herewith two schedules, A and B.

Schedule A presents a statement of all removals of the heads of Departments made by the President of the United States during the session of the Senate so far as the same can be ascertained from the records of this Department.

Schedule B contains a statement of all appointments of heads of Departments at any time made by the President without the advice and consent of the Senate, and while the Senate was in session, so far as the same appears upon the records of the Department of State.

I have the honor to be, very respectfully, your obedient servant,   WILLIAM H. SEWARD.

Hon. JOHN A. BINGHAM, *Chairman.*

Schedule A.

List of removals of heads of Departments made by the President at any time during the session of the Senate:

Timothy Pickering, Secretary of State, removed May 13, 1800.

That is the whole of schedule A. Then comes

Schedule B.

List of appointments of heads of Departments made by the President at any time during the session of the Senate:

Timothy Pickering, Postmaster General, June 1, 1794.

Samuel L. Southard, Acting Secretary of the Treasury, January 26, 1829.

Asbury Dickins, Acting Secretary of the Treasury, March 17, 1832.

John Robb, Acting Secretary of War, June 8, 1832, and July 16, 1832.

McClintock Young, Acting Secretary of the Treasury, June 25, 1834.

Mahlon Dickerson, Acting Secretary of War, January 19, 1835.

C. A. Harris, Acting Secretary of War, April 29, 1836.

Asbury Dickins, Acting Secretary of State, May 19, 1836.

C. A. Harris, Acting Secretary of War, May 27, 1836.

McClintock Young, Acting Secretary of the Treasury, May 14, 1842, and June 30, 1842, and March 1, 1843.

John Nelson, Acting Secretary of State *ad interim*, February 29, 1844.

McClintock Young, Acting Secretary of the Treasury, May 2, 1844.

Nicholas P. Trist, Acting Secretary of State, March 31, 1846.

McClintock Young, Acting Secretary of the Treasury, December 9, 1847.

John Appleton, Acting Secretary of State, April 10, 1848.

Archibald Campbell, Acting Secretary of War, May 26, 1848.

John McGinnis, Acting Secretary of the Treasury, June 20, 1850.

Winfield Scott, Acting Secretary of War *ad interim*, July 23, 1850.

William S. Derrick, Acting Secretary of State, December 23, 1850, and February 20, 1852.

William L. Hodge, Acting Secretary of the Treasury, February 21, 1852.

William Hunter, Acting Secretary of State, March 19, 1852.

William L. Hodge, Acting Secretary of the Treasury, April 26, 1852.

William Hunter, Acting Secretary of State, May 1, 1852.

William L. Hodge, Acting Secretary of the Treasury, May 24, 1852, and June 10, 1852.

William Hunter, Acting Secretary of State, July 6, 1852.

John P. Kennedy, Acting Secretary of War, August 19, 1852.

William L. Hodge, Acting Secretary of the Treasury, August 27, 1852, and December 31, 1852, and January 15, 1853.

William Hunter, Acting Secretary of State, March 3, 1853.

Archibald Campbell, Acting Secretary of War, January 19, 1857.

Samuel Cooper, Acting Secretary of War, March 3, 1857.

Philip Clayton, Acting Secretary of the Treasury, May 30, 1860.

Isaac Toucey, Acting Secretary of the Treasury, December 10, 1860.

Thomas A. Scott, Acting Secretary of War, August 2, 1861.

George Harrington, Acting Secretary of the Treasury, December 18, 1861.

F. W. Seward, Acting Secretary of State, January 4, 1862, and January 25, 1862, and February 6, 1862, and April 9, 1862.

George Harrington, Acting Secretary of the Treasury, April 11, 1862, and May 5, 1862.

William Hunter, Acting Secretary of State, May 14, 1862.

George Harrington, Acting Secretary of the Treasury, May 19, 1862.

F. W. Seward, Acting Secretary of State, June 11, 1862, and June 30, 1862.

George Harrington, Acting Secretary of the Treasury, January 8, 1863.

F. W. Seward, Acting Secretary of State, December 23, 1863, and April 11, 1864.

George Harrington, Acting Secretary of the Treasury, April 14, 1864, and April 27, 1864, and June 7, 1864, and June 30, 1864.

F. W. Seward, Acting Secretary of State, January 4, 1865, and February 1, 1865.

George Harrington, Acting Secretary of the Treasury, March 4, 1865.

William E. Chandler, Acting Secretary of the Treasury, December 20, 1865.

F. W. Seward, Acting Secretary of State, May 15, 1866.

William E. Chandler, Acting Secretary of the Treasury, December 20, 1866.

John T. Hartley, Acting Secretary of the Treasury, September 16, 1867, and November 13, 1867.

F. W. Seward, Acting Secretary of State, March 11, 1868.

Mr. CONKLING. I beg to ask what is the title of the last schedule which has just been read. Will the Manager read it again?

Mr. Manager BUTLER. "List of appointments of heads of Departments made by the President at any time during the session of the Senate." [To the witness.] You told us, Mr. Chew, how long you had been in the State Department. How long was that?

Answer. I was appointed in July, 1834.

Question. We see by the list that there have been certain appointments of Acting Secretaries of State; tell us under what circumstances they were made?

Mr. STANBERY. We must ask that that question be repeated.

Mr. Manager BUTLER. I will repeat the question. [To the witness.] There are in the list certain acting appointments, like those of Mr. Hunter, Mr. Appleton, and Mr. F. W. Seward. I do not ask the authority under which they were made; but I ask the circumstances under which they were made? What was the necessity for making them—the absence of the Secretary or otherwise?

Answer. The absence of the Secretary.

Question. Since 1834, in the thirty-four years you have been there, has there been any appointment of Acting Secretary except on account of the temporary absence of the Secretary, to your knowledge?

Answer. I do not recall any at this time.

Question. By whom were those acting appointments made?

Answer. They were made by the President or by his order.

Question. That is exactly what I want to know. Did the letter of authority in most of these cases—take Hunter's case and Appleton's case, for example—proceed from the head of the Department or from the President?

Mr. EVARTS. We object that the papers must be produced if their form is to be considered as material.

Mr. Manager BUTLER. I am not asking for form; I am asking for fact.

Mr. EVARTS. That is the fact, as we suppose—what the authority or the form of authority was.

Mr. Manager BUTLER. I am asking now from whence and by whom issued; whether the letter, whatever may be its form, came directly from the head of the Department to the Chief Clerk, Mr. Hunter, or to Mr. Appleton, who was the chief clerk, I believe—whether it came directly from the head of the Department or from the President.

Mr. EVARTS. The objection we make is that the letter of authority shows from whom it came, and is the best evidence of from whom it came.

Mr. Manager BUTLER. Suppose it should happen to turn out that there was not any letter?

Mr. EVARTS. Then you would be in a situation where you could prove it by some other evidence. The question is in regard to letters of authority.

Mr. Manager BUTLER. I am asking from whom the authority proceeded, because I do not know now to whom to send to ask to produce the letter until I find out who wrote it.

The CHIEF JUSTICE, (to the witness.) Were any authorities given except in writing and by letter?

The WITNESS. Only in writing.

Mr. Manager BUTLER. I again say, sir, that I am not able to know whom to send to until I can ask from whom those letters came. That is competent always.

The CHIEF JUSTICE. You can ask where the papers are: where these writings are preserved?

Mr. Manager BUTLER. Well, I am inclined, may it please your Honor, to put this question, with the leave of the presiding officer. [To the witness.] From whom did these letters of which you speak come?

Mr. CURTIS and Mr. EVARTS. That we object to.

The CHIEF JUSTICE. The honorable Manager will reduce his question to writing.

Mr. Manager BUTLER. What I propose to ask is whether any of the letters of authority this witness has mentioned came from the Secretary of State or from any other officer. If he says they all came from the President that will end the inquiry. If he says they all came from the Secretary of State then I may want to send for them. I really cannot understand the objection.

The CHIEF JUSTICE. Do the counsel for the President object to that question?

Mr. EVARTS. We object to proof of the authority sought to be proved, except by the production of the writing by which the witness has stated that in all cases it is evidenced. If it is sought to be proved who made a manual delivery of a paper where manual delivery was made to this witness, this witness can speak concerning that, and give such information as pertains to that; but he can go no further.

Mr. Manager BUTLER. I am not now proving the authority; I am proving the source of authority. I am endeavoring to find out from which source of authority these letters came. If they came from the President, that is one thing, and then I can apply there, if I choose, for them; whereas if they came from the Secretary of State, that is another thing, and then I can apply there. I am asking, in the usual course of examination, as I understand the examinations of witnesses, whence certain papers came; were they the papers of the Secretary of State or were they the papers of the President? That does not put in their effect.

Mr. CURTIS. Do you mean to inquire who signed the letters of authority; is that your inquiry?

Mr. Manager BUTLER. I mean to inquire precisely whether the letter of authority came from the Secretary or from the President.

Mr. CURTIS. Do you mean by that who signed the letter, or do you mean out of whose manual possession it came into this gentleman's?

Mr. Manager BUTLER. I mean, sir, who signed the letter, if you put it in that form.

Mr. CURTIS. That we object to.

Mr. Manager BUTLER. I do not do that for the purpose of proving the contents of the letter, but for the purpose of identification of the letter.

Mr. CURTIS. The signature is as much a part of the letter and its contents as anything else.

Mr. EVARTS. Is this offered to prove who signed the letter? We say the paper itself will show who signed it.

Mr. Manager BUTLER. The difficulty is that unless I talk an hour these gentlemen are determined that I never shall have the reply on my proposition. My proposition is not to prove the authority, nor to prove the signature, but it is to prove the identity of the paper; and it is not to prove that it was a letter of authority, because Mr. Seward signed it, for instance, but it is to prove whether I am to look for my evidence in a given direction or in another direction. If the witness says that Mr. Seward signed it, for example, I should have no right to argue to the Senate that, therefore, it was the authority of Mr. Seward; but I am desirous, if I can, to ascertain whether it is worth while for me to go any further than to argue this question; and the objection seems to me over-sensitiveness.

The CHIEF JUSTICE. The Secretary will read the question propounded by the honorable Manager.

The Secretary read as follows:

Question. State whether any of the letters of authority which you have mentioned came from the Secretary of State or from what other officer?

The CHIEF JUSTICE. "Came from the Secretary of State." Do I understand you to mean signed by him?

C. I.—16.

Mr. Manager BUTLER. I am not anxious upon that part of it, sir. I am content with the question as it stands.

The CHIEF JUSTICE. The Chief Justice conceives that the question in the form in which it is put is not objectionable, but——

Mr. Manager BUTLER. I will put it, then, with the leave of the Chief Justice.

The CHIEF JUSTICE. The Chief Justice was about to proceed to say that if it is intended to ask the question whether these documents of which a list is furnished were signed by the Secretary, then he thinks it is clearly incompetent without producing them.

Mr. Manager BUTLER. Under favor, Mr. President, I have no list of these documents; none has been furnished.

The CHIEF JUSTICE. Does not the question relate to the list which has been furnished?

Mr. Manager BUTLER. It relates to the people whose names have been put upon the list; but I have no list of the documents at all. I have only a list of the facts that such appointments were made, but I have no list of the letters, whether they came from the President or from the Secretary or from anybody else.

The CHIEF JUSTICE. In the form in which the question is put the Chief Justice thinks it is not objectionable. If any Senator desires to have the question taken by the Senate he will put it to the Senate. [To the Managers, no Senator speaking.] You can put the question in the form proposed.

Mr. Manager BUTLER, (to the witness.) State whether any of the letters of authority which you have mentioned came from the Secretary of State, or from what other officer?

Mr. CURTIS. I understand the witness is not to answer by whom they were sent.

Mr. Manager BUTLER. I believe I have this witness.

The CHIEF JUSTICE. The Chief Justice will instruct the witness. [To the witness.] You are not to answer at present by whom these documents were signed. You may say from whom they came.

The WITNESS. They came from the President.

By Mr. Manager BUTLER:

Question. All of them?

Answer. Such is the usual course. I know of no exception.

Question. Do you know of any letter of authority for the Chief Clerk acting as Secretary of State which did not come from the President?

Answer. I do not.

Question. Will you upon your return to the office examine if there is any and report to me?

Answer. I will.

By Mr. STANBERY:

Question. Mr. Chew, I see by this list only one instance of the removal by the President of a head of Department during the session of the Senate, and that was an early one, May 13,

1800. You know nothing yourself about the circumstances of that removal?

Answer. Not at all.

Question. You do not know whether that officer had refused to resign when requested, or not?

Answer. I do not.

Question. In your knowledge since you have been in the Department of State in the last thirty-four years, do you know of any instance in which a head of Department, when he has received a request from the President to resign, has refused to resign?

Mr. Manager BUTLER. Stop a moment; I object to that.

The CHIEF JUSTICE. Do the counsel for the President press the question?

Mr. STANBERY. Not now, sir. We have the records.

By Mr. STANBERY:

Question. Have you examined the records of the Department to ascertain under what circumstances it was that President Adams removed Mr. Pickering from the head of the State Department in 1800 while the Senate was in session?

Answer. I have not.

By Mr. Manager BUTLER:

Question. Do you know that he was removed while the Senate was in session of your own knowledge?

Answer. I do not.

Mr. STANBERY, (to the Managers.) You have proved it, gentlemen, yourselves.

Mr. Manager BUTLER. I now offer, sir, from the ninth volume of the works of John Adams——

Mr. STANBERY. There you will find it, I guess.

Mr. Manager BUTLER. I offer from the ninth volume of Little & Brown's edition of 1854 of the works of John Adams by his grandson, Charles Francis Adams,, what purport to be official letters from Timothy Pickering, Secretary of State, to John Adams, President, and from John Adams to him. Is there any objection to my reading them?

Mr. JOHNSON. Will you state the page, Mr. Manager?

Mr. Manager BUTLER. Pages 53, 54, 55. I offer these printed copies as the best evidence of official letters of that date, it is so long ago. We have not been able to find any record of them thus far, but we are still in search. Is there any objection?

Mr. STANBERY. Not at all.

Mr. Manager BUTLER. Then I will read them:

Sir: As I perceive a necessity of introducing a change in the administration of the office of State, I think it proper to make this communication of it to the present Secretary of State, that he may have an opportunity of resigning, if he chooses. I should wish the day on which his resignation is to take place to be named by himself. I wish for an answer to this letter on or before Monday morning, because the nomination of a successor must be sent to the Senate as soon as they sit.

With esteem, I am, sir, your most obedient and humble servant, JOHN ADAMS.

To T. PICKERING, *Secretary of State.*

T. Pickering, Secretary of State, to John Adams.

DEPARTMENT OF STATE,
PHILADELPHIA, 12 *May*, 1800.

Sir: I have to acknowledge the receipt of your letter, dated last Saturday, stating that, "as you perceive a necessity of introducing a change in the administration of the office of State, you think it proper to make this communication of it to the present Secretary of State, that he may have an opportunity of resigning if he chooses;" and that "you would wish the day on which his resignation is to take place to be named by himself."

Several matters of importance in the office, in which my agency will be useful, will require my diligent attention until about the close of the present quarter. I had, indeed, contemplated a continuance in office until the 4th of March next, when, if Mr. Jefferson was elected President, (an event which, in your conversation with me last week, you considered as certain,) I expected to go out, of course. An apprehension of that event first led me to determine not to remove my family this year to the city of Washington; because to establish them there would oblige me to incur an extraordinary expense which I had not the means of defraying; whereas, by separating myself from my family, and living there eight or nine months with strict economy, I hoped to save enough to meet that expense, should the occasion occur. Or, if I then went out of office, that saving would enable me to subsist my family a few months longer, and perhaps aid me in transporting them into the woods, where I had land, though all wild and unproductive, and where, like my first ancestor in New England, I expected to commence a settlement on bare creation. I am happy that I now have this resource, and that those most dear to me have fortitude enough to look at the scene without dismay, and even without regret. Nevertheless, after deliberately reflecting on the overture you have been pleased to make to me, I do not feel it to be my duty to resign.

I have the honor to be, &c.,
TIMOTHY PICKERING.

PHILADELPHIA, 12 *May*, 1800.

Sir: Divers causes and considerations, essential to the administration of the Government, in my judgment, requiring a change in the Department of State, you are hereby discharged from any further service as Secretary of State? JOHN ADAMS, *President of the United States.*

To TIMOTHY PICKERING.

Now, will the Senate allow the Executive Journal of the Senate, of May 12, 1800, to be brought up, by which we propose to show that at the same hour, on the same day, Mr. Adams, the President, sent a nomination to the Senate?

Mr. STANBERY. Do I understand the Manager to say, "the same hour?" Do you expect to prove it?

Mr. Manager BUTLER. I should think, when we come to look at the correspondence, that I am wrong; I think the sending to the Senate was a little previous. [Laughter.]

Mr. STANBERY. You do?

Mr. Manager BUTLER. I do.

Mr. STANBERY. And you expect to prove that?

Mr. Manager BUTLER. I do. [After a pause.] I have not yet heard a decision upon the question whether I am to have the Journal.

Mr. STANBERY. Certainly; we have no objection.

Mr. Manager BUTLER. It is the Executive Journal, and I suppose it cannot be brought in unless the Senate directs it. I will say it is not printed.

Mr. SHERMAN. Mr. President, I move

that the Journal be furnished for that purpose. I suppose there will be no objection.

The motion was agreed to.

CHARLES E. CREECY recalled.

By Mr. Manager BUTLER:

Question. You have been sworn once in this case?

Answer. Yes, sir.

Question, (handing a paper to the witness.) You have told us that you were appointment clerk in the Treasury. Are you familiar with the handwriting of Andrew Johnson.

Answer. I am.

Question. Is that his handwriting?

Answer. It is.

Question. Did you produce this letter from the archives of the Treasury to-day in obedience to a summons?

Answer. I did.

Mr. Manager BUTLER. Mr. President and Senators, it will be remembered that the answer of the President to the first article says, in words:

"And this has ever since remained, and was the opinion of this respondent at the time when he was forced as aforesaid to consider and decide what act or acts should and might lawfully be done by this respondent, as President of the United States, to cause the said Stanton to surrender the said office."

* * * * * * * *

"This respondent was also aware that this act"—

The tenure-of-civil-office act—

"was understood and intended to be an expression of the opinion of the Congress by which that act was passed, that the power to remove executive officers for cause might, by law, be taken from the President and vested in him and the Senate jointly; and although this respondent had arrived at and still retained the opinion above expressed and verily believed, as he still believes, that the said first section of the last-mentioned act was and is wholly inoperative and void by reason of its conflict with the Constitution of the United States."

* * * * * * * *

"And this respondent, further answering, says, that it is provided in and by the second section of 'An act to regulate the tenure of certain civil offices,' that the President may suspend an officer from the performance of the duties of the office held by him, for certain causes therein designated, until the next meeting of the Senate and until the case shall be acted on by the Senate; that this respondent, as President of the United States, was advised, and he verily believed and still believes, that the executive power of removal from office confided to him by the Constitution as aforesaid includes the power of suspension from office at the pleasure of the President; and this respondent, by the order aforesaid, did suspend the said Stanton from office, not until the next meeting of the Senate, or until the Senate should have acted upon the case, but by force of the power and authority vested in him by the Constitution and laws of the United States, indefinitely and at the pleasure of the President."

Now, the second section of the act regulating the tenure of certain civil offices provides:

"That when any officer appointed as aforesaid, excepting judges of the United States courts, shall, during a recess of the Senate, be shown by evidence satisfactory to the President to be guilty of misconduct in office or crime, or for any reason shall become incapable or legally disqualified to perform its duties, in such case, and in no other, the President may suspend such officer and designate some suitable person to perform temporarily the duties of such

office until the next meeting of the Senate, and until the case shall be acted upon by the Senate."

The eighth section provides:

"That whenever the President shall, without the advice and consent of the Senate, designate, authorize, or employ any person to perform the duties of any office, he shall forthwith notify the Secretary of the Treasury thereof."

It will be seen, therefore, Mr. President and Senators, that the President of the United States says in his answer that he suspended Mr. Stanton, under the Constitution, indefinitely and at his pleasure. I propose, now, unless it be objected to, to show that that is false under his own hand, and I have his letter to that effect, which, if there is no objection, I will read, the signature of which was identified by C. E. Creecy.

[The letter was handed to the counsel for the respondent.]

Mr. STANBERY. We see no inconsistency with that part of the act, certainly.

Mr. Manager BUTLER. That was a question I did not put to you. I asked you if you had any objection.

Mr. STANBERY. I tell you we see no inconsistency, much less falsehood, in that letter.

Mr. Manager BUTLER. To that I answer the falsehood is not in the letter, but it is in the answer.

Mr. Manager BUTLER thereupon read the letter, as follows:

EXECUTIVE MANSION,
WASHINGTON, D. C., *August 14, 1867.*

SIR: In compliance with the requirements of the eighth section of the act of Congress of March 2, 1867, entitled "An act regulating the tenure of certain civil offices," you are hereby notified that on the 12th instant Hon. Edwin M. Stanton was suspended from office as Secretary of War and General Ulysses S. Grant authorized and empowered to act as Secretary of War *ad interim.*

I am, sir, very respectfully, yours,
ANDREW JOHNSON.

To Hon. HUGH McCULLOCH,
Secretary of the Treasury.

I wish to call attention again, because it may have escaped the attention of some Senators——

Mr. CURTIS. We object to the gentleman arguing the question.

Mr. STANBERY. It is time certainly we should know what all this discussion means. What question is now before the Senate? What is your question? Let us know whether we have any objection; how it is that this statement is made.

Mr. Manager BUTLER. I am endeavoring to show, sir, that while the President says he did not suspend Mr. Stanton under the tenure-of-office act, and that he had come to the conclusion that he had the right to suspend him before August 12, 1867, without leave of the tenure-of-office act, and without leave of the Senate, yet, acting under the eighth section of the act to which he refers in his letter, he expressly says in that letter that he did suspend him under this act.

Mr. STANBERY. We understand all that.

Mr. CURTIS. He does not say any such thing. We do not object to the honorable Manager offering his evidence; we object to his arguing upon the effect of the evidence at this stage.

Mr. Manager BUTLER. I have argued nothing, sir, except to read the law.

The CHIEF JUSTICE. Gentlemen Managers, the Executive Journal is now here.

Mr. Manager BUTLER. I now produce the Executive Journal of the Senate.

Mr. JOHNSON. Of what date?

Mr. Manager BUTLER. Monday, May 12, 1800. May 9 is the last previous date of executive session:

"MONDAY, May 12, 1800.

"The following written messages were received from the President of the United States by Mr. Shaw, his Secretary:

"Gentlemen of the Senate:

"I nominate the Honorable John Marshall, Esq., of Virginia, to be Secretary of State, in place of the Honorable Timothy Pickering, Esq., removed.

"The Honorable Samuel Dexter, Esq., of Massachusetts, to be Secretary of the Department of War, in the place of the Honorable John Marshall, nominated for promotion to the office of State.

JOHN ADAMS.

"UNITED STATES, May 12, 1800.

"Gentlemen of the Senate:

"I nominate William H. Harrison, of the Northwestern Territory, to be Governor of the Indiana Territory. JOHN ADAMS.

"UNITED STATES, May 12, 1800."

"Gentlemen of the Senate:

"I nominate Israel Ludlow, of the Northwestern Territory, to be Register of the Land Office at Cincinnati.

"JAMES FINDLAY," &c.

Then follows a long list of nominations:

"Gentlemen of the Senate:

"I nominate Seth Lewis, Esq., of Tennessee, to be Chief Justice of the Mississippi Territory, in the place of William McGuire, Esq., resigned.

JOHN ADAMS.

"UNITED STATES, May 12, 1800."

"The messages were read.

"Ordered, That they lie for consideration."

"TUESDAY, May 13, 1800.

"The Senate proceeded to consider the message of the President of the United States of the 12th instant, and the nominations contained therein, of John Marshall and Samuel Dexter, to office, whereupon,

"Resolved, That they do advise and consent to the appointments agreeably to the nomination.

"Ordered, That the Secretary lay this resolution before the President of the United States."

Mr. STANBERY. Will you please to read where it appears there, at what hour, what time of day, that was done?

Mr. Manager BUTLER. I have not undertaken to state the hour. I stated directly to the Senate, in answer to you, that I thought that the letter went to the Senate with the nomination, and I believe it would appear from an examination of the whole case that the nomination of a successor went to the Senate prior to the letter going to Mr. Pickering.

Mr. STANBERY. The honorable Manager will allow me to say he said he expected to prove it.

Mr. Manager BUTLER. The Senate heard what I said. I said I expected it would appear from the whole matter, exactly using that phrase. I am quite sure I know what I said. But, however, as it was the duty of John Adams to send it first to the Senate, I presume he did his duty and sent it first to the Senate before he sent it to Pickering. I mean to say further, that it being all done on the same day, it must be taken to be at the same time in law. But another piece of evidence I adduce is, that he asked Pickering to send in his resignation because it was necessary to send a successor to the Senate as soon as they sat, which he did.

The CHIEF JUSTICE. Do the honorable Managers require the Executive Journal any further?

Mr. Manager BUTLER. No further.

Mr. STANBERY. We have a certified copy of it.

[The Journal was returned to the Secretary's office.]

CHARLES E. CREECY recalled.

By Mr. Manager BUTLER:

Question, (submitting papers to the witness.) Upon receipt of that notification by the President of the United States that he had suspended Mr. Stanton according to the provisions of the civil tenure-of-office act, what was done?

Answer. A copy of the executive communication was sent to the Treasurer, First Comptroller, First Auditor, Second Auditor, and Third Auditor.

Question. Have you the letters of transmissal there?

Answer. I have.

Question. Will you have the kindness to read them?

Answer. Here is one:

TREASURY DEPARTMENT, August 15, 1867.

SIR: In accordance with the requirements of the eighth section of an act entitled "An act regulating the tenure of certain civil officers," I transmit herewith a copy of a letter from the President notifying this Department of the suspension of Hon. E. M. Stanton from the office of Secretary of War and the authorizing of General Ulysses S. Grant to act as Secretary of War ad interim.

I am, very respectfully,

HUGH McCULLOCH,
Secretary of the Treasury.

R. W. TAYLOR, esq., First Comptroller, &c.

The same letter was sent to the others.

Question. Are those officers the proper accounting and disbursing officers of the Department?

Answer. They are for the War Department.

Question. Then, if I understand you, all the disbursing officers of the Treasury for the War Department were notified in pursuance of the act.

Mr. CURTIS. We object to that.

Mr. EVARTS. That is a question of law.

Mr. Manager BUTLER. Were thereupon notified?

Answer. Yes, sir.

Question. Were you there to know of this transmission?

Answer. Yes, sir.

Question. Did you prepare the papers?

Answer. Yes, sir.

Question. Did you prepare them in pursuance of any other act of Congress except the civil tenure-of-office act?

Answer. No, sir.

Mr. Manager BUTLER. That is all. [A pause.]

Mr. CONNESS. I was going to move a recess; but if the witness is to be cross-examined now——

Mr. STANBERY. That will answer. I can wait until the recess.

Mr. HOWARD. Let the examination of this witness be finished.

Mr. Manager BUTLER. I can say to the Senate that we shall reach within a few minutes a place to rest.

The CHIEF JUSTICE. Does the Senator from California withdraw his motion?

Mr. CONNESS. I understand the counsel to wish a recess at this time. I move a recess for fifteen minutes.

The CHIEF JUSTICE. The honorable Manager informs the Senate that he expects to close his evidence within a short time.

Mr. Manager BUTLER. I expect to close it with certain exceptions which I shall name.

Mr. CONNESS. There appears to be a difference of opinion; I only desire to represent the wishes of the body. I think we had better have a recess.

The CHIEF JUSTICE. How long?

Mr. CONNESS. I move that the Senate take a recess for fifteen minutes.

The motion was agreed to; and the Chief Justice resumed the chair at fifteen minutes to three o'clock, and called the Senate to order.

Mr. CONNESS. There seem to be but few Senators present and I move that the Senate adjourn.

Mr. SUMNER. No; I hope not.

Mr. CONNESS. If there is any chance of getting them in, I will withdraw the motion.

Mr. SUMNER. The better motion would be a call of the Senate.

Mr. CONNESS. That is not in order.

Mr. CURTIS. Mr. Chief Justice, it is suggested to me by my colleagues——

The CHIEF JUSTICE. Is the motion withdrawn?

Mr. CONNESS. I will withdraw it at present.

Mr. CURTIS. It is suggested now by my colleagues that I should make known to the Senators that it is our intention, if the testimony on the part of the prosecution should be closed to-day, as we suppose it will be, to ask the Senators to grant to the President's counsel three days in which to prepare and arrange their proofs, and enable themselves to proceed with the defense. We find ourselves in a condition in which it is absolutely necessary to make this request, and I think, and my colleagues agree with me in that——

The CHIEF JUSTICE. The Chief Justice suggests to the counsel that it would be better to postpone that matter until the Senate is full.

Mr. CURTIS. The reason why I thought of making it known at this moment, Mr. Chief Justice, was that I was under the apprehension that there might be some motion for an adjournment, which might in some way interfere with this application, when it would not be in order for me to present it after such a motion to adjourn.

Mr. Manager BOUTWELL. Mr. President and Senators, in the schedule "B," offered a short time since from the State Department, the first name that appears among those appointed during the session of the Senate is that of Timothy Pickering, who from that record appears to have been appointed Postmaster General on the 1st day of June, 1794. We think it a proper time to call the attention of counsel for the respondent to the statutes which we suppose explain the nature of that proceeding. This is the only appointment of the head of a Department which appears from this record as having been made during the session of the Senate. The statutes are first a statute of the 22d of September, 1789, in which it is provided "that there shall be appointed a Postmaster General; his powers and salary, and the compensation to the assistant or clerk and deputies which he may appoint, and the regulations of the Post Office shall be the same as they last were under the resolutions and ordinances of the late Congress." And it was provided in the second section "that this act shall continue in force until the end of the next session of Congress, and no longer." Showing that it was merely a continuance of the post office system that existed under the Continental Congress.

Mr. JOHNSON. Will the Manager give the date of that act?

Mr. Manager BOUTWELL. That act was passed on the 22d of September, 1789. On the 4th day of August, 1790, the Congress passed a supplementary brief act in these words:

"That the act passed the last session of Congress intituled An act for the temporary establishment of the Post Office be, and the same hereby is, continued in force until the end of the next session of Congress, and no longer."

Which was a continuance of the continental system of post office arrangement. On the 3d day of March, 1791, Congress passed another act:

"That the act passed the first session of Congress intituled 'An act for the temporary establishment of the Post Office,' be, and the same is hereby, continued in full force until the end of the next session of Congress, and no longer."

On the 20th day of February, 1792, Congress passed an act making various arrangements in regard to the administration of the post office and establishing certain post routes; and it is provided in that act:

"That the act passed the last session of Congress intituled 'An act to continue in force for a limited time an act entitled "An act for the temporary establishment of the Post Office,"' be, and the same is hereby, continued in full force until the 1st day of June next, and no longer."

This act from which I now read did not contain any provision for the establishment of a Post Office Department as a branch of the Government, but the last section provided:

"That this act shall be in force for the term of two years from the said 1st day of June next, and no longer."

Which would continue this provisional post office system until the 1st day of June, 1794.

On the 8th day of May, 1794, the Congress passed an act covering the whole ground of the post office system, and in that act they provided for the establishment, at the seat of the Government of the United States, of a General Post Office, and that there should be "one Postmaster General," which is the first act which provides for the appointment of a Postmaster General; and then there were all the provisions in regard to the details of the office. The last section of this act which was passed on the 8th day of May, 1794, declared:

"That this act shall be in force from the 1st day of June next."

Which was the day on which the provisional post office department which was the continuance of the continental system terminated. That day was Sunday; but on that day General Washington, who was then President, thought fit, although the Senate was nominally in session, and although it was Sunday, to make the appointment of Timothy Pickering, as Postmaster General. I suppose it will appear from the Journal of the Senate that he was immediately nominated to the Senate and confirmed. This fully explains the nature of the appointment of Mr. Pickering who is, as appears from this record, the only person who was made the head of a Department by an appointment during the session of the Senate.

Mr. Manager WILSON. Mr. President, I wish to call the attention of counsel for the respondent to an entry on the Executive Journal of the Senate of the 10th of May, 1800, also of the 12th of May, 1800, and the 13th, showing that the Senate at that time met at an earlier hour than twelve o'clock. On page 93 of the Journal of the Senate for May 10, 1800, it is entered:

"The Senate adjourned to eleven o'clock on Monday morning."

On Monday morning, May 12, 1800, the Senate met, and the manner of adjournment is as follows:

"After the consideration of the executive business, the Senate adjourned to eleven o'clock to-morrow morning."—Page 94.

"TUESDAY, May 13, 1800.

"The Senate met in pursuance of said adjournment at eleven o'clock."

Mr. Manager BINGHAM. Mr. President and gentlemen of the Senate, we offer in evidence several executive messages of the President of the United States, of dates respectively December 16, 1867; December 17, 1867; again, December 16, 1867; the fourth January 13, 1868, and the fifth December 19, 1867.

[The messages communicate information of the suspension of John H. Patterson from the office of assessor of internal revenue for the fourth district of Virginia; of Charles Lee Moses from the duties of counsel at Brunai, Borneo; of John H. Anderson from the office of collector of internal revenue for the fourth district of Virginia; of Charles H. Hopkins, assessor of internal revenue for the first district of Georgia, and of John B. Lowry, postmaster at Danville, Virginia.]

Mr. Manager BINGHAM. I also offer in evidence, Mr. President and Senators, the communication of the Secretary of State accompanying one of the messages just presented, in which, under date of December 19, 1867, he thus addresses the President of the United States:

"SIR: In compliance with the provisions of section two of the act regulating the tenure of certain civil offices, passed March 2, 1867, I have the honor to report that Charles Lee Moses, United States consul at Brunai, Borneo, was, during the recess of the Senate, suspended from the functions of his office, and that Oliver B. Bradford, consular clerk at Shanghae, was appointed to fill the place temporarily."

I suppose I need not read all the details. We offer in evidence all these messages, with the accompanying papers, as received by the Senate from the President.

Mr. Manager BUTLER. I believe now, sir, that I may inform the Senate that the case on the part of the House of Representatives is substantially closed. There may be a witness or two, who are on their way here, which we shall ask on Monday morning leave to put in. Their testimony is substantially cumulative, not very material; and it is possible that we may have left out a piece or two of documentary evidence in the nature of public documents. Until we can examine carefully all the testimony to see that we have omitted nothing, we should not like to preclude ourselves from offering that. But with these immaterial exceptions, and I trust they will turn out to be no exceptions at all, we have closed the case on the part of the House of Representatives.

Mr. CURTIS. Mr. Chief Justice, the counsel for the President take no exception to what is now proposed by the honorable Managers. It seems to us quite reasonable that they should have opportunity to look over the ground and ascertain whether anything has been omitted, and also if they find that witnesses come here before the next session, whose testimony will be in the nature of cumulative evidence, we shall take no exception to that.

I now desire to submit, Mr. Chief Justice, to the Senate a motion on behalf of the President's counsel that when this court adjourns it adjourn until Thursday next, to allow to the counsel of the President three working days to enable them to collect, collate, and arrange their proofs so as to present the defense to the Senate with as little delay as practicable, and so as to make that consecutive and proper impression which really belongs to it.

We have been wholly unable to do this during the progress of the trial, and before the trial was begun we had no time whatever to apply to this purpose. We think we can assure the Senate that it will very little, if at all, protract the trial, because certainly those gentlemen of the Senate who have been in the habit of practicing law are quite aware of the fact that more time is frequently consumed in the introduction of evidence for the want of having it properly arranged and presented than would have been consumed if the proper efforts had been made outside before the trial was begun. We think, therefore, that we can assure the Senate that a large part, and perhaps all, of this time will be saved if this indulgence can be granted to the President's counsel.

We do not expect to adduce a large amount of oral testimony or a great number of witnesses, but we have a very considerable amount of documentary evidence which we have thus far not been able to collate and arrange, and some portions which we have reason to suppose exist we have not yet been able to search out or find. We request, therefore, that this postponement may take place.

Mr. CONNESS. The rules forbid Senators to make any explanations in the nature of debate. I therefore submit a motion, which is that when the Senate adjourn, or rather that the Senate sitting as a court of impeachment, shall adjourn until Wednesday next at twelve o'clock, which is the time that, in my judgment, should meet the wants of the counsel for the respondent.

Mr. JOHNSON. Mr. Chief Justice, if it is in order, I move to amend the motion made by the honorable member from California by inserting "Thursday" instead of "Wednesday."

Mr. Manager BUTLER. Is that motion debatable by the Managers?

The CHIEF JUSTICE. It is not.

Mr. HOWARD. Mr. President, may I inquire what is the question?

The CHIEF JUSTICE. The Senator from California moves that the Senate sitting as a court of impeachment adjourn until Wednesday next. The Senator from Maryland moves to amend by substituting "Thursday" for "Wednesday." Senators, you who are in favor of agreeing to that motion will say "ay;" those of the contrary opinion "no." [The question being taken.] The ayes have it.

Mr. CAMERON. I call for the yeas and nays. [No, no.]

Mr. Manager BUTLER. I understood, Mr. Chief Justice, and I desire to——

The CHIEF JUSTICE. The question recurs upon the motion of the Senator from California as amended by the motion of the Senator from Maryland, that the Senate adjourn until Thursday next, and upon this question no debate is in order.

Mr. Manager BUTLER. That question is not debatable by the Managers?

The CHIEF JUSTICE. The Chief Justice thinks not.

Mr. SUMNER. On that I ask for the yeas and nays.

The yeas and nays were ordered.

Mr. CONKLING. I rise for information. I wish to inquire whether the Managers want to su m t some remarks upon this motion for delay? i

The CHIEF JUSTICE. The question is upon the motion to adjourn.

Mr. CONKLING. Yes, sir. My purpose is to find out, as influencing my vote, whether they wish the motion disposed of, to the end that they may make some remarks, or not. I presume the Senator from California does not intend to cut them off.

Mr. Manager BUTLER. I had, Mr. President, desired to make a remark or two, and understood it was in order.

Mr. ANTHONY. I understand that the motion is not that the Senate shall now adjourn, but that when the Senate does adjourn it shall adjourn to meet on Thursday.

Several SENATORS. That is it.

Mr. CONKLING. That is certainly debatable.

The CHIEF JUSTICE. Will the Senator from California be good enough to state his motion?

Mr. CONNESS. If the Chair will allow me to state it I will do so. The Chair submitted the question on the amendment before I was aware of it; else I desired to accept the suggestion of Senators around me to make it Thursday in place of Wednesday. What I desired, in other words, was to meet the concurrence of the Senate generally.

The CHIEF JUSTICE. Will the Senator from California allow the Chief Justice to ask if his motion is a motion that the Senate, when it adjourns——

Mr. CONNESS. That was not the form of the motion. I began to make it in that way, but subsequently gave it the other form.

Mr. CAMERON. Now I desire——

The CHIEF JUSTICE. No debate is in order on the motion to adjourn.

Mr. CAMERON. I am not going to debate it. I want to ask the gentlemen Managers whether they will not be prepared to go on with this case on Monday? I can see no reason why the other side should not be as well prepared.

Messrs. Managers BINGHAM and BUTLER. We are ready.

The CHIEF JUSTICE. Order.

Mr. CAMERON. Mr. President, my question is——

The CHIEF JUSTICE. No debate is in order. The Senator from Pennsylvania is out of order.

Mr. CAMERON. I think if you will allow me——

The CHIEF JUSTICE. No debate is in order on a motion to adjourn.

Mr. CAMERON. I am not going to debate it, your Honor; but I have risen to ask the question whether the Managers will be ready to go on with this case on Monday?

Mr. Manager BINGHAM and other Managers. We will be.

Mr. SUMNER. I wish to ask a question, also. I wish to know if the honorable Managers have any views to present to the Senate sitting now on the trial of this impeachment to aid the Senate in determining this question of time? On that I wish to know the views of the honorable Managers.

The CHIEF JUSTICE. The Chief Justice is of opinion that, pending the question of adjournment, no debate is in order from any quarter. It is a question exclusively for the Senate. Senators, you who are in favor of the adjournment of the Senate sitting as a court of impeachment until Thursday next will, as your names are called, answer "yea;" those of the contrary opinion "nay." The Secretary will call the roll.

The question being taken by yeas and nays, resulted—yeas 37, nays 10; as follows:

YEAS—Messrs. Anthony, Bayard, Buckalew, Cattell, Conness, Corbett, Cragin, Davis, Dixon, Edmunds, Ferry, Fowler, Frelinghuysen, Grimes, Henderson, Hendricks, Howard, Howe, Johnson, McCreery, Morrill of Maine, Morrill of Vermont, Norton, Nye, Patterson of New Hampshire, Patterson of Tennessee, Ramsey, Ross, Saulsbury, Sherman, Sprague, Tipton, Trumbull, Van Winkle, Vickers, Willey, and Williams—37.

NAYS—Messrs. Cameron, Chandler, Cole, Conkling, Drake, Morgan, Pomeroy, Stewart, Sumner, and Thayer—10.

NOT VOTING—Messrs. Doolittle, Fessenden, Harlan, Morton, Wade, Wilson, and Yates—7.

The CHIEF JUSTICE. On this question the yeas are 37 and the nays are 10. So the Senate, sitting as a court of impeachment, stands adjourned until Thursday next at twelve o'clock.

Mr. Manager BUTLER. I should like to give notice that all the witnesses may be discharged who have been summoned here on the part of the House of Representatives.

THURSDAY, April 9, 1868.

The Chief Justice of the United States entered the Senate Chamber at twelve o'clock and took the chair.

The usual proclamation having been made by the Sergeant-at-Arms,

The Managers of the impeachment on the part of the House of Representatives appeared and took the seats assigned them.

The counsel for the respondent also appeared and took their seats.

The presence of the House of Representatives was next announced, and the members of the House, as in the Committee of the Whole headed by Mr. E. B. WASHBURNE, the chairman of that committee, and accompanied by the Speaker and Clerk, entered the Senate Chamber, and were conducted to the seats provided for them.

The CHIEF JUSTICE. The Secretary will read the minutes of the last day's proceedings.

The Secretary proceeded to read the Journal of the proceedings of the Senate, sitting for the trial of the impeachment, on Saturday, April 4, 1868, but was interrupted by

Mr. JOHNSON. Mr. Chief Justice, I move that the further reading of the Journal be dispensed with.

The CHIEF JUSTICE. If there be no objection the further reading of the Journal will be dispensed with. The Chair hears no objection.

Gentlemen Managers on the part of the House of Representatives, have you any further evidence to introduce?

Mr. Manager BUTLER. We have a single witness, I believe.

The CHIEF JUSTICE. The Managers will proceed with their evidence.

Mr. H. WOOD sworn and examined.

By Mr. Manager BUTLER:

Question. Where was your place of residence before the war?

Answer. Tuscaloosa, Alabama.

Question. Did you serve in the Union Army during the war?

Answer. I did.

Question. From what time to what time?

Answer. From July, 1861, to July, 1865.

Question. Some time in September, 1866, did you call upon President Johnson, presenting him testimonials for employment in the Government service?

Answer. I did.

Question. What time was it in 1866?

Answer. The 20th or 21st day of September.

Question. How do you fix the time?

Answer. Partially from memory, and partially from the journal of the Ebbitt House.

Question. How long before that had he returned from his trip to Chicago, to the tomb of Douglas?

Answer. My recollection is that he returned on the 15th or 16th. I awaited his return in this city.

Question. Did you present your testimonials to him?

Answer. I did.

Question. Did he examine them?

Answer. Part of them.

Question. What then took place between you?

Mr. STANBERY. What do you propose to prove, Mr. Manager?

Mr. Manager BUTLER. What took place between the President and this witness.

Mr. STANBERY. Has it anything to do with this case?

Mr. Manager BUTLER. Yes, sir.

Mr. STANBERY. Under what article?

Mr. Manager BUTLER. As to the intent of the President in the several articles.

Mr. STANBERY. To do what?

Mr. Manager BUTLER. To oppose Congress. [To the witness.] Will you go on, sir? What did he say?

Answer. He said my claims for Government employment were good, or worthy of attention; I will not fix the words.

Question. What next?

Answer. He inquired about my political sentiments somewhat, noticing that I was not a political man or not a politician. I told him I was a Union man, a loyal man, and in favor of the Administration; that I had confidence in Congress and in the Chief Executive. He then asked me if I knew of any differences between himself and Congress. I told him I did; that I knew some differences on minor points. He then said: "They are not minor points."

Question. Go on, sir?

Answer. And the "influence" or "patronage"—I am not sure which—"of these offices shall be in my favor." That was the meaning.

Question. Were those the words?

Answer. I will not swear that they were the words.

Question. "Shall be in my favor." What did you say to that?

Answer. I remarked that under those conditions I could not accept an appointment of any kind, if my influence was to be used for him in contradistinction to Congress, and retired.

Cross examined by Mr. STANBERY:

Question. Do you know a gentleman in this city by the name of Koppel?

Answer. I do, sir.

Question. Have you talked with him since you have been in the city?

Answer. I have called on him when I first came in the city; I have seen him frequently.

Question. Did you tell Mr. Koppel yesterday morning that all you could say about the President was more in his favor than against him?

Answer. I did not, sir.

Question. Did you tell Mr. Koppel that when you were brought up to be examined since you arrived in this city there was an attempt to make you say things which you would not say?

Answer. I did not, sir. I might, in explanation of that question, say that there was a misunderstanding between the Managers and a gentleman in Boston in regard to an expression that they supposed I could testify to, but that I could not.

Question. Have you been examined before this time since you came into this city?

Answer. By whom?

Question. Have you been examined before, by any one?

Answer. I have.

Question. Under oath?

Answer. Yes, sir.

Question. Who first by?

Answer. By the Managers of the impeachment.

Question. Was your testimony taken down?

Answer. It was.

Question. Were you examined or talked to by any one of them before your examination under oath?

Answer. I had an informal interview with two of them before I was examined. I could hardly call it an examination.

Question. Which two of them, and where?

Answer. By Governor BOUTWELL and General BUTLER.

Question. When?

Answer. Monday of this week.

Question. Did you say to Mr. Koppel that since you have been in the city a proposition was made to you that, in case you would give certain testimony it would be for your benefit?

Answer. I did not, sir.

Reëxamined by Mr. Manager BUTLER:

Question. Who is Mr. Koppel?

Answer. Mr. Koppel is an acquaintance of mine on the avenue—a merchant.

Question. What sort of merchandise, please?

Answer. He is a manufacturer of garments—a tailor. [Laughter.]

Question. Do you know any sympathy between him and the President?

Answer. I have always supposed that Mr. Koppel was a southern man in spirit. He came from Charleston, South Carolina, here—ran the blockade.

Question. Do you mean that as an answer to my question of sympathy between the President and him?

Answer. Yes, sir.

Question. The counsel for the President has asked you if you told Mr. Koppel that you had been asked to say things which you could not say, or words to that effect. In explanation or answer of the question you said there was a misunderstanding which you explained to Mr. Koppel. Will you have the kindness to tell us what that misunderstanding was which you explained to Mr. Koppel?

Mr. STANBERY. We do not care about that.

Mr. Manager BUTLER, (to the counsel for the respondent.) You put in a part of the conversation. I have a right to the whole of it.

Mr. STANBERY. We did not put it in at all—only a certain declaration.

Mr. Manager BUTLER. A certain declaration out of it, that is a part of the conversation.

Mr. STANBERY. Go on in your own way.

Mr. Manager BUTLER, (to the witness.) I will ask, in the first place, did you explain the matter to him?

Answer. I did.

Question. Tell us what the misunderstanding was which you explained to him in that conversation?

Answer. I think, sir, a gentleman from Boston wrote you that the President asked me if I would give twenty-five per cent. of the proceeds of any office for political purposes. I told you that I did not say so; the gentleman in Boston misunderstood me. The President said nothing of the kind to me. I explained that to Mr. Koppel, he probably having misunderstood it.

Question. Did you explain where the misunderstanding arose?

Answer. I told him that I supposed it must have occurred in a conversation between the gentleman in Boston and myself.

Question. In regard to what?

Answer. In regard to the twenty-five per cent.

Question. Where did that arise?

Mr. STANBERY. What about all that?

Mr. Manager BUTLER. I am getting this conversation between Mr. Koppel and this man.

Mr. STANBERY. Not at all. You are speaking about another transaction.

Mr. Manager BUTLER. No; I am asking you if you explained to Mr. Koppel where the idea came from that you were to give twenty-five per cent.

Mr. EVARTS. We object, Mr. Chief Justice. The witness has stated distinctly that nothing occurred between the President and himself, and it is certainly quite unimportant to this court what occurred between this witness and another gentleman in Boston.

Mr. Manager BUTLER. I pray judgment again upon this. The other side put in the conversation between a tailor down in Pennsylvania avenue or somewhere else and this witness. I want the whole of that conversation. I supposed, from the eminence of the gentleman who asked the question, that the conversation between Mr. Koppel, the tailor, and this witness, was put in for some good purpose; and, if it was, I want the whole of it.

Mr. EVARTS. The fact is not exactly as is stated by the learned Manager. In the privilege of cross-examination the counsel for the President asked this witness distinctly whether he had said so and so to a Mr. Koppel. The witness said that he had not, and then volunteered a statement that there might have been some misunderstanding between Mr. Koppel and himself upon that subject, or some misunderstanding somewhere. Our inquiries did not reach or ask for or bring out the misunderstanding. But, passing that point, we stand here distinctly to say that everything which relates to any conversation or interview between the President and this witness, whether as understood or misunderstood, has been gone through, and the present point of inquiry and further testimony is as to the ground of misunderstanding between this witness and some interlocutor in Boston, and we object to its being heard.

Mr. Manager BUTLER. Which he explained to Mr. Koppel, is the point.

Mr. EVARTS. That makes no difference.

Mr. Manager BUTLER. Having put in a part of Mr. Koppel's conversation, whether voluntarily or not, I have the right to the whole of it. I will explain to the gentlemen that I wish to show that the misunderstanding was not that the President said the twenty-five per cent. was to be given, but one of his friends. There is where the misunderstanding arose. Do the gentlemen still object?

Mr. STANBERY and Mr. EVARTS. Of course we object. It has nothing to do with the case.

Mr. Manager BUTLER. I will not press it further. That is all, Mr. Wood.

FOSTER BLODGETT sworn and examined.

By Mr. Manager BUTLER:

Question. Were you an officer of the United States at any time?

Answer. Yes, sir.

Question. Where?

Answer. In Augusta, Georgia.

Question. Holding what office?

Answer. Postmaster.

Question. When did you go into the exercise of the duties of that office?

Answer. I was appointed on the 25th day of July, 1865.

Question. Have you your commission or appointment?

Answer. I have. [Producing it.] I took charge on the 16th day of September, 1865.

Question. Did you receive another commission?

Answer. Yes, sir.

Question. Have you that here?

Answer. Yes, sir. [Producing it.]

Mr. Manager BUTLER, (to the counsel for the respondent, handing them the first commission.) Gentlemen, here is the appointment of Mr. Blodgett from the President in the recess of the Senate. [To the witness.] Is this your other commission?

Answer. Yes, sir.

Question. After you were confirmed by the Senate?

Answer. Yes, sir.

Mr. Manager BUTLER. "To have and to hold for the term of four years from the day of the date hereof unless the President of the United States for the time being shall be pleased sooner to revoke, to determine the commission." This was on the 27th day of July, 1866, issued by the President.

[The commission was handed to the counsel for the President.]

Question. Were you suspended from office?

Answer. Yes, sir.

Question. Have you a copy of the letter of suspension?

Answer. No, sir; I have not a copy of it. It is down with the Committee on Post Offices.

Question. Among the records of the Senate?

Answer. Yes, sir.

Question. When was that?

Answer. On the 3d of January, 1868.

Question. Have you examined to see whether your suspension and the reasons therefor have been sent to the Senate?

Answer. It has been reported to me by the chairman of the Post Office Committee that it had not been sent in.

Question. Can you learn that it has been sent in?

Answer. I have learned that it has not been sent in.

Mr. Manager BUTLER. I suppose Senators can make this certain from their own records, to which we have not access.

Mr. STANBERY. Of course, we know all about it.

Mr. Manager BUTLER. I supposed, sir, you did know all about it. [To the witness.] Has any action been taken on your suspension, except simply that you were suspended?

Answer. None that I know of.

No cross-examination.

Mr. Manager BUTLER. I ask counsel for the President if they desire to be served with notice to produce the original of that letter? [Handing to the counsel a copy of a letter.]

Mr. STANBERY, (having examined the papers.) I see no objection to that. We do not want to put you to the necessity of mere formal proof. Read it.

Mr. Manager BUTLER read as follows:

WAR DEPARTMENT,
ADJUTANT GENERAL'S OFFICE,
WASHINGTON, *February* 21, 1868.

SIR: I have the honor to report that I have delivered the communication addressed by you to Hon. Edwin M. Stanton, removing him from office of Secretary of the War Department, and also to acknowledge the receipt of your letter of this date authorizing and empowering me to act as Secretary of War *ad interim.* I accept this appointment with gratitude for the confidence reposed in me, and will endeavor to discharge the duties to the best of my ability.

I have the honor to be, your obedient servant,
L. THOMAS,
Adjutant General.

To his Excellency ANDREW JOHNSON,
President of the United States.

Mr. Manager BUTLER. I am instructed, Mr. President, by the Managers to give notice that we will ask of the Senate to allow to be put in this case proper certificates from the records of the Senate to show that no report of the reasons for the suspension of Mr. Blodgett has ever been sent to the Senate in conformity with the law.

The CHIEF JUSTICE. Those can be put in at any time.

Mr. Manager BUTLER. Yes, sir. We close here.

Mr. STANBERY. I will ask the honorable Manager under what article this case of Mr. Blodgett comes?

Mr. Manager BUTLER. In the final discussion I have no doubt the gentlemen who close the case will answer that question to the entire satisfaction of the learned gentleman.

Mr. STANBERY. I have no doubt of that myself, but the question is whether we are to be put to the trouble of answering it. That is the point I want to understand.

The CHIEF JUSTICE. The counsel for the President must know that when the Senate has made an order for furnishing to the Managers the certificates which they desire, and they are presented, the introduction of them can then be objected to. At present there is no question before the court.

Mr. STANBERY. My question is to the gentleman under what article this case of Mr. Blodgett comes.

The CHIEF JUSTICE. The Managers of the House of Representatives state that the evidence on their part, with the exception first indicated, is closed. Gentlemen of counsel for the President, you will proceed with the defense.

Mr. CURTIS, of counsel for the respondent, rose and said: Mr. Chief Justice, I am here to speak to the Senate of the United States sitting in its judicial capacity as a court of impeachment, presided over by the Chief Justice of the United States, for the trial of the President of the United States. This statement sufficiently characterizes what I have to say. Here party spirit, political schemes, foregone conclusions, outrageous biases can have no fit operation. The Constitution requires that here should be a "trial," and as in that trial the oath which each one of you has taken is to administer "impartial justice according to the Constitution and the laws," the only appeal which I can make in behalf of the President is an appeal to the conscience and the reason of each judge who sits before me. Upon the law and the facts, upon the judicial merits of the case, upon the duties incumbent on that high officer by virtue of his office, and his honest endeavor to discharge those duties, the President rests his defense. And I pray each one of you to listen to me with that patience which belongs to a judge for his own sake, which I cannot expect to command by any efforts of mine, while I open to you what that defense is.

The honorable Managers, through their associate who has addressed you, [Mr. BUTLER,] has informed you that this is not a court, and that, whatever may be the character of this body, it is bound by no law. Upon those subjects I shall have something hereafter to say. The honorable Manager did not tell you, in terms at least, that here are no articles before you, because a statement of that fact would be in substance to say that here are no honorable Managers before you; inasmuch as the only authority with which the honorable Managers are clothed by the House of Representatives is an authority to present here at your bar certain articles, and, within their limits, conduct this prosecution; and, therefore, I shall make no apology, Senators, for asking your close attention to these articles, one after the other, in manner and form as they are here presented, to ascertain, in the first place, what are the substantial allegations in each of them, what is the legal operation and effect of those allegations, and what proof is necessary to be adduced in order to sustain them; and I shall begin with the first, not merely because the House of Representatives, in arranging these articles, have placed that first in order, but because the subject-matter of that article is of such a character that it forms the foundation of the first eight articles in the series, and enters materially into two of the remaining three.

What, then, is the substance of this first article? What, as the lawyers say, are the *gravamenina* contained in it? There is a great deal of verbiage—I do not mean by that unnecessary verbiage—in the description of the substantive matters set down in this article. Stripped of that verbiage it amounts exactly to these things: first, that the order set out in the article for the removal of Mr. Stanton, if executed, would be a violation of the tenure-of-office act; second, that it was a violation of the tenure-of-office act; third, that it was an intentional violation of the tenure-of-office act; fourth, that it was a violation of the Constitution of the United States; and fifth, was by the President intended to be so. Or, to draw all this into one sentence which yet may be intelligible and clear enough, I suppose the substance of this first article is that the order for the removal of Mr. Stanton was and was intended to be a violation of the tenure-of-office act, and was intended to be a violation of the Constitution of the United States. These are the allegations which it is necessary for the honorable Managers to make out in proof to support that article.

Now, there is a question involved here which enters deeply, as I have already intimated, into the first eight articles in this series, and materially touches two of the others; and to that question I desire in the first place to invite the attention of the court. That question is, whether Mr. Stanton's case comes under the tenure-of-office act. If it does not, if the true construction and effect of the tenure-of-office act when applied to the facts of his case excludes it, then it will be found by honorable Senators when they come to examine this and the other articles that a mortal wound has been inflicted upon them by that decision. I must, therefore, ask your attention to the construction and application of the first section of the tenure-of-office act. It is, as Senators know, but dry work; it requires close, careful attention and reflection; no doubt it will receive them. Allow me, in the first place, to read that section:

"That every person holding any official office to which he has been appointed by and with the advice and consent of the Senate, and every person who shall hereafter be appointed to any such office, and shall become duly qualified to act therein, is and shall be entitled to hold such office until a successor shall have been in like manner appointed and duly qualified, except as herein otherwise provided."

Then comes what is "otherwise provided:"

"*Provided*, That the Secretaries of State, of the Treasury, of War, of the Navy, and of the Interior, the Postmaster General, and the Attorney General, shall hold their offices respectively for and during the term of the President by whom they may have been appointed, and for one month thereafter, subject to removal by and with the advice and consent of the Senate."

Here is a section, then, the body of which applies to all civil officers, as well to those then in office as to those who should thereafter be appointed. The body of that section contains a declaration that every such officer "is," that is, if he is now in office, "and shall be," that is, if he shall hereafter be appointed to office, entitled to hold until a successor is appointed and qualified in his place. That is the body of the section. But out of this body of the section it is explicitly declared that there is to be excepted a particular class of officers "except as herein otherwise provided." There is to be excepted out of this general description of all civil officers a particular class of officers as to whom something is "otherwise provided;" that is, a different rule is to be announced for them.

The Senate will perceive that in the body of the section all officers, as well those then holding office as those thereafter to be appointed, are included. The language is:

"Every person holding any civil office to which he has been appointed." * * * * "and every person who shall hereafter be appointed," * * * "is and shall be entitled," &c.

It affects the present; it sweeps over all who are in office, and come within the body of the section; it includes by its terms as well all those now in office as those who may be hereafter appointed. But when you come to the proviso the first noticeable thing is that this language is changed; it is not that "every Secretary who now is, and hereafter may be, in office shall be entitled to hold that office" by a certain rule which is here prescribed; but the proviso, while it fixes a rule for the future only, makes no declaration of the present right of one of this class of officers, and the question whether any particular Secretary comes within that rule depends on another question, whether his case comes within the description contained in the proviso. There is no language which expressly brings him within the proviso; there is no express declaration, as in the body of the section, that "he is, and hereafter shall be, entitled" merely because he holds the office of Secretary at the time of the passage of the law. There is nothing to bring him within the proviso, I repeat, unless the description which the proviso contains applies to and includes his case. Now, let us see if it does.

"That the Secretaries of State, &c., shall hold their offices respectively for and during the term of the President by whom they may have been appointed."

The first inquiry which arises on this language is as to the meaning of the words "for and during the term of the President." Mr. Stanton, as appears by the commission which has been put into the case by the honorable

Managers, was appointed in January, 1862, during the first term of President Lincoln. Are these words, "during the term of the President," applicable to Mr. Stanton's case? That depends upon whether an expounder of this law judicially, who finds set down in it as a part of the descriptive words "during the term of the President," has any right to add "and any other term for which he may afterward be elected." By what authority short of legislative power can those words be put into the statute so that "during the term of the President" shall be held to mean "and any other term or terms for which the President may be elected?" I respectfully submit no such judicial interpretation can be put on the words.

Then, if you please, take the next step. "During the term of the President by whom he was appointed." At the time when this order was issued for the removal of Mr. Stanton was he holding "during the term of the President by whom he was appointed?" The honorable Managers say yes, because, as they say, Mr. Johnson is merely serving out the residue of Mr. Lincoln's term. But is that so under the provisions of the Constitution of the United States? I pray you to allow me to read two clauses which are applicable to this question. The first is the first section of the second article:

"The executive power shall be vested in a President of the United States of America. He shall hold his office during the term of four years, and, together with the Vice President, chosen for the same term, be elected, as follows."

There is a declaration that the President and the Vice President is each respectively to hold his office for the term of four years; but that does not stand alone; here is its qualification:

"In case of the removal of the President from office, or of his death, resignation, or inability to discharge the powers and duties of the said office, the same shall devolve on the Vice President."

So that although the President, like the Vice President, is elected for a term of four years, and each is elected for the same term, the President is not to hold his office absolutely during four years. The limit of four years is not an absolute limit. Death is a limit. A "conditional limitation," as the lawyers call it, is imposed on his tenure of office. And when, according to this second passage which I have read, the President dies, his term of four years for which he was elected, and during which he was to hold, provided he should so long live, terminates, and the office devolves on the Vice President. For what period of time? For the remainder of the term for which the Vice President was elected. And there is no more propriety, under these provisions of the Constitution of the United States, in calling the time during which Mr. Johnson holds the office of President after it was devolved upon him a part of Mr. Lincoln's term than there would be propriety in saying that one sovereign who succeeded to another sovereign by death holds a part of his predecessor's term. The term

assigned to Mr. Lincoln by the Constitution was conditionally assigned to him. It was to last four years if not sooner ended; but if sooner ended by his death, then the office was devolved on the Vice President, and the term of the Vice President to hold the office then began.

I submit, then, that upon this language of the act it is apparent that Mr. Stanton's case cannot be considered as within it. This law, however, as Senators very well know, had a purpose; there was a practical object in the view of Congress; and, however clear it might seem that the language of the law when applied to Mr. Stanton's case would exclude that case, however clear that might seem on the mere words of the law, if the purpose of the law could be discerned, and that purpose plainly required a different interpretation, that different interpretation should be given. But, on the other hand, if the purpose in view was one requiring that interpretation to which I have been drawing your attention, then it greatly strengthens the argument; because, not only the language of the act itself, but the practical object which the legislature had in view in using that language demands that interpretation.

Now, there can be no dispute concerning what that purpose was, as I suppose. Here is a peculiar class of officers singled out from all others and brought within this provision. Why is this? It is because the Constitution has provided that these principal officers in the several Executive Departments may be called upon by the President for advice "respecting"—for that is the language of the Constitution—"their several duties"—not, as I read the Constitution, that he may call upon the Secretary of War for advice concerning questions arising in the Department of War. He may call upon him for advice concerning questions which are a part of the duty of the President, as well as questions which belong only to the Department of War. Allow me to read that clause of the Constitution, and see if this be not its true interpretation. The language of the Constitution is, that—

"He [the President] may require the opinion in writing of the principal officer in each of the Executive Departments upon any subject relating to the duties of their respective offices."

As I read it, relating to the duties of the offices of these principal officers, or relating to the duties of the President himself. At all events, such was the practical interpretation put upon the Constitution from the beginning of the Government; and every gentleman who listens to me who is familiar, as you all are, with the political history of the country, knows that from an early period of the administration of General Washington his Secretaries were called upon for advice concerning matters not within their respective Departments, and so the practice has continued from that time to this. This is one thing which distinguishes this class of officers from any other embraced within the body of the law.

But there is another. The Constitution undoubtedly contemplated that there should be Executive Departments created, the heads of which were to assist the President in the administration of the laws as well as by their advice. They were to be the hands and the voice of the President; and accordingly that has been so practiced from the beginning, and the legislation of Congress has been framed on this assumption in the organization of the Departments, and emphatically in the act which constituted the Department of War. That provides, as Senators well remember, in so many words, that the Secretary of War is to discharge such duties of a general description there given as shall be assigned to him by the President, and that he is to perform them under the President's instructions and directions.

Let me repeat, that the Secretary of War and the other Secretaries, the Postmaster General and the Attorney General, are deemed to be the assistants of the President in the performance of his great duty to take care that the laws are faithfully executed; that they speak for and act for him. Now, do not these two views furnish the reasons why this class of officers was excepted out of the law? They were to be the advisers of the President; they were to be the immediate confidential assistants of the President, for whom he was to be responsible, but in whom he was expected to repose a great amount of trust and confidence; and therefore it was that this act has connected the tenure of office of these Secretaries to which it applies with the President by whom they were appointed. It says, in the description which the act gives of the future tenure of office of Secretaries, that a controlling regard is to be had to the fact that the Secretary whose tenure is to be regulated was appointed by some particular President; and during the term of that President he shall continue to hold his office; but as for Secretaries who are in office, not appointed by the President, we have nothing to say; we leave them as they heretofore have been. I submit to Senators that this is the natural, and, having regard to the character of these officers, the necessary conclusion, that the tenure of the office of a Secretary here described is a tenure during the term of service of the President by whom he was appointed; that it was not the intention of Congress to compel a President of the United States to continue in office a Secretary not appointed by himself.

We have, however, fortunately, not only the means of interpreting this law which I have alluded to, namely, the language of the act, the evident character and purpose of the act, but we have decisive evidence of what was intended and understood to be the meaning and effect of this law in each branch of Congress at the time when it was passed. In order to make this more apparent and its just weight

more evident allow me to state, what is very familiar, no doubt, to Senators, but which I wish to recall to their minds, the history of this proviso, this exception.

The bill, as Senators will recollect, originally excluded these officers altogether. It made no attempt, indeed it rejected all attempts, to prescribe a tenure of office for them, as inappropriate to the necessities of the Government. So the bill went to the House of Representatives. It was there amended by putting the Secretaries on the same footing as all other civil officers appointed with the advice and consent of the Senate, and, thus amended, came back to this body. This body disagreed to the amendment. Thereupon a committee of conference was appointed, and that committee, on the part of the House, had for its chairman Hon. Mr. SCHENCK, of Ohio, and on the part of this body Hon. Mr. WILLIAMS, of Oregon, and Hon. Mr. SHERMAN, of Ohio. The committee of conference came to an agreement to alter the bill by striking these Secretaries out of the body of the bill and inserting them in the proviso containing the matter now under consideration. Of course when this report was made to the House of Representatives and to this body it was incumbent on the committee charged with looking after its intentions and estimates of the public necessities in reference to that conference—it was expected that they would explain what had been agreed to, with a view that the body itself, thus understanding what had been agreed to be done, could proceed to act intelligently on the matter.

Now, I wish to read to the Senate the explanation given by Hon. Mr. SCHENCK, the chairman of this conference on the part of the House, when he made his report to the House concerning this proviso. After the reading of the report, Mr. SCHENCK said:

"I propose to demand the previous question upon the question of agreeing to the report of the committee of conference. But before doing so, I will explain to the House the condition of the bill and the decision of the conference committee upon it. It will be remembered that by the bill as it passed the Senate it was provided that the concurrence of the Senate should be required in all removals from office, except in the case of the heads of Departments. The House amended the bill of the Senate so as to extend this requirement to the heads of Departments as well as to other officers.

"The committee of conference have agreed that the Senate shall accept the amendment of the House. But, inasmuch as this would compel the President to keep around him heads of Departments until the end of his term, who would hold over to another term, a compromise was made by which a further amendment is added to this portion of the bill, so that the term of office of the heads of Departments shall expire with the term of the President who appointed them, allowing those heads of Departments one month longer, in which, in case of death or otherwise, other heads of Departments can be named. This is the whole effect of the proposition reported by the committee of conference; it is, in fact, an acceptance by the Senate of the position taken by the House."—*Congressional Globe*, Thirty-Ninth Congress, second session, p. 1340.

Then a question was asked, whether it would be necessary that the Senate should concur in all other appointments, &c.; in reply to which Mr. Schenck said:

"That is the case. But their terms of office"—

That is, the Secretaries' terms of office—

"are limited, as they are not now limited by law, so that they expire with the term of service of the President who appoints them, and one month after, in case of death or other accident, until others can be substituted for them by the incoming President."— *Ibid.*

Allow me to repeat that sentence:

"They expire with the term of service of the President who appoints them, and one month after, in case of death or other accident."

In this body, on the report being made, the chairman, Hon. Mr. Williams, made an explanation. That explanation was in substance the same as that made by Mr. Schenck in the House, and thereupon a considerable debate sprang up, which was not the case in the House, for this explanation of Mr. Schenck was accepted by the House as correct, and unquestionably was acted upon by the House as giving the true sense, meaning, and effect of this bill. In this body, as I have said, a considerable debate sprang up. It would take too much of your time and too much of my strength to undertake to read this debate, and there is not a great deal of it which I can select so as to present it fairly and intelligibly without reading the accompanying parts; but I think the whole of it may fairly be summed up in this statement: that it was charged by one of the honorable Senators from Wisconsin that it was the intention of those who favored this bill to keep in office Mr. Stanton and certain other Secretaries. That was directly met by the honorable Senator from Ohio, one of the members of the committee of conference, by this statement:

"I do not understand the logic of the Senator from Wisconsin. He first attributes a purpose to the committee of conference which I say is not true. I say that the Senate have not legislated with a view to any persons or any President, and therefore he commences by asserting what is not true. We do not legislate in order to keep in the Secretary of War, the Secretary of the Navy, or the Secretary of State."—*Ibid.*, p. 1516.

Then a conversation arose between the honorable Senator from Ohio and another honorable Senator, and the honorable Senator from Ohio continued thus:

"That the Senate had.no such purpose is shown by its vote twice to make this exception. That this provision does not apply to the present case is shown by the fact that its language is so framed as not to apply to the present President. The Senator shows that himself, and argues truly that it would not prevent the present President from removing the Secretary of War, the Secretary of the Navy, and the Secretary of State. And if I supposed that either of these gentlemen was so wanting in manhood, in honor, as to hold his place after the politest intimation by the President of the United States that his services were no longer needed, I certainly, as a Senator, would consent to his removal at any time, and so would we all."—*Ibid.*, p, 1516.

I read this, Senators, not as expressing the opinion of an individual Senator concerning the meaning of a law which was under discussion and was about to pass into legislation.

I read it as the report; for it is that in effect— the explanation, rather, of the report of the committee of conference appointed by this body to see whether this body could agree with the House of Representatives in the frame of this bill, which committee came back here with a report that a certain alteration had been made and agreed upon by the committee of conference, and that its effect was what is above stated. And now I ask the Senate, looking at the language of this law, looking at its purpose, looking at the circumstances under which it was passed, the meaning thus attached to it by each of the bodies which consented to it, whether it is possible to hold that Mr. Stanton's case is within the scope of that tenure-of-office act? I submit it is not possible.

I now return to the allegations in this first article; and the first allegation, as Senators will remember, is that the issuing of the order which is set out in the article was a violation of the tenure-of-office act. It is perfectly clear that that is not true. The tenure-of-office act in its sixth section enacts "that every removal, appointment, or employment, made, had, or exercised, contrary to the provisions of this act," &c., shall be deemed a high misdemeanor. "Every removal contrary to the provisions of this act." In the first place no removal has taken place. They set out an order. If Mr. Stanton had obeyed that order there would have been a removal; but, inasmuch as Mr. Stanton disobeyed that order, there was no removal. So it is quite clear that, looking to this sixth section of the act, they have made out no case of a removal within its terms; and, therefore, no case of violation of the act by a removal. But it must not only be a removal, it must be "contrary to the provisions of this act;" and, therefore, if you could hold the order to be in effect a removal, unless Mr. Stanton's case was within this act, unless this act gave Mr. Stanton a tenure of office and protected it, of course the removal, even if it had been actual instead of attempted merely, would not have been "contrary to the provisions of the act," for the act had nothing to do with it.

But this article, as Senators will perceive on looking at it, does not allege simply that the order for the removal of Mr. Stanton was a violation of the tenure-of-office act. The honorable House of Representatives have not, by this article, attempted to erect a mistake into a crime. I have been arguing to you at considerable length, no doubt trying your patience thereby, the construction of that tenure-of-office law. I have a clear idea of what its construction ought to be. Senators, more or less of them who have listened to me, may have a different view of its construction, but I think they will in all candor admit that there is a question of construction; there is a question what the meaning of this law was; a question whether it was applicable to Mr. Stanton's case; a very honest and solid question which any man could entertain, and therefore I repeat it is important to observe that the honorable House of Representatives have not, by this article, endeavored to charge the President with a high misdemeanor because he had been honestly mistaken in construing that law. They go further and take the necessary step. They charge him with intentionally misconstruing it; they say, "Which order was unlawfully issued with intention then and there to violate said act." So that, in order to maintain the substance of this article, without which it was not designed by the House of Representatives to stand and cannot stand, it is necessary for them to show that the President willfully misconstrued this law; that having reason to believe and actually believing, after the use of due inquiry, that Mr. Stanton's case was within the law, he acted as if it was not within the law. That is the substance of the charge.

What is the proof in support of that allegation offered by the honorable Managers? Senators must undoubtedly be familiar with the fact that the office of President of the United States, as well as many other executive offices, and to some extent legislative offices, call upon those who hold them for the exercise of judgment and skill in the construction and application of laws. It is true that the strictly judicial power of the country, technically speaking, is vested in the Supreme Court and such inferior courts as Congress from time to time have established or may establish. But there is a great mass of work to be performed by executive officers in the discharge of their duties, which is of a judicial character. Take, for instance, all that is done in the auditing of accounts; that is judicial whether it be done by an auditor or a comptroller, or whether it be done by a chancellor; and the work has the same character whether done by one or by the other. They must construe and apply the laws; they must investigate and ascertain facts; they must come to some results compounded of the law and of the facts.

Now, this class of duties the President of the United States has to perform. A case is brought before him, which, in his judgment, calls for action; his first inquiry must be, what is the law on the subject? He encounters, among other things, this tenure-of-office law in the course of his inquiry. His first duty is to construe that law; to see whether it applies to the case; to use, of course, in doing so, all those means and appliances which the Constitution and the laws of the country have put into his hands to enable him to come to a correct decision. But after all, he must decide in order either to act or to refrain from action.

That process the President in this case was obliged to go through, and did go through; and he came to the conclusion that the case of Mr. Stanton was not within this law. He came to that conclusion, not merely by an examination of this law himself, but by resorting to the advice which the Constitution and laws of the country enable him to call for to assist him in coming to a correct conclusion. Having done so, are the Senate prepared to say that the conclusion he reached must have been a willful misconstruction—so willful, so wrong, that it can justly and properly, and for the purpose of this prosecution, effectively be termed a high misdemeanor? How does the law read? What are its purposes and objects? How was it understood here at the time when it was passed? How is it possible for this body to convict the President of the United States of a high misdemeanor for construing a law as those who made it construed it at the time when it was made?

I submit to the Senate that thus far no great advance has been made toward the conclusion either that the allegation in this article that this order was a violation of the tenure-of-office act is true, or that there was an intent on the part of the President thus to violate it. And although we have not yet gone over all the allegations in this article, we have met its "head and front," and what remains will be found to be nothing but incidental and circumstantial, and not the principal subject. If Mr. Stanton was not within this act, if he held the office of Secretary for the Department of War at the pleasure of President Johnson as he held it at the pleasure of President Lincoln, if he was bound by law to obey that order which was given to him, and quit the place instead of being sustained by law in resisting that order, I think the honorable Managers will find it extremely difficult to construct out of the broken fragments of this article anything which will amount to a high misdemeanor. What are they? They are, in the first place, that the President did violate, and intended to violate, the Constitution of the United States by giving this order. Why? They say, as I understand it, because the order of removal was made during the session of the Senate; that for that reason the order was a violation of the Constitution of the United States.

I desire to be understood on this subject. If I can make my own ideas of it plain, I think nothing is left of this allegation. In the first place, the case, as Senators will observe, which is now under consideration, is the case of a Secretary of War holding during the pleasure of the President by the terms of his commission; holding under the act of 1789, which created that Department, which, although it does not affect to confer on the President the power to remove the Secretary, does clearly imply that he has that power by making a provision for what shall happen in case he exercises it. That is the case which is under consideration, and the question is this: whether under the law of 1789 and the tenure of office created by that law, designedly created by that law, after the great debate of 1789, and whether under a commission which conforms to it, holding during the pleasure of the President, the President could remove such a

Secretary during the session of the Senate. Why not? Certainly there is nothing in the Constitution of the United States to prohibit it. The Constitution has made two distinct provisions for filling offices. One is by nomination to the Senate and confirmation by them and a commission by the President upon that confirmation. The other is by commissioning an officer when a vacancy happens during a recess of the Senate. But the question now before you is not a question how vacancies shall be filled; that the Constitution has thus provided for; it is a question how they may be created and when they may be created—a totally distinct question.

Whatever may be thought of the soundness of the conclusion arrived at upon the great debate in 1789 concerning the tenure of office, or concerning the power of removal from office, no one, I suppose, will question that a conclusion was arrived at; and that conclusion was that the Constitution had lodged with the President the power of removal from office independently of the Senate. This may be a decision proper to be reversed; it may have been now reversed; of that I say nothing at present; but that it was made, and that the legislation of Congress in 1789 and so on down during the whole period of legislation to 1867 proceeded upon the assumption, express or implied, that that decision had been made, nobody who understands the history of the legislation of the country will deny.

Consider, if you please, what this decision was. It was that the Constitution had lodged this power in the President; that he alone was to exercise it; that the Senate had not and could not have any control whatever over it. If that be so, of what materiality is it whether the Senate is in session or not? If the Senate is not in session, and the President has this power, a vacancy is created, and the Constitution has made provision for filling that vacancy by commission until the end of the next session of the Senate. If the Senate is in session, then the Constitution has made provision for filling a vacancy which is created by a nomination to the Senate; and the laws of the country, as I am presently going to show you somewhat in detail, have made provisions for filling it *ad interim* without any nomination, if the President is not prepared to make a nomination at the moment when he finds the public service requires the removal of an officer. So that if this be a case within the scope of the decision made by Congress in 1789, and within the scope of the legislation which followed upon that decision, it is a case where, either by force of the Constitution the President had the power of removal without consulting the Senate, or else the legislation of Congress had given it to him; and either way neither the Constitution nor the legislation of Congress had made it incumbent on him to consult the Senate on the subject.

I submit, then, that if you look at this matter

C. I.—17.

of Mr. Stanton's removal just as it stands on the decision in 1789 or on the legislation of Congress following upon that decision, and in accordance with which are the terms of the commission under which Mr. Stanton held office, you must come to the conclusion, without any further evidence on the subject, that the Senate had nothing whatever to do with the removal of Mr. Stanton, either to advise for it or to advise against it; that it came either under the constitutional power of the President as it had been interpreted in 1789 or it came under the grant made by the Legislature to the President in regard to all those Secretaries not included within the tenure-of-office bill. This, however, does not rest simply upon this application of the Constitution and of the legislation of Congress. There has been, and we shall bring it before you, a practice by the Government, going back to a very early day, and coming down to a recent period, for the President to make removals from office when the case called for them, without regard to the fact whether the Senate was in session or not. The instances, of course, would not be numerous. If the Senate was in session the President would send a nomination to the Senate saying, "A B in place of C D, removed;" but then there were occasions, not frequent, I agree, but there were occasions, as you will see might naturally happen, when the President, perhaps, had not had time to select a person whom he would nominate, and when he could not trust the officer then in possession of the office to continue in it, when it was necessary for him by a special order to remove him from the office wholly independent of any nomination sent in to the Senate. Let me bring before your consideration for a moment a very striking case which happened recently enough to be within the knowledge of many of you. We were on the eve of a civil war; the War Department was in the hands of a man who was disloyal and unfaithful to his trust; his chief clerk who, on his removal or resignation, would come into the place, was believed to be in the same category with his master. Under those circumstances the President of the United States said to Mr. Floyd, "I must have possession of this office;" and Mr. Floyd had too much good sense or good manners or something else to do anything but resign; and instantly the President put into the place General Holt, the Postmaster General of the United States at the time, without the delay of an hour. It was a time when a delay of twenty-four hours might have been of vast practical consequence to the country. There are classes of cases arising in all the Departments of that character followed by that action; and we shall bring before you evidence showing what those cases have been, so that it will appear that so long as officers held at the pleasure of the President and wholly independent of the advice which he might receive in regard to their removal from the Senate, so long, whenever there was an occasion, the President used the power, whether the Senate was in session or not.

I have now gone over, Senators, the considerations which seem to me to be applicable to the tenure-of-office bill, and to this allegation which is made that the President knowingly violated the Constitution of the United States in the order for the removal of Mr. Stanton from office while the Senate was in session ; and the counsel for the President feel that it is not essential to his vindication from this charge to go further upon this subject. Nevertheless, there is a broader view of this matter, which is an actual part of the case, and it is due to the President it should be brought before you, that I now propose to open to your consideration.

The Constitution requires the President of the United States to take care that the laws be faithfully executed. It also requires of him, as a qualification for his office, to swear that he will faithfully execute the laws, and that, to the best of his ability, he will preserve, protect, and defend the Constitution of the United States. I suppose every one will agree that so long as the President of the United States, in good faith, is endeavoring to take care that the laws be faithfully executed, and in good faith and to the best of his ability is preserving, protecting, and defending the Constitution of the United States, although he may be making mistakes, he is not committing high crimes or misdemeanors.

In the execution of these duties the President found, for reasons which it is not my province at this time to enter upon, but which will be exhibited to you hereafter, that it was impossible to allow Mr. Stanton to continue to hold the office of one of his advisers, and to be responsible for his conduct in the manner he was required by the Constitution and laws to be responsible, any longer. This was intimated to Mr. Stanton, and did not produce the effect which, according to the general judgment of well-informed men, such intimations usually produce. Thereupon the President first suspended Mr. Stanton and reported that to the Senate. Certain proceedings took place which will be adverted to more particularly presently. They resulted in the return of Mr. Stanton to the occupation by him of this office. Then it became necessary for the President to consider, first, whether this tenure-of-office law applied to the case of Mr. Stanton ; secondly, if it did apply to the case of Mr. Stanton, whether the law itself was the law of the land, or was merely inoperative because it exceeded the constitutional power of the Legislature.

I am aware that it is asserted to be the civil and moral duty of all men to obey those laws which have been passed through all the forms of legislation until they shall have been decreed by judicial authority not to be binding ; but this is too broad a statement of the civil and moral duty incumbent either upon private citizens or public officers. If this is the meas-

ure of duty there never could be a judicial decision that a law is unconstitutional, inasmuch as it is only by disregarding a law that any question can be raised judicially under it. I submit to Senators that not only is there no such rule of civil or moral duty, but that it may be and has been a high and patriotic duty of a citizen to raise a question whether a law is within the Constitution of the country. Will any man question the patriotism or the propriety of John Hampden's act when he brought the question whether "ship money" was within the Constitution of England before the courts of England? Not only is there no such rule incumbent upon private citizens which forbids them to raise such questions, but, let me repeat, there may be, as there not unfrequently have been, instances in which the highest patriotism and the purest civil and moral duty require it to be done. Let me ask any one of you, if you were a trustee for the rights of third persons, and those rights of third persons, which they could not defend themselves by reason, perhaps, of sex or age, should be attacked by an unconstitutional law, should you not deem it to be your sacred duty to resist it and have the question tried? And if a private trustee may be subject to such a duty, and impelled by it to such action, how is it possible to maintain that he who is a trustee for the people of powers confided to him for their protection, for their security, for their benefit, may not in that character of trustee defend what has thus been confided to him?

Do not let me be misunderstood on this subject. I am not intending to advance upon or occupy any extreme ground, because no such extreme ground has been advanced upon or occupied by the President of the United States. He is to take care that the laws are faithfully executed. When a law has been passed through the forms of legislation, either with his assent or without his assent, it is his duty to see that that law is faithfully executed so long as nothing is required of him but ministerial action. He is not to erect himself into a judicial court and decide that the law is unconstitutional, and that therefore he will not execute it ; for, if that were done, manifestly there never could be a judicial decision. He would not only veto a law, but he would refuse all action under the law after it had been passed, and thus prevent any judicial decision from being made. He asserts no such power. He has no such idea of his duty. His idea of his duty is that if a law is passed over his veto which he believes to be unconstitutional, and that law affects the interests of third persons, those whose interests are affected must take care of them, vindicate them, raise questions concerning them, if they should be so advised. If such a law affects the general and public interests of the people the people must take care at the polls that it is remedied in a constitutional way.

But, when Senators, a question arises

whether a particular law has cut off a power confided to him by the people through the Constitution, and he alone can raise that question, and he alone can cause a judicial decision to come between the two branches of the Government to say which of them is right, and after due deliberation, with the advice of those who are his proper advisers, he settles down firmly upon the opinion that such is the character of the law, it remains to be decided by you whether there is any violation of his duty when he takes the needful steps to raise that question and have it peacefully decided.

Where shall the line be drawn? Suppose a law should provide that the President of the United States should not make a treaty with England or with any other country? It would be a plain infraction of his constitutional power, and if an occasion arose when such a treaty was in his judgment expedient and necessary it would be his duty to make it; and the fact that it should be declared to be a high misdemeanor if he made it would no more relieve him from the responsibility of acting through the fear of that law than he would be relieved of that responsibility by a bribe not to act.

Suppose a law that he shall not be Commander-in-Chief in part or in whole—a plain case, I will suppose, of an infraction of that provision of the Constitution which has confided to him that command; the Constitution intending that the head of all the military power of the country should be a civil magistrate, to the end that the law may always be superior to arms. Suppose he should resist a statute of that kind in the manner I have spoken of by bringing it to a judicial decision?

It may be said these are plain cases of express infractions of the Constitution; but what is the difference between a power conferred upon the President by the express words of the Constitution and a power conferred upon the President by a clear and sufficient implication in the Constitution? Where does the power to make banks come from? Where does the power come from to limit Congress in assigning original jurisdiction to the Supreme Court of the United States, one of the cases referred to the other day? Where do a multitude of powers upon which Congress acts come from in the Constitution except by fair implications? Whence do you derive the power, while you are limiting the tenure of office, to confer on the Senate the right to prevent removals without their consent? Is that expressly given in the Constitution, or is it an implication which is made from some of its provisions?

I submit it is impossible to draw any line of duty for the President simply because a power is derived from an implication in the Constitution instead of from an express provision. One thing unquestionably is to be expected of the President on all such occasions, that is, that he should carefully consider the question; that he should ascertain that it necessarily arises; that he should be of opinion that it is necessary to the public service that it should be decided; that he should take all competent and proper advice on the subject. When he has done all this, if he finds that he cannot allow the law to operate in the particular case without abandoning a power which he believes has been confided to him by the people, it is his solemn conviction that it is his duty to assert the power and obtain a judicial decision thereon. And although he does not perceive, nor do his counsel perceive, that it is essential to his defense in this case to maintain this part of the argument, nevertheless, if this tribunal should be of that opinion, then before this tribunal, before all the people of the United States, and before the civilized world, he asserts the truth of this position.

I am compelled now to ask your attention, quite briefly, however, to some considerations which weighed upon the mind of the President and led him to the conclusion that this was one of the powers of his office which it was his duty, in the manner I have indicated, to endeavor to preserve.

The question whether the Constitution has lodged the power of removal with the President alone, with the President and Senate, or left it to Congress to be determined at its will in fixing the tenure of offices, was, as all Senators know, debated in 1789 with surpassing ability and knowledge of the frame and necessities of our Government.

Now, it is a rule long settled, existing, I suppose, in all civilized countries, certainly in every system of law that I have any acquaintance with, that a contemporary exposition of a law made by those who were competent to give it a construction is of very great weight; and that when such contemporary exposition has been made of a law, and it has been followed by an actual and practical construction in accordance with that contemporary exposition, continued during a long period of time and applied to great numbers of cases, it is afterward too late to call in question the correctness of such a construction. The rule is laid down, in the quaint language of Lord Coke, in this form:

"Great regard ought, in construing a law, to be paid to the construction which the sages who lived about the time or soon after it was made put upon it, because they were best able to judge of the intention of the makers at the time when the law was made. *Contemporania expositio est fortissima in legem.*"

I desire to bring before the Senate in this connection, inasmuch as I think the subject has been frequently misunderstood, the form taken by that debate of 1789 and the result which was attained. In order to do so, and at the same time to avoid fatiguing your attention by looking minutely into the debate itself, I beg leave to read a passage from Chief Justice Marshall's Life of Washington, where he has summed up the whole. The writer says, on page 162 of the second volume of the Philadelphia edition:

" After an ardent discussion, which consumed several days, the committee divided, and the amendment was negatived by a majority of thirty-four to twenty. The opinion thus expressed by the House of Representatives did not explicitly convey their sense of the Constitution. Indeed, the express grant of the power to the President rather implied a right in the Legislature to give or withhold it at their discretion. To obviate any misunderstanding of the principle on which the question had been decided Mr. Benson moved in the House, when the report of the Committee of the Whole was taken up, to amend the second clause in the bill so as clearly to imply the power of removal to be solely in the President. He gave notice that if he should succeed in this he would move to strike out the words which had been the subject of debate. If those words continued, he said, the power of removal by the President might hereafter appear to be exercised by virtue of a legislative grant only, and consequently be subjected to legislative instability; when he was well satisfied in his own mind that it was by fair construction fixed in the Constitution. The motion was seconded by Mr. Madison, and both amendments were adopted. As the bill passed into a law, it has ever been considered as a full expression of the sense of the Legislature on this important part of the American Constitution."

Some allusion has been made to the fact that this law was passed in the Senate only by the casting vote of the Vice President; and upon that subject I beg leave to refer to the life of Mr. Adams by his grandson, volume one of his works, pages 448 to 450. He here gives an account, so far as could be ascertained from the papers of President Adams, of what that debate was, and finally terminates the subject in this way:

" These reasons," that is, the reasons of Vice President Adams—

" Were not committed to paper, however, and can therefore never be known. But in their soundness it is certain that he never had the shadow of a doubt."

I desire leave, also, to refer on this subject to the first volume of Story's Commentaries on the Constitution, section four hundred and eight, in support of the rule of interpretation which I have stated to the Senate. It will there be found that it is stated by the learned commentator that a contemporaneous construction of the Constitution made under certain circumstances, which he describes, is of very great weight in determining its meaning. He says:

"After all the most unexceptionable source of collateral interpretation is from the practical exposition of the Government itself in its various departments upon particular questions discussed and settled upon their own single merits. These approach the nearest in their own nature to judicial expositions, and have the same general recommendation that belongs to the latter. They are decided upon solemn argument, pro renata, upon a doubt raised, upon a lis mota, upon a deep sense of their importance and difficulty, in the face of the nation, with a view to present action in the midst of jealous interests, and by men capable of urging or repelling the grounds of argument from their exquisite genius, their comprehensive learning, or their deep meditation upon the absorbing topic. How light, compared with these means of instruction, are the private lucubrations of the closet or the retired speculations of ingenious minds, intent on theory or general views, and unused to encounter a practical difficulty at every step!"

On comparing the decision made in 1789 with the tests which are here suggested by the learned commentator, it will be found, in the first place, that the precise question was under discussion; secondly, that there was a deep sense of its importance, for it was seen that the decision was not to affect a few cases lying here and there in the course of the Government, but that it would enter deeply into its practical and daily administration; and in the next place the determination was, so far as such determination could be entertained, thereby to fix a system for the future; and in the last place the men who participated in it must be admitted to have been exceedingly well qualified for their work.

There is another rule to be added to this which is also one of very frequent application, and it is that a long-continued practical application of a decision of this character by those to whom the execution of a law is confided is of decisive weight. To borrow again from Lord Coke on this subject, " Optimus legum interpres consuetudo"—" practice is the best interpreter of law." Now, what followed this original decision? From 1789 down to 1867 every President and every Congress participated in and acted under the construction given in 1789. Not only did the Government so conduct, but it was a subject sufficiently discussed among the people to bring to their consideration that such a question had existed, had been started, had been settled in this manner, had been raised again from time to time, and yet, as everybody knows, so far from the people interfering with this decision, so far from ever expressing in any manner their disapprobation of the practice which had grown up under it, not one party nor two parties but all parties favored and acted upon this system of Government.

Mr. EDMUNDS, (at two o'clock and twenty-five minutes p. m.) Mr. President, if agreeable to the honorable counsel, I will move that the Senate take a recess for fifteen minutes.

The motion was agreed to.

The Chief Justice resumed the Chair at fifteen minutes to three o'clock, and called the Senate to order.

Mr. MORRILL, of Vermont, (after a pause.) I move that the Senate do now adjourn—I see that most of the Senators are away—and on that motion I ask for the yeas and nays.

The yeas and nays were ordered.

Mr. CONKLING. What is the motion? I did not hear it.

The CHIEF JUSTICE. The motion is to adjourn until to-morrow at twelve o'clock, and upon that motion the yeas and nays are ordered.

The question being taken by yeas and nays, resulted—yeas 2, nays 35; as follows:

YEAS—Messrs. McCreery, and Patterson of Tennessee—2.

NAYS—Messrs. Buckalew, Cattell, Chandler, Cole, Conkling, Corbett, Cragin, Davis, Dixon, Doolittle, Drake, Ferry, Fessenden, Frelinghuysen, Grimes, Henderson, Hendricks, Howard, Howe, Johnson,

Morgan, Morrill of Maine, Morrill of Vermont, Morton, Pomeroy, Ross, Sherman, Stewart, Sumner, Thayer, Tipton, Van Winkle, Vickers, Willey, and Yates—35.

NOT VOTING—Messrs. Anthony, Bayard, Cameron, Conness, Edmunds, Fowler, Harlan, Norton, Nye, Patterson of New Hampshire, Ramsey, Saulsbury, Sprague, Trumbull, Wade, Williams, and Wilson—17.

So the Senate refused to adjourn.

The CHIEF JUSTICE. The counsel for the President will proceed with the argument.

Mr. CURTIS. Mr. Chief Justice and Senators, when the Senate adjourned I was asking its attention to the fact that this practical interpretation was put upon the Constitution in 1789, and that it had been continued with the concurrence of the legislative and executive branches of the Government down to 1867, affecting so great a variety of interests, embracing so many offices, so well known not merely to the members of the Goverment themselves, but to the people of the country, that it was impossible to doubt that it had received their sanction as well as the sanction of the executive and the legislative branches of the Government.

This is a subject which has been heretofore examined and passed upon judicially in very numerous cases. I do not speak now, of course, of judicial decisions of this particular question which is under consideration, whether the Constitution has lodged the power of removal in the President alone, or in the President and Senate, or has left it to be a part of the legislative power; but I speak of the judicial exposition of the effect of such a practical construction of the Constitution of the United States originated in the way in which this was originated, continued in the way in which this was continued, and sanctioned in the way in which this has been sanctioned.

There was a very early case that arose soon after the organization of the Government, and which is reported under the name of Stuart vs. Laird, in 1 Cranch's Reports, 299. It was a question concerning the interpretation of the Constitution concerning the power which the Congress had to assign to the judges of the Supreme Court circuit duties. From that time down to the decision in the case of Cooley vs. The Port Wardens of Philadelphia, reported in 12 Howard, 315, a period of more than half a century, there has been a series of decisions upon the effect of such a contemporaneous construction of the Constitution, followed by such a practice in accordance with it; and it is now a fixed and settled rule, which, I think, no lawyer will undertake to controvert, that the effect of such a construction is not merely to give weight to an argument, but to fix an interpretation. And accordingly it will be found by looking into the books written by those who were conversant with this subject that they have so considered and received it. I beg leave to refer to the most eminent of all the commentators on American law, and to

read a line or two from Chancellor Kent's Lectures, found in the first volume, page 310, marginal paging. After considering this subject, and, it should be noted in reference to this very learned and experienced jurist, considering it in an unfavorable light, because he himself thought that as an original question it had better have been settled the other way, that it would have been more logical, more in conformity with his views of what the practical needs of the Government were, that the Senate should participate with the President in the power of removal, nevertheless he sums it all up in these words:

"This amounted to a legislative construction of the Constitution, and it has ever since been acquiesced in and noted upon as of decisive authority in the case. It applies equally to every other officer of the Government appointed by the President and Senate whose term of duration is not specially declared. It is supported by the weighty reason that the subordinate officers in the executive department ought to hold at the pleasure of the head of that department, because he is invested generally with the executive authority, and every participation in that authority by the Senate was an exception to a general principle, and ought to be taken strictly. The President is the great responsible officer for the faithful execution of the law, and the power of removal was incidental to that duty, and might often be requisite to fulfill it."

This, I believe, will be found to be a fair expression of the opinions of those who have had occasion to examine this subject in their closets or as a matter of speculation.

In this case, however, the President of the United States had to consider not merely the general question where this power was lodged, not merely the effect of this decision made in 1789, and the practice of the Government under it since, but he had to consider a particular law, the provisions of which were before him, and might have an application to the case upon which he felt called upon to act; and it is necessary, in order to do justice to the President in reference to this matter, to see what the theory of that law is and what its operation is or must be, if any, upon the case which he had before him; namely, the case of Mr. Stanton.

During the debate in 1789 there were three distinct theories held by different persons in the House of Representatives. One was that the Constitution had lodged the power of removal with the President alone; another was that the Constitution had lodged that power with the President, acting with the advice and consent of the Senate; the third was that the Constitution had lodged it nowhere, but had left it to the legislative power, to be acted upon in connection with the prescription of the tenure of office. The last of these theories was at that day held by comparatively few persons. The first two received not only much the greatest number of votes but much the greatest weight of reasoning in the course of that debate; so much so that when this subject came under the consideration of the Supreme Court of the United States, in the case of ex parte Hennan, collaterally only, Mr. Justice Thompson, who delivered the opinion of the court on that occasion, says that it has never been doubted that the Constitution had lodged the power either in the President alone or in the President and Senate—certainly an inaccuracy; but then it required a very close scrutiny of the debates and a careful examination of the few individual opinions expressed in that debate, in that direction, to ascertain that it ever had been doubted that, one way or the other, the Constitution settled the question.

Nevertheless, as I understand it—I may be mistaken in this—but, as I understand it, it is the theory of this law which the President had before him, that both these opinions were wrong; that the Constitution has not lodged the power anywhere; that it has left it as an incident to the legislative power, which incident may be controlled, of course, by the Legislature itself, according to its own will; because, as Chief Justice Marshall somewhere remarks, (and it is one of those profound remarks which will be found to have been carried by him into many of his decisions,) when it comes to a question whether a power exists the particular mode in which it may be exercised must be left to the will of the body that possesses it; and, therefore, if this be a legislative power, it was very apparent to the President of the United States, as it had been very apparent to Mr. Madison, as was declared by him in the course of his correspondence with Mr. Coles, which is, no doubt, familiar to Senators, that if this be a legislative power the Legislature may lodge it in the Senate, may retain it in the whole body of Congress, the two Houses of Congress, or may give it to the House of Representatives. I repeat, the President had to consider this particular law; and that, as I understand it, is the theory of that law. I do not undertake to say it is an unfounded theory; I do not undertake to say that it may not be maintained successfully; but I do undertake to say that it is one which was originally rejected by the ablest minds that had this subject under consideration in 1789; that whenever the question has been started since it has had, to a recent period, very few advocates; and that no fair and candid mind can deny that it is capable of being doubted and disbelieved after examination. It may be the truth, after all; but it is not a truth which shines with such clear and certain light that a man is guilty of a crime because he does not see it.

The President not only had to consider this particular law, but he had to consider its constitutional application to this particular case, supposing the case of Mr. Stanton to be, what I have endeavored to argue it was not, within its terms. Let us assume, then, that his case was within its terms; let us assume that this proviso, in describing the cases of Secretaries described the case of Mr. Stanton; that Mr. Stanton, having been appointed by President Lincoln in January, 1862, and commissioned to hold during the pleasure of the President, by force of this law acquired a right to hold this office against the will of the President down to April, 1869. Now, there is one thing which has never been doubted under the Constitution, is incapable of being doubted, allow me to say, and that is, that the President is to make the choice of officers. Whether having made the choice, and they being inducted into office, they can be removed by him alone, is another question. But to the President alone is confided the power of choice. In the first place, he alone can nominate. When the Senate has advised the nomination, consented to the nomination, he is not bound to commission the officer. He has a second opportunity for consideration, and acceptance or rejection of the choice he had originally made. On this subject allow me to read from the opinion of Chief Justice Marshall, in the case of Marbury vs. Madison, where it is expressed more clearly than I can express it. After enumerating the different clauses of the Constitution which bear upon this subject, he says:

"These are the clauses of the Constitution and laws of the United States which affect this part of the case. They seem to contemplate three distinct operations:

"1. The nomination. This is the sole act of the President, and is completely voluntary.

"2. The appointment. This is also the act of the President, and is also a voluntary act, though it can only be performed by and with the advice and consent of the Senate.

"3. The commission. To grant a commission to a person appointed might, perhaps, be deemed a duty enjoined by the Constitution. 'He shall,' says that instrument, 'commission all the officers of the United States.'"—1 *Cranch*, 155.

He then goes into various considerations to show that it is not a duty enjoined by the Constitution; that it is optional with him whether he will commission even after an appointment has been confirmed, and he says:

"The last act to be done by the President is the signature of the commission. He has then acted on the advice and consent of the Senate to his own nomination. The time for deliberation has then passed. He has decided. His judgment, on the advice and consent of the Senate concurring with his nomination, has been made, and the officer is appointed."—*Ibid.*, 157.

The choice, then, is with the President. The action of the Senate upon that choice is an advisory action only at a particular stage after the nomination, before the appointment or the commission. Now, as I have said before, Mr. Stanton was appointed under the law of 1789, constituting the War Department, and in accordance with that law he was commissioned to hold during the pleasure of the President. President Lincoln had said to the Senate, "I nominate Mr. Stanton to hold the office of Secretary for the Department of War during the pleasure of the President." The Senate had said, "We assent to Mr. Stanton's holding the office of Secretary for the Department of War during the pleasure of the President." What does this tenure-of-office law say, if it operates on the case of Mr. Stanton? It says Mr. Stanton shall hold office against the will of the President, contrary to the terms of his commission, contrary to the law under which he was appointed, down to the 4th of April, 1869. For this new, fixed, and extended term, where is Mr. Stanton's commission? Who has made the appointment? Who has assented to it? It is a legislative commission; it is a legislative appointment; it is assented to by Congress acting in its legislative capacity. The President has had no voice in the matter. The Senate, as the advisers of the President, have had no voice in the matter. If he holds at all, he holds by force of legislation, and not by any choice-made by the President, or assented to by the Senate. And this was the case, and the only case, which the President had before him, and on which he was called to act.

Now, I ask Senators to consider whether, for having formed an opinion that the Constitution of the United States had lodged this power with the President—an opinion which he shares with every President who has preceded him, with every Congress which has preceded the last; an opinion formed on the grounds which I have imperfectly indicated; an opinion which, when applied to this particular case, raises the difficulties which I have indicated here, arising out of the fact that this law does not pursue either of the opinions which were originally held in this Government, and have occasionally been started and maintained by those who are restless under its administration; an opinion thus supported by the practice of the Government from its origin down to his own day, is he to be impeached for holding that opinion? If not, if he might honestly and properly form such an opinion under the lights which he had, and with the aid of the advice which we shall show you he received, then is he to be impeached for acting upon it to the extent of obtaining a judicial decision whether the executive department of the Government was right in its opinion, or the legislative department was right in its opinion? Strangely enough, as it struck me, the honorable Managers themselves say, "No; he is not to be impeached for that." I beg leave to read a passage from the argument of the honorable Manager by whom the prosecution was opened:

"If the President had really desired solely to test the constitutionality of the law or his legal right to remove Mr. Stanton, instead of his defiant message to the Senate of the 21st of February, informing them of the removal, but not suggesting this purpose, which is thus shown to be an afterthought, he would have said, in substance: 'Gentlemen of the Senate, in order to test the constitutionality of the law entitled "An act regulating the tenure of certain civil offices," which I verily believe to be unconstitutional and void, I have issued an order of removal of E. M. Stanton from the office of Secretary of the Department of War. I felt myself constrained to make this removal lest Mr. Stanton should answer the information in the nature of a quo warranto, which I intend to file, by saying that he holds the office of Secretary of War by the appointment and authority of Mr. Lincoln, which has never been revoked. Anxious that there shall be no collision or disagreement between the several departments of the Government and the Executive, I lay before the Senate this message, that the reasons for my action, as well as the action itself, for the purpose indicated, may meet your concurrence.'"

Thus far are marks of quotation showing the communication which the President should have obtained from the honorable Manager and sent to the Senate in order to make this matter exactly right. Then follows this:

"Had the Senate received such a message the Representatives of the people might never have deemed it necessary to impeach the President for such an act to insure the safety of the country, even if they had denied the accuracy of his legal positions."

So that it seems that it is, after all, not the removal of Mr. Stanton but the manner in which the President communicated the fact of that removal to the Senate after it was made. That manner is called here the "defiant message" of the 21st of February. That is a question of taste. I have read the message as you all have read it. If you can find anything in it but what is decorous and respectful to this body and to all concerned your taste will differ from mine. But whether it be a point of manners well or ill taken, one thing seems to be quite clear: that the President is not impeached here because he entertained an opinion that this law was unconstitutional; he is not impeached here because he acted on that opinion and removed Mr. Stanton; but he is impeached here because the House of Representatives considers that this honorable body was addressed by a "defiant message," when they should have been addressed in the terms which the honorable Manager has dictated.

I now come, Mr. Chief Justice and Senators, to another topic connected with this matter of the removal of Mr. Stanton and the action of the President under this law. The honorable Managers take the ground, among others, that whether upon a true construction of this tenure-of-office act Mr. Stanton be within it, or even if you should believe that the President thought the law unconstitutional and had a right, if not trammeled in some way, to try that question, still by his own conduct and declarations the President, as they phrase it, is estopped. He is not to be permitted here to assert the true interpretation of this law; he is not to be permitted to allege that his purpose was to raise a question concerning its constitutionality; and the reason is that he has done and said certain things. All of us who have read law books know that there is in the common law a doctrine called rules of estoppel, founded, undoubtedly, on good reason, although, as they are called from the time of Lord Coke, or even earlier, down to the present day, odious, because they shut out the truth. Nevertheless there are circumstances when it is proper that the truth should be shut out. What are the circumstances? They are where a question of private right is involved, where on a matter of fact that private right depends, and where one of the parties to the controversy has so conducted himself that he ought not in good conscience to be allowed either to assert or deny that matter of fact.

But did any one ever hear of an estoppel on a matter of law? Did any one ever hear that a party had put himself into such a condition that when he came into a court of justice even to claim a private right, he could not ask the judge correctly to construe a statute, and insist on the construction when it was arrived at in his favor? Did anybody ever hear, last of all, that a man was convicted of crime by reason of an estoppel under any system of law that ever prevailed in any civilized State? That the President of the United States should be impeached and removed from office, not by reason of the truth of his case, but because he is estopped from telling it. would be a spectacle for gods and men. Undoubtedly it would have a place in history, which it is not necessary for me to attempt to foreshadow.

There is no matter of fact here. They have themselves put in Mr. Stanton's commission, which shows the date of the commission and the terms of the commission; and that is the whole matter of fact which is involved. The rest is the construction of the tenure of the tenure-of-office act and the application of it to the case, which they have thus made themselves; and also the construction of the Constitution of the United States, and the abstract public question whether that has lodged the power of removal with the President alone, or with the President and Senate, or left it to Congress. I respectfully submit, therefore, that the ground is untenable that there can be an estoppel by any conduct of the President, who comes here to assert not a private right, but a great public right confided to the office by the people, in which, if anybody is estopped, the people will be estopped. The President never could do or say anything which would put this great public right into that extraordinary predicament.

But what has he done? What are the facts upon which they rely, out of which to work this estoppel, as they call it? In the first place, he sent a message to the Senate on the 12th of December, 1867, in which he informed the Senate that he had suspended Mr. Stanton by a certain order, a copy of which he gave; that he had appointed General Grant to exercise the duties of the office *ad interim* by a certain other order, a copy of which he gave; and then he entered into a discussion in which he showed the existence of this question, whether Mr. Stanton was within the tenure-of-office bill, the existence of the other question, whether this was or was not a constitutional law; and then he invoked the action of the Senate. There was nothing misrepresented. There was nothing concealed which he was bound to state. It is complained of by the honorable Managers that he did not tell the Senate that if their action should be such as to restore Mr. Stanton practically to the possession of the office he should go to law about it. That is the complaint: that he did not tell that to the Senate. It may have been a possible omission, though I rather think not. I rather think that that good taste which is so prevalent among the Managers, and which they so insist upon here, would hardly dictate that the President should have held out to the Senate something which might possibly have been construed into a threat upon that subject. He laid the case before the Senate for their action; and now, forsooth, they say he was too deferential to this law, both by reason of this conduct of his, and also what he did upon other occasions to which I shall presently advert.

Senators, there is no inconsistency in the President's position or conduct in reference to this matter. Suppose this case: a party who has a private right in question submits to the same tribunal in the same proceeding these questions: first, I deny the constitutionality of the law under which the right is claimed against me; second, I assert that the true interpretation of that law will not affect this right which is claimed against me; third, I insist that, even if it is within the law, I make a case within the law—is there any inconsistency in that? Is not that done every day, or something analogous to it, in courts of justice? And where was the inconsistency on this occasion? Suppose the President had summed up the message which he sent to the Senate in this way: "Gentlemen of the Senate, I insist, in the first place, that this law is unconstitutional; I insist, in the second place, that Mr. Stanton is not within it; I respectfully submit for your consideration whether, if it be a constitutional law and Mr. Stanton's case be within it, the facts which I present to you do not make such a case that you will not advise me to receive him back into office." Suppose he had summed up in that way, would there have been any inconsistency then? And why is not the substance of that found in this message? Here it is pointed out that the question existed whether the law was unconstitutional; here it is pointed out that the question existed whether Mr. Stanton was within the law; and then the President goes on to submit for the consideration of the Senate, whom he had reason to believe, and did believe, thought the law was constitutional, though he had no reason to believe that they thought Mr. Stanton was within the law, the facts to be acted upon within the law, if the case was there. It seems the President has not only been thus anxious to avoid a collision with this law; he has not only on this occasion taken this means to avoid it, but it seems that he has actually in some particulars obeyed the law; he has made changes in the commissions, or rather they have been made in the departments, and, as he has signed the commissions, I suppose they must be taken, although his attention does not appear to have been called to the subject at all, to have been made with his sanction, just so far, and because he sanctions that which is done by his Secretaries, if he does not interfere actively to prevent it.

He has done not merely this, but he has also in several cases—four cases, three collectors and one consul, I think they are—sent into the Senate notice of suspension, notice that he had acted under this law and suspended these officers. This objection proceeds upon an entire misapprehension of the position of the President and of the views which he has of his own duty. It assumes that because, when the emergency comes, as it did come in the case of Mr. Stanton, when he must act or else abandon a power which he finds in the particular instance it is necessary for him to insist upon in order to carry on the Government; that because he holds that opinion he must run a muck against the law, and take every possible opportunity to give it a blow, if he can. He holds no such opinion.

So long as it is a question of administrative duty merely he holds that he is bound to obey the law. It is only when the emergency arises, when the question is put to him so that he must answer it, "Can you carry on this department of the Government any longer in this way?" "No." "Have you power to carry it on as the public service demands?" "I believe I have." Then comes the question how he shall act. But whether a consul is to be suspended or removed, whether a defaulting collector is to be suspended or removed, does not involve the execution of the great powers of the Government. It may be carried on; he may be of opinion with less advantage; he may be of opinion not in accordance with the requirements of the Constitution, but it may be carried on without serious embarrassment or difficulty. Until that question is settled he does not find it necessary to make it—settled in some way, by some person who has an interest to raise and have it settled.

I wish to observe, also, (the correctness of which observation I think the Senate will agree with) that these changes which have been made in the forms of the commissions really have nothing to do with this subject; for instance, the change is made in the Department of State, "subject to the conditions prescribed by law." That is the tenure on which I think all commissions should originally have run, and ought to continue to run. It is general enough to embrace all. If it is a condition prescribed by law that the Senate must consent to the removal of the incumbent before he is rightfully out of office, it covers that case. If the tenure-of-office bill be not a law of the land because it is not in accordance with the Constitution, it covers that case. It covers every case necessarily from its terms, for every officer does, and should, and must hold subject to the conditions prescribed by law—not necessarily a law of Congress, but a law of the land—the Constitution being supreme in that particular.

There is another observation, also, and that is, that the change that was made in the Department of the Treasury—"until a successor be appointed and qualified"—has manifestly nothing whatever to do with the subject of removal. Whether the power of removal be vested in the President alone, or vested in the President by and with the advice and consent of the Senate, this clause does not touch it. It is just as inconsistent with removal by the President with the consent of the Senate as it is inconsistent with the removal by the President alone. In other words, it is the general tenure of the office which is described, according to which the officer is to continue to hold; but he and all other officers hold subject to some power of removal vested somewhere, and this change which has been made in the commission does not declare where it is vested, nor has it any influence on the question in whom it is vested.

I wish to add to this, that there is nothing, so far as I see, on this subject of estoppel, growing out of the action of the President, either in sending the message to the Senate of the 12th of December, or in the changes in the commissions, or in his sending to the Senate notices of suspensions of different officers, which has any bearing whatever upon the tenure-of-office act as affecting the case of Mr. Stanton. That is a case that stands by itself. The law may be a constitutional law; it may not only be a law under which the President has acted in this instance, but under which he is bound to act, and is willing to act, if you please, in every instance; still, if Mr. Stanton is not within that law, the case remains as it was originally presented, and that case is, that, not being within that law, the first article is entirely without foundation.

I now, Mr. Chief Justice, have arrived at a point in my argument when, if it be within the pleasure of the Senate to allow me to suspend it, it will be a boon to me to do so. I am unaccustomed to speak in so large a room, and it is fatiguing to me. Still, I would not trespass at all upon the wishes of the Senate if they desire me to proceed further.

Mr. JOHNSON. I move that the court adjourn until to-morrow at twelve o'clock.

The motion was agreed to; and the Senate, sitting for the trial of the impeachment, adjourned.

FRIDAY, *April* 10, 1868.

The Chief Justice of the United States entered the Senate Chamber at twelve o'clock and took the chair.

The usual proclamation having been made by the Sergeant-at-Arms,

The Managers of the impeachment on the part of the House of Representatives appeared and took the seats assigned them.

The counsel for the respondent also appeared and took their seats.

The presence of the House of Representatives was next announced, and the members of the House, as in Committee of the Whole, headed by Mr. E. B. WASHBURNE, the chairman of that committee, and accompanied by the Speaker and Clerk, entered the Senate Chamber, and were conducted to the seats provided for them.

The CHIEF JUSTICE. The Secretary will read the minutes of the last day's proceedings.

The Secretary read the Journal of yesterday's proceedings of the Senate sitting for the trial of the impeachment.

The CHIEF JUSTICE. Senators will please to give their attention. The counsel for the President will proceed with the argument.

Mr. CURTIS. Mr. Chief Justice and Senators, among the points which I accidentally omitted to notice yesterday, was one which seems to me of sufficient importance to return, and for a few moments to ask the attention of the Senate to it. It will best be exhibited by reading from Saturday's proceedings a short passage. In the course of those proceedings Mr. Manager BUTLER said:

"It will be seen, therefore, Mr. President and Senators, that the President of the United States says in his answer that he suspended Mr. Stanton under the Constitution, indefinitely and at his pleasure. I propose, now, unless it be objected to, to show that that is false under his own hand, and I have his letter to that effect, which, if there is no objection, I will read, the signature of which was identified by C. E. Creecy."

Then followed the reading of the letter, which was this:

EXECUTIVE MANSION,
WASHINGTON, D. C., *August* 14, 1867.

SIR: In compliance with the requirements of the eighth section of the act of Congress of March 2, 1867, entitled "An act regulating the tenure of certain civil offices," you are hereby notified that on the 12th instant Hon. Edwin M. Stanton was suspended from office as Secretary of War and General Ulysses S. Grant authorized and empowed to act as Secretary of War *ad interim.*

I am, sir, very respectfully, yours,
ANDREW JOHNSON.

This is the letter which was to show, under the hand of the President, that when he said in his answer he did not suspend Mr. Stanton by virtue of the tenure-of-office act that statement was a falsehood. Allow me now to read the eighth section of that act:

"That whenever the President shall, without the advice and consent of the Senate, designate, authorize, or employ any person to perform the duties of any office he shall forthwith notify the Secretary of the Treasury thereof; and it shall be the duty of the Secretary of the Treasury thereupon to communicate such notice to all the proper accounting and disbursing officers of his Department."

The Senate will perceive that this section has nothing to do with the suspension of an officer and no description of what suspensions are to take place; but the purpose of the section is that if in any case the President, without the advice and consent of the Senate, shall, under any circumstances, designate a third person to perform temporarily the duties of an office he is to make a report of that designation to the Secretary of the Treasury, and that

officer is to give the necessary information of the event to his subordinate officers. The section applies to and to and includes all cases. It applies to and includes cases of designation on account of sickness or absence or resignation or any cause of vacancy, whether temporary or permanent, and whether occurring by reason of a suspension or of a removal from office. And, therefore, when the President says to the Secretary of the Treasury, "I give you notice that I have designated General Thomas to perform the duties *ad interim* of Secretary of War," he makes no allusion, by force of that letter, to the manner in which that vacancy has occurred or the authority by which it has been created; and hence, instead of this letter showing, under the President's own hand, that he had stated a falsehood, it has no reference to the subject-matter of the power or the occasion of Mr. Stanton's removal.

Mr. Manager BUTLER. Read the second section, please; the first clause of it.

Mr. CURTIS. What did the Manager call for?

Mr. Manager BUTLER. Read the first clause of the second section of the act, which says that in no other case except when he suspends shall he appoint.

Mr. CURTIS. The second section provides:

"That when any officer appointed as aforesaid, excepting judges of the United States courts, shall, during a recess of the Senate, be shown by satisfactory evidence," &c.

The President is allowed to suspend such an officer. Now, the President states in his answer that he did not act under that section.

Mr. Manager BUTLER. That is not reading the section. That is not what I desired.

Mr. CURTIS. I am aware that is not reading the section, Mr. Manager. You need not point that out. It is a very long section, and I do not propose to read it.

Mr. Manager BUTLER. The first half a dozen lines.

Mr. CURTIS. This section authorizes the President to suspend in cases of crime and other cases which are described in this section. By force of it the President may suspend an officer. This eighth section applies to all cases of temporary designations and appointments, whether resulting from suspensions under the second section, whether arising from temporary absence or sickness or death or resignation; no matter what the cause may be, if for any reason there is a temporary designation of a person to supply an office *ad interim* notice is to be given to the Secretary of the Treasury; and therefore I repeat, Senators, that the subject-matter of this eighth section and the letter which the President wrote in consequence of it has no reference to the question under what authority he suspended Mr. Stanton.

I now ask the attention of the Senate to the second article in the series; and I will begin as I began before, by stating what the substance of this article is, what allegations it makes, so as to be the subjects of proof, and then the Senate will be prepared to see how far each one of these allegations is supported by what is already in the case, and I shall be enabled to state what we propose to offer by way of proof in respect to each of them. The substantive allegations of this second article are that the delivery of the letter of authority to General Thomas was without authority of law; that it was an intentional violation of the tenure-of-office act; that it was an intentional violation of the Constitution of the United States; that the delivery of this order to General Thomas was made with intent to violate both that act and the Constitution of the United States. That is the substance of the second article. The Senate will at once perceive that if the suspension of Mr. Stanton was not a violation of the tenure-of-office act in point of fact, or, to state it in other terms, if the case of Mr. Stanton is not within the act, then his removal, if he had been removed, could not be a violation of the act.

If his case is not within the act at all, if the act does not apply to the case of Mr. Stanton, of course his removal is not a violation of that act. If Mr. Stanton continued to hold under the commission which he received from President Lincoln, and his tenure continued to be under the act of 1789, and under his only commission, which was at the pleasure of the President, it was no violation of the tenure-of-office act for Mr. Johnson to remove, or attempt to remove, Mr. Stanton; and therefore the Senate will perceive that it is necessary to come back again, to recur under this article, as it will be necessary to recur under the whole of the first eight articles, to the inquiries, first, whether Mr. Stanton's case was within the tenure-of-office act; and secondly, whether it was so clearly and plainly within that act that it can be attributed to the President as a high misdemeanor that he construed it not to include his case. But suppose the case of Mr. Stanton is within the tenure-of-office act, still the inquiry arises, whether what was done in delivering this letter of authority to General Thomas was a violation of that act; and that renders it necessary that I should ask your careful attention to the general subjects-matter of this act and the particular provisions which are inserted in it in reference to each of those subjects.

Senators will recollect undoubtedly that this law, as it was finally passed, differs from the bill as it was originally introduced. The law relates to two distinct subjects. One is removal from office, the other subject is appointments of a certain character made under certain circumstances to fill offices. It seems that a practice had grown up under the Government that where a person was nominated to the Senate to fill an office, and the Senate either did not act on his nomination during their session or rejected the nomination, after the adjournment of the Senate and in the recess it was considered competent for the President by a temporary commission to appoint that same person to that same office; and that was deemed by many Senators, unquestionably by a majority, and I should judge from reading the debates by a large majority of the Senate, to be an abuse of power—not an intentional abuse. But it was a practice which had prevailed under the Government to a very considerable extent. It was not limited to very recent times. It had been supported by the opinions of different Attorneys General given to different Presidents. But still it was considered by many Senators to be a departure from the spirit of the Constitution, and a substantial derogation from the just power of the Senate in respect to nominations for office. That being so, it will be found on an examination of this law that the first and second sections of the act relate exclusively to removals from office and temporary suspensions in the recess of the Senate; while the third section and several of the following sections, to which I shall ask your particular attention, relate exclusively to this other subject of appointments made to office after the Senate had refused to concur in the nomination of the person appointed. Allow me now to read from the third section:

"That the President shall have power to fill all vacancies which may happen during the recess of the Senate, by reason of death or resignation"—

I pause here to remark that this does not include all cases. It does not include any case of the expiration of a commission. It includes simply death and resignation, not cases of the expiration of a commission during the recess of the Senate. Why these were thus omitted I do not know; but it is manifest that the law does not affect to, and in point of fact does not, cover all cases which might arise belonging to this general class to which this section was designed to refer.

The law goes on to say—

"That the President shall have power to fill all vacancies which may happen during the recess of the Senate, by reason of death or resignation, by granting commissions which shall expire at the end of their next session thereafter. And if no appointment, by and with the advice and consent of the Senate, shall be made to such office so vacant or temporarily filled as aforesaid during such next session of the Senate, such office shall remain in abeyance, without any salary, fees, or emoluments attached thereto, until the same shall be filled by appointment thereto, by and with the advice and consent of the Senate; and during such time all the powers and duties belonging to such office shall be exercised by such other officer as may by law exercise such powers and duties in case of a vacancy in such office."

Here all the described vacancies in office occurring during the recess of the Senate and the failure to fill those vacancies in accordance with the advice of the Senate are treated as occasioning an abeyance of such offices. That applies, as I have said, to two classes of cases, vacancies happening by reason of death or resignation. It does not apply to any other vacancies.

The next section of this law does not relate

to this subject of filling offices, but to the subject of removals:

"That nothing in this act contained shall be construed to extend the term of any office the duration of which is limited by law."

The fifth section is:

"That if any person shall, contrary to the provisions of this act, accept any appointment to or employment in any office, or shall hold or exercise, or attempt to hold or exercise, any such office or employment, he shall be deemed, and is hereby declared to be, guilty of a high misdemeanor, and, upon trial and conviction thereof, he shall be punished therefor by a fine not exceeding $10,000, or by imprisonment," &c.

Any person who shall, "contrary to the provisions of this act," accept any appointment. What are the "provisions of this act" in respect to accepting any appointment? They are found in the third section of the act putting certain offices in abeyance under the circumstances which are described in that section. If any person does accept an office which is thus put into abeyance, or any employment or authority in respect to such office, he comes within the penal provisions of the fifth section; but outside of that there is no such thing as accepting an office contrary to the provisions of the act, because the provisions of the act, in respect to filling offices, extend no further than to these cases; and so, in the next section, it is declared:

"That every removal, appointment, or employment made, had, or exercised contrary to the provisions of this act, and the making, signing, sealing, countersigning, or issuing of any commission or letter of authority for or in respect to any such appointment or employment, shall be deemed, and is hereby declared to be, high misdemeanors," &c.

Here, again, the making of a letter of authority, contrary to the provisions of the act, can refer only to those cases which the act itself has described, which the act itself has prohibited; and any other cases which are outside of such prohibition, as this case manifestly is, do not come within its provisions.

The stress of this article, however, does not seem to me to depend at all upon this question of the construction of this law, but upon a totally different matter, which I agree should be fairly and carefully considered. The important allegation of the article is that this letter of authority was given to General Thomas enabling him to perform the duties of Secretary of War *ad interim* without authority of law; that I conceive to be the main inquiry which arises under this article, provided the case of Mr. Stanton and his removal are within the tenure-of-office bill at all.

I wish first to bring to the attention of the Senate the act of 1795, which is found in 1 Statutes-at-Large, page 415. It is a short act, and I will read the whole of it:

"That in case of vacancy in the office of Secretary of State, Secretary of the Treasury, or of the Secretary of the Department of War, or of any officer of either of the said Departments, whose appointment is not in the head thereof, whereby they cannot perform the duties of their said respective offices, it shall be lawful for the President of the United States, in case he shall think it necessary, to authorize any person or persons, at his discretion, to perform the duties of the said respective offices until a successor be appointed or such vacancy be filled: *Provided*, That no one vacancy shall be supplied, in manner aforesaid, for a longer term than six months."

This act, it has been suggested, may have been repealed by the act of February 20, 1863, which is found in 12 Statutes-at-Large, pages 656. This also is a short act, and I will trespass on the patience of the Senate by reading it:

"That in case of the death, resignation, absence from the seat of Government, or sickness of the head of any executive Department of the Government, or of any officer of either of the said Departments whose appointment is not in the head thereof, whereby they cannot perform the duties of their respective offices, it shall be lawful for the President of the United States, in case he shall think it necessary, to authorize the head of any other executive Department, or other officer in either of said Departments whose appointment is vested in the President, at his discretion, to perform the duties of the said respective offices until a successor be appointed, or until such absence or inability by sickness shall cease: *Provided*, That no one vacancy shall be supplied in manner aforesaid for a longer term than six months."

These acts, as the Senate will perceive, although they may be said in some sense to relate to the same general subject-matter, contain very different provisions, and the later law contains no express repeal of the other. If, therefore, the later law operates as a repeal, it is only as a repeal by implication. It says in terms that "all acts and parts of acts inconsistent with this act are hereby repealed." That a general principle of law would say if the statute did not speak those words. The addition of those words adds nothing to its repealing power. The same inquiry arises under them that would arise if they did not exist, namely, how far is this later law inconsistent with the provisions of the earlier law?

There are certain rules which I shall not fatigue the Senate by citing cases to prove, because every lawyer will recognize them as settled rules upon this subject.

In the first place there is a rule that repeals by implication are not favored by the courts. This is, as I understand it, because the courts act on the assumption or the principle that if the Legislature really intended to repeal the law they would have said so; not that they necessarily must say so, because there are repeals by implication; but the presumption is that if the Legislature entertained a clear and fixed purpose to repeal a former law they would be likely at least to have said so; and, therefore, the rule is a settled one that repeals by implication are not favored by the courts. Another rule is that the repugnancy between the two statutes must be clear. It is not enough that under some circumstances one may possibly be repugnant to the other. The repugnancy, as the language of the books is, between the two must be clear, and if the two laws can stand together the latter does not impliedly repeal the former. If Senators have any desire to recur to the authorities on this subject, they will find a sufficient number of them collected in Sedgwick on Statute Law, page 126.

Now, there is no repugnancy whatsoever between these two laws that I can perceive. The act of 1795 applies to all vacancies, however created. The act of 1863 applies only to vacancies, temporary or otherwise, occasioned by death and resignation; removals from office, expiration of commissions, are not included. The act of 1795 applies only to vacancies; the act of 1863 to temporary absences or sickness. The subject-matter, therefore, of the law is different; there is no inconsistency between them; each may stand together and operate upon the cases to which each applies; and therefore I submit that, in the strictest view which may ultimately be taken of this subject, it is not practicable to maintain that the later law here repealed altogether the act of 1795. But, whether it did or not, I state again what I have had so often occasion to repeat before, is it not a fair question, is it a crime to be on one side of that question and not on the other? Is it a high misdemeanor to believe that a certain view taken of the repeal of this earlier law by the later one is a sound view? I submit that that would be altogether too stringent a rule even for the honorable Managers themselves to contend for; and they do not, and the House of Representatives does not, contend for any such rule. Their article alleges as matter of fact that there was a willful intention on the part of the President to issue this letter to General Thomas without authority of law; not on mistaken judgment, not upon an opinion which, after due consideration, lawyers might differ about; but by reason of a willful intention to act without authority; and that, I submit, from the nature of the case, cannot be made out.

The next allegation in this article to which I desire to invite the attention of the Senate is, that the giving of this letter to General Thomas during the session of the Senate was a violation of the Constitution of the United States. That will require your attentive consideration. The Constitution, as you are well aware, has provided for two modes of filling offices. The one is by temporary commissions during the recess of the Senate when the vacancy happens in the recess; the other is by appointment with the advice and consent of the Senate, followed by a commission from the President; but it very early became apparent to those who administered the Government that cases must occur to which neither of those modes dictated by the Constitution would be applicable, but which must be provided for; cases of temporary absence of the head of a Department the business of which, especially during the session of Congress, must, for the public interest, continue to be administered; cases of sickness, cases of resignation or removal, for the power of removal, at any rate in that day, was held to be in the President; cases of resignation or removal in reference to which

the President was not, owing to the suddenness of the occurrence, in a condition immediately to make a nomination to fill the office, or even to issue a commission to fill the office, if such vacancy occurred in vacation; and therefore it became necessary by legislation to supply these administrative defects which existed and were not provided for by the Constitution. And accordingly, beginning in 1792, there will be found to be a series of acts on this subject of filling vacancies by temporary or *ad interim* authority; not appointments, not filling vacancies in offices by a commission in the recess of the Senate, nor by a commission signed by the President in consequence of the advice and consent of the Senate; but a mode of designating a particular person to perform temporarily the duties of some particular office which otherwise, before the office can be filled in accordance with the Constitution, would remain unperformed. These acts are one of May 8, 1792, section 8, (1 Statutes-at-Large, p. 281;) February 17, 1795, (1 Statutes-at-Large, p. 415;) and the last in February 20, 1863, (12 Statutes-at-Large, p. 656.)

The Senate will observe what particular difficulty these laws were designed to meet. This difficulty was the occurrence of some sudden vacancy in office or some sudden inability to perform the duties of an office; and the intention of each of these laws was, each being applied to some particular class of cases, to make provision that notwithstanding there was a vacancy in the office, or notwithstanding there was a temporary disability in the officer without a vacancy, still the duties of the office should be temporarily discharged. That was the purpose of these laws. It is entirely evident that these temporary vacancies are just as liable to occur during the session of the Senate as during the recess of the Senate; that it is just as necessary to have a set of legislative provisions to enable the President to carry on the public service in case of these vacancies and inabilities during the session of the Senate as during the recess of Senate; and, accordingly, it will be found, by looking into these laws, that they make no distinction between the sessions of the Senate and the recesses of the Senate in reference to these temporary authorities. "Whenever a vacancy shall occur" is the language of the law—"whenever there shall be a death or a resignation or an absence or a sickness." The law applies when the event occurs that the law contemplates as an emergency; and the particular time when it occurs is of no consequence in itself, and is deemed by the law of no consequence. In accordance with this view, Senators, has been the uniform and settled and frequent practice of the Government from its very earliest date, as I am instructed we shall prove, not in any one or two or few instances, but in great numbers of instances. That has been the practical construction put upon these laws from the time when the earliest law was passed in 1792, and it has continued down to this day.

The honorable Managers themselves read a list a few days since of temporary appointments during the session of the Senate of heads of Departments, which amounted in number, if I counted them accurately. to upward of thirty; and if you add to these the cases of officers below the heads of Departments the number will be found, of course, to be much increased; and, in the course of exhibiting this evidence, it will be found that, although the instances are not numerous, for they are not very likely to occur in practice, yet instances have occurred on all fours with the one which is now before the Senate, where there has been a removal or a suspension of an officer, sometimes one and sometimes the other, and the designation of a person has been made at the same time temporarily to discharge the duties of that office.

The Senate will see that in practice such things must naturally occur. Take the case, for instance, of Mr. Floyd, which I alluded to yesterday. Mr. Floyd went out of office. His chief clerk was a person believed to be in sympathy with him and under his control. If the third section of the act of 1789 was allowed to operate the control of the office went into the hands of that clerk. The Senate was in session. The public safety did not permit the War Department to be left in that predicament for one hour, if it could be avoided, and President Buchanan sent down to the Post Office Department and brought the Postmaster General to the War Department, and put it in his charge. There was then in this body a sufficient number of persons to look after that matter; they felt an interest in it; and consequently they passed a resolve inquiring of President Buchanan by what authority he had made an appointment of a person to take charge of the War Department without their consent, without a nomination to them, and their advising and consent to it; to which a message was sent in answer containing the facts on this subject, and showing to the Senate of that day the propriety, the necessity, and the long-continued practice under which this authority was exercised by him; and giving a schedule running through the time of General Jackson and his two immediate successors, I think, showing great numbers of *ad interim* appointments of this character, and to those, as I have said, we shall add a very considerable number of others.

I submit, then, that there can be no ground whatever for the allegation that this *ad interim* appointment was a violation of the Constitution of the United States. The legislation of Congress is a sufficient answer to that charge.

I pass, therefore, to the next article which I wish to consider, and that is not the next in number, but the eighth; and I take it in this order because the eighth article, as I have analyzed it, differs from the second only in one particular; and therefore, taking that in connection with the second, of which I have just been speaking, it will be necessary for me to say but a very few words concerning it.

It charges an attempt unlawfully to control the appropriations made by Congress for the military service, and that is all there is in it except what is in the second article.

Upon that, certainly, at this stage of the case, I do not deem it necessary to make any observations. The Senate will remember the offer of proof on the part of the Managers designed, as was stated, to connect the President of the United States, through his Private Secretary, with the Treasury, and thus enable him to use unlawfully appropriations made for the military service. The Senate will recollect the fate of that offer, and that the evidence was not received; and therefore it seems to me quite unnecessary for me to pause to comment any further upon this eighth article.

I advance to the third article, and here the allegations are, that the President appointed General Thomas; second, that he did this without the advice and consent of the Senate; third, that he did it when no vacancy had happened in the recess of the Senate; fourth, that he did it when there was no vacancy at the time of the appointment; and, fifth, that he committed a high misdemeanor by thus intentionally violating the Constitution of the United States.

I desire to say a word or two upon each of these points; and first we deny that he ever appointed General Thomas to an office. An appointment can be made to an office only by the advice and consent of the Senate, and through a commission signed by the President, and bearing the great seal of the Government. That is the only mode in which the appointment can be made. The President, as I have said, may temporarily commission officers when vacancies occur during the recess of the Senate. That is not an appointment. It is not so termed in the Constitution. A clear distinction is drawn between the two. The President also may, under the acts of 1795 and 1863, designate persons who shall temporarily exercise the authority and perform the duties of a certain office when there is a vacancy; but that is not an appointment. The office is not filled by such a designation. Now, all which the President did was to issue a letter of authority to General Thomas, authorizing him *ad interim* to perform the duties of Secretary of War. In no sense was this an appointment.

It is said it was made without the advice and consent of the Senate. Certainly it was. How can the advice and consent of the Senate be obtained to an *ad interim* authority of this kind under any of these acts of Congress? It is not an appointment that is in view. It is to supply temporarily a defect in the administrative machinery of the Government. If he had gone to the Senate for their advice and consent he must have gone on a nomination made by him of General Thomas to this office, a thing he never intended to do, and never made any attempt to carry into effect.

It is said no vacancy happened in the recess. That I have already considered. Temporary appointments are not limited to the temporary supply of vacancies happening in the recess of the Senate, as I have already endeavored to show.

It is said there was no vacancy at the time the act was done. That is begging the question. If Mr. Stanton's case was not within the tenure-of-office act, if, as I have so often repeated, he held under the act of 1789, and at the pleasure of the President, the moment he received that order which General Thomas carried to him there was a vacancy in point of law; however he may have refused to perform his duty and prevented a vacancy from occurring in point of fact. But the Senate will perceive these two letters were to be delivered to General Thomas at the same time. One of them is an order to Mr. Stanton to vacate the office; the other is a direction to General Thomas to take possession when Mr. Stanton obeys the order thus given. Now, may not the President of the United States issue a letter of authority in contemplation that a vacancy is about to occur? Is he bound to take a technical view of this subject, and have the order creating the vacancy first sent and delivered, and then sit down at his table and sign the letter of authority afterward? If he expects a vacancy, if he has done an act which in his judgment is sufficient to create a vacancy, may he not, in contemplation that that vacancy is to happen, sign the necessary paper to give the temporary authority to carry on the duties of the office?

Last of all, it is said he committed a high misdemeanor by intentionally violating the Constitution of the United States when he gave General Thomas this letter of authority. If I have been successful in the argument I have already addressed to you you will be of opinion that in point of fact there was no violation of the Constitution of the United States by delivering this letter of authority, because the Constitution of the United States makes no provision on the subject of these temporary authorities, and the law of Congress has made provision equally applicable to the recess of the Senate and to its session.

Here, also, I beg leave to remind the Senate that if Mr. Stanton's case does not fall within the tenure-of-office act, if the order which the President gave to him to vacate the office was a lawful order and one which he was bound to obey, everything which is contained in this article, as well as in the preceding articles, fails. It is impossible, I submit, for the honorable Managers to construct a case of an intention on the part of the President to violate the Constitution of the United States out of anything which he did in reference to the appointment of General Thomas, provided the order to Mr. Stanton was a lawful order and Mr. Stanton was bound to obey it.

I advance now, Senators, to a different class of articles, and they may properly enough, I suppose, be called the conspiracy articles, because they rest upon charges of conspiracy between the President and General Thomas. There are four of them, the fourth, fifth, sixth, and seventh in number as they stand. The fourth and the sixth are framed under the act of July 31, 1861, which is found in 12 Statutes-at-Large, page 284. The fifth and seventh are framed under no act of Congress. They allege an unlawful conspiracy, but they refer to no law by which the acts charged are made unlawful. The acts charged are called unlawful, but there is no law referred to and no case made by the articles within any law of the United States that is known to the President's counsel. I shall treat these articles, therefore, the fourth and sixth together, and the fifth and seventh together, because I think they belong in that order. In the first place, let me consider the fourth and sixth, which charge a conspiracy within this act which I have just mentioned. It is necessary for me to read the substance of this law in order that you may see whether it can have any possible application to this case. It was passed on the 31st of July, 1861, as a war measure, and is entitled, "An act to define and punish certain conspiracies." It provides—

"That if two or more persons within any State or Territory of the United States shall conspire together to overthrow or to put down or to destroy by force the Government of the United States, or to levy war against the United States, or to oppose by force the authority of the Government of the United States; or by force to prevent, hinder, or delay the execution of any law of the United States; or by force to seize, take, or possess any property of the United States against the will or contrary to the authority of the United States; or by force, or intimidation, or threat to prevent any person from accepting or holding any office or trust or place of confidence under the United States."

These are the descriptions of the offenses. The fourth and sixth articles contain allegations that the President and General Thomas conspired together by force, intimidation, and threats to prevent Mr. Stanton from continuing to hold the office of Secretary for the Department of War; and also that they conspired together by force to obtain possession of property belonging to the United States. These are the two articles which I suppose are designed to be drawn under this act; and these are the allegations which are intended to bring the articles within it.

Now, it does seem to me that the attempt to wrest this law to any bearing whatsoever upon this prosecution is one of the extraordinary things which the case contains. In the first place, so far from having been designed to apply to the President of the United States or to any act he might do in the course of the execution of what he believed to be his duty, it does not apply to any man or any thing within the District of Columbia at all.

"If two or more persons within any State or Territory of the United States."

Not within the District of Columbia. This is a highly penal law, and an indictment found in the very words of this act charging things to have been in the District of Columbia and returned into the proper court of this District, I will undertake to say, would not bear a general demurrer, because there is locality given to those things made penal by this act of Congress. It is made applicable to certain portions of the country, but not made applicable to the District of Columbia.

But not to dwell upon that technical view of the matter, and on which we should not choose to stand, let us see what is this case. The President of the United States is of opinion that Mr. Stanton holds the office of Secretary for the Department of War at his pleasure. He thinks so, first, because he believes the case of Mr. Stanton is not provided for in the tenure-of-office act, and no tenure of office is secured to him. He thinks so, secondly, because he believes that it would be judicially decided, if the question could be raised, that a law depriving the President of the power of removing such an officer at his pleasure is not a constitutional law. He is of opinion that in this case he cannot allow this officer to continue to act as his adviser and as his agent to execute the laws if he has lawful power to remove him; and under these circumstances he gives this order to General Thomas.

I do not view this letter of authority to General Thomas as a purely military order. The service which General Thomas was invoked for is a civil service; but, at the same time, Senators will perceive that the person who gave the order is the Commander-in-Chief of the Army; that the person to whom it was given is the Adjutant General of the Army; that the subject-matter to which the order relates is the performance of services essential to carry on the military service; and, therefore, when such an order was given by the Commander-in-Chief to the Adjutant General respecting a subject of this kind, is it too much to say that there was invoked that spirit of military obedience which constitutes the strength of the service? Not that it was a purely military order; not that General Thomas would have been subject to a court-martial for disobeying it; but that as a faithful Adjutant General of the Army of the United States, interested personally and professionally and patriotically to have the duties of the office of Secretary for the Department of War performed in a temporary vacancy, was it not his duty to accept the appointment unless he saw and knew that it was unlawful to accept it? I do not know how, in fact, he personally considered it; there has been no proof given on the subject; but I have always assumed—I think Senators will assume—that when the distinguished General of the Army of the United States, on a previous occasion, accepted a similar appointment, it was under views of propriety and duty such as those which I have now

been speaking of; and how and why is there to be attributed to General Thomas, as a coconspirator, the guilty intent of designing to overthrow the laws of his country, when a fair and just view of his conduct would leave him entirely without reproach?

And when you come, Senators, to the other coconspirator, the President of the United States, is not the case still clearer. Make it a case of private right, if you please; put it as strongly as possible against the President in order to test the question. One of you has a claim to property; it may be a disputed claim; it is a claim which he believes may prove, when judicially examined, to be sound and good. He says to A B, "Go to C D, who is in possession of that property; I give you this order to him to give it up to you; and if he gives it up take possession." Did anybody ever imagine that that was a conspiracy? Does not every lawyer know that the moment you introduce into any transaction of this kind the element of a claim of right all criminal elements are purged at once; and that this is always true between man and man where it is a simple assertion of private right, the parties to which are at liberty either to assert them or forego them, as they please? But this was not such a case; this was a case of public right, of public duty, of public right claimed upon constitutional grounds and upon the interpretation of the law which had been given to it by the law-makers themselves. How can the President of the United States, under such circumstances, be looked upon by anybody, whether he may or may not be guilty or not guilty of other things as a coconspirator under this act?

These articles say that the conspiracy between the President and General Thomas was to employ force, threats, intimidation. What they have proved against the President is that he issued these orders, and that alone. Now, on the face of these orders, there is no apology for the assertion that it was the design of the President that anybody at any time should use force, threats, or intimidation. The order is to Mr. Stanton to deliver up possession. The order to General Thomas is to receive possession from Mr. Stanton when he delivers it up. No force is assigned to him; no authority is given to him to apply for or use any force, threats, or intimidation. There is not only no express authority, but there is no implication of any authority to apply for or obtain or use anything but the order which was given him to hand to Mr. Stanton; and we shall offer proof, Senators, which we think cannot fail to be satisfactory in point of fact, that the President from the first had in view simply and solely to test this question by the law; that if this was a conspiracy it was a conspiracy to go to law, and that was the whole of it. We shall show you what advice the President received on this subject, what views in concert with his advisers he entertained, which, of course, it is not my province now to comment upon; the evidence must first be adduced, then it will be time to consider it.

The other two conspiracy articles will require very little observation from me, because they contain no new allegations of fact which are not in the fourth and sixth articles, which I have already adverted to; and the only distinction between them and the others is that they are not founded upon this conspiracy act of 1861; they simply allege an unlawful conspiracy, and leave the matter there. They do not allege sufficient facts to bring the case within the act of 1861. In other words, they do not allege force, threats, or intimidation. I shall have occasion to remark upon these articles when I come to speak of the tenth article, because these articles, as you perceive, come within that category which the honorable Manager announced here at an early period of the trial; articles which require no law to support them; and when I come to speak of the tenth article, as I shall have occasion to discuss this subject, I wish that my remarks, so far as they may be deemed applicable, should be applied to these fifth and seventh articles which I have thus passed over.

I shall detain the Senate but a moment upon the ninth article, which is the one relating to the conversation with General Emory. The meaning of this article, as I read it, is that the President brought General Emory before himself as Commander-in-Chief of the Army for the purpose of instructing him to disobey the law, with an intent to induce General Emory to disobey it, and with intent to enable himself unlawfully and by the use of military force through General Emory, to prevent Mr. Stanton from continuing to hold office. Now, I submit that, not only does this article fail of proof in its substance as thus detailed, but that it is disproved by the witness whom they have introduced to support it. In the first place, it appears clearly from General Emory's statement that the President did not bring him there for any purpose connected with this appropriation bill affecting the command of the Army, or the orders given to the Army. This subject General Emory introduced himself, and when the conversation was broken off it was again recurred to by himself asking the President's permission to bring it to his attention. Whatsoever was said upon that subject was said not because the President of the United States had brought the commander of the department of Washington before him for that purpose, but because, having brought him there for another purpose, to which I shall allude in a moment, the commanding General chose himself to introduce that subject and converse upon it, and obtain the President's views upon it.

In the next place, having his attention called to the act of Congress and to the order under it, the President expressed precisely the same opinion to General Emory that he had previously publicly expressed to Congress itself

C. I.—18.

at the time when the act was sent to him for his signature; and there is found set out in his answer on page 32 of the official report of these proceedings what that opinion was; that he considered that this provision interfered with his constitutional right as the Commander-in-Chief of the Army; and that is what he said to General Emory. There is not even probable cause to believe that he said it for any other than the natural reason that General Emory had introduced the subject, had asked leave to call his attention to it, and evidently expected and desired that the President should say something on the subject; and if he said anything was he not to tell the truth? That is exactly what he did say. I mean the truth as he apprehended it. It will appear in proof, as I am instructed, that the reason why the President sent for General Emory was not that he might endeavor to seduce that distinguished officer from his allegiance to the laws and the Constitution of his country, but because he wished to obtain information about military movements which he was informed upon authority which he had a right to and was bound to respect might require his personal attention.

I pass, then, from this article, as being one upon which I ought not to detain the Senate, and I come to the last one, concerning which I shall have much to say, and that is the tenth article, which is all of and concerning the speeches of the President.

In the front of this inquiry the question presents itself: What are impeachable offenses under the Constitution of the United States? Upon this question learned dissertations have been written and printed. One of them is annexed to the argument of the honorable Manager who opened the cause for the prosecution. Another one on the other side of the question, written by one of the honorable Managers themselves, may be found annexed to the proceedings in the House of Representatives upon the occasion of the first attempt to impeach the President. And there have been others written and published by learned jurists touching this subject. I do not propose to vex the ear of the Senate with any of the precedents drawn from the Middle Ages. The framers of our Constitution were quite as familiar with them as the learned authors of these treatises, and the framers of our Constitution, as I conceive, have drawn from them the lesson which I desire the Senate to receive, that these precedents are not fit to govern their conduct on this trial.

In my apprehension, the teachings, the requirements, the prohibitions of the Constitution of the United States prove all that is necessary to be attended to for the purposes of this trial. I propose, therefore, instead of a search through the precedents which were made in the times of the Plantagenets, the Tudors, and the Stuarts, and which have been repeated since, to come nearer home and see what provisions of the Constitution of the

United States bear on this question, and whether they are not sufficient to settle it. If they are it is quite immaterial what exists elsewhere.

My first position is, that when the Constitution speaks of "treason, bribery, and other high crimes and misdemeanors" it refers to, and includes only, high criminal offenses against the United States, made so by some law of the United States existing when the acts complained of were done; and I say that this is plainly to be inferred from each and every provision of the Constitution on the subject of impeachment.

"Treason" and "bribery." Nobody will doubt that these are here designated high crimes and misdemeanors against the United States, made such by the laws of the United States, which the framers of the Constitution knew must be passed in the nature of the Government they were about to create, because these are offenses which strike at the existence of that Government—"other high crimes and misdemeanors." *Noscitur a sociis.* High crimes and misdemeanors; so high that they belong in this company with treason and bribery. That is plain on the face of the Constitution; in the very first step it takes on the subject of impeachment. "High crimes and misdemeanors" against what law? There can be no crime, there can be no misdemeanor without a law, written or unwritten, express or implied. There must be some law; otherwise there is no crime. My interpretation of it is that the language "high crimes and misdemeanors" means "offenses against the laws of the United States." Let us see if the Constitution has not said so.

The first clause of the second section of the second article of the Constitution reads thus: "The President of the United States shall have the power to grant reprieves and pardons for offenses against the United States, except in cases of impeachment." "Offenses against the United States" would include "cases of impeachment," and they might be pardoned by the President if they were not excepted. Then cases of impeachment are, according to the express declaration of the Constitution itself, cases of offenses against the United States.

Still, the learned Manager says that this is not a court, and that, whatever may be the character of this body, it is bound by no law. Very different was the understanding of the fathers of the Constitution on this subject.

Mr. Manager BUTLER. Will you state where it was I said it was bound by no law?

Mr. STANBERY. "A law unto itself."

Mr. Manager BUTLER. "No common or statute law" was my language.

Mr. CURTIS. I desire to refer to the sixty-fourth number of the Federalist, which is found in Dawson's edition, on page 453:

"The remaining powers which the plan of the Convention allots to the Senate, in a distinct capacity, are comprised in their participation with the Executive in the appointment to offices, and in their judicial character as a court for the trial of impeachments, as in the business of appointments the Executive will be the principal agent, the provisions relating to it will most properly be discussed in the examination of that department. We will therefore conclude this head with a view of the judicial character of the Senate."

And then it is discussed. The next position to which I desire the attention of the Senate is, that there is enough written in the Constitution to prove that this is a court in which a judicial trial is now being carried on. "The Senate of the United States shall have the sole power to try all impeachments." "When the President is tried the Chief Justice shall preside." The trial of all crimes, except in case of impeachment, shall be by jury. This, then, is the trial of a crime. You are the triers, presided over by the Chief Justice of the United States in this particular case, and that on the express words of the Constitution. There is also, according to its express words, to be an acquittal or a conviction on this trial for a crime. "No person shall be convicted without the concurrence of two thirds of the members present." There is also to be a judgment in case there shall be a conviction.

"Judgment in cases of impeachment shall not extend further than removal from office and disqualification to hold any office of honor, trust, or profit under the United States."

Here, then, there is the trial of a crime, a trial by a tribunal designated by the Constitution in place of court and jury, a conviction, if guilt is proved, a judgment on that conviction, a punishment inflicted by the judgment for a crime; and this on the express terms of the Constitution itself. And yet, say the honorable Managers, there is no court to try the crime and no law by which the act is to be judged. The honorable Manager interrupted me to say that he qualified that expression of no law; his expression was "no common or statute law." Well, when you get out of that field you are in a limbo, a vacuum, so far as law is concerned, to the best of my knowledge and belief.

I say, then, that it is impossible not to come to the conclusion that the Constitution of the United States has designated impeachable offenses as offenses against the United States, that it has provided for the trial of those offenses, that it has established a tribunal for the purpose of trying them, that it has directed the tribunal in case of conviction to pronounce a judgment upon the conviction and inflict a punishment. All this being provided for, can it be maintained that this is not a court, or that it is bound by no law?

But the argument does not rest mainly, I think, upon the provisions of the Constitution concerning impeachment. It is, at any rate, vastly strengthened by the direct prohibitions of the Constitution. "Congress shall pass no bill of attainder or *ex post facto* law." According to that prohibition of the Constitution, if every member of this body sitting in its legislative capacity and every member of the other body sitting in its legislative capacity, should unite in passing a law to punish an act after the act was done, that law would be a mere nullity. Yet what is claimed by the honorable Managers in behalf of members of this body? As a Congress you cannot create a law to punish these acts if no law existed at the time they were done; but sitting here as judges, not only after the fact but while the case is on trial, you may individually, each one of you, create a law by himself to govern the case.

According to this assumption the same Constitution which has made it a bill of rights of the American citizen, not only as against Congress but as against the Legislature of every State in the Union, that no *ex post facto* law shall be passed—this same Constitution has erected you into a body and empowered every one of you to say *aut inveniam aut faciam viam*: if I cannot find a law I will make one. Nay, it has clothed every one of you with imperial power; it has enabled you to say, *sic volo, sic jubeo, stat pro ratione voluntas*: I am a law unto myself, by which law I shall govern this case. And, more than that, when each one of you before he took his place here called God to witness that he would administer impartial justice in this case according to the Constitution and the laws, he meant such laws as he might make as he went along. The Constitution, which had prohibited anybody from making such laws, he swore to observe; but he also swore to be governed by his own will; his own individual will was the law which he thus swore to observe; and this special provision of the Constitution that when the Senate sits in this capacity to try an impeachment the Senators shall be on oath means merely that they shall swear to follow their own individual wills! I respectfully submit this view cannot consistently and properly be taken of the character of this body or of the duties and powers incumbent upon it.

Look for a moment, if you please, to the other provision. This same search into the English precedents, so far from having made our ancestors who framed and adopted the Constitution in love with them, led them to put into the Constitution a positive and absolute prohibition against any bill of attainder. What is a bill of attainder? It is a case before the Parliament where the Parliament make the law for the facts they find. Each legislator (for it is in their legislative capacity they act, not in a judicial one) is, to use the phrase of the honorable Managers, "a law unto himself;" and according to his discretion, his views of what is politic or proper under the circumstances, he frames a law to meet the case and enacts it or votes in its enactment. According to the doctrine now advanced bills of attainder are not prohibited by this Constitution; they are only slightly modified. It is only necessary for the House

of Representatives by a majority to vote an impeachment and send up certain articles and have two thirds of this body vote in favor of conviction, and there is an attainder; and it is done by the same process and depends on identically the same principles as a bill of attainder in the English Parliament. The individual wills of the legislators, instead of the conscientious discharge of the duty of the judges, settle the result.

I submit, then, Senators, that this view of the honorable Managers of the duties and powers of this body cannot be maintained. But the attempt made by the honorable Managers to obtain a conviction upon this tenth article is attended with some peculiarities which I think it is the duty of the counsel to the President to advert to. So far as regards the preceding articles, the first eight articles are framed upon allegations that the President broke a law. I suppose the honorable Managers do not intend to carry their doctrine so far as to say that unless you find the President did intentionally break a law those articles are supported. As to those articles there is some law unquestionably, the very gist of the charge being that he broke a law. You must find that the law existed; you must construe it and apply it to the case; you must find his criminal intent willfully to break the law, before the articles can be supported. But we come now to this tenth article, which depends upon no law at all, but, as I have said, is attended with some extraordinary peculiarities.

The complaint is that the President made speeches against Congress. The true statement here would be much more restricted than that; for although in those speeches the President used the word "Congress," undoubtedly he did not mean the entire constitutional body organized under the Constitution of the United States; he meant the dominant majority in Congress. Everybody so understood it; everybody must so understand it. But the complaint is that he made speeches against those who governed in Congress. Well, who are the grand jury in this case? One of the parties spoken against. And who are the tryers? The other party spoken against. One would think there was some incongruity in this; some reason for giving pause before taking any very great stride in that direction. The honorable House of Representatives sends its Managers here to take notice of what? That the House of Representatives has erected itself into a school of manners, selecting from its ranks those gentlemen whom it deems most competent by precept and example to teach decorum of speech; and they desire the judgment of this body whether the President has not been guilty of indecorum, whether he has spoken properly, to use the phrase of the honorable Manager. Now, there used to be an old-fashioned notion that although there might be a difference of taste about oral speeches, and, no doubt, always has been and always will be many such differences, there was one very important test in reference to them, and that is whether they are true or false; but it seems that in this case that is no test at all. The honorable Manager, in opening the case, finding, I suppose, that it was necessary, in some manner, to advert to that subject, has done it in terms which I will read to you:

"The words are not alleged to be either false or defamatory, because it is not within the power of any man, however high his official position, in effect to slander the Congress of the United States, in the ordinary sense of that word, so as to call on Congress to answer as to the truth of the accusation."

Considering the nature of our Government, considering the experience which we have gone through on this subject, that is a pretty lofty claim. Why, if the Senate please, if you go back to the time of the Plantagenets and seek for precedents there, you will not find so lofty a claim as that. I beg leave to read from two statutes, the first being 3 Edward I, ch. 34, and the second 2 Richard II, ch. 1, a short passage. The statute, 3 Edward I, ch. 34, after the preamble, enacts—

"That from henceforth none be so hardy to tell or publish any false news or tales, whereby discord or occasion of discord or slander may grow between the king and his people, or the great men of the realm; and he that doeth so shall be taken and kept in until he hath brought him into court which was the first author of the tale."

The statute 2 Richard II, c. 1, s. 5, enacted with some alterations the previous statute. It commenced thus:

"Of devisors of false news and of horrible and false lies of prelates, dukes, earls, barons, and other nobles and great men of the realm; and also of the chancellor, treasurer, clerk of the privy seal, steward of the king's house, justices of the one bench or of the other, and of other great officers of the realm."

The great men of the realm in the time of Richard II were protected only against "horrible and false lies," and when we arrive in the course of our national experience during the war with France and the administration of Mr. Adams to that attempt to check, not free speech, but free writing, Senators will find that although it applied only to written libels it contained an express section that the truth might be given in evidence. That was a law, as Senators know, making it penal by written libels to excite the hatred or contempt of the people against Congress among other offenses; but the estimate of the elevation of Congress above the people was not so high but that it was thought proper to allow a defense of the truth to be given in evidence. I beg leave to read from this sedition act a part of one section and make a reference to another to support the correctness of what I have said. It is found in Statutes-at-Large, page 596:

"That if any person shall write, print, utter, or publish, or shall cause or procure to be written, printed, uttered, or published, or shall knowingly and willingly assist or aid in writing, printing, uttering, or publishing any false, scandalous, and malicious writing or writings against the Government of the United States, or either House of the Congress of the United States, or the President of the United States, with intent to defame the said Government,

or either House of the said Congress, or the said President, or to bring them, or either or any of them the hatred of the good people of the United States, or to stir up sedition within the United States, or to excite any unlawful combinations therein," &c.

Section three provides—

"That if any person shall be prosecuted under this act for the writing or publishing any libel aforesaid, it shall be lawful for the defendant, upon the trial of the cause, to give in evidence in his defense the truth of the matter contained in the publication charged as a libel. And the jury who shall try the cause shall have a right to determine the law and the fact, under the direction of the court, as in other cases."

In contrast with the views expressed here, I desire now to read from the fourth volume of Mr. Madison's works, pages 542 and 547, passages which, in my judgment, are as masterly as anything Mr. Madison ever wrote, upon the relations of the Congress of the United States to the people of the United States in contrast with the relations of the Government of Great Britain to the people of that island; and the necessity which the nature of our Government lays us under to preserve freedom of the press and freedom of speech:

"The essential difference between the British Government and the American Constitution will place this subject in the clearest light.

"In the British Government the danger of encroachments on the rights of the people is understood to be confined to the Executive Magistrate. The Representatives of the people in the Legislature are only exempt themselves from distrust, but are considered as sufficient guardians of the rights of their constituents against the danger from the Executive. Hence it is a principle that the Parliament is unlimited in its power, or, in their own language, is omnipotent. Hence, too, all the ramparts for protecting the rights of the people—such as their Magna Charta, their Bill of Rights, &c.—are not reared against the Parliament, but against the royal prerogative. They are merely legislative precautions against Executive usurpations. Under such a Government as this, an exemption of the press from previous restraint, by licensers appointed by the king, is all the freedom that can be secured to it.

"In the United States the case is altogether different. The people, not the Government, possess the absolute sovereignty. The Legislature, no less than the Executive, is under limitations of power. Encroachments are regarded as possible from the one as well as from the other. Hence, in the United States, the great and essential rights of the people are secured against legislative as well as against executive ambition. They are secured, not by laws paramount to prerogative, but by constitutions paramount to laws. This security of the freedom of the press requires that it should be exempt not only from previous restraint by the Executive, as in Great Britain, but from legislative restraint also; and this exemption, to be effectual, must be an exemption not only from the previous inspection of licenses, but from the subsequent penalty of laws."

One other passage on page 547, which has an extraordinary application to the subject now before you:

"1. The Constitution supposes that the President, the Congress, and each of its Houses may not discharge their trusts, either from defect of judgment or other causes. Hence they are all made responsible to their constituents at the returning periods of election; and the President, who is singly intrusted with very great powers, is, as a further guard, subjected to an intermediate impeachment.

"2. Should it happen, as the Constitution supposes it may happen, that either of these branches of the Government may not have duly discharged its trust, it is natural and proper that, according to the cause and degree of their faults, they should be brought into contempt or disrepute, and incur the hatred of the people.

"3. Whether it has, in any case, happened that the proceedings of either or all of those branches evince such a violation of duty as to justify a contempt, a disrepute, or hatred among the people, can only be determined by a free examination thereof, and a free communication among the people thereon.

"4. Whenever it may have actually happened that proceedings of this sort are chargeable on all or either of the branches of the Government, it is the duty, as well as right, of intelligent and faithful citizens to discuss and promulge them freely, as well to control them by the censorship of the public opinion as to promote a remedy according to the rules of the Constitution. And it cannot be avoided that those who are to apply the remedy must feel, in some degree, a contempt or hatred against the transgressing party."

These observations of Mr. Madison were made in respect to the freedom of the press. There were two views entertained at the time when the sedition law was passed concerning the power of Congress over this subject. The one view was that when the Constitution spoke of freedom of the press it referred to the common-law definition of that freedom. That was the view which Mr. Madison was controverting in one of the passages which I have read to you. The other view was that the common-law definition could not be deemed applicable, and that the freedom provided for by the Constitution, so far as the action of Congress was concerned, was an absolute freedom of the press. But no one ever imagined that freedom of speech, in contradistinction from written libel, could be restrained by a law of Congress; for whether you treat the prohibition in the Constitution as absolute in itself or whether you refer to the common law for a definition of its limits and meaning the result will be the same. Under the common law no man was ever punished criminally for spoken words. If he slandered his neighbor and injured him he must make good in damages to his neighbor the injury he had done; but there was no such thing at the common law as an indictment for spoken words. So that this prohibition in the Constitution against any legislation by Congress in restraint of the freedom of speech is necessarily an absolute prohibition; and therefore this is a case not only where there is no law made prior to the act to punish the act, but a case where Congress is expressly prohibited from making any law to operate even on subsequent acts.

What is the law to be? Suppose it is, as the honorable Managers seem to think it should be, the sense of propriety of each Senator appealed to. What is it to be? The only rule I have heard—the only rule which can be announced—is that you may require the speaker to speak properly. Who are to be the judges whether he speaks properly? In this case the Senate of the United States on the presentation of the House of Representatives of the United States; and that is supposed to be the freedom of speech secured by this absolute prohibition of the Constitution. That is the same free-

dom of speech, Senators, in consequence of which thousands of men went to the scaffold under the Tudors and the Stuarts. That is the same freedom of speech which caused thousands of heads of men and of women to roll from the guillotine in France. That is the same freedom of speech which has caused in our day more than once "order to reign in Warsaw." The persons did not speak properly in the apprehension of the judges before whom they were brought. Is that the freedom of speech intended to be secured by our Constitution?

Mr. Chief Justice and Senators, I have to detain you but a very short time longer, and that is by a few observations concerning the eleventh article, and they will be very few, for the reason that the eleventh article, as I understand it, contains nothing new which needs any notice from me. It appears by the official copy of the articles which is before us, the printed copy, that this article was adopted at a later period than the preceding nine articles, and I suppose it has that appearance, that the honorable Managers, looking over the work they had already performed, perhaps not feeling perfectly satisfied to leave it in the shape in which it then stood, came to the conclusion to add this eleventh article, and they have compounded it out of the materials which they had previously worked up into the others. In the first place, they said, here are the speeches; we will have something about them, and accordingly they begin by the allegation that the President at the Executive Mansion, on a certain occasion, made a speech, and without giving his words, but it is attributed to him that he had an intention to declare that this was not a Congress within the meaning of the Constitution; all of which is denied in his answer, and there is no proof to support it. The President, by his whole course of conduct, has shown that he could have entertained no such intention as that. He has explained that fully in his answer, and I do not think it necessary to repeat the explanation.

Then they come to the old matter of the removal of Mr. Stanton. They say he made this speech denying the competency of Congress to legislate, and following up its intent he endeavored to remove Mr. Stanton. I have sufficiently discussed that, and I shall not weary the patience of the Senate by doing so any further.

Then they say that he made this speech and followed up its intent by endeavoring to get possession of the money appropriated for the military service of the United States. I have said all I desire to say upon that.

Then they say that he made it with the intent to obstruct what is called the law "for the better government of the rebel States," passed in March, 1867, and in support of that they have offered a telegram to him from Governor Parsons and an answer to that telegram from the President, upon the subject of an amendment of the Constitution, sent in January before the March when the law came into existence, and, so far as I know, that is the only evidence which they have offered upon that subject. I leave, therefore, with these remarks, that article for the consideration of the Senate.

It must be unnecessary for me to say anything concerning the importance of this case, not only now but in the future. It must be apparent to every one, in any way connected with or concerned in this trial, that this is and will be the most conspicuous instance which ever has been or can ever be expected to be found of American justice or American injustice, of that justice which Mr. Burke says is the great standing policy of all civilized States, or of that injustice which is sure to be discovered and which makes even the wise man mad, and which, in the fixed and immutable order of God's providence, is certain to return to plague its inventors.

Mr. CONNESS, (at two o'clock and twenty minutes p. m.) Mr. President, I move that the court take a recess for fifteen minutes.

The motion was agreed to; and the Chief Justice resumed the chair at twenty-five minutes to three o'clock.

The CHIEF JUSTICE. Senators will please resume their seats and give their attention. Gentlemen of counsel for the President, you will please proceed with the defense.

Mr. STANBERY. We will call General Thomas first.

LORENZO THOMAS sworn and examined.
By Mr. STANBERY:

Question. General Thomas, will you state how long you have been in the service?

Answer. I went to West Point in the year 1819. I entered the Military Academy in September of that year, and was graduated July 1, 1823, and appointed second lieutenant of the fourth infantry. I have been in the Army since that date.

Question. What is your present rank in the Army?

Answer. I am adjutant general of the Army, with the rank of brigadier general, and major general by brevet.

Question. When was your brevet conferred?

Answer. I really forget. I would have to refer to the Army Register for that.

Question. Can you recollect the year?

Answer. Yes, sir; it was after I returned from one of my southern trips.

Question. During the war?

Answer. Yes, sir.

Question. Toward the close of it?

Answer. Toward the close of it. I was first made a colonel, as adjutant general, on the 7th of March, when Colonel Cooper went out.

Question. When were you first appointed adjutant general?

Answer. On the 7th of March, 1861.

Question. On what service were you during the war, generally? Give us an idea of your service.

Answer. During the administration of the War Department by General Cameron I was on duty as adjutant general in the office. I accompanied him on his western trip to Missouri and to Kentucky and returned with him. Then, after that, after making that report, he left the Department, and Mr. Stanton was appointed. I remained in the Department some time after Mr. Stanton was appointed, several months. The first duty he placed me on from the office—at any rate as one of the duties—he sent me down on the James river to make exchanges of prisoners of war under the arrangement made by General Dix with the rebels.

Mr. Manager BUTLER. To what point is this evidence?

Mr. STANBERY. To bring around the reason why there was the interruption in the Adjutant General's business, and how long it continued and when he returned. It will be through in a moment. [To witness.] What was the next service?

Answer. During the war I was sent once or twice—three times, perhaps—to Harrisburg to organize volunteers and to correct some irregularities there; not irregularities exactly, but in order to put regiments together, skeleton regiments. I was sent there and ordered to bring them together—once at Philadelphia and twice at Harrisburg. I was sent to Harrisburg also about the time that Lee was invading Maryland and Pennsylvania; but my principal duty was down on the Mississippi river.

Question. What was the duty there?

Answer. Threefold. The first was to inspect the armies on the river in that part of the country. The second was to look into cotton lands.

Mr. Manager BUTLER. Will not that appear better by the order?

The WITNESS. I have it.

Mr. STANBERY. The orders are here, but it will take a great while to introduce them.

Mr. Manager BUTLER. Very well.

Mr. STANBERY. I will ask him nothing but what he has performed. [To the witness.] What was the third duty?

Answer. To take charge of the negro population and to organize them as troops.

Question. Were you the first officer who organized negro regiments?

Answer. No, sir.

Question. Who was prior to you?

Answer. I think that General Butler had organized some in New Orleans. Some were organized before I took charge. I was sent down on the Mississippi and in the rebellious States, and I had charge of all of them there.

Question. What number of regiments were organized under your care?

Answer. I organized upwards of eighty thousand colored soldiers. The particular number of regiments I do not recollect, because they were numbered some with those in New Orleans and some with those in the East.

Question. After that service was performed what was the next special duty you were detailed on?

Answer. I returned to this city after I heard of the surrender of Lee. I was then on my way up the river. I came to Washington. The next duty I was placed upon was to make an inspection of the Provost Marshal General's office throughout the country, first at Washington, and then throughout the loyal States. I performed that service.

Question. What next?

Answer. My last service was, I was ordered throughout the United States to examine the national cemeteries under a law passed by Congress. That duty I have performed; but my report is not yet in. It is very voluminous. Those are the duties that I have performed.

Question. Did those duties fall under your proper duties as adjutant general; and in what capacity?

Answer. Perfectly so. As adjutant general I am *ex officio* inspector of the Army, and these duties are germane to it.

Question. This duty of inspection of the cemeteries was the last special duty that you have been called upon to perform?

Answer. Yes, sir.

Question. When did you return from having performed that last special duty?

Answer. I came to Washington on three different occasions. I would come here and then would go back.

Question. When did you return from this last duty or this last detail upon the national cemetery business?

Answer. I do not think I can give the precise date; but it was about the close of last year.

Question. Toward the close of the year 1867?

Answer. Yes, sir.

Question. You say you had then completed this last duty or service?

Answer. I had visited every State where the cemeteries were. The only ones I have not visited are two very small ones near this city. I left them to the last.

Question. You were then ready to make your report?

Answer. Yes, sir; I was writing it out and would have had it ready if it had not been for the interruption of this court. It is nearly completed.

Question. You have not since been detailed upon any other special service except about this War Department?

Answer. No, sir; I was engaged in making this report and I continued on that duty until I was placed in charge of the Adjutant General's office.

Question. At what date were you returned to your Adjutant General's office?

Answer. The President sent for me and gave me a note to General Grant dated the 13th of February. General Grant's note to me in answer to that, putting me in charge, was dated the next day—the 14th.

Question. Who had occupied your office during your absence?

Answer. General E. D. Townsend, Assistant Adjutant General.

Question. Your assistant?

Answer. My first assistant with the rank of colonel.

Question. Then you never lost your position as adjutant general?

Answer. Never.

Question. Did you apply to the President to restore you?

Answer. I spoke to the President on two or three occasions, some months ago, stating that when I got through this particular business I should like to have charge of my office. He knew what my wishes were; but on this occasion I did not mention it to him.

Mr. Manager BUTLER. Stop a moment. I wish to object *in limine* to any conversation between this person and the President.

Mr. STANBERY. This is his application to the President that I am trying to prove, to be restored to his duty as Adjutant General.

Mr. Manager BUTLER. I do not object to that fact; but I do not want this conversation.

Mr. STANBERY. I do not want any conversation now. [To the witness.] You applied once or twice to him before to restore you?

Answer. I stated that that was my wish.

Question. On the 13th of February you received the order which you had requested before restoring you to your position?

Answer. Yes, sir. It was not a note to me; it was a note to General Grant.

Question. But that note restored you to your position?

Answer. Yes, sir.

Question. When, after that, did you see the President, and what did he say to you or did you say to him between that time and the time you received your order on the 21st?

Answer. On one occasion I went over to take him some resignations——

Question. After you had been restored to your office?

Answer. Yes, sir; some resignations that Mr. Stanton gave me which were on his table.

Question. To take over?

Answer. Yes, sir.

Question. Was that the first occasion on which the President spoke to you about taking possession of the War Office?

Mr. Manager BUTLER. Stop a moment. I object to that question; it is leading, and so grossly leading, in my judgment, that it is almost intentional. "Was that the first occasion he spoke to you"—assuming that he had spoken.

Mr. STANBERY. He did speak afterward, we know.

Mr. Manager BUTLER. How do we know?

Mr. STANBERY. We will come to it in

another way. [To the witness.] Do you recollect what occurred on the 21st of February?

Answer. Yes, sir. I thought your question was anterior to that.

Mr. STANBERY. It was. What happened in the War Office on the morning of the 21st of February in regard to closing the office on the succeeding day, the 22d?

Answer. Toward twelve o'clock I went up myself and asked Mr. Stanton, then Secretary of War, if I should close the office the next day, the 22d of February, and he directed me to do it. I issued such a circular and sent it around to the different Departments.

Question. Was that an order made by you as adjutant general?

Answer. Yes, sir; by his order.

Question. Was that before you had seen the President that day?

Answer. Yes, sir.

Question. Now, what took place after you had issued that order?

Answer. Very soon after I had issued it I received a note from Colonel Moore, the Private Secretary of the President, that the President wished to see me. I immediately went over to the White House, and saw the President. He came out of his library with two communications in his hand.

Question. He came out with two papers in his hand?

Answer. Yes, sir. He handed them to Colonel Moore to read. They were read to me.

Question. Read aloud?

Answer. Read aloud. One was addressed to Mr. Stanton, dismissing him from office, and directing him to turn over the books, papers, &c., pertaining to the War Department. The other was addressed to me, appointing me Secretary of War *ad interim*, and stating that Mr. Stanton had been directed to transfer the office to me.

Question. Was that the first time you saw those papers, or either of them?

Answer. The first time.

Question. You had no hand whatever in writing those papers or dictating them?

Answer. Nothing whatever.

Mr. Manager BUTLER. Excuse me; that is very leading again.

Mr. STANBERY. Well. [To the witness.] What was said by the President at that time to you or by you to the President?

Mr. Manager BUTLER. Do you prepose to put in conversations——

Mr. STANBERY. I do.

Mr. Manager BUTLER. Between this party and the President?

Mr. STANBERY. Right there, certainly. [Handing him the papers.]

Mr. EVARTS. Which they put in evidence.

Mr. Manager BUTLER. I will not interpose the objection here, sir.

By Mr. STANBERY:

Question. What, then, was said between you and the President?

Answer. He said he was determined to support the Constitution and the laws, and he desired me to do the same. [Laughter.]

Mr. Manager BUTLER. I do not object.

The WITNESS. I told him I would.

By Mr. STANBERY:

Question. What further took place or was said?

Answer. He then directed me to deliver this paper addressed to Mr. Stanton to him.

Question. Was that all? Did you then leave?

Answer. I told him that I would take an officer in my department with me to see that I delivered it and note what occurred, and I stated that I would take General Williams.

Question. Who is General Williams?

Answer. One of the assistant adjutants general in my department on duty there.

Question. You told the President you would take him along to witness the transaction?

Answer. Yes, sir.

Question. What did you do then?

Answer. I went over to the War Department, went into one of my rooms, and told General Williams I wished him to go with me; I did not say for what purpose. I told him I wanted him to go with me to the Secretary of War and note what occurred.

Question. Without telling him what it was you intended?

Answer. I did not tell him anything about it. I then went to the Secretary's room and handed him the first paper.

Question. When you say the first paper, which was that?

Answer. The paper addressed to him.

Question. What took place then? Did he read it?

Answer. He got up when I came in, and we bade good morning to each other, and I handed him that paper, and he put it down on the corner of his table and sat down. Presently he got up and opened it and read it, and he then said, "Do you wish me to vacate the office at once, or will you give me time to remove my private property?" I said, "Act your pleasure."

Question. Did he say what time he would require?

Answer. No, sir; I did not ask him. I then handed him the paper addressed to me, which he read, and he asked me to give him a copy.

Question. What did you say?

Answer. In the meantime General Grant came in, and I handed it to him. General Grant asked me if that was for him. I said no; merely for his information. I promised a copy, and I went down.

Question. Down where? To your office?

Answer. Into my own room.

Question. Your own room is below that of the Secretary; on the first floor?

Answer. Below General Schriver's room; the one opposite the Secretary's.

Question. It is on the lower floor?

Answer. Yes, sir.

Question. You went down and made a copy of the order?

Answer. I had a copy made, which I certified as Secretary of War *ad interim.* I took that up and handed it to him. He then said, "I do not know whether I will obey your instructions or whether I will resist them." Nothing more passed of any moment, and I left.

Question. Was General Grant there at the second interview?

Answer. No, sir.

Question. The Secretary was alone then?

Answer. He was alone. His son may have been there, because he was generally in the room.

Question. Did General Williams go up with you the second time?

Answer. No, sir.

Question. What time of the day was this?

Answer. I think it was about twelve o'clock that I went up to see the Secretary, and this was just after I came down and wrote the order—it was toward one o'clock, I suppose.

Question. It was immediately after you had written the order to close the office?

Answer. Yes, I got the note immediately after from Colonel Moore.

Question. Was that all that occurred between you and the Secretary on that day, the 21st?

Answer. I think it was. [After a pause.] No, no; I was confounding the 22d with the 21st.

Question. What further?

Answer. I went into the other room and he was there, and I said that I should issue orders as Secretary of War. He said that I should not; he would countermand them, and he turned to General Schriver and also to General Townsend, who were in the room, and directed them not to obey any orders coming from me as Secretary of War.

By Mr. Manager BUTLER:

Question. Do I understand that this was the 21st?

Answer. I think it was the 21st.

By Mr. STANBERY:

Question. The 22d or 21st?

Answer. The 21st, I think. What brings it to my mind is, he wrote a note which he handed me prohibiting me from acting on the subject.

Question. Have you got that note?

Answer. I think I gave it to you. I have some here; probably it may be among them. I will look. The note is dated February 21; I know that.

Question, (presenting a paper to the witness.) See if that is the order that he then gave you?

Answer. That is it.

Question. I see the body of it is not in Mr. Stanton's handwriting?

Answer. He dictated it to General Townsend. That is his handwriting. A copy was made of it, and Mr. Stanton signed it, and handed it to me.

Question. Will you read it, if you please?

Answer. "War Department, Washington city, February 21, 1868——

Mr. Manager BUTLER. Stop a moment, if you please. Let us see that paper.

[The paper was thereupon handed to the Managers and examined by them.]

Mr. Manager BUTLER. We have no objection.

Mr. STANBERY, (to the witness.) Now read it, if you please, General.

The witness read as follows:

WAR DEPARTMENT,
WASHINGTON CITY, *February* 21, 1868.

SIR: I am informed that you presume to issue orders as Secretary of War *ad interim.* Such conduct and orders are illegal, and you are hereby commanded to abstain from issuing any orders other than in your capacity as Adjutant General of the Army.

Your obedient servant,

EDWIN M. STANTON,
Secretary of War.

Brevet Major General L. THOMAS, *Adjutant General.*

Question. Did you see the President after that interview?

Answer. I did.

Question. What took place?

Mr. Manager BUTLER. I object now, Mr. President and Senators, to the conversation between the President and General Thomas. Up to this time I did not object, as you observed, upon reflection, to any orders or directions which the President gave, or any conversation had between the President and General Thomas at the time of issuing the commission. But now the commission has been issued; the demand has been made; it has been refused; and a peremptory order given to General Thomas to mind his own business and keep out of the War Office has been put in evidence. Now, I suppose that the President, by talking with General Thomas, or General Thomas, by talking with the President, cannot put in his own declarations for the purpose of making evidence in favor of himself. The Senate has already ruled by solemn vote, and in consonance, I believe, with the opinion of the presiding officer, that there were such evidence of common intent between these two parties as to allow us to put in the acts of each to bear upon the other; but I challenge any authority that can be shown anywhere that, in trying a man for an act before any tribunal, whether a judicial court or any other body of tryers, testimony can be given of what the respondent said in his own behalf, and especially to his servant, and *a fortiori* to his coconspirator. A conspiracy being alleged, can it be that the President of the United States can call up any officer of the Army, and, by talking to him after the act has been done, justify the act which has been done?

The act which we complain of was the removal of Mr. Stanton and the appointment of Mr. Thomas. That has been done; that is, if he can be removed at all. I understand the argument just presented to us by the learned counsel who is absent, after having delivered his argument, is, that there was no removal at all, and no appointment at all. Then, of course, if there was not, there has not been anything done; we might as well stop here. Assuming, however, the correctness of another part of his argument, to wit, that the only power of removal remained in the President or in the President and the Senate; assuming that to be true, and therefore that he could not be quite right in his idea that the question of removal depended upon Mr. Stanton's legs in walking out, because everything had been done but that; assuming that that portion of his argument is the better one we insist that there was a removal, there was an appointment, and that is the act at any rate which is being inquired about; for whatever the character of that act is there is the end, be it better or worse.

But after that act I mean to say that Mr. Thomas cannot make evidence for himself by going and talking with the President, nor the President with Mr. Thomas. Even supposing that the act was as innocent a thing as a conspiracy to get up a lawsuit, after the conspiracy had taken place and it had eventuated in the act, then they could not put in their declarations. True, there is not much evidence of any such conspiracy, because I should suppose that if the President meant to conspire with anybody to get up a lawsuit he would have conspired with his Attorney General and not his Adjutant General. He is a queer person with whom to make a conspiracy to get up a lawsuit. But even a thing so innocent as that, after it was done, could not be ameliorated, defended, altered, or changed by the declarations of the parties, one to the other. Therefore, in limine, I must object; and I need not go any further now than object to any evidence of what the President says, which is not a part of the thing done, a part of the res gestæ, any conversation which takes place after the thing done, after the act of which we complain.

Mr. STANBERY. Mr. Chief Justice, if I understand the case as the gentleman supposes it to be now, the whole case depends upon the removal of Mr. Stanton.

Mr. Manager BUTLER. I have not said any such thing. I do not know what you understand.

Mr. STANBERY. You say the transaction stops with issuing the order for his removal.

Mr. Manager BUTLER. That transaction stops.

Mr. STANBERY. Does not your conspiracy stop? Does not your case stop? That is the question.

Mr. Manager BUTLER. No.

Mr. STANBERY. I agree myself that your case stops with that order, because I agree with what now seems to be the view taken by the honorable Manager, that that did in fact remove Mr. Stanton per se. If it did, it was the law that give it that effect; for there is no question about a removal merely in fact, no question about an actual ouster by force here;

but it is a question of a legal removal, and that we are upon; and I now understand the honorable Manager to say that that order, according to his judgment, effected a legal removal, and it was not necessary for Mr. Stanton's legs to move him out of office; he was already out by the order. If Mr. Stanton was out by the order, the learned Managers are also out by the order, for then it must be a legal order, making a legal removal, not a forcible, illegal ouster.

But, says the learned Manager, the transaction ended in giving the order and receiving the order, and you are to have no testimony of what was said by the President or General Thomas except what was said just then, because that was the transaction; that was the res gestæ. Does the learned gentleman forget his testimony? Does he forget how he attempted to make a case? Does he forget, not what took place in the afternoon between the President and General Thomas that we are now going into, but what took place that night? Does he forget what sort of a case he attempts to make against the President, not at the time when that order was given, nor before it was given, nor in the afternoon of the 21st, but under his conspiracy counts, the Managers have undertaken to give in evidence that on the night of the 21st General Thomas declared that he was going to enter the War Office by force?

That is the matter charged as illegal; and the articles say that the conspiracy between General Thomas and the President was that the order should be executed by the exhibition of force, intimidation, and threats, and to prove that what has he got here? The declarations of General Thomas, not made under oath, as we propose to have them made, but his mere declarations, when the President was absent and could not contradict him—not, as now, under oath, and all the conversation when the President was present and could contradict or might admit. The honorable Manager has gone into all that to make a case against the President of conspiracy; and not merely that, but proves the acts and declarations of General Thomas on the 22d; and not only that, but as late as the 9th of March, at the presidential levee brings a witness, with the eyes of all Delaware upon him, [laughter,] and proves by that witness, or thinks he has proved, that on that night General Thomas also made a declaration involving the President in this conspiracy, as a party to a conspiracy still existing to keep Mr. Stanton out of office.

Now, how are we to defend against these declarations made on the night of the 21st or the 22d, and again as late as the 9th of March? Does not the transaction run through all that time? How is the President to defend himself if he is allowed to introduce no proof of what he said to General Thomas after the date of the order? May he not call General Thomas?

Is General Thomas impeached here as a co-conspirator? Is his mouth shut by a prosecution? Not at all. He is free as a witness—brought here and sworn. Now, what better testimony can we have to contradict this alleged conspiracy than the testimony of one of the alleged conspirators; for if General Thomas did not conspire, certainly the President did not conspire. A man cannot conspire by himself. And now we contradict by this testimony, and have a right to contradict by this testimony, what was stated on the night of the 21st. Here is an interview on the afternoon of the 21st. We want to show that not only at twelve o'clock on the day when he received the order the President gave him no instructions, no orders, and made no agreement to use force; but that at the subsequent meeting in the afternoon of that day, when General Thomas returned to report to the President that Mr. Stanton refused to surrender the office, the President still gave no directions and entered into no conspiracy of force; and that accordingly on the night of the 21st, when General Thomas spoke of his own intentions, he had no authority to speak for the President; and he did not profess to speak for him.

It is in this point of view, if the court please, that it seems to me this is the very best testimony we can give, and the most legal and admissible. It is not after the transaction is ended; it is not after the proof on the other side is ended as to the conspiracy; but it is long before the time when, according to their proof, the conspiracy ceased. In that point of view, we claim that it is perfectly legal.

Mr. Manager BUTLER. Mr. President, I think I must have made myself very illy understood if what I said has been fairly met or attempted to be met by the learned counsel. This is my objection: not that they shall not prove by Mr. Thomas that he did not say what we proved that he said to Mr. BURLEIGH; he will be a bold man to say he did not say it, however; not that they shall not prove that he did not say what he proved we said to Mr. Karsner, although I should think my learned friend had had enough of Mr. Karsner; not that they shall not show any fact which is competent to be shown; but the proposition I make as a legal proposition, (and it has not been met nor touched by the argument,) is that it is not competent to show that Mr. Thomas did not say to Mr. BURLEIGH that he meant to use force, by proving what was said between Mr. Thomas and the President; that the President cannot put in his declaration; and I challenge again a law book to be brought in before this Senate—common low, parliamentary law, constitutional law, statute law, or "law unto ourselves"—any law that was ever heard of in which any such proposition was ever held. It never was held, sir. Go to your own reading; tell me of the case where after we show that a man has done an act, which act is complained of, when he is on trial for that act, he can bring his servant, his co-conspirator, and show what he said to his servant and his servant to him, in order to his justification. What thief could not defend himself by that, what murderer could not defend himself by that—show what he said, the one to the other, and the other to the one after the thing has happened, after the act has been done?

Now, it is said, as though this case was to be carried on by some little snap-catch of a word, that I said there was a removal, and, therefore, I must have said it was a legal removal. I say there never was a legal removal of Mr. Stanton. There was an act of removal so far as the President of the United States could exercise the power, so far as he could do it, so far as he is criminally responsible for it, so far as he must be held to every intendment of the consequences of it as much as though Mr. Stanton had gone out in obedience to it; because who is the President? He is the Chief Executive, and has the Army and the Navy, and has issued an order to one officer of the Army to take possession.

But, Senators, I am not now insisting that the President shall not ask Mr. Thomas, "Sir, did you conspire?" I am content they shall ask him that and I will ask him in return, "Did you conspire with the President; did you do this, or did you do that?" But my proposition is, that they cannot put in what the President said to Thomas, or what Thomas said to the President after he had given the order. The learned counsel says "Why these gentlemen Managers have put in what Mr. Thomas said all along, and what the President said all along." I understand that; so we can. It is the commonest thing in all courts of justice where I have seen cases tried—and where I have not the books are all one way upon that matter—it is the commonest thing on earth to put in the confession of a criminal made clear down to the time of the trial, down to the hour of the trial. Is it not? If he makes a confession the moment the officer is bringing him and putting him into the dock, it may be used against him. But who ever heard that it gave the prisoner the right to introduce what he said to his associate, what he said to his servant, what he said to his neighbor, after the act was done, be the act whatever it may?

It is said you must allow him to put this in because the President cannot defend himself otherwise. He has all the facts to defend himself with. What I mean to say is that he shall not defend himself by word of mouth. I do not claim that the conspiracy was made between the 21st of February and the 9th of March. I claim that it was made before that time; and I think we shall be able, before we get through, to convince everybody else of it. I claim that we find certain testimony of it between these two dates.

Now, understand me. I do not object to asking Mr. Thomas what he said to Mr. BUR-

LEIGH, what he said to Mr. Wilkeson, what he said to Mr. Karsner, what he said to anybody, where we have put in what he said; but I do object to his putting in any more of the President's declarations after the act done. I do not want any more such exhibitions as this. When a simple order is given by the President to his subordinate, a very harmless thing, quite in common course, it is given to him with a flourish of trumpets. "Now, I want you to sustain the Constitution and laws;" and the officer says, "I will sustain the Constitution and the laws." Do we not understand what all that was done for? It was a part of the defense got up there at the time; a declaration made to be put in here before you or before some court.

Nobody can doubt what that was for. Did he ever give any other order to Thomas or any other officer and say: "Now, sir, here is a little order, and I want you to sustain the Constitution and laws; I am going to sustain the Constitution and laws, and you must sustain the Constitution and laws;" and then solemnly for that officer to say, "I will sustain the Constitution and the laws." Did you ever hear of that in any other case? Why was it done in this case? It was done for the purpose of blinding whatever court should try the case, in order that it might be put in as a justification. "Oh! I did not mean to do anything but sustain the Constitution and the laws, and I said so at the time." That declaration was put in out of the usual and ordinary course, and it is to prevent any more of that sort of declarations got up, manufactured by this criminal at the time when he was going into his crime and after the crime was committed, that I make the objection. Under such circumstances to give him the opportunity to manufacture testimony in this way never was heard of in any court of justice.

Mr. EVARTS. Mr. Chief Justice and Senators, if the crime, as it is called, of the President of the United States was complete when this written order was handed by him to General Thomas and received by General Thomas, why have the Managers occupied your attention with other and later proceedings in his behalf of the removal of Mr. Stanton? The first, the only act in regard to that removal which the Managers introduced, was of the 22d of February, and the presentation of General Thomas, and then with the purpose, as it was said, of forcibly ejecting Mr. Stanton from the office of Secretary of War. That is the act—that is the fact—that is the res gestæ on which they stand; and it was by the combination of the delegate from Dakota invited to attend and take part in that act where the force was sought to be brought into this case in the intention of the President of the United States; and then the evidence connecting the intention of the President of the United States with this act, this fact, this res gestæ of the 22d was drawn from the hearsay evidence of what General Thomas

had said, and upon the pledge of the Managers that they would connect the President with it.

And now, in the presence of a court of justice and in the Senate of the United States, the Managers of the House of Representatives, speaking "in the name of all the people of the United States," object when we seek to show what did occur between the President and General Thomas up to the time of the only act and fact they introduced on the 22d by hearsay evidence of General Thomas's statements of what he meant to do. They sought to implicate the President in the intended force to be used by that hearsay testimony upon the pledge that they would connect the President with it; and we offer the evidence that we said in the first instance should have been brought here under oath of this agent or actor himself to prove what the connection of the President was. When that hearsay has been let in, secondary evidence, and we undertake to show by the oath of the actor, the agent, the officer, what really occurred between him and the President of the United States, they say that is of no consequence, that is no part of the res gestæ, and that is no part of evidence showing what the relation between the parties was. Why, Mr. Chief Justice and Senators, if the learned Managers had objected that General Thomas was not to be received as a witness because he was a coconspirator, a cocriminal, some of the observations of the learned Manager might have some application; but that is not the aspect, and that is not the claim in which the matter is presented to your notice. It is that General Thomas being a competent witness to speak the truth here as to whatever is pertinent to this case is not to be permitted to say what was the agency, what was the instruction, what was the concomitant observation of the President of the United States that attended every interview antecedent to the time which they have put in evidence.

So, too, they have sought to give evidence of intent, gathered from a witness who overheard what General Thomas said, pertinent, as they supposed, on the 9th of March, and that is upon the idea that General Thomas had been empowered by the President to say or do something that made his statements pertinent to commit the President. Now, if they can show, through General Thomas, by hearsay, what they claim is to implicate the President in intent, running up to the 9th of March, we can prove by General Thomas, up to any date in respect to which they offered evidence, all that did occur between the President and himself, in order that if there be connection that may be made accurate and precise, and if there be no connection that disconnection be made absolute and complete.

Mr. Manager BINGHAM. Mr. President and Senators, I desire, to the right understanding of this controversy, that the question to which my associate Manager objected may be reported by the Secretary.

The CHIEF JUSTICE. The counsel will please reduce the question to writing.

The question was reduced to writing, and read as follows:

What occurred between the President and yourself at that second interview on the 21st?

Mr. Manager BINGHAM. The Senators will notice that the attempt is now made for the first time in the progress of this trial, and I think is made here for the first time in the presence of any tribunal of justice in this country by respectable counsel, to introduce in the defense of an accused criminal his own declarations made after the fact. Before this second interview referred to in the question, the crime charged in the first article, if crime it be, was committed and complete. The time has not yet come, Senators, for the full discussion of the question, whether it was a crime for Andrew Johnson, on the 21st day of February, 1868, with intent to violate the act regulating the tenure of certain civil offices, to issue an order for the removal, as averred in the first article—not "removing" as the counsel stated, but "for the removal of"—the Secretary of War from the Department of War not only in contravention of the express terms of that act itself, but in defiance of the action of the Senate then had upon the suspension under the same law, by the same President, of the same Secretary, and whereof he had notice. For myself, I stand ready, as the learned counsel has seen fit to make the challenge in this stage of the case, to say that if the tenure-of-office act be a valid act, the attempt to remove in contravention of the provisions of that act which declares a removal to be a misdemeanor, is itself a misdemeanor, not simply at common law, but by the laws of the United States. I am not surprised that this utterance was made at this stage of the case; for the learned counsel who closed his elaborate and exhaustive argument in the defense had ventured upon the bold declaration here in the presence of the Senate, that an attempt to commit a misdemeanor, made such by the laws of any sovereignty upon the earth, was not itself a crime consummated by the very attempt, and itself a misdemeanor.

I pass that question now; with all respect I say it ought not to have been referred to in this discussion. The only question before the Senate is whether it is competent for an accused criminal, high or low, official or unofficial, President or private citizen, after the fact charged against him, to make evidence for himself by his own declarations either to a co-conspirator or to anybody else. That is all the point there is involved in this question; and I reiterate what was said, doubtless after due reflection, by my associate Manager, that there is not an authority fit to be brought into a court of justice but denounces the proposition as hearsay and violative of the rules of law. Why justice itself is impotent if evidence is to be made by every criminal violator of the law for himself, after the fact, by his own declarations.

I am amazed at the declaration of counsel that the Senate have admitted hearsay in behalf of the prosecution. Senators upon reflection can assent to no such proposition. The declaration of coconspirators made in the prosecution of the common purposes or common design, never was held to be hearsay evidence. On the contrary, it is primary evidence, and in the language of one of our own courts, in most instances, it is the only evidence which the nature of the case ever admits of. It rests upon the simple proposition of the law which addresses itself to the common judgment and the common sense of mankind that what one man does by another he does himself. If the President conspired with Lorenzo Thomas to violate the laws of this country, and by his written letter of authority sent him forth to violate the law, he made him his agent, and in the language of the law, whatever Lorenzo Thomas did in the prosecution of that agreement to do an unlawful act between himself and the President, is evidence not simply against himself, but against his principal.

It is the law of this country and of every other country where the common law is observed; it is a question no longer open for discussion, and I may add that the question that is raised here is one that is not open for discussion, for I venture to say that every text-book that treats of the law of evidence declares that the declarations of an accused after the fact are never admissible upon his own motion. All that is said at any one given time when any part of what is said on that occasion has been admitted for the prosecution, is admissible. But that is not the question before the Senate at all. This is a subsequent conversation between himself and his coconspirator after his crime was complete, after he had sent forth his letter of authority to Thomas, after he had issued the order for the removal of Stanton, after the demand had been made by Thomas for the surrender of the office. On the evening of the 21st day of February there is a conversation between these coconspirators, confessedly conspirators if your law be valid, upon their own answer before the Senate, in order to exculpate themselves. I say to Senators that it is trifling with justice, trifling with that justice which was this day invoked in your presence, to allow any man to make evidence in this manner for himself after the fact.

How easy it was for him to say to Mr. Thomas that night when he found that inquiry was being made in the Capitol touching this criminal agreement between them, "Why, Mr. Thomas, our only object is peacefully and quietly to appeal to the courts of justice;" "Why, Mr. Thomas, you must not touch the hair of the head of the Secretary of War;" "Why, Mr. Thomas, we both have the profoundest respect for the decision of the Senate this day made, notice of which has been served upon us;" "Why, Mr. Thomas, we both recognize the obligations of the tenure-of-office act;" "Why, Mr. Thomas, it is farthest from our intention to violate the act at all." Sir, the law declares that if the order was unlawful, the unlawful intent laid in the averment is proved by the fact itself, and he can never disprove it by his declarations. Why, then, introduce them here? Why trifle with justice here in this way? The rule has been settled in every case that has ever been tried in the Senate of the United States heretofore, that the general rules of evidence according to the common law govern the proceedings. If there is an exception to be found to that in any of the rulings of the Senate in trials of this kind hitherto, I challenge its production.

The CHIEF JUSTICE. The Secretary will read the question once more.

The Secretary read as follows:

What occurred between the President and yourself at that second interview on the 21st.

The CHIEF JUSTICE. The question is, is the question just read admissible?

Mr. DRAKE. On that I ask for the yeas and nays.

The yeas and nays were ordered; and being taken, resulted—yeas 42, nays 10; as follows:

YEAS—Messrs. Anthony, Bayard, Buckalew, Cattell, Cole, Conkling, Corbett, Davis, Dixon, Doolittle, Edmunds, Ferry, Fessenden, Fowler, Frelinghuysen, Grimes, Henderson, Hendricks, Howe, Johnson, McCreery, Morgan, Morrill of Maine, Morrill of Vermont, Morton, Norton, Patterson of New Hampshire, Patterson of Tennessee, Pomeroy, Ross, Sherman, Sprague, Stewart, Sumner, Tipton, Trumbull, Van Winkle, Vickers, Willey, Williams, Wilson, and Yates—42.

NAYS—Messrs. Cameron, Chandler, Conness, Cragin, Drake, Harlan, Howard, Nye, Ramsey, and Thayer—10.

NOT VOTING—Messrs. Saulsbury and Wade—2.

So the Senate determined the question to be admissible.

The CHIEF JUSTICE. The question will be read to the witness.

The Secretary read the question, as follows:

What occurred between the President and yourself at that second interview on the 21st.

The WITNESS. I stated to the President that I had delivered the communication, and that Mr. Stanton gave this answer: "Do you wish me to vacate at once or will you give me time to take away my private property?" and that I replied "act your pleasure." I then said that after delivering the copy of the letter to him he said: "I do not know whether I will obey your instructions or resist them." This I mentioned to the President, and his answer was: "Very well; go and take charge of the office and perform the duties."

By Mr. STANBERY:

Question. Was that all that passed?

Answer. That is about all that passed at that time.

Question. What time in the afternoon was that?

Answer. This was immediately after giving the second letter to Mr. Stanton.

Mr. Manager BUTLER. We withdraw all objection to that conversation. [Laughter.]

Mr. STANBERY. Whether you do or not it is in. The withdrawal is ex post facto. [To the witness.] Was this before or after you got Stanton's order?

Answer. It was after.

Question. Did you see Stanton again that afternoon?

Answer. I did not.

Question. Or the President?

Answer. Not after I left him this time.

Question. What first happened to you the next morning?

Answer. The first thing that happened to me next morning was the appearance at my house of the marshal of the District, with an assistant marshal and a constable, and he arrested me.

Question. What time in the morning was that?

Answer. About eight o'clock, before I had my breakfast. The command was to appear forthwith. I asked if he would permit me to see the President; I simply wanted to inform him that I had been arrested. To that he kindly assented, though he said he must not lose sight of me for a moment. I told him certainly I did not wish to be out of his sight. He went with me to the President's and went into the room where the President was. I stated that I had been arrested, at whose suit I did not know——

Mr. Manager BUTLER. Stop one moment. Does the presiding officer understand the ruling to go to this, to allow what occurred the next day to be brought in?

The CHIEF JUSTICE. The Chief Justice so understands it.

Mr. STANBERY. Go on, General.

The WITNESS. He said "Very well, that is the place I want it in—the courts." He advised me then to go to you, and the marshal permitted me to go to your quarters at the hotel. I told you that I had been arrested and asked what I should do——

Mr. Manager BUTLER. Wait a moment.

Mr. EVARTS. I suppose it is no great matter about that.

Mr. STANBERY, (to the Managers.) Is that part of the conspiracy? [Laughter.]

Mr. Manager BUTLER. I have no doubt of it. [Laughter.]

Mr. STANBERY, (to the witness.) Did you go to court?

Answer. I was presented by the marshal to Judge Cartter.

Question. What happened there?

Answer. Judge Cartter——

Mr. Manager BUTLER. I object.

Mr. STANBERY. Were you held to bail or anything of that kind?

Answer. I was required to give bail in $5,000.

Question. And then discharged from custody?

Answer. I was then discharged; but there is one point that I wish to state if it is admissible; I do not know whether it is or not. I asked him distinctly what that bail meant——

Mr. Manager BUTLER. Stop.

Mr. STANBERY. Do you mean that you asked the judge?

The WITNESS. Yes; I asked the judge what it meant. He said——

Mr. Manager BUTLER. Stop. Does your Honor allow that?

Mr. STANBERY. That is another part of the case, and we will come to that after a while. [To the witness.] How long did you remain there?

Answer. I suppose it took altogether perhaps an hour, because friends came in to give the bail. I had nobody with me, not even a lawyer.

Question. After you were admitted to bail, did you go again to the War Department that day?

Answer. I did.

Question. That was the 22d?

Answer. I am speaking of the 22d; but I think this other matter is important to me.

Mr. Manager BUTLER. I will withdraw the objection if the witness thinks it important to him.

Mr. STANBERY. Very well; go on with the explanation you wished to make.

The WITNESS. I asked the judge what it meant. He said it was simply to present myself there at half past ten the following Wednesday. I then asked him if it suspended me from any of my functions. He said no, it had nothing to do with them. That is the point I want to state.

By Mr. STANBERY:

Question. When did you next go to the War Department that day?

Answer. I went immediately from there, first stopping at the President's on my way, and stating to him that I had given bail. He made the same answer, "Very well; we want it in the courts." I then went over to the War Office and found the east door locked. This was on the 22d the office was closed. I asked the messenger for my key. He told me that he had not got it; the keys had all been taken away, and my door was locked. I then went up to Mr. Stanton's room, the one that he occupies as an office, where he receives. I found him there with some six or eight gentlemen, some of whom I recognized, and I understood afterward that they were all members of Congress. They were all sitting in a semi-ellipsis, the Secretary of War at the apex. I came in the door. I stated that I came in to demand the office. He refused to give it to me, and ordered me to my room as Adjutant General. I refused to obey. I made the demand a second and a third time. He as often refused and as often ordered me to my room. He then said, "You may stand there; stand as long as you please." I saw nothing further was to be

done, and I left the room and went into General Schriver's office, sat down and had a chat with him, he being an old friend. Mr. Stanton followed me in there, and Governor Moorhead, member of Congress from Pittsburg. He told Governor Moorhead to note the conversation, and I think he took notes at a side table. He asked me pretty much the same questions as before.

Question. State what he did ask?

Answer. Whether I insisted upon acting as Secretary of War and should claim the office. I gave a direct answer, "Yes;" and I think it was at that time I said I should also require the mails. I said that on one occasion, and I, think then. I do not know whether it is on the memorandum or not. Then there was some little chat with the Secretary himself.

Question. Between you and the Secretary?

Answer. Between me and the Secretary.

Question. Had these members of Congress withdrawn then?

Answer. Yes, sir.

Question. Now, tell us what happened between you and the Secretary after they withdrew.

Answer. I do not recollect what first occurred; but I said to him, "the next time you have me arrested"—for I had found out it was at his suit I was arrested; I had seen the paper——

Mr. Manager BUTLER. Stop a moment. I propose, Mr. President, to object to the conversation between the Secretary and General Thomas at a time which we have not put in, because we put in only the conversation while the other gentlemen were there. This is something that took place after they had withdrawn.

Mr. STANBERY. What is the difference: they did not stay to hear the whole.

The CHIEF JUSTICE. It appears to have been immediately afterward and part of the same conversation.

Mr. STANBERY. The same conversation went right on.

Mr. Manager BUTLER. Will. General Thomas say it was the same conversation?

The WITNESS. Mr. Stanton turned to me and got talking in a familiar manner.

Mr. Manager BUTLER. Go on, then, sir.

The WITNESS. I said "The next time you have me arrested, please do not do it before I get something to eat." I said I had had nothing to eat or drink that day. He put his hand around my neck, as he sometimes does, and ran his hand through my hair, and turned around to General Schriver and said, "Schriver, you have got a bottle here; bring it out." [Laughter.]

By Mr. STANBERY:

Question. What then took place?

Answer. Schriver unlocked his case and brought out a small vial, containing, I suppose, about a spoonful of whisky, and stated at the same time that he occasionally took a little for dyspepsia. [Laughter.] Mr. Stanton took that and poured it into a tumbler and divided it equally and we drank it together.

Question. A fair division?

Answer. A fair division, because he held up the glasses to the light and saw that they each had about the same, and we each drank. [Laughter.] Presently a messenger came in with a bottle of whisky, a full bottle; the cork was drawn, and he and I took a drink together. "Now," said he, "this, at least, is neutral ground." [Laughter.]

Question. Was that all the force exhibited that day?

Answer. That was all.

Question. Have you ever at any time attempted to exercise any force to get into that office?

Answer. At no time.

Question. Have you ever had any instructions or directions from the President to use force, intimidation, or threats at any time?

Mr. Manager BUTLER. Wait. "At any time?" That would bring it down to to-day. I supposed the ruling did not come down to to-day. Any time prior to the 21st or 22d of February I am content with your inquiring about, but I still must object to putting in what was said yesterday.

Mr. STANBERY. On the 9th of March you say it still continued.

Mr. Manager BUTLER. The 9th of March?

Mr. STANBERY. Then we will inquire prior to the 9th of March.

Mr. Manager BUTLER. I have said nothing about that. I say the 9th of March is just as bad as it would be to-day. I object to any time after the act. He was impeached on the 22d of February, and I suppose got up his case after that.

Mr. EVARTS. We have a right to negative up to the point at which you have given any positive evidence, which is the 9th of March.

Mr. Manager BUTLER. We have given no evidence of what the President has said or the instructions that came from the President. We have given evidence of what Mr. Thomas has said, and that is entirely a different thing. You may ask him if he said so to Mr. Karsner; but if there is anything in any rule of law, if law •is to be held at all, this testimony cannot be put in.

Mr. EVARTS. Mr. Chief Justice, the point, if anything, by which Mr. Karsner was allowed to speak of the interview between General Thomas and himself of the 9th of March was that General Thomas's statements then made might be held to be either from something that had been proved on the part of the Managers, or from something that would be proved on the part of the Managers, a committal of the President. Now, certainly, under the ruling that has been made, as well as under the necessary principles of law and justice, the President is entitled to negative, through the witness who knows, anything that proceeded from him, the witness, as brought in testimony here, having been authorized by anything that occurred between the President and himself.

Mr. Manager BUTLER. I do not propose to argue further. If it is not self-evident to everybody, no argument can make it plainer. I simply object to a question, which is this: "What have been the directions of the President down to the 9th of March," after he had been impeached? Because, if he can put them in down to the 9th of March, he can down to to-day; and to prove that Mr. Karsner did not say a thing to Mr. Thomas they offer to prove that the President did not say a thing to Mr. Thomas.

Mr. EVARTS. That is not the point. The point is not that we can show affirmatively every conversation, but negatively we can show up to and including the date concerning which they have given anything in evidence by which they claim to implicate the President, that he up to that time had never given any instructions or declarations justifying the use of force. It is of the 9th of March they have given evidence that this witness then meant presently, *in futuro*, to kick Mr. Stanton out; and now we propose to show that up to that conversation the President of the United States had never given authority or directions of any kind to use force.

Mr. Manager BUTLER. How does that prove that Mr. Thomas did not say so?

Mr. EVARTS. It does not prove it in the least. It only proves that he said it without authority of the President of the United States, which is the whole point on your point of proving that he said it all.

Mr. Manager BINGHAM. In other words, Mr. President, I desire to say the proposition now is for the witness to swear to conclusions, not to what the President did say, not to what the President did do, but to his conclusion that all he said and all he did did not authorize him to use force.

The CHIEF JUSTICE. The counsel for the President will reduce the question to writing, if they press it.

The question being reduced to writing was read, as follows:

Did the President, at any time prior to or including the 9th of March, authorize or direct you to use force, intimidation, or threats to get possession of the War Office?

The CHIEF JUSTICE. The Chief Justice will submit this question to the Senate. Senators, you who are of opinion that the question is admissible will say "ay," and those of the contrary opinion will say "no."

The question being put, was decided to be admissible.

Mr. STANBERY. Answer the question now, General.

The WITNESS. Read it, if you please.

The Secretary read the question, as follows:

Did the President at any time prior to or including the 9th of March authorize or direct you to use force, intimidation, or threats to get possession of the War Office?

The WITNESS. He did not.

By Mr. STANBERY:

Question. Now please state what conversation you had with Mr. BURLEIGH on the night of the 21st of February?

Answer. He came to my house and asked me in reference to this matter of my being appointed Secretary of War. I told him I was appointed, and I mentioned what occurred between Mr. Stanton and myself, and I think it was that which led him to ask me "What are you going to do?" Mr. Stanton having said he did not know whether he would obey my instructions or resist them. There are two persons I spoke with. To one I said, that if I found my door locked, or if I found the War Office locked, I would break open the door; and to the other I said I would call upon General Grant for force. I have got them mixed up; I do not know which expression I used to Mr. Wilkeson, but one to him and the other to Dr. BURLEIGH. I made use of both expressions that evening however, one to Mr. Wilkeson and one to Dr. BURLEIGH; I do not suppose it makes any difference which. Their testimony shows that better than mine. Mr. BURLEIGH asked me what time I was going to the War Office. I told him I would be there about ten o'clock the next day. This was the night of the 21st I was talking to him. The conversation was a short one; he very soon left me, saying he would call again. I think he said he would come up to the War Office the next morning.

Question. Did you ask him to go?

Answer. I did not. I think he said he would come and see the fun, or something of that kind.

Question. What was the conversation you had with Mr. Karsner on the 9th of March?

Answer. I would like to describe that.

Question. What do you know of Mr. Karsner?

Answer. I knew nothing about him whatever until I had seen him then. If I had been asked the question, I should have said I had never seen him, though my attention was once called to the fact that I did once see him in the spring of 1827, when I happened to be at home with a severe spell of sickness. I did see him on that occasion. I suppose there were circumstances brought it to my mind.

Question. What took place at the President's?

Answer. It was toward the end of the President's reception, and I was walking with General Todd, and was about going out of the door when I found that this person rushed forward and seized me by the hand. I looked surprised, because I did not know him. He mentioned his name, but I could not recollect it. I understood him to say that he was from New Castle, my native village. He certainly used both those words; but he says he did not; it is possible

he did not, as he says he only stated that he was from New Castle county. I may be mistaken; I do not want to do him injustice. He said he knew my father and my brother, and that he had known me forty years before. I suppose that would have been about the time I spoke of; but I have no recollection of it at all. He held on to my hand. I was surprised at the man's manner, because he came up to me as if I had been an intimate relation of his for years.

Mr. Manager BUTLER. Stop a moment. I suppose this is a little improper to give his surprises. Tell us what was done and stated there.

Mr. STANBERY. Go on, General.

The WITNESS. I tried to get away from him, and he then said—he was a Delawarean—"The eyes of all Delaware are upon you, [laughter,] and they expect you to stand fast." I said: "Certainly I shall stand fast," and I was about leaving when he seized my hand again and asked me a second time the same question, saying he expected me to stand fast. Said I: "Certainly I will stand fast." I was smiling all the time. I got away from his hand a second time, and he seized it again and drew me further in the room and asked the same question. I was a little amused, when I raised myself up on my toes in this way [standing on tiptoes] and said: "Why, don't you see I am standing firm?" Then he put this in my mouth: "When are you going to kick that fellow out," or something of that kind. "Oh," said I, "we will kick him out by and by."

Question. Are you certain the "kicking out" came from him?

Answer. Yes, sir—oh yes. [Laughter.] I want to say one thing. I did not intend any disrespect to Mr. Stanton at all. On the contrary, he has always treated me with kindness, and I would do nothing to treat him with disrespect.

Question. Had you ever any idea of kicking Mr. Stanton for any purpose.

Answer. No, sir.

Question. How came you to use the word at all?

Answer. Because it was put in my mouth.

Question. Did you say it seriously or in a jocular way?

Answer. (smilingly.) I was very glad to get away; I went out at once.

Cross-examined by Mr. Manager BUTLER:

Question. Did I understand you to say that there had been no unkind feelings between you and Mr. Stanton ever?

Answer. No. sir; I do not think there ever had been any unkind feeling.

Question. Or difference of opinion?

Answer. There was a difference of opinion, I suppose.

Question. Did you not believe that he sent you away from the office of Adjutant General in order to have General Townsend carry on that office?

C. I.—19.

Answer. I do not.

Question. You do not so believe?

Answer. No, sir.

Question. You have not done anything in the Adjutant General's office as the head of that department for how many years up to the 13th of February last?

Answer. I was a short time absent, as I told you, on the James river making exchanges with the rebel commissioner; but on my return I always went to my office. The first time, perhaps, that I was detached was, I think, on the 23d day of — I ought to have said I had gone three or four times up to Pennsylvania.

Mr. Manager BUTLER. Please answer my question. You ought to do that. Since what time, up to the 13th day of February had you done anything in your office as adjutant general of the Army, not acting inspector general?

Answer. I was in the Adjutant General's office—I have got the date here, if you will let me refer to it——

Mr. STANBERY. Certainly; refer to your papers.

The WITNESS, (producing papers.) These are my original instructions to go down on the Mississippi river.

Mr. Manager BUTLER. I do not care for the precise date. Can you not tell me the month?

Answer. I would rather give you the precise date. I have it—the 25th day of March, 1863.

Question. From that time until the 13th of February, 1868, have you ever conducted the business of the Adjutant General's office?

Answer. The 14th was the date.

Question. Up to the 13th will do for me?

Answer. No, sir.

Question. Have you always been sent upon outside inspecting duty?

Answer. Yes.

Question. Had you been recommended by Mr. Stanton to be retired?

Answer. That I cannot say. I was recommended by General Grant to be retired, and that communication went to Mr. Stanton, and Mr. Stanton took it to the President, as I understood. What he said to the President I do not know.

Question. The President overruled General Grant's recommendation for your retiracy?

Answer. The President did not set me aside.

Question. He overruled that recommendation, did he not? He did not have you retired in pursuance of that recommendation, did he?

Answer. He did not.

Question. Did you ever ask Mr. Stanton to restore you to office?

Answer. No; I did not.

Question. If there was a kindly feeling with him all the time he was a friend of yours, and you would not harm a hair of his head, certainly not kick him, why did you not ask him?

Answer. I knew perfectly well that the services, especially this one that I referred to, were very important, and I knew he said himself that I was the only one who could do the work, and therefore he sent me.

Question. But while you knew the service you were sent on was so important, and you were the only man to do it, you did ask Johnson, and why did you not ask Stanton, to restore you?

Answer. I did not suppose he wanted me in the office, though there was no unkind feeling.

Question. Only he did not want you there?

Answer. I do not suppose he did.

Question. It was perfectly kindly, except that he did not want you about?

Answer. I suppose so. I was in the habit of going to his office whenever I was here; I did it many a time, and he has asked me to do certain things in his office there.

Mr. Manager BUTLER. You have answered all. Now, General Thomas, when did you first receive the intimation from the President that you were to be made Secretary of War?

Answer. The President sent for me on the 18th of February.

Question. Three days before you got the order, was it?

Answer. Yes, sir.

Question. Have you ever stated that you had an intimation that you would be appointed Secretary of War earlier than that?

Answer. I must now refer to a paper which I suppose you have. When I was asked before one of the committees when I first got an intimation I supposed they were referring to my going in the Adjutant General's office, but I never had an intimation before the 18th of February that the President had any idea of making me Secretary of War.

Question. Now, if you will pay attention to my question, General Thomas, and answer it you will oblige me. My question was, whether you ever stated to anybody that you got such an intimation before that time?

Answer. Not to my knowledge, unless it was before that committee, as I tell you, the two things were mixed up.

Question. Did you not swear that before the committee?

Answer. I afterward made a correction on that paper.

Question. Excuse me; I did not ask you what corrections you made; I asked you what you swore to?

Answer. I swore that I had received an intimation, but I found that it was not so, and I had a right to correct my testimony.

Question. You were asked, then, before the committee, not the Managers?

Answer. I am not speaking of the Managers, but of the committee.

Question. You were asked before a committee of the House when you received the first intimation. How early did you swear that to be, whether it was by mistake or otherwise?

Answer. The intimation that I received that I would probably be put in the Adjutant General's office must have been made some two weeks before the occurrence, perhaps.

Question. I ask now, and I want you again to pay attention to my question——

Answer. I know your question.

Question. How early did you swear that you received an intimation that you would be made Secretary of War?

Answer. I should like to divide those two things. I told you that I corrected my evidence.

Question. I am dividing them; now I am getting to what you swore to first; by and by I will come to the correction, perhaps. I have divided them. Now answer my question: what did you swear to first before you took advice?

Mr. STANBERY. "Took advice!" Monstrous!

The WITNESS. I swore that I received an intimation—I think an intimation from Colonel Moore.

Question. I did not ask you who you received it from; I asked the time when?

Answer. I cannot tell the time; I do not know it.

Question. What time did you swear it was?

Answer. I say I do not know; I suppose two or three weeks; I cannot say.

Question. Did you receive it from Colonel Moore, the Military Secretary?

Answer. Receive what?

Question. The intimation that you were to be made Secretary of War?

Answer. No.

Question. Did you so testify?

Answer. I suppose not, because I tell you the two cases were in my mind. I think I have answered it distinctly enough. The honorable Manager is trying to mix two things, when I am trying to separate them.

Question. Now, sir, did you not know or believe you were to be made Secretary of War before you received that order of the 21st of February?

Answer. No, sir.

Question. Did you not believe you were?

Answer. The 18th, I said.

Question. Now listen to the question and answer it. That will be better. I ask you if you did not know you were to be made Secretary of War before you received that order of the 21st—know or believe?

Answer. "Know" positive, no.

Question. Did you not believe you were to be?

Answer. I thought I would be, because it had been intimated to me.

Question. Intimated to you by the President himself?

Answer. Yes, sir.

Question. Did you tell him whether you would be glad to take the office?

Answer. I told him I would take it; I would obey his orders.

Question. What made you tell him that you would obey his orders?

Answer. Because he was my Commander-in-Chief.

Question. Why was it necessary to tell him you would obey his orders?

Answer. I do not know that there was any particular necessity in it.

Question. Why should you say to him, when he asked you to be Secretary of War, that you would, and would obey his orders?

Answer. Certainly, as Secretary of War.

Question. Why did you feel it necessary in your own mind to say that you would obey his orders?

Answer. I do not know that it was particularly necessary.

Question. Why did you do it?

Answer. It was a very natural reply to make.

Question. Tell me any other time, when you were appointed to an office, that you told the appointing power you would obey the orders?

Mr. EVARTS. It does not appear he was appointed at any other time.

Mr. Manager BUTLER. Does it not? [To the witness.] Have you not been appointed adjutant general?

Answer. Certainly; I am adjutant general.

Question. At any other time, when you were appointed to office, tell me whom you told that you would obey the orders?

Answer. I do not know that I told any one. The other appointments I got in the ordinary course.

Question. Then this was an extraordinary appointment?

Answer. Certainly it was; I never had one of that kind before. [Laughter.]

Question. And so extraordinary that you thought it necessary to tell the President before you got it that if he would give it to you you would obey his orders?

Answer. I did not say any such thing.

Question. You did so tell him?

Answer. I did tell him so.

Question. And you thought it was proper so to tell him?

Answer. Certainly.

Question. What orders did you expect to receive that you found it necessary to tell him you would obey them?

Answer. I did not know that I was to expect to receive any particular order.

Question. Then, before you got the appointment you told him you would obey the order. This was on the 18th?

Answer. Yes.

Question. You got a note from Colonel Moore to go to the President's, you say, on the 21st?

Answer. Yes, sir.

Question. Were you sent for on the 18th?

Answer. Yes.

Question. Sent for by Colonel Moore?

Answer. Yes, sir.

Question. And you went up there?

Answer. Yes.

Question. And the President told you he thought of making you Secretary of War?·
Answer. Yes.

Question. And you told him you would be very glad to be made Secretary of War, and would obey his orders?
Answer. I did not say I would be very glad.

Question. That you would accept it?
Answer. The President said that he thought of making me Secretary of War, but that he would consider of the matter.

Question. And you answered to that that you would accept it and obey his orders, did you?
Answer. The time that I said I would obey his orders was when I got the appointment.

Question. Oh! that was the time?
Answer. The other was an intimation from him.

Question. You said this about obeying his orders at the time you got the appointment?
Answer. Yes.

Question. What did you say on the 18th, when the President said he thought of making you Secretary of War?
Answer. He did not say positively he was going to make me so.

Question. He said he was considering it?
Answer. He said he was considering of it.

Question. What did you say then?
Answer. I do not recollect that I said anything in particular.

uestion. Anything in general—anything at all?
Answer. I do not know that I did.

Question. You neither thanked him nor intimated in any form that you would or would not take it?
Answer. No.

Question. Then you want to take it back now?
Answer. I do not want to take back anything I have said.

Question. Do you not? I understood you to say that you told him on the 18th you would obey his orders?
Answer. I meant to say on the 21st, when he gave me the appointment.

Question. Therefore, you want to take it back as to the 18th?
Answer. Certainly.

Question. Then you do want to take back anything?
Mr. EVARTS. He has already corrected it by stating that you misunderstood him.
Mr. Manager BUTLER. If he did, then he stated what was not correct; for I did not misunderstand him.
Mr. EVARTS. He has already made that correction, but you misunderstood him.
Mr. Manager BUTLER. I was competent to hear the correction he made. I am perfectly competent to hear it without any assistance. [To the witness.] Now, General Thomas, on the 21st again you were sent for?
Answer. Yes.

Question. Between the 18th and 21st did you go to your friend Stanton and tell him that you thought of taking his place?
Answer. No, sir.

Question. Were you in the War Office?
Answer. I was there generally every day.

Question. On the 21st you were sent for again by Colonel Moore, were you not?
Answer. Yes, sir.

Question. By a note?
Answer. A note.

Question. He came in person?
Answer. A note.

Question. Have you that note?
Answer. I do not know whether I have or not. I gave one note to the counsel. One I mislaid.

Question. Do you think Mr. Stanbery has got it?
Answer. I think he took one of them.
Mr. Manager BUTLER. We will pass that while the gentlemen are hunting it up.
Mr. EVARTS. We have none of the 21st.
The WITNESS. Then I have mislaid it.
By Mr. Manager BUTLER:

Question. You got a note to go to the President's?
Answer. I got a note to go to the President's.

Question. Did you know for what purpose?
Answer. I did not.

Question. Did you suspect?
Answer. I had no suspicion at all.

Question. Did you not have some belief of what you were going there for?
Answer. I had not.

Question. And you went over?
Answer. I went over, of course.

Question. You went into the President's room, and he was coming out of the library, you say?
Answer. I went into the council room, and he came out of the library with Colonel Moore.

Question. Fetching two papers ready written?
Answer. Yes, sir.

Question. Now, please state to me exactly, in order, what was first said and what was next said by each of you. The President is coming out with two papers in his hand; what next?
Answer. I think the first thing he did was to hand them to Colonel Moore and tell him to read them.

Question. What next? They were read then?
Answer. They were read and handed to me.

Question. What then?
Answer. He said: "I shall uphold the Constitution and the laws, and I expect you to do the same." I said certainly I would do it, and I would obey his orders; that is the time I used that expression.

Question. Let me see if I have got it exactly. He came out with the two papers; handed them to Colonel Moore; Colonel Moore read them. He then said: "I am going to uphold the Constitution and the laws, and I want you to do the same;" and you said, "I will, and I will obey your orders?"
Answer. I did.

Question. Why did you put in you would obey his orders just then?

Answer. I suppose it was very natural, speaking to my Commander-in-Chief.

Question. What next was said then?

Answer. He told me to go over to Mr. Stanton and deliver the paper addressed to him.

Question. Which you did so?

Answer. I did.

Question. In the manner you have told us?

Answer. Yes, sir.

Question. At this first interview before you left the building Mr. Stanton gave you the letter which you have put in here, did he?

Answer. After I delivered him the second one, the one to me, dated the 21st instant.

Question. Before you left the building he gave you that paper?

Answer. Yes, sir; that was when he was sitting in Schriver's room.

Question. Then you knew that he did not mean to give up the office?

Answer. I did.

Question. You so understood fully?

Answer. Certainly.

Question. You went back and reported that to the President, did you?

Answer. Yes, sir.

Question. Did you report to him that Stanton did not mean to give up that office?

Answer. I reported to him exactly what Stanton had said.

Question. Did he ask you what you thought about it, whether he was going to give it up or not?

Answer. He did not.

Question. Did you tell him what you thought about it?

Answer. I did not.

Question. You reported facts to him. You reported the same facts that had made an impression on your mind that Stanton was not going to give up the office?

Mr. EVARTS. You are assuming what facts he stated. You are assuming that he stated something.

Mr. Manager BUTLER. I beg pardon. I assume nothing. [To the witness.] I ask did you report the same facts to the President which had made the impression on you mind that Stanton did not mean to give up the office?

Answer. I reported these facts—his conversation with me.

Question. Did you show him the letter?

Answer. I did not.

Question. Did you not tell him about the letter?

Answer. I did not.

Question. Why not?

Answer. I did not suppose that it was necessary.

Question. Here was a letter ordering you to——

Mr. STANBERY. We object to your arguing it with the witness. Ask your question.

Mr. Manager BUTLER. Wait till the ques-tion is out, and if you have any objection state it. Do not interrupt me.

Mr. STANBERY. We object to argument now; that is all.

Mr. Manager BUTLER, (to the witness.) You had a letter which alleged on its face that your action was illegal, and which convinced you, as you say, with other facts——

Mr. STANBERY. Mr. Chief Justice, we ask that that question be reduced to writing.

Mr. Manager BUTLER. I shall never be able to reduce it to writing if you do not stop interrupting me. I will put the question now once more. [To the witness.] You had a letter from Mr. Stanton which, together with other facts that had happened, convinced you that Stanton meant not to give up the office. Now, sir, with that letter in your pocket, why did you not report it to your chief?

Answer. I did not suppose it was necessary. I reported the conversation that I had said I would give orders, and he said he would counter-mand them and that he gave those orders to both General Schriver and General Townsend.

Question. Then did you tell the President that Mr. Stanton had given orders to Schriver and Townsend not to obey you?

Answer. I think I did.

Question. Have you any doubt about that in your own mind?

Answer. I do not think I have any doubt of that.

Question. After that I understand you to say, he said, "Very well, go on and take possession of the office?"

Answer. He did so.

Question. Was anything more said?

Answer. I think not at that time.

Question. You went away?

Answer. Yes, sir.

Question. About what time in the day was this on the 21st?

Answer. I closed the office about twelve o'clock. I suppose I was absent at the President's a short time for it took but a short time. I imagine it was about one o'clock.

Question. You mean you closed the office as Adjutant General, by your order as Adjutant General about twelve o'clock?

Answer. Yes, sir; by order of the Secretary of War, at twelve o'clock.

Question. After that you went to the President and got your own order as Secretary of War?

Answer. Yes, sir.

Question. And after that you came down to Mr. Stanton and had a conversation with him, got a letter, and went back to the President's?

Answer. Yes, sir.

Question. What time in the afternoon was it when you went back to the President's?

Answer. I think I can call it to mind in this way: the time was noted when I had this conversation that Hon. Mr. MOORHEAD took down; I think it was ten minutes past——

Mr. Manager BUTLER. That was the next day.

The WITNESS. Oh! You are speaking of the 21st?

Question. Was MOORHEAD there on the 21st?

Answer. No, sir.

Question. I am speaking of the 21st?

Answer. I went down and had the copy made, and as soon as the clerk made it I certified it, and then I took it up, and then went to the President's.

Question. What time in the day was it? That is all I desire.

Answer. I suppose it must have been between one and two o'clock, perhaps nearer two than one.

Question. Did you see the President again that day?

Answer. Not after I paid this visit.

Question. Then after he told you to go and take possession of the office you did not see the President? Was it Mr. Wilkeson or Mr. BURLEIGH that you first told about taking possession of the office?

Answer. Wilkeson.

Question. Where was that?

Answer. I think it was in my own office first.

Question. About how long after you left the President's?

Answer. I am not certain whether it was before or after, as Wilkeson came there to see me.

Question. You do not know whether it was before or after that?

Answer. I do not recollect whether it was before I went over to the President's or after. I think it was before, however.

Question. You told Mr. Wilkeson, he tells us, that you meant to call on General Grant for a military force to take possession of the office?

Answer. Yes.

Question. Did you mean that when you told it, or was it merely rhodomontade?

Answer. I suppose I did not mean it, for it never entered my head to use force.

Question. You did not mean it?

Answer. No, sir.

Question. It was mere boast, brag?

Answer. Oh, yes.

Question. How was that? Speak as loud as you did when you began.

Answer. I suppose so.

Question. Very well, then. You saw Wilkeson that evening again, did you not, at Willard's Hotel?

Answer. I think I saw him there for a few moments.

Question. Did you again tell him you meant to use force to get into the office?

Answer. That I do not recollect. I stated it to him once I know.

Question. Can you not tell whether you bragged to him again that evening?

Answer. I did not brag to him.

Question. Did you not tell him at Willard's that you meant to use force to get into that office?

Answer. Either at my office or Willard's, one of the two.

Question. You have already said you told it to him at your office?

Answer. I do not think I told it to him more than once.

Question. Suppose that he testifies that you told it at Willard's to him; was that brag then?

Answer. It would have been the same—yes.

Question. You saw BURLEIGH that evening?

Answer. At my own house.

Question. Did you tell him that you meant to use force?

Answer. I think the expression I used to him was that if I found my doors locked I would break them open.

Question. Did he not put the question to you in this form substantially: "What will you do if Stanton will not go out;" and did you not answer, "We will put him out?"

Answer. I dare say I did.

Question. Do you not know you did?

Answer. I dare say I did; I am not certain.

Question. Did he not then say, "But suppose the doors are barred;" and did you not then say, "I will batter them down," or "We will batter them down?"

Answer. Yes, sir.

Question. Was that brag?

Answer. No, sir. At that time I felt as if I would open the doors if they were locked against me.

Question. Then you had got over bragging at that time, had you?

Answer. I suppose so.

Question. Do you not know whether you had or not?

Answer. When I had this conversation with Mr. BURLEIGH I felt precisely as I said to him.

Question. At that time you really meant to go in and break down the door?

Answer. If it was locked, yes.

Question. And really meant to use force according as you said you would? You meant what you said, did you not?

Answer. I meant what I said.

Question. Do you mean to say that Mr. BURLEIGH has not properly put before the Senate what you did say?

Answer. I do not pretend to say so. He would recollect the conversation better than I.

Question. And whatever you said to him you meant in good, solemn earnest?

Answer. I suppose so.

Question. No rhodomontade there? You had got over playfulness with Wilkeson about writing to Grant entirely, had you not?

Answer. Yes; because I had got home and had time to think the matter over.

Question. And having got over the playful part of it, and thinking the matter over, you had come to the conclusion to use force; and having come to that conclusion, why did you not?

Answer. Because I reflected that it would not answer.

Question. Why not answer?

Answer. It would produce difficulty, and I did not want to bring it on.

Question. What kind of difficulty?

Answer. I supposed bloodshed.

Question. And what else?

Answer. Nothing else.

Question. Then by difficulty you mean bloodshed, do you say?

Answer. If I had used force I suppose I would have been resisted with force, and blood might have been shed. That is my answer.

Question. What time did you leave BURLEIGH or did BURLEIGH leave you?

Answer. It was after night when he came; the visit was a very short one.

Question. About what time did he leave?

Answer. I do not recollect exactly; eight or nine o'clock, I suppose.

Question. Immediately after he left did you go to a masquerade ball?

Answer. Yes, sir.

Question. How late did you stay?

Answer. I stayed until about the time of—I suppose it was toward midnight.

Question. After?

Answer. I cannot be positive of that. About midnight, I presume.

Question. How soon was it after BURLEIGH left before you left for the ball?

Answer. I think it was about nine o'clock or along about half past nine or somewhere there. It was after BURLEIGH left.

Question. Did you see anybody but your own family between the time BURLEIGH left and the time you started for the ball?

Answer. Yes.

Question. Who?

Answer. A little girl living next door, who was going with my daughter to the masquerade ba l.

Question. A young lady?

Answer. Yes, sir.

Question. You did not discuss this matter with her, I take it?

Answer. I did not.

Question. Did you discuss it with anybody after you left BURLEIGH or BURLEIGH left you until you got to the ball?

Answer. I did not. I saw no person to discuss it with.

Question. And you did not discuss it at the ball?

Answer. I did not.

Question. And a masquerade ball—I do not know, but I put it interrogatively—is not a good place for contemplation of high ministerial official duties, is it?

Answer. No; it is not.

Question. You did not contemplate your official duties there, did you?

Answer. I went there, I say, to take charge of two little girls. That was all.

Question. And to throw off care, as we all have a right to do?

Answer. No, sir; I did not go with any such purpose. I had promised them some days before.

Question. You went with them?

Answer. I went with them to take charge of them. I went in my present dress. [The uniform of a major general.]

Question. And when you came home you went to bed immediately?

Answer. I did.

Question. How early in the morning—how long had you been up before this marshal came?

Answer. I generally rise about seven, unless when I go to market. I get up earlier then.

Question. How early did you get up this morning, having been out a little late the night before?

Answer. I got up at seven o'clock; that is my usual hour.

Question. Did the marshal come immediately?

Answer. The marshal came there about eight o'clock.

Question. Before you could get any breakfast?

Answer. Before I had my breakfast.

Question. Did you consult anybody on this question between the time of getting up and the time the marshal came?

Answer. I did not.

Question. Now, sir, before this the last you said to anybody on this question was that you told BURLEIGH in solemn earnest you were going to use force, and then, almost immediately, you went to a ball; from the ball you came home and went to bed; got up, and saw nobody until the marshal came. When did you change your mind from this solemn determination to use force, although it might bring on bloodshed?

Answer. I changed it after I had made use of this to BURLEIGH, undoubtedly.

Question. I know you did after. When?

Answer. I suppose very soon.

Question. I did not ask you what your supposition is. I asked you when you changed your mind.

Answer. I do not know.

Question. When do you first remember having changed your mind?

Answer. I do not know.

Question. What is the first remembrance that you have of a different purpose?

Answer. I do not know. You are asking now as to a point of time.

Question. No; I am asking no point of time. You have now a different purpose in your mind, have you not, from what you told BURLEIGH?

Answer. I have.

Question. You must have obtained that purpose some time. When did you change the purpose? The first time you remember you had a different purpose?

Answer. I certainly changed it before I was arrested, and that was at eight o'clock on the morning of the 22d.

Question. How do you fix that so certainly?

Answer. Because on the 22d I had determined not to do so.

Question. What time on the 22d?

Answer. Before I was arrested, undoubtedly.

Question. Why "undoubtedly?"

Answer. I may have thought it over in bed before I got up.

Question. Will you swear that you did, and that you changed your purpose then?

Answer. I cannot tell the precise moment when I changed my purpose.

Question. Did you not tell Mr. BURLEIGH that the reason why you did not carry out your purpose was the cause of your arrest?

Answer. I did not.

Question. Did you tell him anything to that effect?

Answer. No.

Question. Had you any conversation on that subject with him?

Answer. I did not see Dr. BURLEIGH after that, I do not think.

Question. He testified that within a week of the time he was on the stand you told him that the reason why you did not carry out the purpose which you had told him you would of using force, was that you were arrested?

Answer. He must have misunderstood me then, because the arrest had nothing to do with it.

Question. And you did not tell him that?

Answer. I think not.

Question. Do you know not?

Answer. I will not say I know not; but I am pretty certain I did not.

Question. What makes you certain you did not tell him so?

Answer. Because I had made up my mind not to use force at all.

Question. Were you not asked by the board of Managers, on the 13th of March, after having heard BURLEIGH's testimony read, whether it was not true, and did you not say it was all true?

Answer. Yes, sir; I did. I said that both his and Wilkeson's was true, because what they testified to I said I had no doubt was the fact.

Question. Now, why do you say BURLEIGH's testimony is not true when he says that you told him that the arrest was the cause of your change?

Answer. That I do not think I told him.

Question. And the only reason you have for thinking you did not tell him is that you think you must have come to the conclusion before you were arrested?

Answer. I did; certainly.

Question. But you cannot tell us when you did come to that conclusion from any act of memory of yours?

Answer. Not the particular moment.

Mr. MORRILL, of Maine. If the parties are willing to pause here, as it is now five o'clock——

Several SENATORS. Get through with this witness.

Mr. MORRILL, of Maine. I would move an adjournment, not otherwise.

Mr. Manager BUTLER. We shall be wholly under the direction of the Senate. We have no objection on our part.

The CHIEF JUSTICE. The Senator from Maine moves——

Mr. MORRILL, of Maine. I do not make the motion unless it suits the convenience of parties.

Mr. Manager BUTLER. I will go on. [To the witness.] Now, then, General Thomas, when you came to the solemn conclusion to use force after solemnly thinking of the matter, did you believe in your own mind you were carrying out the President's orders?

Answer. No; quite the reverse.

Question. Then when you came to that conclusion you believed you were going to do it against his orders, did you?

Answer. Not in accordance with them, certainly.

Question. Then, although you had told him the day before that you would obey his orders, you came to a determination to do quite the reverse, did you?

Mr. STANBERY. He has not said that.

Mr. Manager BUTLER. I am asking him if he did.

The WITNESS. Repeat that question.

By Mr. Manager BUTLER:

Question. You say that you came to the solemn determination to use force, and you meant to do it, quite in reverse of the President's orders?

Answer. I said no such thing.

Question. Hear the question. The day before when you received your appointment you told him you would obey his orders?

Answer. I did.

Question. The first act that you came to a solemn conclusion about was that you proposed to act the very reverse of his orders?

Answer. I did not say that was in reverse of his orders. I said that was my idea; if I was resisted I could resist in turn.

Question. Did you mean to do that act in obedience to the President's orders or against them?

Answer. Not in obedience to the President's orders, for he gave me no orders.

Question. You mean to say that you had come to a solemn resolution on your own responsibility to initiate bloodshed?

Answer. I said that I would, if I found the doors locked, break them down, and I afterward said that when I came to think of the matter I found that a difficulty might occur, and 1 would not be the means of bringing about bloodshed. That is what I say.

Question. Did you think you were justified in doing what you came to the conclusion to do by the President's order?

Answer. I would have been justified as my own act.

Question. Did you believe you were so justified by the President's order?

Answer. No; not by the President's order—by the appointment which he gave me, yes.

Question. The appointment he gave you?

Answer. I had a right then to go and take possession of that office.

Question. By force?

Answer. In any way I pleased.

Question. At your pleasure, by force. Now, did you ever ask the President what you should do?

Answer. I did not.

Question. Did you not ever suggest to him that Stanton would resist?

Answer. I reported to him from day to day that every time I asked him he refused.

Question. Anything but the refusal?

Answer. The refusal was the only thing.

Question. Did you ever suggest to him that Stanton would resist?

Answer. Resist by force?

Question. Yes, sir.

Answer. No; I said he refused.

Question. Did you not understand in your own mind that he would resist?

Answer. I did not know what means he would take.

Question. I did not ask what you knew. Did you not in your own mind believe he would resist?

Answer. Yes.

Question. Had you any doubt of it?

Answer. I had not.

Question. Did you not know that, if you got in at all, you must get in by force?

Answer. Yes.

Question. Did you ever report to the President, your superior, that you came to the conclusion that you could not get in, if you got in at all, except by force?

Answer. I said no such thing to him.

Question. Why did you not report to him the conclusion you came to?

Answer. I did not think it necessary at all.

Question. You reported to him every time Stanton refused?

Answer. Yes.

Question. But you did not think it necessary to report to him that you could not get the office without resistance?

Answer. No.

Question. And you never asked his advice what you should do?

Answer. No.

Question. Nor for his command?

Answer. No.

Question. Nor orders in any way?

Answer. No. He merely told me to go on

and take possession of the office, without stating how I was to do it.

Question. And how many times over did he keep telling you that, as you reported to him?

Answer. I think I had three interviews with Mr. Stanton.

Question. One Friday?

Answer. One Saturday, one Monday, and one Tuesday; I think four. Saturday was the time I made the demand.

Question. Each time when you made the demand on Mr. Stanton he refused?

Answer. Yes, sir.

Question. Each time you reported it to the President?

Answer. Yes, sir.

Question. During all the time you were certain he would not give up except by force?

Answer. I was certain he would not give up; he was going to keep it.

Question. And, thinking it important to report each time his refusal, you never asked the President how you should get possession of the office?

Answer. I never did.

Question. Nor never suggested to him that you could not get it except by force?

Answer. I suggested to him that the true plan would be, in order to get possession of the papers, to call upon General Grant——

Question. Leave the papers—the office I am talking about?

Answer. The papers are the thing. You cannot carry on an office unless you have what is inside of it.

Question. I did not ask how you can carry on an office. I ask if you ever reported to him anything more than Mr. Stanton's refusal?

Answer. I never did.

Question. You never asked how you were to get possession of the building?

Answer. No.

Question. Now, let me come to the matter of papers. Did you afterward hit upon a scheme by which you might get possession of the papers without getting possession of the building?

Answer. Yes, sir.

Question. And that was by getting an order of General Grant?

Answer. Yes——

Mr. EVARTS. He has not stated what it was.

By Mr. Manager BUTLER:

Question. Did you write such an order?

Answer. I wrote the draft of a letter; yes, and gave it to the President.

Question. Did you sign it?

Answer. I signed it.

Question. And left it with the President for his——

Answer. For his consideration.

Question. When was that?

Answer. The letter is dated the 10th of March.

Question. That was the morning after you told Karsner you were going to kick him out?

Answer. That was the morning after.

Question. And you carried that letter?

Answer. I had spoken to the President before about that matter.

Question. You did not think any bloodshed would come of that letter?

Answer. None at all.

Question. And the letter was to be issued as your order?

Answer. Yes.

Question. And before you issued that order, took that away to get hold of the mails or papers, you thought it necessary to consult the President?

Answer. I gave that to him for his consideration.

Question. You did think it necessary to consult the President, did you not?

Answer. I had consulted him before.

Question. Either before or after, you thought it necessary?

Answer. It was merely carrying out that consultation.

Question. When you thought of getting possession of the mails and papers through an order as Secretary of War you thought it necessary to consult the President; but you did not think any bloodshed would come from that, did you?

Answer. No, I did not; it was a peaceable mode.

Question. When you were about taking a peaceable mode in issuing your order you consulted him? When you had come to the conclusion to run the risk of bloodshed you did not consult him? Is that so?

Answer. I did not consult him.

Question. Did the President ever give at any of these times any other answer than " Go on, and get possession?"

Answer. No; not in reference to the office.

Question. Did he ever chide you in any way for any means that you were employing?

Answer. Never.

Question. Did he ever find fault that you were doing it differently from what you ought to do?

Answer. No.

Question. Did he ever remark to you in any way about declarations of force until after these impeachment proceedings began?

Answer. No.

Question. They were published and notorious, were they not? Have you acted as Secretary of War *ad interim* since?

Answer. I have given no order whatever.

Question. That may not be all the action of a Secretary of War *ad interim.* Have you acted as Secretary of War *ad interim?*

Answer. I have, in other respects.

Question. What other respects?

Answer. I have attended the councils.

Question. Cabinet meetings, you mean?

Answer. Cabinet meetings.

Question. Have you been recognized as Secretary of War *ad interim?*

Answer. I have been.

Question. Continually?

Answer. Continually.

Question. By the President and the other members of the Cabinet?

Answer. Yes, sir.

Question. Down to the present hour?

Answer. Down to the present hour.

Question. All your action as Secretary of War *ad interim* has been confined, has it not, to attending Cabinet meetings?

Answer. It has. I have given no order whatever.

Question. Have you given any advice to the President? You being one of his constitutional advisers, have you given him advice as to the duties of his office, or the duties of yours?

Answer. The ordinary conversation that takes place at meetings of that kind. I do not know that I gave him any particular advice.

Question. Did he ever call you in?

Answer. He has asked me if I had any business to lay before him several times.

Question. You never had any?

Answer. I never had any except the case of the note I proposed sending to General Grant.

Question. I want to inquire a little further about that. He did not agree to send that notice, did he?

Answer. When I first spoke to him about it I told him what the mode of getting possession of the papers was, to write a note to General Grant to issue an order calling upon the heads of bureaus, as they were military men, to send to me communications designed either for the President or the Secretary of War. That was one mode.

Question. What was the other mode you suggested?

Answer. The other mode would be to require the mails to be delivered from the city post office.

Question. And he told you to draw the order?

Answer. No; he did not.

Question. But you did?

Answer. I did it of myself, after having this talk?

Question. Did he agree to that suggestion of yours?

Answer. He said he would take it and put it on his own desk. He would think about it.

Question. When was that?

Answer. On the 10th.

Question. Has it been lying there ever since as far as you know?

Answer. It has been.

Question. He has been considering ever since on that subject?

Answer. I do not know what he has been doing.

Question. Has he ever spoken to you or you to him about that order since?

Answer. Yes.

Question. When?

Answer. I may have mentioned it one day at the council, and he said we had better let the matter rest until after the impeachment. I think that was it.

Question. Until after the impeachment trial was over? So it is resting there awaiting this trial, as you understand?

Answer. Yes, sir.

Question. Not to be brought up till then?

Answer. I so understand.

Question. With the exception of that, attending those meetings has been your entire business as Secretary *ad interim?*

Answer. Yes, sir.

Question. Now, has he ever asked you to know where the troops were about Washington?

Answer. He never did.

Question. Or whether there had been any changes of troops?

Answer. He never did.

Question. You tell us you attended a masquerade ball that night. Did you keep the President advised of where you were?

•*Answer.* I did not.

Question. Did you tell Colonel Moore where you were?

Answer. I did not.

Question. Did you tell him where you were going?

Answer. I think not—no.

Question. You are pretty sure about that?

Answer. He might have known I was going to the masquerade ball. I had procured tickets for my children some days before.

Question. Did the President in any of these interviews with you, his Cabinet counselor, his constitutional adviser, ever suggest to you that he had not removed Mr. Stanton?

Answer. Never. He always said that Mr. Stanton was out of office; he took that ground at once?

Question. Were you not somewhat surprised when you heard Mr. Curtis say here yesterday that he was not removed?

Answer. I do not know anything about that.

Question. Did he ever tell you that you were not appointed?

Answer. No.

Question. Have you not always known you were appointed?

Answer. Yes.

Question. Has he not over and over again told you you were appointed?

Answer. No; not over and over again.

Question. But two or three times?

Answer. I do not know that it has come up at all. He may have done it two or three times.

Question. He never suggested to you from the day he gave you that paper, when he was going to support the Constitution and the laws, down to to-day, he never intimated to you that you were not appointed regularly as Secretary of War, did he?

Answer. No.

Question. And that he had not appointed you.

Answer. No.

Question. Nor none of the Cabinet, his constitutional advisers say, "You are not appointed, General; you are only here by sufferance?" None of them ever said that, did they?

Answer. None of them ever said that to me.

Question. Tell us, if you can, what you meant when you told the President you were going to uphold the Constitution and the laws?

Answer. Why, to be governed by the Constitution and the laws made in pursuance thereof, of course.

Question. You were going to be governed by the Constitution and the laws made in pursuance thereof. Did you include in that the tenure-of-office bill?

Answer. Yes, sir; so far as it applied to me.

Question. You were going to uphold the Constitution and that particular law; you had that in your mind at the time, had you not?

Answer. Not particularly in my mind at the time.

Question. You did not make any exception of that?

Answer. No; I made no exception; you have got my language.

Question. Has not the President given you directions about other things than taking possession of the War Office?

Answer. He has told me on several occasions what he wanted. He wanted to get some nominations sent up here. They were on the Secretary's table, on Mr. Stanton's table.

Question. And he could not get them?

Answer. He did not get them.

Question. Well, he could not?

Answer. I do not say that.

Question. What did he tell you, whether he could or could not get them?

Answer. I do not know whether he could or could not. I could not get them.

Question. And he could not as far as you know?

Answer. I do not know that he could not.

Question. And he complained to you?

Answer. He did not complain to me, but he said that cases were lying over, and some of them military cases, that ought to be disposed of. I mentioned it to Mr. Stanton twice that the President wanted those nominations and he said he would see to it. This was while I was acting as Adjutant General, not as Secretary of War.

By Mr. STANBERY:

Question. Did he send them to the President?

Answer. He did not, to my knowledge.

By Mr. Manager BUTLER:

Question. Now, at any other of these times, when he has given you directions, has he ever told you he was going to uphold the Constitution and the laws?

Answer. No; I think not.

Question. Did he ever tell you he was going to uphold the Constitution and the laws?

Answer. That is the only time that conversation occurred between us.

Question. Can you give any reason why both of you should come to the conclusion that the Constitution and the laws wanted upholding about that time?

Answer. No.

Question. What had happened to the Constitution and the laws, or was about to happen, that required you both to uphold them?

Answer. I do not know that anything was about to happen.

Question. Well, what had happened?

Answer. Nothing had happened.

Question. Why did he so solemnly tell you there, upon this occasion, that he was going to uphold the Constitution and laws, and why did you say, "I will uphold the Constitution and laws?"

Answer. Why, it was the most natural thing in the world. He made the remark to me.

Question. Now, about Mr. Karsner, and I will not trouble you much further. Were you examined before the Managers about Mr. Karsner's testimony?

Answer. It was read to me there.

Question. As taken down from his lips?

Answer. I suppose so.

Question. Was it not substantially almost exactly as he gave it here?

Answer. I do not know how he gave it here exactly.

Question. Did not you hear him?

Answer. There was one point in it I did not agree to.

Question. Did you hear him give it here?

Answer. Partially. I could not hear all where I was sitting.

Question. As it was read over to you there, were you not asked in Karsner's presence if there was anything that he said that was not true?

Answer. That question was asked me and I answered yes.

Question. What did you say it was he said that was not true?

Answer. I think he testified here——

Question. No; there?

Answer. I do not know there. I am speaking now of a portion of the testimony here.

Question. You told me you did not hear here, and therefore I confine my question to what occurred before the Managers. Keep your mind, if you can, to the time when you were before the Managers. Did you not sit down before the Managers and there have Mr. Karsner's testimony read over to you in his presence?

Answer. It was read over, but not at my instance at all. It was read to me, and I was asked if it was correct, and I said "Yes."

Question. You were asked if it were correct and you said "Yes." Did you object that any single word was not correct?

Answer. I did not object to any word. I objected to his manner.

Question. How could you see his manner on paper?

Answer. You asked him to get up and show it.

Question. Then, after you got there, when that was read over to you, did you say, "I did not say 'kicking;' Karsner said 'kicking' to me." Did you say that?

Answer. No; I did not.

Question. Then did you not say, when asked for any explanation, that it was playful; was not that the only explanation you gave?

Answer. I said it was playful on my part.

Question. Was not that the only explanation you gave before the Managers?

Answer. I do not recollect; I suppose it was, though.

Question. Was not Mr. Karsner then called up and asked whether it appeared playful to him?

Answer. Yes; he was.

Question. And did not he testify to you that it was not playful at all, but that you seemed to be very earnest?

Answer. Yes; he did.

Question. And did he not illustrate your earnestness by the way you brought yourself down?

Answer. That is one point where I say he was mistaken. He applied that to the time I said we would kick him out. He applied it to that, which was not the case. It was the third time he asked me to stand firm; then I straightened myself up in that way.

Question. And you think he applied it to the time you were to kick him out?

Answer. Yes, sir.

Question. Did you object then that you yourself did not use the words "Kick him out?"

Answer. No; I did not. I said it was in answer to a question from him. I have had time to think that matter over after I was called up there, and I have gone over the whole in my own mind after I got home.

Question. That was the 13th of March you were asked before us, was it not?

Mr. EVARTS. Allow me to ask if you will allow us to have a copy of the testimony to which you are now referring—Mr. Karsner's testimony before the Managers.

Mr. Manager BUTLER. With great pleasure. I gave it to Mr. Stanbery when Mr. Karsner was here.

Mr. SHERMAN. I was about to make a motion to adjourn.

Mr. Manager BUTLER. I am about through. I will be through in a minute. [To the witness.] Upon your reinstatement in office as adjutant general did you address the clerks?

Answer. I did make a short address to each section of them. I sent for the officers in charge and told them I would like to see the clerks.

Question. Was that within three days of the

time you were appointed Secretary of War *ad interim?*

Answer. It was between the time I was reinstated as adjutant general and the time I was appointed Secretary of War; I do not recollect what particular day.

Mr. Manager BUTLER, (to the counsel for the respondent.) The witness is yours, gentlemen.

Mr. STANBERY. We will ask some questions.

Mr. HENDERSON. Mr. President, I move that the Senate sitting as a court do now adjourn.

The motion was agreed to; and the Senate sitting for the trial of the impeachment adjourned.

SATURDAY, *April* 11, 1868.

The Chief Justice of the United States entered the Senate Chamber at twelve o'clock and five minutes p. m., and took the chair.

The usual proclamation having been made by the Sergeant-at-Arms,

The Managers of the impeachment on the part of the House of Representatives appeared and took the seats assigned them.

The counsel for the respondent also appeared and took their seats.

The presence of the House of Representatives was next announced, and the members of the House, as in Committee of the Whole, headed by Mr. E. B. WASHBURNE, the chairman of that committee, and accompanied by the Speaker and Clerk, entered the Senate Chamber and were conducted to the seats provided for them.

The CHIEF JUSTICE. The Secretary will read the minutes of the last day's proceedings.

The Secretary read the Journal of yesterday's proceedings of the Senate sitting for the trial of the impeachment.

The CHIEF JUSTICE. Gentlemen of counsel for the President, you will proceed with your evidence.

Mr. Manager BINGHAM. Mr. President, before the counsel for the accused proceed, I desire to say that the Managers wish to move the Senate for such change of rule twenty-one of the proceedings in this trial as will allow the Managers and the counsel for the President to be heard on the final argument, subject to the provision of the rule as it stands that the argument shall be opened and closed by the Managers on the part of the House.

Mr. SHERMAN. I should like to have the proposition repeated. I could not hear it distinctly.

The CHIEF JUSTICE. The honorable Manager will please reduce his proposition to writing.

Mr. Manager BINGHAM. I will. [After writing the proposition.] Mr. President, I desire to read the motion as reduced to writing.

Mr. CONKLING. I beg to state that the voice of the Manager is entirely inaudible here.

Mr. Manager BINGHAM. "The Managers move the Senate to so amend rule twenty-one as to allow such of the Managers as desire to be heard, and also such of the counsel for the President as desire to be heard, to speak on the final argument, subject to the provision of the rule that the final argument shall be opened and closed by the Managers on the part of 'the House."

The CHIEF JUSTICE. Senators, it is moved by the Managers on the part of the House of Representatives, that the twenty-first rule be so modified as to allow as many on the part of the Managers and as many on the part of the counsel for the President to be heard as may see fit to address the Senate in the final argument.

Mr. POMEROY. Mr. President, as that is in the nature of a resolution, under our general rule it should lie over one day for consideration.

The CHIEF JUSTICE. The Chief Justice was about to observe that the proposition required some answer on the part of the Senate, and that it would be proper for some Senator to make a motion in respect to it.

Mr. BUCKALEW. I move that the resolution be laid over for consideration until to-morrow.

The CHIEF JUSTICE. It goes over, of course, if there be objection.

Mr. EDMUNDS. I would inquire of the Chair whether the twenty-first rule does not now provide by its terms that this privilege may be extended to the Managers and the counsel if the Senate so order; and I would therefore inquire whether any amendment of the rule be necessary if the Senate should desire to extend that privilege?

The CHIEF JUSTICE. Certainly not. . It is competent for any Senator to move such an order; but the Chair has yet heard no motion to that effect.

Mr. FRELINGHUYSEN. Mr. President, I make the motion that the order be adopted. It of course is not necessary that it should lie over, as it is provided for in the rule that this order may be adopted.

Mr. POMEROY. I have no objection to taking the vote now, if it is desired. I do not care to have it lie over to another day.

The CHIEF JUSTICE. The Senator from New Jersey will please reduce his order to writing.

Mr. SHERMAN. If it is in order, I will move that the twenty-first rule be relaxed so as to allow three persons on each side to speak under the rule, instead of two.

The CHIEF JUSTICE. That motion will be in order as an amendment to the order proposed by the Senator from New Jersey.

Mr. SHERMAN. I withdraw it for the present to allow the vote to be taken on that.

The order proposed by Mr. FRELINGHUYSEN

having been reduced to writing and sent to the desk—

The CHIEF JUSTICE. The Secretary will read the order proposed by the Senator from New Jersey.

The Secretary read as follows:

Ordered, That as many of the Managers and of the counsel for the respondent be permitted to speak on the final argument as shall choose to do so.

The CHIEF JUSTICE. That order will be considered now unless objected to.

Mr. HOWARD. Mr. President, I hope that order will be laid over until the next day's session.

The CHIEF JUSTICE. If objected to, it will lie over.

Mr. HOWARD. I object.

Mr. TRUMBULL. An objection does not carry it over, does it?

The CHIEF JUSTICE. The Chair thinks it does.

Mr. TRUMBULL. It does not change the rule. The rule provides for this very thing being done, if the Senate choose to allow it.

Mr. CONKLING. Mr. President, may I inquire under what rule of the Senate thus organized it is that this motion lies over upon the objection of a single Senator?

The CHIEF JUSTICE. The Chief Justice in conducting the business of the court adopts for his general guidance the rules of the Senate sitting in legislative session as far as they are applicable. That is the ground of his decision.

Mr. CONKLING. The reason for my inquiry was this: the very rule we are discussing provides that a certain thing shall happen "unless otherwise ordered;" and I supposed that a motion otherwise to order was always in order.

The CHIEF JUSTICE. It is competent for the Senator from New York to appeal from the decision of the Chief Justice.

Mr. CONKLING. Oh, no, sir; I merely made the point by way of suggestion to the Chair.

Mr. JOHNSON. Mr. Chief Justice, I appeal to the honorable member from Michigan to withdraw——

The CHIEF JUSTICE. No debate is in order.

Mr. JOHNSON. I am not about to debate it, sir. If they are to have an opportunity of addressing the Senate they ought at once to know it on both sides.

The CHIEF JUSTICE. Gentlemen of counsel for the President, you will please to proceed with the defense.

LORENZO THOMAS—examination continued.

Mr. STANBERY. General Thomas wishes to make some explanatory statements.

The WITNESS. I wish to correct my testimony yesterday in one or two particulars. I read a letter signed by Mr. Stanton addressed to me on the 21st of February. The date misled me; I did not receive a copy of that letter until the next day after I had made the demand

for the office. The Secretary came in and handed me the original, and my impression is that I noted on that original its receipt. It was then handed to General Townsend, who made the copy that I read here, and handed it to me. I had it not until after the demand on the 22d of February.

By Mr. STANBERY:

Question. Then, when you saw the President on the afternoon of the 21st you had not yet received that letter from Mr. Stanton?

Answer. I had not.

Question. You then stood upon the interview which you referred to?

Answer. I did. The next correction I want to make is that I am made to say here that the President told me "to take possession of the office." His expression was "take charge of the office."

Question. Are you certain that that was his expression?

Answer. Positive. I was asked if I could give the date of my brevet commission. I do not know whether it is important or not, but I have it here.

Question. What is the date?

Answer. The brevet of major general 13th of March, 1865.

Question. Upon whose recommendation was that? Who first suggested it?

Answer. Mr. Stanton gave it to me.

Question. Did you ask him for it or did he volunteer it?

Mr. Manager BUTLER. That is not in the nature of correction or of explanation.

Mr. STANBERY. He could not get it yesterday. It was an omitted fact, and he passed it until he could get his commission.

Mr. Manager BUTLER. Very good.

By Mr. STANBERY:

Question. How was it—asked for or voluntarily tendered?

Answer. He had more than once said he intended to give it to me, and on this occasion, when I came from some important duty, I said that the time had arrived when I ought to have this commission. He said "certainly," and gave it to me at once. I do not think he ever intended to withhold it.

There is another point I want to state. When I was before the committee, or the honorable Managers, General BUTLER asked the clerk, I think it was, for the testimony of Dr. BURLEIGH. He said he had it not, that it was at his home. I do not know whether I said or he said, "It makes no difference." He asked me a number of questions in reference to that. I assented to them all. I never heard that testimony read.

Question. You never heard Dr. BURLEIGH's testimony read?

Answer. No, sir; nor do I recollect the particular questions, except that they were asked me and I assented. I said that Dr. BURLEIGH, no doubt, would recollect the conversation better than I.

By Mr. Manager BUTLER:

Question. General Thomas, how many times yesterday did you answer that the President told you each time to "take possession of the office?"

Answer. I have not read over my testimony particularly. I do not know how many times.

Question. Was that untrue each time you said it?

Answer. If I said so it was. "Take charge" were the words of the President.

Question. Have you any memorandum by which you can correct that expression? If so, produce it.

Answer. I have no memorandum with me here; I do not know that I have any.

Question. Have you looked at one since you were on the stand?

Answer. I have not.

Question. How can you tell better to-day than you could yesterday?

Answer. Because I read that evidence as recorded.

Question. You gave it yesterday yourself?

Answer. I did.

Question. And you could know better what it was by reading it than when you testified to it?

Answer. Yes, sir.

Question. And you are sure the word was "charge" each time?

Answer. "Take charge of."

Question. And then the three times when you reported to him that Stanton would not go out, refused to go out, each time he said, "Take charge of the office?"

Answer. He did.

Question. Was your attention called at the time he said that to the difference between taking "charge" of the office and taking "possession" of it?

Answer. My attention was not called to it.

Question. How, then, do you so carefully make that distinction now in your mind?

Answer. Because I know that that was his expression. I have thought the matter over.

Question. You have always known that that was his expression, have you not?

Answer. Yes.

Question. And you have thought the matter over?

Answer. Yes.

Question. Well, then, how could you make such a mistake yesterday?

Answer. I think the words were put into my mouth; I do not recollect distinctly.

Question. The same as Karsner put in about the "kicking out?"

Answer. Yes.

Question. And you are rather in the habit, are you, when words are put into your mouth, of using them?

Answer. I am not always in the habit.

Question. Why was yesterday an exception?

Answer. I do not know why it was an exception.

Question. I want to ask you another question on another subject which was omitted yesterday?

Answer. Certainly.

Question. After you and Karsner were summoned here as witnesses, did you go and quarrel with him?

Answer. I had some words with him in the room here adjoining.

Question. Did you call him a liar and a perjurer?

Answer. I did.

Question. You called him a liar and perjurer, did you?

Answer. I think I did both; I certainly did call him a liar.

Question. And a perjurer?

Answer. I think it is probable I did; but the "liar," I know.

Question. You knew that he and you both were in the witness-room waiting to be called?

Answer. I was here.

Question. And you knew he was here for that purpose?

Answer. I presume I did; yes.

Question. And while he was there you undertook to talk with him about his testimony?

Answer. I stated to him in the two instances: I will give them to you——

Question. Just answer my question, sir; I have not asked you what you said. I only ask you this question, whether you undertook to talk with him about his testimony?

Answer. I do not know who introduced the conversation. It was certainly not I, I do not think, for he was there some time before I spoke to him.

Question. Did you speak first or he?

Answer. That I do not recollect.

Question. Now, then, did you tell him that he was a liar and a perjurer at that time?

Answer. I did tell him he was a liar, and I may have said he was a perjurer.

Question. Did you offer violence to him?

Answer. I did not.

Question. Did you speak violently to him?

Answer. I did not, except in that way.

Question. Were you then in full uniform as now?

Answer. As I am now.

Question. There is another question I want to ask you which was omitted. Do you still intend to take charge or possession of the office of Secretary of War?

Answer. I do.

Question. Have you said to any person within a few days, "We'll have that fellow," meaning Stanton, "out, if it sinks the ship?"

Answer. Never.

Question. Did you say so to Mr. Johnson?

Answer. I did not.

Question. Anything to that effect?

Answer. Not that I have any recollection of.

Question. Do you know whether you did or not?

Answer. What Mr. Johnson do you mean?

Question. Mr. B. B. Johnson.

Answer. There was a Mr. Johnson came to see me at my house in reference to another matter, and we may have had some conversation about this.

Question. When was it that that Mr. Johnson came to your house to see you about another matter?

Answer. That I hardly recollect.

Question. About how long ago?

Answer. I am trying to recollect now. He came to me about the business——

Question. Never mind what his business was. When was it?

Answer. But I want to call it to mind. I have a right to do that, I think.

Question. But not to state it?

Answer. I took no note of the time, and I can hardly tell. It was recently, not very long ago.

Question. Within two or three days?

Answer. No, sir; before that time.

Question. Within a week?

Answer. I think it is more than a week.

Question. Let me give you the date—on Friday, a week ago yesterday?

Answer. I cannot give the date. I do not know it.

Question. Was it longer than that?

Answer. Well, I did not charge my memory with it. It was a familiar conversation we had.

Question. Were you joking then?

Answer. Certainly.

Question. Oh, joking?

Answer. Yes.

Question. Did you, jokingly or otherwise, say these words: "and we'll have Stanton out of there if we have to sink the ship?"

Answer. I have no recollection of making use of that expression.

Question. Did you make use of one equivalent to that in substance?

Answer. I have no recollection of it.

Question. Have you such a recollection of what you say as to know whether you did or not?

Answer. I have not. I would rather he would testify himself; he knows it better than I. I cannot recollect all the conversation I had.

Question. Do you deny that you said so?

Answer. I cannot deny it, because I do not know that I did.

Question. You say you would rather he would testify; and I will try to oblige you in that respect; but if you did say so, was it true or merely more brag?

Answer. You may call it as you please; brag, if you say so.

Question. I do not want to put words into your mouth; what do you call it?

Answer. I do not call it "brag."

Question. What was it?

Answer. It was a mere conversation, whatever it may have been.

Question. Did you mean what you said, or did you say what you did not mean?

Answer. I did not mean to use any violence against Mr. Stanton to get him out of office.

Question. What did you mean by the expression "We'll have him out if it sinks the ship?"

Answer. I have said I do not know that I used that expression.

Question. You have told me also that Mr. Johnson can tell better. I am assuming now you did say it?

Mr. EVARTS. That you have no right to do. Mr. Johnson has not said so yet.

Mr. Manager BUTLER. This witness does not say that he did not say so.

Mr. EVARTS. That is another matter. You have not proved it yet.

The WITNESS. I cannot say. He was there on official business in reference to an officer dismissed from the Army.

Question. Official business?

Answer. I mean business connected with an officer dismissed from the Army.

Question. Then you were joking on this subject?

Answer. Certainly.

Question. Did you ever see Mr. Johnson before?

Answer. I have no recollection. It is possible I may have seen him.

Question. Have you seen him since?

Answer. I have not to my knowledge.

Question. Now, here was a stranger who called on you on official business, business pertaining to your office?

Answer. No, sir.

Question. Official business about getting a man reinstated who had been dismissed?

Answer. Yes.

Question. Very good. He called upon you on business connected with the Army?

Answer. That had nothing to do with my office.

Question. Now, did you go to joking with him, a total stranger, in this way?

Answer. I knew him as the lawyer employed by Colonel Belger to get him reinstated, and Colonel Belger sent him to me. Now you have got it.

Question. Was he a stranger to you?

Answer. I think he was.

Question. Now, then, being a stranger, having that fixed, will you answer did you go to joking with this stranger on such a subject?

Answer. Certainly. We had quite a familiar talk when he was there. He sat with me for some time.

Question. And that is the only explanation you can give of that expression?

Answer. That is sufficient, I think.

Question. Whether it is sufficient or not somebody else will judge; is it the only one you can give?

Answer. It is the only one I do give.

Question. And it is the only one you can give?

Answer. Yes.

Question. A single word now upon another

subject: did anybody talk with you about your testimony since you left the stand?

Answer. Since I left the stand?

Question. Yes; since yesterday?

Answer. Well, I suppose I have talked with a dozen persons.

Question. Such as whom?

Answer. Several persons met me and said they were very glad to hear my testimony. We did not enter into any particulars about it. I have been met to-day jocularly about taking an equal drink with the Secretary of War by two or three persons. I have talked in my own family about it.

Question. Has anybody talked to you about these points, or have you talked to anybody about these points where you have changed your testimony?

Answer. I came here this morning and saw the Managers, and told them wherein I wanted——

Mr. Manager BUTLER. The Managers! You do not mean that quite?

Mr. EVARTS. The counsel for the President.

The WITNESS. I saw the counsel for the President, and told them I wished to make corrections.

By Mr. Manager BUTLER:

Question. You did not mean the Managers; you meant the counsel?

Answer. I meant the counsel; these gentlemen sitting here, [pointing to the counsel for the President.]

Question. That you had a perfect right to do. Had you talked with anybody before that about these points?

Answer. Yes.

Question. Whom?

Answer. General Townsend this morning.

Question. The Assistant Adjutant General?

Answer. Yes.

Question. Anybody else?

Answer. About these points?

Question. Exactly.

Answer. No.

Question. Are you sure?

Answer. I have said no. I am sure.

Question. Now, sir, did you not receive a letter from Mr. Stanton, whether a copy or not, on the 21st of February?

Answer. I did not.

Question. You said that he gave you the original, and the date is noted. Have you seen that original?

Answer. Since?

Question. Yes.

Answer. I have not.

Question. The date was noted on that original. When was that original given you?

Answer. The one I read here on the 22d?

Question. I did not ask you, "the one you read here"—the original; when was that given you?

Answer. On the 22d.

C. I.—20.

Question. Did you have more than one paper given you?

Answer. That was handed to me, and then it was handed to General Townsend, who made a copy, and the Secretary gave me the copy which I read here. The other paper I have not seen.

Question. And that was the 22d?

Answer. On the 22d, dated the 21st.

Question. Prepared, then, the day before?

Answer. I suppose so. It has the date of the day before.

Question. Then do you mean to take all back that was said in the room of Mr. Schriver about your not going on with the office or their not obeying you on the afternoon of the 21st?

Answer. Oh, yes; it was the 22d, because General Townsend was not there on the 21st.

Question. Then on the 21st there was nothing said about his not obeying you?

Answer. I think not.

Question. Nothing said to Schriver about not obeying you?

Answer. I think not.

Question. Then there was nothing said about not obeying you on the 21st at all?

Answer. I think not.

Question. And you never reported to the President that Stanton would not obey you on the 21st?

Answer. I reported to the President the two conversations I had with him.

Question. What were the two? The one in Schriver's room seems to have gone out. What were the two?

Mr. EVARTS. There were two besides that, Mr. BUTLER.

Mr. Manager BUTLER. The witness will tell me.

Mr. EVARTS. But you said it was not so.

Mr. Manager BUTLER. I did not. I said that one seemed to have gone out.

Mr. EVARTS. One of the conversations. That was not one of the two.

Mr. Manager BUTLER. I do not know that.

The WITNESS. General Schriver did not hear either of these conversations.

Question. Then on the 21st there was no such conversation that you testified to?

Answer. Not in reference to that letter—no.

Question. Was there any conversation at all as to General Townsend's not obeying you, or General Schriver's not obeying you, on the 21st?

Answer. None.

Question. Then what you told us yesterday, that you reported that to the President and got his answer to that, all that was not so, was it?

Answer. All that was not so.

Question. Now, upon another matter. When you were examined before the committee——

Answer. Which committee?

Question. The committee——

Answer. I have been examined twice. I only want to know.

Question. The committee of the House, not

the Managers. You were asked this question: "Did you make any report to the President on Friday of what had transpired," and did you not answer in these words: "Yes, sir; I saw the President and told him of what had occurred." He said, "Well, go along and administer the Department." When I stated what had occurred with Mr. Stanton, he said to me, "You must just take possession of the Department and carry on the business." Did you so swear before the committee?

The witness not replying—

Question. Let me give you the words again?

Answer. I thought you were waiting for somebody else. I say, as I said before, the words were: "Take charge"——

Question. That is not the question.

Answer. What is the question?

Question. The question is this: in answer to a question which I will read again to show you that the words were not put in your mouth, in these words, "Did you make any report to the President on Friday of what had transpired," did you not answer in these words, "Yes, sir; I saw the President, and told him of what had occurred." He said, "Well, go along and administer the Department." And did you not proceed to state, "When I stated what had occurred with Mr. Stanton, he said 'You must just take possession of the Department and carry on the business.'" Now, sir, did you swear that? That is the only thing I asked you.

Answer. If that is there I suppose I swore to it. I want to make one statement, though.

Question. Was it true?

Answer. No; the word used was the other.

Mr. Manager BUTLER. That is all.

The WITNESS. I wish to make one statement in reference to that very thing. I think I ought to do it. I was called there hastily. There were a good many events that had transpired. I requested on two occasions that committee to let me wait and consider, and they refused, would not let me do it, pressed me with questions all the time.

By Mr. Manager BUTLER:

Question. How was that?

Answer. When I was called before that committee on the evening of——

Mr. Manager BUTLER. February 26.

The WITNESS. On the evening of the day of my trial. I went there after getting through with that trial. I on two occasions requested them to postpone the examination until next morning, or until I could go over the matter. That was not allowed me.

Question. Did you make any such request?

Answer. I did twice.

Question. Of whom did you make it?

Answer. To those who were there.

Question. Who was there?

Answer. I think the committee was pretty full.

Question. The committee on preparing the articles of impeachment were there?

Answer. Yes, sir.

Question. That committee you mean, and the committee was full?

Answer. I do not know whether Mr. STEVENS was there. He was there a portion of the time. I do not know whether he was there at this particular time.

Question. And you tell the Senate now on your oath that you requested the committee to give you time to answer the questions, and they refused you?

Answer. I requested that it might be deferred until the next morning, when I could have an opportunity to go over in my own mind those things. It was not granted. There was no refusal given, but I was still pressed with questions.

Then there is another matter I want to speak about—when I came to correct that testimony. There are two things there that are confounded in reference to dates; the first part of it, the date of my appointment as Adjutant General and that of my appointment as Secretary of War *ad interim*—I supposed they were asking me in reference to the former, and that is the reason those two questions got mixed up. Then when I went there to correct my testimony I wished to do it. I read it over and found that some of it was not in English, and I thought there was something taken down, and I believe there was, that I did not say. They would not permit me to correct the manuscript, but I put something at the bottom just in a hasty way. I suppose it is on that paper, [pointing to a manuscript in the hand of Mr. Manager BUTLER.] I do not know.

Question. I will come to that. Now, then, have you got through with your statement?

Answer. I have.

Question. Very well, then, you will answer me a few questions. Did you not come and ask to see your testimony as it was taken down by that committee?

Answer. I went to the clerk and saw him.

Question. Did he give you the report which I hold in my hand?

Answer. He was not in; and I came the next day, the second day, and he handed it to me; and twice he went, I think, to some member of the committee, I do not know who. I said I wished to correct it; I wanted to make it at least decent English in some respects; but I was informed that I could not correct the manuscript, that I might——

Question. He reported to you that you might make any corrections in writing?

Answer. Yes, sir.

Question. Then, did you read the whole testimony over?

Answer. I think I did; I am not certain about that.

Question. Do you not know you did?

Answer. No; I do not know that I did.

Question. What were you there for?

Answer. I came there to correct the first part of it particularly, and that was the reason

I went there. I took it for granted that the rest was correct.

Question. You did not want to correct any other portion of it?

Answer. No.

Question. And the first part of it only referred to the mistake in the time about your being made Adjutant General or being made Secretary of War?

Answer. It had reference to the notification given me more particularly?

Question. By the President?

Answer. I had stated the notification——

Question. The notification by the President to be Secretary of War or Adjutant General that was mixed?

Answer. That was mixed.

Question. That was what you wanted to correct?

Answer. I stated that I received that notification from Colonel Moore. Colonel Moore did give me the notification that I would probably be put back as Adjutant General, but he did not as Secretary of War.

Question. That was what you wished to correct?

Answer. That was the principal correction I wished to make.

Question. And you did not want to correct anything else?

Answer. If there was anything wrong, I did. My corrections are there, whatever they may be. I suppose that is the paper.

Question. You then went over your testimony, did you not, and corrected such portions as you pleased?

Answer. Oh, I had full privilege to do that, of course.

Question. And wrote out here portions of two sheets which are in your handwriting, are they not, of corrections? [Showing the pages to the witness.]

Answer. Yes, sir, I corrected in my own handwriting.

Question. And signed it "L. Thomas, Adjutant General?"

Answer. Yes, sir. There are not two sheets, however. There is one sheet and a little more.

Question. I said portions of two sheets. Now, sir, having read over your testimony and attempted to correct it, did you correct anything in this portion in which you are reported as saying that the President ordered you to go forward and take possession and administer the office?

Answer. I do not think I made any such correction as that.

Question. You have sworn that that was not true. Why did you not correct it?

Answer. I have said so because I know his expression.

Question. Why did you not correct it before?

Answer. Well, I have thought the matter over.

By Mr. STANBERY:

Question. General Thomas, I find a report

of your testimony as given yesterday, as you gave it originally, on the examination as to the first interview with the President, which I will now read to you and see whether it is correctly reported:

"*Question.* What occurred between the President and yourself at the second interview on the 21st of February?

"WITNESS. I stated to the President that I had delivered the communication, and that he gave this answer.

"Mr. STANBERY. What answer?

"WITNESS. The answer, 'Do you wish me to vacate at once, or will you give me time to take away my private property,' and that I answered, 'at your pleasure.' I then stated that, after delivering the copy of the letter to him, he said, 'I do not know whether I will obey your instructions or resist them.'"

The WITNESS. I said "act your pleasure."

Mr. STANBERY. Now, the point of your answer I wish to bring to your attention is this:

"This I mentioned to the President. His answer was, 'Very well; go on and take charge of the office and perform the duty.'"

Did you say that?

Answer. I said that.

Question. It was in the cross-examination that this "possession" came out, was it not?

Answer. Yes, sir.

By Mr. Manager BUTLER:

Question. Then you mean to say that in answer to Mr. Stanbery you put it all right yesterday, and in the answer to me you got it all wrong?

Answer. In reference to your examination.

Mr. STANBERY. We will see how your examination was by and by. We shall want General Thomas as to what took place on the trial after we put in the record.

Mr. Manager BUTLER. Call him in at any time; we shall always be glad to see him. [Laughter.]

General THOMAS. Thank you, sir.

WILLIAM T. SHERMAN sworn and examined.

By Mr. STANBERY:

Question. General Sherman, were you in Washington last winter?

Answer. I was.

Question. What time did you arrive here?

Answer. About the 4th of December last.

Question. How long did you remain here?

Answer. Two months.

Question. Till the 4th of February, or about that time?

Answer. Until about the 3d or 4th of February.

Question. On what business had you come?

Answer. I came as a member of the Indian peace commission by adjournment.

Question. Any other business at that time?

Answer. At that time no other business. Subsequently, by order, I was assigned to a board of officers organized under the laws of Congress to submit articles of war and regulations for the Army.

Question. At what date was that assignment?

Answer. I could procure the order, which

would be perfect evidence of its date; but I must now state that it was within ten days of my arrival here; about ten days.

Question. About ten days after your arrival here?

Answer. About the middle of December that order was issued.

Question. Then you had a double duty?

Answer. I had a double duty for a few days.

Question. During that time, from the 4th of December until the 3d or 4th of February, had you several interviews with the President?

Answer. I had.

Question. Did you see him alone, when there was no person present but the President and yourself?

Answer. Yes, sir.

Question. Did you see him also in company with General Grant?

Answer. I saw him in company with General Grant once, and I think twice.

Question. Had you several interviews with him in relation to the case of Mr. Stanton?

Answer. I had.

Mr. Manager BINGHAM. Mr. President, we desire, without delaying the Senate, to respectfully submit our objections here again, without desiring to argue it. We believe it our duty, as the representatives of the House, to object——

Mr. STANBERY. Object to what?

Mr. Manager BINGHAM. That the declarations of the President touching any matter involved in this issue, not made at the time when we have called them out ourselves, are not competent evidence, and desire to submit the point, if such is the pleasure of the Senate, to the ruling of the presiding officer.

Mr. STANBERY. Allow me to come to some question that we can get started upon. This is introductory.

Mr. Manager BINGHAM. I understand it so.

Mr. STANBERY. You will soon see what our object is with General Sherman. There will be no mistake about it when we come to it.

Mr. Manager BINGHAM. I understand the object is to call out conversations with the President.

The CHIEF JUSTICE. At present no such question has been asked.

Mr. STANBERY. Now we will come to the point very quick. [To the witness.] General, while you were here, did the President ask you if you would take charge of the office of the Department of War in case of the removal of Mr. Stanton?

Mr. Manager BUTLER. I object to the question, and ask that it be reduced to writing.

The CHIEF JUSTICE. The counsel will reduce the question to writing.

Mr. STANBERY. Do you object because it is leading or because of the substance of it?

Mr. Manager BUTLER. I object to it for every reason.

Mr. STANBERY. Then I will put it in a form——

Mr. Manager BUTLER. I beg your pardon; put it in writing.

Mr. STANBERY. I will lay a foundation first. [To the witness.] At what time were those interviews? Have you a memorandum?

The WITNESS, (consulting his memoranda.) The interview with General Grant and the President, do you refer to?

Mr. STANBERY. No; any interview. I will ask you a question that will relieve you, perhaps. Had you interviews with the President before Mr. Stanton came back to the office, while General Grant was yet in it?

The WITNESS. Yes, sir; of a social nature entirely, before that time.

Question. Had you interviews with him after that?

Answer. I had.

Question. How long after that; after Mr. Stanton came back?

Answer. The day following, I think.

Question. Were you and the President alone at that interview the day after?

Answer. General Grant was also present?

Question. What did that interview relate to?

Answer. The removal——

Mr. Manager BUTLER. Stop a moment. Do not get it in indirectly. Meet the question man fashion, please.

Mr. STANBERY. What did it relate to?

Mr. Manager BUTLER. That gives the substance of it. I object. Meet the question.

Mr. STANBERY, (to the witness.) Did it relate to the occupation of the War Department by Mr. Stanton?

The WITNESS. It did.

Question. Now, what was it?

Mr. Manager BUTLER. Stop a moment. We object. We ask that it be put in writing.

By Mr. STANBERY:

Question. What conversation passed between you and the President?

Mr. Manager BUTLER. Excuse me. I asked to have the question in writing. Shall I have it? I have three times attempted, and each time failed.

The CHIEF JUSTICE. The counsel will please reduce the question to writing.

The question, having been reduced to writing, was handed to and read by the Secretary, as follows:

In that interview what conversation took place between the President and you in regard to the removal of Mr. Stanton?

Mr. Manager BUTLER. To that we object. I suppose we can agree on the day. That must have been the 14th of January last. On the 13th Mr. Stanton was reinstated; and the 14th, if it was the day after, would be the date.

Mr. STANBERY, (to the witness.) Can you give us the day of that conversation, General?

The WITNESS. Yes, sir. [Consulting a memorandum.] According to a memorandum which I hold Mr. Stanton reëntered on the possession of his office of Secretary of War on Tuesday, the 13th. Monday was the 12th, Tuesday the 13th. The conversation occurred on Wednesday, the 14th of January.

The CHIEF JUSTICE. The Chief Justice thinks the question admissible within the principle of the decision made by the Senate relating to a conversation between General Thomas and the President; but he will put the question to the Senate, if any Senator desires it.

Mr. CONNESS. On that I ask for a vote and for the yeas and nays.

The yeas and nays were ordered.

Mr. Manager BUTLER. We should like to hear the grounds on which the offer is made stated.

Mr. STANBERY. The Managers ask me to state the grounds upon which we expect this testimony——

Mr. Manager BUTLER. No, sir.

Mr. STANBERY. What, then?

Mr. Manager BUTLER. I ask you simply for the ground on which you put it—not the testimony; the grounds on which you can put in any possible declaration, not the declaration itself.

Mr. STANBERY. This ground: we expect to prove by General Sherman——

Mr. Manager BUTLER. I object, sir. I have not asked that.

Mr. STANBERY. Is it not admissible to say what we expect to prove?

Mr. Manager BUTLER. No, sir; that is to get before the court, Mr. Chief Justice——

Mr. STANBERY. "Get before the court!"

Mr. Manager BUTLER. Get before the court or the Senate—that I should fall into bad habits sometimes is not wonderful. [laughter] —it is to get before the Senate the testimony by statements of the counsel. The question wholly and solely is whether the declarations of the President can be given in evidence. What those declarations are, in my judgment, it would be improper to state and unprofessional to state, because that is begging the whole question and attempting to get them before the Senate and the country by the recital of the counsel. That never is permitted. The sole question is, whatever the declarations are, if any possible declaration can be competent at that time. If the declaration asked for can be competent you may assume that any possible conversation can be competent, and then we will assume that this——

Mr. STANBERY. Exactly; then you come to the point.

Mr. Manager BUTLER. That this can be, and therefore there is no occasion to state what it is.

Mr. STANBERY. Take it in that way, any possible declaration can be evidence. Do you propose to argue this?

Mr. Manager BUTLER. We do not want to argue it.

Mr. STANBERY. We do.

Mr. Manager BUTLER. If the Senate will vote that it is competent we cannot alter it by argument.

Mr. STANBERY. Mr. Chief Justice and Senators, the testimony which we expect to elicit from General Sherman I look upon as vital upon the question of intent, as testimony we are entitled to have upon legal grounds perfectly well settled and perfectly unanswerable. I can say now in argument, I presume, what I expect to prove. "If," says the honorable Manager, "any declarations you choose to call out are admissible, you may make them as strong as you please—imagine any that you please—and still no declaration of the President made on that 14th of January can be admitted here!"

Now, first of all, what is the issue here? Let the Managers speak for themselves. I first read from the honorable Manager who opened this case, at page 94 of his argument.

Mr. Manager BUTLER. You read from page 94 of the record, not of the argument.

Mr. STANBERY. The Manager said:

"Having shown that the President willfully violated an act of Congress, without justification, both in the removal of Stanton and the appointment of Thomas, for the purpose of obtaining wrongfully the possession of the War Office by force, if need be, and certainly by threats and intimidations, for the purpose of controlling its appropriations through its *ad interim* chief, who shall say that Andrew Johnson is not guilty of the high crime and misdemeanors charged against him in the first eight articles?"

Again, on page 109, speaking of the orders of removal:

"These and his concurrent acts show conclusively that his attempt to get the control of the military force of the Government, by the seizing of the Department of War, was done in pursuance of his general design, if it were possible, to overthrow the Congress of the United States; and he now claims by his answer the right to control at his own will, for the execution of this very design, every officer of the Army, Navy, civil, and diplomatic service of the United States."

Again, on page 99:

"Failing in his attempt to get full possession of the office through the Senate, he had determined, as he admits, to remove Stanton at all hazards, and endeavored to prevail on the General to aid him in so doing. He declines. For that the respondent quarrels with him, denounces him in the newspapers, and accuses him of bad faith and untruthfulness. Thereupon, asserting his prerogatives as Commander-in-Chief, he creates a new military department of the Atlantic. He attempts to bribe Lieutenant General Sherman to take command of it by promotion to the rank of general by brevet, trusting that his military services would compel the Senate to confirm him.

"If the respondent can get a general by brevet appointed, he can then by simple order put him on duty according to his brevet rank, and thus have a general of the Army in command at Washington, through whom he can transmit his orders and comply with the act which he did not dare transgress, as he had approved it, and get rid of the hated General Grant. Sherman spurned the bribe. The respondent, not discouraged, appointed Major General George H. Thomas to the same brevet rank, but Thomas declined.

"What stimulated the ardor of the President just at that time, almost three years after the war closed, but just after the Senate had reinstated Stanton, to reward military service by the appointment of generals by brevet? Why did his zeal of promotion take that form and no other? There were many other meritorious officers of lower rank desirous of promotion. The purpose is evident to every thinking mind. He had determined to set aside Grant, with whom he had quarreled, either by force or fraud, either in conformity with or in spite of the act of Congress, and control the military power of the country. On the 21st of February—for all these events cluster nearly about the same point of time—he appoints Lorenzo Thomas Secretary of War and orders Stanton out of the office. Stanton refuses to go; Thomas is about the streets declaring that he will put him out by force, 'kick him out.'"

But, still more closely to the point, we will come to the testimony of intent, on page 251. This is upon the introduction of the case of Mr. Cooper. To show the intent of the President, the learned Managers have gone back to the fall of 1867, and begin their proof with an intention commenced in the fall, carried along, says the honorable Manager, to the very date of the 21st of February, of the appointment of Thomas. Most of the proof, he says, "clusters about that time," but it begins, he says, in the fall; and he calls Chandler to prove what? That Cooper was inducted into office by the President, being his own Private Secretary, for the purpose of carrying out what? His intention to get his own man first into the War Office to control the requisitions there, and then to get his own man into the Treasury Department to meet those requisitions and to pay them, and thereby control the purse as well as the sword of the nation.

"The only question"—

says the learned Manager—

"is, is this competent, if we can show it was one of the ways and means? The difficulty that rests in the minds of my learned friends on the other side is that they cluster everything about the 21st of February, 1868. They seem to forget that the act of the 21st of February, 1868, was only the culmination of a purpose formed long before, as in the President's answer he sets forth, to wit: as early as the 12th of August, 1867."

* * * * * * * * *

"To carry it out there are various things to do. He must get control of the War Office; but what good does that do if he cannot get somebody who shall be his servant, his slave, dependent on his breath, to answer the requisitions of his pseudo officer whom he may appoint; and therefore he began when? Stanton was suspended, and as early as the 12th of December he had got to put that suspension and the reasons for it before the Senate, and he knew it would not live there one moment after it got fairly considered. Now he begins. What is the first thing he does? 'To get somebody in the Treasury Department that will mind me precisely as Thomas will, if I can get him in the War Department.' That is the first thing; and thereupon, without any vacancy, he must make an appointment. The difficulty that we find is that we are obliged to argue our case step by step upon a single point of evidence. It is one of the infelicities always of putting in a case that sharp, keen, ingenious counsel can insist at all steps on impaling you upon a point of evidence; and therefore I have got to proceed a little further.

"Now, our evidence, if you allow it to come in is, first, that he made this appointment; that this failing, he sent it to the Senate, and Cooper was rejected. Still determined to have Cooper in, he appointed him ad interim, precisely as this ad interim Thomas was appointed, without law and against right. We put it as a part of the whole machinery by which to get hold, to get, if he could, his hand into the Treasury of the United States, although Mr. Chandler has just stated there was no way to get it except by a requisition through the War Department; and at the same moment, to show that this was part of the same illegal means, we show you that although Mr. McCulloch, the Secretary of the Treasury, must have known that Thomas was appointed, yet the President took pains—we have put in the paper—to serve on Mr. McCulloch an attested copy of the appointment of Thomas ad interim, in order that he and Cooper might recognize his warrants."

That is what they put in. They have got that testimony for that purpose, as they say, to show the intent of the President, began, they say, as early as the 12th of August, 1867, progressed in by the appointment of Cooper in the fall of 1867, going all through the subsequent time until it "culminated" on the 21st of February by at last finding the proper tool to do this work in the War Office. He was looking, according to the argument, for a proper tool—for a servant—for one who would do his bidding, and, forsooth, after a search, he found the very man in what the Manager has called "a disgraced officer."

Now, Mr. Chief Justice and Senators, and especially those of you who are lawyers, what case are they attempting to make against the President? Not simply that he did certain acts that would make him criminal, but that he did these acts mala fide, with an unlawful intent and criminal purpose. They do not prove that purpose, or attempt to prove it, by any positive testimony; but they say, "we prove certain facts from which we raise a presumption that that was the purpose." It is upon proof, founded on presumption, and such proof is admissible, that the gentlemen rest the essential part of their case; that is to say, the criminal intent. They prove certain acts that may be criminal or stand indifferent, according to the intent of the party. Then they prove certain other acts and declarations which, as they say, raise the presumption that the thing done, the order given, the appointment made, was made with that criminal intent laid, and they say, "we not only show that criminal intent then, but," they say, "it was conceived months before," and that all the machinery was put in motion, and that the President, from the 12th of August, 1867, was pursuing that intent, looking for tools, agents to carry out that intent, and it did not culminate until the 21st of February, 1868, although the gentleman says most of the facts happened to cluster about that period, but not all of them.

This being so, Senators, what is the rule to rebut this presumption of intention? When a prosecution is allowed to raise the presumption of guilt from the intent of the accused, by proving circumstances which raised that presumption against him, may he not rebut it by proof of other circumstances which show that he could not have had such a criminal intent? Was anything ever plainer than that?

Why, consider what a latitude one charged with crime is allowed under such circumstances. Take the case of a man charged with passing counterfeit money. You must prove his intent; you must prove his scienter; you must prove circumstances from which a presumption arises; did he know the bill was counterfeit. You may prove that he had been told so; prove that he had seen other money of the same kind, and raise the intent in that way. Even when you make such proof against him arising from presumptions, how may he rebut that presumption of intent from circumstances proved against him? In the first place, by the most general of all presumptions, proof of good character generally. That he is allowed to do to rebut a presumption—the most general of all presumptions, not that he did what was right in that transaction, not that he did certain things or made certain declarations about the same time which explained that the intent was honest, but going beyond that through the whole field of presumptions, for it is all open to him, he may rebut the presumption arising from proof of express facts by the proof of general good character, raising the presumption that he is not a man who would have such an intent.

Mr. Manager BUTLER. We do not object to that proof.

Mr. STANBERY. You do not!

Mr. Manager BUTLER. Put in his good character.

Mr. STANBERY. Such a general thing as that! And yet you object to this?

Mr. Manager BUTLER. Put in his good character, and we will take issue on that.

Mr. STANBERY. Now, what evidence is a defendant entitled to who is charged with crime where it is necessary to make out an intent against him where the intent is not positively proved by his own declarations, but where the intent to be gathered by proof of other facts, which may be guilty or indifferent according to the intent. What proof is allowed against him to raise this presumption of intent? Proof of those facts from which the mind itself infers a guilty intention. But while the prosecution may make such a case against him by such testimony, may he not rebut the case by exactly the same sort of testimony? If it is a declaration that they rely upon as made by him at one time, may he not meet it by declarations made about the same time with regard to the same transaction? Undoubtedly. They cannot be too remote; I admit that; but if they are about the time, if they are connected with the transaction, if they do not appear to have been manufactured, then the declarations of the defendant from which the inference of innocence would be presumed are, under reasonable limitations, just as admissible as the declarations of the defendant from which the prosecution has attempted to deduce the inference of criminal purpose. Now let us look at the authorities on this point. In the trial of Hardy, reported in State Trials, volume twenty-four, page 1065, Mr. Erskine, who defended Hardy, called a Mr. Daniel Stuart as a witness. The case is so fully in point that I will read from it pretty largely:

"*Mr. Erskine.* I call back this gentleman only for the purpose of asking him one question, which I could not with propriety ask him before; you stated, in your former examination, your personal acquaintance with the prisoner at the bar, and your

transactions with him before; did your ever hear him state what his plan of reform was?

"Yes, I have; he always stated it to be the Duke of Richmond's plan, universal suffrage and annual Parliaments.

"Was that said to you publicly, or in the privacy of confidence?

"It was said publicly. And he sold me some copies of the Duke of Richmond's letter.

"*Mr. Attorney General.* I really must object to this sort of examination.

"*Mr. Erskine.* Then I will not defend this question. I am persuaded your lordships will not refuse to the unfortunate man at the bar that evidence which has been received for every prisoner, under similar circumstances, from the earliest times of our history to the present moment. I am sorry to consume the time of the court, but if I am called upon I will repeat to your lordships, *verbatim,* from the State Trials, various questions, upon similar occasions, put by different prisoners, by consent of all the judges, all the attorney generals and solicitor generals, and counsel for the Crown. I only wish to know whether the question is objected to or not.

"*Mr. Attorney General.* It is.

"*Mr. Erskine.* I will proceed, and I have much more pleasure in doing it from the manner in which the attorney general conducted himself recently, because the moment that it was stated as a proceeding which, we thought, might be serviceable to the prisoner, and consistent with the rules of evidence, he instantly acceded to its production; therefore, independent of satisfying your lordships, if I can satisfy my learned friend that we are in the regular course, I am persuaded he would be sorry himself that this prisoner should be deprived of the advantage which all others have enjoyed."

Then this great advocate proceeds to give the cases from the State Trials upon the point that I am now considering—the declarations of a prisoner as evidence of his intent, whether it were unlawful or lawful, in the matter as to which he is charged.

I read from page 1068:

"Now, what is the present case? The prisoner is charged with the overt acts, which I need not repeat, because we are so well acquainted with the nature of them."

We are charged with overt acts in issuing this order.

"But he is not charged with the commission of those acts as substantive acts, but he is charged with having in his mind the wicked and detestable purpose of aiming at the destruction of the king, to put down and bring the king to death, and that in the fulfillment of that most detestable imagination he did the specific acts charged upon the record."

As we are charged here with intent, not to put down the king, but to put down Congress, and our detestable acts are to put a tool in the War Department to control the requisitions, and another tool in the Treasury Department to get hold of the money.

Mr. Erskine continues:

"That is to say, that he agreed to assemble a convention to be held which was not held—that he conspired to hold it, for the purpose of subverting the rule and authority of the country, and not that alone, but that he consented to hold such convention, which convention, in his mind, was to accomplish the purpose of the subversion of the Government, and that he did agree to assemble that convention for the purpose of that subversion in fulfillment, not that the other is the consequence of it, but in fulfillment of the detestable purpose of compassing the king's death.

"Here, then, the intention of the mind is the question which the jury have to try; and I think I may appeal to what passed in the court on Saturday, that I did not seek to lay down other rules of evidence than those that have been most recently stated, and those that have been determined in ancient times."

Now he comes to the cases:

"The counsel for Lord George Gordon were the present Lord Kenyon, lord chief justice of the king's bench, and myself, who have now the honor to speak to the court; and I was permitted to ask the Rev. Erasmus Middleton (the first witness, and therefore his examination fell to me as junior in the case) these questions—I should tell your lordships, to make it more intelligible, that the great object was to see what intention Lord George Gordon had, which could be collected only from what passed before—'Did you, at any of these numerous meetings of this Protestant Association, which you attended from the time Lord George Gordon became president of that society,' (which was two years before,) 'till the 29th of May'"—

That was the "culmination" of Lord George Gordon's conduct:

"'till the 29th of May;' did you ever hear Lord George Gordon, in his public speeches in that association, make use of any expressions which showed any disloyal or unconstitutional intentions in him?"

"Not in the least," says the witness; "the very reverse." Now, continues Erskine:

"Now, compare this with the question I am going to ask; a cunning, artful man might stand up in a Protestant association, and hold forth great professions when he meant the contrary; but no man who reposes confidence in the bosom of a friend, building himself upon the honor and honesty of his friend, when he tells him what his object is, will deceive him. Good God! if I were to ask people, did not Mr. Hardy, in the Corresponding Society, say that the Duke of Richmond's plan was his object, he might say it there, for the purpose of its afterwards being given in evidence, that he had publicly avowed that; if that may be asked, how is it possible to oppose the other? The examination then goes on: 'Did all his speeches, delivered as president, meet with your approbation; and did it appear to you that his views were the same as those of the whole associated body?' 'Quite so.' 'Did you ever hear Lord George Gordon make use of any expressions as if he meant to repeal this bill by force of arms?' 'Not in the least.' 'Were the meetings open?' and so on."

Again:

"The next case I shall state is that of my Lord Russell, who was indicted for compassing the king's death, and the overt act was consulting to raise rebellion and to seize the king's guards. In his defense he called many persons of quality to speak to his affection toward the Government, and his detestation of risings against it—I will pause here a minute. Why, a man might have a great deal of affection to the Government in the year 1780 and might change upon the subject, but yet the criminal law of England looks out industriously to see how it can interfere in favor of liberty and life, not trying how it can shut out the light, but how it can let it shine in; even that question, which I do not think one of the strictest, was suffered to be let in, because Dr. Burnet had had a long acquaintance with Lord Russell, and Lord Russell might not have conceived the purpose of rebellion till a short time before; but I shall ask as to the time when they say this man's mind was full of this conspiracy"—

As we do here—the time of this intent; no other time—

"but I shall ask, as to the time when they say this man's mind was full of conspiracy, so horrible in its nature, what were the sentiments which he was pouring into the bosom of his friend as the object of all these societies?

"'Doctor Burnet,' (says Lord Russell,) 'if you please to give some account of my conversation?' Doctor Burnet says: 'I have had the honor to be known to my Lord Russell several years, and he hath declared himself with much confidence to me, and he always, upon all occasions, expressed himself against all risings.' Now, this is not character to say that Lord Russell was a quiet, peaceable man; no, this is

evidence of conversation; my Lord Russell declared it so; therefore it is not that you are to raise a probability upon the subject by the general nature of a man's character, or what you think of him; but it shall be allowed to witnesses to say what the person trying has expressed, because it raises an intrinsic improbability of his being guilty of the crime imputed to him. Doctor Burnet says: 'He always expressed himself against all risings; and when he spoke of some people that would provoke to it he expressed himself so determined against that matter I think no man could do more.'"

Now, what we expect to prove is, that, so far from there being any intent on the part of the President to select a tool to take possession of that War Office, he asked first the General of the Army, Grant, and when he failed him, who next? The next most honored soldier that we have, Sherman. He was a tool! It was the President's purpose, they say, to put a tool there! That was his intent, to find a man who could take a bribe, by brevet perhaps, and, having found such a man as that, put him there! They say he did find such a man in Thomas, "a disgraced officer." Well, if that was his intent in the fall; if with that intent he put Cooper in the Treasury, it must have been with that intent he would put Sherman in the War Office. Before he thought of Thomas at all, before he thought of any subordinate, he took one of the most honored officers of the land, and said to him: "Come now, take this office; you are fit to be my tool—take this office, not to carry it on as you carried on this great war, not to remain a trusted and honorable man, but to become my subordinate and my tool!" Will the gentleman say that the President at that time had an intent to seize upon the requisitions of that Department, to get a man there who would send an improper requisition over to the Treasury, as they say, a man in the Treasury, as they say, to honor an improper requisition—that the President had put him there to drive Congress out of these Halls, and that he intended to put Sherman there to become his tool? Would the gentleman dare to say that? Would the President, in the first place, have dared to make such a proposition to such a man as General Sherman?

Gentlemen of the Senate, if you are to raise a presumption that the President intended to carry out an unlawful purpose by appointing Cooper, that he intended to carry out the same unlawful purpose by appointing Thomas, how does it happen that you do not give him the benefit of the presumption arising from his attempt to get such a man as General Sherman, that could not be made a tool of? And yet this is all to be shut out from the defense of the President!

In the cases that I have put, the case, for instance, of Lord George Gordon, who was indicted for a treasonable speech made on a certain day—I forget the date—before a certain association, he was allowed to go into proof running through a period of two years before that in meetings of that same association, that, instead of encouraging risings or insurrections, he had set his face against them. All that was admitted, although it was begun two years prior to the declaration for which he was indicted, and, indeed, more than two years before, certainly not clustering about the same time, not during the time when they say the intent arose, but long prior to that time, when in fact his intent may have been honest; for in two years a man may change his intent. They might have said at that time, "You have gone too far back; the question is as to your intent at the time of the transaction, as to your intent at the time when we have given evidence against you.' Lord George Gordon went back two years behind that. We stop within the time which they have fixed themselves. We do not ask to give any testimony as to the President's intent before the acts which they have brought forward to raise a presumption of guilt against him.

They began in the fall of 1867 with the appointment of Cooper, as they say. This is in the subsequent winter, when Sherman is here, right in the middle of this transaction. The President, as they say, had this intent all along before the act had culminated; that is, had ended, had reached its consummation— all that time, they say, the bad intent was in the President's mind, and they use every circumstance they can against him to raise the presumption that he intended to carry it out. Now, we want to show his acts and his declarations during that time to dissipate this idea that the President had any unlawful intent, to show that he was not seeking after a tool, but seeking for an honest, honorable, high-minded soldier—to do what? That which was unlawful? No; but to do that which the President thought belonged to him. We will show you that he asked General Sherman if he would take that office upon the removal of Mr. Stanton, and then said to General Sherman——

Mr. Manager BUTLER. That is not allowable.

Mr. STANBERY. What! that I cannot state what we are going to prove? I insist on it as a right.

Mr. Manager BUTLER. I insist that it is never done in any court.

Mr. STANBERY. If the Senate choose to stop me, I will stop; but I hope I shall be allowed to state what I expect to prove. I have been too long at the bar not to know that I have that right. The gentleman may answer my argument, but I hope he will not stop it.

Mr. Manager BUTLER. If you look at the book you hold in your hand you will find that Erskine stopped the Attorney General in precisely the same case from which you have quoted, and said, "You must not read a letter."

Mr. STANBERY. "Must not read a letter!" I am not reading a letter; I am stating what I expect to prove, and the gentleman takes me up. He does not understand where he is or where I am. He puts an intent into

my mind that I have not got, as he seems to have the very good faculty of putting intents into every man's mind. We expect to show that the President not only asked General Sherman to take this position, but told him then distinctly what his purpose was, and that was to put that office in such a situation as to drive Mr. Stanton into the courts of law.

Mr. Manager BUTLER. This is wholly unprofessional and improper.

Mr. STANBERY. I will judge of that. Erskine in this argument introduces a great many cases, which it would take too long to read; but finally the question which he put was allowed to be put and was answered; and I understand the decision in Hardy's case has gone into the text-books as law. But it was not necessary to have Hardy's case. I will ask any lawyer who has ever tried a case where the question was the intention, and where the case made against his client was of facts from which a presumption of intention was pretended to be raised by the prosecution, may he not show contemporaneous acts, acts covering the same time as those used against him, declarations within the same time with those used against him; may he not be allowed to resort to these to rebut the criminal intention, and to show that his intention was fair, honest, and legal? Undoubtedly such is the law; and it is upon this ground that we ask the introduction of the testimony of General Sherman.

Mr. Manager BUTLER. Mr. President, Senators, I was quite willing to put this case to the judgment of both lawyers and laymen of the Senate without a word of argument; and I only speak now to "the lawyers," because the learned counsel for the President emphasizes that word as though he expected some peculiar advantage from speaking to the lawyers of the Senate. All the rules of evidence are founded upon the good sense of mankind, as experience in the courts of law has shown what is most likely or unlikely to elicit truth, and they address themselves just as well to the layman as they do to the lawyer. There is no gentleman in the Senate, nay, there is no gentleman anywhere, that cannot understand this question of evidence; and if the plain rules of fair judgment and fair examination are applied to it, as I doubt not they will be, there can be no difficulty in the matter.

I agree that I labor, not under any weight of the argument that has just been put forward against me, but labor under the weight of the opinion of the presiding officer, who, deciding without argument, has told the Senate that in his opinion this came within the previous ruling, which I suppose to be the ruling of yesterday. If it did I should not for a moment have troubled the Senate, because I have long since learned, however they may be against me, to bow to the decisions of the tribunal before which I am.

But this is entirely another and a different case. In order to understand it let us see what is the exact question. The exact question is "In that interview," to wit, on the 14th of January, "what conversations took place between the President and you in regard to the removal of Mr. Stanton?" "What conversation;" it does not ask for acts now; pray, gentlemen, keep the distinction. "What conversation took place between you?" is the question, and upon that the Senate will vote.

Now, how is this attempted to be supported? I agree that the first part of the argument made by the learned Attorney General was the very best one he ever made in his life, because it consisted mostly in reading what I had said. [Laughter.] He put the question, and I have a right to say so, I trust, without any immodesty, because he adopted all I said as his own, which is one of the highest compliments I ever had paid to me. I thought it was a good argument, Senators, when I made it to you; I hoped it would convince you that it was right; but it failed. If it can be any better now in the mouth of the Attorney General I desire to see the result. I was arguing about putting in the President's act in appointing Mr. Cooper. I tried in every way I could to get it before you; I tried to show you that you ought to permit me to do so; but by an almost solid vote you said I should not. I said, "I can prove the intent." My argument failed to convince you. Will it do any better when read by the musical voice of my friend from Ohio? I think not. Of course you will allow me to have so much self-gratulation as still to say that I think it ought to have convinced you. I only bow to the fact that it did not.

But the point was there that I was attempting to prove, not a declaration of Mr. Johnson, but his act in putting in Cooper; here they ask for conversations. We failed; the Senate decided that we could not put in any act except such as was charged in the articles. We do not charge in the articles an attempt to bribe, or use as a tool, the gentleman who is on the stand, for whom we all have so high a respect. I do not think that we have that appreciation of him. Whatever appreciation the President might have, we never had that. What do we charge? We charge that he used the man whom we saw on the stand here before us a tool, and judge ye on your consciences whether he is not on his appearance here a fit instrument. Judge ye! Judge ye! You have seen him—a weak, vacillating, vain old man, just fit to be pampered by a little pride to do things which no man and no patriot would dare do. Why, let me call your attention for a moment to him. On this stand here yesterday he was going on to say that his conversation was playful to Karsner, playful to Wilkeson; but when he saw that that was not so, that that did not put him in a dignified position, he swung back to the truth and told us he meant to have force to the shedding of blood.

Mr. EVARTS. He said exactly the contrary.

Mr. Manager BUTLER. I do not understand the gentleman.

Mr. EVARTS. He said exactly the contrary.

Mr. Manager BUTLER. He said that he had made up his mind to use force to the shedding of blood.

Mr. EVARTS. No; to break a door; but when he thought of shedding blood he retracted his opinion.

Mr. Manager BUTLER. And he remained of that mind until the next morning.

Mr. EVARTS. No; he did not say that.

Mr. Manager BUTLER. What he found at the masquerade ball or elsewhere to change his mind he has not told us; nor can he tell us when he changed his mind. Am I not right? But I pass from that; I am only calling the attention of the Senate to the distinction between the two.

Now, then, how is this attempted to be supported? The learned gentleman from Ohio says what? He says "in a counterfeiter's case we have to prove the *scienter*." Yes, true; and how? By showing the passage of other counterfeit bills? Yes; but, gentlemen, did you ever hear, in a case of counterfeiting, the counterfeiter prove that he did not know the bill was bad by proving that at some other time he passed a good bill? Is not that the proposition? We try the counterfeit bill, which we have nailed to the counter, of the 21st of February; and, in order to prove that he did not issue it, he wants to show that he passed a good bill on the 14th of January. It does not take a lawyer to understand that. That is the proposition.

We prove that a counterfeiter passed a bad bill: I am following the illustration of my learned opponent. Having proved that he passed a bad bill, what is the evidence he proposes? That at some other time he told somebody else, a good man, that he would not pass bad money, to give it the strongest form; and you are asked to vote it on that reason. I take the illustration. Is there any authority brought for that? No.

What is the next ground? The next is that it is in order to show Andrew Johnson's good character. If they will put that in testimony I will open the door widely. We shall have no objection whenever they offer that. I will take all that is said of him by all good and loyal men, whether for probity, patriotism, or any other matter that they choose to put in issue. But how do they propose to prove good character? By showing what he said to a gentleman. Did you ever hear of good character, lawyers of the Senate; laymen of the Senate, did you ever hear a good character proved in that way? A man's character is in issue. Does he call up one of his neighbors and ask what the man told him about his character? No; the general speech of people in the community, what was publicly known and said of him, is the point, and upon that went Hardy's case.

Now, then, lawyers of the Senate, I have never seen before cited in the course of an argument on the law the speeches of counsel. I thought it was not within the common usage of the profession. Am I not right, lawyers of the Senate; and yet page after page of the argument of Mr. Erskine, who was going forward in every way that he could to save the life of his client, has been cited here to the Senate to govern them as a precedent. A more unprofessional act I never knew.

Mr. STANBERY. Mr. Chief Justice, I must ask the gentleman to cease these statements of "unprofessional" matter. I read —I wish the gentleman to attend to what I say now—I read only so much of the argument of Erskine as showed the application of the cases which I read from Erskine's speech. That was all.

Mr. Manager BUTLER. I attended with care to what was said; I had the book in my hand and followed the gentleman; the argument of the counsel only was read; and now, to show the application of that particular case, let me ask what the question there was. The question was, what were the public declarations of Mr. Hardy? He was accused of having made a speech and made a series of speeches which were held to be treasonable. Then the question was, what was his character as a loyal man, and upon that the discussion arose from which citations have been made; and when the discussion finally terminated, gentlemen of the Senate, what was the question? I read from page 1096 of the twenty-fourth volume of the State Trials:

"Did you before the time of this convention being held, which is imputed to Mr. Hardy, ever hear from him what his objects were—whether he has at all mixed himself in that business?

"I have very often conversed with him, as I mentioned before, about his plan of reform; he always adhered to the Duke of Richmond's plan, and said that will be the plan that will be adopted in the end. I disagreed with him about that, and that occasioned it more particularly to be marked in my memory; we disputed about it, and he always obstinately adhered to it, and stated that to be the object of the society, and his whole object.

"Was this said in the confidence of private regard or in public company, where it might be said ostentatiously?

"I was never in public company with him; he and another person were with me one night, and I have had long and frequent conversations with him upon the subject.

"From all that you have seen of him, what is his character for sincerity and truth?

"I have every reason to believe him to be a very sincere, simple, honest man.

"Mr. Attorney General. If this had been stated at first to be the question meant to be asked, I do not see what possible objection I could have to it."

. And if they will ask General Sherman or anybody else what is Andrew Johnson's character for sincerity and truth I will not object. I assure you. That was the whole question about which the dispute arose in Hardy's case; and the Attorney General finally said "if I had known that was what you are after I never should have objected."

What was Lord George Gordon's case? This is an illustration of the difficulty of reading from the arguments of counsel, whether they are made here by me or made by Lord Erskine in regard to Gordon's trial. We are on one side when we are arguing our cause, and we are apt to get our minds somewhat biased. What was Lord George Gordon's case? Lord George Gordon was accused of treason in leading a mob of Protestants against the House of Parliament; and there, in order to show his intention, there were allowed to be put in evidence against him the cries of the mob made publicly and orally as part of the *res gestæ.* To meet that, what was the defense? The defense was the insanity of Lord George Gordon, and upon that defense, and upon the whole case they went into the widest possible range. Let the gentlemen on the other side come in and prove—which is the best defense they have got—that Andrew Johnson is insane, and we shall then go into all his conversations to see whether he talked or acted like a sane man, on which idea in that case the defense went into Lord George Gordon's acts and sayings, but in no other way.

Then, what is the next thing that is said about this? They then go into Lord William Russell's case. Lord Russell's case was one of those so eloquently denounced by the gentleman who opened for the President yesterday as one of those cases occurring under the Plantagenets and Tudors which he would not appeal to for authority. They do drink at our fountain sometimes. They have got back now to those cases which they would lay aside yesterday. They have come back to them to-day; but what was there? The whole question was, what was Lord William Russell's character for loyalty. The question asked the witness was, what was his character for loyalty, to which the reply was "Good." Then he was asked "How long have you known him?" and he replied "I have known him some time." Then came the question "Did you ever hear him express himself against the king and against the Government?" to which the answer was "No;" and then followed the question, "Did you ever hear him express himself in favor of insurrection?" and the answer was "No." That is precisely as every lawyer here has heard the question of character inquired into. The question is "What is the character of such a man for truth?" The witness says "Good." That is not putting in hearsay. That is to get a negative. In that case they were not asking for what Lord Russell said, but they were offering to prove that he did not say anything that was treasonable, not what he did say; and that was upon the question of his good character.

Let me call your attention to the other point upon which this is pressed, and that seems to be the strong point of the case, because my friend said as he opened it "this is very vital," hoping, I suppose, that by possibility he might in some way be able to fright you from your propriety. If it is a very vital matter you will pardon me for arguing it at some length.

Mr. STANBERY. Will the learned Manager allow me one moment? In regard to Mr. Hardy's case, he has fallen into an error in reading the question, which was not the one at all I was upon. He read as to general character.

Mr. Manager BUTLER. To that I say I have fallen into no such error.

Mr. STANBERY. One moment, if you please.

Mr. Manager BUTLER. No; I cannot allow you to interpolate for the purpose of stating that I did not cite correctly.

Mr. STANBERY. One moment for a correction.

Mr. Manager BUTLER. I cannot spare a moment, sir.

Mr. STANBERY. I wish to show only that the very question was put and answered under the decision of the court in that case.

Mr. Manager BUTLER. Allow me to say that I read the only question that was put and directly after it was allowed to be put——

Mr. STANBERY. I shall have to leave it to my associate.

Mr. Manager BUTLER. Certainly. If you will turn to the case you will find it, sir. I began with "Mr. Daniel Stuart examined by Mr. Erskine," and I read from there to where the attorney general said, "If this had been stated at first to be the question meant to be asked, I do not see what possible objection I could have to it." I read from where the court decided down to where the question was put and answered, and to what the attorney general said about it. Therefore I made no mistake. I am not in the habit of reading a portion and leaving out a portion of a man's speech, and then commenting upon it.

Now, Senators, what is the other point; and it is the only one I feel any trouble about? That is that some gentlemen may think that this question comes within the decision of yesterday. Yesterday we objected to the President's declaration after we said the conspiracy had culminated. It was claimed that they had a right to put in what he said when Thomas reported back to him, and the Senate decided that it should be put in; but now they propose to go a month prior to that time and they propose to go over a space of time where we offered evidence to prove the President's bad intent, and the Senate of the United States ruled it out. I allude to Cooper's case. We offered to prove that in December he put Cooper in, and what Cooper was doing in order to show the President's bad intent; and the Senate of the United States, upon the offer of the Representatives of the people of the United States, ruled that out; and now the gentlemen propose to go on and show what the President said to General Sherman.

One argument which I used to appeal to prejudice is that I stated that the President was seeking for tools. I said so; but, at the same time, I said that he never found one in General Sherman. What I mean to say, and

what will appear to you and the country, is that he was seeking for somebody by whom he might get Mr. Stanton out; some gentleman of the Army. First he tried Grant; then he wanted to get General Sherman in, so that when General Sherman, not wanting the cares of office upon him for a moment, ready to get rid of them at any time, should resign and leave, so as to get rid of it, as he doubtless would, he could then put in somebody else. He went along; he began with Grant, and he went down through Grant and down through Sherman and George H. Thomas, and down, down, until he struck Lorenzo Thomas, and then he found the man who could be put in. Now, the gentlemen propose to offer to prove that he did not find a tool in General Sherman, in order to satisfy the Senate that he did not find one in Thomas! Do these two things hold together? Does one belong to the other? Because he did not find a tool, a proper man to be made an *ad interim* Secretary, and to sit in his Cabinet as an *ad interim* Secretary, in General Sherman, does that prove that therefore he did not find a proper man in Thomas?

But, then, look at the vehicle of proof. What is the vehicle of proof? They do not propose to prove it by his acts. When they are offered I shall be willing to let them go in. Let them offer any act of the President about that time, either prior or since, and I shall not object, although the Senate ruled out an act in Cooper's case. But how do they propose to prove it? "What conversations took place between the President and you?" I agree, gentlemen of the Senate—I repeat it even after the criticisms that have been made—that you are a law unto yourselves. You have a right to receive or reject any testimony. All the common law can do for you is, that being the accumulation of the experience of thousands of years of trial, it may afford some guide to you; but you can override it. You have no right, however, to override the principles of justice and equity, and to allow the case of the people of the United States to be prejudiced by the conversations of the criminal they present at your bar, made in his own defense before the acts done, which the people complain of. That I may, I trust, without offense say; because there is a law that must govern us at any and all times, and the single question is—I did not mean to trouble the Senate with it before, and never will again on this question of conversation—what limit is there? If this is allowable you may put in his conversations with everybody; you may put in his conversations with newspaper reporters—and he is very free with those if we are to believe the newspapers. If he has a right to converse with General Sherman about this case and put that in, I do not see why he has not a right to converse with Mack, and John, and Joe, and J. B., and J. B. S., and T. R. S., and X. L. W., or whoever he may talk with, and put all that in.

I take it there is no law which makes a conversation with General Sherman any more competent than a conversation with any other man. And where are you going to stop in this trial? Go on thus and they will get the forty, the sixty, the ninety, the one hundred days—more than the forty they first asked, by simply calling everybody with whom the President has had conversation; for I believe I may say without offense that he is understood to be a great conversationalist, and on this principle they may introduce proof of all that he has said to everybody else about that time about the case; and if we may believe report, we are to have reporters and everybody else with whom the President has engaged in conversation.

Allow me to say one thing further. Gentlemen of the Senate, I said in your hearing to the learned counsel that I did not think it right for him to state what he expected to prove; and in order to prevent his stating it I said he might imagine any possible conversation. I objected to it, because he thereby gets before the court, before the court and jury, before the court and the country, a supposition that he could prove that thing. That is what it is done for; it is an argument to the prejudice; and I thought it then unprofessional, and I state that in that very book which he held in his hand in Hardy's case the attorney general of England offered to read a letter found in Hardy's possession and he began to read it. Erskine objected, and said "You must not read it until it is allowed to go in evidence." Said he, "I want the court to understand what is in the letter. It cannot be read for that purpose. Argue from its situation, argue from where it was found, argue from who signed it, what its pertinency or relevancy is; but you cannot read the letter and put it in before the court and jury until after it is ruled to be in evidence." The gentleman in his practice—I charge it upon him here—has seen hundreds of times a court stop counsel and say, "Hand it to me; hand the paper up to me; you must not read it until after it is ruled upon." I objected all that I could, but an aggregate body like this of course could not stop him if he chose to go on. Now, what was said after he had argued it? He said he wanted to show that the President had tried to get this officer of the Army to take the War Department, so that he could get Stanton out. That is what we charge, that he would take anybody, do anything, to get Stanton out. That is the very thing we charge. He would be glad to get General Sherman to aid him. He would have been glad to get General Grant. Failing in him he tries General Sherman. Failing in him he tries Major General George H. Thomas, the hero of Nashville. He failing, he is willing then even to take Lorenzo Thomas to get Stanton out. What for? The late Attorney General has said the purpose was to drive Stanton into the courts. The President knew, or his counsel knew, that Stanton could not go into the courts to get back again. There is no proper process.

Let them state the process, if they can, by which Mr. Stanton was to be reinstated in office. I think they will find it as difficult to show to the Senate such a process as they will to show that where a general law applies to the States and Territories of the United States it does not apply to the District of Columbia. It will be as difficult and fully as troublesome to show the one as the other.

Now, the simple question comes back to us, and it is the only one on which you are to rule, Are the conversations of the President with General Sherman evidence? If the conversations with him are evidence, is not every conversation that the President has had at any time with anybody evidence in this case? Where is the distinction?

Mr. EVARTS. Mr. Chief Justice and Senators, some incidental questions, partly of professional propriety, have arisen and been discussed at some length by the learned Manager. Let me read from page 165 of the record of this trial on the question of stating what is intended to be proved.

We objected to certain testimony, and then this occurred:

"Mr. Manager BUTLER. The object is to show the intent and purpose with which General Thomas went to the War Department on the morning of the 22d of February; that he went with the intent and purpose of taking possession by force; that he alleged that intent and purpose; that in consequence of that allegation Mr. BURLEIGH invited General MOORHEAD and went up to the War Office. The conversation which I expect to prove is this: after the President of the United States had appointed General Thomas and given him directions to take the War Office, and after he had made a quiet visit there on the 21st, on the evening of the 21st he told Mr. BURLEIGH that the next day he was going to take possession by force. Mr. BURLEIGH said to him——

"Mr. STANBERY. No matter about that. We object to that testimony.

"Mr. Manager BUTLER. You do not know what you object to if you do not hear what I offer.

Mr. Manager BUTLER. Read on: "We object to it," and I stopped.

Mr. EVARTS. I have read what I have read, sir.

Mr. Manager BUTLER. But stopped a little short.

Mr. EVARTS. I have read what I have read. Now, sir, we come to the impropriety of my learned associate's having drawn attention to the pertinency of what appeared in argument and in the citation of authorities upon the trial of Hardy, and whether that question was pertinent to this or not. Now, I understand the question which was there discussed related exactly to the introduction of conversations between the accused and the witness produced to prove them, antecedent to the period of the alleged treason; and it all resulted in this, on page 1096 of 24 State Trials:

"*Lord Chief Justice Eyre.* You may put the question exactly as you propose. I confess I wished by interposing to avoid all discussion, because I consider what we are doing, and whom we have at that bar, and in that box, who are suffering by every moment's unnecessary delay in such a case as this.

"*Mr. Erskine.* I am sure the jury will excuse it; I

meant to set myself right at this bar; this is a very public place.

"*Mr. Daniel Stuart* examined by *Mr. Erskine.*"

The question was put exactly as he proposed:

"Did you before the time of this conversation being held, which is imputed to Mr. Hardy, over hear from him what his objects were—whether he has at all mixed himself in that business?

"I have very often conversed with him."

And then he goes on to state the conversations.

Now, Mr. Chief Justice and Senators, I come to the merits of this question of evidence. This is a very peculiar case. Whenever evidence is sought to be made applicable to it, it is a crime of the narrowest dimensions and of the must puny proportions; it exists for its completion and for its guilt, for its enormity and for its claim to punishment, upon the delivery of a written paper by the President to General Thomas, to be communicated to the Secretary of War; and that offense, in those naked proportions, if contrary to a valid law and if done with intent which makes it criminal under that law, the Congress in the enactment which makes it indictable has permitted to be punished by a fine of six cents and no more! That is the naked dimension of the mere technical statutory offense, and that is included within the mere act of the delivery of a paper unattended by any grave public considerations of guilt and of consequence that should attend it to bring it into judgment here. When we come to evidence, I say thus puny are the proportions of the offense and thus limited the range to which the defendant is permitted to call witnesses. But when we come to the magnificence of the accusation, as found on page 75, italicised by the Managers, we will see what it is:

"We define, therefore, an impeachable high crime or misdemeanor to be *one in its nature or consequences subversive of some fundamental or essential principle of government or highly prejudicial to the public interest, and this may consist of a violation of the Constitution, of law, of an official oath, or of duty, by an act committed or omitted, or, without violating a positive law, by the abuse of discretionary powers from improper motives, or for any improper purpose.*"

Without any violation of law, an act may be done in abuse of discretionary authority with improper motives or for an improper purpose; and thus the widest possible range is opened to this inquiry on the part of the accusation, to bring within the range of guilt the President of the United States. But further, the claim is that it is a mistake, on the whole, to think that it is a question of guilt or of innocence, but, in the phrase of the learned Managers, "Is it not rather more in the nature of an inquest of office;" and then, on page 77 :

"We suggest, therefore, that we are in the presence of the Senate of the United States, convened as a constitutional tribunal, to inquire into and determine whether Andrew Johnson, because of malversation in office, is longer fit to retain the office of President of the United States."

At page 97 we come a little more definitely to matter bearing upon this question, and I beg the attention of Senators to this :

"It may be said that the President removed Mr. Stanton for the very purpose of testing the constitutionality of this law before the courts, and the question is asked, Will you condemn him as for a crime for so doing? If this plea were a true one it ought not to avail; but it is a subterfuge. We shall show you that he has taken no step to submit the question to any court, although more than a year has elapsed since the passage of the act."

Then, at page 108, we are told:

"Upon the first reading of the articles of impeachment the question might have arisen in the mind of some Senator, Why are these acts of the President only presented by the House when history informs us that others equally dangerous to the liberties of the people, if not more so and others of equal usurpation of powers, if not greater, are passed by in silence?

"To such possible inquiry we reply: that the acts set out in the first eight articles are but the culmination of a series of wrongs, malfeasances, and usurpations committed by the respondent, and therefore need to be examined in the light of his precedent and concomitant acts to grasp their scope and design."

And then common fame and current history are referred to, and confirmed by a citation of cases two hundred and forty years old from the British reports, to show that they are good ground for you to proceed upon in your verdict. Bringing, then, this to a head, the honorable Manager says:

"Who does not know that from the hour he began these his usurpations of power he everywhere denounced Congress, the legality and constitutionality of its action, and defied its legitimate powers, and, for that purpose, announced his intentions and carried out his purpose, as far as he was able, of removing every true man from office who sustained the Congress of the United States? And it is to carry out this plan of action that he claims the unlimited power of removal, for the illegal exercise of which he stands before you this day."

These are the pretensions and these the dimensions of public inculpation of the Chief Magistrate of this nation which are of such grave import. From their intent and design, from their involving the public interests and the fundamental principles of the Government, they are worthy of this great tribunal's attention, and of a judgment that deposes him from his office and calls upon the people for a reëlection. All the eleven articles are upon trial, and if this evidence be pertinent and admissible under any of them it is pertinent and admissible now. And now I should like to look first to the question of the point of time as bearing upon the admissibility of this evidence. Under the eleventh article the speech of the 18th of August, 1866, is alleged as laying the foundation of the illegal purposes that culminated in 1868, to point the criminality, that is what made the subject of accusation in that article. Proof, then, of the speeches of 1866 is made evidence under this article eleven, that imputes not criminality in making the speech, but in the action afterward pointed by the purpose of the speech. So, too, a telegram to Governor Parsons, in January, 1867, is supposed to be evidence as bearing upon the guilt completed in the year 1868.

So, too, the interview between Wood, the office-seeker, and the President of the United States, in September, 1866, is supposed to bear in evidence upon the question of intent in the consummation of the crime alleged to have been completed in 1868. I apprehend, therefore, that on the question of time this interview between General Sherman and the President of the United States, in the very matter of the public transaction of the President of the United States changing the head of the War Department, which was actually completed in February, 1868, is near enough to point intent and to show honest purpose, if these transactions, thus in evidence, are near enough to bear upon the same attributed crimes.

There remains, then, only this consideration, whether it is open to the imputation that it is a mere proof of declarations of the President concerning what his motives and objects were in reference to his subsequent act in the removal of Stanton. It certainly is not limited to that force or effect. Whenever evidence of that mere character is offered that question will arise to be disposed of; but as a part of the public action and conduct of the President of the United States in reference to this very office, and his duty and purpose in dealing with it, and on the very point, too, as to whether that object was to fill it by unwarrantable characters tending to a perversion or betrayal of the public trust, we propose to show his consultations with the Lieutenant General of the armies of the United States to induce him to take the place.

On the other question of whether his efforts are to create by violence a civil war or bloodshed, or even a breach of the peace, in the removal of the Secretary of War, we show that in this same consultation it was his desire that the Lieutenant General should take the place in order that by that means the opportunity might be given to decide the differences between the Executive and Congress as to the constitutional powers of the former by the courts of law. If the conduct of the President in relation to matters that are made the subject of inculpation, and of inculpation through motives attributed through designs supposed to be proved, cannot be made the subject of evidence, if his public action, if his public conduct, if the efforts and the means that he used in the selection of agents are not to be received to rebut the intentions or presumptions that are sought to be raised against him, well, indeed, was my learned associate justified in saying that this is a vital question. Vital in the interests of justice, I mean, rather than vital to any important considerations of the cause. Vital undoubtedly on the merest principles of common justice, that when the Chief Magistrate of the nation is brought under inculpation from a series of charges of this complexion and of this comprehension, and when the motives are assigned,

when the presumptions and innuendoes are alleged which I have treated of, that he shall not be permitted, in the presence of this great council sitting upon his case and doing justice to him as an individual, but more, sitting in this case and doing justice in respect to his office of President of the United States, doing justice to the great public questions proposed to be affected by your judgment—whether the chosen head of the nation shall be deposed from authority by the action of this court composed of a branch of the Congress, and the people resorted to again through the mode of election for a new Chief Magistrate. I apprehend that this learned court of lawyers and laymen will not permit this "fast and loose" game of limited crime for purposes of proof and unlimited crime for purposes of accusation, that they will not permit this enlargement and contraction, phrases sometimes replaced by a more definite and shorter Saxon description.

Mr. SPRAGUE, (at twenty minutes before three o'clock.) I move that the Senate take a recess for fifteen minutes.

The motion was agreed to; and the Chief Justice resumed the chair at five minutes to three o'clock.

The CHIEF JUSTICE. Senators will please to give their attention. The counsel for the President will proceed. [After a pause.] Do the counsel for the President desire to be heard further?

Mr. CURTIS. No, Mr. Chief Justice.

Mr. Manager WILSON. Mr. President, I shall claim the attention of the Senate but for a few minutes. My principal purpose is to get before the minds of Senators the truth in the Hardy case as it fell from the lips of the chief justice. when he passed upon the question which had been propounded by Mr. Erskine and objected to by the attorney general. The ruling is in these words:

"*Lord Chief Justice Eyre.* Mr. Erskine, I do not know whether you can be content to acquiesce in the opinion that we are inclined to form upon the subject, in which we go a certain way with you. Nothing is so clear as that all declarations which apply to facts, and even apply to the particular case that is charged, though the intent should make a part of that charge, are evidence against a prisoner and are not evidence for him, because the presumption upon which declarations are evidence is, that no man would declare anything against himself unless it were true; but every man, if he was in a difficulty, or in the view to any difficulty, would make declarations for himself. Those declarations, if offered as evidence, would be offered, therefore, upon no ground which entitled them to credit. That is the general rule. But if the question be—as I really think it is in this case, which is my reason now for interposing—if the question be, what was the political speculative opinion which this man entertained touching a reform of Parliament, I believe we all think that opinion may very well be learned and discovered by the conversations which he has held at any time, or in any place.

"*Mr. Erskine.* Just so, that is my question; only that I may not get into another debate, I beg your lordship will hear me a few words.

"*Lord Chief Justice Eyre.* I think I have already anticipated a misapprehension of what I am now stating, by saying that if the declaration was meant to apply to a disavowal of the particular charge made against this man that declaration could not be received: as, for instance, if he had said to some friend of his, When I planned this convention I did not mean to use this convention to destroy the king and his Government, but I did mean to get, by means of this convention, the Duke of Richmond's plan of reform—that would fall within the rule I first laid down; that would be a declaration, which being for him, he could not be admitted to make, though the law will allow a contrary declaration to have been given in evidence. Now, if you take it so, I believe there is no difficulty."

And upon that ruling the question was changed as read by my associate Manager, and correctly read by him, and all that followed this ruling of the chief justice and the subsequent discussion was read by my associate Manager. The lord chief justice further said:

"You may put the question exactly as you propose."

That is after discussion had occurred subsequent to the ruling of the chief justice to which I have referred, and in which a change in the character of the original question was disclosed.

"I confess I wished by interposing to avoid all discussion, because I consider what we are doing, and whom we have at that bar, and in that box, who are suffering by every moment's unnecessary delay in such a cause as this.

"Mr. Erskine. I am sure the jury will excuse it; I meant to set myself right at this bar; this is a very public place."

Then follows the question—

"Mr. Daniel Stuart examined by Mr. Erskine.

"Did you before the time of this convention being held, which is imputed to Mr. Hardy, ever hear from him what his objects were, whether he has at all mixed himself in that business?

"I have very often conversed with him, as I mentioned before, about his plan of reform; he always adhered to the Duke of Richmond's plan."

And which declaration——

Mr. FESSENDEN. Is that the answer?

Mr. Manager WILSON. That is the answer. And which declaration came within the exception to the rule laid down by the chief justice. The final question was then put:

"From all that you have seen of him, what is his character for sincerity and truth?

"I have every reason to believe him to be a very sincere, simple, honest man."

To which the attorney general said:

"If this had been stated at first to the question meant to be asked I do not see what possible objection I could have to it."

Mr. FESSENDEN. Does not that remark apply to both questions?

Mr. Manager WILSON. That remark applies to the last question. The remark was made after the last question was put; but, as I understand it, the two questions are substantially the same, and are connected, and the remark of the attorney general applied to both, as the first was but the basis, the inducement to the last.

Mr. FESSENDEN. They were put consecutively?

Mr. Manager BUTLER. Nothing between. One was inducement to the other.

Mr. Manager WILSON. Now, what is the question which has been propounded by the counsel on the part of the President to General Sherman? It is this:

"In that interview what conversation took place between the President and you in regard to the removal of Mr. Stanton?"

Now, I contend that that calls for just such declarations on the part of the President as fall within the rule laid down by the chief justice in the Hardy case, and, therefore, must be excluded. If this conversation can be admitted, where are we to stop? Who may not be put upon the witness-stand and asked for conversations had between him and the President, and at any time since the President entered upon the duties of the presidential office, to show the general intent and drift of his mind and conduct during the whole period of his official existence? And if this be competent and may be introduced, may it not be followed by an attempt to introduce conversations occurring between the President, his Cabinet, and General Grant, by way of inducing this Senate, under pretense of merely defending the respondent. to try a question of veracity between the General of the Army and the President of the United States? The interview out of which that question sprung occurred about the same time that this one did; and I suppose the next offer will be to put in the conversation between the President, his several Secretaries, Cabinet officers, and the General of the Army, in order that the preponderance of testimony (considered numerically, at least,) submitted here in this trial may weigh down the General of the Army, he being no party concerned in this proceeding. Such an offer may meet us at the next step, because it was a conversation which transpired about that time.

Mr. Manager BUTLER. Only the day before.

Mr. Manager WILSON. Yes; only the day before. We certainly must insist upon the well known and long established rule of evidence being applied to this particular objection, for the purpose of ending now and forever, so far as this case is concerned, these attempts to put in evidence the declarations of the President, made, it may be, for the purpose of meeting an impeachment by such weapons of defense.

It is offered to be proved now, as the counsel inform us, that the President told General Sherman that he desired him to accept an appointment of Secretary for the Department of War to the end that Mr. Stanton might be driven to the courts of law for the purpose of testing his title to that office; and, inasmuch as the counsel have referred to the opening argument of my associate Manager, and seem to delight in reading therefrom, let me read a brief paragraph or two from that opening applying to this pretended purpose of the President of driving the Secretary of War to the courts to test his title. On that occasion the Manager said:

"The President knew, or ought to have known,

his official adviser, who now appears as his counsel, could and did tell him, doubtless, that he alone, as Attorney General, could file an information in the nature of a *quo warranto* to determine this question of the validity of the law.

"Mr. Stanton, if ejected from office, was without remedy, because a series of decisions has settled the law to be that an ejected officer cannot reinstate himself either by *quo warranto, mandamus,* or other appropriate remedy in the courts."

The counsel refrain from noticing this answer to the President's assertion so often made that he was only endeavoring to manufacture a lawsuit and get a case into the courts; and I am led to believe that the purpose was not the harmless one of getting the Lieutenant General of the Army into the position of Secretary of War, by way of enabling the respondent to secure a judicial decision of the contested question to which the President and Secretary Stanton were parties, but for the purpose of getting possession, as we have charged, of that Department for his, the respondent's, own purposes, and putting Mr. Stanton in a position where he could not get into court and secure a judgment upon his title to that office—not, I beg counsel to remember, not that we charge that the President believed or expected that he could make a tool of General Sherman; but that he might oust Mr. Stanton from the actual possession of his office by getting General Sherman to accept it, and thus putting Stanton in a position where he could not have his claim to the office tested; and further expecting and believing, doubtless, that General Sherman would not long desire to occupy the position; and when he might ask to be relieved from the thankless position, to escape from the never-ending political contests of this city, then the Adjutant General of the Army, or some other person equally pliant, could be put into the place vacated by General Sherman. The President did not succeed in that effort. General Sherman declined the position tendered, and, as has been said, the respondent wandered on down with his offer of place and power until he came to Adjutant General Thomas. Then he found the person who was willing to undertake this work, who was willing to use force, as he declared, to get possession of that office, and obey the orders of the President; and now, with that proof of the President's criminal acts and intents in and before the Senate, it is proposed by his counsel to make apparent his innocence and effectuate his defense by giving in evidence his own declarations at a time not embraced in any of the former rulings of the Senate. If a case can be defended in this way, no civil officer of the United States can ever be convicted on impeachment; and if the same rule should apply in the courts of justice, no criminal will ever be convicted for any offense therein. If the officer or the criminal may make his own defense by his own declarations, he will always have one which will meet his case and work his acquittal.

I do not desire longer to detain the Senate by prolonging this discussion. I am willing to

C. I.—21.

let this objection rest upon the authority produced by the learned counsel for the President, for under it, and by force of it, the testimony now offered must be excluded.

The CHIEF JUSTICE. Senators, the Chief Justice has expressed the opinion that the question now proposed is admissible within the vote of the Senate of yesterday. He will state briefly the grounds of that opinion. The question yesterday had reference to a conversation between the President and General Thomas after the note addressed to Mr. Stanton was written and delivered, and the Senate held it admissible. The question to-day has reference to a conversation relating to the same subject-matter, between the President and General Sherman, which occurred before the note of removal was written and delivered. Both questions were asked for the purpose of proving the intent of the President in the attempt to remove Mr. Stanton. The Chief Justice thinks that proof of a conversation shortly before a transaction is better evidence of the intent of an actor in it than proof of a conversation shortly after the transaction. The Secretary will call the roll.

Mr. DRAKE. Will the Chief Justice be so kind as to state the question submitted to the Senate and about to be voted on?

The CHIEF JUSTICE. The Secretary will read the question.

The Secretary read as follows:

Question. In that interview what conversation took place between the President and you in regard to the removal of Mr. Stanton?

The CHIEF JUSTICE. Upon this question the yeas and nays have been demanded, and have been ordered. Senators, you who are of opinion that the question is admissible will, as your names are called, answer yea; those of the contrary, nay.

The question being taken by yeas and nays, resulted—yeas 23, nays 28; as follows:

YEAS—Messrs. Anthony, Bayard, Buckalew, Cole, Davis, Dixon, Doolittle, Fessenden, Fowler, Grimes, Hendricks, Johnson, McCreery, Morgan, Norton, Patterson of Tennessee, Ross, Sprague, Sumner, Trumbull, Van Winkle, Vickers, and Willey—23.

NAYS—Messrs. Cameron, Cattell, Chandler, Conkling, Conness, Corbett, Cragin, Drake, Edmunds, Ferry, Frelinghuysen, Harlan, Henderson, Howard, Morrill of Maine, Morrill of Vermont, Morton, Nye, Patterson of New Hampshire, Pomeroy, Ramsey, Sherman, Stewart, Thayer, Tipton, Williams, Wilson, and Yates—28.

NOT VOTING—Messrs. Howe, Saulsbury, and Wade—3.

So the question was ruled to be inadmissible.

Mr. STANBERY, (to the witness.) General Sherman, in any of the conversations of the President while you were here, what was said about the department of the Atlantic?

Mr. Manager BUTLER. Stay a moment. I submit that that falls within the ruling just made. They cannot put in these declarations.

The CHIEF JUSTICE. The counsel will reduce his question to writing.

Mr. STANBERY. I will vary the question.

The question was reduced to writing and sent to the desk.

The CHIEF JUSTICE. The Secretary will read the question:

The Secretary read it, as follows:

What do you know about the creation of the department of the Atlantic?

Mr. Manager BUTLER. We have no objection to what General Sherman knows about the creation of the department of the Atlantic, provided he speaks of knowledge and not from the declarations of the President. All orders, papers, his own knowledge, if he has any, if it does not come from declarations, we do not object to. Although we do not see how this is in issue, if the presiding officer will instruct the witness, as in the other case, to separate knowledge from hearsay, we shall make no objection. I have no doubt the general knows the distinction himself. I desire to ask do these gentlemen ask for the President's declarations under this?

The CHIEF JUSTICE. Do the counsel for the President ask for the President's declarations?

Mr. STANBERY. I may misunderstand the honorable Managers, but I understood them to claim that the President created the department of the Atlantic as a part of his unlawful intent by military force to oust Congress, or something of that kind. Do I understand the gentleman to abandon all claim in regard to the department of the Atlantic?

Mr. Manager BUTLER. I am not on the stand, Mr. President. When I am I will answer questions to the best of my ability. The presiding officer asked the learned counsel a question. If the presiding officer does not want an answer, that is another matter. The question put was, do you ask for the President's declarations, and thereupon the counsel undertakes to quiz me.

The CHIEF JUSTICE. The counsel for the President will be good enough to state whether in this question they include statements made by the President.

Mr. STANBERY. Not merely that; what we expect to prove is in what manner the department of the Atlantic was created; who defined the bounds of the department of the Atlantic; what was the purpose for which the department was arranged.

The CHIEF JUSTICE. Is this conversation subsequent to the time of the removal or attempted removal?

Mr. STANBERY. I do not know whether it was subsequent. It was about the time——

Mr. EVARTS. Prior.

Mr. STANBERY. Prior to the time, I believe.

The CHIEF JUSTICE. The Chief Justice will submit the question to the Senate.

Mr. Manager BUTLER. I do not see that there is any question. I stated——

The CHIEF JUSTICE. The Secretary will read the question.

The Secretary read it, as follows:

What do you know about the creation of the department of the Atlantic?

Mr. Manager BUTLER. I suppose a department can only be created by an order.

The CHIEF JUSTICE. Does the honorable Manager object to the question as put?

Mr. Manager BUTLER. I object to the question altogether; but, if it is to be put at all, I want it expressly, carefully guarded, not to put in any declarations or any information learned from the President.

The CHIEF JUSTICE. The Chief Justice will submit the question to the Senate, whether the question shall be put.

The question being put, it was determined in the negative. So the Senate ruled the question was inadmissible.

Mr. STANBERY, (to the witness.) I will ask you this question, General Sherman: did the President make any application to you respecting the acceptance of the duties of Secretary of War *ad interim?* Did he make a proposition to you—not a declaration—but did he make an offer to you?

Mr. Manager BUTLER. Have you the question in writing?

Mr. STANBERY. Yes, sir, [handing it to Mr. Manager BUTLER.] Now, we propose to prove an act, not a declaration.

Mr. Manager BUTLER. I am instructed, Mr. President, to object to this, because an application cannot be made without being either in writing or in conversation, and then either would be the written or oral declaration of the President, and it is entirely immaterial to this issue.

Mr. EVARTS. Mr. Chief Justice and Senators, the ground, as we understand it, upon which the offer, in the form and to the extent in which our question which was overruled sought to put it, was overruled, was because it proposed to put in evidence declarations of the President as if statements of what he was to do or what he had done. We offer this present evidence as executive action of the President at the time and in the direct form of a proposed devolution of office then presently upon General Sherman.

Mr. Manager BUTLER. To that we simply say this is not the way to prove executive action. Anything done by the Executive we do not object to. Applications made in a closet cannot be put in, whether in the form of declarations or otherwise.

Mr. STANBERY. Of course, Mr. Chief Justice and Senators, if we offer to prove the actual appointment of General Sherman to be Secretary of War *ad interim,* we must produce the paper, the executive order. That is not what we are about to offer now, for the proffer was not accepted. What we offer now is, not a declaration, but an act; a thing proposed by the President to General Sherman, unconnected, if you please, with any declaration of any intention. Let the act speak for itself.

Mr. Manager BUTLER. Verbal or written?

Mr. STANBERY. Verbal. Would it have been any better if it had been in writing by a note? Is it a question under the statute of frauds that you must have it in writing, a thing that can only be made in writing, and is not good when made by parol? What we are upon now we have not discussed at all. It is an act; a thing proposed; an office tendered to a party, unaccompanied by any declaration at all. "General Sherman, will you take the position of Secretary of War *ad interim?*" Is not that an act? Is that a declaration merely of intention? Is not that the offer of the office? We claim that it is; and we say, therefore, it does not come within the question of declarations at all. He is not declaring anything about it; he is not saying what his intention is; but he is doing an act. "Will you take this office, General? I offer it to you." That is the question. Let us have that act in, and then let it speak for itself, whether it makes for us or makes against us.

Mr. Manager BUTLER. I propose only to claim my right to close the discussion just to call the attention of the Senate to this. Suppose he did offer it, what does that prove? Suppose he did not offer it, what does that prove? If you mean to deal fairly with the Senate, and not get in a conversation under the guise of putting in an act, what does it prove? It would rather prove in our favor that he was trying to get General Sherman to take this office in order to get out Stanton. And if it was the mere act I should not object perhaps. The difficulty is, while it is not within the statute of frauds, I think it is within everything but the statute. I think it is an attempt under the guise of an act to get in a conversation.

The CHIEF JUSTICE. The Secretary will read the question.

The Secretary read as follows:

Did the President make any application to you respecting your acceptance of the duties of Secretary of War *ad interim?*

The CHIEF JUSTICE. The Chief Justice will put the question to the Senate.

The question being put was determined in the affirmative. So the Senate decided the question to be admissible.

By Mr. STANBERY.

Question. Answer the question, if you please, General Sherman?

The WITNESS, (to the Secretary.) Will you read it again, sir?

The Secretary read the question, as follows:

Did the President make any application to you respecting your acceptance of the duties of Secretary of War *ad interim?*

Answer. The President tendered me the office of Secretary of War *ad interim* on two occasions; the first was on the afternoon of January 25 and the second on Thursday, the 30th of January.

Question. Mr. Stanton was then in office, was he?

Answer. Mr. Stanton was then in office as now.

Question. Was any one else present?

Answer. I think not, sir. Mr. Moore may have been called in to show some papers, but I think was not present when the President made me this tender. To both of them—shall I go on?

Mr. STANBERY. There is no objection.

Answer. To both of them I replied in writing. My answer to the first is dated on the 27th of January; my answer to the second is dated on the 31st of January.

Question. Did you receive any communication in writing from the President on that subject?

Answer. I did not.

Question. What was the date of your first letter?

Answer. The 27th.

Question. Is that the letter to the President or to General Grant?

Answer. According to my notes, the letter to the President; and I think my notes are correct, for I took them from my record-book this morning. The second letter I know to be dated the 31st, also taken from the same record-book.

Question. Now, referring to the time when the offer was first made to you by the President, did anything further take place between you in reference to that matter. Besides the tender by him and the acceptance or non-acceptance by you, what took place concomitant with that act?

Mr. Manager BUTLER. I suppose you mean to except the answer?

Mr. STANBERY. I ask in reference to that very thing as concomitant with the act.

Mr. Manager BUTLER. We object, for the very plain reason that this is now getting in the conversations again.

Mr. STANBERY. You have got the act.

Mr. Manager BUTLER. Ah, yes, Senators; I call your attention to the manner in which this case is tried. I warned you that if you let in the act they would attempt to get in the declaration under it. That was the opening wedge. Now, they say they have got in the act and they are going for the declaration, to see if by chance they cannot get around your ruling.

Mr. EVARTS. What is your proposition now to the Senators?

Mr. Manager BUTLER. My proposition is, objecting to this evidence, that the evidence is incompetent and is based upon first getting in an act which proved nothing and looked to be immaterial, so that it was quite liberal for Senators to vote it in, but that liberality is taken advantage of to endeavor to get by the ruling of the Senate and put in declarations which the Senate has ruled out.

Mr. EVARTS. The tender of the War

Office by the Chief Executive of the United States to a general in the position of General Sherman is an executive act, and as such has been admitted in evidence by this court. Like every other act thus admitted in evidence as an act, it is competent to attend it by whatever was expressed from one to the other in the course of that act to the termination of it. And on that proposition the learned Manager shakes his finger of warning at the Senators of the United States against the malpractices of the counsel for the President. Now, Senators, if there be anything clear, anything plain in the law of evidence, without which truth is shut out, the form and features of the fact permitted to be proved excluded, it is this rule that the spoken act is a part of the attending qualifying trait and character of the act itself.

Mr. Manager BUTLER. To that I answer, Senators, that here was an immaterial act—mark, an act wholly immaterial. The only qualification that could be put in would be the answer, perhaps, of General Sherman; that is not offered; but the offer is to put in an incompetent conversation as explaining an immaterial act. What is the proposition put forward here? It is that the Executive can make offers of office to any man in the country, general or other, and then put in the fact that he made the offer of the office, and, as illustrative of that fact, put in everything he said about it. That is the proposition. I did not use the word "malpractice" about that proposition; but it is a most remarkable proposition. He makes an act himself, insists upon putting it in, and then says, "I have got in the act; now you must let me explain it." He could have saved himself the explanation by keeping the act out. But that is the proposition; and I undertake—no; it is not worthy of words or asseveration. A criminal on trial puts in his act, presses it in, and then says, "I have got the act in; now I must show what I said about it in order to explain that act." It argues itself.

The CHIEF JUSTICE. The counsel will reduce their question to writing.

The counsel for the respondent reduced the question to writing and presented it to Mr. Manager BUTLER.

Mr. Manager BUTLER, having read the question, passed it up to the Secretary's desk, saying: I assume that it asks for conversations.

The CHIEF JUSTICE. The Secretary will read the question.

The Secretary read the question, as follows:

At the first interview at which the tender of the duties of the Secretary of War *ad interim* was made to you by the President did anything further pass between you and the President in reference to the tender or your acceptance of it?

Mr. Manager BUTLER. The President will ask the counsel whether they expect, under that, to put in the declarations of the President or the conversations of the President?

The CHIEF JUSTICE. The Chief Justice will submit the question to the Senate as it is proposed.

Mr. DRAKE. On that question I ask for the yeas and nays.

The yeas and nays were ordered.

Mr. ANTHONY. Let the question be read.

The Secretary again read the question.

The question being taken by yeas and nays, resulted—yeas 23, nays 29; as follows:

YEAS—Messrs. Anthony, Bayard, Buckalew, Cole, Davis, Dixon, Doolittle, Fessenden, Fowler, Grimes, Hendricks, Johnson, McCreery, Morgan, Norton, Patterson of Tennessee, Ross, Sprague, Sumner, Trumbull, Van Winkle, Vickers, and Willey—23.

NAYS—Messrs. Cameron, Cattell, Chandler, Conkling, Conness, Corbett, Cragin, Drake, Edmunds, Ferry, Frelinghuysen, Harlan, Henderson, Howard, Howe, Morrill of Maine, Morrill of Vermont, Morton, Nye, Patterson of New Hampshire, Pomeroy, Ramsey, Sherman, Stewart, Thayer, Tipton, Williams, Wilson, and Yates—29.

NOT VOTING—Messrs. Saulsbury and Wade—2.

So the Senate decided the question to be inadmissible.

By Mr. STANBERY:

Question. Now, the second interview, General Sherman; when did you say that was?

Answer. The second interview, wherein he offered me that appointment, was on the 30th of January.

Question. In that interview did he again make an offer to you to be Secretary of War *ad interim*?

Answer. Very distinctly, sir.

Question. At that interview was anything said in explanation of that offer?

Mr. Manager BINGHAM and Mr. Manager BUTLER. We object.

Mr. EVARTS. The same ruling, of course.

Mr. STANBERY. I only want it to be ruled out, if you object to it. Let us have the ruling upon it.

Mr. Manager BUTLER. I would ask the presiding officer whether that does not exactly fall within the ruling just made?

Mr. EVARTS. We understand that it does, Mr. BUTLER, and have so stated to the Chair. We have asked our question, and we take the ruling of the court against it.

By Mr. STANBERY:

Question. In these conversations did the President state to you that his object was to take the question before the courts?

Mr. Manager BINGHAM and Mr. Manager BUTLER. Stop a moment. We object to that.

The CHIEF JUSTICE. The counsel will please reduce their question to writing.

Mr. Manager BUTLER. I suppose they do not propose——

Mr. STANBERY. We have a right to offer it.

Mr. Manager BINGHAM. We have a right to object to it.

Mr. STANBERY. That we understand perfectly. We may state what we propose to prove.

Mr. Manager BUTLER. But then, Mr.

President, the courts sometimes say, after they have ruled a question, that it is not within the proprieties of the trial to offer the same thing over and over again. It is sometimes done in a court for the purpose of taking a bill of exceptions, or a writ of error on the rulings. If the counsel say that that is the purpose here, we shall not object, because they ought to preserve their rights in all forms. But supposing this to be the court of last resort, if court at all, there can be no proper occasion over and over for throwing themselves against the rulings.

Mr. STANBERY. I do not understand that the ruling was upon this specific question. It was the general question, what was said, that was ruled out those times. I want to make the specific question now to indicate what we desire to prove. I now put the specific question whether in any of those interviews the President said what was his intention in regard to making the question at law? I have not put that question before.

Mr. Manager BUTLER. And, Mr. President, my remarks were in reply to the distinct admission of the counsel that the question came within the ruling and that he expected it to be ruled out, but still intended to make the offer.

Mr. EVARTS. That was the previous question.

Mr. Manager BUTLER. Oh, no; this last one.

Mr. EVARTS. No; you are mistaken about it. Besides, Mr. Chief Justice and Senators, although there is no review by any court of your determinations of interlocutory or of final questions, yet, as the learned Managers know, it is entirely competent to bring to the notice of the court that is to pass upon the question in the final judgment the evidence that is supposed to be admissible, in order that it may be, as it is always if properly originated, a matter of argument, that the case is to be disposed of on the ground as if it were admitted; and that we have a right to do, and not be limited to abstractions in the determination of these questions.

The CHIEF JUSTICE. The counsel for the President will please reduce their question to writing.

Mr. EVARTS. And the difference we make between this specific question and the general question which has been excluded, and in regard to which we do not propose to trouble the Senate further, is, that when a general conversation cannot be admitted, if the objection be applicable, and it has been successfully made here, then to exclude a conclusion on a definite point the specific question may be put.

The CHIEF JUSTICE. The counsel will reduce their question to writing.

The question being reduced to writing, it was handed by the counsel for the respondent to Mr. Manager BUTLER, and after inspection, handed by him to the Secretary.

Mr. Manager BUTLER. I object, Mr. President, to the question, both as leading in form, outrageously so, and incompetent under the previous rulings.

The CHIEF JUSTICE. The Secretary will read the question.

The Secretary read the question as reduced to writing, as follows:

In either of these conversations did the President say to you that his object in appointing you was that he might thus get the question of Mr. Stanton's right to the office before the Supreme Court?

The CHIEF JUSTICE. Senators, you who are of opinion that the question just read——

Mr. HOWARD. I ask for the yeas and nays on that question.

The yeas and nays were ordered.

The CHIEF JUSTICE. Senators, you who are of opinion that the question just read is admissible will, as your names are called, answer yea. Those of the contrary opinion will answer nay. The Secretary will call the roll.

Mr. Manager BUTLER. Let the question be again read.

The CHIEF JUSTICE. The Secretary will read the question again.

The Secretary read as follows:

In either of these conversations did the President say to you that his object in appointing you was that he might thus get the question of Mr. Stanton's right to the office before the Supreme Court?

Mr. DOOLITTLE. Mr. Chief Justice, I do not know that I understood the ground of objection of the Managers.

Mr. Manager BUTLER. As outrageously leading and utterly incompetent and entirely against the ruling of the Senate.

The CHIEF JUSTICE. The Secretary will call the roll.

The Secretary proceeded with and concluded the calling of the roll.

Mr. JOHNSON, (who had not voted.) I ask for the reading of the question. I did not hear it distinctly, and that was the reason I declined to vote.

The CHIEF JUSTICE. The Secretary will read the question.

The Secretary read as follows:

In either of these conversations did the President say to you——

Mr. JOHNSON. That will do, sir. I vote in the negative.

Mr. DAVIS, (who had first voted in the affirmative.) Mr. Chief Justice, the question is leading. I vote in the negative.

The result was announced—yeas 7, nays 44; as follows:

YEAS—Messrs. Anthony, Bayard, Fowler, McCreery, Patterson of Tennessee, Ross, and Vickers—7.

NAYS—Messrs. Buckalew, Cameron, Cattell, Chandler, Cole, Conkling, Conness, Corbett, Cragin, Davis, Dixon, Doolittle, Drake, Edmunds, Ferry, Fessenden, Frelinghuysen, Grimes, Harlan, Henderson, Hendricks, Howard, Howe, Johnson, Morgan, Morrill of Maine, Morrill of Vermont, Morton, Norton, Nye, Patterson of New Hampshire, Pomeroy, Ramsey, Sherman, Sprague, Stewart, Thayer, Tipton,

Trumbull, Van Winkle, Willey, Williams, Wilson, and Yates—44.

NOT VOTING—Messrs. Saulsbury, Sumner, and Wade—3.

So the question was decided to be inadmissible.

Mr. STANBERY. Mr. Chief Justice and Senators, this question undoubtedly has been overruled upon matter of form at least. I now propose to change the form of it. I do not want to be thrown out upon a mere technicality. I therefore change it.

Mr. Manager BUTLER. Let me see it.

Mr. STANBERY handed the question as written by him to Mr. Manager BUTLER.

Mr. Manager BUTLER. Mr. President and Senators, the question as presented to me is:

Was anything said at that conversation by the President as to any purpose of getting the question of Mr. Stanton's right to the office before the courts?

Now, Mr. President and Senators, this is the last question precisely, without the leading part of it, I so understand. Now, then, I understand it to be a very well settled rule of trials that where a counsel deliberately puts a question leading in form, and has it passed upon, he cannot afterward withdraw the leading part and put the same question without it. Sometimes this rule has been relaxed in favor of very young counsel, [laughter,] who did not know what a leading question was, but not otherwise. I have seen very young men make mistakes by accident, and I have known the courts to let them up and say, "We will not hold the rule, if you made an accident."

Mr. President, I call your and the Senate's attention to the fact that I three times over objected to the last question as being outrageously leading, and I did it so that there should be no mistake; yet the counsel for the President went on and insisted not only on not withdrawing it, but on putting the Senate to the delay of having the yeas and nays taken. If I had not called their attention to it I agree that perhaps the rule might not be enforced; but I called their attention to it. They are five gentlemen of the oldest men in the profession, to whom this rule was well known. They chose to submit to the Senate a tentative question, and now they propose to try that over again, keeping you voting on forms of questions until your patience is wearied out. That is what they may do.

I had the honor to say to the Senate a little while ago that all the rules of evidence are founded upon good sense, and this rule is founded on good sense. It would do no harm in the case of this witness; but the rule is founded on this proposition: that counsel shall not put a leading question to a witness, and thus instruct him what they want him to say, and then have it overruled and withdraw it, and put the same question in substance, because you could always instruct a witness in that way. Of course, that was not meant here, because I assume it would do no harm in any form, and the counsel would not do it; but I think the Senate

should hold itself not to be played with in this way. If you choose to sit here and have the yeas and nays called, I can sit here as long as anybody.

Mr. STANBERY. Mr. Chief Justice, this is quite too serious a business that we are engaged in, and the responsibility is too great, the issues are too important, to descend to the sort of controversy that would be introduced here. The gentleman says I am an old lawyer, long at the bar. I hope I never have disgraced the position. I hope I am not in the habit of making factious opposition before any court, high or low, especially not before this body, which has treated us with so much courtesy.

But the learned Manager intimates here that I have deliberately put a leading question, resorting to the low tactics of an Old Bailey court, for the purpose of getting time and making factious opposition. I scorn any such imputation.

Leading questions! Undoubtedly the previous question was leading; but was it intended to be leading, intended to draw General Sherman out to say something that otherwise would not be said? The learned Manager says Oh no, it was not intended, so far as General Sherman is concerned, to be a leading question; but so far as the counsel is concerned the purpose was to put it in that form that the counsel might have another opportunity of putting it in a legal form, thus insinuating that deliberately that question was manufactured in a leading form, knowing that it would be rejected on account of form, for the purpose of getting ten or fifteen minutes of time in order to put it in a proper form!

Leading questions! Will the honorable Manager please to read over the record of this case and see hundreds of leading questions put by him again and again. We got tired of objecting to them. I must be permitted to disclaim any such intention as this.

This is a matter of great importance to us. We deem it to be so. The interests of our client are in our hands, to defend him the best way we can. We wish it to appear what we desire to prove and what we are anxious to prove. We do not want to make any more argument upon it. We submit it to the judgment of the Senate. We put the question as to the matter which we seek to prove, that it may appear what it is that we seek to prove, to use every effort in our power, not factiously but honorably, properly, not to argue again and again the same point, but simply to have the opportunity of having our questions put before the Senate and decided.

The CHIEF JUSTICE. The Secretary will read the question.

The Secretary read as follows:

Was anything said at that conversation by the President as to any purpose of getting the question of Mr. Stanton's right to the office before the courts?

Mr. EVARTS. We desire to alter the first phrase by striking out the words "at that conversation," and inserting " at either of these interviews," so as to cover the same ground as before.

The CHIEF JUSTICE. The question will be so modified. The Secretary will read the question as modified.

The Secretary read as follows:

Was anything said at either of those interviews by the President as to any purpose of getting the question of Mr. Stanton's right to the office before the courts?

The CHIEF JUSTICE put the question on the admissibility of this question; and it was determined in the negative.

Mr. HENDERSON. I desire to ask a question of the witness, and I send it to the desk in writing.

The CHIEF JUSTICE. The Secretary will read the question proposed by the Senator from Missouri.

The Secretary read as follows:

Did the President, in tendering you the appointment of Secretary of War *ad interim*, express the object or purpose of so doing?

Mr. Manager BINGHAM. Mr. President, we must object to that question, as being within the ruling already settled by the court, and submit it to the Senate. It is both leading and incompetent.

The CHIEF JUSTICE. The Chief Justice will submit the question to the Senate. Senators, you who are of the opinion that the question proposed by the Senator from Missouri——

Messrs. DOOLITTLE and THAYER called for the yeas and nays; and they were ordered.

Mr. DRAKE. I ask for the reading of the question again.

The Secretary again read the question propounded by Mr. HENDERSON.

Mr. DOOLITTLE. Mr. Chief Justice, I have risen for the purpose of moving that the Senate go into consultation on this important question; but, as I see that there may not be time to-night to go into consultation, I move that the court adjourn until Monday at twelve o'clock. ["No!" "No!"]

The CHIEF JUSTICE. The question is on the motion of the Senator from Wisconsin, that the Senate, sitting as a court of impeachment, adjourn until Monday at twelve o'clock.

The motion was not agreed to.

The CHIEF JUSTICE. The question recurs on the admissibility of the question proposed by the Senator from Missouri, [Mr. HENDERSON.] Senators, you who are of opinion that the question is admissible and should be put to the witness will, as your names are called, answer yea; those of the contrary opinion will answer nay. The Secretary will call the roll.

The question being taken by yeas and nays, resulted—yeas 25, nays 27; as follows:

YEAS—Messrs. Anthony, Bayard, Buckalew, Davis, Dixon, Doolittle, Fessenden, Fowler, Grimes, Henderson, Hendricks, Johnson, McCreery, Morrill of Maine, Morton, Norton, Patterson of Tennessee, Ross, Sherman, Sprague, Sumner, Trumbull, Van Winkle, Vickers, and Willey—25.

NAYS—Messrs. Cameron, Cattell, Chandler, Cole, Conkling, Conness, Corbett, Cragin, Drake, Edmunds, Ferry, Frelinghuysen, Harlan, Howard, Howe, Morgan, Morrill of Vermont, Nye, Patterson of New Hampshire, Pomeroy, Ramsey, Stewart, Thayer, Tipton, Williams, Wilson, and Yates—27.

NOT VOTING—Messrs. Saulsbury and Wade—2.

So the question proposed by Mr. HENDERSON was decided to be inadmissible.

Mr. TRUMBULL, (at half-past four o'clock.) I move that the Senate, sitting as a court of impeachment, adjourn until Monday at twelve o'clock.

Mr. STEWART, Mr. SUMNER, and Mr. THAYER called for the yeas and nays, and they were ordered; and being taken, resulted—yeas 25, nays 27; as follows:

YEAS—Messrs. Bayard, Buckalew, Cameron, Cattell, Corbett, Davis, Dixon, Doolittle, Fessenden, Fowler, Frelinghuysen, Grimes, Henderson, Hendricks, Howe, Johnson, McCreery, Morton, Norton, Patterson of Tennessee, Ramsey, Sprague, Trumbull, Van Winkle, and Vickers—25.

NAYS—Messrs. Anthony, Chandler, Cole, Conkling, Conness, Cragin, Drake, Edmunds, Ferry, Harlan, Howard, Morgan, Morrill of Maine, Morrill of Vermont, Nye, Patterson of New Hampshire, Pomeroy, Ross, Sherman, Stewart, Sumner, Thayer, Tipton, Willey, Williams, Wilson, and Yates—27.

NOT VOTING—Messrs. Saulsbury and Wade—2.

So the Senate refused to adjourn.

Mr. Manager BUTLER, (to the counsel for the respondent.) Have you anything further with this witness, gentlemen?

Mr. STANBERY. I propose to put a question, which I will send to the Managers.

The question was sent in writing to Mr. Manager BUTLER.

Mr. Manager BUTLER. The question proposed is:

At either of those interviews was anything said in reference to the use of threats, intimidation, or force to get possession of the War Office, or the contrary?

We object for the reason that it is leading, and the substance of it has been voted upon at least three times.

Mr. EVARTS. Do you say it is leading?

Mr. STANBERY. I do not understand that it is leading.

Mr. Manager BUTLER. We do not care much about the "leading" point.

Mr. EVARTS. You do not object to it as leading?

Mr. Manager BUTLER. No, sir.

The CHIEF JUSTICE. The question will be read by the Secretary.

The Secretary read as follows:

At either of these interviews was anything said in reference to the use of threats, intimidation, or force to get possession of the War Office, or the contrary?

The CHIEF JUSTICE put the question on the admissibility of the question; and it was determined in the negative.

After a pause—

The CHIEF JUSTICE. Have the counsel for the President any further questions?

Mr. STANBERY. We are considering, Mr. Chief Justice, whether there is any other question we have to put to General Sherman.

Mr. ANTHONY, (at four o'clock and thirty-seven minutes p. m.) I move that the Senate, sitting as a court of impeachment, do now adjourn.

Mr. Manager BUTLER. Let us finish with this witness.

The CHIEF JUSTICE put the question on the motion to adjourn, and declared that it appeared to be agreed to.

Mr. DRAKE called for the yeas and nays; and they were ordered.

Mr. CONKLING. I beg to inquire whether the Managers mean to cross-examine this witness.

Mr. Manager BUTLER. Not at all, if we can only get the other side through with him.

Mr. CONKLING. I thought they were through with him.

Mr. Manager BUTLER. No; they will not finish with him.

The CHIEF JUSTICE. The Secretary will call the roll.

The Secretary called the name of Mr. ANTHONY, and he responded.

Mr. THAYER. Mr. President, I rise for information. I desire——

The CHIEF JUSTICE. The roll is being called, and no debate is in order.

Mr. THAYER. I desire to inquire what we are voting on?

The CHIEF JUSTICE. On a motion to adjourn.

Mr. THAYER. I did not hear what the counsel for the defense said in regard——

The CHIEF JUSTICE. Debate is not in order. The Secretary will proceed with the call.

The Secretary concluded the call of the roll, and the result was announced—yeas 20, nays 32; as follows:

YEAS—Messrs. Anthony, Bayard, Buckalew, Davis, Dixon, Doolittle, Edmunds, Fowler, Grimes, Henderson, Hendricks, Howe, Johnson, McCreery, Morton, Norton, Patterson of Tennessee, Trumbull, Van Winkle, and Vickers—20.

NAYS—Messrs. Cameron, Cattell, Chandler, Cole, Conkling, Conness, Corbett, Cragin, Drake, Ferry, Fessenden, Frelinghuysen, Harlan, Howard, Morgan, Morrill of Maine, Morrill of Vermont, Nye, Patterson of New Hampshire, Pomeroy, Ramsey, Ross, Sherman, Sprague, Stewart, Sumner, Thayer, Tipton, Willey, Williams, Wilson, and Yates—32.

NOT VOTING—Messrs. Saulsbury and Wade—2.

So the Senate refused to adjourn.

Mr. STANBERY. Mr. Chief Justice, I will state to the Managers and to the Senate that under these rulings we are not now prepared to say that we have any further questions to put to General Sherman; but it is a matter of so much importance that we desire to be allowed to recall General Sherman on Monday if we deem it proper further to examine him.

Mr. Manager BUTLER. We are very desirous that the examination of this witness should be closed, if possible——

Mr. Manager BINGHAM. Oh, no; we have no objection.

Mr. HOWE. I move that the Senate, sitting as a court, adjourn.

The motion was agreed to; and the Senate, sitting for the trial of the impeachment, adjourned until Monday next at twelve o'clock.

MONDAY, *April* 13, 1868.

The Chief Justice of the United States entered the Senate Chamber at twelve o'clock and five minutes p. m., and took the chair.

The usual proclamation having been made by the Sergeant-at-Arms,

The Managers of the impeachment on the part of the House of Representatives appeared and took the seats assigned them.

The counsel for the respondent also appeared and took their seats.

The presence of the House of Representatives was next announced, and the members of the House, as in Committee of the Whole, headed by Mr. E. B. WASHBURNE, the chairman of that committee, and accompanied by the Speaker and Clerk, entered the Senate Chamber, and were conducted to the seats provided for them.

The CHIEF JUSTICE. The Journal of the last day's proceedings will be read by the Secretary.

The Secretary proceeded to read the Journal of the proceedings of the Senate sitting for the trial of the impeachment on Saturday last; but was interrupted at fifteen minutes past twelve o'clock.

Mr. STEWART. I move that the further reading of the Journal be dispensed with.

The CHIEF JUSTICE. If there be no objection, the further reading of the Journal will be dispensed with. The Chair hears no objection. Before the counsel for the President proceed, the Chief Justice will state that on Saturday last the Senator from New Jersey [Mr. FRELINGHUYSEN] had submitted a motion for an order to remove the limit fixed by Rule 21 as to the number who may participate in the final argument of the cause. That order is before the Senate unless objected to.

Mr. SUMNER. Mr. President, I send to the Chair an amendment to that order to come in at the end:

Provided, That the trial shall proceed without any further delay or postponement on this account.

The CHIEF JUSTICE. The order which is proposed by the Senator from New Jersey will be read.

The SECRETARY. The order is as follows:

Ordered, That as many of the Managers and of the counsel for the President be permitted to speak on the final argument as shall choose to do so.

It is proposed to amend the order by adding the following proviso:

Provided, That the trial shall proceed without any further delay or postponement on this account.

Mr. FRELINGHUYSEN. I accept the amendment of the Senator from Massachusetts.

The CHIEF JUSTICE. The question will be on the order as modified.

Mr. Manager WILLIAMS. Mr. President, with your leave, and yours, gentlemen of the Senate, before taking the vote on this question, and in default of any remarks in support of the motion submitted by the honorable Managers on the part of the House, I feel constrained to ask your indulgence for a word or two, not so much in the way of argument or remonstrance as for the purpose of inviting your attention to the precedents in cases of this sort.

It has pleased the Senate to adopt a rule limiting the discussion upon the final argument of this case to two counsel on each side; and this I may say is in conformity with the rule which I believe prevails almost universally in ordinary cases in the trial of all civil actions, and in the trial of indictments in the criminal courts, even though those cases may be of very small magnitude, and concern the public at large to none, or but a very trifling extent. I am not here to contest the right of this tribunal sitting as a court, or of any other judicial tribunal, to impose such reasonable limitations upon the freedom of speech as the interests of justice may require, or as may be necessary to facilitate its proper administration. I admit that time is legitimate consideration; but in the text of Magna Charta, comes, I think, after justice: " we will not sell, we will not deny, we will not delay right or justice."

It struck me, however, that the effect of this rule was to create a condition of things which was calculated, in some degree, to embarrass the gentlemen who have been sent here to conduct this case on the part of the House and the people. The House, acting upon its discretion and upon a full consciousness of the importance of this case, has devolved this responsible task upon seven of its members. In this particular, although the case is one without a precedent, they certainly have not deviated from the ordinary rule. I know no cases in which the number has been less than five. There are many, I think, where it has amounted to as much as eleven. The effect, however, of this rule will then be to exclude from the debate upon this question—I mean the final debate, and I take that to be really and substantially the only important one—at least four of the Managers appointed by the House.

If time were a matter of importance—and I am now willing to admit that it is, as the House concedes in its proceedings here, in the articles which it has presented, and in the whole conduct of its Managers, as exhibited before you—it would have seemed to me, that while a reasonable limitation would be proper it would, perhaps, have relieved us to some extent and enabled all the Managers to perform what they might conceive to be their duties as imposed upon them by the House of Representatives, if this honorable body had undertaken to say how much time, or, in other words, how many hours, the public convenience and the

interests of the State would allow them to give to the prosecution in this case. In that event the time allowed could have been divided and apportioned among the Managers, and that would have been in conformity with the terms of the rule in regard to interlocutory motions where an hour has been assigned to each side, and the privilege left to members of saying by whom the several questions may be discussed. If the rule had been modified in this way the Managers, as I have observed, would have been relieved, because they could then have distributed the several parts among themselves.

It struck me, however—and I rose merely for the purpose of calling your attention to the precedents—that the rule was an unusual one. It did not meet the approbation of the Managers in the first instance; and when, as they did, under a sort of compulsion imposed upon them, distribute the parts in this drama, if I may be allowed to call it so, they directed their chairman to make this application. It has been postponed; it is now made, and is now before you. They thought the rule was unusual. I think they all shared in that opinion. I have taken very little time myself to look into the precedents; but since the motion has been made I have thought it was my duty so to do, and I desire to state now to this honorable Senate what is the result in ordinary cases; and this, I think, will not be considered one of that description.

There have been but five cases within our history of impeachments before the Senate of the United States. The first of them was the case of Blount, which was tried, I think, in the year 1798. That was the impeachment of a Senator; it went off upon a collateral question, which was as to the fact whether a member of the Senate was an officer impeachable under the Constitution. The next case was the case of Judge Pickering, of New Hampshire. The charge there was drunkenness. The defense put in—if there can be said to have been a defense put in regularly, where the respondent did not appear by counsel—was insanity. That question was tried in advance; it was ruled against him; and thereupon, upon the motion of the members of the House, at the special instance and upon the special order of the House itself, to whom, I believe, the question was then referred, the case was submitted without argument, and a judgment rendered against the defendant.

The third case was that of Justice Chase. There the number of managers was seven. They were all heard except one, and yet the number of arguments made was equal to the number of managers, because the default of that one, if it was a default, was supplied by two speeches from Mr. Randolph, the chairman, who opened the case and closed it.

The next case was that of Judge Peck. There the number of managers was five. They all participated in the argument.

In none of these cases does there seem to

have been—I may be mistaken, and stand subject to correction if I am wrong—any question as to the right of the House to be heard, if it desired, through all its managers. If there was any discussion then, or any rule adopted on the subject at that or any other time, members of the Senate who have participated in the framing of these rules must be of course aware of it, and will be able to make the answer in their votes. There, however, as I have already remarked, the course was the same as in the case of Justice Chase.

The last case was the case of Judge Humphreys. That took place at the commencement of the war. Then there was no appearance, and of course no defense, and a sort of judgment was taken by default, something, perhaps, in the nature of a judgment of outlawry.

It seems, then, that in the only two cases that have been contested in this country before this Senate, the rule has been that all the managers appointed by the House should be allowed to participate in the discussion.

How is it elsewhere? I have not chosen to go beyond the waters to look into the precedents ; but there is one case in British history which is familiar to all of us, which is associated, I may say, with the school-boy recollection of every man in this nation, of every man, indeed, who is familiar with our language, a case made memorable, I suppose, mainly, not by the peculiar interest which it involved, but by the fact that it was illustrated by the splendid genius of some of the greatest men that England has ever produced. It was not because Warren Hastings was the Governor General of Bengal—that was a small matter, held, I believe, by the grace of the British East India Company—but because such men as Edmund Burke and Richard Brinsley Sheridan were among the managers. It was such men as those who made the case an epoch in parliamentary history.

It may be said, however, that there was another reason for it, and that was its long duration. It continued, I believe, for as long a period as seven years. I beg Senators to understand that I do not quote it as an authority on that point ; but I think it will be remembered by all of them that the labor of argumentation was distributed among all the managers, the articles being numerous, complicated, and elaborate, though I suppose that the fact of all the managers participating had nothing to do possibly with the prolongation of the time.

And now, in view of these precedents, I would desire to ask how does the present case compare with them? Is it an ordinary one? Why, it dwarfs them all into absolute nothingness. There is nothing in the world's history that compares with this. It makes an epoch in history, and therefore I may well say that you are making history to-day. And therefore, too, I think it is, that upon questions of this sort you should so rule as to show to posterity that you do properly appreciate the magnitude of the interests involved. Senators, I feel myself the difficulty of realizing its magnitude. I know how hard it is for us, even, who are the actors in this great drama, to rise to the height of this great argument. Why, what is the case? That of a judge of the Supreme Court or of the district court of the United States? That of a custom-house officer? No. It is the case of the Chief Magistrate of a great people, of an empire reaching from ocean to ocean, and comprehending within its circumference forty millions of free, intelligent, thinking people, who are looking upon your doings and waiting in breathless suspense for your verdict. That is the case now before you ; and if, in the case of a judge of the Supreme Court—and from my habitual respect for that tribunal, I would not be understood to speak disparagingly of the position—or if in the case of a judge of the district court, it was thought improper to impose any limitations, where the number of managers was the same as now, what shall be said of the application in a case like this of a rule which prevails, as I have already remarked, in all the courts, even in the most indifferent causes? It can only be accounted for in one way : either that the case was of small consequence, or that it was so plain that the judges required no professional research and no argument to aid them.

And now I desire only to say in conclusion, in order that I may not be misunderstood, that in the remarks which I have made I have not been moved by any considerations that were personal to myself. I have lived long enough to outlive the time when the ambition to be heard is felt by men ; I have lived too long, at all events, to think it worth while to press an argument upon an unwilling judge, whatever may be the reasons by which he may be influenced, whether he may regard the case as too clear a one, or whether he may consider it as so unimportant as not to be entitled to a reasonable amount of time. I do not know, if you relax this rule, whether I shall be personally able to take advantage of it or not. That will depend upon my strength ; that will depend again upon the feeling that I may have as to the necessity of anything additional to what may be said by others. I felt it, however, to be my duty to enter my protest—and I do it most respectfully—against what may be drawn into a precedent hereafter. If in a case like this the argument may be limited to two, how will it be when another supreme judge is arraigned before another Senate for high crimes and misdemeanors? I take it for granted that, measuring things by their comparative proportions, another Senate would feel authorized to reduce the number of counsel to one ; and if it came to a district judge or a custom-house officer I do not know whether they might not feel authorized to deny that privilege altogether.

Mr. Manager STEVENS. Mr. Chief Justice, I have but a word to say, and that is of very little importance. I do not expect to be able, if allowed, to say many words upon this subject. There is one single article which I am somewhere held responsible for for introducing, and a single article only, which I wish to argue at a very brief length; but I desire that my colleagues should have full opportunity to exercise such liberty as they deem proper in the argument.

I have no objection myself—I do not speak for my colleagues—if the Senate choose to limit our time, to their doing so, and fixing it at what they think reasonable, what one gentleman here would occupy, for I find they occupy three days sometimes here. I am willing to allow the Senate to fix the time and let the Managers, those who are not already expected to speak in conclusion, to divide that time among themselves. However, sir, this is a mere suggestion.

I merely wish to say that I trust some further time will be given, as there are two or three subjects on which for a short time, perhaps an hour or three quarters of an hour, some of us may be anxious to give the reasons why we were so pertinacious in the House in insisting upon their introduction after the House had reported leaving them out. I confess I feel in that awkward position that I owe it to myself and to the country to give the reasons why I insisted with what is called obstinacy in introducing one of the articles; but I am willing to be confined to any length of time which the Senate may deem proper. What I have to say I can say very briefly. Indeed, I cannot say it at any great length if I would. I merely make this suggestion, and beg the pardon of the Senate for having obtruded thus long upon their time when they ought to proceed.

The CHIEF JUSTICE. Do the counsel for the President desire to submit any remarks to the Senate?

Mr. SHERMAN. Mr. President, I submit an amendment, which I desire to be added to the order as it stands.

The CHIEF JUSTICE. The amendment will be read by the Clerk.

Mr. FRELINGHUYSEN. Mr. President, before the amendment of the Senator from Ohio is submitted, I desire, if I am at liberty, to modify the resolution somewhat by adding a further proviso that only one counsel on the part of the Managers shall be heard in the close. It was not the purpose of the resolution to change the rule, excepting as to the number who should speak.

The CHIEF JUSTICE. The Secretary will read the order as modified by the Senator from New Jersey.

The SECRETARY. The order, as modified by the mover, now reads:

Ordered, That as many of the Managers and of the counsel for the President be permitted to speak on the final argument as shall choose to do so: *Provided,* That the trial shall proceed without any further delay or postponement on this account: *And provided further,* That only one Manager shall be heard in the close.

The amendment of the Senator from Ohio [Mr. SHERMAN] is to add:

But the additional time allowed by this order to each side shall not exceed three hours.

Mr. Manager BOUTWELL. Mr. President and Senators, I am very unwilling myself to make any remarks upon this resolution, because I am so situated, upon the judgment of the Managers, that it is a delicate matter for me to do so; and had it not been for the qualification made by the honorable Senator from New Jersey I should have said nothing. But if the Senate will consider that in the case of Judge Peck, after the testimony was submitted to the Senate, it was first summed up by two managers on the part of the House; that then the counsel for the respondent argued the cause of the respondent by two of their number, and that then the case was closed for the House of Representatives by two arguments made by the managers; if the Senate will consider that in the trial of Judge Chase the argument on the part of the House of Representatives and of the people of the United States was closed by three managers after the testimony had been submitted and the arguments in favor of the respondent had been closed; if they will consider that in the trial of Judge Prescott, in Massachusetts, (which I venture to say in this presence was one of the most ably conducted trials in the history of impeachments, either in this country or in Great Britain, on the part of the managers sustained by Chief Justice Shaw and on the part of the respondent by Mr. Webster,) that two arguments were made by the managers of the House of Representatives on the part of the House and on the part of the people of that Commonwealth after the case of the respondent had been closed both upon the evidence and upon the argument, I think, it needs no further illustration to satisfy this tribunal that the cause of the people, the cause of the House of Representatives, if this case should be opened to full debate on the part of the five gentlemen who represent the respondent here, ought not to be left to the close of a single individual.

Mr. JOHNSON. Mr. Chief Justice, I ask for the reading of the order as moved by the mover, and as proposed to be modified by the member from Ohio.

The Secretary read the order as modified by Mr. FRELINGHUYSEN, and the amendment of Mr. SHERMAN.

Mr. STANBERY. Mr. Chief Justice and Senators, we hope this extension of time will not be an injury to us in disguise. We have neither asked it nor objected to it; it comes from the opposite side to have more counsel than are already assigned by the rules which have been adopted. We make no objection; no objection if all seven of my learned friends argue this case; but as I understand the amendment offered by the Senator from Ohio, it is that in the final argument, as to which as yet there is no limitation of time, but only of the number of counsel, the provision as to the addition of counsel shall be amended by a proviso that the additional time shall not be more than three hours. The time already is indefinite. The rule fixes only the number of counsel, not the time that they shall occupy. As yet the Senate have not said that in the final summing up, or indeed in the opening which we have had, counsel shall be limited as to time. I do not know in what position we should be if this amendment of the Senator from Ohio is adopted. Three hours in addition to what? Three hours in addition to a time that is made indefinite by the rule! I cannot understand it. I only call the attention of the Senate to it that there may be no misunderstanding hereafter; and as to that matter of a limit as to time, I hope we may say that not one of us has any idea of lengthening out time for any purpose of delay. I think the Senate can have enough confidence in us to know that when we are through we will stop; that we will only take as much time as in this great case we may deem to be necessary. I know if we go beyond that we shall lose the attention of the court. Not an instant do we mean to speak after we have concluded what is material to us in the case. If we attempt to take time beyond that for something out of the case we shall very soon see, Senators, in the expression of your faces, that you are not listening to us with attention. For one I can say, and I think I can speak for my learned associates, that we shall not take a moment more than we consider necessary; every moment necessary for the case, not a moment unnecessarily in our best judgment as to how we are to present the case. I know it is the custom of courts to limit the time of counsel—they must do it—in their ordinary business. It is done in the Supreme Court of the United States; but when there is an important case even before that court which limits each argument of counsel to two hours generally, whenever the court is asked in an important case to enlarge the time, they do it and give four hours. On one occasion I had myself two entire days for an argument in that court; but that case, important as it was, has no sort of comparison with the case now before you. Counsel, when they are limited to an exact time, are embarrassed by it. It is a rule that keeps our attention continually on the clock and not on the case; we are afraid to begin and follow up an argument for fear we shall exhaust too much time on that and will be caught by the punctual hour before we come to other important matters. Now, I hope it is not necessary to suggest that counsel are not here to use unnecessary time, who have a reputation to sustain before the world and before this Senate. I beg them not to decide this question upon any idea that we have abused the liberty which is or may be accorded to us.

Mr. SHERMAN. Mr. President, I will withdraw my amendment, as I see there will be difficulty in discriminating between those who are limited by time and those who are not.

The CHIEF JUSTICE. The Senator from Ohio withdraws his amendment. The question recurs on the order proposed by the Senator from New Jersey, as modified by him.

Mr. Manager BUTLER. I do not rise, sir, to debate this question, but simply to ask the counsel for the President, while they do not ask for this, whether they desire it? I should like to know whether they desire this extension? They may think that they would not ask it, but the question is whether they would wish it, because if they do not wish it it would make a very decided impression on my mind as to whether it should be granted. I want to say here, however, Mr. President, that I speak without prejudice to anybody, because, from the very kind attention I have received from the Senate in the opening argument, which, unfortunately, fell upon me, I do not, in any event, under any relaxation of the rule, propose to trespass a single moment in the closing argument upon the attention of the Senate, but to leave it to the very much better argumentation of my associates. Therefore I speak wholly without any wish upon my own part except that such argumentation may be had as shall convince the country that the case has been fully stated on the one side and the other.

Mr. SUMNER. Mr. President, I should like to have the resolution reported.

The CHIEF JUSTICE. The Secretary will read the resolution again.

The Secretary read as follows:

Ordered, That as many of the Managers and of the counsel for the President be permitted to speak on the final argument as shall choose to do so: *Provided*, That the trial shall proceed without any further delay or postponement on this account: *And provided further*, That only one Manager shall be heard in the close.

Mr. SUMNER. Mr. President, I move to strike out the last proviso and insert the substitute which I send to the Chair.

The CHIEF JUSTICE. The Secretary will read the amendment proposed by the Senator from Massachusetts.

The SECRETARY. It is proposed to strike out the last proviso in the following words:

And provided further, That only one Manager shall be heard in the close.

And in lieu thereof to insert:

And provided, That according to the practice in cases of impeachment the several Managers who speak shall close.

Mr. CONKLING. I beg to ask an answer from the counsel for the President to the question propounded by Mr. Manager BUTLER.

Mr. EVARTS. I was rising, Mr. Chief Justice and Senators, to say a word in reference to this question when the Senator from Massachusetts sent up an amendment to the Clerk. It will not be in the power of the counsel for the President, if the rule shall now be enlarged, to contribute the aid of more than two additional advocates in behalf of the President. The rule was early adopted and known to us, and the arrangement of the number of counsel was accommodated to the rule. Beyond that we have nothing to say. If the rule shall be enlarged, all of us will with pleasure take advantage of the liberality of the Senate.

In regard, however, to the arrangement of six against four as would then be the odds which we should need to meet, we naturally might feel some interest, particularly if it is a proposition to be entertained by the court that all of our opponents should speak after we had got through and we should hear nobody to reply to before we made our arguments. The last speech hitherto has been made in behalf of the President; but if there is any value in debate whatever, it is that when it begins and is of controversy between two sides each as fairly as may be should have an opportunity to know and reply to the argument of the other. Now, the present rule, very properly as it seems to us, and wholly in accordance with the custom in all matters of forensic debate, thus disposes of the matter by requiring that the Managers shall open by one of their number, and the two counsel for the President allowed to speak and make their reply, and then the second Manager appearing in that behalf to close. So, too, if the number should be enlarged, it would seem, especially if there should be the disparity of six against four, an equal and equally just arrangement should be made in the distribution of the arguments of the Managers and of the counsel. Beyond that, we have nothing to say.

The CHIEF JUSTICE. Senators, the question is on the amendment proposed by the Senator from Massachusetts.

Mr. WILLIAMS. Mr. President, I move to lay the order and the amendment upon the table, with a view of having a test vote as to whether the original rule shall or shall not be changed.

Mr. DRAKE. I raise a question of order, Mr. President, that in this Senate, sitting for the trial of an impeachment, there is no authority for moving to lay any proposition on the table. We must come to a direct vote, I think, one way or the other.

Mr. HOWARD. Debate is out of order.

The CHIEF JUSTICE. The Chief Justice cannot undertake to limit the Senate in respect to its mode of disposing of a question; and as the Senator from Oregon [Mr. WILLIAMS] announced his purpose to test the sense of the Senate, in regard to whether they will alter the rule at all the Chief Justice conceives his motion to be in order.

Mr. WILLIAMS. I ask for the yeas and nays on the motion.

The yeas and nays were ordered, and taken.

Mr. ANTHONY. My colleague [Mr. SPRAGUE] has been called away by a summons to attend the bedside of a friend with whom he has held the most intimate relations for twenty years, and who sent a request by telegraph that he would come and see him before he died. I make this explanation, as, under no ordinary circumstances would he have been absent from the service of the Senate even for a single day, under these circumstances.

The result was announced—yeas 38, nays 10; as follows:

YEAS—Messrs. Buckalew, Cameron, Cattell, Chandler, Cole, Conkling, Conness, Corbett, Cragin, Drake, Edmunds, Ferry, Fessenden, Harlan, Henderson, Hendricks, Howard, Howe, Johnson, Morgan, Morrill of Maine, Morrill of Vermont, Morton, Norton, Patterson of New Hampshire, Pomeroy, Ramsey, Ross, Sherman, Stewart, Sumner, Thayer, Tipton, Van Winkle, Vickers, Williams, Wilson, and Yates—38.

NAYS—Messrs. Anthony, Davis, Dixon, Doolittle, Fowler, Grimes, McCreery, Patterson of Tennessee, Trumbull, and Willey—10.

NOT VOTING—Messrs. Bayard, Frelinghuysen, Nye, Saulsbury, Sprague, and Wade—6.

So the order, with the pending amendment, was laid on the table.

The CHIEF JUSTICE. Gentlemen of counsel for the President, you will proceed with the defense.

WILLIAM T. SHERMAN'S examination continued.

By Mr. STANBERY:

Question. After the restoration of Mr. Stanton to the War Office upon the vote of the Senate, did you form an opinion as to whether the good of the service required another man in that office than Mr. Stanton?

Mr. Manager BUTLER. Stay a moment. We object. Will you reduce the question to writing?

The CHIEF JUSTICE. The counsel for the President will please reduce the question to writing.

Mr. STANBERY. I am perfectly willing to do so, though I can hardly be called to do so at the request of the learned Manager. I made a similar request to him more than once, and it was never complied with.

The CHIEF JUSTICE. The rule requires that it be done.

Mr. Manager BUTLER. I beg a thousand pardons. Whenever it was intimated by the Chief Justice it was done. It is not a matter of kindness; it is a matter of rule.

Mr. STANBERY. Mr. Chief Justice, my impression was that that rule applied to a question put by a Senator, not to the questions of counsel. Otherwise we should never get through. It is a question put by a Senator that must be in writing. I may be mistaken, however.

The CHIEF JUSTICE. The Secretary will read the rule.

The Secretary read Rule 15, as follows:

"XV. All motions made by the parties or their counsel shall be addressed to the presiding officer, and if he or any Senator shall require it, they shall be committed to writing and read at the Secretary's table."

The CHIEF JUSTICE. The counsel will please reduce their question to writing.

The question was reduced to writing.

The CHIEF JUSTICE. The Secretary will read the question proposed by the counsel for the President.

The Secretary read as follows:

Question. After the restoration of Mr. Stanton to office did you form an opinion whether the good of the service required a Secretary of War other than Mr. Stanton; and if so, did you communicate that opinion to the President?

Mr. Manager BINGHAM. Mr. President and Senators, we desire to state very briefly to the Senate the ground upon which we object to this question. It is that matters of opinion are never admissible in judicial proceedings, but in certain exceptional cases, cases involving professional skill, &c.; it is not necessary that I should enumerate them. It is not to be supposed for a moment that there is a member of the Senate who can entertain the opinion that a question of the kind now presented is competent under any possible circumstances in any tribunal of justice. It must occur to Senators that the ordinary tests of truth cannot be applied to it at all; and in saying that, my remark has no relation at all to the truthfulness or veracity of the witness. There is nothing upon which the Senate could pronounce any judgment whatever. Are they to decide a question upon the opinions of forty or forty thousand men what might be for the good of the service? The question involved here is a violation of the laws of the land. It is a question of fact that is to be dealt with by witnesses; and it is a question of law and fact that is to be dealt with by the Senate.

Now, this matter of opinion may just as well be extended one step further, if it is to be allowed at all. After giving his opinion of what might be requisite to the public service, the next thing in order would be the witness's opinion as to the obligations of the law, the restrictions of the law, the prohibitions of the law. We cannot suppose that the Senate will entertain such a question for a moment. It must occur to the Senate that by adopting such a rule as this it is impossible to see the limit of the inquiry or the end of the investigation. If it be competent for this witness to deliver this opinion, it is equally competent for forty thousand other men in this country to deliver their opinions to the Senate; and then, when is the inquiry to end? We object to it as utterly incompetent.

Mr. STANBERY. Mr. Chief Justice and Senators, if ever there was a case involving a question of intention, a question of conduct, a question as to acts which might be criminal or might be indifferent according to the intent of the party who committed them, this is one of that class. It is upon that question of intent (which the gentlemen know is vital to their case, which they know as well as we know they must make out by some proof or other) that a great deal of their testimony has been offered, whether successfully or not I leave the Senate to determine; but with that view much of their testimony has been offered and has been insisted upon. That is, it has been to show with what intent did the President remove Mr. Stanton. They say the intent was against the public good, in the way of usurpation, to get possession of that War Office and drive out a meritorious officer, and put a tool, or as they say in one of their statements a slave, in his place.

Upon that question of conduct, Senators, what now do we propose to offer to you? That the second officer of the Army—and we do not propose to stop with him—that this high officer of the Army, seeing the complication and difficulty in which that office was, by the restoration of Mr. Stanton to it, formed the opinion himself that for the good of the service Mr. Stanton ought to go out and some one else take the place. Who could be a better judge of the good of the service than the distinguished officer who is now about to speak?

But the gentlemen say what are his opinions more than another man's opinions, if they are merely given as abstract opinions? We do not intend to use them as abstract opinions. The gentlemen did not read the whole question. It is not merely what opinion had you, General Sherman; but having formed that opinion, did you communicate it to the President, that the good of the service required Mr. Stanton to leave that Department; and that in your judgment, acting for the good of the service, some other man ought to be there.

This is no declaration of the President we are upon now. This is a communication made to him to regulate his conduct, to justify him, indeed to call upon him to look to the good of the service, and to be rid, if possible, in some way of that unpleasant complication. Any one can see there was a complication there that must in some way or other be got rid of; for look at what the Managers have put in evidence! It appears by Mr. Stanton's own statement that from the 12th of August, 1867, Mr. Stanton has never seen the President, has never entered the Executive Mansion, has never sat at that board where the President's legal advisers, the heads of Departments, are bound to be under the Constitution.

Will they say that the relations between him and the President had got to that pitch that Mr. Stanton was unwilling to go there lest he might not be admitted? He never made that attempt; but that is not all: Mr. Stanton says deliberately on the 4th of March in his communication to the House of Representatives, when he sent the correspondence between the President and General Grant, "I have not only not seen the President, but I have had no official communication with the President since the 12th of August, 1867." How is the Army to get along with that sort of thing? How is the service to be benefited in that way? Certainly it is for the benefit of the service that the President should have there some one with whom he can advise as to what is to be done in regard to the Army.

But what has the Secretary of War become? One of two things is inevitable: he is running the War Department without any advice or consultation with the President or he is doing nothing. Ought that to be the position of a Secretary of War? The President could not get out of that difficulty. He might have got out of it, perhaps, by humbling himself before Mr. Stanton, by sending him a note of apology that he had ever suspended him. By humbling himself to his subordinate it might have been that Mr. Stanton would have forgiven him. Would you ask him to do that, Senators?

Now, when you are looking to motives, when you consider the provocations that the President has had, when beyond that you see the necessities of the public service placed in that situation that no longer can there be any communication between the Secretary of War and the President, is it fit that the public service should be carried on in that way, just to enable the Secretary of War to hold on to his office and become a mere *locum tenens?* Then, when you are considering the conduct, the intentions, and the matter that is in the mind of the President to get rid of Stanton—undoubtedly he had that matter in his mind—when you find that he has been advised, not only as we propose to prove, by General Sherman himself, that the good of the service required that that difficulty should be ended, but that General Sherman, as I shall undertake to prove, communicated also the opinion of General Grant to the very same point, and when, as I tell you, we shall follow it up by the agreement of these two distinguished generals to go to Mr. Stanton and to tell him that, for the good of the service, he ought to resign, as he had intimated when the President first suspended him that he would resign, the Senate being here to take care that the President get no improper man there—now, when you are trying the President for his intentions, whether he acted in good faith or bad faith, Senators, will you shut out from him the advice that he received from these two distinguished officers, and will you allow the Managers still to say that he acted without advice, that he acted for the very purpose of removing a faithful officer and getting in his place some tool or slave of his? When it was said to him that there should be a change for the benefit of the service, can you not extend to him so much charity as to believe that he would be impressed by the opinions of these two distinguished generals? They say they did not intend to make themselves parties to the controversy, but they saw, as things stood there, that either the President must go out or Mr. Stanton. That was the character of it. It is with this view that we offer this testimony, and I trust this is not to be ruled out.

Mr. Manager BUTLER. Mr. President, Senators, I foresaw if we did not remain long enough in session, which the late hour of the night on Saturday warned us not to do, to finish this witness, so that only the usual rule of recalling would be enforced, that the struggle would be renewed again in some form to-day to get in the declarations of the President or declarations to the President; and now the proposition is to ask General Sherman whether he did not form an opinion that it was necessary that Mr. Stanton should be removed.

Mr. STANBERY. I did not say "remove."

Mr. Manager BUTLER, (to the Secretary.) Allow me to have the question. I believe I am correct. [Obtaining the question.] What is it?

Whether the good of the service required a Secretary of War other than Mr. Stanton, and if so did you not communicate that opinion to the President.

Of course there could not be any other Secretary of War but Mr. Stanton, unless Mr. Stanton resigned or was removed. It would be a good deal more to the purpose to ask him whether he communicated that opinion to Mr. Stanton, if it may be put in at all, because Mr. Stanton could have resigned.

Mr. EVARTS. We will follow it up with that.

Mr. Manager BUTLER. *Quousque tandem abutere nostra patientia?* I am not able to say to what extent you will go in offers; but I am very glad we are told that is to be done and these tentative experiments are to go on, for what purpose, Senators, you will judge; certainly for no legal purpose. Now, it is said that it is necessary to put this in, and the argument is pressed that was used on Saturday, "We must show that, or we cannot defend the President." Well, if you cannot defend the President without another breach of the law for his breach of the law, I do not see any necessity for his being defended. You are breaking the law to defend him, because you are putting in testimony that has no relevancy, no pertinency, no competency under the law. After you have let this come in, Senators, if you can do so, will you allow me to ask General Sherman whether he did not come to an equally firm opinion that it was for the good of the service, or for the good of the country, that Johnson should be removed? The learned Attorney General says that he came to the opinion that this complication, as he called it, should be broken up. I think most of us came to that conclusion—but how? General Sherman might think it was by removing Mr. Stanton; General Grant might think it was by removing Johnson. The House of Representatives have thought that the complication could be broken up by the removal of Johnson. Are you going to put in General Sherman's opinion to counterbalance the weight of the opinion of the House of Representatives?

Again, will the next question be put to General Sherman whether if he thought it was better to remove Stanton and put in Thomas, that would be a good change for the good of the service; or shall we be allowed on another article to show that General Sherman did not think it was a good plan to put in Thomas, and so convict the President of a wrong intent, because General Sherman thought Thomas was a bad man, and, therefore, the President is guilty if he put him in? Because General Sherman thought that Mr. Stanton was a bad man, therefore it was for the good of the service to put Stanton out, and therefore the President is innocent in putting him out—that seems to be the proposition. Can we go into this region of opinion? I speak wholly without reference to the witness. I am now speaking wholly upon the general principle of opinions of men. That will send us into another region of inquiry which we do not want to go into. If this testimony comes in, we shall then have to ask General Sherman what were your relations with Mr. Stanton? Have you had a quarrel with him? Did you not think it would be better for the service if you could get rid of your enemy? Was not that the thing? Was there not an unfortunate difficulty between you? If you allow this opinion to go in, you cannot prevent our going into the various considerations which would make this opinion of little value. It is that kind of inquiry into which I have no desire to enter, and I pray this Senate not to enter for the good of the country and for the integrity of the law. That is the next question we shall have to ask, what were the grounds of your opinion?

Again, we shall have to go further. We shall have to call as many men on the other side as we can. If General Sherman is put in here as an expert, we shall have to call General Sheridan and General Thomas—I mean George H. Thomas always—and General Meade, and other men of equal experience, to say whether upon the whole they did not think it was for the best to keep Mr. Stanton in, and whether they communicated their opinions to the President and to Mr. Stanton. But I think nothing can more clearly demonstrate the fact that this cannot be evidence. If it is put on the ground that he is an expert as an Army officer, then we have Army officers, if not quite as expert, yet as much experts in the eye of the law as he is, and the struggle will be here on which side would be the most of them.

There is another purpose on which this is put in. It is said it is put in to show that the President had not a wrong intent. There has been a great deal said here about intent which, I think, deserves a word of comment, as though the intent has got to be proved by somebody that the President told he had a wrong intent. That seems to be the proposition as put forward, that you have to bring some direct proof, some man who heard the President say he had a bad intent, or something equivalent to that. The question before you is, did Mr. Johnson break the law of the land when he removed Mr. Stanton? If he did break the law of the land when he removed Mr. Stanton, what then? Then the law supplies the intent, and says that no man can do wrong intending right. That

illustrates this question in another view; because suppose it is for the good of the service and it is demonstrated that it is best for the good of the service that Mr. Stanton should be put out, does that justify the President in breaking the law of the land to get him out? Does that aid his intent? Shall you do evil that good may come? Can you do that under any state of circumstances? The question is not whether it was best to have Mr. Stanton out. Upon that question Senators may be divided in opinion. There may be many men, for aught I know or aught I care, there may be Senators who think that it would be best to have Stanton out; but that is not the question at all. Admit it, the question is, is it best to break the law of the land by the chief executive officer in order to get him out? Is it best to strain the Constitution and the laws in order to get him out? However much he may desire to do it the fact that the Secretary is a bad officer does not give the President a right to do an illegal thing to get him out? See where you are coming, Senators. It is this, that it is a justification for the President or any other executive officer to break the law of the land if he can show that he did what he thought was a good thing by doing it.

I am aware that the executive office, if I go to history, has been carried on a little upon that idea. Let me illustrate: you Senators and the House of Representatives agreeing together as the Congress of the United States passed a law that no man should hold office in the southern States that could not take the oath of loyalty; and I am aware that the President of the United States—he ought to have been impeached for it—boldly put men into office who could not take that oath in the South, and paid them their salaries, and justified it before the Senate and the House of Representatives on the ground that he thought he was doing the best for the service to do it—a breach of the law which, if the House and the country had had time to follow him in the innumerable things he has done, would and ought to have been presented as ground for impeachment. It is one of his crimes. And now he comes here and before the Senate of the United States, says, "Well, I got advice that such a man was not a good officer, and, therefore, I broke the law to put him out, and that is my excuse." Is it an excuse?

But one other thing to which I wish to call your attention, because you have heard it here over and over again, is this: it is said that Mr. Stanton has not had a seat in that board, that Cabinet council, since the 12th of August last. Whose fault was that? He attended every meeting up to within a week of the 12th of August. He did his duty up to within a week of the 12th of August. He was notified that suspension was coming. He was then suspended until the 13th of January; and when he came back into the office it was not for the President to humble himself, but it was for him to notify him as the head of a Department to come and take his seat if he so desired; but that notice never came. It was not for him to thrust himself upon the President, but it was for him to go when he understood his presence would be agreeable.

But that is put forward here as though this Government could not go on without a Cabinet board; and the learned counsel has just told us that it is a constitutional board. Upon that I want to take issue, once for all, Senators, it is an unconstitutional board. There is not one word in the Constitution about a Cabinet or a board. Jeremy Bentham said, years ago, that a board was always a shield, and there has been an attempt in some of the later Presidents to get these boards around them to shield them in their acts as a board. The Constitution says that the principal officers of the Departments may be called upon in their respective offices, in regard to their duties, to give opinions in writing to the President; and the earlier Presidents called upon their Cabinet officers for opinions in writing. I have on my table here an opinion that Thomas Jefferson gave to Washington, about his right to appoint embassadors, in writing. They are not to be a board, not to sit down and consult, not to have executive councils. That is an assumption of executive power that has grown up little by little from the cabinets of the Old World. These heads of Departments were given to the President as aids, and not as a shield; and he now will attempt to shield himself, perhaps, under their advice and under their action. It is not mere form. The opinion in writing was required by the Constitution—why? Because the framers of the Constitution well knew that there were Cabinet councils, and from the initials of a Cabinet council in England came that celebrated word "cabal," which has been the synonym of all that was vile in political combination from that day to this; and knowing that, it would seem almost with prescience that they required not that there should be verbal consultations semi-weekly by which things might be arranged and by which a secret conclave might be held, but that there should be what? That there should be written opinions asked and given, so that they might be known of all men; so that the President could not say, "Why, I got this advice from my Cabinet counselor," unless he showed it in writing, and so that the Cabinet counselor should not say that he failed to give this advice, because the President might show it in writing. Think of this Cabinet and what it has got to be! Picture to yourselves, Senators, President Johnson and Lorenzo Thomas in Cabinet consultation to shield the President! If Lorenzo Thomas was rightly appointed, then of course he can go into Cabinet consultation. If they have a right to put in consultation one Cabinet officer they have a right to put in another. If they have a right to put in the opinion of the Attorney General, who, by the

C. I.—22.

way, is not by the law a Cabinet officer in the sense in which it is said a head of a Department is—if they have a right to put in the opinion of one head of a Department they have a right to put in another; if a permanent, then a temporary Cabinet officer; if a temporary head of a Department, then an *ad interim* one. I find no dereliction of duty on the part of Mr. Stanton in this; nothing showing that the War Department could not go on. Let them show that the President has ever done according to the Constitution, asked Mr. Stanton any opinion in writing as to the duties of his Department, or that he has ever sent an order to him which he disobeyed; and that will be pertinent, that will show a reason; but I pray the Senate not to let us go into the region of opinion.

I have taken this much time, Senators, because I think we save time by taking it, if we come to the right decision to-day to keep out this range of opinion. This case is to be tried by your opinion; not upon your opinion as to whether Stanton is a good or a bad officer, but upon the opinion that, whether good or bad, the President broke the law in removing him, and must take the consequences of that breach of the law. It is said here that he broke it in order to get into court. I agree that if his counsel are correct he is in court, and in a court where he will have the full benefit of having the law settled forever.

Mr. EVARTS rose.

Mr. CONKLING. Before the counsel proceeds I beg to submit a question, which I send to the desk in writing.

The CHIEF JUSTICE. The question propounded by the Senator from New York will be read.

The Secretary read as follows:

Question. Do the counsel for the respondent offer at this point to show by the witness that he advised the President to remove Mr. Stanton in the manner adopted by the President, or merely that he advised the President to nominate for the action of the Senate some person other than Mr. Stanton?

Mr. STANBERY. We do not propose either. We propose simply to show that he gave his opinion that for the good of the service somebody else ought to be there.

Mr. Manager BUTLER. Without regard to the mode?

Mr. STANBERY. We do not propose to show that he advised him about the mode of removal; but we propose to show this opinion communicated to the President.

Mr. EVARTS. Mr. Chief Justice and Senators, I do not propose, upon this question of evidence, to discuss the constitutional relations of the President of the United States to his Cabinet, nor to anticipate in the least the consideration of the merits of this case, as they shall finally be the subject of discussion. If the accusations against the President of the United States upon which he is on trial here, and judgment upon which must result in his deposition from his great office and a call upon the people of the United

States to choose his successor, turn wholly upon the mere question of whether the President has been guilty of a formal violation of a statute law, which might subject him to a six cents' fine or a ten days' imprisonment, if he were indicted for it—if that is the measure and the strength (as, when it comes to question of evidence, is constantly urged upon you) of this accusation, I think that the honorable Manager who so eloquently and warmly pressed upon you the consideration that Warren Hastings's trial was nothing to this was a little out of place. If they will make it just as it would be if the President had been indicted under the civil-tenure act, when he could have been found guilty or innocent under the circumstances of the act, and then the punishment could have been made appropriate to the circumstances of its actual formal technical infraction, we could understand that trial; and that is open to the House of Representatives or to any informer at any time. On the contrary, through hours and pages of eloquence, the mere act and fact of the removal of Mr. Stanton is made the circumstance or *corpus delicti* upon which, in respect of its motives, its purposes, its tendencies, its results, the "high crime," in the constitutional sense of that term, which would call for a removal from office of the Chief Magistrate by reason of some grave public interest being injured, is made the topic of argument and of proof.

Now, Mr. Chief Justice and Senators, you cannot fail to see that General Sherman is not called here as an expert to give an opinion whether Mr. Stanton is a good Secretary of War or not. He is not called here as an expert to assist your judgment in determining whether or no it was for the public interest that Mr. Stanton should be removed, in the sense of determining whether this form of removal was legal or not. He is introduced here as the second in command over the armies of the United States, and to show an opinion on his part, as a military man and in that position, that the military service required for its proper conduct that a Secretary should take the place of Mr. Stanton whose relations to that service and to the Commander-in-Chief were not such as those of Mr. Stanton were, that that opinion was communicated to the President. We shall enlarge the area by showing that it was shared in by other competent military authority.

And, now, if a President of the United States, when brought under trial before a court of impeachment upon impeachment, is not at liberty in his defense to show that the acts which are brought in question as against the public interest and with bad motives, and to obstruct laws, and to disturb the public peace, acts wantonly done, recklessly done, violently done, were proper and necessary in the judgment of those most competent to think, most competent to advise, most responsible to the country in every sense for their opinions and their advice, what can he show? Is it not

proper for him to prove that, furnished with those opinions and supported by those opinions, (whether, in fact, which is yet to be determined, he adopted a mode that was unjustifiable or not; and whether you shall adjudge the mode to be criminal or not, is not now important,) he acted in such a manner that the motives and the objects which he had in view were of the public service, and for the public service, and based upon the intelligent and responsible opinion and advice of those in whom the service and the community generally had, and upon the best foundations, the most abiding confidence.

Now, Senators, reflect; you are taking part in a solemn transaction which is to effect, in your unfavorable judgment, a removal of the Chief Magistrate of the nation for some offense that he has committed against the public welfare with bad motives and for an improper purpose; and we offer to show you that upon consultations and deliberations and advice from those wholly unconnected with any matters of personal controversy and any matters of political controversy, and occupying solely the position of duty and responsibility in the military service of the country, he acted and desired to accomplish this change. We cannot prove everything in a breath; nor is it a criticism on testimony justly to exclude it, that it does not in itself prove all; but if it shall be followed, as it will be, by evidence of equal authority and weight and by efforts of the President, or authority to make efforts given by the President to secure a change in the control of this office which the military service of the country thus demanded, we shall have shown you by an absolute negative that this intention, this motive, this public injury, so vehemently, so profusely imputed in the course of the arguments, so definitely charged in the articles, had no foundation whatever.

Mr. Manager BINGHAM. Mr. President and Senators, after the very pertinent question that was propounded by one of the Senators to the counsel for the President had been put, nothing more would have been said by the Managers but for the argument that has since been interposed. The suggestion made by the honorable Senator shows the utter incompetency and absurdity of the proposition that is presented here now: that was whether you proposed to ask of the witness that he formed the opinion and expressed it to the Executive that he ought to remove the Secretary of War in the mode and manner that he did remove him or attempt to remove him. Is there any one here bold enough to say that if he had formed the opinion against the legality of the proceeding and had so expressed himself to the President it would be competent for us to introduce any such matter here as a mere matter of opinion to prove intent or to prove any thing else against the President.

But, apart from that, the reason chiefly why I rose to reply to the utterances of the gentleman who has just taken his seat is this: he intimates here the extraordinary opinion for himself that the trial in a court of justice of a beggar arrested in your streets for a crime punishable with six cents of fine or, perchance, five hours' imprisonment, is subject to a very different rule of evidence and of administrative justice from that which prevails and applies when you come to prosecute the Chief Magistrate of the nation. The American people will entertain no opinions of that sort; nor will their Senators. We have the same rule of justice and the same rule of evidence for the trial of the President of the United States and for the trial of the most defenseless and the weakest of all our citizens.

Mr. EVARTS. Will the honorable Manager allow me to say that the only illustration I used was of an indictment against the Chief Magistrate of the Union on trial before a police court?

Mr. Manager BINGHAM. I supposed myself that when the gentleman made use of the remark he intended certainly to have the Senate understand that there was a different rule of evidence and of administrative justice in the prosecution of an indictment in a court where the penalty might be six cents from that which applied in the prosecution of the President before the Senate.

Mr. EVARTS. When the issues are different the evidence will be different. It does not depend on the dignity of the defendant.

Mr. Manager BINGHAM. It is very difficult to see how the gentleman can escape from the position which he has assumed here before the Senate by making the remark that he supposed the President to be prosecuted. It is a very grave question in this country whether the President can be prosecuted in the courts of the United States for an indictable offense before he is impeached. It has been incorporated in your Constitution that after he has been impeached and removed he may be indicted and prosecuted for the crime. I do not, however, stop to argue that question now. I do not care who is prosecuted upon an indictment, whether the President or a beggar, the same rule of evidence applies to each. I do not care who is impeached, whether it be the President of the United States or the lowest civil officer in the service of the United States before the Senate, the same rule of evidence obtains, and the common-law maxim applies that where an offense is charged which is unlawful in itself, and it is proved to have been committed, (as alleged in every one of these articles, and established, I say, by the proof as to all of them,) the law itself declares that the intent was criminal, and it is for the accused to show justification. That is the language of the books. I so read it in the volume lying before me, the third of Greenleaf.

I do not stop to delay the Senate by reading the words further than I have recited them, that where the act is unlawful the intent is established by the proof of the fact that he did commit the unlawful act. As I intimated before, that being the rule of evidence as to the intent, which was very adroitly suggested as the reason for asking this extraordinary question, this kind of testimony could be of no avail unless, indeed, we were to have the opinion of the Lieutenant General as to the legality of the act.

I remarked before—and upon that remark I stand—that the question of the legality of the President's conduct is not to be settled by the opinions of any witness called at this bar; it is to be settled by the judgment of this Senate; and it is to be settled by the judgment of the Senate to the exclusion of every other tribunal on the earth, for it is so written in your Constitution. Intents are not to be proved in any conceivable form or shape by the opinions of any number of witnesses about the legality of an act. The law and the judges of the law will determine whether the act was unlawful; and opinions, though ever so often formed and expressed by a third person, cannot make an unlawful act a legal or a lawful act, and cannot get rid of the intention which the law says necessarily follows the commission of an unlawful act.

Well, say the gentlemen again, the President was taking the advice of honored and honorable gentlemen in the public service. The Constitution, as the Senate well know, indicates who shall be the President's advisers in such a case as this of the removal of the head of a Department. That Constitution expressly declares that he may appoint, and thereby necessarily remove, the present incumbent by and with the advice and consent of the Senate. The tenure-of-office act, following the Constitution, provided further that he may for sufficient reasons to him appearing suspend the incumbent and take the advice of the Senate, laying the facts before the Senate, with the evidence upon which he acted, whether the suspension should be made absolute. The President did take the advice of the Senate; he did suspend this officer whose removal he undertakes to prove now by individual opinions the public service requires. He sent notice of that suspension to the Senate. The Senate, as his constitutional adviser, acted upon it. They gave him notice that they advised him not to attempt any further interference with the Secretary for the Department of War. They gave him notice that under the law he could not go a step further. He thereupon falls back upon his assumed right, and undertakes to defy the Constitution, to defy the tenure-of-office act, to defy the Senate, and to remove the Secretary of War, and appoint another in his place without the advice and consent of anybody except such as he chose to call into his councils; and now he undertakes to justify by having them swear to their opinions. We protest against it in the name of the Constitution; we protest against it in the name of the laws enacted in pursuance of the Constitution; and we protest against it in the name of that great people whom we this day represent, and whose rights have been outrageously betrayed, and are now being audaciously defied before this tribunal.

The CHIEF JUSTICE. The Secretary will read the question.

The Secretary read as follows:

Question. After the restoration of Mr. Stanton to office did you form an opinion whether the good of the service required a Secretary of War other than Mr. Stanton; and if so, did you communicate that opinion to the President?

The CHIEF JUSTICE. The Chief Justice will submit the question to the Senate.

Mr. CONNESS called for the yeas and nays, and they were ordered; and being taken, resulted—yeas 15, nays 35; as follows:

YEAS — Messrs. Anthony, Bayard, Buckalew, Dixon, Doolittle, Fowler, Grimes, Hendricks, Johnson, McCreery, Patterson of Tennessee, Ross, Trumbull, Van Winkle, and Vickers—15.

NAYS—Messrs. Cameron, Cattell, Chandler, Cole, Conkling, Conness, Corbett, Cragin, Davis, Drake, Edmunds, Ferry, Fessenden, Frelinghuysen, Harlan, Henderson, Howard, Howe, Morgan, Morrill of Maine, Morrill of Vermont, Morton, Norton, Nye, Patterson of New Hampshire, Pomeroy, Ramsey, Sherman, Stewart, Thayer, Tipton, Willey, Williams, Wilson, and Yates—35.

NOT VOTING—Messrs. Saulsbury, Sprague, Sumner, and Wade—4.

So the question was decided to be inadmissible.

Mr. JOHNSON. Mr. President, I send to the Chair a question.

The CHIEF JUSTICE. The Secretary will read the question proposed by the Senator from Maryland.

The Secretary read as follows:

Did you at any time, and when, before the President gave the order for the removal of Mr. Stanton as Secretary of War, advise the President to appoint some other person in the place of Mr. Stanton?

Mr. Manager BUTLER. To that we have the honor to object as being leading in form, and not only in form bad, but being covered by the vote just taken.

Mr. EVARTS. I suggest, Mr. Chief Justice, that the objection of a question being leading in form cannot be made when it is put by a member of the court. I have never understood that such an objection could be made. It imputes to the court the idea of putting words into the witness's mouth to lead him.

Mr. Manager BUTLER. I do not know, Mr. President——

Mr. DAVIS. Mr. Chief Justice, I suggest whether the Managers or the counsel for the defense can interpose any objection to a question made by a member of the court?

The CHIEF JUSTICE. The Chief Justice thinks that any objection to the putting of a question by a member of the court must come from the court itself.

Mr. Manager BUTLER. Whenever that question arises, the Managers wish to be heard upon it.

Mr. DRAKE. I object to the putting of the question.

The CHIEF JUSTICE. The only mode in which an objection to the question can be decided properly is to rule the question admissible or inadmissible; and that is for the Senate. The question of the Senator from Maryland has been proposed unquestionably in good faith, and it addresses itself to the witness in the first instance, and it is for the Senate to determine whether it shall be answered by the witness or not. Senators, the question is whether the question propounded by the Senator from Maryland is admissible.

Mr. HOWE. Mr. President, I should like to have the question read again. I did not understand it.

The CHIEF JUSTICE. The Secretary will read the question propounded to the witness by the Senator from Maryland.

The Secretary read as follows:

Question. Did you at any time, and when, before the President gave the order for the removal of Mr. Stanton as Secretary of War, advise the President to appoint some other person than Mr. Stanton?

Mr. DRAKE. On that question I ask for the yeas and nays.

The yeas and nays were ordered; and being taken, resulted—yeas 18, nays 32; as follows:

YEAS — Messrs. Anthony, Bayard, Buckalew, Dixon, Doolittle, Edmunds, Fessenden, Fowler, Grimes, Henderson, Hendricks, Johnson, Patterson of Tennessee, Ross, Trumbull, Van Winkle, and Vickers—18.

NAYS—Messrs. Cameron, Cattell, Chandler, Cole, Conkling, Conness, Corbett, Cragin, Davis, Drake, Ferry, Frelinghuysen, Harlan, Howard, Howe, Morgan, Morrill of Maine, Morrill of Vermont, Morton, Norton, Nye, Patterson of New Hampshire, Pomeroy, Ramsey, Sherman, Stewart, Thayer, Tipton, Willey, Williams, Wilson, and Yates—32.

NOT VOTING—Messrs. Saulsbury, Sprague, Sumner, and Wade—4.

So the Senate decided the question to be inadmissible.

Mr. STANBERY. We have nothing further to ask of General Sherman.

Mr. Manager BINGHAM. We have nothing to ask of General Sherman.

The CHIEF JUSTICE. The Chief Justice desires to ask whether the counsel for the President will require General Sherman again at all?

To this question no response was made; but Mr. Stanbery and Mr. Manager BUTLER each engaged in conversation with the witness.

Mr. COLE, (at two o'clock and fifteen minutes p. m.) I move that the Senate take a recess for fifteen minutes.

The motion was agreed to; and the Chief Justice resumed the chair at half past two o'clock, and called the Senate to order.

The CHIEF JUSTICE. Gentlemen counsel for the President, please proceed with your evidence.

R. J. MEIGS sworn and examined.

By Mr. STANBERY:

Question. What office do you hold?

Answer. I am clerk of the supreme court of the District of Columbia.

Question. Were you clerk of that court in February last?

Answer. Yes.

Question. Have you with you the affidavit and warrant under which Lorenzo Thomas was arrested?

Answer. I have. [Producing some papers.]

Question. Are these the original papers?

Answer. The original papers.

Question. Did you affix the seal of the court to the warrant?

Answer. I did.

Question. On what day?

Answer. On the 22d of February last.

Question. At what hour of the day?

Answer. It was between two and three o'clock in the morning of that day?

Question. At what place?

Answer. At the clerk's office, where the seal is.

Question. Did you sit up in that office all night?

Answer. No, sir.

Question. Who brought that warrant to you?

Answer. I do not know the gentleman who brought it; he said he was a member of Congress, Mr. PILE, of Missouri.

Question. He announced himself as Mr. PILE, of Missouri?

Answer. Yes, sir.

Question. He then brought that warrant to you at your house at that hour in the morning?

Answer. Yes, sir.

Question. And you went then to the clerk's office?

Answer. I went to the clerk's office and affixed the seal and attested it.

Question. To whom did you deliver the warrant?

Answer. To Mr. PILE, if that was the gentleman. I did not know him, and do not know him now.

Question. The marshal was not there at that time?

Answer. No, sir.

Mr. Manager BUTLER. May I ask to what article this applies?

Mr. STANBERY. What article! It does not apply to any article. It applies very conclusively to some of your proof, and it applies very much to our answer, as you will find when we are a little further along in the case. [To the witness.] Have you the warrant here?

Answer. Yes, sir, I have.

Question. Did he bring the affidavit upon which the warrant was founded, or did you get that afterward?

Answer. I believe all the papers he gave me. I think so; but I am not sure of it. I cannot recollect.

Mr. STANBERY. We propose to read these papers, gentlemen, [handing the warrant and affidavit to the Managers.]

Mr. Manager BUTLER, (having examined the papers.) I understand, Mr. President, that the counsel for the President offer the affi-

davit and warrant in evidence. Before coming to them, I should like to ask a question or two of the witness. I suppose that is our right.

Mr. STANBERY. About the papers or what?

Mr. Manager BUTLER. About the thing you have been examining in regard to.

Mr. EVARTS. That is all we have been examining about.

Mr. Manager BUTLER. I propose to examine about the proof you have already put in.

Mr. STANBERY. We are through with the witness as soon as we get the papers. You can take him now and cross-examine him.

Mr. Manager BUTLER. Very well.

Cross-examined by Mr. Manager BUTLER:

Question. You say you affixed the seal about two o'clock in the morning of the 22d of February?

Answer. Between two and three o'clock in the morning.

Question. Were you called upon to get up and go to the office to do that?

Answer. I was.

Question. In cases where great crimes have been committed, and it is necessary to stop the further progress of crime, you have been accustomed to do that, I suppose?

Answer. I do not know of any case where that was necessary to prevent a crime. I have done the same thing in *habeas corpus* cases, and in one replevin case I remember.

Question. Where it is a matter of consequence you do these things when called upon?

Answer. Certainly.

Question. It is nothing unusual for you to do it in such cases?

Answer. It cannot be said to be unusual. I would do it at any time.

By Mr. STANBERY:

Question. Have you often been called upon in the course of your experience at night?

Answer. Only three times, and this is one of them.

Question. Do you know what became of this extreme case? What was done with this criminal?

Answer. I was not present at the examination.

Mr. STANBERY, (to the Managers.) Are you through with the papers?

Mr. Manager BUTLER. I am through with the papers.

Mr. STANBERY. Very well.

Mr. Manager BUTLER. I have the honor to object, Mr. President, to the warrant and affidavit of Mr. Stanton being received as evidence in this cause. I do not think Mr. Stanton can make testimony against the President by any affidavit that he can put in, or for him by any proceedings between him and Lorenzo Thomas. I do not think the warrant is relevant to this case in any form. The fact that Thomas was arrested has gone in, and that is all. To put in the affidavit upon which he was arrested certainly is putting in *res inter alios*. It is not a proceeding between Thomas and the President; but this is between Thomas and Stanton, and in no view is it either pertinent or relevant to this case or competent in any form, so far as I am instructed.

Mr. EVARTS. Mr. Chief Justice and Senators, the arrest of General Thomas was brought into testimony by the Managers and they argued, I believe in their opening, before they had proved it, that that was what prevented General Thomas using force to take possession of the War Office. We now propose to show what that arrest was in form and substance by the authentic documents of it, which are the warrant and the affidavit on which it was based. The affidavit, of course, does not prove the facts stated in it; but the proof of the affidavit shows the fact upon which, as a judicial foundation, the warrant proceeded. We then propose to follow the opening thus laid, of this proceeding, by showing how it took place and how efforts were made on behalf of General Thomas by *habeas corpus* to raise the question for the determination of the Supreme Court of the United States in regard to this act.

Mr. Manager BUTLER. I understand, Mr. President, that if this affidavit goes in at all, it is then evidence of all that it states, if the gentlemen have a right to put it in.

Mr. EVARTS. I said otherwise; but you can have your own conclusion. We do not admit it to be so.

Mr. Manager BUTLER. That is my conclusion, and that is what we should claim; and I think nothing more clearly shows that it cannot be evidence than that fact. This was not an attempt of the President to get this matter before the court; it was an attempt of Mr. Stanton to protect himself from violence which had been threatened in two instances before. This was late at night. Mr. Stanton, we can easily judge from the evidence, was informed *that night of the threats made to* BURLEIGH, *the* threats made to Wilkeson, and the threats made at Willard's Hotel, and being informed of them he did not know at what hour this man might bring his masqueraders upon him, and thereupon he took care to protect himself at the earliest possible hour.

But how that can relieve the President from crime, how that shows that he did or did not commit the act complained of, because Stanton arrested Thomas or Thomas arrested Stanton, is more than I can conceive. Suppose Stanton had not arrested Thomas, would it show that the President is not guilty here? Suppose he did arrest him, does it show that he is guilty here? Is it not merely, in the language of the law, well known to every lawyer in the Senate, *res inter alios acta*—things done between other parties than the parties to this record. We only adverted to the arrest in putting in Thomas's declaration to show what effect it had on his mind.

Mr. EVARTS. It has already been put in

proof by General Thomas that before he went to the court upon this arrest he saw the President and told him of his arrest, and the President immediately replied "that is as it should be;" or "that is as we wish it to be, the question in the court." Now, I propose to show that this is the question that was in the courts, to wit: the question of the criminality of a person accused and this civil-tenure bill. And I then propose to sustain the answer of the President, and also the sincerity and substance of this his statement already in evidence, by showing that this proceeding, having been commenced as it was by Mr. Stanton against General Thomas, was immediately taken hold of as the speediest and most rapid mode, through a *habeas corpus*, in which the President or the Attorney General, or General Thomas acting in that behalf, would be the actor, in order to bring at once before this court, the supreme court of the District, the question of the validity of his arrest and confinement under an act claimed to be unconstitutional, with an immediate opportunity of appeal to the Supreme Court of the United States then in session, from which at once there could have been obtained a determination of the point.

Mr. Manager BUTLER. And whenever that is proposed to be shown I propose to show that Mr. Thomas was discharged on the motion of his own counsel from arrest by the judge.

Mr. EVARTS. Very well; that is afterward; we will see about that; we will prove our case: you can prove yours.

Mr. Manager BUTLER. Admit this and the Senate will be traveling into the question of the various facts taking place in another court; and I have not yet heard any of the learned counsel say that this did not come within the rule of *res inter alios acta*—things done between others than parties to the record.

Mr. EVARTS. I did not think it necessary.

Mr. Manager BUTLER. That may be a very good answer; but, whether it is necessary or not, is it not so? Is there a lawyer anywhere who does not understand that, and who does not know that the proceedings between two other persons after a crime is committed, never yet were offered in evidence to show that a crime was not committed.

It is said that the President was glad to get this matter before a court. Did he see that affidavit? No. Did he know what was in it? No. All he knew was that his man was carried into court on some process which the man himself, Thomas, did not even know what it was. He was simply arrested. Mr. Thomas himself did not see the affidavit at that time, did not know anything of the matter except that he was taken by the marshal. He had never seen the paper on the evidence here; he did not even know for what he was arrested. All he knew was that he was arrested for something or other; whether it was for being at the masquerade ball the night before, masked, or-what it was he could not tell; he does not pretend to have told here in evidence; but when he said to the President, "they have arrested me"—for which of his virtues or for which of his crimes nobody knew—he did not, he does not say that he ever saw any paper in any form; but he simply went to the President and told him "I am arrested." And what, then, did the President say? "That is where I want you to be, in court." I should have thought he wanted him anywhere else except in the War Office; and that is all the testimony shows so far.

Now, they propose to put in Mr. Stanton's affidavit. It is exceedingly good reading, gentlemen of the Senate, and sets forth the case with great luminousness. It shows the terror and alarm of the good citizens of the District of Columbia when at night men who are known to be men of constancy and steadfastness, men representing important districts in Congress, felt it was their duty to call upon the chief justice of the supreme court of this District to interpose, felt that it was their duty to call up the venerable clerk of that court in the dead of night to get a warrant, and felt that it was their duty to take immediate means to prevent the consummation of this crime. It shows the terror and alarm which the unauthorized, illegal, and criminal acts of this respondent had thrown this city into at that hour. Undoubtedly all that is in the affidavit; undoubtedly all that can be shown; and then, thank God, we have before the Senate and the people of America this appeal to the laws by Mr. Stanton, which this criminal respondent never undertook, either before or since, although furnished with all the panoply of legal attack and defense in the Attorney General. He never brought his *quo warranto;* he never brought any process; he never took any step of himself, nor had he for a year.

All that will appear doubtless, and we should be glad to have it in, provided it did not open us into regions of unexplored and uncertain, diffuse and improper evidence, opening entirely new issues. If you are ready to go into it I am; but I say it does not belong to this case. I think we can make quite as much out of it as they can, but it is no portion of this case. It is not the act of the President; it has nothing to do with the President; the President never saw these papers upon any evidence here; and what Mr. Thomas did, and what Mr. Stanton did, they themselves must stand by.

Mr. STANBERY. I believe our hour has not expired, and I wish upon this matter to address, Mr. Chief Justice, a few words to the Senate.

Senators, there are two grounds upon which we ask the admission of this testimony. First of all, there are already in evidence the declarations of the President that he made this removal to bring the question of that law to the consideration of the courts. That is already in evidence, and as to that the Managers say it is all pretense, all a subterfuge.

Mr. Manager BUTLER. Where in evidence?

Mr. STANBERY. Among other things in a place that I need not refer to now, the speech of the honorable Manager who opened the case.

Mr. Manager BUTLER. If you will take my speech as evidence I am very glad. That is the best evidence.

Mr. STANBERY. Not, except as a last resort, for anything. The gentleman has repeated that this is all pretense of asking to get into the courts, that it is a subterfuge, an afterthought, a mere scheme on the part of the President to avoid the consequences of an act done with another intention than that. Again, what sort of a case have the Managers attempted to make against the President upon his intentions with regard to the occupation of the War Office by Thomas? They have sought to prove that the intentions of the President were not to get it by law but to get it by intimidation, threats, and force; they have gone into this themselves to show the intent of the President, and how? They have given the declarations of Thomas as to his purpose of using threats, intimidation, or force, and claim that those declarations bind the President, and you, Senators, have admitted them against the President. The mere declarations of Thomas as to his intention to enter the office by force and intimidation are to be considered the declarations of the President, and as evidence of his intent. Oh! say the gentlemen, that thing was stopped by this prosecution; the prompt arrest of General Thomas next morning was the only thing that defeated the accomplishment of the purpose that was in the mind of the President and in the mind of General Thomas.

Mr. Manager BUTLER. I did not say so. Thomas said so.

Mr. STANBERY. Thomas said so! The Senate will bear me witness who said so, who called that a subterfuge, and who called that a pretense! We wish to show what was this proceeding got up at midnight, as the learned Manager says, in view of a great crime just committed or about to be committed; got up under the most pressing necessity, with a judge, as we will show, summoned from his bed at an early hour on that winter morning, the 22d of February, at two o'clock—a judge brought from the bench, such was the urgent and pressing necessity, either pretended or real, on the part of Mr. Stanton to avoid the use of force and intimidation to remove him from that office. We shall show that having had him arrested, held to bail in $5,000, the time of the trial or further hearing of this great criminal having been fixed for the next Wednesday, all this being done on the prior Saturday, when he got there on that day it turned out thus: "Why we have got no criminal at all; General Thomas is just as good a citizen as we have in this community." General Thomas's counsel say to the court, "He is surrendered; he is in custody; and we do that for the purpose of moving a *habeas corpus.*" As soon as that purpose was announced, all at once this great criminal and this great criminal act immediately disappear, and the judge says, "This is all nothing at all that we have had against you, General Thomas; we do not even want to ask you to give bail; on the contrary, I dismiss you." And the counsel for Mr. Stanton, who were there on that morning, and who had seen this great criminal punished, or, at any rate, put under bonds for good behavior, expressly consent to what? Not merely that he shall be put at large under bonds; not merely that he shall give bonds for his good behavior, but that he shall be absolutely discharged and go free, just as if there was no prosecution at all; not bound over to the next term of the court, but totally discharged, and, as we shall show you, discharged for the very purpose of preventing what was then in preparation, the presentation of a *habeas corpus,* that the case might be got immediately to the Supreme Court of the United States, then in session, the only ready way in which the question could be brought before the courts and decided for any purpose of any value. Senators, is that, too, to be excluded? I trust not.

Mr. Manager BUTLER. I did not mean to trouble the Senate again; but one or two statements of fact have been made to which, I think, I must call your attention. First, it is said that Mr. Thomas was discharged wholly. That depended upon the chief justice of that court. If you are going to try him by impeachment, wait until after we get through with this case. One trial at a time is sufficient. Is he to be tried because he did not do his duty under the circumstances? Neither Mr. Stanton, nor your Honor, nor anybody else has any right to judge of the act of that court until he is here to defend himself, which the chief justice of the supreme court of the District of Columbia is amply able to do.

Then there is another point which I wish to take into consideration. It is said that Thomas had become a good citizen. I have not agreed to that. I do not believe anybody else has; but he himself testifies that the fight was all out of him the next morning after this process, and they put in then that he agreed to remain neutral. Then there was no occasion to hold him any longer. He took a drink to seal the neutrality. Do they not remember the testimony that on the next morning after this he and Stanton took a drink and agreed to remain neutral, and they held up the glasses and said, "This is neutral ground now?" What was the use of holding him any further?

Mr. STANBERY. That is, he took a drink with the great criminal!

Mr. Manager BUTLER. He took a drink with the President's tool; that is all. The thing was settled. The poor old man came and complained that he had not had anything to eat or drink, and in tender mercy to him

Mr. Stanton gave him something to drink; and he says that from that hour, if he had not before, he has never had an idea of force. What, then, was the use of holding him?

Now, I wish to call the attention of the Senate to another statement of fact, and that is, that they did not hold him to keep the peace. Why, the next morning he was told that he was not held to keep the peace. He said that here to the Senate upon his oath, and he insisted upon putting it in; I objected, but he said it was necessary for him to make that point, and then I yielded that he might do it. He said to the Senate that the judge told him, "This does not interfere in any way with your duties as Secretary of War."

But there is still another thing. This unconstitutional law has been on the statute-book since a year ago last March. The learned Attorney General of the United States stands before me. Where is the writ of *quo warranto* which it was his duty to file?

Mr. STANBERY. I will show it to you right away, as soon as I get through this testimony.

Mr. Manager BUTLER. Then it will be the first exhibition that has ever been made to any court in the United States of it, if it is shown to me. I suppose it has been prepared since as part of this defense. Where is the *quo warranto* filed in any court, Judge Carter's court, or anybody else's court? Where is the proceeding taken? He—I put it to him as a lawyer, dare he deny it?—he is the only man in the United States that could file a *quo warranto,* and he knows it. He is the only man who could initiate this proceeding, and he knows it. And yet it was not done; and still he comes here and talks about putting in the quarrels between Mr. Stanton and Mr. Thomas over this matter. They are *res inter alios,* I say again—things done between others— and they have nothing more to do with this case, and hardly as much as the fact which the President with his excellent taste, and the excellent taste of his counsel, drew out here against my objection, that Mr. Stanton when this man Thomas claimed that he was fainting for want of his breakfast and his drink, gave him a drink.

The CHIEF JUSTICE. The counsel will please reduce their question to writing.

Mr. STANBERY. It is the affidavit, if the court please, that we offer in evidence.

The CHIEF JUSTICE. What does the affidavit relate to?

Mr. STANBERY. It is that upon which the warrant was issued—the affidavit by Mr. Stanton, and the warrant for the arrest of Thomas founded on that affidavit. We offer the two papers.

Mr. EVARTS. To be followed by the other proof which we have stated.

The CHIEF JUSTICE. The Chief Justice thinks the affidavit upon which the arrest was made is competent testimony, as it relates to a transaction upon which Mr. Thomas has already been examined, and as it may be material to show the purpose of the President to resort to a court of law. He will be happy to put the question to the Senate if any member desires it. (No Senator being heard to speak.) Read the affidavit.

Mr. Manager BUTLER. Does your Honor understand that the affidavit is admitted?

The CHIEF JUSTICE. Yes, sir.

Mr. Manager BUTLER. I heard one Senator ask for the question to be put.

The CHIEF JUSTICE. Does any Senator ask the question to be put?

Mr. CONNESS. I asked that the question be put, and I now ask for the yeas and nays upon it.

The yeas and nays were ordered.

Mr. HOWARD. I wish the question might be read. We do not fully understand it.

The CHIEF JUSTICE. The Chair will state that the counsel for the President propose to put in the affidavit upon which the arrest of General Thomas was made on the morning, I think, of the 22d of February.

Mr. JOHNSON. It is impossible to decide without knowing what the paper is.

The CHIEF JUSTICE. Will the counsel state what they propose to prove in writing?

Mr. EVARTS. I will read the affidavit.

Mr. Manager BUTLER. We object to that. Then it is in.

The CHIEF JUSTICE. Objection is made to reading the affidavit. If the counsel will state what they propose to prove in writing it will be better.

Mr. STANBERY. We propose to offer an affidavit made by Mr. Stanton on the night of the 21st or morning of the 22d of February.

The CHIEF JUSTICE. You will state it in writing.

The proposition having been reduced to writing,

The CHIEF JUSTICE. The Secretary will read the proposition of the counsel for the President.

The Secretary read as follows:

We offer a warrant of arrest of General Thomas, dated February 22, 1868, and the affidavit on which the warrant issued.

The CHIEF JUSTICE. Senators, you who are of opinion that the evidence proposed to be offered by the counsel for the President is admissible, will, as your names are called, answer yea; those of the contrary opinion, nay. The Secretary will call the roll.

The question being taken by yeas and nays, resulted—yeas 34, nays 17; as follows:

YEAS.—Messrs. Anthony, Bayard, Buckalew, Cattell, Cole, Corbett, Cragin, Davis, Dixon, Doolittle, Fessenden, Fowler, Frelinghuysen, Grimes, Henderson, Hendricks, Johnson, McCreery, Morrill of Maine, Morrill of Vermont, Morton, Norton, Patterson of New Hampshire, Patterson of Tennessee, Pomeroy, Ross, Sherman, Sumner, Trumbull, Van Winkle, Vickers, Willey, Williams, and Yates—34.

NAYS.—Messrs. Cameron, Chandler, Conkling, Conness, Drake, Edmunds, Ferry, Harlan, Howard,

Howe, Morgan, Nye, Ramsey, Stewart, Thayer, Tipton, and Wilson—17.

NOT VOTING.—Messrs. Saulsbury, Sprague, and Wade—3.

So the Senate decided that the offer of the counsel should be admitted.

Mr. EVARTS. I will read the papers. The affidavit is:

To Hon. DAVID K. CARTTER, *Chief Justice of the Supreme Court for the District of Columbia:*

Comes Edwin M. Stanton, of the city of Washington, in the said District, and upon oath says that on the 21st day of February, A. D. 1868, he, the said Edwin M. Stanton, duly held the office of Secretary for the Department of War, under and according to the Constitution and laws of the United States; that he had, prior to said 21st day of February, A. D. 1868, been duly nominated and appointed to the said office of Secretary of War by the President of the United States, and that his said nomination had been submitted in due form of law to the Senate of the United States, and his said nomination had been duly assented to and confirmed by and with the advice of the Senate; and he, the said Edwin M. Stanton, had duly accepted said office, and taken out and subscribed all the oaths required by law, upon his induction into said office, and was in the actual possession of said office and performing the duties thereof on said 21st day of February, A. D. 1868, and he had never resigned said office, or been legally dismissed therefrom, and he claims that he does now legally hold said office, and is entitled to all the rights, privileges, and powers thereof.

And the said Edwin M. Stanton on oath further states that on said 21st day of February, 1868, in the city of Washington aforesaid, Andrew Johnson, President of the United States, made and issued an order in writing under his hand, with intent and purpose of removing him, the said Edwin M. Stanton, from the said office of Secretary for the Department of War, and authorizing and empowering Lorenzo Thomas, Adjutant General of the Army of the United States, to act as Secretary of War *ad interim*, and directing him, the said Thomas, to immediately enter upon the discharge of the duties pertaining to that office. And your affiant further states that the said pretended order of removal of him from the said office of Secretary of War is wholly illegal and void and contrary to the express provisions of an act duly passed by the Congress of the United States on the 2d day of March, A. D. 1867, entitled "An act regulating the tenure of certain civil offices." And your affiant on oath further states that the said Lorenzo Thomas did, on said 21st day of February, A. D. 1868, in said city of Washington, accept the said pretended appointment as Secretary of War *ad interim*, and on the same day left with your affiant a copy of the said pretended order of the President removing your affiant as Secretary of War, and appointing the said Lorenzo Thomas Secretary of War *ad interim*, certified by the said Lorenzo Thomas under his own hand as Secretary of War *ad interim*. And on the same 21st day of February, A. D. 1868, in the city of Washington aforesaid, the said Lorenzo Thomas delivered to your affiant the said pretended order of Andrew Johnson, with intent to cause your affiant to deliver to him, the said Thomas, all the records, books, papers, and other public property now in his (the affiant's) custody and charge as Secretary of War. And your affiant further states on oath, and that he is informed and believes that the said Thomas has, in said city of Washington and District aforesaid, exercised and attempted to exercise the duties of Secretary of War, and to issue orders as such, and your affiant is also informed and believes that the said Lorenzo Thomas gives out and threatens that he will forcibly remove your complainant from the building and apartments of the Secretary of War in the War Department, and forcibly take the possession and control thereof under his said pretended appointment by the President of the United States as Secretary of War *ad interim*.

And your affiant alleges that the appointment under which the said Thomas claims to act, and to hold and perform the duties of Secretary of War, is wholly unauthorized and illegal, and that the said

Thomas, by accepting such appointment, and thereunder exercising and attempting to exercise the duties of Secretary of War, has violated the provisions of the fifth section of the act above referred to, and thereby has been guilty of a high misdemeanor, and subjected himself to the pains and penalties prescribed in said fifth section against any person committing such offense.

Whereupon your affiant prays that a warrant may be issued against Lorenzo Thomas, and that he may be thereupon arrested and brought before your Honor and thereupon that he may be dealt with as the law and justice in such case appertains.

EDWIN M. STANTON.

Sworn and subscribed before me this 21st day of February, A. D. 1868.

D. K. CARTTER, *Chief Justice.*

Sworn to and subscribed before me by Edwin M. Stanton at the city of Washington, in the District of Columbia, this 22d day of February, 1868.

D. K. CARTTER, *Chief Justice.*

The warrant is dated the 22d of February, 1868.

Mr. STANBERY. First the 21st and then the 22d. It is dated before twelve o'clock, and then after twelve o'clock.

Mr. EVARTS. It is sworn to twice, once on the 21st and once on the 22d. The warrant is as follows:

United States of America, District of Columbia, ss.—To David S. Gooding, United States marshal for the District of Columbia: I, David K. Cartter, Chief Justice of the supreme court of the District of Columbia, hereby command you to arrest Lorenzo Thomas of said District forthwith, and that you have the said Lorenzo Thomas before me at the chambers of the said supreme court in the city of Washington, forthwith, to answer to the charge of a high misdemeanor in this, that on the 21st day of February, 1868, in the District of Columbia, he did unlawfully accept the appointment of the office of Secretary of War *ad interim,* and did then and there unlawfully hold and exercise and attempt to hold and exercise the said office contrary to the provisions of the act entitled "An act regulating the tenure of certain civil offices," passed March 2, 1867, and hereof fail not but make due return.

Given under my hand and seal of said court this 22d day of February, 1868,

[L. S.] D. K. CARTTER,

Chief Justice of the Supreme Court of the District of Columbia.

Attest: R. J. MEIGS, *Clerk.*

The marshal's return is as follows:

WASHINGTON CITY, D. C., *February* 22, 1868.

The within writ came to hand at seven o'clock a. m., and was served by me on the said Lorenzo Thomas at eight o'clock a. m., and I now return this writ and bring him before Chief Justice Cartter at nine o'clock a. m. of to-day.

DAVID S. GOODING,

United States Marshal, D. C.

By Mr. STANBERY:

Question. Mr. Meigs, I perceive this is a judge's warrant at chambers?

Answer. Yes, sir.

Question. Are you in the habit of keeping any record further than filing the papers, or did you make any record further than filing the papers of that proceeding?

Answer. When the recognizance was executed, that was put upon the docket of the court. You will see that the warrants are marked with a number.

Question. The recognizance of bail?

Answer. As soon as that is done the cases are all put upon the docket of the court in order that it may appear how the defendant is discharged, or what becomes of him.

Question. Well, has this defendant been discharged?

Mr. Manager BUTLER. Stay a moment. That will appear by the record.

The WITNESS. Yes; that will appear by the record.

By Mr. STANBERY:

Question. Have you a record of the discharge also?

Answer. The docket shows that.

Question. Is that the docket of the judge or the docket of the court?

Answer. The docket of the court.

Question. Does the judge return the case into court?

Answer. The recognizance of course is returned into court.

Question. I am not speaking of the recognizance; I am speaking of this case?

Answer. The recognizance was taken upon that case, and was returned into court, and was entered upon the docket of the court.

Question. You make no record of these papers?

Answer. No; no record of those papers. They are filed, and constitute a part of the record of the case at court.

Question. Have you got your docket with you?

Answer. No, sir. The subpœna did not require it to be brought, and of course it was not brought.

Mr. STANBERY, (to the Managers.) We will have the docket if you require it, gentlemen. Do you want that formal matter?

Mr. Manager BUTLER. A little more than that.

Mr. STANBERY. Do you want us to produce——

Mr. Manager BUTLER. I do not want anything, except I shall object to any incompetent testimony.

Mr. STANBERY. You can take this witness.

Mr. Manager BUTLER. That is all, Mr. Meigs.

Mr. STANBERY. Mr. Meigs, will you bring this docket that contains this entry?

Answer. Yes, sir.

Mr. Manager BUTLER, (to the witness.) A single word. Will you not extend the record as far as you can, and bring us a certified copy of this case as it will appear after being extended?

Mr. STANBERY. Call Mr. Clephane.

Mr. JOHNSON, (sending a question to the desk.) Mr. Chief Justice, I desire to put a question to General Sherman. He is in the room, I believe.

The CHIEF JUSTICE. The Secretary will read the question. To whom does the Senator from Maryland address it?

Mr. JOHNSON. General Sherman. He is in the court, I understand.

WILLIAM T. SHERMAN recalled.

The Secretary read the question of Mr. JOHNSON, as follows:

When the President tendered to you the office of Secretary of War *ad interim* on the 27th of January, 1868, and on the 31st of the same month and year, did he, at the very time of making such tender, state to you what his purpose in so doing was?

Mr. Manager BINGHAM. We object to the question as being within the ruling of the Senate, and incompetent.

The CHIEF JUSTICE. The Chief Justice will submit that question to the Senate.

Mr. DRAKE. Upon that question I ask for the yeas and nays.

The yeas and nays were ordered.

The CHIEF JUSTICE. Senators, you who are of opinion that the question proposed by the honorable Senator from Maryland is admissible, will, as your names are called, answer yea; those of a contrary opinion, nay.

Mr. JOHNSON. Before the roll is called I ask that the question be read again.

The Secretary again read the question.

The question being taken by yeas and nays, resulted—yeas 26, nays 22; as follows:

YEAS—Messrs. Anthony, Bayard, Buckalew, Cole, Davis, Dixon, Doolittle, Fessenden, Fowler, Frelinghuysen, Grimes, Henderson, Johnson, McCreery, Morrill of Maine, Morrill of Vermont, Morton, Norton, Patterson of Tennessee, Ross, Sherman, Sumner, Trumbull, Van Winkle, Vickers, and Willey—26.

NAYS—Messrs. Cattell, Chandler, Conkling, Conness, Corbett, Cragin, Drake, Edmunds, Ferry, Harlan, Howard, Howe, Morgan, Nye, Pomeroy, Ramsey, Stewart, Thayer, Tipton, Williams, Wilson, and Yates—22.

NOT VOTING—Messrs. Cameron, Hendricks, Patterson of New Hampshire, Saulsbury, Sprague, and Wade—6.

The CHIEF JUSTICE. On this question the yeas are 26 and the nays 22. So the question is admitted and will be put to the witness. The Secretary will read the question again.

The Secretary read the question to the witness, as follows:

When the President tendered to you the office of Secretary of War *ad interim* on the 27th of January, 1868 and on the 31st of the same month and year, did he, at the very time of making such tender, state to you what his purpose in so doing was?

The WITNESS. He stated to me that his purpose——

Mr. Manager BUTLER. Stay a moment. The question, Mr. Chief Justice, was whether he did state, not what he stated. We want to object to what he stated.

Mr. EVARTS. Answer yes or no, General. *Answer.* Yes.

The CHIEF JUSTICE. The witness answers that he did.

By Mr. STANBERY:

Question. What purpose did he state?

Mr. Manager BINGHAM. To that we object.

Mr. Manager BUTLER. The counsel had dismissed this witness, and he is not to be brought back, on a question of the court, for the purpose of counsel opening the case again.

The CHIEF JUSTICE. The Chief Justice thinks it is entirely competent for the Senate to recall any witness.

Mr. Manager BUTLER. I have not objected to the Senate recalling a witness.

The CHIEF JUSTICE. The Senate has decided that the question shall be put to the witness. That amounts to a recalling of him, and the Chief Justice is of opinion that the witness is bound to answer the questions. Does any Senator object?

Mr. Manager BUTLER. We understand that the only question he has been recalled for has been answered.

Mr. EVARTS. We have asked another question.

Mr. JOHNSON. I propose to add to it—I thought my question included that—if the President did, what did he state that his purpose was?

Mr. Manager BINGHAM. To that we object; and we ask the Senate to consider that the last clause suggested now by the honorable Senator from Maryland, "And what did the President say," is the very question which the Senate this day did solemnly decide adversely to its being put, and it so decided on Saturday; in short, the last clause now put to the witness by the honorable Senator from Maryland is, What did the President say? making the President's declarations evidence for himself when they are not called out by the Government. It was suggested by my associate in argument on Saturday that if that method were pursued in the administration of justice, and the declarations of the accused were made evidence for himself at his pleasure, the administration of justice would be impossible in any court.

Mr. DAVIS. I rise to a question of order.

The CHIEF JUSTICE. The Senator from Kentucky.

Mr. DAVIS. It is that one of the Managers has no right to object to a question propounded by a member of the court.

Mr. Manager BUTLER. We might as well meet that question now.

Mr. Manager BINGHAM. I desire to say on that subject, if I may be allowed to do so, without trespassing——

The CHIEF JUSTICE. The honorable Manager will wait one moment. When a member of the court propounds a question it seems to the Chief Justice that it is clearly within the competency of the Managers to object to the question being put and state the grounds for that objection, as a legal question. It is not competent for the Managers to object to a member of the court asking a question; but after the question is asked, it seems to the Chief Justice, that it is clearly competent for the Managers to state their objections to the questions being answered.

Mr. CONNESS. I ask that the question now put be reduced to writing.

The CHIEF JUSTICE. The Clerk has it reduced to writing. It will be read.

The Secretary read it, as follows:

If he did, state what he said his purpose was?

Mr. CONNESS. Do I understand that to be a part of, or an addition made to the other question?

Mr. JOHNSON. Part of the same question.

The CHIEF JUSTICE. It must be regarded at present as an independent question.

Mr. CONNESS. And therefore I ask that the independent question be reduced to writing. It has nothing to do with the other.

The CHIEF JUSTICE. The Chief Justice understands the question which has just been read by the Clerk to be the question.

Mr. CONNESS. Then I call for its reading again.

The CHIEF JUSTICE, (to the Secretary.) Read the question.

The Secretary read as follows:

If he did, state what he said his purpose was?

Mr. CONNESS. "Did" what?

Mr. DRAKE. I would inquire for information, Mr. President, whether, in order to test the introduction of that question, it is necessary that a Senator should object to its being put?

Mr. EDMUNDS. No; the Chief Justice has decided that it is not.

Mr. DRAKE. Very well.

The CHIEF JUSTICE. The Chief Justice has said that it does not seem to him competent for the Managers or the counsel to object to a question being put by a Senator; but after it has been put, the question whether it shall be answered must necessarily depend upon the judgment of the court, and either the counsel for the President or the honorable Managers are quite at liberty to address any observations they see fit to the court upon that point.

Several SENATORS. That is right.

Mr. JOHNSON. Certainly; I do not doubt that.

Mr. Manager BINGHAM. Upon that statement I may be pardoned for saying our only purpose is to object to the answer being taken by the Senate to the question, and not to object to the right of the honorable gentleman from Maryland to offer his question.

Mr. JOHNSON. I so understand.

Mr. Manager BINGHAM. And that is the question that is before the Senate. The question that we raise before the Senate is, that it is incompetent for the accused to make his own declarations evidence for himself.

The CHIEF JUSTICE. The Chief Justice has already said upon a former occasion that he thinks that, for the purpose of proving the intent, this question is admissible; and he thinks, also, that it comes within the rule which has been adopted by the Senate as a guide for its own action. This is not an ordinary court, but it is a court composed largely of lawyers and gentlemen of great experience in the business transactions of life, and they are quite

competent to determine upon the effect of any evidence which may be submitted to them; and the Chief Justice thought that the rule which the Senate adopted for itself was founded on this fact; and in accordance with that rule, by which he determined the question submitted on Saturday, he now determines this question in the same way.

Mr. DRAKE. I ask for a vote of the Senate upon the question.

The CHIEF JUSTICE. The Secretary will read the question.

Mr. Manager BUTLER. I only want to ask a single question. The Chief Justice understands this, as does the board of Managers, as I understand, to be precisely the same question that was ruled upon on last Saturday evening, when the Chief Justice ruled.

Mr. Manager BINGHAM. And this morning, too.

The CHIEF JUSTICE. The Chief Justice does not say that. What he does say is, that it is a question of the same general import, to show the intent of the President during these transactions. The Secretary will read the question again.

Mr. JOHNSON. I ask that both questions be read, the first and the second, taken in connection with each other. The witness has answered the first.

The CHIEF JUSTICE. The Secretary will read the original question, and then he will read the present question before the Senate.

The SECRETARY. The first question was:

When the President tendered to you the office of Secretary of War *ad interim* on the 27th of January, 1868, and on the 31st of the same month and year, did he, at the very time of making such tender, state to you what his purpose in so doing was?

The witness having answered this, the question now is:

If he did, state what he said his purpose was?

The CHIEF JUSTICE. Senators, you who are of opinion that the question just read, "if he did, state what he said his purpose was," is admissible, and should be put to the witness, will, as your names are called, answer yea; those of a contrary opinion, nay. The Secretary will call the roll.

Mr. HOWE. Before I vote upon the admissibility of this answer, I wish, if there is any regular mode of doing so, to ascertain the state of the record upon another point; and that is, whether the fact that this office was tendered to the witness on the stand was a fact put in by the defense or by the prosecution. My own recollection is not very distinct about it, and I am not sure that I am right.

The CHIEF JUSTICE. The Chief Justice must remind the Senator that no debate is in order unless there be a motion to retire for conference.

Mr. EVARTS. I may be permitted, as counsel, to state that it was put in by the defense.

Mr. Manager BINGHAM. It was put in by the defense.

Mr. EVARTS. I have so stated.

Mr. Manager BINGHAM. I wish it to be understood distinctly.

Mr. HOWE. The Chief Justice will allow me to remark that putting a question to ascertain the state of the record was entering into debate by no manner of means.

The CHIEF JUSTICE. It may be, however.

Mr. HOWE. It may not be.

The CHIEF JUSTICE. The Secretary will call the roll.

The question being taken by yeas and nays, resulted—yeas 26, nays 25; as follows:

YEAS—Messrs. Anthony, Bayard, Buckalew, Cole, Corbett, Davis, Dixon, Doolittle, Fessenden, Fowler, Frelinghuysen, Grimes, Henderson, Hendricks, Johnson, McCreery, Morton, Norton, Patterson of Tennessee, Ross, Sherman, Sumner, Trumbull, Van Winkle, Vickers, and Willey—26.

NAYS—Messrs. Cameron, Cattell, Chandler, Conkling, Conness, Cragin, Drake, Edmunds, Ferry, Harlan, Howard, Howe, Morgan, Morrill of Maine, Morrill of Vermont, Nye, Patterson of New Hampshire, Pomeroy, Ramsey, Stewart, Thayer, Tipton, Williams, Wilson, and Yates—25.

NOT VOTING.—Messrs. Saulsbury, Sprague, and Wade—3.

So the question propounded by Mr. JOHNSON was held to be admissible.

The WITNESS. May I take the question in my hand? [The question was handed to the witness and examined by him.] The first question was as to "both occasions." [The previous question was handed to the witness and examined by him.]

Mr. EVARTS. It covers both occasions.

The WITNESS. The conversations were long and covered a great deal of ground; but I will endeavor to be as precise to the point as possible. The President stated to me that the relations which had grown up between the Secretary of War, Mr. Stanton, and himself——

Mr. Manager BUTLER. Stay a moment. I must again interpose, Mr. President. The question is simply what the President stated his purpose was, and not to put in his whole declarations.

Mr. JOHNSON. That is all that is asked. This is preliminary to that.

Mr. CURTIS. That is all he is going to answer.

Mr. Manager BUTLER. I pray that that may be submitted to the Senate, whether they will have the whole of the long conversation, which is nothing to the purpose.

Mr. Manager BINGHAM. His purpose in offering General Sherman a commission.

Mr. Manager BUTLER. Yes, sir.

Mr. JOHNSON. That is it.

The WITNESS. I intended to be very precise and very short; but it appeared to me necessary to state what I began to state, that the President told me that the relations between himself and Mr. Stanton, and between Mr. Stanton and the other members of the Cabinet, were such that he could not execute the office which he filled as President of the United States without making provision *ad*

interim for that office; that he had the right under the law; he claimed to have the right, and his purpose was to have the office administered in the interest of the Army and of the country; and he offered me the office in that view. He did not state to me then that his purpose was to bring it to the courts directly; but for the purpose of having the office administered properly in the interest of the Army and of the whole country.

Mr. STANBERY. On both occasions, General, or the other occasion?

The WITNESS. I asked him why lawyers could not make a case; that I did not wish to be brought as an officer of the Army into any controversy.

Mr. CONKLING. Will you not repeat that last answer, General?

The WITNESS. I asked him why lawyers could not make a case, and not bring me, or an officer, into the controversy. His answer was that it was found impossible, or a case could not be made up; but, said he, "If we can bring the case to the courts it would not stand half an hour." I think that is all that he stated to me then.

By Mr. STANBERY:

Question. On either occasion?

Mr. JOHNSON. That is my question.

The WITNESS. The conversation was very long and covered a great deal of ground——

Mr. Manager BUTLER. I object to this examination being renewed by the counsel for the President.

Mr. STANBERY. There were two occasions. Has the witness got through both? That is the question.

Mr. Manager BUTLER. Whatever may be the pretense under which it is to be renewed, I hold that, according to the due order of trials, it ought not to be allowed. Let us see how it is to be done. Mr. President. The counsel dismissed this witness and he was gone, and he is brought back at the request of one of the judges, and that judge——

Mr. STANBERY. I must interrupt the learned Manager to say that we did not dismiss him. On the contrary, both sides asked to retain him, the learned Manager saying at the time that he wanted to give him a private examination.

Mr. Manager BUTLER. To that I must interpose a denial. I have asked for no private examination. I say the counsel dismissed him from the stand, dismissed him as a witness in this case from the stand. Then he is called back by one of the judges. In any court that anybody ever practiced in before, or in any tribunal, when that is done and a question is put by a judge, that never yet opened the case to have the witness examined by the counsel who had dismissed him.

Mr. JOHNSON. I ask for the reading of the question. I think I asked him to answer as to both of the occasions when the office was tendered to him.

The CHIEF JUSTICE. The Secretary will read the question proposed by the Senator from Maryland.

The SECRETARY. The witness having answered "yes" to the previous question, the question is, "State what he said his purpose was?"

The CHIEF JUSTICE. Nothing is more usual in courts of justice than to recall witnesses for further examination, especially at the instance of one of the members of the court. It is very often done at the instance of counsel. It is, however, a matter wholly within the discretion of the court; and if any Senator desires it the Chief Justice will be happy to put it to the court, whether the witness shall be further examined. If not——

Mr. WILLIAMS. I ask for the opinion of the court on that subject, whether the counsel can renew the examination of this witness and go beyond the question propounded by a member of the court.

The CHIEF JUSTICE. The counsel will please reduce the question they propose to put to writing.

The question having been reduced to writing was sent to the Secretary's desk, and read as follows:

Have you answered as to both occasions?

The CHIEF JUSTICE. The question is objected to, and the decision of the question will determine whether the counsel can put any further questions to the witness.

Mr. EVARTS. We may be heard upon that, I suppose.

The CHIEF JUSTICE. Certainly.

Mr. EVARTS. The question, Senators, whether a witness may be recalled is a question of the practice of courts. It is a practice almost universal, unless there is a suspicion of bad faith, to permit it to be done, and it is always in the discretion of the court. In special circumstances, where collusion is suspected between the witness and counsel for wrong purposes adverse to the administration of justice, a strict rule may be laid down. Whatever rule this court in the future shall lay down as peremptory, if it be that neither party shall recall a witness that has been once dismissed from the stand, of course will be obligatory upon us; but we are not aware that anything has occurred in the progress of this trial to intimate to counsel that any such rule had been adopted, or would be applied by this court.

Mr. Manager BUTLER. Mr. President, on Saturday this took place: this question was asked:

"In that interview"—

That is, when the offer was made—

"what conversation took place between the President and you in regard to the removal of Mr. Stanton?"

That question was offered to be put, and after argument, and upon a solemn ruling, twenty-eight gentlemen of the Senate decided that it could not be put. That was exactly the same question as this, asking for the same conversation at the same time. Then certain other proceedings were had, and after those were had the counsel waited some considerable time at the table in consultation, and then got up and asked leave to recall this witness this morning for the purpose of putting questions. The Senate gave that leave and adjourned. This morning they recalled the witness and put such questions as they pleased, and we spent as many hours, as you remember, in doing that. On Saturday they had got through with him, except that they wanted a little time to consider whether they would recall him; they did recall him this morning, and after getting through with him the witness was sent away. Then he was again recalled to enable one of the judges to put a question, to satisfy his mind. Of course, he was not acting as counsel for the President in so doing; that could not be supposed possible. He wanted to satisfy his mind.

Mr. JOHNSON. What does the honorable Manager mean?

Mr. Manager BUTLER. I mean precisely what I say, that it cannot be supposed possibly that he was acting as counsel for the President.

Mr. JOHNSON. Mr. Chief Justice, if the honorable Manager means to impute that in anything I have done in this trial I have been acting as counsel, or in the spirit of counsel, he does not know the man of whom he speaks. I am here to discharge a duty; and that I propose to do legally. And permit me to say to the honorable Manager that I know what the law is as well as he does, and it is not my purpose in any way to depart from it.

Mr. Manager BUTLER. Again I repeat, so that my language may not be misunderstood, that it is not to be supposed that he was acting as counsel for the President. Having put his question and satisfied his mind of something that he wanted satisfied, something that he wanted to know, how can it be that that opens the case to allow the President's counsel to go into a new examination of the witness? How do they know, if he is not acting as counsel for the President, and there is not some understanding between them, which I do not charge— how can the President's counsel know that his mind is not satisfied? He recalled the witness for the purpose of satisfying his own mind, and only for that reason. I agree it is common to recall witnesses for something that has been overlooked or forgotten; but I appeal to the presiding officer that while—and I never have said otherwise—a member of the court who wants to satisfy himself by putting some question may recall a witness for that purpose, it never is understood that that having been done the case was opened to the counsel on either side to go on and put other questions. The court is allowed to put the question, because it is supposed that the judge wants to satisfy his mind on a particular point. After the judge has satisfied his mind on that particular point then there is to be an end, and it is not to open the case anew. I trust I have answered the honorable Senator from Maryland that I meant no imputation. I was putting it right the other way.

Mr. JOHNSON. I am satisfied, Mr. Chief Justice; and I only rise to say that I did not know that the counsel proposed to ask any question, and I agree with the honorable Manager that they have no right to do any such thing.

Mr. EVARTS. Mr. Chief Justice, one moment will, I tnink, show that——

Mr. Manager BINGHAM. Will the gentleman from New York yield to me a single moment, without pretending to interrupt him? Mr. President, I desire, on behalf of the Managers, here, so that there may be no possible misunderstanding about it, to disclaim, once for all, that it was either intended by my associate, who has taken his seat, or is intended by the Managers, at any time, or in any way to question the right and the entire propriety of any Senator recalling any witness and putting any question to him that he sees fit. We impute no improper motives to any Senator for doing so; and we wish it distinctly understood that it is furthest from our purpose. But we recognize his perfect right to do so and the entire propriety of it.

Mr. EVARTS. A moment's consideration, I think, will satisfy the Senate, Mr. Chief Justice, that the question is not precisely of our right to recall the witness, but the question of right, if it be important to be discussed—and it may be in some future applications of the rule—is, that when the court have introduced, by their right of questioning, new matter of evidence that had previously been excluded, then the counsel upon either side are not obliged to leave that portion of the evidence incomplete or without cross-examination; for some piece of evidence might be drawn out that, as it stood, nakedly, it would be prejudicial to one side or the other, prejudicial to the side whose witness was recalled, if you please; and certainly it would be competent, in the ordinary rules of examination, that the counsel should be permitted to place the whole of the fact and the truth—within the proper rules of evidence, of course—before the court.

Mr. WILLIAMS. If I may be allowed to state, I do not, of course, object, under the decision made by the Senate, to a full answer to the question propounded by the Senator from Maryland; but my objection is made upon the ground that the Senate has repeatedly decided that the conversations of the President were not admissible in evidence, and the witness having answered the question of the Senator from Maryland, it is not competent for the counsel for the President to proceed to examine him upon that point, because it is contrary to the decision already made.

The CHIEF JUSTICE. The Secretary will again read both the questions, so that the Senate may understand precisely what is before it.

The SECRETARY. The first question was as follows:

When the President tendered to you the office of Secretary of War *ad interim* on the 27th of January, 1868, and on the 31st of the same month and year, did he, at the very time of making such tender, state to you what his purpose in so doing was?

The witness having answered "yes," the next question was:

State what he said his purpose was.

The question now is:

Have you answered as to both occasions?

Mr. JOHNSON. That is not my question.

Mr. STANBERY. That is mine; and I want to say one word as to that. Notwithstanding the honorable Senator from Maryland has put this question, he has put it about our client and our case. They belong to us. He has put it so that a new door is opened that was closed to us before, and the court has gone into that new evidence that was a sealed book to us, about which we could neither examine nor cross-examine. That which was closed to us by the decision of the court on Saturday is now opened by the question of the Senator to-day. Now, I understand the doctrine contended for to be that we must take that answer, for better or worse, to a question we did not put. Now, Senators, if in that answer the matter had been condemnatory of the President; if the Senator had got as an answer that the President told the witness expressly that he intended to violate any law; that he was acting in bad faith; that he meant to use force, I am told the doctrine here now is, "inasmuch as it was brought out by a Senator, not by yourselves, although it is fatal testimony to your client, you cannot cross-examine him one word about it." It is not testimony of our asking. Suppose it had been brought out by the Managers, could we not cross-examine. Suppose it is brought out by a Senator, does that make it any more sacred against the pursuit of truth and the sacred right of cross-examination? Does the doctrine of estoppel come here, that wherever any question is answered upon the interrogatory of a Senator you must take that answer, without any opportunity to contradict the witness or to cross-examine the witness; that that sacred right cannot be exercised: that we are estopped not by our own act, not by testimony we have called out, but we are estopped by the act of another, and shut out from the pursuit of truth, because a Senator has put the question and the answer to that question is condemnatory of our client? I say the moment that door is opened and new testimony introduced in the cause we have a right to cross-examine the witness; a right to explain it if we can, to contradict it if we can, to impeach the very witness who testifies to it if we can. Every weapon that a defendant has in pursuit of truth as to testimony against him is put into our hands the moment such a question is put and such a question is answered.

Mr. Manager BINGHAM. Mr. President, I think Senators cannot fail to have observed the most extraordinary remarks that have just fallen from the lips of the honorable counsel for the President. It is perfectly apparent to intelligent men, whether on the floor of the Senate or in these galleries, that they have attempted, through this witness, to obtain the mere naked declaration of the accused to rebut the legal presumption of his guilt arising from his having done an unlawful act.

I am not surprised at the feeling with which the honorable gentleman has just discussed this question. If I heard aright the testimony which fell from the lips of the witness, the Lieutenant General, it was testimony that utterly disappointed and confounded the counsel for the accused. What was it? Nothing was said, said the witness, in the first conversation about an appeal to the courts, and finally this was said, that it was impossible to make up a case by which to appeal to the courts. These declarations of the President, standing in that form, are not satisfactory to the counsel. They are brought out, to be sure, upon the question of the honorable gentleman from Maryland; but they are not satisfactory to the counsel; and now he tells the Senate that he has the right to cross-examine. To cross-examine whom, sir? To cross-examine his own witness. To cross-examine him for what purpose? "In search of the truth!" Well, he is in pursuit of the truth under difficulties. The witness has already sworn to matter of fact that shows the naked, bald falsity of the defense interposed here by the President in his answer, that his only purpose in violating the law was to test the validity of the law in the courts. Why did not he test the validity of the law in the courts? It will not do to say to the Senate of the United States that he has accounted for it in telling this witness that the case could not be made up. The learned counsel who has just taken his seat is too familiar with the law of this country, too familiar with the absolute adjudication of this very case in the Supreme Court, to venture to indorse for a moment this utterance of his client made to the Lieutenant General that it was impossible to make up a case.

I stand here and assert what the learned counsel knows right well, that all that was needful to make up a case was for the President of the United States to do just what he did do in the first instance, to issue an order directing Mr. Stanton to surrender the office of Secretary for the Department of War to "Lorenzo Thomas, whom he had that day appointed Secretary of War *ad interim*," and to surrender all the records of the office to him, to surrender the property of the office to him, and upon the refusal of the Secretary of War to obey his command through his Attorney General,

who now appears as his attorney in the trial and defense of this case, to sue out a writ of *quo warranto*. That is the law which we undertake to say is settled in this case, notwithstanding his statement to the witness whom they have called here. It is settled in the case of Wallace *vs.* Anderson, as the Senate will recollect, reported in 5 Wheaton, page 291. The opinion of the court, from which no dissent was expressed by any member of the bench, was delivered by Chief Justice Marshall, and I will read the opinion:

"Mr. Chief Justice Marshall delivered the opinion of the court, that a writ of *quo warranto* could not be maintained except at the instance of the Government; and as this writ was issued by a private individual, without the authority of the Government, it could not be sustained, whatever might be the right of the prosecutor or of the person claiming to exercise the office in question. The information must, therefore, be dismissed."

That power was not employed by the Executive through the Attorney General. Let him answer in some other way than by these declarations, sought to be reached through a cross-examination of their own witness, why he did not follow up his illegal order for the removal of Stanton and for the appointment of Lorenzo Thomas as Secretary of War *ad interim* by illegally suing out his writ of *quo warranto* and trying the question in the courts.

But, gentlemen Senators, there is something more than that in this case—and I desire merely to refer to it in passing—that the question which the gentlemen raise here in argument now is, in substance and in fact, whether, having violated the Constitution and laws of the United States, in the manner shown by the testimony here, beyond question, they cannot at last strip the people of the power which they retained to themselves by impeachment—to hold such malefactors to answer before the Senate of the United States, to the exclusion of the interposition of every other tribunal of justice upon God's footstool. What has this question to do with the final decision of the case before the Senate? I say if your Supreme Court sat to-day in judgment upon this question it has no power and can have none over this Senate. The question belongs to the Senate, in the language of the Constitution, exclusively. The words are that "the Senate shall have the sole power to try all impeachments."

The sole or only power to try impeachments includes the power to try and determine every question of law and fact arising in a case of impeachment. It is in vain that the decision of the Supreme Court or of the circuit court or of the district court or of any court outside of this is invoked for the decision of any question arising in this trial between the people and their guilty President. We protest, then, against a speech that has been made here in this matter. We protest, also, against the attempt here to cross-examine their own witness and get rid of the matter already stated so truthfully and so fairly by the witness, which clearly makes against their client and strips him of every feather, and leaves him naked for the avenging hand of justice to reach him without let or hinderance.

Mr. EVARTS. Mr. Chief Justice and Senators, I shall enter into no discussions irrelevant to this matter; but we cannot consent to have matters so misrepresented. My learned associate, arguing upon a hypothetical case as to the injustice of the rule sought to be laid down when it should happen that the evidence was injurious to a party, that he should be restricted from cross-examination undertook, by way of argument, to influence the opinion of the Senate. It had not the remotest application, and, as must have been apparent to every intelligent observer, was not connected in the least with the actual evidence given. The evidence given, if it is agreeable to the Managers, is extremely satisfactory to us presenting the very point of the inquiry of the Lieutenant General to the President why the lawyers could not make up a case without bringing in an *ad interim* appointment. The answer of the President was that it could not be done, but when on the effect of an *ad interim* appointment the matter was brought up, the case would not stand half an hour, agreeing with Mr. Manager BUT-LER in his hypothetical case in the note that he wrote for the President to send to the Senate: "I felt myself constrained to make this removal lest Mr. Stanton should answer the information in the nature of a *quo warranto*, which I intend the Attorney General shall file at an early day, by saying that he holds the office of Secretary of War by the appointment and authority of Mr. Lincoln which has never been revoked."

Mr. Manager BINGHAM. Mr. President, I desire, in response to the gentleman's remarks, very briefly to state to the Senate that instead of bettering his client's case he has made it worse by his attempt to explain this declaration of the President to the witness that it was impossible to make up a case without an *ad interim* appointment. I agree and stated myself in the remarks which I made before, that it was necessary that he should issue his order of removal as he did issue it, and that it was necessary he should issue his order of appointment to Lorenzo Thomas or somebody else as Secretary of War *ad interim*, as he did issue it; but now how does the case stand? Had he not made an *ad interim* appointment six months before this conversation with the Lieutenant General? Had he not made an *ad interim* appointment in August, 1867, of General Grant? Ah! says the gentleman, he only suspended Mr. Stanton then under the tenure-of-office act, and therefore the question could not very well be raised. I have no doubt that will be the answer of the counsel; it is all the answer they can make; but gentlemen Senators, how does such an answer stand with the corrupt answer put in here by the President that he did not make that suspension under the tenure-of-office act but under the Constitution

C. I.—23.

of the United States, and by virtue of the powers vested in him by that Constitution? He cannot play "fast and loose" in this way in the presence of the Senate and the people of this country.

Why did he not issue out his writ of *quo warranto* in August when he had his appointment of Secretary *ad interim*, casting your statute aside, going into courts, forestalling the power of the people to try him by impeachment for this violation of law, for this unlawful act, which by the law of every country where the common law obtains, carries the criminal intent with it on its face, and which he cannot talk from the record by any false statement, nor swear from the record in any shape or form by any mere declarations of his own.

One word more, and I have done with this matter. They got in evidence of what he told Thomas, and now they want to contradict that evidence. After the refusal of the office to him by Stanton, after Stanton refused to obey Thomas's orders, after he had ordered Thomas to go to his own place, and Thomas refused to obey his orders and declared himself Secretary and his purpose to control the office, to take possession of the records, and seize upon its mails, you have had offered here by this defense the declarations of the accused to Thomas when he went back and reported to him this refusal "Go on, take possession of the office;" not "I am going to appeal to the courts," not "Go to the Attorney General for a writ of *quo warranto;*" there was no intimation of that sort then; but that declaration of the accused to Lorenzo Thomas on the night of the 21st of February after he had committed this crime against the laws and Constitution of his country is to be got rid of here to-day by his declaration at another time, that they are seeking after now, to the Lieutenant General.

We are not trying the President here for having offered the Lieutenant General an appointment of Secretary *ad interim*, or an absolute appointment either. We are trying the President here for issuing an order, in violation of law, for the removal of Mr. Stanton and another letter of authority, in violation of the law, directing Lorenzo Thomas to take possession of the War Department, its records, and its property, and to discharge the functions of the office of Secretary of War *ad interim*, in utter contempt of the Constitution, of his own oath of office, of the statutes of the United States, and of the solemn decision of the Senate. And these gentlemen come here to get rid of this matter in this way by cross-examining, to use their own word, their own witness, because, after failing to get anything from him themselves, and the Senate having succeeded in getting words from him that do not suit their purpose, they seek to get rid of the whole matter by a further examination.

Mr. DAVIS. Mr. Chief Justice, I ask for information if the question propounded by the honorable Senator from Maryland has been fully answered?

The CHIEF JUSTICE. The Senator from Kentucky will reduce his question to writing.

Mr. DAVIS. I do not propose——

The CHIEF JUSTICE. The rule requires that the question shall be reduced to writing.

Mr. DAVIS. I do not propound any question to the witness at all. I merely make the suggestion to the Chief Justice whether the question, as drafted by the honorable Senator from Maryland, has been fully answered by the witness or not?

The CHIEF JUSTICE. It is impossible for the Chief Justice to reply to that question. The witness only can reply.

The WITNESS. Where is my answer?

Mr. TRUMBULL. I ask is there not a question pending?

Mr. DAVIS. I ask that the question be read.

The CHIEF JUSTICE. The Chief Justice will explain the position of the matter to the Senate. The Senator from Maryland desired that the following question should be put to the witness, (General Sherman:) "When the President tendered to you the office of Secretary of War ad interim on the 27th of January, 1868, and on the 31st of the same month and year, did he, at the very time of making such tender, state to you what his purpose in so doing was?" To that question the witness replied, "he did" or "yes." That answer having been given, the Senator from Maryland propounded the further question, "The witness having answered yes, will he state what he said his purpose was?" The witness having made an answer to that question either partial or full, the Chief Justice is unable to decide which, the counsel for the President propose this question: "Have you answered as to both occasions?" That is the same question which the Senator from Kentucky now proposes to the Chief Justice, and which he is unable to answer. The Senator from Oregon [Mr. WILLIAMS] objects to the question proposed by the counsel for the President upon the ground that General Sherman having been recalled at the instance of a Senator, and having been examined by him, he cannot be examined by counsel for the President. The Chief Justice thinks that that is a matter entirely within the discretion of the Senate, but that it is usual, under such circumstances, to allow counsel to proceed with their inquiries relating to the same subject-matter.

Mr. WILLIAMS. Mr. President, I withdraw my objection to this question. When the question was orally put I understood it to be another and different question. I am willing a full answer shall be given to the question propounded by the Senator from Maryland, but object to new questions.

The CHIEF JUSTICE. The Secretary will read the question, and the witness will answer.

The SECRETARY. The question is, "have you answered as to both occasions?"

The WITNESS. I should like to hear my answer as far as it had gone.

Mr. JOHNSON. I move that the reporter read the answer.

The CHIEF JUSTICE. That will be done.

Mr. J. J. MURPHY, one of the reporters for the Globe, read the previous answer of the witness from the short-hand notes, as follows:

"I intended to be very precise and very short; but it appeared to me necessary to state what I began to state, that the President told me that the relations between himself and Mr. Stanton, and between Mr. Stanton and the other members of the Cabinet, were such that he could not execute the office which he filled as President of the United States without making provision ad interim for that office; that he had the right under the law; he claimed to have the right; and his purpose was to have the office administered in the interest of the Army and of the country; and he offered me the office in that view. He did not state to me then that his purpose was to bring it to the courts directly; but for the purpose of having the office administered properly in the interest of the Army and of the whole country.

"Mr. STANBERY. On both occasions, General, or the other occasion?

"The WITNESS. I asked him why lawyers could not make a case; that I did not wish to be brought as an officer of the Army into any controversy."

"Mr. CONKLING. Will you not repeat that last answer, General?"

"The WITNESS. I asked him why lawyers could not make a case, and not bring me, or an officer, into the controversy? His answer was, that it was found impossible, or a case could not be made up; 'but,' said he, 'if we can bring the case to the courts, it would not stand half an hour.' I think that is all that he stated to me then."

Mr. DRAKE. Now read the pending question.

The SECRETARY. The question is: "Have you answered as to both occasions."

The WITNESS. The question first asked me seemed to restrict me so close to the purpose that I endeavored to confine myself to that point alone. On the first day or the first interview in which the President offered me the appointment ad interim he confined himself to very general terms, and I gave him no definite answer. The second interview, which was on the afternoon of the 30th, not the 31st, was the interview during which he made the points which I have testified to. In speaking he referred to the constitutionality of the bill known as the civil tenure-of-office bill, I think, or the tenure of civil-office bill; and it was the constitutionality of that bill which he seemed desirous of having tested, and which, he said, if it could be brought before the Supreme Court properly, would not stand half an hour. We also spoke of force. I first stated that if Mr. Stanton would simply retire, although it was against my interest, against my desire, against my personal wishes, and against my official wishes, I might be willing to undertake to administer the office ad interim. Then he supposed that the point was yielded; and I made this point, "Suppose Mr. Stanton do not yield?" He answered, "Oh! he will make no objection; you present the order, and he will retire." I expressed my doubt and he remarked, "I know him better than you do; he is cowardly.'' I then begged to be excused from giving him an answer to give the subject more reflection, and I gave him my final answer in writing. I think that letter, if you insist upon knowing my views, should come into evidence, and not parol testimony taken up; but my reasons for declining the office were mostly personal in their nature.

Mr. JOHNSON. Mr. Chief Justice, with the permission of the Senate I desire to correct a mistake of fact. I thought General Sherman said the 31st, but it is the 30th of January, and therefore I desire to have that correction made in my written question.

The CHIEF JUSTICE. If there be no objection that correction will be made. The 30th will be substituted for the 31st in the record of the question of the Senator from Maryland.

Mr. HENDERSON. I desire to ask the witness a question which I send to the Chair in writing.

The CHIEF JUSTICE. The Secretary will read the question of the Senator from Missouri.

The Secretary read as follows:

Did the President, on either of the occasions alluded to, express to you a fixed resolution or determination to remove Stanton from his office?

The WITNESS. If by removal is meant a removal by force, he never conveyed to my mind such an impression; but he did most unmistakably say that he could have no more intercourse with him in the relation of President and Secretary of War.

Mr. HOWARD. I wish to put a question to the witness. I send it to the Chair.

The CHIEF JUSTICE. The Secretary will read the question proposed by the Senator from Michigan.

The Secretary read as follows:

You say the President spoke of force. What did he say about force?

The WITNESS. I inquired, "Suppose Mr. Stanton do not yield, what then shall be done?" "Oh," said he, "there is no necessity of considering that question; upon the presentation of an order he will simply go away," or "retire."

Mr. HOWARD. Is that a full answer to the question?

The WITNESS. I think it is, sir.

Mr. HENDERSON. Mr. President, I desire to submit another question. I send it to the desk.

The CHIEF JUSTICE. The Secretary will read the question proposed by the Senator from Missouri.

The Secretary read as follows:

Did you give any opinion or advice to the President on either of those occasions in regard to the legality or propriety of an *ad interim* appointment; and if so, what advice did you give, or what opinion did you express to him?

Mr. Manager BINGHAM. Mr. President, we must object to that.

Mr. Manager BUTLER. It has been overruled once to-day. I suppose the Senate means to adhere to some rule.

The CHIEF JUSTICE. Do the honorable Managers object to the question being answered?

Mr. Manager BINGHAM and Mr. Manager BUTLER. We do.

The CHIEF JUSTICE. The Chief Justice will put the question to the Senate whether the question proposed by the Senator from Missouri is admissible and should be put to the witness.

The question being put, was determined in the negative.

So the question propounded by Mr. HENDERSON was decided to be inadmissible.

Mr. STANBERY. If no other questions are sought to be put to General Sherman, I believe we are through with him.

The CHIEF JUSTICE. Do the honorable Managers desire to put any questions?

Mr. Manager BUTLER. I did not know that the counsel for the President had anything to do with this examination.

Mr. STANBERY. I have said we are through. We do not propose to argue that point.

The CHIEF JUSTICE. Gentlemen, General Sherman desires to know if you are through with him on both sides?

Mr. Manager BINGHAM. We may desire to recall the Lieutenant General to-morrow.

The WITNESS. I have a summons to appear before your committee to-morrow.

Mr. EVARTS. We must insist, Mr. Chief Justice, that the cross-examination must be finished before the witness is allowed to leave the stand.

Mr. Manager BINGHAM. We do not propose to make any cross-examination at present.

Mr. EVARTS. No cross-examination " at present !" We insist that the cross-examination must be made now if it is to be made at all.

The CHIEF JUSTICE. Undoubtedly that is the rule.

Mr. Manager BINGHAM. We submit that the gentlemen themselves on Saturday made an appeal for leave to recall the witness; and for myself, and as I understood it to be for my associate Managers, I made no objection. It is for the Senate to determine whether we shall recall him to-morrow.

Mr. EVARTS. We have no desire to be strict about these rules, but we desire that they shall be equally strict on both sides.

The CHIEF JUSTICE. Undoubtedly the general rule is that if the Managers desire to cross-examine they must cross-examine before dismissing the witness; but that will be a question for the Senate when General Sherman is recalled.

Mr. Manager BUTLER. This witness has not been called now by the counsel, and therefore we do not cross-examine at present about the matter inquired of by the court. The court's questions are all very well; we cannot interfere with those; we do not propose to do so. We will take our own course in our own way.

Mr. EVARTS. Very well.

Mr. Manager BUTLER. And let you know what it is when we get ready.

R. J. MEIGS recalled.

By Mr. STANBERY:

Question. Have you the docket of the supreme court of the District with you now?

Answer. I have.

Question. Will you read the docket entries in the case of the United States *vs.* Lorenzo Thomas?

Mr. Manager BUTLER. Is that evidence? I have no belief that the docket entry of a court, until the record is made up, is anything more than a minute from which the record may be extended. I directed that the record should be extended in this case for the use of the Senate.

Mr. STANBERY. It is not a case in which any record was made, as the witness has already told us; but it was a proceeding before a judge at chambers, and the only entry on the books is the entry on the docket.

The CHIEF JUSTICE. The witness will proceed, unless the question be objected to.

Mr. Manager BUTLER. I have objected.

Mr. Manager BINGHAM. We must object to the evidence as incompetent.

The CHIEF JUSTICE. The counsel for the President will please state in writing what they propose to prove.

The offer of the counsel for the President was reduced in writing in the form of a question to the witness, as follows:

Have you got the docket entries as to the disposition of the case of the United States *vs.* Lorenzo Thomas, and if so will you produce and read them?

The CHIEF JUSTICE. The Chief Justice thinks that this is a part of the same transaction, and is competent evidence; but he will put the question to the Senate if any Senator desires it. [After a pause.] The witness will answer the question.

The WITNESS. The examining magistrate or the judge took the recognizance of General Thomas for his appearance on a subsequent day, and when that recognizance was taken it was put on the docket of the court, because there might be a *scire facias* upon it on one supposition, and there might be an indictment. Therefore it was put upon the docket of the court.

Mr. STANBERY. Read the docket entries.

The WITNESS. The case is numbered 5711.

"THE UNITED STATES *vs.* LORENZO THOMAS:

"Warrant for his arrest issued by Hon. Chief Justice Cartter, on the oath of E. M. Stanton, to answer the charge of high misdemeanor, in that he did unlawfully accept the appointment of the office of Secretary of War *ad interim*, February 22, 1868.

"Warrant served by the marshal February 22, 1868.

"Recognizance for his appearance on the 26th instant, February 22, 1868.

"Discharged by Chief Justice Cartter, on the motion of the defendant's counsel, February 26, 1868."

Mr. STANBERY. That is all.

The CHIEF JUSTICE. Do the honorable Managers desire to cross-examine this witness?

Mr. Manager BUTLER. We have nothing to ask of this witness, sir.

Mr. JOHNSON. I move that the court adjourn.

Mr. STEWART. On that motion I call for the yeas and nays.

The CHIEF JUSTICE. The Senator from Maryland moves that the Senate, sitting as a court of impeachment, adjourn until to-morrow at twelve o'clock. On this question the yeas and nays are asked for.

The yeas and nays were not ordered, one fifth of the Senators present not sustaining the call.

The question being put on the motion to adjourn, there were, on a division—ayes 24, noes 18; and the Senate, sitting for the trial of the impeachment, adjourned until to-morrow at twelve o'clock.

TUESDAY, *April* 14, 1868.

The Chief Justice of the United States entered the Senate Chamber at twelve o'clock and five minutes p. m., and took the chair.

The usual proclamation having been made by the Sergeant-at-Arms,

The Managers of the impeachment on the part of the House of Representatives appeared and took the seats assigned them.

The counsel for the respondent, with the exception of Mr. Stanbery, also appeared and took their seats.

The presence of the House of Representatives was next announced, and the members of the House, as in Committee of the Whole, headed by Mr. E. B. WASHBURNE, the chairman of that committee, and accompanied by the Speaker and Clerk, entered the Senate Chamber, and were conducted to the seats provided for them.

The CHIEF JUSTICE. The Secretary will read the Journal.

Mr. STEWART. I move that the reading of the Journal be dispensed with.

The CHIEF JUSTICE. If there be no objection the reading of the Journal will be dispensed with. The Chair hears no objection.

Mr. SUMNER. I send to the Chair an order.

The CHIEF JUSTICE. The Secretary will read the order.

The Secretary read as follows:

Ordered, In answer to the motion of the Managers, that, under the rule limiting the argument to two on a side unless otherwise ordered, such other Managers and counsel as choose may print and file arguments at any time before the argument of the closing Manager.

The CHIEF JUSTICE. If there be no objection the order will be considered now.

Mr. CONNESS. I object, Mr. President.

The CHIEF JUSTICE. Objection is made. The order will lie over for one day.

Mr. SUMNER. I beg leave most respectfully to inquire under what rule such an objection can be made.

The CHIEF JUSTICE. The Chief Justice stated on Saturday that in conducting the business of the court he applied, as far as they were applicable, the general rules of the Senate. This has been done upon several occasions, and when objection has been made orders have been laid over to the next day for consideration.

Mr. SUMNER. Of course it is not for me to argue the question; but I beg to remind the Chair of the rule under which this order is moved.

The CHIEF JUSTICE. It will lie over. Gentlemen of counsel for the President, you will please proceed with the defense.

Mr. EVARTS. Mr. Chief Justice and Senators, it is our misfortune to be obliged to state to the court that since the adjournment yesterday, and not coming to our knowledge until just before we came into court this morning, our associate, Mr. Stanbery, is prevented by illness, which confines him, wholly from attending upon the court to-day. I have seen him, and have learned the opinion of his physician that he will undoubtedly, in expectation, be able to resume his duty within forty-eight hours, and there may be some hope that he will be able to do so by to-morrow. In the suddenness of this knowledge to us, and in the actual arrangement in reference to the proofs, it would be very difficult for us, and almost impossible with any proper attention to the justice of the case, to proceed to-day; and we suppose that an indulgence, at least for the day, would lessen the chance of longer procrastination. The gentlemen of the Senate and the Chief Justice will be so good as to bear in mind that much of the matter to be produced in evidence is within the personal knowledge of our associate, Mr. Stanbery, and not within our own, and we have to say that the conduct of the proofs has been accorded to him.

It is, of course, not pleasant for us, and not pleasant for Mr. Stanbery especially, that such an occasion as this should arise for the introduction of personal considerations; but in our best judgment we can only present it to the court in the aspect that I have named, and submit it to their discretion whether the facility and the indulgence that may be needed on our part should be limited to this day or whether it should extend over the two days that we suppose would assure the restoration of Mr. Stanbery to health. I saw Mr. Stanbery last evening, and, although he had been a little affected by a cold which he had contracted, I supposed him to be, as he supposed himself to be, in a condition of health that would permit him to go on as usual; and it was only as we were preparing to come to court this morning that he himself was obliged to submit to the confinement of his physician and to inform us of his situation.

Mr. DRAKE. Mr. President, I would ask a question of the counsel for the defense.

The CHIEF JUSTICE. The Secretary will read the question proposed by the Senator from Missouri.

The Secretary read the question, as follows:

Cannot the day be occupied by counsel for the respondent in giving in documentary evidence?

Mr. EVARTS. It cannot, as we understand the situation of the proofs and our duty in regard to them.

Mr. HOWE. Mr. President, I move that the Senate, sitting as a court of impeachment, adjourn until to-morrow at twelve o'clock.

The motion was agreed to.

The CHIEF JUSTICE. The Senate, sitting as a court of impeachment, stands adjourned until to-morrow at twelve o'clock.

WEDNESDAY, *April* 15, 1868.

The Chief Justice of the United States took the chair.

The usual proclamation having been made by the Sergeant-at-Arms,

The Managers of the impeachment on the part of the House of Representatives and the counsel for the respondent, except Mr. Stanbery, appeared, and took the seats assigned them respectively.

The members of the House of Representatives, as in Committee of the Whole, preceded by Mr. WASHBURNE, chairman of that committee, and accompanied by the Speaker and Clerk, appeared and were conducted to the seats provided for them.

The CHIEF JUSTICE. The Secretary will read the Journal of yesterday's proceedings.

The Secretary read the Journal of yesterday's proceedings of the Senate sitting for the trial of the impeachment.

The CHIEF JUSTICE. The first business in order is the consideration of the order submitted by the Senator from Massachusetts [Mr. SUMNER] yesterday.

Mr. SUMNER. I should like to have it reported.

The CHIEF JUSTICE. The Secretary will read the order.

The Secretary read as follows:

Ordered, In answer to the motion of the Managers, that, under the rule limiting the argument to two on a side, "unless otherwise ordered," such other Managers and counsel as choose may print and file arguments at any time before the argument of the closing Manager.

The CHIEF JUSTICE. The question is on agreeing to the order.

Mr. EDMUNDS. I move to amend the order so that it will read, "May print and file arguments at any time before the argument of the opening Manager shall be concluded," in order that the counsel for the defense may have an opportunity to see what arguments they are to reply to.

Mr. SUMNER. I have no objections to that.

Mr. JOHNSON. I ask for the reading of the order as proposed to be amended.

The CHIEF JUSTICE. The Secretary will read the order.

The SECRETARY. The order submitted reads as follows:

Ordered, In answer to the motion of the Managers, that, under the rule limiting the argument to two on a side, unless otherwise ordered, such other Managers and counsel as choose may print and file arguments at any time before the argument of the closing Manager.

It is proposed to strike out the words "argument of the closing Manager" and insert "argument of the opening Manager shall be concluded."

Mr. EVARTS. Mr. Chief Justice, may we be allowed to make a suggestion in reference to this order?

The·CHIEF JUSTICE. Certainly.

Mr. EVARTS. The amendment offered and accepted places, I suppose, the proper restriction upon the arguments to be furnished in print on the part of the Managers. That puts the matter in pro er shape, I suppose, as regards the printed briefs that may be put in on the part of the Managers; that is to say, that they shall be filed before we make our reply. On our part, however, it would be proper that we should have the liberty of filing the briefs at any time before the closing Manager makes his final reply, as a part of our new briefs may be in reply to the new briefs that are put in on the part of the prosecution.

Mr. Manager BINGHAM. Mr. President and Senators, I desire to say, in regard to the remark which has just been made by the honorable gentleman on behalf of the accused, that it would seem, if the order be entered as he suggests, that additional arguments made by counsel on behalf of the President need not be filed until the close of the arguments on behalf of the accused made orally to the Senate, the repliant on behalf of the Congress of the United States and of the people would have no opportunity to see those arguments not delivered, and therefore could not reply to them. I would suggest that the order as it stands is right. It gives the counsel for the President the opportunity to review what may be filed before they argue, and it gives the counsel for the people the opportunity to review before he argues whatever may be filed here on behalf of the President.

Mr. EVARTS. Undoubtedly there are inconveniences in this enlargement of the rule, however applied; but there seems to be an equality in requiring each side to furnish its arguments in time to have replying counsel answer them; and the same rule upon my suggestion would be applied to us that by this present amendment is applied to the Managers for the impeachment, for they are not required to file their additional briefs except at the very moment that they close their oral argument,

and then we are obliged to commence our oral argument.

Mr. NELSON. Mr. Chief Justice and Senators, I desire to say on this motion that it was agreed between the counsel for the President that the three of our number who have hitherto managed the case should take upon themselves the continuous management and the argument of the case before the Senate. In consequence of the imputation made by the Managers, that we desired unnecessarily to consume the time of the Senate, those of us who, under this arrangement, had not intended to argue the cause did not intend, either by ourselves or through others, to make any application to the Senate for an enlargement of the rule; but, inasmuch as that application has been made in behalf of the Managers, I desire to say to the Senate that if we are permitted to argue the cause I think it would be more fair to the two counsel who did not expect to argue the case to permit us to make an extemporaneous argument before the Senate. We have not made any preparation whatever in view of written arguments. We suppose, though we do not know how the fact is, that the Managers on the part of the House, who have had this subject before them for a much longer period than we have had, are much more familiar with this subject and are better prepared with written addresses than we are, so that if the rule is to be extended I respectfully ask the Senate to allow us to address the Senate in such mode, either oral or written, as we may desire. I beg leave to say to the Senate that while I do not, speaking for myself, expect to be able to interest the Senate as much as the learned gentlemen to whom the management of the cause has been hitherto confided on the part of the President, yet, as I reside in the President's own State, as I have practiced my profession in his town, the town of his domicile, for the last thirty years, and as he saw proper to ask my services in his behalf, and as I fully concur with him in the leading measures of his Administration I desire, if I am heard at all, to be heard in the mode which I have suggested.

Mr. CONNESS. I offer the following as a substitute for the order now pending.

The CHIEF JUSTICE. The Secretary will read the substitute proposed by the Senator from California.

The Secretary read it, as follows:

Strike out all after the word "ordered" and insert: That the twenty-first rule be so amended as to allow as many of the Managers and of the counsel for the President to speak on the final argument as shall choose to do so: *Provided*, That not more than four days on each side shall be allowed; but the Managers shall make the opening and the closing argument.

Mr. DRAKE. On that question I ask for the yeas and nays.

The yeas and nays were ordered.

Mr. Manager BOUTWELL. I should like to have the substitute read once more.

The CHIEF JUSTICE. The Secretary will read the proposed substitute.

The Secretary again read it.

The CHIEF JUSTICE. Does the honorable Manager desire to address the Senate?

Mr. Manager BOUTWELL. No, sir.

The CHIEF JUSTICE. The question is on the substitute proposed by the Senator from California.

The question being taken by yeas and nays, resulted—yeas 19, nays 27; as follows:

YEAS—Messrs. Cameron, Conness, Cragin, Dixon, Doolittle, Fowler, Harlan, Henderson, Hendricks, McCreery, Patterson of Tennessee, Ramsey, Sherman, Stewart, Trumbull, Van Winkle, Willey, Wilson, and Yates—19.

NAYS—Messrs. Anthony, Buckalew, Cattell, Chandler, Cole, Conkling, Davis, Drake, Edmunds, Ferry, Frelinghuysen, Howard, Howe, Johnson, Morgan, Morrill of Maine, Morrill of Vermont, Morton, Patterson of New Hampshire, Pomeroy, Ross, Saulsbury, Sumner, Thayer, Tipton, Vickers, and Williams—27.

NOT VOTING—Messrs. Bayard, Corbett, Fessenden, Grimes, Norton, Nye, Sprague, and Wade—8.

So the substitute was rejected.

Mr. DOOLITTLE. Mr. Chief Justice, I prefer altogether oral arguments to these printed ones, and I submit the following as a substitute, understanding that there are six Managers on the part of the House and four counsel for the respondent. ["Order!" "Order!"] I have drawn an order which— ["Order!" "Order!"]

The CHIEF JUSTICE. Order! There can be no debate.

Mr. DOOLITTLE. Which I ask to have read.

The CHIEF JUSTICE. The Secretary will read the amendment proposed by the Senator from Wisconsin.

The Secretary read as follows:

Strike out all after the word "ordered" and insert:

That upon the final argument two Managers of the House open, two counsel for the respondent reply; that two other Managers rejoin, to be followed by two other counsel for the respondent; and they, in turn, to be followed by two other Managers of the House, who shall conclude the argument.

Mr. DRAKE. I move the indefinite postponement of the whole proposition, together with the substitute.

The CHIEF JUSTICE. The Senator from Missouri moves the indefinite postponement of the order and the proposed substitute.

Mr. SUMNER. Let us have the yeas and nays on that.

The yeas and nays were ordered; and being taken, resulted—yeas 34, nays 15; as follows:

YEAS—Messrs. Anthony, Buckalew, Chandler, Cole, Conkling, Conness, Corbett, Davis, Dixon, Drake, Edmunds, Ferry, Fessenden, Grimes, Harlan, Henderson, Hendricks, Howard, Howe, Johnson, Morgan, Morrill of Maine, Morrill of Vermont, Morton, Patterson of New Hampshire, Pomeroy, Ross, Saulsbury, Sherman, Stewart, Thayer, Tipton, Williams, and Yates—34.

NAYS—Messrs. Cameron, Cattell, Cragin, Doolittle, Fowler, Frelinghuysen, McCreery, Patterson of Tennessee, Ramsey, Sumner, Trumbull, Van Winkle, Vickers, Willey, and Wilson—15.

NOT VOTING—Messrs. Bayard, Norton, Nye, Sprague, and Wade—5.

So the order and substitute were indefinitely postponed.

Mr. FERRY. I now submit an order on which I desire action.

The CHIEF JUSTICE. The Secretary will read the order proposed by the Senator from Connecticut.

The Secretary read as follows:

Ordered, That the twelfth rule be so modified as that the hour of the day at which the Senate shall sit upon the trial now pending shall be, unless otherwise ordered, at eleven o'clock forenoon; and that there shall be a recess of thirty minutes each day commencing at two o'clock p. m.

The CHIEF JUSTICE. This order is for present consideration unless objected to.

The CHIEF JUSTICE put the question, and declared that the noes appeared to have it.

Mr. THAYER, Mr. DRAKE, and others called for the yeas and nays, and they were ordered; and being taken, resulted—yeas 24, nays 26; as follows:

YEAS—Messrs. Cameron, Cattell, Chandler, Cole, Conkling, Conness, Corbett, Cragin, Drake, Ferry, Frelinghuysen, Harlan, Howard, Howe, Morgan, Morrill of Maine, Morrill of Vermont, Ramsey, Sherman, Stewart, Sumner, Thayer, Williams, and Wilson—24.

NAYS—Messrs. Anthony, Bayard, Buckalew, Davis, Dixon, Doolittle, Edmunds, Fessenden, Fowler, Grimes, Henderson, Hendricks, Johnson, McCreery, Morton, Patterson of New Hampshire, Patterson of Tennessee, Pomeroy, Ross, Saulsbury, Tipton, Trumbull, Van Winkle, Vickers, Willey, and Yates—26.

NOT VOTING—Messrs. Norton, Nye, Sprague, and Wade—4.

So the order was rejected.

The CHIEF JUSTICE. Gentlemen of counsel for the President, please proceed with the defense.

Mr. EVARTS. Mr. Chief Justice and Senators, although I am not able to announce, as I should be very glad to do, that our associate, Mr. Stanbery, had, according to his hopes, been able to come out to-day, yet I am happy to say that he is quite convalescent, and cannot be long interrupted from giving the proper attention to the proper conduct of the case. Under these circumstances, and from a desire to do whatever we may properly do in advancing the trial of the cause, we propose, with the permission of the court, to proceed to-day in putting in the documentary evidence, which will take a very considerable time, and probably we shall not wish to be called upon to proceed with any oral testimony until to-morrow, when we shall be happy to do so.

Mr. CURTIS. Mr. Chief Justice, we desire to bring before the Senate the nomination sent by the President of the United States to the Senate on the 21st of February, as I am instructed, of Hon. Thomas Ewing for the office of Secretary for the Department of War. We wish the executive clerk to be instructed to produce that, in order that we may put it in evidence.

Mr. CONKLING. Mr. President, I beg to say that counsel is entirely inaudible here.

Mr. CURTIS. My request, Senators, was

that the executive clerk might be instructed to bring in and exhibit here in evidence the nomination sent by the President of the United States under the date of the 21st of February last, as I am instructed, the nomination of Hon. Thomas Ewing for the place of Secretary for the Department of War.

The CHIEF JUSTICE. The Chief Justice is informed by the Secretary that the injunction of secrecy has not been removed from this proceeding. It will be necessary that it should be removed.

Mr. JOHNSON. Does that apply to a nomination?

Mr. EDMUNDS. I ask unanimous consent to say, if I am permitted, on that point——

The CHIEF JUSTICE. If there be no objection, the Senator can proceed by unanimous consent.

Mr. EDMUNDS. I desire to say that under the new rules the fact of a nomination being made, it is provided, shall not be a secret communication, and hence I think there can be no impropriety in ordering the production of the paper.

Mr. CURTIS. I was so instructed on inquiry, and supposed no motion to remove the injunction of secrecy was necessary.

Mr. SHERMAN. Mr. Chief Justice, if a motion is necessary, I will move that the executive clerk be sworn as a witness in the case.

Mr. EDMUNDS. With the consent of the Chief Justice I will read the fortieth rule, recently adopted:

"All information or remarks concerning the character or qualifications of any person nominated by the President to office shall be kept a secret. But the fact that a nomination has been made shall not be regarded as a secret."

The CHIEF JUSTICE. The executive clerk will be sworn.

D. W. C. CLARKE sworn and examined.

By Mr. CURTIS:

Question. Will you state what document you have before you?

Answer. I have the original nomination by the President of Thomas Ewing, sen., to be Secretary for the Department of War.

Question. Will you please to read it?

Answer. The witness read as follows:

To the Senate of the United States:
I nominate Thomas Ewing, sen., of Ohio, to be Secretary for the Department of War.
ANDREW JOHNSON.
WASHINGTON, D. C., *February 22, 1868.*

Question. On what day was that actually received by you?

Answer. On the 22d of February.

Mr. CURTIS. Now, I desire to put in evidence, Mr. Chief Justice, a copy of the message of the President of the United States to the Senate of the United States, which bears date on the 24th of February, 1868. I have the printed copy, which is the authorized copy. I suppose it will not be objected that we have not obtained it from the proper source?

Mr. Manager BUTLER. The mere vehicle of proof, Mr. President, will not be objected to; but the proof itself will be, for a very plain reason. It was after the President was impeached by the House, and, of course, it is his declaration attempted to be put in. A declaration by him, after he was impeached, whether made to the Senate or anybody else, it seems to us, cannot be evidence.

The exact order of time, if it may not be in the mind of Senators, was this: on the 21st of February a resolution was offered to the House of Representatives looking to the impeachment of the President, bringing it before the House; on the 22d it was acted upon and actually voted. Impeachment was actually voted on the 22d. Then intervened Sunday, the 23d. Any message sent on the 24th, therefore, must have been known to the President to have been after the impeachment.

Mr. CURTIS. It will be remembered that the honorable Managers put in evidence in the course of their proceedings a resolve passed by the Senate to which this message is a response; so that the question is whether the honorable Managers can put in evidence a resolve of the Senate transmitted to the President of the United States in reference to the removal of Mr. Stanton, and the Senate will refuse to receive the reply which the President made to that resolve. That is the question which is now before the court.

Mr. Manager BUTLER. I have only to say, Mr. President, that that is an argument to the prejudice, and not to the law. Suppose he offers his answer here to-day, is that to be received as evidence? This message is said to be the answer to the resolve of the Senate. I pray you to remember that our learned friends insist that the rules of law should govern. Will they dare to say to the Senate that they ever heard of a case where, after indictment of the criminal, the respondent was allowed to put in evidence his statement of his defense? If so, when is that right to cease? We put in the resolve because it was a part of the transaction of removing Mr. Stanton, made before the impeachment was determined upon. We cannot put in his declarations down to to-day. That is a familiar rule of law. They cannot. I only ask the Senate to consider of it as a precedent hereafter, as well as being a great wrong upon the people, that after they indict, if you use that word, after they impeach an officer, then he can send in a message which shall be taken as evidence for him.

Mr. EVARTS. Mr. Chief Justice and Senators, the learned Manager asks whether we dare do something. We have not been in the habit of considering the measure for the conduct of forensic disputations to be a question of daring. We are not in the habit of applying such epithets to opponents, nor hitherto of receiving them from them. The measure of duty of counsel to the law and the facts is the measure we shall strive to obey, and not the measure of daring, if for no other reason for this: that on the rule of law and fact and evidence we might, perhaps, expect sometimes a superiority, but on the measure of daring, never.

Now, this question arises thus: is the learned Manager entirely right in saying that the impeachment was voted on the 22d? The 22d was Saturday, and, unless I am mistaken, the vote was not taken until Monday.

Mr. Manager BUTLER. I was entirely right—on Saturday. The vote was taken on the 22d of February.

Mr. EVARTS. That is, that articles should be brought in. The articles, however, were not voted until the 24th.

Mr. Manager BUTLER. The articles could not be prepared until some time afterward.

Mr. EVARTS. I am merely stating a fact, not complaining. They were found soon enough. Now, it is said that because the vote that impeachment should proceed was taken on the 22d that impairs the credit or the admissibility of the piece of evidence that is laid before the Senate. My learned associate has distinctly told the situation of the matter. Perhaps both of these transactions were public at the time, or were made public soon afterward. This message, the injunction of secrecy in respect to which has been removed, might be within the range of recourse on the one side or the other for argument, and for the knowledge of the court. But our learned opponents have put in the language of the resolution of the Senate. Exactly what bearing that has as part of the *res gestæ* of the removal of Mr. Stanton which had taken place so far as the criminality of the President was concerned before this resolution was passed by the Senate it was not easy to see. It was, however, received as proper evidence. The one reason that we did not consider it objectionable was that we supposed, as a matter of course and of right, that this message, which is an answer to that resolution, upon the introduction of the topic by the resolution being offered in evidence, would be admissible in itself. We submit, therefore, that on every principle, both of law and of discretion, if it may be so said, in regard to the completeness of the record upon the point, this message of the President should be allowed to be read and given in evidence.

Mr. Manager BUTLER. I simply desire to call the attention of the Senate to the fact that whether it is a matter of daring or professional knowledge, neither of the counsel has stated any possible precedent. I desire also to call the attention of the Senate to the fact, so that the counsel may never be in doubt hereafter, what was the legal effect of the resolution of the Senate in our minds, that we put in that resolution to show that, notwithstanding 'the resolution of the Senate served on the President at eleven o'clock at night on the night of the 21st, he still went on and treated this Lorenzo Thomas as Secretary, and took him

into his Cabinet consultation, and Lorenzo Thomas was recognized after that by him as the Secretary *ad interim*, and after that Lorenzo Thomas was breathing out his own designs to take possession of the office by force. It was in order to show that the President of the United States was determined to disobey the law of the land, that it was known to him—the Senate served it upon him for the purpose of having him know it, and did not leave it to the slow channels of communication in print, but served a certified copy on him to stay his hand, and he refused to stay his hand.

Now, can it be that a prepared argument after that, and after he was impeached by the House of Representatives, can be put in evidence? One ounce of action on his part in obedience to the law and the resolution of the Senate would have been a great deal better than pages of argument; but there was none. The gentlemen will not use the word "dare," for they would dare do all that good lawyers would dare do in favor of their client, but I will say the gentlemen have not shown a single legal position upon which this can stand.

The CHIEF JUSTICE. The counsel for the President will please put in writing what they propose to prove.

Mr. Manager BUTLER. We have sent the Clerk to look at the House Journal to correct us if we are wrong.

Mr. EVARTS. It will delay the question, then, somewhat.

Mr. Manager BUTLER. The report of the committee was made on the 22d. All of us were of opinion that the resolution was passed on the 22d. We think we are right; but we will make that certain.

After the lapse of a few minutes—

Mr. Manager BUTLER. We find, Mr. President, on examination, the state of the record is this: that on the 21st of February a resolution was proposed for impeachment and referred to a committee; on the 22d the committee reported, and that was debated through the 22d and into Monday, the 24th, and the actual vote was taken on Monday, the 24th.

Mr. EVARTS. Late in the afternoon—five o'clock in the afternoon; so that I was right in the fact. Is there any further objection made now?

Mr. Manager BUTLER. Certainly.

Mr. Manager BINGHAM. I desire to state the reasons why we insist upon this objection. The House of Representatives, as appears by the Journal which has now been furnished us, on the 22d of February, through its committee, reported "that Andrew Johnson be impeached of high crimes and misdemeanors." The discussion proceeded on that day. On the day preceding, however, the 21st of February, it appeared that the Senate of the United States, as is already in evidence from the Journal of the Senate itself, proceeded to consider another message of the President of the United States, in which he had reported to the Senate that he had removed from the Department of War Edwin M. Stanton, then Secretary of War, by the previous action of the Senate. The Senate having refused to concur in the suspension, refused to acquiesce in the reasons assigned by the President under the tenure-of-office act. Having given the President notice thereof, the President thereupon proceeds, after this notice, to remove him and to appoint a Secretary of War *ad interim*, in direct contravention of the express words of the act itself and of the action of the Senate. On that day, the 21st of February, the Senate, it seems, considered the action of the President in this matter of removal and in this matter of appointment of the head of a Department in direct contravention of the prohibitions of existing law and of the action of the Senate under it and the notice which it had served on the President.

On that night, as the record also shows, the 21st of February, 1868, the Senate of the United States passed a resolution reciting the action of the President in the premises, to wit, his removal of the Secretary of War, his appointment of a Secretary *ad interim*, and declaring by solemn resolve that under the Constitution and laws of the United States the President had no power to make the removal or to make the appointment. That was the action of the Senate, which has been given in evidence here in support of the prosecution. It was all concluded, as the Senate will notice from what I have said, on the 21st and 22d of February, 1868. My impression is that the notice was served on the night of the 21st, but, that I may not make a mistake in this matter, I say it was not served later than the 22d day of February.

Now, what takes place? Here is a presentment made on the 21st or 22d day of February, 1868, against this President before the grand inquest of the nation, and he seeks to put in a declaration made after presentment made, which is certainly tantamount to a warrant for his arrest, for from that moment he was within the power of the people. Although he fled to the remotest ends of the earth he could never stop for a moment the progress of this inquiry to final judgment, although personal process never reached him. It is so provided in the text of your Constitution. It is to be challenged by no man.

After these proceedings had been thus instituted, two days after the fact of the action of the Senate and three days after the fact of his commission of the crime, he enters upon the task of justifying himself before the nation for a violation of its laws, for a violation of its Constitution, for a violation of his oath of office, for his defiance of the Senate, for his defiance of the people, by sending a message to the Senate of the United States on the 24th day of February, 1868. What is it, Senators? Is it any more than a volunteer declaration of the criminal, after the fact, in his own behalf? Does it alter the case in law? Does it alter the case in the reason or judgment of any

man living, either within the Senate or out of the Senate, that he chose to put his declaration in his own defense in writing? The law makes no such distinctions. I undertake to assert it here, regardless of any attempt to contradict my statement, that there is no law that enables any accused criminal, after the fact, to make declarations, either orally or in writing, either by message to the Senate or a speech to a mob, to acquit himself or to affect in any manner his criminality before the tribunals of justice, or to make evidence which shall be admitted under any form of law upon his own motion to justify his own criminal conduct.

I do not hesitate to say that every authority which the gentlemen can bring into court regulating the rule of evidence in procedures of this sort is directly against the proposition, and for the simple reason that it is a written declaration made by the accused voluntarily, after the fact, in his own behalf. I read for the information of the Senate the testimony touching this fact of the service of the notice of the action had by the Senate upon the conduct of the President whereof he stands accused before the Senate. It is as follows. On page 109 of the trial Mr. McDonald testified:

"An attested copy of the foregoing resolution was delivered by me into the hands of the President of the United States at his office in the Executive Mansion at ten o'clock p. m. on the 21st of February, 1868."

On the 24th of February, three days afterward, he volunteers a written declaration which he now proposes to make evidence in his own behalf before this tribunal of justice. Of course it is evidence for no purpose whatever, except for the purpose of exculpating him from the criminal accusation preferred against him. It is for no other purpose.

Senators will bear with me while I make a further remark. The proposition is to introduce his whole message, not simply what he says for himself, not simply the arguments that he chooses to present in the form of a written declaration, in vindication of his criminal conduct, in violation of the clearest and plainest provisions of law, and in direct defiance of the action of the Senate' and of the notice it had served on him on the night of the 21st of February; but the Senate will bear with me when I say, what they do know, that this message reports the declarations of third persons, and of course the Senate are asked to accept these, too, as evidence in the trial of the accused at their bar.

He reports in this message the declarations of third persons whom he has pleased to call his "constitutional advisers." He states their opinions. Without giving their language he gives the conclusions, and those conclusions are to be drawn before the Senate as matter of evidence. I beg leave to say here, in the presence of the Senate, that there is no colorable excuse for the President or for his counsel coming before the Senate to say to them, whether it be communicated in his written message or otherwise, that he has any right to attempt to shelter himself for a violation of the laws of the country under the opinions of any member of his Cabinet. The Constitution never vested his Cabinet counselors with any such authority, as it never vested the President with authority to suspend the laws or to violate the laws or to disregard the laws or to make appointments in direct contravention of the laws, and in defiance of the final action of the Senate acting in express obedience to the requirement of the law.

Mr. Manager BUTLER, (after examining the message.) You are right. He reports the opinion of his Cabinet.

Mr. Manager BINGHAM. I was aware that I was right. There is no colorable excuse for this proceeding. I say it with all respect to the learned counsel, and I challenge now the production of authority from any respectable court that ever allowed any man, high or low, official or unofficial, to introduce his own declarations, written or unwritten, made after the fact, in his defense. That is the point I take here. I beg the pardon of the Senate for having detained them so long in the statement of a proposition so simple, and the law of which is so clearly settled running through centuries. I submit the question to them.

Mr. EVARTS. Mr. Chief Justice and Senators——

Mr. Manager BUTLER. Do we ever have the close here?

Mr. EVARTS. I dare say you have; but I also have the opportunity to speak. No question arises of my irregularity, I take it.

Mr. Manager BINGHAM. No, no.

Mr. EVARTS. Mr. Chief Justice and Senators, the only apology that the learned Manager has made for the course of his remarks is the consumption of your time, and yet he has not hesitated to say, and again to repeat, that there is not a color of justification for the attempt of the President of the United States to defend himself or for the efforts that his counsel make.

Mr. Manager BINGHAM. Will the gentleman allow me to correct him? I do not think the gentleman intends to misrepresent me here.

Mr. EVARTS. I do not misrepresent you.

Mr. Manager BINGHAM. I did not say, then, if the gentleman pleases, that there was no colorable excuse for the President to attempt to defend himself or for his counsel to defend him. I did not say that.

Mr. EVARTS. It all comes to the same thing. Everything that is attempted upon our view or line of the subject in controversy, unless it conforms to the preliminary view that the learned Managers choose to throw down, is regarded as outside of the color of law or of right on the part of the President or his counsel, and so it is repeatedly charged.

Now, if the crime was completed on the 21st of February, which is not only the whole basis of this argument of the learned Managers, but of every other argument upon the evidence that I have had the honor of hearing from them, I should like to know what application or relevancy the resolution passed by the Senate on the 21st of February, after the act of the President had been completed, and after that act had been communicated to the Senate, has on the issue of whether that act was right or wrong? And if the fact that it is an expression of opinion relieves the testimony from the possibility of admission, what was this but an expression of the opinion of the Senate of the United States in the form of a resolution regarding a past act of the President? There could be, then, no single principle of the law of evidence upon which this fact put in proof in behalf of the Managers could be admitted, except as a communication from this branch of the Government to the President of the United States of its opinion concerning the legality of his action; and in the same line and in immediate reply the President communicates to the Senate of the United States, openly and in a proper message, his opinions concerning the legality of the act. What would be thought of the Government that, in a criminal prosecution, by way of inculpating a prisoner, should give in evidence what a magistrate or a sheriff had said to him concerning the crime imputed, and then shut the mouth of the prisoner as to what he had said then and there in reply? Why, the only possibility, the only argument for affecting the prisoner with criminality for what had been said to him, was that, unreplied to, it might be construed into admission or submission: and to say that the prisoner, when told "You stole that watch," could not give in evidence his reply, "It was my own watch, and I took it because it was mine," is precisely the same proposition that is being applied here by the learned Managers to this communication back and forth between the Senate and the President.

Mr. Manager BUTLER. A single word, Mr. President, upon that proposition. I think if any sheriff should say to a thief, "Sir, whose watch is that?" and the thief could not make a reply until four days afterward, after he was indicted, a written statement, then, as to whose watch it was, and putting in what his neighbors said about it, would never be received. I take the illustration; it is a good one, an excellent illustration. A sheriff says to a prisoner, "Where did you get that watch?" Four days afterward—after he has been in jail, after the indictment is being found against him, and while the court is in session, he sends an answer to the sheriff and says that answer must be given in evidence, and not only that, but he puts in that answer what everybody else said, what four or five men said to him, as is the case in this message. He is not content with putting in his own answer, but he puts in the view of the Cabinet. Now, we object. If they will fetch the Cabinet here and let us cross-examine them and find out what they meant when they gave him any advice, and how they came to give it to him, and under what circumstances they gave it to him, we shall have a different reply to make to that. But at present we do not want them to put in (to carry out the parallel) what, after he got into jail and consulted with the prisoners in the same room, he says was his answer, and what the prisoners who were with him said about it.

Mr. EVARTS. Mr. Chief Justice and Senators, every case is to be regarded according to its circumstances, and you will judge whether a communication from you to the President of the United States, communicated to him on the 22d of February——

Mr. Manager BUTLER. The 21st.

Mr. EVARTS. I understood you to say that you could not say that.

Mr. Manager BUTLER. Ten o'clock at night on the 21st.

Mr. EVARTS. You got at it then. You did not have it before.

Mr. Manager BINGHAM. I read it.

Mr. EVARTS. Ten o'clock at night on the 21st the communication was sent to him. The Senate was not in session on the 22d, as I am informed, more than an hour, it being a holiday, and this message sent in on Monday, Sunday intervening, is not an answer according to the ordinary course of prompt and candid treaty between the Senate and President concerning a matter in difference, or an answer to imputation communicated to him. As for the simile of the President being in prison, we have removed that by showing that he was not impeached until five o'clock in the afternoon of Monday the 24th; and as to the simile that the Cabinet were his fellow-prisoners in the same cell, the answer is that they have not been impeached at all. But we do not pursue these trivial illustrations. The matter is within the intelligence of the court, and must be disposed of by it.

Mr. Manager BINGHAM. Mr. President and Senators, I desire to say, once for all, to the Senate that I have said no word, and intend to say no word, during the progress of this trial, that justifies the assertion of counsel for the President that I deny his right to make a defense either in person or by his counsel. What I insist upon here, and ask the Senate to act upon, is that he shall make a defense precisely as unofficial citizens of the United States make defenses, according to the law of the land and not otherwise; that he shall not after the commission of crime manufacture evidence in his own behalf, either oral or written, by his own declaration, and incorporate in it, too, the declarations of third persons and throw it upon the court as testimony. It has never been allowed in any respectable court in this country upon any occasion. When men stood upon trial for their lives they never were permitted after the fact to manufacture testimony by their own declarations, either written or un-

written, and on their own motion introduce it in the courts of justice.

I have another word or two to say in the light of what has dropped from the lips of the counsel. He has evaded most skillfully the point I took occasion to make in the hearing of the Senate, that here is an attempt to introduce not only the written declarations of the accused in his own behalf after the fact, but the declarations of third persons, not under oath, and their conclusions reported in this message of the 24th of February, 1868. I venture to say that a proposition of the extent of this never was made before in any tribunal of justice in the United States where any man stood accused of crime, not simply to give his own declarations, but to report the declarations of third persons in his own behalf and throw them before the Senate as testimony.

One other remark. The gentleman seems to think that the President had a right to send a message to the Senate of the United States which should operate as evidence. I concede that the President of the United States has the right under the Constitution to communicate from time to time to the two Houses of Congress such matters as he thinks pertain to the public interest; and if he thinks that is of the public interest he may do so; but I deny that there is any colorable excuse (I repeat those words here) for intimating that the President of the United States, charged with the commission of crime on the 21st of February, 1868, and proved guilty, I undertake to say, by his written confession, to the satisfaction of every intelligent and unprejudiced mind in and out of the Senate in this country, could proceed to manufacture a defense three days after the fact in the form of a message. That is the point I make on the gentleman here. He says "What importance, then, do you attach to the action of the Senate." We attach precisely this importance to it: that the law of the land enjoined upon the President of the United States the duty to notify the Senate of the suspension of this officer and the reasons therefor, and the evidence upon which he made the suspension. The law of the land enjoined upon the Senate the duty to act upon the report of the President so made, together with his reasons and the evidence which he adduced, and come to a decision. In pursuance of the requirement of the second section of the tenure-of-office act the Senate of the United States, by an almost unanimous decision, came to the conclusion that the reasons furnished by the President and the evidence adduced by him for the suspension of the Secretary of War were insufficient, and in accordance with that law the Senate non-concurred in the suspension. The law expressly provides that if they concur they shall notify the President. The law, by every intendment, provides that if they non-concur they shall notify the Secretary of War that he may, in obedience to the express requirement of the act, forthwith resume the functions of the office from which he has been suspended. They did give him that notice. Why should they not notify the Executive that he may know with whom to communicate, and not be longer communicating with the Secretary of War *ad interim*, General Grant, who had been appointed, in accordance with the provisions of the act, Secretary of War *ad interim* in August, 1867?

The gentleman, I trust, is answered as to the importance and propriety of introducing this evidence; but there was further reason for it, to leave the President without excuse before the Senate and before the people for persisting in his unlawful attempt, in violation of the law of the land, to execute the duties of the office of the Secretary of War through another person than Edwin M. Stanton. It was his business to submit to the final decision of that arbiter constituted by the tenure-of-office act to decide the question whether the suspension should become absolute or whether it should be rejected.

But here is a man defying the action of the Senate, defying the express letter of the law, that the Secretary of War, in whose suspension they had refused to concur, should forthwith resume the functions of that office, proceeding with his conspiracy with Thomas to remove him and to confer the functions of this office upon another, regardless of the action of the Senate, regardless of the law regulating the tenure of civil offices, regardless of the Constitution, regardless of his oath, regardless of the rights of the American people; and he winds up the farce and the defiant guilt of which he stands convicted by act before the Senate with his written declaration, which is of no higher authority than his oral declaration, made three days after the fact, and asks the Senate to receive it as evidence.

The CHIEF JUSTICE. There is, perhaps, Senators, no branch of the law in which it is more difficult to lay down precise rules than that which relates to evidence of the intent with which an act is done. In the present case it appears that the Senate, on the 21st of February, passed a resolution, which I will take the liberty of reading:

"Whereas the Senate have received and considered the communication of the President stating that he has removed Edwin M. Stanton, Secretary of War, and had designated the Adjutant General of the Army to act as Secretary of War *ad interim:* Therefore,

"*Resolved by the Senate of the United States,* That under the Constitution and laws of the United States the President has no power to remove the Secretary of War, and to designate any other officer to perform the duties of the office *ad interim.*"

That resolution was adopted on the 21st of February, and was served, as the evidence before you shows, on the evening of the same day. The message which is now proposed to be introduced was sent to the Senate on the 24th day of February. It does not appear to the Chief Justice that the resolution of the Senate called for an answer, or that there was any call upon the President to answer from the Senate itself; and therefore he must regard the message which was sent to the Senate on the 24th of February as a vindication of the President's act addressed by him to the Senate; and it does not appear to the Chief Justice to come within any of the rules which have been applied to the introduction of evidence upon this trial. He will, however, take pleasure in submitting the question to the Senate if any Senator desires it. [After a pause.] If no Senator desires that the question be submitted to the Senate, the Chief Justice rules the evidence to be inadmissible.

Mr. CURTIS. Mr. Chief Justice, we wish to put in evidence a table which has been compiled in the office of the Attorney General, which will be found to be, I believe, a convenience in the progress of the trial in the examination of the documentary evidence which will be put in.

Mr. DRAKE. Mr. President, we cannot hear the honorable counsel.

Mr. CURTIS. I will endeavor to make myself heard.

The CHIEF JUSTICE. If Senators will observe the rules of the Senate, and the gentlemen who are in the Chamber and the persons in the galleries will abstain from conversation, it will be much easier to hear the counsel.

Mr. CURTIS. I will read the headings of this table, so that the nature of its contents may be perceived. It excludes all military and naval officers, all judges of the constitutional judiciary of the United States, all judges of the Court of Claims, all officers whose appointment is vested in the President alone, the heads of Departments, or the courts of law, and all public ministers, consuls, and other agents of foreign intercourse. They are excluded, and with these exceptions "the following is an approximate list of all other executive and territorial offices of the United States now and heretofore established by statutory designation, with their respective statutory tenures."

Then follows the list of officers the table contains. In the first place the date of the act of Congress by which the office was created, the volume and page of the Statutes-at-Large, and next comes the name or title of the office. The fourth column shows whether the tenure of the office was for a definite term. Then there is another column showing whether it was for a term definite "unless sooner removed," the first column being for a definite term without any qualification whatever, the second column being for a term definite unless sooner removed, the third column for a term indefinite and not expressly during pleasure, and the fourth for a term indefinite, but expressly "during pleasure."

Mr. Manager BUTLER. Before you put that in we wish to object.

Mr. CURTIS. One moment. The names of the offices are given, and then there are carried out in these columns what tenure belongs to each of them. Of course this is not offered as strictly evidence, but it has been compiled as a table which it will be found very convenient to refer to in argument, but which it would be necessary to consult and turn over a great number of statutes of the United States in order to make use of or arrive at these results. Here they are all brought under the eye, and we desire to have the table printed so that it may be used in argument by counsel on all sides.

Mr. Manager BUTLER. I observe, Mr. President and Senators, that there is one important column missing in this table, if it is to have any effect on anybody's mind, and that is a column showing whether the Senate was or was not in session at the time any one of these officers was removed.

Mr. CURTIS. It has nothing to do, allow me to say, Mr. Manager, with removals at all. It is the tenure of office merely. It has no bearing on any question of removal. It merely gives the statute tenures of these different offices; and there are no facts here stated; everything is derived from the statutes. All that is in the table is derived from the statutes of the United States.

Mr. Manager BUTLER. The difficulty that we find is that this is proposed to be made a portion of the evidence. It may be printed and appended to the argument of either gentleman or sent as argument to the table of any Senator—precisely as (if I may use it as an illustration) I sent my brief—as an abstract from the laws; but to offer it in evidence and to have it printed except in that way is what we object to. The reason for the objection must be obvious. Who has any surety that this is correct? The commissions are not kept by the Attorney General. They are in the Department of State.

Mr. EVARTS. This has nothing to do with commissions.

Mr. Manager BUTLER. Then this is a mere abstract of the laws?

Mr. EVARTS. That is what we have stated exactly.

Mr. Manager BUTLER. Put it, then, in your argument. Why should your abstract of the laws be put in evidence any more than anybody else's? The difference is this: if either of my friends on the other side under their hand and upon their examination put in their brief an abstract of law I should believe that the law was exactly as it purports to be abstracted. But they do not claim that they have examined this table—that this is their work. It is done in the Attorney General's office. Now, I have not so much confidence in everybody in the Attorney General's office that I am willing to take his abstract of laws and have it put in these solemn proceedings. If Mr. Binckley, for instance, the Assistant Attorney General, should prepare any paper of this sort, I should look it over a great while before I should give it great weight, and, I think, the country would from their knowledge. If Mr. Stanbery, if either of the learned gentlemen

before me, will examine this and say that from their examination it is correct, and they make it a part of their argument, I am content; but until that is done I object to its going in evidence. Until that is done I object, and, as my associate says, we shall object then. It is not evidence in any form.

Mr. EVARTS. Mr. Chief Justice and Senators, there is but a word to be said on this subject. It imparts into the case no primary evidence. It can be verified by oath as being correctly or honestly made up, if that is required. We upon our professional credit present it as in our belief a correct statement in a tabular form of the distribution of the statutory provisions concerning the tenure of office that are in force under the Government of the United States.

Mr. Manager BUTLER. Allow me, without interrupting the gentleman, here to ask whether he has examined it so as to know of his own knowledge that it is so, because that will make a great difference to my mind.

Mr. EVARTS. So presenting it, the question is, whether you will receive it as the proper and necessary tabular introduction to the documentary evidence concerning these different classes of offices in respect to the conduct of the Government in filling or in vacating the places. We did not expect an objection to be made, least of all upon so vague a notion as Mr. Binckley's political character, which we are not prepared to defend, and he is not present to defend himself. We submit it to the Senate. They can treat it, if you please, as a presentation by us now presently of the distribution of the offices of the United States according to statute, in order to introduce our practical and actual legal testimony appropriate to each class. It is submitted to the discretion of the Senate.

Mr. Manager BOUTWELL. Mr. President and Senators, this paper, upon examination, does not show that any person was ever appointed to office or was removed from office.

Mr. EVARTS. So we have stated, over and over again, that it comes out of the statutes bodily.

Mr. Manager BOUTWELL. Then I am utterly unable to see how it can be regarded as testimony upon any issue that is before this tribunal.

Mr. TRUMBULL. Mr. President, I move that the paper be printed as a part of the proceedings of the Senate.

Mr. EVARTS. That is all we desire.

The CHIEF JUSTICE. It will be necessarily printed, having been offered by the counsel for the President. The Chair will put the question, however. You who are of opinion that the paper be printed will say "ay;" those of contrary opinion will say "no."

The motion was agreed to.

The table thus ordered to be printed is as follows:

Exclusively of all Military and Naval Officers; all Judges of the constitutional Judiciary of the United States; all Judges of the Court of Claims; all Officers whose appointment is vested in the President alone: the Heads of Departments or the courts of law; and all public Ministers, Consuls, and other agents of foreign intercourse; the following is an approximate list of all other Executive and Territorial Officers of the United States now and heretofore, by statutory designation, with their respective statutory tenure, namely:

Date of act creating the office.	Statutes-at-Large Volume.	Page.	Name or Title of Office.	For a term definite.	For a term definite unless sooner removed.	For a term indefinite, and not expressly during pleasure.	For a term indefinite, but expressly during pleasure.	Remarks.
September 2, 1789	1	65	Secretary of the Treasury			do.		
March 3, 1857	11	220	Assistant Secretary of the Treasury			do.		
March 14, 1864	13	28	Additional Assistant Secretary of the Treasury			do.		
September 2, 1789	1	65	Comptroller			do.		
September 2, 1789	1	65	Auditor			do.		
September 2, 1789	1	65	Treasurer		do.			
August 6, 1846	9	59	Assistant Treasurers			do.		
March 3, 1863	12	761	Assistant Treasurers			do.		
September 2, 1789	1	65	Register of Treasury			do.		
February 20, 1863	12	656	Assistant Register			do.		
May 8, 1792	1	280	Commissioner of the Revenue			do.		This office was discontinued by act of April 6, 1802; reëstablished by act of July 24, 1813; and finally abolished by act of December 23, 1817.
February 23, 1795	1	419	Purveyor of Public Supplies			do.		Abolished by act of March 28, 1812.
April 25, 1812	2	716	Commissioner of General Land Office			do.		
March 3, 1817	3	366	Second Auditor			do.		
March 3, 1817	3	366	Third Auditor			do.		
March 3, 1817	3	366	Fourth Auditor			do.		
March 3, 1817	3	366	Fifth Auditor			do.		
July 2, 1836	5	80	Sixth Auditor			do.		
March 3, 1817	3	366	Second Comptroller			do.		
May 29, 1830	4	414	Solicitor of the Treasury			do.		
March 3, 1849	9	395	Commissioner of Customs		do.			
June 3, 1864	13	99	Comptroller of Currency			do.		
July 1, 1862	12	432	Commissioner of Internal Revenue			do.		
March 3, 1863	12	725	Deputy Commissioner of Internal Revenue			do.		
July 31, 1789	1	29	Naval officer / Collector of customs			do.		
March 2, 1799	1	627	Surveyor of customs			do.		By act of May 15, 1820, 3 Statutes, 582, these offices are limited to a term of four years, and the incumbents are declared to be removable therefrom at pleasure.
March 2, 1799	1	627	Navy agent			do.		
March 3, 1809	2	536	Receiver of public moneys for lands			do.		
May 10, 1800	2	75	Register of Land Office			do.		
May 10, 1800	2	73	District attorneys			do.		
September 24, 1789	1	92				do.		

STATEMENT—Continued.

Date of act creating the office.	Statutes-at-Large. Volume.	Statutes-at-Large. Page.	Name or Title of Office.	For a term definite.	For a term definite unless sooner removed.	For a term indefinite, and not expressly during pleasure.	For a term indefinite, but expressly during pleasure.	Remarks.
September 24, 1789	1	87	Marshals		do.			Removable at pleasure.
September 24, 1789	1	93	Attorney General			do.		
March 1, 1823	3	735	Appraisers (for certain ports)			do.		
May 28, 1830	4	409	Additional appraiser (for New York)			do.		
March 3, 1851	9	629	General appraiser			do.		
March 3, 1863	12	276	Cashier of internal revenue			do.		
July 1, 1862	12	433	Assessors of internal revenue			do.		
July 1, 1863	12	433	Collectors of internal revenue			do.		
April 2, 1792 and	1	296	{ Director of Mint			do.		
	5	133	{ Treasurer of Mint			do.		
January 18, 1837	5	133	Assayer of Mint			do.		
January 18, 1837	5	133	Mr and refiner of Mint			do.		
January 18, 1837	5	133	Chief coiner of Mint			do.		
January 18, 1837	5	133	Engraver of Mint			do.		
March 2, 1799	1	700	Captain revenue cutter			do.		
March 2, 1799	1	700	Lieutenants revenue cutter			do.		
March 3, 1845	5	794	Engineers revenue cutter			do.		
July 16, 1798	1	694	Directors of marine hospitals			do.		
July 27, 1789	1	29	Secretary of State				do.	
March 3, 1853	10	212	Assistant Secretary of State			do.		
July 4, 1864	13	386	Commissioner of immigration				do.	
July 4, 1864	13	386	Superintendent of immigration	do.				
July 11, 1862	12	531	Judges and arbitrators under treaty of April 7, 1862					Tenure "during good behavior."
August 7, 1789	1	53	Governor of Northwest Territory		do.	do.		
August 7, 1789	1	53	Secretary of Northwest Territory		do.	do.		
Mh 26, 1804 and Mh 3, 1805	2	283	Judges of Northwest Territory					
			Governor of Territory of Orleans and Territory of Louisiana	do.	do.			
March 3, 1805	2	331	Secretary of Territory of Orleans and Territory of Louisiana		do.			
March 3, 1805	2	331	Judges of Territory of Orleans and Territory of Louisiana	do.				
March 3, 1805	2	331	District attorney of Territory of Orleans and Territory of Louisiana					
			Marshal of Territory of Orleans and Territory of Louisiana					
April 7, 1798	1	559	Officers for Territory of Mississippi			do.		
May 7, 1800	2	59	Officers for Territory of Indiana			do.		
January 11, 1805	2	309	Officers for Territory of Michigan			do.		

Date	No.	No.	Officers				Remarks
February 3, 1809	514	2	Officers for Territory of Illinois				
June 4, 1812	744	2	Governor of Territory of Missouri				
June ...	744	2	Secretary of Territory of Missouri	do.	do.		
March 2, 1819	746	2	Judges of Territory of Missouri				
Mch 2, 18..	494	3	Secretary of Arkansas Territory				
March 3, 1817	495	3	Judges of Arkansas Territory				
Mch 3, 1817	372	3	Secretary of ... Territory				
Mch 30, 1822	655	3	Secretary of ... Territory				
Mch 30, 1822	655	3	Secretary of ... Territory				
Mch 30, 1822	656	3	Judges of Florida Territory	do.	do.	do.	
Mch 30, 1822	656	3	... of Florida Territory				
March 3, 1825	126	4	Judges of Florida Territory				
April 20, 1836	11	5	Governor of Wisconsin Territory				
April 20, 1836	11	5	Secretary of Wisconsin Territory				
April 20, 1836	14	5	Chief justice and ...	do.	do.		
September 9, 1850	447	9	Attorney and marshal	do.	do.		
Sept ber 9, 1850	48	9	Governor of Territory of New Mexico				Act vests appointment in the President alone.
Sept ber 9, 1850	449	9	Secretary of Territory of New Mexico	do.	do.	do.	
Sept ber 9, 1850	450	9	... and ... justices				Tenure "during good behavior."
September 9, 1850	450	9	Marshal for Territory of New Mexico	do.	do.		
Sept ber 9, 1850	453	9	... of New Mexico	do.	do.	do.	
September 9, 1850	453	9	Secretary of Utah Territory				
September 9, 1850	455	9	... and marshal				
September 9, 1850	456	9	... and marshal				
June 12, 1838	296	5	Secretary of Iowa Territory				
June 12, 1838	238	5	... and associate justices	do.	do.	to.	
June 12, 1838	238	5	Attorney and marshal				
August 14, 1848	324	9	... of Oregon Territory	do.	do.		
August 14, 1848	328	9	Chief and associate justices				
August 14, 1848	327	9	Attorney and ...	do.	do.		
Mch 3, 1849	404	9	... Territory				
Mch 3, 1849	404	9	Secretary of Minnesota Territory	do.	do.	do.	
Mch 3, 1849	406	9	Chief and associate justices				
Mch 3, 1849	406	9	... and marshal				
March 2, 1853	173	10	... of Washington Territory				
Mch 2, 1853	175	10	Secretary of ... Territory	do.	do.		
Mch 2, 1853	176	10	Chief and ...				
May 30, 1854	278	10	... and marshal				
May 30, 1854	278	10	... of Nebraska Territory	do.	do.	do.	
May 30, 1854	290	10	Secretary of Nebraska Territory				
May 30, 1854	281	10	Chief and associate ...				
May 30, 1854	281	10	Marshal for Nebraska ...	do.	do.		
May 30, 1854	284	10	... Territory				
May 30, 1854	284	10	Secretary of ... Territory	do.	do.	do.	
May 30, 1854	286	10	Chief and ... justices				
May 30, 1854	287	10	... and marshal				
February 24, 1863	665	12	... of Arizona Territory	do.	do.	do.	
February 24, 1863	665	12	Secretary of Arizona Territory				
February 24, 1863	665	12	Judges for ...				

STATEMENT—Continued.

Date of act creating the office.	Statutes-at-Large Volume.	Statutes-at-Large Page.	Name or title of office.	For a term definite.	For a term definite unless sooner removed.	For a term indefinite, and not expressly during pleasure.	For a term indefinite, but not expressly during pleasure.	Remarks.
February 24, 1863	12	665	Surveyor general of Arizona Territory		do.			
February 28, 1861	12	172	███ of ███ Territory		do.			
February 28, 1861	12	172	Secretary of ███ Territory		do.			
February 28, 1861	12	174	Chief and associate justices	do.				
February 28, 1861	12	175	███ney and ███		do.			
March 2, 1861	12	239	███ of Dakota Territory		do.			
March 2, 1861	12	240	Secretary of Dakota Territory		do.			
March 2, 1861	12	241	Chief and ███ justices	do.				
March 2, 1861	12	242	Attorney and marshal		do.			
March 2, 1861	12	210	███ of ███ Territory		do.			
March 2, 1861	12	210	Secretary of ███ Territory		do.			
March 2, 1861	12	212	Chief and associate justices	do.				
March 2, 1861	12	213	Attorney and marshal		do.			
March 3, 1863	12	809	███ of Idaho Territory		do.			
March 3, 1863	12	809	Secretary of Idaho Territory		do.			
March 3, 1863	12	811	Chief and associate justices	do.				
March 3, 1863	12	812	Attorney and marshal		do.			
May 26, 1864	13	86	Governor of Mo███ ███na Territory		do.			
May 26, 1864	13	86	Secretary of ███na Territory		do.			
May 26, 1864	13	89	███ ███ associate justices	do.				
May 26, 1864	13	89	Attorney for ███na Territory		do.			
May 18, 1796	1	464	███ for			do.		
March 3, 1803	2	233	Surveyor general ███ of Tennessee			do.		
April 29, 1816	3	325	Surveyor of ███ south of Tennessee			do.		
March 3, 1823	3	755	Surveyor for Territories of Illinois and Missouri			do.		
March 3, 1831	4	492	Surveyor general for Territory of Florida			do.		
June 12, 1838	5	243	Surveyor for Territory of Louisiana			do.		
September 27, 1850	9	496	Surveyor for Territory of Wisconsin			do.		
March 3, 1851 and	9	617	Surveyor general for Territory of Oregon			do.		
March 3, 1853	10	244	Surveyor general for California			do.		
July 17, 1854	10	306	Surveyor general for Washington Territory			do.		And until successor qualified.
July 22, 1854	10	308	Surveyor general for New Mexico			do.		And until successors qualified.
February 21, 1855	10	611	Surveyor general for Kansas and Nebraska			do.		And until successors qualified.
February 21, 1855	10	176	Surveyor General for Utah Territory			do.		
March 2, 1861	12	214	Surveyor General for Colorado Territory			do.		
March 2, 1861	12	244	Surveyor General for Nevada Territory			do.		
March 3, 1817	3	375	Surveyor General for Dakota Territory			do.		
			Surveyor for North Mississippi Territory			do.		

Date			Office					Remarks
May 26, 184_	13	89	Surveyor General for ... Territory		......	......	......	
July 4, 1836	15	117	... of ...		do.			
Mh 2, 1861	12	246	... of Indian Affairs		do.			
July 9, 1832	4	564	Superintendent of Indian trade		do.			
April 16, 18_	3	428	Indian agents		do.			
Mh 16, 1819	3	514	Indian agent		do.			
Mh 3, 1819	3	519	Indian agent		do.			
May 6, 1822	3	683	Superintendent of Indian Affairs		do.			
June 30, 1834	4	735	... of Indian Affairs		do.			
June 30, 1834	4	163	Indian agents		do.			
March 3, 1837	5	437	... of Indian Affairs					
... 5, 1850	9	586	Indian					
June 5, 1850	9	86-7	... of Indian Affairs	do.	do.	do.	do.	See act February 27, 1851.
February 27, 1851	9	3	Superintendent of Indian Affairs		do.		do.	See act February 27, 1851.
Mh 3, 1852	10	700	Indian	do.	do.	do.	do.	
Mh 3, 1855	10	185	Indian agents		do.			
August 18, 186_	11	81	Superintendent of Indian Affairs		do.			
March 3, 1857	11	185	Indian agents		do.			
June 25, 1860	12	113	Superintendent of Indian Affairs		do.			
February 8, 1861	12	130	Indian					
February 8, 1861	12	130	Superintendent of Indian Affairs					
July 1	12	489	Indian agents	do.	do.	do.	do.	
April 8, 1864	13	39	Superintendent of Indian Affairs					
April 8, 1864	13	40	Indian agents					
Mh 2, 1833	4	622	... of Pensions		do.			
Mh 3, 1835	4	779	... of Pensions					
Mch 3, 1837	5	187	Commissioner of Pensions					
Mh 4, 1840	5	589	Commissioner of Pensions		do.		do.	
January 20, 1843	5	697	... of Pensions					
January 11, 1846	9	3	... of Pensions					
January 19, 1849	9	341	... of Pensions		do.		do.	Abolished, act—
Mh 29, 1816	3	324	... of Public Buildings		d.			
July 1	10	30	... of Pensions					
Mh 26, 1862	12	387	Superintendent of Public Printing					
September 22, 1789	1	70	... of Agriculture					
Ast 4, 190_	1	178	Master General		d.			
Mh 3, ...	1	218	... ter		d.			
February 20, 1792	1	234	Postmaster		d.			
My 8, 1794	1	357	... ter		d.		do.	
Mh 2, 1799	1	733	Post master General		d.			
pAil 30, 1810	2	593	Post master		d.			
March 3, 1825	4	102	Post master					
July 2, 1836	5	87	Deputy Postmasters					
March 3, 1853	10	255	Assistant ... Generals					
April 30, 1798	12	553	Secretary of the Navy		d.		do.	Abolished by act of March 3, 1817.
July 31, 1861	12	292	... Secretary of the ...		d.			
July 5, 1862	12	510	... of Bureaus in ... Department		d.			For four years, "unless sooner removed by the President."
May 8, 1792	1	49	Secretary of War					
May 8, 1792	1	280	Accountant of War		do.			}"Shall hereafter be appointed," &c.
... 6, 1856	11	30	Solicitor Court of Claims		do.	do.		
March 3, 1863	12	766	Assistant soli ... ... urt of Claims					
March 3, 1863	12	766	Solicitor Court of Claims					
March 3, 1863	12	766	Assistant solicitor Court of Claims					
	12	766	Deputy solicitor Court of Claims					

STATEMENT—Continued.

Date of act creating the office.	Volume	Page	Name or Title of Office.	For a term definite.	For a term definite unless sooner removed.	For a term indefinite, and not expressly during pleasure.	For a term indefinite, but not expressly during pleasure.	Remarks.
July 4, 1836	5	109	Principal clerk public lands	.....	.....	do.	.....	
July 4, 1836	5	109	Principal clerk of private land claims	.....	.....	do.	.....	
July 4, 1836	5	110	Principal clerk of Surveys	.....	.....	do.	.....	
July 4, 1836	5	111	Recorder of General Land Office	.....	.....	do.	.....	
July 4, 1836	5	111	Solicitor of same	.....	.....	do.	.....	
July 4, 1836	5	111	Secretary to sign Land Patents	.....	.....	do.	.....	
March 3, 1849	9	395	Secretary of the Interior	.....	.....	do.	.....	
March 14, 1862	12	369	Assistant Secretary of the Interior	.....	.....	do.	.....	
February 20, 1863	12	656	Solicitor of War Department	.....	.....	do.	.....	
March 2, 1865	13	468	Solicitor of Navy Department	.....	.....	do.	.....	
March 3, 1865	13	508	Commissioner Freedmen's Bureau	do.	.....	do.	.....	Abolished by act of—
March 3, 1865	13	508	Assistant Commissioners of Freedmen's Bureau	.....	.....	do.	.....	Abolished by act of—
February 13, 1837	4	774 / 147	Superintendents, treasurers, and other officers of branch mints	.....	.....	do.	.....	
July 3, 1852	10	11	Commissioner of Education	do.	.....	do.	.....	
April 21, 1862	12	382	Assistant Secretary of War	do.	.....	do.	.....	
March 3, 1863	13	770	Second Assistant Secretary of War	do.	.....	do.	.....	
July 4, 1864	13	382	Commissioners to revise statutes	do.	.....	.....	.....	
March 2, 1867	14	434	Commissioners Emancipation, District of Columbia	do.	.....	.....	.....	
August 3, 1861	13	287	Warden of jail, District of Columbia	.....	.....	.....	.....	
June 27, 1866	14	74	Commissioners to codify laws, District of Columbia	.....	.....	.....	.....	
April 16, 1862	12	376	Justices of peace for District of Columbia	do.	.....	do.	.....	
May 20, 1862	12	12	Register of wills, District of Columbia	.....	.....	do.	.....	
February 27, 1801	2	103	Register of deeds, District of Columbia	.....	.....	do.	.....	
May 17, 1848	9	229	Commissioner (reciprocity treaty)	.....	.....	.....	.....	
February 14, 1863	12	651	Commissioner, chief astronomer and surveyor to carry into effect treaty of June 15, 1846	.....	.....	.....	.....	
Treaty June 5, 1854	10	1090	Commissioner (Hudson Bay and Puget Sound)	.....	do.	.....	.....	
August 11, 1856	11	42		.....	.....	do.	.....	
June 27, 1864	13	195	Commissioners under treaties with Colombia, &c.	.....	.....	do.	.....	
February 29, 1861	13	145		.....	.....	.....	.....	
June 30, 1864	13	323		.....	.....	do.	.....	
March 3, 1851	9	631	Commissioner California Land Claims	.....	.....	.....	.....	

Mr. CURTIS. Mr. Chief Justice, we now desire to put in evidence rather in a more formal manner than has been done heretofore, although the substantial facts have been brought before the Senate, we believe, by the honorable Managers themselves, the proceedings which took place at the time of the removal of Mr. Pickering by Mr. Adams, accompanied by a certificate that the letters to and from various persons between the 29th of June, 1799, and the 1st of May, 1802, have been for many years missing from the files of the Department of State. The correspondence itself, therefore, cannot be produced from the originals, or from copies of the originals, but no doubt they are correct, as those letters were read the other day by the honorable Managers from a volume of Mr. Adams's works. They are the same letters. The letters are not here; they are not in the Department; but they are printed in that volume and were read from the volume the other day.

Mr. Manager BUTLER. Wait a moment. We are not certain about this. [After an examination of the documents offered in evidence.] Do I understand the counsel for the President to say that these papers show anything different from what was shown by the Managers?

Mr. CURTIS. No. I stated that in substance the matter was now before the Senate, but we wanted the formal documents to be put in.

Mr. Manager BUTLER. The only difficulty I find is this: that you do not put in all; you do not put in what was done on the 12th of May as well as the 13th of May, 1800.

Mr. CURTIS. We put in what there is here.

Mr. EVARTS. You have already put in the other.

Mr. Manager BUTLER. Very good.

Mr. CURTIS. We offer these documents from the Department of State.

Mr. Manager BUTLER. Very well.

The documents thus offered in evidence are as follows:

UNITED STATES OF AMERICA,
Department of State:

To all to whom these presents shall come, greeting:

I certify that the document hereunto annexed is a true copy, carefully examined and compared with the original resolution of the Senate, dated 13th May, 1800, and filed in this Department, confirming John Marshall, of Virginia, to be Secretary of State, and Samuel Dexter, of Massachusetts, to be Secretary of the Department of War.

In testimony whereof I, William H. Seward, Secretary of State of the United States, have hereunto subscribed my name and caused the seal of the Department of State to be affixed.

Done at the city of Washington this 5th day of March, A. D. 1868, and of the independence of the United States of America the ninety-second.

[L. S.]

WILLIAM H. SEWARD.

UNITED STATES OF AMERICA,
IN SENATE, *May 13, 1800.*

The Senate proceeded to consider the message of the President of the United States of the 12th instant, and the nominations contained therein, of

The Hon. John Marshall, esq., of Virginia, to be Secretary of State, in the place of the Hon. Timothy Pickering, esq., removed.

The Hon. Samuel Dexter, esq., of Massachusetts, to be Secretary of the Department of War, in the place of the Hon. John Marshall, nominated for promotion to the office of State.

Whereupon,

Resolved, That they do advise and consent to the appointments agreeably to the nominations respectively.

Attest: SAMUEL A. OTIS, *Secretary.*

The CHIEF JUSTICE. The executive clerk of the Senate desires to correct a statement made in respect to the nomination of Mr. Ewing. Mr. Clarke will make the correction.

D. W. C. CLARKE recalled.

The WITNESS. I stated in my examination that the nomination of Mr. Ewing was brought to the Senate on the 22d of February. I did so in consequence of a memorandum which I found at the bottom of my sheet. I find, by investigation since, that I made that memorandum from the fact that it was brought to the Senate Chamber on the 22d of February by Mr. Moore, but the Senate was not in session, and he returned with it to the Executive Mansion. He brought it up with one other message and the message of the President in relation to the removal of Mr. Stanton on the 24th, and it was then submitted to the Senate.

By Mr. CURTIS:

Question. I want to see if I correctly understand you. I understand your statement now to be that Colonel Moore brought it and delivered it to you on the 22d, but the Senate had adjourned?

Answer. No, sir. He brought it up on the 22d; he did not deliver it to me.

Question. He brought it?

Answer. He brought it on the 22d, but the Senate was not in session, and he took it back to the Executive Mansion.

Question. And on the 24th he returned, and then it was formally brought in?

Answer. That is it.

By Mr. Manager BUTLER:

Question. How do you know that he brought it here; of your own knowledge?

Answer. Only by the information of Colonel Moore.

Question. Then all you have been telling us is what Colonel Moore told you?

Answer. Yes, sir; that is, all in regard to the nomination.

Mr. Manager BUTLER. Very well, sir; we do not want any more of Colonel Moore's information from you.

Mr. CURTIS. We will call Colonel Moore.

WILLIAM G. MOORE recalled.

By Mr. CURTIS:

Question. (handing to the witness the message nominating Thomas Ewing, sen., as Secretary of War.) What is the document you hold in your hand?

Answer. The nomination to the Senate of Thomas Ewing, sen., of Ohio, to be Secretary for the Department of War.

Question. Did you receive that from the President of the United States?

Answer. I did.

Question. On what day?

Answer. On the 22d day of February, 1868.

Question. About what hour in the day?

Answer. I think it was after twelve o'clock.

Question. And before what hour?

Answer. And before one.

Question. Between twelve and one?

Answer. Between twelve and one.

Question. What did you do with it?

Answer. By the direction of the President I brought it to the Capitol to present it to the Senate.

Question. About what time did you arrive here?

Answer. I cannot state definitely, but I presume about a quarter past one.

Question. Was the Senate then in session, or had it adjourned?

Answer. It had, after a very brief session, adjourned.

Question. What did you do with the document, in consequence?

Answer. I returned with it to the Executive Mansion, after a visit to the House of Representatives.

Question. Were you apprised before you reached the Capitol that the Senate had adjourned?

Answer. I was not.

Question. What did you do with the document subsequently?

Answer. I returned with it to the Executive Mansion, after having visited the House of Representatives.

Question. Was anything more done with the document by you, and if so, when, and what did you do?

Answer. I was directed by the President on Monday, the 24th day of February, 1868, to return and deliver it to the Senate.

Question. What did you do in consequence?

Answer. I obeyed the order.

Cross-examined by Mr. Manager BUTLER:

Question. Was that open and as it is now, or in a sealed envelope, when you took it?

Answer. In a sealed envelope.

Question. Did you put it in yourself?

Answer. I did not.

Question. Did you see it put in?

Answer. I did not.

Question. How do you know what was in the envelope?

Answer. It was, I believe, the only message I brought that day; I gave it to the clerk, who sealed it and handed it to me.

Question. And then did you unseal it again at all; or did you examine it to see what was in it until you left it here on the 24th?

Answer. I did not, to my recollection.

Question. Did you show it to anybody here in the House on that day?

Answer. No, sir; it was sealed.

Question. Have you spoken this morning with Mr. Clarke here upon this subject?

Answer. He asked me upon what date I had delivered the message. I told him the 24th.

Mr. CURTIS. I now offer in evidence, Mr. Chief Justice, a document which I desire to be read by the Clerk.

Mr. Manager BUTLER. Allow me to see it before it is read.

Mr. CURTIS. Certainly.

[The document was handed to Mr. Manager BUTLER and examined by him.]

Mr. Manager BUTLER. We have no objection.

The CHIEF JUSTICE. The Secretary will read the document.

The Secretary read as follows:

UNITED STATES OF AMERICA,
Department of State:
To all to whom these presents shall come, greeting:

I certify that the document hereunto annexed is a true copy, carefully examined and compared with the original record of this Department, authorizing "John Nelson, Attorney General, to discharge the duties of Secretary of State *ad interim* until a successor to A. P. Upshur shall be appointed," and that this appointment was made during the session of the Senate.

I further certify that the confirmation by the Senate of John C. Calhoun to succeed Mr. Nelson is a true copy of the original filed in this Department.

In testimony whereof I, William H. Seward, Secretary of State of the United States, have hereunto subscribed my name and caused the seal of the Department of State to be affixed.

Done at the city of Washington the 6th day of [L. S.] April, A. D. 1868, and of the independence of the United States of America the ninety-second. WILLIAM H. SEWARD.

The Hon. John Nelson, Attorney General of the United States, will discharge the duties of Secretary of State *ad interim* until a successor to the Hon. A. P. Upshur be appointed.

The Department of State will be put into mourning for the death of the Hon. Abel P. Upshur, late Secretary of State; and all foreign envoys and ministers of the United States, and other officers connected with the Department of State, whether at home or abroad, will wear the usual badges in token of grief and respect for his memory, during the period of thirty days from the time of receiving this order.

February 29, 1844. JOHN TYLER.

IN SENATE OF THE UNITED STATES,
March 6, 1844.

Resolved, That the Senate advise and consent to the appointment of John C. Calhoun, of South Carolina, to be Secretary of State in place of Abel P. Upshur, deceased, agreeably to the nomination.

Attest: ASBURY DICKINS,
Secretary.

Mr. CURTIS. I now offer in evidence another document, which I also wish to be read by the Clerk after it has been inspected.

[The document was handed to the Managers.]

Mr. Manager BUTLER. We have no objection to this.

The CHIEF JUSTICE. The Secretary will read the document.

The Secretary read as follows:

UNITED STATES OF AMERICA,
Department of State:
To all to whom these presents shall come, greeting:

I certify that the document hereunto annexed is a true copy, carefully examined and compared with the original record of this Department, authorizing Winfield Scott to act as Secretary of War *ad interim,* during the vacancy occasioned by the resignation of George W. Crawford, and that this appointment was made during the session of the Senate.

I further certify that the confirmation by the Senate of Charles M. Conrad as Secretary of War to succeed General Scott is a true copy of the original filed in this Department.

In testimony whereof I, William H. Seward, Secretary of State of the United States, have hereunto subscribed my name and caused the seal of the Department of State to be affixed.

Done at the city of Washington this 6th day of [L. S.] April, A. D. 1868, and of the independence of the United States of America the ninety-second.   WILLIAM H. SEWARD.

I hereby appoint Major General Winfield Scott to act as Secretary of War *ad interim* during the vacancy occasioned by the resignation of the Hon. George W. Crawford.   MILLARD FILLMORE.
July 23, 1850.

—

[Extract.]
IN EXECUTIVE SESSION,
SENATE OF THE UNITED STATES,
August 15, 1850.
Resolved, That the Senate advise and consent to the appointment of the following named persons agreeably to their nominations respectively:

*　　*　　*　　*　　*　　*　　*

Charles M. Conrad, of the State of Louisiana, to be Secretary of War.
Attest: ASBURY DICKINS,
Secretary.

Mr. CURTIS. I now offer in evidence three papers, all of which relate to the same transaction. I have put them in an envelope, so that they may be kept together.

[The papers were handed to the Managers and examined by them.]

Mr. Manager BUTLER, (selecting one of the papers.) We object to this memorandum. We do not object to the other papers. The memorandum of Mr. Browning is not any better than anybody else's memorandum.

Mr. CURTIS. It merely states a fact which appears by a comparison of the date of the commission with the date of the *ad interim* appointment. It is immaterial.

Mr. Manager BUTLER. Very good. We have no objection to the other papers.

The CHIEF JUSTICE. The Secretary will read the documents.

Mr. CURTIS. We offer those which are not objected to.

The Secretary read the documents, as follows:

DEPARTMENT OF THE INTERIOR,
WASHINGTON, D. C., *April* 7, 1868.
I, O. H. Browning, Secretary of the Interior, do hereby certify that the annexed paper is a true copy from the records of this Department.

In testimony whereof I have hereunto subscribed [L. S.] my name and caused the seal of the Department to be affixed the day and year above written.
O. H. BROWNING,
Secretary of the Interior.

[Copy.]
EXECUTIVE MANSION,
WASHINGTON, *January* 10, 1861.
I hereby appoint Moses Kelley to be acting Secretary of the Interior until other arrangements can be made in the premises.   JAMES BUCHANAN.

Mr. Manager BUTLER. May I ask the counsel if they have any record there of what became of the Secretary of the Interior at the time this acting appointment was made, whether he had resigned or ran away, or what?

Mr. CURTIS. I am not informed. I cannot speak either from the record or from recollection. There was a commission sent up which has not yet been read.

The Secretary read as follows:

UNITED STATES OF AMERICA,
Department of State:
To all to whom these presents shall come, greeting:
I certify that the document hereunto annexed is a true copy, carefully examined and compared with the original record in this Department.

In testimony whereof I, William H. Seward, Secretary of State of the United States, have hereunto subscribed my name and caused the seal of the Department of State to be affixed.

Done at the city of Washington this 6th day of April A. D., 1868, and of the independence of [L. S.] the United States of America the ninety-second.   WM. H. SEWARD.

—

ABRAHAM LINCOLN,
President of the United States of America:
To all who shall see these presents, greeting:
Know ye, that reposing special trust and confidence in the patriotism, integrity, and abilities of Caleb B. Smith, of Indiana, I have nominated, and by and with the advice and consent of the Senate do appoint, him to be Secretary of the Interior of the United States, and do authorize and empower him to execute and fulfil the duties of that office according to law. And to have and to hold the said office with all the powers, privileges, and emoluments thereunto of right appertaining unto him, the said Caleb B. Smith, during the pleasure of the President of the United States for the time being.

In testimony whereof I have caused these letters to be made patent and the seal of the United States to be hereunto affixed.

Given under my hand, at the city of Washington, the 5th day of March, in the year of our Lord [L. S.] 1861, and of the independence of the United States of America the eighty-fifth.
ABRAHAM LINCOLN.
By the President:
WILLIAM H. SEWARD, *Secretary of State.*

Mr. CURTIS. I now offer in evidence a document which relates to the removal from office of the collector and appraiser of merchandise at the city of Philadelphia, and also a copy of the commissions issued to their successors.

[The documents were handed to the Managers and examined by them.]

Mr. Manager BUTLER. Our objection to this, Mr. President, is that this is not an act of any President or any person having authority to discharge officers. What is offered is a letter of one McClintock Young, acting Secretary of the Treasury, directed to the appraiser in Philadelphia, in which he recites a fact. That is what is offered in evidence—the act of McClintock Young, acting Secretary of the Treasury—which he writes to the collector of customs at Philadelphia, asking him to hand a letter to Richard Coe, Esq., saying that he is directed to say that he does not want his services any longer. I do not see how it bears on this issue. The fact that somebody was commissioned we do not object to; but we do object to this letter of acting Assistant Secretary McClintock Young.

Mr. CURTIS. Do you want evidence of the fact that he was acting Secretary?

Mr. Manager BUTLER. No, sir; I have that fact among these commissions of my own.

Mr. CURTIS. The documents are certified regularly by the Secretary of the Treasury as coming from the records of that Department. The documents themselves consist of two letters signed by McClintock Young, who it is admitted was the acting Secretary of the Treasury at the time when he signed these letters. We offer them in evidence to show acts of removal of these Treasury officers, the appraiser and the collector in Philadelphia, by the act of McClintock Young, acting Secretary of the Treasury, who says that he proceeds "by the direction of the President."

Mr. Manager BUTLER. The difficulty we find is not removed. It is an attempt by McClintock Young, acting Secretary of the Treasury, to remove an officer by reciting that he is directed by the President so to do. If this is evidence, we have to go on and try the question of the right of McClintock Young to do this act, to see whether an appraiser is one of the "inferior officers" that a Secretary of the Treasury may remove, or the President may remove without the advice and consent of the Senate; we have to go into a new series of investigations. It is not an act of the President; it is not an act of the head of a Department; and it is remarkable as the only case that can be found of the kind so far as we know; and if it was evidence at all, it would rather prove the rule by being the exception.

Mr. CURTIS. I understand it to be admitted that McClintock Young was the acting Secretary of the Treasury.

Mr. Manager BUTLER. Yes, sir; I have his appointment.

Mr. CURTIS. I take this act of his, therefore, as if it had been done by a Secretary of the Treasury.

Mr. Manager BUTLER. Yes, sir.

Mr. CURTIS. He says that he proceeds by the order of the President, and I take it to be well settled judicially and practically that wherever the head of a Department says he acts by the order of the President he is presumed to tell the truth, and it requires no evidence to show that he acts by the order of the President. No such evidence is ever preserved, no record is ever made of the direction which the President gives to one of the heads of Departments, as I understand, to proceed in a transaction of this kind. But when a head of a Department says "by order of the President I say so and so" all courts and all bodies presume that he tells the truth.

The CHIEF JUSTICE. The Chief Justice thinks that this evidence is admissible. The act of a Secretary of the Treasury is the act of the President unless the contrary be shown. He will put the question to the Senate, however, if any Senator desires it. [After a pause.] The evidence is admitted. Do you desire to have it read?

Mr. CURTIS. If you please, your Honor.

The Secretary read as follows:

UNITED STATES OF AMERIKA,
TREASURY DEPARTMENT, *April* 7, 1868.

Pursuant to the act of Congress of the 22d of February, 1849, I hereby certify that the annexed are true and correct copies from the records of this Department of the commissions issued to Richard Coe and Charles Francis Breuil, as appraisers of merchandise for the port of Philadelphia, in the State of Pennsylvania.

In witness whereof I have hereunto set my hand and caused the seal of the Treasury Department to be affixed on the day and year first above written. H. McCULLOCH,
[L. S.]
Secretary of the Treasury.

Mr. CURTIS. It is only necessary to give the dates of those commissions; you need not read them at large.

The SECRETARY. The commission of Richard Coe is dated the 25th day of June, 1841; the commission of Charles Francis Breuil is dated the 30th day of August, 1842.

Mr. CURTIS. Now read the letters.

The Secretary read as follows:

TREASURY DEPARTMENT, *August* 17, 1842.

SIR: I am directed by the President to inform you that your services as appraiser of merchandise for the port of Philadelphia are no longer required.

I am, very respectfully, &c.,
McCLINTOCK YOUNG,
Acting Secretary of the Treasury.
RICHARD COE,
Appraiser of Merchandise, Philadelphia.

TREASURY DEPARTMENT, *August* 17, 1842.

SIR: I have to request that you will deliver the inclosed letter to Richard Coe, Esq., appraiser at Philadelphia.

I am, &c.,
McCLINTOCK YOUNG,
Acting Secretary of the Treasury.
Collector of the Customs, Philadelphia.

Mr. CURTIS. I now offer in evidence documents from the Navy Department.

[The documents were handed to the Managers for examination.]

Mr. STEWART, (at two o'clock and fifteen minutes p. m.) I move that the Senate take a recess for fifteen minutes.

Mr. SUMNER. I move an amendment to that, that business be resumed forthwith after the expiration of fifteen minutes.

The CHIEF JUSTICE. The Chief Justice, before putting the question on that amendment, begs leave to remind Senators how extremely difficult it is to resume the business of the Senate unless the Senators are present. The Chief Justice will put the question on the amendment.

The amendment was rejected.

The CHIEF JUSTICE. The question now is on the motion of the Senator from Nevada.

The motion was agreed to.

The CHIEF JUSTICE resumed the chair at the expiration of fifteen minutes, but there not being many Senators present business was not resumed till two o'clock and forty-five minutes p. m., when the Chief Justice said:

Senators will please give their attention. Counsel for the President will proceed with the defense.

Mr. Manager BUTLER. At the adjournment

I was about objecting to the papers offered from the Navy Department. The ground of my objection is this: the certificate appended does not certify them to be copies of records from the Navy Department, but simply certifies "that the annexed is a true statement from the records of this Department" signed by "Edgar T. Welles, chief clerk," and then there is an attestation that he is chief clerk. Then the heading of the paper is "memoranda," so that the paper is not an official copy of the record, but is a statement made up by the chief clerk of the Navy Department of certain matters which he has either been asked or volunteered to do; and the difficulty about it is that it is informal, and they leave out here many of the things which are necessary to ascertain what bearing this has on the case. For instance, Thomas Eastin, Navy agent at Pensacola, it is stated, was, on the 19th of December, 1840, dismissed by direction of the President for failing to render his accounts and Purser So-and-So was ordered to take his place. It does not appear what then was done, whether the Senate was in session and whether the President sent at the same moment an appointment to the Senate. All that appears is that on the 29th of April, 1841, the President appointed Jackson Morton, Navy agent at Pensacola. He might have sent in Jackson Morton's name at the very moment that he dismissed this man. *Non constat;* it does not appear at all.

I only put this as an illustration. These are not copies of records, but they are certified to be a statement made up from the records by somebody not under oath, and who has no right to make statements, and they are wholly illusory. Occasionally there are memoranda in pencil upon these papers made by other persons.

Mr. CURTIS. We can apply India-rubber there, and that would remove that objection.

Mr. Manager BUTLER. Yes, sir. The difficulty is not so much what is stated here as what is left out. Everything is left out that is of value to the understanding of this case. Here are memoranda made up from the records that A B was removed, but the circumstances under which he was removed, who was nominated in his place, and when that person was nominated do not appear. It only appears that somebody was appointed at Pensacola.

Mr. JOHNSON. Are the dates given, Mr. Manager?

Mr. Manager BUTLER. The dates are given in this way: it is stated that on the 19th of December, 1840, a person is removed, and then on the 5th of January one Johnston was informed that he had been appointed. He must have been nominated and gone through the Senate and been confirmed in the meantime. *Non constat* but that he was nominated at this very moment; and if he was nominated at the very moment the other man was removed, the value of it is gone as a precedent.

Then Johnston was lost on the voyage, and on the 29th of April, 1841, another man was appointed; but the whole value, I say, is gone because they have not given us the record; they have only given us memoranda, and it is so stated, "memoranda of records." Who has any commission to make memoranda from the records for evidence before the Senate? And then in the certificate the word "copies" is stricken out, and the words are written in: "A true statement of the records"—a statement such as Mr. Edgar T. Welles chooses to make, or such as anybody else chooses to make. I never heard before that anybody had a right to come and certify memoranda of records, and put it in as evidence. That is one paper.

Then the next paper, although it purports to contain true copies of records from the office, consists of nothing but letters about the appointment and removal of officers, Navy agents again; but being so removed and appointed only a portion of the correspondence is given us. When the nominations were sent in is not given us. I do not mean to say that my friends on the other side chose to leave anything out; but whoever prepared this for them has chosen to leave out the material facts whether the Senate was in session, or whether other names were sent in. Now, the question is if you are going to take excerpts from the records.

I want to call the attention of the Senate still further to the fact that all the officers who are covered by these papers they have offered are appointed under the act of May 15, 1820, for four years. That act provided that:

"All district attorneys, collectors of the customs, naval officers and surveyors of the customs, Navy agents, receivers of public moneys for lands, registers of the land offices, paymasters in the Army, the apothecary general, the assistant apothecaries general, and the commissary general of purchases, to be appointed under the laws of the United States, shall be appointed for the term of four years, but shall be removable from office at pleasure."

So that their very tenure of office settles it that they are removable "at pleasure," so enacted by the law which creates them; and now the gentlemen are going to show that under that, in some particular instances, officers were removed at pleasure, but not to show how they were removed, the manner of their removal, and then to attempt to show that by memoranda made by Edgar T. Welles, certified by Gideon Welles to be chief clerk. Is that evidence?

Mr. CURTIS. I understand the substance of the objections made to these documents to be two. The first is that these are only memoranda from the records and not copies, not full and formal copies from the records. It is said that it is not proper to adduce in evidence such statements of the results shown by the records; that instead of giving a table containing the name of the officer, the office which he held, the day when removed, and the person by whose order he was removed there should be an extended copy of the entire act and all the papers relating to it. Well, in the first place, I wish the Senate to call to mind that the only document of this character relating to removals from office which has been put in by the honorable Managers is a document from the Department of State, which contains exactly this memorandum of facts:

" *Schedule B.*

"List of appointments of heads of Departments made by the President at any time during the session of the Senate:

"Timothy Pickering, Postmaster General, June 1, 1794.

"Samuel L. Southard, Acting Secretary of the Treasury, January 26, 1829."

And so on. That is, it is a list extracted out of the records in the Department of the Secretary of State containing the names of the officers, the offices they held, the date when they were removed, and the authority by which they were removed.

Mr. JOHNSON. How is it certified?

Mr. CURTIS. It is simply certified by the Secretary of State himself.

Mr. Manager BUTLER. In what language?

Mr. CURTIS. This is a copy which I hold in my hand, and I am not prepared to say how it is certified; but it is in evidence, and can be seen. I think it will be found to be simply a letter from the Secretary of State saying that there were found on the records of his Department these facts, not any formal certificate of extracts from the records. If, however, the Senate should think that it is absolutely necessary, or, under the circumstances of this case, proper to require these certified copies of the entire acts, instead of taking the names, dates, and other particulars from the records in the form which we have thought most convenient, and which certainly takes up less time and space than the other would, we must apply for and obtain them. If there is a technical difficulty of that sort it is one which we must remove.

Mr. JOHNSON. Will the counsel state what the act of Congress is which makes these certificates evidence?

Mr. CURTIS. There are several acts of Congress; but in regard to the Navy Department, if I recollect aright, it is in effect that copies of the records and extracts from the records may be certified. I think that is the law.

The substantial objection which the learned Manager undertook to state was that this paper which we now offer would be illusory, and the reason is, because, although it shows the name of the officer, the office he held, the fact of his removal, and the date of the removal, it does not show whether the Senate was then in session, and it does not show what the President did in connection with or in consequence of that removal in the form of a nomination to the Senate. How can the records of the Department of the Navy show those facts? They appear here on your records, and we propose when we have closed the offer of this species of proof to ask the Senate to direct its proper officer to make a certificate from its records of the beginning and end of each session of the Senate from the origin of the Government down to the present time. That is what we shall call for at the proper time, and that will supply that part of the difficulty which the gentleman suggests. The other part of the difficulty which he suggests is, that it does not appear that the President did not fill up these removals by immediate nominations when they were made during the session of the Senate. It does not appear either way. If he desires to argue that the President did fill them up by immediate nominations, he will find the nominations and put them in undoubtedly. The records of the Navy Department, from which this statement comes, can furnish no information on that subject, and therefore it is not defective in that particular.

Mr. Manager BUTLER. The counsel for the President, I think, judge well, that when they can find that we have taken any particular course that must be the right course and the one they ought to follow. We certainly accept that as being the very best exposition of the law so far as we are concerned. But the difficulty is this: we offer testimony sometimes that is not objected to; and I asked my learned friends, I think, in the case referred to, whether they objected to that evidence, and they made no objection. If they had, I might have been more formal; but that does not meet the difficulty quite. The difficulty I find is that they go to the wrong sources of evidence. Evidence of the removal and appointment of officers and the affixing of the seal to commissions is to be sought for only in the State Department. No officer who is removed or appointed by and with the advice and consent of the Senate, who holds his commission under that tenure, can be appointed or can be removed without all the circumstances appearing in the State Department; and there is the place they should go for this evidence. If they would go to the State Department, they would get it all; they would find out when he was appointed, when he was removed, when his successor was appointed, when he was nominated, and everything precisely as they have in the case of Mr. Pickering.

Mr. CURTIS. Does the honorable Manager understand that under the laws of the United States all these officers must be commissioned by the Secretary of State, and that the facts appear in his Department, including the officers under the Interior, the Treasury, the War, and the Navy Departments?

Mr. Manager BUTLER. With the single exception of the Treasury, I do.

Mr. CURTIS. I do not.

Mr. Manager BUTLER. I do so understand it, and it will so appear, I think. But at any rate when the gentleman takes these commissions he will find that the commissions all emanate with the seal of the United States and the signature of the Secretary of State upon them. The testimony that he offers is not the commissions of these officers; and to show that that is the fact I only appeal to his own papers here. Instead of sending us the commissions of these officers, what is the evidence of the appointment?

NAVY DEPARTMENT, *March* 24, 1838.

SIR: The President of the United States, by and with the advice and consent of the Senate, having appointed you Navy agent for four years from the 22d of March, 1838, I have the pleasure to inclose herewith your commission, dated the 24th of March, 1838.

I am, respectfully, yours, M. DICKERSON. LEONARD JARVIS, esq., *Navy Agent, Boston.*

The evidence that they give us of the appointment is a letter of the Secretary, reciting the fact of the commission. If they had gone to the State Department they would have found the record of the commission. Why I complain of it, and that is all the reason I complain of it, is that again it is illusory. If it was a mere matter of form I would not care about it. If my friend will tell me that they will put in the exact dates when these parties were nominated I shall have no objection; but they place either upon the Senate or upon me the burden of going to the records and looking up these dates and looking up the evidence to control their evidence. That is to say, the Senate allow them to put in memoranda of part of a transaction, and put upon the Managers of the House of Representatives the burden of going and looking up the rest of it. I say it is not right to do so; that where they put in the transaction they ought to put in the whole record of the transaction, and then we can all see exactly what the transaction was.

Mr. President, I have so much respect for my learned friends that whenever they state a matter of law as they stated it to the learned Senator from Maryland, that extracts from records might be certified, I am almost afraid to object; but I beg leave to read from Brightly's Digest, the seventeenth section, on page 267, although it is a very bad practice to read from digests:

" All books, papers, documents, and records in the War, Navy, Treasury, and Post Office Departments, and the Attorney General's office, may be copied and certified under seal in the same manner as those in the State Department may now by law be, and with the same force and effect, and the said Attorney General shall cause a seal to be made and provided for his office, with such device as the President of the United States shall approve."

Mr. JOHNSON. What is the date of that act?

Mr. Manager BUTLER. That act is dated February 22, 1849.

Mr. JOHNSON. Thank you, sir.

Mr. Manager BUTLER. And that act refers to the act of September 15, 1789, which provides:

" That all copies of records and papers in the office of the Department of State, authenticated under the seal of the said Department, shall be evidence equally as the original record or paper."

I have not seen any statute which gives any right to certify extracts of records. If these were extracts of entire records they would do; but these are memoranda: that is, the gloss, the interpretation, the collation, the *diegesis* of the clerk of that Department of the records.

The CHIEF JUSTICE. The Chief Justice will submit the question to the Senate.

The Chief Justice put the question, and declared that the noes appeared to have it.

Mr. SHERMAN. I call for the yeas and nays. I think proof of this kind ought not to be kept out on a technical ground.

Mr. HENDRICKS. I wish to inquire whether the objection on the part of the Managers requires that the entire documents relating to the subject in the Departments shall be produced; whether the objection goes upon that proposition?

The CHIEF JUSTICE. The rule requires that a question asked by a Senator shall be reduced to writing.

Mr. HENDRICKS. The question I asked was for information of the Managers themselves, whether the objection goes upon the ground that the documents are not certified in full?

The CHIEF JUSTICE. If there be no objection, the Senator from Indiana can put his question. Otherwise, the rule requires that it shall be in writing.

Mr. Manager BUTLER. I did not understand the question.

The CHIEF JUSTICE. The Senator from Indiana will repeat his question.

Mr. HENDRICKS. The question which I wished answered by the Managers was whether it be required, in the progress of this trial, that the records shall be given in full so far as they relate to any particular question?

Mr. Manager BUTLER. That is what we desire, or, otherwise, it sets us to looking up the same record.

Mr. CONKLING. I wish to put a question to the counsel for the respondent, which I am reducing to writing, and will have prepared in a single moment.

The CHIEF JUSTICE. The counsel will please reduce their proposition to writing.

Mr. CONKLING. I beg the counsel for the respondent to answer the question which I send to the Chair.

The CHIEF JUSTICE. The Secretary will read the question proposed by the Senator from New York.

The Secretary read as follows:

Do the counsel for the respondent rely upon any statute other than that referred to?

Mr. CURTIS. I am not aware that there is any other statute bearing on it. By extracts from the records—of course I do not mean that any officer was authorized to state what he believed the substance of a record to be—I meant that he might extract out of the record a particular document.

Mr. CONKLING. Provided it was a copy so far as it went.

Mr. CURTIS. Provided it was a copy so far as it went.

In that same connection, perhaps, I ought to state, Mr. Chief Justice and Senators, that we do not offer these documents as copies of the records relating to the cases which are named in the documents themselves. They are documents, as I stated at the beginning, of a similar character to that which the Managers put in, containing the substance of each case, the name, the date, the office, the fact of removal. It is true as the honorable Manager has said that, when he offered that he asked us if we objected. We said no; for we knew it would take, perhaps, weeks to make out all those records in full.

Mr. EDMUNDS. With permission, I should like to make an oral inquiry, to save time, of counsel.

The CHIEF JUSTICE. If there be no objection the Senator from Vermont will put his inquiry without reducing it to writing.

Mr. EDMUNDS. I desire to know whether this is offered as touching any question or final conclusion of fact, or whether it is offered merely as giving us a history of practice under the statutes with a view to the law?

Mr. CURTIS. Entirely for the last purpose.

Mr. Manager BUTLER. After the statement of counsel, that this does not go to any issue of fact, but only of practice under the law, we have no objection to it.

The CHIEF JUSTICE. The objection on the part of the Managers is withdrawn. If there be no objection on the part of the Senate the evidence will be admitted.

Mr. CURTIS. I wish there should be no misapprehension. This document goes to matters of fact; but those matters of fact are matters of practice under the law, which I supposed was what the Senator meant.

Mr. EDMUNDS. That is what I understood.

Mr. Manager BUTLER. Then, if it is proof of matter of fact, we object that it is not proper evidence.

Mr. CURTIS. Very well.

The CHIEF JUSTICE. Gentlemen of counsel for the President, have you reduced your proposition to writing?

Mr. CURTIS. Yes, sir.

The CHIEF JUSTICE. The Secretary will read the proposition.

Mr. HOWARD. I desire to ask a question of the learned counsel for the accused.

The CHIEF JUSTICE. The Secretary will read the question proposed by the Senator from Michigan.

Mr. EVARTS. Before that question is read, perhaps it may be of service that I should ask attention to what I have turned to in the record, and that is the letter of the Secretary of State which, at page 351 of the record, introduced

the schedule that was put in evidence by the Managers.

Mr. JOHNSON. What is the schedule?

Mr. EVARTS. Of heads of Departments.

Mr. Manager BUTLER said:

"It is accompanied with a letter simply describing the list, which I will read, as mere inducement.

"Mr. CURTIS. We have no objection.

"Mr. Manager BUTLER. I will read it:

"DEPARTMENT OF STATE,
"WASHINGTON, March 26, 1868.

"SIR: In reply to the note which you addressed to me on the 23d instant, in behalf of the House of Representatives in the matter of the impeachment of the President, I have the honor to submit herewith two schedules, A and B.

"Schedule A presents a statement of all removals of the heads of Departments made by the President of the United States during the session of the Senate so far as the same can be ascertained from the records of this Department.

"Schedule B contains a statement of all appointments of heads of Departments at any time made by the President without the advice and consent of the Senate, and while the Senate was in session, so far as the same appears upon the records of the Department of State.

"I have the honor to be, very respectfully, your obedient servant, WILLIAM H. SEWARD.

"Hon. JOHN A. BINGHAM, Chairman."

Then follows the list, the production of the documents of which would have occupied a considerable length of time.

The CHIEF JUSTICE. The Secretary will read the question proposed by the Senator from Michigan.

The Secretary read as follows:

Do the counsel regard these memoranda as legal evidence of the practice of the Government, and are they offered as such?

Mr. CURTIS. The documents I offer are not full copies of any record. They are, therefore, not strictly and technically legal evidence for any purpose. They are extracts of facts from those records. Allow me, by way of illustration, to read one, so that the Senate may see the nature of the document:

"Navy Agency at New York.

"1864, June 20. Isaac Henderson was, by direction of the President, removed from the office of Navy agent at New York, and instructed to transfer to Paymaster John D. Gibson, of United States Navy, all the public funds and other property in his charge."

We do not offer that as technically legal evidence of the fact that is there stated; but having in view simply to prove, not the case of Mr. Henderson, with its merits and the causes of his removal, &c., all of which would appear on the records, but the practice of the Government under the laws of the United States; instead of taking from the records the entire documents necessary to exhibit his whole case, we have taken the only fact which is of any importance in reference to this inquiry. If the Senate consider that they must adhere to the technical rule of evidence, we must go to the records and have the records copied in full, and of course, for the same reason, read in full.

Mr. Manager BOUTWELL. The honorable counsel for the respondent must see that if they do not prove a case they do not prove any practice. The first thing to be done in order to prove a practice is to prove one or more cases going to show what the practice is. But the vital objection to this testimony which is now offered is, if my examination of it is thorough and accurate, that it relates to a class of officers who are and were, at the time the transactions spoken of in this memoranda occurred, under a special provision of law by which they were created, which takes them entirely out of the line of precedents for the purpose of this trial. That is the vital objection to the introduction of this testimony. As I have read the papers hastily, they all relate to Navy agents and officers who were created by a statute of the year 1820, and in that statute a tenure of office was established for the officers so created—four years, removable at pleasure ; and it is not necessary for me to go into any statement here of the reasons which likely controlled the Congress of the United States in 1820, which led them to make that provision. But having made that provision, created these officers, removable at pleasure, a practice shown by facts, few or many, does not tend in any degree to enlighten this tribunal upon the issues on which they are now called to pass, because these officers were created by a special statute, had a special tenure, and by that tenure were made removable at the pleasure of the President ; and in various cases undoubtedly the President of the United States, acting in conformity to that statute, has removed those officers. Unless the counsel for the respondent are prepared to say that in this file of papers which they now submit there is evidence to show that a practice has prevailed relating to officers not enumerated in the statute of 1820, then I say it is but a waste of the time of this tribunal, knowing what those papers contain, and knowing what the statute is, to permit the introduction of any testimony showing a practice which, if prevailing and admitted, does not enlighten us at all upon the matters in issue here.

Mr. CURTIS. This objection, Mr. Chief Justice and Senators, has reference to the merits of this case and to the weight and effect which the evidence is to have, if it be admitted. We may have been under an entire misapprehension as to the views of the honorable Managers who are conducting this prosecution respecting those merits ; but unless we have been under such a misapprehension we have supposed they meant to attempt to maintain that even if Mr. Stanton at the time when he was removed held at the pleasure of the President, even if he was not within the tenure-of-office act, still, inasmuch as the Senate was in session, it was not competent for the President to remove him ; and, secondly, that although Mr. Stanton might have been removed by the President, not being within the tenure-of-office act, his place could not be even temporarily supplied by an order to General Thomas, because the Senate was in session, and there could be, therefore, no *ad interim* appointment made. It is with

a view to meet that that we introduce this practice of the Government. It is with a view to show that when the President had the right to remove, it mattered not whether the Senate was in session or not, that right might be exercised, and that if that right should be exercised, it mattered not whether the Senate was in session or not, he might make an *ad interim* appointment. If the learned Managers will concede all those grounds to us, if they will agree that the sole question here is whether Mr. Stanton's tenure of office was fixed by that act, and if it was not fixed by that act, that the President might remove him during the session of the Senate, and might lawfully make an *ad interim* appointment during the session of the Senate, then we do not desire to put in this evidence.

Mr. SHERMAN. I should like to ask the honorable Managers a simple question.

The CHIEF JUSTICE. If no objection be interposed, the Senator from Ohio will put his question without reducing it to writing.

Mr. SHERMAN. It is whether the papers now offered in evidence contain the date of appointment and the character of the office?

Mr. EVARTS. That is a question which you put to us.

Mr. JOHNSON, (to Mr. SHERMAN.) You said "Managers."

Mr. SHERMAN. I beg pardon.

Mr. Manager BUTLER. And to that we say that they only contain the date of the removal, but do not give us the date of the nomination, which may have been weeks and months before the date of appointment, as nobody knows better than the Senate. That is the trouble about it.

Mr. CURTIS. These documents are the records of the Navy Department. Allow me to read once more, to give you an illustration of what they contain :

"*Navy Agency at New York.*

"1864, *June* 20. Isaac Henderson was, by direction of the President, removed from the office of Navy agent at New York, and instructed to transfer to Paymaster John D. Gibson, United States Navy, all the public funds and other property in his charge."

That is the character of the document.

Mr. JOHNSON. Does it give the date?

Mr. CURTIS. It gives the date of the removal.

The CHIEF JUSTICE. The counsel for the President propose to offer in evidence two documents from the Navy Department, exhibiting the practice which has existed in that Department in respect to removals from office. To the introduction of this evidence the honorable Managers object. The Chief Justice thinks that the evidence is competent in substance, but that the question of form is entirely subject to the discretion of the Senate, and of the Senate alone. The whole question, therefore, is submitted to the Senate. Senators, you who are of opinion that this evidence should be received will, as your names are called, answer yea; those of the contrary opinion, nay.

The question being then taken by yeas and nays, resulted—yeas 36, nays 15; as follows:

YEAS—Messrs. Anthony, Bayard, Buckalew, Cole, Conkling, Corbett, Davis, Dixon, Doolittle, Edmunds, Ferry, Fessenden, Fowler, Frelinghuysen, Grimes, Henderson, Hendricks, Howe, Johnson, McCreery, Morrill of Maine, Morrill of Vermont, Morton, Patterson of New Hampshire, Patterson of Tennessee, Ross, Saulsbury, Sherman, Stewart, Sumner, Trumbull, Van Winkle, Vickers, Willey, Wilson, and Yates—36.

NAYS—Messrs. Cameron, Cattell, Chandler, Conness, Cragin, Drake, Harlan, Howard, Morgan, Nye, Pomeroy, Ramsey, Thayer, Tipton, and Williams—15.

NOT VOTING—Messrs. Norton, Sprague, and Wade—3.

So the evidence was admitted.

Mr. CURTIS. Unless the honorable Managers desire those documents to be read at length we do not insist upon it on our part.

Mr. Manager BUTLER. We do not desire it.

Mr. CURTIS. Very well; but I suppose they will be printed. ["Certainly."]

The documents thus offered in evidence are as follows:

UNITED STATES NAVY DEPARTMENT,
April 9, 1868.

I hereby certify that the annexed are true statements from the records of this Department.
EDGAR T. WELLES,
Chief Clerk.

Be it known that Edgar T. Welles, whose name is signed to the above certificate, is now and was at the time of so signing, chief clerk in the Navy Department, and that full faith and credit are due to all his official attestations as such.

In testimony whereof, I have hereunto subscribed my name and caused the seal of the Navy Department of the United States to be affixed at the city of Washington, this 9th day of [L. S.] April, in the year of our Lord 1868, and of the independence of the United States the ninety-second.
G. WELLES,
Secretary of the Navy.

Navy Agency at Pensacola.

Thomas Eastin, Navy agent at Pensacola, was on 19th December, 1840, dismissed by direction of the President.

On the same day Purser Dudley Walker, United States Navy, was instructed until otherwise directed to act as Navy agent in addition to his duties as purser of the yard and station.

January 5, 1841. George Johnston was informed that he had been appointed, by and with the advice and consent of the Senate, Navy agent at Pensacola from December 28, 1840.

Johnston, it appears, was lost on the passage to Pensacola.

April 29, 1841. The President appointed Jackson Morton Navy agent at Pensacola.

Navy Agency at Boston.

February 1, 1838. Purser John N. Todd, United States Navy, was directed to assume the duties of Navy agent for the port of Boston and continue in the performance thereof until further orders from the Department.

February 1, 1838. D. D. Brodhead, Navy agent, Boston, was informed that his requisition for $10,000 had been received and the amount remitted to John N. Todd, purser of the Boston station, who had been directed to discharge the duties of Navy agent until further orders.

The Department alluded to reported embarrassments of his private affairs, and as the legal term of his appointment would shortly expire, stated that it felt compelled, under the circumstances of the case, to suggest to him the propriety of tendering at this time his resignation as Navy agent.

March 3, 1838. Daniel D. Brodhead, late Navy agent at Boston, was requested to pay over to John

N. Todd, acting Navy agent at Boston, the amount of public funds remaining in his hands as Navy agent.

Daniel D. Brodhead, having, in a letter dated Boston, February 28, 1838, tendered his resignation as Navy agent, it was acknowledged and accepted by the Department, March 5, 1838.

March 24, 1838. Leonard Jarvis was informed of his having been appointed by the President, by and with the advice and consent of the Senate, Navy agent for the port of Boston from March 22, 1838, and John N. Todd was instructed to pay over to him the amount of public funds in his hands as acting Navy agent.

Navy Agency at New York.

June 20, 1864. Isaac Henderson was, by direction of the President, removed from the office of Navy agent at New York, and instructed to transfer to paymaster John D. Gibson, United States Navy, all the public funds and other property in his charge.

Navy Agency at Philadelphia.

December 26, 1864. James S. Chambers was removed from the office of Navy agent at Philadelphia, and instructed to transfer to paymaster A. E. Watson, United States Navy, all the public funds and other property in his charge.

UNITED STATES NAVY DEPARTMENT,
April 9, 1868.

I hereby certify that the annexed are true copies from the records of the Department.
EDGAR T. WELLES,
Chief Clerk.

Be it known that Edgar T. Welles, whose name is signed to the above certificate, is now, and was at the time of so signing, chief clerk in the Navy Department, and that full faith and credit are due to all his official attestations as such.

In testimony whereof, I have hereunto subscribed my name, and caused the seal of the Navy Department of the United States to be affixed [L. S.] at the city of Washington, this 9th day of April, in the year of Lord 1868, and of the independence of the United States, the ninety-second.
G. WELLES,
Secretary of the Navy.

NAVY DEPARTMENT, *December* 19, 1840.

SIR: The painful duty devolves upon me of informing you that having failed to render and settle your accounts as reqired by law and the frequent calls of the Department, the President has directed that you be dismissed the service of the United States.

You will, therefore, upon the receipt of this communication, consider your functions as Navy agent at Pensacola to have ceased.

Until the arrival of your successor, Purser Dudley Walker has been directed to act as Navy agent, to whom you will turn over the funds, books, and papers belonging to the agency at Pensacola.

I am, respectfully, &c., J. K. PAULDING.
THOMAS EASTIN, esq., *late Navy Agent, Pensacola.*

NAVY DEPARTMENT, *December,* 19, 1840.

SIR: I have directed $9,881 to be remitted to you, being the amount of your requisition of the 1st November.

You will, until otherwise directed, act as Navy agent at Pensacola, in addition to your duties as purser of the yard and station.

A further remittance of $5,000 will be made to you for the use of the United States steamer Warren.

I am, respectfully, &c., J. K. PAULDING.
Purser, DUDLEY WALKER,
Care Commodore A. J. Dallas, Navy-yard, Pensacola.

NAVY DEPARTMENT, *January* 5, 1841.

SIR: The President of the United States, by and with the advice and consent of the Senate, having appointed you Navy agent for the port of Pensacola, West Florida, for four years, from the 28th December, 1840, I have the pleasure to inclose herewith your commission, dated the 5th of January, 1841.

I am, respectfully, &c., J. K. PAULDING.
GEORGE JOHNSTON, esq., *Navy Agent, Washington.*

NAVY DEPARTMENT, *April* 29, 1841.

SIR: The President of the United States having appointed you Navy agent for the port of Pensacola, West Florida, I have the pleasure to inclose herewith your commission.

I inclose to you also a blank bond, which you will execute with at least two sureties, in the sum of $30,000, to be approved by the United States judge or district attorney for the district in which you reside, and return to this Department as soon as practicable.

I am, respectfully, &c., GEORGE E. BADGER.
JACKSON MORTON, esq., *Navy Agent, Pensacola.*

NAVY DEPARTMENT, *July* 16, 1841.

SIR: The President of the United States, by and with the advice and consent of the Senate, having appointed you Navy agent for the port of Pensacola, Florida, from the 29th of April, 1841, I have the pleasure to inclose herewith your commission.

I am, respectfully, &c., GEORGE E. BADGER.
JACKSON MORTON, esq., *Navy Agent, Pensacola.*

NAVY DEPARTMENT, *October* 2, 1841.

SIR: Jackson Morton, Esq., Navy agent for Pensacola, has apprised the Department of his intention to proceed immediately to that place to enter on the discharge of his duties.

Upon his arrival you will transfer to him all the moneys and property belonging to the agency, and take his receipt for the same, which will be a sufficient voucher in the settlement of your accounts in the office of the Fourth Auditor.

I am, respectfully, &c., J. D. SIMMS,
Acting Secretary of the Navy.
Purser D. WALKER, *Acting Navy Agent, Pensacola.*

NAVY DEPARTMENT, *February* 1, 1838.

SIR: Your requisition for $10,000 has been received, and the amount remitted to John N. Todd, purser of the Boston station, who has been directed to discharge the duties of Navy agent until further orders.

The Department regrets that the reported embarrassment of your private affairs, and the condition of the banks in Boston, particularly that in which you have kept your public accounts, renders this course necessary.

As the legal term of your appointment will shortly expire, the Department feels compelled, under the circumstances of the case, to suggest to you the propriety of tendering at this time your resignation as Navy agent.

I am, very respectfully, your obedient servant,
M. DICKERSON.
D. D. BRODHEAD, esq., *Navy Agent, Boston.*

NAVY DEPARTMENT, *February* 1, 1838.

SIR: I have this day authorized to be remitted to you $10,000 under pay and Sub.—

This remittance is made to you with a view to your assumption of the duties of Navy agent for the port of Boston, in addition to your present duty, which you will do on receipt of this, and continue in the performance thereof until further orders from the Department.

I am, respectfully, your obedient servant,
M. DICKERSON.
JOHN N. TODD,
Purser, United States Navy-yard, Boston.

BOSTON, *February* 28, 1838.

SIR: Some time since I received a letter from you stating that Purser Todd was charged with the duties of Navy agent in my place, and giving the reasons of the Department therefor. Without concurring in the opinions of the Department, but solely to relieve it and the Government from any supposed responsibility or embarrassment in relation to my position, I have the honor to tender you my resignation as Navy agent for this port, believing that you as well as all others having official business with me can bear testimony that I have faithfully and satisfactorily performed all my duties as a public officer.

I have the honor to be, with great respect, your obedient servant, DANIEL D. BRODHEAD.
Hon. M. DICKERSON,
Secretary of the Navy, Washington, D. C.

NAVY DEPARTMENT, *March* 3, 1838.

SIR: I request that you will pay over to John N. Todd, acting Navy agent at Boston, the amount of public funds remaining in your hands as Navy agent, for which his receipt will be to you a sufficient voucher.

When I last saw you you assured me that I should hear from you in twenty-four hours.

I regret very much being left in the condition I am as to the Navy agent at Boston.

I am, very respectfully, your obedient servant,
M. DICKERSON.
DANIEL D. BRODHEAD, *late Navy Agent, Boston.*

NAVY DEPARTMENT, *March* 5, 1838.

SIR: Your letter of the 28th ultimo, resigning your office of Navy agent for the port of Boston, has been received, and your resignation is accepted.

I am, very respectfully, your obedient servant,
M. DICKERSON.
D. D. BRODHEAD, esq., *late Navy Agent, Boston.*

NAVY DEPARTMENT, *March* 24, 1838.

SIR: Leonard Jarvis, Esq., of Boston, has been appointed Navy agent for that port in place of D. D. Brodhead, resigned. You will therefore pay over to Mr. Jarvis the amount of public money in your hands as acting Navy agent, and his receipt will be to you a proper voucher in the settlement of your accounts.

So much of your requisition of the 13th instant as has been approved will be remitted to the new agent with as little delay as practicable.

I am, very respectfully, your obedient servant,
M. DICKERSON.
JOHN N. TODD, esq., *Acting Navy Agent, Boston.*

NAVY DEPARTMENT, *March* 24, 1838.

SIR: You having been appointed Navy agent for the port of Boston, I have this day authorized to be remitted to you $53,614 51, under various heads of appropriations, being the amount of the requisitions of the acting Navy agent of the 13th instant, so far as the same were approved.

The acting Navy agent, Purser John N. Todd, I as been instructed to pay over to you the public money in his hands as agent.

Instructions with regard to your duties as Navy agent will be transmitted to you by the Fourth Auditor of the Treasury.

I am, very respectfully, your obedient servant,
M. DICKERSON.
LEONARD JARVIS, esq., *Navy Agent, Boston.*

NAVY DEPARTMENT, *March* 24, 1838.

SIR: The President of the United States, by and with the advice and consent of the Senate, having appointed you Navy agent for four years from the 22d of March, 1838, I have the pleasure to inclose herewith your commission, dated the 24th of March, 1838.

I am, respectfully, yours, M. DICKERSON.
LEONARD JARVIS, Esq., *Navy Agent, Boston.*

NAVY DEPARTMENT, *June* 20, 1864.

SIR: By direction of the President of the United States, you are hereby removed from the office of Navy agent at New York, and you will immediately transfer to Paymaster John D. Gibson, paymaster United States Navy, all the public funds and other property in your charge.

Very respectfully, GIDEON WELLES,
Secretary of the Navy.
ISAAC HENDERSON, Esq., *Navy Agent, New York.*

NAVY DEPARTMENT, *June* 20, 1864.

SIR: You are hereby relieved from the inspection of provisions and clothing at the Brooklyn navy-yard, and will at once assume the duties usually appertaining to the office of Navy agent at the city of New York.

Mr. Henderson has been instructed to turn over to you the public funds and other property in his possession, for which you will receipt to him. You will not permit him to remove from the office any of the books, papers, or vouchers, until the further order of the Department, but you will allow him to place in the office an agent (should he desire to do so) to protect his interests and see that the books and papers necessary to the settlement of his accounts are not used in a manner to destroy their value as vouchers. You will be careful to do nothing to affect in any way the liability of Mr. Henderson or his sureties to the Government.

The chief of the Bureau of Provisions and Clothing will explain to you in person the views of the Department.

Very respectfully, GIDEON WELLES,
Secretary of the Navy.

Paymaster JOHN D. GIBSON,
United States Navy, Brooklyn, New York.

—

NAVY DEPARTMENT, December 26, 1864.

SIR: By direction of the President of the United States you are hereby removed from the office of the Navy agent at Philadelphia, and you will immediately transfer to Paymaster A. E. Watson, United States Navy, all the public funds and other property in your charge.

Very respectfully, GIDEON WELLES,
Secretary of the Navy.

JAMES S. CHAMBERS, Esq., Navy Agent, Philadelphia.

—

NAVY DEPARTMENT, December 26, 1864.

SIR: Mr. James S. Chambers, Navy agent, Philadelphia, has been instructed to turn over to you the public funds and other Government property in his possession, for which you will receipt to him, and you will at once assume the duties usually appertaining to the office of Navy agent. You will not permit Mr. Chambers to remove from the office any of the books, papers, or vouchers until the further order of the Department, but you will allow him to place in the office an agent (should he desire to do so) to protect his interests and see that the books and papers necessary to the settlement of his accounts are not used in a manner to destroy their value as vouchers. You will be careful to do nothing to affect in any way the liability of Mr. Chambers or his sureties to the Government.

Should Mr. Chambers reserve a portion of the funds in his possession to meet outstanding checks, the Assistant Treasurer has been requested not to honor them unless indorsed by you as correct. You will see that they have been given for actual Government dues.

Your office will be kept open at least during the ordinary banking hours in Philadelphia.

Very respectfully, GIDEON WELLES,
Secretary of the Navy.

Paymaster A. E. WATSON,
United States Navy, Philadelphia.

Mr. CURTIS. There is one other document from the Navy Department which I suppose is not distinguishable from those that have just been admitted. It purports to be a list of all civil officers of that Department appointed for four years under the statute of May 15, 1820, and removable from office at pleasure, who were removed as indicated, their terms of office not having expired. Then comes a list giving the name of the officer, the date of his original appointment, the date of his removal, and by whom removed, in a tabular form.

Mr. JOHNSON. Does it give the date of the appointment of his successor?

Mr. CURTIS. No: there is nothing said about his successor. It is merely the act of removal of the officer.

[The document was presented to the Managers and examined by them.]

Mr. Manager BUTLER. We only want to call the attention of the Senate to the fact that it does not contain a very material thing which our schedule contains, to wit: a statement whether the Senate was or was not in session.

Mr. CURTIS. We shall get that in another form.

Mr. Manager BUTLER. Nor who was nominated in the place.

The CHIEF JUSTICE. The evidence is admitted unless there be some objection.

The document is (with the same attestation from the Navy Department as the two preceding ones) as follows:

Civil Officers Appointed for Four Years under the Statute of May 15, 1820, and "Removable from Office at Pleasure" who were removed as indicated, their terms of office not having expired.

NAVY AGENTS.

Names.	Date of original appointment.	Term.	Date of removal.	By whom removed.
R. Swartout	17 October, 1818	-	18 March, 1827	The President.
Amos Binney	Not known	-	6 May, 1826	The President.
James Beatty	17 May, 1810	-	3 March, 1829	The President.
Miles King	27 March, 1816	-	4 March, 1829	The President.
J. M. Sherburne	25 June, 1828	4 years	1 July, 1829	The President.
N. Amory	31 October, 1827	4 years	11 July, 1829	The President.
George Harrison	21 November, 1799	-	3 March, 1833	The President.
John Laighton	27 April, 1830	4 years	29 April, 1841	The President.
John Thomas	11 October, 1833	-	31 August, 1841	The President.
R. C. Wetmore	18 March, 1841	4 years	1 July, 1844	The President.
I. V. Browne	20 September, 1841	4 years	1 April, 1845	The President.
S. McClellan	31 August, 1841	4 years	8 April, 1845	The President.
William B. Scott	8 October, 1848	4 years	5 June, 1849	The President.
Joseph Hale	19 June, 1846	4 years	27 June, 1849	The President.
S. W. Smith	8 July, 1846	4 years	27 June, 1849	The President.
Walker Anderson	3 July, 1848	4 years	24 September, 1849	The President.
George Layall	13 March, 1849	4 years	1 November, 1850	The President.
O. H. Ladd	28 June, 1852	4 years	5 April, 1853	The President.
William Hindman	28 June, 1852	4 years	5 April, 1853	The President.
B. D. Wright	10 August, 1850	4 years	12 April, 1853	The President.
E. O. Perrin	28 August, 1850	4 years	28 May, 1853	The President.
William Flinn	1 April, 1858	4 years	19 April, 1861	The President.
N. F. Ammidown	8 February, 1859	4 years	12 April, 1861	The President.
H. G. S. Key	27 February, 1860	4 years	16 April, 1861	The President.
H. F. Wardell	20 May, 1858	4 years	18 April, 1861	The President.
William Badger	20 May, 1858	4 years	1 May, 1861	The President.
William F. Russell	27 June, 1860	4 years	6 May, 1861	The President.
A. E. Smith	16 December, 1857	4 years	2 May, 1861	The President.
Isaac Henderson	19 July, 1861	4 years	20 June, 1864	The President.
J. S. Chambers	19 July, 1861	4 years	26 December, 1864	The President.

385

[Mr. Curtis sent a large mass of documents to the Managers to be examined.]

The CHIEF JUSTICE. Will the counsel state what he proposes to offer?

Mr. CURTIS. These are documents from the Department of State showing the removal of officers not only during the session of the Senate but during the recess, and covering all cases of vacancy, the purpose of the evidence being to show the practice of the Government coextensive with the necessity that arises out of the different cases—death, resignation, sickness, absence, removal. It differs from the schedule which has been put in by the learned Managers, which covered certain heads of Departments only, because that applies only to removals during the session of the Senate. It includes that, but it includes a great deal more matter.

Mr. Manager BUTLER. I have prepared for myself the same list. In order that the Senate may see exactly what the character is, and may judge then how far this may be competent, I call the attention of the Senate to one, the first one that opens—not by any manner the first in order, but the first one that happens:

I hereby appoint C. A. Harris to perform the duties of acting Secretary of War during the temporary absence of the Secretary for the Department of War. ANDREW JACKSON.
May 27, 1836.

Now I will turn over to the next page:

I hereby authorize and appoint Aaron O. Dayton, chief clerk of the Department of State, to discharge the duties of Secretary of State during the temporary absence of that officer from the seat of Government. M. VAN BUREN.

Mr. Manager BINGHAM. What is the date?
Mr. Manager BUTLER. June 28, 1837. Again:

I authorize J. L. Martin, chief clerk of the Department of State, to perform the duties of Secretary of State during the absence of that officer from the seat of Government. MARTIN VAN BUREN.

That is dated October 16, 1840. Again:

I appoint John Boyle, chief clerk of the Navy Department, acting Secretary of the Navy, to perform, during the absence of the Secretary of the Navy, the duties of Secretary of the Navy Department. ANDREW JACKSON.
WASHINGTON CITY, July 5, 1834.

There are but two exceptions in all these cases to the form I have given, in various modes of expression.

Mr. CURTIS. I suppose it is not a question now what is to be the effect of the evidence; but do you object to it?

Mr. Manager BUTLER. We object to it for any purpose. It is handed to me as a mass, and I want to state what it is, and then I will tell you what I object to; I cannot do so before. I have now given you all the forms with two single exceptions. The first exception is that frequently the language of the letter of appointment, like the one I have read, has been given to cover possible contingencies. For

C. I.—25.

instance, Asbury Dickens is appointed to act as Secretary of the Treasury, "when the Secretary shall be absent," looking to the future, expecting that he would be absent on such a day. Then there are three other cases, one a case in President Monroe's time, where he appointed an acting Secretary, reciting the act of 1792. There is one in John Quincy Adams's time, reciting the act of 1792. There is one in General Jackson's time, reciting that the appointment was under the act of 1792. These are the only three in all this list that recite the act under which they are made. All the others are temporary, are in cases of death or temporary absences from the seat of Government coming within the exact terms of the law of 1792 or 1795.

I have stated what these cases are. Now, the simple question is—I am not going to argue it—will the Senate permit a series of acts, done under the law, and exactly in conformity with the law of 1792 and 1795, reciting, where they recited any law, the act of 1792, to be introduced as evidence upon the trial of a case for an act which is in violation of the act of March 2, 1867, and in violation of the act of February 20, 1868. Does it throw any light—that is to say, is there such a practice of the Government shown by this as throws any light upon the question now in hearing? It goes to the country, it goes to the Senate, that here are a large lot of appointments. True; but these appointments are in conformity with the law, reciting the law when they recite any law at all, and always reciting the exact circumstances to which the law applies. Now, are these to go in for the purpose of justifying what is admitted in the answer to be a breach of the law, if the law is constitutional?

Mr. CURTIS. I do not wish to reply, Mr. Chief Justice. I take it for granted that the Senate will not settle any question as to the merits of this case under the acts of Congress when we are putting in evidence.

The CHIEF JUSTICE. The Chief Justice thinks that the evidence is admissible within the decisions already made. Of the value of it, when admitted, the Senate will judge. If any Senator desires the question to be put to the Senate the Chief Justice will be happy to put it. [After a pause.] The evidence is admitted.

Mr. CURTIS. We do not desire to have these documents read. They are very voluminous and will take time, and it is quite unnecessary to read them, we think, or have them read.

The documents thus offered in evidence are attested by the Secretary of State in the usual form to be copied from the records of his Department, and contain the letters of authority, designation, or appointment in the following cases:

On the 23d of November, 1819, Christopher Vandeventer, chief clerk of the War Department, was authorized by President Monroe, under the act of May 8, 1792, to perform the duties of Secretary of War during the illness of John C. Calhoun, Secretary for that Department.

On the 7th of March, 1825, President J. Q. Adams appointed Samuel L. Southard, Secretary of the Navy, to perform the duties of Secretary of War, that office having become vacant, until the vacancy should be filled.

On the 26th of January, 1829, President J. Q. Adams appointed Samuel L. Southard, Secretary of the Navy, under the authority conferred by the act of May 8, 1792, to perform the duties of Secretary of the Treasury until a successor should be appointed to Richard Rush, Secretary of the Treasury, he being unable to perform his duties by severe illness, or until the inability should cease.

On the 4th of March, 1829, President Jackson appointed James A. Hamilton to take charge of the Department of State until Governor Van Buren should arrive in the city.

On the 24th of April, 1829, President Jackson appointed Asbury Dickins Secretary of the Treasury until the return of Mr. Ingham to the city.

On the 7th of July, 1829, President Jackson appointed William B. Lewis acting Secretary of War during the absence of the Secretary.

On the 8th of July, 1829, President Jackson appointed Richard H. Bradford to take charge of the Navy Department and perform the duties thereof in the absence of the Secretary of the Navy.

On the 19th of August, 1829, President Jackson appointed William B. Lewis Acting Secretary of War during the absence of the Secretary of War.

On the 7th of November, 1829, President Jackson appointed J. G. Randolph to perform the duties of Secretary of War until the return of the Secretary, John H. Eaton, he being absent.

On the 12th of June, 1830, President Jackson authorized Philip G. Randolph to act as Secretary of War while John H. Eaton, the Secretary, should be absent.

On the 8th of March, 1831, President Jackson authorized Philip G. Randolph to act as Secretary of War during the confinement of the Secretary by sickness.

On the 19th of March, 1831, President Jackson authorized John Boyle, chief clerk of the Navy Department, to act as Secretary of the Navy during the necessary absence of Mr. Branch, the Secretary, from the duties of the Department.

On the 12th of May, 1831, President Jackson authorized John Boyle to take charge of the office of Secretary of the Navy and perform its duties until a successor to Mr. John Branch, the Secretary, who had notified the President that he should leave the city "this day," could be appointed, and arrive and take charge of the office.

On the 16th of June, 1831, President Jackson authorized John Boyle, chief clerk of the Navy Department, to act as Secretary of the Navy during the absence from the seat of Government of Levi Woodbury, the Secretary.

On the 18th of June, 1831, President Jackson authorized Philip G. Randolph, chief clerk in the War Office, to discharge the duties of that office until a successor to Major Eaton should be appointed.

On the 21st of June, 1831, President Jackson appointed Asbury Dickins, chief clerk of the Treasury Department, to perform the duties required by law of the Secretary of the Treasury until the arrival of Mr. McLane, appointed successor to Mr. Ingham.

On the 20th of July, 1831, President Jackson appointed Roger B. Taney, Attorney General, to take charge of the Department of War "on the 21st instant, and execute the duties thereof until the arrival of Governor Cass."

On the 10th of August, 1831, President Jackson authorized John Boyle, chief clerk of the Navy Department, to act as Secretary of Navy in the absence of the Secretary, Levi Woodbury, from the seat of Government.

On the 10th of August, 1831, President Jackson appointed Daniel Brent, chief clerk of the Department of State, to act as Secretary of State during the absence of the Secretary from the seat of Government.

On the 12th of September, 1831, President Jackson authorized Roger B. Taney, Attorney General, to act as Secretary of War during the absence from the seat of Government of Governor Cass.

On the 13th of September, 1831, President Jackson appointed Louis McLane, Secretary of the Treasury, to take charge of the War Department during the absence of Governor Cass, Secretary, and Roger B. Taney, acting Secretary.

On the 18th of October, 1831, President Jackson authorized Asbury Dickins, chief clerk of the Treasury Department, to perform the duties of Secretary of the Treasury during the absence of the Secretary.

On the 18th of October, 1831, President Jackson authorized Levi Woodbury, Secretary of the Navy, to take charge of the Department of War and perform the duties of Secretary of War during the absence of the Secretary of War.

On the 17th of March, 1832, President Jackson authorized Asbury Dickins, chief clerk of the Treasury Department, to take charge of that Department and perform the duties of Secretary of the Treasury during the indisposition of Mr. McLane.

On the 8th of June, 1832, President Jackson authorized John Robb, chief clerk of the War Department, to perform the duties of Secretary of War during the absence of the Secretary.

On the 16th of July, 1832, President Jackson appointed John Robb, chief clerk of the War Department, to act as Secretary of War during the absence of the Secretary.

On the 21st of July, 1833, President Jackson appointed Daniel Brent, chief clerk of the Department of State, to exercise the duties and perform the functions of Secretary of State "in the event of the absence from the seat of Government of the Secretary during the present summer or approaching autumn, and during the continuance of such absence."

On the 23d of July, 1832, President Jackson appointed John Boyle to discharge the duties of Secretary of the Navy "in the absence of the Secretary at any time between this date and the 1st of October next."

On the 18th of July, 1833, President Jackson authorized Asbury Dickins, chief clerk of the Treasury Department, to perform the duties of Secretary of the Treasury in case of the absence from the seat of Government or sickness of the Secretary.

On the 8th of November, 1832, President Jackson authorized Asbury Dickins, chief clerk of the Treasury Department, during the absence of the Secretary of the Treasury, to perform the duties of that office.

On the 12th of November, 1832, President Jackson authorized John Robb, chief clerk of the War Department, to act as Secretary of War during the absence of the Secretary.

On the 6th of May, 1833, President Jackson appointed Asbury Dickins, chief clerk of the Treasury Department, to perform the duties of Secretary of the Treasury in the absence of that officer from the seat of Government.

On the 6th of May, 1833, President Jackson appointed John Robb acting Secretary of War during the absence of the Secretary.

On the 13th of May, 1833, President Jackson authorized Louis McLane, Secretary of the Treasury, to perform the duties and functions of Secretary of State during the absence of Edward Livingston from the seat of Government.

On the 29th of May, 1833, President Jackson authorized Asbury Dickins, chief clerk of the Treasury Department, to perform the duties of Secretary of the Treasury for and during the absence of that officer from the seat of Government.

On the 5th of June, 1833, President Jackson authorized Daniel Brent, chief clerk in the Department of State, to act as Secretary of State during the absence of the Secretary from the seat of Government.

On the 6th of June, 1833, President Jackson appointed John Robb to be acting Secretary of War during the absence of the Secretary.

On the 5th of June, 1833, President Jackson appointed John Boyle to be acting Secretary of the Navy "during the absence at any time within the present year of the honorable Levi Woodbury."

On the 13th of June, 1833, President Jackson appointed Daniel Brent to perform the duties of Secretary of State if the Secretary should "be at any time indisposed or absent from the seat of Government."

On the 10th of August, 1833, President Jackson authorized Asbury Dickins, "should the Secretary of State be sick or absent from the seat of Government before my return to Washington," to perform the duties during such sickness or absence.

On the 28th of September, 1833, President Jackson appointed John Robb acting Secretary of War in the absence of the Secretary.

On the 11th of November, 1833, President Jackson authorized Asbury Dickins, chief clerk of the Department of State, to perform the duties of Secretary of State during the absence of the Secretary from the seat of Government.

On the 25th of June, 1834, President Jackson authorized McClintock Young to take charge of the Department of the Treasury until a successor to Mr. Taney, resigned, should be appointed.

On the 5th of July, 1834, President Jackson appointed John Boyle, chief clerk of the Navy Department, to be acting Secretary of the Navy during the absence of the Secretary.

On the 8th of July, 1834, President Jackson authorized Asbury Dickins, chief clerk of the Department of State, to perform the duties of Secretary of State in case of the death, absence from the seat of Government, or sickness of the Secretary of State "during my absence."

On — ——, President Jackson authorized John Forsyth to discharge the duties of Secretary of War during the absence of the Secretary.

On the — ——, President Jackson authorized M. Dickerson to discharge the duties of Secretary of War during the absence of the Secretary.

On the 8th of May, 1834, President Jackson appointed Mahlon Dickerson acting Secretary of War during the absence of the Secretary.

On the 11th of October, 1834, President Jackson appointed Asbury Dickins, chief clerk of the Department of State, to act as Secretary of State during the absence of that officer from the seat of Government.

On the 19th of January, 1835, President Jackson authorized Mahlon Dickerson, Secretary of the Navy, to perform the duties of Secretary of War during the illness of that officer.

On the 2d of May, 1835, President Jackson authorized Asbury Dickins to perform the duties of Secretary of State during the absence of Mr. Forsyth from the seat of Government.

On the 7th of May, 1835, President Jackson appointed John Boyle, chief clerk of the Navy Department, to act as Secretary of the Navy during the absence of Mr. Dickerson from the seat of Government.

On the 18th of May, 1835, President Jackson appointed Carey A. Harris to act as Secretary of War during the absence of the Secretary.

On the 6th of July, 1835, President Jackson appointed Asbury Dickins to act as Secretary of State during the absence of Mr. Forsyth.

On the 1st of July, 1835, President Jackson designated McClintock Young to perform the duties of Secretary of the Treasury "at any periods of absence by the present Secretary during the ensuing months."

On the 31st of August, 1835, President Jackson authorized Asbury Dickins to act as Secretary of State during the absence of Mr. Forsyth from the seat of Government.

On the 28th of September, 1835, President Jackson authorized Asbury Dickins to act as Secretary of State during the absence of Mr. Forsyth from the seat of Government.

On the 20th of October, 1835, President Jackson empowered McClintock Young to perform the duties of Secretary of State "while the present Secretary is absent from the city of Washington."

On the 23d of October, 1835, C. A. Harris was appointed by President Jackson to act as Secretary of War during the temporary absence of the Secretary.

On April 29, 1836, C. A. Harris was appointed by President Jackson to act as Secretary of War during the temporary absence of the Secretary.

On the 27th of May, 1836, President Jackson authorized C. A. Harris to act as Secretary of War during the temporary absence of the Secretary.

On the 7th of July, 1836, President Jackson empowered Asbury Dickins, chief clerk of the Department of State, to act as Secretary of State "in case of the death, absence from the seat of Government, or inability of the Secretary during my absence from the seat of Government."

On the 9th of July, 1836, President Jackson appointed John Boyle, chief clerk of the Navy Department, to discharge the duties of Secretary of the Navy during the absence of Mahlon Dickerson, Secretary, from the seat of Government.

On the 18th of July, 1836, President Jackson authorized C. A. Harris to act as Secretary of War during the temporary absence of that officer from the seat of Government.

On the 8th of September, 1836, President Jackson authorized C. A. Harris to act as Secretary of War during the temporary absence of that officer from the seat of Government.

On the 5th of October, 1836, President Jackson authorized C. A. Harris to act as Secretary of War during the temporary absence of that officer from the seat of Government.

On the 25th of October, 1836, President Jackson authorized Benjamin F. Butler, Attorney General, to act as Secretary of War, that office having become vacant, until the vacancy should be filled.

On the 28th of June, 1837, President Van Buren authorized Aaron O. Dayton, chief clerk of the Department of State, to discharge the duties of Secretary of State during the temporary absence of that officer from the seat of Government.

On the 20th of October, 1837, President Van Buren authorized McClintock Young to discharge the duties of Secretary of the Treasury "whenever that officer may be absent from the seat of Government."

On the 27th of October, 1837, President Van Buren authorized John Boyle, chief clerk of the Navy Department, to act as Secretary of the Navy during the absence of the Secretary.

On the 21st of July, 1838, President Van Buren authorized John Boyle, chief clerk of the Navy Department, to act as Secretary of the Navy during the absence of the Secretary.

On the 1st of July, 1838, President Van Buren authorized McC. Young to act as Secretary of the Treasury during the absence of the Secretary, and in case of the illness or absence of Mr. Young, Samuel McKean to perform the duties.

On the 21st of July, 1838, President Van Buren authorized Aaron Vail, chief clerk of the Department of State, to discharge the functions of Secretary of State "in the event of the absence of the Secretary from the seat of Government."

On the 6th of October, 1838, President Van Buren authorized John Boyle, chief clerk of the Navy Department, to act as Secretary of the Navy during the absence of the Secretary.

On the 24th of April, 1839, President Van Buren authorized McClintock Young to perform the duties of Secretary of the Treasury during the absence of the Secretary.

On the 8th of June, 1839, President Van Buren authorized Aaron Vail, chief clerk of the State Department, to act as Secretary of State during the absence of the Secretary from the seat of Government.

On the 15th of June, 1839, President Van Buren authorized McClintock Young to act as Secretary "in the event of the sickness or absence of Levi Woodbury between this date and the 10th of October next."

On the 28th of August, 1840, President Van Buren authorized J. L. Martin, chief clerk of the Department of State, to perform the duties of Secretary of State during the absence of that officer from the seat of Government.

On the 16th of October, 1840, President Van Buren authorized J. L. Martin, chief clerk of the Department of State to perform the duties of Secretary of State during the absence of that officer from the seat of Government.

On the 3d of March, 1841, President Van Buren appointed McClintock Young, chief clerk of the Treasury Department, to perform temporarily the duties of Secretary of the Treasury until a successor to Mr. Woodbury, resigned, should be sworn into office according to law.

On the 19th of March, 1841, President Harrison appointed John D. Simms acting Secretary of the Navy during the absence of the Secretary from the seat of Government.

On the 27th of April, 1841, President Tyler appointed Daniel Fletcher Webster, chief clerk of the Department of State, to perform the duties of Secretary of State in the absence of that officer from the seat of Government.

On the 13th of September, 1841, President Tyler appointed McClintock Young to perform the duties of Secretary of the Treasury until a successor to Mr. Ewing, late Secretary, should be appointed, qualified, and enter upon the discharge of the duties of head of the Treasury Department.

On the 20th of October, 1841, President Tyler appointed William S. Derrick to perform the duties of acting Secretary of State during the absence of Daniel Fletcher Webster, "now performing those duties," from the seat of Government.

On the 30th of October, 1841, President Tyler appointed McClintock Young acting Secretary of the Treasury.

On the 14th of December, 1842, President Tyler appointed McClintock Young to perform the duties of Secretary of the Treasury during the absence of Hon. Walter Forward from the city of Washington.

On the 30th of June, 1842, President Tyler appointed McClintock Young to perform the duties of Secretary of the Treasury during the absence of Hon. Walter Forward from the city of Washington.

On the 20th of July, 1842, President Tyler appointed McClintock Young to perform the duties of Secretary of the Treasury during the sickness of Hon. Walter Forward.

On the 1st of November, 1842,' President Tyler appointed McClintock Young to perform the duties of Secretary of the Treasury during the absence of Hon. Walter Forward from the city of Washington.

On the 1st of March, 1843, President Tyler appointed McClintock Young to act as Secretary of the Treasury until a successor to Mr. Forward should be appointed and enter upon the discharge of his duties.

On the 7th of June, 1842, President Tyler appointed McClintock Young to perform the duties of Secretary of the Treasury "during the absence of the Secretary after the 8th instant."

On the 9th of May, 1843, President Tyler appointed Hugh S. Legaré to act as Secretary of State until a successor to Mr. Webster, late Secretary of State, should be appointed, qualified, and enter on the discharge of the duties.

On the 8th of June, 1843, President Tyler appointed William S. Derrick to perform the duties of Secretary of State during the absence of Mr. Legaré, acting Secretary.

On the 24th of June, 1843, President Tyler appointed Abel P. Upshur Secretary of State ad interim until a successor should be appointed.

On the 31st of May, 1843, President Tyler appointed Samuel Hume Porter acting Secretary of War during the absence of the Secretary.

On the 17th of August, 1843, President Tyler appointed William S. Derrick acting Secretary of State during the absence of A. P. Upshur from the seat of Government.

On the 28th of August, 1843, President Tyler (John C. Spencer, Secretary of the Treasury, "intending to be absent from the seat of Government on and after the 29th instant for two weeks") appointed McClintock Young to act as Secretary of the Treasury "during such period, should the Secretary be so long absent."

On the 29th of February, 1844, President Tyler appointed John Nelson, Attorney General, Secretary of State ad interim until a successor to Mr. Upshur should be appointed.

On the 2d of May, 1844, President Tyler appointed McClintock Young to perform the duties of Secretary of the Treasury until a successor to J. C. Spencer should be appointed and qualified.

On the 28th of September, 1844, President Tyler appointed Richard K. Crallé acting Secretary of State during the absence of John C. Calhoun from the seat of Government.

On the 2d of April, 1845, President Polk appointed John Y. Mason, Attorney General, to be Secretary of State ad interim during the temporary absence of James Buchanan, Secretary of that Department, from the seat of Government.

On the 4th of August, 1845, President Polk appointed John Y. Mason, Attorney General, to be acting Secretary of State during the temporary absence of Mr. Buchanan from the seat of Government.

On the 31st of March, 1846, President Polk appointed Nicholas P. Trist to be acting Secretary of State during the absence of Mr. Buchanan from the seat of Government.

On the 2d of September, 1846, President Polk appointed Nicholas P. Trist to be acting Secretary of State during the absence of Mr. Buchanan from the seat of Government.

On the 7th of October, 1846, President Polk appointed McClintock Young to perform the duties of Secretary of the Treasury during the absence from the city of Robert J. Walker, Secretary of the Treasury.

On the 4th of March, 1847, President Polk appointed Nicholas P. Trist acting Secretary of State during the absence of Mr. Buchanan from the seat of Government.

On the 31st of March, 1847, President Polk appointed Nicholas P. Trist acting Secretary of State during the absence of Mr. Buchanan from the seat of Government.

On the 4th of August, 1847, President Polk appointed William S. Derrick to be acting Secretary of State during the absence of Mr. Buchanan from the seat of Government.

On the 22d of June, 1847, President Polk appointed John Y. Mason, Secretary of the Navy, to be acting Secretary of State during the absence of Mr. Buchanan, "to take effect the 28th instant."

On the 21st of July, 1847, President Polk appointed McClintock Young to perform the duties of Secretary of the Treasury during the absence from the seat of Government of Robert J. Walker, "he intending to be absent after the 22d instant."

On the 15th of October, 1847, President Polk appointed McClintock Young to perform the duties appertaining to the office of Secretary of the Treasury during the absence of Robert J. Walker.

On the 9th of December, 1847, President Polk appointed McClintock Young to perform the duties appertaining to the office of Secretary of the Treasury during the sickness of Robert J. Walker.

On the 10th of April, 1848, President Polk appointed John Appleton, chief clerk of the State Department, to be acting Secretary of State during the absence of the Secretary from the seat of Government.

On the 26th of May, 1848, President Polk appointed Archibald Campbell, chief clerk of the War Department, to be acting Secretary of War during the temporary absence of the Secretary from the seat of Government.

On the 17th of August, 1848, President Polk appointed McClintock Young to act as Secretary of the Treasury during the temporary absence of Secretary Walker from the seat of Government.

On the 2d of September, 1848, President Polk appointed Isaac Toucey Attorney General, to act as Secretary of State during the temporary absence of the Secretary.

On the 2d of September, 1848, President Polk appointed John Y. Mason, Secretary of the Navy, to act as Secretary of War during the temporary absence of the Secretary.

On the 20th of November, 1848, President Polk appointed Isaac Toucey acting Secretary of State during the temporary absence of Mr. Buchanan from the seat of Government.

On the 6th of March, 1849, President Taylor appointed McClintock Young to act as Secretary of the Treasury until a successor to Mr. Walker should be duly appointed.

On the 8th of March, 1849, President Taylor appointed Reverdy Johnson, Attorney General, to act as Secretary of War during the temporary absence of the Secretary from the seat of Government.

On the 1st of October, 1849, President Taylor appointed William S. Derrick, chief clerk of the Department of State, to act as Secretary of State in the absence of the Secretary.

On the 8th of October, 1849, President Taylor appointed John D. McPherson acting Secretary of War during the temporary absence of Mr. Crawford "for the ensuing ten days."

On the 20th of June, 1850, President Taylor appointed John McGinnis, chief clerk of the Treasury Department, to act as Secretary of the Treasury during the absence of the Secretary from Washington.

On the 23d of July, 1850, President Fill-

more appointed Major General Winfield Scott Secretary of War *ad interim* during the vacancy occasioned by the resignation of George W. Crawford.

On the 4th of October, 1850, President Fillmore appointed William S. Derrick, chief clerk of the State Department, to be acting Secretary of State during the temporary absence of Mr. Webster from the seat of Government.

On the 23d of December, 1850, President Fillmore appointed William S. Derrick, chief clerk of the State Department, to be acting Secretary of State, during the temporary absence of Mr. Webster from the seat of Government.

On the 1st of March, 1851, President Fillmore appointed William L. Hodge to be acting Secretary of the Treasury *ad interim* during the illness of the Secretary.

On the 31st of March, 1851, President Fillmore appointed William S. Derrick, chief clerk of the Department of State, to be acting Secretary of State during the absence of Mr. Webster.

On the 10th of May, 1851, President Fillmore appointed William S. Derrick, chief clerk of the Department of State, to be acting Secretary of State during the absence of Mr. Webster.

On the 13th of May, 1851, President Fillmore appointed C. M. Conrad, Secretary of War, to be acting Secretary of the Navy *ad interim* during the absence of the Secretary.

On the 16th of June, 1851, President Fillmore appointed William L. Hodge, Assistant Secretary, to act as Secretary of the Treasury during the absence of the Secretary.

On the 20th of June, 1851, President Fillmore appointed William S. Derrick, chief clerk of the Department of State, to be acting Secretary of State during the temporary absence of Mr. Webster.

On the 11th of July, 1851, President Fillmore appointed Charles M. Conrad, Secretary of War, to act as Secretary of the Navy during the temporary absence of Mr. Graham from the seat of Government.

On the 14th of July, 1851, President Fillmore appointed William S. Derrick, chief clerk of the Department of State to be acting Secretary of State during the absence of Mr. Webster.

On the 4th of August, 1851, President Fillmore appointed W. A. Graham, Secretary of the Navy, to be acting Secretary of War during the temporary absence of Mr. Conrad.

On the 4th of August, 1851, President Fillmore appointed William L. Hodge to act as Secretary of the Treasury during the absence of the Secretary.

On the 3d of August, 1851, President Fillmore appointed W. A. Graham, Secretary of the Navy, to be acting Secretary of the Interior during the absence of Secretary A. H. H. Stuart from the city.

On the 13th of September, 1851, President

Fillmore appointed William A. Graham, Secretary of the Navy, to act as Secretary of War during the absence of that Secretary.

On the 13th of September, 1851, President Fillmore appointed William L. Hodge acting Secretary of the Treasury during the absence of the Secretary.

On the 22d of September, 1851, President Fillmore appointed Major General Winfield Scott acting Secretary of War during the temporary absence of the Secretary.

On the 25th of September, 1851, President Fillmore appointed John J. Crittenden, Attorney General, to perform the duties of Secretary of State until the return to the seat of Government of Daniel Webster, Secretary of State.

On the 26th of November, 1851, President Fillmore appointed William L. Hodge to act as Secretary of the Treasury until the return of Secretary Corwin.

On the 20th of February, 1852, President Fillmore appointed William S. Derrick, chief clerk of the Department of State, acting Secretary of State in the absence of Mr. Webster.

On the 21st of February, 1852, President Fillmore appointed William L. Hodge to be acting Secretary of the Treasury in the absence of Secretary Corwin.

On the 1st of March, 1852, President Fillmore appointed William L. Hodge acting Secretary of the Treasury in the absence of Secretary Corwin.

On the 19th of March, 1852, President Fillmore appointed William Hunter acting Secretary of State in the absence of Mr. Webster.

On the 26th of April, 1852, President Fillmore appointed William L. Hodge acting Secretary of the Treasury during the indisposition of Secretary Corwin.

On the 2d of November, 1850, President Fillmore appointed Charles M. Conrad, Secretary of War, to act as Secretary of the Navy during the absence of that Secretary.

On the 1st of May, 1852, President Fillmore appointed William Hunter to act as Secretary of State in the absence of Mr. Webster.

On the 19th of May, 1852, President Fillmore appointed William A. Graham, Secretary of the Navy, to act as Secretary of War in the absence of Mr. Conrad.

On the 24th of May, 1852, President Fillmore appointed William L. Hodge to act as Secretary of the Treasury in the absence of Secretary Corwin.

On the 10th of June, 1852, President Fillmore appointed William L. Hodge to act as Secretary of the Treasury in the absence of Secretary Corwin.

On the 6th of July, 1852, President Fillmore appointed William Hunter, chief clerk of the Department of State, to act as Secretary of State in the absence of Mr. Webster.

On the 19th of August, 1852, President Fillmore appointed John P. Kennedy acting Secretary of War during the absence of Secretary Conrad.

On the 27th of August, 1852, President Fillmore appointed William L. Hodge acting Secretary of the Treasury in the absence of Secretary Corwin.

On the 2d of September, 1852, President Fillmore appointed Charles M. Conrad, Secretary of War, to be acting Secretary of State in the absence of Mr. Webster.

On the 4th of October, 1852, President Fillmore appointed William L. Hodge to be acting Secretary of the Treasury, Mr. Secretary Corwin being unable by sickness to perform the duties of the office.

On the 28th of October, 1852, President Fillmore appointed William L. Hodge acting Secretary of the Treasury in the absence of Mr. Corwin.

On the 31st of December, 1852, President Fillmore appointed William L. Hodge to act as Secretary of the Treasury during the sickness of Mr. Corwin.

On the 15th of January, 1853, President Fillmore appointed William L. Hodge to act as Secretary of the Treasury during the sickness of Mr. Corwin.

On the 3d of March, 1853, President Fillmore appointed William L. Hodge to act as Secretary of the Treasury in the absence of Mr. Corwin.

Mr. CURTIS. I now offer documents from the Department of the Postmaster General. They are all in one envelope, (sending some papers in an envelope to the Managers.)

The CHIEF JUSTICE. The counsel will state the nature of the documents.

Mr. CURTIS. They are documents which show the removals of postmasters during the session of the Senate and *ad interim* appointments to fill the places. I believe they are all of that character, though I am not quite sure. Some of them I know are.

Mr. Manager BUTLER. They are exactly of the same kind that the Senate has just admitted.

Mr. CURTIS. I should like to have those read. They are short.

The CHIEF JUSTICE. The Secretary will read the documents.

The Secretary read as follows:

I hereby appoint St. John B. L. Skinner to be acting First Assistant Postmaster General *ad interim* in place of Horatio King, now acting Postmaster General under the law.   JAMES BUCHANAN.
WASHINGTON, *February* 8, 1861.

POST OFFICE DEPARTMENT,
WASHINGTON, D. C., *April* 7, 1868.

I, Alexander W. Randall, Postmaster General of the United States of America, certify that the foregoing is a true copy of the original order on file in this Department, together with extracts from the records in said case.

In testimony whereof I have hereunto set my hand and caused the seal of the Post Office Department to be affixed at the General Post Office [L. S.] in the city of Washington the day and year above written.   ALEX. W. RANDALL,
Postmaster General.

NEW ORLEANS POST OFFICE, ORLEANS PARISH, LOUISIANA, *June 29, 1860.*
Samuel F. Marks, Postmaster: Let this office be placed temporarily in the hands of a special agent of the Department, to be appointed by the Postmaster General, in place of Samuel F. Marks, removed.
JAMES BUCHANAN.
Hon. JOSEPH HOLT, *Postmaster General.*

June 29, 1860.
Instructions sent to D. P. Blair, special agent, to take possession of the office and remove Deutzel, chief clerk.
D. P. Blair held the office from 9th July to September 4, 1860.

Defalcation of the late Postmaster of New York City.
(Ex. Doc. No. 91, Thirty-Sixth Congress, First Session, House of Representatives.)
Letter of Postmaster General Holt, transmitting report in reply to resolution of the House of the 5th June, 1860.

Order of the President.

WASHINGTON. *May 10, 1860.*
New York Post Office, New York county, New York State—Isaac V. Fowler, Postmaster; $75,000 bond.
Let this office be placed temporarily in the hands of a special agent of the Post Office Department, to be appointed by the Postmaster General, in place of Isaac V. Fowler, removed.
JAMES BUCHANAN,
Hon. JOSEPH HOLT, *Postmaster General.*
H. ST. GEORGE OFFUTT, *Special Agent.*
See printed report for further proceedings.

January 21, 1861.
Milwaukee Post Office, Wisconsin, Milwaukee county—Mitchell Steever, postmaster, (failed to pay draft.)
Let this office be placed temporarily in the hands of a special agent of the Post Office Department, to be appointed by the Post Office Department.
JAMES BUCHANAN.
January 25, 1861.
D. M. Bull, special agent, took charge 6th February, 1861, and subsequently handed over the same to W. A. Brynnt, special agent, who remained in charge up to 31st March, 1861.

I hereby appoint St. John B. L. Skinner, now acting First Assistant Postmaster General, to be acting Postmaster General *ad interim* in place of Hon. Montgomery Blair, now temporarily absent.
ABRAHAM LINCOLN.
WASHINGTON, *September 22, 1862.*
[Each of these documents is attested by Postmaster General Randall according to the form before given.]
Mr. CURTIS. I now offer in evidence, reading from the published Executive Documents of the Senate, volume four, second session, Thirty-Sixth Congress, page one, a message of President Buchanan to the Senate in respect to the office of Secretary for the Department of War, and the manner in which he had filled that office in place of Mr. Floyd, and accompanying that message is a list of the names of those persons, as shown by the records of the Department of State, who had discharged the duties of officers of the Cabinet by appointment made in the recess, and those confirmed by the Senate, as well as those acting *ad interim*, or simply acting. This list is printed as an appendix to the message, and was sent into the Senate. I wish that message to be read.
Mr. Manager BUTLER. The difficulty that

I find with this message, Senators, is, that it is the message of Mr. Buchanan, and cannot be put in evidence any more than the declaration of anybody else. We should like to have Mr. Buchanan brought here under oath, and to cross-examine him as to this. There are a great many questions I should like to ask him about his state of mind at this time; whether he had that clearness of perception just then of his duties which would make his messages evidence. But there is a still further objection, and that is, that most of the message is composed of the statements of Mr. "J. S. Black"—Jeremiah S. Black—who refused to have anything to do with this case anyhow. [Laughter.] And I do not think that the statements of those gentlemen, however respectable, are to be taken here as evidence. They may be referred to as public documents, perhaps, but I do not think they can be put in as evidence. How do we know how correctly Mr. Black made up this list or his clerks? Are you going to put in his statements of what was done, and put it upon us or yourselves to examine to see whether they are not all illusory and calculated to mislead? I do not care to argue it any further.
Mr. JOHNSON. What is it offered for?
Mr. CURTIS. I only wish the Senate to understand the purpose with which we offer this, and that will be, as I view it, argument enough. We offer it for the purpose of showing the practice of the Government. This is an act done by the head of the Government in connection with the Senate of the United States. We offer to show that act as a part of the practice of the Government.
Mr. Manager BUTLER. The practice of the Government! I object, once for all, to the practice of this Government being shown by the acts of James Buchanan and Jeremiah S. Black. If you choose to take it, I have no objection.
The CHIEF JUSTICE. The Chief Justice will submit the question to the Senate. Senators, you who are of opinion that the evidence just offered shall be received will please say ay; those of the contrary opinion, no. [Putting the question.] The ayes appear to have it—the ayes have it. The evidence is admitted.
Mr. CURTIS. The message is short, and I desire it to be read.
The Secretary read as follows:

Message from the President of the United States in answer to a resolution of the Senate respecting the vacancy in the office of Secretary of War.
To the Senate of the United States:
In compliance with the resolution of the Senate, passed on the 10th instant, requesting me to inform that body, if not incompatible with the public interest, "whether John B. Floyd, whose appointment as Secretary of War was confirmed by the Senate on the 6th of March, 1857, still continues to hold said office, and if not, when and how said office became vacant; and further to inform the Senate how and by whom the duties of said office are now discharged; and if an appointment of an acting or provisional Secretary of War has been made, how, when, and by what authority it was so made, and why the fact of

said appointment has not been communicated to the Senate," I have to inform the Senate that John B. Floyd, the late Secretary of the War Department, resigned that office on the 29th day of December last, and that on the 1st day of January instant Joseph Holt was authorized by me to perform the duties of the said office until a successor should be appointed or the vacancy filled. Under this authority the duties of the War Department have been performed by Mr. Holt from the day last mentioned to the present time.

The power to carry on the business of the Government by means of a provisional appointment when a vacancy occurs is expressly given by the act of February 13, 1795, which enacts "that in case of vacancy in the office of Secretary of State, Secretary of the Treasury, or of the Secretary of the Department of War, or any officer of either of the said Departments, whose appointment is not in the head thereof, whereby they cannot perform the duties of their said respective offices, it shall be lawful for the President of the United States, in case he shall think it necessary, to authorize any person or persons, at his discretion, to perform the duties of the said respective offices until a successor be appointed or such vacancy be filled: *Provided*, That no one vacancy shall be supplied, in manner aforesaid, for a longer period than six months."

It is manifest that if the power which this law gives had been withheld the public interest would frequently suffer very serious detriment. Vacancies may occur at any time in the most important offices which cannot be immediately and permanently filled in a manner satisfactory to the appointing power. It was wise to make a provision which would enable the President to avoid a total suspension of business in the interval, and equally wise so to limit the executive discretion as to prevent any serious abuse of it. This is what the framers of the act of 1795 did, and neither the policy nor the constitutional validity of their law has been questioned for sixty-five years.

The practice of making such appointments, whether in a vacation or during the session of Congress, has been constantly followed during every Administration from the earliest period of the Government, and its perfect lawfulness has never, to my knowledge, been questioned or denied. Without going back further than the year 1829, and without taking into the calculation any but the chief officers of the several Departments, it will be found that provisional appointments to fill vacancies were made to the number of one hundred and seventy-nine, from the commencement of General Jackson's administration to the close of General Pierce's. This number would probably be greatly increased if all the cases which occurred in the subordinate offices and bureaus were added to the count. Some of them were made while the Senate was in session: some which were made in vacation were continued in force long after the Senate assembled. Sometimes the temporary officer was the commissioned head of another Department, sometimes a subordinate in the same Department. Sometimes the affairs of the Navy Department have been directed *ad interim* by a commodore, and those of the War Department by a general. In most, if not all, of the cases which occurred previous to 1852 it is be-

lieved that the compensation provided by law for the officer regularly commissioned was paid to the person who discharged the duties *ad interim*. To give the Senate a more detailed and satisfactory view of the subject I send the accompanying tabular statement certified by the Secretary of State, in which the instances are all set forth in which provisional, as well as permanent, appointments were made to the highest executive offices from 1829 nearly to the present time, with their respective dates.

It must be allowed that these precedents, so numerous and so long continued, are entitled to great respect, since we can scarcely suppose that the wise and eminent men by whom they were made could have been mistaken on a point which was brought to their attention so often. Still less can it be supposed that any of them willfully violated the law or the Constitution.

The lawfulness of the practice rests upon the exigencies of the public service, which require that the movements of the Government shall not be arrested by an accidental vacancy in one of the Departments; upon an act of Congress expressly and plainly giving and regulating the power; and upon long and uninterrupted usage of the Executive, which has never been challenged as illegal by Congress.

This answers the inquiry of the Senate so far as it is necessary to show "how and by whom the duties of said office are now discharged." Nor is it necessary to explain further than I have done "how, when, and by what authority" the provisional appointment has been made. But the resolution makes the additional inquiry "why the fact of said appointment has not been communicated to the Senate."

I take it for granted that the Senate did not mean to call for the reasons upon which I acted in performing an executive duty, nor to demand an account of the motives which governed me in an act which the law and the Constitution left to my own discretion. It is sufficient, therefore, for that part of the resolution to say that a provisional or temporary appointment like that in question is not required by law to be communicated to the Senate, and that there is no instance on record where such communication ever has been made. JAMES BUCHANAN.

WASHINGTON, *January* 15, 1861.

UNITED STATES OF AMERICA,
Department of State:

To all to whom these presents shall come, greeting:

I certify that the document hereunto annexed contains a correct list, duly examined and compared with the record in this Department, of those persons who have been commissioned by the President of the United States as heads of Departments, during the recess of the Senate, as confirmed by that body, as acting *ad interim* or merely acting, from March 4, 1829, to December 20, 1860, both inclusive.

In testimony whereof I, J. S. Black, Secretary of State of the United States, have hereunto subscribed my name and caused the seal of the Department of State to be affixed.

Done at the city of Washington, this 15th day of January, A. D. 1861, and of the independence of the United States of America the eighty-fifth. J. S. BLACK.

[L. S.]

A list of the names of those persons, as shown by the records of the Department of State, who discharged the duties of officers of the Cabinet, whether by appointment made in recess and those confirmed by the Senate, as well as those acting ad interim or simply acting.

Names.	Office.	Date of appointment.	Character of appointment.
Under President Jackson.			
James A. Hamilton	Secretary of State	March 4, 1829	Acting.
Martin Van Buren	Secretary of State	March 6, 1829	Regular.
Samuel D. Ingham	Secretary of the Treasury	March 6, 1829	Regular.
John Macpherson Berrien	Attorney General	Mh 9, 1829	Regular.
John Branch	Secretary of the Navy	March 9, 1829	Regular.
William T. Barry	Postmaster General	March 9, 1829	Regular.
John H. Eaton	Secretary of War	March 9, 1829	Regular.
Asbury Dickins	Secretary of the Navy	July 24, 1829	Acting.
Wm. B. Lewis	Secretary of War	July 7, 1829	Acting.
Richard H. Bradford	Secretary of the Navy	July 8, 1829	Acting.
William B. Lewis	Secretary of War	August 19, 1829	Acting.
J. G. Randolph	Secretary of War	November 7, 1829	Acting.
Philip G. Randolph	Secretary of War	June 12, 1830	Acting.
J. G. Randolph	Secretary of War	March 8, 1831	Acting.
John Boyle	Secretary of the Navy	May 12, 1831	Acting.
Edward Livingston	Secretary of State	May 24, 1831	Regular.
Levi Woodbury	Secretary of the Navy	May 23, 1831	Reg'r at.
John Boyle	Secretary of the Navy	June 16, 1831	Acting.
Blip G. Randolph	Secretary of War	June 21, 1831	Ad interim.
Asbury Dickins	Secretary of the Treasury	July 21, 1831	Ad interim.
Roger B. Taney	Attorney General	August 1, 1831	Regular.
Lewis Cass	Secretary of War	July 20, 1831	Acting.
Roger B. Taney	Secretary of War	August 8, 1831	Regular.
Louis McLane	Secretary of the Treasury	August 10, 1831	Acting.
John Boyle	Secretary of State	August 10, 1831	Acting.
Daniel Brent	Secretary of War	September 12, 1831	Acting.
Roger B. Taney	Secretary of War	September 13, 1831	Acting.
Louis McLane	Secretary of the Treasury	October 18, 1831	Acting.
Levi Woodbury	Secretary of the Treasury	October 18, 1831	Acting.
Asbury Dickins	Secretary of the Treasury	March 17, 1832	Acting.
John Robb	Secretary of War	June 8, 1832	Acting.
John Robb	Secretary of State	July 16, 1832	Acting.
Daniel Brent	Secretary of War	July 21, 1832	Acting.
John Boyle	Secretary of the Navy	July 23, 1832	Acting.
Asbury Dickins	Secretary of the Treasury	July 18, 1832	Acting.
Asbury Dickins	Secretary of War	November 8, 1832	Acting.
John Robb	Secretary of the Treasury	November 12, 1832	Acting.
John Robb	Secretary of War	March 26, 1833	Acting.
John Robb	Secretary of the Navy	May 6, 1833	Acting.
Asbury Dickins	Secretary of the Treasury	May 13, 1833	Acting.
Louis McLane	Secretary of State	May 29, 1833	Acting.
Asbury Dickins	Secretary of the Treasury	May 29, 1833	Acting.
Louis McLane	Secretary of State	May 29, 1833	Regular.

William J. Duane	Secretary of the Treasury	May 9, 1833	Regular.
Daniel Brent	Secretary of State	June 5, 1833	
John Robb	Secretary of the Navy	June 6, 1833	
... Dickins	Secretary of State	June 5, 1833	Acting.
...	Secretary of State	...e 13, 18...	Acting.
Roger B. Taney	Secretary of the ...	September 23, 1833	Acting.
John Robb	Secretary of ...	September 23, 1833	
Peter V. ...	Secretary of State	...r 1, 1833	Regular.
...v Dickins	Secretary of the ...	...r 15, 1833	
Benjamin F. Butler	Secretary of State	...r 22, 18...	Ad ... imm.
McCli...	Secretary of the ...	J...ne 25, 1834	
Levi ...	Secretary of State	June 27, 1834	
M...	Secretary of the Treasury	June 27, 1834	Regular.
John Forsyth	Secretary of the Navy	...e 30, 1834	
John Boyle	Secretary of the Navy	...ly 5, 1834	Acting.
Asbury Dickins	Secretary of War	No date.	Act.
...h F. Butler	Secretary of War	No d...	Acting.
John Forsyth	Secretary of War	October 11, 1834	Act ...
M... Dickerson	Secretary of State	...y 19, 1835	Acting.
M... Dickerson	Secretary of War	May 1, 1835	Act ...
... Diel...	Secretary of State	May 2, 1835	
...s Kendall	Secretary of War	May 7, 1835	
...y Dickins	Secretary of the Treasury	May 18, 1835	
J hn Boyle	Secretary of State	July 6, 1835	
...y C...	Secretary of the ...	August 31, 1835	Acting.
...y Dickins	Secretary of State	September 28, 1835	
... Young	Secretary of the ...	...r 20, 1835	Acting.
...y Dickins	Secretary of the ...	...r 23, 1835	Acting.
...y Dickins	Secretary of the ...	April 29, 1836	Acting.
...y C.	Secretary of War	May 19, 1836	
...y C.	Secretary of State	July 27, 1836	
...y ...	Secretary of War	July 9, 1836	
...y C.	Secretary of State	July 18, 1836	At ...
...y Dickins	Secretary of War	September 8, 1836	
John Boyle	Secretary of War	M...rch 3, 18...	Regular.
C. A. Harris			
C. A. Harris			
B. F. Butler			
B. F. Butler			

Under President Van Buren.

...l R. Poinsett	Secretary of War	March 7, 1837	Regul...
A. O. Dayton	Secretary of State	June 28, 1837	
McCli... & Young	Secretary of the Treasury	October 20, 1837	Acting.
John Boyle	Secretary of the Navy	October 23, 1837	Regular.
Fel x Grundy	Attorney General	June 25, 1838	Regular.
... Boyle	Secretary of the Navy	...ly 21, 1838	
...n Vail	Secretary of the Treasury	July 10, 1838	
...v Vail	Secretary of State	July 2, 1838	
Aaron Vail	Secretary of the Treasury	April 24, 1839	Acting.
M... Ok Young	Secretary of State	June 8, 1839	Acting.
	Secretary of the Treasury	...ne 15, 1839	Acting.

STATEMENT—Continued.

Names.	Office.		Date of appointment.	Character of appointment.
Under Presidents Harrison and Tyler.				
?y D. Gilpin	?y ?l		?y 11, 1840.	Regul ?.
?n M. Niles	?l		?y 9, 1840	Regul ?.
J. L. Martin	?y of State		?t 8, ?0.	?.
J. L. Martin	?y of State		?r 16, 1840.	*Ad interim.*
MCli ?k Young	?y ?o Treasury		?r 2, ?1	?r.
J. L. Martin ?k Young	Secretary of State		?h 5, 1841	Regul ?.
Thomas Ewing	Secretary of ?o		?h 5, 1841	Regul ?.
?l Webster	Secretary of State		?h 5, 1841	Regul ?.
John Bell	Secretary of War		?h 5, 1841	Regular.
?e E. ?r	?y of ?o Navy		?h 5, ?1	Regular.
An. I. Crittenden	?y of ?o		?h 6, 1841.	Regul ?.
?r			?h 9, 1841.	Acting.
?n D. Simms ?	?r of ?o Navy		?l 27 ?1.	Acting.
?n F. ?k Young	?ky of State			*Ad interim.*
?r	Secretary of ?o ?ury		?r 13, 1841	Regul ?.
A. P. Upshur ?	?r of ?o Navy		?r 3, 1841	Regul ?.
?les A. ?klitfe ?	Secretary of ?o		?r 13, 1841	Regul ?.
?h S. ?r	?r General		?r 13, 1841	Regul ?.
?n D McLean	?y General		?r 3, 1841	Regular.
John C. Spencer	Secretary of War.		October 12, 1841	Act ?.
William S. Derrick	Secretary of State		?r 6, 1841	Aci ?.
?lk ?r	Secretary of ?o Treasury		?r 20, 1841	Aci ?.
?lk Young	Secretary of ?o Treasury			Acting.
?k	?y of ?o		May 14, 1842.	Act ?.
?k Young	?ky of ?o		June 30, 1842	*Ad interim.*
?	?y of ?o		?v 20, 1842.	Regular.
?n C.	?ky of ?o		?h 1, 1843.	*Ad interim.*
?s ?n ?r	Secretary of War.		?h 8, ?3.	Acting.
Hugh S. Legare	Secretary of ?o		?n 8, ?3.	*Ad interim.*
William S. ?k	?y of State		May 9, 1843	Acting.
Abel P. Upshur	?y of State		?n 8, 18.	Acting.
Samuel ?e ?er	Secretary of ?a.		June 24, 1843	*Ad ?im.*
William S. Derrick	?y of State		May 31, 1843.	Amg.
A. ?. ?	?y of State.		?t 17.	?3
?n ?d ?naw	Secretary of State		?y 24, 1843	Regul ?r.
?	?o Navy		July 24, 1843	?s ?.
?n ?s ?k Gilmer	Secretary of State		August 28, ?3	
William Wilkins	?o N ?y		?y 29, 1844	*Ad interim.*
J ?n C. Mason ?	Secretary of War.		?y 15, 1844	Regular.
John ?. ?	?o Navy		?h 14, ?4	?r.
?e M. Bbb	?y of ?o		?e 6,1 ?4.	*Ad interim.*

Under President Polk.

James Buchanan	Secretary of State	March 6, 1845.	Regular.
Robert J. Walker	Secretary of the Treasury	Mh 6, 1845.	Regular.
William L. Marcy	Secretary of War	Mh 6, 1845.	Regular.
...e Johnson	Postmaster General	March 6, 1845.	Regular.
John Y. Mason	Attorney General	March 10, 1845.	Regular.
George Bancroft	Secretary of the Navy	April 2, 1845.	Ac.
J hnoY. Mason	Secretary of State	August 4, 1845.	Ac.
J hn Y. Mason	Secretary of State	March 31, 1846.	Acting.
N. P. Trist	Secretary of State	September 9, 1846.	Regular.
J hnoY. Mason	Secretary of the Navy	September 2, 1846.	Acting.
McClintock Young	Secretary of the Treasury	ber 7, 1846.	Regular.
Nathan Clifford	Attorney General	ber 17, 1846.	Regular.
N. P. Trist	Secretary of State	Mh 11, 1847.	Acting.
N. P. Trist	Secretary of State	Mch 31, 1847.	Ac.
J hnoY. ...	Secretary of the Treasury	June 23, 1847.	Acting.
McClintock Young	Secretary of State	July 21, 1847.	Ac.
William S. ...ck	Secretary of the Treasury	August 4, 1847.	Ac.
McClintock Young	Secretary of the Treasury	ber 15, 1847.	Ac.
John A. Appleton	Secretary of State	December 9, 1847.	Acting.
...hibald Campbell, Jr.	Secretary of War	April 10, 1848.	Regular.
Isaac Toucey	Attorney General	May 26, 1848.	Ac.
Isaac Toucey	Secretary of State	June 21, 1848.	Ac.
J hnoY. Mason	Secretary of War	September 2, 1848.	Ac.
Isaac Toucey	Secretary of State	November 20, 1848.	Ac.

Under Presidents Taylor and Fillmore.

McClintock Young	Secretary of the Treasury	Mh 6, 1849.	Ad interim.
John M. Clayton	Secretary of State	Mh 7, 1849.	Regular.
William M. Meredith	Secretary of the ...ury	March 8, 1849.	Regular.
George W. Crawford	Secretary of War	Mh 8, 1849.	Regular.
William B. Preston	Secretary of the ...vy	Mh 8, 1849.	Regular.
James Collamer	Postmaster General	Feb 8, 1849.	Regular.
Reverdy Johnson	Attorney General	March 8, 1849.	Regular.
Thomas Ewing	Secretary of the Interior	March 8, 1849.	Acting.
Reverdy Johnson	Secretary of War	ber 1, 1849.	Acting.
William S. Derrick	Secretary of State	ber 8, 1849.	Acting.
John D. McPherson	Secretary of the Treasury	June 20, 1850.	Ad ...
J hnoMcGinnis	Secretary of War	July 23, 1850.	Regular.
Wi field Scott	Secretary of War	July 23, 1850.	Regular.
...an P. Hall	Postmaster General	July 22, 1850.	Regular.
Thomas Corwin	Secretary of the Treasury	July 22, 1850.	Regular.
Daniel Webster	Secretary of State	July 22, 1850.	Regular.
W. A. ...an	Secretary of the Navy	...t 15, 1850.	Ac.
J hnoJ. Crittenden	Attorney General	September 12, 1850.	Regular.
Charles M. Conrad	Secretary of the Interior	October 7, 1850.	Regular.
Alexander H. H. Stuart	Secretary of War	...r 7, 1850.	Ac.
W. S. Derrick	Secretary of State	December 6, 1850.	Ac.
Allen A. Hall	Secretary of the Treasury	M nth 11, 1851.	Ac.
W. L. Ho ged	Secretary of State	M nth 31, 1851.	Ac.
W. S. Derrick	...ary of State	May 10, 1851.	Acting.
W. S. Derrick	...ary of State		

STATEMENT—Continued.

Names.	Office.	Date of appointment.	Character of appointment.
C. M. Conrad	Secretary of the Navy	May 15, 1851	Acting.
W. L. Hodge	Secretary of the Treasury	June 16, 1851	Acting.
W. S. Derrick	Secretary of State	June 20, 1851	Acting.
C. M. Conrad	Secretary of the	July 11, 1851	Acting.
W. S. Derrick	Secretary of State	July 14, 1851	Acting.
W. A. Graham	Secretary of War	August 4, 1851	Acting.
W. A. do	Secretary of the Interior	August 4, 1851	Acting.
W. A. Graham	Secretary of War	September 13, 1851	Acting.
W. L. Hodge	Secretary of the Treasury	September 13, 1851	Acting.
Winfield Scott	Secretary of War	September 22, 1851	Acting.
J. J. Crittenden	Secretary of State	September 25, 1851	Acting.
W. L. Hodge	Secretary of State	November 26, 1851	Acting.
W. S. Derrick	Secretary of the Treasury	February 20, 1852	Acting.
W. L. Hodge	Secretary of the Treasury	February 21, 1852	Regular.
William Hunter	Secretary of State	March 1, 1852	Acting.
William L. Hodge	Secretary of the Treasury	Mch 19, 1852	Acting.
C. M. Conrad	Secretary of the Navy	April 26, 1852	Acting.
Wm Hunter	Secretary of State	November 2, 1850	Acting.
M. Conrad	Secretary of the Navy	May 1, 1852	Acting.
William L. Hodge	Secretary of the	May 19, 1852	Acting.
William L. do	Secretary of the	May 24, 1852	Acting.
William Hunter	Secretary of State	June 21, 1852	Acting.
John P. Kennedy	Secretary of the Navy	July 6, 1852	Regular.
John P. Kennedy	Secretary of War	July 22, 1852	Acting.
W. L. Hodge	Secretary of the Treasury	August 19, 1852	Acting.
Samuel D. Hubbard	Postmaster General	August 27, 1852	Regular.
C. M. Conrad	Secretary of State	August 31, 1852	Regular.
W. L. Hodge	Secretary of the Treasury	September 2, 1852	Acting.
W. L. Hodge	Secretary of the Treasury	October 4, 1852	Acting.
Edward Everett	Secretary of State	October 28, 1852	Regular.
W. L. Hodge	Secretary of the Treasury	November 6, 1852	Regular.
W. L. Hodge	Secretary of the	January 15, 1853	Acting.
Wm Hunter	Secretary of State	March 3, 1853	Acting.
W. L. Hodge	Secretary of the Treasury	March 3, 1853	Ad interim.
Under President Pierce.			
W. L. Marcy	Secretary of State	March 7, 1853	Regular.
James Guthrie	Secretary of the Treasury	March 7, 1853	Regular.
Robert McClelland	Secretary of the Interior	March 7, 1853	Regular.
Jefferson Davis	Secretary of War	March 7, 1853	Regular.
J. C. Dobbin	Secretary of the Navy	March 7, 1853	Regular.
James Campbell	Postmaster General	March 7, 1853	Regular.
Caleb Cushing	Attorney General	March 7, 1853	Regular.
P. G. Washington	Secretary of the Treasury	July 11, 1853	Acting.
J. C. Dobbin	Secretary of War	July 11, 1853	Acting.
A. D. Mann	Secretary of State	July 29, 1853	Acting.

Name	Office	Date	Status
P. G. Washington	Secretary of the Treasury	September 23, 1853	Acting.
A. D. Mann	Secretary of State	September 28, 1853	Acting.
P. G. Washington	Secretary of the Treasury	April 12, 1854	Acting.
William Hunter	Secretary of State	August 21, 1854	Acting.
Archibald Campbell	Secretary of War	August 29, 1854	Acting.
P. G. Washington	Secretary of the Treasury	October 5, 1854	Acting.
Archibald Campbell	Secretary of War	October 30, 1854	Acting.
P. G. Washington	Secretary of the Treasury	May 5, 1855	Acting.
Samuel Cooper	Secretary of War	May 26, 1855	Acting.
William Hunter	Secretary of State	July 21, 1855	Acting.
P. G. Washington	Secretary of the Treasury	August 6, 1855	Acting.
Archibald Campbell	Secretary of War	October 9, 1855	Acting.
Archibald Campbell	Secretary of War	January 19, 1857	Acting.
Samuel Cooper	Secretary of War	March 3, 1857	Acting.

Under President Buchanan.

Name	Office	Date	Status
Lewis Cass	Secretary of State	March 6, 1857	Regular.
Howell Cobb	Secretary of the Treasury	March 6, 1857	Regular.
Jacob Thompson	Secretary of the Interior	March 6, 1857	Regular.
John B. Floyd	Secretary of War	March 6, 1857	Regular.
Isaac Toucey	Secretary of the Navy	March 6, 1857	Regular.
Aaron V. Brown	Postmaster General	March 6, 1857	Regular.
J. S. Black	Attorney General	March 6, 1857	Regular.
Philip Clayton	Secretary of the Treasury	April 23, 1857	Acting.
John Appleton	Secretary of State	June 1, 1857	Acting.
Philip Clayton	Secretary of the Treasury	June 23, 1858	Acting.
Philip Clayton	Secretary of the Treasury	July 13, 1858	Acting.
John Appleton	Secretary of State	August 20, 1858	Acting.
Joseph Holt	Postmaster General	March 14, 1859	Regular.
Philip Clayton	Secretary of the Treasury	July 28, 1859	Acting.
William R. Drinkard	Secretary of War	July 5, 1859	Acting.
Philip Clayton	Secretary of the Treasury	July 28, 1859	Acting.
Philip Clayton	Secretary of the Treasury	August 30, 1859	Acting.
Philip Clayton	Secretary of the Treasury	May 30, 1860	Acting.
William H. Trescott	Secretary of State	June 28, 1860	Acting.
Philip Clayton	Secretary of the Treasury	July 27, 1860	Acting.
Philip Clayton	Secretary of the Treasury	October 6, 1860	Acting.
Philip Clayton	Secretary of the Treasury	October 22, 1860	Acting.
Isaac Toucey	Secretary of the Treasury	November 26, 1860	Ad interim.
Philip F. Thomas	Secretary of the Treasury	December 10, 1860	Regular.
W. Hunter	Secretary of State	December 12, 1860	Acting.
J. S. Black	Secretary of State	December 13, 1860	Regular.
Edwin M. Stanton	Attorney General	December 20, 1860	Regular.

Mr. CURTIS. I now desire to move for an order on the proper officer of the Senate to furnish, so that we may put into the case, a statement of the dates of the beginning and end of each session of the Senate, including, of course, its executive sessions as well as its legislative, from the origin of the Government down to the present time. That will enable us, by comparing those dates with these facts which we put into the case, to see what was done within and what was done without the session of the Senate.

The CHIEF JUSTICE. The Chief Justice is of opinion that that is an application which can only be addressed to the Senate in legislative session. If the court desire it he will vacate the chair in order that the President *pro tempore* may take it.

Mr. CURTIS. I would state, Mr. Chief Justice, that we have now concluded our documentary evidence as at present advised; we may possibly desire hereafter to offer some additional evidence of this character, but as we now understand it we shall not.

Mr. JOHNSON. Mr. Chief Justice, I move that the Senate, sitting as a court of impeachment, adjourn until to-morrow at twelve o'clock.

The motion was agreed to; and the Senate sitting for the trial of the impeachment adjourned.

THURSDAY, *April* 16, 1868.

The Chief Justice of the United States took the chair.

The usual proclamation having been made by the Sergeant-at-Arms,

The Managers of the impeachment on the part of the House of Representatives and the counsel for the respondent, except Mr. Stanbery, appeared and took the seats assigned them respectively.

The members of the House of Representatives, as in Committee of the Whole, preceded by Mr. E. B. WASHBURNE, chairman of that committee, and accompanied by the Speaker and Clerk, appeared and were conducted to the seats provided for them.

The CHIEF JUSTICE. The Secretary will read the Journal of yesterday's proceedings.

The Secretary proceeded to read the Journal, but was interrupted by

Mr. SHERMAN. I move that the reading of the Journal be dispensed with.

The CHIEF JUSTICE. If there be no objection the reading of the Journal will be dispensed with. There being no objection, it is so ordered.

Mr. SUMNER. Mr. President, I send to the Chair a declaration of opinion to be adopted by the Senate as an answer to the constantly recurring questions on the admissibility of testimony.

The CHIEF JUSTICE. The Secretary will read the paper submitted by the Senator from Massachusetts.

The Secretary read as follows:

Considering the character of this proceeding, that it is a trial of impeachment before the Senate of the United States, and not a proceeding by indictment in an inferior court;

Considering that Senators are, from beginning to end, judges of law as well as fact, and that they are judges from whom there is no appeal;

Considering that the reasons for the exclusion of evidence on an ordinary trial where the judge responds to the law and the jury to the fact are not applicable to such a proceeding;

Considering that, according to parliamentary usage, which is the guide in all such cases, there is on trials of impeachment a certain latitude of inquiry and a freedom from technicality;

And considering, finally, that already in the course of this trial there have been differences of opinion as to the admissibility of evidence;

Therefore, in order to remove all such differences and to hasten the dispatch of business, it is deemed advisable that all evidence offered on either side not trivial or obviously irrelevant in nature shall be received without objection, it being understood that the same when admitted shall be open to question and comparison at the bar in order to determine its competency and value, and shall be carefully sifted and weighed by Senators in the final judgment.

Mr. CONNESS. Mr. President, I move to lay that paper on the table, and on that motion I ask for the yeas and nays.

The yeas and nays were ordered; and being taken, resulted—yeas 33, nays 11; as follows:

YEAS—Messrs. Buckalew, Cameron, Cattell, Chandler, Cole, Conkling, Conness, Corbett, Cragin, Davis, Dixon, Doolittle, Drake, Edmunds, Ferry, Fessenden, Frelinghuysen, Harlan, Howard, Howe, Johnson, Morgan, Morrill of Maine, Morrill of Vermont, Patterson of New Hampshire, Pomeroy, Ramsey, Saulsbury, Stewart, Thayer, Tipton, Williams, and Yates—33.

NAYS—Messrs. Anthony, Fowler, Grimes, Morton, Patterson of Tennessee, Sherman, Sumner, Van Winkle, Vickers, Willey, and Wilson—11.

NOT VOTING—Messrs. Bayard, Henderson, Hendricks, McCreery, Norton, Nye, Ross, Sprague, Trumbull, and Wade—10.

So the proposition was laid upon the table.

The CHIEF JUSTICE. Gentlemen of counsel for the President, you will please proceed with the defense.

Mr. EVARTS. Mr. Chief Justice and Senators, I am not able to announce the recovery of Mr. Stanbery, but I think had not the weather been so entirely unfavorable he would have been able to be out, perhaps, to-day. He is, however, convalescent, but, nevertheless, the situation of his health and proper care for his complete recovery prevents us from having much opportunity of consultation with him during the intervals of the sessions of this court. We shall desire to-day to proceed with such evidence as we think properly we can produce in his absence, and may occupy the session of the court with that evidence during the usual hours of its sitting. We shall not desire to protract, however, the examinations with any such object or view, and if before the close of the ordinary period of the session we should come to that portion of the testimony in which we regard Mr. Stanbery's presence as indispensable we shall submit that to the discretion of the court.

Mr. CURTIS. Mr. Chief Justice, I desire to offer in evidence two documents received this mornipg from the Department of State of a character, I believe, entirely similar to some of those which were received yesterday. They are in continuation chronologically of what was put in yesterday, and merely complete the series.

Mr. Manager BUTLER. Under the decision of yesterday we do not object. We understand them to be the same thing. You do not desire them read, I suppose.

Mr. CURTIS. No, I do not desire them read.

Mr. JOHNSON. State what they are.

Mr. CURTIS. They are a continuation of the documents put in yesterday, so as to bring the evidence of the practice down to a more recent period.

The documents thus offered in evidence are attested by the Secretary of State in the usual form to be copied from the records of his Department, and contain the letters of authority, designation, or appointment in the following cases:

On the 11th of July, 1853, President Pierce appointed Peter G. Washington to take charge of the Treasury Department "during the expected absence of the Secretary of the Treasury from the seat of Government."

On the 11th of July, 1853, President Pierce appointed James C. Dobbin to be acting Secretary of War in the absence of Jefferson Davis.

On the 29th of July, 1853, President Pierce appointed A. Dudley Mann, Assistant Secretary of State, to be acting Secretary of State during the temporary absence of Secretary W. L. Marcy from the seat of Government.

On the 23d of September, 1853, President Pierce appointed Peter G. Washington to discharge the duties of Secretary of the Treasury during the absence of Secretary Guthrie from the seat of Government.

On the 28th of September, 1853, President Pierce appointed A. Dudley Mann, Assistant Secretary of State, to be acting Secretary of State during the temporary absence of Mr. Marcy from the seat of Government.

On the 12th of April, 1854, President Pierce appointed Peter G. Washington to discharge the duties of Secretary of the Treasury during the temporary absence of Secretary Guthrie from Washington.

On the 21st of August, 1854, President Pierce appointed William Hunter to perform the duties of Secretary of State during the absence of Mr. Marcy from the seat of Government.

On the 29th of August, 1854, President Pierce appointed Archibald Campbell to be acting Secretary of War during the absence of the Secretary from the seat of Government.

On the 5th of October, 1854, President Pierce appointed Peter G. Washington to discharge the duties of Secretary of the Treasury during the absence of Secretary Guthrie from Washington.

C. I.—26.

On the 30th of October, 1854, President Pierce appointed Archibald Campbell, chief clerk of the War Department, to be acting Secretary of War during the temporary absence of the Secretary.

On the 3d of May, 1855, President Pierce appointed Peter G. Washington to discharge the duties of Secretary of the Treasury during the absence of Secretary Guthrie from Washington.

On the 26th of May, 1855, President Pierce appointed Colonel Samuel Cooper, United States Army, acting Secretary of War, during the temporary absence of the Secretary from the seat of Government.

On the 21st of July, 1855, President Pierce appointed William Hunter, Assistant Secretary of State, to perform the duties of Secretary of State, Mr. Marcy being absent from the seat of Government.

On the 6th of August, 1855, President Pierce appointed Peter G. Washington to discharge the duties of Secretary of the Treasury during the absence of Secretary Guthrie from Washington.

On the 9th of October, 1856, President Pierce appointed A. Campbell, acting Secretary of War, during the temporary absence of the Secretary.

On the 19th of January, 1857, President Pierce appointed Archibald Campbell, acting Secretary of War, during the temporary absence of the Secretary.

On the 3d of March, 1857, President Pierce appointed Colonel Samuel Cooper, Adjutant General of the Army, to be acting Secretary of War.

On the 23d of April, 1857, President Buchanan appointed Philip Clayton to discharge the duties of Secretary of the Treasury during the absence from Washington of Secretary Cobb.

On the 1st of June, 1857, President Buchanan appointed John Appleton to be acting Secretary of State during the absence of Secretary Cass from the seat of Government.

On the 28th June, 1858, President Buchanan appointed Philip Clayton to perform the duties of Secretary of the Treasury during the absence of Secretary Cobb from Washington.

On the 13th of July, 1858, President Buchanan appointed Philip Clayton to discharge the duties of Secretary of the Treasury during the absence from Washington of Secretary Cobb.

On the 20th of August, 1858, President Buchanan appointed John Appleton, Assistant Secretary of State, to discharge the duties of Secretary of State during the absence of Secretary Cass from Washington.

On the 26th of April 1859, President Buchanan appointed Philip Clayton to act as

Secretary of the Treasury during the temporary absence of the Secretary of the Treasury.

On the 5th of July, 1859, President Buchanan appointed William K. Drinkard to be acting Secretary of War during the absence of the Secretary from his office.

On the 26th July, 1859, President Buchanan appointed Philip Clayton to act as Secretary of the Treasury during the temporary absence of Secretary Cobb from Washington, "from and after the 1st of August."

On the 30th of August, 1859, President Buchanan appointed Philip Clayton to act as Secretary of the Treasury during the absence of Secretary Cobb from Washington.

On the 30th August, 1859, President Buchanan appointed Philip Clayton to act as Secretary of the Treasury during the absence from Washington of Secretary Cobb.

On the 30th May, 1860, President Buchanan appointed Philip Clayton to act as Secretary of the Treasury during the absence from Washington of Secretary Cobb.

On the 26th June, 1860, President Buchanan appointed William H. Trescott to discharge the duties of Secretary of State during the absence of the Secretary of State from Washington.

On the 27th July, 1860, President Buchanan appointed Philip Clayton to discharge the duties of Secretary of the Treasury during the absence of Secretary Cobb from Washington.

On the 6th October, 1860, President Buchanan appointed Philip Clayton to discharge the duties of Secretary of the Treasury during the absence of Secretary Cobb from Washington.

On the 22d of October, 1860, President Buchanan appointed Philip Clayton to discharge the duties of Secretary of the Treasury during the absence of Secretary Cobb from Washington.

On the 26th of November, 1860, President Buchanan appointed Philip Clayton to discharge the duties of Secretary of the Treasury during the sickness of Secretary Cobb.

On the 13th of December, 1860, President Buchanan appointed William Hunter, chief clerk of the Department of State, to act as Secretary of State until an appointee should be regularly commissioned.

On the 10th of December, 1860, President Buchanan, by virtue of the act of Congress approved February 13, 1795, authorized Isaac Toucey, Secretary of the Navy, to perform the duties of Secretary of the Treasury, "now vacant by the resignation of Howell Cobb," until a successor should be appointed and the vacancy filled.

On the 2d of August, 1861, President Lincoln appointed Thomas A. Scott to act as Secretary of War during the temporary absence of Secretary Cameron from the seat of Government.

On the 8th of August, 1861, President Lincoln appointed George Harrington to discharge the duties of Secretary of the Treasury during the temporary absence from Washington of Salmon P. Chase.

On the 27th of August, 1861, President Lincoln appointed Frederick W. Seward, Assistant Secretary of State, to be acting Secretary of State during the temporary absence from the seat of Government of William H. Seward.

On the 3d of September, 1861, President Lincoln appointed George Harrington to act as Secretary of the Treasury during the absence of S. P. Chase from Washington.

On the 26th of September, 1861, President Lincoln appointed William L. Hodge to be acting Secretary of the Treasury during the absence of the Secretary, "commencing from the 27th instant."

On the 2d of November, 1861, President Lincoln appointed George Harrington to discharge the duties of Secretary of the Treasury during the absence of Salmon P. Chase from Washington.

On the 4th of November, 1861, President Lincoln appointed Frederick W. Seward, Assistant Secretary of State, to be acting Secretary of State during the temporary absence of William H. Seward from the seat of Government.

On the 13th of November, 1861, President Lincoln appointed George Harrington to discharge the duties of Secretary of the Treasury during the absence of S. P. Chase from Washington.

On the 18th of December, 1861, President Lincoln appointed George Harrington to discharge the duties of Secretary of the Treasury during the absence of S. P. Chase from Washington.

On the 4th of January, 1862, President Lincoln, "pursuant to the act of Congress in such case made and provided," the Secretary of State being absent from the seat of Government, appointed Frederick W. Seward, Assistant Secretary, to be Secretary of State.

On the 28th of January, 1862, the Secretary of State being absent from the seat of Government, President Lincoln, "pursuant to the authority in such case provided," authorized Assistant Secretary F. W. Seward to act as Secretary of State.

On the 6th of February, 1862, the Secretary of State being absent from the seat of Government, President Lincoln, "pursuant to the authority in such case provided," authorized Assistant Secretary F. W. Seward to act as Secretary of State.

On the 9th of April, 1862, the Secretary of State being absent from the seat of Government, President Lincoln, "pursuant to the authority in such case provided," authorized Assistant Secretary F. W. Seward to act as Secretary of State.

On the 11th of April, 1862, President Lincoln appointed George Harrington to discharge the duties of Secretary of the Treasury during the absence of Salmon P. Chase from Washington.

On the 5th of May, 1862, President Lincoln appointed George Harrington to discharge the duties of Secretary of the Treasury during the absence of Salmon P. Chase from Washington.

On the 14th of May, 1862, the Secretary of State being absent from the seat of Government, President Lincoln authorized William Hunter, chief clerk of the Department of State, to perform the duties of Secretary until his return.

On the 19th of May, 1862, President Lincoln appointed George Harrington to discharge the duties of Secretary of the Treasury during the absence of Salmon P. Chase from Washington.

On the 11th of June, 1862, President Lincoln authorized Frederick W. Seward, Assistant Secretary of State, to discharge the duties of Secretary of State, the Secretary of State being absent from the seat of Government.

On the 30th of June, 1862, President Lincoln authorized Frederick W. Seward, Assistant Secretary of State, to discharge the duties of Secretary of State, the Secretary of State being absent from the seat of Government.

On the 27th of August, 1862, President Lincoln authorized Frederick W. Seward, Assistant Secretary of State, to discharge the duties of Secretary of State, the Secretary of State being absent from the seat of Government.

On the 8th of January, 1863, President Lincoln appointed George Harrington to discharge the duties of Secretary of the Treasury during the absence of the Secretary, Salmon P. Chase.

On the 13th of March, 1863, President Lincoln appointed George Harrington to discharge the duties of Secretary of the Treasury during the absence of the Secretary, Salmon P. Chase.

On the 18th of April, 1863, President Lincoln appointed George Harrington to discharge the duties of Secretary of the Treasury during the absence of the Secretary, Salmon P. Chase.

On the 27th of April, 1863, President Lincoln, the Secretary of State being absent, appointed William Hunter, chief clerk of the Department of State, to perform the duties of Secretary of State until the return of the Secretary.

On the 21st of May, 1863, President Lincoln appointed George Harrington to perform the duties of Secretary of the Treasury during the absence of the Secretary, Salmon P. Chase.

On the 25th of May, 1863, President Lincoln, the Secretary of State being absent, authorized Frederick W. Seward, Assistant Secretary, to discharge the duties of Secretary of State.

On the 27th of July, 1863, President Lincoln appointed George Harrington to act as Secretary of the Treasury during the absence of the Secretary, Salmon P. Chase.

On the 15th of August, 1863, President Lincoln, the Secretary of State being absent, authorized Frederick W. Seward, Assistant Secretary, to act as Secretary of State.

On the 10th of October, 1863, President Lincoln appointed Lucius E. Chittenden to discharge the duties of Secretary of the Treasury during the absence of Salmon P. Chase, Secretary.

On the 2d of November, 1863, President Lincoln, the Secretary of State being absent, authorized Frederick W. Seward, Assistant Secretary, to act as Secretary of State.

On the 23d of December, 1863, President Lincoln, the Secretary of State being absent, authorized Frederick W. Seward, Assistant Secretary, to act as Secretary of State.

On the 11th of April, 1864, President Lincoln, the Secretary of State being absent, authorized Frederick W. Seward, Assistant Secretary, to act as Secretary of State.

On the 14th of April, 1864, President Lincoln appointed George Harrington to discharge the duties of Secretary of the Treasury during the absence of the Secretary, Salmon P. Chase.

On the 27th of April, 1864, President Lincoln appointed George Harrington to discharge the duties of Secretary of the Treasury during the absence of Secretary Salmon P. Chase.

On the 7th of June, 1864, President Lincoln appointed George Harrington to discharge the duties of Secretary of the Treasury during the absence of Secretary Salmon P. Chase.

On the 30th of June, 1864, President Lincoln authorized George Harrington, Assistant Secretary of the Treasury, to perform all and singular the duties of Secretary of the Treasury until a successor to Mr. Chase, resigned, should be commissioned, or until further order.

On the 11th of July, 1864, President Lincoln appointed George Harrington to discharge the duties of Secretary of the Treasury during the absence of William P. Fessenden, Secretary.

On the 30th of July, 1864, President Lincoln appointed George Harrington to discharge the duties of Secretary of the Treasury during the absence of Secretary Fessenden.

On the 29th of August, 1864, President Lincoln authorized Frederick W. Seward, Assistant Secretary of State, to discharge the duties of Secretary of State during the absence of the Secretary, W. H. Seward.

On the 26th of September, 1864, President Lincoln authorized Frederick W. Seward, Assistant Secretary of State, to discharge the duties of Secretary of State during the absence of the Secretary, W. H. Seward.

On the 17th of October, 1864, President Lincoln appointed George Harrington to act as Secretary of the Treasury during the absence of Secretary Fessenden.

On the 4th of November, 1864, President Lincoln authorized William Hunter, chief clerk of the Department of State, to act as Secretary of State until the return of the Secretary, he being absent.

On the 4th of January, 1865, President Lincoln authorized Frederick W. Seward, Assistant Secretary of State, to act as Secretary of State "during the present temporary absence of William H. Seward."

On the 1st of February, 1865, President Lincoln authorized Frederick W. Seward, Assistant Secretary of State, to discharge the duties of Secretary of State during the absence of William H. Seward.

On the 4th of March, 1865, President Lincoln authorized George Harrington, Assistant Secretary of the Treasury, to perform the duties of Secretary of the Treasury until a successor to Mr. Fessenden should be commissioned and qualified or until further order.

On the 10th of April, 1865, President Lincoln authorized Frederick W. Seward, Assistant Secretary of State, to discharge the duties of Secretary of State during the illness of William H. Seward.

On the 15th of April, 1865, President Johnson appointed William Hunter to perform the duties of Secretary of State until otherwise ordered, Secretary Seward being sick.

On the 26th of July, 1865, President Johnson appointed William Hunter to be acting Secretary of State in the absence of William H. Seward.

On the 15th of August, 1865, President Johnson authorized William Hunter to discharge the duties of Secretary of State in consequence of the absence of the Secretary from the seat of Government.

On the 29th of September, 1865, President Johnson appointed William E. Chandler, Assistant Secretary of the Treasury, to perform the duties of Secretary of the Treasury during the absence of Secretary McCulloch.

On the 4th of October, 1865, President Johnson authorized William Hunter, chief clerk of the Department of State, to discharge the duties of Secretary of State until the return of the Secretary, he being absent.

On the 6th of November, 1865, President Johnson appointed William E. Chandler to discharge the duties of Secretary of the Treasury during the absence of Secretary McCulloch.

On the 20th of December, 1865, President Johnson appointed William E. Chandler to discharge the duties of Secretary of the Treasury during the absence of Secretary McCulloch.

On the 20th of December, 1865, President Johnson appointed William E. Chandler to discharge the duties of Secretary of the Treasury during the absence of Secretary McCulloch.

On the 30th of December, 1865, President Johnson authorized William Hunter to discharge the duties of Secretary of State, the Secretary being absent.

On the 15th of May, 1866, President Johnson authorized F. W. Seward, Assistant Secretary of State, to discharge the duties of Secretary of State, the Secretary being absent.

On the 4th of August, 1866, President Johnson appointed William E. Chandler to discharge the duties of Secretary of the Treasury during the temporary absence of Secretary McCulloch.

On the 10th of August, 1866, President Johnson authorized Henry Stanbery, Attorney General, to discharge the duties of Secretary of State during the absence of that Secretary.

On the 18th of September, 1866, President Johnson authorized Frederick W. Seward, Assistant Secretary of State, to discharge the duties of Secretary of State during the illness of William H. Seward.

On the 5th of October, 1866, President Johnson authorized Frederick W. Seward, Assistant Secretary of State, to discharge the duties of Secretary of State during the illness of William H. Seward.

On the 29th of October, 1866, President Johnson authorized William Hunter, Second Assistant Secretary of State, to discharge the duties of Secretary of State during the absence of William H. Seward.

On the 5th of November, 1866, President Johnson authorized William E. Chandler to perform the duties of Secretary of the Treasury during the temporary absence of Secretary McCulloch.

On the 20th of December, 1866, President Johnson authorized William E. Chandler to perform the duties of Secretary of the Treasury during the temporary absence of Secretary McCulloch.

On the 23d of April, 1867, President Johnson authorized Frederick W. Seward, Assistant Secretary of State, to act as Secretary of State during the absence of William H. Seward.

On the 1st of June, 1867, President Johnson authorized F. W. Seward, Assistant Secretary of State, to act as Secretary of State during the absence of Secretary W. H. Seward.

On the 23d of July, 1867, President Johnson authorized William Hunter, Second Assistant Secretary of State, to discharge the duties of Secretary of State during the absence of William H. Seward.

On the 16th of September, 1867, President Johnson authorized John F. Hartley to discharge the duties of Secretary of the Treasury during the temporary absence of Secretary McCulloch.

On the 9th of October, 1867, President Johnson authorized Frederick W. Seward, Assistant Secretary of State, to discharge the duties of Secretary of State during the absence of the Secretary, W. H. Seward, from the seat of Government.

On the 13th of November, 1867, President Johnson appointed John F. Hartley to discharge the duties of Secretary of the Treasury during the absence of Secretary McCulloch "at any time in the month of November, 1867."

On the 11th of March, 1868, President Johnson appointed F. W. Seward, Assistant Secretary of State, to discharge the duties of Secretary of State during the absence from the seat of Government of Secretary W. H. Seward.

Mr. CURTIS. I will now put in evidence, so that it may be printed in connection with this documentary evidence, statements furnished by the Secretary of the Senate under the order of the Senate, one showing the beginning and ending of each legislative session of Congress from 1789 to 1868; and the other being a statement of the beginning and ending of each special session of the Senate from 1789 to 1868.

Mr. Manager BUTLER. We have no objection.

The CHIEF JUSTICE. The evidence is received.

The documents are as follows:

Statement of the beginning and ending of each Legislative Session of Congress, from 1789 to 1868.

Congress.	Session.	Began.	Ended.
1st	1st	March 4, 1789..	Sept. 29, 1789.
1st	2d	Jan. 4, 1790....	Aug. 12, 1790.
1st	3d	Dec. 6, 1790....	March 3, 1791.
2d	1st	Oct. 24, 1791..	May 8, 1792.
2d	2d	Nov. 5, 1792....	March 2, 1793.
3d	1st	Dec. 2, 1793....	June 9, 1794.
3d	2d	Nov. 3, 1794....	March 3, 1795.
4th	1st	Dec. 7, 1795....	June 1, 1796.
4th	2d	Dec. 5, 1796....	March 3, 1797.
5th	1st	May 15, 1797...	July 10, 1797.
5th	2d	Nov. 13, 1797...	July 16, 1798.
5th	3d	Dec. 3, 1798....	March 3, 1799.
6th	1st	Dec. 2, 1799....	May 14, 1800.
6th	2d	Nov. 17, 1800...	March 3, 1801.
7th	1st	Dec. 7, 1801....	May 3, 1802.
7th	2d	Dec. 6, 1802....	March 3, 1803.
8th	1st	Oct. 17, 1803...	March 27, 1804.
8th	2d	Nov. 5, 1804....	March 3, 1805.
9th	1st	Dec. 2, 1805....	April 21, 1806.
9th	2d	Dec. 1, 1806....	March 3, 1807.
10th	1st	Oct. 26, 1807...	April 25, 1808.
10th	2d	Nov. 7, 1808....	March 3, 1809.
11th	1st	May 22, 1809...	June 28, 1809.
11th	2d	Nov. 27, 1809...	May 1, 1810.
11th	3d	Dec. 3, 1810....	March 3, 1811.
12th	1st	Nov. 4, 1811....	July 6, 1812.
12th	2d	Nov. 2, 1812....	March 3, 1813.
13th	1st	*May 24, 1813.*	*Aug. 2, 1813.*
13th	2d	Dec. 6, 1813....	April 18, 1814.
13th	3d	Sept. 19, 1814..	March 3, 1815.
14th	1st	Dec. 4, 1815....	April 30, 1816.
14th	2d	Dec. 2, 1816....	March 3, 1817.
15th	1st	Dec. 1, 1817....	April 20, 1818.
15th	2d	Nov. 16, 1818...	March 3, 1819.
16th	1st	Dec. 6, 1819....	May 15, 1820.
16th	2d	Nov. 13, 1820...	March 3, 1821.
17th	1st	Dec. 3, 1821....	May 8, 1822.
17th	2d	Dec. 2, 1822....	March 3, 1823.
18th	1st	Dec. 1, 1823....	May 27, 1824.
18th	2d	Dec. 6, 1824....	March 3, 1825.
19th	1st	Dec. 5, 1825....	May 22, 1826.
19th	2d	Dec. 4, 1826....	March 3, 1827.
20th	1st	Dec. 3, 1827....	May 26, 1828.

STATEMENT—Continued.

Congress.	Session.	Began.	Ended.
20th	2d	Dec. 1, 1828....	March 3, 1829.
21st	1st	Dec. 7, 1829....	May 31, 1830.
21st	2d	Dec. 6, 1830....	March 3, 1831.
22d	1st	Dec. 5, 1831....	July 16, 1832.
22d	2d	Dec. 3, 1832....	March 2, 1833.
23d	1st	Dec. 2, 1833....	June 30, 1834.
23d	2d	Dec. 1, 1834....	March 3, 1835.
24th	1st	Dec. 7, 1835....	July 4, 1836.
24th	2d	Dec. 5, 1836....	March 3, 1837.
25th	1st	Sept. 4, 1837...	Oct. 16, 1837.
25th	2d	Dec. 4, 1837....	July 9, 1838.
25th	3d	Dec. 3, 1838....	March 3, 1839.
26th	1st	Dec. 2, 1839....	July 21, 1840.
26th	2d	Dec. 7, 1840....	March 3, 1841.
27th	1st	May 31, 1841...	Sept. 13, 1841.
27th	2d	Dec. 6, 1841....	Aug. 31, 1842.
27th	3d	Dec. 5, 1842....	March 3, 1843.
28th	1st	Dec. 4, 1843....	June 11, 1844.
28th	2d	Dec. 2, 1844....	March 3, 1845.
29th	1st	Dec. 1, 1845....	Aug. 10, 1846.
29th	2d	Dec. 7, 1846....	March 3, 1847.
30th	1st	Dec. 6, 1847....	Aug. 14, 1848.
30th	2d	Dec. 4, 1848....	March 3, 1849.
31st	1st	Dec. 3, 1849....	Sept. 30, 1850.
31st	2d	Dec. 2, 1850....	March 3, 1851.
32d	1st	Dec. 1, 1851....	Aug. 31, 1852.
32d	2d	Dec. 6, 1852....	March 3, 1853.
33d	1st	Dec. 5, 1853....	Aug. 7, 1854.
33d	2d	Dec. 4, 1854....	March 3, 1855.
34th	1st	Dec. 3, 1855....	Aug. 18, 1856.
34th	2d	Aug. 21, 1856...	Aug. 30, 1856.
34th	3d	Dec. 1, 1856....	March 3, 1857.
35th	1st	Dec. 7, 1857....	June 14, 1858.
35th	2d	Dec. 6, 1858....	March 3, 1859.
36th	1st	Dec. 5, 1859....	June 25, 1860.
36th	2d	Dec. 3, 1860....	March 2 1861.
37th	1st	July 4, 1861....	Aug. 6, 1861.
37th	2d	Dec. 2, 1861....	July 17, 1862.
37th	3d	Dec. 1, 1862....	March 3, 1863.
38th	1st	Dec. 7, 1863....	July 4, 1864.
38th	2d	Dec. 5, 1864....	March 3, 1865.
39th	1st	Dec. 4, 1865....	July 25, 1866.
39th	2d	Dec. 3, 1866....	March 2, 1867.
40th	1st	March 4, 1867..	Dec. 2, 1867.
40th	2d	Dec. 2, 1867...	-

OFFICE SECRETARY OF THE SENATE,
April 16, 1868.

I certify that the foregoing statement is correct as appears by the records of the Senate.

J. W. FORNEY, *Secretary.*

—

Statement of the Beginning and Ending of each Special Session of the Senate from 1789 to 1868.

Begun.	Ended.
March 4, 1797	March 4, 1797.
March 4, 1801	March 5, 1801.
March 4, 1809	March 7, 1809.
March 4, 1817	March 6, 1817.
March 4, 1825	March 9, 1825.
March 4, 1829	March 17, 1829.
March 4, 1837	March 10, 1837.
March 4, 1841	March 15, 1841.
March 4, 1845	March 20, 1845.
March 5, 1849	March 23, 1849.
March 4, 1851	March 13, 1851.
March 4, 1853	April 11, 1853.
March 4, 1857	March 14, 1857.
June 15, 1858	June 16, 1858.
March 4, 1859	March 10, 1859.
June 26, 1860	June 28, 1860.
March 4, 1861	March 28, 1861.
March 4, 1863	March 14, 1863.
March 4, 1865	March 11, 1865.
April 1, 1867	April 20, 1867.

OFFICE SECRETARY OF THE SENATE,
April 16, 1868.

I certify that the foregoing statement is correct as appears by the records of the Senate.

J. W. FORNEY, *Secretary.*

Mr. CURTIS. The Sergeant-at-Arms will now please call Walter S. Cox.

WALTER S. Cox sworn and examined.

By Mr. CURTIS:

Question. State what is your residence and what is your profession?

Answer. I reside in Georgetown, in this District. I am a lawyer by profession.

Question. How long have you been in the practice of the law?

Answer. Some twenty years, I think.

Question. In this city?

Answer. Yes, sir.

Question. In what courts?

Answer. In the courts of this District and, most of the time, in the Supreme Court of the United States.

Question. Were you connected professionally with the matter of General Thomas before the criminal court of this District or before a magistrate?

Answer. I was.

Question. When and under what circumstances did your connection with that matter begin?

Answer. On Saturday, the 22d of February—

Mr. Manager BUTLER. Stop a moment, please. If I heard the question correctly, the inquiry put to the witness was, when and under what circumstances did your connection with the case of Thomas before the Supreme Court, or the chief justice of the District, commence?

Mr. CURTIS. That was the question in substance.

Mr. Manager BUTLER. To that we must object. It is impossible to see how the employment of Mr. Cox to defend Mr. Thomas can have anything to do with this case. It stands in this way: we put in that Mr. Thomas said that if it had not been for the arrest he should have taken the War Office by force as he had threatened. The defense then produced the warrant and affidavit and the record of his acquittal. I do not propose to argue it; but I ask the attention of the Senate to the question whether the employment of Mr. Cox by Mr. Thomas as counsel, the circumstances under which he was employed, and the declaration of Mr. Thomas to his counsel, can be put in evidence under any rule, even the one which the Senate has just voted should not be the governing rule of this body—the exception to evidence as too trivial—if it were not legally incompetent?

Mr. CURTIS. I understand the objection to be that we cannot show that General Thomas employed Mr. Cox as his counsel; that we cannot show declarations made by Mr. Thomas to Mr. Cox as his counsel. We do not propose to prove either of those facts. If the gentleman will wait long enough to see what we do propose to prove, he will see that that objection is not applicable. [To the witness.] Will you now state, sir, when, and by whom, and under what circumstances you were employed in that matter?

Mr. Manager BUTLER. Stop one moment. I object. The question is, when, and by whom, and under what circumstances this gentleman was employed? If he was employed by the President that is worse than the other, in my judgment, as a legal proposition. I desire that the question be put in writing that we may have a ruling upon it; or, to save time, if the learned counsel will put in exactly what he proposes to prove by this witness we can meet the whole of it.

The CHIEF JUSTICE. The Chief Justice sees no objection to the question as an introductory question, but will submit it to the Senate if it is desired. [After a pause, to the witness.] You can answer the question.

Answer. On Saturday, the 22d of February, a messenger called at my house with a carriage and stated that Mr. Seward desired to see me immediately——

Mr. Manager BUTLER. I object to the declarations of any person there.

The CHIEF JUSTICE, (to the witness.) You need not state anything that Mr. Seward said to you.

The WITNESS. Nothing was said by Mr. Seward. The messenger stated further that he was directed to take me immediately to the President's House. I accompanied him to the President's House and found the President and General Thomas there alone.

By Mr. CURTIS:

Question. At what hour or about what hour?

Answer. At about five o'clock in the afternoon. After I was seated the President stated——

Mr. Manager BUTLER. Stop a moment. I object to the statement of the President at five o'clock in the afternoon. [Laughter.]

The CHIEF JUSTICE. Will the counsel for the President state the object of this testimony?

Mr. CURTIS rose.

Mr. Manager BUTLER. We desire that that may be put in writing, Mr. Chief Justice.

The CHIEF JUSTICE. The offer to prove will be put in writing if any Senator requires it.

Mr. EDMUNDS. I ask that the offer to prove may be put in writing, that we may all understand precisely what the question is.

The CHIEF JUSTICE. The counsel will please put what they propose to prove in writing.

The offer was reduced to writing and sent to the desk.

The CHIEF JUSTICE. The Secretary will read the proposition.

The Secretary read as follows:

We offer to prove that Mr. Cox was employed professionally by the President, in the presence of General Thomas, to take such legal proceedings in the case that had been commenced against General Thomas as would be effectual to raise judicially the question of Mr. Stanton's legal right to continue to hold the office of Secretary for the Department of

War against the authority of the President, and also in reference to obtaining a writ of *quo warranto* for the same purpose; and we shall expect to follow up this proof by evidence of what was done by the witness in pursuance of the above employment.

Mr. EDMUNDS. Mr. President, I should like to ask an oral question, if there be no objection.

The CHIEF JUSTICE. If there be no objection the Senator from Vermont will ask his question.

Mr. EDMUNDS. I wish to ask at what date this interview is alleged to have taken place?

Mr. CURTIS. The 22d of February.

Mr. Manager BUTLER. This testimony is liable to two objections, if not more, but two sufficient, Mr. President and Senators. The first is that after the act done, and after the matter was in course of impeachment, was in proceeding before the House, and after Mr. Stanton had, to protect himself, made an affidavit that he expected to be turned out of his office by force, the President sent, as is proposed to be proved, for Mr. Cox, the witness, and gave him certain directions. It is alleged that those directions were that he should prepare a *quo warranto*. I had supposed that such a *quo warranto* was to be filed by the Attorney General, if at all, but that that process had substantially gone out of use, and an information in the nature of a writ of *quo warranto* would have been the proper proceeding, and that information must be exhibited by the Attorney General.

Now, then, let us see just here how the case stands. The President had told General Sherman that the reason why he did not apply to lawyers, and why he took Army officers into this trouble, was that it was impossible to make up a case. One of the Senators asked him to repeat that answer, and he repeated it. The President said to him, "I am told by the lawyers that it is impossible to make up a case." After he had been told that, and after he had been convinced of that, he still went on to make the removal, and he undertakes to show to you here that he made the removal to make up a case which he himself declared was impossible to be made up. It is apparent that no case would by possibility have got into court except for the declarations and the threats of this officer Thomas to turn by force Stanton out of the War Office. That having been done, he sends for a very proper counsel, as I have no doubt the Senate will be quite convinced before we get through. He sends for a very proper counsel for Mr. Thomas, and having got him there he undertakes then to make up a case for the Senate, before which he was to be brought by impeachment. Now they say they expect to prove that the President wanted a case made up to go to the courts, and that in pursuance of that Mr. Cox so acted.

Mr. Cox cannot be allowed to testify to that for another reason. They themselves have put in the record (which imports absolute verity and cannot be contradicted by parol or other evidence) that General Thomas was dismissed upon the motion of his counsel. Upon the motion of his counsel the case was dismissed. Therefore we object, in the first place, that this declaration of the President to his lawyer after the fact and after he was in process of being impeached for that fact, shall not be put in evidence in view of the circumstances. We object, then, that what was done in court shall not be proved except by the record, which I believe there is no lawyer in the Senate, and no layman either, will ever believe for a moment can be allowed. Then we object further on this matter that this whole proceeding was between other parties in the court. There is no evidence from the record, so far as it has been put in here, (and the whole record is put in,) that the President went into that court and asked to have that case carried on, that he showed his hand, or that he made himself apparent. He does not appear upon the record. He does not appear as employing counsel. It looks as though it was the case of General Thomas, and the court dealt with it as the case of General Thomas.

If the President had gone and asked that the case might be decided as a great constitutional question, *non constat* but that the court would have decided it; but they did not do so. All that appears on the record is that this gentleman or some other appeared as counsel for General Thomas; and the question was one whether General Thomas should be held under bonds or whether, under the circumstances, he was likely to appear and answer further when the grand jury sat, it being then found that there was no danger from his personal action by violence.

Mr. EVARTS. Mr. Chief Justice and Senators, I will first notice some of the suggestions made by the learned and honorable Manager that seem to us not to have any particular bearing upon the question of evidence now submitted to you, but which may be noticed.

He says that the Attorney General alone can institute a *quo warranto*. The Attorney General has by law no official function in any court except the Supreme Court of the United States, and a *quo warranto* proceeding would need to be commenced in the court of the District. A *quo warranto* proceeding, as has heretofore been contended on the part of the Managers, and in regard to which no dispute has arisen, can only be made, it is supposed by them, on the part of the Government, and not on the part of the officer who has been detruded from office. That is one thing; but the question whether that action of the Government can be taken in any court only by the Attorney General is quite a different matter, and it might appear that if this adhesion of the Attorney General, or his approval that the proceeding should be taken by the professional advisers employed to that end, was necessary, we should be able to produce that proof.

Now, it is said that after the President told

General Sherman that it was impossible to make up a case it is now impossible for us to show that he did attempt to make up a case. This is, I suppose, a new application of the doctrine of estoppel. It is impossible for us to see any other appropriateness in it. But the fact is simply this: that when, in advance of the official action of the President to or towards the removal of Mr. Stanton, and when General Sherman was asked to receive from the Chief Executive the authority to discharge the duties of this office *ad interim*, and when General Sherman was revolving in his own mind his duty as a citizen and as a friend and servant of the Government and sought to inquire why this matter which the President desired to test and to have his presence in the controversy to enable him to test it could not be tested by the lawyers alone, without bringing in a deposit of the *ad interim* authority in any officer, the President replied that it was impossible to make up a case except by such executive action as should lay the basis for judicial interference and determination. Then, in advance, the President did not anticipate the necessity of being driven to this judicial controversy, because, in the alternative of General Sherman's accepting this trust thus reposed in him, the President expected the retirement of Mr. Stanton, and thus by that acquiescence no need would arise for further controversy in court or elsewhere. That is the condition of the proof as it now stands before the Senate, or as we upon it shall contend that it now stands in the judgment of the Senate, in regard to what occurred between the President and General Sherman.

We have already seen in proof that General Thomas received from the President on the 21st of February this designation to take charge of the office from Mr. Stanton if he retired, and his report to the President in the first instance of what was regarded as an equivalent to an acquiescence by Mr. Stanton in this demand of the office and its surrender to the charge of General Thomas. It has then been shown in evidence that General Thomas was arrested on the morning of the 22d, and that before he went into court he communicated that fact to the President and received the President's response that that was as they wished it should be, to have the matter in court.

Now, we propose to show that on the afternoon of the same day, the matter then being in court, (and which the President had said was according to his desire, always supposing that there was not a retirement which rendered further controversy and trouble unnecessary to the parties and the country,) the President did take it up as his controversy between the Constitution and the law, to be determined by the highest judicial tribunal of the country by the most rapid method that the law and competent advisers as to the law should permit. And we are met by the novelty of objection that when the matter to be proved is not the state of the record between the United States and General Thomas in that criminal complaint, but the state of facts as regards the action and purpose of the President of the United States in attempting to produce before the tribunals of the country for solemn judicial determination the matter in controversy, as the record of the criminal charge made and dismissed does not contain the name and action of the President of the United States, in this behalf we cannot show what did occur and what was the action of the President.

The learned Manager says it does not appear by the record that the President made this his controversy and attempted these objects and pursued this purpose. Certainly it does not; and if any lawyer can see how and why and in what possible method of application in the record of a prosecution of General Thomas by the United States for an infraction criminally of the civil tenure-of-office bill the action of the President should appear we might, perhaps, be precluded by some of these suggestions and arguments; but still the matter would be wholly aside from the real point of inquiry here.

Now, Mr. Chief Justice and Senators, we are not to be judged by the measure of the proof that we are able to offer through this witness, as regards the effect and value of the entire evidence bearing upon this point as it shall be drawn from this witness and from other witnesses and from other forms of testimony. We stand here definitely, and so as not to be misunderstood on this proposition, that when the alternative, not expected by the President, of the resistance of Mr. Stanton to this form of resignation or retirement demanded or removal claimed, whatever you choose to call it, was presented, so that he was obliged to find resources in the law, which he had contemplated as a thing greatly to be desired but impossible without the antecedent proceedings upon which a proper footing could be gained in the courts, he then did, with such promptness and such decision and such clear and unequivocal purpose as will be indicated in the evidence, assume immediately that service and that duty ; and it will appear that the opportunity thus presented to him for a more rapid determination than a *quo warranto* or an information in the nature of a *quo warranto* would permit being seized, it was prevented by the action of Mr. Stanton, the prosecutor, and of the court upon the movements of the prosecution to get the case out of court as frivolous and unimportant in its proceeding against General Thomas, and becoming formidable and offensive when it gave an opportunity for the President of the United States by *habeas corpus* to get a prompt decision of the Supreme Court of the United States; and then to show that, this opportunity being thus evaded, the President proceeded as he might with instructions that the only other recourse of judicial determination by an information in the nature of *quo warranto* was resorted to.

Mr. Manager BUTLER. Mr. President, I am very glad for an opportunity afforded me by the remarks of the learned counsel for the President to deal a moment with the doctrine of estoppel. I premise that an argument has been founded to the prejudice of my cause by a use of remarks which I made, to which I want to call the attention of the Senate, as bearing upon what is the doctrine of estoppel as put forward here now by the counsel who has just sat down. I will not be long. I pray you, Senators, to remember that I have never referred to this argument, although it has been a sort of *vade mecum* with the counsel of the defense ever since it was delivered. When I was discussing the obloquy thrown upon Mr. Stanton about his deserting his office I said these words:

"To desert it now, therefore, would be to imitate the treachery of his accidental Chief. But whatever may be the construction of the 'tenure-of-civil-office act' by others, or as regards others, Andrew Johnson, the respondent, is concluded upon it.

"He permitted Mr. Stanton to exercise the duties of his office in spite of it, if that office were affected by it. He suspended him under its provision; he reported that suspension to the Senate with his reasons therefor in accordance with its provisions; and the Senate, acting under it, declined to concur with him, whereby Mr. Stanton was reinstated. In the well-known language of the law, is not the respondent estopped by his solemn official acts from denying the legality and constitutional propriety of Mr. Stanton's position?"

That is all I said. I never said, nor intended to say, nor do the words honestly bear out any man in assuming that I said that the President was estopped from trying his case before the Senate of the United States and showing the unconstitutionality of the law, as was argued in the opening and as has been more than once referred to since. I said that, as between him and Mr. Stanton, Mr. Stanton's position was such that he was estopped from denying the legal propriety of that position or the constitutional propriety of it; and thereupon it was argued that I claimed on behalf of the Managers of the House of Representatives that the President was estopped from trying his case or denying the constitutionality of the law here; and we have had a learned argument, starting from Coke and brought downward, to show that the doctrine of estoppel did not apply to the law. Who ever thought it did? I think there is only one point where the doctrine of estoppel should apply, Senators, in this case, and that is that counsel should be estopped from misrepresenting the argument of their opponents and then making an argument to the prejudice of them. That is an application of the doctrine of estoppel that I want carried out through this trial.

I have not said that the President was estopped from showing that he attempted to put this man forward as his counsel by his declaration to General Thomas. I have only said that the fact that he spoke to Sherman and said to him, "It is impossible to make up a case," shows that he should not be allowed, after the fact, to attempt, if possible, to get up a defense by calling this counsel in.

It is asked what lawyer could suppose that it would appear of record that the President of the United States was engaged in this controversy? Fair dealing, honesty of purpose, uprightness of action, frankness of official position, would have made it apparent. The President of the United States, if he employed counsel for Mr. Thomas in this case, should have sent his counsel into court, and they should have there said, "Mr. Chief Justice, we are here appearing at the instance of the President of the United States for the purpose of trying a great constitutional question which he has endeavored to raise here, and for that purpose we want to get a decision of the Supreme Court of the United States." If then the chief justice of this District had refused to hear that case, there might be some ground for the harsh word "evasion" which the counsel has applied to him, for he says the question was evaded. By whom? It must have been by the chief justice of this District, for he alone made the decision. He says that Mr. Stanton had this case so conducted as to evade this decision. The record of the court shows that this man Thomas was discharged on the motion of his counsel. If they had not moved that he be discharged I venture to say he would not have been discharged; certainly there is no evidence that he would have been, and it is not to be supposed that he would have been. Now they have put in the fact that he was discharged at the motion of his own counsel, and they come back to us and tell us—what? That they want to show through Mr. Cox that the chief justice evaded this point, for nobody else made that decision. If you allow Mr. Cox to come in and say what the President told him, if you can put in his declarations made to Mr. Cox, then I suppose we shall next have his declarations made to Mr. Merrick and Mr. Aiken, and all that class of counsel whom the President brings about him; and having got them in, we shall have to bring before you the chief justice to give his account of the matter, and we shall have to get up a side-bar issue here to try whether the proceedings in the supreme court of this District were regular or otherwise. It is—I will not say designedly—but artistically contrived for the purpose of leading us away from the issue. We are to go to some other issue and some other point, and I never have heard in any court such a proposition.

A single word, now, about this matter of *quo warranto*. A reasonable degree of frankness on this question, I think, as it is a very plain one to lawyers, would not harm anybody. I undertake to say that every lawyer knows that an information in the nature of a *quo warranto* cannot be prosecuted, except in the name of the Attorney General, for any public office; and if any case can be found and shown in this country where it has been prosecuted differently I will beg my friend's pardon, and that is a thing I should not like to do upon this question.

Do they say that this *quo warranto*, whether by Cox or by Stanbery, has ever been presented to any court? No; not at all. Has anybody ever heard of that writ of *quo warranto* until it becomes a necessity for this defense? Ay, and until I put it into that opening speech, which has taught my friends so much, if I may take their continual reference to it? Up to that time had we ever heard of a *quo warranto* from any source? Has it ever been said here until since that time? Never, never. I will not object to any writ of *quo warranto*, or information in the nature of a *quo warranto*, filed in any court from a justice of the peace up to the Supreme Court of the United States, if they will show it was filed before the 21st day of February, or prepared, or that it has been filed since, until this man was impeached. But I want that to come from the record and not from the memory of Mr. Cox.

You may say, Senators, that I am taking too much time upon this matter; but it is really aiding you, because if you open this sort of declaration from the President he can keep the trial going from now until next July, ay, and from next July until the following March, precisely as his defenders in the House of Representatives threatened they would if we carried on this impeachment. "Forewarned, forearmed," Senators. His defenders in the House of Representatives when we were arguing this matter—it has gone into history—said, "You may impeach him, but if you do we will make you take all the forms, and his official life will be ended before you can get through the forms of impeachment; we will protract it till next March." That was the threat, and then, in pursuance of that threat, although your summons required him to file his answer on the day of appearance, as every other summons did, he came into this Senate and asked for forty days. He got ten. He then first asked for delay, so that forty-three days have been expended since he ought to have filed his answer by the order, and thirty-three since he actually filed it, and of those but six on the part of the Managers have been expended in the trial, and but a part of six have been expended on the trial by the counsel for the defense; and the rest, twenty-odd working days, with the whole country pausing while this is going on, with murders going through the southern country in every State unrebuked; twenty odd days have been used up in lenity to him and his counsel, and now we are asked to go into entirely a side-bar issue. It is neither relevant, in my judgment, nor competent under any legal rule, and if it were here it could have no effect.

Mr. FERRY. Mr. President, I desire to put a question to the counsel for the President. I send it to the Chair.

The CHIEF JUSTICE. The Secretary will read the question proposed by the Senator from Connecticut.

The Secretary read it, as follows:

Do the counsel for the President propose to contradict or vary the statement of the docket entries produced by them to the effect that General Thomas was discharged by Chief Justice Cartter on the motion of the defendant's counsel?

Mr. CURTIS. Mr. Chief Justice, I will respond to the question of the Senator that the counsel do not expect or desire to contradict anything which appears on the docket entries. The evidence which we offer of the employment by the President of this professional gentleman for the purposes indicated is entirely consistent with everything that appears on the docket. This is evidence, not of declarations, as the Senators must perceive, but of acts, because it is well settled, as all lawyers know, that there may be verbal acts as well as other bodily acts, and a verbal act is as much capable of proof as a physical act of a different quality or character. Now, an employment for a particular purpose of an agent, whether professional or otherwise, is an act, and may always be proved *valeat quantum* by the only evidence of which it is susceptible, namely, what was said by the party in order to create that employment, and that is what we desire to prove on this occasion.

The dismissal of General Thomas, which has been referred to, and which appears on the docket, was entirely subsequent to all these proceedings, and we shall show that that motion was made and that dismissal took place after it had become certain in the mind of Mr. Cox and his associate counsel that it was of no use further to follow or endeavor to follow these proceedings.

As to the argument, or rather the remarks, which have been addressed by the honorable Manager to the Senate, I have nothing to say. It does not seem to me, however pertinent they may be, that they require any reply.

Mr. Manager WILSON. Mr. President, I beg the indulgence of the Senate for a moment, and I must ask the members of this body to pass upon what we regard to be the real question involved in the objection which has been interposed to the testimony now offered by the counsel from the respondent.

On the 21st day of February, 1868, the President of the United States issued an order removing Edwin M. Stanton from the office of the Secretary for the Department of War. On that same day he issued a letter of authority to Lorenzo Thomas directing him to take charge of the Department of War and to discharge the duties of the office of Secretary of War *ad interim*. The articles, based upon a violation of the tenure-of-office act, are founded upon these two acts of the President on the 21st day of February. The counsel for the respondent now propose to break the force of those acts and that violation of the law by showing that on the 22d day of February, after the fact, the President employed an attorney to raise in the courts the question of the constitutionality of the tenure-of-office act.

Now, I submit to this honorable body that no act, no declaration of the President made after the fact can be introduced for the purpose of explaining the intent with which he acted. And upon this question of intent let me direct your minds to this consideration : the issuing of the orders referred to constitute the body of the crime with which the President stands charged. Did he purposely and willfully issue an order to remove the Secretary of War? Did he purposely and willfully issue an order appointing Lorenzo Thomas Secretary of War *ad interim?* If he did thus issue the orders the law raises the presumption of guilty intent, and no act done by the President after these orders were issued can be introduced for the purpose of rebutting that intent. The orders themselves were in violation of the terms of the tenure-of-office act. Being in violation of that act, they constitute an offense under and by virtue of its provisions, and the offense thus being established must stand upon the intent which controlled the action of the President at the time that he issued the orders. If, after this subject was introduced into the House of Representatives, the President became alarmed at the state of affairs, and concluded that it was best to attempt by some means to secure a decision of the court upon the question of the constitutionality or unconstitutionality of the tenure-of-office act, it cannot avail him in this case. We are inquiring as to the intent which controlled and directed the action of the President at the time the act was done; and if we succeed in establishing that intent, either by proof or by presumption of law, no subsequent act can interfere with it or remove from him the responsibility which the law places upon him because of the act done.

Mr. EVARTS. Mr. Chief Justice and Senators, we have here the oft-repeated argument that the crime against the act of Congress was complete by the papers drawn and delivered by the President; that the law presumes that those papers were made with the intent that appears on their face, which, it is alleged, is a violation of that act; and as that would be enough in an indictment against the President of the United States to affect him with a punishment, in the discretion of the judge, of six cents fine, so by peremptory necessity it becomes in this court a complete and perfect crime under the Constitution, which must require his removal from office, and that anything beyond the intent that the papers should accomplish what they tend to accomplish is not the subject of inquiry here. Well, it is the subject of imputation in the articles; it is the subject of the imputation in the arguments; it is the subject, and the only subject, that gives gravity to this trial, that there was a purpose of injury to the public interest and to the public safety in this proceeding.

Now, we seek to put this prosecution in its proper place on this point, and to show that our intent was no violence, no interruption of the public service, no seizure of the military appropriations, nothing but the purpose by this movement either to procure Mr. Stanton's retirement, as was desired, or to have the necessary footing for judicial proceedings. If this evidence is excluded, then, when you come to the summing up of this cause, you must take the crime of the dimensions and of the completeness that is here avowed, and I shall be entitled before this court and before this country to treat this accusation as if the article had read that he issued that order for Mr. Stanton's retirement, and that direction to General Thomas to take charge *ad interim,* with the intent and purpose of raising a case for the decision of the Supreme Court of the United States between the Constitution and the act of Congress; and if such an article had been produced by the House of Representatives and submitted to the Senate it would have been a laughing stock of the whole country.

The gentlemen shall not make their arguments and escape from them at the same breath. I offer this evidence to prove that the whole purpose and intent of the President of the United States in his action in reference to the occupancy of the office of Secretary of War had this extent and no more: to obtain a peaceable delivery of that trust from one holding it at pleasure to the Chief Executive, or, in the absence of that peaceable retirement, to have a case for the decision of the Supreme Court of the United States; and if the evidence is excluded you must treat every one of these articles as if the intent were limited to an open averment in the articles themselves that the intent of the President was such as I propose to prove it.

Mr. Manager BUTLER. I desire, Mr. Chief Justice, simply to read an authority to settle the question as to a *quo warranto.* I read from 5 Wheaton's Reports, page 291, the case of Wallace *vs.* Anderson:

"Error to the Circuit Court of Ohio.

"This was an information for a *quo warranto,* brought to try the title of the defendant to the office of principal surveyor of the Virginia military bounty lands north of the river Ohio, and between the rivers Scioto and Little Miami. The defendant had been appointed to the office by the State of Virginia, and continued to exercise its duties until the year 1818, during all which time his official acts were recognized by the United States. In that year he was removed by the Governor and council of Virginia, and the plaintiff appointed in his place. The writ was brought, by consent of parties, to try the title to the office, waiving all questions of form and of jurisdiction."

* * * * * * *

"Mr. Chief Justice Marshall delivered the opinion of the court, that a writ of *quo warranto* could not be maintained except at the instance of the Government; and as this writ was issued by a private individual, without the authority of the Government, it could not be sustained, whatever might be the right of the prosecutor or of the person claiming to exercise the office in question. The information must therefore be dismissed.

"Judgment reversed."

Mr. CURTIS. I wish to remark, Mr. Chief

Justice, in reference to that authority, that it is undoubtedly the law in this District and, so far as I know, in all the States, and certainly is the law in England, that there can be no writ of *quo warranto*, or information in the nature of such a writ, except in behalf of the public. But what officer is to represent the public, in whose name the information is to be filed, of course depends upon the particular statutes applicable to the case. These statutes, as lawyers know, differ in the different States. Under the laws of the United States all proceedings in behalf of the United States, in the circuit and district courts, are taken by the district attorneys in their own names; all proceedings in behalf of the United States in the Supreme Court are taken by the Attorney General in his name. In all cases of these public proceedings they are in the name and in behalf of the United States. What particular officer shall represent the United States depends on the court where the proceeding is had. Now, in reference to Mr. Cox, we expect to show an application by Mr. Cox to the district attorney to obtain his signature to the proper information and the obtaining of that signature.

The CHIEF JUSTICE. Senators, the counsel for the President offer to prove that the witness, Mr. Cox, was employed professionally by the President in the presence of General Thomas to take such legal proceedings in the case that had been commenced against General Thomas as would be effectual to raise judicially the question of Mr. Stanton's legal right to continue to hold the office of Secretary for the Department of War against the authority of the President, and also in reference to obtaining a writ of *quo warranto* for the same purpose, and they state that they expect to follow up this proof by evidence of what was done by the witness in pursuance of the above employment. The first article of impeachment, which may, perhaps, for this purpose, be taken as a sample of the rest relating to the same subject, after charging that "Andrew Johnson, President of the United States," in violation of the Constitution and laws, issued the order which has been so frequently read for the removal of Mr. Stanton, proceeds:

"Which order was unlawfully issued with intent then and there to violate the act entitled 'An act regulating the tenure of certain civil offices,'" &c.

The article charges, first, that the act was done unlawfully, and then it charges that it was done with intent to accomplish a certain result. That intent the President denies, and it is to establish that denial by proof that the Chief Justice understands this evidence now to be offered. It is evidence of an attempt to employ counsel by the President in the presence of General Thomas. It is the evidence so far of a fact; and it may be evidence also of declarations connected with that fact. This fact and these declarations, which the Chief Justice understands to be in the nature of facts,

he thinks are admissible in evidence. The Senate has already, upon a former occasion, decided by a solemn vote that evidence of the declarations by the President to General Thomas and by General Thomas to the President, after this order was sent to Mr. Stanton, were admissible in evidence. It has also admitted evidence of the same effect, on the 22d, offered by the honorable Managers. It seems to me that the evidence now offered comes within the principle of those decisions; and, as the Chief Justice has already had occasion to say, he thinks that the principle of those decisions is right, and that they are decisions which are proper to be made by the Senate sitting in its high capacity as a court of impeachment, and composed, as it is, of lawyers and gentlemen thoroughly acquainted with the business transactions of life and entirely competent to judge of the weight of any evidence which may be submitted. He therefore holds the evidence to be admissible, but will submit the question to the Senate, if desired.

Mr. DRAKE. I ask a vote upon the question, sir, by yeas and nays.

The yeas and nays were ordered; and being taken, resulted—yeas 29, nays 21; as follows:

YEAS—Messrs. Anthony, Bayard, Buckalew, Corbett, Davis, Dixon, Doolittle, Fessenden, Fowler, Frelinghuysen, Grimes, Hendricks, Howe, Johnson, McCreery, Morrill of Maine, Morton, Norton, Patterson of New Hampshire, Patterson of Tennessee, Ross, Saulsbury, Sherman, Sprague, Sumner, Trumbull, Van Winkle, Vickers, and Willey—29.

NAYS—Messrs. Cameron, Cattell, Chandler, Conkling, Cragin, Drake, Edmunds, Ferry, Harlan, Howard, Morgan, Morrill of Vermont, Nye, Pomeroy, Ramsey, Stewart, Thayer, Tipton, Williams, Wilson, and Yates—21.

NOT VOTING—Messrs. Cole, Conness, Henderson, and Wade—4.

So the Senate decided the evidence offered by the counsel for the President to be admissible.

Mr. CURTIS, (to the witness.) Will you now answer what occurred between the President, General Thomas, and yourself on that occasion?

Answer. In referring to the appointment of General Thomas as Secretary of War *ad interim* the President stated that Mr. Stanton had refused to surrender possession of the Department to General Thomas, and that he desired the necessary legal proceedings to be instituted without delay to test General Thomas's right to the office and to put him in possession. I inquired if the Attorney General was to act in the matter, and whether I should consult with him. He stated that the Attorney General had been very much occupied in the Supreme Court and had not had time to look into the authorities, but that he would be glad if I would confer with him. I promised to do so, and stated that I would examine the subject immediately, and soon after took leave.

Question. When you left did you leave the President and General Thomas there?

Answer. I did.

Question. About what time in the day was it that you left?

Answer. I do not suppose I was there more than twenty minutes. I left home about five o'clock, I think, in a carriage. I was admitted immediately.

Question. State now anything which you did subsequently in consequence of this employment?

Mr. Manager BUTLER. Does the presiding officer rule that anything that Mr. Cox did afterward tends to show the President's intent?

The CHIEF JUSTICE. The Chief Justice considers it within the principle of the ruling of the Senate.

The WITNESS. After reflecting upon the subject, supposing that the President's desire was to have the questions in controversy——

Mr. Manager BUTLER. I take it the witness's suppositions are not to go in, are they, Mr. President?

The CHIEF JUSTICE, (to the witness.) State what was done?

Mr. CURTIS. In view of which he was acting.

Mr. Manager BUTLER. I never heard of any man's supposition being put in before.

The WITNESS. I came to the conclusion that——

Mr. Manager BUTLER. Now, your "conclusions!" The witness is asked what did he do, not what his conclusions were.

Mr. CURTIS. That is an act for a lawyer, a pretty important act for a lawyer, to come to a conclusion.

Mr. Manager BUTLER. It may or may not be.

The WITNESS. I am stating what course I determined to pursue.

Mr. Manager BUTLER. What the witness did is the only thing inquired about, and I wish him kept to that.

Mr. CURTIS. One thing was that he came to a conclusion. I want to know what that was.

Mr. Manager BUTLER. I object to the conclusion, and should like to have the ruling of the presiding officer upon that.

The WITNESS. On Monday——

Mr. Manager BUTLER. I wish to have that settled.

The CHIEF JUSTICE. The Chief Justice has no doubt that the witness may state his conclusions; but he will put the question to the Senate if desired. [After a pause, to the witness.] Go on.

The WITNESS. The proceeding by *quo warranto* being a very tedious one, which could not be brought to a conclusion within even a year, and General Thomas having been arrested for a violation of the tenure-of-office act, I thought the best mode of proceeding was in the first instance——

Mr. Manager BUTLER. I object now to his thoughts. Stop somewhere. .

The CHIEF JUSTICE, (to the witness.) State your conclusions.

The WITNESS. I determined then to proceed in the first instance in the case of General Thomas. I had a brief interview with the Attorney General on Monday morning.

By Mr. CURTIS:

Question. To proceed how?

Answer. To proceed before the examining judge in that case (as I was about to explain) if the case was in proper condition for it, by applying to the Supreme Court of the United States for a writ of *habeas corpus*, so that the Supreme Court, upon the return of the writ, could examine and see whether——

Mr. Manager BUTLER. These are not acts that are now being given, Mr. President. They are thoughts and conclusions and reasonings of this party, what he would do if something else happened. I object.

The CHIEF JUSTICE. The Chief Justice supposes that the counsel employed by the President may state what course he pursued, and why he pursued it.

Mr. Manager BUTLER. You think he can put in his own determinations and reasonings?

The CHIEF JUSTICE. In reference to that matter, yes.

Mr. Manager BUTLER. I would like the judgment of the Senate upon that.

The CHIEF JUSTICE. The counsel will please put the question they address to the witness in writing, if any Senator desires the judgment of the Senate; if not, the witness will proceed.

Mr. THAYER. I ask——

Mr. HOWARD. I ask that the question may be reduced to writing, so that we may understand it.

The CHIEF JUSTICE. The counsel will reduce their question to writing.

The question propounded to the witness by the counsel for the respondent was read, as follows:

State what conclusions you arrived at as to the proper course to be taken to accomplish the instruction given you by the President.

Mr. Manager BUTLER. That is not what I objected to, Mr. President, and asked to have a ruling upon. Conclusions I did not object to. I objected to his putting in his thoughts and his reasonings by which he came to his conclusions. What he did was one thing, what he thought, and what he determined, and what he wished, and what he hoped depend so much on the state of his mind, whether he was loyally or disloyally disposed to the Government, that I do not think it competent.

The CHIEF JUSTICE. The Chief Justice will direct the witness to confine himself to the conclusions to which he came and the steps which he took.

The WITNESS. Having come to the conclusion, then, that the most expeditious way of raising the questions in controversy before the Supreme Court was to apply for a writ of *habeas corpus* in case General Thomas's case was in proper shape for that, I had a brief interview with the Attorney General on Monday morning, and this course met with his approval. I then proceeded to act in conjunction with the counsel whom General Thomas had engaged to act in his defense in the first instance.

By Mr. CURTIS:

Question. Who was that?

Answer. Mr. Merrick, of Washington. In order, however, to procure a writ of *habeas corpus* from the Supreme Court of the United States it was necessary that the commitment should be made by a court, and not by a judge at chambers or a justice of the peace, whereas General Thomas had been arrested and partially examined before one of the justices of the supreme court of the District of Columbia at chambers, and had been held to appear for further examination on Wednesday the 26th of February. On Wednesday the 26th the criminal court was opened, if I recollect aright, the chief justice presiding, and he announced that he would then proceed to the examination of the case against General Thomas.

Mr. Manager BUTLER. I have the honor to object now, Mr. President, to any proceedings of any description in court being proved other than by the record of the court.

Mr. CURTIS. I ask the witness to state what he did in court. It may have resulted in a record, or it may not have resulted in a record. Until we know what he did we cannot tell whether it would result in a record or not. We do not know that it ever got into a court where there could be a record. It may have been an ineffectual attempt to get it into a court where there could be a record.

Mr. Manager BUTLER. Now, I call the attention of you, Mr. President and the Senators, to the ingenuousness of that speech. The witness has exactly testified that the court had opened and was going on to say what was done in court, what Chief Justice Cartter announced in court, in the criminal court.

Mr. CURTIS. If the honorable Manager will give way for a moment, I say—I intended to be so understood before—that here was the chief justice of the District sitting in a magisterial capacity; he also, as Mr. Cox has said, was there holding the criminal court. Now, we desire to prove that there was an effort made by Mr. Cox to get this case transferred from the chief justice in his capacity of a magistrate into and before the criminal court, and we wish to show what Mr. Cox did in order to obtain that.

Mr. Manager BUTLER. Now, then, I again say that we have found that we have got into court and the record has been produced here. The witness himself has said that Chief Justice Cartter announced that he was going to open the court. Now, if the Senate want to try Chief Justice Cartter, and whether he has done

rightly or wrongly, I only desire that he should have counsel here to defend him. I never before heard the proceeding of a court or a magistrate sitting in a case undertaken to be proved in a tribunal where he was not on trial by the declarations of the counsel of the criminal who got beaten, or who succeeded, either.

The CHIEF JUSTICE. The Chief Justice will submit the question to the Senate. Counsel will please reduce the question to writing.

The question having been reduced to writing was read by the Secretary, as follows:

What did you do toward getting out a writ of *habeas corpus* under the employment of the President?

Mr. Manager BUTLER. That is not the question we have been debating at all. I wish the proprieties of the place would allow me to characterize that as I think it ought to be; but that was not the question we were debating. I made an objection, Mr. President, that the witness should not state what took place in court, and now they put a general question which evades that.

Mr. EVARTS. Our general question is intended to draw out what took place in court.

Mr. Manager BUTLER. Then we object.

Mr. EVARTS. Very well; that we understand. We do not wish to be characterized about it, though.

The CHIEF JUSTICE. Senators, you who are of opinion that the question is admissible——

Mr. GRIMES called for the yeas and nays; and they were ordered.

Mr. HOWE. I wish to have the question reported again.

The Secretary read the question, as follows:

What did you do toward getting out a writ of *habeas corpus* under the employment of the President?

Mr. Manager BUTLER. I wish that the statement of counsel may be added to that, "this being intended to ask what the witness did in court."

Mr. EVARTS. It covers what he did everywhere, which includes "in court."

Mr. Manager BUTLER. That is another change.

Mr. EVARTS. No change whatever. The question has been read three times. It is intended to call out what the witness did toward getting out a writ of *habeas corpus*, and it covers what he did in court, which was the very place to do it.

Mr. CURTIS. If any change or addition is to be made to the question we do not wish to have any equivocation about the word "court," because that may have a double meaning. What was done or attempted to be done was before the magistrate; we meant by that in the court.

Mr. Manager BUTLER. A judge or magistrate sitting judicially, which is the court for all purposes.

Mr. CURTIS. "Sitting judicially," but not as a court.

The CHIEF JUSTICE. The Secretary will read the question once more.

The Secretary read as follows:

What did you do toward getting out a writ of *habeas corpus* under the employment of the President?

The Secretary proceeded to call the roll.

Mr. SHERMAN. Mr. Chief Justice, I desire to state that my friend from Missouri [Mr. HENDERSON] is sick and unable to attend in his place in the Senate to-day. He wished me to make that announcement.

The call of the roll having been concluded, the result was announced—yeas 27, nays 23; as follows:

YEAS—Messrs. Anthony, Bayard, Buckalew, Davis, Dixon, Doolittle, Fessenden, Fowler, Frelinghuysen, Grimes, Hendricks, Johnson, McCreery, Morrill of Maine, Morgan, Norton, Patterson of New Hampshire, Patterson of Tennessee, Ross, Saulsbury, Sherman, Sprague, Sumner, Trumbull, Van Winkle, Vickers, and Willey—27.

NAYS—Messrs. Cameron, Cattell, Chandler, Conkling, Conness, Cragin, Drake, Edmunds, Ferry, Harlan, Howard, Howe, Morgan, Morrill of Vermont, Nye, Pomeroy, Ramsey, Stewart, Thayer, Tipton, Williams, Wilson, and Yates—23.

NOT VOTING—Messrs. Cole, Corbett, Henderson, and Wade—4.

So the Senate decided the question to be admissible.

Mr. CURTIS, (to the witness.) State now, Mr. Cox, what you did in order to obtain a writ of *habeas corpus*, pursuant to the instruction of the President?

Answer. When the chief justice announced that he would proceed as an examining judge to investigate the case of General Thomas, and not as holding court, our first application to him was to adjourn the investigation into the criminal court then in session, in order to have the action of that court. After some little discussion this request was refused. Our next effort was to have General Thomas committed to prison, in order that we might apply to that court for a *habeas corpus*, and upon his being remanded by that court, if that should be done, we might follow up the application by one to the Supreme Court of the United States; but the counsel who represented the Government, Messrs. Carpenter and Riddle, applied to the judge then for a postponement of the examination——

Mr. Manager BUTLER. Stop a moment. Does this also include what was done by the other people there?

The CHIEF JUSTICE. It is an account of the general transaction, as the Chief Justice conceives, and comes within the rule. The witness will proceed.

The WITNESS. The chief justice having indicated an intention to postpone the examination, we directed General Thomas to decline giving any bail for further appearance and to surrender himself into custody, and announce to the judge that he was in custody, and then presented to the criminal court an application for a writ of *habeas corpus*. The counsel on the other side objected that General Thomas could not put himself into custody, and they did not desire that he should be detained in custody. The chief judge also declared that he would not restrain General Thomas of his liberty and would not hold him or allow him to be held in custody. Supposing that he must either be committed or finally discharged, we then claimed that he be discharged, not supposing that the counsel on the other side would consent to it, and supposing that would bring about his commitment, and that we should then have an opportunity of getting a *habeas corpus*. They made no objection, however, to his final discharge, and accordingly the chief justice did discharge him. Immediately after that I went, in company with the counsel whom he had employed, Mr. Merrick, to the President's House, and reported our proceedings and the result to the President. He then urged us to proceed——

Mr. Manager BUTLER. Stay a moment. Shall we have another interview with the President put in, Mr President?

The CHIEF JUSTICE, (to the witness.) What date was this?

The WITNESS. On the 26th, immediately after the proceeding before the judge.

Mr. CURTIS. We propose to show that, having made his report to the President of the failure of this attempt, he then received from the President other instructions upon this subject to follow up the attempt in another way.

Mr. Manager BINGHAM. Do I understand—I ask for information of the counsel—that this interview with the President was on the 26th?

The WITNESS. It was.

Mr. Manager BINGHAM. Two days after he was impeached by the House of Representatives?

Mr. CURTIS. Yes.

Mr. Manager BINGHAM. Two days after he was presented here?

Mr. CURTIS. Yes.

Mr. Manager BINGHAM. And you are asking for the President's declarations after he was arraigned here for this crime to prove his innocence? We ask the vote of the Senate on it.

Mr. CURTIS. We do not ask for declarations, Mr. Manager; we ask for acts.

Mr. Manager BINGHAM. Acts consisting in words two days after his arraignment at this bar. We ask the vote of the Senate on the question.

Mr. YATES. Mr. President, I ask for the vote of the Senate on this question.

The CHIEF JUSTICE. The Chief Justice thinks this evidence incompetent. The declarations of parties——

Mr. EVARTS. Mr. Chief Justice, will you allow us to say a word?

The CHIEF JUSTICE. Certainly.

Mr. EVARTS. If it is to turn on that point, which has not been discussed in immediate reference to this question, we desire to be heard. The offer which the Chief Justice and Senators will remember was read, and upon which the vote of the Senate was taken for admission, included the efforts to have a *habeas corpus* proceeding taken, and also the efforts to have a *quo warranto.* The reasons why, and the time at which, and the circumstances under which the *habeas corpus* effort was made, and its termination, have been given. Thereupon the efforts were attempted at the *quo warranto.* It is in reference to that that the President gave these instructions. We suppose it is covered by the ruling already made.

Mr. Manager BUTLER. A single word, sir. The witness has informed the court that it was not done before because such a proceeding could not be brought to a decision under a year. The President was going to be impeached in the course of ten or fifteen days, and so he started a proceeding, if we are to believe this offer, which was to have a conclusion a year hence!

The CHIEF JUSTICE. The Chief Justice may have misapprehended the intention of the Senate; but he understands their ruling to be in substance this: that acts in respect to the attempt and intention of the President to obtain a legal decision, commencing on the 22d of February, may be pursued to the legitimate termination of that particular transaction; and, therefore, the Senate has ruled that Mr. Cox, the witness, may go on and testify until that particular transaction came to a close. Now, the offer is to prove conversations with the President after the termination of that effort in the supreme court of the District of Columbia. The Chief Justice does not think that is within the intent of the previous ruling; but he will submit the question to the Senate. Senators, you who are of the opinion that this testimony should be received will please say "ay;" those of the contrary opinion, "no." [Putting the question.] The question is determined in the negative. The evidence is not received.

Mr. CURTIS, (to the witness.) Mr. Cox, after you had reported to the President in the manner you have already stated, did you take any further step, did you do any further act in reference to raising the question of the constitutionality of the tenure-of-office act?

Mr. Manager BUTLER. Wait. If what the President did himself, after he was impeached, after the 26th of February, cannot be given in evidence, I do not see that what his counsel did for him may be. That is only one step further.

Mr. EVARTS. We may at least be allowed to put the question, Mr. Chief Justice.

Mr. Manager BUTLER. The question was put and I objected to it.

Mr. EVARTS. It has not been reduced to writing.

The CHIEF JUSTICE. The counsel for the President will reduce their question to writing.

The question having been reduced to writing was read by the Secretary, as follows:

After you had reported to the President the result of your efforts to obtain a writ of *habeas corpus,* did you do any act in pursuance of the original instructions you had received from the President on Saturday, to test the right of Mr. Stanton to continue in the office; and if so, state what the acts were?

The CHIEF JUSTICE. The Chief Justice thinks that this question is inadmissable within the last vote of the Senate; but will put the question to the Senate if any Senator desires it.

Mr. DOOLITTLE. Mr. Chief Justice, I should like to have that question put to the Senate; I think it a different one——

The CHIEF JUSTICE. No debate is allowable. Does the Senator desire the vote of the Senate on the question?

Mr. DOOLITTLE. Yes, sir.

The CHIEF JUSTICE. The question will be read again.

The Secretary read the last question put by the counsel for the respondent.

Mr. SHERMAN. Now, I should like to have the fifth article read.

The CHIEF JUSTICE. The article of the impeachment, the reading of which is called for by the Senator from Ohio, will be read.

The Secretary read article five, as follows:

"That said Andrew Johnson, President of the United States, unmindful of the high duties of his office and of his oath of office, on the 21st day of February, in the year of our Lord 1868, and on divers other days and times in said year, before the 2d day of March, in the year of our Lord 1868, at Washington, in the District of Columbia, did unlawfully conspire with one Lorenzo Thomas, and with other persons to the House of Representatives unknown, to prevent and hinder the execution of an act entitled 'An act regulating the tenure of certain civil offices,' passed March 2, 1867, and in pursuance of said conspiracy did unlawfully attempt to prevent Edwin M. Stanton, then and there being Secretary for the Department of War, duly appointed and commissioned under the laws of the United States from holding said office, whereby the said Andrew Johnson, President of the United States, did then and there commit and was guilty of a high misdemeanor in office."

The CHIEF JUSTICE. The Chief Justice will inquire of the counsel for the President whether they understand the question to be applicable to that article?

Mr. EVARTS. We certainly do.

The CHIEF JUSTICE. Is it asked with a view to obtain evidence bearing upon that article of the impeachment?

Mr. EVARTS. Yes, any article whatever that indicates as part of his intent or within any time alleged to be with an unlawful purpose; we propose to show the lawful and peaceful purpose.

Mr. HOWE. Mr. President, if proper I should like to have the first question addressed to the witness on the stand read again.

The CHIEF JUSTICE. The question upon which the ruling has just taken place?

Mr. HOWE. No, the offer to prove. I should like to have that read again.

The CHIEF JUSTICE. The offer which was made by the counsel, and which the Senate admitted, will be read by the Secretary.

The Secretary read as follows:

We offer to prove that Mr. Cox was employed professionally by the President in the presence of General Thomas, to take such legal proceedings in the case that had been commenced against General Thomas as would be effectual to raise judicially the question of Mr. Stanton's legal right to continue to hold the office of Secretary for the Department of War against the authority of the President, and also in reference to obtaining a writ of *quo warranto* for the same purpose, and we shall expect to follow up this proof by evidence of what was done by the witness in pursuance of the above employment.

The CHIEF JUSTICE. The discussion and the ruling of the Chief Justice in respect to the first article of the impeachment. Nothing had been said about the fifth article in the discussion, so far as the Chief Justice recollects. The question is now asked with reference to the fifth article and the intent alleged in that article to conspire. The Chief Justice thinks it is admissible with that view under the ruling upon the first offer. He will, however, put the question to the Senate if any Senator desires it.

Mr. CONNESS. The vote of the Senate is asked.

The CHIEF JUSTICE. The Senator from California asks for the vote of the Senate. Senators, you who are of the opinion that the question is admissible, and shall be put to the witness, will say ay——

Mr. HOWARD called for the yeas and nays; and they were ordered,

Mr. JOHNSON. I ask for the reading of the fifth article. I was not in when it was read.

The Secretary read the fifth article, as follows:

"That said Andrew Johnson, President of the United States, unmindful of the high duties of his office, and of his oath of office, on the 21st day of February, in the year of our Lord 1868, and on divers other days and times in said year, before the 2d day of March, in the year of our Lord 1868, at Washington, in the District of Columbia, did unlawfully conspire with one Lorenzo Thomas, and with other persons to the House of Representatives unknown, to prevent and hinder the execution of an act entitled 'An act regulating the tenure of certain civil offices,' passed March 2, 1867; and in pursuance of said conspiracy did unlawfully attempt to prevent Edwin M. Stanton, then and there being Secretary for the Department of War, duly appointed and commissioned under the laws of the United States, from holding said office, whereby the said Andrew Johnson, President of the United States, did then and there commit, and was guilty of a high misdemeanor in office."

The CHIEF JUSTICE. The Secretary will now read the question proposed to be put to the witness.

The Secretary read as follows:

After you had reported to the President the result of your efforts to obtain a writ of *habeas corpus*, did you do any other act in pursuance of the original instructions you had received from the President on Saturday to test the right of Mr. Stanton to continue in the office; and, if so, state what the acts were?

The question being taken by yeas and nays, resulted—yeas 27, nays 23; as follows:

YEAS—Messrs. Anthony, Bayard, Buckalew, Davis, Dixon, Doolittle, Fessenden, Fowler, Grimes, Hendricks, Howe, Johnson, McCreery, Morrill of Maine, Morton, Norton, Patterson of New Hampshire, Patterson of Tennessee, Ross, Saulsbury, Sherman, Sprague, Sumner, Trumbull, Van Winkle, Vickers, and Willey—27.

NAYS—Messrs. Cameron, Cattell, Chandler, Conkling, Conness, Cragin, Drake, Edmunds, Ferry, Frelinghuysen, Harlan, Howard, Morgan, Morrill of Vermont, Nye, Pomeroy, Ramsey, Stewart, Thayer, Tipton, Williams, Wilson, and Yates—23.

NOT VOTING—Messrs. Cole, Corbett, Henderson, and Wade—4.

So the question was decided to be admissible.

Mr. CURTIS, (to the witness.) Now you may state it, Mr. Cox.

The WITNESS. On the same day or the next, I forget which, I prepared an information in the nature of a *quo warranto*. I think a delay of one day occurred in the effort to procure certified copies of General Thomas's commission as Secretary of War *ad interim* and of the order to Mr. Stanton. I then applied to the district attorney to sign the information in the nature of a *quo warranto*, and he declined to do so without instructions or a request from the President or the Attorney General. This fact was communicated to the Attorney General and the papers were sent to him. We also gave it as our opinion to him that it would not be——

Mr. Manager BUTLER. Stop. We object to the opinion given by these gentlemen to the Attorney General as tending to show the President's motives or intent.

Mr. CURTIS. We do not insist upon it if the other side object. [To the witness.] You can now proceed to state anything that was done after this time.

The WITNESS. Nothing was done after this time by me. The papers were returned to me recently.

Mr. CURTIS, (to the Managers.) The witness is now yours, gentlemen, for cross-examination.

Mr. CONNESS. I move that the Senate take a recess for fifteen minutes.

The motion was agreed to; and at the expiration of the recess the Chief Justice resumed the chair and called the Senate to order.

WALTER S. Cox cross-examined.

By Mr. Manager BUTLER:

Question. You stated that you had been practicing law here in Washington some twenty years?

Answer. Yes, sir.

Question. Here all the time?

Answer. Always.

Question. Was any other counsel associated with you by the President?

Answer. No, sir; not to my knowledge.

Question. Were you counsel in that case for the President or for General Thomas?

Answer. I considered myself counsel for the President.

Question. Did you so announce yourself to Chief Justice Cartter?

Answer. I did not.

Question. Then you appeared before him as counsel for Thomas?

C. I.—27.

Answer. I did in that proceeding.

Question. And he did not understand in any way, so far as you know, that you were desiring to do anything there on behalf of the President?

Answer. I had mentioned the fact to Judge Cartter privately, out of court, that I had been sent for and directed to take charge of or institute proceedings.

Question. As counsel for the President?

Answer. Yes, sir; that I had been sent for by the President.

Question. But did you tell him that you were coming into his court as counsel for the President?

Answer. I did not. I do not know whether, when I told him, I had then determined to proceed in that way.

Question. In any of the discussions or your action before the court did you inform either the court or the counsel on the other side that you desired to have the case put in train so that you could get a decision of the Supreme Court of the United States?

Answer. I do not think I did.

Question. Had either the court or the counsel any means of knowing that that was your purpose or the President's purpose, so far as you were concerned?

Answer. In no other way than from our application for the *habeas corpus* upon our announcement of General Thomas's surrender into custody, so far as I am advised.

Question. Nothing only what they might infer?

Answer. Precisely.

Question. They might infer that?

Answer. I had no conversation with them before the result.

Question. I am not speaking now of conversations with counsel outside of the court, but I am speaking of proceedings in court?

Answer. Precisely so.

Question. And so far as the proceedings in court were concerned—and I ask for nothing else—there was no intimation, direct or indirect, that there was any wish on the part of the President or the Attorney General to make a case to test the constitutionality or the propriety of any law?

Answer. There was none that I remember in the presence of the judge on the bench acting at that time—no other than private information.

Question. Your private information to the judge I have not asked for. Was there any in court to the counsel who appeared on the other side?

Answer. None.

Question. Then, so far as you know, the counsel on the other side could only treat this as a question of the rights of personal liberty of Mr. Thomas? [No answer.] Well, sir, it being your desire to have that question tested, and as you, appearing for the Government, could do so by consent of the prosecutor, why

did you not speak to the prosecutor's counsel and ask to have it put in train for that?

Answer. Because I did not think they would consent to it. We did not desire to let them know our object at the time.

Question. Then, as I understand you, you concealed your object from them?

Answer. We rather did, I think.

Question. Then they acted as they did act, whether rightly or wrongly, under that concealment, did they?

Answer. They seemed to divine the object before we got through and to endeavor to defeat it.

Question. And they only seemed to divine it from the course they took. That is the only reason they had for seeming to divine it?

Answer. Yes, sir.

Question. You say you prepared the papers for an information in the nature of a *quo warranto?*

Answer. Yes, sir.

Question. On what day was that?

Answer. That was either on Wednesday, the 26th, or the next day.

Question. The 26th or 27th of February?

Answer. Yes, sir; I think it was the 27th.

Question. That was after the President was impeached?

Answer. Yes, sir.

Question. Did you see the President between the time that you reported to him and the time when you prepared this paper?

Answer. I did not. I have never seen him since.

Question. You prepared that paper and carried it to the Attorney General, did you not?

Answer. First, to the district attorney, or rather, I spoke to him without presenting the paper.

Question. You spoke to him and he said he must have some order from the Attorney General or the President before he could act?

Answer. Yes, sir.

Question. And then you went to the Attorney General?

Answer. I did not go in person; I sent the papers.

Question. Did you send a note with them?

Answer. I do not remember.

Question. You simply sent the papers?

Answer. I sent a message, either written or verbal; I do not know which.

Question. By whom?

Answer. I think by Mr. Merrick or Mr. Bradley; I cannot now say which.

Question. What Bradley?

Answer. Joseph H.

Question. The elder or younger?

Answer. The elder.

Question. Was he concerned in the matter?

Answer. He appeared in court with us merely as an adviser, as a friend of General Thomas.

Question. Joseph H. Bradley appeared in the courts of the District?

Answer. He did not appear in his character

as attorney of the court. He appeared in person, not in the character of an attorney.

Question. He appeared in person, but did not appear as an attorney?

Answer. Yes, sir.

Question. Did he say anything?

Answer. Nothing to the court or to the judge.

Question. Is this Mr. Bradley the same man who was disbarred?

Answer. The same.

Question. So that he could not appear. Now, since you sent those papers to the Attorney General, have you ever received them back?

Answer. I have.

Question. When?

Answer. A few days ago.

Question. By "a few days ago" when do you mean? Since you have been summoned as a witness?

Answer. I think not—just before, I believe.

Question. Just before?

Answer. I believe so.

Question. Preparatory to your being summoned as a witness?

Answer. Not that I am aware of.

Question. After or before this case was opened; before or after the trial began?

Answer. After.

Question. How long after.

Answer. I cannot say. I think it was four or five days ago, as near as I can come to it.

Question. Had you any communication with the Attorney General about them between the time you sent them and the time when you received them; I do not ask what the communication was; I only ask the fact whether you had any communication?

Answer. None in person.

Question. Had you any in writing?

Answer. No, sir.

Question. Then you had none in any way, if you had none either in person or in writing?

Answer. Yes, sir; through Mr. Merrick, to whom it was more convenient to see him than it was to me.

Question. So you can only know by what Mr. Merrick said?

Answer. That is all.

Question. Of that I will not ask you; you say the papers were returned to you. Where are they now?

Answer. I have them in my pocket.

Question. Were they not returned to you for the purpose of your having them when you should be called as a witness? Do you not so understand it?

Answer. No, sir; they came with a message?

Question. How soon before you were summoned?

Answer. Not more than a day or two, I think.

Question. On the same day?

Answer. I think a day or two before; I am not very sure.

Question. To your knowledge have those papers, up to the hour in which we are speaking, been presented to any judge of any court?

Answer. They have not.

Question. Up to the hour that we are speaking have you been directed either by the Attorney General or the President to present that application to any judge of any court?

Answer. The papers came to me with a direction that Mr. Merrick and myself should use our discretion.

Question. They came with a written message?

Answer. No; a verbal one, through Mr. Merrick to me, or rather it was communicated to him, and by him to me.

Question. But Mr. Merrick, if I understand you, was not associated with you in this proceeding as counsel for the President, because I asked you if the President had any other counsel?

Answer. He was not, as I understood it; he was counsel for General Thomas.

Question. Was this a movement on the part of General Thomas?

The WITNESS. Which movement?

Mr. Manager BUTLER. This movement for an information in the nature of a *quo warranto?*

Answer. It was not. It would be on the part of the United States on his relation.

Question. On the relation of General Thomas?

Answer. Yes, sir.

Question. Now, sir, have you received in writing, or verbally to yourself, any directions, either from the President or the Attorney General, to file those papers?

Answer. No positive directions.

Question. Any positive or unpositive from him to you?

Answer. Not immediately.

Question. I do not mean through Mr. Merrick?

Answer. The only communication I received was through him.

Question. Now, sir, if you please, state from whom did Mr. Merrick bring you a direction or communication?

Answer. From the Attorney General.

Question. Who? Use names, if you please.

Answer. The Attorney General, Mr. Stanbery.

Question. Five days ago! Mr. Stanbery resigned as Attorney General, we have heard, some fortnight ago or more. How could it come to you from the Attorney General five days ago?

Answer. I mean Mr. Stanbery.

Question. You have never received any direction, even through Mr. Merrick, from the Attorney General, but some sort of direction from the President's counsel, through Mr. Merrick?

Answer. All I received was——

Question. Excuse me; just hear my question?

The WITNESS. Repeat it, if you please.

Mr. Manager BUTLER. Have you received any communication, through Mr. Merrick or anybody else; from the Attorney General of the

United States—not the resigned Attorney General of the United States?

Answer. I have not from any other person than Mr. Stanbery.

Question. And you have not received any from him, either verbally or otherwise, while he was Attorney General?

Answer. I have not.

Question. When you sent in the papers was he then Attorney General?

Answer. I believe so.

Question. Will you not think, and make yourself certain on that point?

Answer. I do not know when he resigned. If you can inform me when that was I can answer.

Question. And the resignation made no difference in your action, so that you do not remember it?

Answer. I do not think he could have resigned at that time. I am very sure that the papers were sent to him within two or three days after the discharge of General Thomas.

Question. And were returned by him to you four or five days ago?

Answer. I cannot be precise as to that—five or six days, or four or five days.

Question. Long after he resigned, at any rate?

Answer. I believe it was.

Question. So that when you told us that Mr. Merrick had brought a communication from the Attorney General you meant from Mr. Stanbery?

Answer. I did.

Question. And you have received no communication from the President or from the Attorney General as to what should be done with those proceedings?

Answer. No, sir.

Question. Then, so far as you know, since you have prepared those papers, there has not been any direction or any effort from the President or the Attorney General—leaving out Mr. Stanbery, for he is not Attorney General now—from the President or the Attorney General to have anything done with those papers?

Answer. There has been no direction, and there has been no——

Question. Communication?

Answer. Communication to me since the papers were forwarded to the office of the Attorney General.

Question. Now, sir, we will go to the court for a moment. Did not Mr. Merrick or yourself make the motion to have Mr. Thomas discharged?

Answer. We did.

Question. Had he not been in custody under his recognizance up to the time of that motion?

Answer. We claimed that he was, but the other side denied it.

Question. And to settle that question you moved his discharge?

Answer. Yes, sir.

Question. And that was granted?

Answer. It was.

Question. Did you make that motion?

Answer. I did.

Question. So that, in fact, General Thomas was discharged by the court from custody on the motion of the President's counsel?

Mr. CURTIS. He has not said "from custody."

The WITNESS. Discharged from further attendance.

By Mr. Manager BUTLER:

Question. Excuse me. If he was not discharged from custody, what was he discharged from?

Answer. He was discharged from the complaint or from any further detention or examination, I suppose.

Question. From "further detention!" He could not be detained without being in custody?

Answer. Not very well.

Mr. Manager BUTLER. I thought not, when I was interrupted by the learned counsel on that point.

The WITNESS. He was discharged from the complaint, I presume.

Question. Then I will repeat the question at the point at which I was interrupted: whether, in fact, Mr. Thomas was not discharged from custody, from detention, from further being held to answer upon that complaint, by the motion of the President's counsel?

Answer. He was.

Question. Now, then, was that information signed by any Attorney General, past, current, or to come, so far as you know?

Answer. It was not.

RICHARD T. MERRICK sworn and examined.

By Mr. CURTIS:

Question. Where do you reside?

Answer. In Washington city.

Question. And what is your profession?

Answer. I am a lawyer by profession.

Question. How long have you been in that profession?

Answer. Nineteen or twenty years, or over. In 1847 I was admitted.

Question. Were you employed professionally in any way in connection with the matter of General Thomas before Chief Justice Cartter?

Answer. I was employed by General Thomas on the morning of the 22d of February, to conduct the proceeding instituted against him, and which brought him before Chief Justice Cartter.

Question. In the course of that day, the 22d of February, did you have an interview, in company with General Thomas or otherwise, with the President of the United States?

Answer. After the action taken by the Chief Justice on the case sitting at chambers on the morning of the 22d, at the instance of General Thomas, I went to the President's House for the purpose of taking to the President the affidavit and the bond filed by General Thomas, and communicating to the President what had transpired in regard to the case.

Question. Did you communicate to him what had transpired?

Answer. I did.

Mr. Manager BUTLER. I did not understand what the question was.

Mr. CURTIS. The question is, did he communicate to the President what had transpired in regard to the case?

Mr. Manager BUTLER. I submit, Mr. President, that that is wholly immaterial. The Senate ruled in the President's acts in employing Mr. Cox as his counsel. Those were his acts. But what communication took place between him and Mr. Merrick, who very frankly tells us here he was employed by General Thomas as his counsel, I think cannot be evidence.

The CHIEF JUSTICE. The Chief Justice thinks the evidence is cumulative only, and is admissible. He will put the question to the Senate if any Senator desires it. The counsel will reduce their question to writing.

Mr. Manager BUTLER. Upon the whole I will not press the objection.

The CHIEF JUSTICE. The objection is withdrawn.

Mr. CURTIS, (to the witness.) State whether you communicated to the President, in the presence of General Thomas, what had transpired in reference to the case?

Answer. My recollection is that I communicated what had transpired to the President in the absence of General Thomas in the first instance, for he was not at the Executive Mansion when I called; but during the interview General Thomas arrived, and the same communication was again made in a general conversation, in which the Attorney General, Mr. Stanbery, the President, General Thomas, and myself participated.

Question. I wish now you would state whether, either from the President himself, or from the Attorney General in his presence, you received any instructions or suggestions as to the course to be pursued by you in reference to General Thomas's case?

Mr. Manager BUTLER. Stay a moment.

By Mr. CURTIS:

Question. In the first place you may fix, if you please. the hour of the day when this occurred on the 22d?

The WITNESS. The Manager signified to me to stop.

Mr. Manager BUTLER. What date was it?

The WITNESS. The 22d of February.

By Mr. CURTIS:

Question. Now, the hour of the day, as near as you can fix it?

Answer. I think the proceedings before Chief Justice Cartter at chambers took place between ten and half past ten o'clock; to the best of my recollection about ten o'clock. Immediately after they terminated, (and they extended through only a very brief period, for

it was simply to give a bond,) I ordered copies of the papers to be made, and as soon as they were made I took them to the Executive Mansion. I think it occupied probably from thirty minutes to an hour to make the copies, and my impression is that I reached the Executive Mansion by noon.

Question. Now, you can answer the residue of the question, whether you received either from the President himself, or the Attorney General in the presence of the President, any directions or suggestions as to the course to be taken by you as counsel in that case?

Mr. Manager BUTLER. Do you ask now for the conversations?

Mr. CURTIS. I ask for suggestions or directions to this gentleman. I do not go outside of those.

Mr. Manager BUTLER. I think those are conversations, and I do not think they can be put in. This was not employing, as was the other case, a counsel to do anything; but it was giving directions as to how Thomas's counsel should try his case.

Mr. CURTIS. I suppose it depends entirely upon what was said. They might amount to verbal acts, as they are called in the books; and if this gentleman so received and acted upon them I suppose they then pass out of the range of mere talk or declarations. The question is whether he received instructions or suggestions from the President or the Attorney General.

Mr. Manager BUTLER. It will be perceived that the difficulty is this: it is not a mere question of the difference between acts and declarations, although declarations make it a remove further off; but my proposition is that the President's acts in directing General Thomas's counsel to defend General Thomas, his client, not being employed by him, the President, cannot be evidence, whether regarded as acts or as declarations. That is all.

Mr. EVARTS. It does not follow that these instructions were to defend Mr. Thomas. The point of the inquiry is that the instructions were to make investigations in this proceeding whether steps could be taken in behalf of the President. You cannot anticipate what the answer is to be by the objections. We offer to show that the Attorney General, in the presence of the President, after this report of the situation that was opened by the existence of this case of General Thomas, gave certain directions to this gentleman of the profession in reference to grafting upon that case the means of having a *habeas corpus.*

Mr. Manager BUTLER. I do not propose to argue it. The statement of it is enough. General Thomas's lawyer goes to the President; the President has no more right to direct General Thomas's lawyer than he has to direct me; and thereupon they do not offer even the declarations of the President, but they offer now the declarations of the President's lawyer, Attorney General Stanbery, and you are asked

to allow his counsel to put his declarations as part of this defense. If that is allowed to go in no argument on earth can be of any avail.
. The CHIEF JUSTICE. The counsel will please reduce their question to writing.

The offer of proof was reduced to writing and sent to the desk.

The CHIEF JUSTICE. The Secretary will read the question propounded by the counsel for the President.

The Secretary read as follows:

We offer to prove that about the hour of twelve noon, on the 22d of February, upon the first communication to the President of the situation of General Thomas's case, the President, or the Attorney General in his presence, gave the attorneys certain directions as to obtaining a writ of *hobeas corpus* for the purpose of testing judicially the right of Mr. Stanton to continue to hold the office of Secretary of War against the authority of the President.

The CHIEF JUSTICE. The Chief Justice thinks this evidence admissible within the rule already determined by the Senate. He will submit the question to the Senate if any Senator desires it. [After a pause.] The witness may answer the question.

The WITNESS. I should like to have the question read.

Mr. CURTIS. The question is, whether the President, or the Attorney General in his presence, gave you any instructions in respect to proceedings to obtain a writ of *habeas corpus* to test the right of Mr. Stanton to hold the office of Secretary contrary to the will of the President?

Answer. The Attorney General, upon learning from me the situation of the case, asked if it was possible in any way to get it to the Supreme Court immediately. I told him I was not prepared to answer that question. He then said: "Look at it and see whether you can take it up to the Supreme Court immediately upon a *habeas corpus* and have a decision from that tribunal." I told him I would.

Question. Subsequent to this time did you come in communication with any gentleman acting as counsel for the President in reference to this matter, and who was that gentleman, if any?

Mr. JOHNSON. What is the question? We did not hear it.

Mr. CURTIS. The question is, whether, subsequent to this time, he came into communication with any other legal gentleman acting as counsel for the President, and who he was?

Answer. I examined the question as requested by the Attorney General, and on the evening or afternoon of the 22d, and I think within two or three hours after I had seen him, I wrote him a note.

Mr. Manager BUTLER. We will not have the contents of that note unless it is ruled in.

The WITNESS. I paused, sir, that you might object.

By Mr. CURTIS:

Question. Stating the result of that examination?

Answer. Stating the result of that examination.

Mr. Manager BUTLER. Whatever was in that note, you will not state it.

The WITNESS. That was all the contents.

Mr. Manager BUTLER. Nothing will be stated unless the Senate rules it in.

By Mr. CURTIS:

Question. You wrote him a note on this subject?

Answer. I wrote him a note on this subject, and on the following Monday or Tuesday, this being Saturday, I met Mr. Cox, who was the counsel of the President, as I understood, and in consultation with him I communicated to him the conclusions to which I had arrived in the course of my examination on the Saturday previous, and we, having come to the same conclusion, agreed to conduct the case together in harmony with a view of accomplishing the contemplated result of getting it to the Supreme Court on a *habeas corpus.*

Question. State now anything which you and Mr. Cox did for the purpose of accomplishing that result?

Answer. Having formed our plan of proceeding, we went into court on the day on which, according to the bond, General Thomas was to appear before Judge Cartter at chambers.

Mr. JOHNSON. What day was that?

The WITNESS. That was, I think, on Wednesday, the 26th, if I am not mistaken. Shall I state what transpired?

Mr. CURTIS. Yes, so far as it regards your acts.

Mr. Manager BUTLER. I respectfully submit once again, Mr. President, that the acts of General Thomas's counsel under the direction of the Attorney General, after the President was impeached, cannot be put in evidence.

The WITNESS, (to counsel.) Will you allow me to make a correction?

Mr. CURTIS and Mr. EVARTS. Certainly.

The WITNESS. You asked when I next came in contact with any one representing the President. I should have stated that on Tuesday night, by appointment, I had an interview with the Attorney General upon the subject of this case and the proceedings to be taken on the following day.

Mr. Manager BUTLER. I do not see that that alters the question, which I desire may be reduced to writing, if it is ever to be done, before I argue it; because I have argued one or two questions here, and then another question appeared when it came to be reduced to writing.

The CHIEF JUSTICE. The counsel will please reduce their question to writing.

The question was reduced to writing, and read by the Secretary, as follows:

What, if anything, did you and Mr. Cox do in reference to accomplishing the result you have spoken of?

Mr. Manager BUTLER. Does that include what was done in court?

Mr. CURTIS. It includes what was done

by the chief justice as a magistrate or in court, if it is so termed.

Mr. Manager BUTLER. I suppose that that must be termed a court.

Mr. EVARTS. It is the same question which was put to the other witness.

Mr. Manager BUTLER. No; it is another person.

The CHIEF JUSTICE. Does the Manager object to the question as proposed?

Mr. Manager BUTLER. Yes, sir.

The CHIEF JUSTICE. The Chief Justice thinks it is competent, but he will put the question to the Senate if any Senator desires it. [After a pause, to the witness.] Answer the question.

The WITNESS, (to the Secretary.) Read me the question.

The Secretary read the question.

The WITNESS. To answer that question it is necessary that I should state what transpired before the judge at chambers and in court on Wednesday; for all that we did was done to accomplish that result.

Mr. CURTIS. Go on.

The WITNESS. Shall I state it?

Mr. CURTIS. Yes.

Answer. We went into the room in the City Hall in which the criminal court holds its session in the morning. Chief Justice Cartter was then holding the term of the criminal court, and the criminal court was regularly opened. After some business in the criminal court was discharged the chief justice announced that he was ready to hear the case of General Thomas. The question was then suggested whether it was to be heard in chambers or before the court. The chief justice said he would hear it as at chambers, the criminal court not having then been adjourned. The case was thereupon called up. The counsel appearing for Mr. Stanton or for the Government, Messrs. Carpenter and Riddle, moved that the case be continued or postponed until the following day on the ground of the absence of one or two witnesses, I think, and on the additional plea of Mr. Carpenter's indisposition. To that motion, after consultation with my associate, Mr. Cox, and Mr. Joseph H. Bradley, who appeared in person as advisory counsel for General Thomas, I rose and objected to the postponement, stating that I was constrained to object, notwithstanding the plea of personal indisposition, to which I always yielded; but I objected now for the reason that this was a case involving a question of great public interest, which the harmonious action of the Government rendered it necessary should be speedily determined. I elaborated the view. Mr. Carpenter replied, representing that there could be no detriment to the public service, and he earnestly urged the court to a postponement. The chief justice thereupon said—I think he remarked that it was the first time he knew of a case in which the plea of a personal indisposition of counsel was not acceded to by the other side, that it was generally

sufficient, and went on to remark upon the motion further in such a manner that I concluded he would continue the case until the following day; and as soon as we saw that he would continue the case until the following day we brought forward a motion that it be then adjourned from before the chief justice at chambers to the chief justice holding the criminal court. That question was argued by counsel, and overruled by the court.

Mr. JOHNSON. By the court?

The WITNESS. By the judge at chambers, not by the court. I then submitted to the judge——

Mr. Manager BUTLER. Mr. President, I wish it simply understood, that I may clear my skirts of this matter, that this all goes in under our objection, and under the ruling of the presiding officer.

The CHIEF JUSTICE. It goes in under the direction of the Senate of the United States. [To the witness.] Proceed, sir.

The WITNESS. We then announced to the judge that General Thomas's bail had surrendered him, or that he was in custody of the marshal, and the marshal was advancing toward him at the time. I think that Mr. Bradley or Mr. Cox handed me, while on my feet, and while I was making that announcement, the petition for a *habeas corpus*, which, I then presented to the criminal court, which having opened in the morning, had not yet adjourned, and over which Chief Justice Cartter was presiding. I presented the *habeas corpus* to the criminal court.

Mr. CURTIS. The petition?

The WITNESS. The petition for a *habeas corpus* to the criminal court, representing that General Thomas was in custody of the marshal, and asked that it should be heard.

Mr. Manager BUTLER. Was that petition in writing?

The WITNESS. That petition was in writing, I believe. As I said, it was handed to me by one of my associates, and if my recollection serves me aright I have seen the petition since, and it was not signed. When handed to me General Thomas and Mr. Bradley were sitting immediately behind me, and after reading it I laid it down, and I believe it was taken up by some of the reporters and not regained for half an hour.

By Mr. CURTIS:

Question. Well, sir, after you had read it what occurred?

Answer. After I had read it a discussion arose upon the propriety of the petition and the regularity of the time, in regard to the time of its presentation. The counsel upon the other side contended that General Thomas was not in custody, and that it was a remarkable case—I remember that expression, I think, of Mr. Carpenter's—for an accused party to insist upon putting himself in jail or in custody. We contended that he was in custody. The chief justice ruled that he was not in custody at all, and that he did not purpose to put him in custody. The counsel upon the other side further stated that they desired neither that he should be put in custody nor that he should give bond, because they were certain, from his character and position, that he would be here to answer any charge that might be brought against him. The chief justice replied that, in view of the statements made by the counsel, he should neither put him in custody nor demand bond, and was himself satisfied there was no necessity for pursuing either course. We then remarked, "If he is not in custody and not under bond he is discharged." I think some one said, "He is then discharged;" and thereupon, in order that there might be a decision in reference to the alternatives presented of his being placed in custody or discharged upon the record, we moved for his discharge in order to bring up the question officially of his commitment. He was thereupon discharged.

Mr. CURTIS. I believe that is all we wish to examine Mr. Merrick upon.

Cross-examined by Mr. Manager BUTLER:
Question. Were you counsel, Mr. Merrick, for Surratt?
Answer. I was, sir.
Question. Was Mr. Cox?
Answer. He was not.
Question. Was Mr. Bradley, who was advisory counsel in this proceeding?
Answer. He was.
Question. When you got to the Executive Mansion that morning Thomas was not there, you tell us?
Answer. I think not. That is my recollection.
Question. Did you learn whether he had been there?
Answer. I do not recollect whether I did or not. Had I so learned I probably should have recollected it.
Question. Did you not learn that Thomas was then over at the War Department?
Answer. I do not recollect that I did, and think I did not.
Question. Did you not learn when he returned that he had come from the War Department?
Answer. I do not recollect.

Mr. Manager BUTLER. I will not tax your want of recollection any further. [Laughter.]

EDWIN O. PERRIN sworn and examined.
By Mr. EVARTS:
Question. Where do you reside?
Answer. I reside on Long Island, near Jamaica.
Question. How long have you been a resident of that region?
Answer. I have been a resident of Long Island over ten years.
Question. Previous to that time where had you resided?
Answer. Memphis, Tennessee.
Question. Are you personally acquainted with the President of the United States?
Answer. I am.

Question. And for how long a time have you been so personally acquainted with him?
Answer. I knew Mr. Johnson in Tennessee for several years before I left the State, having met him more particularly upon the stump in political campaigns, I being a Whig and he a Democrat.
Question. And has that acquaintance continued until the present time?
Answer. It has.
Question. Were you in the city of Washington in the month of February last?
Answer. I was.
Question. And for what period of time?
Answer. I came here, I think, about the 1st day of February, or near that time, and remained until about the 1st of March or last of February.
Question. During that time were you at a hotel or at a private residence?
Answer. At a private boarding-house.
Question. Did you have an interview with the President of the United States on the 21st of February?
Answer. I did.
Question. Alone, or in company with whom?
Answer. In company with a member of the House of Representatives.
Question. Who was he?
Answer. Mr. SELYE, of Rochester, New York.
Question. How did it happen that you made this visit?

Mr. Manager BUTLER. I pray judgment on that.

Mr. EVARTS. It is merely introductory. It is nothing material. You have no ground to object, as the answer will show.

Mr. Manager BUTLER. Very well.

The WITNESS. Mr. SELYE said that while he knew the President he never had been formally presented to him; and understanding that I was a friend of the President, and well acquainted with him, he asked me if I would not go up with him to the President's and introduce him.

By Mr. EVARTS:
Question. When did this occur?
Answer. On the 20th.
Question. The day before?
Answer. The day before—on the 20th.
Question. Your visit, then, on the 21st was on this inducement?
Answer. I made the appointment for the next day. I informed Mr. SELYE that it was Cabinet day, and it would be no use to go until after two o'clock, as we probably would not be permitted to enter, and appointed two o'clock, at his rooms in Twelfth street, to meet him for that purpose.
Question. You went there, and you took up Mr. SELYE?
Answer. I went to Mr. SELYE'S room. He called a carriage, and we got in and drove to the President's house, a little after two o'clock, or perhaps nearly three. I did not note the hour.

Question. Did you have any difficulty in getting in?

Answer. We had. Mr. Kershaw, the usher at the door, when I handed him Mr. SELYE'S card and mine, said that the President had some of his Cabinet with him yet, and no one would be admitted. I told him I wished that he would go in and say to the President or say to Colonel Moore, with my compliments——

Mr. Manager BUTLER. Excuse me; are you going to put in Colonel Moore?

Mr. EVARTS. It is no matter; we are only getting at the fact how he got in. [To the witness.] Was the fact that Mr. SELYE was a member of Congress mentioned?

Answer. That was mentioned that Mr. SELYE was a member of Congress.

Question. And so you got in?

Answer. And so we got in.

Question. When you went up-stairs; and were you immediately admitted, or otherwise?

Answer. We were up-stairs then when this took place; in the ante-room near the President's reception-room.

Question. Very well; then you went in after awhile?

Answer. Yes, sir; we went in.

Question. Was the President alone when you went in?

Answer. He was alone.

Question. And did you introduce Mr. SELYE?

Answer. I introduced Mr. SELYE.

Question. As a member of Congress?

Answer. As a member of Congress from the Rochester district.

Question. Before this time had you heard that any order for the removal of Mr. Stanton had been made?

Answer. I had heard nothing of it.

Question. Nor had Mr. SELYE, so far as you know?

Answer. He had not. I found him lying down when I got to his room, about two o'clock, and he complained of being unwell.

Question. So far as you know, he had heard nothing of it?

Answer. So far as I know, he had heard nothing of it.

Question. Did you then hear from the President of the removal of Mr. Stanton?

Mr. Manager BUTLER. Stay a moment. We feel it our duty to object to the statement of the President to this person or Mr. SELYE or anybody else, declarations made to parties in the country generally. There can be no end to this kind of evidence; everybody may be brought here. Where are we to stop, if there is to be any stop? If not, the time of the country will be consumed in hearing every conversation between the President and every person that he chooses to introduce.

Mr. EVARTS. If the evidence is proper the time to have considered about the public interest was when the trial was commenced or promoted. We are not to be excluded from a defense because it takes time to put it in. Of course it would be more convenient to stop a cause at the end of the prosecution's case and save the time of the country or of the court. We are reducing to writing our offer.

Mr. Manager BUTLER. The question simply is what was said between the President and Mr. SELYE and Mr. Perrin. That is the question that I had the honor to object to.

Mr. EVARTS. We are reducing it to form in order that it may be passed upon.

The offer, having been reduced to writing, was read by the Secretary, as follows:

We offer to prove that the President then stated that he had issued an order for the removal of Mr. Stanton and the employment of General Thomas to perform the duties *ad interim;* that thereupon Mr. Perrin said "Supposing Mr. Stanton should oppose the order;" the President replied "There is no danger of that, for General Thomas is already in the office." He then added, "It is only a temporary arrangement; I shall send in to the Senate at once a good name for the office."

Mr. Manager BUTLER. I find it, Mr. President and Senators, my duty to object to this. There is no end to declarations of this sort. The admission of those to Sherman and to Thomas was advocated on the ground that the office was tendered to them and that it was a part of the *res gestæ.* This is mere narration, mere statement of what he had done and what he intended to do. It never was evidence and never will be evidence in any organized court, so far as any experience in court has taught me. I do not see why you limit it. If Mr. Perrin, who says that he has heretofore been on the stump, can go there and ask him questions, and the answers can be received, why not anybody else? If Mr. SELYE could go there why not everybody else? Why could he not make declarations to every man, ay, and woman, too, and bring them in here, as to what he intended to do and what he had done to instruct the Senate of the United States in their duties sitting as a high court of impeachment?

Mr. EVARTS. Mr. Chief Justice, I am not aware that the credit of this testimony is at all affected by the fact that Mr. Perrin has been engaged in political canvasses, nor do I suppose that it assists us in determining whether this should be admitted, because a declaration might be made even to a female. The question, then, is, whether the declaration, at this time and under these circumstances, of the President's intent in what he had done was and is proper to be heard.

It will be observed that this was an interview between the President of the United States and a member of Congress, one of "the grand inquest of the nation," holding, therefore, an official duty and having access, by reason of his official privilege, to the person of the President; that at this hour of the day the President was in the attitude of supposing, upon the report of General Thomas, that Mr. Stanton was ready to yield the office, desiring only the time necessary to accommodate his private convenience, and that he then stated to these gentlemen, "I have removed Mr. Stanton and appointed General Thomas *ad interim,*" which was their first intelligence of the occurrence; that upon the suggestion, "Will there not be trouble or difficulty?" the President answered (showing thus the bearing on any question of threats or purpose of force as to be imputed to him from the declarations that General Thomas was making at about the same hour to Mr. Wilkeson) that there was no occasion for or "no danger of that as General Thomas was already in." Then, as to the motive or purpose entertained by the President at the time of this act of providing anybody that should control the War Department or the military appropriations, or by combination with the Treasury Department suck the public funds, or to have, though I regret to repeat the words as used by the honorable Manager, a tool or a slave to carry on the office to the detriment of the public service, we propose to show that at the very moment he asserts, "This is but a temporary arrangement; I shall at once send in a good name for the office to the Senate."

Now, you will perceive that this bears upon the President's condition of purpose in this matter, both in respect to any force as threatened or suggested by anybody else being imputable to him at this time, and upon the question of whether this appointment of General Thomas had any other purpose than what appeared upon its face, a nominal appointment, to raise the question of whether Mr. Stanton would retire or not, and determined, as it seemed to be for the moment, by the acquiescence of Mr. Stanton, was then only to be maintained until a name was sent into the Senate, as by proof hitherto given we have shown was done on the following day before one o'clock.

Mr. JOHNSON. Mr. Chief Justice, I ask that the question be read.

The CHIEF JUSTICE. The proposal of the counsel for the President will be read.

The Secretary read as follows:

We offer to prove that the President then stated that he had issued an order for the removal of Mr. Stanton and the employment of Mr. Thomas to perform the duties *ad interim;* that thereupon Mr. Perrin said, "Supposing Mr. Stanton should oppose the order." The President replied: "There is no danger of that, for General Thomas is already in the office." He then added: "It is only a temporary arrangement; I shall send into the Senate at once a good name for the office."

Mr. Manager WILSON. Mr. President, as this objection is outside of any former ruling of the Senate, and is perfectly within the rule laid down in Hardy's case, I wish to call the attention of the Senate to that rule again, not for the purpose of entering upon any considerable discussion, but to leave this objection under that rule to the decision of the Senate:

"Nothing is so clear as that all declarations which apply to facts, and even apply to the particular case that is charged, though the intent should make a part of that charge, are evidence against a prisoner, and are not evidence for him, because the presump-

tion upon which declarations are evidence is that no man would declare anything against himself unless it were true; but every man, if he was in a difficulty, or in the view to any difficulty, would make declarations for himself."—24 *State Trials,* p. 1096.

If this offer of proof does not come perfectly within that rule then I never met a case within my experience that would come within its provisions. I leave this objection to the decision of the Senate upon that rule.

Mr. EVARTS. It may truly be said, I suppose, Mr. Chief Justice and Senators, that the question now proposed is not entirely covered by any previous ruling of the Senate, because there were circumstances in regard to the attitude of the persons between whom and the President those conferences took place that are not precisely reproduced here in the relation of a member of Congress toward the President. But, Senators, you will perceive that before the controversy arose, and at a time when, in the President's opinion, there was to be no controversy, he made this statement in the course of his proper intercourse with this member of Congress, thus introduced to him, concerning his public action. It is applicable in reference both to the point of why the appointment of General Thomas was made and with what limitation of purpose in so appointing him, and as bearing also upon the question of whether he was using or justifying force. May not declarations that are drawn from supposed coadjutors of his, with a view of fixing upon him the responsibility of the same, be rebutted by his statements at the same period in this open and apparently truthful manner, unconnected with any agitation or any questions of difficulty or any *lis mota?* And then it is important, as bearing upon this precise fact, that the next day having sent in, as we have proved, the nomination of Mr. Ewing, senior, of Ohio, for the place of Secretary of War, to show that that was not a purpose or an act that was formed after the occasion of difficulty or after the appearance of danger or threat to himself; but that at the very moment that he was performing the act of removing Mr. Stanton and appointing General Thomas, and had supposed that it had quietly been acceded to, he then and there had the purpose not of making an appointment of General Thomas that was to hold, which should supersede proper action of the Senate; but at the very moment, having used this necessary appointment for the purpose of testing the question of the Constitution and of the law, he then proposed to send to the Senate of the United States a nomination for the office.

Mr. Manager BUTLER. Mr. President, there are one or two new facts now put in, or pretended facts, upon which this evidence is pressed. The more material one is that this was before any controversy arose between the President and Congress upon the subject of Mr. Stanton. If that were so, then it might possibly have some color of a shadow of a shade of bearing. But had there not been a controversy going on? Had he not known that the Senate had restored Mr. Stanton? Had he not tried to get him out and had they not put him back? Had he not been beseeching and beseeching General Sherman to take the office weeks, ay, months before, and had not General Sherman told him, "I cannot take it without getting into difficulty; there will be trouble; why mix me, an Army officer, up in this trouble?" And yet the President's counsel rise here in their place and put this evidence before us, because it was his declaration before any controversy arose or was likely to arise!

Another proposition is put in here, and that is that this must be evidence because it was said to a member of Congress. I am aware that we have many rights, privileges, and appurtenances belonging to our official position, but I never was aware before that one of them was that what was said to us was evidence because it was said to us by anybody. I have had a great many things said to me that I should be very unwilling to have regarded as evidence. For instance, here is a written declaration sent to me to-day. "Butler, prepare to meet your God." [Laughter.] "The avenger is abroad on your track." "Hell is your portion." [Laughter.] Now, I trust that is not evidence because it is said to a member of Congress. And yet it is just as pertinent, just as competent, in my judgment, as this declaration. We are to have these kinds of declarations made to us by the enemies of the country, and we are to sit here and admit the President's declarations in justification of his conduct, which brings out such a condition of this country.

I did not mean by any manner of means when I was up before to suggest that the fact of this being made to a gentleman who is on the stump would make it more or less competent; only to show that so far as the evidence goes, so far as they choose to put in his profession, it is utterly outside of this case. I do not think it would make it more or less evidence because it should have been made to a woman, I was only foreseeing what might come—quite as probable as this—that some of the lady friends—I beg pardon the woman friends of the President might have gone to the White House on that day and he might have told them what his purpose was. It would be just as much evidence, in my judgment, as this; and it was only in that view, to show the innumerableness of the persons to whom these competent declarations could be made, that I brought up the illustration which produced the answer on the part of the learned counsel.

Mr. EVARTS. The *lis mota*, Mr. Chief Justice and Senators, so far as it has been alluded to as bringing discredit upon the President's statements is the controversy between Congress and himself in regard to the removal of Mr. Stanton. What political differences there are or may have been between the President and the Houses of Congress, it is of no consequence to inquire, nor is it of the least consequence to inquire into the period during which the suspension of Mr. Stanton had taken place, for that certainly was within any view of the law that can be suggested. I referred, therefore, as has often been referred, to the controversy produced by the threat of the House and its very prompt execution of impeachment; and that had not occurred in any point to ask the President's attention at the moment of this statement. It was therefore a statement by him unaffected by any such considerations as those.

The CHIEF JUSTICE. Senators, the Chief Justice is unable to determine the precise extent to which the Senate regards its own decision as applicable. He has understood the decision to be that, for the purpose of showing intent, evidence may be given of conversations with the President at or near the time of the transaction. It is said that this evidence is distinguishable from that which has been already introduced. The Chief Justice is not able to to distinguish it; but he will submit directly to the Senate the question whether it is admissible or not.

Mr. CONNESS. I ask for the yeas and nays on that question.

The yeas and were ordered.

The question being taken by yeas and nays, resulted—yeas 9, nays 37; as follows:

YEAS—Messrs. Bayard, Buckalew, Davis, Dixon, Doolittle, Hendricks, McCreery, Patterson of Tennessee, and Vickers—9.

NAYS—Messrs. Cameron, Cattell, Chandler, Conkling, Conness, Corbett, Cragin, Drake, Ferry, Fessenden, Fowler, Frelinghuysen, Grimes, Harlan, Howard, Howe, Johnson, Morgan, Morrill of Maine, Morrill of Vermont, Morton, Nye, Patterson of New Hampshire, Pomeroy, Ramsey, Ross, Sherman, Sprague, Stewart, Thayer, Tipton, Trumbull, Van Winkle, Willey, Williams, Wilson, and Yates—37.

NOT VOTING.—Messrs. Anthony, Cole, Edmunds, Henderson, Norton, Saulsbury, Sumner, and Wade—8.

So the Senate decided the question to be inadmissible.

Mr. EVARTS. This evidence being excluded, we have no other questions to ask of the witness.

Mr. Manager BUTLER. We have none, sir.

Mr. EVARTS. We have reached a point, Mr. Chief Justice and Senators, at which it will be convenient to us that we should not be required to produce more evidence to-day.

Mr. Manager BUTLER. Mr. President, I hope upon this movement for delay the President's counsel will be called upon to go on with their case, and I have only to put to them the exact thing that the President's counsel, Cox and Mr. Merrick, used in the case of General Thomas before the criminal court of this District, according to Merrick's testimony. It is always ungracious to object to delay because of the sickness of counsel. We should have been glad to have Mr. Stanbery here, but these gentlemen present can try this case.

There are four of them. When a motion to postpone the case of Thomas before Chief Justice Cartter was made to postpone the case because of the sickness of Mr. Carpenter, for a single day, the President's counsel, arguing his case, trying his case before the court said "No; a case involving so much of public administration cannot wait for the sickness of counsel." "I thank thee, Jew, for teaching me that word." The President's counsel there well told us what we ought to do. In the case of Mr. Thomas the President could not wait for sick men or sick women. The case must go through. We cannot wait now, on the same ground, for the sickness of the learned Attorney General; and why should we? Why should not this President be called upon now to go on? We have been here thirty-three working days since the President actually filed his answer, and we, the Managers, have used but six days of them, and the counsel but part of seven. Twenty-one of them have been given to delays on motion of the President, and there have been four adjournments on the days we have worked earlier than the usual time of adjournment, in order to accommodate the President.

Now, the whole legislation of this country is stopping; the House of Representatives has to be, day by day, here at your bar. The taxes of the country cannot be revised because this trial is in the way. The appropriations for carrying on the Government cannot be passed because this trial is in the way. Nothing can be done, and the whole country waits upon us and our action, and it is not time now for the exhibitions of courtesy. Larger, higher, greater interests are at stake than such questions of ceremony. Far be it from me not to desire to be courteous, and not to desire that we should have our absent and sick friend here to take part with us; but the interests of the people are greater than the interests of any one individual. Gentlemen of the Senate, this is the closing up of a war wherein three hundred thousand men laid down their lives to save the country. In one day we sacrificed them by tens and twenties of thousands on the field of battle, and shall the country wait now in its march to safety because of the sickness of one man and pause for an indefinite time, because the duration of sickness is always indefinite? More than that, I have here in my hand testimony of what is going on this day and this hour in the South.

Mr. CURTIS. We object to the introduction of any testimony.

Mr. EVARTS. We object to the relevancy of it here.

Mr. Manager BUTLER. The relevancy of it is this, that while we are waiting for the Attorney General to get well, and you are asked to delay this trial for that reason, numbers of our fellow-citizens are being murdered day by day. There is not a man here who does not know that the moment justice is done on this great criminal these murders will cease.

Mr. CURTIS rose.

Mr. Manager BUTLER. I cannot be interrupted. This is the great fact which stands here before us, and we are asked "Why stand ye here idle?" by every true man in the country. Mr. Chief Justice, in Alabama your register of bankruptcy, appointed by yourself, General Spencer, of Tuscaloosa, is driven to-day from his duties and his home by the Ku-Klux-Klan, upon fear of his life, and I have the evidence of it lying on our table; and shall we here delay this trial any longer, under our responsibility to our countrymen, to our consciences, and to our God, because of a question of courtesy? While we are being courteous, the true Union men of the South are being murdered, and on our heads and on our skirts is this blood, if we remain any longer idle.

Again, sir, since you have begun this trial—I hold the sworn evidence of what I say in my hand—since the 20th day of February last and up to the 4th day of this present April—and no gold had been sold by the Treasury prior to that time since December 12—$10,800,-000 of your gold has been sold at a sacrifice to your Treasury, and by whom? More than one-half of it, $5,600,000, by one McGinnis, whom the Senate would not permit to hold office, and over ten thousand dollars in currency, of which I have the official evidence here, under the sworn oath of the Assistant Treasurer at New York, has been paid to him, after the Senate had refused to have him hold any office and had rejected him as a minister to Sweden. He now takes charge of the sale of your gold by order of the Executive, as a broker, and we are to wait day by day while he puts into his pocket, from the Treasury of the country, money by the thousands, because this gold is sold from one and one eighth per cent. to three per cent. lower than the market rates at different dates, as taken from the best tables. The commissions alone amount to what I have said, supposing the gold to be sold honestly by this rejected diplomat.

Worse still, sir; I have here from the same source the fact that since the 1st day of January last there have been bought in the city of New York alone, on behalf of the Treasury, $27,058,100 of the bonds of the United States, by men who return them from three eighths, one half, five eighths to three quarters above the market price, and since February 20, $14,181,600 worth.

Mr. Manager LOGAN. Below.

Mr. Manager BUTLER. No; I mean what I say, above. I never make mistakes in such matters. I know what I say. From the 3d of January to the 28th of January, by such purchases, the price of bonds was run up and the people were made to pay that difference—run up from one hundred and four and three quarters to one hundred and eight per cent., and still the purchases went on, and they have gone on from that of February down to the 4th of April, when the Managers of impeachment on the part of the House of Representatives felt it their duty to take this testimony of the Assistant Treasurer at New York under oath, and the result of it I here lay in detail before you:

Sales of Gold from January 1, 1868, *to April* 4, 1868, *inclusive.*

Date.	By whom sold.	Amount.	Rate.	Commission.	Quotations from Hunt's Merchants' Magazine.	
					Highest.	Closing.
February 20, 1868...	Jay Cooke & Co..........	$200,000	140¼	$250 00	40¼	40⅜
February 21, 1868...	P. M. Meyers & Co..........	100,000	140⅝	-	41¼	41⅛
February 21, 1868...	P. M. Meyers & Co..........	100,000	140¾	-	-	-
February 21, 1868...	P. M. Meyers & Co..........	50,000	141⅛	-	-	-
February 21, 1868...	P. M. Meyers & Co..........	150,000	141	-	-	-
February 21, 1868...	P. M. Meyers & Co..........	100,000	141⅜	625 00	-	-
February 26, 1868...	P. M. Meyers & Co..........	100,000	141⅛	-	41⅜	41⅛
February 26, 1868...	P. M. Meyers & Co..........	120,000	141⅛	-	-	-
February 26, 1868...	P. M. Meyers & Co..........	30,000	141¼	312 50	-	-
March 10, 1868..........	McGinnis Brothers & Smith..........	200,000	140½	250 00	140⅜	39⅞
March 11, 1868..........	P. M. Meyers & Co..........	100,000	139⅞	125 00	39¾	39⅛
March 12, 1868..........	McGinnis Brothers & Smith..........	100,000	140	125 00	40⅛	39⅞
March 14, 1868..........	P. M. Meyers & Co..........	100,000	139⅛	125 00	39⅜	39¼
March 14, 1868..........	McGinnis Brothers & Smith..........	200,000	139¼	-	-	-
March 14, 1868..........	McGinnis Brothers & Smith..........	50,000	139	312 50	-	-
March 16, 1868..........	P. M. Meyers & Co..........	65,000	139⅜	-	39⅞	39¼
March 16, 1868..........	P. M. Meyers & Co..........	35,000	139⅛	-	-	-
March 16, 1868..........	P. M. Meyers & Co..........	40,000	139¾	-	-	-
March 16, 1868..........	P. M. Meyers & Co..........	60,000	139⅜	250 00	-	-
March 16, 1868..........	McGinnis Brothers & Smith..........	100,000	139½	-	-	-
March 16, 1868..........	....	100,000	139⅜	250 00	-	-
March 18, 1868..........	P. M. Meyers & Co..........	100,000	138½	125 00	38⅞	38⅜
March 18, 1868..........	McGinnis Brothers & Smith..........	80,000	138½	-	-	-
March 18, 1868..........	....	120,000	138⅜	250 00	-	-
March 19, 1868..........	McGinnis Brothers & Smith..........	95,000	138¾	-	38¾	38½
March 19, 1868..........	McGinnis Brothers & Smith..........	105,000	138½	-	-	-
March 19, 1868..........	McGinnis Brothers & Smith..........	100,000	138⅝	375 00	-	-
March 19, 1868..........	P. M. Meyers & Co..........	25,000	138¾	-	-	-
March 19, 1868..........	P. M. Meyers & Co..........	75,000	138¼	-	-	-
March 19, 1868..........	P. M. Meyers & Co..........	100,000	138⅜	250 00	-	-
March 20, 1868..........	Jay Cooke & Co..........	100,000	138⅝	125 00	38¾	38¾
March 20, 1868..........	P. M. Meyers & Co..........	200,000	138⅞	250 00	-	-
March 20, 1868..........	McGinnis Brothers & Smith..........	50,000	138¼	-	-	-
March 20, 1868..........	McGinnis Brothers & Smith..........	150,000	138⅜	-	-	-
March 20, 1868..........	McGinnis Brothers & Smith..........	100,000	138⅝	375 00	-	-
March 21, 1868..........	McGinnis Brothers & Smith..........	200,000	138⅞	-	39⅜	39¼
March 21, 1868..........	McGinnis Brothers & Smith..........	100,000	139	375 00	-	-
March 21, 1868..........	P. M. Meyers & Co..........	100,000	138⅞	-	-	-
March 21, 1868..........	P. M. Meyers & Co..........	100,000	138¾	250 00	-	-
March 21, 1868..........	Jay Cooke & Co..........	50,000	139⅛	-	-	-
March 21, 1868..........	Jay Cooke & Co..........	50,000	139⅛	125 00	-	-
March 23, 1868..........	McGinnis Brothers & Smith..........	100,000	139½	125 00	39½	38¾
March 23, 1868..........	Jay Cooke & Co..........	100,000	138¼	125 00	-	-
March 24, 1868..........	P. M. Meyers & Co..........	50,000	138⅛	-	-	-
March 24, 1868..........	P. M. Meyers & Co..........	50,000	138¼	125 00	38⅜	38
March 24, 1868..........	McGinnis Brothers & Smith..........	175,000	138¼	-	-	-
March 24, 1868..........	McGinnis Brothers & Smith..........	25,000	138⅛	250 00	-	-
March 24, 1868..........	P. M. Meyers & Co..........	100,000	138⅛	125 00	-	-
March 25, 1868..........	McGinnis Brothers & Smith..........	100,000	138⅛	-	38¾	38⅜
March 25, 1868..........	McGinnis Brothers & Smith..........	100,000	138⅜	-	-	-
March 25, 1868..........	McGinnis Brothers & Smith..........	60,000	138¾	-	-	-
March 25, 1868..........	McGinnis Brothers & Smith..........	40,000	138¼	375 00	-	-
March 26, 1868..........	McGinnis Brothers & Smith..........	400,000	138⅜	500 00	38½	38⅜
March 26, 1868..........	P. M. Meyers & Co..........	300,000	138⅜	375 00	-	-
March 27, 1868..........	Jay Cooke & Co..........	200,000	138½	250 00	38⅝	38⅜
March 27, 1868..........	McGinnis Brothers & Smith..........	190,000	138¼	-	-	-
March 27, 1868..........	McGinnis Brothers & Smith..........	10,000	138⅛	-	-	-
March 27, 1868..........	McGinnis Brothers & Smith..........	50,000	138½	-	-	-
March 27, 1868..........	McGinnis Brothers & Smith..........	150,000	138⅝	500 00	-	-
March 27, 1868..........	P. M. Meyers & Co..........	100,000	138⅜	-	-	-
March 27, 1868..........	P. M. Meyers & Co..........	300,000	138¼	500 00	-	-
March 28, 1868..........	McGinnis Brothers & Smith..........	300,000	138½	-	38⅝	38⅝
March 28, 1868..........	McGinnis Brothers & Smith..........	200,000	138⅜	-	-	-
March 28, 1868..........	McGinnis Brothers & Smith..........	100,000	138¾	-	-	-
March 28, 1868..........	McGinnis Brothers & Smith..........	100,000	138⅞	875 00	-	-
March 28, 1868..........	Jay Cooke & Co..........	100,000	138⅞	125 00	-	-
March 28, 1868..........	P. M. Meyers & Co..........	50,000	138⅝	-	-	-
March 28, 1868..........	P. M. Meyers & Co..........	250,000	138⅛	375 00	-	-
March 28, 1868..........	P. M. Meyers & Co..........	50,000	139	-	-	-
March 28, 1868..........	....	50,000	138⅞	125 00	-	-
	Carried forward..........	$7,900,000				

STATEMENT—Continued.

Date.	By whom sold.	Amount.	Rate.	Commission.*	Quotations from Hunt's Merchants' Magazine.	
					Highest.	Closing.
	Brought forward	$7,900,000				
March 30, 1868	McGinnis Brothers & Smith	300,000	139	-	39⅞	38¾
March 30, 1868	McGinnis Brothers & Smith	100,000	138⅞	500 00	-	-
March 30, 1868	Jay Cooke & Co	100,000	138½	125 00	-	-
March 31, 1868	P. M. Meyers & Co	135,000	138½	-	38¾	38⅝
March 31, 1868	P. M. Meyers & Co	40,000	138⅝	-	-	-
March 31, 1868	P. M. Meyers & Co	25,000	138¾	250 00	-	-
March 31, 1868	McGinnis Brothers & Smith	85,000	138⅝	-	-	-
March 31, 1868	McGinnis Brothers & Smith	115,000	138½	-	-	-
March 31, 1868	McGinnis Brothers & Smith	100,000	138⅝	375 00	-	-
April 1, 1868	McGinnis Brothers & Smith	100,000	138½	-	-	-
April 1, 1868	McGinnis Brothers & Smith	100,000	138¾	250 00	-	-
April 1, 1868	P. M. Meyers & Co	100,000	138½	125 00	-	-
April 2, 1868	P. M. Meyers & Co	200,000	138	250 00	-	-
April 2, 1868	McGinnis Brothers & Smith	200,000	138	250 00	-	-
April 3, 1868	McGinnis Brothers & Smith	200,000	138	250 00	-	-
April 3, 1868	Jay Cooke & Co	100,000	138	125 00	-	-
April 3, 1868	P. M. Meyers & Co	100,000	138⅛	125 00	-	-
April 4, 1868	P. M. Meyers & Co	250,000	138¼	312 50	-	-
April 4, 1868	McGinnis Brothers & Smith	250,000	138¼	312 50	-	-
April 4, 1868	Fisk & Hatch	300,000	138¼	*	-	-
		$10,800,000				

*Sold direct without commission.

UNITED STATES TREASURY, NEW YORK, *April* 7, 1868.

I certify the accompanying statement to be a correct transcript from the books of this Department.

H. H. VAN DYCK, *Assistant Treasurer.*

NOTE.—Quotations not certified by Mr. Van Dyck.

Purchases of Seven-Thirty Notes.

Date.	Of whom purchased.	Amount.	Rate.
1868.			
January 3	Vermilye & Co	$250,000	104¾
January 6	Jay Cooke & Co	250,000	104¾
January 8	Vermilye & Co	250,000	104¾
January 11	Fisk & Hatch	200,000	105⅜
January 11	Vermilye & Co	300,000	105⅛
January 13	Vermilye & Co	300,000	105¼
January 15	P. M. Myers & Co	999,500	105⅞
January 16	Vermilye & Co	250,000	105¼
January 17	Jay Cooke & Co	500,000	105¾
January 17	Fisk & Hatch	200,000	105¾
January 17	H. A. Heiser's Sons	27,000	105⅜
January 17	Vermilye & Co	250,000	105¼
January 17	P. M. Myers & Co	300,000	105⅞
January 18	Rodman, Fisk & Co	100,000	105½
January 20	Jay Cooke & Co	250,000	105⅞
January 20	Hatch, Foote & Co	100,000	105½
January 21	T. S. Quackenbush	50,000	105⅞
January 21	Vermilye & Co	400,000	105⅞
January 21	Edward Sweet & Co	100,000	105⅞
January 21	Fisk & Hatch	250,000	106
January 24	Jay Cooke & Co	500,000	107
January 27	Fisk & Hatch	500,000	107⅜
January 28	Jay Cooke & Co	350,000	108
January 28	Rodman, Fisk & Co	300,000	108
January 29	Vermilye & Co	500,000	107¾
January 30	Vermilye & Co	200,000	107¾
January 30	Vermilye & Co	200,000	107½
January 31	Fisk & Hatch	2,500,000	107¾
January 31	Jay Cook & Co	2,000,000	107¾
January 31	Vermilye & Co	500,000	107¾
Feb'y 20	Rodman, Fisk & Co	5,400	107½
Feb'y 20	White, Morris & Co	50,000	107½
Feb'y 21	Fisk & Hatch	300,000	107½
	Carried forward	$13,231,900	
1868.	Brought forward	$13,231,900	
Feb'y 21	Vermilye & Co	600,000	107½
Feb'y 21	P. V. Myers & Co	100,000	107⅛
Feb'y 24	Vermilye & Co	300,000	107⅜
Feb'y 24	Jay Cooke & Co	250,000	107⅜
Feb'y 24	Vermilye & Co	300,000	107¼
Feb'y 24	Jay Cooke & Co	250,000	107¼
Feb'y 25	Jay Cooke & Co	300,000	107¼
Feb'y 25	Vermilye & Co	200,000	107⅛
Feb'y 25	Vermilye & Co	300,000	107
Feb'y 25	Jay Cooke & Co	200,000	107
Feb'y 26	Jay Cooke & Co	500,000	106⅞
Feb'y 26	Vermilye & Co	250,000	106⅞
Feb'y 26	Vermilye & Co	250,000	106¾
Feb'y 26	Fisk & Hatch	200,000	106¾
March 18	Fisk & Hatch	1,000,000	105¾
March 18	Jay Cooke & Co	200,000	105¾
March 19	Vermilye & Co	300,000	105¾
March 19	First National Bank	200,000	105¾
March 19	Rodman, Fisk & Co	30,000	105¾
March 20	Central National B'k	100,000	105¾
March 24	Frank & Gantz	300,000	105¾
March 24	First National Bank	98,600	105½
March 24	Hatch, Foote & Co	200,000	105½
March 24	Smith, Randolph & Co	50,000	105½
March 24	Fisk & Hatch	250,000	105½
March 24	H. A. Heiser's Sons	17,500	105½
March 25	H. A. Heiser's Sons	350,000	105½
March 25	Fisk & Hatch	300,000	105½
March 25	Vermilye & Co	500,000	105½
March 26	Smith, Randolph & Co	100,000	105½
March 26	First National Bank	50,000	105½
	Carried forward	$21,278,000	

STATEMENT—Continued.

Date.	Of whom purchased.	Amount.	Rate.
1868.	Brought forward...	$21,278,000	
March 26...	Rodman, Fisk & Co...	26,600	105½
March 26...	Fisk & Hatch............	300,000	105½
March 31...	Rodman, Fisk & Co...	50,000	105½
March 31...	H. A. Heiser's Sons...	300,000	105¾
March 31...	Hatch, Foote & Co.....	250,000	105¾
March 31...	H. Clews & Co...........	12,100	105¾
March 31...	Lounsbury & Fanshaw.....................	50,000	105¾
March 31...	Vermilye & Co..........	300,000	105¾
March 31...	Jay Cooke & Co.........	300,000	105⅞
April 1.......	Smith, Randolph & Co........................	100,000	105⅞
April 1.......	First National Bank of Brooklyn...........	50,000	105¾
April 1.......	Mechanics' Bank......	50,000	105¾
April 1.......	Dorr Russell..............	15,000	105¾
April 1.......	H. A. Heiser's Sons...	67,000	105¾
April 1.......	Vermilye & Co...........	250,000	105¾
April 1.......	Fisk & Hatch.............	300,000	105¾
April 2.......	Jay Cooke & Co.........	300,000	105¾
April 2.......	Torrey, Gidding & Torrey....................	40,000	105¾
April 2.......	Smith, Randolph & Co........................	50,000	105¾
April 2.......	Central National B'k..	25,000	105¾
April 2.......	Frank & Gantz..........	100,000	105¾
April 2.......	Drexel, Winthrop & Co........................	50,000	105¾
April 2.......	Fisk & Hatch...........	200,000	105¾
April 2.......	Hatch, Foote & Co.....	200,000	105¾
April 2.......	Phœnix Bank............	100,000	105¾
April 2.......	Rodman, Fisk & Co...	175,000	105¾
April 2.......	Ocean Bank..............	100,000	105¾
April 2.......	H. A. Heiser's Sons...	300,000	105¾
April 2.......	Trademan's Bank......	50,000	105¾
April 2.......	P. M. Meyers & Co....	55,000	105¾
April 2.......	J. L. Brownell & Co...	50,000	105¾
April 2.......	Stone & Downer........	55,000	105¾
April 3.......	Vermilye & Co...........	250,000	105¾
April 3.......	Jay Cook & Co...........	300,000	105¾
April 3.......	Lockwood & Co.........	560,000	105¾
April 3.......	Newton, Russell & Co	25,000	105¾
April 3.......	Howes & Macy...........	5,000	105¾
April 3.......	Fisk & Hatch............	250,000	105¾
April 3.......	Central National B'k..	10,000	105¾
April 3.......	Hatch, Foote & Co.....	25,000	105¾
April 3.......	Baker & Kitchen.......	34,000	105¾
April 3.......	Rodman, Fisk & Co...	35,000	105¾
April 4.......	Rodman, Fisk & Co...	25,000	105¾
April 4.......	Ninth National B'k...	50,000	105¾
Total.......	....	$27,058,100	

OFFICE OF ASSISTANT TREASURER UNITED STATES, NEW YORK, *April* 6, 1868.

H. H. VAN DYCK, *Assistant Treasurer.*

Now, I say, for the safety of the finances of the people, for the progress of the legislation of the people, for the safety of the true and loyal men, black and white, in the South who have periled their lives for four years; yea, five years; yea, six years; yea, seven years, in your behalf for the good of the country, for all that is dear to any man and patriot, I pray let this trial proceed; let us come to a determination of this issue. If the President of the United States goes free and acquit, then the country must deal with that state of facts as it arises; but if he, as the House of Representatives instructs me, and as I believe, is guilty; if on his head rests the responsibility; if from his policy, from his obstruction of the peace of the country, all this corruption and all these murders come, in the name of Heaven let us have an end of them and see to it that we can sit at least four hours a day to attend to this the great business of the people.

Sir, it may be supposed here that I am mistaken as to time wasted; but let us see; let me give you day and date. The articles of impeachment were presented on March 4, and the summons was returnable March 13, at which time the President, by its terms, was requested to answer. Delay was given, on his application for forty days, to the 23d—ten days, when the answer was filed, and a motion was made for thirty days' delay, which failed. Then a motion for a reasonable time after replication was filed, which was done on the 24th. Time was given, on motion of the President's counsel, until the 30th—six days. On that day the Managers opened their case, and proceeded without delay with their evidence till April 4—six days. Then, at the request of President's counsel, adjourned to April 9—five days. Mr. Curtis opened a part of a day, and asked for an adjournment till the 10th, wherein we lost half a day. They continued putting in evidence till the 11th (12th being Sunday) and 13th. Because of sickness, adjourned again over till Wednesday, 14th. Wednesday adjourned early, because counsel could go no further. Thursday, now another motion to adjourn, because counsel cannot go on. Thirty-four days since the President filed his answer; six days used by the Managers in putting in their case; parts of seven used by the counsel for the President, and twenty-one given as delay to the President on his motion.

I do not speak of all this to complain of the Senate, but only that you and the country may see exactly how courteous and how kind you have been to the criminal and to his counsel. Yielding to the request of the counsel who opened you lost half a day. Then the opening consumed parts of two days. On the next day they said they were not quite ready to go through with General Sherman, and you again adjourned earlier than usual. Then we lost almost all of Monday in discussing the questions which were raised. We adjourned early on Monday, as you remember, and on the next day there was an adjournment almost immediately after the Senate met, because of the learned Attorney General. Now, all we ask is that this case may go on.

If it be said that we are hard in our demands that this trial go on, let me contrast for a moment this case with a great State trial in England, at which were present Lord Chief Justice Eyre, Lord Chief Baron McDonald, Baron Hotham, Mr. Justice Buller, Sir Nash Grose, Mr. Justice Lawrence, and others of her majesty's judges in the trial of Thomas Hardy for treason. There the court sat from nine o'clock in the morning until one o'clock at night, and they thus sat there from Tuesday until Friday night at one o'clock, and then, when Mr. Erskine, afterward Lord Chancellor Erskine, asked of that court that they would not come in so early by an hour the next day because he was unwell and wanted time, the court after argument refused it, and would not give him even that hour in which to reflect upon his opening which he was to make, and which occupied nine hours in its delivery, until the jury asked it, and then they gave him but a single hour, although he said upon his honor to the court that every night he had not got to his house until between two and three o'clock in the morning, and he was regularly in court at nine o'clock on the following morning.

That is the way cases of great consequence are tried in England. That is the way other courts sit. I am not complaining here, Senators, understand me. I am only contrasting the delays given, the kindnesses shown, the courtesies extended in this greatest of all cases, and where the greatest interests are at stake, compared with every other case ever tried elsewhere. The Managers are ready. We have been ready; at all hazards and sacrifices we would be ready. We only ask that now the counsel for the President shall be likewise ready, and go on without these interminable delays with which, when the House began this impeachment, the friends of the President there rose up and threatened. You will find such threats in the Globe. Mr. JAMES BROOKS, of New York, said, in substance, "You can go on with your impeachment, but I warn you that we will make you go through all the forms, and if you go through all the forms we will keep it going until the end of Mr. Johnson's term, and it will be fruitless." Having thus threatened you, Senators, I had supposed that you would not allow the threat to be carried out, as it is attempted to be carried out, by these continued delays.

Mr. President and Senators, I have thus given you the reasons pressing upon my mind why this delay should not be had; and I admit I have done it with considerable warmth, because I feel warmly. I open no mail of mine that I do not take up an account from the South of some murder or worse of some friend of the country. I want these things to stop. Many a man whom I have known standing by my side for the Union I can hear of now only as laid in the cold grave by the assassin's hand. This has stirred my feelings, I admit. The loss of my friends, the loss to the country of those who have stood by it, has, perhaps, very much stirred my heart, so that I have not been able with that coolness with which judicial proceedings should be carried on to address you upon this agonizing topic. I say nothing of the threats of assassination made every hour and upon every occasion, even when objection to testimony is made by the Managers. I say nothing of the threats made against the lives of the great officers of the Senate and against the Managers. We are all free. There is an old Scotch proverb in our favor: "The threatened dog a' lives the longest." We have not the slightest fear

of these cowardly menaces; but all these threats, these unseemly libels on our former government will go away when this man goes out of the White House.

Mr. CONNESS. Mr. President, I offer the following order:

Ordered, That on each day hereafter the Senate, sitting as a court of impeachment, shall meet at eleven o'clock a. m.

Mr. SUMNER. I send to the Chair a substitute for that order.

The CHIEF JUSTICE. The Secretary will read the substitute proposed by the Senator from Massachusetts.

The Secretary read as follows:

That, considering the public interests which suffer from the delay of this trial, and in pursuance of the order already adopted to proceed with all convenient dispatch, the Senate will sit from ten o'clock in the forenoon to six o'clock in the afternoon, with such brief recess as may be ordered.

Mr. TRUMBULL. I rise to a question of order, whether it is in order to consider these propositions to-day under the ruling of the Chair.

The CHIEF JUSTICE. They are not in order if anybody objects.

Mr. TRUMBULL. I object to their consideration.

The CHIEF JUSTICE. They will go over until to-morrow.

Mr. EVARTS. Mr. Chief Justice and Senators, I am not aware how much of the address of the honorable Manager is appropriate to anything that has proceeded from me. I, at the opening of the court this morning, stated how we might be situated, and added that when that point of time arrived I should submit the matter to the discretion of the Senate. I have never heard such a harangue before in a court of justice; but I cannot say that I may not hear it again in this court. All these delays and the ill consequences seem to press upon the honorable Managers except at the precise point of time when some of their mouths are open occupying your attention with their long harangues. If you will look at the reports of the discussions on questions of evidence, as they appear in the newspapers, while all that we have to say is embraced within the briefest paragraphs, long columns are taken up with the views of the learned Managers, and hour after hour is taken up with debates on the production of our evidence by these prolonged discussions, and now twenty minutes by the watch with this harangue of the honorable Manager about the Ku-Klux-Klan. I have said what I have said to the Senate.

Mr. CAMERON. Mr. President, I should like to inquire whether the word "harangue" be in order here?

Mr. Manager BUTLER. So far as I am concerned it is of no consequence.

Mr. DOOLITTLE. Mr. Chief Justice, I should like to know whether the harangue itself was in order, not the word?

Mr. FERRY. Mr. President, I move that the Senate, sitting as a court of impeachment, adjourn.

Mr. SUMNER. I move that the adjournment be until ten o'clock.

Mr. TRUMBULL. That is not in order.

The CHIEF JUSTICE. It is not in order. The motion to adjourn is, under the rule, to the usual time.

Mr. SUMNER. On that I ask for the yeas and nays.

The yeas and nays were not ordered.

The motion was agreed to; and the Senate, sitting for the trial of the impeachment, adjourned until to-morrow at twelve o'clock.

FRIDAY, *April* 17, 1868.

The Chief Justice of the United States took the chair.

The usual proclamation having been made by the Sergeant-at-Arms,

The Managers of the impeachment on the part of the House of Representatives, and the counsel for the respondent, except Mr. Stanbery, appeared and took the seats assigned them respectively.

The members of the House of Representatives, as in Committee of the Whole, preceded by Mr. E. B. WASHBURNE, chairman of that committee, and accompanied by the Speaker and Clerk, appeared and were conducted to the seats provided for them.

The CHIEF JUSTICE. The Secretary will read the Journal of yesterday's proceedings.

Mr. STEWART. I move that the reading of the Journal be dispensed with.

The CHIEF JUSTICE. If there be no objection it will be so ordered. The Chair hears none. It is so ordered. During the sitting of yesterday the Senator from California [Mr. CONNESS] offered an order that the Senate, sitting as a court of impeachment, meet hereafter at eleven o'clock a. m. That will be before the Senate unless objected to. The Secretary will read the order.

The Secretary read as follows:

Ordered, That on each day hereafter the Senate, sitting as a court of impeachment, shall meet at eleven o'clock a. m.

The CHIEF JUSTICE. Does the Senator from Massachusetts desire to offer his amendment?

Mr. SUMNER. I did offer it, Mr. President, yesterday.

The CHIEF JUSTICE. The amendment offered by the Senator from Massachusetts will be read.

The Secretary read the amendment, as follows:

Strike out all after the word "ordered" and insert:

That considering the public interests which suffer from the delay of this trial, and in pursuance of the order already adopted to proceed with all convenient dispatch, the Senate will sit from ten o'clock in the forenoon to six o'clock in the afternoon, with such brief recess as may be ordered.

C. I.—28.

Mr. SUMNER. On that I should like to have the yeas and nays.

The yeas and nays were ordered; and being taken, resulted—yeas 13, nays 30; as follows:

YEAS—Messrs. Cameron, Chandler, Cole, Corbett, Harlan, Morrill of Maine, Pomeroy, Ramsey, Stewart, Sumner, Thayer, Tipton, and Yates—13.

NAYS—Messrs. Anthony, Cattell, Conness, Davis, Dixon, Doolittle, Drake, Ferry, Fessenden, Fowler, Frelinghuysen, Grimes, Hendricks, Howard, Howe, Johnson, Morgan, Morrill of Vermont, Morton, Patterson of New Hampshire, Patterson of Tennessee, Ross, Saulsbury, Sherman, Trumbull, Van Winkle, Vickers, Willey, Williams, and Wilson—30.

NOT VOTING—Messrs. Bayard, Buckalew, Conkling, Cragin, Edmunds, Henderson, McCreery, Norton, Nye, Sprague, and Wade—11.

So the amendment was rejected.

The CHIEF JUSTICE. The question recurs on the order proposed by the Senator from California.

Mr. CONNESS. On that I ask for the yeas and nays.

The yeas and nays were ordered.

Mr. CONNESS. Now let it be read.

The Secretary read as follows:

Ordered, That on each day hereafter the Senate, sitting as a court of impeachment, shall meet at eleven o'clock a. m.

The question, being taken by yeas and nays, resulted—yeas 29, nays 14; as follows:

YEAS—Messrs. Cameron, Cattell, Chandler, Cole, Conkling, Conness, Corbett, Cragin, Drake, Ferry, Frelinghuysen, Harlan, Howard, Howe, Morgan, Morrill of Maine, Morrill of Vermont, Patterson of New Hampshire, Pomeroy, Ramsey, Sherman, Stewart, Sumner, Thayer, Tipton, Willey, Williams, Wilson, and Yates—29.

NAYS—Messrs. Anthony, Davis, Dixon, Doolittle, Fowler, Grimes, Hendricks, Johnson, Patterson of Tennessee, Ross, Saulsbury, Trumbull, Van Winkle, and Vickers—14.

NOT VOTING—Messrs. Bayard, Buckalew, Edmunds, Fessenden, Henderson, McCreery, Morton, Norton, Nye, Sprague, and Wade—11.

So the order was adopted.

Mr. FERRY. I send an order to the Chair.

The CHIEF JUSTICE. The Secretary will read the order proposed by the Senator from Connecticut.

The Secretary read as follows:

Whereas there appear in the proceedings of the Senate of yesterday as published in the Globe of this morning certain tabular statements incorporated in the remarks of Mr. Manager BUTLER upon the question of adjournment, which tabular statements were neither spoken of in the discussion, nor offered or received in evidence: Therefore,

Ordered, That such tabular statements be omitted from the proceedings of the trial as published by rule of the Senate.

Mr. Manager BUTLER. Is that a matter for discussion?

The CHIEF JUSTICE. The order will be for present consideration unless objected to.

Mr. FERRY. I ask its present consideration.

The CHIEF JUSTICE. There is no objection. It is before the Senate.

Mr. Manager BUTLER. I only desire to say, sir, that I stated the effect of the tabular statements yesterday. I did not read them at length, because it would take too much time.

Mr. HENDRICKS. Mr. President, I rise to a question of order and propriety. I wish to know whether it is the right of any Senator to defend the Secretary of the Treasury against attacks that are here made upon him, or whether our mouths are closed while these attacks are made; and if it is not the province and right of a Senator to defend him in his office, whether it is the right of the Manager to make an attack upon him?

The CHIEF JUSTICE. The question of order is made by the resolution proposed by the Senator from Connecticut. Upon that question of order, if the Senate desire to debate, it will be proper that it should retire for consultation. If no Senator moves that order, the Chair conceives that it is proper that the honorable Manager should be heard in explanation.

Mr. Manager BUTLER. I wish to say, sir, that I did not read the tables because they would be too voluminous. I had them in my hands; I made them a part of my argument; I read the conclusions of them, and stated the inferences to be drawn from them, and I thought it was due to myself and due to the Senate that they should be put exactly as they were, and I therefore incorporated them in the Globe.

To the remark of the honorable Senator, I simply say that I made no attack on the Secretary of the Treasury; I said nothing of him; I did not know that he was here at all to be discussed; but I dealt with the act as the act of the Executive simply, and whenever called upon to show I can show the reasons why I dealt with that.

The CHIEF JUSTICE. The Secretary will read the order submitted by the Senator from Connecticut.

The Secretary again read the order.

Mr. ANTHONY. Mr. President, I understood the Senator from Indiana to inquire if under the rules he could be permitted to make an explanation, or to make a defense of the Secretary of the Treasury?

The CHIEF JUSTICE. The rules positively prohibit debate.

Mr. ANTHONY. But by unanimous consent I suppose the rule could be suspended.

Mr. WILLIAMS. I object.

The CHIEF JUSTICE. Objection is made. Senators, you who are in favor of agreeing to the order proposed by the Senator from Connecticut will please say ay, those of the contrary opinion no. [Putting the question.] The ayes appear to have it. The ayes have it, and the order is adopted.

The CHIEF JUSTICE. Gentlemen of counsel for the President, you will please proceed with the defense.

Mr. CURTIS. The Sergeant-at-Arms will call William W. Armstrong.

WM. W. ARMSTRONG sworn and examined.
By Mr. CURTIS:

Question. Please state your name in full?

Answer. William W. Armstrong.

Question. Where do you reside?

Answer. I reside in Cleveland, Ohio.

Mr. DRAKE. I ask permission to make a suggestion to the Chair, in reference to our hearing on this side of the Chamber. Will the Chair instruct the witness to turn his face in this direction?

Mr. EVARTS. Mr. Chief Justice, if we may be allowed a suggestion, there is not so much silence in the Chamber as would be possible, and we must take witnesses with such natural powers as they possess.

Mr. CURTIS, (to the witness.) Speak as loud as you can.

The CHIEF JUSTICE. Conversation in the Senate Chamber must be suspended.

By Mr. CURTIS:

Question. Repeat, if you please, what is your residence?

Answer. Cleveland, Ohio.

Question. And what is your occupation or business?

Answer. I am one of the editors and proprietors of the Cleveland Plaindealer.

Question. Were you at Cleveland at the time of the visit made to that city by President Johnson in the summer of 1866?

Answer. I was.

Question. Were you present at the formal reception of the President by any committee or body of men?

Answer. I was.

Question. State by whom he was received?

Answer. The President and his party arrived at Cleveland about half past eight o'clock in the evening, and were escorted to the Kennard House. After partaking of a supper the President was escorted on to the balcony of the Kennard House, and there was formally welcomed to the city of Cleveland, on behalf of the municipal authorities and the citizens, by the president of the city council.

Question. Did the President respond to that address of welcome?

Answer. He did.

Question. What was the situation of this balcony in reference to the street, in reference to its exposure and publicity, and whether or not there was a large crowd of persons present?

Answer. There was a very large crowd of persons present, and there were quite a large number of people on the balcony.

Question. How did it proceed after the President began to respond?

Answer. For a few moments there were no interruptions, and I judge from what the President said that he did not intend——

Mr. Manager BUTLER. Excuse me. Stop a moment, if you please. I object to what the witness supposed were the President's intentions.

By Mr. CURTIS:

Question. From what you heard and saw

was the President in the act of making a continuous address to the assembly, or was he interrupted by the crowd, and describe how the affair proceeded?

Answer. Well, sir, the President commenced his speech by saying that he did not intend to make a speech. I think, to the best of my recollection, he said that he had simply come there to make the acquaintance of the people, and bid them good-bye. I think that was about the substance of the first paragraphs of his speech. He apologized for the non-appearance of General Grant, and then proceeded with his speech.

Question. How did he proceed, sir? Was it a part of his address, or.was it in response to calls made upon him by the people? Describe what occurred?

Answer. Well, sir, I did not hear all of the speech.

Question. Did you hear calls upon him from the crowd and interruptions?

Answer. I did, quite a number of them.

Question. From what you saw and heard the President say, and all that occurred, was the President closing his remarks at the time when these interruptions began?

Answer. That I cannot say.

Question. Can you say whether these interruptions and calls upon the President were responded to by his remarks?

Answer. Some of them were.

Question. Were the interruptions kept up during the continuance of the address, or was he allowed to proceed without interruption?

Answer. They were kept up very nearly to the conclusion of the President's speech.

Question. What was the character of the crowd? Was it orderly or disorderly?

Answer. Well, sir, the large majority of the crowd were orderly.

Question. As to the rest?

Answer. There was a good deal of disorder.

Question. Was that disorder confined to one or two persons, or did it affect enough to give a character to the interruptions?

Answer. I have no means of ascertaining how many were engaged in the interruptions.

Question. That is not what I asked you. I asked you whether there was enough to give a general character to the interruptions?

Answer. There were quite a number of voices. Whether they were all from the same persons or not I am not able to say.

Cross-examined by Mr. Manager BUTLER:

Question. F. W. Pelton, esq., was the president of the city council, was he not?

Answer. I believe so.

Question. Was not his address on the balcony to the President simply in the hearing of those who were on the balcony, and did not the President after he had received that welcome address then step forward to speak to the multitude?

Answer. I believe that after Mr. Pelton addressed the President several of the distinguished gentlemen who accompanied the party were presented, and then, in response to calls, the President presented himself.

Question. Presented himself in response to the crowd?

Answer. In response to the——

Mr. CURTIS. In response to what?

The WITNESS. In response to the calls.

By Mr. Manager BUTLER:

Question. Would you say that this was a correct or incorrect report of that proceeding:

"About ten o'clock, the supper being over, the party retired to the balcony, where the President was formally welcomed to the Forest City by F. W. Pelton, esq., president of the city council, as follows:

"'Mr. PRESIDENT: On behalf of the municipal authorities of the city I cordially extend to you the hospitalities of the citizens of Cleveland. We recognize you as the Chief Magistrate of this now free Republic and the chosen guardian of their rights and liberties. We are grateful for the opportunity afforded by your visit to our city to honor you as our Chief Magistrate, and again I extend to you and to the distinguished members of your party a hearty welcome.'"

Was that about the substance of Mr. Pelton's address?

Answer. That was about the substance, I think.

Question. Then:

"The President and several members of his party then appeared at the front of the balcony and were introduced to the people?"

Answer. Yes, sir.

Question. Then:

"The vast multitude that filled the streets below was boisterous, and sometimes bitter and sarcastic in their calls, interludes, and replies, though sometimes exceedingly apt."

Would you say that was about a fair representation?

Answer. I do not think there were any calls or any interruptions of the President's speech until after he had proceeded some five or ten minutes.

Question. But, whenever they did come, would that be a fair representation of them?

Answer. What is your question, sir?

Question. "The vast multitude that filled the streets below was boisterous, and sometimes bitter and sarcastic in their calls?"

Answer. They were to some extent.

Question. "They listened with attention part of the time, and at other times completely drowned the President's voice with their vociferations." Was that so?

Answer. Yes, sir, that was so.

Question. "After all the presentations had been made loud calls were made for the President, who appeared and spoke as follows."

Now I will only read the first part to see if you will agree with me as to how soon the interruptions came in:

"FELLOW-CITIZENS: It is not for the purpose of making a speech that I now appear before you. I am aware of the great curiosity which prevails to see strangers who have notoriety and distinction in the country. I know a large number of you desire to see

General Grant, and to hear what he has to say. [A voice: 'Three cheers for Grant.']"

Was not that the first-interruption?

Answer. That was the first interruption.

Question. "But you cannot see him to-night. He is extremely ill." Now, then, was there any interruption after that until he spoke of Stephen A. Douglas, and was not that simply the introduction of applause?

Answer. There were three cheers, I believe, given for Stephen A. Douglas at that time.

Question. Then he went on without interruption, did he not, until these words came in:

"I come before you as an American citizen simply, and not as the Chief Magistrate clothed in the insignia and paraphernalia of State; being an inhabitant of a State of this Union. I know it has been said that I was an alien."

Was not that the next interruption?

Answer. I do not remember that paragraph in the speech.

Question. You do not remember whether that was there or not. Now, sir, do you remember any other interruption until he came to the paragraph:

"There was, two years ago, a ticket before you for the Presidency. I was placed upon that ticket with a distinguished citizen, now no more."

Then did not the voices come in, "Unfortunate!" "Too bad!"?

Answer. I did not hear them.

Question. Do you know whether they were or were not said?

Answer. I do not.

Mr. Manager BUTLER. I will not trouble you any further.

BARTON ABLE sworn and examined.

By Mr. CURTIS:

Question. State your full name.

Answer. Barton Able.

Question. Where do you reside?

Answer. In St. Louis.

Question. What is your occupation?

Answer. I am engaged in the mercantile business, and collector of internal revenue for the first district of Missouri.

Question. Were you at St. Louis in the summer of 1866, at the time when President Johnson visited that city?

Answer. Yes, sir.

Question. Were you upon any committee connected with the reception of the President?

Answer. I was upon the committee of reception from the Merchants' Union Exchange.

Question. Where did the reception take place?

Answer. The citizens of St. Louis met the President and party at Alton, in Illinois, some twenty-four miles above St. Louis. My recollection is that the mayor of the city received him at the Lindell Hotel, in St. Louis.

Question. You speak of being on a committee of some mercantile association. What was that association?

Answer. The merchants and business men of the city had an exchange for doing business, where they met daily.

Question. Not a political association?

Answer. No, sir.

Question. Did the President make a public address or an address to the people in St. Louis while he was there?

Answer. He made a speech in the evening at the Southern Hotel to the citizens.

Question. Were you present at the hotel before the speech was made?

Answer. Yes, sir.

Question. As one of the committee you have spoken of?

Answer. Yes, sir.

Question. Please to state under what circumstances the President was called upon to speak?

Answer. I was in one of the parlors of the hotel with the committee and the President, when some of the citizens came in and asked him to go out and respond to a call from the citizens to speak. He declined, or rather said that he did not care to make any speech. The same thing was repeated two or three times by other citizens coming in, and he finally said that he was in the hands of his friends, or of the committee, and if they said so he would go out and respond to the call, which he did do.

Question. What did the committee say? Did they say anything?

Answer. A portion of the committee, two or three of them, said after some consultation that they presumed he might as well do it. There was a large crowd of citizens on the outside in front of the hotel.

Question. Did the President say anything before he went out as to whether he went out to make a long speech or a short speech, or anything to characterizing the speech he intended to make?

Answer. My understanding of it was that he did not care to make a speech at all.

Mr. CURTIS. That you have already explained.

Mr. Manager BUTLER. Mr. Able, please not give your opinion, but give facts.

By Mr. CURTIS:

Question. You have already explained that he manifested reluctance, and how he manifested it. Now, I want to know if he said anything as to his purpose in going out? If so, I should like to have you state it, if you remember.

Answer. I understood from his acceptance that his intention was to make a short speech when he went out.

Question. Did you or not hear what he said, or were you in a position so that you could hear what he said?

Answer. I heard his conversation with the committee?

Question. I do not mean that; I mean after he went out and began to speak?

Answer. Very little of it.

Question. Was it a large crowd or a small one?
Answer. A large crowd.
Question. Were you present far enough to be able to state what the demeanor of the crowd was toward the President?
Answer. I heard from the inside—I was not on the balcony of the hotel at all; but I heard from the parlor one or two interruptions. I do not recollect but one of them.
Question. You remained in the parlor all the time, I understand you?
Answer. Between the parlor and the dining-room, where the banquet was spread.
Question. You were not on the balcony?
Answer. No, sir.

Cross-examined by Mr. Manager BUTLER:

Question. You met the President at Alton, and you, yourself, as one of this committee, made him an address on board the steamer where he was received, did you not?
Answer. I introduced him to the committee of reception from St. Louis.
Question. The committee of reception from St. Louis met him, then, on board the steamer?
Answer. On board the steamer.
Question. And you introduced him with a little speech?
Answer. Yes, sir.
Question. Then Captain Eads, who was the chairman of the citizens or the spokesman of the citizens, made him an address, did he?
Answer. Yes, sir.
Question. An address of welcome, and to that the President made a response, did he?
Answer. Yes, sir.
Question. And in that address he was listened to with propriety by them, as became his place and the ceremony?
Answer. I observed nothing to the contrary.
Question. You so supposed. Then you went to the Lindell Hotel?
Answer. I did not go to the Lindell Hotel at the time.
Question. The President went, did he not?
Answer. Yes, sir; the President was entertained at the Lindell Hotel.
Question. And en route to the Lindell Hotel he was escorted by a procession, was he not, of the military and civic societies?
Answer. From the landing; yes, sir.
Question. A procession of the benevolent societies?
Answer. I do not recollect what societies they were. There was a very large turn-out; perhaps most of the societies of the city were present.
Question. Were you at the Lindell Hotel at all?
Answer. Yes, sir.
Question. When he got there he was received by the mayor, was he not?
Answer. I was not there when he arrived at the Lindell Hotel.
Question. Were you there when he was received by the mayor?

Answer. No, sir.
Question. You do not know whether the mayor made him a speech of welcome or not there?
Answer. Only from what I saw in the press.
Question. Nor do you know whether the President responded there?
Answer. I was not present.
Question. What time in the day was this when he got to the Lindell Hotel, as near as you can say?
Answer. It was in the afternoon when they left the steamboat landing. I do not know what time they were at the hotel, because I was not present on their arrival.
Question. Can you not tell about what time they got there?
Answer. Well, it was probably between one and five o'clock.
Question. After that did you go with the President from the Lindell Hotel to the Southern Hotel?
Answer. I do not recollect whether I accompanied him from the one hotel to the other or not.
Question. He did go from the one to the other?
Answer. Yes, sir.
Question. There was to be a banquet for him and his suite at the Southern Hotel that night, was there not?
Answer. Yes, sir.
Question. At which there was intended to be speaking to him and by him, I suppose?
Answer. There were to be toasts and responses; yes, sir.
Question. And what time was that banquet to come off?
Answer. I do not recollect the exact hour; I think somewhere about nine o'clock.
Question. At the time the President was called upon by the crowd were you waiting for the banquet?
Answer. When the President was called upon by the crowd I do not think the banquet was ready. He was in the parlors with the committee of citizens.
Question. The citizens being introduced to him, I suppose?
Answer. Yes, sir.
Question. He then went out on to the balcony. Did you hear any portion of the speech?
Answer. Only such portions of it as I could catch from the inside occasionally. I did not go on to the balcony at all.
Question. Could you see on to the balcony where he stood from where you were?
Answer. I could see on to the balcony, but I do not know whether I could see precisely where he stood or not.
Question. While he was making that speech and when he came to the sentence, "I will neither be bullied by my enemies nor overawed by my friends," was there anybody on the balcony trying to get him back?

Answer. I could hardly answer that question. I was not there to see.

Question. You said you could see on to the balcony, but you were not certain that you could see him. You might have seen such an occurrence as that.

Answer. I did not.

Question. You did not see. Can you tell whether it was so or not from your own knowledge?

Answer. I should think if I could not see it I could not tell.

Question. I only wanted to make certain upon that point.

Answer. Well, sir, I am positive on that point.

Question. You have no knowledge on the subject. Who was on the balcony beside him?

Answer. I suppose the balcony will hold perhaps two hundred people. There was a good many people on there; I could not tell how many.

Question. Give me some one of the two hundred, if you know anybody who was there?

Answer. I think Mr. Howe was there. My recollection is that the President walked out with Mr. Howe.

Question. Was General Frank Blair there at any time?

Answer. I have no recollection of it if he was.

Question. Did the President afterward make a speech at the banquet?

Answer. A short one.

Question. Was the crowd a noisy and boisterous one after awhile?

Answer. I heard a good deal of noise from the crowd from where I stood—I stood inside—or where I was moving about, for I was not standing still a great portion of the time.

GEORGE KNAPP sworn and examined.

By Mr. CURTIS:

Question. What is your full name?

Answer. George Knapp.

Question. Where do you reside?

Answer. St. Louis.

Question. What is your business?

Answer. I am one of the publishers and proprietors of the Missouri Republican.

Question. Were you in St. Louis at the time the President visited that city in the summer of 1866?

Answer. I was.

Question. Were you present at the Southern Hotel before Mr. Johnson went out to make a speech to the people?

Answer. I was.

Question. Were you in the room where the President was?

Answer. I was.

Question. Please state what occurred between the President and citizens, or the committee of citizens, in respect to his going out to make a speech?

Answer. The crowd on the outside had called repeatedly for the President, and some conversation ensued between those present. I think I recollect Captain Able and Captain Taylor and myself at any rate were together. The crowd continued to call. Probably some one suggested, I think I suggested, that he ought to go out. Some further conversation occurred, I think, between him and Captain Able——

Question. The gentleman who has just left the stand?

Answer. Yes, sir; Captain Barton Able, and I think I said to him that he ought to go out and show himself to the people and say a few words at any rate. He seemed reluctant to go out, and we walked out together. He walked out on the balcony, and we walked out with him, and he commenced addressing the assembled multitude as it seemed.

Question. What was the character of the crowd? Was it a large crowd, a large number of people?

Answer. I do not think I looked at the crowd. I do not think I got far enough on the balcony to look on the magnitude of the crowd. I think I stood back some distance.

Question. About what number of people were on the balcony itself?

Answer. I suppose there were probably fifteen or twenty; there may have been twenty-five.

Question. Could you hear the cries from the crowd?

Answer. I could not.

Question. What was the character of the proceedings so far as the crowd was concerned?

Answer. Well, I do not recollect distinctly. My impressions are that occasional or repeated questions were apparently put to the President, but I do not now exactly recollect what they were.

Question. Was the crowd orderly or otherwise, so far as you could hear?

Answer. At times it seemed to be somewhat disorderly; but of that I am not very sure.

Cross-examined by Mr. Manager BUTLER:

Question. Did you go on to the balcony at all?

Answer. Yes, sir; I stepped out. It is a wide balcony; it is probably twelve or fifteen feet; it covers the whole of the side wall. I stepped out. I think I was probably only two or three feet back of the President part of the time while he was speaking. Then there are a number of doors or windows leading out to this balcony. You could stand in these windows or doors and hear every word that was said.

Question. Did you listen to the speech so as to hear every word that was said?

Answer. I am not sure that I stayed during the whole time. I listened pretty attentively to the speech while I stood there, but whether I stood there during the whole time or not I do not now recollect.

Question. You told us there were from fifteen to twenty persons, if I understood you aright, on the balcony?

Answer. That is my impression. I am not certain about that, because I did not pay any attention to the number.

Question. How many would the balcony hold?

Answer. I suppose the balcony would hold one hundred.

Question. Then it was not at all crowded on the balcony?

Answer. I do not recollect. I say about that whether it was or not. I did not charge my mind with it, nor do I now recollect. The parlors were full. There was a crowd there waiting to go into the banquet, and I think it is very likely that a large number of them crowded on the balcony to hear the speech. Whether it was crowded or not I do not recollect.

Question. Who were present at the time so as to remember distinctly when he said he would not be overawed by his friends or bullied by his enemies. Do you remember that phrase?

Answer. I do not recollect it.

Question. This confusion in the crowd sometimes prevented his going on, did it not?

Answer. I think it likely; but in that I must only draw from my present impression. I do not recollect.

Question. Did you hear him say anything about "Judas," do you remember?

Answer. No, sir; I do not recollect.

Question. You do not recollect that about Judas? Did you hear him say anything about John Bull, and about attending to him after a while?

Answer. I have no recollection as to the points of the speech.

Question. Then, so far as you know, all you know that would be of advantage to us here is that you were present when some of the citizens asked the President to go out and answer the calls of the crowd?

Answer. Yes; some citizens then present in the parlor asked him.

Question. While the banquet was waiting? At what time was the banquet to take place?

Answer. I think it was to take place at eight o'clock.

Question. What time had this got to be?

Answer. I do not recollect that.

Question. Was it not very near eight o'clock at that time?

Answer. I think when the President went out it was near the time the banquet was to take place, and I think, also, I know, in fact, that while the President was speaking several persons, in speaking about it, said it was time for the banquet to commence, or something to that effect.

Question. The banquet had to wait for him while the crowd outside got the speech?

Answer. I do not know that.

Question. Was not that your impression at the time?

Answer. I think the hour, probably, had passed; but in attending banquets it often happens that they do not take place exactly at the hour fixed.

Question. It appears that this did not; but was that because they waited for the President or because the banquet was not ready?

Answer. I think it was because they waited for the President.

Question. Did you publish that speech the next morning in your paper?

Answer. Yes, sir; it was published.

Question. Did you again republish it on Monday morning?

Answer. Yes, sir.

Question. While your paper is called the Republican it is really the Democrat, and the Democrat is the Republican?

Answer. The Republican was commenced in early times, for I have been connected with it over forty years myself, and at the time——

Mr. Manager BUTLER. I do not care to go back forty years at this time.

The WITNESS. You asked why it was called——

By Mr. Manager BUTLER:

Question. Not why, but as to the fact. Was it in fact the Democratic paper at that time when the President was there?

Answer. Yes, sir.

Question. And the St. Louis Democrat, so called, was really the Republican paper?

Answer. Yes, sir.

Question. Now, in the Democratic paper, called by the name of Republican, the speech was published on Sunday and on Monday?

Answer. Yes, sir.

Question. Has it never been republished since?

Answer. No, sir; not to my knowledge.

Question. State whether you caused an edition of the speech to be corrected for Monday morning's publication?

Answer. I met our principal reporter, Mr. Zider——

Question. Please do not state what took place between you and your reporter; it is only the fact I want, not the conversation. Did you cause it to be done?

Answer. I gave directions to Mr. Zider after complaining about the report of the speech——

Question. Excuse me; I have not asked you about your directions?

Answer. I did. I gave directions on reading the speech——

Question. Please answer the question?

Answer. Well, I gave directions to have it corrected, if that is your question.

Question. Were your directions followed so far as you know?

Answer. I do not recollect the extent of the corrections. I never read the speech afterward, and I have forgotten.

Question. Did you ever complain afterward to any man, Mr. Zider or any other, that the speech was not as it ought to be as it was published on Monday morning in the Republican?

Answer. I cannot draw the distinction between Monday and Sunday. I have repeatedly spoken of the imperfect manner in which I conceived the speech was reported and published in the Republican on Sunday. Whether I spoke of its imperfections for Monday or not I do not recollect.

Question. Will you not let me call your attention, Mr. Witness? You say that you directed a revised publication on Monday, and it was so published. Now, did you ever complain after that revised publication was made to anybody that that publication was not a true one within the next three months following?

Answer. It is possible I might have complained on Monday morning, if the corrections were not made, but I do not recollect.

Question. Excuse me; I did not ask for a possibility?

Answer. I tell you I do not recollect.

Question. But it is possible you did not?

Answer. That I say again I cannot recollect.

Question. Now, sir, will you say that in any important particular the speech as published in your paper differs from the speech as put in evidence here?

Answer. I could not point out a solitary case, because I have not read the speech as put in evidence here, nor have I read the speech since the morning after it was delivered; so I know nothing about what you have put in evidence here.

HENRY F. ZIDER sworn and examined.

By Mr. CURTIS:

Question. Where did you reside in the summer of 1866 when the President visited St. Louis?

Answer. At St. Louis, Missouri.

Question. What was then your business?

Answer. I was then engaged as short-hand writer and reporter for the Missouri Republican, a paper published at St. Louis.

Question. Had you anything to do with making a report of the speech of the President delivered from the balcony of the Southern Hotel?

Answer. I made a short-hand report of the speech. I was authorized to employ all the assistance that I needed, for it was known that the President was to be received at St. Louis. I employed Mr. Walbridge and Mr. Allen to assist me. Mr. Walbridge wrote out the report for publication in the Sunday morning Republican. I went over the same report on Sunday afternoon and made several alterations in it for the Monday morning paper.

Question. The Monday morning Republican?

Answer. Yes, sir. I made the corrections from my own notes.

Question. Did you make any corrections except those which you found were required by your own notes?

Answer. There were three or four corrections that the printers did not make that I had marked on the proof sheets that I made on the paper the following morning in the counting-room.

Question. With those exceptions, did you make any corrections except what were called for by your own notes?

Answer. Those were called for by my own notes.

Question. But they were not in fact made?

Answer. They were not in fact made in the printed copy on Monday.

Question. Now, answer my question whether the corrections were called for by your own notes?

Answer. Oh, yes; all of them.

Question. Have you compared the report which you made, and which was published in the Republican on Monday, with the report published in the St. Louis Democrat?

Answer. I have more particularly compared the report published in the Monday Democrat with the Sunday Republican.

Question. You compared those two?

Answer. Yes, sir. There are about sixty changes.

Mr. JOHNSON. Differences?

The WITNESS. Yes, sir.

By Mr. CURTIS:

Question. Describe the character of those differences?

Mr. Manager BUTLER. "State the differences." I object to that.

Mr. CURTIS. Do you want him to repeat the sixty differences?

Mr. Manager BUTLER. Certainly; if he can.

By Mr. CURTIS:

Question. Have you a memorandum of those differences?

Answer. I have.

Question. Read it, if you please?

Mr. Manager BUTLER. Before he reads it I should like to know when it was made.

By Mr. CURTIS:

Question. When did you make this comparison?

The WITNESS. The exact date?

Mr. CURTIS. If you can give it to us.

Answer, (after consulting a memorandum-book.) Saturday, April 11.

Question. When did you make the memorandum?

Answer. On the Sunday following.

By Mr. Manager BUTLER:

Question. Last Sunday?

Answer. Yes, sir.

Question. This month?

Answer. Yes, sir.

By Mr. CURTIS:

Question. From what did you make the memorandum?

Answer. I had been here before the board of managers twenty-four days, and was discharged and had just returned to St. Louis. I got telegraphic dispatches stating that I was summoned again to appear before the Senate. I then went to the Republican office, took the bound files of the Republican and the bound files of the Democrat for the latter part of 1866, and in company with Mr. James Monaghan, one of the assistant editors, I made a comparison of the two papers, noted the differences, compared those differences twice afterward to see that they were accurate. That was on Saturday. I started for Washington on Sunday afternoon at three o'clock, the first through train.

Question. When was this paper that you call the memorandum, which contains these differences, made?

Answer. On Saturday.

Question. Was it made at the same time when you made this comparison or at a different time?

Answer. The same day.

Mr. CURTIS. Now, you can tell us the nature of the differences; or, if the honorable Manager desires that all those differences should be read, you can read them.

Mr. Manager BUTLER. Stay a moment. Any on which you rely we should like to have read.

Mr. CURTIS. We rely on all of them, more or less.

Mr. Manager BUTLER. Then all of them, more or less, we want read.

Mr. CURTIS. We should prefer to save time by giving specimens; but then, if you prefer to have them all read, we will have them read.

Mr. Manager BUTLER. There is a question back of this, I think, and that is, that we have not the standard of comparison. Surely, then, this cannot be evidence. This witness goes to the Republican office and there takes a paper—he cannot tell whether it was the true one or not, whether made properly or not, or what edition it was—and he compares it with a copy of the Democrat, and having made that comparison he now proposes to put in the results of it. I do not see how that can be evidence. He may state anything that he has a recollection of; but to make the memorandum evidence, to read the memorandum, never was such a thing heard of, I think.

Let me restate it and I have done. He goes to the Republican office, gets a Republican; what Republican, how genuine, what edition it was, is not identified; he says it was in a bound volume. He takes the Democrat, of what edition we do not know, and compares that, and then comes here and attempts to put in the results of a comparison made in which Monaghan held one end of the matter and he held the other. Now, can that be evidence?

Mr. CURTIS. I want to ask the witness a question, and then I will make an observation on the objection. [To the witness.] Who made the report in the Republican which you examined—the one which you examined and

compared with the report in the Democrat; who made that report?

Answer. Mr. Walbridge made that report on Saturday night, September 8, 1866. It was published in the Sunday morning Republican of September 9, 1866.

By Mr. CURTIS:

Question. Have you looked at the proceedings in this case to see whether that has been put in evidence?

Answer. The Sunday morning Republican was mentioned in Mr. Walbridge's testimony, in which he states that he made one or two simple corrections for the Monday morning Democrat.

Question. Now, I wish to inquire, Mr. Zider, whether the report which you saw in the files of the Republican and which you compared with the report in the Democrat was the report which Mr. Walbridge made?

Answer. Undoubtedly it was.

Mr. CURTIS. Now, Mr. Chief Justice, it is suggested by the learned Manager——

Mr. Manager BUTLER. I will save you all trouble. You may put it in as much as you choose. I do not care, on reflection, if you leave it unread. It is of no consequence.

Mr. CURTIS. We will simply put it into the case to save time and have it printed.

Mr. Manager BUTLER. I think there should not be anything printed that is not read. We have got a very severe lesson upon that.

Mr. CURTIS. We understood you to dispense with the reading.

The CHIEF JUSTICE. If the honorable Manager desires to have the paper read it will be read.

Mr. Manager BUTLER. I do not desire it to be read.

Mr. EVARTS. Is it to go in as evidence, Mr. Chief Justice, or not.

The CHIEF JUSTICE. Certainly.

Mr. Manager BUTLER. It may go in for aught I care.

Mr. CURTIS. That is all, Mr. Zider.

The paper thus admitted in evidence, containing a memorandum of the differences between the two reports of President Johnson's speech at St. Louis, is as follows:

Sunday REPUBLICAN, Sept. 9, 1866.	DEMOCRAT, Monday, Sept. 10, 1866.
I *am*	I *was*
Questions *which*	Questions *that*
that we have	∧ we have
as *this* we have	as *those* we have
that they *then* knew	that they *there* knew
its *power* having expired	its *powers* having expired
of ∧ population	of *the* population
without the *will* of the people	without the *consent* of the people
∧ Then when	*And* then when
it *does not* provoke me	it *don't* provoke me
things that *have* been done	things that *has* been done
that *were* intended to be enforced *upon*	that *was* intended to be enforced *on*
abandoned the *party*	abandoned the *power*
that I was a traitor	that I was a t-r-ai-t-o-r
Judas Iscariot ∧ a traitor	*Judas*—Judas Iscariot a t-r-ai-t-o-r
Judas Iscariot! Judas!	*Judaas*, Judas Iscariot, Jud-a-a-s
the twelve apostles	*and these* twelve apostles

he *never could have*
and *that* try to stay
when there *were*
there *was* a Christ
there *were* unbelievers
to day *who* would
———
for years
bear all the *expenses*
———^
Yes, Yes, •
^ a decided majority
What?
Stimulating this
So far as offences are concerned
Upon this subject of offences
and *battled* more for
It has been my peculiar misfortune ^ to have fierce opposition
(a voice why did'nt you do it)
The law was executed,
The law was executed
to *give* somebody else a bounty
he can get $50 bounty
(*Great* cheering)
are ^ entitled to
equal representation in the
Congress of the United States without violating the Constitution (cheers)

Among *this* people. I have labored for it I am for it now. I deny
manner pointed *out* by and sometimes having^
re-
pented makes him a better man than he was before
Yes, I have,
Yes I have,
(Voice "bully for you"^ and *cheers*)
on either side
a kind of over-righteousness
—*over righteousness*—better
than any body else and *although* wanting
He went upon the cross and there was^ nailed by
unbelievers^ and there shed
his blood that you and I might live (cheers

nor the judge^

I know there *are* some that talk
And manage *all* the affairs of State
The people of Missouri as well as other States know that *all* my efforts have
all this
traduction and de-traction that *have*
let us fight *the* enemies
And in parting with you now *I* leave the government in your hands

recognized

---

he *could'nt* have
and ^ try to stay
when there *ware*
there *ware* a Christ
there *ware* unbelievers
to day ^ would
Now what is the plan?
four years
bear all the *expense,*
So much for this question.
Y-a-s, Y-a-s;
as decided a majority
Wha-t?
elevating themselves
So far as the Fenians are concerned
Upon this subject of *Fenians,*
and *sacrificed* more for,
It has been my peculiar misfortune *always* to have fierce opposition
———^—
———
to *vote* somebody else a bounty.
^ can get $50. bounty,
(*Loud* cheering)
are *constitutionally* entitled to
equal suffrage in the
Senate and no power has the
right to deprive them of it without violating the constitution. (cheers)

Among *the* people. I have labored for it. Now I deny,
manner pointed^ by and sometimes *having sinned* and having re-pented
makes him a better man than he was before
Y-a-s I have
Y-a-s I have
Voice (bully for you *old fellow* and *laughter*)
on the *other* side
a kind of over righteous-ness—better than any
body else and *always* wanting,
He went upon the cross & there was *painfully* nailed by
these unbelievers *that I have spoken of heretonight,*
and there shed his blood that you and I might live (cheers)
nor the judge (voice nor the Moses,"
I know there *is* some that talk
And manage^ the affairs of State,
The people of Missouri as well as other States know that^ my efforts have
all this traduction and detraction that *has*
let us fight^ enemies
And in parting with you now leave^ the Government in your hands,

re-cog nized

Cross-examined by Mr. Manager BUTLER:

Question. How long have you been troubled with your unfortunate affliction?

Answer. To what do you refer.

Question. I understood you were a little deaf. Is that so?

Answer. I have been sick the greater part of this year, and was compelled to come here a month ago almost, before I was able to come. I have not got well yet.

Question. Did you hear my question?

Answer. Yes.

Question. How long have you been deaf, if you have been deaf at all?

Answer. Partially deaf for the last two years, I should think.

Question. About what time did it commence?

Answer. I cannot state that.

Question. As near as you can. You know when you became deaf, do you not?

Answer. I know I was not deaf when you made your St. Louis speech in 1866.

Question. That is a very good date to reckon from; but as these gentlemen do not all know when that was, and you and I do, suppose you try it by the almanac and tell us when that was?

Answer. That was on the 13th of October, 1866.

Question. You were not deaf then?

Answer. No.

Question. How soon after that did you become deaf?

Answer. Perhaps a month. [Laughter.]

Question. You are quite sure it was not at that time?

Answer. Quite sure it was not that time, because I heard some remarks the crowd made which you did not. [Laughter.]

Question. I have no doubt you heard very much that I did not. Now, suppose we confine ourselves to this matter. About a month after that you became deaf?

Answer. Partially.

Question. Partially deaf, as now.

Answer. I recovered from that sickness. I became sick again the first part of this year.

Question. Now, will you have the kindness to state whether you have your notes?

The WITNESS. Of the President's speech?

Mr. Manager BUTLER. Yes, sir.

Answer. I have not.

Question. When did you see them last?

Answer. The last recollection I have of them is when Mr. Walbridge was summoned before the Reconstruction Committee to give testimony on the New Orleans riot.

Question. Did you and he then go over that speech together?

Answer. We went over only a part of it.

Question. The part that referred to New Orleans?

Answer. Yes, sir.

Question. But the part that referred to New Orleans you went over with him?

Answer. I did.

Question. Was there any material difference between you and him when you had your notes together in that part of the speech, and if so, state what?

Answer. There was.

Question. What was it?

Answer. He asked me to compare notes with him——

Question. Excuse me; I am not asking what he said. I am asking what difference there was between your report and his report upon that comparison; what material difference?

Mr. EVARTS. I submit, Mr. Chief Justice, that as he is asked the precise question what the difference was that arose upon that comparison, he is to be permitted to state what it was and how it arose.

Mr. Manager BUTLER. I have not asked any difference that arose between him and Mr. Walbridge. Far be it from me to go into that. I have asked what the difference was between the two speeches.

Mr. EVARTS. As it appeared in that comparison.

Mr. Manager BUTLER. As found at that time.

The WITNESS. That is what I was going to answer. If you will possess your soul in patience a moment I will answer.

The CHIEF JUSTICE. The witness will confine himself entirely to what is asked and make no remarks.

The WITNESS. When we proceeded to compare that part relating to the New Orleans riot Mr. Walbridge read from his notes; I looked on, and when he came to this passage, as near as I can remember: "When you read the speeches that were made, and take up the facts, if they are as stated, you will find that speeches were made incendiary in their character, exciting that population called the black population to take up arms and prepare for the shedding of blood;" I called Mr. Walbridge's attention to the qualifying words, "if the facts are as stated." He replied to me, "You are mistaken; I know I am right," and went on. As he was summoned to swear to his notes, and not to mine, I did not argue the question with him further, but let him go on.

By Mr. Manager BUTLER:

Question. What other difference was there?

Answer. There was another difference.

Question. In the New Orleans matter?

Answer. Yes sir. The President's words, I think, were that they there knew a convention was to be called which was extinct by reason of its power having expired. There was a difference in the words "by reason of."

Question. What was that difference?

Answer. The words "by reason of."

Question. Were they in or out of Walbridge's report?

Answer. They were in my report.

Question. And were not in Walbridge's report?

Answer. They were not.

Question. Any other difference?

Answer. No other. That was as far as we proceeded with the report as to the New Orleans riot. The latter part of the report was not compared at all, nor was the first part.

Question. Now, have you the report as it appeared in the Republican of Monday morning before you?

Answer. I have.

Question. Let me read the first few sentences of the report put in evidence, and tell me how many errors there are in that. Have you it?

Answer. Yes, sir; I have it. [The witness produced a new paper.]

Question. Now, I will read from the report put in evidence here:

"Fellow-citizens of St. Louis: In being introduced to you to-night, it is not for the purpose of making a speech. It is true I am proud to meet so many of my fellow-citizens here on this occasion, and under the favorable circumstances that I do. [Cry, 'How about British subjects?'] We will attend to John Bull after a while, so far as that is concerned. [Laughter and loud cheers.] I have just stated that I was not here for the purpose of making a speech."

The WITNESS. "*Am* not here."

Mr. Manager BUTLER. The difference is, here "I was," and there "I am." Now, do you know that the President used the word "am" instead of "was?"

Answer. Of course I do.

Question. I will read on:

"I was not here for the purpose of making a speech; but after being introduced simply to tender my cordial thanks for the welcome you have given me in your midst. [A voice: 'Ten thousand welcomes;' hurrahs and cheers.] Thank you, sir. I wish it was in my power to address you under favorable circumstances upon some of the questions that agitate and distract the public mind at this time"——

Answer. "Questions *which* agitate."

Question. "*Which* agitate" instead of "*that* agitate?"

Answer. Yes.

Question. And then it goes on:

"Questions that have grown out of a fiery ordeal we have just passed through, and which I think as important as those we have just passed by. The time has come when it seems to me that all ought to be prepared for peace—the rebellion being suppressed, and the shedding of blood being stopped, the sacrifice of life being suspended and stayed, it seems that the time has arrived when we should have peace; when the bleeding arteries should be tied up. [A voice: 'New Orleans;' 'Go on.']"

It is so far all right except those two corrections?

Answer. Yes, sir.

Question. Now we will try another part?

The WITNESS. Go over the New Orleans part, if you please. I wish to make a correction in that part.

Question. Are you dealing with a memorandum?

Answer. It is the official proceedings.

Question. You are comparing yourself with the official proceedings as you go on, where you have noted these corrections?

Answer. Yes, sir, in the official proceedings.

Question. Then you are going on with a copy of the official proceedings and noting the differences?

Answer. Yes; but I can make the memoranda without the official proceedings before me. Do you want it? [Offering the printed official report of the trial, with manuscript corrections, to the honorable Manager.]

Mr. Manager BUTLER. No; I do not care for it. You told me that you wished I should go on with the New Orleans part. Why do you wish anything about it?

The WITNESS. You were proceeding to make corrections, and when you came to the New Orleans part you stopped.

By Mr. Manager BUTLER:

Question. Well, I will take this portion of it——

The WITNESS. Any portion.

Question. "Judaas, Judas Iscariot, Judaas?"

Answer. One Judas too many there. [Laughter.]

Question. "There was a Judas once." You are sure he did not speak Judas four times, are you?

Answer. Yes, sir.

Question. How many times did he speak it?

Answer. Please read it again.

Question. I asked how many times did he speak Judas?

Answer. Three times.

Question. Well, I believe we have got "Judaas, Judas Iscariot, Judaas." That is only three times. Why did you say one too many?

Answer. You have it four times there.

Question. I beg your pardon. I have only said it three times. "Judaas, Judas Iscariot, Judaas."

The WITNESS. Are not those words italicized there?

Mr. Manager BUTLER. Yes, sir.

The WITNESS. Are they not stretched out to make it appear ridiculous?

Mr. Manager BUTLER. I really think two of the Judases are spelt with the pronunciation —"J-u-d-a-a-s."

The WITNESS. Yes, and italicized.

Question. Do you mean to say that the President did not speak those words with emphasis?

Answer. I mean to say that he did not speak them in that way.

Question. I read:

"There was a Judas once, one of the twelve apostles. Oh! yes, and these twelve apostles had a Christ. [A voice, 'And a Moses, too.' Great laughter.] The twelve apostles had a Christ, and he could not have had a Judas unless he had had twelve apostles."

See if I am right.

Answer. The word "yes" should not be stretched out with dashes between each letter, as there.

Mr. Manager BUTLER. The "yes" is not here stretched out. Is there any other question you would like to ask me, sir? [Laughter.]

The WITNESS. All I wish is that you shall read it as it is there.

Mr. Manager BUTLER. Now, sir, will you attend to your business and see what differences there are as I read?

"If I have played the Judas, who has been my Christ that I have played the Judas with? Was it Thad. Stevens? Was it Wendell Phillips? Was it Charles Sumner? [Hisses and cheers.] Are these the men that set up and compare themselves with the Saviour of men, and everybody that differs with them in opinion, and try to stay & arrest their diabolical and nefarious policy, is to be denounced as a Judas."

Answer. "And that try."

Question. "Differ with them in opinion, and *that* try to stay and arrest their diabolical and nefarious policy is to be denounced as a Judas. [' Hurrah for Andy and cheers.'"] Am I right so far, sir?

Answer. I think so.

Question. Is that a fair specimen of the sixty corrections?

Answer. There are four in the next three lines.

Question. Is that a fair specimen of the sixty corrections. Answer the question?

Mr. EVARTS. Mr. Chief Justice, I suppose the corrections, the whole of which we have put in evidence, will show for themselves.

Mr. Manager BUTLER. I am cross-examining the witness.

Mr. EVARTS. It has nothing to do with the matter of evidence.

Mr. Manager BUTLER. I am asking a question of the witness on cross-examination, and I prefer that he should not be instructed.

Mr. EVARTS. No instruction. We thought we should save time by putting in the memorandum; but it seems that the cross-examination is to go over every item. We insist that it be confined to questions that are proper. Whether this is a fair specimen or not, compared with the whole paper, will appear by the comparison the court make between the two pieces of evidence.

Mr. Manager BUTLER. I am testing the credibility of this witness, and I do not care to have him instructed.

The CHIEF JUSTICE. If the question is objected to, the honorable Manager will please put it in writing.

Mr. Manager BUTLER. I will put it in writing if the Chief Justice desires.

Mr. EVARTS. It is no question of credibility; it is a mere question of judgment asked of him between two papers, whether one is a fair specimen of the other.

Mr. Manager BUTLER. I will put the question in writing if the Chief Justice desires. The question is this: whether all the corrections which you have indicated in answer to my questions are of the same average character with the other corrections of the sixty?

The WITNESS. There are two or three corrections in that which you have read.

The CHIEF JUSTICE. Is the question objected to?

Mr. EVARTS. We object to the question. It requires a reëxamination of the whole subject.

The CHIEF JUSTICE. The question will be put in writing, objection being made.

Mr. Manager BUTLER. I will pass from that rather than take time, because I shall be accused of having taken up too much time. [To the witness.] Mr. Witness, you have told us that in the next few lines there were corrections, I think four in the next three lines. Now I will read the succeeding lines:

"In the days when there ware twelve apostles and when there ware a Christ, while there ware Judases, there ware unbelievers, too. Y-a-s; while there were Judases, there ware unbelievers. [Voices: 'Hear,' 'Three groans for Fletcher.'] Yes, oh yes! unbelievers in Christ."

The WITNESS. Do you wish me to make corrections there?

Mr. Manager BUTLER. I want you to stop me when there is anything wrong.

The WITNESS. "In the days when there ware;" were is right.

Mr. Manager BUTLER. It reads in mine "ware," and in yours it reads "were?"

Answer. Yes; and then in the next line there is a "ware" again. It should be "were."

Question. What is the next?

Answer. There is another "ware."

Question. That is, it should be "were" instead of "ware?"

Answer. Yes, sir.

Question. Those are the three corrections you want to make there? Are those the only corrections there?

Answer. Then there is one before "unbelievers."

Question. What is it?

Answer. "Were" for "ware."

Question. Are those all?

The WITNESS. Does it read in yours "Voices, 'Hear!' 'Three groans for Fletcher?'"

Mr. Manager BUTLER. Yes, sir. It is all right, is it not? What is the trouble with that?

The WITNESS. There are four "wares" there, are there not?

Mr. Manager BUTLER. What do you mean by "wares?" We have corrected the "e" for the "a;" that is the whole change.

The WITNESS. Yours reads "there ware a Christ;" the "ware" should be "was."

Question. Then all your corrections are of pronunciation and grammar, are they not?

Answer. The President did not use those words.

Question. Do you say that the President does not pronounce "were" broadly, as is sometimes the southern fashion?

Answer. I say that he did not use it as used in that paper.

Question. Did he not speak broadly the word "were" when he used it?

Answer. Not so that it could be distinguished for "ware."

Question. Then it is a matter of how you would spell pronunciation that you want to correct, is it?

Answer. The tone of voice cannot be represented in print.

Question. And still you think "were" best represents his tone of voice, do you?

Answer. I think it did.

Question. Although it cannot be represented in print. Now, sir, with the exception of these corrections in pronunciation and grammar, is there any correction as the speech was printed in the Democrat on Monday from that which was printed in the Republican?

Answer. Of what date?

Question. The Republican of Sunday.

Answer. Yes, sir.

Question. Or of Monday? With the exception of corrections of grammar and pronunciation, is there any correction of substance between the two reports as printed that morning?

Answer. Specify which papers you want compared, the Sunday Republican and Monday Democrat, or the Monday Republican and Monday Democrat?

Question. The Monday Republican and Monday Democrat.

Answer. Yes, sir.

Question. What are they as printed?

Answer. One is "Let the Government be restored. I have labored for it. I am for it now. I deny this doctrine of secession, come from what quarter it may."

Question. What is the change as printed?

Answer. "Let the Government be restored. I have labored for it." So far it is the same in both papers; and then the words "I am for it now" are omitted in the Democrat, and the punctuation is changed so as to begin the next sentence "Now, I deny this doctrine of secession," and then words are omitted and the punctuation changed.

Question. There are four words omitted, "I am for it," before now. What else?

Answer. Speaking of the neutrality law he said, "I am sworn to support the Constitution and to execute the law." Some one halloed out "Why didn't you do it?" and he answered, "The law was executed; the law was executed." Those words "Why didn't you do it" and "The law was executed; the law was executed," are omitted in the Democrat.

Question. What else of substance?

Answer. I do not know that I can point out any others without the memorandum.

Question. Use the memorandum to point out substance, not grammar, not punctuation, not pronunciation.

Answer, (referring to the memorandum.) One expression he used was, "Allow me to ask if there is a man here to-night who in the dark days of Know-Nothingism stood and battled more for their rights"——

Question. What is the word left out or put in there?

Answer. The word "sacrificed" is used in the Democrat, and the word "battled" is the one that was employed.

Mr. Manager BUTLER. I will not trouble you further, sir.

The WITNESS. Oh, I can point out more.

Mr. Manager BUTLER. That is all, sir.

Mr. CURTIS. We now desire, Mr. Chief Justice, to put in evidence a document certified from the Department of State.

[The document was handed to the Managers.]

The CHIEF JUSTICE. The counsel will state the object of this evidence.

Mr. CURTIS. It is the commission issued by President Adams to General Washington, constituting him Lieutenant General of the Army of the United States. The purpose is to show the form in which commissions were issued at that date to high military officers, and we have selected the most conspicuous instance in our history as regards the person, the office, and the occasion.

Mr. Manager BUTLER. There were two commissions issued to General Washington, two appointments made. Was this the one he accepted, or the one he rejected; do you remember?

Mr. EVARTS. We understood it to be the one actually issued, and received by him.

Mr. Manager BUTLER. And accepted by him?

Mr. EVARTS. We suppose so.

Mr. CURTIS. We understand so.

Mr. EVARTS. We desire to have the commission read.

Mr. Manager BUTLER. I see no objection to it. I thought perhaps you could tell me what I inquired about.

Mr. EVARTS. Will the Clerk be good enough to read it?

The CHIEF JUSTICE. The Secretary will read the paper.

The Chief Clerk read the following commission, which is accompanied by a certificate from the Secretary of State, that it is a carefully compared and exact copy of the original on file in his Department:

JOHN ADAMS,
President of the United States of America:

To all who shall see these presents, greeting:

Know ye, that reposing special trust and confidence in the patriotism, valor, fidelity, and abilities of George Washington, I have nominated, and by and with the advice and consent of the Senate do appoint, him Lieutenant General and Commander-in-Chief of all the armies raised or to be raised for the service of the United States. He is therefore carefully and diligently to discharge the duty of Lieutenant General and Commander-in-Chief by doing and performing all manner of things thereunto belonging. And I do strictly charge and require all officers and soldiers under his command, to be obedient to his orders as Lieutenant General and Commander-in-Chief. And he is to observe and follow such orders and directions from time to time as he shall receive from me or the future President of the United States of America. This commission to continue in force during the pleasure of the President of the United States for the time being.

Given under my hand at Philadelphia, this 4th day of July, in the year of our Lord 1798, [L. S.] and in the twenty-third year of the independence of the United States.

JOHN ADAMS.

By command of the President of the United States of America:

JAMES McHENRY, _Secretary of War._

Mr. CURTIS. I now desire, Mr. Chief Justice, to put in a document from the Department of the Interior, showing the removals of superintendents of Indian affairs, and of Indian agents, of land officers, receivers of public moneys, surveyors general, and certain miscellaneous officers who are not brought under any one of those classes. The document which I hold shows the date of the removal, the name of the officer, the office he held, and also contains a memorandum whether the removal was during the recess of the Senate or in the session of the Senate.

Mr. Manager BUTLER. I have but one objection to this species of evidence without anybody brought here to testify to it, and that is this: I have learned that in the case of the Treasury Department, which I allowed to come in without objection, there were other cases not reported where the power was refused to be exercised. I do not know whether it is so in the Interior Department or not. But most of these cases, upon our examination, appear to be simply under the law fixing their tenure during the pleasure of the President for the time being, and some of them are inferior officers originally made appointable by the heads of Departments. If the presiding officer thinks they have any bearing we have no objection.

Mr. CURTIS. I understand the matter of the application of the law to these offices somewhat differently from that which is stated by the honorable Manager. I have not had an opportunity minutely to examine these lists, for they were only handed to me this morning; but I understand that a very large number of these officers held for a fixed tenure of four years. That, however, must be a matter of argument hereafter.

Mr. Manager BUTLER. What class of officers do you speak of?

Mr. CURTIS. Receivers of public moneys is one of the classes.

Mr. JOHNSON. What is the date of the first removal and of the last?

Mr. CURTIS. These tables, I think, extend through the whole period of the existence of that Department. I do not remember the date when the Department was established, but I think they run through the whole history of the Department.

The CHIEF JUSTICE. No objection is made to the reception of this document in evidence.

The document is as follows:

DEPARTMENT OF THE INTERIOR,
WASHINGTON, D. C., _April 17, 1868._

I, Orville H. Browning, Secretary of the Interior, do hereby certify that the annexed thirteen sheets contain full, true, complete, and perfect transcripts from the records of this Department, so far as the same relate to the removals from office of the persons therein named.

In testimony whereof, I have hereunto subscribed my name and caused the seal of the Department [L. S.] to be affixed the day and year above written.

O. H. BROWNING,
Secretary of the Interior.

Removals of Superintendents of Indian Affairs and of Indian Agents.

Date.	Name.	Office.	Remarks.
Mch 13, 1849.	Thos P. Harvey	Superintendent at Saint Louis, Missouri.	During the recess.
June 9, 1865.	W. H. Albin	Central superintendency.	During the recess.
April 18, 1853.	Elias Murray	4th superintendency.	During the recess.
Mch 13, 1857.	Francis Huebschman	4th superintendency.	During the recess.
March 27, 1861.	W. J. Cullen	4th superintendency.	During the recess.
October 29, 1866.	E. B.	ey.	During the recess.
April 8, 1853.	John Dresman	South superintendency.	Senate consented to appointment of his successor.
March 3, 1855.	Thomas S. Drew	South superintendency.	During the recess.
March 17, 1857.	G. W. Denn	ney.	During the recess.
April 11, 1861.	Elias Rector	South superintendency.	During the recess.
Mch 16, 1863.	J. L. Collins	New Mexico superintendency.	During the recess.
March 3, 1865.	Michael Steck	New Mexico superintendency	During the recess.
March 17, 1866.	Filipe Delgado	New Mexico superintendency	Senate consented to appointment of his successor.
August 9, 1866.	G. W. Leiby	Arizona superintendency.	Senate consented to appointment of his successor.
March 31, 1854.	E. F. Beale	California superintendency.	During the recess.
April 16, 1861.	A. D. Rightmire.	Southern District California superintendency	During the recess.
August 10, 1866.	G. M. Hanson	North District California superintendency	During the recess.
Mch 22, 1853.	Austin Wiley	rey.	Senate consented to appointment of his successor.
March 17, 1853.	Jos Park	Oregon superintendency.	Senate consented to appointment of his successor.
June — 1856.	Joel Palmer	Oregon superintendency.	During the recess.
March 22, 1859.	J. W. Nesmith.	Oregon superintendency.	During the recess.
June 30, 1861.	E. R. Geary.	Oregon superintendency.	Senate consented to appointment of his successor.
July 18, 1861.	W. H. Rector.	Washington Territory superintendency.	Senate consented to appointment of his successor.
May —, 1862.	W. W. Mer.	Washington Territory superintendency	Senate consented to appointment of his successor.
6th 30, 1864.	B. F. Kendall	Washington Territory superintendency	Senate consented to appointment of his successor.
September 25, 1866.	C. H. Hale	Washington Territory superintendency	During the recess.
April 18, 1853.	W. H. Waterman	Great Nemaha agency.	During the recess.
March 25, 1861.	W. P. Richardson.	Great N maha agency.	Senate consented to appointment of his successor.
April 15, 1867.	Daniel Vanderslice.	Omaha agency.	Senate consented to appointment of his successor.
May 27, 1861.	R. W. Turnas.	Winnebago agency.	Senate consented to appointment of his successor.
September 7, 1865.	C. H. Mix.	Winnebago agency.	During the recess.
April 29, 1861.	St. A. D. Balcombe.	Pawnee agency.	During the recess.
March 16, 1862.	James L. Gillis.	Pawnee agency.	Senate consented to appointment of his successor.
August 13, 1856.	H. W. De Puy.	St. Peter's agency.	Senate consented to appointment of his successor.
September 11, 1857.	R. G. Mey.	St. Peter's agency.	During the recess.
March 23, 1861.	Charles E. Flanders.	Pottawattomie agency.	Senate consented to appointment of his successor.
September 20, 1864.	Joseph R. Brown.	Otoe and Missouri agency.	During the recess.
January 4, 1859.	W. W. Ross	Upper Arkansas agency.	During the recess.
April 27, 1866.	William Daily	Kansas agency.	Senate consented to appointment of his successor.
April 18, 1861.	R. C. Miley	Kickapoo agency	During the recess.
June 3, 1858.	M. C. Dickey	Kickapoo agency	Senate consented to appointment of his successor.
May 7, 1864.	Royal Baldwin.	Kickapoo agency	During the recess.
March 16, 1865.	Abram Bennett.	Delaware agency.	Senate consented to appointment of his successor.
March 27, 1861.	Thomas B. Sykes.	Shawnee agency.	Senate consented to appointment of his successor.
April 18, 1861.	Fielding Johnson.	Sac and Fox agency.	Senate consented to appointment of his successor.
June 6, 1858.	A. Arnold	Osage river agency.	Senate consented to appointment of his successor.
March 13, 1859.	Francis Tymony.		During the recess.
April 3, 1858.	Max. McCauslin.		During the recess.
April 15, 1861.	Seth Clover.		During the recess.

STATEMENT—Continued.

Date.	Name.	Office.	Remarks.
[illegible] —, [illegible]	F. Fitzpatrick	[illegible] agency	During the [illegible]
April 14, 1862	J. A. Cady	[illegible] Platte [illegible] agency	[illegible] to appointment of his successor.
[illegible] 3, [illegible]	[illegible] Jarot	Upper [illegible] agency	During the [illegible]
[illegible] 29 [illegible]	R. C. S. Brown	[illegible] agency	During the [illegible]
April 5, [illegible]	R. J. Cowart	[illegible] agency	During the [illegible]
March 6, [illegible]	[illegible] Crawford	[illegible] agency	Senate [illegible] to appointment of his successor.
[illegible] 25, 1866	Justin Harland	[illegible] agency	During the [illegible]
April 18, [illegible]	William Wilson	[illegible]	During the [illegible]
July 31, 1861	D. H. [illegible]	[illegible] and [illegible]ckasaw agency	Senate [illegible] to appointment of his successor.
August 22 [illegible]	[illegible]	Choctaw and [illegible]ckasaw agency	During the [illegible]
[illegible] 16, [illegible]	P. P. Elder	[illegible]	During the [illegible]
July 6, 1858	A. I. [illegible]	[illegible] agency	[illegible] the [illegible]
[illegible] 26, [illegible]	Samuel A. [illegible]	[illegible]	Senate [illegible] to appointment of his successor.
April 19, 1861	[illegible]	[illegible]	During the [illegible]
[illegible] 6, [illegible]	J. J. Humphreys	[illegible] agency	Senate [illegible] to appointment of his successor.
April 5, 1849	James [illegible]	[illegible] agency	During the [illegible]
[illegible]	P. [illegible]	[illegible] agency	During the [illegible]
April 5, [illegible]	W. H. [illegible]	[illegible]	During the [illegible]
April 16, [illegible]	Wi[illegible]	[illegible] agency	Senate [illegible] to appointment of his successor.
June 9 [illegible]	G. A. Cutler	[illegible] agency	During the [illegible]
[illegible] 11, [illegible]	Elias [illegible]	[illegible] ([illegible]) agency	[illegible] to appointment of his successor.
June 3, 1861	A. P. Dennison	[illegible] ([illegible]) agency	During the [illegible]
[illegible] 2, 1854	S. H. Culver	[illegible] Ronde ([illegible]) agency	During the [illegible]
[illegible] 16, [illegible]	I. F. Miller	[illegible] ([illegible]) agency	Senate [illegible] to appointment of his successor.
[illegible]	[illegible] Spalding	Siletz (Oregon) [illegible]	During the [illegible]
August 13, 1856	[illegible]	Siletz [illegible]	During the [illegible]
July [illegible], 1861	Daniel [illegible]	[illegible] agency	Senate [illegible] to appointment of his successor.
[illegible] 21, 1863	[illegible] R. Biddle	[illegible]	Senate [illegible] to appointment of his successor.
[illegible] 17, [illegible]	[illegible] B. [illegible]	Umatilla [illegible]	Senate [illegible] to appointment of his successor.
[illegible] 1, 1852	A. R. Wooley	An [illegible] in [illegible] Mo[illegible]	[illegible] [illegible] to appointment of his successor.
[illegible] 1, 1853	[illegible]	An Indian [illegible] in [illegible] Mo[illegible]	During the [illegible]
[illegible] 3, [illegible]	[illegible]	An Indian [illegible] in New [illegible]	During the [illegible]
[illegible] 21, [illegible]	José A. [illegible]	An Indian [illegible] in [illegible] Mo[illegible]	During the [illegible]
May 3, 1853	E. H. Wingfield	An [illegible] in [illegible]	During the [illegible]
July 26, 1861	Michael Steck	An Indian [illegible] in New [illegible]	Sen[illegible] [illegible] to appointment of his successor.
[illegible] 30, [illegible]	I. T. Russell	An Indian [illegible] in New [illegible]	Senate [illegible] to appointment of his successor.
[illegible] 2, [illegible]	Toribio Ro[illegible]	An Indian [illegible] in New [illegible]	Senate [illegible] to appointment of his successor.
[illegible] 22, [illegible]	R. H. Wei[illegible]	An Indian [illegible] in New [illegible]	Senate [illegible] to appointment of his successor.
[illegible] 1, [illegible]	S. M. Baird	An Indian [illegible] in [illegible]	[illegible] [illegible] to appointment of his successor.
[illegible] 6, [illegible]	S. F. K[illegible]	An Indian [illegible] in [illegible]	During the [illegible]
March 24, [illegible]	John Ward	An Indian [illegible] in New [illegible]	During the [illegible]
[illegible] 4, [illegible]	W. F. M. Arny	An Indian [illegible] in [illegible]	During the [illegible]
March 21, [illegible]	L. J. Keithly	An Indian [illegible] in [illegible]	During the [illegible]
April [illegible], 1853	R. B. Lambdin	[illegible] agency	[illegible] the [illegible]
March 28, [illegible]	A. H. Redfield	[illegible] agency	Senate [illegible] to appointment of his successor.
July [illegible], 1861	J. S. Gregory	[illegible] agency	Senate [illegible] to appointment of his successor.
April 26, [illegible]	[illegible] Humphreys	[illegible] Valley ([illegible]) agency	During the [illegible]
[illegible] 7, 1864	F. W. Catch	[illegible] Valley ([illegible]) agency	Senate [illegible] to appointment of his successor.
[illegible] 22, 1865	Charles Hutchings	Flat[illegible] ([illegible]) agency	During the [illegible]
[illegible] 7, [illegible]	Lut[illegible] L. [illegible]	[illegible] feet ([illegible]) agency	Senate [illegible] to appointment of his successor.

			During the
Oct. ... dr ... 1863	H. W. Reed	... feet	... agency	During the
... 1, 1851	R. H. Lansdale	... (Washington Territory) agency	... agency	... the
... 7,	A. A. Bancroft	Indian ... at in	During the
May 11, ... 865	Simeon Whitely	... ter	Senate
April 2 ... 1833	William Bryson	... agency
... 25, 1 ...	William Sprague	... agency	During the
March 22, 1851	J. W. I ... rule	... of the Mississippi	During the
... 65	A. C. Morrill	... of the Mississippi	Senate
November 9, 1856	Edwin Clark	... of the
April ... 1853	L. S. Watrous	... of Lake
Mh 25, ... 51	Cyrus K. Drew	... of Lake

C. ...—2 .

Registers of Land Offices removed during the recess of the Senate.

Date.	Name of officer.	Location of office.	State.	Remarks.
... il 5, ... 49	... n	Winn ... no	Indiana
... il 7, ... 9	Thomas Tiger	Fort W	Indiana
... il 12, 1849	J. H. McBride	Springfield	
... il 14, 1840	... rds	Kalamazoo	Indiana
... y ... 9	... n F. Reed		Arkansas
... y 8	... n Bruton	... o	Arkansas
... y 8, 1849	... n Miller		
... y 8, 1 ...	E. L. Dickson	Champagnole	Arkansas
... y 8, 1849	B. P. Jett	Helena	Arkansas
... y 8, 1849	Hiram Smith	Dixon	Arkansas
May 8, 1849	H ... y L. ... lie		
... y 9, 1849	S. B. Farwell		
... y 9, 1849	B. R. Cowherd	St ... t. Marie	Indiana
May 12, ... 9	J. W. Rush		Louisiana
... y ... 1849	J. S. ... and, Jr.	Vincennes	Iowa
... y 18, 1 ...	Dernhart	... a	Iowa
... y 18, 1849	... r	Iowa City	Iowa
May 21, 1849	W. W. Barrett	Dubuque	Illinois
... y 22, ... 9	... n Barlow	... ild	Wisconsin
May 24, ... 9	... . W. Parris	Detroit Point	Michigan
... y 31, ... 9	Elisha Taylor	Monroe	Louisiana
June 1, ... 9	D. P ...		Louisiana
June 1, ... 9	M. McIntire		Illinois
... e 11, ... 9	J. C. Sloo	Tallahassee	Illinois
... e 14, 1849	... ns J. ... im		Florida
... e 14, ... 9	... e H. Walker		
June 25, 1849	... h P.	Defiance	Ohio
June 25, ...	John Foster		Illinois
... y 12, ...	R. K. McLaughlin	New ...	Louisiana
... y 12, ... 9	Lewis St ...	Ionia ... a	
... y 12, 1849	Benjamin ... man	D ... no	Illinois
	Willi ... am E. ... Bell		

STATEMENT—Continued.

Date.	Name of officer.	Location of office.	State.	Remarks.
July 16, 1849	Harmon Alexander	Palestine	Illinois	
July 27, 1849	Samuel Holmes	Quincy	Illinois	
October 10, 1849	Nathaniel Bolton	Indianapolis	Indiana	
October 10, 1849	Jacob Fresman	Kaskaskia	Illinois	
October 10, 1849	Franklin Cannon	Jackson	Missouri	
November 1, 1849	William McNair	Fayette	Missouri	
October 13, 1850	Alanson Saltmarsh	Cahaba	Alabama	
October 13, 1850	D. B. Graham	Montgomery	Alabama	
June 13, 1861	La Fayette Mosher	Roseburg	Oregon	
July 14, 1855	E. W. Martin	Elba	Alabama	
July 24, 1855	W. P. Davis	Danville	Illinois	
March 2, 1855	Henry J. Biscoe	Helena	Arkansas	
April 3, 1856	Fielding L. Dowsing	Columbus	Mississippi	
April 3, 1857	Deidrick Upson	Winona	Minnesota	
March 19, 1857	George W. Sweet	Sank Rapids	Minnesota	
March 20, 1857	James H. Birch	Platsburg	Missouri	
March 28, 1857	J. O. Henning	Hudson	Wisconsin	
September 22, 1858	Abner C. Smith	Forest City	Minnesota	
April 16, 1859	Samuel Clark	Buchanan	Wisconsin	
May 3, 1859	Daniel Shaw	Superior	Wisconsin	
September 19, 1860	John McEnery	Monroe	Louisiana	
	W. T. dis	Eau Claire	Wisconsin	
April 1, 1861	Ira Munson	San Francisco	California	
April 9, 1861	E. P. Hart	Visalia	California	
	New Keller	Los Angeles	California	
April 9, 1861	William McDaniels	Humboldt	California	
April 9, 1861	J. R. Bennett	Chatfield	Ma	
May 15, 1861	Peter White	Marquette	Michigan	
April 2, 1861	Isaac W. Griffith	Des Moines	Iowa	
April 2, 1861	Lewis S. Hills	Council Bluffs	Iowa	
April 2, 1861	J. M. dis	Fort Dodge	Iowa	
April 2, 1861	S. P. Yeomans	Sioux City	Iowa	
April 9, 1861	E. Q. F. Hastings	Marysville	California	
April 10, 1861	A. C. Bradford	Stockton	California	
April 15, 1861	Isaac W. Smith	Omapia	Washington Territory	
April 15, 1861	Charles S. Benton	La Crosse	Wisconsin	
April 15, 1861	James C. Dow	Henderson	Missouri	
April 18, 1861	Jesse Morin	Fort Scott	Kansas	
April 18, 1861	James B. Jones	Lecompton	Kansas	
April 22, 1861	David R. Curran	Mensha	Kansas	
April 26, 1861	Samuel B. Garrett	Junction City	Kansas	
April 26, 1861	John A. Parker		Nebraska	
April 30, 1861	O. P. Richardson	Santa Fe	New Mexico	
May 1, 1861	Henry T. Brown	Booneville	Missouri	
May 30, 1861	Warren H. Graves	Springfield	Missouri	
June 13, 1861	Benjamin Jennings	Oregon City	Oregon	
June 22, 1861	George McOut	Indianapolis	Indiana	
September 9, 1861	Thomas Walke		Ohio	
August 7, 1861	William E. Keeper	Springfield	Illinois	
March 18, 1895	G. W. Boardman	Booneville	Missouri	

Date	Name	Location	State
September 28, 1866	Simon Jones	New Orleans	Louisiana
September 24, 1866	Royal Buck	Nebraska City	Nebraska
September 24, 1866	H. C. Driggs	East Saginaw	Michigan
October 5, 1866	S. T. Davis	Sioux City	Iowa
October 27, 1866	G. W. Martin	Junction City	Kansas
November 5, 1866	C. R. Dorsey	Brownsville	Nebraska

The above dates are those upon which the successors of the above-named persons were appointed.

Receivers of Public Moneys removed during the recess of the Senate.

Date	Name of officer	Location of office	State	Remarks
March 28, 1849	John G. Won	Lebanon	Alabama	
March 30, 1849	Elisha Morrow	Green Bay	Wisconsin	
April 7, 1849	J. D. ʼelson	Fort Wayne	Indiana	
April 12, 1849	James P. Drake	Indianapolis	Indiana	
April 12, 1849	Mitchell Hinshill	Kalamazoo	Michigan	
April 7, 1849	Thomas Dyer	Chicago	Illinois	
May 7, 1849	Lemuel R. Lincoln	Little Rock	Arkansas	
May 8, 1849	W. J. Adams	Clarksville	Arkansas	
May 8, 1849	D. J. Chapman	Batesville	Arkansas	
May 8, 1849	Matthew Leeper	Fayetteville	Arkansas	
May 8, 1849	D. T. ʼker	Washington	Arkansas	
May 8, 1849	M. F. ʼaey	Champagnole	Arkansas	
May 8, 1849	George Jeffries	Helena	Wis.	
May 9, 1849	John Doment	Dixon	Mississippi	
May 9, 1849	W. W. Leland	Pontotoc	Michigan	
May 9, 1849	M. A. Patterson	Sault Ste. Marie	Mississippi	
May 9, 1849	ʼM C. ʼim	Jackson	Wisconsin	
May 9, 1849	Paschal Bequette	Mineral Point	Wisconsin	
May 12, 1849	Bennett W. Engle	Crawfordsville	Indiana	
May 12, 1849	Samuel Wise	Vincennes	Indiana	
May 18, 1849	ʼhe Gillespie	Greensburg	Louisiana	
May 18, 1849	Verplanck Van Antwerp	Fairfield	Iowa	
May 18, 1849	Enos Lowe	Iowa City	Iowa	
May 18, 1849	George McHenry	Dubuque	Iowa	
May 18, 1849	A. G. Herndon	Springfield	Illinois	
May 21, 1849	John Parsons	Shawneetown	Florida	
May 24, 1849	J. A. Hinestine	Milwaukee	Wisconsin	
June 4, 1849	Braxton Parrish	Shawneetown	Illinois	
June 4, 1849	J. H. Westbrook	Columbus	Mississippi	
June 14, 1849	Frederick Hall	Ionia	Michigan	
June 25, 1849	W. L. Henderson	Defiance	Ohio	
June 25, 1849	Samuel Leech	Stillwater	Minnesota	
June 30, 1849	Daniel Gregory	Vandalia	Illinois	
July 12, 1849	John B. Filhiol	Monroe	Louisiana	
July 27, 1849	Hiram Rodgers	Quincy	Illinois	
August 9, 1849	Niles B. Smith	Springfield	Mesouri	
August 25, 1849	J. M. B. ʼilker	ʼimes	Louisiana	
August 25, 1849	Daniel Ashby	Clinton	Missouri	

STATEMENT—Continued.

Date.	Name of officer.	Location of office.	State.	Remarks.
October 10, 1849	L. R. Noell	Danville	Illinois	
October 10, 1849	John G. Cameron	Edwardsville	Illinois	
December 1, 1849	H. W. Palfrey	New Orleans	Louisiana	
September 4, 1855	James Larkins	Elba	Alabama	
October 8, 1855	A. S. Bryant	Sioux City	Iowa	
October 10, 1855	J. C. Clarborne	Batesville	Arkansas	
September 13, 1856	Thomas C. Shoemaker		Territory of Kansas	
August 19, 1858	E. B. Dean, Jr	Superior	Wisconsin	
September 19, 1860	Christopher H. Dobbs	Monroe	Louisiana	
September 21, 1860	John D. Evans	Forest City	Minnesota	
April 1, 1861	John E. Perkins	Eau Claire	Wisconsin	
March 30, 1861	J. H. McKenny	Chatfield	Minnesota	
June 13, 1861	William J. Martin	Roseburg	Oregon	
March 30, 1861	Thomas McNulty	Chillicothe	Ohio	
April 2, 1861	Isaac Cooper	Des Moines	Iowa	
April 2, 1861	A. H. Palmer	Council Bluffs	Iowa	
April 2, 1861	Thomas Sargent	Fort Dodge	Iowa	
April 2, 1861	Robert Means	Sioux City	Iowa	
April 9, 1861	Joseph Hopkins	Marysville	California	
April 9, 1861	Thomas Baker	Visalia	California	
April 9, 1861	George W. Hook	Humboldt	California	
April 9, 1861	Augustin Olivera	Les Angeles	California	
April 9, 1861	Paschal Bequette	San Francisco	California	
April 9, 1861	W. B. Norman	Stockton	California	
April 10, 1861	M. S. Van Cleare	Olympia	Washington Territory	
April 15, 1861	C. Graham	Henderson	Missouri	
November 10, 1860	Ebenezer Warren	Marquette	Michigan	
April 22, 1861	Samuel Ryan	Menasha	Wisconsin	
April 26, 1861	Findley Patterson	Junction City	Kansas	
April 28, 1861	George J. Clark	Fort Scott	Kansas	
May 24, 1861	W. A. Street	Santa Fé	New Mexico	
May 18, 1861	E. Rush Spencer	Bayfield	Wisconsin	
May 20, 1861	E. E. Buckner	Boonville	Missouri	
May 30, 1861	Thomas J. Bishop	Springfield	Missouri	
June 11, 1861	George E. Greene	Vincennes	Indiana	
June 13, 1861	A. L. Lovejoy	Oregon City	Oregon	
May 27, 1861	C. B. Smith	Brownsville	Nebraska	
June 22, 1861	Charles C. Campbell	Indianapolis	Indiana	
September 9, 1861	A. G. Herndon	Springfield	Illinois	
October 1, 1861	John J. McClelland	Menasha	Wisconsin	
July 30, 1863	Franklin Stewart	Nebraska City	Nebraska	
March 16, 1864	John Greiner	Santa Fé	New Mexico	
September 18, 1866	W. B. Mitchell	St. Cloud	Minnesota	
September 18, 1866	J. S. McFarland	Santa Fé	New Mexico	
September 24, 1866	W. H. H. Waters	Boonville	Missouri	
March 30, 1865	Charles A. Gillman	St. Cloud	Minnesota	
September 9, 1865	J. L. Collins	Santa Fé	New Mexico	

The above dates are those upon which the successors of the above-named persons were appointed.

Receivers of Public Moneys removed during sessions of the Senate, that body advising and consenting to the appointments of their successors.

Date.	Name of officer.	Location of office.	State.	Remarks.
July 31, 1852	Henry Acker	Sault Ste. Marie	Michigan	
December 22, 1857	Harvey Whittington	Platsburg	Missouri	
May 17, 1858	James P. Downer	Ogden	Kansas	
June 3, 1858	Edward	der	Illinois	
December 22, 1858	E. B. Dean, jr.	Springfield	Wisconsin	
Mh 8, 1859	Robert J. Graveriat	Marquette	Michigan	
January 16, 1859	John C. Turk	Dakota City	Nebraska	
February 14, 1860	Thos C. Mnt.	Natchitoches	Louisiana	
February 14, 1860	Milton H. Matt.	Cambridge	Mo	
May 28, 1860	Samuel L. Hayes	St. Cloud	Mo	
January 16, 1860	Dave Shaw	Superior		
Mh 18, 1861	Peter F. Wilson	Omaha	Nebraska	
March 25, 1861	Gear A. Sterens	Traverse City	Mn	
Mh 25, 1861	W. L. P. Little	East Saginaw	Michigan	
March 23, 1861	John F. Tillotson	St. Peter	Minnesota	
Mh 23, 1861	Albert G. Rt	Stevens's Point	Minnesota	
Mh 23, 1861	W. H.	Sunrise City	Mo	
March 25, 1861	Gary J. Wilson	Ionia	Michigan	
March 27, 1861	James D. olds.	Falls St. Croix	Mn	
	Suel E. dms	St. Cloud	Minnesota	
July 19, 1861	Theodore Rodolf	La Crosse	Wisconsin	
July 22, 1861	Jan J. Turnbraugh	Ironton	Missouri	
July 16, 1861	Nathaniel C. Holden	Nebraska City	Missouri	
Mh 6, 1862	Richard C. Vaughn	Nebraska City	Nebraska	
Mh 12, 1863	Enos	Marysville	California	
January 7, 1864	George E. Briggs	Roseburg	Oreg n	
June 7, 1864	B. F. Reynolds	Falls of St. Croix	Wisconsin	
May 4, 1866	John Griemer	Santa Fé	New Mexico	
July 14, 1866	Alfred H. Carrigan	Washington	Arkansas	

The above dates are the dates of confirmation by the Senate.

Registers of Land Offices removed during session of the Senate, that body advising and consenting to the appointment of their successors.

Date.	Name of officer.	Location of office.	State.	Remarks.
March 14, 1849	Joel S. Fiske	Green Bay	Wisconsin	
July 31, 1852	Andrew Backus	Sault Ste. Marie	Michigan	
March 12, 1857	Deidrich Upman	Faribault	Minnesota	
April 14, 1858	Robert Brown	Des Moines	Iowa	
May 17, 1858	Fredwick Emory	Ogden	Kansas	
May 17, 1858	W. H. Doak	Fort Scott	Kansas	
June 3, 1858	J. Rush Spencer	Hudson	Wisconsin	
June 3, 1858	John Connelly, Jr.	Springfield	Illinois	
June 15, 1858	W. V. Gift	San Francisco	California	
March 1, 1859	A. C. Smith	Forest City	Minnesota	
February 14, 1860	John B. Cloutier	Natchitoches	Louisiana	
March 23, 1860	Charles F. Hyerman	Detroit	Michigan	
March 25, 1860	Jacob Barns	Traverse City	Michigan	
March 25, 1860	Moses B. Hess	East Saginaw	Michigan	
March 27, 1861	Orpheus Everts	Falls St. Croix	Wisconsin	
March 23, 1861	Joshua B. Culver	Portland	Minnesota	
March 23, 1861	Oscar Taylor	Otter Tail City	Minnesota	
March 23, 1861	Hugh Brawley	Steven's Point	Wisconsin	
March 23, 1861	Henry N. Setzer	Sunrise City	Minnesota	
March 27, 1861	Thomas E. Massey	Forest City	Minnesota	
March 27, 1861	J. D. Crutendon	St. Cloud	Minnesota	
March 25, 1861	John C. Blanchard	Ionia	Michigan	
March 27, 1861	Samuel Plumer	St. Peter	Minnesota	
July 19, 1861	Charles S. Benton	La Crosse	Wisconsin	
March 6, 1862	Adolph Renard	Recorder of land titles, St. Louis	Missouri	
March 31, 1862	George Webster	Stockton	California	
July 17, 1862	W. H. Lewis	Batesville	Arkansas	
March 9, 1865	D. H. Ball	Marquette	Michigan	
February 10, 1865	Joseph W. Edwards	Marquette	Michigan	

The above dates are the dates of confirmation by the Senate.

Surveyor Generals removed during recess of the Senate.

Date.	Name of officer.	Location of office.	Remarks.
April 11, 1849	Robert Butler	Florida	
May 8, 1849	William Pelham	Arkansas	
May 14, 1849	F. R. Landry	Louisiana	
June 14, 1849	P. K. Conway	Illinois and Missouri	
March 22, 1859	John S. Zieber	Oregon	
April 3, 1861	John Loughborough	Illinois and Missouri	
April 15, 1861	J. W. Mandeville	California	
April 29, 1861	H. B. Burnett	Kansas and Nebraska	
May 11, 1861	Warner Lewis	Iowa and Missouri	
June 13, 1861	W. H. Chapman	Oregon	
March 16, 1865	Daniel W. Wilder	Kansas and Nebraska	

Surveyor Generals removed during session of the Senate, that body advising and consenting to the appointments of their successors.

Date.	Name of officer.	Location of office.	Remarks.
March 3, 1855	George Milbourne	Arkansas	
March 27, 1861	Charles L. Emerson	Minnesota	
July 22, 1861	A. P. Wilbar	New Mexico	
July 15, 1861	James Tilton	Washington Territory	
March 13, 1863	Francis M. Case	Colorado	
February 23, 1864	Edward F. Beale	California	
May 12, 1866	George D. Hill	Dakota	
July 15, 1861	Samuel C. Stambaugh	Utah	

Miscellaneous Removals.

Date.	Name of officer.	Office.	Remarks.
July 23, 1849	S. H. Laughlin	Recorder of General Land Office	During recess.
July 1, 1849	William Medill	Commissioner of Indian Affairs	During recess.
April 7, 1849	Charles Douglas	Commissioner of Public Buildings	During recess.
April 5, 1849	C. P. Sengstack	Warden of the penitentiary, District of Columbia	During recess.
May 9, 1849	Edmond Burke	Commissioner of Patents	During recess.
November 10, 1850	James L. Edwards	Commissioner of Pensions	During recess.
August 12, 1865	Robert Beale	Warden of the jail	During recess.
September 7, 1865	N. C. Towle	Register of deeds, District of Columbia	During recess.
November 3, 1866	Z. C. Robbins	Register of wills, District of Columbia	During recess.
October 21, 1862	S. J. Dallas	Principal clerk of surveys General Land Office	During recess.
June 29, 1850	Jonas B. Ellis	Iowa and clerk of surveys, District of Columbia	Senate consented to appointment of successor.
March 28, 1859	Luke Lea	Commissioner of Indian Affairs	Senate consented to appointment of successor.
December 23, 1859	Thomas Thornley	Warden of the penitentiary, District of Columbia	Senate consented to appointment of successor.
March 19, 1861	Joseph S. Wilson	Commissioner of General Land Office	Senate consented to appointment of successor.
March 6, 1867	R. M. Hall	Register of deeds	Senate consented to appointment of successor.
July 20, 1867	Thomas B. Brown	Warden of the jail, District of Columbia	Senate consented to appointment of successor.

Frederick W. Seward sworn and examined.

By Mr. Curtis:

Question. State what office you hold under the Government?

Answer. Assistant Secretary of State.

Question. How long have you held the office?

Answer. Since March, 1861.

Question. In whose charge in that Department is the subject of consuls and consular and vice consular appointments?

Answer. Under my general supervision.

Question. Please state the practice in making appointments of vice consuls in case of the death, resignation, incapacity, or absence of consuls?

Answer. Usually——

Mr. Manager BUTLER. Stop a moment. Is not that regulated by law?

Mr. CURTIS. That is a matter of argument. We think it is.

Mr. Manager BUTLER. So do we. There cannot be any dispute on that question.

Mr. CURTIS. Now we are going to show the practice under the law.

Mr. Manager BUTLER. Different from the law?

Mr. CURTIS. Just as we have done in other cases. I have a document here to offer, but it requires some explanations to make the document intelligible.

Mr. Manager BUTLER. We do not object if the offer is to show the practice under the law.

Mr. CURTIS, (to the witness.) Proceed, if you please, Mr. Seward.

The Witness. When the vacancy is foreseen the consul nominates a vice consul, who enters upon the discharge of his duties at once during the time that the nomination is sent to the Department of State. The Department approves or disapproves when it receives the nomination. In case the vacancy has not been foreseen and the consul is dead, absent, or sick, unable to discharge the duties or to designate his temporary substitute, then the minister in the country will make a nomination and send that to the Department of State; or if there be no minister, the naval commander will not infrequently make a nomination and send that to the Department of State, and the vice consul so designated will act until the Department shall approve or disapprove. In other cases the Department itself will designate a vice consul without any previous nomination of either minister, consul, or naval commander, and he enters upon the discharge of his duties in the same manner.

Question. How is he authorized or commissioned?

Answer. He receives a certificate of his appointment signed by the Secretary of State.

Question. Running for a definite time, or how?

Answer. Running "subject to the conditions prescribed by law."

Question. Is this appointment of vice consul made temporarily to fill a vacancy, or how otherwise?

Answer. It is made to fill the office during the period which necessarily elapses in the time that it takes for the news of the vacancy to reach the Department for a successor to be appointed.

Question. That is for a succeeding consul to be appointed?

Answer. For a succeeding full officer to be appointed. Sometimes a period of weeks or months may elapse before the news can reach this country, and a similar period before the newly-appointed successor can reach the post.

Question. It is, then, in its character an *ad interim* appointment to fill the vacancy?

Answer. Yes.

Cross-examined by Mr. Manager Butler:

Question. Is there anything said in their commissions or letters of appointment about their being *ad interim?*

Answer. Their letter of appointment says "subject to the conditions prescribed by law."

Question. That is the only limitation there is?

Answer. That is the only limitation I remember.

Question. Are not these appointments made under the fifteenth section of the act of August 18, 1856?

Answer. I think the act of 1856 does not create the office nor give the power of appointment, but it recognizes the office as already in existence, and the power as already in the President.

Mr. Manager BUTLER. We will see about that in a moment, sir.

Mr. JOHNSON. Has the Manager the statute before him?

Mr. Manager BUTLER. I have.

Mr. JOHNSON. What is the volume?

Mr. Manager BUTLER. The volume is the 11th Statutes-at-Large. This statute begins on page 35 of the 11th Statutes-at-Large; but the fourteenth and fifteenth sections are those that relate to the matter. The fourteenth section I will read, for I want to ask some further questions in regard to it: •

"That the President be, and he is hereby, authorized to define the extent of country to be embraced within any consulate or commercial agency, and to provide for the appointment of vice consuls, vice commercial agents, deputy consuls, and consular agents therein, in such manner and under such regulations as he shall deem proper; but no compensation shall be allowed for the service of any such vice consul or vice commercial agent beyond nor except out of the allowance made by his act for the principal consular officer in whose place such appointment shall be made; and no vice consul, vice commercial agent, deputy consul, or consular agent shall be appointed otherwise than in such manner and under such regulations as the President shall prescribe pursuant to the provisions of this act."

[To the witness.] Now, sir, in the Department of State, have they ever undertaken to make a vice consul against the provisions of this act?

The WITNESS. I am not aware that they ever have.

Question. Or attempted it in any way?

Answer. Not that I know of.

Mr. CURTIS. I now offer from the Department of State the document I hold in my hand, which contains a list of consular offices appointed during the session of the Senate when vacancies existed at the time such appointments were made. The earliest instance of it in this list is in 1837, and the latest one does not come down to the law which the honorable Manager has read. They are all prior to that law, and after the year 1837.*

[The document was handed to the Managers for examination.]

Mr. CURTIS. I was mistaken in a date. I thought the honorable Manager read the date of the law as 1866.

Mr. Manager BUTLER. Eighteen hundred and fifty-six. August 18, 1856.

Mr. CURTIS. Then there are some which are subsequent to the law. They begin in 1837, and they come down to about 1862, if I remember rightly. I have not examined it minutely.

Mr. Manager BUTLER. There was a prior statute of 1848 which was partly revived in the law of 1856.

Mr. Manager. BOUTWELL. Mr. Chief Justice, I wish to call the attention of the counsel for the respondent to the fact that it does not appear from this paper that these vacancies did not happen during the recess of the Senate. It merely states that they were filled during the session. As these were offices existing in remote countries the probability is that the vacancies happened during the recess of the Senate.

Mr. CURTIS. It does not appear when the vacancies happened. The purpose for which we offer the evidence is to show that these temporary appointments were made to fill vacancies during the session of the Senate.

Mr. Manager BOUTWELL. I only wish to give notice that we treat them as cases where vacancies happened during the recess of the Senate, it being perfectly understood that, according to the practice, vacancies happening during the recess of the Senate might be filled during the session of the Senate. There is no evidence to the contrary in the papers.

Mr. EVARTS. We understand, then, that the Managers hold that a vacancy that happens in the recess may be filled during the session without sending a nomination to the Senate.

Mr. Manager BOUTWELL. No.

Mr. EVARTS. I thought that was what you stated. Is it not your proposition?

Mr. Manager BOUTWELL. I only give notice that on that record we propose to treat these as vacancies happening during the recess of the Senate.

Mr. EVARTS. And filled during the session.

Mr. Manager BOUTWELL. That we do not know anything about; when they were filled. It does not appear that they did not happen during the recess.

Mr. EVARTS. The certificate is to the effect that they were filled during the session of the Senate.

Mr. Manager BINGHAM. We do not propose to settle the law of the case now.

The CHIEF JUSTICE. The Chief Justice does not understand the honorable Managers as objecting to the reception of this document in evidence.

Mr. Manager BOUTWELL. We do not object to the paper. I only give notice how we propose to treat it, on the face of the paper, as not showing that the vacancies happened during the session of the Senate.

The document is as follows:

UNITED STATES OF AMERICA,
Department of State:

To all to whom these presents shall come, greeting:

I certify that the document hereunto annexed contains a list of consular officers appointed during the session of the Senate, where vacancies existed at the time such appointments were made.

In testimony whereof I, William H. Seward, Secretary of State of the United States, have hereunto subscribed my name and caused the seal of the Department of State to be affixed.

Done at the city of Washington, this 11th day of
[L. S.] April, A. D. 1868, and of the independence of the United States of America the ninety-second. WILLIAM H. SEWARD.

Henry C. Bridges, appointed vice consul at Kin-Kiang, China, May 16, 1864, on the resignation of W. Breck, consul.

D. Thurston, appointed vice consul general at Montreal, May 31, 1864, on the death of J. R. Giddings, consul general.

A. Duff, appointed vice consul at Demerara, 7th January, 1865, on the death of C. G. Hannah, consul.

George W. Healy, appointed vice consul at Bombay, December 28, 1861, on death of L. H. Hatfield, consul.

Robert Bayman, appointed vice consul at Funchal, March 24, 1864, on death of G. True, consul.

E. Bremt, appointed vice consul at Hanover, February 18, 1861, on the resignation of J. S. Holton, consul.

Alexander Thompson, appointed vice consul general at Constantinople, January 7, 1860, awaiting the arrival of M. M. Smith, appointed consul general.

Bernardo J. Arcanques, appointed vice consul at Bayonne, April 19, 1856, on resignation of John P. Sullivan, consul.

Joseph Ayton, appointed vice consul at Carthagena, February 20, 1838, on the resignation of J. M. McPherson, consul.

Thomas V. Clark, appointed vice consul at Guayaquil, December 31, 1857, on resignation of M. P. Gaine, consul.

A. Lacombe, appointed vice consul at Puerto Cabello, January 23, 1865, on the transfer of C. H. Loehr to Laguayra.

John Gardner, appointed vice consul at Rio Janeiro, September 15, 1839, on the removal of J. M. Baker.

H. F. Fitch, appointed vice consul at Pernambuco, April 13, 1860, on death of W. W. Stepp.

August Peixoto, appointed acting consul, December 7, 1864, on the removal of Thomas F. Wilson, consul, at Bahia.

Samuel G. Pond, appointed acting consul at Para, December 2, 1862, on the death of M. R. Williams.

Robert H. Robinson, appointed acting vice consul at Montevideo, March 12, 1858, on resignation of R. M. Hamilton.

Amory Edwards, appointed acting consul at Buenos Ayres, December 28, 1840, on death of Slade.

William L. Hobson, appointed vice consul at Valparaiso, July 17, 1840, on resignation of George G. Hobson.

George B. Merwin, appointed vice consul at Valparaiso, December 5, 1854, on the resignation of Reuben Wood.

W. H. Kelley, appointed vice consul at Otaheite, December 31, 1848. Mr. Hawes not having exequatur.

D. B. Van Brundt, appointed United States consul at Acapulco, May 26, 1860, by Flag Officer Montgomery, on death of McMicken.

GIDEON WELLES sworn and examined.

By Mr. EVARTS:

Question. You are now Secretary of the Navy?

Answer. I am.

Question. At what time and from whom did you receive that appointment?

Answer. I was appointed in March, 1861, by Abraham Lincoln.

Question. And have held office continuously until now?

Answer. From that date.

Question. Do you remember on the 21st of February last your attention being drawn to some movements of troops or military officers?

Answer. On the evening of the 21st of February my attention was called to some movements that were being made.

Question. How was this brought to your attention?

Answer. My son brought it to my attention. He had been attending a party at which there had been an application from a son of General Emory, I think, and from one or two others, for any officer belonging to the fifth regiment or under the command of General Emory to repair forthwith to headquarters.

Question. Your son had observed that and had reported it to you?

Answer. He reported that to me.

Question. Did you, in consequence of that, seek or have an interview with the President of the United States?

Answer. I requested my son to go over that evening; but he did not see the President.

Mr. Manager BUTLER. Stay a moment. We object to what was said.

Mr. EVARTS. He says he sent his son, and his son failed to see the President. His attempt was first to send a message.

The WITNESS. I was not well, and could not go myself.

By Mr. EVARTS:

Question. You attempted to send a message that night?

Answer. I did.

Question. State what happened on the following day?

Answer. On Saturday, the 22d, I went myself, in the morning or about noon, to the President on that subject. I told him what I had heard, and asked him what it meant——

Mr. Manager BUTLER. We object to that conversation.

The WITNESS. Very good.

Mr. EVARTS. Is objection made to this?

Mr. Manager BUTLER. Yes, sir; and before we speak to the objection I should like to ask the witness to fix the time a little more carefully.

Mr. EVARTS. He has stated it exactly; about noon.

The WITNESS. About twelve o'clock on the 22d of February.

By Mr. Manager BUTLER:

Question. How close to twelve, before or after?

Answer. I should think it was a little before twelve o'clock. I will state a circumstance or two. The Attorney General was there when I went in. While I was there the nomination of Mr. Ewing was made out for Secretary of War, and was delivered to the Private Secretary to be carried to the Senate.

Mr. Manager BUTLER. Stay a moment. Let us see what time he said that was.

Mr. EVARTS. It is not time for cross-examination now.

Mr. Manager BUTLER. No; but I submit, Mr. President, it is time for cross-examination upon the question whether the thing is admissible in order to ascertain the time. At one point of time it may be, while at another point of time it clearly is not admissible.

Mr. EVARTS. It is quite immaterial, if you will go on and get through.

Mr. Manager BUTLER. Quite immaterial what point of time?

Mr. EVARTS. Immaterial whether you cross-examine now or hereafter.

Mr. Manager BUTLER. I only want to fix it. [To the witness.] You think it was very near twelve?

The WITNESS. About twelve o'clock.

Question. Could it have been as early as half past eleven?

Answer. No, sir; I do not think it was.

Question. But between that and half past twelve some time?

Answer. Yes, sir.

Question. Within that hour?

Answer. Yes, sir.

Mr. Manager BUTLER. Now, our objection——

Mr. EVARTS. Now I will proceed with my questions, if you please.

Mr. Manager BUTLER. Very well.

Mr. EVARTS. How far have we got now? Let the answer on this point as far as it has gone be read, Mr. Stenographer.

The CHIEF JUSTICE. The stenographer will read what is desired.

D. F. MURPHY, one of the reporters for the Globe, read from the short-hand notes of Mr. Welles's testimony, as follows:

"On Saturday, the 22d, I went myself in the morning or about noon to the President on that subject. I told him what I had heard; asked him what it meant——

"Mr. Manager BUTLER. We object to that conversation."

Mr. EVARTS. Very good.

The CHIEF JUSTICE. If the question be objected to the counsel will please reduce it to writing.

Mr. Manager BUTLER. We object to any conversation of the President at that time.

Mr. EVARTS, (to the witness.) What passed between you and the President after that in regard to that communication which you had made to him?

Mr. Manager BUTLER. Wait a moment. The Chief Justice desired the question to be put in writing.

Mr. EVARTS. That is being done now.

The question was reduced to writing, and read by the Secretary, as follows:

What passed between you and the President after you made that communication and in reference to that communication?

Mr. EVARTS. I would state, Mr. Chief Justice and Senators, before any argument is commenced on this subject, if there is to be one, that this evidence is offered in regard to the article that relates to the conversation between the President and General Emory.

Mr. Manager BUTLER. That is precisely as we understand it, Mr. President; but we also understand the fact to be that General Emory had been sent for before Mr. Welles appears on the scene. That is why I was anxious to fix the time. I am instructed by my associate Managers, and we are now endeavoring to get the matter certain, that General Emory received a note to come to the President's at ten o'clock in the morning, and that he got there before even the Secretary of the Navy. But, however that may be, he was called there before; we cannot at this moment ascertain exactly how that is; but it does not appear, at any rate, that this conversation was before Emory was sent for.

Mr. CURTIS. We shall see about that.

Mr. EVARTS. That is part of the matter of proof that is to be considered of when it is all in, as to which is right in hours and which in facts.

Mr. Manager BUTLER. The question of what was said in the conversation is not to be considered as proof which was right in fact. I suppose my learned opponents would not claim that if this was before General Emory came there they have a right to put in the testimony.

Mr. EVARTS. It is precisely in that view that we offer it.

Mr. Manager BUTLER. I should have said subsequent.

Mr. EVARTS. I beg your pardon.

Mr. Manager BUTLER. I made a mistake as to the comparative date for which I am very glad that you corrected me. If it was subsequent I suppose the gentlemen would not claim that it could be admitted. Therefore it must appear affirmatively that it was before in order to make it competent. That is my proposition. It does not appear affirmatively to have been before, and I think it was after-

ward; but of that I am trying to make myself certain by an examination.

The CHIEF JUSTICE. The Chief Justice thinks the evidence is competent. It will be for the Senate to judge of its value. He will, however, put the question to the Senate if any Senator desires. [After a pause.] You will proceed, Mr. Welles.

Mr. EVARTS. You will be so good as to answer the question, Mr. Welles.

The WITNESS. I should like to have it read.

The CHIEF CLERK. The question is:

What passed between you and the President after you made that communication and in reference to that communication?

The WITNESS. I cannot repeat the words, perhaps, exactly; but yet I should think the first words of the President were: "I do not know what Emory means;" or "I do not know what Emory is about." I remarked that I thought he ought to know; that if he was summoning high officers at such a time the evening before it must be for a reason, and it was his duty, I thought, to send for General Emory, and to inquire into the facts. He hesitated somewhat. We had a little conversation, and I think he said that he would send for him. He either said he would send for Emory or that he would send and inquire into this. I think he said he would send for him. That was about the conversation.

By Mr. EVARTS:

Question. Now, Mr. Welles, I will call your attention to the 21st of February of this year at the time of the close of the Cabinet meeting on that day. At what hour was the Cabinet meeting held on that day, Friday, the 21st of February?

Answer. At twelve. Twelve is the regular hour of meeting.

Question. That is the usual hour and that is the usual day for Cabinet meetings?

Answer. Yes, sir. Tuesdays and Fridays.

Question. Did you at that time have any interview with the President of the United States at which the subject of Mr. Stanton's removal was mentioned?

Answer. I did.

Question. At about what hour of the day was that?

Answer. I cannot fix it. It must have been, perhaps, in the neighborhood of two o'clock.

Question. Had you, up to that time, heard of the removal of Mr. Stanton?

Answer. I had not until the close of Cabinet business that day.

Question. When the Cabinet meeting was closed this interview took place at which the subject was mentioned?

Answer. The President remarked—

Mr. Manager BUTLER. Stop a moment.

Mr. EVARTS, (to the witness.) You need not state now what it was the President said; but that is the time he made the communication?

The WITNESS. Yes, sir.

By Mr. EVARTS:

Question. What passed between you and the President at that time?

Mr. Manager BUTLER. We object to that.

The CHIEF JUSTICE. Counsel will please reduce their question to writing.

Mr. EVARTS. I will state what I propose to prove.

Mr. CONNESS. I move that the Senate take a recess for fifteen minutes.

The motion was agreed to: and at the expiration of the recess the Chief Justice resumed the chair.

Mr. EVARTS. Before presenting in writing the question which was objected to I wish to ask one or two preliminary questions of Mr. Welles before going further. [To the witness.] Did the President proceed to make any communication to you on this occasion concerning the removal of Mr. Stanton and the appointment of General Thomas?

Answer. Yes; he did.

Question. Was this before the Cabinet meeting had broken up; or at what stage of your meeting was it?

Answer. We had concluded the departmental business and were about separating when the President remarked——

Mr. Manager BINGHAM. You need not state anything he said.

Mr. EVARTS. It was then that he made the communication, whatever it was?

The WITNESS. At that time he made the communication.

Question. Who were present?

Answer. I believe all the Cabinet were present. Perhaps Mr. Stanbery, the Attorney General, was not. He was a good deal absent during the session of the Supreme Court.

Question. All were present, unless it be Mr. Stanbery, you think?

Answer. I think so.

Mr. EVARTS. Now, Mr. Chief Justice and Senators, I offer to prove that communication and submit it in this form:

We offer to prove that on this occasion the President communicated to Mr. Welles and the other members of his Cabinet, before the meeting broke up, that he had removed Mr. Stanton and appointed General Thomas Secretary of War *ad interim*, and that upon the inquiry by Mr. Welles whether General Thomas was in possession of the office the President replied that he was; and upon further question of Mr. Welles whether Mr. Stanton acquiesced the President replied that he did; all that he required was time to remove his papers.

Is that objected to?

Mr. Manager BUTLER. Yes, sir. In reference to this question I want to call the counsel's attention to the state of the fact. I understood Mr. Welles said that after the Cabinet meeting broke up——

Mr. EVARTS. No. I have put that according to the fact. You were out, I believe, when it was brought out. It was after they had got through what he calls their departmental business, but before the meeting broke up, that the President made the communication.

Mr. Manager WILSON. Before they separated.

Mr. EVARTS. Before the meeting broke up. It was in the Cabinet meeting not yet broken up.

Mr. Manager BUTLER. We have the honor to object to this.

The CHIEF JUSTICE. The Secretary will read the proposition so that it can be heard by the Senate.

The Secretary read the offer, as follows:

We offer to prove that on this occasion the President communicated to Mr. Welles and the other members of his Cabinet, before the meeting broke up, that he had removed Mr. Stanton and appointed General Thomas Secretary of War *ad interim*, and that upon the inquiry by Mr. Welles whether General Thomas was in possession of the office the President replied that he was; and upon further question of Mr. Welles whether Mr. Stanton acquiesced the President replied that he did; all that he required was time to remove his papers.

Mr. Manager BUTLER. Mr. President and Senators, as it seems to us, this does not come within any possible proposition of law to render it admissible. It is now made certain that this act was done without any consultation of his Cabinet by the President, whether that consultation was to be held verbally, as I think is against the constitutional provision, or whether the theory is to be adopted that the President has a right to consult with his Cabinet upon questions of his conduct. I should hardly have dared, perhaps, to speak upon this question of constitutional law with any confidence, except so far as to bring to the mind of the Senate that the President has no right to call upon his Cabinet save through the constitutional method, were I not borne out in it by the opinion of Jefferson. Early in the Government he took the same view that I have heretofore had the honor incidentally of stating to the Senate. There seems to be good reason for it, because the heads of Departments were in the first place never expected to be a Cabinet; there were but three of them. There has been a gradual growing up of this practice. The Constitution wisely, for good purposes, required that when the President wanted the advice of any one of his principal officers he should ask that advice in writing, and it should be given in writing, so that it should remain for all time exactly what the advice was which he received, and exactly the point made.

And the reason of that was, there had been an attempt in the various trials of impeachment of members of cabinets to put in the fact of the order of the king to the cabinet, or the advice of various members of the cabinet to each other. That had been exploded in the Earl of Danby's case. That question used to arise under that state of facts before courts of impeachment, but our fathers evidently did not mean that it should arise here.

But that is not this case, and I have only adverted to this to make the clear distinction: whatever may be the character of the act of removal of Edwin M. Stanton and the act of appointment of Lorenzo Thomas, I am glad that it is now made quite certain by the testimony of the Secretary of the Navy (who declares he never heard of it until after it was done) that it was not done by the advice of the Cabinet; that the President was solely responsible for it; and upon that, his own sole responsibility, he acted. Now, the question is, after he has done the act, after he has thought it was successful, after he thought Mr. Stanton had yielded the office, can he, by his narration of what he had done and what he intended to do, shield himself before a tribunal from the consequences of that act? Is it not exactly the same question which you decided yesterday by almost unexampled unanimity in the case of Mr. Perrin and Mr. SELYE, the member of Congress, on that same day, a few minutes earlier or a few minutes later. They offered in evidence here what he told Mr. Perrin and what he told Mr. SELYE; they complicated it by the fact that Mr. SELYE was a member of Congress; and the Senate decided by a vote which indicated a very great strength of opinion that that sort of narration could not be put in.

Now, is this any more than narration? It was not to take the advice of Mr. Welles as to what he should do in the future, or upon any question; it was mere information given to Mr. Welles or to the other members of the Cabinet after they had separated in their Cabinet consultation, and while they were meeting together as any other citizens might meet. It would be as if, after you adjourned here, some question should be attempted to be put in as to the action of the Senate because the Senators had not left the room. Again, I say it was simply a narration, and that narration of his intent and purposes, his thoughts, expectations, and feelings.

I do not propose to argue it further until I hear something showing why we are to distinguish this case from the case of Mr. Perrin, on which you voted yesterday. Mr. Perrin tells you that on the 22d he waited for the Cabinet meeting to break up, and as soon as it broke up he went in with Mr. SELYE, and then the President undertook to tell him. You said that was no evidence. Now, when he undertook to tell Mr. Welles is that any more evidence? I cannot distinguish the cases, and I desire to hear them distinguished before I attempt an answer to any such distinction.

Mr. EVARTS. Mr. Chief Justice and Senators, certainly nothing has yet proceeded from the mouth of this witness which has shown that the act of removal of Mr. Stanton or of appointment of General Thomas had taken place without previous advice from the Cabinet. However that fact may be, nothing as yet has been said to show it. All that has been proved is that Mr. Welles had not before that heard of the fact that he had been removed. That is all as it now stands. I merely correct that impression for the moment.

So, too, I wish no misunderstanding as to the situation of the members of the Cabinet toward the President, as being still in their Cabinet meeting with unfinished, unadjourned counsel. I think the honorable Manager is a little in difficulty on that point from having an impression beyond the case as it was left by the witness when he left the stand before the recess, and not attending to the differences made by his answers to my questions since he returned, my desire being to get at the precise fact.

Now, then, it stands thus: that at a Cabinet meeting held on Friday, the 21st of February, when the routine business of the different Departments was over, and when it was in order for the President to communicate to his Cabinet whatever he desired to lay before them, the President did communicate this fact of the removal of Mr. Stanton and the appointment of General Thomas *ad interim*, and that thereupon his Cabinet officers inquired as to the posture in which the matter stood, and as to the situation of the office and of the conduct of the retiring officer. Here we get rid of the suggestion that it is a mere communication to a casual visitor which made the staple of the argument yesterday against the introduction of the evidence as to the conversation with Mr. Perrin and Mr. SELYE. We now present you the communication made by the President of the United States while this act was in the very process of execution, while it was yet, as we say in law, *in fieri*, being done.

It being *in fieri*, the President communicates the fact how this public transaction has been performed and is going on, and we are entitled to that as a part of the *res gestæ* in its sense of a governmental act, with all the benefit that can come from it in any future consideration you are to give to the matter as bearing upon the merits and the guilt or innocence of the President in the premises. It bears, as we say, directly upon the question whether there had been any other purpose than the placing of the office in a proper condition for the public service according to the announcement of the President as his intention when he conversed with General Sherman in the January preceding; and it negatives all idea that at the time that General Thomas to Mr. Wilkeson or to the Dakota delegate, Mr. BURLEIGH, was saying or suggesting anything of force, the President was the author of, or was responsible for, his statements. The truth is, it presents the transaction as wholly and completely an orderly and peaceful movement of the President of the United States, as in fact it was, and no evidence has been given to the contrary, of any occurrence disturbing that peaceful order and as the situation in which its completion left the matter in the mind of the President up to that point of time.

Mr. CURTIS. Mr. Chief Justice, I desire to add to what my colleague has said a very few observations of a slightly different character from those which he has addressed to the Senate. We are anxious that this testimony now offered should be distinguished in the apprehension of the Senate, as it is in our own, from an offer of advice, or from the giving of advice by the Cabinet to the President. We do not place our application for the admission of this evidence upon the ground that it is an act of giving advice by his councilors to the President. We place it upon the ground that this was an official act done by the President himself when he made a communication to his councilors concerning this change which he had made in one of their number; that that was strictly and purely an official act of the President, done in a proper manner, the subject-matter of which each of those councilors was interested in in his public capacity, and which it was proper for the President to make known to them at the earliest moment when he could make such a communication.

Now, I wish to say a word in respect to the character of this council, in reply to the remarks of the honorable Manager concerning the constitutional rights and powers of the President in respect to them. I understand the honorable Manager to have rested his views concerning the constitutional character of those councilors upon what he understands to be Mr. Jefferson's opinions and practice. I wish to bring before the Senate, in this connection, and somewhat in advance of the question which will presently arise respecting advice given by these officers, the practice of this Government concerning such a council; and I beg to refer the Senate, in the first place, to a passage from the Federalist. In its commentary upon that provision of the Constitution which enables the President to require the opinion in writing "of the principal officer in each of the Executive Departments upon any subject relating to the duties of their respective offices"—I read from Dawson's edition of the Federalist, pages 516–17.

Mr. JOHNSON. What is the number?

Mr. CURTIS. Number 73. The author, in the first place, quotes what I have read from the Constitution, and then makes this remark, and passes from the subject as requiring no further discussion or examination.

"This I consider as a mere redundancy in the plan; as the right for which it provides would result of itself from the office."

Mr. JOHNSON. That is by Mr. Hamilton.

Mr. CURTIS. That is Mr. Hamilton. Now, in respect to the practice of this Government, and particularly the practice of Mr. Jefferson, in its relations to what had preceded under other Presidents, I beg leave to refer to Mr. G. T. Curtis's History of the Constitution, volume 2, page 409, note:

"Those who are not familiar with the precise structure of the American Government will probably be surprised to learn that what is in practice sometimes called the 'Cabinet' has no constitutional existence as a directory body, or one that can decide anything. The theory of our Government is, that what belongs to the executive power is to be exercised by the uncontrolled will of the President. Acting upon the clause of the Constitution which empowers the President to call for the opinions in writing of the heads of Departments, Washington, the first President, commenced the practice of taking their opinions in separate consultation; and he also, upon important occasions, assembled them for oral discussion in the form of a council. After having heard the reasons and opinions of each he decided the course to be pursued."

And I may mention here in passing that if Senators have the curiosity to look into the history of the period they will find that the latter course was pursued by General Washington, especially toward the close of his first and during his second administrations on very important occasions, one of the most prominent of which was the difficulty with the French minister, M. Genet, and the course that was pursued by the Government growing out of those complications. The author proceeds:

"The second President, Mr. John Adams, followed substantially the same practice. The third President, Mr. Jefferson, adopted a somewhat different practice. When a question occurred of sufficient magnitude to require the opinions of all the heads of Departments he called them together, had the subject discussed, and a vote taken, in which he counted himself but as one. But he always seems to have considered that he had the power to decide against the opinion of his Cabinet. That he never or rarely exercised it was owing partly to the unanimity in sentiment that prevailed in his Cabinet and to his desire to preserve that unanimity, and partly to his disinclination to the exercise of personal power. When there were differences of opinion he aimed to produce a unanimous result by discussion, and almost always succeeded. But he admits that this practice made the Executive, in fact, a directory."

And then references are given to Mr. Jefferson's works in support of this statement. The author does not continue to speak of the subsequent practice of the Government, as that, no doubt, was considered to be very familiar, his purpose being merely to point out the origin of these two practices; the one being that the members of the Cabinet were called together and a consultation held, and then, as the result of that consultation, the President decided; the other practice being that a vote was taken in the Cabinet, the President himself ordinarily counting as one in that vote, but always understanding that he had the power, if he thought proper to exert it, to decide the question independently of the votes of the Cabinet. That, I understand, has continued to be the practice from Mr. Jefferson's time to the present day, and including all the Presidents who have intervened during that period.

I have made these remarks because they seem to me to have an application, not merely to the testimony now offered, but to other evidence which we shall have occasion to present to the Senate subsequently. They are pertinent to the question now under consideration, for they go to show that, under the Constitution and laws of the United States, as practiced on by every President, including General Washington and Mr. Adams, Cabinet ministers were assembled by them as a council for the purposes of consultation and decision; and, of course, when thus assembled, a communication made to them by the President of the United States concerning an important official act which was then *in fieri*, in process of being executed and not yet completed, is itself an official act of the President, and we submit to the Senate that we have a right to prove it in that character.

A reference has been made by the honorable Manager to attempts which have sometimes been made in England by ministers to defend themselves under the orders of the king. Everybody who understands the British constitution knows that that is in the nature of the Government an absurdity. The king is not responsible; the ministers are; and therefore any order which the king gives contrary to law is executed by his ministers on their own responsibility, and not upon that of the sovereign. In the United States it is wholly otherwise; the responsibility is on the President; but among other responsibilities which it involves is the responsibility to seek and weigh and consider the advice which it is proper for him to receive.

Mr. Manager BUTLER. Mr. President, I shall not pursue the discussion as to whether advice given by the Cabinet to the President would be competent, because it is agreed by the counsel for the President last up that this was neither to get advice, nor was there anything in the nature of advice.

It is said that it is an official act. I had supposed up to this moment—ay, and I suppose now—that there is no act that can be called an official act of an officer which is not an act required by some law or some duty imposed upon that officer. Am I right in my ideas of what is an official act? It is not every volunteer act by an officer that is official. Frequently such acts are officious, not official. An official act, allow me to say, is an act which the law requires, or a duty which is enjoined upon the officer by some law, or some regulation, or in some manner as a duty. Will the learned counsel tell the Senate what constitutional provision, what statute provision, what practice of the Government requires the President at any time to inform his Cabinet or any member of them whatever that he has removed one man and put in another, and that that other man is in office? If there is any such law it has escaped my attention. I am not aware of it.

The only law that ever has been made on this subject is the law of March 2, 1867, which requires the President to inform one member of his Cabinet, to wit, the Secretary of the Treasury, when he suspends an officer, and then requires the Secretary of the Treasury to inform the accounting officers of the Treasury, so that that suspended officer shall by no accident get his salary. Up to that time there never was any law requiring any such information, and that law is a special one for a special purpose; and, in the case of the suspension of Mr. Stanton, was carried out by the President, he sending to the Secretary privately—specially, I should say, rather than privately—sending to the Secretary specially the fact that there had been such removal, and the Secretary, as we have proved by Mr. Creecy, informed his subordinates as the act of March 2, 1867, the tenure of civil office act required.

If I am right, Senators, and there is no official duty on the President to inform his Cabinet, whether in session or out of session, whether just as they broke up or after they had got through the routine of business, or at any other time, as to such a proceeding on his part, then I undertake to say it is not an official act; it is an act required by no law, by no practice, so far as it is in evidence here, and by no duty.

Now, then, what is offered? He had done the act. While the counsel took exception to my stating to the Senate that it was in evidence that this was not a consultion of the Cabinet, that the Cabinet had never consulted upon the removal of Mr. Stanton in the manner and form in which it was done, and that was fairly to be gathered from Mr. Secretary Welles's testimony, yet, I observe that he did not state to the Senate that the Cabinet ever was consulted with upon the question of removing Mr. Stanton in manner and form as it was done; and whenever he or anybody does state it, I have the President's declarations, which I can prove, that it was not so. Therefore, I assume it never will be stated.

Now, then, what is offered? Stanton has been removed by the act of the President; and thereupon, without asking advice—because that is expressly waived by the learned counsel last addressing us—not as a matter of advice, the President gives information. Now, how can that information be evidence? How can he make it evidence? The information is required by no law, was given for no purpose to carry out any official duty, was the mere narration of what the President chose to narrate at that time.

More than that, sir; it is said that this must prove the case of the President; and the gravity with which it was argued by both counsel shows the importance they place upon it. It is said this must prove the case of the President, because it proves that then he had no idea of using force. I should have no objection to grant that at that moment he had no idea of using force, because he at that time supposed that Mr. Stanton had yielded the office, and there was no occasion to use force.

Therefore he had no idea of force at that moment of time, if he told the truth. He says, "Stanton is out and Thomas is in; and it is all settled." Then he did not mean to use force. But what did he mean to do in case Stanton resisted, as Stanton did resist? That is the question for the Senate. What did he contemplate? What had been in his mind? General Sherman lets it out here that he and the President said something about force. General Sherman uses the word "force." Where did he get that idea? Sherman, with great caution, says, "I agree that I do not know that he said anything from which I got the idea of force; so that I could say what he said, or that he said anything from which I had a right to infer it." But he said something from which Sherman did infer it, and he put the word "force" here before you of his own free will and accord. It bore on his mind; and when the learned Senator [Mr. HOWARD] asked what force was meant, what did the President say about force, Sherman said—I give the substance now—"I cannot say what he said that would justify me in using the word 'force.'" The record is before you, Senators. You will correct me if I am wrong; but I think I am exactly right in substance.

That testimony being in, and other testimony, how does the President's narration, after he thought Stanton had given up the office peaceably, (when, if I may use a common phrase, he was chuckling over the fact to his Cabinet that he had got possession of the office easier than he expected to do,) form a piece of evidence in this case? How can it be put in? Senators, you may think this piece of evidence, and perhaps you in some of your decisions have proceeded upon that hypothesis—I have no right to know, but I trust without offense I may suggest it—you may think that this particular piece of evidence does not weigh much, and that, perhaps, it is best to let it in because it does not weigh much. But the counsel on the other side think it weighs heavily, for both of them argue it with great care. I say you may put it upon that ground; but it lays the foundation for other information, other declarations to the other members of the Cabinet; and I do not know where you can stop; and whenever you attempt to stop you simply involve yourselves, I respectfully submit, in an inconsistency, that you ruled in what was said to Mr. Welles and refused to rule in what was said to Mr. A or Mr. B thereafter; for it is impossible, in my judgment, to distinguish the cases.

As yet I have not heard any legal distinction between the case of Perrin and the case of Welles, between what was said to Perrin and what was said to Welles. The only distinction is, that one was a Cabinet officer and the other was not; but is that a legal distinction, when they themselves admit that it was not submitted to the Cabinet officer for the purpose of asking advice, or for any like purpose? It is a mere piece of information. Nor do they stop there. They then propose to put in what the President thought he would do. That is the offer. Now can that be evidence? Can you distinguish it from the cause of Perrin yesterday; I mean by any legal distinction?

Mr. EVARTS. Mr. Chief Justice and Senators, I connected this piece of evidence, which I suppose may rightfully be introduced as a part of the action of the President, with previous testimony that had been given as to what his expectation was would happen on the part of Mr. Stanton when he should make an order for his removal, as made known to us in the testimony of General Sherman; and I cannot consent to that testimony being either misconceived or misrepresented. That witness said "something was said about force, and then the President said there will be no occasion for that, because Mr. Stanton will retire;" and in answer to the question of the honorable Senator from Michigan as to what was said about force the witness assumed to himself that all that was said about force, all that had the idea of force in it, proceeded from himself in the form of his question as to what would happen in case Mr. Stanton should resist or refuse, and then, not only by an absolute exclusion of the idea that the President used any words of force from his, the President's, mouth, or raised a notion that there might be an opportunity or occasion for force, proceeded to say, with that precision which marked all his reflective and deliberate testimony, "The President did not convey to my mind any idea that force was to be used."

The CHIEF JUSTICE. Senators, the Chief Justice thinks that this evidence is admissible. It has, as he thinks, important relation to the *res gesta*, the very transaction which forms the basis of several of the articles of impeachment, and he thinks it also entirely proper to be taken into consideration in forming an enlightened judgment upon the intent of the President. He will put the question to the Senate if any Senator desires it.

Mr. CRAGIN. I ask for the yeas and nays upon it. If it is in order I will ask that the offer to prove made yesterday in the case of the witness Perrin may be read.

The yeas and nays were ordered.

The CHIEF JUSTICE. No debate is in order. The Secretary will call the roll.

Mr. CONNESS. The Senator from New Hampshire calls for the reading of a question.

The CHIEF JUSTICE. What question?

Mr. CONNESS. The question proposed to be put yesterday to another witness, which was then voted upon.

The CHIEF JUSTICE. The Secretary will read the question.

The Chief Clerk being unable to find the written offer yesterday submitted,

Mr. Manager BUTLER. Here is the Globe. You can read it from that.

The Chief Clerk read the offer to prove in the case of the witness E. O. Perrin, yesterday, from the Globe, as follows:

"We offer to prove that the President then stated that he had issued an order for the removal of Mr. Stanton and the employment of General Thomas to perform the duties *ad interim;* that thereupon Mr. Perrin said, 'Supposing Mr. Stanton should oppose the order.' The President replied, 'There is no danger of that, for General Thomas is already in the office.' He then added, 'It is only a temporary arrangement; I shall send in to the Senate at once a good name for the office.'"

Mr. CONKLING. What was the time referred to in that question?

Mr. SUMNER. What was the vote of the Senate on that?

The CHIEF JUSTICE. The Secretary will read the vote of the Senate on that subject.

The SECRETARY. On this question the yeas were 9 and the nays 37.

Mr. TRUMBULL. I should like to know how the Senator from Massachusetts voted upon it. [Laughter.]

The CHIEF JUSTICE. The Secretary will read, in answer to the question, the vote in full.

Mr. SHERMAN. I object. All this is in the nature of argument.

The CHIEF JUSTICE. The Chief Justice thinks it all out of order; but lest there might be some misapprehension he did not interpose.

Mr. HOWARD. I should like to hear a word further from the counsel for the accused upon the subjects embraced in the questions which I send to the desk and ask the Secretary to read before I vote on the question under consideration.

The Chief Clerk read as follows:

In what way does the evidence the counsel for the accused now offer meet any of the allegations contained in the impeachment? How does it affect the *gravamen* of any one of the charges?

Mr. EVARTS. The Senators will perceive that this question anticipates a very extensive field of inquiry, first as to what the *gravamen* of all these articles is; and secondly, as to what shall properly be determined to be the limits of law and fact that properly press upon the issues here; but it is enough to say, probably, as we have every desire to meet the question with all the intelligence that we can command, at the present stage of the matter, without going into these anticipations, that it bears upon the question of the intent with which this act was done, as being a qualification of the act in the President's mind at the time he announces it as complete. It bears on the conspiracy articles, and it bears upon the eleventh article, even if it should be held that the earlier articles, upon the mere removal of Mr. Stanton and the appointment of General Thomas, are to cease in the point of their inquiry, intent, and all, with the consummation of the acts.

Mr. Manager WILSON. A question was asked by a member of the Senate as to the date of the conversation between the President and Mr. Perrin. That was on the 21st; but a few moments after the conversation between the President and Mr. Welles.

The CHIEF JUSTICE. The Chief Justice will restate to the Senate the question as it presents itself to his mind. The question yesterday had reference to the intention of the

C. I.—30.

President, not in relation to the removal of Mr. Stanton, as the Chief Justice understood it, but in relation to the immediate appointment of a successor by sending in the nomination of Mr. Ewing. The question to-day relates to the intention of the President in the removal of Mr. Stanton; and it relates to a communication made to his Cabinet after the departmental business had closed, but before the Cabinet had separated. The Chief Justice is clearly of opinion that this is a part of the transaction, and that it is entirely proper to take this evidence into consideration as showing the intent of the President in his acts. The Secretary will call the roll.

Mr. MORTON. I should like to hear the proposition read. I was not in.

The CHIEF JUSTICE, (to the Secretary.) Read the proposition.

The Chief Clerk read as follows:

We offer to prove that on this occasion the President communicated to Mr. Welles, and the other members of his Cabinet, before the meeting broke up, that he had removed Mr. Stanton and appointed General Thomas Secretary of War *ad interim*; and that, upon the inquiry by Mr. Welles whether General Thomas was in possession of the office, the President replied that he was; and upon further question of Mr. Welles, whether Mr. Stanton acquiesced, the President replied that he did; all that he required was time to remove his papers.

The question being taken by yeas and nays, resulted—yeas 26, nays 23; as follows:

YEAS—Messrs. Anthony, Bayard, Buckalew, Cole, Conkling, Corbett, Davis, Dixon, Doolittle, Fessenden, Fowler, Grimes, Hendricks, Johnson, McCreery, Morton, Patterson of Tennessee, Ross, Saulsbury, Sherman, Sprague, Sumner, Trumbull, Van Winkle, Vickers, and Willey—26.

NAYS—Messrs. Cameron, Cattell, Conness, Cragin, Drake, Edmunds, Ferry, Frelinghuysen, Harlan, Howard, Howe, Morgan, Morrill of Maine, Morrill of Vermont, Patterson of New Hampshire, Pomeroy, Ramsey, Stewart, Thayer, Tipton, Williams, Wilson, and Yates—23.

NOT VOTING—Messrs. Chandler, Henderson, Norton, Nye, and Wade—5.

The CHIEF JUSTICE. On this question the yeas are 26, and the nays are 23.

Mr. CHANDLER, (who had just entered the Chamber.) Mr. President——

The CHIEF JUSTICE. It is too late. The result has been announced. The yeas have it; and the question is admitted.

Mr. EVARTS, (to the witness.) Please state, Mr. Welles, what communication was made by the President to the Cabinet on the subject of the removal of Mr. Stanton and the appointment of General Thomas, and what passed at that time?

The WITNESS. As I remarked, after the departmental business had been disposed of, the President remarked, as usual, when he has anything to communicate himself, that before they separated, it would be proper for him to say that he had removed Mr. Stanton and appointed the Adjutant General, Lorenzo Thomas, Secretary *ad interim*. I asked whether General Thomas was in possession. The President said he was; that Mr. Stanton required some little time to remove his writings, his papers. I said perhaps, or I asked, "Mr. Stanton, then, acquiesces." He said he did, as he understood it.

Question. Was it a part of the President's answer that all he required was time to remove his papers?

Answer. The President made that remark when I inquired in relation to possession, that he merely wanted time to remove his papers—some private papers and matters, I think.

Question. Was the time at which this announcement of the President was made in accordance with the ordinary routine of your meetings as to such matters?

Answer. It was. The President usually communicates after we have got through.

Question. After you have got through of the several departmental affairs?

Answer. Yes, sir; he then states what he has to communicate.

Question. Now, sir, one moment to a matter which you spoke of incidentally. You were there the next morning about noon?

Answer. I was.

Question. Did you then see the appointment of Mr. Ewing?

Answer. I did.

Question. Was it made out before you came there, or after, or while you were there?

Answer. While I was there.

Question. And you then saw it?

Answer. I saw it.

Mr. JOHNSON. What time of the day was that?

The WITNESS. It was about twelve. The Attorney General was there and said that he must be at the Supreme Court. He had not more than time to get to the court.

By Mr. EVARTS:

Question. Did not the Supreme Court meet at eleven?

Answer. I do not know. He had business which required him to be at the Supreme Court at twelve o'clock, I think. He was there up to that time.

Question. Did you become aware of the passage of the civil-tenure act, as it is called, at or about the time that it passed Congress?

Answer. I was aware of it.

Question. Were you present at any Cabinet meeting at which, after the passage of that act, it became the subject of consideration?

Answer. Yes; on two occasions.

Question. Who were present, and when was the first occasion?

Answer. The first occasion when it was brought before the Cabinet was on Friday, I think, the 26th February, 1867. It was at a Cabinet meeting on Friday.

Question Who were present?

Answer. I think all the Cabinet were.

Question. Was Mr. Stanton there?

Answer. Mr. Stanton was there, I think, on that occasion. I might state, perhaps, that the President said he had two bills which he wanted

the advice of the Cabinet about. One of them consumed most of the time that day.

Mr. Manager BUTLER. The point, I believe, is as to what took place there?

By Mr. EVARTS:

Question. This civil-tenure act was the subject of consideration there?

Answer. It was submitted.

Question. How was it brought to the attention of the Cabinet?

Answer. By the President.

Question. As a matter of consideration in the Cabinet?

Answer. For consultation for the advice and the opinion of the members.

Question. How did he submit the matter to your consideration?

Mr. Manager BUTLER. If that involves anything that he said——

Mr. EVARTS. Yes, it does.

Mr. Manager BUTLER. Now, we should like to have, so that we may not discuss this matter in the dark, the offer put in writing: but we object to anything that took place in the Cabinet consultation, and in order to have this matter brought to a point, we desire to have the offer of proof put in writing.

Mr. EVARTS. We will put the whole matter in writing.

The offer was reduced to writing and read by the Secretary, as follows:

We offer to prove that the President at a meeting of the Cabinet while the bill was before the President for his approval, laid before the Cabinet the tenure-of-civil-office bill for their consideration and advice to the President respecting his approval of the bill; and thereupon the members of the Cabinet then present gave their advice to the President that the bill was unconstitutional and should be returned to Congress with his objections, and that the duty of preparing a message, setting forth the objections to the constitutionality of the bill, was devolved on Mr. Seward and Mr. Stanton; to be followed by proof as to what was done by the President and Cabinet up to the time of sending in the message.

Mr. SHERMAN. Does that give the date?

Mr. EVARTS. It gives the date as being the time the bill was before them for consideration.

Mr. CONKLING. During the ten days succeeding its first passage?

Mr. EVARTS. I omitted the precise date because there were two meetings.

Mr. JOHNSON. Within the ten days, I suppose?

Mr. EVARTS. Within the time fixed by the Constitution.

Mr. Manager BUTLER. I assumed, Mr. President and Senators, for the purpose of the objection, that the time to which this offer of proof refers itself is during the ten days between the first passage of the bill by the two Houses and the time of its return, with the objections of the President, for redeliberation and reconsideration.

Mr. EVARTS. It is so stated.

Mr. Manager BUTLER. Upon this question I only propose to open the debate in order that my learned friends may be possessed, so far as I may be able to possess them, of the grounds of our objection.

The question is whether, after a law has been passed, under the due forms of law, the President can show what his opinions were, and the opinions of his Cabinet, before it was passed, as a justification for refusing to obey it and execute it. That is the first proposition.

Let me restate it and see if I have made any mistake. It is whether the President can show his opinions and those of his Cabinet as to the constitutionality of a law before the law is passed, in order to justify himself for refusing to obey it and execute it after it is passed.

I am not now, in stating this objection, dealing with the vehicle of proof, but with the question whether declarations in the Cabinet can or cannot be a mode of proof. I ventured to say to you, Senators, that heretofore the struggle has been, on the trial of impeachments, whether the king's order should sustain the minister; and I was somewhat sharply reminded how familiar it was to everybody that the king could do no wrong in the eye of the British constitution, and therefore that, of course, the ministers were responsible. But the question which I brought to your attention was that the struggle in impeachments in former times was whether the king, not being able to do anything wrong, when he gave his express order or advice to the minister, could shield the minister; and the British Parliament, in the Earl of Danby's case, decided that it could not, for he produced for his justification the order of the king, and that was thought to be a great point.

Now, the proposition is, we having got a king who is responsible, to see if we cannot have the ministers shield the king. That is the proposition; whether the advice of the Cabinet ministers can shield the Chief; in other words, whether the Constitution has placed these heads of Departments around him as aids or shields. That is the question; because if that can be done then impeachment is ended in this country for any breach of law, for there will be no President who cannot find Cabinets subservient enough to advise him as he wants to be advised, especially if they are dependent upon his will, and he cannot be restrained by law from removing them. If he has this power, as he said he had, in a message which is appended as one of his exhibits, in which he also says that if Mr. Stanton had told him that he thought that law was constitutional, he would have removed him before it went into effect, then any President can find a Cabinet subservient enough to him to give him advice, and if that advice can shield him there is an end——

Mr. CURTIS. Allow me to interrupt you, Mr. Manager, to understand what you are saying. What message do you refer to?

Mr. Manager BUTLER. Lest I should make any mistake, perhaps I had better read it.

Mr. CURTIS. I only want to know what message you refer to.

Mr. Manager BUTLER. I am perfectly willing to read it; if you will spare me a moment, I will give you the page. [Examining the official report.] I do not find it. I am certain, however, it is in one of the messages; I think in the message of December 12, 1867, you will find the phrase. I refer to one of the messages given in evidence in this case in which (and with the leave of the counsel and the Senate I will take care that the exact quotation appears in my remarks,) he says, in substance, that if Mr. Stanton had informed him that he would not leave upon being asked under this law, he would have taken care to remove him before it went into operation, or words to that effect. I say if that unlimited power can be held by the President, then he can always defend himself by his Cabinet. Let us look at it in the light of another great criminal whom you, sir, may be called upon to try some time or other. I have no doubt he had a Cabinet around him by whose advice he can defend himself for most of the treasons which he committed. I have no doubt at all upon that proposition.

Let us take it in another view. I have had gentlemen say to me upon this question "Why, would you not allow a military commander, who should either make a battle or forbear a battle, to show that he called a council of officers and what their advice was to justify him in the case of his refusal to give battle or of his giving battle improvidently." To that I answer that I would do so, but I make a wide distinction: I would not let any general call around him his staff officers, dependent on his breath for their official existence, and allow them to show their opinions as a shield for his acts.

I do not, as I said, propose by any means to argue this question. I proposed simply when I rose to open the proposition, and I desire to put in a single authority as a justification why I did myself the honor to say that Jefferson thought it the better opinion that the constitutional right of the Cabinet was to give opinions in writing, and that is the better constitutional principle. I hold in my hand Story's Commentaries on the Constitution, second volume, and I read the third note to section fourteen hundred and ninety-four.

"Mr. Jefferson has informed us that in Washington's administration for measures of difficulty a consultation was held with the heads of Departments either assembled or taking their opinions separately in conversation or in writing. In his own administration he followed the practice of assembling the heads of Departments as a Cabinet council; but he has added that he thinks the course of requiring the separate opinion in writing of each head of a Department is most strictly within the spirit of the Constitution, for the other does in fact transform the Executive into a directory."—4 *Jefferson's Correspondence,* 143, 144.

I have here, and I only propose to refer to it, in the third volume of Adams's works, in the appendix, an opinion of Mr. Jefferson furnished to General Washington upon the question of Washington's right to fix the grade of embassadors, the right to appoint being in the

Constitution, and whether the Senate had a right to negative that grade so fixed by the President. There is an example of one of the opinions that President Washington required of his Secretary of State as early as April 24, 1790, upon this very question of appointment to office, and we have it now to be seen and read of all men; whereas if it had not been for this trial we never should have known what the opinion of the Secretary of the Navy was on this great constitutional question.

Before I sit down I will call the attention of the learned counsel [Mr. Curtis] to the message to which I referred. It will be found on the 46th page of the proceedings of this trial, and the words are:

"If any one of these gentlemen had then said to me that he would avail himself of the provisions of that bill in case it became a law, I should not have hesitated a moment as to his removal."

Mr. CURTIS. What message is that?

Mr. Manager BUTLER. Of the 12th of December, 1867, on the suspension of Mr. Stanton. It is in evidence, and will be found on the 46th page of the proceedings.

Mr. EVARTS. We understand that the Managers have exhausted their opening argument on this point?

Mr. Manager BUTLER. Yes, sir.

Mr. EVARTS. The difference, as we understood, between the honorable Manager's statement of what was contained in the message and what is really in the message, is that he put it upon the President's statement that if it had been pronounced a constitutional law by Mr. Stanton he would have removed him. The point of the President's statement was that there was a concurrence of all the Secretaries who were appointed by Mr. Lincoln that they were not within the law; and if they had taken the opposite ground there would then have been an opportunity for him to have Cabinet ministers of his own appointment for the law to take effect upon.

The question as stated by the honorable Manager is, whether the President can show his opinions and the advice of his Cabinet as to the unconstitutionality of a law as a justification of his refusal to obey the law. That is the proposition on which they rest their argument. Now, Mr. Chief Justice and Senators, this involves more or less the general merits of this case, as they have, necessarily, perhaps, somewhat anticipated by incidental arguments; but we do not propose to occupy your time with preliminary discussions of what must form a very large and important part of the final considerations to be disposed of in this case. It is enough in reference to the question of evidence when it is introduced in a trial, that it should be apparent that the premises of consideration both of fact and of law in the different views that are to be insisted upon, and in the different views that may be maintained by the court within those premises, permit the introduction of evidence authentic in itself and trustworthy, to be used and applied according to the final theory of law and fact as the court shall adopt it.

Now, the proposition in this matter on the part of the Managers may be stated briefly thus, as it has often been repeated, that in regard to the civil tenure act, if what was done by the President on the 21st of February, 1868, in the writing out and delivery of these two orders, one upon Mr. Stanton to surrender, and one to General Thomas to take charge of the surrendered office, if those two papers make a consummate crime, then the law imports an intent to do the thing done, and so to commit the crime, and that all else is inapplicable legally within the purview of an impeachment and its trial as much as it might or would be upon a question of a formal infraction of a statute under an indictment punishable by fine. That is one view. It will be for you to determine hereafter whether a violation of a statute, however complete, is necessarily a high crime and misdemeanor within the meaning of the Constitution for which this remedy of impeachment must be sought, and must carry its punishments.

So, too, it is not to be forgotten that in the matter of defense the bearing of all the circumstances of intent and of deliberation and inquiry and pursuit of duty on the part of a great official to arrive at and determine what is his official duty, under an apparent conflict between the Constitution and the law, forms a part of the general issue of impeachment and defense. Our answer, undoubtedly, does set forth and claim that whatever we have done in the premises has been done upon the President's judgment of his duty under the Constitution of the United States, and after that deliberate and responsible, upright and sincere effort to get all the aid and light on the subject of his duty that was accessible within his powers. One of this most important, one always recognized as among the most important of the aids and guides, supports, and defenses which the Chief Magistrate of the country is to have in the opinion of the people at large, in the opinion of the two Houses of Congress, in the opinion even of judicial consideration, when a case shall properly come before a court, of whether he has pursued his duty or attempted to pursue his duty, is the view that these chief officers of the Government (under his constitutional right to call upon them for their opinions, and under the practice of this Government to convene them in council for the purpose of arriving at those opinions) have given him in regard to the proposed matter of conduct and duty.

And this matter of evidence here touches that part of the case, and is to supply that portion of the evidence of what care, what deliberation, what advice attended the steps of the President as he proceeded in the stress in which he was placed of the obligation of the

Constitution in respect to an act of Congress which had received the constitutional majorities of the two Houses in the very matter in which he was called upon to proceed, not by a voluntary case assumed by him, but in a matter pressing upon his duty as President in regard to the conduct of one of the chief Departments of the Government.

That is the range of the issue, and that is the application of this evidence. That it bears upon the issue, and is authentic testimony within the range of the President's right and duty to aid and support himself in the performance of his office cannot be doubted.

But it is said that this involves matter of grave constitutional difficulty, and that if this kind of evidence is to be adduced that will be the end of all impeachment trials, for it will be equivalent to the authority claimed under the British Constitution, but denied, that the king's order should shield the minister. Whenever any such pretension as that is set forth here, that the order of the Cabinet in council for any act of the President is to shield him from his amenability under the Constitution for trial and judgment upon his act before this constitutional tribunal, it will be time enough to insist upon the argument, or to attempt an answer. But it is produced here as being a part of the conduct of the President, the whole of whose conduct, as it shall be displayed before you in evidence, is to furnish the basis in fact for your judgment and sentence concerning it under the view of the Constitution and the law. Nor is there any fear that any such privilege, or any such right, as we call it, should interfere with the due power of this tribunal and the proper responsibility of all great officers of the Government to it. On the questions that, as we suppose, make up the sum and catalogue of crimes against the State within the general proposition of impeachable offenses, it is impossible that matters of this kind should come in to play. On treason or bribery or offenses involving turpitude, and sinning against the public welfare, no such matters can properly ever come in play. Of course, in some matters of conduct of foreign affairs, if our Constitution permitted the implication of doubtful conduct as within the range of treason, which it does not, it might be supposed that the constitutional advisers might by their opinions support the President in his conduct, if that was made the subject of accusation.

But here it will be perceived that the very matter that is in controversy must be regarded by the court in determining whether this species of evidence is applicable; and in determining its applicability I need not repeat before so learned a court what the question of its weight and force is not to be anticipated.

Mr. CONNESS. I move that the Senate sitting as a court now adjourn. ["No, no."] I will say that I make this motion at request, because this question will be argued at length, and it is now late.

The motion was agreed to—ayes thirty, noes not counted; and the Senate sitting for the trial of the impeachment adjourned until to-morrow at eleven o'clock.

SATURDAY, *April* 18, 1868.

The Chief Justice of the United States took the chair at eleven o'clock a. m.

The usual proclamation having been made by the Sergeant-at-Arms,

The Managers of the impeachment on the part of the House of Representatives and the counsel for the respondent, except Mr. Stanbery, appeared and took the seats assigned them respectively.

The members of the House of Representatives, as in Committee of the Whole, preceded by Mr. E. B. WASHBURNE, chairman of that committee, and accompanied by the Speaker and Clerk, appeared and were conducted to the seats provided for them.

The CHIEF JUSTICE. The Secretary will read the Journal of yesterday's proceedings.

Mr. STEWART. I move to dispense with the reading of the Journal.

Mr. DRAKE. I object.

The CHIEF JUSTICE. The Senator from Missouri objects. The Secretary will proceed with the reading.

The Chief Clerk read the Journal of yesterday's proceedings of the Senate sitting for the trial of the impeachment.

The CHIEF JUSTICE. At the adjournment yesterday the Senate had under consideration an offer to prove on the part of the counsel for the President. The offer will now be read.

The Secretary read as follows:

We offer to prove that the President at a meeting of the Cabinet, while the bill was before the President for his approval, laid before the Cabinet the tenure of civil office bill for their consideration and advice to the President respecting his approval of the bill; and thereupon the members of the Cabinet then present gave their advice to the President that the bill was unconstitutional and should be returned to Congress with his objections, and that the duty of preparing a message, setting forth the objections to the constitutionality of the bill, was devolved on Mr. Seward and Mr. Stanton, to be followed by proof as to what was done by the President and Cabinet up to the time of sending in the message.

The CHIEF JUSTICE. Do the honorable Managers desire to be heard further?

Mr. Manager WILSON. Yes, sir.

Mr. JOHNSON. Mr. Chief Justice, I wish to put a question to the counsel for the President.

The question was sent to the desk and read, as follows:

Do the counsel understand that the Managers deny the statement made by the President in his message of December 12, 1867, in evidence as given by the Managers at page 45 of the official report of the trial, that the members of the Cabinet gave him the opinion there stated as to the tenure-of-office act; and is the evidence offered to corroborate that statement, or for what other object is it offered?

Mr. HOWARD. I have a query to propound to the counsel, also.

Mr. CURTIS. Mr. Secretary, will you send me that question, please?

The question of Mr. Johnson was sent to the counsel.

The CHIEF JUSTICE. The Secretary will read the question proposed by the Senator from Michigan.

The Chief Clerk read as follows:

Do the counsel for the accused not consider that the validity of the tenure-of-office bill was purely a question of law, to be determined on this trial by the Senate: and if so, do they claim that the opinion of Cabinet officers touching that question is competent evidence by which the judgment of the Senate ought to be influenced?

Mr. EDMUNDS, (after a pause.) I inquire of the Chair whether the argument on the part of the Managers cannot proceed while the gentlemen for the defense are considering their answers to these questions, which may take some time?

The CHIEF JUSTICE. The Chief Justice thinks that the argument on the part of the honorable Managers may proceed, and that the counsel can reply to these questions in their argument. That course will be taken if there be no objection.

Mr. CURTIS. That is the course we should prefer, Mr. Chief Justice. We will reply to the question of the honorable Senator from Maryland, and also to that of the honorable Senator from Michigan in the course of the remarks which we desire to address to the Senate.

Mr. Manager WILSON. Mr. President and Senators, as the pending objection confronts one of the most important questions involved in this case, I wish to present the views of the Managers respecting it with such care and exactness as I may be able to command.

The respondent now offers to prove, doubtless as a foundation for other Cabinet action of more recent date, that he was advised by the members of his Cabinet that the act of Congress upon which rest several of the articles to which he has made answer, to wit : "An act regulating the tenure of certain civil offices," passed March 2, 1867, was and is unconstitutional, and therefore void. That he was so advised he has alleged in his answer. Whether he was so advised or not we hold to be immaterial to this case, and irrelevant to the issue joined. The House of Representatives were not to be entrapped, in the preparation of their replication, by any such cunning devise, nor by the kindred one, whereby the respondent affirms that he was not bound to execute said act because he believed it to be unconstitutional. The replication says that the House of Representatives—

"Do deny each and every averment in said several answers, or either of them, which denies or traverses the acts, intents, crimes, or misdemeanors charged against said Andrew Johnson in the said articles of impeachment, or either of them; and for replication to said answer do say that said Andrew Johnson, President of the United States, is guilty of the high crimes and misdemeanors mentioned in said articles," &c.

There is no acceptance here of the issue tendered by the respondent, and in support of which he offers the immaterial, incompetent, and irrelevant testimony to which we object. The advice which he may have received, and the belief which he may have formed touching the constitutionality of said act, cannot be allowed to shield him from the consequences of his criminal acts. Nor can his mistaken view of the Constitution relative to his right to require the opinions of the heads of the several Executive Departments upon certain questions aid his efforts to escape from the just demands of violated law. In his answer to the first article he alleges : .

"This respondent had, in pursuance of the Constitution, required the opinion of each principal officer of the Executive Departments upon this question of constitutional executive power and duty, and had been advised by each of them, including the said Stanton, Secretary for the Department of War, that, under the Constitution of the United States, this power [of removal] was lodged by the Constitution in the President of the United States, and that, consequently, it could be lawfully exercised by him, and the Congress could not deprive him thereof."

The respondent found no provision in the Constitution authorizing him to pursue any such course. The Constitution says the President—

" May require the opinion, in writing, of the principal officer in each of the Executive Departments upon any subject relating to the duties of their respective offices."—*Article 2, section 2.*

Not of his office, not of the legislative department, nor of the judicial department. But when did he require the opinions and receive the advice under cover of which he now seeks to escape? His answer informs us that this all transpired prior to his veto of the bill "regulating the tenure of certain civil officers." Upon those unwritten opinions and that advice he based his veto of said bill and fashioned the character of his message. He communicated his objections to Congress, they were overruled by both Houses, and the bill was enacted into a law in manner and form as prescribed by the Constitution. He does not say that since the final passage of the act he has been further advised by the principal officer of each of the Executive Departments that he is not bound to enforce it. And if he had done so he would have achieved a result of no possible benefit to himself, but dangerous to his advisers, for it will be borne in mind that the articles charge that he "did unlawfully conspire with one Lorenzo Thomas, and with other persons to the House of Representatives unknown." He might have disclosed that these unknown persons were the members of his Cabinet. This disclosure might have placed them in jeopardy without diminishing the peril which attends upon his own predicament.

It is not difficult to see that the line of defense to which we have directed the present objection involves the great question of this case. It tends to matters more weighty than a mere resolution of the technical offenses which float on the surface of this prosecution. Whoever attempts to measure the magnitude of the case by the comparatively insignificant acts which constitute the technical crimes and misdemeanors with which the respondent stands charged, will attain a result far short of its true character, and be rewarded with a most beggarly appreciation of the immensity of its real proportions. Far above and below and beyond these mere technical offenses, grave as they undoubtedly are, the great question which you are to settle is to be found. It envelops the whole case and everything pertaining thereto. It is the great circle which bounds the sphere composed of the multitude of questions and issues presented for your determination. The respondent is arraigned for a violation of and a refusal to execute the law. He offers to prove that his Cabinet advised him that a certain bill presented for his approval was in violation of the Constitution; that he accepted their advice and vetoed the bill; and upon that, and such additional advice as they may have given him, claims the right to resist and defy the provisions of the bill, notwithstanding its enactment into a law by two thirds of both Houses over his objections. In other words, he claims, substantially, that he may determine for himself what laws he will obey and execute, and what laws he will disregard and refuse to enforce. In support of this claim he offers the testimony which, for the time being, is excluded by the objection now under discussion. If I am correct in this, then I was not mistaken when I asserted that this objection confronts one of the most important questions involved in this case. It may be said that this testimony is offered merely to disprove the intent alleged and charged in the articles; but it goes beyond this and reaches the main question, as will clearly appear to the mind of any one who will read with care the answer to the first article. The testimony is improper for any purpose and in every view of the case.

The Constitution of the United States (article two, section one) provides that—

"The executive power shall be vested in a President of the United States of America."

The person at present exercising the functions of the executive office is the respondent who stands at your bar to-day, charged with the commission of high crimes and misdemeanors in office. Before he entered upon the discharge of the duties devolved on him as President he took and subscribed the constitutionally prescribed oath of office, in words as follows:

"I do solemnly swear that I will faithfully execute the office of President of the United States, and will to the best of my ability preserve, protect, and defend the Constitution of the United States."

This oath covers every part of the Constitution, imposes the duty of observing every section and clause thereof, and includes the distribution of powers therein made. The powers embraced and distributed are legislative, executive, and judicial. Of the first the Constitution declares that—

"All legislative powers herein granted shall be vested in a Congress of the United States, which shall consist of a Senate and House of Representatives."—Article 1, section 1.

This encircles the entire range of legislative action. The will of the legislative department is made known by the terms of the bills which it may pass. Of these expressions of the legislative will the Constitution says:

"Every bill which shall have passed the House of Representatives and the Senate, shall, before it become a law, be presented to the President of the United States, and if he approve he shall sign it, but if not he shall return it with his objections to that House in which it shall have originated, who shall enter the objections at large on their Journal, and proceed to reconsider it. If, after such reconsideration, two thirds of that House shall agree to pass the bill it shall be sent, together with the objections, to the other House, by which it shall likewise be reconsidered, and, if approved by two thirds of that House, it shall become a law."—Article 1, section 7.

Thus laws are made. But laws cannot execute themselves. However wise, just, necessary they may be, they are lifeless declarations of the legislative will, until clothed with the power of action by other Departments of the Government.

The builders of our Constitution understood with great exactness the philosophy of government, and provided for every contingency. They knew that laws to be effective must be executed; that the best and purest law could not perform its proper office in the absence of executive power; therefore they created that power and vested it in a President of the United States. To insure a due execution of the power, they imposed the duty of taking and subscribing the oath above quoted on every person elected to the presidential office, and declared that he should comply with the condition "before he enter on the execution of his office." Chief among the executive duties imposed by the Constitution and secured by the oath is the one contained in the injunction that the President "shall take care that the laws be faithfully executed." (Article 2, section 3.) What laws? Those which may have been passed by the legislative department in manner and form as declared by that section of the Constitution heretofore recited. The President is clothed with no discretion in this regard. Whatever is declared by the legislative power to be the law the President is bound to execute. By his power to veto a bill passed by both Houses of Congress he may challenge the legislative will, but if he be overruled by the two-third voice of the Houses he must respect the decision and execute the law which that constitutional voice has spoken into existence. If this be not true, then the executive power is superior to the legislative power. If the executive will may declare what is and what is not law, why was a legislative department established at all? Why impose on the President the constitutional obligation to "take care that the laws be faithfully executed," if he may determine what acts are and what are not laws? It is absurd to say that he has any discretion in this regard. He must execute the law.

"The great object of the executive department is to accomplish this purpose; and without it, be the form of government whatever it may, it will be utterly worthless for offense or defense; for the redress of grievances or the protection of rights; for the happiness or good order or safety of the people."—*Story on the Constitution*, vol. 2, p. 419.

De Tocqueville, in his work on Democracy in America, in opening the chapter on executive power, very truly remarks that—

"The American legislators undertook a difficult task in attempting to create an executive power dependent on the majority of the people, and nevertheless sufficiently strong to act without restraint in its own sphere. It was indispensable to the maintenance of the republican form of government that the representative of the executive power should be subject to the will of the nation."—*Volume* 1, p. 128.

The task was a difficult one, but the great minds from which our Constitution sprung were equal to its severest demands. They created an executive power strong enough to execute the will of the nation, and yet sufficiently weak to be controlled by that will. They knew that "power will intoxicate the best of hearts, as wine the strongest heads," and therefore they surrounded the executive agent with such proper restraints and limitations as would confine him to the boundaries prescribed by the national will or crush him by its power if he stepped beyond. The plan adopted was most perfect. It created the executive power; provided for the selection of the person to be intrusted with its exercise; determined the restraints and limitations which should rest upon, guide, and control it and him, and, out of abundant caution, decreed that—

"The President" * * * * "of the United States shall be removed from office on impeachment for, and conviction of, treason, bribery, or other high crimes and misdemeanors."—*Article* 3, *section* 4.

It is preposterous for the respondent to attempt to defend himself against the corrective power of this grand remedy by interposing the opinions or advice of the principal officers of the Executive Departments, either as to the body of his offense or the intent with which he committed it. His highest duty is to "take care that the laws be faithfully executed;" and if he fail in this particular he must fail in all, and anarchy will usurp the throne of order. The laws are but expressions of the national will, which can be made known only through the enactments of the legislative department of the Government. A criminal failure to execute that will (and every willful failure, no matter what its inducement may be, is criminal) may justly call into action the remedial power of impeachment. This power is, by the express terms of the Constitution, confided to one branch of the legislative department, in these words:

"The House of Representatives" * * * * "shall have the sole power of impeachment."—*Article* 1, *section* 2.

This lodgment of the most delicate power known to the Constitution is most wise and proper, because of the frequency with which those who may exercise it are called to account for their conduct at the bar of the people, and this is the check balanced against a possible abuse of the power, and it has been most effectual. But the wisdom which fashioned our Constitution did not stop here. It next declared that:

"The Senate shall have the sole power to try all impeachments."—*Article* 1, *section* 3.

In the theory of our Constitution the Senate represents the States, and its members being removed from direct accountability to the people are supposed to be beyond the reach of those excitements and passions which so frequently change the political complexion of the House of Representatives; and this is the more immediate check provided to balance the possible hasty action of the Representatives. Wise, considerate, and safe to the perfect work of demonstration is this admirable adjustment of the powers with which we are now dealing. The executive power was created to enforce the will of the nation; the will of the nation appears in its laws; the two Houses of Congress are intrusted with the power to enact laws, the objections of the Executive to the contrary notwithstanding; laws thus enacted, as well as those which receive the executive sanction, are the voice of the people. If the person clothed for the time being with the executive power—the only power which can give effect to the people's will—refuses or neglects to enforce the legislative decrees of the nation, or willfully violates the same, what constituent elements of governmental power could be more properly charged with the right to present and the means to try and remove the contumacious Executive than those intrusted with the power to enact the laws of the people, guided by the checks and balances to which I have directed the attention of the Senate? What other constituent parts of the Government could so well understand and adjudge of a perverse and criminal refusal to obey, or a willful declination to execute, the national will, than those joining in its expression? There can be but one answer to these questions. The provisions of the Constitution are wise and just beyond the power of disputation in leaving the entire subject of the responsibility of the Executive to faithfully execute his office and enforce the laws to the charge, trial, and judgment of the two several branches of the legislative department, regardless of the opinions of Cabinet officers or of the decisions of the judicial department. The respondent has placed himself within this power of impeachment by trampling on the constitutional duty of the Executive and violating the penal laws of the land.

I readily admit that the Constitution of the United States is, in almost every respect, different from the constitution of Great Britain.

The latter is, to a great extent, unwritten, and is, in all regards, subject to such changes as Parliament may enact. An act of Parliament may change the constitution of England. In this country the rule is different. The Congress may enact no law in conflict with the Constitution. The enactments of Parliament become a part of the British constitution. The will of Parliament is supreme. The will of Congress is subordinate to the written Constitution of the United States, but not to be judged of by the executive department. But the theories upon which the two constitutions rest at the present time are almost identical. In both the executive is made subordinate to the legislative power. The Commons of England tolerate no encroachments on their powers from any other estate of the realm. The Parliament is the supreme power of the kingdom, in spite of the doctrine that "the king can do no wrong," and in spite of the assertion that the exercise of the sovereignty rests in the several estates.

The kindred character of the theories permeating the two constitutions may be illustrated by certain parliamentary and ministerial action connected with the American Revolution, and which will well serve the purposes of my argument. On the 27th day of February, 1782, General Conway moved in the House of Commons the following resolution:

"That it is the opinion of this House, that the further prosecution of offensive war on the continent of North America, for the purpose of reducing the revolted Colonies to obedience by force, will be the means of weakening the efforts of this country against her European enemies, dangerously to increase the mutual enmity, so fatal to the interests both of Great Britain and America; and by preventing a happy reconciliation with that country, to frustrate the earnest desire graciously expressed by his majesty to restore the blessing of public tranquillity."—*Hansard*, volume 22, p. 1071.

The Commons passed the resolution. The ministry did not seem to catch its true spirit, and, therefore, on March the 4th next following, General Conway moved another resolution in these more express and emphatic terms, to wit:

"That after the solemn declaration of the opinion of this House in their humble address presented to his majesty on Friday last, and his majesty's assurance of his gracious intention, in pursuance of their advice, to take such measures as shall appear to his majesty to be most conducive to the restoration of harmony between Great Britain and the revolted Colonies, so essential to the prosperity of both, this House will consider as enemies to his majesty and this country all those who shall endeavor to frustrate his majesty's paternal care for the ease and happiness of his people, by advising or by any means attempting the further prosecution of offensive war on the continent of North America, for the purpose of reducing the revolted Colonies to obedience by force."—*Ibid.*, p. 1089.

This resolution led to an animated debate. The temper of the Commons was equal to the directness of the resolution. The ministry saw this and understood exactly its meaning. They were disposed to avoid the implied censure, and attempted to show, by expressions of a determination to observe and respect the opinion of the House as declared in the first resolution, that no necessity existed for the adoption of the second. To effectuate this end Lord North, the Premier, in the course of his remarks, said:

"The majority of that House had resolved that peace should be made with America; and the answer given from the throne was so satisfactory that the House had just concurred in a motion to return thanks to his majesty for making it; where, therefore, could be the ground for coming to a resolution which seemed to doubt the propriety or sincerity of that answer? He was not of the disposition of those who complained of majorities in that House, who condemned them, and by factious and seditious misrepresentations, held them out to the public in the most odious colors; a majority of that House was, in parliamentary language, the House itself; it could never make him change a single opinion, yet he bowed to that opinion which was sanctioned by the majority; though he might not be a convert to such opinion, still he held it to be his indispensable duty to obey it, and never once to lose sight of it, in the advice which, as the servant of the crown, he should have occasion to give his sovereign. It was the right of that House to command: it was the duty of a minister to obey its resolutions; Parliament had already expressed its desires or its orders; and as it was scarcely possible that a minister should be found hardy, daring, infamous enough to advise his sovereign to differ in opinion from his Parliament, so he could not think the present motion, which must suppose the existence of such a minister, could be at all necessary."—*Ibid.*, p. 1090.

And again he said:

"To the policy of that resolution he could not subscribe, but as Parliament had thought proper to pass it, and as ministers were bound to obey the orders of Parliament, so he should make that resolution the standard of his future conduct."—*Ibid.*, p. 1107.

These protestations of Lord North did not arrest the action of the Commons. The resolution passed, and peace followed.

It will be observed that these proceedings on the part of the Commons trenched on ground covered by the prerogatives of the Crown, and affected to some extent the powers of declaring war, making peace, and entering into treaties. Still the ministry bowed in obedience to the command of the House, and declared that—

"It was scarcely possible that a minister should be found hardy, daring, infamous enough to advise his sovereign to differ in opinion from his Parliament."

This grand action of the Commons and its results disclosed the sublimest feature of the British constitution. It was made to appear how thoroughly, under that constitution, the executive power was dependent on the legislative will of the nation. The doctrine that "the king can do no wrong," while it protected his person, was resolved into an almost perfect subordination of the ministers, through whom the powers of the Crown are exerted, to the acts and resolutions of the Parliament, until at last the roar of the lion of England is no more than the voice of the Commons of the realm. So completely had this principle asserted itself in the British constitution that the veto power had passed into disuse for nearly a century, and it has not been exercised since. The last instance of its use was in April, 1696, when William III refused the royal assent to a "bill to regulate elections of members to serve in Parliament." (Hansard, vol. 5, p. 998.)

The men who formed our Constitution in 1787 were not untaught of these facts in English history; and they fashioned our Government on the plan of the subordination of the executive power to the written law of the land. They did not deny the veto power to the President; but they did declare that it should be subject to a legislative limitation, under the operation of which it might, in any given case, be overruled by the Congress, and when this happens, and the vetoed bill becomes a law, the President must yield the convictions of his own judgment, as an individual, to the demands of the higher duty of the officer, and execute the law. His oath binds him to this, and he cannot pursue any other course of action without endangering the public weal. The Constitution regards him in a double capacity—as citizen and public officer. In the first it leaves him to the same accountability to the law in its ordinary processes as would attach to and apply in case he were a mere civilian or the humblest citizen; while in the latter it subjects him to the power of the House of Representatives to impeach, and that of the Senate to remove him from office, if he be guilty of "treason, bribery, or other high crimes and misdemeanors." If the citizen disobeys the law, and be convicted thereof, he may be relieved by pardon; but the officer who brings upon himself a conviction on impeachment cannot receive the executive clemency. For while it is provided that the President "shall have power to grant reprieves and pardons for offenses against the United States," it is also expressly declared that this power shall not extend to "cases of impeachment." (Article 2, section 2.) The same person, if he be a civil officer, may be indicted for a violation of law and impeached for the same act. If convicted in both cases he may be pardoned in the former, but in the latter he is beyond the reach of forgiveness. The relief provided for the disobedient citizen is denied to the offending officer.

I have already observed that the Constitution of the United States distributes the powers of the Government among three departments. First in the order of constitutional arrangement is the legislative department; and this, doubtless, because the law-making power is the supreme power of the land through which the will of the nation is expressed. The legislative power, in other words, the law-making power, is "vested in a Congress of the United States." The acts of Congress constitute the municipal law of the Republic.

"Municipal law is a rule of action prescribed by the supreme power of a State, commanding what is right and prohibiting what is wrong."—1 *Blackstone*, p. 44.

The supreme power of a State is that which is highest in authority, and therefore it was proper that the Constitution should name first the legislative department in the distribution of powers, as through it alone the State can speak. Its voice is the law, the rule of action to be respected and obeyed by every person subject to its direction or amenable to its requirements.

Next in the order of its distribution of powers the Constitution names the executive department. This is proper and logical; for the will—the law—of the nation cannot act except through agents or instrumentalities charged with its execution. The Congress can enact a law, but it cannot execute it. It can express the will of the nation, but some other agencies are required to give it effect. The Constitution resolves these agencies and instrumentalities into an executive department. At the head of this department, charged imperatively with the due execution of its great powers, appears the President of the United States, duly enjoined to "take care that the laws be faithfully executed." If the law which he is to execute does not invest him with discretionary power, he has no election—he must execute the will of the nation as expressed by Congress. In no case can he indulge in the uncertainties and irresponsibilities of an official discretion unless it be conceded to him by express enactment. In all other cases he must follow and enforce the legislative will. "The office of executing a law excludes the right to judge of it;" and as the Constitution charges the President with the execution of the laws, it thereby "declares what is his duty, and gives him no power beyond." (Rawle on the Constitution, p. 134.) Undoubtedly he possesses the right to recommend the enactment and to advise the repeal of laws. He may also, as I have before remarked, obstruct the passage of laws by interposing his veto. Beyond these means of changing, directing, or obstructing the national will he may not go. When the law-making power has resolved, his "opposition must be at an end. That resolution is a law, and resistance to it punishable." (Federalist, No. 70.)

The judgment of the individual intrusted, for the time being, with the executive power of the Republic may reject as utterly erroneous the conclusions arrived at by those invested with the legislative power; but the officer must submit and execute the law. He has no discretion in the premises except such as the particular statute confers on him; and even this he must exercise in obedience to the rules which the act provides. A high officer of the Government once gave to a President of the United States an opinion relative to this doctrine in these words:

"To the Chief Executive Magistrate of the Union is confided the solemn duty of seeing the laws faithfully executed. That he may be able to meet this duty with a power equal to its performance he nominates his own subordinates and removes them at his pleasure."

This opinion was given prior to the passage of the act of March 2, 1867, which requires the concurrence of the Senate in removals from office, which, while denying to the President the power of absolute removal, concedes to him the power to suspend officers and to supply their places temporarily.

"For the same reason the land and naval forces are under his orders as their Commander-in-Chief; but his power is to be used only in the manner prescribed by the legislative department. He cannot accomplish a legal purpose by illegal means, or break the laws himself to prevent them from being violated by others.

"The acts of Congress sometimes give the President a broad discretion in the use of the means by which they are to be executed, and sometimes limit his power so that he can exercise it only in a certain prescribed manner. Where the law directs a thing to be done, without saying how, that implies the power to use such means as may be necessary and proper to accomplish the end of the Legislature. But where the mode of performing a duty is pointed out by statute, that is the exclusive mode, and no other can be followed. The United States have no common law to fall back upon when the written law is defective. If, therefore, an act of Congress declares that a certain thing shall be done by a particular officer, it cannot be done by a different officer. The agency which the law furnishes for its own execution must be used to the exclusion of all others."—*Opinion of Attorney General Black*, Nov. 20, 1860.

This is a very clear statement of the doctrine which I have been endeavoring to enforce, and on which the particular branch of this case now commanding our attention rests. If we drift away from it we unsettle the very foundations of the Government, and endanger its stability to a degree which may well alarm the most hopeful minds and appal the most courageous. A departure from this view of the character of the executive power, and from the nature of the duty and obligation resting upon the officer charged therewith, would surround this nation with perils of most fearful proportions. Such a departure would not only justify the respondent in his refusal to obey and execute the law, but also approve his usurpation of the judicial power when he resolved that he would not observe the legislative will, because, in his judgment, it did not conform to the provisions of the Constitution of the United States touching the subjects embraced in the articles of impeachment on which he is now being tried at your bar. Concede this to him, and when and where may we look for the end? To what result shall we arrive? Will it not naturally and inevitably lead to a consolidation of the several powers of the Government in the executive department? And would this be the end? Would it not rather be but the beginning? If the President may defy and usurp the powers of the legislative and judicial departments of the Government, as his caprices or the advice of his Cabinet may incline him, why may not his subordinates, each for himself, and touching his own sphere of action, determine how far the directions of his superior accord with the Constitution of the United States, and reject and refuse to obey all that come short of the standard erected by his judgment? It was remarked by the Supreme Court of the United States in the case of Martin *vs.* Mott (12 Wheaton, 19) that—

"If a superior officer has a right to contest the orders of the President, upon his own doubts as to the exigency [referred to by the statute] having arisen it must be equally the right of every inferior, and soldier; and any act done by any person in furtherance of such orders would subject him to responsibility in a civil suit, in which his defense must finally rest upon his ability to establish the facts by competent proofs. Such a course would be subversive of all discipline, and expose the best disposed officers to the chances of ruinous litigation." * * * * " The power itself is confined to the Executive of the Union, to him who is, by the Constitution, the commander of the militia, when called into the actual service of the United States; whose duty it is 'to take care that the laws be faithfully executed,' and whose responsibility for an honest discharge of his official obligations is secured by the highest sanction. He is necessarily constituted the judge of the existence of the exigency in the first instance, and is bound to call forth the militia; his orders for this purpose are in strict conformity with the provisions of the law, and it would seem to follow, as a necessary consequence, that every act done by a subordinate officer, in obedience to such orders, is equally justifiable. The law contemplates that, under such circumstances, orders will be given to carry the power into effect; and it cannot, therefore, be a correct inference that any other person has a just right to disobey them."

Apply the principles here enunciated to the case at bar, and they become its perfect supports. If the President has a right to contest and refuse to obey the laws enacted by Congress, his subordinates may exercise the same right and refuse to obey his orders. If he may exercise it in one case, they may assert it in any other. If he may challenge the laws of Congress, they may question the orders of the President. It is his duty to enforce the laws of the nation, and it is their duty to obey his orders. If he may be allowed to defy the legislative will, they may be allowed to disregard the executive order. This begets confusion; and the affairs of the public are made the sport of the contending factions and conflicting agents. No such power belongs to either. To Congress is given the power to enact laws, and while they remain on the statute-book it is the constitutional duty of the President to see to their faithful execution. This duty rests upon all of his subordinates. Its observance by all, the President included, makes the executive department, though it be acting through ten thousand agents, a unit. Unity produces harmony, harmony effects directness of action, and this secures a due execution of the laws. But if the President may disregard the law because he has been advised by his Cabinet and believes that the Congress violated the Constitution in its enactment, and his subordinates may, following his example, disobey his orders and directions, the object and end of an executive unity is defeated, anarchy succeeds order, force, irresponsible and vicious, supplants law, and ruin envelops the Republic and its institutions. If the views which I have imperfectly presented are correct, and such I believe them to be, the testimony to which we object must be excluded from your consideration, and thus will be determined one of the most important questions encircled by this case.

If I have been able to arrest your attention, and to center it upon the question which I have imperfectly discussed, the time occupied by me will not be without profit to the nation. I have endeavored to show that the royal fiction which asserts that "the king can do no wrong" cannot be applied to the President of the United States in such manner as to shield him from the just condemnation of violated law. The king's crimes may be expiated by the vicarious atonement of his ministers; but the President is held personally amenable to the impeaching power of the House of Representatives. Concede to the President immunity through the advice of his Cabinet officers, and you reverse by your decision the theory of our Constitution. Let those who will, assume this responsibility. I leave it to the decision of the Senate.

Mr. CURTIS. Mr. Chief Justice and Senators, I have no intention of attempting to make a reply to the elaborate argument which has now been addressed to you by one of the honorable Managers touching the merits of this case. The time for that has not come. The testimony is not yet before you. The case is not in a condition for you to consider and pass upon those merits, whether they consist in law or fact. The simple question now before the Senate is whether a certain offer of proof which we have placed before you shall be carried out into evidence. Of course that inquiry involves another. That other inquiry is whether the evidence which is offered is pertinent to any matter in issue in this case, and when it is ascertained that the evidence is pertinent I suppose it is to be received. Its credibility, its weight, its effect finally upon the merits of the case or upon any question involved in the case, is a subject which cannot be considered and decided upon preliminarily to the reception of the evidence. And, therefore, leaving on one side the whole of this elaborate argument which has now been addressed to you, I propose to make a few observations to show that this evidence is pertinent to the matter in issue in this case.

The honorable Manager has read a portion of the answer of the President, and has stated that the House of Representatives has taken no issue upon that part of the answer. As to that, and as to the effect of that admission by the honorable Manager, I shall have a word or two to say presently. But the honorable Manager has not told you that the House of Representatives, when the honorable Managers brought to your bar these articles, did not intend to assert and prove the allegations in them which are matters of fact. One of these allegations, Mr. Chief Justice, as you will find by reference to the first article and to the second article and to the third article, is that the President of the United States in removing Mr. Stanton and in appointing General Thomas intentionally violated the Constitution of the United States, that he did these acts with the intention of violating the Constitution of the United States. Instead of saying, "it is wholly immaterial what intention the President had;

it is wholly immaterial whether he honestly believed that this act of Congress was unconstitutional; it is wholly immaterial whether he believed that he was acting in accordance with his oath of office, to preserve, protect, and defend the Constitution when he did this act"—instead of averring that, they aver that he acted with an intention to violate the Constitution of the United States.

Now, when we introduce evidence here, or offer to introduce evidence here, bearing on this question of intent, evidence that before forming any opinion upon this subject he resorted to proper advice to enable him to form a correct one, and that when he did form and fix opinions on this subject it was under the influence of this proper advice, and that consequently when he did this act, whether it was lawful or unlawful, it was not done with the intention to violate the Constitution—when we offer evidence of that character, the honorable Manager gets up here and argues an hour by the clock that it is wholly immaterial what his intention was, what his opinion was, what advice he had received and in conformity with which he acted in this matter.

The honorable Manager's argument may be a sound one; the Senate may ultimately come to that conclusion after they have heard this cause; that is of discussion into which I do not enter; but before the Senate can come to the consideration of those questions they must pass over this allegation; they must either say, as the honorable Manager says, that it is wholly immaterial what opinion the President formed or under what advice or circumstances he formed it, or else it must be admitted by Senators that it is material, and the evidence must be considered.

Now, how is it possible at this stage of the inquiry to determine which of these courses is to be taken by the honorable Senate? If the Senate should finally come to the conclusion that it is wholly immaterial this evidence will do no harm. On the other hand, if the Senate should finally come to the conclusion that it is material what the intention of the President was in doing these acts, that they are to look to see whether there was or not a willful violation of the Constitution, then they will have excluded the evidence upon which they could have determined that question, if it should thus prove to be material.

I respectfully submit, therefore, that whether the argument of the honorable Manager is sound or unsound, whether it will finally prove in the judgment of the Senate that this evidence is immaterial or not, this is not the time to exclude it upon the ground that an examination of the merits hereafter and a decision upon those merits will show that it is immaterial. When that is shown the evidence can be laid aside. If the other conclusion should be arrived at by any one Senator, or by the body generally, then they will be in want of this evidence which we now offer.

In reference to this question, Senators, is it not pertinent evidence? I do not intend to enter into the constitutional inquiry which was started yesterday by an honorable Manager as to the particular character of this Cabinet council. One thing is certain: that every President from the origin of the Government has resorted to oral consultations with the members of his Cabinet and oral discussions in his presence of questions of public importance arising in the course of his official duty. Another thing is equally certain, and that is, that although the written letter remains, and therefore it would appear with more certainty what the advice of a Cabinet councilor was if it were put in writing, yet that every practical man who has had occasion in the business affairs of life and every lawyer and every legislator knows that there is no so satisfactory mode of bringing out the truth as an oral discussion, face to face, of those who are engaged in the subject; that it is the most suggestive, the most searching, the most satisfactory mode of arriving at a conclusion; and that solitary written opinions, composed in the closet, away from the collision between mind and mind which brings out new thoughts, new conceptions, more accurate views, are not the best mode of arriving at a safe result. And under the influence of these practical considerations undoubtedly it is that this habit, beginning with General Washington—not becoming universal by any means until Mr. Jefferson's time, but from that day to this continuing a constant practice—has been formed. President Johnson found it in existence when he went into office, and he continued it.

I therefore say that when the question of his intention comes to be considered by the Senate, when the question arises in their minds whether the President honestly believed that this was an unconstitutional law, when the particular emergency arose, when if he carried out or obeyed that law he must quit one of the powers which he believed were conferred upon him by the Constitution, and not be able to carry on one of the departments of the Government in the manner the public interests required—when that question arises for the consideration of the Senate, then they ought to have before them the fact that he acted by the advice of the usual and proper advisers that he resorted to the best means within his reach to form a safe opinion upon this subject, and that therefore it is a fair conclusion that when he did form that opinion it was an honest and fixed opinion which he felt he must carry out in practice if the proper occasion should arise. It is in this point of view, and this point of view only, that we offer this evidence.

The honorable Senator from Michigan has proposed a question to the counsel for the President, which is this:

Do not the counsel for the accused consider that the validity of the tenure-of-office bill was purely a question of law?

I will answer that part of the question first. The constitutional validity of any bill is of course a question of law which depends upon a comparison of the provisions of the bill with the law enacted by the people for the government of their agents. It depends upon whether those agents have transcended the authority which the people gave them, and that comparison of the Constitution with the law is, in the sense that was intended undoubtedly by the honorable Senator, a question of law.

The next branch of the question is "whether that question is to be determined on this trial by the Senate."

That is a question I cannot answer. That is a question that can be determined only by the Senate themselves. If the Senate should find that Mr. Stanton's case was not within this law, then no such question arises, then there is no question in this particular case of a conflict between the law and the Constitution. If the Senate should find that these articles have so charged the President that it is necessary for the Senate to believe that there was some act of turpitude on his part connected with this matter, some *mala fides*, some bad intent, and that he did honestly believe, as he states in his answer, that this was an unconstitutional law, that an occasion had arisen when he must act accordingly under his oath of office, then it is immaterial whether this was a constitutional or unconstitutional law; be it the one or be it the other, be it true or false that the President has committed a legal offense by an infraction of the law, he has not committed the impeachable offense with which he is charged by the House of Representatives. And, therefore, we must advance beyond these two questions before we reach the third branch of the question which the honorable Senator from Michigan propounds, whether the question of the constitutionality of this law must be determined on this trial by the Senate. In the view of the President's counsel there is no necessity for the Senate to determine that question. The residue of the inquiry is:

Do the counsel claim that the opinion of the Cabinet officers touching that question—

That is, the constitutionality of the law—

is competent evidence by which the judgment of the Senate might be influenced?

Certainly not. We do not put them on the stand as experts on questions of constitutional law. The judges will determine that out of their own breasts. We put them on the stand as advisers of the President to state what advice, in point of fact, they gave him, with a view to show that he was guilty of no improper intent to violate the Constitution. We put them on the stand, the honorable Senator from Michigan will allow me to answer, for the same purpose for which he doubtless, in his extensive practice, has often put lawyers on the stand. A man is proceeded against by another for an improper arrest, for a malicious prosecution. It is necessary to prove malice and want of probable cause. When the want of probable cause is proved the malice is inferable from it; but then it is perfectly well settled that if the defendant can show that he fairly laid his case before counsel, and that counsel informed him that that was a probable case, he must be acquitted; the malice is gone. That is the purpose for which we propose to put these gentlemen on the stand, to prove that they acted as advisers, that the advice was given, that it was acted under; and that purges the malice, the improper intent.

To respond to the question of the honorable Senator from Maryland, he will allow me to say that it is a question which the Managers can answer much better than the President's counsel.

Mr. JOHNSON. Will you read it, please?

Mr. CURTIS. It is:

Do the counsel for the President understand that the Managers deny the statement made by the President in his message of December 12, 1867, to the Senate, as given in evidence by the Managers at page 45 of the official report of the trial that the members of the Cabinet gave him—

That is, the President—

the opinion there stated as to the tenure-of-office act; and is the evidence offered to corroborate that statement, or for what other object is it offered?

We now understand, from what the honorable Manager has said this morning, that the House of Representatives has taken no issue on that part of our answer; that the honorable Managers do not understand that they have traversed or denied that part of our answer. We did also understand before this question was proposed to us that the honorable Managers had themselves put in evidence the message of the President of the 12th of December, 1867, to the Senate, in which he states that he was advised by the members of the Cabinet unanimously, including Mr. Stanton, that this law would be unconstitutional if enacted. They have put that in evidence themselves.

Nevertheless, Senators, this is an affair, as you perceive, of the utmost gravity in any possible aspect of it; and we did not feel at liberty to avoid or abstain from the offering of the members of the President's Cabinet that they might state to you, under the sanction of their oaths, what advice was given. I suppose all that the Managers would be prepared to admit might be—certainly they have made no broader admission—that the President said these things in a message to the Senate; but from the experience we have had thus far in this trial we thought it not impossible that the Managers, or some one of them speaking in behalf of himself and the others, might say that the President had told a falsehood, and we wish therefore to place ourselves right before the Senate on this subject. We desire to examine these gentlemen to show what passed on this subject, and we wish to do it for the purposes I have stated.

Mr. WILLIAMS. Before the learned gen-

tleman concludes I desire to submit a question to him.

The CHIEF JUSTICE. The Secretary will read the question proposed by the Senator from Oregon.

The Chief Clerk read as follows:

Is the advice given to the President by his Cabinet with a view of preparing a veto message pertinent to prove the right of the President to disregard the law after it was passed over his veto?

Mr. CURTIS. I consider it to be strictly pertinent. It is not of itself sufficient; it is not enough that the President received such advice; he must show that an occasion arose for him to act upon it which in the judgment of the Senate was such an occasion that you could not impute to him wrong intention in acting. But the first step is to show that he honestly believed that this was an unconstitutional law. Whether he should treat it as such in a particular instance is a matter depending upon his own personal responsibility without advice. That is the answer which I suppose is consistent with the views we have of this case.

And I wish, in closing, merely to say that the Senators will perceive how entirely aside this view which I have now presented to the Senate is from any claim on behalf of the President that he may disregard a law simply because he believes it to be unconstitutional. He makes no such claim. He must make a case beyond that—a case such as is stated in his answer; but in order to make a case beyond that it is necessary for him to begin by satisfying the Senate that he honestly believed the law to be unconstitutional; and it is with a view to that that we now offer this evidence.

The CHIEF JUSTICE. Senators, the question now before the Senate, as the Chief Justice conceives, respects not the weight but the admissibility of the evidence offered. To determine that question it is necessary to see what is charged in the articles of impeachment. The first article charges that on the 21st day of February, 1868, the President issued an order for the removal of Mr. Stanton from the office of Secretary of War, and that this order was made unlawfully, and that it was made with intent to violate the tenure-of-office act and in violation of the Constitution of the United States. The same charge in substance is repeated in the articles which relate to the appointment of Mr. Thomas, which was necessarily connected with the transaction. The intent, then, is the subject to which much of the evidence on both sides has been directed; and the Chief Justice conceives that this testimony is admissible for the purpose of showing the intent with which the President has acted in this transaction. He will submit the question to the Senate if any Senator desires it.

Mr. HOWARD. I call for the yeas and nays.

The CHIEF JUSTICE. The Senator from Michigan desires that the question be submitted to the Senate, and calls for the yeas and nays.

The yeas and nays were ordered.

The CHIEF JUSTICE. Senators, you who are of opinion that the proposed evidence is admissible will, as your names are called, answer yea; those of the contrary opinion, nay.

Mr. DRAKE. I ask for the reading of the offer of counsel.

The CHIEF JUSTICE. The Secretary will read the offer.

The Chief Clerk read the offer.

The question being taken by yeas and nays, resulted—yeas 20, nays 29; as follows:

YEAS—Messrs. Anthony, Bayard, Buckalew, Davis, Dixon, Doolittle, Fessenden, Fowler, Grimes, Henderson, Hendricks, Johnson, McCreery, Patterson of Tennessee, Ross, Saulsbury, Trumbull, Van Winkle, Vickers, and Willey—20.

NAYS—Messrs. Cameron, Cattell, Chandler, Cole, Conkling, Conness, Corbett, Cragin, Drake, Edmunds, Ferry, Frelinghuysen, Harlan, Howard, Howe, Morgan, Morrill of Maine, Morrill of Vermont, Patterson of New Hampshire, Pomeroy, Ramsey, Sherman, Sprague, Stewart, Thayer, Tipton, Williams, Wilson, and Yates—29.

NOT VOTING—Messrs. Morton, Norton, Nye, Sumner, and Wade—5.

So the Senate decided the evidence to be inadmissible.

GIDEON WELLES—examination continued.

By Mr. EVARTS:

Question. At the Cabinet meetings held at the period from the presentation of the bill to the President until his message sending in his objections was completed was the question whether Mr. Stanton was within the operation of the civil-tenure act the subject of consideration and determination?

Mr. Manager BUTLER. Stop a moment. We object.

The CHIEF JUSTICE. The counsel will please propose their question in writing.

Mr. EVARTS. I will make an offer, with the permission of the Chief Justice.

The offer was reduced to writing, and read by the Chief Clerk, as follows:

We offer to prove that at the meetings of the Cabinet at which Mr. Stanton was present, held while the tenure-of-office bill was before the President for approval, the advice of the Cabinet in regard to the same was asked by the President and given by the Cabinet; and thereupon the question whether Mr. Stanton and the other Secretaries who had received their appointment from Mr. Lincoln were within the restrictions upon the President's power of removal from office created by said act was considered, and the opinion expressed that the Secretaries appointed by Mr. Lincoln were not within such restrictions.

Mr. Manager BUTLER. We object, Mr. President and Senators, that this is only asking the advice of the Cabinet as to the construction of a law. The last question was as to the constitutionality of a law, and advice as to law we suppose to be wholly included within the last ruling of the Senate. We do not propose to argue it.

Mr. EVARTS. We do not so regard the matter; and even if the ruling should be so rightly construed, still, Mr. Chief Justice and Senators, it would be proper for us to make this offer accepting your ruling, if it were not a matter for debate. We understand that the disposition of the question of evidence already made may turn upon any one of several considerations quite outside of the present inquiry; as, for instance, if it should be held to have turned upon considerations suggested by some of the questions put by one or more of the Senators of this body, as to the importance or pertinence of evidence as bearing upon the question of the constitutionality of a law, as tending to justify or explain or affect with intent the act alleged of a violation of the law.

The present evidence sought to be introduced is quite of another complexion, and has this purpose and object in reference to several views that may be applied to the President's conduct; in the first place, as respects the law itself; that a new law confessedly reversing, or, as was frequently expressed in the debates of the Houses which passed the law, "revolutionizing the action of the Government" in respect to this exercise of executive power, and in respect to this particular point also of whether it had any efficacy or was intended to have any application which should fasten upon the President's Secretaries whom he never had selected or appointed, which formed the subject of so much opinion in the Senate, and also in the House of Representatives, was made a subject of inquiry and opinion by the President himself, and that his action concerning which he is now brought in question here in the removal of Mr. Stanton, was based upon his opinion after proper and diligent efforts to get at a correct opinion, whether Mr. Stanton was within the law; and, therefore, that his conduct and action was not in the intent of violating the law which, it is said here, cannot be qualified even under these charges by showing that he did not do it with intention of violating the Constitution.

The point now is that he did not do it with intent of violating the law, but that he did it with the intent of exercising a well-known, perfectly established constitutional power, deemed by him, on the advice of these his Cabinet, not to be embraced within the law; and if the question of the intent of his violation of duty, of the purpose and the motive and the object and the result, the injury to the public service or the order of the State is to form a part of the inquiry, then we bring him by one mode of inquiry within obedience to the Constitution as he was advised, and by this present object of inquiry within obedience to the law as he was advised.

So, too, it has a bearing from the presence of Mr. Stanton and his assent to these opinions, on the attitude in which the President stood in regard to his right to expect from Mr. Stanton an acquiescence in the exercise of the power of removal, which stood upon the Constitution in Mr. Stanton's opinion, and which was not affected by the law in Mr. Stanton's opinion; and thus to raise precisely and definitely in this aspect the qualifications of the President's course and conduct in this behalf as intending an application of force, or contemplating the possibility of the need of an application of force.

Mr. Manager BUTLER. Without intending to debate this proposition, I desire to call the attention of the Senate to the fact that the question seeks to inquire whether the Cabinet, including Mr. Stanton, did not advise the President that the bill as presented for his consideration did not apply to Mr. Stanton and those in like situation with him. I desire to call the attention of the Senate to Exhibit A, on the 38th page, which is the veto message, wherein the President vetoes the bill expressly upon the ground that it does include all his Cabinet, so that if they advised him to the contrary, the advice does not seem to have had operation on his mind.

Mr. Manager BOUTWELL. Read the words.

Mr. Manager BUTLER. I will.

" To the Senate of the United States:

"I have carefully examined the bill to regulate the tenure of certain civil offices. The material portion of the bill is contained in the first section, and is of the effect following, namely:

"That every person holding any civil office to which he has been appointed by and with the advice and consent of the Senate, and every person who shall hereafter be appointed to any such office, and shall become duly qualified to act therein, is, and shall be, entitled to hold such office until a successor shall have been appointed by the President, with the advice and consent of the Senate, and duly qualified; and that the Secretaries of State, of the Treasury, of War, of the Navy, and of the Interior, the Postmaster General, and the Attorney General, shall hold their offices respectively for and during the term of the President by whom they may have been appointed, and for one month thereafter, subject to removal by and with the advice and consent of the Senate.

"These provisions are qualified by a reservation in the fourth section, 'that nothing contained in the bill shall be construed to extend the term of any office the duration of which is limited by law.' In effect the bill provides that the President shall not remove from their places any of the civil officers whose terms of service are not limited by law without the advice and consent of the Senate of the United States. The bill, in this respect, conflicts, in my judgment, with the Constitution of the United States. The question, as Congress is well aware, is by no means a new one."

And then he goes on to argue upon the debate of 1789, which wholly applied to Cabinet officers, and you will find that that is the gist of the President's whole argument. Then, on the forty-first page, after having exhausted the argument as to the Cabinet officers, he says:

"It applies equally to every other officer of the Government appointed by the President whose term of duration is not specially declared. It is supported by the weighty reason that the subordinate officers in the executive department ought to hold at the pleasure of the head of the department, because he is invested generally with the executive authority, and the participation in that authority by the Senate was an exception to a general principle, and ought to be taken strictly. The President is the great responsible officer for the execution of the laws."

But I must ask attention to the point that there is some additional reason to have this evidence go in because Mr. Stanton gave such construction to the law. It was offered in the last proposition voted upon to show that Mr. Stanton gave advice as to the constitutionality of the law; so that in this respect the two propositions stand precisely alike in principle, and cannot be distinguished.

It is said this evidence should be admitted to show that the President when he removed Stanton and put in Thomas, supposed that Stanton did not believe himself to be within the law and protected in office by its enactments. Mr. Stanton had just been reinstated under the law; had refused to resign because he could not be touched under the law; had put the President's power to defiance, as the President says in his message, because he believed that the law did not allow him to be touched. Now, does this evidence tend to show that the President thought Mr. Stanton would agree that he was not kept in office by the law, and go out when he put in Mr. Thomas? Does any sane man believe that the President thought that Mr. Stanton would yield on the ground that he was not covered by the law when he was removed and Mr. Thomas appointed? The President did not put his belief on any such ground; he put it on the ground that Stanton was a coward, and would not dare resist; not that he did not believe himself within the law and protected by it, but that his nerve would not be sufficient to meet General Thomas. That was the President's proposition to General Sherman; it was a reliance on the nerves of the man, not upon his construction of the law. Therefore, I must call your attention to the fact that these offers are wholly illusory and deceptive. They do not show the thing contended for; they cannot show it; they have no tendency to show it, and whether they have or have not, the Senate, by solemn decision, have said that the advice of Cabinet officers is not the legal vehicle of proof by which the fact is to be shown to the Senate, even if it were competent to be proved in any manner.

Mr. EVARTS. Mr. Chief Justice and Senators, the reference to the argument of the President's message, which is contained on page 38 and the following pages of the record, seems hardly to require any attention. The President is there arguing against the bill as a matter of legislation, and rightly regards it in its general application to the officers of the Government, including the principal officers of the Departments. The minor consideration of whether or not it by its own terms reached the particular persons who held their commissions from President Lincoln could not by any possibility have been the subject of discussion by the President of the United States in sending in his objections to the bill on constitutional grounds. It was not a constitutional question whether the bill included the officers who had received their commissions from President Lincoln, or did not exclude them.

The learned Manager seems equally unfortunate in his reference to the conduct of Mr. Stanton upon the preliminary proceeding of his suspension under the civil-tenure act, for no construction can be put upon Mr. Stanton's conduct there except that he did not think he was under the act, I suppose, because he said he did not yield to the act which authorized suspension, but yielded to force. So much for that.

Now, I come to the principal inquiry; and that is whether or not it bears either upon the President's conduct in attempting a removal of Mr. Stanton because he was not under the bill, or whether it bears upon the rightful expectation and calculation of the President that the attempt would be recognized as suitable by Mr. Stanton because he, Mr. Stanton, did not believe he was within the bill.

It will be observed that the President had a perfect right to suppose that Mr. Stanton would not attempt to oppose him, the President, in the exercise of an accustomed authority of the Chief Executive since he, Mr. Stanton, believed it to be unlawful; and if the Executive had been advised by Mr. Stanton on this very point that he, Mr. Stanton, was not protected by the restrictions of the civil tenure-of-office bill, then the President had a right to suppose that when the executive authority given by the Constitution, as it was understood by Mr. Stanton, was not impeded by the operation of the special act of Congress, Mr. Stanton of course would yield to this unimpeded constitutional power.

The CHIEF JUSTICE. Senators, the Chief Justice is of opinion that this testimony is proper to be taken into consideration by the Senate sitting as a court of impeachment; but he is unable to determine what extent the Senate is disposed to give to its previous ruling, or how far they consider that ruling applicable to the present question. He will therefore direct the Secretary to read the offer to prove, and then will submit the question directly to the Senate.

Mr. DRAKE. On that I ask for the yeas and nays.

The Chief Clerk read the offer, as follows:

We offer to prove that at the meetings of the Cabinet at which Mr. Stanton was present, held while the tenure-of-civil-office bill was before the President for approval, the advice of the Cabinet in regard to the same was asked by the President and given by the Cabinet, and thereupon the question whether Mr. Stanton and the other Secretaries who had received their appointment from Mr. Lincoln were within the restrictions upon the President's power of removal from office created by said act, was considered and the opinion expressed that the Secretaries appointed by Mr. Lincoln were not within such restrictions.

The CHIEF JUSTICE. On this question the Senator from Missouri asks for the yeas and nays.

The yeas and nays were ordered; and being taken, resulted—yeas 22, nays 26; as follows:

YEAS—Messrs. Anthony, Bayard, Buckalew, Davis, Dixon, Doolittle, Fessenden, Fowler, Grimes, Henderson, Hendricks, Johnson, McCreery, Patterson of Tennessee, Ross, Saulsbury, Sherman, Sprague, Trumbull, Van Winkle, Vickers, and Willey—22.

NAYS—Messrs. Cameron, Cattell, Chandler, Cole, Conness, Corbett, Cragin, Drake, Edmunds, Ferry, Frelinghuysen, Harlan, Howard, Howe, Morgan, Morrill of Maine, Morrill of Vermont, Patterson of

C. I.—31.

New Hampshire, Pomeroy, Ramsey, Stewart, Thayer, Tipton, Williams, Wilson, and Yates—26.

NOT VOTING—Messrs. Conkling, Morton, Norton, Nye, Sumner, and Wade—6.

So the evidence proposed to be offered was decided to be inadmissible.

Mr. EVARTS, (to the witness.) Mr. Welles, at any of the Cabinet meetings held between the time of the passage of the civil-tenure act and the removal of Mr. Stanton did the subject of the public service as affected by the operation of that act come up for the consideration of the Cabinet.

Mr. Manager BUTLER. I object.

Mr. EVARTS. This is merely introductory.

Mr. Manager BUTLER. "Yes" or "no?"

Mr. EVARTS. Yes.

Mr. Manager BUTLER. We do not object to that.

The WITNESS. I answer yes.

By Mr. EVARTS:

Question. Was it considered repeatedly.

Answer. It was on two occasions, if not more.

Question. During those considerations and discussions was the question of the importance of having some determination judicial in its character of the constitutionality of this law considered?

Mr. Manager BUTLER. Stay a moment; we object.

Mr. EVARTS. It only calls for "yes" or "no."

Mr. Manager BUTLER. If it means only to get in "yes" or "no," whether it was considered, it is not very important.

Mr. EVARTS. That is all.

Mr. Manager BUTLER. Then it is not to get in that there was any particular consideration on a given point. In other words, to make myself plain, by asking a series of well-contrived questions, one might get in pretty much what was done in the Cabinet by "yes" or "no" answers. We object to it as immaterial; and now we, perhaps, might have it settled at once, as well as ever. If this line of testimony is immaterial, then it is immaterial whether the matter was considered in the Cabinet. If the determination of the Senate is that what was done in the Cabinet should not come in here, then whether it was done is wholly immaterial, and is as objectionable as what was done.

Mr. EVARTS. Yes; but the honorable Manager will be so good as to remember that the rulings of the Senate have expressly determined that all that properly bears upon the question of the intent of the President in making the removal and appointing the *ad interim* holder of the office with a view of raising the judicial question is admissible, and has been admitted.

Mr. Manager BUTLER. We never have heard that ruling. It may have escaped us, perhaps.

Mr. EVARTS. By examining the record you will find it.

Mr. Manager BUTLER. We have examined it with great care; but we shall not find that, we think. Will you have the kindness to read that ruling?

Mr. EVARTS. It is in the memory of the court.

Mr. Manager BUTLER. The ruling is on the record.

The CHIEF JUSTICE. If the question be objected to it will be reduced to writing.

The offer of the counsel for the respondent was reduced to writing and handed to the Managers.

Mr. Manager BUTLER. By "the removal" do I understand down to the 21st of February, 1868?

Mr. EVARTS. Yes, sir.

Mr. Manager BUTLER. May I insert these words: "21st of February, 1868?"

Mr. EVARTS. You may alter the word "removal" to "order of the 21st of February, 1868, for the removal."

The CHIEF JUSTICE. The Secretary will read the offer made by the counsel for the President.

The offer was handed to the desk and read, as follows:

We offer to prove that at the Cabinet meetings between the passage of the tenure-of-civil-office bill and the order of the 21st of February, 1868, for the removal of Mr. Stanton upon occasions when the condition of the public service was affected by the operation of that bill came up for the consideration and advice of the Cabinet it was considered by the President and Cabinet that a proper regard to the public service made it desirable that upon some proper case a judicial determination on the constitutionality of the law should be obtained.

Mr. Manager BUTLER. Mr. President and Senators, we, of the Managers, object, and we should like to have this question determined in the minds of the Senators upon this principle. We understand here that the determination of the Senate is, that Cabinet discussions, of whatever nature, shall not be put in as a shield to the President. That I understand, for one, to be the broad principle upon which this class of questions stand and upon which the Senate has voted; and, therefore, these attempts to get around it, to get in by detail and at retail—if I may use that expression—evidence which in its wholesale character cannot be admitted, are simply tiring out and wearing out the patience of the Senate. I should like to have it settled, once for all, if it can be, whether the Cabinet consultations upon any subject are to be a shield. Upon this particular offer, however, I will leave the matter with the Senate after a single suggestion.

It is offered to show that the Cabinet consulted upon the desirability of getting up a case to test the constitutionality of the law. It is either material or immaterial. It might possibly be material in one view if they mean to say that they consulted upon getting up this case in the mode and manner that it is brought here, and only in that event could it be material. Does the question mean to ask if they consulted and agreed together to bring up this

case in the form in which it has been done? If they agreed upon any other proceeding it is wholly immaterial; but if they agreed upon this case, then we are in this condition of things, that they propose to justify the President's act by the advice of his subordinates, and substitute their opinion upon the legality of his action in this case for yours.

Senators, you passed this tenure-of-office act. That might have been done by inadvertence. The President then presented it to you for your revision, and you passed it again notwithstanding his constitutional argument upon it. The President then removed Mr. Stanton, and presented its unconstitutionality again, and presented also the question whether Mr. Stanton was within it, and you, after solemn deliberation and argument, again decided that Mr. Stanton was within its provisions so as to be protected by it, and that the law was constitutional. Then he removed Mr. Stanton on the 21st of February, and presented the same question to you again, and again, after solemn argument, you decided that Mr. Stanton was within its provisions and that the law was constitutional. Now they offer to show the discussions of the Cabinet upon its constitutionality to overrule the quadruple opinion solemnly expressed by the Senate upon these very questions—four times upon the constitutionality of the law, and twice upon its constitutionality and upon the fact that Mr. Stanton was within it. Is that testimony to be put in here? The proposition whether it was desirable to have this constitutional question raised is the one presented. If it was any other constitutional question in any other case, then it is wholly immaterial. If it is this case, then you are trying that question, and they propose to substitute the judgment of the Cabinet for the judgment of the Senate.

Mr. EVARTS. I must, I think, be allowed to say that the patience of the Senate, which is so frequently referred to by the learned Managers as being taxed, seems to be, in their judgment, a sort of unilateral patience, and not open to impressions upon opposite sides. Now, Senators, the proposition can be very briefly submitted to you.

By decisive determinations upon certain questions of evidence arising in this cause you have decided that, at least, what in point of time is so near to this action of the President as may fairly import to show that in his action he was governed by a desire to raise a question for judicial determination shall be admitted. About that there can be no question that the record will confirm my statement. Now, my present inquiry is to show that within this period, thus extensively and comprehensively named for the present, in his official duty and in his consultations concerning his official duty with the heads of Departments, it became apparent that the operation of this law raised embarrassments in the public service and rendered it important as a practical matter that there should be a determination concerning the constitutionality of the law, and that it was desirable that upon a proper case such a determination should be had. I submit the matter to the Senate with these observations.

The CHIEF JUSTICE. The Secretary will read the offer to prove.

The Chief Clerk read the offer.

The CHIEF JUSTICE. The Chief Justice will submit the question to the Senate.

Mr. CONNESS called for the yeas and nays, and they were ordered.

Mr. HENDERSON. Mr. President, I desire to submit a question to the Managers before I vote. I send it to the desk.

The CHIEF JUSTICE. The question propounded to the honorable Managers by the Senator from Missouri will be read.

The Chief Clerk read as follows:

If the President shall be convicted, he must be removed from office.

If his guilt should be so great as to demand such punishment, he may be disqualified to hold and enjoy any office under the United States.

Is not the evidence now offered competent to go before the court in mitigation?

Mr. Manager BUTLER. Mr. President and Senators, I am instructed to answer to that, that we do not believe this would be evidence in any event; but all evidence in mitigation of punishment must be submitted after verdict and before judgment, save where the jury fix the punishment in their verdict, which is not the case here. Evidence in mitigation never is put in to influence the verdict; but if a verdict of guilty is rendered, then circumstances of mitigation, such as good character or possible commission of the crime by inadvertence, can be given, but not upon the issue.

Mr. CONKLING. Is that the rule of practice before this tribunal?

Mr. Manager BUTLER. I do not know as there are any rules of practice here.

Mr. CONKLING. Would that be applicable to this tribunal?

Mr. Manager BUTLER. I am asked by the honorable Senator from New York whether it would be applicable before this tribunal. Under the general practice of impeachments judgment is never given by the House of Peers until demanded by the Commons. Whether that may be applicable here or not I do not mean at this moment to determine. I say judgment never is given until demanded, and as this judgment is to be given as a separate act, if evidence in mitigation is applicable at all, it must be given to influence that event. There is an appreciable time in this tribunal, as in all others, between a verdict of guilty and the act of judgment; and if any such evidence can be given at all it must, in my judgment, be given at that time. It certainly cannot be given for any other purpose.

I have already stated that we do not believe it to be competent at all, and I am so instructed by my associates; but, if ever competent, it cannot be competent until the time arrives for the consideration of the judgment. If I may ask a question, I would inquire do the President's counsel offer this evidence in mitigation, because if they do that will raise another question. We shall not object to it, perhaps, even now, in mitigation, because that will be a confession of guilt. [Laughter.]

The CHIEF JUSTICE. The Secretary will read the offer to prove once more.

The offer was read as follows:

We offer to prove that at the Cabinet meetings between the passage of the tenure-of-civil-office bill and the order of the 21st of February, 1868, for the removal of Mr. Stanton, upon occasions when the condition of the public service was affected by the operation of that bill came up for the consideration and advice of the Cabinet, it was considered by the President and Cabinet that a proper regard to the public service made it desirable that upon some proper case a judicial determination on the constitutionality of the law should be obtained.

The CHIEF JUSTICE. Senators, you who are of opinion that the evidence offered by the counsel for the President should be received will, when your names are called, answer yea; those of the contrary opinion, nay. The Secretary will call the roll.

The question being taken by yeas and nays, resulted—yeas 19, nays 30; as follows:

YEAS—Messrs. Anthony, Bayard, Buckalew, Davis, Dixon, Doolittle, Fessenden, Fowler, Grimes, Henderson, Hendricks, Johnson, McCreery, Patterson of Tennessee, Ross, Saulsbury, Trumbull, Van Winkle, and Vickers—19.

NAYS—Messrs. Cameron, Cattell, Chandler, Cole, Conkling, Conness, Corbett, Cragin, Drake, Edmunds, Ferry, Frelinghuysen, Harlan, Howard, Howe, Morgan, Morrill of Maine, Morrill of Vermont, Patterson of New Hampshire, Pomeroy, Ramsey, Sherman, Sprague, Stewart, Thayer, Tipton, Willey, Williams, Wilson, and Yates—30.

NOT VOTING—Messrs. Morton, Norton, Nye, Sumner, and Wade—5.

So the Senate ruled the offer to be inadmissible.

Mr. ANTHONY, (at two o'clock p. m.) I move that the Senate take a recess for fifteen minutes.

The motion was agreed to; and at the expiration of the recess the Chief Justice resumed the chair.

GIDEON WELLES'S examination continued.

By Mr. EVARTS:

Question. Mr. Welles, was there within the period embraced in the inquiry in the last question, and at any discussions or deliberations of the Cabinet concerning the operations of the civil tenure act, or the requirements of the public service in respect to the same, any suggestion or intimation of any kind touching or looking to the vacation of any office, or obtaining possession of the same by force?

Answer. Never, on any occasion——

Mr. Manager BUTLER. Stop a moment. We object.

The CHIEF JUSTICE. The counsel for the President will please reduce the question to writing.

The question was reduced to writing and sent to the desk and read, as follows:

Was there, within the period embraced in the inquiry in the last question, and at any discussions or deliberations of the Cabinet concerning the operation of the tenure of civil office act and the requirements of the public service in regard to the same, any suggestion or intimation whatever touching or looking to the vacation of any office by force or getting possession of the same by force?

Mr. Manager BUTLER. To that we object. We think it wholly within the previous ruling; and if it were not, it would be incompetent upon another ground—that to show that the President did not state to A, B, or C that he meant to use force by no means proves that he did not tell E, F, and G.

Mr. EVARTS. We may hereafter call persons to testify that he did not tell E, F, and G, and that would not prove that he did not tell A, B, and C.

Mr. Manager BUTLER. And so on to the end of the alphabet.

Mr. EVARTS. Yes; and so on to the end of time. The question is, Mr. Chief Justice and Senators, a negative to exclude a conclusion; and if the subject of force or the purpose of force is within the premises of this issue and trial, evidence on the part of the President to show that in all the deliberations for his official conduct force never entered into contemplation is, as I suppose, rightfully offered on our part.

Mr. Manager BUTLER. We object to the question, whether he told his Cabinet he would or would not use force, as wholly immaterial and as within the last ruling.

The CHIEF JUSTICE. The Chief Justice does not understand the honorable Manager to object to it as leading.

Mr. Manager BUTLER. No; it is not worth while to take that objection. We wish to come to substance.

The CHIEF JUSTICE. The Chief Justice will submit the question to the Senate.

Mr. GRIMES. I ask for the yeas and nays.

The yeas and nays were ordered.

The CHIEF JUSTICE. The Secretary will read the question.

The Chief Clerk again read the question.

The CHIEF JUSTICE. Senators, you who are of opinion that this question is admissible, will, as your names are called, answer yea; those of the contrary opinion, nay.

Mr. FERRY. I was requested by the Senator from Missouri [Mr. DRAKE] to state that he was called away by sickness in his family.

The question being taken by yeas and nays, resulted—yeas 18, nays 26; as follows:

YEAS—Messrs. Anthony, Bayard, Buckalew, Davis; Dixon, Edmunds, Fessenden, Fowler, Grimes, Hendricks, Johnson, McCreery, Patterson of Tennessee, Ross, Saulsbury, Trumbull, Van Winkle, and Vickers—18.

NAYS—Messrs. Cattell, Chandler, Cole, Conkling, Conness, Corbett, Cragin, Ferry, Frelinghuysen, Harlan, Howard, Howe, Morgan, Morrill of Maine, Morrill of Vermont, Patterson of New Hampshire, Pomeroy, Ramsey, Sherman, Stewart, Thayer, Tipton, Willey, Williams, Wilson, and Yates—26.

NOT VOTING—Messrs. Cameron, Doolittle, Drake, Henderson, Morton, Norton, Nye, Sprague, Sumner, and Wade—10.

So the Senate decided the question to be inadmissible.

Mr. EVARTS. We are through with the witness.

Cross-examined by Mr. Manager BUTLER:

Question. Mr. Welles you were asked if you were Secretary of the Navy, and you said you held under a commission, and you gave the date of the commission?

Answer. March, 1861.

Question. You have had no other?

Answer. No other.

Question. And you have been Secretary of the Navy down to to-day?

Answer. I have continued to this time.

Question. Has Lorenzo Thomas acted as a member of the Cabinet down to to day from the 21st of February?

Answer. He has met in the Cabinet since that time.

Question. Did he meet as a member or outsider?

Mr. EVARTS. I submit, Mr. Chief Justice, that this is no cross-examination upon any matter we have examined upon, as far as General Thomas is concerned.

Mr. Manager BUTLER. I waive it. I will not have a word upon that.

By Mr. Manager BUTLER:

Question. Now, then, you told us of something said between you and the President about a movement of troops. I want to know a little more accurately when that was. In the first place what day was it?

Answer. It was on the 22d of February.

Question. Is there any doubt about that in your mind?

Answer. None at all.

Question. What time was it?

Answer. It was not far from twelve o'clock.

Question. I understood you to fix that time of day by something that happened with the Attorney General. What was that?

Answer. I called on the President on the 22d, about twelve o'clock. The reception for official business at the Navy Department is from eleven to twelve. I left as soon as I well could, after that matter was over, and therefore it was a little before twelve, I suppose. When I arrived at the President's and called on him, the Attorney General was there. While there, the nomination of Mr. Ewing was made out.

Question. Never mind about that; I am not now speaking of that.

Answer. I am speaking of that. The Private Secretary wished to get it up to the Senate as early as he could; and Mr. Stanbery remarked that he wished to be here, I think, about twelve; that he had some appointment about twelve; and it had got to be nearly that time then.

Question. I understood you to say that he

had some appointment in the Supreme Court. Was that so?

Answer. I will not be sure that it was.

Question. Did you not state yesterday that he had an appointment in the Supreme Court?

Answer. Perhaps I inferred that it was there; I cannot say that he said it was at the Supreme Court, or where it was.

Question. Did you not so testify yesterday?

Answer. Perhaps I did.

Question. How was the fact?

Answer. He had an engagement.

Question. How was the fact as to your testimony yesterday—not what perhaps you did, but how do you remember you testified on that point yesterday?

Answer. I presume I testified that he was to come here at twelve o'clock to the Supreme Court, because that was my inference. I supposed it was so. He had an engagement at twelve o'clock, and wanted to get away as soon as he could; and it was in connection with the nomination of Mr. Ewing, which went up at the same time.

Question. Have you not heard since yesterday that the court did not sit on Saturdays?

Answer. No, sir.

Question. Have you heard anything on that subject?

Answer. No, sir.

Question. Do you know whether they sit on Saturdays, or not?

Answer. I do not.

Question. You do not know upon that matter?

Answer. I do not.

Question. Now, sir, did you learn that there was any other movement of troops, except an order upon one officer of the regiment to meet General Emory?

Answer. Well, I heard of two or three things that evening.

Question. I am now speaking of the officers of the regiment?

Answer. I understand.

Question. Did you learn that there was any other movement of troops except an order to an officer of the regiment to meet General Emory?

Answer. I heard that the officers of the regiment were required to meet at headquarters that evening.

Question. At what time?

Answer. That evening.

Mr. EVARTS. The 21st.

By Mr. Manager BUTLER:

Question. The evening of the 21st?

Answer. The evening of the 21st.

Question. And that the officers were called to headquarters?

Answer. The officers were called to headquarters.

Question. Did you learn whether it was to give them directions about keeping away from a masquerade or going to it as a reason why they were called to headquarters?

Answer. I did not hear the reasons. If I had heard the reasons perhaps they would have satisfied me. I do not know how that may be.

Question. You did not hear the reasons?

Answer. No; I knew the fact that they had been called to meet at headquarters that evening, which was an unusual order, and were called from a party, I believe.

Question. What party?

Answer. A party that was in F or G street, I think; a reception.

Question. That they were called from a party to go to headquarters. Now, sir, that was all the movement of troops you spoke of yesterday to us, was it not?

Answer. I do not recollect that I spoke of others. I spoke of that.

Question. Had you any other in your mind yesterday but that?

Answer. There were some other movements in my mind; but perhaps not connected with General Emory, unless they were called there for a purpose.

Question. There was none communicated to you, whatever might have been in your mind, was there?

Answer. What do you mean by "none communicated?"

Question. No other movements were communicated to you, whatever may have been in your mind, that evening?

Answer. I heard of movements that evening, or heard of appearances. I heard that the War Department was lighted up, which was an unusual matter.

Question. You heard that the War Department was lighted up?

Answer. I did. I do not know that I alluded to that to President Johnson; but that was one of the circumstances that I heard of the evening before.

Question. Then the movement was the call of the officers of one regiment to meet General Emory. How many officers did you hear were called?

Answer. I did not hear the number of officers. I heard that General Emory's son and his orderlies, one or two, had called at a party, requesting that any officers belonging to the fifth regiment, and, I believe, to his own, should repair forthwith to headquarters; which was thought to be a very unusual movement.

Question. I did not ask for your thoughts about it?

Answer. Well, I thought it was.

Question. Those officers were asked to come to headquarters. That was all you stated to the President of movements of troops?

Answer. I will not say that that was all.

Question. Is it all that you remember you did?

Answer. I will not be sure whether I stated to him the fact of the lighting up of the War Department that night, for that was the first of the intrenchment there, or whether I alluded to the fact that there was a company, or part of a company, reported to me as being seen in the——

Question. Excuse me; I am only asking what you stated, not what you think you did not state.

Answer. I say I do not know that I stated that.

Question. And I am asking for what you stated?

Answer. I say I do not know that I stated to the President that the War Department was lighted up that night.

Question. I do not ask you for what you do not know you stated, but what you know you did state?

Mr. EVARTS. Your question was, whether that was all he stated, and he says he cannot say whether it was all or not.

Mr. Manager BUTLER. I am asking if it was all he stated, and I am asking not for what he did not state, but for what he did.

Mr. EVARTS. He says he cannot say but that he did.

The WITNESS. I stated to him in relation to General Emory and what I heard in regard to him. Whether I alluded to the other facts in my mind I cannot say now.

Mr. Manager BUTLER. Very well; that is exactly what I want; but I did not want to get at what the facts were. The 22d was to be kept as a holiday?

Answer. It is a half holiday, I believe. The War Department closed that office; but I suppose that is in violation of law. The law is that the Departments shall be kept open, each of them every day of the year, save Sundays and the Fourth of July and the 25th of December. The War Department has sometimes——

Mr. Manager BUTLER. Excuse me; I did not ask you for your legal opinion.

The WITNESS. I am not giving a legal opinion. I am stating facts.

Mr. Manager BUTLER. You say it is in violation of law. I suppose that is a legal opinion?

The WITNESS. You can read the law and see what it is.

Question. I am only asking you whether, in fact, it is kept as a holiday?

Answer. We did not keep it as a holiday, as we keep the Fourth of July. The clerks were at the Department and were required to clear their desks before they left.

Question. How was it in the War Department?

Answer. I understood—if you will allow me to state that—that the War Department was closed on that day. I have understood it was closed on other days; but the Navy Department had not been closed in that way.

Question. I do not want any comparison between the Navy and War Departments. I only ask the fact if it was closed on that day. Did you inquire whether the officers were called together to notify them that the next day was to be a holiday or not?

Answer. I made no inquiries on the subject

of others, but communicated to the President what I had learned.

EDGAR T. WELLES sworn and examined.

By Mr. EVARTS:

Question. You are the son of Mr. Secretary Welles?

Answer. Yes, sir.

Question. Are you employed in the Navy Department?

Answer. Yes, sir; I am chief clerk of the Department.

Question, (presenting a paper to the witness.) Please look at this paper and say if that is a blank form of Navy agent's commissions as used in the Department?

Answer. It is the blank form that was used.

Question. Before the civil tenure bill?

Answer. Yes, sir.

Mr. EVARTS. We propose to offer it in evidence.

[The document was handed to Mr. Manager BUTLER.]

Mr. Manager BUTLER. We have no objection to that. Do you want it read?

Mr. EVARTS. No.

The document thus put in evidence is as follows:

President of the United States of America:
To all who shall see these presents, greeting:

Know ye, that reposing special trust and confidence in the patriotism, fidelity, and abilities of ——, I do, by and with the advice and consent of the Senate of the United States, appoint him Navy agent for the ——.

He is therefore carefully and diligently to discharge the duties of Navy agent, by doing and performing all manner of things thereunto appertaining, and he is to observe and follow the orders and directions which he may from time to time receive from the President of the United States and Secretary of the Navy.

This commission to continue in force during the term of four years from the ——.

Given under my hand at Washington, this — day of ——, in the year of our Lord one thousand [L. S.] eight hundred and ——, and in the —— year of the independence of the United States.

By the President:
                                   Secretary of the Navy.

Registered.

By Mr. EVARTS:

Question. Do you remember, on Friday, the 21st of February, that your attention was drawn to some movement, or supposed movement, connected with military organization here?

Answer. I do.

Question. At what hour of the day was that?

Answer. I should suppose it was about five o'clock.

Question. What was it, and how was it brought to your attention?

Answer. I was attending a small reception, and the lady of the house informed me——

Mr. Manager BUTLER. Excuse me. You need not state what the lady of the house said.

Mr. EVARTS. It does not prove the truth of the lady's statement, but only what it was.

Mr. Manager BUTLER. I beg your pardon; but as nothing but the truth is to be in evidence we do not want the lady's statement.

Mr. EVARTS. It came to his notice and he acted upon it. That is the truth to be proved.

Mr. Manager BUTLER. In answer to that, the truth is that this is not the proper way to prove the truth of a case of impeachment, by putting in what the lady said to this man. No matter how he got the information; let him give the information he gave to his father.

Mr. EVARTS. Very well. [To the witness.] What information did you get, whether it was from a lady or not, I do not care?

Mr. Manager BUTLER. No, sir; the question should be, what information did he give to his father?

Mr. EVARTS. I want to prove that he gave the same that he got; that he did not make it up. I certainly am permitted to prove what occurred. It will all be over in three minutes. [To the witness.] Did you gain any information concerning it?

Mr. Manager BUTLER. On the whole, I think it had better come in; I will not object.

Mr. EVARTS. It is utterly immaterial.

Mr. Manager BUTLER. I think it is.

The WITNESS. General Emory had sent his orderlies there that afternoon requesting certain officers named to me to report to headquarters immediately, and that after that General Emory's son, Dr. Tom. Emory, had come there with the request that any officers of two branches of the service—I do not recall what two branches; cavalry and infantry or cavalry and artillery—should report at headquarters immediately.

Mr. CONNESS. Mr. President, we cannot hear the witness. We did not hear the answer to the last question.

Mr. EVARTS. Does the Senator desire it to be repeated?

Mr. CONNESS. Yes, sir.

Mr. EVARTS, (to the witness.) Be so good as to repeat it.

Answer. That General Emory had sent certain orderlies requesting officers, who were named, to report at headquarters without delay, and had also sent his son, requesting that any officers of two branches of the service, cavalry and infantry, or cavalry and artillery, should report at headquarters immediately.

Question. After this, did you communicate this to your father?

Answer. I did, sir.

Question. At what time?

Answer. I should suppose it was about seven o'clock.

Question. The same evening?

Answer. The same evening, between seven and eight o'clock.

Question. Were you sent on any message to the President concerning this?

Answer. I was.

Question. By your father?

Answer. I was sent by him over to the President's.

Question. Did you go?

Answer. I did.

Question. At what hour in the evening?

Answer. Between eight and nine o'clock; shortly after I went home.

Question. Was it on an occasion of any engagement of the President?

Answer. The President was engaged at dinner.

Question. Was it a diplomatic dinner?

Answer. It was a State dinner. I do not remember precisely the character of it.

Question. Did you see him?

Answer. I did not see him on that account.

Question. And you reported to your father?

Answer. I reported to him that I did not see him; that there was nobody at the President's Mansion to communicate with.

Question. Was anything further done that night that you know of on the subject?

Answer. Nothing further that I know of.

No cross-examination.

Mr. EVARTS. Mr. Chief Justice and Senators, we have in attendance, to give their evidence, the Secretary of State, the Secretary of the Treasury, the Secretary of the Interior, and the Postmaster General, and we offer them as witnesses to the same points that we have inquired of from Mr. Welles, and that have been covered by the rulings of the court. If objection is made to their examination, of course it must be considered as covered by the rulings already made.

Mr. WILLIAMS. I did not fully understand the last witness, and I should like to have him recalled for a moment.

EDGAR T. WELLES recalled.

Mr. WILLIAMS. If allowable, I should like to inquire of the witness whether what he communicated to his father was told to him by this lady, or whether it was communicated to him by the officers?

Answer. It was told to me by this lady.

Mr. EVARTS. We tender the witnesses I have named for examination upon the points that Mr. Secretary Welles has been interrogated concerning, and that the rulings of the Senate have covered. If the objection is made, it must be considered as covered by that ruling.

Mr. Manager BUTLER. We object. We have not objected that Mr. Welles was not a credible witness, but only that the testimony to be given was not proper.

Mr. EVARTS. I understand that.

ALEXANDER W. RANDALL sworn and examined.

By Mr. EVARTS:

Question. Mr. Randall, you are Postmaster General?

Answer. I am, sir.

Question. From what time have you held that office?

Answer. I was appointed in July, 1866; I have held it from that time.

Question. Before that time had you been in the Department; and if so, in what capacity?

Answer. I had been from the fall of 1862. I was First Assistant Postmaster General.

Question. Since the passage of the civil-tenure act, have cases arisen in the postal service in which officers came in question for their conduct and duty in the service?

Answer. They have.

Question. Do you remember the case of Foster Blodgett?

Answer. I do.

Question. What was he?

Answer. He was postmaster at Augusta, in Georgia.

Question. Was there any suspension of Mr. Blodgett in his office or in its duties?

Mr. Manager BUTLER. That suspension must have been evidenced by some writing.

Mr. EVARTS. I have asked the question whether there was one.

Mr. Manager BUTLER. If it was in writing I desire it to be produced.

Mr. EVARTS. I expect to produce it.

The WITNESS. There was.

Question. By whom was it made?

Answer. It was made by me.

Question. As Postmaster General?

Answer. As Postmaster General.

Question. Had the President anything to do with it?

Answer. Nothing at all.

Question. Did he know of it?

Answer. Not when it was done, nor before it.

Question, (handing some papers to the witness.) Please look at these papers and say if they are the official papers of that act?

Answer. Yes, sir; they are certified to be by me as Postmaster General.

Question. Did you receive a complaint against Mr. Blodgett?

Answer. There was one; yes, sir.

Question. And was it upon that complaint that your action was taken?

Answer. It was.

Question. In what form did the complaint come to you, and of what fact?

Mr. Manager BUTLER. Let the complaint itself state.

Mr. EVARTS. I have asked in what form it came.

Mr. Manager BUTLER. The complaint will speak for itself. This form is in writing.

Mr. EVARTS. I do not know that.

Mr. Manager BUTLER. Then I object to the information of others.

Mr. EVARTS. I have asked in what form the complaint came to him. Is that objected to?

Mr. Manager BUTLER. No, sir; that is not objected to; whether it was in writing or verbal.

The WITNESS. It came in writing and verbally, both.

Mr. Manager BUTLER. We shall have the writing, I suppose.

Mr. EVARTS. Yes, sir. [To the witness.] And on the complaint, verbally and in writing, this action was taken?

Answer. Yes, sir.

Mr. EVARTS. I propose to put in evidence these papers.

Mr. Manager BUTLER. Let me see them first.

After an examination of the papers.

Mr. Manager BUTLER. Have you a copy of the indictment referred to in these papers?

Mr. EVARTS. It is not here.

Mr. CURTIS. Governor Randall has it here.

Mr. EVARTS, (to the witness.) Have you it here?

The WITNESS. I do not think a copy of the indictment is here.

Mr. Manager BUTLER. That is all there is of it.

Mr. EVARTS. Very well.

Mr. Manager BUTLER. We object to these papers, because, very carefully, there has been left out the only thing that is of any consequence.

Mr. EVARTS. Whose care do you refer to?

Mr. Manager BUTLER. The man who did it.

Mr. EVARTS. Who is that?

Mr. Manager BUTLER. I do not know. This Mr. Blodgett is now attempted to be affected in his absence, and I feel a little bound to take care of him, because, being called as a witness here, he must be dealt justly with. The papers they now offer refer to the evidence of Mr. Blodgett's misconduct, and the evidence is not produced here, not even a recital of it; and therefore I say it is unjust to put in Mr. Randall's recital of a fact that happened when he has in his Department the fact itself, and which has been, by somebody to me unknown, carefully kept away from here.

Mr. EVARTS. Mr. Chief Justice and Senators, the honorable Managers chose, for some reason and ground best known to themselves, to offer in evidence as a part of this incrimination an act of the President of the United States in the removal of Foster Blodgett. I propose to show what that act was.

Mr. Manager BUTLER. I do not object, if you will show what that act was, and not keep back the paper which is the inculpation of Mr. Blodgett.

Mr. EVARTS. I am not inculpating Mr. Blodgett. I am proving what the act of the Executive Officer of the United States was that you have sought to put in evidence by oral testimony.

Mr. Manager BUTLER. You have put in the fact that Mr. Blodgett was removed upon a complaint in writing of misconduct, and you keep back that complaint in writing.

Mr. EVARTS. And you said that if the act was in writing it must be proved by the letters, and I agreed to it, and now produce them.

Mr. Manager BUTLER. You do not produce the complaint.

Mr. EVARTS. Well, we will not wrangle about it. I offer the official act of the Department in the removal of Mr. Blodgett.

Mr. Manager BUTLER. And I object that it is not fair play unless you bring in the complaint.

Mr. EVARTS. The learned Manager treats this as if it were a question of impeaching Mr. Blodgett. I am giving in evidence the act of the executive department which you brought in testimony.

Mr. Manager BUTLER. We proved the act ourselves. We proved that they removed Blodgett. Now, then, there is no occasion to prove that over again, if they are going to stop there.

Mr. EVARTS. You made it inculpation, and we want to prove what the act was.

Mr. Manager BUTLER. Then produce the whole thing on which it was grounded.

Mr. JOHNSON. What is the paper?

Mr. GRIMES. I call for the reading of the paper.

Mr. EVARTS. If you want the indictment produced it may certainly be produced; but the fact that it is not here is no legal objection to these papers.

Mr. JOHNSON. What is the paper produced?

The CHIEF JUSTICE. The counsel for the President will state what they propose to prove in writing.

Mr. EVARTS. I offer in evidence the order and letters handed to the Clerk, and desire that they may be read.

The CHIEF JUSTICE. It will be necessary to state what the order and letters are; otherwise the court will be unable to judge of their admissibility.

Mr. EVARTS. The testimony of Governor Randall has described them as the official action of the Department. I offer in evidence the official action of the Post Office Department in accomplishing the removal of Foster Blodgett, which removal was put in evidence by the Managers.

The CHIEF JUSTICE. The counsel will please reduce their offer to writing.

Mr. SHERMAN. I think we have a right to ask for the reading of the letters to know what we are called upon to vote.

The CHIEF JUSTICE. The Senate undoubtedly have a right to order the letters to be read.

Mr. SHERMAN. We are called upon to decide a question of evidence, and I should like to know what is offered from the papers themselves.

The CHIEF JUSTICE. The usual mode of proposing to prove is by stating the nature of the proof proposed to be offered, and then, upon an objection, the Senate decides whether proof of that description can be introduced. It is not usual to read the proof itself. Un-

doubtedly it is competent for the Senate to order it to be read.

Mr. SHERMAN. If the counsel will state the matter so that we can act upon it without taking time in reading the papers, I have no objection.

The offer to prove of the counsel for the respondent was reduced to writing and sent to the desk.

The CHIEF JUSTICE. The Secretary will read the offer to prove made by the counsel for the President.

The Secretary read as follows:

We offer in evidence the official action of the Post Office Department in the removal of Mr. Blodgett, which removal was put in evidence by oral testimony by the Managers.

Mr. Manager BUTLER. We will not object further. We think we can get in the indictment somehow.

The CHIEF JUSTICE. The objection is withdrawn.

Mr. EVARTS. I ask the Clerk to read the papers in their order.

The CHIEF JUSTICE. The Clerk will read the papers offered by the counsel.

The Chief Clerk read the papers, as follows:

A.

POST OFFICE DEPARTMENT,
January 3, 1868.

It appearing from an exemplified copy of the bill of indictment now on file in this Department, against Foster Blodgett, postmaster at Augusta, Georgia, that he has been indicted in the United States district court for the southern district of Georgia for perjury: it is *Ordered* that said Foster Blodgett be suspended from the office of postmaster at Augusta, Georgia, aforesaid; and that George W. Summers be designated as special agent of this Department to take charge of the post office thereat and discharge all its duties until further action shall be had by the President and Senate of the United States.

ALEX. W. RANDALL,
Postmaster General.

—

POST OFFICE DEPARTMENT,
WASHINGTON, D. C., *April 17, 1868.*

This is to certify that the foregoing, marked A, is a true copy of an original order on file in this Department:

In witness whereof I have hereunto set my hand and caused the seal of the Post Office Department to be affixed, at the General Post Office [L. S.] in the city of Washington, District of Columbia, the day and year first above written.

ALEX. W. RANDALL,
Postmaster General.

—

B.

THE POST OFFICE DEPARTMENT:
To whom it may concern:

Know ye, that Foster Blodgett having been suspended from the office of postmaster at Augusta, Georgia, under a bill of indictment for perjury, George W. Summers is hereby designated a special agent of this Department to take charge of the post office and public property thereat, and to discharge all the duties of the aforesaid office.

Witness my hand and the seal of said Department [L. S.] at Washington this 3d day of January, A. D. 1868.

ALEX. W. RANDALL,
Postmaster General.

—

POST OFFICE DEPARTMENT,
WASHINGTON, D. C., *April 17, 1868.*

This is to certify that the foregoing, marked B, is

a true copy of an original commission on record in this Department.

In witness whereof I have hereunto set my hand and caused the seal of the Post Office Department to be affixed at the General Post
[L. S.]   Office in the city of Washington, District of Columbia, the day and year first above written.
ALEX. W. RANDALL,
Postmaster General.

C.

Post Office Department,
Appointment Office, *January 3, 1868.*

Sir: Inclosed please find blank oath and bond to be executed by yourself and sureties as special agent of this Department to take charge of the post office at Augusta, Richmond county, Georgia. So soon as the same shall have been executed and placed in the mail addressed to this Department, you will then exhibit the inclosed commission to Foster Blodgett, or to the person in charge of the post office at Augusta aforesaid, take possession of the public property thereat, and enter on the full discharge of all the duties thereof, as required by the postal laws and regulations.

You will continue to conduct the office in the same manner as though you were postmaster until the President and Senate shall have taken further action in the premises.

Your salary will be at the rate of $1,800 a year, with three dollars per diem for subsistence.

Very respectfully, your obedient servant,
ST. JOHN B. L. SKINNER,
First Assistant Postmaster General.
George W. Summers, esq., *Augusta, Georgia.*

Post Office Department,
Washington, *April 17, 1868.*

This is to certify that the foregoing, marked C, is a true copy of a letter on record in this Department.

In witness whereof I have hereunto set my hand and caused the seal of the Post Office Department
[L. S.]   to be affixed at the General Post Office in the city of Washington, District of Columbia, the day and year first above written.
ALEX. W. RANDALL,
Postmaster General.

D.

Post Office Department,
Appointment Office, *January 3, 1868.*

Sir: A copy of the bill of indictment found against you in the United States district court for the southern district of Georgia, for perjury, has been placed on file in this Department, and in consequence thereof the Postmaster General has made an order suspending you from the office of postmaster at Augusta, Georgia, and designated George W. Summers as special agent of this Department, to take charge of the aforesaid post office and all the public property thereat.

You are, therefore, required to deliver to said George W. Summers the mail key and all the public property in your possession, upon the exhibition of his commission and demand for the mail key and property aforesaid; take from him duplicate receipts for the same; retain one and forward the other to this Department.

Very respectfully, yours, &c.,
ST. JOHN B. L. SKINNER,
First Assistant Postmaster General.
Foster Blodgett, esq., *Augusta, Georgia.*

Post Office Department,
Washington, *April 17, 1868.*

This is to certify that the foregoing, marked D, is a true copy of a letter on record in this Department.

In witness whereof I have hereunto set my hand and caused the seal of the Post Office Department
[L. S.]   to be affixed at the General Post Office, in the city of Washington, District of Columbia, the day and the year first above mentioned.
ALEX. W. RANDALL,
Postmaster General.

Cross-examined by Mr. Manager BUTLER:

Question. Is the post office in Augusta, Georgia, one that is within the appointment of the President under the law?

Answer. It is.

Question. Was Mr. Blodgett appointed by the President?

Answer. He was.

Question. When?

Answer. I cannot tell you that.

Question. Some time ago?

Answer. Yes, sir; some time ago; and confirmed by the Senate.

Question. Under what law did you, as Postmaster General, suspend him?

Answer. Under the law of necessity.

Question. Any other?

Answer. Under the law authorizing me to put special agents in charge of offices where I was satisfied that injustice was being done by the postmaster, and under the practice of the Department.

Question. I am asking you now as to the law. We will come to the practice by and by. Cannot you tell us whereabouts that law will be found?

Answer. No, sir; not without referring to my notes.

Question. Well, sir, refer to your notes. Of course I do not mean that unwritten law—the law of necessity?

Answer. No. It was a question whether I would close up the office, or appoint a special agent. [Holding a letter in his hand.] I have there, in a letter I wrote——

Question. I do not care about your letters. I am asking you to refer me to the law under which you did it, if you can?

Answer. I can make no further reference than I did to that law, except my authority to appoint special agents.

Question. What statute did you do this under?

Answer. Appoint the special agent?

Question. What statute did you do this act under? What statute do you justify yourself by?

Answer. I do not justify myself under any particular statute.

Question. What general statute?

Answer. No general statute.

Question. Then under no statute whatever, either particular or general, do you justify yourself. Now, sir, do you mean to say that this took place on the 3d of January?

Answer. The fore part of January.

Question. The paper is dated the 3d.

Answer. The fore part of January.

Mr. JOHNSON. What is the date of the paper, Mr. Manager?

Mr. Manager BUTLER. They are all dated the 3d of January, 1868. [To the witness.] Now, sir, have you ever communicated this case to the President?

Answer. I did.

Question. When?

Answer. I do not recollect; some time after it was done.

Question. About how long?

Answer. Perhaps a week.

Question. More?

Answer. I do not remember about that; a few days afterward.

Question. Did you take any advice of the President, or consent, or order before you made this removal?

Answer. I did not.

Question. Was the verbal complaint the same, or different from the written complaint against Foster Blodgett?

Answer. It was the same. It was the statement that he had been indicted by the district attorney.

Question. The statement that he had been indicted?

Answer. Yes, sir.

Question. And was there any other complaint?

Answer. And a copy of the indictment.

Question. Was there any other complaint than that?

Answer. I do not remember now whether there was any other or not.

Question. Who made the complaint to you?

Answer. The district attorney of that district stated to me the fact that an indictment had been found against him.

Question. Did he state it to you in person?

Answer. Yes, sir.

Question. Did you ask him to forward you a copy?

Answer. No, sir.

Question. Did he do so?

Answer. He did, or somebody did.

Question. Somebody did. Do you know who?

Answer. I cannot tell, unless he did.

Question. Did you prepare these papers here?

Answer. I ordered them to be prepared.

Question. You ordered all the papers to be prepared?

Answer. I did.

Question. Why is not a copy of the indictment here, then?

Answer. It was not inquired for, and I did not think of it.

Question. If it was not inquired for, who made the inquiry for the papers?

Answer. One of the attorneys asked me about the case.

Question. One of the counsel asked you about the case, the papers I am talking about now?

Answer. He asked me what was the condition of the case, what the testimony of Mr. Blodgett meant, and I told him, and told him I could furnish all the orders that were made in the case; and I did so.

Question. Then you volunteered to furnish him the orders?

Answer. I did?

Question. Why did you not furnish us a copy of the indictment?

Answer. I cannot tell about that. I did not think anything about it. I would have furnished it to you if you had asked me for it. You did not ask me for any copies.

Question. Now, sir, had you any other complaint against Foster Blodgett except the fact that he was indicted?

Answer. I do not remember any now.

Question. Have you any inclination of your mind; anything in your mind, in any way, of anything else brought against him?

Answer. I cannot tell you now. I do not remember anything else. There may be something in the papers.

Question. Have you any remembrance of acting upon any other, which you have forgotten?

Answer. I do not remember anything now. The papers are quite voluminous, and there may be something else in them. I do not remember now.

Question. Did you act upon any other than this?

Answer. Not that I remember.

Question. Now, sir, was not that an indictment brought by the grand jury of that county against him for taking the test-oath?

Answer. Yes, sir.

Question. Was it for anything else except that he was supposed to have sworn falsely when he swore the test-oath?

Answer. Not that I remember.

Question. It was taking the test-oath as an officer of the United States that he had not been in the rebellion?

Answer. Yes.

Question. And you removed him for that?

Answer. No, sir; I did not remove him.

Question. You suspended him for that?

Answer. Yes.

Question. Did you give him any notice of the suspension?

Answer. I did.

Question. That you were going to do it?

Answer. No, sir; not that I was going to do it. I sent him the notice you see there, or directed it to be sent.

Question. You sent a notice suspending him?

Answer. I directed notice to be sent to him that he was suspended, a copy of which is in the papers.

Question. That was the order of suspension?

Answer. Yes, sir.

Question. You did not give him any means of defending himself, or showing what had happened to him, or how it came on?

Answer. No, sir.

Question. But you suspended him at once?

Answer. I did.

Question. Is there any complaint on your books that he had not properly administered this office?

Answer. I do not remember any.

Question. Certainly none upon which you acted?

Answer. Not that I remember.

Question. And a competent officer, acting properly, because somebody found an indictment against him for taking the test-oath, swearing he was a Union man, you suspended, without any hearing or trial at all?

Answer. I do not swear to any such statement as that. Part of it is incorrect. If you will ask me to state what there is about this case, I shall be glad to do it.

Question. I will ask this question, and you will answer it——

The WITNESS. Ask your questions and I will answer them.

Question. I will put this question: Did you not suspend this officer, without investigation or trial, upon the simple fact of an indictment being found against him for having taken the test-oath to qualify him for that office, against whom no other complaint stood in your office?

Answer. I do not remember any other complaint now, as I have stated before.

Question. And therefore if you answer upon what you know, you will have to answer yes; you did suspend him?

Answer. Yes, I did suspend him; and if he had been convicted I should have asked to have him removed.

Question. This case has been pending since the 3d of January?

Answer. Yes, sir.

Question. Has it ever been communicated by the President to the Senate?

Answer. Not that I know of.

Question. Did he direct you so to do?

Answer. No, sir.

Question. Did you suspend him under the civil-tenure act?

Answer. No, sir.

Question. You took no notice of that?

Answer. Yes, sir; I took notice of it. That was the difficulty in the case, if you will allow me.

Question. You took no notice of it to act under it?

Answer. I could not act under it.

Question. How many hundreds of men have you appointed who could not take the test-oath?

Answer. I do not know of any—none that I know of.

Question. Do you not know that there are men appointed to office who have not taken the test-oath?

The WITNESS. As postmasters?

Mr. Manager BUTLER. Yes, sir.

The WITNESS. No, sir; I do not know of one—never one with my consent.

Mr. JOHNSON. What is your last answer?

The WITNESS. I say there never has been such an appointment with my consent.

By Mr. Manager BUTLER:

Question. Did you learn who were the prosecutors under this indictment?

Answer. No, sir; I did not.

Question. Did you inquire?

Answer. I did not.

Question. Whether they were rebels or Union men?

Answer. I did not.

Question. Did you not ask whether it was a prosecution by rebels down there against Mr. Blodgett?

Answer. No, sir; that was not my business. I simply inquired as to the fact of his being indicted for perjury in taking the oath of office.

Mr. Manager BUTLER. Will you have the kindness to furnish me with a copy of that indictment, duly certified?

The WITNESS. I will do so, certainly.

Mr. Manager BUTLER. And of any other complaint you can find against Foster Blodgett before his trial commenced?

The WITNESS. I will do so.

Mr. CURTIS. We should prefer to have it furnished to the court, and it can be directed to be put into the case. I suppose that will answer the purpose.

Mr. Manager BUTLER. I do not know that until I see it. If you had wanted it very much you could have had it.

Mr. CURTIS. It was a mere inadvertence.

The WITNESS. I presume they did not think of it, for I did not.

Mr. CURTIS. It was a mere inadvertence that it was not produced.

Mr. Manager BUTLER. Perhaps.

Mr. CURTIS. I wish it now produced. [To the witness.] Will you furnish to the Secretary of the Senate a copy of that indictment?

The WITNESS. Yes, sir.

Mr. Manager BUTLER. Furnishing it to the Secretary without my seeing it will not put it into the case. If you desire it to be furnished to him, very well; but I object to anything being put on the files without my seeing it; and I shall want the witness after that.

Mr. EVARTS. If it is objected to as evidence, perhaps it is not worth while to produce it. The only object of having it here is as evidence.

Mr. Manager BUTLER. I cannot tell whether I shall object to it or not until I see it.

Mr. EVARTS. That will be a private matter, then, between you and Governor Randall.

Mr. Manager BUTLER. We shall want the Postmaster General with it. I shall want to ask him some more questions after I get it.

Mr. EVARTS. You can do so.

The WITNESS. There is another similar case in which I suspended a man last week.

Mr. Manager BUTLER. Never mind about the other case. I do not care about what you have done since.

The WITNESS. I thought you might want that.

Reëxamined by Mr. EVARTS:

Question. I understand your judgment as

Postmaster General was that this suspension should be made.

Answer. Yes, sir.

Question. It occurred not during a recess of the Senate?

Answer. No, sir; it was during the session of the Senate.

Question. So that it was not under the civil-tenure act?

Answer. Not as I understand it.

Mr. EVARTS. It would not be a suspension under the civil-tenure act.

Mr. Manager WILLIAMS. It was during the recess.

Mr. EVARTS. It was not in the recess, and the civil-tenure act does not apply to the case. [To the witness.] Now, sir, this oath, for perjury in taking which he was indicted, as you were informed by the indictment, was in taking the oath to this office that he held?

Answer. Yes, sir.

Mr. Manager BUTLER. I object to what was done as to the indictment until that can be produced.

Mr. EVARTS. I said as you stated. You asked him the question whether the indictment was not for taking a false oath. I ask him if that false oath was not in qualifying for this office which he held?

The WITNESS. Yes, sir.

Question. And in which you suspended him?

Answer. Yes, sir; that is what I understand.

Mr. EVARTS. That is all, sir.

Mr. Manager BUTLER. That is all until you bring the indictment.

Mr. SHERMAN. I desire to submit, if the Senate think the question admissible, this question to this witness, or any other member of the Cabinet that may be called. It may be contravened by the decision already made, and I should like to have the question decided by the Senate.

The CHIEF JUSTICE. The Secretary will read the question proposed by the Senator from Ohio.

The Secretary read as follows:

State if, after the 2d of March, 1867, the date of the passage of the tenure-of-office act, the question whether the Secretaries appointed by President Lincoln were included within the provisons of that act, came before the Cabinet for discussion; and if so, what opinion was given on this question by members of the Cabinet to the President.

Mr. Manager BINGHAM. We desire to object to that on the ground of its incompe-,tency, and that we deem it directly within the ruling of the Senate twice or three times made this day.

Mr. Manager BUTLER. The very same question was voted upon.

Mr. Manager BINGHAM. The very same question.

Mr. SHERMAN. I should like to have the question taken by the Senate upon that by yeas and nays.

Mr. HOWARD. I raise a question of order

upon that question of the Senator, that it has been once decided by the Senate.

The CHIEF JUSTICE. The Chief Justice has no doubt that the question may be properly put to the witness. Whether it shall be answered is a question for the Senate to judge.

Mr. Manager BUTLER. I should like, before that question is put, to have the question which was decided by the Senate to-day, the third question I think it is, read from the minutes. It was an offer covering exactly the same ground.

The CHIEF JUSTICE. The offer will be read.

Mr. SHERMAN. If the Senate will allow me, I can tell in a word the difference between the two.

Mr. CONNESS and others. I object.

Mr. CONKLING. Let us hear that offer read.

The CHIEF JUSTICE. The Secretary will read the offer to prove, the reading of which is requested by Mr. Manager BUTLER.

The Secretary read as follows:

We offer to prove that at the meetings of the Cabinet at which Stanton was present, held while the tenure-of-civil-office bill was before the President for approval, the advice of the Cabinet in regard to the same was asked by the President, and given by the Cabinet, and thereupon the question whether Mr. Stanton and the other Secretaries who had received their appointments from Mr. Lincoln were within the restrictions upon the President's power of removal from office created by said act, was considered and the opinion expressed that the Secretaries appointed by Mr. Lincoln were not within such restrictions.

Mr. JOHNSON. I ask that the question propounded by the Senator from Ohio shall now be read.

The Secretary read the question, as follows:

State if, after the 2d of March, 1867, the date of the passage of the tenure-of-office act, the question whether the Secretaries appointed by President Lincoln were included within the provisions of that act, came before the Cabinet for discussion; and if so, what opinion was given on this question by members of the Cabinet to the President?

Mr. FERRY. I call for the yeas and nays on that question.

The yeas and nays were ordered; and being taken, resulted—yeas 20, nays 26; as follows:

YEAS — Messrs. Anthony, Bayard, Buckalew, Davis, Dixon, Doolittle, Fessenden, Fowler, Grimes, Hendricks, Johnson, McCreery, Patterson of Tennessee, Ross, Saulsbury, Sherman, Trumbull, Van Winkle, Vickers, and Willey—20.

NAYS—Messrs. Cameron, Cattell, Chandler, Cole, Conkling, Conness, Corbett, Cragin, Edmunds, Ferry, Frelinghuysen,: Harlan, Howard, Howe, Morgan, Morrill of Maine, Morrill of Vermont, Patterson of New Hampshire, Pomeroy, Ramsey, Stewart, Thayer, Tipton, Williams, Wilson, and Yates—26.

NOT VOTING—Messrs. Drake, Henderson, Morton, Norton, Nye, Sprague, Sumner, and Wade—8.

So the question was not admitted.

Mr. EVARTS. Mr. Chief Justice and Senators, the counsel for the President are now able to state that the evidence on his part is now closed, as they understand their duty in the matter. The conduct of the proofs, however, has been mainly intrusted to Mr. Stanbery, both on the part of the counsel and for some particular reasons in reference to his previous knowledge concerning the conduct of the controversy and the matters to be given in evidence which belonged to his official familiarity with them. Mr. Stanbery's health, we are sorry to say, is still such as to have precluded anything like a serious conference with them since he was taken ill. We submit it, therefore, to the Senate that, upon such consideration, it is possible some other proof may need to be offered. We do not at present expect that it will be so.

Mr. JOHNSON. Mr. Chief Justice, I ask the Managers if they have any proof to offer to-day?

Mr. Manager BUTLER. Not till the other side get through.

Mr. JOHNSON. I move, then, that the court adjourn until eleven o'clock on Monday.

Mr. EVARTS. Mr. Chief Justice, we have made this announcement. We suppose ourselves to be through. I have only stated that in the absence of Mr. Stanbery, it may be possible that some further evidence may need to be offered, which we do not at all expect.

Mr. Manager BUTLER. When you are entirely through we will commence.

The CHIEF JUSTICE. The Senator from Maryland moves that the Senate, sitting as a court of impeachment, adjourn until Monday at eleven o'clock.

The motion, was agreed to; and the Senate, sitting for the trial of the impeachment, adjourned.

MONDAY, *April* 20, 1868.

The Chief Justice of the United States took the chair.

The usual proclamation having been made by the Sergeant-at-Arms,

The Managers of the impeachment on the part of the House of Representatives and the counsel for the respondent, except Mr. Stanbery, appeared and took the seats assigned to them respectively.

The members of the House of Representatives, as in Committee of the Whole, preceded by Mr. E. B. WASHBURNE, chairman of that committee, and accompanied by the Speaker and Clerk, appeared and were conducted to the seats provided for them.

The CHIEF JUSTICE. The Secretary will read the Journal of Saturday's proceedings.

The Secretary proceeded to read the Journal of the Senate sitting on Saturday last for the trial of the impeachment; but before concluding was interrupted by

Mr. STEWART. I move that the further reading of the Journal be dispensed with.

The CHIEF JUSTICE. If there be no objection it will be so ordered. The Chair hears no objection. It is so ordered. Gentlemen of counsel for the President, do you propose to put in any further evidence?

Mr. CURTIS. No, Mr. Chief Justice; we consider that we have closed the evidence on the part of the defense.

The CHIEF JUSTICE. Do the honorable Managers propose to put in any rebutting evidence?

Mr. Manager BINGHAM. As we are advised at present, Mr. President and Senators, we may desire, in case one or two witnesses subpœnaed early in this trial should appear, to call them. I will desire, however, to consult my associates, two of whom are absent and who are expected within a few minutes at the table, in regard to any further statement about it.

The CHIEF JUSTICE. In case the honorable Managers desire to put in further evidence after the argument it will be necessary to obtain an order of the Senate; at least it would be proper to obtain such order before the argument proceeds.

Mr. Manager BINGHAM. I wish to be understood as suggesting to the presiding officer of the Senate that I desire to consult my associates further about it.

The CHIEF JUSTICE. Certainly.

Mr. Manager BINGHAM. So far as the order is concerned, I took it for granted that upon the suggestion made at the time the evidence was closed on the part of the Managers it would be competent for us without further order, if these witnesses should appear, to introduce them upon the stand, because the Senate will recollect, although I have not referred myself to the Journal of proceedings since, it was stated by my associate Manager, Mr. BUTLER, in the hearing of the Senate, that we considered our case closed, reserving our right to call rebutting testimony or to offer some documentary testimony that might have escaped our notice. Some such statement, I believe, was entered upon the Journal.

Mr. JOHNSON. I am not sure that I heard correctly the honorable Manager. I rise merely for the purpose of inquiring whether the Managers desire to have the privilege of offering evidence after the argument begins?

Mr. Manager BINGHAM. Not as at present advised, although on that subject, as doubtless is known to honorable Senators, in proceedings of this sort, (though I am not prepared to say that it has happened in this country; I am not sure but it did, however, in the case of Justice Chase,) such orders have been made after the final argument has been opened. I am not advised, however, that the Managers have any desire of that sort. I wish it to be understood simply by the Senate that there are one or two witnesses who were deemed important on the part of the Managers who were early subpœnaed to attend this trial, and neither of whom we have been able yet to see, although we are advised that they have been in the capital for the last forty-eight hours, or twenty-four hours at least.

Mr. YATES. I do not still understand—I could not hear the Manager—whether he proposes to introduce evidence after the examination is closed and after the argument begins.

Mr. Manager BINGHAM. As at present advised, we have no purpose of the sort. I only made the remark I did in response to the honorable gentleman from Maryland. I do not know what may occur in the progress of this trial, and I do not wish to be concluded by any statement I have made here touching the rights of the people under the usage and practice in proceedings of this kind.

Mr. JOHNSON. I do not think there is any such practice in the United States.

After a pause,

Mr. Manager BUTLER. I desire, Mr. President, to offer the Journal of Congress of 1774–75, of the First Congress, pages 121–22, which is a report of the committee appointed to draft a commission to the General, George Washington, who had just been theretofor appointed:

"SATURDAY, *June* 17, 1775.

* * * * * * * *

"The committee appointed to draft a commission to the General reported the same, which, being read by paragraphs and debated, was agreed to as follows:

"IN CONGRESS.

"The delegates of the United Colonies of New Hampshire, Massachusetts Bay, Rhode Island, Connecticut, New York, New Jersey, Pennsylvania, the counties of New Castle, Kent, and Sussex on Delaware, Maryland, Virginia, North Carolina, and South Carolina.

"To GEORGE WASHINGTON, esq.:

"We, reposing special trust and confidence in your patriotism, valor, conduct, and fidelity, do, by these presents, constitute and appoint you to be General and Commander-in-Chief of the Army of the United Colonies, and of all the forces now raised or to be raised by them, and of all others who shall voluntarily offer their service and join the said Army for the defense of American liberty, and for repelling every hostile invasion thereof. And you are hereby vested with full power and authority to act as you shall think for the good and welfare of the service.

"And we do hereby strictly charge and require all officers and soldiers under your command to be obedient to your orders and diligent in the exercise of their several duties.

"And we do also enjoin and require you to be careful in executing the good trust reposed in you, by causing strict discipline and order to be observed in the Army, and that the soldiers be duly exercised and provided with all convenient necessaries.

"And you are to regulate your conduct in every respect by the rules and discipline of wars, (as herewith given you,) and punctually to observe and follow such orders and directions, from time to time, as you shall receive from this or a future Congress of these United Colonies or Committee of Congress.

"This commission to continue in force until revoked by this or a future Congress.

"By order of the Congress."

The point to which I offer this is that this is the only form of commission ever prescribed by law in this country to a military officer, and in drafting commissions under the Constitution of the United States "the pleasure of the President" was inserted instead of "the pleasure of Congress."

The CHIEF JUSTICE. Is there any objection?

Mr. CURTIS and Mr. EVARTS. No objection.

Mr. Manager BUTLER. I now offer, Mr.

President and Senators, a letter from the Treasury Department in answer to what has been put in as the practice of the Government to appoint officers during the recess. [The letter was handed to the counsel for the respondent.] It is one of a series of letters which were not brought to your attention in the schedules which you allowed to come in. Only so much of the practice, as I charge, as would make on one side was put in.

[The letter was returned to the Manager.]

Mr. EVARTS. The letter we do not consider as applicable to any point that we have made either in argument or in evidence; nor do we regard it as an act of the Treasury Department, but simply as an expression of an opinion of the then existing Secretary of the Treasury. It is simply an immaterial piece of evidence; it is not worth while to occupy time in discussing it.

Mr. Manager BUTLER. I only ask whether you object?

Mr. EVARTS. I have stated all I have to say.

Mr. Manager BUTLER. You do not.

Mr. EVARTS. No. I have stated what it applied to.

Mr. Manager BUTLER. Very well. I will read the letter:

TREASURY DEPARTMENT, *August* 23, 1855.

SIR: Your letter of the 18th instant, recommending William Irving Crandall for the appointment of surveyor of the customs at Chattanooga, Tennessee, is received. The office not having been filled before the adjournment of the Senate, it must necessarily remain vacant until its next session, when your recommendation of Mr. Crandall will receive respectful consideration.

I have the honor to be, very respectfully, your obedient servant,
                                    JAMES GUTHRIE,
                            Secretary of the Treasury.
Hon. J. H. SMITH, *Charleston, South Carolina.*

After a pause,

Mr. Manager BUTLER. If the President will grant me a moment. Mr. Randall did not bring the papers which I called for to me until since we have come into the Senate, and I want to examine them to see what I will and what I will not offer. [After an examination of the papers.] Mr. Randall, you will take the stand.

ALEXANDER W. RANDALL examined.

By Mr. Manager BUTLER:

Question. Had you any copy of the indictment against Foster Blodgett on file in your office?

Answer. What purported to be.

Question. When was it made?

Answer. That I cannot tell you; I suppose about the time the original copy was filed there.

Question. Have you produced it here?

Answer. No, sir.

Question. What did you do with it?

Answer. It is in the office.

Question. Have you produced copies here?

Answer. Yes, sir; there is a copy there before you.

Question. A copy from where?

Answer. From the Treasury Department.

Question. Why did you not produce the copy from your office, as I asked you?

Answer. Because that would not prove anything; I could not certify that it was a copy without having the original.

Question. Have you produced the original?

Answer. I understand it is here. The reason I did not produce it was I understood it was here.

Question. Where?

Answer. Before some committee. It was sent up here with the case. The letter of Mr. McCulloch there explains that.

Question. The letter of Mr. McCulloch explains about Mr. Hopkins's case, which I do not mean to put in; but I mean now to deal with Mr. Blodgett's case?

Answer. You will find the copy of two indictments fastened together in the original as they are there, and I understand they are here. That is the reason I did not bring that, for I could not, without the original, certify that it was a copy.

Question. And you got a copy from the Treasury Department this morning?

Answer. Yes, sir.

Question. Which you produce here, but do not from your own office?

Answer. No, sir; I do not produce that because I could not certify without having the original that it was a true copy; and, understanding the others were here in the Senate, I did not bring it.

Question. But you brought this copy?

Answer. I had forgotten how the case came here.

Mr. Manager BUTLER, (to the counsel for the respondent.) Gentlemen, I will detach these, or only put in one paper, just as you please.

Mr. EVARTS. Of course, we understand.

Mr. Manager BUTLER. I do not care to go through detaching the copy in this one case.

Mr. EVARTS. It is Mr. Blodgett's indictment?

Mr. Manager BUTLER. Yes, sir. I now offer simply the indictment in Blodgett's case, which I will read, without detaching it from the other paper:

UNITED STATES OF AMERICA,
Southern District of Georgia:
District court of the United States for the southern district of Georgia.

NOVEMBER TERM, 1867, *A. D.*

The grand jurors of the United States, chosen, selected, and sworn in, and for the southern district of Georgia, being good and lawful men of the said southern district of Georgia, and being charged to inquire for the United States and for the body of the said district upon their oaths;

Present: that heretofore, that is to say, on the 27th day of July, in the year of our Lord 1866, one Foster Blodgett, of the city of Augusta and county of Richmond, in the State of Georgia, and in the southern district of Georgia aforesaid, was appointed by the President of the United States to the office of deputy postmaster at Augusta aforesaid, the said office, that is to say, the office of deputy postmaster, being an office of profit under the Government of the United States aforesaid, in the civil department of the public service, and that, after said appointment and before entering upon the duties of the said office, and before he, the said Foster Blodgett, was entitled to any salary or other emoluments arising from the said office, to wit, the office of deputy postmaster aforesaid, he, the said Foster Blodgett, was then and there required by law to take and subscribe the oath hereinafter set forth, the said oath being by law made material and necessary to be taken and subscribed by him, the said Foster Blodgett, before entering upon the duties of the office aforesaid, to wit, the office of deputy postmaster at Augusta aforesaid, and, being so required by law, he, the said Foster Blodgett, came in his own proper person before David S. Roath, a judge of the court of ordinary for the county of Richmond, in the State of Georgia and within the district aforesaid, and within the jurisdiction of this court, on the 5th day of September, in the year of our Lord 1866, at Augusta aforesaid, within the county, State, and district aforesaid, and then and there was duly sworn and took his corporal oath before the said David S. Roath, a judge of the court of ordinary for the county of Richmond, in the State of Georgia and district aforesaid, he, the said David S. Roath, being then and there duly authorized by law, and having then and there sufficient and competent power, to administer the said oath to the said Foster Blodgett in that behalf, and that thereupon the said Foster Blodgett, having so sworn as aforesaid, and not having the fear of God before his eyes, but having been moved and seduced by the instigation of the devil, then and there, to wit, on the day and year aforesaid and at the place last aforesaid, before the said David S. Roath, judge of the court of ordinary as aforesaid, (he, the said Roath, having then and there competent authority to administer the said oath as aforesaid,) upon his oath aforesaid, sworn to before the said David S. Roath, on the 5th day of September, in the year of our Lord 1866, falsely, willfully, and corruptly did swear to the purport and effect following, that is to say:

"I, Foster Blodgett, (meaning the said Foster Blodgett,) being appointed deputy postmaster at Augusta, in the county of Richmond and State of Georgia, do swear that I will faithfully perform all the duties required of me and abstain from anything forbidden by the laws in relation to the establishment of the post office and post roads within the United States; and that I will honestly and truly account for and pay over any moneys belonging to the said United States which may come into my possession or control, and I do further solemnly swear that I have never voluntarily borne arms against the United States since I have been a citizen thereof; that I have voluntarily given no aid, countenance, counsel, or encouragement to persons engaged in armed hostility thereto; that I have neither sought nor accepted nor attempted to exercise the functions of any office whatever, under any authority or pretended authority, in hostility to the United States; that I have not yielded a voluntary support to any pretended government, authority, power, or constitution within the United States hostile or inimical thereto; and I do further swear that to the best of my knowledge and ability I will support and defend the Constitution of the United States against all enemies, foreign or domestic; that I will bear true faith and allegiance to the same; that I take this obligation freely, without any mental reservation or purpose of evasion; and that I will well and faithfully discharge the duties of the office on which I am about to enter; so help me God."

Whereas in truth and in fact, the said Foster Blodgett before the time of taking the said oath as aforesaid, had voluntarily borne arms against the United States aforesaid, he the said Foster Blodgett having been at that time, that is to say, at the time when he bore arms as aforesaid, a citizen of the United States aforesaid; and whereas in truth and in fact he the said Foster Blodgett being a citizen as aforesaid, before that time, that is to say, before the time of the taking of the oath, voluntarily had given aid to persons engaged in armed hostility to the United States aforesaid, and had voluntarily as aforesaid given countenance, counsel, and encouragement to persons engaged in armed hostility to the United

States aforesaid; and whereas, in truth and fact, he the said Foster Blodgett being a citizen of the United States as aforesaid had before that time, that is to say before the time of the taking of the said oath as aforesaid, accepted an office, to wit, the office of the captaincy of an artillery company in the service of and under the authority of the so-called confederate States, the so-called confederate States being then and there an authority or a pretended authority in hostility to the United States aforesaid; and whereas in truth and fact he, the said Foster Blodgett, being a citizen as aforesaid, had before that time, that is to say, before the time of the taking of the said oath, yielded a voluntary support to a pretended government of Georgia, the same being at that time, that is to say at the time he, said Foster Blodgett, yielded a voluntary support thereto, a pretended authority in power within the United States and hostile thereto. And so the jurors aforesaid, upon their oaths aforesaid, do say that the said Foster Blodgett, by his oath aforesaid taken and subscribed on the day and year aforesaid, by David S. Roath, a judge of the court of ordinary as aforesaid, falsely, willfully, and corruptly, in manner and form aforesaid did, in the southern district of Georgia, and within the jurisdiction of this court, commit willful and corrupt perjury, contrary to the forms of the statute in such case made and provided, and against the peace and dignity of the United States,

HENRY S. FITCH,
United States Attorney for Georgia.

—

Indorsement.

United States of America, Southern District of Georgia, United States District Court, November Term, 1867.

United States
    vs.   } Indictment for perjury.
Foster Blodgett.

Witnesses: James A. Bennett, Ambrose R. Wright, Dr. M. J. Jones, John N. Wray, Avera D'Antiguac, George W. Vennurey, Allen Phillips, John L. Ellis. A true bill.

HENRY BINGHAM, *Foreman.*

SAVANNAH, *November 26, 1867.*
Filed November 29, 1867.

JAMES McPHERSON, *Clerk.*

Mr. JOHNSON. Does it charge that he was a captain in the rebel service?

Mr. Manager BUTLER. He was charged with being a captain in a volunteer company. [To the witness.] Now, Mr. Randall, upon notice which you have put in as given to Mr. Blodgett being sent to him, did he return an answer, and is this paper that answer or a copy of it? [Handing a paper to the witness.]

Answer. These are copies of the papers that are on file. I can only swear to them as copies of papers on file. I believe these are correct copies.

Question. And that is a copy of his answer? Will you look at it.

Answer. Yes, sir. I have read it all over; I think it is.

Question. The notice left here on the 3d of January, we have learned by the paper which was put in on Saturday?

Answer. I think it was the 3d of January.

Question. And on the 10th he returned this answer?

Answer. Yes, sir.

Mr. Manager BUTLER. I propose to offer it. It is:

WASHINGTON, D. C., *January* 10, 1868.
Hon. A. W. RANDALL:
SIR—

C. I.—32.

Mr. EVARTS. One moment, Mr. Manager. We suppose that there is no inquiry before this Senate sitting as a court of impeachment as to the truth of the charges against Mr. Blodgett, nor as to his defenses. We put in evidence nothing but the official action of the Government through the Post Office Department, and that only in answer to an oral statement concerning it which Mr. Blodgett had himself given. Now, the Manager brings in the indictment, and having got that in claims the right to repel it and thus produce evidence on both sides of the question of the reason of Mr. Blodgett's suspension. We submit to the Senate that the proof is irrelevant.

Mr. Manager BUTLER. Mr. President, the case stands thus: Mr. Foster Blodgett, who is mayor of the city of Augusta, appointed by General Pope, and a member of the constitutional convention—

Mr. EVARTS. No part of that statement is in evidence.

Mr. Manager BUTLER. I propose to put it in evidence, and am stating my case. I have got it all here. He was a member of the constitutional convention and an active Union man—

The CHIEF JUSTICE. The honorable Manager will please reduce his offer to prove to writing.

Mr. Manager BUTLER. I will after I state the grounds of it. I will put—

The CHIEF JUSTICE. The Chief Justice thinks it ought to be reduced to writing now, in order that the Senate may pass upon the question whether they will receive the evidence.

Mr. Manager BUTLER. They cannot until I make the statement, sir.

The CHIEF JUSTICE. The Chief Justice thinks that the same rule which was applied to the counsel for the President yesterday ought to be applied to the honorable Managers to-day. The Managers should state in writing the nature of the evidence which they propose to introduce, and the Senate can then pass upon the question whether they desire to hear evidence of that description.

Mr. JOHNSON. Does the Manager propose to offer that paper in evidence itself?

Mr. Manager BUTLER. I do.

Mr. JOHNSON. And nothing else?

Mr. Manager BUTLER. I propose to offer something else besides. At present I propose to offer this, and it is the first time any counsel has been thus stopped. I assume, Mr. President—I never have assumed any different—that the same rule will be applied to-day as yesterday. I do not want to be understood as asking anything different.

The CHIEF JUSTICE. The honorable Manager appears to the Chief Justice to be making a statement of matters which are not in proof, and of which the Senate has as yet heard nothing. He states that he intends to put them in proof. The Chief Justice therefore requires that the nature of the evidence that he proposes to put before the Senate shall be reduced to writing as has been done heretofore. He will make the ordinary offer to prove, and then the Senate will judge whether they will receive the evidence or not.

Mr. Manager BUTLER. I was trying to state that this was a part of the record produced by the other side. It is the first time, I have a right to say, that any counsel has been interrupted in this way. This——

The CHIEF JUSTICE. Does the honorable Manager decline to put his statement in writing?

Mr. Manager BUTLER. I am not declining to put the statement in writing, sir.

The CHIEF JUSTICE. Then the honorable Manager will have the goodness to put it in writing.

Mr. Manager BUTLER. I can do it, sir, by taking sufficient time.

The CHIEF JUSTICE. It will be allowed.

The proposition having been reduced to writing,

Mr. Manager BUTLER. This is the offer, sir:

We offer to show that Foster Blodgett, the mayor of Augusta, Georgia, appointed by General Pope, and a member of the constitutional convention of Georgia, being, because of his loyalty, obnoxious to some portion of the citizens lately in rebellion against the United States, by the testimony of such citizens an indictment was procured to be found against him; that said indictment being sent to the Postmaster General, he thereupon, without authority of law, suspended said Foster Blodgett from office indefinitely, without any other complaint against him and without any hearing and did not send to the Senate the report of such suspension, the office being one within the appointment of the President by and with the advice and consent of the Senate; this to be proved in part by the answer of Blodgett to the Postmaster General's notice of such suspension, being a portion of the papers on file in the Post Office Department upon which the action of the Postmaster General was taken, a portion of which have been put in evidence by the counsel of the President, and that Mr. Blodgett is shown by the evidence in the record to have always been friendly to the United States and loyal to the Government.

That is the offer. On this we wish to be heard at such time as the Chair will permit.

Mr. EVARTS. We object to the evidence, Mr. Chief Justice and Senators, as being wholly irrelevant to this case. The evidence concerning Foster Blodgett was produced on the part of the Managers, and on their part was confined to his oral testimony that he had received certain commissions under which he held the office of postmaster at Augusta; that he had been suspended in that office by the Executive of the United States in some form of its action, and there was a superadded negative conclusion of his that his case had not been sent to the Senate. In taking up that case the defense offered nothing but the official action of the Post Office Department, coupled with the evidence of the head of that Department that it was his own act, without previous knowledge or subsequent direction of the President of the United States. In that official order, thus a part of the action of the Department, it appears that the ground of it was an

indictment against Mr. Blodgett. A complaint was made that that indictment was not produced. The Managers having procured it, having put it in evidence, they now propose to put in evidence his answer to that indictment or to the accusation made before the Postmaster General.

Mr. Manager BUTLER. I know you do not mean to misstate—his answer to the Postmaster General's notice, not to the indictment.

Mr. EVARTS. His answer to the accusation and the evidence concerning the accusation as placed before the Postmaster General, I understood.

Mr. Manager BUTLER. Not an answer to the indictment.

Mr. EVARTS. An answer to the indictment so far as it was the accusation before the Post Office Department. I understood you to say so; that is, you propose to prove that he was friendly to the United States, and always had been, notwithstanding he had been a captain in the rebel troops. I understood you to say so; and now the honorable Manager states that this paper, which is part of his evidence to sustain Mr. Blodgett's loyalty and defeat the accusation against him, in which Mr. Blodgett may be entirely right for aught I know, is a letter written by him ten days after his suspension; and the honorable Manager states that that letter of his, written to the Postmaster General ten days after his suspension, was a part of the papers upon which the Postmaster General acted in suspending him. How that could be, in the nature of things, it is difficult for me to see. He was suspended on the 3d. Ten days after he wrote an answer to the incrimination; and that is one of the papers on which the Postmaster General suspended him, it is said.

The honorable court can see that this is not evidence introduced by us in disparagement of Foster Blodgett. It is evidence introduced by us to show the action of the Post Office Department in the suspension, which suspension the Managers had put in by oral testimony; and under cover of that the learned Manager first seeks to introduce the accusations against Blodgett, and then to rebut them. If this evidence is rightly put in on their part we of course can meet it on ours; and we shall have an interesting excursion from the impeachment trial of the President to the trial of Mr. Foster Blodgett on the question of loyalty; and I am instructed to say that there is a witness in the city who can testify that he was a captain in the rebel army; and we are ready to go on with that proof if it is desired.

Mr. Manager BUTLER. Mr. President and Senators, I think now it will not be out of any order either of to-day or yesterday or the day before for me to state the grounds upon which I offer this evidence.

Foster Blodgett was called here to show that, holding an office which required the advice and consent of the Senate, he had been suspended indefinitely by the President of the United States, as he supposed, and as we supposed, on the 3d of January, 1868, without any fault on his part, so far as his official duties were concerned, and without any adjudication or conviction of any crime, and a man placed in his office as special agent with the same salary and a little more; so that it amounted to a removal and putting in a man into the office as now appears by the papers presented. Mr. Blodgett testified that up to the day he testified he had not had his case before the Senate; he could get no redress. We thought that upon the proposition that the President desired to obey the law, except that he wanted to make a case to test the constitutionality of it, this was quite pertinent evidence. He having put forward broadly in his answer that he was exceedingly desirous to obey the laws, the civil-tenure act and all other laws, except that he wanted to make a case to test the constitutionality of the law, these facts are put in, and these facts are yet undisputed. They called Mr. Postmaster General Randall on Saturday, and he produced, and they put in, a letter of appointment of one Summers, special agent, with a salary therein set out. They also put in a letter informing Mr. Blodgett that he had been suspended from office. That letter states precisely that it was upon an indictment for perjury, not setting out the indictment, so as to leave us to infer that Foster Blodgett had in some controversy between neighbor and neighbor, or citizen and citizen, somewhere committed willful and corrupt perjury, and that it was so heinous a case that the Postmaster General felt obliged instantly to suspend him; and it was a case, he said, where the great law of necessity compelled him to suspend him at once. In order to meet that we asked for the indictment. We got it at last from the Treasury Department, a copy of it. The indictment then makes certain statements against Mr. Foster Blodgett. Now, Mr. Foster Blodgett instantly upon being notified—this being the 3d of January, and the paper, which I shall show you, being dated the 10th—seven days only, three from ten leaves seven, not ten, Mr. Counsel, so that inadvertences can take place as well on the one side as the other——

Mr. EVARTS. If you consider it material, I will retract.

Mr. Manager BUTLER. I do not consider it material only as a matter of correctness; that is all. As I say, seven days afterward, being in Washington, he instantly answers and puts on file his justification, that this was all a rebel plot and treason against the United States in fact. Having put that on file, that is a part of the case.

Now, I have not said to the Senate that this paper was that upon which Mr. Randall acted in suspending him, but I do say it is a part of the proceedings in the case, and it is a paper on which Mr. Randall acted in not returning that suspension through the President to the Senate. It may be said that Mr. Randall had no business to return it to the Senate. He had just as much business to return it to the Senate as he had to suspend him.

We are answered, too, that they put in only the official act of the Department. · I had the honor to explain to the Senate some days ago that I understood an official act to be that which was made a man's duty by law to do. I never understood that there was any other official act. I have always understood that the kind of acts which a man does where the law does not require him to do them are officious acts and not official, and I think this was the most officious act I have ever known, one which the Postmaster General says there is no law for, which was justified by no statute. A man is suspended; his reputation is ruined as far as it can be; the tribunal the law has appointed before which he could have a hearing, the Senate of the United States, is not informed of it in the regular way. It affects the President of the United States, because he was informed of it after it was done, and he has taken no action; and then when we put him on to say to us "I have been suspended and cannot go before the Senate," the answer is what? When he simply says that the answer is to put in the fact that he was indicted in order to blacken his reputation and send it out to the country.

I never saw Foster Blodgett until the day he was brought upon this stand. I have no interest in him any more than any other gentleman of position in the South. I put it to you, if you had been treated in that way when here as a witness under the summons of the Senate by the Managers of the House of Representatives to testify to a fact, and then the President, after refusing you any hearing before the constitutional tribunal and legal tribunal, had put in the fact to blacken your character that you had been indicted, would you not like to have the privilege of putting in at least your answer on record in the case, that which you did instantly? It is said to be the letter of Mr. Blodgett. True, it is; but it also contains exhibits and other papers which establish the facts beyond controversy.

It is said here, with a slur, that they have got a witness to prove that he was in the rebel army. I do not doubt it—plenty of them—whether he was or not. But what I say is, that he was only a captain in a militia company, and called into service and bound to obey the powers that be; and he was indicted because he yielded to the power of the State of Georgia. to compel him to hold the commission; and taking no commission, he had either to go or lose his life; and he could well swear, although he went as a militia captain into the service, that he did not voluntarily go. But, however that may be, he has a right to have before the country that he has been traduced—a man among his neighbors so well known that they elected him to make the constitutional law for them; a man among his neighbors so well known that General Pope appointed him mayor of this very town where he held the office; a man so well known that when the State of Georgia shall come here and demand a place in this Chamber I have no doubt Foster Blodgett will come and take his place beside the proudest of you.

I say under these circumstances I feel it my duty to put this testimony before you; and if the mere objection is want of relevancy I put it as a matter of justice to a witness that the House of Representatives brought here and who is now being oppressed by the entire power of the executive Government of the United States, who has been confessedly, without law, against right, suspended from his office and so removed, can get no hearing before this tribunal or any other, because the President controls his district attorney and he cannot get a trial down there, and they will not report him up here, and he cannot get a trial here. It appeals to your justice. I do not propose to go into any excursion in trying the case of Foster Blodgett. I only propose to put in all the papers that were on file in the Post Office Department about this case that bear on my side of the case. They have put in such papers as bear on their side of the case, and I propose to put in such papers as bear on my side of the case out of the same bundle, that they shall not pick out such as please them and have them put in without my picking out and putting in from the same bundle such as please us.

Mr. EVARTS. We do not put anything from the bundle. We put in merely the action of the Department. You have taken a paper from the bundle and now propose to put in an answer to it. That is now the statement of the evidence. We have as little to do with and as little care for Foster Blodgett as possible; but you brought him here and compelled us to state the circumstances of the Department's action. We have stated them. If his case is to be tried by this court because it cannot be tried by any other, and if that is a ground of jurisdiction, of course you may have plenty of work.

The CHIEF JUSTICE. The Secretary will read the offer to prove made by the honorable Managers.

The Chief Clerk read:

We offer to show——

Mr. Manager BUTLER. Stop a moment. Perhaps I will amend the offer a little, though not in substance. With leave, sir, I will withdraw that and take one which covers the same points, but is much shorter, which has been drawn up by one of my associates.

The CHIEF JUSTICE. The Secretary will read the offer to prove now made by the honorable Managers.

The Chief Clerk read as follows:

The defendant's counsel having produced from the files of the Post Office Department a part of the record showing the alleged causes for the suspension of Foster Blodgett as deputy postmaster at Augusta, Georgia, we now propose to give in evidence the residue of said record, including the papers on file in the said case, for the purpose of showing the whole of the case as the same was presented to the Postmaster General before and at the time of the suspension of the said Blodgett.

Mr. EVARTS. Our objection to that offer, as we have already stated, is that it does not present correctly the relation of the papers.

The CHIEF JUSTICE. The Chief Justice will submit the question to the Senate. The original offer to prove has been withdrawn. The offer which has just been read has been substituted. Senators, you who are of opinion that the evidence now proposed to be offered should be received will say ay; contrary opinion no. [Putting the question.] The noes have it. The evidence is not received.

Mr. ANTHONY. I should like to have the yeas and nays on that, if not too late.

The CHIEF JUSTICE. It is too late. If there be no objection, however, the Chief Justice will again put the question on taking the yeas and nays. There seems to be no objection.

Mr. CAMERON. I object.

Mr. Manager BUTLER, (to the witness.) Mr. Randall, I have been informed that you desire to make some statement about this removal. If it does not put in anything that the President said or anybody else I shall not object.

The WITNESS. I expressed to a gentleman this morning a wish to explain the circumstances under which I made this suspension. It was one of those cases which there is no provision of law to meet, like several others that we have, and one that I passed upon this last week. The copy of this indictment was brought to me, and the district attorney at the same time or about the same time, soon afterward at any rate, came to me and made statements of the circumstances under which it was found. Under the tenure-of-office law, if we acted under that, the President would have no power, as I understood it, to suspend any officer during the session of the Senate. The only thing he could do would be to send up the name of some man in his place, removing Mr. Blodgett. It occurred to me that this violation of the law by Mr. Blodgett might be merely a technical violation of the law. If it was a technical violation of the law—I am telling now what my reasoning was on the subject—if it was true that he was forced into the rebel service and got out of it as soon as he could, and this violation of the oath of office law, in taking that oath was merely a technical violation for which he was indicted, I did not want him turned out; and for that reason I took the responsibility of doing this thing, of making this suspension and putting a special agent in temporary charge of the office until we could ascertain more fully what the facts were in the case and what action ought to be taken. Those are the circumstances under which this thing was done.

By Mr. Manager BUTLER:

Question. Why did you not report it to the President for his action?

Answer. I told the President what I had done.

Question. When?

Answer. Afterward; as I stated before.

Question. Why did you not report it before you undertook to take the responsibility. Did you not suppose he would turn him out?

Answer. Because the only thing he could do, if he did anything, was to send to the Senate some other nomination, turning this man out.

Question. That is to say, if I understand you, following the law, the only thing he could do was to send to the Senate the name of somebody in place of this man, removed; and you thought, breaking the law, you could do something better?

Answer. I do not put it in any such shape as that. I stated it just exactly as it occurred. I did not want the man turned out if this was a mere technical violation of the law on which he was indicted, and if he was an honest man. That was the reason I was disposed to ascertain the facts. It may have been a technical violation of the law; but I assumed the doing of it for the purpose of not having an act of injustice done to him if he was an honest man.

Question. Was the Senate in session on the 3d of January last?

Answer. I cannot tell you whether it was in session on that day or not.

Question. Was there not a recess?

Answer. There may have been; I do not remember now.

Question. Then the reason that the Senate was in session did not apply to the case?

Answer. I considered the Senate in session. I do not look upon a recess for two or three or five days as a recess of the Senate, in the sense of the Constitution. I do not remember whether the Senate was actually in session on that particular day.

Question. You deemed it to be in session, and you treated it as if in session?

Answer. I considered the session as continuing.

Mr. Manager BUTLER. That is all.

Mr. CONNESS. I should like to ask a question of the witness. I will reduce it to writing.

The WITNESS. One suggestion I forgot to make which I wish to mention. The reason why something was not further done in the case is that I was trying to get information on this subject, and then this trouble began, and this case has lain long without any intention to delay it, and no further action has been had.

Mr. Manager BUTLER. By trouble you mean the impeachment, I suppose?

The WITNESS. Yes, sir; I had no time to have copies made, but I have brought here the original papers which were filed at the time he was appointed. I did not know whether you would want them.

Mr. Manager BUTLER. No, sir; I do not want to see them.

The CHIEF JUSTICE. The question proposed by the Senator from California has been submitted in writing, and will be read by the Secretary.

The question propounded by Mr. CONNESS was read, as follows:

Have you ever taken any step since your act suspending Foster Blodgett in further investigation of his case?

Answer. Yes, sir; in trying to secure information. There is considerable information among the papers here on the subject.

Mr. Manager BUTLER. That is what we offered to put in.

The WITNESS. Beyond what you offered to put in.

Mr. Manager BUTLER. I only offered one thing at a time. We have no more questions to ask the witness.

Mr. CURTIS. Nor we.

Mr. Manager BUTLER. I now offer, Mr. President, an official copy of the order creating the military department of the Atlantic, and putting General Sherman into charge of it.

Mr. EVARTS. What does that rebut? I am not aware that we have given any evidence on that subject.

Mr. Manager BUTLER. Do you object?

Mr. EVARTS. We do, unless it is relevant and rebutting. I do not recall any evidence that we have given concerning the department of the Atlantic.

Mr. Manager BUTLER. It is put in to show part of the action of the President at the same time, on the same day that he restored General Thomas. That date was not fixed until after General Thomas came on to the stand. The object is to show what was done militarily on that same day. That is the reason why it is put in.

Mr. EVARTS. I do not see any connection with General Thomas's testimony. The only connection the honorable Manager states is that he learned from General Thomas when he was restored, as if he did not know that before. It was all public when he was restored. It does not connect itself at all with any evidence we have produced. If it is put on the ground that it was forgotten or overlooked, that is another matter; but to bring it in as rebutting is a consideration which we cannot consider well suggested.

Mr. Manager BUTLER. Mr. President, when I speak of learning a thing in the trial of a cause I mean learning it in the course of the evidence during the trial, not what I know in the country from the newspapers, because they are not always the best sources of knowledge. I say that General Thomas testifies that on the 18th of February the President made an order that he should be restored to his position as Adjutant General. That was fixed by his testimony; it was not fixed before. That was an order given on the 18th to General Grant, which was not published, a private letter or order. Now, I want to show that on that same day, or the day before, this new military division was made here, and General Sherman ordered to the command of it, showing the acts of the

President at or about the same time. The presiding officer has so well told us heretofore the competency of the acts of a party about the same time as being a part of the *res gestæ*, and the Senate has so often allowed testimony to come in to that effect, that I cannot conceive why this cannot be competent. It is part of the things done by the President on the same day, or the day before Thomas was restored. I do not mean to say a word on the question whether it is rebutting; I do not understand that that rule belongs here.

The CHIEF JUSTICE. On the part of the honorable Managers, it is proposed to give in evidence an order establishing the department of the Atlantic. The Chief Justice will submit the question to the Senate.

Mr. ANTHONY. I ask for the yeas and nays.

The yeas and nays were ordered.

Mr. BUCKALEW. Mr. President, I ask for the reading of a question submitted to General Sherman by the counsel for the defense in reference to this very matter. If our Clerk will turn to the record he will find that a question was put to General Sherman as to the establishment of the department of the Atlantic, which was ruled out.

The CHIEF JUSTICE. The Secretary will read the question referred to.

Mr. Manager BUTLER. We shall not trouble the Senate. This being a matter of public document, I suppose we can refer to it in the argument. We withdraw the offer.

The CHIEF JUSTICE. The offer to prove made by the honorable Managers is withdrawn.

Mr. Manager BUTLER. I have now, Mr. President and Senators, a list prepared as carefully as we were able to prepare it in the time given us, from the laws, of the various officers in the United States who would be affected by the President's claim here of a right to remove at pleasure and appoint *ad interim*, this is a list of officers taken from the laws, with their salaries, being a correlative list to that put in by the counsel, showing the number of officers and the amount of salaries which would be affected by the President. In order to bring it before the Senate I will read the recapitulation only thus:

"In the Navy, War, State, Interior, Post Office, Attorney General, Agriculture, Education, and Treasury, the officers are 41,558; the grand total of their emoluments is $21,180,736 87 a year."

I propose that the same course shall be taken with this as with the like schedule, this being a compilation from the laws, that it be printed as part of the proceedings.

The CHIEF JUSTICE. Is there any objection?

Mr. EVARTS. If it shows what it is there is no objection.

The document is as follows:

Navy Department as per Navy Register for 1868.

Office.	Number.	Annual pay.	Total.
Secretary	1	$8,000 00	$8,000 00
Assistant Secretary	1	3,500 00	3,500 00
Solicitor and judge advocate general	1	3,500 00	3,500 00
Admiral	1	10,000 00	10,000 00
Vice admiral	1	7,000 00	7,000 00
Rear admiral	9*	5,000 00	45,000 00
Commodores	24*	4,000 00	96,000 00
Captains	49*	3,500 00	171,500 00
Commanders	90*	2,800 00	252,000 00
Lieutenant commanders	136*	2,343 00	318,648 00
Lieutenants	45*	1,875 00	84,375 00
Masters	29*	1,500 00	43,500 00
Ensigns	52*	1,200 00	62,400 00
Midshipmen	157*	800 00	125,600 00
Surgeons as captains	14*	3,500 00	49,000 00
Surgeons as commanders	38*	2,800 00	106,400 00
Surgeons as lieutenant commanders	28*	2,343 00	65,301 00
Passed assistant surgeons as lieutenants	42*	1,875 00	78,750 00
Assistant surgeons as masters	28*	1,500 00	42,000 00
Paymaster as commodore	1*	4,000 00	4,000 00
Paymasters as captains	12*	3,500 00	30,000 00
Paymasters as commanders	30*	2,800 00	84,000 00
Paymasters as lieutenant commanders	36*	2,343 00	84,348 00
Passed assistant paymasters as lieutenants	39*	1,875 00	73,125 00
Assistant paymasters as masters	26*	1,500 00	39,000 00
Chief engineer as commodore	1*	4,000 00	4,000 00
Chief engineers as captains	4*	3,500 00	14,000 00
Chief engineers as commanders	34*	2,800 00	95,200 00
Chief engineers as lieutenant commanders	11*	2,343 00	25,773 00
First assistant engineers as lieutenants	88*	1,875 00	165,000 00
Second assistant engineers as masters	131*	1,500 00	196,500 00
Third assistant engineers as midshipmen after graduation	24*	800 00	19,200 00
Chaplains as commanders	7*	2,800 00	19,600 00
Chaplains as lieutenant commanders	11*	2,343 00	25,773 00
Professors of mathematics as commanders	4*	2,800 00	11,200 00
Professors of mathematics as lieutenant commanders,	7*	2,343 00	16,401 00
	1,210		$2,464,594 00

* Active list.

Warrant Officers.

Officer.	Number.	Annual pay.	Total.
Boatswains..	52	$1,000 00	$52,000 00
Gunners..	55	1,000 00	55,000 00
Carpenters as gunners.........................	36	1,000 00	36,000 00
Sailmakers as gunners.........................	31	1,000 00	31,000 00
	174		$174,000 00

Constructors.

Officer.	Number.	Annual pay.	Total.
Naval constructor as commodore..................	1	$4,000 00	$4,000 00
Naval constructor as captain....................	1	3,500 00	3,500 00
Naval constructors as commanders...............	3	2,800 00	8,400 00
Naval constructor as lieutenant commander......	1	2,343 00	2,343 00
Assistant naval constructors as masters.........	5	1,500 00	7,500 00
	11		$25,743 00

Retired and Reserved List.

Officer.	Number.	Annual pay.	Total.
Rear admiral....................................	17	$2,000 00	$34,000 00
Commodores	65	1,800 00	117,000 00
Captains..	32	1,600 00	51,200 00
Commanders.....................................	17	1,400 00	23,800 00
Lieutenant commanders...........................	3	1,300 00	3,900 00
Masters (not in the line of promotion).........	6	800 00	4,800 00
Midshipman......................................	1	500 00	500 00
Surgeons as captains............................	18	1,600 00	28,800 00
Surgeons as commanders..........................	3	1,400 00	4,200 00
Surgeons as lieutenant commanders...............	3	1,300 00	3,900 00
Passed assistant surgeons as lieutenants........	3	1,000 00	3,000 00
Assistant surgeons as masters...................	4	800 00	3,200 00
Paymasters as captains..........................	15	1,600 00	24,000 00
Paymaster as commander..........................	1	1,400 00	1,400 00
Chief engineer as lieutenant commander..........	1	1,300 00	1,300 00
First assistant engineers as lieutenants........	4	1,000 00	4,000 00
Second assistant engineers as masters...........	8	800 00	6,400 00
Chaplains as commanders.........................	8	1,400 00	11,200 00
Chaplain as lieutenant commander................	1	1,300 00	1,300 00
Professor as commander..........................	1	1,400 00	1,400 00
Professor as lieutenant commander...............	1	1,300 00	1,300 00
Naval constructor as captain....................	1	1,600 00	1,600 00
Boatswains......................................	6	600 00	3,600 00
Gunners...	6	600 00	3,600 00
Carpenters.....................................	6	600 00	3,600 00
Sailmakers.....................................	5	600 00	3,600 00
	236		$346,000 00

Marine Corps.

Officer.	Number.	Annual pay.	Total.
Brigadier general and commandant................	1	$6,130 00	$6,130 00
Majors (staff)..................................	3	2,666 00	7,998 00
Captains (staff)................................	2	1,776 00	3,552 00
Colonel (line)..................................	1	3,365 00	3,365 00
Lieutenant colonels (line)......................	2	3,015 50	6,031 00
Majors (line)...................................	4	2,666 00	10,664 00
Captains (line).................................	19	1,776 00	33,744 00
First lieutenants (line)........................	30	1,616 00	48,480 00
Second lieutenants (line).......................	27	1,536 00	41,472 00
	89		$161,436 00

RECAPITULATION—NAVY DEPARTMENT.

Office.	Number.	Total annual pay.
Secretary of War, &c., and active list..........................	1,210	$2,464,594 00
Warrant officers..	174	174,000 00
Naval constructors...	11	25,743 00
Retired and reserved list...	236	346,000 00
Marine corps..	89	161,436 00
Total...	1,720	$3,171,773 00

Tabular statement of officers of the Army appointed by the President.

Secretary of War..$8,000

General officers.

Rank.	Number.	Annual pay.	Total.
General...	1	$10,632 00	$10,632 00
Lieutenant General...	1	9,072 00	9,072 00
Major generals	5	5,772 00	28,860 00
Brigadier generals	10	3,918 00	39,180 00
			$87,744 00

Adjutant General's Department.

Rank.	Number.	Annual pay.	Total.
Adjutant General—brigadier general..........................	1	$3,918 00	$3,918 00
Assistant adjutant generals—colonels........................	2	2,724 00	5,448 00
Assistant adjutant generals—lieutenant colonels	4	2,436 00	9,744 00
Assistant adjutant generals—majors	13	2,148 00	27,924 00
			$47,024 00

Inspector General's Department.

Rank.	Number.	Annual pay.	Total.
Colonels..	4	$2,724 00	$10,896 00
Lieutenant colonels...........	3	2,436 00	7,308 00
Majors	3	2,148 00	6,444 00
			$24,648 00

Bureau Military Justice.

Rank.	Number.	Annual pay.	Total.
Brigadier general—Judge Advocate General.............	1	$3,918 00	$3,918 00
Colonel..	1	2,724 00	2,724 00
Majors	9	2,148 00	19,332 00
			$25,974 00

Quartermaster's Department.

Rank.	Number.	Annual pay.	Total.
Brigadier general—Quartermaster General	1	$3,918 00	$3,918 00
Colonels—assistant quartermaster generals	6	2,724 00	16,344 00
Lieutenant colonels—deputy quartermaster generals.	10	2,436 00	24,360 00
Majors—quartermasters	15	2,148 00	32,220 00
Captains—assistant quartermasters	44	1,650 00	72,600 00
Military storekeepers	16	1,650 00	26,400 00
			$175,842 00

Subsistence Department.

Rank.	Number.	Annual pay.	Total.
Brigadier general—Commissary General Subsistence.	1	$3,918 00	$3,918 00
Colonels—assistant commissary generals subsistence.	2	2,724 00	5,448 00
Lieutenant colonels—assistant commissary generals subsistence.	2	2,436 00	4,872 00
Majors	8	2,148 00	17,184 00
Captains	16	1,650 00	26,400 00
			$57,822 00

Medical Department.

Rank.	Number.	Annual pay.	Total.
Brigadier general—Surgeon General	1	$3,918 00	$3,918 00
Colonel—assistant surgeon general	1	2,724 00	2,724 00
Chief medical purveyor—lieutenant colonel	1	2,436 00	2,436 00
Assistant medical purveyors—lieutenant colonels	4	2,436 00	9,744 00
Surgeons—majors	60	2,148 00	128,880 00
Assistant surgeons—first lieutenants	150	1,449 96	217,494 00
Medical storekeepers	5	1,650 00	6,600 00
			$371,796 00

Pay Department.

Rank.	Number.	Annual pay.	Total.
Brigadier general—Paymaster General	1	$3,918 00	$3,918 00
Colonels	2	2,724 00	5,448 00
Lieutenant colonels	2	2,436 00	4,872 00
Majors	60	2,148 00	128,880 00
			$143,118 00

Engineer Department.

Rank.	Number.	Annual pay.	Total.
Chief Engineer—brigadier general	1	$3,918 00	$3,918 00
Colonels	6	2,724 00	16,344 00
Lieutenant colonels	12	2,436 00	29,232 00
Majors	24	2,148 00	51,552 00
Captains	30	1,650 00	49,500 00
Lieutenants	38	1,449 96	55,098 48
			$205,642 48

Ordnance Department.

Rank.	*Number.	Annual pay.	Total.
Brigadier general—Chief of Ordnance	1	$3,918 00	$3,918 00
Colonels.........	3	2,724 00 .	8,172 00
Lieutenant colonels..............................	4	2,436 00	9,744 00
Majors	10	2,148 00	21,480 00
Captains.........	20	1,650 00	33,000 00
Lieutenants.........	26	1,449 96	37,698 96
Military storekeepers.................................	13	1,650 00	21,450 00
			$135,466 96

Signal Corps.

Rank.	Number.	Annual pay.	Total.
Chief—colonel.................	1	$2,724 00	$2,724 00

Post Chaplains.

Rank.	Number.	Annual pay.	Total.
Chaplains...	30	$1,416 00	$42,480 00

Regimental officers—Cavalry.

Rank.	Number.	Annual pay.	Total.
Colonels...............	10	$2,724 00	$27,240 00
Lieutenant colonels............	10	2,436 00	24,360 00
Majors...........	30	2,148 00	64,440 00
Captains...........	120	1,650 00	198,000 00
Adjutants...................	10	1,569 96	15,699 60
Quartermasters...............	10	1,569 96	15,699 60
Commissaries..........	10	1,569 96	15,699 60
First lieutenants...............	120	1,449 96	173,995 20
Second lieutenants......	120	1,449 96	173,995 20
			$709,129 60

Artillery.

Rank.	Number.	Annual pay.	Total.
Colonels.........	5	$2,544 00	$12,720 00
Lieutenant colonels.................	5	2,256 00	11,280 00
Majors...........	15	2,028 00	30,420 00
Captains...........	60	1,530 00	91,840 00
Adjutants...........	5	1,530 00	7,650 00
Quartermasters...........	5	1,530 00	7,650 00
First lieutenants...........	120	1,410 00	169,200 00
Second lieutenants	120	1,350 00	162,000 00
			$492,720 00

Infantry.

Rank.	Number.	Annual pay.	Total.
Colonels..................	45	$2,544 00	$114,480 00
Lieutenant colonels	45	2,256 00	101,520 00
Majors...........	45	2,028 00	91,260 00
Captains...........	450	1,530 00	688,500 00
Adjutants...........	45	1,530 00	68,850 00
Quartermasters...........	45	1,530 00	68,850 00
First lieutenants...........	450	1,410 00	634,500 00
Second lieutenants...........................	450	1,350 00	607,500 00
			$2,375,460 00

West Point.

Rank.	Number.	Annual pay.	Total.
Professors...	8	$2,240 00	$17,920 00

SUMMARY.

Total number of officers, 3,033. Total amount of their salaries, $4,907,831 04.

Department of State as per Official Register of 1865.

Officer.	Number.	Annual salary.	Total annual salary.
Secretary..	1	$8,000 00	$8,000 00
Assistant Secretary..	2	3,500 00	7,000 00
Envoy extraordinary, &c...................................	2	17,500 00	35,000 00
Envoy extraordinary, &c...................................	7	12,000 00	84,000 00
Envoy extraordinary, &c...................................	2	10,000 00	20,000 00
Ministers resident...	21	7,500 00	157,000 00
Secretaries of legation....................................	2	2,625 60	5,250 00
Secretaries of legation....................................	7	1,800 00	12,600 00
Secretaries of legation....................................	17	1,500 00	25,500 00
Assistant secretaries of legation........................	2	1,500 00	3,000 00
Interpreter and secretary of legation...................	1	5,000 00	5,000 00
Dragoman and secretary of legation....................	1	3,000 00	3,000 00
Interpreter...	1	2,500 00	2,500 00
Interpreters...	2	1,500 00	3,000 00
Interpreters...	2	1,000 00	2,000 00
Commissioner and consul general.......................	1	7,500 00	7,500 00
Commissioner and consul general.......................	1	4,000 00	4,000 00
Consul general...	1	5,000 00	5,000 00.
Consul general...	1	6,000 00	6,000 00
Consul generals..	2	3,000 00	6,000 00
Consul general...	1	Fees	
Consul general...	1	3,500 00	3,500 00
Consul generals..	2	4,000 00	8,000 00
Consul general...	1	1,500 00	1,500 00
Consuls...	2	7,500 00	15,500 00
Consuls...	23	2,000 00	46,000 00
Consuls...	12	3,000 00	36,000 00
Consuls...	78	1,500 00	117,000 00
Consuls...	6	3,500 00	21,000 00
Consuls...	9	2,500 00	22,500 00
Consuls...	5	4,000 00	20,000 00
Consuls...	18	1,000 00	18,000 00
Consuls...	3	750 00	2,250 00
Consuls...	5	500 00	2,500 00
Consuls...	84	Fees	
Vice consul..	1	1,500 00	1,500 00
Vice consuls..	11	Fees	
Commercial agents...	3	2,000 00	6,000 00
Commercial agents...	3	1,500 00	4,500 00
Commercial agents...	7	1,000 00	7,000 00
Commercial agents...	7	Fees	
Marshals to consular courts..............................	7	1,000 & fees	7,000 00
Consular clerks...	3	1,000 00	3,000 00
Judges under provisions of treaty with Great Britain of April 7, 1862..	3	2,500 00	7,500 00
Arbitrator under provisions of treaty with Great Britain of April 7, 1862..................................	1	1,000 00	1,000 00
Arbitrator under provisions of treaty with Great Britain of April 2, 1862..................................	1	2,000 00	,000 00
Commissioner..	1	2,000 00	2,000 00
Commissioner..	1	3,000 00	3,000 00
Commissioner..	1	5,000 00	5,000 00
Secretary of commissioner...............................	1	2,000 00	2,000 00
Governors of Territory....................................	6	1,500 00	9,000 00
Governors of Territory....................................	2	2,500 00	5,000 00
Secretaries of Territory...................................	5	1,800 00	9,000 00
Secretary of Territory.....................................	1	1,500 00	1,500 00
Secretaries of Territory...................................	2	2,000 00	4,000 00
	394		$797,600 00

RECAPITULATION—DEPARTMENT OF STATE.

Total number of officers, 394. Total annual salary, $797,600.

Interior Department as per Official Register, 1865.

Officer.	Number.	Annual salary.	Total annual salary.
Secretary	1	$8,000 00	$8,000 00
Assistant Secretary	1	3,500 00	3,500 00
Commissioner General Land Office	1	3,000 00	3,000 00
Registers	73	500 & fees	36,500 00
Receivers	73	500 & fees	36,500 00
Surveyors of public lands	4	2,000 00	8,000 00
Surveyors of public lands	3	3,000 00	9,000 00
Surveyor of public lands	1	2,500 00	2,500 00
Surveyor of public lands	1	1,800 00	1,800 00
Commissioner of Patents	1	4,500 00	4,500 00
Examiners-in-chief	3	3,000 00	9,000 00
Examiners	14	2,500 00	35,000 00
Assistant examiners	12	1,800 00	21,600 00
Second assistant examiners	6	1,600 00	9,600 00
Commissioner of Indian Affairs	1	3,000 00	3,000 00
Superintendents	7	2,000 00	14,000 00
Agents	4	1,800 00	7,200 00
Agents	48	1,500 00	72,000 00
Special agents	7	1,500 00	10,500 00
Sub-agents	1	1,500 00	1,500 00
Sub-agents	3	1,000 00	3,000 00
Commissioner of Pensions	1	3,000 00	3,000 00
Agents for paying Army and Navy pensions in the several States and Territories	45	4,000 00*	—
Captain of Capitol police	1	1,740 00	1,740 00
Police officers	27	1,320 00	35,640 00
President Columbia Institution for Deaf and Dumb	1	2,500 00	2,500 00
Professor Columbia Institution for Deaf and Dumb	1	1,600 00	1,600 00
Professor Columbia Institution for Deaf and Dumb	1	1,800 00	1,800 00
Engineer in charge of Washington aqueduct	1	1,800 00	1,800 00
Superintendent of Hospital for Insane of the Army, Navy, revenue-cutter service	1	2,500 00	2,500 00
Superintendent of police	1	1,500 00	1,500 00
Superintendent of Public Printing	1	3,000 00	3,000 00
Commissioners of police	5	250 00	1,250 00
Ex-officio commissioners of police	2	250 00	500 00
Surgeons of police	3	300 00	900 00
Police magistrates	5	800 00	4,000 00
Corps of detectives	5	840 00	4,200 00
Sergeants of police	10	600 00	6,000 00
Police patrolmen	140	480 00	67,200 00
Sanitary police commissioners	9	480 00	4,320 00
Policeman at President's House	1	1,320 00	1,320 00
Watchman in the crypt	1	960 00	960 00
Gatekeeper at Capitol	1	1,000 00	1,000 00
Watchmen on the grounds	2	720 00	1,440 00
Watchman at public stables	1	1,000 00	1,000 00
Watchmen at President's House	2	720 00	1,440 00
Watchman at reservation No. 2	1	720 00	720 00
Doorkeeper at President's House	1	720 00	720 00
Assistant doorkeeper at President's House	1	720 00	720 00
Public gardener	1	1,440 00	1,440 00
Gardener at President's	1	960 00	960 00
	548		$457,870 00

*Fees: whole compensation not to exceed $4,000 per annum.

RECAPITULATION—INTERIOR DEPARTMENT.

Total number of officers, 548. Total annual salary, $457,870.

Post Office Department as per Official Register, 1865.

Officer.	Number.	Annual salary.	Total annual salary.
Postmaster General	1	$8,000 00	$8,000 00
Assistant Postmaster Generals	3	3,500 00	10,500 00
Postmasters	26,619*	†	4,250,000 00‡
Special agents	29	1,600 00	46,400 00
Special agents	3	1,200 00	3,600 00
Special agent	1	2,500 00	2,500 00
Route agents	410	-	approx. 287,000 00
Local agents	51	-	25,353 00
Mail contractors	3,926	-	5,001,315 00
Local mail agency	67	-	13,541 27
Mail messenger service	1,776	-	111,492 32
Special mail messenger service	1,836	-	51,997 68
	34,722		$9,811,699 27

* As per special list corrected by Post Office Department to October 20, 1867.
† Too varied for speedy classification.   ‡ As per report of Postmaster General.

Attorney General's Office and Judiciary as per Official Register, 1865.

Officer.	Number.	Annual salary.	Total annual salary.
Attorney General	1	$8,000 00	$8,000 00
Assistant Attorney General	1	3,500 00	3,500 00
District attorneys, States and Territories	60	250 & fees.	15,000 00
Marshals courts	60	250 & fees.	15,000 00
Chief justices, Territories	2	2,500 00	5,000 00
Chief justices, Territories	3	2,000 00	6,000 00
Chief justices, Territories	3	1,800 00	5,400 00
Associate justices, Territories	4	2,500 00	10,000 00
Associate justices, Territories	6	2,000 00	12,000 00
Associate justices, Territories	6	1,800 00	10,800 00
	146		$90,700 00

Department of Agriculture as per Official Register, 1865.

Officer.	Number.	Annual salary.	Total annual salary.
Commissioner	1	$3,000 00	$3,000 00

Department of Education as per law creating Department.

Officer.	Number.	Annual salary.	Total annual salary.
Commissioner	1	$4,000 00	$4,000 00

Treasury Department as per Official Register of 1865.

Office.	Number.	Annual salary.	Total annual salary.
Secretary	1	$8,000 00	$8,000 00
Assistant Secretaries	2	3,500 00	7,000 00
Comptroller	1	3,500 00	3,500 00
Comptroller	1	3,000 00	3,000 00
Commissioner of Customs	1	3,000 00	3,000 00
Auditor	6	3,000 00	18,000 00
Treasurer	1	5,000 00	5,000 00
Assistant Treasurer	1	2,800 00	2,800 00
Assistant Treasurer	1	6,000 00	6,000 00
Assistant Treasurer	1	4,500 00	4,500 00
Assistant Treasurer	2	4,000 00	8,000 00
Assistant Treasurer	1	1,000 00	1,000 00
United States depositaries	1	2,500 00	2,500 00
United States depositaries	3	2,000 00	6,000 00
United States depositaries	2	1,800 00	3,600 00
United States depositaries	1	1,600 00	1,600 00
United States depositaries	1	1,500 00	1,500 00
United States depositaries	2	1,400 00	2,800 00
United States depositaries	6	1,300 00	7,800 00
United States depositaries	4	1,200 00	4,800 00
United States depositaries	1	1,000 00	1,000 00
United States depositaries	1	750 00	750 00
United States depositaries	1	480 00	480 00
Register	1	3,000 00	3,000 00
Assistant register	1	2,000 00	2,000 00
Chief of loan branch	1	2,000 00	2,000 00
Comptroller National Currency Bureau	1	5,000 00	5,000 00
Deputy comptroller	1	2,500 00	2,500 00
Solicitor	1	3,500 00	3,500 00
Chief of first division	1	3,000 00	3,000 00
Assistant of first division	1	2,500 00	2,500 00
Commissioner of Internal Revenue	1	4,000 00	4,000 00
Deputy commissioner of internal revenue	1	2,750 00	2,750 00
Assessors of internal revenue	226	1,500 & fees.	602,008 90
Collectors of internal revenue	216	1,500 & fees.	498,239 66
Deputy collectors	216	1,500 00	324,000 00
Supervising architect of Bureau of Construction, (Coast Survey)	1	3,000 00	3,000 00
Assistant supervising architect of Bureau of Construction, (Coast Survey)	1	2,000 00	2,000 00

STATEMENT—Continued.

Office.	Number.	Annual salary.	Total annual salary.
Superintendent of United States Coast Survey	1	6,000 00	6,000 00
First assistant superintendent	1	3,500 00	3,500 00
Second assistant superintendent	2	2,500 00	5,000 00
Hydrographic inspector	1	2,825 00	2,825 00
Disbursing agent of Coast Survey	1	2,500 00	2,500 00
Assistant and foreman of weights and measures	1	2,500 00	2,500 00
Director of Mint at Philadelphia	1	3,500 00	3,500 00
Treasurer of Mint at Philadelphia	1	2,000 00	2,000 00
Melter and refiner of Mint at Philadelphia	1	2,000 00	2,000 00
Assayer of Mint at Philadelphia	1	2,000 00	2,000 00
Chief coiner of Mint at Philadelphia	1	2,000 00	2,000 00
Engraver of Mint at Philadelphia	1	2,000 00	2,000 00
Superintendent of branch mint at San Francisco	1	4,500 00	4,500 00
Treasurer of branch mint at San Francisco	1	4,500 00	4,500 00
Assayer of branch mint at San Francisco	1	3,000 00	3,000 00
Melter and refiner of branch mint at San Francisco	1	3,000 00	3,000 00
Coiner of branch mint at San Francisco	1	3,000 00	3,000 00
Superintendent of branch mint at Denver	1	2,000 00	2,000 00
Assayer of branch mint at Denver	1	1,800 00	1,800 00
Chief coiner of branch mint at Denver	1	1,800 00	1,800 00
Melter and refiner of branch mint at Denver	1	1,800 00	1,800 00
Assistant treasurer at Denver	1	500 00	500 00
Superintendent of assay office at New York	1	3,500 00	3,500 00
Assayer of assay office at New York	1	3,000 00	3,000 00
Melter and refiner of assay office at New York	1	3,000 00	3,000 00
Deputy treasurer of assay office at New York	1	3,000 00	3,000 00
Accountant of assay office at New York	1	2,500 00	2,500 00
Weigh clerk of assay office at New York	1	2,500 00	2,500 00
Special agent	1	5,000 00	5,000 00
Special agents	7	3,000 00	21,000 00
Special agents	2	2,500 00	5,000 00
Special agents	24	$6 per day.	52,560 00
Special agents	2	5 per day.	3,650 00
Supervising inspectors of steamboats	9	1,500 00	13,500 00
Local inspectors of steamboat hulls	28	-	23,900 00
Local inspectors of steamboat boilers	28	-	23,900 00
Captains revenue-cutter service	34	1,800 00	61,200 00
First lieutenants revenue-cutter service	27	1,400 00	37,800 00
Second lieutenants revenue-cutter service	16	1,200 00	19,200 00
Third lieutenants revenue-cutter service	48	900 00	43,200 00
Chief engineer revenue-cutter service	18	1,400 00	25,200 00
First assistant engineer revenue-cutter service	19	1,200 00	22,800 00
Second assistant engineer revenue-cutter service	18	900 00	16,200 00
Chief clerk of Light-House Board	1	2,000 00	2,000 00
Physicians, &c., at marine hospitals	-	-	18,800 00
	1,023		$2,036,263 56

RECAPITULATION—TREASURY DEPARTMENT.

Total number of officers, 1,023. Total annual salary, $2,036,263 56.

RECAPITULATION TOTAL.

Department.	Number of officers.	Total annual salary.
Navy	1,720	$3,171,773 00
War	3,033	4,907,831 04
State	394	797,600 00
Interior	548	457,870 00
Post Office	34,722	9,811,699 27
Attorney General	146	90,700 00
Agricultural	1	3,000 00
Education	1	4,000 00
Treasury	1,023	2,036,263 56
Grand totals	41,588	$21,180,736 87

Errors excepted.

Mr. Manager BUTLER. Mr. President, I have the honor to offer now from the files of the Senate, in the first place, the message of Andrew Johnson nominating Lieutenant General William T. Sherman to be general by brevet in the Army of the United States on the 13th day of February, 1868.

Mr. EVARTS. Under what article is that offered? With what intent?

Mr. Manager BUTLER. That is under the eleventh article and under the tenth.

Mr. EVARTS. The tenth is the speeches.

Mr. Manager BUTLER. I should say the ninth; I beg pardon.

Mr. EVARTS. That is the Emory article.

Mr. Manager BUTLER. That is the General Emory article.

Mr. EVARTS. Do you offer this on the ground that the conferring the brevet on General Sherman was with intent to obstruct the reconstruction act?

Mr. Manager BUTLER. I offer it *valeat quantum.* I referred to it in the argument I have already made. The statement which I made in the opening upon that question has been twice read—once, I believe, by yourself, and once, I am certain, by Mr. Curtis.

Mr. EVARTS. It does not seem to us, Mr. Chief Justice and Senators, to be relevant, and it certainly is not rebutting. We have offered no evidence bearing upon the only evidence you offered under the eleventh article, which was the telegrams between Governor Parsons and the President on the subject of reconstruction. We have offered no evidence on that subject, and we do not see that this appointment——

Mr. Manager BUTLER. They may be both passed upon at once to save time. I offer, also, the appointment by brevet of George H. Thomas to be lieutenant general and then general by brevet, two brevets on the 21st, the same day that Mr. Stanton was removed.

Mr. EVARTS. What was the last paper?

Mr. Manager BUTLER. The last paper was the appointment by brevet of Major General George H. Thomas first to be lieutenant general by brevet and then general by brevet; and that was done on the same day that Mr. Stanton was removed, the 21st of February.

Mr. EVARTS. Mr. Chief Justice and Senators, it is very apparent that this does not rebut any evidence we have offered. It is then offered as evidence-in-chief that the conferring of brevets on these two officers is in some way within the evil intents that are alleged in these articles. We submit that on that question there is nothing in this evidence that imports any such evil intent.

Mr. Manager BUTLER. I only wish to say upon this that we do not understand that this case is to be tried upon the question of whether evidence is rebutting evidence or otherwise, because we understand that to-day the House of Representatives may bring in a new article of impeachment if they choose, and go on with it; but we have a right to put in any evidence which would be competent at any stage of the cause anywhere.

Mr. EVARTS rose.

Mr. Manager BUTLER. Excuse me a moment.

Mr. EVARTS. I wish to ask a question. When does our right to give in evidence end?

Mr. Manager BUTLER. When you get through with competent and pertinent evidence, I suppose.

Mr. EVARTS. I supposed there was a different rule for us?

Mr. Manager BUTLER. No, sir; that is the rule that I am claiming now, putting in competent and pertinent evidence, not a different rule. I beg you will not misunderstand me. In many of the States—I can instance the State of New Hampshire—I am sure the rule of rebutting evidence does not obtain in their courts at all. Each party calls such pertinent and competent evidence as he has up to the hour when he says he has got through from time to time; and in some other of the States it is so applicable, and no injustice is done to anybody.

The CHIEF JUSTICE. The Chief Justice will submit the question to the Senate. The honorable Managers propose to put in evidence the nomination sent by the President to the Senate on the 13th of February, 1868, of Lieutenant General Sherman to be general by brevet, and the nomination of Major General George H. Thomas, sent to the Senate on the 21st of February, 1868, to be lieutenant general by brevet and general by brevet.

Mr. ANTHONY called for the yeas and nays; and they were ordered.

Mr. HOWARD. I ask that the offer may be again read. It is not understood.

The CHIEF JUSTICE. The Chief Justice will state it. The offer was not reduced to writing. It is very brief, and the Chief Justice will state it.

Mr. HOWARD. I respectfully ask that the Chair will again announce it to the Senate.

The CHIEF JUSTICE. He was about to do so. The honorable Managers propose to put in evidence the nomination of Lieutenant General Sherman to be general by brevet, sent to the Senate on the 13th of February, 1868; also, the nomination of Major General George H. Thomas to be lieutenant general by brevet and to be general by brevet, sent to the Senate on the 21st of February, 1868. Senators, you who are of opinion that this evidence shall be received will, as your names are called, answer yea; those of the contrary opinion, nay.

The question being taken by yeas and nays, resulted—yeas 14, nays 35; as follows:

YEAS—Messrs. Anthony, Cole, Fessenden, Fowler, Grimes, Henderson, Morton, Ross, Sumner, Tipton, Trumbull, Van Winkle, Willey, and Yates—14.

NAYS—Messrs. Buckalew, Cameron, Cattell, Chandler, Conkling, Conness, Corbett, Cragin, Davis, Dixon, Doolittle, Drake, Edmunds, Ferry, Frelinghuysen, Harlan, Hendricks, Howard, Howe, Johnson, Mc-

Creery, Morgan, Morrill of Maine, Morrill of Vermont, Patterson of New Hampshire, Patterson of Tennessee, Pomeroy, Ramsey, Sherman, Sprague, Stewart, Thayer, Vickers, Williams, and Wilson—35.

NOT VOTING—Messrs. Bayard, Norton, Nye, Saulsbury, and Wade—5.

So the Senate refused to receive the evidence offered.

Mr. Manager BUTLER. Mr. President, I have the honor to say that the case on the part of the Managers is closed, and all witnesses who are here under the subpœna of the Senate, at the instance of the Managers, may be discharged.

The CHIEF JUSTICE. Does the Chief Justice understand that the case on the part of the President is closed?

Mr. EVARTS. We are able to make the same announcement as regards witnesses who are attending on the part of the defense under subpœna; and this announcement on both sides, we assume, precludes almost necessarily any attempt to proceed with evidence again.

The CHIEF JUSTICE. The honorable Managers will please proceed with their argument.

Mr. Manager BOUTWELL. Mr. Chief Justice and Senators, it has fallen to me, upon the judgment of the Managers, to make the first argument on the part of the House of Representatives in the close. It is very likely that I shall be obliged to occupy the larger part of a day in presenting to the honorable Senate the views which I shall feel it my duty to offer. Under these circumstances, I have to ask that the Senate will do me the favor to adjourn until to-morrow morning at the usual hour, when I shall be prepared to proceed.

Mr. JOHNSON. Mr. Chief Justice, I move that the Senate, as a court of impeachment, adjourn until eleven o'clock to-morrow.

Several SENATORS. Say twelve o'clock.

The CHIEF JUSTICE. The rule now fixes eleven as the hour of meeting.

Mr. EVARTS. Mr. Chief Justice, may I be heard a moment?

The CHIEF JUSTICE. On a motion to adjourn no debate is in order.

Mr. JOHNSON. I withdraw the motion.

Mr. EVARTS. Of course I do not rise with the view of making the least objection to the suggestion on the part of the honorable Managers, which seems to us to be entirely reasonable, but to couple with it a statement to which I beg the attention of the court for a moment. Our learned associate, Mr. Stanbery, has, from the outset, been relied upon by the President and by the associate counsel to make the final argument in this cause; and there are many reasons, professional and others, why we should all wish that this purpose should be carried out. It has been his misfortune, in the midst of this trial and after it had proceeded for a fortnight, to be taken suddenly ill. The illness, of no great gravity, is yielding to the remedies prescribed and to the progress of time, so that he now occupies his parlor, as we found

him this morning. The summing up of a cause of this weight in many aspects, regarding the testimony and the subject and the situation, is, of course, a labor of no ordinary magnitude, physical and otherwise, and Mr. Stanbery is of the opinion, in which we concur, that he will need an interval of two days, added to what in the course of the trial would probably bring him to his feet in the argument, to have the adequate strength for that purpose. It might have been left until the day on which he should have appeared, and then have the request made for a day or two's relief in this regard; but it occurred to us to be fairer to the Managers that the interval of repose should be interposed at a time when it would be useful and valuable to them also, as the proofs are not entirely printed in the proper form for reference, and the latter voluminous evidence on the subject of appointments and the routine of the practice of the Government is such as to require considerable investigation in order to point out to the Senate the efficacy on the one side of, or the answer on the other to, the proofs. It is, therefore, our duty now to suggest (coupling it with the suggestion of the Managers, that until to-morrow should be given for the propriety of the mere agreeable introduction of the argument on their part,) that we ask that you consider this statement which I have made to you, and see whether it is not better in all respects that the matter should now be disposed of. I think the Managers will concur that this is the proper time to consider it and accommodate matters to the providential interference with the leader of the President's counsel and his confidential friend and adviser.

Mr. JOHNSON. What is the motion?

Mr. EVARTS. The suggestion is that an interval of two days should be given now, instead of waiting till Mr. Stanbery shall come in; and I understand the Managers will agree it is better it should occur now than later.

Mr. YATES. I move that the Senate adjourn until Wednesday.

Mr. Manager BOUTWELL. Mr. President——

Mr. YATES. I withdraw the motion if the Managers desire to be heard.

Mr. Manager BOUTWELL. Mr. President, if it shall be the pleasure of the Senate to consider favorably the request made by the learned counsel for the respondent, which is a question of public duty on which I can express no opinion, I certainly should desire that the time to be granted should be granted at once. I may say that if I had consulted my own feelings exclusively I should have made the request for a day more of time for further examination of the record and more careful preparation than I have yet been able to make; but under the circumstances of the trial I did not feel at liberty to ask that favor or consideration upon my own account. I have only now to say that if it is the judgment of the Senate that time should be granted to the learned counsel who is to close for the respondent it would certainly be very desirable on my part that the time should be granted at once, and that we may all have the benefit of it in preparing what we deem it proper to say.

Mr. EVARTS. One word, if I may be indulged. The honorable Senators will also perceive that if Mr. Stanbery's resolution and expectation should be disappointed, it is then a matter of some importance for us of the defense to supply his place as well as we may on an unexpected emergency, and a little time in that behalf also would be valuable to us.

Mr. JOHNSON. Mr. Chief Justice, I move that the Senate, sitting as a court of impeachment, adjourn until Thursday morning.

Several SENATORS. Say Wednesday.

Mr. Manager LOGAN. If the gentleman will withdraw the motion for a moment, I desire to make a request of the Senate.

Mr. JOHNSON. Certainly; or rather I would submit the motion in this form: that when the Senate, sitting as a court of impeachment, adjourn to-day, it adjourn to meet at eleven o'clock on Wednesday morning.

Mr. DOOLITTLE. I suggest twelve o'clock instead of eleven. ["No, no."]

The CHIEF JUSTICE. The rule now fixes eleven as the hour of meeting.

Mr. Manager LOGAN. I merely desire to make a request. Is this the proper time to do it, sir?

The CHIEF JUSTICE. It is.

Mr. Manager LOGAN. Mr. President and Senators, I desire to make a request of the Senate before the adjournment, as doubtless that will be granted upon the statement of the honorable counsel for the President and the Managers, as they both seem to desire this extension of time. I have not presumption enough to ask of the Senate permission to address them on the issues presented for their consideration, nor do I desire to do so; but I ask that I may be permitted to file to-day the printed argument which I have prepared that it may become a part of the record, without taking the time of the Senate, inasmuch as the evidence on both sides, for the prosecution on the part of the people and for the respondent, has been closed.

Mr. STEWART. Mr. President, I move that leave be granted to the Manager to file his argument.

The CHIEF JUSTICE. That involves a change of the rules, and it cannot be done if there is any objection.

Mr. BUCKALEW. I object.

Mr. JOHNSON. May I ask the honorable Manager whether the argument is now in print?

Mr. Manager LOGAN. It is, and I am ready to file it at once.

Mr. STEWART. I make the motion that leave be granted, and that the Manager furnish a copy of his argument to the other side.

The CHIEF JUSTICE. The order cannot be made except by unanimous consent, as it

C. I.—33.

involves a change of the rules. Is there unanimous consent?

Mr. BUCKALEW. I object.

Mr. WILSON. I ask that the rule bearing on this matter be read.

The CHIEF JUSTICE. The Secretary will read the twenty-first rule.

The Chief Clerk read as follows:

"XXI. The case, on each side, shall be opened by one person. The final argument on the merits may be made by two persons on each side, (unless otherwise ordered by the Senate, upon application for that purpose,) and the argument shall be opened and closed on the part of the House of Representatives."

Mr. Manager LOGAN. Mr. President, the reason I made the request to-day—if it is denied, as a matter of course I shall not renew it—was that I might present the argument I have prepared, to the counsel for the respondent, that they, if they saw anything worthy of reply in it, might have an opportunity of replying in their argument.

The CHIEF JUSTICE. The rule permits argument by but two counsel, one in opening and one in the close on the part of the Managers and two on the part of the President. The question of changing the rule has been frequently before the Senate and the Senate has uniformly refused to alter it. An order can be submitted to-day to be considered on the next day of meeting, but not for present consideration except by unanimous consent.

Mr. HOWE. I did not hear any objection.

The CHIEF JUSTICE. Objection has been made.

Mr. DOOLITTLE. I object.

Mr. Manager BOUTWELL. Mr. President, before the adjournment of the Senate I should like to call the attention of the counsel for the respondent to a feature of the testimony. It happens that the Managers, as I suppose, under the construction given to the rule, are to proceed first in the argument. A large mass of testimony has been introduced upon the subject of removals and appointments. At the present time I am not informed whether there are special cases on which the counsel for the President rely. I think it may be proper for me at this time to ask them whether there are cases upon which they purpose to rely as furnishing precedents for the course pursued by the President on the 21st of February.

Mr. ANTHONY. Mr. President, I will make a motion, to lie over until to-morrow, that the twenty-first rule be so modified as to allow the honorable Manager——

The CHIEF JUSTICE. The order will be reduced to writing.

Mr. STEWART. I have drawn up an order which I submit in writing.

The CHIEF JUSTICE. The Senator from Nevada submits an order, which will be read by the Secretary.

The Chief Clerk read as follows:

Ordered, That the honorable Manager LOGAN have leave to file his written argument to-day and furnish a copy to each of the counsel for the respondent.

Mr. SHERMAN. Mr. President, I submit, as a substitute for that, to go over with it, the following:

That the Managers on the part of the House of Representatives and the counsel for the respondent have leave to file written or printed arguments before the oral argument commences.

The CHIEF JUSTICE. The order submitted by the Senator from Nevada is under consideration unless objected to.

Mr. BUCKALEW. I mean my objection to apply to all this.

The CHIEF JUSTICE. It is objected to. For information, the amendment proposed by the Senator from Ohio will be read.

Mr. STEWART. I will accept the amendment offered by the Senator from Ohio as a substitute for my proposition.

The CHIEF JUSTICE. The order as now proposed will be read for information.

The Chief Clerk read as follows:

Ordered, That the Managers on the part of the House of Representatives and the counsel for the respondent have leave to file written or printed arguments before the oral argument commences.

The CHIEF JUSTICE. The present consideration of the order is objected to; it will lie over until to-morrow.

Mr. DOOLITTLE. Mr. Chief Justice, the motion now made is a change of the rule, and I object to it.

The CHIEF JUSTICE. It is already objected to.

Mr. JOHNSON. I now renew the motion that when the Senate, sitting as a court of impeachment, adjourns, it adjourn to meet at eleven o'clock on Wednesday.

The motion was agreed to.

Mr. EDMUNDS. I move that the Senate sitting for this trial do now adjourn.

The motion was agreed to; and the Senate, sitting for the trial of the impeachment, adjourned until Wednesday, the 22d instant.

WEDNESDAY, *April* 22, 1868.

The Chief Justice of the United States took the chair.

The usual proclamation having been made by the Sergeant-at-Arms,

The Managers of the impeachment on the part of the House of Representatives and the counsel for the respondent, except Mr. Stanbery, appeared and took the seats assigned to them respectively.

The members of the House of Representatives, as in Committee of the Whole, preceded by Mr. E. B. WASHBURNE, chairman of that committee, and accompanied by the Speaker and Clerk, appeared and were conducted to the seats provided for them.

The CHIEF JUSTICE. The Secretary will read the minutes of Monday's proceedings.

Mr. EDMUNDS. Mr. President, I move that the reading of the Journal be dispensed with.

The CHIEF JUSTICE. Unless there be some objection it will be so ordered. The Chair

hears no objection. It is so ordered. Senators, the business under consideration when the Senate adjourned on Monday was an order offered by the Senator from Nevada, [Mr. STEWART,] which the Clerk will read.

The Chief Clerk read as follows:

Ordered, That the Managers on the part of the House of Representatives and the counsel of the respondent have leave to file written or printed arguments before the oral argument commences.

Mr. VICKERS. Mr. President, I beg leave to offer this as a substitute.

The CHIEF JUSTICE. The Secretary will read the substitute.

The CHIEF CLERK. It is proposed to strike out all of the proposed order, and insert in lieu thereof:

As the counsel for the President have signified to the Senate, sitting as a court for the trial of the impeachment, that they did not desire to file written or printed arguments, but preferred to argue orally, if allowed to do so: Therefore,

Resolved, That any two of the Managers other than those who under the present rule are to open and close the discussion, and who have not already addressed the Senate, be permitted to file written arguments at or before the adjournment of to-day, or to make oral addresses after the opening by one of the Managers and the first reply of the President's counsel, and that other two of the counsel for the President who have not spoken may have the privilege of reply, but alternating with the said two Managers, leaving the closing argument for the President and the Managers' final reply to be made under the original rule.

Mr. CURTIS. Mr. Chief Justice, it may have some bearing possibly on the vote which is to be taken on this proposition if I were to state what I am now authorized to state, that the extent of Mr. Stanbery's indisposition is such that it will be impracticable for him to take any further part in this trial.

The CHIEF JUSTICE. Senators, you who agree to the amendment proposed by way of substitute by the Senator from Maryland will say ay.

Mr. CONNESS called for the yeas and nays, and they were ordered.

Mr. YATES. I ask for the reading of the amendment.

The CHIEF JUSTICE. The Secretary will read the original proposition and also the substitute.

The Chief Clerk read the order proposed by Mr. STEWART and the amendment of Mr. VICKERS.

The question on the amendment being taken by yeas and nays, resulted—yeas 26, nays 20; as follows:

YEAS—Messrs. Buckalew, Cragin, Davis, Doolittle, Edmunds, Fessenden, Fowler, Frelinghuysen, Grimes, Hendricks, Johnson, McCreery, Morrill of Maine, Morton, Norton, Patterson of New Hampshire, Patterson of Tennessee, Saulsbury, Sprague, Tipton, Trumbull, Van Winkle, Vickers, Willey, Wilson, and Yates—26.

NAYS—Messrs. Cameron, Cattell, Chandler, Conness, Corbett, Drake, Ferry, Henderson, Howard, Howe, Morgan, Morrill of Vermont, Pomeroy, Ramsey, Ross, Sherman, Stewart, Sumner, Thayer, and Williams—20.

NOT VOTING—Messrs. Anthony, Bayard, Cole, Conkling, Dixon, Harlan, Nye, and Wade—8.

Mr. POMEROY. The Senator from California, [Mr. COLE,] who sits by my side, has been called suddenly to leave the city on account of a matter of deep interest to his family. He wished me to say this to the Senate in explanation of his absence.

So the amendment was agreed to.

The CHIEF JUSTICE. The question recurs on the order as amended.

Mr. CONNESS called for the yeas and nays, and they were ordered; and being taken, resulted—yeas 20, nays 26; as follows:

YEAS—Messrs. Buckalew, Cragin, Davis, Doolittle, Fowler, Hendricks, Johnson, McCreery, Morton, Norton, Patterson of New Hampshire, Patterson of Tennessee, Saulsbury, Sumner, Tipton, Trumbull, Vickers, Willey, Wilson, and Yates—20.

NAYS—Messrs. Cameron, Cattell, Chandler, Conness, Corbett, Drake, Edmunds, Ferry, Fessenden, Frelinghuysen, Grimes, Henderson, Howard, Howe, Morgan, Morrill of Maine, Morrill of Vermont, Pomeroy, Ramsey, Ross, Sherman, Sprague, Stewart, Thayer, Van Winkle, and Williams—26.

NOT VOTING—Messrs. Anthony, Bayard, Cole, Conkling, Dixon, Harlan, Nye, and Wade—8.

So the amendment was disagreed to.

Mr. VICKERS. Mr. President, I send an order to the chair.

Mr. Manager STEVENS. Mr. Chief Justice, I desire to make an inquiry; and that is whether there is any impropriety in any Manager's publishing a short argument after this vote. After the motion made here on Monday some few of us, I among the rest, commenced to write out a short argument. I expect to finish it to-night, and, if the first vote had passed, I meant to file it. I do not know that there is any impropriety now in printing it except that it will not go into the proceedings. I would not like to do anything which would be improper, and I inquire whether there would be any impropriety?

Mr. FERRY. Mr. President, I inquire whether it would be in order to move the original order upon which we have taken no vote, introduced, I think, by the Senator from Massachusetts, [Mr. SUMNER.]

The CHIEF JUSTICE. It would not. As the Chief Justice understands the matter is finally disposed of. A proposition has been offered by the Senator from Maryland, [Mr. VICKERS,] which will be read for information.

The Chief Clerk read the order proposed by Mr. VICKERS, as follows:

That one of the Managers on the part of the House be permitted to file his printed argument before the adjournment of to-day, and that after an oral opening by a Manager and the reply of one of the President's counsel, another of the President's counsel shall have the privilege of filing a written or of making an oral address, to be followed by the closing speech of one of the President's counsel and the final reply of a Manager under the existing rule.

The CHIEF JUSTICE. This order is in the nature of an amendment of the rules, and cannot be considered now unless by unanimous consent.

Mr. CONNESS. That was offered, I believe, two days since, if I am not mistaken, by the Senator from Nevada.

The CHIEF JUSTICE. It has just been offered by the Senator from Maryland. If there is no objection it will be now considered.

Mr. CONNESS. I offer a substitute for it.

The CHIEF JUSTICE. It is before the Senate for consideration, and the Senator from California proposes a substitute.

Mr. SHERMAN. I should like to have it read again. It was not heard.

The CHIEF JUSTICE. In a moment. The Secretary will read the order proposed by the Senator from Maryland, and also the substitute proposed by the Senator from California.

The CHIEF CLERK The order as proposed by the Senator from Maryland is:

Ordered, That one of the Managers on the part of the House be permitted to file his printed argument before the adjournment of to-day, and that after an oral opening by a Manager, and the reply of one of the President's counsel, another of the President's counsel shall have the privilege of filing a written or of making an oral address, to be followed by the closing speech of one of the President's counsel, and the final reply of a Manager under the existing rule.

The Senator from California proposes to amend by striking out all after the word "ordered" and inserting:

That such of the Managers and counsel for the President as may choose to do so have leave to file arguments before Friday, April 24.

The CHIEF JUSTICE. The question is on the amendment proposed by way of substitute.

Mr. CONNESS called for the yeas and nays, and they were ordered.

Mr. BUCKALEW. I would move to lay the resolution and amendment on the table; but I desire to have the order and amendment read again.

The CHIEF JUSTICE. The order and proposed amendment will be read again.

The Chief Clerk read the order and the amendment.

Mr. CONNESS. Mr. President, I wish to modify my amendment so as to read "on or before Friday, April 24."

The CHIEF JUSTICE. That modification will be made if there be no objection. The question is on the motion of the Senator from Pennsylvania, [Mr. BUCKALEW,] to lay on the table the proposition and pending amendment.

The motion was not agreed to.

The CHIEF JUSTICE. The question recurs on the amendment proposed by the Senator from California. Upon that question the yeas and nays have been ordered.

The question being taken by yeas and nays, resulted—yeas 24, nays 25; as follows:

YEAS—Messrs. Cameron, Cattell, Chandler, Conkling, Conness, Corbett, Cragin, Drake, Ferry, Henderson, Howard, Morrill of Vermont, Patterson of New Hampshire, Pomeroy, Ramsey, Sherman, Stewart, Sumner, Thayer, Tipton, Willey, Williams, Wilson, and Yates—24.

NAYS—Messrs. Anthony, Bayard, Buckalew, Davis, Dixon, Doolittle, Edmunds, Fessenden, Fowler, Frelinghuysen, Grimes, Hendricks, Howe, Johnson, McCreery, Morgan, Morton, Norton, Patterson of

Tennessee, Ross, Saulsbury, Sprague, Trumbull, Van Winkle, and Vickers—25.
NOT VOTING—Messrs. Cole, Harlan, Morrill of Maine, Nye, and Wade—5.

So the amendment was not agreed to.

The CHIEF JUSTICE. The question recurs on the order proposed by the Senator from Maryland, [Mr. VICKERS.]

Mr. JOHNSON. I move to amend the order by inserting "two" instead of "one" before the words "of the Managers," at the beginning of the order.

Mr. SHERMAN. Say "all."

Mr. JOHNSON. No; I will not say all; that would be objectionable.

The CHIEF JUSTICE. The question is on the amendment of the Senator from Maryland, [Mr. JOHNSON,] to strike out "one" and insert "two."

The question being put, the Chief Justice declared that the amendment appeared to be agreed to.

Mr. CONKLING called for a division.

Mr. HOWARD. I ask how the order will read if amended?

The CHIEF JUSTICE. It is proposed to strike out "one" in the first line and insert "two;" so as to read: "That two of the Managers on the part of the House be permitted to file, &c."

Mr. CONKLING. I beg to withdraw the call for a division; I made it under a misapprehension of the amendment.

The CHIEF JUSTICE. The Chief Justice announced the vote as agreed to. The amendment, then, stands as agreed to.

Mr. CONNESS. What is the state of the question now, the amendment adopted?

The CHIEF JUSTICE. The amendment is adopted. The question is on the order as amended.

Mr. Manager WILLIAMS. Mr. President and Senators, I beg leave to suggest, as I do very respectfully, that the effect of this order as it now stands, requiring that any argument which may be presented shall be in print to-day, will be to leave the matter substantially as it was before, because there is but one of the Managers, as I believe is well understood, although three of them would like to put in arguments, there is but one of them who is so prepared just now; that is to say, whose argument is in print. So that, in this shape, it would be keeping the word of promise to the ear and breaking it to the hope.

Mr. JOHNSON. What time would the Manager like?

Mr. Manager WILLIAMS. If you would say "written" instead of "printed," it would be satisfactory.

Mr. SHERMAN. I move that the order be so amended that "the Managers shall have leave to file written or printed arguments."

The CHIEF JUSTICE. It is moved to strike out the word "two"——

Mr. SHERMAN. No, sir.

The CHIEF JUSTICE. The Chief Justice does not understand the amendment.

Mr. SHERMAN. Will the Secretary read the first clause, and I will submit an amendment.

The CHIEF JUSTICE. The Secretary will read the first clause.

The Chief Clerk read as follows:

Ordered, That two of the Managers on the part of the House be permitted to file their printed argument.

Mr. SHERMAN. I move that the language be, "The Managers on the part of the House be permitted to file printed or written arguments."

Mr. FESSENDEN. That cannot be done without reconsidering the vote by which we inserted the word "two."

The CHIEF JUSTICE. A motion to strike out the word "two" and insert anything else will not be in order; but a motion to add the words "or written" will be in order.

Mr. SHERMAN. I will then move to reconsider the vote adopting the amendment of the Senator from Maryland, [Mr. JOHNSON,] inserting the word "two."

The CHIEF JUSTICE. The Senator from Ohio moves to reconsider the vote by which the word "one" was stricken out and "two" was inserted.

The motion was not agreed to.

The CHIEF JUSTICE. The question recurs on the amendment to insert after the word "printed" the words "or written."

Mr. GRIMES. I wish to have the order reported, so as to know when these written arguments are to be filed. ["To-day."] Then I ask unanimous consent to inquire whether or not it is expected that the counsel for the President will examine these written arguments to-day and be able to make a reply to them to-morrow morning?

The CHIEF JUSTICE. The question is upon adding after the word "printed" the words "or written."

The amendment was agreed to.

Mr. WILSON. I ask that the order be read, as modified.

The Chief Clerk read as follows:

Ordered, That two of the Managers on the part of the House be permitted to file their printed or written arguments before the adjournment of to-day, and that after an oral argument by one Manager and the reply of one of the President's counsel, another of the President's counsel shall have the privilege of filing a written or of making an oral address, to be followed by the closing speech of one of the President's counsel and the final reply of a Manager under the existing rule.

Mr. CORBETT. Mr. President, I move to insert in place of the word "another" the word "two," so as to make it the same on the part of the President's counsel as on the part of the Managers.

The CHIEF JUSTICE. The Clerk will read the order as it stands now, and as it will be if amended as proposed.

Mr. FOWLER. Mr. Chief Justice, the noise is so great in the Hall that we cannot hear.

The CHIEF JUSTICE. Conversation in the Senate Chamber must be suspended.

Mr. FOWLER. Particularly in the galleries.

The CHIEF JUSTICE. Conversation in the Senate Chamber must be suspended, including the galleries.

The CHIEF CLERK. It is proposed to strike out the word "another" before the words "of the President's counsel," and to insert "two;" so that the order will read:

Ordered, That two of the Managers on the part of the House be permitted to file their printed or written arguments before the adjournment of to-day, and that after an oral opening by a Manager and the reply of one of the President's counsel, two of the President's counsel shall have the privilege of filing a written or of making an oral address, to be followed by the closing speech of one of the President's counsel and the final reply of a Manager under the existing rule.

Mr. EVARTS. Mr. Chief Justice and Senators, if you will allow me to say one word on this question, as the rule now stands two of the President's counsel are permitted to make oral arguments. By the amendment, without the modification of inserting "two", instead of "another," we understand that three of the President's counsel will be enabled to make oral arguments to the Senate. That is as many as, under any circumstances, would wish or be able to do so.

Mr. Manager STEVENS. Mr. Chief Justice, this would embarrass the Managers among themselves very much. Would it not do to say that "the Managers and the counsel for the President may file written or printed arguments between this and the meeting of the court to-morrow?" That would disembarrass us of all our difficulties, and I cannot perceive its inconvenience.

Mr. BAYARD. Mr. Chief Justice, I move to lay the resolution on the table, and I ask for the yeas and nays.

Mr. NELSON rose.

Mr. BAYARD. I withdraw the motion.

Mr. FESSENDEN. Mr. President, I ask if the order was not adopted.

The CHIEF JUSTICE. It has not been.

Mr. FESSENDEN. I understood it to be adopted.

The CHIEF JUSTICE. It has not yet been adopted. An amendment was adopted, but the vote has not been taken on the order.

Mr. TRUMBULL. Mr. President, I should like to inquire what the question before the Senate is prior to the motion to lay on the table?

The CHIEF JUSTICE. The motion to lay on the table is withdrawn.

Mr. TRUMBULL. What is the motion pending?

The CHIEF JUSTICE. The motion pending is to strike out the word "another" and insert the word "two."

Mr. TRUMBULL. I would ask the unanimous consent of the Senate to appeal to the Senator from Oregon to withdraw that amendment. The counsel do not ask it.

Mr. CORBETT. Mr. President, as the order is satisfactory to the President's counsel as it now stands without the amendment I withdraw the amendment.

The CHIEF JUSTICE. The question is on adopting the order. The Clerk will read it as it now stands.

The Chief Clerk read as follows:

Ordered, That two of the Managers on the part of the House be permitted to file their printed or written arguments before the adjournment of to-day, and that after an oral opening by a Manager and the reply of one of the President's counsel, another of the President's counsel shall have the privilege of filing a written or of making an oral address, to be followed by the closing speech of one of the President's counsel and the final reply by a Manager under the existing rule.

Mr. CONNESS. I ask for the reading again of the first part of the order.

The Chief Clerk read the order.

Mr. CONNESS. That, Mr. President, I desire to suggest——

The CHIEF JUSTICE. The Senator from California can speak by unanimous consent.

Mr. CONNESS. I will not ask consent, nor speak. I move, at the instance of one of the Managers, to amend so that it will read "before to-morrow noon," that that length of time be given to file either written or printed arguments, as they are not ready to-day.

Mr. GRIMES. How can the other side reply to-morrow?

Mr. HENDERSON. I desire to offer a substitute.

The CHIEF JUSTICE. The first question is on the amendment proposed by the Senator from California, [Mr. CONNESS.]

The amendment was agreed to.

The CHIEF JUSTICE. The question now is on the substitute proposed by the Senator from Missouri, [Mr. HENDERSON.] The Clerk will read it.

The Chief Clerk read as follows:

Strike out all after the word "Ordered" in the original proposition, and insert:

That all the Managers not delivering oral arguments may be permitted to file written arguments at any time before the 24th instant, and the counsel for the President not making oral arguments may file written arguments at any time before Tuesday, the 28th instant.

Mr. HENDERSON called for the yeas and nays on the amendment, and they were ordered.

Mr. THAYER. I move to lay the whole subject on the table.

Mr. SPRAGUE called for the yeas and nays, and they were ordered; and being taken, resulted—yeas 13, nays 37; as follows:

YEAS—Messrs. Buckalew, Conkling, Dixon, Doolittle, Edmunds, Grimes, Henderson, McCreery, Norton, Ross, Sprague, Thayer, and Williams—13.

NAYS—Messrs. Anthony, Cameron, Cattell, Chandler, Conness, Corbett, Cragin, Davis, Drake, Ferry, Fessenden, Fowler, Frelinghuysen, Harlan, Hendricks, Howard, Howe, Johnson, Morgan, Morrill of Maine, Morrill of Vermont, Morton, Patterson of New Hampshire, Patterson of Tennessee, Pomeroy,

Ramsey, Saulsbury, Sherman, Stewart, Sumner, Tipton, Trumbull, Van Winkle, Vickers, Willey, Wilson, and Yates—37.

NOT VOTING—Messrs. Bayard, Cole, Nye, and Wade—4.

So the motion to lay on the table was not agreed to.

The CHIEF JUSTICE. The question is on the amendment proposed by the Senator from Missouri, to strike out all after the word "Ordered" and to insert what will be read by the Secretary.

Mr. HENDERSON. Before it is read I desire to modify it so as to make it read, "Monday, the 27th," instead of "Tuesday, the 28th."

The CHIEF JUSTICE. The Secretary will read the amendment, as modified.

The Chief Clerk read as follows:

Strike out all after the word "Ordered," and insert:

That all the Managers not delivering oral arguments may be permitted to file written arguments at any time before the 24th instant, and the counsel for the President not making oral arguments may file written arguments at any time before Monday, the 27th instant.

Mr. HENDERSON. I will say "before eleven o'clock on Monday, the 27th instant," so that they will be in at the time of meeting.

Mr. DOOLITTLE. Mr. Chief Justice, I desire to inquire of the Chief Justice whether under that rule all the Managers would not be permitted to deliver oral arguments?

Mr. HENDERSON. It does not change the present rule.

The CHIEF JUSTICE. The Secretary will read the order proposed.

Mr. EVARTS. Mr. Chief Justice and Senators, as we understand the order now proposed, it would not enlarge the privilege of the President's counsel in addressing the court. Any liberality that should be shown by the Senate, so far as it could be availed of by the President's counsel under the peculiar circumstances in which they are placed, would probably need to include an opportunity on their part to make oral addresses.

Mr. NELSON. Mr. Chief Justice and Senators, I have felt and still feel an almost irresistible repugnance to saying anything to the Senate upon this subject. In the first place, in the view which I entertained of the Constitution and laws of our country, I regard it as a matter of right in the President of the United States to appear by counsel. I suppose, following the analogies of courts of justice, that the Senate, sitting as a court, have the right to regulate the number of counsel and to confine it within reasonable limits. Inasmuch as the Senate had indicated, by a rule which was adopted before the commencement of the trial, the number of persons who were to address the Senate in the progress of the trial, I felt reluctant to ask that any alteration of that rule should be made in behalf of the President's counsel for the very simple reason that it has never been to me a source of satisfaction to

attempt to address an unwilling audience, and much less would it be a source of gratification for me to attempt to address the Senate when they had indicated by a rule that they were unwilling to hear further argument. On a former occasion I stated to the Senate that intending on our part faithfully to adhere to the rule which you had prescribed for the conduct and management of the trial, two of the President's counsel had determined not to address the Senate; that three others of the President's counsel had assumed, with our consent, the management and direction of the case, and that in our arrangement it was left to them to make the argument before the Senate. As an application was made on the side of the Managers to enlarge the number, I thought that it would not be improper on our part to ask to be permitted to appear for the cause and to argue it. Since I made a few brief observations to the Senate the other day, Mr. Stanbery, upon whom we relied to make the leading argument in behalf of the President, has been confined by sickness. It is uncertain whether he will be able to address the Senate at all; the probabilities at present are that he will not; and even if he should make the effort, the chances are that he will be unable to make that argument to the Senate which he had intended to make.

Under these circumstances I desire to say to the Senate that I would like to be permitted to address the Senate in behalf of the President. Indeed, I desire that the rule shall be so enlarged as to give all the President's counsel the privilege of addressing the Senate, either orally or in writing, as we may find convenient to do. I have stated that, owing to the circumstances indicated, we have not prepared written arguments; and it is too late now for the two counsel who had not intended to address the Senate to make such preparation; but in the progress of the case I have made such notes and memoranda that I think I could argue the case before you; and I feel constrained by a sense of duty to ask the Senate, under these circumstances, to allow the whole of the counsel to make addresses.

I beg leave to assure you, Senators, that in doing this I am not animated, as I trust, by a spirit of idle vanity, and by the desire to make an address in a great cause like this. I have lived long enough in the world to know that sometimes we can make more by our silence than by an effort to make a public address. I am satisfied from my experience that great risks attend such an effort, especially when we attempt to address the Senate or any other assembly extemporaneously; and were I to consult my own feelings and inclinations, I would not make this request; but, under the peculiar circumstances by which we are surrounded, if the Senate are willing to enlarge the rule, I choose to take the risk and to take my chances of endeavoring to argue the case before you, and I feel, Senators, that, under existing circumstances, this is not an unreasonable request.

I may say, although I am not expressly authorized to do so, that I am satisfied the President desires that his cause shall be augued by the two additional counsel whom he has provided in the case, besides the three counsel who were heretofore selected for that purpose; and I trust you will not deny us this right. I trust that you will feel at liberty to extend it to all the counsel in the case. If we choose to avail ourselves of it we will do so. I have no sort of objection, so far as I am concerned, that the same right shall be extended to all or to more than an equal number of the Managers on the other side. I trust that the resolution will be so shaped as to embrace all the counsel who are engaged in the cause in behalf of the President. I do not know that under these circumstances I shall be able to interest the Senate at all. But it is a case of great importance. On the trial of Judge Chase, six of the managers were permitted to address the Senate, and five of the counsel for the defendant were permitted to address the Senate; and in a great case like this, one of such momentous magnitude, a case in which the whole country is interested, is it asking, Senators, too much at your hands, that you will enable us to present his case in the best manner that we may be able to do under the circumstances by which we are surrounded?

The CHIEF JUSTICE. The question is on the amendment proposed by the Senator from Missouri, [Mr. HENDERSON.] The Secretary will read the original proposition again, and also the amendment.

The CHIEF CLERK. The original order is as follows:

Ordered, That two of the Managers on the part of the House be permitted to file their printed or written arguments on or before eleven o'clock to-morrow, and that after an oral opening by a Manager and the reply of one of the President's counsel, another of the President's counsel shall have the privilege of filing a written or making an oral address, to be followed by the closing speech of one of the President's counsel and the final reply of a Manager under the existing rule.

The amendment of the Senator from Missouri is to strike out all after the word "ordered" and insert:

That all the Managers not delivering oral arguments may be permitted to file written arguments at any time before the 24th instant, and the counsel for the President not making oral arguments may file written arguments at any time before eleven o'clock of Monday, the 27th instant.

Mr. HOWARD. Mr. President, I rise to make an inquiry, whether the proper construction of the amendment offered by the honorable Senator from Missouri does not open the door and repeal the twenty-first rule; in short, whether it does not allow all the counsel on the part of the accused and all the Managers who may see fit to make oral arguments in the final summing up?

Mr. CONNESS. To make that——

Mr. EDMUNDS. I object to debate.

Mr. CONNESS. To make that entirely clear, I move to insert the words "in accordance with the twenty-first rule."

The CHIEF JUSTICE. "Subject to the twenty-first rule."

Mr. CONNESS. Yes, "subject to the twenty-first rule."

Mr. HENDERSON. I accept the modification. That is what it means now.

The CHIEF JUSTICE. The Secretary will read the substitute, as modified.

The Chief Clerk read as follows:

Ordered, That all the Managers not delivering oral arguments may be permitted to file written arguments at any time before the 24th instant, and the counsel for the President not making oral arguments may file written arguments at any time after eleven o'clock of Monday, the 27th instant, subject, however, to the twenty-first rule.

Mr. CONNESS. I wish to insert that language at the beginning after the word "that;" so that it will read "that subject to the twenty-first rule" so and so shall be done.

Mr. HENDERSON. I suggest, after the words "oral arguments," to insert "except the two Managers delivering oral arguments under the twenty-first rule."

The CHIEF JUSTICE. The Chief Justice will suggest to the Senator from Missouri that his object will be attained by accepting the amendment proposed by the Senator from California, inserting the words "subject to the twenty-first rule."

Mr. CONNESS. I ask if it was my privilege to offer it as an amendment. I do not know why it was not accepted.

The CHIEF JUSTICE. The Chief Justice understood it to be accepted.

Mr. CONNESS. I suggest to the Secretary to write it.

The CHIEF JUSTICE. It was written and was accepted, as the Chief Justice understood, and then after it was accepted the Senator from Missouri proceeded still further to modify his amendment.

Mr. CONNESS. I ask the Secretary to read it again as I moved it.

The Chief Clerk read as follows:

Ordered, That, subject to the twenty-first rule, all the Managers not delivering oral arguments may be permitted to file written arguments at any time before the 24th instant, and the counsel for the President not making oral arguments may file written arguments at any time before eleven o'clock of Monday, the 27th instant.

The CHIEF JUSTICE. The Senator from California moves to amend the amendment proposed by the Senator from Missouri by inserting after the word "that" the words "subject to the twenty-first rule."

The amendment to the amendment was agreed to.

Mr. TRUMBULL. Is an amendment still in order?

The CHIEF JUSTICE. It is.

Mr. TRUMBULL. I move to strike out all

after the word "that " and insert what I send to the Chair.

The CHIEF CLERK. It is proposed to amend the amendment by striking out all after the word "that " and inserting:

As many of the Managers and of the counsel for the President as desire to do so be permitted to file arguments or to address the Senate orally.

Mr. EDMUNDS, Mr. STEWART, and others called for the yeas and nays, and they were ordered.

Mr. CORBETT. I call for the reading again.

The CHIEF JUSTICE. The Clerk will report the order, the amendment proposed, and the proposed amendment to the amendment.

The CHIEF CLERK. The order originally proposed is as follows:

Ordered, That two of the Managers on the part of the House be permitted to file their printed or written arguments on or before eleven o'clock to-morrow; and that after an oral opening by a Manager and the reply of one of the President's counsel another of the President's counsel shall have the privilege of filing a written or of making an oral address, to be followed by the closing speech of one of the President's counsel and the final reply of a Manager under the existing rule.

The Senator from Missouri [Mr. HENDERSON] proposes to amend that by striking out all after the word "Ordered" and inserting:

That, subject to the twenty-first rule, all the Managers not delivering oral arguments may be permitted to file written arguments at any time before the 24th instant, and the counsel for the President not making oral arguments may file written arguments at any time before eleven o'clock of Monday, the 27th instant.

The Senator from Illinois [Mr. TRUMBULL] proposes to amend the amendment by striking out all after the word "that" and inserting:

As many of the Managers and of the counsel for the President as desire to do so be permitted to file arguments or to address the Senate orally.

The CHIEF JUSTICE. The question is on the amendment proposed by the Senator from Illinois to the amendment of the Senator from Missouri.

The question being taken by yeas and nays, resulted—yeas 29, nays 20; as follows:

YEAS—Messrs. Anthony, Buckalew, Conkling, Cragin, Davis, Doolittle, Edmunds, Ferry, Fessenden, Fowler, Grimes, Henderson, Hendricks, Johnson, McCreery, Morrill of Maine, Norton, Patterson of New Hampshire, Patterson of Tennessee, Ramsey, Saulsbury, Sherman, Sprague, Tipton, Trumbull, Van Winkle, Vickers, Willey, and Yates—29.

NAYS—Messrs. Cameron, Cattell, Chandler, Conness, Corbett, Dixon, Drake, Frelinghuysen, Harlan, Howard, Howe, Morgan, Morrill of Vermont, Morton, Pomeroy, Ross, Stewart, Sumner, Thayer, and Williams—20.

NOT VOTING—Messrs. Bayard, Cole, Nye, Wade, and Wilson—5.

So the amendment to the amendment was agreed to.

The CHIEF JUSTICE. The question recurs on the amendment as amended.

Mr. BUCKALEW. I move to amend further by adding at the end of the amendment the following words:

But the conclusion of the oral argument shall be by one Manager, as provided in the twenty-first rule.

Mr. TRUMBULL. That would be so necessarily.

The amendment to the amendment was agreed to.

The CHIEF JUSTICE. The question recurs on the amendment of the Senator from Missouri [Mr. HENDERSON,] as amended on the motion of the Senator from Illinois, [Mr. TRUMBULL.]

Mr. CAMERON. I rise to inquire whether a substitute would be in order now.

The CHIEF JUSTICE. An amendment to either proposition will be in order. Does the Senator from Pennsylvania propose to offer an amendment?

Mr. CAMERON. Yes, sir, by way of substitute.

The CHIEF JUSTICE. It will be in order to move a substitute to strike out all after the word "that" in the amendment.

Mr. CAMERON. I send my amendment to the Chair.

The CHIEF CLERK. It is proposed to strike out all after the word "that" in the amendment as amended and to insert:

All the Managers and all the counsel for the President be permitted to file written or printed arguments by eleven o'clock to-morrow.

Mr. EDMUNDS. Mr. President, I wish to inquire whether that is offered as a substitute for the original proposition or for the amendment.

The CHIEF JUSTICE. For the amendment.

Mr. EDMUNDS. Then I rise to a point of order, that it is not in order on account of our having voted that the amendment should stand as it is.

The CHIEF JUSTICE. The Chief Justice is of opinion that it is in order as an amendment. The question is on the amendment proposed by the Senator from Pennsylvania, [Mr. CAMERON,] to strike out all after the word "that" in the amendment as amended and insert what has been read.

Mr. HOWE. I move to lay the order and the amendment on the table.

The motion was not agreed to.

The CHIEF JUSTICE. The question recurs on the amendment proposed by the Senator from Pennsylvania, [Mr. CAMERON.]

The amendment was rejected.

The CHIEF JUSTICE. The question recurs on the amendment of the Senator from Missouri as amended on the motion of the Senator from Illinois.

Mr. YATES. I move to strike out all after the word "that" and insert the following.

The CHIEF JUSTICE. The Secretary will read the amendment proposed by the Senator from Illinois, [Mr. YATES.]

The CHIEF CLERK read the amendment, which was to strike out all after the word "that" and to insert:

Four of the Managers and four of the counsel for the respondent be permitted to make printed or written or oral arguments, the Managers to have the opening and closing.

Mr. YATES called for the yeas and nays, and they were ordered.

Mr. JOHNSON. I move to amend by inserting at the close "subject to the limitation in the twenty-first rule" as to the closing of the case, because otherwise all the Managers might close.

The CHIEF JUSTICE. The amendment is not in order, unless it is accepted by the Senator from Illinois. The Senator from Maryland proposes to add "subject to the limitation of the twenty-first rule." Does the Senator from Illinois accept the amendment?

Mr. YATES. Yes, sir.

Mr. ANTHONY. I ask unanimous consent to make an inquiry. Does not this order allow all four of the Managers to reply after all four of the President's counsel have spoken?

Mr. JOHNSON. Not as it is now amended.

The CHIEF JUSTICE. The Chief Justice thinks it does not. The Secretary will read the amendment as it now stands.

The CHIEF CLERK. It is proposed to amend the amendment by striking out all after the word "that" and inserting:

Four of the Managers and four of the counsel for the respondent be permitted to make printed or written or oral arguments, the Managers to have the opening and closing, subject to the limitation of the twenty-first rule.

Mr. GRIMES. I call for the reading of the twenty-first rule.

The CHIEF JUSTICE. The Secretary will read the twenty-first rule.

The Chief Clerk read as follows:

"XXI. The case on each side shall be opened by one person. The final argument on the merits may be made by two persons on each side, (unless otherwise ordered by the Senate upon application for that purpose,) and the argument shall be opened and closed on the part of the House of Representatives."

The CHIEF JUSTICE. The question is on the amendment proposed by the Senator from Illinois [Mr. YATES] to the amendment as amended proposed by the Senator from Missouri, [Mr. HENDERSON.] Upon this question the yeas and nays have been ordered.

The question being taken by yeas and nays, resulted—yeas 18, nays 31; as follows:

YEAS—Messrs. Buckalew, Conkling, Corbett, Cragin, Davis, Doolittle, Fowler, Hendricks, Howard, McCreery, Morgan, Morton, Norton, Saulsbury, Sprague, Van Winkle, Vickers, and Yates—18.

NAYS—Messrs. Anthony, Bayard, Cameron, Cattell, Chandler, Dixon, Drake, Edmunds, Ferry, Fessenden, Frelinghuysen, Grimes, Harlan, Henderson, Howe, Johnson, Morrill of Maine, Morrill of Vermont, Patterson of Tennessee, Pomeroy, Ramsey, Ross, Sherman, Stewart, Sumner, Thayer, Tipton, Trumbull, Willey, Williams, and Wilson—31.

NOT VOTING.—Messrs. Cole, Conness, Nye, Patterson of New Hampshire, and Wade—5.

So the amendment to the amendment was rejected.

The CHIEF JUSTICE. The question recurs on the amendment as amended.

Mr. FRELINGHUYSEN. I should like to hear the original proposition, as moved, I believe, by the Senator from California, read.

Mr. HENDRICKS. Mr. President, I move to postpone the further consideration of this subject until the close of the first argument on the part of the Managers. I think that argument ought to proceed.

The motion was not agreed to; there being on a division—ayes 19, noes 22.

The CHIEF JUSTICE. The question recurs on the amendment of the Senator from Missouri [Mr. HENDERSON] as amended on motion of the Senator from Illinois [Mr. TRUMBULL] to the original proposition made by the Senator from Maryland, [Mr. VICKERS.] Both the original order and the proposed amendment will be read.

The CHIEF CLERK. The original order is as follows:

Ordered, That two of the Managers on the part of the House be permitted to file their printed or written arguments on or before eleven o'clock to-morrow, and that after an oral opening by a Manager and the reply of one of the President's counsel another of the President's counsel shall have the privilege of filing a written or of making an oral address, to be followed by the closing speech of one of the President's counsel and the final reply of a Manager under the existing rule.

The amendment as amended proposes to strike out all after the word "Ordered" and to insert:

That as many of the Managers and of the counsel for the President as desire to do so be permitted to file arguments or to address the Senate orally, but the conclusion of the oral argument shall be by one Manager as provided in the twenty-first rule.

The CHIEF JUSTICE put the question on the amendment as amended and declared himself at a loss to decide the result.

Mr. HOWARD called for the yeas and nays, and they were ordered; and being taken, resulted—yeas 28, nays 22; as follows:

YEAS—Messrs. Anthony, Conkling, Cragin, Davis, Dixon, Doolittle, Edmunds, Ferry, Fessenden, Fowler, Grimes, Henderson, Hendricks, Johnson, McCreery, Morrill of Maine, Morton, Norton, Patterson of Tennessee, Saulsbury, Sherman, Sprague, Tipton, Trumbull, Van Winkle, Vickers, Willey, and Yates—28.

NAYS—Messrs. Bayard, Buckalew, Cameron, Cattell, Chandler, Corbett, Drake, Frelinghuysen, Harlan, Howard, Howe, Morgan, Morrill of Vermont, Patterson of New Hampshire, Pomeroy, Ramsey, Ross, Stewart, Sumner, Thayer, Williams, and Wilson—22.

NOT VOTING—Messrs. Cole, Conness, Nye, and Wade—4.

So the amendment as amended was agreed to.

The CHIEF JUSTICE. The question recurs on the order as amended.

Mr. EDMUNDS. I ask for the yeas and nays on that question.

The yeas and nays were ordered; and being taken, resulted—yeas 28, nays 22; as follows:

YEAS—Messrs. Anthony, Cragin, Davis, Doolittle, Ferry, Fessenden, Fowler, Grimes, Henderson, Hendricks, Johnson, McCreery, Morgan, Morrill of Maine, Morton, Norton, Patterson of Tennessee, Ramsey, Saulsbury, Sherman, Sumner, Tipton, Trumbull, Van Winkle, Vickers, Willey, Wilson, and Yates—28.

NAYS—Messrs. Bayard, Buckalew, Cameron, Cattell, Chandler, Conkling, Corbett, Dixon, Drake, Edmunds, Frelinghuysen, Harlan, Howard, Howe, Morrill of Vermont, Patterson of New Hampshire, Pomeroy, Ross, Sprague, Stewart, Thayer, and Williams—22.

NOT VOTING—Messrs. Cole, Conness, Nye, and Wade—4.

So it was

Ordered, That as many of the Managers as desire to do so be permitted to file arguments or to address the Senate orally; but the conclusion of the oral argument shall be by one Manager, as provided in the twenty-first rule.

The CHIEF JUSTICE. Gentlemen Managers on the part of the House of Representatives, you will please to proceed with the argument.

Hon. JOHN A. LOGAN, one of the Managers of the impeachment on the part of the House of Representatives, thereupon, under the order just adopted by the Senate, filed the following argument:

Mr. PRESIDENT and SENATORS: When one in public life is suddenly called to the discharge of a novel and important public duty whose consequences will be great and whose effects will be historical, he must betray an inordinate self-esteem and an unpardonable lack of modesty if he do not at the outset acknowledge his diffidence and solicit forbearance.

And, sirs, more than any other man do I feel that it becomes me to invoke the charity and to ask the leniency of this honorable tribunal. For surely never since the foundation of this Government has there been cast upon any of its servants a duty so high and important in its nature, so unusual and unexpected in its character, and so full of good or ill in its consequences as the duty with which the Managers on behalf of the people now find themselves charged, and one part of which I now reluctantly find myself called upon to perform. I shall be sustained throughout my effort by the consciousness that the cause I in part represent is too great to be weakened by my weakness, and by the sincere hope that however feeble may be my efforts, and however apparent may be my imperfections, I shall not be accused of a want of fairness, or found lacking in concession and candor.

I wish to assure you, Senators—I wish most earnestly and sincerely to assure the learned and honorable counsel for the defense—that we speak not only for ourselves but for the great body of the people when we say that we regret this occasion, and we regret the necessity which has devolved this duty upon us. Heretofore, sirs, it has been the pride of every American to point to the Chief Magistrate of his nation. It has been his boast that to that great office have always been brought the most preëminent purity, the most undoubted integrity, and the most unquestioned loyalty which the country could produce. However fierce might be the strife of party; however clamorous might be the cry of politics; however desperate might be the struggles of leaders and of factions, it has always been felt that the President of the United States was an administrator of the law in all its force and example, and would be a promoter of the welfare of his country in all its perils and adversities. Such have been the hopes and such has been the reliance of the people at large; and in consequence the chief executive chair has come to assume in the hearts of Americans a form so sacred and a name so spotless that nothing impure could attach to the one and nothing dishonorable could taint the other. To do aught or to say aught which will disturb this cherished feeling will be to destroy one of the dearest impressions to which our people cling.

And yet, sirs, this is our duty to-day. We are here to show that President Johnson, the man whom this country once honored, is unfitted for his place. We are here to show that in his person he has violated the honor and sanctity of his office. We are here to show that he usurped the power of his position and the emoluments of his patronage. We are here to show that he has not only willfully violated the law, but has maliciously commanded its infringement. We are here to show that he has deliberately done those things which he ought not to have done, and that he has criminally left undone those things which he ought to have done.

He has betrayed his countrymen that he might perpetuate his power, and has sacrificed their interests that he might swell his authority. He has made the good of the people subordinate to his ambition, and the harmony of the community second to his desires. He has stood in the way which would have led the dismembered States back to prosperity and peace, and has instigated them to the path which led to discord and to strife. He has obstructed acts which were intended to heal, and has counseled the course which was intended to separate. The differences which he might have reconciled by his voice he has stimulated by his example. The questions which might have been amicably settled by his acquiescence have been aggravated by his insolence; and in all those instances whereof in our articles we complain, he has made his prerogatives a burden to the Commonwealth instead of a blessing to his constituents.

And it is not alone that in his public course he has been shameless and guilty, but that his private conduct has been incendiary and malignant. It is not only that he has notoriously broken the law, but that he has criminally scoffed at the framers of the law. By public harangue and by political arts he has sought to cast odium upon Congress and to insure credit for himself; and thus, in a Government where equal respect and dignity should be observed in reference to the power and authority conferred upon each of its several departments, he has attempted to subvert their just proportions and to arrogate to himself their respective jurisdictions. It is for these things, Senators, that to-day he stands impeached; and it is because of these that the people have bid us prosecute. That we regret it, I have said; that they regret it, I repeat; and though it tears away the beautiful belief with which, like a drapery, they had invested the altar, yet they feel that the time has come when they must expose and expel the sacrilegious priest in order to protect and preserve the purity of the temple.

Yes, Senators, Andrew Johnson, President of the United States, now stands arraigned at this bar to answer to the high crimes and misdemeanors which an indignant and outraged people have at length alleged against him. This trial has given us many surprises, but no one fact has given us more surprise than the tone of complaint which by his counsel he has assumed. Of what should he complain? Did he think that he could proceed in his unwarrantable course forever with impunity? Did he suppose that he could break down every rule and safeguard in the land and that none should say him nay? Did he believe that because the people were for a time stricken into silence by the audacity of his acts they would suffer in sadness and continue to be dumb? Did he not know that they were jealous of their liberties and rights, and in the end would punish him who attempted to tamper with either; and now that they are visiting upon him the inevitable result of his misdeeds is it of this that he complains? He should rather give them thanks that they have spared him so long, and be grateful that their magnanimity has preserved him to this hour. Is it of the articles alleged against him that he complains?

Sirs, the people have selected the latest but not the greatest instance of his dereliction. They have hesitated, in the first instance, to think that the actions which they knew were insidious were intended to be revolutionary. They preferred to attribute to the frailty of his mind what they should have ascribed to the duplicity of his heart; and when, day after day, the evidences of his falsehood became stronger and stronger, when month after month the baseness of his purpose became more and more palpable, and when session after session the proof of his desertion became more and more convincing, still they hesitated, until further hesitation as to him would have been certain destruction to them, and they presented through us, not his most flagrant offenses, but only his last offendings. Should he complain that they denounce for the lesser when he is equally guilty of the greater crimes? Is it of this tribunal that he complains? You, Mr. President, preside, and most worthily preside, over the Supreme Court, which is the court of last resort in all this land. To you and your associates is left the final arbitrament of the most grave and important controversies which concern our people. By your education and habit you are fitted to pass upon serious issues. You are raised by your jurisdiction above the ordinary passions and prejudices of the lesser courts; and

this of itself is a guaranty of your impartiality in a forum like this. And you, Senators, by the theory and structure of our Government, are constituted its most select and responsible legislators. By the arrangement and disposition of the functions of our Federal powers, you occupy a sphere the exact parallel to which is found in no other Government of the world. You are of the President, and yet so far separated from him that you are beyond his flatteries and above his threats. You are of the people, and yet so far removed from them that you are not affected by their local excitements; you are not swayed by their passions, nor influenced by their tumults. When the Constitution fixed the age of eligibility to the Senate it was that your minds should be matured and that your judgments should be ripened; it was that you should have come to that period when reason is not obscured by passion and wisdom is gathered of experience. To such an august body have the people committed their grievances; and of this he certainly should not complain. Does he complain of us? Sirs, it may be that he does; but yet I feel that he should not. What we have done we have done promptly, but none the less reluctantly. We felt, as citizens, the irresistible conviction that this man was false to every citizen; and we felt, as Managers, that we did not dare to jeopardize, by unseemly delay or fatal favors, the safety of a nation. We thought—

"If it were done, when 'tis done, then 'twere well
It were done quickly."

There had been too much dallying with treason already. If but a few short years ago traitors had been quickly seized and speedily punished there would never have been a shot fired in rebellion. If plotters had been made to feel the early gripe of the law there never would have been a resort to arms. When we looked back and recalled the memories of our battle-fields; when we saw the carnage amid the slain, the unutterable woe of the wounded; when we remembered the shriek of the widow and the sob of the orphan; when we reflected on the devastation of our land and the burdens now on our people; when we turned us about and saw in every direction the miseries and the mischiefs which follow every war, no matter how just, and when we remind ourselves that all this would not have been had treason been executed for its overt acts before yet its hands were red; and when we felt, as we do all feel, that to delay might bring all this and more upon us, we could not and did not pause. We urged this trial at "railroad speed." In view of such results self-preservation would have dictated that we should ask for "lightning speed." Ought he to complain? If he is guilty, then there is no speed too great for his deserts. If he is innocent, there is none too great for his deliverance. It is the fact, then, that we have desired to advance this case with all possible speed; but it is not the fact that we have advanced with all possible rigor. We only desired to be just; we did not wish to be severe. If we had been actuated by any spirit other than a sense of our high duty we might have given the President cause to complain. We might have asked, and asked it in the strength of authority, too, that pending the trial he should have been placed under arrest, or at least suspended from his office. The English practice would have sanctioned this. May, in his treatise on the law, privilege, &c., of Parliament, says:

"If the accused be a peer he is attached or retained in custody by order of the House of Lords; if a commoner, he is taken into custody by the sergeant-at-arms attending the Commons, by whom he is delivered to the gentleman usher of the black rod, in whose custody he remains until he is admitted to bail by the House of Lords, or otherwise disposed of by their order."—*Chapter* 23.

In Wooddeson we find it was customary for the Commons to request the Lords that the person impeached "may be sequestered from his seat in Parliament or be committed, or that the peers will take order for his appearance, according as the degree of the imputation justifies more or less severity." The Commons demanded that Clarendon be sequestered from Parliament and committed. (6 Howell's State Trials, 395; 11 Howell, 733.)

Lord Stafford was sequestered in 1641. (2 Nalson's Collections, 7.)

In the matter of the impeachment of Blount it was ordered by the Senate as follows, July 7, 1797:

"That the said William Blount be taken into the custody of the messenger of this House until he shall enter into recognizance, himself in the sum of $20,-000, with two sufficient sureties in the sum of $15,000 each, to appear and answer such articles of impeachment as may be exhibited against him."

On the 18th day of June, 1788, in the Virginia convention, George Mason objected to the pardoning power vested in the President for ordinary crimes. Mr. Madison, in reply, said:

"There is one security in this case to which gentlemen may not have adverted; if the President be connected in any suspicious manner with any person, and there be grounds to believe he will shelter him, the House of Representatives can impeach him; they [evidently referring to the Senate, or the Senate in connection with the House] can remove him if found guilty; *they can suspend him when suspected,* and the power will devolve upon the Vice President."

Therefore, as we have not asked what we might have so consistently demanded, I feel that he has no ground of discontent with us. What, then, is he to answer? He is to make defense to the charge of high crimes and misdemeanors which the people of the United States, in virtue of their sovereignty, do proclaim against him. I wish to be distinctly understood when I say that the allegation comes from the people in their sovereignty—in their supreme capacity as the rulers of us all. By remembering this we may escape from the narrow confines of legal technicalities, and be governed by more extended and liberal rules than prevail in the courts of the common law. It shall not be truthfully said that the charges which come from a whole people are frivolous and vain; it shall not longer be claimed that that which a community in its aggregate capacity asserts is insufficient and of no avail; the mighty mass of men who are the nation—the great unit of minds who are this Union—of minds enlightened, of thoughts profound, of discrimination quick, and purpose steady, of hearts free, of souls resolved, of all the elements which make this nation what it is—a nation young in years, but mature in action. The murmur of this nation is mighty, and its accusations cannot be ignored. Here, at least, it may be said: "*Vox populi vox Dei*"—"the voice of the people is the voice of God."

It is for this reason that neither a demurrer to test any questions of law or a motion to quash to decide any questions of fact has ever been permitted to be interposed against any article of impeachment, no matter where ever or whenever such has been presented. And yet, before issue joined upon the present occasion, it was asseverated against those who favored this proceeding that they were about to pervert the Constitution, to submerge the law, and further their partisan ambitions by the proclamation of charges which on their face are fabulous and weak, if not absurd and contumacious; and in the answer which this respondent has made he has announced, as one of the issues upon which you are to pass, that several of our articles are insufficient in law and inadequate in fact. I repeat, sirs, that this is an anomalous answer. The fiat of a people when solemnly pronounced against one to whom they have delegated official favors and whom they have charged with derelictions of official duty can never be treated as an empty sound, nor their inquiry regarded as an idle ceremony. And here I wish to impress upon these triers the important fact that every article which we here present stands in the light of a separate count in an indictment, and must be decided as a separate issue on its own merits. It should not be permitted, where any count is found to contain matter of substance, that the accused should have a verdict of not guilty because of insufficiency in matters of form.

It is the rule that all questions of law or of fact are to be decided in these proceedings by the final vote upon the guilt or innocence of the accused. It is also the rule that in determining this general issue Senators must consider the sufficiency or insufficiency in law or in fact of every article of accusation. But the insufficiency which they are to consider is not the technical insufficiency by which indictments are measured. No mere insufficiency of statement, no mere want of precision, no mere lack of relative averments, no mere absence of legal verbiage can inure to the benefit of the accused. The insufficiency which will avail him must be such an entire want of substance as takes all soul and body from the charge and leaves it nothing but a shadow. Neither shall the respondent be allowed to escape because of any immaterial variance between the averment and the proof. If we have succeeded in sustaining the principal weight of each separate article, then we are entitled to a finding upon each. These are the propositions which I gather from the following authorities: Trial of Judge Peck, page 232, (Mr. Wirt, counsel for respondent;) Mr. Webster, in the trial of Judge Prescott, page 25; Mr. Shaw, in the same case, page 45; report from the committee of the House of Commons appointed to inspect the Lords journals, April 30, 1794.

Story, on the Constitution, says:

"It is obvious that the strictness of the forms of proceeding in cases of offenses at common law are ill adapted to impeachments. The very habits growing out of judicial employments, the rigid manner in which the discretion of judges is limited and fenced in on all sides, in order to protect persons accused of crimes, by rules and precedents, and the adherence to technical principles which, perhaps, distinguishes this branch of the law more than any other, are all ill adapted to the trial of political offenses in the broad course of impeachments." * * * *
"There is little technical in the mode of proceeding; the charges are sufficiently clear, and yet, in a general form, there are few exceptions which arise in the application of evidence which grow out of mere technical rules and quibbles; and it has repeatedly been seen that the functions have been better understood and more liberally and justly expounded by statesmen than by mere lawyers. An illustrious instance of this sort is upon record in the case of the trial of Warren Hastings, where the question whether an impeachment was abated by a dissolution of Parliament was decided in the negative by the House of Lords as well as the House of Commons, against what seemed to be the weight of professional opinion."—*Story*, secs. 762, 763.

WHAT ARE IMPEACHABLE OFFENSES?

The next question which it is proper to ask is, for what crimes and misdemeanors may an officer be impeached? Can he be impeached for any other than an indictable offense? The authorities certainly sustain the Managers in asserting that he may be. We cannot search through all the cases, as they are too numerous, but will call the attention of the Senate to some that should be regarded as good authority, and the opinions of those who should be regarded as learned in the law.

Mr. Madison, in discussing the power of the President, used the following language:

"What will be the motives which the President can feel for the abuse of his power and the restraints that operate to prevent it? In the first place he will be impeachable by this House before the Senate for such an act of maladministration; and I contend that the wanton removal of meritorious officers would subject him to impeachment and removal from his own high trust."—*Annals of Congress*, 1804-5, vol. 1, p. 517.

The trial of Blount, 1788-89. Story, in speaking of that case, says:

"In the argument upon Blount's impeachment it was pressed with great earnestness that there is not a syllable in the Constitution which confines impeachment to official acts, and it is against the plainest dictates of common sense that such a restraint should be imposed."—*Story*, sec. 802.

Trial of Judge Chase, February 26, 1805. Mr. Manager Nicholson says:

"If, therefore, the President of the United States should accept a bribe he certainly cannot be indicted for it, and yet no man can doubt that he might be impeached. If one of the heads of Departments should undertake to recommend to office for pay he certainly might be impeached for it, and yet I would ask under what law and in what court could he be indicted."—*Judge Chase's Trial*, p. 564.

In the trial of Judge Chase Mr. Manager Randolph says:

"It has been contended that an offense to be impeachable must be indictable. For what, then, I pray you, was it that this provision of impeachment found its way into the Constitution." * * *
"If the Constitution did not contemplate a distinction between an impeachable and an indictable offense whence this cumbrous and expensive process, which has cost us so much labor and so much anxiety to the nation? Whence this idle parade, this wanton waste of time and treasure, when the ready intervention of a court and jury alone was wanting to rectify the evil?"—*Annals of Congress*, 1804-5, p. 642.

By permission of the Senators I will read some extracts that I have made from the speeches of some of the most learned men of England on this same question, which was discussed in the trial of Queen Caroline, in the year 1820.

Earl Grey, in speaking of the powers of Parliament, said:

"He must maintain this principle, supported on the ground of parliamentary law, and bottomed on the constitution of the country, that on all occasions, when a great State necessity or a matter of great State expediency exists, Parliament were vested with extraordinary powers, and it became their duty to exercise those extraordinary powers in order to procure that remedy commensurate with such State necessity or expediency, which no proceeding in a court of law could effect."—*Trial Queen Caroline*, vol. 1, p. 8.

In the same case Brougham (since made a lord) said:

"Impeachment was a remedy for cases not cognizable by the ordinary jurisdiction." * * * *
"The House of Commons might impeach for whatever was indictable, but they also might impeach in cases where no indictment could be found. He submitted, therefore, that some satisfactory reason ought to be stated why impeachment was not resorted to in this instance."—*Vol.* 1, p. 22.

Again, he says:

"The learned attorney general has held that no impeachment could lie unless some law was violated; but the opinion was contrary to the doctrine laid down by the greatest writers on the law of impeachment. Lord Coke did not so limit the power of Parliament. He regarded this power as most extensive, and in describing it quoted this remarkable expression: 'That it was so large and capacious that he could not place bounds to it either in space or time.' In short, this maxim has been laid down as irrefragable, that whatever mischief is done, and no remedy could otherwise be obtained, it is competent for Parliament to impeach." * * * * "Why was impeachment competent in the case of the misdemeanor of a public functionary? Expressly because no remedy was to be found by any other means; because an act had been committed which justice required should be punished, but which could only be reached by Parliament." * * * *
"It happened that the very first impeachment which occurred in the history of Parliament was one which neither related to a public officer nor to any offense known to the law. It was the case of Richard Lyons and others, who were complained of for removing the staple of wool to Paris, for lending money to the king on usurious contracts. The statute against usury had not then been passed, and there were various other charges against the parties which formed

no legal offense. The case was one in which merchants were, among other things, charged with compounding duties with the king for a small percentage."

Also, the "case of Sir Giles Mompessen, for the sale of patents." This was not an indictable offense, and is the more remarkable from being recorded in "Coke's Institutes." Hence we find that in the very inception of trials of impeachment no indictable offense need have been committed.

Again, we find Mr. Brougham stating:

"That the House would exercise the right of impeachment, not because the offense was liable to a five pounds penalty, not because it was indictable, but because some evil had been committed which the ordinary courts of law could not reach. This he conceived was the only constitutional principle upon which impeachment rested." * * * * "The case of Mr. Hastings illustrates his argument, for of the articles of impeachment preferred against him four out of five were for offenses of a nature of which no court of law could take cognizance."—*Vol.* 1, pp. 62 and 63.

I again call attention to the arguments and opinions of learned men of our own country, which most clearly sustain our view on the point now under discussion.

On the trial of Judge Peck Mr. Manager Buchanan says:

"A gross abuse of granted power and an usurpation of power not granted are offenses equally worthy of and liable to impeachment."—*Page* 428.

In the same case Mr. Manager Wickliffe's remarks are so applicable to the conduct of the respondent that I may be pardoned for giving them in this connection. He says:

"Take the case of the President of the United States. Suppose him base enough or foolish enough, if you please, to refuse his sanction to any and every act which Congress may pass. This is a power which, according to the Constitution, he can exercise. Will it be contended that he could be indicted for it as a misdemeanor in any court, State or Federal? Yet, where is the man who would hesitate to remove him from office by impeachment?"—*Peck's Trial,* 1831, p. 309.

In the same case Mr. Wirt, of counsel for the respondent, said:

"The President, Vice President, and all civil officers shall be removed from office on impeachment for and on conviction of treason, bribery, or other high crimes or misdemeanors.' (Constitution, art. 2, sec. 4.) The Constitution itself defines treason, but it does not define bribery, nor does it define those other high crimes and misdemeanors for which these officers may be impeached and removed. Now, what does the Constitution mean by the expression high crimes and misdemeanors? It has a meaning; what is it? and where are you to look for it? The phrase is obviously borrowed from the common law. This instrument thus, by its own terms, connects itself in this instance with the common law, and authorizes you to go to that law for an explanation of its meaning. In the very proceeding, therefore, in which you are now engaged, the common law is in force for the definition of the high crime or misdemeanor which you are called on to punish."—*Peck's Trial,* pp. 498 and 499.

Mr. Story, in discussing what are the functions to be performed in impeachments, says:

"The offenses to which the power of impeachment has been and is ordinarily applied as a remedy, are of a political character," * * * * "what are aptly termed political offenses, growing out of personal misconduct or gross neglect, or usurpations, or habitual disregard of the public interests, in the discharge of duties of political office. These are so various in their character, and so indefinable in their actual involutions, that it is almost impossible to provide systematically for them by positive law. They must be examined upon very broad and comprehensive principles of public policy and duty. They must be judged of by the habits and rules and principles of diplomacy, of departmental operations and arrangements; in short, by a great variety of circumstances, as well those which aggravate as those which extenuate or justify the offensive acts; which do not properly belong to the judicial character in the ordinary administration of justice, and are far removed from the reach of municipal jurisprudence."—*Story on Constitution,* sec. 762.

Treason is defined in the Constitution itself; bribery is defined by common law; and Mr. Story, in discussing the definition of impeachable crimes, says:

"The only practical question is, What are deemed high crimes and misdemeanors? Now, neither the Constitution nor any statute of the United States has in any manner defined any crimes except treason and bribery to be high crimes and misdemeanors, and as such impeachable. In what manner, then, are they to be ascertained? Is the silence of the statute-book to be deemed conclusive in favor of the party until Congress have made a legislative declaration and enumeration of the offenses which shall be deemed high crimes and misdemeanors? If so, then, as has been truly remarked, the power of impeachment, except as to the two expressed cases, is a complete nullity; and the party is wholly dispunishable, however enormous may be his corruption or criminality.—*Story's Com.,* sec. 794.

In further reasoning upon the same subject, he says:

"There are many offenses, purely political, which have been held to be within the reach of parliamentary impeachments, not one of which is in the slightest manner alluded to in our statute-books. And, indeed, political offenses are of so various and complex a character, so utterly incapable of being defined or classified, that the task of positive legislation would be impracticable, if not almost absurd to attempt it." * * * * "The only safe guide, in such cases, must be the common law, which is the guardian at once of private rights and public liberties; and however much it may fall in with the political theories of certain statesmen and jurists, to deny the existence of a common law belonging to and applicable to the nation in ordinary cases, no one yet has been bold enough to assert that the power of impeachment is limited to offenses positively defined in the statute-book of the Union, as impeachable high crimes and misdemeanors."—*Section* 798.

Also, same authority:

"In examining the parliamentary history of impeachments it will be found that many offenses not easily definable by law, and many of a purely political character, have been deemed high crimes and misdemeanors, worthy of this extraordinary remedy. Thus lord chancellors and judges and other magistrates have not only been impeached for bribery and acting grossly contrary to the duties of their office, but for misleading their sovereign by unconstitutional opinions, and for attempts to subvert the fundamental laws, and introduce arbitrary power. So, where a lord chancellor has been thought to have put the great seal to an ignominious treaty; a lord admiral to have neglected the safeguard of the sea; an embassador to have betrayed his trust; a privy counselor to have propounded or supported pernicious and dishonorable measures; or a confidential adviser of his sovereign to have obtained exorbitant grants or incompatible employments—these have been all deemed impeachable offenses."—*Story's Com.,* book 3, chap. 10, sec. 798.

Mr. Story, after his examination of impeachment trials in England and the few cases in this country, came to the following conclusion in regard to the rule applicable to trials of impeachment before the Senate of the United States:

"Congress have unhesitatingly adopted the conclusion that no previous statute is necessary to authorize an impeachment for any official misconduct, and the rules of proceeding and the rules of evidence, as well as the principles of decision, have been uniformly promulgated by the known doctrines of the common law and parliamentary usage. In the few cases of impeachment which have hitherto been tried no one of the charges has rested upon any statutable misdemeanor."—*Story's Com.*, book 3, chap. 10, sec. 797.

Although we have shown that both English and American authorities sustain us in the position that an offense need not be punishable or indictable by statute law to be an impeachable offense, yet we are told that British precedent should not influence the case, because they hold the ministers of the Crown accountable for the honesty, legality, and utility of measures proposed by them, and punishable by impeachment for failure in any of these particulars; yet that construction of the law of impeachable offenses has obtained because Parliament in Great Britain is substantially omnipotent; they may pass *ex post facto*, retroactive laws, bills of attainder, and even change the constitution itself; therefore, that when the Commons present any officer of the Government for any claimed offense, it is not to be considered whether it is made so by any preexisting laws; because, if the Commons impeach and the Peers adjudge the party presented guilty, the joint action of the two Houses would only be in effect to declare the act complained of to be noxious or injurious, although not so enacted by any previous legislation, and that this would be within their clear right. But that our Constitution, by prohibiting the passage of any retroactive or *ex post facto* law or any bill of attainder, has limited impeachment for high crimes and misdemeanors to those acts only which have been declared to be such crimes and misdemeanors by preexisting laws; and, therefore, in this country, whatever might be the case in England, impeachment must be limited to such offenses only as are made so by statute or at common law. There is force and speciousness, to say no more, in this view, and it deserves a careful and candid consideration.

The weight of the argument is derived from the suggestion that the judgment following impeachment is in truth a punishment of crime: that failing the argument fails. True it is, our Constitution forbids the passage of any retroactive or *ex post facto* law, or bill of attainder, as a punishment for crime; but it is equally true that it says that "judgment is cases of impeachment shall not extend further than to removal from office and disqualification to hold and enjoy any office of honor, trust, or profit under the United States; but the party convicted shall, nevertheless, be liable and subject to indictment, trial, judgment, and punishment, according to law." Thus it appears that the judgment of impeachment is not a punishment

for crimes nor misdemeanors, but extends only to removal from office or disqualification to hold office, leaving the party (if a crime is committed) to be punished therefor by other provisions of law, which shall neither be retroactive, *ex post facto*, nor in the nature of a bill of attainder.

This provision would seem, therefore, to make it clear that impeachment is *not* a punishment for crime. True, an officer may be impeached for a crime, technically, either by common or statute law, but he cannot be punished therefor as a part of the judgment of impeachment. He can only be removed from office, and his punishment, if any, is left to the ordinary courts. We are led to consider, therefore, whether, in the language of the Constitution and laws of the United States, the term "removal from office" is anywhere used as the penalty for a crime. Of course that phrase must have the same construction, whether found in the Constitution, which is paramount law only, or in the statutes enacted in conformity with the Constitution, which are equally laws of the United States.

Now, it is admitted by all sides that any officer may be removed under our laws for any reason, no reason, or for political reasons simply, the contest between the Executive and Congress being as to the person or body by whom such removal shall be exercised—whether by the President alone or by the President and Senate in concurrence, or whether such right of removal may be restrained by legislation.

This power of removal by somebody is recognized in a variety of statutes, but nowhere as the penalty for crime. The phrase "removal from office" appears only once in the Constitution. Must it not, therefore, have the same meaning and construction there as it does in the other laws of the United States? Is not this construction of the phrase "removal from office" made certain by the uniform legislation and practice of the Government? And as the phrase "removal from office" is only found in the Constitution as the consequence of conviction upon impeachment, the judgment of which can extend no further than such removal or disqualification for office, is it not equally certain that such judgment is not a punishment for crime, and, therefore, that an officer may be removed by impeachment for political reasons, as he may be for the same reasons by any department of the Government in which the right of removal is vested?

Is not this view of the constitutional provision strengthened by this consideration: that by the theory of and practice under the Constitution, every officer, other than the President and Vice President, may be, and in practice is, removable by the power that appointed him at pleasure; or, in other words, when the service of the Government, in the judgment of the appointing power, seems to make such removal necessary and proper? Is it not, therefore, more consonant with the theory of the Constitution to hold that the President may be removed from office by presentment of the House, who represent in his case the people who appointed him, if the reasons for the removal shall be found sufficient by two thirds of the Senate, who, by the Constitution, are to adjudicate thereupon? Can we not illustrate this by supposing a case of inability in the President to perform the duties of his office because of his insanity? Now, insanity is not a crime, but every act of an insane man might, and almost necessarily would, be a misdemeanor in office.

Is the phrase "misdemeanor in office" any more than the Norman French translation of the English word misbehavior? Judges are to hold office during good behavior. Is not that equivalent to saying they hold office during good demeanor, i. e., while they demean themselves well in office? Are not both phrases the equivalent of the Latin one "dum se bene gesserit?"

How is an insane President or an insane judge to be removed under our Constitution? Clearly not until his insanity is ascertained. By whom is that to be ascertained? The Constitution makes no provision save by presentment by the House, and adjudication by the Senate. And it is remarkable, as sustaining this argument, that the first case of impeachment of a judge under our Constitution, Judge Pickering's, was of an insane man, as the defense allege, and clearly made out by evidence. Judge Pickering was removed, the defense of insanity apparently not being considered by the Senate. Is it not clear that the process of impeachment, under the English constitution, being a mode of punishment of all crimes, as well as a method by which an officer whose official or personal conduct was hurtful to the State might be removed, that our Constitution limiting the form of impeachment to removal only takes away from it its punitive element which it vests in the ordinary courts of law alone; thus leaving the process of impeachment an inquisition of office for any act of the officer or cause which the House of Representatives might present as, and the Senate adjudicate to be, hurtful to the State or injurious to the common weal.

Will any one say that if the President should veto every bill that should pass the Congress—and there not be a two-thirds vote against his veto—and thereby defeat all appropriations, so as to completely block the wheels of Government, that he could not be impeached for an improper use of said power, although he is authorized by the Constitution to use such power? Here would be a case wherein the exercise of lawful power was done in such a way as to become so oppressive and obviously wrong that there must be a remedy, and impeachment would be the only one.

DEFINITION OF CRIMES AND MISDEMEANORS.

Having thus shown that a party can be impeached for offenses not punishable by statute law, it behooves us next to inquire what have been the definitions of crimes and misdemeanors as used by writers of acknowledged authority. It is by the light of these definitions that we are to inquire and determine what culpability, if any, attaches to each and all of the acts by the President of which we complain, and how far he may palliate or justify the act after having admitted its performance. These which I shall read are but few among the many authoritative definitions of crimes and misdemeanors.

What is a crime? Blackstone defines a crime or misdemeanor as being—

"An act committed or omitted in violation of a public law either forbidding or commanding it. This general definition comprehends both crimes and misdemeanors, which, properly speaking, are mere synonymous terms; though in common usage the word crimes is made to denote such offenses as are of deeper and more atrocious dye; while smaller faults and omissions of less consequence are comprised under the gentler name of misdemeanors only."—Blackstone's Commentaries, book 4, p. 5.

"The distinction of public wrongs from private crimes and misdemeanors from civil injuries seems principally to consist in this: that private wrongs or civil injuries are an infringement or privation of the civil rights which belong to individuals merely as individuals; public wrongs or crimes and misdemeanors are a breach and violation of the public rights and duties due to the whole community considered as a community in its social aggregate capacity."—Blackstone's Commentaries, book 4, p. 5.

"When the words high crimes and misdemeanors are used in prosecutions by impeachment, the words high crimes and misdemeanors have no definite signification, but are used merely to give greater solemnity to the charge."—Sentence from a note to Blackstone's Commentaries, 5 Christian.

Or, to state it stronger even than Blackstone does, that the defendant may have the benefit of it, a crime or misdemeanor is the violation of a public law where there shall be a joint operation of act and intention in the perpetration of the act.

Mr. Blake, in discussing Prescott's case, defines a misdemeanor perhaps better than I have heretofore stated it. I will therefore give his definition:

"To misconduct is to misbehave: to misbehave is to misdemean; to misdemean is to be guilty of a misdemeanor—nothing more—nothing less. The term is technical, signifying a crime; hence it follows, as a conclusion from these premises, that misconduct or misbehavior, in its legal interpretation, can signify nothing less.

INTENTION—HOW DETERMINED.

When the unlawful act is shown, how, then, do we gather the intention? It can only be done from all the circumstances surrounding the commission of the act.

I believe it is a rule, both in law and morals, that every man is presumed to intend the natural and probable consequences of his own act. A good motive never accompanies a bad act, nor a bad one a good act.

Mr. Buchanan, in the trial of Judge Peck, states this proposition so clearly that I will adopt his language, (with his quotations):

"'Out of the abundance of the heart the mouth speaketh,' 'The tree is known by the fruit,' are axioms which we have derived from the fountain of all truth. Actions speak louder than words, and it is from the criminal actions the judges must infer the criminal intention."

Speaking of the respondent, Peck, he says:

"If he shall, in an arbitrary manner and without the authority of law, imprison a citizen of this country and thus consign him to infamy, are you not to infer his intention from the act? Is not the act itself the best source from which to draw the inference? Must we, without any evidence, in the spirit of false charity and mercy ramble out of the record to imagine a good motive for this bad conduct? Such rule of decision would defeat the execution of all human laws. No man can doubt but that many a traitor during the American Revolution believed in his conscience that he owed allegiance to the king of Great Britain and would violate his duty to God if he should lend the least aid in the cause of freedom. But if such a man had committed treasonable acts, will any person say he was not guilty of treason because in his secret heart he *might* have had a good intention? Does a poor, hungry, naked wretch filch from my pocket a single dollar to satisfy the cravings of appetite, the law infers a felonious intent, and he must be convicted and punished as a thief, though he may have had no other purpose but that of saving himself and his children from starvation. And shall a man who has been selected to fill a high judicial position on account of his knowledge of the laws of the land be permitted to come before the Senate and say: 'It is very true that I *did*, against law, imprison an American citizen and deprive him for eighteen months of practising that profession by which he lived; it is true that I violated the Constitution of the United States by inflicting on him unusual punishment, but I did not know any better; I had a good intention.'"

And, Mr. President, in the case at bar are we to be told that this violation of law carries with it no bad motive, that the law was broken merely to test its strength? Is a man to be permitted to break a law under the pretense of testing its constitutionality? Are the opinions of a man against the soundness of a law to shield him from punishment for the violation of said law? If so, the opinion of the criminal becomes the rule by which you are to try him, instead of the law which he has broken. If this doctrine be established every traitor in the land will find a complete justification for his many crimes against the Government of the United States in this: that he believed that secession was no violation of the Constitution. Doubtless every robber and murderer has some reason by which he justifies himself in his own mind for the commission of his crimes. But is that a justification or excuse in law? Had Booth (the assassin) been captured alive, doubtless on his trial he would have said that he thought he was doing no wrong in murdering the President, could he thereby have advanced the interests of his friends in the South; and would have also stated, no doubt, that he was advised by his friends to commit the act. And the accused claims the same as an excuse for his conduct. He claims that he was advised by his ministers at the heads of the different branches of the executive department. But, sir, in neither case can such an excuse be considered as in the least manner forming any justification or excuse in law. This plea, answer, or excuse pleaded, if believed by the President and his

C. I.—34.

learned counsel as being any excuse whatever for his violations of law, we may here get some clue to the hesitancy in the trial of Jefferson Davis, the great criminal of the rebellion, (inasmuch as he certainly believed he was doing no wrong in breaking the law, as his opinion was that he was maintaining a great principle.) As the counsel, or a part of them, who now defend the President on this principle, must prosecute Jeff. Davis against this principle, it would seem that, by adopting this theory, they will succeed in releasing both instead of convicting either.

Sirs, adopt this new theory, and you thereby unhinge the law, open wide the prison gates, and give safe conduct to every criminal in the land, no matter how high or low his position, or how grave or small his offenses.

Having thus shown what are impeachable offenses, the definition of crimes and misdemeanors, and how we are to gather the intention of the accused in the violation of a law, it becomes necessary to examine somewhat the basis of the justification stated by the defendant for his action.

RESPONDENT'S DEFENSE TO FIRST TWO CHARGES.

The respondent admits the facts upon which the first charge rests, but denies that they constitute an offense for which he is answerable to this Senate, sitting as a court of impeachment. This denial involves two inquiries:

1. HAD THE PRESIDENT THE POWER TO REMOVE THE SECRETARY OF WAR UNDER THE CIRCUMSTANCES BY VIRTUE OF THE CONSTITUTION AND THE LAWS AS THEY STOOD PRIOR TO THE PASSAGE OF THE TENURE-OF-OFFICE ACT?

2. HAD HE THE RIGHT TO REMOVE THAT OFFICER UNDER THE TENURE-OF-OFFICE ACT?

It must be conceded that a negative answer to either of these propositions is equivalent to a verdict of guilty. The respondent has stated his defense upon the highest possible grounds, and it is of the first importance that his reasons be put to the severest test, for they underlie the whole network of our admirable system of Government. The question here involved was crowded into the smallest compass by the respondent's distinguished premier, on a memorable occasion, when he put to a gaping multitude, heated by the inflammatory speech of this respondent, this question: "Will you have Andrew Johnson President or king?"

Sir, it was gratuitous in this respondent to attempt to purge himself by his answer of an intent to violate the Constitution and laws of the land. His answer stands upon a right which he claims began with his high office, and has clung to the President as an undisputed prerogative since the days of .Washington by virtue of the Constitution. If he is right, the motive, whether good or bad, cannot make him answerable; if he was wrong, the motive follows. The innocent violation of a law is not supposable. If there was in this action of the President the exercise of a rightful power he must be acquitted of this charge; if he acted outside and in violation of law he must be convicted, whatever his motive. Let us, then, examine the two inquiries suggested:

Sirs, I think there exists a widespread and dangerous misapprehension as to the powers and prerogatives of the President. We have been in the habit of speaking of three coördinate branches of Government in such connection and in such manner as to imply that each possesses coequal power with the other. One of the transcendently valuable results of the late war has been the fixing the powers of our three branches of Government where they properly belong, the resolving of hitherto blended powers into the original elements of Government. The rebellion was a war of encroachments upon the rights of the people. The people triumphed, and they now insist that the victory shall not be a barren one.

I hold that the President of the United States possesses no power other than that given him by the Constitution and the laws; and I mean by this that there are no *inherent* powers in the Executive, no *reserved* authority, no *implied* prerogatives other than those which are necessarily dependent upon and derivable from the expressed constitutional provisions and the laws.

With the evils of a monarchy so fresh in their memory the framers of the Constitution sought to surround the President with such checks as to make him a mere *executive officer*—the *servant* of the people. His powers were specifically defined and confined to the narrowest compass; except the high honor of receiving embassies as the representative of the Government, he was stripped of all attributes of sovereignty; he was given no jurisdiction over the legislative or judicial branches, but, on the contrary, was made amenable to the former for his unofficial as well as official conduct; he can create no office, and his appointing power is only conditional; he is unable to declare war or alone make treaties; his authority is mainly *negative*, confined chiefly to offering suggestions to Congress; granting pardons and reprieves, to concluding treaties and appointing embassadors and other public officers " by and with the advice and consent of the Senate." He is the Executive *only*, and "*shall* take care that *the laws* be faithfully executed." He is without the least judicial attribute; and Mr. Kent says:

"When laws are duly made and promulgated they only remain to be executed. No discretion is submitted to the executive officer. It is not for him to deliberate and decide upon the expediency of the law. *What has been once declared to be law under all the cautious forms of deliberation prescribed by the Constitution ought to receive prompt obedience.*"—*Kent's Commentaries*, vol. 1, p. 291.

To the legislative is given the power of supervising the Executive's acts, and to remove him from office for " high crimes and misdemeanors." At the time of the formation of our Government so jealous were the people of their rights and so fearful lest the President might assume undue authority and obtain the power of a monarch, that it was only by the most strenuous exertions of the friends of the proposed Constitution, in triumphantly showing that this power of removal made him subservient to Congress, that the public mind became reconciled, and the Constitution was finally accepted by the people. They seemed even then to well understand their rights. The great danger attending the appointing power was perceived. Then, as now, the people feared the enormous patronage of the Executive if left unrestricted, and they appreciated the fact so patent to-day that lust for power would be likely to corrupt officials and cause them to

"Crook the pregnant hinges of the knee, Where thrift may follow fawning."

Hence, as was thought, " effective measures of keeping officials virtuous while they continue to hold their public trusts" were interposed by making the appointing power a dependency upon the Senate. However we may guard this power, it will ever be liable to be made a source of corruption. Office will be the bribe held out by unprincipled Executives: and at all times there will be found men base enough to accept that bribe. This evil is unavoidable, and to save the nation as far as possible from this curse is appointment made a joint power. The second clause of section two, article two, of the Constitution, says:

"He shall have power, by and with the advice and consent of the Senate, to make treaties, provided two thirds of the Senators present concur; and he shall nominate, and by and with the advice and consent of the Senate shall appoint, embassadors, other public ministers and consuls, judges of the Supreme Court, and all other officers of the United States whose appointments are not herein otherwise provided for."

No shadow of authority is here given to the President alone to appoint any officer whatever, not even the most inferior, except as invested with power by Congress; on the contrary, it is made a joint act of the President *and Senate*. And why was this made a joint power? In order to protect public interests, to prevent a vicious Executive from displacing faithful officers and supplanting them with his own tools and confederates; to prevent the consummation of just such a conspiracy as was conceived by the respondent to obtain possession of all departments of Government, and to use the power thus obtained against the people, even if it involved another great national strife and appeal to arms. But, whatever may have been the reasons which led to this being made a coöperative power of the President and Senate, the *fact* that it is thus made stands uncontroverted, and cannot be explained away. Words have lost their meaning if other construction be put upon it. I wish, however, to direct attention to the remarkable connection of the appointing with another—the treaty-making power. Manifestly the framers of the Constitution had some object in thus blending the two powers; and the reasons given for making the President and Senate parties to treaties apply with equal force to the appointing power. Both the Senate and President are necessary to make a treaty; and in the same sentence the same parties are made the appointing power. Reckless of his acts as has been the respondent in this case, and regardless as he has proved of the Constitution, he has never yet dared to assume to be the sole treaty-making power in this Government; that, without the concurrence of the Senate, he can conclude treaties and annul them. Sirs, under the Constitution the treaty-making and appointing powers are identical; the same parties that make treaties make appointments; the President and Senate are both as essential in perfecting appointments as in making a treaty. And happy for the American people is this so, or would we again have the din of battle ringing in our ears and war once more sweeping over the land.

Human genius has not yet been able to frame a rule for government in which all the powers are so perfectly defined and balanced as to be literally equal. Our own Constitution more nearly approaches such a form than any other that has been given to the world; but even in this instrument, framed by the wisest patriots of the age, one branch in the Government is made superior to the others. This superiority follows from the nature of the duties with which each branch is intrusted and the necessity of some controlling influence—the exponent of the people's will—in order to check usurpations and correct abuses, which in a republic are likely to arise in departments not directly responsible to the people. The grand object to be attained by our Constitution was the consolidation of the several States into one nation by such a compact as would secure "the greatest good to the greatest number." It was to be a Government *of* the people, *for the people.* The experience of ages had shown the necessity of a division of powers, and that one of these powers should possess an influence superior to that of the others; but no one power was made supreme or wholly independent of its contemporaries. The judiciary is eminently "conservative" in its character; it is dependent upon the executive and legislative for its existence and perpetuity, is without creative authority, and its duties are mainly those of an advisory character.

That controlling influence in this great trinity of powers which form our Government is the people, acting through their chosen Representatives in Congress assembled. Even the most casual reader of the Constitution must see that such was the intent of its framers from the wide range of authority delegated, even to regulating the executive and judiciary.

The Constitution lays down this great fundamental principle: "All power is derived from the people." Congress is the only branch in our Government chosen directly from and by the people. The frequency of elections enables the people to change or ratify any policy that Congress may adopt by retiring its members or indorsing their acts by reëlection. This makes the legislative the mouth-piece of the people; to the people alone is Congress responsible, and it is through Congress the people are immediately represented in the Government. The magnitude of the duties assigned to the legislative, and the authority given that branch over the executive and judiciary, aside from the imperative necessity, fully sustain the assumption that the legislative is the superior power in the three departments of Government mentioned in our Constitution. Indeed, upon no other theory could the Government be sustained. This control of the people in their Government is the great feature in republicanism; this power of the many is the distinctive character of our Constitution. While the power of the executive is qualified and restricted by the legislative, the authority of the latter is uncontrolled by any other department. It makes and unmakes; it removes presidents, judges, and other civil officers who may be guilty of high crimes and misdemeanors, and sweeps away all obstacles in the way of the nation's advancement and prosperity, and from its verdict, in a case of trial as this, there is no appeal.

A further examination of section two, article two, will disclose a peculiarity of expression which is important. "He shall nominate, and by and with the advice and consent of the Senate shall appoint," "all officers," &c. The very first step in the matter of appointment is by the Constitution given to the President to "nominate." The appointment is still inchoate. The next step is the concurrence of the Senate, and this completes the ceremony of appointment. It then becomes the duty of the President to issue the commission. In the case of Marbury *vs.* Madison (1 Cranch, 137, 156) it was distinctly affirmed in the opinion of the court that the President could not withhold a commission from an officer nominated and confirmed. (See, also, Story on the Constitution, section 1537.) It is the essence of all contracts or matters in which two or more are to act that their minds must meet and concur, and when this is done the act is complete, and is thenceforward beyond the control of one without the consent of the other. But note again, the Constitution does not confer the power on the President to "appoint." His power is to "nominate," and when the Senate concur, and not till then, is he empowered to "appoint," and in doing this he merely carries out the previously determined wish of both parties to the appointment. In Marbury *vs.* Madison the court says, to "appoint and commission are not one and the same thing."

In the United States *vs.* LeBaron (19 Howard, 74) the court says the commission is not necessarily the appointment, although conclusive evidence of the fact. It would have been the simplest thing to have stripped this question of all doubt when the Constitution was framed had there been a disposition to confer the authority upon the Executive here claimed in the defense. We know that the very matter now before this honorable body was discussed then, so that it cannot now be said we are called upon to decide new questions. By what right, then, or upon what principle of construction, can you interpolate language into the Contution or give the language already there a meaning contrary to its letter?

Mr. Sedgwick, in his work on Construction, says:

"Where there is no obscurity in the effect of the laws, and the object aimed at by the Legislature, we are not permitted to inquire into motives of the Legislature. In order to defeat the law itself, *a fortiori* any law subsequently passed on the same subject."—*Sedgwick*, p. 295; *Dunn vs. Reid*, 10 Peters, 524.

If this is true of statutes, it is much more a just rule in searching for the meaning of a fundamental law. I insist that the Constitution is perfectly clear and unambiguous upon the subject of appointment. There should be no division of opinion on this one point, it does seem to me. Attorney General Legare says:

"The people, however, were wisely jealous of this great power of appointing the agents of the executive department, and chose to restrain it by requiring it in all cases to *nominate*; but only in case it had the concurrence of the Senate to appoint."—3 *Opinions*, p. 675.

But let us look further into this section. I have already alluded to the matter, but will repeat it in this connection. The language is: "But the Congress may by law vest the appointment of such inferior officers as they think proper in the President alone." Now, sirs, there is a familiar maxim—"*expressio unius est exclusio alterius*"—which here prevails. The President is, by this clause, empowered to appoint such inferior officers as Congress may by law direct. Is it too much to urge that, by naming these particularly, and no others, it was intended he should alone appoint no others? But, sirs, even the maximum of the law need not here be invoked. The Constitution not only expresses one, and thus excludes others, but it expresses all—*i. e.*, it provides for the appointment of all officers of the Government, and prescribes the manner of appointment in this section. First, it gives the President and the Senate the power to appoint a certain class; and second, it gives Congress power to allow the President alone, the courts of law, or the heads of Departments, to appoint certain others; and these cover the whole range of officers of the Government; and, to my mind, it is the wildest reasoning that can vault itself into the position claimed by the respondent.

Chief Justice Best, in 5 Bingham, page 180, gives a rule directly applicable here:

"Where a general intention is expressed, and the act expresses also a particular intention incompatible with the general intention, the particular intention is to be considered an exception."

The general intention of the framers of the Constitution was to make the appointing power joint with the President and Senate, and the exception only makes more imperative the general intention.

The inconvenience of uniting these powers in the multitude of minor officers made the exception necessary, but the general intention was only the more distinctly asserted.

But this power of removal, as implied from the power of appointment, is further shown to rest in the Senate and the President conjointly, by the adoption of the third section of the second article, which provides that—

"The President shall have power to fill up all vacancies that may happen during the recess of the Senate by granting commissions which shall expire at the end of the next session."

Mr. Wirt says:

"The meaning of the Constitution seems to me to result in this: that the President alone cannot make a permanent appointment to those offices; that to render the appointment permanent it must receive the consent of the Senate; but that whenever a vacancy shall exist which the public interests require should be immediately filled, and in filling which the advice and consent of the Senate cannot be immediately asked, because of their recess, the President shall have power of filling it by an appointment which shall continue only until the Senate shall have passed upon it, or, in the language of the Constitution, 'till the end of the next session.'"

I am not here discussing the question of vacancies and the power to fill them under the Constitution, but I desire to show that this particular clause of the Constitution now being noticed furnishes strong and direct evidence that the appointing power was intended to be kept undivided in the Senate and President, except in those cases where the two could not from some uncontrollable necessity act at the time. Hence we find Mr. Story holding what I think to be the undisputed construction of the clause, that—

"If the Senate are in session when offices are created by law, and nominations are not made to them by the President, he cannot appoint to such offices during the recess of the Senate, because a vacancy does not happen during the recess of the Senate. In many instances where offices are created by law special power is on this very account given to the President to fill them during the recess; and it was then said that in no other instances had the President filled such vacant offices without the special authority of law."—2 *Story*, paragraph 1559.

This author says again, in paragraph 1557:

"There was but one of two courses to be adopted, either that the Senate should perpetually be in session, in order to provide for the appointment of officers, or that the President should be authorized to make temporary appointments during the recess, which should expire when the Senate should have had an opportunity to act on the subject."

This distinction between temporary and permanent appointments is recognized in the case of the United States *vs.* Kirkpatrick, 9 Wheaton, page 720. The independent action of the President, in violation of the wishes of the Senate, seems not to have been anticipated. In a long list of casualties given by Mr. Wirt, in the opinion referred to, he had in mind only those causes which could not be foreseen as preventing the coöperation of the Senate.

It has been uniformly held that if vacancies are known to exist during the session of the Senate, and nominations are not then made, they cannot be filled by Executive appointment during a recess of the Senate. (4 Opinions, p. 362.) This would not be true if it were unimportant whether the Senate participated in the appointment.

It is urged here that the President not only has the power to appoint, but that, having that power, he may also remove, as a necessary incident. I will admit that if it can be shown that the President may alone appoint to office, then if the tenure of the office is not fixed but remains at the pleasure of the President he may, unquestionably, remove that officer. But, sir, I shall show hereafter that the doctrine of incidental power goes no further than to extend to the President when he alone has the appointing power. I deny that the President anywhere has that power save when conferred by Congress as prescribed by the Constitution. Besides, Mr. President, I assert that, prior to the opinion rendered by the late Attorney General, there can be nowhere found an authority going so far as did that learned gentleman. What says history upon this subject? Hamilton said, in No. 77 of the Federalist:

"It has been mentioned as one of the advantages to be expected from the coöperation of the Senate, in the business of appointments that it would contribute to the stability of the Administration. The consent of that body would be necessary to displace as well as appoint. The change of the Chief Magistrate, therefore, would not occasion so violent or so general a revolution in the officers of the Government as might be expected if he were the sole disposer of offices. When a man in any station had given satisfactory evidence of his fitness for it a new President would be restrained from attempting a change in favor of a person more agreeable to him by the apprehension that the discountenance of the Senate might frustrate the attempt and bring some degree of discredit upon himself. Those who can best estimate the value of a steady administration will be most disposed to prize a provision which connects the official existence of public men with the approbation or disapprobation of that body which, from the greater permanency of its own composition, will, in all probability, be less subject to inconstancy than any other member of the Government. To this union of the Senate with the President in the article of appointments it has, in some cases, been objected that it would serve to give the President an *undue influence over the Senate*, because the Senate would have the power of *restraining* him. This is an absurdity in terms. It cannot admit of doubt that the entire power of appointment would enable him much more effectually to establish a dangerous empire over that body than a mere power of nomination subject to their control."

Mr. Hamilton then proceeds to review, in a masterly manner, the structure and power of the executive department, and in conclusion refers to the many restraints thrown around the Executive, and, speaking to this matter of appointing power, says: "In the only instance in which the abuse of the executive authority was materially to be feared the Chief Magistrate would, by that plan, (speaking of the Constitution,) be subjected to the control of a branch of the legislative body," and asks: "What more can an enlightened and reasonable people desire?"

In No. 76 of the Federalist the writer examines at more length the reasons which led to the adoption of this joint plan of appointment, instead of conferring the entire power upon the President; and he shows that the power given to the President was solely to *nominate*, while the President and Senate *appoint*. He shows that as the President must first nominate he can always, even if the Senate reject, send back the name of some one of his choice; and this should satisfy those who insist upon giving supreme power of appointment to the Executive. He then asks:

"To what purpose, then, require coöperation of the Senate? I answer that the necessity of the concurrence would have a powerful, though in general silent, operation. It would be an excellent check upon a spirit of favoritism in the President, and would tend greatly to prevent the appointment of unfit characters from State prejudice, from family connection, from personal attachment, or from a view to popularity. In addition to this, it would be an efficacious source of stability in an Administration." * * * * "It will readily be comprehended that a man who had himself the sole disposition of offices would be governed much more by his private inclinations and interests than when he was bound to submit the propriety of his choice to the decision and determination of a different and independent body, and that body an entire branch of the Legislature."

Now, sirs, I aver that at the time Hamilton wrote it will be found in this matter he expressed not only his own views, but the views of the people who adopted the Constitution.

Mr. Madison at this time entertained no other view, and his opinions had a large influence upon the people, and contributed, probably, more than those of any other one public man in bringing about the adoption of the Constitution. In No. 47 of the Federalist he argues at length to show that the maxim of Montesquieu, which requires a separation of the departments of power to secure liberty, is not true, and has not been without exception in any Government other than an absolute monarchy. He then shows that by the British constitution the departments of Government are not distinctive, but that one branch of the legislative forms, like our Senate, a great constitutional council to the chief executive; it is the sole depository of judicial power in impeachment, and is the supreme appellate jurisdiction in other cases. And the judges are so far connected with the legislative as to attend and participate in the deliberations, though not to vote.

Mr. Madison then shows that, notwithstanding the unqualified terms in which the axiom of Montesquieu is laid down by the Constitution of the States of the Confederation, there was not a single instance in which the several departments of power have been kept absolutely separate and distinct.

In New Hampshire the Senate had the right of trial by impeachment. The president, who was the head of the executive department, was the presiding member of the Senate, and had a casting vote. The Legislature elected the executive, and his council were chosen from the Legislature. Some State officers were appointed by the Legislature, while the judiciary were appointed by the executive.

In Massachusetts the judiciary were appointed by the executive, and were removable by him on an address of the two branches of the Legislature. Many officers of the State (some of them executive) were appointed by the Legislature.

He passes over Rhode Island and Connecticut, as their constitutions were adopted before the Revolution and before the principles under examination had become an object of attention.

In New York the powers of government were curiously blended. The executive had a partial control over the legislative, and a like control over the judiciary, and even blended the executive and judiciary in the exercise of this control. There was a council of appointment composed of the executive and partly of the legislative, which appointed both executive and judicial officers.

New Jersey blended the powers of government more than either of the foregoing. The Governor, who was the executive, was appointed by the Legislature, and yet he was not only the executive, but he was chancellor and surrogate of the State; he was a member of the supreme court of appeals and president, with a casting vote, of one of the legislative branches. This same legislative branch acted again as executive council of the Governor, and with him constituted the court of appeals. The judiciary were appointed by the Legislature.

Pennsylvania, Delaware, Maryland, Virginia, North Carolina, South Carolina, and Georgia, all had the same system of blended powers. In some of them even justices of the peace were appointed by the Legislature.

It is scarcely possible to find anywhere in contemporary history a stronger proof of the jealousy with which the people clung to their right to control their own political affairs; and it was a great concession of the States of the Confederacy to the Union under the Constitution when they assented to the clause now being considered. In every State of the Confederacy, at the time they were called upon to adopt the Constitution, the people, through the Legislatures, not only made the laws, but they appointed the officers who were to execute them; and not only this, but provided for their removal in the same manner. They seemed to have regarded the Chief Executive as an officer designated to assist the execution of the laws, but that it was unsafe to give him power to appoint those who were to coöperate with him in this duty.

I say it was a great concession, and a radical change which conferred upon the President of the United States even the prerogatives which are now undisputed.

Sirs, the people who adopted the Constitution were unaccustomed to looking upon their executives as standing high above them and distributing the powers which they alone possessed. They had never been in the habit of clothing them with imperial powers, or permitting them to suppose for a moment that they were a distinct and separate entity of government. They had never, in a single instance, given to a State executive a distinct existence separate from his legislative and judicial departments. He always acted conjointly, and upon the question of appointments to and removal from office, more than upon any other, they seemed to have been cautious.

With the light of this history it is monstrous to suppose that the people parted with their power, as is claimed by the respondent, in adopting the article under discussion, that they gave up without a word of dissent all those checks upon the Executive with which they had been so familiar and which they had so uniformly adopted in their State governments.

They did no such thing, Mr. President, and nowhere can it be shown they intended any such thing. On the contrary, we have seen that this clause of the Constitution was urged upon them for the very reason that it practically secured to them a system with which they had been so long familiar. The debates at that time show that the Constitution was adopted under the impression that this clause gave the power of appointment and removal jointly to the Senate and President, and they show, too, that the clause was framed to meet this view. I say, then, it is unwarrantable, upon any principle of constitutional or statutory construction, to give the instrument any other meaning.

As well might you annul an ordinary contract upon declarations given after it is signed. The most that can be shown is what the parties said at the time it was made, and the written compact is conclusive of the meaning expressed. We have seen how the people felt at the time. We have seen what two great writers upon the subject said at the time, and that their opinions influenced largely the adoption of the Constitution. Upon the question under discussion at that time there seemed but one mind.

Mr. President, I think I do not state it too strongly in saying that prior to the meeting of the First Congress, and at the time the Constitution was adopted, none of the friends of the Constitution claimed the power for the President which is now urged. Some of its enemies made the charge, but it was denied by its friends. No man in this country has studied more carefully the history on the subject than Mr. Story. He says in his Commentaries on the Constitution, (pages 15, 39, 40, 41,) that the doctrine (speaking of the same construction urged by the Managers) was maintained, with great earnestness, by the earliest writers, and says that at this period the friends of the Constitution had no other view. He cites 5 Marshall's Life of Washington, chapter 3, page 198, and 1 Lloyd's Debates, 351, 366, 450.

Of the effect of these opinions upon the public mind at that time this writer says:

"This was the doctrine maintained with great earnestness by the Federalists, and it had a most material tendency to quiet the just alarms of the overwhelming influence and arbitrary exercise of this prerogative of the Executive, which might prove fatal to the personal independence and freedom of opinion of public officers, as well as to the public liberties of the country."—*Story's Commentaries*, sec. 1539; *Story on Constitution*, vol. 2, p. 400.

I have been endeavoring to show that at the adoption of the Constitution the appointing power was regarded and made a joint power between the Senate and the President, as was also the power of removal. I think this position well established.

I have thus fully discussed the appointing power directly with the Senate because the same reasons that required that power to be joint apply with equal force to the power of removal.

Let us come down, however, to a period subsequent to the adoption of the Constitution. Congress met March 4, 1789, and continued until September 29, of the same year. On the 27th of July they passed the act organizing the Department of Foreign Affairs, and on the 6th of August following, was passed the act organizing the Department of War. These two acts are identical in language in every particular, except the assignment of duties to the different principal officers of the Department. As much of the argument hinges on the law organizing the Department of War at this time, it is important to know just what was said and done at the time. There are some peculiarities of the law to which I invite attention.

Section one provides that—

"There shall be an executive Department to be denominated the Department of War, and that there shall be a principal officer therein, to be called the Secretary for the Department of War, who shall perform and execute such duties as shall from time to time be enjoined upon him by the President of the United States, agreeably to the Constitution, relative to military commissions, or to the land or naval forces, ships or warlike stores of the United States, or to such other matters respecting military or naval affairs as the President of the United States shall assign to said Department, or relative to the granting of lands to persons entitled thereto for military services rendered to the United States, or relating to Indian affairs; and furthermore, that the said principal officer shall conduct the business of the said Department in such manner as the President of the United States shall from time to time order or direct."

"Sec. 2. That there shall be in the said Department an inferior officer, to be appointed by the said principal officer, to be employed therein as he shall deem proper, and to be called the chief clerk in the Department of War, and who, whenever the said principal officer shall be removed from office by the President of the United States, or in any other case of vacancy, shall, during such vacancy, have charge and custody of all records, books, and papers appertaining to the said Department."

"Sec. 3. The said principal officer, and every other person to be appointed or employed in the said Department, shall, before he enters on the execution of his office or employment, take an oath or affirmation well and faithfully to execute the trust committed to him."

"Sec. 4. The Secretary for the Department of War, to be appointed in consequence of this act, shall forthwith, after his appointment, be entitled to have the custody and charge of all records, books, and papers in the office of Secretary for the Department of War, heretofore established by the United States in Congress assembled."

It is noticeable that the law nowhere provides how or by whom the principal officer is to be appointed. The language of the law is, in the first section, "there shall be a principal officer;" in the third section, "that the said principal officer and every other person to be appointed or employed in said Department," &c., shall take an oath, &c.; in section four, "that the Secretary for the Department of War, to be appointed in consequence of this act, shall forthwith, after his appointment, be entitled to have custody and charge of all records," &c. It has been uniformly held that where no provision is made in the law for the appointment of the officer, the appointment must be made by and with the advice and consent of the Senate. (6 Attorney Generals' Opinions, p. 1.) This results necessarily from the language of the Constitution. No provision was made in the laws organizing either of the Executive Departments as to how the principal officers were to be appointed; they were, therefore, all appointed by and with the advice and consent of the Senate. Is it not fair to suppose the removal was to take place in the same manner? On the same day the War Department was created Congress passed an act giving the President power expressed to remove the Governor and other officers of the Territory organized under the ordinance of 1787, and yet these officers were by the same act to be appointed by and with the advice and consent of the Senate. Is it probable that Congress would have made special provision for the exercise of power in one case, if they had supposed that power incident to the share the President took in the appointment? The act, it seems to me, clearly indicates that Congress regarded legislation necessary to confer the power, else it was needless to have legislated at all upon the subject.

But it is urged that the second section of the War Department act *does* confer this power, absolutely. I say not. The second section provides for the appointment, by the Secretary of War, of an inferior officer, to be called the "chief clerk," who, whenever the said principal officer (the Secretary) shall be removed by the President of the United States, or in any other case of vacancy, shall, during such vacancy, have charge, &c.

There is a marked difference of expression between the act I have referred to, as passed upon the same day, and this. In the one the absolute power of revoking commissions and removing is conferred; in the other the expression, "whenever the said principal officer shall be removed from office by the President," &c. Now, sirs, I think that the utmost which can be claimed from this grant, is recognition of a qualified and limited power over the Secretary of War, in case his removal should become necessary at a time when by the exercise of it a vacancy would be made at a time when the Senate could not assist in filling it. Provision had to be made for this, as the discussions at the time show, and I think the language means nothing more than that the President was to exercise the same and no more power than would be conceded to him in the entire absence of any provision on the subject. This law did not take the case out of the constitutional limitation, and by no legal interpretation can it be held to do so.

When the bill for organizing the Department of Foreign Affairs was under discussion, the original draft read "to be removed by the President." Upon this arose all the discussion which is chiefly relied upon by the counsel for the respondent. Whatever may or may not be proved by that discussion, one thing is observable, namely, the language of the first draft was materially changed, and, as finally adopted, left the question upon inference merely. Instead of declaring that this officer is removable by the President, in plain and unmistakable phrase, an equivocal expression was finally adopted, which it was thought would partially meet the views of the majority and yet decide nothing absolutely.

But let us notice for a moment this discussion of 1789. I am not inclined to underrate the value of that debate, but as forming any rule or guide for us I cannot give it great importance. The leading mind which controlled the removal party was that of Mr. Madison, and he, it is known, argued against his views expressed before the Constitution was adopted. Whether he began to have glimmering hopes of the Presidency himself I will not say, but it certainly detracts from the value of his opinions to know that his views expressed after the Constitution was adopted were different from those entertained when he was urging its adoption. But, as I understand that discussion, the argument turned largely upon the necessity of this power resting somewhere at a time when there was a pressing emergency for its exercise.

The first proposition was made by Mr. Madison that there be established an Executive Department, comprising the Departments of Foreign Affairs, of the War, and of the Treasury, tne chief officers thereof to be called Secretaries; to be nominated by the President and appointed by and with the advice and consent of the Senate, and "to be removable by the President." This resolution was finally made the basis for three separate bills, couched in similar language, creating the Department of Foreign Affairs, Department of the Treasury, and Department of War. The bill creating the Department of Foreign Affairs was first taken up, and gave rise to a long discussion. This bill was amended by inserting in the second article words implying the right of the President to remove the Secretary, and was subsequently amended by striking out of the first article the authority of the President to make such removals. This last amendment was carried by a vote of 81 ayes to 19 noes, and the bill, as amended, passed the House by a vote of 29 to 22. In the Senate the bill was carried by the casting vote of the Vice President.

It is an easily understood principle that where two or more unite in an act they may delegate the authority in all to any one of the number; and this, we may say, was done inferentially by the vote I have noticed. But, sirs, the Senate has since spoken upon this very subject many times, as I shall show, and on every occasion in unmistakable condemnation of the principle laid down by the respondent.

When John Quincy Adams, in 1826, attempted to entangle the United States in an alliance with the new republics of South America, and to establish what was popularly termed the "Panama mission," this encroachment upon legislative prerogative was sturdily resisted; the Senate insisting upon its rights to the utmost, even to contending that when a new mission is created it creates a new office, which does not come under the class of vacancies, and therefore the President has no right to fill it by a temporary appointment.

Under every Administration since the days of Monroe we observe attempts by the Executive to monopolize the right of appointment; but in every instance these encroachments were resisted, the Senate successfully asserting its joint authority to appoint and remove. In the session of 1825–26, warned by the attempted exercise of this assumed power by Mr. Adams in the case of the Panama mission, a select committee was appointed by the Senate, charged with an inquiry into the expediency of reducing executive patronage, which committee reported six bills, intended to control and regulate different branches of the public service and limit some exercises of executive power. In one of the six bills, to secure in office faithful collectors and disbursers of the revenue, the President was required to report to Congress the causes for each removal. The section of the bill to that effect reads:

"That in all nominations made by the President to the Senate to fill vacancies occasioned by an exercise of the President's power to remove from office the fact of the removal shall be stated to the Senate at the same time that the nomination is made, with a statement of the reasons for which such officer may have been removed."

Benton says this was intended to operate as a restraint upon removals without cause, and—

"Was a recognition of a principle essential to the proper exercise of the appointing power, and entirely consonant with Mr. Jefferson's idea of removals, but never admitted by any Administration nor enforced by the Senate against any one—always waiting the legal enactment. The opinion of nine such Senators as composed the committee who proposed to legalize this principle, all of them democratic and most of them aged and experienced, should stand for a persuasive reason why this principle should be legalized."—Benton's Thirty Years' View, vol. 1, chap. 29.

During Jackson's administration this power

of removal, as claimed by the accused, came before the Senate many times, and never but to receive a decided condemnation. Upon the breaking up of Jackson's first Cabinet Mr. Van Buren was nominated to the Senate as minister to England. His confirmation was opposed for several reasons, and among them it was charged that he introduced, as Jackson's Secretary of State, a system of proscription or removal for opinion's sake, and a formal motion was made by Mr. Holmes, of Maine, to raise a committee, with power to send for persons and papers, to inquire into the charges and report to the Senate. But this looked so much like an impeachment of the President that it was dropped. The same reasons for the rejection were urged, however. Among those who insisted upon the rejection for the reason I have stated, among others, were Clay, Webster, Clayton, Colonel Hayne of South Carolina, Governor Moore of Alabama, and not least on the list was Thomas Ewing of Ohio. Van Buren was rejected, and the right of the Senate and the truth of the principle I now insist upon were vindicated.

During Jackson's second term the question came up before the Senate in a different form. The offices of bank directors to the United States Bank were about to be vacated by limitation of their term. Jackson desired the reappointment of, and accordingly nominated, the incumbents. The Senate, for their own reasons, rejected the nominees. Jackson then attempted to coerce the Senate into the appointment, and accordingly sent the same names back, intimating in his message that he would nominate no others. The nominations were sent to a committee, who reported a resolution recommending rejection, which was immediately adopted. The report was an able review of the power of the Senate, and concludes as follows:

"The Senate perceive, with regret, an intimation in the message that the President may not see fit to send to the Senate the names of any other persons to be directors of the bank except those whose nominations have been already rejected. While the Senate will exercise its own rights according to its own views of duty, it will leave to the other officers of the Government to decide for themselves on the manner they will perform their duties. The committee know no reasons why these offices should not be filled; or why, in this case, no further nominations should be made, after the Senate has exercised its unquestionable right of rejecting particular persons who have been nominated, any more than in other cases. The Senate will be ready at all times to receive and consider any such nominations as the President may present to it."

The Senate had condemned the assumption of the President in presuming to remove for opinion's sake, and here we have a condemnation of his attempt to perpetuate in office his own favorites against the wish of the Senate. But Jackson persisted in putting the question to every conceivable test, and removed his Secretary of the Treasury (Mr. Duane) because he refused to do what he conceived to be a violation of the law and his duty in the removal of the public deposits. This was during a vacation of the Senate. The late Chief Justice Taney was put in charge of the Department, and at once carried out the plans of Jackson. Upon the assembling of Congress Mr. Clay introduced into the Senate two resolutions in relation to the matter. The first one was as follows:

"That by dismissing the late Secretary of the Treasury because he would not, contrary to his sense of his own duty, remove the money of the United States in deposit with the Bank of the United States and its branches, in conformity with the President's opinion, and by appointing his successor to effect such removal, which has been done, the President has assumed the exercise of a power over the Treasury of the United States not granted to him by the Constitution and laws, and dangerous to the liberties of the people."

The resolution was adopted by a vote of 28 to 18.

Jackson held the nomination of Taney as Secretary of the Treasury in his pocket until the last week of the session of Congress; but it was rejected as soon as sent to the Senate. An acceptable name was afterwards presented, and the matter ended.

The next expression of the Senate upon the power of the President to remove a Cabinet minister was even more decided in its condemnation of the false doctrine derived from the debate of 1789. I refer, sir, to the passage of the tenure-of-office act over the veto, and of course by two thirds of both Houses of Congress, on March 2, 1867. Both Senate and House here united in this expression; and in this they spoke for every representative element of this Government and for the whole people.

Need I add to this chain of uniform decision the last vote of the Senate given on the 21st day of February, within twelve hours after the respondent had made the attempt to remove Mr. Stanton?

It is plain to my mind that those who voted with the majority in 1789 were not understood to give license to wholesale and causeless removals by the President. And we have the very highest evidence of this not only in the decisions of the Senate, which I have noticed, but in the uniform practice of the Government throughout all Administrations. I do not find that the first President ever exercised the power of removal, but if he did so, it will be seen, I venture to assert, that he consulted the Senate at the time or at its first session. I do find, however, an example of his great respect for, and deference to, that body which the Constitution had made his aid in making appointments.

Less than a month after the bill had passed organizing the Department of Foreign Affairs he sent to the Senate the name of Benjamin Fishbourne as naval officer at the port of Savannah. The Senate rejected the nomination. The President, fearing that in this there might be some misconception of his motives sent another name, but gave his reasons in justification for nominating Colonel Fishbourne. When John Adams desired to displace Mr.

Pickering, his Secretary of State, and appoint another he notified the incumbent that he would, on a certain day, cease to be Secretary of State. Meanwhile, the Senate being in session, he sent in the nomination of John Marshall, who was confirmed; and thus Mr. Pickering was removed, not by the President under any power the law gave, but under the Constitution and by virtue of the power incident to the appointing power vesting in the Senate and the President. This is a very striking and practical illustration of the doctrine then supposed to be the true one, and it was but following out the true spirit of the opinions expressed in the great debate of 1789.

Jefferson, the President who initiated the practice of removals, and was the first to confine his favors to his own party, made it a fundamental principle that removals were only to be made *for cause*. March 7, 1807, only three days after his induction into office, he writes to Mr. Monroe:

"Some removals, I know, must be made. They must be as few as possible, done gradually, and bottomed on some malversation or inherent disqualification."

On the 23d of the same month he thus writes to the Governor of Virginia, Mr. Giles:

"Good men, to whom there is no objection but a difference of political opinion, practiced only so far as the right of a private citizen will justify, are not proper subjects of removal."

Six days after he writes to Eldridge Gerry, afterward Vice President:

"Mr. Adams's last appointments, when he knew he was appointing counselors and aids for me, not for himself, I set aside as fast as depends on me. Officers who have been guilty of gross abuse of office, such as marshals packing juries, &c., I shall now remove, as my predecessor ought in justice to have done. The instances will be few, and governed by strict rule and not party passion. The right of opinion shall suffer no invasion from me."

How, sir, did Mr. Jefferson proceed to displace incompetent or untrustworthy officers? If there was a vacation of the Senate he appointed successors and gave notice to the incumbent of his action. The successor then became the legal officer, and the incumbent was removed by virtue of the new appointment working a revocation of the old commission. If the Senate was in session when this transpired he sent the nominations to that body, and their concurrence in the new appointment worked the revocation. If the Senate was not in session at the time he sent the nominations to that body at its next meeting, and the confirmation concluded the appointment, its action being an order or approval *nunc pro tunc*. And this has been true of every Administration except the present one. I ask counsel for the respondent to show a single removal from office by any President that was ever held of legal force that was not at the time or at a subsequent date approved by the Senate. When this is done the spirit and the letter of the Constitution are met, and when it is not done both are violated. Jefferson did not create vacancies. In making new appoint-

ments he rewarded his friends, and for cause he displaced incompetent men by appointing successors, but his action was always subject to review by the Senate. The Supreme Court said upon this point in *ex parte* Hennen: "The removal takes place in virtue of the new appointment by mere operation of law." Not the mere nomination, but the appointment.

Mr. Madison's administration will be searched in vain to find an instance where he ran counter to the will of the Senate in this matter of removals and appointments. In every instance where changes were made the Senate legalized them if they were appointments coming within the first clause of the second section, article second, of the Constitution.

I do not find that any occasion arose in Mr. Monroe's administration to present the question. I have elsewhere noticed the opinion of his Attorney General, William Wirt, upon the duties of the President in relation to the execution of laws which by their terms are to be executed by officers named in the law. This opinion completely overthrows the assumption of this respondent.

John Quincy Adams succeeded Mr. Monroe. There was no occasion for removals for political causes at this time. There was no revolution of parties. Mr. Adams had occupied the first place in Mr. Monroe's Cabinet during the whole term of eight years, and stood in concurrence with his appointments. It was called "the era of good feeling." It will be found that he made no change in offices filled by nomination to the Senate which were not concurred in by that body.

When Jackson came in there was an entire political revolution in the country. He formed his Cabinet, as all other Presidents had done, by nomination to the Senate. He displaced officials by nominating successors when the Senate was in session, or issuing commissions during vacation, which stood or fell as the first Senate thereafter decided. We have already seen how quickly the Senate brought this President to account for his first usurpation in the matter of removals when he removed Mr. Duane from the Treasury, although it was done during vacation.

Van Buren succeeded Jackson, and nowhere can I find that he violated the general practice of filling appointments and making removals.

Harrison's administration presents another instance of a complete revolution in party power. President Harrison in no instance ran counter to the will of the Senate or made removals or appointments which were without the Senate's concurrence. Mr. Tyler, who succeeded him but a month after his inauguration, was so impressed with the history of Jackson's attempted usurpation that he made this very subject the occasion for remark in his inaugural message. He said:

"In view of the fact, well avouched in history, that the tendency of all human institutions is to concentrate power in the hands of a single man, and that their ultimate downfall has proceeded from this cause, I deem it to be of the most essential importance that a complete separation should take place between the sword and the purse. No matter where or how the public moneys shall be deposited, so long as the President can exert the power of appointing and removing at his pleasure the agents selected for their custody the Commander-in-Chief of the Army and Navy is, in fact, the Treasurer. A permanent and radical change should therefore be decreed. The patronage incidental to the presidential office, already great, is constantly increasing. Such increase is destined to keep pace with the growth of our population, until, without a figure of speech, an army of office-holders may be spread over the land. The unrestrained power exerted by a selfishly ambitious man, in order either to perpetuate his authority or to hand it over to some favorite as his successor, may lead to the employment of all the means within his control to accomplish his object. The right to remove from office, while subjected to no just restraint, is inevitably destined to produce a spirit of crouching servility with the official corps, which, in order to uphold the hand which feeds them, would lead to direct and active interference with elections, both State and Federal, thereby subjecting the course of State legislation to the dictation of the chief executive officer and making the will of that officer absolute and supreme."

When subsequently he found himself at variance with his Cabinet, instead of removing them he caused scandalous things to be written and published of them in public newspapers, and revealed the Cabinet consultations, which were published in the same way, thus making the position of the Cabinet so unpleasant that they resigned. What I now state is alluded to in Mr. Ewing's letter of resignation. (Benton's Thirty Years View, p. 353.)

I will not pursue the history of removals and appointments in subsequent Administrations, but I assert that there will not be found in the practice pursued in any of them the slightest warrant for overriding the Senate either in appointments or removals without authority of law.

It is well understood that immediately upon the inauguration of a President the Senate is called together in extra session and at once go into executive session to consider any new appointments to be made. Cabinet changes are then made and submitted. If the President could remove and appoint without them such proceeding would be useless. Indeed, the President, having in mind the selection of a Cabinet he had reason to believe would be rejected by the Senate, would accomplish his purpose by withholding all nominations until the Senate adjourned, and thus defeat the very purpose of the Constitution in requiring the concurrence of the Senate.

Much weight has been attached to the judicial decisions upon the power of removal. A close scrutiny of these will show that they do not decide the question here discussed.

The opinion of the Supreme Court in *ex parte* Hennen establishes this simple proposition and no other, namely: the power of removal in the absence of all constitutional or statutory regulation is incident to the power of appointment. Hennen was appointed clerk of a court in Louisiana. The law creating the court gave the judge the power to appoint the clerk, but was silent as to how he might be removed. The judge removed Hennen. The Supreme Court of the United States held, on appeal, that the power of removal was incident to the power of appointment, and sustained the judge of the court accordingly. The court, in remarking upon the clause of the Constitution under discussion, remark:

"No one denied the power of the President and Senate jointly, to remove where the tenure of the office was not fixed by the Constitution; which was a full recognition of the principle that the power of removal was incident to the power of appointment."

Any lawyer will see that this is all the court was called upon to say, and in going beyond this to discuss what had been the opinions expressed in the First Congress was mere *dictum*, and is not to be considered as judicial interpretation. It is no new thing for courts to go outside of the case before them, and the Supreme Court is not an exception. There is not, Mr. President, as no one knows better than yourself, a single decision recorded in the Supreme Court reports, where the power of the President to remove from office in violation of the expressed wish of the Senate was drawn in question. Trace the history of all removals by the President down to the present time, and there will be found no instance where a removal has been made to which the Senate has not made the act its own, expressly or impliedly, by confirming the successor to the office made vacant by removal, and this, sir, takes all decided cases out of this discussion.

What we claim is that the Senate must either be first consulted in the removal, or it must subsequently to the removal assent thereto.

In Marbury *vs.* Madison (1 Cranch) the power of the President to remove was not directly made a question. Marbury was nominated a justice of the peace for the District of Columbia under a law which fixed the tenure of his office at four years. The Senate had concurred in the nomination, and the commission was signed by the President but not yet delivered. Mr. Madison, the Secretary of State, refused to deliver it, and a *mandamus* was sued out to compel him to do so. The court decided that a *mandamus* could not lie against the head of an executive Department. Upon the right of Marbury to his commission, however, the court said:

"Some point of time must be taken when the power of the Executive over an officer, not removable at his will, must cease. The point of time must be when the constitutional power of appointment has been exercised. And this power has been exercised when the last act, required from the person possessing the power, has been performed."

By the act of 1789, creating the Department of Foreign Affairs, it was made the duty of the Secretary of that Department to affix the seal of the United States to all commissions signed by the President. Upon the point as to whether the President could arrest the commission here the court said:

"This is not a proceeding which may be varied if the judgment of the Executive shall suggest one more eligible; *but is a precise course, accurately marked out by law,* and is to be *strictly pursued.* It is the duty of the Secretary of State to conform to the law, and in this he is an officer of the United States, bound to obey the laws. He acts under the authority of the law, and not by the instructions of the President."

If that case bears upon this, it goes only to show that the President cannot interfere with the due progress of the law, under the assumption that he is Chief Executive, and therefore possessed of power to control all executive offices.

If there are any decisions of the Supreme Court directly in point they have escaped me. I assume there are none, for the respondent states that he was governed in his action mainly to make a case for the courts, in order to obtain a judicial decision. For the first time in our history have we a direct issue between the two appointing powers. For the first time have we a case where the Senate, refusing to concur in a removal, the President ignores that body and defies its expressed will, and that, too, in the face of a positive enactment.

Sirs, I contend that the Department of War to-day, of which Edwin M. Stanton is Secretary, is not the Department of War of which Henry Knox was Secretary under George Washington. I have shown that by the act of 1789 the law simply created the Department, but assigned no duties to it except such as might suggest themselves as necessary to the President.

The Department remained thus, without any duties imposed upon it by law, and without any legislation recognizing its importance or its distinctiveness, until May 8, 1798. Meanwhile, the duties pertaining to the Navy had been taken from the War Department and conferred on a separate Department; Congress had given the power to make contracts for war and navy materials to the Secretary of the Treasury.

By the act of July 16, 1798, it was provided that all contracts and all purchases for the military service should be made by direction of the Secretary of War. The law also made it the duty of the public purveyor, who was an important officer and responsible for large sums of money, to report to the Secretary of War. The change here may seem unimportant, but it marks the beginning of that emancipation of the War Department from the manacles of executive control which is now by law made so complete.

The subsequent laws organizing the pay department, the quartermaster and commissary departments, the engineer and ordnance corps, all recognize the Secretary of War as in many respects the chief and sole executive officer for the discharge of specific duties with which the President had nothing whatever to do.

Still later, in 1812, when an army was raised to meet the apprehended war with Great Britain, greater powers were conferred on the Secretary of War. In the Indian wars, in the war with Mexico, and especially in the late war against rebellion, Congress seemed to have treated the Secretary of War as the only executive officer with whom they had anything to do, so far as that Department was concerned, and the legislation does not in many instances recognize the existence of a Chief Executive, so great and powerful an engine of government had the War Department become. Resolutions of inquiry for information in relation to military affairs were all directed to the Secretary of War, and he made answer to Congress himself without consultation with the President. The entire and immense system of purchase and supplies for the Army, the organization and equipment of troops, the moving of troops and military supplies, the sequestration of the enemy's property, the entire internal management of Army affairs, the payment and disbursement of millions of dollars annually, the adjustment of numberless claims against the Government, are all by law imposed upon the Secretary of War. Indeed, the War Department has, by virtue of laws passed since 1789, been completely changed, and instead of being a mere appendage to the executive office, with an amanuensis in it to write what the President might dictate, it is now, next to the Treasury, the most powerful and important Department of the Government.

Take up the statute-books and compare the laws as they now stand and as they stood when Congress spoke the Department into existence by four short sections in the act of 1789. You will find that there is scarcely a vestige of the act of 1789 left in force. That made the Department of War a part of the executive office, with its whole control in the President. The laws now place the specific duties of that vast Department in the hands of the Secretary, and hold him alone responsible. The very necessities of our national growth have wrought this change, and the people have come to hold the President no longer responsible, as they once did, for the conduct of the Executive Departments. Any one who, during the late war, had occasion to appeal from Mr. Stanton's decision in matters appertaining to his legal functions knows that what I state was recognized by the President as true.

This, too, has been recognized by judicial decision. The President has no right to perform executive acts by law given to his Secretaries. He had this right in 1789 because the law made them the executors of his will merely.

Can the President make a contract for the supply of the Army or Navy which the courts would hold binding? Can he give legal effect to an act which the law requires a particular officer of the Government to do? Can he step into the War, Treasury, or Navy Departments and sign official papers which the Secretaries sign and make his acts legal? If he is the chief and only controlling Executive, why has not he cut the Gordian knot by taking the War Department reins into his own hands until the Senate shall confirm his nominees?

There can be no other safe view to take of

this question—any other leads to despotism. In speaking of the Executive Departments during the great discussion upon President Jackson's removal of his Secretary of the Treasury, Mr. Clay said:

"We have established and designated offices, and appointed officers in each of these respective Departments to execute the duties respectively allotted to them. The President, it is true, presides over the whole. Specific duties are often assigned by particular laws to him alone, or to other officers under his superintendence. His parental eye is presumed to survey the whole extent of the system in all its movements; but has he power to come into Congress and say such laws only shall you pass; to go into the courts and prescribe the decisions they may pronounce; or even to enter the offices of administration, and where duties are specially confided to those officers to substitute his will to their duty? Or has he a right, when those functionaries, deliberating upon their own solemn obligations to the people, have moved forward in their assigned spheres, to arrest their lawful progress because they have dared to act contrary to his pleasure? No, sir. No, sir. His is a high and glorious station, but it is one of observation and superintendence. It is to see that obstructions in the forward movement of Government, unlawfully interposed, shall be abated by legitimate and competent means."

Will gentlemen consider for a moment the tremendous consequences of the doctrine claimed by this respondent? If, sirs. this Senate concede the power arrogated to the President, he is henceforward the Government. Even Congress is powerless to arrest his despotic rule.

Suppose he desired to force upon the country a certain policy, and chose the Secretary of the Treasury, with his immense power, for his instrument. That officer might decline to execute the President's will, and claim that the law conferred upon him alone certain specific duties which he could not conscientiously abandon to the dictates of the President. The remedy is at hand, and the official guillotine commences its work. An obsequious tool of the Executive is placed at the head of the Treasury, and the Senate and the people are tied hand and foot. He may remove at any time. He may withhold the name of the appointee till the very close of an intervening Senate, and should the Senate reject he may reappoint the same person or another equally subservient. Indeed, sir, if the absolute power claimed is conceded, he may so arrange the appointment as to avoid submitting it at all to the Senate. Can it be possible that a power so tremendous in its consequences was ever intended?

If the Congress of the United States have no right by legislative enactment to fix the tenure to certain offices, and exercise their joint authority in appointments as well as removals from office, what restriction is there on the President's power?

If he can control the Treasury by this ingenious, not to say despotic means, does his power end there? He may remove the Secretary of War and the General-in-Chief, if they dare dispute his policy. He thus possesses himself of the purse of the nation and next its Army. Let me ask the learned counsel, if they be correct in claiming the inherent right of removal in the President, where is the authority that makes Sherman's, Sheridan's, or Farragut's commissions more than blank parchment before the imperial throne at the White House? Under what authority can the Secretaries of the Navy, of State, Department of Interior, Postmaster General, and the thousands of officers of the several executive branches of Government, scattered all over the land, shield themselves from the withering and corrupting touch of the executive wand, when he chooses to command their removal?

If the President can do these things with impunity, let me ask if we have not that state of government forewarned by Mr. Seward's question, "Will you have Andrew Johnson President or king?"

We hear much said about the so-called Cabinet council of the President. The heads of Executive Departments have become Cabinet ministers, who hover around their chief as aids to a general of the Army, and the argument is used that you might with the same propriety force an obnoxious aid upon a general as an obnoxious Cabinet minister upon the President. Sirs, what is the origin of Cabinet councils, and whence comes the appellation Cabinet minister? I do not find them anywhere in the law which organized the several Departments. Let us not be deceived by names. I know of no authority for convening Cabinet conclaves semi-weekly, and I fear these councils are cabals in which the public weal is much less discussed than the party weal.

Tell me why the Postmaster General need be called to consult as to how the Navy Department should be administered; and what necessary connection is there between the duties of the Attorney General as prescribed by law and those appertaining to the War Department? Sirs, the so-called Cabinet councils are misleading us, and so far has this independent and self-constituted board of Government directors counseled the accused that he sets up the difference existing between him and the Secretary of War as working their loss of the latter's counsel in this cabal, and from this he excuses his attempt to remove him. You are asked to give legal existence to this Cabinet, and say the Secretary of War has duties to perform there, failing in which he must leave his Department. This Cabinet appendage to our executive government is an innovation, and should not be legalized.

The Constitution says the President "may require the opinion, in writing, of the principal officers of each of the Executive Departments *upon any subject relating to the duties of their respective offices.*"

But, sirs, it nowhere authorizes him to consolidate the heads of these Departments into a cabal to discuss party politics, and devise ways to perpetuate their tenure by securing the re-election of their chief. There is danger in our forgetting that the law-making power of this Government has imposed duties and obligations upon these heads of Departments which they cannot delegate to the President, much less the Cabinet, and which neither the President nor the Cabinet can arrogate to themselves.

In this portion of the defense set up I do not find that any breach of duty is charged to the Secretary of War. It does not appear that he has been derelict in anything enjoined upon him by law. No, sirs; he has ceased to be an agreeable companion to the President's Cabinet tea parties, and he must be decapitated. Under all this lies much of that evil growing out of the power arrogated to the President. Here is the seed of executive consolidation, of which the fathers had such dread. These secret meetings tend to destroy that independence of administration which the law contemplates. Napoleon used to say that councils of war never fought battles. I think, sirs, I may say that Cabinet councils do not always execute laws.

I come now to notice the second branch of the offense involved in the first charge, namely:

HAD THE PRESIDENT POWER TO REMOVE THE SECRETARY OF WAR IN VIOLATION OF THE TEN-URE-OF-OFFICE ACT?

The first section of this act reads as follows:

"That every person holding any civil office to which he has been appointed by and with the advice and consent of the Senate, and every person who shall hereafter be appointed to any such office, and shall become duly qualified to act therein, is and shall be entitled to hold such office until a successor shall have been appointed by the President, with the advice and consent of the Senate, and duly qualified; and that the Secretaries of State, of the Treasury, of War, of the Navy, and of the Interior, the Postmaster General and the Attorney General, shall hold their offices respectively for and during the term of the President by whom they may have been appointed, and for one month thereafter, subject to removal by and with the advice and consent of the Senate."

It is urged by the accused, in order to evade the necessary consequences attending a violation of this act, first, that it is unconstitutional; and second, that it does not reach Mr. Stanton's case.

The first of these points goes to the power of Congress to enact any law on the subject of tenure of office, while the second is a legal quibble upon the language of the law, which the respondent knows better than any one else is a plain violation of the spirit and intent, not to say letter of the act. Let us consider briefly these two points.

FIRST: IS THE TENURE ACT CONSTITUTIONAL? It would seem idle to discuss a question which, so far as this Senate is concerned, is *res adjudicata*. I am surprised, sirs, to find counsel of such eminence as those pleading for the accused coming before a court and rearguing with pretentious hopes of reversing a decision deliberately made by over two thirds of this body. Would they thus presume before the Supreme Court of the United States? One of

the counsel once sat upon that bench. Would he have tolerated an argument upon a decision of that court which had been rendered after repeated examinations by the most learned of the country, exhausting every phase of argument on both sides, and which decision was finally concurred in by two thirds of the court?

But the question is before the Senate again; has been elaborately argued, and courtesy to the counsel for the respondent, if no other reason offers, would seem to require for it a passing notice.

I do not observe in the remarks of counsel any argument different from that given in the message vetoing the act of March 2, 1867. This did not prevail before the Senate then, and I see no reason why it should now. We are told there that the question arose and was settled in the discussion of 1789 when the War Department and the Foreign Department were created. I think the question presented then is much misapprehended. It was not whether Congress had the power to legislate upon the subject. It was whether they ought to confer the power of removal on the President. If the power *inheres* in the President the act then passed was wholly gratuitous and unnecessary. To my mind the persistent determination with which the majority (and a small one it was) insisted upon putting into those acts of 1789 a clause impliedly giving the power of removal to the President is the highest proof of their belief in the power of Congress to legislate upon the subject, and that without legislation the President would not possess the authority to remove. If Congress was competent to grant the power to the President, are they not equally competent to withhold it?

The only officers of the Government whose tenure is fixed by the Constitution are the President and Vice President and the judges of the Supreme Court and such inferior officers as Congress may establish. (Art. 2 and 3.) The President and Vice President hold for four years, but Congress may remove them by impeachment. The judges hold "during good behavior," but who can decide the good or bad behavior of judges except Congress? Congress cannot abridge the tenure of the office, but they can abridge the officer's tenure by impeaching him.

This, sirs, is the only limitation upon Congress anywhere to be found in the Constitution upon the subject of controlling official tenure. The Constitution is silent upon the subject of tenure. I hold, therefore, that the whole power is vested in Congress to provide, whenever and however they choose, both for appointment to and removal from office. There is not an officer mentioned in the second clause of the second article over whom Congress has not control in such manner as they may by law provide, except in the cases mentioned. Congress is perfectly competent to fix any tenure it deems best to embassadors, ministers, consuls, or any other officers than those whose term of office is fixed by the Constitution. The section of the Constitution to which I have alluded only provides for the manner of appointment; it does not restrain Congress from giving a tenure to the offices which it establishes, and to impose such restraint by implication is wholly unwarrantable. Nothing but the method of appointment is attempted to be controlled. Suppose Congress should determine that the efficiency of our diplomatic system is greatly impaired by the frequent and causeless changes made among ministers, embassadors, or consuls, and that the practice of putting spies upon them, and crediting such mythical men as McCracken, and recalling ministers upon their statements, should be stopped—could no law be passed fixing their tenure, requiring the President to advise with the Senate before recalling the minister, leaving us unrepresented abroad, except where he did so for good cause?

The object of the Constitution was to provide the means of filling offices which Congress might establish. No intention was expressed to control absolutely the tenure of the office or prohibit Congress from prescribing means of removal.

If Congress cannot do more than make the office and prescribe the duties incumbent upon the person filling it, in the matter of those officers referred to in the first part of section second, article second, how can Congress do more in the creating of inferior officers spoken of in the last part of the section? It says, "Congress may vest the appointment of such inferior officers as they think proper in the President alone, in the courts of law, or in the heads of Departments." Suppose Congress create a board of examiners to examine into the national banks, and give the President the power to appoint them. Congress has then exhausted all the directly-conferred power given them by the letter of the Constitution, and they are powerless to fix the tenure here if they are in the other cases. The argument urged is that the power to remove is incident to the power to appoint. The President by law appoints, and, therefore, he alone can terminate the officer's tenure. Congress, by giving the President the power to appoint, is estopped from fixing the tenure, so as to control the President's removing prerogative. But, sirs, we know this is not true. The country is filled with officers, civil and military, some of them appointed by the President alone, others by and with the advice and consent of the Senate, and yet Congress, in these cases, has never been held to be powerless to fix the tenure.

Wherein is the difference between the Constitution saying the President and Senate may appoint certain officers created by law, or the Constitution saying Congress may provide means of filling certain offices? The will of the people is expressed in the same manner through the Constitution directly to the President and Senate in one case, and indirectly to the President, to courts of law, or heads of Departments in the other case, but in neither case do they say through the Constitution, directly or impliedly, that Congress, who create the office, shall not adjust its tenure. The reason for giving the appointment of inferior officers into other hands than the Senate and President was to provide for speedy execution of the law and for early action in filling the offices. Inferior officers were of less importance; they were numerous; vacancies were constantly occurring, and hence the necessity of relieving the Senate and President from acting jointly. But the reason for giving Congress power to control the tenure of inferior offices applies with much greater weight in the case of higher officers, whose wanton and capricious removal may lead to infinitely more dangerous consequences.

If this view be correct, there can be nothing left of the argument against the constitutionality of the tenure act. In Marbury vs. Madison the case of an officer appointed by the President and Senate is presented, where the law also fixed the tenure of the office at five years. In this case the court said:

"If the officer be removable *at the will of the President*, then a new appointment may be immediately made and the rights of the officer terminated; if the officer is by law not removable at the will of the President, the rights the officer has acquired are protected by the law, and are not resumable by the President. They cannot be extinguished by the Executive."

This would be bad law if Congress were powerless to fix a tenure, and it is no answer to say Congress may fix the number of years the officer is to serve, for if the term of years can be fixed so can the manner of his removal.

If Congress can pass one step beyond the power to create the office and provide for filling it, then they can regulate the tenure in any and all particulars. The question cannot turn upon who are or who are not inferior officers, for here we would be left in a maze and labyrinth, and the President could shield himself behind a will-o'-the-wisp. The Constitution does not pretend to define who are or who are not inferior officers, and the fact that this is left undefined shows that the matter of controlling the tenure by congressional enactment of either the one or the other was not the question the framers had in mind. It was much discussed in 1789 as to whether the heads of Departments are inferior officers, and the result of the discussion is doubtful. and really settled nothing. (1 Lloyd's Debates, 480 to 600; Sergeant on Constitution, ch. 29, (ch. 31;) 2 Lloyd's Debates. 1 to 12.) But whether they are or are not does not affect the question in hand. Because this appointment is to be by both Senate and President does not settle it, else every petty postmaster and collector in the country must be held to rank with embassadors, ministers, and judges of the Supreme Court. What rule determines whether the General-in-Chief and all subordinate military officers are or are not inferior officers? There is none. The Army is a creature of law, and Congress has always regulated it as it chose. Some of its officers were placed under the control of the War Department; some minor ones even appointed by the Secretary. Others were nominated to and confirmed by the Senate. In point of fact, however, officers of the Army are not regarded as inferior officers, yet Congress has regulated the whole Army system, imposing restraints upon the President in many ways with regard to it. The question came up in Mr. Monroe's Administration, and was discussed in his message of April 12, 1822. (1 Ex. Journal, 286.) The Senate disagreed with Mr. Monroe, and held that Congress had the right to fix the rule as to promotions and appointments as well as to reductions in the Army, and that this right had, to that time, never been disputed by any President. It is true this was claimed under the general power to make all needful rules and regulations for the government of the Army, but that clause of the Constitution confers no more executive control on Congress in respect to the Army than does the clause which provides that Congress shall establish post offices and post roads over the manner of appointing postmasters.

Story says, (sec. 1537:)

"As far as Congress possesses the power to regulate and delegate the appointment of inferior officers, so far they may prescribe the term of office, the manner in which and the persons by whom the removal as well as the appointment to office may be made."

But, as we have seen, the clause of the Constitution on this subject does not define who are inferior officers, and does not separate them from other officers, with any view to give Congress greater control over their tenure than in other cases, we are brought back again to my position, that there is no restraint upon Congress to regulate the tenure in the one case more than the other.

The officers of the army then coming within the class titled superior, as distinguished from inferior, they are to be placed beside and are to rank with embassadors, ministers, Cabinet officers, &c., and if Congress is competent to control the tenure of the one it is of the other. Unfortunately for the consistency of the respondent's special plea, he is on the record against himself.

By the act of July 13, 1866, section five, it is provided that—

"No officer in the military or naval service shall, in time of peace, be dismissed from service except upon, and in pursuance of, the sentence of a court-martial to that effect or in commutation therefor."

Here is a direct inroad upon the prerogative of the President as now set up, and admits the whole principle here contended for. Where were the vigilant advisers of the President when he approved the bill and made it law? Was there no genius of executive prerogatives near to whisper "Veto?" Was the facile logic of the law officer of the President reserving itself for this occasion?

But this principle of recognizing the *right* or *power* of Congress to legislate as to how an officer is to be displaced had the sanction of Mr. Lincoln in the act of February 25, 1863, creating the office of Comptroller of the Currency. It provides as follows:

"He shall be appointed by the President, on the nomination of the Secretary of the Treasury, by and with the advice and consent of the Senate, and shall hold his office for the term of two years, unless sooner removed by the President, by and with the advice and consent of the Senate."

This is not a power recently claimed by Congress. I have shown in another part of the argument that many unsuccessful efforts were made at different periods of our national history to pass laws similar to the present tenure act, and they were supported by members of all shades of politics. The constitutionality of such laws was not questioned, but the bills always failed from executive influences brought to bear upon Congress. Mr. Benton was an earnest advocate of a tenure act limiting executive control over appointments and removals. Mr. Clay and Mr. Webster have left upon the records of the Senate arguments not only showing the constitutionality of such laws, but giving the most weighty reasons for passing them upon the grounds of public policy and safety.

In 1835 a lengthy discussion occurred upon an amendment offered by Mr. Clay to a pending bill which embraced every principle of the present tenure act. I will be pardoned for giving a condensed statement of the view taken at that time by three Senators who participated in the discussion, as giving briefly the whole argument upon this question. Mr. Clay supported his position by the following arguments, among others:

"It is legislative authority which creates the office, defines its duties, and may prescribe its duration. I speak, of course, of offices not created by the Constitution, but the law. The office coming into existence by the will of Congress, the same will may provide how and in what manner the office and officer shall cease to exist. It may direct the conditions on which he shall hold the office and when and how he shall be dismissed. Suppose the Constitution had omitted to prescribe the tenure of the judicial oath, could not Congress do it?

"But the Constitution has not fixed the tenure of any subordinate officers, and therefore Congress may supply the omission. It would be unreasonable to contend that although Congress, in pursuance of the public good, brings the office and the officer into being and assigns their purposes, yet the President has a control over the officer which Congress cannot reach and regulate." * * * * "The precedent of 1789 was established in the House of Representatives against the opinion of a large and able minority, and in the Senate by the casting vote of the Vice President, John Adams. It is impossible to read the debate which it occasioned without being impressed with the conviction that the just confidence reposed in the father of his country, then at the head of the Government, had great, if not decisive, influence in establishing it. It has never, prior to the commencement of the present Administration, been submitted to the process of review." * * * * "No one can carefully examine the debate in the House of Representatives in 1789 without being struck with the superiority of the argument on the side of the minority, and the unsatisfactory nature of that of the majority."

Daniel Webster agreed with Mr. Clay in his

position in the following language used by him on the occasion:

"I think, then, sir, that the power of appointment naturally and necessarily includes the power of removal where no limitation is expressed nor any tenure but that at will declared. The power of appointment being conferred on the President and Senate I think the power of removal went along with it, and should have been regarded as a part of it, and exercised by the same hands. I think the Legislature possesses the power of regulating the condition, duration, qualification, and tenure of office in all cases where the Constitution has made no express provision on the subject. I am, therefore, of opinion that it is competent for Congress to decide by law, as one qualification of the tenure of office, that the incumbent shall remain in place till the President shall remove him for reasons to be stated to the Senate. And I am of opinion that this qualification, mild and gentle as it is, will have some effect in arresting the evils which beset the progress of the Government and seriously threaten its future prosperity."

This view was sustained by Hon. Thomas Ewing of Ohio:

"Mr. Ewing spoke at length upon the question of removals, maintaining that the Constitution does not confer on the President alone the power of removal; that is a matter of legislative provision, subject to be vested, modified, changed, or taken away at their will; and if it is not regulated at all by law, it rests in the President, in conjunction with the Senate, as part of the appointing power."

The respondent cannot, I think, find support in any precedent or decision, or by any right construction of the Constitution. What, then, becomes of his reliance upon these in defense of his willful violations of the act? He stands convicted by his own confession. Did he make a mistake in his research, and did he innocently misinterpret the Constitution? These mistakes and these innocent misinterpretations are too serious to be thus condoned. To admit them as a good defense would emasculate every criminal law in the land, and leave all public officers free to misinterpret statutes with impunity, and, no matter what the consequences, they could shield themselves from punishment. Mr. Johnson's pretended prototype, Jackson, did not so understand the law. When the Senate passed the resolution declaring his removal of his Secretary of the Treasury, Mr. Duane, a usurpation, Jackson regarded it as equivalent to impeachment. In his protest to the Senate he said—

"That the resolution does not expressly allege that the assumption of power and authority which it condemns was intentional and corrupt, is no answer to the preceding view of its character and effect. The act thus condemned necessarily implies volition and design in the individual to whom it is imputed, and, being unlawful in its character, the legal conclusion is, that it was prompted by improper motives, and committed with an unlawful intent. The charge is not of a mistake in the exercise of supposed powers, but of the assumption of powers not conferred by the Constitution and laws, but in derogation of both, and nothing is suggested to excuse or palliate the turpitude of the act. In the absence of any such excuse or palliation there is room only for one inference, and that is, that the intent was unlawful and corrupt."

I cannot believe the respondent relies upon this plea of innocent intent as amounting even to a shadow of defense. He not only took the risk of construing the Constitution upon a question not settled by any judicial decision, but

C. I.—35.

he did it in direct defiance of the solemn judgment of this Senate; and he to-day defies this judgment by denouncing the tenure act as unconstitutional. But the accused says even if the tenure act be held constitutional, still he is guiltless, because it does not apply to the case of Mr. Stanton; and this brings me to inquire—

Second. DOES THE TENURE ACT APPLY TO THE PRESENT SECRETARY OF WAR?

It is a new method of ascertaining the meaning of a law, plain upon its face, by resorting to legislative discussions, and giving in evidence opinions of persons affected by the law. As a matter of fact, it is well known the act was intended to prevent the very thing Mr. Johnson attempted in the matter of Mr. Stanton's removal. I think this manner of defense will not avail before this Senate. The law must govern in its natural and plain intendment, and will not be frittered away by extraneous interpretation. The President in his veto message admits substantially this construction.

The proviso does not change the general provisions of the act except by giving a more definite limit to the term of office, but the last paragraph of the act puts the whole question back into the hands of the Senate according to the general intention of the act, and provides that even the Secretaries are "subject to removal by and with the advice and consent of the Senate."

The act first provides that all persons holding civil offices at the date of its passage appointed by and with the advice and consent of the Senate shall only be removed in the same manner. This applies to the Secretary of War. The proviso merely gives a tenure running with the term of the President and one month thereafter, subject to removal by the advice and consent of the Senate. The law clearly gives Mr. Stanton a right to the office from the 4th of March, 1865, till one month after the 4th of March, 1869, and he can only be disturbed in that tenure by the President by and with the advice and consent of the Senate.

Yet, although Mr. Stanton was appointed by Mr. Lincoln in his first term, when there was no tenure to the office fixed by law, and continued by Mr. Lincoln in his second term, it is argued that his term expired one month after the passage of the tenure-of-office act, March 2, 1867, for the reason that Mr. Lincoln's term expired at his death. This is false reasoning; the Constitution fixes the term of the President at four years, and by law the commencement of his term is the 4th of March. Will it be said that when Mr. Johnson is deposed by a verdict of the Senate that the officer who will succeed him will serve for four years? Certainly not. Why? Because he will have no presidential term, and will be merely serving out a part of the unexpired term of Mr. Lincoln, and will go out of office 4th of March, 1869, at the time Mr. Lincoln would have retired by expiration of his term, had he lived.

I give section ten of the act of March 1, 1792, which settles the question whether the term ceases with the death or resignation of the President, which so clearly decides the matter and settles it that no argument is necessary further on the subject:

"SEC. 10. *And be it further enacted*, That whenever the offices of President or Vice President shall both become vacant the Secretary of State shall forthwith cause a notification thereof to be made to the executive of every State, and shall also cause the same to be published in at least one of the newspapers printed in each State, specifying that electors of the President of the United States shall be appointed or chosen in the several States within thirty-four days preceding the first Wednesday in December then next ensuing: *Provided*, There shall be the space of two months between the date of such notification and the said first Wednesday in December; but if there shall not be the space of two months between the date of such notification and the first Wednesday in December, and if the term for which the President and Vice President last in office were elected shall not expire on the 3d day of March next ensuing, then the Secretary of State shall specify in the notification that the electors shall be appointed or chosen within thirty-four days preceding the first Wednesday in December in the year next ensuing, within which time the electors shall accordingly be appointed or chosen, and the electors shall meet and give their votes on the said first Wednesday in December, and the proceedings and duties of the said electors and others shall be pursuant to the directions prescribed in this act."

This law settles certainly the question, if any doubt existed before, that the term does not expire on the death or resignation of the President, but continues as his term the four years.

But I will not argue this question at more length. If the judgment of men, deliberately expressed, can ever be relied upon, I think it safe to assume that this Senate will not reverse its judgment so recently expressed upon the constitutionality and meaning of the tenure act. The only question, then, which remains is simply this: has the accused violated that act? No one knows better than this accused the history of, and the purpose to be secured by, that act. It was ably and exhaustively discussed on both sides, in all aspects. In the debates of Congress it was subsequently reviewed and closely analyzed in a veto message of the respondent. No portion of that act escaped his remark, and no practical application which has been made of it since did he fail to anticipate. He knew before he attempted its violation that more than three fourths of the Representatives of the people in Congress assembled had set their seal of disapprobation upon the reasons given in the veto message and had enacted the law by more than the constitutional number of votes required. Nay, more: he was repeatedly warned, by investigations made looking toward just such a proceeding as is now being witnessed in this court, that the people had instructed their Representatives to tolerate no violation of the laws constitutionally enacted. What, then, is the violation here charged upon this respondent, and what are the proofs to sustain it? Upon the 21st day of February, 1868, the respondent sent

the following official order to Edwin M. Stanton, Secretary of War:

EXECUTIVE MANSION,
WASHINGTON, D. C., *February* 21, 1868.
SIR: By virtue of the power and authority vested in me as President by the Constitution and laws of the United States, you are hereby removed from office as Secretary for the Department of War, and your functions as such will terminate upon the receipt of this communication.
You will transfer to Brevet Major General Lorenzo Thomas, Adjutant General of the Army, who has this day been authorized and empowered to act as Secretary of War *ad interim*, all records, books, papers, and other property now in your custody and charge.
Respectfully, yours, ANDREW JOHNSON.
Hon. EDWIN M. STANTON, *Washington, D. C.*

Upon the same day he sent to Lorenzo Thomas, Adjutant General of the Army, the following order:

EXECUTIVE MANSION,
WASHINGTON, D. C., *February* 21, 1868.
SIR: Hon. Edwin M. Stanton having been this day removed from the office as Secretary for the Department of War, you are hereby authorized and empowered to act as Secretary of War *ad interim*, and will immediately enter upon the discharge of the duties pertaining to that office.
Mr. Stanton has been instructed to transfer to you all the records, books, papers, and other public property now in his custody and charge.
Respectfully, yours, ANDREW JOHNSON.
Brevet Major General LORENZO THOMAS, *Adjutant General United States Army, Washington, D. C.*

"Every person holding any civil office, to which he has appointed by and with the advice and consent of the Senate," * * * * "is and shall be entitled to hold such office until a successor shall have been in like manner appointed and duly qualified."

This plain and not to be misunderstood provision of the law is violated. The order for removal was made absolute and without condition. The President ignored all "advice and consent of the Senate," and planted himself upon his own opinion as to his inherent power to act outside of the law and in violation of it; and his answer so confesses. The proofs of his guilt are therefore placed beyond dispute. What, sirs, says the law with regard to the crime involved in such conduct? The sixth section of the same act declares that "every removal" "made" "contrary to the provisions of this act" "is hereby declared to be a high misdemeanor."

Upon these facts, and in the face of this law, can there be a doubt that the charge is fully sustained? Need we pursue the question of intent, when by the terms of the law the mere act of removal, in violation of it, is declared a "high misdemeanor?" But, sirs, we do not shrink from an examination into the motives which actuated this accused. The history of his public acts since the passage of this law is crowded with evidences of his guilty intent. To-day, with the fear of that law before his eyes, he conforms strictly to its requirements; to-morrow he openly defies it and declares his purpose not to be governed by it: and, with the strangest inconsistency and indecision of character, he wavers between the plainest duty pointed out by law and the rashest contempt of all law. We have shown by the testimony that under his instructions the chiefs of the Departments changed the forms of official bonds of commissions and letters of appointment to adapt them to the requirements of this law. We have seen that within five months after its passage he suspended the Secretary of War and notified the several Executive Departments that he had done so under the provisions of this act. We have seen that hundreds of commissions, to fill various offices, were issued under his sign manual, distinctly recognizing the provisions of this act. Yet, in defiance of the law, and in disregard of his own repeated recognition of it, he asks this Senate to hold him guiltless. Do the annals of criminal trials anywhere present so monstrous an absurdity?

But the circumstances connected with this removal are themselves proof positive of a criminal purpose. Upon the 12th of August, 1867, the President suspended the Secretary of War and appointed General Grant the *ad interim* Secretary. This suspension purported to be in conformity to the law, and was acquiesced in. Under the provisions of the second section of the "tenure act," this removal was reported to the Senate within twenty days after its next meeting. The reasons assigned by the President were duly considered by the Senate, and the following resolution communicated to the President as their decision:

IN EXECUTIVE SESSION,
SENATE OF THE UNITED STATES,
January 13, 1868.

Resolved, That, having considered the evidence and reasons given by the President in his report of the 12th of December, 1867, for the suspension from the office of Secretary of War of Edwin M. Stanton, the Senate do not concur in such suspension.
Attested.

The law says in such case, "but if the Senate shall refuse to concur in such suspension, such officer so suspended shall resume the functions of his office, and the powers of the person so performing its duties shall cease." The Secretary *ad interim* vacated the office accordingly, and the suspended Secretary resumed his duties. I will not stop now to speak of the unmanly and disgraceful attempt made by the President and his Cabinet cabal to trick the General-in-Chief into a violation of the law and to force upon Mr. Stanton the alternative of submitting to an indirect removal from office under cover of his suspension, or resorting to legal proceedings through the courts which could not possibly have ended during the present Administration. The history of all criminals illustrates a constant struggle between crime and cowardice—the desire to commit the crime and the fear of the consequences that may follow. The criminal intent to disregard the law was never more manifest in the mind of the accused than at this time; but his dread of punishment deterred him from the overt act. The answer of the respondent and the proofs spread upon the record show that from the

13th of January to the 21st of February he was scheming and devising means to thwart the vote of this Senate and to dispossess the Secretary of War in disregard of the law, and yet to evade, if possible, the punishment consequent upon its violation. The law told him if he should remove the Secretary he must do so "by and with the advice and consent of the Senate." He knew by the previous vote of that body that no such "advice and consent" would be given. He, therefore, not only admonished by the Senate, but directed by the law, usurped a power nowhere given, and issued his mandate accordingly. With what effrontery then comes in the plea that his only motive was to innocently assert his prerogatives? Was the War Department to be made a mere plaything in the hands of the Executive? Was the machinery of that vast Department to halt and its chief officer to subject himself to a trial for neglect of duty, while Mr. Johnson would amuse himself with preparing a case for the courts? Did he not know that the law enjoined duties upon the Secretary which he could not lay aside? Could he have for a moment supposed that that officer would tamely submit to an order for removal in which he had every reason to believe the Senate would not concur? No, sir; he comprehended fully the length and breadth of the offense he was then committing. He saw then, as plainly as he sees now, what would be the legal consequences of his act, and only hoped to shield himself behind that forbearance which he had mistaken for cowardice on the part of the representatives of the people.

But, Mr. President and Senators, this inquiry is relieved of all doubts; the question is *res adjudicata*, and I have simply to read the decision rendered upon the same day this high-handed attempt at usurpation was made:

IN EXECUTIVE SESSION,
SENATE OF THE UNITED STATES,
February 21, 1868.

Whereas the Senate have received and considered the communication of the President stating that he had removed Edwin M. Stanton, Secretary of War, and had designated the Adjutant General of the Army to act as Secretary of War *ad interim :* Therefore,

Resolved by the Senate of the United States, That, under the Constitution and laws of the United States, the President has no power to remove the Secretary of War and to designate any other officer to perform the duties of that office *ad interim.*

REMARKS UPON ARTICLE SECOND.

Let us pass to notice briefly article second. The respondent is here charged with violating the tenure-of-office act in the appointment of Lorenzo Thomas as Secretary of War on the 21st of February, 1868, there being no vacancy in said office. The letter of appointment is as follows:

EXECUTIVE MANSION,
WASHINGTON, D. C., *February* 21, 1861.

SIR: Hon. Edwin M. Stanton having been this day removed from the office as Secretary for the Department of War, you are hereby authorized and empowered to act as Secretary of War *ad interim,* and will immediately enter upon the discharge of the duties pertaining to that office.

Mr. Stanton has been instructed to transfer to you all the records, books, papers, and other public property now in his custody and charge.

Respectfully yours,   ANDREW JOHNSON.

Brevet Major General LORENZO THOMAS, *Adjutant General United States Army, Washington, D. C.*

This appointment was made simultaneously with the removal of Mr. Stanton; it was made with the full knowledge that no vacancy existed, and that the Senate had so decided; it was made in defiance of all those repeated warnings to which I have alluded—that the Congress of the United States would regard the act as an open violation of law; it was made with every reasonable apprehension on his part that it would lead almost inevitably to his impeachment. Indeed, in this act, as well as others now laid down to his charge, he seems not only to have defied, but to have courted impeachment.

The law told him here, as plainly as it told him in the matter of removal, that his act was denounced as a high misdemeanor in office. It told him more. It said to the person who would accept such appointment and attempt to discharge duties under it, would thereby himself commit a high misdemeanor in office. This respondent was, therefore, guilty of the double crime of himself violating the law and inducing others to join him in the criminal act. Section six of the tenure act says:

"Every removal, appointment, or employment made, had, or received, contrary to the provisions of this act, and the making, signing, counter-signing, or issuing of any commission or letter of authority for or in respect to any such appointment or employment, shall be deemed and are hereby declared to be high misdemeanors."

What defense is made for the palpable violation of the law now shown? The respondent goes back to the act of February 13, 1795, and rests his case upon that law, which provides as follows, (1 Statutes-at-Large, p. 415:)

"*Be it enacted by the Senate and House of Representatives of the United States of America in Congress assembled,* That in case of vacancy in the office of Secretary of State, Secretary of the Treasury, or of the Secretary of the Department of War, or of any officer of either of the said Departments whose appointment is not in the head thereof, whereby they cannot perform the duties of their said respective offices, it shall be lawful for the President of the United States, in case he shall think it necessary, to authorize any person or persons, at his discretion, to perform the duties of the said respective offices until a successor be appointed or such vacancy be filled: *Provided,* That no one vacancy shall be supplied, in manner aforesaid, for a longer term than six months."

But by the very terms of the act of 1795 this respondent can there find no defense; that law says, "*in case of vacancy in the office of Secretary of the Department of War* whereby he cannot perform the duties of said office, it shall be lawful for the President to authorize any person to perform its duties." We see, then, *there must be a vacancy* in the office, or a disability on the part of the Secretary to act before the President can make such an appointment. There was neither a vacancy nor a disability existing at the time Lorenzo Thomas was appointed. This respondent, then, has

not only violated the tenure act, but he has violated the very law under which he claims immunity. Nothing can be plainer, and nothing exhibits more strongly the utter hollowness of his defense.

ARTICLE THIRD.

The next and third article charges the President with a violation of the Constitution of the United States in the appointment of Lorenzo Thomas as Secretary of War while the Senate was in session, no vacancy having occurred during the recess of the Senate, and no vacancy existing at the time. The facts alleged are not controverted; the question presented to the Senate under this article involves the proper construction of our fundamental law. I have previously addressed myself to the Senate upon this subject, and will not again enter upon it.

The line of inquiry is very simple. If this accused has violated a law constitutionally enacted, then has he violated the Constitution itself. He has sworn to support the Constitution, and by that oath he is enjoined to "take care that the laws are faithfully executed." He cannot support the Constitution and defy the laws enacted pursuant to it any more than he can execute the laws faithfully and violate the Constitution. The duties are blended, and he cannot violate one without violating the other. If he be guilty under either the first or second article, he is guilty of the offense charged in the third.

ARTICLES FOURTH, FIFTH, SIXTH, AND SEVENTH.

The four succeeding charges allege conspiracy between the respondent and Lorenzo Thomas and others unknown:

First. By force, intimidation, and threats unlawfully to hinder Edwin M. Stanton, then Secretary of War, from holding said office, contrary to the provisions of an act to prevent and punish certain conspiracies, approved July 31, 1861.

Second. To prevent and hinder the execution of an act regulating the tenure of certain civil offices, passed March 2, 1867, by attempting unlawfully to prevent Edwin M. Stanton, then Secretary of War, from holding said office.

Third. By force to seize, take, and possess the property of the United States in the Department of War, then and there in the custody of Edwin M. Stanton, Secretary of the Department of War, contrary to an act to define and punish certain conspiracies, approved July 31, 1861.

Fourth. To seize, take, and possess the property of the United States in the Department of War, and in custody of said Stanton, with intent to disregard and violate an act regulating the tenure of certain civil offices, passed March 2, 1867.

That part of the conspiracy act which defines the offenses here charged is as follows:

"That if two or more persons, within any State or Territory of the United States, shall conspire together" * * * * "to oppose by force the authority of the Government of the United States, or by force to prevent, hinder, or delay the execution of any law of the United States, or by force to seize, take, or possess any property of the United States, against the will or contrary to the authority of the United States, or by force or intimidation or threat to prevent any person from accepting or holding any office or trust or place of confidence under the United States, each and every person so offending shall be guilty of a high crime."

The acts which he has himself admitted to have done and those proved against him by the undisputed testimony of witnesses bring his conduct within the letter of the law. No other result could have followed his conduct—it tended *directly* to "hinder and delay the execution of" the tenure act. He had no other purpose than to "seize, take, and possess the property of the United States in the War Department," against the will and contrary to the authority of the United States, then in the lawful custody of the Secretary of War, and as placed there by the highest authority in the land. And it is equally evident that his design was to prevent Edwin M. Stanton from holding the office to which he had been legally appointed, and from which he had not been and could not be legally removed. We are not, then, to inquire at this time whether he is guilty of a high misdemeanor in doing these things, which have been made the *gravamen* of the first three articles; but we are to see whether he has unlawfully conspired, by force or intimidation or threat, to attempt the accomplishment of these objects.

What are the evidences of a conspiracy? It may be well first to inquire, what is a conspiracy? Under articles fourth and sixth we are confined in our definition to a conspiracy or agreement by force to do the things alleged. Under the fifth and seventh articles of impeachment the broader rule of the common law is applicable. Leaving the discussion of those articles for their proper place, let us inquire whether there is a conspiracy proved in violation of the act of 1861. To determine this there must be grouped about the accused all the circumstances tending to explain his conduct.

From the very nature of the crime its perpetrators would carefully abstain from leaving any trace of their original purpose. We are, then, to scan the circumstances surrounding the transaction; we are to inquire into the character of the act to be performed, the means and the instrument employed, the declarations of the conspirators before and since, the mind and temper of the accused, as well as his coconspirators, and everything that can throw light upon their motives and intentions. What are these circumstances, acts, and declarations?

Here we find the unmistakable declaration of one of the conspirators that he intended to use force; that should the doors of the Department be barred against him he would break them down. When he made this declaration he had been once refused possession, and if any one

thing appear more clearly than another in the testimony it is that he fully anticipated a forcible contest in order to succeed. He was clothed with ample authority by the President to do this. It will not do to say that General Thomas's order was in the usual form, and therefore the President only expected of him the usual compliance with the order, for Thomas knew that not only in the opinion of his General-in-Chief and the rightful Secretary of War, but in the solemnly declared judgment of Congress, that order was but blank paper; when, therefore, we find him declaring a purpose to resort to force, he only stated what was necessary to make the order of the slightest use. No one knew better than Thomas the consequences of even accepting such an order, and the mere agreement between the President and himself, the one to issue the order and the other to accept it and to enter upon its execution, both knowing it to be unlawful, is of itself enough to hold both responsible for the manner in which either attempted to execute it. But his conversation with Mr. Burleigh was not merely the idle talk of a garrulous old man, drawn out of him by an inquisitive interlocutor, for we find that on the same day, and previous to his conversation with Burleigh, he had a conversation with Samuel Wilkeson, in which, after some hesitation, he told that witness substantially the same thing on two different occasions.

I quote briefly from his testimony, pages 212, 213:

"The WITNESS. I asked him to tell me what had occurred that morning between him and the Secretary of War in his endeavor to take possession of the War Department. He hesitated to do so till I told him that the town was filled with rumors of the change that had been made, of the removal of Mr. Stanton and the appointment of himself. He then said that since the affair had become public he felt relieved to speak to me with freedom about it. He drew from his pocket a copy, or rather the original, of the order of the President of the United States, directing him to take possession of the War Department immediately. He told me that he had taken as a witness of his action General Williams, and had gone up into the War Department and had shown to Edwin M. Stanton the order of the President, and had demanded, by virtue of that order, the possession of the War Department and its books and papers. He told me that Edwin M. Stanton, after reading the order, had asked him if he would allow to him sufficient time for him to gather together his books, papers, and other personal property and take them away with him; that he told him that he would allow to him all necessary time to do so, and had then withdrawn from Mr. Stanton's room. He further told me, that day being Friday, that the next day would be what he called a *dies non*, being the holiday of the anniversary of Washington's birthday, when he had directed that the War Department should be closed; that the day thereafter would be Sunday, and that on Monday morning he should demand possession of the War Department and of its property, and if that demand was refused or resisted he should apply to the General-in-Chief of the Army for a force sufficient to enable him to take possession of the War Department; and he added that he did not see how the General of the Army could refuse to obey his demand for that force. He then added that under the order that the President had given to him he had no election to pursue any other course than the one that he indicated; that he was a subordinate officer directed by an order from a superior officer, and that he must pursue that course."

Here we find not only the purpose to use force distinctly declared, but that, under the " order the President had given him, he had no election to pursue any other course." I ask how he could have spoken truthfully and have made any other declaration, when it is patent that no other course could have been successful? It does not seem to me that this view of the case could be made to appear more clear by illustration; and yet let me put a parallel case.

Suppose Andrew Johnson had determined to possess himself of the Capitol with a view of ousting Congress, and had directed the Speaker of the House of Representatives and the President of the Senate to turn over all the records, and had directed Thomas to take immediate possession. Such an order would be no less unlawful, in one view of the tenure act, than the one he gave. Could anybody doubt that such an order would mean revolution, and that a clash of arms must follow if it were executed; and, if such thing followed, that Mr. Johnson would be directly chargeable with the consequences? Would not *force* appear all over the order, though the word were not written? If the officer charged with executing such order declared, after receiving it, that he intended to use force, would any sane man set up that the President must not be held accountable for the declarations of such officer when they were declarations showing the only means of accomplishing the object? Let me ask wherein this hypothetical case is not covered by that at bar? Mr. Stanton was intrenched behind the law as securely as is Congress; he had frequently declared that he would not yield except to superior force. I say, then, that when the President ordered Thomas to take immediate possession of the War Department he gave him a *carte blanche* to do whatever he thought necessary to accomplish his purpose, and Thomas only echoed his coconspirator when he talked with Burleigh and Wilkeson. But General Thomas not only communicated his purpose to Burleigh, but he afterward told this witness why he had not executed his plan. Witness says (page 210) that he (Thomas) told him that the only thing that prevented his taking possession of the War Department on the morning he had invited Burleigh to be present was because of his arrest by the United States marshal at an unusually early hour.

At this point, before noticing the attempt of Thomas to seize the War Department on the morning of the 22d of February, I desire to call attention to a fact in evidence showing a perfect concurrence of mind between the President and his coconspirator, Thomas. On the morning of the 22d, the President's Private Secretary addressed a note, by direction of the President, to General Emory, in command of the military forces of the department. General Emory responded in person, and met the President about the same hour that Thomas entered the War Department. That interview is made the subject-matter of a separate article, and I will not give it at length in this place. But I urge that no man can read General Emory's narrative of what then transpired in the light of the circumstances surrounding this case and not feel himself driven to the conclusion that the President meant to use the military force of this department through that officer to carry out his unlawful design; and nothing but the indirect rebuke administered by General Emory, and his avowed purpose made to the President to obey no orders except they should come through the General-in-Chief, as by law provided, deterred the accused from then and there directing him to marshal his forces, if necessary, for the expulsion of Mr. Stanton.

While this remarkable scene was transpiring in the Executive Mansion, another not less remarkable was being enacted by the tool of the President at the War Department. There were many witnesses present, most of whom have testified. As they concur substantially in their testimony, I will give that of but one of them, Hon Thomas W. Ferry. (See page 224.)

"In the presence of Secretary Stanton, Judge Kelley, Moorhead, Dodge, Van Wyck, Van Horn, Delano, and Freeman Clarke, at twenty-five minutes past twelve m., General Thomas, Adjutant General, came into the Secretary of War Office, saying, 'Good morning,' the Secretary replying, 'Good morning, sir.' Thomas looked around and said, 'I do not wish to disturb these gentlemen, and will wait.' Stanton said, 'Nothing private here; what do you want, sir?'

"Thomas demanded of Secretary Stanton the surrender of the Secretary of War Office. Stanton denied it to him, and ordered him back to his own office as Adjutant General. Thomas refused to go. 'I claim the office of Secretary of War, and demand it by order of the President.'

"Stanton. 'I deny your authority to act, and order you back to your own office.'

"Thomas. 'I will stand here. I want no unpleasantness in the presence of these gentlemen.'

"Stanton. 'You can stand there if you please, but you cannot act as Secretary of War. I am Secretary of War. I order you out of this office, and to your own.'

"Thomas. 'I refuse to go, and will stand here.'

"Stanton. 'How are you to get possession; do you mean to use force?'

"Thomas. 'I do not care to use force, but my mind is made up as to what I shall do. I want no unpleasantness, though. I shall stay here and act as Secretary of War.'

"Stanton. 'You shall not, and I order you, as your superior, back to your own office.'

"Thomas. 'I will not obey you, but will stand here, and remain here.'

"Stanton. 'You can stand there, as you please. I order you out of this office to your own. I am Secretary of War, and your superior.'

"Thomas then went into opposite room across hall (General Schriver's) and commenced ordering General Schriver and General E. D. Townsend. Stanton entered, followed by Moorhead and Ferry, and ordered these Generals not to obey or pay attention to General Thomas's orders; that he denied his assumed authority as Secretary of War *ad interim*, and forbade their obedience of his directions. 'I am Secretary of War, and I now order you, General Thomas, out of this office to your own quarters.'

"Thomas. 'I will not go. I shall discharge the functions of Secretary of War.'

"Stanton. 'You will not.'

"Thomas. 'I shall require the mails of the War Department to be delivered to me, and shall transact the business of the office.'

"Stanton. 'You shall not have them, and I order you to your own office.'"

Gentlemen of the Senate, was this the method of executing an ordinary command of an officer delivered to him for an ordinary purpose? Did Thomas assume this belligerent attitude and enter upon this despicable business in such violent manner without having been instructed to do so, if necessary, by the man whose orders he was executing? Is it not probable that at the very moment he was bullying the Secretary of War and ordering General Schriver and General Townsend to recognize him as the rightful Secretary he was expecting the force necessary to maintain his authority from General Emory, who, he thought, was receiving instructions from the President to that effect? Sirs, this coincidence and concurrence of action between the President and Thomas on that morning is susceptible of no reasonable solution other than that they meditated the use of force and were availing themselves of every possible means to obtain it.

Now, sirs, I do not desire to pursue this inquiry further. If there was a conspiracy between these parties to take possession of the War Department by force, as I think has been fully shown by the evidence at this trial, then that conspiracy must be held to extend necessarily to the charges laid in the fourth and sixth articles, and they need not be separately discussed.

I will now briefly notice the charge laid in articles five and seven. The President is here charged with conspiring with Lorenzo Thomas and others unknown to seize, take, and possess the property of the United States in the Department of War, and to hinder and prevent Edwin M. Stanton, the Secretary of said Department, from holding his said office; this in violation of the civil-tenure act. In these charges there is no allegation of force being meditated, as was necessary in alleging the violation of the conspiracy act. The offense charged, then, consists simply in an agreement to do an unlawful act in an unlawful manner. It does not matter what means were contemplated nor what used. It is enough to know that the act and the manner of its accomplishment were unlawful.

The evidence already adduced, and the laws cited, show that at the time the accused attempted Mr. Stanton's removal he was lawfully in possession of his office. The evidence and the laws noticed also show that the accused had exhausted every legal means to remove Mr. Stanton. I say, then, that Mr. Johnson could take no step beyond these which would not in itself be an unlawful act. There was no way to remove Mr. Stanton against his will and without the advice and consent of the Senate except by resort to unlawful means. If he is proved to have attempted this by concert or agreement with one or more he is guilty of a conspiracy so to do. There is, sirs, an unwarrantable attempt to throw around this charge of conspiracy a meaning which it has not in law, to clothe this offense with something abhorrent to public sentiment; and we are told that persons may be jointly engaged in the most heinous crimes, and yet we must be cautious before convicting them of a conspiracy. This is an appeal to popular prejudice; and is nowhere to be derived from the books and decisions upon criminal law. The accused could not himself carry out his unlawful purpose; he was forced to select an accomplice. He made that selection, the agreement was entered into, the requisite order issued, the two minds met, and one of the parties entered upon the design to be accomplished, and that design being an unlawful one the conspiracy was complete. The tenure-of-office act, in its fifth and sixth sections, denounces as a high misdemeanor the very acts which are proved to have been committed by the President. Were it not for the rule of law which protects him while in his high office from a criminal prosecution before a jury of his countrymen he could upon his own answer be convicted and sentenced to imprisonment. And so, also, could Lorenzo Thomas. How, then, can he escape conviction before this court which can properly try him, simply because he has united with one or more persons to commit the offense? All the evidence which has been presented under the fourth and sixth articles applies with greater weight to the fifth and seventh. And should it be found not to establish that he conspired by *force* to remove Mr. Stanton, it by no means follows that he did not conspire at all. It would seem to me a work of supererogation to add to the grouping of guilty circumstances already given to intensify the proofs of complicity.

The accused has admitted in his answer that on and before August 5, 1867, "he became satisfied that he could not *allow* the said Stanton to continue to hold the office of Secretary of the War Department;" "that he did necessarily consider and *determine* that the said Stanton ought no longer to hold the said office;" "and to give effect to such his decision and *determination* he did address the said Stanton a note," &c., following:

"SIR: Public considerations of a high character constrain me to say that your resignation as Secretary of War will be accepted."

To which Mr. Stanton, on the same day, said:

"In reply, I have the honor to say that public considerations of a high character, which alone have induced me to continue at the head of this Department, constrain me not to resign the office of Secretary of War before the next meeting of Congress."

Here was the first step pursuant to the plan to dispossess Mr. Stanton peaceably if he could, forcibly if he must. Here he was plainly told that only by resort to the latter means would the Secretary yield. The answer tells us he was forced to consider what "acts could be done to cause the said Stanton to *surrender* the said office." Surrenders, Mr. President, do not often precede force. They usually follow not only its exhibition but its application.

The tenure act pointed out but one way, and Mr. Stanton having declined to resign, the law pointed out the only peaceable way.

He next, on the 12th of August, seven days after Mr. Stanton refused to resign, appointed General Grant *ad interim* and suspended Mr. Stanton; but this was but of temporary duration, for the Senate refused to concur, and Mr. Stanton resumed his functions of office.

Here ended all legal means; here ended all peaceable means; this exhausted every resort except to force, and this he prepared himself to use. He says the next step, although a violation of the law, was taken to raise a question for the courts. This will not do. He had been told in plainest terms by Mr. Stanton that he would not resign; he had been told by that officer that he yielded to superior force in the matter of his suspension, and he knew that the Senate had practically instructed Mr. Stanton that no attempt at removal by unlawful means would be sustained by them. We have Mr. Johnson, then, brought to an alternative which had but one solution in his mind, and that he had already determined upon, namely, to remove Mr. Stanton at all hazards.

To raise a question for the courts forsooth! He could not do this, and he well knew it, except by committing a trespass upon the bailiwick of Mr. Stanton, by law assigned him, and when within his office by forcibly ejecting him therefrom. If, sirs, his design was not to go this far, still if it included a purpose to establish a second Secretary of War in that building, and require subordinates to obey the orders of the pretended Secretary, this was force in the meaning of the act. We are bound to infer that when Mr. Johnson sat out to accomplish an object which he had every reason to believe would be successful only upon the application of force, he meditated that force; and whether he subsequently went to that extreme does not matter; the offense is complete without it. But what did he do? Having failed to secure the General-in-Chief as a tool he selected an officer of the Army, who was nominally Adjutant General, but whom neither Mr. Lincoln while he was President nor Mr. Stanton would trust in charge of the Adjutant General's department. The respondent peremptorily ordered the General-in-Chief to reinstate this man, knowing that he could not show a greater contempt for Mr. Stanton's authority than to thrust upon that Department an officer whom Mr. Stanton himself had suspended from his duties.

He had still another motive: the office of the Adjutant General was in the same building with that of the Secretary of War, and the ulterior purpose to possess himself of the entire building was thus to be more readily accomplished. On the 21st of February General Thomas was directed to take immediate possession of the War Department. He went accordingly and demanded the office. It is in evidence that on that same day the Senate,

upon information furnished them by the Secretary of War, passed a resolution declaring the attempted removal of Mr. Stanton a violation of the Constitution and the laws, and that resolution upon the same day was placed in the hands of the accused and his coconspirator Thomas. Not only this, they both knew that the House of Representatives had, in view of this removal, entered seriously upon the consideration of this respondent's impeachment. With these proceedings well understood, with the consequences certain to await the accused and his coconspirators, the order to Thomas is not countermanded, nor are his instructions changed, but the plan originally entered upon is attempted to be carried out without the slightest deviation, as we learn from Thomas's testimony, and with the plan fresh in his mind as laid before him by the accused, Thomas, on the same night, stated to Mr. BURLEIGH what he was going to do. Let me give a portion of BURLEIGH's testimony, pp. 201–2:

"A. On the evening of the 21st of February last I learned that General Thomas had been appointed Secretary of War *ad interim*, I think while at the Metropolitan Hotel. I invited Mr. Leonard Smith, of Leavenworth, Kansas, to go with me up to his house and see him. We took a carriage and went up. I found the general there getting ready to go out with his daughters to spend the evening at some place of amusement. I told him I would not detain him if he was going out; but he insisted on my sitting down, and I sat down for a few moments. I told him that I had learned he had been appointed Secretary of War. He said he had; that he had been appointed that day, I think; that after receiving his appointment from the President he went to the War Office to show his authority or his appointment to Secretary Stanton, and also his order to take possession of the office; that the Secretary remarked to him that he supposed he would give him time to remove his personal effects or his private papers, something to that effect; and his reply was 'Certainly.' He said that in a short time the Secretary asked him if he would give him a copy of his order, and he replied 'Certainly,' and gave it to him. He said that it was no more than right to give him time to take out his personal effects. I asked him when he was going to assume the duties of the office. He remarked that he should take possession the next morning at ten o'clock, which would be the 22d; and I think in that connection he stated that he had issued some order in regard to the observance of the day; but of that I am not quite sure. I remarked to him that I should be up at that end of the avenue the next day, and he asked me to come in and see him. I asked him where I would find him, and he said in the Secretary's room, up stairs. I told him I would be there. Said he, 'Be there punctual at ten o'clock.' Said I, 'You are going to take possession to-morrow?' 'Yes.' Said I, 'Suppose Stanton objects to it—resists?' 'Well,' said he, 'I expect to meet force by force,' or 'use force.'

"Mr. CONKLING. Repeat that.

"The WITNESS. I asked him what he would do if Stanton objected or resisted? He said he would use force or resort to force. Said I, 'Suppose he bars the doors?' His reply was, 'I will break them down.' I think that was about all the conversation that we had there at that time in that connection."

I have not noticed the sending for General Wallace, the officer second in command of this military department, after the President had failed in his attempted seduction of General Emory. I have not noticed the frequent declarations of the coconspirator Thomas, showing that up to the time this trial was entered upon he had not desisted from his purpose to possess himself of the War Department; that he is, in violation of any other theory than that he is, and has been since his appointment, in perfect accord and agreement with the President, received into Cabinet councils and official communication with the President as Secretary of War; that he has certified papers, one of which is in evidence, as Secretary of War; and in them 'at least, if not practically, is to-day by recognition and order of the President a *de facto* Secretary of War.

But, sirs, casting aside all evidence introduced by the prosecution, and looking at the charge of conspiracy in the light of the testimony which the answer furnishes, there is left us but one of two conclusions: either that this accused and General Thomas are fully sustained by the law in what they did and attempted to do, or they are both guilty, and the one now on trial must be convicted.

I will not here stop to notice the charges laid in article eighth. The offense does not materially differ from that laid in the second and third articles.

ARTICLE NINTH.

We are brought, then, to notice article ninth, which charges that the accused instructed General Emory that the act of Congress approved March 2, 1867, was unconstitutional and in contravention of commission of the said Emory, with intent to induce him, in his official capacity as commander of the military forces of this department, to violate the provisions of that act, and with the further intent thereby to enable the accused to prevent the execution of the tenure act, and also prevent Edwin M. Stanton, the Secretary of War, from discharging the duties of his office by virtue thereof. It would be difficult to read General Emory's testimony under this charge, if it stood unconnected with any other evidence, and not conclude that he was sent for by the President with a view to counsel a violation of this law.

This testimony is brief, and I crave the indulgence of the court to read it as given upon the record. General Emory was summoned by the President's Private Secretary. The note sent him and his testimony I will now read.

General Emory's testimony, pages 227, 228, and 229:

EXECUTIVE MANSION,
WASHINGTON, D. C., *February 22, 1868*.

* GENERAL: The President directs me to say that he will be pleased to have you call on him as early as practicable.

Very respectfully and truly, yours,
WILLIAM G. MOORE,
United States Army.

"Q. How early did you call? A. I called immediately.

"Q. How early in the day? A. I think it was about mid-day.

"Q. Whom did you find with the President, if anybody? A. I found the President alone when I first went in.

"Q. Will you have the kindness to state as nearly as you can what took place there? A. I will try and state the substance of it, but the words I cannot undertake to state exactly. The President asked me if I recollected a conversation he had had with me when I first took command of the department. I told him that I recollected the fact of the conversation distinctly. He then asked me what changes had been made. I told him no material changes; but such as had been made I could state at once. I went on to state that in the fall six companies of the twenty-ninth infantry had been brought to this city to winter; but, as an offset to that, four companies of the twelfth infantry had been detached to South Carolina, on the request of the commander of that district; that two companies of artillery that had been detached by my predecessor, one of them for the purpose of aiding in putting down the Fenian difficulties, had been returned to the command; that, although the number of companies had been increased, the numerical strength of the command was very much the same, growing out of an order reducing the artillery and infantry companies from the maximum of the war establishment to the minimum of the peace establishment. The President said, 'I do not refer to those changes.' I replied that if he would state what changes he referred to, or who made the report of the changes, perhaps I could be more explicit. He said, 'I refer to recent changes, within a day or two,' or something to that effect. I told him I thought I could assure him that no changes had been made; that, under a recent order issued for the government of the armies of the United States, founded upon a law of Congress, all orders had to be transmitted through General Grant to the Army, and, in like manner, all orders coming from General Grant to any of his subordinate officers must necessarily come, if in my department, through me; that if by chance an order had been given to any junior officer of mine it was his duty at once to report the fact. The President asked me, 'What order do you refer to?' I replied, 'To Order No. 17 of the series of 1867.' He said, 'I would like to see the order,' and a messenger was dispatched for it. At this time a gentleman came in who I supposed had business in no way connected with the business that I had in hand, and I withdrew to the further end of the room, and while there the messenger came with the book of orders and handed it to me. As soon as the gentleman had withdrawn I returned to the President with the book in my hand, and said I would take it as a favor if he would permit me to call his attention to that order; that it had been passed in an appropriation bill, and I thought it not unlikely had escaped his attention. He took the order and read it; and observed, 'This is not in conformity to the Constitution of the United States, that makes me Commander-in-Chief, or with the terms of your commission.'

"Mr. HOWARD. Repeat his language, if you please.

"The WITNESS. I cannot repeat it any nearer than I am now doing.

"Mr. CONKLING. Repeat your last answer louder, so that we may hear.

"Mr. JOHNSON. What he said.

"The WITNESS. What who said; the President or me?

"Mr. HOWARD. The President.

"The WITNESS. He said, 'This is not in conformity with the Constitution of the United States, which makes me Commander-in-Chief, or with the terms of your commission.' I replied, 'That is the order which you have approved and issued to the Army for our government,' or something to that effect. I cannot recollect the exact words, nor do I intend to quote the exact words of the President. He said, 'Am I to understand that the President of the United States cannot give an order except through the General of the Army' or 'General Grant?' I said, in reply, that that was my impression; that that was the opinion the Army entertained, and I thought upon that subject they were a unit. I also said, 'I think it is fair, Mr. President, to say to you that when this order came out there was considerable discussion on the subject as to what were the obligations of an officer under that order, and some eminent lawyers were consulted—I myself consulted one—and the opinion was given to me decidedly and unequivocally that we were bound by the order, constitutional or not constitutional. The President observed that the object of the law was evident.

"Mr. Manager BUTLER. Before you pass from that, did you state to him who the lawyers were that had been consulted? A. Yes.

"Q. What did you state on that subject? A. Perhaps, in reference to that, a part of my statement was not altogether correct. In regard to myself, I consulted Mr. Robert J. Walker.

"Q. State what you said to him, whether correct or otherwise? A. I will state it. I stated that I had consulted Mr. Robert J. Walker, in reply to his question as to whom it was I had consulted; and I understand other officers had consulted Mr. REVERDY JOHNSON.

"Q. Did you say to him what opinion had been reported from those consultations? A. I stated before that the lawyer that I had consulted stated to me that we were bound by it undoubtedly; and I understood from some officers, who I supposed had consulted Mr. JOHNSON, that he was of the same opinion.

"Q. What did the President reply to that? A. The President said, 'The object of the law is evident.' There the conversation ended by my thanking him for the courtesy with which he had allowed me to express my own opinion.

"Q. Did you then withdraw? A. I then withdrew."

I have said that this testimony, standing alone, bears upon its face proof of guilt, but we are not permitted to view it from so narrow a stand-point. It is illumined from many sources, and is given a significance not to be misunderstood. There is scarcely a scene or act connected with this remarkable drama of executive usurpation which does not explain this attempt to alienate a gallant officer from his General-in-Chief, and stamp it as scarcely less infamous than the attempt previously made to alienate the General-in-Chief from the whole loyal people of the land.

Sirs, there is not in this the naked procuration to violate law, but a treasonable attempt to poison the mind of a high Army officer to sow dissension, insubordination, and treachery in the Army. This, too, sirs, from the Commander-in-Chief. Such conduct in an officer or soldier is, by the Articles of War, punishable with death. Scores of soldiers have paid this penalty for mutinous conduct not half so aggravating. The moral sense not only of the Army but of the country must be shocked at such an exhibition from a Chief Magistrate; and, sirs, I will be pardoned for saying that General Emory never did a more heroic act than when he spurned the treacherous offer of high command which he knew would await him should he lend himself to the conspiracy already hatched by the President.

Now, sirs, how is this extraordinary interview explained by the accused? He says in his answer that his purpose was to ascertain what changes had been made in the military affairs of this department. That may have been one of his motives, but is it to be believed for a moment that this was all? To do this we must shut our eyes to all the cumulative evidence in this case. No one was threatening to use force against Mr. Johnson. There was no effort being made to oust him from office by force. He had nothing to apprehend from the military forces of this Department. There was no unusual excitement anywhere in the country that made it necessary for him to marshal these forces. The only thing, sirs, which he had any reason to apprehend might happen was, that in the event he persisted in his design to execute his order to remove the Secretary of War, this military force might not be found subservient to his wishes. And here we have a key which unlocks his treasonable designs. Here we have his motive made plain as the sunlight. He could not, by open confession, disclose more certainly what was intended by him when he summoned General Emory to his presence. It was not a proper question to ask that officer, when upon the witness stand, what he understood the President to mean by that cabalistic manner with which he introduced the subject of recent changes in the military forces made within a day or two. That is a question for you, Senators, to answer. General Emory could have answered it but one way. But let us see whether the turn which the conversation took does not of itself show the leading motive which the President had in mind. General Emory had responded fully as to the question put him, and assured the President that there had been no recent changes, and could be none (under the law and orders) without General Emory's first knowing it. There the conversation ought to have ended if the President's answer is held to disclose the whole truth. General Emory read to him the law by which he was guided, and the President himself took it and read it, and immediately observed:

"This is not in conformity with the Constitution of the United States, which makes me Commander-in-Chief, or with the terms of your commission."

General Emory replied, speaking of the order which promulgated that law:

"That is the order which you have approved and issued to the Army for our government."

The Commander-in-Chief being thus baffled by his subordinate, made this reply:

"Am I to understand that the President of the United States cannot give an order except through the General of the Army, or General Grant?"

This last answer is a complete portraiture of the President's motives, and his disappointment in not finding in Emory a willing tool through whom he might prosecute his designs. To put this in other phrase it would read:

"Then, General Emory, I am to understand you will not obey my orders unless I communicate them through General Grant?"

General Emory felt himself called upon to say that with regard to this law the Army were a unit. Of its meaning the President could have no doubt, for after listening to General Emory a moment longer, he remarked, with apparent disappointment at the result of the interview, "The object of the law is evident," and they then separated.

When we remember that this is but one of the links in the chain being forged by the accused with which to manacle the Secretary of War and bind a great department of the Government to the Juggernaut used by him to crush all opposition to executive will, the offense appears in hideous distinctness. That it was such a link to be thus used I am forced to believe, and I leave it to await the judgment of this high court.

I am disinclined, after this protracted discussion. to dwell at any length upon the tenth and eleventh articles; and yet I beg not to be understood as derogating from their importance or their gravity. The accused is here charged not only with improprieties and indecencies of speech; he is not only called to answer intemperate, disgraceful, incendiary, and riotous language, but he is charged with following up the purposes avowed in these speeches by overt acts looking directly to the obstruction of the laws which he had sworn to take care should be faithfully executed. If the conduct of this accused, in his official capacity, in word, act, and deed, has not shown conclusively his guilt under both of these articles then there could be no proof adduced, however strong, that would be sufficient.

The proof does show his unlawful attempt to obstruct the laws as therein charged. I will not again do more than to ask your examination of the facts proved and found in the recorded testimony, which shows how eagerly he entered upon the dangerous business of obstructing and defying the laws of the country. As to his speeches, upon which the tenth article is based, look at them, read them ; there they stand in history as a monument of his everlasting disgrace. The great labor of explaining and justifying such speeches and conduct is certainly in able hands. It is defended and justified as one of the great privileges of the President of the United States to be guilty of such indecency, impropriety, vulgarity, profanity, and impiety of speech as to offend the moral sense of the whole people. It is for them to show how far the liberty of indecent speech in a high official may be indulged before it reaches that unwarrantable license where the only power than can *will* step in and correct the wrong. The idea that a President may so demean himself by indecent speech as to make him a scoff and byword, and place himself so low in the moral scale that none "would stoop to touch his loftiest thought," and yet not be guilty of such misdemeanors as would call for the very action we have taken, is beyond my ken.

"O judgment, thou art fled to brutish beasts,
  And men have lost their reason."

The defense have not, by their evidence, contradicted what we have proven, but have only strengthened our case. There has been no proof adduced on the part of the defendant that either will justify or excuse his unlawful acts. The evidence of General Sherman, and all others put on the stand by the defense, only make his guilt the more manifest. The attempt by documentary evidence to prove the practice of the Government to justify his act proves that the practice has been to obey the law and not violate it, as all appointments and removals proved have been made under some existing law, either the laws of 1789, 1795, 1820, 1856, or some authority in law upon which the act was based. But suppose every other Administration had violated the law, would that justify the violation of a positive enactment making its violation a crime or misdemeanor? Certainly not. If so, a murderer might justify his murder on the grounds that murders were common in the country from the commencement of the Government to the present time. Even the advice of his Cabinet cannot excuse him. By advising a crime they cannot shield their chief, but may be impeachable themselves for advising a disobedience of law. But it is all of record, and I will not pursue it further. We have laid bare his offenses. In all that has been proven, or aught of his conduct since President, which is a matter of history, there is not to be found a good motive for his conduct. He is found without any of the elements necessary to fit him for any official position.

Goodness, clemency, and a proper liberality should be among the virtues that adorn a Chief Magistrate. With the aid of these he should be able to greatly assist in the amelioration of the condition of the whole people. The chief end of all his actions should be to promote peace, safety, prosperity, and happiness to the nation.

This was the idea of the heathen philosophers; they defined a good prince as "one who endeavors to render his subjects happy;" "and a tyrant," on the contrary, "one who only aims at his own private advantage."

An example of the first we had in the lamented Lincoln, and of the latter in Mr. Johnson.

Mr. Lincoln was endowed with one of the most genial souls that Heaven ever gave to man and an intellect of most wonderful power. His apprehension was quick, his judgment sound, his conclusions correct. His mind was sufficiently capacious to comprehend all the vast range of thought to which occasion gave scope. He met the critical hour of duty to his country like a statesman and a man. He sustained loyalty and gave all his strength in crushing treason. Instead of denouncing your Congress, he consulted and advised with them for the good of the country. Instead of vetoing every law, he aided and assisted in giving them force. Instead of openly violating the plain provisions of your enactments, he executed them faithfully, as was his duty.

How a Government is to be administered while peace is smiling is one thing, and how it is to be administered amid the horrors of war is quite another thing. Mr. Lincoln had wants hourly multiplying upon his hands that before or since were unheard of. The difficulties with which the war on our hands was complicated were almost interminable; but with each new-found difficulty he found *new strength, hope,* and *energy*, until all obstacles were overcome and the war ended. But at the very dawn of the nation's new birth, resting from his labors and contemplating that peace that was then breaking through the dark, angry clouds of war, he fell by the hand of an assassin.

Yes, his sun has set forever. Loyalty's gentle voice can no longer wake thrills of joy along the tuneless chords of his moldering heart. Yet the patriots and lovers of liberty, who still linger on the shore of time, rise and bless his memory; and millions yet unborn will in after times rise up to deplore his fate and cherish as a household word his deathless name.

Mr. President and Senators, what patriots that linger behind will rise up and bless the memory of Andrew Johnson? Who will in after times rise up to deplore the fate that now surely awaits him? Who will cherish as a household word his dishonored name? None, none, Mr. President; no, not one! No, sir; the virtues that should adorn a Chief Magistrate fled on the induction of this criminal into that high office. In sadness and sorrow did the people witness this man succeed to the executive chair—not by their spontaneuos voice, not by their free accord, but by the ministration of the murderer's missive. They witnessed him, who had acquired power by such a sorrowful and inauspicious chance, bending blindly to the behests of those whose adherents, if not they themselves, had lately been in rebellious arms against that Constitution which he had sworn to protect and maintain. They saw him, flushed with arrogance and pride, despise the warnings of the people and deride the mandates of their legislators. When an act of the legislative department of the Government would not inure to his advantage politically they saw him openly violate and trample it under foot. When loyalty was supported and peace attempted to be perpetuated they saw him disregard their will and throw all manner of obstructions in the way.

When the officers of the Government would not bend the knee and cry "great and good prince," they saw him attempt to hurl them from his courts. When the commander of the Army would not do his bidding they have seen him conspire to destroy his good name and fame before the country. When the country was at ease they have seen him give it grief and pain. When at peace and rest they have seen his attempt to give it revolution and blood.

They saw him with a ruthless and heavy hand attempt to seize the nation's purse and the nation's sword, and thus, by clutching in his longing grasp all the attributes of power, place himself in a condition where he might with safety announce his views and enforce his designs.

They felt the weight of his great office fall like an enshrouding pall over a suffering people. They marked with alarm and consternation his rapid strides to that point where his sway would have been autocratic and his reign irresistible. It was not alone by force that this was to be accomplished. By appeals which were designing, and all the more dangerous because of apparent candor, he drew to him the careless and unsuspecting. By pledges, all the more reprehensible because of plighted honor, he soothed the suspicions of the cautious and the wise. By profuse disposition of rewards in his hands he gained the mercenary and attracted the unscrupulous; and where the pliant arts of flattery and persuasion failed to accomplish his intended views, by the stern show of his power and authority he awed the timid and overbore the weak.

These, sirs, we have manifested, if by our proof we have made aught manifest. And to all this what does he reply? That, though his acts were bad, his motives were good; that, though his course was unlawful, his heart was well-meaning; that he trampled on the law in order that he might uphold the law; that he disregarded his oath the better to enable him to keep it. When we ask him why he set aside the law of the land he replies that it was because it was opposed to the Constitution of the land; and when we again inquire as to the Constitution of the land we are assured that it is his prerogative to construe it even in violation of the laws of the land. Have I stated this beyond the line of his defense? Have I wronged him by one unjust description of his conduct or his claim? If not, shall this state of things longer exist? Shall we snap the chains that bind us or continue in them longer? Shall we vindicate the law or crouch at the usurper's frown? Shall we vindicate to-day the principle that underlies the very foundation of this Government or allow the laws to be trampled under foot at the will of every tyrant?

It is a fundamental principle of this Government that there shall be a known rule and law by which not only the conduct of the citizen, but all officers, including the Chief Magistrate of the nation, shall be regulated and governed. This is a Government of laws and not of men. It is this principle which distinguishes this republican form of Government of ours from the monarchies of the Old World.

I repeat, sirs, this is a Government of laws and not of men. Never before, I believe, was it known in this enlightened country that the executive head of the nation had the arrogance to take upon himself not only the executive, but the judicial functions of the Government. No, sir; under the smiles of that merciful Providence who had watched over and guided the destinies of the people, we have hitherto been exempt, and I trust in God shall hereafter continue to be, from the affliction of that most direful scourge, a Chief Executive with full discretionary powers to execute a law or declare it unconstitutional at will. It is not that which pleaseth nor that which is most consonant with the humor and inclination of the President, but the law, which should be the rule of his conduct. I trust, sirs, that the time will never again come in the history of this nation when, by elevation to the Presidency, any one will become so infatuated as to imagine himself independent of that rule, or to set up his own private judgment or opinions as the only standard by which he will be guided or governed. Then, sirs, whether we shall in the future witness this attempt in other Executives depends upon your decision upon the issues in this case involved. Being the grand tribunal from which there can be no appeal, you should properly reflect the law and the testimony. The pure stream of public justice should flow gently along, undisturbed by any false pretense on the part of the defendant or false sympathy upon your part. The President should not be permitted to play the necromancer with this Senate as he did with the country through the law department of the executive branch of the Government, whereby he raised a tempest that he himself could not control. Well might he have exclaimed:

> "I am the rider of the wind,
> The stirrer of the storm;
> The hurricane I left behind
> Is yet with lightning warm."

But, thanks to the wisdom of our far-seeing patriot sires, you, Senators, are, by our Constitution, made the great power that shall calm the tempest and so direct the lightning that its strokes shall be warded off from the people and fall only upon the head of their oppressor.

Yes, Senators, we fervently hope and confidently rely upon you to calm the storm, and prevent the Temple of Liberty being dashed to earth by the hurricane. We cannot, will not believe that we are or will be mistaken in those in whom we now place our trust. Methinks I hear a voice coming up from the lowly pillows of patriotism's immortal martyrs, saying, "Be of good cheer, all will yet be well." We cannot, will not believe that the respondent's unjust appeals will avail him now. He appeals to the truth of history to vindicate him in the acts of former Executives; but truth itself rises up from the midst of the mass of testimony here adduced, and says, even in this appeal, he has polluted God's holy sanctuary; and when on justice he relies to protect him, and lift him up out of his difficulties, justice comes forward in all her majesty and declares that he has not only trampled the laws of man but of God under foot. When he indirectly asks that the mantle of charity shall by you be thrown over his shortcomings and violations of law clemency steps forward, and with a loud voice cries, "Forbearance has ceased to be a virtue;" "Mercy to this criminal would be cruelty to the State."

From the 14th day of April, 1865, to this day, as shown by the testimony, he has been consistent only with himself and the evil spirits of his Administration. False to the people who took him from obscurity and conferred on him splendor; who dug him from that oblivion to which he had been consigned by the treason of his State, and gave him that distinction which, as disclosed by his subsequent acts, he never merited and has so fearfully scandalized, disgraced, and dishonored; false to the memory of him whose death made him President; false to the principles of our contest for national life; false to the Constitution and laws of the land and his oath of office; filled with all vanity, lust, and pride; substituting, with the most disgusting self-complacency and ignorance, his own coarse, brutalized will for the will of the people, and substituting his vulgar, vapid, and ignorant utterances for patriotism, statesmanship, and faithful public service, he has completed his circle of high crimes and misdemeanors; and, thanks to Almighty God, by the imbedded wisdom of our fathers found in the Constitution of our country, he stands to-day, with all his crimes upon his head, uncovered before the world, at the bar of this the most august tribunal on earth, to receive the awful sentence that awaits him as a fitting punishment for the crimes and misdemeanors of which he stands impeached by the House of Representatives, in the name and on behalf of all the people.

Here, Senators, we rest our case; here we leave the great criminal of the age. In your hands, as wisely provided by the charter of our liberties, this offender against the Constitution, the laws, liberty, peace, and public decency of our country is now left to be finally and, in the name of all the people, we humbly trust, disposed of forever, in such manner as no more to outrage the memories of an heroic and illustrious past, nor dim the hopes, expectations, and glories of the coming future. Let us, we implore you, no more hear *his* resounding footfalls in the temple of American constitutional liberty, nor have the vessels of the ark of the covenant of our fathers polluted by his unholy hands. Let not the blood of a half million of heroes who went to their deaths on the nation's battle-fields for the nation's life cry from the ground against us on account of the crimes permitted by us, and committed by him whom we now leave in your hands. Standing here to-day for the last time with my brother Managers, to take leave of this case and this great tribunal, I am penetrated and overwhelmed with emotion. Memory is busy with the scenes of the years which have intervened between March 4, 1861, and this day. Our great war, its battles and ten thousand incidents, without mental bidding and beyond control, almost pass in panoramic view before me. As in the presence of those whom I have seen fall in battle as we rushed to victory, or die of wounds or disease in hospital far from home and the loved ones, to be seen no more until the grave gives up its dead, have I endeavored to discharge my humble part in this great trial.

The world in after times will read the history

of the administration of Andrew Johnson as an illustration of the depth to which political and official perfidy can descend. Amid the unhealed ghastly scars of war; surrounded by the weeds of widowhood and cries of orphanage; associating with and sustained by the soldiers of the Republic, of whom at one time he claimed to be one; surrounded by the men who had supported, aided, and cheered Mr. Lincoln through the darkest hours and sorest trials of his sad yet immortal administration—men whose lives had been dedicated to the cause of justice, law, and universal liberty—the men who had nominated and elected him to the second office in the nation at a time when he scarcely dared visit his own home because of the traitorous instincts of his own people; yet, as shown by his official acts, messages, speeches, conversations, and associations, almost from the time when the blood of Lincoln was warm on the floor of Ford's theater, Andrew Johnson was contemplating treason to all the fresh fruits of the overthrown and crushed rebellion, and an affiliation with and a practical official and hearty sympathy for those who had cost hecatombs of slain citizens, billions of treasure, and an almost ruined country. His great aim and purpose has been to subvert law, usurp authority, insult and outrage Congress, reconstruct the rebel States in the interests of treason, insult the memories and resting-places of our heroic dead; outrage the feelings and deride the principles of the living men who aided in saving the Union, and deliver all snatched from wreck and ruin into the hands of unrepentent, but by him pardoned, traitors.

But, all honor to the servants of a brave and loyal people, he has been in strict conformity to the Constitution arrested in his career of crime, impeached, arraigned, tried, and here awaits your sentence. We are not doubtful of your verdict. Andrew Johnson has long since been tried by the whole people and found guilty, and you can but confirm that judgment already pronounced by the sovereign American people.

Henceforth our career of greatness will be unimpeded. Rising from our baptism of fire and blood, purified by our sufferings and trials under the approving smiles of Heaven, and freed, as we are, from the crimes of oppression and wrong, the patriot heart looks outward and onward for long and ever-increasing national prosperity, virtue, and happiness.

Hon. GEORGE S. BOUTWELL, on behalf of the Managers, addressed the Senate, as follows:

Mr. PRESIDENT, SENATORS: The importance of this occasion is due to the unexampled circumstance that the Chief Magistrate of the principal Republic of the world is on trial upon the charge that he is guilty of high crimes and misdemeanors in office. The solemnity of this occasion is due to the circumstance that this trial is a new test to our public national virtue and also of the strength and vigor of popular government. The trial of a great criminal is not an extraordinary event, even when followed by conviction and the severest penalty known to the laws. This respondent is not to be deprived of life, liberty, or property. The object of this proceeding is not the punishment of the offender, but the safety of the State. As the daily life of the wise and just magistrate is an example for good, cheering, encouraging, and strengthening all others, so the trial and conviction of a dishonest or an unfaithful officer is a warning to all men, and especially to such as occupy places of public trust.

ISSUES.

The issues of record between the House of Representatives and Andrew Johnson, President of the United States, are technical and limited. We have met the issues, and, as we believe, maintained the cause of the House of Representatives by evidence direct, clear, and conclusive. Those issues require you to ascertain and declare whether Andrew Johnson, President of the United States, is guilty of high crimes and misdemeanors as set forth in the several articles of impeachment exhibited against him, and especially whether he has violated the laws or the Constitution of the country in the attempt which he made on the 21st of February last to remove Edwin M. Stanton from the office of Secretary for the Department of War, and to appoint Lorenzo Thomas Secretary of War *ad interim.*

These are the issues disclosed by the record. They appear in the statement to be limited in their nature and character; but your final action thereon involves and settles questions of public policy of greater magnitude than any which have been considered in the political or judicial proceedings of the country since the adoption of the Constitution.

DEFENSE.

Mr. Johnson attempts to defend his conduct in the matter of the removal of Mr. Stanton by an assertion of "the power at any and all times of removing from office all executive officers for cause to be judged of by the President alone."

This claim manifestly extends to the officers of the Army and of the Navy, of the civil and the diplomatic service. He thus assumes and demands for himself and for all his successors absolute control over the vast and yearly increasing patronage of this Government. This claim has never been before asserted, and surely it has never been sanctioned; nor is there a law or usage which furnishes any ground for justification, even the least.

Heretofore the Senate has always been consulted in regard to appointments, and during the sessions of the Senate it has always been consulted in regard to removals from office. The claim now made, if sanctioned, strips the Senate of all practical power in the premises, and leaves the patronage of office, the revenues and expenditures of the country in the hands of the President alone. Who does not see that the power of the Senate to act upon and confirm a nomination is a barren power, as a means of protecting the public interests, if the person so confirmed may be removed from his office at once without the advice and consent of the Senate? If this claim shall be conceded the President is clothed with power to remove every person who refuses to become his instrument.

An evil-minded President may remove all loyal and patriotic officers from the Army, the Navy, the civil and the diplomatic service, and nominate only his adherents and friends. None but his friends can remain in office; none but his friends can be appointed to office. What security remains for the fidelity of the Army and the Navy? What security for the collection of the public revenues? What accountability remains in any branch of the public service? Every public officer is henceforth a mere dependent upon the Executive. Heretofore the Senate could say to the President, "You shall not remove a faithful, honest public officer." This power the Senate has possessed and exercised for nearly eighty years, under and by virtue of express authority granted in the Constitution. Is this authority to be surrendered? Is this power of the Senate, this prerogative we may almost call it, to be abandoned? Has the country, has the Senate, in the exercise of its legislative, executive, or judicial functions, fully considered these broader and graver issues touching and affecting vitally our institutions and system of government?

The House of Representatives has brought Andrew Johnson, President of the United States, to the bar of this august tribunal, and has here charged him with high crimes and misdemeanors in office. He meets the charge by denying and assailing the ancient, undoubted, constitutional powers of the Senate. This is the grave, national, historical, constitutional issue. When you decide the issues of record, which appear narrow and technical, you decide these greater issues also.

The Managers on the part of the House of Representatives, as time and their abilities may permit, intend to deal with the criminal and with these his crimes, and also to examine the constitutional powers of the President and of the Senate. I shall first invite your attention, Senators, to the last-mentioned topics.

It is necessary, in this discussion, to consider the character of the Government, and especially the distribution of powers and the limitations placed by the Constitution upon the executive, judicial, and legislative departments.

TENTH AMENDMENT.

The tenth amendment to the Constitution provides that "the powers not delegated to the United States by the Constitution, nor prohibited by it to the States, are reserved to the States respectively, or to the people."

This provision is not to be so construed as to defeat the objects for which the Constitution itself was established; and it follows, necessarily, that the three departments of the Government possess sufficient power collectively to accomplish those objects.

It will be seen from an examination of the grants of power made to the several departments of the Government that there is a difference in the phraseology employed, and that the legislative branch alone is intrusted with discretionary authority. The first section of the first article provides that "all legislative powers *herein granted* shall be vested in a Congress of the United States, which shall consist of a Senate and House of Representatives."

The first section of the second article provides that "executive power shall be vested in a President of the United States of America;" and the first section of the third article provides that "the judicial power of the United States shall be vested in one Supreme Court, and in such inferior courts as the Congress may, from time to time, ordain and establish." The words "herein granted," as used in the first section of the first article of the Constitution, are of themselves words of limitation upon the legislative powers of Congress, confining those powers within the authority expressed in the Constitution. The absence of those words in the provisions relating to the executive and judicial departments does not, as might at first be supposed, justify the inference that unlimited authority is conferred upon those departments. An examination of the Constitution shows that the executive and judicial departments have no inherent vigor by which, under the Constitution, they are enabled to perform the functions delegated to them, while the legislative department, in noticeable contrast, is clothed with authority "to make all laws which shall be necessary and proper for carrying into execution the foregoing powers, *and all other powers vested by this Constitution in the Government of the United States, or any department or officer thereof."*

By virtue of this provision the Constitution devolves upon Congress the duty of providing by legislation for the full execution not only of the powers vested in Congress, but also of providing by legislation for the execution of those powers which, by the Constitution, are vested in the executive and judicial departments. The legislative department has original power derived from the Constitution by which it can set and keep itself in motion as a branch of the Government, while the executive and judicial departments have no self-executing constitutional capacity, but are constantly dependent upon the legislative department. Nor does it follow, as might upon slight attention be assumed, that the executive power given to the President is an unlimited power, or that it answers or corresponds to the powers which have been or may be exercised by the executive of any other Government. The President of the United States is not endowed by the Constitution with the executive power which was possessed by Henry VIII or Queen Elizabeth, or by any ruler in any other country or time, but only with the power expressly granted to him by the Constitution and with such other powers as have been conferred upon him by Congress for the purpose of carrying into effect the powers which are granted to the President by the Constitution. Hence it may be asserted that whenever the President attempts to exercise any power he must, if his right be questioned, find a specific authority in the Constitution or laws. By the Constitution he is Commander-in-Chief of the Army and Navy; but it is for Congress to decide, in the first place, whether there shall be an Army or Navy, and the President must command the Army or Navy as it is created by Congress, and subject, as is every other officer of the Army and Navy, to such rules and regulations as Congress may from time to time establish.

The President "may require the opinion in writing of the principal officer in each of the Executive Departments upon any subject relating to the duties of their respective offices," but the executive offices themselves are created by Congress, and the duties of each officer are prescribed by law. In fine, the power to set the Government in motion and to keep it in motion is lodged exclusively in Congress under the provisions of the Constitution.

By our system of Government the sovereignty is in the people of the United States, and that sovereignty is fully expressed in the preamble to the Constitution. By the Constitution the people have vested discretionary power—limited, it is true—in the Congress of the United States, while they have denied to the executive and judicial departments all discretionary or implied power whatever.

The nature and extent of the powers conferred by the Constitution upon Congress have been clearly and fully set forth by the Supreme Court. (McCulloch vs. The State of Maryland, 4 Wheaton, pp. 409 and 420.) The court, in speaking of the power of Congress, say:

"The Government, which has a right to do an act, and has imposed on it the duty of performing that act, must, according to the dictates of reason, be allowed to select the means."

Again, they say:

"We admit, as all must admit, that the powers of the Government are limited, and that these limits are not to be transcended; but we think tho sound construction of the Constitution must allow to *the national Legislature* that discretion, with respect to the means by which the powers it confers are to be carried into execution, which will enable that body to perform the high duties assigned to it in the manner most beneficial to tho people. Let the thing be legitimate, let it be within the scope of the Constitution, and all means which are appropriate, which are plainly adapted to the end, which are not prohibited, and consistent with the letter and spirit of the Constitution, are constitutional."

It is also worthy of remark, in this connection, that the article which confers legislative powers upon the Congress of the United States declares that *all* legislative powers herein granted—that is, granted in the Constitution—

shall be vested in the Congress of the United States; while in the section relating to the powers of the President it is declared that *the* executive power shall be vested in a President of the United States of America. The inference from this distinction is in harmony with what has been previously stated. "The executive power" spoken of is that which is conferred upon the President by the Constitution, and it is limited by the terms of the Constitution, and must be exercised in the manner prescribed by the Constitution. The words used are to be interpreted according to their ordinary meaning.

It is also worthy of remark that the Constitution, in terms, denies to Congress various legislative powers specified. It denies also to the United States various powers, and various powers enumerated are likewise denied to the States. There is but one denial of power to the President, and that is a limitation of an express power granted. The single instance of a denial of power to the President is in that provision of the Constitution wherein he is authorized " to grant reprieves and pardons for offenses against the United States, except in cases of impeachment." As the powers granted to the President are specified, and as he takes nothing by implication or inference, there was no occasion to recite or enumerate powers not delegated to him. As the Constitution clothes Congress with powers of legislation which are ample for all the necessities of national life, wherein there is opportunity for the exercise of a wide discretion, it was necessary to specify such powers as are prohibited to Congress. The powers of Congress are ascertained by considering as well what is prohibited as what is granted, while the powers of the Executive are to be ascertained clearly and fully by what is granted. Where there is nothing left to inference, implication, or discretion, there is no necessity for clauses or provisions of inhibition. In the single case of the grant of the full power of pardon to the President, a power unlimited in its very nature, the denial of the power to pardon in case of impeachment became necessary. This example fully illustrates and establishes the position to which I now ask your assent. If this view be correct it follows necessarily, as has been before stated, that the President, acting under the Constitution, can exercise those powers only which are specifically conferred upon him, and can take nothing by construction, by implication, or by what is sometimes termed the necessity of the case.

But in every Government there should be in its constitution capacity to adapt the administration of affairs to the changing conditions of national life. In the Government of the United States this capacity is found in Congress, in virtue of the provision already quoted, by which Congress is authorized "to make all laws which shall be necessary and proper for carrying into execution the foregoing powers, (*i. e.*, the powers given to Congress,) and all other powers vested by this Constitution in the Government of the United States, or in any department or officer thereof."

It is made the duty of the President, "from time to time, to give to the Congress information of the state of the Union, and recommend to their consideration such measures as he shall judge necessary and expedient."

Provision is also made in the Constitution for his coöperation in the enactment of laws. Thus it is in his power to lay before Congress the reasons which, in his opinion, may at any time exist for legislative action in aid of the executive powers conferred by the Constitution upon the President; and under the ample legislative powers secured to Congress by the provisions already quoted there is no reason in the nature of the Government why the constitutional and lawful powers of the Executive may not be made adequate to every emergency of the country. In fine, the President may be said to be governed by the principles which govern the judge in a court of law. He must take the law and administer it as he finds it without any inquiry on his part as to the wisdom of the legislation. So the President, with reference to the measure of his own powers, must take the Constitution and the laws of the country as they are, and be governed strictly by them. If, in any particular, by implication or construction, he assumes and exercises authority not granted to him by the Constitution or the laws he violates his oath of office, by which, under the Constitution, it is made his duty " to take care that the laws be faithfully executed," which implies necessarily that he can go into no inquiry as to whether the laws are expedient or otherwise; nor is it within his province, in the execution of the law, to consider whether it is constitutional. In his communications to Congress he may consider and discuss the constitutionality of existing or proposed legislation, and when a bill is passed by the two Houses and submitted to him for approval he may, if in his opinion the same is unconstitutional, return it to the House in which it originated with his reasons. In the performance of these duties he exhausts his constitutional power in the work of legislation. If, notwithstanding his objections, Congress, by a two-thirds majority in each House, shall pass the bill, it is then the duty of the President to obey and execute it, as it is his duty to obey and execute all laws which he or his predecessors may have approved.

If a law be in fact unconstitutional it may be repealed by Congress, or it may, possibly, when a case duly arises, be annulled in its unconstitutional features by the Supreme Court of the United States. The repeal of the law is a legislative act; the declaration by the court that it is unconstitutional is a judicial act; but the power to repeal or to annul or to set aside a law of the United States is in no aspect of the case an executive power. It is made the

duty of the Executive to take care that the laws be faithfully executed—an injunction wholly inconsistent with the theory that it is in the power of the Executive to repeal or annul or dispense with the laws of the land. To the President in the performance of his executive duties all laws are alike. He can enter into no inquiry as to their expediency or constitutionality. All laws are presumed to be constitutional, and, whether in fact constitutional or not, it is the duty of the Executive so to regard them while they have the form of law. When a statute is repealed for its unconstitutionality, or for any other reason, it ceases to be law in form and in fact. When a statute is annulled in whole or in part by the opinion of a competent judicial tribunal, from that moment it ceases to be law. But the respondent and the counsel for the respondent will seek in vain for any authority or color of authority in the Constitution or the laws of the country by which the President is clothed with power to make any distinction upon his own judgment, or upon the judgment of any friends or advisers, whether private or official persons, between the several statutes of the country, each and every one of which he is, by the Constitution and by his oath of office, required faithfully to execute. Hence it follows that the crime of the President is not, either in fact or as set forth in the articles of impeachment, that he has violated a constitutional law, but his crime is that he has violated a law, and in his defense no inquiry can be made whether the law is constitutional; for inasmuch as he had no constitutional power to inquire for himself whether the law was constitutional or not, so it is no excuse for him that he did unlawfully so inquire and came to the conclusion that the law was unconstitutional.

It follows, from the authorities already quoted and the positions founded thereon, that there can be no inquiry here and now by this tribunal whether the act in question—the act entitled "An act regulating the tenure of certain civil offices"—is in fact constitutional or not. It was and is the law of the land. It was enacted by a strict adherence to constitutional forms. It was and is binding upon all the officers and departments of the Government. The Senate, for the purpose of deciding whether the respondent is innocent or guilty, can enter into no inquiry as to the constitutionality of the act, which it was the President's duty to execute, and which, upon his own answer, and by repeated official confessions and admissions, he intentionally, willfully, deliberately set aside and violated.

If the President, in the discharge of his duty "to take care that the laws be faithfully executed," may inquire whether the laws are constitutional, and execute those only which he believes to be so, then, for the purposes of government, his will or opinion is substituted for the action of the law-making power, and the Government is no longer a Government of laws, but the Government of one man. This is also true, if, when arraigned, he may justify by show-ing that he has acted upon advice that the law was unconstitutional. Further, if the Senate sitting for the trial of the President may inquire and decide whether the law is in fact constitutional, and convict the President if he has violated an act believed to be constitutional, and acquit him if the Senate think the law unconstitutional, then the President is in fact tried for his judgment, to be acquitted if in the opinion of the Senate it was a correct judgment, and convicted if in the opinion of the Senate his judgment was erroneous. This doctrine offends every principle of justice. His offense is that he intentionally violated a law. Knowing its terms and requirements, he disregarded them.

With deference I maintain still further that it is not the right of any Senator in this trial to be governed by any opinion he may entertain of the constitutionality or expediency of the law in question. For the purposes of this trial the statute which the President, upon his own confession, has repeatedly violated is the law of the land. His crime is that he violated the law. It has not been repealed by Congress; it has not been annulled by the Supreme Court; it stands upon the statute-book as the law; and for the purposes of this trial it is to be treated by every Senator as a constitutional law. Otherwise it follows that the President of the United States, supported by a minority exceeding by one a third of this Senate, may set aside, disregard, and violate all the laws of the land. It is nothing to this respondent, it is nothing to this Senate, sitting here as a tribunal to try and judge this respondent, that the Senators participated in the passage of the act, or that the respondent, in the exercise of a constitutional power, returned the bill to the Senate with his objections thereto. The act itself is as binding, is as constitutional, is as sacred in the eye of the Constitution as the acts that were passed at the first session of the First Congress. If the President may refuse to execute a law because in his opinion it is unconstitutional, or for the reason that, in the judgment of his friends and advisers, it is unconstitutional, then he and his successors in office may refuse to execute any statute the constitutionality of which has not been affirmatively settled by the Supreme Court of the United States. If a minority, exceeding one third of this Senate by one, may relieve the President from all responsibility for this violation of his oath of office, because they concur with him in the opinion that this legislation is either unconstitutional or of doubtful constitutionality, then there is no security for the execution of the laws. The constitutional injunction upon the President is to take care that the laws be faithfully executed; and upon him no power whatsoever is conferred by the Constitution to inquire whether the law that he is charged to execute is or is not constitutional. The constitutional injunction upon you, in your present capacity, is to hold the respondent faithfully to the exe-

cution of the constitutional trusts and duties imposed upon him. If he has willfully disregarded the obligation resting upon him, to take care that the laws be faithfully executed, then the constitutional duty imposed upon you is to convict him of the crime of having willfully disregarded the laws of the land and violated his oath of office.

I indulge, Senators, in great plainness of speech, and pursue a line of remark which, were the subject less important or the duty resting upon us less solemn, I should studiously avoid. But I speak with every feeling and sentiment of respect for this body and this place of which my nature is capable. In my boyhood, from the gallery of the old Chamber of the Senate, I looked, not with admiration merely, but with something of awe upon the men of that generation who were then in the seats which you now fill. Time and experience may have modified and chastened those impressions, but they are not, they cannot be obliterated. They will remain with me while life remains. But, with my convictions of my own duty, with my convictions of your duty, with my convictions of the danger, the imminent peril, to our country if you should not render a judgment of guilty against this respondent, I have no alternative but to speak with all the plainness and directness which the most earnest convictions of the truth of what I utter can inspire.

MOTIVE.

Nor can the President prove or plead the motive by which he professes to have been governed in his violation of the laws of the country. Where a positive specific duty is imposed upon a public officer his motives cannot be good if he willfully neglects or refuses to discharge his duty in the manner in which it is imposed upon him. In other words, it is not possible for a public officer, and particularly for the President of the United States, who is under a special constitutional injunction to discharge his duty faithfully, to have any motive except a bad motive if he willfully violates his duty. A judge, to be sure, in the exercise of a discretionary power, as in imposing a sentence upon a criminal, where the penalty is not specific, may err in the exercise of that discretion and plead properly his good motives in the discharge of his duty; that is, he may say that he intended, under the law, to impose a proper penalty; and inasmuch as that was his intention, though all other men may think that the penalty was either insufficient or excessive, he is fully justified by his motives.

So the President, having vested in him discretionary power in regard to granting pardons, might, if arraigned for the improper exercise of that power in a particular case, plead and prove his good motives, although his action might be universally condemned as improper or unwise in that particular case. But the circumstances of this respondent are wholly different. The law which, as he admits, he has intentionally and deliberately violated, was mandatory upon him, and left in his hands no discretion as to whether he would, in a given case, execute it or not.

A public officer can neither plead nor prove good motives to refute or control his own admission that he has intentionally violated a public law.

Take the case of the President; his oath is:

"I do solemnly swear that I will faithfully execute the office of President of the United States, and will to the best of my ability preserve, protect, and defend the Constitution of the United States."

One of the provisions of that Constitution is that the President shall "take care that the laws be faithfully executed." In this injunction there are no qualifying words. It is made his duty to take care that the *laws. the laws*, be faithfully executed. A law is well defined to be "a rule laid, set, or established by the law-making power of the country." It is of such rules that the Constitution speaks in this injunction to the President; and in obedience to that injunction, and with reference to his duty under his oath to take care that the laws be faithfully executed, he can enter into no inquiry as to whether those laws are expedient or constitutional, or otherwise. And inasmuch as it is not possible for him, under the Constitution, to enter lawfully into any such inquiry, it is alike impossible for him to plead or to prove that, having entered into such inquiry, which was in itself unlawful, he was governed by a good motive in the result which he reached and in his action thereupon. Having no right to inquire whether the laws were expedient or constitutional, or otherwise, if he did so inquire, and if upon such inquiry he came to the conclusion that, for any reason, he would not execute the law according to the terms of the law, then he willfully violated his oath of office and the Constitution of the United States. The necessary, the inevitable presumption in law is, that he acted under the influence of bad motives in so doing, and no evidence can be introduced controlling or coloring in any degree this necessary presumption of the law.

Having, therefore, no right to entertain any motive contrary to his constitutional obligation to execute the laws, he cannot plead his motive. Inasmuch as he can neither plead nor prove his motive, the presumption of the law must remain that in violating his oath of office and the Constitution of the United States he was influenced by a bad motive. The magistrate who willfully breaks the laws, in violation of his oath to execute them, insults and outrages the common sense and the common nature of his countrymen when he asserts that their laws are so bad that they deserve to be broken. This is the language of a defiant usurper, or of a man who has surrendered himself to the counsel and control of the enemies of his country.

If a President, believing the law to be un-constitutional, may refuse to execute it, then your laws for the reconstruction of the southern States, your laws for the collection of the internal revenue, your laws for the collection of custom-house duties, are dependent for their execution upon the individual opinion of the President as to whether they are constitutional or not; and if these laws are so dependent, all other laws are equally dependent upon the opinion of the Executive. Hence it follows that, whatever the legislation of Congress may be, the laws of the country are to be executed only so far as the President believes them to be constitutional. This respondent avers that his sole object in violating the tenure-of-office act was to obtain the opinion of the Supreme Court upon the question of the constitutionality of that law. In other words, he deliberately violated the law, which was in him a crime, for the purpose of ascertaining judicially whether the law could be violated with impunity or not. At that very time he had resting upon him the obligations of a citizen to obey the laws, and the higher and more solemn obligation, imposed by the Constitution upon the first magistrate of the country, to execute the laws. If a private citizen violates a law, he does so at his peril. If the President or Vice President, or any other civil officer, violates a law, his peril is that he may be impeached by the House of Representatives and convicted by the Senate. This is precisely the responsibility which the respondent has incurred; and it would be no relief to him for his willful violation of the law, in the circumstances in which he is now placed, if the court itself had pronounced the same to be unconstitutional.

But it is not easy to comprehend the audacity, the criminal character of a proceeding by which the President of the United States attempts systematically to undermine the Government itself by drawing purposely into controversy, in the courts and elsewhere, the validity of the laws enacted by the constituted authorities of the country, who, as much as himself, are individually under an obligation to obey the Constitution in all their public acts. With the same reason and for the same object he might violate the reconstruction laws, tax laws, tariff acts, or the neutrality laws of the country; and thus, in a single day of his official life, raise questions which could not be disposed of for years in the courts of the country. The evidence discloses the fact that he has taken no step for the purpose of testing the constitutionality of the law. He suspended numerous officers under, or, if not under, at least, as he himself admits, in conformity with the tenure-of-office law, showing that it was not his sole object to test its constitutionality. He has had opportunity to make application through the Attorney General for a writ of *quo warranto*, which might have tested the validity of the law in the courts. This writ is the writ of the Government, and it can never be granted upon the application of a private person. The

President has never taken one step to test the law in the courts. Since his attempted removal of Mr. Stanton on the 21st of February last he might have instituted proceedings by a writ of *quo warranto*, and by this time have obtained, probably, a judicial opinion covering all the points of the case. But he shrinks from the test he says he sought. Thus is the pretext of the President fully exposed. The evidence shows that he never designed to test the law in the courts. His object was to seize the offices of the Government for purposes of corruption, and by their influence to enable him to reconstruct the Union in the interest of the rebellious States. In short, he resorted to this usurpation as an efficient and necessary means of usurping all power and of restoring the Government to rebel hands.

No criminal was ever arraigned who offered a more unsatisfactory excuse for his crimes. The President had no right to do what he says he designed to do, and the evidence shows that he never has attempted to do what he now assigns as his purpose when he trampled the laws of his country under his feet.

These considerations have prepared the way in some degree, I trust, for an examination of the provisions of the Constitution relating to the appointment of embassadors and other public ministers and consuls, judges of the Supreme Court, and other officers of the United States, for whose appointment provision is made in the second section of the second article of the Constitution. It is there declared that the President "shall nominate," and, by and with the consent of the Senate, shall "appoint embassadors and other public ministers and consuls, judges of the Supreme Court, and all other officers of the United States whose appointments are not herein otherwise provided for and which shall be established by law." The phrase, "are not herein otherwise provided for," is understood to refer to Senators, who, under the Constitution, in case of a vacancy, may be appointed by the Governors of the several States, and to those appointments which might be confided by law to the courts or to the heads of Departments. It is essential to notice the fact that neither in this provision of the Constitution nor in any other is power given to the President to remove any officer. The only power of removal specified in the Constitution is that of the Senate, by its verdict of guilty, to remove the President, Vice President, or other civil officer who may be impeached by the House of Representatives and presented to the Senate for trial.

Upon the premises already laid down it is clear that the power of removal from office is not vested in the President alone, but only in the President by and with the advice and consent of the Senate. Applying the provision of the Constitution already cited to the condition of affairs existing at the time the Government was organized, we find that the course pursued by the First Congress and by the first President was the inevitable result of the operation of this provision of the organic law. In the first instance, several executive Departments were established by acts of Congress, and in those Departments offices of various grades were created. The conduct of foreign affairs required the appointment of embassadors, ministers, and consuls, and consequently those necessary offices were established by law. The President, in conformity with this provision of the Constitution, made nominations to the Senate of persons to fill the various offices so established. These nominations were considered and acted upon by the Senate, and when confirmed by the Senate the persons so nominated were appointed and authorized by commissions under the hand of the President to enter upon the discharge of their respective duties. In the nature of the case it was not possible for the President, during a session of the Senate, to assign to duty in any of the offices so created any person who had not been by him nominated to the Senate and by that body confirmed, and there is no evidence that any such attempt was made. The persons thus nominated and confirmed were in their offices under the Constitution, and by virtue of the concurrent action of the President and the Senate. There is not to be found in the Constitution any provision contemplating the removal of such persons from office. But inasmuch as it is essential to the proper administration of affairs that there should be a power of removal, and inasmuch as the power of nomination and confirmation vested in the President and in the Senate is a continuing power, not exhausted either by a single exercise or by a repeated exercise in reference to a particular office, it follows legitimately and properly that the President might at any time nominate to the Senate a person to fill a particular office, and the Senate, in the exercise of its constitutional power, could confirm that nomination, that the person so nominated and confirmed would have a right to take and enjoy the office to which he had been so appointed, and thus to dispossess the previous incumbent. It is apparent that no removal can be made unless the President takes the initiative, and hence the expression "removal by the President."

As, by a common and universally recognized principle of construction, the most recent statute is obligatory and controlling wherever it contravenes a previous statute, so a recent commission, issued under an appointment made by and with the advice and consent of the Senate, supersedes a previous appointment although made in the same manner. It is thus apparent that there is, under and by virtue of the clause of the Constitution quoted, no power of removal vested either in the President or in the Senate, or in both of them together as an independent power; but it is rather a consequence of the power of appointment. And as the power of appointment is not vested in the President, but only the right to make a nomination, which becomes an appointment only when the nomination has been confirmed by the Senate, the power of removing a public officer cannot be deemed an executive power solely within the meaning of this provision of the Constitution.

This view of the subject is in harmony with the opinion expressed in the seventy-sixth number of the Federalist. After stating with great force the objections which exist to the "exercise of the power of appointing to office by an assembly of men," the writer proceeds to say:

"The truth of the principles here advanced seems to have been felt by the most intelligent of those who have found fault with the provision made in this respect by the convention. They contend that the President ought solely to have been authorized to make the appointments under the Federal Government. But it is easy to show that every advantage to be expected from such an arrangement would in substance be derived from the power of *nomination*, which is proposed to be conferred upon him, while several disadvantages which might attend the absolute power of appointment in the hands of that officer would be avoided. In the act of nominating his judgment alone would be exercised, and as it would be his sole duty to point out the man who with the approbation of the Senate should fill an office, his responsibility would be as complete as if he were to make the final appointment. There can, in this view, be no difference between nominating and appointing. The same motives which would influence a proper discharge of his duty in one case would exist in the other; and as no man could be appointed but upon his previous nomination, every man who might be appointed would be in fact his choice.

"But his nomination may be overruled. This it certainly may, yet it can only be to make place for another nomination by himself. The person ultimately appointed must be the object of his preference, though, perhaps, not in the highest degree. It is also not very probable that his nomination would often be overruled. The Senate could not be tempted by the preference they might feel to another to reject the one proposed, because they could not assure themselves that the person they might wish would be brought forward by a second, or by any subsequent nomination. They could not even be certain that a future nomination would present a candidate in any degree more acceptable to them. And as their dissent might cast a kind of stigma upon the individual rejected, and might have the appearance of a reflection upon the judgment of the Chief Magistrate, it is not likely that their sanction would often be refused, where there were not special and strong reasons for the refusal.

"To what purpose, then, require the coöperation of the Senate? I answer that the necessity of their concurrence would have a powerful, though in general, a silent operation. It would be an excellent check upon the spirit of favoritism in the President, and would tend greatly to preventing the appointment of unfit characters, from State prejudice, from family connection, from personal attachment, or from a view to popularity. And, in addition to this, it would be an efficacious source of stability in the Administration.

"It will readily be comprehended that a man who had himself the sole disposition of office would be governed much more by his private inclinations and interests than when he was bound to submit the propriety of his choice to the dictation and determination of a different and independent body, and that body an entire branch of the Legislature. The possibility of rejection would be a strong motive to care in proposing. The danger of his own reputation, and, in the case of an elective magistrate, to his political existence, from betraying a spirit of favoritism, or an unbecoming pursuit of popularity, to the observation of a body whose opinion would

have great weight in forming that of the public, could not fail to operate as a barrier to one and to the other. He would be both ashamed and afraid to bring forward for the most distinguished or lucrative stations candidates who had no other merit than that of coming from the same State to which he particularly belonged, or of being in some way or other personally allied to him, and possessing the necessary insignificance and pliancy to render them the obsequious instruments of his pleasure."

When the President has made a nomination for a particular office, and that nomination has been confirmed by the Senate, the constitutional power of the President during the session of the Senate is exhausted with reference to that officer. All that he can do under the Constitution is in the same manner to nominate a successor, who may be either confirmed or rejected by the Senate. Considering the powers of the President exclusively with reference to the removal and appointment of civil officers during the session of the Senate it is clear that he can only act in concurrence with the Senate. An office being filled, he can only nominate a successor, who, when confirmed by the Senate, is, by operation of the Constitution, appointed to the office, and it is the duty of the President to issue his commission accordingly. This commission operates as a *supersedeas*, and the previous occupant is thereby removed.

No legislation has attempted to enlarge or diminish the constitutional powers of the President, and no legislation can enlarge or diminish his constitutional powers in this respect, as I shall hereafter show. It is here and now, in the presence of this provision of the Constitution concerning the true meaning of which there neither is nor has ever been any serious doubt in the mind of any lawyer or statesman, that we strip the defense of the President of all the questions and technicalities which the intellects of men, sharpened but not enlarged by the practice of the law, have wrung from the legislation of the country covering three fourths of a century.

On the 21st day of February last Mr. Stanton was *de facto* and *de jure* Secretary for the Department of War. The President's letter to Mr. Stanton of that date is evidence of this fact:

EXECUTIVE MANSION,
WASHINGTON, D. C., *February* 21, 1868.

SIR: By virtue of the power and authority vested in me as President by the Constitution and laws of the United States, you are hereby removed from office as Secretary for the Department of War, and your functions as such will terminate upon receipt of this communication.

You will transfer to Brevet Major General Lorenzo Thomas, Adjutant General of the Army, who has this day been authorized and empowered to act as Secretary of War *ad interim*, all records, books, papers, and other public property now in your custody and charge.

Respectfully, yours,   ANDREW JOHNSON.
Hon. EDWIN M. STANTON, *Washington, D. C.*

This letter is an admission, not only that Mr. Stanton was Secretary of War on the 21st of February, 1868, but also that the suspension of that officer of the 12th of August, A. D. 1867, whether made under the tenure-of-office act or not, was abrogated by the action of the Senate of the 13th of January, 1868, and that then Mr. Stanton thereby was restored lawfully to the office of Secretary for the Department of War.

On the 21st day of February the Senate was in session. There was then but one constitutional way for the removal of Mr. Stanton ; a nomination by the President to the Senate of a successor, and his confirmation by that body. The President attempted to remove Mr. Stanton in a way not known to the Constitution, and in violation thereof, by issuing the said order for his removal. In the first of the articles it is set forth that this order was issued "in violation of the Constitution and of the laws of the United States," and the President is consequently guilty under this article if we have proved a violation either of the Constitution or the laws. If we show that he has violated the Constitution of the United States, we show also that he has violated his oath of office, which pledged him to support the Constitution. Thus is the guilt of the President, under the Constitution and upon admitted facts, established beyond a reasonable doubt. This view is sufficient to justify and require at your hands a verdict of guilty under the first article, and this without any reference to the legislation of the country, and without reference to the constitutionality of the tenure-of-office act or to the question whether the Secretary of War is included within its provisions or not. But I intend in the course of my argument to deal with all these questions of law, and to apply the law as it shall appear to the facts proved or admitted. To be sure, in my judgment, the case presented by the House of Representatives in the name of all the people of the United States might safely be rested here; but the cause of justice, the cause of the country, requires us to expose and demonstrate the guilt of the President in all the particulars set forth in the articles of impeachment. We have no alternative but to proceed. In this connection I refer to a view presented by the counsel for the President in his opening argument. He insists or suggests that inasmuch as the letter to Stanton of the 21st of February did not, in fact, accomplish a removal of the Secretary, that therefore no offense was committed. The technicalities of the law have fallen into disrepute among the people, and sometimes even in the courts. The technicalities proper of the law are the rules developed by human experience, and justly denominated, as is the law itself, the perfection of human reason. These rules, wise though subtle, aid in the administration of justice in all tribunals where the laws are judicially administered. But it often happens that attorneys seek to confuse the minds of men and thwart the administration of justice by the suggestion of nice distinctions which have no foundation in reason and find no support in general principles of right.

The President cannot assume to exercise a power as a power belonging to the office he holds, there being no warrant in law for such exercise, and then plead that he is not guilty because the act undertaken was not fully accomplished. The President is as guilty in contemplation of law as he would have been if Mr. Stanton had submitted to his demand and retired from the office of Secretary for the Department of War. Nothing more possible remained for the President except a resort to force, and what he did and what he contemplated doing to obtain possession of the office by force will be considered hereafter.

If these views are correct, the President is wholly without power, under and by virtue of the Constitution, to suspend a public officer. And most assuredly nothing is found in the Constitution to sustain the arrogant claim which he now makes, that he may during a session of the Senate suspend a public officer indefinitely and make an appointment to the vacancy thus created without asking the advice and consent of the Senate either upon the suspension or the appointment.

I pass now to the consideration of the third clause of the second section of the second article of the Constitution :

"The President shall have power to fill up all vacancies that may happen during the recess of the Senate, by granting commissions which shall expire at the end of their next session."

The phrase, "may happen," construed according to the proper and well-understood meaning of the words when the Constitution was framed, referred to those vacancies which might occur independently of the will of the Government—vacancies arising from death, from resignation, from circumstances not produced by the act of the appointing power. The words "happen" and "happened" are of frequent use in the Bible, "that well of pure English undefiled," and always in the sense of accident, fortuity, chance, without previous expectation, as to befall, to light, to fall, or to come unexpectedly. This clause of the Constitution contains a grant of power to the President, and under and by virtue of it he may take and exercise the power granted, but nothing by construction or by implication. He then, by virtue of his office, may, during the recess of the Senate, grant commissions which shall expire at the end of the next session, and thus fill up any vacancies that may happen ; that is, that come by chance, by accident, without any agency on his part.

If, then, it be necessary and proper, as undoubtedly it is necessary and proper, that provision should be made for the suspension or temporary removal of officers who, in the recess of the Senate, have proved to be incapable or dishonest, or who in the judgment of the President are disqualified for the further discharge of the duties of their offices, it is clearly a legislative right and duty, under the clause of the Constitution which authorizes Congress "to make all laws which shall be necessary and proper to carry into execution the foregoing powers, and all other powers vested in the Government of the United States, or in any department or officer thereof," to provide for the contingency. It is no answer to this view of the case to say that until the 2d of March, 1867, Congress neglected to legislate upon this subject; and that during the long period of such neglect, by the advice of Attorneys General, the practice was introduced and continued, by which the President, during the recess of the Senate, removed from office persons who had been nominated by the President and confirmed by the Senate. This practice having originated in the neglect of Congress to legislate upon a subject clearly within its jurisdiction, and only tolerated by Congress, has, at most, the force of a practice or usage which can at any time be annulled or controlled by statute.

This view is also sustained by the reasoning of Hamilton, in the sixty-seventh number of the Federalist, in which he says:

"The last of these two clauses, it is equally clear, cannot be understood to comprehend the power of filling vacancies in the Senate, for the following reasons: *First*, the relation in which that clause stands to the other, which declares the general mode of appointing officers of the United States, denotes it to be nothing more than a supplement to the other, for the purpose of establishing an auxiliary method of appointment in cases to which the general method was inadequate. The ordinary power of appointment is confided to the President and Senate *jointly*, and can therefore only be exercised during the session of the Senate; but as it would have been improper to oblige this body to be continually in session for the appointment of officers, and as vacancies might happen *in their recess*, which it might be necessary for the public service to fill without delay, the succeeding clause is evidently intended to authorize the President, *singly*, to make temporary appointments 'during the recess of the Senate, by granting commissions which should expire at the end of their next session.'"

The arguments which I have thus offered, and the authorities quoted, show that the President had not the power during the session of the Senate to remove either the Secretary of War or any civil officer from office by virtue of the Constitution. The power of removal during the recess of the Senate was recognized by the act of 1789, and tolerated by the country upon the opinions of Attorneys General till 1867. The President claims, however, and as an incident of the power of removal, the power to suspend from office indefinitely any officer of the Government; but inasmuch as his claim to the power of removal is not supported by the Constitution, he cannot sustain any other claim as an incident of that power. But if the power to remove were admitted, it would by no means follow that the President has the power to suspend indefinitely. The power to suspend indefinitely is a different power from that of removal, and it is in no proper sense necessarily an incident. It might be very well conceived that if the framers of the Constitution had thought fit to confer upon the President the power to remove a public officer ab-

solutely, his removal to be followed by the nomination of a successor to the Senate, they might yet have denied to the President the power to suspend public officers indefinitely and to supply their places by his appointees without the advice and consent of the Senate. But, inasmuch as the power to suspend indefinitely is not a power claimed as a specific grant under the Constitution, and as the claim by the President of the power of removal during a session of the Senate is not sustained by the text of the Constitution or by any good authority under it, it is not important to consider whether, if the power of removal were admitted to exist, the power to suspend indefinitely could be considered as an incident. It is sufficient to say that neither power, in the sense claimed by the President, exists under the Constitution or by any provision of law.

I respectfully submit, Senators, that there can be no reasonable doubt of the soundness of the view I have presented, both of the language and meaning of the Constitution in regard to appointments to office. But, if there were any doubt, it is competent and proper to consider the effects of the claim, if recognized, as set up by the President. And in a matter of doubt as to the construction of the Constitution it would be conclusive of its true interpretation that the claim asserted by the President is fraught with evils of the gravest character. He claims the right, as well when the Senate is in session as when it is not in session, to remove absolutely, or to suspend for an indefinite period of time, according to his own discretion, every officer of the Army, of the Navy, and of the civil service, and to supply their places with creatures and partisans of his own. To be sure, he has not asserted, in direct form, his right to remove and suspend indefinitely officers of the Army and Navy; but when you consider that the Constitution makes no distinction in the tenure of office between military, naval, and civil officers; that all are nominated originally by the President and receive their appointments upon the confirmation of the Senate, and hold their offices under the Constitution by no other title than that which secures to a Cabinet officer or to a revenue collector the office to which he has been appointed, there can be no misunderstanding as to the nature, extent, and dangerous character of the claim which the President makes. The statement of this arrogant and dangerous assumption is a sufficient answer to any doubt which might exist in the mind of any patriot as to the true intent and meaning of the Constitution. It cannot be conceived that the men who framed that instrument, who were devoted to liberty, who had themselves suffered by the exercise of illegal and irresponsible power, would have vested in the President of the United States an authority, to be exercised without the restraint or control of any other branch or department of the Government, which would enable him to corrupt the civil, military, and naval officers of the country by rendering them absolutely dependent for their positions and emoluments upon his will.

At the present time there are forty-one thousand officers, whose aggregate emoluments exceed $21,000,000 per annum. To all these the President's claim applies. These facts express the practical magnitude of the subject. Moreover, this claim was never asserted by any President or by any public man from the beginning of the Government until the present time. It is in violation also of the act of July 13, 1866, which denies to the Executive the power to remove officers of the Army and the Navy, except upon sentence of a court-martial. The history of the career of Andrew Johnson shows that he has been driven to the assertion of this claim by circumstances and events connected with his criminal design to break down the power of Congress, to subvert the institutions of the country, and thereby to restore the Union in the interest of those who participated in the rebellion. Having entered upon this career of crime, he soon found it essential to the accomplishment of his purposes to secure the support of the immense retinue of public officers of every grade and description in the country. This he could not do without making them entirely dependent upon his will; and in order that they might realize their dependence, and thus be made subservient to his purposes, he determined to assert an authority over them unauthorized by the Constitution, and therefore not attempted by any Chief Magistrate. His conversation with Mr. Wood in the autumn of 1866 fully discloses this purpose.

Previous to the passage of the tenure-of-office act he had removed hundreds of faithful and patriotic public officers, to the great detriment of the public service, and followed by an immense loss of the public revenues. At the time of the passage of the act he was so far involved in his mad schemes—schemes of ambition and revenge—that it was, in his view, impossible for him to retrace his steps. He consequently determined, by various artifices and plans, to undermine that law and secure to himself, in defiance of the will of Congress and of the country, entire control of the officers in the civil service and in the Army and the Navy. He thus became gradually involved in an unlawful undertaking from which he could not retreat. In the presence of the proceedings against him by the House of Representatives he had no alternative but to assert that under the Constitution power was vested in the President exclusively, without the advice and consent of the Senate, to remove from office every person in the service of the country. This policy, as yet acted upon in part, and developed chiefly in the civil service, has already produced evils which threaten the overthrow of the Government. When he removed faithful public officers, and appointed others whose only claim to consideration was their unreasoning devotion to his interest and unhesitating obe-

dience to his will, they compensated themselves for this devotion and this obedience by frauds upon the revenues and by crimes against the laws of the land. Hence it has happened that in the internal revenue service alone—chiefly through the corruption of men whom he has thus appointed—the losses have amounted to not less than twenty-five, and probably to more than fifty million dollars during the last two years.

In the presence of these evils, which were then only partially realized, the Congress of the United States passed the tenure-of-office act as a barrier to their further progress. This act thus far has proved ineffectual as a complete remedy; and now the President, by his answer to the articles of impeachment, asserts his right to violate it altogether, and by an interpretation of the Constitution which is alike hostile to its letter and to the peace and welfare of the country he assumes to himself absolute and unqualified power over all the offices and officers of the country. The removal of Mr. Stanton, contrary to the Constitution and the laws, is the particular crime of the President for which we now demand his conviction. The extent, the evil character, and the dangerous nature of the claims by which he seeks to justify his conduct are controlling considerations. By his conviction you purify the Government and restore it to its original character. By his acquittal you surrender the Government into the hands of an usurping and unscrupulous man, who will use all the vast power he now claims for the corruption of every branch of the public service and the final overthrow of the public liberties.

Nor is it any excuse for the President that he has, as stated in his answer, taken the advice of his Cabinet officers in support of his claim. In the first place, he had no right under the Constitution to the advice of the head of a Department except upon subjects relating to the duties of his Department. If the President has chosen to seek the advice of his Cabinet upon other matters, and they have seen fit to give it upon subjects not relating to their respective Departments, it is advice which he had no constitutional authority to ask, advice which they were not bound to give, and that advice is to him, and for all the purposes of this investigation and trial, as the advice of private persons merely. But of what value can be the advice of men who, in the first instance, admit that they hold their offices by the will of the person who seeks their advice, and who understand most clearly that if the advice they give should be contrary to the wishes of their master they would be at once, and in conformity with their own theory of the rights of the President, deprived of the offices which they hold? Having first made these men entirely dependent upon his will, he then solicits their advice as to the application of the principle by which they admit that they hold their places to all the other officers of the

Government. Could it have been expected that they, under such circumstances, would have given advice in any particular disagreeable to the will of him who sought it?

It was the advice of serfs to their lord, of servants to their master, of slaves to their owner.

The Cabinet respond to Mr. Johnson as old Polonius to Hamlet. Hamlet says:

"Do you see yonder cloud, that's almost in shape of a camel?
"*Polonius.* By the mass, and 'tis like a camel, indeed.
"*Hamlet.* Methinks it is like a weasel.
"*Polonius.* It is backed like a weasel.
"*Hamlet.* Or, like a whale?
"*Polonius.* Very like a whale."

The gentlemen of the Cabinet understood the position that they occupied. The President, in his message to the Senate upon the suspension of Mr. Stanton, in which he says that he took the advice of his Cabinet in reference to his action upon the bill regulating the tenure of certain civil offices, speaks thus:

"The bill had then not become a law. The limitation upon the power of removal was not yet imposed, and there was yet time to make any changes. If any one of these gentlemen had then said to me that he would avail himself of the provisions of that bill in case it became a law, I should not have hesitated a moment as to his removal."

Having indulged his Cabinet in such freedom of opinion when he consulted them in reference to the constitutionality of the bill, and having covered himself and them with public odium by its announcement, he now vaunts their opinions, extorted by power and given in subserviency, that the law itself may be violated with impunity. This, says the President, is the exercise of my constitutional right to the opinion of my Cabinet. I, says the President, am responsible for my Cabinet. Yes, the President is responsible for the opinions and conduct of men who give such advice as is demanded, and give it in fear and trembling lest they be at once deprived of their places. This is the President's idea of a Cabinet, but it is an idea not in harmony with the theory of the Constitution.

The President is a man of strong will, of violent passions, of unlimited ambition, with capacity to employ and use timid men, adhesive men, subservient men, and corrupt men, as the instruments of his designs. It is the truth of history that he has injured every person with whom he has had confidential relations, and many have escaped ruin only by withdrawing from his society altogether. He has one rule of life: he attempts to use every man of power, capacity, or influence within his reach. Succeeding in his attempts, they are in time, and usually in a short time, utterly ruined. If the considerate flee from him, if the brave and patriotic resist his schemes or expose his plans, he attacks them with all the enginery and patronage of his office and pursues them with all the violence of his personal hatred. He attacks to destroy all who will not become his instruments, and all who become his instruments are destroyed in the use. He spares no one. Already this purpose of his life is illustrated in the treatment of a gentleman who was of counsel for the respondent, but who has never appeared in his behalf.

The thanks of the country are due to those distinguished soldiers who, tempted by the President by offers of kingdoms which were not his to give, refused to fall down and worship the tempter. And the thanks of the country are not less due to General Emory, who, when brought into the presence of the President by a request which he could not disobey, at once sought to protect himself against his machinations by presenting to him the law upon the subject of military orders.

The experience and the fate of Mr. Johnson's eminent adherents are lessons of warning to the country and to mankind; and the more eminent and distinguished of his adherents have furnished the most melancholy lessons for this and for succeeding generations.

It is not that men are ruined when they abandon a party; but in periods of national trial and peril the people will not tolerate those who, in any degree or under any circumstances, falter in their devotion to the rights and interests of the Republic. In the public judgment, which is seldom erroneous in regard to public duty, devotion to the country and adherence to Mr. Johnson are and have been wholly inconsistent.

Carpenter's historical painting of Emancipation is a fit representation of an event the most illustrious of any in the annals of America since the adoption of the Constitution. Indeed, it is second to the ratification of the Constitution only in the fact that that instrument, as a means of organizing and preserving the nation, rendered emancipation possible. The principal figure of the scene is the immortal Lincoln, whose great virtues endear his name and memory to all mankind, and whose untimely and violent death, then the saddest event in our national experience, but now not deemed so great a calamity to the people who loved him and mourned for him as no public man was ever before loved or lamented, as is the shame, humiliation, disgrace, and suffering caused by the misconduct and crimes of his successor. It was natural and necessary that the artist should arrange the personages of the group on the right hand and on the left of the principal figure. Whether the particular assignment was by chance, by the taste of the artist, or by the influence of a mysterious Providence which works through human agency, we know not. But on the right of Lincoln are two statesmen and patriots who, in all the trials and vicissitudes of these eventful years, have remained steadfast to liberty, to justice, to the principles of constitutional government. Senators and Mr. Chief Justice, in this presence I venture not to pronounce their names.

On the left of Lincoln are five figures representing the other members of his Cabinet. One of these is no longer among the living; he died before the evil days came, and we may indulge the hope that he would have escaped the fate of his associates. Of the other four three have been active in counseling and supporting the President in his attempts to subvert the Government. They are already ruined men. Upon the canvas they are elevated to the summit of virtuous ambition. Yielding to the seductions of power they have fallen. Their example and fate may warn us, but their advice and counsel, whether given to this tribunal or to him who is on trial before this tribunal, cannot be accepted as the judgment of wise or of patriotic men.

On motion of Mr. SPRAGUE, at two o'clock and fifteen minutes p. m., the Senate took a recess for fifteen minutes.

At the expiration of the recess the Chief Justice resumed the chair and called the Senate to order.

Mr. SHERMAN. I move that the roll of the Senators be called, so that we may get their attendance.

Mr. CONNESS. That is never done.

Mr. SHERMAN. It can be done. A motion to adjourn will have the same effect practically.

Mr. CONNESS. The Senator may move an adjournment and get a call in that way.

Mr. SHERMAN. I move a call of the Senators.

The CHIEF JUSTICE. The Senator from Ohio moves that the roll of the Senate be called.

Mr. CONNESS. It never has been done.

Mr. SUMNER. The rule provides for a call of the Senate.

Mr. CONNESS. I should like to hear the rule.

Mr. SUMNER. It is Rule 16.

The CHIEF JUSTICE. The Secretary will read the sixteenth rule of the Senate.

The Chief Clerk read as follows:

"16. When the yeas and nays shall be called for by one fifth of the Senators present, each Senator called upon shall, unless for special reasons he be excused by the Senate, declare openly and without debate his assent or dissent to the question. In taking the yeas and nays, and upon a call of the Senate, the names of the Senators shall be called alphabetically."

The CHIEF JUSTICE. If there be no objection the Secretary will call the roll to ascertain who are present.

Mr. DRAKE. I object, sir.

Mr. SHERMAN. I move that there be a call of the Senate.

The motion was agreed to; and the roll being called, forty-four Senators answered to their names.

The CHIEF JUSTICE. There are forty-four Senators answering to their names. The honorable Manager will proceed.

Mr. Manager BOUTWELL. Mr. President, Senators, leaving the discussion of the provisions of the Constitution, I am now prepared to ask your attention to the character and history of the act of 1789, on which stress has been laid by the President in his answer, and by the learned counsel who opened the case for the respondent. The discussion in the House of Representatives in 1789 related to the bill establishing a Department of Foreign Affairs. The first section of that bill, as it originally passed the House of Representatives, after recapitulating the title of the officer who was to take charge of the Department, and setting forth his duties, contained these words in reference to the Secretary of the Department: "To be removable from office by the President of the United States." The House, in Committee of the Whole, discussed this provision during several days, and all the leading members of the body appear to have taken part in the debate. As is well known, there was a difference of opinion at the time as to the meaning of the Constitution. Some contended that the power of removing civil officers was vested in the President absolutely, to be exercised by him, without consultation with the Senate, and this as well when the Senate was in session as during vacations. Others maintained that the initiative in the removal of a public officer must be taken by the President, but that there could be no actual removal except by the advice and consent of the Senate, and that this rule was applicable to the powers of the President as well during the vacation as during the session of the Senate. Others maintained that during the session of the Senate, while the initiative was in the President, the actual removal of a civil officer could be effected only upon the advice and consent of the Senate, but that during the vacations the President might remove such officers and fill their places temporarily, under commissions, to expire at the end of the next session of the Senate. Mr. Madison maintained the first of these propositions, and he may be said to be the only person of historical reputation at the present day who expressed corresponding opinions, although undoubtedly his views were sustained by a considerable number of members. It is evident from an examination of the debate that Mr. Madison's views were gradually and finally successfully undermined by the discussion on that occasion.

As is well known, Roger Sherman was then one of the most eminent members of that body. He was a signer of the Declaration of Independence, a member of the Convention which framed the Constitution of the United States, and a member of the House of Representatives of the First Congress. He was undoubtedly one of the most illustrious men of the constitutional period of American history; and in each succeeding generation there have been eminent persons of his blood and name; but at no period has his family been more distinguished than at the present time. Mr. Sherman took a leading part in the discussion, and there is no doubt that the views which he entertained and expressed had a large influence in producing the result which was finally reached. The report of the debate is found in the first volume of the Annals of Congress; and I quote from the remarks made by Mr. Sherman, preserved on pages 510 and 511 of that volume:

"Mr. SHERMAN. I consider this a very important subject in every point of view, and therefore worthy of full discussion. In my mind it involves three questions. First. Whether the President has, by the Constitution, the right to remove an officer appointed by and with the advice and consent of the Senate. No gentleman contends but that the advice and consent of the Senate are necessary to make the appointment in all cases, unless in inferior offices where the contrary is established by law; but then they allege that, although the consent of the Senate be necessary to the appointment, the President alone, by the nature of his office, has the power of removal. Now, it appears to me that this opinion is ill-founded, because this provision was intended for some useful purpose, and by that construction would answer none at all. I think the concurrence of the Senate as necessary to appoint an officer as the nomination of the President; they are constituted as mutual checks, each having a negative upon the other.

"I consider it as an established principle that the power which appoints can also remove, unless there are express exceptions made. Now, the power which appoints the judges cannot displace them, because there is a constitutional restriction in their favor; otherwise the President, by and with the advice and consent of the Senate, being the power which appointed them, would be sufficient to remove them. This is the construction in England, where the king has the power of appointing judges; it was declared to be during pleasure, and they might be removed when the monarch thought proper. It is a general principle in law as well as reason that there shall be the same authority to remove as to establish. It is so in legislation, where the several branches whose concurrence is necessary to pass a law must concur in repealing it. Just so I take it to be in cases of appointment, and the President alone may remove when he alone appoints, as in the case of inferior offices to be established by law." * * * *

"As the office is the mere creature of the Legislature we may form it under such regulations as we please, with such powers and duration as we think good policy requires. We may say he shall hold his office during good behavior, or that he shall be annually elected. We may say he shall be displaced for neglect of duty, and point out how he shall be convicted of it without calling upon the President or Senate.

"The third question is, if the Legislature has the power to authorize the President alone to remove this officer whether it is expedient to invest him with it? I do not believe it absolutely necessary that he should have such power, because the power of suspending would answer all the purposes which gentlemen have in view by giving the power of removal. I do not think that the officer is only to be removed by impeachment, as is argued by the gentleman from South Carolina, (Mr. Smith,) because he is the mere creature of the law, and we can direct him to be removed on conviction of mismanagement or inability without calling upon the Senate for their concurrence. But I believe, if we make no such provision, he may constitutionally be removed by the President, by and with the advice and consent of the Senate; and I believe it would be most expedient for us to say nothing in the clause on this subject."

I may be pardoned if I turn aside for a moment, and, addressing myself to the learned gentleman of counsel for the respondent who is to follow me in argument, I request him to refute, to overthrow the constitutional argument of his illustrious ancestor, Roger Sherman. Doing this, he will have overcome the first, but only the first, of a series of obstacles in the path of the President.

In harmony with the views of Mr. Sherman was the opinion expressed by Mr. Jackson, of Georgia, found on page 508 of the same volume. He says:

"I shall agree to give him [that is, the President] the same power in cases of removal that he has in appointing; but nothing more. Upon this principle I would agree to give him the power of suspension during the recess of the Senate. This, in my opinion, would effectually provide against those inconveniences which have been apprehended and not expose the Government to those abuses we have to dread from the wanton and uncontrollable authority of removing officers at pleasure."

It may be well to observe that Mr. Madison, in maintaining the absolute power of the President to remove civil officers, coupled with his opinions upon that point doctrines concerning the power of impeachment which would be wholly unacceptable to this respondent. And, indeed, it is perfectly apparent that without the existence of the power to impeach and remove the President of the United States from office in the manner maintained by Mr. Madison in that debate, that the concession of absolute power of removal would end in the destruction of the Government. Mr. Madison, in that debate, said:

"The danger to liberty, the danger of maladministration, has not yet been found to lie so much in the facility of introducing improper persons into office as in the difficulty of displacing those who are unworthy of the public trust."—*Annals of Congress*, p. 515, vol. 1.

Again, he says:

"Perhaps the great danger, as has been observed, of abuse in the executive power lies in the improper continuance of bad men in office. But the power we contend for will not enable him to do this; for if an unworthy man be continued in office by an unworthy President the House of Representatives can at any time impeach him, and the Senate can remove him, whether the President chooses or not. The danger, then, consists merely in this: the President can displace from office a man whose merits require that he should be continued in it. What will be the motives which the President can feel for such abuse of his power and the restraints that operate to prevent it? In the first place he will be impeachable by this House before the Senate for such an act of maladministration; for I contend that the wanton removal of meritorious officers would subject him to impeachment and removal from his high trust."—*Annals of Congress*, p. 517, vol. 1.

It is thus seen that Mr. Madison took great care to connect his opinions of the power of removal in the President with a distinct declaration that if this power was improperly exercised by the President he would himself be liable to impeachment and removal from office. If Mr. Madison's opinions were to be accepted by the President as a whole, he would be as defenseless as he is at the present time if arraigned upon articles of impeachment based upon acts of maladministration in the removal of public officers. The result of the debate upon the bill for establishing the executive Department of Foreign Affairs was that the phrase in question which made the head of the Department "removable from office by the President of the United States" was stricken out by a vote of 31 in the affirmative to 19 in the negative, and another form of expression was introduced into the second section which is manifestly in harmony with the views expressed by Mr. Sherman and those who entertained corresponding opinions.

The second section is in these words:

"Sec. 2. *And be it further enacted*, That there shall be in the said Department an inferior officer, to be appointed by the said principal officer, and to be employed therein as he shall deem proper, and to be called the chief clerk of the Department of Foreign Affairs, and who, whenever the said principal officer shall be removed from office by the President of the United States, or in other case of vacancy, shall, during such vacancy, have the charge and custody of all records, books, and papers appertaining to said Department."—*United States Statutes-at-Large*, vol. 1, p. 29.

It will be seen that the phrase here employed, "whenever the said principal officer shall be removed from office by the President of the United States," is not a grant of power to the President; nor is it, as was asserted by the counsel for the respondent, a legislative interpretation of a constitutional power. But it is merely at most a *quasi* recognition of a power in the Constitution to be exercised by the President, at some time, under some circumstances, and subject to certain limitations. But there is no statement or declaration of the time when such power could be exercised, the circumstances under which it might be exercised, or the limitations imposed upon its exercise.

All these matters are left subject to the operation of the Constitution and to future legislation. This is in entire harmony with the declaration made by Mr. White, of North Carolina, in the debate of 1789. He says:

"Let us then leave the Constitution to a free operation, and let the President, with or without the consent of the Senate, carry it into execution. Then, if any one supposes himself injured by their determination, let him have recourse to the law, and its decision will establish the true construction of the Constitution."

Mr. Gerry, of Massachusetts, also said:

"Hence all construction of the meaning of the Constitution is dangerous or unnatural, and therefore ought to be avoided. This is our doctrine, that no power of this kind ought to be exercised by the Legislature. But we say, if we must give a construction to the Constitution, it is more natural to give the construction in favor of the power of removal vesting in the President, by and with the advice and consent of the Senate; because it is in the nature of things that the power which appoints removes also."

Again, Mr. Sherman said, speaking of the words which were introduced into the first section and finally stricken out:

"I wish, Mr. Chairman, that the words may be left out of the bill, without giving up the question either way as to the propriety of the measure."

The debate upon the bill relating to the Department for Foreign Affairs occurred in the month of June, 1789; in the following month of August Congress was engaged in considering the bill establishing the Treasury Department. This bill originated in the House, and contained the phrase now found in it, being the same as that contained in the bill establishing the State Department.

The Senate was so far satisfied of the impolicy of making any declaration whatever upon the subject of removal that the clause was struck out by an amendment. The House refused to concur, however, and the Senate, by the casting vote of the Vice President, receded from the amendment.

All this shows that the doctrine of the right of removal by the President survived the debate only as a limited and doubtful right at most.

The results reached by the Congress of 1789 are conclusive upon the following points: that that body was of opinion that the power of removal was not in the President absolutely, to be exercised at all times and under all circumstances; and secondly, that during the sessions of the Senate the power of removal was vested in the President and Senate, to be exercised by their concurrent action; while the debate and the votes indicate that the power of the President to remove from office during the vacation of the Senate was, at best, a doubtful power under the Constitution.

It becomes us next to consider the practice of the Government, under the Constitution, and in the presence of the action of the First Congress, by virtue of which the President now claims an absolute, unqualified, irresponsible power over all public officers, and this without the advice and consent of the Senate or the concurrence of any other branch of the Government. In the early years of the Government the removal of a public officer by the President was a rare occurrence, and it was usually resorted to during the session of the Senate, for misconduct in office only, and accomplished by the appointment of a successor through the advice and consent of the Senate. Gradually a practice was introduced, largely through the example of Mr. Jefferson, of removing officers during the recess of the Senate and filling their places under commissions to expire at the end of the next session. But it cannot be said that this practice became common until the election of General Jackson, in 1828. During his administration the practice of removing officers during the recesses of the Senate was largely increased, and in the year 1832, on the 18th of September, General Jackson removed Mr. Duane from the office of Secretary of the Treasury. This occurred, however, during a recess of the Senate. This act on his part gave rise to a heated debate in Congress and an ardent controversy throughout the country, many of the most eminent men contending that there was no power in the President to remove a civil officer, even during the recess of the Senate. The triumph of General Jackson in that controversy gave a full interpretation to the words which had been employed in the statute of 1789.

But, at the same time, the limitations of that power in the President were clearly settled, both upon the law and upon the Constitution, that whatever might be his power of removal during a recess of the Senate, he had no right to make a removal during a session of the Senate, except upon the advice and consent of that body to the appointment of a successor. This was the opinion of Mr. Johnson himself, as stated by him in a speech made in the Senate on the 10th of January, 1861:

"I meant that the true way to fight the battle was for us to remain here and occupy the places assigned to us by the Constitution of the country. Why did I make that statement? It was because on the 4th day of March next we shall have six majority in this body; and if, as some apprehend, the incoming Administration shall show any disposition to make encroachments upon the institution of slavery, encroachments upon the rights of the States or any other violation of the Constitution, we, by remaining in the Union and standing at our places, will have the power to resist all these encroachments. How? We have the power even to reject the appointment of the Cabinet officers of the incoming President. Then should we not be fighting the battle in the Union by resisting even the organization of the Administration in a constitutional mode, and thus, at the very start, disable an Administration which was likely to encroach on our rights and to violate the Constitution of the country? So far as appointing even a minister abroad is concerned, the incoming Administration will have no power without our consent if we remain here. It comes into office handcuffed, powerless to do harm. We, standing here, hold the balance of power in our hands; we can resist it at the very threshold effectually, and do it inside of the Union and in our house. The incoming Administration has not even the power to appoint a postmaster whose salary exceeds $1,000 a year without consultation with, and the acquiescence of, the Senate of the United States. The President has not even the power to draw his salary, his $25,000 per annum, unless we appropriate it."—*Congressional Globe*, vol.—, page—.

It may be well observed that, for the purposes of this trial, and upon the question whether the President is or is not guilty under the first three articles exhibited against him by the House of Representatives, it is of no consequence whether the President of the United States has power to remove a civil officer during a recess of the Senate. The fact charged and proved against the President, and on which, as one fact proved against him, we demand his conviction, is, that he attempted to remove Mr. Stanton from the office of Secretary of War during a session of the Senate. It cannot be claimed with any propriety that the act of 1789 can be construed as a grant of power to the President to an extent beyond the practice of the Government for three quarters of a century under the Constitution and under the provisions of the law of 1789. None of the predecessors of Mr. Johnson, from General Washington to Mr. Lincoln, although the act of 1789 was in existence during that period, had ever ventured to claim that either under that act or by virtue of the Constitution the President of the United States had power to remove a civil officer during a session of the Senate without its consent and advice. The utmost that can be said is, that for the last forty years it had been the practice of the Executive to remove civil officers at pleasure during the recess of the Senate. While it may be urged that this practice, in the absence of any direct legislation upon the subject, had become the common law of the country, protecting the Executive in a policy corresponding to that practice, it is also true, for stronger reasons, that Mr. Johnson was bound by his oath of office to adhere to the practice of his predecessors in other particulars, none of whom had ever ventured to remove a civil officer from his office during the session of the Senate and appoint a successor, either permanent or *ad interim*, and authorize that successor to enter upon the discharge of the duties of such office. The case of Timothy Pickering has been explained and it constitutes no exception. As far as is known to me the lists of removals and appointments introduced by the respondent do not sustain the claim of the answer in regard to the power of removal.

Hence it is that the act of 1789 is no security to this respondent, and hence it is that we hold him guilty of a violation of the Constitution and of his oath of office under the first and third articles of impeachment exhibited against him by the House of Representatives, and this without availing ourselves of the provisions of the tenure-of-office act of March 2, 1867.

I respectfully ask that the views now submitted in reference to the act of 1789, may be considered in connection with the argument I have already offered upon the true meaning of the provisions of the Constitution relating to the appointment of civil officers.

I pass now to the consideration of the act of the 13th of February, 1795, on which the President relies as a justification for his appointment of Lorenzo Thomas as Secretary of War *ad interim*. By this act it is provided:

"In case of vacancy in the office of Secretary of State, the Secretary of the Treasury, or of the Secretary of the Department of War, or of any other officer of either of the said Departments whose appointment is not in the head thereof, whereby they cannot perform the duties of their said respective offices, it shall be lawful for the President of the United States, in case he shall think it necessary, to authorize any person or persons, at his discretion, to perform the duties of the said respective offices until a successor be appointed or such vacancy be filled: *Provided*, That no one vacancy shall be supplied in manner aforesaid, for a longer term than six months."—1 *Statutes-at-Large*, p. 415.

The ingenuity of the President and his counsel has led them to maintain that the phrase "in case of vacancy," used in this statute, relates to any and every vacancy, however produced. But the reading of the entire section, whether casually or carefully, shows that the purpose of the law was to provide a substitute temporarily in case of vacancy whereby the person in office *could not perform the duties of his office*, and necessarily applied only to those contingencies of official life which put it out of the power of the person in office to discharge the duties of the place; such as sickness, absence, or inability of any sort. And yet the President and his counsel contend that a removal by the President is a case of vacancy contemplated by the law, notwithstanding the limitation of the President in his power of appointing an officer temporarily as to those cases which render it impossible for the duly commissioned officer to perform the duties of his office. When it is considered, as I have shown, that the President had no power—and this without considering the tenure-of-office act of March 2, 1867—to create a vacancy during a session of the Senate, the act of 1795, even upon his construction, furnishes no defense whatever. But we submit that if he had possessed the power which he claims by virtue of the act of 1789, that the vacancy referred to in the act of 1795 is not such a vacancy as is caused by the removal of a public officer, but that that act is limited to those vacancies which arise unavoidably in the public service and without the agency of the President. But there is in the section of the act of 1795, on which the President relies, a proviso which nullifies absolutely the defense which he has set up. This proviso is that no one vacancy shall be supplied in manner aforesaid (that is, by a temporary appointment) for a longer term than six months.

Mr. Johnson maintains that he suspended Mr. Stanton from the office of Secretary of War on the 12th of August last, not by virtue of the tenure-of-office act of March 2, 1867, but under a power incident to the general and unlimited power of removal, which, as he claims, is vested in the President of the United States, and that, from the 12th of August last, Mr. Stanton has not been entitled to the office of Secretary for the Department of War. If he suspended Mr. Stanton as an incident of his general power of removal, then his suspension, upon the President's theory, created a vacancy such as is claimed by the President under the statute of 1795. The suspension of Mr. Stanton put him in such a condition that he '' could not perform the duties of the office.'' The President claims also to have appointed General Grant Secretary of War *ad interim* on the 12th of August last, by virtue of the statute of 1795. The proviso of that statute declares that no one vacancy shall be supplied in manner aforesaid (that is, by temporary appointment) for a longer term than six months. If the act of 1795 were in force, and if the President's theory of his rights under the Constitution and under that act were a valid theory, the six months during which the vacancy might have been supplied temporarily expired by limitation on the 12th day of February, 1868, and yet on the 21st day of February, 1868, the President appointed Lorenzo Thomas Secretary of War *ad interim* to the same vacancy, and this in violation of the statute which he pleads in his own defense. It is too clear for argument that if Mr. Stanton was lawfully suspended, as the President now claims, but not suspended under the tenure-of-office act, then the so-called restoration of Mr. Stanton on the 13th January was wholly illegal. But if the statute of 1795 is applicable to a vacancy created by suspension or removal, then the President has violated it by the appointment of General Thomas Secretary of War *ad interim*. And if the statute of 1795 is not applicable to a vacancy occasioned by a removal, then the appointment of General Thomas Secretary of War *ad interim* is without authority or the color of authority of law.

The fact is, however, that the statute of 1795 is repealed by the operation of the statute of the 20th of February, 1863. (Statutes-at-Large, vol. 12, p. 656.)

If Senators will consider the provisions of the statute of 1863 in connection with the power of removal under the Constitution during a session of the Senate, by and with the advice and consent of the Senate, and the then recognized power of removal by the President during a recess of the Senate to be filled by temporary appointments, as was the practice previous to March 2, 1867, they will find that provision was made by the act of 1863 for every vacancy which could possibly arise in the public service.

The act of February 20, 1863, provides—

"That in case of the death, *resignation*, absence from the seat of Government, or sickness of the head of an executive Department, or of the head of any officer of either of the said Departments whose appointment is not in the head thereof, *whereby they cannot perform the duties of their respective offices*, it shall be lawful for the President of the United States, in case he shall think it necessary, to authorize the head of any other executive Department or other officer in either of said Departments whose appointment is vested in the President, at his discretion, to perform the duties of the said respective offices until a successor be appointed, or until such absence or inability shall cease: *Provided*, That no one vacancy shall be supplied in manner aforesaid for a longer term than six months."

Provision was thus made by the act of 1863 for filling all vacancies which could occur under any circumstances. It is a necessary rule of construction that all previous statutes making other and different provisions for the filling of vacancies are repealed by the operation of more recent statutes; and for the plain reason that it is inconsistent with any theory of government that there should be two legal modes in existence at the same time for doing the same thing.

If the view I have presented be a sound one it is apparent that the President's conduct finds no support either in the Constitution, in the act of 1789, or in the legislation of 1795, on which he chiefly relies as a justification for the appointment of Thomas as Secretary of War *ad interim*. It follows, also, that if the tenure-of-office act had not been passed the President would have been guilty of a high misdemeanor, in that he issued an order for the removal of Mr. Stanton from office during the session of the Senate, in violation of the Constitution and his own oath of office; that he was guilty of a high misdemeanor in the appointment of Lorenzo Thomas as Secretary of War *ad interim*, and this whether the act of the 13th of February, 1795, is in force, or whether the same has been repealed by the statute of 1863. His guilt is thus fully proved and established as charged in the first, second, and third articles of impeachment exhibited against him by the House of Representatives, and this without considering the requirements or constitutionality of the act regulating the tenure of certain civil offices.

I pass now to the consideration of the tenure-of-office act. I preface what I have to say by calling to your attention that portion of my argument already addressed to you, in which I have set forth and maintained, as I was able, the opinion that the President had no right to make any inquiry whether an act of Congress is or is not constitutional; that, having no right to make such inquiry, he could not plead that he had so inquired and reached the conclusion that the act inquired about was invalid. You will also bear in mind the views presented, that this tribunal can take no notice of any argument or suggestion that a law deemed unconstitutional may be willfully violated by the President. The gist of his crime is that he intentionally disregarded a law, and, in the nature of the case, it can be no excuse or defense that such law, in his opinion, or in the opinion of others, was not in conformity with the Constitution.

In this connection I desire to call your attention to suggestions made by the President, and by the President's counsel—by the President in his message of December, 1867, and by the President's counsel in his opening argument—that if Congress were by legislation to abolish a department of the Government, or to declare that the President should not be Commander-in-Chief of the Army or the Navy, that it would be the duty of the President to disregard such legislation. These are extreme cases and not within the range of possibility. Members of Congress are individually bound by an oath to support the Constitution of the United States, and it is not to be presumed, even for the purpose of argument, that they would wantonly disregard the obligations of their oath, and enact in the form of law rules or proceedings in plain violation of the Constitution. Such is not the course of legislation, and such is not the character of the act we are now to consider. The bill regulating the tenure of certain civil offices was passed by a constitutional majority in each of the two Houses, and it is to be presumed that each Senator and Representative who gave it his support did so in the belief that its provisions were in harmony with the provisions of the Constitution. We are now dealing with practical affairs, and conducting the Government within the Constitution; and in reference to measures passed by Congress under such circumstances, it is wholly indefensible for the President to suggest the course that, in his opinion, he would be justified in pursuing if Congress were openly and wantonly to disregard the Constitution and inaugurate revolution in the Government.

It is asserted by the counsel for the President that he took advice as to the constitutionality of the tenure-of-office act, and being of opinion that it was unconstitutional, or so much of it at least as attempted to deprive him of the power of removing the members of the Cabinet, he felt it to be his duty to disregard its provisions; and the question is now put, with feeling and emphasis whether the President is to be impeached, convicted, and removed from office for a mere difference of opinion. True, the President is not to be removed for a *mere* difference of opinion. If he had contented himself with the opinion that the law was unconstitutional, or even with the expression of such an opinion privately or officially to Congress, no exception could have been taken to his conduct. But he has attempted to act in accordance with that opinion, and in that action he has disregarded the requirements of the statute. It is for this action that he is to be arraigned, and is to be convicted. But it is not necessary for us to rest upon the doctrine that it was the duty of the President to accept the law as constitutional and govern himself accordingly in all his official doings. We are prepared to show that the law is in truth in harmony with the Constitution, and that its provisions apply to Mr. Stanton as Secretary for the Department of War.

The tenure-of-office act makes no change in the powers of the President and the Senate, during the session of the Senate, to remove a civil officer upon a nomination by the President, and confirmation by the Senate, of a successor. This was an admitted constitutional power from the very organization of the Government, while the right now claimed by the President to remove a civil officer during a session of the Senate, without the advice and consent of the Senate, was never asserted by any of his predecessors, and certainly never recognized by any law or by any practice. This rule applied to heads of Departments as well as to other civil officers. Indeed, it may be said, once for all, that the tenure by which members of the Cabinet have held their places corresponds in every particular to the tenure by which other civil officers have held theirs. It is undoubtedly true that, in practice, members of the Cabinet have been accustomed to tender their resignations upon a suggestion from the President that such a course would be acceptable to him. But this practice has never changed their legal relations to the President or to the country. There was never a moment of time, since the adoption of the Constitution, when the law or the opinion of the Senate recognized the right of the President to remove a Cabinet officer during a session of the Senate, without the consent of the Senate given through the confirmation of a successor. Hence, in this particular, the tenure-of-office act merely enacted and gave form to a practice existing from the foundation of the Government—a practice in entire harmony with the provisions of the Constitution upon that subject. The chief change produced by the tenure-of-office act had reference to removals during the recess of the Senate. Previous to the 2d of March, 1867, as has been already shown, it was the practice of the President during the recesses of the Senate to remove civil officers and to grant commissions to other persons under the third clause of the second section of the second article of the Constitution. This power, as has been seen, was a doubtful one in the beginning. The practice grew up under the act of 1789, but the right of Congress by legislation to regulate the exercise of that power was not questioned in the great debate of that year, nor can it reasonably be drawn into controversy now.

The act of March 2, 1867, declares that the President shall not exercise the power of removal, absolutely, during the recess of the Senate, but that if any officer shall be shown, by evidence satisfactory to the President, to be guilty of misconduct in office, or of crime, or for any reason shall become incapable or legally disqualified to perform his duties, the President may suspend him from office and designate some suitable person to perform temporarily the duties of such office until the next meeting of the Senate and the action of the Senate thereon.

By this legislation the removal is qualified and is made subject to the final action of the Senate instead of being absolute, as was the fact under the practice theretofore prevailing. It is to be observed, however, that this feature of the act regulating the tenure of certain civil offices is not drawn into controversy by these proceedings, and therefore it is entirely unimportant to the President whether that provision of the act is constitutional or not. I can, however, entertain no doubt of its constitutionality. The record of the case shows that Mr. Stanton was suspended from office during the recess, but was removed from office, as far as an order of the President could effect his removal, during a session of the Senate. It is also wholly immaterial to the present inquiry whether the suspension of Mr. Stanton on the 12th of August, 1867, was made under the tenure-of-office act, or in disregard of it, as the President now asserts. It being thus clear that so much of the act as relates to appointments and removals from office during the session of the Senate is in harmony with the practice of the Government from the first, and in harmony with the provisions of the Constitution on which that practice was based, and it being admitted that the order of the President for the removal of Mr. Stanton was issued during a session of the Senate, it is unnecessary to inquire whether the other parts of the act are constitutional or not, and also unnecessary to inquire what the provisions of the act are in reference to the heads of the several Executive Departments. I presume authorities are not needed to show that a law may be unconstitutional and void in some of its parts, and the remaining portions continue in full force.

The body of the first section of the act regulating the tenure of certain civil offices is in these words:

"Every person holding any civil office to which he has been appointed by and with the advice and consent of the Senate, and every person who shall hereafter be appointed to any such office, and shall become duly qualified to act therein, is, and shall be entitled, to hold such office until a successor shall have been in like manner appointed and duly qualified, except as herein otherwise provided."

Omitting for the moment to notice the exception, there can be no doubt that this provision would have applied to the Secretary of War, and to every other civil officer under the Government; nor can there be any doubt that the removal of Mr. Stanton during a session of the Senate is a misdemeanor by the law, and punishable as such under the sixth section of the act, unless the body of the section quoted is so controlled by the proviso as to take the Secretary of War out of its grasp. The proviso is in these words:

"That the Secretaries of State, of the Treasury, of War, of the Navy, and of the Interior, the Postmaster General, and the Attorney General shall hold their offices respectively for and during the term of the President by whom they may have been appointed and one month thereafter, subject to removal by and with the advice and consent of the Senate."

We maintain that Mr. Stanton, as Secretary of War, was, on the 2d day of March, 1867, within and included under the language of the proviso, and was to hold his office for and during the term of the President by whom he had been appointed, and one month thereafter, subject to removal, however, by and with the advice and consent of the Senate. We maintain that Mr. Stanton was then holding the office of Secretary of War for and in the term of President Lincoln, by whom he had been appointed; that that term commenced on the 4th of March, 1865, and will end on the 4th of March, 1869. The Constitution defines the meaning of the word "term." When speaking of the President, it says:

"He shall hold his office during the term of four years, and, together with the Vice President, chosen for the same term, be elected as follows."

Now, then, although the President first elected may die during his term, the office and the term of the office still remain. Having been established by the Constitution, it is not in any degree dependent upon the circumstance whether the person elected to the term shall survive to the end or not. It still is a presidential term. It still is in law the term of the President who was elected to the office. The Vice President was chosen at the same time and elected for the same term. But it is the term of a different office from that of President—the term of the office of Vice President. Mr. Johnson was elected to the office of Vice President for the term of four years. Mr. Lincoln was elected to the office of President for the term of four years. Mr. Lincoln died in the second month of his term, and Mr. Johnson succeeded to the office.

It was not a new office; it was not a new term. He succeeded to Mr. Lincoln's office, and for the remainder of Mr. Lincoln's term of office. He is serving out Mr. Lincoln's term as President. The law says that the Secretaries shall hold their offices respectively for and during the term of the President by whom they may have been appointed. Mr. Lincoln's term commenced on the 4th of March, 1865. Mr. Stanton was appointed by Mr. Lincoln; he was in office in Mr. Lincoln's term, when the act regulating the tenure of certain civil offices was passed; and by the proviso of that act he was entitled to hold that office until one month after the 4th of March, 1869, unless he should be sooner removed therefrom, by and with the advice and consent of the Senate.

The act of March 1, 1792, concerning the succession, in case the office of President and Vice President both become vacant, recognizes the presidential term of four years as the constitutional term. Any one can understand that in case of vacancy in the office of President and Vice President, and in case of a new election by the people, that it would be desirable to make the election for the remainder of the term. But the act of 1792 recognizes the impossibility of this course in the section which provides that the term of four years for which a President and Vice President shall be elected (that is, in case of a new election, as stated,) shall in all cases commence on the 4th day of March next succeeding the day on which the votes of the electors shall have been given.

It is thus seen that by an election to fill a vacancy the Government would be so far changed in its practical working that the subsequent elections of President, except by an amendment to the Constitution, could never again occur in the years divisible by four, as at present, and might not answer to the election of members to the House of Representatives, for the presidential elections might occur in the years not divisible by two. The Congress of 1792 acted upon the constitutional doctrine that the presidential term is four years and cannot be changed by law.

On the 21st of February, 1868, while the Senate of the United States was in session, Mr. Johnson, in violation of the law—which, as we have already seen, is in strict harmony in this particular with the Constitution and with the practice of every Administration under the Constitution from the beginning of the Government—issued an order for the removal of Mr. Stanton from his office as Secretary for the Department of War. If, however, it be claimed that the proviso does not apply to the Secretary of War, then he does not come within the only exception made in the statute to the general provision in the body of the first section already quoted; and Mr. Stanton, having been appointed to office originally by and with the advice and consent of the Senate, could only be removed by the nomination and appointment of a successor by and with the advice and consent of the Senate. Hence, upon either theory, it is plain that the President violated the tenure-of-office act in the order which he issued on the 21st of February, A. D. 1868, for the

C. I.—37.

removal of Mr. Stanton from the office of Secretary for the Department of War, the Senate of the United States being then in session.

In support of the view I have presented I refer to the official record of the amendments made to the first section of the tenure-of-office act. On the 18th of January, 1867, the bill passed the Senate, and the first section thereof was in these words:

"That every person [excepting the Secretaries of State, of the Treasury, of War, of the Navy, and of the Interior, the Postmaster General, and the Attorney General] holding any civil office to which he has been appointed by and with the advice and consent of the Senate, and every person who shall hereafter be appointed to any such office, and shall become duly qualified to act therein, is, and shall be, entitled to hold such office until a successor shall have been in like manner appointed and duly qualified, except as herein otherwise provided."

On the 2d of February the House passed the bill with an amendment striking out the words included in brackets. This action shows that it was the purpose of the House to include heads of Departments in the body of the bill, and subject them to its provisions as civil officers, who were to hold their places by and with the advice and consent of the Senate, and subject, during the session of the Senate, to removal by and with the advice and consent of the Senate only; but subject to suspension under the second section during a recess of the Senate as other civil officers, by virtue of the words at the close of the section, "except as herein otherwise provided." At the time the bill was pending between the two Houses there was no proviso to the first section, and the phrase "except as otherwise herein provided" related necessarily to the second and to the subsequent sections of the bill. On the 6th of February the Senate refused to agree to the House amendment, and by the action of the two Houses the bill was referred to a committee of conference. The conference committee agreed to strike out the words in brackets agreeably to a vote of the House, but as a recognition of the opinion of the Senate the proviso was inserted which modified in substance the effect of the words stricken out, under the lead of the House, only in this, that the Cabinet officers referred to in the body of the section as it passed the House were to hold their offices as they would have held them if the House amendment had been agreed to without condition, with this exception: that they were to retire from their offices in one month after the end of the term of the President by whom they might have been appointed to office. The object and effect of this qualification of the provision for which the House contended was to avoid fastening, by operation of law, upon an incoming President the Cabinet of his predecessor, with no means of relieving himself from them unless the Senate of the United States was disposed to concur in their removal.

In short, they were to retire by operation of law at the end of one month after the expiration of the term of the President by whom they had been appointed; and in this particular their tenure of office was distinguished by the proviso from the tenure by which other civil officers mentioned in the body of the section were to hold their offices, and their tenure of office is distinguished in no other particular.

The counsel who opened the cause for the President was pleased to read from the Globe the remarks made by Mr. SCHENCK in the House of Representatives, when the report of the conference committee was under discussion. But he read only a portion of the remarks of that gentleman, and connected with them observations of his own, by which he may have led the Senate into the error that Mr. SCHENCK entertained the opinion as to the effect of the proviso which is now urged by the respondent; but, so far from this being the case, the statement made by Mr. SCHENCK to the House is exactly in accordance with the doctrine now maintained by the Managers on the part of the House of Representatives. After Mr. SCHENCK had made the remarks quoted by the counsel for the respondent, Mr. Le Blond, of Ohio, rose and said:

"I would like to inquire of the gentleman who has charge of this report whether it becomes necessary that the Senate shall concur in all appointments of executive officers, and that none of them can be removed after appointment without the concurrence of the Senate?"

Mr. SCHENCK says, in reply:

"That is the case; but their terms of office is limited, (as they are not now limited by law,) so that they expire with the term of service of the President who appoints them, and one month after, in case of death or other accident, until others can be substituted for them by the incoming President."

Mr. Le Blond, continuing, said:

"I understand, then, this to be the effect of the report of the committee of conference: in the event of the President finding himself with a Cabinet officer who does not agree with him, and whom he desires to remove, he cannot do so, and have a Cabinet in keeping with his own views, unless the Senate shall concur."

To this Mr. SCHENCK replies:

"The gentleman certainly does not need that information from me, as this subject has been fully debated in this House."

Mr. Le Blond said, finally:

"Then I hope the House will not agree to the report of the committee of conference."

This debate in the House shows that there was there and then no difference of opinion between Mr. SCHENCK, who represented the friends of the bill, and Mr. Le Blond, who represented the opponents of the bill, that its effect was to confirm the Secretaries who were then in office in their places until one month after the expiration of Mr. Lincoln's term of office, to wit, the 4th day of March, 1869, unless, upon the nomination of successors, they should be removed by and with the advice and consent of the Senate. Nor does the language used by the honorable Senator from Ohio, who reported the result of the conference to the Senate, justify the inference which has been drawn from it by the counsel for the respond-

ent. The charge made by the honorable Senator from Wisconsin, which the honorable Senator from Ohio was refuting, seems to have been, in substance, that the first section of the bill and the proviso to the first section of the bill had been framed with special reference to Mr. Johnson, as President, and to the existing condition of affairs. In response to this the honorable Senator from Ohio said:

"I say that the Senate have not legislated with a view to any persons or any President, and therefore he commences by asserting what is not true. We do not legislate in order to keep in the Secretary of War, the Secretary of the Navy, or the Secretary of State."

It will be observed that this language does not indicate the opinion of the honorable Senator as to the effect of the bill; but it is only a declaration that the object of the legislation was not that which had been intimated or alleged by the honorable Senator from Wisconsin. This view of the remarks of the honorable Senator from Ohio is confirmed by what he afterward said in reply to the suggestion that members of the Cabinet would hold their places against the wishes of the President, when he declares that under such circumstances he, as a Senator, would consent to their removal at any time, showing most clearly that he did not entertain the idea that under the tenure-of-office act it would be in the power of the President to remove a Cabinet officer without the advice and consent of the Senate. And we all agree that in ordinary times, and under ordinary circumstances, it would not only be just and proper for a Cabinet officer to tender his resignation at once, upon the suggestion of the President that it would be acceptable, but we also agree that it would be the height of personal and official indecorum if he were to hesitate for a moment as to his duty in that particular. But the justification of Mr. Stanton, and his claim to the gratitude and encomiums of his countrymen, is, that when the nation was imperiled by the usurpations of a criminally-minded Chief Magistrate, he asserted his constitutional and legal rights to the office of Secretary for the Department of War, and thus by his devotion to principle, and at great personal sacrifices, he has done more than any other man since the close of the rebellion to protect the interests and maintain the rights of the people of the country.

But the strength of the view we entertain of the meaning and scope of the tenure-of-office act is nowhere more satisfactorily demonstrated than in the inconsistencies of the argument which has been presented by the learned counsel for the respondent in support of the President's positions. He says, speaking of the first section of the act regulating the tenure of certain civil offices:

"Here is a section, then, the body of which applies to all civil officers, as well to those then in office as to those who should thereafter be appointed. The body of this section contains a declaration that every such officer 'is,' that is, if he is now in office, and 'shall be,' that is, if he shall hereafter be appointed to office, entitled to hold until a successor is appointed and qualified in his place. That is the body of the section."

This language of the eminent counsel is not only an admission, but it is a declaration that the Secretary for the Department of War, being a civil officer, as is elsewhere admitted in the argument of the counsel for the respondent, is included in and covered and controlled by the language of the body of this section. It is a further admission that in the absence of the proviso the power of the President over the Secretary for the Department of War would correspond exactly to his power over any other civil officer, which would be merely the power to nominate a successor whose confirmation by the Senate, and appointment, would work the removal of the person in office. When the counsel for the respondent, proceeding in his argument, enters upon an examination of the proviso, he maintains that the language of that proviso does not include the Secretary for the Department of War. If he is not included in the language of the proviso, then upon the admission of the counsel he is included in the body of the bill, so that for the purposes of this investigation and trial it is wholly immaterial whether the proviso applies to him or not. If the proviso does not apply to the Secretary for the Department of War, then he holds his office, as in the body of the section expressed, until removed therefrom by and with the advice and consent of the Senate. If he is covered by the language of the proviso, then a limitation is fixed to his office, to wit: that it is to expire one month after the close of the term of the President by whom he has been appointed, subject, however, to previous removal by and with the advice and consent of the Senate.

I have already considered the question of intent on the part of the President, and maintained that in the willful violation of the law he discloses a criminal intent which cannot be controlled or qualified by any testimony on the part of the respondent.

The counsel for the respondent, however, has dwelt so much at length on the question of intent, and such efforts have been made during the trial to introduce testimony upon this point, that I am justified in recurring to it for a brief consideration of the arguments and views bearing upon and relating to that question. If a law passed by Congress be equivocal or ambiguous in its terms, the Executive, being called upon to administer it, may apply his own best judgment to the difficulties before him, or he may seek counsel from his official advisers or other proper persons; and acting thereupon, without evil intent or purpose, he would be fully justified, and upon no principle of right could he be held to answer as for a misdemeanor in office. But that is not this case. The question considered by Mr. Johnson did not relate to the meaning of the tenure-of-office act. He understood perfectly well the intention of Congress, and he admitted in his

veto message that that intention was expressed with sufficient clearness to enable him to comprehend and state it. In his veto message of the 2d of March, 1867, after quoting the first section of the bill to regulate the tenure of certain civil offices, he says:

"In effect the bill provides that the President shall not remove from their places *any civil officers* whose terms of service are not limited by law without the advice and consent of the Senate of the United States The bill, in this respect, conflicts, in my judgment, with the Constitution of the United States."

His statement of the meaning of the bill relates to all civil officers, to the members of his Cabinet as well as to others, and is a declaration that, under that bill, if it became a law, none of those officers could be removed without the advice and consent of the Senate. He was, therefore, in no doubt as to the intention of Congress as expressed in the bill submitted to him for his consideration, and which afterward became the law of the land. He said to the Senate, "If you pass this bill, I cannot remove the members of my Cabinet." The Senate and the House in effect said, "We so intend," and passed the bill by a two-thirds majority. There was then no misunderstanding as to the meaning or intention of the act. His offense, then, is not, that upon an examination of the statute he misunderstood its meaning and acted upon a misinterpretation of its true import, but that understanding its meaning precisely as it was understood by the Congress that passed the law, precisely as it is understood by the House of Representatives to-day, precisely as it is presented in the articles of impeachment, and by the Managers before this Senate, he, upon his own opinion that the same was unconstitutional, deliberately, willfully, and intentionally disregarded it. The learned counsel say that he had a right to violate this law for the purpose of obtaining a judicial determination. This we deny. The constitutional duty of the President is to obey and execute the laws. He has no authority under the Constitution, or by any law, to enter into any schemes or plans for the purpose of testing the validity of the laws of the country, either judicially or otherwise. Every law of Congress may be tested in the courts, but it is not made the duty of any person to so test the laws. It is not specially the right of any person to so test the laws, and the effort is particularly offensive in the Chief Magistrate of the country to attempt by any process to annul, set aside, or defeat the laws which by his oath he is bound to execute. Nor is it any answer to say, as is suggested by the counsel for the respondent, that "there never could be a judicial decision that a law is unconstitutional, inasmuch as it is only by disregarding a law that any question can be raised judicially under it." If this be true, it is no misfortune. But the opposite theory, that it is the duty or the right of the President to disregard a law for the purpose of ascertaining judicially whether he has a right to violate a law, is abhorrent to every just principle of government, and dangerous in the highest degree to the existence of free institutions.

But his alleged purpose to test the law in the courts is shown to be a pretext merely. Upon his own theory of his rights he could have instituted proceedings by information in the nature of a *quo warranto* against Mr. Stanton on the 13th of January, 1868. More than three months have passed, and he has done nothing whatever. When by Mr. Stanton's action Lorenzo Thomas was under arrest, and proceedings were instituted which might have tested the legality of the tenure-of-office act, Mr. Cox, the President's special counsel, moved to have the proceedings dismissed, although Thomas was at large upon his own recognizance. Can anybody believe that it was Mr. Johnson's purpose to test the act in the courts? But the respondent's insincerity, his duplicity, is shown by the statement which he made to General Sherman in January last. Sherman says, "I asked him why lawyers could not make a case, and not bring me, or an officer, into the controversy? His answer was, 'that it was found impossible, or a case could not be made up;' 'but,' said he, 'if we can bring the case to the courts it would not stand half an hour.'" He now says his object was to test the case in the courts. To Sherman he declares that a case could not be made up, but if one could be made up the law would not stand half an hour. When a case was made up which might have tested the law he makes haste to get it dismissed. Did ever audacity and duplicity more clearly appear in the excuses of a criminal?

This brief argument upon the question of intent seems to me conclusive, but I shall incidentally refer to this point in the further progress of my remarks.

The House of Representatives does not demand the conviction of Andrew Johnson unless he is guilty in the manner charged in the articles of impeachment; nor does the House expect the Managers to seek a conviction except upon the law and the facts considered with judicial impartiality. But I am obliged to declare that I have no capacity to understand those processes of the human mind by which this tribunal, or any member of this tribunal, can doubt, can entertain a reasonable doubt, that Andrew Johnson is guilty of high misdemeanors in office, as charged in each of the first three articles exhibited against him by the House of Representatives.

We have charged and proved that Andrew Johnson, President of the United States, issued an order in writing for the removal of Edwin M. Stanton from the office of Secretary for the Department of War while the Senate of the United States was in session, and without the advice and consent of the Senate, in violation of the Constitution of the United States and of his oath of office, and of the provisions of an act passed March 2, 1867, entitled "An act regulating the tenure of certain civil offices,"

and that he did this with intent so to do; and thereupon we demand his conviction under the first of the articles of impeachment exhibited against him by the House of Representatives.

We have charged and proved that Andrew Johnson, President of the United States, violated the Constitution and his oath of office in issuing an order for the removal of Edwin M. Stanton from the office of Secretary for the Department of War during the session of the Senate, and without the advice and consent of the Senate, and this without reference to the tenure-of-office act; and thereupon we demand his conviction under the first of the articles of impeachment exhibited against him by the House of Representatives.

We have charged and proved that Andrew Johnson, President of the United States, did issue and deliver to one Lorenzo Thomas a letter of authority in writing authorizing and empowering said Thomas to act as Secretary of War *ad interim*, there being no vacancy in said office, and this while the Senate of the United States was in session, and without the advice and consent of the Senate, in violation of the Constitution of the United States, of his oath of office, and of the provisions of an act entitled "An act regulating the tenure of certain civil offices," and all this with the intent so to do; and thereupon we demand his conviction under the second of the articles of impeachment exhibited against him by the House of Representatives.

We have charged and proved that Andrew Johnson, President of the United States, in the appointment of Lorenzo Thomas to the office of Secretary of War *ad interim*, acted without authority of law and in violation of the Constitution and of his oath of office; and this without reference to the tenure-of-office act; and thereupon we demand his conviction under the third of the articles of impeachment exhibited against him by the House of Representatives.

At this point the honorable Manager yielded for an adjournment.

Mr. CONKLING. I move that the Senate sitting for this trial adjourn.

The CHIEF JUSTICE. The Senator from New York moves that the Senate sitting as a court of impeachment adjourn until to-morrow at eleven o'clock.

The motion was agreed to; and the Senate sitting for the trial of the impeachment adjourned.

THURSDAY, *April* 23, 1868.

The Chief Justice of the United States took the chair.

The usual proclamation having been made by the Sergeant-at-Arms,

The Managers of the impeachment on the part of the House of Representatives and the counsel for the respondent, except Mr. Stanbery, appeared and took the seats assigned to them respectively.

The members of the House of Representatives, as in Committee of the Whole, preceded by Mr. E. B. WASHBURNE, chairman of that committee, and accompanied by the Speaker and Clerk, appeared and were conducted to the seats provided for them.

The CHIEF JUSTICE. The Secretary will read the minutes of yesterday's proceedings.

The Journal of the Senate sitting yesterday for the trial of the impeachment was read.

Mr. GRIMES. Mr. Chief Justice, I ask leave to offer an order which will lie over if there be any objection made to it.

The CHIEF JUSTICE. The Secretary will read the order proposed by the Senator from Iowa.

The Chief Clerk read as follows:

Ordered, That hereafter the hour for the meeting of the Senate, sitting for the trial of the impeachment of Andrew Johnson, President of the United States, shall be twelve o'clock meridian of each day except Sunday.

The CHIEF JUSTICE. Is there any objection to the present consideration of the proposed order?

Mr. SUMNER. I object.

The CHIEF JUSTICE. Objection is made, and it will lie over. Mr. Manager BOUTWELL will please proceed with his argument.

Mr. Manager BOUTWELL. Mr. President, Senators, the learned counsel for the respondent seems to have involved himself in some difficulty concerning the articles which he terms the conspiracy articles, being articles four, five, six, and seven. The allegations contained in articles four and six are laid under the act of July 31, 1861, known as the conspiracy act. The remarks of the learned counsel seem to imply that articles five and seven are not based upon any law whatever. In this he greatly errs. An examination of articles four and five shows that the substantive allegation is the same in each, the differences being that article four charges the conspiracy with intent, by intimidation and threats, unlawfully to hinder and prevent Edwin M. Stanton from holding the office of Secretary for the Department of War. The persons charged are the respondent and Lorenzo Thomas. And it is alleged that this conspiracy for the purpose set forth was in violation of the Constitution of the United States and of the provisions of an act entitled "An act to punish certain conspiracies," approved July 31, 1861. The fifth article charges that the respondent did unlawfully conspire with one Lorenzo Thomas, and with other persons, to prevent the execution of the act entitled "An act regulating the tenure of certain civil offices," and that in pursuance of that conspiracy they did unlawfully attempt to prevent Edwin M. Stanton from holding the office of Secretary for the Department of War. It is not alleged in the article that this conspiracy is against any particular

law, but it is alleged that the parties charged did unlawfully conspire. It is very well known that conspiracies are of two kinds. Two or more persons may conspire to do a *lawful* act by *unlawful* means; or two or more persons may conspire to do an *unlawful* act by *lawful* means. By the common law of England such conspiracies have always been indictable and punishable as misdemeanors. The State of Maryland was one of the original thirteen States of the Union, and the common law of England has always prevailed in that State, except so far as it has been modified by statute. The city of Washington was originally within the State of Maryland, but it was ceded to the United States under the provisions of the Constitution. By a statute of the United States, passed February 27, 1801, (Statutes-at-Large, vol. 2, p. 103,) it is provided:

"That the laws of the State of Maryland, as they now exist, shall be and continue in force in that part of the said district which was ceded by that State to the United States, and by them accepted as aforesaid."

By force of this statute, although probably the law would have been the same without legislation, the English common law of crimes prevails in the city of Washington. By another statute entitled "An act for the punishment of crimes in the District of Columbia," (Statutes-at-Large, vol. 4, p. 450,) approved March 2, 1831, special punishments are affixed to various crimes enumerated when committed in the District of Columbia. But conspiracy is not one of the crimes mentioned. The fifteenth section of that act provides:

"That every other felony, misdemeanor, or offense not provided for by this act may and shall be punished as heretofore, except that in all cases where whipping is part or the whole of the punishment, except in the cases of slaves, the court shall substitute therefor imprisonment in the county jail for a period not exceeding six months."

And the sixteenth section declares—

"That all definitions and descriptions of crimes, all fines, forfeitures, and incapacities, the restitution of property, or the payment of the value thereof, and every other matter not provided for in this act, be and the same shall remain as heretofore."

There can then be no doubt that, under the English common law of crimes, sanctioned and continued by the statutes of the United States in the District of Columbia, the fifth and seventh articles set forth offenses which are punishable as misdemeanors by the laws of the District.

Article six is laid under the statute of 1861, and charges that the respondent did unlawfully conspire with Lorenzo Thomas, by force, to seize, take, and possess the property of the United States in the Department of War, and this with intent to violate and disregard the act entitled "An act regulating the tenure of certain civil offices." The words used in the conspiracy act of 1861 leave room for argument upon the point raised by the learned counsel for the respondent. I admit that the District of Columbia is not included by specific designation; but the reasons for the law and the natural interpretation of the language justify the view that the act applies to the District. I shall refer to a single authority only upon the point.

The internal-duties act of August 2, 1813, (Statutes, vol. 3, p. 82) subjects, in express terms, the "several Territories of the United States and the District of Columbia" to the payment of the taxes imposed; upon which the question arose whether Congress has power to impose a direct tax on the District of Columbia, in view of the fact that by the Constitution it is provided that "representation and direct taxes shall be apportioned among the several States which may be included within the Union according to their respective numbers."

In the case of Loughborough vs. Blake the Supreme .Court of the United States unanimously decided, in a brief opinion by Chief Justice Marshall, that although the language of the Constitution apparently excepts the District of Columbia from the imposition of direct taxes, yet the reason of the thing requires us to consider the District as being comprehended, in this respect, within the intention of the Constitution. (Loughborough vs. Blake, 5 Wheaton, p. 317.)

The reasoning of the Supreme Court and its conclusion in this case were satisfactory to the bar and the country, and no person has deemed it worth while to raise the question anew under the direct tax act of August 5, 1861, (Statutes 12, 296,) which also comprehends the Territories and the District of Columbia.

But the logical rules of construction applicable to an act of Congress are the same as those applicable to the Constitution. An act of Congress and the Constitution are both laws—nothing more, nothing less—except that the latter is of superior authority. And if, in the construction of the Constitution, it may be satisfactorily maintained that the District of Columbia is to be deemed, because of the reason of things, to be comprehended by a provision of the Constitution which in words, and in their superficial construction, excludes it, must not the same rule of construction produce the same result in the determination of the legal intent and import of an act of Congress, when an obscurity exists in the latter and for the same cause?

The seventh article is laid upon the common law, and charges substantially the same offenses as those charged in the sixth article. The result then is that the fifth and seventh articles, which are based upon the common law, set forth substantially the same offenses which are set forth in the fourth and sixth articles, which are laid upon the statute of July 31, 1861; and as there can be no doubt of the validity of the fifth and seventh articles, it is practically immaterial whether the suggestion made by the counsel for the respondent, that the conspiracy act of 1861 does not include the District of Columbia, is a valid suggestion or not. Not doubting that the Senate will find that the charge of conspiracy is sufficiently laid under existing laws in all the articles, I proceed to an examination of the evidence by which the charge is supported.

It should always be borne in mind that the evidence in proof of conspiracy will generally, from the nature of the crime, be circumstantial; and this case in this particular is no exception to the usual experience in criminal trials. We find, in the first place, if the allegations in the first, second, and third articles have been established, that the President was engaged in an unlawful act. If we find Lorenzo Thomas or any other person coöperating with him upon an agreement or an understanding or an assent on the part of such other person to the prosecution of such unlawful undertaking an actual conspiracy is proved. The existence of the conspiracy being established, it is then competent to introduce the statements and acts of the parties to the conspiracy, made and done while the conspiracy was pending, and in furtherance of the design; and it is upon this ground that testimony has been offered and received of the declarations made by Lorenzo Thomas, one of the parties to the conspiracy, subsequent to the 18th of January, 1868, or perhaps to the 13th of January, 1868—the day on which he was restored to the office of Adjutant General of the Army of the United States by the action of the President, and which appears to have been an initial proceeding on his part for the purpose of accomplishing his unlawful design—the removal of Mr. Stanton from the office of Secretary for the Department of War. The evidence of agreement between the respondent and Thomas is found in the order of the 21st of February, 1868, appointing Thomas, and in the conversation which occurred at the time the order was placed in Thomas's hands. The counsel for the respondent at this point was involved in a very serious difficulty. If he had admitted (which he took care not to do) that the order was purely a military one, he foresaw that the respondent would be involved in the crime of having issued a military order which did not pass through the General of the Army, and thus would be liable to impeachment and removal from office for violating the law of the 2d of March, 1867, entitled "An act making appropriations for the support of the Army for the fiscal year ending June 30, 1868, and for other purposes."

If he had declared that it was not a military order, then the transaction confessedly was in the nature of an agreement between the President and Lorenzo Thomas; and if the act contemplated by that agreement was an unlawful act, or if the act were unlawful, and the means employed for accomplishing it were unlawful, then clearly the charge of conspiracy would be maintained. Hence he was careful to say, in denying that the order was a military order, that it nevertheless "invoked that spirit of military obedience which constitutes the strength of the service." And further, he says of Thomas, that, as a faithful Adjutant General of the Army of the United States, interested personally, professionally, and patriotically to have the office of Secretary of the Department of War performed in a temporary vacancy, was it not his duty to accept the appointment unless he knew that it was unlawful to accept it? The admissions and statements of the learned counsel are to the effect, on the whole, that the order was not a military order, nor do we claim that it was a military order, but it was a letter addressed to General Thomas, which he could have declined altogether without subjecting himself to any punishment by a military tribunal. This is the crucial test of the character of the paper which he received, and on which he proceeded to act. Ignorance of the law, according to the old maxim, excuses no man; and whether General Thomas, at the first interview he had with the President on the 18th of January, 1868, or at his interview with him on the day when he received the letter of appointment, knew that the President was then engaged in an unlawful act, is not material to this inquiry. The President knew that his purpose was an unlawful one, and he then and there induced General Thomas to coöperate with him in the prosecution of the unlawful design. If General Thomas was ignorant of the illegal nature of the transaction, that fact furnishes no legal defense for him, even though morally it might be an excuse for his conduct. But certainly the President, who did know the illegal nature of the proceeding, cannot excuse himself by asserting that his coconspirator was at the time ignorant of the illegal nature of the business in which they were engaged.

It being proved that the respondent was engaged in an unlawful undertaking in his attempt to remove Mr. Stanton from the office of Secretary for the Department of War, that, by an agreement or understanding between General Thomas and himself they were to coöperate in carrying this purpose into execution, and it being proved, also, that the purpose itself was unlawful, all the elements of a conspiracy are fully established; and it only remains to examine the testimony in order that the nature of the conspiracy may more clearly appear and the means by which the purpose was to be accomplished may be more fully understood.

The statement of the President in his message to the Senate under date of 12th of December, 1867, discloses the depth of his feeling and the intensity of his purpose in regard to the removal of Mr. Stanton. In that message he speaks of the bill regulating the tenure of certain civil offices at the time it was before him for consideration. He says:

"The bill had not then become a law; the limitation upon the power of removal was not yet imposed, and there was yet time to make any changes. If any one of those gentlemen [meaning the members of his Cabinet] had then said to me that he would avail himself of the provisions of that bill in case it became a law I should not have hesitated a moment as to his removal."

When, in the summer of 1867, the respondent became satisfied that Mr. Stanton not only did not enter into the President's schemes but was opposed to them, and he determined upon his suspension and final removal from the office of Secretary for the Department of War, he knew well that the confidence of the people in Mr. Stanton was very great, and that they would not accept his removal and an appointment to that important place of any person of doubtful position, or whose qualifications were not known to the country. Hence he sought, through the suspension of Mr. Stanton and the appointment of General Grant as Secretary of War *ad interim*, to satisfy the country for the moment, but with the design to prepare the way thereby for the introduction into the War Department of one of his own creatures. At that time it was supposed that the suspension of Mr. Stanton and the appointment of General Grant were made under and by virtue of the act regulating the tenure of certain civil offices; and although the conduct of the President during a period of nearly six months in reference to that office was in conformity to the provisions of that act, it was finally declared by him that what he had done had been done in conformity to the general power which he claims under the Constitution, and that he did not in any way recognize the act as constitutional or binding upon him. His message to the Senate of the 12th of December was framed apparently in obedience to the tenure-of-office act. He charged Mr. Stanton with misconduct in office, which, by that act, had been made a ground for the suspension of a civil officer; he furnished reasons and evidence of misconduct which, as he alleged, had been satisfactory to him, and he furnished such reasons and evidence within twenty days after the meeting of the Senate next following the day of suspension.

All this was in conformity to the statute of March 2, 1867. The Senate proceeded to consider the evidence and reasons furnished by the President, and in conformity to that act passed a resolution, adopted on the 13th of January, 1868, declaring that the reasons were unsatisfactory to the Senate, and that Mr. Stanton was restored to the office of Secretary for the Department of War. Up to that time there had been no official statement or declaration by the President that he had not acted under the tenure-of-office act; but he now assumed that that act had no binding force, and that Mr. Stanton was not lawfully restored to the office of Secretary for the Department of War.

Upon the adoption of the resolution by the Senate General Grant at once surrendered the office to Mr. Stanton. This act upon his part filled the President with indignation toward both General Grant and Mr. Stanton, and from that day he seems to have been under the influence of a settled and criminal purpose to destroy General Grant and to secure the removal of Mr. Stanton. During the month following the restoration of Mr. Stanton the President attempted to carry out his purpose by various and tortuous methods. First he endeavored to secure the support of General Sherman. On two occasions, as is testified by General Sherman, on the 27th and 31st of January, he tendered him the position of Secretary of War *ad interim*. It occurred very naturally to General Sherman to inquire of the President whether Mr. Stanton would retire voluntarily from the office; and also to ask the President what he was to do, and whether he would resort to force if Mr. Stanton would not yield. The President answered, "Oh, he will make no objection; you present the order and he will retire." Upon a doubt being expressed by General Sherman, the President remarked, "I know him better than you do; he is cowardly." The President knew Mr. Stanton too well to entertain any such opinion of his courage as he gave in his answer to General Sherman; the secret of the proceeding, undoubtedly, was this: he desired in the first place to induce General Sherman to accept the office of Secretary of War *ad interim* upon the assurance on his part that Mr. Stanton would retire willingly from his position, trusting that when General Sherman was appointed to and had accepted the place of Secretary of War *ad interim* he could be induced, either upon the suggestion of the President or under the influence of a natural disinclination on his part to fail in the accomplishment of anything which he had undertaken, to seize the War Department by force. The President very well knew that if General Sherman accepted the office of Secretary of War *ad interim* he would be ready at the earliest moment to relinquish it into the hands of the President, and thus he hoped through the agency of General Sherman to secure the possession of the Department for one of his favorites.

During the period from the 13th day of January to the 21st of February he made an attempt to enlist General George H. Thomas in the same unlawful undertaking. Here, also, he was disappointed. Thus it is seen that from August last, the time when he entered systematically upon his purpose to remove Mr. Stanton from the office of Secretary for the Department of War, he has attempted to secure the purpose he had in view through the personal influence and services of the three principal officers of the Army; and that he has met with disappointment in each case. Under these circumstances nothing remained for the respondent but to seize the office by an open, willful, defiant violation of law; and as it was necessary for the accomplishment of his purpose that he should obtain the support of some one, and as his experience had satisfied him that no person of capacity or respectability or patriotism would unite with him in his unlawful enterprise, he sought the assistance and aid

of Lorenzo Thomas. This man, as you have seen him, is an old man, a broken man, a vain man, a weak man, utterly incapable of performing any important public service in a manner creditable to the country; but possessing, nevertheless, all the qualities and characteristics of a subservient instrument and tool of an ambitious, unscrupulous man. He readily accepted the place which the President offered him, and there is no doubt that the declarations which he made to Wilkeson, Burleigh, and Karsner were made when he entertained the purpose of executing them, and made also in the belief that they were entirely justified by the orders which he had received from the President, and that the execution of his purpose to seize the War Department by force would be acceptable to the President. That he threatened to use force there is no doubt from the testimony, and he has himself confessed substantially the truth of the statements made by all the witnesses for the prosecution who have testified to that fact.

These statements were made by Thomas on and after the 21st of February, when he received his letter of authority, in writing, to take possession of the War Department. The agreement between the President and Thomas was consummated on that day. With one mind they were then and on subsequent days engaged and up to the present time they are engaged in the attempt to get possession of the War Department. Mr. Stanton, as the Senate by its resolution has declared, being the lawful Secretary of War, this proceeding on their part was an unlawful proceeding. It had in view an unlawful purpose; it was therefore in contemplation of the law a conspiracy, and the President is consequently bound by the declarations made by Thomas in regard to taking possession of the War Department by force. Thomas admits that on the night of the 21st it was his purpose to use force; but on the morning of the 22d his mind had undergone a change and he then resolved not to use force. We do not know precisely the hour when his mind underwent this change, but the evidence discloses that upon his return from the supreme court of the District, where he had been arraigned upon a complaint made by Mr. Stanton, which, according to the testimony, was twelve o'clock or thereabouts, he had an interview with the President; and it is also in evidence that at or about the same time the President had an interview with General Emory, from whom he learned that that officer would not obey a command of the President unless it passed through General Grant, as required by law.

The President understood perfectly well that he could neither obtain force from General Grant nor transmit an order through General Grant for the accomplishment of a purpose manifestly unlawful; and inasmuch as General Emory had indicated to him in the most distinct and emphatic manner his opinion that the law requiring all orders to pass through the headquarters of the General commanding was constitutional, indicating also his purpose to obey the law, it was apparent that at that moment the President could have had no hope of obtaining possession of the Department of War by force. It is a singular coincidence in the history of this case that at or about the same time General Thomas had an interview with the President and came to the conclusion that it would not be wise to resort to force.

The President has sought to show his good intention by the fact that, on the 22d or the 24th of February, he nominated Hon. Thomas Ewing, senior, as Secretary for the Department of War. Mr. Ewing is not an unknown man. He has been a member of the Senate and the head of the Treasury Department. His abilities are undoubted, but at the time of his nomination he was in the seventy-ninth year of his age, and there was no probability that he would hold the office a moment longer than his sense of public duty required. It was the old game of the President—the office in the hands of his own tool or in the hands of a man who would gladly vacate it at any moment. This was the necessity of his position, and throws light upon that part of his crime which is set forth in the eleventh article.

For, in fact, his crime is one—the subversion of the Government. From the nature of the case we are compelled to deal with minor acts of criminality by which he hoped to consummate this greatest of crimes.

In obedience to this necessity he appointed Grant, hoping to use him and his influence with the Army, and failing in this, to get possession of the place and fill it with one of his own satellites. Foiled and disappointed in this scheme, he sought to use, first, General Sherman, then General George H. Thomas, then Hon. Thomas Ewing, senior, knowing that neither of these gentlemen would retain the office for any length of time. There were men in the country who would have accepted the office and continued in it and obeyed the Constitution and the laws. Has he named any such person; has he suggested any such person? His appointments and suggestions of appointments have been of two sorts—honorable men, who would not continue in the office, or dishonorable, worthless men, who were not fit to hold the office.

The name of General Cox, of Ohio, was mentioned in the public journals; it was mentioned, probably, to the President. Did it meet with favor? Did he send his name to the Senate? No.

General Cox, if he had accepted the office at all, would have done so with the expectation of holding it till March, 1869, and with the purpose of executing the duties of the trust according to the laws and the Constitution. These were purposes wholly inconsistent with the President's schemes of usurpation. But is it to be presumed or imagined that when the President issued his order for the removal of Mr. Stanton, and his letter of authority to Lorenzo Thomas, on the 21st of February, he had any purpose of appointing Mr. Ewing Secretary of War? Certainly not. On the afternoon of the 21st he informs his Cabinet that Stanton was removed and that Thomas had possession of the office. He then so believed. Thomas had deceived or misled him. On the 22d instant he had discovered that Stanton held on to the place, and that Emory could not be relied upon for force.

What was now his necessity? Simply a resort to his old policy. He saw that it was necessary to avoid impeachment if possible, and also to obtain the sanction of the Senate to a nomination which would work the removal of Mr. Stanton, and thus he would triumph over his enemies and obtain condonation for his crimes of the 21st of February. A well-laid scheme, but destined to fail and to furnish evidence of his own guilty purposes. With the office in the possession of Mr. Ewing he foresaw that for the prosecution of his own plans the place would always be vacant.

Thus has this artful man pursued the great purpose of his life. Consider the other circumstances. On the 1st of September last General Emory was appointed to the command of the department of Washington. He has exhibited such sterling honesty and vigorous patriotism in these recent troubles and during the war that he can bear a reference to his previous history. He was born in Maryland, and in the early part of the war the public mind of the North questioned his fidelity to the Union. His great services and untarnished record during the war are a complete defense against all suspicion, but is it too much to believe that Mr. Johnson entertained the hope that General Emory might be made an instrument of his ambition? Nobly has General Emory undeceived the President and gained additional renown in the country. In General Lorenzo Thomas the President was not deceived. His complicity in recent unlawful proceedings justifies the suspicions entertained by the country in 1861 and 1862 touching his loyalty. Thomas and the President are in accord. In case of the acquittal of the President, they are to issue an order to General Grant putting Thomas in possession of the reports of the Army to the War Department.

Is there not in all this evidence of the President's criminal intention? Is not his whole course marked by duplicity, deception, and fraud? "All things are construed against the wrong-doer" is the wise and just maxim of the law. Has he not trifled with and deceived the Senate? Has he not attempted to accomplish an unlawful purpose by disingenuous, tortuous, criminal means? His criminal intent is in his willful violation of the law, and his criminal intent is, moreover, abundantly proved by all the circumstances attending the violation of the law.

His final resort for safety was the Senate, praying for the confirmation of Mr. Ewing. On the 21st of February he hoped that Stanton would yield willingly or that Emory could be used to remove him. On the 22d he knew that Stanton was determined to remain, that Emory would not furnish assistance, that it was useless to appeal to Grant. He returns to his old plan of filling the War Office by the appointment of a man who would yield the place at any moment; and now he asks you to accept as his justification an act which was the last resort of a criminal attempting to escape the judgment due to his crimes. Upon this view of the law and the facts we demand a conviction of the respondent upon articles four, five, six, and seven exhibited against him by the House of Representatives.

The evidence introduced tending to show a conspiracy between Johnson and Thomas to get possession of the War Department tends also, connected with other facts, to show the purpose of the President to obtain possession of the Treasury Department. Bearing in mind his claim that he can suspend or remove from office, without the advice and consent of the Senate, any civil officer, and bearing in mind, also, that the present Secretary of the Treasury supports this claim, and every obstacle to the possession of the Treasury Department is removed. If the Secretary should decline to coöperate it would only be necessary for the President to remove him from office and place the Treasury Department in the hands of one of his own creatures.

Upon the appointment of Thomas as Secretary of War *ad interim* the President caused notice to be given thereof to the Secretary of the Treasury, accompanied with the direction, under the President's own hand, to that officer to govern himself accordingly. It is also proved that on the 22d day of December Mr. Johnson appointed Mr. Cooper, who had been his Private Secretary and intimate friend, Assistant Secretary of the Treasury.

The evidence fully sustains the statements made in the opening argument of Manager BUTLER in support of article nine. The facts in regard to General Emory's interview with the President were then well known to the Managers, and the argument and view presented in the opening contain all that is necessary to be said upon that article.

The learned counsel who opened the case for the President seems not to have comprehended the nature of the offense set forth in the tenth article. His remarks upon that article proceeded upon the idea that the House of Representatives arraign the President for slandering or libeling the Congress of the United States; no such offense is charged, nor is it claimed by the Managers that it would be possible for Mr. Johnson or any other person to libel or slander the Government. It is for no purpose of protection or indemnity or punishment that we arraign Mr. Johnson for words

spoken in Washington, Cleveland, and St. Louis. We do not arraign him for the words spoken; but the charge in substance is, that a man who could utter the words which as is proved were uttered by him is unfit for the office he holds. We claim that the common law of crimes, as understood and enforced by Parliament in cases of impeachment, is in substance this: That no person in office shall do any act contrary to the good morals of the office; and that, when any officer is guilty of an act contrary to the good morals of the office which he holds, that act is a misdemeanor for the purpose of impeachment and removal from office.

Judge Chase was impeached and escaped conviction by four votes only for words spoken from the bench of the circuit court sitting in Baltimore; words which are decorous and reputable when compared with the utterances of Mr. Johnson. Judge Humphreys was convicted and removed from office for words spoken treasonable in character, but not as much calculated to weaken and bring the Government of the United States into contempt as were the words uttered by Mr. Johnson in his speech of the 18th of August, 1866. Judge Humphreys was convicted by the unanimous vote of the Senators, nineteen of whom now sit on this trial. If a magistrate can ever be guilty, for words spoken, of an impeachable misdemeanor, there can be no doubt that Mr. Johnson is so guilty.

I ask you to consider in comparison, or in contrast, the nature of the language used by Chase, Humphreys, and Johnson, as set forth in the articles of impeachment preferred in the several cases.

The eighth article in the case of Chase is in these words:

"And whereas mutual respect and confidence between the Government of the United States and those of the individual States, and between the people and those governments, respectively, are highly conducive to that public harmony without which there can be no public happiness, yet the said Samuel Chase, disregarding the duties and dignity of his judicial character, did, at the circuit court for the district of Maryland, held at Baltimore in the month of May, 1803, pervert his official right and duty to address the grand jury then and there assembled on the matters coming within the province of the said jury, for the purpose of delivering to the said grand jury an intemperate and inflammatory political harangue, with intent to excite the fears and resentment of the said grand jury and of the good people of Maryland against their State government and constitution, a conduct highly censurable in any, but peculiarly indecent and unbecoming in a judge of the Supreme Court of the United States; and, moreover, that the said Samuel Chase, then and there, under pretence of exercising his judicial right to address the said grand jury as aforesaid, did, in a manner highly unwarrantable, endeavor to excite the odium of the said grand jury and of the good people of Maryland against the Government of the United States, by delivering opinions which, even if the judiciary were competent to their expression on a suitable occasion and in a proper manner, were at that time, and as delivered by him, highly indecent, extra-judicial, and tending to prostitute the high judicial character with which he was invested to the low purpose of an electioneering partisan."

The first article against Humphreys was as follows:

"That, regardless of his duties as a citizen of the United States, and unmindful of the duties of his said office, and in violation of the sacred obligation of his official oath, 'to administer justice without respect to persons,' and faithfully and impartially discharge all the duties incumbent upon him as judge of the district court of the United States for the several districts of the State of Tennessee, agreeable to the Constitution and laws of the United States,' the said West H. Humphreys, on the 29th day of December, A. D. 1860, in the city of Nashville, in said State, the said West H. Humphreys then being a citizen of the United States, and owing allegiance thereto, and then and there being judge of the district court of the United States for the several districts of said State, at a public meeting on the day and year last aforesaid, held in said city of Nashville, and in the hearing of divers persons then and there present, did endeavor by public speech to incite revolt and rebellion within said State against the Constitution and Government of the United States, and did then and there publicly declare that it was the right of the people of said State, by an ordinance of secession, to absolve themselves from all allegiance to the Government of the United States, the Constitution, and laws thereof."

The offense with which Humphreys is charged in this article was committed on the 29th day of December, 1860, before the fall of Sumter, and when only one State had passed an ordinance of secession. The declaration was merely a declaration in a public speech that the State of Tennessee had the right to secede from the Union.

The President, in his speech of the 18th of August, 1866, at Washington, says:

"We have witnessed in one department of the Government every effort, as it were, to prevent the restoration of peace, harmony, and union; we have seen, as it were, hanging upon the verge of the Government, as it were, a body calling or assuming to be the Congress of the United States, when it was but a Congress of a part of the States; we have seen Congress assuming to be for the Union when every step they took was to perpetuate dissolution and make dissolution permanent. We have seen every step that has been taken, instead of bringing about reconciliation and harmony, has been legislation that took the character of penalties, retaliation, and revenge. This has been the course; this has been the policy of one department of your Government."

These words have been repeated so frequently, and the public ear is so much accustomed to them, that they have apparently lost their influence upon the public mind. But it should be observed that these words, as has been proved by the experience of two years, were but the expression of a fixed purpose of the President. His design was to impair, to undermine, and, if possible, to destroy the influence of Congress in the country. Having accomplished this result, the way would then have been open to him for the prosecution of his criminal design to reconstruct the Government in the interest of the rebels, and, through his influence with them, to secure his own election to the Presidency in 1868. It must, however, be apparent that the words in the speech of Mr. Johnson are of graver import than the words which were spoken by Judge Chase to the grand jury at Baltimore, or those uttered by Judge Humphreys to the people of Tennessee. And yet the latter was convicted by a unanimous

vote of this Senate; and the former escaped conviction by four votes only. These words are of graver import, not merely in the circumstance that they assail a department of the Government, but in the circumstance that they were uttered by the President of the United States in the Executive Mansion, and in his capacity as President of the United States, when receiving the congratulations and support of a portion of the people of the country, tendered to him in his office as Chief Magistrate. Judge Chase, although a high officer of the Government, was without political influence and without patronage; his personal and official relations were limited, and his remarks were addressed to the grand jury of a judicial district of the country merely.

Judge Humphreys was comparatively unknown; and although his words were calculated to excite the citizens of Tennessee, and induce them to engage in unconstitutional undertakings, his influence was limited measurably to the people of that State.

Mr. Johnson addressed the whole country; and holding in his hands the immense patronage and influence belonging to the office of President, he was able to give practical effect to the declarations he then made. The nature of the respondent's offense is illustrated by the law in reference to the duty of officers and soldiers of the Army, although the law is not applicable to the President:

"Any officer or soldier who shall use contemptuous or disrespectful words against the President of the United States, against the Vice President thereof, against the Congress of the United States, shall be cashiered or otherwise punished, as a court-martial shall direct."—Statutes-at-Large, vol. 2, p. 360, April 10, 1806.

Moreover, in the case of Judge Chase, as is stated by Mr. Dane in his "Abridgment," (vol. 7, chap. 222:)

"On the whole evidence it remained in doubt what words he did utter. The proof of seditious intent rested solely on the words themselves; and as the words were not clearly proved the intent was in doubt."

In the case of Mr. Johnson there is no doubt about the words uttered; they have been fully and explicitly proved. Indeed, they are not denied by the respondent. The unlawful intent with which he uttered the words not only appears from the character of the language employed, but it is proved by the history of his Administration. In his message of the 22d of June, 1866, relating to the constitutional amendment, in his annual message of December, 1866, and in numerous other declarations, he has questioned and substantially denied the legality of the Congress of the United States.

In the trial of Judge Chase it was admitted by the respondent "that for a judge to utter seditious sentiments with intent to excite sedition would be an impeachable offense." (Dane's Abridgment, vol. 7, chap. 222.) And this not under the act known as the "sedition act;" for that had been previously repealed; but upon the general principle that an officer whose duty it is to administer the law has no right to use language calculated to stir up resistance to the law. If this be true of a judge, with stronger reason it is true of the President of the United States, that he should set an example of respect for all the departments of the Government and of reverence for and obedience to the laws of the land.

The speeches made by the President at Cleveland and St. Louis, which have been proved and are found in the record of the case, contain numerous passages similar in character to that extracted from his speech of the 18th of August, 1866, and all calculated and designed to impair the just authority of Congress. While these declarations have not been made the basis of substantive charges in the articles of impeachment, they furnish evidence of the unlawful intent of the President in his utterance of the 18th of August, and also of the fact that that utterance was not due to any temporary excitement or transient purpose which passed away with the occasion which had called it forth. It was a declaration made in accordance with a fixed design, which had obtained such entire control of his nature that whenever he addressed public assemblies he gave expression to it. The evidence which has been submitted by the respondent bearing upon the tenth article indicates a purpose, in argument, to excuse the President upon the ground that the remarks of the people stimulated, irritated, and excited him to such an extent that he was not wholly responsible for what he said. If this were true, it would exhibit great weakness of character; but as a matter of fact it is not true. The taunts and gibes of the people served only to draw from him those declarations which were in accord with the purposes of his life. This is shown by the fact that all his political declarations made at Cleveland and at St. Louis, though made under excitement, are in entire harmony with the declarations made by him in the East Room of the Executive Mansion, on the 18th of August, 1866, when he was free from any disturbing influence, and expressed himself with all the reserve of which his nature is capable.

The blasphemous utterances at St. Louis cannot be aggravated by me, nor can they be extenuated by anything which counsel for the respondent can offer. They exhibit the character of the speaker.

Upon these facts thus proved and the views presented we demand the conviction of the respondent of the misdemeanors charged in the tenth article.

Article eleven sets forth that the object of the President in most of the offenses alleged in the preceding articles was to prevent the execution of the act passed March 2, 1867, entitled, "An act for the more efficient government of the rebel States." It is well known, officially and publicly, that on the 29th of May, 1865, Mr. Johnson issued a proclamation for the reorganization of the government of North Carolina, and that that proclamation was followed by other proclamations, issued during the next four months, for the government of the several States which had been engaged in the rebellion. Upon the death of Mr. Lincoln Mr. Johnson entered upon the office of President in a manner which indicated that, in his judgment, he had been long destined to fill the place, and that the powers of the office were to be exercised by him without regard to the other departments of the Government. In his proclamation of the 29th of May, and in all the proclamations relating to the same subject, he had assumed that in his office as President he was the "United States," for the purpose of deciding whether, under the Constitution, the government of a State was republican in form or not; although by a decision of the Supreme Court it is declared that this power is specially vested in the two Houses of Congress. In these proclamations he assumed, without authority of law, to appoint, and he did appoint, Governors of the several States thus organized. In fine, between the 29th of May, 1865, and the assembling of Congress in December of that year, he exercised sovereign power over the territory and people of the eleven States that had been engaged in the rebellion.

On the assembling of Congress in the month of December he informed the Senate and House of Representatives that the Union was restored, and that nothing remained for the two Houses but severally to accept as Senators and Representatives such loyal men as had been elected by the Legislatures and people of the several States. Congress refused to ratify or to recognize those proceedings upon the part of the President as legal or proper proceedings, and from that time forward he has been engaged in various projects for the purpose of preventing the reconstruction of the Union on any other plan than that which he had inaugurated. In the execution of this design he attempted to deprive Congress of the confidence of the people of the country; hence it was that, among other things, on the 18th day of August, 1866, at the city of Washington, as set forth in the tenth and eleventh articles, he did in a public speech declare and affirm in substance that the Thirty-Ninth Congress of the United States was not a Congress authorized by the Constitution to exercise legislative power under the same; but, on the contrary, was a Congress of only a part of the States.

In the further execution of his purpose to prevent the reconstruction of the Union upon any plan except that which he had inaugurated, he attempted to prevent the ratification by the several States of the amendment to the Constitution known as article fourteen. By the Constitution the President has no power to participate in amendments or in propositions for amendments thereto; yet, availing himself of the circumstance of the passage of a resolution by the House of Representatives on the 13th day of June, 1866, requesting the President to submit to the Legislatures of the several States the said additional article to the Constitution of the United States, he sent to the Senate and House of Representatives a message in writing, in which he says:

"Even in ordinary times any question of amending the Constitution must be justly regarded as of paramount importance. This importance is at the present time enhanced by the fact that the joint resolution was not submitted by the two Houses for the approval of the President, and that of the thirty-six States which constitute the Union eleven are excluded from representation in either House of Congress, although, with the single exception of Texas, they have been entirely restored to all their functions as States, in conformity with the organic law of the land, and have appeared at the national Capitol by Senators and Representatives who have applied for and have been refused admission to the vacant seats. Nor have the sovereign people of the nation been afforded an opportunity of expressing their views upon the important questions which the amendment involves. Grave doubts, therefore, may naturally and justly arise as to whether the action of Congress is in harmony with the sentiments of the people, and whether State Legislatures, elected without reference to such an issue, should be called upon by Congress to decide respecting the ratification of the proposed amendment."

He also says:

"A proper appreciation of the letter and spirit of the Constitution, as well as of the interests of national order, harmony, and union, and a due deference for an enlightened public judgment, may at this time well suggest a doubt whether any amendment to the Constitution ought to be proposed by Congress and pressed upon the Legislatures of the several States for final decision until after the admission of such loyal Senators and Representatives of the now unrepresented States as have been, or as may hereafter be, chosen in conformity with the Constitution and laws of the United States."

This message was an extra-official proceeding, inasmuch as his agency in the work of amending the Constitution is not required; and it was also a very clear indication of an opinion on his part that, inasmuch as the eleven States were not represented, the Congress of the United States had no power to act in the matter of amending the Constitution.

The proposed amendment to the Constitution contained provisions which were to be made the basis of reconstruction. The laws subsequently passed by Congress recognize the amendment as essential to the welfare and safety of the Union. It is alleged in the eleventh article that one of the purposes of the President in the various unlawful acts charged in the several articles of impeachment, and proved against him, was to prevent the execution of the act entitled "An act for the more efficient government of the rebel States," passed March 2, 1867. In the nature of the case it has not been easy to obtain testimony upon this point, nor upon any other point touching the misconduct and crimes of the President. His declarations and his usurpations of power have rendered a large portion of the officeholders of the country for the time being subservient to his purposes; they have been ready to conceal and reluctant to communicate any evidence calculated to implicate the President. His communications with the South have been generally, and it may be said almost exclusively, with the men who had participated in the rebellion, and who are now hoping for final success through his aid. They have looked to him as their leader, by whose efforts and agency in the office of President of the United States they were either to accomplish the objects for which the war was undertaken, or at least to secure a restoration to the Union under such circumstances that, as a section of the country and an interest in the country, they should possess and exercise that power which the slaveholders of the South possessed and exercised previous to the rebellion. These men have been bound to him by the strong bonds of hope, fear, and ambition. The corruptions of the public service have enriched multitudes of his adherents and quickened and strengthened the passion of avarice in multitudes more. These classes of men, possessing wealth and influence in many cases, have exerted their power to close up every avenue of information. Hence the efforts of the committees of the House of Representatives and the efforts of the Managers to ascertain the truth and to procure testimony which they were satisfied was in existence have been defeated often by the devices and machinations of those who in the North and in the South are supposed to be allied to the President. There can, however, be no doubt that the President in every way open to him used his personal and official influence to defeat the ratification of the constitutional amendment. Evidence of such disposition and of the fact also is found in the telegraphic correspondence of January, 1867, between Mr. Johnson and Lewis E. Parsons, who had been previously appointed Governor of Alabama by the President. It is as follows:

MONTGOMERY, ALABAMA, *January* 17, 1867.

Legislature in session. Efforts making to reconsider vote on constitutional amendment. Report from Washington says it is probable an enabling act will pass. We do not know what to believe. I find nothing here. LEWIS E. PARSONS,
Exchange Hotel.

His Excellency ANDREW JOHNSON, *President.*

UNITED STATES MILITARY TELEGRAPH,
EXECUTIVE OFFICE,
WASHINGTON, D. C., *January* 17, 1867.

What possible good can be obtained by reconsidering the constitutional amendment? I know of none in the present posture of affairs; and I do not believe the people of the whole country will sustain any set of individuals in attempts to change the whole character of our Government by enabling acts or otherwise. I believe, on the contrary, that they will eventually uphold all who have patriotism and courage to stand by the Constitution and who place their confidence in the people. There should be no faltering on the part of those who are honest in their determination to sustain the several coördinate departments of the Government in accordance with its original design. ANDREW JOHNSON.

Hon. LEWIS E. PARSONS, *Montgomery, Alabama.*

This correspondence shows his fixed purpose to defeat the congressional plan of reconstruction. Pursuing the subject further it is easy to discover and comprehend his entire scheme of criminal ambition. It was no less than this: to obtain command of the War Department and of the Army, and by their combined power to control the elections of 1868 in the ten States not yet restored to the Union. The congressional plan of reconstruction contained as an essential condition the extension of the elective franchise to all loyal male citizens, and the exclusion from the franchise of a portion of those who had been most active in originating and carrying on the rebellion. The purpose of Mr. Johnson was to limit the elective franchise to white male citizens, and to permit the exercise of it by all such persons without regard to their disloyalty. If he could secure the control of the War Department and of the Army it would be entirely practicable, and not only practicable but easy, for him in the coming elections quietly to inaugurate a policy throughout the ten States by which the former rebels, strengthened by the support of the Executive here, and by the military forces distributed over the South, would exclude from the polls every colored man and permit the exercise of the elective franchise by every white rebel. By these means he would be able to control the entire vote of the ten rebel States; by the same means, or indeed by the force of the facts, he would be able to secure the election of delegates to the Democratic national convention favorable to his own nomination to the Presidency. The vote of these ten States in the convention, considered in connection with the fact that he and his friends could assure delegates from other sections of the country that, if he were nominated, he could control beyond peradventure the electoral vote of these ten States, would have secured his nomination. This he confidently anticipated. Nor, indeed, can there be much doubt that this scheme would have been successful; but it was apparent that there was no possibility of his obtaining the control of the War Department and of the Army unless he could disregard and break down the act regulating the tenure of certain civil offices, passed March 2, 1867. If, however, he could annul or disregard or set aside the provisions of that act, then the way was open for the successful consummation of his plan. With thousands and tens of thousands of office holders, scattered all over the country, depending upon him for their offices and for the emoluments of their offices, he would be able to exert a large influence, if not absolutely to control the nominations of the Democratic party in every State of the Union. With the War Department in his hands, and the tenure-of-office act broken down, he would be able to remove General Grant, General Sherman, General Sheridan, or any other officer, high or low, who, in his opinion, or upon the facts, might be an obstacle in his way. With the Army thus corrupted and humiliated, its trusted leaders either driven from the service or sent into exile in distant parts of the country, he would be able to wield the power of that vast organization for his own personal advantage.

Under these circumstances it was not probable merely, but it was as certain as anything in the future could be, that he would secure, first, the nomination of the Democratic party in the national nominating convention; and secondly, that he would secure the electoral votes of these ten States. This being done, he had only to obtain enough votes from the States now represented in Congress to make a majority of electoral votes, and he would defy the House and Senate should they attempt to reject the votes of the ten States, and this whether those States had been previously restored to the Union or not. In a contest with the two Houses he and his friends and supporters, including the War Department, the Treasury Department, and the Army and Navy, would insist that he had been duly elected President, and by the support of the War Department, the Treasury Department, the Army, and the Navy, he would have been inaugurated on the 4th of March next President of the United States for four years.

That the President was and is hostile to Mr. Stanton, and that he desired his removal from office, there is no doubt; but he has not assumed the responsibility which now rests upon him, he has not incurred the hazard of his present position, for the mere purpose of gratifying his personal feelings toward Mr. Stanton. He disregarded the tenure-of-office act; he first suspended and then removed Mr. Stanton from the office of Secretary for the Department of War; he defied the judgment of and the advice and authority of the Senate; he incurred the risk of impeachment by the House of Representatives, and trial and conviction by this tribunal, under the influence of an ambition unlimited and unscrupulous, which dares anything and everything necessary to its gratification. For the purpose of defeating the congressional plan of reconstruction he has advised and encouraged the people of the South in the idea that he would restore them to their former privileges and power; that he would establish a white man's Government; that he would exclude the negroes from all participation in political affairs; and, finally, that he would accomplish in their behalf what they had sought by rebellion, but by rebellion had failed to secure. Hence it is through his agency and by his influence the South has been given up to disorder, rapine, and bloodshed; hence it is that since the surrender of Lee and Johnston thousands of loyal men, black and white, have been murdered in cold blood or subjected to cruelties and tortures such as in modern times have been perpetrated only by savage nations and in remote parts of the world; hence it is that twelve million people are without law, without order, unprotected in their industry or their rights; hence it is that ten States are without government and unrepresented in Congress; hence it is that the people of the North are even now uncertain whether the rebellion, vanquished in the field, is not finally to be victorious in the councils and in the Cabinet of the country; hence it is that the loyal people of the entire Union look upon Andrew Johnson as their worst enemy; hence it is that those who participated in the rebellion, and still hope that its power may once more be established in the country, look upon Andrew Johnson as their best friend, and as the last and chief supporter of the views which they entertain.

The House of Representatives has brought this respondent to your bar for trial, for conviction, and for judgment; but the House of Representatives, as a branch of the legislative department of the Government, has no special interest in these proceedings. It entered upon them with great reluctance, after laborious and continued investigation, and only upon a conviction that the interests of the country were in peril, and that there was no way of relief except through the exercise of the highest constitutional power vested in that body. We do not appeal to this tribunal because any special right of the House of Representatives has been infringed, or because the just powers of or the existence of the House are in danger, except as that body must always participate in the good or ill fortune of the country. They have brought this respondent to your bar, and here demand his conviction in the belief, as the result of much investigation, of much deliberation, that the interests of this country are no longer safe in his hands.

But the House of Representatives, representing the people of the country, may very properly appeal to this tribunal, constituted, as it is, exclusively of Senators representing the different States of this Union, to maintain the constitutional powers of the Senate. To be sure, nothing can injuriously affect the powers and the rights of the Senate which does not affect injuriously the rights of the House of Representatives, and of the people of the whole country; but it may be said with great truth that this contest is first for the preservation of the constitutional powers of this branch of the Government. By your votes and action, in concurrence with the House of Representatives, the bill "regulating the tenure of certain civil offices" was passed and became a law, and this notwithstanding the objections of the President thereto and his argument against its passage. On a subsequent occasion, when you considered the suspension of Mr. Stanton and the message of the President, in which, by argument and by statements, he assailed the law in question, you asserted its validity and its constitutionality by refusing to concur in the suspension of Mr. Stanton. On a more recent occasion, when he attempted to remove Mr. Stanton from office, you, by solemn resolution, declared that his action therein was contrary to the laws and to the Constitution of the country.

From the beginning of the Government this body has participated under the Constitution and by virtue of the Constitution in all matters pertaining to appointments to office; and, by the universal practice of the country, as well before the passage of the tenure-of-office act as since, no removal of any officer whose appointment was by and with the advice and consent of the Senate, has been made during a session of the Senate, with your knowledge and sanction, except by the nomination of a successor, whose nomination was confirmed by and with the advice and consent of the Senate. Mr. Johnson, in presence of this uniform constitutional practice of three quarters of a century and against the express provisions of the tenure-of-office act, made in this particular in entire harmony with that practice, asserts now, absolutely, the unqualified power to remove every officer in the country without the advice or consent of the Senate.

Never in the history of any free government has there been so base, so gross, so unjustifiable an attempt upon the part of an executive, whether emperor, king, or President, to destroy the just authority of another department of the Government.

The House of Representatives has not been indifferent to this assault; it has not been unmindful of the danger to which you have been exposed; it has seen, what you must admit, that without its agency and support you were powerless to resist these aggressions, or to thwart, in any degree, the purposes of this usurper. In the exercise of their constitutional power of impeachment they have brought him to your bar; they have laid before you the evidence showing conclusively the nature, the extent, and the depth of his guilt. You hold this great power in trust, not for yourselves merely, but for all your successors in these high places, and for all the people of this country. You cannot fail to discharge your duty; that duty is clear. On the one hand it is your duty to protect, to preserve, and to defend your own constitutional rights, but it is equally your duty to preserve the laws and institutions of the country. It is your duty to protect and defend the Constitution of the United States, and the rights of the people under it; it is your duty to preserve and to transmit unimpaired to your successors in these places all the constitutional rights and privileges guarantied to this body by the form of government under which we live. On the other hand, it is your duty to try and convict the accused, if guilty, and to pronounce judgment upon the respondent, that all his successors, and all men who aspire to the office of President in time to come, may understand that the House of Representatives and the Senate will demand the strictest observance of the Constitution; that they will hold every man in the presidential office responsible for a rigid performance of his public duties.

Nothing, literally nothing, can be said in defense of this respondent. Upon his own admissions he is guilty, in substance, of the gravest charges contained in the articles of impeachment exhibited against him by the House of Representatives. In his personal conduct and character he presents no quality or attribute which enlists the sympathy or the regard of men. The exhibition which he made in this Chamber on the 4th of March, 1865, by which the nation was humiliated and republican institutions disgraced, in the presence of the representatives of the civilized nations of the earth, is a truthful exhibition of his character. His violent, denunciatory, blasphemous declarations made to the people on various occasions, and proved by the testimony submitted to the Senate, illustrate other qualities of his nature. His cold indifference to the desolation, disorder, and crimes in the ten States of the South exhibit yet other and darker features.

Can any one entertain the opinion that Mr. Johnson is not guilty of such crimes as justify his removal from office and his disqualification to hold any office of trust or profit under the Government of the United States? William Blount, Senator of the United States, was impeached by the House of Representatives and declared guilty of a high misdemeanor, and though not tried by the Senate the Senate did, nevertheless, expel him from his seat by a vote of 25 to 1, and, in the resolution of expulsion, declared that he had been guilty of a high misdemeanor. The crime of William Blount was that he wrote a letter and participated in conversations, from which it appeared probable that he was engaged in an immature scheme to alienate the Indians of the Southwest from the President and the Congress of the United States; and also, incidentally, to disturb the friendly relations between this Government and the Governments of Spain and Great Britain. This, at most, was but an arrangement, never consummated into any overt act, by which he contemplated, under possible circumstances which never occurred, that he would violate the neutrality laws of the United States.

Andrew Johnson is guilty, upon the proof in part and upon his own admissions, of having intentionally violated a public law, of usurping and exercising powers not exercised nor even asserted by any of his predecessors in office.

Judge Pickering, of the district court of New Hampshire, was impeached by the House of Representatives, convicted by the Senate, and removed from office, for the crime of having appeared upon the bench in a state of intoxication. I need not draw any parallel between Judge Pickering and this respondent.

Judge Prescott, of Massachusetts, was impeached and removed from office for receiving illegal fees in his office to the amount of $10 70 only. Judge Prescott belonged to one of the oldest and most eminent families of the State, and he was himself a distinguished lawyer. But such was the respect of the Senate of that state for the law, and such the public opinion

that it was the duty of magistrates to obey the law, that they did not hesitate, to convict him and remove him from office.

The Earl of Macclesfield was impeached and convicted for the misuse of his official powers in regard to trust funds, an offense in itself of a grave character, but a trivial crime compared with the open, wanton, and defiant violation of law by a Chief Magistrate whose highest duty is the execution of the laws.

If the charges preferred against Warren Hastings had been fully sustained by the testimony, he would be regarded in history as an unimportant criminal when compared with the respondent. Warren Hastings, as governor general of Bengal, extended the territory of the British empire, and brought millions of the natives of India under British rule. If he exercised power in India for which there was no authority in British laws or British customs—if in the exercise of that power he acquired wealth for himself or permitted others to accumulate fortunes by outrages and wrongs perpetrated upon that distant people, he still acted in his public policy in the interest of the British empire and in harmony with the ideas and purposes of the British people.

Andrew Johnson has disregarded and violated the laws and Constitution of his own country. Under his administration the Government has not been strengthened, but weakened. Its reputation and influence at home and abroad have been injured and diminished. He has not outraged a distant people bound to us by no ties, but those which result from conquest and the exercise of arbitrary power on our part; but through his violation of the laws and the influence of his evil example upon the men of the South, in whose hearts the purposes and the passions of the war yet linger, he has brought disorder, confusion, and bloodshed to the homes of twelve millions of people, many of whom are of our own blood and all of whom are our countrymen. Ten States of this Union are without law, without security, without safety; public order everywhere violated, public justice nowhere respected; and all in consequence of the evil purposes and machinations of the President. Forty millions of people have been rendered anxious and uncertain as to the preservation of public peace and the perpetuity of the institutions of freedom in this country.

There are no limits to the consequences of this man's evil example. A member of his Cabinet in your presence avows, proclaims, indeed, that he suspended from office indefinitely a faithful public officer who was appointed by your advice and consent; an act which he does not attempt to justify by any law or usage, except what he is pleased to call the law of necessity. Is it strange that in the presence of these examples the ignorant, the vicious, and the criminal are everywhere swift to violate the laws? Is it strange that the loyal people of the South, most of them poor, dependent, not yet confident of their newly-acquired rights, exercising their just privileges in fear and trembling, should thus be made the victims of the worst passions of men who have freed themselves from all the restraints of civil government? Under the influence of these examples good men in the South have everything to fear, and bad men have everything to hope.

Caius Verres is the great political criminal of history. For two years he was prætor and the scourge of Sicily. The area of that country does not much exceed ten thousand square miles, and in modern times it has had a population of about two million souls. The respondent at your bar has been the scourge of a country many times the area of Sicily and containing a population six times as great. Verres enriched himself and his friends; he seized the public paintings and statues and carried them to Rome. But at the end of his brief rule of two years he left Sicily as he had found it; in comparative peace, and in the possession of its industries and its laws. This respondent has not ravaged States nor enriched himself by the plunder of their treasures; but he has inaugurated and adhered to a policy which has deprived the people of the blessings of peace, of the protection of law, of the just rewards of honest industry. A vast and important portion of the Republic, a portion whose prosperity is essential to the prosperity of the country at large, is prostrate and helpless under the evils which his Administration has brought upon it. When Verres was arraigned before his judges at Rome, and the exposure of his crimes began, his counsel abandoned his cause and the criminal fled from the city. Yet Verres had friends in Sicily, and they erected a gilded statue to his name in the streets of Syracuse. This respondent will look in vain, even in the South, for any testimonials to his virtues or to his public conduct. All classes are oppressed by the private and public calamities which he has brought upon them. They appeal to you for relief. The nation waits in anxiety for the conclusion of these proceedings. Forty millions of people, whose interest in public affairs is in the wise and just administration of the laws, look to this tribunal as a sure defense against the encroachments of a criminally-minded Chief Magistrate.

Will any one say that the heaviest judgment which you can render is any adequate punishment for these crimes? Your office is not punishment, but to secure the safety of the Republic. But human tribunals are inadequate to punish those criminals who, as rulers or magistrates, by their example, conduct, policy, and crimes, become the scourge of communities and nations. No picture, no power of the imagination can illustrate or conceive the suffering of the poor but loyal people of the South. A patriotic, virtuous, law-abiding Chief Magistrate would have healed the wounds of war, soothed private and public sorrows, protected the weak, encouraged the strong, and lifted from the southern people the burdens which now are greater than they can bear.

Travelers and astronomers inform us that in the southern heavens, near the Southern Cross, there is a vast space which the uneducated call the hole in the sky, where the eye of man with the aid of the powers of the telescope has been unable to discover nebulæ, or asteroid, or comet, or planet, or star, or sun. In that dreary, cold, dark region of space, which is only known to be less than infinite by the evidences of creation elsewhere, the Great Author of celestial mechanism has left the chaos which was in the beginning. If this earth were capable of the sentiments and emotions of justice and virtue, which in human mortal beings are the evidences and the pledge of our divine origin and immortal destiny, it would heave and throe, with the energy of the elemental forces of nature, and project this enemy of two races of men into that vast region, there forever to exist in a solitude eternal as life, or as the absence of life, emblematical of, if not really, that "outer darkness" of which the Saviour of man spoke in warning to those who are the enemies of themselves, of their race, and of their God. But it is yours to relieve, not to punish. This done and our country is again advanced in the intelligent opinion of mankind. In other Governments an unfaithful ruler can be removed only by revolution, violence, or force. The proceeding here is judicial, and according to the forms of law. Your judgment will be enforced without the aid of a policeman or a soldier. What other evidence will be needed of the value of republican institutions? What other test of the strength and vigor of our Government? What other assurance that the virtue of the people is equal to any emergency of national life?

The contest which the House of Representatives carries on at your bar is a contest in defense of the constitutional rights of the Congress of the United States, representing the people of the United States against the arbitrary, unjust, illegal claims of the Executive.

This is the old contest of Europe revived in America. England, France, and Spain have each been the theater of this strife. In France and Spain the executive triumphed. In England the people were victorious. The people of France gradually but slowly regain their rights. But even yet there is no freedom of the press in France; there is no freedom of the legislative will; the emperor is supreme.

Spain is wholly unregenerated. England alone has a free Parliament and a government of laws emanating from the enfranchised people. These laws are everywhere executed, and a sovereign who should willfully interpose any obstacle would be dethroned without delay. In England the law is more mighty than the king. In America a President claims to be mightier than the law.

This result in England was reached by slow movements, and after a struggle which lasted through many centuries. John Hampden was not the first nor the last of the patriots who resisted executive usurpation, but nothing could have been more inapplicable to the present circumstances than the introduction of his name as an apology for the usurpations of Andrew Johnson.

"No man will question John Hampden's patriotism or the propriety of his acts when he brought the question whether ship-money was within the constitution of England before the courts;" but no man will admit that there is any parallel between Andrew Johnson and John Hampden. Andrew Johnson takes the place of Charles I, and seeks to substitute his own will for the laws of the land. In 1636 John Hampden resisted the demands of an usurping and unprincipled king, as does Edwin M. Stanton to-day resist the claims and demands of an unprincipled and usurping President.

The people of England have successfully resisted executive encroachments upon their rights. Let not their example be lost upon us. We suppressed the rebellion in arms, and we are now to expel it from the executive councils. This done, republican institutions need no further illustration or defense. All things then relating to the national welfare and life are made as secure as can be any future events. The freedom, prosperity, and power of America are established. The friends of constitutional liberty throughout Europe will hail with joy the assured greatness and glory of the new Republic. Our internal difficulties will rapidly disappear. Peace and prosperity will return to every portion of the country. In a few weeks or months we shall celebrate a restored Union upon the basis of the equal rights of the States, in each of which equality of the people will be recognized and established. This respondent is not to be convicted that these things may come, but justice being done, these things are to come.

At your bar the House of Representatives demand justice—justice for the people, justice to the accused. Justice is of God, and it cannot perish. By and through justice comes obedience to the law by all magistrates and people. By and through justice comes the liberty of the law, which is freedom without license.

Senators, as far as I am concerned, the case is now in your hands, and it is soon to be closed by my associate. The House of Representatives have presented this criminal at your bar with equal confidence in his guilt and in your disposition to administer exact justice between him and the people of the United States.

His conviction is the triumph of law, of order, of justice. I do not contemplate his acquittal—it is impossible. Therefore I do not look beyond. But, Senators, the people of America will never permit an usurping Executive to break down the securities for liberty provided by the Constitution. The cause of the Republic is in your hands. Your verdict of *guilty* is *peace* to our beloved country.

Mr. JOHNSON. Mr. Chief Justice, I understand from the counsel for the President who is next to address the Senate that he would be very much obliged to the Senate if they would take their usual recess now, he being anxious to make a continuing argument. I move, therefore, that the court take a recess for fifteen minutes.

The motion was agreed to; and at the expiration of the recess the Chief Justice resumed the chair.

Hon. THOMAS A. R. NELSON, counsel for the respondent, addressed the Senate, as follows:

Mr. CHIEF JUSTICE and SENATORS: I have been engaged in the practice of my profession as a lawyer for the last thirty years. I have been concerned in every variety of cause which can be tried under the laws of the State in which I reside. I have, in the course of my somewhat lengthy professional life, argued cases involving life, liberty, property, and character. I have prosecuted and defended every species of criminal cause, from murder in the first degree down to a simple assault. But in rising to address you to-day I feel that all the causes in which I ever was concerned sink into comparative insignificance when compared with this; and a painful sense of the magnitude of the case in which I am now engaged, and of my inability to meet and to defend it as it should be defended, oppresses me as I rise to address you; and I would humbly invoke the great Disposer of events to give me a mind to conceive, a heart to feel, and a tongue to express those words which should be properly and fitly expressed on this great occasion. I would humbly invoke that assistance which comes from on high; for when I look at the results which may follow from this trial; when I endeavor to contemplate in imagination how it is to affect our country and the world, I start back, feeling that I am utterly incapable of comprehending its results, and that I cannot look into the future and foretell them.

I feel, Senators, that it will be necessary upon this occasion for me to notice many things which, as I suppose, have but little bearing upon the specific articles of impeachment which have been presented. In doing so, to borrow the language of Mr. Wirt upon the trial of Judge Peck, "If we pursue the opening arguments of the honorable Managers more closely than may seem necessary to some of the court, it will be remembered that it would be presumptuous in us to slight any topic which the learned and honorable Managers may have deemed it important to press on the consideration of the court."

It has been charged that the President was "trifling" with the Senate. Scarcely had we entered upon this trial before charges were made against him of seeking, and improperly seeking, to gain time; to effect an unworthy and improper procrastination. I shall dwell but a moment on that. We supposed that there was no impropriety in our asking at the hands of the Senate a reasonable indulgence to prepare for our defense, when the subject of impeachment had been before the House of Representatives in some form or other for more than a twelvemonth, and when the worthy and able Managers who have been selected to conduct it in this Senate were armed at all points and ready to contest the cause on the one hand, and we, upon the other, were suddenly summoned from our professional pursuits; we, who are not politicians, but lawyers engaged in the practice of our profession, were summoned here to measure arms with gentlemen who are skilled in political gladiation and are well posted upon all the subjects that may be involved in this investigation.

But it is not merely the complaint as to time and as to trifling with the Senate that it will become my duty to notice. A great many things have been said, Senators, and among the rest an effort has been made to draw "a picture of the President's mind and heart;" he has been stigmatized as a "usurper," as a "traitor to his party," as "disgracing the position held by some of the most illustrious in the land," as "a dangerous person, a criminal, but not an ordinary one," as "encouraging murders, assassinations, and robberies all over the southern States;" and finally, by way of proving that there is one step between the sublime and the ridiculous, he has been charged with being "a common scold" and a "ribald, scurrilous blasphemer, bandying epithets and taunts with a jeering mob."

Such are some of the many accusations which have been made here from time to time in the progress of this protracted investigation. Nothing or next to nothing has been said in vindication of the President against these charges. It will be my duty, Senators, to pay some attention to them to-day. We have borne it long enough, and I propose before I enter upon the investigation of the articles of impeachment to pay some attention to these accusations which have been heaped upon us almost every day from the commencement of the trial and which have hitherto passed unanswered and unnoticed on the side of the President of the United States.

If it be true, as alleged, that the President is guilty of all these things, or if he has been guilty of one tithe of the offenses which have been imputed to him in the opening argument, and which have been iterated and reiterated in the argument of to-day, then I am willing to confess that he is—

"A monster of such frightful mien
As to be hated needs but to be seen."

I am willing to admit that if he is guilty of any of the charges which have been made against him he is not only worthy of the censure of this Senate, but a whip should be put in every honest hand to lash him around the world as a man unworthy of the notice of gentlemen and unfit for the association of any of his race; he should be pointed at everywhere and shown as a monster; he should be banished from society; his very name should become a word to frighten children with throughout the land from one end of it to the other, so that when one should meet him his sight would cause—

"Each particular hair to stand on end
Like quills upon the fretful porcupine."

If he be a man such as is represented on the other side, then, Senators, we agree that neither I, nor any of those who are associated with me, can defend him.

But who is Andrew Johnson? Who is the man that you have upon trial now, and in regard to whom the gaze not of little Delaware, but of the whole Union and of the civilized world is directed at the present moment? Who is Andrew Johnson? That is a question which a few years ago many of those whom I now address could have answered, and could have answered with pleasure and delight and joy. Who is Andrew Johnson? Go to the town of Greenville but a few short years ago, a little village situate in the mountains of East Tennessee, and you will see a poor boy entering that village a stranger, without friends, without acquaintances, following an humble mechanical pursuit, scarcely able to read, unable to write, but yet industrious in his calling, honest and faithful in his dealings, and having a mind such as the God of heaven had implanted within him, and which it was intended and designed should be called into exercise and displayed before the American people. He goes there, and I may say, almost in the language of Mr. Clay in reference to the State of Kentucky, he enters the State of Tennessee an orphan, poor, penniless, without the favor of the great; "but scarce had he set his foot upon her generous soil when he was seized and embraced with parental fondness, caressed as though he had been a favorite child, and patronized with liberal and unbounded munificence." In the first instance he applies to the people of his county to honor him by giving him a seat in the lower branch of the State Legislature. That wish is granted. Next he is sent to the State Senate; then to the House of Representatives of the American Congress; then, by the voice of the people in two hard fought contests, he was elected Governor of the State; then he was sent to the Senate of the United States, and his whole career thus far was a career in which he had been honored and respected by the people, and it has only been within some two or three years that charges have been preferred against him such as those which are presented now.

Never since the days of Warren Hastings, ay, never since the days of Sir Walter Raleigh, has any man been stigmatized with more severe reprobation than the President of the United States. All the powers of invective which the able and ingenious Managers can command have been brought into requisition to fire your hearts and to prejudice your minds against him. A perfect storm has been raised around him. All the elements have been agitated.

"Far along,
From peak to peak the rattling crags among
Leaps the live thunder! Not from one lone cloud,
But every mountain now hath found a tongue,
And Jura answers through her misty shroud,
Back to the joyous Alps, who call to her aloud!"

The storm is playing around him; the pitiless rain is beating upon him; the lightnings are flashing around him; but I have the pleasure to state to you, Senators, to-day, and I hope that my voice will reach the whole country, that in the midst of it all he still stands firm, serene, unbent, unbroken, unsubdued, unawed, unterrified, hurling no words of threat or menace at the Senate of the United States, threatening no civil war to deluge his country with blood; but feeling a proud consciousness of his own integrity, appealing to heaven to witness the purity of his motives in his public administration, and calling upon you, Senators, in the name of the living God, to whom you have made an appeal, that you will do equal and impartial justice in this case according to the Constitution and the laws, to pronounce him innocent of the offenses which have been charged against him.

Who is Andrew Johnson? Are there not Senators here who are well acquainted with him? Are there not men here whose minds go back to the stirring times of 1860 and 1861, when treason was rife in this Capitol, when men's faces turned pale, when dispatch after dispatch was sent from this Chamber and from the House of Representatives to the people of the southern States to "fire the southern heart," to prepare the southern mind for that revolution which agitated our country and which cost the lives and the treasure of the nation to such an alarming extent? Where was Andrew Johnson then? Standing here, almost within ten feet of the place in which I stand now, solitary and alone, in this magnificent Chamber, when "bloody treason flourished over us," his voice was heard arousing the nation. Some of you heard it. I only heard its echoes as they rolled along from one end of the land to the other, to excite and arouse the patriotism of our common country. Yes, he stood "solitary and alone," the only member from the South who was disposed to battle against treason then; and he now is called a traitor himself! He who has periled his life in a thousand forms to put down treason; he who has been reckless of danger; he who has periled his life, his fortune, and his sacred honor to save this land from destruction and ruin—he now is stigmatized and denounced as a traitor; and from one end of the country to the other that accusation is made, and it rings and rings again until the echoes even

come back to the Capitol, and are intended, if possible, to influence the judgment of Senators!

Who is Andrew Johnson? Not a man who is disposed to betray any trust that had been reposed in him; but a man who, whenever he has been before the people who know him best, has upon all occasions been sustained—sustained by his neighbors, sustained by his State, sustained by his country—and who on all occasions has shown himself worthy of the high confidence and trust that have been reposed in him.

I know, Senators, that when I state these things in your presence and in your hearing they may excite a smile of derision among some of those who differ with him in opinion. I know that an unfortunate difference of opinion exists between the Congress of the United States and the President, and I feel, in attempting to address you in his behalf upon some of the very questions about which this difference exists, that, in the language of Mr. Adams, I am walking in the midst of burning plowshares; but I pray Almighty God to direct me and to lead me aright, for I believe in His presence this day that my distinguished client is innocent of the charges that are preferred against him; and I hope that God's blessing, that has followed him thus far in life, will follow him now, and that he will at the end of this trial come out of the fiery furnace through which he is passing without the smell of fire upon his garments.

Who is Andrew Johnson? Why, Senators, when the battle of Manassas, as we called it in the South, or of Bull Run, as I believe it is called in the North, was fought, when our troops were defeated, when they rushed in hot haste and awful confusion to this capital, when men's faces turned pale and their hearts grew faint, where was Andrew Johnson then, this traitor, this usurper, this tyrant? Again he was heard in his place in the Senate, and he rises with a resolution in his hand, undismayed, unfaltering, believing in the justice of the great cause in which the country was engaged, and once more his voice was heard proclaiming to the whole land and to all the world the objects and purposes of the war and the determination of the Congress of the United States, in the fear of God and in the confidence of the justice of their cause, to pursue it to an honorable and a safe conclusion. Then it was that his voice was heard, and again the plaudits of hundreds and thousands shook the very walls of this Capitol in his favor, as they had done on former occasions when he stood here and vindicated the American Constitution and proclaimed the determination of the Government to uphold and to maintain it.

One word more, Senators, in regard to the President of the United States. It is admitted upon all hands that we are addressing gentlemen of the highest intelligence and position in the land, many of whom, as has been repeatedly said, are judges and lawyers well skilled in the law. What has been your rule of conduct either as judges or lawyers when you came to pronounce judgment upon the conduct of a fellow-man? You endeavored to place yourselves in his position; you endeavored to look at things from his stand-point; you endeavored to judge of them as he judged of them; and when you thus act you are enabled understandingly to determine whether the particular act in question be right or wrong. I only ask you here to-day, if it be possible for you to do so, to place yourselves in Andrew Johnson's position, and to look from his stand-point, and judge in the manner in which he judged. I know, Senators, that this is asking a great deal at your hands. I know it is asking a great deal of men who have fixed opinions upon subjects like these to review their own opinions and to consider them, especially where they are different from those of the man whose conduct they are endeavoring to judge. But I feel, when I am addressing you here to-day, that I am not addressing a Senate such as the honorable Managers spoke of the other day; I am not addressing mere politicians. I feel that I am addressing judges—the most eminent judges known to the laws and the Constitution of our country—judges sitting upon the greatest trial known to the Constitution; judges who have prescribed an oath for themselves; and while I know, while we all feel, the power of passion and of prejudice and preconceived opinion, and know the difficulty of laying them aside, yet, Senators, I would humbly and respectfully invoke you this day, in the name of that God to whom you have appealed, to make one honest, faithful effort to banish from your mind, as far as possible, all preconceived opinions; to sink the politician in the judge; to rise to the dignity and majesty of this great occasion; and, though it be like cutting off a right arm or plucking out a right eye, I ask you, Senators, to rise to that superhuman, God-like effort which shall enable you to banish these opinions and to do that equal and impartial justice which you have sworn to do.

Some people think that this cannot be done. It is impossible to close our eyes against what is taking place out of doors. It is impossible not to know that the newspapers have discussed this case. The press of this country is now the most tremendous power that belongs to it, a power greater than the power of Presidents and Senators and Representatives, the mightiest power known to the land. It is impossible for us to close our eyes against the fact that this case has been discussed and discussed over and over again in every form by those who favor impeachment and by those who are opposed to it, and all manner of opinions have been expressed. Some have said that they can calculate just exactly what is to be the result of this trial. Senators, I have made no such calculation. I declare to you here most solemnly, I declare to this country most solemnly, that I make no such calculation. No such unworthy investigation has for a moment agitated my mind. No, Senators; I would not do a thing so unworthy of the lofty position which you hold in the land. I say to you, and I say to the whole country, that whatever others may think, whatever they may believe, I for one do not believe that impeachment is a foregone conclusion. If I thought so, humble as I am, and exalted as you are, I would scorn the idea of addressing myself to this honorable court; but I do not believe it. No, sirs, no; nothing but a result which I trust in God never will happen will bring me to the conclusion that any such state of things exists with honorable men, the representatives of the sovereignty of the States; for, Senators, we all know enough about the history of our country to know that it requires no ordinary talent, no ordinary character, no ordinary experience to get to this Chamber in which you are acting as the representatives of the States. It requires standing, character, age, talent, to enable men to come here and to occupy the positions that you now occupy; and, for the honor of our common country, for the honor of American Senators, for the honor of our noble ancestors who framed this tribunal with a view to do equal and impartial justice, I cannot for one moment credit such things. I would say now, as I have seen it said on some few occasions, I would say now as ever to the American people, place no confidence in these things; believe that the Senators of the American nation are all honest and honorable men; and in every time of trial and of danger, when the billows of excitement roll high, when human passions are aroused and agitated in the highest degree, look to the Senate; look with hope and with confidence; look to those men who are in some degree elevated above dependence upon mere popular clamor and hasty and temporary excitement; look to the Senate; look to it with confidence, and thus looking your hope shall not be in vain.

Thus it is, Senators, that I shall endeavor to address you on this occasion. It is with this hope and with this confidence that I approach the consideration of some of the other topics which have been raised in this cause. I asked you a moment ago, if possible, to place yourselves in the condition of the President of the United States, to divest yourselves, so far as you can, of all preconceived opinions—and I admitted that it is an almost superhuman effort to do so—and to place yourselves, as far as you can, in his position, to look at his acts in the manner in which he looked at them. And now trace the history of his life in another view, his life as a politician.

Who is the President of the United States? A Democrat of the straightest of strict constructionists; an old Jacksonian, Jeffersonian Democrat; a man who proclaimed his Democracy in the very letter of acceptance which he wrote at the time when he was nominated for the Vice Presidency ; a man who told you and who told the whole country in that letter that he was a Democrat, and who endeavored to arouse the old Democracy to what he called the pure and correct Democracy of the country to rally around the national flag, and to sustain the country in the great conflict through which it was passing. Now, when you look at this, and when you consider all the public speeches that he ever made, examine the records of Congress, examine your debates everywhere, look to any question in which an inquiry into the Constitution of the United States was ever involved, where do you find the President? You find him under all circumstances a strict constructionist of the Constitution, adhering with tenacity to the principles of that party faith in which he had been trained and educated ; and when you look at the great difference of opinion that exists between him and yourselves and him and the House of Representatives upon the great questions that are agitating the country, while you may differ from him in opinion, while you do differ with him in opinion, yet, Senators, I ask you if he may not honestly entertain an opinion different from yours? Do accord to him something of those motives that you accord to every other human being upon a trial; accord to him at least what the laws of the land grant to the meanest criminal who ever was arraigned at the bar of justice ; accord to him the benefit of the legal presumption that he shall be presumed innocent until the contrary appears. Look at his motives, look at the manner in which he has acted ; and if there has been, as there is, an unfortunate difference of opinion between him and the Congress of the United States upon great constitutional questions, why, Senators, attribute that difference, if you please, to the training, to the education, to the habits of thought of his whole life ; but do not, in the absence of proof, attribute it to unworthy, base, mean, dishonorable motives, as you are asked to do on the other side.

I beg leave, Senators, to remind you of the resolution to which I adverted a few moments ago ; for, in the view which I take of this case, that resolution furnishes a key to the whole conduct of the President in the controversy out of which this unfortunate prosecution has arisen. How was that resolution of 1861? It is familiar to you all:

"*Resolved*, That the present deplorable civil war has been forced upon the country by the disunionists of the southern States now in revolt against the constitutional Government and in arms around the capital; that in this national emergency Congress, banishing all feeling of mere passion or resentment, will recollect only its duty to the whole country; that this war is not prosecuted on our part in any spirit of oppression, nor for any purpose of conquest or subjugation, nor for the purpose of overthrowing the rights or established institutions of those States, but to defend and maintain the supremacy of the Constitution and all laws made in pursuance thereof, and to preserve the Union with all the dignity, equality, and rights of the several States unimpaired; that as soon as these objects are accomplished the war ought to cease."

There is the chart that has guided the President of the United States in the discharge of his official duty ; there is the platform on which he has stood; and if he has not viewed it in the light in which others regarded it, still, Senators, we ask you if it is not capable of being regarded in the light in which he viewed it? If it is, then, as I shall maintain, we deprive this prosecution of all improper motive. I declare here to you to-day that in view of all the testimony which has been offered on the other side, in view of all that is known to the history of the country, with the exception of one solitary circumstance, the President of the United States has stood up in letter and in spirit to what he believed to be the terms of this resolution which was adopted with something approaching unanimity in both Houses of Congress in 1861. In the progress of the war he felt that it was necessary for him to yield the question of slavery so far as he had any influence in the State or section of country in which he resided. He did yield, and he went as far as the farthest to proclaim emancipation in the State over which he had been placed as military governor; but in all other respects he has endeavored to carry out the terms of this resolution, which was introduced by himself in the Senate, and into the other House by the venerable Crittenden, known to you all, who now is no more, but whose memory will be cherished with veneration and respect so long as America shall have a name. So long as talent and genius and independence and faithfulness and firmness shall be venerated and respected, the name of that great and good man will be honored in our own and all other lands.

Do not misunderstand me, Senators. It is not my purpose to enter to-day upon any discussion of the differences of opinion between the Congress of the United States and the President in regard to the different reconstruction policy which has been pursued by each. I only advert to it for the purpose of showing that there was a pledge that the dignity, equality, and rights of the States should be preserved; and in 1860 and in 1861, when the galleries of this Senate rang with shouts and applause of the multitude, when fair women and brave men were not ashamed to express their admiration for and gratitude to him who is now on trial before you, he advocated a doctrine which was exceedingly obnoxious to the people of the southern States. What was that doctrine? It was that the Congress of the United States had the power to compel obedience to the Constitution and laws of the United States. He denounced the doctrine of secession. He denied that any State had the right to withdraw from the Union without the consent of all the States. He insisted that the whole power of the Government should be brought into requisition to keep those States within the Union.

He faithfully maintained his principles during the war. When the war was over; when

Lee surrendered suddenly and unexpectedly; when the Government was cast upon him by an act beyond his control; when all its responsibilities were devolved upon him, and in the sudden emergency in which he was called upon to act it was necessary for him to act promptly, to act hastily, to act speedily, so as to bring the state of hostilities to a final termination as soon as possible, Senators, what did he do? There was no time to call Congress together, no time to assemble the representatives of the nation, for the situation of the country, upon Lee's surrender, demanded immediate and prompt action. What did the President do? According to the testimony of Mr. Stanton himself, which is now known and familiar through all the land, the President of the United States undertook to carry out what he believed to be the policy of his lamented predecessor. He undertook this in good faith. He retained the Cabinet which Mr. Lincoln left. He manifested no desire to segregate himself from the party by whom he had been elevated to power. He endeavored faithfully to carry out the provisions of the resolution of 1861 to preserve the dignity, equality, and rights of the States, and not to impair them in the slightest degree.

And now the question which I put before this Senate and before the whole country is this: suppose he committed an error; suppose he is wrong; suppose Congress is right; in the name of all that is sacred, I ask can you predicate guilt of any acts like these? In the name of all that is sacred, I ask can any one say that he is a traitor to his principles, or a traitor to the party that elected him? It is a mere difference of opinion, an unfortunate, a very unfortunate one, between him and the Congress of the United States; but who can say in the spirit of candor and truth that he was not endeavoring and did not in all his acts strive to carry out what he believed to be the policy of the party by whom he was elevated to power? When he did everything that he thought it was necessary to do; when, following the example of Mr. Lincoln in regard to Arkansas and Louisiana, and certainly following the spirit of Mr. Lincoln's proclamations and efforts, he sought to restore the other southern States to the relations which they had maintained to our common Union before the civil war commenced, I ask who can say that there was guilt in all this? You may differ with him in opinion; you may think he was wrong; I have no doubt that a large majority of the Senators whom I address do conscientiously and honestly believe that he was wrong; but still, Senators, does the mere fact that you think he was wrong disrobe this case of that part of our defense which rests upon the honesty and the integrity of the judgment which he exercised? In the name of all that is sensible I ask, is a judge to be tried because he mistakes the law in a charge to a jury? I need not turn to authorities; I need not read law books to satisfy the honorable Senate that every man acting in a judicial

capacity, from a simple justice of the peace up to the Chief Justice of the highest court in the United States, is protected by the laws of the land in the faithful and honest exercise of the judgment that is conferred upon him.

You have heard a great deal, Senators, about the doctrine of implied powers. I may have occasion to speak of that again in another part of my observations to you; but now let me put one plain, simple question to this Senate and to the whole country: can any man put his finger upon any sentence or clause in the Constitution of our country which says who is to restore the relations of peace in the land when they have been disturbed by a civil war? You have the power to suppress rebellion; but the very moment you go beyond the language of the Constitution you launch out into implied powers. The very moment you depart from the language of the Constitution you are obliged to resort to the doctrine of implication, and the very moment you admit the doctrine of implication then I maintain that that doctrine is just as applicable to the President of the United States as it is to any Senator or to any Representative.

I know to whom I am addressing myself; I know the intelligence and the high respectability of this great tribunal; but I put the question with fearless confidence to every Senator, where do you get the power in the Constitution to pass your reconstruction laws? Where do you get it unless you get it under the power to suppress insurrection? Where do you get it unless you obtain it under those general powers by which the war was carried on, and under which it was declared that a Government has an inherent right to protect itself against dissolution? Where do you get the power elsewhere? In the name of law and order and justice that you have inscribed upon the tablet over the door that enters into this magnificent Chamber, and which I trust will be inscribed in characters of living light upon the mind and the heart of every Senator I address to-day, I ask you, Senators, where do you get this power if you do not get it by implication? The Constitution is silent. It does not say that Congress shall pass laws to reconstruct States that have been in rebellion. It does not say that the President of the United States shall do this. You are obliged to resort to implication. He is the Commander-in-Chief of your armies. The country was in a state of war; peace had not been declared when these measures of his were undertaken. It was necessary to protect the country against disbanded armies, against the ravage and the ruin that were likely to follow in the wake of thousands upon thousands of soldiers who were discharged and turned loose upon the country. I repeat, there was no time to falter, no time to hesitate, no time in which even to ask the judgment and the aid of the Congress of the United States. He was forced to act; and if, in the construction of the powers and duties that belong to him as President of the United States, as Commander-in-Chief of your Army, as the principal executive officer in the land, your President mistook his powers, if he misconceived them, if he fell into the error into which you may say that Mr. Lincoln, his lamented predecessor, had fallen, I ask you, gentlemen, is there to be no charity, no toleration, no license, no liberality for a difference of opinion? Have we gone back two hundred years in the history of the world to the period when, as you all know, it was customary, especially in regard to religious opinions, to burn at the stake for differences in opinion; or do we live in the midst of the light of the nineteenth century, when the Gospel is spread abroad, when a liberal and enlightened spirit characterizes the age, when the human mind has been developed in such form and to such extent as the world never witnessed before? I ask you, Senators, is he to be judged in the spirit of the dark and the Middle Ages; are you to go back to the history of the midnight of mankind in order to find a rule for his conduct; or are you to judge him with a liberal, enlightened, patriotic judgment, and give his conduct the weight to which it is entitled?

I maintain on this great subject that the President in his position as the chief executive officer of the land was entitled to form a judgment; that he was compelled to form it; and that even if his actions were erroneous and contrary to the Constitution, if he was governed by honest and correct and upright motives, his honesty and integrity of motive in this court or any court under the heavens is a shield and a protection to him against all the darts that may be leveled at him from any quarter, high or low. The servant that knew his master's will and did it not was punished; but never the servant who did not know his master's will or who erred, and honestly erred, in the exercise of the best judgment and reason he possessed.

Senators, I maintain that this cursory glance at the history of the country and of the difference of opinion that exists between Congress and the President is sufficient to show that he was animated by upright and correct motives, and that he ought not to be judged in the spirit in which the honorable Managers ask that he shall be judged; his acts ought not to be condemned; but you ought to give him at least the merit of having had reason to act in the manner in which he did act.

Without dicussing the questions, but merely for the purpose of recalling the attention of Senators to certain dates, I beg leave to remind you, as I have already done, that, according to Mr. Stanton's own testimony in another investigation, which has been published under the authority of Congress, the President of the United States endeavored to carry out what he believed to be the policy of Mr. Lincoln; and after referring to some few dates and circumstances I shall pass from this part of the history of our country without undertaking to discuss the merits of the difference of opinion between Congress and the President. I only allude to it for the purpose of relieving him from the charge of being a usurper, a traitor, a tyrant, a man guilty of every crime known under the heavens!

Mr. Lincoln, in his proclamation of July 8, 1864, stated that he had failed to approve the first reconstruction bill passed by Congress on the 2d of July, 1864, and had expressed an unwillingness to set aside the constitutions of Arkansas and Louisiana. In his proclamation of December 8, 1863, he had invited—mark my language—he had invited the people of the rebellious States to form new constitutions, to be adopted by not less than one tenth of the voters who had voted at the presidential election of 1860, each of whom should take the oath of amnesty prescribed by his proclamation. President Johnson, as you know, when he came into power, recognized Governor Peirpoint's government in Virginia, a government, if I am correctly informed as to its history, actually embracing only a few counties of the State of Virginia during the war; but which the Congress of the United States thought, and rightfully thought, was sufficiently well organized to justify it in consenting to the formation of a new State, now known as the State of West Virginia.

This is the correct statement of the case, if I am not misinformed as to the facts of history; and, Senators, you will pardon me if I should fall into errors on these subjects, because, as I have stated to you, I am no politician. It is like carrying coals to Newcastle or telling a thrice-told tale for any of us to argue these questions before Senators and Representatives who are much more familiar with them than we are, and if I should fall into any errors I beg you to believe that they are errors of ignorance and not of design. I know the great superiority that the gentlemen who are Managers in this cause have over us in their knowledge of these matters, because each member of the House of Representatives and every Senator in reference to these subjects may say of himself *"pars fui;"* you have all been concerned in them and they are much more familiar to you than they are to me. Still, Senators, I beg leave to remind you that President Johnson recognized the Peirpoint government. That government was recognized as the State government of Virginia under an election held by the people of that State, and under that election West Virginia was formed into a new State, and all this was done, if I am not misinformed, without any act of reconstruction being passed by the Congress of the United States.

When President Johnson came into power, and saw that the Congress of the United States had recognized the existence of the State of Virginia and had formed West Virginia into a new State within her jurisdiction, was he not justified in the belief that by recognizing the Peirpoint government he was pursuing not only the policy of Mr. Lincoln and the party that elevated him to power, but the policy of the Senate and House of Representatives of the United States? Surely so; and if he committed an error it was an error of the head and not an error of the heart, and it ought not to be made a matter of railing accusation against him.

The President when he came into office was guided by these precedents, and, if you allow me to coin a word, by the unapproved act of 1864, (Mr. Davis's bill,) which recognized the right of the President to appoint military governors. Now, without dwelling upon that point I simply recall to your recollection the fact that by a proclamation he recognized Francis H. Peirpoint as Governor of Virginia on the 9th of May, 1865. Between the 29th of May and the 13th of July, 1865, he appointed provisional governors for North Carolina, Mississippi, Georgia, Texas, Alabama, South Carolina, and Florida. In October, 1865, he sent dispatches to Governor Perry, of South Carolina, and others, urging the adoption of the anti-slavery amendment. And on the 4th of December, 1865, he communicated his action to Congress, denying that secession had segregated the rebellious States from the Union, and leaving it to each a House to judge of the elections, qualifications, and returns of its own members.

Now, Senators, let me pause a moment and ask you the question here. up to that time, up to the assembling of the Congress of the United States in December, 1865, who was there in all this broad land, from one end of it to the other, that dared to point "the slow, unmoving finger of scorn" at Andrew Johnson and say that he was a traitor to his party, or say that he had betrayed any trust reposed in him? He was faithfully carrying out what I repeat he believed to be the policy of Congress and of his predecessor. He was anxious that this Union should be restored. He was anxious to pour oil upon the troubled waters and heal the wounds of his distracted and divided country. If he erred in this it was almost a divine error. If he erred in this it was a noble error. It was an error which was intended to restore peace and harmony to our bleeding country. It was an error which was designed to banish the recollection of the war. It was an error which was intended to bring into fraternal embrace the fathers and the sons, the brothers and the sisters, the husbands and the wives who had been separated through that awful calamity which overshadowed our country and that terrible civil war which drenched the land in human gore.

I say that if he committed an error in this, it is not an error that should be imputed as a crime; and however greatly you may differ from him, if you will pronounce upon his conduct that judgment which I invoke elevated judges to pronounce; if you pronounce that cool, calm, dispassionate judgment which must be exercised by every one of you who intends faithfully to redeem the pledge which he has made to God and the country, I think, Senators, you will surely acquit him of many of the accusations that have been made against him.

One other thought before I leave this branch of the subject. On the 20th of August, 1866, the President of the United States proclaimed the rebellion at an end, and on the 2d of March, 1867, an act was approved entitled "An act to provide for the temporary increase of the pay of officers in the Army of the United States," by the second section of which it is enacted:

"That section one of an act entitled 'An act to increase the pay of soldiers in the United States Army, and for other purposes,' approved June 20, 1864, be, and the same is hereby, continued in full force and effect for three years from"—

Mark the language—

"from and after the close of the rebellion as announced by the President of the United States by proclamation bearing date the 20th day of August, 1866."

There is a legislative, a congressional recognition of the fact that the war is at an end; there is a recognition of the President's power so to proclaim it, and without discussing the question, (for I have said I will not enter upon the discussion of it, though I am invited to it, I might almost say by the repeated remarks which have been made by the honorable Managers,) I maintain that this legislative recognition of the President's proclamation announcing the termination of the civil war, the close of the rebellion, was a recognition of the fact that the southern States were not out of the Union and that it goes far to extenuate, if not to justify, the view which the President of the United States took in reference to the restoration of these States to their harmonious relations with the Government of the country.

And now, Senators, having disposed to some extent, but not entirely, of these personal charges which have been made against the President, having reviewed briefly and imperfectly something of his personal and political history, I invite you to look back upon the record of his whole life, and in his name I ask you, and I ask the country to-day, as Samuel asked the people of Israel in the olden time:

"Behold, here I am; witness against me before the Lord and before His anointed, whose ox have I taken? or whose ass have I taken? or whom have I defrauded? whom have I oppressed? or of whose hand have I received any bribe to blind mine eyes therewith? and I will restore it to you."

And I trust that the answer of this Senate, and the answer of the whole country, will be such as the people of Israel gave; for—

"They said, thou hast not defrauded us, nor oppressed us; neither hast thou taken aught of any man's hand. And he said unto them, the Lord is witness against you and His anointed is witness this day that ye have not found aught in my hand. And they answered, he is witness."

The President appeals with proud confidence to the Senate and the whole country to attest the purity and integrity of his motives; and while he does not claim that his judgment is infallible, while he does not claim that he may not have committed errors—and who in his position may not have committed great and grievous errors—while he claims no such attributes as these, he does claim, before this Senate and before the world, that he is an honest man, that he is a man of integrity, that he is a man of pure and upright motives; and notwithstanding the clamor that has been raised against him, he feels it, and he appeals to the judgment of this Senate and of the world to vindicate him in it.

Mr. Chief Justice and Senators, one of the first questions which, as I respectfully think, is of importance in this cause is a question which I have barely touched in passing along but have not attempted to consider. That question is, what sort of tribunal is this? Is this a court or is it not? Some votes have been taken, Senators, as you know, in the progress of this cause upon this question. It has not been discussed according to my recollection by any of the counsel for the President. At an early period of the trial you retired to your Chamber to consider of it. What debates you had there I know not. Whether they have been published I know not. Your votes were announced by the Chief Justice, but whether the discussions in the secret session of the Senate have been published I confess I am ignorant. All that I have to say is that if they have been published I have not seen them. While I do not know to what extent the opinion of Senators may be fixed and formed upon this question, I ask, as a matter of right, whether you consider yourselves as having decided it or not, that you will allow me to address myself for a short time to the consideration of this which I regard as one of the greatest questions that ever has been presented since the formation of our Government. I think I am not asking too much at the hands of the Senate when I ask to be heard upon this subject; for even if you have decided the question, if you follow the analogy furnished from courts of law and equity, where a rule for a new trial may be entered at *nisi prius* or a petition for a rehearing may be filed in a court of chancery, or a bill of review or a reargument or anything that a judge may deem proper to be heard upon a subject that is before him, it will not be asking too much for me to request you to hear me for a few moments upon this subject.

It was argued by the honorable Manager who opened this cause that this is a mere Senate; that it is not a court. I will call your attention to a single paragraph or two in the learned argument of the able gentleman who has managed this cause with such consummate tact and ability on the side of the prosecution, and from whom we have had so many fine examples of the decency and propriety of speech. He says:

"I trust, Mr. President and Senators, I may be pardoned for making some suggestions upon these topics, because to us it seems these are questions not of form, but of substance. If this body here is a court in any manner as contradistinguished from the Senate, then we agree that many, if not all, the analogies of the procedures of courts must obtain; that the common-law incidents of a trial in court must have place; that you may be bound in your proceedings and adjudication by the rules and precedents of the common or statute law."

* * * * * * * * *

"We claim and respectfully insist that this tribunal has none of the attributes of a judicial court as they are commonly received and understood. Of course, this question must be largely determined by the express provisions of the Constitution, and in it there is no word, as is well known to you, Senators, which gives the slightest coloring to the idea that this is a court, save that in the trial of this particular respondent, the Chief Justice of the Supreme Court must preside."

That position has been affirmed again in argument by others; and treatises, I had almost said volumes, have been written upon this subject. Able and learned arguments have been presented to the Senate, and through the newspapers to the public, upon this question. Gentlemen in their researches have gone back to the black-letter learning of the English law books and the English Parliament to search for precedents, to search for authorities in reference to this great question; and the position which they have assumed and most learnedly and persistently insisted upon is that this high court of impeachment possesses all the powers of a court of impeachment in England; that it is to be governed by the same rules and the same regulations; that you are not to go to the common law for precedents or principles to guide your judgment, but that you are, in the language of two of the ablest gentlemen on the other side, "a law unto yourselves." Let us consider this position for a moment. I have but one answer to make to it.

It is not my purpose to follow the industrious and careful and diligent and learned Managers on the other side, and I do not utter these as words of vain and empty compliment, for they have bestowed a degree of labor, industry, and research in the investigation of this cause that is in the highest degree creditable to their talents and to the integrity and fidelity with which they are endeavoring to discharge the trust that has been reposed in them by the House of Representatives. But, with the greatest respect for the ability and learning which have been displayed upon the other side, I beg leave, Mr. Chief Justice and Senators, to submit to your consideration one or two arguments which it strikes me are pertinent and appropriate.

In the first place, I deny that you are to go to the law of Parliament, the *lex parliamentaria*, for the authority which is to guide and govern and control in this great trial; and why do I say so? Because I maintain that this tribunal is different from any tribunal that the world ever saw. No such tribunal is known in history. It never had a parallel. It never had an existence until it sprang into being, full-armed, like Minerva from the brain of

Jove, under the creative hand of those who framed the Constitution of the United States. You are to interpret it, as I maintain, not by the lights of English history alone, but by the light of the circumstances under which the Constitution of the United States was adopted.

I do not say, Mr. Chief Justice, that you are to ignore history. I do not say that you are to ignore a knowledge of the decisions that have been made in Parliament or that have been made in the courts of justice of England. I grant that upon some subjects it is perfectly right and proper to go to English history, to examine English law books, to investigate English causes, with a view of interpreting phrases and terms that were known to our fathers, and that have been incorporated into the Constitution of the country; but none of them afford any clue to this investigation, none of them afford any light upon this subject; and why? Because, I repeat, this tribunal has no exemplar in the history of the world. It is the tribunal of the American Constitution, and we must look to the language of the American Constitution in order to ascertain what it means; and I ask, and I hope your Honor will not take any offense at my using phraseology which I am sure is not intended to give any, I respectfully ask this Senate, whether it was the intention of the framers of the Constitution that the Chief Justice of the United States should be called down from the most elevated tribunal upon the face of the earth to preside over your deliberations, and that when he comes here he shall have no more power than an ordinary speaker of an ordinary House of Representatives, and hardly so much; that he shall be a mere automaton, a machine, a conduit through whom the votes of the Senate are to pass to the records of the country?

I insist that there was an object, a high object and purpose in the framers of the Constitution when they called the Chief Justice from his lofty position to preside over the deliberations of the Senate. There was an object and a purpose, an object such as never had been attained in English history; an object such as was unknown to the British constitution; for, may it please your Honor, under the British constitution, as I understand its history, Parliament did not consider themselves bound by the judgment of the judges, although they often consulted them upon legal questions. I maintain that instead of that fact furnishing an argument, as they have attempted to use it on the other side to prove that it was the intention of the framers of the Constitution that the Chief Justice should be a mere automaton or cipher in this trial, when you look to the history of the formation of the Constitution every intendment is to be taken to the contrary.

Now, without taking up too much time, Senators, on this question, interesting and important as it is, I beg leave to remind you of some facts connected with the history of this subject. I do not consider that it is necessary for me to bring in volumes here and to read page after page to the Senate upon this subject. I take it for granted that Senators are informed, and no doubt a great deal better informed upon it than I am. All that I deem it material and important to do is to refresh your recollection in regard to some of the circumstances connected with the incorporation of this provision into the Constitution of the United States. You will recollect, Senators, that when the Constitution was about to be formed various plans of government were offered. Without bringing in the volumes or taking up the time of the Senate to read at length the different plans of government which were proposed by different members of the Convention that formed the Constitution. I only call your attention to so much as I think is pertinent to this question. You remember that Colonel Hamilton introduced what was called a plan of government, and in the ninth section of that it was provided that—

"Governors, Senators, and all officers of the United States to be liable to impeachment for mal and corrupt conduct, and upon conviction to be removed from office and disqualified from holding any place of trust or profit; all impeachments to be tried by a court."

Mark the proposition, for it is in the light of these propositions that I maintain we are to arrive at a true and correct interpretation of the Constitution itself:

"All impeachments to be tried by a court, to consist of the chief or senior judge of the superior court of law in each State: Provided, That such judge hold his place during good behavior, and have a permanent salary."

That was introduced on the 18th of June, 1787, and will be found in 1 Eliot's Debates on the Federal Constitution, page 180. Mr. Randolph had a plan of government; and the thirteenth proposition contained in Mr. Randolph's plan was in these words:

"Resolved, That the jurisdiction of the national judiciary shall extend to cases which respect the collection of the national revenue, impeachment of any officer, and questions which involve the national peace and harmony."

That was introduced on the 19th of June, 1787, and is set out in 1 Eliot's Debates, page 182. In Mr. Charles Pinckney's plan, introduced on the 19th of May, 1787, four days after the Convention was organized, it was provided that—

"The jurisdiction of the court to be termed the Supreme Court should extend to the trial or impeachment of officers of the United States."

That is set out in the first volume of the Madison Papers, page 131. Mr. Madison preferred the Supreme Court for the trial of impeachments, or rather a tribunal of which that should form a part. (See the Supplement to Eliot and 5 Madison Papers, p. 528.) Mr. Jefferson, in his letter of the 22d of February, 1798, to Mr. Madison, alludes to Mr. Tazewell's attempt to have a jury trial of impeachments. That will be found in the fourth volume of Jefferson's Works, page 215.

Mr. Hamilton, in the Federalist, No. 65, says:

"Would it have been an improvement of the plan to have united the Supreme Court with the Senate in the formation of the *court of impeachments?* This union would certainly have been attended with several advantages; but would they not have been overbalanced by the signal disadvantage already stated, arising from the agency of the same judges in the double prosecution to which the offender would be liable? To a certain extent the benefits of that union will be obtained from making the Chief Justice of the Supreme Court the president of the court of impeachments, as is proposed to be done in the plan of the convention; while the inconveniences of an entire incorporation of the former into the latter will be substantially avoided. This was perhaps the prudent mean."

Messrs. Madison, Mason, Morris, Pinckney, Williamson, and Sherman discussed the impeachment question, and in lieu of the words "bribery and maladministration," Colonel Mason substituted the words "other high crimes and misdemeanors against the State," as is shown in 5 Eliot's Debates, and Madison Papers, 528, 529. On the same day a committee of style and arrangement was appointed, consisting of Messrs. Johnson, Hamilton, Morris, and King. On Wednesday, the 12th of September, 1787, Dr. Johnson reported a digest of the plan. On Monday, the 17th of September, 1787, the engrossed Constitution was read and signed, as will be seen in 5 Madison Papers, page 553.

So far, Senators, as I have examined this question it does not appear when or how the words "when the President of the United States is tried the Chief Justice shall preside," now in the Constitution, were inserted. No doubt you are much better informed upon this subject than myself. I have, however, seen it stated that they must have been introduced upon a compromise in a committee, and that this fact is shown by Mr. Madison's writings; but in the researches which I have been able to make in the comparatively short time during which this investigation has been going on I have not been able to ascertain whether that reference is correct or not. I have not had the long period of twelve months' incubation which the gentlemen on the other side have had within which to prepare myself upon this great subject. But so far as I do comprehend or understand it I maintain the following propositions, to which I ask the attention of the Chief Justice and of the Senate; I shall not dwell upon them at any great length; it will be for you, Senators, and for him, to judge and decide whether any, and if any, how many of them are founded in sound reason.

I say that the law of Parliament furnishes no satisfactory exposition as to the office and duty of the Chief Justice on an impeachment trial. The interpretation must have been found in the light of the circumstance under which the provision was inserted. The anxiety of many members of the Convention to intrust impeachment to a judicial tribunal proves that they believed the learning and intelligence of the judges were essential elements to a fair determination. I think that is one of the most important considerations in the investigation of this great question. You have seen that one of the plans was to have impeachment tried by a court to be constituted of judges from each of the States; another plan was to have them tried by the Supreme Court of the United States; and another plan was to have the Supreme Court associated with the Senate upon the trial. Mark you, every one of these plans of impeachment looked to judicial aid and assistance in the trial of the cause; and when the Convention finally determined that the Chief Justice should preside, I maintain, Senators, they determined that he should come here as a judge, that he should come here clothed as he is in his robes of office, that he should declare the law and pronounce a judicial opinion upon any question arising in the cause. And while, sir, I know it is for your Honor to determine what course you will pursue, while I do not presume to dictate to this honorable court or to the Chief Justice who presides over it—it is my province to argue; it is your province, sir, to decide and to determine—I yet respectfully insist before the Senate and the world that I have the right, as one of the counsel for the President of the United States, to call, as I do call, upon the venerable Chief Justice who presides over your deliberations for an expression of his judgment and opinion upon any question of law which may arise in this case.

And how, in the name of common sense, does this doctrine of mine trench in the slightest degree upon any right or privilege of the American Senate? Does it conflict with any duty or with any power that is imposed upon you by the Constitution of our common country? Senators, learned as you are, respectable as is your standing at home, high as is the position which the States that have placed you here have conferred upon you, you may still derive instruction from the opinions of a gentleman learned in the law and holding the highest judicial office in the land. Does it invade any privilege or any prerogative—though I do not like to use that word—or any power of the American Senate to say that we ask that they may be guided in their deliberations by the profound and dispassionate judgment of one who is presumed to hold the scales of justice in an unfaltering and untrembling hand, one who holds his office independent of popular excitement and popular commotion, one who has been elevated to his high and lofty position because of his learning, his integrity, his talents, his character? Is it, I ask, any disparagement even to the American Senate, to respectfully request of him that he shall deliver an opinion to you upon any of the questions that may arise in this cause?

Then, Senators, it will be for you to judge and determine for yourselves, under such opinion, what may be the duty that you have to perform in this case. I insist that so far from this being an argument in disparagement either of the power or of the intelligence of the Senate, it is an argument which in its nature is calculated to aid the Senate as a court in arriving at a correct conclusion; and that no man who regards the Constitution and the laws of the land, no man who is in search of justice, no man who is willing to see the laws faithfully and honestly and impartially administered, can for one moment deny the right of this great civil magistrate, clothed in his judicial robes and armed with all the power and authority of the Constitution, to declare what he believes to be the law upon questions arising in this cause.

I hope you will pardon me for dwelling on this point for a few moments, as it has not been discussed, I believe, by any of the gentlemen who are counsel for the President. Indeed, I do not know that I represent the opinion of any gentleman who is counsel for the President except myself; but I think that as one of his counsel I have a right to submit any views or opinions that I entertain in reference to the case to the consideration of the Chief Justice and the Senators. When you look to the clause of the Constitution under which this power is conferred I say that every word in it is a technical word. The Senate shall try an impeachment. I do not quote the words literally, and it is not necessary to turn to them. They are familiar to you all. The Senate is to try an impeachment; and upon this trial the Senators shall be upon oath or affirmation; and when the President is tried the Chief Justice shall preside.

What is the meaning of the word "trial?" It is unnecessary for me to enter into any elaborate definition of it. It is enough for me to say that it is not used in the Constitution in the sense of suffering; it is not used in the Constitution in many of the senses that it is used in common parlance; but it is used in the sense of a judicial proceeding, and here, as I have admitted, you must go to the fountains of the English law, you must go to the terms that were in existence at the time when the Constitution was adopted, for the purpose of ascertaining and determining what is the meaning of the word "trial." It is a word dear to every Englishman; it is a word dear to every American. The idea of a judicial trial, a trial in which a judge is to preside, a trial in which a man skilled in the law and supposed to be a man of integrity and independence is to preside, is a proceeding that is dear to every Englishman and dear to every American; because for centuries it has been regarded in England, and ever since the formation of our own Government here, as essential to the preservation of the liberty of the citizen that a trial is to be conducted with all the aid of judicial interpretation that can be afforded.

Mr. Worcester defines "preside" to be "set aside or placed over others; to have authority over others; to preside over an assemblage." "Trial" is not used, as I say, in the sense of temptation or suffering, but to convey the idea of a judicial proceeding similar to a court and jury. And I insist that when the term "Chief Justice" is used as it is the term "Chief Justice" is itself a technical word. What does it mean? It means a judicial officer. The Constitution does not say in so many words that there shall be a judicial tribunal in which there shall be a chief justice. It authorizes Congress to create judicial tribunals. It took it for granted that there would be a court; it assumed that in that court there would be a chief justice, and that he should be a judge; and when it assumed that it assumed that he should act in the capacity which I have insisted upon.

Without dwelling upon this argument further, I can only say that in the views which I entertain of the question I conceive it to be one of the most important questions that ever were presented for consideration in this or any other country. So far, we all know, Senators, that this is the first case under the American Constitution in which the Senate has been called upon as a court of impeachment to try the Chief Magistrate of the land. If our Government survives the throes of revolution, if our Government continues as it is, undiminished, unimpaired in the hands of posterity, the precedent which you are to form now will last for a thousand years to come, and the decision which is made now is a decision that will be quoted in after ages and that will be of the very utmost and highest importance; and I maintain that in the view which has been presented we have a right to call upon the Chief Justice to act not merely as presiding officer, but to act as a judge in the conduct and management of this trial.

I have already referred to some startling and extraordinary propositions which are made by the Managers; I must notice some others. Mr. Manager BINGHAM says—I quoted the expression awhile ago—that you are "a rule and a law unto yourselves." Mr. Manager BUTLER proclaims that, "a constitutional tribunal, you are bound by no law, either statute or common." He says, further, that "common fame and current history may be relied on to prove the facts;" that is, to prove the President's course of administration; and, further, that "the momentous question" is raised "whether the presidential office ought in fact to exist."

Senators, in the whole progress of American history I have never read or heard or seen three such startling propositions as these which are insisted upon by the honorable Managers on the other side. They are dangerous to liberty. They are dangerous to the perpetuity of the Constitution and the American Government. They would overthrow every principle of justice and of law which is known to the civilized world if they were carried out to the extent which the honorable gentlemen insist upon. In this land of liberty, this land of law, this land where we have a written Constitution, who ever heard or dreamed that such doctrines would be asserted here?

If I do not misunderstand the language of the honorable gentleman who opened the case, he thinks that this Senate has the power to set aside the Constitution of the United States itself. Many of the most eminent and learned writers in England and our own country, in treating on the subject of the distribution of powers between the three departments of the Government, the executive; the legislative, and the judicial tribunal, have sounded a note of warning that the danger is to be apprehended from the executive; it is not to be apprehended from the judicial department, but it is to be apprehended from the encroachments of the Legislature, from the popular branch of the Government; and now we hear a learned, able, and distinguished leader of the House of Representatives, the chief Manager in this impeachment trial, boldly assuming, as I understand his argument before the American Senate, that you have the right to judge and determine for yourselves whether the American Constitution shall last.

Senators, such a notion is not in conformity to the heathful doctrines of the American Constitution. The real true sovereignty in this land is not in you; it is not in the President; it is not in the Chief Justice; it is in the American people, and they, and they only, can alter their Constitution. No Senate, no House of Representatives, no judge, no Congress can alter the American Constitution. I know that now-a-days it excites almost ridicule with some to hear anything said in behalf of the American Constitution. On one occasion since the commencement of this trial, when a witness spoke of the President of the United States, saying that he intended to support the Constitution of the country, it excited a universal smile in the Senate and in the gallery. That venerable instrument which was established by the wisdom of some of the bravest and best men that the world ever saw, that noble instrument which was purchased with the blood and the treasure of the Revolution, and which we have been accustomed to regard with sacred reverence, seems to have been so often trampled upon and violated in this land that when one dares to mention it with something of the reverence of ancient times, something of the respect which we have been accustomed to cherish for it, it excites a smile of derision and laughter in the land. God grant that a more healthful sentiment may animate and inspire the hearts of the American people, and that we shall return, now that this war has passed away, to something of our former veneration and respect for the American Constitution, and that we shall teach our children who are to come after us to love and revere it, as was taught in times past, as the political bible of the country; that it is not to be treated with aught but that respect and that reverence and

that high consideration which we were formerly accustomed to bestow on it.

"Common fame" you are to resort to! Is it possible that this great impeachment trial has reached so "lame and impotent a conclusion" as this, that the honorable Manager is driven to the necessity of insisting before you that common fame is to be regarded as evidence by Senators? I hope it will not grate harshly upon your ears when I repeat the old and familiar adage that "common fame is a common liar." Are the Senators of the United States to try the Chief Executive Magistrate upon rumor, the most dangerous, the most uncertain, the most unreliable, the most fatal and destructive proof that ever was offered under the sun? Why, the glory and boast of the English law and of the American Constitution are that we have certain fixed principles of law, fixed principles of evidence that are to guide, to govern, to control in the investigation of causes; and one of the beauties, one of the greatest perfections of the system of American jurisprudence, is that when you go into a court of justice nothing scarcely is taken by intent. There sits the judge; there are the jury; here are the witnesses who are called upon to testify; they are not allowed to give in evidence any rumor that may have been afloat in the country; they are compelled to speak of facts within their own knowledge. The case is investigated slowly, cautiously, deliberately. The truth is arrived at, not by any hasty conclusion, but it is arrived at upon solemn trial and upon patient and faithful investigation; and when the result is attained it commands the confidence of the country, it secures the approbation of the world, and that result is acquiesced in by the citizen; and if it be in a higher court it passes into the history of law and goes down to posterity as a precedent to be followed in all time to come; and herein, Senators, is the great security of the liberty that the American people enjoy.

I hope you will pardon me for giving utterance to one thought in this connection. I shall not say that it is original, but it is a thought which I have often cherished and indulged in. It is this: that the liberty of the American people is not that liberty merely which is defined in written constitutions; it is not that liberty which is enforced by congressional enactment; but, little as the American people think of it—and would to God that they would think of it a thousand times more intensely than they do—the only liberty that we have now or ever have had, so far as the American citizen is concerned, is that liberty which is enforced and secured in the judicial tribunals of the country. We talk about our social equality. We talk about all being free and equal. It is an idle song, it is a worthless tale, it is a vain and empty expression unless that liberty and that equality are enforced in a court of justice. There it is; I have seen it there, and so have you. It is the only place that I ever did see it. The poor man, the humblest man upon the face of the earth, I have seen come there as a plaintiff or a defendant; I have seen a thousand times the impartial judge, sitting blind to all external emotions and impressions, declare the law and try the cause and administer justice to this poor, ignorant, unfortunate man against the richest and the most powerful of the land. There is your law, there is your justice, there is the only liberty that is worthy of enjoyment; and to talk about common fame and common rumor being admitted before the highest tribunal known to the Constitution as a criterion of judgment would be, if admitted, to overthrow the Constitution itself, and to destroy the liberty which has thus far been enjoyed in the land.

"A law unto yourselves!" Senators, if this be so our Constitution has been written in vain. If this be so, all the volumes that swell the public libraries of the country and the private libraries of lawyers and statesmen have been written and published in vain. "A law unto yourselves!" That carries us back almost in imagination to the days of the Spanish Inquisition, to some of those dark, secret, unknown tribunals in England, in Venice, in the Old World, whose proceedings were hidden from mankind and whose judgments were most awful and terrible and fearful in their results. No, sirs; no. I deny that you are a law unto yourselves. I maintain that you have a Constitution. I insist that you must look not to parliamentary history for the reasons that I have already stated, but look to the common law, not as an authoritative exposition of all the duties which are incumbent on you, but as a guide to enlighten your judgments and your understandings, and that you must be governed by those great eternal principles of justice and of reason which have grown up with the growth of centuries and which lie at the very foundation of all the liberty we enjoy. This, Senators, is what I insist is the true doctrine of the American Constitution; and that this wild, latitudinarian, unauthorized interpretation of the honorable Manager can find no lodgment anywhere in view of the correct and eternal principles of justice that are incorporated into the American Constitution and form part of the law in every State.

If that be so, if you are governed by no law, if you are "a law unto yourselves," if the Constitution has nothing to do with it, if "common fame" and "common rumor" are to govern and control here, then the very oath that you have solemnly taken is an extra-judicial oath, not binding upon the conscience, not binding according to the laws of the land, and it would invest the most dangerous power in the Senate of the United States that ever was invested in any tribunal upon the face of the earth. It would enable the Senate of the United States, under the pretext of being "a law unto yourselves," to defeat the will of the American people and remove from office any man who might be displeasing to you, to set at naught their election, and to engross into your own hands all the power of the Constitution. Senators, I can conceive of no despotism worse than this. I can conceive of no danger menacing the liberties of the American people more awful and fearful than the danger that menaces them now, if this doctrine finds any sort of favor in the mind or the heart of any Senator to whom it is addressed. I repeat, in regard to this, as I did in regard to some other matters awhile ago, that I do not believe the American Senate will, for one moment, cherish any such doctrine or act upon it in the slightest degree. The doctrine would prostrate all the ramparts of the Constitution, destroy the will of the American people, and it would engross into the hands of the Congress of the United States all those powers which were intended to be confided to the other departments and distributed among them.

Mr. Chief Justice, in considering the case now before us, there is a preliminary question underlying it which is of very considerable interest; and it is, what are crimes and misdemeanors under the Constitution? But, before I pass to that, I desire, while considering some of the extraordinary arguments that have been presented by the honorable Managers on the other side, to remind the Senate and the Chief Justice of one proposition which was paraded at an early day of this trial. I regretted almost the moment I took my seat, after it was announced, that I had not answered it then; but it is in your record, and it is not too late to give a passing remark to it now.

The honorable Manager [Mr. BUTLER] made use of the expression that "The great pulse of the nation beats perturbedly, pauses fitfully when we pause, and goes forward when we go forward." And you have been told time and again that the honorable Managers are acting for "all the people of the United States." I may have something to say about that, Senators, before I close the remarks I have to make to you; but I shall postpone the consideration of that for the present.

Yes, the public pulse beats perturbedly; it pauses when you pause; it goes forward when you go forward; and you have been told time and again that the people out of doors are anxious for the conviction of the President of the United States. Will you permit me, Senators, to be guilty of the indecorum almost of saying one word about myself, and I only say it by way of stating an argument. In the whole course of my professional career, from the time I first obtained, as a young man, a license to practice law, down to the present moment, I never had the impudence or the presumption to talk to a judge out of court about any case in which I was concerned. My arguments before him have always been made in court, always made in public. I have had sufficient respect for the independence of the judges before whom I have had the honor to practice my profession to take it for granted that they were men of honor, men of intelligence, and that they would not hear any remarks that I would attempt to infuse into their understandings out of doors and not in the presence of my adversary.

But the doctrine here is that the public pulse beats in a particular direction. Have we come to this? Is this case to be tried by the greatest court in Christendom, not upon law, not upon evidence, not under the instructions of the Chief Justice of the United States, But tried upon common rumor; and is it to become interesting or cease to be interesting just according to the beating of the public pulse? Why, Senators, if it were not that I do not intend to say one word that is designed to be offensive to any of the gentlemen on the other side or to any Senator, I would say that I would almost regard this as an insulting argument to them; but I shall not make use of that expression. It is not my intention, in anything I have said or may say, to wound the sensibilities of any one or to give any just cause of offense to anybody who is in any way connected with this case. But you are to try it according to the public pulse! What an argument to advance to the American Senate! What an argument to put forth to the American nation! All history teems with examples of the gross, outrageous injustice that has been done in criminal trials, high and low, in parliamentary tribunals, and in the courts of justice; and I am afraid that our own country is not entirely exempt from some notable instances of it, where popular clamor was allowed to influence the judgment of judges; and those instances which are recorded in history, those instances of blood and of murder and of outrage and of wrong that have been perpetrated in the name of justice, are an admonition to us that the public pulse should have nothing to do with your judgment.

Senators, regarding every man whom I address as a judge, as a sworn judge, allow me for one moment to call your attention to one great trial in this country which I hope in some of its principles will be a guide to you; and I do not think it will be an unworthy guide in the investigation which you have to make here. There was a case which occurred in the early history of the American nation where there was a great political trial. The waves of popular excitement ran high. It was understood that the President of the United States himself desired the conviction of the offender. The public pulse beat fitfully then. It went forward as the judge went forward, and it went backward as the judge went backward. It was a great occasion. It was one of the most illustrious trials that ever occurred in English or American jurisprudence.

There was the great criminal, morally guilty no doubt, for so he has been held in the judgment of posterity. There sat the judge, one of the illustrious predecessors of the distinguished gentleman who presides over your deliberations now. There he sat calm, unmoved, unawed, unmindful of the beating of the public pulse, the very impersonation of Justice, having no motive under heaven except to administer the law and to administer it faithfully; and he had the nerve and the firmness to declare the law in the fear of God rather than in the fear of man; and although the criminal was acquitted, and although there was some popular clamor in regard to the acquittal, the judgment of posterity has sanctioned the course of the judicial determination, and every American citizen who has any regard for his country, every judge and every lawyer who has any respect for judicial independence and integrity, looks back with veneration and respect to the name and to the conduct of John Marshall.

So long as judicial independence shall be admired, so long as judicial integrity shall be respected, the name of John Marshall will be esteemed in our own country and throughout the civilized world as one of the brightest luminaries of the law, as one of the most faithful judges that ever presided in a court. It is true that clouds and darkness gathered around him for the moment, but they soon passed away and were forgotten—

"As some tall cliff that lifts its awful form,
Swells from the vale and midway leaves the storm,
Though round its breast the rolling clouds are spread,
Eternal sunshine settles on its head."

Such was the name and such the fame of John Marshall, and God grant that his spirit may fall, like the mantle of Elijah, upon the illustrious magistrate who presides and every judge who sits here, that you may catch its inspiration, Senators, and that you may throw to the moles and bats all appeals to your prejudices, all appeals from without, and that you may discharge your whole duty in the fear of that God to whom you appealed. If I might propose such a low, groveling, contemptible consideration on the minds of Senators here, if I might be pardoned for alluding to it, (for the very thought almost makes me shrink back with horror from myself,) I would say to you that if you were to rise above these prejudices, cast these clamors away from your thoughts, do your duty like Marshall did, in the fear of God, even in a low, pitiful, contemptible party point of view, it would make you stand higher with your own party and with the world than you would stand doing an act of gross injustice. Forgive me, though, for mentioning such a consideration, for I really think it is beneath the dignity of the Senate to entertain it for a moment. No, sirs; I treat you as judges; I treat you as honorable men; I treat you as sworn officers of the law; and thus treating you, I say that I banish all such thoughts from my mind, and I come before you as an impartial tribunal, believing before God and my country that you will try to do your duty in this case irrespective of popular clamors and regardless of opinions from without.

Such, I trust, will be the judgment of the whole land ; and when you and I and all of us shall pass away from the scene of human action, when the memory of the stirring events which now agitate the public mind shall almost be forgotten, I trust that the after ages will look back with wonder and admiration and love and respect and honor to the American Senate for the manner in which they shall have discharged their duty in this case. I trust, Senators, that the result will be such as will command the approbation not only of your own consciences, not only of the States that you have the honor to represent, but the approbation of Him who is a greater judge than you are, and the approbation of posterity who are to come after you.

Now, Mr. Chief Justice, I desire briefly to present to your consideration and that of the Senate this proposition : while we cannot go to the British constitution or the British Parliament or British law to ascertain the meaning of a court such as they never had, consisting of a Senate and Chief Justice, yet "treason, bribery, or other high crimes and misdeameanors" were words well known and defined at the date of the adoption of the Constitution ; and in order to ascertain their meaning a most excellent rule of interpretation was adverted to by Chief Justice Marshall in the trial to which I have referred. In Burr's trial, speaking of the term "levying war," used by the Constitution in the definition of treason, he says :

"But the term is not for the first time applied to treason by the Constitution of the United States. It is a technical term. It is used in a very old statute of that country whose language is our language, and whose laws form the substratum of our law. It is scarcely conceivable that the term was not employed by the framers of our Constitution in the sense which had been affixed to it by those from whom we borrowed it. So far as the meaning of any terms, particularly terms of art, is completely ascertained, those by whom they are employed must be considered as employing them in that ascertained meaning, unless the contrary be proved by the context. It is, therefore, reasonable to suppose, unless it be incompatible with other expressions of the Constitution, that the term "levying war" is used in that instrument in the same sense in which it was understood in England and in this country, to have been used in the statute of the 25th of Edward III, from which it was borrowed."—Burr's Trial, p. 308.

The words "treason, liberty, or other high crimes and misdemeanors" were words just as familiar to the framers of the Constitution as they are to us. One of the honorable Managers made an argument here, if I understood it, to show that because Dr. Franklin was in London about the time of Warren Hastings' trial, that had a great deal to do with the proper mode of construing the American Constitution on the subject of the powers of the Chief Justice. But Blackstone's Commentaries no doubt were as familiar to the lawyer at the date of the formation of the American Constitution as that venerable work is to the lawyers and

C. I.—39.

judges of the present day. "Crimes and misdemeanors" are the offenses for which impeachment may be resorted to. You all know that in one passage of his work he says that crimes and misdemeanors are almost synonymous words; but in another and further exposition of it he undertakes to show, and does show, that the word "crime" is used in the sense of charging higher offenses such as usually fall within the denomination of felonies and the word "misdemeanors," and those trivial and lighter offenses which are not punishable with death, but by fine and imprisonment, or either, or both.

What is the rule of interpretation ? It is unnecessary for me to turn to authorities on this question. You are to construe words in the connection in which they are used ; you are to construe them in the sense of their being of the same kind or nature of other words. Now, if I correctly apprehend the law at the date of the American Constitution, treason by the law of England was a felony punishable with death ; bribery was a misdemeanor not punishable with death, but punishable by fine and imprisonment. When the word "crimes," therefore, is used in the Constitution, the argument that I make is, and it has been made by one of the learned Managers, I think, in a much more able manner than I can present it—I am willing to say I borrow it from the gentleman—that the word "crimes" is to be construed in the same sense as the word "treason ;" it is to be understood as embracing felonious offenses, offenses punishable with death or with imprisonment in the penitentiary where they have penitentiaries in the different States. The word "misdemeanors" has reference to other and different offenses altogether. It does not mean a simple assault, for the expression of the Constitution is "high crimes and misdemeanors"—"high crimes" referring, of course, to such crimes as are punishable with death ; high misdemeanors referring to such misdemeanors as were punishable by fine and imprisonment, and not to such simple misdemeanors as an assault.

What, then, is the argument from that? I know there is a great difference of opinion on this question, and if I correctly apprehend Mr. Story's treatise on it in his admirable work upon the Constitution, he regards it as an open question to this day, or at least to the day at which he wrote, what is the true meaning of the term "crimes and misdemeanors" as employed in the Constitution of the United States. One party of constructionists, if I may so express myself, hold that you are not to look to the common law to ascertain the meaning of the words "crimes and misdemeanors," but you are to look to the parliamentary law in order to ascertain it. So far as I have any knowledge on the subject, the parliamentary law does not define and never did undertake to define what is the meaning of "crimes and misdemeanors." What did the parliamentary law undertake to do? It undertook to punish not only office-holders but citizens for offenses which were regarded as offenses against the Government. Often, without turning the offender over to the courts, the party was impeached or attainted by a proceeding in Parliament; but there is no definition there, so far as I know, of "crimes and misdemeanors;" they were, to use the language of the gentlemen, in great part "a law unto themselves."

But when the framers of the Constitution incorporated these words into our charter, did they borrow them from the parliamentary law or did they get them from Blackstone and from Hale, and from other writers upon criminal law in England? Where did they obtain these words, "crimes and misdemeanors?" They got them from the common law of England and not from the law of Parliament, as I insist; and then the proposition follows as a corollary from the premises I have laid down, if the premises be correct—it follows inevitably if the proposition which I have assumed be a correct one, that the words "crimes and misdemeanors" are used in the sense in which they were employed by writers upon criminal law in England at the date of the Constitution, that nothing is an impeachable offense under the American Constitution except that which was known as a crime or misdemeanor within the definition of those words under the British law and that which may be created as such by the Constitution of the United States. I doubt even—and I submit that to the consideration of Senators, I respectfully submit it as a doubt, and one well worthy of your consideration—whether the Congress of the United States, within the meaning of the American Constitution, has a right to create a new crime, a new misdemeanor, something that was not known as a crime or as a misdemeanor at the date of the adoption of the Constitution?

I think it is a matter of great doubt, to say the least of it; and in entertaining this opinion I at least am warranted by the doubts which have been thrown on the subject by some of the ablest text-writers upon the American Constitution. It is, Mr. Chief Justice, upon this and upon kindred questions—no matter whether the views I have presented are right or wrong—that I submit that we have the right respectfully to demand at the hands of your Honor a judicial exposition of the meaning of the Constitution. It will, as I said before, be for you, sir, under your sense of duty, under your own construction of the powers that are conferred upon you by the Constitution of our common country—it will be for you, in the discharge of your duty, to decide for yourself whether this respectful request will be answered or not.

Mr. YATES. If the gentleman does not desire to finish his speech to-night, I will move that the Senate, sitting for this trial, adjourn.

Mr. NELSON. It is my business and duty, of course, to be governed and controlled altogether by the pleasure of the Senate. I am free to say that I feel somewhat fatigued, and I would be much obliged to the Senate, if it would not interfere with their duties, for an adjournment at this time; but if they do not choose to do so I will go on. It is my wish to conform exactly to the will of the Senate, whatever it may be.

Mr. YATES. I submit the motion.

The CHIEF JUSTICE. The Senator from Illinois moves that the Senate, sitting as a court of impeachment, adjourn until to-morrow at eleven o'clock.

The motion was agreed to; and the Senate, sitting for the trial of the impeachment, adjourned.

FRIDAY, *April* 24, 1868.

The Chief Justice of the United States took the chair.

The usual proclamation having been made by the Sergeant-at-Arms,

The Managers of the impeachment on the part of the House of Representatives and the counsel for the respondent, except Mr. Stanbery, appeared and took the seats assigned to them respectively.

The members of the House of Representatives, as in Committee of the Whole, preceded by Mr. E. B. WASHBURNE, chairman of that committee, and accompanied by the Speaker and Clerk, appeared, and were conducted to the seats provided for them.

The CHIEF JUSTICE. The Secretary will read the Journal of yesterday's proceedings.

The Journal of yesterday's proceedings of the Senate, sitting for the trial of the impeachment, was read.

The CHIEF JUSTICE. The first business this morning is the order proposed by the Senator from Iowa, [Mr. GRIMES,] changing the hour of meeting. The Clerk will read the order.

The Chief Clerk read as follows:

Ordered, That hereafter the hour for the meeting of the Senate, sitting for the trial of the impeachment of Andrew Johnson, President of the United States, shall be twelve o'clock meridian of each day except Sunday.

Mr. WILSON. Mr. President, I ask for the yeas and nays upon that.

The yeas and nays were ordered; and being taken, resulted—yeas 21, nays 13; as follows:

YEAS—Messrs. Anthony, Davis, Doolittle, Ferry, Fessenden, Fowler, Grimes, Hendricks, Johnson, McCreery, Morgan, Morrill of Vermont, Norton, Patterson of Tennessee, Ramsey, Saulsbury, Trumbull, Van Winkle, Vickers, Willey, and Yates—21.

NAYS—Messrs. Conkling, Conness, Cragin, Edmunds, Harlan, Howe, Pomeroy, Sprague, Stewart, Sumner, Thayer, Tipton, and Wilson—13.

NOT VOTING.—Messrs. Bayard, Buckalew, Cameron, Cattell, Chandler, Cole, Corbett, Dixon, Drake, Frelinghuysen, Henderson, Howard, Morrill of Maine, Morton, Nye, Patterson of New Hampshire, Ross, Sherman, Wade, and Williams—20.

So the order was adopted.

Mr. EDMUNDS. Mr. President, I offer the following order.

The CHIEF JUSTICE. The order proposed by the Senator from Vermont will be read.

The Chief Clerk read as follows:

Ordered, That after the arguments shall be concluded, and when the doors shall be closed for deliberation upon the final question the official reporters of the Senate shall take down the debates upon the final question, to be reported in the proceedings.

Mr. SUMNER. I object.

The CHIEF JUSTICE. The order will lie over if objected to. Mr. Nelson, of counsel for the respondent, will please proceed.

Mr. NELSON. Mr. Chief Justice and Senators, in the progress of my remarks yesterday I alluded to certain opinions expressed by one of the honorable Managers [Mr. WILSON] in a report to which his name is affixed made to the House of Representatives. Lest any misunderstanding should arise from that reference I desire to state that while I shall read a part of the report—that portion of it which I adopt as my argument—I do not consider that there is any inconsistency in the position which the honorable Manager assumed in his report to the House of Representatives and the position which he has assumed here in argument. If I correctly understand the honorable Manager's position, while he insists, as I insist in this case, that you are to look to the common law, and not merely to the law of Parliament, in order to ascertain the meaning of the words "crimes and misdemeanors" in the Constitution, yet he insists that it is competent for Congress to create a crime or misdemeanor under the Constitution by legislation, and that such crime or misdemeanor is an impeachable offense. I hope neither that honorable gentleman nor the Senate will misunderstand me with this explanation when I call attention only to those parts of the argument contained in his report which I rely upon, and because the definitions which he gives are in more appropriate language than any which I can furnish. In his report, at page 60, he says:

"As was very pertinently remarked by Hopkinson on the trial of Chase, 'The power of impeachment is with the House of Representatives, but only for impeachable offenses. They are to proceed against the offense, but not to *create* the offense, and make any act criminal and impeachable at their will and pleasure. What is an offense is a question to be decided by the Constitution and the law, not by the opinion of a single branch of the Legislature, and when the offense thus described by the Constitution or the law has been committed then, and not till then, has the House of Representatives power to impeach the offender.'"

The honorable Manager proceeds:

"A civil officer may be impeached for a high crime. What is a crime? It is such a violation of some known law as will render the offender liable to be prosecuted and punished. Though all willful violations of rights come under the generic name of wrongs, only certain of those made penal are called crimes.'"

In another passage he says:

"All that has been said herein concerning the term 'crimes' may be applied with equal force to the term 'misdemeanors,' as used in the Constitution. The latter term in nowise extends the jurisdiction of the House of Representatives beyond the range of indictable offenses. Indeed, the terms 'crime' and 'misdemeanor' are, in their general sense, synonymous, both being such violations of law as expose the persons committing them to some prescribed punishment; and, although it cannot be claimed that all crimes are misdemeanors, it may be properly said that all misdemeanors are crimes."

Adopting that definition of the honorable Manager, [Mr. WILSON,] the point which I endeavor to make in argument is, that the definition given by the honorable Manager who opened the argument [Mr. BUTLER] is not a correct definition. That opening, as the Senate will remember, is accompanied by a very carefully prepared and elaborate argument on the part of Mr. LAWRENCE, who agrees in the following definition given by the honorable Manager:

"We define, therefore, an impeachable high crime or misdemeanor to be one in its nature or consequences subversive of some fundamental or essential principle of government, or highly prejudicial to the public interest, and this may consist of a violation of the Constitution, of law, of an official oath, or of duty, by an act committed or omitted, or, without violating a positive law, by the abuse of discretionary powers from improper motives or for any improper purpose."

If you go to the law of Parliament for a definition of "treason, bribery, or other crimes and misdemeanors," as I have already said, you will not find it. If you go to the law of Parliament for the purpose of ascertaining what is an impeachable offense, then you go to a law which is not in force in our country at all. Every species of offense which the Parliament chose to treat as such, whether it was declared by statute or not, was the subject-matter of impeachment by the Commons before the House of Lords. Their frame of government is different from ours. Persons were tried in England for very slight and very trivial offenses, and very severe punishments were inflicted in various instances in the progress of English history upon the persons who were supposed to have been guilty of offenses. This process of impeachment is such that we have no very accurate account of it in history, so far as I have been able to examine the authorities upon the subject. It is true, as the gentleman said, that nearly five hundred years ago the subject was introduced in the English Parliament, and that they considered it there and claimed that the House of Lords had jurisdiction over it in consequence of the law of Parliament; but how that law of Parliament arose, whence it originated, neither the House of Lords nor Mr. Burke in his elaborate report and argument in the House of Commons undertook to state. It arose from what they assumed to be usage; and if you go to the parliamentary law in order to determine that usage in this country, then you will be obliged to punish anything as an offense that might be said of any person or of any authority whatever. In Stephen's History of the English Constitution, page 347, he says that—

"The revival of impeachment is a remarkable

event in our constitutional annals. The earliest instance of parliamentary impeachment or of a solemn accusation of any individual by the Commons at the bar of the Lords was that of Lord Latimer, in the year 1376."

Which, as I understood the honorable Manager's argument, is the period to which he refers.

"The latest hitherto was that of the Duke of Suffolk, in 1449."

And, as the honorable Manager told the Senate, he states that this practice of impeachment had for a long time given way to attainder. In the same work Mr. Stephen comments on Floyd's case as a proof of "the disregard which popular assemblies entertain for principles of justice when satiating their reckless appetites for revenge." He says, in describing Floyd's case, "that a few words spoken as to being pleased with the misfortunes of the Elector Palatine and his wife" were the offense which he had committed; and the punishment that was inflicted upon him was to ride from the Fleet to Cheapside without a saddle and holding by the horse's tail, two hours in the pillory, to be branded with the letter K in the forehead, another ride and pillory to be taken in four days, with the words on a paper in his hat showing his offense; that he was to be whipped at the cart's tail from the Fleet to Westminster Hall; that a fine of £5,000 and imprisonment for life at Newgate were imposed upon him.

If there be anything in the argument that you are to look to the parliamentary law for the definition of the phrase "high crimes and misdemeanors," and for the definition of impeachable offenses, then an offense such as was attributed to him, or an offense such as was attributed to other parties afterwards who were tried for making speculations in the public revenue, would be the subject-matter of impeachment in this country; but, as I maintain, this is limited by the Constitution, and you can only look to the common law for the purpose of ascertaining the definition of crimes and misdemeanors. Mr. Story, I know, says in his work upon the Constitution that in one case it was settled in this country that the term "crimes and misdemeanors" did not have the signification which I insist upon; but at the same time in his treatise he asserts that there is a contrariety of opinion on the subject, one set of interpreters of the Constitution holding the doctrine to be one way, and another and a different set holding it to be a different way; and, as I understand him, he does not regard the question as being by any means finally and authoritatively settled. So then I recur to the proposition with which I set out, that in order to ascertain what are impeachable crimes and misdemeanors it is necessary to go to the common law for the definition, and when you go to the common law for the definition nothing is impeachable in this country within the meaning of the Constitution except a crime or misdemeanor known as such at the time when the

Constitution was adopted. In other words, I respectfully maintain that Congress has no power to create a crime or misdemeanor in its nature different from crimes and misdemeanors as known and understood at the time of the adoption of the Constitution.

Feebly and imperfectly as this argument has been presented, I will not undertake to dwell upon it further.

I desire, although it is not exactly in the order which I had prescribed for my remarks, to call the attention of the Senate now to some observations made by the honorable gentleman who addressed the Senate yesterday, [Mr. Manager BOUTWELL,] and in order that there may be no misunderstanding as to the observations to which I desire to call your attention I will read a paragraph from the gentleman's speech of the day before yesterday:

"The President is a man of strong will, of violent passions, of unlimited ambition, with capacity to employ and use timid men, adhesive men, subservient men and corrupt men, as the instruments of his designs. It is the truth of history that he has injured every person with whom he has had confidential relations, and many have escaped ruin only by withdrawing from his society altogether. He has one rule of life: he attempts to use every man of power, capacity, or influence within his reach. Succeeding in his attempts, they are in time, and usually in a short time, utterly ruined. If the considerate flee from him, if the brave and patriotic resist his schemes or expose his plans, he attacks them with all the enginery and patronage of his office and pursues them with all the violence of his personal hatred. He attacks to destroy all who will not become his instruments, and all who become his instruments are destroyed in the use. He spares no one."

The particular sentence to which I desire to call your attention is in the close of that paragraph:

"Already this purpose of his life is illustrated in the treatment of a gentleman who was of counsel for the respondent, but who has never appeared in his behalf."

It is to me, Senators, a source of much embarrassment how to speak in reply to the accusation which has thus been preferred against the President of the United States. The honorable Manager treats him as if he were a political leper, and as if his very touch would communicate contagion, and as if almost the very sight of him would produce death. But I respectfully insist that upon a statement of facts, which I will make to you in a moment, and which I deem to be called for by the accusation which he has made in reference to Judge Black, it will appear that injustice has been done, no doubt unintentionally, by the honorable Manager, in the remarks which he has made. I regret that this topic has been introduced here; but, as it is brought forward, I must meet it. I am not aware that I ever saw Judge Black in my life until I met him in consultation in the President's council chamber. In the few interviews which we had there our intercourse, though brief, was pleasant and agreeable; and it is with a feeling of embarrassment that, under those circumstances, I deem it necessary to say anything upon this subject at all. In order that you may understand what I have to say about it I desire to refer the Senate to a brief statement which I have prepared on account of the delicacy of the subject; and, although I have not had time to write it out as I would have desired to do, it will be sufficient to enable you to comprehend the facts which I am about to state. You will understand, Senators, that I do not purport to give a full history of what I may call the Alta Vela case, as to which a report was made to the Senate by the Secretary of State upon your call. A mere outline of the case will be sufficient to explain what I have to say in reference to Judge Black.

Under the guano act of 1856, William T. Kendall on the one side, and Patterson and Marguiendo on the other, filed claims in the Secretary of State's office to the island which is claimed by the Government of St. Domingo. (Report, pp. 2, 3.)

On the 17th of June, 1867, the examiner of claims submitted a report adverse to the claim for damages against the Dominican Government. On the 22d of July, 1867, Mr. Black addressed a letter to the President, (page 10,) and another on the 7th August, 1867. On page 13 it is said that Patterson and Marguiendo acquiesce in the decision. On page 13 it is shown that other parties are in adverse possession. On page 15 it is asserted that the contest is between citizens of the United States, and can be settled in the courts of the United States. The contest now seems to be between Patterson and Marguiendo and Thomas B. Webster & Co. (Report, p. 15.)

On the 14th December, 1859, Judge Black, as Attorney General, rejected the claim of W. J. Kendall to an island in the Caribbean sea, called Cayo Verde, (page 24,) and Mr. Seward seems to regard the two cases as resting on the same principle in his report of 17th of January, 1867.

On the 22d July, 1867, Judge Black addressed a letter to the President inclosing a brief, (page 53.) On the 7th August, 1867, he addressed another communication to the President, (page 55.) On the 7th February, 1868, an elaborate and able communication was sent to the President, signed J. W. Shaffer, attorney for Patterson & Marguiendo, and Black, Lamon & Co., of counsel, in which they criticised with severity the report of Mr. Seward and asked the President to review his decision. (Report, p. 65.)

These citations are made from Executive Document No. 39, Fortieth Congress, second session.

According to the best information I can obtain I state that *on the 9th March*, 1868, General BENJAMIN F. BUTLER addressed a letter to J. W. Shaffer, in which he stated that he was "clearly of opinion that, under the claim of the United States, its citizens have the exclusive right to take guano there," and that he had never been able to understand why the

Executive did not long since assert the rights of the Government and sustain the rightful claims of its citizens to the possession of the island *in the most forcible manner* consistent with the dignity and honor of the nation.

This letter was concurred in and approved of by JOHN A. LOGAN, J. A. GARFIELD, W. H. KOONTZ, J. K. MOORHEAD, THADDEUS STEVENS, J. G. BLAINE, and JOHN A. BINGHAM, on the same day, 9th March, 1868.

The letter expressing the opinion of Generals BUTLER, LOGAN, and GARFIELD was placed in the hands of the President by Chauncey F. Black, who, on the 16th March, 1868, addressed a letter to him in which he inclosed a copy of the same with the concurrence of THADDEUS STEVENS, JOHN A. BINGHAM, J. G. BLAINE, J. K. MOORHEAD, and WILLIAM H. KOONTZ.

After the date of this letter, and while Judge Black was the counsel of the respondent in this cause, he had an interview with the President, in which he urged immediate action on his part and the sending an armed vessel to take possession of the island; and because the President refused to do so Judge Black, on the 19th March, 1868, declined to appear further as his counsel in this case.

Such are the facts in regard to the withdrawal of Judge Black, according to the best information I can obtain. So far as the President is concerned, "the head and front of his offending hath this extent, no more."

It is not necessary to my purpose that I should censure Judge Black or make any reflection upon or imputation against any of the honorable Managers.

The island of Alta Vela, or the claim for damages, is said to amount in value to more than a million dollars, and it is quite likely that an extensive speculation is on foot. I have no reason to charge that any of the Managers are engaged in it, and presume that the letters were signed, as such communications are often signed by members of Congress, through the importunity of friends.

Judge Black no doubt thought it was his duty to other clients to press this claim; but how did the President view it?

Senators, I ask you for a moment to put yourself in the place of the President of the United States, and as this is made a matter of railing accusation against him, to consider how the President of the United States felt it. I am willing that the facts in this case shall be spread not only before the Senate, but before the whole country, and that his enemies shall be the judges of the purity of his conduct and motives in regard to it.

There are two or three facts to which I desire to call the attention of the Senate and the country in connection with these recommendations. They are, first, that they were all gotten up after this impeachment proceeding was commenced against the President of the United States. Keep the dates in mind, and you will see that such is the fact. Every one of them was gotten up after this impeachment proceeding was commenced against him.

Another strong and powerful fact to be noticed in vindication of the President of the United States, in reference to this case which has been so strongly preferred against him, is that while I have not made, and will not make, any imputation whatever upon the honorable Managers in the cause, these recommendations were signed by four of the honorable gentlemen to whom the House of Representatives have intrusted the duty of managing this great impeachment against him.

Now, let me present to you in my plain language a single idea, Senators, in regard to this matter. If the President went to war with a weak and feeble Power to gain the island, it would seem that he had done so in fear of the Managers and in the fear of losing the highly valued services of Judge Black. If he failed to do the thing which he was called upon to do by his eminent and distinguished counsel, there was danger that he would exasperate Judge Black and his friends, and their influence would be turned against him on the trial. It was under these delicate circumstances that this petition was presented to the President of the United States. He was between Scylla and Charybdis. In forming his own determination, no matter which way it might be formed, his motives might be impugned and his integrity might be assailed; but they know little of the President of the United States, far less than your humble speaker knows, who imagine that they can force or drive or compel him, under any imaginable state of circumstances, to do what he believes to be wrong. He is a man of peculiar temperament and disposition. By careful management and proper manipulation he may, perhaps, be gently led; but it is a pretty difficult thing to do that. But with his temperament and his disposition, no man, no power under the heavens can compel him to go one inch beyond what he believes to be right; and although he knew that in rejecting this claim in the peculiar situation in which he was placed he might raise up enemies against him, although he was well aware that a powerful influence might be brought to bear against him in this trial, and that it would be trumpeted abroad from one end of the Union to the other that Judge Black had become disgusted with his cause and dissatisfied with it, and had deserted it and abandoned it on account of his full conviction of his guilt—although the President, I say, knew this, and although he knew that a black cloud would be raised against him, yet his feeling was that

"Although that cloud were thunder's worst,
And charged to crush him—let it burst."

And he acted like a noble-hearted man, as he is; he acted like a sentinel placed, if I may so express myself, upon the watch-tower of the Constitution, faithful to the rights of the people who had exalted him to that lofty position; unmindful of self, regardless of consequences, he was determined not to do an act which he believed to be wrong. He was determined not to employ the whole power of the United States in a war against a little Power down here that had no capacity of resistance. He was determined not, under these painful and difficult circumstances, to be used as an instrument in the hands of anybody, or any set of men under heaven, to carry on a speculation which he believed might be carried on with dishonor to the Government or with disgrace to himself if he consented to be concerned in it.

And I ask you, Senators, to weigh his conduct; let the impartial judgment of the world look this statement of facts in the face and pronounce upon it as you have to pronounce upon this impeachment; and when you come, in the cool moments of calm deliberation, to look over the President's conduct and these articles of impeachment that are preferred against him, I think you will find that, like the grave charge which was presented by the honorable Manager the day before yesterday, these charges vanish away,

"And, like the baseless fabric of a vision,
Leave not a rack behind."

Such, I trust, Senators, will be the result; such, I trust, will be the conclusion of this trial; and, although the President is now passing through the fiery furnace, although now every act and every motive of his public life is being investigated, yet he fears it not. He challenges the utmost scrutiny; he challenges the strongest investigation that may be made into his conduct; and while, as I said yesterday, he hurls no defiance at the Senate, and does not authorize me to say one word that will be offensive to his judges, yet he defies his enemies now as he has always defied them; and he appeals to the purity and honesty of his own motives and of his own principles to shield him against this charge, as he does against every other of the charges that have been preferred. No, Senators, instead of this being a matter of accusation against the President of the United States, in the view which I entertain of it, and in the view which I think every honorable and high-minded man will entertain of it, it will elevate him a head and shoulders taller than he ever stood before in the estimation of his friends; and it will be regarded as one of the proudest and noblest acts of his life that he could not be coaxed or driven to do what he believed to be a wrong in the name of the Government of the United States. This is preferred here as if the President had done some wrong to Judge Black. What wrong did he do? How did any pollution result from Judge Black's contact with him as counsel? Did he discard Judge Black and tell him he did not want him to appear as his counsel any more in the cause? No, sir; it was upon his own voluntary motion that he withdrew from the case. If the President of the United States has done him any injury the

President knows it not; his counsel know it not; and I leave it to the judgment of the world to determine upon this statement how much of justice there is in the accusation which was so strongly made against him.

Senators, allow me to call your attention to another paragraph in the speech of the honorable Manager who last addressed you. It is not my purpose or intention to undertake the duty at present of answering at length that able and carefully-prepared argument which the honorable Manager has made. I must leave the notice of it to those who are to follow me in the argument on the side of the President. But there is another paragraph which reads in this language:

"Having indulged his Cabinet in such freedom of opinion when he consulted them in reference to the constitutionality of the bill, and having covered himself and them with public odium by its announcement, he now vaunts their opinions, extorted by power and given in subserviency, that the law itself may be violated with impunity."

You remember how elegantly the honorable gentleman introduced the dialogue between Hamlet and Polonius, when speaking upon this subject, and you may remember that he goes on and says:

"This, says the President, is the exercise of my constitutional right to the opinion of my Cabinet. I, says the President, am responsible for my Cabinet. Yes, the President is responsible for the opinions and conduct of men who give such advice as is demanded, and give it in fear and trembling lest they be at once deprived of their places. This is the President's idea of a Cabinet, but it is an idea not in harmony with the theory of the Constitution."

And in another place, I believe, the gentleman spoke of the members of the Cabinet being serfs:

"It was the advice of serfs to their lord, of servants to their master, of slaves to their owner."

I desire, Senators, to refresh your recollection by reading a single paragraph from the message of the President of the United States which was put in evidence upon the side of the prosecution, the famous message dated December 12, 1867; and lest I should forget to present the idea to your consideration, I wish to state now, in reference to this message, as well as in reference to all other documents signed by the President of the United States which they have introduced upon the other side as evidence against him, that if any rule of law is to obtain in this high and honorable tribunal, when they put these documents in evidence before the Senate they make them, so to speak, their witnesses, and they cannot discredit them. They have not undertaken to discredit them at all. When we offered to introduce the members of the Cabinet as witnesses to prove certain statements which were made by the President in these messages, the Senate refused to do so, and while at the moment I regretted the decision of the Senate, yet upon sober second thought I was inclined to the opinion that the Senate had probably settled the question exactly right, that it was unnecessary for us to introduce the members of the Cabinet, unnecessary for us to introduce their testimony to sustain these statements, when these statements are not impugned in the slightest degree by any evidence which is offered by the other side. What does the President say in that message? I read from page 138 of the record of the trial:

"This was not the first occasion in which Mr. Stanton, in discharge of a public duty, was called upon to consider the provisions of that law. That tenure-of-office law did not pass without notice. Like other acts, it was sent to the President for approval. As is my custom, I submitted its consideration to my Cabinet for their advice upon the question whether I should approve it or not. It was a grave question of constitutional law, in which I would of course rely most upon the opinion of the Attorney General and of Mr. Stanton, who had once been Attorney General."

Now, you see, to use the elegant word of the honorable Manager on the other side, he calls these serfs around him to see what these serfs will say in reference to the constitutionality of the law which he has under consideration:

"Every member of my Cabinet advised me that the proposed law was unconstitutional. All spoke without doubt or reservation; but Mr. Stanton's condemnation of the law was the most elaborate and emphatic. He referred to the constitutional provisions, the debates in Congress, especially to the speech of Mr. Buchanan when a Senator, to the decisions of the Supreme Court, and to the usage from the beginning of the Government through every successive Administration, all concurring to establish the right of removal as vested by the Constitution in the President. To all these he added the weight of his own deliberate judgment, and advised me that it was my duty to defend the power of the President from usurpation, and to veto the law."

There is in the "plain, unvarnished" statement of the President of the United States, uncontradicted by any witnesses called here, a statement that we offered to verify by the introduction of the members of the Cabinet as witnesses. We offered to prove every word, at least the substance of every word that is contained in that paragraph of the message, and had the members of the Cabinet here, and were ready and willing to put them upon oath; but their testimony was not admitted; and so, in view of the two things, first that this message was offered in evidence upon the side of the prosecution, and second that we offered to prove the truth of the statements contained here, I assume as an indisputable fact in the case that Mr. Stanton, about whom the whole world seems to be set on fire now, did give to the President the advice that this civil-tenure bill, about which such a great cry has been raised in the land, was an unconstitutional law, and that it was his duty to veto it. While I never saw Mr. Stanton to my knowledge, and have no sort of personal acquaintance with him, I think that if I were in his place I should exclaim as somebody exclaimed—I forget who it was, but I know these honorable Senators will remember it a great deal better than I do—"Save me from my friends, and I will take care of my enemies." I think if ever a man on the face of the earth had reason to exclaim "Save me from my friends," Mr. Stanton has reason to exclaim "Save me from the description which is given here of a Cabinet officer, and of the mean, low, debasing, mercenary motive by which a Cabinet officer is supposed to act." But this is a sort of family quarrel, and I shall not undertake to interfere in it.

One other thing in this connection about Mr. Stanton. Mr. Stanton as one of the President's Cabinet advised him to veto the civil tenure-of-office bill; but before Mr. Johnson became President Mr. Stanton placed on record an opinion which I think it proper for me to read under existing circumstances; and it is an opinion which does not stand in the category of the action of Mr. Stanton as one of the members of President Johnson's Cabinet. On the 3d of March, 1865, Mr. Stanton addressed the following letter to "His Excellency Andrew Johnson, Vice President-elect:"

WAR DEPARTMENT,
WASHINGTON CITY, *March* 3, 1865.

SIR: This Department has accepted your resignation as brigadier general and military governor of Tennessee.

Permit me on this occasion to render to you the thanks of this Department for your patriotic and able services during the eventful period through which you have exercised the high trusts committed to your charge.

In one of the darkest hours of the great struggle for national existence against rebellious foes the Government called you from the Senate, and from the comparatively safe and easy duties of civil life, to place you in the front of the enemy, and in a position of personal toil and danger perhaps more hazardous than was encountered by any other citizen or military officer of the United States.

With patriotic promptness you assumed the post, and maintained it under circumstances of unparalleled trial, until recent events have brought safety and deliverance to your State and to the integrity of that constitutional Union for which you so long and so gallantly periled all that is dear to man on earth.

That you may be spared to enjoy the new honors and perform the high duties to which you have been called by the people of the United States is the sincere wish of one who, in every official and personal relation, has found you worthy of the confidence of the Government and the honor and esteem of your fellow-citizens.   EDWIN M. STANTON,
Secretary of War.
His Excellency ANDREW JOHNSON,
Vice President-elect.

Mr. Chief Justice and Senators, but three short years have elapsed since that letter of indorsement was written by Mr. Secretary Stanton to the present President of the United States; and I read it for a twofold purpose: first, to show that when I spoke to you yesterday in regard to the services of the President of the United States in behalf of the Union I did speak the words of truth and soberness, and I show you, out of the mouth of Mr. Stanton himself, that he deserved all the encomiums which I endeavored to pass upon him in the progress of my remarks yesterday for his faithful devotion to the Union and for having exposed himself in the hour of danger in its behalf; and, second, to show that in three short years it is scarcely possible, in the nature of things, that the President of the United States should be so suddenly changed as they insist he is in behalf of the prosecution. It is hardly conceivable that in a period of three

short years a gentleman of whom the Secretary of War spoke in the highest terms of commendation which I have read should become the monster, the tyrant, the usurper, the wicked man that he is represented to be upon the other side. Mr. Stanton runs through this whole trial; his name is almost everywhere. Mr. Stanton's name is, at least, substantially embodied in the charges that are contained in these articles. Here you have Mr. Stanton in two positions indorsing the President of the United States: first, when he ceased to hold the office of military governor of Tennessee and was elevated to the high position of Vice President-elect, you have him saying—

"That you may be spared to enjoy the new honors and perform the high duties to which you have been called by the people of the United States is the sincere wish of one who in every official and personal relation has found you worthy of the confidence of the Government and the honor and esteem of your fellow-citizens."

That is Mr. Stanton's indorsement in 1865; and then you have Mr. Stanton's act as one of the President's advisers when the civil tenure bill was passed in February, 1867. You have him then indorsing the action of the President in both forms up to the time that the civil tenure bill was passed; and if a difference of opinion afterward grew up between them, if unkind feelings existed between them, if there was a loss of confidence on the part of the President, and if their relations toward each became less harmonious than they had been before, all that I have to say about it is that it furnishes no ground of impeachment that should in the slightest degree affect his character or his motives.

There is one other thing, before I come to the consideration in detail of the various articles of impeachment, that I desire, Senators, to call your attention to, and that is to this same proceeding which was had in the House of Representatives upon the subject of impeachment. I know not how it has struck the minds of Senators; I know not how it has impressed the minds of the people of the United States; but one of the strangest anomalies in the political history of our Government is that these articles of impeachment should have been gotten up against the President of the United States after twelve months' examination, and that some of the leading charges against him, of which I will speak after awhile, should be founded upon acts which were done in reference to the Thirty-Ninth Congress. If the President of the United States is the guilty culprit that they represent him to be on the other side, if he has defamed and slandered Congress, if he has done acts which are worthy of impeachment, is it not passing strange that the Thirty-Ninth Congress took no notice of them, and that after that Congress is defunct, after it has passed out of existence, after its name and its memory have gone into history, another Congress should take up offenses against that Congress and make them matter of grave accusation against the President of the United States? I will read one of the charges investigated by that Congress. This is rather by anticipation and a little out of the order that I had designed; but as I have the book before me I will read it now. One of the grounds of accusation then presented against him by the committee in the House of Representatives—and they had seventeen of them—the last of the file was this:

"That he has been guilty of acts calculated, if not intended, to subvert the Government of the United States, by denying that the Thirty-Ninth Congress was a constitutional body, and fostering a spirit of disaffection and disobedience to the law and rebellion against its authority, by endeavoring, in public speeches, to bring it into odium and contempt."

I have in my possession the actual vote which was taken in the House of Representatives upon the subject. My memory may fail me; I may have been misinformed about it; but I have been informed and believe, and you know much better than I do how the fact is, that the House of Representatives, by a considerable majority, refused to entertain these accusations as ground of impeachment against the President of the United States by a solemn vote. And if there were any law in this tribunal (and the gentlemen say there is not unless it be that mysterious and wonderful law of Parliament which they rely upon, and which after all the definitions they give to it amounts at last to no law at all) or any application by analogy of the principles of law, I would avail myself of the doctrine of estoppel which was so learnedly insisted upon by one of the honorable Managers on the other side, and I would insist, with all due deference and respect, that the House of Representatives, after having voted down this charge that the President of the United States had slandered and maligned the Thirty-Ninth Congress, was estopped from making any accusation of that kind against the President now.

But I hope I may say without offense, and before proceeding to notice some of the charges more specifically that have been preferred here, that I think the Senate of the United States, sitting as a judicial tribunal, can look to the circumstances under which these charges are preferred without any disrespect whatever to the House of Representatives; and when you come to look at the circumstances under which these charges were preferred, after the President of the United States had been virtually acquitted in the House of Representatives, you have at least evidence that it was done without any great amount of deliberation in the House, possibly under the influence of that excitement which legislative assemblies as well as individuals are liable to; and that very circumstance, without imputing any wrong or improper motive to the House of Representatives, is one to which I maintain that this Senate, this assembly of grave and reverend seniors, who are impaneled, as it were, here under the Constitution to try these articles of impeachment, may

look, and may look with propriety—for they do not come before you, Senators, like those articles which were preferred against Warren Hastings in England, and which were the subject of long and earnest debate in the House of Commons before they were presented. They were prepared in hot haste after the President had removed Mr. Stanton; they were passed upon very brief debate in the House of Representatives, and thus they come here. If the House has acted, as I hope it has, hastily, Senators, it is your province and your duty, as I maintain most respectfully, to look to that fact, and not to give the same importance to accusations made under such circumstances as you would to those which were made under more careful deliberation, and especially when the House of Representatives, but a very short time before, had acquitted the President of a large number of the charges which were preferred against him in the able and ingenious report presented by its Judiciary Committee. Surely, under these circumstances, it will be no disparagement of the House, it will be no disparagement to you to look to the fact that these charges were hastily presented, and if, upon sober review here, you should believe that these charges come to you in at least a questionable shape, so far as the swift circumstances under which they were adopted are concerned, it will be no reflection upon the House any more than it would upon an individual. I trust that, as the House of Representatives is composed of men, at least men of flesh and blood like yourselves, it will be no disparagement to them to say that even a House of Representatives, composed of honorable men, acting under the impulses of feeling, and acting hastily and without any great amount of deliberation, acting, as it were, in passion, may do a thing which, upon "sober second thought," they would not do over again. We all know human nature well enough, at least in our own persons and in our own characters, to know that when we act in passion, when we act in haste, when we act in excitement, we are apt to do things which, upon reflection, we have reason to regret; and those actions, while they are in a great measure excusable, on account of the haste and passion in which they are committed, are yet actions which do not command the same power and influence in society that they would do if they were the result of grave and careful and deliberate and mature consideration.

Now, Senators, I shall have to call your attention to the articles of impeachment somewhat in detail; and though it is rather a disagreeable duty to tread this mill-horse round, to go to these articles of impeachment and take them up one by one and make brief comments on them, as it is my purpose to do; though I know that the subject is becoming stale and weary, not only to the Senate, but to those who are gathered around to hear this investigation; yet I cannot, in accordance with my sense of duty in this case, take my seat until I offer some considerations to the Senate on each one of the articles of impeachment. Although it must necessarily be to some extent a tedious business, yet I do so because, Senators, if you follow the precedents which we have had in other cases, you will be required to vote upon each one of the articles of impeachment separately, and you will have to form your judgment and opinion upon each in a separate way.

In regard to the first article of impeachment it may not be out of place to look to that article as it is presented, and to state very briefly the article itself and the answer to it. I do not propose to go through all the verbiage of that article, nor to repeat in detail all the facts stated in the answer; but the article charges in substance that on the 21st of February, 1868, the President unlawfully issued an order for the removal of Edwin M. Stanton, without saying anything in this part of the article about the Senate being or not being in session. It alleges that on the 12th of August, 1867, during the recess of the Senate, he suspended Mr. Stanton; that on the 12th of December, 1867, and within twenty days after the meeting of the Senate, he reported the suspension and his reasons, and that the Senate refused to concur in the suspension; that Stanton, by virtue of the act "regulating the tenure of certain civil offices," forthwith resumed the office; and that on the 21st of February, 1868, the President issued the order of removal to Stanton, and that this was done, first, in violation of the "act regulating the tenure of certain civil offices," passed March 2, 1867; and second, in violation of the Constitution, and without the consent of the Senate, then in session; and that it was a high misdemeanor in office.

Without going into all the details the answer substantially states that Mr. Stanton was appointed Secretary during pleasure by Mr. Lincoln on the 15th of January, 1862; that the office was created by the act passed on the 7th of August, 1789; that Stanton became one of the advisers of the President and subject to his general control; that the respondent succeeded to the Presidency on the 15th of April, 1865, and Mr. Stanton continued to hold the office; that the respondent being satisfied that he could not let Mr. Stanton continue in office without detriment to the public interest he decided to suspend him on the 5th of August, 1867. The invitation to Mr. Stanton to resign his office is set out in the answer; also his reply declining to do so. It is further stated that the respondent required and acted upon the opinion as to the civil tenure-of-office act of each principal officer of the Executive Departments; that this action was made known to the Senate on the 2d of March, 1867; that although he believed the tenure-of-office act was void the respondent, in his capacity as President, formed the opinion that Stanton's case was in fact by the first section; that notwithstanding respondent's opinion on that subject, he was anxious that Stanton's removal should be acquiesced in by the Senate or that the question should be judicially determined; that the right of suspension is provided for by the tenure-of-office law in the second section, and that Mr. Stanton was not suspended until the next meeting or action of the Senate, but indefinitely and at the President's pleasure; that a vacancy thus existing General Thomas was appointed *ad interim* under the act of 13th February, 1795; that the purpose to obtain a judicial decision was made known at or near the date of this order; that, not intending to abandon his rights as President, but anxious to avoid any question, the respondent did send his message to the Senate on the 12th of December, 1867; that his hopes not being realized, the respondent, in order to raise the question for judicial decision, and to that end only, issued the order removing Stanton and appointing Thomas *ad interim* on the 21st of February, 1868. There is besides an answer to each specific allegation.

Now, Senators, allow me to present one thought before entering upon the consideration of this first article, which, as I conceive, is applicable to all the articles; indeed, much of what we have to say upon the first article applies to all the other articles, and it involves to some extent a necessary repetition to consider them in detail, but I shall endeavor, as far as I can possibly do so, to avoid such repetition.

All the articles of impeachment, or nearly all of them, charge a removal. One of the Managers spoke a good deal, and very much to the purpose, upon the subject of technical law. I did not understand the gentleman as making any objection to it. He regarded it as a proper means of enforcing the rights of parties and as a legitimate portion of legal science. Well, although I know that technical rules are not to be observed in this Senate, if you follow the precedents of trials of impeachment which we have already had in the United States, and especially if you follow the decisions in the British Parliament, yet there ought to be something at least substantial in the articles that are preferred against a man. Now, what is it that is provided for by the civil-tenure bill? Before I come to consider that bill at all in its details, let me ask what is provided for there? It is the removal of a person; and that is the thing which is charged in each one of what I may, for want of a better word, call the counts of this indictment, each one of the articles that are preferred here. Senators, if you follow the law and the rules of law that have been adopted in other cases, if at any rate you look to them as being a guide to some extent, although not binding and obligatory to all intents and purposes as judicial decisions, what is a familiar rule of law? There is not a judge or a lawyer in this Senate who does not know that in every law-book which has been written in two hundred years a distinction is taken between a crime and an attempt to commit a crime. The distinction is just as broad and as wide as Pennsylvania avenue. According to statutory regulations almost everywhere, and even according to the common law, murder is one thing, an attempt to commit murder is another and a different thing. Burglary is one thing; an attempt to commit that offense is another and a different thing.

Now, I ask, and I ask in all earnestness, of this Senate as lawyers and judges, when these articles of impeachment charge the President with the removal of Mr. Stanton. is it not a solecism in language that they should ask this Senate on their oaths to say that the President of the United States is guilty of a violation of the civil-tenure bill, or guilty of either of the offenses that are charged here? That there was an attempt to remove there is no sort of question; but if the doctrine contended for by the learned Managers be the true doctrine, if this civil-tenure bill be a constitutional law, as they insist it is, if the President has no power to remove except on the advice and consent of the Senate of the United States, then, Senators, I ask you how is it that he can be found guilty of removing Mr. Stanton from office, taking the premises of the honorable gentlemen to be correct, when there was no removal at all? If their doctrine be the true doctrine, there was no removal from office at all; you do not bring it within the civil-tenure bill unless you have a case of removal, and even under the civil-tenure bill it is not a case of removal; but if either construction be the true one it is a case of an attempt to remove a person from office; sq that it seems to me it is utterly impossible for the honorable Managers to escape the dilemma in which the nature of their accusation places them.

Upon the first article, Mr. Chief Justice and Senators, I desire to maintain briefly three propositions.

First. That the tenure-of-office bill is unconstitutional and void. Gentlemen have intimated a doubt whether the Senate ought to hear any argument upon that subject, but for the reasons indicated yesterday that a court at *nisi prius* would hear an argument on a rule for a new trial, or that a chancery court will allow a bill of review on a petition for a rehearing, while I do not intend to argue the question at any great length, I respectfully ask the Senate to hear what we have to say on this subject, as it is material and important to our defense.

Second. That if the civil-tenure bill is not constitutional, it does not embrace such a case as the removal of Mr. Stanton.

Third. That if both these propositions are erroneous, the President acted from laudable and honest motives, and is not, therefore, guilty of any crime or misdemeanor.

Upon the first proposition as to the unconstitutionality of the civil-tenure act, as it has not been done already in behalf of the President of the United States, I feel myself constrained to remind you of certain things which occurred in the debate of 1789. Although I know they are familiar probably to every Senator I address, yet I regard these things as material and important to our defense, and at the expense of telling "a thrice-told tale," and of wearying the patience of the honorable Senate, I must ask the privilege of presenting as briefly as I can the views which I entertain upon that subject.

In the House debate which occurred on the 16th of June, 1789, on the bill to establish the Department of Foreign Affairs, Mr. White moved to strike out the words "to be removable from office by the President of the United States." He advocated this because the Senate had the joint power of appointment. His views were sustained, as you recollect, in that argument by Messrs. Smith of South Carolina, Huntington, White, Sherman, Page, Jackson, Gerry, and Livermore, and were opposed by Messrs. Vining, Madison, Boudinot, and Ames, as is seen in Gales & Seaton's Debates in Congress, old series, volume one, page 473 to 608. Mr. Madison said in that debate:

"It is evidently the intention of the Constitution that the first magistrate should be responsible for the executive department; so far, therefore, as we do not make the officers who are to aid him in the duties of that department responsible to him, he is not responsible to his country."

He placed the discussion mainly on the constitutional provision that—

"The executive power shall be vested in the President."—*Ibid.,* 481.

Mr. Sedgwick said :

"If expediency is at all to be considered, gentlemen will perceive that this man is as much an instrument in the hands of the President as the pen is the instrument of the Secretary in corresponding with foreign courts. If, then, the Secretary of Foreign Affairs is the mere instrument of the President, one would suppose, on the principle of expediency, this officer should be dependent upon him. It would seem incongruous and absurd that an officer, who, in the reason and nature of things, is dependent on his principal and appointed merely to execute such business as is committed to the charge of his superior, (for the business, I contend, is committed solely to his charge) I say it would be absurd, in the highest degree, to continue such person in office contrary to the will of the President, who is responsible that the business be conducted with propriety and for the general interests of the nation."—1 *Debates in Congress, old series,* 542.

In that same debate Mr. Sedgwick seems to have anticipated just such a state of affairs as existed between the President and Mr. Stanton. A part of Mr. Sedgwick's remarks is copied in one of the President's messages to Congress; but I desire to read the whole paragraph from which the President in his message took the extract that was submitted to Congress. He discussed the subject in an admirable and unanswerable manner. And when you keep it in mind, as has been, I believe, already stated in argument, that this debate was had soon after the adoption of the Constitution, that several gentlemen who had participated in the formation of the Constitution were members of Congress, and among them Mr. Madison, one of the ablest writers who ever wrote upon that subject, not even excepting Alexander Hamilton himself; when you take it into consideration that this discussion was at that early period and by persons who were concerned in the formation of the Constitution itself, the opinions which they expressed are deserving of the very highest consideration. And if there be anything in the doctrine of the law which is applied to every other case; if there be anything in the idea that when a decision upon a legal question is once made that decision should stand; if there be anything in the doctrine of *stare decisis*, then, Senators, I maintain that an opinion which so far as I know anything of our history as a Government has never been seriously controverted at any time except during the administration of Jackson, and the decision of which at that time was in favor of the view that we entertain now, is to be considered as entitled to respect. If an opinion that was acquiesced in for nearly eighty years is not an authority to a man for doing an act, then I can conceive of nothing that is sufficient authority.

If, according to the English law, a man would be protected in an action as to real property by sixty years' possession, if according to the statute law of the State in which I reside seven years' adverse possession under a color of title would give him an absolute title to his tract of land, if these healing statutes which have been passed from time to time, both in England and in our own country, and which are intended for the repose of society to secure titles to property, are administered every day, as they are, I presume, in all the courts of the United States, why may we not argue, and argue with propriety before the American Senate, that when a question was settled eighty years ago, and when the decision was never controverted until the present time except on the occasion to which I have referred, the conclusion at which Congress then arrived is upon principle binding and obligatory upon this Senate, and that you should follow it upon the same principle that the judges are in the habit of following judicial determinations in regard to the rights of property that have been long acquiesced in and have become rules of law.

If Mr. Sedgwick had been a prophet, if he had been Daniel, or Isaiah, or Jeremiah, or any one of the old prophets, and had undertaken to describe the difference between the President of the United States and Mr. Stanton, he could not have done it better than he has done in the language which I am about to read to you:

"The President is made responsible, and shall he not judge of the talents, ability, and integrity of his instruments? Will you depend on a man who has imposed upon the President and continue him in office when he is evidently disqualified unless he can be removed by impeachment? If this idea should prevail—which God forbid—what would be the result? Suppose, even, that he should be removable by and with the advice and consent of the Senate, what a wretched situation might not our public councils be involved in? Suppose the President has a Secretary in whom he discovers a great degree of ignorance, or a total incapacity to conduct the business he has assigned him; *suppose him inimical to the President*"—

There Mr. Stanton looms right up and he is the very man that this political prophet had in his mind when he was making this argument before the House of Representatives:

"Or suppose any of the great variety of cases which would be good cause for removal, and impress the propriety of such a measure strongly on the mind of the President, *without any other evidence than what exists in his own ideas* from a contemplation of the man's conduct and character, day by day, what, let me ask, is to be the consequence if the Senate are to be applied to? If they are to do anything in this business, I presume they are to deliberate, because they are to advise and consent. *If they are to deliberate, you put them between the officer and the President*"—

Just as the Managers of the impeachment and the impeachment itself are attempting to do in this case:

"They are, then, to inquire into the causes of removal; the President must produce his testimony. How is the question to be investigated? Because, I presume, there must be some rational rule for conducting this business? Is the President to be sworn to declare the whole truth and to bring forward facts; or are they to admit suspicion as testimony; or, is the word of the President to be taken at all events? If so, this check is not of the least efficacy in nature."

And then Mr. Sedgwick goes on with this paragraph, which is quoted in the message to which I have referred:

"But, if proof be necessary, what is then the consequence? Why, in nine cases out of ten, where the case is very clear to the mind of the President that the man ought to be removed, the effect cannot be produced, because it is absolutely impossible to produce the necessary evidence. Are the Senate to proceed without evidence? Some gentlemen contend not. Then the object will be lost. *Shall a man, under these circumstances, be saddled upon the President,* who has been appointed for no other purpose but to aid the President in performing certain duties? Shall he be continued, I ask again, against the will of the President? If he is, where is the responsibility? Are you to look for it in the President, who has no control over the officer, no power to remove him if he acts unfeelingly or unfaithfully? Without you make him responsible, you weaken and destroy the strength and beauty of your system. What is to be done in cases which can only be known from a long acquaintance with the conduct of an officer?"

Never did more sensible remarks proceed from the lips of mortal man than the observations which I have read in your hearing, Senators, and which are just as descriptive as it is possible for language to be of the circumstances under which the removal of Mr. Stanton occurred. This is extracted from the same authority, 1 Debates in Congress, old series, page 543.

Now, I ask your special attention to the next step. Mr. Benson, of New York, moved to amend by inserting in place of the words "to be removable from office by the President of the United States" the words "that the chief clerk, whenever the said principal officer shall be removed from office by the President of the United States, as in any other case of vacancy, shall, during such vacancy, have the custody and charge of all records, books, and papers."

This was carried by a vote of yeas 30, nays 18. (1 Debates, old series, 601, 602, 603.)

Mr. Benson now moved (page 604) to strike out of the first clause the words "to be removable by the President;" which was carried—yeas 31, nays 19.

The honorable Manager who opened the cause made an argument, as I remember—I shall not take time to turn to it—that this debate occurred in Committee of the Whole, and that what transpired in the House is not shown in any report of the debates. If that be so, does it in the slightest degree affect the force and validity of the argument itself? Is it not to be presumed that the very same men who had adopted this principle in Committee of the Whole would, when they came to act in the House proper, vote under the same views which they had expressed in committee?

Mr. Benson said that his objection to the clause arose from an idea that the power of removal by the President hereafter might appear to be exercised by a legislative grant only, and consequently be subjected to legislative instability, when he was well satisfied in his own mind it was fixed by a fair legislative construction of the Constitution. (Ibid., 603.)

Mr. Madison's reasons for sustaining the motion to strike out were, "First, altering the mode of expression tends to give satisfaction to those gentlemen who think it not an object of legislative discretion; and second, because the amendment already agreed to fully contains the sense of this House upon the doctrine of the Constitution, and therefore the words are unnecessary as they stand here."

Now, indulge me, if you please, while I call your attention and refresh your recollection by the remarks of Chancellor Kent upon this general subject. He quotes the following words from the act creating the Treasury Department: "That whenever the Secretary shall be removed from office by the President of the United States, or in any other case of vacancy," &c., and says, "This amounted to a legislative construction," &c., as quoted by the President in his message; and Kent continues:

"This question has never been made the subject of judicial discussion, and the construction given to the Constitution in 1789 has continued to rest on this loose, incidental, declaratory opinion of Congress and the sense and practice of the Government since that time."

You see, from these remarks, that Chancellor Kent, if the question had been presented to him as an original question, if he had been called upon to determine it as a judge, would have said that he thought this construction rested on ground altogether too loose to justify him as a judge in giving that opinion; but what does he say as to the effect of the settlement thus made? He says:

"It may now be considered as firmly and definitely settled, and there is good sense and practical utility in the construction."—Kent's Commentaries, p. 310.

Part of this is quoted by the President, part of it is not; but I read you the whole paragraph. Judge Story, in his Commentaries, volume three, section fifteen hundred and thirty-seven, says:

"The public, however, acquiesced in this decision; and it continues, perhaps, the most extraordinary case in the history of the Government of a power conferred by implication on the Executive by the assent of a bare majority of Congress, which has not been questioned on many other occasions."

That much is enacted in the President's message. But what does Judge Story say further in the same connection and in the same paragraph?

"Even the most jealous advocates of State rights seem to have slumbered over this vast reach of authority, and have left it untouched as the neutral ground of controversy, in which they desired to reap no harvest, and from which they retired without leaving any protestations of title or contest."

It will thus be seen that although the Federalist opposed the power of removal, Mr. Madison and Judge Story and Chancellor Kent regarded it as firmly settled and established; and now, Senators, if authority is worth anything, if precedent is worth anything, if the opinions of two of the ablest judges we ever had in this country are worth anything, I maintain that it follows inevitably that the civil tenure bill is unconstitutional, and that the President was justified in exercising his veto power against it.

Whether, however, that view of the case be correct or not, there is still another view of it. If the President were wrong; if he were erroneously advised by his Cabinet; if he came to an improper conclusion; if the view which was taken by Congress on this subject were the correct view, still this argument is pertinent and appropriate as to the question of intention, because, as I have already said, in each of these articles an unlawful intention is charged against the President of the United States; and upon whose opinions, I respectfully ask, could this Senate, sitting as judges, rely with greater confidence than upon the opinions of two of the most eminent jurists that our country has ever produced, Kent and Story? They are names familiar to every judge and every lawyer in the United States as household words; and not here alone are these names distinguished. Far across the sea, in Westminster Hall, in that country from whence we borrowed our laws, the names of Kent and Story are almost as familiar as they are in the Chamber where his Honor presides as Chief Justice of the United States. Their works are quoted by British judges, by British lawyers, and by text-writers, and no two names in English or American jurisprudence stand higher than the names of these two distinguished citizens of our country. If they are not a sufficient authority to settle in the mind of the Senate, as they probably would not be in view of your action hitherto on the subject, that the law is unconstitutional, yet I ask you, Senators, if the advice of two such distinguished men as these might not well guide the action of the President of the United States, and relieve him from the criminality which is imputed to him in these articles of impeachment?

I hope you will allow me, Senators, to call your attention to some other opinions than these. This subject of appointments to and removals from office has been a matter of investigation in various forms by Attorneys General of the United States. The learned Manager who opened the cause was well aware of this; and how did he meet it? Nobody is more astute than him in the management of a cause. I will do him the justice to say that, although I do not exactly agree with him in his notions about decency and propriety of speech, I have not seen a gentleman in my life who manages a cause with more skill and art and ability than he has managed this prosecution from the very commencement of it. With that astuteness for which he has distinguished himself in the investigation of this cause, when he came to speak of the opinions of the Attorney General he made use of an observation to this effect—I shall not undertake to quote him literally—that after that office had become political he did not consider it a matter of any very great importance to quote the opinions of its incumbents. I had a slight suspicion—I hope the gentleman will forgive me if it were an erroneous one—that possibly the authority of the Attorneys General might not be just exactly the kind of authority he wanted; and so, although I did not know much about the subject, and had never had occasion to examine the opinions of the Attorneys General, I concluded that I would look into them, and I find several opinions there to which I wish to call your attention.

Before I do this let me invite you, Senators, to consider the provision in the Constitution of the United States that the President may require the opinion in writing of the principal officer of each of the Executive Departments upon any subject relating to the duties of their respective offices, and to the act of September 24, 1789, which provides that the Attorney General shall give his advice upon questions of law when required by the President. It may be that I place an exaggerated construction upon this provision of the Constitution and upon the act of 1789. It will be for you as judges to decide how that is. I will state my proposition before I read the section *in extenso*, and I will state it in such manner as to direct your attention to the point which I am endeavoring to demonstrate.

I maintain, in view of the proper construction of the act of 1789, that it is a matter of perfect indifference whether the President of the United States is advised by the particular Attorney General who may belong to his Cabinet in reference to a particular act or not. I maintain that the opinions delivered by the Attorney General are in the nature of judicial decisions. I do not say that they are to all intents and purposes judicial decisions; but, in the view which I entertain of the act of 1789, I insist that they should be as operative and effectual in this high and honorable court as a judicial decision of respectable authority would be in the court over which your Honor usually presides. Why do I say so? I will tell you. Unless I have misread the Constitution of the United States there is no provision there declaring that the decisions of the Supreme Court of the United States shall be final and conclusive and authoritative upon questions of law. There is no such provision in the Constitution; if there is, it has escaped me. The framers of the Constitution assumed that there was a certain state of things at the time they made it. They assumed that the history of the world would be before the country. They assumed that the history of English jurisprudence would be known or could be known to American citizens. In other words, they assumed that there was and would continue to be a certain amount of knowledge and information in the world, and therefore that it was not necessary for them to provide in the Constitution that the decisions made by the members of the Supreme Court of the United States should be binding upon their successors in office. They knew just as well as you know that the practice of English judges had been for centuries to regard a decision by a judicial tribunal in a case carefully considered, and especially in a case that had continued for any length of time, as an authority from which it was not safe in the administration of the law to depart.

Now, the argument I make before you is, that as the Constitution of the United States does not specify that the decision of the judges shall have all the binding force of authority in the land—and yet it has that force—this act of Congress, although it does not say so in reference to the opinions of the Attorneys General any more than the Constitution does in reference to the decisions of the judges of the Supreme Court of the United States, yet, upon any fair construction, upon any legal intendment, under this act of 1789, the opinion of the Attorney General may be regarded by the President, and by all others who have anything to do with that opinion, as a valid authority, and that it is sufficient to justify his action in any given case that may be covered by that opinion.

What is the provision of the act of September 24, 1789, section thirty-five? (1st volume Statutes-at-Large, page 93, and 1st volume of Brightly's Digest, page 92.) It is provided by that section—

"That there shall be appointed an Attorney General for the United States, who shall be sworn or affirmed to a faithful execution of his office, whose duty it shall be to prosecute and conduct all suits in the Supreme Court in which the United States shall be concerned, and to give his advice and opinions upon questions of law when required by the President of the United States, or when requested by the heads of any of the Departments touching any matters that may concern their Departments," &c.

When you take the two provisions together;

first, the provision of the Constitution that the President may call upon the principal officer in each executive department for advice and opinion, and second, the provision of the act of 1789 that he may call upon this officer of the law, the Attorney General, for advice and opinion, I maintain that when that advice and opinion are given they are by virtue of the Constitution and the law binding upon the President of the United States; and that even if they were not given in reference to the particular removal of Mr. Stanton, yet if they were given in any case on all fours with his, if they were given in any similar case, these opinions are in the nature of judicial opinions, and they are a perfect shield and protection to the President, if I can bring his act in this particular case within the spirit and meaning of any of them. Now, without commenting on these opinions or detaining the Senate by reading them at length, I will present a few without comment; for if I were to undertake to comment upon each opinion as to the power of appointment and the power of removal it might take up more time than would be advisable. Trusting to and believing in the intelligence and discrimination of the Senate, I will give them the substance of the positions assumed, as I understand, by the different Attorneys General who have given their opinions upon the question.

In the first volume of the Opinions of the Attorney General, page 631, it will be seen that General Swartwout's commission (under the act of May 15, 1820, to limit the tenure of certain offices) as navy agent at New York expired during the preceding session of the Senate, and Mr. Wirt, Attorney General, gave an opinion, on the 22d of October, 1823, addressed to the Secretary of the Navy, in which he held that the words in the Constitution, "happen during the recess of the Senate"—and this, I think, will be a good answer to a portion of the argument offered by the honorable Manager who spoke yesterday—are equivalent to the words "happen to exist," and that "the President has power to fill during the recess of the Senate, by temporary commission, a vacancy that occurred by expiration of a commission during a previous session of that body."

In the same volume, page 213, will be found another opinion of Mr. Wirt. The register of wills held his office under a commission during the pleasure of the President. Mr. Wirt in his opinion, delivered on the 15th of June, 1818, held that where an act of Congress gives the President the power to appoint without designating the tenure by which the office is to be held it is during the pleasure of the President. That is the advice and opinion of one of the most eminent lawyers, and one of the most gifted orators, that ever lived in the United States. He says:

"If the President had no right to issue such a commission the commission is void, the office vacant, and the President has now a right to commission another person anew. If, on the contrary, the President had the right to issue such a commission, he has on the face of that commission the power of removal and the authority to reappoint."

In the second volume of Opinions of Attorneys General, page 333, will be found an opinion of Mr. Berrien, given on the 2d April, 1830, in which he held that—

"The appointment of a navy agent during the recess of the Senate, made in the case of a vacancy occurring during the recess, is in the exercise of the constitutional power of the President, and not by force of the act of 3d March, 1809; and the constitutional limitation of such appointment is to the end of the succeeding session of Congress, unless it be sooner determined by the acceptance of a new commission made, under an appointment by and with the advice and consent of the Senate."

Mr. Legaré, in an opinion, on the 22d October, 1841, declared that—

"The Constitution authorizes the President to fill vacancies that may happen during the recess of the Senate, even though a vacancy should occur after a session of the Senate has intervened. The executive power of removal from office, as indicated in the argument of Mr. Madison, delivered in the First Congress, drawn from the character of executive power and executive responsibility and the irresistible necessity of the case, has been acquiesced in by the whole country."

Again, in the fourth volume of Opinions of Attorneys General, page 218, will be found the opinion of Mr. Attorney General John Nelson, on the 9th of August, 1843, in Lieutenant Coxe's case, where the applicant was heard by counsel, a proceeding, as I suppose, somewhat rare in the Attorney General's office. In that opinion he declared, referring to the case of Marbury vs. Madison, that—

"Even after confirmation by the Senate the President may, in his discretion, withhold a commission from the applicant; and until a commission to signify that the purpose of the President has not been changed the appointment is not fully consummated."

All of these cases, without stopping to comment upon them, you will see have more or less bearing on the question under consideration. Now indulge me, if you please, while I read extracts from an opinion of Mr. Crittenden, to be found in the fifth volume of the Opinions of the Attorneys General, page 290. It is infinitely a better argument than any which I can present. You will see that he necessarily travels over the same beaten path that we are compelled to travel over in this case; and I think it is a matter of very great consequence that in this case we do show that the path is so well known and so much traveled that there can be no mistake about it.

Upon the question submitted by the President whether he had authority to remove from office the chief justice of the Territory of Minnesota, erected by the act of March 3, 1849, who had been appointed for four years, Mr. Crittenden, in his opinion of the 23d of January, 1851, after referring to Chief Justice Marshall's opinion in the American Insurance Company vs. Canter, (1 Peters, 546,) where it was held that these were not constitutional but legislative courts, created in virtue of the general right of sovereignty which exists in the Government, said what I will now read. I propose to give you the language of Mr. Crittenden, one of the ablest statesmen who ever sat in these Halls, a man without fear and without reproach, a man of a splendid, gigantic ii.tellect, "faithful among the faithless" under all circumstances; one whose opinions, as I respectfully think, are entitled to the highest degree of credit. This opinion was delivered in the meridian of his life, when he was in the full possession of his mental powers, and when there could be no mistake as to the force and effect to which any production of his mind was entitled. He said:

"Being civil officers appointed by the President by and with the advice and consent of the Senate, and commissioned by the President, they are not excepted from that executive power which, by the Constitution, is vested in the President of the United States over all civil officers appointed by him, and whose tenures of office are not made by the Constitution itself more stable than during the pleasure of the President of the United States. That the President of the United States has, by the Constitution of the United States, the power of removing civil officers appointed and commissioned by him, by and with the advice and consent of the Senate, where the Constitution has not otherwise provided by fixing the tenures during good behavior, has been long since settled, and has ceased to be a subject of controversy or doubt. In the great debate which arose upon that question in the House of Representatives shortly after the adoption of the Constitution, Mr. Madison is reported to have said 'it is absolutely necessary that the President should have the power of removing from office; it will make him, in a peculiar manner, responsible for their conduct and subject him to impeachment himself if he suffers them to perpetrate, with impunity, high crimes or misdemeanors against the United States, or neglects to superintend their conduct, so as to check their excesses. On the constitutionality of the declaration I have no manner of doubt.' And the determination of Congress was in accordance with his views and has since been invariably followed in practice by every President of the United States."

And in the same opinion (page 291 of the same volume) Mr. Crittenden said:

"The power of removal is vested by the Constitution in the President of the United States to promote the public welfare; to enable him to take care that the laws be faithfully executed; to make him responsible if he suffers those to remain in office who are manifestly unfit and unworthy of public confidence."

Again, Mr. Cushing in the 8th volume of Opinions, page 233, in an elaborate opinion in regard to the Navy efficiency act of the 28th February, 1855, held—

"That the President of the United States possesses constitutional power to dismiss officers of the Army or Navy coextensive with his power to dismiss executive or administrative officers in the civil service of the Government."

Again, Mr. Speed, in his opinion of April 25, 1865, addressed to Secretary McCulloch, declaring that the act of 1865, vesting the power of appointment of assistant assessors in the respective assessors is unconstitutional, argues that it is the duty of the President to make the appointment; and I ask you, Senators, to pay special attention to this opinion, for I suppose that Mr. Speed stands very high in some quarters of the United States. This opinion is not in any of the printed volumes of opinions; I have a certified copy of it which I placed in the possession of Mr. Stanbery, and which can be at any time produced before the Senate; but

I vouch for the correctness of the extract which I am about to read:

"It is his [the President's] duty to do all he has lawful power to do when the occasion requires an exercise of authority. To do less on such an occasion would be pro tanto to abdicate his high office. The Constitution is the supreme law—a law superior and paramount to any other. If any law be repugnant to the Constitution it is void."

This bears not only on the civil-tenure bill, but it is square up to all the questions the gentlemen on the other side have argued in connection with it. Here is the opinion of the adviser of the President's predecessor, a man whose opinion was on file, a man in whose judgment he had the right to confide, for be it known and always kept in remembrance that the President of the United States is not himself a lawyer; he never studied the legal profession; he has no claims or pretensions to know anything about it; but in the discharge of his official duties he has the right to consult the legal adviser who is placed there to guide and direct him upon questions of law by the Constitution of the country and by the act of 1789. If he finds an opinion on file in his office, or if he finds it recorded in any reported volume of the opinions of the Attorneys General, it is, and is properly, a guide, a precedent which he may safely follow; and it is such an opinion as will protect him against any imputations of unlawful or improper motives. Pardon me for reading this again, so that you may have the whole of it in unbroken connection:

"It is his duty to do all he has lawful power to do when the occasion requires an exercise of his authority. To do less on such an occasion would be, pro tanto, to abdicate his high office. The Constitution is the supreme law—a law superior and paramount to any other. If any law be repugnant to the Constitution, it is void; in other words, it is no law."

And, Mr. Chief Justice, if you see proper in the discharge of your duty to comply with the respectful request which has been presented to you to deliver an opinion upon any of the legal questions which are involved in this case, I most respectfully ask you to consider this opinion of the Attorney General, and to declare that it is sound doctrine "that if any law be repugnant to the Constitution it is void; in other words, it is no law." Now, allow me, Mr. Chief Justice, to call your attention to the closing sentence of this opinion of Mr. Speed, which I think is the very essence of the law:

"It is the peculiar province of the judicial department to say what the law is in particular cases. But before such case arises, and in the absence of authoritative exposition of the law by that department, it is equally the duty of the officer holding the executive power of the Government to determine for the purposes of his own conduct and action as well the operation of conflicting laws as the unconstitutionality of any one."

There is an opinion from an Attorney General who is not a member of the Cabinet, not a "serf" of the President, who gave his opinion before or about the time the present incumbent came into the presidential office. There is his opinion placed upon the records of one of the departments of this Government, to stand and to stand forever, so far as his opinion will go, as a guide to the highest executive officer in the Government, declaring that if a law is unconstitutional in the view of the President it is no law at all, and he is not bound to follow it. He declares that the President has the right, in the absence of any judicial exposition, to construe the law for himself. I need not tell this Senate that this is no new doctrine. Senators, within your day and mine there was an executive officer of the United States who was, as they say the present incumbent is, a man of strong will, a man not possessing any great advantages of education or of mental culture, but still a man of strong intellect and of determination just as strong as his intellect. You all remember Andrew Jackson, a name that was once potent in the United States. No name was ever more powerful in this Government of ours from the time of its foundation down to the present day than the name of Andrew Jackson. "There were giants in those days" when Andrew Jackson was at the head of the Government of the United States. Andrew Jackson exercised the power of removal, and his right to do so was called in question by some of the ablest men who ever sat within the Senate of the United States. It was discussed and learnedly discussed; and yet he persevered in his determination. He maintained the power and authority of the President of the United States to remove from office and to make appointments, and you all recollect the scene that occurred and which made the history of this body memorable.

A resolution was introduced into the Senate—I believe it was occasioned, in part at least, by the removal of Mr. Duane—to the effect that the President of the United States, in his late proceedings, had violated the Constitution of the United States. That resolution passed the Senate; and a gentleman who is now no more, one whose name is well known in the political history of the United States, Mr. Benton, took up that subject. I have not recurred to the history of the debates with sufficient accuracy to tell how long it was that he continued to agitate the question, but my recollection is that it was for several years; and I remember, as all these Senators will remember, the remarkable expression which Mr. Benton used: "Solitary and alone I set this ball in motion." He determined that that resolution censuring the President of the United States should be expunged from the records of the Senate; and he debated it time and again with tremendous energy and power, until at last the resolution was expunged from the Journal of the Senate of the United States. So far as there is any recorded judgment within my knowledge that is the last record. It is a record in favor of the power of removal. There was "the sober, second thought" of the Senate. There was a recision of a resolution that reflected upon the character and upon the action of General Jackson; and, so far as that

C. I.—40.

record goes, it is in favor of the power and authority which I have argued for. There can be no controversy in regard to this.

Now let us see how far we have progressed in this argument. I have shown you the opinions of Mr. Madison and Mr. Sedgwick and others in the debate of 1789. I have shown you the opinions of Kent and Story, two of our ablest American commentators. I have shown you opinions of Attorneys General, eminent in their profession and standing high in the confidence of the country. I have shown you the action of the American Senate in the expunging resolution. I thus present to you what I may call, in the language of Judge Story, an unbroken current of authority in favor of the proposition that not only the civil-tenure bill is unconstitutional, but that the President has the right to remove from office. I mean to say that the principles maintained by them would lead to that result, that he has the power of removal which he claims in his answer. And I maintain, Senators—forgive the repetition—that whether he is right or wrong in this, this current of authority for near eighty years is sufficient to throw protection around him; and when I show you, as I have done from the opinion of Mr. Speed, that in the absence of any judicial determination it is the sworn and bounden duty of the President of the United States to judge of a constitutional question for himself, I do not present to the Senate any novel doctrine. It is not for me to say whether the doctrine is right or wrong. My opinions are of no sort of consequence in this Senate. If my arguments are well founded, and if they are well supported, they will have weight and influence with you; if not, they will be rejected. So it is not necessary for me to say what I think upon these questions; but I maintain that this is not a novel doctrine in the United States. I told you yesterday that the present President is a Democrat of the straightest sect. I told you that he was really nominated as a Democrat in the convention that nominated Mr. Lincoln and himself for President and Vice President. That was not a Democratic convention, I know. It was a convention composed of Union men without any reference to the old lines of demarkation between Whigs and Democrats. That was a convention which had assembled together for the purpose of sustaining Mr. Lincoln, and whose view and opinion was that by sustaining Mr. Lincoln and the measures of his administration they would sustain the strong arm of the Government in putting down the rebellion, which had not then been brought to a conclusion. In his letter accepting the nomination, as I told you yesterday, President Johnson remarked that he was a Democrat!

Senators, I will read to you the opinions of Mr. Jefferson and General Jackson presently; but before I do that let me call your attention to the effect of this political training of the President of the United States. You must always bear that in mind. You must go to his stand-point and look at things as he looked at them and judge of them as he judged of them, for you are now in search of motive; that is what you are trying to determine in this case. You are in search of the question of intention; and when you judge of his conduct in that way, and when you remember that he is a Democrat of the Jeffersonian and Jacksonian school, if I can show you, as I will presently show you, that Mr. Jefferson and General Jackson undertook to construe the Constitution of the United States for themselves, and claimed that as executive officers they had the right to do so, I show you that according to the political training and education of the President of the United States it is a doctrine in which he might well believe; and especially when you have Mr. Speed's opinion that I have read confirmatory of that doctrine, it furnishes a sufficient vindication and protection of the President as to the exercise of his judgment.

Let us see what Mr. Jefferson and General Jackson said on this subject. Mr. Jefferson, if I understand him correctly, carried his doctrine much further than the present President of the United States carries it. I will refer to the sixth volume of Mr. Jefferson's works, page 461, and I will read a part of a letter of his there to be found, from which you will see he goes a bar's length beyond the present President of the United States in the views that he entertains. The President has told you that he was anxious to have the question between him and Congress settled by the judicial department. But what were Mr. Jefferson's views? He, as you all very well know, and the world knows, was the author of the Declaration of Independence and one of the greatest of the revolutionary minds. In the letter to which I have referred, to Mr. Torrance, he said:

"The second question, whether the judges are invested with exclusive authority to decide on the constitutionality of a law, has been heretofore a subject of consideration with me in the exercise of official duties. Certainly there is not a word in the Constitution which has given that power to them more than to the executive or legislative branches. Questions of property, of character, and of crime being ascribed to the judges, through a definite course of legal proceedings, laws involving such questions belong, of course, to them; and as they decide on them ultimately and without appeal, they, of course, decide *or themselves.* The constitutional validity of the law or laws again prescribing executive action, and to be administered by that branch ultimately and without appeal, the executive must decide for *themselves* also whether under the Constitution they are valid or not. So also as to laws governing the proceedings of the Legislature, that body must judge *for itself* the constitutionality of the law, and equally without appeal or control from its coördinate branches. And, in general, that branch which is to act ultimately and without appeal on any law is the rightful expositor of the validity of the law, uncontrolled by the opinions of the other coördinate authorities."

So that, if I correctly apprehend Mr. Jefferson's meaning in this letter, he goes a bar's length beyond the right asserted by Mr. Johnson in his answer in this case:

"It may be said that contradictory decisions may arise in such case, and produce inconvenience. This is possible, and is a necessary failing in all human proceedings."

He goes on to show, in this letter to Mr. Torrance, that such contradictory decisions had arisen and no special harm had resulted; but I do not deem it material to occupy your time with reading at length. In the seventh volume of Mr. Jefferson's Works, page 135, he says, in a letter to Judge Roane:

"My construction of the Constitution is very different from that you quote."

I do not read the rest, because there is so much reading necessary to be done in the argument of the case that I am really fearful of wearying your patience, and I take it that it is not necessary for me to do so, because the mere mention of this letter will call it up to the recollection of Senators, and you will remember the connection. I only read so much of it as bears upon the point which I am endeavoring to illustrate:

"My construction of the Constitution is very different from that you quote. It is that each department is truly independent of the others, and has an equal right to decide for itself what is the meaning of the Constitution in the cases submitted to its action: and especially where it is to act ultimately and without appeal. I will explain myself by examples which, having occurred while I was in office, are better known to me, and the principles which governed them."

I deem it unnecessary to read further from this letter. The point is, that in this letter he asserts that "each department is truly independent of the others, and has an equal right to decide for itself what is the meaning of the Constitution in the cases submitted to its action; and especially where it is to act ultimately and without appeal." If that doctrine be correct the President of the United States had the right to decide this question for himself, independent of any intention or design to have a case made and prepared for the adjudication of the judicial tribunals of the country. But, even if that be not correct, it certainly goes far to explain, if not to justify, the action of the President of the United States in the removal of Mr. Stanton.

Although it is not precisely in connection with this point, yet, as it may have a bearing upon the question, I will quote a sentence from General Jackson's Maysville road bill veto. Of course that can be found anywhere and everywhere in your records; but for the sake of convenience I quote it from the Statesman's Manual, volume two, page 726:

"When an honest observance of constitutional compacts cannot be obtained from communities like ours it need not be anticipated elsewhere; and the cause in which there has been so much martyrdom, and from which so much was expected by the friends of liberty, may be abandoned and the degrading truth, that man is unfit for self-government, admitted. And this will be the case if *expediency* be made a rule of construction in interpreting the Constitution. Power in no Government could desire a better shield for the insidious advances which it is ever ready to make upon the checks that are designed to restrain its action."

On page 772, in General Jackson's veto of the bank bill, he said:

"If the opinion of the Supreme Court covered the whole ground of this act, it ought not to control the coördinate authorities of this Government."

I want you, now, to notice these assertions, for you will see that such great men as Jefferson and Jackson went beyond the present President of the United States in their assertions, for they denied the right of the Supreme Court even to adjudge a question:

"The Congress, the Executive, and the court must each for itself be guided by its own opinion of the Constitution. Each public officer who takes an oath to support the Constitution swears that he will support as he understands it, and not as it is understood by others."

I remember very well that there was a great deal of criticism at that day about this principle asserted by General Jackson in his veto of the bank bill; but it is enough for me to show that he asserted the power.

"It is as much the duty of the House of Representatives, of the Senate, and of the President to decide upon the constitutionality of any bill or resolution which may be presented to them for passage or approval as it is of the supreme judges when it may be brought before them for judicial decision. The opinion of the judges has no more authority over Congress than the opinion of Congress has over the judges; and on that point the President is independent of both. The authority of the Supreme Court must not, therefore, be permitted to control the Congress or the Executive when acting in their legislative capacities, but to have only such influence as the force of their reasoning may deserve."

That was prerogative! We have heard a great deal of talk here about prerogative. That was prerogative when General Jackson asserted that he had the right to construe the Constitution of the United States for himself, and independent of the judicial tribunals of the country. If General Jackson and Mr. Jefferson asserted this extraordinary power while they were filling the executive office, how much more may Andrew Johnson, the present President of the United States, say, "Here is a question about which there is a difference of opinion between the Congress of the United States and myself; here is a question that is distracting and dividing the country; I desire to have this question settled; I do not wish to settle it by my own strong hand; I desire to submit it to the judicial tribunals of the country; and in order to do that I will exercise a power which has been exercised from the foundation of the Government; I will remove Mr. Stanton; I will place this question in a condition in which it can be settled by the judicial tribunals of the United States; I will endeavor to do this; I will invoke the action of the highest judicial tribunal in the country." Of course this idea was involved: "If the Supreme Court of the United States decide this question in favor of the view which Congress has presented I will acquiesce in and submit to the decision; if the Supreme Court decide the question the other way I will persevere in the determination to appoint some one else in the place of an officer in my Cabinet who is obnoxious to me." Now, I maintain, Senators, that there was nothing wrong in this; nothing illegal in it.

Oh, but it is argued on the other side that after the President of the United States has vetoed a bill, and after it has been again passed by two thirds of both Houses of Congress, it is then placed in such a situation that he has no right to put any construction upon it different from that which Congress has placed upon it. I cannot see the logic of the difference between the two cases. A law, when passed by Congress and approved by the President of the United States and placed upon the statute-book, is nothing more than a law. If the President of the United States exercises his veto power and attempts to prevent the passage of a law, or, in other words, refuses that assent which the Constitution empowers him to give or to withhold, and the Congress of the United States passes it over the veto and it goes upon the statute-book, is it anything more than a law? Has it any greater or more binding force in the one case than it has in the other? And if the President of the United States has any power of judgment, and especially of judgment in cases where duties are confided to him by the Constitution and where it is his business to act, may he not exert in the one case just as much as in the other? I cannot for the life of me see the force of the distinction which the learned and honorable Managers are attempting to take in this case.

Senators, there are questions peculiarly belonging to the executive department which the President of the United States of necessity must have the right of determining for himself. Specious and ingenious as the argument of the honorable Manager yesterday was, that there may be an implication in favor of Congress as to the exercise of its powers enumerated in the Constitution, and that there can be no implication in favor of the President as to the duties that are imposed upon him by the same instrument, it still has no foundation in sound reason or in any authority known to the law. The very term "executive power" is, like most of the other terms employed in the Constitution, a technical phrase. I have shown you how Mr. Madison understood it in the debate of 1789. I have shown you what a wide latitude of interpretation he took in giving a meaning to the words "executive power," and that he held that in virtue of those very words the President was responsible for the action of the Cabinet that he had called around him.

If you can get from the Constitution an implication in any case; if you can derive from the words "executive power," or from the words "he shall take care that the laws be faithfully executed," or from his oath, or from any other words in the Constitution relating to his functions, any power by implication in any case, the doctrine of implication arises as to all other powers that may be conferred upon him; and I can see no reason why you may not imply anything that is necessary to be done as much in favor of the President as you may imply it in favor of Congress. When you take the Constitution of the United States and look to the enumerated powers, there is not one of them that tells how any power is to be executed. Congress may create a Navy; Congress may declare war; Congress may levy taxes. It does not say how you are to create a Navy; it does not say whether you are to do that particular act by taxation or not; it does not prescribe whether your vessels are to be iron-clad vessels or sail vessels; it does not prescribe how much tonnage they shall have.

All these and a thousand other things are left to the discretion of Congress. You derive the power which you have exercised time and again, from the foundation of the Government, in regard to the Army and the Navy and every other branch of the public service, as a necessary incident under the general provision of the Constitution to do anything that may be necessary and proper to carry any of the granted powers into effect. Now, if this doctrine of implication which is absolutely necessary and essential to the legitimate and proper exercise of the powers conferred on Congress by the Constitution has been acquiesced in and practiced on from the foundation of the Government by Congress, why may it not be acquiesced in as to the President of the United States? There is no force, as I maintain, in the distinction which the honorable Manager insists upon.

Mr. JOHNSON. Mr. Chief Justice, I move that the court take a recess of fifteen minutes.

The motion was agreed to; and at the expiration of the recess the Chief Justice resumed the chair and called the Senate to order.

Mr. NELSON. Mr. Chief Justice and Senators, I have been reminded of one thing which I should have stated to you before; and before I proceed further I desire to call your attention to it. I have not had opportunity to consult the works upon the subject, but I presume the fact is well known to the Senate that Mr. Clay and Mr. Webster, in the progress of the debate upon General Jackson's conduct in reference to the removal of Mr. Duane and the removal of the deposits, conceded the power of the President to remove the Secretary, but their opposition to his course was founded mainly upon objections growing out of the law upon the subject of the Treasury Department. This, if I am correctly informed, and I believe I am, is an additional and very strong opinion in favor of the proposition for which I have contended before you.

Upon the question on which I was addressing you, I have not only the opinion of Mr. Jefferson and General Jackson, but I have the high authority of Mr. Madison himself. In the fourth volume of Madison's Works, page 349, is a letter which was written by him in 1834. Without reading the whole letter, I will only read so much of it as I think is pertinent to the question before you.

Mr. JOHNSON. Who is the letter to? To Mr. Coles?

Mr. NELSON. It is not stated, sir; it is blank. It is dated 1834, and will be found on page 349 of the fourth volume of his works. The letter is not very long, and is as follows:

"DEAR SIR: Having alluded to the Supreme Court of the United States as a constitutional resort in deciding questions of jurisdiction between the United States and the individual States, a few remarks may be proper, showing the sense and degree in which that character is more particularly ascribed to that department of the Government.

"As the legislative, executive, and judicial departments of the United States are coördinate, and each equally bound to support the Constitution, it follows that each must, in the exercise of its functions, be guided by the text of the Constitution according to its own interpretation of it, and, consequently, that in the event of irreconcileable interpretations, the prevalence of the one or the other Department must depend on the nature of the case, as receiving its final decision from the one or the other, and passing from that decision into effect without involving the functions of any other."

The argument upon the other side is that the President of the United States, under the Constitution, is a mere man in buckram; that he has no power or authority to decide anything; that he can do nothing on the face of the earth unless it is nominated in the bond; that he must be the passive instrument of Congress; and that he must be subjected to the government and control of the legislative department of the Government. The argument which we make is, that under the Constitution there are living, moving, acting powers and duties vested in and imposed upon the President of the United States, and that he must, of necessity, have the right, in cases appropriately belonging to his department of the Government, to exercise something like judicial discretion; that he must act upon his own authority and upon his own construction of the Constitution; and when he thus acts in reference to the removal of an officer or anything else, I maintain that it is different from the action of a private individual. A private individual, if he violates the laws of the land, is amenable for their violation under the principle that "ignorance of the law excuseth no man;" but the President of the United States having the executive power vested in him by the Constitution has the right to exercise his best judgment in the situation in which he is placed, and if he exercises that judgment honestly and faithfully, not from corrupt motives, then his action cannot be reviewed by Congress or by any other tribunal than the tribunal of the people in the presidential election should he be a candidate before them again, and he is protected by the powers imposed by the Constitution. Mr. Madison proceeds:

"It is certainly due from the functionaries of the several departments to pay much respect to the opinions of each other; and, as far as official independence and obligation will permit, to consult the means of adjusting differences and avoiding practical embarrassments growing out of them, as must be done in like cases between the different coördinate branches of the legislative department.

"But notwithstanding this abstract view of the coördinate and independent right of the three departments to expound the Constitution "—

Mark his phraseology there. One of the makers of the Constitution, hoary with age, venerable at the time when this letter was written, having no motive except to leave to posterity the mature judgment of a patriot in regard to the true and proper construction of that sacred instrument which he had an agency in making, Mr. Madison says:

"But notwithstanding this abstract view of the coördinate and independent right of the three departments to expound the Constitution, the judicial department most familiarizes itself to the public attention as the expositor by the order of its functions in relation to the other departments, and attracts most the public confidence by the composition of the tribunal.

"It is the judicial department in which questions of constitutionality, as well as of legality, generally find their ultimate discussion and operative decision; and the public deference to and confidence in the judgment of the body are peculiarly inspired by the qualities implied in its members, by the gravity and deliberation of their proceedings, and by the advantage their plurality gives them over the unity of the executive department, and their fewness over the multitudinous composition of the legislative department.

"Without losing sight, therefore, of the coördinate relations of the three departments to each other, it may always be expected that the judicial bench, when happily filled, will, for the reasons suggested, most engage the respect and reliance of the public as the surest expositor of the Constitution, as well in questions within its cognizance concerning the boundaries between the several departments of the Government as in those between the Union and its members."

And it was, as I said before, to that department that the President of the United States desired that an appeal should be made. But you will observe here that the idea is distinctly presented by this venerable and patriotic man that the coördinate and independent departments of the Government have the right, each for itself and each within its appropriate sphere and in relation to its own appropriate duties, to construe the Constitution. If this view be correct the President of the United States had the right to construe the Constitution for himself, notwithstanding the passage of the civil-tenure bill, and he had the right to act under it in the manner in which he did, and you cannot make a crime, you cannot make an offense out of such an action. You cannot justify it in the view of the American people; you cannot justify it to the civilized world; Senators, I maintain that you cannot justify it to your own consciences to place such a construction as that upon the act of the President, and to deny him the powers which he has attempted to exercise in this case.

Now, let me call your attention to the famous protest of General Jackson, and you will see that the same doctrine is carried out there:

"By the Constitution the 'executive power is vested in the President of the United States.' Among the duties imposed upon him, and which he is sworn to perform, is that of 'taking care that the laws be faithfully executed.' Being thus made responsible for the entire action of the executive department, it was but reasonable that the power of appointing, overseeing, and controlling those who execute the laws—a power in its nature executive—should remain in his hands. It is, therefore, not only his right, but the Constitution makes it his duty, to 'nominate, and by and with the advice and consent of the Senate, appoint' all 'officers of the United States whose appointments are not in the Constitution otherwise provided for,' with the proviso that the appointment of inferior officers may be vested in the President alone, in the courts of justice, or in the heads of Departments.

"The executive power vested in the Senate is neither that of 'nominating' nor 'appointing.'"

You will see that General Jackson, with characteristic energy and courage, stood up faithfully in vindication of his executive power while he was President of the United States:

"The executive power vested in the Senate is neither that of 'nominating' nor 'appointing.' It is merely a check upon the executive power of appointment. If individuals are proposed for appointment by the President, by them deemed incompetent or unworthy, they may withhold their consent and the appointment cannot be made. They check the action of the Executive, but cannot in relation to these very subjects act themselves nor direct him. Selections are still made by the President; and the negative given to the Senate, without diminishing his responsibility, furnishes an additional guarantee to the country that the subordinate executive, as well as the judicial offices, shall be filled with worthy and competent men.

"The whole executive power being vested in the President, who is responsible for its exercise, it is a necessary consequence that he should have a right to employ agents of his own choice to aid him in the performance of his duties, and to discharge them when he is no longer willing to be responsible for their acts."

The very idea that one of the Senators I now address, Senator SHERMAN, must have had in his mind at the time when he made those remarks which were quoted by Judge Curtis in the opening upon our side:

"In strict accordance with this principle the power of removal, which, like that of appointment, is an original executive power, is left unchecked by the Constitution in relation to all executive officers for whose conduct the President is responsible, while it is taken from him in relation to judicial officers for whose acts he is not responsible. In the Government from which many of the fundamental principles of our system are derived the head of the executive department originally had power to appoint and remove at will all officers, executive and judicial. It was to take the judges out of this general power of removal, and thus make them independent of the Executive that the tenure of their offices was changed to good behavior. Nor is it conceivable why they are placed in our Constitution upon a tenure different from that of all other officers appointed by the Executive, unless it be for the same purpose."

Now, Senators, at the hazard of some repetition, allow me at this point to sum up as far as I have gone. I have shown you that in the debate of 1789 some of the ablest men this country ever produced, and some of the very men who had an agency in framing the Constitution itself, conceded the power of removal, as claimed by the President. I have shown you that for nearly eighty years, with the single exception of the struggle which took place in General Jackson's time, that power has been acquiesced in. I have shown you that two of the most eminent writers on American jurisprudence, Kent and Story, have treated the question as settled. I have shown you, from the opinions of some of the ablest Attorneys General who have ever been in office in this country, that the power of removal existed in the manner in which it was exercised by the President. I have shown you that, from this opinion and practice during the long period of time to which I have adverted, it was conceded that the power of removal belonged to the President in virtue of the Constitution, and that the Senate had no constitutional right or power to interfere with him. Having shown you all this, I have now a few words to say in regard to the President's act in removing Mr. Stanton and in further answer to the first article against him.

As you have observed, the first proposition which I have endeavored to demonstrate is, that the civil-tenure bill is unconstitutional and void; for if the doctrines be correct which I have endeavored to maintain before you, and if this long chain of authority is entitled to the slightest degree of respect, it follows inevitably that Congress had no power to pass the law; and it follows, furthermore, that the President had the right to exercise a judgment in regard to retaining or removing one of the councilors whom the Constitution had placed around him for the purpose of aiding him in the administration of public affairs.

But the other view in which I wish to argue the case—and it has already been indicated in various statements from time to time made by me in the progress of my remarks—is this: suppose that the proposition I have endeavored to maintain before you is erroneous; suppose that Congress are right and that the President is wrong; suppose that Congress had the power to pass the civil-tenure bill; suppose that he had no right to act contrary to that; then the question comes up whether or not he is guilty upon any of these articles of impeachment. The first eight articles charge in different forms an intent to violate the Constitution of the United States, or to violate the civil-tenure bill, or to violate the conspiracy act of 1861. Every one of those articles contains a charge of an unlawful intention; they do not charge an unlawful act simply, with the exception of the fifth article, which says nothing about the intent. Now, recurring to what I have already said on this subject, I desire to sustain what I have said by a reference to some of the decisions or some of the opinions in the law books, and I ask the question how can any unlawful intent be predicated of his act? According to Foster and Hale and other writers upon criminal law, and I quote this from 1 Bouvier's Dictionary, page 647, who cites Foster and Hale and others for the definition:

"Every crime must have, necessarily, two constituent parts, namely, an act forbidden by law and an intention."

And that is as applicable, I take it, to a high misdemeanor as it is to a high crime.

"The act is innocent or guilty just as there was or

was not an intention to commit a crime; for example: a man embarks on board a ship at New York for the purpose of going to New Orleans; if he went with an intention to perform a lawful act he is perfectly innocent; but if his intention was to levy war against the United States he is guilty of an overt act of treason."

Mr. Bishop, in his work on criminal law, section 252, says:

"Intent is not always inferable from the act done."

I maintain that, there being no unlawful or improper intention there can be no crime or misdemeanor; and although I did not read this yesterday I substantially cited it; but having it here I ask your indulgence to repeat it again in the language of the book itself. I refer to Wharton's Criminal Law, page 733, and Roscoe's Criminal Evidence, page 804, to sustain this proposition:

"An indictment against an officer of justice for misbehavior in office must charge that the act was done with corrupt, partial, malicious, or improper motives, and, above all, with a knowledge that it was wrong."

In Wharton, page 269, and 2 Russell, 732, this principle is stated:

"As to acts of an official nature, everything is presumed to be rightfully done until the contrary appears."

Again, Mr. Bishop, in his Criminal Law, section 80, says:

"A case of overwhelming necessity (as to intent) or honest mistake of fact will be excepted out of a general statute."

Now, Senators, if these are the rules that prevail in courts of law—and they are rules founded in wisdom, in common sense, in justice —if these rules obtain in criminal trials every day in courts of law, what is there to prevent them from being enforced in this court, and what is there to prevent them from shielding this respondent from the imputation which is made upon him? How can it be said that he had any wrongful or unlawful intent when the Constitution gave him the power to judge for himself in reference to the particular act? How can it be said that he had any wrongful or unlawful intent when the practice of the Government for the long period of time to which I have adverted was sufficient to justify him in exercising the power which he attempted to exercise? How can it be said that there was any wrongful or unlawful intent when he had all these opinions of the Attorneys General to guide and lead and direct him? How can it be said that there was any unlawful intent when he had the very opinions of the Senators and Representatives at the time when the law was passed as a guide to lead and direct him in the performance of his duty? It does seem to me that it beggars all belief to say that the President intended anything wrong. It outrages our ideas of common justice and of common sense to say that there was any purpose or intent upon his part either to violate the Constitution or to violate the civil-tenure bill. If Mr. Speed is correct, and if the other writers are correct, and the President believed that the law was unconstitutional, then, until the question at least was adjudicated by the highest court in the United States, the President had the right to exercise his judgment, and you cannot hold that he was guilty of any criminal intention.

Was ever such a case presented ? How bald, how naked do these charges appear when you look at the proof! I will not take up time, Senators, to turn to the evidence of witnesses which you all have fresh in your recollection. Was there ever such a scene in the history of the world among men claiming to have intelligence, among persons in the exercise of ordinary reason and judgment as the scene that occurred in reference to Mr. Stanton's removal and the attempt to bring the question before the courts of justice. There is old General Thomas, whom they stigmatize a good deal on the other side; but I take him to be a plain, simple-hearted, honest old gentleman, who has been forty years in the military service of the country. If there were any suspicions about him, such as the gentleman [Mr. Manager BOUTWELL] alluded to yesterday, as to whether he was in favor of the rebellion or against it, it is a very extraordinary thing that Mr. Stanton should send him down to the southern States, and that he should organize some seventy or eighty thousand negroes there to fight the battles of the Union. He is a plain, simple-hearted, honest old man, whose very countenance is a recommendation to him before anybody under the heavens hears him speak. Perhaps his vanity was a little tickled by the idea of being appointed Secretary of War. No doubt the old man felt very comfortable at that elevation for a little while. But who that heard his testimony in this court can doubt for a moment his intention to speak the truth in regard to everything he said ? He goes to the War Department, and you have that wonderful scene at the time when he attempts to take possession of the office of Secretary of War. This he was going to do with force and violence ! Was there ever such a thing since the world began, such an act of force as you had there between Mr. Thomas and Mr. Stanton when this proceeding was going on? They met together like twin brothers. They almost embraced each other. I believe he said Mr. Stanton did hug him, or something like that. [Laughter.] He came very near it, if he did not actually do it; and in the fullness of his heart Mr. Stanton became exceedingly kind and liberal upon the occasion, and he called for liquor, and had it brought out, and there was that great dram, containing about one spoonful, fairly, honestly, equally divided between these two aspiring Secretaries, and done in a spirit of fraternity and of love such as I suppose never was witnessed in a forcible contest on the face of the earth before. [Laughter.]

An attempt was made to have this question settled. Stanton puts his arm around him and says, "This is neutral ground, Thomas,

between you and me; there is no war here when we have this liquor on hand ;" and not only divided that spoonful, but he felt so good after he took that that he sent out and got a bottle full more. [Laughter.] I suspect, Senators—I do not know how the fact is—but I suspect that old friend Thomas not only felt a little elevated by the idea of being Secretary of War *ad interim*, after having served his country in a somewhat inferior capacity for a good while, but I imagine the old man took so much of that good liquor on that occasion that he felt his spirits very much elevated, and was disposed to talk to Mr. Karsner and all these other men in the manner in which he did talk.

And yet they tell you this was force ! Oh, yes, force; attempting forcibly to eject Mr. Stanton from the office of Secretary of War— by drinking a spoonful of liquor and helping to divide a bottle with him ! Was there ever such an idea of force before ? This is the "lame and impotent conclusion" of the proceeding which we have upon the other side.

Well, they conclude that they will depart from that neutral ground. After they got out of the building Mr. Stanton goes along and he wakes up Mr. Meigs in the dark hours of the night—he or some of his friends. It is *idem sonans;* it is the same thing, I reckon. Whatever he did by others he did by himself. His friends go and arouse Mr. Meigs in the dark hours of the night, as if some felony were about to be committed. They go there as if they were attempting to raise the hue and cry. They wake him from the slumbers of the night and require him to go to his office to make out a warrant against old man Thomas for trying to violate the civil-tenure bill. He rises and goes to his office with hot haste, something like the haste in which this impeachment proceeding was gotten up. He goes to his office. He issues his warrant with all proper gravity and decorum, and it is placed in the hands of an officer, and poor old Thomas, with about a pint or a quart of liquor in him, [laughter,] is arrested and taken before a judge to be tried for this great offense of violating the civil-tenure bill! He is placed in the custody of an officer as if he had committed some horrible outrage, some terrible offense. The officer follows him over to the President's. He sticks to him like a leech, closer a good deal than a brother. [Laughter.] He follows him over there, and will not allow poor old Thomas to get out of his sight at all. "Oh, you have committed a terrible offense; you have violated the civil-tenure bill; you are liable to fine and liable to imprisonment, and I cannot permit you, sir, to escape out of my clutches." But at last the old man gets a lawyer and comes along before the judge. The lawyers get to discussing the question before the judge, and strange to say this terrible offense which it took a midnight warrant to reach, this terrible offense which it required a marshal or some other officer with his tipstaff to take care should not be committed with impunity, and to hold on to the person of Thomas so that he could not escape—when these lawyers came to argue it before the judge, and they began to find out there was some idea of taking the thing up to the Supreme Court, the tune was changed. "A change came o'er the spirit of their dream," and this offense, which was so terrible a few hours before, sinks into insignificance, and old than Thomas is discharged, as the judge discharged the turkey at the table that had been there for a week, upon his own recognizance. [Laughter.] No case is to be permitted to be made out for the settlement and adjudication of the Supreme Court of the United States.

Mr. Secretary Stanton's great warrant reminds me of an anecdote, Senators. I am a very poor hand at telling one, but I believe I will try it. I do not know whether I shall succeed in telling it or not. It is one I used to hear a gentleman in our State of Tennessee tell about two Irishmen. They came over to this country and were very ignorant of our habits and manners and customs, and particularly in reference to the "varmints" that belonged to the United States. They were walking along one day, and they saw a little ground squirrel run up on a stump and then go down into the hollow of the stump. One of the Irishmen concluded he would catch him and see what kind of a "baste" it was. So he put his hand down in the hollow, and the other one said to him, "Have you got him, Pat?" "No," he replied, "by the powers, he has got me!" [Laughter.] And that was just exactly the way, Senators, with Mr. Stanton and this great warrant. Instead of getting Mr. Thomas, they found he was likely to get them, and therefore he was discharged upon his own recognizance, and we hear nothing more of his great offense. Whoever heard of such a proceeding as this intended to be converted into a grave and terrible and awful charge against the President of the United States "or any other man?" [Laughter.]

Before I pass, Senators, from this view of the case, allow me to read an authority here, without comment, in support of a proposition which I assumed before you awhile ago as to the force and effect of the long-continued usage and practice of the Government and the universal interpretation of the Constitution. I should have read it before. Chancellor Kent, in the first volume of his Commentaries, page 528, says:

"A solemn decision upon a point of law arising in any given case becomes an authority in a like case, because it is the highest evidence which we can have of the law applicable to the subject, and the judges are bound to follow that decision so long as it stands unreversed, unless it can be shown that the law was misunderstood or misapplied in that particular case. If a decision has been made upon solemn argument and mature deliberation, the presumption is in favor of its correctness, and the community have a right to regard it as a just declaration or exposition of the law and to regulate their actions and contracts by it. It would, therefore, be extremely inconvenient

to the public if precedents were not duly regarded and implicitly followed. It is by the notoriety and stability of such rules that professional men can give safe advice to those who consult them, and people in general can venture with confidence to buy and trust and to deal with each other. If judicial decisions were to be lightly disregarded, we should disturb and unsettle the great landmarks of property. When a rule has been once deliberately adopted and declared, it ought not to be disturbed unless by a court of appeal or review, and never by the same court except for very cogent reasons and upon a clear manifestation of error, and if the practice were otherwise it would be leaving us in a state of perplexing uncertainty as to the law,"

And the very same thing can be said about the construction of the Constitution and the acts of the Executive for a long time.

"The language of Sir William Jones is exceedingly forcible on this point. 'No man,' says he, ' who is not a lawyer would ever know how to act, and no man who is a lawyer would, in many instances, know what to advise unless courts were bound by authority as firmly as the pagan deities were supposed to be bound by the decrees of fate.'"

I shall not repeat, Senators, what I esteem to be the unanswerable argument of Judge Curtis, that the removal of Mr. Stanton is not a case embraced, or intended to be embraced, in the tenure-of-civil-office bill according to the terms of the bill itself. It is enough for me to refer you to that argument without repeating it.

And so, having on this branch of the case considered the three propositions with which I set out, having endeavored to demonstrate upon the first article, first, that the civil-tenure act is unconstitutional; second, that the action of the President was not a violation of the terms of the civil-tenure bill itself, because, from what occurred at the time that bill was passed it is manifest that it was not intended to embrace the Secretaries, as Judge Curtis showed in his extracts from the remarks that were made at the time when the bill was passed; and having shown, third, that if both these propositions be incorrect, still there was no intent, so as to maintain the accusation that is made upon the first article. I pass to the second article, and will endeavor to make my argument as brief as possible upon it.

The second article charges, in substance, that the President was guilty of a high misdemeanor in office by delivering the letter of authority to General Thomas while the Senate was in session, without its advice and consent, when there was no vacancy, and contrary to the tenure-of-civil-office act. In our answer we show that a vacancy existed when the letter of authority was delivered; that the appointment ad interim was justified by long usage, though the Senate was in session; that the tenure-of-civil-office act was not violated, even if it is a constitutional law, because the notification to the Senate of the removal and the appointment of Mr. Ewing shows that there was no criminal intent, no design to prevent the Senate from the exercise of its concurrent power in the appointment of a successor to the man who was attempted to be removed by the President.

The third article sets out the letter to Thomas, charges that he was appointed during the session when there was no vacancy, and that this was a high misdemeanor in office. In our answer we rely on the answer to the first article; deny that Thomas was "appointed" in the sense of the term used there, and insist that he was only temporarily designated; that there was no intent to violate the Constitution or make a permanent appointment; and we deny that there was no vacancy. Mr. Story says, in the third volume of his Commentaries, section 1553, that the Senate are said to have protested against the creation and appointment of ministers to Ghent, made during recess; that on the 20th of April, 1822, they held that the President could not create the office of minister and make appointments during the recess, and that—

"By vacancies they understood to be meant vacancies occurring from death, resignation, promotion, and *removal.* The word 'happen' had relation to some casualty not provided for by law."

If the Senate are in session when an office is created and no nomination is made, the President cannot fill the vacancy (for there is none) during the 'recess; and upon that question there is, as already shown, some difference of opinion.

The fourth article charges the President with conspiring with Thomas and other persons unknown with an intent, by intimidation and threats, unlawfully to hinder and prevent Stanton from holding the office, contrary to the act of July 31, 1861, and the Constitution, and charges that in this he was guilty of a "high crime in office." It is not necessary for me to do more than to refer to the answers in connection with these charges, and make an occasional passing remark upon some of them. The answer contains a general and specific denial; protests that Mr. Stanton was not Secretary; that the act was done to try Mr. Stanton's right; that there was no intimidation or threats, either to prevent Stanton or to induce Thomas, by such means, to obtain the office; that Mr. Thomas proceeded in a peaceful manner; that Stanton still retains undisturbed possession; and that the fourth article charges no agreement with Thomas to use threats, and does not state the threats.

Upon this article I have to say: 1. "Conspiracy at common law is an agreement between two or more persons to do an unlawful act, or an act which may become in the combination injurious to others." (1 Bouvier, 281.) "The indictment must show that it was intended to effect an unlawful purpose, or a lawful purpose by unlawful means." (Wharton, 669; Roscoe, 406.) In 3 Burrowe, page 1321, it was held that conspiracies may endanger public health, violate public morals, insult public justice, destroy the public peace, or affect public trade or business. It is not necessary that any act should

be done or that any one should be defrauded or injured. (1 Bouvier, 281, 282.)

2. The act entitled "An act to define and punish certain conspiracies," approved July 31, 1861, was passed soon after the rebellion commenced. It provides—I am not reading the act; for the sentences of these acts are very long, as are the sentences of most of the acts of Congress that I have read; I only read in connection the phraseology that pertains, as I think, to the particular matter charged—it provides that—

"If two or more persons, within any State or Territory of the United States, shall conspire together" * * * * by force, to prevent, hinder, or delay the execution of any law of the United States," * * * "each and every person so offending shall be guilty of a high crime," &c.

On this statute and the fourth article—for I wish to run over them as rapidly as I can—I remark,

1. That it is doubtful whether the word "Territory," as was argued by Judge Curtis, embraces the District of Columbia acquired after the Constitution, according to Scott vs. Sandford, 19 Howard, 615; 2 Story on the Constitution, 196; the United States vs. Gratiot, 14 Peters, 537.

2. The Constitution, article one, section eight, clause seventeen, confers the power to acquire a district not exceeding ten miles square, and does not use the word "Territory," so far as I know, in reference to the District of Columbia, or the district that was to be acquired under that provision of the Constitution.

3. The article does not charge that the act was done "by force," but uses the words "intimidation and threats," without setting out the threats. Although we do not insist here upon the technicality that it is required in a declaration or an indictment, yet upon any principle of correct pleading there ought to be enough alleged at least to show what is the offense that the party is charged with, and to bring the offense within the terms of the statute, which, as I say, is not done.

4. It charges that the object was to prevent Stanton from holding the office of Secretary of War, but does not allege how this was done to prevent, hinder, or delay the execution of any law of the United States. It does not set out or refer to the tenure-of-civil-office act.

5. I maintain, without dwelling upon the argument, that there is no proof of conspiracy so as to let in Thomas's declarations, according to the principle stated in Roscoe, 414, 417.

6. There is no proof of intimidation and threats to Stanton.

7. There is no pretense of a high crime in office as charged in this fourth article.

8. Sergeant Talfourd says a conspiracy is more difficult to be ascertained precisely than any other offense for which an indictment lies—

"An indictment against an officer of justice"—

And this is a mere repetition, with slightly

different phraseology, of a principle I relied on a while ago—

> "An indictment against an officer of justice for misbehavior in office must charge that the act was done with corrupt, partial, malicious, or improper motives, and, above all, with a knowledge that it was wrong."—*Wharton*, 733; *Roscoe*, 804.

The fifth article charges an unlawful conspiracy with Thomas and others unknown to hinder and prevent the execution of the tenure-of-civil-office act, and attempting to prevent Stanton from holding the office of Secretary of War. In our answer we deny the charge in its own terms; refer to the answer to the fourth article; deny that Stanton was Secretary; and except to the sufficiency of the fifth article as not showing by what means or what agreement the alleged conspiracy was formed or carried out.

In regard to this fifth article I maintain:

1. As to indictments for conspiracy, one person cannot be convicted. It must be by two, unless charged "with persons unknown;" and for that I refer to Wharton, 693, though that proposition is doubted by Roscoe in his Criminal Evidence, 418. He says that the record of acquittal of one is evidence for another.

2. The tenure-of-civil-office act of March 2, 1867, contains no provision as to "conspiracy."

3. The fifth section makes it a high misdemeanor to accept or hold any employment contrary to its provisions, &c. And the sixth section makes every removal, appointment, or employment contrary to the provisions of the act a high misdemeanor.

4. No force is charged in this article under the act of 1861.

5. We say that no conspiracy is proved. There is no agreement between the President and General Thomas to do any unlawful act whatever. The President, in virtue of his power as President, appoints Mr. Thomas, or attempts to appoint him, to the office of Secretary of War *ad interim.* He does not direct that any force shall be used. He does not direct that any unlawful act shall be done. All that he does is simply to make the appointment, and he does it with a view, as you may infer from all the testimony in the case, of having the question judicially settled.

Something was said by one of the Managers about General Sherman's testimony in this connection. General Sherman, in his testimony, spoke of the thought of force having crossed his own mind when he was reflecting about what it might be necessary for him to do; but when he was examined the second time, he distinctly and explicitly acquitted the President of the United States of ever having intimated to him any design or purpose whatever to employ force in the ejection of Mr. Stanton from the office of Secretary of War.

6. We say on this fifth article that if the tenure-of-office act is unconstitutional no misdemeanor can arise out of it.

7. A mere conspiracy to prevent the execution of the act of 1861 is not indictable. It must be a forcible conspiracy, or a conspiracy to act by force.

The sixth article, which I shall consider briefly, charges that the President did unlawfully conspire with Lorenzo Thomas by force to seize, take, and possess the property of the United States in the Department of War, then in the custody of Stanton, contrary to the act of July 31, 1861, and with intent then and there to violate "an act regulating the tenure of certain civil offices," and that he was thereby guilty of a "high crime in office." The denial to this article is brief and general. It denies that Stanton was Secretary; denies the conspiracy and unlawful intent; and refers to former answers. The first section of the conspiracy act of 1861 declares that—

> "If two or more persons within any State or Territory of the United States shall conspire together" * * * "by force to seize, take, or possess any property of the United States against the will or contrary to the authority of the United States," * * * "each and every person so offending shall be guilty of a high crime," &c.

On this act and article I argue:

1. That the President is not "a person" within the meaning of the act, and that official delinquency is always appropriately designated.

2. He is Commander-in-Chief of the Army and Navy, may recommend laws, command the Army and Navy and the militia when called into active service, require opinions in writing from his Cabinet officers, and he is required to take care that the laws be faithfully executed.

3. From these powers it results that the Department of War and the Secretary are under his control, and that he cannot be charged with seizing a thing which he had the right to take or to control by means of his authority over the Secretary of War.

4. The article does not charge that he attempted to seize, take, and possess the property "against the will or contrary to the authority of the United States," so as to bring the crime within the definition of the act of 1861.

The seventh article charges the President with conspiring with Thomas unlawfully to seize, take, and possess the property of the United States in the Department of War in the custody of Stanton, Secretary for the Department, with intent to violate the act regulating the tenure of certain civil offices, as a "high misdemeanor in office." The answer denies and negatives the terms of the charge, refers to former answers, and alleges that the allegations are insufficient.

I scarcely think any argument is necessary upon this seventh article, though I will say briefly that I do not see any violation of the President's oath of office in this or any other case; that, for the reasons already indicated, in view of the authorities which have already been read, there was no conspiracy; that the intent to seize, take, and possess the property in the War Department is not an offense within the tenure-of-civil-office act; that Thomas's declarations are no evidence of the conspiracy, as shown in Roscoe, 414, 417. Mr. Starkie says that mere detached declarations and confessions of persons not defendants, not made in the prosecution of the objects of the conspiracy, are not evidence even to prove the existence of a conspiracy.

In reference to the eighth article, which charges that the President committed and was guilty of a high misdemeanor in issuing and delivering to Thomas a letter of authority "with intent unlawfully to control the disbursements of the moneys appropriated for the military service and for the Department of War," contrary to the act regulating the tenure of certain civil offices, without the consent of the Senate, while the Senate was in session, and there being no vacancy, the answer admits the issuance of the letter of authority, but denies any unlawful intent; insists that there was a vacancy, and that his object was to bring the question to a decision before the Supreme Court.

Upon this article, I remark: 1. There is no provision in the tenure-of-civil-office act against "an intent unlawfully to con'rol the disbursements of the moneys appropriated for the military service and the Department of War," and no offense can be lawfully imputed of such an intention.

2. Under the constitutional provision that the President shall "take care that the laws be faithfully executed," the President may make and repeal Army rules and regulations as to pay for extra service, there being no legislation on the subject, and he may lawfully exercise a general supervision and control over the acts of the Secretary and other subordinates as to the disbursement of moneys, as was determined by the Supreme Court of the United States in the case of the United States vs. Eliason, 16 Peters, 291; 14 Curtis, 304.

3. The President's powers, as declared by the Supreme Court of the United States, time and again, are such as we maintain that no offense can be predicated of these acts. Without citing all the decisions, I refer to the case of Wilcox vs. Jackson, 13 Peters, 498, where it is said that the President acts in many cases through the heads of Departments, and the Secretary of War, having directed a section of land to be reserved for military purposes, the court presumed it to have been done by direction of the President, and held it to be by law his act; which, by the way, if I deemed it necessary, would be a very good authority to comment upon, in answer to the argument of the honorable Managers, that no implication results in favor of the powers which are conferred upon the President under the Constitution. There is a case where, to all intents and purposes, the Supreme Court enforced the doctrine of implication in his favor, and held that it would be presumed that the Secretary had acted by direction of the President himself,

and that that would be a sufficient protection to him.

The ninth article takes us into a somewhat different field; and I believe when we get there we part for a season at least with Mr. Stanton. The ninth article charges the President with instructing Brevet Major General Emory that a part of the act passed March 2, 1867, entitled "An act making appropriations," &c., and especially the second section thereof, directing that all orders from the President shall be issued through the General of the Army, which had been promulgated by general orders for the government of the Army of the United States, was unconstitutional, with intent to induce Emory, as commander of the department of Washington, to violate the provisions of said act, and to obey the orders of the President, and also with intent to violate the act regulating the tenure of civil offices, and to prevent Stanton from holding the office of Secretary of War.

The answer to this ninth article sets out, in substance, the note of the 22d of February, requesting Emory to call, the object being to be advised as to the military changes made in the department of Washington which had not been brought to the respondent's notice. Emory called respondent's attention to the second section of the appropriation act. Respondent said it was not constitutional. The conversation is stated, and you have seen that there is no substantial difference, as I understand it, between the conversation as set out in the President's answer and the conversation as stated by General Emory himself. The President says that he did not order or request Emory to disobey any law; that he merely expressed an opinion that the law was in conflict with the Constitution; and General Emory sustains that to all intents and purposes, for, when the subject was introduced, General Emory interrupted the President, and called his attention to this appropriation act.

I have to say in reference to this ninth article, that the Constitution, article two, section two, with which you are all familiar, provides that "the President shall be Commander-in-Chief of the Army and Navy of the United States and of the militia of the several States when called into the actual service of the United States." The object of this provision, without turning to the cases and taking up your time in reading them, as is stated in 1 Kent, 283; 8 Eliot's Debates, 103; Story on the Constitution, sections 1491, 1492; and 5 Marshall's Life of Washington, pages 583 to 588, was to give the exercise of power to a single hand. In Captain Meigs's case Mr. Attorney General Black—and I presume from the eulogy passed upon Mr. Attorney General Black by the honorable Manager yesterday, his opinion now, at any rate, ought to be a very authoritative opinion—in 9 Opinions, 468, says:

"As Commander-in-Chief of the Army, it is your right to decide, according to your judgment, what officer shall perform any particular duty, and as the supreme Executive Magistrate you have the power of appointment. Congress could not, if it would, take away from the President, or in any wise diminish the authority conferred on him by the Constitution."

Mr. Story, in his Commentaries, volume three, section fourteen hundred and eighty-five, quoting from the Federalist, No. 74, says that—

"Of all the cases and concerns of Government, the direction of war most peculiarly demands those qualities which distinguish the exercise of power by a single hand. Unity of plan, promptitude, activity, and decision are indispensable to success; and these can scarcely exist except when a single magistrate is intrusted exclusively with the power."

In section fourteen hundred and eighty-six, he says:

"The power of the President, too, might well be deemed safe, since he could not of himself declare war, raise armies, or call forth the militia, or appropriate money for the purpose; for these powers all belong to Congress."

Chancellor Kent, in his Commentaries, page 282, says:

"The command and application of the public force to execute law, maintain peace, and resist foreign invasion, are powers so obviously of an executive nature and require the exercise of qualities so characteristical of this department that they have always been exclusively appropriated to it in every well-organized Government upon the earth."

He shows the absurdity of Hume's plan of giving the direction of the army and navy to one hundred Senators; of Milton's, of giving the whole executive and legislative power to a single permanent council of senators; and Locke's, to a small oligarchical assembly.

In the case of the United States vs. Eliason, already cited, (16 Peters, 291,) it is said:

"The President has unquestioned power to establish rules for the government of the Army, and the Secretary of War is his regular organ to administer the military establishment of the nation, and rules and orders promulgated through him must be received as the acts of the Executive, and as such are binding on all within the sphere of his authority."

Senators, I maintain that there is no proof here to show, in the first place, that there was any unlawful or improper conversation between the President and General Emory. Mr. Manager BUTLER, with that fertility of invention which he has so eminently displayed at every stage of this proceeding, argues that it was either to bring about a civil war by resisting a law of Congress by force, or to recognize a Congress composed of rebels and northern sympathizers, that this conversation was had. Now, let us look to the circumstances under which the conversation took place. Mark you, an angry correspondence with General Grant had occurred from the 25th of January to the 11th of February, 1868. The President had charged, or intimated, at least, in the course of that correspondence, that he regarded General Grant as manifesting a spirit of insubordination. The removal of Mr. Stanton took place on the 21st of February. The Senate's resolution of the 21st of February, disapproving of the removal of Stanton, was sent to the President and the President sent a formal protest or message in response on the 24th of February.

I have not brought in newspapers here, Senators, and I do not intend to bring them in, because the facts that I am about to state are so fresh in your recollection. Without going into any minutiæ of detail, it is enough for me to say, in general terms, that on the manifestation of this unfortunate difference, for, no matter who is right or who is wrong about it, it is an unfortunate thing that there is a difference of opinion between the Chief Executive of the nation and the Congress, or or any part of the Congress, of the United States; it is a matter to be regretted that such a difference of opinion exists among you; but when this correspondence occurred, when these resolutions were offered in the Senate and in the House, if my memory does not fail me, and I do not think it possible it can in the short interval of time that has elapsed, there was telegram upon telegram, offer upon offer, made on the one side to Congress to support them, and on the other side to support the President.

The Grand Army of the Republic—the "G. A. R."—seemed to be figuring upon a large scale, and if there had not been the exercise of a very great prudence on the part of Congress and very great prudence on the part of the President of the United States himself we should have had this country enveloped in the flames of civil war. I hope, Senators, no matter what opinion you may entertain upon that subject; no matter who you may think was the strongest—and God forbid that the country should ever have any occasion to test who has the greatest military power at its command, the Congress of the United States or the President of the United States—I say, without entering upon such a question as that, which we all ought to view with horror, do give to the President of the United States the poor credit of believing that he has some friends in this country, that there are persons in the different States who would have been willing to rally around him. If an unfortunate military contest had occurred in the country, how it would have resulted the Great Being above us only knows.

All that I claim for the President of the United States is that whether he had few or many forces at his command, your President, as I told you upon the first day I came here, has manifested a degree of patriotic forbearance for which the worst enemy he has on the face of the earth ought to give him credit. If he was a tyrant, if he was a usurper, if he had the spirit of a Cæsar or of a Napoleon, if his object was to wrest the liberties of this country, your President could very easily have sounded the tocsin of war, and he could have had some kind of a force, great or small, perhaps to rally around him. But, instead of doing that, he comes here through his counsel before the Senate of the United States; and although he and his counsel, or at least I as one of them—I do not undertake to speak for the other gentlemen—honestly believe that under the Constitution of the United States organizing the Senate and the House of Representatives, the House of Representatives as at present constituted, with fifty Representatives from ten of the southern States absent, has no power to present articles of impeachment; and although he believes, as I do most conscientiously, that the Senate, as at present constituted, with twenty Senators absent from this Chamber who have a right to be here, has no power to try this impeachment, he makes no objection to your proceeding to try him. I shall not argue the question I have just suggested, for, in view of the almost unanimous vote against the resolution of Senator Davis, I think it would be an idle consumption of time to do so. I only advert to it so that I may place upon record this fact.

I say that, although the President and one, at least, of his counsel entertained this opinion, and doubt whether the House of Representatives, as organized, has the right to present the charges, or the Senate, as organized, has the right to try them under the Constitution, which says that "no State shall be deprived of its equal suffrage in the Senate," yet the President, instead of resorting to war, the President, instead of resorting to any of those acts of arbitrary tyranny and oppression which are resorted to by the ambitious man such as he is described to be, has come here; and while he states the objection, through me, at least, as one of his counsel, yet, in a peaceable manner, in a quiet manner, he submits this question, as well as all others, to be judged by the Senate of the United States in its present organization. And will you not at least give him credit for some degree of forbearance? When gentlemen talk of his being a tyrant and a usurper, when they talk of his object and purpose in sending for General Emory, Senators, do they prove any improper design upon his part? None on the face of the earth.

In this state of things, when the whole country was agitated and excited; when men's minds were aroused everywhere in the unfortunate division of parties in the United States to such an extent that they were offering troops on the one hand to sustain Congress and troops on the other hand to sustain the President, and when the General of the Army and the President had differed in their opinions, I maintain that the very fact that the President has done nothing of a military character shows that he had no intention to do the acts which are imputed to him. But when he saw these dispatches, when he knew that there was a difference between General Grant and himself, when he knew that there were persons sending dispatches through the newspapers, Governors, it was said, and leading men in the various States, as to how they would stand up to the Congress of the United States in this controversy, it was natural, right, proper, within the legitimate scope of the powers conferred upon him by the Constitution, that he should send for this officer, that he should inquire what was the meaning of these new troops that were brought into the city of Washington.

He had a right to do it, and the fact that he did do it is no evidence of any unlawful intention or design upon his part; but it proves that he was endeavoring to understand, as it was his duty to understand as the Commander-in-Chief of the Army of the United States, what was the meaning of the introduction of these forces. How did he know but that General Grant in the progress of this quarrel might attempt to assume the powers of a military dictator? How did he know but that General Grant might be endeavoring to envelop, to surround him by troops, and to have him arrested? Had he not a right to send for an officer? Had he not a right to inquire into the introduction of these military forces here? When he found that it was only a trivial force, when he found that there was no particular design on the part of anybody to violate the Constitution of the United States, his inquiry stopped; no effort was made upon his part to gather an Army or to rally a force to go to war with the Congress of the United States, but he retains counsel, comes here by his counsel, and in a peaceful manner submits himself to the judgment of the American Senate. I said it to you on the first day that his counsel appeared here, that the history of the whole world does not furnish anything in moral sublimity and grandeur surpassing the trial in which you are now engaged.

I said then, and I repeat it now, that I was delighted and rejoiced to see that this unfortunate controversy was taking this turn. I regretted that any such controversy had originated, regretted that there was any such unhappy difference of opinion between the Congress of the United States and the President; but in view of these red-hot dispatches that were pouring in upon both sides from every quarter of the United States, I did felicitate my country and I felicitated you upon the thought that the President of the United States had come here through his counsel and that he was willing to abide the arbitrament of the American Senate, the sworn men of the Constitution, the judges of your own constitutional powers. You judge as any other court judges that undertakes to determine the question of its jurisdiction. Let you judge for yourselves whether you have the constitutional power to try him. He comes before you in this peaceable and quiet mode; and I maintain, Senators, that he is not justly chargeable with the imputations that are made against him, and that his conduct is a full answer to the entire argument that has been made by the gentlemen upon the other side. They may impute motives; they may say just as much as they please about the conversation with General Emory or anybody else; the President has brought no force here; he has not attempted in any manner whatever to over-awe Congress; he has not attempted in any manner whatever to plunge this country into a revolution; he has acted peaceably and quietly, and the imputations that are made against him, as I insist, have no just foundation in the facts of the case. All the testimony shows—I shall not go into it in detail—that the President of the United States had it in view to have this question settled in a peaceable and amicable mode, that he contemplated no force, but de-signed that it should go before the Supreme Court.

The tenth article charges the President with making intemperate, scandalous, and inflam-matory harangues and uttering loud threats and bitter menaces against Congress and the laws of the United States, which are particu-larly indecent and unbecoming in the Chief Magistrate of the United States, and have brought the high office of President into con-tempt, ridicule, and disgrace. The charge is that he did this and was guilty of a high mis-demeanor in office; and the article specifies three speeches—one at the Executive Mansion, one at Cleveland, and one at St. Louis.

A great deal of testimony has been taken about those speeches. I might make an argu-ment as to whether they are faithful represent-ations of what the President said or not. I shall not weary your patience after having delayed you so long with any argument upon that point.

The answer says that the first amendment of the Constitution provides that "Congress shall make no law abridging the freedom of speech or of the press." "Freedom" is de-fined to be personal and private; "liberty" to be public. We say, therefore, that this is a personal right in the President as a citizen. I say further that his speeches were not offi-cial, like his communications to Congress, but were private and personal and in answer to the call of his fellow-citizens.

Ten years ago it would have struck the American people with astonishment that such a charge should be preferred against the Pres-ident of the United States. Almost from my boyhood down to the commencement of the war I have heard politicians talking time and again about what was known as the old sedition law; and if there ever was anything that stunk in the nostrils of the American people it was what was called the sedition law, the object of which was to prevent the publication of matter that might affect the President or the Govern-ment of the United States. We in this coun-try like to exercise the freedom of speech. Our fathers guarantied it to us in the Constitution, and, like the liberty of the press, which is also another cherished right dear to every American citizen, we like to have the largest liberty in the exercise of the right. The American peo-ple have been accustomed to it ever since they were a nation; and it is a great deal better to tolerate even impropriety and indecency of

speech, and to tolerate the licentiousness of the press, than it is to impose such restrictions as are imposed in other countries. Public opinion, as a general rule, will regulate and con-trol the indecency of speech, and it will regu-late and control the licentiousness of the press. If public opinion does not do it as a general rule, in a great many cases the arm of the law is long enough and it is strong enough to apply any corrective that may be necessary.

But the American people love to exercise the freedom of speech; and let it be known and remembered always that great as the powers of Congress may be, great as the powers of the President of the United States are, there is in a technical sense a body of men who have ever been admitted by all politicians and public men in the United States to be the sovereigns, the masters of both; that is, the people; they are the common constituents of Congress and of the President. Members of Congress have the right to speak and to talk with perfect freedom of the conduct of the President, and, as we maintain, the President in turn has the right to "carry the war into Africa," and to speak about Congress whenever he is assailed; and if he does this in his private intercourse with the citizens of the United States, not in official intercourse, he has just the same right to do it that any other citizen has in our Government; and whenever you destroy the right of the President of the United States to defend him-self against charges that may be made against him either in Congress or out of Congress, then you put the President at the feet of Congress and you destroy that independence which was intended by the Constitution to be secured to each of the coördinate departments of the Gov-ernment in their appropriate sphere.

It was intended that the legislative depart-ment should be independent here and within the circle of its appropriate duties; that the judicial department should be, in like manner, independent in the exercise of the functions and powers properly and appropriately belong-ing to it, and that the President of the United States, as to all executive matters, should be equally independent, both of the judiciary and of the Congress of the United States; and to hold otherwise is to enable Congress, as we insist, to monopolize all the powers of the Constitution and to become ultimately a des-potism such as never was contemplated by the fathers.

Now, Senators, I do not intend to go mi-nutely into this question, for I desire to close my remarks this evening, if you will have the patience to hear me to a close, and I shall try to close them at as early a period as I can. I do not intend to go minutely into the discussion of this question; but I have to say in regard to the President of the United States just as I said in regard to the House of Representatives: he is a mortal man; he is made of flesh and blood. The President of the United States has temper, passion, just like any other man.

When things are said about him in Congress or anywhere else, pray let us know why it is that he may not defend himself. I believe it was the 31st of January, 1866, but I may be mistaken in the date, when the venerable leader, as he is called, of the House of Representatives, who had opposed the President's nomination at Baltimore, and who, if I am not mistaken in the history of the country, had insisted there that the President was out of the United States, who never did favor him under any circumstances whatever, spoke in the House of Representatives of Charles I.

This was a few days before the President made one of the speeches that he has made in the course of this controversy. The President made a speech at the Executive Mansion on the 22d of February, 1866, in which he alluded to that, and in which he treated it as a sort of invitation to assassination. That imputation, so far as I know, was never noticed by the venerable Manager in the House of Representatives at all. Other members of Congress assailed him. You had the right to do it, a perfect right to do it, in the exercise of that freedom of speech and of that power of deliberation that belonged to you, a perfect right to say anything you pleased of the President of the United States.

But when these things were said by members of Congress, when they were published and circulated all over the land, spread broadcast in the newspapers, what is there in the Constitution, what is there in the position of the President of the United States, that ties his hands and prevents him from exercising the ordinary right of self-defense that belongs to any other citizen of the land? I admit that the President of the United States in a communication made officially to Congress ought to observe proper decorum, that he ought to observe that amenity of expression, if I may use such a phrase, as should be employed in the intercourse between one department of the Government and another; but I maintain that when Andrew Johnson makes a tour from Washington city to Chicago and Cleveland and St. Louis and Cincinnati, and returns to the city of Washington, he is nothing but a private citizen.

To be sure, he is President of the United States; but nothing in the Constitution, nothing in the laws of the land, undertakes to regulate his movements under such circumstances. He goes as a private citizen; and when he goes, if he is called out to make a speech as he was called out to make it by the people, and he chooses to answer the call, and if some severe philippics have been uttered against him by members of Congress, and he chooses to answer them; if members of Congress have insisted in the strongest sort of terms on their right to hold this doctrine or that doctrine or the other doctrine, why may not the President of the United States answer these things in the same way, appealing as he does to the

people, who are the common constituents of both? Who would deny to any Senator or any Representative the right when he goes home, or when he goes anywhere else within the limits of the magnificent territory that now constitutes the United States of America—who would have the assurance and the presumption to deny the power of any one of you, either in what is ordinarily called a stump speech or in any other mode of communication, to assail the conduct of the President of the United States? Why, Senators, this very thing of the freedom of discussion, although in heated political contests it is often carried to an improper extent, is the very life and salvation of the Republic. This thing of having parties in our land, although party spirit seems to have culminated in some of those dangers which were apprehended by Washington in his Farewell Address, and having parties a little more equally divided than they have been within the last three or four years in the United States, is essential to the preservation of the liberty of the American citizen. When parties are nearly equally balanced they watch each other, and they are sedulously cautious in regard to anything that may violate the Constitution of the United States.

I will not, as I have said, go minutely into the testimony on this matter; but I believe it has been proved, in regard to every one of those occasions, that it was an occasion sought not by the President, but by others. It is fresh in your recollection that when Mr. Senator JOHNSON and others called upon the President at the Executive Mansion they called upon him in their character of citizens, and he replied to them as he had a right to reply to them. When he went to Cleveland the proof shows that he did not desire to do anything more than to make a brief salutation to the people and leave them, but he was urged by his friends to do more; and I think it very likely, Senators, from my knowledge—and I am appealing to your own knowledge of the manner in which things are done in our country—I think it very likely, from the circumstances which are detailed here in evidence, and especially from the report of the speech itself, that there was a mob there at Cleveland, ready cut and dried, and prepared to insult and to assail the President of the United States in the manner they did do and to prevent him, if possible, from being heard. So, when they gave him provocation, he replied just as any other man would do and just as any other man had the right to do; and if he did make use of strong expressions in regard to the Congress of the United States, his expressions were not stronger than he had the right to use. Without discussing the question who was right or who was wrong, and insisting as I do upon the freedom of speech, I maintain this. So when he went to St. Louis he was again urged by his friends, according to the testimony, to go out and address the people. He had no desire to do so; he was urged and urged again by his friends, under whose control he had placed himself, to go there and answer their call; and is it not natural in a free Government like ours that the President of the United States should associate with the people; and when they make a call on him to address them is there anything improper and unreasonable in his doing it? And if when he addresses them a prepared mob intends to insult him; if they excite his passions, as the passions of any man would be excited under the circumstances, and he answers them a little intemperately and somewhat in their own way, speaks about the Congress of the United States pretty freely, pray tell us what sort of treason is committed? Does the Congress of the United States hold itself up so far above the President and the people of the United States as to say that your acts are not subject to criticism either by the President or by anybody else that chooses to criticise them? I tell you, Senators, we have not got that far yet. The President, any citizen of the United States of America, from the President down to the humblest citizen, has the right to criticise any act of Congress that he chooses to criticise, and he has the right to speak of any act of Congress in any mode that he sees proper to speak; and if the people will tolerate it there is no law and nothing in the Constitution to prevent it; and if this power of free speech, as I said before, is improperly exercised, then the corrective must be in the people themselves. So I say that one of the greatest rights secured to the people under the Constitution of this country would be invaded if this article was sustained.

The eleventh article charges that on the 18th of August, 1866, the defendant asserted that the Thirty-Ninth Congress was not a lawful Congress, denied that it had the right to recommend constitutional amendments, and in pursuance thereof removed Stanton on the 21st of February, 1868, to prevent the execution of the tenure-of-civil-office act, and to prevent the execution of the Army appropriation bill, and prevent the execution of the act for the more efficient government of the rebel States. The honorable Manager, Mr. BUTLER, referred to the President's admission that he attempted to prevail on General Grant to disobey the law, to his admission that he intended from the first to oust Mr. Stanton, his order to Grant not to recognize Stanton, his order to Thomas to take possession, &c. In answer to all this I have to say that the honorable Manager admits that if the Senate shall have decided that all the acts charged in the preceding articles are justified by law, then so large a part of the intent and purpose with which the respondent is charged in this article would fail of proof that it would be difficult to say whether he might not with equal impunity violate the laws known as the reconstruction acts; and as we have shown that the President is entitled to an acquittal on the other charges, he must be entitled to a judgment or verdict of not guilty upon this. But we say that none of the acts charged amount to a high crime or misdemeanor; that he had the right to deny the authority of Congress as he had previously done in his messages. I have them here, but I shall not turn to them.

Time and again the President, in his veto messages especially, has asserted, in his communications to Congress, his views and opinions as to the rights of the southern States that are excluded from representation; and although the phraseology is a little more courtly and elegant in the messages than it was in the several speeches which have been referred to, yet, so far as the substance is concerned, the President, in almost every one of those communications, has asserted his belief that the southern States are entitled to representation, and that they ought not to be excluded by Congress.

We say that none of the acts charged amount to a high crime or misdemeanor; that he had the right to deny the authority of Congress as he had previously done in his messages; that he had the right, as President, to instruct General Grant, who is his subordinate, bound to obey his commands, to disobey a law which he believed to be unconstitutional, or test its validity in the courts of law; that he had the right to remove Stanton and to order Thomas to take possession of the War Office; that he had the right to differ in opinion with Congress, and to answer the telegraphic dispatch of Governor Parsons as he did.

I ask, have not members of Congress during all Administrations, commencing with the Administration of General Washington, been accustomed to assail the measures of every President, both in Congress and out of it? And may not the President vindicate and endeavor to sustain his own views before the people in opposition to Congress? And can he not with propriety say to members of Congress when they oppose his views, "You are assailing the executive department," with just as much propriety as they can say that he is assailing the legislative department? The obligation to support the Constitution is equally obligatory on both, and both have the right under this and all other circumstances to appeal to their common sovereigns, the people, with a view of procuring a final and authoritative settlement of the controversy.

Senators, I had intended to notice, and I will now, with your indulgence, very briefly notice, one or two of the observations of the honorable Manager who last addressed you. He said that the President's object was to obtain control of the Army and Navy, and regulate the elections of 1868 in the ten southern States, so as to let the rebels exercise the elective franchise and exclude negroes from voting. What authority in the proof in this case had the honorable gentleman upon which to make that assertion? He said that the South had been given up to rapine, bloodshed, and murder by the President's policy. Why, Senators, under whose control is the South? Is not the South under the control of Congress? Is it not under the control of Army officers appointed by the President of the United States in pursuance of an act of Congress which he had attempted to veto? And who was responsible for this? I live in the South; and the statement which I am about to make will go just for what you think it is worth, much or little; but my observation ever since the close of the war is, that although there has been a bad state of things in some portions of the southern States, nine tenths of the murders and assassinations that have been reported in the newspapers and talked about here in Congress are made to order, got up for political effect, with a view of keeping up agitation and excitement, and that there is no warrant or foundation for the charge that the President has given up the South to any such condition of affairs.

It has been said, Senators, that the President takes the place of Charles I and Stanton the place of John Hampden. I am glad that the Manager did some justice to Mr. Stanton before he got through. He placed him in the condition of a "serf," as I showed you awhile ago, and I am glad that he wound up with Mr. Stanton by showing or asserting that he was entitled to the reputation of John Hampden; but as to the President being Charles I, or as to his assuming any powers that are not warranted by the Constitution of the country, I have endeavored in my feeble and imperfect way to show you that he is not guilty.

Senators, many other things might be said; but I have already occupied your time much longer than I had designed to do, or would have done if I had had a little more notice beforehand that I should be permitted to address you at all. I stated to you when I asked for the privilege of addressing you that I had no written speech, nothing but notes and memoranda which I had not an opportunity even to regulate or to put into something like order to address you. Therefore, what I have said has been said under some disadvantages. I only regret that it has not been more worthily said. Now, before I take my seat let me say to you. you have this whole case before you. I say to you now toward its conclusion, as I said at its commencement, that a high and solemn duty rests upon you, Senators of the United States. I have the same faith now that I have expressed ever since I undertook this case and that I expressed so fully yesterday. I do believe that confidence ought to be reposed in the American Senate. I do believe that men of your character and of your position in the world have the ability to decide a case impartially and to set aside all party considerations in its determination. I believe it, and I trust that the result will show that the country has a right to believe it.

Every lawyer, every judge in the United

C. I.—41.

States, is familiar with the fact that a great many cases are put in the law books, and especially in works on evidence, rather as a caution to judges and jurors than anything else, as to improper and unjust verdicts that have been rendered in times past. Every lawyer knows that cases are reported in the books where men, especially upon circumstantial evidence, have been tried and executed for murder and other offenses, and who it afterward appeared upon a more careful investigation, were not guilty of the offenses imputed to them. These cases are not put in the books for the purpose of frightening judges and juries from their propriety, but they are put in for the purpose of causing them to exercise a salutary degree of caution in the powers which are conferred upon them. So without going over these things in detail, I may say that I think even the Senate of the United States may look back upon the history of the world for the purpose of deriving the same instructive lessons that are intended in law books to be impressed upon the courts and juries of the land. Without undertaking to travel along the whole course of history, some three or four examples have occurred that are not unworthy of a passing notice before I take my seat.

Without going into the details, every Senator is fully informed of the account which has been transmitted to us in history of the murder of Cæsar by Brutus; and for nearly twenty centuries it has been a question whether that act was an act of patriotism, and whether it was justified or not. The execution of Charles I is another of the historical problems which have probably not been settled, and never will be satisfactorily settled in the opinions of mankind. Some regard Cromwell as a patriot, as a man animated by the purest and most correct motives; others look upon him as being an ambitious man, who designed to engross power improperly into his own hand. That question still remains open. But these deeds of violence which have been done in the world have not always been followed by peace or quiet to those who have done them. A few short years after the execution of Charles I, the bodies of Cromwell and Bradshaw, and one or two others who were concerned in that execution, were, in consequence of a change of public sentiment in England, taken from their graves and they were hung in terror and in hate and execration by the party that came into power.

Louis XVI was executed by the people of France. Did that act give peace and quiet to the French kingdom? No; it was soon followed by deeds of bloodshed such as the world never saw before. The guillotine was put in motion, and the streets of Paris, it is said, literally ran with human gore. Most of those who were concerned in the trial of Charles I were executed. Three of them came to America and sought refuge in the vicinity of New Haven. They were compelled to hide themselves in caves. Their graves were not known to those in whose midst they lived, or are but little known.

These deeds of violence, done in times of high party and political excitement, are deeds that should admonish you as to the manner in which you discharge the duty that devolves upon you here. This thing of being rid of the Chief Magistrate of the land in the mode that is attempted here may be fraught with consequences that no man can foresee. I have no idea that it will be fraught with such consequences as those I have described; and yet deeds that are done in excitement often come back in future years, and cause a degree of feeling which it is not, perhaps, proper for me, on this occasion, to describe; it has been done a great deal better by a master hand, who tells us:

"But ever and anon of grief subdued,
  There comes a token like a scorpion's sting,
Scarce seen, but with fresh bitterness imbued.
  And slight withal may be the things which bring
Back on the heart the weight which it would fling
  Aside forever: it may be a sound—
A tone of music—summer's eve—or spring—
  A flower, the wind, the ocean which shall wound,
Striking the electric chain wherewith we are darkly
      bound;
  And how and why we know not, nor can trace
Home to its cloud this lightning of the mind,
  But feel the shock renewed—nor can efface
The blight and blackening which it leaves behind."

God grant that the American Senate shall never have such feelings as these. God grant that you may so act in the discharge of your duty here that there shall be no painful remembrance, Senators, to come back on you in your dying hour. God grant that you may so act that you cannot only look death, but eternity in the face, and feel that you have discharged your duty and your whole duty to God and your country. And if you thus act, you will, I am sure, act in such manner as to command the approbation of angels and of men, and the admiration and applause of the world and of posterity who are to come after us.

Mr. Chief Justice and Senators, you and each of you, personally and individually, have struggled through life until you have reached the positions of eminence you now occupy. It has required time and study and labor and diligence to do so; but, after all, the fame which you have acquired is not your own. It belongs to me; it belongs to others. Forty million American citizens are tenants in common of this priceless property. It is not owned alone by you and your children. We all have a direct and immediate interest in it. Whatever strife may have existed among us as a people; whatever of crimination and recrimination may have been engendered amid the fierceness of party passion, yet in the cool moments of calm reflection every true patriot loves his country as our common mother, and points with just pride to the hard-earned reputation of all her children. Let me invoke you, therefore, in the name of all the American people, to do nothing that may even seem to be a stain upon the judicial ermine, or to dim, for

a moment, the bright escutcheon of the American Senate. The honorable Manager who addressed you on yesterday [Mr. BOUTWELL] referred in eloquent terms to Carpenter's historical painting of emancipation. Following at an humble distance his example, may I be permitted to say that I have never entered the Rotunda of this magnificent and gorgeous Capitol when I have not felt as if I were treading upon holy ground; and I have sometimes wished that every American sire could be compelled by law and at the public expense to bring his children here, at least once in their early years, and to cause them to gaze upon and to study the statuary and paintings which, at every entrance and in every hall and chamber and niche and stairway, are redolent with the history of our beloved country. Columbus studying the unsolved problem of a new world, and the white man and Indian as types of the march of civilization, arouse attention and reflection at the threshold. Within, the speaking canvas proclaims the embarkation of the Pilgrim Fathers; their sublime appeal to the God of oceans and of storms; their stern determination to seek a "faith's pure shrine" among the "sounding aisles of the dim woods," and "freedom to worship God;" and the divine, the angelic countenance of Rose Standish as she leans, with woman's love, upon the shoulder of her husband, and looks up, with woman's faith, for more than mortal aid and guardianship, so fixes and rivets attention,

"That, as you gaze upon the vermil cheek,
  The lifeless figure almost seems to speak."

And there is the grand painting that represents Washington, the victor, surrendering his sword after having long before refused a a crown—one of the sublimest scenes that earth has ever seen, presenting, as it nobly does, to all the world the greatest and best example of pure and unselfish love of country. Not to speak of other teeming memories which everywhere meet the eye and stir the soul, as I sat a few days since gazing upward upon the group (Washington and the sisterhood of early States) who look down from the topmost height of the Dome, methought I saw the spirits of departed patriots rallying in misty throngs from their blissful abode and clustering near the wondrous scene that is transpiring now; and as I sat, with face upturned, I seemed to see the shadowy forms descend into the building and arrange themselves with silent but stately preparation in and around this gorgeous apartment. I have seen them, in imagination, ever since. I see them now! Above and all around us. *There* in the galleries, amid those living forms of loveliness and beauty, are Martha Washington and Dolly Madison and hundreds of the maids and matrons of the Revolution, looking down with intense interest and anxious expectation, and watching with profoundest solicitude the progress of the grandest trial of the nineteenth century. And *there*, in your very midst and at your sides, are sitting the shades of Sherman and Hamilton, Washington and Madison, Jefferson and Jackson, Clay and Webster, who in years that are past bent every energy and employed every effort to build our own great temple of liberty, which has been and will continue in all time to be the wonder, the admiration, and the astonishment of the world. If there be joy in heaven over one sinner that repenteth, and if the shades of Dives and Lazarus could commune across the great gulf with each other, it is no wonder that the spirits of departed patriots are gathered to witness this mighty inquest, and that they are now sitting with you upon this, the most solemn of all earthly investigations. Behind the Chief Justice I see the grave and solemn face of the intrepid Marshall; and above, among, and all around us are the impalpable forms of all the artists of our former grandeur! Mr. Chief Justice and Senators, if you cannot clasp their shadows to your souls, let me entreat you to feel the inspiration of their sacred presence; and as you love the memory of departed greatness; as you revere the names of the patriot fathers; and as you remember the thrilling tones of the patriot voices that were wont to speak "the thoughts that breathed and the words that burned" with deathless love for our institutions and our laws, so may you be enabled to banish from your hearts every vestige of prejudice and of feeling, and to determine this great issue in the lofty spirit of impartial justice, and with that patriotic regard for our present and future glory that ever prompted the action of the purest and best and greatest names that, in adorning our own history, have illuminated the history of the world. And when the day shall come—and may it be far distant—when each of you shall "shuffle off this mortal coil," may no thorn be planted in the pillow of death to embitter your recollection of the scene that is being enacted now; and when the time shall come, as come it may, in some future age, when your own spirits shall flit among the hoary columns and chambers of this edifice, may each of you be then enabled to exclaim—

"Here I faithfully discharged the highest duty of earth; here I nobly discarded all passion, prejudice, and feeling; here I did my duty and my whole duty, regardless of consequences; and here I find my own name inscribed in letters of gold, flashing and shining, upon the immortal roll where the names of all just men and true patriots are recorded!"

I do not know, Mr. Chief Justice, that it is exactly in accordance with the etiquette of a court of justice for me to do what I propose to do now; but I trust that you and the Senate will take the will for the deed, and if there is anything improper in it you will overlook it. I cannot close, sir, the remarks which I have to make in this case, without returning my profound thanks to the Chief Justice and the Senators for the very kind and patient attention with which they have listened to me on this occasion. Imperfect as the argument has been, and lengthy as it has been, you have extended to me the patient attention which I had little reason to expect, and I cannot, Senators, take my seat without returning my thanks to you, whether it be according to the usage of a court like this or not.

On motion of Mr. TIPTON, the Senate, sitting for the trial of the impeachment, adjourned.

SATURDAY, *April* 25, 1868.

The Chief Justice of the United States took the chair.

The usual proclamation having been made by the Sergeant-at-Arms,

The Managers of the impeachment on the part of the House of Representatives and the counsel for the respondent, except Mr. Stanbery, appeared and took the seats assigned to them respectively.

The members of the House of Representatives, as in Committee of the Whole, preceded by Mr. E. B. WASHBURNE, chairman of that committee, and accompanied by the Speaker and Clerk, appeared and were conducted to the seats provided for them.

The CHIEF JUSTICE. The Secretary will read the Journal of yesterday's proceedings.

The Journal of yesterday's proceedings of the Senate, sitting for the trial of the impeachment, was read.

The CHIEF JUSTICE. The first business this morning is the order proposed by the Senator from Vermont, [Mr. EDMUNDS.] The Clerk will read the order.

Mr. EDMUNDS. Mr. President, at the request of several Senators who desire to consider the question, I move that the consideration of the order be postponed until Monday morning.

Mr. DRAKE. Mr. President, I move that the order be indefinitely postponed.

Mr. SUMNER. That is better.

Mr. DRAKE. And on that motion I call for the yeas and nays.

Mr. EDMUNDS. So do I, Mr. President.

The CHIEF JUSTICE. The motion for indefinite postponement takes precedence of the motion to postpone to a day certain; and upon that question the yeas and nays are demanded.

The yeas and nays were ordered.

Mr. CONKLING. I wish to inquire what was the motion of the Senator from Vermont?

The CHIEF JUSTICE. The Senator from Vermont moved to postpone until Monday; the Senator from Missouri moves to postpone indefinitely; and the question now is upon the indefinite postponement.

Mr. SHERMAN. I should like to have the order read.

The CHIEF JUSTICE. The Clerk will read the order.

The Chief Clerk read as follows:

Ordered, That after the arguments shall be concluded, and when the doors shall be closed for deliberation upon the final question, the official reporters of the Senate shall take down the debates upon the final question, to be reported in the proceedings.

The question being taken by yeas and nays on Mr. DRAKE's motion, resulted—yeas 20, nays 27; as follows:

YEAS—Messrs.Cameron, Chandler, Conkling, Corbett, Drake, Ferry, Harlan, Howard, Morrill of Maine, Morrill of Vermont, Mortòn, Nye, Pomeroy, Ramsey, Ross, Stewart, Sumner, Thayer, Tipton, and Yates—20.

NAYS—Messrs. Anthony, Buckalew, Cragin, Davis, Dixon, Doolittle, Edmunds, Fessenden, Fowler, Frelinghuysen, Grimes, Henderson, Hendricks, Howe, Johnson, McCreery, Morgan, Norton, Patterson of Tennessee, Saulsbury, Sherman, Trumbull, Van Winkle, Vickers, Willey, Williams, and Wilson—27.

NOT VOTING—Messrs. Bayard, Cattell, Cole, Conness, Patterson of New Hampshire, Sprague, and Wade—7.

So the order was not indefinitely postponed.

The CHIEF JUSTICE. The question recurs on the motion of the Senator from Vermont to postpone the order until Monday.

The motion was agreed to.

Mr. SUMNER. Mr. President, I send to the Chair an order which I desire to have read.

The CHIEF JUSTICE. The Secretary will read the order.

The Chief Clerk read as follows:

Ordered, That the Senate, sitting for the trial of Andrew Johnson, President of the United States, will proceed to vote on the several articles of impeachment at twelve o'clock on the day after the close of the arguments.

Mr. SUMNER. If the Senate is ready to act on it——

The CHIEF JUSTICE. The order is for present consideration, unless objected to.

Mr. JOHNSON. I object.

The CHIEF JUSTICE. Being objected to it lies over.

Mr. SUMNER. Mr. President, I send to the Chair two additional rules, the first of which is derived from the practice of the Senate on the trials of Judge Chase and Judge Peck.

The CHIEF JUSTICE. The Secretary will read both of the additional rules proposed.

The Chief Clerk read as follows:

RULE 23. In taking the votes of the Senate on the articles of impeachment the presiding officer shall call each Senator by his name, and upon each article propose the following question, in the manner following: "Mr. ——, how say you, is the respondent, ——, guilty or not guilty as charged in the —— article of impeachment?" whereupon each Senator shall rise in his place and answer "guilty" or "not guilty."

RULE 24. On a conviction by the Senate it shall be the duty of the presiding officer forthwith to pronounce the removal from office of the convicted person according to the requirement of the Constitution. Any further judgment shall be on the order of the Senate.

The CHIEF JUSTICE. Is the Senate ready for the consideration of these rules now?

Mr. JOHNSON. I object.

The CHIEF JUSTICE. Objection is made; they will lie over. [After a pause.] Gentlemen of counsel for the President, you will please proceed with the argument in his defense.

Hon. WILLIAM S. GROESBECK, on behalf of the respondent, addressed the Senate as follows:

Mr. CHIEF JUSTICE and SENATORS: I am sorry that I am not so well to-day as I should like to be; but I know the desire of the Senate to get on with this argument, and I have, therefore, preferred to come here this morning in the condition I am and attempt to present an outline, at least, of the views I have formed of the respondent's case.

Since the organization of our Government we have had five trials of impeachment—one of a Senator, and four of judges, who held their office by appointment and for a tenure that lasted during life or good behavior. It has not been the practice, nor is it the wise policy, of a republican or representative Government to avail itself of the remedy of impeachment for the control and regulation of its elective officers. Impeachment was not invented for that purpose, but rather to lay hold of offices that were held by inheritance and for life. And the true policy of a republican Government, according to my apprehension, is to leave these matters to the people. They are the great and supreme tribunal to try such questions, and they assemble statedly with the single object to decide whether an officer shall be continued or whether he shall be removed from office.

I may be allowed, Senators, to express my regret that such a case as this is before you; but it is here, and it must be tried, and therefore I proceed, as I promised at the outset, to say what I may feel able to say in behalf of the respondent.

In the argument of one of the Managers the question was propounded:

"Is this body, now sitting to determine the accusation of the House of Representatives against the President of the United States, the Senate of the United States or a court?"

The argument goes on to admit:

"If this body here is a court in any manner as contradistinguished from the Senate, then we agree" * * * * "that the accused may claim the benefit of the rule in criminal cases, that he may only be convicted when the evidence makes the case clear beyond reasonable doubt."

In view of this statement, and in view of the effort that has been made by the Managers in this cause, I ask, Senators, your attention to the question, in what character do you sit on this trial? We have heard labored and protracted discussion to show that you did not sit as a court; and the Managers have even taken offense at any such recognition of your character. For some reason I will not allude to they have done even more, and claimed for this body the most extraordinary jurisdiction. Admitting that it was a constitutional tribunal, they have yet claimed that it knew no law, either statute or common; that it consulted no precedents save those of parliamentary bodies; that it was a law unto itself; in a word, that its jurisdiction was without bounds; that it may impeach for any cause, and there is no appeal from its judgment. The Constitution would appear to limit somewhat its jurisdiction, but everything this tribunal may deem impeachable becomes such at once, and when the words "high crimes or misdemeanors" are used in that instrument they are without signification and intended merely to give solemnity to the charge.

To sustain this extraordinary view of the character of this tribunal we have been referred to English precedents, and especially to early English precedents, when, according to my recollection, impeachment and attainder and bills of pains and penalties labored together in the work of murder and confiscation. Senators, I do not propose to linger about these English cases. We have cases of our own upon this subject; we have teachings of our own. This we know: our fathers, in framing the Constitution, were jealous of delegating their power, and tried to make a limited constitutional Government; tried to enumerate all the power they were willing to intrust to any department of it. The executive department is limited; the judicial department is limited; and the legislative department, we have supposed, was also limited; but according to the argument made here on this trial it is otherwise, and it has in its service and at its command an institution that is above all law and acknowledges no restraint; an institution worse than a court-martial, in that it has a broader and more dangerous jurisdiction. Senators, I cannot believe for one moment that there is lying in the heart of the Constitution any such tribunal as this; and I invite your attention to a brief examination of our own authorities and of our own teachings upon this subject.

It was with much doubt and hesitation that the jurisdiction to try impeachment at all was intrusted to the Senate of the United States. The grant of this power to this body was deferred to the last moment of time. Nor was your jurisdiction overlooked. Allow me to call your attention very briefly to the proceedings of the Federal Convention upon this subject as recorded in the Journal of that body. In the first report that was presented it was proposed to allow impeachment for "malpractice or neglect of duty." It will be observed that this was very English-like and very broad in the jurisdiction proposed to be conferred. There is not necessarily any crime in the jurisdiction here proposed to be conferred. In the next report it was proposed to allow the tribunal jurisdiction for "treason, bribery, and corruption." It will be observed that they began to get away from the English precedents and to approach the final result at which they arrived. The jurisdiction here proposed was partly criminal and partly broad and open, not necessarily involving penal liability. In the next report it was proposed that impeachment should be allowed for "treason or bribery"—nothing else. It will be observed that here was nothing but gross, flagrant crime. This jurisdiction was considered too limited and was opened, and that gives us the jurisdiction we have in the present. Constitution,

"treason, bribery, or other high crimes and misdemeanors"—no malpractice, no neglect of duty, nothing that left the jurisdiction open. The jurisdiction is shut and limited by any fair construction of this language; and it was intended to be shut. It is impossible to observe the progress of the deliberations of the Convention upon this single question, beginning with the broadest and most open jurisdiction and ending in a jurisdiction defined in these technical terms of law, without coming to the conclusion that it was their determination that the jurisdiction should be circumscribed and limited.

But in what character, Senators, do you sit here? You have heard the argument of the Managers; you have heard their frequent discussions upon this subject all through the progress of the cause, appealing to English precedents to maintain the position that you sit here not as a court, but as an inquest of office or as some nameless tribunal with unbounded and illimitable jurisdiction. Now. we have precedents, we have our own precedents upon this subject; and let me call your attention to them for a few moments.

But, before doing so, I desire to say that it has been heard for the first time in this trial that this tribunal, sitting as you are sitting, was anything else than a court. I challenge the gentlemen in all the investigations they may have made of the action of the constitutional Convention, of the utterances of jurists, or of anything that has been said or done to throw light upon this inquiry, to produce anything calculated to make the impression that the tribunal that tried impeachment was anything else than a court.

Let us look, Senators, to our own precedents. We have had five trials of impeachment in the United States. The first was the case of Blount. What was the language of the tribunal in that trial—not of counsel, but of the tribunal itself? What was its language upon this identical question? Hear it. When they came to give their final decision they did it in this language:

"The *court* is of opinion that the matter alleged in the plea of the defendant is sufficient in law to show that this *court* ought not to hold jurisdiction of the said impeachment, and that the said impeachment be dismissed."

That is good authority. It is good American precedent upon this question. It is the deliberate opinion of the Senate of the United States in the first trial in which it sat in this capacity, declaring itself, in the most solemn language it uttered throughout the trial, its final decision, to be a court and not an inquest of office or some nameless thing that by reason of its mystery is calculated to frighten, or at least to confuse.

What was the next case? The Pickering case. I am referring now to the appendix to volume three of the Senate Journal. On pages 489 and 507 the language of the body will be found on this subject in the following form: in its process, its own language, it styles itself "the Senate sitting in their capacity of a court of impeachment," and the last action of the body, their decision, was upon the question in this form:

"Is the *court* of opinion that John Pickering be removed?"

So, too, in the next, the Chase trial. The President in that case styles the body a "court," and, more fortunate than the Chief Justice in this, escaped all censure from the Managers of the House of Representatives.

In the next, the case of Peck, the tribunal itself took the final vote under its own resolution in this language:

"*Resolved*, That this court will now pronounce judgment in the case of James H. Peck, judge of the United States court for the district of Missouri."

In the case of Judge Humphreys, in 1862, the Senate styled itself in all its proceedings "the high court of impeachment."

Senators, I have gone over every precedent we have in our own history upon this question, and I show that in every instance the body, the Senate, in those trials solemnly declared itself to be a court. If we are to go for precedents let us take our own rather than the precedents from abroad which have been so liberally quoted by the Managers on this occasion.

In what spirit, Senators, should you try this case? Allow me to refer you upon this subject to the language of Story in his Commentaries on the Constitution, to be found on page 216, section seven hundred and forty-three. I beg your attention to this language of Justice Story upon the question which I have just propounded:

"The great objects to be attained in the selection of a tribunal for the trial of impeachments are impartiality, integrity, intelligence, and independence. If either of these be wanting the trial must be radically imperfect. To secure impartiality the body must be in some degree removed from popular power and passions, from the influence of sectional prejudice, and from the more dangerous influence of party spirit. To secure integrity there must be a lofty sense of duty and a deep responsibility to future times and to God. To secure intelligence there must be age, experience, and high intellectual powers as well as attainments. To secure independence there must be numbers as well as talents, and a confidence resulting at once from permanency of place, dignity of station, and enlightened patriotism."

On the next page he adds:

"Strictly speaking, the power"—

That is, the power of impeachment—

"partakes of a political character; and on this account it requires to be guarded in its exercise against the spirit of faction, the intolerance of party, and the sudden movements of popular feeling."

Senators, this is not my language; it is the language of a distinguished jurist whom you all respect. While it is not mine, I affirm, by all our own authorities, by our own teachings on this subject, that it is a true and faithful portraiture of what is meant in the Constitution by the tribunal which tries impeachments. And for this very purpose you have been sworn anew to prepare you for this new duty. The oath which you took when you entered this Chamber as Senators was a political, legislative oath. The oath that is now upon you is purely judicial, to do impartial justice.

We are, then, Senators, in a court. What are you to try? You are to try the charges contained in these articles of impeachment, and nothing else. Upon what are you to try them? Not upon common fame; not upon the price of gold in New York, or upon any question of finance; not upon newspaper rumor; not upon any views of party policy; you are to try them upon the evidence offered here and nothing else, by the obligation of your oaths.

What is the issue before you? Allow me to say it is not a question whether this or that thing were done. You are not here to try a mere act. By the very terms of the Constitution you can only try in this tribunal crime. Let me repeat the jurisdiction:

"Treason, bribery, and other high crimes and misdemeanors."

The jurisdiction is shut within that language, and the issue that this court can try is only the issue of crime or no crime. What is crime? In every grade of it, Senators, there must be unlawful purpose and intention. Where these are wanting there cannot be crime. There must be behind the act the unlawful purpose prompting its commission; otherwise there can be no crime.

Let me illustrate. Suppose a crazy man should burst into this Chamber and kill one of us. He has committed the act of homicide; he has not committed a crime.

Let me put the case in a different form. Suppose a President should become deranged, and while in that condition should plot treason, attempt to bribe, and break law upon law, would you impeach him? You have no jurisdiction to try him upon impeachment.

Let me put another case not supposititious. President Lincoln claimed and exercised the power of organizing military commissions, under which he arrested and imprisoned citizens within the loyal States. He had no act of Congress warranting it; and the Supreme Court has decided that the act was against the express provisions of the Constitution. Now comes the question, and I beg your attention to it: suppose he did violate the express provisions of the Constitution, according to the gentlemen on the other side he must be convicted. I beg to read from the argument of one of the Managers upon that subject. Says the Manager who addressed you on the day before yesterday:

"Nor can the President prove or plead the motive by which he professes to have been governed in his violation of the laws of the country." * * * "The necessary, the inevitable presumption in law is, that he acted under the influence of bad motives in so doing, and no evidence can be introduced controlling or coloring in any degree this necessary presumption of the law.

"Having, therefore, no right to entertain any motive contrary to his constitutional obligation to execute the laws he cannot plead his motive. Inasmuch as he can neither plead nor prove his motive, the presumption of the law must remain that in violating his oath of office and the Constitution of the United States he was influenced by a bad motive."

The gentleman seems to acknowledge that there must be motive. There can be no crime without motive. But when the party comes forward and offers to prove it his answer is, "You shall not prove it." When he comes forward and offers to prove it from his warm, living heart, the answer is, "We will make up your motive out of the presumptions of law, and conclude you upon that subject; we will not hear you." The command is "silence" when you propose to prove the exact motive by which you were prompted in the act.

No, Senators; the jurisdiction of this body is to try crime. There is no crime without unlawful intention and purpose. You cannot get it without the unlawful intent or purpose behind the act prompting its commission. Why, what is the judgment that you shall render in this case? Not did the President do this or that act; that is not your inquiry; but was he guilty of a high misdemeanor in the purpose with which he did the act?

With these preliminary observations, I propose to proceed to a brief examination of the merits of the case.

You are now all of you, Senators, familiar with the articles of impeachment, and I need not attempt to go over them article by article. I have this to say, and you will all concur with me instantly upon making the statement: the first eight articles are built upon two acts of the President; the one, the removal of Stanton, the other the letter of authority given to Thomas. Now, if you will take up these eight articles, and then the last, the eleventh, and notice the substantial part of them, around which they throw their charges of bad intent and their averments, you will see that in the whole eight articles there are but these two acts, the removal of Stanton and the letter of authority to Thomas, so that we have only to inquire in reference to these two acts in order to ascertain the merits of this case upon these eight articles, and in fact I may say the eleventh also.

If the President of the United States had the right to remove Edwin M. Stanton, then these eight articles are without support. If, in addition to that, he had the right to give that letter of authority to Lorenzo Thomas, the eight articles fall in ruins instantly. There is no Senator who has studied this case who will not see the accuracy of this statement at once; and it relieves us from the necessity of going through them, article by article, and step by step. Give me these two propositions, the right to remove Stanton and the right to issue the letter of authority to Thomas, and the articles fall instantly; there is nothing left of them. So that we have at last, in the consideration of these articles, but two inquiries to make:

1. Had the President the right to remove Stanton?

2. Had he the right to issue the letter of authority to Thomas?

I propose, as well as I am able in my condition, to examine these two questions.

Taking up the questions in their order, first, had the President the right to remove Edwin M. Stanton? I propose to examine that question in the first instance in connection with the act regulating the tenure of certain civil offices. It is claimed on the one side that by the operations of this law Mr. Stanton was withdrawn from his previous position and covered and protected here. It is claimed upon the other side that the law does not apply to his case; and if it do not, I think it will be acknowledged by the Senators that the President had the right to remove him. Allow me to call your attention, therefore, to one section of this law in which the question is presented:

"That every person holding any civil office to which he has been appointed by and with the advice and consent of the Senate, and every person who shall hereafter be appointed to any such office, and shall become duly qualified to act therein, is, and shall be, entitled to hold such office until a successor shall have been in like manner appointed and duly qualified, except as herein otherwise provided: *Provided*, That the Secretaries of State, of the Treasury, of War, of the Navy, and of the Interior, the Postmaster General, and the Attorney General, shall hold their offices respectively for and during the term of the President by whom they may have been appointed, and for one month thereafter, subject to removal by and with the advice and consent of the Senate."

Now, gentlemen, let me state a few facts before we proceed to the consideration of the construction of this section. The first fact to which I call your attention is that the act was passed on the 2d of March 1867. I further call your attention to the fact that Stanton's commission is dated on the 15th of January, 1862. It is a commission given to him by President Lincoln, by which he was to hold the office of Secretary for the Department of War "during the pleasure of the President of the United States for the time being." Mr. Johnson became President on the 15th of April, 1865. He has not in any manner commissioned Mr. Stanton. Upon these facts, Senators, I claim it is clear that Mr. Stanton is not protected by this bill. Let us inquire. The law proposed to grant to the Cabinet officers, as they are called, a term that shall last during the term of the President by whom they were appointed, and one month thereafter. Mr. Johnson has not appointed Mr. Stanton. He was appointed during the first term of Mr. Lincoln. He was not appointed at all during the current presidential term. He holds his office by a commission which would send him through Administration after Administration until it is recalled. Now, what is the meaning of this language, " he shall hold his office during the term of the President by whom he was appointed?" and he was not appointed during the present term. I think that is enough. It does seem to me that that simple statement settles this question.

The gentleman has said this is Mr. Lincoln's term. The dead have no ownership in office or estate of any kind. Mr. Johnson is the President of the United States with a term, and this is his term. But it would make no difference if Mr. Lincoln were living to-day; if Mr. Lincoln were the President to-day he could remove Mr. Stanton. Mr. Lincoln would not have appointed him during this term. It was during the last term that Mr. Stanton received his appointment and not this; and an appointment by a President during one term, by the operation of this law will not extend the appointee through another term because that same party may happen to be reëlected to the Presidency. Stanton, therefore, holds under his commission, and not under the law.

Again, Senators, his tenure of office cannot be extended or changed from his commission to the law. What is the proposition of this law? Mr. Stanton held, before its passage, "during the pleasure of the President for the time being." This law proposes to give him, in place of a term at pleasure, a term of years and one month thereafter. By what authority can the Congress of the United States extend the term in this manner? That office can only be held by the appointment of the President. His nomination and his appointment must cover the whole term which the appointee claims. On any other theory the Congress of the United States might extend the offices of persons who had been appointed indefinitely through years and years, and thus defeat the constitutional provision that the President shall nominate and shall appoint for the office, for the whole term of the office. There is no other construction that can be put upon it.

And in this view of it, it appears to me, Senators, that the law we have under consideration cannot be made to apply to any offices which were occupied at the time of its passage. Take the case of a general office held at pleasure. What is the character of that tenure? The lowest tenure known to the law is a tenure at pleasure, at suffrance, at will. To convert that into a tenure for a fixed term is to enlarge it, to extend it, to increase it, to make it a larger estate than it was before. If the office be one that cannot be filled without presidential nomination and appointment it does seem to me, whatever may be the office, it cannot be extended as to those who were in office at the time. If this be a right construction of the act of March 2, 1867, and I am compelled to leave it with this brief examination, Mr. Stanton is left where he was before its passage.

It is further to be observed that the act of March 2, 1867, has no repealing clause. We are, therefore, remitted to the previous laws applicable to his case, and this refers us to the Constitution and the act of August 7, 1789. By the provisions of this law it is provided among other things that—

"There shall be an executive Department to be denominated the Department of War; and there shall be a principal officer therein to be called the Secretary for the Department of War, who shall perform and execute such duties as shall from time to time be enjoined on or intrusted to him by the President of the United States, and the said principal officer shall conduct the business of the said Department in such manner as the President of the United States shall from time to time order and instruct.

"There shall be in the said Department an inferior officer, to be appointed by said principal officer, to be employed therein as he shall deem proper, and to be called the chief clerk of the Department of War; and whenever the said principal officer shall be removed from office by the President of the United States, and in any other case of vacancy, shall, during the same, have charge of the records, books," &c.

This is the law to which we are referred, unless the act to regulate the tenure of certain civil offices covers the case of Mr. Stanton. By the terms of this law, by the commission that was issued to Mr. Stanton to hold "during the pleasure of the President of the United States for the time being" framed upon this law, by the uniform construction of it, as I shall show, the President had the right to remove Mr. Stanton according to his pleasure.

Mr. FESSENDEN. Mr. President, the counsel will excuse me. I wish to observe, if I may be permitted to do so, that the counsel is evidently laboring under very severe difficulty in endeavoring to go on, and if he finds himself very much oppressed I feel disposed to move an adjournment unless one of the Managers wishes to occupy the day.

Mr. GROESBECK. I am very much obliged to the Senator, if he will allow me to answer him. I thank him for the suggestion; but I came here indisposed this morning, and I have apprehensions that I shall not be any better if this matter is postponed. Hence I do not know but that I had better go on as best I can. I shall be very thankful for the attention of the Senate to what I shall say in the condition in which I find myself.

But we are told, Senators, by the gentlemen who argue this cause on the other side that there has been no such case as the removal of a head of a Department without the coöperation of the Senate, and that the construction which we claim as applicable to this law is unsound. Allow me, upon that subject, to call your attention to pages 357 and 359 of the proceedings. I now refer to the letter of John Adams, written under one of these three laws that were passed in the First Congress under the Constitution. I give you the letter:

PHILADELPHIA, *May* 12, 1800.

SIR: Divers causes and considerations, essential to the administration of the Government, in my judgment, requiring a change in the Department of State, you are hereby discharged from any further service as Secretary of State.

JOHN ADAMS,
President of the United States.

That was the act of John Adams, by whose casting vote the bill of 1789 was passed; that act was done according to the construction that was given to the bill; and it is an outright removal during the session of the Senate without the coöperation of the Senate. The letter is addressed to the Secretary of State in his office, declaring him removed; and when Mr. Adams comes to communicate with the Senate he sends his communication nominating John Marshall, not "in place of Mr. Pickering, to be removed with your assent," but "in place of Mr. Pickering, removed by my will, and according to the law and the language of his commission." Why, Senators, there is no doubt about it. If John Adams, who passed this law in the Senate by his casting vote, had had the least idea that the power of removal was not, as it is said to be in the law, in his own hand, do the gentlemen suppose that he would have taken the course he did, and that he would not have taken some such course as this: "Senators, I propose, with your consent, to remove Timothy Pickering and appoint John Marshall in his place." That was not the right construction of the law. His act is the true construction according to his own interpretation and according to the interpretation that has been given from that day to this, down to the passage of the act of March 2, 1867, done in session, done by himself, done without consultation or coöperation with the Senate; and that very form which he adopted when he did remove, as a distinct and independent act, has been followed from that day to this.

Senators, let me call your attention, too, while I am upon this subject, and lest I forget it, to the language of John Marshall in the case of Marbury vs. Madison. He was there discussing the question when an appointment was made, when it was complete, so that it was withdrawn from the control of the President; and he held in the decision of that case that it was complete when the commission was made out; but in the course of his decision he goes on to remark:

"When the officer is removal at the will of the Executive the circumstance with completes his appointment is of no concern, because the act is at any time revocable."

So it was always held and so it has been always understood, "removable by the President;" that is the language; so the commission runs, "removable at the pleasure of the President for the time being." When? In recess? no, at his pleasure; in session? no, at his pleasure, is the language of the commission and the authority given by the commission and by the law. Who will attempt to construe a commission in such language, holding at pleasure, into a commission that he may remove this month or that month or the next month, or in recess or in session? It is, Senators, at pleasure; so it has always been understood and construed.

If I am right in the view which I have very briefly taken of the operations of this law, Mr. Stanton was not covered by it, and he is subject to removal under the commission which he received from Mr. Lincoln and under the law of 1789. I beg you to observe that that

law is in full force. There is no attempt to repeal it in the act of March 2, 1867. That act in fact has no repealing clause. What then? What becomes of the first eight articles of this case?

Let us stand at this point and look over the case; it is an excellent point of observation from which to look at it. We have removed one difficulty; we have ascertained one fact: Edwin M. Stanton could be removed by the President. I should like to linger on this question longer. I should like, if I had voice and health to-day, to call your attention to many other points which I had intended to present in this discussion. I should like to read to you the language of your own Senators upon this question, especially the pertinent language of the Senator who from the conference committee reported this bill for your consideration. I should like to read that language, for it was the last utterance in this Chamber before the bill was passed; and it was received with no dissenting voice. It was the true, sound, accepted construction of the law.

But I pass on. We have torn down the main structure of these eight articles. Take out the question of the power to remove Stanton from these eight articles and they are without support. All you have left to consider is the single question of the right to confer the *ad interim* authority upon Lorenzo Thomas. Senators, we see more than that, if this be so. All these questions of intent—all these questions of force—all these questions of whether we intended to go into court—all these questions that occupied us so much in the course of this investigation, vanish out of sight; for if we had this authority, Edwin M. Stanton was a trespasser; we had the right to remove him, and we were not bound to go to court to ascertain that right.

But, Senators, let me ask you still one other question before I proceed. Suppose Mr. Stanton is within the tenure-of-office act—what then? The inquiry then comes for your consideration whether the President is criminal in acting upon the supposition that he was not within it. This inquiry does not challenge the constitutionality of the law. It is a question of construction of a doubtful law. Is there a Senator here who will not admit, whatever his view may be upon this subject, that it was a law about which any one might reasonably adopt this construction? I believe that the majority of the Senators in this Chamber are of the opinion that it does not apply to the case of Mr. Stanton; and even if it did, there is no majority of Senators, intelligent Senators as you are, who would say that there was not room for doubt in the construction of the law. What then? Let me in this connection refer you to the act creating the office of Attorney General. It is to be found on page 93 of 1 Statutes-at-Large, and reads as follows:

"And there shall also be appointed a meet person, learned in the law, to act as Attorney General for the United States, who shall be sworn or affirmed to a faithful execution of his office; whose duty it shall be to prosecute and conduct all suits in the Supreme Court in which the United States shall be concerned, and to give his advice and opinion upon questions of law when required by the President of the United States."

I need not read any further. Here was a law, the tenure-of-office act, construe it as you will, about which no Senator will differ as to the fact that it might be reasonably interpreted as not covering Mr. Stanton by its provisions. And now suppose that the President of the United States did take counsel upon this subject, and did construe the law as Senator SHERMAN and other Senators in this Chamber have construed it; I am putting this case now upon the theory that it covered Mr. Stanton; yet a law of doubtful construction as it is, if the President availed himself of the counsels of this officer, who is designated for this special duty, he is harmless by this impeachment, goes acquit of all charge of lawlessness, and cannot be censured for following such counsel.

What is the testimony on that subject? We have a little. It was offered by the Managers themselves. You remember, Senators, when we were introducing the testimony in this cause, it was offered by the defense to give you the fullest measure of light upon all these questions. The Managers shut it out. You consented that the evidence which we proposed to offer of consultations that were held in the presence of the President by his Cabinet, where every word was an act, business consultations, not idle conversations, but consultations for the purpose of deciding upon these grave and important matters; consultations which, if you individually were to undertake to investigate this question of motive and what was done, you could not pass by—when we offered to bring these in and they were excluded we thought for a time we were without any light on this question. But, Senators, I will refer you to some evidence bearing on this very point and to a meeting of the Cabinet, as set forth in evidence offered by the Managers, where all the members of the Cabinet were present, and where it appears that this subject came up for consideration, and it was "taken for granted that as to those members of the Cabinet who had been appointed by Mr. Lincoln their tenure of office was not fixed by the provisions of the act. I do not remember, says the President, that the point was distinctly stated; but I well recollect that it was suggested by one member of the Cabinet who was appointed by Mr. Lincoln and that no dissent was expressed."

The Attorney General was there; the entire Cabinet was there; and this subject was considered; this very question of construction came up, and the opinion was expressed that Mr. Stanton was not included. So that even if the law covered him, yet by the authority of the statute appointing an Attorney General and requiring him to give advice upon questions of law, the President, acting upon the consultation that occurred in his presence, had the right to do what he did in this instance; and even, as I said, if the law covers Mr. Stanton, it being a question of construction, the respondent is protected.

In this view I desire to repeat that we get rid of a large portion of this cause, and therefore it is that I would like to linger at this point; for it seems to me that it is the most important point in the cause. But I pass on.

Suppose, Senators, that the view which I have been presenting is not correct, and that the law does apply to Mr. Stanton, what then? The next inquiry is whether that act be constitutional, or rather let me say, if it be constitutional, whether the conduct of the President in the removal of Mr. Stanton was criminal. I am aware, that very many of you participated as legislators in the passage of that very law, and that you have affirmed its constitutionality. In the unfortunate condition of this case the law makers become the judges, and therefore I would not be understood as arguing the point that I now propose to present with a view to change your opinions or to show that the law was unconstitutional. It is not that; but I beg you to observe that my whole object is to present this inquiry to your consideration, whether, in the condition of this question and in the condition of the President, he had the right to take the steps that he did take without incurring the charge of criminality?

And now, passing as I shall, although I had intended to take it up, all discussion of this as an original question; passing by the inquiry what is the right interpretation of the Constitution as to the place where this power of removal is lodged, I proceed to consider the question in the aspect which I have suggested. I start from this point. The question is at least doubtful; and from that point of view I propose to examine it as it stood on the 2d of March, 1867, or at the time the President acted in this case, to ascertain the question of criminality on his part in the act which he did.

Our Government is composed of three departments, which, according to the theory of their structure, are to last through all time and under all trials and are to be preserved in their entireness and integrity. The power has been carefully divided and distributed among them with a view to preserve each one in its separateness and independence. They are each independent of the other. No one is responsible to the other. They are responsible to the people or to the States. All this is carefully set down in the Constitution. Those who have charge of these various departments, by the theory and structure of the Government, are enjoined each to take care of its own prerogative, if I may use such a word, and to protect itself against all possible encroachment from the others. This they do, each and every department, by observing with the utmost fidelity the provisions of the written Constitution.

At the head of one of these departments, the executive, stands the President of the United States. He is sworn by an oath, the most solemn and obligatory that could be administered, "faithfully to execute the office of President of the United States, and to preserve, protect, and defend the Constitution of the United States." This is not an oath merely to execute the laws. The laws are not named in it. The first part of this oath, "faithfully to execute the office of President," would cover his obligation to execute the law and his obligation to discharge all other executive duties imposed upon him. There would seem to be something more than this; and he is required, in addition to this oath that covers his ordinary executive duties, to swear to the best of his ability to preserve, protect, and defend the Constitution of the United States. That oath is administered to the President alone of all the officers of the Government. I do not say, Senators, that it has any extraordinary significance; but I do say that there is enough in it for admonition, at least; there is enough in it for constant caution as a duty of the President in reference to the Constitution. It does seem to me that the terms of such an oath solemnly imposed upon him would impress him with the idea, or any of us with the idea, that it was the first paramount duty that he should ever, in all his executive conduct, keep his eye upon the Constitution of the United States; in all trial that he should look to it; in all doubt that he should lean toward it; in all difficulty that he should take shelter under it.

I heard the eloquent argument of the Manager [Mr. BOUTWELL] who addressed us but two days ago. I heard what he said about the executive department. I should be pleased if I had strength of voice to answer it. The sum and substance of it was that the President of the United States is but the constable of Congress; no more; that he is put into his place merely to execute the laws of Congress. Why, Senators, this is not the right interpretation of the Constitution. He is the Chief Magistrate of this nation, having charge of one of its great departments; and he is faithless to his trust if he do not protect the powers conferred by the Constitution upon that department.

But without delaying upon this question, let me proceed at once to what is more vital to the matter in hand. Shall he disregard law? Never. He should never in mere wantonness disregard any law of Congress that may be passed. Shall he execute all law? Let me answer that question by referring you to the argument of the gentleman whom I have just named. I refer to pages 814, 815, and 817; and I beg leave to say that I take issue with the Manager in the positions which he has taken on this subject, almost entirely. He says:

"If a law be in fact unconstitutional it may be repealed by Congress, or it may, possibly"—

Just possibly—

"when a case duly arises, be annulled in its unconstitutional features by the Supreme Court of the United States. The repeal of the law is a legislative act; the declaration by the court that it is unconstitutional is a judicial act; but the power to repeal or to annul or to set aside a law of the United States is in no aspect of the case an executive power. It is made the duty of the Executive to take care that the laws be faithfully executed—an injunction wholly inconsistent with the theory that it is in the power of the Executive to repeal or annul or dispense with the laws of the land. To the President in the performance of his executive duties all laws are alike. He can enter into no inquiry as to their expediency or constitutionality. All laws are presumed to be constitutional, and, whether in fact constitutional or not, it is the duty of the Executive so to regard them while they have the form of law."

That is the last congressional theory I have heard. Let me read further:

"Hence it follows that the crime of the President is not, either in fact or as set forth in the articles of impeachment, that he has violated a constitutional law, but his crime is that he has violated a law, and in his defense no inquiry can be made whether the law is constitutional."

So that, according to the reasoning of the Manager, if now here on this inquiry you should be of the unanimous opinion that the law for the alleged violation of which the President is impeached was unconstitutional, yet you would have to go on and convict him of the commission of a crime in the fact that he did not execute what was not law. I desire to read a little further on this question. Hear the Manager:

"The Senate, for the purpose of deciding whether the respondent is innocent or guilty, can enter into no inquiry as to the constitutionality of the act, which it was the President's duty to execute, and which, upon his own answer, and by repeated official confessions and admissions, he intentionally, willfully, deliberately set aside and violated."

Let me read again:

"With deference I maintain still further that it is not the right of any Senator in this trial to be governed by any opinion he may entertain of the constitutionality or expediency of the law in question. For the purposes of this trial the statute which the President, upon his own confession, has repeatedly violated is the law of the land. His crime is that he violated the law."

I wish to read one other passage from this speech, to show the startling doctrines which the Manager has put forth, and upon which it seems the President is to be convicted, according to his theory! Hear this:

"If the President or Vice President, or any other civil officer, violates a law, his peril is that he may be impeached by the House of Representatives and convicted by the Senate. This is precisely the responsibility which the respondent has incurred; and it would be no relief to him for his willful violation of the law, in the circumstances in which he is now placed, if the court itself had pronounced the same to be unconstitutional."

Senators, in answering the question whether the President shall execute all law, I beg to be understood as differing in toto cœlo from the gentleman from whose argument I have just read. If a law be declared by the Supreme Court, the third department of this Government, and, by the very terms of the Constitution itself, the highest and final interpreter of the constitutionality of congressional enactments, to be unconstitutional, the President is untrue to his position if he execute it in letter or in spirit, or one jot or tittle of it. Let me tell the gentleman, in answer to his long argumentation upon this point, that he makes no distinction between law whatever, that if an act of Congress be unconstitutional it is no law; it never was law; it never had a particle of validity, although it went through the forms of congressional enactment; from the beginning *ab initio* it was null and void, and to execute it is to violate that higher law, the Constitution of the United States, which declares that to be no law which is in conflict with its provisions.

What shall I say, then, in answer to this argument? Shall he execute all law? No. If a law be declared by the Supreme Court unconstitutional he should not execute it. If the law be upon its very face in flat contradiction to plain express provisions of the Constitution, as if a law should forbid the President to grant a pardon in any case, or if a law should declare that he should not be Commander-in-Chief, or if a law should declare that he should take no part in the making of a treaty, I say the President without going to the Supreme Court of the United States, maintaining the integrity of his department, which for the time being is intrusted to him, is bound to execute no such legislation, and he is cowardly and untrue to the responsibilities of his position if he should execute it.

But, Senators, the difficulty is not here. The difficulty arises in doubtful cases, in cases where the powers are not plainly and expressly stated in the Constitution; and here it is that we come to the question in inquiry between us in this case. Suppose an act of Congress interpret the Constitution in a doubtful case for the first time, shall the President execute it? I say yes. Suppose an act, instead of giving an interpretation for the first time in a doubtful case, contradicts a long accepted previous interpretation—in this supposition we are approaching the case before us—what is to be done? To follow the Constitution is the first and paramount duty of the President, and to maintain the integrity of his department is also a duty; and if an act of to-day is contrary to a long established interpretation of the Constitution upon a question of power, and a fit case presents itself where he is required to act, it is right and proper in a peaceable way, with a due regard to the public welfare, to test the accuracy of the new interpretation in the forum which is the highest and final interpreter of such questions.

Senators, with this preliminary observation I propose to examine the condition of this question at the time the President performed these acts; but before I do so allow me to call your attention to a few rules of interpretation. They are these:

Acquiescence by the people and the various Departments of the Government gives force to any interpretation. (15 Maryland Reports, p. 458.)

Let me state another. It may be a grave question whether a first interpretation is right; but long acquiescence in it, if it be a statute, makes another statute necessary to change it; if it be a constitution it would require an amendment of the Constitution to change it. (4 Gill and Johnson, p. 345.)

Let me give you another. A long and uniform interpretation becomes a fixed interpretation. When a constitution early undergoes legislative interpretation, and a series of acts are passed according to such interpretation, covering say seventy years, even if it were doubtful, such constant, long and uniform interpretation should remove the doubt. (1 Maryland Reports, p. 351.)

I desire to refer you to one other rule before I pass to the argument, to be found in 1 Story, section four hundred and eight:

"And, after all, the *most unexceptional* source of *collateral interpretation* is from the practical exposition of the Government itself in its various Departments upon particular questions discussed and settled upon their own single merits. These approach the nearest in their own nature to *judicial* expositions, *and have the same general recommendation* that belongs to the latter. They are decided upon solemn argument, *pro re nata,* upon a doubt raised, upon a *lis mota,* upon a deep sense of their importance and difficulty, in the face of the nation, with a view to present action, in the midst of jealous interests, and by men capable of urging or repelling the grounds of argument by their genius, their comprehensive learning, or their deep meditation upon the absorbing topic."

With these preliminary observations, I desire that you will bear with me while I present the question in this form—not the question of the constitutionality of your tenure-of-office act; I will not challenge its constitutionality here in your very faces; you have affirmed it. I beg you to notice, however, that the question which I propose to consider is what was right and proper for the President, the condition of this question and his own condition at the time he did the act which is set forth in these articles. Observe, before I start upon this inquiry, the law of March 2, 1867, is *constitutional interpretation.* By that law of March 2, 1867, you interpreted the Constitution that the power of removal was lodged in the President and Senate. The previous law that was passed in 1789, was also, as we know from the frequent utterances of those who participated in its passage, *constitutional interpretation;* and the question before us is what was the condition of this question at the period of time to which we are calling your attention, when the President acted. Observe the purpose for which I have cited these rules. A long acquiescence by the people and the Departments of the Government in any interpretation becomes a fixed interpretation; a long and uniform interpretation of the Constitution for a period of seventy years, even if it were a doubtful question, removes the doubt; and it is in the light of those rules of interpretation that I propose to make the inquiry; and I will briefly take it up in all the departments of the Government. How stands the question in the judicial department? I admit, Senators, that we have no *res adjudicata* upon this question; the exact question has never been presented to the Supreme Court of the United States; but we have opinions from the Supreme Court, which I proceed now to read.

In 1839, in the case of *ex parte* Hennen, it was declared by the court, Mr. Justice Thompson delivering the opinion:

"No one denied the power of the President and Senate jointly to remove where the tenure of the office was not fixed by the Constitution, which was a full recognition of the principle that the power of removal was incident to the power of appointment; but it was very early adopted as a practical construction of the Constitution that this power was vested in the President alone, and such would appear to have been the legislative construction of the Constitution, for in the organization of the three great Departments of State, War, and Treasury, in 1789, provision was made for the appointment of a subordinate officer by the head of the Department, who should have charge of the records, books, and papers appertaining to the office when the head of the Department should be removed from office by the President of the United States. When the Navy Department was established, in the year 1798, provision was made for the charge and custody of the books, records, and documents of the Department in case of vacancy in the office of Secretary, by removal or otherwise. It is not here said 'by removal of the President,' as is done with respect to the heads of the other Departments; yet there can be no doubt that he holds his office with the same tenure as the other Secretaries, and is removable by the President. The change of phraseology arose probably from its having become the settled and well-understood construction of the Constitution that the power of removal was vested in the President alone in such cases, although the appointment of the officer is by the President and Senate."—13 *Peters*, p. 139.

This is a voice at least, an opinion at least, from the Supreme Court upon this question; not an adjudication, I acknowledge, but an opinion, in reference to which we might have the right to say that it was pronounced with the concurrence of the other members of the bench.

Let me call your attention to another case where we have an utterance from one of the justices of the Supreme Court. I refer to the case of the United States *vs.* Guthrie. (17 Howard, 284.) The case went off upon another point, but in the course of his dissenting opinion Mr. Justice McLean said he thought "the construction" (the one referred to and the one claimed in behalf of the respondent in this case) "wrong, and that the late Supreme Court so thought, with Marshall at its head." He adds, however, and to this I call special attention: "But this power of removal has been, perhaps, too long established and exercised to be now questioned."

It will be observed that Judge McLean refers to Marshall. Let us see what Marshall himself says. I refer you to 2 Marshall's Life of Washington, page 162—the second, or Philadelphia edition, as it is called. I ask Senators to observe the language of Marshall upon this occasion, for it is a complete answer to the argument of the Manager the day before yesterday in regard to the right interpretation of the debate of 1789. Marshall says:

"After an ardent discussion, which consumed several days, the committee divided, and the amendment was negatived by a majority of thirty-four to twenty. The opinion thus expressed by the House of Representatives did not explicitly convey their sense of the Constitution. Indeed, the express grant of the power to the President rather implied a right in the Legislature to give or withhold it at their discretion. To obviate any misunderstanding of the principle on which the question had been decided, Mr. Benson moved in the House, when the report of the Committee of the Whole was taken up, to amend the second clause in the bill so as clearly to imply the power of removal to be solely in the President. He gave notice that if he should succeed in this he would move to strike out the words which had been the subject of debate. If those words continued, he said, the power of removal by the President might hereafter appear to be exercised by virtue of a legislative grant only, and consequently be subjected to legislative instability; when he was well satisfied in his own mind that it was by fair construction fixed in the Constitution. The motion was seconded by Mr. Madison, and both amendments were adopted."

Now, let me give you Marshall's own words as to the result of that debate:

"As the bill passed into a law it has ever been considered as a full expression of the sense of the Legislature on this important part of the American Constitution."

That is Marshall to whom McLean referred in his dissenting opinion; that is his own language. I have no other references to make directly to the Supreme Court or to the judges of that court; but while I am upon the judicial aspect of the question allow me also to refer you to the opinion of Chancellor Kent, to be found in 1 Kent, page 310. There, treating of the act of 1789, he says:

"This amounted to a legislative construction of the Constitution, and it has ever since been acquiesced in and acted upon as of decisive authority in the case. It applies equally to every other officer of the Government appointed by the President and Senate whose term of duration is not specially declared. It is supported by the weighty reason that the subordinate officers in the executive Department ought to hold at the pleasure of the head of that department, because he is invested generally with the executive authority, and every participation in that authority by the Senate was an exception to a general principle, and ought to be taken strictly. The President is the great responsible officer for the faithful execution of the law, and the power of removal was incidental to that duty, and might often be requisite to fulfill it."

Senators, you observe I call your attention to the condition of this question at the time in the court; I give you two utterances from the bench of the court; I give you the opinion of Marshall; I give you the opinion of Kent upon the point whether, doubtful as the question was, it had been interpreted and fixed at the time they gave those utterances. Now, let me refer to the action of the executive Department.

From the beginning of the Government to March 2, 1867, this has been the uniform construction and practice of every Administration. Washington approved the bill; Adams's vote passed it; Jefferson maintained the same position; Madison drew the bill; Monroe and Jackson and the Presidents that followed them all maintained the same construction, and every President, including President Lincoln, through all our history of eighty years and twenty Administrations, maintained this construction upon the question of where the power of removal is lodged? Observe the judicial department every time its voice has been heard on this question, from the foundation of the Government until now, as far as it has expressed itself, has affirmed that the power is lodged by the Constitution in the President. The executive department, from Washington, who put his name to the bill that affirmed it, through Adams, who helped to pass it, and Madison, who drew it; through all the Presidents we have had from the very start of the Government under the Constitution down to the present hour, every one has acted upon this construction and affirmed this practice from the beginning until now.

I now take you, gentlemen, into the legislative department of the Government. The First Congress assembled under the present Constitution on the 4th day of March, 1789. The Constitution provided, you will remember, for Executive Departments, and associated them with the President as councilors and advisers. It became the duty of this Congress to organize them. Very early in the session Mr. Boudinot rose in his place and called the attention of Congress to the fact that the Executive Departments under the old Confederation had come to an end; that it was necessary now to organize new and corresponding ones under the new Constitution, and he suggested in the first instance that before they legislated on the subject they should in debate fix the principles and determine the number of the Departments which it was necessary to create. They at once entered upon the subject, and they agreed to establish three Departments.

If the Senate intends to go into recess, I would be pleased if it would do so now.

Mr. CONKLING. I make the ordinary motion.

Mr. SUMNER. I move that the Senate take a recess for fifteen minutes.

The motion was agreed to; and at the expiration of the allotted time the Chief Justice resumed the chair and called the Senate to order.

Mr. GROESBECK. When the Senate went into recess it will be remembered that I had just begun to present the condition of this question in the legislative department of the Government. It was brought to the attention of Congress in the first session that was held under the Constitution. Very early in that session Mr. Boudinot, of New Jersey, rose and presented the question for consideration, and expressed his desire, as I have intimated, that before the bills should be passed the House should settle the principles upon which they

should be constructed and the number of Departments that should be created. Mr. Madison moved with him in this matter, and I think it was his pen that drew the bills that were afterward vitalized into the laws establishing the Departments of Foreign Affairs, of War, and of the Treasury. I need scarcely state to the Senators here present, who must all of them have examined this debate, the principles upon which those bills were constructed and eventually vitalized. I must be allowed, however, in this connection, to refer to the argument of the Manager [Mr. BOUTWELL] on the day before yesterday, in which he undertakes to state the results which were reached in the Congress that passed these laws, and he states them in this language:

"The results reached by the Congress of 1789 are conclusive upon the following points: that that body was of opinion that the power of removal was not in the President absolutely, to be exercised at all times and under all circumstances; and secondly, that during the sessions of the Senate the power of removal was vested in the President and Senate, to be exercised by their concurrent action, while the debate and the votes indicate that the power of the President to remove from office during the vacation of the Senate was, at best, a doubtful power under the Constitution."

I must be allowed also to express my astonishment at this summing up of the results of that debate in 1789. I have read to you the language of John Marshall as to the purpose of that debate. I have read to you the utterances of Justice Thompson from the bench of the Supreme Court as to the results of that debate. I have cited you also to the opinions of Story and of Kent as to the results of that debate. And I here say, with all respect to the honorable Manager, that the statement of its results which he presents in his argument is not authorized (allow me to say it with entire respect) by anything that occurred. I say here in the presence of the Senate, all of whom have examined more or less that great debate running through a period of seven or eight days upon the single question where is the power of removal lodged, that the only point which was discussed and finally settled was this: is this power lodged in the President alone, or is it lodged in the President and Senate; and they closed the debate deciding that the power was in the President alone, and changed the phraseology of the bills as they were originally drawn so that all appearance of grant from the Legislature might be avoided, and from the face of the bills it would appear that the Legislature intended to express themselves as recognizing the power to be by the Constitution directly in the President, and therefore not necessary to be conferred by legislative grant.

I have stated accurately, Senators, the substance of that debate. I challenge all contradiction from anything that transpired or from anything that was said.

What passed? They passed the three bills establishing three Departments with these features incorporated into each and all of them.

They called them Executive Departments; they made a principal officer called the Secretary, who was to perform such duties as should "from time to time be enjoined on him or intrusted to him by the President" and should "conduct the business of the Department in such manner as the President should from time to time order and instruct." They provided a chief clerk, who, "when the said principal officer should be removed from office by the President," should take charge of the books, papers, &c. This is the general tenor of the bills in reference to those three Departments. Such was the action of the First Congress of the United States, a Congress divested of all party animosity, of all party view, I may say comparatively disinterested, at the very opening of the Government just starting under the new Constitution. Such was the action of the Congress who intended to fix for all time, as far as they might fix it, the policy upon which this particular power should be regulated in the future; and in the language of Marshall, as he expressed it in the quotation which I read, in order "*to avoid legislative instability*" upon this very question, they took care to so frame the bills as that they should not take the form of grant from the Legislature, and so that it might appear as constitutional interpretation only. They passed three laws during that session as I have referred to them. Those laws are in force to this day. They are professedly an interpretation of the Constitution, so declared by the Supreme Court, as I have read to you, not in a *res adjudicata* utterance, but in an opinion upon an incidental question, so declared and treated by all the Presidents we have had, so declared by that Congress which passed them, and so regarded by every subsequent Congress down to the Thirty-Ninth.

Senators, I will now pass on nine years, to 1798. They then framed another executive Department called the Navy Department; and they recognized the power of removal in that under this phraseology: "In case of vacancy by removal or otherwise," not "by the President;" still more strongly conveying the idea that it was a power lodged by the Constitution in the President, and needing no legislative interference. Upon that theory they framed the fourth Department, the Navy Department.

I now step down twenty-seven years, to the creation of the Post Office Department; and in that law they recognized this arrangement in language like this: "provided, that in case of death, resignation, or removal from office of the Postmaster General," without saying by whom; but they had all these laws before them, and others to which I shall refer which had received construction, and in reference to which it was distinctly understood that they were interpretations of the Constitution, acknowledging the power to be lodged in the President, and, therefore, it was not necessary that it should be conferred by express grant.

I pass on to the Interior Department, created in March, 1840. We find in that law language like this:

"Who [the Secretary] shall hold his office by the same tenure and receive the same salary as the Secretaries of the other Departments."

Under that language, also, he was removable at pleasure. He held his office by the same tenure as the other Secretaries, and could be removed in the same way.

Let me call your attention to the seventh Department, if I may call it that, the Attorney General's Department. That office was established on the 24th day of September, 1789, and in the law establishing it there is not one word said upon the subject of removal or vacancy. The law is as silent as the grave; and yet, under the interpretation given to these laws from the beginning until now, the Attorney General has taken his commission "during the pleasure of the President for the time being," and has been subject to removal by the President, just as any other of the heads of these Executive Departments.

I have now gone through the legislation establishing the seven Executive Departments, ranging from 1789 down to 1849, a period of sixty years. But this is not all. I might cite you to numberless other offices, assistants to these, revenue officers, postmasters, and I know not what, established all through this period from Congress to Congress, with different terms; some at pleasure, some for a fixed term unless sooner removed, some indefinitely; and yet all regarded as removable by the President under phraseology like this.

Now, what shall we say of all this legislation? I began with the First Congress that met under the Constitution; I come down with you to the Thirty-Ninth Congress that passed the civil-tenure act; and I point you, by the way, from Congress to Congress, to laws that were passed by these Congresses affirming—every law of this kind being an affirmance—the construction that was started in 1789, that the power of removal was lodged by the Constitution in the President of the United States. I say here by virtue of imperfect examination myself, but of information upon which I rely, that if you were to gather the laws of Congress from 1789 to March, 1867, which expressly affirm this construction, they would average some two or three to every Congress.

Now, how stands the question? What have we? Here is a question of constitutional interpretation. I beg the Senate to observe that these laws which I have read are in force; they are constitutional interpretations. The civil-tenure act of 1867 may be in force. That, too, is constitutional interpretation. Now, we come to the question of duty on the part of the President in that condition of legislation. Every department of the Government had been down to March, 1867, of that opinion; all the Presidents, the Supreme Court to the extent I have stated, and every Congress. I probably ought to modify that statement, but there were some seventy or eighty laws upon this subject between 1789 and 1867 affirming the same doctrine by the form in which they acknowledged the power of removal. All this occurred; this was the condition of the question; and now I submit it to you Senators. The law of March, 1867, is constitutional interpretation; all these other laws are constitutional interpretation. May not human reason pause here? May not human judgment doubt? What is the condition of the question? All the Presidents, every revered name that ever filled the office, affirming this doctrine; the Supreme Court uttering itself upon this doctrine; thirty-eight Congresses affirming this doctrine; this on one side, and one Congress on the other. May not human reason pause? May not human judgment doubt? With this great preponderance of testimony and of construction running through a period of nearly eighty years, was it criminal to stand with this great mass of precedents around him and believe as the thirty-eight Congresses had believed, as all the President's had believed, as all that had gone before him had believed; was it criminal, I say, that he, too, believed in that way, and thought that it was a proper case, it being simply a question of constitutional interpretation, to pass to that tribunal which has a right higher than the Executive and higher than Congress upon the subject of interpretation?

Do you believe, Senators—this is the question which I desire to propound to you—that Andrew Johnson at the time I have referred to honestly thought that the Constitution lodged this power of removal in the hands of the President? Look back upon what he had before him upon which to form the opinion, and I put again the question to you, do you believe he honestly thought it was so? Your law was before him; these other laws were before him; and what did he propose to do? Just this: to take up your law as it was and go to that tribunal that could inform him finally and effectually how the question stood.

But what, Senators, shall be the effect upon the very question, admitting it as an original question to be one of doubt, of this long line of interpretation in every department of the Government? I read you the rule that a long and uniform interpretation makes a fixed interpretation. A long and uniform interpretation, say for seventy years, of a doubtful question under the Constitution, would remove the doubt. What rule shall we apply? We are now upon the subject of a power not expressed, and yet we want stability in reference to these powers just as much as if they were expressed. *Stare decisis*, that is the rule; and without it your Government has no stability whatever. Can you fix the interpretation of one of these powers by construction? When shall it be accomplished? In five hundred years? I think you would all say that. In four hundred years?

I think you would all agree to that. In two hundred years? Yes. In one hundred? Well, it had run on this very question seventy-eight years of the history of the United States; in fact, the whole of its political existence. *Stare decisis*, if we are to have any stability in reference to our Constitution. There is not one half of it written. *Stare decisis* is the rule that has preserved the English Government, that has no written constitution. In this rule it has found firm anchorage through century after century and through revolution after revolution. Are we to have any stability whatever in our institutions? *Stare decisis* is the rule we must adopt and adhere to; and on this rule this question stands.

The Thirty-Ninth Congress alone—very solitary in the midst of all this array—has given its interpretation to the Constitution. Was it any better than that of 1789? Say it was as good; I do not propose to institute any comparison; I do not say that it was not just as dispassionate, just as cool, in just as good a condition as the other; but it was no better than the Congresses which preceded it.

And this brings me now to the question: is this Senate prepared to drag a President in here and convict him of crime, because he believed as every other President believed, as the Supreme Court believed, as thirty-eight of the thirty-nine Congresses believed? That is the question. Senators, that is the state of the question, and in the condition of Andrew Johnson you can find no criminality in what he did. I have put the question to myself, putting myself in his place, with the views which I entertain of the President's duty, not to lie down with his hand on his mouth, and his mouth in the dust before Congress, but to stand up as the Chief Magistrate of a nation whose walls are the shores of a great continent, and maintain the integrity of his department. He shall execute your laws; he shall execute even the doubtful laws; but when you bring to him a question like this; when he has all this precedent behind him and around him, all these voices sounding in his ears, as to what is the right interpretation of the Constitution, and only one the other way, I say you are going too far to undertake to brand him with criminality because he proposed to go to the Supreme Court and ascertain how it is. To go there is peaceable, is constitutional, is lawful. What is that tribunal there for? For this very purpose.

I did not state the entire case in what I have said. I should have referred you also to the President's care, to the proprieties of his conduct in reference to consulting those who, by long usage, are the advisers and councilors of the President. You shut out many of those inquiries. You would not hear from the defense upon these questions. Suppose this: suppose it to have been brought to your attention, Senators, that upon a question of moment like this, a serious question, in which you yourselves were interested, the President of the United States disregarded all the usages that had prevailed in the conduct of the Administration among other Presidents, turned his back upon his Cabinet, held no consultations, but going alone in willfulness and disregard of those around him, did the act; it would have been a sorry thing for President Johnson if that proof could have been made upon him; and yet the fact that he could prove just the contrary was shut out. Is not that a matter to be considered in determining, not upon the constitutionality of the law, but upon the question of guilt, for that is the question we have before this tribunal?

Now, what was Mr. Johnson's condition? He had a Cabinet officer who was unfriendly to him, personally and politically. All the confidential relations between them were broken up. That Cabinet officer himself tells you, in a letter to Congress, dated as late as 4th of February—I read from page 235 of the proceedings—that he "has had no correspondence with the President since the 12th of August last;" and he further says that since he resumed the duties of the office he has continued to discharge them "without any personal or written communication with the President;" and he adds:

"No orders have been issued from this Department in the name of the President, with my knowledge, and I have received no orders from him."

It thus appears that this Cabinet officer was really a new Executive, repudiating the President, having no official communication with him, and proposing to have none; administering the duties of his Department without recognizing even the President's name; his enemy. I will not canvass the merits of these officers; but the relation of confidence was gone which you will acknowledge should exist; for it not unfrequently happens, I may venture to say, that you ask for what takes place in those Cabinet consultations if the President is willing to remove the seal of secrecy; I think such a request as that has been made within six months from the lower House, if not from the upper; but we know this, that it is a confidential relation, and that when the confidence is gone the relation is destroyed. That was the President's condition. Here was a Cabinet officer, in fact, who was a sort of executive running the office in his own name, not even proposing to communicate with the President. In this condition of things Mr. Johnson found it to be his duty, as he communicated it to General Sherman, to make a change in that Department. Let me refer to General Sherman's language on that subject. General Sherman says on page 519, in answer to a question that was put to him:

"I intended to be very precise and very short; but it appeared to me necessary to state what I began to state, that the President told me that the relations between himself and Mr. Stanton, and between Mr. Stanton and the other members of the Cabinet, were such that he could not execute the office which he filled as President of the United States without mak-

ing provision *ad interim* for that office; that he had the right under the law; he claimed to have the right, and his purpose was to have the office administered in the interest of the Army and of the country; and he offered me the office in that view. He did not state to me then that his purpose was to bring it to the court directly, but for the purpose of having the office administered properly in the interest of the Army and of the whole country."

That was the condition of things. Here was a Cabinet officer who refused all intercourse. Observe, Senators, I do not intend to go into any inquiry as to right or wrong. I merely state the naked fact. He refused all intercourse. He carried on the Department without communication with the President; a sort of secondary executive. The unity of the Cabinet was gone. In that condition of things the President felt it to be his duty, as Chief Magistrate, to make a change in that Department. I see before me here this afternoon more than one man who, if he were in that executive chair, would not tolerate such a condition of things in his Cabinet. It is utterly impossible to administer the executive part of the Government with division and wrangling and controversy and want of confidence between all the members of it; and in this necessity it was that Mr. Johnson moved to procure a change in that Department. That was the case, his own case, a case pressing upon him, not sought; and in executing the duty, as he conceived it to be, to effect that change he came in conflict with this law, and proposed to have its constitutional validity tested.

But, says the gentleman, [Mr. BOUTWELL,] he did not. I answer that he did. The petition for a writ of *quo warranto* was prepared; and if these proceedings had not been instituted it would have been filed. But how would he have been laughed at, how would he have been ridiculed if he were now conducting in the Supreme Court proceedings on *quo warranto*, a termination of which could be reached by no possibility for about a year, when at the time this thing was inaugurated it was reported that he was to be impeached and evicted within ten, twenty, or thirty days? The case was brought here. He did prepare, but he had no opportunity to put it to a constitutional test. Mr. Stanton brought a suit against Mr. Lorenzo Thomas. He had him arrested. There was the opportunity. By reason of that he could reach the decision instantly, and how the President snatched at it; and how it was snatched away from him that he might not have the opportunity of testing the constitutionality of the law! So that the President stands fairly on this question.

Talk of force here! Where is the force? Where is even one single bitter personal interview in all this transaction? Not a quarrel of words anywhere. And this is the performance of the Executive who started off to take possession of one of the Departments under his charge by force! Well, Senators, we have force in the pictures that might easily be drawn of the termination of this transaction. Force is exhibited, if I may so express myself, in that cordial embrace of Thomas and Stanton, when the one stood with his arm around the other, and ran his fingers affectionately through his silver locks. That is the force, the concentration of "force, intimidation, and threats!" And that is about all you can make of it.

We offered to bring in here the Cabinet to testify as to what their advice was upon that subject, and you would not hear that. Although it was *res gestœ*, if there were such a thing to be found in any transaction, although they had consulted upon this very question, although their words were deeds, yet you would not hear them; you shut their mouths, and remitted us to the man from Delaware and the empty utterances and boastings of Lorenzo Thomas. What great truth-searchers are these Managers in this case! They want us to find force, to find this evil intent in the utterances of this man from Delaware and in the idle conversations at an evening reception, or a midnight masquerade, of a man "dressed in a little brief authority;" and yet they will not hear the deliberations, the consultations that are held upon this very question, when the transaction is hot in the mind of the party who is about to perform it. There is no rescuing this trial from the manifest imperfection of the testimony on that point.

Now, what was the President's purpose? Why did the President—I put the question to myself while this matter was in progress—appoint—no; it is not an appointment—why did he give this letter of authority to Lorenzo Thomas? He had to do it, Senators; there was no other way he could adopt by which he could put the case in condition to test the law. If he had nominated to you the office would have remained in the exact condition in which it was without a nomination; and therefore it was necessary, by an arrangement of this kind, to get some one who could represent the Government on that question; and that was the whole purpose of it. What was his intention in all these movements? Just to get rid of this defiant, unfriendly Secretary. Allow me to use this expression without conveying any personal censure; but that was the relation in which he stood to the President?

What did he do? In the first place he applied to General Grant; and the honorable Manager had the assurance to interpret that as a mischievous movement—selecting a man whom the country delights to honor, in whom it has the utmost confidence; ay, in whom the gentleman himself intends to express, ere long, still greater confidence. Selecting such a man as that is to be regarded as a mischievous transaction.

What next? The very next step he took was, not to get a dangerous man, not to get a man in whom you had no confidence. The next man was General Sherman. Who dare charge wickedness or bad purpose upon such movements?

What next? General Sherman would not take it. Did the President run then after somebody that was mischievous, somebody that would excite your apprehensions, and give reason to fear that mischief might come out of the movement? No. The next application was to Major General Thomas. It seems that the President picked out the three men of all others in the nation who should command your favor in regard to the purposes he had in view. No; you cannot make his conduct mischievous. He had one purpose, and that was to change that War Department, and it would have delighted him to make the change and to put there permanently any competent man whom you would select; anything to get rid of the poisoned condition of his Cabinet, and that he might have unity and peace restored to it.

But, say the gentlemen, he executed this law in other respects; he changed the forms of his commissions; he reported suspensions under this law. So he did; and, Senators, it is one of the strongest facts in this case. He did not take up this law and tear it to pieces. That is lawlessness. He did not trample it under his feet. That is lawlessness. He took it up to have it interpreted in the case that pressed upon him individually, and in all other respects he executed it without the surrender of his own convictions. It was said in the suspension of Mr. Stanton, for instance, that he acted under your law. He did. I can adjust that suspension to the terms of your law: I can adjust it also to his own views; and instead of seizing upon that as a subject of censure, I tell you it was an overture from the President, I know, to get out of this difficulty, and to conciliate you in the hope that you would relieve and let him have a Cabinet such as any of you would demand if you were in his place.

Look at that suspension; look at the message of suspension. He tells you, "My Cabinet—and Mr. Stanton is the most emphatic of all of them—believe this law is unconstitutional." Mr. Stanton was the one who was selected, as he tells you in the letter, to draw the veto. I wish he had not had a lame arm and he could have drawn it. It would have been sharper than the one you received. But he tells you in that act of suspension what his views were about the law. He goes on and tells you further, in that very message, "We had this matter up in Cabinet meeting; one of the Secretaries appointed by Mr. Lincoln said it did not apply to him, or to any one of those who held over from the previous term, and there was no dissent." All those opinions were in his mind. He communicated them in the very message where you say he surrendered himself utterly to the terms of the tenure-of-civil-office bill. He did all that; and it is to his credit that he has not rushed into heedless and reckless controversy with the law, but has suffered it to be executed until the question of its constitutionality is in some way determined.

Now, gentlemen, I cannot believe—I have been sitting here and listening to the evidence presented in this case for a long time and reading more or less about it, and I have never been able to come to the conclusion that, when all these matters were laid before the Senate and understood, they could convict the President of criminality for what he has done. There is no force. Where is it? Where is the threat? Where is the intimidation? Nowhere. He did try to get into the courts. That we know. He did his best to get there; ran after a case by which he could have carried it there. Where is his criminality? Is he criminal because he did not surrender the convictions of his mind on the constitutionality of the act of March 2, 1867? So was General Washington criminal; so was Adams criminal. The voices of all these Presidents sustain him; the voices of all the Congresses behind him sustain him; the whole history of the Government sustains him in the position which he took. How, then, can you find criminality in his conduct?

But I will hurry on to the second question. Let us go back a moment before I go forward. Return with me for an instant to the end of that brief examination which I made of the right construction of the tenure-of-civil-office act. I told you then that if Stanton were not included the first eight articles of this impeachment substantially fell; and, even if he were included, there could be no criminality if the President acted upon a question of law under the advice of the Attorney General, who was officially designated for the very purpose of giving him that advice. So that from that point of view the great portion of the case falls. I have been examining it, however, in this other aspect. Suppose Stanton were under the law and we had not observed it. I then presented the question, where is the power of removal lodged? Although you have your own opinions, Senators, upon the question, differing from that of the President, I see around me gentlemen who argued upon it ably. There is yet the other question which I have presented, and which must be met; and will you, can you, condemn as criminal the President because with such light as he had he thought differently, and acted as I have described?

I come now to the next question, about the *ad interim* appointment; and I beg you to observe that if you shall come to the conclusion that the President had the right to make an *ad interim* appointment, then there is a great shipwreck of this impeachment; it nearly all tumbles into ruin. I beg you again, when you come to examine these articles, to see how many of them are built upon the two facts, the removal of Stanton and the *ad interim* letter given to Thomas. Now, had he the right to make that temporary appointment? He made it under the act of February 13, 1795. Allow me to read it:

"That in case of vacancy in the office of Secretary of State, Secretary of the Treasury, or of the Secretary of the Department of War, or of any officer of either of the said Departments whose appointment is not in the head thereof, whereby they cannot perform the duties of their said respective offices, it shall be lawful for the President of the United States, in case he shall think it necessary, to authorize any person or persons, at his discretion, to perform the duties of the said respective offices until a successor be appointed or such vacancy be filled: *Provided*, That no one vacancy shall be supplied, in manner aforesaid, for a longer term than six months."

You will be pleased to observe that all possible conditions of the Departments requiring temporary supply are expressed under the single word "vacancy." It covers removal; it covers the expiration of the term of office; it covers a resignation; it covers absence; it covers sickness; it covers every possible condition of the Department in which it may be necessary *ad interim* to supply the service. This law was passed February 13, 1795. There has been another act passed, partly covering the same ground, under the date of February 20, 1863. The question is now, does the act of February 20, 1863, repeal the act of February 13, 1795?

Senators, allow me to call your attention to a few rules of interpretation in reference to statutes before I compare these.

1. The law does not favor repeals by implication. Again, if statutes can be construed together they are to stand. Further, a latter statute, in order to repeal a former one by implication, must fully embrace the whole subject-matter of it. Still again, to effect an entire repeal, all the provisions of the previous statute, the whole subject-matter of it, must be covered.

Let me illustrate. Suppose the reach of a statute extended from myself to yonder door, if I might illustrate it in that way; if a subsequent statute were passed which reached half way, it would repeal as much of the former statute as it overlaid and leave the balance in force. What lies beyond is legislative will, still unrecalled, and is just as binding as the new statute.

Now, we come to the comparison of these statutes. The statute of 1795 I have read. The statute of February 20, 1863, (12 Statutes-at-Large, p. 656,) provides for the case of "death, resignation, absence from the seat of Government, or sickness." Death, resignation, absence, and sickness are the only cases covered by this statute. There are two cases that are not provided for by it, and they are covered by the statute of 1795—removal, expiration of term. We are advised by this simple statement that the reach of the statute of 1795 was beyond that of the statute of February 20, 1863, and so much as lies outside, beyond the latter statute, is still valid legislative will by all fair rules upon the subject of the repeal of statutes.

With these few remarks upon that subject I come to the consideration of the *ad interim* question, and I will endeavor to consider it very briefly. From the foundation of the Government, as you have been advised by my colleague [Mr. Curtis] and others, it has been the policy of the Government to provide for these *ad interim* necessities. They are not appointments. No commission goes. There is no commission issued under the seal of the United States in such cases. There is a mere letter of authority. Such appointees are not considered as filling the office. I will state a case to illustrate the character of an *ad interim* appointment and the hold it takes upon the office. When Mr. Upshur was killed in 1844 an *ad interim* appointment was made to supply the vacancy occasioned by that accident, and soon afterward the President nominated to the Senate a gentleman to fill the place permanently.

When he made that nomination he nominated Mr. Calhoun in the place of Mr. Upshur, deceased, not even noticing the *ad interim* appointee. That fairly illustrates the condition of an *ad interim* occupant of an office. It has been the policy of the Government from the beginning to furnish these supplies to the necessities of the Departments for sickness, for absence, for resignation, for any of these causes. An officer at the head of a Department dies; the President may wish to appoint some one at a distance; he may wish to inquire before he finally selects the person who is to fill the place. He waits, and in the mean time the Department—say the Treasury Department, and others I might name, must be carried on, and the *ad interim* appointee steps in and carries it on. This occurs just as well during the session of the Senate as in the recess. There is not one particle of difference between a session and a recess in the application of this policy. The law makes no difference. Take the law of February 20, 1863; it does not say in the recess you may act, but at any time according to the necessity you may act. That is the rule.

Now, Senators, I will dismiss this part of the subject by calling your attention to *ad interim* appointments that have been made during the session of heads of Departments. In the first place I give you the case of Mr. Nelson, who was appointed *ad interim* Secretary of State during the session of the Senate. I give you the case of General Scott, who was appointed *ad interim* Secretary of War during the session of the Senate. I give you the case of Mr. Moses Kelly, who was appointed *ad interim* Secretary of the Interior Department during the session of the Senate. I give you the case of Mr. Holt, who was appointed during the session of the Senate Secretary of War *ad interim*; but I intend to linger a little at the case of Mr. Holt. I call the attention of the Senate especially to that case, for it is worthy of especial attention and consideration. The case is presented in a message communicated to the Senate by President Buchanan on the 15th of January, 1861, which has been put in evidence and will be found on page 583 of our proceedings. I will read the message:

"*To the Senate of the United States:*

"In compliance with the resolution of the Senate, passed on the 10th instant, requesting me to inform that body, if not incompatible with the public interest, 'whether John B. Floyd, whose appointment as Secretary of War was confirmed by the Senate on the 6th of March, 1857, still continues to hold said office, and if not, when and how said office became vacant; and further to inform the Senate how and by whom the duties of said office are now discharged; and if an appointment of an acting or provisional Secretary of War has been made, how, when, and by what authority it was so made, and why the fact of said appointment has not been communicated to the Senate,' I have to inform the Senate that John B. Floyd, the late Secretary of the War Department, resigned that office on the 29th day of December last, and that on the 1st day of January instant Joseph Holt was authorized by me to perform the duties of the said office until a successor should be appointed or the vacancy filled. Under this authority the duties of the War Department have been performed by Mr. Holt from the day last mentioned to the present time."

I call your attention, Senators, to this case especially, for this single reason, and it is important: the Senate itself took the matter under consideration, and inquired of the President what he had done, why he had done it, and by what authority he had done it. In other words, in the case of Holt the Senate went into an actual investigation of the question, and that is the reason why I linger upon it. The Senate asked the President, "Why did you do it, and why did you not report to us?" Full inquiry was made by the Senate in that case into this *ad interim* question, and Mr. Buchanan replied as follows:

"The power to carry on the business of the Government by means of a provisional appointment when a vacancy occurs is expressly given by the act of February 13, 1795, which enacts 'that in case of vacancy in the office of Secretary of State, Secretary of the Treasury, or of the Secretary of the Department of War, or any officer of either of the said Departments, whose appointment is not in the head thereof, whereby they cannot perform the duties of their said respective offices, it shall be lawful for the President of the United States, in case he shall think it necessary, to authorize any person or persons, at his discretion, to perform the duties of the said respective offices until a successor be appointed or such vacancy be filled: *Provided,* That no one vacancy shall be supplied in manner aforesaid for a longer period than six months.'"

He replies that he did it under the law of 1795, Senators will observe. He communicated that fact to the Senate. The Senate received his communication, and were satisfied. That is good *res adjudicata* on this question. The Senate took up on that occasion this identical question of *ad interim* appointments during the session, investigated it thoroughly, received Mr. Buchanan's reply that he did it under the very law under which we acted, and the Senate concurred. There was no censure. If the Senate did not censure that act, will they drag President Johnson here as a criminal and brand him with crime for his act? I think not. The cases are identical. You cannot discriminate between them. Both were done under the same law, both done during the session, both exactly alike. The one was not censured.

Shall the other be made the ground of criminal condemnation of President Johnson?

I proceed now to glance at the Emory article, and I shall simply glance at it, Senators. I do not intend to linger upon such a charge as this. It makes a great noise in the articles; but it is very harmless in the proof. What is the proof to sustain it? The President had an interview with General Emory, and in the course of that interview General Emory informed him of the passage of a certain law by which he as Commander-in-Chief was divested of the authority to issue commands directly, but they must pass through the General-in-Chief. They had a conversation upon the subject, and the President remarked in the course of that conversation that the law was unconstitutional. He had said it to you; he did not say anything more to Emory; and that is the enormous crime he committed under article nine. He said the law was unconstitutional. What of that? It is in evidence before you, and uncontradicted. Secretary Welles tells you that the President had been informed that there were unusual movements of troops going on in the city the night before, and Secretary Welles called upon the President to advise him of that fact, and the President said he would inquire about it. He did. He sent a note to General Emory; General Emory waited upon him and gave him the information. That is all. Is it not explained why he sent for General Emory? Does anybody contradict it? No. The time, the occasion, everything in the transaction, adjusts itself to that explanation and to no other. Here was a President whom you had subordinated to an inferior officer—I mean to the extent of requiring him to pass his orders through an inferior officer—who having heard these rumors of military movements going on, and being called upon by one of his Cabinet officers to look into it, responded, "I will inquire;" and he did. That is all there is of article nine. I will not delay upon it any longer.

I now come to article ten. I shall leave the labored discussion of this article to my colleague [Mr. Evarts] who is to come after me. But I wish to say just a few words about it. I refer you in reply to this whole article to the constitutional bearing upon this subject, denying to Congress the right to abridge the freedom of speech. Are there any limitations to this privilege? Does it belong only to the private citizen? Is it denied to officers of the Government? May not the Executive freely canvass the measures of any other department? May Congress set itself up as the standard of good taste? Has it authority to prescribe the rules of presidential decorum? Will it not be quite enough if Congress will preserve its own dignity? Shall it dictate the forms of expression in which it may be referred to? Can you punish in the forum of impeachment what Congress cannot forbid in the form of law? These are pertinent questions bearing upon article ten.

But I do not propose to discuss it. I wish to present to you, Senators, a little history which article ten very forcibly suggests to my mind.

In 1798 some good people in the country seem to have been operated upon very much as the Managers, or rather the House of Representatives were in this instance, and they took it into their heads to get up what is called a sedition law, which is very like article ten. I propose to read it. The act of July 14, 1798, provided:

"That if any person shall write, print, utter or publish, or shall cause or procure to be written, printed, uttered or published, or shall knowingly and willingly assist or aid in writing, printing, uttering, or publishing any false, scandalous, and malicious writing or writings against the Government of the United States, or either House of the Congress of the United States, or the President of the United States, with intent to defame the said Government, or either House of the said Congress, or the said President, or to bring them, or either of them, into contempt or disrepute, or to excite against them, or either or any of them, the hatred of the good people of the United States, or to stir up sedition within the United States, or to excite any unlawful combinations therein, for opposing or resisting any law of the United States, or any act of the President of the United States, done in pursuance of any such law, or of the powers in him vested by the Constitution of the United States, or to resist, oppose, or defeat any such law or act, or to aid, encourage or abet any hostile designs of any foreign nation against the United States, their people or Government, then such person, being thereof convicted before any court of the United States having jurisdiction thereof, shall be punished by a fine not exceeding $2,000, and by imprisonment not exceeding two years."

I need not explain, Senators, the purpose of this act. It expired by its own limitation. It was the most offensive law that has ever been passed since the Government was organized. So offensive was it that the people would not rest under it, although it was passed to last but three years. They started, as it were, the hue and cry against everybody who defended it or was concerned in it, and hunted them to a political death. But it was a good law compared with article ten. The sedition law of 1798 condemned what? It condemned the act of cooly and under no provocation or excitement preparing and publishing a libel against the Government or any department thereof; but so clamorous and indignant were the people over such legislation that they broke it down; and the consequence has been, so unpopular was it, that Congress has not ventured to pass a law upon the subject of libel against the Government or any department from that day to this. It has been reserved for the House of Representatives, through its Managers, to renew the practice in a more objectionable form. And I take it upon myself to suggest that before we are to be condemned in a court of impeachment we shall have some law upon the subject; and I have ventured to draw up, and I shall close my examination of this particular question by presenting to you the draft of a bill which I have made on article ten of this impeachment. It should have a preamble, of course. I will proceed to read it:

Whereas it is highly improper for the President of

the United States or any other officer of the executive department or of any department to say anything tending to bring ridicule or contempt upon the Congress of the United States, or to impair the regard of the good people of the United States for the Congress and the legislative power thereof, (which all officers of the Government ought inviolably to preserve and maintain;) and whereas (quoting in part from an argument of the Managers) the dignity of station, the proprieties of position, the courtesies of office, all of which are a part of the common law of the land, require the President of the United States to observe that gravity of deportment, that fitness of conduct, that appropriateness of demeanor, and those amenities of behavior which are a part of his high official functions; and whereas he stands before the youth of the country as the exemplar of all that is of worth in ambition, or that is to be sought in aspiration, and before the men of the country as a grave magistrate, and before the world as the representative of free institutions; and whereas it is the duty of Congress, and especially of the House of Representatives, as the fountain of national dignity, to lay down rules of decorum, and to regulate the manners and etiquette proper for this and every other high officer of the Government: Therefore,

Be it enacted, &c., That if the President or any other officer shall say anything displeasing to Congress, or either branch thereof, or shall in any addresses, extemporaneous or written, which he may be required to make in response to calls from the people, say anything tending to impair the regard of the people for Congress, or either branch thereof, or if he shall use any unintelligible phrases, such as that "Congress is a body hanging as it were on the verge of the Government," or say that it is "a Congress of only a part of the States," because ten States are not represented therein; or if he shall charge it in such addresses with encroaching upon constitutional rights, however he may think; or if he shall misquote or carelessly quote the sacred Scriptures, or in any of said extemporaneous addresses use bad grammar, then, and in either of such cases, he shall be guilty of a high misdemeanor, and upon trial and conviction thereof shall be fined in any sum not exceeding $10,000, or imprisoned not exceeding ten years. [Laughter.]

That is article ten. [Laughter.]

The next, and last, is article eleven. Senators, I have discussed article eleven already with the exception of one single feature, and that is the part of it which charges obstruction or interference with the law for the reconstruction of the rebel States. That is the only feature in article eleven I have not fully answered in the remarks I have made in connection with other articles. Now, what shall I say of that? I am glad, Senators, that I have nothing to say upon the subject. What testimony has the prosecution offered in support of that charge? They offer this single testimony, and no other: a telegram from Parsons, and a reply from the President, dated in the January preceding the March when the law was passed. Need I pause upon such proof of the violation or obstruction of a thing not *in esse* when the act was done?

We heard a magnificent oration from one of the honorable Managers two days ago; but the defect of it was, it had nothing to support it. He made his magnificent oration, sounding with sonorous sentences through this Hall, for about three hours, on that telegram of January 15, 1867, which was sent two months before the law was passed. That is all the proof. If we intend to judge this case upon proof here presented, that is all the proof he had for a large portion of his speech.

Now, Senators, I have gone over this case as far as I intend to do in my condition, though not so far as I proposed to do when I prepared my brief. But I know I am to be followed by a gentleman who will go over it step by step, article by article, in all probability, and therefore I feel the more safe in omitting a part of what I have prepared to say and what under other circumstances I should have been glad to say. I stand now beyond article eleven, beyond all the articles, and I ask you to look back with me upon the case. What questions are involved in it? I am happy to be able to say that there is no political question; that there is no party question. I was glad, the defense was glad, the counsel were glad of the opportunity of relieving you from the embarrassment of any such questions. The questions presented are these:

1. Where is the power of removal lodged by the Constitution?

2. Is Stanton covered by the civil-tenure act?

3. Could the President make an *ad interim* appointment?

4. Did he do anything mischievous in his interview with General Emory?

And then there is this matter of the liberty of speech, which, I apprehend, nobody intends to take on his back and carry as a heavy load for the rest of his life, so that we have no political questions here. I am glad it is so. They are dry questions of practice and of law; one of them the oldest question in the history of the Government. And on this statement of the case, when you strip it of all the verbiage and rumor and talk of every kind, standing almost naked upon a few technical propositions, upon such a case we ask your judgment of acquittal. We are entitled to it beyond all peradventure. It almost shocks me to think that the President of the United States is to be dragged out of his office on these miserable little questions, whether he could make an *ad interim* appointment for a single day, or whether in anything he did there was so great a crime that you should break the even flow of the Administrations of the country, disturb the quiet of the people, and impair their confidence in a great degree in the stability of their Government; that you should, in a word, take possession of the Executive, and, what is worse and most unfortunate in the condition of things, empty the office and fill it with one of your own number. Not on this case. Surely not on this case, Senators. I cannot understand how such a thing can possibly be done. How miserable is this case! An *ad interim* appointment for a single day, an attempt to remove Edwin M. Stanton, who stood defiantly, and, right or wrong, had destroyed the harmony and unity of the Cabinet. I do not speak in censure of Mr. Stanton—such is the fact. That is all!

Senators, we have been referred to a great many precedents. I heard one of the honorable Managers talk two days ago about Charles I, and we have had abundance of precedents submitted on the subject of expediency and things like that; policy, if you please, as if this were a measure and not a trial. We have nothing to do with measures in the high court of impeachment. You are trying the defendant on the charges set forth in these articles and upon the proof offered from the witness-stand, and upon nothing else. I, too, can point to those precedents to which the gentlemen have called your attention—the miserable precedents which they have brought up on the subject of impeachment, even from centuries back; and they are to me, as they should be to all of us, not examples for imitation, but "beacon lights to warn us from the dangerous rocks on which they are kindled." Let us shun all unnecessary violence. As we sow, so shall we reap; like begets like; violence, violence, and the practice of to-day shall be the precedent for to-morrow.

What shall be your judgment? What is to be your judgment, Senators, in this case? Removal from office and perpetual disqualification? If the President has committed that for which he should be ejected from office it were judicial mockery to stop short of the largest disqualification you can impose. It will be a heavy judgment. What is his crime, in its moral aspects, to merit such a judgment? Let us look at it.

He tried to pluck a thorn out of his very heart, for the condition of things in the War Department, and consequently in his Cabinet, did pain him as a thorn in his heart. You fastened it there, and you are now asked to punish him for attempting to extract it. What more? He made an *ad interim* appointment to last for a single day. You could have terminated it whenever you saw fit. You had only to take up the nomination which he sent to you, which was a good nomination, and act upon it and the *ad interim* appointment vanished like smoke. He had no idea of fastening it upon the Department. He had no intention to do anything of that kind. He merely proposed that for the purpose, if the opportunity should occur, of subjecting this law to a constitutional test. That is all the purpose it was to answer. It is all for which it was intended. The thing was in your hand from the beginning to the end. You had only to act upon the nomination, and the matter was settled. Surely that is no crime.

I point you to the cases that have occurred of *ad interim* appointment after *ad interim* appointment; but I point especially to the case of Mr. Holt where the Senate in its legislative capacity examined it, weighed it, decided upon it, heard the report of the President, and received it as satisfactory. That is, for the purposes of this trial, before the same tribunal *res adjudicata*, I think, and it will be so regarded.

What else did he do? He talked with an officer about the law. That is the Emory article. He made intemperate speeches, though

full of honest, patriotic sentiments; when reviled he should not revile again, when smitten upon one cheek he should turn the other.

But, says the gentleman who spoke last on behalf of the Managers, he tried to defeat pacification and restoration. I deny it in the sense in which he presented it—that is, as a criminal act. Here, too, he followed precedent and trod the path on which were the footprints of Lincoln, and which was bright with the radiance of his divine utterance, "charity for all, malice toward none." He was eager for pacification. He thought that the war was ended. The drums were all silent; the arsenals were all shut; the roar of the cannon had died away to the last reverberations; the armies were disbanded; not a single enemy confronted us in the field. Ah, he was too eager, too forgiving, too kind. The hand of conciliation was stretched out to him and he took it. It may be he should have put it away, but was it a crime to take it? Kindness, forgiveness a crime? Kindness a crime? Kindness is omnipotent for good, more powerful than gunpowder or cannon. Kindness is statesmanship. Kindness is the high statesmanship of heaven itself. The thunders of Sinai do but terrify and distract; alone they accomplish little; it is the kindness of Calvary that subdues and pacifies.

What shall I say of this man? He is no theorist; he is no reformer; I have looked over his life. He has ever walked in beaten paths, and by the light of the Constitution. The mariner, tempest tossed at mid-sea, does not more certainly turn to his star for guidance than does this man in trial and difficulty to the star of the Constitution. He loves the Constitution. It has been the study of his life. He is not learned and scholarly, like many of you; he is not a man of many ideas or of much speculation; but by a law of the mind he is only the truer to that he does know. He is a patriot, second to no one of you in the measure of his patriotism. He loves his country; he may be full of error; I will not canvass now his views; but he loves his country; he has the courage to defend it, and I believe to die for it if need be. His courage and his patriotism are not without illustration.

My colleague [Mr. Nelson] referred the other day to the scenes which occurred in this Chamber when he alone of twenty-two Senators remained; even his State seceded, but he remained. That was a trial of his patriotism, of which many of you, by reason of your locality your and life-long association, know nothing. How his voice rang out in this Hall in the hour of alarm for the good cause, and in denunciation of the rebellion. But he did not remain here; it was a pleasant, honorable, safe, and easy position; but he was wanted for a more difficult and arduous and perilous service. He faltered not, but entered upon it. That was a trial of his courage and patriotism of which some of you who now sit in judgment on more than his life know nothing. I have often thought that those who dwelt at the North, safely distant from the collisions and strife of the war, knew but little of its actual, trying dangers. We who lived on the border know more. Our horizon was always red with its flame; and it sometimes burned so near us that we could feel its heat upon the outstretched hand. But he was wanted for greater peril, and went into the very furnace of the war, and there served his country long and well. Who of you have done more? Not one. There is one here whose services cannot be over-estimated, as I well know, and I withdraw all comparison.

But it is enough to say that his services were great and needed; and it seems hard, it seems cruel, Senators, that he should be dragged here as a criminal, or that any one who served his country and bore himself well and bravely through that trying ordeal, should be condemned upon miserable technicalities.

If he has committed any gross crime, shocking alike and indiscriminately the entire public mind, then condemn him; but he has rendered service to the country that entitles him to kind and respectful consideration. He has precedents for everything he has done, and what excellent precedents! The voices of the great dead come to us from the grave sanctioning his course. All our past history approves it. How can you single out this man now, in this condition of things, and brand him before the world, put your brand of infamy upon him because he made an *ad interim* appointment for a day; and possibly may have made a mistake in attempting to remove Stanton? I can at a glance put my eye on Senators here who would not endure the position which he occupied. You do not think it is right yourselves. You framed this civil-tenure law to give each President his own Cabinet, and yet his whole crime is that he wants harmony and peace in his.

Senators, I will not go on. There is a great deal that is crowding on my tongue for utterance, but it is not from my head; it is rather from my heart; and it would be but a repetition of the vain things I have been saying the past half hour. But I do hope you will not drive the President out and take possession of his office. I hope this not merely as counsel for Andrew Johnson—for Andrew Johnson's administration is to me but as a moment, and himself as nothing in comparison with the possible consequences of such an act. No good can come of it, Senators, and how much will the heart of the nation be refreshed if at last the Senate of the United States can, in its judgment upon this case, maintain its ancient dignity and high character in the midst of storm and passion and strife.

Mr. GRIMES. Mr. Chief Justice, I move that the Senate, sitting as a court of impeachment, adjourn.

The motion was agreed to; and the Senate, sitting for the trial of the impeachment, adjourned.

MONDAY, *April* 27, 1868.

The Chief Justice of the United States took the chair.

The usual proclamation having been made by the Sergeant-at-Arms,

The Managers of the impeachment on the part of the House of Representatives and the counsel for the respondent, except Mr. Stanbery, appeared and took the seats assigned to them respectively.

The members of the House of Representatives, as in Committee of the Whole, preceded by Mr. E. B. WASHBURNE, chairman of that committee, and accompanied by the Speaker and Clerk, appeared and were conducted to the seats provided for them.

The Journal of last Saturday's proceedings of the Senate sitting for the trial of impeachment was read.

The CHIEF JUSTICE. The first business in order is the consideration of the order submitted by the Senator from Vermont, [Mr. EDMUNDS.] The Secretary will read the order.

The Chief Clerk read as follows:

Ordered, That after the arguments shall be concluded, and when the doors shall be closed for deliberation upon the final question, the official reporters of the Senate shall take down the debates upon the final question, to be reported in the proceedings.

Mr. WILLIAMS. Mr. President, I propose an amendment to the resolution, which I send to the Chair.

The Chief Justice read the amendment, which was to add to the proposed order the following words:

But no Senator shall speak more than once, nor to exceed fifteen minutes, during such deliberation.

Mr. JOHNSON. Mr. Chief Justice, I ask for the reading of the rule in relation to the time Senators are permitted to speak. I think it is fifteen minutes upon each article.

The CHIEF JUSTICE. The Secretary will read the rule.

The Chief Clerk read rule twenty-three, as follows:

"XXIII. All the orders and decisions shall be made and had by yeas and nays, which shall be entered on the record, and without debate, except when the doors shall be closed for deliberation, and in that case no member shall speak more than once on one question, and for not more than ten minutes on an interlocutory question, and for not more than fifteen minutes on the final question, unless by consent of the Senate, to be had without debate; but a motion to adjourn may be decided without the yeas and nays, unless they be demanded by one fifth of the members present."

Mr. JOHNSON. That is upon each article, as I supposed.

Mr. EDMUNDS. No, sir; it is not.

The CHIEF JUSTICE. The question is on the amendment proposed by the Senator from Oregon, [Mr. WILLIAMS.]

Mr. HOWARD. I move to amend the amendment by adding after the words "fifteen minutes" the words "on one question."

The CHIEF JUSTICE. The question is on the amendment proposed by the Senator from

Michigan to the amendment of the Senator from Oregon.

Mr. SUMNER called for the yeas and nays, and they were ordered ; and being taken, resulted—yeas 19, nays 30 ; as follows:

YEAS—Messrs. Bayard, Buckalew, Davis, Dixon, Doolittle, Fessenden, Fowler, Frelinghuysen, Grimes, Hendricks, Howard, Johnson, McCreery, Norton, Patterson of Tennessee, Saulsbury, Trumbull, Vickers, and Willey—19.

NAYS—Messrs. Cameron, Cattell, Chandler, Conkling, Corbett, Cragin, Drake, Edmunds, Ferry, Harlan, Henderson, Howe, Morgan, Morrill of Maine, Morrill of Vermont, Morton, Nye, Patterson of New Hampshire, Pomeroy, Ramsey, Ross, Sherman, Stewart, Sumner, Thayer, Tipton, Van Winkle, Williams, Wilson, and Yates—30.

NOT VOTING—Messrs. Anthony, Cole, Conness, Sprague, and Wade—5.

So the amendment to the amendment was rejected.

The CHIEF JUSTICE. The question recurs on the amendment offered by the Senator from Oregon.

Mr. BAYARD. I move to amend the amendment by striking out "fifteen" and inserting "thirty;" and on that I ask for the yeas and nays.

The yeas and nays were ordered ; and being taken, resulted—yeas 16, nays 34 ; as follows:

YEAS—Messrs. Bayard, Buckalew, Corbett, Davis, Dixon, Doolittle, Fessenden, Fowler, Grimes, Hendricks, Johnson, McCreery, Norton, Patterson of Tennessee, Saulsbury, and Vickers—16.

NAYS—Messrs. Anthony, Cameron, Cattell, Chandler, Conkling, Cragin, Drake, Edmunds, Ferry, Frelinghuysen, Harlan, Henderson, Howard, Howe, Morgan, Morrill of Maine, Morrill of Vermont, Morton, Nye, Patterson of New Hampshire, Pomeroy, Ramsey, Ross, Sherman, Stewart, Sumner, Thayer, Tipton, Trumbull, Van Winkle, Willey, Williams, Wilson, and Yates—34.

NOT VOTING—Messrs. Cole, Conness, Sprague, and Wade—4.

So the amendment to the amendment was rejected.

The CHIEF JUSTICE. The question recurs on the amendment of the Senator from Oregon.

Mr. MORTON. I move the postponement of the further consideration of this subject until after the argument is concluded by the counsel and the Managers.

Mr. HOWARD. I second that motion.

The motion to postpone was agreed to.

The CHIEF JUSTICE. The next business in order is the consideration of the proposed new rules submitted by the Senator from Massachusetts, [Mr. SUMNER.] The first one of them will be read.

Mr. SUMNER. Mr. President, I ask that those propositions, which were moved by me on Saturday, may go over until after the close of the argument.

The CHIEF JUSTICE. If there be no objection the proposition of the Senator from Massachusetts will be considered as agreed to, and the proposed rules will go over. Gentlemen Managers on the part of the House of Representatives, you will please proceed with the argument.

Hon. THADDEUS STEVENS, one of the Managers on behalf of the House of Representatives, addressed the Senate as follows :

Mr. Chief Justice, may it please the court, I trust to be able to be brief in my remarks, unless I should find myself less master of the subject which I propose to discuss than I hope. Experience has taught that nothing is so prolix as ignorance. I fear I may prove thus ignorant, as I had not expected to take part in this debate until very lately.

I shall discuss but a single article—the one that was finally adopted upon my earnest solicitation, and which, if proved, I considered then, and still consider, as quite sufficient for the ample conviction of the distinguished respondent and for his removal from office, which is the only legitimate object for which this impeachment could be instituted.

During the very brief period which I shall occupy I desire to discuss the charges against the respondent in no mean spirit of malignity or vituperation, but to argue them in a manner worthy of the high tribunal before which I appear and of the exalted position of the accused. Whatever may be thought of his character or condition, he has been made respectable and his condition has been dignified by the action of his fellow-citizens. Railing accusation, therefore, would ill become this occasion, this tribunal, or a proper sense of the position of those who discuss this question on the one side or the other.

To see the chief servant of a trusting community arraigned before the bar of public justice, charged with high delinquencies, is interesting. To behold the Chief Executive Magistrate of a powerful people charged with the betrayal of his trust, and arraigned for high crimes and misdemeanors, is always a most interesting spectacle. When the charges against such public servant accuse him of an attempt to betray the high trust confided in him and usurp the power of a whole people, that he may become their ruler, it is intensely interesting to millions of men, and should be discussed with a calm determination, which nothing can divert and nothing can reduce to mockery. Such is the condition of this great Republic, as looked upon by an astonished and wondering world.

The offices of impeachment in England and America are very different from each other in the uses made of them for the punishment of offenses; and he will greatly err who undertakes to make out an analogy between them, either in the mode of trial or the final result.

In England the highest crimes may be tried before the high court of impeachment, and the severest punishments, even to imprisonment, fine, and death, may be inflicted.

When our Constitution was framed all these personal punishments were excluded from the judgment, and the defendant was to be dealt with just so far as the public safety required, and no further. Hence it was made to apply simply to political offenses—to persons holding political positions, either by appointment or election by the people.

Thus it is apparent that no crime containing malignant or indictable offenses higher than misdemeanors was necessary either to be alleged or proved. If the respondent was shown to be abusing his official trust to the injury of the people for whom he was discharging public duties, and persevered in such abuse to the injury of his constituents, the true mode of dealing with him was to impeach him for crimes or misdemeanors, (and only the latter is necessary,) and thus remove him from the office which he was abusing. Nor does it make a particle of difference whether such abuse arose from malignity, from unwarranted negligence, or from depravity, so repeated as to make his continuance in office injurious to the people and dangerous to the public welfare.

The punishment which the law, under our Constitution, authorizes to be inflicted fully demonstrates this argument: that punishment upon conviction extends only to removal from office, and if the crime or misdemeanor charged be one of a deep and wicked dye the culprit is allowed to run at large, unless he should be pursued by a new prosecution in the ordinary courts. What does it matter, then, what the motive of the respondent might be in his repeated acts of malfeasance in office? Mere mistake in intention, if so persevered in after proper warning as to bring mischief upon the community, is quite sufficient to warrant the removal of the officer from the place where he is working mischief by his continuance in power.

The only question to be considered is: is the respondent violating the law? His perseverance in such a violation, although it shows a perverseness, is not absolutely necessary to his conviction. The great object is the removal from office and the arrest of the public injuries which he is inflicting upon those with whose interests he is intrusted.

The single charge which I had the honor to suggest I am expected to maintain. That duty is a light one, easily performed, and which, I apprehend, it will be found impossible for the respondent to answer or evade.

When Andrew Johnson took upon himself the duties of his high office he swore to obey the Constitution and take care that the laws be faithfully executed? That, indeed, is and has always been the chief duty of the President of the United States. The duties of legislation and adjudicating the laws of his country fall in no way to his lot. To obey the commands of the sovereign power of the nation, and to see that others should obey them, was his whole duty—a duty which he could not escape, and any attempt to do so would be in direct violation of his official oath ; in other words, a *misprision of perjury.*

I accuse him, in the name of the House of Representatives, of having perpetrated that foul offense against the laws and interests of his country.

On the 2d day of March, 1867, Congress passed a law, over the veto of the President, entitled "An act to regulate the tenure of certain civil offices," the first section of which is as follows:

"*Be it enacted by the Senate and House of Representatives of the United States of America in Congress assembled,* That every person holding any civil office to which he has been appointed by and with the advice and consent of the Senate, and every person who may hereafter be appointed to any such office and shall become duly qualified to act therein, is and shall be entitled to hold such office until a successor shall have been in like manner appointed and duly qualified, except as herein otherwise provided: *Provided,* That the Secretaries of State, of the Treasury, of War, of the Navy, and of the Interior, the Postmaster General, and the Attorney General, shall hold their offices respectively for and during the term of the President by whom they may have been appointed, and for one month thereafter, subject to removal by and with the advice and consent of the Senate."

The second section provides that when the Senate is not in session, if the President shall deem the officer guilty of acts which require his removal or suspension, he may be suspended until the next meeting of the Senate ; and that within twenty days after the meeting of the Senate the reasons for such suspension shall be reported to that body ; and, if the Senate shall deem such reasons sufficient for such suspension or removal, the officer shall be considered removed from his office ; but if the Senate shall not deem the reasons sufficient for such suspension or removal, the officer shall forthwith resume the functions of his office. and the person appointed in his place shall cease to discharge such duties.

On the 12th day of August, 1867, the Senate then not being in session, the President suspended Edwin M. Stanton, Secretary of the Department of War, and appointed U. S. Grant, General, Secretary of War *ad interim.* On the 12th day of December, 1867, the Senate being then in session, he reported, according to the requirements of the act, the causes of such suspension to the Senate, which duly took the same into consideration. Before the Senate had concluded its examination of the question of the sufficiency of such reasons he attempted to enter into arrangements by which he might obstruct the due execution of the law, and thus prevent Edwin M. Stanton from forthwith resuming the functions of his office as Secretary of War, according to the provisions of the act, even if the Senate should decide in his favor.

And in furtherance of said attempt, on the 21st day of February, 1868, he appointed one Lorenzo Thomas, by letter of authority or commission, Secretary of War *ad interim,* without the advice and consent of the Senate, although the same was then in session, and ordered him (the said Thomas) to take possession of the Department of War and the public property appertaining thereto, and to discharge the duties thereof.

We charge that, in defiance of frequent warnings, he has since repeatedly attempted to carry those orders into execution, and to prevent Edwin M. Stanton from executing the laws appertaining to the Department of War and from discharging the duties of the office.

The very able gentleman who argued this case for the respondent has contended that Mr. Stanton's case is not within the provisions of the act regulating the tenure of certain civil offices, and that therefore the President cannot be convicted of violating that act. His argument in demonstrating that position was not, I think, quite equal to his sagacity in discovering where the great strength of the prosecution was lodged. He contended that the proviso which embraced the Secretary of War did not include Mr. Stanton, because he was not appointed by the President in whose term the acts charged as misdemeanors were perpetrated; and in order to show that, he contended that the *term* of office mentioned during which he was entitled to hold meant the time during which the President who appointed him actually did hold, whether dead or alive; that Mr. Lincoln, who appointed Mr. Stanton, and under whose commission he was holding indefinitely, being dead, his *term* of office referred to had expired, and that Mr. Johnson was not holding during a part of that *term*. That depends upon the Constitution and the laws made under it. By the Constitution, the whole time from the adoption of the Government was intended to be divided into equal presidential periods, and the word "*term*" was technically used to designate the time of each. The first section of the second article of the Constitution provides—

"That the executive power shall be vested in a President of the United States of America. He shall hold his office during the *term* of four years, and together with the Vice President, chosen for the same *term*, be elected as follows," &c.

Then it provides that—

"In cases of removal from office, or of his death, resignation, or inability to discharge the duties of said office, the same shall devolve on the Vice President, and Congress may by law provide for the case of removal, death, resignation, or inability both of the President and Vice President, designating what officer shall then act as President, and such officer shall act accordingly until the disability be removed or a President shall be elected."

The learned counsel contends that the Vice President who accidentally accedes to the duties of President, is serving out a new presidential term of his own, and that, unless Mr. Stanton was appointed by him, he is not within the provisions of the act. It happened that Mr. Stanton was appointed by Mr. Lincoln in 1862 for an indefinite period of time, and was still serving as *his* appointee, by and with the advice and consent of the Senate. Mr. Johnson never appointed him, and, unless he held a valid commission by virtue of Mr. Lincoln's appointment, he was acting for three years, during which time he expended billions of money and raised hundreds of thousands of men, without any commission at all. To permit this to be done without any valid commis-

sion would have been a misdemeanor in itself. But if he held a valid commission, whose commission was it? Not Andrew Johnson's. Then in whose term was he serving, for he must have been in somebody's term? Even if it was in Johnson's term, he would hold for four years unless sooner removed, for there is no term spoken of in the Constitution of a shorter period for a presidential term than four years. But it makes no difference in the operation of the law whether he was holding in Lincoln's or Johnson's term. Was it not in Mr. Lincoln's term? Lincoln had been elected and reëlected, the second term to commence in 1865, and the Constitution expressly declared that that term should be four years.

By virtue of his previous commission and the uniform custom of the country, Mr. Stanton continued to hold during the term of Mr. Lincoln, unless sooner removed. Now, does any one pretend that from the 4th of March, 1865, a new presidential term did not commence? For it will be seen upon close examination that the word "*term*" alone marks the time of the presidential existence, so that it may divide the different periods of office by a well recognized rule. Instead of saying that the Vice President shall become President upon his death the Constitution says:

"In case of the removal of the President from office, or of his death, resignation, or inability to discharge the *powers and duties* of the said office, the same shall devolve on the Vice President."

What is to devolve on the Vice President? Not the presidential commission held by his predecessor, but the "duties" which were incumbent on him. If he were to take Mr. Lincoln's term he would serve for four years, for term is the only limitation to that office, defined in the Constitution, as I have said before. But the learned counsel has contended that the word "*term*" of the presidential office means the death of the President. Then it would have been better expressed by saying that the President shall hold his office during the *term* between two assassinations, and then the assassination of the President would mark the period of the operations of this law.

If, then, Mr. Johnson was serving out one of Mr. Lincoln's terms, there seems to be no argument against including Mr. Stanton within the meaning of the law. He was so included by the President in his notice of removal, in his reasons therefor given to the Senate, and in his notification to the Secretary of the Treasury; and it is too late, when he is caught violating the very law under which he professes to act, to turn round and deny that that law affects the case. The gentleman treats lightly the question of estoppel; and yet really nothing is more powerful, for it is an argument by the party himself against himself, and although not pleadable in the same way is just as potential in a case *in pais* as when pleaded in a case of *record*.

But there is a still more conclusive answer.

The first section provides that *every* person holding civil office who has been appointed with the advice and consent of the Senate, and every person that hereafter shall be appointed to any such office, shall be entitled to hold such office until a successor shall have been in like manner appointed and duly qualified, except as herein otherwise provided. Then comes the proviso which the defendant's counsel say does not embrace Mr. Stanton, because he was not appointed by the President in whose term he was removed. If he was not embraced in the proviso, then he was nowhere specially provided for, and was consequently embraced in the first clause of the first section, which declares that every person holding any civil office not otherwise provided for comes within the provisions of this act.

The respondent, in violation of this law, appointed General Thomas to office, whereby, according to the express terms of the act, he was guilty of a high misdemeanor. But whatever may have been his views with regard to the tenure-of-office act he knew it was a law, and so recorded upon the statutes. I disclaim all necessity in a trial of impeachment to prove the wicked or unlawful intention of the respondent, and it is unwise ever to aver it. In impeachments, more than in indictments, the averring of the fact charged carries with it all that it is necessary to say about intent. In indictments you charge that the defendant, "instigated by the devil," and so on ; and you might as well call on the prosecution to prove the presence, shape, and color of his majesty, as to call upon the Managers in impeachment to prove intention. I go further than some, and contend that no corrupt or wicked motive need instigate the acts for which impeachment is brought. It is enough that they were official violations of law. The counsel have placed great stress upon the necessity of proving that they were willfully done. If by that he means that they were voluntarily done I agree with him. A mere accidental trespass would not be sufficient to convict. But that which is *voluntarily* done is *willfully* done, according to every honest definition ; and whatever malfeasance is willingly perpetrated by an office-holder in office, whatever he may allege was his intention.

The President justifies himself by asserting that all previous Presidents had exercised the same right of removing officers, for cause to be judged of by the President alone. Had there been no law to prohibit it when Mr. Stanton was removed the cases would have been parallel, and the one might be adduced as an argument in favor of the other. But, since the action of any of the Presidents to which he refers, a law had been passed by Congress, after a stubborn controversy with the Executive, denying that right and prohibiting it in future, and imposing a severe penalty upon any executive officer who should exercise it; and that, too, after the President

had himself made issue on its constitutionality and been defeated. No pretext, therefore, any longer existed that such right was vested in the President by virtue of his office. Hence the attempt to shield himself under such practice is a most lame evasion of the question at issue. Did he "take care that this law should be faithfully" executed? He answers that acts that would have violated the law, had it existed, were practiced by his predecessors. How does that justify his own malfeasance ?

The President says that he removed Mr. Stanton simply to test the constitutionality of the tenure-of-office law by a judicial decision. He has already seen it tested and decided by the votes, twice given, of two thirds of the Senators and of the House of Representatives. It stood as a law upon the statute-books. No case had arisen under that law, or is referred to by the President, which required any judicial interposition. If there had been, or should be, the courts were open to any one who felt aggrieved by the action of Mr. Stanton. But instead of enforcing that law he takes advantage of the name and the funds of the United States to resist it, and to induce others to resist it. Instead of attempting, as the Executive of the United States, to see that that law was faithfully executed, he took great pains and perpetrated the acts alleged in this article, not only to resist it himself, but to seduce others to do the same. He sought to induce the General-in-Chief of the Army to aid him in an open, avowed obstruction of the law as it stood unrepealed upon the statute-book. He could find no one to unite with him in perpetrating such an act until he sunk down upon the unfortunate individual bearing the title of Adjutant General of the Army. Is this taking care that the laws shall be faithfully executed? Is this attempting to carry them into effect, by upholding their validity, according to his oath? On the other hand, was it not a high and bold attempt to obstruct the laws and take care that they should not be executed? He must not excuse himself by saying that he had doubts of its constitutionality and wished to test it. What right had he to be hunting up excuses for others, as well as himself, to violate this law? Is not this confession a misdemeanor in itself?

The President asserts that he did not remove Stanton under the tenure-of-office law. This is a direct contradiction of his own letter to the Secretary of the Treasury, in which, as he was bound by law, he communicated to that officer the fact of the removal. This portion of the answer may, therefore, be considered as disposed of by the non-existence of the fact, as well as by his subsequent report to the Senate.

The following is the letter just alluded to, dated August 14, 1867 :

Sir: In compliance with the requirements of the act entitled "An act to regulate the tenure of certain civil offices," you are hereby notified that on the 12th instant Hon. Edwin M. Stanton was suspended from his office as Secretary of War, and General U. S. Grant authorized and empowered to act as Secretary *ad interim.*

Hon. SECRETARY OF THE TREASURY.

Wretched man! A direct contradiction of his solemn answer! How necessary that a man should have a good conscience or a good memory! Both would not be out of place. How lovely to contemplate what was so assiduously inculcated by a celebrated Pagan into the mind of his son: *"* Virtue is truth, and truth is virtue." And still more, virtue of every kind charms us, yet that virtue is strongest which is effected by justice and generosity. Good deeds will never be done, wise acts will never be executed, except by the virtuous and the conscientious.

May the good people of this Republic remember this good old doctrine when they next meet to select their rulers, and may they select only the brave and the virtuous.

Has it been proved, as charged in this article, that Andrew Johnson in vacation suspended from office Edwin M. Stanton, who had been duly appointed and was then executing the duties of Secretary of the Department of War, without the advice and consent of the Senate; did he report the reasons for such suspension to the Senate within twenty days from the meeting of the Senate; and did the Senate proceed to consider the sufficiency of such reasons? Did the Senate declare such reasons insufficient, whereby the said Edwin M. Stanton became authorized to forthwith resume and exercise the functions of Secretary of War, and displace the Secretary *ad interim,* whose duties were then to cease and terminate; did the said Andrew Johnson, in his official character of President of the United States, attempt to obstruct the return of the said Edwin M. Stanton and his resumption forthwith of the functions of his office as Secretary of the Department of War; and has he continued to attempt to prevent the discharge of the duties of said office by said Edwin M. Stanton, Secretary of War, notwithstanding the Senate decided in his favor? If he has, then the acts in violation of law, charged in this article, are full and complete.

The proof lies in a very narrow compass, and depends upon the credibility of one or two witnesses, who, upon this point, corroborate each other's evidence.

Andrew Johnson, in his letter of the 31st of January, 1868, not only declared that such was his intention, but reproached U. S. Grant, General, in the following language:

"You had found in our first conference 'that the President was desirous of keeping Mr. Stanton out of office, *whether sustained in the suspension or not.'* You knew what reasons had induced the President to ask from you a promise; you also knew that in case your views of duty did not accord with his own convictions it was his purpose to fill your place by another appointment. Even ignoring the existence of a positive understanding between us, these conclusions were plainly deducible from our various conversations. It is certain, however, that even under these circumstances you did not offer to return the

place to my possession, but, according to your own statement, placed yourself in a position where, could I have anticipated your action, I would have been compelled to ask of you, as I was compelled to ask of your predecessor in the War Department, a letter of resignation, or else to resort to the more disagreeable expedient of suspending you by a successor."

He thus distinctly alleges that the General had a full knowledge that such was his deliberate intention. Hard words and injurious epithets can do nothing to corroborate or to injure the character of a witness; but if Andrew Johnson be not wholly destitute of truth and a shameless falsifier then this article and all its charges are clearly made out by his own evidence.

Whatever the respondent may say of the reply of U. S. Grant, General, only goes to confirm the fact of the President's lawless attempt to obstruct the execution of the act specified in the article.

If General Grant's recollection of his conversation with the President is correct, then it goes affirmatively to prove the same fact stated by the President, although it shows that the President persevered in his course of determined obstruction of the law, while the General refused to aid in its consummation. No differences as to the main fact of the attempt to violate and prevent the execution of the law exist in either statement; both compel the conviction of the respondent, unless he should escape through other means than the facts proving the article. He cannot hope to escape by asking this high court to declare the "law for regulating the tenure of certain civil offices" unconstitutional and void; for it so happens—to the hopeless misfortune of the respondent—that almost every member of this high tribunal has more than once—twice, perhaps three times—declared upon his official oath that law constitutional and valid. The unhappy man is in this condition: he has declared himself determined to obstruct that act; he has, by two several letters of authority, ordered Lorenzo Thomas to violate that law; and he has issued commissions during the session of the Senate without the advice and consent of the Senate, in violation of law, to said Thomas. He must therefore either deny his own solemn declarations and falsify the testimony of General Grant and Lorenzo Thomas, or expect that verdict whose least punishment is removal from office.

But the President denies in his answer to the first and the eleventh articles (which he intends as a joint answer to the two charges) that he had attempted to contrive means to prevent the due execution of the law regulating the tenure of certain civil offices, or had violated his oath "to take care that the laws be faithfully executed." Yet while he denies such attempt to defeat the execution of the laws, in his letter of the 31st of January, 1868, he asserts, and reproaches General Grant by the assertion, that the General knew that his object was to prevent Edwin M. Stanton from forthwith resuming the functions of his office, notwithstanding that the Senate might decide in his favor; and the President and U. S. Grant, General, in their angry correspondence of the date heretofore referred to, made an issue of veracity—the President asserting that the General had promised to aid him in defeating the execution of the laws by preventing the immediate resumption of the functions of Secretary of War by Edwin M. Stanton, and that the General violated his promise; and U. S. Grant, General, denying ever having finally made such promise, although he agrees with the President that the President did attempt to induce him to make such promise and to enter into such an arrangement.

Now, whichever of these gentlemen may have lost his memory, and found in lieu of the truth the vision which issues from the Ivory Gate—though who can hesitate to choose between the words of a gallant soldier and the pettifogging of a political trickster?—is wholly immaterial, so far as the charge against the President is concerned. That charge is, that the President did attempt to prevent the due execution of the tenure-of-office law by entangling the General in the arrangement; and unless both the President and the General have lost their memory and mistaken the truth with regard to the promises with each other, then this charge is made out. In short, if either of these gentlemen has correctly stated these facts of attempting the obstruction of the law the President has been guilty of violating the law and of *misprision of official perjury*.

But, again, the President alleges his right to violate the act regulating the tenure of certain civil offices, because, he says, the same was inoperative and void as being in violation of the Constitution of the United States. Does it lie in his mouth to interpose this plea? He had acted under that law and issued letters of authority, both for the long and short term, to several persons under it, and it would hardly lie in his mouth after that to deny its validity unless he confessed himself guilty of lawbreaking by issuing such commissions.

Let us here look at Andrew Johnson accepting the oath "to take care that the laws be faithfully executed."

On the 2d of March, 1867, he returned to the Senate the "tenure-of-office bill"—where it originated and had passed by a majority of more than two thirds—with reasons elaborately given why it should not pass finally. Among these was the allegation of its unconstitutionality. It passed by a vote of 35 yeas to 11 nays. In the House of Representatives it passed by more than a two-thirds majority; and when the vote was announced the Speaker, as was his custom, proclaimed the vote, and declared in the language of the Constitution, "that two-thirds of each House having voted for it, notwithstanding the objections of the President, it has become a law."

I am supposing that Andrew Johnson was at this moment waiting to take the oath of office, as President of the United States, "that he would obey the Constitution and take care that the laws be faithfully executed." Having been sworn on the Holy Evangels to obey the Constitution, and being about to depart, he turns to the person administering the oath and says, "Stop; I have a further oath. I do solemnly swear that I will not allow the act entitled 'An act regulating the tenure of certain civil offices,' just passed by Congress over the presidential veto, to be executed; but I will prevent its execution by virtue of my own constitutional power."

How shocked Congress would have been—what would the country have said to a scene equalled only by the unparalleled action of this same official, when sworn into office on that fatal 5th day of March which made him the successor of Abraham Lincoln! Certainly he would not have been permitted to be inaugurated as Vice President or President. Yet, such in effect has been his conduct, if not under oath at least with less excuse, since the fatal day which inflicted him upon the people of the United States. Can the President hope to escape if the fact of his violating that law be proved or confessed by him, as has been done? Can he expect a sufficient number of his tryers to pronounce that law unconstitutional and void—those same triers having passed upon its validity upon several occasions? The act was originally passed by a vote of 29 yeas to 9 nays.

Subsequently the House of Representatives passed the bill with amendments, which the Senate disagreed to, and the bill was afterward referred to a committee of conference of the two Houses, whose agreement was reported to the Senate by the managers and was adopted by a vote of 22 yeas to 10 nays.

After the veto, upon reconsideration of the bill in the Senate, and after all the arguments against its validity were spread before that body, it passed by a vote of 35 yeas to 11 nays.

The President contends that by virtue of the Constitution he had the right to remove heads of Departments, and cites a large number of cases where his predecessor had done so. It must be observed that all those cases were before the passage of the tenure-of-office act, March 2, 1867. Will the respondent say how, the having done an act when there was no law to forbid it justifies the repetition of the same act after a law has been passed expressly prohibiting the same. It is not the suspension or removal of Mr. Stanton that is complained of, but the manner of the suspension. If the President thought he had good reasons for suspending or removing Mr. Stanton, and had done so, sending those reasons to the Senate, and then obeyed the decision of the Senate in their finding, there would have been no complaint; but instead of that he suspends him in direct defiance of the tenure-of-office law, and then enters into an arrangement, or attempts to do so. in which he thought he had succeeded, to prevent the due execution of the law after the decision of the Senate. And when the Senate ordered him to restore Mr. Stanton he makes a second removal by virtue of what he calls the power vested in him by the Constitution.

The action of the Senate on the message of the President, communicating his reasons for the suspension of E. M. Stanton, Secretary of War, under the act entitled "An act to regulate the tenure of certain civil offices," was as follows:

IN EXECUTIVE SESSION,
SENATE OF THE UNITED STATES,
January 13, 1868.

Resolved, That having considered the evidence and reasons given by the President in his report of December 12, 1867, for the suspension from the office of Secretary of War of Edwin M. Stanton, the Senate do not concur in such suspension.

And the same was duly certified to the President, in the face of which he, with an impudence and brazen determination to usurp the powers of the Senate, again removed Edwin M. Stanton, and appointed Lorenzo Thomas Secretary *ad interim* in his stead. The Senate, with calm manliness, rebuked the usurper by the following resolution:

IN EXECUTIVE SESSION,
SENATE OF THE UNITED STATES,
February 21, 1868.

Whereas the Senate has received and considered the communication of the President stating that he had removed Edwin M. Stanton, Secretary of War, and had designated the Adjutant General of the Army to act as Secretary of War *ad interim:* Therefore,

Resolved by the Senate of the United States, That under the Constitution and laws of the United States the President has no power to remove the Secretary of War and to designate any other officer to perform the duties of that office *ad interim.*

Yet he continued him in office. And now this offspring of assassination turns upon the Senate, who have thus rebuked him in a constitutional manner, and bids them defiance. How can he escape the just vengeance of the law? Wretched man, standing at bay, surrounded by a cordon of living men, each with the ax of an executioner uplifted for his just punishment. Every Senator now trying him, except such as had already adopted his policy, voted for this same resolution, pronouncing his solemn doom. Will any one of them vote for his acquittal on the ground of its unconstitutionality? I know that Senators would venture to do any necessary act if indorsed by an honest conscience of an enlightened public opinion; but neither for the sake of the President nor of any one else would one of them suffer himself to be tortured on the gibbet of everlasting obloquy How long and dark would be the track of infamy which must mark his name, and that of his posterity! Nothing is therefore more certain than that it requires no gift of prophecy to predict the fate of this unhappy victim.

I have now discussed but one of the numerous articles, all of which I believe to be fully sustained, and few of the almost innumerable offenses charged to this wayward, unhappy official. I have alluded to two or three others which I could have wished to have had time to present and discuss, not for the sake of punishment, but for the benefit of the country. One of these was an article charging the President with usurping the legislative power of the nation, and attempting still his usurpations.

With regard to usurpation, one single word will explain my meaning. A civil war of gigantic proportions, covering sufficient territory to constitute many States and nations, broke out, and embraced more than ten millions of men, who formed an independent government, called the Confederate States of America. They rose to the dignity of an independent belligerent, and were so acknowledged by all civilized nations, as well as by ourselves. After expensive and bloody strife we conquered them, and they submitted to our arms. By the law of nations, well understood and undisputed, the conquerors in this unjust war had the right to deal with the vanquished as to them might seem good, subject only to the laws of humanity. They had a right to confiscate their property to the extent of indemnifying themselves and their citizens; to annex them to the victorious nation, and pass just such laws for their government as they might think proper.

This doctrine is as old as Grotius, and as fresh as the Dorr rebellion. Neither the President nor the judiciary had any right to interfere, to dictate any terms, or to aid in reconstruction further than they were directed by the sovereign power. That sovereign power in this Republic is the Congress of the United States. Whoever, besides Congress, undertakes to create new States or to rebuild old ones, and fix the condition of their citizenship and union, usurps powers which do not belong to him, and is dangerous or not dangerous, according to the extent of his power and his pretensions. Andrew Johnson did usurp the legislative power of the nation by building new States, and reconstructing, as far as in him lay, this empire. He directed the defunct States to come forth and live by virtue of his breathing into their nostrils the breath of life. He directed them what constitutions to form, and fixed the qualifications of electors and of office-holders. He directed them to send forward members to each branch of Congress, and to aid him in representing the nation. When Congress passed a law declaring all these doings unconstitutional and fixed a mode for the admission of this new territory into the nation he proclaimed it unconstitutional, and advised the people not to submit to it nor to obey the commands of Congress. I have not time to enumerate the particular acts which constitute his high-handed usurpations. Suffice it to say that he seized all the powers of the Government within these States, and, had he been permitted, would have become their absolute ruler. This he persevered in attempting notwithstanding Congress declared more than once all the governments which he thus created to be void and of none effect.

But I promised to be brief, and must abide by the promise, although I should like the judgment of the Senate upon this, to me, seeming vital phase and real purpose of all his misdemeanors. To me this seems a sublime spectacle. A nation, not free, but as nearly approaching it as human institutions will permit of, consisting of thirty millions of people, had fallen into conflict, which among other people always ends in anarchy or despotism, and had laid down their arms, the mutineers submitting to the conquerors. The laws were about to regain their accustomed sway, and again to govern the nation by the punishment of treason and the reward of virtue. Her old institutions were about to be reinstated so far as they were applicable, according to the judgment of the conquerors. Then one of their inferior servants, instigated by unholy ambition, sought to seize a portion of the territory according to the fashion of neighboring anarchies, and to convert a land of freedom into a land of slaves. This people spurned the traitors, and have put the chief of them upon his trial, and demand judgment upon his misconduct. He will be condemned, and his sentence inflicted without turmoil, tumult, or bloodshed, and the nation will continue its accustomed course of freedom and prosperity without the shedding any further of human blood and with a milder punishment than the world has been accustomed to see, or perhaps than ought now to be inflicted.

Now, even if the pretext of the President were true and not a mere subterfuge to justify the chief act of violation with which he stands charged, still that would be such an abuse of the patronage of the Government as would demand his impeachment for a high misdemeanor. Let us again for a moment examine into some of the circumstances of that act. Mr. Stanton was appointed Secretary of War by Mr. Lincoln in 1862, and continued to hold under Mr. Johnson, which, by all usage, is considered a reappointment. Was he a faithful officer, or was he removed for corrupt purposes? After the death of Mr. Lincoln, Andrew Johnson had changed his whole code of politics and policy, and instead of obeying the will of those who put him into power he determined to create a party for himself to carry out his own ambitious purposes. For every honest purpose of Government, and for every honest purpose for which Mr. Stanton was appointed by Mr. Lincoln, where could a better man be found? None ever organized an army of a million of men and provided for its subsistence and efficient action more rapidly than Mr. Stanton and his predecessor.

It might, with more propriety, be said of this officer than of the celebrated Frenchman, that he "organized victory." He raised and by his requisitions distributed more than a billion dollars annually, without ever having been charged or suspected with the malappropriation of a single dollar; and when victory crowned his efforts he disbanded that immense Army as quietly and peacefully as if it had been a summer parade. He would not, I suppose, adopt the personal views of the President; and for this he was suspended until restored by the emphatic verdict of the Senate. Now, if we are right in our narrative of the conduct of these parties and the motives of the President, the very effort at removal was a high-handed usurpation as well as a corrupt misdemeanor for which of itself he ought to be impeached and thrown from the place he was abusing. But he says that he did not remove Mr. Stanton for the purpose of defeating the tenure-of-office law. Then he forgot the truth in his controversy with the General of the Army. And because the General did not aid him, and finally admit that he had agreed to aid him in resisting that law, he railed upon him like a very drab.

The counsel for the respondent allege that no removal of Mr. Stanton ever took place, and that therefore the sixth section of the act was not violated. They admit that there was an order of removal and a recision of his commission; but as he did not obey it, they say it was no removal. That suggests the old saying that it used to be thought that "when the brains were out the man was dead." That idea is proved by learned counsel to be absolutely fallacious. The brain of Mr. Stanton's commission was taken out by the order of removal—the recision of his commission—and his head was absolutely cut off by that gallant soldier, General Thomas, the night after the masquerade. And yet, according to the learned and delicate counsel, until the mortal remains, everything which could putrify, was shoveled out and hauled into the muck-yard there was no removal. But it is said that this took place merely as an experiment to make a judicial case. Now, suppose there is anybody who, with the facts before him, can believe that this was not an afterthought, let us see if that palliates the offense.

The President is sworn to take care that the laws be faithfully executed. In what part of the Constitution or laws does he find it to be his duty to search out for defective laws that stand recorded upon the statutes in order that he may advise their infraction? Who was aggrieved by the tenure-of-office bill that he was authorized to use the name and the funds of the Government to relieve? Will he be so good as to tell us by what authority he became the obstructor of an unrepealed law instead of its executor, especially a law whose constitutionality he had twice tested? If there were nothing else than his own statement he deserves the contempt of the American people, and the punishment of its highest tribunal. If he were not willing to execute the laws passed by the American Congress and unrepealed, .

let him resign the office which was thrown upon him by a horrible convulsion and retire to his village obscurity. Let him not be so swollen by pride and arrogance, which sprang from the deep misfortune of his country, as to attempt an entire revolution of its internal machinery, and the disgrace of the trusted servants of his lamented predecessor.

The gentleman [Mr. Groesbeck] in his peroration on Saturday implored the sympathy of the Senate with all the elegance and pathos of a Roman Senator pleading for virtue ; and it is to be feared that his grace and eloquence turned the attention of the Senate upon the orator rather than upon the accused. Had he been pleading for innocence his great powers would have been well exerted. Had he been arguing with equal eloquence before a Roman Senate for such a delinquent, and Cato, the Censor, had been one of the judges, his client would have soon found himself in the stocks in the middle of the forum instead of receiving the sympathy of a virtuous and patriotic audience. [Mr. Manager STEVENS read a portion of his argument standing at the Secretary's desk; but after proceeding a few minutes, being too feeble to stand, obtained permission to take a seat, and having read nearly half an hour from a chair until his voice became almost too weak to be heard, handed over his manuscript to Mr. Manager BUTLER, who concluded the reading.]

Hon. THOMAS WILLIAMS, one of the Managers on behalf of the House of Representatives, next addressed the Senate as follows:

Mr. PRESIDENT AND SENATORS OF THE UNITED STATES: Not unused to the conflicts of the forum I appear in your presence to-day in obedience to the command of the Representatives of the American people, under a sense of responsibility which I have never felt before. This august tribunal whose judges are the elect of mighty provinces—the presence at your bar of the Representatives of a domain that rivals in extent the dominion of the Cæsars, and of a civilization that transcends any that the world has ever seen, to demand judgment upon the high delinquent whom they have arraigned in the name of the American people for high crimes and misdemeanors against the State, the dignity of the delinquent himself, a king in everything but the name and paraphernalia and inheritance of royalty, these crowded galleries, and, more than all, that greater world outside which stands on tiptoe as it strains its ears to catch from the electric messenger the first tidings of a verdict which is either to send a thrill of joy through an afflicted land, or to rack it anew with the throes of anarchy and the convulsions of despair, all remind me of the collossal proportions of the issue you are assembled to try. I cannot but remember, too, that the scene before me is without example or parallel in human history. Kings, it is true, have been uncrowned, and royal heads have

C. I.—43.

fallen upon the scaffold; but in two single instances only, as I think, have the formalities of law been ostensibly invoked to give a coloring of order and of justice to the bloody tragedy. It is only in this free land that a constitutional tribunal has been charged for the first time with the sublime task of vindicating an outraged law against the highest of its ministers, and passing judgment upon the question whether the ruler of a nation shall be stripped, under the law and without shock or violence, of the power which he has abused.

This great occasion was not sought by us. The world will bear the Representatives of the people witness that they have not come here for light and transient causes, but for the reason only that this issue has been forced upon them by a long series of bold assumptions of power on the part of the Executive, following each other with almost the blazing and blinding continuity of the lightning of the tropics, and culminating at last in a mortal challenge, which in the defense of their constitutional power as a branch of the American Congress, and as faithful sentinels over the liberties of the people, it was impossible for them to decline. With the first, open defiance of the legislative will they were left, of course, with no alternative but to abdicate their rule or to vindicate their right to make the law and see that it was obeyed. To this imperious necessity the people, in whose name they speak—a branch of that race whose quick sensibility to public danger has ever kept a sleepless vigil over its liberties—have yielded at last with a reluctance which nothing but the weariness of civil strife, the natural longing for repose, the apprehensive sense that it was "better, perhaps, to bear the ills we had than fly to others that we knew not of"—the reflection that this Administration must have an end, and above all, perhaps, the delusive hope that its law-defying head himself would ultimately submit to a necessity which was as strong as fate, could have brought about, or would have, perhaps, excused. He has misunderstood their reasons, as his counsel show that they do now, mistaken their temper, and presumed upon their forbearance. He has forgotten that there was a point at which the conflict must end in the shock of two opposing forces, and the overthrow of one or other of the antagonistic elements. It was necessary, perhaps, in the order of Providence that he should reach that point by striking such a blow at the public liberties as should awaken the people as with an earthquake shock to the consciousness that the toleration of usurpation brings no security to nations.

To show, however, how much they have borne and forborne, perhaps forgiven, for the sake of peace, and how much they now pass over for the sake of a speedy solution of the impending trouble which has impeded the onward and upward movement of this great Government, and spread confusion and disorder through many of its Departments, and what, moreover, is the true import and significance of the acts for which the President is now arraigned, I must be allowed, with your indulgence, to take up for a moment the key which is required to unlock the mysteries of the position. The man who supposes that this is but a question of the removal of an obnoxious officer, a mere private quarrel between two belligerents at the other end of the avenue, wherein it is of no great national consequence which of the opposing parties shall prevail, has no adequate apprehension of the gravity of the case, and greatly disparages the position and the motives of the high accusers. The House of Representatives espouses no man's quarrel, however considerable he may be. It has but singled out from many others of equal weight the facts now charged, as facts for the most part of recent occurrence, of great notoriety, and of easy proof, by way of testing a much greater question without loss of time. The issue here is between two mightier antagonists, one the Chief Executive Magistrate of this nation and the other the people of the United States, for whom the Secretary of War now holds almost the only strong position of which they have not been dispossessed. It is but a renewal on American soil of the old battle between the royal prerogative and the privileges of the Commons, which was closed in England with the reigns of the Stuarts—a struggle for the mastery between a temporary Executive and the legislative power of a free State over the most momentous question that has ever challenged the attention of a people. The counsel for the President, reflecting, of course, the views of their employer, would have you to believe that the removal of a departmental head is an affair of State too small to be worthy of such an avenger as this which we propose. Standing alone, stripped of all the attendant circumstances that explain the act and show the deadly *animus* by which it was inspired, it is not improbable that there are some who might have been induced to think, with them, that a remedy so extreme as this was more than adequate. It is only under the light shed upon the particular issue by antecedent facts which have now passed into history that the giant proportions of this controversy can be fully seen, if they are not made sufficiently apparent now by the defiant tone of the President and the formidable pretensions set up by him in his thoughtfully considered and painfully elaborated plea.

The not irrelevant question "Who is Andrew Johnson?" has been asked by one of his counsel, as it has often been by himself, and answered in the same way, by showing who he *was* and what he had done before the people of the loyal States so generously intrusted him with that contingent power which was made absolute only for the advantage of defeated and discomforted treason by the murderous pistol of an assassin. I will not stop now to inquire as to scenes enacted on this floor so eloquently rehearsed by the counsel for the President, with two pictures of so opposite a character before me, or even to inquire whether his resistance to the hegira of the southern Senators was not merely a question, himself being the witness, as to the propriety and wisdom of such a step at that particular time. The opportunity occurs just here to answer it as it is put, by showing who Andrew Johnson *is*, and what he has been since the unhappy hour of that improvident and unreflecting gift. *Eheu! quantum mutatus ab illo!* Alas, how changed, how fallen from that high estate that won for him the support of a too confiding people! Would that it could have been said of him as of that apostate spirit who was hurled in hideous ruin and combustion down from Heaven's crystal battlements, that even in his fall he "had not yet lost all his original brightness nor appeared less than Archangel ruined."

The master-key to the whole history of his administration, which has involved not a mere harmless difference of opinion, as one of his counsel seems to think, on a question where gentlemen might afford to disagree without a quarrel, but one long and unseemly struggle by the Executive against the legislative power, is to be found in the fact of an early and persistent purpose of forcing the rebel States into the Union by means of his executive authority, in the interests of the men who had lifted their parricidal hands against it, on terms dictated by himself, and in defiance of the will of the loyal people of the United States as declared through their Representatives. To accomplish this object, how much has he not done and how much has a long-suffering people not passed over without punishment and almost without rebuke? Let history, let your public records, which are the only authentic materials of history, answer, and they will say that—

For this, instead of convening the Congress in the most momentous crisis of the State, he had issued his royal proclamations for the assembling of conventions and the erection of State governments, prescribing the qualifications of the voters, and settling the conditions of their admission into the Union.

For this he had created offices unknown to the law, and filled them with men notoriously disqualified by law, at salaries fixed by his own mere will.

For this he had paid those officers in contemptuous disregard of law, and paid them, too, out of the contingent fund of one of the Departments of the Government.

For this he had supplied the expenses of his new governments by turning over to them the spoils of the dead confederacy, and authorizing his satraps to levy taxes from the conquered people.

For this he had passed away unnumbered millions of the public property to rebel railroad companies without consideration, or sold it to them in clear violation of law, on long credits, at a valuation of his own and without any security whatever.

For this he had stripped the Bureau of Freedmen and Refugees of its munificent endowment, by tearing from it the lands appropriated by Congress to the loyal wards of the Republic, and restoring to the rebels their justly forfeited estates after the same had been vested by law in the Government of the United States.

For this he had invaded with a ruthless hand the very penetralia of the Treasury, and plundered its contents for the benefit of favored rebels by ordering the restoration of the proceeds of sales of captured and abandoned property which had been placed in its custody by law.

For this he had grossly abused the pardoning power conferred on him by the Constitution in releasing the most active and formidable of the leaders of the rebellion with a view to their service in the furtherance of his policy, and even delegated that power for the same objects to men who were indebted to its exercise for their own escape from punishment.

For this he had obstructed the course of public justice not only by refusing to enforce the laws enacted for the suppression of the rebellion and the punishment of treason, but by going into the courts and turning the greatest of the public malefactors loose, and surrendering all control over them by the restoration of their estates.

For this he had abused the appointing power by the removal on system of meritorious public officers for no other reason than because they would not assist him in his attempt to overthrow the Constitution and usurp the legislative power of the Government.

For this he had invaded the rightful privileges of the Senate by refusing to send in nominations of officers appointed by him during the recess of that body, and after their adjournment reappointing others who had been rejected by them as unfit for the places for which they had been appointed.

For this he had broken the privileges of, and insulted the Congress of the United States by instructing them that the work of reconstruction belonged to him only, and that they had no legislative right or duty in the premises, but only to register his will by throwing open their doors to such claimants as might come there with commissions from his pretended governments, that were substantially his own.

For this, on their refusal to obey his imperial rescript, he had arraigned them publicly as a revolutionary assembly and not a Congress, without the power to legislate for the States excluded, and as "traitors, at the other end of the line," in actual rebellion against the people they had subdued.

For this he had grossly abused the veto power, by disapproving every important measure of legislation that concerned the rebel States, in accordance with his public declaration that he would veto all the measures of the law-making power whenever they came to him.

For this he had deliberately and confessedly exercised a dispensing power over the test-oath law, by appointing notorious rebels to important places in the revenue service, on the avowed ground that the policy of Congress, in that regard, was not in accordance with his opinions.

For this he had obstructed the settlement of the nation, by exerting all his influence to prevent the people of the rebel States from accepting the constitutional amendment or organizing under the laws of Congress, and impressing them with the opinion that Congress was blood thirsty and implacable, and that their only refuge was with him.

For this he had brought the patronage of his office into conflict with the freedom of elections, by allowing and encouraging his official retainers to travel over the country, attending political conventions and addressing the people in support of his policy.

For this, if he did not enact the part of a Cromwell, by striding into the Halls of the Representatives of the people and saying to one man, "You are a hypocrite;" to another, "You are a whoremonger;" to a third, "You are an adulterer;" and to the whole, "You are no longer a Parliament;" he had rehearsed the same part substantially outside, by traveling over the country, and, in indecent harangues, assailing the conduct and impeaching the motives of its Congress, inculcating disobedience to its authority by endeavoring to bring it into disrepute, declaring publicly of one of its members that he was a traitor, of another that he was an assassin, and of the whole that they were no longer a Congress.

For this, in addition to the oppression and bloodshed that had everywhere resulted from his known partiality for traitors, he had winked at, if not encouraged, the murder of loyal citizens in New Orleans by a confederate mob by holding correspondence with its leaders, denouncing the exercise of the right of a political convention to assemble peacefully in that city as an act of treason proper to be suppressed by violence, and commanding the military to assist, instead of preventing, the execution of the avowed purpose of dispersing them.

For this, it is not too much to say, in view of the wrong and outrage and the cry of suffering that have come up to us upon every southern breeze, that he had in effect reopened the war, inaugurated anarchy, turned loose once more the incarnate devil of baffled treason and unappeasable hate, whom, as we fondly thought, our victories had overthrown and bound in chains, ordained rapine and murder from the Potomac to the Gulf, and deluged the streets of Memphis as well as of New Orleans, and the green fields of the South, already dotted with so many patriot graves, with the blood of martyred citizens.

And because for all he has not been called to render an account, for the reasons that have been already named, it is now assumed and argued by his counsel that he stands acquitted by a judgment which disapproves its truth, although it rests for the most part on record evidence, importing that "absolute verity" which is, of course, not open to dispute. This extraordinary assumption is but another instance of that incorrigible blindness on the part of the President in regard to the feelings and motives of Congress that has helped to hurry him into his present humiliating predicament as a criminal at your bar.

But all these things were not enough. It wanted one drop more to make the cup of forbearance overflow—one other act that should reach the sensorium of the nation, and make even those who might be slow to comprehend a principle, to understand that further forbearance was ruin to us all; and that act was done in the attempt to seize by force or stratagem on that Department of the Government through which its armies were controlled. It was but a logical sequence of what had gone before—the last of a series of usurpations, all looking to the same great object. It did not rise, perhaps, beyond the height of many of the crimes by which it was ushered in. But its meaning could not be mistaken. It was an act that smote upon the nerve of the nation in such a way as to render it impossible that it could be either concealed, disparaged, or excused, as were the muffled blows of the pick-ax that had been so long silently undermining the bastions of the Republic. It has been heard and felt through all our wide domain like the reverberation of the guns that opened their iron throats upon our flag at Sumter; and it has stirred the loyal heart of the people again with the electric power that lifted it to the height of the sublimest issue that ever led a martyr to the stake or a patriot to the battle-field. That people is here to-day, through its Representatives on your floor and in your galleries, in the persons alike of the veterans who have been scarred by the iron hail of battle, and of the mothers and wives and daughters of those who have died that the Republic might live, as well as of the commissioned exponents of the public will, to demand the rewards of their sacrifices and the consummation of their triumph in the award of a nation's justice upon this high offender.

And now as to the immediate issue, which I propose to discuss only in its constitutional and legal aspects.

The great crime of Andrew Johnson, as already remarked, running through all his administration, is that he has violated his oath of office and his constitutional duties by the obstruction and infraction of the Constitution and the laws, and an endeavor to set up his own will against that of the law-making power, with a view to a settled and persistent purpose of forcing the rebel States into Congress on his own terms, in the interests of the traitors, and in defiance of the will of the loyal people of the United States.

The specific offenses charged here, which are but the culminating facts, and only the last of a long series of usurpations, are an unlawful attempt to remove the rightful Secretary of War and to substitute in his place a creature of his own, without the advice and consent of the Senate, although then in session ; a conspiracy to hinder and prevent him from resuming or holding the said office after the refusal of the Senate to concur in his suspension, and to seize, take, and possess the property of the United States in said Department ; an attempt to debauch an officer of the Army from his allegiance by inculcating insubordination to the law in furtherance of the same object ; the attempt to set aside the rightful authority of Congress and to bring it into public odium and contempt, and to encourage resistance to its laws by the open and public delivery of indecent harangues, impeaching its acts and purposes and full of threats and menaces against it and the laws enacted by it, to the great scandal and degradation of his own high office as President ; and the devising and contriving of unlawful means to prevent the execution of the tenure-of-office, Army appropriation, and reconstruction acts of March 2, 1867.

To all of these which relate to the attempted removal of the Secretary of War the answer is :

1. That the case of Mr. Stanton is not within the meaning of the first section of the tenure-of-office act.

Second. That if it be, the act is unconstitutional and void so far as it undertakes to abridge the power claimed by him of " removing at any and all times all executive officers for causes to be judged of by himself alone," as well as of suspending them indefinitely at his sovereign will and pleasure ; and,

Third, That whether the act be constitutional or otherwise, it was his right, as he claims it to have been his purpose, to disobey and violate it with a view to the settlement of the question of its validity by the judiciary of the United States.

And first, as to the question whether the present Secretary of War was intended to be comprehended within the first section of the act referred to.

The defendant insists that he was not, for the reason that he derived his commission from Mr. Lincoln, and not being removed on his accession, continued by reason thereof to hold the office and administer its duties at his pleasure only, without having at any time received any appointment from himself: assuming, as I understand, either that under the proviso to the first section of this act the case was not provided for, or that by force of its express language, his office was determined by the expiration of the first term of the President who appointed him.

The body, or enacting clause of this section,

677

provides that *every* person then holding any
civil office who had been appointed thereto by
and with the advice and consent of the Senate,
or who should be thereafter appointed to any
such office, should be entitled to hold until a
successor is appointed in the like manner.

It is clear, therefore, that its general object
was to provide for all cases, either then existing or to happen in the future.

It is objected, however, that so much of this
clause as refers to the heads of Departments is
substantially repealed by the saving clause,
which is in the following words:

"*Provided*, That the Secretaries of State, of the
Treasury, of War, of the Navy, and of the Interior,
the Postmaster General, and the Attorney General,
shall hold their offices respectively for and during
the term of the President by whom they may have
been appointed, and for one month thereafter, subject to removal by and with the advice and consent
of the Senate."

This proviso was the result of a conference
on the disagreeing votes on the amendment of
the House striking out the exception in favor
of the heads of Departments, and was suggested—if he may be excused the egotism—by
the individual who now addresses you, and to
whom, as the mover and advocate of the
amendment, was very naturally assigned the
duty of conducting the negotiation on the part
of the House, for the purpose of obviating the
objection taken in debate on this floor by one
of the Senate managers, that the effect of the
amendment would be to impose on an incoming President a Cabinet that was not of his own
selection. I may be excused for speaking of
its actual history, because that has been made
the subject of comment by the learned counsel
who opened this case on behalf of the President. If it was intended or expected that it
should so operate as to create exceptions in
favor of an officer whose notorious abuse of
power was the proximate cause, if not the im-
pelling motive for the enactment of the law, I
did not know it. It will be judged, however,
by itself, without reference either to the particular intent of him who may have penned it,
or to any hasty opinion that may have been expressed in either House as to the construction
of which it might be possibly susceptible.

The argument of the defendant rests upon
the meaning of the word "appointed." That
word has both a technical and a popular one.
In the former, which involves the idea of a
nomination and confirmation in the constitutional way, there was no appointment certainly
by Mr. Johnson. In the latter, which is the
sense in which the people will read it, there
unquestionably was. What, then, was meant
by the employment of this word?

It is a sound and well-accepted rule in all
the courts, in exploring the meaning of the
law-giver, especially in cases of remedial statutes, as I think this is, if it is not rather to be
considered as only a declaratory one in this particular, to look to the old law, the mischief
and the remedy, and to give a liberal construc-

tion to the language *in favorem libertatis*, in
order to repress the mischief and advance the
remedy; taking the words used in their ordinary and familiar sense, and varying the meaning as the intent, which is always the polar
star, may require. Testing the case by this
rule what is to be the construction here?

The old law was—not the Constitution—but a
vicious practice that had grown out of a precedent involving an early and erroneous construction of that instrument, if it was intended
so to operate. The mischief was that this practice had rendered the officers of the Government,
and among them the heads of Departments, the
most powerful and dangerous of them all, from
their assumed position of advisers of the President, by the very dependency of their tenure,
the mere ministers of his pleasure, and the
slaves of his imperial will, that could at any
moment, and as the reward of an honest and
independent opinion, strip them of their employments, and send them back into the ranks
of the people. The remedy was to change
them from minions and flatterers into *men*, by
making them free, and to secure their loyalty
to the law by protecting them from the power
that might constrain their assent to its violation. To accomplish this object it was necessary that the law should cover all of them,
high and low, present and prospective. That
it could have been intended to except the most
important and formidable of these functionaries, either with a view to favor the present
Executive, or for the purpose of subjecting the
only head of a Department who had the confidence of Congress to his arbitrary will, is as
unreasonable and improbable, as it is at variance with the truth of the fact and with the
obvious general purposes of the act.

For the President of the United States to
say, however, now, after having voluntarily
retained Mr. Stanton for more than two years
of his administration, that he was there only
by sufferance, or as a mere *movable*, or heir-
loom, or incumbrance that had passed to him
with the estate, and not by virtue of his own
special appointment, if not "paltering with the
people in a double sense," has very much the
appearance of a not very respectable quibble.
The unlearned man who reads the proviso—as
they for whose perusal it is intended will read
it—and who is not accustomed to handle the
metaphysic scissors of the professional casuists
who are able "to divide a hair 'twixt north
and northwest side," while he admits the ingenuity of the advocate, will stand amazed, if
he does not scorn the officer who would stoop
to the use of such a subterfuge.

Assuming, however, for the sake of argument, that the technical sense is to prevail,
what is to be its effect? Why only to make the
law-giver enact a very unreasonable and impossible thing, by providing in words of the *future*
tense, that the commission of the officer shall
expire nearly two years *before* the passage of
the law, which is a construction that the gen-

eral rule of law forbids! To test this let us substitute for the general denominational phrases of "Secretary of War, of State, and of the Navy," the names of Messrs. Seward, Stanton, and Welles, and for that of the President who appointed them, the name of Lincoln, and the clause will read: "*Provided*, That Messrs. Seward, Stanton, and Welles, shall hold their offices respectively for and during the term of Abraham Lincoln, and for one month thereafter." The effect will then be to put you in the position of having enacted not only an *absurdity*, but an *impossibility*. But on this there are at least two rules of interpretation that start up in the way of the solution. The first is that it is not respectful to the Legislature to presume that it ever intended to enact an absurdity, if the case is susceptible of any other construction; and the second that—

"Acts of Parliament that are impossible to be performed are of no validity; and if there arise out of them collaterally any absurd consequences manifestly contradictory to common reason, they are, with regard to these collateral consequences, void."—1 *Blackstone's Commentaries,* 91.

If the effect of the proviso, however, upon something analogous to the doctrine of *cy pres*, or, in other words, of getting as near to its meaning as possible, was to determine the office at the time of the passage of the law, then, on the other hand, the retention of the officer by the President for five months afterward, and through an intervening Congress, without a commission or even a nomination, was a breach of the law, and therefore a misdemeanor in itself; which he could hardly plead, and would scarcely ask you to affirm, against the general presumption of the faithful performance of official duty for the purpose of sheltering him from the consequences of still another violation of the law.

Assuming again, however, that, as is claimed by the defense, the case of Mr. Stanton does not fall within the proviso, what, then, is the result? Is it the predicament of a *casus omissus* altogether? Is he to be hung up, like Mahomet's coffin, between the body of the act and the proviso, the latter nullifying the former on the pretext of an exception, and then repudiating the exception itself as to the particular case; or is the obvious and indisputable purpose of providing for all cases whatever, to be carried out by falling back on the general enacting clause which would make him irremovable by the President alone, and leaving him outside of the provision as to *tenure*, which was the sole object of the exception? There is nothing in the saving clause which is at all inconsistent with what goes before. The provision that takes every officer out of the power of the President is not departed from in that clause. All it enacts is that the tenure shall be a determinate one in cases that fall within it. If Mr. Stanton was appointed by President Johnson within the meaning of the proviso, he holds, of course, until the expiration of his term. If not, he holds subject to removal like other officers under the enacting clause. It has been so often asserted publicly as to have become a generally accredited truth, that the special purpose of the act was to protect him. I do not affirm this, and do not consider it necessary that I should, or important to the case whether he favored the passage of the law or not. It will be hardly pretended, however, by anybody, that he was intended to be excluded entirely from its operation.

Nor is the case helped by the reference to the fourth section of the act, which provides that nothing therein contained shall be construed to extend the term of any office the duration of which is limited by law. The office in question was one of those of which the tenure was indefinite. The construction insisted on by me does not extend it. The only effect is to take away the power of removal from the President alone and restore it to the parties by whom the Constitution intended that it should be exercised.

Assuming, then, that the case of Mr. Stanton is within the law, the next question is as to the validity of the law itself. And here we are met, for the first time in our history as a nation, by the assertion, on the part of the President, of the illimitable and uncontrollable power under the Constitution, in accordance, as he insists, with the judicial opinion, the professional sentiment, and the settled practice under the Government of removing at any and all times all executive officers whatever, without responsibility to anybody, and as included therein the equally uncontrollable power of suspending them indefinitely and supplying their places from time to time by appointments made by himself *ad interim*. If there be any case where the claim has heretofore extended, even in theory, beyond the mere power to create a vacancy by removal during the recess of the Senate, I do not know it. If there be any wherein the power to suspend indefinitely, which goes even beyond this, has been asserted, it is equally new to me. This truly regal pretension has been fitly reserved for the first President who has ever claimed the imperial prerogative of founding governments by proclamation, of taxing without a Congress, of disposing of the public property by millions at his own will, and of exercising a dispensing power over the laws. It is but a logical sequence of what he has been already permitted to do with absolute impunity and almost without complaint. If he could be tolerated thus far, why not consummate the work which was to render him supreme, and crown his victory over the legislative power by setting this body aside as an advisory council, and claiming himself to be the rightful interpreter of the laws? The defense made here is a defiance, a challenge to the Senate and the nation, that must be met and answered just now in such a way as shall determine which, if any, is to be the master.

If the claim asserted is to be maintained by your decision, all that will remain for you will be only the formal abdication of your high trust as part of the appointing power, because there will be then absolutely nothing left of it that is worth preserving.

But let us see what there is in the Constitution to warrant these extravagant pretensions, or to prevent the passage of a law to restore the practice of this Government to the true theory of that instrument.

I do not propose to weary you with a protracted examination of this question. I could not add to what I have already said on the same subject in the discussion in the House of the bill relating to removals from office in December, 1866, to which I would have ventured to invite your attention, if the same point had not been so fully elaborated here. You have already passed upon it in the enactment of the present law by a vote so decisive and overwhelming, and there is so little objection on the part of the counsel for the President to the validity of that law, that I may content myself with condensing the arguments on both sides into a few general propositions which will comprehend their capital features.

The case may be stated, as I think, analytically and synoptically thus:

The first great fact to be observed is, that while the Constitution enumerates sundry offices, and provides the manner of appointment in those cases, as well as in "all others to be created by law," it prescribes no tenure except that of good behavior in the case of the judges, and is entirely silent on the subject of removal by any other process than that of impeachment.

From this the inferences are:

1. That the tenure of good behavior, being substantially equivalent to that for life, the office must in all other cases be determinable at the will of some department of the Government, unless limited by law; which is, however, but another name for the will of the lawmaker himself. And this is settled by authority.

2. That the power of removal at will, being an implied one only, is to be confined to those cases where the tenure is not ascertained by law; the right of removal in any other form than by the process of impeachment depending entirely on the hypothesis of a will of which the essential condition always is that it is free to act without reason and without responsibility.

3. That the power of removal, being implied as a necessity of state to secure the dependence of the officer on the Government, is not to be extended by construction so as to take him out of the control of the Legislature, and make him dependent on the will of the Executive.

The next point is that the President is by the terms of the Constitution to "nominate, and by and with the advice and consent of the Senate appoint," to all offices, and that without this concurrence he appoints to none except when authorized by Congress. And this may be described as the *rule* of the Constitution.

The exceptions are:

1. That in the cases of inferior offices the Congress may lodge this power with the President alone or with the courts or the heads of Departments ; and

2. That in cases of vacancy happening during the recess of the Senate he may—not *appoint*—but *fill them up* by granting commissions to expire at the end of the next session of that body.

From which it appears—

1. That the President cannot, as already stated, in any case, appoint alone without the express authority of Congress, and then only in the case of inferior offices.

2. That the power to supply even an accidental vacancy was only to continue until the Senate was in a condition to be consulted and to advise and act upon the case ; and

3. As a corollary from these two propositions, that if the power to remove in cases where the tenure is indefinite be, as it is solemnly conceded by the Supreme Court of the United States *in re* Heenan (13 Peters) an incident to the power to appoint, it belongs to the President and Senate, and not to the President alone, as it was held in that case to be in the judge who made the appointment.

The argument upon which this implied and merely inferential power, not of "filling up," but of *making* a vacancy during the recess— which is now claimed to extend to the making of a vacancy at any time—has been defended, is—

First. The possible necessity for the exercise of such a power during the recess of the Senate, or, in other words, the argument *ab inconvenienti.*

Second. That the power of removal is a purely executive function, which, passed by the general grant in the first section of the second article of the Constitution, would have carried the power to appoint, if unprovided for, and is to be considered in him in all cases wherein it has not been expressly denied or lodged in other hands ; while the association of the Senate, the same not being an executive body, is an exception to the general principle, and must be taken strictly so as not to extend thereto.

Third. That it is essential to the President as the responsible *head* of the Government, charged by his oath with the execution of the laws, that he should control his own subordinates by making their tenure of office to depend upon his will, so as to make a unit of the Administration.

The answer to the *first* of these propositions is that there is no necessity for the exercise of the power during the recess, because the case supposed may be provided for by Congress— as it has been by the act now in question— under its express constitutional authority "to make all laws which shall be necessary or proper for carrying into execution all powers vested in the Government, or in any Department thereof," a power which, by the, way is very strangely claimed by one of the President's counsel to be an implied one.

To the *second* the answer is that whether an executive power or not depends on the structure of the Government, or, in other words, on what the Constitution makes it; that the clause in question is but a distributive one; that if all executive power is in the President, then by parity of reason all legislative power is in Congress without reference to the Constitution; that the Senate is not only associated with the President in the general appointing power, but that the power itself may be withdrawn by Congress almost entirely from both, under the provision in regard to inferior offices, which would involve a repugnancy to the general grant relied on, if the power be an executive one; that if no provision had been made for appointment in the Constitution the power to supply the omission would have resulted to the law-maker under the authority just quoted, to make "all laws that might be necessary or proper for carrying into execution all powers vested in the Government or any department thereof," which carries with it the power to create all offices; and that, moreover, this power of removal, in the only case wherein it is referred to, is made a *judicial* one.

To the *third* the answer is—

1. That however natural it may be for the President, after an unchecked career of usurpation for three long years, during which he has used his subordinates generally as the slavish ministers of his will, and dealt with the affairs of this nation as if he had been its master also as well as theirs, he greatly mistakes and magnifies his office, as has been already shown in the fact that under the Constitution he may be stripped at any time by Congress of nearly the whole of the appointing power; and,

2. That the responsibility of the President is to be graduated by, and can be only commensurate with, the power that is assigned to him; that the obligation imposed on him is to take care that the *laws* are faithfully executed, and not his *will*, which is so strangely assumed to be the only law of the exalted functionaries who surround him; and that it is not only *not* essential to the performance of their duty under the law that the heads of Departments should be the mere passive instruments of his will, but the very contrary.

Upon this brief statement of the argument it would seem as if there could be no reasonable doubt as to the meaning of the Constitution. But the high delinquent who is now on trial, feeling that he cannot safely rest his case here, and shrinking from the inexorable logic that rules it against him, takes refuge in the past, and claims to have found a new Constitution that suits him better than the old one, in the judicial authorities, in the opinion of the

commentators, in the enlightened professional and public sentiment of the nation, and in a legislative practice and construction that are coeval with the Government, and have continued without interruption until the present time. A little inquiry, however, will show that there is no altar of sanctuary, no city of refuge here, to shelter the greatest of the nation's malefactors from the just vengeance of a betrayed and indignant people.

And first, as to judicial authority. There are but three cases, I think, wherein these questions have ever come up for adjudication before the Supreme Court of the United States, and in all of them the decisions have been directly in conflict with the theory and pretensions of the President.

The first was the familiar one of Marbury *vs.* Madison, 1 Cranch, 256, made doubly memorable by the fact that it arose out of one of the so-called midnight appointments made by the elder Adams—the same, by the way, whose casting vote as an executive officer turned the scale in favor of the power to which he was destined to succeed in the First Congress of 1789, on the eve of his retirement—under a law which had been approved only the day before, authorizing the appointment of five justices of the peace for the District of Columbia, to serve respectively for the term of five years. The commission in question had been duly signed and registered, but was withheld by his successor (Jefferson) on the ground that the act was incomplete without a delivery. It was not claimed by him that the appointment was revocable if once consummated. If it had been, the resistance would have been unnecessary, and the assertion of the right to the office an idle one. Chief Justice Marshall, in delivering the opinion of the court, holds this language:

"Where an officer is removable at the will of the Executive, the circumstance which completed his appointment is of no consequence, because the act is at any time revocable. But where the officer is not removable at the will of the Executive, the appointment is not revocable and cannot be annulled. Having once made the appointment his power over the office is terminated in all cases where by law the officer is not removable by him. Then, as the law creating the office gave the right to hold for five years independent of the Executive, the appointment was not revocable, but vested in the officer legal rights that are protected by the laws of his country."

The point ruled here is precisely the same as that involved in the tenure-of-office act, to wit: that Congress may define the tenure of any office it creates, and that once fixed by law it is no longer determinable at the will of anybody—the act being a mere substitution of the will of the nation for that of the Executive, by giving that will the form of law, which is, indeed, the only form that is consistently admissible in a government of law. The present Executive insists—as Jefferson did not—that he has the power under the Constitution to remove or suspend at any and all times any executive officer whatever for causes to be judged of by himself alone; and that, in the opinion of his advisers, this power cannot be lawfully restrained; which is in effect to claim the power to *appoint* without the advice and consent of the Senate, as he has just now done, as well as to *remove*.

The next case in order is that of *ex parte* Heenan, reported in 13 Peters, which involved a question as to the right of the judge of the district court of Louisiana to remove, at his discretion, a clerk appointed by him indefinitely under the law. The court say there—Thompson, Justice, delivering the opinion—that—

"All offices, the tenure of which is not fixed by the Constitution or limited by law, must be held either during good behavior or at the will and discretion of some department of the Government, and subject to removal at pleasure."

And again that—

"In the absence of all constitutional provisions or statutory regulation it would seem to be a sound and necessary rule to consider the power of removal as an incident to the power to appoint."

They add, however—

"*But* it was very early adopted as the *practical* construction that the power was vested in the President alone, and that such would appear to have been the *legislative* construction, because in establishing the three principal Departments of State, War, and Treasury, they recognized the power of removal in the President, although by the act of 1798, establishing the Navy Department, the reference was not by name to him."

The result was that upon the principles thus enunciated, involving the exception as to cases where the tenure was limited by law, as laid down in Marbury *vs.* Madison, they declared the power of removal to have been well exercised by the judge who made the appointment under the law, for the reason only that it was an incident thereto.

It is well worthy of remark, however, in this connection, that although what is thus gratuitously said as to the practical construction in opposition to the rule there recognized does not conflict in any way with the doctrine of Marbury *vs.* Madison, it is entirely at variance, as seems to be confessed, with the decision itself, which, on the doctrine of Mr. Madison in the debate of 1789, that the power of removal was a strictly executive one, and passed by the general grant of the Constitution, unless expressly denied or elsewhere lodged, must have been inevitably the other way, because in that case it must have resulted, not to the judge, but to the President. Whether a mere permissive, *sub silentio*, exercise of a power like this, or even a temporary surrender on grounds of personal confidence or party favor, where it perhaps violated no constitutional interdict, and was, in point of fact, authorized as to all but the superior offices, can raise a prescription against a constitutional right, or how many laws it will require to abrogate the fundamental law, I will not stop now to inquire. It is sufficient for my purpose that the case decides that the power of removal is but an incident to the power of appointment, and that, of course, it can be exercised only by the same agencies, as the tenure-of-office act exactly provides.

The next and last case is that of the United States *ex relatione vs.* Guthrie, reported in 17 Howard, 284, which was an application for a *mandamus* to the Secretary of the Treasury to compel him to pay the salary of a territorial judge in Minnesota, who had been removed by the President before the expiration of his term, which was fixed by law at four years. The case was dismissed upon the doctrine that the proceeding was not a proper one to try the title to an office, and therefore the question of the power to remove was not disposed of or discussed, except by Justice McLain, who dissented on the main point and felt called upon, of course, to pass upon the other. I refer to his opinion mainly for the purpose of borrowing, with a part of the argument, an important statement in relation to the views of the bench that was almost coeval with the Constitution itself on this question. He says, on page 806:

"There was great contrariety of opinion in Congress on this power. With the experience we now have in regard to its exercise there is great doubt whether the most enlightened statesman would not come to a different conclusion."

The power referred to was that of the removal by the President of the heads of the principal Departments of the Government, as conceded by the acts of 1789.

"The Attorney General calls this a constitutional power. There is no such power given in the Constitution. It is presumed to be in the President from the power of appointment. This presumption, I think, is unwise and illogical. The reasoning is: The President and Senate appoint to office; therefore the President may remove from office. Now, the argument would be legitimate if the power to remove were inferred to be the same that appoints.

"It was supposed that the exercise of this power by the President was necessary for the efficient discharge of executive duties; that to consult the Senate in making removals the same as making appointments would be too tardy for the correction of abuses. By a temporary appointment the public service is now provided for in-case of death; and the same provision could be made where immediate removals are necessary. The Senate, when called upon to fill the vacancy, would pass upon the demerits of the late incumbent.

"This, I have never doubted, was the true construction of the Constitution: and I am able to say it was the opinion of the late Supreme Court with Marshall at its head."

And again:

"If the power to remove from office may be inferred from the power to appoint, both the elements of the appointing power are necessarily included. The Constitution has declared what shall be the executive power to appoint, and, by consequence, the same power should be exercised in a removal."

It will be said, perhaps, that all this is qualified by the remark that "this power of removal has been, perhaps, too long established and exercised to be now questioned." It is enough, however, to refer to the observation which follows, that "the voluntary action of the Senate and the President would be necessary to change the practice," to show what was meant by him. Such events as our eyes have witnessed, and such a conjuncture of affairs following fast upon their heels as would leave the Executive with all his formidable patronage and all the prestige of his place, without even the meager support of a third in either House, were scarcely within the range of human probability. When he remarks, therefore, that it was "*perhaps* too late to question it," he means, of course, "to question it *successfully*," as the context shows. If he had meant otherwise he would not have referred to a voluntary change of practice as operating a corresponding change of the Constitution. He was too good a lawyer and too large a statesman to affirm that the fundamental law of a great State could be wrested from its true construction either by the errors of the Legislature, or the toleration of a mischievous practice and a monster vice for less than eighty years.

It is apparent, then, from all the cases, that the judicial opinion, so far from sustaining the view of the President, settles at least two points which are fatal to his pretensions: *first*, that Congress may so limit the tenure of an office as to render the incumbent irremovable except by the process of impeachment; and *second*, that the power to remove, so far as it exists, is but an incident to the power to appoint.

Nor is it any answer to say, as has been claimed in debate on this floor, that these were cases of *inferior* offices where, under the Constitution, it was within the power of Congress to regulate them at its discretion: There is nothing in the provision as to inferior offices to distinguish them from others beyond the mere article of *appointment*. This is a question of *tenure*, and that is equally undefined as to both, except in the few cases specially enumerated therein. It was equally within the power of Congress to regulate in one case as in the other. The right to regulate is a necessary result of the right to create. When it establishes an office, as it has established the departmental bureaus, by law, it has, of necessity, the right to prescribe its duties and say how long it shall be held and when it shall determine. When it does say so, it can hardly be maintained with any show of reason that a power which is only implied from the fact that the tenure of office has been left indefinite in the Constitution which has vested the establishment of offices in Congress, shall be held to operate to defeat its will and shorten the life of its own creature in cases where its legislation is express.

And so, too, as to the doctrine that the power of removal is but an incident to the power to appoint. That is settled upon grounds of reason, as a general principle, which has no more application to inferior offices than to superior ones. The idea is that the power of removal wherever it exists is in the very nature of things but part and parcel of the power to appoint, and that as a consequence the power that makes, and none other, must unmake; and on this idea it was ruled in the particular case that the power to remove was in the judge, because the authority to appoint was there. It equally rules, however,

that where the appointment is in the head of a Department the power of removal belongs to him; that where it is lodged by Congress in the President alone it is in him only; and where it is in the President and Senate conjointly there it is in both; which is precisely the doctrine maintained by the minority in the Congress of 1789. It ought to be a sufficient answer, however, that no such distinction was taken by Justice Thompson in the Heenan case, although he referred to the departure from this rule in the practical construction which had assigned the power to the President alone.

The judicial opinion having thus signally failed to support the dangerous heresies of the President, the next resort is to that of the statesmen, lawyers, and publicists who have from time to time illustrated our history. And here, too, it will be found that the great criminal who is at your bar has no better support than he has found in higher quarters.

I am not here to question the doctrine which has been so strongly urged, upon the authority of Lord Coke, that contemporaneous exposition is entitled to great weight in law. Taking it to be sound, however, it will hardly be pretended, I suppose, that there is anything of this description which will compare in value with the authoritative, and, I might almost say, oracular utterances of the Federalist, which was the main agent, under Providence, in securing for the Constitution the support of the people of the several States, and has since occupied the rank of a classic in the political literature of America. And yet, in the seventy-seventh number of that series, which is ascribed to the pen of Alexander Hamilton, himself perhaps "the first among his peers" in the Convention which framed that instrument, it is assumed as an unquestionable proposition and that, too, in the way of answer to the objection of instability arising from frequent changes of administration, that inasmuch "as the Senate was to participate in the business of appointments, its consent would therefore be necessary to displace as well as to appoint." Nor was it considered even necessary to reason out a conclusion that was so obvious and inevitable. It does not seem to have been supposed by anybody that a power so eminently regal could ever be raised in the executive of a limited Government out of the mere fact of the silence of the Constitution on that subject and the failure to provide any other mode of removal than by the process of impeachment. If the conclusion, however, was not a sound one, then it was no better than a false pretense, which those at least who concurred in its presentation were morally estopped from controverting. And yet it is to one of the distinguished authors of these papers, in his quality of a legislator, that the nation is mainly indebted for the vote which inaugurated and fastened so long upon it the mischievous and anti-republican doctrine and practice which it has cost a revolution to overthrow. It does not seem, however, to have effected any change in the opinions of the distinguished author, as we find him insisting in a letter written ten years afterward to James McHenry, then Secretary of War, that even the power to fill vacancies happening during the recess of the Senate is to be confined to "such offices as having been once filled have become vacant by accidental circumstances."

From the time of the settlement of the policy of the Government on this subject by its first Congress down till the accession of the younger Adams in 1826, a period of nearly forty years, the question does not seem to have been agitated, for the very satisfactory reason that the patronage was so inconsiderable, and the cases of abuse so rare, as to attract no attention on the part of public men. In the last named year, however, a committee was raised by the Senate, headed by Mr. Benton, and composed of nine of the most eminent statesmen of that day, to consider the subject of restraining this power by legislation. That committee agreed in the opinion that the practice of dismissing from office was a dangerous violation of the Constitution, which had in their view been "*changed* in this regard *by construction* and *legislation*," which were only another name for legislative construction, and reported sundry bills for its correction not unlike in some respects to the present law. Those bills failed of course, but with the public recognition of the new and alarming doctrine which followed the accession of the next Administration, that the public offices, like the plunder of a camp, were the legitimate spoils of the victorious party, the subject was revived in 1835 by the appointment of another committee, embracing the great names of Calhoun, Webster, and Benton, for the same object. The result of their labors was the introduction of a bill requiring the President in all cases of removal to state the reasons thereof, which passed the Senate by a vote of 31 to 16, or nearly two thirds of that body. In the course of the debate on that bill, Mr. Webster, whose unsurpassed, and, as I think, unequaled ability as a constitutional lawyer will be contested by nobody, held this emphatic language:

"After considering the question again and again within the last six years I am willing to say that, in my deliberate judgment, the original decision was wrong. I cannot but think that those who denied the power in 1789 had the best of the argument. It appears to me, after thorough and repeated and conscientious examination that an erroneous interpretation was given to the Constitution in this respect by the decision of the First Congress."

And again:

"I have the clearest conviction that they (the Convention) looked to no other mode of displacing an officer than by impeachment or the regular appointment of another person to the same place."

And further:

"I believe it to be within the just power of Congress to reverse the decision of 1789, and I mean to hold myself at liberty to act hereafter upon that question as the safety of the Government and of the Constitution may require."

Mr. Calhoun was equally emphatic in his condemnation of the power and speaks of previous cases of removal as "rather exceptions than constituting a practice."

The like opinion was obviously entertained by both Kent and Story, the two most distinguished of the commentators on the Constitution, and certainly among the highest authorities in the country. The former, after referring to the construction of 1789 as but "a loose, incidental, and declaratory opinion of Congress," is constrained to speak of it as "a striking fact in the constitutional history of our Government that a power so transcendent as that which places at the disposal of the President alone the tenure of every executive officer appointed by the President and Senate, should depend on *inference* merely, and should have been gratuitously declared by the First Congress in opposition to the high authority of the Federalist, and supported or acquiesced in by some of those distinguished men who questioned or denied the power of Congress to incorporate a national bank." (1 Kent's Commentaries, sec. 16, p. 308.) The latter speaks of it with equal emphasis as "constituting the most extraordinary case in the history of the Government of a power conferred by *implication* in the Executive by the assent of a bare majority in Congress which has not been questioned on many other occasions." (2 Commentaries, sec. 1543.)

The same opinion, too, is already shown upon the testimony of Judge McLain, as cited above, to have been shared by "the old Supreme Court, with Marshall at its head." It seems, indeed, as though there had been an unbroken current of sentiment from sources such as these through all our history against the existence of this power. If there be any apparently exceptional cases of any note but the equivocal one of Mr. Madison, they will be found to rest only, as I think, upon the legislation of 1789 and the long practice that is supposed to have followed it. I make no account of the opinions of Attorneys General, although I might have quoted that of Mr. Wirt, in 1818, to the effect that it was only when Congress had not undertaken to fix the tenure of the office that the commission could run during the pleasure of the President. They belong to the same category as those of Cabinet officers. It may not be amiss, however, to add just here that although this question was elaborately argued by myself upon the introduction of the bill to regulate removals from office in the House of Representatives, which was substantially the same as the present law, which was depending at that time, no voice but one was lifted up in the course of a protracted debate against the constitutionality of the measure itself.

What, then, is there in the legislation of 1789, which is claimed to be not only a contemporary but an authoritative exposition of the meaning of the Constitution, and has no value whatever except as the expression of an opinion as to the policy of making the heads of Departments dependent on the President, unless the acts of that small and inexperienced Congress are to be taken as of binding force upon their successors and as a sort of oracular outgiving upon the meaning of the Constitution?

Whatever may have been the material provisions of the several acts passed at that session, for the establishment of these Departments, it is not to be supposed that it was intended to accomplish a result so clearly not within the province of the law-maker as the binding settlement of the sense of that instrument on so grave a question. The effect of these acts has, I think, been greatly misunderstood by those who rely on them for such a purpose. All that they amount to is the concession to the President, in such a form as was agreeable to his friends, of a power of removal which the majority was disposed to accord to him in cases where the tenure of the officer was left indefinite, and the office was therefore determinable at will, but which those friends declined to accept as a grant, because they claimed it as a right. The result was but a compromise, which evaded the issue by substituting an *implied* grant for an *express* one, and left the question in dispute just where it found it. The record shows, however, that even in this shape the bill finally passed the House by a vote of only 29 to 22. In the Senate, however, where the debate does not appear, it was carried only by the casting vote of the Vice President, not properly himself a legislative but an *executive* officer, who had a very direct interest in the decision.

The case shows, moreover, as already suggested, that there was no question involved as to the duration of the office. Whether it could be so limited, as has been done in the tenure-of-office law, was not a point in controversy, and is not, of course, decided. That it might be so, is not disputed as to the "inferior" offices. The thing itself was done, and the right to do it acquiesced in and affirmed, as shown already in the case of Marbury *vs.* Madison, as early as 1801. It cannot be shown, however, that there is any difference between the cases of *inferior* and *superior* offices in this respect. There is no word in the Constitution to require that the latter shall hold only *at pleasure.* Both are created by law, and Mr. Madison himself admits, in the debate of 1789, that "the legislative power creates the office, defines the power, *limits its duration,* and annexes the compensation." All that the Constitution contains is the exception from the general power of appointment in the authority to Congress to vest that power in inferior cases in the President alone, in the courts of law, or in the heads of Departments. But there is nothing here as to the power of removal—nothing but as to the

privilege of dispensing with the Senate in the matter of appointments, and no limitation whatever upon its power over the office itself in the one case more than in the other.

And now let me ask what did the decision amount to, supposing it had even ruled the question at issue, but the act of a mere Legislature with no greater powers than ourselves? Is there anything in the proceedings of the Congress of 1789 to indicate that it ever assumed to itself the prerogative of setting itself up as an interpreter of the fundamental law? The men who composed it understood their functions better than to suppose that it had any jurisdiction over questions of this sort. If it had, so have we, and *judgments* may be reversed on a rehearing, as constitutions cannot be. But if it did exist whence was it derived? How was the Congress to bind the people by altering the law to which it owed its own existence, and all its powers? It could not bind its successors by making even its own enactments irrepealable. If it had a right to give an opinion upon the meaning of the Constitution, why may we not do the same thing? The President obviously assumes that they were both wiser and better than ourselves. If the respect which he professes for their opinions had animated him in regard to the Congresses which have sat under his administration, the nation would have been spared much tribulation and we relieved of the painful necessity of arraigning the Chief Magistrate of the Republic at your bar for his crimes against order, and liberty, and his open defiance of law.

However it may be with others, I am not one of those who think that all wisdom and virtue have perished with our fathers, or that they were better able to comprehend the import of an instrument with whose practical workings they were unfamiliar than we who are sitting under the light of an experience of eighty years, and suffering from the mistakes which they made in regard to the future. They made none greater than the illusion of supposing that it was impossible for our institutions to throw up to the surface a man like Andrew Johnson; and yet it was this mistake—perhaps no other—that settled the first precedent, which was so likely to be followed, in regard to the mischievous power of removal from office. But if twenty-nine votes in the House at that day, making a meager majority of only seven, and nine only in a Senate that was equally divided, in the first hours of constitutional life, and with such a President as Washington, to fling a rose-colored light over the future of the Republic, had even intended to give, and did give, a construction to our great charter of freedom, what is to be said of 133 votes to 37, constituting more than three fourths of one House, and of 35 to 11, or nearly a like proportion of the other, in the maturity of our strength, with a population of nearly forty millions, and under the light of an experience which has proved that even the short period of eighty years was capable of producing what our progenitors supposed to be impossible even in the long tract of time?

But there is one other consideration that presents itself just here, and it is this: it does not strike me by any means as clear that there was anything in the act of 1789, aside from any supposed attempt to give it the force of an authoritative exposition of the Constitution, that was necessarily inconsistent with the view of that instrument which I have been endeavoring to maintain. Taking the authority lodged by it with the President as a mere *general grant* of power, there was nothing certainly in its terms to prevent it. So far at least as regarded the *inferior* officers, it resulted from the express authority of Congress to vest the power of *appointment* in the President alone, that they might have even left the power of removal in the same hands also as an incident. And so, too, as to the superior ones. The power to remove in any case was but an implied one. If it was necessary, as claimed, to enable the Executive to perform his proper functions under the Constitution, instead of raising the power in himself by the illogical inference, that it must belong to him *qua* Executive, it presented one of the very cases for which it is provided expressly that Congress shall "make all laws that shall be necessary and proper for carrying into execution all power vested by the Constitution in the Government of the United States, or in any Department or officer thereof." To infer in the face of such a provision as this, that any or all powers necessary to either department of the Government belong to them, of course, because they are necessary, is a reflection on the understandings of the framers of the Constitution, and is in effect to nullify the provision itself, by enabling the other Departments of the Government to dispense entirely with the action of the law-maker.

But, admitting the act of 1789 to import, in its full extent, all that it is claimed to have decided, it is further insisted that this untoward precedent has been ripened into unalterable law by a long and uninterrupted practice in conformity with it. If it were even true, as stated, there would be nothing marvelous in the fact that it has been followed up by other legislation of a kindred character. It is not to be doubted that a general opinion did prevail for many years that all the offices of the Government not otherwise provided for in the Constitution ought to be held at will, for the obvious reason, among others, that it rendered the process of removal easy by making an impeachment unnecessary. The only question in dispute was in whose hands this power could be most appropriately lodged. It so happened, however, that the first of our Presidents brought with him into the office an elevation of character that placed him above all suspicion, and assured to him a confidence so unbounded that it would have been considered entirely safe to vest him with unlimited command; and it was but natural, as it was certainly highly convenient, that the exercise of that will, which was to determine the life of the officer, should be lodged with him. It was so lodged.

But is there anything remarkable in the fact that the precedent thus set should have been followed up in the practice of the Government? It would have been still more remarkable if it had been otherwise. It was a question of patronage and power—of rewarding friends, and punishing enemies. A successful candidate for the Presidency was always sure to bring in with him a majority in the popular branch at least, along with a host of hungry followers flushed with their victory and hungering after the spoils. Was it expected that they should abridge his power to reward his friends, or air their own virtue by self-denying ordinances? That would have been too much for men, and politicians, too. No. Though the wisest statesmen of the country had realized and deplored for forty years at least the giant vice which had been gnawing into the very entrails of the state, and threatened to corrupt it in all its members, there was no remedy left, but the intervention of that Providence which has purified the heart of the nation through the blood of its children, and cast down the man who "but yesterday might have stood against the world," so low, that with all his royal patronage there are none left—no, I think not one—"so poor as to do him reverence."

It is not even true, however, that the precedent of the Congress of 1789 has been followed invariably and without interruption since that time. The history of our legislation shows not only repeated instances wherein the tenure of office has been so precisely defined as to take the case entirely out of the control of the Executive, but some in which even the power of removal itself has been substantially exercised by Congress, as one would suppose it might reasonably be, where it creates and may destroy, makes and may unmake, even the subject of controversy itself.

The act of 1801, already referred to in connection with the case of Marbury and Madison, assigning a tenure of five years absolutely to the officer, involves a manifest departure from it.

The five several acts of August 14, 1848, March 3, 1849, September, 1850, and May 3, 1854, providing for the appointment of judges in the Territories of Oregon, Minnesota, New Mexico, Kansas, and Nebraska, and fixing their terms of office at four years absolutely, are all within the same category.

The act of 25th February, 1863, followed by that of June 3, 1864, establishing the office of Comptroller of the Currency, defining his term and making him irremovable except by and with the advice and consent of the Senate, and upon reasons to be shown, is another of the same description.

The act of March 3, 1865, which authorizes

any military or naval officer who has been dismissed by the authority of the President to demand a trial by court-martial, and in default of its allowance within six months, or of a sentence of dismissal or death thereby, avoids the order of the Executive; and the act of July 13, 1866, which provides that no officer in time of peace shall be dismissed except in pursuance of a sentence of a court-martial, are both examples of like deviation of the strongest kind, for the double reason that the President is, under the Constitution, the Commander-in-Chief of the Army and Navy of the United States, and none but *civil* officers are amenable to the process of impeachment, and that the officer dismissed is absolutely restored, awakened into new life, and raised to his feet by the omnipotent fiat of the legislative power.

And, lastly, the act of 15th May, 1820, (3 Statutes, 582,) which dismisses by wholesale a very large and important class of officers at periods specially indicated therein, not only fixes the tenure prospectively, but involves a clear exercise of the power of removal itself on the part of the Legislature.

Further developments in the same direction would no doubt reward the diligence of the more pains-taking inquirer. That, however, would only be a work of supererogation. Enough have been shown to demonstrate beyond denial that the practice relied on has been anything but uniform.

To establish even a local custom or prescription the element of continuity is as important as that of time. Any break in that continuity by an adverse entry or even a continual claim, would arrest the flow of a statute of limitations against the rightful owner of a tenement. An interruption of the enjoyment would be equally fatal to a prescription. But are we to be told that a case which in this view would not even be sufficient to establish a composition for tithes, or a trifling easement as between individuals, is sufficient to raise a prescription against a constitutional right or to abrogate the fundamental law of a nation and bar the inappreciable inheritance of its people? The very statement of the proposition would seem to furnish its own refutation.

But this is not all. If the case had even been one of uninterrupted continuity, how is it as to the element of time? To settle a custom, either public or private, it must have the hoar of antiquity upon it; its origin must be traced far back into the night of time, so far that no living memory can measure it, and no man can say that he has drunk at its head-springs or stood beside its cradle. What is the case here? It is a question of the fundamental law of a people whose dominions embrace a continent, and whose numbers are multitudinous as the stars of heaven. A little more than three quarters of a century will measure the career that they have thus far run. What a mere span is this? Why I have seen on this floor, a not uninterested

spectator of this great drama, a veteran states-man, known by fame, and perhaps personally, to all of you, whose years go back behind your Constitution itself. But what is a century but the briefest hour in the life of a State? How is a mere non-user for seventy-five of its infant years to be set up either to bar a fundamental right, or to prove that it never existed? It required six centuries of struggle with the prerogative to settle the British constitution firmly upon the foundations of Magna Charta, and no hostile precedent of the reigns of either the Plantagenets or Tudors was allowed to stand in the way of the onward movement that culminated in the revolution of 1688. And yet it is gravely urged on us, that the conduct of our national life is to be regulated by the mistakes of its childhood, and that the grand patrimony of the Revolution has been squandered beyond recovery by the thoughtless improvidence, or too generous and trustful prodigality of an earlier heir who had just come to his estate.

And now I may venture to say, I think, that it has been shown abundantly that all the resources of the President on this point have failed him. The awards of reason, the judgments of the courts, the opinions of statesmen, lawyers, and publicists, the precedent of 1789, and the practice of the Government, are all against him.

Mr. MORRILL, of Vermont, (at four o'clock and five minutes p. m.) I understand that the Manager is extremely ill to-day, and would not be able to finish his argument if he were well. I therefore move that the Senate, sitting as a court, adjourn until to-morrow.

The motion was agreed to; and the Senate, sitting for the trial of the impeachment, adjourned until to-morrow at twelve o'clock.

TUESDAY, *April* 28, 1868.

The Chief Justice of the United States took the chair.

The usual proclamation having been made by the Sergeant-at-Arms,

The Managers of the impeachment on the part of the House of Representatives and the counsel for the respondent, except Mr. Stanbery, appeared and took the seats assigned to them respectively.

The members of the House of Representatives, as in Committee of the Whole, preceded by Mr. E. B. WASHBURNE, chairman of that committee, and accompanied by the Speaker and Clerk, appeared, and were conducted to the seats provided for them.

The Journal of yesterday's proceedings of the Senate, sitting for the trial of the impeachment, was read.

Mr. SUMNER. Mr. President, I send to the Chair an amendment to the rules of the Senate, sitting for the trial of impeachments. When that has been read, if there be no objection, I will ask that it go over until the close of the arguments, to take its place with the other matters which will come up for consideration at that time.

The CHIEF JUSTICE. The Secretary will read the proposed rule for information.

The Chief Clerk read as follows:

Whereas it is provided in the Constitution of the United States that on trials of impeachment by the Senate no person shall be convicted without the concurrence of two thirds of the members present, and the person so convicted shall be removed from office; but this requirement of two thirds is not extended to any further judgment, which remains subject to the general law that a majority prevails; therefore, in order to remove any doubt thereupon:

Ordered, That after removal, which necessarily follows conviction, any question which may arise with regard to disqualification or any further judgment shall be determined by a majority of the members present.

Mr. DAVIS. I object to the consideration of it.

The CHIEF JUSTICE. The proposed order will lie over. That is the disposition proposed by the Senator from Massachusetts. Mr. Manager WILLIAMS will proceed on the part of the House of Representatives.

Mr. Manager WILLIAMS. Mr. President and Senators, I have to thank you for the indulgence which you were kind enough to extend to me yesterday at a time when I very much wanted it. I shall endeavor, however, to testify my gratitude by not abusing it.

Before I closed yesterday I was referring to the position taken by me, and, as I thought, sufficiently demonstrated, that the President had failed in all his supports; that the reason of the thing, the natural reason, the cultivated reason of the law, the judicial sentiment, the opinions of commentators, the precedent of 1789, and even the practice, were all against him; but then I suggested that there was one resource still left, and to that I now come, and that is in the opinion of what is sometimes called his Cabinet, the trusted counselors whom he is pleased to quote as the advisers whom the Constitution and the practice of the Government have assigned to him. If all the world has forsaken him, they, at least, are still faithful to the chief whom they have so long accompanied, and so largely comforted and encouraged through all his manifold usurpations.

It is true that these gentlemen have not been allowed to prove, as they would have desired to do, that maugre all the reasoning of judges, lawyers, and publicists, they were implicitly of the opinion, and so advised the President, that the tenure-of-office law, not being in accordance with his will, was, of course, unconstitutional. It may be guessed, I suppose, without damage to our case, that if allowed they would have proved it. With large opportunies for information I have not heard of any occasion wherein they have ever given any opinion to the President, except the one that was wanted by him, or known to be agreeable to his will. If there had been time I should have been glad to hear from some of these functionaries on that question. It would have been

pleasant to hear the witness on the stand at least, discourse of constitutional law. If the public interest has not suffered, the public curiosity has at least been balked by the denial of the high privilege of listening to the luminous expositions which some of these learned Thebans, whose training has been so high as to warrant them in denouncing us all—the legislators of the nation—as no better than "Constitution tinkers," would have been able to help us with.

It is a large part of the defense of the President, as set forth in his voluminous special plea, and elaborated in the argument of the opening counsel, not only that his Cabinet agreed with him in his views as to the law, but that if he has erred, it was under the advice received from those whom the law had placed around him. It is not shown, however, and was not attempted to be shown, that in regard to the particular offense for which he is now arraigned before you they were ever consulted by him. But to clear this part of the case of all possible cavil or exception, I feel that it will not be amiss to ask your attention to a few remarks upon the relations of the President with this illegitimate body, this excrescence, this mere fungus, born of decay, which has been compounded in process of time out of the heads of the Departments, and has shot up within the last few years into the formidable proportions of a directory for the general government of the State.

The first observation that suggests itself is that this reference to the advice of others proceeds on the hypothesis that the President himself is not responsible, and is therefore at war with the principal theory of the defense, which is that he is the sole responsible head of the executive department, and must therefore, ex necessitate, in order to the performance of his appropriate duties, have the undisputed right to control and govern and remove them at his own mere will—as he has just done in the case of Mr. Stanton—a theory which precludes the idea of advice in the fact that it makes the adviser a slave. What, then, does the President intend? Does he propose to abandon this line of defense? He cannot do it without surrendering his case.

Is it his purpose, then, to divert us from the track by doubling on his pursuers, and leading them off on a false scent, or does he intend the offer of a vicarious sacrifice? Does he think to make mere scapegoats of his counselors by laying all his multitudinous sins upon their backs? Does he propose to enact the part of another Charles, by surrendering another Strafford to the vengeance of the Commons? We must decline to accept the offer. We want no ministerial heads. We do not choose in the pursuit of higher game to stoop to any ignobler quarry either on the land or on the sea. It would be anything but magnanimous in us to take, as it would be base in him to offer, the heads of those whom our own past legislation has degraded into slaves. When Cæsar falls his counselors will disappear along with him. Perhaps he thinks, however, that *nobody* is responsible. But shall we allow him to justify in one breath the removal of Mr. Stanton on the ground that under the law he was his master, and then in another, when arraigned for this, to say that he is not responsible because he took advice from those who are but mere automata—only his "hands and voice," in the language of his counsel—and no more than the mere creatures of his imperial will? This would be a sad condition, indeed, for the people of a Republic claiming to be free. We can all understand the theory of the British constitution. The king can do no wrong. The person of majesty is sacred. But then the irresponsibility of the sovereign is beautifully reconciled with the liberty of the subject, by holding the ministry responsible, and thus taking care that he shall get no bad advice from them. But what is to be our condition, with no recourse between the two, to either king or minister? It will be not unlike what is said in the touching plaint of the Britons, "The barbarians drive us to the sea, and the sea drives us back again on the barbarians."

But who made these men the advisers of the President? Not the Constitution, certainly; not the laws, or they would have made them free. The Constitution has given to him no *advisers* but the Senate, whose opinion he scouts at and defies, because he cannot get from it the advice he wants, and would obtain, no doubt, if it were reduced to the condition of that of imperial Rome. All it provides in regard to the heads of Departments is that he may require the opinion in writing of each of them upon any subject relating to the duties of *his own special office*, and no more. He cannot require it as to other matters, and by the strongest implication it was not intended that he should take it on any matter outside of their own respective offices and duties. He has undoubtedly the privilege which belongs to other men, of seeking for advice wherever he may want it; but if he is wise, and would be honestly advised—as he does not apparently wish to be—he will go to those who are in a condition to tell him the truth without the risk of being turned out of office, as Mr. Stanton has been, for doing so. No tyrant who has held the lives of those around him in his hands, has ever enjoyed the counsels of any but minions and sycophants. If it had been the purpose of the framers of the Constitution to provide a council for the President, they would have looked to it that he was not to be surrounded with creatures such as these.

But then it is said that the practice of holding Cabinet councils was inaugurated by President Washington, and has since continued without interruption. It is unquestionable that he did take the opinions in writing of all the heads of Departments, on bills that were submitted to him in the constitutional way, and not un-

likely that he may have consulted them as to appointments, and other matters of executive duty that involved anything like discretion. They may have met occasionally in after times upon the special invitation of the President. It was not, however, as I think, until the period of the war, when the responsibilities of the President, as Commander-in-Chief of the armies, were so largely magnified as to make it necessary that he should take counsel from day to day, that they crystallized into their present form, as a sort of institution of state; and not till the accession of Andrew Johnson, that they began to do the work of Congress, in a condition of peace, by legislating for the restoration of the rebel States. From that time forward, through all that long and unhappy interregnum of the law-making power, while the telegraph was waiting upon the action of those mysterious councils, that dark tribunal which was erecting States by proclamation, taxing the people, and surrendering up the public property is to keep them on their feet, and exercising a dispensing power over the laws, had apparently taken the place of the Congress of the nation, with powers quite as great as any that the true Congress has ever claimed. To say that the acts of this mere cabal, which looked for all the world, like some dark conclave of conspirators plotting against the liberties of the people, were the results of free consultation and comparison of views, is to speak without knowledge. I for one mistrusted them from the beginning, and, if I may be excused the egotism again, it was under the inspiration of the conviction that they could not have held together so long under an imperious, self-willed man like the present Executive, without a thorough submission to all his views, that I was moved to introduce and urge, as I did, through great discouragements, but, thank God, successfully, the amendment to the tenure-of-office bill, that brings about this conflict. It has come sooner than I expected, but not too soon to vindicate, by its timely rescue of the most important of the Departments of the Government from the grasp of the President, the wisdom of a measure which, if it had been the law at the time of Mr. Johnson's accession, would, in my humble judgment, have set his policy aside, and made his resistance to the will of the loyal people, and his project of governing the nation without a Congress, impossible. The veil has been lifted since the passage of this law, and those who wish, may now read in letters of living light the great fact, that during the progress of all this usurpation that has convulsed the nation, and kept the South in anarchy for three long years, there was scarce a ripple of dissent to ruffle the stagnant surface of those law-making and law-breaking cabals, those mere beds of justice, where, in accordance with the theory of the President himself, there was but one will that reigned undisputed and supreme.

To insist, then, that any apology is to be found

for the delinquencies of the President, in the advice of a Cabinet, where a difference of opinion was considered treason to the head, and loyalty to the law, instead of to the will of the President, punished by dismissal, is, as it seems to me, on his part, the very climax of effrontery. What adequate cause does the President now assign for the removal of Mr. Stanton? His counsel promised us in their opening, that they would exhibit reasons to show that it was impossible to allow him to continue to hold the office. They have failed to do it. They have not even attempted it. Was it because he had failed to perform his duties, or had in any way offended against the law? The President alleges nothing of the kind. Was it even a personal quarrel? Nothing of this sort is pretended either. All that we can hear of, is that there was a "want of mutual confidence;" that "his relations to Mr. Stanton were such as to preclude him from resorting to him for *advice*," (Heaven save the mark!) and that he did not think he could be any longer safely responsible for him. His counsel say that Mr. Stanton is a thorn in his side. Well a thorn in the flesh is sometimes good for the spirit. But so are Grant and Sherman and Sheridan, and so is Congress, and so is every loyal man in the country who questions or resists his will. The trouble is, as everybody knows, that Mr. Stanton does not indorse his policy, and cannot be relied on to assist him in obstructing the laws of Congress; and that is just the reason why you want this thorn to "stick," and, if need be, prick and fester a little there, and must maintain it there, if you would be faithful to the nation and to yourselves. You cannot let Mr. Stanton go, by an acquittal of the President, without surrendering into his hands the very last fortress that you still hold, and are now holding only at the point of the bayonet.

But there is a point just here that seems to have been entirely overlooked by the counsel for the President, to which I desire especially to invite your attention. It seems to have been assumed by them throughout—if it is not, indeed, distinctly asserted in the defendant's plea—that if they shall be able to succeed in establishing a power of removal in the President, either under the Constitution or the act of 1789, erecting the Department now in question, he may exercise that power at his mere will and pleasure, without reason and without responsibility; and having failed to show any adequate cause, or indeed any cause whatever for the act done here, he stands, of course, on this hypothesis. But is this the law? Is there no such thing as an abuse of power, and a just responsibility as its attendant? Was it intended in either case—whether the power flowed from one source, or from the other—that it should be exerciseable without restraint? That doctrine would be proper in a monarchy, perhaps, but is ill suited to the genius of institutions like our own. Nor was it the opinion of Mr. Madison, or those who voted

C. I.—44.

and acted with him in the Congress of 1789. No man there who asserted the power of removal to be in the President, or concurred in bestowing it on him for the occasion, ever supposed that its exercise was to be a question of mere caprice, or whim, or will. To the objection that this would be the effect of the doctrine of removal, it was answered by Mr. Madison himself in these words:

"The danger consists merely in this: that the President can displace from office a man whose merits require that he should be continued in it. What will be the motive which the President can feel for such abuse of his power, and the restraints that operate to prevent it? In the first place he will be impeached by the House before the Senate for such an act of maladministration; for I contend that the wanton removal of meritorious officers would subject him to impeachment and removal from his own high trust."

And it was, no doubt, mainly on this argument that the power of removal was embodied in the law.

What, then, have the President and his counsel to say in answer to this? Is the President impeachable on his own case, or does he expect to realize the fruits of the argument, and then repudiate the very grounds on which the alleged construction rests? Was Mr. Stanton a meritorious officer? Did his merits require that he should be continued in the place? No loyal man, I think, disputes that they did, and this Senate has already solemnly adjudged it, in their decision that, upon the reasons stated by the President, there was no sufficient cause for his removal, while none other have been since shown by the accused himself. What, then, was the motive for this act of *maladministration*, as Mr. Madison denominates it? Nothing that we are aware of, except the fact that the President cannot control the War Office in the interests of his policy, so long as he is there. Was this, then, a wanton removal? It was something more—it was a wicked one. And are we to be told now that he is bound to show no reasons, and cannot be compelled to answer for it to the nation, by those who claim the power of removal for him on the very footing that its abuse would be impeachable?

But it is further strenuously argued, that although the law may be constitutional, and the case of Mr. Stanton within it, as it has been already held to be by this Senate, the case was not so clear a one as to authorize a charge of crime against the President, unless it can be shown that he has willfully misconstrued it; and that although wherever a law is passed through the forms of legislation, it is his duty to see that it is faithfully executed so long as it requires no more than ministerial action on his part, yet, where it is a question of cutting off a power confided to him by the Constitution, and he alone can bring about a judicial decision for its settlement; if, on due deliberation and advice, he should be of the opinion that the law was unconstitutional, it would be no violation of duty to take the needful steps to raise that question, so as to have it peacefully decided.

Allow me to say in answer, that if even ignorance of the law, which excuses nobody else, can be held to excuse the very last man in the nation who ought to be allowed to plead it, the testimony shows, I think, that he did not misunderstand its meaning. His suspension of Mr. Stanton, which was an entirely new procedure, followed, as it was, by his report of the case to the Senate within twenty days after its next meeting, is evidence that he *did* understand the law as comprehending that case, and did not intend to violate it, if he could get rid of the obnoxious officer without resorting to so extreme and hazardous a remedy.

But the question here is not so much whether he ignorantly and innocently mistook the law, as whether in the case referred to of an interference with the power claimed by him under the Constitution, he may suspend the operation of a law by assuming it to be unconstitutional, and setting it aside until the courts shall have decided that it is a constitutional and valid one. In the case at issue, it was not necessary to violate the law, either by contriving to prevent the incumbent from resuming his place under it, or turning him out by violence after he had been duly reinstated by the Senate, if he honestly desired to test its validity in the judicial forum. All that it was necessary for him to do, was to issue his order of removal, and give the officer a notice of that order, and its object. If he refused to obey, the next and obvious step would have been to direct the Attorney General to sue out a writ of *quo warranto*, on his own relation. This was not his course. The remedy was not summary enough for his uses, as his special counsel, employed only after the arrest of his pseudo Secretary Thomas, testifies, because it would have allowed the law to reign in the meanwhile, instead of creating an interregnum of mere will by which he hoped to supersede it. His project was to seize the place; by craft, if possible; by force, if necessary. For this purpose he claims to have made an arrangement with General Grant for its surrender to himself, in case the judgment of the Senate should restore the officer, and now taxes that distinguished officer with bad faith to him individually, for his obedience to the law.

It stands, therefore, upon his own confession, that he intended to prevent Mr. Stanton from resuming his position, in which case—as he well knew, and as his Attorney General knew, and must have informed him, there was no remedy at law for the ejected officer. Foiled and baffled by the integrity of Grant, after full deliberation he issues his order of removal on the 21st of February, and sends it by his lieutenant, Thomas, with a commission to himself to act as Secretary *ad interim*, and enter upon the duties of the office. He does not fail to suggest to him at the same time, that Stanton is a coward, and may be easily frightened out of the place with a proper show of energy on his part. He tells him also that he expects him to support the Constitution and the laws—as he understands them, of course. Thomas is a martinet. He knows no law, as he confesses, but the order of his Commander-in-Chief. He has been taught no argument but arms—no logic but the dialectics of hard knocks. Instructed by the President, he hopes to frighten Stanton by his big looks and horrent arms. He proceeds upon his warlike errand in all the panoply of a brigadier, and loftily demands the keys of the fortress from the stern warder, who only stipulates for twenty-four hours to remove his camp equipage and baggage. The conquest is apparently an easy one. He reports forthwith to his chief with the brevity of a Cæsar: "*Veni, vidi, vici.*" They rejoice, no doubt, together over the pusillanimity of the Secretary; and the puissant Adjutant then unbends, and flies for relaxation, after his heroic and successful feat, to the delights and mysteries of the masquerade; not, however, until he has "fought his battle o'er again," and invited his friends to be present at the surrender on the following morning, which he advises them that he intends to compel by force, if necessary.

The masquerade opens. "Fair women and brave men" are there, and—

"Music ascends with its voluptuous swell,
 And eyes look love to eyes that speak again
 And all goes merry as a marriage bell."

The Adjutant himself is there. The epaulette has modestly retired behind the domino. The gentleman from Tennessee at least will excuse me, if after his own example, I borrow from the celestial armory, on which he draws so copiously, a little of that *light* artillery, with which he blazes along his track, like a November midnight sky with all its flaming asteroids. The Adjutant, I repeat, is there.

"Grim-visaged war hath smoothed his wrinkled front,
And now, instead of mounting barbed steeds
To fright the souls of fearful adversaries,
He capers nimbly in a lady's chamber
To the lascivious pleasing of a lute."

But lo! a hand is laid upon his shoulder, which startles him in the midst of the festivities, like the summons to "Brunswick's fated chieftain" at the ball in Brussels, on the night before the battle in which he fell. It is the messenger of the Senate, who comes to warn him that his enterprise is an unlawful one. On the following morning he is waited upon again by another officer, with a warrant for his arrest for threats which looked to a disturbance of the peace. This double warning chills his martial ardor. Visions of impending trouble pass before his eyes. He sees, or thinks he sees, the return of civil strife, the floors of the Department dabbled, perhaps, like those of the royal palace at Holyrood, with red spots of blood. But, above all, he feels that the hand of the law-maker and of the law itself, which is stronger than the sword, is on him, and he puts up his weapon, and repairs, in peaceful guise, to take possession of his conquest. I do not propose, however, to describe the interview which followed. That will be the task of the future dramatist. It will be sufficient for us to accompany him back to the White House, where he receives the order to "Go on and take possession," which he was so unhappily called back to contradict, and which it was then well understood, of course, that he could not obtain except by force; and he continues to be recognized as Secretary of War, without a portfolio or a *cure*, while he waits under the direction of the President, not upon the law, but only to see, like Micawber, what may turn up here, and to be inducted and installed in proper form, as soon as your previous decision shall have been reversed, and his title affirmed, by your votes in favor of an acquittal. The idea of a suit, in which direction no single step was ever taken, is now abandoned, if it was ever seriously entertained.

The conversation, however, with General Sherman, who was called as a witness by the President himself, settles the fact conclusively, if not already demonstrated by all the attendant circumstances, that it was not his purpose at any time to bring the case into the courts for adjudication. He preferred the dexterous finesse, or the strong hand, to a reference which every sensible lawyer would have told him could be attended with only one result, and that a judgment in favor of the law.

But in this great strait, instead of a resort to the Attorney General himself, his special counsel Cox, employed only after the arrest of Thomas, is called to prove that he advised against the writ of *quo warranto*, because of "the law's delay," and endeavored to seek a remedy more summary through a *habeas corpus*, in the event of the commitment of the Secretary *ad interim*. Supposing it all true, however, the movement came too late to help his employer's case, by showing a desire to put the issue in the way of a judicial decision upon the law. Nor is it clear by any means that such a process could have achieved the desired results. With a warrant good upon its face, and charging a threatened disturbance of the peace, or an offense against a statute of the United States, I doubt whether any court would venture to declare the warrant void, or to discharge upon such a hearing, on the footing of the unconstitutionality of the law, which had received nearly three fourths of the votes of both Houses, or, indeed, of any law whatever; while I do not see how even a decision against it, could have had either the effect of ousting Stanton or putting Thomas in his place. It is enough, however, for the present purpose that the prisoner was discharged on the motion of his own attorney.

The counsel for the President admits that he cannot in ordinary cases erect himself into a judicial tribunal, and decide that a law is unconstitutional, because the effect would be that there could never be any judicial decision upon it; but insists, as already stated, that where a particular law has cut off a power confided to him by the Constitution, he alone has the power to raise the question for the courts, and there is no objection to his doing it; and instances the cases of a law to prevent the making of a treaty, or one to declare that he shall not exercise the functions of Commander-in-Chief.

It has been already very fully answered that there is no evidence here to show that there was any honest purpose whatever to bring this case into the courts, but that, on the contrary, there is very conclusive testimony to prove that he intended to keep it out of them. But had he a right to hold this law a nullity until it was affirmed by another tribunal, whether it was constitutional or not? The Constitution gives to him the power of passing upon the acts of the two Houses, by returning a bill with his objections thereto, but if it is afterwards enacted by two thirds of both it is provided that "it shall become a law." What is a law? It is a rule of civil conduct prescribed by the supreme power of a State. Is there any higher power than the Legislature? Is it essential to the operation of a law that it should have the approval of the judiciary, as well as of the President? It is as obligatory on th President as upon the humblest citizen. Nay, it is, if possible, more so. He is its minister. The Constitution requires that he shall take care that it be faithfully executed. It is for others to controvert it, if aggrieved, in a legal way, but not for him. If they do, however, it is at their peril, as it would be at his, even in the cases put, where it is asked, with great emphasis, whether he would be bound to obey? Those cases are extreme ones. But if hard cases are said to make bad precedents, it may be equally remarked that extreme cases make bad illustrations. They are, moreover, of express powers, as this is not. But it will be time enough to answer them when they arise. It is not a supposable contingency, that two thirds of both Houses of Congress will flatly violate their oaths in a clear case. Thus far in their history, they have passed no law, I believe, that has been adjudged invalid. Whenever they shall be prepared to do what is now supposed, constitutions will be useless, faith will have perished among men, and limited representative government become impossible. When it comes to this, we shall have revolution, with bloody conflicts in our streets, with a Congress legislating behind bayonets, and that anarchy prevailing everywhere, which is already foreshadowed by the aspect of a Department of this great Government beleaguered by the minions of despotism, with its head a prisoner, and armed sentinels pacing before its doors. Who shall say that the President shall be permitted to disobey even a doubtful law, in the assertion of a power that is only implied? If he may, why not also set aside the obnoxious section of the appropriation bill, upon which he has endeavored unsuccessfully to debauch the officers of the Army by teaching them insubordination to the law? Why not openly disregard your reconstruction acts, as he will assuredly do, if you shall teach him by your verdict here that he can do it with impunity? The legal rule is that the presumption is in every case in favor of the law, and that is a *violent* one, where none has ever been reversed. The President claims that this presumption shall not stand as against him. If it may not here, it cannot elsewhere. To allow this revolutionary pretension, is to dethrone the law and substitute his will. To say that he may hold his office, and disregard the law, is to proclaim either anarchy or despotism. It is but a short step from one extreme to the other. To. be without law, and to leave the law dependent on a single will, are in effect but one and the same thing. The man who can declare what is law, and what is not, is already the absolute master of the State.

But who is to try this case? The President insists that it belongs to the jurisdiction of the Supreme Court, where, as he untruly says, he endeavored to carry it. So it would, if the question involved were one of merely private right. But in his eccentric efforts to get into one court, by turning his back upon it, he has stumbled very unexpectedly into another. It is not the one he sought, but it is the one the Constitution has provided for just such delinquencies as his, and he cannot decline its cognizance. I beg pardon. He has sent you word, through the special counsel whom he sends here with his personal protest, that he might have declined it, on the opinion still entertained by both of them, that this is no Congress, and you are no court of competent jurisdiction to bring before you and try a President of the United States, by the logic of which argument he proves equally, of course, that he is no President. To avoid a bloody conflict, however, although he has been tendered the necessary aid in men, and inasmuch, I suppose, as you have been so indulgent as not to put him to the humiliation of appearing in person at your bar, he waives his sufficient plea to the jurisdiction, and condescends, only out of the abundance of his grace, and in a spirit of forbearance, for which he claims due credit at your hands, to make answer before a tribunal which he might rightfully have defied.

But he is here now by attorney, in what his other counsel have taken great pains to prove to you to be a court indeed, although they insist, not very consistently, in almost the same breath, that it has only the functions of a jury. I shall not dispute that question with them. I am willing to agree that the Senate, *pro hac vice*, is a court, and that, too, of exclusive jurisdiction over the subject-matter in dispute, from which it follows by a necessary logic, as I think, that it is fully competent to try and decide the whole case for itself, taking such advice as it thinks proper as to the law, and then rejecting it if it is not satisfactory. If it cannot do this, it is but the shadow and mockery of what the defendant's counsel claim it to be in force and fact. But by what name soever it may be called, it will solve for the President the problem which

he has desired to carry into another tribunal, without waiting for any extraneous opinion. It has already determined upon the constitutionality of the tenure-of-office law, by enacting it over his objections, as it has already passed upon its meaning, by its condemnation of the act for which he is now to answer at its bar. It will say, too, if I mistake not, that whether constitutional or not, it will allow no executive officer, and much less the Chief Magistrate of the nation, to assume that it is not so, and set up his own opinion in its place, until its previous and well-considered judgment upon the same opinion has been judicially affirmed.

But does it make any difference whether Mr. Stanton's case is within the tenure-of-office act or not. Had the Executive the power at any time, either during the session or the recess, to create a vacancy to be filled up by an appointment *ad interim*, to continue during his own pleasure; or if he had, could he prolong a vacancy so created beyond the period of six months?

The Constitution provides—and it required such a provision, in view of the general clause which associates the Senate with the President, and makes their advice and consent necessary in all cases of appointment, to authorize it—that he shall have power to fill up all vacancies happening during the recess, by temporary commissions to expire at the end of the next session; and by a necessary implication of course he cannot do it in the same way, or without their advice and consent while the Senate is at hand to afford it. The word *happen*, as used here, imports accident or casualty only, according to the best authorities. If this is the correct interpretation he cannot, of course, create a vacancy for that purpose during the recess, under the Constitution, although he may claim to do so under the law establishing the Department, which places the power of removal in his hands. If he does, however, the case then falls within the constitutional provision, and the vacancy thus created must be filled by a commission to expire at the end of the next session.

He did create a vacancy in this case by the suspension during the recess, which he proceeded to supply by the appointment of General Grant as Secretary of War *ad interim* at his pleasure. And this he now defends, not under the provisions of the tenure-of-office law, which would have authorized it, but which he expressly repudiates, but upon the footing, in the first place, of his constitutional power.

Nothing is clearer, however, than the proposition, that there was no authority to do this thing except what is to be found in the act which he repudiates. There are no laws and no precedents, so far as I am advised, to justify or excuse it. If he may suspend indefinitely, and appoint at pleasure a Secretary *ad interim*, he may not only change the terms of the commission, but strip the Senate of all participation in the appointing power.

But then he says, again, that he did this under the authority, also, of the act of 13th February, 1795, for filling temporary vacancies. The tenor of that act is, that in a case of vacancy it shall be lawful for the President, if he deem it necessary, to authorize any person or persons to perform the duties until a successor is appointed or such vacancy is filled: with the proviso, however, that no one vacancy shall be supplied in that manner for a longer term than six months; which proves, of course, that the exigency provided for was only to be a temporary one.

We maintain that this act has been repealed by the more recent one of 13th February, 1863, which confines the choice of the President to the heads of the other Departments. It is insisted, however, that while the former covers all cases of vacancy, the latter is confined to some particular instances, not including those of removal, or such as may be brought about by efflux of time, and does not, therefore, operate as a repeal to that extent. Granting this, for the sake of the argument, to be true, how is it to apply to a vacancy occuring during the recess, without a repeal of the constitutional provision which is intended expressly for just such cases? Was it intended to supersede it, and is it to be so interpreted? This will hardly be pretended, if it were even clear that the Legislature had such a power. The intent and meaning of the act are so transparent from the context, from the words of tenure, and from the six months' limitation, that it is impossible to mistake them, or even to doubt, that it was designed for merely accidental and transient cases, that were left unprovided for in the Constitution. The President's claim would perpetuate the vacancy by enabling him to refuse to fill it, or to nominate a successor.

If it be even true, however, that he might have appointed General Grant during the recess, under the law of 1795, it is equally clear that he could not continue him in office, or protract the vacancy beyond six months; and yet he insists, in his special plea in answer to the averment of the absence of the condition of vacancy on the 21st of February, when he appointed General Thomas—which was more than six months after the appointment of General Grant—that there was a continuing vacancy at that time; intending, of course, that the act of the Senate in refusing to approve his suspension, and his resumption of the duties of the office, were to be treated as of no account whatever. From the premises of the President, that the civil-tenure act was invalid on constitutional grounds, and did not, at all events, embrace that case, his inference of a continuing vacancy is undeniable, and his appointment of General Thomas, therefore, entirely unauthorized by the act on which he relies.

But there is more in this aspect of the case than the mere failure of the authority. Taking it that, although he might possibly remove during the recess, he could not suspend and appoint a Secretary *ad interim* except by virtue of the tenure-of-office law, and that it may be well pleaded in his defense, even though he may have insisted that he did not refer to, or follow, or recognize it, I think it cannot be a question among lawyers, that all the acts of a public officer are to be conclusively presumed to have been done under the law which authorized them. But then it will be said, as it has been in regard to the proof of changes made in the forms of commissions to make them harmonize with the now disputed law, and of other evidence of a kindred character, that this is only to set up the doctrine of estoppel, which, though not unreasonable, has been so often characterized as odious in the civil courts, against a defendant in a criminal proceeding.

I am ready to admit that estoppels are odious, because they exclude the truth, but have never supposed that they were so, when their effect was only to shut out falsehood. It was not for this purpose, however, in my view at least, that such evidence was offered; but only to contradict the President's assertions by his acts, and to show that when he pleads through his counsel, that if the law was valid he honestly believed the contrary, and that if it embraced the case of Mr. Stanton he innocently mistook its meaning, and did not intend willfully to misconstrue it, he stated what was not true.

And now, a few words only upon the general question of intent itself, which has been made to figure so largely in this cause, under the shadow of the multiplied averments in regard to it. I do not look upon those averments as at all material; and if not material, they are, as every lawyer knows, but mere surplusage which never vitiates, and it is never necessary to prove. I do not speak as a criminal lawyer, but there is no professional man, I think, who reads these charges, that will not detect in them something more, perhaps by way of abundant caution, than even the technical nicety of the criminal pleader. I do not know that even in the criminal courts, where an act is charged in clear violation of a law forbidding it, and especially if it involve the case of a public officer, that it is any more necessary to allege that he violated the law, with the *intent* to violate it, than to aver that he was not ignorant of the law, which every man is bound to know. The law presumes the intent from the act itself, which is a necessary inference, if the law is to be observed and its infraction punished; and the party committing it, is responsible for all the consequences, whether he intended them or not. It makes no difference about the motive, for wherever a statute forbids the doing of a thing, the doing it willfully, although without any corrupt motive, is indictable. (2 Dwarris, 677; 4 Term Rep., 457.) So when the President is solemnly arraigned to answer here to the charge that he has infringed the Constitution, or disobeyed the commands or violated any of the provisions of the tenure of office or any other law, he cannot plead either that he did it ignorantly or by mistake, because ignorance of the law excuses nobody, or that he did it only from the best of motives, and for the purpose of bringing the question of its efficacy, or his obligation to conform to it, to a legal test, even though he could prove the fact, as he has most signally failed to do in the case before you. The motives of men, which are hidden away in their own breasts, cannot generally be scrutinized, or taken into the account, where there is a violation of the law. An old Spanish proverb says, that there is a place—not to be named to ears polite—which is "paved with good intentions." If they, or even bad advice can be pleaded hereafter, in excuse for either neglect or violation of duty here, it will be something comfortable to die upon at least, and few tyrants will ever suffer for their crimes. If Andrew Johnson could plead, as he has actually done, in apology for his own dispensation with the test-oath law, or any other feature of his law-defying policy, that his only aim was to conciliate the rebels and facilitate the work of restoration, his great exemplar, whom he has so closely copied—the ill-advised and headstrong James II—might equally have pleaded that he did the very same thing in the interests of universal tolerance. The English monarch forfeited his throne and disinherited his heirs upon that cast. It remains to be seen whether our king is to run out the parallel.

I beg to say, however, in this connection, that I do not by any means admit, that a case like this is to be tried or judged by the rigid rules and narrow interpretations of the criminal courts. There is no question here of the life or liberty or property of the delinquent; it is a question only of official delinquency, involving, however, the life of a great State, and with it the liberties of a great people. If the defendant is convicted, he forfeits only his official place, and is, perhaps, disqualified from taking upon himself any other, which will be no very severe infliction, I suppose, unless the rebels themselves should be so fortunate as to come once more into the possession of the Government, and so weak as to trust a man who had been untrue to those who had honored him so generously before. The accusers here are forty millions of freemen, the accused but one, who claims to be their master; the issue, whether he shall be allowed to defy their will, under the pretext that he can govern them more wisely than their Congress, and to take the sword, and, in effect, the purse of the nation into his own hands.

On such an issue, and before such a tribunal, I should not have hesitated to stand upon the plain, unvarnished, untechnical narration of the facts, leaving the question as to their effect upon the interests of the nation, and their bearing upon the fitness of Andrew Johnson to hold the helm of this great State, to be decided by statesmen, instead of turning it over either to the quibbles of the lawyer, or the subtleties of the casuist. I have no patience for the disquisitions of the special pleader in a case like this. I take a broader view, one that, I think, is fully sustained by the authorities, and that is, that in cases such as this, the safety of the people, which is the supreme law, is the true rule, and the only rule that ought to govern. I do not propose to reargue that question now, because it seems to me something very like a self-evident proposition. If Andrew Johnson, in the performance of the duties of his high office, has so demeaned himself as to show that he is no respecter of the laws; that he defies the will of those who make them, and has encouraged disobedience to their behests; that he has fostered disaffection and discontent throughout the lately revolted States; that he is a standing obstacle to the restoration of the peace and tranquillity of this nation; that he claims and asserts the power of a dictator, by holding one of your great departments in abeyance, and arrogating to himself the absolute and uncontrollable right to remove, or suspend at his mere will, every executive officer of the Government, on the land and on the seas, and to supply their places without your agency, if, for any or all of these reasons, the Republic is no longer safe in his hands; then before heaven and earth, as the conservators of the nation's weal, as the trusted guardians of its most invaluable rights, as the depositaries of the most sacred and exalted trust that has ever been placed in the hands of man, it becomes your high and solemn and imperious duty, to see that the Republic shall take no detriment, and to speak peace to a disturbed and suffering land, by removing him from the trust he has abused, and the office that he has disgraced.

There are other points in this case on which I would have desired to comment if time and strength had been allowed to me for that purpose. It is only within the last few days that I have entertained the hope that the Senate would so far relax its rule as to enable me to obtain what, under the circumstances, is at best but an imperfect hearing, and I have felt it necessary, therefore, to confine myself to the leading arguments connected with the removal of the Secretary of War. I wish it to be understood, however, that I do not underrate the value of such of the articles as I have been obliged to pretermit. There is nothing in the whole case, I think, of graver import to the nation than the means adopted by the President for overthrowing the legislative power by fostering disobedience to its enactments and bringing its accepted organ into disrepute.

To this charge there are three answers. The first is the supposed constitutional right to the use of an unbridled tongue, which knows no difference between licentiousness and liberty. The second is the provocation supposed to have been offered in the language used by members of Congress in debate, in what seems to be forgotten to be their constitutional right, which not only protects them from challenge anywhere, but gives to them the right freely to criticise the public conduct of the President, over whom the law has placed them, by making him amenable to them for all his errors, as they are not to him. The third is the harmless jest, in the suggestion of a law to regulate the speech and manners of the President. If his counsel can find food for mirth in such a picture as the evidence has shown, I have no quarrel with their taste. The President may enjoy the joke, perhaps, himself. I do not think he can afford it, but history informs us that Nero. fiddled while Rome was burning. Whether he does or not, however, I trust that he will find a *censor morum* here as stern as Cato, in the judicial opinion of this body, that the man who so outrages public decency, either in his public or private character, in the pursuit of an object so treasonable as his, has demonstrated his unfitness longer to hold the high place of a Chief Magistrate of a free, intelligent, and moral people. I take leave of this unpalatable theme by remarking only that even the advocate of the people must feel, as a child of the Republic himself, while he is compelled to say thus much, that he would rather have turned his back, if it had been possible, on such a spectacle, and thrown a mantle over the nakedness that shames us all.

And now, American Senators, Representatives, and judges upon this mighty issue—joint heirs yourselves of that great inheritance of liberty that has descended to us all, and has just been ransomed and repurchased by a second baptism of blood—a few words more, and I have done.

If the responsibilities of the lawyer are such as to oppress him with their weight how immeasurably greater are your own! The House of Representatives has done its duty. The rest is now with you. While I have a trust in that God who went before our hosts, as he did before the armies of Israel, through the fiery trials that led so many of the flower of our youth to distant graves on southern battle-fields, which has never failed me in the darkest hour of the nation's agony, I cannot but realize that He has placed the destinies of this nation in your hands. Your decision here will either fall upon the public heart like a genial sunbeam, or fling a disastrous twilight, full of the gloomiest portents of coming evil, over the land. Say not that I exaggerate the issue or overcolor the picture. This, if it were true, would be but an error of much smaller consequence than the perilous mistake of underrating its importance. It is, indeed, but the catastrophe of the great drama which began three years ago with murder—the denouement of the mortal struggle between the power that makes the law and that which executes it—between the people themselves, and the chief of their own servants, who now undertakes to defy their will. What is your verdict to decide? Go to the evidence, to the plea of the President himself, and to the

defiant answer that he sends by his Tennessee counsel, and they will give you the true measure of the interests involved. It is not a question only whether or not Andrew Johnson is to be allowed to serve as President of the United States for the remainder of his term. It is the greater question whether you shall hold so long yourselves the power that the Constitution gives you by surrendering the higher one to him of suspending, dismissing, and appointing at his will and pleasure every executive officer in the Government from the highest to the lowest without your consent, and if possible the still higher one of disregarding your laws for the purpose of putting those laws on trial before they can be recognized. He has made this issue with you voluntarily and defiantly. If you acquit him upon it, you affirm all his imperial pretensions, and decide that no amount of usurpation will ever bring a Chief Magistrate to justice, because you will have laid down at his feet your own high dignity, along with your double function of legislators and advisers, which will be followed of course by that of your other, I will not say greater, office as judges. It will be a victory over you and us which will stir the heart of rebeldom with joy, while your dead soldiers will turn uneasily in their graves ; a victory to be celebrated by the exultant ascent of Andrew Johnson to the Capitol, like the conqueror in a Roman triumph, dragging not captive kings, but a captive Senate at his chariot wheels, and to be crowned by his reëntry into the possession of that Department of the Government over which this great battle has been fought. It is shown in evidence that he has already intimated that he would wait on your action here for that purpose. But is this all? Hug not to your bosoms, I entreat you, the fond illusion that it is all to end there. It is but the beginning of the end. If his pretensions are sustained, the next head that will fall as a propitiatory offering to the conquered South, will be that of the great chief who humbled the pride of the chivalry by beating down its serried battalions in the field, and dragging its traitor standard in the dust ; to be followed by the return of the rebel office-holders, and a general convulsion of the State which shall cast loose your reconstruction laws, and deliver over the whole theater of past disturbances to anarchy and ruin. Is this an exaggerated picture? Look to the history of the past and judge.

And, now, let me ask you, in conclusion, to turn your eyes but for a moment to the other side of the question, and see what are to be the consequences of a conviction—of such a verdict as, I think, the loyal people of this nation, with one united voice. demand at your hands. Do you shrink from the consequences? Are your minds disturbed by visions of impending trouble? The nation has already, within a few short years, been called to mourn the loss of a great Chief Magistrate, through the bloody catastrophe by which a rebel hand has been, unfortunately, enabled to lift this man into his place, and the jar has not been felt as the mighty machine of State, freighted with all the hopes of humanity, moved onward in its high career. This nation is too great to be affected seriously by the loss of any one man. Are your hearts softened by the touching appeals of the defendant's counsel, who say to you that you are asked to punish this man only for his divine mercy, his exalted charity to others? Mercy to whom? To the murdered Dostie and his fellows? To the loyal men whose carcases were piled in carts like those of swine, with the gore dripping from the wheels, in that holocaust of blood, that carnival of murder which was enacted in New Orleans? To those who perished in that second St. Bartholomew at Memphis, where the streets were reddened with the lurid light of burning dwellings, and the loyal occupants, who would have escaped, were cast back into the flames? The divine mercy itself is seasoned by justice, and waits only on contrition. This is no place for such emotions. If it be, it is mercy to loyalty and innocence, that cries aloud for the removal of this bold, bad man. If it be, remember, that while your loyal brethren are falling from day to day in southern cities by the assassin's knife, and the reports of the Freedmen's Bureau are replete with horrors at which the very cheek turns pale, your judgment here stains no scaffold with the blood of the victim. No lictor waits at your doors to execute your stern decree. It is but the crown that falls, while none but the historian stands by to gibbet the delinquent for the ages that are to come. No wail of woe will disturb your slumbers, unless it comes up from the disaffected and disappointed South, which will have lost the foremost of its friends. Your act will be a spectacle and an example to the nations, that will eclipse even the triumph of your arms, in the vindication of the public justice in the sublimer and more peaceful triumph of the law. The eyes of an expectant people are upon you. You have but to do your duty, and the patriot will realize that the good genius of the nation, the angel of our deliverance, is still about us and around us, as in the darkest hour of the nation's trial.

Mr. JOHNSON. Mr. Chief Justice, I move that the Senate take a recess for fifteen minutes.

The motion was agreed to; and at the expiration of the recess the Chief Justice resumed the chair and called the Senate to order.

Mr. Manager BUTLER. I ask leave of the President and Senators to make a short narration of facts, rendered necessary by what fell from Mr. Nelson, of counsel for the President, in his speech on Friday last, which will be found on pages 888, 889, and 890 of the record.

The CHIEF JUSTICE. If there be no objection the honorable Manager will proceed.

Mr. Manager BUTLER. This narration is, as I say, rendered necessary by what was said by Mr. Nelson, of counsel for the President, in his argument on Friday last, contained in pages 888, 889, and 890 of the record, in relation to Hon. J. S. Black, and the supposed connection of some of the Managers and members of the House with him in regard to the island of Alta Vela. This explanation becomes necessary because of the very anomalous course taken by the learned counsel in introducing in his argument what he calls a "statement of facts," not one of which would have been competent if offered in evidence, and upon which he founds an attack upon a gentleman not present, and from which he deduces insinuations injurious to some of the Managers and other gentlemen, members of the House of Representatives, who are not parties to the issue here, and who have no opportunity to be heard.

The learned counsel was strenuous in argument to prove that this was a court, and its proceedings were to be such only as are had in judicial tribunals. He therefore ought to have constrained himself, at least, to act in accordance with his theory. The veriest tyro in the law in the most benighted portion of the southern country ought to know that in no court, however rude or humble, would an attack be allowed upon the absent or counsel engaged in a cause upon a statement of pretended facts, unsupported by oath, unsifted by cross-examination, and which those to be affected by them had no opportunity either to verify or dispute.

After extracting the details of a document sent by his client to the Senate, the counsel proceeds in relation to a dispute concerning the island of Alta Vela:

"According to the best information I can obtain I state that on *the 9th of March,* 1868, General BENJAMIN F. BUTLER addressed a letter to J. W. Shaffer, in which he stated that he was 'clearly of opinion that, under the claim of the United States, its citizens have the exclusive right to take guano there,' and that he had never been able to understand why the Executive did not long since assert the rights of the Government and sustain the rightful claims of its citizens to the possession of the island *in the most forcible manner* consistent with the dignity and honor of the nation.

"This letter was concurred in and approved of by JOHN A. LOGAN, J. A. GARFIELD, W. H. KOONTZ, J. K. MOORHEAD, THADDEUS STEVENS, J. G. BLAINE, and JOHN A. BINGHAM, on the same day, 9th March, 1868.

"The letter expressing the opinion of Generals BUTLER, LOGAN, and GARFIELD was placed in the hands of the President by Chauncey F. Black, who, on the 16th March, 1868, addressed a letter to him in which he inclosed a copy of the same with the concurrence of THADDEUS STEVENS, JOHN A. BINGHAM, J. G. BLAINE, J. K. MOORHEAD, and WILLIAM H. KOONTZ.

"After the date of this letter, and while Judge Black was the counsel of the respondent in this cause, he had an interview with the President, in which he urged immediate action on his part and the sending an armed vessel to take possession of the island; and because the President refused to do so Judge Black, on the 19th March, 1868, declined to appear further as his counsel in this case.

"Such are the facts in regard to the withdrawal of Judge Black, according to the best information I can obtain. So far as the President is concerned, 'the head and front of his offending hath this extent—no more.'

"It is not necessary to my purpose that I should censure Judge Black or make any reflection upon or imputation against any of the honorable Managers.

"The island of Alta Vela, or the claim for damages, is said to amount in value to more than a million dollars, and it is quite likely that an extensive speculation is on foot. I have no reason to charge that any of the Managers are engaged in it, and presume that the letters were signed, as such communications are often signed, by members of Congress, through the importunity of friends.

"Judge Black, no doubt, thought it was his duty to other clients to press this claim; but how did the President view it?" * * * * * * *

"There are two or three facts to which I desire to call the attention of the Senate and the country in connection with these recommendations. They are, first, that they were all gotten up after this impeachment proceeding was commenced against the President of the United States. Keep the dates in mind, and you will see that such is the fact. Every one of them was gotten up after this impeachment proceeding was commenced against him."

It cannot fail to be evident, that while the counsel disclaims any imputation either upon Judge Black or the Managers in words, he so states what he claims to be the facts as to convey the very imputation disclaimed. Therefore it is that I have felt called upon to notice the insinuated calumny.

My personal knowledge of matters connected with the island of Alta Vela is very limited.

Some time in the summer of 1867, being in waiting on other business in the office of the Attorney General, Mr. Stanbery, I was present at an argument by Judge Black in behalf of the American citizens claiming an interest in that island. I there, for the first time, learned the facts agreed and in dispute concerning it by listening to and incidentally taking a part, on being appealed to, in the discussion. In February last my attention was next drawn to the matter of the spoliation and imprisonment of American citizens upon the island of Alta Vela by an inquiry of a personal friend, Colonel Shaffer, if I had any acquaintance with the question, and if so, would give him my opinion as a lawyer upon the merits of the controversy. To serve a friend simply, upon recollection of the discussion with the Attorney General, I gave him such "opinion," the rough draft of which I hold in my hand, which is without date, and which, being copied, I signed and placed in his hands. This I believe to have been in the early part of February; certainly before the act was committed by Andrew Johnson which brought on this impeachment. From that time until I saw my "opinion" published in the New York Herald, purporting to come from President Johnson, I never saw it or communicated with either of the gentlemen whose names appear in the counsel's statement attached thereto in any manner, directly or indirectly, in regard to it or the subject-matter of it, or the island of Alta Vela, or the claims of any person arising out of it or because of it. Thus far I am able to speak of my own knowledge.

Since the statement of the counsel "according to the best information he can obtain," I have made inquiry and from the best informa-

tion I can obtain find the facts to be as follows: that soon after the "opinion" was signed Colonel Shaffer asked Hon. JOHN A. LOGAN to examine the same question, presented him his brief of the facts, and asked him if he could concur in the opinion, which, after examination, Mr. LOGAN consented to do, and signed the original paper signed by myself. I may here remark that the recollection of General LOGAN and Colonel Shaffer concur with my own as to the time of these transactions. I have learned and believe that my "opinion" with the signature of General LOGAN attached was placed in the hands of Chauncey F. Black, esq., and by him handed to the President of the United States with other papers in the case. Mr. Black made a copy of my "opinion," and afterward at his convenience procured a member of Congress, a personal friend of his, one of the signers, to get the names of other members of Congress, two of whom happened to be Managers of the impeachment. This was done by a separate application to each without any concert of action whatever, or knowledge or belief that the paper was to be used in any way or for any purpose other than the expression of their opinions upon the subject-matter. This copy of my "opinion," when so signed, was a very considerable time after the original given to the President. I desire further to declare that I have no knowledge of or interest, directly or indirectly, in any claim whatever arising in any manner out of the island of Alta Vela other than as above stated.

In justice to the other gentlemen who signed the copy of the paper, I desire to annex hereto the affidavits of Chauncey F. Black, esq., and Colonel J. W. Shaffer, showing that neither of the gentlemen signing the paper had any interest or concern in the subject-matter thereof other than as above set forth.

While I acquit the learned counsel of any intentional falsity of statement as he makes it to his "best information," which must have been obtained from Andrew Johnson, yet the statement contains every element of falsehood, being both the *suppressio veri* and the *suggestio falsi* in that it says that on the 9th of March General BENJAMIN F. BUTLER addressed a letter to J. W. Shaffer, and that "this letter was concurred in and approved of by JOHN A. LOGAN, J. A. GARFIELD, W. H. KOONTZ, J. K. MOORHEAD, THADDEUS STEVENS, J. G. BLAINE, and JOHN A. BINGHAM on the same day, 9th March, 1868," when the President knew that the names of the five last-mentioned gentlemen were procured on a copy of the letter long after the original was in his hands.

Again, there is another deliberate falsehood in the thrice reiterated statement that these signatures were procured and sent to him for the purpose of intimidating him into doing an act after he was impeached, the propriety and legality of which was contrary to his judgment, when, in truth and in fact, the signatures were procured and sent to him in order, as he averred, to sustain him in doing what he himself declared was just and legal in the premises, and which he intended to do.

The use made of these papers is characteristic of Andrew Johnson, who usually raises issues of veracity with both friend and foe with whom he comes in contact:

I, Chauncey F. Black, attorney and counselor-at-law, do depose and say that the law firm of Black, Lamont & Co., have been counsel for years on behalf of Patterson & Marguiondo to recover their rights in the guano discovered by them in the island of Alta Vela, of which they had been deprived by force, and the imprisonment of their agents by some of the inhabitants of Dominica. As such counsel, we have argued the cause to the Secretary of State, and also to the President, before whom the question has been pending since July 19, 1867.

We have in various forms pressed the matter upon his attention, and he has expressed himself fully and freely satisfied with the justice of the claims of our clients and his conviction of his own duty to afford the desired relief, but had declined to act because of the opposition of the Secretary of State. General J. W. Shaffer having become associated with us in the case and having learned that General BUTLER had become acquainted with the merits of the case, procured his legal opinion upon it, and also a concurrence by General LOGAN. After receiving this opinion I inclosed it to the President. The time when this opinion was received, and whether it was dated, I do not recollect. The time that it was presented to the President by me can be established by the date of my letter inclosing it. Learning from a mutual friend that it would be desirable for the President to receive the recommendations of other members of Congress I carried a copy of the opinion to the House of Representatives and procured the signatures of some of my personal friends and asked them to procure the signatures of others which were attached to the copy. Some considerable time after I had forwarded the original I sent this copy so signed to the President. These signatures were procured upon personal application to the gentlemen severally, without any concert of action whatever on their part, and without any reference to any proceedings then pending in the then present action of Congress in regard to the President whatever.

From my relation to the case of Alta Vela, I have knowledge of all the rights and interest in it, or in relation to it, so that I am certain that neither of the gentlemen who signed the paper or copy have any interest in the claim or matter in dispute or in any part thereof, or arising therefrom in any manner, directly or indirectly, or contingently, and that all averment to the contrary from any source whatever is untrue in fact.   CHAUNCEY F. BLACK.

Sworn and subscribed before me this 28th day of April, A. D. 1868.   N. CALLAN,
[L. S.]   *Notary Public.*

To the best of my knowledge and belief the facts contained in the above affidavit are true in every particular.   J. W. SHAFFER.

Sworn and subscribed before me this 28th day of April, A. D. 1868.   N. CALLAN,
[L. S.]   *Notary Public.*

With this simple statement of the facts, Mr. President and Senators, I am content to leave the question of the history of Alta Vela.

Mr. NELSON. Mr. Chief Justice and Senators, as you have heard the statement of the honorable Manager, I trust you will permit me to make such reply as I deem fitting and appropriate to the present occasion. The honorable gentleman speaks——

The CHIEF JUSTICE. The counsel can proceed by unanimous consent. If there be no objection he will proceed.

Mr. NELSON. Of course I will not presume to proceed without leave of the Chief Justice and the Senate. I inferred from their silence that the Senate were willing to hear me.

The honorable gentleman speaks as to what he supposes to be the knowledge and the duty of a tyro in the law, and animadverts with some severity upon the introduction of this foreign subject by him in the course of the investigation. I beg leave to remind the honorable Senators that, so far as I am concerned, I did not introduce the topic without having, as I believed, just cause and just reason to do it; and whatever may be the gentleman's view in regard to a tyro in the legal profession, I beg leave to say to him, and to this Senate, that I never have seen the day in my life—not from the earliest moment when my license was signed down to the present time—when a client of mine was assailed, and assailed as I believed unjustly, that I did not feel it the very highest professional duty I owed upon the face of the earth to vindicate and defend him against the assault. My views may be, and probably are, different from those of the honorable gentleman and from the views of others. Without casting any censure upon my associates, I will say that if the duty had devolved on me to lead and conduct the investigation in this case, as it did not devolve, but upon those of longer and higher standing in the profession than myself, I would have met the gentleman on every occasion when he made his assaults upon the President of the United States, and I would have answered them from time to time as those charges were made; and I would not have permitted one of his insinuations to go unanswered, so far as an answer could be furnished on our side. When the honorable Manager—I am not alluding to the one who has just addressed the Senate, but to the honorable Manager who closed the argument so far as it has progressed [Mr. BOUTWELL]—addressed the Senate on the other side, and saw fit to draw in dark and gloomy colors a picture of the President of the United States, and of the influence he has over his Cabinet, and when he saw fit to represent them as serfs obedient to the control of their master, and to make allusion to the withdrawal of Judge Black, I deemed that a fitting and proper occasion, and so consider it still upon the most calm and mature reflection, for me, as one of the counsel for the President, to meet and answer it, and nail it to the counter, as I think I have done successfully.

You all know—and if need be I can hunt up the newspapers and can furnish the testimony —that when Judge Black retired from the President's cause it was published and proclaimed in newspapers hostile to the President that Judge Black, seeing that the case of the President was a desperate case, had withdrawn from it in disgust; and the very highest professional duty that can animate counsel under the heavens devolved on me when this imputation was contained in the address of the honorable Manager and alluded to in the connection in which it was, to vindicate the President of the United States against the public aspersions which had been made upon him. It was for that reason and no other that I spoke of it, not with any desire to make an assault upon the Managers.

While I treated them with civility, while I treated them with kindness, and, as I think, with very great forbearance, the honorable gentleman to-day has made imputations upon me which I hurl back with indignation and with scorn—undeserved imputations. I treated the gentlemen on the other side with courtesy and with kindness. He has rewarded me with insult and with outrage in the presence of the American Senate. It will be for you, Senators, to judge whose demeanor is most proper before you, that of the honorable gentleman who foully and falsely charges me with insinuating calumny, or my course in vindicating the President of the United States in the discharge of my professional duty here. So far as any question that the gentleman desires to make of a personal character with me is concerned this is not the place to make it. Let him make it elsewhere if he desires to do it.

Mr. YATES. Mr. President, I rise to call the counselor to order.

Mr. NELSON. Mr. Chief Justice and Senators, I will endeavor to comply with the suggestion of the Senator. I do not wish to make use of any language improper in this tribunal, but I hope that Senators will pardon me for repelling the strong remarks made by the gentleman on the other side. But let it pass. What I desire to say to you, Senators, and that is much more important than anything else, is this: when I made the statement which I did to the Senate, I made it with a full knowledge, as I believed, of what I was doing. It may be possible, Senators, that I may have committed an error as to the date of the paper which was signed by Messrs. LOGAN and the other Managers. My recollection is that that paper is without date, and I took it for granted that it was signed on the same day, the 9th of March, that was mentioned by the honorable gentleman; but that is an immaterial error, if it be one. I had the letters in my possession on the day I addressed you, and if the gentleman had seen fit to deny any statement contained in those letters upon that day I had them here ready to read to the Senate. I had no knowledge that this subject would be called up to-day until the honorable gentleman told me during your adjournment of a few minutes. Since that notification I have sent for the letters. I was fearful, however, that they would not be here in time for me to read them now; but if it becomes necessary I shall ask the leave of the Senate to read those letters to-morrow before my associate shall resume his argument in the case. I shall have them, and as this topic is introduced by the honorable gentleman, and introduced, too, in terms of censure of me, I shall ask the honorable Senate to allow me to read those letters.

What is the point? If there be any point in connection with this matter, what is it, and why did I introduce the matter here at all in vindication of the President of the United States against the imputation that was made about Judge Black? Why did I refer to the letters at all? It was for the purpose of showing, in answer to the honorable Manager, Mr. BOUTWELL, this great fact in explanation of the conduct with Judge Black, that the President of the United States had been placed in a dilemma such as no man under accusation had ever been placed in before, for the purpose of showing that, so far as that correspondence is concerned, it was a correspondence which arose after the articles of impeachment had been agreed upon, and probably after they had been preferred to the Senate. It was for that purpose that I introduced the correspondence. It has excited, awakened, and aroused the attention of this whole nation that the counsel for the President of the United States should abandon his cause, and that the true secret of that abandonment has not grown out of any insult the President of the United States rendered to the counsel, out of any injury which he did to them, but has grown out of the fact that a claim was pressed to the island referred to under the circumstances stated. Now, I will go further than I did the other day, and I will answer for it here and anywhere else ; I believe that Judge Black acted improperly, under those circumstances, in withdrawing his services from the President of the United States, according to the best lights I have on the subject. Here is this accusation presented against him, and here is this astonishing claim presented to him, signed by four of the Managers of this impeachment, presented at this extraordinary period of time, presented when this impeachment was hanging over him ; and I maintain still that I had the right, and that it was my solemn and bounden duty, to vindicate him against the charge that was preferred.

Mr. Manager BUTLER. Does the gentleman know what he is saying; "a claim signed by four of the Managers?"

Mr. NELSON. I meant to say letter. If I said "claim" I meant to say there was an indorsement. I am glad the gentleman has corrected me. What I mean to say, Senators—I may have used some word I did not intend to use—the idea that I intend to convey is that a letter was in the first instance signed by the honorable Manager, General BUTLER, that there was an indorsement of that letter by three other members of the House of Representatives who are Managers in this case; that this letter and the indorsement of it had relation to the Alta Vela claim, that the subject was brought up to the consideration of the President of the United States pending this impeachment, and that whether the letter in-dorsing General BUTLER'S letter was signed on the 9th of March or at a later period is wholly immaterial. It was signed after this impeach-ment proceeding was commenced, and Judge Black endeavored to get the attention of the President to the claim and to have him decide upon it, as I am informed and believe, though I have no written evidence of that fact; Judge Black urged it upon him after this impeach-ment proceeding commenced and after Judge Black had met some of the other counsel and myself in the council chamber of the President. I was not present at that time, but I have it, I may say, from the lips of the President him-self, and I believe it to be true, that Judge Black urged upon him a decision of this claim, and that his answer, among others, was that he did not think it a proper time for him to act on the claim, because the Congress of the Uni-ted States was in session, and that if it was right and proper for a vessel to be sent down there or any act of public hostility to take place, the President of the United States answered Judge Black, as I am informed and believe, by tell-ing him that Congress was in session, and by asking him to call upon Congress to pass any law that might be necessary for that purpose, and that it was not proper for him to interfere in it. This is all—

Mr. GRIMES rose.

Mr. NELSON. I will relieve the gentleman by stating that I have said as much as I desired to say. I will ask permission, when I receive those letters, in some form to put them before the Senate, and with this remark I will take my seat.

Mr. Manager BUTLER. I trust not until they are shown not to have been mutilated.

Mr. NELSON. Sir!

Mr. Manager LOGAN rose.

Mr. EDMUNDS. Mr. President, I ask that the argument in the cause may proceed. This matter has nothing to do with any question before us.

The CHIEF JUSTICE. The argument on behalf of the President will proceed.

Mr. CAMERON. Mr. President, I trust the Manager from Illinois will be allowed to be heard.

Mr. Manager LOGAN. Mr. President, if there is no objection I merely desire to say—

The CHIEF JUSTICE. The honorable Manager can proceed, if there be no objection.

Mr. Manager LOGAN. Just a moment. I merely wish to correct the gentleman from Tennessee, the counsel for the respondent, by saying that he is mistaken about this letter having been signed after the impeachment commenced by either General BUTLER or my-self. I know well when I signed it, and the gentleman will find the correction, if he will examine thoroughly, and will certainly be kind enough to make it. I signed the letter long before there was anything thought of impeach-ment.

Mr. NELSON. If you will let me do so, I will say with great pleasure that I had no de-sign to misrepresent any gentleman concerned in the cause; and in order that the matter may be decided I will have the letter brought here. I may have fallen into an error about the date, but my understanding was that it was after the impeachment proceedings were commenced; but to obviate all difficulty I will produce the letter itself, no matter whether it shows I am mistaken or not. If it shows that I am mis-taken I will bring it here in fairness to the Senate; and if it shows that I am right I will bring it again in fairness to the Senate. That is all the gentleman can ask, I am sure. I may possibly be mistaken.

Several SENATORS. Let the argument pro-ceed.

The CHIEF JUSTICE. The argument on the part of the President will proceed.

WILLIAM M. EVARTS, esq., of counsel for the respondent, addressed the Senate as follows:

I am sure, Mr. Chief Justice and Senators, that no man of a thoughtful and considerate temper would wish to take any part in the sol-emn transaction which proceeds to-day unless held to it by some quite perfect obligation of duty. Even if we were at liberty to confine our solicitudes within the horizon of politics; even if the interests of the country and of the party in power, and if duty to the country and duty to the party in power, (as is sometimes the case, and as public men so easily persuade themselves is, or may be, the case in any junc-ture,) were commensurate and equivalent, who will provide a chart and compass for the wide, uncertain sea that lies before us in the imme-diate future? Who shall determine the cur-rents that shall flow from the event of this stu-pendous political controversy; who measure their force; and who assume to control the storms that it may breed?

But if we enlarge the scope of our responsi-bility and of our vision, and take in the great subjects that have been constantly pressing upon our minds, who is there so sagacious in human affairs, who so confident of his sagacity, who so circumspect in treading among grave responsibilities and so assured of his circum-spection, who so bold in his forecast of the fu-ture, and so approved in his prescience, as to see, and to see clearly, through this day's busi-ness?

Let us be sure, then, that no man should be here as a volunteer or lift a little finger to jostle the struggle and contest between the great forces of our Government, of which we are witnesses, in which we take part, and which we, in our several vocations, are to assist in determining.

Of the absolute and complete obligation which convenes the Chief Justice of the United States and its Senators in this court for the trial of this impeachment, and of its authentic commission from the Constitution, there can be no doubt. So, too, of the deputed authority of these honorable Managers, and their presence in obedience to it, and the attendance of the House of Representatives itself in aid of their argument and their appeal, there is as little doubt. The President of the United States is here, in submission to the same Constitution, in obedience to it, and in the duty which he owes by the obligation he has assumed to preserve, protect, and defend it. The right of the President to appear by counsel of his choice makes it as clearly proper, under the obligations of a liberal profession, and under the duty of a citizen of a free State of sworn fidelity to the Constitution and the laws, that we should attend upon his defense; for though no distinct vocation and no particular devotion to the more established forms of public service hovers our presence, yet no man can be familiar with the course of the struggles of law, of government, of liberty in the world, not to know that the defense of the accused becomes the trial of the Constitution and the protection of the public safety.

It is neither by a careless nor capricious distribution of the most authentic service to the State that Cicero divides it among those who manage political candidacies, among those who defend the accused, and among those who in the Senate determined the grave issues of war and peace and all the business of the State; for it is in facts and instances that the people are taught their Constitution and their laws, and it is by fact and on instances that their laws and their Constitutions are upheld and improved. Constitutions are framed; laws established; institutions built up; the processes of society go on until at length by some opposing, some competing, some contending forces in the State, an individual is brought into the point of collision, and the clouds surcharged with the great forces of the public welfare burst over his head. It is then that he who defends the accused, in the language of Cicero, and in our own recognition of the pregnant instances of English and American history, is held to a distinct public service.

As, then, duty has brought us all here to this august procedure and has assigned to each of us his part in it, so through all its responsibilities and to the end we must surrender ourselves to its guidance. Thus following, our footsteps shall never falter or be misled; and leaning upon its staff, no man need fear that it will break or pierce his side.

The service of the constitutional procedure of impeachment in our brief history as a nation has really touched none of the grave interests that are involved in the present trial. Discarding the first occasion in which it was moved, being against a member of the Senate, as coming to nothing important, political or judicial, unless to determine that a member of this body was not an officer of the United States; and the next trial, wherein the accusa-

tion against Judge Pickering partook of no qualities except of personal delinquency or misfortune, and whose result gives us nothing to be proud of, and to constitutional law gives no precedent except that an insane man may be convicted of crime by a party vote; and the last trial of Judge Humphreys, where there was no defense, and where the matters of accusation were so plain and the guilt so clear that it was understood to be, by accused, accusers, and court, but a mere formality, and we have trials, doubtless of interest, of Judge Chase and of Judge Peck. Neither of these ever went for a moment beyond the gravity of an important and solemn accusation of men holding dignified, valuable, eminent, public judicial trusts; and their determination in favor of the accused left nothing to be illustrated by their trials except that even when the matter in imputation and under investigation is wholly of personal fault and misconduct in office politics will force itself into the tribunal.

But what do we behold here? Why, Mr. Chief Justice and Senators, all the political power of the United States of America is here. The House of Representatives is here as accuser; the President of the United States is here as the accused; and the Senate of the United States is here as the court to try him, presided over by the Chief Justice, under the special constitutional duty attributed to him. These powers of our Government are here, this our Government is here, not for a pageant or a ceremony; not for concord of action in any of the duties assigned to the Government in the conduct of the affairs of the nation; but here in the struggle and contest as to whether one of them shall be made to bow by virtue of constitutional authority confided to the others, and this branch of the political power of the United States shall prove his master. Crime and violence have placed all portions of our political Government at some disadvantage. The crime and violence of the rebellion have deprived this House of Representatives and this Senate of the full attendance of members that might make up the body under the Constitution of the United States, when it shall have been fully reëstablished over the whole country. The crime and violence of assassination have placed the executive office in the last stage of its maintenance under mere constitutional authority. There is no constitutional elected successor of the President of the United States, taking his power under the terms of the Constitution and by the authority of the suffrage; and you have now before you the matter to which I shall call your attention, not intending to anticipate here the discussion of constitutional views and doctrines, but simply the result upon the Government of the country which may flow from your determination of this cause under the peculiar circumstances in which, for the first time, too, in the history of the Government, a true political trial takes place.

If you shall acquit the President of the United States from this accusation all things will be as they were before. The House of Representatives will retire to discharge their usual duties in legislation, and you will remain to act with them in those duties and to divide with the President of the United States the other associated duties of an executive character which the Constitution attributes to you. The President of the United States, too, dismissed from your presence uncondemned, will occupy through the constitutional term his place of authority, and however ill the course of politics may go or however well, the Government and its Constitution will have received no shock. But if the President shall be condemned, and if by authority under the Constitution necessarily to be exerted upon such condemnation he shall be removed from office, there will be no President of the United States; for that name and title is accorded by the Constitution to no man who has not received the suffrages of the people for the primary or the alternative elevation to that place. A new thing will have occurred to us; the duties of the office will have been annexed to some other office, will be discharged *virtute officii* and by the tenure which belongs to the first office. Under the legislation of the country early adopted, and a great puzzle to the Congress, that designation belongs to this Senate itself to determine by an officer of its own gaining the right under the legislation of 1792 to add to his office conferred by the Senate the performance of the duties of President of the United States, the two offices running along. Whatever there may be of novelty, whatever of disturbance, in the course of public affairs thus to arise from a novel situation, is involved in the termination of this cause; and therefore there is directly proposed to you, as a necessary result from one determination of this cause, this novelty in our Constitution: a great nation whose whole frame of government, whose whole scheme and theory of politics rest upon the suffrage of the people, will be without a President, and the office sequestered will be discharged by a member of the body whose judgment has sequestered it.

I need not attract your attention, long since called to it, doubtless, in your own reflections, *more familiar than I am with the routine, to what will follow in the exercise of those duties; and you will see at once that the situation, from circumstances for which no man is responsible, is such as to bring into the gravest possible consequences the act that you are to perform. If the President of the United States, elected by the people, and having standing behind him the second officer of the people's choice, were under trial, no such disturbance or confusion of constitutional duties, and no such shock upon the feelings and traditions of the people, would be effected; but, as I have said, crime and violence, for which none of the agents of the Government are responsible, have

brought us into this situation of solicitude and of difficulty.

It will be seen, then, that as this trial brings the legislative power of the Government confronted with the executive authority, and its result is to deprive the nation of a President and to vest the office in the Senate, it is indeed the trial of the Constitution; over the head and in the person of the Chief Magistrate who fills the great office the forces of this contest are gathered, and this is the trial of the Constitution; and neither the dignity of the great office which he holds, nor any personal interest that may be felt in one so high in station, nor the great name and force of these accusers, the House of Representatives, speaking for "all the people of the United States," nor the august composition of this tribunal, which brings together the Chief Justice of the great court of the country and the Senators who have States for their constituents, which recalls to us in the mere etiquette of our address the combined splendors of Roman and of English jurisprudence and power—not even this spectacle forms any important part in the watchful solicitude with which the people of this country are gazing upon this procedure. The sober, thoughtful people of this country, never fond of pageants when pageants are the proper thing, never attending to pageants when they cover real issues and interests, are thinking of far other things than these.

Mr. Chief Justice, it is but a few weeks since the great tribunal in which you habitually preside, and where the law speaks with authority for the whole nation, adjourned. Embracing, as it does, the great province of international law, the great responsibility of adjusting between State and General Government, the conflicting interests and passions belonging to our composite system, and with determining the limits between the coördinate branches of the Government, there is one other duty assigned to it in which the people of the country feel a nearer and a deeper interest. It is as the guardian of the bill of rights of the Constitution, as the watchful protector of the liberties of the people against the encroachments of law and government, that the people of the United States look to the Supreme Court with the greatest attention and with the greatest affection. That court having before it a subject touching the liberty of the citizen finds the hamstring of its endeavor and its energy to interpose the power of the Constitution in the protection of the Constitution cut by the sharp edge of a congressional enactment, and in its breast carries away from the judgment-seat the Constitution and the law to be determined, if ever, at some future time and under some happier circumstances.

Now, in regard to this matter, the people of the United States give grave attention. They exercise their supervision of the conduct of all their agents, of whom, in any form and in any capacity and in any majesty, they have not yet learned to be afraid. The people of this country have had nothing in their experience of the last six years to make them fear anybody's oppression, anybody's encroachments, anybody's assaults, anybody's violence, anybody's war. Masters of this country, and masters of every agent and agency in it, they bow to nothing but the Constitution, and they honor every public servant that bows to the Constitution. And at the same time, by the action of the same Congress, the people see the President of the United States brought as a criminal to your bar, accused by one branch of Congress, to be tried by the other, his office, as I have said, to be put in commission and an election ordered. He greatly mistakes who supposes that the people of the United States look upon the office of President, the great name and power that represents them in their collective capacity, in their united power, in their combined interests, with less attachment than upon any other of the departments of this Government. The President is, in the apprehension and in the custom of the people of the United States, the Magistrate, the authority for whom they have that homage and that respect which belong to the elective office. His oath of office is as familiar to the people of this country as it is to you, for they heard it during the perils of the war from lips that they revered, and they have seen its immense power under the resources of this Constitution of theirs and supported by their fidelity to maintain the contest of this Government against all comers to sustain the Constitution and the law.

It has been spoken of here as if the President's oath were simply an oath to discharge faithfully the duties of his office, and as if the principal duty of the office was to execute the laws of Congress. Why, that is not the President's oath; that portion of it is the common oath of everybody in authority to discharge the duties of his office; but the peculiar oath of the President, the oath of the Constitution, is in the larger portion of it which makes him the sworn preserver, protector, and defender of the Constitution itself; and that is an office and that is an oath which the people of the United States have intrusted and exacted to and from no other public servant but the President of the United States. And when they conferred that power and exacted that duty they understood its tremendous responsibilities, the tremendous oppositions it might encounter, and they understood their duty implied in the suffrage that had conferred the authority and exacted the obligation to maintain him in it—to maintain him in it as against foreign aggression, as against domestic violence, as against encroachments from whatever quarter, under the guise of congressional or whatever authority, upon the true vigor of the Constitution of the United States.

President Lincoln's solemn declaration upon which he gained strength for himself and by which he gave strength to the people, "I have a solemn vow registered in heaven that I will preserve, protect, and defend the Constitution of the United States," carried him and carried the people following him through the struggles, the dangers, the vicissitudes of the rebellion; and that vow, as a legend, now adorns the halls of legislation in more than one State of the Union. This oath of the President, this duty of the President, the people of this country do not in the least regard as personal to him; but it is an oath and a duty assumed and to be performed as their representative, in their interest, and for their honor; and they have determined, and they will adhere to their determination, that the oath shall not be taken in vain, for that little phrase "to the best of my ability," which is the modest form in which the personal obligation is assumed, means, when conferred upon the ability of the President, the ability of the country; and most magnificently did the people pour out its resources in aid of that oath of President Lincoln; and so when the shock comes, not in the form of violence, of war, of rebellion, but of a struggle between the forces of the Government in regard to constitutional authority, the people of the United States regard the President as then bound to the special fidelity of watching that all the departments of this Government obey the Constitution as well as that he obeys it himself.

They give him no assumption of authority beyond the laws and the Constitution, but all the authority and all the resources of the laws and the Constitution are open to him, and they will see to it that the President of the United States, whoever he may be, in regard to the office and its duty shall not take this oath in vain if they have the power to maintain him in its performance. That indeed the Constitution is above him, as it is above all of the servants of the people, as it is above the people themselves until their sovereignty shall choose to change it, they do not doubt. And thus all their servants, President and Congress and whatever authority, are watched by the people of the United States in regard to obedience to the Constitution.

And not disputing the regularity, the complete authenticity, and the adequate authority of this entire procedure, from accusation through trial and down to sentence, the people yet claim the right to see and to know that it is duty to the Constitution observed and felt throughout that brings the result, whatever it may be. Thus satisfied, they adhere to the Constitution, but they do not purpose to change it. They are converts of no theories of congressional omnipotence. They understand none of the nonsense of the Constitution being superior to the law except that the law must be obeyed and the Constitution not. They know their Government, and they mean to maintain it; and when they hear that this tremendous enginery of impeachment and trial and threatened conviction or sentence, if the law and the facts will justify it, has been brought into play, that this power which has lain in the Constitution, like a sword in its sheath, is now drawn, they wish to know what the crime is that the President is accused of. They understand that treason and bribery are great offenses, and that a ruler guilty of them should be brought into question and deposed. They are ready to believe that, following the law of that enumeration, there may be other great crimes and misdemeanors touching the conduct of Government and the welfare of the State that may equally fall within the jurisdiction and the duty. But they wish to know what the crimes are. They wish to know whether the President has betrayed our liberties or our possessions to a foreign State. They wish to know whether he has delivered up a fortress or surrendered a fleet. They wish to know whether he has made merchandise of the public trust and turned authority to private gain. And when informed that none of these things are charged, imputed, or even declaimed about, they yet seek further information and are told that he has removed a member of his Cabinet.

The people of this country are familiar with the removal of members of Cabinets and all persons in authority. That on its mere statement does not strike them as a grave offense needing the interposition of this special jurisdiction. Removal from office is not with the people of this country, especially those engaged in politics, a terror or a disagreeable subject; indeed it may be said that it maintains a great part of the political forces of this country; that removal from office is a thing in the Constitution, in the habit of its administration. I remember to have heard it said that an old lady once summed up an earnest defense of a stern dogma of Calvinism, that if you took away her "total depravity" you took away her religion, [laughter;] and there are a great many people in this country that if you take away removal from office you take away all their politics. So that, on that mere statement, it does not strike them as either an unprecedented occurrence or as one involving any great danger to the State.

"Well, but how comes it to be a crime?" they inquire. Why, Congress passed a law for the first time in the history of the Government undertaking to control by law this matter of removal from office; and they provided that if the President should violate it it should be a misdemeanor, and a high misdemeanor; and now he has removed, or undertaken to remove, a member of his Cabinet, and he is to be removed himself for that cause. He undertook to make an *ad interim* Secretary of War, and you are to have made for you an *ad interim* President in consequence!

That is the situation. "Was the Secretary of War removed?" they inquire. No; he was not removed, he is still Secretary, still in possession of the Department. Was force used? Was violence meditated, prepared, attempted, applied? No; it was all on paper, and all

went no further than making the official attitude out of which a judgment of the Supreme Court could be got. And here the Congress intercepting again and in reference to this great office, this great authority of the Government instead of the liberty of the private citizen, recourse to the Supreme Court, has interposed the procedure of trial and impeachment of the President to settle by its own authority this question between it and the Executive. The people see and the people feel that under this attitude of Congress there seems to be a claim of right and an exercise of what is supposed to be a duty, to prevent the Supreme Court of the United States interposing its serene judgment in the collisions of Government and of laws upon either the framework of the Government or upon the condition and liberty of the citizen. And they are not slow to understand, without the aid of the very lucid and very brave arguments of these honorable Managers, that it is a question between the omnipotence of Congress and the supremacy of the Constitution of the United States; and that is an issue on which the people have no doubt, and from the beginning of their liberties they have had a clear notion that tyranny was as likely to be exercised by a Parliament or a Congress as by anybody else.

The honorable Managers have attracted our notice to the principles and the motives of the American Revolution as having shown a determination to throw off the tyranny of a king, and they have told us that that people will not bend its neck to the usurpations of a President. That people will not bend its neck to the usurpations of anybody. But the people of the United States know that their fathers went to war against the tyranny of Parliament, claiming to be good subjects of the king and ready to recognize his authority, preserving their own legislative independence, and against the tyranny of Parliament they rebelled; and, as a necessity finally of securing liberty against Parliament, severed their connection with the mother country; and if any honorable member of either House will trace the working of the ideas in the Convention that framed the Constitution of the United States he will discover that inordinate power which should grow up to tyranny in the Congress was more feared, more watched, more provided against than any other extravagance that the workings of our Government might be supposed possible to lead to.

Our people, then, are unwilling that our Government should be changed; they are unwilling that the date of our Constitution's supremacy should be fixed, and that any department of this Government should grow too strong or claim to be too strong for the restraints of the Constitution. If men are wise they will attain to what was sagacious, and if obeyed in England might have saved great political shocks, and which is true for our obedience and for the adoption of our people now as it was then.

Said Lord Bacon to Buckingham, the arbitrary minister of James I:

"As far as it may lie in you, let no arbitrary power be intruded; the people of this kingdom love the laws thereof, and nothing will oblige them more than a confidence of the free enjoyment of them; what the nobles upon an occasion once said in Parliament, '*Nolumus leges Angliæ mutari*,' is imprinted in the hearts of all the people."—1 *Bacon's Works*, p. 712.

And in the hearts of all the people of this country the supremacy of the Constitution and obedience to it are imprinted, and whatever progress new ideas of parliamentary government instead of executive authority dependent upon the direct suffrage to the people may have been made with theorists or with statesmen, they have made no advance whatever in the hearts or in the heads of the people of this country.

I know that there are a good many persons who believe that a written constitution for this country, as for any other nation, is only for a nascent state and not for one that has acquired the pith and vigor of manhood. I know that it is spoken of as the swathing bands that may support and strengthen the puny limbs of infancy, but shame and encumber the maturity of vigor. This I know, and in either House I imagine sentiments of that kind have been heard during the debates of the last two Congresses; but that is not the feeling or the judgment of the people; and this in their eyes, in the eyes of foreign nations, in the eyes of the enlightened opinion of mankind is the trial of the Constitution, not merely in that inferior sense of the 'determination whether its powers accorded to one branch or other of the Government have this or that scope and impression and force, but whether a Government of a written constitution can maintain itself in the forces prescribed and attributed by the fundamental law, or whether the immense passions and interests of a wealthy and powerful and populous nation will force asunder all the bonds of the Constitution, and in the struggle of strength and weight the natural forces, uncurbed by the supreme reason of the State, will determine the success of one and the subjection of the other.

Now, Senators, let us see to it that in this trial and in this controversy we understand what is at stake and what is to be determined. Let us see to it that we play our part as it should be played and under the motives and for the interests that should control statesmen and judges. If, indeed, this, our closely cinctured Liberty, is at last to loosen her zone and her stern monitor, Law, debauched and drunken with this new wine of opinion that is crushed daily from ten thousand presses throughout this land, is to withdraw its guardianship, let us be counted with those who with averted eye and reverent step backward seek to veil this shameless revelry, and not with those who exult and cheer at its excesses. Let us so act as that what we do and what we purpose and what we wish shall be to build up the State, to give

C. I.—45.

new stability to the forces of the Government, to cure the rash passions of the people, so that it may be said of each one of us, *ad Rempublicam firmandam et ad stabiliendas vires et sanandum populum omnis ejus purgebat institutio.*

Thus acting, thus supported, doubt not the result shall be in accord with these high aspirations, these noble impulses, these exalted duties; and whether or no the forces of this Government shall feel the shock of this special jurisdiction in obedience to law, to evidence, to justice, to duty, then you will have built up the Government, amplified its authority, and taught the people renewed homage to authority.

And now, this brings me, Mr. Chief Justice and Senators, to an inquiry asked very early in this cause with emphasis and discussed with force, with learning, and with persistence, and that is, is this a court? I must confess that I have heard defendants arguing that they were *coram non judice* before somebody that was not a judge, but I never heard till now of a plaintiff or a prosecutor coming in and arguing that there was not any court, that his case was *coram non judice.* Nobody is wiser than the intrepid Manager who assumed the first assault upon this court, and he knew that the only way he could prevent his cause from being turned out of court was to turn the court out of his cause, [laughter;] and if the expedient succeeds his wisdom will be justified by the result, and yet it would be a novelty. It is said:

"There is no word in the Constitution which gives the slightest coloring to the idea that this is a court, except that in this particular case the Chief Justice must preside."

So that the Chief Justice's gown is the only shred or patch of justice that there is within these Halls; and it is only accidentally that that is here owing to the peculiar character of the inculpated defendant.

"This is a Senate to hold an inquest of office upon Andrew Johnson."

And I suppose, therefore, to find a verdict of "office found." Certainly, it is sought for. I have not observed in your rule that each Senator is to rise in his place and say "office found," or "office not found." Probably every Senator does not expect to find it. Your rules, your Constitution, your habit, your etiquette call it a court, assume that there is some procedure here of a judicial nature; and we found out finally on our side of this controversy that it was so much of a court at least that we could not put a leading question in it; and that is about the extreme exercise of the authority of a court in regard to the conduct of procedure that we lawyers habitually discover.

The Constitution, as has been pointed out to you, makes this a court; it makes its proceeding a trial; it assigns a judgment; it accords a power of punishment to its procedure; and it provides that a jury in all judicial proceedings of a criminal character shall be necessary except in this court and on this form of procedure. We may assume, then, that so far as words go, it is a court and nothing but a court.

But it is a question the honorable Manager says, "of substance and not of form." He concedes that if it be a court you must find upon the evidence something to make out the guilt of the offender to secure a judgment, and he argues against its being a court, not from any nice criticism of words or forms, but, as he expresses it, for the substance. He has instructed you, by many references and by an interesting and learned brief appended to his opening speech, in English precedents and authority to show that it is almost anything but a court; and perhaps during the hundreds of years in which the instrument of impeachment was used as a political engine, if you look only to the judgment and the reasons of the judgment you would not think it was really a very judicial proceeding; but that through all the English history, it was a proceeding in court, controlled by the rules of the court as a court, cannot be doubted.

Indeed, as we all know, though the learned Manager has not insisted upon it, the presence of the trial under the peculiar procedure and jurisdiction of impeachment in the House of Lords was but a part of the general jurisdiction of the House of Lords as the great court of the kingdom in all matters civil and criminal; and one of the favorite titles of the Lords of Parliament in these earlier days was "judges of Parliament." And now the House of Lords in England is the supreme court of that country as distinctly as our great tribunal of that name is of this country.

But one page of pretty sound authority, I take it, will put to flight all these dreamy, misty notions about a law and procedure of Parliament in this country and in this tribunal that is to supersede the Constitution and the laws of our country, when I show you what Lord Chancellor Thurlow thought of that subject as prevalent or expected to prevail in England. In Hastings's trial, Lord Loughborough having endeavored to demonstrate that the ordinary rules of proceeding in criminal cases did not apply to parliamentary impeachments, which could not be shackled by the forms observed in the courts below, Lord Thurlow said:

"My lords, with respect to the laws and usage of Parliament, I utterly disclaim all knowledge of such laws. It has no existence. True it is, in times of despotism and popular fury, when to impeach an individual was to crush him by the strong hand of power, of tumult, or of violence, the laws and usage of Parliament were quoted in order to justify the most iniquitous or atrocious acts. But in these days of light and constitutional government, I trust that no man will be tried except by the laws of the land, a system admirably calculated to protect innocence and to punish crime."

And after showing that in all the State trials under the Stuart reigns, and even down to that of Sacheverel, in every instance were to be found the strongest marks of tyranny, injustice, and oppression. Lord Thurlow continued:

"I trust your lordships will not depart from recognized, established laws of the land. The Commons may impeach, your lordships are to try the cause; and the same rules of evidence, the same legal forms which obtain in the courts below, will, I am confident, be observed in this assembly."—Wraxall's Memoirs, p. 275.

But the learned Manager did not tell us what this was if it was not a court. It is true he said it was a Senate, but that conveys no idea. It is not a Senate conducting legislative business; it is not a Senate acting upon executive business; it is not a Senate acting in caucus on political affairs; and the question remains, if it is not a court what is it? If this is not an altar of justice which we stand about, if we are not all ministers here of justice, to feed its sacred flame, what is the altar and what do we do here about it? It is an altar of sacrifice if it is not an altar of justice; and to what divinity is this altar erected? What but the divinity of party hate and party rage, a divinity to which we may ascribe the Greek character given of Envy, that it is at once the worst and the justest divinity, for it dwarfs and withers its worshipers. That, then, is the altar that you are to minister about, and that the savage demon you are to exalt here in displacing Justice.

Our learned Managers, representing the House of Representatives, do not seem to have been at all at pains to conceal the party spirit and the party hate which displayed itself in the haste, in the record, and in the maintenance of this impeachment. To show you what progress may make in the course of thirty years in the true ideas of the Constitution, and of the nature of impeachments, let me read to you what the managers of the impeachment of Judge Peck had to say in this behalf. And a pretty solid body of managers they were, too—Judge Ambrose Spencer, of New York; Mr. Henry R. Storrs, of New York; Mr. McDuffie, of South Carolina; Mr. Buchanan, of Pennsylvania, and Mr. Wickliffe, of Kentucky. Ambrose Spencer, as stern a politician as he was an upright judge, opened the case, and had a word to say on the subject of party spirit and party hate. Let me ask your attention to it:

"There is, however, one cheering and consolatory reflection. The House of Representatives, after a patient and full examination, came to the resolution to impeach Judge Peck by a very large majority; and the record will show an absence of all party feeling. Could I believe that that baleful influence had mingled itself with and predominated in that vote no earthly consideration could have prevailed on me to appear here as one of the prosecutors of this impeachment. I have not language to express the abhorrence of my soul at the indulgence of such unhallowed feelings on such a solemn procedure."—Peck's Trial, p. 289.

Mr. Manager BUTLER talked to you many hours. Did he say anything wiser, or juster, or safer for the Republic than that? Judge Spencer knew what it was to be a judge and to be a politician. For twenty years while he was on the bench of New York, the great judicial light in the common-law jurisdiction of that State, he was a head and leader of a political party, vehement and earnest and unflinching in support of its measures and in the conduct of its discipline; and yet no lawyer, no suitor, no critic ever ventured to say, or to think, or to feel that Judge Spencer on the bench was a politician or carried any trait or trace of party feeling or interest there. Judge Spencer was a politician in the House of Representatives then; but Judge Spencer in the management of an impeachment could only say that if party feeling mingled in it he would have nothing to do with it, for his soul abhorred it in relation to so solemn a procedure. Yes, indeed, this divinity of party hate, when it possess a man, throws him now into the fire and now into the water, and he is unsuitable to be a judge until he can come again clothed and in his right mind to hear the evidence and administer the law.

But to come down to the words of our English history and experience, if this is not a court it is a scaffold, and an honorable Manager, yesterday told you so, that each one of you brandished now a headsman's ax to execute vengeance, you having tried the offender on the night of the 21st of February already. I would not introduce these bold words that should make this a scaffold, in the eyes of the people of this country, and you headsmen brandishing your axes, but the honorable Manager has done so, and I have no difficulty in saying to you that if you are not a court, then you are that which he described and nothing else. If it be true that on the night of the 21st of February, upon a crime committed by the President at midday of that date and on an impeachment moving already forward to this Chamber from the House of Representatives, you did hold a court and did condemn, then you are here standing about the scaffold of execution, and the part that you are to play is only that which was assigned you by the honorable Manager, Mr. STEVENS, and he wanted you held by fealty to your own judgments, not to blench at the sight of the blood.

Now, to what end is this prodigious effort to expel from this tribunal all ideas of court and of justice? What is it but a bold, reckless, rash, and foolish avowal, that if it be a court there is no cause here that, upon judicial reason, upon judicial scrutiny, upon judicial weighing and balancing of fact and of law, can result in a judgment which the impeaching party here, the Managers and House of Representatives, demand, and constitutionally may demand, to be done by this court? At last, to what end are the wisdom, and the courage, the civil prudence and the knowledge of history which our fathers brought to the framing of the Constitution; of what service this wise, this honest frown in the Constitution upon *ex post facto* laws and bills of attainder? What is a bill of attainder; what is a bill of pains and penalties in the experience and in the learning of English jurisprudence and parliamentary history? It is a proceeding by the legislature as a legislature to enact crime, sentence, punishment, all in one. And certainly there is no alternative for you if you do not sit here under law to examine evidence, to be impartial, and to regard it as a question of personal guilt to be followed by personal punishment and personal consequences upon the alleged delinquent, then you are enacting a bill of pains and penalties upon the simple form that a majority of the House and two thirds of the Senate must concur, and the Constitution and the wisdom of our ancestors all pass for naught.

Our ancestors were brave and wise, but they were not indifferent to the dangers that attended this tribunal. They had no resource in the Constitution where they could so well fix this necessary duty in a free Government to hold all its servants amenable to public justice for the public service except to devolve it upon this Senate; but let me show you within the brief compass of the debate, and the only material debate, in the Journal of the Convention that framed the Constitution, how the fears and the doubts predominated:

"Mr. Madison objected to a trial of the President by the Senate, especially as he was to be impeached by the other branch of the Legislature; and for any act which might be called a misdemeanor. The President, under these circumstances, was made improperly dependent. He would prefer the Supreme Court for the trial of impeachments; or, rather, a tribunal of which that should form a part.

Mr. Gouverneur Morris thought no other tribunal than the Senate could be trusted. The Supreme Court were too few in numbers, and might be warped or corrupted. He was against a dependence of the Executive on the Legislature, considering the legislative tyranny the great danger to be apprehended; but there could be no danger that the Senate would say untruly, on their oaths, that the President was guilty of crimes or facts, especially as in four years he can be turned out."

That was Gouverneur Morris's wisdom as to the extent to which the Senate might be trusted under the sanctions and obligations of judicial oaths; but—

"Mr. Pinckney disapproved of making the Senate the court of impeachments, as rendering the President too dependent on the Legislature. If he opposes a favorite law the two Houses will combine against him, and, under the influence of heat and faction, throw him out of office."—5 *Madison Papers*, p. 528.

There is the sum and substance of the wisdom that our ancestors could bring to the subject of whether this was to be or could be a court. It is undoubtedly a very great burden and a very exhaustive test upon a political body to turn it into a court for the trial of an executive official in ordinary circumstances. I shall hereafter point out to you the very peculiar, the very comprehensive and oppressive concurrence and combination of circumstances as bearing on this trial that require of you to brace yourselves upon all the virtue that belongs to you and to hold on to this oath for the Divine aid that may support you under this most extraordinary test of human conduct to which our Constitution subjects you to-day.

Now, what could the Constitution do for us? A few little words, and that is all—truth, justice, oath, duty. And what does the whole scope of our moral nature and the whole support we may hope from a higher aid extend to in any of the affairs of life but these? Truth, justice, oath, duty control the fate, life, liberty, character, and property of every citizen. Truth, justice, oath, duty are the ideas that the Constitution has forced upon your souls to-day. You receive them or you neglect them; whichever way you turn you cannot be the same men afterward that you were before. Accepted, embraced, obeyed, you are nobler and stronger and better. Spurned, rejected, you are worse and baser and weaker and wickeder than before. And it is thus that by strong ideas a free Government must always be held to the path of duty and to the maintenance of its own authority and to the prevalence of its own strength for its perpetual existence.

They are little words, but they have great power. Truth is to the moral world what gravitation is to the material; it is the principle upon which it is established and coheres; and justice in the adaptation of truth to the affairs of men is in human life what the mechanism of the heavens is to the principle that sustains the forces of the globe. Duty is acceptance, obedience to these ideas, and this once gained secures the operation which was intended. When, then, you bend submissive to this oath, that faith among men which, as Burke says, "holds the moral elements of the world together," and that faith in God which binds that world to His throne, subdue you to the service of truth and justice; and the ever-living guardian of human rights and interests does not neglect what is essential to the preservation of the human race and its advancement. The purity of the family and the sanctity of justice have ever been cared for, and will ever be cared for. The furies of the Greek mythology had charge of the sanctions of an oath. The imaginations of the prophets of the world have sanctioned the solemnity of an oath, and peopled the place of punishment with oath-breakers; and all the tortures and torments of history are applied to public servants who, in betrayal of sworn trust, have disobeyed those high, those necessitous obligations without which the whole fabric of society falls in pieces.

I do not know why or how it is that we are so constituted, but so it is. The moral world has its laws as well as the material. Why a point of steel lifted above temple or dome should draw the thunderbolt and speed it safely to the ground I know not. How, in our moral constitution, an oath lifted to heaven can draw from the great swollen cloud of passion and of interest and of hate its charge I know not, but so it is. And be sure that loud and long as these honorable Managers may talk, although they speak in the voice of "all the people of the United States," with their bold persuasions that you shall not obey a judicial oath, I can bring against it but a single sentence and a single voice; but that sentence is a commandment and that voice speaks with authority: "Thou shalt not take the name of the Lord thy God in vain, for the Lord will not hold him guiltless that taketh his name in vain."

The moth may consume the ermine of that supreme justice whose robes you wear; rust, Senators, may corrode the sceptre of your power; nay, Messrs. Managers, time even shall devour the people whose presence beating against the doors of this Senate House you so much love to vaunt and menace, but of the word that I have spoken "heaven and earth shall pass away and no jot or tittle of it fail."

I have now reached, Mr. Chief Justice and Senators, a point where an adjournment would be agreeable, if such is the pleasure of the Senate.

Mr. CONKLING. I move that the Senate sitting as a court of impeachment adjourn until to-morrow.

The motion was agreed to; and the Senate, sitting for the trial of the impeachment, adjourned.

WEDNESDAY, *April 29*, 1868.

The Chief Justice of the United States took the chair.

The usual proclamation having been made by the Sergeant-at-Arms,

The Managers of the impeachment on the part of the House of Representatives and the counsel for the respondent, except Mr. Stanbery, appeared and took the seats assigned to them respectively.

The members of the House of Representatives, as in Committee of the Whole, preceded by Mr. E. B. WASHBURNE, chairman of that committee, and accompanied by the Speaker and Clerk, appeared and were conducted to the seats provided for them.

The Journal of yesterday's proceeding of the Senate, sitting for the trial of the impeachment, was read.

Mr. NELSON. Mr. Chief Justice and Senators——

Mr. SUMNER. Mr. President, before the gentleman makes a motion I send an order to the Chair.

The CHIEF JUSTICE. The Secretary will read the order.

The Chief Clerk read the order, as follows:

Whereas Mr. Nelson, one of the counsel for the President, in addressing the Senate, has used disorderly words, as follows, namely: beginning with personalities directed to one of the Managers he proceeded to say, "So far as any question that the gentleman desires to make of a personal character with me is concerned, this is not the place to make it. Let him make it elsewhere if he desires to do it;" and whereas such language, besides being discreditable to these proceedings, is apparently intended to provoke a duel or to signify a willingness to fight a duel, contrary to law and good morals: Therefore,

Ordered, That Mr. Nelson, one of the counsel of the President, has justly deserved the disapprobation of the Senate.

Mr. NELSON. Mr. Chief Justice and Senators——

The CHIEF JUSTICE. The counsel can proceed only by unanimous consent.

Mr. NELSON. I was just going to ask permission, Mr. Chief Justice.

Mr. SUMNER. I must object, unless it is in direct explanation.

Mr. NELSON. All I desire to say this morning to the Senate——

Mr. SUMNER. I must object, unless it is in direct explanation.

Mr. SHERMAN. I object to the consideration of the resolution.

Mr. NELSON. If you will permit, I will simply state this much——

Mr. SHERMAN. I have no objection to the explanation, but I object to the consideration of the resolution.

The CHIEF JUSTICE. I will ask the counsel whether he proposes to make an explanation.

Mr. NELSON. All that I desired to do, Mr. Chief Justice, this morning was to read the letters as I indicated to the Senate yesterday that I should ask permission to do. That is all I desire to do, with a single word of explanation.

The CHIEF JUSTICE. The resolution proposed by the Senator from Massachusetts is not before the Senate if it is objected to.

Mr. SHERMAN. I object to its consideration now.

Mr. Manager BUTLER. If the President and Senate will spare me a single word, I trust, so far as I am concerned, that anything that arose out of what occurred yesterday may be ended from any language that the learned counsel used toward me, and I hope that no further action may be taken upon that matter. As to the reading of the letters, I propose to object to that until they can be proved in the usual course of judicial proceedings.

Mr. JOHNSON. Mr. Chief Justice, I move to lay the resolution offered by the Senator from Massachusetts upon the table.

The CHIEF JUSTICE. It is not before the Senate.

Mr. NELSON. Senators, will you allow me to say one word?

Mr. SUMNER. Mr. President, I wish to inquire whether the gentleman can proceed except by unanimous consent.

The CHIEF JUSTICE. He cannot.

Mr. SUMNER. I must object to any person proceeding who has used the language in this Chamber used by that gentleman.

Mr. TRUMBULL. Mr. President——

The CHIEF JUSTICE. The Chief Justice, perhaps, erred through inadvertence in responding to the Senator from Massachusetts. The Senate undoubtedly can give leave to the counsel to proceed if it sees fit; but if any objection is made the question whether he have leave or not must be submitted to the Senate.

Mr. TRUMBULL. Mr. President, after

what has occurred, a statement having been received from the Managers, I think it proper that the counsel should have permission also to make a statement in explanation; and I move that he have such leave.

The CHIEF JUSTICE. Senators, you who are in favor——

Mr. Manager BUTLER. Is that debatable?

The CHIEF JUSTICE signified that it was not.

Mr. SUMNER. Mr. President, I wish to understand the nature of the motion made by the Senator from Illinois. Is it that the counsel have leave to explain his language of yesterday, or that he have leave to introduce the letter?

Mr. JOHNSON. No debate is in order.

The CHIEF JUSTICE. Debate is not in order.

Mr. TRUMBULL. It is not in reference to letters. My motion is that he have leave to make his explanation; I do not know what it is. Inasmuch as one of the Managers has made an explanation, I think it due to the counsel that he be allowed to make an explanation.

Mr. Manager BUTLER. Do you mean to have the letters read?

The CHIEF JUSTICE. Senators, you who agree that the counsel shall have leave to make an explanation to the Senate will say ay; contrary, no. [Putting the question.] The ayes appear to have it. The ayes have it.

Mr. NELSON. Mr. Chief Justice and Senators, I hope you will allow me before I make this explanation to say a single word in answer to the resolution offered by the honorable Senator, [Mr. SUMNER,] not for the purpose of censuring the Senator, but for the purpose of saying to the Senate that the remarks which I made in the Senate yesterday were made under the heat of what I esteemed to be very great provocation. I intended no offense to the Senate in what I said. If anything is to be done with the gentleman's resolution I hope the Senate will permit me, before disposing of that, to defend myself against this imputation, and to show the reason why I indulged in the remarks I did. But as the honorable Manager has signified a willingness that this thing shall end, I meet him in the same way. So far as I am concerned, I desire to say nothing more of a personal character whatever.

The letters which I desire to read——

Mr. Manager BUTLER. I object that they are not genuine nor proved.

Mr. NELSON. I read them merely as a part of my explanation.

Mr. Manager BUTLER. I do not think that can be done.

The CHIEF JUSTICE. The Chief Justice is under the impression that the leave does not extend to the reading of the letters. If he is wrong the Senate will correct him. If any Senator chooses to make a motion that leave be given that will be put to the Senate.

Mr. DAVIS. Mr. Chief Justice, I rise to a point of order. After the Senate has permitted one of the counsel to make an explanation, I make the question whether a Manager has any right to interpose an objection. I concede that a Senator may have such a right; but I deny that a Manager has any such right as that.

The CHIEF JUSTICE. The Chief Justice understood the motion of the Senator from Illinois to be confined to an explanation of the personal matter which arose yesterday, and that it did not extend to the reading of the letters which the counsel proposed to submit to the Senate; but leave can be given if the Senate sees fit.

Mr. HOWARD. Mr. President, I beg leave respectfully to object to the reading of the letters which are proposed to be read by the counsel.

The CHIEF JUSTICE. No debate is in order; and no motion is at present before the Senate.

Mr. HOWARD. I raise the objection until after they have been presented to the Managers for examination.

Mr. HENDRICKS. Mr. President, I move that the counsel be allowed to read so much of the letter as will show to the Senate what date it bears.

Mr. NELSON. That is all I want.

Mr. TIPTON. Mr. President, I call for the regular order of the morning, the defense of the President.

The CHIEF JUSTICE. The regular order is the motion of the Senator from Indiana, [Mr. HENDRICKS.]

Mr. HOWE. I should like to hear the motion stated. I did not understand it.

The CHIEF JUSTICE. The Senator from Indiana will restate his motion.

Mr. HENDRICKS. The motion which I made is that the attorney for the President be allowed to read so much of the letter as will show its date and the place at which it was written.

The CHIEF JUSTICE. Senators, the question is on the motion of the Senator from Indiana.

The motion was agreed to.

Mr. NELSON. The first letter to which I alluded is a letter bearing date March 9, 1868, addressed by BENJAMIN F. BUTLER to "Colonel J. W. Shaffer, Washington, District of Columbia."

Mr. JOHNSON. Does that purport to be an original letter or a copy?

Mr. NELSON. I understand it to purport to be an original letter. My understanding is that this is the genuine signature of BENJAMIN F. BUTLER, and these are the genuine and original signatures of JOHN A. LOGAN and J. A. GARFIELD. I am not acquainted with the handwriting of the gentlemen, but only speak from information. If the Senate would allow me to read this letter, it is a very short one;

I do not want to make any comment on it except merely to explain the matter about the dates.

Mr. Manager BUTLER. I have no objection if you allow me to reply to it.

Mr. HOWE. I must object.

Mr. HOWARD. I object to the reading of the letter.

The CHIEF JUSTICE. It cannot be read under the order which has been made.

Mr. NELSON. The fact to which I desire to call the attention of the Senate, and it is necessary for me to do so, is, that this letter in the caption bears date, as I have shown, on the 9th of March, 1868. It is signed here "BENJAMIN F. BUTLER." Below the signature of BENJAMIN F. BUTLER are the words, "I concur in the opinion above expressed by General BUTLER," signed "JOHN A. LOGAN." Below that are the words "And I," signed "J. A. GARFIELD." There is no other date in that letter from beginning to end except the 9th of March, 1868.

Mr. JOHNSON. Will the counsel permit me to ask whether the handwriting in which the date is written is the same apparently in which the letter is?

Mr. NELSON. The handwriting in which the date is written is precisely the same handwriting as the address and body of the letter; but the signature to the letter, as I take it, is in a different handwriting from the body of the letter. On the 16th of March, 1868, Mr. Chauncey F. Black addressed a letter to the President stating that he inclosed a copy of the letter to which I have just adverted; and in order that the Senate may understand that, you will observe that the copy is, as I believe, identical with the original letter which I have just produced——

Mr. HOWE. Mr. President——

The CHIEF JUSTICE. The gentleman will confine himself exclusively to the dates.

Mr. NELSON. Altogether to the dates; but I cannot, if your Honor please, explain this thing about the dates without this reference, as the Senate will see. I am not trying to make an argument; I do not intend to violate any rule of the Senate knowingly; and your Honor will see in a moment that I am not trying to make an argument.

Mr. HENDRICKS. Mr. President, my motion was that the attorney be allowed to read so much of the letter as would show the date. I think that is all that it is important for the Senate to know in this personal explanation, and I object to an explanation in regard to the letter going further except so far as it is in direct response to the points made against him.

Mr. NELSON. If the honorable Senate and the Chief Justice will allow me to say a word there, I cannot explain about the date of this copy unless I tell you the difference between this paper and the other paper which I have read. It is impossible for me to explain the date otherwise. All I can say is that this copy bears the same date as the original, and has the additional signatures of Mr. KOONTZ, J. K. MOORHEAD, THADDEUS STEVENS, J. G. BLAINE, and JOHN A. BINGHAM; and that there is no other date to this letter except the date in the caption of the letter. That is the only explanation I can make. You will see that the copy is precisely like the original down to the words. "And I, J. A. GARFIELD." Then come in this letter, which as to these names is an original, the words "I concur. W. H. KOONTZ;" followed by the names "J. K. MOORHEAD, THADDEUS STEVENS, J. G. BLAINE," and "JOHN A. BINGHAM;" and in that paper, from beginning to end, there is no date but the 9th of March. That is the explanation I have to make.

The CHIEF JUSTICE. The counsel for the President will please proceed with the argument in defense.

Mr. CAMERON. Before the counsel proceeds I desire to submit an order.

The CHIEF JUSTICE. The Secretary will read the order proposed by the Senator from Pennsylvania.

The Chief Clerk read the order, as follows:

That the Senate, sitting as a court of impeachment, shall hereafter hold night sessions, commencing at eight o'clock p. m. to-day and continuing until eleven o'clock p. m., until the arguments of the counsel for the President and of the Managers on the part of the House of Representatives shall be concluded.

Mr. JOHNSON. I object.

The CHIEF JUSTICE. The present consideration being objected to, the order will lie upon the table.

Mr. Manager BUTLER. Shall these papers, Mr. President, which have been read be placed upon the records of the court now, so that we can get at them? The originals I desire.

The CHIEF JUSTICE. The Chief Justice is unable to answer that question. He takes it for granted that the counsel will submit them to the honorable Managers.

Mr. Manager BUTLER. I beg your pardon. They were only submitted under insult.

Mr. NELSON. All I desired to do was this: the honorable gentleman asked me to submit the letters to them. I said I would most assuredly let them have them if he would return the originals; and I would hand the letters and copies to them. The gentleman can take them with the understanding that he returns them to me.

The CHIEF JUSTICE. There can be no further discussion of this matter except with the consent of the Senate.

Mr. NELSON. There are the letters, [sending the papers to Mr. Manager BUTLER.]

Mr. Manager BUTLER. No, sir; let them go on the files.

Mr. NELSON. I will deposit them with the Secretary for the present.

Mr. Manager BUTLER. Let them go on the files.

[The papers were handed to the Secretary.]

The CHIEF JUSTICE. The counsel for the President will proceed with the argument.

Mr. EVARTS. Mr. Chief Justice and Senators, if indeed we have arrived at a settled conclusion that this is a court, that it is governed by the law, that it is to confine its attention to the facts applicable to the law, and regard the sole evidence of those facts to be embraced within the testimony of witnesses or documents produced in court, we have made great progress in separating, at least, from your further consideration much that has been impressed upon your attention heretofore.

If the idea of power and will is driven from this assembly, if the President is here no longer exposed to attacks upon the same principle on which men claim to hunt the lion and harpoon the whale, then, indeed, much that has been said by the honorable Managers, and much that is urged upon your attention from so many quarters, falls harmless in your midst. It cannot be said of this Senate, *fertur numeris leges solutis*, that it is carried by numbers unrestrained by law. On the contrary, right here is might and power; and, as its servants and in its investigation and pursuit, your sole duty is exhausted. It follows from this that the President is to be tried upon the charges which are produced here, and not upon common fame, and, least of all, is he to be charged in your judgment, as he has been inveighed against hour after hour in argument, upon charges which the impeaching authority of the House of Representatives deliberately threw out as unworthy of impeachment and unsuitable for trial. We, at least, when we have an indictment brought into court and another indictment ignored and thrown out are to be tried upon the former and not upon the latter. And, if on the 9th of December, of the last year, the House of Representatives, with whom, by the Constitution, rests the sole impeaching power under this Government, by a vote of one hundred and seven to fifty-seven, threw out all the topics that fill up the declamatory addresses of the learned Managers, it is enough for me to say, that for reasons satisfactory to that authority, the House of Representatives, that bill was thrown out and those charges were withheld.

So, too, if it be a trial on public prosecution, and with the ends of public justice alone in view, the ordinary rule of restraint of the conduct of the prosecuting authorities applies here; and I do not hesitate to say that this trial—to be, in our annals, the most conspicuous that our history will present; to be scrutinized by more professional eyes, by the attention of more scholars at home and abroad; to be preserved in more libraries; to be judged of as a national trait, a national scale, a national criterion forever—presents an unexampled spectacle of a prosecution that overreaches judgment from the very beginning and inveighs and selects and impugns and oppresses as if already convicted, at every stage, the victim they pursue. The duty, the constraint upon a prosecuting authority under a government of law pursuing only the public justice is scarcely less strict and severe than that which rests upon the judge himself. To select evidence, having possession of better; to exclude evidence, knowing that it bears upon the inquiry; to restrict evidence, knowing that the field is thus closed against the true point of justice, is no part of a prosecuting authority's duty or power. Whatever may be permitted in the private contests of the forum, in the zeal of contending lawyers for contending clients, there is no such authority, no such duty, no such permission by our laws in a public prosecution. Much less, when the proofs have been thus kept narrow, when the charges are thus precise and technical, is it permissible for a prosecuting authority to enlarge the area of declamation and invective. Much less is it suitable for a public prosecution to inspire in the minds of the court prejudice and extravagance of jurisdiction beyond the points properly submitted.

It has usually been supposed that upon actual trials involving serious consequences forensic discussion was the true method of dealing with the subject, and we lawyers appearing for the President being, as Mr. Manager BOUTWELL has been polite enough to say, "attorneys whose practice of the law has sharpened but not enlarged their intellects," have confined ourselves to that method of forensic discussion. But we have learned here that there is another method of forensic controversy which may be called the method of concussion. I understand the method of concussion to be to make a violent, noisy, and explosive demonstration in the vicinity of the object of attack, whereas the method of discussion is to penetrate the position and if successful to capture it. The Chinese method of warfare is the method of concussion, and consists of a great braying of trumpets, sounding of gongs, shouts, and shrieks in the neighborhood of the opposing force, which rolled away and the air clear and calm again the effect is to be watched for. But it has been reserved for us in our modern warfare, as illustrated during the rebellion, to present a more singular and notable instance of the method of warfare by concussion than has ever been known before. A fort impregnable by the method of discussion, that is, penetrating and capturing it, has been on the largest scale attempted by the method of concussion, and some two hundred and fifty tons of gunpowder in a hulk moored near the stone walls of the fort has been made the means and the occasion of this vast experiment. Unsatisfied with that trial and its result the honorable Manager who opened this case [Mr. BUTLER] seems to have repeated the experiment in the vicinity of the Senate. [Laughter.] The air was filled with epithets, the dome shook with invective. Wretchedness and misery and suffering and blood, not included within the record, were made the means of this explosive mixture. And here we are surviving the concussion, and after all reduced to the humble and homely method of discussion which belongs to "attorneys whose intellects have been sharpened but not enlarged by the practice of the law." [Laughter.]

In approaching, then, the consideration of what constitutes impeachable offenses, within the true method and duty of that solemn and unusual procedure and within the Constitution, we see why it was that the effort was to make this an inquisition of office instead of a trial of personal and constitutional guilt; for if it is an inquest of office "crowner's quest law" will do throughout for us, instead of the more solemn precedents and the more dignified authorities and duties which belong to solemn trial. Mr. Manager BUTLER has given us a very thorough and well-considered suggestion of what constitutes an impeachable offense. Let me ask your attention to it; and every one of these words is underscored by the honorable Manager:

"We define, therefore, an impeachable high crime or misdemeanor to be one in its nature or consequences subversive of some fundamental or essential principle of government, or highly prejudicial to the public interest, and this may consist of a violation of the Constitution, of law, of an official oath, or of duty, by an act committed or omitted, or, without violating a positive law, by the abuse of discretionary powers from improper motives or for any improper purpose."

See what large elements are included in this, the Manager's definition! It must be "subversive of some fundamental or essential principle of government," "highly prejudicial to the public interest," and must proceed "from improper motives" and for an "improper purpose." That was intended, in the generality of its terms, to avoid the necessity of actual and positive crime; but it has given us in one regard everything that is needed to lift the peccability of these technical offenses of mere statutory infraction out of the region of impeachable offense. It is not that you may accuse of a definite and formal crime, and then have outside of your indictment, not covered by charge or admitted for proof or countervailing proof, large accusations that touch these general subjects, but that the act under inquiry, charged and proved or refuted by proof, must be of itself such as, within its terms and regular and natural consequence, thus touches vital interests or fundamental principles. The fallacy of these general qualifying terms is in making them the substance of the crime instead of the conditions of impeachability. You must have the crime definite under law and Constitution, and even then it is not impeachable unless you affect it with some of the public and general and important qualities that are indicated in this definition of the learned and honorable Manager.

We may look, perhaps, at the statement made by the Managers of the House of Representatives on this subject of what constitutes an impeachable offense in the trial of Judge Peck, Mr. Buchanan, of Pennsylvania, chairman of the managers, being the speaker:

"What is an impeachable offense? This is a preliminary question which demands attention. It must be decided before the court can rightly understand what it is they have to try. The Constitution of the United States declares the tenure of the judicial office to be 'during good behavior.' Official misbehavior, therefore, in a judge is a forfeiture of his office. But when we say this we have advanced only a small distance. Another question meets us. What is misbehavior in office? In answer to this question, and without pretending to furnish a definition, I freely admit we are bound to prove that the respondent has violated the Constitution or some known law of the land. This, I think, was the principle fairly to be deduced from all the arguments on the trial of Judge Chase and from the votes of the Senate in the articles of impeachment against him."—*Peck's Trial,* p. 427.

That crime, in the sense of substantial guiltiness, personal delinquency, moral opprobrious blame, is included even under the largest and most liberal accusation that was espoused and defended by the managers in Hastings's impeachment, is to be gathered from one of the many splendid passages of Burke's invective in that cause:

"As to the crime which we charge, we first considered well what it was in its nature, and under all the circumstances which attended it. We weighed it with all its extenuations and with all its aggravations. On that review we are warranted to assert that the crimes with which we charge the prisoner at the bar are substantial crimes; that they are no errors or mistakes, such as wise and good men might possibly fall into; which may even produce very pernicious effects, without being, in fact, great offenses. The Commons are too liberal not to allow for the difficulties of a great and arduous public situation. They know too well the domineering necessities which frequently occur in all great affairs. They know the exigency of a pressing occasion which in its precipitate career bears everything down before it, which does not give time to the mind to recollect its faculties, to reënforce its reason, and to have recourse to fixed principles, but by compelling an instant and tumultuous decision too often obliges men to decide in a manner that calm judgment would certainly have rejected. We know, as we are to be served by men, that the persons who serve us must be tried as men, and with a very large allowance indeed to human infirmity and human error. This, my lords, we knew, and we weighed before we came before you. But the crimes which we charge in these articles are not lapses, defects, errors of common human frailty, which, as we know and feel, we can allow for. We charge this offender with no crimes that have not arisen from passions which it is criminal to harbor; with no offenses that have not their root in avarice, rapacity, pride, insolence, ferocity, treachery, cruelty, malignity of temper; in short, in nothing that does not argue a total extinction of all moral principle, that does not manifest an inveterate blackness, dyed ingrain with malice, vitiated, corrupted, gangrened to the very core. If we do not plant his crimes in those vices which the heart of man is made to abhor, and the spirit of all laws, human and divine, to interdict, we desire no longer to be heard on this occasion. Let everything that can be pleaded on the ground of surprise or error upon those grounds be pleaded with success; we give up the whole of those predicaments. We urge no crimes that are not crimes of forethought. We charge him with nothing that he did not commit upon deliberation; that he did not commit against advice, supplication, and remonstrance; that he did not commit against the direct command of lawful authority; that he did not commit after reproof and reprimand, the reproof and reprimand of those who are authorized by the laws to reprove and reprimand him. The crimes of Mr. Hastings are crimes not only in themselves, but aggravated by being crimes of contumacy. They were crimes not against forms, but against those eternal laws of justice which are our rule and our birthright. His offenses are not in formal, technical language, but in reality, in substance and effect, *high* crimes and high misdemeanors."—*Burke's Works,* vol. 7, pp. 13, 14.

And so the articles charged them, not leaving it to the declamation or invention of the orators of that great occasion. I need not insist, in repetition of the very definite, concise, and I must think effective argument of the learned counsel who opened this case for the respondent, [Mr. Curtis,] upon the strict constitutional necessity, under the clause prohibiting *ex post facto* laws, and under the clause prohibiting bills of attainder, and under the clauses that fix the trial as for crime in the Constitution under the designation in the articles of enumeration of "treason" and "bribery" alone, the highest great crimes against the State that can be imagined, that you should have here what is crime against the Constitution and crime against the law, and then that it should have those public proportions that are indicated in the definition of the opening Manager, and those traits of freedom from error and mistake and doubt and difficulty which belong, in the language of Mr. Burke, to an arduous public station. And then you will perceive that under these necessary conditions either this judgment must be arrived at, that there is no impeachable offense here which covers and carries with it these conditions, or else that the evidence offered on the part of the respondent that was to negative, that was to countervail, that was to reduce, that was to refute all these qualifications should have been admitted; and when a court like this has excluded the whole range of evidence relating to the public character of the accused and the difficulties of an arduous public situation, it must have determined that the crimes charged do not partake of that quality, or else it would have required them to have been affirmatively supported by proofs giving those qualifications, and permitted them to be reduced by countervailing evidence. And when a court sits only for a special trial, when its proceedings are incapable of review, when neither its law nor its fact can be dissected, even by reconsideration within its own tribunal, the necessary consequence is that, when you come to make up your judgment, either you must take as for granted all that we offered to prove, all that can fairly be embraced as to come in, in form, in substance, in color, and in fact, by the actual production of such proof, so that your judgment may thus proceed; or else it is your duty before you reach the irrevocable step of judgment and sentence to resume the trial and call in the rejected evidence. I submit to it to you that a court without review, without new trial, without exception, and without possible correction of errors, must deal with evidence in this spirit and upon this rule.

And unless you arrive, as I suppose you must, at the conclusion that the dimensions of this trial relate to the formal, technical infraction of the statute law that has been adduced in evidence here, it will be your duty to reopen your doors, call the respondent again before you, and go into the field of inquiry that has been touched in declamation, but has not been permitted in proof.

But, Mr. Chief Justice and Senators, there is no better mode of determining whether a crime accorded to a particular jurisdiction and embraced within a particular prohibition is to be a high crime and misdemeanor, and what a high crime and misdemeanor means, and what the lowest level and the narrowest limit of its magnitude and of its height must be, than to look at its punishment. Epithets, newly-invented epithets, used in laws do not alter the substance of things. Your legislation of the 2d of March, 1867, introducing into a statute law the qualifying word "high," applied to a misdemeanor, is its first appearance in the statute law of this country or of the parent country from whom we draw our jurisprudence. It means nothing to a lawyer. There is in the conspiracy act of 1861 the same introduction of the word "high" as applied to the body of the offense there called "a crime." A "high crime" it is called in this little conspiracy act of 1861, and there in the one instance and here in the other an epithet is thrown into an act of Congress. But, Mr. Chief Justice and Senators, when the legislative authority in its scale of punishment makes it, as the common sense of mankind considers, great in its penalty, terrible in its consequences, that is a legislative statement of what the quality of the crime is. When you put into a statute that the offense shall be punished by death you need no epithet to show that that is a great, a heinous crime; and when the framers of this Constitution put into it, as the necessary result of the trial of the President of the United States and his conviction, that his punishment should be deprivation of office, and that the public should suffer the necessity of a new election, that showed you what they meant by "high crime or misdemeanor."

I know that soft words have been used by every Manager here on the subject of the mercy of our Constitution and the smallness of the punishment, that it does not touch life, limb, or property. Is that the sum of penalties? Is that the measure of oppression of punishment? Why, you might as well say that when the mother feels for the first time her new-born infant's breath, and it is snatched from her and destroyed before her eyes, she has not been deprived of life, liberty, or property. In a Republic, where public spirit is the life and where public virtue is the glory of the State, and in the presence of public men possessing great public talents, high public passions, and ambitions, made up, as this body is, of men sprung, many of them, from the ordinary condition of American life, and by the force of their native talents and by the high qualities of endurance and devotion to the public service, who have lifted themselves into this eminent position, if not the envy the admiration of all their countrymen, it is gravely proposed to you, some of whom from this elevated position do not disdain to look upon the Presidency of the United States as still a higher, a nobler, a greater office, if not of pride yet of duty, that you shall feel and say that it is a little thing to take a President from his public station and strike him to the ground, branded with high crime and misdemeanor, to be a byword and reproach through the long gauntlet of history forever and forever. In the great hall of Venice, where long rows of doges cover with their portraits the walls, the one erased, the one defeatured canvas attracts to it every eye; and one who has shown his devotion to the public service from the earliest beginning, and you who have attended in equal steps that same ascent upward, and now, in the very height and flight of your ambition, feel your pinions scorched and the firm sockets of your flight melted under this horrid blaze of impeachment, are to be told, as you sink forever, not into a pool of oblivion but of infamy, and as you carry with you to your posterity to the latest generation this infamy, that it is a trifling matter, and does not touch life, liberty, or property! If these are the estimates of public character, of public fame, and of public disgrace by which you, the leaders of this country, the most honored men in it, are to record your estimate of the public spirit and of the public virtue of the American State, you have indeed written for the youth of this country the solemn lesson that it is dust and ashes.

Now, what escape is there from this conclusion, in every true estimate of the character of this procedure and of the result that you seek to fasten upon this President if justice requires it, to say that it is trifling and trivial and that formal and technical crime may lead to it? Do the people of this country expect to be called to a presidential election in the middle of a term, altering the whole calendar, it may be, of the Government, because there has been an infraction of a penal statute carrying no consequences beyond? It is accidental, to be sure, that the enforced and irregular election that may follow upon your sentence at this time concurs with the usual period of the quadrennial election; but it it is merely accidental. And yet these, Senators, are gravely proposed to you as trivial results that are to follow from a judgment on an accusation of the character and of the quality that I have stated in fact, as compared with the quality and the character that it should bear in truth.

In reference to this criminality of the infraction of the statute, which in the general remarks that I am making you will see furnishes the principal basis of charge that I am regarding, we may see from the statute itself what the measure of criminality there given is, what the measure under indictment would be or might be, and then you will see that that infraction, if it occurred, and if it were against the law and punishable by the law under the ordinary methods and procedures of our common courts of justice, furnishes not only no vindication of, but no support to, the notion that upon it can be ingrafted the accusation of impeachment, the accusation of criminality that is impeachable, any more than any other topic of comparatively limited and trivial interest and concern.' The provision is not that there must be a necessary penalty of gravity, but that under the scale of imprisonment and fine the only limit is that it shall not exceed $10,000 of pecuniary liability and five years of imprisonment. Six cents fine, one day's imprisonment, according to the nature of the offense, within the discretion of the court, may satisfy the public justice under indictment in regard to this offense which is claimed as the footing and front of the President's fault.

Nor was this open, unrestricted mercy of the law unattended to in debate. The honorable Senator from Massachusetts, [Mr. SUMNER,] in the course of the discussion of this section of the bill, having suggested that it would be well, at least, to have a moderate minimum of punishment that would secure something like substance necessarily in the penal infliction and having suggested $1,000 or $500 as the lower limit, basing upon this wise intimation that some time or other there might be a trial under this section before a court that had a political bias and the judge might let the man off without any substantial punishment, he was met by the honorable Senator from Vermont [Mr. EDMUNDS] and the honorable Senator from Oregon, [Mr. WILLIAMS,] who seemed to have the conduct of the bill, at least in respect to these particular provisions, in the way to which I will attract your attention. Mr. SUMNER said:

"Shall we not in this case, where political opinion may intrude on the bench, make a provision that shall at least secure a certain degree of punishment?"

Mr. EDMUNDS defended the unlimited discretion of punishment.

Mr. WILLIAMS said:

"I concur in the views expressed by the Senator from Vermont, for the reason, in the first place, that this is a new offense created by statute, and it does not define a crime involving moral turpitude, but rather a political offense; and there is some ground to suppose that mistakes may be made under this law by persons in office; and I think that in such case there should be a large discretion left to the court."

So much for indictment; so much for the wise reasons of our legislators; and then, that being the measure and the reason, there is clamped upon this a necessary, an inevitable, an inexorable result that is to bring these vast consequences to the State and to the respondent. But even then you do not know or understand the full measure of discretion, unless you attend to the fact that such formal, technical crimes when made the subject of conviction and of sentence in obedience to the law are, under a principle of our Constitution and of every other just, I will not say merciful, Government in the world, made subjects of pardon; but under this process of impeachment, with but one punishment, and that the highest in the public fame and character of men that is known or that can be conceived, we have this further, this terrible additional quality, that the punishment is immitigable, immutable, irreversible, unpardonable, and no power whatever can lighten or relieve the load with which an impeached and convicted public servant goes forth from your Chambers in a just exercise of this power of impeachment with a punishment heavier than he can bear.

And now, what answer is there to this but an answer that will take a load of punishment and of infamy from him and place it somewhere else? True it is that if he be unjustly convicted, if he be convicted for technical and formal faults, then the judgment of the great nation, of intelligent and independent men, stamps upon his judges the consequences that they have failed to inflict upon the victim of their power. Then it is that the maxim *si innocens damnatur, judex bis damnatur* finds its realization in the terrors of public opinion and the recorded truths of history.

I have introduced these considerations simply to show you that these notions that if you can prove that a man has stumbled over the statute it is essential that he should bear these penalties and these consequences find no support in reason, none in law, none in the Constitution, none in the good sense of this high tribunal, none in the habits and views of the great people whom we represent. Indeed, we should come under the condemnation of the speaker in Terrence if we were to seek upon this narrow, necessary view, as it is urged, of law such consequences as I have stated: *Summum jus sæpe summa est malitia*—an extremity of the law is often the extremity of wickedness.

And now I am prepared to consider the general traits and qualities of this offense charged, and I shall endeavor to pursue in the course of my argument a consideration, perhaps not always formal nor always exactly defined, of three propositions:

1. That the alleged infractions of these penal statutes are not in themselves, nor in any quality or color that has been fastened upon them by the evidence in this cause, impeachable offenses.

2. Having an application to the same conclusion, that whatever else there is attendant, appurtenant, or in the neighborhood of the subjects thus presented to your consideration they are wholly political and not the subject of jurisdiction in this court or in any court, but only in the great forum of the popular judgment, to be debated there at the hustings and in the newspapers by the orators and the

writers to whom we are always so much indebted for correct and accurate views on subjects presented for such determination. If I
shall have accomplished this I shall have
accomplished everything. I shall have drawn
attention to the true dimensions in a constitutional view of the crime alleged even if it has
been committed, and shall have shown by a
reflex application of the argument that it is
mere error and confusion, perhaps pardonable
in an impeaching authority, but unpardonable
in a court of judgment, to confound things
political with things criminal.

And then, third, I shall ask your attention
to the precise traits and facts as disclosed in
the evidence charged in the articles, and bring
you, I think, to a safe, an indisputable, firm,
and thorough conclusion that even the alleged
infractions of penal law have none of them, in
fact, taken place.

Now, let us look at this criminality in the
point upon which, in the largest view of any
evidence in support of it given on the part of
the Managers, it must turn. We must separate, at least for the purpose of argument,
the innuendoes, the imputations, the aggravations that find their place only in the oratory of the Managers, or only in your own
minds as conversant with the political situation and enlisted zealously in the rightful
controversies which belong to it as a political
situation, and we are then to treat the subject
in this method: that up to twelve o'clock on
February the 21st, 1868, the President was innocent and unimpeachable, and at one o'clock
on the same day he was guilty and impeachable of the string of offenses that fill up all the
articles except that devoted to the speeches,
the tenth; for whatever he did was done then
at that point of time, leaving out the Emory
article, which relates to a conversation on the
morning of the 22d, and which I also should
have excepted from these observations. What
he did was all in writing. What he did was
all public and official. What he did was communicated to all the authorities of the Government having relation to the subject. Therefore you have at once proposed for your consideration a fault, not of personal delinquency,
not of immorality or turpitude, not one that
disparages in the judgment of mankind, not
one that degrades or affects the position of the
malefactor; it is, as Mr. Senator WILLIAMS
truly said, a "new offense," also, an offense
"not involving turpitude, and rather of a
political character."

Now, too, upon these proofs the offense carries no consequences beyond what its action
indicates, to wit: a change in the head of a
Department. It is not a change of the Department. It is not an attempt to wrest a
Department or apply an office against the law,
contrary to the regulations of the Government,
and turn its power against the safety or peace
of the State; not in the least. Whatever imaginations may suggest, whatever invective and

opprobrium may intimate, the fact is that it
had no other object, had no other plan, would
have had no other consequences—I mean within
the limits of this indictment and of this proof—
than to substitute for Mr. Stanton some other
citizen of the United States that by and with
the advice and consent of the Senate should be
approved for that high place, or to fill it until
that advice and consent should be given by
some legal *ad interim* holder of the office, not
filling it, but discharging its duties.

If, then, the removal had been effected, if
the effort to assert a constitutional authority
by the President had been effectual, no pretense is made, or can be made, that anything
would have been accomplished that could be
considered as a turning of the Government or
any branch of its service out of the authority
of law. Neither did it in purpose or consequences involve any change in the policy of the
Executive of the United States in the War
Department or in its management. Whatever
there might have been of favor or support in
public opinion, in political opinion, in the
wishes and feelings of the Congresses of the
United States in favor of Mr. Stanton for that
post, and however well deserved all that might
be, Senators cannot refuse to understand that
that does not furnish a reason why the offense
committed by a change of the head of a Department should be exaggerated into a crime against
the safety of the State.

But I think we may go further than that, and
say that however great may have been the
credit with the Houses of Congress and with
the people or with the men of his own party
which the Secretary of War, Mr. Stanton,
enjoyed, it cannot be denied that there was a
general and substantial concurrence of feeling
in this body, among all the public men in the
service of the Government, and among the
citizens in general, that the situation disclosed
to public view and public criticism of an antagonism between the head of a Department and the
President of the United States was not suitable
to the public service, and was not to be encouraged as a situation in the conduct of the executive government, and that there was a general
opinion among thoughtful and considerate people that however much the politics of the
Secretary of War might be regarded as better
than the politics of the President, if we would
uphold the frame of government and recognize
the official rights that belong to the two positions, it was a fair and just thing for the President to expect that the retirement should take
place on the part of the Secretary rather than
that he, the President, should be driven to a
forced resignation himself, or to the necessity
of being maimed and crippled in the conduct
of the public service.

It follows necessarily, then, that the whole
criminality, in act, in purpose, and in consequence, that in this general survey we can
attach to the imputed offense, is a formal contravention of a statute. I will not say how

criminal that may be. I will not say whether absolute, undeviating, inflexible, perfect obedience to every law of the land may not be exacted under the penalty of death from everybody holding public station. That is matter of judgment for legislators; but nevertheless the morality, the policy, the quality of the transaction cannot be otherwise affected than so far as the actual punishments of the statute are made applicable. When you consider that this new law, thus passed, really "reverses the whole action of this Government" in the language of Senators and Representatives who spoke in its behalf during its passage; that in the language of the same debaters it "revolutionizes the practice of the Government;" and when you consider that the only person in the United States that this law, in respect to removal from office, was intended or by its terms could affect was the President of the United States; that nobody else was subject to the law; that it was made a rule, a control, a restraint, a mandate, a direction to nobody else in the United States except the President, just as distinctly as if it had said in its terms, "If the President of the United States shall remove from office he shall be punished by fine and imprisonment;" and when you know that by at least debated and disputed contests it was claimed that the President of the United States had the right to remove, and that an inhibition upon that right was a direct assertion of congressional authority aimed at the President in his public trust, duty, and authority of carrying on the executive government, you can then at once see that by a necessary exclusion and conclusion, however much the act may have been against the law in fact as on subsequent judgment may be held by this or any other court, yet it was an act of that nature, forbidden under those circumstances, and to be attempted under those obligations of duty, if attempted at all, which give it this quality, and you see at once that no rhetoric, that no argument, that no politics whatever can fix upon the offense, completed or attempted, any other quality than this: a violation of a law, if it shall be so held, in support of and in obedience to the higher obligation of the Constitution. Whenever anybody puts himself in that position, nobody can make a crime of it in the moral judgment, in the judicial determination. In sentence and measure of punishment, at least, if not in formal decision and judgment, no man can make a crime of it.

We are treated to the most extraordinary view on the subject of violating what is called an unconstitutional law. Why, nobody ever violates an unconstitutional law, because there never is any such obstacle to a man's action, freedom, duty, right, as an unconstitutional law. The question is whether he violates law, not whether he violates a written paper published in a statute-book, but whether he violates law; and the first lessons under a written Constitution are and must be that a law un-

constitutional is no law at all. The learned Manager, Mr. BOUTWELL, speaks of a law being, possibly he says, capable of being annulled by the judgment of the Supreme Court. Why, the Supreme Court never annuls a law. There is not any difference in the binding force of the law after the Supreme Court has annulled it, as he calls it, from what there was before. The Supreme Court has no political function; it has no authority of will or power to annul a law. It has the faculty of judgment, to discern what the law is, and what it always has been, and so to declare it.

Apply it to an indictment under this very statute, and supposing the law is unconstitutional for the purpose of argument, what is the result? Is the man to be punished because he has violated the law and the Supreme Court has not as yet declared it unconstitutional? No; he comes into court and says, "I have violated no law." The statute is read; the Constitution is read; and the judge says, "You have violated no law." That is the end of the matter; and he does not want to appeal to the discretion of the court in the measure of punishment or to the mercy of the Executive in the matter of pardon. He has done what was right, and he needs to make no apology to Congress or anybody else, and Congress, in so far as it has not protected the public servant, rather owes an apology to him. I shall consider this matter more fully hereafter; and now look at it only in the view of fixing such reduced and necessarily reduced estimate of the criminality imputed as makes it impossible that this should be an impeachable offense.

Much has been said about the duty of the people to obey and of officers to execute unconstitutional laws. I claim for the President no greater right in respect to a law that operates upon him in his public duty, and to him exclusively, to raise a question under the Constitution to determine what his right and what his duty is, than I claim for every citizen in his private capacity when a law infringes upon his constitutional and civil and personal rights; for to say that Congress has no right to pass unconstitutional laws, and yet that everybody is to obey them just as if they were constitutional and to be punished for breaking them just as if they were constitutional, and to be prevented from raising the question whether they are constitutional by penal inflictions that are to fall upon them whether they succeed in proving them unconstitutional or not, is, of course, trampling the Constitution and its defense of those who obey it in the dust. Who will obey the Constitution as against an act of Congress that invades it if the act of Congress with the sword of its justice can cut off his head and the Constitution has no power to save him, and nothing but debate hereafter as to whether he was properly punished or not? The gentlemen neglect the first, the necessary conditions of all constitutional government, when they press upon us **arguments** of this nature.

But again, the form alleged of infraction of this law, whether it was constitutional or unconstitutional, is not such as to bring any person within any imputation, I will not say of formal infraction of the law, but of any violent, willful use and extent of resistance to or contempt of the law. Nothing was done whatever but to issue a paper and have it delivered, which puts the posture of the thing in this condition and nothing else : the Constitution, we will suppose, says that the President has a right to remove the Secretary of War; the act of Congress says the President shall not remove the Secretary of War; the President says, "I will issue an official order which will raise the same question between my conduct and the statute that the statute raises between itself and the Constitution." As there is not and cannot be and never should be a reference of a law abstractly to the revision and determination of the Supreme Court or of any other court, which would be making it a council of revision and of superior and paramount political and legislative authority, so when the Constitution and a law are or are supposed to be at variance and inconsistent everybody upon whose right this inconsistency intrudes has a right under the usual ethical conditions of conduct of good citizenship to put himself in a position to act under the Constitution and not under the law. And thus the President of the United States, as it is all on paper thus far—the Constitution is on paper, the law is on paper—issues an order on paper which is but an assertion of the Constitution and a denial of the law, and that paper has legal validity if the Constitution sustains it, and is legally invalid and ineffectual, a mere *imbelle telum*, if the law prohibits it and the law is conformed to the Constitution. Therefore it appears that nothing was done but the mere course and process of the exercise of right claimed under the Constitution without force, without violence, and making nothing but the attitude, the assertion which, if questioned, might raise the point for judicial determination.

Now, Senators, you are not, you cannot be unfamiliar with the principle of our criminal law, the good sense, the common justice of which, although it sometimes is pushed to extremes, approves itself to every honest mind, that criminal punishments, under any form of statute definitions of crime, shall never be made to operate upon acts even of force and violation that are or honestly may be believed to be done under a claim of right. It is for this purpose that the *animus*, the intent, the *animus furandi* in case of larceny, the malice prepense in a case of murder, the intent necessary in every crime, is made the very substance of the crime, and nothing is felt to be more oppressive, and nothing has fewer precedents in the history of our legislation or of our judicial decisions, than any attempt to coerce the assertion of peaceable and civil claims of right by penal enactments. It is for that reason that our communities and our law-givers have always frowned upon any attempt to coerce the right of appeal under any restrictions or any penalties of costs of a character oppressive. Civil rights are rights valuable and practical just according as people can avail themselves of them, they keeping the peace ; and the moment you put the coercion of punishment upon the assertion of a right, a claimed right, in a manner not violating the peace and not touching the public safety, you infringe one of the necessary liberties of every citizen.

Although I confess that I feel great reluctance, and it is contrary to my own taste and judgment very much to mingle what is but a low level of illustration and argument with so grave and general a subject as determining the dimensions and qualities of an impeachable offense, yet, on the other hand, day after day it is pressed upon you that a formal violation of a statute, although made under the claim of a constitutional right and duty honestly felt and possessed by the President, is nevertheless a ground of impeachment, not to be impeded or prevented by any of these considerations ; and hence I am induced to ask your attention to what is but an illustration of the general principle, that penal laws shall not be enforced in regard to an intent which is governed by a claim of right. And this singular case occurred : a poacher who had set his wires within the domain of a lord of the manor had caught a pheasant in his wires ; the gamekeeper took possession of the wires and of the dead pheasant, and then the poacher approaches him by threats of violence, which would amount to robbery, not larceny, takes from him the wires and the dead pheasant, and the poacher situated in that way on other's dominions, and thus putting himself in a condition where the humanity of the law can hardly reach and protect him, is brought into question and tried for robbery ; and Vaughan, Baron, says:

"If the prisoner demanded the wires under the honest impression that he had a right to them, though he might be liable to a trespass in setting them, it would not be a robbery. The gamekeeper had a right to take them, and when so taken they never could have been recovered from him by the prisoner; yet still, if the prisoner acted under the honest belief that the property in them continued in himself, I think it is not a robbery. If, however, he used it merely as a pretense, it would be robbery. The question for the jury is, whether the prisoner did honestly believe he had a property in the snares and pheasant or not."—1 *Russell on Crimes*, 872.

Thus does the criminal law of a free people distinguish between technical and actual fault ; and what mean the guarantees of the Constitution, and what mean the principles and the habits of English liberty, that will not allow anybody enjoying those liberties to be drawn into question criminally upon any technical or formal view of the law to be administered by hide-bound authority or judges established and devoted to the prosecution of crime ; what mean those fundamental provisions of our liberty, that no man shall be put on trial on an accusation of crime, though formally committed, unless the grand jury shall choose to bring him under inculpation, and that when thus brought under inculpation he shall not be condemned by any judge or magistrate, but the warm and living condemnation of his peers shall be added to the judicial determination, or he shall go free? Surely we have not forgotten our rights and our liberties and upon what they rest, that we should bring a President of the United States under a formal apparatus of iron operation that by necessity if you set it agoing shall, without crime, without fault, without turpitude, without moral fault even of violating a statute that he believed to be a statute binding upon him, bring about this monstrous conclusion—I do not mean in any condemnation of it, but monstrous in its dimensions—of depriving him of his office and the people of the country of an executive head?

Mr. CONKLING. Mr. President, I move an intermission of fifteen minutes.

The motion was agreed to; and at the expiration of the recess the Chief Justice resumed the chair and called the Senate to order.

Mr. EVARTS. I am quite amazed, Mr. Chief Justice and Senators, at the manner in which these learned Managers are disposed to bear down upon people that obey the Constitution to the neglect or avoidance of a law. It is the commonest duty of the profession to advise, it is the commonest duty of the profession to maintain and defend the violation of a law in obedience to the Constitution; and in the case of an officer whose duty is ministerial, whose whole obligation in his official capacity is to execute or to give free course to a law, even when the law does not bear at all upon him or his rights, the officer may appeal to the courts if he acts in good faith and for the purpose of the public service, and with a view of ascertaining by the ultimate tribunal in season to prevent public mischiefs, whether the Constitution or the law is to be the rule of his conduct and whether they be at variance.

Let me ask your attention to a case in Selden's Reports in the New York court of appeals, (3 Selden, page 9,) the case of Newell, the auditor of the canal department, in error, against the People. The constitution of the State of New York contains provisions restrictive upon the capacity or power of the Legislature to incur public debt. The Legislature, deeming it, however, within its right to raise money for the completion of the canals upon a pledge of the canals and their revenues, not including what may be called the personal obligation of the State, a dry mortgage as it were, not involving debt, but only carrying the pledge, undertook to and did raise a loan of $6,000,000. Mr. Newell, the canal auditor, when a draft was drawn upon him in his official capacity, which it became him as a ministerial officer, obedient to the law, to honor and proceed upon, refused it honor, and raised the question whether this act was constitutional. Well, now, he ought to have been impeached! He ought to have had the Senate and the court of appeals of New York convened on him and been removed from office! The idea of a canal auditor setting himself up against what the learned Manager calls law! He set himself up in favor of law and against its contravention, and the question was carried through the supreme court of that State, and the supreme court of that State, decided that the law was constitutional, but upon an appeal to the court of appeals that court held it unconstitutional, and the $6,000,000 loan was rolled away as a scroll, needing to be fortified by an indemnifying proceeding amending the constitution and extending its provisions.

Now, I should like to know if the President of the United States, who has taken an oath to preserve, protect, and defend the Constitution of the United States, in reference to a law that is made over his head and on his right, and over and on nothing else in this nation, cannot appeal to the Constitution? And when he does make the appeal is the Constitution to answer him, through the House of Representatives, "We admit, for argument, that the law is unconstitutional; we admit it operates on you and your trust-right, and nothing else; we admit that you were going to raise the constitutional question, and yet the process of impeachment is the peril under which you do that, and its ax is to cut off your head for questioning an unconstitutional law that operates upon your right and contravenes that Constitution which you have sworn to protect and defend in every department of the Government, on and for the Legislature, on and for the judiciary, on and for the people, on and for the executive power?" How will our learned Managers dispose of this case of Newell, the auditor, against the people of the State of New York—a worthy, an upright, a useful, a prosperous assertion in the common interest and for the maintenance of the constitution, of a duty to the people?

And are we such bad citizens when we advise that the Constitution of the United States may be upheld, and that anybody, without a breach of the peace and in an honest purpose, may make a case that the instance may be given whereby the judgment of the court may be had and the Constitution saved from violation? Not long since the State of New York passed a law laying a tax on brokerage sales in the city of New York of a half or three fourths per cent. on all goods that should be sold by brokers, seeking to raise for the revenue purposes of the State of New York about ten million dollars on the brokers' sales of merchandise, which sales distribute through the operations of that emporium the commerce of the whole country for consumption through all the States of the Union. Your sugar, your tea, your coffee that you consume in the valley of the Mississippi was to be made to pay a tax in the city of New York, to support the State of New York in its government by that tax; and they made it penal for any broker to sell without giving a bond and paying the tax. Was it very wicked for me when all the brokers were in this distress, to advise them that the shortest way to settle that matter was not to give the bond; and when one of them, one of the most respectable citizens of the city, was indicted by the grand jury for selling coffee without giving a bond, and it came before the courts, instead of having, as I supposed when I gave my advice, to come up to the Supreme Court of the United States, to vindicate the Constitution of the United States, I had the good fortune to succeed in the court of appeals of the State of New York itself, that court holding that the law was unconstitutional, and the indictment failed. Was I a bad citizen for saving the Constitution of the United States against these infractions of law? Was the defendant in the indictment a bad citizen for undertaking to obey the Constitution of the United States? Where are your constitutional decisions—McCulloch *vs.* Maryland; Brown *vs.* Maryland; the bank-tax cases—all these instances by which a constitution is arrayed for the protection of the rights which it secures? It is always by instances, it is always by acts, and the only ethical condition is that it shall be done without a breach of the peace and in good faith.

How is it with people in office that violate, sometimes, the law? Is it true that they must necessarily be punished for it? Mr. Lincoln, before the "invasion" or "insurrection" broke out, had raised the case of the Constitution for the suspension of the *habeas corpus*, undertook to arrest a mischief that was going on at Key West, where, through the forms of peace, an attack was made upon the Government fort there through the *habeas corpus*. An excellent way to take a fort! I do not know whether the honorable Manager, [Mr. BUTLER,] who is so good a lawyer, tried that in all his military experience or not, [laughter;] but the *habeas corpus* was resorted to down in Florida to empty that fort of all its soldiers, and was succeeding admirably. A judge issued the *habeas corpus*; the soldier was brought out, and then he was free: and so the fort would have been taken by *habeas corpus*. President Lincoln suspended the *habeas corpus*, violating the law, violating the Constitution. Should he have been impeached? Is it necessary that a man should be impeached? What did he do? He suspended it by proclamation of the 10th of May, 1861, to be found in volume twelve Statutes-at-Large, page 1260; and at the opening of the next session he referred to the fact that the legality of the measures was questioned, and said they were ventured upon under a public necessity, and submitted to the judgment of Congress whether there should be legislation or not. That is found on pages 12 and 13 of the Senate Journal, first session, Thirty-Seventh Congress, 1861.

There were various other acts of this great, heroic, good President—the arrest of the members of the Legislature of Maryland, never justified by any law or any constitution that I know of, but wholly justified by duty to the country. And it so happens, what every statesman knows as the experience of government, that public action is to be judged by public men and public officers as private actions are to be judged by private men, according to the quality of the act, whether it shall be impeached or whether it shall be indemnified.

I do not seek this argument as going further than to meet the necessity which I understand these learned Managers put forth that an infraction of a statute must carry out of office any President of the United States who is so guilty. Why, the very next statute in the book before me, after the civil-office-tenure act, on page 232 of the volume, is an act to declare valid and conclusive certain proclamations of the President and acts done in pursuance thereof, or of his orders, for the suppression of the late rebellion against the United States. The military commissions had been declared invalid by the Supreme Court, and we have an act of indemnity covering a multitude of formal, technical sins by indemnity and protection to have the same effect as if the law had been passed before they were performed. So, therefore, this dry, dead interpretation of law and duty by which act, act, act, unqualified, unscrutinized, unweighed, unmeasured, is to form the basis of necessary action of the guillotine of impeachment, disappears wholly under the clear, bright, and honest light which true statesmanship sheds upon the subject.

I may as conveniently at this point of the argument as at any other pay some attention to the astronomical punishment which the learned and honorable Manager [Mr. BOUTWELL] thinks should be applied to this novel case of impeachment of the President. Cicero, I think it is, who says that a lawyer should know everything, for sooner or later there is no fact in history, in science, or of human knowledge that will not come into play in his arguments. Painfully sensible of my ignorance, being devoted to a profession which "sharpens and does not enlarge the mind," [laughter,] I yet can admire without envy the superior knowledge evinced by the honorable Manager. Indeed, upon my soul, I believe he is aware of an astronomical fact which many professors of that science are wholly ignorant of. But nevertheless, while some of his honorable colleagues were paying attention to an unoccupied and unappropriated island on the surface of the seas, Mr. Manager BOUTWELL, more ambitious, had discovered an untenanted and unappropriated region in the skies, reserved, he would have us think, in the final councils of the Almighty, as the place of punishment for convicted and deposed American Presidents. [Laughter.]

At first I thought that his mind had become so "enlarged" that it was not "sharp" enough to observe that the Constitution had limited the punishment; but on reflection I saw that he was as legal and logical as he was ambitious and astronomical, [laughter,] for the Constitution has said "removal from office," and has put no limit to the distance of the removal, [laughter,] so that it may be, without shedding a drop of his blood, or taking a penny of his property, or confining his limbs, instant removal from office and transportation to the skies. [Laughter.] Truly, this is a great undertaking; and if the learned Manager can only get over the obstacles of the laws of nature the Constitution will not stand in his way. He can contrive no method but that of a convulsion of the earth that shall project the deposed President to this infinitely distant space; but a shock of nature of so vast an energy and for so great a result on him might unsettle even the footing of the firm members of Congress. We certainly need not resort to so perilous a method as that., How shall we accomplish it? Why, in the first place, nobody knows where that space is but the learned Manager himself, and he is the necessary deputy to execute the judgment of the court. [Laughter.]

Let it then be provided that in case of your sentence of deposition and removal from office the honorable and astronomical Manager shall take into his own hands the execution of the sentence. With the President made fast to his broad and strong shoulders, and, having already essayed the flight by imagination, better prepared than anybody else to execute it in form, taking the advantage of ladders as far as ladders will go to the top of this great Capitol, and spurning then with his foot the crest of Liberty, let him set out upon his. flight, [laughter,] while the two Houses of Congress and all the people of the United States shall shout "Sic itur ad astra." [Laughter.]

But here a distressing doubt strikes me; how will the Manager get back? [Laughter.] He will have got far beyond the reach of gravitation to restore him, and so ambitious a wing as his could never stoop to a downward flight. Indeed, as he passes through the constellations, that famous question of Carlyle by which he derides the littleness of human affairs upon the scale of the measure of the Heavens, "What thinks Böotes as he drives his hunting dogs up the zenith in their leash of sidereal fire?" will force itself on his notice. What, indeed, would Böotes think of this new constellation? [Laughter.]

Besides, reaching this space, beyond the power of Congress even "to send for persons and papers," [laughter,] how shall he return, and how decide in the contest, there become personal and perpetual, the struggle of strength between him and the President? [Laughter.] In this new revolution, thus established forever, who shall decide which is the sun and which is the moon? Who determine the only scientific

test which reflects the hardest upon the other? [Laughter.]

If I have been successful at all in determining the general latitude of the imputed offense as not bringing it, under the circumstances which this evidence attaches to it, to the quality and grade of impeachable offenses, I may now be prepared, and I hope with some commendable brevity, to notice what I yet regard as important to the course of my argument, and what I assigned as the second topic of it, to show that all else is political; but I wish to draw your attention also to what I think is a matter of great moment, a matter of great concern and influence for all statesmen, and for all lovers of the Constitution and of the country—to the particular circumstances under which the two departments of the Government now brought in controversy are placed. I speak not of persons, but of the actual constitutional possession of the two departments.

The office of President of the United States, in the view of the framers of the Constitution, and in the experience of our national history, and in the esteem of the people, and in the ambition of all who aspire to that great place by worthy means, is an office of great trust and power. It has great powers. They are not monarchical or tending to monarchy, because the tenure of the office, its source of original commission, and its return of the trust to those who control it, and its amenability under the Constitution to this process of impeachment and the authority of Congress, save it from being at all dangerous to the liberties of the nation. Yet it is, and is intended to be, an office of great authority, and the Constitution in its coördinate department cannot be sustained without maintaining all the authority that the Constitution has intended for this executive office. But it depends for its place in the Constitution upon the fact, the practical fact, that its authority is committed by the suffrage of the people, and that when this authority is exerted it is not by individual purpose or will, or upon the mere strength which a single individual can oppose to the collective power of the Congress of the United States. It is because and as the people, who by their suffrage have raised the President to his place, are behind him, holding up his hands, speaking with his voice, sustaining him in his high duties, that the President has the place and can maintain it under the Constitution.

This great power is safe, then, to the people for the reasons I have stated, and it is safe to the President because the people are behind him and have just exhibited their confidence by the suffrage that has promoted him. When, however, alas, our Constitution comes to this trial that one is lifted to the presidential office who has not received the suffrage of the people for that office, then at once discord, dislocation, deficiency, difficulty show themselves; then at once the great powers of the office which were consonant with a free Constitution and with the supremacy of popular will, by the fact that for a brief term the breath of life of the continuing favor of the people gave them efficacy and strength, find no support in fact. Then it is that in the criticisms of the press, in the estimates of public men, in the views of the people, these great powers, strictly in trust and within the Constitution, seem to be despotic and personal. And then, if we will give due force to another difficulty that our system of vicious politics has introduced, and that is that in the nomination for the two offices, selecting always the true leader of the popular sentiment of the time for the place of President, we look about for a candidate for the Vice Presidency to attract minority and to assuage differences and to bring in inconsistent support, and make him different from the President in political position and in general circumstances for popular support, and couple with the fact that I have spoken of in the Constitution and which belongs to it this vice in our politics, then when the Vice President becomes President of the United States, not only is he in the attitude of not having the popular support for the great powers of the Constitution, but he is in the condition of not having the party support for the fidelity and maintenance of his authority that are necessary. Then, adhering to his original opinions, to the very opinions and political attitude which form the argument for placing him in the second place of authority, he is denounced as a traitor to his party and is watched and criticised by all the leaders of that party.

I speak not particularly in reference to the present presidential term and its incumbent, and the actual condition of politics here; I speak of the very nature of the case. All the public men, all the ambitious men, nay, all the men interested in the public service, in carrying on the Government for the purposes and with the views, in the interest of duty, of the party, have made their connections, and formed their views, established their relations with the President who has disappeared. They then are not in the attitude of support, personal or political, that may properly be maintained among the leaders of a party, and that is implied in the fact that an election has taken place by the joint efforts, crowning in the final result the President of the selection of the people. Then it is that high words are interchanged. Then it is that ambitious men, who had framed their purposes, both for the present and for the future, upon the footing of the presidential predomination that had been secured by the election, find these plans dislocated and disturbed; and then it is that if wisdom and prudence and the personal qualities of pacification and of accommodation and of attraction are wanting upon the one side and the other, terrible evils threaten the conduct of the Government and the peace of the State. It was thus, as we all know by looking back to the experience of the Whig party, that differ-

ences, even in time of peace and of quiet, had been urged so far in the Presidency of Mr. Tyler, that an impeachment was moved against him in the House of Representatives, and had more than one hundred supporters; and yet, when it was all over, nobody, I think, could have dreamed that there was anything in the conduct of Mr. Tyler, in the matter complained of, that was just ground for impeachment. So, too, in great part during the incumbency of Mr. Fillmore, elevated to the Presidency, his action and his course, tempered and moderated as it was by some of the personal qualities that I have stated, was yet carried on in resistance to the leading ideas of the party that had raised him to power.

Then the Opposition, seizing upon this opportunity, encourage the controversy, urge on the quarrel, but do not espouse it, and thus it ends in the President being left without the support of the currents of authority that underlie and vivify the Constitution of the United States—the favor of the people; and so when this unfortunate, this irregular condition of the executive office concurs with times of great national juncture, of great and serious oppression and difficulty of public affairs, then at once you have at work the special, the peculiar, the irregular operation of forces that expose the Constitution, left unprotected and undefended with the full measure of support that every department of the Government should have to resist the other, pressing on to dangers and to difficulties that may shake and bring down the pillars of the Constitution itself.

I suggest this to you as wise men, to understand how out of circumstances for which no man is responsible, attributable to the working of the Constitution itself, in this effort to provide a successor, and to the inattention paid to it in the suffrages of the people and the selections of the politicians, how there is a weakness, and a special weakness, that the Presidency is as it were an undefended fort, and see to it that the invasion is not urged and made successful by the temptation thus presented.

This exception, weakness of the Presidency under our Constitution, is encountered in the present state of affairs by an extraordinary development of party strength in the Congress. There are in the Constitution but three barriers against the will of a majority of Congress within the terms of their authority. One is that it requires a two-thirds vote to expel a member of either House; another that a two-thirds vote is necessary to pass a law over the objections of the President; and another, that a two-thirds vote of the Senate, sitting as a court for the trial of impeachment, is requisite to a sentence. And now how have these two last protections of the executive office disappeared from the Constitution in its practical working by the condition of parties that has given to one the firm possession by a three-fourths vote, I think in both Houses, of the control of the action of each body of the Legislature? Reflect upon this. I do not touch upon the particular circumstance that the nonrestoration of the southern States has left your numbers in both Houses of Congress less than they might under other circumstances be. I do not calculate whether that absence diminishes or increases the disproportion that there would be. Possibly their presence might even aggravate the political majority which is thus arrayed and thus overrides practically all the calculations of the presidental protection through the guarantes of the Constitution ; for, what do the two-thirds provisions mean? They meant that in a free country, where elections were diffused over a vast area, no Congressman having a constituency of over seventy or eighty thousand people, it was impossible to suppose that there would not be a somewhat equal division of parties, or impossible to suppose that the excitements and zeal of party could carry all the members of it into any extravagance. I do not call them extravagances in any sense of reproach ; I merely speak of them as the extreme measures that parties in politics, and under whatever motives, may be disposed to adopt.

Certainly, then, there is ground to pause and consider before you bring to a determination this great struggle between the coördinate branches of the Government, this agitation and this conclusion in a certain event of the question whether the coördination of the Constitution can be preserved. Attend to these special circumstances and determine for yourselves whether under these influences it is best to urge a contest which must operate upon the framework of the Constitution, and its future unattended by any exceptions of a peculiar nature that govern the actual situation. Ah, that is the misery of human affairs, that the stress comes and has its consequence when the system is least prepared to receive it. It is the misery that disease, casual, circumstantial, invades the frame when health is depressed and the powers of the constitution to resist it are at the lowest ebb. It is that the gale rises and sweeps the ship to destruction when there is no sea-room for it and when it is upon a leeshore. And if concurrent with that danger to the good ship, her crew be short, her helm unsettled, and disorder begins to prevail, there comes to be a final struggle for the maintenance of mastery against the elements and over the only chances of safety, how wretched is the condition of that people whose fortunes are embarked in that ship of state !

What other protection is there for the presidential office than these two-thirds guarantees of the Constitution that have disappeared? The Supreme Court placed there to determine, among the remarkable provinces of its jurisdiction, the lines of separation and of duty and of power under our Constitution between the Legislature and the President. Ah! under this evidence, received and rejected, the very effort of the President was, when the two-thirds majorities had urged the contest against him, to raise a case for the Supreme Court to decide ; and then the Legislature, coming in by its special condition of impeachment, intercepts the effort and brings his head again within the mere power of Congress where the two-thirds rule is equally ineffectual as between the parties to the contest.

This is matter of grave import, of necessary consideration, and which, with the people of this country, with watchful foreign nations, and in the eyes of history, will be one of the determining features of this great controversy ; for great as is the question in the estimate of the Managers or of ourselves or of the public intelligence of this people, of how great the power should be on one side or the other, with Congress or with the President, that question sinks into absolute insignificance compared with the greater and higher question, the question that has been in the Constitution, that has been in the minds of philosophers, of publicists, and of statesmen since it was founded, whether it was in the power of a written constitution to draw lines of separation and put up buttresses of defense between the coördinate branches of the Government? And with that question settled adversely with a determination that one can devour, and having the power, will devour the other, then the balances of the American Constitution are lost and lost forever. Nobody can reinstate in paper what has once been struck down in fact. Mankind are governed by instances, not by resolutions.

And then, indeed, there is placed before the people of this country either despair at the theory of paper constitutions, which have been derided by many foreign statesmen, or else an attempt to establish new balances of power by which, the poise of the different departments being more firmly placed, one can be safe against the other. But who can be wiser than our fathers? Who can be juster than they? Who can be more considerate or more disinterested than they? And if their descendants have not the virtue to maintain what they so wisely and so nobly established, how can these same descendants hope to have the virtue and the wisdom to make a better establishment for their posterity?

Nay, Senators, I urge upon you to consider whether you will not recoil from settling so tremendous a subject under so special, so disadvantageous, so disastrous circumstances as I have portrayed to you in the particular situation of these branches of the Government. A stronger Executive, with an absolute veto, with a longer term, with more permanent possession and control of official patronage, will be necessary for the support of this executive department, if the wise and just and considerate measure of our ancestors shall not prove, in your judgment, sufficient; or, if that be distasteful, if that be unacceptable, if that be inadmissible, then we must swing it all over into the omnipotence of Congress, and recur to the exploded experiment of the Confederation, where Congress was executive and legislative, all in one.

There is one other general topic, not to be left unnoticed for the very serious impression that it brings upon the political situation which forms the staple—I must say it—of the pressure on the part of the Managers to make out a crime, a fault, a danger that should enlist your action in the terrible machinery of impeachment and condemnation. I mean the very peculiar political situation in the country itself and in the administration of this Government over the people of the country which has been the womb from which has sprung this disorder and conflict between the departments of the Government. I can, I think, be quite brief about it, and certainly shall not infringe upon any of the political proprieties of the occasion.

The suppression of an armed rebellion and the reduction of the revolted States to the power of the Government, when the region and the population embraced in the rebellion were so vast, and the head to which the revolt had come was so great, and the resistance so continuous, left a problem of as great difficulty in human affairs as was ever proposed to the actions of any Government. The work of pacification would have been a severe task for any Government after so great a struggle, when so great passions were enlisted, when so great wounds had been inflicted, when so great discontents had urged the controversy, and so much bitterness had survived its formal settlement; but wonderful to say, with his situation, so difficult as to surpass almost the powers of Government as exhibited in any former instance in the history of the world, there occurred a special circumstance that by itself would have tasked all the resources of statesmanship under even a simple Government. I mean the emancipation of the slaves, which had thrown four millions of human beings, not by the processes of peace but by the sudden blow of war, into the possession of their freedom, which had changed at once, against their will, the relation of all the rest of the population to these men that had been their slaves.

The process of adaptation of society and of law to so grave a social change as that, even when accomplished in peace, and when not disturbed by the operations of war and by the discontents of a suppressed rebellion, are as much as any wisdom or any courage, or any prosperity that is given to government, can expect to ride through in safety and peace. When, then, these two great political facts concur and press upon the Government that is responsible for their conduct, how vast, how difficult, how intractable, and unmanageable seems the posture!

But this does not represent the measure or even the principal feature of the difficulty. When the Government whose arms have triumphed and suppressed resistance is itself, by

the theory and action of the Constitution, the Government that by peaceful law is to maintain its authority, the process is simple; but under our complex Government, according to the theory and the practice, the interests and the feelings, the restored Constitution surrenders their domestic affairs at once to the local governments of the people who have been in rebellion. And then arises what has formed the staple of our politics for the last four years, what has tried the theory, the wisdom, the courage, the patriotism of all. It is how far under the Constitution as it stands the General Government can exercise absolute control in the transition period between war and absolute restored peace, and how much found to be thus unmanageable shall be committed to changes of the Constitution. And when we understand that the great controversy in the formation of the Constitution itself was how far the General Government should be intrusted with domestic concerns, and when the final triumph and the general features of the Constitution that the people of the States were not willing, in the language of Mr. Ellsworth, to intrust the General Government with their domestic interests, we see at once how wide, how dangerous, how difficult the arena of controversy of constitutional law and of difference of opinion as to what was or is constitutional, and if it be not of what changes shall be or ought to be made in the Constitution to meet the practical situation.

Then when you add to this that as people divide on these questions, and as the practical forces on one side and the other are the loyal masses and the rebel masses, whoever divides from his neighbor, from his associate, from his party adherents in that line of constitutional opinion and in that line of governmental action, which seems to press least changes upon the Constitution and least control upon the masses lately in rebellion, will be suspected and charged and named and called an ally of traitors and rebels, you have at once disclosed how our dangerous politics have been brought to the head in which these names of "traitor" and of "rebel," which belong to war, have been made the current phrases of political discussion.

I do not question the rectitude nor do I question the wisdom of any positions that have been taken as matter of argument or as matter of faith or as matter of action in the disposition of this peculiar situation. I only attract your attention to the necessities and dangers of the situation itself. We were in the condition in which the question of the surrender to the local communities of their domestic affairs, which the order of the Constitution had arranged for the peaceful situation, became impossible without the gravest dangers to the State both in respect to the public order and in respect to this changed condition of the slaves.

In English history the Commons were urged,

after they had rejected the king from the British constitution and found the difficulty of making things work smoothly, *stare super antiquas vias;* but, said Sergeant Maynard, "It is not the question of standing upon the ancient ways, for we are not on them." The problem of the Constitution is, as it was then, how to get upon the ancient ways from these paths that disorder and violence and rebellion had forced us into; and here it was that the exasperations and the exacerbations of politics came up mingling with charges of infidelity to party and with treason, moral treason, political treason, I suppose, to the State. How many theories did we have?

In this Senate, if I am not mistaken, one very influential and able and eloquent Senator was disposed to press the doctrines of the Declaration of Independence into being working forces of our constituted liberty, and a sort of pre-constitutional theory was adopted to suit the logical and political difficulties of the case. In another House a great leader was disposed to put it upon the transconstitutional necessities that the situation itself imposed in perfect peace as in absolute and flagrant war. And thus it was that minds trained in the old school, attached to the Constitution, unable as rhetoricians or as reasoners to adopt these learned phrases and these working theories of pre-constitutional or transconstitutional authority and obligation, were puzzled among the ruins of society that the war had produced; and thus, as it seems to me, we find these concurring dangers leading ever to an important and necessary recognition by whoever has to deal with them of the actual and practical influences that they have upon the controversy.

And now let me urge here that all this is within the province of politics; and a free people are unworthy of their freedom and cannot maintain it if their public men, their chosen servants, are not able to draw distinctions between legal and constitutional offense and odious or even abominable politics. Certainly it is so. *Idem sentire de republicâ,* to agree in opinion concerning the public interest, is the bond of one party, and diversity from those opinions the bond of the other; and where passions and struggles of force in any form of violence or of impeachment as an engine of power come into play, then freedom has become license, and then party has become faction, and those who do not withhold their hand until the ruin is accomplished will be subject to that judgment that temperance and fortitude and patience were not the adequate qualities for their conduct in the situation in which they were placed. Oh, why not wise enough to stay the pressure till adverse circumstances shall not weigh down the State? Why not in time remember the political wisdom—

"Beware of desperate steps. The darkest day,
Live till to-morrow, will have passed away."

I hold in my hand an article from the Tribune, written under the instructions of this trial and put with great force and skill. I do not propose to read it. I bring it here to show and to say that it is an excellent series of articles of impeachment against the President of the United States within the forum of politics for political repugnancy and obstruction, and an honest confession that the technical and formal crimes included in these articles are of very paltry consideration. That is an excellent article of impeachment demanding by process suitable to the forum an answer; and for the discussions of the hustings and of the election, there it belongs; there it must be kept. But this being a court, we are not to be tried for that in which we are not inculpated. How wretched the condition of him who is to be thus oppressed by a vague, uncertain shadow which he cannot oppose or resist! If the honorable . Managers will go back to the source of their authority, if they will obtain what was once denied them, a general and open political charge, it may, for aught I know, be maintainable in law; it may be maintainable in fact; but then it would be brought here; it would be written down; its dimensions would be known and understood; its weight would be estimated; the answer could be made.

And then your leisure and that of the nation being occupied with hearing witnesses about political differences and the question of political repugnance and obstruction upon the side of the President, those who should be honored with his defense in that political trial would at least have the opportunity of reducing the force of the testimony against them and of bringing opposing and contravening proofs; and then, at least, if you would have a political trial, you would have it with name and with substance to rest upon. But while that a President of the United States is to be brought into the procedure of this court by a limited accusation, found "not guilty" under that, and convicted on an indictment that the House refused to sustain, or upon that wider indictment of the newspaper press, and without an opportunity to bring proof or to make arguments on the subject, seems to us too monstrous for any intelligence within or without this political circle, this arena of controversy, to maintain for a moment.

I may hope, somewhat briefly, to draw your attention to what lies at the basis of this discussion of the power and authority that may be rightfully exercised or reasonably be assumed in the action of the President to be exercised, even if it should prove erroneous within the premises of this matter between the two branches of the Government.

The coördination of the powers of Government is not only the greatest effort in the frame of a written constitution, but I think it must be conceded that as it occupies the main portion of the Constitution itself, so it has been regarded by all competent critics at home and abroad to have been a work most successfully accom plished by the framers of our Government. Indeed, if you will look at the Constitution, you will find that beyond that very limited though very important service, of dividing what belongs to Government and what shall be left to the liberties of the people, and then discriminating between what shall be accorded to the General Government and what shall be left to the domestic governments of the States, the whole service of the Constitution is to build up these three departments of the Government so that they shall have strength to stand as against the others, and not strength to encroach or overthrow.

Much has been said about Congress as being the great repository of power. Why, of course it is. It is the repository of power and of will, and there is not any difficulty in making Congress strong enough. Congress, that must be intrusted with all the strings of power and furnished with all its resources, the effort of the Constitution is to curb and restrain; and so you will find that almost all the inhibitions of the Constitution are placed upon Congress—upon Congress in withholding it from power over the people; from Congress in withholding it from power over the States; from Congress in withholding it from power over the coördinate branches; and, nevertheless, by a necessary and absolute deposit of authority in Congress, it is left master of the whole. This power of Parliament in the British constitution makes the Commons masters of the Government. To what purpose is it to provide that the justices of the Supreme Court shall hold their tenure for life, and that their salaries shall not be diminished during the term of their service, when Congress, by an undoubted constitutional power, may omit and refuse to appropriate one dollar to the support of any particular justice during any particular year or series of years? Nevertheless, the Government is to be administered by men, and in an elective government the trust is that the selected agents of the people will be faithful to their interest and will be endowed with sufficient intelligence to protect them.

But simple as is the constitution of the judiciary, and needing no care, when you come to the executive authority arises the problem which has puzzled, does puzzle, will puzzle, all framers of government having no source and no ideas of authority except what springs from the elective suffrage. You have the balance of the British constitution between the Crown and the Parliament, because it rests upon ideas and traditions and experience which have framed one portion of the Government as springing up from the people and in their right, and the other portion of the Government as descending from Divine authority and in its right; and you have no difficulty in enlarging, confirming, and bracing up the authority of Parliament, provided you leave standing the authority and majesty of the throne. But here the problem is, how, without the support

of nobility, of the fountain of honor, of time, of strength, of inheritance, how under a suffrage and for a brief period to make an Executive that is strong enough to maintain itself against the contentions of the Constitution?

Under these circumstances, and adjusting the balance as it is found in the Constitution, our ancestors disposed of the question. It has served us to this time. Sometimes, in the heat of party, the Executive has seemed too strong; sometimes, in the heat of party, Congress has seemed too strong; yet every contest and every danger passes away, managed, administered, controlled, protected by the great, superior, predominant interest and power of the people themselves. And the essence of the Constitution is, that there is no period granted by it of. authority to the Senate in their six years' term, to the President in his four years' term, to the House of Representatives in their two years' term, no period that cannot be lived through in patience subordinate and obedient to the Constitution; and that, as was said in the debate which I read from the Convention, applied to the particular topic of impeachment, there will be no danger when a four years' recurring election restores to the common master of Congress and the Executive the trust reposed, that there will be a temptation to carry for political controversy and upon political offense the sword of the Constitution, and make it peremptory and final in the destruction of the office.

I beg leave, in connection with this subject, its delicacy, its solicitudes in the arrangement of constitutional power, to read two passages from a great statesman, whose words when he was alive were as good as anybody's, and since his death have not lost their wisdom with his countrymen; I mean Mr. Webster. In his debate upon the Panama mission he said, in speaking of the question of the confidence of Congress in the Executive:

"This seems a singular notion of confidence, and certainly is not my notion of that confidence which the Constitution requires one branch of the Government to repose in another. The President is not our agent, but, like ourselves, the agent of the people. They have trusted to his hands the proper duties of his office; and we are not to take those duties out of his hands from any opinion of our own that we should execute them better ourselves. The confidence which is due from us to the Executive and from the Executive to us is not personal, but official and constitutional. It has nothing to do with individual likings or dislikings; but results from that division of power among departments and those limitations on the authority of each which belong to the nature and frame of our Government. It would be unfortunate, indeed, if our line of constitutional action were to vibrate backward and forward according to our opinions of persons, swerving this way to-day from undue attachment, and the other way to-morrow from distrust or dislike. This may sometimes happen from the weakness of our virtues or the excitement of our passions; but I trust it will not be coolly recommended to us as the rightful course of public conduct."—*Webster's Works*, vol. 3, p. 187.

Again, in his speech on the presidential protest in the Senate in 1834, he said:

"The first object of a free people is the preservation of their liberty, and liberty is only to be pre-.

served by maintaining constitutional restraints and just division of political power. Nothing is more deceptive or more dangerous than the pretense of a desire to simplify government. The simplest Governments are despotisms; the next simplest, limited monarchies; but all republics, all Governments of law, must impose numerous limitations and qualifications of authority and give many positive and many qualified rights. In other words, they must be subject to rule and regulation. This is the very essence of free political institutions. The spirit of liberty is, indeed, a bold and fearless spirit; but it is also a sharp-sighted spirit; it is a cautious, sagacious, discriminating, far-seeing intelligence; it is jealous of encroachment, jealous of power, jealous of man. It demands checks; it seeks for guards; it insists on securities; it intrenches itself behind strong defenses, and fortifies itself, with all possible care, against the assaults of ambition and passion. It does not trust the amiable weaknesses of human nature, and, therefore, it will not permit power to overstep its prescribed limits, though benevolence, good intent, and patriotic purpose come along with it. Neither does it satisfy itself with flashy and temporary resistance to illegal authority. Far otherwise. It seeks for duration and permanence; it looks before and after; and, building on the experience of ages which are past, it labors diligently for the benefit of ages to come. This is the nature of constitutional liberty; and this is *our* liberty, if we will rightly understand and preserve it. Every free Government is necessarily complicated, because all such Governments establish restraints, as well on the power of Government itself as on that of individuals. If we will abolish the distinction of branches, and have but one branch; if we will abolish jury trials, and leave all to the judge; if we will then ordain that the legislator shall himself be that judge; and if we will place the executive power in the same hands, we may readily simplify government. We may easily bring it to the simplest of all possible forms, a pure despotism. But a separation of departments, so far as practicable, and the preservation of clear lines of division between them, is the fundamental idea in the creation of all our constitutions; and, doubtless, the continuance of regulated liberty depends on maintaining these boundaries."— *Webster's Works,* vol. 4, p. 122.

I think I need to add nothing to these wise, these discriminating, these absolute and peremptory instructions of this distinguished statesman. The difficulty and the danger are exactly where this Government now finds them in the withholding of the strength of one department from working the ruin of another.

Mr. CONKLING. Mr. President, I move an adjournment of the Senate.

The motion was agreed to; and the Senate, sitting for the trial of the impeachment, adjourned.

Thursday, *April* 30, 1868.

The Chief Justice of the United States took the chair.

The usual proclamation having been made by the Sergeant-at-Arms,

The Managers of the impeachment on the part of the House of Representatives and the counsel for the respondent, except Mr. Stanbery and Mr. Curtis, appeared and took the seats assigned to them respectively.

The members of the House of Representatives, as in Committee of the Whole, preceded by Mr. E. B. WASHBURNE, chairman of that committee, and accompanied by the Speaker and Clerk, appeared and were conducted to the seats provided for them.

The Journal of yesterday's proceedings of the Senate, sitting for the trial of the impeachment, was read.

The CHIEF JUSTICE. The first business in order is the motion of the Senator from Massachusetts, [Mr. SUMNER,] which the Secretary will read.

The Chief Clerk read as follows:

Whereas Mr. Nelson, one of the counsel for the President, in addressing the Senate, has used disorderly words, as follows, namely: beginning with personalities directed to one of the Managers he proceeded to say: "So far as any question that the gentleman desires to make of a personal character with me is concerned, this is not the place to make it. Let him make it elsewhere if he desires to do it;" and whereas such language, besides being discreditable to these proceedings, is apparently intended to provoke a duel or to signify a willingness to fight a duel, contrary to law and good morals: Therefore,

Ordered, That Mr. Nelson, one of the counsel of the President, has justly deserved the disapprobation of the Senate.

Mr. JOHNSON. Mr. Chief Justice, I move to lay the resolution on the table.

Mr. SUMNER. On that I ask for the yeas and nays.

The yeas and nays were ordered; and the Chief Clerk called Mr. ANTHONY's name.

Mr. ANTHONY. Before voting on this I should like to propose a question to the counsel, and I will do it in writing, or, if the Senate will allow me, I will do it verbally.

The CHIEF JUSTICE. If there is no objection the Senator from Rhode Island can propose a question.

Mr. ANTHONY. I wish to ask of the counsel if, in the remark which has been quoted in the resolution, it was his intention to challenge the Manager alluded to to a mortal combat?

Mr. NELSON. It is a very difficult question for me to answer. During the recess of the Senate the day before yesterday the honorable gentleman [Mr. Manager BUTLER] remarked to me that he was going to say something upon the subject of Alta Vela, and desired me to remain. When the gentleman read his remarks to the Senate I regarded them as charging me with dishonorable conduct before the Senate, and in the heat of the discussion I made use of language which was intended to signify that I hurled back the gentleman's charge upon him, and that I would answer that charge in any way in which the gentleman desired to call me to account for it. I cannot say I had particularly the idea of a duel in my mind, as I am not a duelist by profession; but, nevertheless, my idea was that I would answer the gentleman in any way in which he chose to call upon me for it. I did not intend to claim any exemption on account of age or any exemption on account of other things that are apparent to the Senate. That was all that I meant to signify, and I hope the Senate will recollect the circumstances under which this thing was done. The Senate has treated me and every other gentleman concerned in this case with the utmost kindness and politeness, and has given marked attention to what we

have said, and the idea of insulting the Senate
is a thing that never entered my mind. I had
no such thought or design. I entertain the
kindest feelings and the most respectful feelings toward the Senate, and would be as far
as any man upon the face of the earth from
saying anything which would justly give offense
to the gentlemen of the Senate whom I was
addressing.

Mr. SUMNER. Mr. President, I ask that
the resolution be read again.

The Chief Clerk read the resolution.

The CHIEF JUSTICE. The Secretary will
proceed with the call of the roll on the motion
to lay on the table. .

The question being taken by yeas and nays,
resulted—yeas 35, nays 10; as follows:

YEAS—Messrs. Anthony, Bayard, Buckalew, Cattell, Chandler, Corbett, Cragin, Davis, Dixon, Doolittle, Drake, Edmunds, Ferry, Fessenden, Fowler,
Frelinghuysen, Grimes, Harlan, Hendricks, Howe,
Johnson, Morrill of Maine, Morton, Norton, Patterson of New Hampshire, Patterson of Tennessee,
Ramsey, Ross, Saulsbury, Sherman, Tipton, Trumbull, Van Winkle, Vickers, and Williams—35.

NAYS—Messrs. Cameron, Howard, Morgan, Morrill of Vermont, Pomeroy, Stewart, Sumner, Thayer,
Wilson, and Yates—10.

NOT VOTING—Messrs. Cole, Conkling, Conness,
Henderson, McCreery, Nye, Sprague, Wade, and
Willey—9.

So the resolution was laid upon the table.

The CHIEF JUSTICE. The next business
in order is the order proposed by the Senator
from Pennsylvania, [Mr. CAMERON,] which the
Secretary will read.

The Chief Clerk read as follows:

Ordered, That the Senate, sitting as a court of impeachment, shall hereafter hold night sessions, commencing at eight o'clock p. m. to-day, and continuing until eleven o'clock p. m., until the arguments
of the counsel for the President and of the Managers on the part of the House of Representatives
shall be concluded.

Mr. SUMNER. I move to strike out all
after the word "Ordered," and insert what I
send to the Chair.

The CHIEF JUSTICE. The words proposed to be inserted will be read.

The Chief Clerk read as follows:

That the Senate will sit during the remainder of
the trial from ten o'clock in the forenoon to six
o'clock in the afternoon, with such brief recess as may
be ordered.

Mr. SUMNER. On that I should like to
have the yeas and nays.

Mr. TRUMBULL. Mr. President, I move
to lay this whole subject on the table.

Mr. SUMNER. On that I ask for the yeas
and nays.

The yeas and nays were ordered; and being
taken, resulted—yeas 32, nays 17; as follows:

YEAS—Messrs. Anthony, Bayard, Buckalew, Cat-
tell, Corbett, Davis, Dixon, Doolittle, Drake, Ferry,
Fessenden, Fowler, Frelinghuysen, Grimes, Hend-
ricks, Howe, Johnson, McCreery, Morrill of Maine,
Morrill of Vermont, Morton, Norton, Patterson of
New Hampshire, Patterson of Tennessee, Ramsey,
Ross, Saulsbury, Sprague, Trumbull, Van Winkle,
Vickers, and Willey—32.

NAYS—Messrs. Cameron, Chandler, Conkling,
Cragin, Edmunds, Harlan, Howard, Morgan, Pom-

eroy, Sherman, Stewart, Sumner, Thayer, Tipton,
Williams, Wilson, and Yates—17.

NOT VOTING—Messrs. Cole, Conness, Henderson,
Nye, and Wade—5.

So the order and amendment were laid upon
the table.

The CHIEF JUSTICE. Mr. Evarts will
proceed with the argument for the President.

Mr. EVARTS. We perceive then, Mr. Chief
Justice and Senators, that the subject out of
which this controversy has arisen between the
two branches of the Government, executive
and legislative, touches the very foundations
of the balanced powers of the Constitution;
and in the arguments of the honorable Managers it has to some extent been so pressed upon
your attention. You have been made to believe that so weighty and important is the
point in controversy as to the allocation of the
power over office included in the function of
removal that if it is carried to the credit of
the executive department of this Government
it makes it a monarchy. Why, Mr. Chief Justice and Senators, what grave reproach is this
upon the wisdom and foresight and civil prudence of our ancestors that have left unexamined and unexplored and unsatisfied these
doubts or measures of the strength of the Executive as upon so severe a test or inquiry of
being a monarchy or a free republic? I ask
your attention to a passage from the Federalist,
in one of the papers by Alexander Hamilton,
who meets in advance these aspersions that
were sought to be thrown upon the establishment of the executive power in a President.
He there suggests in brief and solid discriminations the distinctions between the Presidency:

"The President of the United States would be an
officer elected by the people for four years; the king
of Great Britain is a perpetual and hereditary prince.
The one would be amenable to personal punishment
and disgrace; the person of the other is sacred and
inviolable. The one would have a qualified negative
upon the acts of the legislative body; the other has
an absolute negative. The one would have a right to
command the military and naval forces of the nation;
the other, in addition to this right, possesses that of
declaring war and of raising and regulating fleets and
armies by his own authority. The one would have a
concurrent power with a branch of the Legislature in
the formation of treaties; the other is the sole possessor of the power of making treaties. The one
would have a like concurrent authority in appointing
to offices; the other is the sole author of all appointments. The one can confer no privileges whatever;
the other can make denizens of aliens, noblemen of
commoners, can erect corporations with all the rights
incident to corporate bodies. The one can prescribe
no rules concerning the commerce or currency of the
nation; the other is in several respects the arbiter of
commerce, and in this capacity can establish markets
and fairs, can regulate weights and measures, can lay
embargoes for a limited time, can coin money, can
authorize or prohibit the circulation of foreign coin.
The one has no particle of spiritual jurisdiction; the
other is the supreme head and governor of the national church! What answer shall we give to those
who would persuade us that things so unlike resem-
ble each other? The same that ought to be given to
those who tell us that a Government, the whole power
of which would be in the hands of the elective and
periodical servants of the people, is an aristocracy,
a monarchy, and a despotism."

But a little closer attention both to the history of the framing of the Constitution and to the opinions that maintained a contest in the body of the Convention which should finally determine the general character and nature of the Constitution will show us that this matter of the power of removal or the control of office, as disputable between the Executive and the Senate, touches more nearly one of the other great balances of the Constitution; I mean that balance between the weight of numbers in the people and the equality of States, irrespective of population, of wealth, and of size. Here it is, if I may be allowed to say so, that the opinions to which my particular attention was drawn by the honorable Manager, [Mr. BOUTWELL,] the opinions of Roger Sherman, had their origin. One of the most eminent statesmen of the last generation said to me that it was to Mr. Sherman and to his young colleague, Mr. Ellsworth, and to Judge Paterson, of New Jersey, that we owed it, more than to all else in that Convention, that our Government was made what that statesman pronounced it to be, the best Government in the world, a Federal Republic, instead of being what it would have been but for those members of the Convention, as this same statesman of the last generation expressed it, a consolidated empire, the worst Government in the world.

Between these two opinions it was that the controversy whether the Senate should be admitted into a share of the executive power of official appointment, the great arm and strength of the Government came into play; and as a part of his firm maintenance of the equality of the States Mr. Sherman insisted that this participation should be accorded to the Senate; and others resisted as too great a subtraction from the sum of executive power to be capable safely of this distribution and frittering away. Mr. Adams, the first President of that name, I am informed upon authority not doubted, bringing it to me from the opinion of his grandson, died in the conviction that even the participation in appointment that the Constitution, as construed and maintained in the practice of this Government, accorded to the Senate, would be the point upon which the Constitution would fail; that this attraction of power to comparatively irresponsible and unnoticed administration in the Senate would ultimately so destroy the strength of the Executive with the people and create so great discontent with the people themselves that the Executive of their own choice upon the Federal forces and numbers which the Constitution gives to that election would not submit to the executive power thus bestowed being given to a body that had its constitution without any popular election whatever, and had its members and strength made up not by the wealth and power and strength of the people, but by the equality of the States.

When you add to that this change which gives to the Senate a voice in the removal from office, and thus gives them the first hold upon the question of the maintenance of official power in the country, you change wholly the question of the Constitution; and instead of giving the Senate only the advisory force which that instrument commits to it, and only under the conditions that the office being to be filled they have nothing to say but who shall fill it, and if they do not concur still leave it to the Executive to name another and another and another, always proceeding from his original and principal motion in the matter, you change it to the absolute preliminary power of this body to say to the Executive of the United States that every administrative office under him shall remain as it is, and these officers shall be over him and against him provided they be with and for you; and when you add to that the power to say "until we know and determine who the successor will be, until we get the first move by the Executive's concession to us of the successor, we hold the reins of power that the office shall not be vacated," you do indeed break down at once the balance between the executive and the legislative power as represented in this body of the latter department of the Government, and you break down the Federal election of President at once, and commit to the equality of States the partition and distribution of the executive power of this country.

I would like to know how it is that the people of this country are to be made to adopt this principle of their Constitution that the executive power attributed to the Federal members, made up of Senators and Representatives added together for each State, is to go through the formality of the election of a President upon that principle and upon that calculation, and then find that the executive power that they supposed was involved in that primary choice and expression of the public will is to be administered and controlled by a body made up of the equality of States. I would like to know on what plan our politics are to be carried on; how can you make the combinations, how the forces, how the interests, how the efforts that are to throw themselves into a popular election to raise a presidential control of executive power, and then find that that executive power is all administered on the principle of equality of States. I would like to know how it is that New York and Pennsylvania and Ohio and Indiana and Illinois and Missouri and the great and growing States are to carry the force of popular will into the executive chair upon the Federal numbers of the Electoral Colleges, and then find that Rhode Island and Delaware and the distant States unpeopled are to control the whole possession and administration of executive power. I would like to know how long we are to keep up the form of electing a President with the will of the people behind him and then find him stripped of the power thus committed to him in the partition between the States without regard to numbers or to popular opinion. There is the grave dislocation of the balances of the Constitution; there is the absolute destruction of the power of the people over the presidential authority, keeping up the form of an election, but depriving it of all its results. And I would like to know, if by law or by will this body thus assumes to itself this derangement of the balances of the Constitution as between the States and popular numbers, how long New England can maintain in its share of executive power, as administered here, as large a proportion as belongs to New York, to Pennsylvania, to Ohio, to Indiana, to Illinois, and to Missouri together.

I must think, Mr. Chief Justice and Senators, that there has not been sufficiently considered how far these principles thus debated reach, and how the framers of the Constitution, when they came to debate in the year 1789 in Congress what was or should be the actual and practical allocation of this authority, understood the question perfectly in its bearing and in its future necessities.

True, indeed, Mr. Sherman was always a stern and persistent advocate for the strength of the Senate as against the power of the Executive. It was there, on that point, that the Senate represented the equality of States; and he and Mr. Ellsworth, holding their places in the Convention as the representatives of Connecticut, a State then a small State, between the powerful State of Massachusetts on the one side and New York on the other; and Judge Paterson, of New Jersey, the representative of that State, a small State, between the great State of New York on the one side and the great State of Pennsylvania on the other, were the advocates, undoubtedly, of this distribution of power to the Senate; and, as is well known in the history of the times, a correspondence of some importance took place between the elder Mr. Adams and Mr. Sherman, in the early days of the working of the Government, as to whether the fears of Mr. Adams that the Executive would prove too weak or the purposes of Mr. Sherman that the Senate should be strong enough were or were not most in accord with the principles of the Government. But all that was based upon the idea that the concurrence of the Senate, under the terms of the Constitution, in appointment, was the only detraction from the supremacy and independence of executive authority.

Now, this question comes up in this form, the power of removal is, and always has been, claimed and exercised by the Executive in this Government separately and independently of the Senate. Until the act of March 2, 1867, the actual power of removal by the Senate never has been claimed. Some constructions upon the affirmative exercise of the power of appointment by the Executive have at different times been suggested, and received more or less support, tending to the conclusion that thus the Senate might have some

hold of the question of removals; and now this act, which we are to consider more definitely hereafter, does not assume in terms to give the Senate a participation in the distinct and separate act of an executive nature, the removal from office. Indeed, the manner that the Congress has dealt with the subject is quite peculiar. Unable, apparently, to find adequate support for the pretension that the Senate could claim a share in the distinct act of removal or vacating of office, the scheme of the law is to change the tenure of office, so that removability as a separate and independent governmental act, by whomever to be exerted, is obliterated from the powers of this Government. Look at that, now, that you do absolutely strike out of the capacity and resources of this Government the power of removing an officer as a separate executive act; I mean an executive act in which you participate. You have determined by law that there shall be no vacation of an office possible, except when and as and by the operation of completely filling it. And so far have you carried that principle that you do not even make it possible to vacate it by the concurrence of the Senate and the President; but you have deliberately and firmly determined that the office shall remain full as an estate and possession of the incumbent, from which he can be removed under no stress of the public necessity except by the fact occurring of a complete appointment for permanent tenure of a successor concurred in by the Senate and made operative by the new appointee going into and qualifying himself in the office.

This seems at the first sight a very extraordinary provision for all the exigencies of a Government like ours, with its forty thousand officers, whose list is paraded here before you, with their twenty-one millions of emoluments, to show the magnitude of the great prize contended for between the Presidency and the Senate. It is a very singular provision, doubtless, that in a Government which includes under it forty thousand officers there should be no governmental possibility of stopping a man in or removing him from an office except by the deliberate succession of a permanent successor approved by the Senate and concurred in by the appointee himself going to the place and qualifying and assuming its duties.

I speak the language of the act, and while the Senate is in session there is not any power of temporary suspension or arrest of fraud or violence, of danger or menace, in the conduct of the subsisting officer. When you are in recess there is a power of suspension given to the Executive, and we are better off in that respect when you are in office than when you are in session, for we can, by a peremptory and definite and appropriate action, arrest misconduct by suspension. But as I said before, I repeat, under this act the incumbents of all these offices have a permanent estate until a successor, with your consent and his own, is inducted into the office.

I do not propose to discuss (as quite unnecessary to any decision of any matter to be passed on in your judgment) at any very great length the question of the constitutionality of this law. A very deliberate expression of opinion, after a very valuable and thorough debate, conducted in this body, in which the reasons on each side were ably maintained by your most distinguished members, and a very thorough consideration in the House of Representatives, where able and eminent lawyers, some of whom appear among the Managers to-day, gave the country the benefit of their knowledge and their acuteness, have placed this matter upon a legislative judgment of constitutionality. But I think all will agree that a legislative judgment of constitutionality does not conclude a court, and that when legislative judgments have differed, and when the practice of the Government for eighty years has been on one side and the new ideas introduced are confessedly of reversal and revolution in those ideas, it is not saying too much to say that after the expression of the legislative will, and after the expression of the opinion of the Legislature implied in their action, there yet would remain for debate among jurists and lawyers, among statesmen, among thoughtful citizens, and certainly properly within the province of the Supreme Court of the United States, the question whether the one or the other construction of the Constitution, so vital in its influence upon the Government, was the correct and the safe course for the conduct of the Government.

Let me ask your attention for a moment upon two points, to the question as presenting itself to the minds of the Senators, as to whether this was or was not a reversal and revolution in the practice and theories of the Government, and also as to the weight of a legislative opinion. In the Senate, the Senator from Oregon [Mr. WILLIAMS] said:

"This bill undertakes to reverse what has heretofore been the admitted practice of the Government; and it seemed to me that it was due to the exalted office of the President of the United States, the Chief Magistrate of the nation, that he should exercise this power; that he should be left to choose his own Cabinet, and that he should be held responsible, as he will be, to the country for whatever acts that Cabinet may perform."—*Congressional Globe*, Thirty-Ninth Congress, second session, p. 384.

This Senator touches the very marrow of the matter, that when you are passing this bill, which in the whole official service of this country reverses the practice, you should at least leave the exception of the Cabinet officers in. That was the point; leaving them entirely in, and that, with that exception in, it was a reversal of the practice of the Government to all the rest, and the Cabinet should be left as they were, because, as he said wisely, the country will hold the Executive responsible for what his Cabinet does; and they will so hold him until they find out that you have robbed

the Executive of all responsibility by robbing it of what is the pith of responsibility, discretion.

The same honorable Senator proceeds, in another point of the debate:

"I know there is room for disagreement of opinion; but it seemed to me that if we revolutionize the practice of the Government in all other respects, we might let this power remain in the hands of the President of the United States"—

That is, the Cabinet officers' appointment—

"that we ought not to strip him of this power, which is one that it seems to me it is necessary and reasonable that he should exercise."—*Ibid.*, p. 384.

The honorable Senator from Michigan [Mr. HOWARD] says:

"I agree with him"—

Referring to the Senator from Indiana [Mr. HENDRICKS]—

"that the practical precedents of the Government thus far lead to this interpretation of the Constitution, that it is competent for the President during the recess of the Senate to turn out of office a present incumbent and to fill his place by commissioning another. This has been, I admit, the practice for long years and many generations; but it is to be observed at the same time that this claim of power on the part of the Executive has been uniformly contested by some of the best minds of the country."—*Ibid.*, p. 407.

And now, as to the weight of mere legislative construction, even in the mind of a legislator himself, as compared with other sources of authoritative determination, let me ask your attention to some other very pertinent observations of the honorable Senator from Oregon, [Mr. WILLIAMS:]

"Those who advocate the executive power of removal rely altogether upon the legislative construction of the Constitution, sustained by the practice and opinions of individual men. I need not argue that the legislative construction of the Constitution has no binding force. It is to be treated with proper respect; but few constructions have been put upon the Constitution by Congress at one time that have not been modified or overruled at other or subsequent times; so that, so far as the legislative construction of the Constitution upon this question is concerned, it is entitled to very little consideration."—*Ibid.*, p. 439.

The point in the debate was that the legislative construction of 1789 has worked into the bones of the Government by the indurating process of practice and exercise was a construction of powerful influence on the matter; and yet the honorable Senator from Oregon justly pushes the proposition that legislative construction *per se*—that I may not speak disrespectfully, I speak his words—"that legislative construction is entitled to very little consideration;" that it has "no binding force." Shall we be told that a legislative construction of March 2, 1867, and a practice under it for one year that has brought the Congress face to face with the Executive and introduced the sword of impeachment between the two branches upon a removal from office, raising the precise question that an attempt by the President to remove a Secretary and appoint an *ad interim* discharge of its duties is to result in a removal by the Senate of the Executive itself and the appointment of one of its own members to the *ad interim* discharge of the duties of the Presidency? That is the issue made by a recent legislative construction.

But the honorable Senator from Oregon, with great force and wisdom, as it seems to me, proceeded in the debate to say that the courts of law, and, above all, the Supreme Court of the United States, were the place to look for authoritative, for permanent determinations of these constitutional questions; and it will be found that in this he but followed the wisdom shown in the debate in 1789 and in the final result of it, in which Mr. Sherman concurred as much as any member of that Congress, that it was not for Congress to name or assign the limits upon executive power by enactment nor to appropriate and confer executive power by endowment through an act of Congress, but to leave it, as Mr. White, of North Carolina, said, and as Mr. Gerry, of Massachusetts, said, and as Mr. Sherman, of Connecticut, said, for the Constitution itself to operate upon the Foreign-Secretary act, and let the action be made under it by virtue of a claim of right under the Constitution, and whoever was aggrieved let him raise his question in the courts of law. And upon that resolution and upon that situation of the thing the final vote was taken, and the matter was disposed of in that Congress; but it was then and ever since has been regarded as an authentic and authoritative determination of that Congress that the power was in the President, and it has been so insisted upon, so acted upon ever since, and nobody has been aggrieved, and nobody has raised the question in the courts of law. That is the force and the weight of the resolution of that First Congress and of the practice of the Government under it.

In the House of Representatives, also, it was a conceded point in the debate upon this bill, when one of the ablest lawyers in that body, as I understand by repute, Mr. WILLIAMS, one of the honorable Managers, in his argument for the bill, said:

"It aims at the reformation of a giant vice in the administration of this Government by bringing its practice back from a rule of its infancy and inexperience."—*Ibid.*, p. 18.

He thought it was a faulty practice, but that it was a practice, and that, from its infancy to the day of the passage of the bill it was a vice inherent in the system and exercising its power over its action he did not doubt. He admits, subsequently, in the same debate that the Congress of 1789 decided, and their successors for three quarters of a century acquiesced in this doctrine.

I will not weary the Senate with a thorough analysis of the debate of 1789. It is, I believe, decidedly the most important debate in the history of Congress. It is, I think, the best considered debate in the history of the Government. I think it included among its debaters as many of the able men and of the wise men, the benefit of whose public service this nation has ever enjoyed, as any debate or measure that this Government has ever entertained or canvassed. And it was a debate in which the civil prudence and forecast of the debaters manifested itself, whichever side they took of the question, in wonderful wisdom, for the premises of the Constitution were very narrow. Most probably the question of removal from office as a distinct subject had never occurred to the minds of men in the Convention. The tenure of office as not to be made permanent except in the case of the justices of the Supreme Court, and the periodicity of the House of Representatives, of the Senate, and of the Executive were fixed. Then there was an attribution of the whole inferior administrative official power of the Government to the Executive as being an executive act, with the single qualification, exceptional in itself, that the advice and consent of the Senate should be interposed as a negative upon presidential nomination carrying him back to a substitute if they should not agree on the first nominee.

The point raised was exactly this, and may be very briefly stated: those who, with Mr. Sherman, maintained that the concurrence in removals was as necessary as the concurrence in appointments put themselves on a proposition that the same power that appointed should have the removal. That was a little begging of the question—speaking it with all respect—as to who the appointing power was really under the terms and in the intent of the Constitution. But, conceding that the connection of the Senate with the matter really made them a part of the appointing power, the answer to the argument, triumphant as it seems to me, as it came from the distinguished speakers, Mr. Madison, Mr. Boudinot, Fisher Ames, and other supporters of the doctrine that finally triumphed, was this: primarily the whole business of official subordinate executive action is a part of the executive function; that being attributed *in solido* to the President, we look to exceptions to serve the turn and precise measure of their own definition, and discard that falsest principle of reasoning in regard to laws or in regard to conduct, that exception is to breed exception or amplification of exception. The general mass is to lose what is subtracted from it by exception, and the general mass is to remain with its whole weight not thus separately and definitely reduced. When, therefore, these statesmen said you find the freedom of executive action and its solid authority reduced by an exception of advice and consent in appointment you must understand that that is the limit of the exception, and the executive power in all other respects stands unimpaired.

What, then, is the test of the consideration? Whether removal from office belongs to the executive power, if the Constitution has not attributed it elsewhere; and then the question was of statesmanship, whether this debate was important, whether it was vital, whether its determination one way or the other did affect seriously the character of the Government and its working; and I think all agreed that it did, and all so agreeing, and all coming to the resolution that I have stated, what weight, what significance is there in the fact that the party that was defeated in the argument submitted to the conclusion and to the practice of the Government under it, and did not raise a voice or take a vote in derogation of it during the whole course of the Government?

But it does not stand upon this. After forty-five years' working of this system, between the years 1830 and 1835, the great party exacerbations between the Democracy, under the lead of General Jackson, and the Whigs, under the mastery of the eminent men that then filled these Halls, the only survivor of whom, eminent then himself and eminent ever since, now does me the honor to listen to my remarks, [referring to Hon. Thomas Ewing, of Ohio,] then under that antagonism there was renewed the great debate; and what was the measure which the contesting party, under the influence of party spirit, brought the matter to? Mr. Webster said while he led the forces in a great array, which, perhaps, for the single instance combined the triumvirate of himself, Mr. Calhoun, and Mr. Clay, that the contrary opinion and the contrary practice was settled. He said: "I regard it as a settled point; settled by construction, settled by precedent, settled by the practice of the Government, settled by legislation;" and he did not seek to disturb it. He knew the force of those forty-five years, the whole existence of the nation under its Constitution upon a question of that kind; and he sought only to interpose a moral restraint upon the President in requiring him, when he removed from office, to assign the reasons of the removal.

General Jackson and the Democratic party met the point promptly with firmness and with thoroughness, and in his protest against a resolution which the Senate had adopted in 1834, I think, that his action in the removal of Mr. Duane (though they brought it down finally, I believe, to the point of the removal of the deposits) had been in derogation of the Constitution and the laws, he met it with a defiance in his protest which brought two great topics of debate up; one the independence of the Executive in its right to judge of constitutional questions, and the other the great point that the conferring by choice of the people upon the President of their representation through Federal numbers, was an important part of the Constitution, and that he was not a man of his own will, but endued and reënforced by the will of the people. That debate was carried on and that debate was determined by the Senate passing a vote which enacted its opinion that his conduct had been in derogation of the Constitution and the laws; and on this very point a reference was made to the common master of them all, the people of the United States; and upon a reëlection of General Jackson and upon a confirmation of opinion from the people themselves, they in their primary capacity acting through the authentic changes of their Government, by election, brought into the Senate, upon this challenge, a majority that expunged the resolution censuring the action of the Executive. You talk about power to decide constitutional questions by Congress, power to decide them by the Supreme Court, power to decide them by the Executive. I show you the superior power of all that has been drawn into the great debate, of public opinion and the determination of the suffrage, and I say that the history of free countries, the history of popular liberty, the history of the power of the people, not by passion or by violence, but by reason, by discretion and peaceful, silent, patient exercise of their power, was never shown more distinctly and more definitely than on this very matter, whether it is a part of the executive power of this country or of the legislative or senatorial power, that removal from office should remain in the Executive or be distributed among the Senators. It was not my party that was pleased or that was triumphant, but of the fact of what the people thought there was not any doubt, and there never has been since until the new situation has produced new interests and resulted in new conclusions.

Honorable Senators and Representatives will remember how in the debate which led to the passage of the civil-tenure act it was represented that the authority of the First Congress of 1789 ought to be somewhat scrutinized because of the influence upon their debates and conclusions that the great character of the Chief Magistrate, President Washington, might have produced upon their minds. Senators, why can we not look at the present as we look at the past? Why can we not see in ourselves what we so easily discern as possible with others? Why can we not appreciate it that perhaps the judgments of Senators and of Representatives now may have been warped or misled somewhat by their opinions and feelings toward the Executive as it is now filled? I apprehend, therefore, that this matter of party influence is one that is quite as wise to consider, and this matter of personal power in authority of character and conduct is quite as suitable to be weighed when we are acting as when we are criticising the action of others.

Two passages I may be permitted to quote from this great debate as carried on in the Congress of 1789. One is from Mr. Madison at page 480 of the first volume of the Annals of Congress:

"It is evidently the intention of the Constitution that the first magistrate should be responsible for the executive department. So far, therefore, as we do not make the officers who are to aid him in the duties of that department responsible to him, he is not responsible to his country. Again, is there no danger that an officer, when he is appointed by the concurrence of the Senate, and has friends in that body, may choose rather to risk his establishment on the favor of that branch than rest it upon the discharge of his duties to the satisfaction of the executive branch, which is constitutionally authorized to inspect and control his conduct? And if it should happen that the officers connect themselves with the Senate, they may mutually support each other, and for want of efficacy reduce the power of the President to a mere vapor; in which case his responsibility would be annihilated, and the expectation of it unjust. The high executive officers, joined in cabal with the Senate, would lay the foundation of discord, and end in an assumption of the executive power, only to be removed by a revolution in the Government. I believe no principle is more clearly laid down in the Constitution than that of responsibility."

Mr. Boudinot, (page 487,) said:

"Neither this clause [of impeachment] nor any other goes so far as to say it shall be the only mode of removal; therefore, we may proceed to inquire what the other is. Let us examine whether it belongs to the Senate and President. Certainly, sir, there is nothing that gives the Senate this right in express terms; but they are authorized, in express words, to be concerned in the appointment. And does this necessarily include the power of removal? If the President complains to the Senate of the misconduct of an officer, and desires their advice and consent to the removal, what are the Senate to do? Most certainly they will inquire if the complaint is well founded. To do this they must call the officer before them to answer. Who, then, are the parties? The supreme executive officer against his assistant; and the Senate are to sit as judges to determine whether sufficient cause of removal exists. Does not this set the Senate over the head of the President? But suppose they shall decide in favor of the officer, what a situation is the President then in, surrounded by officers with whom, by his situation, he is compelled to act, but in whom he can have no confidence, reversing the privilege given him by the Constitution, to prevent his having officers imposed upon him who do not meet his approbation?"

In these weighty words of Mr. Boudinot and Mr. Madison is found the marrow of the whole controversy. There is no escaping from it. If this body pursue the method now adopted they must be responsible to the country for the action of the executive department; and if officers are to be maintained, as these wise statesmen say, over the head of the President, then that power of the Constitution which allowed him to have a voice in their selection is entirely gone; for I need not say that if it is to be dependent upon an instantaneous selection, and thereafter there is to be no space of repentance or no change of purpose on the part of the Executive as new acts shall develop themselves and new traits of character shall show themselves in the incumbent, it is idle to say that he has the power of appointment. It must be the power of appointment from day to day; that is the power, of appointment for which he should be held responsible, if he is to be responsible at all. I wish to ask your attention to the opinions expressed by some of the statesmen who took part in this determination of what the effect, and the important effect, of this conclusion of the Congress of 1789 was. None of them overlooked its importance on one side or the other; and I beg leave to read from the life and works of the elder Adams, at page 448 of the first volume, the interesting comments of one, himself a distinguished statesman, in whom we all have confidence, Mr. Charles Francis Adams:

"The question most earnestly disputed turned upon the power vested by the Constitution in the President to remove the person at the head of that bureau at his pleasure. One party maintained it was an absolute right. The other insisted that it was subject to the same restriction of a ratification by the Senate which is required when the officer is appointed. After a long contest in the House of Representatives, terminating in favor of the unrestricted construction, the bill came up to the Senate for its approbation.

"This case was peculiar and highly important. By an anomaly in the Constitution, which, upon any recognized theory, it is difficult to defend, the Senate, which, in the last resort, is made the judicial tribunal to try the President for malversation in office, is likewise clothed with the power of denying him the agents in whom he may choose most to confide for the faithful execution of the duties of his station, and forcing him to select such as they may prefer. If, in addition to this, the power of displacing such as he found unworthy of trust had been subjected to the same control, it cannot admit of a doubt that the Government must, in course of time, have become an oligarchy, in which the President would sink into a mere instrument of any faction that might happen to be in the ascendant in the Senate; this, too, at the same time that he would be subject to be tried by them for offenses in his department, over which he could exercise no effective restraint whatever. In such case the alternative is inevitable, either that he would have become a confederate with that faction, and therefore utterly beyond the reach of punishment by impeachment at their hands for offenses committed with their privity, if not at their dictation, or else, in case of his refusal, that he would have been powerless to defend himself against the paralyzing operation of their ill-will. Such a state of subjection in the executive head to the Legislature is subversive of all ideas of a balance of powers drawn from the theory of the British Constitution, and renders probable at any moment a collision, in which one side or the other, and it is most likely to be the Legislature, must be ultimately annihilated.

"Yet, however true these views may be in the abstract, it would scarcely have caused surprise if their soundness had not been appreciated in the Senate. The temptation to magnify their authority is commonly all-powerful with public bodies of every kind. In any other stage of the present Government than the first it would have proved quite irresistible. But throughout the administration of General Washington there is visible among public men a degree of indifference to power and place which forms one of the most marked features of that time. More than once the highest Cabinet and foreign appointments went begging to suitable candidates, and begged in vain. To this fact it is owing that public questions of such moment were then discussed with as much of personal disinterestedness as can probably ever be expected to enter into them anywhere. Yet even with all these favoring circumstances it soon became clear that the republican jealousy of a centralization of power in the President would combine with the *esprit du corps* to rally at least half the Senate in favor of subjecting removals to their control. In such a case the responsibility of deciding the point devolved, by the terms of the Constitution, upon Mr. Adams, as Vice President. The debate was continued from the 15th to the 18th of July, a very long time for that day in an assembly comprising only twenty-two members when full, but seldom more than twenty in attendance. A very brief abstract, the only one that has yet seen the light, is furnished in the third Volume of the present work. Mr. Adams appears to have made it for the purpose of framing his own judgment in the contingency which he must have foreseen as likely to occur. The final vote was taken on the 18th. Nine Senators voted to subject the President's power of removal to the will of the Senate: Messrs. Few, Grayson, Gunn, Johnson, Izard, Langdon, Lee, Maclay, and Wingate. On the other hand, nine Senators voted against claiming the restriction: Messrs. Bassett, Carroll, Dalton, Elmer, Henry, Morris, Paterson, Read, and Strong. The result depended upon the voice of the Vice President. It was the first time that he had been summoned to such a duty. It was the only time during his eight years of service in that place that he felt the case to be of such importance as to justify his assigning reasons for his vote. These reasons were not committed to paper, however, and can, therefore, never be known. But in their soundness it is certain that he never had the shadow of a doubt. His decision settled the question of constitutional power in favor of the President, and, consequently, established the practice under the Government, which has continued down to this day. Although there have been occasional exceptions taken to it in argument, especially at moments when the executive power, wielded by a strong hand, seemed to encroach upon the limits of the coördinate departments, its substantial correctness has been, on the whole, quite generally acquiesced in. And all have agreed that no single act of the First Congress has been attended with more important effects upon the working of every part of the Government."

It is thus that this was regarded at the time that the transaction took place. I beg now to call the attention of the Senate to the opinions of Fisher Ames, as expressed in letters written by him concurrently with the action of the Congress to his correspondent, an intelligent lawyer of Boston, Mr. George Richards Minot. In a letter to Mr. Minot, dated the 31st of May, 1789, to be found in the first volume of the life of Mr. Ames, page 51, he writes:

"You dislike the responsibility of the President in the case of the Minister of Foreign Affairs. I would have the President responsible for his appointments; and if those whom he puts in are unfit they may be impeached on misconduct, or he may remove them when he finds them obnoxious. It would be easier for a minister to secure a faction in the Senate or get the protection of the Senators of his own State than to secure the protection of the President, whose character would suffer by it. The number of the Senators, the secrecy of their doings, would shelter *them*, and a corrupt connection between those who appoint *to* office and who also maintain *in* office and the officers themselves would be created. The meddling of the Senate in appointments is one of the least defensible parts of the Constitution. I would not extend their power any further."

And again, under date of June 23, 1789, page 55 of the same volume:

"The debate in relation to the President's power of removal from office is an instance. Four days' unceasing speechifying has furnished you with the merits of the question. The transaction of yesterday may need some elucidation. In the Committee of the Whole it was moved to strike out the words 'to be removable by the President,' &c. This did not pass, and the words were retained. The bill was reported to the House, and a motion made to insert in the second clause, 'whenever an officer shall be removed by the President, or a vacancy shall happen in any other way,' to the intent to strike out the first words. The first words, 'to be removable,' &c., were supposed to amount to a legislative disposal of the power of removal. If the Constitution had vested it in the President, it was improper to use such words as would imply that the power was to be exercised by him in virtue of this act. The mover and supporters of the amendment supposed that a grant by the Legislature might be resumed, and that as the Constitution had already given it to the President it was putting it on better ground, and, if once gained by the declaration of both Houses, would be a construction of the Constitution, and not liable to future encroachments. Others, who contended against the advisory part of the Senate in removals, supposed the first ground the most tenable, that it would include the latter, and operate as a declaration of the Constitution, and at the same time expressly dispose of the power. They further apprehended that any change of position would divide the victors and endanger the final decision in both Houses. There was certainly weight in this last opinion. Yet, the amendment being actually proposed, it remained only to choose between the two clauses. I think the latter, which passed, and which seems to imply the legal (rather constitutional) power of the President, is the safest doctrine. This prevailed, and the first words

were expunged. This has produced discontent, and possibly in the event it will be found disagreement, among those who voted with the majority.

"This is in fact a great question, and I feel perfectly satisfied with the President's right to exercise the power, either by the Constitution or the authority of an act. The arguments in favor of the former fall short of full proof, but in my mind they greatly preponderate.

"You will say that I have expressed my sentiments with some moderation. You will be deceived, for my whole heart has been engaged in this debate. Indeed, it has ached. It has kept me agitated, and in no small degree unhappy. I am commonly opposed to those who modestly assume the rank of champions of liberty and make a very patriotic noise about the people. It is the stale artifice which has duped the world a thousand times, and yet, though detected, it is still successful. I love liberty as well as anybody. I am proud of it, as the true title of our people to distinction above others; but so are others, for they have an interest and a pride in the same thing. But I would guard it by making the laws strong enough to protect it. In this debate a stroke was aimed at the vitals of the Government, perhaps with the best intentions, but I have no doubt of the tendency to a true aristocracy."

It will thus be seen, Senators, that the statesmen whom we most revere regarded this as, so to speak, a construction of the Constitution as important as the framing of itself had been. And now, a law of Congress having introduced a revolution in the doctrine and in the practice of the Government, a legislative construction binding no one and being entitled to little respect from the changeableness of legislative constructions, in the language of the honorable Senator from Oregon, the question arises whether a doubt, whether an act in reference to the unconstitutionality of this law on the part of the executive department is a ground of impeachment. The doctrine of unconstitutional law seems to me—and I speak with great respect—to be wholly misunderstood by the honorable Managers in the propositions which they present. Nobody can ever violate an unconstitutional law, for it is not a rule binding upon him or anybody else. His conduct in violating it or in contravening it may be at variance with other ethical and civil conditions of duty; and for the violation of those ethical and civil conditions he may be responsible. If a marshal of the United States, executing an unconstitutional fugitive slave bill, enters with the process of the authority of law, it does not follow that resistance may be carried to the extent of shooting the marshal; but it is not because it is a violation of that law; for if it is unconstitutional there can be no violation of it. It is because civil duty does not permit civil contests to be raised by force and violence. So, too, if a subordinate executive officer, who has nothing but ministerial duty to perform, as a United States marshal in the service of process under an unconstitutional law, undertakes to deal with the question of its unconstitutionality, the ethical and civil duty on his part is, as it is merely ministerial on his part to have his conscience determine whether he will execute it in this ministerial capacity or whether he will resign his office. He cannot, under proper ethical rules,

determine whether the execution of the law
shall be defeated by the resistance of the apparatus provided for its execution; but if the law
bears upon his personal rights or official emoluments, then, without a violation of the peace,
he may raise the question of the law and resist
it consistently with all civil and ethical duties.

Thus we see at once that we are brought face
to face with the fundamental propositions, and
I ask attention to a passage from the Federalist, at page 549, where there is a very vigorous
discussion by Mr. Hamilton of the question of
unconstitutional laws; and to the case of Marbury *vs.* Madison in 1 Cranch. The subject is
old, but it is there discussed with a luminous
wisdom, both in advance of the adoption of the
Constitution and of its construction by the Supreme Court of the United States, that may
well displace the more inconsiderate and loose
views that have been presented in debate here.
In the Federalist, No. 78, page 541, Mr. Hamilton says:

"Some perplexity respecting the rights of the courts
to pronounce legislative acts void, because contrary
to the Constitution, has arisen from an imagination
that the doctrine would imply a superiority of the
judiciary to the legislative power. It is urged that
the authority which can declare the acts of another
void must necessarily be superior to the one whose
acts may be declared void. As this doctrine is of
great importance in all the American Constitutions,
a brief discussion of the ground on which it rests cannot be unacceptable.

"There is no position which depends on clearer principles than that every act of a delegated authority
contrary to the tenor of the commission under which
it is exercised is void. No legislative act, therefore,
contrary to the Constitution, can be valid. To deny
this would be to affirm that the deputy is greater
than his principal; that the servant is above his
master; that the representatives of the people are
superior to the people themselves; that men acting
by virtue of powers may do not only what their powers
do not authorize, but what they forbid.

"If it be said that the legislative body are themselves the constitutional judges of their own powers,
and that the construction they put upon them is conclusive upon the other departments, it may be answered that this cannot be the natural presumption,
where it is not to be collected from any particular
provisions in the Constitution. It is not otherwise
to be supposed that the Constitution could intend to
enable the representatives of the people to substitute their *will* to that of their constituents. It is far
more rational to suppose that the courts were designed to be an intermediate body between the people and the Legislature, in order, among other things,
to keep the latter within the limits assigned to their
authority. The interpretation of the laws is the
proper and peculiar province of the courts. A Constitution is, in fact, and must be regarded by the
judges as a fundamental law. It therefore belongs
to them to ascertain its meaning, as well as the meaning of any particular act proceeding from the legislative body. If there should happen to be an irreconcilable variance between the two, that which has
the superior obligation and validity ought, of course,
to be preferred; or, in other words, the Constitution
ought to be preferred to the statute, the intention of
the people to the intention of their agents.

"Nor does this conclusion, by any means, suppose
a superiority of the judicial to the legislative power.
It only supposes that the power of the people is superior to both, and that where the will of the Legislature, declared in its statutes, stands in opposition
to that of the people, declared in the Constitution,
the judges ought to be governed by the latter rather
than the former. They ought to regulate their decisions by the fundamental laws, rather than by those
which are not fundamental."

Again:

"If, then, the courts of justice are to be considered
as the bulwarks of a limited Constitution, against
legislative encroachments, this consideration will
afford a strong argument for the permanent tenure
of judicial offices, since nothing will contribute so
much as this to that independent spirit in the judges,
which must be essential to the faithful performance
of so arduous a duty."—*Ibid.*, 544.

In the case of Marbury *vs.* Madison, (1
Cranch, pp. 175, 178,) the Supreme Court of
the United States, speaking through the great
Chief Justice Marshall, said:

"The question whether an act repugnant to the
Constitution can become the law of the land is a
question deeply interesting to the United States; but
happily not of an intricacy proportioned to its interests. It seems only necessary to recognize certain principles, supposed to have been long and well established, to decide it.

"That the people have an original right to establish for their future government such principles as,
in their opinion, shall most conduce to their own
happiness is the basis on which the whole American
fabric has been erected. The exercise of this original right is a very great exertion; nor can it, nor
ought it, to be frequently repeated. The principles,
therefore, so established are deemed fundamental,
and as the authority from which they proceed is
supreme and can seldom act they are designed to be
permanent.

"This original and supreme will organizes the
Government and assigns to different departments
their respective powers. It may either stop here or
establish certain limits not to be transcended by those
departments.

"The Government of the United States is of the
latter description. The powers of the Legislature
are defined and limited; and that those limits may
not be mistaken or forgotten the Constitution is
written. To what purpose are powers limited, and
to what purpose is that limitation committed to
writing if these limits may at any time be passed by
those intended to be restrained? The distinction
between a Government with limited and unlimited
powers is abolished if those limits do not confine the
persons on whom they are imposed, and if acts prohibited and acts allowed are of equal obligation. It
is a proposition too plain to be contested that the
Constitution controls any legislative act repugnant
to it; or that the Legislature may alter the Constitution by an ordinary act.

"Between these alternatives there is no middle
ground. The Constitution is either a superior, paramount law, unchangeable by ordinary means, or it
is on a level with ordinary legislative acts, and, like
other acts, is alterable when the Legislature shall
please to alter it.

"If the former part of the alternative be true,
then a legislative act contrary to the Constitution is
not law; if the latter part be true, then written constitutions are absurd attempts on the part of the people to limit a power in its own nature illimitable.

"Certainly all those who have framed written
constitutions contemplate them as forming the fundamental and paramount law of the nation, and,
consequently, the theory of every such government
must be that an act of the legislature, repugnant to
the constitution, is void.

"This theory is essentially attached to a written
constitution, and is, consequently, to be considered
by the court as one of the fundamental principles
of our society. It is not, therefore, to be lost sight
of in the further consideration of this subject.

"If an act of the Legislature repugnant to the
Constitution is void, does it, notwithstanding its invalidity, bind the courts and oblige them to give it
effect? Or, in other words, though it be not law, does
it constitute a rule as operative as if it was a law?
This would be to overthrow in fact what was established in theory, and would seem, at first view, an
absurdity too gross to be insisted on. It shall, however, receive a more attentive consideration.

"It is emphatically the province and duty of the
judicial department to say what the law is. Those

who apply the rule to particular cases must of necessity expound and interpret that rule. If two laws conflict with each other the courts must decide on the operation of each.

"So if a law be in opposition to the Constitution; if both the law and the Constitution apply to a particular case, so that the court must either decide that case conformably to the law, disregarding the Constitution; or conformably to the Constitution, disregarding the law, the court must determine which of these conflicting rules governs the case. This is of the very essence of judicial duty.

"If, then, the courts are to regard the Constitution—and the Constitution is superior to any ordinary act of the Legislature—the Constitution, and not such ordinary act, must govern the case to which they both apply.

"Those, then, who controvert the principle that the Constitution is to be considered, in court, as a paramount law, are reduced to the necessity of maintaining that courts must close their eyes on the Constitution and see only the law.

"This doctrine would subvert the very foundation of all written constitutions. It would declare that an act which, according to the principles and theory of our Government, is entirely void, is yet, in practice, completely obligatory. It would declare that if the Legislature shall do what is expressly forbidden, such act, notwithstanding the express prohibition, is in reality effectual. It would be giving to the Legislature a practical and real omnipotence with the same breath which professes to restrict their powers within narrow limits. It is prescribing limits, and declaring that those limits may be passed at pleasure.

"That it thus reduces to nothing what we have deemed the greatest improvement on political institutions—a written constitution—would of itself be sufficient in America, where written constitutions have been viewed with so much reverence for rejecting the construction."

Undoubtedly it is a question of very grave consideration how far the different departments of the Government, legislative, judicial, and executive, are at liberty to act in reference to unconstitutional laws. The judicial duty, perhaps, may be plain. They wait for a case; they volunteer no advice; they exercise no supervision. But as between the Legislature and the Executive, even when the Supreme Court has passed upon the question, it is one of the gravest constitutional points for public men to determine when and how the Legislature may raise the question again by passing a law against the decision of the Supreme Court, and the Executive may raise the question again by undertaking an executive duty under the Constitution against the decision of the Supreme Court and against the determination of Congress. We in this case have been accused of insisting upon extravagant pretensions. We have never suggested anything further than this, for the case only requires it, that whatever may be the doubtful or debatable region of the coördinate authority of the different departments of Government to judge for themselves of the constitutionality or unconstitutionality of laws, to raise the question anew in their authentic and responsible public action, when the President of the United States, in common with the humblest citizen, finds a law passed over his right, and binding upon his action in the matter of his right, then all reasons of duty to self, to the public, to the Constitution, to the laws, require that the matter should be put in the train of judicial decision, in order that the light of the

C. I.—47.

serene reason of the Supreme Court may be shed upon it, to the end that Congress even may reconsider its action and retract its encroachment upon the Constitution.

But Senators will not have forgotten that General Jackson, in his celebrated controversy with the Whig party, claimed that no department of the Government should receive its final and necessary and perpetual exclusion and conclusion on a constitutional question from the judgment even of the Supreme Court, and that under the obligations of each one's oath, yours as Senators, yours as Representatives, and the President's as Chief Executive, each must act in a new juncture and in reference to a new matter arising to raise again the question of constitutional authority. Now, let me read in a form which I have ready for quotation a short passage on which General Jackson in his protest sets this forth. I read from a debate on the fugitive slave law as conducted in this body in the year 1852, when the honorable Senator from Massachusetts [Mr. SUMNER] was the spokesman and champion of the right for every department of the Government to judge the constitutionality of law and of duty:

"But whatever may be the influence of this judgment"—

That is, the judgment of the Supreme Court of the United States in the case of Prigg vs. Pennsylvania—

"But whatever may be the influence of this judgment as a rule to the judiciary it cannot arrest our duty as legislators. And here I adopt, with entire assent, the language of President Jackson, in his memorable veto, in 1832, of the Bank of the United States. To his course was opposed the authority of the Supreme Court, and this is his reply:

"'If the opinion of the Supreme Court covers the whole ground of this act it ought not to control the coördinate authorities of this Government. The Congress, the Executive, and the court, must each for itself be guided by its own opinion of the Constitution. *Each public officer who takes an oath to support the Constitution swears that he will support it as he understands it, and not as it is understood by others.* It is as much the duty of the House of Representatives, of the Senate, and of the President, to decide upon the constitutionality of any bill or resolution which may be presented to them for passage or approval as it is of the supreme judges when it may be brought before them for judicial decision. The authority of the Supreme Court must not, therefore, be permitted to control the Congress or the Executive when acting in their several legislative capacities, but to have only such influence as the force of their reasoning may deserve.'

"With these authoritative words of Andrew Jackson I dismiss this topic."—*Appendix to Congressional Globe*, Thirty-Second Congress, first session, p. 1108.

"Times change and we change with them." Nevertheless, principles remain; duties remain; the powers of Government remain; their coördination remains; the conscience of men remains, and everybody that has taken an oath, and everybody that is subject to the Constitution without taking an oath, by peaceful means has a right to revere the Constitution in derogation of unconstitutional laws; and any legislative will or any judicial authority that shall deny the supremacy of the Constitution in its power to protect men who thus conscientiously, thus peacefully raise questions for determination in a conflict between the Constitution and the law, will not be consistent with written constitutions or with the maintenance of the liberties of this people as established by and dependent upon the preservation of written constitutions.

Now let us see whether upon every ethical, constitutional, and legal rule the President of the United States was not the person upon whom this civil-tenure act operated, not as an executive officer to carry out the law, but as one of the coördinate departments of the Government over whom in that official relation the authority of the act was sought to be asserted. The language is general. "Every removal from office contrary to the provisions of this act shall be a high misdemeanor." Who could remove from office but the President of the United States? Who had the authority? Who could be governed by the law but he? And it was in an official constitutional duty, not a personal right, not a matter of personal value or choice or interest with him.

When, therefore, it is said and claimed that by force of a legislative enactment the President of the United States should not remove from office, whether the act of Congress was constitutional or not, that he was absolutely prohibited from removing from office, and if he did remove from office, although the Constitution allowed him to remove, yet the Constitution could not protect him for removing, but that the act of Congress seizing upon him could draw him in here by impeachment and subject him to judgment for violating the law though maintaining the Constitution, and that the Constitution pronounced sentence of condemnation and infamy upon him for having worshiped its authority and sought to maintain it, and that the authority of Congress has that power and extent practically, you tear asunder your Constitution, and (if on these grounds you dismiss this President from this court convicted and deposed) you dismiss him the victim of the Congress and the martyr of the Constitution by the very terms of your judgment, and you throw open for the masters of us all in the great debates of an intelligent, instructed, populous, patriotic nation of freemen the division of sentiment to shake this country to its center, "the omnipotence of Congress" as the rallying cry on one side, and "the supremacy of the Constitution" on the other.

Mr. CONKLING. Mr. President, I move an intermission for fifteen minutes.

The motion was agreed to; and after the expiration of the recess the Chief Justice resumed the chair and called the Senate to order.

Mr. GRIMES. Mr. Chief Justice, I move a call of the Senate.

The motion was agreed to.

The CHIEF JUSTICE. The Secretary will call the roll.

The Chief Clerk called the roll.

The CHIEF JUSTICE. There are forty-two Senators answering to their names. A quorum is present. The counsel for the President will proceed.

Mr. EVARTS. There is but one other topic that I need to insist upon here as bearing upon that part of my argument which is intended to exhibit to the clear apprehension, and I hope adoption, of this court, the view that all here that possesses weight and dignity, that really presents the agitating contest which has been proceeding between the departments of our Government, is political and not criminal, or suitable for judicial cognizance; and that is what seems to me the decisive test in your judgments and in your consciences; and that is the attitude that every one of you already in your public action occupies toward this subject.

The Constitution of the United States never intended so to coerce and constrain the consciences and the duties of men as to bring them into the position of judges between themselves and another branch of government in regard to matters of difference between themselves and that other branch of government in matters which concerned wholly the partition of authority under the Constitution between themselves and that other department of the Government. The eternal principles of justice are implied in the constitution of every court, and there are no more immutable, no more inevitable principles than these, that no man shall be a judge in his own cause, and that no man shall be a judge in a matter in which he has already given judgment. It is abhorrent to the natural sense of justice that men should judge in their own cause. It is inconsistent with nature itself that man should assume an oath and hope to perform it by being impartial in his judgment when he has already formed it. The crimes that a President may have imputed to him that may bring him into judgment of the Senate are crimes against the Constitution or the laws involving turpitude or personal delinquency.

They are crimes in which it is inadmissable to imagine that the Senate should be committed as parties at all. They are crimes which, however much the necessary reflection of political opinions may bias the personal judgment of this or that member, or all the members of the body—an infirmity in the court which cannot be avoided—yet it must be possible only that they should give a color or a turn and not be themselves the very basis and substance of the judgment to be rendered. When, therefore, I show you as from the records of the Senate that you yourselves have voted upon this law whose constitutionality is to be determined, and that the question of guilt or innocence arises upon constitutionality or judgment of constitutionality, when you have in your capacity of a Senate undertaken after the alleged crime committed, as an act suitable in your judgment to be performed by you in your relation to the executive authority and your duty under this Government to pronounce, as you did by resolution, that the removal of Mr. Stanton and the appointment of General Thomas were not authorized by the Constitution and the laws, you either did or did not regard that as a matter of political action; and if you regarded it as a matter of political action, then you regarded it as a matter that could not possibly be brought before you in your judicial capacity for you to determine upon any personal consequences to the Executive. How was it a matter for political action unless it was a matter of his political action and the controversy was wholly of a political nature? If you, on the other hand, had in your minds the possibility of this extraordinary jurisdiction being brought into play by a complaint to be moved by the House of Representatives before you, what an extraordinary spectacle do you present to yourselves and to the country? No; the controlling, the necessary feeling upon which you acted must have been that "it is a stage and a step in governmental action concerning which we give this admonition and this suggestion and this reproof."

In 1834, when the Senate of the United States was debating the question of the resolution condemnatory of General Jackson's proceedings in reference to the deposits and Mr. Duane, the question was raised, "Can you, will you, should you pronounce opinion upon a matter of this kind when possibly it may be made the occasion, if your views are right, of an impeachment and of a necessary trial?" The answer of the great and trusted statesmen of the Whig party of that day was, "If there was in the atmosphere a whisper, if there was in the future a menace, if there was a hope or a fear, accordingly as we may think or feel, that impeachment was to come, debate must be silenced and the resolution suppressed." But they recognized the fact that it was mere political action that was being resorted to, and that was or was to be possible; but the complexion of the House, and the sentiment of the the House, and the attitude of the Senate as claiming it only to be matter of political discussion and determination, absolutely rejected the notion of impeachment, and labored, therefore, the debate a political debate and the conclusion a political conclusion.

There is but óne proposition that consists with the truth of the case and with the situation of you, Senators, here, and that is that you regarded this as political action and political decision, not by possibility a matter of judgment on a subject to be introduced for judicial consideration. It is not true that that resolution does not cover guilt; it only expresses an opinion that the state of the law and the authority of the Constitution did not cover the action of the President, but it does not impute violence or design or wickedness of purpose, or other than a justifiable difference of opinion to resort to an arbiter between you. But, even in that limited view, I take it no Sen-

ator can think or feel that, as a preliminary part of the judgment of a court that was to end in acquittal or conviction, this proceeding could be for a moment justified.

The two gravest articles of impeachment against the weightiest trial ever introduced into this court, those on which as large a vote of condemnation was gained as upon any others, were the two articles against Judge Chase, one of which brought him in question for coming to the trial of Fries, in Pennsylvania, with a formed and pronounced opinion; and another, the third, was for allowing a juryman to enter the box on the trial of Callender, at Richmond, who stated that he had formed an opinion.

I would like to see a court of impeachment that regards this as great matter that a judge should come to a trial and pronounce a condemnation of the prisoner before the counsel are heard, and should allow a juryman to enter the box who excused himself from having a free mind on the point discussed as he had formed an opinion, and yet that should tell us that you having formed and expressed an opinion are to sit here judges on such a matter as this. What is there but an answer of this kind necessary? the Constitution never brings a Senate into an inculpation and a condemnation of a President upon matters in which and of which the two departments of the Government in their political capacities have formed and expressed political opinions. It is of other matter and of other fault, in which there are no parties and no discriminations of opinion. It is of offense, of crime, in which the common rules held by all of duty, of obligation, of excess, or of sin, are not determinable upon political opinions formed and expressed in debate.

But the other principle is equally contravened, and this aids my argument that it is political and not personal or criminal; it is that you are to pass judgment of and concerning the question of the partition of the offices of this Government between the President and yourselves. The very matter of his fault is that he claims them; the very matter of his condemnation is that you have a right to them; and you, aided by the list furnished by the Managers, of forty-one thousand in number and $21,000,000 of annual emolument, are to sit here as judges whether his false claim and his appeal to a common arbiter in a matter of this kind is to be imputed to him as personal guilt and followed by personal punishment.

How would any of us like to be tried before a judge who, if he condemned us, would have our houses, and if he acquitted us we should have his? So sensitive is the natural sense of justice on this point that the whole country was in a blaze by a provision in the fugitive slave law that a commissioner should have but five dollars if he set the slave free and ten dollars if he remanded him. Have honorable judges of this court forgotten that crisis of the public mind as to allowing a judge to have an interest in the subject of his judgment? Have they forgotten that the honorable Senator from Massachusetts in the debate upon this tenure-of-office act thought that political bias might affect a court so that it might give judgment of but nominal punishment for an infraction of the act; and yet you are full of politics. Why? Because the question is political; and the whole point of my reference is as an absolute demonstration that the Constitution of the United States never forces honorable men into a position where they are judges in their own cause or where they have in the course of their previous duties expressed a judgment.

I have omitted from this consideration the fact that the great office itself, if by your judgment it shall be taken from the elected head of this Republic, is to be put in commission with a member of your own body chosen to-day, and to-morrow, at any time, by yourselves, and that you are taking the crown of the people's magistracy and of the people's glory to decorate the honor of the Senate. An officer who by virtue of your favor holds the place of President *pro tempore* of your body adds the Presidency to its duties by the way; and an officer changeable from day to day by you as you choose to have a new President *pro tempore*, who by the same title takes from day to day the discharge of the duties of President of the United States.

When the prize is that, and when the circumstances are as I have stated, Senators must decline a jurisdiction upon this demonstration that human nature and human virtue cannot endure that men should be judges in such a strife. I will agree your duty keeps you here. You have no right to resign or avoid it; but it is a duty consistent with judicial fairness, and only to be assumed as such; and the subject itself, thus illustrated, snatches from you at once, as wholly political, the topics that you have been asked to examine.

It will suit my convenience and sense of the better consideration of the separate articles of impeachment to treat them at first somewhat generally, and then, by such distribution as seems most to bring us finally to what, if it shall not before that time have disappeared, appears to be the gravest matter of consideration.

Let me ask you at the outset to see how little as matter of evidence this case is. Certainly this President of the United States has been placed under as trying and as hot a gaze of political opposition as ever a man was or could be. Certainly for two years there has been no partial construction of his conduct. Certainly for two years he has been sifted as wheat by one of the most powerful winnowing machines that I have ever heard of—the House of Representatives of the United States of America. Certainly the wealth of the nation, certainly the urgency of party, certainly the zeal of political ambition, have pressed into the service of imputation, of inculpation, and

of proof all that this country affords, all that the power "to send for persons and papers" includes.

They have none of the risks that attend ordinary litigants of bringing their witnesses in court to stand the test of open examination and cross-examination; but they can put them under the constriction of an oath and an exploration in advance and see what they can prove, and so determine whom they will bring and whom they will reject. They can take our witness from the stand already under oath, and even of so great and high a character as the Lieutenant General of your armies, and out of court ply him with a new oath and a new examination to see whether he will help or hurt them by being cross-examined in court. Every arm and every heart is at their service, stayed by no sense except of public duty to unnerve their power or control its exercise.

And yet here is the evidence. The people of this country have been made to believe that all sorts of personal vice and wickedness, that all sorts of official misconduct and folly, that all sorts of usurpation and oppression, practiced, meditated, plotted, and executed on the part of this Executive, were to be explored and exposed by the prosecution and certainly set down in the record of this court for the public judgment. Here you have for violence, oppression, and usurpation a telegram between the President and Governor Parsons, long public, two years ago. You have for his desire to suppress the power of Congress the testimony of Wood, the office-seeker, that when the President said he thought the points were important he said that he thought they were minor, and that he was willing to take an office from the President and yet uphold Congress; that the President said they were important and he thought the patronage of the Government should be in support of those principles which he maintained, and Wood, the office-seeker, went home and was supposed to have said that the President had used some very violent and offensive words on the subject, and he was brought here to prove them, and he disproved them.

Now, weigh the testimony upon the scale that a nation looks at it, upon the scale that foreign nations look at it, upon the scale that history will apply to it, upon the scale that posterity will in retrospect regard it. It depends a good deal upon how large a selection a few specimens of testimony could offer. If I bring a handful of wheat marked by rust and weevil, and show it to my neighbor, he will say, "Why, what a wretched crop of wheat you have had;" but if I tell him "these few kernels are what I have taken from the bins of my whole harvest," he will answer, "What a splendid crop of wheat you have had." And now answer, answer if there is anything wrong in this? Mr. Manager WILSON, from the Judiciary Committee that had examined for more than a year this subject, made a report to the

House. It is the wisest, the clearest, and also one of the most entertaining views of the whole subject of impeachment in the past and in the present that I have ever seen or can ever expect to see, and what is the result? That it is all political. All these thunder-clouds are political, and it is only this little petty pattering of rain and these infractions of statutes that are personal or criminal. And "the grand inquest of the nation" summoned to the final determination upon the whole array, on the 9th of December, 1867, votes, 107 to 57, "no impeachment." If these honorable Managers had limited their addresses to this court to matters that in purpose, in character, in intent, and in guilt occurred after that bill of impeachment was thrown out by their House, how much you would have been entertained in this cause! I have not heard anything that had not occurred before that. The speeches were made eighteen months before. The telegram occurred a year before. Wood, the office-seeker, came into play long before. What is there, then, not covered by this view?

The honorable Managers, too, do not draw together always about these articles. There seem to have been an original production, and then a sort of afterbirth that is added to the compilation, and as I understand the opening Manager, [Mr. BUTLER,] if there is not anything in the first article you need not trouble yourself to think there is anything in the eleventh; and Mr. Manager STEVENS thinks that if there is not anything in the eleventh you had better not bother yourself in looking for anything in the first ten, for he says a county-court lawyer, I think, could get rid of them. Let me give you his exact words:

"I wish this to be particularly noticed, for I intend to offer it as an amendment. I wish gentlemen to examine and see that this charge is nowhere contained in any of the articles reported, and unless it be inserted there can be no trial upon it; and if there be the shrewd lawyers, as I know there will be, and caviling judges"—

He did not state that he felt sure of that—

"and without this article they do not acquit him, they are greener than I was in any case I ever undertook before the court of quarter sessions."

It will not be too vain in us to think that we come up perhaps to this estimate on our side and at this table of these quarter-session lawyers that would be adequate to dispose of these articles of impeachment; and they are right about it, quite right about it. If you cannot get in what is political and nothing but political, you cannot get hold of anything that is criminal or personal.

Now, with that general estimate of the limit and feebleness of the proofs and of the charges, I begin with the consideration of an article in regard to which, and the subject-matter of which, I am disposed to concede more than I imagine can be claimed fairly in regard to the other articles, that some proof to the point of demonstration has been presented, and that is the speeches. I think that it has been fairly proved here that the speeches charged upon the President, in substance and in general, were made. My first difficulty about them is that they were made in 1866, and related to a Congress that has passed out of existence, and were a subject in the report of the Judiciary Committee to the House, upon which the House voted that they would not impeach. My next is that they are crimes against rhetoric, against oratory, against taste, and perhaps against logic, but that the Constitution of the United States, neither in itself or by any subsequent amendments, has provided for the government of the people of this country in these regards. It is a novelty in this country to try anybody for making a speech.

There are a great many speeches made in this country, and therefore the case undoubtedly would have arisen in the course of eighty years of our Government. Indeed, I believe, if there is anything that marks us, and to the approval, at least in ability, of other nations, it is that any man in this country not only has a right to make a speech, but can make a speech and a good one, and that he does some time or other in his life actually accomplish it. Why, the very lowest epithet for speech-making in the American public adopted by the newspapers is "able and eloquent." [Laughter.] I have seen applied to the efforts of the honorable Managers here the epithet, in advance in the newspapers, of "tremendous" [laughter] before they have been delivered here, of "tremendous force;" and I saw once an accurate arithmetical statement of the force of one of them in advance that it contained thirty-three thousand words. [Laughter.]

We are speech-makers; therefore the case must have arisen for a question of propriety; and now for the first time we begin with the President, and accuse him; we take him before no ordinary court, but organize a court for the purpose which adjourns the moment it is over with him, furnishes no precedent, and must remove him from office and order a new election. That is a great deal to turn on a speech. Only think of it! To be able to make a speech that should require a new election of a President to be held! Well, if the trial is to take place, let the proclamation issue to this speech-making people, "let him that is without sin among you cast the first stone;" and see how the nation on tiptoe waits; but who will answer that dainty challenge and who assume that fastidious duty? We see in advance the necessary requirements. It must be one who by long discipline has learned always to speak within bounds, one whose lips would stammer at an imputation, whose cheek would blush at a reproach, whose ears would tingle at an invective, and whose eyes would close at an indecorum. It must be one who by strict continence of speech and by control over the tongue, that unruly member, has gained with all his countrymen the praise of ruling his own spirit, which is greater than one who taketh a city.

And now the challenge is answered; and it seems that the honorable Manager to whom this duty is assigned is one who would be recognized at once in the judgment of all as first in war, first in peace in boldness of words, first in the hearts of all his countrymen that love this wordy intrepidity. [Laughter.] Now, the champion being gained, we ask for the rule, and in answer to an interlocutory inquiry which I had the honor to address to him he said the rule was the opinion of the court that was to try the case.

Now, let us see whether we can get any guidance as to what your opinions are on this subject of freedom of speech; for we are brought down to that, having no law or precedent besides. I find that the matter of charge against the President is that he has been "unmindful of the harmony and courtesies which ought to exist and be maintained between the executive and legislative branches of the Government." If it prevails from the executive toward the legislative, it should prevail from the legislative toward the executive, upon the same standard, unless I am to be met with what I must regard as a most novel view presented by Mr. Manager WILLIAMS in his argument the other day, that as the Constitution of the United States prevents your being drawn in question anywhere for what you say, therefore it is a rule that does not work both ways. [Laughter.] Well, that is a remarkable view of personal duty, that if I wore an impenetrable shirt of mail, it is just the thing for me to be drawing daggers against everybody else that is met in the street. "Noblesse oblige" seems to be a law which the honorable Manager does not think applicable to the Houses of Congress. If there be anything in that suggestion how should it guard, reduce, and regulate your use of freedom of speech? I have not gone outside of the debates that relate to this civil-tenure act; my time has been sufficiently occupied in reading all that was said in both Houses on that subject; but I find now a well-recorded precedent, not merely in the observations of a single Senator, but in a direct determination of the Senate itself passing upon the question what certain bounds at least of freedom of speech as between the two departments of the Government permitted. The honorable Senator from Massachusetts, in the course of the debate, using this form of expression in regard to the President, said, and on the subject of this very law:

"You may ask protection, against whom? I answer plainly, protection against the President of the United States. There, sir, is the duty of the hour. Ponder it well, and do not forget it. There was no such duty on our fathers; there was no such duty on our recent predecessors in this Chamber, because there was no President of the United States who had become the enemy of his country."—*Congressional Globe*, second session Thirty-Ninth Congress, p. 525.

The President had said that Congress was "hanging on the verge of the Government;" but here is a direct charge that the President of the United States is an enemy of the country. Mr. SUMNER being called to order for this expression, the honorable Senator from Rhode Island, [Mr. ANTHONY,] who not infrequently presides with so much urbanity and so much control over your deliberations, gave this aid to us as to what the common law of this tribunal was on the subject of the harmonies and courtesies that should prevail between the legislative and the executive departments. He said:

"It is the impression of the Chair that those words do not exceed the usual latitude of debate which has been permitted here."

Is not that a good authority, the custom of the tribunal established by the presiding officer? Mr. SHERMAN, the honorable Senator from Ohio, said:

"I think the words objected to are clearly in order. I have heard similar remarks fifty times without any question of order being raised."

Communis error facit jus. That is the principle of this view; and the Senate came to a vote, the opposing numbers of which remind me of some of the votes on evidence that we have had in this trial; the appeal was laid on the table by twenty-nine yeas to ten nays. [Laughter.]

We shall get off pretty easy from a tribunal whose "usual latitude of debate" permits the legislative branch to call the Executive an enemy of his country. But that is not all. Proceeding in the same debate, after being allowed to be in order, Mr. SUMNER goes on with a speech the eloquence of which I cannot be permitted to compliment, as it is out of place, but certainly it is of the highest order, and of course I make no criticism upon it; but he begins with an announcement of a very good principle:

"Meanwhile I shall insist always upon complete freedom of debate, and I shall exercise it. John Milton, in his glorious aspirations, said, "Give me the liberty to know, to utter, and to argue freely above all liberties." Thank God, now that slave-masters have been driven from this Chamber, such is the liberty of an American Senator! Of course there can be no citizen of a Republic too high for exposure, as there can be none too low for protection. The exposure of the powerful and the protection of the weak; these are not only invaluable liberties but commanding duties."

Is there anything in the President's answer that is nobler or more thoroughgoing than that? And if the President is not too high, but that it should be not only an invaluable liberty but a commanding duty to call him an enemy of the country, may not the House of Representatives be exposed to an imputation of a most unintelligible aspersion upon them that they "hang on the verge of the Government?" Then the honorable Senator proceeds with a style of observation upon which I shall make no observation whatever, and I feel none, but Cicero *in Catilinam, in Verrem, et pro Milonem*, does not contain more eloquence against the objects of his invective than this speech of the honorable Senator. Here are his words:

"At last the country is opening its eyes to the actual condition of things. Already it sees that Andrew Johnson, who came to supreme power by a bloody accident, has become the successor of Jefferson Davis in the spirit by which he is governed and in the mischief he is inflicting on his country. It sees the president of the rebellion revived in the President of the United States. It sees that the violence which took the life of his illustrious predecessor is now by his perverse complicity extending throughout the rebel States, making all who love the Union its victims and filling the land with tragedy. It sees that the war upon the faithful Unionists is still continued under his powerful auspices, without any distinction of color, so that all, both white and black, are sacrificed. It sees that he is the minister of discord, and not the minister of peace. It sees that, so long as his influence prevails, there is small chance of tranquillity, security, or reconciliation; that the restoration of prosperity in the rebel States, so much longed for, must be arrested; that the business of the whole country must be embarrassed, and that those conditions on which a sound currency depends must be postponed. All these things the country now sees. But indignation assumes the form of judgment when it is seen also that this incredible, unparalleled, and far-reaching mischief, second only to the rebellion itself, of which it is a continuation, is invigorated and extended through a plain usurpation." * * * * "The President has usurped the powers of Congress on a colossal scale, and he has employed these usurped powers in fomenting the rebel spirit and awakening anew the dying fires of the rebellion. Though the head of the executive, he has rapaciously seized the powers of the legislative, and made himself a whole Congress in defiance of a cardinal principle of republican government that each branch must act for itself without assuming the powers of the other; and, in the exercise of these illegitimate powers, he has become a terror to the good and a support to the wicked. This is his great and unpardonable offense, for which history must condemn him if you do not. He is a usurper, through whom infinite wrong has been done to his country. He is a usurper, who, promising to be a Moses, has become a Pharaoh."—*Congressional Globe*, Thirty-Ninth Congress, second session, p. 541.

And then it all ends in a wonderfully sensible—if the honorable Senator will allow me to say so—and pithy observation of the honorable Senator from Wisconsin, [Mr. HOWE:]

"The Senator from Massachusetts has advanced the idea that the President has become an enemy to his country." * * * * "But I suppose that not only to be the condition of the sentiment in this Senate touching the present President of the United States, but I suppose we never had a President who was not in communication with a Senate divided upon just that question, some thinking that he was an enemy of the country and others thinking that he was not; and I respectfully submit, therefore, that the Senator from Massachusetts will be competent to try an impeachment if it should be sent here against the President, as I conceive the Senator from Maryland would be competent to try that question in spite of the opinions which he has pronounced here."—*Ibid.*, p. 545.

That is good sense. Senatorial license must, if it goes so wide as this, sometimes with good-natured Senators be properly described as a little Pickwickian.

We have also a rule provided for us in the House of Representatives, and I have selected a very brief one, because it is one that the honorable Managers will not question at all, as it gives their standard on the subject. I find that there this rule of license in speech, in a very brief, pithy form, is thus conducted between two of the most distinguished members of that body, who can, as well as any others, for the purpose of this trial, furnish a standard of what is called by the honorable Manager "propriety of speech." I read from page 263 of the Congressional Globe for the Fortieth Congress, first session:

"Mr. BINGHAM. I desire to say, Mr. Chairman, that it does not become a gentleman who recorded his vote fifty times for Jefferson Davis, the arch traitor in this rebellion, as his candidate for President of the United States, to undertake to damage this cause by attempting to cast an imputation either upon my integrity or my honor. I repel with scorn and contempt any utterance of that sort from any man, whether he be the hero of Fort Fisher not taken or of Fort Fisher taken." [Laughter.]

Now, for the reply:

"Mr. BUTLER. But if during the war the gentleman from Ohio did as much as I did in that direction I shall be glad to recognize that much done. But the only victim of the gentleman's prowess that I know of was an innocent woman hung upon the scaffold, one Mrs. Surratt. And I can sustain the memory of Fort Fisher if he and his present associates can sustain him in shedding the blood of a woman tried by a military commission and convicted without sufficient evidence in my judgment."

To which, on page 364, Mr. BINGHAM responds with spirit:

"I challenge the gentleman, I dare him here or anywhere in this tribunal, or in any tribunal, to assert that I spoliated or mutilated any book. Why, sir, such a charge, without one tittle of evidence, is only fit to come from a man who lives in a bottle and is fed with a spoon." [Laughter.]

Now, what under Heaven that means I am sure I do not know, [laughter,] but it is within the common law of courtesy in the judgment of the House of Representatives. We have attempted to show that in the President's addresses to the populace there was something of irritation, something in the subjects, something in the manner of the crowd that excused and explained, if it did not justify, the style of his speech. You might suppose that this interchange in debate grew out of some subject that was irritating, that was itself savage and ferocious; but what do you think was the subject these honorable gentlemen were debating upon? Why, it was charity. [Laughter.] The question of charity to the South was the whole staple of the debate; "charity," which "suffereth long and is kind." "Charity envieth not." "Charity vaunteth not itself, is not puffed up." [Laughter.] Charity "doth not behave itself unseemly, seeketh not her own, is not easily provoked, thinketh no evil; rejoiceth not in iniquity, but rejoiceth in the truth, beareth all things, believeth all things, hopeth all things, endureth all things; charity never faileth." But, then, the Apostle adds, which I fear might not be proved here, "Tongues may fail." [Laughter.]

Now, to be serious, in a free Republic who will tolerate this fanfaronade about speech-making? "*Quis tulerit Gracchos de seditione querentes.*"

Who will tolerate public orators prating about propriety of speech. Why cannot we learn that our estimate of others must proceed upon general views, and not vary according to particular passions or antipathies? When Cromwell in his career through Ireland, in the name of the Parliament, had set himself down before the town of Ross and summoned it to surrender, exhausted in its resistance this Papist community asked to surrender only upon the conditions of freedom of conscience. Cromwell replied: "As to freedom of conscience, I meddle with no man's conscience, but if you mean by that liberty to celebrate the mass, I would have you understand that in no place where the power of the Parliament of England prevails shall that be permitted." So, freedom of speech the honorable Managers in their imputation do not complain of; but if anybody says that the House of Representatives hangs upon the verge of the Government we are to understand that in no place where the power of the two Houses of Congress prevails shall that degree of liberty be enjoyed, though they meddle with no man's propriety or freedom of speech.

Mr. Jefferson had occasion to give his views about the infractions upon freedom of writing that the sedition law introduced in the Legislature of this country, and at the same time some opinion about the right of an Executive to have an opinion about the constitutionality of a law and to act accordingly; and I will ask your attention to brief extracts from his views. Mr. Jefferson, in a letter to Mr. President Adams, written in 1804, (Jefferson's Works, vol. 3, p. 555,) says:

"I discharged every person under the punishment or prosecution under the sedition law, because I considered and now consider that law to be a nullity as absolute and as palpable as if Congress had ordered us to fall down and worship a golden image, and that it was as much my duty to arrest its execution in every stage as it would have been to have rescued from the fiery furnace those who should have been cast into it for refusing to worship the image. It was accordingly done in every instance, without asking what the offenders had done or against whom they had offended, but whether the pains they were suffering were inflicted under the pretended sedition law."

And in another letter he replies to some observations against this freedom of the Executive about the constitutionality of laws:

"You seem to think it devolved on the judges to decide on the validity of the sedition law; but nothing in the Constitution has given them a right to decide for the Executive more than to the Executive to decide for them. Both magistrates are equally independent in the sphere of action assigned to them. The judges believing the law constitutional had a right to pass a sentence of fine and imprisonment, because the power was placed in their hands by the Constitution; but the Executives believing the the law to be unconstitutional, were bound to remit the execution of it, because that power had been confided to them by the Constitution. That instrument meant that its coördinate branches should be checks on each other; but the opinion which gives the judges the right to decide what laws are constitutional and what not, not only for themselves in their own sphere of action, but for the Legislature and Executive also in their sphere, would render the judiciary a despotic branch."

We have no occasion and have not asserted the right to resort to these extreme opinions which it is known Jefferson entertained. The opinions of Madison, more temperate but equally thorough, were to the same effect. The coördinate branches of the Government must surrender their coördination whenever they allow a past rescript to be a final bar to renewing or presenting constitutional questions for reconsideration and redetermination, if necessary, even by the Supreme Court.

But we have here some instances of the courtesy prevailing in the different branches of the Government in the very severe expression of opinion that Mr. Manager BOUTWELL indulged in in reference to the heads of Departments. That is an executive branch of the Government; and here you are sitting in these Halls, and the language used was as much severer, as much more degrading to that branch of the Government than anything said by the President in reference to Congress as can be imagined. Exception here is taken to the fact that the President called Congressmen, it is said, in a telegram, "a set of individuals." We have heard of an old lady not well instructed in long words who got very violent at being called an individual, because she supposed it was opprobrious. But here we have an imputation in so many words that the heads of Departments are "serfs of a lord, servants of a master, slaves of an owner." And yet in this very presence sits the eminent Chief Justice of the United States, and the eminent Senator from Maine, [Mr. FESSENDEN,] and the distinguished Senator from Pennsylvania, [Mr. CAMERON,] all of whom have held Cabinet offices by this tenure, thus decried and derided; and if I were to name the Senators who aspire in the future to hold these degraded positions, I am afraid I should not leave judges enough here to determine this cause. [Laughter.] All know that this is all extravagance. "*Est modus in rebus; sunt certi denique fines.*"

There is some measure in things. There is some limit to the bounds of debate and discussion and imputation. I will agree that nothing could be more unfortunate than the language used by the President as offending the serious and religious tastes and feelings of a community, in the observations which he was drawn into by a very faulty method of reasoning, in a speech that he made at St Louis. The difficulty is, undoubtedly, that the President is not familiar with the graces taught at schools, the costly ornaments and studied contrivances of speech, but that he speaks right on; and when an obstacle is presented in his path he proceeds right over it. But here is a rhetorical difficulty for a man not a rhetorician. An illusive metaphorical suggestion has been made that he is a Judas. If anybody—I do not care how practiced he is—undertakes to become logical with a metaphor, he will get into trouble at once; and that was the President's difficulty. He looked around with the eye of a logician and said, "Judas's fault was the betrayal of all goodness. Where is the goodness that I have betrayed?" And the moment, therefore, that you seek to be logical by introducing the name of the Divinity against whom he had thus sinned, of course you would produce that offense and shock to our senses which otherwise would not have been occasioned.

I am not entirely sure that when you make allowances for the difference between an *extempore* speech of the President to a mob, and a written, prepared, and printed speech to this court, by an honorable Manager, but that there may be some little trace of the same impropriety in that figure of argument which presented Mr. Carpenter to your observation as an inspired painter, whose pencil was guided by the hand of Providence to the apportionment of Mr. Stanton to perpetual bliss and of Governor Seward to eternal pains. [Laughter.] But all that is matter of taste, matter of feeling, matter of discretion, matter of judgment.

The serious views impressed upon you with so much force by the counsel for the President who opened this cause for us, and supported by the quotations from Mr. Madison, present this whole subject in its proper aspect to an American audience. I think that if our newspapers would find some more discriminating scale of comment on speeches than to make the lowest scale "able and eloquent" we should have a better state of things in public addresses.

Our position in regard to the speeches is that the circumstances produced in truth should be considered, that words put into the speaker's mouth from the calls of the crowd, ideas suddenly raised by their unfriendly and impolite suggestions are to have their weight, and that without apologizing, for no man is bound to apologize before the law or before the court for the exercise of freedom of speech, it may be freely admitted that it would be very well if all men were accomplished rhetoricians, finished logicians, and had a bridle on their tongues.

And now, without pausing at all upon the eleventh article, which I leave to the observations of the honorable Managers among themselves to dispose of, I will take up the Emory article. The Emory article is an offense which began and ended on the 22d of February, and is comprised within a half hour's conversation between the President and a General of our armies.

I dare say that in the rapid and heated course of this impeachment through the House of Representatives it may have been supposed by rumor, uncertain and amplified, that there had occurred some kind of military purpose or intention on the part of the President that looked to the use of force; but under these proofs what can we say of it but that the President received an intimation from Secretary Welles that all the officers were being called away from what doubtless is their principal occupation in time of peace, attendance upon levees, were summoned, as they were from the halls of revelry at Brussels to the battle of Waterloo, and it was natural to inquire when and where this battle was to take place; and the President, treating it with very great indifference, said he did not know anything about General Emory, and did not seem to care anything about it; but finally when Secretary Welles said "you had better look into it," he did look into it, and there was a conversation which ended in a discussion of constitutional law between the President and the General, in which the General, reinforced by Mr. REVERDY JOHNSON, a lawyer, and Mr. Robert J. Walker, a lawyer, actually put down the President entirely! [Laughter.] Now, if he ought to be removed from office for that and a new election ordered for that, you will so determine in your judgment; and if any other President can go through four years without doing something worse than that, we shall have to be more careful in the preliminary examinations in our nominating conventions. [Laughter.] I understand this article to be hardly insisted upon.

Then come the conspiracy articles. The conspiracy consists in this: it was all commenced and completed in writing; the documents were public; they were immediately promulgated, and that is the conspiracy, if it be one. It is quite true that the honorable Manager who conducted with so much force and skill the examinations of the witnesses did succeed in proving that besides the written orders handed by the President of the United States to General Thomas, there were a few words of attendant conversation, and those words were, "I wish to uphold the Constitution and the laws," and an assent of General Thomas to the propriety of that course. But by the power of our profession the learned Manager made it evident, by the course of his examination, in which he asked the witness if he had ever heard those words used before when a commission was delivered to him and receive for reply that it had not, and that it was not routine, that they carried infinite *gravity of suspicion!*

What is there that we cannot believe in the power of counsel to affix upon innocent and apparently laudable expressions these infinite consequences of evil surmise, when we remember how, in a very celebrated trial, "chops and tomato sauce" were to go through the service of getting a verdict from a jury on a question of a breach of promise of marriage? [Laughter.] Now, "chops and tomato sauce" do not import a promise of marriage; there is not the least savor of courtship nor the least flavor of flirtation, even, in them; but it is in "the hidden meaning." And so "the Constitution and the laws," by these two men, at midday, and in writing, entering into a conspiracy, mean, we are told, bloodshed, civil commotion, and war! Well, I cannot argue against it. Cardinal Wolsey said that in political times you could get a jury that would bring in a verdict that Abel killed Cain; and it may be that an American Senate will find that in this allusion to the Constitution and the laws is found sufficient evidence to breed from it a purpose of commotion and civil war.

But the conspiracy articles have but a trivial

foundation to rest upon. Here we have a statute passed at the eve of the insurrection intended to guard the possession of the offices of the United States from the intrusion of intimidation, threats, and force, to disable the public service. It is, in fact, a reproduction of the first section of the sedition act of 1798 somewhat amplified and extended. It is a law wholly improper in time of peace, for, in the extravagance of its comprehension, it may include much more than should be made criminal except in times of public danger. But the idea that a law intended to prevent rebels at the South, or rebel sympathizers as they were called at the North, from intimidating officers in the discharge of their public duty, should be wrested to an indictment and trial of a President of the United States and an officer of the Army under a written arrangement of orders to take possession of and administer one of the Departments of the Government according to law, is wresting a statute wholly from its application. We are all familiar with the illustration that Blackstone gives us of the impropriety of following the literal words of a statute as against a necessary implication, when he says that a statute against letting blood in the street could not properly support an indictment against a surgeon for tapping the vein of an apoplectic patient who happened to have fallen on the sidewalk. And there is no greater perversity or contrariety in this effort to make this statute applicable to orderly and regular proceedings between recognized officers of the United States in the disposition of an office than there would be in punishing the surgeon for relieving the apoplectic patient.

I did not fully understand, though I carefully attended to, the point of the argument of the learned Manager, [Mr. BOUTWELL,] who, with great precision and detail, brought into view the common law of Maryland as adopted by Congress for the government in the domestic and ordinary affairs of life of the people in this District; but if I did rightly understand it, it was that, though there was nothing in the penal code of the District, and although the act of 1801 did not attempt to make a penal code for the District, yet somehow or other it became a misdemeanor for the President of the United States, in his official functions, to do what he did do about this office, because it was against the common law of Maryland as applied in this District.

I take it that I need not proceed on this subject any further. The common law has a principle that when the common law stigmatizes a *malum in se* and a felony it may be a misdemeanor at common law to attempt it and to use the means. But the idea that when a statute makes *malum prohibitum*, and affixes a punishment to it if executed the common law adds to that statutory *malum prohibitum* and punishment a common law punishment, for attempting it, when the statute itself has not

included an attempt within it, I apprehend is not supported by any authority or any view of the law; and I must think that it cannot be supposed in the high forum of a court of impeachment as making a high crime and misdemeanor, that the President of the United States, in determining what his powers and duties were in regard to filling offices, should have looked into the common law of the District of Columbia because the offices are inside of the District.

Then, upon the views presented of the conspiracy articles, let us see what the evidence is. There was no preparation or meditation of force; there was no application of force; there was no threat of force authorized on the part of the President; and there was no expectation of force, for he expected and desired nothing more and nothing less than that, by the peaceful and regular exercise of authority on his part, through the ordinary means of its exercise, he should secure obedience, and if, disappointed in that, obedience should not be rendered, all that the President desired or expected was that, upon that legal basis thus furnished by his official action, there should be an opportunity of taking the judgment of the courts of law.

Now, there seems to be left nothing but those articles that relate to the *ad interim* appointment of General Thomas and to the removal of Mr. Stanton. I will consider the *ad interim* appointment first, meaning to assume, for the purpose of examining it as a possible crime, that the office had been vacated and was open to the action of the President. If the office was full, then there could be no appointment by the authority of the President or otherwise. The whole action of the President manifestly was based upon the idea that the office was to be vacated before an *ad interim* appointment could possibly be made, or was intended to take effect.

The letter of authority accompanied the order of removal and was of course secondary and ancillary to the order of removal, and was only to take up the duties of the office and discharge them if the Secretary of War should leave the office in need of such temporary charge.

I think that the only circumstance we have to attend to before we look precisely at the law governing *ad interim* appointments is some suggestion as to any difference between *ad interim* appointments during the session of the Senate and during the recess. The honorable Managers, perhaps all of them, but certainly the honorable Manager, Mr. BOUTWELL, has contended that the practice of the Government in regard to removals from office covered only the case of removals during the recess of the Senate. It will be part of my duty and labor when I come to consider definitely the question of the removal of Mr. Stanton to consider that point, but for the purpose of Mr. Thomas's appointment no such discrimination needs to be made. The question about the right of the

Executive to vacate an office, as to be discriminated between recess and session, arises out of the constitutional distinction that is taken, to wit: that he can only fill an office during session by and with the advice and consent of the Senate, and that he can during the recess commission—it is not called filling the office, or appointing, but commission by authority, to expire with the next session.

But *ad interim* appointments do not rest upon the Constitution at all. They are not regarded, they never have been regarded as an exercise of the appointing power in the sense of filling an office. They are regarded as falling within either the executive or legislative duty of providing for a management of the duties of the office before an appointment is or can properly be made. In the absence of legislation it might be said that this power belonged to the Executive; that a part of his duty was, when he saw that accident had vacated an office or that necessity had required a removal, under his general authority and duty to see that the laws are executed, he should provide that the public service should be temporarily taken up and carried on. I do not think that that is an inadmissible constitutional conclusion.

But it might equally well be determined that it was a *casus omissus*, for which the Constitution had provided no rules and which the legislation of Congress might properly occupy. From the beginning, therefore, as early as 1792 and 1789, indeed, provision is made for temporary occupation of the duties of an office, and the course of legislation was this: the eighth section of the act of 1792, regulating three of the Departments, provided that temporary absence and disabilities of the heads of Departments, leaving the office still full, might be met by appointments of temporary persons to take charge. The act of 1795 provided that in case of a vacancy in the office there might be power in the Executive which would not require him to fill the office by the constitutional method but temporarily to provide for a discharge of its duties. Then came the act of 1863, which in terms covers to a certain extent but not fully both of these predicaments; and I wish to ask your attention to some circumstances in regard to the passage of that act of 1863. I have said that the eighth section of the act of 1792 provides for filling temporarily, not vacancies but disabilities. In January, 1863, the President sent to Congress this brief message, and Senators will perceive that it relates to this particular subject:

To the Senate and House of Representatives:

I submit to Congress the expediency of extending to other Departments of the Government the authority conferred on the President by the eighth section of the act of the 8th of May, 1792, to appoint a person to temporarily discharge the duties of Secretary of State, Secretary of the Treasury, and Secretary of War, in case of the death, absence from the seat of Government, or sickness of either of those officers.   ABRAHAM LINCOLN.

WASHINGTON, *January* 2, 1863.

That is to say, the temporary disability provision of the act of 1792, which covered all the Departments then in existence, had never been extended by law to cover the other Departments, and the President desired to have that act extended. The act of 1795 did not need to be extended, for it covered "vacancies" in its terms and was applicable to other Departments, and vacancies were not in the mind of the President, nor was there any need of a provision of law for them. This message having been referred to the Judiciary Committee, the honorable Senator from Illinois, [Mr. TRUMBULL,] the chairman of that committee, made a very brief report; I believe this is the whole of it, or rather a brief statement in his place concerning it, in which he said:

"There have been several statutes on the subject, and as the laws now exist the President of the United States has authority temporarily to fill the office of Secretary of State and Secretary of War with one of the other Secretaries by calling some person to discharge the duties."

The other Department was the Treasury.

"We received communications from the President of the United States asking that the law be extended to the other Executive Departments of the Government, which seems to be proper; and we have framed a bill to cover all of those cases, so that whenever there is a vacancy the President may temporarily devolve the duty of one of the Cabinet ministers on another Cabinet minister, or upon the chief officer in the Department for the time being."

Here there does not seem to have been brought to the notice in terms of the Senate or of the honorable Senator the act of 1795; nothing is said of it; and it would appear, therefore, as if the whole legislation of 1863 proceeded upon the proposition of extending the act of 1792 as to disabilities in office, not vacancies, except that the honorable Senator uses the phrase "vacancies" and that he speaks of having provided for the occasions that might arise. The act of 1863 does not cover the case of vacancies except by resignation, and it is not, therefore, a vacancy act in full. It does add to the disabilities which the President had asked to have covered, a case of resignation which he did not ask to have covered, and which did not need to be covered by new legislation, because the act of 1794 embraced it. But this act of 1863 does not cover all the cases of vacancy. It does not cover vacancies by removal, if removal could be made, and we supposed it could in 1863; it does not cover the case of expiration of office, which is a case of vacancy provided there are terms to office.

Under that additional light it seems as if the only question presented of guilt on the part of the President in respect to the appointment to office *ad interim* was a question of whether he violated a law. But Senators will remark the very limited form in which that question arises. It is not pretended that the appointment of Thomas, if the office was vacant, was a violation of the civil-tenure act; that is, it is not pretended in argument, although perhaps it may be so charged in the articles;

because an examination of the act shows that the only appointments prohibited there and the infringement of which is made penal is appointing contrary to the provisions of that act, as was pointed out by my colleague, Judge Curtis, and seems to have been assented to in the argument on the other side; that an appointment prohibited or an attempt at an appointment prohibited relates to the infraction of the policy and provisions of that act as applied to the attempt to fill the offices that are declared to be in abeyance under certain predicaments. I believe that to be a sound construction of the law, whether assented to or not, not to be questioned anywhere.

Very well, then, supposing that the appointment of General Thomas was not according to law, it is not against any law that prohibits it in terms, nor against any law that has a penal clause or a criminal qualification upon the act. What would it be if attempted without authority of the act of 1795, because that was repealed, and without authority of the act of 1863, because General Thomas was not an officer that was eligible for this temporary employment? It would simply be that the President, in the confusion among these statutes, had appointed or attempted to appoint an *ad interim* discharge of the office without authority of law. You could not indict him very well for it, and I do not think you can impeach him for it. There are an abundance of mandatory laws upon the President of the United States, and it never has been customary to put a penal clause in them till the civil-tenure act of 1867.

But on this subject, the *ad interim* appointments, there is no penal clause and no positive prohibition in any statute. There would be, then, simply a defect of authority in the President to make the appointment. What, then, would be the consequence? General Thomas might not be entitled to discharge the duties of the office; and if he had undertaken to give a certificate as Secretary *ad interim* to a paper that was to be read in evidence in a court, and a lawyer had got up and objected that General Thomas was not Secretary *ad interim*, and had brought the statutes, the certificate might have failed. That is all that can be claimed or pretended in that regard.

But we have insisted, and we do now insist, that the act of 1795 was in force; and that whether the act of 1795 was or was not in force, is one of those questions of dubious interpretation of implied repeal upon which no officer, humble or high, could be brought into blame for having an opinion one way or the other. And if you proceed upon these articles to execute a sentence of removal from office of a President of the United States, you will proceed upon an infliction of the highest possible measure of civil condemnation upon him personally, and of the highest possible degree of interference with the constitutionally elected Executive dependent on suffrage that it is possible for a court to inflict, and you will rest it on the basis either that the act of 1795 was repealed or upon the basis that there was not a doubt or difficulty or an ignorance upon which a President of the United States might make an *ad interim* appointment of General Thomas for a day, followed by a nomination of a permanent successor on the succeeding day. Truly, indeed, we are getting very nice in our measure and criticism of the absolute obligations and of the absolute acuteness and thoroughness of executive functions when we seek to apply the process of impeachment and removal to a question whether an act of Congress required him to name a head of a Department to take the vacant place *ad interim*, or an act of Congress not repealed permitted him to take a suitable person. You certainly do not, in the ordinary affairs of life, rig up a trip-hammer to crack a walnut.

I think, Mr. Chief Justice, that I shall be able to conclude what I may have to say to the Senate further within certainly the compass of an hour; and as the customary hour of adjournment has been reached, I may, perhaps, be permitted to say that I feel somewhat sensibly the impression of a long argument.

Several SENATORS. Go on, go on.

Mr. HENDERSON. I move that the Senate adjourn.

The CHIEF JUSTICE. The Senator from Missouri moves that the Senate, sitting as a court of impeachment, adjourn until to-morrow at twelve o'clock.

The motion was agreed to; and the Senate, sitting for the trial of the impeachment, adjourned.

FRIDAY, *May* 1, 1868.

The Chief Justice of the United States took the chair.

The usual proclamation having been made by the Sergeant-at-Arms,

The Managers of the impeachment on the part of the House of Representatives and the counsel for the respondent, except Mr. Stanbery and Mr. Curtis, appeared and took the seats assigned to them respectively.

The members of the House of Representatives, as in Committee of the Whole, preceded by Mr. E. B. WASHBURNE, chairman of that committee, and accompanied by the Speaker and Clerk, appeared and were conducted to the seats provided for them.

The Journal of yesterday's proceedings of the Senate, sitting for the trial of the impeachment, was read.

The CHIEF JUSTICE. Senators will please give their attention. The counsel for the President will proceed with the argument.

Mr. EVARTS. Mr. Chief Justice and Senators, I cannot but feel that notwithstanding the unfailing courtesy and the long-suffering patience which for myself and my colleagues I have every reason cheerfully to acknowledge on the part of the court in the progress of this trial and in the long argument, you had at the adjournment yesterday reached somewhat of the condition of feeling of a very celebrated judge, Lord Ellenborough, who, when a very celebrated lawyer, Mr. Fearne, had conducted an argument upon the interesting subject of contingent remainders to the ordinary hour of adjournment, and suggested that he would proceed whenever it should be his lordship's pleasure to hear him, responded, "The court will hear you, sir, to-morrow; but as to pleasure, that has been long out of the question." [Laughter.]

Be that as it may, duties must be done, however arduous, and certainly your kindness and encouragement relieve from all unnecessary fatigue in the progress of the cause. We will look for a moment, under the light which I have sought to throw upon the subject, a little more particularly at the two acts, the one of 1795 and the other of 1863, that have relation to this subject of *ad interim* appointments. The act of 1795 provides:

"That in case of vacancy in the office of Secretary of State, Secretary of the Treasury, or of the Secretary of the Department of War, or of any officer of either of the said Departments, whose appointment is in the head thereof, whereby they cannot perform the duties of their said respective offices, it shall be lawful for the President of the United States, in case he shall think it necessary, to authorize any person or persons, at his discretion, to perform the duties of the said respective offices until a successor be appointed or such vacancy be filled: *Provided*, That no one vacancy shall be supplied in manner aforesaid for a longer term than six months."

The act of 1863, which was passed under a suggestion of the President of the United States, not for the extension of the vacancy act which I have read to the other Departments, but for the extension of the temporary-disability provision of the act of 1792, does provide as follows:

" In case of the death, resignation, absence from the seat of Government, or sickness of the head of any executive Department of the Government, or of any officer of either of the said Departments whose appointment is not in the head thereof, whereby they cannot perform the duties of their respective offices, it shall be lawful for the President of the United States, in case he shall think it necessary, to authorize"—

Not "any person or persons," as is the act of 1795, but—

"to authorize the head of any other executive Department or other officer in either of said Departments whose appointment is vested in the President, at his discretion, to perform the duties of the said respective offices until a successor be appointed, or until such absence or disability by sickness shall cease: *Provided*, That no one vacancy shall be supplied in manner aforesaid for a longer term than six months."

It will be observed that the eighth section of the act of 1792, to which I will now call attention, being in 1 Statutes-at-Large, page 281, provides thus:

"*That in case of the death, absence from the seat* of Government, or sickness of the Secretary of State, Secretary of the Treasury, or of the Secretary of the War Department, or of any officer of either of the said Departments, whose appointment is not in the head thereof, whereby they cannot perform the du-

ties of their respective offices, it shall be lawful for the President of the United States, in case he shall think it necessary, to authorize any person or persons, at his discretion, to perform the duties of the said respective offices until a successor be appointed, or until such absence or inability by sickness shall cease."

I am told, or I understand from the argument, that if there was a vacancy in the office of Secretary of War by the competent and effective removal of Mr. Stanton by the exercise of the President's authority in his paper order, there has come to be some infraction of law by reason of the President's designating General Thomas to the *ad interim* charge of the office, because it is said that though under the act of 1795, or under the act of 1792, General Thomas, under the comprehension of "any person or persons," might be open to the presidential choice and appointment, yet that he does not come within the limited and restricted right of selection for *ad interim* duties which is imposed by the act of 1863; and it seems to have been assumed in the argument that the whole range of selection permitted under that act was of the heads of Departments. But your attention is drawn to the fact that it permits the President to designate any person who is either the head of a Department, or who holds any office in any Department the appointment of which is from the President; and I would like to know why General Thomas, Adjutant General of the armies of the United States, holding his position in that Department of War, is not an officer appointed by the President, and open to his selection for this temporary duty; and I would like to know upon what principle of ordinary succession or recourse for the devolution of the principal duty any officer could stand better suited to assume for a day or for a week the discharge of the *ad interim* trust than the Adjutant General of the armies of the United States, being the staff officer of the President, and the person who stands there as the principal directory and immediate agent of the War Department in the exercise of its ordinary functions?

I cannot but think it is too absurd for me to argue to a Senate that the removal of a President of the United States should not depend upon the question whether an Adjutant General was a proper *locum tenens* or not, or whether entangled between the horns of the repealed and unrepealed statutes the President may have erred in that on which he hung his rightful authority.

Let me call your attention now to an exercise of this power of *ad interim* appointment as held in the administration of President Lincoln, at page 582 of the record, before the enactment of the statute of 1863. You will observe that before the passing of the act of 1863 there was in force no statutory authority for the appointment of *ad interim* discharge of the offices except the acts of 1792 and 1795, which were limited in their terms to the Departments of War, of State, and of the Treasury. You have, therefore, directly in this action of President Lincoln the question of *ultra vires*, not of an infraction of a prohibitory statute with a penalty, but of an assumption to make an appointment without the adequate support of an enabling act of Congress to cover it, for he proceeded, as will be found at the very top of that page:

I hereby appoint St. John B. L. Skinner, now acting First Assistant Postmaster General, to be acting Postmaster General *ad interim*, in place of Hon. Montgomery Blair, now temporarily absent.
ABRAHAM LINCOLN.
WASHINGTON, *September* 22, 1862.

The Department of the Post Office was not covered by the acts of 1792 or 1795, and the absence of authority in respect to it and the other later organized Departments formed the occasion of the President's message which led to the enactment of 1863. I would like to know whether, when President Lincoln appointed Mr. Skinner to be Postmaster General, without an enabling and supporting act of Congress to justify him, he deserved to be impeached, whether that was a crime against the Constitution and his oath of office, whether it was a duty due to the Constitution that he should be impeached, removed, and a new election ordered?

I cannot but insist upon always separating from these crimes alleged in articles the guilt that is outside of articles and that has not been proved, and that I have not answered for the respondent nor have been permitted to rebut by testimony. I take the thing as it is, and I regard each article as including the whole compass of a crime, the whole range of imputation, the whole scope of testimony and consideration; and unless there be some measure of guilt, some purpose or some act of force, of violence, of fraud, of corruption, of injury, of evil, I cannot find in mistaken, erroneous, careless, or even indifferent excesses of authority, making·no impression upon the fabric of the Government and giving neither menace nor injury to the public service, any foundation for this extraordinary proceeding of impeachment.

Am I right in saying that an article is to contain guilt enough in itself for a verdict to be pronounced by the honorable members of the court "guilty" or "not guilty" on that article; guilty not of an act as named, but "guilty of a high crime and misdemeanor as charged," and as the form of question adopted in the Peck and Chase trials is distinctly set down and not the question used in the Pickering trial for a particular purpose, which has led the honorable Manager [Mr. WILSON] to denounce it as a mockery of justice, a finding of immaterial facts, leaving no conclusions of law or judgment to be found by anybody.

There is another point of limitation on the authority of the President, as contained both in the act of 1795 and of 1863, which has been made the subject of some comment by the learned and honorable Manager, [Mr. BOUTWELL:] it is that anyhow and anyway the President has been guilty of a high crime and misdemeanor, however innocent otherwise, because the six months' ability accorded to him by the act of 1795 or 1863 had already expired before he appointed General Thomas.

The reasoning I do not exactly understand; it is definitely written down and the words have their ordinary meaning, I suppose; but how it is that the President is chargeable with having filled a vacancy thus occurring on the 21st of February, 1868, if it occurred at all, by an appointment that he made *ad interim* on that day which was to run in the future, what the suggestion that the six months' right had expired rests upon, I do not understand. It is attempted to connect it in some way with a preceding suspension·of Mr. Stanton under the civil-tenure act, which certainly did not create a vacancy in the office as by law it was prohibited from doing, nor did it create in any form or manner a vacancy in the office. No matter, then, whether the suspension was under the civil-tenure-office act or the act of 1795, the office was not vacant until the removal; and whatever there may have been wanting in authority in that preceding action of the President as not sufficiently supported by his constitutional authority to suspend, which he claims, and as covered necessarily by the act of 1867, as is argued on the part of the Managers, I cannot see that it has anything to do with cutting short the term during which it was competent for the President to make an *ad interim* appointment.

There remains nothing to be considered except about an *ad interim* appointment as occurring during a session of the Senate. An effort has been made to connect a discrimination between the session and the recess of the Senate in its operation upon the right of *ad interim* or temporary appointments, with the discrimination which the Constitution makes between the filling of an office during the session and the limited commission which is permitted during the recess. But sufficiently, I imagine, for the purposes of conviction in your minds, it has been shown that temporary appointment does not rest upon the constitutional provisions at all; that it is not a filling of the office, which remains just as vacant, as far as the constitutional right and duty remains or is divided in the different Departments of the Government, as if the temporary appointment had not been made. When the final appointment is made it dates as from and to supply the place of the person whose vacancy led to the *ad interim* appointment. That in the very nature of things there should be no difference in this capacity between recess and session sufficiently appears, and the acts of Congress draw no distinction, and the practice of the Government makes not the least difference.

We are able to present to your notice on the

pages of this record cases enough applicable to the very heads of Departments to make it unnecessary to argue the matter upon general principles any further. Mr. Nelson, on the 29th of February, 1844, was appointed *ad interim* in the State Department during the session of the Senate. This is to be found on page 556. General Scott was appointed in the War Department July 23, 1850, page 537, during the session of the Senate; Moses Kelly, Secretary of the Interior, January 10, 1861, during the session of the Senate, at page 558; and Joseph Holt Secretary of War on the 1st of January, 1861, during the session of the Senate, at page 583. Whether these were to fill vacancies or for temporary disabilities makes no difference on the question; nor how the vacancy arose, whether by removal or resignation or death.

The question of the *ad interim* faculty of appointment depends upon no such considerations. They were actual vacancies filled by *ad interim* appointment, and related all, except that of Moses Kelly, to Departments that were covered by the legislation of 1792 and 1795. That of Moses Kelly to the Department of the Interior was not covered by that legislation, and would come within the same principle with the appointment of Mr. Skinner which I have noticed on page 582.

I now come with the utmost confidence, as having passed through all possible allegations of independent infraction of the statute, to the consideration of the removal of Mr. Stanton as charged as a high crime and misdemeanor in the first article, and as to be passed upon by this court under that imputation and under the President's defense. The crime as charged must be regarded as the one to be considered, and the crime as charged and also proved to be the only one upon which the judgment has to pass. Your necessary concession to these obvious suggestions relieves very much of any difficulty and of any protracted discussion this very simple subject as it will appear to be.

Before taking up the terms of the article and the consideration of the facts of the procedure I ask your attention now, for we shall need to use them as we proceed, to some general light to be thrown both upon the construction of the act by the debates of Congress and upon the relation of the Cabinet as proper witnesses or proper aids in reference to the intent and purpose of the President within the practice of this Government, and with the latter first.

Most extraordinary, as I think, views have been presented in behalf of the House of Representatives in relation to Cabinet ministers. The personal degradation fastened upon them by the observations of the honorable Manager [Mr. BOUTWELL] I have sufficiently referred to; but I recollect that there are in your number two other honorable Senators, the honorable Senator from Maryland [Mr. JOHNSON] and the honorable Senator from Iowa, [Mr. HARLAN,] who must take their share of the oppro-

brium which yesterday I divided among three members of this court alone.

But as matter of constitutional right, of ability of the President to receive aid and direction from these heads of Departments, it has been presented as a dangerous innovation, of a sort of Star Chamber council, I suppose, intruded into the Constitution, that was to devour our liberties. Well, men's minds change rapidly on all these public questions, and perhaps some members of this honorable Senate may have altered their views on that point from the time of the date of the paper I hold in my hand, to which I wish to ask your attention. It is a representation that was made to Mr. President Lincoln by a very considerable number of Senators as to the propriety of his having a Cabinet that could aid him in the discharge of his arduous executive duties:

"The theory of our Government, the early and uniform practical construction thereof, is that the President should be aided by a Cabinet council agreeing with him in political principle and general policy, and that all important measures and appointments should be the result of their combined wisdom and deliberation. The most obvious and necessary condition of things, without which no Administration can succeed, we and the public believe does not exist; and, therefore, such selections and changes in its members should be made as will secure to the country unity of purpose and action in all material and essential respects. More especially in the present crisis of public affairs the Cabinet should be exclusively composed of statesmen who are cordial, resolute, unwavering supporters of the principles and purposes above mentioned."

There are appended to this paper as it comes to me the signatures of twenty-five Senators. Whether it was so signed or not I am not advised; but that it was the action of those Senators, I believe, is not doubted, and among them there are some fifteen or more that are members of this present court. The paper has no date, but the occurrence was, I think, some time in the year 1862 or 1863, a transaction and a juncture which is familiar to the recollection of Senators who took part in it, and doubtless of all the public men who I have the honor now to address.

These honorable Managers in behalf of the House of Representatives do not hold to these ideas at all, and I must think that the course of this court in its administration of the laws of evidence as not enabling the President to produce the supporting aid of his Cabinet, which you said he ought to have in all his measures and views, has either proceeded upon the ground that his action, in your judgment, did not need any explanation or support, or else you had not sufficiently attended to these valuable and useful views about a Cabinet which were presented to the notice of President Lincoln. Public rumor has said, the truth of which I do not vouch, as I have no knowledge, but there are many who well know that the President rather turned the edge of this representation by a suggestion whether in fact the meaning of the honorable Senators was not that his Cabinet should agree with them rather than with him, Mr. Lincoln. However that may be, the doctrines are good and are according to the custom of the country and the law of our Government.

We may then find it quite unnecessary to refute by any very serious and prolonged argument the imputations and invectives against Cabinet agreement with the President which have been urged upon your attention.

And now, as bearing both on the question of a fair right to doubt and deliberate on the part of the President on the constitutionality of this law, the civil-tenure act, and on the construction of its first section as embracing or not embracing Mr. Stanton, I may be permitted to attract your attention to some points in the debates in the Congress which have not yet been alluded to, as well as to repeat some very brief quotations which have once been presented to your attention. I will not recall the history of the action of the House on the general frame and purpose of the bill, nor the persistence with which the Senate, as one of the advisers of the President in the matters of appointment as well as a member of the legislative branch of the Government, pressed the exclusion of Cabinet ministers from the purview of the bill altogether; but when it was found that the House was persistent also in its view, the Senate concurred with it on conference in a measure of accommodation concerning this special matter of the Cabinet which is now to be found in the text of the first section of the act. In the debate on the tenure-of-office bill the honorable Senator from Oregon, [Mr. WILLIAMS,] who seems to have had, with the honorable Senator from Vermont, [Mr. EDMUNDS,] some particular conduct of the debate according to a practice apparently quite prevalent now in our legislative halls, said this:

"I do not regard the exception as of any great practical consequence"—

That is, the exception of Cabinet ministers—
"because I suppose if the President and any head of a Department should disagree so as to make their relations unpleasant, and the President should signify a desire that that head of Department should retire from the Cabinet, that would follow without any positive act of removal on the part of the President."—*Congressional Globe*, Thirty-Ninth Congress, second session, p. 383.

Mr. SHERMAN, bearing on the same point, said:

"Any gentleman fit to be a Cabinet minister, who receives an intimation from his chief that his longer continuance in that office is unpleasant to him, would necessarily resign. If he did not resign it would show he was unfit to be there. I cannot imagine a case where a Cabinet officer would hold on to his place in defiance and against the wishes of his chief."—*Ibid.*, p. 1046.

But, nevertheless, this practical lack of importance in the measure, which induced the Senate to yield their opinions of regularity of governmental proceedings and permit a modification of the bill, led to the enactment as it now appears; and the question is how this matter was understood, not by one man, not by one speaker, but, so far as the record goes,

by the whole Senate on the question of construction of the act as inclusive of Mr. Stanton in his personal incumbency of office or not. When the conference committee reported the section as it now reads as the result of a compromise between the Senate in its firm views and the House in its firm purposes the honorable Senator from Michigan [Mr. HOWARD] asked that the proviso might be explained. Now you are at the very point of finding out what it means when a Senator gets so far as to feel a doubt and wants to know and asks those who have charge of the matter and are fully competent to advise him. The honorable Senator [Mr. WILLIAMS] states:

"Their terms of office shall expire when the term of office of the President *by whom they were* appointed expires.

"I have from the beginning of this controversy regarded this as quite an immaterial matter, for I have no doubt that any Cabinet minister who has a particle of self-respect—and we can hardly suppose that any man would occupy so responsible an office without having that feeling—would decline to remain in the Cabinet after the President had signified to him that his presence was no longer needed. As a matter of course the effect of this provision will amount to very little one way or the other; for I presume that whenever the President sees proper to rid himself of an offensive or disagreeable Cabinet minister, he will only have to signify that desire and the minister will retire and a new appointment be made."—*Ibid.*, p. 1515.

Mr. SHERMAN, one of the committee of conference, states:

"I agreed to the report of the conference committee with a great deal of reluctance.

"I think that no gentleman, no man of any sense of honor, would hold a position as a Cabinet officer after his chief desired his removal, and, therefore, the slightest intimation on the part of the President would always secure the resignation of a Cabinet officer. For this reason I do not wish to jeopard this bill by an unimportant and collateral question."

He proceeds further:

"The proposition now submitted by the conference committee"—

And this was in answer to the demand of the Senate to know from the committee what they had done and what the operation of it was to be. The answer of Mr. SHERMAN is:

"The proposition now submitted by the conference committee is that a Cabinet minister shall hold his office during the LIFE or TERM of the President who appointed him. *If the President dies* the Cabinet goes out; if the *President is removed for* cause by impeachment the Cabinet goes out; *at the expiration of the term of the President's office* the Cabinet goes out."

This is found at page 1515 of the Globe of that year. Now, how in the face of this can we with patience listen to long arguments to show that, in regard to Cabinet ministers situated as Mr. Stanton is, the whole object of limitation of the proviso and the bill to which the Senate was ready to assent becomes nugatory and unprotective of the President's necessary right, by a constructive enforcement against him of a continuing Cabinet officer whom he never appointed at all? And how shall we tolerate this argument that the term of a President lasts after he is dead, and that the term in which Mr. Stanton was appointed by Mr. Lincoln lasts through the succeeding term to which Mr. Lincoln was subsequently elected? But that is not the point. You are asked to remove a President from office under the stigma of impeachment for crime, to strike down the only elected head of the Government that the actual circumstances permit the Constitution to have recourse to, and to assume to yourselves the sequestration, and administration of that office *ad interim* upon the guilt of a President in thinking that Mr. SHERMAN, in behalf of the conference committee, was right in explaining to the Senate what the conference committee had done. Nobody contradicted him; nobody wanted any further explanation; nobody doubted that there was no vice or folly in this act that, in undertaking to recognize a limited right of the President not to have ministers retained in office that he had not had some voice in appointing, gave it the shape, and upon these reasons, that it bears to-day.

And I would like to know who it is in this honorable Senate that will bear the issue of the scrutiny of the revising people of the United States on a removal from office of the President for his removal of an officer that the Senate has thus declared not to be within the protection of the civil-tenure act. Agree that, judicially, afterward it may be determined anywhere that he is, who will pronounce a judgment that it is wrong to doubt? *Ego assentior eo*, the President might well say in deference to the opinion of Mr. SHERMAN, even if that judgment of some inferior court, to say nothing even of the highest, the Supreme Court, or the highest special jurisdiction, this court, should determine otherwise.

But the matter was brought up a little more distinctly. Mr. DOOLITTLE having said that this proviso would not keep in the Secretary of War and that that had been asserted in debate as its object, Mr. SHERMAN, still having charge of the matter, as representing the conference committee, proceeds:

"That the Senate had no such purpose was shown by its vote twice to make this exception. That this provision does not apply to the present case is shown by the fact that its language is so framed as *not to apply to the present President.* The Senator shows that himself, and argues truly that it would not prevent the present President from removing the Secretary of War, the Secretary of the Navy, and the Secretary of State. And if I supposed that either of these gentlemen was so wanting in manhood, in honor, as to hold his place after the politest intimation by the President of the United States that his services were no longer needed, I, certainly, as a Senator, would consent to his removal, and so would we all."

That is at page 1516 of the Globe; and yet later, in continuation of the explanation, the same honorable Senator says thus definitely:

"We provide that a Cabinet minister shall hold his office, not for a fixed term, NOT until the Senate shall consent to his removal, *but as long as the power that appoints him holds office. If the principal office is* vacated, *the Cabinet minister goes* out."—*Page* 1517.

And if the principal office is not vacated by death under our Government, we certainly belong to the race of the immortals. Now, senators, I press upon your consideration the inevitable. the inestimable weight of this senatorial discussion and conclusion. I do not press it upon particular Senators who took part in it, especially. I press it upon the concurring, unresisting, assenting, agreeing, confirming, corroborating silence of the whole Senate. And I would ask if a President of the United States and his Cabinet, having before them the question upon their own solution of the ambiguities or difficulties, if there be any, and I think there are not, in this section, might not well repose upon the sense of the Senate that they would not have agreed to the bill if it had any such efficacy as is now pretended for it, and the explanation of the committee, and the acceptance of it by the Senate that it had no such possible construction or force. Nevertheless, if the President must be convicted of a high crime and misdemeanor for this concurrence with your united judgments, and that sentence proceeds also from your united judgments, we shall have great difficulty in knowing which of your united judgments is entitled to the most regard.

In the House this matter was considered in the statements of Mr. SCHENCK, who, with Mr. WILLIAMS and Mr. WILSON, now among the Managers, constituted the conference committee, Mr. WILLIAMS having been, as is well known, one of the principal promoters of the original measure. Mr. SCHENCK states upon a similar inquiry made in the House as to what they had all done on conference:

"A compromise was made by which a further amendment is added to this portion of the bill, so that the term of office of the heads of Departments shall expire with the term of the President who appointed them. allowing those heads of Departments one month longer, in which, in case of death or otherwise, other heads of Departments can be named. This is the whole effect of the proposition reported by the committee of conference."

And again :

"Their terms of office are limited, as they are not now limited by law, so that they expire with the term of service of the President who appoints them and one month after."—*Congressional Globe*, second session Thirty-Ninth Congress, page 1340.

Not the elected term, but "the term of service;" and if removal by impeachment terminates the term of service, as it certainly does, or death by a higher power equally terminates it, upon Mr. SCHENCK's view, in which apparently Messrs. Managers WILSON and WILLIAMS concurred, the House is presented as coming to the same conclusion with the Senate. Nevertheless, the whole grave matter left of crime is an impeachment of the House for making the removal, and a condemnation sought from the Senate upon the same ground; and we are brought, therefore, to a consideration of the meaning of the act, of its constitutionality, of the right of the President to put its constitutionality in issue by proper and peaceful proceedings, or of his right to doubt and differ on the construction, and honestly, peacefully to proceed, as he might feel himself best advised, to learn what it truly meant.

And now I may here at once dispose of what I may have to say definitely in answer to some proposition insisted on by the honorable Manager, [Mr. BOUTWELL.] He has undertaken to disclose to you his views of the result of the debate of 1789, and of the doctrines of the Government as there developed, and has not hesitated to claim that the limitation of those doctrines was confined to appointments during the recess of the Senate. Nothing could be less supported by the debate or by the practice of the Government. In the whole of that debate, from beginning to end, there is not found any suggestion of the distinction that the honorable Manager has not hesitated to lay down in print for your guidance as its result. The whole question was otherwise, whether or no the power of removal resided in the President absolutely. If it did, why should he not remove at one time as well as at another? The power of appointment was restricted in the Constitution by a distinction between recess and session. If, on the other hand, the power of removal was administerable by Congress, it needed to provide for its deposit with the President, if that was the idea, as well in time of session as in time of recess, because the whole question and action of the separate exercise of the power of removal from the power of appointment would arise when the emergency of removal dictated instant action. We understand that when the removal is political, or on the plan of rotation in office, as we call it, the whole motive of the removal is the new appointment.

The new appointment is the first thought and wish. There is no desire to get rid of the old officer except for the purpose of getting in the new. And therefore the general practice of the Government in its mass of action, since the times of rotation in office began, is of this political removal, which is not getting rid of the old officer from any objection to him, but because his place is wanted for the new. Hence all this parade of the action of the Government showing that it has been the habit in those political appointments to send in the name of the new man, and by that action put him in the place of the old, serves no purpose of argument, and carries not a penny's weight on the question. The form of the notice as in the last one on your table, the appointment of General Schofield, and so from the beginning of the office, is "in place of A B," not "to be removed by the Senate," but "of A B, removed," meaning this: "I, as President, have no power to appoint unless there is a vacancy; I tell you that I have made a vacancy or present to you a case of vacancy created by my will, by removal; not death or resignation; and I name to you C D to be appointed in the place of A B, removed." That is the meaning of that action of the Government.

You will observe that in finding cases in the practice of the Government where there has been a separate act of removal, during session or during recess either, we are under two necessary restrictions as to their abundance or frequency, which the nature of the circumstances imposes. The first is that in regard to Cabinet officers you can hardly suppose an instant in which a removal can be possible, because in the language, honorable Senators, you can hardly conceive of the possibility of a Cabinet officer's not resigning when it is intimated to him that his place is wanted; and, therefore, all this tirade of exultation that we found no case of removal of a Cabinet officer save that of Timothy Pickering rests upon Senator SHERMAN's proposition and Senator WILLIAMS's proposition that you cannot conceive of the possibility of there being a Cabinet minister that would need to be removed, and the practice of our Government has shown that these honorable Senators were right in their proposition, and that there never have been, from the foundation of the Government to the present time, but two cases where there were Cabinet ministers that on the slightest intimation of their chief did not resign. Now, do not urge on us the paucity of the cases of removal of heads of Departments as not helping the practice of the Government when that paucity rests upon retirement whenever a President desires it.

Mr. Pickering, having nothing but wild land for his support and a family to sustain, flatly told Mr. Adams that he would not resign, because it would not be convenient for him to make any other arrangements for a living until the end of his term; and the President, without that consideration of domestic reasons which perhaps Mr. Pickering hoped would obtain with him, told him that he removed him, and he did; and he went, I believe, to his wild land and was imprisoned there by the squatters, and came into very great disaster from this removal. Mr. Mr. Stanton, under the motives of public duty, it is said, takes the position that for public reasons he will not resign. These are the only two cases in our Government in which the question has arisen, and in one of them, before the passage of the civil-tenure act, the Secretary was instantly removed by the power of the President, and in the other it was attempted after long sufferance.

We can find in the history of the Government—for we should hardly expect to escape the occurrence when we have so many officers—instances enough of removal by executive authority during the session of the Senate of subordinate officers of the Government who derived their appointment from the President, by the advice and consent of the Senate, and every one of those cases is pertinent and an instance. You will observe in regard to them, as I said before, how peculiar must be the situation of the officer and office and of the President toward them when this separate, independent, and condemnatory removal needs to take place. In the first place, there must be some fault in the conduct of the officer, not necessarily crime, and not necessarily neglect of office, but some fault in manner at least, as of that collector down in Alabama, who, when he was asked by the Secretary of the Department how far the Tombigbee ran up, answered that it did not run up at all, [laughter;] and he was removed from office for his joke on the subject of the Tombigbee river not running up, but, as other rivers do, running down. It does not do to have these asperities on the part of inferior officers. So, too, when the fault arises of peculation, of deficiency of funds, or what not, the sureties know of it, come forward and say to the officer, "You must resign; we cannot be sureties any longer here;" and in nine cases out of ten, where an occurrence would lead to removal, it is met by the resignation of the inferior officer. Therefore the practice of the Government can expect to suggest only the peculiar cases where promptitude and necessity of the rough method of removal are alike demanded from the Executive. I will ask the attention of this honorable court to the cases we have presented in our proofs, with the page and instance of each removal during the session of the Senate. That is the condition of this list—the whole of it:

	Year.	Page.
Timothy Pickering	1800	357
Thomas Eastin, navy agent at Pensacola	1840	569
Isaac Henderson, navy agent	1864	571
James S. Chambers, navy agent	1864	572
Amos Binney	1826	573
John Thomas	1841	573
Samuel F. Marks	1860	581
Isaac V. Fowler	1860	581
Mitchell Steever	1861	581

. I think the honorable Senators must give their assent to the propositions I have made that in regard to Cabinet officers it is almost impossible to expect removal as a separate act; that political removals necessarily have for their first step the selection and presentation of the new man for whose enjoyment of office the removal is to take place; that in regard to criminality and necessity requiring instant removal of subordinate officers, resignation will then be required by their sureties or by their sense of shame or their disposition to give the easiest issue to the difficulty in which they are placed; and when with the circumstances of the matter reducing the dimensions of the possibility and of the frequency within these narrow limits I present to you in behalf of the respondent these evidences of the action of this Government during the session of the Senate, I think you must be satisfied with the proposition assented to by every statesman—I think assented to by every debater on the passage of this civil-tenure act: that the doctrine and the action and the practice of the Government had been that the President removed in session or in recess, though some discrimination of that kind was attempted; but the facts, the arguments, the reasons all show that removal, if a right and if a power, is not discriminated between session and recess.

Look at it in regard to this point: the Senate is in session, and a public officer is carrying on his frauds at San Francisco or at New York or wheresoever else, perhaps in Hong Kong or Liverpool, and it comes to the knowledge of the Executive; the session of the Senate goes on; the fact of his knowledge does not put him in possession of a good man to succeed him either in his own approval or in the assent of the new nominee; and if it is necessary under our Constitution that the consul at Hong Kong or at Liverpool, or the sub-Treasurer at New York or the master of the mint at San Francisco, should go on with his frauds until you and the President can find a man and send him there and get his assent and his qualifications, very well. It is not a kind of legislation that is adapted to the circumstances of the case is all that I shall venture to suggest. Whatever your positive legislation has done or attempted to do, no construction and no practice of the Government while the executive department was untrammeled by this positive restriction has ever shown a discrimination between session and recess. Of course, the difference between session and recess is shown in the political appointments where, the object being the new appointment, the commission goes out in the recess; where, during the session, the object being the new appointment, it must proceed through the concurrence of the Senate.

And now that I come to consider the actual merits of the proceeding of the President and give a precise construction to the first section of the bill, I need to ask your attention to a remarkable concession made by Mr. Manager BUTLER in his opening, as we regarded it, that if the President, having this wish of removal, had accomplished it in a method the precise terms of which the honorable Manager was so good as to furnish, then there would have been no occasion to have impeached him. It is not then, after all, the *fortiter in re* on the part of the President that is complained of, but the absence of the *suaviter in modo*; and you, as a court, upon the honorable Manager's own argument, are reduced to the necessity of removing the President of the United States not for the act, but for the form and style in which it was done, just as the collector at Mobile was removed for saying that the river Tombigbee did not run up at all.

But more definitely the honorable Manager [Mr. BOUTWELL] has laid down two firm and strong propositions—I will ask your attention to them—bearing on the very merits of this case. We argue that if this act be unconstitutional we had a right to obey the Constitution, at least in the intent and purpose of a peaceful submission of the matter to a court, and that our judgment on the matter, if deliberate, honest, and supported by diligent application to the proper sources of guidance, is entitled to support us against an incrimination. To meet that, and to protect the case against the injury from the exclusion of evidence that tends to that effect, the honorable Manager [Mr. BOUTWELL] does not hesitate to say that the question of the constitutionality or unconstitutionality of the law does not make the least difference in the world where the point is that an unconstitutional law has been violated, and for a President to violate an unconstitutional law is worthy of removal from office. Now, mark the desperate result to which the reasoning of the honorable Managers, under the pressure of our argument, has reduced them. That is their proposition, and the reason for that proposition is given in terms. If that is not so ; if the question of constitutionality or unconstitutionality in fact is permitted to come into your considerations of crime, then you would be punishing the President for an error of judgment, releasing him or condemning him according as he happened to have decided right or wrong, and that the honorable Manager tells us is contrary to the first principles of justice. Let us, before we get through with this matter, have some definite meeting of minds on this subject between these honorable Managers and ourselves.

At page 814, in the argument of the honorable Manager, [Mr. BOUTWELL,] we are told that "the crime of the President is not, either in fact or as set forth in the articles of impeachment, that he has violated a constitutional law; but his crime is that he has violated a law, and in his defense no inquiry can be made whether the law is constitutional," and that the Senate in determining innocence or guilt is to render no judgment as to the constitutionality of the act. I quote the results of his propositions, not the full language. At page 815 this is the idea :

"If the President may inquire whether the laws are constitutional, and execute those only which he believes to be so, then the Government is the Government of one man. If the Senate may inquire and decide whether the law is in fact constitutional, and convict the President if he has violated an act believed to be constitutional, and acquit him if the Senate think the law unconstitutional, then the President is, in fact, tried for his judgment, to be acquitted if, in the opinion of the Senate, it was a correct judgment, and convicted if, in the opinion of the Senate, his judgment was erroneous. This doctrine offends every principle of justice."

That doctrine does with us offend every principle of justice that a President of the United States should be convicted when honestly, with proper advice, peacefully and deliberately, he has sought to raise a question between the Constitution and the law ; and the honorable Manager can escape from our argument on that point in no other mode than by the desperate recourse of saying that constitutional laws and unconstitutional laws are all alike in this country of a written Constitution, and that anybody who violates an unconstitutional law meets with some kind of punishment or other. This confusion of ideas as to a law being valid for any purpose that is unconstitutional I have already sufficiently exposed in a general argument. At page 815 he says :

"It is not the right of any Senator in this trial to be governed by any opinion he may entertain of the constitutionality of the law in question."

You may all of you think the law is unconstitutional, and yet you have got to remove the President ! "It has not been annulled by the Supreme Court." And you may simply inquire whether he has violated the law.

That is pretty hard on us that we cannot even go to the Supreme Court to find out whether it is unconstitutional, and we cannot regard it on our own oath of office as unconstitutional and proceed to maintain the obligation to sustain the Constitution, and you cannot look into the matter at all. but the unconstitutional law must be upheld !

"Nor can the President prove or plead the motive by which he professes to have been governed in his violation of the laws of the country."

What is the reason for that? He has taken an oath to preserve the Constitution, and therefore he cannot say that he acted under the Constitution and not under the law ! His oath strikes him so that he cannot maintain the Constitution, and the Constitution cannot protect him !

A man who breaks an unconstitutional law on the ground that it is unconstitutional, and that he has a right to break it, is "a defiant usurper."

Those are the propositions, and I think the honorable Manager is logical ; but the difficulty is that his logic drives him to an absurdity which, instead of rejecting, he adopts—a fault in reasoning which certainly we should not expect.

On the question of construction of the law what are the views of the honorable Managers as to the point of guilt or innocence? We have claimed that if the President in good faith construed this law as not including Mr. Stanton under its protection, and he went on upon that opinion, he cannot be found guilty. The honorable Manager, [Mr. BOUTWELL,] at page 889, takes up this question and disposes of it in this very peculiar manner:

"If a law"—

I ask your attention to this:

"If a law passed by Congress be equivocal or ambiguous in its terms the Executive, being called upon to administer it, may apply his own best judgment to the difficulties before him, or he may seek counsel of his advisers or other persons; and acting thereupon without evil intent or purpose he would be fully justified"—

We never contended for anything stronger than that—

"he would be fully justified, and upon no principle of right could he be held to answer, as for a misdemeanor in office."

Logic is a good thing, an excellent thing ; it operates upon the mind without altogether yielding to the bias of feeling ; and as we press an argument, however narrow it may be, if it be logical, the honorable Managers seem obliged to bend to it, and in both cases have thrown away their accusation. Tell me what more do we need than this, an ambiguous and equivocal law which the President was called on to act under, and might, as we tried to prove, "seek counsel from his official advisers or other proper persons, and acting thereupon without evil intent or purpose he would be fully justified, and upon no principle of right could he be held to answer as for a misdemeanor in office?" And what is the answer which the honorable Managers make to this logical proposition? Why, that this act is not of that sort; it is as plain as the nose on a man's face, and it was nothing but violent resistance of light that led anybody outside of this Senate to doubt what it meant! The honorable Manager who follows me [Mr. BINGHAM] will have an opportunity to correct me in my statements of their propositions, and to furnish an adequate answer, I doubt not, to the views I have had the honor now to present.

And now take the act itself, which is found at page 430 of the edition of the statutes I have before me. It is provided—

"That every person holding any civil office to which he has been appointed by and with the advice and consent of the Senate, and every person who shall hereafter be appointed to any such office, and shall become duly qualified to act therein, is and shall be entitled to hold such office until a successor shall have been in like manner appointed and duly qualified, except as herein otherwise provided."

Then the "provision otherwise" is:

"*Provided*, That the Secretaries of State, of the Treasury, of War, of the Navy, and of the Interior, the Postmaster General, and the Attorney General, shall hold their offices respectively for and during the term of the President by whom they may have been appointed, and for one month thereafter, subject to removal by and with the advice and consent of the Senate."

That is the operative section of this act of erecting and limiting the new arrangement of offices. The section of incrimination, so far as it relates to removal, I will read, omitting all that relates to any other matter; the sixth section:

"That every removal" * * * "contrary to the provisions of this act" * * * "shall be deemed, and is hereby declared to be, a high misdemeanor"—

I alter the plural to singular—

"And upon trial and conviction thereof, every person guilty thereof shall be punished by a fine not exceeding $10,000, or by imprisonment not exceeding five years, or both said punishments, in the discretion of the court."

You will observe that this act does not affix a penalty to anything but a "removal," an accomplished removal. Acts of a penal nature are to be construed strictly; and yet whenever we ask that necessary protection of the liberty and of the property and of the life of a citizen of the United States under a penal statute, we are told that we are doing something very extraordinary for a lawyer in behalf of his client. All principles, it seems, are to be changed when you have a President

for a defendant; all the law retires, and will and object and politics assume their complete predominance and sway, and everything of law, of evidence, and of justice is narrow and not enlarged. That may be. All I can say is that if the President had been indicted under this act, or should hereafter be indicted under this act, then the law of the land would apply to his case as usually administered, and if he has not removed Mr. Stanton he cannot be punished for having done it. You might have punished an attempt to remove. See what you have done in regard to appointments:

"Every appointment or employment, made, had, or exercised, contrary to the provisions of this act, and the making, signing, sealing, countersigning, or issuing of any commission or letter of authority for, or in respect to any such appointment or employment, shall be deemed, and is hereby declared to be, a high misdemeanor."

There you have made not only an appointment, but an attempt on movement of the pen toward an appointment a crime, and you will punish it, I suppose, some day or other. But removal stands on act and fact. Now, what does the article charge in this behalf, for I believe as yet it has not been claimed that it is too narrow to insist that the crime as charged in the article shall be the one you are to try. "Removal" is not charged in the articles anywhere; the allegation is that Andrew Johnson did unlawfully and in violation of the Constitution "issue an order in writing for the removal of Edwin M. Stanton, with intent to violate" the civil-tenure act, and "with intent to remove him, the Senate being in session." If you had had a section of this statute that said "any removal, or the signing of any letter, or order, or paper, or mandate of removal, shall be a crime," then you would have had an indictment and a crime before you; but you have neither crime nor indictment as appears from this first article. And yet it may be said that in so small a matter as the question of the removal of a President it does not do to insist upon the usual rules of construction of a criminal law. I understand the proposition to be this: that here is a criminal law which has been violated; that by the law of the land it has been violated, so that indictment could inculpate, verdict would find guilt, and sentence would follow at law; and that thereupon, upon that predicament of guiltiness, the President of the United States is exposed to this peculiar process of impeachment; and if I show that your law does not make punishable an attempt to remove or a letter of removal, and that your article does not charge a removal, and that is good at law, then it is good against impeachment, or else you must come back to the proposition that you do not need a legal crime.

So much for the law. What is the true attitude of Mr. Stanton and of the President of the United States toward this office and this officer at the time of the alleged infraction of the law? Mr. Stanton held a perfectly good title to that office by the commission of a President of the United States to hold it, according to the terms of the commission, "during the pleasure of the President for the time being." That is the language of the commission. He held a good title to the office. A *quo warranto* moved against him while he held that commission unrevoked, unannulled, and undetermined would have been answered by the production of the commission, "I hold this office during the pleasure of the President of the United States for the time being, and I have not been removed by the President of the United States." That was the only title he held up to the passage of the civil-tenure act. By the passage of the civil-tenure act it is said that a statutory title was vested in him not proceeding from the executive power of the United States at all, not commissioned by the Executive of the United States at all, not to be found, ascertained, or delegated by the Executive of the United States at all, but a statutory title superadded to his title from the executive authority which he held during pleasure, which gave him a durable office determinable only one month after the expiration of some term of years or other.

We are not now discussing the question whether he is within it or not. That being so, the first question to which I ask your attention is this, that the act is wholly unconstitutional and inoperative in conferring upon Mr. Stanton or anybody else a durable office to which he has never been appointed. Appointment to all office proceeds from the President of the United States, or such heads of Department or such courts of law as your Legislature may repose it in. You cannot administer appointment to office yourselves, for what the Constitution requires the President to have control of you cannot confer anywhere else. The appointment of Secretary of War is one which cannot be taken from the President and conferred upon the courts of law or the heads of Department. Whatever may be the action of Congress limiting or contriving the office, as you please, the office itself is conferable only by the action of the Executive. And when Mr. Stanton holds or anybody else holds an office during pleasure, which he has received by commission and authority of the President of the United States, a sufficient title to, you can no more confer upon him by your authority and appointment a title durable and *in invitum* as against the President of the United States, you can no·more confer it upon him because he happens to be holding an office during pleasure, than you could if he was out of office altogether. I challenge contradiction from the lawyers who oppose us and from the judgment of honorable and intelligent lawyers here. Where are you going to carry this doctrine of legislative appointment to office if you can carry it to find a man who the President has never asked to hold an office except from day to day and can enact him into a durable

office for life? You may determine tenures if you please; I am not now discussing that; you may determine tenures for life; but you cannot enact people into tenures for life. The President must appoint; and his discretion and his judgment in appointing to an office for life are very different from his discretion and his judgment in appointing to an office during his pleasure, which he can change at will. Now you will sweep all the offices of the country not only into the Senate but into Congress if you adopt this principle of enacting people into office; and if, upon the peg that there is an office at sufferance or at will, you can convert it in favor of the holder by an act of Congress into an estate for life or for years, you will appoint to office; and of that there can be no doubt.

The next question, and the only question, of constitutionality or construction (for the general question of the constitutional power to restrict appointments I shall not further trouble the Senate with) is, whether the Secretary of War is within the first section. The office of the Secretary of War is within the first section undoubtedly. The question, therefore, is whether the provisions concerning the office of Secretary of War applicable to that office are in their terms, giving them full course and effect, such as to hold Mr. Stanton in that office against the will of the President by the statutory term that is applicable to that office, and is or is not applied to him.

The argument that if Mr. Stanton is no within the proviso then he is within the body of the section stumbles over this transparent and very obvious, as we suppose, fallacy; the question of the law is whether the office of Secretary of War is within the proviso or not. You have not made a law about Mr. Stanton by name. The question, then, whether he is within one or the other terms of the alternative, is whether the office of Secretary of War is within the section or within the proviso; and will anybody doubt about that? It is on the same footing with the other Secretaryships; it is on the same footing as an office with every other Department. The question whether the office of Mr. Stanton or the office of Mr. Browning is within one or the other alternative of the section is not a question of construction of law, but a question of whether the facts of the tenure and holding of the actual incumbency of the one or the other bring him within the proviso. If he is not brought within the proviso, his office being there, the fact that he is not in does not carry his office back into the first part, because his office would be back there for the future as well as for the past and for the present.

It is a statute made for permanent endurance, and the office of Secretary of War, now and forever, as long as the statute remains upon the book, is disposed of one way or the other within the first part or within the proviso. And yet we have been entertained, in public discussions as well as in arguments here, with what is supposed to be a sort of triumphant refutation, that Mr. Stanton's office in his actual incumbency is not protected by the proviso; that then his office is carried back under the body of the section. There is no doubt about the office being under the proviso. It says so:

"*Provided*, That the Secretaries of State, of the Treasury, of War, of the Navy, and of the Interior, the Postmaster General, and the Attorney General shall hold their offices respectively," &c.

That does not mean the men; it means the offices shall have that tenure. Having got along so far that this office of Secretary of War, like the office of Secretary of the Interior, must always remain under that proviso, and is never governable or to be governed by the body of the section, we have but one other consideration, and that is whether the proviso, which is the only part of the section that can operate upon the office of Secretary of War, so operates upon that office as to cover Mr. Stanton in a durable tenure for the future; and that turns upon the question whether the durability of tenure provided as a general rule for the office is in the terms of its limitation such as to carry him forward, or whether its bound has already been reached and he is out of it. That is a question of fact in the construction of the proviso. He either stays in the proviso or he drops out of the proviso; and if he personally drops out of the proviso in his present incumbency he cannot get back into the operative clause, because he cannot get back there without carrying his office there, and his office never can get back.

Is it not true that this proviso provides a different tenure for the Cabinet officers from what the first and operative part of the section provides? If this office or this officer goes back, this very incumbent goes back; he gets a tenure that will last forever, that is, until the Senate consents to his removal. How absurd a result that is, to give to this poor President control of his Cabinet, that those that he appointed himself, if he should happen to be reëlected, he could get rid of in a month, and those that Mr. Lincoln appointed for him from the beginning, and before he had any choice in it, he must hold on to forever till you consent that they shall go out; that those in regard to whom he had the choice of nomination he may by the expiration of the statutory term be freed from, but those that he had nothing to do with the appointment of shall last forever till you consent to release him specifically from them. That is the necessary result of carrying him personally back, and Mr. Stanton would hold under the next President—if any of you can name him, I will supply in the argument his name—I can name several; whether it is the President that is to come in by removal from office, or the President by the election of the people in the autumn. Either way he would have a choice to relieve himself from the Secretaries. No; I think they would all then be in shape for him, all having been appointed by somebody that had preceded him, and he would not have any chance at all.

Such absurdity, either in reasoning or in practical result, can never be countenanced by the judgment of this court. If the office of Secretary of War is within the proviso, and it certainly is, as it is not contended that the other Secretaries are not in their offices within it, then Mr. Stanton is or is not protected by the proviso. If he is not protected by the proviso his case is not provided for. Now, suppose that this proviso had contained a second proviso following after the first, "and provided further, that the persons now holding the offices of Secretary of War, &c., who were appointed and commissioned by Mr. Lincoln, shall not be deemed within the above proviso, which regulates the tenure of those offices," that would not have carried the offices back under the new tenure of the operative section, but simply have provided that, the offices being governed by the proviso, the incumbents, under the particular circumstances of their case, should not be even protected by the proviso; and this is the necessary construction of the act.

If this be the real construction, there is the end of the crime. If the construction be equivocal or ambiguous, the honorable Manager [Mr. Boutwell] says it would be abhorrent to every sense of justice to punish the President for having erred in its construction; but being so plain a case that nobody can say two words on one side or the other of it, it is mere assumption to say that there is a doubt or difficulty, and that an argument is necessary. Well, we certainly have belied on the one side and the other the proposition of this absolute plainness, for we have spent a great many words on this subject on the one side and the other. This being so, let us consider what the President did; and assuming that the statute covers Mr. Stanton's case, assuming that the removal of Mr. Stanton is prohibited by it under the penalties, let us see what the President did.

I have said to you that Mr. Stanton had a title to this office dependent on the President's pleasure. He claimed, or others claimed for him, that he had a tenure dependent on the statute. The question of dependence on the statute was a question to be mooted and determined as a novel one; the question of tenure by appointment was indubitable; and the President proposed to put himself in the attitude of reducing the tenure of Mr. Stanton to his statutory tenure at least. He therefore issues a paper which is a revocation of his commission, a recall of his office, as it depends on presidential appointment. Without that no question ever could be raised by any person upon the statutory tenure, because the presidential tenure would be an adequate answer to a *quo warranto.* The President then, peaceably and in writing, issued a paper which is served upon Mr. Stanton, saying, in effect, "I, the President of the United States, by such authority as I possess, relieve or remove you from the office of Secretary of War;" and that that recalled and terminated the commission and the title that was derived from presidential appointment nobody can deny.

Did the President proceed further? When Mr. Stanton, as he might reasonably have expected; when, as upon the evidence he did probably calculate, instead of adhering to his opinion that the tenure-of-office act was unconstitutional and that the tenure-of-office act did not include his title, refused to yield the only title that on Mr. Stanton's profession he held, to wit, the presidential appointment, to this recall, did the President then interpose force to terminate his statutory title, or did he, having thus reduced him to the condition of his statutory title, then propose and then act either in submission to the power which Mr. Stanton had over him, or did he wish to have the question of the statutory title determined at law? It is enough to say that he did not do anything in the way of force; that he expected in advance, as appears by his statements to General Sherman, that Mr. Stanton would yield the office. Why should Mr. Stanton not yield it? The grounds on which he had put himself in August were that his duty required him to hold the office until Congress met; that is, to hold it so that the presidential appointment could not take effect without your concurrence. Congress had met and was in session, and this "public duty" of Mr. Stanton, on his own statement had expired. Mr. Stanton had told him the act was unconstitutional and had aided in writing the message that so disclosed the presidential opinion to you.

He had concurred in the opinion that he was not within the act. His retirement on this order would be in submission to these views, if not in submission to the views Senators here had expressed that no man could be imagined who would refuse to give up office in the Cabinet when desired by the President; but if that predicament was excusable while this Senate was not in session to prevent a bad appointment, if that were feared, how could it be a reason when this Senate was in session? Mr. Stanton having stated to General Thomas on the first presentation of his credential that he wanted to know whether he desired him to vacate at once or would give him time to remove his private papers, and that having been reported to the President the President regarded it as all settled, and so informed his Cabinet, as you have permitted to be given in evidence. After that, after the 21st, what act is charged in this article? Up to and through the 21st and the written order of removal and its delivery to Mr. Stanton, and the repose of the President upon that posture in which Mr. Stanton left it, what was done by the President about that office? Nothing whatever. There was a desire, an effort to seize upon a movement made by Mr. Stanton, based upon an affidavit, not that he had removed from office, but sworn to on the 21st, and again on the early morning of the 22d that he was still in the office and held it against General Thomas, and instantly the President said, "Very well, the matter is in court."

It might have gone into court on the trial of an indictment against Thomas; but a speedier method was arrived at in the consultations of the President with his counsel, to have a *habeas corpus* carried forward before the Supreme Court, and jump at that. Then Mr. Chief Justice Cartter, who, I take it, all who know him understand to be one who sees as far into a millstone as most people, put that cause out of his court by its own weight and the *habeas corpus* fell with it. That is all that is proved and all that is done. I submit to you, therefore, that the case of a resistance or violation of law does not at all arise. We do not even get to the position of whether a formal and peaceable violation for the purpose of raising the question before the Supreme Court was allowable. A revocation of the presidential title of Stanton was allowable; a resistance of the statutory title was not attempted; and the matter stood precisely as it would stand if a person was in the habit of cutting wood on your lot, and claimed a title to it, and meant to have a right to cut wood there, and before you went to law with him to determine the right in an action of trespass you were careful to withdraw a license terminable at will which you had given him and under which he was cutting wood. Withdraw your license before you bring your action of trespass or you will be beaten in it. Withdraw your license, and then he cuts upon his claim of right, and your action of trespass has its course and determines title. That was the situation.

All that is said about the right to violate unconstitutional laws never can have the footing for consideration, where all that is done by anybody is to put upon paper the case out of which, as an instance, the judgment of a court can be called for as to a violation or no violation. If there must be an intervention of force, then a law may be said to be violated and an offender must suffer, accordingly as it shall prove to be constitutional or unconstitutional. But where there is a Constitution as the predominant law, the statute as an inferior law, and an executive mandate is issued by the President in pursuance of either one law or the other, according to which is in force, for they both cannot be, we suppose, then, he commits no violation of the law in thus presenting for consideration and determination the case.

We must, then, come either to intent, purpose, motive, some force prepared, meditated, threatened, or applied, or some evil invasion of the actual working of the department of the Government in order to give substance to this allegation of fault. No such fact, no such intent, no such purpose is shown. We are prevented from showing the attendant views, information, and purpose upon which the President proceeded; and if so, it must be upon the ground that views, intent, and purpose do not qualify the act. Very well, then, carry it through so; let the Managers be held to the narrowness of their charges when they ask for judgment as they are when they exclude testimony, and let it be determined upon their reasoning on an article framed upon this plan, "that the President of the United States, well knowing the act to be unconstitutional, as in fact it is, undertook to make an appointment contrary to its provisions and conformable to the Constitution of the United States, with the intent that the Constitution of the United States should prevail in regard to the office in overthrow of the authority of the act of Congress, and thereupon and thereby, with an intent against which there can be no presumption, for he is presumed to have intended to do what he did do, we ask that for that purpose of obeying the Constitution rather than an invalid law he should be removed from office!"

And this absurdity is no greater than—for it is but a statement of—the propositions of law and of fact to which the honorable Managers have reduced themselves in their theories of this cause, which exclude all evidence of intent or purpose and of effect and conduct, and take hold upon mere personal infraction of a statute of the United States, granting, for the purpose of argument, that it may be unconstitutional, and insisting that, under your judgments, it shall not make any difference whether it is unconstitutional or not. If that be so, then we have a right to claim that it is unconstitutional for the purposes of your judgment; and they agree that if you cannot so treat it and find us guilty, then it would be against the first principles of justice to punish us for an erroneous or mistaken opinion concerning constitutionality.

Now, the review of the evidence I do not purpose to weary you with. It all lies within the grasp of a handful on either side and it will astonish you, if you have not already perused the record, how much of it depends upon the arguments or the debates of counsel, how little upon what is included in the testimony. Already your attention has been turned to the simplicity and folly, perhaps, of the conduct of General Thomas; already your attention must have fixed itself upon the fact that to prove this threatened *coup d'état* to overthrow the Government of the United States and control the Treasury and the War Department you had to go to Delaware to prove a statement by Mr. Karsner that twenty days afterward Thomas said he would kick Stanton out. That is the fact; there is no getting over it. A *coup d'état* in Washington on the 21st of February, meditated, prepared, planned by military force, is proved by Karsner, brought from Delaware to say that on the 9th of March, in the East Room, General Thomas said he meant to kick Stanton out. That phrase, disrespectful as it is, and undoubtedly intimating force, is rather of a personal than of a national act. [Laughter.] I submit that criticism is well founded. I think so. It comes up to a breach of the peace, provided it has been perpetrated. [Laughter.] But it does not come up to that kind of proceeding by which Louis Napoleon seized the liberties of the French republic; and we expected, under the heats under which this impeachment was found, that we should find something of that kind. The Managers do not neglect little pieces of evidence, as is shown by their production of Mr. Karsner; and if they find this needle in a hay-stack and produce it as the sharp point of their case, there is nothing else, there is no bristling of bayonets under the haymow, you may be sure. Are there, then, any limits or discriminations in transactions of State? Are there public prosecutions, public dangers, public force, public menace? Undoubtedly there might be, and undoubtedly many who voted for impeachment supposed there were; and undoubtedly the people of the United States, when they heard there had been an impeachment voted, took it for granted there was something to appear. We have gone through it all. There is no defect of power nor of will. Every channel of the public information, even the newspapers, seem to be ardent and eager enough to aid this prosecution. Everybody in this country, all the people of the United States, are interested. They love their liberties; they love their Government; and if anybody knew of anything that would bear on that question of force, the *coup d'état*, we should have heard it. We must, then, submit, with great respect, that upon this evidence and upon these allegations there is no case made out of evil purpose, of large design of any kind, and no act that in form is an infraction of any law.

Now, what is the attitude which you must occupy toward each particular charge in these articles? Guilty or not guilty of a high crime and misdemeanor by reason of charges made and proved in that article; guilty of what the Constitution means as sufficient cause for removal of a President from office within that article. You are not to reach over from one article to another; you are to say guilty or not guilty of each as it comes along; and you are to take the first one as it appears; you are to treat it as within the premises charged and proved; you are to treat the President of the United States, for the purpose of that determination, as if he were innocent of everything else, of good politics and good conduct; you are to deal with him under your oath to administer impartial justice within the premises of accusation and proof as if President Lincoln were charged with the same thing, or General Grant, if the proposition that political gratitude is a lively sense of benefits expected leads men's minds forward rather than backward in the list of Presidents; you are to treat it as if the respondent were innocent, as if he were your friend, as if you agreed in public sentiment, in public policy; and nevertheless the crime charged and proved is such as that you will remove General Washington or President Lincoln for the same offense.

I am not to be told that it was competent for the Managers to prove that there were *coup d'états*, hidden purposes of evil to the State, threatened in this innocent and formal act apparently. Let them prove it and then let us disprove it, and then judge us within the compass of the testimony and according to the law governing these considerations. But I ask you if I do not put it to you truly that within the premises of a charge and proof the same judgment must go against President Lincoln with his good politics, and General Washington with his majestic character, as against the respondent?

And so, as you go along from the first to the second article will you remove him for having made an error about the repeal or non-repeal of statutes in regard to appointments to office, if you can find a fault? I cannot see any fault under any of the forms of the statutes. If the power of removal of Mr. Stanton under the former practice of the Government and unrestricted by this civil-tenure act existed it existed during the session as well as during the recess. If that were debatable and disputable the prevailing opinion was that it covered, and the practice of the Government shows that it covered, the removal during the session. At any rate, you must judge of this as you would have judged of Mr. Lincoln, if he had been charged with a high crime in appointing Mr. Skinner to be Postmaster General when there was not any authority under the appointment acts of the United States.

And this brings me very properly to consider, as I shall very briefly, in what attitude the President stands before you when the discussion of vicious politics or of repugnant politics, whichever may be right or wrong, is removed from the case. I do not hesitate to say that if, you separate your feelings and your conduct, his feelings and his conduct, from the aggravations of politics as they have been bred since his elevation to the Presidency, under the peculiar circumstances which placed him there, and your views in their severity, governed, undoubtedly, by the grave juncture of the affairs of the country, are reduced to the ordinary standard and style of estimate that should prevail between the departments of this Government, I do not hesitate to say that upon the impeachment investigations and upon the impeachment evidence you leave the general standing of the President unimpaired in his conduct and character as a man or as a magistrate. Agree that his policy has thwarted and opposed your policy, and agree that yours is the rightful policy: nevertheless, within the Constitution and within his right, and within

his principles as belonging to him and known and understood when he was elevated to the office, I apprehend that no reasonable man can find it in his heart to say that evil has been proved against him here. And how much is there in his conduct toward and for his country that up to this period of division commends itself not only to your but to the approval and applause of his countrymen? I do not insist upon this topic; but I ask you to agree with me in this: that his personal traits of character and the circumstances of his career have made him in opinion what he is: without learning, as it is said by his biographers, never having enjoyed a day's schooling in his life, devoted always to such energetic pursuits in the service of the State as commended him to the favor of his fellow-citizens and raised him step by step through all the gradations of the public service, and in every trial of fidelity to his origin and to the common interests proved faithful, struggling always in his public life against the aristocratic influences and oppressions which domineered so much in the section of country from which he came. He was always faithful to the common interest of the common people, and carried by his aid and efforts as much as any one else the popular measure of the homestead act against the southern policy and the aristocratic purposes of the governing interests of the South.

And I ask you to notice that, bred in a school of Tennessee Democratic politics, he had always learned to believe that the Constitution must and should be preserved; and I ask you to recognize that when it was in peril, and all men south of a certain line took up arms against it, and all men north ought to have taken up arms in politics or in war for it, he loved the country and the Constitution more than he loved his section and the glories that were promised by the evil spirits of the rebellion. I ask you whether he was not as firm in his devotion to the Constitution when he said, in December, 1860:

"Then let us stand by the Constitution; and, in saving the Union, we save this, the greatest Government on earth."

And whether, after the battle of Bull Run, he did not show as great an adhesion to the Constitution when he said:

"The Constitution—which is based on principles immutable, and upon which rest the rights of men and the hopes and expectations of those who love freedom throughout the civilized world—must be maintained."

He is no rhetorician and no theorist, no sophist and no philosopher. The Constitution is to him the only political book that he reads. The Constitution is to him the only great authority which he obeys. His mind may not expand; his views may not be so plastic as those of many of his countrymen; he may not think we have outlived the Constitution, and he may not be able to embrace the Declaration of Independence as superior and predominant to it. But to the Constitution he adheres. For it and under it he has served the State from boyhood up, labored for, loved it. For it he has stood in arms against the frowns of a Senate; for it he has stood in arms against the rebellious forces of the enemy; and to it he has bowed three times a day with a more than eastern devotion.

And when I have heard drawn from the past cases of impeachment and attempts at deposition, and five hundred years have been spoken of as furnishing the precedents explored by the honorable Managers, I have thought they found no case where one was impeached for obeying a higher duty rather than a written law regarded as repugnant to it, and yet, familiar to every child in this country, as well as to every scholar, a precedent much older comes much nearer to this expected entanglement. When the princes came to king Darius and asked that a law should be made that "whosoever shall ask any petition" "for thirty days, save of thee, O king, he shall be cast into the den of lions;" and when the plea was made that " the law of the Medes and Persians altereth not," and the minister of that day, the great head and manager of the affairs of the empire, was found still to maintain his devotion to the superior law, which made an infraction of the lower law, then was the case when the question was whether the power to which he had been obedient was adequate to his protection against the power that he had disobeyed; and now the question is whether the Constitution is adequate to the protection of the President for his obedience to it against a law that the princes have ordained that seeks to assert itself against it. The result of that impeachment we all know, and the protection of the higher power was not withheld from the obedient servant.

The honorable Manager, [Mr. WILSON,] in the very interesting and valuable report of the minority of the Judiciary Committee, entertains and warns the House of the fate of impeachment as turning always upon those who were ready with its ax and sword to destroy. He gives, in the language of Lord Caernarvon on Lord Danby's trial, a history of the whole force of them, and everybody is turned against in his turn that draws this sword. In this older case that I have referred to you may remember in the brief narrative that we have a history of the sequel of the impeachers:

"And they brought those men which had accused Daniel, and they cast them into the den of lions, them, their children, and their wives; and the lions had the mastery of them, and brake all their bones in pieces or ever they came at the bottom of the den."

This, then, Senators, is an issue not of political but of personal guilt within the limits of the charge and within the limits of the proof. Whoever decides it must so decide, and must decide upon that responsibility which belongs to an infliction of actual and real punishment upon the respondent. We all hold one or the other in trust; and when the natural life is taken he who framed it demands " Where is thy brother?" and when under our frame of Government, whereby the creation of all departments proceeds from the people which breathes into these departments, executive and judicial, the breath of life, whose favor is yours as well as the President's continuing force and strength, asks of you, as your sentence is promulgated, " Where is thy brother in this Government whom we created and maintained alive?" no answer can be given that will satisfy them or will satisfy you, unless it be in truth and in fact that for his guilt he was slain by the sword of Constitution upon the altar of Justice. If that be the answer you are acquit; he is condemned; and the Constitution has triumphed, for he has disobeyed and not obeyed it, and you have obeyed and not disobeyed it.

Power does not always sway and swing from the same center. I have seen great changes and great evils come from this matter of unconstitutional laws not attended to as unconstitutional, but asserted, and prevailing, too, against the Constitution, till at last the power of the Constitution took other form than that of peaceful, judicial determination and execution. I will put some instances of the wickedness of disobeying unconstitutional laws and of the triumph who maintained it to be right and proper.

I knew a case where the State of Georgia undertook to make it penal for a Christian missionary to preach the gospel to the Indians, and I knew by whose advice the missionary determined that he would preach the gospel and not obey the law of Georgia, on the assurance that the Constitution of the United States would bear him out in it; and the missionary, as gentle as a woman, but as firm as every free citizen of the United States ought to be, kept on the teaching to the Cherokees.

And I knew the great leader of the moral and religious sentiment of the United States, who, representing in this body, and by the same name and of the blood of one of its distinguished Senators now, [Mr. FRELINGHUYSEN,] the State of New Jersey, tried hard to save his country from the degradation of the oppression of the Indians at the instance of the haughty planters of Georgia. The Supreme Court of the United States held the law unconstitutional and issued its mandate, and the State of Georgia laughed at it and kept the missionary in prison, and Chief Justice Marshall and Judge Story and their colleagues hung their heads at the want of power in the Constitution to maintain the departments of it. But the war came, and as from the clouds from Lookout Mountain swooping down upon Missionary Ridge the thunders of the violated Constitution of the United States and the lightnings of its power over the still home of the missionary Worcester and the grave of the missionary Worcester taught the State of Georgia what comes of violating the Constitution of the United States.

I have seen an honored citizen of the State

of Massachusetts, in behalf of its colored seamen, seek to make a case by visiting South Carolina to extend over those poor and feeble people the protection of the Constitution of the United States. I have seen him attended by a daughter and grandchild of a signer of the Declaration of Independence and a framer of the Constitution, who might be supposed to have a right to its protection, driven by the power of Charleston and the power of South Carolina, and the mob and the gentlemen alike, out of that State and prevented from making a case to take to the Supreme Court to assert the protection of the Constitution. And I have lived to see the case thus made up determined that if the Massachusetts seamen, for the support of slavery, could not have a case made up, then slavery must cease; and I have lived to see a great captain of our armies, a general of the name and blood of Sherman, sweep his tempestuous war from the mountain to the sea, and returning home trample the State of South Carolina beneath the tread of his soldiery; and I have thought that the Constitution of the United States had some processes stronger than civil mandates that no resistance could meet. I do not think the people of Massachusetts suppose that efforts to set aside unconstitutional laws and to make cases for the Supreme Court of the United States, are so wicked as is urged here by some of its representatives; and I believe that if we cannot be taught by the lessons we have learned of obedience to the Constitution in peaceful methods of finding out its meaning, we shall yet need to receive some other instruction on the subject.

The strength of every system is in its weakest part. Alas for that rule? But when the weakest part breaks, the whole is broken. The chain lets slip the ship when the weak link breaks, and the ship founders. The body fails when the weak function is vitally attacked; and so with every structure, social and political, the weak point is the point of danger, and the weak point of the Constitution is now before you in the maintenance of the coördination of the departments of the Government, and if one cannot be kept from devouring another then the experiment of our ancestors will fail. They attempted to interpose justice. If that fails, what can endure?

We have come all at once to the great experiences and trials of a full-grown nation, all of which we thought we should escape. We never dreamed that an instructed and equal people, with freedom in every form, with a Government yielding to the touch of popular will so readily, ever would come to the trials of force against it. We never thought that what other systems from oppression had developed—civil war—would be our fate without oppression. We never thought that the remedy to get rid of a despotic ruler fixed by a Constitution against the will of the people, would ever bring assassination into our political experience. We never thought that political differences under an elective Presidency would bring in array the departments of the Government against one another to anticipate by ten months the operation of the regular election. And yet we take them all, one after another, and we take them because we have grown to the full vigor of manhood, when the strong passions and interests that have destroyed other nations, composed of human nature like ourselves, have overthrown them. But we have met by the powers of the Constitution these great dangers—prophesied when they would arise as likely to be our doom—the distractions of civil strife, the exhaustions of powerful war, the intervention of the regularity of power through the violence of assassination. We could summon from the people a million of men and inexhaustible treasure to help the Constitution in its time of need. Can we summon now resources enough of civil prudence and of restraint of passion to carry us through this trial so that whatever result may follow, in whatever form, the people may feel that the Constitution has received no wound? To this court, the last and best resort for this determination, it is to be left. And Oh, if you could only carry yourselves back to the spirit and the purpose and the wisdom and the courage of the framers of the Government, how safe would it be in your hands! How safe is it now in your hands, for you who have entered into their labors will see to it that the structure of your work comports in durability and excellency with theirs. Indeed, so familiar has the course of the argument made us with the names of the men of the Convention and of the First Congress that I could sometimes seem to think that the presence even of the Chief Justice was replaced by the serene majesty of Washington, and that from Massachusetts we had Adams and Ames, from Connecticut Sherman and Ellsworth, from New Jersey Paterson and Boudinot, and from New York Hamilton and Benson, and that they were to determine this case for us. Act, then, as if under this serene and majestic presence your deliberations were to be conducted to their close and the Constitution was to come out from the watchful solicitude of these great guardians of it as if from their own judgment in this high court of impeachment.

Mr. POMEROY. I move that the Senate take a recess for fifteen minutes.

The motion was agreed to; and at the expiration of the recess the Chief Justice resumed the chair and called the Senate to order.

Mr. Stanbery appeared with the counsel for the respondent.

Mr. SHERMAN. I move a call of the Senate.

The motion was agreed to; and the roll of Senators was called.

The CHIEF JUSTICE. Forty Senators have answered to their names. Senators will please give their attention. The counsel for the President will proceed.

Hon. HENRY STANBERY, on behalf of the respondent, addressed the Senate as follows:

Mr. CHIEF JUSTICE AND SENATORS: It may seem an act of indiscretion almost amounting to temerity that in my present state of health I should attempt the great labor of this case. I feel that in my best estate I could hardly attain to the height of the great argument. Careful friends have advised me against it. My watchful physician has yielded a half reluctant consent to my request, accompanied with many a caution that I fear I shall not observe. But, Senators, an irresistible impulse hurries me forward. The flesh indeed is weak; the spirit is willing. Unseen and friendly hands seem to support me. Voices inaudible to all others, I hear, or seem to hear. · They whisper words of consolation, of hope, of confidence. They say, or seem to say to me, "Feeble champion of the right, hold not back; remember that the race is not always to the swift nor the battle to the strong; remember in a just cause a single pebble from the brook was enough in the sling of the young shepherd."

Senators, in all our history as a people, never before have the three great departments of the Government been brought on the scene together for such an occasion as this. We have had party strifes in our history before. Many a time the executive and legislative departments have been in fierce and bitter antagonism. Many a time before a favorite legislative policy has been thwarted and defeated by the persistent and obstinate efforts of an Executive. Many a time before extreme party men have advised a resort to impeachment. Even as far back as the time of Washington his grand and tranquil soul was disturbed in that noted year, 1795, when he stood in antagonism with a majority in the House of Representatives upon that famous British treaty, when, upon their demand, he refused to surrender the correspondence, impeachment by the bad men of the party was then threatened. So, too, in many a subsequent day of our party contests. Oftentimes in the remembrance of men not older than myself, oftentimes when to accomplish the purposes of the party there seemed to be this way and no other way have we heard this same advice given, "This is the remedy to follow;" but, happily for us, such bad counsels never heretofore have prevailed.

This undoubtedly is a remedy within the contemplation of the Constitution, a remedy for a great mischief. Our wise forefathers saw that a time might come, an emergency might happen when nothing but the removal of the Chief Magistrate could save the nation; but they never made it to be used for party purposes. Has the time come now? Has, after the lapse of eighty years, the time at last come when this extreme remedy of the Constitution must be applied? If so, all just men will say, amen. But if, on the contrary, bad advice has

at last prevailed, if this is a step at last in the interests of party, carried by the bad advice of the worst men of the party, if at last this great and august tribunal is to be degraded to carry out a party purpose, Oh, then, there remains a day of retribution for every man that participates in this great wrong, sure to come, nor long to be delayed.

But let me not anticipate the character of the case. Let us look at it as it develops itself. I listened with great attention to the persistent efforts of my learned friends, the Managers, to convince you, Senators, that you are not sitting in a judicial capacity, that all the ordinary forms in the administration of justice are laid aside. They told you again and again there was no right of challenge here. What if there was not? Ah, does not your duty then become the more solemn, your obligation the stronger to take care when the accused cannot protect himself that you will protect him? With the greatest care and perseverance they strike out all the forms that pertains to judicial proceeding; they say they do not belong here. What if they do not? What is that to you, Senators, who with your upraised hands have invoked your God to witness that you will impartially try and decide this case? What are these forms to you? Strike them all out, and deeper and deeper that oath strikes in.

It is the habit of the advocate to magnify his case; but this case best speaks for itself. For the first time in our political existence, the three great departments of our Government are brought upon the scene together; the House of Representatives as the accusers; the President of the United States as the accused; the judiciary department, represented by its head, in the person of the Chief Justice; and the Senate of the United States as the tribunal to hear the accusation and the defense, and to render the final judgment. The Constitution has anticipated that so extreme a remedy as this might be necessary, even in the case of the highest officer of the Government. It was seen that it was a dangerous power to give one department to be used against another department. Yet, it was anticipated that an emergency might arise in which nothing but such a power could be effectual to preserve the Republic. Happily for the eighty years of our political existence which have passed no such emergency has hitherto arisen. During that time we have witnessed the fiercest contests of party. Again and again the executive and the legislative departments have been in open and bitter antagonism. A favorite legislative policy has more than once been defeated by the obstinate and determined resistance of the President, upon some of the gravest and most important issues that we have ever had, or are ever likely to have. The presidential policy and the legislative policy have stood in direct antagonism. During all that time this fearful power was in the hands of the legislative department, and more than once a resort to it has been advised by extreme party men as a sure remedy for party purposes; but, happily, that evil hitherto has not come upon us.

What new and unheard of conduct by a President has at last made a resort to this extreme remedy unavoidable? What presidential acts have happened so flagrant that all just men of all parties are ready to say "the time has come when the mischief has been committed; the evil is at work so enormous and so pressing that in the last year of his term of office it is not safe to await the coming action of the people?" If such a case has happened, all honorable and just men of all parties will say amen; but if, on the contrary, it should appear that this fearful power has at last been degraded and perverted to the use of a party; if it appears that at last bad advice, often before given by the bad men of party, has found acceptance, this great tribunal of justice, now regarded with so much awe, will speedily come to be considered as a monstrous sham. If it should be found to be the willing instrument to carry out the purposes of its party, then there remains for it and for every one of its members who participates in the great wrong a day of awful retribution sure to come nor long to be delayed. But I will not anticipate nor speak further of the case itself until its true features are fully developed.

THE ARTICLES.

I now proceed to a consideration of the articles of impeachment:

They are eleven in number. Nine of them charge acts which are alleged to amount to a *high misdemeanor in office*. The other two, namely, the *fourth* and *sixth*, charge acts which are alleged to amount to a *high crime in office*. It seems to be taken for granted that, in the phrase used in the Constitution, "other high crimes and misdemeanors," the term *high* is properly applicable as well to misdemeanors as to crimes.

The acts alleged in the eleven articles as amounting to high misdemeanors or high crimes are as follows:

In article one, the issuing of the order of February 21, 1868, addressed to Stanton, "for the removal" of Stanton from office, with intent to violate the tenure-of-office act and the Constitution of the United States, and to remove Stanton.

In article two, the issuing and delivering to Thomas of the letter of authority of February 21, 1868, addressed to Thomas, with intent to violate the Constitution of the United States and the tenure-of-office act.

In article three, the appointing of Thomas by the letter addressed to him of the 21st of February, 1868, to be Secretary of War *ad interim*, with intent to violate the Constitution of the United States.

In article four, conspiring with Thomas with intent, by intimidation and threats, to hinder Stanton from holding his office, in violation of the Constitution of the United States and the conspiracy act of July 31, 1861.

In article five, conspiring with Thomas to hinder the execution of the tenure-of-office act, and, in pursuance of the conspiracy, attempting to prevent Stanton from holding his office.

In article six, conspiring with Thomas to seize by force the property of the United States in the War Department, then in Stanton's custody, contrary to the conspiracy act of 1861, and with intent to violate the tenure-of-office act.

In article seven, conspiring with Thomas with intent to seize the property of the United States in Stanton's custody, with intent to violate the tenure-of-office act.

In article eight, issuing and delivering to Thomas the letter of authority of February 21, 1868, with intent to control the disbursements of the money appropriated for the military service and for the War Department, contrary to the tenure-of-office act and the Constitution of the United States, and with intent to violate the tenure-of-office act.

In article nine, declaring to General Emory that the second section of the Army appropriation act of March 2, 1867, providing that orders for military operations issued by the President or Secretary of War should be issued through the General of the Army, was unconstitutional and in contravention of Emory's commission, with intent to induce Emory to obey such orders as the President might give him directly and not through the General of the Army, with intent to enable the President to prevent the execution of the tenure-of-office act, and with intent to prevent Stanton from holding his office.

In article ten, that, with intent to bring in disgrace and contempt the Congress of the United States and the several branches thereof, and to excite the odium of the people against Congress and the laws by it enacted, he made three public addresses, one at the Executive Mansion on the 18th of August, 1866, one at Cleveland on the 3d of September, 1866, and one at St. Louis on the 8th of September, 1866, which speeches are alleged to be peculiarly indecent and unbecoming in the Chief Magistrate of the United States, and by means thereof the President brought his office into contempt, ridicule, and disgrace, and thereby committed and was guilty of a high misdemeanor in office.

In article eleven, that, by the same speech made on the 18th of August, at the Executive Mansion, he did, in violation of the Constitution, attempt to prevent the execution of the tenure-of-office act, by unlawfully contriving means to prevent Stanton from resuming the office of Secretary for the Department of War, after the refusal of the Senate to concur in his suspension, and by unlawfully contriving and attempting to contrive means to prevent the execution of the *act making appropriations for the support of the Army*, passed March 2, 1867, and to prevent the execution of the *act to provide for the more efficient government of the rebel States*, passed March 2, 1867.

It will be seen that all of these articles, except the tenth, charge violations either of the Constitution of the United States, of the tenure-of-office act, of the conspiracy act of 1861, of the military appropriation act of 1867, or of the reconstruction act of March 2, 1867. The tenth article, which is founded on the three speeches of the President, does not charge a violation either of the Constitution of the United States or of any act of Congress. Five of these articles charge a violation of the Constitution, to wit, articles one, two, three, four, and eight. Seven of the articles charge violations of the tenure-of-office act, to wit, articles one, two, five, six, seven, eight, nine, and eleven. Two of the articles charge a violation of the conspiracy act of 1861, to wit, articles four and six. Two of them charge violations of the appropriation act of March 2, 1867, to wit, articles nine and eleven. One only charges a violation of the reconstruction act of March 2, 1867, and that is article eleven.

We see, then, that four statutes of the United States are alleged to have been violated. Three of these provide for penalties for their violation, that is to say, the tenure-of-office act, the conspiracy act of 1861, and the military appropriation act of March 2, 1867. The violation of the tenure-of-office act is declared by the act itself to be a "high misdemeanor." The violation of the conspiracy act is declared to be "a high crime." The violation of the second section of the military appropriation act is declared to be simply "a misdemeanor in office."

It will be observed that the first eight articles all relate to the War Department, and to that alone. Article one sets out an attempted removal of the head of that Department. Three others relate to the *ad interim* appointment of Thomas to be acting Secretary of that Department. The four others relate to conspiracies to prevent Stanton from holding his office as Secretary for the Department of War, or to seize the public property in that Department, or to control the disbursements of moneys appropriated for the services of that Department.

Now, first of all, it must not escape notice that these articles are founded upon the express averment that from the moment of his reinstatement on the non-concurrence of the Senate Mr. Stanton became the lawful Secretary for that Department; that, upon such order of the Senate, he at once entered into possession of the War Department and into the lawful exercise of its duties as Secretary, and that up to the date of the articles of impeachment that lawful right and actual possession had remained undisturbed; that all the acts charged in these eight articles were committed during that time; that, notwithstanding these acts, Stanton remains lawfully and actually in possession; and that the office has been at no time vacant.

We see, then, that, according to the case made in these eight articles, the President did not succeed in getting Mr. Stanton out of office or of putting General Thomas in, either in law or in fact. We see, according to these articles, that the President did not succeed, either by force or otherwise, in preventing Mr. Stanton from holding his office or in getting possession of the public property in that Department or in controlling the disbursements of public money appropriated for the use of that Department. There has been, according to the very case made in these articles, no public mischief. The lawful officer has not been disturbed; the lawful custody of the public property and public money of the Department has not been changed. No injury has been done either to the public service or the public officer. There has been no removal of Mr. Stanton—only an abortive attempt at removal. There has been no acting Secretary put in an office vacant by death, resignation, or disability—put there during the time of such actual vacancy or temporary absence. All the time the Secretary himself has been there in the actual performance of his duties. No *ad interim* officer has, in law or fact, been constituted, for in law or fact there has been no *interim* as to the Secretary himself. There has been no moment of time in which there could be an acting Secretary or an *ad interim* Secretary, either in law or fact, for it is impossible to conceive of an *ad interim* Secretary of War when there is no *interim*, that is, when the lawful Secretary is in his place and in the actual discharge of his duties.

Mark it, then, Senators, that the acts charged as high crimes and misdemeanors in these eight articles, in respect to putting Mr. Stanton out and General Thomas in, are things *attempted* and *not* things *accomplished*. It is the attempt, and the unlawful intent with which it was formed, that the President is to be held responsible for. So that it comes to be a question of vital consequence in reference to this part of the case whether the high crimes and misdemeanors provided for in the tenure-of-office act and in the second section of the military appropriation act purport to punish not only the commission of the acts, but to punish as well the abortive attempt to commit them.

I limit myself in what has been said to the four articles touching the removal of Mr. Stanton and the appointment of General Thomas. As to the four conspiracy articles, there can be no question that the actual accomplishment of the thing intended is not made necessary to constitute the offense; for the statute against conspiracies expressly provides for the punishment of the unlawful intent, the unlawful conspiracy itself, without reference to any further act done in pursuance of it, or to the partial or complete accomplishment of the unlawful design. But, contrariwise, the other two acts do not punish the intent alone, but only the commission of the thing intended; and the offense provided for in these two acts, while it requires the unlawful intent to be a part of the crime, requires something else to supplement it, and that is the actual commission of the thing intended.

And here, Senators, before I proceed to consider these articles in detail, seems to me the proper time to bring your attention to another consideration, which I deem of very great moment. What is the subject-matter which constitutes these high crimes and misdemeanors? Under what legislation does it happen that the President of the United States is brought under all this penal liability? What are these high crimes and misdemeanors? Has he committed treason or bribery? Has he been guilty of peculation or oppression in office? Has he appropriated the public funds or the public property unlawfully to his own use? Has he committed any crime of violence against any person, public officer or private individual? Is he charged with any act which amounts to the *crimen falsi* or was done *causa lucri*? Nothing of the sort. These alleged high crimes and misdemeanors are all founded upon mere forms of executive administration. For the violation, they say, of the rules laid down by the legislative department to regulate the conduct of the executive department in the manner of the administration of executive functions belonging to that department.

The regulations so made purport to change what theretofore had been the established rule and order of administration. Before the passage of the second section of the military appropriation act the President of the United States, as Commander-in-Chief of the Army and head of the executive department, issued his orders for military operations either directly to the officer who is charged with the execution of the order or through any intermediate channel that he deemed necessary or convenient. No subordinate had a right to supervise his order before it was sent to its destination. He was not compelled to consult his Secretary of War, who was merely his agent, nor the General next to himself in rank as to that important thing, the subject-matter of his order, or, that merely formal thing, the manner of its transmission. But, by this second section, the mere matter of form is attempted to be changed. The great power of the President as Commander-in-Chief to issue orders to all his military subordinates is respected. The act tacitly admits that over these great powers Congress has no authority. The substance is not touched, but only the form is provided for; and it is a departure from this mere form that is to make the President guilty of a high crime and misdemeanor.

Then, again, as to the tenure-of-office act, that also purports to introduce a new rule in the administration of the executive powers. It does not purport to take away the President's power of appointment or power of removal absolutely; but it purports to fix the mode in which he shall execute that power, not as theretofore by his own independent action, but thereafter, only by the concurrence of the Senate. It is a regulation by the Legislature of the manner in which an executive power is to be performed.

So, too, as to *ad interim* appointments, it does not purport to take away that power from the President; it only attempts to regulate the execution of the power in a special instance.

Mr. Burke, on the impeachment of Warren Hastings, speaking of the crimes for which he stood impeached, uses this significant language:

"They were crimes, *not* against *forms*, but against those eternal laws of justice which are our rule and our birthright. His offenses are *not* in *formal, technical* language, but in *reality*, in *substance*, and effect, high crimes and high misdemeanors."

Now, Senators, if the legislative department had a constitutional right thus to regulate the performance of executive duties, and to change the mode and form of exercising an executive power which had been followed from the beginning of the Government down to the present day, is a refusal of the Executive to follow a new rule, and, notwithstanding that, to adhere to the ancient ways, that sort of high crime and misdemeanor which the Constitution contemplates? Is it just ground for impeachment? Does the fact that such an act is called by the Legislature a high crime and misdemeanor necessarily make it such a high crime and misdemeanor as is contemplated by the Constitution? If, for instance, the President should send a military order to the Secretary of War, is that an offense worthy of impeachment? If he should remove an officer on the 21st of February and nominate another on the 22d, would that be an impeachable misdemeanor? Now, it must be admitted that if the President had sent the name of Mr. Ewing to the Senate on the 21st, in the usual way, in place of Mr. Stanton removed, and had not absolutely ejected Mr. Stanton from office, but had left him to await the action of the Senate upon the nomination, certainly in mere matter of form there would have been no violation of this tenure-of-office act.

Now, what did he do? He made an order for the removal of Mr. Stanton on the 21st, but did not eject him from office, and sent a nomination of Mr. Ewing to the Senate on the 22d. Is it possible that thereby he had committed an act that amounted to a high crime and misdemeanor, and deserved removal from office? And yet that is just what the President has done. He has more closely followed the mere matter of form prescribed by the tenure-of-office act than, according to the learned Manager who opened this prosecution, was necessary. For, if he had made an order of removal, and at once had sent to the Senate his reasons for making such removal, and had stated to them that his purpose was to make this removal in order to test the constitutionality of the tenure-of-office act, then, says the honorable Manager, "Had the Senate received such a message, the Representatives of the people might never have deemed it necessary to impeach the President for such an act, to insure the safety of the country, even if they had denied the accuracy of his legal positions." How, then, can it be deemed necessary to impeach the President for making an order of removal on one day, advising the Senate of it the same day, and sending the nomination of a successor the next day? Was ever a matter more purely formal than this? And yet this is the only act. Is this, in the words of Mr. Burke, not in merely *technical* language, "but in reality, in substance, and effect," a high crime and misdemeanor within the meaning of the Constitution?

I dislike very much to ask favors, but if it be the pleasure of the Senate to adjourn, I shall detain them but a short time to-morrow, and it will be a great favor to me, a very great favor.

Mr. GRIMES. Mr. Chief Justice, I move that the Senate, sitting as a court of impeachment, now adjourn.

The motion was agreed to; and the Senate, sitting for the trial of the impeachment, adjourned.

SATURDAY, *May* 2, 1868.

The Chief Justice of the United States took the chair.

The usual proclamation having been made by the Sergeant-at-Arms,

The Managers of the impeachment on the part of the House of Representatives and the counsel for the respondent, except Mr. Curtis, appeared and took the seats assigned to them respectively.

The members of the House of Representatives, as in Committee of the Whole, preceded by Mr. E. B. WASHBURNE, chairman of that committee, and accompanied by the Speaker and Clerk, appeared and were conducted to the seats provided for them.

The Journal of yesterday's proceeding of the Senate, sitting for the trial of the impeachment, was read.

The CHIEF JUSTICE. The counsel will proceed with the argument. Senators will please give their attention.

Mr. STANBERY. Mr. Chief Justice, first of all, Senators, I must return my thanks for the very great kindness shown me yesterday. I was greatly in need of it. I am greatly benefited by the rest it has afforded me. I feel refreshed and better prepared, though at last how poorly, for the work that yet lies before me. Nevertheless your courtesy so kindly, so cheerfully extended, I shall not soon forget.

And now, Senators, before I enter upon this case I must be allowed to speak in advance my deliberate opinion of the case itself, not in the way of rhodomontade, not that I hope to carry anything before a body like this by the

C. I.—49.

mere expression of confidence; not at all; but still having examined this case from beginning to end, having looked through it in all its parts, I feel ready to say that there is not only no case, but no shadow of a case. Oh! for an hour of my ancient vigor that I might make this declaration good; but poorly prepared I hope to make it good to the satisfaction of the Senate that now hear me.

STANTON NOT WITHIN THE TENURE-OF-OFFICE ACT.

The first clause of the first section declares that every person then or thereafter holding any civil office under an appointment with the advice and consent of the Senate and due qualification shall hold his office until a successor shall have been in like manner appointed and qualified.

If the act contained no other provisions qualifying this general clause, then it would be clear,

1. That it would apply to all civil officers who held by appointment made by the President with the advice of the Senate, including judicial officers as well as executive officers. It gives all of them the same right to hold, and subjects all of them to the same liability to be removed. From the exercise of the power of *suspension* by the independent act of the President, made applicable to any officer so holding, by the second section, judges of the United States are expressly excepted. We find no such exception, express or implied, as to the exercise of the power of *removal* declared in the first section. Judicial officers, as well as executive officers, are made to hold by the same tenure. They hold during the pleasure of the President and the Senate, and cease to hold when the President and Senate appoint a successor.

2. It applies equally to officers whose tenure of office, as fixed prior to the act, was to hold during the pleasure of the President, as to those who were to hold for a fixed term of years, or during good behavior.

3. It purports to take from the President the power to remove any officer, at any time, for any cause, by the exercise of his own power alone. But it leaves him a power of removal with the concurrence of the Senate. In this process of removal the separate action of the President and the Senate is required. The initiatory act must come from the President, and from him alone. It is upon his action *as taken* that the Senate proceeds, and they give or withhold their consent to what he *has* done. The manner in which the President may exercise his part of the process is merely formal. It may be simply by the nomination of a successor to the incumbent or the officer intended to be removed. Then, upon the confirmation by the Senate of such nomination, and the issuance of a commission to him, the removal becomes complete. Or the President may exercise his part of the process by issuing an order of removal, followed by a nomination. Neither the

order for removal or the nomination works a change in itself. Both are necessarily conditional upon the subsequent action of the Senate. So, too, the order of removal, the nomination, and the confirmation of the Senate are not final. A further act remains to be done before the appointment of the successor is complete, and that is an executive act exclusively—the signing of the commission by the President. Up to this point the President has a *locus penitentiæ*; for, although the Senate have advised him to appoint his nominee, the President is not bound by their advice, but may defeat all the prior action by allowing the incumbent to remain in office.

Thus far we have considered the first clause of the first section of the act without reference to the context. Standing alone it seems to have a universal application to all civil officers, and to secure *all* of them who hold by the concurrent action of the President and the Senate against removal otherwise than by the same concurrent action and to make all of them liable to removal by that concurrent action.

Are there exceptions to the universality of the tenure of office so declared? We say there are:

1. Exceptions by *necessary implication*. Judicial officers of the United States come within this exception; for their tenure of office is fixed by the Constitution itself. They cannot be removed either by the President alone or by the President and Senate conjointly. They alone hold for life or during good behavior, subject to only one mode of removal, and that is by impeachment.

2. Exceptions *made expressly* by the provisions of the act; which make it manifest that it was not intended for all civil officers of the United States. First of all, this purpose is indicated by the *title* of the act. It is entitled "An act regulating the tenure of *certain* civil offices'—not of *all* civil offices. Next, we find, that immediately succeeding the first clause which, as has been shown, is in terms of universal application, comprehending "every person holding any civil office," the purpose of restraining or limiting its generality is expressed in these words, "except as herein otherwise provided for." This puts us at once upon inquiry. It advises us that all persons and all officers are not intended to be embraced in the comprehensive terms used in the first clause; that some persons and some officers are intended to be excepted and to be "otherwise provided for;" that some who do hold by the concurrent action of the President and the Senate are not to be secured against removal by any other process than the same concurrent action.

What class of officers embraced by the general provisions of the first clause are made to come within the clause of exception? The *proviso* which immediately follows answers the question. It is in these words:

"*Provided*, That the Secretaries of State, of the Treasury, of War, of the Navy, and of the Interior, the Postmaster General, and the Attorney General, shall hold their offices respectively for and during the term of the President by whom they may have been appointed, and for one month thereafter, subject to removal by and with the advice and consent of the Senate."

We see that these seven heads of Department are the only civil officers of the United States which are especially designated. We see a clear purpose to make some special provision as to them. Being civil officers holding by the concurrent appointment of the President and the Senate, they would have been embraced by the first general clause of the section, if there had been no exception and no *proviso*. The argument on the other side is, that, notwithstanding the declared purpose to make exceptions, these officers are not made exceptions; that notwithstanding there is a *proviso* as to them, in which express provision is specially for *their* tenure of office, we must still look to the general clause to find their tenure of office. It is a settled rule of construction that every word of a statute is to be taken into account, and that a *proviso* must have effect as much as any other clause of the statute.

Upon looking into this *proviso* we find its purpose to be the fixing a tenure of office for these seven officers. And how is that tenure fixed? We find it thus declared: some of them are given a tenure-of-office, others are not. But as to the favored class, as to that class intended to be made safe and most secure, even *their* tenure is not so ample and permanent as the tenure given to all civil officers who, prior to the act, held by the same tenure as themselves. By the general clause all civil officers are embraced and protected from executive removal, including as well those who hold by no other tenure than "the pleasure of the President." This tenure, "during the pleasure of the President," was the tenure by which all these Cabinet officers held prior to the passage of this law. Now, for the first time, this *proviso* fixed another and safer tenure for certain Cabinet officers, not for all. It gave to some of them the right to hold during the term of one President and for one month of the term of the succeeding President; but it did not give that right to all of them. It was given only to a favored class, and the new tenure so given to the favored class was not so favorable as that given to other civil officers who had theretofore held by precisely the same uncertain tenure, that is to say, "the pleasure of the President," for these other civil officers were not limited to the term of one President and one month afterwards, but their tenure was just as secure from "the pleasure of the President," after the expiration of one presidential term, and after the expiration of the first month of the succeeding presidential term, as it was before.

We see, then, that in fixing a new tenure of office for Cabinet officers, the tenure given to one class of them, and that the most favored, was not as favorable as that given to other civil officers theretofore holding by the same tenure with themselves. This favored class were not to hold one moment after the expiration of the month of the second presidential term. At that punctual time the right of the President to select his Cabinet would, even as to them, return to him. If they were to remain after that, it would be that it was his pleasure to keep them and to give them a new tenure by his choice in the regular mode of appointment.

But, as we have seen, the *proviso* makes a distinction between Cabinet officers and divides them into two classes, those holding by appointment of the President for the time being, and those not appointed by him, but by his predecessor, and holding only by his sufferance or pleasure. If ever an intent was manifest in a statute it is clear in this instance. There is a division into two classes, a tenure of office given to one class and withheld from the other. Before the passage of this act all Cabinet officers holding under any President, whether appointed by him or his predecessor, held by the same tenure, "the pleasure of the President." This *proviso* makes a distinction between them never made before. It gives one class a new and more seecure tenure, and it leaves the other class without such new tenure. One class was intended to be protected, the other not.

Now comes the question. Upon what ground was this distinction made? Why was it that a better title, a stronger tenure was given to one class than to the other? The answer is given by the *proviso* itself. The officers in the Cabinet of a President, who were nominated by him, who were appointed by him with the concurrence of the Senate, are those to whom this new and better tenure is given. They are officers of his own selection; they are his chosen agents. He has once recommended them to the Senate as fit persons for the public trust, and they have obtained their office through his selection and choice. The theory here is, that having had one free opportunity of choice, having once exercised his right of selection, he shall be bound by it. He shall not dismiss his own selected agent upon his own pleasure or caprice. He is, in legal language, "estopped" by the selection he has made, and is made incapable by his own act of dissolving the official relation which he has imposed on himself. Having selected his Cabinet officer, he must take him as a man takes his chosen wife, for better or worse.

But as to such Cabinet officers as are not of a President's selection; as to those who have been selected by a former President; as to those whose title was given by another; as to those he never appointed, and, perhaps, never would have appointed; as to those who came to him by succession and not by his own act; as to those who hold merely by his acquiescence or sufferance—*they* are entitled to no favor, and receive none. They stand as step-children in his political family, and are not placed on the same level with the rightful heirs entitled to the inheritance.

The construction claimed by the Managers leads to this inevitable absurdity: that the class entitled to favor are cut off at the end of the month, while those having a less meritorious title remain indefinitely. What was intended for a benefit becomes a mischief, and the favored class are worse off than if no favor had been shown them. Their condition was intended to be made better than that of their fellows, and has been made worse. From those entitled to protection it is taken away to be given to those not entitled.

Now, when President Johnson was invested with his office, he found Mr. Stanton holding the office of Secretary of War. He had been appointed by Mr. Lincoln during his first term, and was holding in the second month of Mr. Lincoln's second term under the old appointment. Mr. Stanton was neither appointed by Mr. Lincoln or Mr. Johnson for that second term; so that we are relieved from all question whether the fractional term, counting from the accession of Mr. Johnson, is to be called the unexpired term of Mr. Lincoln, or the proper term of Mr. Johnson, and whether, if he had been appointed or reappointed by Mr. Lincoln during his second term, he might not have claimed that he was entitled, as against Mr. Johnson, to hold on to its end. Mr. Stanton never had any tenure of office under the tenure-of-office act for the current presidential term, never having been appointed for that term by either Mr. Lincoln or Mr. Johnson. He, therefore, does not come within the category of those members of Mr. Johnson's Cabinet who have been appointed by Mr. Johnson.

At the date of the passage of the tenure-of-office act, the Cabinet of Mr. Johnson was composed as follows: the Secretaries of State, of the Treasury, of War, and of the Navy, held by appointment of Mr. Lincoln made in his first term; the Secretary of the Interior, the Postmaster General, and the Attorney General, held by the appointment of Mr. Johnson made during his current term. There was, then, as to the entire seven, a difference as to the manner and time of their appointment. Four had been appointed by Mr. Lincoln, and the other three by Mr. Johnson. All of them held by the same tenure, "the pleasure of the President." All of them, without reference to constitutional provisions, were, by existing laws, removable by the independent action of the President. The acts of Congress creating the offices of Secretaries of State, of War, and of the Navy, expressly recognize the executive authority to remove them at pleasure. The acts of Congress creating the four other heads of Departments place them on the same footing as to tenure of office. All these acts remained, in this particular, in full force. This tenure-of-office act introduces a distinction made applicable to Cabinet officers alone, never made before. For the first time it gives to those appointed by the President for the time being a new tenure. It secures them from removal at his pleasure alone. It repeals, as to them, the existing laws, and declares that they shall thereafter be entitled to hold during the remainder of the term of the President by whom they were appointed, and for one month of the succeeding presidential term, exempt from removal by the sole act of the President, and only subject to removal by the concurrent act of the President and Senate.

But it gives them no right to hold against the pleasure of the succeeding President one moment after the expiration of that punctual time of one month. When that time has arrived their right to hold ceases and their offices become vacant. The policy here declared is unmistakable, that notwithstanding anything to the contrary in the act, every President shall have the privilege of his own choice, of his own selection of the members of his Cabinet. The right of selection for himself is, however, qualified. He may not, as theretofore, enjoy this right throughout his term. For the first month he must take the Cabinet of his predecessor, however opposed to him in opinion or obnoxious to him personally. Then, too, while the right is given to him, it cannot be exercised but once. It is a power that does not survive, but expires with a single execution.

Now, as to the three members of Mr. Johnson's Cabinet, appointed by his own exercise of this independent power, he having, as to them, once exercised the power, it is, as to them, exhausted. The consequence is that these three officers no longer remain subject to *his pleasure* alone. They are entitled to hold in defiance of his wishes throughout the remainder of his term, because they are his own selected officers; but their right are not entitled to hold during the whole term of his successor, but only for a modicum of that term, just because they were not selected by that successor. So much for these three.

Now, as to the other four, as to whom Mr. Johnson has not exercised his right of choice even by one appointment. May they hold during the residue of his term in defiance of his wishes? Do they come within that clear policy of giving to every President one opportunity at least to exercise his independent right of choice? Surely not. Then, if, as to them, he has the right, how can he exercise it, if, as in the case of Mr. Stanton, the Cabinet officer holds on after he has been requested to resign? What mode is left to the President to avail himself of his own independent right when such an officer refuses to resign? None other than the process of removal; for he cannot put the man of his choice *in* until he has put the other *out*. So that the independent right of choice cannot under such conditions be exercised at all without the corresponding right of removal; and the one necessarily implies the other.

We have seen that the tenure of office fixed by the *proviso* for Cabinet officers, applies only to those members of Mr. Johnson's Cabinet appointed by himself. It therefore does not apply to Mr. Stanton. If there is any other clause of the act which applies to Mr. Stanton, it must be the first general clause, and if that does not apply to him, then his case does not come within the purview of the act at all, but must be ruled by the preëxisting laws, which made him subject at all times to the pleasure of the President and to the exercise of his independent power of removal. And this is precisely what is claimed by the Managers. They maintain that, although the *proviso* does not give Mr. Stanton a new tenure, yet the first general clause does, and that he is put by that clause on the same footing of all other civil officers who, at the date of the act, held by the concurrent appointment of the President and Senate by no other tenure than "during the pleasure of the President."

But all the officers intended to be embraced by that first clause, who held by that tenure before, are declared to hold by a new tenure. Not one of them can be removed by the President alone. Whether appointed by the President for the time being or by his predecessor, they must remain in defiance of the President until removed by the concurrent action of the President and the Senate. In effect, so far as the power of the President is concerned, *they* may hold for life. If Mr. Stanton comes within the protection of that clause, if his tenure of office is fixed by that clause, it follows inevitably that Mr. Johnson cannot remove him. It follows as inevitably that no succeeding President can remove him. He may defy Mr. Johnson's successor as he now defies Mr. Johnson. He may say to that successor as he has said to Mr. Johnson, "I am compelled to deny your right under the Constitution and laws of the United States, without the advice and consent of the Senate." If the successor of Mr. Johnson should point him to the *proviso*, and at the end of the month require him to leave, his answer, according to the Managers, would run thus: "That *proviso* did not fix my tenure of office. It did not apply to me, but only to those appointed by Mr. Johnson. They must go out with the month; I do not. My tenure is fixed by the first clause, and you cannot get clear of me without the advice and consent of the Senate."

NO REMOVAL OF MR. STANTON.

But if it be held that Mr. Stanton did come within the purview of the tenure-of-office act; if it be held that his removal by the independent action of the President is forbidden by the act, then we maintain that no such removal is charged in the articles or made out in the proof.

It is only in the first article that any charge is made in reference to Mr. Stanton's removal. That article nowhere alleges that Mr. Stanton has been removed, either in law or in fact. It does allege that on the 21st of February Stanton was "lawfully entitled to hold said office of Secretary for the Department of War," and that on that day the President "did, unlawfully and in violation of the Constitution and laws of the United States, issue an order in writing for the removal of Edwin M. Stanton from the office of Secretary for the Department of War." It is the issuance of this order *for a removal* that is made the *gravamen* of the charge. It is not followed by any allegation that it had the effect to work a removal, either in law or in fact. On the contrary, in the very next article, which is founded on the order to Thomas, which purports to be made after the order for the removal of Stanton, it is alleged that Stanton still held the office lawfully, and that notwithstanding the order for removal to Stanton and the order to Thomas to act as Secretary, Stanton still held the office, and no vacancy was created or existed. This is the tenor of every article, that Stanton never has been removed, in law or in fact; that there never has been an *ouster*, either in law or in fact; that there never has been at no time a vacancy. The proof shows that Stanton remains in possession, and that his official acts continue to be recognized.

Now, if the order *per se* operated a removal in law, it must follow that the order was valid and in conformity with the Constitution and laws of the United States, for no order made contrary thereto could take effect in law. If there was a removal *in law* the executive order which accomplished it was a valid, not an unlawful act. But if the order did not operate a removal *per se*, and if a removal *in fact*, though not *in law*, might be held sufficient to constitute an offense, and if it were alleged and were proved that under the illegal order an actual *ouster* or removal was effected by force or threats the answer to be given in this case is conclusive. No *ouster* in fact, no actual or physical removal, is proved or so much as charged. Mr. Stanton has never to this day been put out of actual possession. He remains in possession as fully since the order was made as before, and still holds on.

Now, we look in vain through this tenure-of-office act for any provision forbidding *an attempt* to cause a removal, or making it penal to issue an order for such a purpose. The sixth section is the only one on the subject of removal, and that provides:

"That every removal" "made" "contrary to the provisions of this act" "shall be deemed, and is hereby declared to be, a high misdemeanor;"

and is made punishable by fine not exceeding $10,000, or by imprisonment not exceeding five years, or both, at the discretion of the court.

No latitude of construction can torture an attempt to make a removal into an actual removal, or can turn an abortive effort to do a given thing into the accomplished fact. Such a latitude of construction could not be allowed where the rule of construction is least restricted, and least of all in a penal statute where the rule of construction is the most restricted.

It seems a waste of words to argue this point further. There is a total failure of the case upon the first article on this point, if we had none other. And yet this article is the head and front of the entire case. Strike it out and all that remains is "leather and prunella."

But, Senators, if you should be of opinion that the tenure-of-office act protected Mr. Stanton, and that the attempt to remove him was equivalent to a removal, we next maintain—

First, That the President had a right to construe the law for himself, and if, in the exercise of that right, he committed an error of construction, and acted under that error, he is not to be held responsible.

Second, If he had so construed the law as to be of opinion that Mr. Stanton was intended to be protected by it against his power of removal, and was also of opinion that the law in that respect was contrary to the Constitution, he is not to be held reponsible if he therein committed an error.

I proceed to argue these points in the order in which they have been stated. First, then, is the President responsible for an official act done by him under an erroneous construction of an act of Congress? I agree that ignorance or misconception of the law does not, in general, excuse a party from civil or criminal liability for an act contrary to law. But this well-established rule has exceptions equally well established, and the case here falls within one of the exceptions, and not within the rule. Where a law is passed which concerns the President and touches his official duties it is not only his right but his duty to determine for himself what is the true construction of the law, and to act, or refuse to act, according to that determination, whatever it may be. He is an executive officer, not a mere ministerial officer. He is invested with a discretion, with the right to form a judgment, and to act under his judgment so formed, however erroneous. No such discretion is allowed to a ministerial officer. *His* business is not to construe the law, but merely to perform it, and he acts at his peril if he does not do that which is commanded by reason of an erroneous construction, however honestly entertained.

But, as I have said, the President is not a ministerial officer. His function is not merely to execute laws, but to construe them as well. The Constitution makes this too clear for question. It does not, it is true, vest him with judicial power, which always implies the exercise of discretion. It vests him with the executive power, but, nevertheless, with a discretion as to the mode of its execution. The Constitution contemplates that, in the exercise of that executive power, he may be involved in doubt and perplexity as to the manner of its exercise, and, therefore, gives him the privilege of resorting to his Cabinet officers for advice. The Constitution binds him by an oath not only faithfully to execute his office, not merely to carry into execution laws of Congress, but also, to the best of his ability, to preserve, protect, and defend the Constitution itself. This great trust implies the exercise of a large discretion.

It is sufficient, upon this point, to cite a late opinion of the Supreme Court of the United States, in what is called the Mississippi injunction case, decided in April, 1867. Mr. Chief Justice Chase, delivering the opinion of the court, says :

"It is assumed by the counsel for the State of Mississippi that the President, in the execution of the reconstruction acts, is required to perform a mere ministerial duty. In this assumption there is, we think, a confounding of the terms ministerial and executive, which are by no means equivalent in import. A ministerial duty, the performance of which may, in proper cases, be required of a Department by judicial process, is one in respect to which nothing is left to discretion. It is a simple, definite duty, arising under conditions admitted or proved to exist, or imposed by law."

After citing some cases of merely ministerial duty, the Chief Justice proceeds as follows :

"In each of these cases nothing was left to discretion. There was no room for the exercise of judgment. The law required the performance of a single, specific act, and that performance, it was held, might be required by *mandamus*. Very different is the duty of the President in the exercise of the power to see that the laws are faithfully executed, and among those laws the acts named in the bill. The duty thus imposed on the President is in no just sense ministerial. It is purely executive and political. An attempt on the part of the judicial department of the Government to enjoin the performance of such duties by the President might be justly characterized, in the language of Chief Justice Marshall, as an 'absurd and excessive extravagance.' It is true that, in the instance before us, the interposition of the court is not sought to enforce action by the Executive under constitutional legislation, but to restrain such action under legislation alleged to be unconstitutional. But we are unable to perceive that this circumstance takes the case out of the general principle which forbids judicial interference with the exercise of executive discretion."

When, therefore, this tenure-of-office act came to be considered by the President in reference to his purpose to remove Mr. Stanton from office, he had a right and it was his duty to decide for himself whether the proposed removal of Mr. Stanton was or was not forbidden by the act. As yet that act had received no construction by the judicial department, nor had the President any authority to send the act to the Supreme Court, and require the judgment of that court upon its true meaning. The Constitution gave him no right to resort to the judges for advice. He could not settle his doubts, if he entertained doubts, by asking any other opinions than those of the heads of Departments.

But the President was not even required to ask the advice of his Cabinet, nor even of his Attorney General, to which officer he may resort for advice as a head of Department under the provisions of the Constitution, and whose special duty it is made by an act of Congress to give the President advice when called for by him on any question of law. The President, although such aids are given to him by the Constitution in forming his judgment on a question of law, is not bound to resort to them. He may do so out of abundant caution, but such is his own latitude of discretion that he may act without invoking such aid, or he may reject the advice when asked for and given, and lawfully decide for himself, though perhaps not so wisely or cautiously.

Besides this late authoritative exposition, as to the discretionary power of the President, there is abundance of other authority entitled to the gravest consideration, which might be adduced to the same effect, and which I propose to introduce upon the next point, which I now proceed to consider, and that point is, that if the President had so construed this tenure-of-office act as to be satisfied that Mr. Stanton came within its provisions, but was also of opinion that the law in that respect was contrary to the Constitution, he is not to be held responsible if therein he committed an error. The case in that aspect stood thus : here was an act of Congress which, in the construction given to it by the President, forbade the removal of Mr. Stanton from the War Department. The President, in the exercise of his executive functions and of his duty to see that the laws were faithfully executed, came to the conclusion that in the execution of so much of this executive duty as had relation to the administration of the War Department, it was expedient to place it in the hands of another person. His relations with Mr. Stanton were such that he felt unwilling any longer to be responsible for his acts in the administration of that Department, or to trust him as one of his confidential advisers. The question at once arose whether this right of removal denied to him by this law, was given to him by the Constitution ; or, to state it in other words, whether this law was in this respect in pursuance of the Constitution.

Now, it appears that his opinion upon this question had been made up deliberately. When this same law was on its passage and had been presented to him for his approval, his opinion was formed that it was in violation of the Constitution. He refused to approve it, and returned it to Congress with a message in which this opinion was distinctly announced. It passed, notwithstanding, by a constitutional majority in both Houses. No one doubts that then, at least, he had a perfect right to exercise a discretion, and no one has ever yet asserted that an error in an opinion so formed involved him in any liability.

The exercise of that veto power exhausted all his means of resistance to what he deemed an unconstitutional act, in his legislative capacity ; and so far as the law provided a rule of action for others than himself, no other means of resistance were left to him. But this law was directly aimed at him and the exercise of the executive power vested in him by the Constitution. When, therefore, he came a second time to consider it, it was in thé discharge of an executive duty. Had he then no discretion of any sort? Was he bound to act in a merely ministerial capacity? Having once finally exercised a discretion in his legislative capacity to prevent the passage of the law, was he thereby deprived of his discretion in his executive capacity when he was called upon to act under it?

It has been said, that a law passed over a President's veto by a majority of two thirds, has a greater sanction than a law passed in the ordinary way by a mere majority. I know that there are those who, while they admit that, as to a law passed in the ordinary mode by the concurrent acts of the two Houses and the President, it may be questioned on the score of unconstitutionality, yet maintain that a law not passed by such a concurrence, but by the separate action of the two Houses without the concurrence of the Executive, or against his will, is something superior to ordinary legislation, and takes the character of a fundamental or organic enactment. But this is a modern heresy unsustained by the slightest reason or authority. It is at last but a legislative act. It stands upon an equal footing with other legislative acts. It cannot be put upon higher ground or lower ground. No distinction is allowable between the one and the other. But, if it were, it certainly would seem more reasonable that such a law passed by one coördinate department, would stand on lower ground than a law passed with full concurrence of both departments.

The question then recurs, is the President invested with a discretion in his executive capacity? In the exercise of that discretion may he compare the law with the Constitution, and if, in his opinion, the law vests him with a power not granted by the Constitution, or deprives him of a power which the Constitution does grant, may he refuse to execute the power so given, or proceed to execute the power so taken away? We have already cited a late decision of the Supreme Court directly in point. That presented the direct question whether, as to the reconstruction acts, passed like this tenure-of-civil-office act, by a vote of two thirds in each House, the President had, notwithstanding, in reference to those laws, an executive discretion. The decision maintains that he had.

I now proceed to show that this is no modern doctrine. The authorities which I shall cite go beyond the necessities of this case. Some of them go to the length of asserting that this executive discretion survives even after the passage of the law by the legislative department, it has been construed by the judicial department, and in that extreme case, leave the President at last to act for himself in opposition to the express will of both the other departments. I will first cite some opinions upon this extreme position.

Mr. Jefferson says:

"The second question, whether the judges are invested with exclusive authority to decide on the constitutionality of a law, has been heretofore a subject of consideration with me in the exercise of official duties. Certainly there is not a word in the Constitution which has given that power to them more than to the executive or legislative branches. Questions of property, of character, and of crime, being ascribed to the judges, through a definite course of legal proceedings—laws involving such questions belong of course to them, and as they decide on them ultimately and without appeal they of course decide *for themselves*. The constitutional validity of the law or laws prescribing executive action, and to be administered by that branch ultimately and without appeal, the executive must decide for *themselves* also whether under the Constitution they are valid or not. So, also, as to laws governing the proceedings of the Legislature; that body must judge *for itself* the constitutionality of the law, and, equally, without appeal or control from its coördinate branches. And, in general, that branch which is to act ultimately and without appeal, on any law, is the rightful expositor of the validity of the law, uncontrolled by the opinions of the other coördinate authorities."

President Jackson, in his veto message upon the bank bill, uses this language:

"If the opinion of the Supreme Court covered the whole ground of this act it ought not to control the coördinate authorities of this Government. The Congress, the Executive, and the court must each for itself be guided by its own opinion of the Constitution."

Mr. Van Buren makes use of this language:

"Everybody knows that an act which is contrary to the Constitution is a nullity, although it may have passed according to the forms of the Constitution. That instrument creates several departments, whose duty it may become to act upon such a bill in the performance of their respective functions. The theory of the Constitution is that these departments are coördinate and independent of each other, and that, when they act in their appropriate spheres, they each have a right, and it is the duty of each to judge for themselves in respect to the authority and requirements of the Constitution without being controlled or interfered with by their co-departments, and are each responsible to the people alone for the manner in which they discharge their respective duties in that regard. It is not, therefore, to be presumed that that instrument, after making it the President's especial duty to take an oath to protect and uphold the Constitution and prevent its violation, intended to deny to him the right to withhold his assent from a measure which he might, conscientiously believe would have that effect and to impose upon him the necessity of outraging his conscience by making himself a party to such a violation."

Whether these views are sound or not is not now the question. It happens that as to this tenure-of-civil-office law, it has never been held by the Supreme Court to be constitutional. But, if it had been otherwise, if this law had been pronounced constitutional by a solemn decision of the Supreme Court of the United States, what ground would there be for holding the President guilty of a high misdemeanor in forming an opinion sanctioned by the authority of three of his predecessors?

I will now call attention to certain leading authorities upon the point that a law passed by Congress in violation of the Constitution is totally void, and as to the discretion vested in the President to decide for himself the question of the validity of such a law. I cite first from the Federalist, No. 76:

"There is no position which depends on clearer principles than that every act of a delegated authority contrary to the tenor of the commission under which it is exercised, is void. No legislative act, therefore, contrary to the Constitution, can be valid." "If it be said that the legislative body are themselves the constitutional judges of their own powers, and that the construction they put upon them is conclusive upon *the other departments*, it may be answered that this cannot be the natural presumption where it is not to be collected from any particular provisions in the Constitution."

I cite next from No. 31 of the Federalist, in reference to that clause of the Constitution declaring its supremacy and the supremacy of the laws. It is said:

"It will not, I presume, have escaped observation that it *expressly* confines this supremacy to laws made *pursuant to the Constitution*, which I mention merely as an instance of caution in the Convention; since that limitation would have been to be understood, though it had not been expressed."

Chancellor Kent, in the first volume of his Commentaries, uses this language:

"But in this and all other countries where there is a written constitution designating the powers and duties of the legislative as well as of the *other* departments of the Government, an act of the Legislature may be void as being against the Constitution."

Speaking of the legislative power the Chancellor adds:

"It is liable to be constantly swayed by popular prejudice and passion, and it is difficult to keep it from pressing with injurious weight upon the constitutional rights and privileges of *the other departments*."

In Hayburn's case (2 Dall., page 407) the opinions of the judges of the circuit courts of the United States for the districts of New York, Pennsylvania, and North Carolina, upon the constitutionality of the act of March 23, 1792, are reported. This act purported to confer upon the judges a power which was not judicial. They were of opinion that Congress had no authority to invest them with any power except such as was strictly judicial, and they were not bound to execute the law in their judicial capacity.

In Calder *vs.* Bull, (3 Dall., page 398,) speaking of the paramount authority of Federal and State constitutions, it is said:

"If any act of Congress or of the Legislature of a State violates those constitutional provisions, it is unquestionably void."

In Van Horn's Lessee *vs.* Dorrance (2. Dall., page 308) we find the following:

"What are Legislatures? Creatures of the Constitution; they owe their existence to the Constitution. They derive their powers from the Constitution. It is their commission; and, therefore, all their acts must be conformable to it, or else they will be void." "Whatever may be the case in other countries, yet in this there can be no doubt that every act of the Legislature repugnant to the Constitution is absolutely void."

Chief Justice Marshall, delivering the opinion of the court in Marbury *vs.* Madison, says:

"It is a proposition too plain to be contested that the Constitution controls any legislative act repugnant to it; or, that the Legislature may alter the Constitution by an ordinary act. Between these alternatives, there is no middle ground. The Constitution is either a superior, paramount law, unchangeable by ordinary means, or it is on a level with ordinary legislative acts, and like other acts, is alterable when the Legislature shall please to alter it. If the former part of the alternative be true, then a legislative act contrary to the Constitution is not law; if the latter part be true, then written constitutions are absurd attempts on the part of the people, to limit a power in its nature illimitable." "Certainly all those who have framed written constitutions contemplate them as forming the fundamental and paramount law of the nation, and, consequently, the theory of every such government must be, that an act of the Legislature, repugnant to the Constitution, is void." "Thus the particular phraseology of the Constitution of the United States confirms and strengthens the principle, supposed to be essential to all written constitutions, that a law repugnant to the Constitution is void; and that courts, as well as *other departments*, are bound by that instrument."

In Dodge *vs.* Woolsey (18 Howard, pages 347–8) the court say:

"The departments of the Government are legislative, executive, and judicial. They are coördinate in degree to the extent of the powers delegated to each of them. Each, in the exercise of its powers, is independent of the other, but all, rightfully done by either, is binding upon the others. The Constitution is supreme over all of them, because the people who ratified it have made it so; consequently, anything which may be done unauthorized by it is unlawful."

Again, in 22 Howard, page 242, the nullity of any act inconsistent with the Constitution is produced by the declaration that the Constitution is the supreme law.

I will now refer to some decisions of the Supreme Court of the United States, which relate more particularly to the point, that as an executive officer the President is vested with a discretion.

In Marbury *vs.* Madison (1 Cranch, page 380) is the following:

"By the Constitution of the United States the President is invested with certain important political powers, in the exercise of which he is to use his own discretion, and is accountable only to his country in his political character, and to his own conscience. To aid him in the performance of these duties, he is authorized to appoint certain officers to act by his authority and in conformity with his orders. In such cases their acts are his acts, and whatever opinion may be entertained of the manner in which executive discretion may be used, still there exists, and exist, no power to control this discretion."

And in Martin *vs.* Mott (12 Wheaton, page 31) this:

"The law does not provide for any appeal from the judgment of the President, or for any right in subordinate officers to review his decision, and, in effect, defeat it. Whenever a statute gives a discretionary power to any person to be exercised by him upon his own opinion of certain facts, it is a sound rule of construction that the statute constitutes him the sole and exclusive judge of the existence of those facts."

Quotations from opinions of the Supreme Court maintaining that the executive power of the President is in no sense merely *ministerial* but strictly *discretionary*, might be multiplied indefinitely. And, indeed, it is easy to show, from repeated decisions of the same court, that the heads of Departments, except where the performance of a specific act or duty is required of them by law, are in no sense ministerial officers, but that they too are clothed with a discretion, and protected from responsibility for error in the exercise of that discretion.

Thus, Decatur *vs.* Paulding, 14 Peters; Kendall *vs.* Stokes, 3 Howard; Brashear *vs.* Mason, 6 Howard; in which latter case the court says:

"The duty required of the Secretary by the resolution was to be performed by him as the head of one of the executive Departments of the Government, in the ordinary discharge of his official duties; that in general such duties, whether imposed by act of Congress or by resolution, are not merely ministerial duties; that the head of an executive Department of the Government, in the administration of the various and important concerns of his office, is continually required to exercise judgment and discretion; and that the court could not, by *mandamus*, act directly upon the officer, to guide and control his judgment and discretion in matters committed to his care in the ordinary discharge of his official duties."

I will now ask your attention, Senators, to the remaining articles.

And first the four conspiracy articles. These allege that the President unlawfully conspired with Lorenzo Thomas, and others to the House of Representatives unknown, on the 21st of February, 1868—first, to hinder and prevent Edwin M. Stanton, Secretary of War, from holding the office of Secretary for the Department of War, contrary to the conspiracy act of July 31, 1861, and in violation of the Constitution of the United States; second, to prevent and hinder the execution of the "act regulating the tenure of certain civil offices," and in pursuance of this conspiracy did unlawfully attempt to prevent Edwin M. Stanton from holding the said office; third, by force to seize, take, and possess the property of the United States in the Department of War in the custody and charge of Edwin M. Stanton, Secretary thereof, contrary to the conspiracy act of July 31, 1861, and of the tenure-of-office act; fourth, with intent unlawfully to seize, take, and possess the property of the United States in the Department of War in the custody of Edwin M. Stanton, the Secretary thereof, with intent to violate the "act regulating the tenure of certain civil offices."

It will be seen that these four conspiracy counts all relate to the same subject-matter, the War Office, the Secretary of the War Office, and the public property therein situated. And this is all that is necessary to be said about these articles; for not a scintilla of proof has been adduced in their support. The case attempted to be made out under these conspiracy articles by the Managers was, in the first place, by the production of the two sets of orders issued on the 21st of February. But as these of themselves did not amount to evidence of a conspiracy, as they carried the idea of no unlawful agreement, but simply stood upon the footing of an order given by a President to a subordinate, the Managers, in order to make some show of a case, offered to introduce the declarations of General Thomas, made on the night of the 21st and on the 22d of February and other days, intending to show a purpose on his part to obtain possession of the Department and the property of the Department by intimidation and force. Objection was made at the time to the introduction of these declarations without laying a foundation upon which the President could be made liable by such declaration. Impressed with this objection, the Manager who opened the prosecution, after some consideration, at length answered an inquiry of a Senator, that he expected to follow up the proof of the declarations by proof connecting the President with them. Upon that assurance he was allowed to give the declarations of General Thomas in evidence. But that is the last we have heard of any supporting proof so promised. Not a scintilla of proof has been obtained from General Thomas or from any other quarter, under the conspiracy charge, of any authority given or intended to be given by the President to General Thomas to resort to force, intimidation, or threats in the execution of the order which the President had given. This is quite enough to say with regard to those articles.

Next, as to the ninth article, usually known as the *Emory* article. It had no substance in itself from the beginning, and, since the testimony of Mr. Welles, remains without the slightest foundation.

Next, as to the tenth article, relative to the speeches made at the Executive Mansion, at Cleveland, and at St. Louis, in the months of August and September, 1866. It is in the name of all the people of the United States that you, Senators, are, in this article, called upon to hold the President of the United States criminally responsible, even to the loss of his office, for speaking, as the article has it, with a loud voice to assemblages of American citizens, what is called scandalous matter touching the Thirty-Ninth Congress of the United States.

In the first place, that political body did not deem it necessary to guard their own honor and privileges by taking notice of charges so made against themselves. Every word charged had been brought to their notice, and they were pressed again and again to commence proceedings to vindicate their honor thus aspersed. But they deliberately declined to interfere, and so the slander, if it were a slander, spoken, and the object against which it was spoken, have all passed away, and a new Congress finds it necessary to vindicate the honor of its defunct predecessor by doing that which its predecessor refused to do for itself.

When the statutes of *scandalum magnatum* prevailed and were in full force in England, there happened this case, which will be found reported in Yelverton : a common citizen was prosecuted for scandalous matter spoken of a peer. Pending the prosecution the great man lost his peerage; whereupon it was decided that the prosecution should be dismissed.

It passes comprehension that such an article as this tenth article should be gravely presented in the name of the American people for words spoken to them by one of their servants, the President, against another of their servants, the Congress of the United States. If there is any one precious right which our people value as a jewel beyond price it is the right of free speech with the corresponding right of a free press. Muzzle the one or gag the other, and we are back again to the times when there was no such body in the State as the people.

This tenth article carries us back five hundred years, to the days when the privilege of Parliament meant the privilege of the House of Lords, and no common man dare speak against its authority, or the authority or personal character of what was called the great men of the realm who sat there. A common man said of that proud prelate, the Bishop of Norwich, "You have writ me that which is against the word of God, and the maintenance of superstition." Straightway the privilege of Parliament seized him and punished him. Another said of my Lord Abergavenny, "He sent for me and put me in little ease." That poor man was seized at once and punished for daring to speak thus of one of the magnates of the land.

But the spirit of English liberty, after struggling for years, at last proved victorious over these ancient abuses, and a man in England may now speak his religious sentiments without fear of the fires of Smithfield ; he may discuss the proceedings of the great men of Parliament with at least a fair opportunity of defending the liberty of speech. And at last the press of that country has cleared itself of nearly all the shackles that have been imposed upon it. Nominally the law remains unchanged. Privilege of Parliament has not been expressly repealed ; but, like the sword of the Black Prince in Westminster Abbey, "it lies more honorable in its rust than in its edge ; more glorious in its disuse than in its service."

Upon the formation of the Constitution of the United States our fathers were not unmindful of what had happened in the past. They had brought with them the traditions of suffering and persecution for opinion's sake, and they determined to lay here for themselves the foundations of civil liberty so strong that they never could be changed. When our Constitution was formed and was presented to the various States for adoption, the universal objection made to it was not so much for what it contained as for what it omitted. It was said, we find here no bill of rights ; we find here no guarantee of conscience, of speech, of press. The answer was, that the Constitution itself was, from beginning to end, a bill of rights ; that it conferred upon the Government only certain specified and delegated powers, and among these were not to be found any grant of any power over the conscience or over free speech or a free press. The answer was plausible, but not satisfactory.

The consequence was that at the first Congress held under the Constitution, according to instructions sent from the various State conventions, ten amendments were introduced and adopted, and the first in order among them is this amendment :

"ARTICLE 1. Congress shall make no law respecting an establishment of religion or prohibiting the free exercise thereof ; or abridging the freedom of speech or of the press ; or the right of the people peacefully to assemble and to petition the Government for a redress of grievances."

There, in that article, associated with religious freedom, with the freedom of the press, with the great right of popular assemblage and of petition—there we find safely anchored forever this inestimable right of free speech.

Mark now, Senators, the prescient wisdom of the people! Within ten years after the adoption of the Constitution the Government was entirely in the hands of one party. All of its departments, executive, legislative, and judicial, were concentrated in what was then called the *Federal* party. But a formidable party had begun to show itself, headed by a formidable leader—a party then called the *Republican*, since known as the *Democratic* party. Nothing was left to them but free speech and a free press. All the patronage was upon the other side. But they made the most of these great engines. So much, however, had the dominant party lost discretion, confident in its party strength, that, irritated to folly and madness by the fierce attacks made upon its executive, its judiciary, and its Houses of Congress, in an evil hour it passed an act, July 14, 1798, entitled "An act for the punishment of certain crimes against the United States."

The second section of this act provides :

"That if any person shall write, print, utter, publish" * * * * "any false, scandalous, and malicious writings against the Government of the United States, or either House of the Congress of the United States, or the President of the United States, with intent to defame the said Government or either House of the said Congress, or the said President, or to bring them or either of them into contempt or disrepute, or to excite against them, or either or any of them, the hatred of the good people of the United States," * * * * "such persons" * * * * "shall be punished by a fine not exceeding $2,000 and by imprisonment not exceeding two years."

No act has ever been passed by the Congress of the United States so odious to the people as this. Mr. Hamilton and other great Federalists of the day attempted in vain to defend it before the people. But the authors of the law and the law itself went down together before the popular indignation, and this act, which was gotten up by a great and powerful party in order to preserve itself in power, became the fatal means of driving that party out of power, followed by the maledictions of the people.

History continues to teach, now as heretofore, that "Eternal vigilance is the price of liberty." There is now, as there has been in the past, a constant tendency to transfer power from the many to the few. There the danger lies to the permanence of our political institutions, and its source is in the legislative department, and in the legislative department alone.

Guard that well and we are safe; and to guard it well you must guard the other departments from its encroachments. Without the help of the people they cannot defend themselves. This last attempt manifested in this tenth article to again bring into play the fearful privilege of the legislative department is only a repetition of what has happened from the dawn of history. Wherever that has been the governing element it has always been jealous of free speech and a free press. It has not been so with the absolute monarch. He feels secure, surrounded by physical power, sustained by armies and navies. Accordingly we find that such a monster as Tiberius pardoned a poor wretch who had lampooned his authority and ridiculed his conduct, while the decemvirs remorselessly put to death a Roman satirist who was bold enough to attack and to bring into contempt their authority.

The eleventh article is the only one that remains to be considered. I confess my inability to make anything out of that article. There is, in the first place, a reference to the speech of the 18th of August, 1866, and it then charges substantially the same things contained in the tenth article in reference to that speech, adding a new allegation, not sustained by proof of the speech itself or by any other proof in the case, that by that speech the President denied the power of the Thirty-Ninth Congress to propose amendments to the Constitution of the United States. Then follow indefinite allegations of contriving means or attempting to contrive means to defeat the execution of the tenure-of-civil-office act, the military appropriation act, and the reconstruction act. What things were contrived we are not told, nor what things were attempted to be contrived. I do not feel warranted in taking up the time of the Senate by any further consideration of this anomalous article. So far as it has any reference whatever to the freedom of speech, what I have said in answer to the tenth article seems to be sufficient. As to anything this article contains beyond reference to that speech I, for one, can make nothing out of it.

And now, Senators, after this review of the articles of impeachment, we are prepared to form some idea of the nature of this impeachment itself. Where, now, is the mischief? Where, now, is the injury to any individual or to any officer of the Government brought about by the action of the President? Whether actuated by good motives or bad, no injury has followed; no public interest has suffered; no officer has been changed, either rightfully or wrongfully; not an item of public property or of public money has passed out of the custody of law, or has been appropriated to improper uses.

To all this it is said that it is enough that the law has been violated, that powers have been assumed by the President not conferred upon him by the Constitution of the United States. It is in the order of the 21st of February, 1868, that it is claimed on the part of the Managers that the President usurped a power not granted by the Constitution.

If that proposition could be established the Managers would still be a great way off from a conviction for an impeachable offense. Much more must be made out besides the actual violation by the President of the constitutional provision: first of all, the criminal intent to violate; and secondly, the existence of an act of Congress providing that such violation with criminal intent should amount to a high crime and misdemeanor. But I hasten to meet the Managers upon the main proposition, and I maintain with confidence that the order issued on the 21st of February, 1868, for the removal of Mr. Stanton, was issued by the President in the exercise of an undoubted power vested in him by the Constitution of the United States. No executive order issued by any President, from the time of Washington down to the present, comes to us with a greater sanction or higher authority or stronger indorsement than this order. If this order is indeed, as it is claimed, a usurpation of power not granted by the Constitution, then Washington was a usurper in every month of his administration, and after him every President that ever occupied that high office from his day to that of the present incumbent; for every one of them has exercised, without doubt and without question, this executive power of removal from office.

So far as this question stands upon authority, it may be said to have been more thoroughly and satisfactorily settled than any one that has at any time agitated the country; settled first in 1789 by the very men who framed the Constitution itself; then, after the lapse and acquiescence of some forty years, brought again and again into question in high party times in 1826, in 1830, and in 1835. But in the worst party times it was never changed by the Legislature, but left as it was until the 2d of March, 1867, when, after the lapse of almost *eighty* years, a new rule was attempted to be established which proposes to reverse the whole past.

Now, Senators, let us consider upon the Constitution itself this question of the executive power of removal. No power is expressly given by the Constitution to *remove* any civil officer from office, except what is given by means of impeachment. The power of *appointment* to office, however, is expressly given, and that is given to the President, as to certain officers, by and with the advice and consent of the Senate. That is, in the act of appointing to office the main part is done by the Executive, but there must be a participation therein of the legislative department.

Now, all agree that there must exist somewhere a power to remove officers for other causes and under other circumstances than those which would justify or require impeachment. Somewhere in the executive department, or in the executive and legislative departments combined, there must be lodged this power of removal. Inasmuch as it is not given expressly to the President, does it belong to both; and if not to both, to which of the two does it properly belong?

First of all, then, let us consider the thing that is to be done. It is a contingency that arises, not in the legislative department, but in the executive department. It concerns an officer of that department charged with the execution of the law. He is in the performance of a strictly executive duty. It is found necessary to displace him. Is it in the nature of things, there being an executive power and a legislative power, that there can be a doubt that it is the executive power that must now be called into action?

Consider how carefully these powers are separated in the Constitution, and their functions defined. The legislative power is vested in the Legislature. What is legislative power? It is a power to make laws—a power to legislate; not a power to carry laws into execution after they are made; not a power to give interpretation to laws after they are made. Its function begins and ends in the creation of law itself. Undoubtedly the legislative power has much to do in the matter of offices and of the executive department. It is a part of the legislative function to create these offices, to abolish them, to define the duties of the incumbents, to amend them, and, from time to time, change them, and to fix the salaries of the officers—all these are properly legislative functions having regard to executive offices. But a law which establishes the office and defines its duties does not put the officer in place, or the law in process of execution. All that belongs to the executive department.

Look now at the character of the executive department. The Constitution of the United States vests all executive authority in the President. Wherever you find executive power to be exercised, he is the source and fountain from which it must proceed. This would be enough of itself, but, in addition to this, he alone, and not Congress, is required to see that the laws are faithfully executed, and he alone is required to take an oath to preserve, protect, and defend the Constitution of the United States. But how is he to execute the laws? Certainly not by his own hands. He cannot act as marshal or district attorney, or as a head of Department. He must see that the laws are executed by the proper agents, and he must see to it that they are *faithfully* executed. It is not a barren abstract duty imposed upon him, but a living obligation, with the sanction of an oath, not to be omitted under any circumstances. Wherever there is an unfaithful or improper officer the President of the United States has not only the power but it is his duty to remove him. The truth is, it would be impossible to carry on this Government under any other idea than that.

This idea of a participation of the Senate in all the constantly recurring questions of removal requiring instant action for the safety of the public would involve administration in inextricable confusion and difficulty. It would turn the Senate into the most corrupt of political bodies. It would fill this Senate Chamber with cliques and favoritism. It would lead to constant cabals. One thousandth part of the cases requiring actual investigation could never be reached, and those that could be reached would consume the entire time of the Senate to the exclusion of all other public business. And, again, it would give time to unfaithful officers to defy the Executive, and looking to the Senate, grow bolder and bolder in their peculations.

The more we study our excellent Constitution the clearer it becomes that the wise men who framed it endeavored in all possible ways, by checks and balances, to keep the three great departments coördinate and separate, and, as far as possible, independent of each other. The judiciary department is made incapable of exercising any other than a judicial function; and, in general, such is the case with regard to the other two departments.

But there are cases plainly expressed where, under certain circumstances, the executive and legislative departments combine for certain purposes. A striking instance is in the matter of legislation, where, upon the final passage of a bill, the Executive is given a qualified legislative power. So, too, in the formation of a treaty, which is strictly an executive duty, one branch of the Legislature is allowed a participation. And, lastly, in the executive business of appointments to office one branch of the Legislature, that is to say, the Senate, is also allowed to participate. But, beyond these definite fixed points, there is no authority anywhere in the Constitution for the legislative department to exercise an executive power, or for the executive department to exercise a legislative power. The moment, therefore, the Legislature assumes a right to participate in the executive power of removal it claims a right to exercise an executive power in a matter for which it finds no grant or authority in the Constitution.

I stand, then, Senators, on the constitutional power of the President to remove Mr. Stanton from office. If he did in fact possess that power what becomes of the tenure-of-office act, or anything else in the way of legislation? If it is a constitutional power which he possesses, how can it be taken away by any mode short of a constitutional amendment? Then, too, if he deems it his constitutional power, how can you punish him for following in good faith that oath which he has been compelled to take, that he "will preserve, protect, and defend the Constitution of the United States."

Look, Senators, at what has happened since the beginning of this trial. During the progress of the case, on the 31st of March, 1868, a question arose, in which the Senate, as a court of impeachment, were equally divided.

Thereupon the Chief Justice decided the question in the affirmative by his casting vote. I make now the following extract from the minutes of the next day, April 1:

"Mr. SUMNER. Mr. President, I send to the Chair an order which is in the nature of a correction of the Journal.

"The Secretary read as follows: 'It appearing from the reading of the Journal of yesterday that on a question where the Senate were equally divided, the Chief Justice, presiding on the trial of the President, gave a casting vote, it is hereby declared that, in the judgment of the Senate, such vote was without authority under the Constitution of the United States.'

"Mr. SUMNER. On that question I ask for the yeas and nays.

"The yeas and nays were ordered; and being taken, resulted—yeas 21, nays 27.

"So the proposed order was rejected."

How near, Mr. Chief Justice, did you come to the commission of an impeachable offense, according to this modern doctrine announced here by the Managers!

But it is said on behalf of the Managers that although each department of the Government may have the right to construe the Constitution for itself in the matter of its own action—that being so, the legislative department may carry out its own opinions of the Constitution to all their final results, even if thereby they totally absorb every power of the executive department. They are the sole judges of their own powers when called upon to act, and must decide for themselves. But if they have this ultimate power of decision so also has the Executive; and if they have a right to enforce their construction against the Executive, so also has the Executive a right to enforce its construction against theirs. It was to meet that very contingency, it was to save us from such fatal consequences, that the wisdom of our forefathers introduced the judiciary department as the final arbiter of all such questions. That failing, there is but one alternative—an actual collision or a resort to the people themselves. This last is the great conservative element in our Government. When this fails us all is gone. When the voice of the people ceases to be appealed to, or, being appealed to, ceases to be listened to, then faction and party will have accomplished their perfect work, and this frame of government will, like a worthless thing, be cast away.

Nothing is plainer than the duty of the Executive to resist encroachments of the legislative department. If he submits tamely to one usurpation of his rightful powers he may lose all. What is there to prevent the Congress of the United States from passing a law to take away from the President his veto power, and to make its exercise a high crime and misdemeanor punishable by long imprisonment and made impeachable? What is there to prevent them, if left to the unrestrained exercise of their own power, from transferring the command of the Army and Navy from the President to one of his subordinate officers, and making the attempt on his part to exercise his constitutional function a high crime, and subjecting him to imprisonment? The doctrine asserted by the Managers saps the very foundation of our system, and turns our written Constitution into a mere mockery. Wherever a President is deliberately of opinion that an act of Congress calls upon him to exercise a power not given to him by the Constitution, he violates that Constitution if he follows it. Again, wherever he is called upon to execute a law which deprives him of a constitutional power, he violates the Constitution as well by executing it. A great trust is committed to his hands, sanctioned by a solemn oath, and he cannot surrender the one or violate the other.

And now, Senators, I ask your close attention to what seems to me a most singular characteristic of this case. How does it happen that for the first time in the history of our country the President of the United States has been suddenly subjected to such punitive legislation as that which was passed on the 2d of March, 1867? Laws were passed on that day purporting to change the order of executive action. Such laws have not been uncommon either in our national or State Legislatures. It has often happened that the legislative department has made changes in the manner of administration of the executive department; oftentimes imposing duties never imposed before; oftentimes prescribing action in the most direct and explicit terms. But where before has legislation of this sort been found attended with such pains and penalties as we find here?

Now, observe, Senators, that neither in the punitive clauses of the second section of that military appropriation act, nor in the sixth section of that tenure-of-office act, is the President of the United States so much as mentioned. Whoever drew these acts shrunk from referring to the office by name. It is under the general description of "person" or "civil officer" that he is made liable to fine and imprisonment for failing to carry out the new provisions of law. But there is no question that it is the President, and the President alone, that is meant. The law was made for him; the punishment was made for him. He is left no choice, no chance of appeal to the courts, no mode of testing the validity of the new law. The rule is laid down for him and the consequences of disobedience. The language in effect is, *this or the penitentiary. Do our bidding, or take the consequences of impeachment.* I undertake to say that, in the history of legislation, nothing like this is anywhere to be found.

And now, Senators, how do all these high-sounding phrases, importing high crimes and misdemeanors, found in these two acts of Congress, compare with the actual character of those acts called high crimes and misdemeanors in the text of the Constitution? I do not intend to argue this question upon precedent. That work has been effectually done by the learned Manager, Mr. WILSON, and he has set at rest forever the pretense that there is any precedent that makes anything an impeachable offense but those crimes and misdemeanors punishable by indictment. But precedents here are out of place. The language of the Constitution is too plain to be misunderstood. The President is to be impeached only "on conviction of treason, bribery, or other high crimes and misdemeanors."

In these pregnant words the whole matter is settled. There is, first of all, an enumeration of what crimes are in the contemplation of the Constitution treason and bribery; and they are the highest of official crimes that can be committed. If the Constitution had stopped there no doubt could exist. Would anything short of treason have sufficed for an article of impeachment—anything even amounting to misprision of treason, or even that modern crime in English law, treason-felony? Could any case have been made against the President under an article alleging treason short of actual levying of war or giving aid and comfort to the enemies of the United States? Then, as to bribery, would anything short of actual bribery have sufficed? Would an attempt to bribe—an act almost equal to bribery, yet just short of it? Certainly not.

Besides these two enumerated crimes follows that other phrase, "other high crimes and misdemeanors." What sort of crimes and misdemeanors? Why, such as are assimilated to those that are enumerated; not all crimes and misdemeanors, but such as are of a similar character with those enumerated, and which are raised by express classification to high grades known, recognized, and established. They are crimes and misdemeanors, says Mr. Burke, not of form, but of essence. You cannot call that a high crime and misdemeanor which in the nature of things is not. There is no room for cunning manufacture here. If a legislative act should undertake to declare that the commonest assault and battery should be a high crime and misdemeanor under the Constitution, that would not change its essence or make it the high offense which the Constitution requires.

I hope it may not be found out of place nor unworthy of the occasion to call the attention of the court to a case parallel, in my judgment, to this:

"*First Watch.* This man said, sir, that Don John, the prince's brother, was a villain.
"*Dogberry.* Write down—Prince John, a villain:— why, this is flat perjury, to call a prince's brother—villain.
"*Sexton.* What heard you him say else?
"*Second Watch.* Marry, that he had received a thousand ducats of Don John for accusing the lady Hero wrongfully.
"*Dogberry.* Flat burglary as ever was committed.
"*Verges.* Yea, by the mass, that it is."

Look through all the correlative provisions of the Constitution on the subject, as to trial, conviction, judgment, and punishment, as to pardons, and, last of all, to that provision that

"the trial of all crimes, except in cases of impeachment, shall be by jury," and that other provision, that after conviction on impeachment "the party convicted shall, nevertheless, be liable and subject to indictment, trial, judgment, and punishment, according to law." If you are not yet satisfied, examine the proceedings of the Convention that framed this article, and see how studiously they rejected all impeachment for misbehavior in office, and how steadily they adhered to the requisition that nothing but a high crime and misdemeanor should suffice.

The honorable Managers have put the case of *insanity.* But will you add to that awful visitation of Providence the impious judgment of man, that the sufferer is guilty of a high crime and misdemeanor? As to the President, however, the case of insanity is provided for, not by removal, not by impeachment, but by the temporary devolution of the office upon the Vice President.

Senators, was there ever a more abortive attempt to make a case for impeachment of the President under the Constitution? This bantling of impeachment, from the first, showed few signs of vitality. There was never any real life in it. It has been nursed by the Managers with the greatest care, especially by that honorable Manager whose business it was first to bring it to the notice of the Senate. He dandled the bantling in his arms with consummate skill. He pinched its poor wan cheeks for some show of life, but even then it was too evident that it was *in articulo mortis.* The nurse was skillful, but the subject, with all its care, was beyond his art. Long since this show of vitality vanished, and now it lies, bereft of life, a shapeless mass which gives no sign, scarcely a grim contortion, the counterfeit resemblance of life under the galvanic touch of high party excitement.

There is one other point, Senators, to which it is perhaps proper I should call attention. I understand it to be argued by the Managers that the *ad interim* authority given to General Thomas was in violation of law, and that, aside from any question growing out of the tenure-of-office act, there was no law or authority to justify that appointment. But is it possible, even if such an error as that had been committed by the President, it would make him liable to impeachment? In the course of the administration of the affairs of this Government in the great departments many things are done almost every day for which it is impossible to find warrant of law. They are done, however, in good faith, done sometimes under a great necessity, and finally grow up into usages apparently contrary to law, yet which are even winked at by courts when brought to the test of a decision. But for myself, after the most thorough investigation of the state of the law as to *ad interim* appointments, I am unable to see that there has been any violation of law in this *ad interim* appointment, or rather in this attempt to make an *ad interim* appointment.

The Constitution contains only the following provision as to vacancies:

"The President shall have power to fill up all vacancies that may happen during the recess of the Senate, by granting commissions which shall expire at the end of their next session."

This is a very different thing from an *ad interim* appointment. The case contemplated by the Constitution is in no sense an *acting* or *ad interim* authority. The appointment and commission there required fill the vacancy with a regular officer. But immediately after the formation of the Constitution, in the administration of the Government, emergencies at once arose in the executive department requiring instant action. Suddenly an unexpected vacancy in an office required at once a *locum tenens* to carry on the business, before there was time to select a new officer, to know of his acceptance, or to induct him into office. So, too, there being no vacancy, a temporary disability might occur from sickness or necessary absence, which also required some one to act during the *interim*. It was to meet these unforeseen contingencies, which were nowhere provided for in the Constitution, that acts of Congress were passed in the years 1792, 1795, and 1863.

It is in the review of these various acts of Congress that it is claimed on the part of the Managers that there is no authority of law for making a temporary appointment in case of an office made vacant by removal, which was claimed by the President to be the case as to Mr. Stanton. They maintain that if the order of the President did remove Mr. Stanton, if by its own constitutional power it had that effect, if it was a lawful order, yet the President committed a violation of law in attempting to put an *ad interim* appointee there, just because it was a vacancy caused by removal. They claim that the act of 1863 regulates the whole matter, and, inasmuch as that gives no authority for an *ad interim* appointment to a vacancy caused by removal, no such authority is to be looked for in the other statutes.

A mere reference to the prior legislation will show the fallacy of this argument. The act of 1792 provided for *ad interim* appointments in these cases alone: vacancy occasioned by death or by disability from absence or sickness. It will be observed that this act made no provision for an *ad interim* appointment in case of a vacancy by resignation, by expiration of term, or by removal. Next came the act of 1795, and this provides for an *ad interim* appointment in case of any vacancy whatsoever. It extends, therefore, to all forms of vacancy, whether by death, resignation, or expiration of term of office; and wherever such vacancy exists power is given to the President to authorize any person to perform the official duties until the vacancy is filled, but limits the time for such temporary authority to the period

of six months. Next comes the act of 1863, and this applies to temporary appointments in only two cases of vacancy—those caused by death and by resignation, omitting any provision as to vacancies caused by expiration of term or by removal. Like the act of 1795, it limits the time of the temporary authority to six months.

There is no express repeal in the act of 1863 of any former act. It only purports to repeal such acts and parts of acts as are inconsistent with it. Now, comparing the act of 1795 with the act of 1863, I am unable to see any inconsistency between the two acts. It is true that, as to vacancies occasioned by death or resignation, both acts equally apply; and the most that can be said of the last is that it is cumulative. But as to vacancies occasioned by expiration of term and by removal from office, inasmuch as there is no provision whatever in the act of 1863 as to those vacancies, they remain as fixed by the act of 1795. For certainly, as to those vacancies so provided for by the act of 1795, there is no inconsistency between that and the act of 1863, which is without any provision whatever on those subjects-matter. There is, therefore, not even a pretense here of repeal by implication.

Very much, however, is said as to those *ad interim* appointments made during the session of the Senate, as if that were a circumstance of any weight or consequence whatever with regard to an *ad interim* appointment. It will be seen that not one of these laws distinguishes as to time of recess or time of session in regard to the authority of the President to make these *ad interim* appointments. The question is, when does the necessity arise, not whether it is during the recess or session of the Senate. And such has been the uniform construction given to these acts from the beginning of the Government to this day. These *ad interim* appointments are made indifferently, whether the Senate is in session or in recess.

Hitherto, Senators, I have considered this case in its legal aspects, and it seems to me that the argument may very well stop here. Whatever there is of matter of fact in the case adds greatly to the President's defense. Look through the proof adduced by the Managers outside of the mere formal documentary exhibits. What is there left but the testimony as to the speeches? What is there that has the slightest bearing upon the case of the President except what they have attempted to force into the case by the declarations of General Thomas?

We have heard from the Managers, especially from that Manager who opened the case on the part of the prosecution, many high-sounding declarations of what they expected to prove. But what a total failure we have seen in the way of performances! Look, now, with what a flourish of trumpets the declarations of General Thomas as to his purposes and intents were heralded before the court. On page 180 of the printed record we find the following:

"Mr. Manager BUTLER presented the question in writing at the Secretary's desk.
"The CHIEF JUSTICE. The Secretary will read the question.
"The Secretary read the following question proposed to be put to the witness, WALTER A. BURLEIGH:
"'You said yesterday, in answer to my question, that you had a conversation with General Lorenzo Thomas on the evening of the 21st of February last. State if he said anything as to the means by which he intended to obtain, or was directed by the President to obtain, possession of the War Department. If so, state all he said as nearly as you can.
"Mr. STANBERY. We object, Mr. Chief Justice."
"The CHIEF JUSTICE. Do you desire to make any observations to the Court?
"Mr. STANBERY. We do, sir.
"The CHIEF JUSTICE. The question will be submitted to the Senate.
"Mr. FRELINGHUYSEN. Mr. President, I desire to submit a question.
"The CHIEF JUSTICE. The Secretary will read the question submitted by the Senator from New Jersey [Mr. FRELINGHUYSEN] to the Managers.
"The Secretary read as follows:
"Do the Managers intend to connect the conversation between the witnesses and General Thomas with the respondent?
"The CHIEF JUSTICE. Are the Managers prepared to reply to the question?
"Mr. Manager BUTLER. Mr. President, if the point is to be argued, with the leave of the Senate, we will endeavor to answer that question in the argument.
"The CHIEF JUSTICE. It is to be argued. The Manager will proceed, if he desires.
"Mr. STANBERY. We do not hear the answer.
"Mr. Manager BUTLER. The answer is, Mr. President, if you will allow me to repeat it, that, as I understand the point raised is to be argued on the one side and the other, we will endeavor to answer the question submitted by the Senator from New Jersey in the course of our argument.
"Mr. TRUMBULL. Mr. President, I should like to hear the question read again, as I think the answer to the inquiry of the Senator from New Jersey is in the question propounded by the Managers, as I heard it.
"The CHIEF JUSTICE. The Secretary will read the question again. Senators will please give their attention.
"The Secretary again read the question of Mr. Manager BUTLER.
"The CHIEF JUSTICE. Do the Managers propose to answer the question of the Senator from New Jersey?
"Mr. Manager BUTLER. If there is to be no argument, Mr. President, I will answer the question proposed. If there is to be an argument on the part of the counsel for the President, we propose, as a more convenient method, to answer the question in the course of our argument, because otherwise we might have to make an argument now. I can say that we do propose to connect the respondent with this testimony."

Now, Senators, I ask you whether that pledge under which that testimony was admitted has been redeemed?

I will make one more reference to the proof. It is upon the question as to the intention of the President to bring the constitutionality of the tenure-of-office act to the final arbitrament of the Supreme Court. He sets that defense up in his answer. He alleges that that intention has accompanied every act touching the suspension and removal of Mr. Stanton, and that he has never lost sight of it. If everything else were ruled against the President this great exculpatory fact must shield him.

Now listen to Mr. Manager BUTLER upon this question. On page 96 of the record he says:

"Indeed, will you hear an argument as a Senate of the United States, a majority of whom voted for that very bill, upon its constitutionality, in the trial of an executive officer for willfully violating it before it had been doubted by any court?
"Bearing upon this question, however, it may be said that the President removed Mr. Stanton for the very purpose of testing the constitutionality of this law before the courts, and the question is asked, Will you condemn him as for a crime for so doing? If this plea were a true one it ought not to avail; but it is a subterfuge. We shall show you that he has taken no step to submit the question to any court, although more than a year has elapsed since the passage of the act."

Senators, where has this been shown on the part of the Managers? Where is there even a feeble attempt to show it? But look now to the proof on the part of the President. Cabined, cribbed, and confined as we have been by the rulings of the Senate upon this question, yet what appears? From first to last the great fact forces itself upon our attention that this was no subterfuge of the President, no after-thought to escape the consequences of an act, but, on the contrary, that this wholesome and lawful purpose of a resort to the proper tribunal to settle the difficulty between Congress and himself was in the mind of the President from the very beginning. They proved it by his own declarations introduced by themselves in his letter to General Grant, dated February 10, 1868, which may be found on page 234 of the printed record. One extract from that letter will suffice. The President says:

"You knew the President was unwilling to trust the office with any one who would not, by holding it, compel Mr. Stanton to resort to the courts. You perfectly understood that in this interview, 'some time' after you accepted the office, the President, not content with your silence, desired an expression of your views, and you answered him that Mr. Stanton 'would have to appeal to the courts.'"

If this is not enough, Senators, remember the testimony of General Thomas, of General Sherman, of Mr. Cox, of Mr. Merrick, and see throughout the purpose of the President declared at all times, from first to last, to bring this question to judicial arbitrament. After all this, what a shocking perversion of testimony it is to pronounce it an after-thought or a subterfuge! And after the proof of what took place on that trial of Thomas, how can the Managers be bold enough to say that they will "show you that he has taken no step to submit the question to any court, although more than a year has elapsed since the passage of the act?"

Senators, it was not at all necessary for the defense of the President that, in the exercise of that discretion which the law allows to him, he should be put to prove that his intentions were all right. He has gone far beyond the necessities of his case. Never were good intentions and honest motives more thoroughly proved than they have been proved in this case. I repeat it, that, if everything else were made out against him, this great exculpatory fact must absolve him from all criminal liability.

And now, Senators, I have done with the law and the facts of the case. There remains for me, however, a duty yet to be performed—one of solemn import and obligation—a duty to my client, to my former chief, to my friend. There may be those among you, Senators, who cannot find a case of guilt against the President. There may be those among you who, not satisfied that a case for impeachment has yet arisen, are fearful of the consequences of an acquittal. You may entertain vague apprehensions that, flushed with the success of an acquittal, the President will proceed to acts of violence and revolution. Senators, you do not know or understand the man. I cannot say that you willfully misunderstand him; for I, too, though never an extreme party man, have felt more than once, in the heat of party conflicts, the same bitter and uncompromising spirit that may now animate you. The time has been when I looked upon General Jackson as the most dangerous of tyrants. Time has been when, day after day, I expected to see him inaugurate a revolution; and yet, after his•administration was crowned with success and sustained by the people, I lived to see him gracefully surrender his great powers to the hands that conferred them, and, under the softening influences of time, I came to regard him, not as a tyrant, but as one of the most honest and patriotic of men.

Now, listen for a moment to one who, perhaps, understands Andrew Johnson better than most of you; for his opportunities have been greater. When, nearly two years ago, he called me from the pursuits of professional life to take a seat in his Cabinet, I answered the call under a sense of public duty. I came here almost a stranger to him and to every member of his Cabinet except Mr. Stanton. We had been friends for many years. Senators, need I tell you that all my tendencies are conservative? You, Mr. Chief Justice, who have known me for the third of a century, can bear me witness. Law, not arms, is my profession. From the moment that I was honored with a seat in the Cabinet of Mr. Johnson not a step was taken that did not come under my observation, not a word was said that escaped my attention. I regarded him closely in Cabinet, and in still more private and confidential conversation. I saw him often tempted with bad advice. I knew that evil counselors were more than once around him. I observed him with the most intense anxiety. But never, in word, in deed, in thought, in action, did I discover in that man anything but loyalty to the Constitution and the laws. He stood firm as a rock against all temptation to abuse his own powers or to exercise those which were not conferred upon him. Steadfast and self-reliant in the midst of all difficulty, when dangers threatened, when temptations were strong,

C. I.—50.

he looked only to the Constitution of his country and to the people.

Yes, Senators, I have seen that man tried as few have been tried. I have seen his confidence abused. I have seen him endure, day after day, provocations such as few men have ever been called upon to meet. No man could have met them with more sublime patience. Sooner or later, however, I knew the explosion must come. And when it did come my only wonder was that it had been so long delayed. Yes, Senators, with all his faults, the President has been more sinned against than sinning. Fear not, then, to acquit him. The Constitution of the country is as safe in his hands from violence as it was in the hands of Washington. But if, Senators, you condemn him, if you strip him of the robes of his office, if you degrade him to the utmost stretch of your power, mark the prophecy? The strong arms of the people will be about him.. They will find a way to raise him from any depths to which you may consign him, and we shall live to see him redeemed, and to hear the majestic voice of the people, "Well done, faithful servant, you shall have your reward!"

But if, Senators, as I cannot believe, but as has been boldly said with almost official sanction, your votes have been canvassed and the doom of the President is sealed, then let that judgment not be pronounced in this Senate Chamber; not here, where our Camillus in the hour of our greatest peril, single-handed, met and baffled the enemies of the Republic; not here, where he stood faithful among the faithless; not here, where he fought the good fight for the Union and the Constitution; not in this Chamber, whose walls echo with that clarion voice that, in the days of our greatest danger, carried hope and comfort to many a desponding heart, strong as an army with banners. No, not here. Seek out rather the darkest and gloomiest chamber in the subterranean recesses of this Capitol, where the cheerful light of day never enters. There erect the altar and immolate the victim.

Mr. STANBERY, after proceeding some time, said: With the consent of the Senate, Mr. Chief Justice, I would ask permission that my young friend at my side may read from my brief a few pages while I gather a little strength for what I wish to say.

Mr. ANTHONY. The counsel evidently is laboring very painfully in his endeavor to address the Senate, and I move that the Senate, sitting as a court of impeachment, adjourn until Monday at twelve o'clock.

Several SENATORS. Oh, no; let the argument be read.

Mr. STANBERY. I do not ask an adjournment.

Mr. ANTHONY. I withdraw the motion if the counsel does not desire it.

Mr. WILLIAM F. PEDDRICK thereupon proceeded to read the argument, and continued the reading until two minutes to two o'clock.

Mr. JOHNSON. I move that the court take a recess for fifteen minutes.

The motion was agreed to; and at the expiration of the recess the Chief Justice resumed the chair and called the Senate to order.

Mr. PEDDRICK continued to read the argument for some time, when

Mr. STANBERY resumed and concluded.

Mr. HOWARD. I move that the Senate, sitting for the trial of the impeachment, adjourn until Monday at twelve o'clock.

The motion was agreed to; and the Senate, sitting for the trial of the impeachment, adjourned.

MONDAY, *May* 4, 1868.

The Chief Justice of the United States took the chair.

The usual proclamation having been made by the Sergeant-at-Arms,

The Managers of the impeachment on the part of the House of Representatives and Messrs. Nelson and Groesbeck, of counsel for the respondent, appeared and took the seats assigned to them respectively.

The members of the House of Representatives, as in Committee of the Whole, preceded by Mr. E. B. WASHBURNE, chairman of that committee, and accompanied by the Speaker and Clerk, appeared and were conducted to the seats provided for them.

The Journal of Saturday's proceedings of the Senate, sitting for the trial of the impeachment, was read.

The CHIEF JUSTICE. Mr. Manager BINGHAM will proceed with the argument on the part of the House of Representatives.

Hon. JOHN A. BINGHAM, one of the Managers of the impeachment on the part of the House of Representatives, closed the argument, as follows:

Mr. PRESIDENT and SENATORS: I protest, Senators, that in no mere partisan spirit, in no spirit of resentment or prejudice do I come to the argument of this grave issue. A Representative of the people, upon the responsibility and under the obligation of my oath, by order of the people's Representatives, in the name of the people, and for the supremacy of their Constitution and laws, I this day speak. I pray, you, Senators, "hear me for my cause." But yesterday the supremacy of the Constitution and laws was challenged by armed rebellion; to-day the supremacy of the Constitution and laws is challenged by executive usurpation, and is attempted to be defended in the presence of the Senate of the United States by the retained advocates of the accused.

For four years millions of men disputed by arms the supremacy of American law on American soil. Happily for our common country, happily for our common humanity, on the 9th

day of April, in the year of our Lord 1865, the broken battalions of treason and armed resistance to law surrendered to the victorious legions of the Republic. On that day, not without sacrifice, not without suffering, not without martyrdom, the laws were vindicated. On that day the word went out all over our own sorrow stricken land and to every nationality that the Republic. the last refuge of constitutional liberty, the last sanctuary of an inviolable justice, was saved by the virtue and valor of its children.

On the 14th day of April, in the year of our Lord 1865, amid the joy and gladness of the people for their great deliverance, here in the capital, by an assassin's hand, fell Abraham Lincoln, President of the United States, slain not for his crimes, but for his virtues, and especially for his fidelity to duty—that highest word revealed by God to man.

Upon the death of Abraham Lincoln, Andrew Johnson, then Vice President, by force of the Constitution, became President of the United States, upon taking the prescribed oath that he would faithfully execute the office of President, and preserve, protect, and defend the Constitution of the United States. The people, bowing with uncovered head in the presence of the strange, great sorrow which had come upon them, forgot for the moment the disgraceful part which Andrew Johnson had played here upon the tribune of the Senate on the 4th day of March, 1865, and accepted the oath thus taken by him as the successor of Abraham Lincoln as confirmation and assurance that he would take care that the laws be faithfully executed. It is with the people an intuitive judgment, the highest conviction of the human intellect, that the oath faithfully to execute the office of President, and to preserve, protect, and defend the Constitution of the United States, means, and must forever meanwhile the Constitution remains as it is—that the President will himself obey, and compel others to obey, the laws enacted by the legislative department of the Government, until the same shall have been repealed or reversed. This, we may assume, for the purpose of this argument, to be the general judgment of the people of this country. Surely it is the pride of every intelligent American that none are above and none beneath the laws; that the President is as much the subject of law as the humblest peasant on the remotest frontier of our ever advancing civilization. Law is the only sovereign, save God, recognized by the American people; it is a rule of civil action not only to the individual. but to the million; it binds alike each and all. the official and the unofficial, the citizen and the great people themselves.

This, Senators—and I am almost fearful that I may offend in saying it—is of the traditions of the Republic, and is understood from the Atlantic to the Pacific shores by the five and thirty millions of people who dwell between these oceans and hold in their hands to-day the greatest trust ever committed in the providence of God to a political society.

I feel myself justified, entirely justified, in saying that it rests not simply upon the traditions of the people, but is embodied in their written record from the day when they fired the first gun on the field of Lexington to this hour. Is it not declared in that immortal Declaration which will live as long as our language lives, as one of the causes of revolt against the king of Great Britain, whose character was marked by every act which may define a tyrant, that he had forbidden his governors to pass laws, unless suspended in their operation until they should have received his assent—I use the words of the Declaration, which, like the words of Luther, were half battles—the law should be suspended until his assent should be obtained. That was the first utterance against the claim of executive power to suspend the laws by those immortal men with whom God walked through the night and storm and darkness of the Revolution, and whom he taught to lay here at the going down of the sun the foundations of those institutions of civil and religious liberty which have since become the hope of the world.

I follow the written record further, still asking pardon of the Senate, praying them to remember that I speak this day not simply in the presence of Senators, but in the presence of an expecting and waiting people, who have commissioned you to discharge this high trust, and have committed to your hands, Senators, the issues of life and death to the Republic. I refer next to the words of Washington, first of Americans and foremost of men, who declared that the Constitution which at any time exists until changed by the act of the whole people is sacredly obligatory upon all.

I refer next to a still higher authority, which is the expression of the collective power and will of the whole people of the United States, in which it is asserted that—

"This Constitution, and the laws made in pursuance thereof, and all treaties made or which shall be made by the authority of the United States, shall be the supreme law of the land; and the judges in every State shall be bound thereby, anything in the constitution and laws of any State to the contrary notwithstanding."

That is the solemn declaration of the Constitution; and pending this trial, without a parallel in the history of the nation, it should be written upon these walls.

How are these propositions, so plain and simple that "the wayfaring man could not err therein," met by the retained counsel who appear to defend this treason of the President, this betrayal of the great trusts of the people? The proposition is met by stating to the Senate, with an audacity that has scarcely a parallel in the history of judicial proceedings, that every official may challenge at pleasure the supreme law of the land, and especially that the President of the United States, charged by his oath, charged by the express letter of the Constitu-

tion, that "he shall take care that the laws be faithfully executed," is nevertheless invested with the power to interpret the Constitution for himself, and to determine judicially—Senators, I use the word used by the learned gentleman who opened the case for the accused —to determine judicially whether the laws declared by the Constitution to be supreme are after all not null and void, because they do not happen to accord with his judgment.

That is the defense which is presented here before the Senate of the United States, and upon which they are asked to deliberate, that the Executive is clothed with power judicially —I repeat their own word, and I desire that it may be burned into the brain of Senators when they come to deliberate upon this question—that the President may judicially construe the Constitution for himself, and judicially determine finally for himself whether the laws, which by your Constitution are declared to be supreme, are not, after all, null and void and of no effect, and not to be executed, because it suits the pleasure of his highness, Andrew Johnson, first king of the people of the United States, in imitation of George III, to suspend their execution. He ought to remember, when he comes with such a defense as that before the Senate of the United States, that it was said by one of those mighty spirits who put the Revolution in motion and who contributed to the organization of this great and powerful people, that Cæsar had his Brutus, Charles I had his Cromwell, and George III should profit by their example. Nevertheless —and this is the central point of this entire discussion—the position is assumed here in the presence of the Senate, in the presence of the people of the United States, and in the presence of the civilized world, that the President of the United States is invested with the judicial power to determine the force and effect of the Constitution, of his own obligations under it, and the force and effect of every law passed by the Congress of the United States. It must be conceded, if every official may challenge the laws as unconstitutional, and especially if the President may, at his pleasure, declare any act of Congress unconstitutional, reject, disregard, and violate its provisions, and this, too, by the authority of the Constitution, that instrument is itself a Constitution of anarchy, not of order, a Constitution authorizing a violation of law, not enjoining obedience to law. Senators, establish any such rule as this for official conduct, and you will have proved yourselves the architects of your country's ruin; you will have converted this land of law and order, of light and knowledge, into a land of darkness, the very light whereof will be darkness—a land

"Where eldest Night
And Chaos, ancestors of nature, will hold
Eternal anarchy, amidst the noise
Of endless wars, and by confusion stand."

Disguise, gloze over, and, by specious and

ingenious argument, excuse the President's acts, as gentlemen may, the fact is that we are passing upon the question whether the President may not, at his pleasure, and without peril to his official position, set aside or annul both the Constitution and laws of the United States, and in his great office inaugurate anarchy in the land.

The whole defense of the President rests upon the simple but startling proposition that he cannot be held to answer for any violation of the written Constitution and laws of the United States, because of his asserted right under the Constitution, and by the Constitution, to interpret for himself and execute or disregard, at his election, any provision either of the Constitution or statutes of the United States.

No matter what demagogues may say of it outside of this Chamber, no matter what retained counsel may say of it inside of this Chamber, that is the issue; and the recording angel of history has already struck it into the adamant of the past, there to remain forever; and upon that issue, Senators, you and the House of Representatives will stand or fall before the tribunal of the future. That is the issue. It is all there is of it. It is what is embraced in the articles of impeachment. It is all that is embraced in them. In spite of the technicalities, in spite of the lawyer's tricks, in spite of the futile pleas that have been interposed here in the President's defense, that is the issue. It is the head and front of Andrew Johnson's offending, that he has assumed to himself the executive prerogative of interpreting the Constitution and deciding upon the validity of the laws at his pleasure, and suspending them and dispensing with their execution.

I say it again, Senators, with every respect for the gentlemen who sit here as the representatives of States and the representatives as well of that great people who are one people though organized by States, that the man who has heard this prolonged discussion, running through days and weeks, who does not understand this to be the plain, simple proposition made in the hearing of Senators, insisted upon as the President's defense, is one of those unfortunates whom even a thrush might pity, to whom God in his providence has denied the usual measure of that intellectual faculty which we call reason.

In the trial of this case the Senate of the United States is the sole and only tribunal which can judicially determine this question. The power to decide it is with the Senate; the responsibility to decide it aright is upon the Senate. That responsibility can be divided by the Senate with no human being outside of this Chamber. It is all-important to the people of the United States at large as it is all-important to their Representatives in Congress assembled, and surely it is all-important to the Senators, sworn to do justice in the premises between the people and the President, that this great issue which touches the nation's life shall be decided in accordance with the spirit as well as with the letter of the Constitution. It is all-important that it shall be decided in accordance with that justice to establish which the Constitution itself was ordained; that justice before the majesty of which we this day bow as before the majesty of that God whose attribute it is; that justice which dwelt with Him before worlds were, which will abide with Him when worlds perish, and by which we shall be judged for this day's proceeding.

The Senate, having the sole power to try impeachments, must of necessity be vested by every intendment of the Constitution with the sole and exclusive power to decide every question of law and of fact involved in the issue. And yet, Senators, although that would seem to be a self-evident proposition, hours have been spent here to persuade the Senate of the United States that the Senate at last had not the sole power to try every issue of law and fact arising upon this question between the people and the President. The ex-Attorney General well said the other day, for he quoted a familiar canon of interpretation, "Effect must be given to every word in a written statute." Let effect be given to every word in the written statute of the people—their fundamental law, the Constitution of the United States—and there is an end of all controversy about the exclusive power of the Senate to decide every question of law and fact arising upon this issue.

What meant this long-continued discussion on the part of the counsel for the President, resting upon a remark of my colleague [Mr. Manager BUTLER] in his opening on behalf of the people that this was not a court? Was it an attempt to divert the Senate from the express provision of the Constitution that the Senate should be the sole and final arbiters between the people and the President? What meant this empty criticism about the words of my colleague that this was not a court, but the Senate of the United States? My colleague, Mr. Chief Justice, simply followed the plain words of the Constitution, that "the Senate shall have the sole power to try all impeachments."

I propose neither to exhaust my strength nor the patience of the Senate by dwelling upon this miserable device to raise an issue between the Senate and the courts, because that is what it resulted in at last although it came after a good deal of deliberation, after a good many days of incubation, after many utterances on many subjects concerning things both in the heavens above and in the earth beneath and in the waters under the earth! I do not propose to imitate the example of the learned and accomplished counsel of the President on the trial of this grave issue which carries with it so many and so great results to all the people of the United States not only of this day, but of the great hereafter. I trust I shall be saved in the providence of God, by His grace, from becoming, as have some of the counsel for the President in this august presence, a mere eater-up of syllables, a mere snapper-up of unconsidered trifles. I propose to deal in this discussion with principles, not with "trifles light as air." I care not if the gentlemen choose to call the Senate sitting in the trial of an impeachment a court. The Constitution calls it the Senate. I know, as every intelligent man knows, that the Senate of the United States, sitting upon the trial of impeachment, is the highest judicial tribunal of the land. That is conceding enough to put an end to all that was said on that point—some of it most solemnly—by the stately argument of the learned gentleman from Massachusetts, [Mr. Curtis;] some of it most tenderly by the effective and adroit argument of my learned and accomplished friend from Ohio, [Mr. Groesbeck,] and some of it most wittily—so wittily that he held his own sides lest he should explode with laughter at his own wit—by the learned gentleman from New York, [Mr. Evarts,] who displayed more of Latin than of law in his argument, and more of rhetoric than of logic, and more of intellectual pyrotechnics than of either. [Laughter.]

But, Senators, I am not to be diverted by these fireworks, by these Roman candles, by these fiery flying serpents that are let off at pleasure, and to order, by the accomplished gentleman from New York, from the point made here between the people and the President by his advocates. I stand upon the plain, clear letter of the Constitution, which declares that "the Senate shall have the sole power to try all impeachments;" that it necessarily invests the Senate with the sole and exclusive power to determine finally and forever every issue of law and fact arising in the case. This is one of those self evident propositions arising under the Constitution of the United States of which Hamilton spoke in words clear and strong, which must carry conviction to the mind of every man, and which I beg leave to read in the hearing of the Senate.

Said Hamilton, a man who was gifted by Providence with one of those commanding intellects, whose thoughts indelibly impressed themselves wherever they fell:

"This is one of those truths which, to a correct and unprejudiced mind, carries its own evidence along with it, and may be obscured but cannot be made plainer by argument or reasoning. It rests upon axioms as simple as they are universal—the *means* ought to be proportioned to the *end;* the persons from whose agency the attainment of any *end* is expected ought to possess the *means* by which it is to be attained."—*Federalist*, No. 23.

The end required by the letter of your Constitution of the Senate of the United States is that the Senate decide finally and for themselves every issue of law and fact arising between the people and their accused President. What comes then, I want to know, Senators, of the argument of the learned gentleman from New York? The most significant lesson to be gathered from which is this: that the right way and the effectual way by which a man may make his speech immortal is to make it eternal. [Laughter.] What becomes of his long drawn-out sentence here about the right of this accused and guilty man, who stands this day clothed with perjury as with a garment in the presence of the people, to be heard first in the Supreme Court of the United States before the Senate shall proceed to trial and judgment? The Senate is vested with the sole and exclusive power to try this question, and the Supreme Court of the United States has no more power to intervene either before or after judgment in the premises than has the Court of St. Petersburg; and so the people of the United States, I hesitate not to say, will hold.

Nevertheless, clear and manifest as this proposition is, it has been insisted upon here from the opening of this defense to its close by all the counsel who have participated in the discussion, that the Supreme Court is the final arbiter for the decision of all questions arising under the Constitution. I do not state the proposition too broadly, Senators. My occupations have been of such a nature from the commencement of this trial to this hour that I have relied more upon my memory of what counsel said than upon any reading which I have given to their voluminous arguments in defense of the accused; but I venture to say that the proposition is not more broadly stated by me than it has been stated by them.

I submit to the Senate that the proposition for the defense is not warranted by the Constitution; that there are many questions arising under the Constitution of the United States which by no possibility can be considered as original questions either in the Supreme Court or in any other court of the United States. For example, my learned and accomplished friend who honors me with his attention, and represents the great and growing Commonwealth of Illinois upon this floor, [Mr. Trumbull,] is here and is to remain here, not by force of any decision which the Supreme Court of the United States has made, or by force of any decision which the Supreme Court of the United States may hereafter make. It is not a question within their jurisdiction. Illinois is one of those great Commonwealths which, since the organization of the Constitution and within the memory of living men, have sprung up from the shores of the beautiful Ohio away to the golden sands of California, girdling the continent across with a cordon of free Commonwealths under the direct operation of the Constitution of the United States. The people by that Constitution did provide that the Congress shall have power to admit new States into the Union, and when the Congress passed upon the question whether the people of Illinois had organized a government republican in form and were entitled to assume their place in the sisterhood of free Commonwealths the decision was final, and the judge of the Supreme Court who dares to challenge the great seal of the State of Illinois, which the gentleman represents, ought to be instantly ejected from his place, which he would thereby dishonor and disgrace, by the supreme power of the people speaking and acting through the process of impeachment.

It does not belong in any sense of the word to the judicial power of the United States to decide all questions arising under the Constitution and laws. Why, according to this logic, the Supreme Court would come to sit in judgment at last upon the power given exclusively to each House to judge of the election and qualification of its own members. Senators, the judicial power of the United States is entitled to all respect and to all consideration here and everywhere else; but that judicial power, as is well known to Senators, is defined and limited by the terms of the Constitution, and beyond those limitations or outside of those grants that tribunal cannot go. I read from the Constitution the provision in answer to the argument of the gentleman touching the judicial power of the United States:

"The judicial power of the United States shall be vested in one Supreme Court, and in such inferior courts as the Congress may from time to time ordain and establish." * * * * * * *

"The judicial power shall extend to all cases, in law and equity arising under this Constitution, the laws of the United States, and treaties made, or which shall be made, under their authority; to all cases affecting embassadors, other public ministers, and consuls; to all cases of admiralty and maritime jurisdiction; to controversies to which the United States shall be a party; to controversies between two or more States; between a State and citizens of another State; between citizens of different States; between citizens of the same State claiming lands under grants of different States, and between a State, or the citizens thereof, and foreign States, citizens or subjects."

"In all cases affecting embassadors, other public ministers, and consuls, and those in which a State shall be a party, the Supreme Court shall have original jurisdiction. In all the other cases before mentioned the Supreme Court shall have appellate jurisdiction, both as to law and fact, with such exceptions and under such regulations as the Congress shall make."—*Constitution*, article 3.

As I said before, inasmuch as the Senate of the United States has the sole power to try all impeachments, and therefore the exclusive power to finally determine all questions arising therein, it results that its decisions can neither be restricted by judgments in advance, made by either the Supreme Court or any other court of the United States, nor can the final judgment of the Senate upon impeachment be subjected to review by the civil courts of the United States or to reversal by executive pardon. So it is written in the Constitution, that the pardoning power shall not extend to impeachments. Impeachment is not a case in "law or equity," within the meaning of the terms as employed in the third article of the Constitution, which I have just read. It is in no sense a case within the general judicial power of the United States.

Senators, no one is either bold enough or weak enough to stand in the presence of the Senate of the United States and clearly and openly proclaim and avow that the Supreme Court has the power to try impeachments. Nevertheless, the position assumed in this defense for the accused that he may suspend the laws, dispense with their execution, and interpret and construe the Constitution for himself to the hurt of the Republic, without peril to his official position, if he accompanies it either at the time or after the fact with a statement that his only object in violating the Constitution or in suspending the laws and dispensing with their execution was to obtain at some future day a judicial construction of the one or a judicial decision upon the validity of the other, the Senate is not to hold him to answer upon impeachment for high crimes and misdemeanors, does involve the proposition, and no man can get away from it, that the courts at last have a supervising power over this unlimited and unrestricted power of impeachment vested by the people in the House of Representatives, and this unrestricted power to try all impeachments vested by the people in the Senate. On this proposition I am willing to stand, defying any man here or elsewhere to challenge it successfully. The position assumed by the accused means that or it means nothing. If it does not mean that it is like unto—

"A tale told by an idiot,
Full of sound and fury, signifying nothing."

Just nothing. Now, I ask you, Senators, what colorable excuse is there for presenting any such monstrous proposition as this to the consideration of the Senate of the United States? I think myself in this presence justified in reiterating the words of John Marshall upon one occasion, that it is reasonable to presume that the Senate knows something.

The original jurisdiction of the Supreme Court of the United States cannot by any possibility extend to a case of impeachment. Senators will please remember the text of the Constitution which I have just read, that the original jurisdiction of the Supreme Court of the United States is by the express letter of the Constitution restricted to foreign embassadors, other public ministers, and consuls, and to cases in which a State may be a party. The accused is not a foreign embassador; the accused is not a foreign minister; the accused is not a consul; and the accused is not as yet, thank God, "the State." Therefore, the accused is not within the original jurisdiction of the Supreme Court of the United States.

When the gentlemen were dwelling so learnedly and so long upon this question, and reading from the great case of Marbury *vs.* Madison, they ought to have remembered that the Chief Justice who pronounced that decision, and whose intellect, full-orbed, shed a steady and luminous light on the jurisprudence of the country for a third of a century, declared, what no man has since questioned, that the orginal jurisdiction of the Supreme Court as defined in this text of the Constitution could neither be enlarged nor restricted by congressional enactment. These gentlemen ought to have remembered, further, when they invoked the intervention of the Supreme Court or any other court, between the people and this accused President, that the appellate jurisdiction of the Supreme Court, by numerous decisions, depends exclusively under the Constitution upon the will of Congress. It results, therefore, that they must go to some other tribunal for the settlement of this great question between the people and the President, unless Congress chooses to let them go to the Supreme Court by a special enactment for their benefit. The appellate jurisdiction, Senators, of the Supreme Court as defined in the Constitution by words clear and plain and incapable of any misunderstanding or misconstruction, exclude the conclusion that a case of impeachment can by any possibility be within the jurisdiction of any of the courts of the United States, either its district, its circuit, or its Supreme Court. The Senate will notice that by the terms of the Constitution the appellate jurisdiction from the district and circuit courts is limited to the cases in law and equity and the other cases named in the Constitution, none of which embrace a case of impeachment.

There is, therefore, Senators, no room for invoking the decision of the Supreme Court of the United States upon any question touching the liability of the President to answer upon impeachment by the people's Representatives at the bar of the Senate. What excuse, therefore, I ask, is there for the pretense that the President may set aside and dispense with the execution of the laws, all or any of them, enacted by the Congress under the pretext of defending the Constitution by invoking a judicial inquiry in the courts of the United States.

Be it known, Senators, that but two questions which by possibility could become the subject of judicial decision, have been raised by the learned and astute counsel who have attempted to make this defense. The first is that the heads of Departments are the mere registering secretaries of the President of the United States, and are bound to recognize his will as their sworn duty. I deny that proposition; and I think that the learned gentleman from New York did well, remarkably well, as he does everything well, to quote in advance for our instruction when we should come to reply to him upon this point, those divine words of the great Apostle to the Gentiles, wherein he speaks of charity as long patient and suffering. It required a charity, Senators, broader than the charity of the Gospel, to sit patiently by and hear these gentlemen invoke the decision of the Supreme Court upon either of the questions involved in this issue, when we knew that these gentlemen, overflowing as they manifestly are with all learning, ancient and modern, the learning of the dead as well as the learning of the living, knew right well

that the Supreme Court of the United States had solemnly decided both questions against them.

Now for the proof. As to the obligation of the heads of the Departments to learn their duty under the law through the will of an Executive, the Senate will remember that the learned gentleman from New York handled the great case of Marbury vs. Madison with wondrous skill and dexterity. He took care, however, not to quote that part of the decision which absolutely settles this question as to the obligation of the Secretaries to respond to the will of the Executive in questions of law; he took care not to quote it, and to keep it in the back ground. Perhaps, Senators, he assumed that he knew all that the poor Managers of the House knew about this case, and then he knew all that he knew besides, gathered from Tacitus, if you please, and from the phillipics of Cicero against Cataline and from that speech of his in defense of Milo, which it happens he never made until after poor Milo was convicted and banished and was heard to cry out in the agony of his soul if he had made that speech for him on the trial, "I would not be to-day here in Marseilles eating mullets." Laughter.]

I read now in the hearing of the Senate the decision of Chief Justice Marshall in the case of Marbury vs. Madison, touching this alleged obligation of the heads of Departments to take the will of the Executive as their law. Marshall says on page 158 of 1 Cranch:

"It is the duty of the Secretary of State to conform to the law, and in this he is an officer of the United States, bound to obey the laws. He acts in this respect, as has been very properly stated at the bar, under the authority of law and not by the instructions of the President."

If he should disobey the law, does it not logically result that the President's commands cannot excuse him; that the people might well depose him from his office whether the President willed it or not? It only illustrates the proposition with which I started out, that neither the President nor his Secretaries are above the Constitution or above the laws which the people enact.

As for the other proposition, Senators, attempted to be set up here for this accused and guilty President, that he may, with impunity, under the Constitution and laws of the United States, interpret the Constitution and sit in judicial judgment, as the gentleman from Massachusetts [Mr. Curtis] urged it, upon the validity of your laws, that question has also been ruled in the Supreme Court of the United States, and from that hour to this has never been challenged. Although an attempt was made to drag the illustrious name of the Chief Justice who presides, under the Constitution, at this moment over this deliberative and judicial assembly, to their help, it was made in vain, as I shall show before I have done with this argument. I say that the position assumed for the President by all his counsel that he is to judicially interpret the Constitution for himself; that he is to judicially determine the validity of laws, and execute them or suspend them and dispense with their execution at his pleasure and defy the power of the people to bring him to trial and judgment, was settled against him thirty years ago by the Supreme Court of the United States, and that decision has never been questioned since by any authoritative writer upon your Constitution or by any subsequent decision in your tribunals of justice. I read, in the first place, the syllabus as collated by the reporter [Mr. Worthington] from the report itself, and then I will read the decision of the court. It is the case of Kendall *vs.* the United States, 12 Peters. In the syllabus it is stated that—

"By an act for the relief of the relators in the case the Solicitor of the Treasury was directed to audit their claims for certain services, and the Postmaster General was directed to credit them with the sum thus found due. The Postmaster General upon the settlement of the claim by the Solicitor credited the relators with a part of the amount found due, but refused to credit them with the remainder. A *mandamus* was applied for and issued by the circuit court of the District, whereupon the Postmaster General brought the case before the Supreme Court by a writ of error."

Upon the hearing of that case in the Supreme Court, Justice Thompson pronounced the united judgment of the court as follows:

"It was urged at the bar that the Postmaster General was alone subject to the direction and control of the President with respect to the execution of the duty imposed upon him by this law; and this right of the President is claimed as growing out of the obligation imposed upon him by the Constitution to take care that the laws be faithfully executed. This is a doctrine that cannot receive the sanction of this court. It would be vesting in the President a *dispensing power*, which has no countenance for its support in any part of the Constitution, and is asserting a principle which, if carried out in its results to all cases falling within it, would be clothing the President with a power entirely to control the legislation of Congress and paralyze the administration of justice.

"To contend that the obligation imposed on the President to see the laws faithfully executed implies a power to forbid their execution, is a novel construction of the Constitution, and entirely inadmissible."—12 *Peters*, p. 612.

I ask you, Senators, to consider whether I was not justifiable in saying that it was a tax upon one's patience to sit here and listen from day to day and from week to week to these learned arguments made in defense of the President, all resting upon his asserted executive prerogative to dispense with the execution of the laws and protect himself from trial and conviction before this tribunal, because he said that he only violated the laws in order to test their validity in the Supreme Court, when that court had already decided thirty years ago that any such assumed prerogative in the President enabled him to sweep away all the legislation of Congress and prevent the administration of justice itself, and found no countenance in the Constitution? I suppose, Senators, that the learned ex-Attorney General thought that there was something here that might disturb the harmony and the order of their argument in this decision of Kendall *vs.* the United States, and

so in his concluding argument for the accused he attempted to fortify against such consequences by calling to his aid the decision of the present Chief Justice in what is known as the Mississippi case. With all respect to the learned ex-Attorney General, and to all his associates engaged in this trial, I take it upon me to say that the decision pronounced by his honor the Chief Justice of the United States in the Mississippi case has no more to do with the question involved in this controversy than has the Koran of Mohammed, and the gentleman was utterly inexcusable in attempting to force that decision into this case in aid of any such proposition as that involved in this controversy, and made, as I shall show before I have done with it, directly by the President himself in his answer, as well as by the lips of his retained counsel.

What did his honor the Chief Justice decide in the Mississippi case? Nothing in the world but this, as is well known to every lawyer in America, even to every student of the law versed not beyond the horn-books of his profession, that where the law vested the President with discretionary power his judgment in the exercise of his discretion, under the law, until that judgment was overruled by the legislative power of the nation, concluded all parties. We agree to it. The learned Senator from New York, who honors me with his attention, [Mr. Conkling,] knows that before he was born that question was decided precisely in the same way in the great State which he so honorably represents here to-day, and is reported in 12 Wheaton; but it does not touch this question at all, and the proposition is so foreign to the question that it is like one of those suggestions referred to by Webster upon one occasion when he said to make it to a right-minded man is to insult his intelligence. I read, however, from the opinion of the Chief Justice, and in reading from it I wish to be understood that I agree with every word and letter and syllable which the Chief Justice uttered; but it does not touch this question. The Attorney General, in citing, prefaced it with these words:

"It is sufficient upon this point to cite a late opinion of the Supreme Court of the United States, in what is called the Mississippi injunction case, decided April, 1867. Mr. Chief Justice Chase, delivering the opinion of the court, says:

"'It is assumed by the counsel for the State of Mississippi that the President in the execution of the reconstruction acts is required to perform a mere ministerial duty. In this assumption there is, we think, a confounding of the terms ministerial and executive, which are by no means equivalent in import. A ministerial duty, the performance of which may, in proper cases, be required of a head of a Department by judicial process, is one in respect to which nothing is left to discretion. It is a simple, definite duty, arising under conditions admitted or proved to exist, or imposed by law.'"

After citing some cases of merely ministerial duty, the Chief Justice proceeds as follows:

"In each of these cases nothing was left to discretion. There was no room for the exercise of judgment. The law required the performance of a single, specific act, and that performance, it was held, might be required by *mandamus*. Very different is the duty of the President in the exercise of the power to see that the laws are faithfully executed, and among the laws the acts named in the bill."

What acts? The reconstruction act that vested him with a very large discretion to the hurt of the nation:

"The duty thus imposed on the President is in no just sense ministerial. It is purely executive and political. An attempt on the part of the judicial department of the Government to enjoin the performance of such duties by the President might be justly characterized, in the language of Chief Justice Marshall, as an 'absurd and excessive extravagance.' It is true that, in the instance before us, the interposition of the court is not sought to enforce action by the executive under constitutional legislation, but to restrain such action under legislation alleged to be unconstitutional. But we are unable to perceive that this circumstance takes the case out of the general principle which forbids judicial interference with the exercise of executive discretion."

What on earth has that to do with the question in issue here? I may have occasion, Senators, and you will pardon me if I avail myself of the opportunity, to say that the law which is called in question here this day leaves no discretion whatever in the Executive, and, in the language of his honor the Chief Justice, imposed upon him a plain unequivocal duty, about which he was not even mistaken himself. I count myself, therefore, justified, even at this stage of my argument, in reiterating my assertion that the decision in the Mississippi case has nothing whatever to do with the principle involved in this controversy, and that the President has no excuse whatever for attempting to interfere with and set aside the plain mandates and requirements of the law. There was no discretion left in him whatever; and even his counsel had not the audacity to argue here before the Senate that the act of 1867 which is called in question by this Executive, who has violated its provisions, dispensed with its execution, and defied its authority, left any discretion in him. The point they make is that it is unconstitutional and no law; and that is the very point settled in Kendall *vs.* the United States, that the power vested in the President "to take care that the laws be faithfully executed" vests in him no power to set aside a law of the United States, and to direct the head of a Department to disobey it, and authorize the head of the Department to plead his royal mandate in a court of justice in excuse and justification of his refusal to obey the plain requirement of the law. It is written in the Constitution that "he shall take care that the laws be faithfully executed." Are we to mutilate the Constitution, and for the benefit of the accused to interpolate into the Constitution a word which is not there and the introduction of which would annihilate the whole system, that is to say, that "the President shall take care that the laws which he approves, and only the laws which he approves, shall be faithfully executed?" This is at last the position assumed for the President by himself in his answer and assumed for him by his counsel in his defense; and the assumption conflicts with all that I have already read from the Constitution, with all that I have already read of its judicial interpretation and construction; and it conflicts as well with all that remains of the instrument itself. It is useless to multiply words to make plain a self-evident proposition; it is useless to attempt to imply this power in the President to set aside and dispense with the execution of the laws in the face of the express words of the Constitution, that "all legislative power granted by this Constitution shall be vested in a Congress which shall consist of a Senate and a House of Representatives," that he shall be sworn "faithfully to execute the office of President," and therefore faithfully to discharge every obligation which the Constitution enjoins, first and foremost of which obligations is thus written on the very fore-front of the instrument, that he shall take care that the laws enacted by the people's representatives in Congress assembled shall be faithfully executed—not some of the laws; not the laws which he approves; but the laws shall be executed until the same shall have been duly repealed by the power that made them or shall have been constitutionally reversed by the Supreme Court of the United States acting within the limitations and under the restrictions of the Constitution itself.

We have heard much, Senators, in the progress of this discussion, about the established custom of the people of this country; we have heard much about the long-continued practice of eighty years under the Constitution and laws of the United States. You have listened in vain, Senators, for a single citation of a single instance in the history of the Republic where there was an open violation of the written law of this land, either by the Executive, by States, or by combinations of men, which the people did not crush at the outset and put down. That is a fact in our history creditable to the American people, and a fact that ought to be considered by the Senate when they come to sit in judgment upon this case now made before them for the first time under the Constitution of the United States, whether the President is above the laws and can dispense with their execution with impunity in the exercise of what is adroitly called his judicial power of interpretation.

I need not remind Senators of that fact in our early history when, by insurrection, a certain act was attempted to be resisted in the State of Pennsylvania, when Washington took measures promptly to crush the first uprising of insurrection against the majesty of the laws. The gentlemen have attempted to summon to their aid the great name of the hero of New Orleans. It is fresh within the recollection of Senators, as it is fresh within the recollection of millions of the people of this country, that when the

State of South Carolina, in the exercise of what she called her sovereign power as a State, by ordinance attempted to set aside the laws of the United States for the collection of customs, the President of the United States, Andrew Jackson, not unmindful of his oath—although the law was distasteful to him, and it is a fact that has passed into history that he even doubted its constitutionality—yet, nevertheless, issued his proclamation to the insurgents, and, lifting his hand, swore " by the Eternal the Union must and shall be preserved." There was no recognition here of the right either in himself or in a State to set aside the laws.

Gentlemen, there is a case still fresher within the recollection of Senators, and still fresher in the recollection of the people of this country, that attests more significantly than any other the determination of the people to abide by their laws enacted by their Congress, whatever the law may be and however odious it may be. The gentleman from New York—else I might not have alluded to it in this discussion—took occasion to refer to the fugitive slave law of 1850; a law which was disgraceful, (and I say it with all respect to the Congress that enacted it;) a law which was in direct violation of the letter and the spirit of the Constitution; a law of which I can say, at least, although I doubt much whether the gentleman from New York can say as much, that it never found an advocate in me; a law of which Webster spoke when he said, " My judgment always was, and that is my opinion to-day, that it is unwarranted by the Constitution ;" a law which offered a bribe out of the common Treasury of the nation to every magistrate who sat in judgment upon the right of a flying bondman to that liberty which was his by virtue of that same creative energy which breathed into his nostrils the breath of life and he became a living soul; a law which offered a reward to the ministers of justice to shorten the judgment of the poor; a law which, smiting the conscience of the American people and the conscience of the civilized world, made it a crime to give shelter to the houseless, and, in obedience to the utterances of our divine Master, to give a cup of water to him that was ready to perish ; a law enacted for the purpose of sustaining that crime of crimes, that sum of all villainies, which made merchandise of immortality, which transformed a man into a chattel, a thing of trade, which, for want of a better word, we call a slave, with no acknowledged rights in the present, with no hope of a heritage in the great hereafter, to whose darkened soul, under his crushing bondage, the universe was voiceless, and God himself seemed silent; a law under the direct operation of which that horrible tragedy was enacted, my good sir, [addressing Mr. Groesbeck,] within our own noble Commonwealth, in the streets of your beautiful city, (Cincinnati,) when Margaret Garner,

with her babe lashed upon her breast, pursued by the officers by virtue of this law, in her wild frenzy forgot her mother's affection in the joy she felt in sending, before its appointed time, by her own hand, the spotless spirit of her child back to the God who gave it rather than to allow it to be tossed back into this hell of human bondage under the operation of American law; a law sustained by the American people even on that day when Anthony Burns walked in chains under the shadow of Bunker Hill, "where every sod's a soldier's sepulcher," and where sleeps the first great martyr in the cause of American independence, to be tried by a magistrate in a temple of justice girdled itself with chains and guarded by bayonets; and yet the people stood by and said let the law be executed until it be repealed.

Gentlemen talk about the American people recognizing the right of any President to set aside the laws! Who does not know that two years after this enactment, in 1852, the terrible blasphemy was mouthed in Baltimore by the representatives of that same party that to-day insists upon the executive prerogative to set aside your laws and annihilate your Government, touching this fugitive slave law that all discussion in Congress and out of Congress should be suppressed? When they passed that resolution they ought to have remembered that there is something stronger after all than the resolutions of mere partisans in convention assembled. They ought to have remembered that God is not in the earthquake or in the fire, but in "the still, small voice," speaking through the enlightened conscience of enlightened men, and that it is at last omnipotent. But—and I only refer to it: God knows that, for the honor of our country, I would take a step backward and cover the nakedness and shame of the American people in that day of America's dishonor; but when they passed that resolution they nominated their candidate, and he accepted its terms, and he was carried to the presidential chair by the votes of all the States of this Union, except four, upon the basis that he would execute the laws, however odious they might be, however offensive they might be to the judgment and conscience of the people of the United States and of the civilized world.

And now, with such a record as this, these gentlemen dare to come before the Senate and tell the Senate that it is the traditional policy of the American people to allow their own laws to be defied by their own Executive. I deny it. There is not a line in your history but gives a flat denial to the assumption. It has never been done.

In this connection, Senators, I feel constrained, although I deeply regret it, to be compelled to depart from the direct line of my argument to notice another point that was made by the gentleman in order to bolster up this assumption, made for the first time, as I insist, in our history, of the right of the Executive, by his executive prerogative, to suspend and dispense with the execution of the laws, and that was the reference which was made to your lamented and martyred President, Abraham Lincoln. In God's name, Senators, was it not enough that he remembered in the darkest hours of your trial and when the pillars of your holy temple trembled in the storm of battle that oath which, in his own simple words, was "registered in heaven," and which he must obey on the peril of his soul—was it not enough that he kept his faith unto the end and finally laid down his life a beautiful sacrifice in defense of the Republic and the laws without slandering and calumniating his memory now that he is dead, that his tongue is mute, unable to speak for himself, by the bald, naked, and false assertion that he violated the laws of his country? I speak earnestly, I speak warmly on this subject, because the man thus slandered and outraged in the presence of the Senate and the civilized world was not only my own personal friend, but he was the friend of our common country and our common humanity. I deny that, for a single moment, he was regardless of the obligations of his oath or of the requirements of the Constitution. I deny that he ever violated your laws. I deny that he ever assumed to himself the power claimed by this apostate President this day to suspend your laws and dispense with their execution. Though dead, he yet speaks from the grave; and I ask Senators when they come to consider this accusation against their murdered President, to ponder upon the words of his first inaugural, when manifestly alluding to the fugitive slave law, which violated every conviction of his nature, from which he went back with abhorrence, he yet nevertheless in that inaugural said to the American people, however much we may dislike certain laws upon our statute-books, we are not at liberty to defy them, nor to disregard them, nor to set them aside; but we must await the action of the people and their repeal through the law-making power. I do not quote the exact words, but I quote the substance; I doubt not they are as familiar to the minds of Senators as they are to me.

Oh, but said the gentleman, he suspended the *habeas corpus* act. The gentleman was too learned not to know that it has been settled law from the earliest times to this hour that in the midst of arms the laws are silent, and that it is written in the Constitution that "the privilege of the writ of *habeas corpus* shall not be suspended unless when in cases of rebellion or invasion the public safety may require it." It was not Mr. Lincoln that suspended the *habeas corpus* act; it was that great public, solemn, civil war that covered your heavens with blackness and filled the habitations of your people with mourning and lamentation for their beautiful, slain upon the high places of the land. Senators, the best answer that I can make to this assertion that your murdered President was

responsible for what necessarily resulted from this atrocious and unmatched rebellion, I make in the words of that grand and noble man, than whom a purer, a wiser, or better spirit never ascended the chair of civil magistracy in this or in any country, in this age or in any age—I refer to John Quincy Adams—when he said that in the presence of public war, either domestic or foreign, all the limitations of your Constitution are silent, and in the event of insurrection in any of the States, all the institutions of the States within which it rages, to use his own terse, strong words, "go by the board." You cannot prosecute war by a magistrate's warrant and a constable's staff. Abraham Lincoln simply followed the accepted law of the civilized world in doing what he did. I answer further, for I leave no part of it unanswered, I would count myself dishonored, being able to speak here for him when he cannot speak for himself, if I left any colorable excuse for this assault upon his character unanswered and unchallenged.

Why, say the gentlemen, you passed your indemnity acts. Now, who is there in this Senate of the United States so weak as not to know that it is in vain that you pass indemnity acts to protect the President of the United States, if, after all, his acts were unconstitutional—to the hurt of private right. You must go a step further than that; you must deny jurisdiction to the courts, you must shut the doors of your temple of justice, you must silence the ministers of the law before you pass an indemnity act which will protect him if his act at last be unconstitutional. That was not the purpose of the act. If the gentleman referred to the general indemnity act, I had the honor to draft it myself. I claim no particular credit for it. It is not unknown to the legislation of this country and of other countries. The Congress of the United States, as Senators will remember, passed a similar act in 1862. The general act to which I refer was passed in 1867. That act was simply declaring that the acts of the President during the rebellion and of those acting for the President in the premises, should be a bar to prosecutions against them in the courts. What was the object of it? If it be in the power of the nation to defend itself, if it be constitutional to defend the Constitution, if it be constitutional for the President to summon the people to the defense of their own laws and the defense of their own firesides and the defense of their own nationality, the law said that this should be an authority to the courts to dismiss the proceeding, on the ground that the act was done under the order of the President. But how could we make his act valid under the Constitution if it was unconstitutional, if the limitations of the Constitution operated? I do not stop to argue the question. It has been argued by wager of battle, and it has been settled beyond review in this tribunal or in any tribunal that the public safety is the highest law, and that it is a part and parcel of the Constitution of the United States.

I have answered, Senators, and I trust I have answered sufficiently, all that has been aid by the counsel for the President for the purpose of giving some colorable justification for the monstrous plea which they this day interpose for the first time in our history that it pertains to the executive prerogative to interpret the Constitution judicially for himself and to determine judicially the validity of every law passed by Congress and to execute it or suspend it or dispense with its execution at his pleasure.

Mr. SHERMAN. If the honorable Manager will pause at this point of the argument I will submit a motion that the Senate take a recess for fifteen minutes.

The motion was agreed to.

At the expiration of the recess the Chief Justice resumed the chair and called the Senate to order.

Mr. Manager BINGHAM. Mr. President and Senators, the last words which I had the honor to utter in the presence of the Senate were to the effect that I had endeavored to answer what had been said by the counsel for the accused in defense of the monstrous proposition made for the first time in the history of the Republic that the Executive may suspend and dispense with the execution of the people's laws at his pleasure. I beg the pardon of the Senate for having forgotten to notice the very astute argument made by the learned counsel from New York [Mr. Evarts] in behalf of the President touching the broker who refused to pay the license under your revenue laws, and under the advice of the learned counsel was finally protected in the courts. Senators, pardon me for saying again that the introduction of such an argument as that was an insult to the intelligence of the American Senate; it does not touch the question, and the man who does not understand that proposition is not fit to stand in the presence of this tribunal and argue for a moment any issue involved in this controversy.

Nothing is more clearly settled, Senators—and I ought to ask pardon at every step I take in this argument for making such a statement to the Senate—nothing is more clearly settled under the American Constitution in all its interpretations than that the citizen upon whom the law operates is authorized by the Constitution to decline compliance without resistance and appeal to the courts for his protection. That was the case of the New York broker to which the learned counsel referred; and desperate must be the defense of his client if it hangs upon any such slender thread.

Who ever heard of that rule of universal application in this country of the right of the citizen peacefully, quietly, without resistance, without meditating resistance, to appeal to the courts against the oppression of the law being applied to the sworn executor of the law? The learned gentleman from New York would have given us more light on this subject if he had informed us that the collector under your revenue law had dared, under a letter of authority of Andrew Johnson, to set aside a statute, and upon his own authority, coupled with that of his chief, to defy your power. The two questions are as distinct as life and death, as light and darkness, and no further word need be said by me to the American Senate in answer to that proposition.

I may be pardoned now, Senators, for referring to other provisions of the Constitution which do sustain and make clear the position I assumed as the basis of my argument, that the letter of the law passed by the people's Representatives in Congress assembled concludes the Executive. I have given you already the solemn decision of the Supreme Court of the United States upon that subject, unquestioned and unchallenged from that day to this. I now turn to a higher and a more commanding authority, the supreme law of the land ordained by the people and for the people, in which they have settled this question between the people and the Executive beyond the reach of a colorable doubt. I refer to the provisions of the Constitution which declare that—

"Every bill which shall have passed the House of Representatives and the Senate shall, before it become a law, be presented to the President of the United States; if he approve, he shall sign it, but if not, he shall return it with his objections to that House in which it shall have originated, who shall enter the objections at large on their Journal and proceed to reconsider it. If, after such reconsideration, two thirds of that House shall agree to pass the bill, it shall be sent, together with the objections, to the other House, by which it shall likewise be reconsidered, and if approved by two thirds of that House it shall become a law." * * * * *

"If any bill shall not be returned by the President within ten days (Sundays excepted) after it shall have been presented to him the same shall be a law in like manner as if he had signed it, unless the Congress by their adjournment prevent its return, in which case it shall not be a law."

I ask the Senators to please note in this controversy between the Representatives of the people and the advocates of the President that it is there written in the Constitution so plainly that no mortal man can gainsay it, that every bill which shall have passed the Congress of the United States and been presented to the President and shall have received his signature shall be a law; that it further provides that every bill which he shall disapprove and return to the House in which it originated with his objections, if reconsidered and passed by the Congress of the United States by a two-thirds vote, shall become a law; and that every bill which shall have passed the Congress of the United States and shall have been presented to the President for his approval which he shall retain for more than ten days, Sundays excepted, during the session of Congress, shall be a law. That is the language of the Constitution; it shall be a law if he approves it; it shall be a law if he disapproves it and the Congress pass it over his veto; it shall be a law if he retain it for more than ten days during the session of Congress, Sundays excepted. In each such case it shall be a law. It is in vain, altogether in vain, against this bulwark of the Constitution, that gentlemen come, not with their rifled ordnance, but with their small arms playing upon it, and telling the Senate of the United States and the people of the United States in the face of the plain words of the Constitution that it shall *not* be a law. The people meant precisely what they said, that it shall be a law; though the President give never so many reasons, by veto, why he deems it unconstitutional, nevertheless, if Congress by a two-thirds vote pass it over his veto, it shall be the law. That is the language of the Constitution.

What is their answer? "It is not to be a law unless in pursuance of the Constitution." An unconstitutional law, they say, is no law at all. We agree to that; but the executive—and that is the point in controversy here—is not the department of the Government to determine that issue between the people and their Representatives; and the man is inexcusable, absolutely inexcusable, who ever had the advantage of common schools and learned to read the plain text of his native vernacular, who dares to raise the issue in the light of the plain text of the Constitution that the President, in the face of the Constitution, is to say it shall not be a law, though the Constitution says expressly IT SHALL BE A LAW. I admit that when an enactment of Congress shall have been set aside by the constitutional authority of this country it thenceforward ceases to be law, and the President himself might well be protected for not thereafter recognizing it as law. I admit it, although gentlemen on that side of the Chamber will pardon me—and surely I make the allusion for no disrespectful purpose whatever—I say it rather because it has been pressed into this controversy on the other side, in saying that it was the doctrine taught by him who is now called the great apostle of Democracy in America, that the Supreme Court of the United States could not decide the constitutionality of a law for any other department of this Government; that they only decide for themselves and the suitors at their bar. For what earthly use the citation from Jefferson was introduced by the learned gentleman from Tennessee, [Mr. Nelson,] who first referred to it, and by the learned Attorney General, I cannot for the life of me comprehend in the light of the answer here interposed by the President. He tells you, Senators, by his answer that he only violated the law, he only asserted this executive prerogative, that would cost any crowned head in Europe this day his life, innocently for the purpose of taking the judgment of the Supreme Court; and here comes his learned advocate from Tennessee, and his learned advocate, the Attorney General, quoting the opinion of Thomas Jefferson to show

that at last the decision of the Supreme Court could not control him at all; that it could not decide any question for the departments of the Government.

I am not disposed to cast reproach upon Mr. Jefferson. I know well that he was not one of the framers of the Constitution. I know well that he was not one of the builders of the fabric of American empire. While he contributed much to work out the emancipation of the American people from the control and domination of British rule and deserves well of his country, one of the authors of the Declaration of Independence, yet I know well enough that his opinions on that subject are not accepted at this day by the great body of the American people and find no place in the authoritative and commanding writers upon the text of your Constitution. He was a man, doubtless, of fine philosophic mind; he was a man of noble, patriotic impulses; he rendered great service to the country and deserves well of his countrymen; but he is not an authoritative exponent of the principles of your Constitution, and never was.

I may be pardoned further, in passing, for saying in connection with this citation that is made here, right in the face of the answer of the accused, that his only object in violating the law was to have a decision of the Supreme Court on the subject, that another distinguished man of the Democratic party standing in his place in the Senate years ago, in the controversy about the constitutionality of the United States Bank, afterward lifted to the Presidency of the United States, declared in his place here that while he should give a respectful consideration to the decision of the Supreme Court of the United States touching the constitutionality of an act of Congress, he should nevertheless, as a Senator upon his oath, hold himself not bound by it at all. That was Mr. Buchanan.

One thing is very certain: that these authorities quoted by the gentlemen do sustain in some sort, if it needed any support at all, the position that I have ventured to assume before the Senate, that upon all trials of impeachment presented by the House of Representatives the Senate of the United States is the highest judicial tribunal of the land, and is the exclusive judge of the law and fact, no matter what any court may have said touching any question involved in the issue.

Allow me, Senators, now to take one step further in this argument touching this position of the President, for I intend in every step I take to stand with the Constitution of my country, the obligations of which are upon me as a representative of the people. I have already in your hearing cited a text from the Constitution which ought to close this controversy between the people and the President as to his right to challenge a law which the Constitution declares is a law and shall be a law despite his veto. The other provision of the Constitution to which I refer is that provision which defines and limits the executive power of the President. I refer again to the words of the Constitution:

"The President shall be Commander-in-Chief of the Army and Navy of the United States, and of the militia of the several States, when called into the actual service of the United States; he may require the opinion, in writing, of the principal officer in each of the Executive Departments upon any subject relating to the duties of their respective offices, and he shall have power to grant reprieves and pardons for offenses against the United States, except in cases of impeachment.

"He shall have power, by and with the advice and consent of the Senate, to make treaties, provided two thirds of the Senators present concur; and he shall nominate, and by and with the advice and consent of the Senate shall appoint, embassadors, other public ministers and consuls, judges of the Supreme Court, and all other officers of the United States, whose appointments are not herein otherwise provided for, and which shall be established by law; but the Congress may by law vest the appointment of such inferior officers as they think proper in the President alone, in the courts of law, or in the heads of Departments.

"The President shall have power to fill up all vacancies that may happen during the recess of the Senate, by granting commissions which shall expire at the end of their next session.

"He shall from time to time give to the Congress information of the state of the Union, and recommend to their consideration such measures as he shall judge necessary and expedient; he may, on extraordinary occasions, convene both Houses, or either of them, and in case of disagreement between them, with respect to the time of adjournment, he may adjourn them to such time as he shall think proper," &c.

These are the specific powers conferred on the President by the Constitution. I shall have occasion hereafter in the course of this argument to take notice of that other provision which declares that the executive power shall be vested in a President. It is not a grant of power, however, I may be allowed to say in passing, to the President, and never was so held by anybody in this country. The provisions of the Constitution which I have read grant to the President of the United States no legislative nor judicial power. Both of these powers, legislative and judicial, are necessarily involved in the defense this day attempted to be set up by the Executive; first, in the words of his own counsel, that he may judicially interpret the Constitution for himself and judicially determine upon the validity of every enactment of Congress; and second, in the position assumed by himself, and for which he stands charged here at your bar as a criminal, to repeal—I use the word advisedly and considerately—to repeal by his own will and pleasure the laws enacted by the Representatives of the people. This power of suspending the laws, of dispensing with their execution until such time as it may suit his pleasure to test their validity in the courts, is a repeal for the time being, and, if it be sustained by the Senate, may last during his natural life, if so be the American people should so long tolerate him in the office of Chief Magistrate of the nation. Why should I stop to argue the question whether such a power as this, legislative and judicial, may be rightfully assumed by the President of the United States, under the Constitution, when that Constitution expressly declares that all legislative power granted by this Constitution shall be vested in Congress, and that all judicial power shall be vested in a Supreme Court and in such inferior courts as the Congress may by law establish, subject, nevertheless, to the limitations and definitions of power embraced in the Constitution itself? The assumption upon which the defense of the President rests, that he shall only execute such laws as he approves or deems constitutional, is an assumption which invests him with legislative and judicial power in direct contravention of the express words of the Constitution.

If the President may dispense with one act of Congress upon his own discretion, may he not in like manner dispense with every act of Congress? I ask you, Senators, whether this conclusion does not necessarily result, as necessarily as effect follows efficient cause? If not, pray why not? Is the Senate of the United States, in order to shelter this great criminal, to adopt the bold assumption of unrestricted executive prerogative, the wild and guilty fantasy that the king can do no wrong, and thereby clothe the Executive of the American people with power to suspend and dispense with the execution of their laws at his pleasure, to interpret their Constitution for himself, and thereby annihilate their Government?

Senators, I have endeavored to open this question before you in its magnitude. I trust that I have succeeded. Be assured of one thing, that according to the best of my ability, in the presence of the Representatives of the nation, I have not been unmindful of my oath; and I beg leave to say to you, Senators, this day, in all candor, that, in my judgment, no question of mightier import was ever before presented to the American Senate, and to say further, that no question of greater magnitude ever can come by possibility before the American Senate, or any question upon the decision of which greater interests necessarily depend.

In considering this-great question of the power of the President by virtue of his executive office to suspend the laws and dispense with their execution, I pray you, Senators, consider that the Constitution of your country, essential to our national life, cannot exist without legislation duly enacted by the Representatives of the people in Congress assembled and duly executed by their chosen Chief Magistrate. Courts, neither supreme nor inferior, for the administration of justice within the limitations of your Constitution, can exist without legislation. Is the Senate to be told that this Department of the Government, essential to the peace of the Republic, essential to the administration of justice between man and man, those ministers of justice who, in the simple oath of the purer days of the Republic, were sworn to do equal justice between the poor and the rich, shall not administer justice at all if perchance the President of the United States may choose, when the Congress comes to enact a law for the organization of the judiciary, and enact it even despite his objections to the contrary in accordance with the Constitution by a two-thirds vote, to declare that according to his judgment and his convictions it violates the Constitution of the country, and therefore it shall not be put into execution?

Senators, if he has the power to sit in judgment judicially—and I use the word of his advocate—upon the tenure-of-office act of 1867, he has like power to sit in judgment judicially upon every other act of Congress; and in the event of the President of the United States interfering with the execution of a judiciary act establishing for the first time, if you please, in your history, or for the second time, if you please, if by some strange intervention of Providence the existing judges should perish from the earth, I would like to know what becomes of this naked and bald pretense (unfit to be played with by children, much less by full-grown men) of the President, that he only violates the laws innocently and harmlessly, to have the question decided in the courts, when he arrogates to himself the power to prevent any court sitting in judgment upon the question?

Representatives to the Congress of the United States cannot be chosen without legislation; first, the legislation of the Congress apportioning representation among the several States according to the whole number of representative population in each; and second, an enactment either of the Congress or of the Legislatures of the several States fixing the time, place, and manner of holding the elections. Is it possible that the President of the United States, in the event of such legislation by the Congress, clearly authorized by the very terms of the Constitution, and essential to the very existence of the Government, is permitted, in the exercise of his judicial executive authority, to sit in judgment upon your statute and say that it shall not be executed? This power given by your Constitution to the Congress to prescribe the time and place and manner of holding elections for Representatives in Congress in the several States, and to alter as well the provisions of the State Legislatures, in the words of one of the framers of the Constitution, was put into the instrument to enable the people through the national Legislature to perpetuate the legislative department of their own Government in the event of the defection of the State Legislatures; and we are to be told here, and we are to deliberate upon it from day to day and from week to week, that the President of the United States is, by virtue of his executive office and his executive prerogative, clothed with the authority to determine the validity of your law and to suspend it and dispense with its execution at pleasure.

Again, a President of the United States to execute the laws of the people enacted by their Representatives in Congress assembled, cannot be chosen without legislation. Are we again to be told that the President at every step is vested with authority to dispense with the execution of the law and to suspend its operation till he can have a decision, if you please, in the courts of justice? Revenue cannot be raised, in the words of the Constitution, to provide for the common defense and general welfare without legislation. Is the President to intervene with his executive prerogative to declare that your revenue laws do not meet his approval, and in the exercise of his independent coördinate power as one of the departments of this Government chooses to suspend the law and dispense with its execution? If the President may set aside all laws and suspend their execution at pleasure, it results that he may annul the Constitution and annihilate the Government, and that is the issue before the American Senate. I do not go outside of his answer to establish it, as I shall show before I have done with this controversy.

The Constitution itself, according to this assumption, is at his mercy, as well as the laws, and the people of the United States are to stand by and be mocked and derided in their own Capitol when, in accordance with the express provision of their Constitution, they bring him to the bar of the Senate to answer for such a crime than which none greater ever was committed since the day when the first crime was committed upon this planet as it sprung from the hand of the Creator; that crime which covered one manly brow with the ashy paleness and terrible beauty of death, and another with the damning blotch of fratricide. The people are not to be answered at this bar that it is in vain that they have put into the hands of their Representatives the power to impeach such a malefactor, and by the express words of their Constitution they have put the power into the hands of the Senate, the exclusive power, the sole power to try him for his high crimes and misdemeanors.

The question touches the nation's life. Be it known, Senators, that your matchless constitution of government, and the hope of the struggling friends of liberty in all lands, and for the perpetuity and the triumph of which millions of hands are lifted this day in silent prayer to the God of nations, can no more exist without laws duly enacted by the law-making power of the people than can the people themselves exist without air or without that bright heaven which bends above us filled with the life-giving breath of the Almighty. A Constitution and laws which are not and cannot be enforced are dead. The vital principle of your Constitution and laws is that they shall be the supreme law of the land—supreme in every State, supreme in every Territory, supreme in every rood of the Republic, supreme upon every deck covered by your flag, in every zone of the globe. And yet we are debating here to-day whether a man whose breath is in his nostrils, the mere servant of the people, may not suspend the execution both of the Constitution and of the laws at his pleasure, and defy the power of the people. The determination, Senators, of all these questions is involved in this issue, and it is for the Senate, and the Senate alone, to decide them and to decide them aright.

I have dwelt thus long upon this point because it underlies the whole question in issue here between the President and the people, and upon its determination the decision of the whole issue depends. If I am right in the position that the acts of Congress are law, binding upon the President and to be executed by him until repealed by Congress or actually reversed by the courts, it results that the willful violation of such acts of Congress by the President and the persistent refusal to execute them is a high crime or misdemeanor, within the terms of the Constitution, for which he is impeachable, and of which, if he be guilty, he ought to be convicted and removed from the office that he has dishonored. It is not needful to inquire whether only crimes or misdemeanors specifically made such by the statutes of the United States are impeachable, because by the laws of the United States all crimes and misdemeanors at the common law, committed within the District of Columbia, are made indictable. I believe it is conceded on every hand that a crime or misdemeanor made indictable by the laws of the United States, when committed by an officer of the United States in his office, in violation of his sworn duty, is a high crime and misdemeanor within the meaning of the Constitution. At all events, if that be not accepted as a true and self-evident proposition by Senators, it would be in vain that I should argue further with them. And I might as well expect to kindle life under the ribs of death as to persuade a Senate, so lost to every sense of duty and to the voice of reason itself, which comes to the conclusion that after all it is not a high crime and misdemeanor under the Constitution for a President of the United States deliberately and purposely, in violation of his oath, in violation of the plain letter of the Constitution that he shall take care that the laws be faithfully executed, to set the laws aside and defiantly declare that he will not execute them.

Senators, I refer in passing, without stopping to read the statute, for I believe it was read by my associate, [Mr. Manager BOUTWELL,] to the act of February 27, 1801, (2 Statutes-at-Large, 103, 104,) which declares that the common law as it existed in Maryland at the date of the cession shall be in force in the District. I refer also to 4 Statutes-at-Large, page 450, section fifteen, which declares that all crimes and offenses not therein specifically provided for shall be punished as theretofore provided, referring to the act of 1801. I refer also to 12 Statutes-at-Large, page 763, section three, which confers jurisdiction to try all these offenses upon the courts of the District.

That common-law offenses are indictable in the District has been settled by the courts of the District and by the Supreme Court. In the United States vs. Watkins, 3 Cranch, the circuit court of the District ruled—

"In regard to offenses committed within this part of the District the United States have a criminal common law and the court has criminal common-law jurisdiction."

And in the case of the United States vs. Kendall, before referred to in 12 Peters, 614, the court ruled:

"That the common law as it was in force in Maryland when the cession was made remained in force in the District."

It is clear that the offenses charged in the articles, if committed in the District of Columbia, would be indictable, for at the common law an indictment lies for all misdemeanors of a public evil example, for neglecting duties imposed by law, and for offenses against common decency, 4 Bacon's Abridgement, page 302, letter E.

This is all, Senators, that I deem it important at present to say upon the impeachable character of the offenses specified in the articles against the President further than to remark that although the question does not arise upon this trial for the reasons already stated, a crime or misdemeanor committed by a civil officer of the United States not indictable by our own laws or by any laws, has never yet been decided not to be impeachable under the Constitution of the United States; nor can that question ever be decided save by the Senate of the United States. I do not propose to waste words, if the Senate please, in noticing what but for the respect I bear him I would call the mere lawyer's quirk of the learned counsel from Massachusetts upon the defense [Mr. Curtis] that even if the President be guilty of the crimes laid to his charge in the articles presented by the House of Representatives, they are not high crimes and misdemeanors within the meaning of the Constitution, because they are not kindred to the great crimes of treason and bribery. It is enough, Senators, for me to remind you of what I have already said that they are crimes which touch the nation's life, which touch the stability of your institutions; they are crimes which, if tolerated by this highest judicial tribunal in the land, vest the President by solemn judgment with the power under the Constitution to suspend at pleasure all the laws upon your statute-book, and thereby overturn your Government. They have heretofore been held crimes, and crimes of such magnitude that they have cost the perpetrators their lives—not simply their offices, but their lives. Of this I may have more to say hereafter.

But I return to my proposition. The defense of the President is not whether indictable crimes or offenses are laid to his charge, but it rests upon the broad proposition, as already said, that impeachment will not lie against him for any violation of the Constitution and laws because of his asserted constitutional right to judicially interpret every provision of the Constitution for himself, and also to interpret for himself the validity of every law and execute or disregard upon his election any provision of either the Constitution or the laws, especially if he declare at or after the fact that his only purpose in violating the one or the other was to have a true construction of the Constitution in the one case and a judicial determination of the validity of the law in the other, in the courts of the United States.

That I do not state this as the position of the President too strongly, I pray Senators to notice what I now say, for I would count myself a dishonored man if purposely here or elsewhere I should misrepresent the position assumed by the President. The counsel for the President [Mr. Curtis] in his opening attempts to gainsay the statement as I have just made it, that the defense of the President rests upon the assumption as stated in his answer. The counsel, in the opening, states, that—I quote his words from page 382, and they were qualified by none of his associates who followed him; the statement was considerately made; he meant precisely what he said, as follows:

"But when, Senators, the question arises whether a particular law has cut off a power confided to him (the President) by the people through the Constitution, and he alone can raise that question, and he alone can cause a judicial decision to come between the two branches of the Government to say which of them is right, and after due deliberation, with the advice of those who are his proper advisers, he settles down firmly upon the opinion that such is the character of the law"—

That is to say, that it is unconstitutional, that it cuts off a power confided to him by the people—

"it remains to be decided by you whether there is any violation of his duty when he takes the needful steps to raise that question and have it peaceably decided in the courts."

I ask, Senators, in all candor, if the President of the United States, by force of the Constitution, as the learned counsel argue, is vested with judicial authority thus to interpret the Constitution and decide upon the validity of any law of Congress upon this statement of counsel as I have just read it from the report now before you and upon your tables, what is there to hinder the President from saying this of every law of the land; that it cuts off some power confided to him by the people?

Senators, the learned gentleman from Massachusetts was too self-poised; he is, manifestly, too profound a man to launch out upon this wild, stormy sea of anarchy, careless of all consequences, in the manner in which some of his associates did. You may remember—and I quote it only from memory, but it is burned into my brain, and will only perish with my life—you remember the utterance of the gentleman from New York, not so careful of his words, who before you said, in the progress of his argument, that the Constitution had

invested the President with the power to guard the people's rights against congressional encroachments. You remember that as he progressed in his argument he ventured upon the further assertion in the presence of the Senate of the United States, and so you will find it written doubtless in the report, that if you dared to decide against the President upon this issue, the question would be raised before the people under the banner of the supremacy of the Constitution in defense of the President, and the omnipotence of Congress upon the other; the supremacy of the Constitution would be the sign under which the President was to conquer against the omnipotence of Congress to bind him by laws enacted by themselves in the mode prescribed by the Constitution.

Senators, I may be pardoned for summoning the learned counsel from Massachusetts as a witness against the assumption of his client, and against the assumption of his associate counsel, touching this power of the President to dispense with the execution of the laws. In 1862 there was a pamphlet issued bearing the name of the learned gentleman from Massachusetts touching the limitations upon executive power imposed by the Constitution. I read from that pamphlet, and pledge myself to produce the original, so that it may be inspected by the Senate. I regret that my reporter has not brought it into the court. It shows the difference between the current of a learned man's thoughts when he speaks for the people and according to his own convictions, and the thoughts of the same learned man when he speaks for a retainer:

"*Executive Power,*" *by B. R. Curtis: Cambridge,* 1862. "*Dedicated*—" To all persons who have sworn to support the Constitution of the United States, and to all citizens who value the principles of civil liberty which that Constitution embodies, and for the preservation of which it is our only security, these pages are respectfully dedicated"—by the Author.

"The President is the Commander-in-Chief of the Army and Navy, not only by force of the Constitution, but under and subject to the Constitution, and to every restriction therein contained, and to every law enacted by its authority, as completely and clearly as the private in the ranks. *He is General-in-Chief, but can a General-in-Chief disobey any law of his own country? When he can he superadds to his rights as commander the powers of a usurper; and that is military despotism;*" * * * "*the mere authority to command an army is not an authority to disobey the laws of the country.*"

The President has only executive power, not legislative, not judicial. The learned counsel learned that word "judicial" after he entered upon the defense of the President. I may be pardoned in saying that I lay nothing to his charge in this. He bore himself bravely and well in the presence of this tribunal. He discharged his duty and his whole duty to his client. If he has even changed his mind he had a right to change it in the interests of his client; but I have a right to have him bear witness in the interests of the people and in support of the Constitution of my country. I therefore read further from him:

"Besides all the powers of the President are executive merely. He cannot make a law. He cannot

C. I.—51.

repeal one. He can only execute the laws. He can neither make nor suspend nor alter them. He cannot even make an article of war.''

That is good law. It was not good law in the midst of the rebellion, but it is good law, nevertheless, under the Constitution, in the light of the interpretation given to it by that great man, Mr. John Quincy Adams, whom I before cited. When the limitations of the Constitution are operative, when the whole land is covered with the serene light of peace, when every human being, citizen and stranger, within your gates is under the shelter of the limitations of the Constitution, it is the very law and nothing but the law.

Now, Senators, that this alleged judicial executive power of the President to suspend at his discretion all the laws upon your statute-book and to dispense with their execution is the defense and the whole defense of this President seems to me clear—clear as that light of heaven in which we live, and so clear, whatever may be the decision of this tribunal, that it will be apparent to the judgment of the American people. It cannot be otherwise. It is written in his answer. It is written in the arguments of his counsel printed and laid upon your tables. No mortal man can evade it. It is all there is of it; and to establish this assertion that it is all there is of it I ask Senators to consider what article the President has denied? Not one. I ask the Senate to consider what offense charged against him in the articles of the House of Representatives he has not openly by his answer confessed or is not clearly established by the proof? Not one. Who can doubt that while the Senate was in session the President, in direct violation of the express requirement of the law, which, in the language of his honor, the Chief Justice, in the Mississippi case, left no discretion in him, enjoined a special duty on him, did purposely, deliberately, violate the law and defy its authority, in that he issued an order for the removal of the Secretary for the Department of War and issued a letter of authority for the appointment of a successor, the Senate being in session and not consulted in the premises? The order and the letter of authority are written witnesses of the guilt of the accused. They are confessions of record. There is no escape from them.

If this order is a clear violation of the tenure-of-office act, if the letter of authority is also a clear violation of the tenure-of-office act, the President is manifestly guilty, in manner and form, as he stands charged in the first, the second, the third, the eighth, and the eleventh articles of impeachment; and no man can gainsay it except a man who accepts as law the assumption of his answer that it is his executive prerogative judicially to interpret the Constitution for himself; to set aside, to violate, and to defy the law when it vests no discretion in him whatever, and challenge the people to bring him to trial and judgment.

Senators, on this question of the magnitude and character of these offenses charged against the President I shall be permitted, inasmuch as the counsel from New York thought it important to refer to it, to ask your attention to what was ruled and settled, and I think well settled, on the trial of Judge Peck. The counsel took occasion to quote, as you may remember, a certain statement from the record of that trial, but took special pains to avoid any statement of what was actually settled by it. I choose to have the whole of the authority. If the gentleman insists upon the law in this case, I insist upon all the forms and upon all its provisions. In the trial of Peck, from which I read on page 427, Mr. Buchanan, chairman of the Managers on the part of the House of Representatives, made the statement that—

"An impeachable violation of law may consist in the abuse as well as in the usurpation of authority."

Subject, if you please, to the limitations of your own law that the abuse and the usurpation, as is clearly the fact here in the capital, are indictable. I venture to say, Senators, if you look carefully through that record you will find none of the learned gentlemen who appeared in behalf of Judge Peck questioning for a moment the correctness of the proposition. The learned and accomplished and lamented ex-Attorney General of the United States, Mr. Wirt, who appeared on that trial, admitted it. There seemed to have been no question in the Senate upon the subject against it. I think Mr. Buchanan was most happy in his statement of the law in declaring that it may consist in an abuse of power and may consist in a usurpation of authority. For the purposes of this case I think it capable of the clearest demonstration that this is the rule which ought to govern its decision, inasmuch as all the offenses charged, when committed within the District, as already shown, are indictable.

It is conceded that there is a partial exception to this rule, and that exception furnishes all the law which has appeared in this case, so far as I have been able to discover, in the defense of the Executive. It is an exception, however, made exclusively in the interests of judicial officers. The rule is well stated in 5 Johnson, 291, by Chancellor Kent, in the case of Yates vs. Lansing. I read from that authority:

"Judicial exercise of power is imposed upon the courts, and they must decide and act according to their judgment, and therefore the law will protect them."

He adds:

"The doctrine which holds a judge exempt from a civil suit or indictment for any act done or omitted to be done by him sitting as judge has a deep root in the common law. It is to be found in the earliest judicial records, and it has been steadily maintained by an undisturbed current of decisions in the English courts amid every change of policy and through every revolution of their Government."

A judge manifestly, upon this authority, acting within his general authority, cannot be held to answer for an error of judgment. He would only be impeachable, however erroneous his judgment might be, for an abuse, for a usurpation of authority great in itself, and it must be specially averred, and must be proved as averred. No such rule ever was held to apply, since the courts first sat at Westminster, to an executive officer. It is an exception running through all the law in favor of judicial officers. A mere executive officer clothed with no judicial authority would be guilty of usurpation without the averment of corruption. I beg to say that it has never been averred, or held necessary if averred, in any authoritative case against any executive officer whatever. An error of judgment would not excuse him. I refer to the general rule of law on this subject as stated by Sedgwick in his work on statutory and constitutional law, in which he says:

"Good faith is no excuse for the violation of statutes. Ignorance of the law cannot be set up in defense, and this rule holds good in civil as well as in criminal cases."—1 *Sedgwick*, 100.

Mr. CONNESS. Mr. President, I should like to ask the Manager whether he feels able to go on further to-day or not? I make the suggestion to him.

Mr. Manager BINGHAM. I am at the pleasure of the Senate. I will be able to proceed, if it be the pleasure of the Senate, for half an hour or so more with this argument; but I abide the pleasure of the Senate, and will defer to whatever may be their wishes about it.

Several SENATORS. Go on! Go on!

Mr. Manager BINGHAM. Senators, at this point of the argument the gentleman from New York, speaking for the President, knowing that the rule as I have read it from Sedgwick is the rule of universal application to executive officers and to all officers save judicial officers, that ignorance of the law can never be interposed as an excuse either in civil or criminal proceedings for the deliberate violation of the law, entered upon a wonderful adventure when he undertook to tell the Senate of the United States—I really thought it was a slip of the tongue, for I have great respect for his learning, and I could not but think he knew better—but he intimated that this rule, which holds the violator of law answerable and necessarily implies the guilty purpose and the guilty intent from the fact of its violation, was a rule that was restricted to offenses *mala in se*. The gentleman ought to have known when he made that utterance that the highest writer upon the law in America, and second to no writer upon the law who writes in the English language in any country, has truly recorded in his great commentaries upon the laws that the distinction between *mala prohibita* and *mala in se* is long ago exploded, and the same rule applies to the one as to the other. I refer to 1 Kent's Commentaries, page 529, and really I cannot see why it should not be so. I doubt very much whether

it is within the compass of the mind of any Senator within the hearing of my voice to say it should not be so. Chancellor Kent says upon that subject, page 529:

"The distinction between statutory offenses which are *mala prohibita* only, or *mala in se*, is now exploded, and a breach of the statute law in either case is equally unlawful and equally a breach of duty."

The Senate will remember the very curious and ingenious use that the gentleman attempted to make of this statement of his, and that was that it cannot be possible that you are to hold these acts of the President criminal by force of the act of 1801 which, by relation simply, makes common-law offenses indictable crimes within the District of Columbia; but that was not the only use, but that was a part of it and he went on to say to the Senate further that he could not see the force of the remark made by my colleague, [Mr. BOUTWELL,] that the President of the United States in this letter of authority by the appointment *ad interim* of Lorenzo Thomas in the presence of the Senate, during its session, without its advice and consent, twelve days after the expiration of the six months limited by the provisions of the act of 1795, could be held a criminal act. The defense of the President in some sort rested on the provisions of that law which authorized him to supply a vacancy in the several Departments for a period not exceeding six months. Well, I will try to explain it here if I may be pardoned in case I should happen to refer to it again in the progress of my argument.

It is explained by this simple word, that the act of 1795, under which he attempts in his distress to shelter himself, says that no one vacancy shall be so supplied for a longer period than six months; he did supply it, according to the very words of his answer, for he tells you he made a vacancy indefinitely when he suspended Edwin M. Stanton, Secretary of War; he says in his answer it was an indefinite suspension, not simply for six months, but during the time he might occupy the executive power in this country. He indefinitely suspended him, he says, under the Constitution and laws; and he tells you further, in the same answer, that under the act of 1795 he supplied the vacancy. That act told him he should not supply it for a longer period than six months, unless it results that at the end of every six months he may supply it again and the statute thereby be repealed, supply it to the end of the time allotted him under the Constitution to execute the office of President of the United States. I would like some Senator, in your deliberations, to make answer to that suggestion and see how it can be got rid of. He makes a vacancy indefinitely; he appoints General Grant Secretary of War *ad interim;* at the end of six months, and twelve days after the expiration of six months, in utter defiance of the law of 1795, he makes another appointment; and at the end of that six months and twelve days after, if you please, in further defiance of it, he makes another, and so on until the end of the time during which he may exercise the office of President, while the law itself expressly declares that no vacancy shall be so supplied for a longer period than six months. I think the gentleman from New York could have seen it but for the interest he felt in the fate of his client. That is my impression, and everybody else can see it in this country.

But it has been further said, by way of illustration and answer to all this, said by the counsel for the President, "Suppose the Congress of the United States should enact a law in clear violation of the express power conferred upon the President, as, for example, a law declaring that he shall not be Commander-in-Chief of the Army, a law declaring that he shall not exercise the pardoning power in any case whatever, is not the President to intervene and protect the Constitution?" I answer, no; not by repealing the laws. The President is not to intervene and protect the Constitution against the laws. The people of the United States are the guardians of their own honor, the protectors of their own Constitution, and if there be anything in that Constitution more clearly written and defined and established than another, it is the express and clear provision that the legislative department of this Government is responsible to no power on earth for the exercise of their legislative authority and the discharge of their duties during the sessions of the Congress save to the people that appointed them. It is a new doctrine altogether that the Constitution is exclusively in the keeping of the President. When that day comes, Senators, that the Constitution of your country, so essential to your national existence and so essential to the peace, the happiness, and the prosperity of the people, rests exclusively upon the fidelity and patriotism and integrity of Andrew Johnson, may God save the Constitution and save the republic from its defender! No, sirs; there is no such power vested in the President of the United States. It is only coming back to the old proposition.

Why, say the gentlemen, surely it would be unconstitutional for Congress so to legislate. Agreed, agreed; I admit that it would be not only unconstitutional, but it would be criminal. But the question is, before what tribunal is the Congress to answer? Only before the tribunal of the people. Admit that they did it corruptly, admit that they did it upon bribe; and yet every man at all conversant with the Constitution of the country knows well that it is written in that instrument that members of Congress shall not be held to answer in any other place or before any body whatever for their official conduct in Congress assembled save to their respective Houses. That is the end of it. They answer to the people, and the people alone can apply the remedy, and of course ought to apply it. You cannot make them answer in the courts. You have had it

ruled that you cannot try them by impeachment, and of course when a majority vote that way in each House you can hardly expect to expel them. Their only responsibility is to the people, and the people alone have the right to challenge them. That is precisely what the people have written in the Constitution, and every man in this country so understands it.

Senators, I may make another remark which shows here the utter fallacy of any such position as that interposed by the counsel, and that is, that the Congress which would be so lost to all sense of justice and duty as to take away the pardoning power from the Executive in any case whatever have it in their power to take away any appeal to the courts of justice in the United States upon that question, so that there would be an end to it, and there would be no remedy but with the people, unless, indeed, the President is to take up arms to set aside the laws of the Congress of the United States. The Constitution of your country is no such weak or wicked invention.

Having disposed of this proposition, Senators, the next inquiry to be considered before the Senate, and to which I will direct their attention, is, has the President power under the Constitution to remove the heads of Departments and fill vacancies so created during the session of the Senate of the United States without its consent, and against the express authority of law? If he has not this power he is confessedly guilty as charged. If he has, of course he ought to go acquitted as charged in the first, second, and third articles.

Mr. CONNESS. I move that the Senate, sitting as a court, adjourn until to-morrow.

Mr. Manager BINGHAM. I shall be very glad, indeed, for that courtesy.

The motion was agreed to; and the Senate, sitting for the trial of the impeachment, adjourned.

TUESDAY, *May* 5, 1868.

The Chief Justice of the United States took the chair.

The usual proclamation having been made by the Sergeant-at-Arms,

The Managers of the impeachment on the part of the House of Representatives and Messrs. Evarts, Groesbeck, and Nelson, of counsel for the respondent, appeared and took the seats assigned to them respectively.

The members of the House of Representatives, as in Committee of the Whole, preceded by Mr. E. B. WASHBURNE, chairman of that committee, and accompanied by the Speaker and Clerk, appeared and were conducted to the seats provided for them.

The Journal of yesterday's proceedings of the Senate, sitting for the trial of the impeachment, was read.

The CHIEF JUSTICE. Mr. Manager BINGHAM will proceed with the argument in behalf of the House of Representatives.

Mr. Manager BINGHAM. Mr. President and Senators, I would do injustice, Senators, to myself; I would do injustice to the people whom I represent at this bar, if I were not to acknowledge, as I do now, my indebtedness to honorable Senators for the attention which they gave me yesterday while I attempted to demonstrate to the Senate in behalf of the people of the United States, that no man in office or out of office is above the Constitution or above the laws; that all are bound to obey the laws; that the President of the United States, above all other officials in this country, is bound to take care that the laws be faithfully executed; and especially that the suspending power and the dispensing power asserted by the President endangers the existence of the Constitution, is a violation of the rights of the people, and cannot for a moment be tolerated.

When I had the honor to close my remarks yesterday, I stated to the Senate that their inquiry would be directed first to the question whether the President has the power under the Constitution to remove the heads of Departments and fill vacancies so created by himself during the session of the Senate in the absence of an express authority of law authorizing him so to do. If the President has not this power, he is confessedly guilty, as charged in the first, second, third, eighth, and eleventh articles; unless, indeed, the Senate is to come to the conclusion that it is no crime in the President of the United States deliberately and purposely and defiantly to violate the express letter of the Constitution of the United States and the express prohibition of the statutes of the Congress. I have said that the act was criminal if it was done deliberately and purposely. What answer has been made to this, Senators? That the allegation is found in these articles of the criminal intent, and learned counsel have stood here before the Senate arguing from hour to hour and from day to day to show that a criminal intent is to be proved. I deny it. I deny that there is any authority which justifies any such statement. The law declares, and has declared for centuries, that any act done deliberately in violation of the law; that is to say, any unlawful act done by any person of sound mind and understanding, and responsible for his acts, necessarily implies that the party doing it intended the necessary consequences of his own act. I make no apology, Senators, for the insertion of the word "intent" in the articles. I do not treat it as surplusage. It was not needful; but I make no apology for it. It is found in every indictment; and who ever heard of a court where the rules are applied with more strictness than they can be expected to be applied by the Senate of the United States, demanding of the prosecutor, in any instance whatever, that he should offer testimony of the criminal intent specially averred in the indictment, when he had proved that the act was done and the act done was unlawful? It is a

rule, a rule not to be challenged here or elsewhere among intelligent men, that every person, whether in office or out of office, who commits an unlawful act made criminal by the very terms of the statute of the country within which he lives and to the jurisdiction of which he is subject intends all that is involved in the doing of the act, and the intent laid, therefore, is established. No proof is required. Why? To require it would simply defeat the ends of justice.

Who is able to penetrate the human intellect, to follow it to its secret and hidden recesses in the brain or heart of man, and bear witness of that which it meditates and which it purposes? Men, intelligent men, and especially the ministers of justice, judge of men's purposes by their acts, and necessarily hold that they intend exactly that which they do; and it is for them, not for their accusers, to show that they did it by misadventure, to show that they did it under a temporary delirium of the intellect by which in the providence of God they were for the time being deprived of the power of knowing their duty and of doing their duty under the law.

Senators, upon a memorable occasion not unlike this which to-day attracts the attention of the Senate, and attracts the attention of the people of the United States, and attracts the attention of the civilized world, the same question was raised before the tribunal of the people whether intent was to be established, and one of those men on that occasion, when Earl Strafford knelt before the assembled majesty of England, arose in his place and answered that question in words so clear and strong that they ought to satisfy the judgment and satisfy the conscience of every Senator. I read the words of Pym on the trial of Strafford, as to the intent:

"Another excuse is this, that whatsoever he hath spoken was out of good intention. Sometimes, my lords, good and evil, truth and falsehood lie so near together that they are hardly to be distinguished. Matters hurtful and dangerous may be accompanied with such circumstances as may make them appear useful and convenient; and, in all such cases, good intention will justify evil counsel; but where the matters propounded are evil in their own nature, such as the matters are wherewith the Earl of Strafford is charged—as to break a public faith, and to subvert laws and government—they can never be justified by any intentions, how good soever they be pretended."

Is there no endeavor here "to break public faith?" Is there no endeavor here "to subvert laws and Government?" I leave Senators to answer that question upon their own conscience and upon their oaths.

On this subject of intent I might illustrate the utter futility of the position assumed here by the learned counsel, by a reference to a memorable instance in history when certain fanatics, under the reign of Frederick II, put little children to death with the intent of sending them to heaven, because the Master had written, "Of such is the Kingdom." It does not appear that this good intent of slaying the innocents, with their sunny faces and sunny hearts, that they might send them at once to heaven, was of any avail in the courts of justice.

I read also of a Swedish minister who found within the kingdom certain subjects who were the beneficiaries of a charity, upon whose heads Time, with its frosty fingers, had scattered the snows of five and seventy winters, whom he put brutally and cruelly to death, with the good intent of thereby increasing the trust in the interest of the living who had a longer measure of days before them. I never read, Senators, that any such plea as that availed in the courts of justice against the charge of murder with malice aforethought.

I dismiss this subject. It is a puerile conceit, unfit to be uttered in the hearing of Senators, and condemned by every letter and line and word of the common law, "the growth of centuries and the gathered wisdom of a thousand years."

It is suggested by one of my honorable colleagues, [Mr. WILLIAMS,] and it is not unfit that I should notice it in passing, that doubtless Booth, on the 14th day of April, 1865, when he sent the pure spirit of your martyred President back to the God who gave it, thought, declared, if you please—"declared" is the proper word—declared that he did that act in the service of his country, in the service of liberty, in the service of law, in the service of the rights of a common humanity. If the avenging hand of justice had not cut him off upon the spot where he stood, instantly, as though overtaken by the direct judgment of offended Heaven, I suppose we should have had this sort of argument interposed in his behalf that his intentions were good, and therefore the violated law itself ought to justify his act and allow him to go acquit, not a condemned criminal, but a crowned and honored man.

I really feel, Senators, that I ought to ask your pardon for having dwelt upon this proposition; but you know with what pertinacity it has been pressed upon the consideration of Senators, and, with all respect to the learned and accomplished gentlemen who made it, I deem it due to myself to say here that I think it was unworthy of them and unworthy of the place.

I return, Senators, to my proposition: has the President the power under the Constitution and the laws during the session of the Senate to create vacancies in the heads of Departments under your Constitution, and fill them without the authority of express law and without the advice or consent of the Senate? If he has not, he has violated the Constitution, and he has violated, as I shall show hereafter, the express law of the land, and is therefore criminal—criminal in his conduct and in his intention before the tribunal where he stands arraigned by order of the people.

First, then, is the Constitution violated by this act of removal and appointment? And here, Senators, although I may have occasion to notice it hereafter more specifically and especially, I ask you to pardon me for referring to it here at this time, it cannot have escaped your notice that the learned and astute counsel for the President took care all the while from the beginning to the end of this controversy not to connect the two powers of removal and appointment during the session of the Senate in their presence and without their consent together.

Every line and word of the voluminous arguments uttered by the very learned and ingenious counsel of the President bears witness to the truth of that which I now assert. Why was this? Simply, Senators, as I shall presently show you, that the appointing power is by the express terms of the Constitution, during the session of the Senate, put beyond the power of the President, save and except where it is expressly authorized by law. I thank the gentlemen for making this concession, for it is a confession of guilt on the part of their client. When no answer could be made they acted upon the ancient, time-honored, and accepted maxim that silence is gold, and so upon that point they were silent one and all without exception. There was an appointment made here in direct violation of express law; in direct violation of the express letter of the Constitution; in direct violation of every interpretation that has ever been put upon it by any commanding intellect in this country, and the gentlemen knew it.

It is in vain, Senators, that they undertake to meet that point in this case by any reference to the speech of my learned and accomplished friend who represents the State of Ohio upon the floor of the Senate, [Mr. SHERMAN.] Not a word escaped his lips in the speech which they have quoted here touching this power of appointment during the session of the Senate and in direct violation of the express letter of the tenure-of-office act, nor did any such word escape him from the lips of any Senator. I am not surprised; it does credit to the intellectual ability of the learned gentlemen who appear for the President that they kept that question.out of sight in their elaborate and exhaustive arguments. I read for the Senators the provision of the Constitution upon this subject which I read yesterday:

"The President" * * * * "shall nominate,.and by and with the advice and consent of the Senate shall appoint, embassadors, other public ministers and consuls, judges of the Supreme Court, and all other officers of the United States whose appointments are not herein otherwise provided for, and which shall be established by law, but the Congress may by law vest the appointment of such inferior officers as they think proper in the President alone, in the courts of law, or in the heads of Departments."

Can any one doubt that this provision clearly restricts the power of the President over the appointment of heads of Departments in this, that it expressly requires that all appointments not otherwise provided for in this Constitution, enumerating embassadors and others, shall be by and with the advice and consent of the Senate? It is useless to waste words upon the proposition. It is plain and clear. It must be so unless the appointments of the heads of Departments, in the words of the Constitution, are otherwise provided for; and I respectfully ask Senators wherein are they otherwise provided for in the Constitution? The heads of Departments are named by that title, and by the very terms of the Constitution it is provided that the Congress may by law vest in the heads of Departments the power to appoint without the consent of the President, without the consent of anybody but the authority of a law of Congress, all inferior officers. Is any man, in the light of this provision, to stand before the Senate and argue that heads of Departments are inferior officers? If, then, their appointment is not otherwise provided for in the Constitution, which I take for granted, I ask the Senate whether their appointment is otherwise provided for by law, whether it was ever otherwise provided for by law?

I am not unmindful of the fact, in passing, that some of the learned counsel for the President said "here was no appointment; this was only an authority to fill a vacancy." The counsel are not strong enough for their client. They cannot get rid of his answer. He declares that he did make an appointment indefinitely, made a removal and filled it, and followed it with another. The words "appointment *ad interim*" more than once unwittingly escaped the lips of the counsel. But I do not propose to rest this case upon any quibbles, upon any technicalities, upon any controversy about words. I rest it upon the broad spirit of the Constitution, and stand here this day to deny that there ever was an hour since the Constitution went into operation that the President of the United States had authority to authorize anybody, temporarily even, to exercise the functions of a head of a Department of this Government save by the authority of express law. It is surely a self-evident proposition that must be understood by Senators that the power which created the law may repeal it.

I make this remark here and now because the President's defense, as stated in his answer more clearly and distinctly than in any of the arguments of the learned counsel, is that he asserts and exercises this power by virtue of the implied, unwritten executive prerogative judicially to interpret the Constitution for himself and judicially to determine the validity of all the laws of the land for himself, and therefore to appoint just such ministers as he pleases, at such times as he pleases, and for such periods as he pleases, in defiance alike of the Constitution and of the laws. The language is that the removal was indefinite. The language of his answer is that he indefinitely vacated the office, and filled it, of course, indefinitely, and that is his defense. There is no getting away from it.

In the answer, on pages 25 and 26 of the record, this will be found recorded in it:

"And this respondent, further answering, says, that it is provided in and by the second section of an act to regulate the tenure of certain civil offices, that the President may suspend an officer from the performance of the duties of the office held by him, for certain causes therein designated, until the next meeting of the Senate, and until the case shall be acted on by the Senate; that this respondent, as President of the United States, was advised, and he verily believed and still believes, that the executive power of removal from office confided to him by the Constitution, as aforesaid, includes the power of suspension from office at the pleasure of the President, and this respondent, by the order aforesaid, did suspend the said Stanton from office, not until the next meeting of the Senate, or until the Senate should have acted upon the case, but by force of the power and authority vested in him by the Constitution and laws of the United States, indefinitely and at the pleasure of the President."

That is his answer. Under the Constitution he claims this power. On that subject, Senators, I beg leave to say, in addition to what I have already uttered, that it was perfectly well understood when the Constitution was on trial for its deliverance before the American people that no such power as this was lodged in the President of the United States; on the contrary, that for every abuse of power, for every usurpation of authority, for every violation of the Constitution and the laws, he was liable at all times to that unrestricted power of the people to impeach him through its Representatives and to try him before its Senate without let or hinderance from any tribunal in the land. I refer upon this point to the clear utterance of Hamilton as recorded in the seventy-seventh number of the Federalist:

"It has been mentioned as one of the advantages to be expected from the coöperation of the Senate, in the business of appointments, that it would contribute to the stability of the Administration. *The consent of that body would be necessary to displace as well as to appoint.* A change of the Chief Magistrate, therefore, would not occasion so violent or so general a revolution in the officers of the Government as might be expected if he were the sole disposer of offices. Where a man in any station had given satisfactory evidence of his fitness for it, a new President would be restrained from attempting a change in favor of a person more agreeable to him, by the apprehension that a discountenance of the Senate might frustrate the attempt, and bring some degree of discredit upon himself. Those who can best estimate the value of a steady administration will be most disposed to prize a provision which connects the official existence of public men with the approbation or disapprobation of that body, which, from the greater permanency of its own composition, will in all probability be less subject to inconstancy than any other member of the Government."

"To this union of the Senate with the President, in the article of appointments, it has in some cases been objected that it would serve to give the President an undue influence over the Senate; and in others that it would have an opposite tendency; a strong proof that neither suggestion is true.

"To state the first, in its proper form, is to refute it. It amounts to this: the President would have an improper influence over the Senate, because the Senate would have the power of restraining him. This is an absurdity in terms."

And I agree with Hamilton that it is an absurdity in terms after what has been written in the Constitution of your country, for any man, whatever may be his attainments, and whatever may be his pretensions, to say that the President has the power, in the language of his answer, of indefinitely vacating all the executive offices of this country, and indefinitely, therefore, filling them without the advice and consent of the Senate in the absence of an express law authorizing him so to do. And here I leave that point for the consideration of the Senate and for the consideration of that great people whom the Senate represent upon this trial.

I ask, also, the judgment of the Senate upon the weighty words of Webster, whom the gentleman [Mr. Evarts] concedes is entitled to some consideration in this body, who illustrated for long years American institutions by his wisdom, his genius, and his learning; a man who, when living, stood alone among living men by reason of his intellectual stature; a man who, when dead, sleeps alone in his tomb by the sounding sea, meet emblem of the majesty and sweep of his matchless intellect. I ask, Senators, attention to the words of Mr. Webster on this appointing power conferred upon the President under the Constitution, subject to these limitations, by and with the advice and consent of the Senate:

"The appointing power is vested in the President and Senate: this is the general rule of the Constitution. The removing power is part of the appointing power; it cannot be separated from the rest but by supposing that an exception was intended; but all exceptions to general rules are to be taken strictly, even when expressed; and, for a much stronger reason, they are not to be implied, when not expressed, unless inevitable necessity of construction requires it."—4 *Webster's Works*, p. 194.

What answer, I pray you, Senators, has been given, what answer can be given to these interpretations of your Constitution by Hamilton and Webster? None, except to refer to the acts of 1789 and 1795, and the opinions expressed in the debates of the First Congress. Neither those acts nor the debates justify the conclusion that the President during the session of the Senate may vacate and fill the Executive Departments of this Government at his pleasure, and without the advice and consent of the Senate, in the absence of any express authority of law and in direct violation of the prohibitions of the law. The acts themselves will bear no such interpretation. I dismiss, with a single word, all reference to the debate on the occasion, for the Senate are not unadvised that there were differences of opinion expressed in that debate, nor is the Senate unadvised that it has already been ruled from the Supreme Bench of the United States that the opinions expressed by Representatives or Senators in Congress pending the discussion of any bill are not to be received as any authoritative construction or interpretation whatever to be given to the act. It would be a sad day for the American people if the time should ever come when the utterances of excited debate are to be received ever afterward as the true construction and interpretation of law. Senators, look to the acts,

and see whether the gentlemen are justified in attempting to infer either from the legislation of 1789 or from the legislation of 1795 or from any other legislation which at any time existed on the statute-books of this country, this executive prerogative, in direct violation of the express letter of the Constitution, to vacate all the executive offices of this Government at his pleasure, and fill them during the session of the Senate, and thereby control the patronage of the Government, amounting to millions upon millions, at his pleasure, and put it into the hands of irresponsible agents to become only the supple tools of his mad ambition.

Of this act of 1789 Mr. Webster well said—and I am not here even to dispute the proposition; indeed, I would hesitate long before I ventured to dispute any proposition which he accepted for the time being as possible under the Constitution—that he did not condemn the legislation of 1789 as being unconstitutional, but he did condemn it as being highly impolitic, and which had subjected the people of this country to great abuses. He did say, however—and to these words I ask, also, the attention of the Senate—of the legislation of 1789, "that it did separate the power of removal from the power of appointment." It did separate it, subject to its own limitations. It did separate it, and confer it, too, by authority of that act and by no other authority. It is for this purpose, and for this purpose alone, that I cited Mr. Webster in this part of the argument. "It was a grant of power to the President," conferred upon him by the Congress to remove executive officers. I admit, Senators, that during the recess of the Senate such a statute ought to be always upon your statute-book so long as you have a President who can be trusted. A man who is betraying his trusts ought to be suspended from his office, which is a temporary removal, for reasons appearing to the President which justify it; and that is precisely your law to-day. It is within the power of the Congress undoubtedly to confer it upon the President. That is your law to-day.

What one of the counsel now, I ask the Senate to consider, ventured to say here—if it was uttered it certainly escaped my observation—that the President of the United States at any time had power during the session of the Senate to vacate the offices of the heads of the Departments in this country even under the acts of 1789 and fill them indefinitely at his pleasure? What practice in the Government was cited here to support any such pretension of power in the Executive? None whatever. To be sure, reference was made to the case of Pickering; but the gentlemen ought to remember that when reference was made to it, so far as the removal was concerned, it was expressly authorized by the act of 1789; I care not how informally; the words are in that act "unless removed by the President;" it is a grant of power, and Webster so interprets it on page 194 of the fourth volume of his works as an act of Congress which separated the power of removal from the power of appointment. His construction was right. Upon that construction I stand in this argument. But it does not follow by any manner of means because this power was exercised by the elder Adams that he thereby furnished a precedent in justification of the violation of another and a different statute, which by every intendment repealed the act of 1789 and stripped the President of any colorable excuse for asserting any such authority.

That is my first answer to this point made by the counsel, and I make a still further answer to it; and that is this, that the elder Adams himself, as his letter to his Secretary of State clearly discloses, did not consider that it was proper even under the law of 1789 for him to make that removal during the session of the Senate, and therefore these significant words are incorporated in his letter of request to Secretary Pickering that he should resign before the session of the Senate, the resignation, of course, to take effect at a future day, so that upon the incoming of the Senate he might name a successor, showing exactly how he understood the obligations of the Constitution.

Although the record, so far as I have been able to trace it, is somewhat imperfect, I think it but justice to the memory of that distinguished patriot to declare that the whole transaction justifies me in saying here, as my belief, in the presence of the Senate, that he did not issue the order for the removal of Pickering after the Senate had commenced its session. It is true that he issued it on the same day, but he did not issue it after the Senate had commenced its session; he issued it before; and upon the assembling of the Senate and the opening of the Senate on the same day, showing his respect for the Constitution and the laws and the obligation of his oath, he sent to that Senate the name of the successor of Pickering, John Marshall, and on the next day, Tuesday, John Marshall, as Secretary of State, was confirmed to succeed Timothy Pickering, removed by and with the advice and consent of the Senate. Nor does it appear that John Marshall exercised the functions of his office, or attempted to exercise the functions of office, until the Senate had passed upon the question of his appointment, and therefore necessarily passed upon the question of the removal of Pickering. All these facts arise in this case in the removal of Pickering to disprove everything that has been said here by way of apology or justification or even of excuse of the action of the President of the United States in violating the Constitution and the existing laws of the country.

But the other provision of the Constitution, Senators, which I recited yesterday in your hearing, pours a flood of light upon this question as to the power of the President to vacate the executive offices and fill them at his pleasure, and dispels the mists with which counsel have attempted to envelop it, and that is the provision that the President shall have power to fill up all vacancies which may happen during the recess of the Senate and to issue commissions to his appointees to fill such vacancies, which commissions shall expire at the end of the next session of the Senate. I ask Senators what possible sense is there in this express provision of the Constitution that the President shall have power to fill up all vacancies which may happen during the recess of the Senate, his commissions to expire at the end of their next session; if after all, as is claimed in his answer and is asserted by his unlawful acts under the laws of the United States, he is invested by the Constitution with the power to make vacancies at his pleasure even during the session of the Senate? I ask Senators, further, to answer what sense is there in the provision that the commission which he may issue to fill a vacancy happening during the recess of the Senate shall expire at the end of their next session, if after all, notwithstanding this limitation of the Constitution, the President may, during the session, create vacancies and fill them, in the words of his answer, indefinitely? If he has any such power as that, I may be allowed to say here, in the words of John Marshall, your Constitution at last is but a splendid bauble; it is not worth the paper upon which it is written. It is a matter of mathematical demonstration upon the text of this instrument, by necessary implication, that the President's power to fill vacancies is limited to vacancies that arise during the recess of the Senate, save where it is otherwise provided for by express provision of law.

That is my answer to all that has been said here by the gentlemen upon this subject. They have brought a long list of appointments and a long list of removals from the foundation of the Government to this hour, which is answered by a single word, that there was existing law authorizing it all, and that law no longer exists. Not a line or word or tittle of it exists since the 2d day of March, 1867; assuming in what I say now, of course, that the tenure-of-office act is constitutional and valid, I refer to those statutes; I shall not exhaust my strength or the patience of the Senate by stopping to read them here and now, but I shall refer to them in the report of my argument. Those statutes are as follows:

"Act to provide for government of territory north-west of river Ohio. Approved August 7, 1789.

"Be it enacted, &c., That in all cases in which by the said ordinance (for government of territory northwest of river Ohio) any information is to be given or communication made by the Governor of the said Territory to the United States in Congress assembled, or to any of their officers, it shall be the duty of the said Governor to give such information and to make such communication to the President of the United States; and the President shall nominate, and by and with the advice and consent of the Senate shall appoint, all officers who, by the said ordinance, were to have been appointed by the United States in Congress assembled, and all officers so appointed shall be commissioned by him; and in all cases where the United States in Congress assembled might by the said ordinance revoke any commission or remove from any office, the President is hereby declared to have the same powers of revocation and removal."—1 *Statutes*, p. 50, sec. 1.

"Act to amend the act entitled 'An act making alterations in the Treasury and War Departments.' Approved February 13, 1795.

"In case of vacancy in the office of Secretary of State, Secretary of the Treasury, or of the Secretary of the Department of War, or of any officer of either of the said Departments whose appointment is not in the head thereof, whereby they cannot perform the duties of their said respective offices, it shall be lawful for the President of the United States, in case he shall think it necessary, to authorize any person or persons, at his discretion, to perform the duties of the said respective offices until a successor be appointed or such vacancy be filled: *Provided*, That no one vacancy shall be supplied in manner aforesaid for a longer term than six months."—1 *Statutes*, 415; 1 *Brightly's Digest*, 225.

"An act to limit the term of office of certain officers therein named, and for other purposes. Approved May 15, 1820.

"From and after the passage of this act, all district attorneys, collectors of the customs, naval officers and surveyors of the customs, navy agents, receivers of public moneys for lands, registers of the land offices, paymasters in the Army, the apothecary general, the assistant apothecary general, and the commissary general of purchases, to be appointed under the laws of the United States, shall be appointed for the term of four years, but shall be removable from office at pleasure."—3 *Statutes*, 582.

"An act to regulate the diplomatic and consular systems of the United States. Approved August 18, 1856.

Section one regulates the appointment and compensation of consuls.

"It belongs exclusively to the President, by and with the advice and consent of the Senate, to appoint consular officers at such places as he or they deem to be meet. They are officers created by the Constitution and the laws of nations and by acts of Congress."—11 *Statutes*, 52, section 3; 1 *Brightly*, 174, Note a; (and see also the provision touching appointments.)

If this provision of the Constitution, then, means what it expressly declares, that the President's power of appointment in the absence of express law is limited to such vacancies as may happen during the recess of the Senate, it necessarily results that an appointment made during the session of the Senate, without the advice and consent of the Senate, of the head of a Department, in the absence of any law authorizing it to be made temporarily or otherwise, as did the act of 1795, is unconstitutional and unlawful; and that is my answer to all they have said on that subject. But that act of 1795 is repealed by your statute of 1867, as also by your act of 1863, as I shall claim. If the President may issue it, it must be a commission according to his own claim of authority, arising under this unlimited executive prerogative, which can never expire but by and with his consent; and if any man can answer the proposition I should like to have it answered now. If, notwithstanding all that is on your statute-books; if, notwithstanding this limitation of your Constitution which I have read, that his commissions to fill vacan-

cies arising during the recess shall expire with the next session of the Senate, he may nevertheless create the vacancies during the session and fill them without your advice and consent, I reassert my proposition that such commission cannot expire, if his assertion be true, without the consent of the Executive; and if that proposition can be answered by any man, I desire it to be answered now. I want to know by what provision of the Constitution the commission expires upon the claim of this answer; and if it does not expire without the consent of the Executive, I want to know what becomes of the appointing power lodged jointly in the Senate with the Executive for the protection of the people's rights and the protection of the people's interests. It cannot be answered here or anywhere by a retained advocate of the President or by a volunteer advocate of the President, in the Senate or out of the Senate.

I demand to know, again, what provision of the Constitution, under the claim set up in this answer, terminates the commission. I took occasion to read from the answer that I might not be misunderstood. He puts it directly upon the Constitution. Nobody is to be held responsible for it; and I am glad it is so, either by intendment or otherwise—nobody is to be held responsible for this assumption but this guilty and accused President. It was an audacity the like of which has no parallel in centuries for him to come before the custodians of the people's power and thus defy even their written Constitution, its plainest text, and its plainest letter.

Senators, I have thought upon this subject carefully, considerately, conscientiously. I have endeavored to find anywhere within the text of the Constitution any colorable excuse for this claim of power asserted by the President and dangerous to the liberties of the people, and I can find, from beginning to end of that great instrument, no letter or word upon which even the astutest casuist could for a moment fasten, save the words that "the executive power shall be vested in a President."

That gives no colorable excuse for this assumption. What writer upon your Constitution, what decision of your courts, what utterances of all the great statesmen who have in the past illustrated our history, have ever intimated that this provision of the Constitution was a grant of power? It is nothing more, Senators, and no man and no human ingenuity can torture this provision of the Constitution into anything more than a mere designation of the officer or person to whom shall be committed, under the Constitution and subject to its limitations and subject to the further limitations of the law enacted in pursuance of the Constitution, the executive power of the Government. Adopt the construction that it is a grant of power, and why not follow it to its conclusions and see what comes of your Constitution, and what comes of the rights of the

811

people, of their power to limit by a written Constitution every department of the Government? Is it not as plainly written in the Constitution that "all legislative powers herein granted shall be vested in a Congress of the United States, which shall consist of a Senate and House of Representatives?" Is anybody to reason from that designation of the body to whom the legislative power is assigned a grant of power, and especially an indefinite authority. to legislate upon such subjects as they please without regard to the Constitution? Is it not also just as plainly written in the Constitution that "the judicial power of the United States shall be vested in one Supreme Court and in such inferior courts as the Congress may, from time to time, ordain and establish" by law? Is anybody thence to infer that this is an indefinite grant of power authorizing the Supreme Court or the inferior courts of the United States to sit in judgment upon any and all conceivable questions, and even to reverse by their decisions the power of impeachment lodged exclusively in the House of Representatives and the judgment in impeachment authorized to be pronounced exclusively and only by the Senate of the United States?

It will never do for any man to say that this provision of the Constitution is a grant of power. It is simply the designation of the officer to whom the executive power of the Government shall be committed under the limitations of the Constitution and the laws, as "the Congress" is the designation of the department to which shall be committed the legislative power, and as "the courts" is the designation of the department to which shall be committed the judicial power; and upon this subject I refer, also, to what Mr. Webster said touching the limitations of the executive authority:

"It is perfectly plain and manifest, that, although the framers of the Constitution meant to confer executive power on the President, yet they meant to define and limit that power, and to confer no more than they did thus define and limit. When they say it shall be vested in a President, they mean that one magistrate, to be called a President, shall hold the executive authority; but they mean, further, that he shall hold this authority according to the grants and limitations of the Constitution itself."—4 Webster's Works, p. 186.

Does not the Constitution, Senators, define and limit the executive power in this, that it declares that the President shall have power to grant reprieves and pardons, &c. ; in this, that it declares that the President shall have power to appoint by and with the advice and consent of the Senate foreign embassadors and other public officers; in this, that it provides that he shall have power to make treaties by and with the advice and consent of the Senate? And does it not limit his power in this, that it declares that all legislative power shall be vested in a Congress which shall consist of a Senate and House of Representatives; in this, that it declares that the President shall take care that the laws which the Congress enacts shall be faithfully executed; in this, that it declares that every bill which shall have passed the Congress of the United States with or without his consent shall be a law, to remain a law—and that is the very point in controversy here between the President and the people—to be executed as a law until the same shall have been repealed by the power that made it or actually reversed by the Supreme Court of the United States in a case clearly within its jurisdiction and within the limitations of the Constitution itself?

It has been settled law in this country from a very early period that the constitutionality of a law should not be questioned much less adjudged against the validity of the law. by a court clothed by the Constitution with jurisdiction in the premises, unless upon a case so clear as to scarcely admit of a doubt; and what is the result, Senators? That there is not—I feel myself justified in saying it, without recently having very carefully examined the question—one clear, unequivocal decision of the Supreme Court of the United States against the constitutionality of any law whatever enacted by the Congress of the United States—not one. There was no such decision as that in the Dred Scott case. Lawyers will understand, when I use the word "decision," what I mean—the judgment pronounced by the court upon the issue joined upon the record. There was no such decision in that case; nor in any other case, so far as I can recollect. On this subject, however, I may be excused for reading a decision or two from our courts. In the case of Fletcher vs. Peck, 6 Cranch, page 87, Marshall, delivering the opinion, said:

"The question whether a law be void for its repugnancy to the Constitution is, at all times, a question of much delicacy, which ought seldom, if ever, to be decided in the affirmative in a doubtful case."

And again:

"The opposition between the Constitution and the law should be such that the judge feels a clear and strong conviction of their incompatibility with each other."

In ex parte McCollum, 1 Cowen's Reports, 564, Chief Justice Savage says:

"Before the court will deem it their duty to declare an act of the Legislature unconstitutional a case must be presented in which there can be no rational doubt."

In Morris vs. The People, 3 Denio, 381, the court say:

"The presumption is always in favor of the validity of the law, if the contrary is not clearly demonstrated."

I have read these, Senators, not that it was really necessary to my argument, but to answer the pretension of this President that he may come here to set aside a law, and in order to justify himself assume the prerogative to do it in order that he may test its validity in the courts of justice when the courts have never ventured upon that dangerous experiment themselves, and, on the contrary, have thirty years ago, as I showed to the Senate yesterday, solemnly ruled, without a dissenting voice, that the assumption of power claimed by the President would defeat justice itself and annihilate the laws of the people. I have done it also to fortify the text of your Constitution and to make plain its significance, which declares that every bill which shall have passed the Congress with or without the President's approval, even over his veto, shall be a law. The language is plain and simple. It is a law until it is annulled; in the words of Hamilton, as recorded in the seventh volume of his works, a law to the President; a law to every department of the Government, legislative, executive, and judicial; a law to all the people.

It is in vain the gentlemen say that it is only constitutional laws that bind. That is simply begging the question. The presumption, as I have shown you from the authorities, is that every law is constitutional until by authority it is declared otherwise, and the question here is whether that authority is in Andrew Johnson. That is the whole question, whether that authority is in Andrew Johnson. Your Constitution says it shall be a law. It does not mean that it shall remain a law after it shall have been reconsidered by the law-making power and repealed; it does not say that it shall remain a law to the hurt and deprivation of private right after it shall have been adjudged unconstitutional in the Supreme Court of the United States under the limitations of the Constitution and within their express jurisdiction; but it does mean that until judgment be pronounced authoritatively in your tribunals of justice, or that power be exercised authoritatively by the people's Representatives in Congress assembled, it shall be a law to the President, to every head of Department, as the court ruled in the case from which I read yesterday in 12 Peters, to every Representative in Congress, to every Senator, and every human being within the jurisdiction of your laws.

Why do the gentlemen make this distinction at all that it is only laws passed in pursuance of the Constitution that are to bind? Why not follow their premises to their logical conclusions that the President of the United States, as I took occasion to say yesterday, is by virtue of the prerogatives of his office vested with the power judicially to interpret the Constitution for himself and judicially to decide for the time being for himself the validity of every law, and therefore may, with impunity, set aside every law upon your statute-book, in the words of his advocate, for the reason that he has come to the deliberate conclusion that it interferes with some power vested in him by the people?

Senators, considering the operations of the President's mind as manifested in his past official conduct, God only knows to what absurd conclusions he might arrive hereafter, if by your judgment you recognize this unlimited prerogative in him, when he comes to sit in judicial judgment upon all the laws upon the statute-book. He might come to the conclusion that they all interfered with and cut off some power confided to him by the Constitution!

The position conflicts with every principle of law and every principle of common sense. If this discretionary power is in the President no man can lay his hand upon him. That was exactly the ruling of his Honor the Chief Justice, in the Mississippi case, touching the exercise of certain discretionary power vested in the President by the reconstruction act. His judgment concludes everybody; the courts cannot review his decisions, and unless you charge him with corruption there is an end of all inquiry. It was settled more than fifty years ago in the case to which I referred yesterday from memory, reported in 12 Wheaton, and has never been challenged from that day to this. I deny any such discretion in the Executive, because it is a discretion incompatible with the public liberties, because it is a discretion in direct conflict with the express letter of the Constitution, because it is a discretion which vests him with more than kingly prerogative, because it is a discretion which puts the servant above his master, because it is a discretion which clothes the creature with power superior to the power of its creator.

The American people will tolerate no such discretion in the Executive, by whomsoever sanctioned or by whomsoever advocated. When that day comes that the American people will tamely submit to this assumption of authority that their President is above their Constitution and above their laws, and may defy either or both at his pleasure with impunity, they will have proved themselves unfit custodians of the great trust which has been committed to their care in the interests of their children and in the interests of the millions that are to come after them. I have no fear of the results with the people. Their instincts are all right. They understand perfectly well that the President is but their servant to obey their laws in common with themselves, and to execute their laws in mode and manner as the laws themselves prescribe; and not to sit in judgment day by day upon their authority to legislate for themselves and to govern themselves by laws duly enacted through their Representatives in Congress assembled.

And this brings me, Senators, to the point made by the learned gentleman from New York when he talked of that coming struggle in which the President and his friends, headed doubtless by the learned gentleman himself, would march under the banner of the "supremacy of the Constitution" against the "omnipotence of Congress." I have uttered no word, nor have my associates uttered any word, that justified any suggestion about the omnipotence of Congress. I can understand very well something about the omnipotence of a Parliament under the protection of a corrupt hereditary monarch, of whom it may be said, and is said by his retainers, "He rules by the grace of God and of divine right;" but I cannot understand, nor can plain people anywhere understand, what significance is to be attached to this expression, "the omnipotence of Congress"—a Congress the popular branch of which is chosen every second year by the suffrages of freemen. I intend to utter no word, as I have uttered no word from the beginning of this contest to this hour; which will justify any man in intimating that I claim for the Congress of the United States any omnipotence. I claim for it simply the power to do the people's will as required by the people in their written Constitution and enjoined by their oaths.

It does not result, because we deny the power of the Executive to sit in judicial judgment upon the legislation of Congress, that unconstitutional enactments, abuses of power, usurpations of authority, and corrupt practices on the part of a Congress, are without remedy. The first remedy under your Constitution is in the courts of the United States, in the mode and manner prescribed by your Constitution; and the last great remedy under your Constitution is with the people that ordain constitutions, that appoint Senators, that elect Houses of Representatives, that establish courts of justice, and abolish them at their pleasure.

The gentleman can alarm nobody by talking about an omnipotent Congress. If the Congress abuse its trust let it be held to answer for that abuse; but let the Congress answer somewhere else than to the President of the United States. Your Constitution has declared that they shall answer to no man for their legislation or for their words uttered in debate, save to the respective Houses to which they belong, and to that great people who appoint them.

That is my answer to the gentleman's clamor about an omnipotent Congress. Among the American people there is nothing omnipotent and nothing eternal but God, and no law save His and the laws of their own creation, subject to the requirements of those laws to which the gentleman so eloquently referred the other day, which he wrote upon the stone table amid the earthquake and the darkness of the mountain, and a part of which, I deeply regret to say, the gentleman, in his eloquent discourse, both forgot and broke. We are the keepers of our own conscience. It was well enough for the gentleman to remind the Senators of the obligations of their oath. It was well enough for the gentleman to suggest to them, so elegantly as he did, the significance of those great words, "justice, law, oath, duty." It was well enough for him to repeat in the hearing of the Senate and in the hearing of this listening audience those grand words of the common Father of us all, "Thou shalt not take the name of the Lord thy God in vain." But it was not well for the gentleman, in the heat and fire of his argument, to pronounce judgment upon the Senate, to pronounce judg-

ment upon the House of Representatives, and to say, as he did say, that, unmindful of the obligations of our oaths, regardless of the requirements of the Constitution, forgetful of God and forgetful of the rights of our fellowmen, in the spirit of hate, we had preferred these articles of impeachment.

It was not well for the gentleman, either, to intimate that the Senate of the United States had exercised a power that did not belong to them, when, in response to the message of the President of the United States of the 21st of February, 1868, they had resolved that the act done by the President and communicated to the Senate, to wit, the removal of the head of a Department and the appointment of a successor thereto without the advice and consent of the Senate, was not authorized by the Constitution and laws. It was the duty of the Senate, if they had any opinion upon the subject, to express it; and it is not for the President of the United States, either in his own person or in the person of his counsel, to challenge the Senate as disqualified to sit in judgment under the Constitution as his triers upon articles of impeachment, because, in the discharge of another duty, they had pronounced against him. They pronounced aright. The people of the United States will sanction their judgment whatever the Senate may think of it themselves.

Senators, that all that I have said in this general way of the power assumed and exercised by the President and attempted to be justified here is directly involved in this issue, and underlies this whole question between the people and this guilty President, no man can gainsay.

1. He stands charged with a misdemeanor in office in that he issued an order in writing for the removal of the Secretary of War during the session of the Senate, without its advice and consent, in direct violation of express law, and with intent to violate the law.

2. He stands charged, during the session of the Senate, without its advice or consent, in direct violation of the express letter of the Constitution and of the act of March 2, 1867, with issuing a letter of authority to one Lorenzo Thomas, authorizing him and commanding him to assume and exercise the functions of Secretary for the Department of War.

3. He stands charged with an unlawful conspiracy to hinder the Secretary of War from holding the office, in violation of the law, in violation of the Constitution, in violation of his own oath, and with the further conspiracy to prevent the execution of the tenure-of-office act, in direct violation of his oath as well as in direct violation of the express provisions of your statute; and to prevent, also, the Secretary of War from holding the office of Secretary for the Department of War; and with the further conspiracy, by force, threat, or intimidation, to possess the property of the United States and unlawfully control the same contrary to the act of July 20, 1861.

814

He stands charged further with an unlawful attempt to influence Major General Emory to disregard the requirements of the act making appropriations for the support of the Army, passed March 2, 1867, and which expressly provides that a violation of its provisions shall be a high crime and misdemeanor in office.

He stands further charged with a high misdemeanor in this, that on the 18th day of August, 1866, by public speech he attempted to excite resistance to the Thirty-Ninth Congress and to the laws of its enactment.

He stands further charged with a high misdemeanor in this, that he did affirm that the Thirty-Ninth Congress was not a Congress of the United States, thereby denying and intending to deny the validity of its legislation except in so far as he saw fit to approve it, and denying its power to propose an amendment to the Constitution of the United States; with devising and contriving means by which he should prevent the Secretary of War, as required by the act of the 2d of March, 1867, from resuming forthwith the functions of his office, after having suspended him and after the refusal of the Senate to concur in the suspension; and with further devising and contriving to prevent the execution of an act making appropriations for the support of the Army, passed March 2, 1867, and further to prevent the execution of the act to provide for the more efficient government of the rebel States.

That these several acts so charged are impeachable has been shown. To deny that they are impeachable is, as I have said, to place the President above the Constitution and the laws, to change the servant of the people into their master, the executor of their laws into the violator of their laws. The Constitution has otherwise provided, and so it has been otherwise interpreted by one of the first writers upon the law in America; I refer to the text of Chancellor Kent, which the gentlemen were careful not to read:

"In addition to all the precautions which have been mentioned to prevent abuse of the executive trust in the mode of the President's appointment, his term of office and the precise and definite limitations imposed upon the exercise of his power, the Constitution has also rendered him directly amenable by law for maladministration. The inviolability of any officer of Government is incompatible with the republican theory, as well as with the principles of retributive justice. The President, Vice President, and all civil officers of the United States may be impeached by the House of Representatives for treason, bribery, and other high crimes and misdemeanors, and upon conviction by the Senate removed from office. If, then, neither the sense of duty, the force of public opinion, nor the transitory nature of the seat are sufficient to secure a faithful discharge of the executive trust, but the President will use the authority of his station to violate the Constitution or law of the land, the House of Representatives can arrest him in his career by resorting to the power of impeachment.—1 Kent's Commentaries, p. 289.

And what answer is made when we come to your bar to impeach them; when we show him guilty of maladministration as no man ever was before in this country; when we show that he has violated your Constitution; when we show that he has violated your laws; when we show that he has defied the power of the Senate even after they had admonished him of the danger that was impending over him? The answer is, that he is vested with an unlimited prerogative to decide all these questions for himself, and to suspend even your power of impeachment in the courts of justice until some future day, which day may never come, when it will suit his convenience to test the validity of your laws and consequently the uprightness of his own conduct before the Supreme Court of the United States. There never was a balder piece of effrontery practiced since man was upon the face of the earth. I care not if he be President of the United States, it is simply an insult to human understanding to press any such defense in the presence of his triers.

I have said enough and more than enough to show that the matter charged against the President is impeachable. I waste no words upon the frivolous question whether the articles have the technical requisites of an indictment. There is no law anywhere that requires it. There is nothing in the precedents of the Senate of the United States, sitting as a high court of impeachment, but condemns any suggestion of the kind. I read, however, for the perfection of my argument rather than for the instruction of the Senate, from the text of Rawle on the Constitution, (p. 216,) in which he declares "that articles of impeachment need not be drawn up with the precision and strictness of indictments. It is all-sufficient that the charges be distinct and intelligible." They are distinct and intelligible; they are well enough understood, even by the smallest children of the land who are able to read their mother tongue, that the President stands charged with usurpation of power in violation of the Constitution, in violation of his oath, in violation of the laws; that he stands charged with an attempt to subvert the Constitution and laws, and usurp to himself all the powers of the Government vested in the legislative and judicial, as well as in the Executive Departments.

Touching the proofs, Senators, little need be said. The charges are admitted substantially by the answer. Although the guilty intent is formally denied by the answer and attempted to be denied in argument, the accused submits to the judgment of the Senate that, admitting all the charges to be true, admitting them to be established as laid, nevertheless he cannot be held to answer before the Senate for high crimes and misdemeanors, because it is his prerogative to construe the Constitution for himself, to determine the validity of your laws for himself, and to suspend the people's power of impeachment until it suits his convenience to try the question in the courts of justice. That is the whole case; it is all there is to it or of it or about it, after all that has been said here by his counsel, and that was the significance of the opening argument, that he could only be convicted of such high crimes and misdemeanors as are kindred with treason and bribery. I believe I referred to that suggestion yesterday and asked the Senate to consider that the offenses whereof he is charged, whereof he is clearly guilty, and which he confesses himself in his answer are offenses which touch the nation's life and endanger the public liberties, and cannot be tolerated for a day or an hour by the American people. I proceed, then, Senators, as rapidly as possible, for I myself am growing weary of this discussion——

Mr. SHERMAN. Mr. President, if the honorable Manager desires to pause at this moment in his argument, I will move that the Senate take the usual recess.

Mr. Manager BINGHAM. I hope to be able to close my argument to-day, and if it is the pleasure of the Senate to take the recess now I will yield; but——

Mr. EDMUNDS. Would you prefer it now or to proceed half an hour longer?

Mr. Manager BINGHAM. I will proceed for half an hour and then a recess can be taken.

Mr. SHERMAN. Very well; I withdraw my motion.

Mr. Manager BINGHAM. The first question that arises, Senators, under the first article, is whether Mr. Stanton was the Secretary of War. That he was duly appointed in 1862 by and with the advice and consent of the Senate is conceded. About that there is no question. As the law then stood he was entitled to hold the office under his commission until removed by authority of the act of 1789 or by the authority of some other existing act in full force at the time of his removal; or otherwise he was not removable at all without the advice and consent of the Senate. That is the position I take in regard to this matter, and I venture to say before the Senate that there is not one single word in the records of the past history of this country to contradict it. The act of 1789, as I have said before, authorized the removal; but we shall see whether that act authorized his removal in 1867.

The gentlemen seem to think the tenure of his office depended upon the words of a commission. If that were so I would surrender the question; but I deny it. The tenure of his office depended upon the provisions of the Constitution and the existing law then or afterward in force, whatever it might be. There is no vested power in the President of the United States on this subject beyond the reach of legislation; and he never had any power whatever over the question except that joint power with the Senate, to which I have referred, in the Constitution, and the power expressly conferred by the legislation of Congress. The power that conferred it clearly might take it away. The tenure-of-office act changed the law of 1789. The gentlemen have made elaborate arguments, showing that the act of 1863 did not necessarily, by repugnancy, repeal the whole of the act of 1789; and that part of their argument was very significant as proving that it was competent for the Congress of the United States to put an end to all this talk about the tenure of an office depending, in any sense of the word, upon the language of a commission. It depends exclusively upon the provisions of existing laws. The act of 1867 has repealed the act of 1789, and it repealed the act of 1795 as well. That law provided for the suspension of all officers theretofore appointed and commissioned by and with the advice and consent of the Senate, and it provided for the suspension of all civil officers thereafter appointed by and with the advice and consent of the Senate, and no kind of sophistry can evade the plain, clear words of the law.

The gentlemen undertake to get up a distinction here between the office and the person who holds the office. No such distinction will avail them. This act of 1867 puts an end to all such quibbling. The office and the person who fills it are alike under the protection of the law and beyond the reach of the Executive, except as limited and directed by the law, and no man can gainsay it.

"Every person"—

I suppose that does not mean an office merely—

"Every person holding any civil office to which he has been appointed by and with the advice and consent of the Senate, and every person who shall hereafter be appointed to any such office, and shall become duly qualified to act therein, is and shall be entitled to hold such office until a successor shall have been in like manner appointed and duly qualified, except as herein otherwise provided."

"Herein otherwise provided" had relation to the second section, which made provision for temporary removal by suspension:

"Provided, That the Secretaries of State, of the Treasury, of War, of the Navy, and of the Interior, the Postmaster General, and the Attorney General, shall hold their offices respectively for and during the term of the President by whom they may have been appointed and for one month thereafter, subject to removal by and with the advice and consent of the Senate.

"SEC. 2. And be it further enacted, That when any officer appointed as aforesaid, excepting judges of the United States courts, shall, during a recess of the Senate, be shown, by evidence satisfactory to the President, to be guilty of misconduct in office or crime, or for any reason shall become incapable or legally disqualified to perform its duties, in such case, and in no other, the President may suspend such officer and designate some suitable person to perform temporarily the duties of such office."

"In such case, and in no other." What case? That he shall have become temporarily disqualified, incapable, or legally disqualified, or shall be guilty of misdemeanor in office or crime in such case and no other shall the President suspend him. What other condition is there? That it shall be in the recess of the Senate, and so the section says:

"That when any officer" * * * * "shall, during a recess of the Senate, be shown, by evidence satisfactory to the President, to be guilty of misconduct in office or crime, or for any reason shall become incapable or legally disqualified to perform its duties, in such case, and in no other," &c.

During the recess of the Senate, and not at any other time, shall the President suspend him and report within twenty days after their next meeting to the Senate the fact of suspension, the reasons and the evidence upon which it is made. There is a law so plain that no man can misunderstand it—a plain, clear, distinct provision of the law, that in such case and no other, to wit, during the recess and for the reasons, and only the reasons, named in the statute, shall he suspend from office any person heretofore appointed by and with the advice and consent of the Senate, or who may be hereafter appointed by and with the advice and consent of the Senate.

It is admitted that the Secretary of War and every other officer appointed with the advice and consent of the Senate, holding at the time of the enactment of this law, was within the provisions of the body of the act. The President himself is prohibited by the act from removal, as he was authorized by the act of 1789 to make removals. There is no escape from the conclusion if gentlemen admit the validity of the law. What next? It is attempted to be said here that from the body of this act the Secretaries appointed by Mr. Lincoln were excepted. Who, pray, says that? I have just read to you the commanding words of Mr. Webster that exceptions, unless clearly expressed in the law, are never to be implied except where a positive necessity exists for their implication. It is a sound rule of construction. Who says that the heads of Departments appointed by Mr. Lincoln are by the proviso excepted from the body of the act?

The gentlemen, in the absence of any further reason, undertook to quote from the speech of my learned and accomplished friend, the Senator from Ohio, forgetting that one line of his speech declares expressly, by necessary intendment, that the existing Secretaries at the head of Departments were within the provisions of the law, wherein he says that if the Secretary would not withdraw or resign upon the politest suggestion from the President he himself would consent to his removal. What significance can be attached to these words if they do not mean this: that by this law the President after all may not be permitted to remove the Secretary of War, but if he politely requests him to resign, and he should refuse to resign, the Senator would himself consent to his removal?

As the matter then stood, the Senator was doubtless entirely justified before the country in coming to that conclusion, for facts had not sufficiently disclosed themselves to show the necessity of the Secretary of War retaining his office in the light of the solemn decision of the Supreme Court that he was at liberty in spite of the President, under cover of that decision, to interpret the law for himself, to stand by the law for himself, subject to impeachment if he abused the trust, and in the words of the court not to take the law from the President. Times have changed. The Presi-

dent has more fully developed his character. It is understood now by the whole country, by the whole civilized world, that he has undertaken to usurp all the powers of this Government and to betray the trust committed to him by the people through their Constitution.

The Secretary is said to be excepted by the proviso from the body of the statute. It is an afterthought. The President himself in his message, which I will take the liberty to cite, in the report notified the Senate that if he had supposed any member of his Cabinet would have availed himself of the law to retain the office against his will he would have removed him without hesitation before it became a law. He supposed then he was within the law; they all supposed he was within the law.

Again, the President is concluded on this question, Senators, because on the 12th day of August, 1867, he issued an order suspending Edwin M. Stanton, Secretary of War, under this act. What provision is there in the Constitution authorizing the President to suspend anybody for a day or an hour—a head of Department, from office? Nobody ever claimed it; nobody ever exercised it. It is a thing unheard of altogether in the past history of the country. It never was authorized by any law, save the act of March 2, 1867, the tenure-of-office act. The language of the act is "suspension;" and, Senators, pardon me, for I do not intend that this confessedly guilty man shall change front in the presence of the Senate in order to cover up his villainy. In his message to the Senate he not only quotes the word of the statute that he had suspended him, but he quotes the other word of the statute, that the suspension was not yet "revoked." I ask you, Senators, when that word ever before occurred in the executive papers of a President of the United States, that he had "revoked" a suspension. It is the word of the tenure-of-office act that the President may, if he becomes satisfied that the suspension is made without just cause, revoke it; and he communicates to the Senate that the suspension was not yet revoked. He thought he was within the statute when he suspended him. He thought he was within the statute when he communicated to the Senate that he had not yet revoked the suspension. He thought he was within the statute when, in obedience to its express requirement, within twenty days after the next meeting of the Senate, he did, as required by the law, report the suspension to the Senate, together with the reasons and the evidence on which he made the suspension. It is too late for any man to come before the Senate and say that the President of the United States did not himself believe that the Secretary of War was within the operation of the statute; that he believed that he was excepted from its provisions by the operation of the proviso.

Moreover, his letter to the Secretary of the Treasury, reciting the eighth section of the tenure-of-office act, and notifying him that he had suspended Edwin M. Stanton, was a further recognition of the fact on his part that Mr. Stanton was within the provisions of the act.

But that is not all. His own counsel who opened the case, [Mr. Curtis,] as will be seen by a reference to his argument, declares that there are no express words that bring the Secretary of War, Edwin M. Stanton, within the proviso. That is his own position, and that being so, he must be within the body of the statute. There is no escape from it.

There has been further argument, however, on this subject, that the President did not intend to violate the law. If he believed he was within the statute, and suspended him under the statute and by authority of the statute, and reported in obedience to the statute to the Senate within the next twenty days, with the reasons and the evidence upon which he made the suspension, it will not do to come and say now that the President did not intend to violate the law, that he did not think it obligatory upon him. If he did not think it obligatory upon him, why did he obey it in the first instance—why did he exercise power under it at all? There is but one answer, Senators, that can be given, and that answer itself covers the President with ignominy and shame and reproach. It is this: "I will keep my oath; I will obey the law; I will suspend the head of a Department under it by its express authority for the first time in the history of the Republic; I will report the suspension to the Senate, together with the reasons and the evidence upon which the suspension was made; and if the Senate concur in the suspension I will abide by the law; if the Senate non-concur in the suspension I will defy the law, and fling my own record in their face, and tell them that it is my prerogative to sit in judgment judicially upon the validity of the statute." That is the answer, and it is all the answer that can be made to it by any man.

I admit, Senators, upon this construction of the law, for I have not yet done with it, that the President in the first instance, as to the suspension within the limitation of the law, is himself the judge of the sufficiency of the reasons and the evidence in the first instance, and that he is not to be held impeachable for any honest error of judgment in coming to that conclusion. It would be a gross injustice to hold him impeachable for any honest error of judgment in coming to his conclusion that the Secretary of War was guilty of a misdemeanor or crime in office, that he had become incapable or legally disqualified to hold the office. But the President is responsible if, without any of the reasons assigned by the law, he nevertheless availed himself of the power conferred under the law to abuse it and suspend the Secretary of War though he knew he was not disqualified for any reason, though he knew that there was no colorable excuse for charging that he was guilty of misdemeanor or crime or that he had become in any manner

C. I.—52.

legally disqualified; and this is the very crime charged against him in the eleventh article of impeachment, that he did attempt to violate the provisions of the tenure-of-office act, in that he attempted to prevent Edwin M. Stanton, Secretary of War, from resuming the functions of the office or from exercising the office to which he had been appointed by and with the advice and consent of the Senate in direct violation of the provisions of the act itself.

Now, what are his reasons? The President is concluded by his record and in the presence of the American people is condemned upon his record. What are his reasons? Let the Senate answer when they come to deliberate. What evidence did he furnish this Senate, in the communication made to it, that Edwin M. Stanton had become in any manner disqualified to discharge the duties of that office? What evidence did he furnish the Senate that he had been guilty of any misdemeanor or crime in office? What evidence was there that he was legally disqualified, in the words of the statute? None whatever. It results, therefore, Senators, that the President of the United States, upon his own showing, judged by his own record, suspended Edwin M. Stanton from the office of the Secretary of War and appointed a successor without the presence of any of the reasons named in the statute, and he is confessedly guilty before the Senate and before the world, and no man can acquit him.

Mr. WILSON. I move that the Senate take a recess for fifteen minutes.

The motion was agreed to; and, at the expiration of the recess, the Chief Justice resumed the chair and called the Senate to order.

Mr. Manager BINGHAM. Mr. President and Senators, when the recess was taken I had said all that I desired, and all that I think it needful to say, to show that the President of the United States, himself being witness upon his own messages sent to the Senate of the United States, has been guilty, and is guilty, in manner and form as he stands charged in the first, second, third, eighth, and eleventh articles of impeachment. It does seem hard, Senators, and yet the interest involved in this question is so great that I do not feel myself at liberty to fail to utter a word that might, perhaps, be uttered fitly in this presence in the cause of the people, but it seems hard to be compelled to coin one's heart's drops into thoughts to persuade the Senate of the United States that a man who stands self-convicted on their records ought to be pronounced guilty. It touches the concern of every man in this country whether the laws are to be supreme, whether they are to be vindicated, whether they are to be executed, or whether at last, after all that has passed before our eyes, after all the sacrifices that have been made, after the wonderful salvation that has been wrought by the sacrifice of blood in the vindication of the people's laws, their own Chief Magistrate is to renew the rebellion with impunity and violate the laws at his pleasure and set them at defiance.

When the Senate took its recess I had shown, I think, to the satisfaction of every candid mind within the hearing of my voice, that the President without colorable excuse had availed himself of the authority conferred for the first time by the laws of the Republic to suspend the head of a Department and had disregarded at the same time its express limitation, which declares that he shall not suspend him save during the recess of the Senate, and then only for the reason that from some cause he has become incapacitated to fill the office, as by the visitation of Providence, or has become legally disqualified to hold the office, or is guilty of a misdemeanor or of a crime. Without the shadow of evidence that your Secretary of War was incapacitated; without the shadow of evidence that he was legally disqualified; without the shadow of evidence that he was guilty of a misdemeanor or a crime, he dared to suspend him and to defy the people, in the presence of the people's tribunes, who hold him to answer for the violation of his oath, for the violation of the Constitution, and for the violation of the law. Senators, whatever may be the result of this day's proceeding, impartial history, which records and perpetuates what men do and suffer in this life, will do justice to your slandered and calumniated Secretary of War.

The gentleman [Mr. Groesbeck] spoke of him but yesterday as being a thorn in the heart of the President. The people know that for four years of sleepless vigilance he was a thorn in the heart of every traitor in the land who lifted his hands against their flag and against the sanctuary of your liberties. He can afford to wait; his time has not come. His name will survive the trial of this day and be remembered with the names of the demigods and the heroes who, through an unprecedented conflict, saved the Republic alive; and I charge your recusant President with calumny, with slander, when he suspends the Secretary of War under pretense, in the words of your statute, that he was guilty of a misdemeanor or a crime in office or had become legally disqualified. He was legally disqualified, undoubtedly, judging him by the President's standard, if the qualification of office is an utter disregard of the obligations of an oath. He was guilty of a misdemeanor and crime, undoubtedly, if, according to the President's standard, he was guilty of consenting that the Executive of the United States may, at his pleasure, suspend the people's laws and dispense with their execution—those laws which are enacted by themselves and for themselves and are for their protection, both while they wake and while they sleep, at home and abroad, on the land and on the sea.

Your Secretary of War, Senators, whatever may be the result of this day's proceeding, will stand, as I said before, in the great hereafter,

upon the pages of history as one who was "faithful found among the faithless;" a man equal in the discharge of his office, in every quality that can adorn or ennoble or elevate human nature, to any man of our own time or of any time; a man that was "clear in his great office;" a man who "organized victory" for your battalions in the field as man never organized victory before in the Cabinet councils of a people since nations were upon the earth; and this man is to be suspended by a guilty and corrupt and oath-breaking President, under a law which he defies, and under the hollow and hypocritical pretense that he was guilty of misdemeanor or crime or, in the language of the law, had become otherwise legally disqualified from holding the office.

I dismiss the subject. The Secretary needs no defense from me. And yet it was fit, in passing, that I should take this notice of what the President has done, not simply to his hurt, but to the hurt of the Republic. I have said enough, Senators, to satisfy you, and to satisfy all reasonable men in this country, that the President, when he made this suspension of the Secretary of War, had no doubt of the validity of this law, of its obligation upon him, and that the Secretary was within its provisions; and hence, availing himself of its express provisions, he did suspend him and made report, as I have said, to the Senate.

Now, what apology or excuse can be made for this abuse of the powers conferred upon the President, and of which he stands charged by impeachment here this day in that he has abused, in the language of the authority which I read yesterday in the hearing of the Senate, assented to in the Senate on the trial of Justice Peck without a dissenting voice, abused the power conferred upon him by the statute? The counsel may doubt, or affect to doubt, the tenure-of-office act; the President never doubted it until he was put on trial. When it was presented to him for his approval it was a question with him whether it was in accord with the Constitution; but after Congress had passed it by a two-thirds vote over his veto in the mode prescribed by the Constitution the President thenceforward, until he was impeached by the people's Representatives, recognized the obligation of the law and the plain, simple words of the Constitution, that if the bill be passed by a two-thirds vote over his veto it shall become a law to himself and to everybody else in the Republic.

The counsel, however, doubt the validity of the law. They raise the question in the answer; they raise it in the argument. They intimate to the Senate that it is unconstitutional, and they state a very plain and very simple proposition. It is really a grateful thing—it is to me a very grateful thing—to be able to agree with counsel for the President upon any legal proposition whatever. They do state one proposition to which I entirely assent; and that is, that an unconstitutional law is no law. But it is no law to the President, it is no law to the Congress, it is no law to the courts, it is no law to the people, only after its constitutionality shall have been decided in the mode and manner prescribed by the Constitution; and the gentleman who so adroitly handled that text as it came from the mighty brain of Marshall, knew it to be the rule governing the case just as well as anybody else knows it. It is a law until it shall have been reversed. It has not been reversed. To assume any other position would be to subject the country at once to anarchy, because, as I may have occasion to say in the progress of this argument, the humblest citizen in the land is as much entitled to the impunity which that proposition brings as is the President of the United States. It does not result, however, that the humblest citizen of the land, in his cabin upon your western frontier, through whose torn thatch the wintry rains come down, and through whose broken walls the winds blow at pleasure, is at liberty to defy the law upon the hypothesis that it is unconstitutional and to decide it in advance. The same rule applies to your President. Your Constitution is no respecter of persons.

Is, then, this law constitutional, is it valid, and did the President intend to violate its provisions? Senators, I said before that the rule of the common law and the common sense of mankind is, that whenever a man does an unlawful act, himself being a rational, intelligent, responsible agent, he intends precisely what he does, and there is an end to all further controversy. It sometimes happens, however, because in the providence of God truth is stronger than falsehood—it is linked to the Almighty, and partakes in some sort of his omnipotence—that a guilty conscience sometimes makes confessions and thereby contributes to the vindication of violated law and the administration of justice between man and man in support of the rights of an outraged and violated people. So it has happened, Senators, to the accused at your bar. The President of the United States was no exception to that rule that murder will out. He could not keep his secret. It possessed him; it controlled his utterances, and it compelled him, in spite of himself, to stammer out his guilty purpose and his guilty intent, and thereby silence the tongue of every advocate in this Chamber and of every advocate outside of this Chamber who undertakes to excuse him on the ground that he did not intend the necessary consequences of his own act. He did intend them and he confesses it.

And now I ask the Senate to note what is recorded on page 234 in the record, in his letter to General Grant, and see what becomes of this pretense that the intent is not proved; that he did not intend to violate the law; that he did not intend, in defiance of the express words of the law, which are that the Secretary shall forthwith resume the functions of his office in the event that the Senate shall nonconcur in the suspension, and notify the Secretary of the fact of non-concurrence, all of which appears on your record, to prevent the Secretary from so assuming his office. The President, in his letter to General Grant of February 10, 1868, to be found on page 234 of the record, says:

"First of all, you here admit that from the very beginning of what you term 'the whole history' of your connection with Mr. Stanton's suspension, you intended to circumvent the President. It was to carry out that intent that you accepted the appointment. This was in your mind at the time of your acceptance. It was not, then, in obedience to the order of your superior, as has heretofore been supposed, that you assumed the duties of the office. You knew it was the President's purpose to prevent Mr. Stanton from resuming the office of Secretary of War."

How could he know it if that was not the President's purpose? It would be, it seems to me, and I say it with all reverence, beyond the power of Omnipotence itself to know a thing that was not to be at all, and could not by any possibility be, and did not exist. "You knew it was the President's purpose to prevent Mr. Stanton from resuming the office of Secretary of War." And what says the law? That it shall be the duty of the suspended Secretary, if the Senate shall non-concur in the suspension, "forthwith to resume the functions of the office." And yet the Senate are to be told here that we must prove intent! Well, we have proved it; and what more are we to prove before this man is to be convicted and the people justified in the judgment of their own Senators? He says to General Grant in this letter, "It was my purpose, and you knew it, to prevent Mr. Stanton from resuming the functions of his office."

I give him the benefit of his whole confession. There is nothing in this stammering utterance of this violator of oaths and violator of Constitutions and violator of laws, that can help him either before this tribunal or any other tribunal constituted as this is of just and upright men. He says further on:

"You knew the President was unwilling to trust the office with any one who would not, by holding it, compel Mr. Stanton to resort to the courts."

And he knew as well as he knew anything, that if he prevented Mr. Stanton from resuming the office, Mr. Stanton could no more contest that question in your courts of justice than can the unborn; and the man who does not know it ought to be turned out of the office that he disgraces and dishonors for natural stupidity. He has abused the powers that have been given him. A man who has sense enough to find his way to the Capitol ought to have sense enough to know that. And yet this defense goes on here and the people are mocked and insulted day by day by this pretense that we are persecuting an innocent man, a defender of the Constitution, a lover of justice, a respecter of oaths!

I have said, Senators, in the progress of this discussion, that this pretense of the President is an afterthought. The letter which I have just read is of date, you remember, February 10, 1868, in which he says that his object was to prevent Mr. Stanton from resuming the office. Then there is another assertion, which is also an afterthought, that he wished to drive him into the courts to test the validity of the law. If he prevented Mr. Stanton's resumption of the office there was an end of it, he never could get into the courts; and that question has been settled also in this country, and is no longer an open question, and the President knew it. The question has been ruled and settled, as I stated long ago in the progress of this controversy, in the case of Wallace *vs.* Anderson, 5 Wheaton, 291, where Chief Justice Marshall, delivering the opinion of the court, says:

"A writ of *quo warranto*—"

And it is the only writ by which the title to the office could be tested under your present laws—

"could not be maintained except at the instance of the Government, and as this writ was issued by a private individual without the authority of the Government it could not be sustained, whatever might be the right of the prosecutor or of the person claiming the office in question."

This high court of impeachment, Senators, is the only tribunal to which this question could by possibility be referred. Mr. Stanton could not bring the question here; the people could, and the people have, and the people await your judgment.

Senators, I now ask you another question. How does the President's statement that it was to compel Mr. Stanton to resort to the courts that he suspended him stand with the pretense of the President's answer that his, the President's, only purpose was to have the Supreme Court pass upon the constitutionality of the law? A tender regard this for the Constitution. He said this was his only purpose in breaking the law, the validity and the obligation of which, in the most formal and solemn manner, he had recognized by availing himself of its express grant to suspend the head of a Department from the functions of his office, and to appoint temporarily a successor and report the fact to the Senate; and he now comes with his answer and says that his only purpose was to test the validity of the law in the Supreme Court! If that was his sole purpose how comes it that the President did not institute the proceeding? The Senate will answer that question when they come to pass upon the defense which the President has incorporated in his plea. How comes it that he did not institute the proceeding? I think if the venerable Senator from Maryland, [Mr. JOHNSON,] full of learning as he is full of years, were to respond here and now to that inquiry, he would answer: "Because it was impossible for the President to institute the proceeding."

Mr. Chief Justice, it is well known to every jurist of the country, as the question stands and as the President left it, that there is no colorable excuse under the Constitution and laws of this country for saying that he could institute the proceeding. If he could not institute the proceeding, then, I ask again, why insult the people by mocking them with this bald, hypocritical assertion that his only purpose in all he did was to institute a proceeding on his own motion in the Supreme Court of the United States to test the validity of the people's laws? It is only another illustration, surrounded as the President is by gentlemen learned in the law—and I cast no reproach upon them in saying it, for it was their duty to defend him; it was their duty to bring to his defense all their experience, all their learning, and all those great gifts of intellect and of heart with which it has pleased Providence to endow them—but at last it is only another evidence of what I said before, that, notwithstanding the advice and counsel of his learned and accomplished defenders, truth is at last stronger than falsehood, and only illustrates the grand utterances of that immortal man who in his blindness meditated a song so sublime and holy that it would not misbecome the lips of those ethereal virtues that he saw with that inner eye which no calamity could darken or obscure, when he said—

"Who knows not that truth is strong,
Next to the Almighty."

The President simply utters another falsehood when he comes before the Senate and says that his purpose in violating his oath, in violating your Constitution, in violating your laws, was, that he might test the validity of the statute in the Supreme Court of the United States, when he knew he had no power under the Constitution and laws to raise the question at all. There ends that part of the defense, and there I leave it.

The written order for the removal of the Secretary of War and the written letter of authority for the appointment of Lorenzo Thomas to the office of Secretary for the Department of War are simply written confessions of his guilt in the light of that which I have already read from the record, and no man can gainsay it. I dispose, once for all, of this question of intent by a text that doubtless is familiar to Senators. The evidence being in writing the intent necessarily results, if I am right at all in my apprehension of the rule of law. I read from page 15 of 3 Greenleaf:

"For though it is a maxim of law, as well as the dictate of charity, that every person is to be presumed innocent until he is proved to be guilty; yet it is a rule equally sound that every sane person must be supposed to intend that which is the ordinary and natural consequences of his own purposed act. Therefore, 'where an act, *in itself indifferent*, becomes criminal if done' with a particular intent, there the intent must be proved and found; but where the act is *in itself unlawful* the proof of justification or excuse lies on the defendant; and, in failure thereof, the law implies a criminal intent."

Was the act unlawful? If your statute was valid it clearly was, for your statute says, in the sixth section:

"That every removal, appointment, or employment made, had, or exercised contrary to the provisions of this act, and the making, signing, sealing, countersigning, or issuing of any commission or letter of authority for or in respect to any such appointment or employment, shall be deemed, and are hereby declared to be, high misdemeanors; and, upon trial and conviction thereof, every person guilty thereof shall be punished by a fine not exceeding $10,000 or by imprisonment not exceeding five years, or both said punishments, in the discretion of the court."

Senators, is it an unlawful act within the text of Greenleaf? That surely is an unlawful act the doing of which is by the express law of the people declared to be a penal offense punishable by fine and imprisonment in the penitentiary. What answer do the gentlemen make? How do they attempt to escape from this provision of the law? They say, and it did amaze me, the President attempted to remove the Secretary of War, but he did not succeed. Are we to be told that the man who makes an attempt upon your life here in the District of Columbia, although if you are to search never so closely the statutes of the United States you would not find the offense definitely defined and its punishment prescribed by statute—are we to be told that because he did not succeed in murdering you outright he must go acquit to try what success he may have on another day and in another place in accomplishing his purpose? Senators, I have notified you already of that which you do know, that your act of 1801, as well as your act of 1831, declares that all offenses indictable at the common law committed within the District of Columbia shall be crimes or misdemeanors, according to their grade, and shall be indictable and punishable in the District of Columbia in your own courts.

I listened to the learned gentleman from New York the other day upon this point, and for the life of me (and I beg his pardon for saying it) I could not understand what induced the gentleman to venture upon the intimation that there was any such thing possible as a defense for the President if they admit the unlawful attempt to violate this law by admitting the order to be an unlawful attempt. I say, with all respect to the gentlemen, that it has been settled during the current century and longer, by the highest courts of this country and of England, that an attempt to commit a misdemeanor, whether the misdemeanor be one at common law or a misdemeanor by statute law, is itself a misdemeanor; and in support of that I read from 1 Russell:

"An attempt to commit a statutable misdemeanor, is as much indictable as an attempt to commit a common-law misdemeanor; for when an offense is made a misdemeanor by statute, it is made so for all purposes. And the general rule is, that 'an attempt to commit a misdemeanor is a misdemeanor, whether the offense is created by statute, or was an offense at common law.'"—*Russell on Crimes*, p. 84.

I should like to see some authoritative view brought into this Senate to contradict that rule. It is common law as well as common sense. But, further, what use is there for raising a question of this nature when the further provision of the statute is that—

"The making, signing, sealing, countersigning, or issuing of any commission or letter of authority for or in respect to any such appointment or employment shall be deemed, and are hereby declared to be, high misdemeanors."

The issuing of the order, the issuing of the letter of authority of and concerning the appointment is, by the express words of your law, made a high misdemeanor. Who is there to challenge this here or anywhere? What answer has been made to it? What answer can be made to it? None, Senators, none. When the words of a statute are plain there is an end to all controversy; and in this, as in every other part of this discussion touching the written laws of the land, I stand upon that accepted canon of construction cited by the Attorney General in his defense of the President last week, when he said "effect must be given to every word of the written law." Let effect be given to the words that "every letter of authority" shall be a high misdemeanor. Let effect be given to the statute that every commission issued and every order made affecting or referring to the matter of the employment in the office shall be a high misdemeanor. Let the Senate pass upon it. I have nothing further to say about it. I have discharged my duty, my whole duty.

The question now remains, and the only question that now remains, *is this tenure-of-office act valid?* If it is, whatever gentlemen may say about the first article, there is no man but knows that under the second and third and eighth articles, by issuing the letter of authority in the very words of this statute, and in the very light of his own letter, which I have read just now in the hearing of the Senate, as to his intent and purpose, he is guilty of a high misdemeanor. No matter what may be said about the first article, he did issue the letter of authority which is set forth in the second article, and he has written it down in his letter of the 10th of February, that his object and purpose was to violate that very law, and to prevent the Secretary of War from resuming the functions of the office, although the law says he shall forthwith resume the functions of the office in case the Senate shall non-concur in his suspension. And yet gentlemen haggle here about this question as if it were an open question. It is not an open question. It is a settled, closed question at this hour in the judgment of every enlightened, intelligent man who has had access to your record in this country, and it is useless and worse than useless to waste time upon it.

The question now is: is your act valid, is it constitutional? Senators, I ought to consider that question closed; I ought to assume that the Congress of the United States who passed the act will abide by it. They acted upon the responsibility of their oaths. They acted under the limitations of the Constitution. The Thirty-Ninth Congress, not unmindful, I trust, of their obligations, and not incapable of duly considering the grants and limitations of the Constitution, passed this law because, first, they deemed that it was authorized by the Constitution, and because, second, they deemed that its enactment was necessary—that is the word of the Constitution itself—to the public welfare and the public interest. They sent it, in obedience to the requirements of the Constitution, to the President for his approval. The President, in the exercise of his power and his right under the Constitution, considered it and returned it to the House in which it had originated with his objections. When he had done this we claim, and, in claiming it, we stand upon the traditions of the country, that all his power over the question of the validity of this law terminated. He returned it to the House with his objections. He suggested that it was unconstitutional. The Senate and the House reconsidered it, in obedience to the Constitution, in the light of the President's objections, and by a two-thirds vote under the obligation of their oaths reënacted the bill into a law; and, in the words of the Constitution, it thereby became a law, a law for the President, and it will for ever remain a law until it is repealed by the law-making power or reversed by the courts having jurisdiction.

And now, what takes place? These gentlemen come before the Senate with their answer and tell the Senate that it is unconstitutional. They ask the Senate, in other words, to change their record; ask to have this Journal read hereafter at the opening of the court. "The people of the United States against the Senate and House of Representatives, charged with high crimes and misdemeanors in this, that in disregard of the Constitution, in disregard of their oath of office, they did enact a certain law entitled 'An act to regulate the tenure of certain civil offices' to the hurt and injury of the American people, and were thereby guilty of high crimes and misdemeanors in office." Senators, we have had our lessons here upon charity in the progress of this trial, but really it does seem to me that this would be a stretch of that charity which requires you to give away your coat. I never knew before that it went beyond your outer garments, your bread, the money in your purse; but it seems you are to make a voluntary surrender of your good name, of your character, your conscience, in order to accomodate this accused and guilty culprit, and say after all that it is not the President of the United States that is impeached, it is the Senate that is sitting in judgment upon him; and now we will accommodate this poor unfortunate by making a clean breast of it, and making a confession before gods and men that we violated our own oaths, that we violated the Constitution of the country, in that we did enact into a law, despite the President's veto to the

contrary, a certain act entitled "An act to regulate the tenure of certain civil offices," passed March 2, 1867!

When it comes to that, it is not for me to say what becomes of the Senate. There is a power to gibbet us all in eternal infamy for making up records of this kind deliberately to the injury of the rights of a whole people, and to the dishonor and shame and disgrace of human nature itself. And yet the question is made here, and the truth is it had to be made, it is in the answer, that the law is unconstitutional. If the law be valid the President is guilty, and there is no escape for him. It is needful to make the issue, and having made it, it is needful that the Senate decide it. If they decide that the law is constitutional there is the end of it. They have decided it three times. They decided it when they first passed the law. They decided it when they reënacted it over the President's veto. They decided it again, as it was their duty to decide it, when he sent his message to them on the 21st of February, 1868, telling them that he had violated and defied its provisions, that he had disregarded their action; it was their duty to decide it. The Senate need no apology, and I am sure will never offer any apology to any man in this life or to any set of men for what they did on that occasion. What! The President of the United States to deliberately violate the law of the United States, to disregard the solemn action of the Senate, to treat with contempt the notice that the Senate had served upon him in accordance with the law, and send a message to them, deliberately insulting them in their own Chamber by telling them, in so many words, "I have received your notice; I know you have non-concurred in the suspension of the Secretary of War; I was willing to coöperate with you; and without regard to the law, without the slightest evidence that the Secretary of War was in any sense disqualified, without the slightest evidence that he was guilty of a misdemeanor or crime, as required by your statute, I suspended him, agreeing all the while, if you concurred with me, and thereby cast reproach and dishonor unjustly upon a faithful officer and violated as well your own oaths and the law of your country, well and good; I should stand with you; we would strike hands together."

But, sirs, you have seen fit to have regard to your oaths; you have seen fit to act in some sense up to the character of that grand man who illustrated the glory and dignity which sometimes is vouchsafed to this poor human nature of ours when he was asked to violate the most holy law by eating forbidden food, when he answered no. Well, seemingly do it, for surely they will put you to death. He answered again, "No, for that would bring a stain and dishonor upon my gray hairs; take me to the torture; take me to the torture!" The Senate, mindful of the obligations of their oaths, careless of the influence of power and position touching this question, when the message of the President came to them that he had deliberately violated your law and defiantly challenged you to make answer, did make answer, as it was your duty under your oaths and to that great people who commissioned you, "Sir, the thing which you have done is not warranted by the Constitution and laws of your country."

And this, Senators, is my answer to this charge of hate in the prosecution of this impeachment. The Representatives of the people, and all others who thought it worth while to notice my own official conduct touching this matter of impeachment, know well that I kept myself back, and endeavored to keep others back from rushing madly on to this conflict between the people and their President. The Senate, also acting in the same spirit, gave him this notice that he might retrace his steps and thereby save the institutions of the country the peril of this great shock. But no; it was needful that he should illustrate the old Pagan rule, "Whom the gods would destroy they first make mad."

I return to the question of the validity of this law, with the simple statement that by the text of the Constitution, as I have already read it in the hearing of the Senate, it is provided that all appointments not otherwise provided for in the Constitution shall be made by and with the advice and consent of the Senate. It necessarily results, as Mr. Webster said, from this provision that the removing power is incident to the appointing power unless otherwise provided by law. I have shown to the Senate that this removing power has never been otherwise exercised, from the First Congress to this hour, except in obedience to the express provisions of law; that the act of 1789 authorized the removal, that the act of 1795 authorized the temporary appointment. I add further that I have argued in the presence of the Senate the effect of that provision of the Constitution that the President shall have power to fill up all vacancies which may happen during the recess of the Senate by granting commissions which shall expire at the end of their next session, which by necessary implication means, and means nothing else, that he shall not create vacancies, without the authority of law, during the session of the Senate, and fill them at his pleasure without the consent of the Senate.

I have but one word further to add in support of the constitutionality of this law, and that is the express grant of the Constitution itself that the Congress shall have power "to make all laws which shall be necessary and proper," interpreting that word "proper" in the language of Marshall himself, in the great case of McCulloch vs. Maryland, as being "adapted to," "shall have power to make all laws necessary and adapted to carrying into execution" "all" the "powers vested by this Constitution in the Government of the United States or in any department or officer thereof." I think that grant of power is plain enough, and clear enough to sanction the enactment of the tenure-of-office act, even admitting, if you please, that the power of removal and appointment, subject to the law of Congress, was conferred upon the President, which I deny, there is a grant of power that the Congress may pass all laws necessary and proper to regulate every power granted under this Constitution to every officer thereof. Is the President of the United States "an officer thereof?" I do not stop, Senators, to argue the proposition further, but refer to an authority in 4 Webster's Works, 199, in which he recognized the same principle, most distinctly and clearly, that it is competent for the Congress of the United States to regulate this very question by law; and I add that the Congresses of the United States, from the First Congress to this hour, have approved the same thing by their legislation. That is all there is of that question. The law, I take it, is valid enough, and will remain valid forever, if its validity is to depend upon a judgment of reversal by the Senate that twice passed it under the solemn obligations of their oaths.

Something has been said here about a continued practice of eighty years. I have said enough on that subject, I think, to answer, fully answer, all that was said by the learned counsel for the President. I have shown that the act of 1789, by the interpretation and construction of one of the first men of America, Mr. Webster, did really by direct operation separate the removing from the appointing power and was itself a grant of power. I have said already, and have shown to the Senate, that the Constitution confers that power upon the Senate. Then there is no practice of eighty years adverse to this tenure-of-office act; so that I need say no further word on that subject, but leave it there.

All the acts from 1789 down to 1867 bear witness of one thing, and that is that the Congress of the United States have full power under the Constitution by law to confer upon the President the power of temporary or permanent removal or withhold it. That is precisely what they establish, and I stand upon it here as a Representative of the people, prosecuting for the people these articles of impeachment, and declare here, this day, upon my conscience, and risk what reputation I may have in this world upon the assertion that the whole legislation of this country from 1789 to 1867 together, bears one common testimony to the power of the Congress to regulate by law the removal and appointment of all officers within the general limitation of the Constitution of the supervisory power of the Senate. Why, the act of 1789, as Webster said, conferred upon the President the power of removal and thereby separated it from the power of appointment of which it was a necessary incident and subjected this country to great abuses.

The act of 1795, on the other hand, gave him power to make certain temporary appointments, limited, however, to six months for any one vacancy, thereby showing that it was no power under the Constitution and beyond the limitations and the restrictions of law.

The act of 1868 limited and restricted him to certain heads of Departments and other officials of the Government, as did also the act of 1789. If the President of the United States has this power by force of the Constitution, independent of law, pray tell me, Senators, how it comes that the act of 1789 limited and restricted him to the chief clerk of that Department, how it comes that the act of 1795 limited and restricted him to the period of six months only, for any one vacancy? If, as is claimed in this answer, he had the power of indefinite removal and therefore the power of indefinite appointment, how comes it that the act of 1863 limited him to certain officials of the Government and did not leave him at liberty to choose from the body of the people. I waste no further words on the subject. I consider the question fully closed and settled. All the legislation shows the power of the President to be subject to the limitations of the Constitution and subject to the further limitation of such enactments as the Congress may make, which enactments must bind him, as they bind everybody else, whether he approves them or not, until they shall have been duly reversed by the courts of the United States or repealed by the people's Representatives in Congress assembled.

I may be pardoned, Senators, having gone over hastily in this way the general facts in this case, for saying that the President's declarations are here interposed to shield him from his manifest guilt under the first three, the eighth, and the eleventh articles in this matter of removal and appointment during the session of the Senate. These declarations of the President are declarations after the fact. Most of them were excluded by the Senate, and most properly, in my judgment, excluded by the Senate. Some of them were admitted. I do not regret it. It shows that the Senate were willing even to resolve a doubtful question, or, if it were not a doubtful question, to relax the rules of evidence in the exercise of their discretion, to see what explanation the Chief Executive could possibly give for his conduct, and allow him, contrary to all the rules of evidence, to be a witness in his own case, and that, too, not under the obligations of an oath. They introduced his declarations. They amount to no more than that to which I have referred already, that it was his purpose in violating the law to really test its validity in the courts, whenever, of course, he got ready to test it. That is all there was of them. There was nothing more of the declarations of the President as introduced by him in this trial. If that can be any possible excuse in the light of the fact to which I have before

referred, that it was simply impossible for him to test the question in the courts in the form in which he himself put the question, there is an end of it. There is no use in pressing the matter any further, and I dismiss it with this additional remark, that he had no right, no colorable right, to challenge in that way the laws of a free people and suspend their execution until it should suit his pleasure to test their validity in the courts of justice.

But, Senators, what more is there? He is charged here with conspiracy, and conspiracy is proved upon him by his letter of authority to Thomas and Thomas's acceptance under his own hand, both of which papers are before the Senate and in evidence. What is a conspiracy? A simple agreement between two or more persons to do an unlawful act, either with or without force, and the offense is complete the moment the agreement is entered into. That is to say, the moment the mind of each assents to the guilty proposition to do an unlawful act, conspiracy is complete, and the parties are then and there guilty of a misdemeanor. It is a misdemeanor at the common law; it is a misdemeanor under the act of 1801; it is a misdemeanor under the act of 1831. It is a misdemeanor for which Andrew Johnson and Lorenzo Thomas are both indictable after this proceeding shall have closed; and it is a misdemeanor an indictment for which would be worth no more than the paper upon which it would be written until after this impeachment shall have closed and the Senate shall have pronounced the righteous judgment of guilty upon this offender of your laws, and for a very simple reason.

Senators, it is written in your Constitution that the President shall have power to grant reprieves and pardons for all—not *some*, but *all*—offenses against the United States save in cases of impeachment. Indict Lorenzo Thomas to-morrow for his misdemeanor in that he conspired with Andrew Johnson to violate the law of the United States, in that he conspired with him to prevent, contrary to the "act to regulate the tenure of certain civil offices," Edwin M. Stanton from forthwith resuming the functions of his office upon the refusal of the Senate to concur in his suspension; and all that is wanting is for Andrew Johnson, with a mere wave of his hand, to issue a general pardon and dismiss the proceeding. I say again this is the tribunal of the people in which to try this great offender, this violator of oaths, of the Constitution, and of the laws.

Say the gentlemen, that is a very little offense; you might forgive that. The pardoning power does not happen to be conferred upon the Senate, and this tender and tearful appeal to the Senate on the ground of its being a little thing does not amount to very much. But, say the gentlemen, you have also charged him, under the act of 1861, with having conspired with Lorenzo Thomas, in the one count by force, in the other by threat and intimidation, to work out the same result, to prevent the execution of the laws and to violate their provisions. So we have, and we say that he is clearly pro_ed guilty. How? By the confession chiefly of his coconspirator. I have said the conspiracy is established by the written letter of authority and by the written acceptance of that letter of authority by Thomas. The conspiracy is established, and the conspiracy being established, I say that the declarations of his coconspirator, made in the prosecution of the common design, are evidence against them both. And in support of that I refer the Senate to the case of the United States *vs.* Cole, 5 McLane's United States Circuit Court Reports:

"Where *prima facie* evidence has been given of a combination the acts or confessions of one are evidence against all." * * * * "It is reasonable that where a body of men assume the attribute of individuality, whether for commercial business or for the commission of a crime, that the association should be bound by the acts of one of its members in carrying out the design."

You have the testimony of the declaration of this coconspirator. He was conversing with friends; and it is for the Senate to determine whether he was not invoking the aid of friends in the prosecution of this common design. He told one friend that in two or three days he would kick the Secretary of War out; he told that other friend, Dr. BURLEIGH, who visited his house, to come up on to-morrow morning, "and if the doors are closed I will break them down." It was inviting a friend of his own to be there, in case of need, to render him assistance and coöperation. There is something further, however, in this evidence of the purpose to employ force. In the examination (page 440 Impeachment Record) of this coconspirator he is asked in regard to the papers of the Department:

"Did you afterward hit upon a scheme by which you might get possession of the papers without getting possession of the building?
"*Answer.* Yes, sir.
"*Question.* And that was by getting an order of General Grant?
"*Answer.* Yes—
"Mr. EVARTS. He has not stated what it was.
"By Mr. Manager BUTLER:
"*Question.* Did you write such an order?
"*Answer.* I wrote the draft of a letter; yes, and gave it to the President.
"*Question.* Did you sign it?
"*Answer.* I signed it.
"*Question.* And left it with the President for his——
"*Answer.* For his consideration.
"*Question.* When was that?
"*Answer.* The letter is dated the 10th of March."

After he was impeached, defying the power of the people to check him, he left the letter with the President for his consideration.

"*Question.* That was the morning after you told Karsner you were going to kick him out?
"*Answer.* That was the morning after.
"*Question.* And you carried that letter?
"*Answer.* I had spoken to the President before about that matter.
"*Question.* You did not think any bloodshed would come of that letter?
"*Answer.* None at all.
"*Question.* And the letter was to be issued as your order?
"*Answer.* Yes.

"*Question.* And before you issued that order, took that away to get hold of the mails or papers, you thought it necessary to consult the President?
"*Answer.* I gave that to him for his consideration.
"*Question.* You did think it necessary to consult the President, did you not?
"*Answer.* I had consulted him before."

Further on he says:

"*Question.* They were published and notorious, were they not? Have you acted as Secretary of War *ad interim* since?
"*Answer.* I have given no order whatever.
"*Question.* That may not be all the action of a Secretary of War *ad interim.* Have you acted as Secretary of War *ad interim?*
"*Answer.* I have, in other respects.
"*Question.* What other respects?
"*Answer.* I have attended the councils.
"*Question.* Cabinet meetings, you mean.
"*Answer.* Cabinet meetings.
"*Question.* Have you been recognized as Secretary of War *ad interim?*
"*Answer.* I have been.
"*Question.* Continually?
"*Answer.* Continually.
"*Question.* By the President and the other members of the Cabinet?
"*Answer.* Yes, sir.
"*Question.* Down to the present hour?
"*Answer.* Down to the present hour.
"*Question.* All your action as Secretary of War *ad interim* has been confined, has it not, to attending Cabinet meetings?
"*Answer.* It has. I have given no order whatever.
"*Question.* Have you given any advice to the President? You being one of his constitutional advisers, have you given him advice as to the duties of his office or the duties of yours?
"*Answer.* The ordinary conversation that takes place at meetings of that kind, I do not know that I gave him any particular advice.
"*Question.* Did he ever call you in?
"*Answer.* He has asked me if I had any business to lay before him several times.
"*Question.* You never had any?
"*Answer.* I never had any except the case of the note I proposed sending to General Grant.
"*Question.* I want to inquire a little further about that. He did not agree to send that notice, did he?
"*Answer.* When I first spoke to him about it I told him what the mode of getting possession of the papers was, to write a note to General Grant to issue an order calling upon the heads of bureaus, as they were military men, to send to me communications designed either for the President or the Secretary of War. That was one mode.
"*Question.* What was the other mode you suggested?
"*Answer.* The other mode would be to require the mails to be delivered from the city post office.
"*Question.* And he told you to draw the order?
"*Answer.* No; he did not.
"*Question.* But you did?
"*Answer.* I did it of myself, after having this talk.
"*Question.* Did he agree to that suggestion of yours?
"*Answer.* He said he would take it and put it on his own desk. He would think about it.
"*Question.* When was that?
"*Answer.* On the 10th.
"*Question.* Has it been lying there ever since, as far as you know?
"*Answer.* It has been.
"*Question.* He has been considering ever since on that subject?
"*Answer.* I do not know what he has been doing.
"*Question.* Has he ever spoken to you or you to him about that order since?
"*Answer.* Yes.
"*Question.* When?
"*Answer.* I may have mentioned it one day at the council, and he said we had better let the matter rest until after the impeachment."

A notice to the Senate that these two confederates and conspirators have been deliberately conferring together about violating, not simply your tenure-of-office act, but your act making appropriations for the Army of 2d of March, 1867; that one of the conspirators has written out an order for the very purpose of violating the law, and the other conspirator, seeing the handwriting upon the wall, and apprehensive, after all, that the people may pronounce him guilty, concludes to whisper in the ear of his coconspirator, "Let it rest until after the impeachment." Give him, Senators, a letter of authority, and he is ready, then, to renew this contest and again sit in judicial judgment upon all your statutes, and say that he has deliberately settled down in the conviction that your law regulating the Army, fixing the headquarters of its General in the capital, not removable without the consent of the Senate, does nevertheless impair, in the language of that argument made by Judge Curtis, certain rights conferred upon him by the Constitution, and by his profound judicial judgment he will come to the conclusion to set that aside, too, and order General Grant to California or to Oregon or to Maine, and defy you again to try him. Senators, I trust you will spare the people any such exhibition.

And now, Senators, it has been my endeavor to finish all that I desire to say in this matter. I hope, I know really, that I could finish all that I have to say, if I were in possession of my strength, in the course of an hour or an hour and a half. It is now, however, past four o'clock, and if the Senate should be good enough to indulge me I shall promise not to ask a recess to-morrow if it pleases Providence to bring me here to answer further in the case of the people against Andrew Johnson.

Mr. HOWARD. I move that the Senate, sitting for the trial of the impeachment, adjourn until to-morrow at twelve o'clock.

The motion was agreed to; and the Senate, sitting for the trial of the impeachment, adjourned.

WEDNESDAY, *May* 6, 1868.

The Chief Justice of the United States took the chair.

The usual proclamation having been made by the Sergeant-at-Arms,

The Managers of the impeachment on the part of the House of Representatives, and Messrs. Evarts, Groesbeck, and Nelson, of counsel for the respondent, appeared and took the seats assigned to them respectively.

The members of the House of Representatives, as in Committee of the Whole, preceded by Mr. E. B. WASHBURNE, chairman of that committee, and accompanied by the Speaker and Clerk, appeared and were conducted to the seats provided for them.

The Journal of yesterday's proceedings of the Senate, sitting for the trial of the impeachment, was read.

The CHIEF JUSTICE. Senators will please give their attention. Mr. Manager BINGHAM will resume the argument in behalf of the House of Representatives.

Mr. Manager BINGHAM. Mr. President and Senators, yesterday I had said nearly all that I desired to say touching the question of the power of the President under the legislation of the United States to control the executive offices of this Government. To the better understanding, however, of my argument, Senators, I desire to read the provisions of the several statutes and to insist in the presence of the counsel for the President on this trial, the acts of 1789 and of 1795 have ceased to be law, and that the President can no more exercise authority under them to-day than can the humblest citizen of the land. I desire also, Senators, in reading these statutes, to reaffirm the position which I assumed yesterday with perfect confidence that it would command the judgment and assent of every Senator, to wit: that the whole legislation of this country from the first Congress in 1789 to this hour bears a uniform witness to the fact that the President of the United States has no control over the executive officers of this Government, except such control as is given by the text of the Constitution which I read yesterday, to fill up such vacancies as may occur during the recess of the Senate with limited commissions to expire with their next session, or such power as is given to him by express authority of law. I care nothing for the conflicting speeches of Representatives in the First Congress on this question. The statutes of the country conclude them and conclude us, and conclude as well every officer of this Government from the Executive down.

What, then, Senators, is the provision of this act of 1789? I may be allowed, in passing, to remark—for I shall only read one of them—that the act establishing the Department for Foreign Affairs contains precisely the same provision, word for word, as the act of the same session establishing the Department of War. The provision of the act of 1789 is this:

"SEC. 2. That there shall be in the said Department an inferior officer, to be appointed by the said principal officer, and to be employed therein as he shall deem proper, and to be called the chief clerk of the Department of Foreign Affairs, and who, whenever the said principal officer shall be removed from office by the President of the United States"—

Which I showed you yesterday, upon the authority of Webster, was a grant of power without which the President could not have removed him—

"or in any other case of vacancy, shall, during such vacancy, have the charge and custody of all records, books, and papers appertaining to the said Department."

Standing upon that statute, Senators, and standing upon the continued and unbroken practice of eighty years, I want to know, as I inquired yesterday, what practice shows that this vacancy thus created by authority of the act of 1789 could be filled during the session of the Senate by the appointment of a new head to that Department without the consent of the Senate as prescribed in the Constitution. No precedent whatever has been furnished.

I said yesterday all that I have occasion to say touching the case of Pickering. I remarked yesterday, what I but repeat in passing, without delaying the Senate, that the vacancy was not filled without the consent of the Senate, and that is the end of this unbroken current of decisions upon which the gentlemen rely to sustain this assumption of power on the part of the accused President. It cannot avail them. The act of 1789 excludes the conclusion which they have attempted to impress upon the minds of the Senate in defense of the President. The law restricts him to the chief clerk. If he had the power to fill the vacancy, why this restriction? Could he override that law? Could he commit the custody of the papers and records of that Department, on the act of 1789, to any human being on earth during that vacancy but the chief clerk, who was not appointed by him, but by the head of the Department? There stands the law, and in the light of that law the defense made by the President turns to dust and ashes in the presence of the Senate. I say no more upon that point, reminding the Senate that the act of 1789 establishing the War Department contains precisely the same provision and imposes precisely the same limitation, giving him no power to fill the vacancy by appointment during the session of the Senate.

I pass now to the act of 1795. The act of 1792 is obsolete, has been superseded, and was substantially the same as the act of 1795; and what I have to say, therefore, of the act of 1795, applies as well to the act of 1792. I read from 1 Statutes-at-Large, page 415:

"In case of vacancy in the office of Secretary of State, Secretary of the Treasury, or of the Secretary of the Department of War, or of any officer of either of the said Departments whose appointment is not in the head thereof, whereby they cannot perform the duties of their said respective offices, it shall be lawful for the President of the United States, in case he shall think it necessary, to authorize any person or persons, at his discretion, to perform the duties of the said respective offices until a successor be appointed or such vacancy be filled: Provided, That no one vacancy shall be supplied in manner aforesaid for a longer term than six months."

There stood the act of 1789, unrepealed up to this time, I admit, expressly authorizing the President to create the vacancy, but restricting him as to the control of the Department after it was created to the chief clerk of the Department. That is superseded by the act of 1795, in so far as the appointment is concerned, by expressly providing and giving him the additional power:

"It shall be lawful for the President of the United States, in case he shall think it necessary, to authorize any person or persons, at his discretion, to perform the duties of the said respective offices until a successor be appointed."

It was a grant of power to him. No grant of power could be more plainly written. What is the necessity of this grant if the defense made here by the President as stated in his answer and read by me to the Senate yesterday be true—that the power is in him by virtue of the Constitution? If it be, I ask to-day, as I asked yesterday, how comes it that Congress restricted this constitutional power to appointments not to exceed six months for any one vacancy? That is the language of the statute. Am I to argue with Senators that this term "any one vacancy" excludes the conclusion that the President could, upon his own motion, multiply vacancies ad infinitum by creating another at the end of the six months and making a new appointment? Senators, there is no unbroken current of decisions to support any such assumption.

There is no action of the executive department at any time to support it or give color to it, and there I leave it.

I ask the attention of Senators now to the provisions of the act of 1863, which also affirms the absolute control of the legislative departments over this whole question of removal and appointments, save and except always the express provision of the Constitution—which, of course, the Legislature cannot take away—that the President may fill up vacancies which may happen during the recess of the Senate by limited commissions to expire at the end of their next session. The act of 1863 is in these words:

"That in case of the death, resignation, absence from the seat of Government, or sickness of the head of any executive Department of the Government, or of any officer of either of the said Departments whose appointment is not in the head thereof, whereby they cannot perform the duties of their respective offices, it shall be lawful for the President of the United States, in case he shall think it necessary, to authorize the head of any other executive Department or other officer in either of said Departments whose appointment is vested in the President, at his discretion, to perform the duties of the said respective offices until a successor be appointed or until such absence or inability by sickness shall cease: Provided, That no vacancy shall be supplied in manner aforesaid for a longer term than six months."

Senators, what man can read that statute without being forced to the conclusion that the Legislature thereby reaffirmed the power that they affirmed in 1789, the power that they affirmed in 1795, to control and regulate by law this asserted unlimited power of the Executive over either appointments or removals. Look at the statute. Is he permitted to choose at large from the body of the community to fill temporarily these vacancies? Not at all.

"It shall be lawful for the President of the United States, in case he shall think it necessary, to authorize the head of any other executive Department, or other officer of either of said Departments whose appointment is vested in the President"—

that is, the inferior officers—

"at his discretion, to perform the duties of the said respective offices until a successor be appointed."

He is restricted by the very terms of the statute to the heads of Departments or to such inferior officers of the several Departments as are by law subject to his own appointment, and by that act he can appoint no other human being. There is the law; and yet gentlemen stand here and say that the act of 1789 and the act of 1795 were not repealed, when they read the authority themselves to show that when two statutes are repugnant and irreconcilable the last must control and works the repeal of the first. Here is the President by this act restricted expressly to the heads of Departments and to the inferior officers of Departments subject to his appointment under law, and he shall appoint no one else. Was that the provision of 1795? Do these statutes stand together? Are they by any possibility reconcilable. For the purpose of my argument it is not needful that I should insist upon the repeal of the act of 1795 any further than it relates to the vacancies which arise from the cases enumerated in the act of 1863. The act of 1863 is a reassertion of the power of the Legislature to control this whole question; and that is the unbroken current of decisions from the First Congress down to this day, that the President can exercise no control over this question except by authority of law and subject to the express requirements of law.

This brings me then, Senators, to the act of 1867, to which I referred yesterday, and which I refer to now to-day in this connection for the purpose of completing this argument and leaving every man without excuse upon this question as to the limitations imposed by law upon the President of the United States, touching this matter of appointment and removal of the heads of Departments, and of all other officers whose appointment is, under the Constitution, by and with the advice and consent of the Senate; and my chief object in referring again this morning to the act of 1867 is to show to the Senate, what I am sure must have occurred to them already, rather to perfect my own argument than to suggest any new thought to them, that by every rule of interpretation, that by every letter and word of law read in the conduct of this argument on behalf of the President by his counsel, the act of 1867, by necessary implication, beyond the shadow of a doubt repeals the acts of 1789 and of 1795 and leaves the President of the United States subject to the requirements of this law as to all that class of officials. The language of this law is:

"That every person holding any civil office to which he has been appointed by and with the advice and consent of the Senate"—

That is, all past appointments at the time of the passage of this law—

"and every person who shall hereafter be appointed to any such office, and shall become duly qualified to act therein, is, and shall be, entitled to hold such office until a successor shall have been in like manner appointed and duly qualified, except as herein otherwise provided."

How appointed? "In like manner appointed" by and with the advice and consent of the Senate, and duly qualified and commissioned under such appointment. All present officials shall hold these offices. What becomes of this grant of power in the act of 1789 to the President to remove? What becomes of this grant of power in the act of 1795 to make temporary appointments for six months? What becomes of the provision of the act of 1863 which authorized him to fill these vacancies with the heads of Departments or by inferior officers for a period not exceeding six months? They all go by the board. There stands the provision of the statute which no man can get away from, concluding this whole question:

"That every person holding any civil office," * * * * "by and with the advice and consent of the Senate," * * * * "shall be entitled to hold such office until a successor shall have been in like manner appointed and duly qualified."

Nothing could be plainer. There is no room for any controversy about it. There is not an intelligent man in America that will challenge it for a moment. "Every person holding" the office must include all persons holding the office. He shall continue to hold it—so the statute says—until a successor shall, in like manner, that is to say, by and with the advice and consent of the Senate, be not only appointed, but duly qualified. What room is there here, Senators, for any further controversy in this matter? None whatever.

I referred yesterday to the proviso. I asked the attention of Senators yesterday to the fact that the elaborate argument of Mr. Curtis on behalf of the accused declares in words, as you will find it recorded in the report of the case, that the present heads of Departments appointed by Mr. Lincoln are not by any express words whatever within the proviso. He not only made the statement in manner and form as I now reiterate it in the hearing of the Senate, but he proceeded to argue to the Senate to show that they were not even by implication within the proviso. And so his argument stands reported to this hour; and, so far as I observed, really uncontradicted by anything said whatever by any of his associates; but if they did contradict it, if they did depart from it, if they did differ with him in judgment about it, they are entitled to the benefit of the difference. I do not desire to deny them the benefit of it. I only wish to say that it cannot avail them. I only wish to say in the hearing of Senators that the interpretation put upon that proviso by the opening counsel for the President, declaring that it did not extend to nor embrace the existing appointments of the heads of Departments under Mr. Lincoln, is an admission that Mr. Stanton was entitled to hold his office until removed by and with the advice and consent of the Senate. The reason given by Mr. Curtis was that there are no express words embracing the heads of Departments appointed by Mr. Lincoln. The further reason given by Mr. Curtis was that there is nothing which by necessary implication brings them within the operation of the proviso. If they be not within the operation of the proviso, they are, by the very words of the statute, within the body of the act. The counsel who followed him for the President admitted that the offices were within the body of the act. The persons holding the offices, by the very words of the act "every person," are within the body of the act, and they are to retain the office, unless suspended for the special reasons named in the second section, by the express terms of the act, until a successor shall be, in like manner, appointed by and with the advice and consent of the Senate and shall have been duly qualified.

But I return to the proviso. The proviso is:

"*Provided,* That the Secretaries of State, of the Treasury, of War, of the Navy, and of the Interior, the Postmaster General, and the Attorney General, shall hold their offices respectively for and during the term of the President by whom they may have been appointed, and for one month thereafter, subject to removal by and with the advice and consent of the Senate." •

This proviso manifestly, in the last clause of it, stands with the general provisions of the first clause of the section which I have read, that they are at any time subject to removal by and with the advice and consent of the Senate. The residue of the proviso is to limit the tenure of office of the heads of these several Departments appointed by and with the advice and consent of the Senate, by this limitation, that one month after the expiration of the term of the President by whom they were appointed, their office shall expire by mere operation of law, without the intervention of the Senate, without the intervention of the President, without the intervention of anybody. It was said here, very properly, by the Attorney General, that effect must be given to every word in a written statute. It is the law. Effect must be given to it, and such an effect as will carry out the intent of the law itself. Give effect, Senators, if you please, to the words "during the term of the President and for one month thereafter." Give effect to the words "the term of the President," if you please. The Constitution employs this phrase "term of the President." It declares that the President shall hold his office during the term of four years. It is the only presidential term known to the Constitution. The act of March 1, 1792, reaffirms the same principle by law. I read from 1 Statutes-at-Large, page 241 :

"That the term of four years, for which a President and Vice President shall be elected, shall in all cases commence on the 4th day of March next succeeding the day on which the votes of the electors shall have been given."

After making provision for an election in certain contingencies when a vacancy shall have arisen in the office both of President and Vice President of the United States, the statute follows it up with the same words that the term shall commence on the 4th of March next after the election or the counting of the votes. The provision of the Constitution throws some light upon the subject:

"In case of the removal of the President from office, or of his death, resignation, or inability to discharge the powers and duties of the said office, the same shall devolve on the Vice President; and the Congress may by law provide for the case of removal, death, resignation, or inability, both of the President and Vice President, declaring what officer shall then act as President, and such officer shall act accordingly, until the disability be removed or a President shall be elected."

In the light of these provisions of the Constitution, and of this provision of the act of 1792, is it not apparent to the mind of every man within the hearing of my voice that the presidential term named and referred to in the act of 1867 is the constitutional term of four years? It must be so. It must be the term authorized by the Constitution and the laws, for there is no other "term." The position assumed here is that Andrew Johnson has a term answering to the provisions of the Constitution, of the act of 1792 and of the act of 1867, both of which employ the same word—the term of four years under the Constitution. Apply this provision of the Constitution which I have just read, that in the event of the inability of the President of the United States to execute the duties of the office the Vice President shall execute the duties of the office until such disability be removed. That is the language of the Constitution. If the President of the United States elected by the people, and therefore possessed of a constitutional term, and the only person who ever can have a constitutional term while the Constitution remains as it is, shall be overtaken with sickness, and by delirium, if you please, rendered utterly incapable, in the language of the Constitution, of discharging the duties of the office, and his inability continues for the period of four consecutive months, is the Senate to be told that the Vice President, upon whom the duties of the office by this provision devolve, by reason of the construction imposed here upon this statute or attempted to be put upon it by the counsel, is to be said to have a term within the meaning of this law, and therefore by operation of the statute, within one month after the disability arose against the President by reason of his delirium, every executive office by operation of law became vacant; and are you to follow it to the absurd and ridiculous conclusion when, in the language of the Constitution, the disability shall be removed and the President restored to office, the offices filled with the advice and consent of the Senate by the Vice President, upon whom the office in the meantime devolved—for by the terms of the Constitution your President disabled was civilly dead ; you had but the one President, and that was the Vice President, during the four months—on account of vacancies arising by operation of law one month after the office was devolved upon him by the Constitution by reason of the inability of the President, are to become vacant one month after the expiration of this four months' term and the return of the disabled President to his office by reason, in the language of the Constitution, of the removal of his disability.

It will not do. He had no term. No effect is given to the words of your statutes in that way; and more than that, Senators, these learned and astute counsel knew right well that they changed in their own minds, and changed by the words of their own argument, the very language of the statute, so that it should have read to accomplish their purposes: "that the office shall expire within one month after the end of the term *in which* they may have been appointed," not "in one month after the end of the term of the President *by whom* appointed," as the statute does read; but their logic rests upon the assumption that the statute contains words which it does not contain, "that their office shall expire within one month after the term in which they may have been appointed."

Concede that, change the law in that way in order to accommodate this guilty man, and I will admit that you arrive at this conclusion, and that is as about absurd as the other, giving their construction to the law, changing its language from what it is, "that the office shall expire in one month after the term of the President by whom appointed," so that it shall read "after the end of one month from the end of the term in which they were appointed," and it results that ever since the 4th day of April, 1865, the people of the United States have been without a constitutional or lawful Secretary of State, without a constitutional Secretary of the Treasury, without a constitutional Secretary of the Navy, and without a constitutional Secretary of War, because accepting the assumptions of these gentlemen, that by this word "term" in the statute is meant the term in which they were appointed and not the term of the President by whom they were appointed, admit their premises, and no mortal man can escape the conclusion that the offices all became vacant on the 4th day of April, 1865. That is the position assumed by these gentlemen for the simple reason that these four Secretaries were every one of them appointed by Mr. Lincoln in his first term, which first term expired on the 4th day of March, 1865.

Senators, that is not the meaning of your law. "The reason of the law is the life of the law." The reason of the law was simply this: that the Presidents elected by the people for a term—and no other Presidents have a term—should, by operation of law, upon their coming to the office, be relieved, without any intervention of theirs, of all the several heads of Departments who had been appointed by their predecessors. That is the meaning of the law. That is all there is of it. So far as this question of the right of an incoming President to a new Cabinet is concerned, that is the extent of it. The word "term" determines it. Did that mean that a President reëlected for a term and thereby continuing in the office should be relieved from his own appointees by operation of law, and that, too, without his consent, and, if you please, against his wish? It never entered into the mind of a single member of the

Thirty-Ninth Congress. I venture to say that no utterance of that sort is found recorded upon the debates touching this reform in the legislation of the country and controlling executive appointments. What right had Mr. Lincoln to complain that the law did not vacate the heads of Departments by its own operation for his benefit when he had filled them himself? The law was passed for no such purpose. I read the law literally as it is. They were to hold their offices, in the light of the reason of the law, during the entire term, if it should be eight years or twelve years or sixteen years, of the President by whom they were appointed, and their office was to expire within one month after the expiration of the term of the President by whom they were appointed, not within one month after the expiration of the term in which they were appointed.

That is my position in regard to this question. I have no doubt about its being the true construction of the law, neither had the accused; and I stated to the Senate yesterday my reasons for the assertion; I do not propose to repeat them to-day. The Senate did me the honor to listen and attend to my remarks on that subject, wherein the President, by every step he took until this impeachment was instituted, confessed that that was the operation of this law, and these heads of Departments might avail themselves of it.

In the act of 1792 my attention is called to another provision of it, which I did not read, which shows the operation of this word "term" still more strongly than does the provision of the twelfth section, which I did read. It is found in the tenth section of the act, which provides—

"That whenever the offices of President and Vice President shall both become vacant the Secretary of State shall forthwith cause a notification thereof to be made to the Executive of every State, and shall also cause the same to be published in at least one of the newspapers printed in each State, specifying that electors of the President of the United States shall be appointed or chosen in the several States within thirty-four days preceding the first Wednesday in December then next ensuing: *Provided,* There shall be the space of two months between the date of such notification and the said first Wednesday in December; but if there shall not be the space of two months between the date of such notification and the first Wednesday in December, and if the *term* for which the President and Vice President last in office were elected shall not expire on the 3d day of March next ensuing, then the Secretary of State shall specify in the notification that the electors shall be appointed or chosen within thirty-four days preceding the first Wednesday in December in the year next ensuing, at which time the electors shall accordingly be appointed or chosen."

Showing that this term by the express provisions of the law is limited everywhere and intended to be limited everywhere within the meaning and sense of the Constitution. That being so there is no person who has a term but the President elected by the people. There is no person, therefore, whose appointments can, by any possibility, be within the provisions of this proviso but such a President, and in that case the Secretary of War and the other Secretaries of the various Departments are under the operation of the statute within the proviso, so as to limit and determine their offices at the expiration of one month after the inauguration of a successor elected also to a term. It is the only construction which gives effect to all the words of the statute. It must be a successor, not a reëlection of the same President.

There is one other point in this matter, and I have done with it. The gentlemen give this proviso a retroactive operation in order to get along with their case, and, as I showed to the Senate, vacate the offices really by making the statute read as it does not read, that these officers are to go out of office one month after the expiration of the term in which they were appointed. In order to get up this construction they give a retroactive operation to the act, and make it take effect two years before its passage, and make it vacate the four Executive Departments I have named on the 4th day of April, 1865, when in point of fact the act was not passed until the 2d day of March, 1867. I have just this to remark on that subject, that it is a settled rule of the law that a retrospective operation can be given to no statute whatever without express words. The counsel for the President admits there are no express words in the proviso. That is the language of his own argument. I hold him to it, and I ask the Senate to pass upon it. I refer to the authority of Sedgwick on Statutory and Constitutional Law, page 190:

"The effort of the English courts appears indeed always to be to give the statutes of that kingdom a prospective effect only, unless the language is so clear and imperative as not to admit of doubt."

* * * * * * * * *

"In this country the same opposition to giving statutes a retroactive effect has been manifested, and such is the general tenor of our decisions."

I have no doubt of it. The express language of the first clause of the law gives it a retrospective operation in one sense of the word, that is, it embraces every officer heretofore appointed by and with the advice and consent of the Senate, and by express language every officer hereafter to be so appointed. But this proviso, in the words of Mr. Curtis, contains no express language of that kind, and on the contrary, contains words which exclude the conclusion. I leave the question there. If Mr. Lincoln had lived I think every Senator must agree that under this statute and within the reason of the law he could not have availed himself of the acts of 1789 and 1795 to remove a single head of Department appointed by himself at any time during his term; and I do not care how often his term was renewed it was still the term and answered to the statute, and he was still the President by whom these officers were appointed. And when his term expired, whether it was renewed twice or three or four times, when his term had expired the proviso *in futuro* took effect according to its own express language, and the offices by operation of law became vacated one month after

the expiration of that term, and that term never does expire until the end of the time limited.

I have nothing further to say, Senators, upon this point. I think I have made it plain enough.

Having said this, allow me to remark in this connection that I think my honorable and learned friend from Ohio, [Mr. Groesbeck,] in his argument, spoke a little hastily and a little inconsiderately when he ventured to tell the Senate that unless Mr. Stanton was protected by the tenure-of-office act the first eight articles of impeachment must fail. Passing the question of removal, about which I have said enough, and more than enough, how can anybody agree with the honorable gentleman in his conclusion touching this matter of appointment? What man can say one word, one intelligible word in justification of the position that the act of 1867 did not sweep away every line and letter of the power of appointment conferred on the President by the acts of 1789 and 1795, as to every officer, appointable by and with the advice and consent of the Senate? I have asked the attention of the Senate before, and beg pardon for asking their attention again to the express words of the act which settle beyond controversy that point. Those words are:

"That every person holding any civil office to which he has been appointed, by and with the advice and consent of the Senate" * * * * "shall be entitled to hold such office until a successor shall have been in like manner appointed and duly qualified."

The proviso, even allowing it to have the effect and operation which the gentlemen claim, only vacates the office; but it does not allow a successor to be appointed. There is not a word or syllable of that sort in it. The statute then stands declaring in substance that all vacancies in all these Departments shall hereafter be filled only by and with the advice and consent of the Senate, save as it may be qualified by the third section; and what is that?

"That the President shall have power to fill up all vacancies which may happen during the recess of the Senate, by reason of death or resignation, by granting commissions which shall expire at the end of their next session thereafter."

Showing additional reasons in support of my position that this statute necessarily repeals the acts of 1789 and 1795, that he may merely fill up during the recess, reiterating in other words the provision of the Constitution itself, but by law absolutely limiting and restricting his power of appointment to vacancies during the recess.

"And if no appointment, by and with the advice and consent of the Senate, shall be made to such office so vacant or temporarily filled as aforesaid during such next session of the Senate, such office shall remain in abeyance, without any salary, fees or emoluments attached thereto, until the same shall be filled by appointment thereto, by and with the advice and consent of the Senate."

Showing, as plainly as language can show, that the President's power over the premises is by law absolutely excluded.

"And during such time all the powers and duties

belonging to such office shall be exercised by such other officer as may by law exercise such powers and duties in case of a vacancy in such office."

This throws you back upon the provisions of the act of 1863, but there is the express provision that the office shall remain in abeyance. Here is an appointment *ad interim* during the session of the Senate; here is an appointment *ad interim* to fill a vacancy which did not arise during the recess; here is an appointment *ad interim* to fill a vacancy created by an act of removal by himself; and what do the gentlemen say to it? Why it did not succeed, I answered that yesterday, that the very words of the statute declare that the issuance of the letter of authority shall be itself a high misdemeanor. That is answer enough.

But what else is said here about this thing? The gentlemen come here to argue and put it in the answer of the President that the act of 1867 is unconstitutional and void. They have argued for hours here to the Senate to assure them that no man can be guilty of a crime for the violation of an unconstitutional act, because it was no law that he violated. Why all this effort, Senators, made by these learned counsel? Why this solemn averment in this answer of the President that the act of 1867 is unconstitutional and void, if, after all, there was no violation of its provisions; if, after all, it was no crime for him to make this *ad interim* appointment; if, after all, the acts of 1789 and 1795 remain in full force? Senators, I have no patience to pursue an argument of this sort. The position assumed is utterly inexcusable, utterly indefensible. Admitting Mr. Stanton, if you please, to be within the proviso, admitting that the proviso operated retrospectively, admitting that it vacated his office on the 4th day of April, 1865, as also the offices of Mr. Seward and Mr. Welles and Mr. McCulloch, leaving the Republic without any lawful heads to those Departments, accepting the absurd propositions of these gentlemen, and I ask you what answer is that to the second and third and eighth articles of accusation against this President that he committed a high crime and misdemeanor in office in that he issued a letter of authority contrary to the provisions of the sixth section? It is just no answer at all. I think the counsel must so understand it themselves.

What answer is that, I ask you, Senators, to the charges in the fourth, fifth, sixth, and seventh articles, that he entered into conspiracy with Thomas to prevent the execution of the law, and the averment in the eleventh article, which averments are divisible, as every lawyer knows, that he attempted by device and contrivance to prevent the execution of the law and to prevent the Secretary of War, Edwin M. Stanton, from resuming the functions of the office in obedience to the requirements of the act of 1867, which is also made a crime by your act of 1861 touching conspiracies, which is a crime at common law, as I read in

the hearing of the Senate from 4 Bacon, and which crime at common law is made indictable by your act of 1801, and so affirmed by the decisions of the circuit court of your District and by the decision of the Supreme Court of the United States, which I also read in the hearing of the Senate. I ask Senators to consider whether, admitting that the Secretary of War had ceased to be entitled to the office, and was not to be protected in the office by operation of the law, the President must go acquit of these conspiracies into which he has entered and for the very purpose alleged, as confessed by himself in his letter which I read yesterday in the hearing of the Senate, and must go acquit of issuing this letter of authority in direct violation of the sixth section of the act.

There were other words uttered by the counsel here to show that there was a great deal more in this accusation than these gentlemen were willing to concede. The Senate will remember the language of Mr. Attorney General Stanbery, that this act was an odious, offensive, unconstitutional law, in that it attempted to impose penalties upon the Executive for discharging his executive functions, making it a crime or misdemeanor for him to exercise his undoubted discretionary power as claimed in his answer under the Constitution. He affirmed here with emphasis before the Senate that the law was made exclusively for the Executive. He forgot, Senators, that the fifth section of the act makes it apply to every man who participates with the Executive voluntarily in the breach of the law, and makes it a high misdemeanor for any person to accept any such appointment, &c., punishable by fine and imprisonment in the same measure precisely as the President himself is punishable.

I do not understand, Senators, why this line of argument was entered upon, if my friend from Ohio was right in coming to the conclusion that there was nothing in the conspiracy, that there was nothing in issuing the letter of authority in violation of the express penal provisions of the law, if Mr. Stanton was not protected by the law and could be rightfully removed. There is a great deal in it beyond that. The President had no right to make the appointment. That is the express language of your law. And for doing it he is liable to indictment whenever the Senate shall have executed its power over him by his removal from office. I explained yesterday how it is that he is not liable to prosecution before. Your Constitution provides that, after the judgment shall be pronounced upon him of removal from office he may be held to answer by indictment for the crimes and misdemeanors whereof he has been impeached.

I referred yesterday, Senators, to the fact disclosed in the evidence that the President has been pursuing these acts of usurpation in utter defiance and contempt of the people's power to control him since the impeachment was preferred against him. I read in the hearing of the Senate yesterday what was sworn to by Thomas as to the proposition to have an order made upon General Grant to compel the surrender of the papers of the Department of War to his Secretary *ad interim*. I read in the hearing of the Senate yesterday what Thomas swore to, that the President concluded to defer action upon the order which Thomas had written out and left lying upon the table awaiting the result of impeachment. And, Senators, something has transpired here upon the floor in the progress of this case which gives significance to this conversation between the President and Thomas, and that was the language of his veteran and intrepid friend from Tennessee, [Mr. NELSON,] who stood here unmoved while he uttered the strong words in the hearing of the Senate, that it was his own conviction, and it was also the conviction or opinion of the President himself, that the House of Representatives had no power under the Constitution to impeach him, no matter what he was guilty of, and that the Senate of the United States had no power under the Constitution as now organized to try him upon impeachment. We are very thankful that the President, of his grace, permits the Senate to sit quietly and deliberate on this question presented by articles of impeachment through the people's Representatives.

But I ask Senators to consider whether the President—for I observe the counsel did not intimate that the President was willing to abide the judgment—whether the President in this matter, after all, is not playing now the same *rôle* which he did play when he availed himself of the provisions of the tenure of-office act to suspend Edwin M. Stanton from office and appoint a Secretary *ad interim* to await the action of the Senate; whether he is not playing the same *rôle* that he did play further when he availed himself of that act and notified the Senate of the suspension, together with the reasons and the evidence, agreeing to allow the Senate to deliberate, agreeing, if the Senate would concur in the suspension and make it absolute, to abide the judgment; but, nevertheless, reserving to himself that unlimited prerogative of executive power to defy the final judgment of the Senate if it was not in accord with his own. Is that the posture of this case? I think it had been well for the President of the United States, when he was informing us of his opinions on the subject through his learned counsel, to have gone a step further and to have informed us whether he would abide the judgment. He has let us know that we may sit and try him, as he let the Senate know before that they might sit and consider his reasons of suspension; but he let them know, when they came to a conclusion adverse to his own, that he would not abide their judgment.

He issued an order to Thomas. His counsel in the opening—and that is another significant fact in this case—said it could not be strictly

called a military order; yet the habitual custom of the officers of the Army to obey all the orders of a superior, gave it in some sense the force of a military order to Adjutant General Thomas, commanding him to take possession of the Department of War while the Senate was in session and without consulting it. It would not surprise me, Senators, at all, if the President were to issue an order to-morrow to his Adjutant General to disperse the Senate, after sending such an utterance as this here by the lips of his counsel, that the Senate has no constitutional right to try him by reason, he says, of the absence of twenty Senators, excluded by the action of this body, elected by ten States entitled to representation on this floor—a question which the President of the United States has no more right to decide nor to meddle with than has the Czar of Russia. It is a piece of arrogance and impudence for the President of the United States to send to the Senate of the United State a message that they are not constitutionally constituted, and have no right to decide for themselves the qualification and election of their own members when it is the express provision of the Constitution that they shall have that power, and no man on earth shall challenge it.

I trust, Senators, after this utterance of the President, which is substantially an utterance that you shall suspend judgment in the matter and defer to his will to a trial in the courts when it shall suit his convenience to inquire into the rights of the people to have their own laws executed—that the Senate of the United States will prove itself in the *finale* of this controversy with the President possessed of the grand heroic spirit of which the deputies of the nation were possessed in 1789 in France when the king sent to its bar his order that the representatives of the people should disperse. Its illustrious president, Bailly, rising in his place was hailed by the grand master with the inquiry, "You heard the king's order, sir?" "Yes, sir," and immediately turning to the deputies, said, "I cannot adjourn the Assembly until it has deliberated upon the order." "Is that your answer?" said the grand master. "Yes, sir," and "It appears to me that the assembled nation cannot receive an order;" followed by the words of the great tribune of the people, Mirabeau, "Go tell those who sent you that bayonets can do nothing against the will of the nation." That, sir, is our answer to the arrogant words of the President that the Senate has no constitutional right to sit in judgment upon the high crimes and misdemeanors whereof he stands impeached this day by the Representatives of the people.

I have said, Senators, all that I have occasion to say touching the first eight articles preferred against the President. Having entered into this conspiracy, having issued this order for removal unlawfully, having issued this letter of authority unlawfully, it was necessary that the President should take another step in his guilty march; and accordingly he ventured, as conspirators always do, very cautiously upon the experiment of corrupting the conscience and staining the honor of the gallant soldier who was in command of the military forces of the District. He had an interview with him the day after he had issued this order, the day after he had issued this letter of authority, and said to him, "Sir, this act of 1867 making appropriations for the Army which requires all military orders to pass through the General of the Army, whose headquarters are in the District of Columbia, and which declares also that any violation of its provisions shall be a high misdemeanor in office is an unconstitutional law; it is an unconstitutional law, General, and it is not within the purview of your commission." It was simply a suggestion to the General that his Commander-in-Chief would stand by him in violating the law of the land. It was a suggestion to him that it would be a very great accommodation if the commandant of the military forces of the District of Columbia would receive his orders directly from the President and not from the General of the Army.

It was a confession, Senators, by indirection, to be sure—that confession, however, which always syllables itself upon the tongue of guilt when guilt speaks at all—that General Grant, the hero of the century, who led your battalions to victory upon a hundred stricken fields, having vindicated the supremacy of the laws by wager of battle, would surely here in the capital be faithful to the obligations and the requirements of law, and refuse to strike hands with him. More than that; he had put it in writing and confessed, to which I asked the attention of Senators yesterday, to this effect, "You knew, General Grant, that my object and purpose was to violate and defy the law; you accepted the office to circumvent me." That is his language in his letter to Grant of the 10th of February. And yet the gentlemen say it is a miserable accusation! Is it? It is so miserable an accusation that in any other country than this, where the laws are enforced rigidly, it would cost an executive or military officer his head to suggest to any subordinate that he should violate a law, and a penal law at that, touching the movement of troops and military orders; and so plain that no mortal man could mistake its meaning. I say no more upon that point; I leave it with the Senate.

The act itself in its second section declares that a violation of its provisions shall be a high misdemeanor in office, punishable by fine and imprisonment in the penitentiary. The rule of law is that an attempt to commit a misdemeanor is itself a misdemeanor. It is the rule of the common law, and it is the rule of the District happily, and governs the President and ought to govern him and ought to govern everybody else within the District. I heard a sneer about this question, I thought, from one of the counsel that it was limited to the District in its

operations. If the legislation which is limited exclusively to the District is to be sneered at by counsel, what means the provision in the Constitution that the Congress shall have exclusive legislative power over the District? It is for the protection and defense of the nation. But it is not limited altogether to the District at last. The act of 1801 was limited to the District in applying the common-law rule, but the act which it supports is coextensive with the Republic. It is not necessary that the officer himself should be indictable in order to hold him impeachable. It is only necessary that the act he did, by the strict construction that is put upon this question by the counsel for the accused, was a crime or misdemeanor under the laws of the country. That it was such a crime and misdemeanor I have shown.

I leave article nine. I now consider article ten, about which a great deal has been said both by the opening counsel and by the concluding counsel. The President is in that article charged with an indictable offense in this, that in the District of Columbia he uttered seditious words—I am stating now the substance and legal effect of the charge—seditious words tending to incite the people to revolt against the Thirty-Ninth Congress and to disregard their legislation, asserting in terms that it was no Congress, that it was a body "assuming to be a Congress" "hanging upon the verge of the Government," and committing also acts of public indecency which, as I showed to the Senate yesterday upon the authority which I read, is at common law an indictable misdemeanor, showing a purpose to violate the law himself and to encourage and incite others to violate the law. The language of the President was the language of sedition.

What did the counsel say about it? They referred you to the sedition act of 1798, which expired by its own limitation, and talked about its having been a very odious law. I do not know but they intimated that it was a very unconstitutional law. Pray what court of the United States ever so decided? There were prosecutions under it, but what court of the United States ever so decided? What commanding authority upon the Constitution ever ruled that the law was unconstitutional? I admit that no such law as that ought to be upon your statute-book, of general operation and application in this country, except in a day of national peril. That was a day of national peril. There was sedition in the land. The French minister was abroad in the Republic, everywhere attempting to stir up the people to enter into combinations abroad hurtful and dangerous to the security of American institutions.

But I pass it. The gentlemen referred to Mr. Jefferson coming into power through his hostility to the sedition act of 1798; and he had no sooner got into power than he reenacted it as to every officer and soldier of your Army, and it stands the law of your

Republic from that day to this. I read from the act of 1806:

"Any officer or soldier who shall use contemptuous or disrespectful words against the President of the United States, against the Vice President thereof, against the Congress of the United States, or against the Chief Magistrate or Legislature of any of the United States in which he may be quartered, if a commissioned officer, shall be cashiered or otherwise punished as a court-martial shall direct; if a non-commissioned officer or soldier, he shall suffer such punishment as shall be inflicted on him by the sentence of a court-martial."

Even unto death. That has been for more than sixty years the law of the Republic. Using disrespectful language toward the President or using disrespectful language toward the Congress is an offense in an officer or soldier.

The gentlemen read from the Constitution in the hope, I suppose, to show that it was utterly impossible for the Congress of the United States to inflict pains and penalties by law for seditious utterances either by their President or anybody else. If it were competent for the Congress of 1806 to enact that law, it was equally competent for the Congress of 1798 to enact a sedition law; and by the act of 1801 these seditious utterances made in your District are indictable as misdemeanors, whether made by the President or anybody else, and especially in an official charged with the execution of the laws—for, as I read yesterday, a refusal to do an act required by the law of an officer is at common law indictable—the attempt to procure another or others to violate law, on the part of such officer, is also indictable; and, in general, seditious utterances by an executive officer at the common law always were indictable; that is to say, to incite the people to resistance to law or to incite the officers of the Army to mutiny or to disregard law.

But, say counsel, this is his guarantied right under the Constitution. The freedom of speech, says the gentleman, is not to be restricted by a law of Congress. How is that answered by this act of 1806, which subjects every soldier in your Army and every officer in your Army to court-martial for using disrespectful words of the President or of the Congress or of his superior officers? The freedom of speech guarantied by the Constitution to all the people of the United States, is that freedom of speech which respects, first, the right of the nation itself, which respects the supremacy of the nation's laws, and which finally respects the rights of every citizen of the Republic. I believe in that freedom of speech. That is the freedom of speech to which the learned gentleman from New York referred when he quoted the words of Milton: "Give me the liberty to know, to argue, and to utter freely according to conscience above all liberties." That is the liberty which respects the rights of nations and the rights of individuals, which is called that virtuous liberty, a day, an hour of which,

is worth a whole eternity of bondage. That is our American constitutional liberty—the liberty in defense of which the noblest and the best of our race, men of whom the world was not worthy, have suffered hunger and thirst, cold and nakedness, the jeer of hate, the scowl of power, the gloom of the dungeon, the torture of the wheel, the agony of the fagot, the ignominy of the scaffold and the cross, and by their living and their dying glorified human nature and attested its claim to immortality. I stand, Senators, for that freedom of speech; but I stand against that freedom of speech which would disturb the peace of nations and disturb the repose of men even in their graves.

There is, Senators, but one other part of this case that I deem it my duty particularly further to discuss; and that is the allegation contained in the eleventh article, which alleges specifically the attempt, not the accomplishment, of the acts, but rests on all the evidence, which applies to all the other articles preferred against this accused and guilty man—the attempts by devices to incite the people to resistance against their own Congress and its laws by declaring that it was a Congress of only part of the States; the attempt to prevent the ratification by the Legislatures of the several States of the fourteenth article of amendment preferred by the Thirty-Ninth Congress on the same ground that it was not the Congress of the nation and had no power to propose an article of amendment to the Constitution, a position asserted by him even in his messages to the Congress, reasserted in his speech; an attempt to prevent the execution of the tenure-of-office act; an attempt to prevent the execution of the act making appropriations for the support of the Army and the Department of War, passed March 2, 1867; an attempt to defeat the operation and execution of the act for the more efficient government of the rebel States.

Why, said the learned gentleman from Ohio, [Mr. Groesbeck,] the evidence that we introduce to support this last averment of the eleventh article, it appears, was a thing done by the President some months before the act was passed. The gentleman was entirely right in his dates, but he was altogether wrong in his conclusions. We introduced the telegram for no such purpose. We introduced the telegram in order to sustain that averment of the eleventh article that he attempted to defeat the ratification of the fourteenth article of amendment, an amendment essential to the future safety of the Republic, by the judgment of twenty-five million men who have so solemnly declared by its ratification in twenty-three of the organized States of the Union.

This fourteenth article of amendment, as the Senate will recollect, was passed about the month of June, 1866, by the Thirty-Ninth Congress. After it had been passed, and ratified perhaps by some of the States, the President sent this telegram to Governor Parsons, of Alabama, dated January 17, 1867:

"What possible good can be obtained by reconsidering the constitutional amendment?"

It had already been rejected by that Legislature.

"I know of none in the present posture of affairs; and I do not believe the people of the whole country will sustain any set of individuals in attempts to change the whole character of our Government by enabling acts or otherwise."

"Any set of individuals," not a Congress, but a simple mob.

"I believe, on the contrary, that they will eventually uphold all who have patriotism and courage to stand by the Constitution, and to place their confidence in the people. There should be no faltering on the part of those who are honest in their determination to sustain the several coördinate departments of the Government in accordance with its original design."

Coupled with his messages to Congress, coupled with the utterances of his counsel from Tennessee, what is all this but an affirmation on the part of the President that the States lately in insurrection after all hold the power over the people of the organized States of this Union to the extent that they can neither legislate for the government of those disordered communities, nor amend their own Constitution even for the Government and protection of themselves? If it does not mean that, it means nothing. In the language of the learned counsel from New York, who appears as the able advocate of the President at this bar, it is an attempt on the part of the President to revive an expiring rebellion, "the lost cause." It is an utterance of his to the effect that unless the ten States lately in insurrection choose to assent, the people of the organized States shall not amend their Constitution. The President calls on men to rally to his standard in support of the coördinate departments of the Government against these encroachments of a "set of individuals" upon the rights of the people.

Senators, you remember well what the general provisions of the fourteenth article of the amendment were. I desire, however, to the right understanding of this question elsewhere as well as here, that this article of amendment shall go into the record of this case, thus assailed by the President in his conspiracy with those lately in rebellion, in his attempt to revive "the lost cause," in his attempt to impose a fetter upon the nation which at last will work its ruin and crown the rebellion itself with success. The fourteenth article of amendment is in these words:

ARTICLE XIV.

SECTION 1. All persons born or naturalized in the United States, and subject to the jurisdiction thereof, are citizens of the United States and of the State wherein they reside. No State shall make or enforce any law which shall abridge the privileges or immunities of citizens of the United States; nor shall any State deprive any person of life, liberty, or property, without due process of law, nor deny to any person within its jurisdiction the equal protection of the law.

SEC. 2. Representatives shall be apportioned among the several States according to their respective numbers, counting the whole number of persons in each State, excluding Indians not taxed. But when the right to vote at any election for the choice of electors for President and Vice President of the United States, Representatives in Congress, the executive and judicial officers of a State, or the members of the Legislature thereof, is denied to any of the male inhabitants of such State, being twenty-one years of age and citizens of the United States, or in any way abridged, except for participation in rebellion or other crime, the basis of representation therein shall be reduced in the proportion which the number of such male citizens shall bear to the whole number of male citizens twenty-one years of age in such State.

SEC. 3. No person shall be a Senator or Representative in Congress, or elector of President and Vice President, or hold any office, civil or military, under the United States, or under any State, who, having previously taken an oath as a member of Congress, or as an officer of the United States, or as a member of any State Legislature, or as an executive or judicial officer of any State, to support the Constitution of the United States, shall have engaged in insurrection or rebellion against the same, or given aid or comfort to the enemies thereof. But Congress may, by a vote of two thirds of each House, remove such disability.

SEC. 4. The validity of the public debt of the United States authorized by law, including debts incurred for payment of pensions and bounties for services in suppressing insurrection or rebellion, shall not be questioned. But neither the United States nor any State shall assume or pay any debt or obligation incurred in aid of insurrection or rebellion against the United States, or any claim for the loss or emancipation of any slave; but all such debts, obligations, and claims shall be held illegal and void.

SEC. 5. That Congress shall have power to enforce, by appropriate legislation, the provisions of this article.

That is the article which the people desire to adopt, and that which President by coöperation and combination with those lately in rebellion seeks to defeat. What right had he to meddle with it? The gentlemen undertook to draw a distinction between Andrew Johnson the citizen, and Andrew Johnson the President. I thought, Senators, at the time I could see some significance in it. It was a little hard for them to stand here and defend the right of the President under his sworn obligation to take care that the laws be faithfully executed, and to support the Constitution under the law and in accordance with the law and the limitations of the law, to excuse him as President for any of those utterances. It was a much more easy matter, if you will, to excuse him as private citizen Andrew Johnson for saying that the people were without a Congress, and that being without a Congress their legislation was void, and, of course, was not to be enforced except in so far as he saw fit to approve or to enforce it; that being without a Congress, they had no right to propose this article of amendment essential to the future life of the Republic. What was this at last but saying that rebellion works no forfeiture? What was this at last but saying that by acts of secession and acts of rebellion in sufficient numbers among eleven States, or more than one fourth of all the States of the Union, and a persistent refusal to elect members to Congress, they thereby deprive the people of legislative power, and by the same method deprive the people of the power to propose amendments to their own Constitution?

No more offensive words, Senators, ever were uttered by an executive officer in this country or any country; no utterances more offensive could by possibility be made by Andrew Johnson. They are understood by the common, plain people as the utterances of an expiring rebellion in aid of the lost cause. Hostility to the amendment—why? Because, among other things, it forever makes slavery impossible in the land; because, among other things, it makes the repudiation of the plighted faith of this nation, either to its living or to its dead defenders, forever impossible in the land; because, by its further provisions, it makes the assumption of any debt or liability contracted in aid of the rebellion, either by State or congressional legislation, forever impossible in the land; because, by its provisions, it makes compensation for slaves forever impossible in the land, either by congressional enactment or by State legislation. Is that the secret of this hostility? If not, then what is it? Simply that you have no Congress and no right to amend the Constitution; that your nationality is broken up and destroyed. And his own adviser and counselor in this presence took the same ground, only he attempted to qualify it by saying that you might have the power of ordinary legislation, although you had no power of impeachment, and said that was the President's opinion, gave us notice in advance that that was the President's opinion. He will allow you to proceed with the mockery of the trial, giving you notice, however, that you have no right to pronounce judgment unless you pronounce judgment of acquittal!

As I said before, Senators, all the facts of this case support the averment of the eleventh article of impeachment. I do not propose to review them. I have referred already at sufficient length to the facts which do support it. I only ask Senators to remember when they come to deliberate that there are several averments in the eleventh article of these attempts to violate the law which I have shown by your act of 1801 and the rule of common law are indictable as committed in the District; that these were committed within the District; and that the averments are divisible. You might find him not guilty of one of the averments in the eleventh article and find him guilty of another. Surely you will find him guilty, and must find him guilty, upon your consciences, if you hold it to be a crime for the President purposely and deliberately to attempt to prevent the execution of a law of Congress, with or without force, with or without threat or intimidation. You must under the eleventh article find this man guilty of having entered into such combination and having contrived and devised to defeat

and hinder and prevent, as averred in that article, the execution of the tenure-of-office act, especially, as therein averred, to prevent the Secretary of War from forthwith resuming the functions of his office in obedience to the requirements of the act. And it is no matter whether Secretary Stanton was within the act or without it, it was decided by the legislative department of the Government, by the Senate of the United States under the Constitution, and its decision under the law should have controlled the President, as it certainly must control the Secretary.

The law was mandatory—it commanded the Secretary, upon the decision of the Senate and notice given to him, forthwith to resume the functions of that office, and for disobedience to its commands, after such judgment of the Senate and such notice, he himself should be impeached. Now, this fact being established and confessed, how is the Senate to get away from it when the President himself puts it in writing and confesses, on the 10th day of February, 1868, that as early as the 12th day of August, 1867, it was his purpose to prevent Edwin M. Stanton from resuming the functions of that office, and therefore it was his purpose, as alleged in the eleventh article, to prevent, if by possibility he could, the execution of the law? Senators, I can waste no further words upon the subject. It is useless for me to exhaust my strength by further argumentation.

I assume, Senators, after all that I have said on this subject, that I have made it clear to the entire satisfaction of every Senator that the substantive averments of the various articles preferred by the House of Representatives against the President are established by the proof and confessed substantially by his answer. I hold, Senators, that these articles are substantially established upon the proofs in the case, upon the confessions of the President himself of record in his answer, in this, that the President did issue his order for the removal of the Secretary of War during the session of the Senate of the United States in violation of the provisions of the act of March 2, 1867, regulating the tenure of certain civil offices, and with the intent to violate it, which intent the law implies, and which intent the President expressly confesses.

That his guilt is further established in this: that he did issue his letter of authority to Thomas in violation of that act, with the intent, as declared by himself, to prevent the Secretary of War from resuming the functions of the office after he himself had suspended him in pursuance of the provisions of the act, and submitted the same to the judgment of the Senate according to its requirements.

That he is guilty further in this: upon the proofs that he did unlawfully conspire with Lorenzo Thomas, as charged in the fourth, fifth, sixth, and seventh articles, with or without force, with or without intimidation, to prevent and hinder the Secretary of War from holding the office in direct violation of the terms of the tenure-of-office act.

That he is guilty further in this: that he did attempt to induce General Emory to violate the act making appropriations for the support of the Army, the violation of which act is by its second section declared to be a high misdemeanor in office.

That he is guilty further in this: that by his intemperate and scandalous harangues he was guilty of a great public indecency and of the attempt to bring the Congress of the United States into contempt and to incite the people to sedition and anarchy.

That he is guilty in this: that by denying the constitutionality of the Thirty-Ninth Congress, and by his acts before referred to, he did assume to himself the prerogative of dispensing with the laws, of suspending their execution at pleasure, until such time as it might suit his own convenience to test the question of their validity or to ascertain the true construction of the Constitution in the courts of the United States.

And that by contriving with those lately in insurrection he did further attempt to prevent the ratification of the fourteenth article of amendment to the Constitution; and by all these several acts did attempt to prevent the execution of the tenure-of-office act, the execution of the Army appropriation act, and the execution of the act for the more efficient government of the rebel States.

These facts being thus established will not only enforce conviction upon the Senate, in my judgment, but they will enforce conviction as well upon the minds of the great body of the people of this country.

Nothing remains, therefore, Senators, for me further to consider in this discussion than the confession and attempted avoidance of the President as made in his answer. I have anticipated it in the body of my argument. Senators have attended to what I have said. It is only needful for me to remind them that it is answered by the President that he claims the power indefinitely to suspend the heads of Departments during the session of the Senate without their advice and consent, and to fill the vacancies thus made by appointments *ad interim;* that he claims the right to interpret the Constitution for himself; and, in the exercise of that right, to pronounce for himself upon the validity of every act of Congress which may be placed upon the statute book, and therefore, by virtue of his prerogative as the Executive of the United States, in defiance of your laws and in defiance of the transcendent power of impeachment, vested by the people in their House of Representatives, he may suspend the laws and dispense with their execution at his pleasure!

That is the position of the President. These are the offenses with which he stands charged.

They have acquired and taken something of technical form and shape in the articles; but the effect of the charges against the President is usurpation in office, suspending the people's laws, dispensing with the execution thereof purposely, with intent to violate them, and, in the language of the article, to hinder and to prevent their execution.

The attempted avoidance set up is an implied judicial power, as it was called by the learned counsel of the President, to determine for himself the true construction of the Constitution and judicially to determine for himself the validity of all your laws. I have endeavored to show, Senators, that this assumption of the President is incompatible with every provision of your Constitution; that it is at war with all the traditions of the Republic; that it is in direct conflict with the contemporaneous and continued construction of the Constitution by the legislative, executive, and judicial departments. I have endeavored also to impress you, Senators, with my own conviction that this assumption of the President to interpret the Constitution and the laws for himself, to suspend the execution of the laws at his pleasure, is an assumption of power simply to set aside the Constitution, to set aside the laws, and to annihilate the Government of the people. This is the President's crime: that he has assumed this prerogative, dangerous to the people's liberties, violative alike of his oath, of the Constitution, and of the laws enacted under the Constitution. I have also endeavored to show to the Senate that these offenses, as specified in the articles, are impeachable, and are declared by the laws of the land to be high crimes and misdemeanors, indictable and punishable as such.

And yet the President has the audacity in his answer—and I go not beyond it to convict him—to come before the Senate and declare in substance: "Admitting all that is charged against me to be true; admitting that I did suspend the execution of the laws; that I did enter into a conspiracy with intent to prevent the execution of the laws, that it was my purpose to prevent their execution, that I did issue a letter of authority in direct violation of the law; nevertheless, I say it was my right to do so, and it is not your right to hold me to answer, because by force of the Constitution I am entitled to interpret the Constitution for myself, and to decide upon the validity of a law, whether it conflicts with a power conferred upon me by the Constitution, and if it does I must take the necessary steps to test its validity in the courts of justice." That is the President's answer as recorded here.

I have endeavored to show, further, that the civil tribunals of this country, under the Constitution, can by no possibility have any power to determine any such issue between the President and the people. I do not propose to repeat my argument, but I ask the Senate to consider, that if the courts shall be allowed to intervene, and in the first instance decide any question of this sort between the people and the accused President, it necessarily does result that the courts at last, acting upon the suggestions of the President, may decide every question of impeachment which can possibly arise by reason of the malfeasance and guilty acts of a President in office, and defy the power of the people to impeach him and try him in the Senate. What, the Supreme Court to decide a question of this sort for the Senate of the United States, when the Constitution declares that the Senate shall have the sole power to try all impeachments, which I said before necessarily includes the sole power to try every question of law and fact finally and forever between the President and the people!

That is my answer. That is the position we assume here, on behalf of the people, before the Senate. If we are wrong; if, after all, you, Senators, can cast the burden which, in our judgment, the Constitution imposes upon you, and upon you alone, on the courts, thereby depriving the people of the power of removing an accused and guilty President, that is for you. We do not entertain for a moment the belief that the Senate will give any countenance to this position assumed by the President in his answer, and which at last constitutes his sole defense.

These acts charged, then, as I said, are acts of usurpation in office, criminal violations of the Constitution and laws of the land; and inasmuch as they are committed by the Chief Magistrate of the nation, dangerous to the public liberties. The people, Senators, have declared in words too plain to be mistaken and too strong to be evaded by the subtleties of a false logic, that the Constitution ordained by them and the laws enacted by their Representatives in Congress assembled shall be obeyed, and shall be executed and enforced by their servant, the President of the United States, until the same shall be amended or repealed in the mode prescribed by themselves. They have written this decree of theirs all over this land in the tempest and fire of battle.

When twelve million people, standing within the limits of eleven States of this Union, entered into confederation and agreement against the supremacy of the Constitution and laws, and conspired to suspend their execution and to annul them within their respective territorial limits, from ocean to ocean, by a sublime uprising, the people stamped out in blood the atrocious assumption that millions of men were to be permitted, acting under State organizations, to suspend for a moment the supremacy of the Constitution or the execution of the people's laws. Is it to be supposed that this great and triumphant people, who but yesterday wrote this decree of theirs amid the flame of battle, are now at this day tamely to submit to the same assumption of power by a single man, and he their own sworn Executive? Let the people answer that question, as they assuredly will answer it, in the coming elections.

Is it not in vain, I ask you, Senators, that the people have thus vindicated by battle the supremacy of their own Constitution and laws, if, after all, their President is permitted to suspend their laws and dispense with the execution thereof at pleasure, and defy the power of the people to bring him to trial and judgment before the only tribunal authorized by the Constitution to try him? That is the issue which is presented before the Senate for decision by these articles of impeachment. By such acts of usurpation on the part of the ruler of a people, I need not say to the Senate, the peace of nations is broken, as it is only by obedience to law that the peace of nations is maintained and their existence perpetuated. Law is the voice of God and the harmony of the world—

"*It doth preserve the stars from wrong,*
Through it the eternal heavens are fresh and strong."

All history is but philosophy teaching by example. God is in history, and through it teaches to men and nations the profoundest lessons which they learn. It does not surprise me, Senators, that the learned counsel for the accused asked the Senate, in the consideration of this question, to close that volume of instruction, not to look into the past, not to listen to its voices. Senators, from that day when the inscription was written upon the graves of the heroes of Thermopylæ, "Stranger, go tell the Lacedemonians that we lie here in obedience to their laws," to this hour, no profounder lesson has come down to us than this: that through obedience to law comes the strength of nations and the safety of men.

No more fatal provision ever found its way into the constitutions of States than that contended for in this defense which recognizes the right of a single despot or of the many to discriminate in the administration of justice between the ruler and the citizen, between the strong and the weak. It was by this unjust discrimination that Aristides was banished because he was just. It was by this unjust discrimination that Socrates, the wonder of the Pagan world, was doomed to drink the hemlock because of his transcendent virtues. It was in honorable protest against this unjust discrimination that the great Roman Senator, father of his country, declared that the force of law consists in its being made for the whole community.

Senators, it is the pride and boast of that great people from whom we are descended, as it is the pride and boast of every American, that the law is the supreme power of the State and is for the protection of each by the combined power of all. By the constitution of England the hereditary monarch is no more above the law than the humblest subject; and by the Constitution of the United States the President is no more above the law than the poorest and most friendless beggar in your streets. The usurpations of Charles I inflicted untold injuries upon the people of England, and finally cost the usurper his life. The subsequent usurpations of James II—and I only refer to it because there is between his official conduct and that of this accused President the most remarkable parallel that I have ever read in history—filled the brain and heart of England with the conviction that new securities must be taken to restrain the prerogatives asserted by the Crown if they would maintain their ancient constitution and perpetuate their liberties. It is well said by Hallam that the usurpations of James swept away the solemn ordinances of the legislature. Out of those usurpations came the great revolution of 1688, which resulted, as the Senate well know, in the dethronement and banishment of James, in the elevation of William and Mary, in the immortal Declaration of Rights, of which it is well said that it is—

"The germ of the law which gave religious freedom to the Dissenter; which secured the independence of the judges; which limited the duration of Parliaments; which placed the liberty of the press under the protection of juries; which prohibited the slave trade; which abolished the sacramental test; which relieved the Roman Catholics from civil disabilities; which reformed the representative system—of every good law which has been passed during a hundred and sixty years; of every good law which may hereafter in the course of ages be found necessary to promote the public weal and to satisfy the demands of public opinion."

Senators, that great Declaration of Rights contains in substance these words of accusation against this king of England: he has endeavored to subvert the liberties of the kingdom in this, that he has suspended and dispensed with the execution of the laws; in this, that he has issued commissions under the great seal contrary to law; in this, that he has levied money to the use of the Crown contrary to law; in this, that he has caused cases to be tried in the king's bench which are cognizable only in the Parliament. (The Lords Journal of Parliament, vol. 14, p. 125.)

I ask the Senate to notice that these charges against James are substantially the charges presented against this accused President and confessed here of record, that he has suspended the laws and dispensed with the execution of the laws, and in order to do this has usurped authority as the Executive of the nation, declaring himself entitled under the Constitution to suspend the laws and dispense with their execution. He has further, like James, issued a commission contrary to law. He has further, like James, attempted to control the appropriated money of the people contrary to law. And he has further, like James, although it is not alleged against him in the articles of impeachment, it is confessed in his answer, attempted to cause the question of his responsibility to the people to be tried, not in the king's bench, but in the Supreme Court, when that question is alone cognizable in the Senate of the United States. Surely, Senators, if these usurpations, if these endeavors on the part of James thus to subvert the liberties of the people of England cost him his crown and kingdom, the like offenses committed by Andrew Johnson ought to cost him his office and subject him to that perpetual disability pronounced by the people through the Constitution upon him for his high crimes and misdemeanors.

Senators, you will pardon me—but I will detain you but a few moments longer—for asking your attention to another view of this question between the people and the Executive. I use the words of England's brilliant historian when I say had not the legislative power of England triumphed over the usurpations of James, "with what a crash, felt and heard to the farthest ends of the world, would the whole vast fabric of society have fallen." May God forbid that the future historian shall record of this day's proceedings, that by reason of the failure of the legislative power of the people to triumph over the usurpations of an apostate President through the defection of the Senate of the United States, the just fabric of American empire fell and perished from the earth! The great revolution of 1688 in England was a forerunner of your own Constitution. The Declaration of Rights to which I have referred but reasserted the ancient constitution of England, not found in any written instrument, but scattered through the statutes of four centuries.

The great principles thus reasserted by the Declaration of Rights in 1688 were, that no law should be passed without the consent of the Representatives of the nation, no tax should be laid, no regular soldiery should be kept up, no citizen should be deprived for a single day of his liberty by the arbitrary will of the sovereign, no tool of power should plead the royal mandate in justification for the violation of any legal right of the humblest citizen, and forever swept away the assumption that the executive prerogative was above the fundamental law. These were the principles, Senators, involved in that day in the controversy between the people and their recusant sovereign. They are precisely the principles this day involved in this controversy between the people and their recusant President. Without revolution, Senators, like the great Parliament of 1688, you are asked to reassert the principles of the Constitution of your country, not to be searched for through the statutes of centuries, but to be found in that grand, sacred, written instrument given to us by the fathers of the Republic. The Constitution of the United States, as I have said, embodies all that is valuable of England's Declaration of Rights, of England's constitution and laws. It was ordained by the people of the United States amid the convulsions and agonies of nations. By its express provisions all men within its jurisdiction are equal before the law, equally entitled to those rights of person which are as universal as the material structure of man, and equally liable to answer to its tribunals of justice for every injury done either to the citizen or to the State.

It is this spirit of justice, of liberty, of equality, Senators, that makes your Constitution dear to freemen in this and in all lands, in that it secures to every man his rights, and to the people at large the inestimable right of self-government, the right which is this day challenged by this usurping President, for if he be a law to himself the people are no longer their own law makers through their Representatives in Congress assembled. The President thereby simply becomes their dictator. If the President become a dictator he will become so by the judgment of the Senate, not by the text of the Constitution, not by any interpretation heretofore put upon it by any act of the people, nor by any act of the people's Representatives. The Representatives of the people have discharged their duty in his impeachment. They have presented him at the bar of the Senate for trial, in that he has usurped and attempted to combine in himself the legislative and executive powers of this great people, thereby claiming for himself a power by which he may annihilate their Government. We have seen that when the supremacy of their Constitution was challenged in battle the people made such sacrifice to maintain it as has no parallel in history.

Senators, can it be that after this triumph of law over anarchy, of right over wrong, of patriotism over treason, the Constitution and laws are again to be assailed in the capital of the nation in the person of the Chief Magistrate, and by the judgment of the Senate he is to be protected in that usurpation? The President by his answer and by the representations of his counsel asks you, deliberately asks you, by your judgment to set the accused above the Constitution which he has violated and above the people whom he has betrayed; and that, too, upon the pretext that the President has the right judicially to construe the Constitution for himself, judicially to decide for himself the validity of your laws, and to plead in justification at your bar that his only purpose in thus violating the Constitution and the laws is to test their validity and ascertain the construction of the Constitution upon his own motion in the courts of justice, and thereby suspend your further proceeding.

I ask you, Senators, how long men would deliberate upon the question whether a private citizen, arraigned at the bar of one of your tribunals of justice for a criminal violation of the law, should be permitted to interpose a plea in justification of his criminal act that his only purpose was to interpret the Constitution and laws for himself, that he violated the law in the exercise of his prerogative to test its validity hereafter at such day as might suit his own convenience in the courts of justice. Surely, Senators, it is as competent for the private citizen to interpose such justification in answer to crime in one of your tribunals of justice as it is for the President of the United States to interpose

it, and for the simple reason that the Constitution is no respector of persons and vests neither in the President nor in the private citizen judicial power.

Pardon me, Senators, for saying it; I speak it in no offensive spirit; I speak it from a sense of duty; I utter but my own conviction and desire to place it upon the record, that for the Senate to sustain any such plea, would, in my judgment, be a gross violation of the already violated Constitution and laws of a free people.

Can it be, Senators, that by your decree you are at last to make this discrimination between the ruler of the people and the private citizen, and allow him to interpose his assumed right to interpret judicially your Constitution and laws? Are you solemnly to proclaim by your decree:

> "Plate sin with gold,
> And the strong lance of justice hurtless breaks;
> Arm it in rags, a pigmy's straw doth pierce it?"

I put away, Senators, the possibility that the Senate of the United States, equal in dignity to any tribunal in the world, is capable of recording any such decision even upon the petition and prayer of this accused and guilty President. Can it be that by reason of his great office the President is to be protected in his high crimes and misdemeanors, violative alike of his oath, of the Constitution, and of the express letter of your written law enacted by the legislative department of the Government?

Senators, I have said perhaps more than I ought to have said. I have said perhaps more than there was occasion to say. I know that I stand in the presence of men illustrious in our country's history. I know that I stand in the presence of men who for long years have been in the nation's councils. I know that I stand in the presence of men who may, in some sense, be called to-day the living fathers of the Republic. I ask you, Senators, to consider that I speak before you this day in behalf of the violated law of a free people who commission me. I ask you to remember that I speak this day under the obligations of my oath. I ask you to consider that I am not insensible to the significance of the words of which mention was made by the learned counsel from New York: justice, duty, law, oath. I ask you, Senators, to remember that the great principles of constitutional liberty for which I this day speak have been taught to men and nations by all the trials and triumphs, by all the agonies and martyrdoms of the past; that they are the wisdom of the centuries uttered by the elect of the human race who were made perfect through suffering.

I ask you, Senators, to consider that we stand this day pleading for the violated majesty of the law, by the graves of a half million of martyred hero-patriots who made death beautiful by the sacrifice of themselves for their country, the Constitution, and the laws, and who by their sublime example have taught us that all must obey the law; that none are above the law; that no man lives for himself alone, but each for all; that some must die that the State may live; that the citizen is at best but for to-day, while the Commonwealth is for all time; and that position, however high, patronage, however powerful, cannot be permitted to shelter crime to the peril of the Republic.

It only remains for me, Senators, to thank you, as I do, for the honor you have done me by your kind attention, and to demand, in the name of the House of Representatives, and of the people of the United States, judgment against the accused for the high crimes and misdemeanors in office whereof he stands impeached, and of which before God and man he is guilty.

As Mr. Manager BINGHAM concluded there were manifestations of applause in different portions of the galleries, with cheers.

The CHIEF JUSTICE. Order! Order! If this be repeated the Sergeant-at-Arms will clear the galleries.

This announcement was received with laughter and hisses by some persons in the galleries, while others continued the cheering and clapping of hands.

Mr. GRIMES. Mr. Chief Justice, I move that the order of the court to clear the galleries be immediately enforced.

The motion was agreed to.

The CHIEF JUSTICE. The Sergeant-at-Arms will clear the galleries. [Hisses and cheers and clapping of hands in parts of the galleries.] If the offense be repeated the Sergeant-at-Arms will arrest the offenders.

Mr. TRUMBULL. I move that the Sergeant-at-Arms be directed to arrest the persons making the disturbance, if he can find them, as well as to clear the galleries.

The CHIEF JUSTICE. The Chief Justice has already given directions to that effect.

[The Sergeant-at-Arms, by his assistants, continued to execute the order by clearing the galleries.]

Mr. CAMERON. Mr. President, I hope the galleries will not be cleared. A large portion of the persons in the galleries had a very different feeling from that expressed by those who clapped and applauded. It was one of those extraordinary occasions which will happen sometimes——

Several SENATORS. Order.

Mr. FESSENDEN. I call the Senator to order.

The CHIEF JUSTICE. Debate is not in order.

Mr. CAMERON. We all know that such outbursts will occasionally take place——

Mr. JOHNSON. I call the member to order.

The CHIEF JUSTICE. The Senator from Pennsylvania is not in order. The galleries will be cleared.

Mr. CONNESS. Mr. President, I move

that the court take a recess for fifteen minutes.

Several SENATORS. Not until the galleries are cleared.

The CHIEF JUSTICE. The question is on the motion of the Senator from California, that the Senate, sitting as a court of impeachment, take a recess for fifteen minutes.

The motion was not agreed to.

Mr. DAVIS. I ask the presiding officer to have the order to clear the galleries enforced.

The CHIEF JUSTICE. The Sergeant-at-Arms states to the presiding officer that the order is being enforced as fast as practicable.

Mr. SHERMAN. Mr. President, is it in order to move that the Senate retire to its Chamber for deliberation? I will make that motion, if it is in order.

Mr. TRUMBULL. I hope not.

The CHIEF JUSTICE. The Chief Justice thinks that until the order of the Senate is enforced it cannot properly take any other order or proceed with any other matter.

Mr. SHERMAN. Very well.

Mr. TRUMBULL. No order can be made until the galleries are cleared. That order is being executed.

Mr. SHERMAN. I think many persons in the galleries do not understand that they are ordered to leave the galleries. There is some misapprehension, I think.

The CHIEF JUSTICE. The persons in attendance in the galleries are informed that the Senate has made an order that the galleries be cleared, and it is expected that those in the galleries will respect the order.

The galleries having been cleared, with the exception of the diplomatic gallery and the reporters' gallery,

Mr. ANTHONY. Mr. President, I move that the further execution of the order be dispensed with.

Mr. TRUMBULL. I insist that the order be executed.

Several SENATORS. So do I.

The CHIEF JUSTICE. Does the Senator from Rhode Island withdraw his motion?

Mr. ANTHONY. No, sir; I make the motion.

The CHIEF JUSTICE. The Senator from Rhode Island moves that the further execution of the order in regard to clearing the galleries be suspended.

Mr. CONKLING. I wish to ask a question of the Chair. I inquire whether the suspension of the order will open all the galleries for the return of those who have been turned out?

The CHIEF JUSTICE. The Chief Justice thinks it would have that effect.

Mr. TRUMBULL. I hope the order will not be suspended. Let it be executed.

The CHIEF JUSTICE. The question is on the motion to suspend the order clearing the galleries.

The motion was not agreed to.

The CHIEF JUSTICE. The galleries will be cleared.

The diplomatic gallery having been cleared, Mr. MORRILL, of Maine. Mr. Chief Justice, I desire, if it is in order, to submit a motion. It is that when the Senate, sitting for the trial of the impeachment, adjourn to-day, it adjourn to Saturday next at twelve o'clock.

Mr. CAMERON. Before that——

The CHIEF JUSTICE. Debate is not in order.

Mr. CAMERON. I want to say that the motion was made against my judgment for clearing the galleries; but it was agreed to. I perceive that the galleries are not yet cleared; and until that order is carried out I will not consent to any business.

The CHIEF JUSTICE. The Chief Justice sees nobody in the galleries.

Mr. CAMERON. The persons I refer to are behind the Chief Justice. (Referring to the reporters' gallery.)

The CHIEF JUSTICE. Does the Senator from Pennsylvania object to——

Mr. CAMERON. No; but I desire that your order shall be carried out.

The CHIEF JUSTICE. The Chief Justice is informed that the reporters who occupy the reporters' gallery are still there. Is it the pleasure of the Senate that they shall remain?

Mr. CONNESS. I renew the motion for a recess.

The CHIEF JUSTICE. The Chief Justice desires to execute the will of the Senate precisely, and wishes to understand what it is. The Senator from Pennsylvania has very properly called the attention of the Chief Justice to the fact that the reporters still remain in the galleries. Is it the pleasure of the Senate——

Several SENATORS. They are all out now. They are all gone.

The CHIEF JUSTICE. Then the order is completely executed. The Chair will now recognize the Senator from California.

Mr. CONNESS. I move a recess.

Several SENATORS. Oh, no.

Mr. CONNESS. If it is manifestly not the judgment of the Senate, of course I do not want the question put.

The CHIEF JUSTICE. Does the Senator withdraw his motion?

Mr. CONNESS. I withdraw it.

The CHIEF JUSTICE. The question is on the motion of the Senator from Maine, [Mr. MORRILL,] that when the Senate, sitting as a court of impeachment, adjourn to-day, it adjourn to meet on Saturday next at twelve o'clock.

Mr. CONNESS. On that I call for the yeas and nays.

The yeas and nays were ordered; and being taken, resulted—yeas 22, nays 29; as follows:

YEAS—Messrs. Anthony, Cattell, Cragin, Dixon, Doolittle, Fessenden, Fowler, Frelinghuysen, Grimes, Henderson, Howard, Johnson, Morrill of Maine, Norton, Patterson of New Hampshire, Patterson of Tennessee, Ross, Saulsbury, Sprague, Trumbull, Van Winkle, and Willey—22.

NAYS—Messrs. Buckalew, Cameron, Chandler, Conkling, Conness, Corbett, Davis, Drake, Edmunds, Ferry, Harlan, Hendricks, Howe, McCreery, Morgan, Morrill of Vermont, Morton, Nye, Pomeroy, Ramsey, Sherman, Stewart, Sumner, Thayer, Tipton, Vickers, Williams, Wilson, and Yates—29.

NOT VOTING—Messrs. Bayard, Cole, and Wade—3.

So the motion was not agreed to.

Mr. EDMUNDS. I move that when the court adjourns it adjourn to meet on Friday next at twelve o'clock.

Mr. CONNESS. On that I call for the yeas and nays.

Mr. SHERMAN. I ask the Senator from Vermont if he will not postpone his motion until we settle the question of the amount of debate to be allowed.

Mr. EDMUNDS. My motion is that when the court adjourns to-day it adjourn to the time named.

Mr. SHERMAN. I prefer to settle the other question. After that is settled I will vote to adjourn over.

Mr. EDMUNDS. For the time being then, Mr. President, I withdraw the motion.

Mr. SHERMAN. There is a pending resolution, offered, I think, by the Senator from Vermont himself, on that subject.

Mr. EDMUNDS. I have no objection to settling those questions first; indeed, I think it better that we should do so.

Mr. SUMNER. Mr. President, I would suggest that there were several orders that were expressly postponed to the close of the argument. They are, therefore, naturally at this moment in order.

Mr. CONKLING. I call for the regular order of business, Mr. President.

The CHIEF JUSTICE. The first order of business is the motion of the Senator from Vermont, [Mr. EDMUNDS,] that the official reporters take report of the debates upon the final question when the doors shall be closed for deliberation, to be printed in the proceedings. This refers to the closing of the doors for deliberation on the final question. The Secretary will read the order and the amendments to it.

The CHIEF CLERK. The order submitted by the Senator from Vermont, [Mr. EDMUNDS,] on the 24th of April, is as follows:

Ordered, That after the arguments shall be concluded, and when the doors shall be closed for deliberation upon the final question, the official reporters of the Senate shall take down the debates upon the final question, to be reported in the proceedings.

The Senator from Oregon [Mr. WILLIAMS] moved to amend the proposed order by adding to it the words:

But no Senator shall speak more than once, nor to exceed fifteen minutes, during such deliberation.

The CHIEF JUSTICE. The question is on the amendment.

Mr. ANTHONY. I move to amend the amendment by adding to it the words "except by leave of the Senate to be had without debate, as provided in Rule 23." The amendment as it stands seems to cut off the provision of Rule 23. Perhaps the mover of the amendment will accept this modification, for I suppose it is not the intention to cut off that provision.

Mr. CONNESS. I rise for information. I rise to inquire of the Chair whether this is a consultation of the Senate that we are now proceeding with, and consequently open to limited debate, or whether we are sitting as a court, debate not being in order.

The CHIEF JUSTICE. The Senate has made as yet no order for closing the doors for deliberation, nor has it made any order to retire for consultation. Consequently at present there can be no debate.

Mr. CONNESS. Upon the first order presented I ask for the yeas and· nays.

The CHIEF JUSTICE. The question now is on the amendment of the Senator from Rhode Island to the amendment of the Senator from Oregon.

Mr. HOWARD. Mr. President, I ask for the reading of the twenty·third rule.

The CHIEF JUSTICE. The Secretary will read the twenty·third rule.

The rule was read, as follows:

"XXIII. All the orders and decisions shall be made and had by yeas and nays, which shall be entered on the record, and without debate, subject to the operation of Rule VII, except when the doors shall be closed for deliberation, and in that case no member shall speak more than once on one question, and for not more than fifteen minutes on the final question, unless by consent of the Senate, to be had without debate; but a motion to adjourn may be decided without the yeas and nays, unless they be demanded by one-fifth of the members present."

Mr. DRAKE. Is the amendment offered by the Senator from Rhode Island subject to amendment?

The CHIEF JUSTICE. It is not. It is an amendment to an amendment.

Mr. DRAKE. If it be adopted as an amendment can it be amended afterward?

Mr. ANTHONY. The Senator can state what modification he desires.

Mr. DRAKE. I wish, before the word "leave," in the amendment proposed by the Senator from Rhode Island, to insert the word "unanimous."

Mr. ANTHONY. I do not accept that proposition. My amendment merely conforms to the twenty-third rule.

Mr. WILLIAMS. I ask for information if, under this proposed amendment of the Senator from Rhode Island, the rule can be changed without one day's notice, or whether it can be changed at once upon the motion of any member?

Mr. THAYER. Mr. President, I desire to inquire if it is in order now to move that the doors of the galleries be opened.

The CHIEF JUSTICE. It is.

Mr. THAYER. Then I make that motion, and I ask for the reading of the nineteenth rule.

Mr. CONKLING. I hope the reporter's gallery at any rate will be opened, unless we mean to meet in secret conclave.

The CHIEF JUSTICE. The Secretary will read the nineteenth rule.

Rule 19 was read, as follows:

"XIX. At all times while the Senate is sitting upon the trial of an impeachment, the doors of the Senate shall be kept open unless the Senate shall direct the doors to be closed while deliberating upon its decisions."

The CHIEF JUSTICE. That rule does not apply, as the Chief Justice understands, to the clearing of the galleries, but applies to the general closing of the doors for purposes of deliberation.

Mr. THAYER. I make the motion that the doors of the galleries be opened.

The CHIEF JUSTICE. That motion can be made at this time only by unanimous consent, there being another question pending. Is there any objection to the motion?

Mr. CONNESS. I object to it.

The CHIEF JUSTICE. The question is on the amendment of the Senator from Rhode Island, [Mr. ANTHONY.]

Mr. CONKLING. I beg to make an inquiry of the Chair. I beg to inquire whether the order of the Chair included the place where the reporters sit, where no applause was made, and their absence from which leaves us entirely in secret session so far as public reports are concerned.

The CHIEF JUSTICE. The Chief Justice was under the impression that the order of the Senate did not include the reporters' gallery, and put the question distinctly to the Senate whether it did or did not. While the question was being put the reporters left the gallery, and the point was not decided by the Senate.

Mr. CONKLING. Then I submit, as a question of order, that under the order the doors of the reporters' gallery should not have been closed, and are now open, in view of that order, to the reporters.

The CHIEF JUSTICE. If there be no objection——

Mr. CAMERON. It seems to me that while it may be very proper to admit reporters, it is equally proper to admit everybody——

The CHIEF JUSTICE. Debate is not in order.

Mr. CAMERON. I only desire to say a word. I think we ought to admit everybody——

Mr. CONKLING. The Chair did not direct the reporters' gallery to be cleared.

Mr. CAMERON. And the Chair certainly did not direct inoffensive people to be turned out.

Mr. SHERMAN. I move that the pending order be postponed with a view to submit a motion to open the galleries.

Mr. TRUMBULL. If the Senate will allow me, I desire to say that I think the demonstration in the galleries will not be repeated. I hope gentlemen will withdraw their objections and by unanimous consent let the galleries be opened.

Mr. SHERMAN. I think the object is accomplished.

Mr. TRUMBULL. I think we have accomplished all that is necessary. The order has been obeyed. If there is no objection, I hope the presiding officer will order the doors of the galleries to be opened.

The CHIEF JUSTICE. If there be no objection, the doors will be opened. The Chair hears no objection, and he directs the galleries to be opened.

Mr. WILSON. I move that the Senate take a recess for fifteen minutes.

The motion was agreed to; and at the expiration of the recess the Senate resumed its session.

The CHIEF JUSTICE. The Chief Justice understands that the argument on the part of the House of Representatives and also on the part of the defendant, the President of the United States, is closed. If there is anything further to submit the gentlemen on both sides will state it.

Mr. Manager BOUTWELL. Nothing further on the part of the Managers.

Mr. EVARTS. Nothing on our part.

Mr. HENDRICKS. Mr. President, the questions that are now coming before the Senate ought to be discussed and debated. I move, therefore, that the Senate retire to consider of the different propositions that are before us, either to their room or in the Senate Chamber; or if by unanimous consent the debate can be allowed to be extended to ten minutes, we remaining here, I do not want to disturb anybody, and I would rather go on and debate here as we are.

The CHIEF JUSTICE. The only motion in order is that the Senate retire for deliberation, or that the doors be closed for deliberation.

Mr. FESSENDEN. I suggest to the Senator from Indiana to change his motion so that we may consult in this Chamber and let the audience retire.

Mr. HENDRICKS. Mr. President——

The CHIEF JUSTICE. No debate is in order but by unanimous consent.

Mr. HENDRICKS. I was about to suggest that we proceed now as if we had retired, without disturbing anybody. I think we might so regard ourselves, and go on.

Mr. TRUMBULL. I suppose that can be done by unanimous consent.

The CHIEF JUSTICE. Certainly.

Mr. TRUMBULL. I hope it will be done.

Mr. HENDRICKS. By unanimous consent we may be allowed to proceed under the rules as if we had retired for deliberation.

The CHIEF JUSTICE. If there be no objection——

Mr. CONKLING. What is the precise proposition?

Mr. HENDRICKS. That we consider these questions in public as if we had retired, so that what is said in regard to these proposed rules shall be public.

Mr. CONNESS. That is to say that debate shall be allowed.

Mr. HENDRICKS. To the extent of ten minutes as limited by the rules.

The CHIEF JUSTICE. The Chief Justice thinks it proper to say to the Senate that this reverses its whole order of proceeding. It can be done, undoubtedly, by unanimous consent. If there be no objection——

Mr. EDMUNDS and Mr. WILLIAMS. I object.

The CHIEF JUSTICE. Objection is made. The Senator from Indiana moves that the Senate retire for the purpose of considering the pending question.

Mr. EDMUNDS. I move to amend that motion so that it shall be an order, as the rules provide, that the doors shall be closed.

The CHIEF JUSTICE. That is the regular motion in order, that the doors be closed under the rules. The Senate has heretofore varied that proceeding by retiring for conference.

Mr. HENDRICKS. Senators will allow me to say that my only object in making this motion was to relieve ourselves in regard to the limitation of debate. I think there is no necessity for disturbing the audience, or disturbing the audience by going out.

The CHIEF JUSTICE. The Chief Justice must remind the Senator that debate is not in order. The question is on the motion to close the doors for deliberation.

The motion was agreed to.

The Senate Chamber having been cleared and the doors closed,

The CHIEF JUSTICE stated the question to be on the order proposed by Mr. EDMUNDS, with the amendments thereto offered by Mr. WILLIAMS and Mr. ANTHONY.

After debate,

Mr. FRELINGHUYSEN moved to lay the proposed order on the table; which motion was agreed to—yeas 28, nays 20; as follows:

YEAS—Messrs. Cameron, Cattell, Chandler, Conkling, Conness, Corbett, Cragin, Drake, Ferry, Frelinghuysen, Harlan, Henderson, Howe, Morgan, Morrill of Maine, Morton, Norton, Patterson of New Hampshire, Pomeroy, Ramsey, Ross, Stewart, Sumner, Thayer, Tipton, Trumbull, Williams, and Yates—28.

NAYS—Messrs. Anthony, Bayard, Buckalew, Davis, Dixon, Doolittle, Edmunds, Fessenden, Fowler, Grimes, Hendricks, Johnson, McCreery, Morrill of Vermont, Patterson of Tennessee, Saulsbury, Sprague, Van Winkle, Vickers, and Willey—20.

NOT VOTING—Messrs. Cole, Howard, Nye, Sherman, Wade, and Wilson—6.

So the order was laid on the table.

The CHIEF JUSTICE laid before the Senate a letter from the Speaker of the House of Representatives, asking that the House might be notified when the doors of the Senate should be open.

On motion of Mr. EDMUNDS, it was

Ordered, That the Secretary inform the House of Representatives that the Senate, sitting for the trial of the President upon articles of impeachment, will notify the House when it is ready to receive them at the bar.

The CHIEF JUSTICE stated the next business in order to be the following order, submitted by Mr. SUMNER on the 25th of April:

Ordered, That the Senate, sitting for the trial of Andrew Johnson, President of the United States, will proceed to vote on the several articles of impeachment at twelve o'clock on the day after the close of the arguments.

After debate,

Mr. DRAKE submitted the following amendment to Rule 23, to come in at the end of the rule:

The fifteen minutes herein allowed shall be for the whole deliberation on the final question, and not to the final question on each article of impeachment.

The proposed amendment was laid over for future consideration.

On motion of Mr. JOHNSON, the Senate, sitting for the trial of the impeachment, adjourned.

THURSDAY, *May* 7, 1868.

The Chief Justice of the United States took the chair.

The usual proclamation was made by the Sergeant-at-Arms.

Mr. Nelson, of counsel for the respondent, appeared in his seat.

The Journal of yesterday's proceedings of the Senate, sitting for the trial of the impeachment, was read.

The CHIEF JUSTICE. When the Senate was considering the order which is now the unfinished business it was sitting with closed doors, and the doors will now be closed for deliberation, under the rules, unless there be some order to the contrary. [After a pause.] The doors will be closed for deliberation.

Mr. HOWE. Mr. President, I do not see any necessity for closing the doors. Unless Senators do see a necessity for it I hope that order will not be executed.

The CHIEF JUSTICE. There can be no deliberation unless the doors are closed. There can be no debate under the rules, unless the doors be closed.

Mr. SUMNER. Still, Mr. President, I would rise to a question of order. It is whether the Senate can proceed to deliberate now except by a vote. There must be another vote of the Senate in order to proceed to deliberate to-day, I take it. We adjourned last night, and we have now met in open session.

The CHIEF JUSTICE. There can be no debate on the question of order; but the Chief Justice will submit the question to the Senate. The Senator from Massachusetts makes a question of order that before the Senate can proceed to deliberate there must be another formal vote of the Senate. The Chair will submit that question directly to the Senate.

Mr. SHERMAN. I should like to ask the Senator from Massachusetts a question, whether he proposes to act on the pending resolution without debate?

Mr. SUMNER. I did not intend to interpose any opposition to anything. I only wished that whatever we did should be done according to the rules. We have now been sitting—this is merely an answer to the inquiry of the Senator—in open session——

The CHIEF JUSTICE. Debate is out of order. It can go on by unanimous consent, not otherwise.

Mr. SUMNER. And how shall we get from open session into deliberation?

Mr. EDMUNDS. I object to debate.

The CHIEF JUSTICE. There can be no debate until the doors are closed.

Mr. CONKLING. I rise for information from the Chair. I wish to inquire whether, when the presiding officer announces that a certain thing will be done unless objection is made, and no objection is made, that is not tantamount to a vote of the Senate and does not cover in substance the point made by the Senator from Massachusetts.

The CHIEF JUSTICE. The Chief Justice so regards it.

Mr. SUMNER. If that is understood——

Mr. EDMUNDS. I object to all debate.

Mr. TRUMBULL. Mr. President, I wish, before the doors are closed, to raise a question of order under the twenty-third rule, which reads as follows:

"All the orders and decisions shall be made and had by yeas and nays, which shall be entered on the record and.without debate, except when the doors shall be closed for deliberation."

That means deliberation in reference to a matter, as I understand it, connected with the immediate trial. These are rules adopted for the general government of the Senate in all cases of impeachment. I never understood when I agreed to these rules that they would be used as a restraint upon the Senate in reference to any question that might be raised here. Propositions are raised here having no particular bearing upon this trial as to the course of proceeding, and we ought to settle those, it seems to me——

Mr. EDMUNDS. I rise to a question of order. I object to debate until the order of the Chair is complied with.

The CHIEF JUSTICE. There can be no debate until the order of the Chair is executed.

Mr. TRUMBULL. What is the order?

The CHIEF JUSTICE. The Chair stated to the Senate that when deliberation was terminated by adjournment last evening they were sitting with closed doors, and unless some objection should be made he would direct the doors to be closed. He waited, and no objection was made, and he then directed the doors to be closed. Until that order is executed there can be no debate.

The Chamber was thereupon cleared and the doors closed.

The CHIEF JUSTICE stated that the unfinished business before the Senate yesterday at its adjournment, to wit, the motion submitted by Mr. SUMNER on the 25th of April, that the

Senate will proceed to vote on the several articles of impeachment at twelve o'clock m. on the day after the close of the arguments, was the business now before the Senate.

The Senate resumed the consideration of the resolution.

Mr. MORRILL, of Maine, moved to amend the motion of Mr. SUMNER by striking out all after the word "that," in the first line, and inserting the following in lieu thereof:

When the Senate sitting to try impeachment adjourns to-day it will be to Monday next at twelve o'clock m., when the Senate will proceed to take the yeas and nays on the articles of impeachment without debate; any Senator desiring it to have permission to file a written opinion, to go upon the record of the proceedings.

Mr. DRAKE moved to amend the amendment by inserting after the word "permission" the words "at the time of giving his veto."

After debate,

Mr. CONKLING moved that the further consideration of the pending subject be postponed.

After further debate,

Mr. TRUMBULL moved that the pending subject lie on the table; which was agreed to.

Mr. MORRILL, of Vermont, submitted the following motion for consideration:

Ordered, That when the Senate adjourns to-day it adjourn to meet on Monday next, at eleven o'clock a. m., for the purpose of deliberation, under the rules of the Senate sitting on the trial of impeachments; and that on Tuesday, at twelve o'clock m., the Senate shall proceed to vote, without debate, on the several articles of impeachment, and each Senator shall be permitted to file, within two days after the vote shall have been taken, his written opinion, to go on the record.

Mr. ANTHONY moved to amend the motion of Mr. MORRILL, of Vermont, by striking out the words "on Tuesday" and inserting the words "on or before Wednesday."

Mr. CONNESS called for the yeas and nays on the amendment, and they were ordered; and being taken, resulted—yeas 13, nays 37; as follows:

YEAS—Messrs. Anthony, Buckalew, Davis, Dixon, Doolittle, Fowler, Hendricks, McCreery, Patterson of Tennessee, Ross, Saulsbury, Sprague, and Vickers—13.

NAYS—Messrs. Cameron, Cattell, Chandler, Cole, Conkling, Conness, Corbett, Cragin, Drake, Edmunds, Ferry, Frelinghuysen, Harlan, Henderson, Howard, Howe, Johnson, Morgan, Morrill of Maine, Morrill of Vermont, Morton, Norton, Nye, Patterson of New Hampshire, Pomeroy, Ramsey, Stewart, Sumner, Thayer, Tipton, Trumbull, Van Winkle, Willey, Williams, Wilson, and Yates—37.

NOT VOTING — Messrs. Bayard, Fessenden, Grimes, and Wade—4.

So the amendment was not agreed to.

Mr. SUMNER moved that the further consideration of the motion of Mr. MORRILL, of Vermont, be postponed, and that the Senate proceed to consider the articles of impeachment.

After debate,

Mr. SUMNER called for the yeas and nays on his motion, and they were ordered; and

being taken, resulted—yeas 15, nays 38; as follows:

YEAS—Messrs. Cameron, Conkling, Conness, Drake, Harlan, Morgan, Nye, Pomeroy, Stewart, Sumner, Thayer, Tipton, Williams, Wilson, and Yates—15.

NAYS—Messrs. Anthony, Bayard, Buckalew, Cattell, Chandler, Cole, Corbett, Cragin, Davis, Dixon, Doolittle, Edmunds, Ferry, Fessenden, Fowler, Frelinghuysen, Grimes, Henderson, Hendricks, Howard, Howe, Johnson, McCreery, Morrill of Maine, Morrill of Vermont, Morton, Norton, Patterson of New Hampshire, Patterson of Tennessee, Ramsey, Ross, Saulsbury, Sherman, Sprague, Trumbull, Van Winkle, Vickers, and Willey—38.

NOT VOTING—Mr. Wade—1.

So the motion was not agreed to.

Mr. SUMNER moved to amend the motion of Mr. MORRILL, of Vermont, by striking out the word "Monday," and inserting "Saturday."

Mr. SUMNER called for the yeas and nays, and they were ordered; and being taken, resulted—yeas 16, nays 36; as follows:

YEAS—Messrs. Cameron, Chandler, Cole, Conkling, Conness, Drake, Harlan, Howard, Morgan, Pomeroy, Stewart, Sumner, Thayer, Williams, Wilson, and Yates—16.

NAYS—Messrs. Anthony, Bayard, Buckalew, Cattell, Corbett, Cragin, Davis, Dixon, Doolittle, Edmunds, Ferry, Fessenden, Fowler, Frelinghuysen, Grimes, Henderson, Hendricks, Howe, Johnson, McCreery, Morrill of Maine, Morrill of Vermont, Morton, Norton, Patterson of New Hampshire, Patterson of Tennessee, Ramsey, Ross, Saulsbury, Sherman, Sprague, Tipton, Trumbull, Van Winkle, Vickers, and Willey—36.

NOT VOTING—Messrs. Nye and Wade—2.

So the amendment was not agreed to.

Mr. SUMNER moved to amend the motion of Mr. MORRILL, of Vermont, by striking out at the end thereof the following words:

And each Senator shall be permitted to file within two days after the vote shall have been so taken his written opinion, to go on the record.

Mr. DRAKE moved to amend the portion proposed to be stricken out by striking out the words "within two days after the vote shall have been so taken," and inserting in lieu thereof the words "at the time of giving his vote."

Mr. DRAKE called for the yeas and nays on his amendment, and they were ordered; and being taken, resulted—yeas 12, nays 38; as follows:

YEAS—Messrs. Cameron, Chandler, Conkling, Conness, Drake, Harlan, Howard, Morgan, Ramsey, Stewart, Sumner, and Thayer—12.

NAYS—Messrs. Anthony, Bayard, Buckalew, Cattell, Cole, Corbett, Cragin, Davis, Dixon, Doolittle, Edmunds, Ferry, Fessenden, Fowler, Frelinghuysen, Grimes, Henderson, Hendricks, Johnson, McCreery, Morrill of Maine, Morrill of Vermont, Morton, Norton, Patterson of New Hampshire, Patterson of Tennessee, Ross, Saulsbury, Sherman, Sprague, Tipton, Trumbull, Van Winkle, Vickers, Willey, Williams, Wilson, and Yates—38.

NOT VOTING—Messrs. Howe, Nye, Pomeroy, and Wade—4.

So the amendment was not agreed to.

The question recurring on the amendment proposed by Mr. SUMNER to strike out the closing sentence the motion of Mr. MORRILL, of Vermont,

Mr. SUMNER called for the yeas and nays,

and they were ordered; and being taken, resulted—yeas 6, nays 42; as follows:

YEAS—Messrs. Drake, Harlan, Ramsey, Stewart, Sumner, and Thayer—6.

NAYS—Messrs. Bayard, Buckalew, Cameron, Cattell, Chandler, Cole, Corbett, Davis, Dixon, Doolittle, Edmunds, Ferry, Fessenden, Fowler, Frelinghuysen, Grimes, Henderson, Hendricks, Howard, Howe, Johnson, McCreery, Morgan, Morrill of Maine, Morrill of Vermont, Morton, Norton, Patterson of New Hampshire, Patterson of Tennessee, Pomeroy, Ross, Saulsbury, Sherman, Sprague, Tipton, Trumbull, Van Winkle, Vickers, Willey, Williams, Wilson, and Yates—42.

NOT VOTING—Messrs. Anthony, Conkling, Conness, Cragin, Nye. and Wade—6.

So the amendment was not agreed to.

Mr. MORRILL, of Vermont, having modified his motion, it was agreed to, as follows:

Ordered, That when the Senate adjourns to-day, it adjourn to meet on Monday next, at eleven o'clock a. m. for the purpose of deliberation, under the rules of the Senate, sitting on the trial of impeachment, and that on Tuesday next following, at twelve o'clock m., the Senate shall proceed to vote without debate on the several articles of impeachment; and each Senator shall be permitted to file within two days after the vote shall have been so taken his written opinion, to be printed with the proceedings.

The Senate proceeded to consider the resolution submitted by Mr. DRAKE yesterday, to amend the twenty-third rule by adding thereto the following:

The fifteen minutes herein allowed, shall be for the whole deliberation on the final question, and not to the final question on each article of impeachment.

The resolution was adopted.

The Senate proceeded to consider the resolution submitted by Mr. SUMNER on the 25th of April, to amend the rules by inserting the following additional rule:

RULE 23. In taking the votes of the Senate on the articles of impeachment, the presiding officer shall call each Senator by his name, and upon each article propose the following question, in the manner following: "Mr. ——, how say you, is the respondent, ——, guilty or not guilty, as charged in the —— article of impeachment?" whereupon each Senator shall rise in his place and answer "guilty" or "not guilty."

Mr. CONKLING moved to amend the proposed rule by striking out the words "as charged in," and inserting the words " of ·a high crime or misdemeanor (as the case may be) within."

After debate,

Mr. SUMNER modified his proposed rule by inserting after the words " not guilty" the words " of a high crime or misdemeanor."

• Mr. BUCKALEW moved to amend the proposed rule by striking out all after the word "following" where it last occurs and inserting in lieu thereof:

Mr. ——, how say you, is the respondent, Andrew Johnson, President of the United States, guilty or not guilty of a high crime or misdemeanor (as the case may be) as charged in the article of impeachment?

Mr. SUMNER accepted the amendment of Mr. BUCKALEW.

Mr. CONNESS moved further to amend the proposed rule by striking out all after the word "upon" in the fourth line and inserting in lieu thereof the following:

Each of the articles numbered one, two, three, four, five, seven, eight, nine, ten, and eleven propose the following question in the manner following: Mr. Senator, how say you, is the respondent, Andrew Johnson, President of the United States, guilty or not guilty of a high crime or misdemeanor as charged in this article? And upon each of the articles numbered four and six he shall propose the following question: Mr. Senator, how say you, is the respondent, Andrew Johnson, President of the United States, guilty or not guilty of a high crime charged in this article? Whereupon each Senator shall rise in his place and answer "guilty" or "not guilty."

After debate,

Mr. HENDRICKS moved to amend the amendment of Mr. CONNESS by inserting at the end thereof the following:

But in taking down the vote on the eleventh article the question shall be put as to each clause of said article charging a distinct offense.

After debate,

Mr. CONNESS called for the yeas and nays on the amendment to the amendment, and they were ordered; and being taken, resulted—yeas 22, nays 15; as follows:

YEAS—Messrs. Anthony, Davis, Doolittle, Drake, Edmunds, Ferry, Fowler, Frelinghuysen, Harlan, Henderson, Hendricks, Johnson, McCreery, Norton, Patterson of Tennessee, Ross, Sprague, Tipton, Trumbull, Van Winkle, Vickers, and Willey—22.

NAYS—Messrs. Buckalew, Cole, Conness, Corbett, Cragin, Morton, Patterson of New Hampshire, Pomeroy, Ramsey, Stewart, Sumner, Thayer, Williams, Wilson, and Yates—15.

NOT VOTING—Messrs. Bayard, Cameron, Cattell, Chandler, Conkling, Dixon, Fessenden, Grimes, Howard, Howe, Morgan, Morrill of Maine, Morrill of Vermont, Nye, Saulsbury, Sherman, and Wade—17.

So the amendment was agreed to.

After debate,

The question recurring on the amendment proposed by Mr. CONNESS as amended,

Mr. JOHNSON moved that the whole subject lie upon the table.

Mr. SUMNER called for the yeas and nays on the motion, and they were ordered; and being taken, resulted—yeas 24, nays 11; as follows:

YEAS—Messrs. Bayard, Buckalew, Cameron, Cattell, Conness, Davis, Doolittle, Drake, Harlan, Henderson, Hendricks, Johnson, McCreery, Norton, Patterson of Tennessee, Saulsbury, Sprague, Thayer, Tipton, Trumbull, Van Winkle, Vickers, Willey, and Yates—24.

NAYS—Messrs. Cole, Corbett, Cragin, Edmunds, Ferry, Pomeroy, Ramsey, Ross, Sumner, Williams, and Wilson—11.

NOT VOTING—Messrs. Anthony, Chandler, Conkling, Dixon, Fessenden, Fowler, Frelinghuysen, Grimes, Howard, Howe, Morgan, Morrill of Maine, Morrill of Vermont, Morton, Nye, Patterson of New Hampshire, Sherman, Stewart, and Wade—19.

So the motion was agreed to.

On motion of Mr. YATES, it was

Ordered, That when the Senate adjourn it be to Monday next at ten o'clock a. m.

On motion of Mr. COLE, the Senate, sitting for the trial of the impeachment, adjourned.

MONDAY, *May* 11, 1868.

The Chief Justice of the United States took the chair.

The usual proclamation was made by the Sergeant-at-Arms.

The Journal of Thursday's proceedings of

the Senate, sitting for the trial of the impeachment, was read.

The CHIEF JUSTICE. As the Senate meets this morning, under the order, for deliberation, the doors will be closed unless some Senator desires to make a motion.

Mr. SHERMAN. Before the doors are closed I will submit a motion that I believe will receive the unanimous consent of the Senate. To morrow will be a day on which there will be considerable excitement. I move, therefore, that the Sergeant-at-Arms be directed to place his assistants through the gallery, and to arrest, without the order of the Senate, any person who violates the rules of order of the Senate. I do not know but that is the rule now; but it had better be announced publicly and openly so that everybody can understand that to-morrow there shall be no marks of approbation or disapprobation when the vote is cast.

Mr. EDMUNDS. Certainly that is the standing order of the Senate now. I have no objection to the motion, however.

Mr. SHERMAN. I think this will give it more publicity.

Mr. SUMNER. I should say that an intimation made to the Sergeant-at-Arms on that subject ought to be sufficient.

The CHIEF JUSTICE. The Chief Justice will state to the Senate that the Sergeant-at-Arms has already taken the precaution suggested by the Senator from Ohio.

Mr. SHERMAN. Then the Sergeant-at-Arms ought to give notice in the morning papers.

Mr. WILLIAMS. I would suggest, too, that before the Clerk proceeds to call the roll to-morrow morning, as there may be very many persons in the galleries who are strangers, the Chief Justice publicly admonish all persons in the galleries to observe order, and that no manifestations of applause or disapprobation will be allowed in the Senate during the day, otherwise persons so violating the rule will be arrested.

The CHIEF JUSTICE. That will be done.

Mr. SHERMAN. I withdraw my motion.

The CHIEF JUSTICE. The Sergeant-at-Arms will clear the galleries and close the doors.

The Senate Chamber was thereupon cleared and the doors closed.

The CHIEF JUSTICE stated that in compliance with the desire of the Senate he had prepared the question to be addressed to Senators upon each article of impeachment, and that he had reduced his views thereon to writing; which he read.

Mr. BUCKALEW submitted the following motion; which was considered by unanimous consent, and agreed to:

Ordered, That the views of the Chief Justice be entered upon the Journal of the proceedings of the Senate for the trial of impeachments.

C. I.—54.

The following are the views of the Chief Justice:

SENATORS: In conformity with what seemed to be the general wish of the Senate when it adjourned last Thursday, the Chief Justice, in taking the vote on the articles of impeachment, will adopt the mode sanctioned by the practice in the cases of Chase, Peck, and Humphreys.

He will direct the Secretary to read the several articles successively, and after the reading of each article will put the question of guilty or not guilty to each Senator, rising in his place, in the form used in the case of Judge Chase:

" Mr. Senator ——, How say you? Is the respondent, Andrew Johnson, President of the United States, guilty or not guilty of a high misdemeanor, as charged in this article?"

In putting the question on articles four and six, each of which charges a crime, the word " crime" will be substituted for the word " misdemeanor."

The Chief Justice has carefully considered the suggestion of the Senator from Indiana, [Mr HENDRICKS,] which appeared to meet the approval of the Senate, that in taking the vote on the eleventh article, the question should be put on each clause, and has found himself unable to divide the article as suggested. The article charges several facts, but they are so connected that they make but one allegation, and they are charged as constituting one misdemeanor.

The first fact charged is, in substance, that the President publicly declared in August, 1866, that the Thirty-Ninth Congress was a Congress of only part of the States and not a constitutional Congress, intending thereby to deny its constitutional competency to enact laws or propose amendments of the Constitution; and this charge seems to have been made as introductory, and as qualifying that which follows, namely, that the President, in pursuance of this declaration, attempted to prevent the execution of the tenure-of-office act by contriving and attempting to contrive means to prevent Mr. Stanton from resuming the functions of Secretary of War after the refusal of the Senate to concur in his suspension, and also by contriving and attempting to contrive means to prevent the execution of the appropriation act of March 2, 1867, and also to prevent the execution of the rebel States governments act of the same date.

The gravamen of the article seems to be that the President attempted to defeat the execution of the tenure-of-office act, and that he did this in pursuance of a declaration which was intended to deny the constitutional competency of Congress to enact laws or propose constitutional amendments, and by contriving means to prevent Mr. Stanton from resuming his office of Secretary, and also to prevent the execution of the appropriation act and the rebel States governments act.

The single substantive matter charged is the

attempt to prevent the execution of the tenure-of-office act; and the other facts are alleged either as introductory and exhibiting this general purpose, or as showing the means contrived in furtherance of that attempt.

This single matter, connected with the other matters previously and subsequently alleged, is charged as the high misdemeanor of which the President is alleged to have been guilty.

The general question, guilty or not guilty of a high misdemeanor as charged, seems fully to cover the whole charge, and will be put as to this article as well as to the others, unless the Senate direct some mode of division.

In the tenth article the division suggested by the Senator from New York [Mr. CONKLING] may be more easily made. It contains a general allegation, to the effect that on the 18th of August, and on other days, the President, with intent to set aside the rightful authority of Congress and bring it into contempt, delivered certain scandalous harangues, and therein uttered loud threats and bitter menaces against Congress and the laws of the United States enacted by Congress, thereby bringing the office of President into disgrace, to the great scandal of all good citizens, and sets forth, in three distinct specifications, the harangues, threats, and menaces complained of.

In respect to this article, if the Senate sees fit so to direct, the question of guilty or not guilty of the facts charged may be taken in respect to the several specifications, and then the question of guilty or not guilty of a high misdemeanor, as charged in the article, can also be taken.

The Chief Justice, however, sees no objection to putting the general question on this article in the same manner as on the others; for, whether particular questions be put on the specifications or not, the answer to the final question must be determined by the judgment of the Senate, whether or not the facts alleged in the specifications have been sufficiently proved, and whether, if sufficiently proved, they amount to a high misdemeanor within the meaning of the Constitution.

On the whole, therefore, the Chief Justice thinks that the better practice will be to put the general question on each article without attempting to make any subdivision, and will pursue this course if no objection is made. He will, however, be pleased to conform to such directions as the Senate may see fit to give in this respect.

Whereupon,

Mr. SUMNER submitted the following order; which was considered by unanimous consent, and agreed to:

Ordered, That the questions be put as proposed by the presiding officer of the Senate, and each Senator shall rise in his place and answer "guilty" or "not guilty" only.

On motion by Mr. SUMNER, the Senate proceeded to consider the following resolution, submitted on the 25th of April last:

Resolved, That the following be added to the rules of procedure and practice in the Senate when sitting on the trial of impeachments:

On a conviction by the Senate, it shall be the duty of the presiding officer forthwith to pronounce the removal from office of the convicted person according to the requirement of the Constitution. Any further judgment shall be on the order of the Senate.

After debate,

The CHIEF JUSTICE announced that the hour of eleven o'clock a. m., fixed by order of the Senate for deliberation and debate, had arrived, and that Senators could now submit their views on the several articles of impeachment, subject to the limits to debate fixed by the twenty-third rule.

After deliberation,

On motion of Mr. CAMERON, at ten minutes before two o'clock p. m., the Senate took a recess for twenty minutes; at the expiration of which,

After further deliberation and debate,

On motion by Mr. CONNESS, at five o'clock and thirty minutes p. m., the Senate took a recess until half past seven o'clock p. m.

The Senate reassembled at seven o'clock and thirty minutes p. m. and resumed deliberation.

Mr. EDMUNDS submitted the following motion; which was considered by unanimous consent, and agreed to:

Ordered, That the Secretary be directed to inform the House of Representatives that the Senate, sitting for the trial of the President of the United States, will be ready to receive the House of Representatives in the Senate Chamber on Tuesday, the 12th of May, at twelve o'clock m.

After further deliberation,

Mr. EDMUNDS submitted the following motion for consideration:

Ordered, That the standing order of the Senate, that it will proceed at twelve o'clock noon to-morrow to vote on the articles of impeachment, be rescinded.

After further deliberation,

On motion of Mr. EDMUNDS, it was

Ordered, That when the Senate, sitting for the trial of the President upon articles of impeachment, adjourn it be to meet to-morrow at half-past eleven o'clock a. m.

On motion of Mr. CAMERON, the Senate, sitting for the trial of the impeachment, adjourned.

TUESDAY, *May* 12, 1868.

The Chief Justice of the United States took the chair.

The usual proclamation was made by the Sergeant-at-Arms.

Messrs. Managers BINGHAM, BOUTWELL, LOGAN, and STEVENS appeared at the Managers' table.

Messrs. Stanbery, Evarts, and Groesbeck, of counsel for the respondent, appeared in their seats.

The Secretary proceeded to read the Journal of yesterday's proceedings of the Senate sitting for the trial of the impeachment.

Mr. EDMUNDS. As time is rapidly flying, I move that the further reading of the Journal be dispensed with.

The CHIEF JUSTICE. It will be so ordered if there be no objection.

Mr. DAVIS. I object. I want the Journal read.

The Secretary resumed and concluded the reading of the Journal.

Mr. EDMUNDS. I move to take up the order that I offered yesterday.

The CHIEF JUSTICE. The order offered by the Senator from Vermont is the first business for consideration. The Secretary will read the order.

The order was read, as follows:

Ordered, That the standing order of the Senate, that it will proceed at twelve o'clock noon to-morrow to vote on the articles of impeachment, be rescinded.

Mr. CHANDLER. Mr. President——

The CHIEF JUSTICE. The Senator from Michigan. No debate is in order.

Mr. CHANDLER. I desire to make a statement, with the unanimous consent of the Senate, in regard to my colleague. He is very sick——

The CHIEF JUSTICE. The Senator from Michigan can make his statement by unanimous consent. The Chair hears no objection.

Mr. CHANDLER. My colleague [Mr. Howard] was taken suddenly ill, and was delirious yesterday all day, and is very sick, indeed, this morning. He desires to be here. He told me that he would be here, even if it imperiled his life; but both his physicians protested against his coming, and said it would imperil his life. With that statement I desire to move that the Senate, sitting as a court, adjourn until Saturday at twelve o'clock.

Mr. EDMUNDS. Let my order be passed first.

Mr. CHANDLER. Let the order of the Senator from Vermont be acted upon, and after it is agreed to I desire to make the motion I have indicated.

The CHIEF JUSTICE. The question is on the order offered by the Senator from Vermont.

The order was agreed to.

Mr. CHANDLER. I now make the motion that the Senate, sitting as a court, adjourn until Saturday at twelve o'clock.

Mr. HENDRICKS. I move to amend by saying "to-morrow at twelve o'clock."

Mr. CHANDLER. There is no probability, his physicians inform me, that my colleague will be able to be out to-morrow. He had a very high fever and was delirious all day yesterday and last night. I think Saturday the earliest time possible, although he says he will be here to-day if the Senate insist on taking the vote; but it certainly will be at the peril of his life.

Mr. FESSENDEN. I wish to inquire whether rescinding the order as to taking the vote and the postponement until Saturday will leave the order with reference to filing opinions to go over, and whether the time there fixed will apply to the final vote or whether it will apply from to-day?

Mr. JOHNSON and Mr. DRAKE. The final vote.

The CHIEF JUSTICE. The Chief Justice understands that that order applies to the final vote.

Mr. CONNESS. And two days thereafter.

Mr. HENDRICKS. Mr. President——

The CHIEF JUSTICE. Does the Senator from Indiana move his amendment?

Mr. HENDRICKS. Yes, sir. I change my motion to say "on Thursday, at twelve o'clock." To postpone it until Saturday is a matter of great personal inconvenience to me and possibly other Senators. If we can possibly get a vote as early as Thursday it will be a great convenience. If the Senator from Michigan is not well enough to be here on Thursday of course there will be no objection to a further postponement.

Mr. CHANDLER. Mr. President——

The CHIEF JUSTICE. No debate is in order.

Mr. CHANDLER. Would Friday suit?

Several SENATORS. No, no.

The CHIEF JUSTICE. The Senator from Indiana moves to substitute Thursday for Saturday.

The amendment was rejected.

Mr. TIPTON. I move now to amend by saying Friday.

The CHIEF JUSTICE. The Senator from Nebraska moves to amend by substituting Friday for Saturday.

The amendment was rejected.

The CHIEF JUSTICE. The question recurs on the motion of the Senator from Michigan, to adjourn until Saturday at twelve o'clock.

Mr. BUCKALEW. I suggest that we make some order informing the House of Representatives.

Mr. CONNESS, and others. That can be done afterward.

Mr. BUCKALEW. Then the question ought to be put in this form, that when we adjourn to-day we adjourn to meet at that time instead of being an absolute adjournment.

The CHIEF JUSTICE. Does the Senator from Michigan accept that modification, that when the Senate, sitting as a court, adjourns to-day it adjourn to meet on Saturday at twelve o'clock?

Mr. CHANDLER. Certainly.

The CHIEF JUSTICE. Then the question is on that motion.

The motion was agreed to.

Mr. EDMUNDS. I move that the Secretary be directed to inform the House of Representatives that the Senate will proceed further upon this trial on Saturday at twelve o'clock. [After a pause.] On reflection and consultation with the Chief Justice, I think it better to withdraw the motion I made, inasmuch as the illness of Mr. HOWARD is so uncertain; we can notify the House at that time if it shall be necessary that they attend.

Mr. DRAKE. Mr. President, I move that the Senate, sitting upon the trial of the impeachment, do now adjourn.

The motion was agreed to.

The CHIEF JUSTICE. The Senate, sitting as a court of impeachment, stands adjourned until Saturday at twelve o'clock.

SATURDAY, *May* 16, 1868.

The Chief Justice of the United States took the chair at twelve o'clock m.

The usual proclamation was made by the Sergeant-at-Arms.

Messrs. Managers BINGHAM, BOUTWELL, WILSON, BUTLER, LOGAN, WILLIAMS, and STEVENS appeared at the Manager's table.

Messrs. Stanbery, Nelson, Evarts, and Groesbeck, of counsel for the respondent, appeared in their seats.

The Secretary read the Journal of last Tuesday's proceedings of the Senate, sitting for the trial of the impeachment.

Mr. EDMUNDS. Mr. President, I offer the following resolution to notify the House of Representatives.

The CHIEF JUSTICE. The order will be read.

The Chief Clerk read as follows:

Ordered, That the Secretary be directed to inform the House of Representatives that the Senate, sitting for the trial of the President upon articles of impeachment, is now ready to receive them in the Senate Chamber.

The order was agreed to.

The CHIEF JUSTICE. The Secretary will notify the House of Representatives.

Mr. WILLIAMS. Mr. President, I move that the Senate proceed to the consideration of the order that I submitted the other day as to reading the articles.

The CHIEF JUSTICE. The Secretary will read the order which the Senator from Oregon proposes to take up.

The Executive Clerk read as follows:

Ordered, That the Chief Justice, in directing the Secretary to read the several articles of impeachment, shall direct him to read the eleventh article first, and the question shall then be taken on that article, and thereafter the other ten successively as they stand.

Mr. JOHNSON. That is not debatable, I suppose.

The CHIEF JUSTICE. It is not debatable.

Mr. JOHNSON. But I rise to inquire the reason for changing the order of the articles?

Mr. CONNESS. I object to debate.

The CHIEF JUSTICE. Debate is not in order.

Mr. EDMUNDS. Sickness is the reason.

Mr. HENDRICKS and Mr. JOHNSON called for the yeas and nays, and they were ordered.

The CHIEF JUSTICE. The Secretary will read the order again.

The Chief Clerk read the proposed order.

The CHIEF JUSTICE. The question is on taking up the order for consideration, upon which the yeas and nays have been ordered.

The question being taken by yeas and nays, resulted—yeas 34, nays 19; as follows:

YEAS—Messrs. Anthony, Cameron, Cattell, Chandler, Cole, Conkling, Conness, Corbett, Cragin, Drake, Edmunds, Ferry, Frelinghuysen, Harlan, Howard, Howe, Morgan, Morrill of Maine, Morrill of Vermont, Morton, Nye, Patterson of New Hampshire, Pomeroy, Ramsey, Sherman, Sprague, Stewart, Sumner, Thayer, Tipton, Wade, Williams, Wilson, and Yates—34.

NAYS—Messrs. Bayard, Buckalew, Davis, Dixon, Doolittle, Fessenden, Fowler, Henderson, Hendricks, Johnson, McCreery, Norton, Patterson of Tennessee, Ross, Saulsbury, Trumbull, Van Winkle, Vickers, and Willey—19.

NOT VOTING—Mr. Grimes—1.

So the order was taken up for consideration.

The CHIEF JUSTICE. The question now is on the adoption of the order proposed by the Senator from Oregon.

Mr. FESSENDEN. I ask for the yeas and nays on the adoption of that order.

The yeas and nays were ordered.

The Sergeant-at-Arms announced the presence of the House of Representatives at the bar, and the members of the House of Representatives, as in Committee of the Whole, preceded by Mr. E. B. WASHBURNE, chairman of that committee, and accompanied by the Speaker and Clerk, appeared and were conducted to the seats provided for them.

Mr. MORTON. I desire to have the question stated.

The CHIEF JUSTICE. The Secretary will read the order.

The Chief Clerk read the order submitted by Mr. WILLIAMS.

The question being taken by yeas and nays, resulted—yeas 34, nays 19; as follows:

YEAS—Messrs. Anthony, Cameron, Cattell, Chandler, Cole, Conkling, Conness, Corbett, Cragin, Drake, Edmunds, Ferry, Frelinghuysen, Harlan, Howard, Howe, Morgan, Morrill of Maine, Morrill of Vermont, Morton, Nye, Patterson of New Hampshire, Pomeroy, Ramsey, Sherman, Sprague, Stewart, Sumner, Thayer, Tipton, Wade, Williams, Wilson, and Yates—34.

NAYS—Messrs. Bayard, Buckalew, Davis, Dixon, Doolittle, Fessenden, Fowler, Henderson, Hendricks, Johnson, McCreery, Norton, Patterson of Tennessee, Ross, Saulsbury, Trumbull, Van Winkle, Vickers, and Willey—19.

NOT VOTING—Mr. Grimes—1.

So the order was agreed to.

Mr. HOWARD. Mr. President, if it be in order, I desire to place on the files of the Senate my opinion.

The CHIEF JUSTICE. It is in order.

Mr. HOWARD. I will then send it to the Secretary to be filed. I have not had an opportunity to do so until this time in consequence of my ill health.

Mr. EDMUNDS. Mr. President, I move that the Senate now proceed to vote upon the articles according to the order of the Senate just adopted.

Mr. FESSENDEN. Before that motion is made, I wish to make a motion that the voting be postponed for half an hour, and I will state the reason why I make it as the Senator from

Michigan [Mr. CHANDLER] 'stated the other day. I saw Mr. GRIMES last evening, and he told me that he should certainly be here this morning. It was his intention——

Mr. JOHNSON. Will the honorable member permit me to interrupt him for a moment? He is here.

Mr. FESSENDEN. I thought he was not.

Mr. JOHNSON. I have sent for him. He is down stairs. He will be in the Chamber in a moment. Here he is.

Mr. GRIMES entered the Senate Chamber.

Mr: FESSENDEN. I withdraw the motion.

The CHIEF JUSTICE. The question is on the motion submitted by the Senator from Vermont.

Mr. DAVIS. We do not know what the motion is.

The CHIEF JUSTICE. The Senator from yermont will please to put his motion in writing.

Mr. DAVIS, (after a pause.) Mr. Chief Justice, we understand the motion made by the Senator from Vermont, and there is no necessity for having it reduced to writing.

Mr. EDMUNDS. I have reduced it to writing, and send it to the Chair.

The CHIEF JUSTICE. The motion will be read.

The Chief Clerk read as follows:

Ordered, That the Senate now proceed to vote upon the articles, according to the rules of the Senate.

The order was agreed to.

The CHIEF JUSTICE. By direction of the Senate the Chief Justice admonishes the citizens and strangers in the galleries that absolute silence and perfect order are required. It will be matter of unfeigned regret if any violation of the order of the Senate should necessitate the execution of its further order, that the persons guilty of disturbance be immediately arrested.

Senators, in conformity with the order of the Senate, the Chair will now proceed to take the vote on the eleventh article, as directed by the rule. The Secretary will read the eleventh article.

The Chief Clerk read as follows:

ARTICLE XI.

That said Andrew Johnson, President of the United States, unmindful of the high duties of his office, and of his oath of office, and in disregard of the Constitution and laws of the United States, did heretofore, to wit, on the 18th day of August, A. D. 1866, at the city of Washington, and the District of Columbia, by public speech, declare and affirm, in substance, that the Thirty-Ninth Congress of the United States was not a Congress of the United States authorized by the Constitution to exercise legislative power under the same, but, on the contrary, was a Congress of only part of the States, thereby denying, and intending to deny, that the legislation of said Congress was valid or obligatory upon him, the said Andrew Johnson, except in so far as he saw fit to approve the same, and also thereby denying, and intending to deny, the power of the said Thirty-Ninth Congress to propose amendments to the Constitution of the United States; and, in pursuance of said declaration, the said Andrew Johnson, President of the United States, afterwards, to wit, on the 21st day of February, A. D. 1868, at the city of Washington, in the District of Columbia, did, unlawfully, and in disregard of the requirements of the Constitution that he should take care that the laws be faithfully executed, attempt to prevent the execution of an act entitled "An act regulating the tenure of certain civil offices," passed March 2, 1867, by unlawfully devising and contriving, and attempting to devise and contrive, means by which he should prevent Edwin M. Stanton from forthwith resuming the functions of the office of Secretary for the Department of War, notwithstanding the refusal of the Senate to concur in the suspension theretofore made by said Andrew Johnson of said Edwin M. Stanton from said office of Secretary for the Department of War; and, also, by further unlawfully devising and contriving, and attempting to devise and contrive, means, then and there, to prevent the execution of an act entitled "An act making appropriations for the support of the Army for the fiscal year ending June 30, 1868, and for other purposes," approved March 2, 1867; and, also, to prevent the execution of an act entitled, "An act to provide for the more efficient government of the rebel States," passed March 2d, 1867, whereby the said Andrew Johnson, President of the United States, did then, to wit, on the 21st day of February, A. D. 1868, at the city of Washington, commit and was guilty of a high crime and misdemeanor in office.

The CHIEF JUSTICE. Call the roll.

The Chief Clerk called the name of Mr. ANTHONY.

Mr. ANTHONY rose in his place.

The CHIEF JUSTICE. Mr. Senator ANTHONY, how say you? Is the respondent, Andrew Johnson, President of the United States, guilty or not guilty of a high misdemeanor, as charged in this article?

Mr. ANTHONY. Guilty.

[This form was continued in regard to each Senator as the roll was called alphabetically, each rising in his place as his name was called and answering "Guilty" or "Not guilty." When the name of Mr. GRIMES was called, he being very feeble, the Chief Justice said he might remain seated; he, however, with the assistance of friends rose and answered. The Chief Justice also suggested to Mr. HOWARD that he might answer in his seat, but he preferred to rise.]

The call of the roll was completed with the following result:

The Senators who voted "Guilty" are Messrs. ANTHONY, CAMERON, CATTELL, CHANDLER, COLE, CONKLING, CONNESS, CORBETT, CRAGIN, DRAKE, EDMUNDS, FERRY, FRELINGHUYSEN, HARLAN, HOWARD, HOWE, MORGAN, MORRILL of Maine, MORRILL of Vermont, MORTON, NYE, PATTERSON of New Hampshire, POMEROY, RAMSEY, SHERMAN, SPRAGUE, STEWART, SUMNER, THAYER, TIPTON, WADE, WILEY, WILLIAMS, WILSON, and YATES—35.

The Senators who voted "Not Guilty" are Messrs. BAYARD, BUCKALEW, DAVIS, DIXON, DOOLITTLE, FESSENDEN, FOWLER, GRIMES, HENDERSON, HENDRICKS, JOHNSON, McCREERY, NORTON, PATTERSON of Tennessee, ROSS, SAULSBURY, TRUMBULL, VAN WINKLE, and VICKERS—19.

The CHIEF JUSTICE. The Secretary will now read the first article.

Mr. WILLIAMS. Mr. Chief Justice, I move that the Senate take a recess for fifteen minutes.

The motion was not agreed to.

The CHIEF JUSTICE, (to the Chief Clerk.) Read the first article.

Mr. WILLIAMS. Mr. President, I move that the Senate, sitting as a court of impeachment, adjourn until the 26th day of this month at twelve o'clock.

The CHIEF JUSTICE. The Senator from Oregon moves that the Senate sitting as a court of impeachment adjourn, until what day?

Mr. WILLIAMS. Tuesday, the 26th instant, at twelve o'clock.

Mr. JOHNSON. Mr. Chief Justice——

The CHIEF JUSTICE. No debate is in order.

Mr. JOHNSON. I only ask if it is in order to adjourn the Senate when it is pronouncing judgment? It has already decided upon one of the articles.

The CHIEF JUSTICE. The precedents seem to be, except in one case, and that is the case of Humphreys, that the announcement be not made by the presiding officer until after the vote has been taken on all the articles. The Chair will, however, take the direction of the Senate. If they desire the announcement of the vote which has been taken to be now made he will make it.

Mr. SHERMAN. That announcement had better be made. The yeas and nays should be read over first, however.

Mr. JOHNSON. There may be some mistake in the count.

The CHIEF JUSTICE. The Secretary will read the list, if there be no objection.

Mr. DRAKE. I rise to a question of order, that a motion to adjourn is pending, and that that motion takes precedence of all other things.

Mr. HENDRICKS. I suggest, sir, as a modification well known of that rule, that a motion to adjourn cannot be made pending the taking of a vote. The vote is not completed until it is announced. It is not in order pending the call of the roll, and that is not completed until the result is announced.

The CHIEF JUSTICE. The Chair stated that if such was the desire of the Senate the vote would be announced, and no objection was heard to that course.

Mr. DOOLITTLE. On the question of order, I submit that a motion to adjourn to some other day is not a privileged motion.

Mr. JOHNSON. I move, Mr. Chief Justice, that the vote be announced. That is in order, certainly.

The CHIEF JUSTICE. If there be no objection, the vote on the eleventh article will be announced.

The Chief Clerk read the list of those voting "Guilty" and "Not guilty," respectively, as follows:

GUILTY—Messrs. Anthony, Cameron, Cattell, Chandler, Cole, Conkling, Conness, Corbett, Cragin, Drake, Edmunds, Ferry, Frelinghuysen, Harlan, Howard, Howe, Morgan, Morrill of Maine, Morrill of Vermont, Morton, Nye, Patterson of New Hampshire, Pomeroy, Ramsey, Sherman, Sprague, Stewart, Sumner, Thayer, Tipton, Wade, Willey, Williams, Wilson, and Yates—35.

NOT GUILTY—Messrs. Bayard, Buckalew, Davis, Dixon, Doolittle, Fessenden, Fowler, Grimes, Henderson, Hendricks, Johnson, McCreery, Norton, Patterson of Tennessee, Ross, Saulsbury, Trumbull, Van Winkle, and Vickers—19.

The CHIEF JUSTICE. Upon this article thirty-five Senators vote "Guilty," and nineteen Senators vote "Not guilty." Two thirds not having pronounced guilty, the President is, therefore, acquitted upon this article.

Mr. CAMERON. Now, Mr. President, I renew the motion that the Senate adjourn until Tuesday, the 26th instant.

The CHIEF JUSTICE. That is the pending motion.

Mr. HENDRICKS. I ask what is the motion?

The CHIEF JUSTICE. The motion is that the Senate, sitting as a court of impeachment, adjourn to meet at twelve o'clock on Tuesday, the 26th instant.

Mr. HENDRICKS. Then, Mr. President, I submit, as a question of order, that the Senate is now executing an order already made, which is in the nature and has the effect of the previous question, and therefore a motion to adjourn otherwise than simply to adjourn at once is not in order.

The CHIEF JUSTICE. A motion that when the Senate adjourns it adjourn to meet at a certain day could not now be entertained, because the Senate is in process of executing an order. A motion to adjourn to a certain day seems to the Chair to come under the same rule. He will, therefore, decide the motion not to be in order.

Mr. CONNESS. Mr. President, from that decision of the Chair I appeal.

The CHIEF JUSTICE. The Chief Justice decides that a motion to adjourn to a day certain is within the principle of a motion that when the Senate adjourns it adjourn to meet upon a certain day, and that this motion is not in order pending the execution of an order already made by the Senate. That the Senate may understand the ground of the decision he will direct the Clerk to read the order under which the Senate is now acting.

The Chief Clerk read as follows:

Ordered, That the Senate now proceed to vote upon the articles, according to the rules of the Senate.

Mr. CONKLING. I rise for information from the Chair. Is the order just read by the Secretary the order adopted this morning on the motion of the Senator from Vermont, [Mr. EDMUNDS?]

The CHIEF JUSTICE. It is. From the ruling of the Chief Justice an appeal is taken to the Senate. Senators, you who agree to sustain the ruling of the Chair will say ay, those of the contrary opinion will say no——

Mr. CONNESS. Upon that question I call for the yeas and nays.

The yeas and nays were ordered; and being

taken, resulted—yeas 24, nays 30; as follows:

YEAS—Messrs. Anthony, Bayard, Buckalew, Conkling, Davis, Dixon, Doolittle, Ferry, Fessenden, Fowler, Grimes, Henderson, Hendricks, Johnson, McCreery, Morgan, Norton, Patterson of Tennessee, Saulsbury, Sherman, Trumbull, Van Winkle, Vickers, and Willey—24.

NAYS—Messrs. Cameron, Cattell, Chandler, Cole, Conness, Corbett, Cragin, Drake, Edmunds, Frelinghuysen, Harlan, Howard, Howe, Morrill of Maine, Morrill of Vermont, Morton, Nye, Patterson of New Hampshire, Pomeroy, Ramsey, Ross, Sprague, Stewart, Sumner, Thayer, Tipton, Wade, Williams, Wilson, and Yates—30.

The CHIEF JUSTICE. The decision of the Chair is not sustained; and the motion of the Senator from Oregon is in order.

Mr. HENDERSON. The motion, I believe, is to adjourn the court until the 25th instant. I move to strike out the date and insert "Wednesday, the 1st day of July next."

The CHIEF JUSTICE. The question is on the amendment of the Senator from Missouri.

Mr. TRUMBULL called for the yeas and nays, and they were ordered.

The CHIEF JUSTICE. Senators, you who agree that "Tuesday, the 26th instant," shall be stricken out, and the words "Wednesday, the 1st of July," be inserted, will, as your names are called, answer yea; those of the contrary opinion nay.

The yeas and nays being taken, resulted—yeas 20, nays 34; as follows:

YEAS—Messrs. Bayard, Buckalew, Davis, Dixon, Doolittle, Fessenden, Fowler, Grimes, Henderson, Hendricks, Johnson, McCreery, Norton, Patterson of Tennessee, Ross, Saulsbury, Trumbull, Van Winkle, Vickers, and Willey—20.

NAYS—Messrs. Anthony, Cameron, Cattell, Chandler, Cole, Conkling, Conness, Corbett, Cragin, Drake, Edmunds, Ferry, Frelinghuysen, Harlan, Howard, Howe, Morgan, Morrill of Maine, Morrill of Vermont, Morton, Nye, Patterson of New Hampshire, Pomeroy, Ramsey, Sherman, Sprague, Stewart, Sumner, Thayer, Tipton, Wade, Williams, Wilson, and Yates—34.

So the amendment was rejected.

The CHIEF JUSTICE. The question recurs on the motion submitted by the Senator from Oregon, that the Senate, sitting as a court of impeachment, adjourn until Tuesday, the 26th instant.

Mr. McCREERY. Is an amendment in order?

The CHIEF JUSTICE. It is.

Mr. McCREERY. I move to amend by providing that when the Senate, sitting as a court of impeachment, adjourns to-day, it adjourn without day.

The CHIEF JUSTICE. The Senator from Kentucky moves to strike out the words "Tuesday, the 26th instant," and insert "without day."

Mr. McCREERY. I call for the yeas and nays on that amendment.

The yeas and nays were ordered; and being taken, resulted—yeas 6, nays 47; as follows:

YEAS—Messrs. Bayard, Davis, Dixon, Doolittle, McCreery, and Vickers—6.

NAYS—Messrs. Anthony, Buckalew, Cameron, Cattell, Chandler, Cole, Conkling, Conness, Corbett, Cragin, Drake, Edmunds, Ferry, Fessenden, Fowler, Frelinghuysen, Harlan, Henderson, Hendricks, Howard, Howe, Johnson, Morgan, Morrill of Maine, Morrill of Vermont, Morton, Norton, Nye, Patterson of New Hampshire, Patterson of Tennessee, Pomeroy, Ramsey, Ross, Saulsbury, Sherman, Sprague, Stewart, Sumner, Thayer, Tipton, Trumbull, Van Winkle, Wade, Willey, Williams, Wilson, and Yates—47.

NOT VOTING—Mr. Grimes—1.

So the amendment was rejected.

Mr. BUCKALEW. Mr. President, I move to strike out the date named and insert "Monday next."

The CHIEF JUSTICE. The question is on the amendment of the Senator from Pennsylvania.

The amendment was rejected.

The CHIEF JUSTICE. The question recurs on the motion of the Senator from Oregon.

Mr. HENDRICKS. On that I ask for the yeas and nays.

The yeas and nays were ordered.

The CHIEF JUSTICE. The question is on the motion of the Senator from Oregon for an adjournment of the Senate sitting as a court of impeachment until Tuesday, the 26th instant.

Mr. CONKLING. What is the motion; that when the Senate adjourns to-day it adjourn to that time, or that it now adjourn until that time?

The CHIEF JUSTICE. That the Senate, sitting as a court of impeachment, do now adjourn until Tuesday, the 26th instant.

The question being taken by yeas and nays, resulted—yeas 32, nays 21; as follows:

YEAS—Messrs. Anthony, Cameron, Cattell, Chandler, Cole, Conness, Corbett, Cragin, Drake, Edmunds, Frelinghuysen, Harlan, Howard, Howe, Morrill of Maine, Morrill of Vermont, Morton, Nye, Patterson of New Hampshire, Pomeroy, Ramsey, Ross, Sprague, Stewart, Sumner, Thayer, Tipton, Van Winkle, Wade, Williams, Wilson, and Yates—32.

NAYS—Messrs. Bayard, Buckalew, Conkling, Davis, Dixon, Doolittle, Ferry, Fessenden, Fowler, Henderson, Hendricks, Johnson, McCreery, Morgan, Norton, Patterson of Tennessee, Saulsbury, Sherman, Trumbull, Vickers, and Willey—21.

NOT VOTING—Mr. Grimes—1.

The CHIEF JUSTICE. On this question the yeas are 32 and the nays are 21. So the Senate, sitting as a court of impeachment, stands adjourned until Tuesday, the 26th instant, at twelve o'clock.

TUESDAY, May 26, 1868.

The Chief Justice of the United States took the chair at twelve o'clock m.

The usual proclamation was made by the Sergeant-at-Arms.

Messrs. Stanbery, Evarts, and Nelson, of counsel for the respondent, appeared in their seats.

Mr. WILLIAMS. I offer the following order.

The CHIEF JUSTICE. The Secretary will read the order.

The Chief Clerk read as follows:

Resolved, That the resolution heretofore adopted as to the order of reading and voting upon the articles of impeachment be rescinded.

Mr. SUMNER. Mr. President——

Mr. JOHNSON. Is that debatable?

The CHIEF JUSTICE. It is not debatable.

Mr. SUMNER. I do not wish to debate; but I would like to have it amended so that it may operate from this day. For instance, leave to file opinions goes on for two days from the vote.

The CHIEF JUSTICE. The Senator from Massachusetts can move an amendment, but it is not debatable. The question is on the adoption of the resolution.

Mr. SUMNER. I should like to have it read again, for I may have misunderstood it.

The Chief Clerk read as follows:

Resolved, That the resolution heretofore adopted as to the order of reading and voting upon the articles of impeachment be rescinded.

Mr. SUMNER. That is a different order from what I supposed.

Mr. JOHNSON. Mr. Chief Justice, I do not rise to debate it, but merely to ask the mover what will be the effect of the adoption of that order?

The CHIEF JUSTICE. Explanation implies debate. It is not in order.

Mr. TRUMBULL. Mr. President, I should like to hear the resolution read which is to be rescinded.

The CHIEF JUSTICE. The Secretary will read the order heretofore adopted by the Senate.

Mr. POMEROY. I think the proceedings of the last day should be read first; then we shall know what the order is that is to be rescinded, and we can proceed to vote intelligently. I move that we have the proceedings read.

The CHIEF JUSTICE. The Chief Justice thinks the first business in order is to notify the House of Representatives that the Senate is ready to receive them at its bar. After that has been done the course has been to read the Journal of the proceedings, and then the regular business of the Senate will be in order. No objection having been made to entertaining the order proposed by the Senator from Oregon, the Chief Justice submitted it to the Senate.

Mr. JOHNSON. I object.

Mr. EDMUNDS. I move that the House of Representatives be notified that the Senate is ready to receive them.

The motion was agreed to.

The CHIEF JUSTICE. The Sergeant-at-Arms will notify the House of Representatives.

The Sergeant-at-Arms presently appeared at the bar and announced the Managers of impeachment on the part of the House of Representatives.

The CHIEF JUSTICE. The Managers will take their seats within the bar.

The Managers took the seats provided for them.

The members of the House of Representatives, as in Committee of the Whole, preceded by Mr. E. B. WASHBURNE, chairman of that committee, and accompanied by the Speaker and Clerk, next appeared and were conducted to the seats provided for them.

The CHIEF JUSTICE. The Secretary will read the Journal of the last day's proceedings.

The Chief Clerk read the Journal of the proceedings of the Senate, sitting for the trial of the impeachment, of Saturday, the 16th instant.

Mr. JOHNSON. Mr. Chief Justice, there is an omission, I think, in the Journal. It is not stated that Mr. Stanbery, who is one of the counsel for the President, was present on the occasion of the proceedings just read. I move that the omission be supplied. We know he was present.

The CHIEF JUSTICE. That statement is made in the Journal as it stands. There was an omission in the reading. The Secretary will now read the order submitted by the Senator from Oregon.

The Chief Clerk read Mr. WILLIAMS's resolution, as follows:

Resolved, That the resolution heretofore adopted as to the order of reading and voting upon the articles of impeachment be rescinded.

Mr. BUCKALEW. Mr. President, if it requires unanimous consent to change the rule in the manner proposed, I object.

The CHIEF JUSTICE. The Chief Justice is under the impression that it changes the rule, and he will state the case to the Senate, in order that the Senate may correct him if he is wrong. The twenty-second rule of the Senate provides that—

" On the final question, whether the impeachment is sustained, the yeas and nays shall be taken on each article of impeachment separately."

That necessarily implies that they be taken in their order unless it is otherwise prescribed by the Senate. Subsequently the framing of a question to be addressed to the Senators was left to the Chief Justice, and he stated the views which seemed to him proper to be observed. In the course of that statement he said that "he will direct the Secretary to read the articles successively, and after the reading of each article will put the question of guilty or not guilty to each Senator, rising in his place, in the form used in the case of Judge Chase," and then stated the form.

After the statement was made—

"Mr. SUMNER submitted the following order; which was considered by unanimous consent, and agreed to:
"*Ordered,* That the questions be put as proposed by the presiding officer of the Senate, and each Senator shall rise in his place and answer guilty or not not guilty, only."

That was the order under which the Senate was acting until on the 16th of May the Senate adopted the following order moved by the Senator from Oregon, [Mr. WILLIAMS:]

"*Ordered,* That the Chief Justice, in directing the Secretary to read the several articles of impeachment, shall direct him to read the eleventh article first, and the question shall then be taken on that article, and thereafter the other ten successively as they stand."

This order changing the rule was in order on the 16th of May, having been moved some days before. Subsequently, after the House had been notified that the Senate was ready to receive them, the Senator from Vermont [Mr. EDMUNDS] moved—

"That the Senate do now proceed to vote upon the articles according to the order of the Senate just adopted."

The Senate proceeded to vote upon the eleventh article, and after that adjourned until to-day. The present motion is to change the whole of these orders, for changing only the order of the 16th will not reach the effect intended. It must change, also, the order adopted on the motion of the Senator from Massachusetts, [Mr. SUMNER,] and also, as the Chief Justice conceives, the rule. He is of opinion, therefore, that a single objection will take it over this day, but will submit the question directly to the Senate without undertaking to decide it, as it is a matter which relates especially to the present order of business. [Putting the question.] Senators, you who are of the opinion that the motion of the Senator from Oregon is now in order will say ay; those of the contrary opinion no. The noes appear to have it.

Mr. DRAKE called for a division.

Mr. HENDERSON called for the yeas and nays, and they were ordered; and being taken, resulted—yeas 29, nays 25 ; as follows:

YEAS—Messrs. Cameron, Cattell, Chandler, Cole, Conkling, Conness, Cragin, Drake. Frelinghuysen, Harlan, Howard. Howe, Morgan, Morrill of Maine, Morton, Nye, Pomeroy, Ramsey, Ross, Sherman, Sprague, Stewart, Sumner, Thayer, Tipton, Wade, Williams, Wilson, and Yates—29.

NAYS—Messrs Anthony, Bayard, Buckalew, Corbett, Davis, Dixon, Doolittle, Edmunds, Ferry, Fessenden, Fowler, Grimes, Henderson, Hendricks, Johnson, McCreery, Morrill of Vermont, Norton, Patterson of New Hampshire, Patterson of Tennessee, Saulsbury, Trumbull, Van Winkle, Vickers, and Willey—25.

The CHIEF JUSTICE. The Senate decides that the resolution of the Senator from Oregon is now in order. The Secretary will read the resolution.

The Chief Clerk read as follows :

Resolved, That the resolution heretofore adopted as to the order of reading and voting upon the articles of impeachment be rescinded.

Mr. CONKLING. I offer the following as a substitute for the pending order.

The CHIEF JUSTICE. The Secretary will read the amendment of the Senator from New York.

The Chief Clerk read as follows :

Strike out all after the word "Resolved," and insert :

That the Senate, sitting for the trial of Andrew Johnson, President of the United States, will now proceed, in manner prescribed by the rules in that behalf, to vote upon the remaining articles of impeachment.

Mr. TRUMBULL called for the yeas and nays on the amendment, and they were ordered ; and being taken resulted—yeas 26, nays 28 ; as follows :

YEAS—Messrs. Bayard, Buckalew, Cole, Conkling, Davis, Dixon, Doolittle, Ferry, Fessenden. Fowler. Grimes, Henderson, Hendricks, Johnson, McCreery, Morgan, Morrill of Vermont, Morton, Norton, Patterson of New Hampshire, Patterson of Tennessee. Saulsbury, Trumbull, Van Winkle, Vickers, and Willey—26.

NAYS—Messrs. Anthony, Cameron, Cattell, Chandler, Conness, Corbett, Cragin, Drake, Edmunds, Frelinghuysen, Harlan, Howard, Howe, Morrill of Maine, Nye, Pomeroy, Ramsey, Ross, Sherman, Sprague, Stewart, Sumner, Thayer, Tipton, Wade, Williams, Wilson, and Yates—28.

So the amendment was rejected.

The CHIEF JUSTICE. The question recurs on the resolution proposed by the Senator from Oregon.

Mr. WILLIAMS. I suggest an amendment to the phraseology of that resolution so as to refer to the rules as well as the resolution heretofore adopted.

The CHIEF JUSTICE. The Senator will reach his object by saying "The several orders heretofore adopted."

Mr. WILLIAMS. Very well; let that phraseology be adopted.

The CHIEF JUSTICE. The Secretary will read the resolution, as modified.

The Chief Clerk read as follows:

Resolved, That the several orders heretofore adopted as to the order of reading and voting upon the articles of impeachment be rescinded.

Mr. TRUMBULL. Mr. President, I wish to inquire whether it is in order to rescind an order partly executed. What would be the effect of it? It seems to me not to be in order to rescind an order which has been partly executed.

The CHIEF JUSTICE. If the Senator from Illinois makes that question of order, the Chief Justice will submit it to the Senate.

Mr. TRUMBULL. I make that question, that you cannot rescind an order that is partly executed. We have voted under that order. It might be rescinded as to what remains unexecuted; but the effect of rescinding an order would be a reconsideration.

Mr. CONNESS. Mr. President, I object to discussion of this subject.

The CHIEF JUSTICE. No debate is in order.

Mr. CONNESS. I supposed the Senate had already decided that this resolution was in order.

Mr. DOOLITTLE. Mr. Chief Justice, whatever might have been the ruling on the order as it stood——

The CHIEF JUSTICE. No debate is in order.

Mr. DOOLITTLE. This proposition I object

to as out of order. On its face it proposes to change the rules of the Senate.

Mr. THAYER. I call the Senator to order.

The CHIEF JUSTICE. The Senator cannot debate the question.

Mr. DOOLITTLE. I object to the proposition as out of order.

Mr. CONKLING. That has been done already.

The CHIEF JUSTICE. That has been done.

Mr. DOOLITTLE. If the Chief Justice will allow me to say, not in its present form.

Mr. SPRAGUE. The Senator is out of order.

Mr. DOOLITTLE. I object that this resolution is out of order.

The CHIEF JUSTICE. The Senator is out of order.

Mr. DOOLITTLE. I object to the resolution.

The CHIEF JUSTICE. The Senator from Illinois [Mr. TRUMBULL] objects that the order proposed by the Senator from Oregon [Mr. WILLIAMS] is not in order, because it rescinds an order which is already in process of execution.

Mr. TRUMBULL. Which has been already partly executed.

The CHIEF JUSTICE. And that question the Chief Justice will submit to the Senate as a question of order.

Mr. EDMUNDS. Mr. President, I move that the Senate withdraw for consultation on this question.

Several SENATORS. No, no.

The CHIEF JUSTICE. The Senator from Vermont moves that the Senate do now withdraw for consultation.

The motion was not agreed to.

Mr. MORRILL, of Maine. Will the Chair entertain a motion at this time?

The CHIEF JUSTICE. The objection of the Senator from Illinois is not yet disposed of.

Mr. TRUMBULL. Mr. President, I desire to put it upon two grounds: one that it is partly executed——

Mr. CONNESS. I object.

Mr. TRUMBULL. I take it that it is in order to state my question of order.

The CHIEF JUSTICE. The Senator can state his question of order.

Mr. TRUMBULL. My objection is twofold; first, that it is out of order to undertake to rescind an order partly executed; and secondly, that it is a violation of the rule which requires one day's notice to change a rule, and it expressly now proposes to change a rule.

The CHIEF JUSTICE. Senators, you who are of opinion that the point of order made by the Senator from Illinois should be sustained will say ay; those of the contrary opinion, no. [Putting the question.] The noes appear to have it.

Mr. TRUMBULL. I ask for the yeas and nays.

The yeas and nays were ordered.

The CHIEF JUSTICE. The Senator from Illinois makes the point of order that the resolution moved by the Senator from Oregon is not now in order for consideration, because it relates to an order partly executed, and because—will the Senator oblige the Chair by stating his other reason?

Mr. CONNESS. I object to two points of order at a time. One will be sufficient.

The CHIEF JUSTICE. Will the Senator from Illinois be kind enough to state his other reason?

Mr. TRUMBULL. My other reason is that, as now amended, the resolution proposes to change a standing rule of the Senate, which cannot be done without a day's notice.

The CHIEF JUSTICE. Senators, you who are of opinion that the point of order should be sustained as stated will answer yea; those of the contrary opinion nay.

The Chief Clerk proceeded to call the roll, and having concluded the call—

Mr. CONKLING, (who had voted yea.) Mr. President, I rise to a question of order, if that be the proper form. I think I voted myself under a misapprehension, and I understand other Senators have done so. Will the Chief Justice be kind enough to restate the question in the form in which it was put? I understand from other Senators that the question propounded was in this form: those in favor of sustaining the point of order will vote yea. I had supposed that the question was as put before: those deeming the proposition in order will say yea; and I voted affirmatively, meaning to vote against the point raised by the Senator from Illinois, but I am told that the effect of the record is to make me vote in favor of the point of order. I want to know what the form of the question was, if the Chair will be kind enough to state it.

The CHIEF JUSTICE. The Chief Justice stated the question in the form supposed by the Senator from New York, that those who voted to sustain the point of order made by the Senator from Illinois would say yea; those of the contrary opinion nay. If there be a misunderstanding the question will be again submitted to the Senate. ["No!" "No!"]

Mr. CONKLING. I beg to change my vote, if that is the form. I voted under an entire misapprehension. I vote nay.

The result was announced—yeas 24, nays 30; as follows:

YEAS—Messrs. Anthony, Bayard, Buckalew, Davis, Dixon, Doolittle, Edmunds, Ferry, Fessenden, Fowler, Grimes, Henderson, Hendricks, Johnson, McCreery, Morgan, Morrill of Vermont, Norton, Patterson of Tennessee, Saulsbury, Trumbull, Van Winkle, Vickers, and Willey—24.

NAYS—Messrs. Cameron, Cattell, Chandler, Cole, Conkling, Conness, Corbett, Cragin, Drake, Frelinghuysen, Harlan, Howard, Howe, Morrill of Maine, Morton, Nye, Patterson of New Hampshire, Pomeroy, Ramsey, Ross, Sherman, Sprague, Stewart, Sumner, Thayer, Tipton, Wade, Williams, Wilson, and Yates—30.

So the point of order was not sustained.

Mr. MORRILL, of Maine. Mr. President, I rise to inquire whether the Chair will entertain a motion at the present time?

The CHIEF JUSTICE. Any motion to amend this resolution. The question now is on the resolution offered by the Senator from Oregon. Any motion to amend that resolution is in order, or a motion to postpone it is in order.

Mr. MORRILL, of Maine. I move that the Senate sitting to try the impeachment of Andrew Johnson, President of the United States, do now adjourn to the 23d day of June next at twelve o'clock, and on that question I demand the yeas and nays.

The CHIEF JUSTICE. The Chief Justice has heretofore ruled that that motion was not in order, but he was not sustained by the Senate. He will now submit the question whether this motion is in order directly to the Senate. Senators, you who are of opinion that the motion of the Senator from Maine, that the Senate do now adjourn until the 23d day of June——

Mr. CONNESS. Mr. President, I rise to inquire of the Chair whether a ruling made by the Senate upon a given point does not stand as the rule of the Senate until the Senate reverses it?

The CHIEF JUSTICE. Undoubtedly; but the Chief Justice cannot undertake to say how soon the Senate may reverse its rulings. Senators, you who are of opinion that the motion of the Senator from Maine, that the Senate do now adjourn until the 23d day of June, is in order, will say ay; those of the contrary opinion, no. [Putting the question.] The ayes appear to have it.

Mr. HENDERSON called for the yeas and nays, and they were ordered; and being taken, resulted—yeas 35, nays 18; as follows:

YEAS—Messrs. Anthony, Cameron, Cattell, Chandler, Cole, Conkling, Conness, Corbett, Cragin, Drake, Edmunds, Ferry, Frelinghuysen, Harlan, Howard, Howe, Morrill of Maine, Morrill of Vermont, Morton, Nye, Patterson of New Hampshire, Pomeroy, Ramsey, Ross, Sherman, Sprague, Stewart, Sumner, Thayer, Tipton, Wade, Willey, Williams, Wilson, and Yates—35.

NAYS—Messrs. Bayard, Buckalew, Davis, Dixon, Doolittle, Fessenden, Fowler, Henderson, Hendricks, Johnson, McCreery, Morgan, Norton, Patterson of Tennessee, Saulsbury, Trumbull, Van Winkle, and Vickers—18.

NOT VOTING—Mr. Grimes—1.

So the Senate decided the motion to be in order.

Mr. MORRILL, of Maine. I now renew my motion that the Senate, sitting for the trial of the impeachment of Andrew Johnson, President of the United States, adjourn to Tuesday, the 23d day of June, at twelve o'clock.

Mr. FERRY called for the yeas and nays, and they were ordered.

Mr. ROSS. Mr. President, I move to amend the motion by striking out "the 23d day of June" and inserting "the 1st day of September," and on that amendment I ask for the yeas and nays.

The yeas and nays were ordered; and being taken, resulted—yeas 15, nays 39; as follows:

YEAS—Messrs. Bayard, Davis, Dixon, Doolittle, Fessenden, Fowler, Henderson, Johnson, McCreery, Norton, Ross, Saulsbury, Trumbull, Van Winkle, and Vickers—15.

NAYS—Messrs. Anthony, Buckalew, Cameron, Cattell, Chandler, Cole, Conkling, Conness, Corbett, Cragin, Drake, Edmunds, Ferry, Frelinghuysen, Grimes, Harlan, Hendricks, Howard, Howe, Morgan, Morrill of Maine, Morrill of Vermont, Morton, Nye, Patterson of New Hampshire, Patterson of Tennessee, Pomeroy, Ramsey, Sherman, Sprague, Stewart, Sumner, Thayer, Tipton, Wade, Willey, Williams, Wilson, and Yates—39.

So the amendment was rejected.

The CHIEF JUSTICE. The question recurs on the motion of the Senator from Maine, that the Senate sitting as a court of impeachment do now adjourn until Tuesday, the 23d day of June, and upon that question the yeas and nays have been ordered.

The question being taken by yeas and nays, resulted—yeas 27, nays 27; as follows:

YEAS—Messrs. Anthony, Cameron, Cattell, Chandler, Conness, Corbett, Cragin, Drake, Harlan, Howard, Howe, Morrill of Maine, Nye, Pomeroy, Ramsey, Ross, Sherman, Sprague, Stewart, Sumner, Thayer, Tipton, Wade, Willey, Williams, Wilson, and Yates—27.

NAYS—Messrs. Bayard, Buckalew, Cole, Conkling, Davis, Dixon, Doolittle, Edmunds, Ferry, Fessenden, Fowler, Frelinghuysen, Grimes, Henderson, Hendricks, Johnson, McCreery, Morgan, Morrill of Vermont, Morton, Norton, Patterson of New Hampshire, Patterson of Tennessee, Saulsbury, Trumbull, Van Winkle, and Vickers—27.

The CHIEF JUSTICE. Upon this question the yeas are 27 and the nays are 27; so the motion is not agreed to.

Mr. WILLIAMS. Mr. President, I move that the Senate proceed to vote upon the second article of impeachment.

The CHIEF JUSTICE. The Senator from Oregon moves that the Senate do now proceed to vote upon the second article.

Mr. WILLIAMS. I withdraw the motion that I have just made until the other order is adopted. I was under the misapprehension that it had been adopted.

The CHIEF JUSTICE. The question recurs on the resolution already submitted by the Senator from Oregon, which the Clerk will again read.

The Chief Clerk read as follows:

Resolved, That the several orders heretofore adopted as to the order of reading and voting upon the second article of impeachment be rescinded.

The resolution was agreed to.

Mr. WILLIAMS. Mr. President, I now move that the Senate proceed to vote upon the second article of impeachment.

The CHIEF JUSTICE. The Senator from Oregon moves that the Senate now proceed to vote upon the second article of impeachment.

Mr. TRUMBULL. Is that in order, I rise to inquire?

The CHIEF JUSTICE. There being now no order relating to the order in which the articles shall be taken, the Chief Justice thinks it is in order. Senators, you who agree to the motion proposed by the Senator from Oregon, that the Senate do now proceed to vote upon the second article of impeachment, will say ay; those of the contrary opinion no. [Putting the question.] The ayes appear to have it. The ayes have it, and the motion is agreed to.

The Chief Justice will again admonish strangers and citizens in the galleries of the necessity of observing perfect order and profound silence. The Clerk will now read the second article of impeachment.

The Chief Clerk read as follows:

ARTICLE II.

That on the said 21st day of February, in the year of our Lord 1868, at Washington, in the District of Columbia, said Andrew Johnson, President of the United States, unmindful of the high duties of his office, of his oath of office, and in violation of the Constitution of the United States, and contrary to the provisions of an act entitled "An act regulating the tenure of certain civil offices," passed March 2, 1867, without the advice and consent of the Senate of the United States, said Senate then and there being in session, and without authority of law, did, with intent to violate the Constitution of the United States, and the act aforesaid, issue and deliver to one Lorenzo Thomas a letter of authority in substance as follows, that is to say:

EXECUTIVE MANSION,
WASHINGTON, D. C., *February* 21, 1868.

SIR: The Hon. Edwin M. Stanton having been this day removed from office as Secretary for the Department of War, you are hereby authorized and empowered to act as Secretary of War *ad interim*, and will immediately enter upon the discharge of the duties pertaining to that office.

Mr. Stanton has been instructed to transfer to you all the records, books, papers, and other public property now in his custody and charge.

Respectfully yours, ANDREW JOHNSON.
To Brevet Major General LORENZO THOMAS, *Adjutant General United States Army, Washington, D. C.*

Then and there being no vacancy in said office of Secretary for the Department of War, whereby said Andrew Johnson, President of the United States, did then and there commit and was guilty of a high misdemeanor in office.

The name of each Senator was called in alphabetical order by the Chief Clerk; and as he rose in his place the Chief Justice propounded the following question:

Mr. Senator ——, how say you, is the respondent, Andrew Johnson, President of the United States, guilty or not guilty of a high misdemeanor as charged in this article of impeachment?

The call of the roll having been concluded, The Senators who voted "Guilty" are: Messrs. ANTHONY, CAMERON, CATTELL, CHANDLER, COLE, CONKLING, CONNESS, CORBETT, CRAGIN, DRAKE, EDMUNDS, FERRY, FRELINGHUYSEN, HARLAN, HOWARD, HOWE, MORGAN, MORRILL of Maine, MORRILL of Vermont, MORTON, NYE, PATTERSON of New Hampshire, POMEROY, RAMSEY, SHERMAN, SPRAGUE, STEWART, SUMNER, THAYER, TIPTON, WADE, WILLEY, WILLIAMS, WILSON, and YATES—35.

The Senators who voted "Not guilty" are: Messrs. BAYARD, BUCKALEW, DAVIS, DIXON, DOOLITTLE, FESSENDEN, FOWLER, GRIMES, HENDERSON, HENDRICKS, JOHNSON, McCREERY, NORTON, PATTERSON of Tennessee, ROSS,

SAULSBURY, TRUMBULL, VAN WINKLE, and VICKERS—19.

The CHIEF JUSTICE. Thirty-five Senators have pronounced the respondent, Andrew Johnson, President of the United States, guilty; nineteen have pronounced him not guilty. Two thirds not having pronounced him guilty, he stands acquitted upon this article.

Mr. WILLIAMS. Mr. President, I move that the Senate now proceed to vote upon the third article.

The motion was agreed to.

The CHIEF JUSTICE. The Secretary will read the third article.

The Chief Clerk read the third article of impeachment, as follows:

ARTICLE III.

That said Andrew Johnson, President of the United States, on the 21st day of February, in the year of our Lord, 1868, at Washington, in the District of Columbia, did commit and was guilty of a high misdemeanor in office, in this, that, without authority of law, while the Senate of the United States was then and there in session, he did appoint one Lorenzo Thomas to be Secretary for the Department of War *ad interim*, without the advice and consent of the Senate, and with intent to violate the Constitution of the United States, no vacancy having happened in said office of Secretary for the Department of War during the recess of the Senate, and no vacancy existing in said office at the time, and which said appointment, so made by said Andrew Johnson, of said Lorenzo Thomas, is in substance as follows, that is to say:

EXECUTIVE MANSION,
WASHINGTON, D. C., *February* 21, 1868.

SIR: The Hon. Edwin M. Stanton having been this day removed from office as Secretary for the Department of War, you are hereby authorized and empowered to act as Secretary of War *ad interim*, and will immediately enter upon the discharge of the duties pertaining to that office.

Mr. Stanton has been instructed to transfer to you all the records, books, papers, and other public property now in his custody and charge.

Respectfully yours, ANDREW JOHNSON.
To Brevet Major General LORENZO THOMAS, *Adjutant General United States Army, Washington, D. C.*

The roll was called as before, and as each Senator rose in his place the Chief Justice propounded this question:

Mr. Senator ——, how say you, is the respondent, Andrew Johnson, President of the United States, guilty or not guilty of a high misdemeanor, as charged in this article?

The result was as follows:

Those who voted "Guilty" are: Messrs. ANTHONY, CAMERON, CATTELL, CHANDLER, COLE, CONKLING, CONNESS, CORBETT, CRAGIN, DRAKE, EDMUNDS, FERRY, FRELINGHUYSEN, HARLAN, HOWARD, HOWE, MORGAN, MORRILL of Maine, MORRILL of Vermont, MORTON, NYE, PATTERSON of New Hampshire, POMEROY, RAMSEY, SHERMAN, SPRAGUE, STEWART, SUMNER, THAYER, TIPTON, WADE, WILLEY, WILLIAMS, WILSON, and YATES—35.

Those who voted "Not guilty" are: Messrs. BAYARD, BUCKALEW, DAVIS, DIXON, DOOLITTLE, FESSENDEN, FOWLER, GRIMES, HENDERSON, HENDRICKS, JOHNSON, McCREERY, NORTON, PATTERSON of Tennessee, ROSS, SAULSBURY, TRUMBULL, VAN WINKLE, and VICKERS—19.

The CHIEF JUSTICE. Thirty-five Senators have pronounced Andrew Johnson, President of the United States, guilty, as charged in this article; nineteen have pronounced him not guilty. Two thirds not having pronounced him guilty, the President of the United States stands acquitted upon this article.

Mr. WILLIAMS. Mr. President, I move that the Senate, sitting as a court of impeachment, do now adjourn *sine die*.

Mr. BUCKALEW. I ask for the yeas and nays on that motion.

The yeas and nays were ordered and taken.

The roll was called, and the result was as follows:

YEAS—Messrs. Anthony, Cameron, Cattell, Chandler, Cole, Conkling, Corbett, Cragin, Drake, Edmunds, Ferry, Frelinghuysen, Harlan, Howard, Morgan, Morrill of Maine, Morrill of Vermont, Morton, Nye, Patterson of New Hampshire, Pomeroy, Ramsey, Sherman, Sprague, Stewart, Sumner, Thayer, Tipton, Van Winkle, Wade, Willey, Williams, Wilson, and Yates—34.

NAYS—Messrs. Bayard, Buckalew, Davis, Dixon, Doolittle, Fowler, Henderson, Hendricks, Johnson, McCreery, Norton, Patterson of Tennessee, Ross, Saulsbury, Trumbull, and Vickers—16.

NOT VOTING — Messrs. Conness, Fessenden, Grimes, and Howe—4.

The CHIEF JUSTICE. Before announcing the vote the Chief Justice will remind the Senate that the twenty-second rule provides that if "upon any of the articles presented" the impeachment shall not "be sustained by the votes of two thirds of the members present" a judgment of acquittal shall be entered.

Several SENATORS. We cannot hear.

The CHIEF JUSTICE. The Chief Justice begs leave to remind the Senate that the twenty-second rule provides that "if the impeachment shall not, upon any of the articles presented, be sustained by the votes of two thirds of the members present, a judgment of acquittal shall be entered."

Mr. DRAKE. I suggest, Mr. President, that that was done when the President of the Senate declared the acquittal upon each article.

The CHIEF JUSTICE. That is not the judgment of the Senate; but if there be no objection, the judgment will be entered by the Clerk.

Mr. HOWARD. Not at all.

Mr. SUMNER. Of course not.

Several SENATORS. There is no objection.

Mr. HOWARD. Let the vote on adjournment be announced.

Mr. JOHNSON. Judgment must be entered.

Mr. SUMNER. There seems to be a misunderstanding as to the entry which it is proposed to make in the Journal.

The CHIEF JUSTICE. The Clerk will enter, if there be no objection, a judgment according to the rules—a judgment of acquittal.

Mr. CONNESS. I simply desire to say to the Chair that the very rule which has been read implies a vote before such a judgment can be entered; and unless a vote be taken no such judgment can be entered under the rule.

The CHIEF JUSTICE. The Chief Justice spoke of those articles upon which the vote has been taken. The rule is express.

Mr. CONNESS. Certainly; judgment must be entered on them.

Mr. DRAKE. I would suggest to the Chair that in the case of Judge Peck the only entry of acquittal was the declaration by the presiding officer that he was acquitted.

The CHIEF JUSTICE. The Chief Justice simply follows the rules which have been ordained for their own government by the Senate. He does not follow a precedent; he follows the rule.

Mr. SUMNER. Mr. President, as I understand, the Chair has already, on each vote, made a declaration of acquittal, and that is of record.

The CHIEF JUSTICE. That, however, is not the judgment of the Senate contemplated by the rule; it is simply the result of the particular vote upon each article, and the rules provide that the judgment shall be entered.

Mr. CONNESS. There can be no objection to that.

The CHIEF JUSTICE. Upon the question of adjournment without day the yeas are 34 and the nays are 16. So the Senate sitting as a court of impeachment for the trial of Andrew Johnson upon articles of impeachment presented by the House of Representatives stands adjourned without day.

OPINIONS FILED UNDER THE ORDER OF THE SENATE.

Ordered, That when the Senate adjourns to-day, it adjourn to meet on Monday next, at eleven o'clock, a. m., for the purpose of deliberation, under the rules of the Senate, sitting on the trial of impeachments, and that on Tuesday next following, at twelve o'clock m., the Senate shall proceed to vote without debate on the several articles of impeachment; and each Senator shall be permitted to file within two days after the vote shall have been so taken his written opinion, to be printed with the proceedings.—*In Senate, Thursday, May 7, 1868.*

OPINION

OF

HON. LYMAN TRUMBULL.

To do impartial justice in all things appertaining to the present trial, according to the Constitution and laws, is the duty imposed on each Senator by the position he holds and the oath he has taken, and he who falters in the discharge of that duty, either from personal or party considerations, is unworthy his position, and merits the scorn and contempt of all just men.

The question to be decided is not whether Andrew Johnson is a proper person to fill the presidential office, nor whether it is fit that he should remain in it, nor, indeed, whether he has violated the Constitution and laws in other respects than those alleged against him. As well might any other fifty-four persons take upon themselves by violence to rid the country of Andrew Johnson because they believed him a bad man as to call upon fifty-four Senators, in violation of their sworn duty, to convict and depose him for any other causes than those alleged in the articles of impeachment. As well might any citizen take the law into his own hands, and become its executioner, as to ask the Senate to convict outside of the case made. To sanction such a principle would be destructive of all law and all liberty worth the name, since liberty unregulated by law is but another name for anarchy.

Unfit for President as the people may regard Andrew Johnson, and much as they may desire his removal, in a legal and constitutional way, all save the unprincipled and depraved would brand with infamy and contempt the name of any Senator who should violate his sworn convictions of duty to accomplish such a result.

Keeping in view the principles by which, as honest men, we are to be guided, let us inquire what the case is.

The first article charges Andrew Johnson, President of the United States, with unlawfully issuing an order, while the Senate was in session, and without its advice and consent, with the intent to remove Edwin M. Stanton from the office of Secretary for the Department of War, contrary to the Constitution and the "act regulating the tenure of certain civil offices," passed March 2, 1867. It will be observed that this article does not charge a removal of the Secretary, but only an intent to remove, which is not made an offense by the tenure-of-office act or any other statute; but, treating it as if the President's order had been obeyed, and an actual removal had taken place, would such removal, had it been consummated, have been a violation of the Constitution irrespective of the tenure-of-office act? The question of the power to remove from office arose in 1789, in the First Congress which assembled under the Constitution, and except as to offices whose tenure was fixed by that instrument, was then recognized as belonging to the President; but whether as a constitutional right, or one which the Congress might confer, was left an open question. Under this recognition by the Congress of 1789, every President, from that day till 1867, had exercised this power of removal, and its exercise during all that time had been acquiesced in by the other departments of the Government, both legislative and judicial. Nor was this power of removal by the President exercised only in the recess of the Senate, as some have supposed, but it was frequently exercised when the Senate was in session, and without its consent.

Indeed, there is not an instance on record prior to the passage of the tenure-of-office act, in which the consent of the Senate had been invoked simply for the removal of an officer. It is *appointments to*, and not *removals from*, office that the Constitution requires to be made by and with the advice and consent of the Senate. It is true that an appointment to an office, when the appointee becomes duly qualified, authorizes him to oust the prior incum-

868

bent, if there be one, and in that way effects his removal; but this is a different thing from a simple removal. The Constitution makes no distinction between the power of the President to remove during the recess and the sessions of the Senate, nor has there been any in practice. The elder Adams, on the 12th of December, 1800, the Senate having been in session from the 17th of November preceding, in a communication to Timothy Pickering, used this language, "You are hereby discharged from any further service as Secretary of State." Here was a positive dismissal of a Cabinet officer by the President, while the Senate was in session, and without its consent. It is no answer to say that President Adams the same day nominated John Marshall to be Secretary of State in place of "Timothy Pickering, removed."

The nomination of a person for an office does not, and never did, effect the removal of an incumbent. And such incumbent, unless removed by a distinct order, holds on till the nominee is confirmed and qualified. The Senate might never have given its advice and consent to the appointment of John Marshall, and did not in fact do so until the following day. The removal of Pickering was complete before Marshall was nominated to the Senate, as the message nominating him shows; but whether this was so or not we all know that a person in office is never removed by the mere nomination of a successor.

Thomas Eastin, navy agent at Pensacola, was removed from office by President Van Buren on the 19th of December, 1840, while the Senate was in session, and the office the same day placed temporarily in charge of Dudley Walker, and it was not till the 5th of January following that George Johnson was, by and with the advice and consent of the Senate, appointed navy agent to succeed Eastin.

June 20, 1864, and while the Senate was in session, President Lincoln removed Isaac Henderson, navy agent at New York, an officer appointed by and with the advice and consent of the Senate, and placed the office in charge temporarily of Paymaster John D. Gibson.

Isaac V. Fowler, postmaster at New York; Samuel F. Marks, postmaster at New Orleans; and Mitchell Steever, postmaster at Milwaukee, all of whom had previously been appointed by and with the advice and consent of the Senate, were severally removed by the President during the sessions of the Senate in 1860 and 1861, the offices placed temporarily in charge of special agents, and it was not till some time after the removals that nominations were made to fill the vacancies.

Other cases, during other Administrations, might be referred to, but these are sufficient to show that removals from office by the President during the session of the Senate have been no unusual thing in the history of the Government.

Of the power of Congress to define the tenure of the offices it establishes and make them determinable either at the will of the President alone, of the President and Senate together, or at the expiration of a fixed period, I entertain no doubt. The Constitution is silent on the subject of removals except by impeachment, which it must be admitted only applies to removals for crimes and misdemeanors; and if the Constitution admits of removals in no other way, then a person once in office would hold for life unless impeached, a construction which all would admit to be inadmissible under our form of Government. The right of removal must, then, exist somewhere. The First Congress, in the creation of the Department of War, in 1789, recognized it as existing in the President, by providing that the chief clerk should perform the duties of the principal officer, called a Secretary, "whenever the said principal officer shall be removed from office by the President of the United States, or in any other case of vacancy." Under this act the power of the President to remove the Secretary of War, either during the recess or session of the Senate, is manifest. The law makes no distinction in that respect, and whether it was an inherent power belonging to the President, under the Constitution as President, or was derived from the statute creating the office, is not material so far as relates to the power of the President to remove that officer.

This continued to be the law until the passage of the tenure-of-office act, March 2, 1867; and had the President issued the order for the removal of the Secretary of War prior to the passage of that act, it would hardly be contended by any one that, in so doing, he violated any law constitutional or statutory. The act of March 2, 1867, was passed to correct the previous practice, and had there been no such practice there would have been no occasion for such a law. Did that act, constitutional and valid as it is believed to be, change the law so far as it related to a Secretary then in office, by virtue of an appointment made by a former President during a presidential term which ended March 4, 1865?

The language of the first section of the act is:

"That every person holding any civil office to which he has been appointed by and with the advice and consent of the Senate, and every person who shall hereafter be appointed to any such office, and shall become duly qualified to act therein, is and shall be entitled to hold such office until a successor shall have been in like manner appointed and duly qualified, except as herein otherwise provided: *Provided*, That the Secretaries of State, of the Treasury, of War, of the Navy, and of the Interior, the Postmaster General, and the Attorney General, shall hold their offices respectively for and during the term of the President by whom they may have been appointed, and one month thereafter, subject to removal by and with the advice and consent of the Senate."

Mr. Lincoln, by and with the advice and consent of the Senate, appointed Mr. Stanton Secretary of War on the 15th of January, 1862, and commissioned him to hold the office "during the pleasure of the President of the United

States for the time being." He was never re-appointed, either by Mr. Lincoln after his re-election, or by Mr. Johnson since Mr. Lincoln's death. The continuance of Mr. Stanton in office by Mr. Lincoln after his second term commenced, and by Mr. Johnson after Mr. Lincoln's death, cannot be construed as a reappointment during that term, because the word "appointed" in the tenure-of-office act must be construed to mean a legal appointment, which could only be made by and with the advice and consent of the Senate. The term of the President by whom Mr. Stanton was appointed, and the one month thereafter, expired nearly two years before the passage of the tenure-of-office act. It will not do to say that because Mr. Lincoln was elected for a second term that therefore the term of the President by whom Mr. Stanton was appointed has not expired. The fact that Mr. Lincoln was his own successor in 1865 did not make the two terms one any more than if any other person had succeeded him, and were he now alive the presidential term during which he appointed Mr. Stanton would long since have expired. But Mr. Lincoln, in fact, deceased soon after his second term commenced, and was succeeded by the Vice President, elected for the same term, on whom the office of President was by the Constitution devolved.

It has been argued that this is Mr. Lincoln's term. If this be so, it is his second term, and not the term during which Mr. Stanton was appointed; but if this be Mr. Lincoln's and not Mr. Johnson's term, when will the "term of the President" by whom Mr. Browning and the other Cabinet officers appointed since Mr. Lincoln's death expire? Mr. Lincoln never appointed them, and if they are to hold "during the term of the President by whom they were appointed and for one month thereafter" they hold indefinitely, because, according to this theory, Mr. Johnson, the President by whom they were appointed, never had a term, and we have the anomaly of a person on whom the office of President is devolved, and who is impeached as President, and whom the Senate is asked to convict as President, who has no term of office. The clause of the Constitution which declares that the President "shall hold his office during the term of four years" does not mean that the person holding the office shall not die, resign, or be removed during that period, but to fix a term or limit during which he may, but beyond which he cannot, hold the office. If he die, resign, or be removed in the mean time, manifestly the term, so far as he is concerned, has come to an end. The term of the presidential *office* is four years, but the Constitution expressly provides that different persons may fill the office during that period, and in popular language it is called the term of the person who happens for the time being to be in the office. It is just as impossible for Mr. Stanton to now serve as Secretary of War for the term of the President by whom

he was appointed as it is for Mr. Lincoln to serve out the second term for which he was elected. Both the presidential term of the President who appointed Mr. Stanton and the person who made the appointment have passed away, never to return; but the presidential office remains, filled, however, by another person, and not Mr. Lincoln.

It being apparent that so much of the proviso to the first section of the tenure-of-civil-office act of March 2, 1867, as authorizes the Secretary of War to hold the office for and during the term of the President by whom he was appointed is inapplicable to the case of Mr. Stanton, by what tenure did he hold the office on the 21st of February last, when the President issued the order for his removal?

Originally appointed *to hold office during the pleasure of the President for the time being*, and, as has already been shown, removable at the will of the President, according to the act of 1789, there would seem to be no escape from the conclusion that the President had the right to issue the order for his removal. It has, however, been insisted that if the proviso which secures to the Secretaries the right to hold their respective offices during the term of the President by whom they may have been appointed and for one month thereafter does not embrace Mr. Stanton, because Mr. Johnson did not appoint him, that then, as a civil officer, he is within the body of the first section of the act and entitled to hold his office until by and with the advice and consent of the Senate a successor shall have been appointed and duly qualified. Not so; for the reason that the body of the first section can have no reference to the tenure of an office expressly excepted from it by the words "except as herein otherwise provided," and the provision which follows, fixing a different tenure for the Secretary of War. Can any one doubt that the law was intended to make, and does make a distinction between the tenure of office given to the Secretaries and that given to other civil officers? How, then, can it be said that the tenures are the same, or the same as to any particular Secretaries?

The meaning of the section is not different from what it would be if instead of the words, "every person holding any civil office," there had been inserted the words *marshal, district attorney, postmaster*, and so on, enumerating and fixing the tenure of all other civil officers except the Secretaries; and then had proceeded to enumerate the different Secretaries and fix for them a different tenure from that given to the other enumerated officers. Had the section been thus written, would any one think, in case a particular Secretary for some personal reason was unable to avail himself of the benefit of the law securing to Secretaries a certain tenure of office, that he would therefore have the right to the benefit of the law in which Secretaries were not mentioned, securing to marshals and others a different tenure of office? The object of an exception or proviso in a statute is to limit or take something out of the body of the act, and is usually resorted to for convenience, as a briefer mode of declaring the object than to enumerate everything embraced in the general terms of the act, and then provide for the excepted matter. The fact that the terms of the proviso which fix the tenure of office of all Secretaries are such that a particular Secretary, for reasons personal to himself, cannot take advantage of them, does not operate to take from the proviso the office of a Secretary, and the tenure attached to it, and transfer them to the body of the section which provides a tenure for holding office from which the office of Secretary is expressly excepted.

The meaning of this first section will be still more apparent by supposing a case involving the same principle but wholly disconnected with the one under consideration. Suppose Congress were to-day, May 16, 1868, to pass an act declaring that "two terms of the district court in every judicial district of the United States shall be held during the year 1868, commencing on the first Monday of June and November, except as herein otherwise provided; provided, that two terms of the district court in each of the judicial districts in the State of New York shall be held during the year 1868, commencing on the first Monday of April and September:" manifestly it would at this time be as impossible to comply with so much of the proviso as requires a court to be held in the New York districts in April, 1868, as it now is for Mr. Stanton to serve out the term of the President by whom he was appointed, which ended March 4, 1865.

Would that circumstance take the provision for the New York districts out of the proviso, and because, by the body of the act, two terms are required to be held in every judicial district in the United States on the first Monday of June and November, authorize the holding of courts in the New York districts at those periods? It is believed that no judge would for a moment think of giving such a construction to such an act; and yet this is precisely the construction of an act believed to be analogous in principle which must be resorted to to bring Mr. Stanton within the body of the first section of the tenure-of-office act.

Laying out of view what was said at the time of the passage of the tenure-of-office act, as to its not interfering with Mr. Johnson's right to remove the Secretaries appointed by his predecessor, and the unreasonableness of a construction of the act which would secure them in office longer than the Secretaries he had himself appointed, and fasten them for life on all future Presidents, unless the Senate consented to the appointment of successors, the conclusion seems inevitable, from the terms of the tenure-of-office act itself, that the President's right to remove Mr. Stanton, the Secretary of War appointed by his predecessor, is not affected by it, and that, having the author-

ity to remove that officer under the act of 1789, he did not violate either the Constitution or any statute in issuing the order for that purpose. But even if a different construction could be put upon the law, I could never consent to convict the Chief Magistrate of a great people of a high misdemeanor and remove him from office for a misconstruction of what must be admitted to be a doubtful statute, and particularly when the misconstruction was the same put upon it by the authors of the law at the time of its passage.

The second article charges that the President, in violation of the Constitution, and contrary to the tenure-of-office act, and with intent to violate the same, issued to Lorenzo Thomas a letter of authority empowering him to act as Secretary of War *ad interim*, there being no vacancy in the office of Secretary of War. There is nothing in the tenure-of-office act, or any other statute, prohibiting the issuing of such a letter, much less making it a crime or misdemeanor. The most that can be said is that it was issued without authority of law.

The Senate is required to pass judgment upon each article separately, and each must stand or fall by itself. There is no allegation in this article of any design or attempt to use the letter of authority, or that any harm came from it; and any Senator might well hesitate to find the President guilty of a high misdemeanor for simply issuing such a letter, although issued without authority of law. The proof, however, shows that the letter was issued by the President in connection with the order for the removal of Mr. Stanton, which, as has already been shown, was a valid order. The question, then, arises whether the President was guilty of a high misdemeanor in issuing to the Adjutant General of the Army a letter authorizing him, in view of the contemplated vacancy, temporarily to discharge the duties of Secretary of War.

Several statutes have been passed providing for the temporary discharge of the duties of an office by some other person in case of a vacancy, or when the officer himself is unable to perform them. The first was the eighth section of the act of May 8, 1792, and is as follows:

"That in case of the death, absence from the seat of Government, or sickness of the Secretary of State, Secretary of the Treasury, or of the Secretary of the Department of War, or of any other officer of either of the said Departments whose appointment is not in the head thereof, whereby they cannot perform the duties of their respective offices, it shall be lawful for the President of the United States, in case he shall think it necessary, to authorize any person or persons, at his discretion, to perform the duties of the said respective offices until a successor be appointed, or until such absence or inability by sickness shall cease."

The second act, passed February 13, 1795, declares:

"That in case of vacancy in the office of Secretary of State, Secretary of the Treasury, or of the Secretary of the Department of War, or of any officer of either of the said Departments whose appointment is not in the head thereof, whereby they cannot perform the duties of their said respective offices, it shall be lawful for the President of the United States, in case he shall think it necessary, to authorize any person or persons, at his discretion, to perform the duties of the said respective offices, until a successor be appointed or such vacancy be filled: *Provided*, That no one vacancy shall be supplied in manner aforesaid for a longer term than six months."

Neither of these acts provided for vacancies in the Navy, Interior or Post Office Department. Mr. Lincoln, in 1863, called attention to this defect in a special message, as follows:

To the Senate and House of Representatives:

I submit to Congress the expediency of extending to other Departments of the Government the authority conferred on the President by the eighth section of the act of the 8th of May, 1792, to appoint a person to temporarily discharge the duties of Secretary of State, of the Treasury, and the Secretary of War, in case of the death, absence from the seat of Government, or sickness of either of those officers.

ABRAHAM LINCOLN.

WASHINGTON, *January* 2, 1863.

February 20, 1863, Congress passed a third act on this subject, which declares:

"In case of the death, resignation, absence from the seat of Government, or sickness of the head of any executive Department of the Government, or of any officer of either of the said Departments whose appointment is not in the head thereof, whereby they cannot perform the duties of their respective offices, it shall be lawful for the President of the United States, in case he shall think it necessary, to authorize the head of any other executive Department, or other officer in either of said Departments whose appointment is vested in the President, at his discretion, to perform the duties of the said respective offices until a successor be appointed, or until such absence or disability by sickness shall cease: *Provided*, That no one vacancy shall be supplied in manner aforesaid for a longer term than six months."

These statutes contain all the legislation of Congress on the subject to which they relate. It has been insisted that, inasmuch as under the act of 1863 the President had no authority to designate any other person to perform the duties of Secretary of War than an officer in that or some of the other Executive Departments, and then in case of vacancy to supply such only as are occasioned by death or resignation, his designation of the Adjutant General of the Army to supply temporarily a vacancy occasioned by *removal* was without authority. If the act of 1863 repealed the act of 1795 this would doubtless be so; but if it did not repeal it, then the President clearly had the right, under that act, which provided for the temporary discharge of the duties of Secretary of War in *any* vacancy by *any* person, to authorize General Thomas temporarily to discharge those duties. The law of 1863, embracing, as it does, all the Departments, and containing provisions from both the previous statutes, may, however, be construed to embrace the whole subject on which it treats, and operate as a repeal of all prior laws on the same subject. It must, however, be admitted that it is by no means clear that the act of 1863 does repeal so much of the act of 1795 as authorizes the President to provide for the temporary discharge of the duties of an office from which an incumbent has been removed, or whose term

of office has expired by limitation before the regular appointment of a successor.

It has been argued that the tenure-of-office act of March 2, 1867, repealed both the act of 1795 and that of 1863, authorizing the temporary supplying of vacancies in the Departments. This is an entire misapprehension. The eighth section of the tenure-of-office act recognizes that authority by making it the duty of the President, when such designations are made, to notify the Secretary of the Treasury thereof; and if any one of the Secretaries were to die or resign to-morrow the authority of the President to detail an officer in one of the Departments to temporarily perform the duties of the vacant office, under the act of 1863, would be unquestioned. This would not be the appointment of an officer while the Senate was in session without its consent, but simply directing a person already in office to discharge temporarily, in no one case exceeding six months, the duties of another office not then filled.

It is the issuing of a letter of authority in respect to a removal, appointment, or employment "*contrary to the provisions*" of the tenure-of-office act that is made a high misdemeanor. As the order for the removal of Mr. Stanton has already been shown not to have been "contrary to the provisions of this act," any letter of authority in regard to it is not forbidden by the sixth section thereof.

Admitting, however, that there was no statute in existence expressly authorizing the President to designate the Adjutant General of the Army temporarily to discharge the duties of the office of Secretary of War, made vacant by removal, till a successor, whose nomination was proposed the next day, could be confirmed, does it follow that he was guilty of a high misdemeanor in making such temporary designation when there was no law making it a penal offense or prohibiting it? Prior to 1863, as Mr. Lincoln's message shows, there was no law authorizing these temporary designations in any other than the three Departments of State, Treasury, and War; and yet President Lincoln himself, on the 22d of September, 1862, prior to any law authorizing it, issued the following letter of authority appointing a Postmaster-General *ad interim*:

I hereby appoint St. John B. L. Skinner, now acting First Assistant Postmaster General, to be acting Postmaster General *ad interim*, in place of Hon. Montgomery Blair, now temporarily absent.

ABRAHAM LINCOLN.

WASHINGTON, *September* 22, 1862.

To provide for temporary disabilities or vacancies in the Navy Department, and for which no law at the time existed, President Jackson, during his administration, made ten different designations or appointments of Secretaries of the Navy *ad interim*. Similar *ad interim* designations in the Navy Department were made by Presidents Van Buren, Harrison, Tyler, Polk, Filmore, and others; and these appointments were made indiscriminately during the sessions of the Senate as well as during its recess. As no law authorizing them existed at the time these *ad interim* appointments were made in the Navy and Post Office Departments, it must be admitted that they were made without authority of law; and yet, who then thought, or would now think, of impeaching for high crimes and misdemeanors the Presidents who made them? President Buchanan, in a communication to the Senate made January 15, 1861, on the subject of *ad interim* appointments, used this language:

"Vacancies may occur at any time in the most important offices which cannot be immediately and permanently filled in a manner satisfactory to the appointing power. It was wise to make a provision which would enable the President to avoid a total suspension of business in the interval, and equally wise so to limit the executive discretion as to prevent any serious abuse of it. This is what the framers of the act of 1795 did, and neither the policy nor the constitutional validity of their law has been questioned for sixty-five years.

The practice of making such appointments, whether in a vacation or during the session of Congress, has been constantly followed during every Administration from the earliest period of the Government, and its perfect lawfulness has never, to my knowledge, been questioned or denied. Without going back further than the year 1829, and without taking into the calculation any but the chief officers of the several Departments, it will be found that provisional appointments to fill vacancies were made to the number of one hundred and seventy-nine from the commencement of General Jackson's administration to the close of General Pierce's. This number would probably be greatly increased if all the cases which occurred in the subordinate offices and bureaus were added to the count. Some of them were made while the Senate was in session; some which were made in vacation were continued in force long after the Senate assembled. Sometimes the temporary officer was the commissioned head of another Department, sometimes a subordinate in the same Department. Sometimes the affairs of the Navy Department have been directed *ad interim* by a commodore, and those of the War Department by a general."

Importance is sought to be given to the passage by the Senate, before the impeachment articles were found by the House of Representatives, of the following resolution:

"*Resolved by the Senate of the United States*, That under the Constitution and laws of the United States the President has no power to remove the Secretary of War and designate any other officer to perform the duties of that office *ad interim*"—

as if Senators sitting as a court on the trial of the President for high crimes and misdemeanors would feel bound or influenced in any degree by a resolution introduced and hastily passed before an adjournment on the very day the orders to Stanton and Thomas were issued. Let him who would be governed by such considerations in passing on the guilt or innocence of the accused, and not by the law and the facts as they have been developed on the trial, shelter himself under such a resolution. I am sure no honest man could. It is known, however, that the resolution coupled the two things, the removal of the Secretary of War and the designation of an officer *ad interim*, together, so that those who believed either without authority were compelled to vote for the resolution.

My understanding at the time was, that the act of 1863 repealed that of 1795 authorizing the designation of a Secretary of War *ad interim* in the place of a Secretary *removed*; but

I never entertained the opinion that the President had not power to remove the Secretary of War appointed by Mr. Lincoln during his first term. Believing the act of 1795 to have been repealed, I was bound to vote that the President had no power under the law to designate a Secretary of War *ad interim* to fill a vacancy caused by removal, just as I would feel bound to vote for a resolution that neither President Jackson nor any of his successors had the power, under the law, to designate *ad interim* Postmasters General or Secretaries of the Navy and Interior prior to the act of 1863; but it by no means follows that they were guilty of high crimes and misdemeanors in making such temporary designations. They acted without the shadow of statutory authority in making such appointments. Johnson claims, and not without plausibility, that he had authority under the act of 1795 to authorize the Adjutant General of the Army to perform temporarily the duties of Secretary of War; but if that act was repealed, even then he simply acted as his predecessors had done with the acquiescence of the nation for forty years before. Considering that the facts charged against the President in the second article are in no respect contrary to any provision of the tenure-of-office act; that they do not constitute a misdemeanor, and are not forbidden by any statute; that it is a matter of grave doubt whether so much of the act of 1795 as would expressly authorize the issuing of the letter of authority to General Thomas is not in force, and if it is not, that President Johnson still had the same authority for issuing it as his predecessors had exercised for many years without objection in the Navy, Interior, and Post Office Departments, it is impossible for me to hold him guilty of a high misdemeanor under that article. To do so would, in my opinion, be to disregard, rather than recognize, that impartial justice I am sworn to administer.

What has been said in regard to the second article applies with equal force to the third and eighth articles: there being no proof of an unlawful intent to control the disbursements of the moneys appropriated for the military service, as charged in the eighth article.

Articles four, five, six, and seven, taken together, charge in substance that the President conspired with Lorenzo Thomas and other persons with intent, by intimidation and threats, to prevent Edwin M. Stanton from holding the office of Secretary of War, and by force to seize and possess the property of the United States in the Department of War; also that he conspired to do the same things contrary to the tenure-of-office act, without any allegation of force or threats. The record contains no sufficient proof of the intimidation, threats, or force charged; and as the President had, in my opinion, the right to remove Mr. Stanton, his order for that purpose, as also that to General Thomas to take possession, both peacefully issued, have, in my judgment, none of the elements of a conspiracy about them.

The ninth article, known as the Emory article, is wholly unsupported by evidence.

The tenth article, relating to the speeches of the President, is substantially proven, but the speeches, although discreditable to the high office he holds, do not, in my opinion, afford just ground for impeachment.

So much of the eleventh article as relates to the speech of the President made August 18, 1866, is disposed of by what has been said on the tenth article.

The only proof to sustain the allegation of unlawfully attempting to devise means to prevent Edwin M. Stanton from resuming the office of Secretary of War is to be found in a letter from the President to General Grant, dated February 10, 1868, written long after Mr. Stanton had been restored. This letter, referring to a controversy between the President and General Grant in regard to certain communications, oral and written, which had passed between them, shows that it was the President's intent, in case the Senate did not concur in Stanton's suspension, to compel him to resort to the courts to regain possession of the War Department, with a view of obtaining a judicial decision on the validity of the tenure-of-office act; but the intention was never carried out, and Stanton took possession by the voluntary surrender of the office by General Grant. Was this intent or purpose of the President to obtain a judicial decision in the only way then practicable a high misdemeanor?

It is unnecessary to inquire whether the President would have been justified in carrying his intention into effect. It was not done and his entertaining an intention to do it constituted, in my opinion, no offense. There is, however, to my mind another conclusive answer to this charge in the eleventh article. The President, in my view, had authority to remove Mr. Stanton, and this being so, he could by removal at any time have lawfully kept him from again taking possession of the office.

There is no proof to sustain the other charges of this article. In coming to the conclusion that the President is not guilty of any of the high crimes and misdemeanors with which he stands charged, I have endeavored to be governed by the case made without reference to other acts of his not contained in the record, and without giving the least heed to the clamor of intemperate zealots who demand the conviction of Andrew Johnson as a test of party faith, or seek to identify with and make responsible for his acts those who from convictions of duty feel compelled on the case made to vote for his acquittal. His speeches and the general course of his administration have been as distasteful to me as to any one, and I should consider it the great calamity of the age if the disloyal element, so often encouraged by his measures, should gain political ascendency. If the question was, Is Andrew Johnson a fit person for President? I should answer, *no;* but it is not a party question, nor upon Andrew Johnson's deeds and acts, except so far as they are made to appear in the record, that I am to decide.

Painful as it is to disagree with so many political associates and friends whose conscientious convictions have led them to a different result, I must, nevertheless, in the discharge of the high responsibility under which I act, be governed by what my reason and judgment tell me is the truth, and the justice and the law of this case. What law does this record show the President to have violated? Is it the tenure-of-office act? I believe in the constitutionality of that act, and stand ready to punish its violators; but neither the removal of that faithful and efficient officer, Edwin M. Stanton, which I deeply regret, nor the *ad interim* designation of Lorenzo Thomas, were, as has been shown, forbidden by it. Is it the reconstruction acts? Whatever the facts may be, this record does not contain a particle of evidence of their violation. Is it the conspiracy act? No facts are shown to sustain such a charge, and the same may be said of the charge of a violation of the appropriation act of March 2, 1867; and these are all the laws alleged to have been violated. It is, however, charged that Andrew Johnson has violated the Constitution. The fact may be so, but where is the evidence of it to be found in this record? Others may, but I cannot find it. To convict and depose the Chief Magistrate of a great nation, when his guilt was not made palpable by the record, and for insufficient cause, would be fraught with far greater danger to the future of the country than can arise from leaving Mr. Johnson in office for the remaining months of his term, with powers curtailed and limited as they have been by recent legislation.

Once set the example of impeaching a President for what, when the excitement of the hour shall have subsided, will be regarded as insufficient causes, as several of those now alleged against the President were decided to be by the House of Representatives only a few months since, and no future President will be safe who happens to differ with a majority of the House and two thirds of the Senate on any measure deemed by them important, particularly if of a political character. Blinded by partisan zeal, with such an example before them, they will not scruple to remove out of the way any obstacle to the accomplishment of their purposes, and what then becomes of the checks and balances of the Constitution, so carefully devised and so vital to its perpetuity? They are all gone. In view of the consequences likely to flow from this day's proceedings, should they result in conviction on what my judgment tells me are insufficient charges and proofs, I tremble for the future of my country. I cannot be an instrument to produce such a result; and at the hazard of the ties even of friendship and affection, till calmer times shall do justice to my motives, no alternative is left me but the inflexible discharge of duty.

OPINION
OF
HON. JAMES W. GRIMES.

The President of the United States stands at the bar of the Senate charged with the commission of high crimes and misdemeanors. The principal offense charged against him is embodied in various forms in the first eight articles of impeachment. This offense is alleged to consist in a violation of the provisions of the first section of an act of Congress entitled "An act regulating the tenure of certain civil offices," approved March 2, 1867, in this, that on the 21st day of February, 1868, the President removed, or attempted to remove, Edwin M. Stanton from the office of Secretary for the Department of War, and issued a letter of authority to General Lorenzo Thomas as Secretary for the Department of War *ad interim.*

The House of Representatives charge in their three first articles that the President attempted to remove Mr. Stanton, and that he issued his letter of authority to General Thomas with an intent to violate the law of Congress, and with the further "intent to violate the Constitution of the United States." The President, by his answer, admits that he sought to substitute General Thomas for Mr. Stanton at the head of the Department of War; but insists that he had the right to make such substitution under the laws then and now in force, and denies that in anything that he has done or attempted to do he intended to violate the laws or the Constitution of the United States.

To this answer there is a general traverse by the House of Representatives, and thereon issue is joined; of that issue we are the triers, and have sworn that in that capacity we will do "impartial justice according to the Constitution and the laws."

It will be perceived that there is nothing involved in the first eight articles of impeachment but pure questions of law growing out of the construction of statutes. Mr. Johnson's guilt or innocence upon those articles depends wholly on the fact whether or not he had the power, after the passage of the tenure-of-office act of March 2, 1867, to remove Mr. Stanton and issue the letter of appointment to General Thomas, and upon the further fact, whether, having no such legal authority, he nevertheless attempted to exercise it "with intent to violate the Constitution of the United States."

Mr. Stanton was appointed Secretary for the Department of War by Mr. Lincoln on the 15th day of January, 1862, and has not since been reappointed or recommissioned. His commission was issued to continue "for and during the pleasure of the President." His appointment was made under the act of August 7, 1789, the first two sections of which read as follows:

"There shall be an executive Department to be denominated the Department of War; and there shall be a principal officer therein, to be called the Secretary for the Department of War, who shall perform and execute such duties as shall from time to time be enjoined on or intrusted to him by the President of the United States, and the said principal officer shall conduct the business of the said Department in such manner as the President of the United States shall from time to time order and instruct.

"There shall be in the said Department an inferior officer, to be appointed by said principal officer, to be employed therein as he shall deem proper, and to be called the chief clerk of the Department of War; *and whenever the said principal officer shall be removed from office by the President of the United States, and in any* other case of vacancy, shall, during the same, have charge of the records, books," &c.

At the same session of Congress was passed the act of July 27, 1789, creating the Department of Foreign Affairs. The two first sections of the two acts are precisely similar except in the designations of the two Departments. Upon the passage of this last act occurred one of the most memorable and one of the ablest debates that ever took place in Congress. The subject under discussion was the tenure of public officers, and especially the tenure by which the Secretaries of the Executive Departments should hold their offices. Without going into the particulars of that great debate, it is sufficient to say that the reasons assigned by Mr. Madison and his associates in favor of a "tenure during the pleasure of the President" were adopted as the true constitutional theory on this subject. That great man, with almost a prophetic anticipation of this case, declared on the 16th June, 1789, in his speech in the House of Representatives, of which he was a member from Virginia, that—

"It is evidently the intention of the Constitution that the First Magistrate should be responsible for the executive department. So far, therefore, as we do not make the officers who are to aid him in the duties of that department responsible to him he is not responsible to the country. Again, is there no danger that an officer, when he is appointed by the concurrence of the Senate and his friends in that body, may choose rather to risk his establishment on the favor of that branch than rest it upon the discharge of his duties to the satisfaction of the executive branch, which is constitutionally authorized to inspect and control his conduct? And if it should happen that the officers connect themselves with the Senate, they may mutually support each other, and for want of efficacy reduce the power of the President to a mere vapor, in which case his responsibility would be annihilated, and the expectation of it unjust. The high executive officers joined in cabal with the Senate would lay the foundation of discord, and end in an assumption of the executive power, only to be removed by a revolution of the Government."

It will be observed that it is here contended that it is the Constitution that establishes the tenure of office. And in order to put this question beyond future cavil, Chief Justice Marshall, in his Life of Washington, volume 2, page 162, says:

"After an ardent discussion, which consumed several days, the committee divided, and the amendment was negatived by a majority of thirty-four to twenty. The opinion thus expressed by the House of Representatives did not explicitly convey their sense of the Constitution. Indeed, the express grant of the power to the President rather implied a right in the Legislature to give or withhold it at their discretion. To obviate any misunderstanding of the principle on which the question had been decided, Mr. Benson moved in the House, when the report of the Committee of the Whole was taken up, to amend the second clause in the bill so as clearly to imply the power of removal to be solely in the President. He gave notice that if he should succeed in this he would move to strike out the words which had been the subject of debate. If those words continued, he said, the power of removal by the President might hereafter appear to be exercised by virtue of a legislative grant only, and consequently be subjected to legislative instability, when he was well satisfied in his own mind that it was by fair construction fixed in the Constitution. The motion was seconded by Mr. Madison, and both amendments were adopted."

And Judge Marshall adds:

"As the bill passed into a law it has ever been considered as a full expression of the sense of the Legislature on this important part of the American Constitution."

And Chancellor Kent says, when speaking of the action of this Congress, many of the members of which had been members of the Convention that framed the Constitution, the chiefest among them, perhaps, being Madison, who has been called the father of that instrument:

"This amounted to a legislative construction of the Constitution, and it has ever since been acquiesced in and acted upon as of decisive authority in the case. It applies equally to every other officer of the Government appointed by the President and Senate whose term of duration is not specially declared. It is supported by the weighty reason that the subordinate officers in the executive department ought to hold at the pleasure of the head of that department, because he is invested generally with the executive authority, and every participation in that authority by the Senate was an exception to a general principle, and ought to be taken strictly. The President is the great responsible officer for the faithful execution of the law, and the power of removal was incidental to that duty, and might often be requisite to fulfill it."—1 *Kent. Com.*, 310.

Thus the Constitution and the law stood as expounded by the courts, as construed by commentators and publicists, as acted on by all the Presidents, and acquiesced in by all of the Congresses from 1789 until the 2d March, 1867, when the tenure-of-office act was passed. The first section of this act reads as follows:

"That every person holding any civil office to which he has been appointed by and with the advice and consent of the Senate, and every person who shall hereafter be appointed to any such office, and shall become duly qualified to act therein, is and shall be entitled to hold such office until a successor shall have been in a like manner appointed and duly qualified, except as herein otherwise provided."

Then comes what is "otherwise provided:"

"*Provided*, That the Secretaries of State, of the Treasury, of War, of the Navy, and of the Interior, the Postmaster General, and the Attorney General shall hold their offices respectively for and during the term of the President by whom they may have been appointed, and for one month thereafter, subject to removal by and with the advice and consent of the Senate."

The controversy in this case grows out of the construction of this section. How does it affect the act of 1789, and does it change the tenure of office of the Secretary for the Department of War as established by that act? To that inquiry I propose to address myself. I shall not deny the constitutional validity of the act of March 2, 1867. That question is not necessarily in this case.

The first question presented is, is Mr. Stanton's case within the provisions of the tenure-of-office act of March 2, 1867?

Certainly it is not within the body of the first section. The tenure which that provides for is not the tenure of *any* Secretary. *All* Secretaries whose tenure is regulated by this law at all are to go out of office at the end of the term of the President by whom they shall be appointed, and one month thereafter, unless sooner removed by the President, by and with the advice and consent of the Senate, while all other civil officers are to hold until a successor shall be appointed and duly qualified. The office of Secretary has attached to it one tenure; other civil officers another and different tenure, and no one who holds the office of Secretary can, *by force of this law*, hold by any other tenure than the one which the law specially assigns to that office. The plain intent of the proviso to the first section is to prescribe a tenure for the office of Secretary different from the tenure fixed for other civil officers. This is known to have been done on account of the marked difference between the heads of Departments and all other officers, which made it desirable and necessary for the public service that the heads of Departments should go out of office with the President by whom they were appointed. It would, indeed, be a strange result of the law if those Secretaries appointed by Mr. Lincoln should hold by the tenure fixed by the act for ordinary civil officers, while all the other Secretaries should hold by a different tenure; that those appointed by the present and all future Presidents should hold only during the term of the President by whom they may have been appointed, while those not appointed by him should hold indefinitely; and this under a law which undertakes to define the tenure of all the Secretaries who are to hold their offices under the law. I cannot come to that conclusion. My opinion is, that if Mr. Stanton's tenure of office is prescribed by this law at all, it is prescribed to him as Secretary of War, under and by force of the proviso to the first section; and if his case is not included in that proviso it is not included in the law at all.

It is clear to my mind that the *proviso* does not include, and was not intended to include, Mr. Stanton's case. It is not possible to apply to his case the language of the proviso unless we suppose it to have been intended to legislate him out of office; a conclusion, I consider, wholly inadmissable. He was appointed by President Lincoln during his first term of office. He cannot hereafter go out of office at the end of the term of the President by whom he was appointed. That term was ended before the law was passed. The proviso, therefore, cannot have been intended to make a rule for his case; and it is shown that it was not intended. This was plainly declared in debate by the conference committee, both in the Senate and in the House of Representatives, when the proviso was introduced and its effect explained.

The meaning and effect of the *proviso* were then explained and understood to be that the only tenure of the Secretaries provided for by this law was a tenure to end with the term of service of the President by whom they were appointed, and as this new tenure could not include Mr. Stanton's case, it was here explicitly declared that it did not include it. When this subject was under consideration in the House of Representatives on the report of the conference committee on the disagreeing vote of the two Houses, Mr. SCHENCK, of Ohio, chairman of the conference committee on the part of the House, said :

"It will be remembered that by the bill as it passed the Senate it was provided that the concurrence of the Senate should be required in all removals from office, except in the case of the heads of Departments. The House amended the bill of the Senate so as to extend this requirement to the heads of Departments as well as to their officers.

"The committee of conference have agreed that the Senate shall accept the amendment of the House. *But, inasmuch as this would compel the President to keep around him heads of Departments until the end of his term who would hold over to another term, a compromise was made by which a further amendment is added to this portion of the bill, so that the term of office of the heads of Departments shall expire with the term of the President who appointed them,* allowing these heads of Departments one month longer."

When the bill came to the Senate and was considered on the disagreeing vote of the two Houses, and Mr. DOOLITTLE, of Wisconsin, charged that although the purpose of the measure was, in his opinion, to force the President against his will to retain the Secretaries appointed by Mr. Lincoln, yet that the phraseology was such that the bill, if passed, would not accomplish that object, Mr. SHERMAN, of Ohio, who was a member of the conference committee and assisted to frame the proviso, said :

"I do not understand the logic of the Senator from Wisconsin. He first attributes a purpose to the committee of conference which I say is not true. I say that the Senate have not legislated with a view to any persons or any President, and therefore he commences by asserting what is not true. We do not legislate in order to keep in the Secretary of War, the Secretary of the Navy, or the Secretary of State."

Then a conversation arose between the Senator from Ohio and another Senator, and the Senator from Ohio continued thus :

"That the Senate had no such purpose is shown by its vote twice to make this exception. That this pro- vision does not apply to the present case is shown by the fact that its language is so framed as not to apply to the present President. The Senator shows that himself, and argues truly that it would not prevent the present President from removing the Secretary of War, the Secretary of the Navy, and the Secretary of State. And if I supposed that either of these gentlemen was so wanting in manhood, in honor, as to hold his place after the politest intimation by the President of the United States that his services were no longer needed, I certainly, as a Senator, would consent to his removal at any time, and so would we all."

Did any one here doubt the correctness of Mr. SHERMAN's interpretation of the act when he declared that it "*would not prevent the present President from removing the Secretary of War, the Secretary of the Navy, and the Secre-tary of State?*" Was there any dissent from his position? Was there not entire acquiescence in it?

Again, said Mr. SHERMAN :

"In this case the committee of conference—I agreed to it, I confess, with some reluctance—came to the conclusion to qualify to some extent the power of removal over a Cabinet minister. We provide that a Cabinet minister shall hold his office not for a fixed term, not until the Senate shall consent to his removal, *but as long as the power that appoints him holds office.*"

But whatever may have been the character of the debates at the time of the passage of the law, or whatever may have been the contemporaneous exposition of it, I am clearly convinced that the three Secretaries holding over from Mr. Lincoln's administration do not fall within its provisions under any fair judicial interpretation of the act; that Mr. Stanton held his office under the act of 1789, and under his only commission, issued in 1862, which was at the pleasure of the President; and I am, consequently, constrained to decide that the order for his removal was a lawful order. Any other construction would involve us in the absurdity of ostensibly attempting to limit the tenure of all Cabinet officers to the term of the officer having the power to appoint them, yet giving to three of the present Cabinet ministers an unlimited tenure; for, if the construction contended for by the Managers be the correct one, while four of the present Cabinet officers will go out of office absolutely, and without any action by the Senate, on the 4th of April next, they having been appointed by Mr. Johnson, the three Cabinet officers appointed by Mr. Lincoln will hold by another and different tenure, and cannot be removed until the incoming President and the Senate shall mutually agree to their removal.

If I have not erred thus far in my judgment, then it follows that the order for the removal of Mr. Stanton was not a violation of the Constitution of the United States by reason of its having been issued during the session of the Senate. If Mr. Stanton held his office at the pleasure of the President alone under the act of 1789, as I think he did, it necessarily follows that the President alone could remove him. The Senate had no power in reference to his continuance in office. I am wholly unable to perceive, therefore, that the power of the President to remove him was affected or qualified by the fact that the Senate was in session.

It has sometimes been put forward, as it was by Mr. Webster in the debate of 1835, that the usual mode of removal from office by the President during a session of the Senate had been by the nomination of a successor in place of A B, removed. This would naturally be so in all cases except the few in which the officer could not be allowed, consistently with the public safety, to continue in office until his successor should be appointed and qualified and also should refuse to resign. Such cases cannot often have occurred. But when they have occurred, I believe the President has exercised that power which was understood to belong to him alone, and which in the statute tenure of most offices is recognized by the acts of Congress creating them to be the pleasure of the President of the United States. A number of cases of this kind have been put in evidence. I do not find, either in the debates which have been had on the power of removal, or in the legislation of Congress on the tenure of offices, any trace of a distinction between the power of the President to remove in recess and his power to remove during a session of the Senate an officer who held solely by his pleasure; and I do not see how such a distinction could exist without some positive and distinct provision of law to make and define it. I know of no such provision. If that was the tenure by which Mr. Stanton held the office of Secretary for the Department of War, and I think it was, then I am also of the opinion that it was not a violation of the Constitution to remove him during a session of the Senate.

If Mr. Stanton held under the act of 1789 no permission of the President to continue in office, no adoption of him as Secretary for the Department of War, could change the legal tenure of his office as fixed by law or deprive the President of the power to remove him.

My opinion on the matter of the first article is not affected by the facts contained in it, that the President suspended Mr. Stanton and sent notice of the suspension to the Senate, and the Senate refused to concur in that suspension. In my opinion that action of the President could not and did not change the tenure of Mr. Stanton's office, as it subsisted by law at the pleasure of the President, or deprive the President of that authority to remove him which necessarily arose from that tenure of office.

If the order of the President to Mr. Stanton was a lawful order, as I have already said I thought it was, the first question under the second article is whether the President did anything unlawful in giving the order to General Thomas to perform the duties of Secretary for the Department of War ad interim.

This was not an appointment to office. It was a temporary designation of a person to discharge the duties of an office until the office could be filled. The distinction between such a designation and an appointment to office is in itself clear enough, and has been recognized certainly since the act of February 13, 1795. Many cases have occurred in which this authority has been exercised. The necessity of some such provision of law, in cases of vacancy in offices which the Executive cannot instantly fill, must be apparent to every one acquainted with the workings of our Government, and I do not suppose that a reasonable question can be made of the constitutional validity of a law providing for such cases.

The law of 1795 did provide for such cases; and the President, in his answer, says he was advised that this was a subsisting law not re-

pealed. It may be a question whether it has been repealed; but from the best examination I have been able to bestow upon the subject I am satisfied it has not been repealed.

I do not propose to enter into the technical rules as to implied repeals. It is a subject of great difficulty, and I do not profess to be able to apply those rules; I take only this practical view of the subject: when the act of February 20, 1863, was passed, which it is supposed may have repealed the act of 1795, it is beyond all dispute that vacancies in office might be created by the President; and there might be the same necessity for making temporary provision for discharging the duties of such vacant offices as was provided for by the act of 1795. The act of 1863 is wholly silent on this subject. Why should I say that a public necessity provided for in 1795 and not negatived in 1863 was not then recognized; or why should I say that if recognized it was intended by the act of 1863 that it should not thereafter have any provision made for it? Comparing the act of 1863 and the cases it provided for, I see no sufficient reason to say that it was the intention of Congress in 1863 to deprive the President of the power given by the act of 1795 to supply the temporary necessities of the public service in case of vacancy caused by removal.

But if I thought otherwise I should be unable to convict the President of a crime because he had acted under the law of 1795. Many cases of ad interim appointments have been brought before us in evidence. It appears to have been a constant and frequent practice of the Government, in all cases when the President was not prepared to fill an office at the moment when the vacancy occurred, to make an ad interim appointment. There were one hundred and seventy-nine such appointments specified in the schedule annexed to the message of President Buchanan, found on page 584 of the printed record, as having occurred in little more than the space of thirty years. I have not minutely examined the evidence to follow the practice further, because it seems to me that if, as I think, the President had the power to remove Mr. Stanton, he might well conclude, and that it cannot be attributed to him as a high crime and misdemeanor that he did conclude, that he might designate some proper officer to take charge of the War Department until he could send a nomination of a suitable person to be Secretary; and when I add that on the next day after this designation the President did nominate for that office an eminent citizen in whose loyalty to our country and in whose fitness for any duties he might be willing to undertake the people would be willing to confide, I can find no sufficient reason to doubt that the President acted in good faith and believed that he was acting within the laws of the United States. Surely the mere signing of that letter of appointment, "neither attended or followed by the possession of the office named in it or by any act of force, of violence, of fraud, of corruption, of injury, or of evil, will not justify us in depriving the President of his office."

I have omitted to notice one fact stated in the second article. It is that the designation of General Thomas to act *ad interim* as Secretary of War was made during a session of the Senate. This requires but few words. The acts of Congress, and the nature of the cases to which they apply, admit of no distinction between *ad interim* appointments in the sessions or the recess of the Senate. A designation is to be made when necessary, and the necessity may occur either in session or in recess.

I do not deem it necessary to state any additional views concerning the third article, for I find in it no allegations upon which I have not already sufficiently indicated my opinion.

The fourth, fifth, sixth, and seventh articles charge a conspiracy. I deem it sufficient to say that, in my judgment, the evidence adduced by the House of Representatives not only fails to prove a conspiracy between the President and General Thomas to remove Mr. Stanton from office by force or threats, but it fails to prove any conspiracy in any sense I can attach to that word.

The President, by a written order committed to General Thomas, required Mr. Stanton to cease to act as Secretary for the Department of War, and informed him that he had empowered General Thomas to act as Secretary *ad interim.* The order to General Thomas empowered him to enter on the duties of the office and receive from Mr. Stanton the public property in his charge. There is no evidence that the President contemplated the use of force, threats, or intimidation; still less that he authorized General Thomas to use any. I do not regard the declarations of General Thomas, as explained by himself, as having any *tendency* even to fix on the President any purpose beyond what the orders on their face import. Believing, as I do, that the orders of the President for the removal of Mr. Stanton, and the designation of General Thomas to act *ad interim*, were legal orders, it is manifestly impossible for me to attach to them any idea of criminal conspiracy. If those orders had not been, in my judgment, lawful, I should not have come to the conclusion, upon the evidence, that any actual intent to do an unlawful act was proved.

The eighth article does not require any particular notice after what I have said of the first, second, and third articles, because the only additional matter contained in it is the allegation of an intent to unlawfully control the appropriations made by Congress for the military service by unlawfully removing Mr. Stanton from the office of Secretary for the Department of War.

In my opinion, no evidence whatever, tending to prove this intent, has been given. The Managers offered some evidence which they supposed might have some tendency to prove this allegation, but it appeared to the Senate that the supposed means could not, under any circumstances, be adequate to the supposed end, and the evidence was rejected. Holding that the order for the removal of Mr. Stanton was not an infraction of the law, of course this article is, in my opinion, wholly unsupported.

I find no evidence sufficient to support the *ninth* article.

The President, as Commander-in-Chief of the Army, had a right to be informed of any details of the military service concerning which he thought proper to inquire. His attention was called by one of his Secretaries to some unusual orders. He sent to General Emory to make inquiry concerning them. In the course of the conversation General Emory himself introduced the subject which is the gist of the ninth article, and I find in what the President said to him nothing which he might not naturally say in response to General Emory's inquiries and remarks without the criminal intent charged in this ninth article.

I come now to the question of intent. Admitting that the President had no power under the law to issue the order to remove Mr. Stanton and appoint General Thomas for Secretary the Department of War *ad interim*, did he issue those orders with a manifest *intent* to violate the laws and "the Constitution of the United States," as charged in the articles, or did he issue them, as he says he did, with a view to have the constitutionality of the tenure-of-office act judicially decided?

It is apparent to my mind that the President thoroughly believed the tenure-of-office act to be unconstitutional and void. He was so advised by every member of his Cabinet when the bill was presented to him for his approval in February, 1867. The Managers on the part of the House of Representatives have put before us and made legal evidence in this case the message of the President to the Senate, dated December 12, 1867. In that message the President declared—

"That tenure-of-office law did not pass without notice. Like other acts it was sent to the President for approval. As is my custom, I submitted its consideration to my Cabinet for their advice upon the question, whether I should approve it or not. It was a grave question of constitutional law, in which I would of course rely most upon the opinion of the Attorney General and of Mr. Stanton, who had once been Attorney General. Every member of my Cabinet advised me that the proposed law was unconstitutional. All spoke without doubt or reservation, but Mr. Stanton's condemnation of the law was the most elaborate and emphatic. He referred to the constitutional provisions, the debates in Congress—especially to the speech of Mr. Buchanan when a Senator—to the decisions of the Supreme Court, and to the usage from the beginning of the Government through every successive Administration, all concurring to establish the right of removal as vested by the Constitution in the President. To all these he added the weight of his own deliberate judgment, and advised me that it was my duty to defend the power of the President from usurpation and to veto the law."

The counsel for the respondent not only

offered to prove the truth of this statement of the President by members of the Cabinet, but they tendered in addition thereto the proof "that the duty of preparing a message, setting forth the objections to the constitutionality of the bill, was devolved on Mr. Seward and Mr. Stanton." They also offered to prove—

"That at the meetings of the Cabinet, at which Mr. Stanton was present, held while the tenure-of-office bill was before the President for approval, the advice of the Cabinet in regard to the same was asked by the President and given by the Cabinet; and thereupon the question whether Mr. Stanton and the other Secretaries who had received their appointment from Mr. Lincoln were within the restrictions upon the President's power of removal from office created by said act was considered, and the opinion expressed that the Secretaries appointed by Mr. Lincoln were not within such restrictions."

And,

"That at the Cabinet meetings between the passage of the tenure-of-civil-office bill and the order of the 21st of February, 1868, for the removal of Mr. Stanton, upon occasions when the condition of the public service as affected by the operation of that bill came up for the consideration and advice of the Cabinet, it was considered by the President and Cabinet that a proper regard to the public service made it desirable that upon some proper case a judicial determination on the constitutionality of the law should be obtained."

This evidence was, in my opinion, clearly admissible as cumulative of, or to explain or disprove, the message of the President, which narrates substantially the same facts, and which the Managers have introduced and made a part of their case; but it was rejected as incompetent testimony by a vote of the Senate. I believe that decision was erroneous; and inasmuch as there is no tribunal to revise the errors of this, and it is impossible to order a new trial of this case, I deem it proper to regard these offers to prove as having been proved.

We have in addition to this testimony as to the intent of the President the evidence of General Sherman. The President desired to appoint General Sherman Secretary *ad interim* for the Department of War, and tendered to him the office. The complications in which the office was then involved was talked over between them. General Sherman says that the subject of using force to eject Mr. Stanton from the office was only mentioned by the President to repel the idea. When General Sherman asked him why the lawyers could not make up a case and have the conflicting questions decided by the courts, his reply was "that it was found impossible, or a case could not be made up; but," said he, "if we can bring the case to the courts it would not stand half an hour."

Here, then, we have the President advised by all of the members of his Cabinet, including the Attorney General, whose duty it is made by law to give legal advice to him, including the Secretary for the Department of War, also an eminent lawyer and an Attorney General of the United States under a former Administration, that the act of March 2, 1867, was unconstitutional and void, that the three members of the Cabinet holding over from Mr. Lincoln's administration were not included within its provisions, and that it was desirable that upon some proper case a judicial determination on the constitutionality of the law should be obtained.

Now, when it is remembered that, according to Chief Justice Marshall, the act of 1789, creating the Department of War, was intentionally framed "so as to clearly imply the power of removal to be solely in the President," and that "as the bill passed into a law, it has ever been considered as a full expression of the sense of the Legislature on this important part of the American Constitution;" when it is remembered that this construction has been acquiesced in and acted on by every President from Washington to Johnson, by the Supreme Court, by every Congress of the United States from the first that ever assembled under the Constitution down to the Thirty-Ninth; and when it is remembered that all of the President's Cabinet and the most eminent counselors within his reach advised him that the preceding Congresses, the past Presidents and statesmen, and Story and Kent and Thompson and Marshall were right in their construction of the Constitution, and the Thirty-Ninth Congress wrong, is it strange that he should doubt or dispute the constitutionality of the tenure-of-office act?

But all this is aside from the question whether Mr. Stanton's case is included in the provisions of that act. If it was not, as I think it clearly was not, then the question of intent is not in issue, for he did no unlawful act. If it was included then I ask whether, in view of those facts, the President's *guilty intent* to do an unlawful act "shines with such a clear and certain light" as to justify, to require, us to pronounce him guilty of a high constitutional crime or misdemeanor? The Manager, Mr. BOUTWELL, admits that—

"If a law passed by Congress be equivocal or ambiguous in its terms, the Executive, being called upon to administer it, may apply his own best judgment to the difficulties before him, or he may seek counsel of his advisers or other persons; and acting thereupon without evil intent or purpose, he would be fully justified, and upon no principle of right could he be held to answer as for a misdemeanor in office."

Does not this admission cover this case? Is there not doubt about the legal construction of the tenure-of-office act? Shall we condemn the President for following the counsel of his advisers and for putting precisely the same construction upon the first section of the act that we put upon it when we enacted it into a law?

It is not necessary for me to refer to another statement made by a Manager in order to sustain my view of this case; but I allude to it only to put on record my reprobation of the doctrine announced. It was said that—

"The Senate, for the purpose of deciding whether the respondent is innocent or guilty, can enter into no inquiry as to the constitutionality of the act, which it was the President's duty to execute, and which, upon his own answer, and by repeated official confessions and admissions, he intentionally, willfully, deliberately set aside and violated."

I cannot believe it to be our duty to convict

the President of an infraction of a law, when in our consciences we believe the law itself to be invalid, and therefore having no binding effect. If the law is unconstitutional it is null and void, and the President has committed no offense and done no act deserving of impeachment.

Again, the Manager said :

"The constitutional duty of the President is to obey and execute the laws. He has no authority under the Constitution, or by any law, to enter into any schemes or plans for the purpose of testing the validity of the laws of the country, either judicially or otherwise. Every law of Congress may be tested in the courts, but it is not made the duty of any person to so test the laws."

Is this so? It is not denied, I think, that the constitutional validity of this law could not be tested before the courts unless a case was made and presented to them. No such case could be made unless the President made a removal. That act of his would necessarily be the basis on which the case would rest. He is sworn to "preserve, protect, and defend the Constitution of the United States." He must *defend* it against all encroachments, from whatever quarter. A question arose between the legislative and executive departments as to their relative powers in the matter of removals and appointments to office. That question was, Does the Constitution confer on the President the power which the tenure-of-office act seeks to take away? It was a question manifestly of construction and interpretation. The Constitution has provided a common arbiter in such cases of controversy—the Supreme Court of the United States. Before that tribunal can take jurisdiction a removal must be made. The President attempted to give the court jurisdiction in that way. For doing so he is impeached, and for the reason, as the Managers say, that—

"He has no authority under the Constitution, or by any law, to enter into any schemes or plans for the purpose of testing the validity of the laws of the country, either judicially or otherwise."

If this be true, then if the two Houses of Congress should pass by a two-thirds vote over the President's veto an act depriving the President of the right to exercise the pardoning power, and he should exercise that power nevertheless, or if he should exercise it only in a single case for the purpose of testing the constitutionality of the law, he would be guilty of a high crime and misdemeanor and impeachable accordingly. The Manager's theory establishes at once the complete supremacy of Congress over the other branches of Government. I can give my assent to no such doctrine. This was a *punitive* statute. It was directed against the President alone. It interfered with the prerogatives of his department as recognized from the foundation of the Government. It wrested from him powers which, according to the legislative and judicial construction of eighty years, had been bestowed upon him by the Constitution itself. In my opinion it was not only proper, but it was his duty to cause

the disputed question to be determined in the manner and by the tribunal established for such purposes. This Government can only be preserved and the liberty of the people maintained by preserving intact the coördinate branches of it—legislative, executive, judicial—alike. I am no convert to any doctrine of the omnipotence of Congress.

But it is said that in our legislative capacity we have several times decided this question, and that our judgments on this trial are therefore foreclosed. As for myself, I have done no act, given no vote, uttered no word, inconsistent with my present position. I never believed Mr. Stanton came within the provisions of the tenure-of-office act, and I never did any act, or gave any vote, indicating such a belief. If I had done so, I should not consider myself precluded from revising any judgment then expressed, for I am now acting in another capacity, under the sanction of a new oath, after a full examination of the facts, and with the aid of a thorough discussion of the law as applicable to them. The hasty and inconsiderate action of the Senate on the 21st February may have been, and probably was, a sufficient justification for the action of the House of Representatives, as the grand inquest of the nation, in presenting their articles of impeachment, but it furnishes no reason or apology to us for acting otherwise than under the responsibilities of our judicial oath, since assumed.

The *tenth* article charges that, in order to

"bring into disgrace, ridicule, hatred, contempt, and reproach the Congress of the United States, and the several branches thereof, to impair and destroy the regard and respect of all the good people of the United States for the Congress and legislative power thereof, (which all officers of the Government ought inviolably to preserve and maintain,) and to excite the odium and resentment of all the good people of the United States against Congress, and the laws by it duly and constitutionally enacted; and in pursuance of his said design and intent, openly and publicly, and before divers assemblages of the citizens of the United States convened in divers parts thereof to meet and receive said Andrew Johnson as the Chief Magistrate of the United States, did, on the 18th day of August, in the year of our Lord 1866, and on divers other days and times, as well before as afterward, make and deliver with a loud voice certain intemperate, inflammatory, and scandalous harangues, and did therein utter loud threats and bitter menaces."

These speeches were made in 1866. They were addressed to promiscuous popular assemblies, and were unattended by any official act. They were made by the President in his character of a citizen. They were uttered against the Thirty-Ninth Congress, which ceased to exist more than a year ago. That body deemed them to be unworthy of their attention, and the present House of Representatives decided by an overwhelming majority that they, too, did not consider them worthy to be made the ground of impeachment.

The first amendment to the Constitution of the United States declares that "Congress shall make no law" "abridging the freedom of speech." Congress, therefore, could pass no law to punish the utterance of those speeches before their delivery; but according to the theory of this prosecution, we, sitting as a court *after* their delivery, can make a law, each for himself, to govern this case and to punish the President.

I have no apology to make for the President's speeches. Grant that they were indiscreet, indecorous, improper, vulgar, shall we not, by his conviction on this article, violate the spirit of the Constitution which guaranties to him the freedom of speech? And would we not also violate the spirit of that other clause of the Constitution which forbids the passage of *ex post facto* laws? We are sworn to render impartial justice in this case according to the Constitution and the laws. According to what laws? Is it to be, in the absence of any written law on the subject, according to the law of each Senator's judgment, enacted in his own bosom, after the alleged commission of the offense? To what absurd violations of the rights of the citizen would this theory lead us? For my own part I cannot consent to go beyond the worst British Parliaments in the time of the Plantagenets in efforts to repress the freedom of speech.

The *eleventh* article contains no matter not already included in one or more of the preceding articles, except the allegation of an intent to prevent the execution of the act of March 2, 1867, for the more efficient government of the rebel States. Concerning this a telegraphic dispatch from General Parsons, of Alabama, and the reply of the President thereto, each dated in January preceding the passage of the law, appears to be the only evidence adduced. These dispatches are as follows:

MONTGOMERY, ALABAMA, *January* 17, 1867.

Legislature in session. Efforts making to reconsider vote on constitutional amendment. Report from Washington says it is probable an enabling act will pass. We do not know what to believe. I find nothing here. LEWIS E. PARSONS,
Exchange Hotel.
His Excellency ANDREW JOHNSON, *President.*

The response is:

UNITED STATES MILITARY TELEGRAPH,
EXECUTIVE OFFICE, WASHINGTON, D. C.,
January 17, 1867.

What possible good can be obtained by reconsidering the constitutional amendment? I know of none in the present posture of affairs; and I do not believe the people of the whole country will sustain any set of individuals in attempts to change the whole character of our Government by enabling acts or otherwise. I believe, on the contrary, that they will eventually uphold all who have patriotism and courage to stand by the Constitution and who place their confidence in the people. There should be no faltering on the part of those who are honest in their determination to sustain the several coördinate departments of the Government in accordance with its original design. ANDREW JOHNSON.
Hon. LEWIS E. PARSONS, *Montgomery, Alabama.*

I am wholly unable, from these dispatches, to deduce any criminal intent. They manifest a diversity of political views between the President and Congress. The case contains ample evidence outside of these dispatches of that diversity of opinion. I do not perceive that these dispatches change the nature of that well-known, and, in my opinion, much to be deplored diversity.

I have thus, as briefly as possible, stated my views of this case. I have expressed no views upon any of the questions upon which the President has been arraigned at the bar of public opinion outside of the charges. I have no right to travel out of the record.

Mr. Johnson's character as a statesman, his relations to political parties, his conduct as a citizen, his efforts at reconstruction, the exercise of his pardoning power, the character of his appointments, and the influences under which they were made, are not before us on any charges, and are not impugned by any testimony.

Nor can I suffer my judgment of the law governing this case to be influenced by political considerations. I cannot agree to destroy the harmonious working of the Constitution for the sake of getting rid of an unacceptable President. Whatever may be my opinion of the incumbent, I cannot consent to trifle with the high office he holds. I can do nothing which, by implication, may be construed into an approval of impeachments as a part of future political machinery.

However widely, therefore, I may and do differ with the President respecting his political views and measures, and however deeply I have regretted, and do regret, the differences between himself and the Congress of the United States, I am not able to record my vote that he is guilty of high crimes and misdemeanors by reason of those differences. I am acting in a judicial capacity, under conditions whose binding obligation can hardly be exceeded, and I must act according to the best of my ability and judgment, and as they require. If, according to their dictates, the President is guilty, I *must* say so; if, according to their dictates, the President is not guilty, I *must* say so.

In my opinion the President has not been guilty of an impeachable offense by reason of anything alleged in either of the articles preferred against him at the bar of the Senate by the House of Representatives.

OPINION
OF
HON. GEORGE F. EDMUNDS.

I had hoped that the formal consideration of the subject would be officially reported in order that the world might know, without diminution or exaggeration, the reasons and views upon which we proceed to our judgment. But as the Senate has, for causes satisfactory to itself, decided otherwise, I have reduced to writing all that I expected to have said here, that it may be, so far as of any interest to them, exposed to the examination of my countrymen.

I can only, within the time allotted by the rules, state briefly the grounds upon which my judgment in this case rests. All the arguments on either side cannot be reviewed in detail, and they must therefore be dismissed with the general observation that in those respects in which they are not in harmony with the reasons or conclusions I now state, they appear to me to be unsound.

As my duties are clearly judicial, "impartially" to try the respondent upon the accusations contained in the articles of impeachment, and to decide "according to the Constitution and the laws," I have only conscientiously to discharge that duty, and so doing I have no concern with or responsibility for the consequences, political or other, that may flow from my decision. If the respondent has been guilty of a violation of law, the Representatives of the people in the House of Representatives, like a grand jury in ordinary cases, are the sole judges whether that violation of law is of such enormity or of such consequence as a precedent, if permitted to pass without notice, as to require the prosecution of the offender. As they have presented the cause for our action, we have only to apply the law as it is to the facts proved. We have no discretion to say guilty or not guilty according to our views of expediency or our personal wishes. Whatever they may be they can have no tendency to show that the respondent is either innocent or guilty. These propositions are fundamental elements in all civilized systems of jurisprudence. Any other would be a mockery of justice, and soon result in the destruction of liberty and free government. The truth and the law are the only stable foundations of society, and whoever, for any cause or motive, however worthy apparently, departs from these, commits a great wrong upon what all good men unite in wishing to preserve.

The statement of these principles would have been a work of entire supererogation but for the fact that the appeals and remonstrances of the press of the country, touching our disposition of the case, have been urgent, and which, if extended to all trials, would poison the fountains of justice.

The first three articles, taken collectively, charge the respondent with an illegal removal of Mr. Stanton from office as Secretary of War and the illegal appointment of Adjutant General Thomas *ad interim* in his place. These articles also aver that these acts were done with intent to violate the Constitution and the law. The answer asserts that although the acts charged were designedly done, they are justifiable, because,

1. If the act of March 2, 1867, prohibited them, it was in conflict with the Constitution, and therefore void.

2. The Constitution and the laws under it in force prior to March 2, 1867, conferred the power of removal upon the respondent, and that act did not in this instance purport to take it away.

3. If Mr. Stanton was lawfully removed, the power to appoint General Thomas was conferred by the act of 1795, which for that purpose was still in force.

4. If either the removal or appointment was in violation of law, still it was done in good faith, under a sincere claim of right, and therefore it could not be the basis of or amount to a crime or misdemeanor.

Upon the allegations and proofs the commission of the acts charged is indisputable, and hence the main question is, do either of them constitute a high crime or misdemeanor?

The Constitution made express provision for the *appointment* of officers, as follows:

"And he [the President] shall nominate and, by and with the advice and consent of the Senate, shall appoint embassadors, other public ministers and consuls, judges of the Supreme Court, and all other officers of the United States, whose appointments are not herein otherwise provided for, and which shall be established by law; but the Congress may, by law, vest the appointment of such inferior officers as they shall think proper in the President alone, in the courts of law, or in the heads of Departments."

And power was also conferred upon the President "to fill up all vacancies that may happen during the recess of the Senate, by granting commissions which shall expire at the end of their next session."

"*The* executive power" named as to be vested in the President, must of necessity be *that* power and no other which the Constitution grants to him. So speaking, it proceeds at once to define and describe it. All the *powers* of the President are specifically enumerated, with apparently the utmost precision, even those most clearly within the general definition of "executive power." Two of these, namely, the power to be Commander-in-Chief and the power to grant reprieves and pardons, are perfect illustrations of this. On the other hand, his *duties* are partly detailed, as to "receive embassadors," and partly generalized, as "to take care that the laws be faithfully executed." This difference arose from the nature of things. The limited *powers* which the framers of the Constitution thought fit to grant to the person who was to take the place of kings and emperors in systems of government hostile to liberty, could be easily named, and ought to be jealously defined. The *duties* relating to seeing the *laws* faithfully executed could not all be foreseen in detail, and from them there could scarcely arise any danger to the Republic, for he was not to execute the laws himself, but to "take care" that they *be* "faithfully executed." This could only be done by just such and only the methods and agencies provided for that purpose by the laws themselves. He could not, rightfully, violate the laws in order to enforce them. This is, I believe unquestioned; and it was perfectly stated by Attorney General Black, on the 20th of November, 1860, in advising President Buchanan touching his duties relating to some of the first acts of the rebellion, as follows:

"To the Chief Executive Magistrate of the Union is confided the solemn duty of seeing the laws faithfully executed. That he may be able to meet this duty with a power equal to its performance he nominates his own subordinates and removes them at pleasure. For the same reason, the land and naval forces are under his orders as their Commander-in-Chief. *But his power is to be used only in the manner prescribed by the legislative department. He cannot accomplish a legal purpose by illegal means, or break the laws himself to prevent them from being violated by others."—9 Opinions Attorneys General, 516.*

The Constitution expressly provides, on the other hand, that *Congress* shall have power—

"To make all laws which shall be necessary and proper for carrying into execution the foregoing powers, and all other powers vested by the Constitution in the Government of the United States, *or in any department thereof.*"

In view of these provisions I cannot doubt that the regulation of the tenure of the offices to be established by law was not confided by the Constitution to the President, but was left to be provided for by legislation.

The scheme, plainly, was to leave the *selection* of persons to fill offices to the President, acting with the advice and consent of the Senate, and to leave to the *whole* Government—that is to the law-making power—full discretion as to the establishment of offices, and as to the terms upon which and the tenure by which they should be held by the persons so selected. Any other construction would defeat, as for several years prior to the recent act it has defeated in many instances, entirely the express declaration of the Constitution that the offices shall be filled by such persons as shall be advised by the Senate; for temporary commissions could be issued from session to session, even to the very persons rejected by the Senate, as has been the case. And if officers by the Constitution are removable at the will of the President, why, when once appointed, should they not hold at his pleasure, and if so, how can the law put a period to their holding, as has been in various instances from the first, without question from any source?

Certainly if, when the Constitution is silent, the legislative power may declare that whoever is appointed to a particular office shall *cease* to hold it at the end of four years, it may also declare that the appointee shall enjoy it during that time. The two things are complementary to each other, and logically inseparable.

These views as to what in general belongs to legislative power are fully sustained by many decisions of the Supreme Court, among which, Martin *vs.* Hunter's lessee, 1 Wheat., 326 ; Wayman *vs.* Southard, 10–1; 16 Peters, 89 ; Jones *vs.* Van Zandt, 5 How., may be read with profit.

It was to establish a reign of law, the only safeguard of society and the only means of liberty, that the Constitution was formed. We must, therefore, suppose that the cases not specifically provided for and the implied powers generally were intended to be left to the provisions of law, in making which both the President and Congress must always participate, and usually concur, and not to the un-

controlled will of the Executive. Indeed, the counsel for the respondent do not seem very seriously to question this interpretation of the Constitution considered independently of a construction which they insist has been by legislative discussion and enactment, and by long practice of Executives, put upon it.

I will dispose, very briefly, of this construction, as it is called. Extended examination, for which there is not time, would make the fallacy of it clear to demonstration. So far as legislative discussion is concerned, (although that is no safe or admissible guide to the construction of law as law, for no member is bound by the opinions or words of any other, and so his silence is no acquiescence,) the pretension has been from the beginning the subject of dispute between adherents of a President and the representatives of the States and people, not as to the right of a President to resist a legislative rule, which has rarely, if ever before, been asserted, but as to the propriety of enacting one; and even Mr. Madison himself, whose opinions are so much relied upon by the counsel for the respondent, was, at different times, on both sides of the question; and Mr. Adams, whose casting vote in the Senate passed the act of 1789, was strongly opposed to the provision of the Constitution requiring the Senate to confirm any appointment, and he was by the public so generally supposed to have been influenced by his expectation of becoming President himself that he thought it necessary to repel the accusation of (to use his own words) "deciding in favor of the powers of the prime because I look up to that goal."

An analysis of the debates and votes upon the act of 1789, creating the Department of Foreign Affairs, will demonstrate the inconclusiveness of tests of this sort. Of the fifty-four members of the House of Representatives present, those who argued that the power of removal was, by the Constitution, in the President, were Sedgwick, Madison, (who had maintained the opposite,) Vining, Boudinot, Clymer, Benson, Scott, Goodhue, and Baldwin. Those who contended that the President had not the power, but that it might be conferred by law, but ought not to be, were Jackson, Stone, and Tucker. Those who believed that the President had not the power, and that it could not be conferred, were White, Smith of South Carolina, Livemore, and Page. Those who maintained that the President had not the inherent power, but that it might be bestowed by law, and that it was expedient to bestow it, were Huntington, Madison at first, Gerry, Ames, Hartly, Lawrence, Sherman, Lee, and Sylvester—twenty-four in all speaking. Of these fifteen thought the Constitution did not confer this power upon the President, while only nine thought otherwise. But those who thought he had the power and those who thought the law ought to confer it were seventeen.

Thirty did not speak at all, and in voting

upon the words conferring or recognizing the power they were just as likely to vote upon the grounds of Roger Sherman as upon the reasons of those who merely intended to admit the power. On the motion to strike out the words "to be removable by the President," the ayes were twenty and the noes thirty-four; but no guess, even, can be formed that this majority took one view rather than the other. Indeed, adding only the eight who spoke against the inherent power, but for the provisions of law, to the twenty opponents of both, and there is a clear majority adverse to any such inherent power in the President. And when on the next day it was proposed to change the language to that which became the law, among the ayes are the names of White, Smith of South Carolina, Livemore, Page, Huntington, Gerry, Ames, and Sherman, all of whom, as we have seen, were of opinion against the claim of an inherent power of removal in the President. All this, with a possible error as to one or two persons, arising from the vagueness or contradictory character of their language, is in the record of the proceedings, obvious to any one who will undergo the labor of its examination.

The construction, then, claimed to be derived from this source ceases to have any foundation in point of fact.

On the other hand, a select committee of the Senate, of which Thomas H. Benton was chairman, and having among its members Mr. Van Buren and Mr. Hayne, made a report in 1826, in which they say:

"Not being able to reform the Constitution in the election of President, they must go to work upon his powers, and trim down these by statutory enactments whenever it can be done by law, and with a just regard to the proper efficiency of the Government. For this purpose they have reported six bills," &c.

One of these bills was a bill entitled "A bill to prevent military and naval officers from being dismissed the service at the pleasure of the President;" and it prohibited any dismissal except on the sentence of a court-martial, or on address of both Houses of Congress. The substance of this bill became a law by the approval of the respondent himself, on the 13th day of July, 1866. In 1835, on the favorable report of a select committee, of which Mr. Calhoun, Mr. Webster, and Mr. Benton were members, on the same subject of executive patronage, analogous measures were agitated, but I have not space to detail them. Aside from actual legislation appearing in the statutes, there has been no general recognition of these claims, but a constant protest by all parties, in their turn, against them.

As to the supposed recognition by the laws themselves, and a practice under them, it need only be said that the whole course of legislation, comprised in more than twenty statutes, has until 1863 *authorized* the President to make removals; and hence *they furnish no evidence of his powers, independently of the law, but the contrary*. It needs no argument to show that what the laws have *authorized* they may *forbid*. No law can become so old that the legislative power cannot change it; and even as to legislative construction it is the same. A later Congress has just as much power in that respect as an earlier.

The acts of 1792, 1795, and 1863, relating to *ad interim* appointments, which have always been acquiesced in without question from any source, are decisive utterances, so far as legislative action can possibly be so, of the power of the *law* to regulate the exercise of powers and duties *expressly conferred* by the Constitution upon the President and Senate. Our own statutes and those of all States having written constitutions are full of similar or analogous instances.

Can it be said, then, that where the letter of the Constitution is silent upon another branch of the same subject the law has no power to speak, and that behind that veil of silence sleeps a kingly prerogative of the President?

The act of 1863, providing for a national currency, expressly declared that the Comptroller of the Currency should hold his office for five years, and should not be removed without the advice and consent of the Senate. It was passed by votes irrespective of party, receiving, among others, that of the honorable Senator from Wisconsin who sits farthest from me, [Mr. DOOLITTLE,] without any objection from any source to this feature of it. It was approved by President Lincoln. The law and practice of the Government were thus changed, and in that instance restored to the letter and true spirit of the Constitution, with the concurrence of all parties, full five years before this case arose. And, as I have said, substantially, and, indeed, identically, the same principle was, with the official approval of the respondent himself, applied to military and naval officers by the act of July 13, 1866, relating to the Army, prohibiting their removal without the sentence of a court-martial, which power had been exercised during the war, *under the authority of law*, and not under claim of prerogative. (Act of July 17, 1862.)

The judicial decisions and opinions touching this subject support the same view.

Marbury *vs.* Madison, 1 Cranch, is, as I understand it, expressly in point; and in the late case of Mr. Guthrie, (17 How.,) the only judge whose views of jurisdiction made it proper for him to speak, upheld the same doctrine.

For these reasons, and many others that the time does not permit me to state, I conclude that the act of March 2, 1867, is perfectly constitutional.

Does the act apply to the case of Mr. Stanton, and forbid his removal at the will of the President?

It is conceded that the leading clause of the section does include him, but it is claimed that he is taken out of it by a proviso which not only effects that, but which also excludes him from the proviso itself or fails to mention him at all! In construing a statute it is always necessary to look at the whole scope of the law in all its sections, and at the state of facts existing at the time of its passage, in order to make a proper application of the law, and to search through the language of the act for the design to which it was devoted.

These facts are that Mr. Stanton was then the Secretary of War, subject to removal from office under the act of 1789 at the pleasure of the respondent. On that state of facts the proviso said that "the Secretary of War," &c., "*shall hold*" their offices, respectively, for and during the term of the President by whom they may have been appointed," &c. Now, as Mr. Stanton was then Secretary of War, he must be the person included in that description. That Secretary is (with the others) by name the very subject of which the proviso speaks. And it will be noticed that the language as to the appointment is in the past tense, "*may have been* appointed" are the words. That the proviso declared something touching the tenure of Mr. Stanton cannot truly be denied. But if it did not declare *anything* as to him, then, confessedly, the leading and sweeping opening clause embraces him, for then as to him it is not "otherwise provided." Having ascertained, then, that the proviso speaks of Mr. Stanton, we find that it says that he "*shall hold*" his office, &c., for a described period. These words, it will be seen, apply only to the *future*, and import, if language has any meaning, that he shall, after the passage of the act, *continue and remain in office by force of the law.* The respondent's counsel insist, however, that the real meaning of this language is (if applicable to him) that he shall *not* hold the office at all!

If, as we have shown, when the act passed he was the Secretary of War named in and affected by the proviso, the question is was he, on the 21st day of February, 1868, holding office in the same way and under the same tenure that he was at the passage of the act, which said he *should hold*, and not that he should not? It is not disputed that he was. Was he then, at the passage of the act holding his office "during the term of the President by whom he was appointed?" He was appointed by President Lincoln. Then was March 2, 1867, the time of the passage of the act, during the term of Mr. Lincoln, who was, so far as relates to Mr. Stanton, the President named in the proviso?

The Constitution says the President "shall hold his office during the *term of four years*," and that the Vice President shall be "chosen for the same term." It creates and permits no other term or period whatever, but provides only, in case of death, &c., for the devolution of "duties" or "*office*," not the term, upon the Vice President.

Mr. Lincoln began a regular term on March 4, 1865, and died in April of that year, when

C. I.—56.

the office devolved on the respondent. Now, if the respondent became thereby invested with a constitutional "*term*" *of his own* as President, he must be in for *four years* from April 15, 1865, which is not pretended by any one. Hence, he must take the office for the *unexpired term of Mr. Lincoln,* his predecessor. It was the *office* and not the *term*, which are distinct things, that Mr. Lincoln held when he died. The *office* did not die with him, but survived in all its current identity and force to his successor, the respondent, measured by precisely the same "*term*" that it was before. When, therefore, the statute speaks of "the term of the President," it does not refer to ownership or possession, which a man cannot be said to have after his death, but it plainly refers to the term *for and in relation to which* that President was elected, and which, by the Constitution, was attributed to him. A reference to any lexicon will show that this is the principal and most frequent meaning of the word " of."

To claim that at the death of Mr. Lincoln the "term" applicable to him thereby expired and ended would be as erroneous as to claim that the death of a tenant for a term of years not yet expired produces an end of the term, and that his legal representative either takes a new term or none at all.

But it is truly said that Mr. Lincoln had a prior term *in which*, in the language of counsel, Mr. Stanton was appointed, which had expired two years before the passage of the law; and it is claimed that that *first term* is the one named in the act, and that it meant, therefore, that Mr. Stanton should hold for one month after March 4, 1865, instead of one month after March 4, 1869. The answer (if any be needful) is that the act passed in the middle of Mr. Lincoln's second *and then existing term*, and to reject that term, and apply the words of the statute to a past and completed term, which had then no existence either in law or fact, would be contrary not only to any supposable intention of the lawmakers, but in direct violation of the words of the statute, which declare that he "shall hold" (instead of not holding) not during the term "in which" he "may have been appointed," as counsel use the words, but "during the term of the President *by whom* he may have been appointed." Any other construction would involve the gross absurdity that Congress by that act, on the 2d of March, 1867, legislated out of office virtually, as of April 4, 1865, those Secretaries who had been appointed by Mr. Lincoln, and intended to declare that officers then legally holding should go out of office two years before the passage of the act!

This result was sought to be avoided by the distinguished counsel who opened the defence, if I rightly understood him, by advancing the idea that the proviso should be construed to read and apply to *future* Secretaries, &c., and to have no reference to the then present ones.

This is, perhaps, sufficiently answered already. I know of no rule of construction by which that word can be interpolated into the statute, and if it were the proviso would be made thereby to have no reference at all to the present Secretaries, who would then fall within the very letter and protection of the body of the section.

The proviso cannot fairly be made to take the case out of the general clause of the section, on the ground that this is a case therein "otherwise provided" for, as is claimed, and then be construed not to affect the case itself, and to leave it under the act of 1789, on the ground that it does not apply to the case at all! That would be saying that it did and did not speak of the case.

The idea that the proviso does not speak of the present Secretary of War arises, on the very reasoning of those who maintain it, out of the fallacy of confounding the *subject* of the proviso, (the Secretary of War,) with what is *affirmed of that subject*, thus: "What is declared or affirmed in the proviso of the Secretary of War is, under the circumstances, erroneous or non-existing; therefore nothing is declared of the subject, (the Secretary of War,)" which is absurd. The second section plainly points out, also, the *only* way of removal of *all* officers, but with my views of the first it is not necessary to enlarge upon it.

It is said that this was not the intention in fact when the law passed; and to prove this the expression of one or two Senators, made upon the spur and in the hurry of the moment, are cited. I dissent entirely from any such inference, and from any such rule of interpreting or administering law, as law. With the exception of certain questions appealing to the will of the whole law-making power, and not necessary to be now enumerated, the body is responsible for, and its will is found in, what it declares in its laws, and not for, or in the opinions of its individual members. The Journals of the Houses, even, cannot be resorted to for any such purpose. This is the rule in all civilized countries, and is, with the solid reasons for it, known to every lawyer.

It is urged, as touching in some degree the probable intent of this proviso, that the construction I have put upon it would work an inequality in the duration of the offices of the various Secretaries, some having been appointed by Mr. Lincoln, and some by Mr. Johnson. If that were the effect, it could not alter the plain construction of the law as applied to the first-named Secretaries. But no such result follows. The evident meaning of the word "of," used in the phrase "during the term of the President by whom they may have been appointed," being "relating, or having reference to," the word "*term*" as there used and applied, under the circumstances existing, to *all the Secretaries*—which embraced both classes—related both to Mr. Lincoln and Mr. Johnson. It related, as I have shown, to Mr. Lincoln primarily and expressly, and it related to Mr. Johnson *sub modo*, who, as Vice President, was chosen for, and who succeeded as President for, the "*same* term," and who was, under the qualifications of the Constitution, filling out the unexpired term relating to Mr. Lincoln. Thus, and in no other way, can all the words of the proviso be made effective, and a rational and just result be reached. It appears to me, therefore, without any doubt, that the law in question covers the case.

The act, then, prohibited the removal of Mr. Stanton and the appointment of General Thomas, and it declared such removal or appointment to be a high misdemeanor, and denounced a punishment against it.

But it is contended that, as the articles charge not only an intentional doing of the acts forbidden—which the respondent admits—but also an intent thereby to violate the law and the Constitution—which he denies—he cannot be found guilty unless it is also proved that such intent existed in point of fact. I do not understand that to be the law, and I think no authority for such a proposition can be found anywhere. Certainly the cases cited by the counsel for the respondent do not maintain it, unless it be conceded that the discretion therein spoken of as existing in the course of exercising constitutional executive powers, or authority delegated by law, means a discretion to decide what powers are executive, and what authority is delegated, in spite of the Constitution that measures and defines the powers, and the law that confers the authority; a proposition so contrary to justice and reason and so subversive of government that it carries its own refutation.

The philosophy and experience of ages concur in the propriety of the maxim that "ignorance of the law excuseth no man." For obvious reasons a government of laws could not exist if any man or officer were to be left to put his own construction upon, or to form and act upon his own views of the validity of the laws framed for the benefit and protection of all. Every citizen, either in or out of office, acts in the peril of the law. If the respondent really believed that this case was not within the act of Congress, or that the act was unconstitutional, he could do what he did at the risk of being condemned if he proved to be wrong, or of being justified if he proved to be right, in the judgment of the tribunal of last resort before which he might be brought for trial, and to which tribunal, the same Constitution, which he claims the right to judge of for himself, has committed by express command the high duty to try *him* for such acts, upon the same principles of law, impartial and immutable, as apply to the humblest citizen in the land.

· In general, it is only when the motive or intention is an element in the description or definition of the very act forbidden that it becomes material on the trial of a person accused of crime. Murder, larceny, and robbery, like the case cited by Mr. Evarts, are instances of this kind. Treason, violations of the fugitive slave laws, and the liquor laws, are illustrations of the other class of cases, which embraces so much of this one as relates to removal and appointment, the unlawful doing of which the statute declares to be a misdemeanor, and punishes as such. All that is required in such cases is the voluntary commission of the act forbidden. An erroneous belief that it was lawful is no defense. Upon this all writers upon criminal law, all decisions, all systems of jurisprudence, and the practice of all countries, agree. It is true that the morally innocent sometimes suffer from this necessary rule, but in such cases the hardship necessary to the stability of society is usually mitigated by a remission of penalties.

In this case there is no penalty in the legal or constitutional sense to be inflicted by this tribunal. *Punishment* by impeachment does not exist under our Constitution. The accused cannot thereby be deprived of life, liberty, or property. He can only be removed from the office he fills and prevented from holding office, not as a punishment, but as a means merely of protection to the community against the danger to be apprehended from having a criminal in office. It merely does what the respondent himself claims the power to do, at his own pleasure, in respect to Mr. Stanton and every other officer in the land. The only difference is that this body does it under oath, upon a trial, under an authority expressly conferred, while the respondent claims it and has done it without any such sanctions of justice and at his mere will.

The "indictment, trial, judgment, and punishment" of the respondent are, by the Constitution, expressly reserved to the ordinary criminal courts.

It has been said that there is injustice in condemning an officer for infractions of law committed under the supposition that they were legal acts. There may be hardship, but there can be no injustice, in vindicating the supremacy of the law. We do not make the law, we only adjudge what it is. It is the law that speaks to the offender through us, and the same law imposes upon us the duty to declare it. Were it material, however, to inquire into the motive and purposes of the respondent in these transactions, it would be an easy task to show that they are not above criticism, resting, as they seem to do, upon his dislike to a system of laws which he wished to overthrow, but which the Secretary was unwilling to assist in. It is enough, for the present, to say that if the respondent be legally guilty, to acquit him upon any such grounds as are claimed would be to sanction a disregard of law and to invite him, as well as future Presidents, to try more forcible and dangerous experiments upon the Government, instead of teaching the great lesson that, in some form,

all nations must learn at last, that its highest officers ought to be most careful and scrupulous in the observance of its laws.

I conclude, then, that the intents charged in these three articles are either immaterial or such as the law conclusively infers from the acts proved, although I should have no hesitation in finding, as a matter of fact, that in the removal of Mr. Stanton the respondent did intend to violate the act of March 2, 1867, if not the Constitution. While it is probable that he and many of the heads of Departments thought at the time the act passed, as did some members of Congress, that the Secretaries appointed by Mr. Lincoln were not within it, I am fully satisfied that, either upon or without advice, he thought, when he suspended Mr. Stanton in August, 1867, and has since thought, that the statute covered the case. His conduct is, to my mind, reconcilable with no other hypothesis. He had then determined (as he says himself) that he could no longer tolerate Mr. Stanton in the office; yet, instead of removing him, as he had, if he acted with a view to the faithful execution of the laws, a perfect legal right to do under the act of 1789, if the act of March 2, 1867, did not protect him, he *suspended* him, as that act permitted, designated another to act, for which designation, upon a suspension, there was no pretense or color of law save that same act, and reported his action to the Senate within the time and in the manner required by it. And, as he now claims, he also took these and subsequent steps, in order to test in the courts the validity of this law, which he believed to invade the constitutional rights of the Executive, and which he was, therefore, bound to test judicially. If he thought the case was not within the law, why did he not remove Mr. Stanton in August? And how could he think that the case could be made to try the validity of a law that did not apply to it?

But the respondent insists that, although the law may be valid and cover the case, inasmuch as his act of dismissal of Mr. Stanton was illegal and void, it was no removal of Mr. Stanton, and no violation of the law prohibiting removals. If this novel notion could be popularized into all criminal trials it would be of vast benefit to offenders. The result would be that, as no act in violation of law changes the rights of innocent persons, all such acts must be guiltless, because void. The statute does not forbid or punish *legal* acts of removal, (it would be strange if it did,) but *illegal* ones like this, which, so far as anything the respondent could do, was complete; for, had it been legal, Mr. Stanton by that act alone would have been out of office. The respondent's position, put in the forms of logic, would stand thus: the statute punishes all removals; illegal removals are void and not removals at all; therefore the statute punishes no illegal removals.

It has been made a question, in respect to

the appointment of Thomas, (supposing Mr. Stanton had been lawfully removed so as to create a vacancy,) whether that appointment was lawful. No power for that appointment is claimed under the Constitution; but the act of 1795 is relied upon as authority for it. It is so if it be still in force; but it seems clear to my mind, after a careful investigation of the three acts on the same subject, and the decisions of courts upon analogous questions, that the act of 1863 is a substitute for both the acts of 1792 and 1795, and that it was intended to take the place of both these acts entirely. In statutes, as in contracts, the intention of the framers, drawn from the words of the acts and the facts to which they apply, and under which they were made, is the pole star of construction.

The act of 1792 applied to cases of "death," "absence," and "sickness," in the three then existing Departments, and provided for temporary appointment, without limitation as to the choice of persons, till the cause therefor should cease.

The act of 1795 provided in the same way for cases of "vacancy" in the same three Departments only, but limited the supply to six months. These might happen in four modes, as the law then stood: by death, expiration of term, removal from office, and resignation.

The act of 1863 covered *all* the Departments, and described two cases of vacancy, those by death and by resignation, and also sickness and absence, and required the temporary service to be performed by some officer of some Department other than the one in which the case might arise, and for six month's only. The last act, therefore, is on the same subject as both the former ones, and changes the provisions of each. It provides for all the *classes* of cases embraced in both those acts, though not for every *instance* in each class, and it requires a *totally different* and *restricted method of supply*. It is impossible to imagine any reason for requiring a vacancy caused by death or resignation, both of which must be independent of the President's will, and fortuitous as to him, to be supplied in a particular and limited manner, while a vacancy caused by removal at the will of the President, or expiration of term, neither of which could be fortuitous, should be left to be filled at the mere pleasure of the President, without any guard or limitation whatever. It must be presumed, therefore, that the intention was to substitute a more carefully guarded and limited system in the place of the old one, and not to allow vacancies made by the law or the will of the President to be so filled. This is made the more probable when we consider that even this is going to the utmost verge of legislative power in such cases.

The law upon the subject of repeals, by implication, is well summed up by the supreme court of Massachusetts, in Bartlett *vs.* King, (12 Mass., 563,) as follows:

"A subsequent statute revising the whole subject-matter of a former one, and evidently intended as a substitute for it, although it contains no express words to that effect, must, on the principles of law, as well as in reason and common sense, operate to repeal the former."

And in Leighton *vs.* Walker (9 N. H., 61,) it is decided that—

"When the design to revise a statute clearly appears the former statutes are to be considered as no longer in force, though not expressly repealed."

I am of opinion, therefore, that the respondent is guilty as charged in the first three articles. There is another view of this removal and appointment not necessary, as I construe the law, to a decision, but which is of too much importance to be passed by in silence. It is this, whether, if the case stood upon the acts of 1789 and 1795 alone, one of which authorizes a removal at pleasure, and the other an appointment *ad interim*, the respondent can justify his conduct upon the evidence before us. The inducing and controlling *motive* of these acts of the respondent was displeasure because the Secretary of War was not so subservient to him in his avowed and determined opposition to the laws of the land respecting the southern States as some other heads of Departments; and the undisputed *design* of the respondent, in his efforts to displace Mr. Stanton, was to replace him by some one more pliant to his wishes and less earnest in his administration of the laws. This was the "harmony" desired in the "Cabinet." These were the "public considerations of a high character" which made Mr. Stanton's resignation desirable to the respondent, and which have led him to commit the acts appearing in the evidence.

The case, then, is the removal of a faithful officer, neither accused nor suspected of any other wrong than adherence to the duty the law imposed upon him, *because* of that faithfulness and adherence to duty, by a President of the United States who was determined thereby to counteract and defeat the law, because he believed or professed to believe in a different "policy" of his own! In my opinion no higher crime, no graver violation of constitutional duty, no act more dangerous to law or to the liberties of the nation can be found within the reach of the Executive. Surely the opinion of Mr. Madison, so much referred to by the counsel, cannot be questioned on this point. He says:

"The danger, then, consists merely in this: The President can displace from office a man whose merits require that he should be continued in it; what will be the motive which the President can have for such abuse of his power and the authority that operates to prevent it? In the first place he will be impeachable by the House for such an act of maladministration," &c.—*Annals of Congress, VI*, p. 517.

It is, perhaps, proper in this connection that I should say expressly, what is implied in what I have stated, that I entirely disagree with the doctrine advanced in the argument, that we may find the respondent guilty although the statute he has violated affecting his rights is itself a nullity, and in violating it he has only done what the Constitution, the supreme law, permitted. If such be the law the Constitution, instead of being a guard, guide, and warning to officers, is a snare.

The fourth article is denied by the answer, and I do not think that it is proved.

The fifth article charges an unlawful conspiracy to prevent the execution of the act of March 2, 1867, and an unlawful attempt to prevent Mr. Stanton from holding the office. The conspiracy is denied, but the act is admitted, with a claim of its legality. This article is, I think, embodied within the same principles as the first, and I am of opinion, upon the grounds already stated, that the respondent is guilty; for, although the mere attempt to do an unlawful act is not within the penal section of that act, I think that an attempt to commit an unlawful act of such grave character as this, is in law, a high misdemeanor.

The Supreme Court of the United States (United States *vs.* Quincy, 6 Pet., 465) has correctly defined a criminal attempt as follows:

"To attempt to do an act does not, either in law or in common parlance, imply the completion of the act or any definite progress toward it. Any effort or endeavor to effect it will satisfy the terms of the law."

The sixth and seventh articles allege a conspiracy to seize (the sixth) by force, (the seventh,) unlawfully, the War Department, property, &c. This is denied by the answer. It seems to be properly conceded by the defense, even if the respondent had a lawful right to remove Mr. Stanton and to appoint General Thomas, that if that right was in honest dispute he could not justify resorting to force instead of the law to dispossess an officer from an office which he had legally held, and which he still claimed in good faith to hold legally.

The question, then, on this article is purely one of fact. Did the respondent, upon the facts proved, and what we may lawfully take notice of public history in connection with those facts, combine with Thomas to get possession of the War Office at the expense of resorting to violence, or physical power, if that should be needful to reach the result? At the expense of repetition, to a certain extent, I will state the case upon this question. It is matter of history that prior to the July session of Congress in 1867, the opposition of the respondent to the laws relating to the rebel States was so great that every obstacle that legal ingenuity could suggest was, under his sanction, thrown in the way of their operating in the spirit intended by Congress, and that their effect was thus almost paralyzed. It is also historic that Mr. Stanton, through whose Department these laws were to be carried into execution or to be obstructed, was earnestly in favor of carrying them out according to the manifest will of Congress and the fair meaning of the laws themselves. Nevertheless, obstructive interpretations and orders were issued which led to the session of July, 1867, and the explanatory act of that session. The personal relations of the respondent and Mr. Stanton had been theretofore always friendly, and it has never been suggested, even, that Mr. Stanton had or has committed any wrong toward the President personally or otherwise, save in his conduct before mentioned, and in his refusal to resign. "Public consideration" alone, as the President himself stated, were the cause of the difference. The difference as to these laws, then, existed at that session. The respondent, in his answer, says that prior to August 5, 1867, which was only two weeks after the adjournment, "he became satisfied that he could not allow the said Stanton to continue to hold the office without hazard to the public interest." In other words, the President was opposed to the law in all its parts, and determined to defeat it. Mr. Stanton was for it. This was the sole *casus belli.* There was a clear opportunity to resort to legal means to displace the Secretary then by nominating another suitable person in his place.

It may be said that the President knew that there would be no hope of the confirmation of any one who would not disagree with him about the full execution of laws as greatly as Mr. Stanton, and hence it was useless for him to resort to that method of relief. This is doubtless true, and it places the respondent in the position of refusing to take a clear legal method of change because it would not answer his purpose. This necessarily leads to the presumption that if the respondent was in earnest he would try some other way. He did so. No sooner had Congress adjourned than he "suspended" Mr. Stanton, as he had a legal right to do under the act of 1867, provided he acted in good faith in so doing, and not as a mere cover to get rid of an obstacle in the way of his own opposition to law. Had he believed in his power of removal, he could have exercised it then, and if Mr. Stanton would not yield, he could have instantly resorted to the courts of law. This he did not do, but on the contrary excluded Mr. Stanton from the office *under the law* for nearly six months, and then endeavored to arrange for defeating the same law, by preventing Mr. Stanton from resuming possession under the vote of the Senate of January, 1868. At that time, then, his design was plainly to *prevent* Mr. Stanton, not, by law, but by some other expedient, from holding the office, and forcing *him*, if he could, to resort to legal measures for redress.

During all this period down to the 21st of February, when the act in question was committed, no one was nominated to succeed Mr. Stanton; and from the vote of January to that date no step whatever was taken to resort to any legal mode to procure the change he was determined to bring about. There was no need to make an *ad interim* appointment if the sole object was to put things in process of judicial decision, for the order of dismissal alone, if not obeyed, would do that; and if obeyed, there would be no further steps in that respect for the President to take; the desired end would be accomplished. In this state of things, with the Senate in session and presumably ready to confirm an irreproachable man, he turns his back upon it and makes overtures to General Sherman to take the office under his fiat. This is declined. Then General Thomas, a man who, judging from his appearance in court, must have been known to the respondent not to be suited to the place of Secretary of War, is suddenly restored to place as Adjutant General, the principal executive officer in the Army, and is then at once appointed Secretary *ad interim*, with instructions to "enter immediately upon the discharge of the duties," &c., which General Thomas agrees to do, with a formal mutual *salvo* that "the Constitution and the laws" under which the President had professed at the same time to dismiss Mr. Stanton, should be maintained. I cannot believe that the respondent expected that Mr. Stanton would yield to anything less than force. He had been formally notified in writing in August by Mr. Stanton himself that he denied his power to remove him, or to suspend him without legal cause, and that he would only yield when he had "no alternative but to submit, under protest, to superior force." Thomas confesses on the stand that at some time in the course of the effort to get possession, he expected to use force. In view of all these circumstances I cannot resist the conclusion that the sixth and seventh articles are proved, and that the respondent is guilty, as therein charged.

The gravamen of the eighth article seems to be the alleged attempt, by certain means alleged, to get unlawful control of the public moneys. If this be the meaning of that article, and I think it is, I think the proof does not sustain the charge, and that the respondent is not guilty upon that article.

The ninth article appears to me also to be wholly unsustained by proof.

The tenth and eleventh articles, so far as they relate to the sayings and speeches of the respondent, require for their support under the rule I have before adverted to, an unlawful and criminal design and intent. However disgraceful these speeches may be—and they certainly do not need any comment in that respect—fairly considered they were, I think, only intended to appeal to the political prejudices of the people, and to induce them to overturn the party of Congress by a revolution at the polls, and not by illegal violence. As such, I think them, in a legal sense, within the liberty of speech secured by the Constitution and by the spirit of our institutions; a liberty so essential to the welfare and permanency of a free Government in a state of peace and under the rule of municipal law, that it were better to tolerate a considerable abuse of it rather than to subject it to legal repression or condemnation.

Besides the accusation of criminal speech, article eleven seems to contain three charges:

a contriving of means to defeat the act of March 2, 1867; to defeat the Army appropriation bill of 1867; and to defeat the act for the more efficient government of the rebel States. The first and third of these charges, I think, for the reasons already stated, are proved by the evidence already referred to as to the causes for and the attempt to remove Mr. Stanton. The second, I think, is not. But upon the construction put upon this article by the Senate, that it only contains an accusation touching Mr. Stanton, I feel bound to vote guilty upon it.

Much has been said in the course of the trial upon the nature of this proceeding, and the nature of the offenses which can fairly be embraced with the terms of the Constitution. In my opinion this high tribunal is the sole and exclusive judge of its own jurisdiction in such cases, and that, as the Constitution did not establish this procedure for the punishment of crime, but for the secure and faithful administration of the law, it was not intended to cramp it by any specific definition of high crimes and misdemeanors, but to leave each case to be defined by law, or, when not defined, to be decided upon its own circumstances, in the patriotic and judicial good sense of the Representatives of the States. Like the jurisdiction of chancery in cases of fraud, it ought not to be limited in advance, but kept open as a great bulwark for the preservation of purity and fidelity in the administration of affairs, when undermined by the cunning and corrupt practices of low offenders, or assailed by bold and high-handed usurpation or defiance; a shield for the honest and law-abiding official; a sword to those who pervert or abuse their powers, teaching the maxim which rulers endowed with the spirit of a Trojan can listen to without emotion, that "kings may be cashiered for misconduct."

Two exceptions that go, practically, to the jurisdiction of this tribunal over such a cause as this have been so much insisted upon in argument that their bravery challenges admiration as much as their error does condemnation. The first is that the Senate has no right to judge in what is called its own case; that such an act is contrary to the first principles of justice, &c.

In any proper sense it is not its own case. Its members have no personal interest in it. It is the case of the *law* violated by the usurpation of power under color of office. As well might it be said that a court could not try a contempt, or punish a breach of injunction, or sit in judgment in a case in which the community of which the judges were members had an interest. To countenance such a doctrine would be to defeat this great but gentle remedy of the Constitution almost entirely; for most of the powers capable of easy usurpation are those granted to this body.

The second is that the three great departments of the Government created by the Con-

887

stitution, being coördinate, neither has the power to bring into review the acts of the other, and each is the supreme judge for itself of its own rights under the Constitution. If each of the departments were in all respects the equal of the other, this would be true, and the only method of correcting the misconduct or aggression of either would be the *ultima ratio regum*—force. But the fathers, whose wisdom has been so much and justly praised by the counsel for the respondent, foresaw that such an arbitrament would destroy the Government and the liberty that the Constitution was intended to perpetuate.

They, therefore, in the Constitution defined and measured, so far as was possible, the respective powers of each. To this they superadded the last and only means possible to human agency, a tribunal composed of the Representatives of equal States, chosen for periods long enough to remove them from the sudden impulses of popular excitement, and short enough to make them feel responsible to the settled convictions of the community they represented. To this tribunal, sworn to impartiality and conscientious adherence to the Constitution and the laws, they committed the high powers indispensable to such a frame of Government, of sitting in judgment upon the crimes and misdemeanors of the President, as well as all other officers of the United States. These faculties of the Senate fill up the measure of that description of it given by Mr. Madison as the "great sheet anchor of the Government." August, benignant, and supreme, upon the complaint of the people's Representatives, it brings to its judgment seat judges and Presidents and all the ministers of the law—no station too lofty or powerful for its reach, none too low to escape its notice—and subjects them, alike, to the serene and steadfast justice of the law. The mechanism of government can do no more for society than this. These great powers, at once the emblem, the ideal, and the realization of that orderly justice which is the law, we must this day exercise without fear. And so acting, there can follow to us no possible reproach and no detriment to the Republic.

<hr>

OPINION
OF
HON. REVERDY JOHNSON.

Time does not permit an examination in detail of the several articles of impeachment. I content myself, therefore, with considering the legal questions upon which the most of them depend.

I. For what can the President be impeached? If the power was given without assigning the causes it is obvious that he would be almost wholly dependent upon Congress, and that was clearly not designed. The Constitution consequently provides that impeachment can only be for "treason, bribery, or other high crimes and misdemeanors." For no act which does not fall within the legal meaning of those terms can impeachment be maintained. Political opinions, whatever they may be, when not made crimes or misdemeanors, are not the subjects of the power. If any such opinions can be legally declared crimes or misdemeanors, what are spoken, no matter by whom, when no force is used disturbing the public peace, certainly cannot be, such legislation being prohibited, not only by reason of the absence of any delegated authority to Congress, but because that department is expressly prohibited from so legislating by the very terms of the first of the amendments of the Constitution, providing that "Congress shall make no law" "abridging the freedom of speech."

This guarantee extends to every citizen, whether he be in public or private life. Whatever a private citizen can say without responsibility to Congress the President or any other official can say. The provision is intended to secure such freedom to all without regard to official station. The right is a personal one, for the exercise of which there is no responsibility. It is secured as absolutely to every person as the right of freedom of speech is secured to members of Congress by the sixth section of the first article of the Constitution, which says that "for any speech or debate in either House they shall not be questioned in any other place." Both provisions are upon the theory, proved to be correct by history, that a free Government is ever best maintained (if, indeed, it can be maintained without it) by such unfettered freedom. Its possession by others than members of Congress is a necessary restraint upon that department, while its possession by its members is equally necessary to a proper exercise of their power. In both instances the right is placed beyond restraint.

If members of Congress in debate assail the President in disparaging and vituperative language; if they charge him with treason, a violation of every duty, a want of every virtue, and with every vice; if they even charge him with having been accessory to the murder of his lamented predecessor—charges calculated to bring him "into disgrace," "hatred," "contempt, and reproach"—they are exempt from responsibility, by any legal proceeding, because "freedom of speech and debate" is their right—how can it be that the President is responsible for the speeches alleged to have been made by him at the places and times referred to in the tenth and eleventh articles, when freedom of speech is equally secured to him. That such speeches, whether made by members of Congress or the President, are in bad taste, and tend to disturb the harmony which should prevail between the two departments of the Government, may be conceded, but there is no law making them crimes or misdemeanors. This was attempted to be done, as far as printed publications were concerned, by the second section of the act of the 14th of July, 1798, (the sedition act.) The constitutionality of that law was denied by many of the most eminent men of the day, and the party which passed it was driven from power by an overwhelming majority of the people of the country, upon the ground that it palpably violated the Constitution. By its own terms it was to continue but for a brief period, and no one in or out of Congress has ever suggested its revival. But the passage of the act proves that without such a law oral speeches or written publications in regard to any department of the Government are not criminal offenses.

If these views be sound, the articles which charge the President with having committed a high misdemeanor by the speeches made in Washington, St. Louis, and Cleveland, in 1866, are not supported, first, because there is no law which makes them misdemeanors; and second, because if there was any such law it would be absolutely void.

II. That the terms crimes and misdemeanors in the quoted clause mean legal crimes and misdemeanors (if there could be any doubt upon the point) is further obvious from the provision in the third section of the first article of the Constitution, that, notwithstanding the judgment on impeachment, the party is liable to "indictment, trial, judgment, and punishment according to law." This proves that an officer can only be impeached for acts for which he is liable to a criminal prosecution. Whatever acts, therefore, could not be criminally prosecuted under the general law cannot be the grounds of an impeachment. Nor is this doctrine peculiar to the United States. It was held in the case of the impeachment of Lord Melville, as far back as 1806, and has never since been judicially controverted in England. The charges in that case were the alleged improper withdrawal and use of public funds intrusted to him as treasurer of the Navy. By the managers it was contended that these were by law crimes and misdemeanors, and denied by his lordship's counsel. The impeachment evidently turned upon the decision of the question. The opinion of the judges was requested by the House of Lords, and their answer was, that they were not crimes or misdemeanors, and his lordship, on a vote, in the aggregate upon all the articles, of thirteen hundred and fifty, was acquitted by a majority of eight hundred and twenty-four.

III. Are, then, the acts alleged in the first eight articles crimes and misdemeanors?

1. Are they so independent of the actual intent with which they were done?

2. If not, are they without criminality because of such actual intent?

I. The acts charged are the orders of the President of the 21st of February, 1868, removing Mr. Stanton as Secretary of War and appointing General Thomas as Secretary *ad interim.* The President's authority for the first, his counsel contend, is vested in him by the Constitution, and not subject to the power of Congress; and that if it was, and Congress had a right to pass the act of the 22d of March, 1867, "regulating the tenure of certain civil offices," that act did not take from him the power to remove Mr. Stanton. I will consider the second question first. What, then, in regard to Mr. Stanton, is the true construction of that act? Did it leave the President's right to remove him as he possessed it before the act was passed? With all respect to the contrary opinion, I think that it clearly did.

Without referring now to the different views entertained by the House of Representatives and the Senate as to the propriety of including Cabinet officers within the restriction which the law imposes upon the President in relation to other civil officers, it seems to me to be perfectly clear, from the language of the act itself, that Mr. Stanton's case is not within such restriction. In the first place, the title of the act is the regulation of the tenure of CERTAIN (not of ALL) civil offices. In the second, the tenure prescribed in the body of the first section is, that every person holding a civil office under an appointment made by the President, with the advice and consent of the Senate, and who has duly qualified, is to hold his office until his successor shall in like manner be appointed and qualified. If the law stopped here, the Cabinet would be embraced and hold by the same tenure. But from this tenure certain exceptions are made. The concluding part of the section is in these words: "except as herein otherwise provided." These latter words mean the same thing as if they were in the beginning instead of the close of the section. Place them in the beginning, and no one could doubt their meaning.

It would then be clear that it was not the purpose to prescribe the tenure of all officers appointed by the President with the consent of the Senate, and that in regard to some a different one was to be provided. If this be right, and I do not see that it can be questioned, it follows that whatever tenure is differently prescribed, as to other offices, these are not to be held by the tenure in the first section. Immediately succeeding the words of exception before quoted, follows the provision to which the exception refers, "that the Secretaries of State, of the Treasury, of War, of the Navy, and of the Interior, the Postmaster General, and the Attorney General," are to hold by a different tenure from that before defined. And this is, that they are to "hold their offices respectively for and during the term of the President by whom they may have been appointed, and for one month thereafter," subject, of course, to removal by the President with the approval of the Senate. That this proviso withdraws the offices specially enumerated from the operations of the enacting clause cannot be doubted. It has the same effect in this regard as if it had been the first section of the act instead of a proviso to that section. If it had been itself the first section, and what is now the first section without the proviso had been the second, then all would admit that the tenure of office provided by the first section as it stands would have nothing to do with the tenure of Cabinet officers. In other words, that it was the object of the act to assign to these offices a tenure entirely distinct from that assigned to other civil offices.

The only inquiry that remains is, what is the tenure by which Cabinet officers hold their places? That they are not to hold them for an unlimited period is evident. What, then, is the limitation of their title?

I. It commences, necessarily, with the date of their appointments.

II. It expires at the end of the term of the President by whom they may have been appointed, and one month thereafter. Mr. Stanton was appointed by President Lincoln during his first term, by and with the advice and consent of the Senate. By virtue of that appointment, and by that alone, he was commissioned. He never received any other appointment or commission. If the act of the 2d of March, 1867, had passed during Mr. Lincoln's first term, and was constitutional, Mr. Stanton's term of office would have expired at the end of one month succeeding the termination of Mr. Lincoln's first term, with no other right afterward to the office than in the nature of a tenantcy at sufferance.

The title which he could claim under the act of 1867 has long since ended. To enable him to hold the office against the wish of the President by whom he was not appointed, in my judgment, would be a palpable violation of the law, equally inconsistent with its language and its object. Inconsistent with its language, because that says that the office is to be held "for and during the term of the President by whom" he was appointed, and Mr. Lincoln's term necessarily terminated with his life. Inconsistent with its object, because that clearly is to leave a President who comes into office at the termination, by whatever cause, of the term of his predecessor, the unfettered right at the end of one month after such termination to select his own Cabinet.

If the propriety (conceding Congress to have the power) be admitted of denying to the President the right exercised by all of his predecessors of removing a Cabinet officer at pleasure, it would seem to be most improper and impolitic in regard to any such officer not appointed by himself. Responsible for the preservation of the Constitution and the faithful execution of the laws, nothing could be more unjust and unwise than to force upon him a Cabinet in whom he might have no confidence whatever, either for want of integrity or capacity, or both, and in whose selection he had no choice.

III. If there could be any doubt that the construction I give to the act is correct, it would be removed by the explanation of Senators

SHERMAN and WILLIAMS, members of the committee of conference on the part of the Senate, when making their report. The Senate had by two votes decided that Cabinet officers should, as always before, hold their places at the pleasure of the President, and that such was evidently the design of Congress when organizing the several Departments. The Senate, therefore, excluded them altogether from the provisions of the bill, but the House insisted upon including them. It was this difference between the two Houses which the conference committee was appointed to settle. In making the report Mr. SHERMAN stated that to include them would, in his opinion, be practically unimportant, because "*No gentleman, no man with any sense of honor, would hold a position as a Cabinet officer after his chief desired his removal; and, therefore, the slightest intimation on the part of the President would always secure*" his resignation. And he added that, by the proposition of the committee, such an officer would hold "HIS OFFICE DURING THE LIFE OR THE TERM OF THE PRESIDENT WHO APPOINTED HIM," and that "*if the President dies the Cabinet goes out; if the President is removed for cause by impeachment the Cabinet goes out; at the expiration of the term of the President's office the Cabinet goes out; so that the Government will not be embarrassed by an attempt by a Cabinet officer to hold on to his office, despite the wish of the President or a change in the Presidency;*" and that this provision obviated "*the great danger that might have arisen from the bill as it stood amended by the House.*"

Mr. WILLIAMS said that the House by its amendment had placed "the heads of Departments on the same footing with other civil officers, and provided that they should not at any time be removed, without the advice and consent of the Senate;" that this was objected to, because when "*a new President came into office he might be compelled to have a Cabinet not of his own selection;*" and that the amendment proposed by the committee was, "*that when the term of office expires the offices of the members of the Cabinet shall also expire,*" at the end of one month thereafter. He further added, that "the report of the committee is intended to put the heads of Departments upon the same footing with all the other officers named in the bill, *with this exception, that their terms shall expire when the term of office of the President by whom they were appointed expires; that is the effect of the provision.*" Relying upon these statements, the Senate adopted the report of the committee, and the bill passed with the proviso. No Senator intimated that these gentlemen had not placed a proper construction upon the proviso, and consequently no Senator suggested that the then members of the Cabinet of the President, who were not appointed by him, but by Mr. Lincoln, were either within the protection of the body of the section or of the proviso, and I do not think I am mistaken in the impression that the bill could not have been passed by the Senate without the understanding that Messrs. SHERMAN· and WILLIAMS were right in their interpretation of it.

It also appears by the President's message of the 12th of December, 1867, given in evidence by the managers, that it was construed in the same way by every member of the Cabinet, Mr. Stanton included. That gentleman being appointed by Mr. Lincoln, and not by Mr. Johnson, his tenure of office ended one month succeeding the death of the former. In the language of Mr. SHERMAN, when the President who appoints a Cabinet officer "dies," the officer "goes out." How, then, can the Senate convict the President of having criminally violated the act in question, when what he did in relation to Mr. Stanton was not within the prohibition of the act, according to the interpretation put upon it at the time it was being passed by the Senate itself? and· yet this they will do if they find him guilty upon the articles which relate to his attempt to remove Mr. Stanton on the 21st of February, 1868.

IV. Did the President commit a crime or misdemeanor by his order of the 21st of February, 1868, appointing General Thomas Secretary *ad interim?* That appointment forms the subject of the charges in the second, third, and eighth articles. If I am right, that Mr. Stanton was not within the protection of the act of 1867, and could be removed at pleasure by the President, then the legal effect of his order of the 21st of February worked a removal, and, of course, made a vacancy in that Department.

There being a vacancy, had not the President a right to fill it by an *ad interim* appointment? If he had, the articles in question are unsupported. 1. Independent of legislation, the President being, with a few exceptions, vested with the executive power of the Government, and responsible for the faithful execution of the laws, he must have the power by implication to provide against their temporary failure. And if this be so, then, upon the occurrence of a vacancy in office, which, if not at once supplied, will cause such a failure, he must have the right to guard against it. 2. But there is legislation which, in my judgment, clearly gives him the power to make the appointment.

On the contingency ·" of the death, absence from the seat of Government, or sickness of the Secretary of State, Secretary of the Treasury, or of the Secretary of War," &c., the President, by the act of the 8th of May, 1792, section eight, was authorized to appoint any person or persons to perform the duties of the said offices respectively "until a successor be appointed, or until such absence or inability by sickness shall cease."

This act provided for a vacancy caused by death in either of the three departments named, and not for one produced ·by any other cause.

A vacancy, therefore, arising from resignation or removal or expiration of term of office, was not provided for. The omission was supplied by the act of the 13th of February, 1795, which gives the President the same authority in the case of a vacancy, however produced. Like the act of 1792, it is confined to the State, Treasury, and War Departments, and differs from it in limiting the authority to a period of six months succeeding the vacancy. Both laws left unprovided for vacancies occurring in the other Departments. But it appears by the evidence that such appointments were made by all the predecessors of Mr. Johnson in the Departments not included within the acts referred to, as well as in those that were included. And there is nothing to show that their validity was at any time questioned by Congress. On such an appointment by President Buchanan of Judge Holt to the War Department, made during the session of the Senate, a resolution was passed calling upon him to state the authority under which he acted. This he did by the message of January 15, 1861. In that message many instances are mentioned of appointments of the kind in all the Departments as well during the session as in the recess of the Senate: and from that time to this impeachment the authority of the President had been considered established.

For the appointment of Thomas, then, the President had the example of all his predecessors. To hold that he committed a crime or misdemeanor in making it would, I think, shock a proper sense of justice, and· impute to every President, from Washington to Lincoln, offenses for which they should have been impeached and removed from office. Such an imputation could not fail to meet the severe rebuke and condemnation of the country. But it is said that the act of 1795 was repealed by that of the 20th of February, 1863. This seems to me a palpable error. That act contains no words of express repeal, nor even of reference to the one of 1795.

If it does repeal that act, it is only because its provisions are so inconsistent with it that the two cannot in any particular stand together. If they can, upon a well-settled rule of interpretation, they must so stand. Are they so inconsistent that this cannot be done? 1. The legal presumption is that Congress, when they passed the latter act, had the former one before them, and that they intended only to repeal the former in the particulars for which the former provides. The policy of such legislation was adopted in 1789 by the act organizing the several Departments. By the second section of the one relating to the War Department, (and the same provision is made as to the other Departments,) on the removal from office by the President of the Secretary, or a vacancy arising from any cause, the chief clerk was to have charge and custody of all the papers, &c., of the office. ·It was also adopted in 1792, 1795, and 1863, and is in words recognized by the eighth section of the act of the 2d of March, 1867, itself, in the provision "that whenever the President shall, without the advice and consent of the Senate, designate, authorize, or employ any person to perform the duties of any office," he shall inform the Secretary of the Treasury. This provision evidently implies that the President had the right to make such an appointment, and subject it to no other qualification (and that was unnecessary, as it was always done before) than that he advise the Secretary.

This policy is not only conducive, but absolutely necessary to the good of the public service. The act of 1863 does not embrace the case of a vacancy arising from removal, or expiration of term. These two cases, therefore, if the act of 1795 is not in force, and the President has not the power independent of legislation, are without remedy, and the office, although the event may occur the day after the termination of a Congress, must remain in abeyance, and all business connected with it so remain until the commencement of a succeeding Congress, which, when the act of 1863 was passed, would have been a period of eight months. The disastrous condition in which this might place the country is of itself sufficient to prove that the act of 1795, by which such a condition would be averted, was not intended to be repealed by the one of 1863. And this court, as well as any other court before whom the question may arise, is bound to rule against such an appeal.

V. Thus far I have considered the act of 1867 as constitutional. I will now examine that question. As regards this case, the inquiry is only material upon the assumption (which I have endeavored to show is unfounded) that Mr. Stanton was within the act so as to deprive the President of the power to remove him. Is the act constitutional? The Constitution is framed upon the theory (the correctness of which no political student will deny) that a free constitutional government cannot exist without a separation of legislative, executive, and judicial powers, and that the complete success of such a separation depends upon the absolute independence of each. Under this conviction, the legislative department, within the limits of its delegated powers, is made supreme; and the executive department, with a few exceptions, not necessary to be mentioned, is also made supreme; and the same is true of the judicial department.

The object of the supremacy of each would be defeated if either were subordinate to the others. To avoid this each must necessarily have the right of self-protection. This is obvious. To put it in the power of the Executive to defeat constitutional laws passed by Congress in due form would be to destroy the independence of that department; and to put it in the powers of Congress to take away or limit the constitutional powers of the Executive would likewise be to destroy the complete independence of that department. How, then, are they to maintain their respective rights? To submit would be to abandon them, and be a violation of duty. If the Executive interferes with the rightful authority of Congress that body must defend itself; and for this purpose it may resort to impeachment, if the interference be a high crime and misdemeanor.

1. Has the President, by the Constitution, the power to remove officers appointed with the advice of the Senate? Whatever doubts were originally entertained upon the point, the power is too firmly established to be shaken, if a constitutional question can be settled by the authority of time and precedent. It was clearly held to exist when the Departments were established in 1789 by the laws creating them, and by the congressional debates of the day. Until lately this was conceded. Every commentator upon the Constitution has so stated. The Supreme Court of the United States have also so held.

In a letter of Mr. Madison to Edward Coles, of the 15th of October, 1834, (4 Madison's Writings, 368,) in referring to the question of the right of the Senate to participate in removals, that distinguished statesman writes thus:

"*The claim on* CONSTITUTIONAL *ground to a share in the removal as well as appointment of officers is in direct opposition to the uniform practice of the Government from its commencement. It is clear that the innovation would not only vary essentially the existing balance of power, but expose the Executive occasionally to a total inaction, and at all times to delays fatal to the due execution of the laws.*"

And on the 16th of February, 1835, in a speech in the Senate, Mr. Webster, while questioning the correctness of the decision of 1789, says:

"*I do not mean to deny*" "*that at the present moment the President may remove these officers at will, because the early decision adopted that construction, and the laws have since uniformly sanctioned it.*"

If any supposed doubtful constitutional question can be conclusively solved, is not this so solved? Mr. Madison, in his message of January 30, 1815, adverting to the power of Congress to incorporate a bank of the United States, which he, while a member of Congress, with great ability had denied, said that he waived the question as "precluded in (his) judgment by repeated recognitions under varied circumstances of the validity of such an institution in acts of the legislative, executive, and judicial branches of the Government." Are not these observations even more applicable to the present question than to the one before him?

VI. Admitting, however, for argument sake, that I am in error as to the construction of the act of 2d of March, 1867, or its constitutionality, this can hardly be disputed—that differences of opinion in regard to each may be honestly entertained. Conceding this, it necessarily follows that there can be no criminality in the holding of either opinion. The President thought and still thinks, as he tells us, that Mr. Stanton is not so within the act as to be beyond his right to remove him; or, if he is, that the act in that respect is unconstitutional. As to the first, he has the express sanction of Senators WILLIAMS and SHERMAN, announced when the law was being passed, and the implied sanction of every member of the Senate who voted for it, without questioning the construction given to it by the two Senators. And as to the second, he has the sanction of the doctrine established in 1789, and acted upon by every one of his predecessors from Washington to Lincoln, admitted as established by Mr. Webster in 1835, and vindicated as essential to the public service by Mr. Madison in 1834. Entertaining these opinions, what were his rights and his duty?

If by the Constitution the power of removal was vested in him, he was bound by the very terms of his official oath to maintain it. Not to have done so would have been to violate the obligation of that oath to "preserve, protect, and defend the Constitution." But two courses were left open to him—that of forcible resistance, or of a resort to the judiciary. The first might have produced civil commotion, and that he is proved never to have contemplated. The judicial department of the Government was established for the very purpose, among others, of deciding such a question, it being given jurisdiction in "all cases in law and equity arising under (the) Constitution." It was to this tribunal that the evidence shows that he intended to resort. Was that a crime? He believed, and had a right to believe, that the constitutional authority of the Executive was violated by the act, if Mr. Stanton was protected by it; and he sought to have that question peacefully settled by the judgment of the very tribunal created for such a purpose. And there was no one else who could appeal to it with that view. It was the authority of the executive department of the Government, not any individual right of his own, which was assailed. He, and no one else, represented that department and could institute legal proceedings for its vindication. This, therefore, was not only his right, but his sworn duty. The doctrine that the President is forced to execute any statute that Congress may pass according to the forms of law, upon subjects not only not within their delegated powers, but expressly denied to them, is to compel him to abandon his office and submit all its functions to the unlimited control of Congress, and thus defeat the very object of its creation. Such a doctrine has no support in the Constitution, and would in the end be its destruction.

It has been contended on the part of the managers that the President has no right to question the constitutionality of an act of Congress because of his duty faithfully to execute the laws. But what is the law which he is to execute if the act is in conflict with the Constitution? Is not that also a law? The Con-

stitution declares it not only to be one, but to be the supreme law, and prescribes no such supremacy to acts of Congress, except to such as are passed in "pursuance thereof." The execution, therefore, by him of an act not passed in pursuance of the Constitution, but in violation of it, instead of being a duty, would be a breach of his sworn obligation to preserve the Constitution. Nor is there any inconsistency between his duty to protect the Constitution, and to see to the faithful execution of the laws—the Constitution itself prohibiting the enactment of any law which it does not authorize Congress to pass. Were it otherwise the Constitution might become a dead letter, as its effect from time to time would depend upon Congress; in other words, that body would be the Government, possessing practically all powers—legislative, executive, and judicial—a result clearly destructive of liberty.

VII. Each of the articles charged that the enumerated acts were done by the President "with intent" "to violate" the acts of Congress specially mentioned, and were "contrary to the provision of the Constitution," and that he was, therefore, "guilty of a high misdemeanor in office."

The alleged offenses, then, are made to consist of acts and intent. The latter is as material as the former. Now, what doubt can reasonably be entertained that the President had not the intent imputed? On the contrary, is it not manifest that his purpose was to preserve both from violation? This is certainly true, unless it be supposed that he believed that the Supreme Court of the United States would aid him in such a violation. Assuming that he believed that tribunal to be honest and capable, the very fact of his wishing to obtain its decision upon the questions before him demonstrates that his design was not to subvert, but to uphold the Constitution, and obtain a correct construction of the act of March, 1867.

VIII. I deem it wholly unnecessary to consider the fourth, fifth, sixth, and seventh—the conspiracy articles—or the ninth, the Emory article, no evidence whatever having been offered even tending, as I think, to their support.

IX. It has been said that the Senate, by their resolution of February, 1868, having declared that the President's removal of Mr. Stanton was contrary to the Constitution and the law, the Senators voting for it are concluded upon both points. This is a great error. That resolution was passed by the Senate in its legislative capacity, and without much deliberation. The questions were scarcely debated. To hold that any Senator who voted for it is not at perfect liberty to reconsider his opinion on this trial is to confound things entirely distinct. That resolution the Senate at any time, in its legislative character, can reverse when convinced of its error. But this is not so in relation to any error of law or fact into which this court may now fall. It is now acting in a judicial character. The judgment which it may pronounce as regards the respondent will be final. To suppose, then, that a Senator, when he is satisfied that his former opinion upon the legal questions now before him is erroneous, may not correct it, but is bound to pronounce a judgment which he is convinced would be illegal, is to force him to violate the oath he has taken to decide the case impartially, according to law and justice. The resolution of February was not a law. That everybody will admit. To act in virtue of it, disregarding what he is convinced is the law, would be a gross abandonment of duty. It has also been said by some inconsiderate persons that our judgment should be influenced by party consideration. We have been told in substance that party necessity requires a conviction; and the same is invoked to avoid what it is madly said will be the result of acquittal—civil commotion and bloodshed. Miserable insanity, a degrading dereliction of patriotism. These appeals are made evidently from the apprehension that Senators may conscientiously be convinced that the President is innocent of each of the crimes and misdemeanors alleged in the several articles, and are intended to force him to a judgment of guilt. No more dishonoring efforts were ever made to corrupt a judicial tribunal. They are disgraceful to the parties resorting to them, and should they be successful, as I am sure they will not, they would forever destroy the heretofore unblemished honor of this body, and inflict a wound upon the Constitution itself which, perhaps, no time could heal.

OPINION
OF
HON. PETER G. VAN WINKLE.

In the following remarks I have endeavored to state the conclusions to which I have arrived, with some reasons for them, and not to review the whole case. I have, therefore, omitted the consideration of all questions raised in the course of the proceedings which do not affect those conclusions:

Conceding the constitutionality of the tenure-of-office act of March 2, 1867, there yet remains some questions to be disposed of before an intelligent answer can be given to the accusation or charge contained in the first article of impeachment. Senators are to pronounce upon this, as well as the charges in the other articles, by replying, under the oaths they have respectively taken, to the question, " Is the respondent, Andrew Johnson, President of the United States, guilty or not guilty of a high misdemeanor, (or crime, as the case may be,) *as charged in this article?*" I have, therefore, in each case, where I deemed it at all necessary, endeavored to present the charge stripped of immaterial verbiage, in order to ascertain more readily and certainly whether it describes a misdemeanor or crime.

The first article alleges that the respondent did, unlawfully and in violation of the Constitution and laws, issue an order in writing for the removal of Edwin M. Stanton from the office of Secretary *for* the Department of War, with the intent to violate the act above referred to, and with the further intent, contrary to and in violation of the provisions of the said act, and contrary to the provisions of the Constitution, and without the advice and consent of the Senate, then in session, remove the said Stanton from his said office.

The Constitution is silent on the subject of removals from office, unless a rule on the subject may be inferred from the provisions it contains relating to offices and officers. The only authoritative interpretation of its meaning in this relation previous to the passage of the tenure-of-office act is found in an act of Congress passed in 1789, and this concedes to the President alone the right to remove. The provisions of the tenure-of-office act must therefore be examined in order to determine whether what is charged to have been done by the respondent was a violation of that act and of the Constitution.

The plain and evident intention of the act just referred to is that no person appointed to any office by and with the advice and consent of the Senate shall be removed therefrom, although he may be suspended in certain specified cases, without the like advice and consent. There is no question that Mr. Stanton was so appointed to the office of Secretary of War, and was duly qualified to act therein. In order to prevent a removal from any such office the act provides, in effect, that the incumbent shall hold it until his successor is in like manner appointed and duly qualified, unless the time is limited by law, and shall expire before such appointment and qualification. The proviso in the first section does not, in my opinion, except any of the Cabinet officers from the operation of the preceding clause of the same section, although, for the first time, it specifically limits their respective terms. If, as is alleged, the proviso leaves it doubtful as to the duration of Mr. Stanton's term, it is, in my opinion, certain that at the time the said order in writing was issued his tenure was protected by the preceding clause. In its very language he was, and is still, "holding *a* civil office to which he has been appointed by and with the advice and consent of the Senate," and the order in writing not only addresses him as Secretary *for* the Department of War, but asserts that his "functions as such will terminate on receipt of that communication."

The sixth and only penal section of the act which refers to a case like that under consideration provides that every removal, appointment, or employment made, had, or exercised contrary to the provisions of that act shall be

894

deemed, and is thereby declared to be, a high misdemeanor. It therefore appears that the act of the respondent complained of, if it was criminal, must be obnoxious to the provisions of this section.

The charge made by the first article is, that the respondent did "issue an order in writing (which is set out at full length) for the removal of Edwin M. Stanton from the office of Secretary *for* the Department of War." This is the whole of it, so far as the acts as distinguished from the intentions of the respondent are concerned. There is not even an allegation that the order in writing was ever delivered to, or served on, Mr. Stanton, or ever directed to be so delivered or served, or that any attempt was made to deliver or serve it; or, in fact, that Mr. Stanton ever saw or heard of it.

As the order in writing is neither an appointment or employment it must have effected a removal, or have been, at least, an attempt to remove, in order to constitute a violation of the act; but no removal or attempt to remove is charged, and consequently the respondent could not have been guilty "of a high misdemeanor, as charged in this (first) article." Had an attempt to remove been charged there was still no averment of even attempted delivery or service of the order in writing. "To issue," which means simply to send forth, cannot imply a delivery or service; and if there is evidence of a delivery to be found in the proceedings it cannot be applicable to this article, in which there is no charge or averment. This objection may seem technical, but a consideration of the whole article will show that it is substantial, and that a service or delivery was, in fact, necessary to complete the alleged offense, especially if it is observed that the order in writing addressed to Mr. Stanton says, "Your functions as such (Secretary of War) will terminate upon receipt of this communication," and consequently not till then. It is, therefore, evident that the delivery to and receipt by Mr. Stanton of the order in writing was necessary to complete his removal from office, if any mere writing could have that effect.

Admitting that the intents of the respondent in issuing the order in writing were precisely as charged, it may be questioned whether they, together with the act done, constitute a high misdemeanor. Of course the intent alone does not. It merely qualifies or characterizes the act, and however reprehensible the former may be the latter must be of itself unlawful. There is no clause in the act that forbids or denounces the mere issue, without some further act, of such a paper as the order in writing, and such an issue could not be even an attempt to remove from office. By the very terms of the order any intention to remove Mr. Stanton until he had received it is negatived, and there is no charge or allegation that he did receive it.

It has been suggested that the answer of the respondent to the first article contains confessions which cure the defects above indicated. To this I reply that the answer cannot confess what is not charged.

The second article is based upon the letter of authority issued and delivered by the respondent to General Lorenzo Thomas. It charges that the respondent, with intent to violate the Constitution and the tenure-of-office act, the Senate being then in session, and there being no vacancy in the office of Secretary of War, did issue and deliver to the said Thomas the aforesaid letter of authority, which is set out at full length. Referring to some remarks made above on the first article, it is plain that the issue and delivery of the letter of authority cannot be a violation of the Constitution unless it is also a violation of the tenure-of-office act, which is charged. In order, therefore, to ascertain whether the charge made in the second article covers a misdemeanor the act itself must be reviewed.

The most rigid examination of that act will fail to disclose that its provisions anywhere refer to an *ad interim* appointment, except in its second section, where, in case of a suspension, such an appointment is authorized. The language, after stating what offense or misconduct will authorize a suspension, is that "in such case, and in no other," "the President may suspend such officer, and designate some suitable person to perform temporarily the duties of such office," &c. Here the suspension is the principal thing, and the temporary designation the subordinate. This justifies the construction that the words "in such case, and no other," mean that only such cases as are specified in the beginning of the section, occurring in a recess of the Senate, will authorize suspension. They do not and cannot mean that in no other case shall there be a temporary designation or appointment. Such a conclusion is forbidden by the fact that temporary designations were, at the passage of the act, and still are, authorized by both law and custom.

Turning to the penal sections of the tenure-of-office act it will be seen that the fifth applies only to those who accept, hold, or exercise any office or employment contrary to the provisions of that act; and, as General Thomas is not upon trial, its further consideration may be dismissed. If, then, the respondent committed a misdemeanor under this article, the act or acts done by him must have been such as are described in the sixth section.

That section declares that "every removal, appointment, or employment made, had, or exercised, contrary to the provisions of this act, and the making, signing, sealing, countersigning, or issuing of any commission or letter of authority, for or in respect to any such appointment or employment," shall be deemed a high misdemeanor. Leaving out of consideration the word removal, which is not involved in the charge, the section includes only appointments and employments made, had, or exercised, contrary to the provisions of the tenure-of-office act, and certain acts relating to such appointments and employments. As the latter are a consequence of the former, and as if the former was legal, the latter, in the same case, would be legal also ; and, in fact, there could be no employment without a previous appointment—the former may be considered as included in the latter—so that if the appointment of General Thomas was legal, or the reverse, his employment would bear the same character.

It may be fairly questioned whether the authority conferred on General Thomas was in its nature an appointment, in the strict legal sense of that term. The letter set out in the article simply empowers and authorizes him to act, and does not use the word appoint, or any equivalent term. In the case of a suspension, authorized by the second section, it is not said that the President may appoint, but that he may "designate some suitable person," &c. The term appointment may be familiarly used in such cases ; but what is questioned is whether such is its proper legal application. Conceding this, however, it remains to inquire whether the appointment of General Thomas was, in the language of the penal sections, "contrary to the provisions of the act." It is very evident that the act refers everywhere to appointments made by and with the consent of the Senate, except in the second section, and there so far only as the same relates to the designation of a person to act *ad interim* in the case of a suspension, which has been already noticed. It is very certain that an *ad interim* appointment, designation, or authorization has never been held, or, so far as I am informed, even supposed to require the advice and consent of the Senate. It does not seem, therefore, that the letter of authority, as it is called in the article, is contrary to the provisions of the tenure-of-office act. As the making, signing, &c., of any letter of authority, made penal by the sixth section, must be for or in respect to such an appointment, &c., as is contrary to the provisions of the act, and it has been shown that the letter of authority to General Thomas did not relate to such an appointment, the issue and delivery of it did not constitute a misdemeanor, as charged in the second article.

The third article is also based upon the letter to General Thomas, which is set forth at length, but is not here called a letter of authority, but an appointment. It is not charged to have been issued contrary to the tenure-of-office act; but the remarks on the preceding article may properly be referred to here. The charge is that, under circumstances precisely similar to those stated in the second article, the respondent did, without authority of law, the Senate being in session, appoint one Lorenzo Thomas to be Secretary for the Department of War *ad interim*, without the advice

and consent of the Senate, with intent to violate the Constitution, no vacancy having happened in the said office during the recess of the Senate or existing at the time.

It will be observed that it is not charged that the Secretary was not temporarily absent from the office, or sick, in which cases the so-called appointment would have been legal. The act of the respondent is alleged to have been done without authority of law, with intent to violate the Constitution. If it can be deemed a full appointment it was such a violation, for such appointments require the advice and consent of the Senate; but as the letter, the only evidence on the subject, shows it to have been only *ad interim*, and the Constitution makes no mention of such appointments, it does not appear that it can be such a violation. As to its being done "without authority of law," it can hardly be intended to assert that every act for which a special or general permission of law is not shown is unlawful and a misdemeanor. Yet this is the only ground on which the alleged act of the respondent is charged to be the latter.

The fourth, fifth, sixth, and seventh articles are severally based on an alleged conspiracy of the respondent and General Thomas. It is sufficient to say as to these that there is no evidence before the Senate which furnishes proof of even a technical conspiracy.

As to the eighth article, it may be remarked that the evidence relating to its subject clearly shows that the *ad interim* appointment of General Thomas, or of any other person, would not have enabled the respondent "to control the disbursements of the moneys appropriated for the military service and the Department of War" any further than he legally might with Mr. Stanton or any other acceptable person in the office. This negatives the alleged criminal intent.

The ninth article is supported by evidence, and the alleged intents may be said to be disproved.

The tenth article charges, in substance, that the respondent, designing and intending to set aside the rightful authorities and powers of Congress, attempts to bring Congress and its several branches into disgrace, ridicule, hatred, contempt, and reproach ; to impair and destroy the respect of the people for Congress and its legislative power and to excite the odium and resentment of the people against Congress and the laws enacted by it ; in pursuance of such design and intent, openly and publicly made and delivered, with a loud voice, certain intemperate, inflammatory, and scandalous harangues, the particulars of which are set forth in the three specifications found in this article. It is pleasant to learn, as is disclosed at the end, that this design and intent of the respondent was in some manner frustrated, for it is there said that by means of the said utterances, declarations, threats, and harangues, the respondent had brought, not Congress, but "the high office of the President of the United States into contempt, ridicule, and disgrace, to the great scandal of all good citizens." There may be more truth than poetry in this, and if so, it is not the first case of an engineer "hoist by his own petard." It may, nevertheless, be difficult to determine whether the ineffectual design and intention, or the accomplished result, constitutes the alleged misdemeanor.

The difficulty, however, may be obviated by remembering that several of the original States, almost as a condition of their respective ratifications of the Constitution, insisted that certain amendments of that instrument should be adopted, which, as to the most of them, was speedily done. The first provides that "Congress shall make no law abridging the freedom of speech." This remains in the Constitution, and is unquestionably of universal application. It seems, therefore, that no such misdemeanor as is charged in this article can be committed in this country.

The eleventh article alleges in substance that the respondent, by public speech, declared and affirmed that the Thirty-Ninth Congress was not a constitutional Congress, authorized to exercise legislative power, but a Congress of only part of the States, thereby denying and intending to deny that its legislation was valid or obligatory upon him, except in so far as he saw fit to approve the same, and also thereby denying and intending to deny the power of the said Thirty-Ninth Congress to propose amendments to the Constitution of the United States.

I do not perceive or admit that these alleged intentions are proved, and in my remarks on the preceding article have expressed the opinion that declarations and affirmations made by public speech cannot constitute a criminal offense. This, however, is of little importance, as the whole is merely introductory, and does not constitute or greatly, if at all, affect the charge which follows, on which the judgment of the Senate must be predicated.

Giving to the language used its ordinary meaning and construction, it is somewhat difficult to state the charge with entire certainty, as when stated it will be seen to involve the apparent anomaly of asserting that the respondent attempted to prevent the execution of an act of Congress by attempting to prevent the execution of two other acts of Congress, or rather by devising and contriving, and attempting to devise and contrive, means so to do. But I will endeavor to state in terms what the charge is, as it appears to me, after a careful and critical examination of the language used.

The charge, in effect, is that, in pursuance of the said declaration, the respondent, did unlawfully, and in disregard of the requirement of the Constitution, that he should take care that the laws be faithfully executed, attempt to prevent the execution of the tenure-of-office act by unlawfully devising and contriving, and attempting to devise and contrive, means by which he should prevent Mr. Stanton from forthwith resuming the functions of his office, notwithstanding the refusal of the Senate to concur in his suspension; and also attempted to prevent the execution of the said act by further unlawfully devising and contriving, and attempting to devise and contrive, means to prevent the execution of the Army appropriation act of 1867, and also to prevent the execution of the reconstruction act of the 2d of March, in the same year.

As there is no specification of any "means" so devised and contrived, and no sufficient proof of any attempt to interfere with the execution of the two last-mentioned acts, their further consideration may be dismissed. The only specific charge remaining is the devising and contriving, and attempting to devise and contrive, means by which he should prevent Mr. Stanton resuming his office under the circumstances stated; and, in fact, as the *attempting to attempt* to commit a misdemeanor is rather too remote to be in itself a misdemeanor the naked charge is that the respondent attempted to prevent the execution of the tenure-of-office act by devising and contriving means, which are nowhere specified or described, by which he should prevent Mr. Stanton from forthwith resuming the functions of his office. The proof of this charge rests wholly upon the respondent's correspondence with General Grant, which is in evidence, and by which it appears that the respondent endeavored to induce the General, at a time previous to the correspondence, but while that officer was authorized to perform, and was performing, the duties of Secretary of War *ad interim*, to keep possession of that office, and thereby prevent Mr. Stanton's resumption of it, or to surrender it in time to permit the induction of a successor for that purpose.

This evidence, as far as it goes, is sufficiently explicit, but it remains to be determined whether the respondent is, in the words of the question to be proposed to every Senator, and to be answered by him under the oath he has taken, "guilty or not guilty of a high misdemeanor, as charged in this article." It is, therefore, necessary to consider whether the charge it contains describes a high misdemeanor, and, if so, whether the respondent is guilty as charged.

There can be no doubt that an actual prevention of the execution of a law by one whose duty it is to take care that the laws be faithfully executed is a misdemeanor, and it may be conceded that an attempted prevention by such a person is also a misdemeanor; but it may be doubted whether merely devising and contriving means by which such prevention might be effected is an attempt to commit the act which constitutes the offense. "Devising" is simply a mental operation, and while "contriving" may have a broader signification the connection in which it is used here seems to restrict it. Even with the light thrown upon these words by the evidence, as above cited, they appear to imply nothing more than an intention to effect the alleged prevention. An intention, not followed by any act, cannot constitute an attempt to commit a misdemeanor,' and the question to be proposed must be answered negatively.

It may be remarked that the evidence further discloses that the object of the respondent in his proposal to General Grant was to compel Mr. Stanton to institute legal proceedings, by which his right to the office, denied by the respondent, could be tested. This would not have justified the alleged attempt had it been actually made, but it would have qualified the intention, by showing that the object was not primarily to violate the law, and thus have at least tended to diminish the criminality involved in the illegal act.

OPINION
OF
HON. WILLIAM M. STEWART.

A brief examination of the law will determine the character of the President's conduct in removing Stanton and appointing Thomas *ad interim*. The act to regulate the tenure of certain civil offices supersedes all former legislation on the questions involved in that removal and appointment. The sixth section of the act declares—

"That every removal, appointment, or employment made, had, or exercised contrary to the provisions of this act, and the making, signing, sealing, countersigning, or issuing of any commission or letter of authority for or in respect to any such appointment or employment, shall be deemed, and are hereby declared to be, high misdemeanors, and, upon trial and conviction thereof, every person guilty thereof shall be punished by a fine not exceeding $10,000, or by imprisonment not exceeding five years, or both said punishments, in the discretion of the courts."

The same penalties are imposed for issuing orders or giving letters of authority for or in respect to removals and appointments which are prohibited by law that are imposed in cases of actual removals and appointments. It matters not whether Stanton was actually removed or Thomas actually appointed *ad interim*, the issuance of the order for the removal and the giving of the letter of authority to Thomas are admitted. If the power was wanting either to remove Stanton or to appoint Thomas, the President is guilty of a high misdemeanor, on the admitted facts. The questions, then, to be determined are, was the removal of Stanton and the appointment or employment of Thomas, or either of them, unlawful? The body of the first section declares—

"That every person holding any civil office to which he has been appointed by and with the advice and consent of the Senate, and every person who shall hereafter be appointed to any such office and shall become duly qualified to act therein, is, and shall be, entitled to hold such office until a successor shall have been in like manner appointed and duly qualified, except as *herein otherwise provided.*"

C. I.—57.

This language, if unqualified by any other provisions of the act, would extend the term of all officers therein described (including Mr. Stanton, Secretary of War,) until a removal by the appointment and qualification of 'a successor as *therein provided*. It also prescribes the manner in which removals and appointments may be effected, and prohibits all other modes of removals and appointments. The term of office and the mode of vacating and filling office are the three distinct propositions of the body of the first section of the act. There must be no departure from these propositions, except as therein (that is, in that act) otherwise provided. All former acts of Congress providing a different term or a different mode of appointment or removal are by this section repealed. Any practice of the Government inconsistent with the provisions of this law is prohibited. This dispenses with the necessity of examining former acts or former practice concerning any matter within the scope and meaning of this section. There can be no qualification to this language not found in the act itself. It does not read, except as the practice of the Government or former acts of Congress may prescribe, but it does read, *except as herein otherwise provided*. Can the legislative will, in repealing former acts or changing existing practice, be more clearly expressed than to declare a rule and also to declare that it shall be the only rule? The body of the first section clearly prohibited the removal of Stanton and the appointment of Thomas *ad interim*. If these acts were not in violation of law, it was because they were authorized by other provisions in the act itself. The interpretation of the act, then, so far as it affects the President, depends upon the question, what is *therein otherwise provided*? Is it *therein provided* that he may do the acts complained of? If so, he obeyed the law ; if not, he violated it. The limitations or exceptions upon the first section are four. One relates to removals, one to appointments, and two relate to the term of office. The former are contained in the second section, and the latter are found in the fourth section and the proviso to the first. The second section reads as follows :

"That when any officer appointed as aforesaid, excepting judges of the United States courts, shall during a recess of the Senate be shown, by evidence satisfactory to the President, to be guilty of misconduct in office or crime, or for any reason shall become incapable or legally disqualified to perform its duties, in such case, *and in no other*, the President may suspend such officer and designate some suitable person to perform temporarily the duties of such office until the next meeting of the Senate, and until the case shall be acted upon by the Senate ; and such person so designated shall take the oaths and give the bonds required by law, to be taken and given by the person duly appointed to fill such office; and in such case it shall be the duty of the President within twenty days after the first day of such next meeting of the Senate, to report to the Senate such suspension, with the evidence and reasons for his action in the case, and the name of the person so designated to perform the duties of such office. And if the Senate shall concur in such suspension and advise and consent to the removal of such officer, they shall so certify to the President, who may thereupon remove such officer, and by and with the advice and consent of the Senate, appoint another person to such office. But if the Senate shall refuse to concur in such suspension, such officer so suspended shall forthwith resume the functions of his office, and the powers of the person so performing its duties in his stead shall cease, and the official salary and emoluments of such officer shall, during such suspension, belong to the person so performing the duties thereof, and not to the officer so suspended."

The emphatic language is "*in such case and no other*" the President may suspend and designate a person to perform the duties of said office temporarily. This suspension and temporary appointment limit two of the general propositions in the first section, first, a temporary removal may be made by the President alone at the times and in the cases therein provided, but in no other. This limits the first section, so that in substance the act declares that no person now in office, or who may hereafter be in office by and with the advice and consent of the Senate, shall be removed by the President alone without the advice and consent of the Senate to the appointment of a successor, except in recess of the Senate, when the President may suspend for the causes set forth in the second section of this act, and in no other case whatever. The other general proposition of the first section, which is limited by the second section, relates to appointments.

Upon the question of appointment to an office held by another, the first and second sections contain all existing statutory regulations. The substance of these two sections bearing upon the question under consideration is, that no person shall be appointed by the President alone to an office where there is no vacancy, and which office is, by law, to be filled by and with the advice and consent of the Senate, without such advice and consent, except in cases of suspension in the *recess* of the Senate arising under the provisions of the second section of this act, and in such *case and no other* the President may make temporary appointment, as therein provided. The temporary suspension and appointment are limitations upon the positive language of the first section, and are qualifications therein otherwise provided, and the only qualifications anywhere appearing in the act to the general rule requiring the advice and consent of the Senate to an appointment, and prohibiting all removals, except through such appointment. It is true the removal is not complete, but it is the first step towards it, and is an actual suspension from office without the advice and consent of the Senate to the appointment of a successor; and it is also true that the appointment is only temporary, but the appointee, contrary to the provisions of the first section, enters upon the discharge of the duties of the office without any action of the Senate.

This is all the statutory law which bears upon the question under consideration, namely, the removal of Stanton and the appointment of Thomas *ad interim*, and it positively prohibits that removal and appointment by the President alone. The President recognized the binding force of this law in the suspension of Stanton and appointment of General Grant *ad interim*, and in several other cases, and his subsequent disregard of its plain provisions cannot be pleaded as an inadvertence. The two other exceptions to the first section do not relate to the mode of vacating or filling office, which is the subject of inquiry, but to the term of office. The only reason for an examination of these exceptions in this connection is to exclude any inference that provision is made in the act either for removing Stanton or appointing Thomas *ad interim*.

The fourth section reads as follows:

"That nothing in this act contained shall be construed to extend the term of any office the duration of which is limited by law."

This section leaves unchanged the term of office as fixed by law, notwithstanding the general language of the first section that such term shall extend until the appointment and qualification of a successor. The proviso contains the other limitation, and relates to the term of certain designated offices, but contains no exception to the general rule as to removals or appointments. The language is:

"*Provided*, That the Secretary of State, of the Treasury, of War, of the Navy, and of the Interior, the Postmaster General, and the Attorney General, shall hold their offices respectively for and during the term of the President by whom they may have been appointed, and for one month thereafter, subject to removal by and with the advice and consent of the Senate."

Nothing is more certain than that this proviso is silent both as to removals and appointments by the President alone. The proviso fixes a limit on the term of the offices therein named, but makes no other exception. If it be contended that the language is obscured, how does that obscurity help the President, for no possible construction can make it confer the authority to do what is prohibited in the body of the section, namely, to remove an officer and appoint another to fill his place *ad interim* without the advice and consent of ·the Senate. When the President found that he was prohibited from removing, suspending, or appointing, except as in said act provided, it was enough for him to know that nothing in the act authorized him to remove Stanton and appoint Thomas *ad interim*. Stanton's appointment was for an indefinite term, and he was still in office on the 21st day of February, 1868. It makes no difference what his term of office was, or by whom appointed. The mode adopted to put him out was prohibited. There is no reason, in view of the conduct of the parties or the language of the law, to support the suggestion that the law was retroactive, and operated to terminate Stanton's office one month after Johnson became President. Such a construction would not only be inconsistent with the whole conduct of the President in recognizing Stanton as Secretary of War, but would be in violation of the well-established rule of statutory construction that no law shall have a retroactive effect, unless the will of the law-making power be so clearly expressed as to be wholly inconsistent with any other interpretation. This law, without any violation of language or principles of construction, applies to the present and to the future, and was so understood, until it became important to change or pervert its obvious meaning.

The President understood the law on the 2d of March, 1867, when he sent his veto message to Congress. (Page 38 of Record.)

He says in that message, ''In effect the bill provides that the President shall not remove from their places any of the civil officers whose terms of service are not limited by law without the advice and consent of the Senate of the United States.' Then it included any civil officers whatever. Now it includes some and excludes others.

I am aware that a constitutional question has been raised upon the denial of the right of the President to remove from office, which I need not discuss after the repeated votes of the Senate affirming the constitutional validity of such a law. But no one has contended or will contend that the President could make any appointment, for any temporary purpose whatever, without the authority of law, and he certainly cannot do so against a plain statute. The issuance of the letter of authority for the appointment or employment of Thomas is expressly declared to be a misdemeanor. It is no answer to the admitted constitutional power of Congress to pass the law to say that cases might arise in which it might be inconvenient if the President were deprived of the right to fill temporary vacancies. That would be a matter for the legislative department to decide, and besides no such case had arisen when Thomas was appointed or employed, but, on the contrary, Mr. Stanton was in office and fully qualified to discharge the duties of the Department of War. It is no excuse for violating a law to say that cases may arise when the law would work inconveniences, particularly when no inconvenience exists in the given case. No precedent has been found in the history of the Government for the removal of Stanton and the appointment of Thomas *ad interim*. They are in direct violation of the Constitution and cannot be justified or excused by practice, if such practice has existed.

Usurpation is not to be tolerated against the express provisions of written law and against the protest of the Senate after mature consideration. I regard the removal of Stanton and the appointment of Thomas as parts of the same transaction. The two acts, taken together, in defiance of law and the decision of the Senate, constitute a bold and deliberate attempt to dispense with the provision of the Constitution which makes the advice and consent of the Senate necessary to the appointment to office. For if the President can remove the Secretary of War and appoint a person *ad interim* to fill the place the advice and consent of the Senate are of no consequence. This would authorize him to remove all executive officers, civil and military, and put persons into these offices suitable to his purposes, who might remain in office indefinitely. He might or he might not nominate to the Senate. If he should condescend to do so he might nominate the persons holding *ad interim*, and the Senate could only choose whether it would confirm the nominees or let the same persons continue *ad interim*. The Senate could in that case choose as to the character of the commissions, but would have no voice as to the character of the officers. But suppose the President should nominate different persons from the *ad interim* appointees, which persons would, of course, be also the choice of the Executive, and in that event the Senate might confirm or allow the *ad interim* officers to continue to discharge the duties of the respective offices. In that case the Senate would have the poor privilege of choosing between two instruments of the President. If this can be done in the case of the Secretary of War it can be done in all cases of executive offices, civil and military. The whole power of the Government would then be in the hands of one man. He could then have his tools in all the offices, through whom alone the civil and military power of the United States could be exercised. To acquit Andrew Johnson is to affirm this power in the present and all future Presidents.

The motives of the President in deliberately violating law cannot be considered. Such a defense might be set up in every criminal case. He does not claim that he did not intend to issue the order for the removal of Stanton and issue the letter for the appointment of Thomas *ad interim*. If either of these acts was a misdemeanor, he intended to commit a misdemeanor. The question of intention or motive can only be material where doubt exists as to voluntary or deliberate character of the offense. My conclusion is that the President deliberately violated the law both in issuing the order for the removal of Stanton and in giving the letter of authority to Thomas, and that all the articles involving a charge of either of those acts ought to be sustained if we desire to preserve the just balance of the coördinate departments of the Government and vindicate the authority of law.

OPINION
OF
HON. JAMES HARLAN.
—

In the first article of impeachment the House of Representatives accuse Andrew Johnson, President of the United States, of the commission of "a high misdemeanor in office," in issuing an order, during the session of the

Senate, for the removal of Edwin M. Stanton, Secretary of the Department of War, from said office, February 21, 1868, in violation of the Constitution and of an act entitled "An act regulating the tenure of certain civil offices," approved March 2, 1867.

The President in his answer to this article, presented to the Senate March 23, 1868, admits that he did remove said Stanton from said office by suspending him August 12, 1867, and by making it absolute and perpetual, as per order dated February 21, 1868; and justifies the act of removal by asserting—

"That the *Constitution* of the United States confers on the President" * * * "*the power at any and all times of removing from office all executive officers for cause, to be judged of by the President alone,*" and that "*the Congress could not deprive him thereof.*"—*Impeachment Record*, p. 23.

It is proper to observe in the beginning that the President does not justify under any existing statute—that of 1789, creating the Department of War, or any other. He admits the act of removal, and claims that it was not "a high misdemeanor in office;" alleging that the *Constitution* confers on him the absolute and exclusive right to remove all executive officers at discretion, whether the Senate be in session or not, and admitting the existence of an act of Congress prohibiting it, the act of removal was, nevertheless, legal, because, in his opinion, Congress had no right, under the Constitution, to prohibit, to regulate, or in any way to interfere with the exercise of this executive function.

That is the issue joined under the first article, which brings us necessarily to an examination of the provisions of the Constitution which are supposed to clothe the President with this exclusive authority to make *removals* from office.

The Constitution does not anywhere, in terms, confer on the *President* the authority to make *removals;* nor does it anywhere confer on him this right by *necessary implication.* It does confer on him the *qualified right* to *make appointments.*

The second clause of the second section of article two of the Constitution provides that—

"He shall *nominate,* and by and with *the advice and consent of the Senate* shall appoint, embassadors, other public ministers and consuls, judges of the Supreme Court, and all *other* officers of the United States, whose appointments are not herein otherwise provided for, and which shall be established by law."

It also provides that—

"Congress may by law vest the appointment of such inferior officers as they think proper in the President alone, in the courts of law, or in the heads of Departments."

And the last clause of this section provides that—

"The President shall have power to fill up all vacancies that may happen during the recess of the Senate, by granting commissions which shall expire at the end of their next session."

It is therefore clear that the President is clothed by direct grant of the Constitution with the absolute, unrestrained, and exclusive right to make *appointments* to fill *vacancies* temporarily which may *happen* during the *recess* of the Senate, and with the *qualified* right to make permanent *appointments* during the sessions of the Senate; but he is not clothed with the authority by direct grant to make *removals* either in the recess or during the sessions of the Senate.

Nor does the President appear to be vested with the exclusive authority to make removals by *any necessary implication,* or by any necessary construction of any other clause of the Constitution.

It is sometimes argued that the right to remove is a necessary incident or concomitant of the right to appoint. But this is begging the very question at issue. Is it a necessary incident of the power to appoint? If so, why is it so? May not the act of *appointment* be distinct and separate from the act of removal? If not—if they must necessarily go together—if they must necessarily be performed by the same party or parties—if they are necessary concomitants of each other, it will follow irresistibly that the President, having the exclusive and absolute authority to make temporary appointments to fill vacancies during the recess of the Senate, may make removals during the recess; and as he is clothed only with a *qualified* right to make appointments during the session, the right to *remove* during the session of the Senate must be *qualified* by the same limitations. To assert the contrary would involve the absurdity of insisting that the *incident* is superior to the *principle;* that the implied power is greater than the *direct grant;* or, to apply the reasoning in physics, it would be to assert that the *reflected* light from another surface may be superior to the direct solar ray—that the momentum of a flying projectile is greater than the original force from which it derived its motion. It is clear, therefore, as it seems to me, if the right of removal is an incident of the right to appoint—if the two acts must go together—if all the authority possessed by the President to *remove* an officer is *derived* from the grant of authority *to appoint,* and if the power to appoint during the sessions of the Senate is qualified depending on the "advice and consent of the Senate," it must follow that the authority to remove during the sessions is in like manner qualified and dependent on the advice and consent of the Senate.

But if the power of *appointment* and the power of *removal* are separate functions, it would have been possible for the framers of the Constitution to have conferred on the President the authority to perform the one and to have withheld from him the authority to perform the other. Conferring on him the right *to appoint,* they might have left the power *to remove* in abeyance, to be regulated by law, or might have conferred the latter authority on some other officer or department of the Government.

And, if it should be found on examination

that the authority to remove officers of the United States or any of them has been vested by the Constitution in some other organ of the Government, it would seem to raise a very strong presumption that it was not the intention of the framers to confer this authority, as to them, on the President.

Now, by reference to the fourth section of article two of the Constitution it will be seen that the authority to remove all civil officers is vested in the Senate. It directs that—

"The President, Vice President, and *all* civil officers of the United States shall be *removed from office* on impeachment for and conviction of treason, bribery, or other high crimes and misdemeanors."

The sixth clause of the third section of article one provides that—

"The Senate shall have the sole power to try all impeachments."

This, if it were a new question, would seem to make it clear that the President could not make removal of *civil* officers. The Constitution does not confer the right on him by any direct grant, and does confer the power in direct terms on the Senate to remove all civil officers, and, if they should see proper, to disqualify them ever afterward from the right to hold office under the United States.

The implied right of the President to make removals at discretion is sometimes claimed under the third section of article three of the Constitution, which provides that the President "shall take care that the laws be faithfully executed." It is insisted that the President must exercise the power of removing unfaithful, incompetent, and corrupt officers in order to secure "the faithful execution of the laws." But if this is a correct construction, if being charged with seeing that the laws are faithfully executed necessarily vests in him the right to remove unfaithful officers at his own discretion, he may remove *judicial* as well as *executive* officers; the judges of the Supreme Court as well as the heads of Executive Departments. If not, why not? It may be said that the Constitution provides that "the judges, both of the Supreme and inferior courts, shall hold their offices during good behavior." But who shall judge of their "behavior," whether it be good or bad? If in the President's opinion the judges do behave badly; if in his opinion, on account of their malfeasance or misfeasance in office, he could not faithfully execute the laws, why may he not remove them? It may be said that the Constitution does not in terms confer on the President the right to remove them even for *cause*, however flagrant, and does confer the power on the Senate by impeachment. I answer that it does not confer on the President in express terms the right to remove other officers, even for *cause*, and that it does confer this right on the Senate to remove the latter as well as judges. In this respect the judges are not exceptional.

It may be said, however, that, although the Constitution does not vest the power to remove all *other* civil officers for impeachable offenses in the Senate, it does not provide that they shall not be removed in some other mode or by some other officer or department of the Government. I answer, nor does the Constitution provide that judges shall not be removed in any other mode, or by any other officer or department of the Government. It simply says that the judges shall hold their offices during good behavior. When they behave badly they may be removed. They may be removed for impeachable offenses, like all other civil officers, by the Senate. And if clothing the Senate with power to remove other civil officers does not, by implication, *deprive* the President of the authority to remove them when, in his opinion, the faithful execution of the laws may require it, by what process of reasoning can it be claimed that the judges can be removed by the Senate *only?* The Constitution does not say so. It does not prohibit the removal of the judges by the President. And if he find that a judge is corrupt, willfully misinterprets the laws, or refuses to adjudicate cause, and if Congress should not be in session, or, being in session, should refuse or neglect to remove him by impeachment, why may not the President do it? If it is conceded that he may remove a Secretary of War at discretion, either during the session of the Senate or in the recess, under that clause of the Constitution which makes it his duty "to see that the laws are faithfully executed," why may he not, under the same clause, remove a judge for what he may consider gross misconduct?

There can be but one answer. The practice of the Government has sanctioned the removal of other civil officers by the President at will during the recess of the Senate, and by and with the advice and consent of the Senate during its session; and no President has yet ventured on the exercise of the authority to remove judges of the courts of the United States. The distinction has no sanction, or in the well-settled rules of legal construction.

But if the President is clothed by the Constitution "with power at any and *all times* (during the session as well as in the recess) of removing from office all executive officers for cause to be judged of by the President alone," and if, as he claims in his answer, "the Congress could not deprive him thereof," may he not also remove at discretion officers of the Army and Navy? And if not, why not?

The Constitution does not fix their tenure of office. It makes no distinction between them and civil officers (other than judges) in this respect. They are all appointed under that clause of the Constitution, heretofore recited, which provides that the President "shall nominate, and by and with the advice and consent of the Senate shall appoint," "all officers of the United States," and all other provisions which say that Congress shall have power "to raise and support armies" and "to provide and maintain a navy." It does not provide that the officers shall hold for life or good behavior. So far as the Constitution provides, if the President is vested with authority to remove Mr. Stanton, the Secretary of War, he may also remove any officer of the Army or Navy; and if Congress cannot by law regulate the tenure of office of the former, Congress cannot regulate the tenure of the latter. It is true Congress has from time to time by law regulated the tenure of military officers and provided the mode of their removal.

During nearly the whole period of the existence of the Government they have been removable for cause alone, in pursuance of the finding of a court-martial, subject, however, to the approval of the President. During the late war Congress authorized the President to drop any military officer from the rolls at discretion; at the close of the war this act was repealed. But if it should be conceded that Congress cannot by law regulate the tenure of civil officers and the manner of their removal, it must be conceded also that Congress cannot, under the Constitution, regulate the tenure of officers of the Army and Navy. If the act regulating the tenure of certain civil officers is void by reason of conflict with the Constitution, then all the acts regulating the tenure of military officers are also void. And if the President may innocently violate the former, he may with impunity trample under foot the latter; if he can remove Secretary Stanton, he may dismiss General Grant or Admiral Farragut.

I cannot bring myself to believe that the framers of the Constitution could have intended to vest in the President a purely discretionary power so vast and far-reaching in its consequences, which if exercised by a bad or a weak President would enable him to bring to his feet all the officers of the Government, military and civil, judicial and executive, to strike down the republican character of our institutions and establish all the distasteful characteristics of a monarchy. For the participation of the Senate in appointments during its sessions would become nugatory, if the President may legally remove them at discretion, and fill up the vacancies thus made by temporary appointments. And the people would be without remedy if, as he avers in his answer, Congress has not the right to restrain or by law regulate the exercise of this executive function.

This leads me to notice in consecutive order the argument presented by several Senators during this consultation, tending to justify this act of removal, drawn from their construction of the statute of August 7, 1789, creating the War Department.

The first section of this act, after creating this Department, provides—

"That there shall be a principal officer therein, to be called the Secretary for the Department of War."

The second section authorizes the appointment by the Secretary of an inferior officer, to be called the chief clerk—

"Who, whenever the said principal officer shall be removed from office by the President of the United States, or in any other case of vacancy, shall, during such vacancy, have the charge and custody of all records, books, and papers appertaining to the said Department."—*Statutes-at-Large*, vol. 1, p. 50.

The phrase "whenever the said principal officer shall be removed from office by the President" is in itself, they think, a grant of power to remove the Secretary of War; that this law was not repealed by the act of March 2, 1867, "to regulate the tenure of certain civil offices," but is still in force, and consequently that the removal of Mr. Stanton was legal and innocent.

Before proceeding to examine the law of March 2, 1867, I will express my doubt of the correctness of the construction placed by these Senators on the statute of August 7, 1789.

I doubt it because the President, although advised by counsel of the highest professional standing, does not claim protection under this law, but under the Constitution itself; asserting, in his answer to this article, that his authority to make removals is derived from that instrument, and that "the Congress could not deprive him thereof." He does not even so much as name this act of 1789. I doubt it, because a careful examination of the debates of the Congress by whom this law was enacted will show that the members who insisted on placing this phraseology in the text of the act, did not construe it as a grant of authority to make removals. In fact, Marshall, in his Life of Washington, (vol. 2, page 162,) referring to the debate on this subject, says that after words had been incorporated into the bill explicitly authorizing the President to remove the head of the Department they were stricken out and the foregoing words substituted for the express purpose of avoiding the inference that, in the opinion of Mr. Madison and those who agreed with him, Congress could either grant to or withhold this authority from the President. It is perfectly clear that they wished to leave this question of authority to remove where the Constitution left it, with a legislative expression of opinion that the President could make removals. This was doubtless Mr. Madison's opinion and the opinion of a majority of the members of the House, concurred in by one half of the Senators present, as the record shows that the bill passed by the casting vote of the Vice President. Hence the President's counsel, who doubtless examined this case thoroughly, do not claim authority under this law. They knew its intent was not a grant, but an expression of opinion on a constitutional construction. And as such it is entitled to the weight which may properly attach to the utterances made in congressional debates by members of Congress; which, judging from what I have heard from the President's counsel and Senators in this consultation, are not considered infallible—even less authoritative than judicial opinions—and, in my opinion, neither is entitled to any more respect than is required by the weight of the reasoning by which their opinions are supported. In the forum of reason is the tribunal where they and we, all are compelled to bring our opinions for arbitrament. As a legislative declaration of opinion injected into the body of a law, granting nothing and denying nothing, commanding nothing and prohibiting nothing, it is no more authoritative than the resolution of the Senate of February 21, 1868, informing the President that, by the removal of Mr. Stanton and the appointment of Mr. Thomas, he violated the Constitution and laws; and, in fact, is not entitled to so much respect as an authority, because in adopting the declaration in the law of 1779 there was in the House a very small majority in the affirmative, and the Senators were *equally divided*; while in the adoption of the declaration in the resolution twenty-eight Senators voted in the affirmative, and but six Senators voted in the negative; and in the House of Representatives the substantive allegation of the resolution, as set forth in the first and second articles of impeachment, was affirmed by a three-fourths majority.

Nor can the declaration cited by Senators from Kent's Commentaries, in which, referring to this debate, he is made to say that this legislative construction of the Constitution "has ever since been acquiesced in and acted upon as of decisive authority in the case," be adopted unquestioned. For he proceeds to say:

"It applies to *every other officer of the Government* appointed by the President and Senate whose term of duration is not specially declared."—*Kent's Commentaries*, page 19.

This would include all the officers of the Army and Navy; and it is known to every reader of the statutes that Congress has from the beginning of the Government to the present hour regulated by law the removals of this entire class of officers; and that Congress has, at various times, enacted laws regulating the mode of removal of civilians. Nor has it been held at any time that "declaring" by law the tenure of office—that is the term of years during which the commission may run—affects in any way the power of removal. For example, the law creating land officers, postmasters, territorial governors, judges, &c., and many others authorize appointments for fixed periods, and yet it has been uniformly maintained in practice that the President could at any time during the recess of the Senate remove them at will, and during the sessions with the concurrence of the Senate. It has been thus settled in practice that the limitation of a tenure to a fixed period does not affect the question of removal. Hence, as the commentator's facts prove to be untrue, his conclusions cease to have weight. So far as the uniform legislative action of the Government can settle a construction of the Constitution, it has been decided that Congress has the power to fix the tenure of all officers except judges, and also the manner of their removal.

And the executive construction is equally uniform and conclusive. It has been definitely settled in practice that the President may in the recess *remove* all officers at will except judges and other officers whose tenure and mode of removal is regulated by law, and that during the session removals may be made by the President only with the concurrence of the Senate.

It is extremely doubtful whether the framers of the Constitution intended to confer the power on the President to make removals during the recess. The language used, "*to fill up* vacancies which may *happen*," seems to imply the contrary. And they seem to have carefully provided against the assumption of this power under the plea of necessity, to protect the public interests from unworthy officers during the recess, by authorizing the President to convene the Senate in extra session *whenever* in his judgment the public interests require it, thus enabling him at all times to submit the question of changes to the judgment of that body.

But removals have been made in the civil service during the recess of the Senate by all the Presidents. This power under the Constitution has been during the whole period gravely questioned by the ablest statesmen and jurists. The practice has, nevertheless, obtained. No law existed until recently prohibiting it. It may, therefore, be conceded as settled that the President may, in the absence of law to the contrary, during the recess of the Senate, make removals from office. It is, however, equally well settled by precedent that the President cannot make removals, except in pursuance of law, during the session, otherwise than by appointments of successors, to be made "by and with the advice and consent of the Senate;" and that in making removals in the military service he must follow the mode indicated in the Articles of War and Army Regulations established by law.

This construction has been so uniform as to render it impossible for the learned counsel for the President during this protracted trial to produce even one well-authenticated case to the contrary. The case cited by them of the removal of Timothy Pickering, Secretary of State, by the elder Adams, is the only one which they claim to be an exception. And in that case the letter removing Mr. Pickering and the President's message nominating Mr. Marshall as his successor bear the same date. But if this case were admitted to be an exception to the general rule, it would violate all established principles of correct reasoning to assume that one exceptional case establishes the true construction of the Constitution, it being in direct conflict with the otherwise uniform practice, extending over the entire period of the history of the Government.

I therefore conclude that Andrew Johnson, President, violated the Constitution of the

United States and his oath of office in issuing his order, February 21, 1868, the Senate being in session, removing Edwin M. Stanton, Secretary of the Department of War, from said office; and that he is guilty of a high misdemeanor in office as charged in this article of impeachment, even if the law "regulating the tenure of certain civil offices," approved March 2, 1867, had never been enacted.

But I am unable to perceive any serious ambiguity in that statute. The authorities all agree that it is legitimate in construing any apparently obscure passage in the text of a new law to ascertain, first, the old law or usage; secondly, the evil or matter of complaint; thirdly, the remedy proposed in the new law. Now let us apply these rules to the statute of March 2, 1867:

First. Under the old law or usage the President had the right, as we have seen, to make removals at will during the recess of the Senate.

Secondly. The evil or subject-matter of complaint was that the President, now arraigned at your bar, had been, during the previous recess of the Senate, removing multitudes of faithful officers from their respective posts of duty and appointing untrustworthy successors, for purely partisan purposes, to aid him in making war on the measures adopted by Congress to secure the restoration of peace, harmony, and good government in the recently insurrectionary States.

Thirdly. The remedy proposed was to fix by law the tenure of civil offices and regulate the manner of removals, as had been done from the beginning in relation to military officers, so as to prevent the President from making removals at discretion, even during the recess, without the approval of the Senate. Hence the first section enacts:

"That every person holding any civil office to which he has been appointed, by and with the advice and consent of the Senate, and every person who shall hereafter be appointed to any such office, and shall become duly qualified to act therein, is, and shall be, entitled to hold such office until a successor shall have been in like manner appointed and duly qualified, except as herein otherwise provided: *Provided,* That the Secretaries of State, of the Treasury, of War, of the Navy, and of the Interior, the Postmaster General, and the Attorney General, shall hold their offices respectively for and during the term of • the President by whom they may have been appointed, and for one month thereafter, subject to removal by and with the advice and consent of the Senate."

Does it effect the objects proposed? It evidently embraces all existing civil officers appointed by the President, by and with the advice and consent of the Senate, as well as all who may hereafter be appointed. It is evidently not its purpose to *extend* the legal term of service of any of them, for section four provides:

"That nothing in this act contained shall be construed to extend the term of any office the duration of which is fixed by law."

But its intent is clearly twofold. *First,*

to prohibit *removals; secondly, to limit the. terms of service.* The prohibition to remove evidently applies to *all.* The limitation of the term is applied to the Secretaries of State, of the Treasury, of War, of the Navy, of the Interior, the Postmaster General, and the Attorney General, and none others. This analysis removes all ambiguity. The section provides that every civil officer appointed by the President, with the approval of the Senate, shall hold his office until his successor shall be in like manner appointed; that is, no removal shall take place except by the appointment, with the concurrence of the Senate, of a successor; provided, however, that the offices of heads of Departments shall terminate by operation of law in one month after the expiration of the presidential term. The assumption that any of the seven officers were intended to be excepted out of the general prohibition of removal at the will of the President alone is clearly inconsistent with the last clause of the proviso, which declares that those seven officers shall also be "subject to removal by and with the advice and consent of the Senate." For, if it was in fact, as contended, the intent of this proviso to except any of these officers from the general prohibition to remove by the President alone, why should it confer the authority to remove them with the concurrence of the Senate?

The learned casuistry to which we have listened over the construction of the phrase "term of the President by whom they may have been appointed" has, according to my apprehension, no application to the vital point in this controversy—*the prohibition of removal.* It relates to the *limitation of the term of service,* and nothing else.

I have not been able to perceive anything in the legislative history attending the passage of this act inconsistent with this construction. It is substantially this: the Senate passed the bill prohibiting the removal of all civil officers except the heads of Departments. The House struck out the exceptions; the Senate declined to concur; the House insisted. The bill was then sent to a joint committee of conference of the two Houses. They proposed a compromise, the House yielding something and the Senate yielding something. They finally agreed that the prohibition of removals by the President at discretion should apply to all, including heads of Departments, but that the termination of the period of service of the latter should be fixed at one month after the close of each presidential term. They so reported, and their report was adopted by both Houses.

I have now only to state that the President has officially construed the law as applicable to Secretary Stanton in his order of August 12, 1867, suspending him from office, as provided in the second section of this act, and in his letter addressed to the Secretary of the Treasury, informing that officer that he had suspended said Stanton, as directed by the eighth section of this act. The letter is in these words:

EXECUTIVE MANSION,
WASHINGTON, D. C., *August* 14, 1867.

SIR: In compliance with the requirements of the eighth section of the act of Congress of March 2, 1867, entitled "An act regulating the tenure of certain civil offices," you are hereby notified that on the 12th instant Hon. Edwin M. Stanton was suspended from office as Secretary of War and General Ulysses S. Grant authorized and empowered to act as Secretary of War *ad interim.*

I am, sir, very respectfully yours,
ANDREW JOHNSON.

Hon. HUGH McCULLOCH, *Secretary of the Treasury.*

He also admits its application to Stanton by sending to the Senate his message dated December 12, 1867, communicating to that body his reasons for the suspension, as directed by the second section. That he construed this law as applicable to Secretary Stanton, and willfully violated it, is also established by his answer to the first article of impeachment, as found in the record of the trial. He responds in these words:

"The respondent was also aware that this act [of March 2, 1867] was understood and intended to be an expression of the opinion of the Congress by which that act was passed, that the power to remove executive officers for cause might by law be taken from the President and vested in him and the Senate jointly."—*Impeachment Trial*, p. 24.

This would seem to settle the question of the President's *purpose.* He admits that he "was *aware*" that this act was understood and *intended* to be an expression of the opinion of Congress" that he could not remove executive officers without the concurrence of the Senate. Now, no one will be so hardy as to deny that the *intent* of a law is *the law* in very *essence* and *truth*, for the only object of the analysis of any law by court or commentaries is to ascertain, if possible, the *intent* of the Legislature enacting it.

That the President did proceed to inquire, as he asserts in this connection, whether the act was not capable of some other construction, and if in the course of this inquiry he did honestly conclude, as he asserts, that it was susceptible of another construction different from the admitted intent of Congress, so far from being a palliation, was a grave aggravation of his offense; for it is a declaration of a *purpose*to bend the law from its *true intent* to suit his wishes. He thus confesses that he *sought to evade* and did, as he thinks, evade the declared and admitted will of the Legislature.

With this admission in his official answer to this article before our eyes, there can be no doubt that he did with *malice prepense* violate the *true, known,* and *admitted intent* of this law. Believing as I do that the President did thus officially place the correct construction on said law, and that said law is in harmony with the Constitution, and that he did willfully violate its provisions, which violation is declared by said law to be a "high misdemeanor," I do not perceive how it is possible for a Senator, on his oath, to avoid finding him guilty as charged in the first article of impeachment.

In relation to the second article of impeachment, I may observe, the House of Representatives accuse the President of the committal of a high misdemeanor in office in appointing Lorenzo Thomas, Adjutant General United States Army, Secretary of War *ad interim* on the 21st day of February, 1868, there being no vacancy in said office, without the advice and consent of the Senate, the Senate being in session.

The President in his answer admits that he did issue the order of appointment, as charged, without the advice and consent of the Senate, the Senate being in session, (Impeachment Trial, p. 27,) and justifies it by declaring that there was at the time a vacancy in said office, and that—

"It was lawful according to a long and well-established usage to empower and authorize the said Thomas to act as Secretary of War *ad interim.*"

To support this justification, his counsel in the argument of this cause, and several Senators during this consultation, have cited two statutes which authorize temporary appointments. The first one was enacted May 8, 1792, and the second February 13, 1795. The first one is marked "obsolete" on the statute-book, and is admitted to have been repealed (if not before) by the act of February 20, 1863, which covers all the matter contained in the act of 1792, and is also inconsistent with it. This brings us to the consideration of the plea of authority to appoint Mr. Thomas to the office of Secretary of War *ad interim* during the session and without the consent of the Senate under the statute of 1795, even if a vacancy did legally exist. These are the exact words of the law:

"That in case of vacancy in the office of Secretary of State, Secretary of the Treasury, or of the Secretary of the Department of War, or of any officer of either of the said Departments, whose appointment is not in the head thereof, whereby they cannot perform the duties of their said respective offices, it shall be lawful for the President of the United States, in case he shall think it necessary, to authorize any person or persons, at his discretion, to perform the duties of the said respective offices until a successor be appointed or such vacancies be filled: *Provided*, That no one vacancy shall be supplied, in manner aforesaid, for a longer term than six months. Approved February 13, 1795."—*Statutes-at-Large*, vol. 1, page 415.

I notice that the Senator from Maine, [Mr. FESSENDEN,] in the observations submitted by him, has, as I think, misconstrued this law by omitting in the text, as cited by him, an entire clause, necessary to be considered in arriving at a correct construction. It is in these words: "Whereby they cannot perform the duties of their said respective offices." These are words of limitation which the judge or commentator has no right to ignore or erase. Had they been omitted by Congress in enacting the law—did they not stand as a part of it—the Senator's rendering would be less vulnerable. But, giving these words their usual meaning and force, his rendering is manifestly erroneous. Applying this law to the actual case at bar, and omitting unnecessary descriptive phrases, it will read:

"That in case of *vacancy* in the office of the Secretary of War, *whereby he cannot perform the duties* of his said office, it shall be lawful for the President of the United States, *in case he shall think it necessary*, to authorize any person, at his discretion, to perform the duties of the said office, &c.: *Provided*, That no one vacancy shall be supplied, in manner aforesaid, for a longer term than six months."

Now, it may be observed that there are two classes of vacancies known to the statutes, and which may occur in the administration of the Departments: *absolute legal vacancies* in office by death, resignation, or expiration of term of service, whereby there are no officers in existence for the respective offices; and *vacancies* occasioned by the *absence of officers* from their respective offices, on account of sickness or absence from the seat of Government. The question therefore arises *whether* the *vacancies* contemplated and provided for by this statute are of the first or of the second class, or whether both are included.

It appears to my mind perfectly clear that the first class are not intended to be included, and that the law is applicable only to cases of vacancy by the absence of officers from their offices, the said offices being legally filled, but the incumbents being incapable, for any sufficient reason, to perform their official duties.

To construe this statute so as to apply to absolute vacancies in office would, as it appears to me, make it both useless and unconstitutional. For, in case of an absolute legal vacancy in the recess of the Senate, the Constitution itself, in direct terms, authorizes the President to fill it temporarily, to continue for as long or as short a period as he may desire, not extending beyond the end of the next session of the Senate. Hence, if this law was intended to confer on the President the power to fill *legal* vacancies in office, occurring in the recess, it is nugatory—it is perfectly useless—for the President was previously vested by the Constitution with this authority.

And to assume that the intent of this law was to provide for absolute legal vacancies in office occurring during the session of the Senate would be clearly unconstitutional; for the Constitution provides, as we have seen, that the President "shall nominate, and by *and with the advice and consent of the Senate* shall appoint, all officers" whose appointment are not otherwise provided for in the Constitution itself, whether created by the Constitution or by law. The President must, therefore, obtain the consent of the Senate when in session before he can make an appointment to fill an absolute legal vacancy, with the exception of one class of officers only, *inferior* officers, who may be appointed by the President alone when Congress shall so provide by law. But the office of Secretary of War is not of this class. It is not an inferior office, and is declared by the law of 1789 to be a superior office, and the Secretary is styled "a principal officer." Congress could not, therefore, by law vest the appointment of this and similar officers exclusively in the President either for a short or a long period. To maintain that Congress could by law dispense with the advisory power of the Senate would be equivalent to a declaration that Congress could by law amend the Constitution or abolish it entirely; for if Congress could suspend one of its provisions, they may suspend any or all of them. This would be reducing the authority of that great charter to the grade of a statute only.

The limitation of such appointments to a period not exceeding six months could not change the constitutionality of the provision. For, if Congress could by a statute dispense with the advisory power over appointments during the sessions of the Senate for a single day, they could for a year or ten years or forever. It is not a question of *time* during which such appointment may run, but of constitutional power to deprive the Senate of an opportunity to exercise a judgment in the case. The Constitution vests this authority in the Senate, without regard to the length of *time* of the service of the appointee; and it does not confer the authority on the President to disregard it, nor on Congress the power to set aside either for a long or a short period.

Congress could, of course, abolish the War or any other Department created by law. They could also abolish the office of Secretary of War, or unite the War Department with some other Department temporarily or permanently, and require the head of that other Department to perform the duties of both, or might reduce it to the grade of a bureau in another Department, and authorize an inferior officer to perform the duties now devolving on the Secretary; and probably might, by law, authorize the President to do this at his discretion; but this is not what is claimed by the President under the law of 1795. He does not claim that this authorizes him to abolish the War Department or the office of Secretary of War, or to unite it with any other Department temporarily, or to devolve the duties of Secretary of War on the head of another Department, or to reduce it in grade and devolve its duties on an inferior officer. He claims that Congress has by this law, approved August 7, 1789, vested in him the right "to authorize *any person*" (adopting the words of the statute) "*at his discretion* to perform the duties of" Secretary of War during the session of the Senate, there being an actual legal vacancy in said office, for a period not exceeding six months.

Now, if this is the true meaning of this law,

it authorizes the President, as we have seen, to dispense with the advisory power of the Senate, when in session, in the appointment of a *great* officer to fill "a principal" office for a period of six months; and, as this would be in direct conflict with the Constitution, the law as thus construed must be void.

To give this law force, we are therefore compelled to construe the word "vacancy" mentioned in the act as meaning a *corporeal* vacancy—the *absence* of the *officer* from his office—the legal tenure still continuing in him as when the officer is out of the city; is disabled by insanity or sickness; is in custody or in prison, or is necessarily occupied with other duties. This interpretation is in perfect harmony with the literal and usual meaning of the word of the statute itself, "in case of vacancy in the office of Secretary" * * * * "of the Department of War" * * * * "*whereby 'he cannot perform the duties of'* his 'said office it shall be lawful for the President of the United States, in case he shall think it necessary, to authorize any person, at his discretion, to perform the duties of the said office,'" &c. And any other construction would render the qualifying phrase, "whereby they cannot perform the duties of their said respective offices," meaningless. It is a settled rule of construction that you must, if possible, give every word of a statute meaning and force.

But what meaning can be attached to this clause if applied to an actual legal vacancy, as by death, resignation, removal, or expiration of legal term of service. In such cases the officer, and his legal functions as such, have ceased to exist. There is no *officer* in existence. To apply these qualifying words in such cases, "whereby they cannot perform the duties of their said respective offices," is sheer nonsense. The law does not provide that in case of *any* vacancy, or *all* vacancies, but in case of vacancies of this description, "whereby the officers cannot perform the duties of their offices."

The same reasoning would apply to another qualifying phrase in this act, authorizing the President to make temporary appointments. It is in these words: "In case he shall think it necessary." How is it possible to apply this language to an actual legal vacancy in a superior office, such as Secretary of State, Secretary of War, &c. The necessity of having an officer to fill these great offices was settled by Congress when the law was enacted creating them. If an actual vacancy occurred the necessity of filling it could not be a question. But if the officer was sick or absent from the city, "whereby he could not perform the duties of his said office," the question of *necessity* for the appointment of some one, by detail or otherwise, to perform these duties, until he recovered or returned to his post, would arise. And no one would be a more fit person to judge of that necessity than the President.

I may observe here, in passing, that the allegation so frequently made during this trial by the President's counsel, and by Senators in this consultation, that "the practice" of making temporary appointments, the Senate being in session, to fill absolute legal vacancies in office, "has been frequent and unbroken, almost from the formation of the Government," is not supported by facts. I have examined, as carefully as my time would permit, all that long list of cases of temporary appointments, supposed by the President's counsel to bear on this case, as they stand recorded in the printed record of this trial, beginning on page 575 and ending on page 582, and find that nearly all of them were made, as the list itself shows, on account of the absence or sickness of the regularly appointed officer. And nearly all of the residue were made to fill vacancies occurring during the recess of the Senate, and I do not find a single case of temporary appointment to fill a vacancy occasioned by a removal made during the session of the Senate. I therefore conclude that no such case exists, or it would have been produced, as the learned and numerous counsel had full access to the records of the Departments and of the chief executive office.

Should it appear, therefore, that a case or two of temporary appointments had been made by previous Presidents, in a period of nearly eighty years, on account of an actual vacancy occurring by death or resignation, during the session of the Senate, it would not justify the unaccountable allegation of counsel and of Senators that the precedents were almost numberless, and that the chain was unbroken. Nor would one case or many of violated law, by others, if they really existed, justify the President in the performance of an illegal act. But, when his act is unsupported by a single case this attempt at justification is most remarkable and startling.

After giving this subject the most careful examination of which I am capable, I am compelled to come to the conclusion that if there had been an existing legal vacancy in the office of Secretary of War, the President had no authority under the statute of 1795, or any other law, the Senate being in session, to fill it in the mode charged in the second article of impeachment and admitted in the President's answer. Much less had he the right to both create and fill a vacancy as charged in the first and second articles.

These acts, whether taken jointly or separately, seem to me to be a clear violation both of the Constitution and the law. That they were performed by the President deliberately and willfully for the purpose of defeating the execution of the latter, according to its true intent and meaning, is, according to my judgment, fully established. I do not, therefore, see my way clear, under the solemnities of my oath, to find him innocent.

OPINION
OF
HON. GARRETT DAVIS.

The subject of impeachment is provided for in the Constitution by several clauses, which I will quote:

"The House of Representatives shall have the sole power of impeachment."

"The Senate shall have the sole power to try all impeachments. When sitting for that purpose they shall be on oath or affirmation. When the President of the United States is tried the Chief Justice shall preside; and no person shall be convicted without the concurrence of two thirds of the members present."

"The President, Vice President, and all civil officers of the United States, shall be removed from office on impeachment for and conviction of treason, bribery, or other high crimes and misdemeanors."

"Judgment in cases of impeachment shall not extend further than to removal from office and disqualification to hold and enjoy any office of honor, trust, or profit under the United States; but the party convicted shall, nevertheless, be liable and subject to indictment, trial, judgment, and punishment according to law."

Our system of impeachment has not been transferred from any other Government, nor was its organization confided to Congress; but the cautious statesmen who founded our Government incorporated it in and built it up as part of the Constitution itself. They enumerated its essential features and made it *sui generis.* 1. No person but civil officers of the United States are subject to impeachment. 2. The Senate is constituted the court of impeachment. 3. The Chief Justice of the United States is to preside over the court when the President is under trial, and the Vice President or President *pro tempore* of the Senate in all other cases. 4. No conviction can take place unless two thirds of the Senators present concur. 5. No impeachment can be made but for treason, bribery, or other high crimes and misdemeanors against the United States. 6. Judgment of impeachment cannot extend to death or other corporal punishment, or fine or imprisonment; but is restricted to removal from and disqualification to hold office; but the party convicted, nevertheless, to be liable and subject to indictment, trial, judgment, and punishment according to law. The offenders, offenses, court, and punishment are all distinctly impressed with political features.

But the prosecution has assumed two strange and untenable positions in the course of this trial. 1. That the Senate, in the performance of the present most important office and duty, is not a court. It is certainly not a *legislative* body, nor *exercising legislative* powers; it is not an advisory council connected in a common function with the President. What, then, is it? Most of the States had previously to the formation of the Constitution organized their several tribunals to try cases of impeachment, and by some they had been denominated *courts of impeachment*, and all had invested them with the powers and attributes of courts. They, were universally held to be courts. The Constitution invests the Senate with the *sole* power to try all impeachments. *To try* is to examine a case judicially by the rules of law, and to apply them to the legal evidence taken in the trial, and to render the judgment of the law upon the claims of the parties according to the evidence. The phrases "to try," "tried," "convicted," "conviction," and "judgment" are all used in the Constitution in connection with impeachment and the proceedings in it. Those words, in connection with their context, establish, organize, and describe a court; and, as applied to the Senate necessarily constitute it a court with jurisdiction to try all cases of impeachment.

The Senate now and for this occasion is a *court* of impeachment for the trial of the President of the United States, and, like all other courts, is bound by the law and the evidence properly applicable to the case.

The other novel position of the prosecution, that on this trial the Senate "is a law to itself," is still more extraordinary. The power conferred by the Constitution on the Senate when trying impeachments is limited and wholly judicial, and the idea of combining with it any legislative power whatever is not only without any warrant, but is in direct hostility to the fundamental principle of our Government, which separates and makes mutually impassable all its legislative and judicial power. But the position that the Senate, when trying an impeachment, is "a law to itself," is bound by no law, may decide the case as it wills, is illimitable and absolute in the performance of special, restricted, judicial functions in a limited government, is revoltingly absurd. On the trial of any impeachment the Senate has no more authority to make or disregard law than it has to make or disregard facts; and it would be as legitimate and proper and decorous for the Managers, in relation to the evidence in this case, to announce to the Senate, "You are witnesses to yourselves" as "You are a law to yourselves." No court has any right or power to make or disregard either law or evidence in the trial of any case; and a court which would act upon and avow that rule of conduct would be execrated by mankind. There is a particular and emphatic contrary obligation on this court, for each one of its members has individually made a solemn appeal to God "that in all things appertaining to the trial of the impeachment of Andrew Johnson, President of the United States, now pending, he will do impartial justice according to the Constitution and the laws."

One of the leading and inflexible laws which bind this court is embodied in the Constitution in these words:

"No person shall be removed from office but on impeachment for and conviction of treason, bribery, or other high crimes and misdemeanors."

That is the category of all impeachable offenses, and they must be acts declared by the law of the United States to be treason or bribery, or some other offense which it denominates a "high crime or misdemeanor." The laws which define impeachable offenses may be the Constitution, or acts of Congress, or the common law, or some other code, if adopted either by the Constitution or act of Congress. No common-law offense, as such merely, can sustain the impeachment of any officer; but to have that authority, it must have become a part of the law of the United States by being adopted by the Constitution or some act of Congress, and would have operation and effect only to the extent that it was consistent with the provisions, principles, and general spirit of the Constitution.

No respectable authority has ever maintained that all offenses merely against the common law, or merely against public morals or decency were impeachable under our Constitution. Story has argued, in support of the position, that some offenses against the common law, and not made so by act of Congress, are impeachable; but he states his premises so generally and vaguely that it is impossible to obtain a full and clear comprehension of his meaning. He neither asserts the broad proposition that all common-law offenses are impeachable, nor does he attempt to define or describe generally those that are; but contents himself with the position, vaguely and hesitatingly taken and maintained, that there are common-law offenses which are offenses against the United States and which are impeachable; but how or where or by what language of the Constitution, or law of Congress they become offenses against the United States he does not attempt to show. But he distinctly admits that to be impeachable the offense must be against the United States.

The idea of prosecuting and punishing an act as an offense, which no law has made an offense, all must reject. *Treason, bribery, high crimes, and misdemeanors* are technical terms, found in the common law, and that express certain classes of offenses. But the common law, in whole or part, is not *necessarily,* or *per se,* the law of the United States, and to become so must be adopted by the Constitution or an act of Congress, and not otherwise. There is no provision or words in the Constitution which expressly or by implication adopts the common law. When it was before the conventions of the States on the question of their ratification of it, that it did not adopt the common law was frequently and strenuously objected to, especially in the convention of Virginia; and no one denied the truth of that position. The courts, Federal and State, and the profession generally, have up to the present time held that there is no adoption of the common law by the Constitution of the United States, and there never has been any by act of Congress.

But this precise question has been decided by the Supreme Court in the negative, and more than once. Hudson & Goodwin were indicted under the common law, in the circuit court of the district of Connecticut, for a libel against the Government of the United States; and the case was taken up to the Supreme Court, which decided without any announced difference of opinion among its members, and with the full approbation of Pinckney, Attorney General, that the courts of the United States have no *common-law* jurisdiction in cases of *libel* or *any other crimes* against the United States; but, that by the principles of general law, they have the power to fine for contempt, to imprison for contumacy, and to enforce the observance of their orders, &c.; that the legislative authority of the Union must first make an act a *crime,* affix a punishment to it, and declare the court that shall have jurisdiction.— (7 Cranch, 32.) The court, in the case of the United States *vs.* Coolidge, (1 Wharton, 415,) being an indictment under the common law, for rescuing a prize at sea, recognized the authority of the previous case, and dismissed the indictment. Judge Story sat in both cases, and was the only judge who expressed a dissent in the latter case from the ruling of that court.

The common law, in whole or part, has been adopted by the constitutions or statutes of most of the States; but in Louisiana it has never been made to supersede the civil law, nor the Partidas in Florida. The courts of the United States recognize and adopt, not the criminal, but the civil portion of the common law, generally to the extent to which it has been appropriated by a State, in all cases arising in that State within their jurisdiction; but not as the *common law,* nor as the *law of the United States,* but as the law of the particular State. In States that have not appropriated the common law in whole or part, the United States courts adopt such other law generally as they have established for the government of cases arising in them respectively. But this adoption by the courts of the United States of the laws of the States never extends to criminal or penal cases, but is restricted to those of a civil nature. No State ever executes in any form the penal laws of another State, and the United States only their own penal laws, and they exist in no other form than acts of Congress.

The State of Maryland adopted the common law, and on the organization of the District of Columbia, Congress recognized and continued the laws of that State in so much of it as had been ceded by Maryland. But the laws so adopted by Congress were local to the Maryland portion of the District; they did not extend to the part of it ceded by the State of Virginia, in which Congress adopted and continued in the same way the laws of Virginia. As the laws of each State are local and distinctive, so are the laws of Maryland and Virginia which were adopted by Congress for the District of Columbia on its organization, local and distinctive to the portions of the District that were ceded by those States respectively.

Treason, bribery, and other offenses of the nature of high crimes and misdemeanors, to be impeachable, must be crimes against the general law of the United States, and punishable in their courts of the localities where committed. Thus, treason against the United States is an impeachable offense, whether it be committed in any State or Territory, or the District of Columbia; and so of any other act to be impeachable, it must be an offense by the laws of the United States, if perpetrated anywhere within its boundary. That an act done in the portion of this District, ceded by the State of Maryland, would be an impeachable offense, and a similar act done in any place beside in the United States, would not be impeachable, is sustained by neither law nor reason. Such an offense would be against the District of Columbia, not against the United States. The law of impeachment is uniform and general, not various and local, and it has no phase restricted to the District of Columbia as has been assumed by the prosecution.

Then, besides treason and bribery, which are impeachable by the Constitution, to make any other act an impeachable offense it must not only be defined and declared to be an offense, but it must be stamped as a *high crime or misdemeanor* by an act of Congress. The words "high crimes and misdemeanors" do not define and create any offense, but express, generally and vaguely, criminal nature ; and of themselves could not be made to sustain an indictment or other proceeding for any offense whatever; but a law must define an offense, and affix one of those terms to it, to make it a constitutional ground of impeachment. And this is not all; the offense in its nature must have the type of heinous moral delinquency, or grave political viciousness, to make an officer committing it amenable to so weighty and unfrequent a responsibility as impeachment. He may have been guilty of a violation of the Sabbath or of profane swearing, or of breaches of the mere forms of law ; and if they had been declared offenses by act of Congress, with the prefix of "high crime" or "high misdemeanor" attached to them, they would not be impeachable offenses. They would be too trival, too much wanting in weight and State importance to evoke so grave, so great a remedy. Nor would any crime or offense whatever against a State, or against religion or morality, be a cause for impeachment, unless such an act had been previously declared by a law of Congress to be a *high crime* or a *high misdemeanor*, and was in its character of deep turpitude.

It results from this view of the law of impeachment that, as none of the articles against the President charge him with treason or bribery, which are made impeachable offenses by the Constitution, they, or some one of them, must allege against him the doing of an act or acts which a law of Congress has declared to be an offense against the United States, and denominated it to be, and in its vicious nature it must be, a high crime or high misdemeanor, and that the President did that act with a criminal intent to violate the law, to authorize this court to convict him and pronounce judgment that he be removed from office.

I will now proceed to the examination of the offenses charged in the several articles. The first charges the President with the commission of a high misdemeanor in having sent a letter to Edwin M. Stanton, Secretary of the Department of War, dismissing him from office while the Senate was in session, in violation of the act of Congress "to regulate the tenure of certain civil offices."

Article two charges the President with the commission of a high misdemeanor, in having delivered his letter to Lorenzo Thomas directing him to assume possession of the War Department, and to perform its duties *ad interim*, the Senate being then in session, and without its advice and consent, there being no vacancy in the office of Secretary of the Department of War, in violation of his oath of office, the Constitution of the United States, and the act of Congress aforesaid.

Article four charges the President of unlawfully conspiring with Lorenzo Thomas, with intent, by intimidation and threats, to prevent Edwin M. Stanton, Secretary of War, from holding said office, in violation of the Constitution of the United States and the "act to define and punish certain conspiracies," whereby he committed a high crime in office.

Article six charges the President of having conspired with Lorenzo Thomas, by force, to seize, take, and possess the property of the United States, in the Department of War, in violation of the civil office tenure act, whereby he committed a high crime in office.

The third, fifth, seventh, and eighth articles charge the same matter, in somewhat different form, as is embodied in the other four articles; and I propose to consider the charges of the whole eight as growing out of the act of the President in sending his letter to Stanton removing him from the office of Secretary of War, and his letter to Thomas to take charge *ad interim* of it. Those two letters comprehend the substance of all the offenses charged against the President in the first eight articles.

The ninth article charges the President, as Commander-in-Chief of the Army, of having attempted to induce General Emory, an army officer, to disobey the law of Congress requiring army orders from the President, or Secretary of War, to be transmitted through the General of the Army, and was guilty thereby of a high misdemeanor in office.

To this article three answers may be made :

1. The act does not make an attempt to induce a military officer to disobey it, whether committed by the President or other person, any offense.

2. The evidence not only does not sustain, but disproves that charge against the President.

3. If the charge had been sustained by the proof, the President, as Commander-in-Chief, has the absolute and unquestionable right to issue military orders directly, and without the intervention of another officer, to any officer or soldier whatever; and the provision of the act on which this article is based, is an unconstitutional and flagitious attempt by Congress to subordinate, in a measure, the Commander-in-Chief to the General of the Army.

The tenth article is based wholly on passages taken from several public speeches made by the President, not in his official character but as a private citizen, to assembled crowds of the people, by whom he was called out and urged to address them. Whatever of improper matter, manner, or spirit are in those public addresses was provoked by gross insults then offered to him, which, though not a justification, is much palliation. The President was then exercising a right which our fathers held inviolable, and which they intended should never be invaded, and for the protection of which they made this special amendment to the Constitution:

"Congress shall make no law abridging the freedom of speech or the press."

For the Senate, as a court of impeachment, to set up to be "a law to itself," and impeach the President as guilty of a high crime and misdemeanor for exercising a liberty which the founders of our Government deemed so valuable, so necessary to the preservation of their freedom, as to declare in their fundamental law should never be abridged, would violate that fundamental law and shock the free spirit of America. The basing of an article of impeachment on those speeches of the President, is calculated to bring down upon the whole proceeding the suspicion and revulsion of a free people, and it ought to be dismissed from this court as containing no impeachable matter.

The eleventh article charges that Andrew Johnson, President of the United States, was guilty of a high misdemeanor in declaring and affirming in substance "that the Thirty-Ninth Congress of the United States was not a Congress of the United States authorized by the Constitution to exercise legislative power under the same, but, on the contrary, was a Congress of only part of the States." This is not the language proved in the case to have been used by the President on any occasion; and if he had used it, he could not be impeached for it, because there is no law which makes the use of such language by the President, or any person, a high crime or misdemeanor or any offense, and any act of Congress declaring it to be an offense would be unconstitutional and void as abridging the freedom of speech. This article also charges—

"That the said Andrew Johnson, President of the United States, did, unlawfully and in disregard of the requirement of the Constitution that he should take care that the laws be faithfully executed, attempt to prevent the execution of an act entitled 'An act regulating the tenure of certain civil offices,' by unlawfully devising and contriving means by which he should prevent Edwin M. Stanton from forthwith resuming the functions of the office of Secretary for the Department of War, notwithstanding the refusal of the Senate to concur in the suspension theretofore made by said Andrew Johnson of said Edwin M. Stanton from said office."

To this charge it may be answered—it is made in terms too general and vague to require any answer—that the unlawful means which the President devised and contrived to prevent Edwin M. Stanton from forthwith resuming the functions of the office of Secretary of War, are not described or set out by any language whatever; and that act or any law of Congress does not make the devising or contriving of any means to prevent Edwin M. Stanton or any other civil officer whom the President has removed from office, and in whose removal the Senate has refused to concur, from resuming the duties of the office from which he has been so removed, a high crime or misdemeanor, or any offense; and said civil-office-tenure bill, so far as it restricts the President's power to remove said Stanton, is not consistent with, but in derogation of, the Constitution, and null and void.

And the eleventh article charges also that Andrew Johnson, President of the United States, devised and contrived other unlawful means to prevent the execution of an act entitled "An act making appropriations for the support of the Army for the fiscal year ending June 30, 1868, and for other purposes;" and also to prevent the execution of an act entitled "An act to provide for the more efficient government of the rebel States." Upon this last charge it may be observed—there is no description or facts setting out the means which the President devised and contrived to prevent the execution of either of the acts therein referred to—that the devising and contriving means to prevent the execution of said acts, or either of them, is not made a high crime or misdemeanor by them, or any law; that there is no evidence that he did devise and contrive any means to prevent the execution of said acts, or either of them; and that the act first referred to, in the part which the President is charged to have violated, and the last act, wholly, are unconstitutional, null, and void. Thus, it is shown on these several grounds, that there is nothing in the eleventh article on which the President, can be impeached.

Some of the articles charge the President with the commission of high misdemeanors, and others of high crimes in the violation of his official oath and of the Constitution generally. The Constitution has no provision declaring a violation of any of its provisions to be a crime; that is a function of the legislative power, and it has passed no law to make violations of the Constitution, or of official oaths by the President, or any other officers crimes.

The articles of impeachment seem to be drawn with studied looseness, duplicity, and vagueness, as with the purpose to mislead; certain it is, if their matter charged to be criminal had been separately, concisely, and distinctly stated, this court, and especially its many members who are not lawyers, would have had a much more ready comprehension of it. I will not take up and consider the other articles *seriatim*, but will group their matter under three heads: 1. The removal of Mr. Stanton from the office of Secretary of War; 2. the designation of General Thomas to take charge of that office *ad interim*; 3. the alleged conspiracies of the President with Thomas to prevent by intimidation and force Stanton from acting as Secretary of War, and to take possession of the property of the United States in his custody. The letter of the President to Mr. Stanton, informing him that he was thereby removed from office as Secretary of War, is charged to be a high misdemeanor, and in violation of the act to regulate the tenure of certain civil offices.

The fifth and sixth sections of that act are the only parts of it which define and create any offenses, and I will quote them both in their order:

"If any person shall, contrary to the provisions of this act, accept any appointment to, or employment in any office, or shall hold or exercise, or attempt to hold or exercise any such office or employment, he shall be deemed, and is hereby declared to be guilty of a high misdemeanor," &c.

This provision might apply to General Thomas, the *ad interim* employé, but cannot include the President.

The sixth section enacts—

"That every removal, appointment, or employment made, had, or exercised, contrary to the provisions of this act, and the making, signing, sealing, countersigning, or issuing of any commission or letter of authority for or in respect to any such appointment or employment, shall be deemed, and are hereby declared to be, high misdemeanors," &c.

The President's letter to Mr. Stanton is not, in fact, his removal from office, though it was intended to procure it; but he refused obedience to it, persisted in holding the office of Secretary of War, and still continues in it and • the actual discharge of its duties. The President's letter to him did not remove him in fact, and if the civil-office-tenure act be constitutional it did not in law; and he is now, and has been ever since, notwithstanding the President's letter, dismissing him, in fact and law, in office. It is contended by the prosecution that the letter of dismission is against the Constitution and the law, and has no legal effect whatever. Stanton was at its date in fact in possession of the office and performing its duties, and has so continued to the present time, and on this theory of the prosecution there has been no removal of him in fact or in law. And if that theory be unsound, and the President have the

power by the Constitution to remove him, and the act of Congress proposing to restrict that power is consequently void, his removal was and is *de jure* valid. In one aspect there is a removal proper and constitutional; in the other there is no removal of Mr. Stanton.

But these are the great questions in the case? Is the first section of the civil-office-tenure act in conflict with the Constitution, void, and of no effect? Does that section cover the case of the removal of Mr. Stanton? Did the President, in writing the letter of removal from office to Mr. Stanton, and the letter to General Thomas, directing him to take charge of the office *ad interim*, willfully and with criminal intent violate the civil-office-tenure bill? These propositions comprehend the substance matter of the first eight articles.

The first section of that act is in these words:

"That every person holding any civil office to which he shall have been appointed by and with the advice and consent of the Senate, and every person who shall hereafter be appointed to any such office, and shall become duly qualified to act therein, is, and shall be entitled to hold such office until a successor shall have been in like manner appointed and duly qualified, except as hereinafter provided: *Provided*, That the Secretary of State, of the Treasury, of War, of the Navy, and of the Interior, the Postmaster General and the Attorney General shall hold their offices respectively for and during the term of the President by whom they may have been appointed, and for one month thereafter, subject to removal by and with the advice and consent of the Senate."

The Constitution creates a Congress in which it vests all the legislative power of the Government of the United States; a President in whom it vests all the executive power, and a Supreme Court, and authorizes inferior courts to be established by Congress, in which it vests all the judicial power—except that it provides that the Senate shall constitute a court of impeachment, with jurisdiction to try all civil officers who might be impeached by the House of Representatives, and to adjudge amotion from and disqualification to hold office. Neither department can rightfully, or without usurpation exercise any powers which the Constitution has vested in either of the other departments. Congress has the power, and is bound in duty to pass all laws necessary and proper to enable the President to execute the powers intrusted to him by the Constitution, and without which legislation there are many he could not execute, but it cannot confer on him any additional power, nor can it divest him of any. He forms a separate and coördinate department of the Government with Congress as another, and the courts as the third, and each derive all their powers from the Constitution alone. Neither is subordinate to the others, though the powers vested in Congress are the most various, extensive, vigorous, and popular, and necessarily it is the most aggressive and effective in its aggressions upon the other departments; the judiciary is the least so, though the inevitable tendency of all power, however lodged, is to augment itself.

The power of appointment to office exists

necessarily in all Governments, and is of an executive nature ; and if the Constitution had contained no particular provision on this subject its language, "the executive power shall be vested in a President of the United States of America," would have imported the power of appointing to office, and by implication would have vested it wholly in the President. But the effect of this general language is qualified by a special provision:

"And he [the President] shall nominate, and by and with the advice and consent of the Senate shall appoint, embassadors," &c.

This is restrictive and exceptional of the general power of appointment, previously by implication conferred on the President, and has no other operation than what is expressed in its words, and they being exceptional no implied power results from them against the general grant of power from which they make an exception. But the power of removal from office also, as necessarily as the power of appointment, exists in all Governments, and is no less an executive power. It is located somewhere in the Government of the United States, but being an executive power it cannot be in Congress, for legislative powers only are vested in that body. It is not established, or vested by any express or special provision of the Constitution, but is by the general language:

"The executive power shall be vested in a President of the United States of America."

The Constitution leaves the power of removal just as this general provision vests it, with the President alone. The power of Congress to make all laws which shall be necessary and proper for carrying into execution its enumerated powers, and all other powers vested by the Constitution in the Government of the United States, or any department or officer thereof, is purely a legislative power; and gives no authority to assume or interfere with any powers of the President, or the judicial department. Instead of being a power to assail them, its legitimate and literal office is to uphold their powers and to give facilities in their execution. That, or any other provision of the Constitution gives to Congress no warrant or pretext to interfere with the executive power of removal from office, vested by the Constitution in the President alone.

The power of removal and the power of appointment to office, though both executive, are in their nature distinct and independent of each other. One, the power of appointment, was treated specially and separately from the other in the Constitution, it associating the Senate with the President in its exercise. But for this particular regulation of the power of appointment, it is most probable that no question as to the other distinct power of removal from office would ever have been made ; and that all would have silently conceded that both powers being executive in their character, and all the executive power of the Government having been vested by the

C. I.—58.

Constitution in the President, they properly appertained to him alone, and he would never have been challenged in the sole and exclusive exercise of either. But however that may be, the truth of this proposition cannot be successfully controverted: the provision of the Constitution associating the Senate with the President in the power of *appointment*, does not invest it with the same, or any connection with the power of *removal*: or authorize Congress to pass the civil-office-tenure act, or any other act that would impair the President's sole power and right to exercise it.

But the whole subject of the power of removal from office came up for consideration in the First Congress, on the organization of the Department of Foreign Affairs, in 1789, and elicited a debate of great ability among the ablest men of the body, many of whom had been members of the Convention which framed the Constitution. Congress was much divided on the subject, but a majority of both Houses sustained the position that the Constitution conferred on the President the power to remove from office, and the contending parties made a compromise, by which the act organizing the Department recognized the power of the President to remove the head of this Department, in this language:

"The chief clerk, whenever the principal officer shall be *removed* from office by the *President* of the United States, or in any other case of vacancy, shall, during such vacancy, have the charge and custody of all records, books, and papers appertaining to the said Department."

The supporters of the exclusive power of the President were opposed to any language being used in the act that *seemed to confer* this power on the President, and its opponents accepted language that conceded and recognized the President's power of removal without expressly deducing it from the Constitution.

The act establishing the Department of War, with a provision in the same language recognizing the power of the President to remove the Secretary, was passed at a subsequent day of the same session, with but little and no serious opposition.

Both those acts formally admit the sole power of the President to remove the heads of the respective Departments, but neither of them contains any language to confer that power on the President. The supporters of the principle that the Constitution vested it solely in him rejected from the bill organizing the Department of Foreign Affairs all language that seemed to confer it upon the President, and claimed and determined to maintain it as one of his powers solely from the Constitution; and the opponents of this principle, being willing to concede the power to the President, if the acts did not expressly state the power to be conferred on him by the Constitution, they were passed in their existing form, recognizing it as a presidential power to remove both Secretaries. The acts were not intended to confer this power on the President; they have no language whatever to that effect, yet they concede that he possessed it; and he could derive it only from the Constitution. This was as certain an assertion and establishment of the sole constitutional power of the President to remove from office, as if it had been expressed in the most direct terms; and no attempt has ever, before the passage of the civil-office-tenure bill, been made in Congress to disturb this question as thus settled.

From that time, every President has claimed and exercised the sole power of removal at all times as an executive power conferred by the Constitution. The great commentators on it, Kent, Story, and Rawle, have treated this power as belonging to the President alone by the provisions and effect of the Constitution itself, settled by the acts of Congress of 1789, the uniform and unchallenged practice of the Government, and the general acquiescence of the country. The Supreme Court has repeatedly, and without doubt or hesitation, recognized it as an established constitutional principle; and Chief Justice Marshall many times, in his opinions, refers to it, as he does to the other and unquestioned powers of the President. Hamilton and Madison were among its great authors and firm defenders; it was conceded to be a settled principle by Clay, Calhoun, Benton, Wright, Clayton, and all the statesmen of America down to the passage of the civil-rights bill; and Mr. Webster maintained, adhered to it, and advocated its exercise, while the Senate was in session and at all times, as Secretary of State under President Tyler. No attempt had ever before been made to arrest or qualify its unconditional exercise by the President, as well when the Senate was in session as when it was not. The reason of America, guided by principle, authority, and experience, was unwilling to divest, unsettle, or change this presidential power by act of Congress or alteration of the Constitution because of being satisfied that it was essentially of the nature of an executive power and absolutely necessary to enable the President to perform his greatest duty, to see that the laws be faithfully executed. If a controverted constitutional question can ever be settled, the power of the President to remove from office at his own will has been beyond further legitimate question.

The sixth section of the civil-office-tenure act before quoted declares that—

"Every removal, appointment, or employment, made, had, or exercised contrary to the provisions of this act, and the making, signing, sealing, or countersigning of any commission or letter of authority for or in respect to any such appointment or employment, shall be deemed, and are hereby declared to be, high misdemeanors," &c.

But, if the Constitution invests the President with the sole and exclusive power to remove all the officers referred to in said act, his exercise of that power at all times is legitimate and makes a vacancy in the office, which his duty requires him to fill according to the Constitution and the laws; and an act of Congress which by its terms so provides as to strip him of that power, in whole or part, and to make his performance of duty after its exercise a crime, is unconstitutional and void. The exercise of a constitutional power and the performance of constitutional duty by the President can be made neither criminal nor punishable either by impeachment, or fine and imprisonment.

If President Johnson has from the Constitution the sole power to remove from office, his letter to Mr. Stanton dismissing him from the office of Secretary of War could not be made a crime by any act which Congress could pass; and it produced a vacancy in the office which his action, in some form, was necessary to fill; and, in the meantime, it was his duty to supply the vacancy in the office temporarily according to law.

Very soon after the Government went into operation, vacancies by death and otherwise occurred in various offices; and, whether it was during the recess or session of the Senate, the President was frequently not prepared to fill them properly by appointment and commissions to terminate at the end of its next ensuing session, or to make a nomination to it for its advice and consent, from a want of a knowledge of men, and many other causes. To meet this temporary exigence Congress, in an act passed in May, 1792, made this provision:

"That in case of the death, absence from the seat of Government, or sickness of the Secretary of State, Secretary of the Treasury, or of the Secretary of the Department of War, or of any officer of either of said Departments whose appointment is not in the head thereof, whereby they cannot perform the duties of their respective offices, it shall be lawful for the President of the United States, in case he shall think it necessary, to authorize any person or persons, at his discretion, to perform the duties of the said respective offices until a successor shall be appointed."

This law is strictly within the power of Congress:

"To make all laws which shall be necessary and proper for carrying into execution the powers vested by the Constitution in the President."

It confers no new power upon him; all the executive power of the Government had been vested in him by the Constitution, and this act only furnished him facilities for its proper and convenient execution.

But this law was essentially defective; it was limited to the three Departments first organized—State, Treasury, and War—and to vacancies in office occasioned by death, absence from the seat of Government, or sickness. Other legislation was necessary, and in February, 1795, Congress passed this other law:

"That in case of vacancy in the office of Secretary of State, Secretary of the Treasury, or of the Secretary of the Department of War, or of any officer of either of the said Departments whose appointment is not in the head thereof, whereby they cannot perform the duties of their respective offices, it shall be lawful for the President of the United States, in case he shall think it necessary, to authorize any person or persons, at his discretion, to perform the duties of said respective offices, until a successor be appointed or such vacancy filled: *Provided,* That no one vacancy shall be supplied in manner aforesaid for a longer period than six months."

It will be observed, that this second law covers the whole ground, and more, occupied by the first; it applies to the same three Departments, none others being then organized; but it is extended beyond vacancies occasioned by death, absence from the seat of Government, or sickness, and provides for *all vacancies, from whatever causes produced,* and limits the continuance of such supplies to six months.

But this legislation in time became incomplete, as it did not provide for this supply of temporary service in the Navy, Post Office, and Interior Departments, and the office of Attorney General, when vacancies should occur in them. But, nevertheless, in consideration of the special requisition of the Constitution, that the President should see that the laws be faithfully executed, that all the executive power of the Government was vested in him, and from the necessity of the case, every President from the passage of the first act of 1792 exercised the power of designating some person for the supply temporarily, when vacancies occurred, not only in the Foreign, Treasury, and War Departments, but also in all the other Departments; and there are many instances of such appointments spreading over that whole period. These temporary appointments were not provided for by the Constitution, but from time to time by the laws of Congress which regulated them; and they were in truth not *appointments to office,* but a designation of persons to supply the places and perform the duties temporarily of offices, in which vacancies occurred, until they could be filled by regular appointments; and their necessity and validity were questioned by no one.

But in February, 1863, Montgomery Blair, Postmaster General, resigned his office during the session of the Senate, and President Lincoln designated an Assistant Postmaster General to perform the duties *ad interim* of Postmaster General, and afterwards sent a special message to Congress, then in session, asking its attention to the fact, that the laws of Congress in relation to such appointments, applied only to the Foreign, Treasury, and War Departments, and recommended the passage of an act to extend them to the other Departments of the Government. Thereupon Congress passed the act containing these provisions:

"That in case of the death, resignation, absence from the seat of Government, or sickness of the head of any executive Department of the Government, or of any officer of either of said Departments whose appointment is not in the head thereof, whereby they cannot perform the duties of their respective offices, it shall be lawful for the President of the United States, in case he shall think it necessary, to authorize the head of any other executive Department, or other officer in either of said Departments whose appointment is vested in the President, at his discretion, to perform the duties of the said respective offices until a successor be appointed, or until such absence or

inability by sickness shall cease: *Provided,* That no one vacancy shall be supplied in manner aforesaid for a longer period than six months.

"Sec. 2. *And be it further enacted,* That all acts or parts of acts inconsistent with the provisions of this act are hereby repealed."

I have embodied in this opinion the whole of the three acts of Congress, authorizing the temporary supply, or *ad interim* appointments to the several Departments of the Government. The last act only has express words of repeal, and they are restricted to acts or parts of acts that are inconsistent with its provisions. It provides in general language for the supply of vacancies occurring in all the Departments, and the spirit and meaning of the provision will also include the office of Attorney General; it, however, does not apply to *all vacancies* that may occur in them, but only to such as are caused by "death, resignation, absence from the seat of Government, or sickness." It makes no provision whatever for vacancies resulting from other causes, but, like the act of 1792, is defective in this respect; that act having provided only for vacancies produced by death, absence from the seat of Government, or sickness, and this act making provision but for one additional class of vacancies, by death; both omitted vacancies by removal and expiration of term of office.

The chief purpose of the act of 1795 was to supply the defect of the act of 1792, in the class of vacancies, and it was made to extend to vacancies generally, all vacancies that might occur from any cause; but, like the previous act, it extended only to the Departments of Foreign Affairs, of the Treasury, and of War, being all the Departments then organized. If this provision of the act of 1795, had embodied words which would have applied it to such other Departments of the Government as might thereafter be created, there would have been no necessity for the act of 1863, and there never would have been any thought of it. The act of 1795, comprehending vacancies from *every cause*—expiration of the term of office, removal, or any other possible cause—and the act of 1863 providing only for such as were produced by death, resignation, absence from the seat of Government, and sickness, the act of 1795, so far as it provides for vacancies from expiration of official term or removal from office, is not inconsistent with the act of 1863, and therefore, to that extent, is not repealed by it, and governs the case of the removal of Stanton and the letter of the President to General Thomas directing him to take charge *ad interim* of the War Department. If there was a vacancy it was produced by presidential *removal;* and the designation by the President of General Thomas or *any other person* for the temporary performance of its duties was authorized by the law of 1795, and if there was no vacancy in the office there could be and was no appointment to or employment of Thomas in it, as Stanton was never out and he never in actually; and the letter of the President to him being neither appointment to or employment in the office, and having no validity or effect, its simple delivery to Thomas constitutes no crime for punishment by impeachment, or trial, judgment, and sentence in a criminal court. It is the *appointment* or *employment*, not the abortive effort to do either, by the President that is the offense.

It is admitted, that if the President's letter to Thomas had been addressed to any officer of either of the Departments, or he had filled an office in one of them, it would not have been in conflict with the act of 1863, and would have been authorized by the act of 1795. As it had no effect to put Stanton out or Thomas in office, and no more results were produced by it than if it had never been written, can statesmen, Senators, and judges announce to the nation and the world that the writing of this letter is a high crime and misdemeanor, and sufficient ground for the impeachment of the President of the United States?

There is another constitutional principle which prevents the civil-office-tenure act from governing the case of Stanton. He was appointed by President Lincoln in his first term, and by the language of his commission was to hold his office during the pleasure of the President. All concede that the law, constitutional or statutory at that time, and down to the passage of the civil-office-tenure bill, authorized the President to remove Stanton from office whenever he willed to do so.

But it is contended, that this act changed the tenure and conditions by which Stanton held his office, from an indefinite term and presidential will to a certain term, and the overruling of the presidential by the senatorial will; that he held his office until the expiration of one month from the 4th of March, 1869, when the four years for which Mr. Lincoln was elected the second time would end, and Mr. Stanton's term as Secretary of War would thus continue until April 6, 1869, during which period he could not be removed by the President without the permission of the Senate. This is not the appointment, the ordination into the office of Secretary of War of Stanton as President Lincoln made it, but a new and essentially different one; and who conferred it upon him? Not the President, by and with the advice and consent of the Senate, but Congress, by the form of a legislative act. It is an indirect attempt by the legislative department of the Government to strip the executive department, of a material portion of the power of appointment to office, and to invest one of its own branches with it, and this against the presidential veto. To give Mr. Stanton, or any officer in office, the benefits of the new conditions and tenure organized by the civil-office-tenure act, requires a new appointment to be made by the President, with the advice and consent of the Senate, and not by Congress in the form of an act of legislation. To confer on him these cumulative benefits would require a cumulative appointment and commission, in the form and by the authority prescribed by the Constitution.

But another ground of the defense against the articles based on the removal of Mr. Stanton is, that his case does not, and was not, intended to come within the language and operation of the civil-office-tenure act.

From the terms, provisions, and history of the passage of that act through the two Houses of Congress, it is plain that that body adopted the general purpose of requiring the concurrent action of the Senate to enable the President to remove the officers designated in it; but intended so far to modify that purpose as to allow to every President, as his personal and official prerogative, to make *one* selection of *all* the members of his Cabinet. No one will deny that this is the general rule established by the act; and to give it practical effect it provides that the term of office of the chiefs of the several Departments, shall end one month after the term of the President by whom they may have been appointed. The obvious intention was that no President should be bound to continue officers between whom and himself such important and confidential relations must necessarily subsist, who had not been chosen by him, but that he should have one choice for each office, and be held to it until the Senate should give its consent that he might make another.

This right is accorded to him not by express language, but by implication so clear as to admit of no doubt; and he possesses it as the portion of his before general power of removal, of which this act does not attempts to deprive him—it does not confer, or attempt to confer it upon him, but leaves him in possession of it. The act is framed on the concession of the then existing power of the President, to remove the officers for whose cases it provides; and after declaring a general rule for them, excepts from its operation the Cabinet officers, and makes for them a special rule, which is to continue to operate in relation to each one for one month after the expiration of the term of the President by whom he was appointed; and then leaves him subject to the President's sole and unqualified power of removal as it existed before the act. The President may then permit him to remain in office, or may remove him at his pleasure, whether the Senate is in session or not. After removing him the President may designate *any person* to perform the duties of the office *ad interim* for six months, by which time he must make a nomination to the Senate for its advice and consent.

The general and unrestricted power to remove from office had been exercised, without question, by every President of the United States up to the date of the civil-office-tenure act, including Tyler, Fillmore, and Johnson, Vice Presidents, on whom the Constitution had devolved the office of President.

The first section of the civil-office-tenure act embodies all of it that bears upon the question, whether the case of Mr. Stanton is comprehended by it. By this law each Cabinet officer holds his place for one month after the expiration "of the term of the President by whom he was appointed;" it is, therefore, necessary to know what is meant by the words, "the term of the President."

Section one, article two, of the Constitution, is in these words:

"The executive power shall be vested in a President of the United States of America. He shall hold his office during the term of four years, and, together with the Vice President, chosen for the same time, be elected as follows."

All authorities say that "term is the time for which anything lasts." In our Government no office lasts after the death of the termor, or passes to heirs, devisees, or executors, but reverts immediately to the State. The tenure of some offices is for life, others for a definite number of years, and some during the pleasure of the appointing power; but the term of all ends also inexorably upon the death of the incumbent. The term of the many marshals and other officers, who are appointed for four years could, with as much reason and truth, be said to continue to the end of that time, though the incumbents died before its lapse, as it can be said that the term of a President, who died early in the four years for which he was elected, runs on until the expiration of the four years. When a man in office dies that closes his term; and so soon as another is appointed to it his term commences.

Mr. Lincoln was elected President and Mr. Hamlin Vice President for a common term of four years, commencing on the 4th of March, 1861, and as both survived it the term of each ended by lapse of time, March 3, 1865. The second term of Mr. Lincoln for four years, and Mr. Johnson's term for the same time, began the 4th of March, 1865, and both ended April following; Mr. Lincoln's by his death, and Mr. Johnson's by the office of President being devolved on him, and he thereby ceasing to be Vice President under this provision of the Constitution:

"In case of the removal of the President from office, or of his death, resignation, or inability to discharge the powers and duties of the said office, the same shall devolve on the Vice President."

Mr. Johnson become President by having been elected Vice President, and by the operation of the Constitution, upon the death of the President, Mr. Lincoln. He is as much the President as if he had been elected to that office instead of to the Vice Presidency. His presidential term commenced when he was inaugurated into the office, and is to continue to *last* for the residue of the term for which Mr. Lincoln was elected President and he Vice President. His presidential term, though not so long, is as definite as Mr. Lincoln's was; both by the Constitution were to continue until the 4th of March, 1869, and both, by the same law, were subject to be determined before that time by their "removal from office, death, res-

ignation, or inability to discharge the powers and duties of the office." The Presidency, while Mr. Johnson has been filling it and performing its duties under the Constitution, is as much his office as it was Mr. Lincoln's when he held the same relation to it; and the proposition that this time of Mr. Johnson in the office is not his *term* but a *continuation of Mr. Lincoln's term*, is not sustained by the Constitution, fact, or reason.

But if it were a continuation of Mr. Lincoln's term, it would be of his second, not his first term, which the Constitution inexorably closed on the 3d March, 1865; and he having been reëlected his second term commenced the next day. If Mr. Johnson be serving out Mr. Lincoln's term, it is not his *first one*, for that is "with the years before the flood," but his second term; and Mr. Johnson would be invested with every right and power in it to which Mr. Lincoln would be entitled; and among them would be the power and the right to remove Mr. Stanton from the office of Secretary of War. This act provides, that the chief officer of the seven principal Departments of the Government, shall respectively hold their offices according to the tenure established by it, for and during *the term* of the President by whom they may have been appointed. This is a permanent and uniform law, and the measure established by it being the term of the President by whom the officer was appointed, and one month thereafter, and Mr. Stanton having been appointed Secretary of War by Mr. Lincoln during his first term in January, 1862, and that term having expired with the 3d of March, 1865, if Mr. Lincoln had lived until the passage of this act, under it he would have had the power to remove Mr. Stanton, and any other of his Cabinet officers whom he had not appointed in his second term, and this right passed to President Johnson.

There are several purposes apparent on the face of the civil-office-tenure bill: 1. That all officers appointed by and with the advice and consent of the Senate should hold their places until it should approve their removal. 2. That the Cabinet officers of the President should be so far exceptional to this rule, that all Presidents should have the privilege and the power to make one selection for each of those offices. 3. That, having made a choice, he shall be held to it until the Senate shall have given him its consent to make another choice. This arrangement in relation to the President and his Cabinet was, doubtless, made upon some reasons; and all concede that it applies to every President chosen by the Electoral College; and what reasons are there that make it necessary and proper for the administration of a President so elected that do not apply with equal force to one upon whom the Constitution has devolved the office on the death of a President with whom he was elected to the Vice Presidency? The plain letter and meaning of the Constitution and this act of Congress, assure this right to President Johnson, and it cannot be wrested from him without doing violence to both Constitution and law. If he had given in his adhesion, and plainly and palpably exercised this power for the benefit of the party which passed the law, by removing one of his Secretaries who is opposed to that party, and had, nominated to the place one of their faithful and trusted men, would his right to make the removal have been questioned?

After the best inquiry of which I am capable, I think these positions to be true beyond reasonable doubt:

1. That the President, by the well-settled principle of the Constitution, possesses, as one of his executive powers, the sole and exclusive power of removing all officers, as well when the Senate is in session as when it is not.

2. That the provision of the civil-office-tenure act, which requires the President to report to the Senate his removal of certain officers, and its advice and concurrence to make the removal complete and effective, is in derogation of that constitutional power of the President, and is, therefore, unconstitutional and void.

3. That the case of the removal of Stanton does not come within the provision, spirit, and meaning of the civil-office-tenure act.

4. That President Johnson had the power and the right to remove Stanton as Secretary of War; and having removed him, and thereby caused a vacancy, he had the power, under the act of 1795, and it was his duty to supply that vacancy temporarily; and his designation of General Thomas to take charge of the office *ad interim* was a proper exercise of power. Consequently neither the removal of Stanton, nor the *ad interim* appointment of Thomas by President Johnson, was an impeachable offense, but a legitimate exercise of power.

There is then left for my examination, only those articles of impeachment which embrace the matter of the conspiracies with General Thomas charged against the President. There is but one law of Congress against conspiracies, which was passed in 1861, and is in these words:

"That if two or more persons within any State or Territory of the United States shall conspire together to overthrow or to put down or to destroy by force the Government of the United States, or to levy war against the United States, or to oppose by force the authority of the Government of the United States, or by force to prevent, hinder, or delay the execution of any law of the United States, or by force to seize, take, or possess any property of the United States against the will or contrary to the authority of the United States, or by force or intimidation or threats to prevent any person from accepting or holding any office or trust or place of confidence under the United States; each and every person so offending shall be guilty of a high crime, and upon conviction thereof in any district or circuit court of the United States having jurisdiction thereof, or district or supreme court of any Territory of the United States having jurisdiction thereof, shall be punished by a fine not less than $500 and not more than $5,000, or by imprisonment, with or without hard labor, as the court shall determine, for a period not less than six months nor greater than six years, or by both such fine and imprisonment."

This was a war measure passed at the beginning of the rebellion, and was directed against rebels and traitors, and their abettors at that time and in the future. It was never intended, and is a perversion of that law to attempt to apply it to the case of a removal by the President of an officer of the Government, and his direction to the person whom he had designated to supply temporarily the vacancy to take possession of the office, and his application to the person removed to turn over to him the books, property, &c., appertaining to the office.

All the offenses enacted by that law require, as an essential constituent of them, that the persons committing them shall conspire together to do the several acts which are made criminal with force or intimidation or threats; and in the absence of that purpose there is no crime. The charges against the President are, in the fourth article, that he did unlawfully conspire with one Lorenzo Thomas, and with other persons to the House of Representatives unknown, with intent, by intimidation and threats, unlawfully to hinder and prevent Edwin M. Stanton, Secretary of War, from holding said office; in the fifth article, that he did unlawfully conspire with one Lorenzo Thomas, and with other persons to the House of Representatives unknown, to prevent and hinder the execution of an act entitled "An act regulating the tenure of certain civil offices;" in the sixth article, that he did unlawfully conspire with one Lorenzo Thomas by force to seize, take, and possess the property of the United States in the Department of War; in the seventh article, that he did unlawfully conspire with one Lorenzo Thomas with intent unlawfully to seize, take, and possess the property of the United States in the Department of War.

As to the fifth and seventh articles, they charge no intent or purpose on the part of the President of doing the things therein specified with force, intimidation, or threats; which being of the essence of said offenses and omitted, no offenses are charged; and as to those articles, and also the fourth and sixth, there is no evidence that the President entered into any conspiracy with General Thomas, or any persons, to do the things set forth in said articles; or that he intended, advised, or sanctioned the use of any force, intimidation, or threats in doing them. The whole case against the President in connection with the matters charged in those four articles is, that he wrote a letter of the usual tenor to Mr. Stanton, removing him from the office of Secretary of War, and a letter to General Thomas, notifying him of his designation to supply the vacancy temporarily, and directing him to take charge of the office and enter upon its duties; all of which, by the Constitution and laws, he had the power and the right to do. There is no evidence that he intended, advised, or sanctioned the use of any force, intimidation, or threats in connection with these transactions.

There is nothing in the case to sustain the fourth, fifth, sixth, and seventh articles, and with the others they all fall together.

Upon the grounds I have stated I reach the conclusion, that the defense of the President is full and complete; but there are other grave and weighty reasons why this court should not proceed to his conviction, that I will now proceed to consider.

The Senate is sitting as a court of impeachment, to try articles preferred by the House of Representatives against the President of the United States. Each member has taken a special oath prescribed by the Constitution, and in these words:

"I solemnly swear that in all things appertaining to the trial of the impeachment of Andrew Johnson, President of the United States, now pending, I will do impartial justice according to the Constitution and the law: so help me God."

None of his acts can be considered but those which are set forth against him in the articles as offenses, and he can be convicted only upon such as are defined and declared by the laws of the United States to be high crimes or misdemeanors, and which are in their nature and essence offenses of that character. This court is bound to try these articles of impeachment by the same laws and rules of evidence, substantially, which would govern an ordinary criminal court on the trial of indictments against Andrew Johnson for the same offenses—except in the matter of judgment against him, which here would be more grievous.

I will quote from Blackstone's Commentaries a fundamental principle, which is found in all works on criminal law, is recognized in every criminal court in America, and which should guide and control this court in the pending trial:

"And as vicious will without a vicious act is no civil crime, so, on the other hand, an unwarrantable act without a vicious will is no crime at all. So that to constitute a crime against human laws there must be first a vicious will, and secondly, an unlawful act consequent upon such vicious will."

This principle, that to the unlawful act there must attach a criminal intent or purpose, which prompted the commission of the act, is the guiding light of all courts: a person doing the act charged to be a crime, in its absence, might be guilty, but it would be without criminality. The law generally infers the criminal intent from the unlawful act, but it always permits the accused party to show by proof the absence of the criminal intent, which is generally an easier task in relation to offenses merely *mala prohibita*, than in those which are also *mala se*. All the offenses charged against the President are merely and strictly *mala prohibita*.

If the civil-office-tenure bill on its face is so ambiguous and uncertain as not to inform an officer of Government possessed of a good common understanding, with reasonable certainty, whether or not it did comprehend the case of Mr. Stanton, and forbid his removal from office by the President, that act being new and never having received a judicial construction; and Andrew Johnson was under trial on indictment in an ordinary criminal court for the violation of that act, in the removal of Mr. Stanton, the court on motion would instruct the jury to acquit.

If the question whether that act does not trench on a great constitutional power of the President, and is not therefore void, be one of doubt and difficulty, and President Johnson desired to have that question solved correctly; and to that end consulted the Attorney General and all the other members of his Cabinet, and their opinion was unanimous that it was unconstitutional; and he was counseled by them all, including Mr. Stanton, to veto the act upon that ground, and one of his purposes in removing Mr. Stanton was to make a case for the Supreme Court, in which its constitutionality should be decided, universal reason and justice would pronounce, that in writing his letter to Mr. Stanton dismissing him from office, the President had no criminal intent, and did not commit an impeachable offense.

The evidence on this point which the prosecution presented, and which was admitted without objection, would probably be sufficient with most minds to exculpate the President from all criminal intent; but the most satisfactory proof that could have been made upon it, and which was clearly competent, was the evidence of the members of the Cabinet, which a majority of this court ruled it would not hear. A criminal court would not have excluded this evidence, or, if having done so inadvertently, on conviction by the jury, it would of its own motion award a new trial. In the face of so grave an error committed by this court, and affecting so materially the defense of the respondent, it would be a great wrong to him and the country to proceed to his conviction.

The powers of our Government are carefully and wisely divided out among the three departments, and the lines of separation are in some cases so indistinct that it is difficult to avoid overstepping them. A just and patriotic President would not willfully infringe the constitutional powers and rights of Congress; nor would that body, if composed of such men, make any intentional aggression upon those confided to the President. I have observed no such disposition on the part of the present executive head; and the question between him and Congress growing out of the civil-office-tenure bill, he desired to have submitted to and decided by the Supreme Court, as has been satisfactorily proved in this case. He took legal advice, and was informed that under existing laws he could not have any proceeding instituted to determine it, which could be taken to the Supreme Court and be tried by it until about the time or after the expiration of his presidential term. He had no remedy by which he could test the question in a reasonable time.

Congress and the President both should have desired and have sought the settlement of this, and all other questions of controverted power between them, by the judgment of that tribunal which the Constitution had designed for that purpose. In a few hours of any day, Congress could have framed and passed a law which would have enabled the Supreme Court summarily to have got possession of and to decide promptly this, and all other questions between it and the President; and such settlement of the disputed boundaries of their respective powers, would have been accepted by the people generally, and as to those questions would have given repose to the country. But instead of such wise and peaceful legislation, Congress was exhausting all its ingenuity and all its resources to make its aggressions upon the Executive Departments successful and complete; and so to organize, fetter, and intimidate the Supreme Court, as to prevent it from interfering to perform its great office of settling such questions by the Constitution, law, and reason.

But Mr. Stanton sued out a criminal warrant against General Thomas to protect himself against intrusion into the War Office; and when the President heard of this proceeding he expressed his gratification, knowing that the question of the validity of his removal of Mr. Stanton would come up on the hearing of a writ of *habeas corpus* that might be sued out by General Thomas. The latter executed bond with surety to appear before Judge Cartter to answer the complaint of Stanton, and at the appointed time appeared before the Judge with his surety, who surrendered him to the court. It was the plain duty of Judge Cartter to have ordered General Thomas into the custody of the marshal, or to prison; but he did neither, because either would have been a restraint of his liberty and have made a ground for suing out a writ of *habeas corpus* for a judicial inquiry into the cause of his detention. The case, immediately after hearing by the judge before whom the writ might be returned, could be taken to the Supreme Court, heard at once, and the questions of right between Stanton and Thomas to the War Office and the constitutionality of the civil-office-tenure bill, would be before the court for its decision.

This was the purpose of Thomas, and by this time it had become apparent; and the *impartial and patriotic* judge determined to defeat it by the disregard of his own official duty; and he refused to order Thomas into custody, and consequently there ceased to be any ground for Thomas to sue out a writ of *habeas corpus.* Here a corrupt judge revealed himself, and afforded to the House of Representatives an opportunity to impeach him for corruption in office, palpable and flagitious. But it was their bull that had gored the ox.

The purpose and desire of the President, to have the question of the constitutionality of the civil-rights bill decided by the Supreme Court is manifest; that it, and all other questions between them have not been submitted to that test is due to the default of Congress.

But the exclusion of important evidence by this court involves another and very grave error. The Constitution says of impeachment, "No person shall be convicted without the concurrence of two thirds of the members present." *Convicted* does not mean *simply condemned*, for a man may be condemned of a crime without or against evidence; but *convicted* means *proved and determined to be guilty.* There may be *condemnation*, but cannot be *conviction* without *proof.* One of the necessary elements of *conviction* is evidence, and it might be impossible on all the evidence of the defense in a case, and yet practicable and easy upon the residue after excluding a material part of it. The exclusion of material evidence is a *part of conviction*, and may be *substantially* and *practically the conviction.*

But conviction is a totality, can exist only *in solido*, and in all its parts and processes, and as a whole, it requires two thirds of the Senators present. To demand two thirds to *convict*, and to *permit* a majority to exclude all or a material part of the evidence which might produce conviction, would not only be a hollow mockery, but an absurdity and contradiction. The constitutional rule, which requires two thirds to convict, by necessary implication, makes the same number necessary to rule out the defendant's evidence, in whole or part, and so produce conviction. If this court, by a majority of its members, had excluded the whole of the defendant's evidence, it would have shocked the country, and there would have been a general exclamation, that a rule of practice which would enable a bare majority indirectly to effect what a great constitutional principle required two thirds to do, to convict in all cases of impeachment, was both mischievous and unsound. This court should correct this erroneous ruling of an important constitutional principle by its judgment in favor of the President.

There are still other cogent considerations against the impeachment of the President, one of the most weighty of which I made at the opening of the trial, and will here restate. This court is not constituted according to the requirements of the Constitution, and, therefore, is incompetent to try the case before it.

The Constitution provides that—

"The Senate of the United States shall be composed of two Senators from each State, chosen by the Legislature thereof for six years; and each Senator shall have one vote." * * * "No State, without its consent, shall be deprived of its equal suffrage in the Senate." * * * "The Senate shall have the sole power to try all impeachments," &c.

Every State has an equal right to have two members of the Senate, and to choose them by her Legislature, and to organize her government and elect that Legislature by her own people, with whom rests her political power, without any dictation or interference by Congress. When a State has chosen her Senators, and they apply at the bar of the Senate for admission as members, it is the right of the State and of her Senators-elect, if they have the qualifications required by the Constitution, to be admitted, and this body cannot, without violating it, keep them out. The Senate has the right to reject an applicant who does not present himself with qualifications, election, and return in conformity to the Constitution, but every one who comes so arrayed is entitled to admission.

In time of peace, when there is no rebellion or insurrection in a State against the United States, a majority or any number of the Senate or of the two Houses of Congress have no right or power to deny to such or any State representation in them; and its exercise is destructive of the Constitution, and overthrows the Government which it created. Such a power would at all times enable a faction, that happened to hold a majority in the two Houses to mutilate them at will, and control the whole Government by excluding the Senators and Representatives from as many States as might be needful for their purposes. All this has been inaugurated and is in course of successful enactment by the dominant party.

When the rebellion was crushed out and those engaged in it made their submission, the Constitution, by its own force, reinstated the States involved in it *de jure* to their previous position in the Union, with all the rights and duties of the other States. They conformed their constitutions and governments, so far as they had been estranged by secession and rebellion, to the Constitution and Government of the United States, and elected their Senators and Representatives.

Congress by many of its laws, the Executive by multitudinous appointments and other acts, and the Supreme Court by hearing all cases coming up from them and allotting its members to hold circuit courts in them, recognized them as States; but still the Senate and House persisted in keeping out their Senators and Representatives. At length Tennessee extended the right of suffrage to her negro population, and disfranchised a large portion of her white men that had been implicated in the rebellion, and forthwith the majority in the two Houses admitted her Senators and Representatives; but the other southern States continued to be contumacious on the vital, radical party question of negro suffrage, and therefore were continued to be denied their great constitutional right of representation in the two Houses of Congress. It was thus demonstrated, that the cause of denying to the southern States representation in Congress, in violation of the Constitution, was their not having conferred the right to vote on their negro population, and that they were to continue unrepresented until they surrendered that point, or until means could be devised to fasten it upon them. A Senate from which almost one third of its members is excluded, and who, if present, would probably differ from the majority of those here in their judgment of this important case, cannot form a constitutional court of impeachment for its trial.

The impeachment of the President of the United States is the arraignment of the executive department of the Government by one branch of the legislative department and its trial by the other. The incongruity of such a responsibility and consequent danger of the ultimate subordination of the executive to the legislative department excited the gravest apprehensions of that wisest political sage, Mr. Madison, when the Constitution was being framed. Short of the sword, it is the extreme remedy, and was intended for the worst political disorders of the executive department. Nothing but treason, official bribery, or other high crimes and misdemeanors, made so by law, and also in their nature of deep moral turpitude, which are dangerous to the safety of the State, and which palpably disqualify and make unfit an incumbent to remain in the office of President, can justify its application to him. Cases that do not come up to this measure of delinquency, those who made the Constitution intended should be remedied in the frequency of our elections by the people at the ballot-box, and the public repose and welfare require that they should be referred to that most appropriate tribunal.

Impeachment was not intended to be used as an engine to gratify private malice, to avenge disappointed expectations, to forward schemes of personal ambition, to strengthen the measures or continue the power of a party, to punish partisan infidelity, to repress and crush its dissensions, to build up or put down opposing factions. By our system all that sort of work is to be done in popular canvasses; and to bring the great and extraordinary remedy of impeachment to do any of it, is the vile prostitution of what was intended to be a rare and august remedy for great evils of state.

The impeachment of a President of the United States, for a difference of political policy between him and Congress, is a monstrous perversion of power. Is the present prosecution anything but that? President Johnson and Congress agreed in their policy and measures to put down the rebellion, and they were signally successful; and after it was crushed out these departments of the Government did many formal and important official acts relating to each and all of them engaged in the rebellion as States in the Union, and as having the same relations as the other States with the Government of the United States.

Those States complied with conditions insisted upon both by the President and Congress, and by their constitutions and laws they respectively abolished slavery, renounced the principle of secession, repudiated their debts created by their rebellion, and ratified the thirteenth amendment of the Constitution, by which slavery was abolished throughout the United States. For the masses of the people of those States, the President thought all this was submission and expiation enough, and refused to insist that they should, in addition, confer on their late slaves, who in two States exceeded the whites, and in all of them were a large portion of the aggregate population, the right of suffrage, nor would he consent to unite in unconstitutional measures to force negro suffrage upon those States. This is the real head and front of the President's offending: he would not coöperate with the Radicals in their scheme to get possession of and control the governments and all the political power of the southern States by the agency of voting negroes against the will of the white people, and to all their unconstitutional measures to effect it he opposed the power with which the Constitution had invested him.

A subordinate ground of their ire against the President was, that to many of the people of the southern States who were engaged in the rebellion, he extended the magnanimity and clemency of the people of the United States in the exercise of the pardoning power, the noblest of all the great powers with which they have intrusted him. But there were no rebels, however vile, that were willing to become the liegemen of the Radical party, whose pardon they did not favor; and they have trenched further upon the powers of the President by assuming that of pardon, in bills introduced in both Houses to remove the disabilities of a great number of rebels, since become Radicals. But it is time all were pardoned!

Among the many strange positions assumed by the prosecution are: 1. The President has no right to inquire into and act upon his conclusion that the civil-office-tenure act, or any other act of Congress, is unconstitutional. 2. That it was his duty to execute that act without any question of its constitutionality. 3. That this court of impeachment has no right or power to inquire into the constitutionality of that act.

The latter position is so palpably and flagitiously unsound as to deserve no other answer than a simple denial. The others are entitled to some consideration, though they are negatived by the Constitution itself, to prove which I will quote from it:

"This Constitution and the laws of the United States which shall be made in *pursuance thereof*" * * * * "shall be the supreme law of the land; and the judges in every State shall be bound thereby, anything in the constitutions or laws of any State to the contrary notwithstanding."

"The Senators and Representatives before mentioned, and the members of the several State Legislatures, and all executive and judicial officers, both of the United States and of the several States, shall be bound by oath or affirmation to support this Constitution."

"The President, before he enter on the execution of his office, shall take the following oath or affirmation:

"I do solemnly swear (or affirm) that I will faithfully execute the office of President of the United States, and will to the best of my ability preserve, protect, and defend the Constitution of the United States."

The plain sequences of these provisions of the Constitution are some very important principles:

1. The Constitution is the paramount law of the land throughout the United States.

2. Every constitution and law of the States and every act of Congress, so far as they may be inconsistent with the Constitution of the United States, fall before its predominant authority and force, and from their origin are void and of no effect.

3. While it is the right of every citizen to oppose unconstitutional acts of Congress by every proper means, it is the especial duty of the President to make that resistance, as the chief executive officer of the Government, who has taken an official oath before entering on the execution of his office that he will faithfully execute the office of President of the United States, and will to the best of his ability preserve, protect, and defend the Constitution of the United States. He has no more important duty to perform, and none more obligatory upon him, than to preserve, protect, and defend the Constitution against all assailants, against Congress, and all comers. In doing this, he is not to make war, or any civil convulsion; but he is to resort to every appropriate means with which the Constitution and the laws have intrusted him; and none could be more fit than his removal of Mr. Stanton from office, with the purpose of making a case for the Supreme Court, in which the constitutionality of the civil-office-tenure bill should be decided by the tribunal appointed by the Constitution for the final judgment of all such questions.

The right of each department of the Government to interpret and construe the Constitution for itself, and by it to determine the validity of all acts of Congress, within the scope of the performance of their respective functions in the Government as to all questions not adjudged by the Supreme Court, has heretofore been a generally received principle, and has always been acted upon in the administration of the Government. That a President was bound to execute an unconstitutional act of Congress without any question, until it was so decided by the Supreme Court, and by taking steps to have it subjected to that test, committed an impeachable crime, is one of the absurd and mischievous heresies of this day.

In relation to this matter Mr. Madison so clearly expresses the true principles of the Constitution that I will dismiss it with a quotation from him, with the remark that the principles which he expresses have always been generally held by all the statesmen, courts, and jurists of America. Madison Papers, volume four, page 394, dated in 1834, says:

"As the legislative, executive, and judicial departments of the United States are coördinate, and each equally bound to support the Constitution, it follows that each must, in the exercise of its functions, be guided by the text of the Constitution according to its own interpretation of it; and consequently that in the event of irreconcilable interpretations the prevalence of the one or the other department must depend on the nature of the case as receiving the final decision from one or the other, and passing from that decision into effect without involving the functions of any other.

"But notwithstanding this abstract view of the coördinate and independent right of the three departments to expound the Constitution, the judicial department most familiarizes to the public attention as the expositor, by the order of its functions in relation to the other departments, and attracts most the public confidence by the composition of the tribunal.

In the judicial department, in which constitutionality as well as legality generally find their ultimate discussion and operative decision; and the public deference to and confidence in the judgment of that body are peculiarly inspired by the qualities implied in its members and by the gravity and deliberation of their proceedings, and by the advantage their plurality gives them over the unity of the executive department, and their firmness over the multitudinous composition of the legislative department.

"Without losing sight, therefore, of the coördinate relations of the three departments to each other, it may always be expected that the judicial bench, when happily filled, will, for the reasons suggested, most engage the respect and reliance of the public as the surest expositor of the Constitution, as well in questions within its cognizance concerning the boundaries between the several departments of the Government as in those between the Union and its members."

· Mr. Chief Justice, I believe these propositions to be true:

1. The power of removal from office is an executive power, and is vested by the Constitution in the President solely; and, consequently, that so much of the act to regulate the tenure of certain civil offices as proposes to restrict the President's exercise of that power, is unconstitutional and void.

2. That the case of Edwin M. Stanton, Secretary of War, does not come within the operation of that act, and it presented no obstruction to his removal by the President if constitutional.

3. That the removal of Stanton produced a vacancy in the office of Secretary of the Department of War, which the President was authorized by the laws of Congress to supply for six months, by the designation of any person to perform its duties for that period.

4. That there is no evidence that the President violated, or attempted to violate the "act to define and punish certain conspiracies," the act which directs "all orders and instructions relating to military operations by the President or Secretary of War to be issued through the General of the Army, and in case of his inability through the next in rank," or the act "to provide for the more efficient government of the rebel States." And, moreover, I believe the two acts last referred to were in conflict with the Constitution and void and of no effect.

5. I believe the President has the same freedom of speech which the Constitution guarantees to every American citizen; and if he had not, he has been guilty of no such abuse of it, as to constitute an impeachable offense.

Upon these propositions, the truth of which

I do not doubt, I conclude that there is no ground whatever for the impeachment of the President, and pronounce my opinion that all the articles be dismissed.

In conclusion, I will express condemnation of the harsh spirit and flagrant violations of decorum with which this case has been prosecuted in court; and especially of the violent and unjustifiable denunciations and opprobrious epithets with which some of the Managers have indulged themselves toward the respondent. Such exhibitions certainly do not commend proceedings by impeachment before the Senate of the United States to the respect and high consideration of our countrymen or the world.

OPINION
OF
HON. JOHN SHERMAN.

This cause must be decided upon the reasons and presumptions which by law apply to all other criminal accusations. Justice is blind to the official station of the respondent and to the attitude of the accusers speaking in the name of all the people of the United States. It only demands of the Senate the application to this cause of the principles and safeguards provided for every human being accused of crime. For the proper application of these principles we ourselves are on trial before the bar of public opinion. The novelty of this proceeding, the historical character of the trial, and the grave interests involved, only deepen the obligation of the special oath we have taken to do impartial justice according to the Constitution and laws.

And this case must be tried upon the charges now made by the House of Representatives. We cannot consider other offenses. An appeal is made to the conscience of each Senator of guilty or not guilty by the President of eleven specific offenses. In answering this appeal a Senator cannot justify himself by public opinion or by political, personal, or partisan demands, or even grave considerations of public policy. His conscientious conviction of the truth of these charges is the only test that will justify a verdict of guilty. God forbid that any other should prevail here. In forming this conviction we are not limited merely to the rules of evidence, which by the experience of ages have been found best adapted to the trial of offenses in the double tribunal of court and jury, but we may seek light from history, from personal knowledge, and from all sources that will tend to form a conscientious conviction of the truth. And we are not bound to technical definitions of crimes and misdemeanors. A willful violation of the law, a gross and palpable breach of moral obligations tending to unfit an officer for the proper discharge of his office, or to bring the office into public contempt and derision, is, when charged and proved, an impeachable offense. And the nature and criminality of the offense may depend on the official character of the accused. A judge would be held to higher official purity, and an executive officer to a stricter observance of the letter of the law. The President, bound as a citizen to obey the law, and specially sworn to execute the law, may properly in his high office as Chief Magistrate, be held to a stricter responsibility than if his example was less dangerous to the public safety. Still, to justify the conviction of the President, there must be specific allegations of some crime or misdemeanor involving moral turpitude, gross misconduct, or a willful violation of law, and the proof must be such as to satisfy the conscience of the truth of the charge.

The principal charges against the President are that he willfully and purposely violated the Constitution and the laws, in the order for the removal of Mr. Stanton, and in the order for the appointment of General Thomas as Secretary of War *ad interim*. These two orders were contemporaneous—part of the same transaction—but are distinct acts, and are made the basis of separate articles of impeachment.

Their common purpose, however, was to place the Department of War under the control of General Thomas without the advice and consent of the Senate.

On these charges certain leading facts are either admitted, or are so clearly proved that they may be assumed to be admitted. It thus appears that during the session of the Senate, and without the advice and consent of the Senate, the President did make these orders with the avowed purpose of gaining possession of the Department of War. That he knew that his power to remove Mr. Stanton was denied and contested both by the Senate and Mr. Stanton; that this act was committed after full deliberation, and with the expectation that it would be effective in expelling Mr. Stanton from the Department of War, and that this act of removal was in no way connected with the power of the President to appoint or remove a Secretary of War by and with the advice and consent of the Senate, but was the act of the President alone, done by him under claim that it was within his power under the Constitution and the laws. It is, therefore, not so much a question of intention as a question of lawful power.

If the President has the power, during the session of the Senate, and without her consent, to remove the Secretary of War, he is not guilty under the first, fourth, fifth, and sixth articles presented by the House; while, if the exercise of such a power is in violation of the Constitution and the laws, and was done by him willfully, and with the intent to violate the law, he is guilty, not only of malfeasance in office, but of a technical crime, as charged by the first article, and upon further proof of the conspiracy alleged, is guilty, as charged by the fourth, fifth, and sixth articles.

The power to remove Mr. Stanton is claimed by the President—*first*, under the Constitution of the United States; and *second*, under the act of 1789 creating the Department of War.

First. Has the President, under and by virtue of the Constitution, the power to remove executive officers?

The question involved is one of the gravest importance. It was fully discussed in the first session of the First Congress; and latterly has been so often discussed in the Senate that it is only necessary for me to state the general principles upon which my own judgment in this case rests.

The power to remove officers is not expressly conferred upon the President by the Constitution. If he possesses it it must be—1. From his general duty to see that the laws are faithfully executed; or, 2. As an incident to his appointing power; or, 3. By authority from time to time conferred upon him by law. Is it derived from his general executive authority? The first section of the second article of the Constitution provides that "the executive power shall be vested in the President." Section three of the same article provides "that he shall take care that the laws be faithfully executed." This duty to execute the laws no more includes the power to remove an officer than it does to create an office. The President cannot add a soldier to the Army, a sailor to the Navy, or a messenger to his office, unless that power is conferred upon him by law; yet he cannot execute the laws without soldiers, sailors, and officers. His general power to execute the laws is subordinate to his duty to execute them with the agencies and in the mode and according to the terms of the law. The law prescribes the means and the limit of his duty, and the limitations and restrictions of the law are as binding upon him as the mandatory parts of the law.

The power of removal at his will is not a necessary part of his executive authority. It may often be wise to confer it upon him; but, if so, it is the law that invests him with discretionary power, and it is not a part, or a necessary incident, of his executive power. It may be, and often is, conferred upon others.

That the power of removal is not incident to the executive authority is shown by the provisions of the Constitution relating to impeachment. The power of removal is expressly conferred by the Constitution only in cases of impeachment, and then upon the Senate, and not upon the President. The electors may elect a President and Vice President, but the Senate only can remove them. The President and the Senate can appoint judges, but the Senate only can remove them. These are the constitutional officers, and their tenure and mode of removal is fixed by the Constitution. All other officers are created by law. Their duties are defined, their pay is prescribed, and their tenure and mode and manner of removal may be regulated by law.

The sole power of the President conferred by

the Constitution as to officers of the Government is the power to appoint, and that must be by and with the advice and consent of the Senate. Does the power of appointment imply the power of removal? It is conferred by two clauses of section two of article two of the Constitution, as follows:

"He shall have power, by and with the advice and consent of the Senate, to make treaties, provided two thirds of the Senators present concur; and he shall nominate, and by and with the advice and consent of the Senate shall appoint, embassadors, other public ministers and consuls, judges of the Supreme Court, and all other officers of the United States whose appointments are not herein otherwise provided for, and which shall be established by law; but the Congress may by law vest the appointment of such inferior officers as they think proper in the President alone, in the courts of law, or in the heads of Departments.

"The President shall have power to fill up all vacancies that may happen during the recess of the Senate by granting commissions which shall expire at the end of their next session."

If the power to remove is incident to the power to appoint, it can only be coextensive with the power to appoint. In that case, during the session of the Senate, the removal must be "by and with the advice and consent of the Senate." By any other construction the implied power would defeat the express power. In all arguments on this subject it is assumed that the power to remove an officer must exist somewhere; that removal by impeachment could not have been intended to be the only mode of removing an officer, and therefore the power to remove must, from the necessity of its exercise, be held to exist in some Department of the Government, and must be implied from some express grant of power. By this reasoning some have implied the power to remove from the power to appoint, and a distinction has been made between a removal during the session of the Senate and one made during the recess. If the power to remove is derived from the power to appoint, then the President during the recess may exercise it, and may then fill the vacancy by a temporary appointment. But, if this argument is tenable, he cannot remove an officer during the session of the Senate without they consent. Then they share with him in the power to appoint, and in all the power that is derived from the power to appoint. Therefore, the removal of one officer during the session of the Senate, except in and by the appointment of another, or by the consent of the Senate, would be clearly unconstitutional, unless the power to remove is derived from some other than the appointing power.

In this case the removal of Mr. Stanton is not claimed by the President to be derived from the appointing power; but it is asserted as a distinct exercise of an independent constitutional and legal power incident to his executive office or conferred upon it by law. In the early discussions on this subject, especially by Mr. Madison, the alleged power of the President to remove all officers at pleasure was based upon the general clauses already quoted conferring executive authority. If this is tenable all limitations upon his power of removal are unconstitutional. A constitutional power can only be limited by the Constitution, and yet Congress has repeatedly limited and regulated the removal of officers. Officers of the Army and Navy can only be removed upon conviction by court-martial; in some cases the assent of the Senate is required, and in others the tenure of office is fixed for a term of years. A careful examination of the debate of 1789 on the organization of the Executive Departments will show that while a majority of the House decided that the power of removal was with the President yet they were not agreed upon the basis of this power. The debate was only as to heads of Departments, as to whom there are peculiar reasons why they should only hold their offices at the pleasure of the President. The Government was new; the President commanded the entire confidence of all classes and parties, and the wisest could not then foresee the rapid and vast extension in territory and population of the new nation, making necessary a multitude of new offices, and increasing to a dangerous degree the power, patronage, and influence inherent in the executive office. Who can believe that if the great men who were then willing that Washington should remove his heads of Departments at pleasure could have foreseen the dangerous growth of executive power would have been willing by mere inference to extend his power so as to remove at pleasure all executive officers. This power unrestricted and unlimited by law is greater and more dangerous than all the executive authority conferred upon the President by express grant of the Constitution. His command of the Army and Navy is limited by the power of Congress to raise armies and navies, to declare war, and to make rules and regulations for the government of the Army and Navy. His power to pardon is limited to cases other than of impeachment. His power to appoint officers and make treaties is limited by the consent of the Senate. Surely when these express powers, far less important, are so carefully limited by the Constitution, an implied power to remove at pleasure the multitude of officers created by law cannot be inferred from that instrument. If so the implied power swallows up and overshadows all that are expressly given. What need he care for the Senate when he may remove in a moment, without cause, all officers appointed with their consent? What need he care for the law when all the officers of the law are instruments of his will, holding office, not under the tenure of the law, but at his pleasure alone? The logical effect of this power, if admitted to exist under and by virtue of the Constitution, is revolution. However much respect is due to the decision of the first Congress, yet the actual working of civil government is a safer guide than the reasoning of the wisest men unaided by experience.

Their judgment that the head of a Department should be removable by the President may be wise, but the power to remove is not conferred by the Constitution, but, like the office itself, is to be conferred, created, controlled, limited, and enforced by the law. That such was the judgment of Marshall, Kent, Story, McLean, Webster, Calhoun, and other eminent jurists and statesmen, is shown by their opinions quoted in the argument; but they regarded the legislative construction as controlling for the time the natural and proper construction of the Constitution. The legislative construction given by the first Congress has been gradually changed. Army and Navy officers have long been placed beyond the unlimited power of the President. Postmasters and others have a fixed term of office. Various legislative limitations have been put upon the power and mode of removal. The Comptroller of the Currency holds his office for five years, and can only be removed by the President upon reasons to be communicated to the Senate. Finally, when the derangement of the revenue service became imminent, and the abuse of the power of removal produced a disgraceful scramble for office, the legislative authority asserted its power to regulate the tenure of civil offices by the passage, on the 2d of March, 1867, of the tenure-of-civil-office act. That this measure is constitutional, and that it is in the highest degree expedient, we have asserted by our vote for the law. The President had the right to demand of us a review of this opinion under the sanction of the special oath we have taken. Aided by the very able argument in this cause, and by a careful review of the authorities, I am still of the opinion that the Constitution does not confer upon the President as a part of or as incident to his executive authority the power to remove an officer, but that the removal of an officer, like the creation of an office, is the subject of legislative authority, to be exercised in each particular case in accordance with the law.

I therefore regard the tenure-of-office act as constitutional and as binding upon the President to the same extent as if it had been approved by him. He has no more right to disregard the law passed according to the Constitution without his assent than a Senator could disregard it if passed without his vote. The veto power is a vast addition to executive authority, and experience has shown the necessity to limit rather than extend it. But, if in addition to his veto power he may still disregard a law passed over it, or discriminate against such a law, his veto becomes absolute. No such doctrine is consistent with a republican form of government. The law, when passed in the mode prescribed, must be binding on all or on none. He who violates it violates it at his peril. If, therefore, the removal of Mr. Stanton is within the penal clauses of that act the President is guilty not only of an impeachable but an indictable offense. He cannot excuse himself by showing that he believed it unconstitutional, or that he was advised that it was unconstitutional. If a citizen assumes that an act is unconstitutional and violates it he does it at his peril. He may on his trial assert its unconstitutionality, and if the court of last resort in his case pronounces the law unconstitutional he will be acquitted. He takes that risk at his peril. If the law is held constitutional his belief to the contrary will not acquit him. Ignorance of the law does not excuse crime, and he who undertakes to violate it on the pretense that it is unconstitutional—thus setting up his opinions against that of the law-making power—must take the consequences of his crime.

The same rule applies much stronger to the President when he violates a law on the claim that it is unconstitutional. He is not only bound to obey the law, but he is sworn to execute the law. In resisting it he violates his duty as a citizen and his oath as an officer. If he may protect himself by an honest opinion of its unconstitutionality, then all his responsibility ceases. He may assert it on his trial like all other persons accused of crime, but the court having final jurisdiction of his case must decide this question like all others, and if that court affirms the law his guilt is complete.

In this case the President knew that a breach of this law by him could only be tried by the Senate. His pardoning power exempts him from all punishment, except by and after impeachment. His case can only be tried by the Senate, and it is a court of last resort. His violation of this law might enable others to get the opinion of the Supreme Court, by creating rights or claims to office; but his offense could not be tried before the Supreme Court, but must be tried before a court that in its legislative and executive capacity had already thrice considered this law and held it valid. A violation of it, then, on the pretext of its unconstitutionality, would be in the face of these well-considered judgments of the court that alone was competent to try his cause, and would be in the highest sense willful, deliberate, and premeditated.

It remains to consider whether, under the law as it existed on the 21st of February, 1868, the removal of Mr. Stanton was authorized, and this involves only the construction of two acts, namely:

1. The act entitled "An act to establish an executive Department, to be denominated the Department of War," approved August 7, 1789; and

2. The act of March 2, 1867, entitled "An act regulating the tenure of certain civil offices."

The second section of the act of 1789 provides—

"That there shall be in the said Department an inferior officer, to be appointed by the said principal officer, to be employed therein as he shall deem proper, and to be called the chief clerk in the Department of War, and who, whenever the said principal officer shall be removed from office by the

President of the United States, or in any other case of vacancy, shall, during such vacancy, have the charge and custody of all records, books, and papers appertaining to the said Department."

This was copied from the act organizing the Department of Foreign Affairs, which was the subject of the debate so often quoted in this cause. Whatever differences of opinion existed as to the constitutional power of the removal by the President, no one questioned the purpose of this act to declare and affirm the right of the President to remove the Secretary of War. Some who denied the constitutional power were willing to confer it by law as to heads of Departments, and the first draft of the bill expressly conferred the power of removal on the President. This was changed so as to declare the power to exist and to provide for the vacancy caused by its exercise. This act stands unaltered and unrepealed, unless it is modified by the tenure-of-office act. Under it the power of removal by the President of a Cabinet officer has been conceded by each branch of the Government during every Administration—though disputes have existed as to the origin of the power—some deriving it from the Constitution and others from the plain intent of the act of 1789. The power to remove Cabinet officers since the passage of that act was repeatedly recognized by all who took part in the debate in the Senate on the tenure-of-office bill—the only question being as to the propriety of continuing the power. I do not understand the managers to question the correctness of this construction, but they claim—

1. That the power of removal was limited to during the recess of the Senate and did not exist during the session of the Senate; and

2. That the power to remove Mr. Stanton was taken from the President by the tenure-of-office act.

Does the act of 1789 make a distinction between removals during the session and during the recess of the Senate? Upon this point, at the opening of this trial, I had impressions founded upon a distinction that I think ought to have been made in the law; but a full examination of the several acts cited, and the debates upon them, show that in fact no such distinction was made. If such had been the intention of the framers of the act of 1789, instead of stating the unlimited power of removal, they would have provided for a removal or vacancy "during the recess of the Senate." The debates show that no such distinction was claimed, and that the majority held that the unlimited power of removal was with the President by virtue of the Constitution.

The subsequent acts of 1792 and 1795, in providing for vacancies, made no distinction between vacancies during the session and during the recess, and in the numerous acts cited by counsel, providing for the creation and tenure of offices, passed prior to March 2, 1867, no distinction is made between a removal during the session and during the recess. The practice has corresponded with this construction. In two cases the power to remove heads of Departments has been exercised; the one by John Adams, in the removal of Timothy Pickering; the other by Andrew Jackson, in the removal of Mr. Duane. The first case occurred during the session and the latter during the recess. In compliance with this construction, the commissions of heads of Departments declare their tenure to be during the pleasure of the President, and the commisson under which Mr. Stanton now holds the Department of War limits his tenure "during the pleasure of the President of the United States for the time being." This form of commission, used without question for seventy years through memorable political contests, is entirely inconsistent with a construction of the act of 1789 limiting the power of removal to the recess of the Senate.

The distinction made by the Managers between *removals* during the session and during the recess is derived from the distinction made by the Constitution between *appointments* made during the session and during the recess; but this claim is inconsistent with the foundation upon which the tenure-of-office act rests. If removals are governed by the constitutional rule as to appointments, then the President may remove at pleasure during the recess, for he may then appoint temporarily without the consent of the Senate, and Congress may not limit this constitutional power. But Congress has wisely, as I have shown, rejected this claim. It has repeatedly dissevered removals from appointments, and has treated the power of removal not as a constitutional power, but as one to be regulated by law in the creation, tenure, pay, and regulation of offices and officers; and therefore, in ascertaining whether the law makes a distinction between a removal during the session and during the recess, we must ascertain the intention of the law as gathered from its language, history, and construction, and from these we can derive no trace of such a distinction. Nor can this distinction be derived from the rarity of removals of Cabinet officers during the session of the Senate, for the argument applies as well to removals during the recess. Removals of heads of Departments are rare indeed; for when the tenure-of-office bill was pending it was not considered possible that a case would occur where a head of a Department would decline to resign when requested to by his chief.

The multitude of Cabinet ministers who have held office recognized this duty with but two exceptions. I do not question the patriotism of Mr. Stanton in declining to resign during the recess; but cases of that kind must be of rare occurrence and dangerous example. It was held by us all that the public safety and the public service demands unity, efficiency, and harmony between the heads of Departments and the President. To legislate against this, and yet hold the President responsible for their acts, would be unexampled in our history, and therefore the law always gave the President the power to remove at his pleasure these and most other executive officers until we were compelled by the evil example of a bad President to limit this power. I therefore conclude that, prior to the 2d of March, 1867, the law invested the President with the power at his pleasure to remove Mr. Stanton both during the session and during the recess, and the question remains whether by the tenure-of-office act that power was taken away from him.

To determine the proper construction of this act we must examine its history and the particular evil it was intended to remedy. It was introduced on the 8d day of December, 1866, being the first day of the second session of the Thirty-Ninth Congress. The President having formally abandoned the political party that elected him, undertook, by general removals, to coerce the officers of the Government to support his policy. The revenue service especially was deranged, and widespread demoralization threatened that branch of the public service. At that time nearly all civil officers of the Government held at the pleasure of the President; some by the express provision of law; others under this general practice of the Government.

The President, for political reasons, during the then last recess, created vacancies by removal, and filled them by temporary appointments. It was to check this evil that Congress undertook to regulate the tenure of civil offices, and to protect officers in the discharge of their duties. The bill originated in the Senate, and, as introduced, excepted from its operation the heads of Departments. The bill was referred to a committee, and, as reported, the first section was as follows:

"That every person (excepting the Secretaries of State, of the Treasury, of War, of the Navy, of the Interior, the Postmaster General, and the Attorney General) holding any civil office to which he has been appointed by and with the advice and consent of the Senate, and every person who shall hereafter be appointed to any such office, and shall become duly qualified to act therein, is, and shall be, entitled to hold such office until a successor shall have been in like manner appointed and duly qualified, except as herein otherwise provided."

On the 10th of January, 1867, a motion was made to strike out the exception of the heads of Departments, and was discussed at length. The exception did not rest upon any want of power in Congress to extend the operation of the bill to the heads of Departments, but upon the necessity of giving the President control over these officers in order to secure unity and efficiency in his executive authority. Nearly all the duties of heads of Departments are by law required to be performed "as the President of the United States shall from time to time direct." They are rarely prescribed by law. This is especially so as to the Secretary of War, who issues all orders "by command

of the President," and by virtue of his office is invested by law with less power than an accounting officer. His duty prescribed by the Constitution is to give his opinion in writing when called for by the President. His prescribed legal duty is to make requisitions upon the Secretary of the Treasury for the service of the Army. All his other duties rest upon the discretion, order, and command of the President. As the President is responsible for the acts of heads of Departments, as they exercise a part of his executive authority, as their duties are not defined by law, as is the case with most civil officers, it was deemed unwise to take from the presidential office the power to remove such heads of Departments as did not possess his confidence. After debate the motion to strike out the exception was lost without a division. At a subsequent stage of the bill the motion was renewed and was lost by the decisive vote of 18 yeas and 27 nays, and the bill was then passed.

In the House of Representatives the motion to strike out the exception was made and lost, but was subsequently reconsidered, and the motion was carried, and with this amendment the bill passed the House.

The question again came before the Senate upon a motion to concur with the House in striking out the exception of the heads of Departments, and was fully debated, and again the Senate refused to concur with this amendment by a vote of 17 yeas to 28 nays. In this condition the disagreement between the two Houses came before a committee of conference, where it was the bounden duty of the conferees to maintain as far as possible the view taken by their respective Houses. The usual course in such a case, where the disagreement does not extend to the whole of the bill, or to the principle upon which it is founded, is to report an agreement upon so much as has been concurred in by both Houses, thus limiting the change in existing law to those provisions which meet the concurrence of both Houses; therefore, the Senate conferees might properly have declined to extend the change of the law beyond the vote of the Senate, and certainly would not have been justified in agreeing to a proposition thrice defeated by the vote of the Senate. The difference between the two Houses was confined to the sole question whether that bill should regulate the tenure of office of the heads of Departments. The Senate left them subject to removal at the pleasure of the President. The House secured their tenure subject to removal only at the pleasure of the Senate. After a long conference, the act as it now stands was reported. The first section is as follows:

"That every person holding any civil office to which he has been appointed by and with the advice and consent of the Senate, and every person who shall hereafter be appointed to such office, and shall become duly qualified to act therein, is and shall be entitled to hold such office until a successor shall have been in like manner appointed and duly qualified, 'except as herein otherwise provided: *Provided*, That the Secretaries of State, of the Treasury, of War, of the Navy, and of the Interior, the Postmaster General, and the Attorney General, shall hold their offices respectively for and during the term of the President by whom they may have been appointed and for one month thereafter, subject to removal by and with the advice and consent of the Senate."

What is a fair and legal construction of this section? First. That the tenure of civil offices generally should be left as in the original bill, but a special provision should be made for the tenure of heads of Departments. Second. That the President appointing a head of a Department should not, during his term, without the consent of the Senate, remove him. Third. That after thirty days from the expiration of the term of the President who appointed a head of a Department, the office of the latter would expire by limitation. To this extent, and to this extent alone, did the Senate conferees agree to change the existing law. The general clause prohibiting removals of civil officers is confined to those who have been appointed by and with the advice and consent of the Senate. The special clause prohibiting removals of Cabinet officers is that those who have been appointed by a President during his term shall not be removed without the consent of the Senate.

The distinction is kept up between heads of Departments and other civil officers, and the only limitation upon the power of the President already conferred by law is, that having appointed such an officer he shall not remove him during his term, without the advice and consent of the Senate. In all other respects the law of 1789 remains unaltered.

Was, then, Mr. Stanton appointed by the President during his term of office? If not, he holds his office under his original commission and tenure, and not under this act. If he is included in this act its effect is to declare his office vacant April 4, 1865, for that was thirty days after the expiration of the term of the President who appointed him. No such absurd purpose was intended. The plain purpose was to leave him to stand upon his then tenure and commission and to allow each President for each term to appoint his heads of Departments, with the consent of the Senate, and to secure them in their tenure during that term and thirty days thereafter, unless the Senate sooner consented to their removal. If the purpose was to protect Mr. Stanton against removal why select the language that excludes him? He was not appointed by this President nor during this presidential term. How easy, if such was the purpose, to say that "heads of Departments holding office or hereafter appointed should hold their offices," &c. To hold that the words inserted were intended to warn the President not to remove Mr. Stanton upon peril of being convicted of a high misdemeanor, is to punish the President as a criminal for the violation of a Delphic oracle. It impugns the capacity of the conferees to express a plain idea in plain words.

C. I.—59.

I can only say, as one of the Senate conferees under the solemn obligations that now rest upon us in construing this act, that I did not understand it to include members of the Cabinet not appointed by the President, and that it was with extreme reluctance and only to secure the passage of the bill that, in the face of the votes of the Senate, I agreed to the report limiting at all the power of the President to remove heads of Departments. What I stated to the Senate is shown by your records. One of your conferees [Mr. BUCKALEW] refused to agree to the report. Another [Mr. WILLIAMS] thought that a case of a Cabinet office refusing to resign when requested by the President was not likely to occur. I stated explicitly that the act as reported did not protect from removal the members of the Cabinet appointed by Mr. Lincoln, that President Johnson might remove them at his pleasure; and I named the Secretary of War as one that might be removed. I yielded to the opinion of the Senate that no limitation should be made upon the power of the President to remove heads of Departments solely to secure the passage of the bill. I could not conceive a case where the Senate would require the President to perform his great executive office upon the advice and through heads of Departments personally obnoxious to him, and whom he had not appointed, and, therefore, no such case was provided for. You did not expressly assent to this construction, but you did not dissent. If either of you had dissented, I leave to each Senator to say whether, in the face of his previous vote, he would have approved the report. This construction of the law, made when this proceeding could not have been contemplated, when the President and each member of his Cabinet were supposed to believe the act unconstitutional, made here in the Senate as an explanation for my yielding so much of your opinions, is binding upon no one but myself. But can I, who made it and declared it to you, and still believe it to be the true and legal interpretation of those words, can I pronounce the President guilty of crime, and by that vote aid to remove him from his high office for doing what I declared and still believe he had a legal right to do? God forbid!

A Roman emperor attained immortal infamy by posting his laws above the reach of the people and then punishing their violation as a crime. An American Senator would excel this refinement of tyranny, if, when passing a law, he declared an act to be innocent, and then as a judge punished the same act as a crime. For this reason I could not vote for the resolution of the 21st of February, and cannot say "guilty" to these articles.

What the President did do in the removal of Mr. Stanton he did under a power which you repeatedly refused to take from the office of the President—a power that has been held by that officer since the formation of the Government, and is now limited only by the words of an act the literal construction of which does not include Mr. Stanton. This construction was put upon the act by the Cabinet when it was pending for the approval of the President. In my judgment it is not shaken by the ingenious arguments of the Managers.

The original exception was in the body of the section; it was inserted by the conferees in a modified form, as a proviso at the close of the section. The first clause relates to all civil officers, except heads of Departments. The second clause relates to heads of Departments and no other officers. The first clause expressly excepts the officers named in the proviso, and also those described in the fourth section. To consider both classes of officers as within both clauses of the section is, it seems to me, an unnatural and forced construction of language, and certainly, when construed on a criminal trial, is too doubtful upon which to base criminal guilt.

It follows, that as Mr. Stanton is not protected by the tenure-of-civil-office act, his removal rests upon the act of 1789, and he, according to the terms of that act and of the commission held by him, and in compliance with the numerous precedents cited in this cause, was lawfully removed by the President, and his removal not being contrary to the provisions of the act of March 2, 1867, the first, fourth, fifth, and sixth articles, based upon his removal, must fail.

The only question remaining in the first eight articles is whether the appointment of General Thomas as Secretary of War ad interim, as charged in the second, third, seventh, and eighth articles is in violation of the Constitution and the laws, and comes within the penal clauses of the tenure-of-office act, and was done with the intent alleged, if so, the President is guilty upon these articles. This depends upon the construction of the clauses of the Constitution already quoted and of the several acts approved February 13, 1795, February 20, 1863, and the tenure-of-office act.

Under the Constitution no appointment can be made by the President during the session of the Senate, except by and with the advice and consent of the Senate, unless of such inferior officers as Congress may by law invest in the President alone.

By the act of February 13, 1795, it is provided—

"That in case of vacancy in the office of Secretary of State, Secretary of the Treasury, or of the Secretary of the Department of War, or of any officer of either of the said Departments whose appointment is not in the head thereof, whereby they cannot perform the duties of their said respective offices, itshall be lawful for the President of the United States, in case he shall think it necessary, to authorize any person or persons, at his discretion, to perform the duties of the said respective offices until a successor be appointed or such vacancy be filled: Provided, That no one vacancy shall be supplied in manner aforesaid for a longer term than six months."

A grave question might arise whether this act is constitutional; whether the head of a Department is an officer whose appointment even for a time might be delegated to the President alone during the session of the Senate. Its existence unrepealed would relieve the President from all criminal fault in acting upon it; but it is in derogation of the plain constitutional right of the Senate to participate in all important appointments, and if abused would utterly destroy their power. This act applied only to the three Departments then existing, and was only intended to apply to vacancies existing, and not to vacancies to be made. Its sole purpose was to provide for a temporary vacancy until the constitutional mode of appointment could be exercised, and could not infringe upon or impair the right of the Senate to participate in appointments. In the Statutes-at-Large it is designated as "obsolete;" and is, in fact, superseded by the act approved February 20, 1863, (vol. 12, p. 656.) This act, in its title, shows its plain object and purpose. It is entitled "An act temporarily to supply vacancies in the Executive Departments in certain cases." It provides—

"That in case of the death, resignation, absence from the seat of Government, or sickness of the head of any executive Department of the Government, or of any officer of either of the said Departments whose appointment is not in the head thereof, whereby they cannot perform the duties of their respective offices, it shall be lawful for the President of the United States, in case he shall think it necessary, to authorize the head of any other executive Department, or other officer in either of said Departments whose appointment is vested in the President, at his discretion, to perform the duties of the said respective offices until a successor be appointed, or until such absence or inability by sickness shall cease: Provided, That no one vacancy shall be supplied in manner aforesaid for a longer term than six months.

"SEC. 2. And be it further enacted, That all acts or parts of acts inconsistent with the provisions of this act are hereby repealed."

This act, together with the clause of the Constitution providing for vacancies during the recess, provides for all cases of vacancy except the one of removal during the session of the Senate, and that is left to be exercised as a part of the constitutional power of appointment by and with the advice and consent of the Senate. This act is complete in itself, and by its second section repeals the act of 1795, and all other acts providing for temporary appointments. It is in harmony with the Constitution, for it avoids the doubtful power conferred by the act of 1795, of appointing a new officer without the consent of the Senate, but delegates to another officer, already confirmed by the Senate, the power temporarily to perform the duties of the vacant place.

Under the authority of this act in the case of the vacancies provided for the President might have authorized the head of any other executive Department to perform temporarily the duties of Secretary of War, and the country would have had the responsibility of a high officer already approved by the Senate. In that event no new officer would have been appointed, no new salary conferred, no new agent of unauthorized power substituted in the place of an officer of approved merit, no mere instrument to execute executive will would have been thrust in the face of the Senate during their session, to hold the office in spite of the constitutional power of the Senate and against their advice and consent. Under this act the President had no more power to appoint General Thomas Secretary of War *ad interim* than he had to appoint any of the leaders of the late rebellion. General Thomas is an officer of the Army, subject to court-martial, and not an officer of the Department, or in any sense a civil or Department officer.

Did the act of March 2, 1867, confer this authority? On the contrary, it plainly prohibits all temporary appointments except as specially provided for. The third section repeats the constitutional authority of the President to fill all vacancies happening during the recess of the Senate by death or resignation; and that if no appointment is made during the following session to fill such vacancy, the office shall remain in abeyance until an appointment is duly made and confirmed; and provision is made for the discharge of the duties of the office in the mean time. The second section provides for the suspension of an officer during the recess, and for a temporary appointment *during the recess.* This power was exercised and fully exhausted by the suspension of Mr. Stanton until restored by the Senate, in compliance with the law. No authority whatever is conferred by this act for any temporary appointment during the session of the Senate, but, on the contrary, such an appointment is plainly inconsistent with the act, and could not be inferred or implied from it. The sixth section further provides:

"That every removal, appointment, or employment made, had, or exercised contrary to the provisions of this act, and the making, signing, sealing, countersigning, or issuing of any commission or letter of authority for or in respect to any such appointment or employment, shall be deemed, and are hereby declared to be, high misdemeanors, and, upon trial and conviction thereof, every person guilty thereof shall be punished by a fine not exceeding $10,000, or by imprisonment not exceeding five years, or both said punishments, in the discretion of the court."

The language is plain, explicit, and was inserted not only to prohibit all temporary appointments except during the recess, and in the mode provided for in the second section, but the unusual course was taken of affixing a penalty to a law defining the official duty of the President. The original bill did not contain penal clauses; but it was objected in the Senate that the President had already disregarded mandatory provisions of the law, and would this; and, therefore, after debate, these penal sections were added to secure obedience to the law and to give to it the highest sanction.

Was not this act willfully violated by the President during the session of the Senate?

It appears from the letter of the President to General Grant, from his conversation with General Sherman, and from his answer, that he had formed a fixed resolve to get rid of Mr. Stanton and fill the vacancy without the advice of the Senate. He might have secured a new Secretary of War by sending a proper nomination to the Senate. This he neglected and refused to do. He cannot allege that the Senate refused to relieve him from an obnoxious minister. He could not say that the Senate refused to confirm a proper appointee, for he would make no appointment to them. The Senate had declared that the reasons assigned for suspending Mr. Stanton did not make the case required by the tenure-of-office act, but I affirm as my conviction that the Senate would have confirmed any one of a great number of patriotic citizens if nominated to the Senate. I cannot resist the conclusion, from the evidence before us, that he was resolved to obtain a vacancy in the Department of War in such a way that he might fill the vacancy by an appointment without the consent of the Senate and in violation of the Constitution and the law. This was the purpose of the offer to General Sherman. This was the purpose of the appointment of General Thomas. If he had succeeded as he hoped he could have changed his temporary appointment at pleasure, and thus have defied the authority of the Senate and the mandatory provisions of the Constitution and the law. I cannot in any other way account for his refusal to send a nomination to the Senate until after the appointment of General Thomas. The removal of Mr. Stanton by a new appointment, confirmed by the Senate, would have complied with the Constitution. The absolute removal of Mr. Stanton would have created a temporary vacancy, but the Senate was in session to share in the appointment of another. An *ad interim* appointment without authority of law, during the session of the Senate, would place the Department of War at his control in defiance of the Senate and the law, and would have set an evil example, dangerous to the public safety—one which, if allowed to pass unchallenged, would place the President above and beyond the law.

The claim now made that it was the sole desire of the President to test the constitutionality of the tenure-of-office act, is not supported by reason or by proof. He might, in August last, or at any time since, without an *ad interim* appointment, have tested this law by a writ of *quo warranto.* He might have done so by an order of removal, and a refusal of Mr. Stanton's requisitions. He might have done so by assigning a head of a Department to the place made vacant by the order of removal. Such was not his purpose or expectation. He expected by the appointment of General Sherman at once to get possession of the War Department, so when General Thomas was appointed there was no suggestion of a suit at law until the unexpected resistance of Mr. Stanton, supported by the action of the Senate, indicated that as the only way left.

Nor is this a minor and unimportant violation of law. If upon claim that the tenure-of-

office act was unconstitutional, he might remove an officer and place his instrument or agent in possession of it, he might in the same way and by the same means take possession of all the Executive Departments, of all the bureaus, of the offices of the Auditors, Comptrollers, Treasurer, collectors, and assessors, and thus contról, by his will, the purse and the sword. He knew that his power was contested, and he defied it. It is clearly shown that his purpose was deliberately formed and deliberately executed, and the means for its execution were carefully selected. I therefore conclude that the appointment of General Thomas was a willful violation of the law in derogation of the rights of the Senate, and that the charges contained in the second, third, seventh, and eighth articles are true.

The criminal intent alleged in the ninth article is not sustained by the proof. All the President did do in connection with General Emory is reconcilable with his innocence, and therefore I cannot say he is guilty as charged in this article.

The tenth article alleges intemperate speeches improper and unbecoming a Chief Magistrate, and the seditious arraignment of the legislative branch of the Government. It does not allege a specific violation of law, but only personal and political offenses for which he has justly forfeited the confidence of the people.

Am I, as a Senator, at liberty to decide this cause against the President even if guilty of such offenses. That a President in his personal conduct may so demean himself by vice, gross immorality, habitual intoxication, gross neglect of official duties, or the tyrannous exercise of power, as to justify his removal from office is clear enough; but the Senate is bound to take care that the offense is gross and palpable, justifying in its enormity the application of the strong words "high crime or misdemeanor." And above all, we must guard against making crimes out of mere political differences, or the abuse of the freedom of speech, or of the exhibition of personal weakness, wrath, or imbecility. We do not confer the office of President, and may not take it away except for crime or misdemeanor. The people alone may convict and condemn for such offenses. The Senate may not trespass upon the jurisdiction of the people without itself being guilty of usurpation and tyranny. Better far to submit to a temporary evil than to shake the foundations of the civil superstructure established by the Constitution by enlarging our jurisdiction so as to punish by removal from office the utmost latitude of discussion, crimination and recrimination, which, so long as it is unaccompanied by unlawful acts, is but the foolish vaporing of liberty.

The House of Representatives of the Thirty-Ninth Congress refused to rest an accusation upon these speeches, and so of the present House, until other acts of a different character induced these articles of impeachment. We must pass upon this article separately, and upon it my judgment is that it does not allege a crime or misdemeanor within the meaning of the Constitution.

The great offense of the President consists of his opposition, and thus far successful opposition, to the constitutional amendment proposed by the Thirty-Ninth Congress, which, approved by nearly all the loyal States, would, if adopted, have restored the rebel States, and thus have strengthened and restored the Union convulsed by civil war. Using the scaffoldings of civil governments, formed by him in those States without authority of law, he has defeated this amendment; has prolonged civil strife; postponed reconstruction and reunion; and aroused again the spirit of rebellion overcome and subdued by war. He alone, of all the citizens of the United States, by the wise provisions of the Constitution, is not to have a voice in adopting amendments to the Constitution; and yet he, by the exercise of a baleful influence and unauthorized power, has defeated an amendment demanded by the result of the war. He has obstructed as far as he could all the efforts of Congress to restore law and civil government to the rebel States. He has abandoned the party which trusted him with power, and the principles so often avowed by him which induced their trust.

Instead of coöperating with Congress, by the execution of laws passed by it, he has thwarted and delayed their execution, and sought to bring the laws and the legislative power into contempt. Armed by the Constitution and the laws, with vast powers, he has neglected to protect loyal people in the rebel States, so that assassination is organized all over those States, as a political power to murder, banish, and maltreat loyal people, and to destroy their property. All these he might have ascribed to alleged want of power, or to difference of opinion in questions of policy, and for these reasons no such charges were exhibited against him, though they affected the peace and safety of the nation. When he adds to those political offenses the willful violation of a law by the appointment of a high officer during the session of the Senate, and without its consent, and with the palpable purpose to gain possession of the Department of War, for an indefinite time, a case is made not only within the express language of the law a high misdemeanor, but one which includes all the elements of a crime, to wit: a violation of express law, willfully and deliberately done with the intent to subvert the constitutional power of the Senate, and having the evil effect of placing in the hands of the President unlimited power over all the officers of the Government.

This I understand to be the substance of the eleventh article. It contains many allegations which I regard in the nature of the inducement, but it includes within it the charge of the willful violation of law more specifically set out in the second, third, seventh, and eighth articles, and I shall therefore vote for it.

The power of impeachment of all the officers of the Government, vested in the Senate of the United States, is the highest trust reposed in any branch of our Government. Its exercise is indispensable at times to the safety of the nation, while its abuse, especially under political excitement, would subordinate the executive and the judiciary to the legislative department. The guards against such a result are in the love of justice inherent in the people who would not tolerate an abuse of power, and also in the solemn appeal each of us has made to Almighty God to do impartial justice in this cause. We dare not for any human consideration disregard this oath, but guided by conscience and reason will, no doubt, each for himself, render his verdict upon these charges according to the law and the testimony, and without bias from personal, political, or popular influence. This done we may disregard personal consequences and leave our judgment and conduct in this great historical trial to the test of time.

OPINION
OF
HON. ORRIS S. FERRY.

Eleven articles of impeachment are preferred by the House of Representatives against the President of the United States.

The first, second, third, eighth, and eleventh depend, wholly or in part, upon the validity and construction of the act of March 2, 1867, "regulating the tenure of certain civil offices," and will be considered together in a subsequent portion of this opinion.

The fourth, fifth, sixth, and seventh charge the commission of the offense technically known as "conspiracy," either as defined by statute or by common law. It is sufficient to say, in regard to these articles, that the proof does not sustain the charge. No testimony has been adduced to show a "conspiracy" by the President with any person other than Lorenzo Thomas, and the evidence exhibited is substantially confined to the letter of authority of February 21, 1868, signed by the former, and the acceptance of the place of Secretary of War *ad interim* by the latter. The conduct of General Thomas seems to have been influenced by a mistaken idea of the obligation of military obedience, (to which, indeed, the phraseology of the letter of authority affords some countenance,) while the President treats him as a subordinate rather than as a confederate.

So, also, the proof fails to sustain the ninth article, which is based upon the conversation between the President and General Emory on the 22d of February, 1868. The only evidence before us is the testimony of General Emory himself, which discloses the declaration by the President of his opinion of the validity of an act of Congress, but affords no reason to infer that it was given as charged, "with intent thereby to induce said Emory, as commander of the department of Washington, to violate the provisions of said act," &c.

The specifications of the tenth article, as to the delivery of the speeches, are substantially proved, but the legal conclusion, that thereby "said Andrew Johnson, President of the United States, did commit and was then and there guilty of a high misdemeanor in office," does not result from the establishment of the truth of the specifications. The speeches proved were certainly not indictable, either at common law or by statute, nor were they in any sense acts of official misconduct or omissions of official duty. They were vain, foolish, vulgar, and unbecoming, but the Constitution does not provide that a President may be impeached for the exhibition of these qualities.

Contenting myself with these observations upon the fourth, fifth, sixth, seventh, ninth, and tenth articles of impeachment, I find the respondent *not guilty* upon each and all of them.

The first, second, third, eighth, and eleventh articles remain to be considered, and upon these I am constrained to arrive at a different result. I accept, preliminarily, the construction given by the Chief Justice to the eleventh article:

"The gravamen of this article seems to be that the President attempted to defeat the execution of the tenure-of-office act." * * * * "The single substantive matter charged is the attempt to prevent the execution of the tenure-of-office act." * * * * "This single matter, connected with the other matters, previously and subsequently alleged, is charged as the high misdemeanor of which the President is alleged to have been guilty. The general question, guilty or not guilty of a high misdemeanor as charged, seems fully to cover the whole charge."— *Remarks of the Chief Justice*, Impeachment Trial, p. 1236.

If an actual violation of the tenure-of-office act is a high misdemeanor, as declared by the act itself, then, in my judgment, the attempt to "defeat," to "prevent" the execution of that act by the President of the United States, charged with the whole responsibility of executive duty, is a high misdemeanor in office, for whose commission the Constitution subjects him to impeachment and removal from office.

With this preliminary statement I observe that my opinion upon the second, third, eighth, and eleventh articles arises out of and must stand or fall with the opinion which I have formed upon the first. The greater portion of my remaining observations will therefore be directed to that article.

The substantive charge in the first article is the removal of Mr. Stanton, contrary to the provisions of the tenure-of-office act. It is true that the removal is alleged only indirectly, but it is familiar law that the technicality of an indictment is unnecessary in articles of impeachment. The first article states in detail what the President did and the intent with which it was done, namely, to violate the act;

and the facts stated constitute in effect an actual removal, with which statement the evidence also accords.

On the 21st of February, 1868, the President sends written notice to Mr. Stanton stating to him "you are hereby removed." On the same day the President informs Lorenzo Thomas that Mr. Stanton has "been this day removed," and appoints the Adjutant General Secretary *ad interim*. The Secretary *ad interim* is invited to take and does take his place as Secretary of War in the Cabinet councils from that day to the present; is recognized there as Secretary by the President and Cabinet, and Mr. Stanton is carefully excluded; and finally, two nominations of a permanent Secretary have been sent to the Senate by the President "in place of Edwin M. Stanton, removed." By these acts the President must stand or fall; according to them he is to be tried, and he accepts the issue.

Was, then, the removal of Mr. Stanton a high misdemeanor as charged? The sixth section of the tenure-of-office act is as follows:

"Every removal, appointment, or employment made, had, or exercised contrary to the provisions of this act, and the making, signing, sealing, countersigning, or issuing of any commission or letter of authority for or in respect to any such appointment or employment shall be deemed, and are hereby declared to be, high misdemeanors, and upon trial and conviction thereof every person guilty thereof shall be punished by a fine not exceeding $10,000, or by imprisonment not exceeding five years, or both said punishments, in the discretion of the court."

If the statute is valid, and Mr. Stanton is within its provisions, the character of the offense would seem to be unmistakable.

The President denies its validity, asserting—

"That the Constitution of the United States confers on him as part of the executive power, and as one of the necessary means and instruments of performing the executive duty expressly imposed upon him by the Constitution, of taking care that the laws be faithfully executed, *the power at any and all times of removing from office all executive officers for cause to be judged of by the President alone.*"—*Answer to Article 4.*

Of course this claim would extend not only to the act of March 2, 1867, but would sweep from the statute-book every act fixing any tenure of office except the pleasure of the President. The assertion of these extraordinary prerogatives rests upon the following words of the Constitution:

"The executive power shall be vested in a President of the United States of America."

It is not pretended that there is a word in the Constitution besides these that confers upon anybody the power of removal from office, except in cases of impeachment. It behooves us, then, to inquire what is this "*executive power*" which is "*vested*" in the President of the United States of America?

Executive powers differ in different nations. A Russian czar has executive power quite unlike that of a British sovereign, and we have hitherto supposed that of the latter to be equally dissimilar to the authority of a republican President. How, then, shall we measure the executive function in the United States? Simply by the Constitution. Does that instrument expressly confer a power? We must submit. Is it silent, and is it necessary to place the power somewhere for the well-ordering of the state? We must search the Constitution to find the authority which is clothed with the function of creating or designating the proper depositary.

The Constitution is silent upon the power of removal; but this is a power that may be needful for the well-ordering of the State; and turning to the last clause of the eighth section of the first article of the Constitution we find the authority given to Congress "to make all laws which shall be necessary and proper for carrying into execution all powers vested by this Constitution in the *Government of the United States, or in any Department or officer thereof.*"

It would certainly seem too plain for argument that the "act regulating the tenure of certain civil offices" is within the very letter of this constitutional authority. The judgment of the Senate, three times definitely expressed, has been in conformity with these views, and to that judgment I adhere.

The inquiry whether Mr. Stanton is within the provisions of the law has been complicated by the ingenuity of counsel, but, upon a fair consideration of the act, presents little difficulty. The first section is as follows:

"*Every person* holding any civil office to which he has been appointed by and with the advice and consent of the Senate, and every person who shall hereafter be appointed to any such office, and shall become duly qualified to act therein, is, and shall be, entitled to hold such office until a successor shall have been in like manner appointed and duly qualified, except as herein otherwise provided: *Provided,* That the Secretaries of State, of the Treasury, of War, of the Navy, and of the Interior, the Postmaster General, and the Attorney General, shall hold their offices respectively for and during the term of the President by whom they may have been appointed, and for one month thereafter, subject to removal by and with the advice and consent of the Senate."

It is claimed that the debates in Congress, and especially in the Senate, upon the passage of the act, demand a construction which shall exclude Mr. Stanton from its provisions. I remark here that these debates should not be confounded with what is termed "contemporaneous construction." I shall have occasion to consider the latter in another place. The debates may properly be examined in order to ascertain the intent of the makers of the law. I was not in Congress at the passage of the act, and must consider it in its historic and legal aspect. The counsel who opened the case for the President very truly remarked, (page 375, Impeachment Trial:)

"This law, as Senators very well know, had a purpose; there was a practical object in the view of Congress; and however clear it might seem that the language of the law, when applied to Mr. Stanton's case, would exclude that case; however clear that might seem on the mere words of the law, if the purpose of the law could be discerned, and that purpose plainly required a different interpretation, that different interpretation should be given."

What, now, was the practical object of this

law so far as it refers to Cabinet officers? I think that no candid reader of the debates in the House of Representatives can doubt that that body intended to protect all the members of Mr. Johnson's Cabinet against removal by the President alone. Rightly or wrongly, they felt that it would be safer for the country to have the Departments in the hands of the existing Cabinet officers until the Senate should consent to their removal. I think that it is also evident that the Senate was willing to leave with the President the power of removing all Cabinet officers as theretofore practiced.

Here the two Houses disagreed, and in the bill as reported by the conference committee there was a compromise. I think that the House supposed that it had attained its object by the bill as reported by the conference committee, by keeping in *all* the Cabinet officers until one month after the close of the current presidential term, unless the Senate should sooner consent to their removal. I think that the Senate supposed that it had gained its point so far as the Secretaries appointed by Mr. Lincoln were concerned. I am thus brought to the necessity of construing a law passed by one House with a different intention from that which animated the other. I am, of course, left to determine the true intent and meaning of the law by the law itself, giving to its language its ordinary legal scope and signification.

Coming thus to the consideration of the first section of the act, (which alone is material to this inquiry,) it will be observed that it does not deal with the incidents of *offices*, but with the franchises of *persons*. It regulates *tenures*, not *terms*, of office. It is only the opposite view, which has no sanction in the statute, that can lead to a misconception of its scope.

The word *tenure* comes to us from the law of real estate:

"The thing holden is styled a *tenement*, the possessors *tenants*, and the manner of their possession a *tenure*."—2 *Bla. Com.*, 60.

Webster defines the word as follows:

"Tenure: the act or right of holding as property. Manner of holding in general."

It is a right or title pertaining to a *person*, and as such is treated throughout the statute. The body of the section comprehends "*every person holding civil office,*" and is restricted only by a single exception, namely, the persons described in the proviso as holding their offices during the term of the President by whom they were appointed. The counsel for the President (page 1099, Impeachment Trial) quotes the proviso:

"*Provided*, That the Secretaries of State, of the Treasury, of War, of the Navy, and of the Interior, the Postmaster General, and the Attorney General, shall hold their offices respectively," &c.

And adds:

"That does not mean the men; it means the offices shall have that tenure."

This certainly sounds like absurdity. The Secretary of State or of War is not an *office*, but an *officer*; a person holding an office. An office has no tenure; the possessor of an office has that "manner of possession," that "act or right of holding," that "manner of holding," which is a *tenure*. The absurdity becomes apparent if we read the proviso according to the construction of the ingenious counsel for the President;

"The offices of Secretary of State, of War, &c., shall hold their respective offices," &c.

It follows, therefore, as suggested by one of the Managers, that it is immaterial whether we consider Mr. Stanton as holding his office during the term of the President by whom he was appointed or not; all agree that he was holding the office; if within the term of the President by whom he was appointed he is embraced in the proviso; if not within such term, he was a "person holding civil office," and protected by the body of the section.

If, now, I turn to contemporaneous construction to ascertain the meaning of the law, I find such a construction given both by the executive and legislative departments of the Government. Whatever the President or his Cabinet may have thought before the final passage of the act of its effect upon Mr. Stanton, a period arrived within a few months after its passage when it became necessary for Mr. Johnson to give it a practical construction. He informs us that he proceeded with great and anxious deliberation, and the evidence before us demonstrates that he arrived at the conclusion that Mr. Stanton was within the act.

On the 12th of August, 1867, the President suspended the Secretary of War from office, in conformity with the provisions of the act. By the same authority he appointed General Grant Secretary *ad interim*. He notified the Secretary of the Treasury of his action, citing the act by name as the authority for such notification. He sent in his reasons to the Senate, pursuant to the law, and, as he informs us, hoped for the concurrence of the Senate and the removal of the Secretary, in accordance with the law.

It is too late now to do away with the effect of this executive construction by the assertion that a power of suspension has been discovered in the Constitution which has never been exercised and never thought of before since the foundation of the Government.

Upon the presentation of the President's reasons for the removal of the Secretary the Senate gave a legislative construction to the statute. It proceeded in exact conformity with the terms of the law; it considered the reasons; it debated them; it refused to concur in them, and sent notice thereof to the President. I am not aware that a single Senator in that debate suggested that Mr. Stanton was suspended by virtue of the Constitution, or that he was not embraced in the protection of the tenure-of-office act.

Upon, then, a fair consideration of the debates accompanying the passage of the act-upon the proper construction of the language of the act itself, and upon the contemporaneous construction given to it by the executive and legislative branches of the Government, I find Mr. Stanton to be embraced within the provisions of the first section.

I find, therefore, the act to be valid, and that it includes Mr. Stanton in its protection against the presidential power of removal without the consent of the Senate.

I find that the President has deliberately broken this law, and, by its express terms, has, in so doing, committed a high misdemeanor.

It is urged, however, that the offense is not complete because the criminal intent was absent. It is said that the law was broken to test its constitutionality. To this the obvious answer is, he who breaks a law for this purpose must take the risk of its being held to be constitutional by the proper tribunals. In this case the Senate is the proper tribunal for the trial of the question, and it affirms the constitutionality of the law.

But I do not find, in fact, that it was the intention of the President to try the constitutional question. The means adopted were not adapted to that end. Upon the removal of Mr. Stanton the latter could have no remedy in the courts, and the President, though time and opportunity have been ample since the passage of the law, has never attempted to initiate legal proceedings himself.

The evidence in this case exhibits the real intent with perfect clearness. The declarations of the President at different periods during the last two years, as proved before us; his intermeddling with the southern Legislatures in opposition to Congress, as shown by the Alabama telegram; his conversation with Wood, unfolding his purpose of distributing a patronage, whose emoluments exceed twenty-one million dollars a year, for the purpose of creating a party hostile to the measures of Congress—all these demonstrate a fixed and unconstitutional design to "defeat" and "prevent" the execution of the laws. Grant that he was honest in all this, and that he believed that the laws ought to have been defeated. So were Charles I and James II honest in their ideas of the royal prerogative; but those ideas brought one to the block and cost the other his crown. In this country the Legislature is the organ of the people, and the laws are the people's will. For the Executive to set his own will in opposition to the will of the people, expressed through Congress, and employ the powers vested in him for other purposes to that end, is repugnant to the whole spirit of the Constitution.

Yet the evidence leaves no doubt that such has been the persistent course of the President for more than two years. In this course Mr. Stanton had become a formidable obstacle to the designs of Mr. Johnson. The message of the latter of December 12, 1867, communicating the reasons for the suspension of the Secretary, and the answer to the first article of impeachment, disclose the irreconcilable nature of their differences, and, as is evident from the President's letter to General Grant, these differences culminated soon after the passage of the supplementary reconstruction bill of March 23, 1867. From the time of the passage of that bill the possession of the Department of War would confer vast influence either in favor of or against the whole system of reconstruction adopted by Congress, according to the views of the possessor. Mr. Stanton was known to favor that system, as the President himself declares in the letter to General Grant.

And herein I find the intent of the President in this removal of the Secretary an intent to defeat the will of the people already crystalized into law, and substitute his own will instead; an intent unlawful, unconstitutional, and revolutionary, and which, breaking out into overt act, in the removal of Mr. Stanton, gives to that act a deeper tinge of guilt than attaches to any mere violation of a penal statute.

Complaint has been made because upon this question of intent the Senate refused to hear the testimony of Cabinet officers as to the advice given by them to the President. I cannot conceive of any proposition more dangerous to the stability of our institutions than that the President may shield himself from impeachment for high crimes and misdemeanors behind the advice of his Secretaries. Apart from the common-law objection of irrelevancy, such evidence should be excluded upon the gravest considerations of public policy.

Upon this review of the law and the testimony I find that the President is guilty of a high misdemeanor as charged in the first article of impeachment.

It is a necessary result of this opinion that I also find him guilty of high misdemeanors as charged in the second, third, eighth, and eleventh articles of impeachment. I do not think it needful to elaborate the legal and logical connection, as it will be obvious to any careful reader of the articles themselves, keeping in mind that the construction suggested by the Chief Justice is applied to the eleventh article, as before stated.

OPINION

OF

HON. WILLIAM P. FESSENDEN.

The House of Representatives have, under the Constitution of the United States, presented to the Senate eleven distinct articles of impeachment for high crimes and misdemeanors against the President. Each Senator has solemnly sworn, as required by the Constitution, to "do impartial justice according to the Constitution and the laws," upon the trial. It needs no argument to show that the President is on

937

trial for the specific offenses charged, and for none other. It would be contrary to every principle of justice, to the clearest dictates of right, to try and condemn any man, however guilty he may be thought, for an offense not charged, of which no notice has been given to him, and against which he has had no opportunity to defend himself. The question then is, as proposed to every Senator, sitting as a judge, and sworn to do impartial justice, "Is the President guilty or not guilty of a high crime or misdemeanor, as charged in all or either of the articles exhibited against him?"

The first article of the series substantially charges the President with having attempted to remove Edwin M. Stanton from the office of Secretary of War, which he rightfully held, in violation of law and of the Constitution of the United States. Granting that an illegal and unconstitutional attempt to remove Mr. Stanton in the manner alleged in the article, whether successful or not, is a high misdemeanor in office, the first obvious inquiry presents itself, whether under the Constitution and the laws the President had or had not a right to remove that officer at the time such attempt was made, the Senate being then in session. To answer this inquiry it is necessary to examine the several provisions of the Constitution bearing upon the question, and the laws of Congress applicable thereto, together with the practice, if any, which has prevailed since the formation of the Government upon the subject of removals from office.

The provisions of the Constitution applicable to the question are very few. They are as follows:

ARTICLE 11, SECTION 1. "The executive power shall be vested in a President of the United States of America.

"ART. 11, SEC. 2. He[the President]" * * * * "shall nominate, and, by and with the advice and consent of the Senate, shall appoint, embassadors, other public ministers and consuls, judges of the Supreme Court, and all other officers of the United States, whose appointments are not herein otherwise provided for, and which shall be established by law."

Same section:

"The President shall have power to fill up all vacancies that may happen during the recess of the Senate by granting commissions which shall expire at the end of their next session.

"ART. 11, SEC. 4. The President, Vice President, and all civil officers of the United States shall be removed from office on impeachment for and conviction of treason, bribery, or other high crimes and misdemeanors."

The whole question of removals from office came under the consideration of the First Congress assembled after the adoption of the Constitution and was much discussed by the able men of that day, among whom were several who took a prominent part in framing that instrument. It was noticed by them that the only provision which touched in express terms upon the subject of removals from office was found in the clause which related to impeachment; and it was contended that, consequently, there was no other mode of removal. This

idea, however, found no favor at the time, and seems never since to have been entertained. It is quite obvious that as such a construction would lead to a life tenure of office, a supposition at war with the nature of our Government, and must of necessity involve insuperable difficulties in the conduct of affairs it could not be entertained.

But it was equally obvious that a power of removal must be found somewhere, and as it was not expressly given except in the impeachment clause, it must exist among the implied powers of the Constitution. It was conceded by all to be in its nature an executive power; and while some, and among them Mr. Madison, contended that it belonged to the President alone, because he alone was vested with the executive power, and, from the nature of his obligations to execute the law and to defend the Constitution, ought to have the control of his subordinates, others thought that as he could only appoint officers "by and with the advice and consent of the Senate" the same advice and consent should be required to authorize their removal. The first of these constructions finally prevailed, as those who have read the debates of that period well know. This was understood and avowed at the time to be a legislative construction of the Constitution, by which the power of removal from office was recognized as exclusively vested in the President. Whether right or wrong, wise or unwise, such was the decision, and several laws were immediately enacted in terms recognizing this construction of the Constitution.

The debate referred to arose upon a bill for establishing what is known as the Department of State. And in accordance with the decision of that First Congress the right and power of the President to remove the chief officer of that Department expressly recognized in the second section, as follows:

"SEC. 2. And be it further enacted, That there shall be in the said Department an inferior officer," &c., * * * "who, whenever the said principal officer shall be removed from office by the President of the United States, or in any other case of vacancy, shall, during such vacancy, have the charge," &c.—Act approved July 27, 1789.

The same provision is found in totidim verbis in the act establishing the Department of War, approved August 7, 1789; and terms equally definite are found in the act to establish the Treasury Department, approved September 2, 1789. These several acts have continued in force to the present day; and although the correctness of the legislative construction then established has more than once been questioned by eminent statesmen since that early period, yet it has been uniformly recognized in practice, so long and so uniformly as to give it the force of constitutional authority. A striking illustration of this practical construction arose in the administration of John Adams, who, when the Senate was in session, removed Mr. Pickering from the office of Secretary of State without asking the advice and consent of the Senate, nominating to that body for appointment on the same day John Marshall, in the place of Timothy Pickering, *removed*. No question seems to have been made at the time of this exercise of power. The form of all commissions issued to the heads of Departments, and to other officers whose tenure was not limited by statute, has been "during the pleasure of the President for the time being." And the right to remove has been exercised without restraint, as well upon officers who were appointed for a definite term as upon those who held during the pleasure of the President.

It has been argued that even if this right of removal by the President may be supposed to exist during the recess of the Senate, it is otherwise when that body is in session. I am unable to perceive the grounds of this distinction, or to find any proof that it has been recognized in practice. The Constitution makes no such distinction, as it says nothing of removal in either of the clauses making distinct provisions for appointment in recess and during the session. Probably this idea had its origin in the fact that in recess the President could appoint for a definite period without the advice and consent of the Senate, while in the other case no appointment could be made without that advice and consent. It has been uniformly held that a vacancy occurring in time of a session can only be filled during session by and with the advice and consent of the Senate, and cannot be lawfully filled during recess. But I am not aware that the President's power of removal during the session has ever been seriously questioned while I have been a member of the Senate. The custom has undoubtedly been to make the nomination of a successor the first step in a removal, so that the two acts were substantially one and the same. But instances have not unfrequently occurred during session where the President thought it proper to remove an officer at once, before sending the name of his successor to the Senate. And during my time of service previous to the passage of the act of March 2, 1867, I never heard his right to do so seriously questioned. The passage of that act is, indeed, in itself an admission that such were understood to be the law and the practice.

I will not attempt to discuss the question here whether the construction of the Constitution thus early adopted is sound or unsound. Probably it was thought that while the restraining power of the Senate over appointments was a sufficient protection against the danger of executive usurpation from this source, the President's responsibility for the execution of the laws required a prompt and vigorous check upon his subordinates. Judging from the short experience we have had under the act of March 2, 1867, the supervising power of the Senate over removals is poorly calculated to secure a prompt and vigorous correction of abuses in office, especially upon the modern claim that where offices are of a local character the representative has a right to designate the officer; under which claim this branch of executive authority, instead of being lodged where the Constitution placed it, passes to one of the legislative branches of the Government.

Such as I have described was the legislative construction of the Constitution on the subject of removals from office, and the practice under it, and such was the statute establishing the Department of War, distinctly recognizing the President's power to remove the principal officer of that Department at pleasure, down to the passage of the act regulating the tenure of certain civil offices, which became a law March 2, 1867. Although that act did not receive my vote originally, I did vote to overrule the President's veto, because I was not then, and am not now, convinced of its unconstitutionality, although I did doubt its expediency, and feared that it would be productive of more evil than good. This is not the occasion, however, to criticise the act itself. The proper inquiry is, whether the President, in removing, or attempting to remove, Mr. Stanton from the office of Secretary of War, violated its provisions; or, in other words, whether, if the President had a legal right to remove Mr. Stanton before the passage of that act, as I think he clearly had, he was deprived of that right by the terms of the act itself. The answer to this question must depend upon the legal construction of the first section, which reads as follows, namely:

"*Be it enacted, &c.*, That every person holding any civil office, to which he has been appointed by and with the advice and consent of the Senate, and every person who shall hereafter be appointed to any such office, and shall become duly qualified to act therein, is, and shall be, entitled to hold such office until a successor shall have been in like manner appointed and duly qualified, *except as herein otherwise provided: Provided,* That the Secretaries of State, of the Treasury, of War, of the Navy, and of the Interior, the Postmaster General, and the Attorney General, shall hold their offices respectively for and during the term of the President by whom they may have been appointed, and for one month thereafter, subject to removal by and with the advice and consent of the Senate."

In considering how far these provisions apply to the case of Mr. Stanton, the state of existing facts must be carefully borne in mind.

Mr. Stanton was appointed by President Lincoln during his first term, which expired on the 4th of March, A. D. 1865. By the terms of his commission he was to hold "during the pleasure of the President for the time being." President Lincoln took the oath of office, and commenced his second term on the same 4th day of March, and expired on the 15th day of the succeeding April. Mr. Johnson took the oath of office as President on the day of the death of President Lincoln. Mr. Stanton was not appointed Secretary of War by either, but continued to hold under his original commission, not having been removed. How, under these circumstances, did the act of March 2, 1867, affect him?

A preliminary question as to the character under which Mr. Johnson administered the office of President is worthy of consideration, and may have a material bearing.

The fifth clause of section one, article eleven, of the Constitution, provides as follows, namely:

"In case of the removal of the President from office, or of his death, resignation, or inability to discharge the powers and duties of the said office, the same shall devolve upon the Vice President."

What shall devolve upon the Vice President? The powers and duties of the office simply, or the office itself? Some light is thrown upon this question by the remainder of the same clause, making provision for the death, &c., of both the President and Vice President, enabling Congress to provide by law for such a contingency, as to declare "what officer shall *act as President*," and that "such officer shall *act* accordingly"—a very striking change of phraseology. The question has, however, in two previous instances, received a practical construction. In the case of Mr. Tyler, and again in that of Mr. Fillmore, the Vice President took the oath as President, assumed the name and designation, and was recognized as constitutionally President of the United States, with the universal assent and consent of the nation. Each was fully recognized and acknowledged to be President, as fully and completely, and to all intents, as if elected to that office.

Mr. Johnson then became *President*. Did *he* have a term of office? Was he merely the tenant or holder of the term of another, and that other his predecessor, President Lincoln? Did Mr. Lincoln's term continue after his death, as has been argued? It is quite manifest that two persons cannot be said to have one and the same term of the Presidency at the same time. If it was Mr. Lincoln's term, it was not Mr. Johnson's. If it was Mr. Johnson's, it was not Mr. Lincoln's. If Mr. Johnson had no term, when do the Secretaries appointed by him go out of office, under the act of March 2, 1867? When does the one month after "the expiration of the term of the President by whom *they* have been appointed" expire? A President without a term of office would, under our system, be a singular anomaly, and yet to such a result does this argument lead. I am unable to give my assent to such a proposition.

If Mr. Stanton was legally entitled to hold the office of Secretary of War on the 21st of February, 1868, as averred in the first article, he must have been so entitled by virtue of his original appointment by President Lincoln, for he had received no other appointment. If the act of March 2, 1867, terminated his office, he must, to be legally in office on the 21st of February, 1868, have been again appointed and confirmed by the Senate. He must, therefore, be assumed to have held under the commission by the terms of which he held "during the pleasure of the President for the time being." After the death of President Lin-

coln, then, he held at the pleasure of President Johnson, by his permission, up to the passage of the act of March 2, 1867, and might have been removed by him at any time. Did that act change his tenure of office without a new appointment, and transform what was before a tenure at will into a tenure for a fixed period? Granting that this could legally be done by an act of Congress, which may well be questioned, the answer to this inquiry must depend upon the terms of the act itself. Let us examine it.

It is obvious to my mind that the intention was to provide for two classes of officers; one, the heads of Departments, and the other comprising all other officers, appointed by and with the advice and consent of the Senate. The act provides a distinct tenure for each of these classes; for the heads of Departments a fixed term, ending in one month after the expiration of the term of the President by whom they were appointed; for all others an indefinite term, ending when a successor shall have been appointed and duly qualified. These two provisions are wholly unlike each other. Both are intended to apply to the present and the future, and to include all who may come within their scope. Does Mr. Stanton, by any fair construction, come within either? How can he be included in the general clause, when the Secretary of War is expressly excepted from its operation? The language is, "Every person holding any civil office, &c., shall be entitled to hold such office," "*except as herein otherwise provided.*" Then follows the proviso, in which the Secretary of War is specifically designated, and by which another and a different tenure is provided for the Secretary of War. Surely, it would be violating every rule of construction to hold that either an office or an individual expressly excluded from the operation of a law can be subject to its provisions.

Again, does Mr. Stanton come within the proviso? What is the term therein fixed and established for the Secretary of War? Specifically, the term of the President by whom he was appointed, and one month thereafter. *He* was appointed by President Lincoln, and the term of President Lincoln existing at the time of his appointment expired on the 4th of March, 1865. Can any one doubt that had a law been in existence on that day similar to that of March 2, 1867, Mr. Stanton would have gone out of office in one month thereafter? The two terms of Mr. Lincoln were as distinct as if held by different persons. Had he been then reappointed by Mr. Lincoln, and confirmed, and a law similar to that of March 2, 1867, been then in existence, is it not equally clear that he would have again gone out of office in one month after the expiration of Mr. Lincoln's second term? If so, the only question would have been whether Mr. Lincoln's term expired with him, or continued, notwithstanding his death, until the 4th day of March,

1869, although he could no longer hold and execute the office, and although his successor, elected and qualified according to all the forms of the Constitution, was, in fact and in law, President of the United States. How could all that be, and yet that successor be held to have no term at all? To my apprehension such a construction of the law is more and worse than untenable.

The word "term," as used in the proviso, when considered in connection with the obvious design to allow to each person holding the presidential office the choice of his own confidential advisers, must, I think, refer to the period of actual service. Any other construction might lead to strange conclusions. For instance, suppose a President and Vice President should both die within the first year of the term for which they were elected. As the law now stands, a new election must be held within thirty-four days preceding the first Wednesday of December then next ensuing. A new term of four years would commence with the inauguration of the new President before the term for which the preceding President was elected had expired. Do the heads of Departments appointed by that preceding President hold their offices for three years of the term of the new President and until one month after the expiration of the term for which such preceding President was elected? Such would be the consequence of giving to the word "term" any other meaning than the term of actual service. It must be evident, therefore, that the word "term" of the President, as used in the proviso, is inseparable from the individual, and dies with him.

If I am right in this conclusion, Mr. Stanton, as Secretary of War, comes neither within the body of the section nor within the proviso, unless he can be considered as having been *appointed* by Mr. Johnson.

Words used in a statute must, by all rules of construction, be taken and understood in their ordinary meaning, unless a contrary intention clearly appears. As used in the Constitution, *appointment* implies a designation—an act. And with regard to certain officers, including the Secretary of War, it implies a nomination to the Senate and a confirmation by that body. A Secretary of War can be *appointed* in no other manner. This is the legal meaning of the word *appointed*. Is there any evidence in the act itself that the word *appointed*, as used in the proviso, was intended to have any other meaning? The same word occurs three times in the body of the section, and in each case of its use evidently has its ordinary constitutional and legal signification. There is nothing whatever to show that it had, or was intended to have, any other sense when used in the proviso. If so, then it cannot be contended that Mr. Stanton was ever appointed Secretary of War by Mr. Johnson, and he cannot, therefore, be considered as included in the proviso. The result is, that he is excluded from the general provision because expressly excepted from its operation, and from the proviso by not coming within the terms of description.

It not unfrequently happens, as every lawyer is aware, that a statute fails to accomplish all the purposes of those who penned it, from an inaccurate use of language, or an imperfect description. This may be the case here. But when it is considered that this proviso was drawn and adopted by eminent lawyers accustomed to legal phraseology, who perfectly well knew and understood the position in which certain members of Mr. Johnson's Cabinet stood, not appointed by him, but only suffered to remain in office under their original commissions from President Lincoln; and when it is further considered that the object of that proviso was to secure to each President the right of selecting his own Cabinet officers, it is difficult to suppose the intention not to have been to leave those officers who had been appointed by President Lincoln to hold under their original commissions, and to be removable at pleasure. Had they intended otherwise it was easy so to provide. That they did not do so is in accordance with the explanation given when the proviso was reported to the Senate, and which was received with unanimous acquiescence.

It has been argued that Mr. Johnson has recognized Mr. Stanton as coming within the first section of the act of March 2, 1867, by suspending him under the provisions of the second section. Even if the President did so believe, it by no means follows that he is guilty of a misdemeanor in attempting to remove him, if that view was erroneous. The President is not impeached for acting contrary to his belief, but for violating the Constitution and the law. And it may be replied that, if the President did entertain that opinion, testimony was offered to show that his Cabinet entertained a different view. Whatever respect the opinion of either may be entitled to, it does not settle the question of construction. But a sufficient answer to the argument is that, whether Mr. Stanton comes within the first section of the statute or not, the President had a clear right to suspend him under the second section. That section applies to all civil officers, except judges of the United States courts, "appointed as aforesaid;" that is, "by and with the advice and consent of the Senate;" and Mr. Stanton was such an officer, whatever might have been his tenure of office. The same remark applies to the eighth section, in relation to the designation of General Thomas. That section covers every "person" designated to perform the duties of any office, without the advice and consent of the Senate. Both of these sections are general in their terms and cover all persons coming within their purview, whether included in the first section or not.

I conclude, then, as Mr. Stanton was appointed to hold "during the pleasure of the

President for the time being," and his tenure was not affected by the act of March 2, 1867, the President had a right to remove him from office on the 21st of February, 1868, and, consequently, cannot be held guilty under the first article.

Even, however, if I were not satisfied of the construction given herein of the act of March 2, 1867, I should still hesitate to convict the President of a high misdemeanor for what was done by him on the 21st of February. The least that could be said of the application of the first section of that act to the case of Mr. Stanton is that its application is doubtful. If, in fact, Mr. Stanton comes within it, the act done by the President did not remove him, and he is still Secretary of War. It was, at most, an attempt on the part of the President, which he might well believe he had a right to make. The evidence utterly fails to show any design on the part of the President to effect his purpose by force or violence. It was but the simple issuance of a written order, which failed of its intended effect. To depose the constitutional chief magistrate of a great nation, elected by the people, on grounds so slight, would, in my judgment, be an abuse of the power conferred upon the Senate, which could not be justified to the country or the world. To construe such an act as a high misdemeanor, within the meaning of the Constitution, would, when the passions of the hour have had time to cool, be looked upon with wonder, if not with derision. Worse than this, it would inflict a wound upon the very structure of our Government, which time would fail to cure, and which might eventually destroy it.

It may be further remarked that the President is not charged in the first article with any offense punishable, or even prohibited, by statute. The *removal* of an officer contrary to the provisions of the act of March 2, 1867, is punishable, under the sixth section, as a high misdemeanor. The *attempt* so to remove is not declared to be an offense. The charge is, that the President issued the order of February 21, 1868, *with intent* to violate the act, by removing Mr. Stanton. If, therefore, this attempt is adjudged to be a high misdemeanor, it must be so adjudged, not because the President has violated any law or constitutional provision, but because, in the judgment of the Senate, the attempt to violate the law is in itself such a misdemeanor as was contemplated by the Constitution, and justifies the removal of the President from his high office.

The second article is founded upon the letter of authority addressed by the President to General Lorenzo Thomas, dated February 21, 1868. The substantial allegations of the article are, that this letter was issued in violation of the Constitution and contrary to the provisions of the "act regulating the tenure of certain civil offices," without the advice and consent of the Senate, that body being then in session; and without the authority of law, there being at the time *no vacancy* in the office of Secretary of War.

In the view I have taken of the first article there was legally a vacancy in the Department of War, Mr. Stanton having been removed on that same day, and the letter of authority states the fact, and is predicated thereon. It is a well-established principle of law that where two acts are done at the same time, one of which in its nature precedes the other, they must be held as intended to take effect in their natural order. The question then is whether, a vacancy existing, the President had a legal right to fill it by a designation of some person to act temporarily as Secretary *ad interim*. The answer to this question will depend, to a great extent, upon an examination of the statutes.

The first provision of statute law upon this subject is found in section eight of an act approved May 8, 1792, entitled "An act making alterations in the Treasury and War Departments."

That section empowers the President, "in case of *death, absence from the seat of Government, or sickness*" of the Secretaries of State, War, or the Treasury, "or of any officer of either of said Departments, whose appointment is not in the head thereof, in case he shall think it necessary, to *authorize* any person or persons, at his discretion, to perform the duties of the said respective offices until a successor be appointed, or such absence or inability by sickness may cease."

It will be noticed that this act provides for one case of vacancy and two of temporary disability, making the same provision for each case. In neither case does it require any consent of the Senate, or make any allusion to the question whether it is or is not in session. It is viewed as a mere temporary arrangement in each case, and fixes no specific limit of time to the exercise of authority thus conferred. Nor does it restrict the President in his choice of a person to whom he may confide such a trust.

By an act approved February 13, 1795, chapter twenty-one, to amend the act before cited, it is provided "*that in case of vacancy*" in either of the several Departments of State, War, or the Treasury, or of any officer of either, &c.,

"it shall be lawful for the President," * * * * "in case he shall think it necessary, to *authorize* any person or persons, at his discretion, to perform the duties of the said respective offices until a successor be appointed or such vacancy be filled: *Provided*, That no one vacancy shall be supplied in manner aforesaid for a longer term than six months."

This act, it will be observed, applies only to vacancies, and does not touch temporary disabilities, leaving the latter to stand as before, under the act of 1792. It still leaves to the President his choice of the person, without restriction, to supply a vacancy; and while it provides for all vacancies, arising from whatever cause, like the law of 1792, it makes no allusion to the Senate, or to whether or not that body is in session. But this act differs from its predecessor in this, that it specifically limits the time during which any one vacancy can be supplied to six months.

Thus stood the law down to the passage of the act of February 20, 1863. (Statutes-at-Large, vol. 12, page 656.) In the meantime four other Departments had been created, to neither of which were the provisions before cited applicable. And yet it appears from the record that almost every President in office since the creation of those Departments had, in repeated instances, exercised the same power and authority in supplying temporary vacancies and disabilities in the new Departments which he was authorized to exercise in those originally created, without objection, and even without remark.

The act of February 20, 1863, provides—

"That in case of the death, resignation, absence from the head of Government, or sickness of the head of any executive Department, or of any officer of either of said Departments," &c., "it shall be lawful for the President" * * * * "to *authorize* the head of any other executive Department, or other officer in either of said Departments whose appointment is vested in the President," " to perform the duties" * * * * "until a successor be appointed, or until such absence or disability shall cease: *Provided*, That no one vacancy shall be supplied in manner aforesaid for a longer term than six months."

Section two repeals all acts or parts of acts inconsistent, &c.

This act, it will be observed, covers, in terms, the cases provided for in the act of 1792, and one more—a vacancy by *resignation*. It limits the range of selection, by confining it to certain specified classes of persons. It limits the time for which any *vacancy* may be supplied to six months, and it extends the power of so supplying vacancies and temporary absence and disability to all the Departments. Clearly, therefore, it repeals the act of 1792, covering all the cases therein enumerated, and being in several important particulars inconsistent with it. There was nothing left for the act of 1792 which was not regulated and controlled by the act of 1863.

How was it with the act of 1795? That act covered all cases of vacancy. Had it repealed the prior act of 1792? It had applied the limitation of six months for any one *vacancy*, and to that extent was inconsistent with the act of 1792, so far as a vacancy by death was concerned. But it left the cases of sickness and absence untouched. The power conferred by the act of 1792 in those cases remained, and was exercised, without question, in a multitude of cases, by all the Presidents, down to the passage of the act of 1863.

In like manner, the act of 1863, while it took out of the operation of the act of 1795 the case of vacancy by resignation, and made a new provision for it, left untouched vacancies by removal and by expiration of a limited tenure of office. Suppose the act of 1863 had provided in terms for only the two cases of absence and sickness specified in the act of 1792, will it be contended that in such a case the power conferred in that act in case of death would have been repealed by the act of 1863? If not, by parity of reasoning the enumeration of a vacancy by *resignation* in the act of 1863, would extend no further than to take that case out of the act of 1795, leaving the cases of removal and expiration of term still subject to its operation. The conclusion, therefore, is, that whatever power the President had by the act of 1795 to appoint any person *ad interim*, in case of removal, remains unaffected by the act of 1863.

It has been argued that the authority vested in the President by the act of 1795 is repealed by the sixth section of the act of March 2, 1867, which prohibits and punishes "the making, signing, sealing, countersigning, or issuing of any commission, *or letter of authority*, for or in respect to any such appointment or employment." If the act of 1795 is repealed by this section, it must operate in like manner upon the act of 1863. The consequence would be that in no case, neither in recess nor in session, neither in case of vacancy, however arising, absence or sickness, would the President have power, even for a day, to authorize any person to discharge the duties of any office in any of the Departments, which is filled by presidential appointment. All must remain as they are, and all business must stop, during session or in recess, until they can be filled by legal appointment. This could not have been intended. The words above cited from the sixth section of the act of 1867 are qualified by the words "contrary to the provisions of this act." The language is "commission or letter of authority for or in respect to any *such* appointment or employment;" to wit, a "removal, appointment, or employment made, had, or exercised contrary to the provisions of this act." If, therefore, the removal is not contrary to the act, neither is the designation of a person to discharge the duties temporarily; and a letter of authority issued in such a case is not prohibited.

In confirmation of this view it will be noticed that the eighth section of the act of March 2, 1867, expressly recognizes the power of the President, "without the advice and consent of the Senate," to "designate, authorize, or employ" persons to perform the duties of certain offices temporarily—thus confirming the authority conferred by the preceding acts.

My conclusion, therefore, is that, as the President had a legal right to remove Mr. Stanton, notwithstanding the act of March 2, 1867, he had a right to issue the letter of authority to General Thomas to discharge the duties of the Department of War, under and by virtue of the act of 1795.

It has been urged, however, that the six months' limitation in the act of 1795 had expired before the 21st of February, 1868, in consequence of the appointment of General

Grant as Secretary of War *ad interim* on the 12th day of August, 1867. I am unable to see the force of this argument. Whatever may have been the opinion of the President, as to his power of suspending an officer under the Constitution, (and I am of the opinion that he had no such power,) he clearly had the right to suspend Mr. Stanton under the second section of the act of March 2, 1867, and must be held in law to have acted by virtue of the lawful authority thereby conferred; more especially as he saw fit to conform in all respects to its provisions. The action of the Senate upon that suspension restored Mr. Stanton to his office of Secretary of War. This suspension cannot be considered as a removal, and the subsequent removal on the 21st of February created a vacancy in the office from that date. The designation of General Thomas cannot, therefore, be considered as a continuation of the original designation of General Grant on the 12th day of August, 1867.

But even if I am wrong in this conclusion, and the President had no power by existing laws to appoint a Secretary of War *ad interim*, yet if Mr. Stanton did not come within the first section of the act of 1867 the second article fails. The gravamen of that article is the violation of the Constitution and the act of March 2, 1867, by issuing the letter of authority, with intent to violate the Constitution, &c., "there being no vacancy in the office of the Secretary of War." If a legal vacancy existed the material part of the accusation is gone. A letter of authority, such as that issued to Thomas, is in no sense an appointment to office as understood by the Constitution. If it be, then the power to issue such a letter in any case without the assent of the Senate cannot be conferred by Congress. If it be, the acts of 1792, 1795, and 1863 are unconstitutional. The sixth section of the act of March 2, 1867, recognizes the distinction between an appointment and a letter of authority. The practice has been frequent and unbroken, both with and without the authority of statute law, to issue letters of authority in cases of vacancy and temporary disability almost from the formation of the Government. It has been called for by the necessity of always having some one at the head of a Department. There is no law prohibiting such a designation in case of a vacancy in a Department. If the President had no authority to issue the letter in this individual case, it was, at most, a paper having no force and conferring no power. It was no violation either of the Constitution or the law. The fact that on the very next day a nomination was actually sent to the Senate, though, as the Senate had adjourned, it was not communicated until the succeeding day, goes to show that there might have been no design to give anything but the most temporary character to the appointment. To hold that an act of such a character, prohibited by no law, having the sanction of long practice necessary for the

transaction of business, and which the President might well be justified in believing authorized by existing law, was a high misdemeanor justifying the removal of the President of the United States from office, would, in my judgment, be, in itself, a monstrous perversion of justice, if not of itself a violation of the Constitution.

The first two articles failing, the third, fourth, fifth, sixth, seventh, and eighth must fail with them.

The third differs from the second only in the allegation that the President *appointed* Lorenzo Thomas Secretary *ad interim* without the assent of the Senate, that body being then in session and there being no vacancy in said office. The answer to this allegation is, first, it was not an appointment requiring the assent of the Senate, but a simple authority to act temporarily; and second, there was a legal vacancy in the office existing at the time.

Of article four it is sufficient to say that there is no evidence to sustain it. There is nothing bearing upon it except the idle vaporing of Thomas himself of what he intended to do; and he testifies under oath that the President never authorized or suggested the use of force. What was said by Thomas was said out of doors, not to Mr. Stanton, nor communicated to him by message. The interviews between General Thomas and Mr. Stanton were of the most pacific character. The reply of Mr. Stanton when the letter of the President was delivered to him was of a nature to repel the idea of resistance, and the testimony of General Sherman shows that the President did not anticipate resistance.

It is essential to the support of this fourth article, and also of article sixth, that *intimidation and threats* should have been contemplated by the parties charged with the conspiracy, under the act of July 31, 1861. These failing, the charge fails with them in both articles.

As to the fifth and seventh articles, the attempt is made to sustain them under a law of Congress, passed February 27, 1804, extending the criminal laws of Maryland over so much of the District as was part of that State. Inasmuch as the common law was, so far as it had not been changed by statute, the law of Maryland, and conspiracy a misdemeanor, the President is charged with a misdemeanor by conspiring with Thomas to do an act made unlawful by the act of March 2, 1867. This is the only interpretation which I am able, with the aid of the arguments of the Managers, to place upon these articles. Granting the positions assumed as the foundation for the charges in these articles, they must fail if the act which the President proposed to do was a lawful act, and he did not propose to accomplish it by unlawful means. The removal of Mr. Stanton is the means proposed in order to prevent him from holding his office, as charged in the fifth, and to take and possess the property of the United States in his custody, as charged in the seventh article. The right to remove him, therefore, disposes of both articles.

Outside of any of these considerations, I have been unable to look upon either of these four articles as justifying a charge of conspiracy. The legal idea of a conspiracy is totally inapplicable to the facts proved. The President, if you please, intends to remove a person from office by an open exercise of power, against the provisions of a law, contending that he has a right so to do, notwithstanding the law, and temporarily to supply the vacancy thus created. He issues an order to that effect, and at the same time orders another person to take charge of the office, who agrees to do so. How these acts, done under a claim of right, can be tortured into a conspiracy, in the absence of any specific provision of law declaring them to be such, is beyond my comprehension.

Article eight is disposed of by what has been said on the preceding articles.

Article nine is, in my judgment, not only without proof to support it, but actually disproved by the evidence.

With regard to the tenth article, the specifications are sufficiently established by proof. They are three in number, and are extracts from speeches of the President on different occasions. It is not pretended that in speaking any of the words the President violated the Constitution, or any provision of the statute or common law, either in letter or spirit. If such utterance was a misdemeanor, it must be found in the nature of the words themselves.

I am not prepared to say that the President might not, within the meaning of the Constitution, be guilty of a misdemeanor in the use of words. Being sworn "to preserve, protect, and defend the Constitution," if he should in words persistently deny its authority and endeavor by derisive and contemptuous language to bring it into contempt and impair the respect and regard of the people for their form of government, he might, perhaps, justly be considered as guilty of a high misdemeanor in office. Other cases might be supposed of a like character and leading to similar results. It remains to inquire what was the character of the words proved.

Those spoken on the 18th day of August, 1866, contained nothing calculated to impair the confidence of the country in our form of government or in our cherished institutions. They did not contain severe reflections upon the conduct of a coördinate branch of the Government. They were not an attack upon Congress as a branch of the Government, but upon the conduct of the individuals composing the Thirty-Ninth Congress. He did not speak of *Congress* generally as "hanging upon the verge of the Government, as it were," but of a particular Congress, of which he spoke as assuming to be "a Congress of the United States, while in fact it is a Congress of only a part of the States," and which particular Congress he accused of encroaching upon constitutional rights and violating the fundamental principles of government.

It may be remarked that those words were not official. They were spoken in reply to an address made to him by a committee of his fellow-citizens—spoken *of* the Congress and not *to* it. The words did not in terms deny that it was a constitutional Congress or assert that it had no power to pass laws. He asserted what was true in point of fact, that it was a Congress of only a part of the States. Granting that the words spoken would seem to imply that he had doubts, to some extent, of the true character of that Congress and the extent of its powers, so long as several States were excluded from representation, he did not, in fact or in substance, deny its constitutional existence; while in all his official communications with that Congress he has ever treated it as a constitutional body. Is there another man in the Republic, in office or out of office, who had not on that day a perfect right to say what the President said? Would any one think of punishing any member of Congress for saying out of doors precisely the same things of the body of which he was a member? Is the President alone excluded from the privilege of expressing his opinions of the constitution of a particular Congress and of denouncing its acts as encroachments upon "constitutional rights" and the "fundamental principles of government?" In process of time there might possibly be a Congress which would be justly liable to the same criminations of a President. In such a case is he to remain silent, and is he forbidden by the Constitution, on pain of removal from office, to warn the people of the United States of their danger?

It is not alleged that the President did not believe what he said on this occasion to be true. Whether he did, or not is a question between him and his conscience. If he did, he had a perfect moral right so to speak. If he did not, his offense is against good morals, and not against any human law. There is, in my judgment, nothing in these words to prove the allegation that the President's intent in speaking them was to impair and destroy the respect of the people for the legislative power of Congress, or the laws by it duly and constitutionally enacted, or to set aside its rightful authority and powers. If the words were designed to bring that particular Congress into contempt, and to excite the resentment of the people against it, however much I may disapprove both words and intention, I do not think them an impeachable offense.

The remarks contained in the second and third specifications present themselves to my mind in the same light. They, too, contain severe reflections upon the Thirty-Ninth Congress; nothing more. I have not been able to discover any menaces or threats against Congress, unless they are found in the declaration that he would veto their measures; and this, I think, must in fairness be taken as applying to measures of a certain character, of which he had been speaking. The speeches at Cleveland and St. Louis, though highly objectionable in style, and unbecoming a President of the United States, afford nothing to justify the allegation that they were menacing toward Congress or to the laws of the country. To consider their utterance a high misdemeanor, within the meaning of the Constitution, would, in my view, be entirely without justification.

So highly did the people of this country estimate the importance of liberty of speech to a free people, that, not finding it to be specifically guarantied in the Constitution, they provided for it in the first amendment to that instrument. "Congress shall make no law abridging the freedom of speech." Undoubtedly there are great inconveniences, and perhaps positive evils, arising from the too frequent abuse of that freedom; more, perhaps, and greater from an equally protected freedom of the press. But the people of the United States consider both as essential to the preservation of their rights and liberties. They, therefore, have chosen to leave both entirely unrestrained, subjecting the abuse of that liberty only to remedies provided by law for individual wrongs. To deny the President a right to comment freely upon the conduct of coördinate branches of the Government would not only be denying him a right secured to every other citizen of the Republic, but might deprive the people of the benefit of his opinion of public affairs; and of his watchfulness of their interests and welfare. That under circumstances where he was called upon by a large body of his fellow-citizens to address them, and when he was goaded by contumely and insult, he permitted himself to transcend the limits of proper and dignified speech, such as was becoming the dignity of his station, is matter of deep regret and highly censurable. But, in my opinion, it can receive no other punishment than public sentiment alone can inflict.

If I rightly understand the accusation contained in the eleventh article it is substantially this:

"That, on the 18th day of August, 1866, the President, by public speech, declared, in substance, that the Thirty-Ninth Congress was not a Congress of the United States, authorized to exercise legislative power, thereby intending to deny that the legislation of said Congress was valid or obligatory on him, except so far as he saw fit to approve the same, and thereby denying, and intending to deny, the power of said Thirty-Ninth Congress to propose amendments to the Constitution."

And "in pursuance of said declaration" the President, on the 21st day of February, 1868, attempted to prevent the execution of the act of March 2, 1867:

First. By unlawfully attempting to devise means to prevent Mr. Stanton from resuming the functions of Secretary of War, after the Senate had refused to concur in his suspension.

C. I.—60.

Second. By unlawfully attempting to devise means to prevent the execution of the appropriation act for the support of the Army for the fiscal year ending June 30, 1868.

And that further, in pursuance of said declaration, he unlawfully attempted to prevent the execution of the so-called reconstruction act of March 2, 1868.

Whereby he was guilty of a high misdemeanor in office on the 21st day of February, 1868.

I have already stated, in commenting on the tenth article, that I do not consider the President's declaration, on the 18th of August, 1866, as fairly liable to the construction there put upon it and repeated in this article. There were no such words said, nor can they be fairly implied. The words were that it was not a Congress of the United States, but only of a part of the States. Taken literally, these words were true. But a Congress of a part of the States may be a constitutional Congress, capable of passing valid laws, and as such the President has uniformly recognized the Thirty-Ninth Congress. The declaration being perfectly susceptible of an innocent meaning, and all his official acts being consistent with that meaning, it would be unjust to suppose a different one, which he did not express.

In this view the foundation of the article fails.

But whether in pursuance of that declaration or not, did he *unlawfully* devise means to prevent the execution of the law of March 2, 1867, in the manner charged?

The first specification rests, if upon anything, upon the letter to General Grant, dated February 10, 1868. This letter must be taken as a whole, and not considered by detached parts.

From that letter I am satisfied that the President expected General Grant, in case the Senate should not concur in the suspension of Mr. Stanton, to resign the office to him, so that he might have an opportunity to fill the office before Mr. Stanton resumed the performance of its duties, with a view of compelling Mr. Stanton to seek his remedy in the court. If the President had such a design, it could only be carried out legally by removing Mr. Stanton before he should have time to resume the functions of Secretary of War, if the President had a right to remove him. It has been seen by my remarks upon the first article, that I think the President had such right. The design, then, if the President entertained it, was not unlawful.

As to the second specification, it has not, that I can see, any proof to sustain it; and if it had, it is not quite apparent how an attempt to prevent the execution of the act for the support of the Army can be considered as proof of an intention to violate the civil-tenure act, which seems to be the gravamen of this article.

No evidence whatever was adduced to show

that the President had devised means, or in any way attempted, to prevent the execution of the "act to provide for the more efficient government of the rebel States."

It has been assumed in argument by the managers that the President, in his answer, claims not only the right under the Constitution to remove officers at his pleasure, and to suspend officers for indefinite periods, but also to fill offices thus vacated for indefinite periods—a claim which, if admitted, would practically deprive the Senate of all power over appointments, and leave them in the President alone. The President does claim the power of removal, and that this includes the power of suspension. But a careful examination of his answer will show that he claims no other power than that conferred by the act of 1795, to fill vacancies in the Departments temporarily, and for a period not exceeding six months, not by appointment without the consent of the Senate, but by designation, as described in the act—a power conferred by Congress, and which can be taken away at any time, if it should be found injurious to the public interest.

Even, however, if the claim of the President did go to the extent alleged, it is not made a charge against him in the articles of impeachment. And however objectionable and reprehensible any such claim might be, he cannot be convicted of a high misdemeanor for asserting an unconstitutional doctrine, if he has made no attempt to give it practical effect, especially without a charge against him and a trial upon it.

I am unwilling to close the consideration of this remarkable proceeding before adverting to some other points which have been presented in the argument.

The power of impeachment is conferred by the Constitution in terms so general as to occasion great diversity of opinion with regard to the nature of offenses which may be held to constitute crimes or misdemeanors within its intent and meaning. Some contend, and with great force of argument, both upon principle and authority, that only such crimes and misdemeanors are intended as are subject to indictment and punishment as a violation of some known law. Others contend that anything is a crime or misdemeanor within the meaning of the Constitution which the appointed judges choose to consider so; and they argue that the provision was left indefinite from the necessity of the case, as offenses of public officers, injurious to the public interest, and for which the offender ought to be removed, cannot be accurately defined beforehand; that the remedy provided by impeachment is of a political character, and designed for the protection of the public against unfaithful and corrupt officials. Granting, for the sake of the argument, that this latter construction is the true one, it must be conceded that the power thus conferred might be liable to very great abuse, especially

in times of high party excitement, when the passions of the people are inflamed against a perverse and obnoxious public officer. If so, it is a power to be exercised with extreme caution when you once get beyond the line of specific criminal offenses. The tenure of public offices, except those of judges, is so limited in this country, and the ability to change them by popular suffrage so great, that it would seem hardly worth while to resort to so harsh a remedy, except in extreme cases, and then only upon clear and unquestionable grounds.

In the case of an elective Chief Magistrate of a great and powerful people, living under a written Constitution, there is much more at stake in such a proceeding than the fate of the individual. The office of President is one of the great coördinate branches of the Government, having its defined powers, privileges, and duties; as essential to the very framework of the Government as any other, and to be touched with as careful a hand. Anything which conduces to weaken its hold upon the respect of the people, to break down the barriers which surround it, to make it the mere sport of temporary majorities, tends to the great injury of our Government, and inflicts a wound upon constitutional liberty. It is evident, then, as it seems to me, that the offense for which a Chief Magistrate is removed from office, and the power intrusted to him by the people transferred to other hands, and especially where the hands which receive it are to be the same which take it from him, should be of such a character as to commend itself at once to the minds of all right-thinking men as, beyond all question, an adequate cause. It should be free from the taint of party; leave no reasonable ground of suspicion upon the motives of those who inflict the penalty, and address itself to the country and the civilized world as a measure justly called for by the gravity of the crime and the necessity for its punishment. Anything less than this, especially where the offense is one not defined by any law, would, in my judgment, not be justified by a calm and considerate public opinion as a cause for removal of a President of the United States. And its inevitable tendency would be to shake the faith of the friends of constitutional liberty in the permanency of our free institutions and the capacity of man for self-government.

Other offenses of the President, not specified in the articles of impeachment, have been pressed by the managers as showing the necessity for his removal. It might be sufficient to reply that all such were long prior in date to those charged in the articles, have been fully investigated in the House of Representatives, were at one time decided by a majority of the learned Committee on the Judiciary in that body to present no sufficient ground for impeachment, and were finally dismissed by the House as not affording adequate cause for such a proceeding, by a vote of nearly, if not quite, two to one. But it is enough to say that they are not before the Senate, and that body has no right to consider them. Against them the President has had no opportunity to defend himself, or even to enter his denial. To go outside of the charges preferred, and to convict him because, in our belief, he committed offenses for which he is not on trial, would be to disregard every principle which regulates judicial proceedings, and would be not only a gross wrong in itself, but a shame and humiliation to those by whom it was perpetrated.

It has been further intimated by the Managers that public opinion calls with a loud voice for the conviction and removal of the President. One Manager has even gone so far as to threaten with infamy every Senator who voted for the resolution passed by the Senate touching the removal of Mr. Stanton, and who shall now vote for the President's acquittal. Omitting to comment upon the propriety of this remark, it is sufficient to say, with regard to myself, that I not only did not vote for that resolution, but opposed its adoption. Had I so voted, however, it would afford no justification for convicting the President, if I did not, on examination and reflection, believe him guilty. A desire to be consistent would not excuse a violation of my oath to do "impartial justice." A vote given in haste and with little opportunity for consideration would be a lame apology for doing injustice to another, after full examination and reflection.

To the suggestion that popular opinion demands the conviction of the President on these charges, I reply that he is not now on trial before the people, but before the Senate. In the words of Lord Eldon, upon the trial of the Queen, "I take no notice of what is passing out of doors, because I am supposed constitutionally not to be acquainted with it." And again, "It is the duty of those on whom a judicial task is imposed to meet reproach and not court popularity." The people have not heard the evidence as we have heard it. The responsibility is not on them, but upon us. They have not taken an oath to "do impartial justice according to the Constitution and the laws." I have taken that oath. I cannot render judgment upon their convictions, nor can they transfer to themselves my punishment if I violate my own. And I should consider myself undeserving the confidence of that just and intelligent people who imposed upon me this great responsibility, and unworthy a place among honorable men, if for any fear of public reprobation, and for the sake of securing popular favor, I should disregard the conviction of my judgment and my conscience.

The consequences which may follow either from conviction or acquittal are not for me, with my convictions, to consider. The future is in the hands of Him who made and governs the universe, and the fear that He will not govern it wisely and well would not excuse me for a violation of His law.

OPINION
OF
HON. GEORGE H. WILLIAMS.

Deeply impressed with a sense of my responsibility and duty in the case now before the Senate, I shall vote for the conviction of the President upon the first three articles of impeachment upon the ground that the removal of Secretary Stanton and the appointment of Adjutant General Thomas, as charged in said articles, were in violation of the Constitution of the United States.

To decide otherwise would be to say that the President has the absolute and unlimited power, at all times and under all circumstances, to remove from and appoint to office, and that so much of the Constitution as provides that the President "shall nominate, and by and with the advice and consent of the Senate appoint," is of no effect. Nothing would be necessary to annihilate all participation by the Senate in appointments, except to call the appointee, in case of removal, an officer *ad interim*—that is, an officer to hold until it suits the purposes of the President to send a nomination to the Senate to which it is willing to agree.

Untiring and exhaustive researches on behalf of the President do not show, and I venture to assert that not one single instance can be found in the history of the Government, where the head of a Department has been removed and a successor appointed while the Senate was in session without the advice and consent of that body. Nothing is clearer to my mind than that the power of the President over the offices of the country during the session of the Senate is one thing, and his power during the recess of the Senate is another and a different thing.

When the Constitution says that the President may fill up all vacancies that may happen during the recess of the Senate it certainly confers upon him a power which he does not possess and cannot exercise while the Senate is in session.

When removals have been made during the recess of the Senate it has been argued that vacancies made in this way have happened; therefore they could be filled temporarily by the President; but now it is proposed, by building one inference upon another, to include a session as well as a recess, and so abrogate the authority of the Senate and invest the Executive with absolute and despotic power. I am very certain that the practice of removals and temporary appointments stands upon that clause of the Constitution which refers to the recess of the Senate, and in my judgment it is not only a total departure from the precedents, but a plain violation of the Constitution, to make one of its sections which applies exclusively to a recess apply also and equally to a session of the Senate.

Congress, if it should try, could not delegate

any such power to the President. Congress may vest the appointment of certain inferior officers in the President alone, in the courts of law, or in the heads of Departments; but Congress can no more vest the power in the President of removing and appointing the head of a Department without the advice of the Senate than it can vest the power in the President to make a treaty without the concurrence of the Senate.

The practice of the Government has not been inconsistent with this view of the Constitution. Pickering's case, in 1800, is cited, but there the removal and nomination to the Senate were simultaneous acts. President Adams did not attempt to make any appointment.

Some cases of *ad interim* appointments to provide for casualties have been produced, but no case can be found where the President, *uno flatu*, removed and appointed the head of a Department while the Senate was in session without its consent.

President Johnson cannot say that he was mistaken as to this point, for, in addition to what he must have learned from many years of public service, he declared in a speech which he delivered in the Senate on the 10th of January, 1861, in the most emphatic manner, that the President had no such power as he has exercised in the removal of Stanton and the appointment of Thomas.

I do not find that the act of 1789 or subsequent acts upon this subject have ever been so construed as to warrant the executive acts in question, and they could not be so construed without ignoring the clear distinction which the Constitution makes between a recess and a session of the Senate. Concerning the decision of 1789, which is the head and front of the defense in this case, it may be said that it was brought about by the arguments of James Madison in the House and the casting vote of Vice President Adams in the Senate, both of whom at the time expected to fill the executive office, and both of whom, it has been said, looked upon a contrary decision as expressing a want of confidence in the then administration of Washington. Most, if not all, of the distinguished legislators and judges of the nation, such as Webster, Clay, Calhoun, Kent, Story, and the Supreme Court of the United States, with Marshall at its head, have affirmed the incorrectness of that decision, and experience has demonstrated its mischievous and corrupting tendencies and effects. Webster, commenting on this decision, and speaking of the framers of the Constitution, in 1835, said:

"I have the clearest conviction that they looked to no other mode of displacing an officer than by impeachment, or by the regular appointment of another person to the same place."

I think it wholly unnecessary to discuss the acts of 1792, 1795, and 1863, because they have been swept out of existence by the tenure-of-office act of March 2, 1867. This is established by the application of two familiar rules of law. One is, that the act of March 2, 1867, embraced and provided for the temporary and permanent appointment and removal of every officer whose appointment is vested in the President and the Senate; and the other is, its clear repugnancy to all preceding legislation on the subject.

Great effort has been made to show that the removal of Stanton and the appointment of Thomas were unimportant infractions of the statute, and therefore the President ought to be acquitted.

Adopting the views of the President that this Senate is a court, and finding that the accused has committed an act which the law declares to be a high misdemeanor, then it follows, according to all rules governing judicial tribunals, that a judgment for conviction must be given, no matter what Senators may think of the wisdom of the law or the nature of the offense. Much of the argument for the defense proceeds upon the ground that the President has a right to decide for himself as to the constitutionality of an act of Congress. Whatever may be the correct view of this question, it must be admitted that if the President violates a penal law of Congress he does so at his peril. When impeached for such an act, if the Senate upon the trial holds the law to be unconstitutional and void, he must, of course, be acquitted; but if the Senate holds the law to be constitutional and valid, it must necessarily convict. Any public officer or private citizen may test the validity of a criminal statute by its violation, but in so doing he undertakes to suffer its penalties, if, upon his trial, it is upheld and enforced by judicial authority.

To allow any person not acting judicially when arraigned for crime to plead, in bar of the prosecution, his mistaken opinion of the justice or validity of the law, would be to deliver over the land to anarchy and crime.

Two questions only as to this law are before the Senate. One is, Is it constitutional? and the other is, Has it been violated by the President? Webster said, in one of his great speeches, that "the regulation of the tenure of office is a common exercise of legislative authority, and the power of Congress in this particular is not at all restrained or limited by anything contained in the Constitution, except as to judicial officers;" and I am very sure that the Senate, after having three times decided by more than a two-thirds vote of the members present each time that the tenure-of-office act is constitutional, will now regard that question as *res adjudicata*.

Has the President broken any of the provisions of the act? Nobody denies that the body of the first section, which provides that every person appointed to office by and with the advice and consent of the Senate shall hold until his successor is in like manner appointed and qualified, embraces the Secretary of War; but an attempt is made to construe the proviso to the section so as to exclude that officer from the protection of the act. To maintain this construction reliance is chiefly placed upon some remarks of Senator SHERMAN, in connection with the bill. I presume, on this account, it may be proper for me to say that I introduced the original bill, and had the honor to be chairman of the committee of conference by whom this proviso was reported. When the bill passed the Senate the heads of Departments were expressly excepted, but the House of Representatives amended it by striking out that exception, and the conference committee agreed to the House amendment, with a modification as to the time during which such officers should be under the protection of the law. There was no suggestion or intimation in the committee that the act did not apply to Mr. Johnson's Cabinet, and the only purpose of the proviso was to put a limitation upon the holding of Cabinet officers, and that is its fair construction.

Great stress has been put upon the words "except as herein otherwise provided" just preceding the proviso, but the fact is that these words were in the bill before the proviso was attached and refer to the fourth section, and, therefore, instead of being an exception, the proviso is a mere qualification of the general words of the section. I do not see how it is possible to conclude that Mr. Stanton is not protected by the body of the section or the proviso. If he is within the proviso, then he has a right to hold for one month after the end of some presidential term, and cannot in the mean time be removed without the consent of the Senate. That is the time expressly fixed by the proviso when a Secretary ceases to be under the protection of the Senate, and it makes no difference whether the present is Lincoln's or Johnson's presidential term. If Mr. Stanton is not affected by the proviso, then he is necessarily within the body of the section, for that includes every officer in the United States appointed by and with the advice and consent of the Senate, which is exactly Stanton's case.

The idea that this act took effect two years before it was enacted, so as to remove anybody from office at that time, is a simple absurdity. Considerable discussion has taken place as to whether or not the present is Mr. Lincoln's or Mr. Johnson's presidential term. This, as it seems to me, is an unimportant but not doubtful question. When the Constitution speaks of the term of the President, it means a definite period of four years, not an uncertain time dependent upon the death, resignation or removal of the person who takes possession of the office; and therefore the present is Mr. Lincoln's term, unless there can be two presidential terms between the 4th of March, 1865, and the 4th of March, 1869.

Let us look at the second section of the tenure-of-office act. That provides that when any officer appointed as aforesaid, that is, by and with the advice and consent of the Senate, is suspended, and the Senate do not concur in the suspension, such officer shall forthwith resume the functions of his office.

E. M. Stanton was appointed by and with the advice and consent of the Senate. He was suspended. The Senate did not concur in his suspension. It was then his right and duty forthwith to resume the functions of his office; but the President would not allow him so to do, for he not only cut off all official relations with Mr. Stanton, but appointed, received, and recognized another person as Secretary of War. What quibble can be found to excuse this plain violation of the law? Admitting, for the sake of argument, that the President could legally remove Mr. Stanton, then I deny that he could legally appoint Thomas *ad interim*, for the reason that the second section of the tenure-of-office act declares that upon the suspension of an officer an *ad interim* appointment may be made, "and in no other case." When Stanton was suspended, the *ad interim* appointment of General Grant was legal; but any *ad interim* appointment upon a removal is absolutely prohibited. Vacancies in office can only be filled in two ways under the tenure-of-office act. One is by temporary appointment, as provided in the Constitution, during the recess of the Senate, and the other is by an appointment by and with the advice and consent of the Senate during the session.

One might reasonably suppose that the construction of this act was settled, so far as the Senate was concerned.

On the 12th of December the President communicated to the Senate the fact that, on the 12th of the preceding August, he had suspended Mr. Stanton, and gave his reasons therefor; and the Senate, assuming that Mr. Stanton was within the protection of the tenure-of-office act, proceeded to consider the President's reasons, and, under the leadership of the distinguished Senator from Maine, [Mr. FESSENDEN,] refused, by an overwhelming vote of thirty-five to six, to concur in the suspension. Every one of the majority then understood that the effect of that vote was to reëstablish Mr. Stanton in his office under the provisions of the tenure-of-office act.

On the 21st of February, 1868, the President informed the Senate that he had removed Mr. Stanton and appointed Adjutant General Thomas Secretary of War *ad interim*, and the Senate proceeded to consider that communication, and, after protracted argument, decided, by a vote of twenty-seven to six, "that, under the Constitution and laws of the United States, the President has no power to remove the Secretary of War and to designate any other officer to perform the duties of that office *ad interim*."

Among those who voted to affirm this doctrine was the distinguished Senator from Illinois, [Mr. TRUMBULL.]

Now, after these proceedings, which go upon

the express ground that Mr. Stanton is within the provisions of the tenure-of-office act, we are asked to eat up our own words and resolutions and stultify ourselves by holding that the act did not apply to Mr. Stanton.

President Johnson is also fully committed to the same construction of the act. On the 12th of August he suspended Mr. Stanton, a proceeding provided for by said act, but otherwise unwarranted by law and unknown to the practice of the Government.

On the 14th day of August, 1867, he notified the Secretary of the Treasury, as follows:

"Sir: In compliance with the requirements of the act entitled 'An act to regulate the tenure of certain civil offices,' you are hereby notified that on the 12th instant, Hon. Edwin M. Stanton was suspended from his office as Secretary of War and General U. S. Grant authorized and empowered to act as Secretary ad interim."

He also reported his reasons to the Senate for the suspension of Mr. Stanton within twenty days from its meeting, as required by said act. Having vainly tried to oust Mr. Stanton by an observance of the act, he boldly determined upon its violation by Stanton's removal. This he admits, but says it was with a view to test the constitutionality of the act, forgetting, as it seems, that such a question could not possibly arise if the act did not apply to Mr. Stanton. To argue, in view of these facts, that the President removed Stanton through a mistaken idea that the law did not apply to him, is trifling with common sense.

Taking the ground of the President that the present is his presidential term, then, I say, to all intents and purposes, he has appointed Stanton Secretary of War. Time and again, in official communications to the Senate, he has declared Mr. Stanton to be Secretary of War, and in his message of December 12, 1867, he submitted to the Senate the question as to whether or not Mr. Stanton should continue to be Secretary of War, and the Senate confirmed him in that position; so that, without the usual forms, there has been that concurrence between the Executive and the Senate as to the Secretaryship of Mr. Stanton which the Constitution contemplates. The commission is no part of the appointment. The President cannot hold and treat Mr. Stanton as his Secretary of War for two or three years, and then, when questioned for an illegal act upon or through such Secretary, deny his official character and relations. If he was the President's Secretary of War for executive purposes he was such Secretary of War for the purposes of Congress.

Much discussion has taken place in this case as to the intent of the President. There is nothing of this question. His intent was to transfer the War Department from E. M. Stanton to some other person of his choice without the consent and in defiance of the will of the Senate. This is obvious and undeniable, and every Senator must believe it. The pretext that all his proceedings for the removal of

Stanton and the appointment of Thomas were to get up a law-suit is a shallow and miserable subterfuge.

One question made is that the President has not removed Mr. Stanton. Stanton was either removed or he was not. If he was not removed, then the appointment of Thomas was a clear violation of the sixth section of the tenure-of-office act, for it was an appointment to fill a vacancy where no vacancy existed.

Assuming that the tenure-of-office act is valid, and applicable to Mr. Stanton, then the President could not remove him.

Suppose Stanton, to avoid conflict under the orders of the 21st of February, had given possession of the War Office to Thomas. He would still have been Secretary of War, because those orders were illegal and void. What the tenure-of-office law intended to prohibit and punish was the action of the President as to removals and appointments without the consent of the Senate, though, of course, such action, being in contravention of law, would have no force. Great effort has been made to show that the removal of Stanton and the appointment of Thomas were insignificant acts. They might possibly be so regarded if there were harmony and peace in the country.

Congress has passed laws for the reconstruction of the States lately in rebellion, and the execution of these falls within the jurisdiction of the War Department. The President holds them to be unconstitutional, and is bitterly opposed to their existence. Stanton is understood to be friendly to this legislation. He stands, therefore, in the way of the President, and his removal and the appointment of an executive puppet in his place may involve the lives and liberties of thousands of citizens, and perchance the peace and integrity of the nation.

During this trial we have been treated to much from the writings of James Madison. Arguing about executive power in the Congress of 1789, he said:

"If an unworthy officer be continued in office by an unworthy President, the House of Representatives can at any time impeach him and the Senate can remove him, whether the President chooses or not."

Speaking again of the President, he says:

"I contend that the wanton removal of meritorious officers would subject him to impeachment and removal from his high trust."

No man can deny that E. M. Stanton, by his ability and experience, his patriotism and personal integrity, is eminently fitted for the head of the War Department.

Andrew Johnson has removed him because his unbending loyalty made him an obstacle to the President's ambitious and partisan purposes, and appointed to his place a man wholly incompetent, whose only merit is abject servility to the will of his master. If James Madison was a judge here to-day he would vote for impeachment upon that ground alone.

We have been earnestly warned by the President's counsel not to encroach upon the execative department of the Government. Considering that the President usurped the legislative control and reconstruction of the States lately in rebellion ; that he has vetoed fifteen acts of Congress, to say nothing of those he has pocketed ; that he comes now by his confidential counsel to say what he has before said, that there is no Congress and we are no Senate ; that, without acknowledging our authority, he appears simply to avoid civil commotion, and we are prepared to appreciate the modesty and grace of this admonition.

I am surprised to find so many holding the opinion that the President is not impeachable for anything that the law does not declare a crime or a misdemeanor. Cannot he be impeached for a violation of the Constitution ? Suppose he should declare war or borrow money or levy taxes without authority of law ? Is there no remedy ? Suppose, for partisan purposes, he should veto all the acts of Congress, or in some mad freak pardon all the criminals of the United States. Suppose by drunkenness and debauchery he should become incompetent to perform the duties of the office. Is Congress bound to tolerate wickedness, corruption, and treachery in the executive office so long as there is no violation of a penal statute ?

I shall vote for conviction on the tenth article.

Whenever the Chief Magistrate of this country, whose wisdom and virtue ought to exalt the nation, makes a public blasphemer of himself, and going about the country in speeches excites resistance to law and defends mob violence and murder, I think he ought to be removed from office.

This is no question of taste or good manners or of unfriendly criticism upon Congress. Those speeches were crimes. When they were delivered they took the wings of the wind. They were published and read throughout the turbulent South. They imparted boldness to violence and revenge, and I have little doubt that many a poor man is sleeping in a bloody grave in consequence of those speeches. Official duties and relations impose restraint upon freedom of speech as well as upon freedom of action.

Suppose a judge of the Supreme Court should go about making speeches and telling the people that the reconstruction or other acts of Congress were void, and that he would so decide when opportunity should arise, is there any doubt that he could be impeached for conduct so indecent and so disastrous to the peace and good order of society ?

West H. Humphreys, United States district judge for Tennessee, was convicted by the unanimous vote of this Senate of high crimes and misdemeanors for what he said in a public speech in the city of Nashville on the 29th December, 1860.

Whether Andrew Johnson shall be removed from office or not is the least question in this case. Made up as the issues are, to acquit is to decide that the President may at any time, irrespective of the provisions of the Constitution, and in open and undisguised contempt of the authority and will of the Senate, remove from and appoint to office.

To acquit is to hold that the laws of the land are not what they are written down in the statute-books of the country to be, but are the unwritten and, it may be, unknown will of one man who happens to fill the executive office of the nation.

All courts may take judicial notice of history, and by what I have a right to know in this case I have been sorrowfully and reluctantly brought to the conclusion that Andrew Johnson is a bad man ; that the policy of his administration has been to rule or ruin ; that he has endeavored by usurpation and the abuse of his veto to subordinate the legislative power to his personal views and purposes, and that his official career and example have been to injure, degrade, and demoralize the country ; and I believe that his removal from office will invigorate the laws, vindicate the Constitution, and tend greatly to restore unity and peace to the nation.

OPINION
OF
HON. HENRY WILSON.

The past seven years have been to gentlemen occupying seats in this Chamber years of pressing duties and stern trials. In the trying times through which the nation has passed and is passing it has sometimes happened that Senators of large capacity, ripe experience, and eminent public service have widely differed in the interpretation of the Constitution and the construction of the laws. Whenever the high duties imposed upon Senators by the exigencies of the country have pressed for action, and our deliberations have been distracted by the diverse opinions of Senators learned in the law, I have striven to discharge my duty by giving whatever doubts clouded my judgment or embarrassed my action to patriotism, to liberty, and to justice—to the security of my country and the rights of all its citizens. In glancing back over these years I find few votes I would recall by following this rule of action. In this great trial, imposed upon the Senate by the Constitution of our country and the Representatives of the people, I shall give whatever doubts have arisen to perplex or embarrass to my country rather than to its Chief Magistrate, now arraigned as a violator of the Constitution, a violator of the laws, and a violator of his oath to faithfully execute the laws. By a too rigid adherence to forms and technicalities the substance is often lost. Discarding forms and technicalities and looking only to the substance, I shall so vote as to secure the ends of justice.

I am not, I trust, unmindful of the gravity of the occasion, of the solemnity of my oath, nor of the obligation ever resting upon me "to be just and fear not." I know that the vote I shall give in this great trial will be criticised sharply in our age and in ages to come. The President is on trial before the Senate—the Senate is on trial before the present age and before the coming ages. I intend to vote for the conviction of the President and for his removal from his high office, and to submit my motives and my action to the judgment of the present and of the future. From the verdict of the Senate the President has no appeal; from the verdict of posterity the Senate has no appeal. I propose to state, with brevity, some of the reasons why I shall vote for the conviction of the President of the United States upon the charges preferred by the Representatives of the people.

The framers of the Constitution well knew the seductive, grasping, and aggressive nature of executive power. They knew that for ages the contest had been "to rescue," in the words of Daniel Webster, "liberty from the grasp of executive power," and that "our security was in our watchfulness of executive power." They knew that the champions of human freedom in the Old World, though often baffled, had struggled for generations to limit and restrain executive power. They sought to make the executive power of the nation useful to the country, but not dangerous to the liberties of the people. They gave to the President a short term of office, and clothed the Representatives of the people with power to arraign him before the Senate, not only for high crimes, but for high misdemeanors, too. Jealous of executive power, the framers of the Constitution gave to the House of Representatives—a body representing the interests, the sentiments, the opinions of the people, and their passions, too—complete authority to arraign the Chief Magistrate of the nation before the tribunal of the Senate. They clothed the Senate of the United States, composed of gentlemen quite as liable as are the members of the House of Representatives to be influenced by the interests, the opinions, the sentiments, and the passions of the people, with ample power to try, convict, and remove the President, not only for the commission of high crimes, but for high misdemeanors.

High misdemeanors may or may not be violations of the laws. High misdemeanors may, in my judgment, be misbehavior in office detrimental to the interests of the nation, dangerous to the rights of the people, or dishonoring to the Government. I entertain the conviction that the framers of the Constitution intended to impose the high duty upon the House of Representatives to arraign the Chief Magistrate for such misbehavior in office as injured, dishonored, or endangered the nation, and to impose upon the Senate the duty of trying, convicting, and removing the Chief Magistrate proved guilty of such misbehavior. Believing this to be the intention of the framers of the

Constitution and its true meaning; believing that the power should be exercised whenever the security of the country and the liberties of the people imperatively demand it; and believing by the evidence adduced to prove the charges of violating the Constitution and the tenure-of-office act, and by the confessed and justified acts of the President, that he is guilty of high misdemeanors, I unhesitatingly vote for his conviction and removal from his high office.

The President is charged by the House of Representatives with violating the Constitution and the tenure-of-office act in removing Mr. Stanton from the office of Secretary of War and in appointing Adjutant General Thomas Secretary of War *ad interim*. The removal of Mr. Stanton and the appointment of Adjutant General Thomas, and the violation of the tenure-of-office act, if Mr. Stanton be within that act, stand confessed and justified in the answer of the President to the charges of the House of Representatives. The answer of the President, without any other evidence, is to my mind conclusive evidence of his guilt. Upon his answer, confessions, assumptions, and justifications I have no hesitation in recording my vote of "guilty." The assumptions of power put forth by the President in his defense cannot but startle and alarm all men who would maintain the just powers of all branches of the Government. Had the President inadvertently violated the Constitution and the laws; had he pleaded in justification misconstruction of the Constitution and the laws, I might have hesitated to vote for his conviction. But he claims the right to remove civil officers and appoint others *ad interim* during the session of the Senate. If that claim of power is admitted by a vote of acquittal, the President can remove during the session of the Senate tens of thousands of civil officers, with their millions of compensation, and appoint his own creatures to fill their places without the advice and consent of the Senate, and thus nullify that provision of the Constitution that empowers the Senate to give its advice and consent to appointments.

Not content with this assumption of power, the President claims the right to pronounce a law of Congress unconstitutional, to refuse to execute it, although he is sworn to do so, and to openly violate it with a view of testing its constitutionality in the courts, although no means may exist for months or years to come to test the constitutionality of the law so violated in the judicial tribunals of the country. The President claims and has exercised the right to declare Congress an unconstitutional body, incapable of enacting laws or of proposing amendments to the Constitution; to hold the laws in abeyance; to refuse to execute them, and to defiantly violate them in order to test their constitutionality. These are the positions assumed by Andrew Johnson. These assumptions, if admitted, radically change the character of our Government. If they are sustained by a verdict of acquittal the President ceases to be the servant of the law and becomes the master of the people, and a law-non-executing power, a law-defying power, a law-breaking power is created within the Government. Instead of an Executive bound to the faithful execution of the laws of Congress the nation has an Executive bound only to execute the laws according to his own caprices, whims, and sovereign pleasure. Never can I assent, by a vote of acquittal, to executive assumptions so unconstitutional, so subversive of the Government, so revolutionary in their scope and tendency. These assumptions will introduce into our constitutional system, into our Government of nicely-adjusted parts, derangement, disorganization, and anarchy.

Criminal acts raise the presumption of wrong motives, intentions, and purposes. The President's acts, claims, and assumptions, made against the well-known protests of vast masses of the people, the organs of public opinion, the Congress of the United States, and the laws of the land,.afford ample evidence that his motives, intentions, and purposes were unworthy, if not criminal. We are sworn to give this arraigned President a trial as impartial as the lot of humanity will permit. But we cannot close our eyes to the records of the past three years, nor can we wholly shut out from all influences our personal knowledge of his intentions, purposes, and acts. The framers of the Constitution, when they empowered Senators to sit in judgment upon an arraigned Chief Magistrate, must have presumed that Senators would know something of the motives, intentions, and purposes, and be familiar with the public record of him who should exercise executive power in their time. The framers of the Constitution knew, when they gave Senators the power to try an arraigned Chief Magistrate, the country knows, and we know, that personal knowledge and the historic records of the country cannot but influence in some degree the feelings and judgments of men.

Four years ago eleven States were wrenched from the Union, their governments were arrayed against the country, the land was desolated with civil war, the nation was struggling to restore and maintain the unity of the country, the supremacy of the Government, and the freedom of millions made free by executive proclamation and a constitutional amendment. The faith of the nation was plighted to restore the broken Union on the basis of loyalty, and to maintain the freedom of millions of emancipated bondmen. The men pledged to liberty and union accepted Andrew Johnson, supported and trusted him. Coming into power, he at once, in spite of the fears and protests of the loyal men who had confided in him, entered upon a policy that placed the conquered rebel States in the keeping of traitors, and put loyal men and the freedmen completely under the authority of men who had striven for four years on bloody fields to destroy their country, to perpetuate the slavery of the very men surrendered to their control.

To lighten the burdens and partially protect and defend the endangered rights of the freedmen, Congress passed a Freedmen's Bureau bill; the President arrested it by a veto. Congress passed another Freedmen's Bureau bill; the President endeavored to defeat it by another veto, and when it passed into law he strove to embarrass and thwart its operations. To protect the freedmen he had wickedly abandoned to the control of their enemies and the nation's enemies, Congress passed a civil-rights bill; the President attempted to arrest it by a veto; and failing in that, he has utterly neglected to enforce it. Congress endeavored, by submitting an amendment to the Constitution, to secure the reconstruction of the Union; the President met it by a denial of the authority of Congress to submit an amendment, and by an invocation to his governments in the rebel States to reject it. The rebel States having failed to adopt the constitutional amendment, Congress passed the reconstruction measures over Executive vetoes. Those measures of restoration have encountered in their execution the hostility of the President. Faithful generals have been removed for their fidelity and efficiency, and others have been rebuked and thwarted.

The history of the past three years records it, and our personal knowledge attests it, that the President has sought to prevent the enforcement of the laws passed over his vetoes. In every form he has striven to prevent the restoration of the Union on a basis of loyalty to the country and the equal rights and privileges of the people. The evidences legally before us, the records of the country, the personal knowledge of Senators, show the motives, intentions, and designs of President Johnson.

To accomplish his purposes and designs, Mr. Johnson sought, by the use of executive patronage, to corrupt the American people. When Congress, by the casting vote of Vice President Adams, decided, in the beginning of Washington's Administration, that the Senate was a part of the appointing power, but not of the removing power, the office-holders of the country were but a few hundred in number, and received a compensation amounting to but a few thousand dollars. In our time the Federal office-holders are counted by tens of thousands, and their compensation amounts to many millions. To defeat the will of the people, the President, in the interests of disloyalty, inequality, and injustice, sought to use the corrupt and corrupting influences of executive patronage. The Postmaster General made the shameless declaration, that officers who ate the President's bread should support the President's policy. To maintain the cause of the country, as well as to protect honest public officers who would not betray their country, Congress enacted the civil-tenure act. It met the executive veto, the executive denunciation of unconstitutionality, and the executive violation. Mr. WILLIAMS, of the House of Representatives, who drew the proviso to the first section of the act, tells us that he intended that the act should protect Mr. Stanton.

The Senator from Oregon, [Mr. WILLIAMS,] who introduced the original bill, and who was on the committee of conference, and the Senator from Vermont, [Mr. EDMUNDS,] who reported the bill from the Committee on the Judiciary, and who was also on the committee of conference, both claim that Mr. Stanton is protected by the act. A fair and logical construction of the language of the act gives its protection to Mr. Stanton. A large majority in Congress voted for the bill in the belief that it threw its protection over the great War Secretary, who stood before the country one of the foremost champions of Congress in its struggle against the anarchical, disorganizing, and unpatriotic action of the Executive. Mr. Stanton was suspended by Mr. Johnson; the reasons for his suspension were submitted to Congress; the reasons were pronounced insufficient by more than a three fourths vote of the Senate; Mr. Stanton returned to his office; the President refused to acknowledge him; and, after several days, issued the order for his removal, and he appointed Adjutant General Thomas Secretary of War *ad interim*—all in direct violation of the tenure-of-office act.

The President refused to send a nomination to the Senate, knowing that it was the will of the Senate and of the nation that Mr. Stanton should remain at the head of the War Department. He had vainly sought to induce General Grant to be a party in thwarting the will of the Senate by preventing the return of Mr. Stanton to the War Office. He had failed to persuade Lieutenant General Sherman to aid him in removing Mr. Stanton from his office. He then took Adjutant General Thomas, through whom all communications must go to the Army, and made him Secretary of War *ad interim*. The law requires all communications to the Army to go through General Grant. Might it not have been, by placing Thomas in the War Department, while holding the office of Adjutant General, the purpose of the President to have the means of communication with the Army under his control, and substantially to set aside the law requiring such communications to go through the General of the Army?

In support of the acts of the President, claims are made and powers asserted by Mr. Johnson and his counsel hostile to the spirit and genius of our institutions, to the integrity of the Government, and to the security of public liberty. The acquittal of the President will give the sanction of the Senate to the monstrous powers assumed, claimed, and exercised by the President, and will, in my judgment, increase the lawlessness, disorder, and outrage now so prevalent in the States lately in rebellion. His conviction and removal from office will rebuke lawlessness, disorder, and crime, and inspire hope and courage among loyal and law-abiding men. I cannot contemplate without the deepest anxiety the fatal effects, the suffering and sorrow that must follow the acquittal of the President. The disastrous consequences of his acquittal seem to flash upon me whichsoever way I turn. Conscious of the responsibilities that rest upon me, I shall unhesitatingly vote for the conviction of the President, for his removal from office, and for his disqualification from hereafter holding any office under the Constitution he has violated and the Government he has dishonored.

OPINION

OF

HON. GEORGE VICKERS.

The Constitution secures to the President of the United States the nomination of civil officers and their appointment, if the Senate shall advise and concur. He is the initiating and acting power, and gives character and form to the proceeding before it is presented to the consideration of the Senate, which body has no power to present the name of any one to the President as an object of official favor. The act of 1789, which created the Department of War, does not limit the tenure of the office of the Secretary of that Department, but assigns such duties as shall be enjoined upon and intrusted to him by the President, agreeably to the Constitution.

Soon after the Government went into operation the power of removal from office was exercised by the Executive during the session as well as in the recess of the Senate; the commissions to the Secretaries and many other officers contained the statement that they held at the pleasure of the President. A practice immediately arose and prevailed, and was continued down to the year 1867, of removal from office by the Executive; the power of removal was claimed as an incident to that of appointment; and as essential to a faithful execution of the laws, on the ground that unless the President possessed it he could not remove a faithless officer who might be engaged in obstructing the execution of the laws or in embezzling the public funds; the duty of the President under the Constitution, to take care that the laws should be faithfully executed, could not be efficiently discharged unattended by the power of removal. Although differences of opinion may have existed upon this as well as other provisions of that instrument, yet the practice uninterruptedly continued, with the implied assent of the Legislature, for upward of seventy-five years, and constituted a legislative construction which was affirmed by different Attorneys General of the United States, whose attention had been specially called to the subject.

The acquiescence by Congress in that construction, whether originally correct or not, was fully sufficient to justify President Johnson in its exercise. Although it may be termed an implied power, it is as valuable and essential to a coördinate department as an express grant. The power to create banks and of erecting custom and light-houses is derived by implication. The concurrent authorities of Kent and Story refer to the power of removal of officers by the President, as established by usage and acquiescence, as well as by the opinions of the most eminent lawyers, judges, and statesmen, as the settled construction of the Constitution. It was advocated and practiced by Jefferson, Madison, Monroe, Jackson, Van Buren, and other Presidents, down to Mr. Johnson. The elder Adams removed Mr. Pickering, Secretary of State, during the session of Congress, and without consulting it; he requested Mr. Pickering to resign, and on his refusal removed him by a peremptory order, and nominated John Marshall his successor. The right of Mr. Adams does not seem to have been questioned. The act of 1789, in its second section, provides for the appointment of a chief clerk in the Department of War, who, whenever the principal officer, the Secretary, shall be removed by the President, or in any other case of vacancy, shall have the charge and custody of all the records and papers in the office. The language of this act recognizes an existing right in the President, under the Constitution, to remove a Secretary at his discretion.

The debates in Congress in 1789, by the ablest men of the nation, show that the power of removal from office was conceded to be in the President, and the bills establishing the Departments and regulating the duties to be performed were framed purposely to conform to that construction of the Constitution. Thus, in the act relating to the Treasury Department, the seventh section provides that the assistant 'shall take charge of the records, books, and papers "whenever the Secretary shall be removed from office by the President of the United States, or in any other case of vacancy." In the same year the Department of Foreign Affairs was created, and in the second section of the act it is declared that there shall be appointed an inferior officer, to be called the chief clerk, and who, "whenever the said principal officer shall be removed from office by the President of the United States, or in any other case of vacancy, shall, during such vacancy, have the charge and custody of the records," &c. These three statutes do not confer the power of removal, but they treat it as existing in the executive department, and were designed and drafted to exclude the presumption of implication of a grant of that power to the President by legislative authority.

The act of the 2d March, 1867, regulating the tenure of civil offices, and passed over the President's veto, was intended to alter and change the settled construction of the Constitution, and to empower the Senate to continue a Cabinet officer in commission against the will and wishes of the Executive, and to restrain and check his wonted power of removal; the statute trenched upon and materially impaired what the President and his legal advisers, including the Secretary of War, believed and declared to be a constitutional right and prerogative of the executive department. The President having sworn to "preserve, protect, and defend the Constitution of the United States," considered it to be his duty, as custodian of the executive department, to treat the act as unconstitutional, and to exert the power claimed and exercised by all his predecessors. The statute of 2d March, 1867, essays to create an offense of high misdemeanor in any one who may attempt to violate it, and for this effort of the President to maintain the integrity of his department until the judiciary, the only arbiter to determine a question of such magnitude in the last resort, should decide, the impeachment is predicated.

If one department shall attempt or do what another department shall believe to be an essential and vital encroachment upon its high powers or functions, the law of self-defense is as applicable as it would be to a personal attack by one upon another. It cannot be expected that the executive department is to be the agent for executing a statute upon itself which is to dismember and deprive it of half its vigor or vitality; the duty enjoined upon the President to see that the laws are executed was not designed to operate in such a case, for the practical recognition of such a principle might be used to work the destruction of the whole frame of the Government and make the Constitution its own destroyer. The allegation that if the President shall be permitted to contravene a statute which he and his Cabinet believe invades and infracts the constitutional limits and powers of the department over which he presides, and feels bound to preserve, that he may be at equal liberty to disregard any law of a different character and object, has no more force than that the right of self-defense may be extended to justify an individual in assaulting every person he may chance to meet. If it is in the lawful competency of Congress to punish the infraction of every law by pains and penalties, and to deprive the courts of the United States of their jurisdiction over the same, Congress would soon become omnipotent, the coördination of the departments be destroyed, and the structure and genius of our Government be changed by the action of one department.

It may well be questioned if the Cabinet officers who were appointed by a former President, and not reappointed in a second term, either by that President or by Mr. Johnson, his successor, were intended to be embraced by the act of 2d March, 1867; if it were a matter of doubt the accused would be entitled to the benefit of it. From a careful examination of the act, taken in connection with the avowed purpose of it, as declared in the Senate and House of Representatives by the committees of conference at the time of its final passage, my opinion is that such officers were not, nor intended to be, included in it. Entertaining the views I have expressed, I do not consider that the first and eighth articles of impeachment are sustained.

The act of Congress of 1795, chapter twenty-one, provides for the filling of all vacancies by the President, by appointments *ad interim* for a period not exceeding six months. The power of removal or suspension necessarily carries with it the right to fill the vacancy temporarily on the ground of public necessity ; the exigency may exist at any time, whether during the session or in the recess of the Senate, and the public interest and service may require the promptest action by the President. The acts of 1863 and 1867 do not, by implication, repeal the cases provided for and covered by the act of 1795, which embraces all cases of vacancy from whatever cause, and authorizes *ad interim* employments, but only such as are occasioned by death, resignation, absence, or sickness, leaving the vacancies occasioned by removal and expiration of commission unrepealed.

The act of 1867, regulating the tenure of certain civil offices, by its second section, empowers the President to fill vacancies which may happen during the recess of the Senate, by reason of death or resignation, and in such cases to grant commissions, which shall expire at the end of the next session thereafter, but makes no provision for filling vacancies which may occur during the session of the Senate, leaving such to be filled under existing laws and the usages of the department. The eighth section of the tenure-of-office act declares that whenever the President shall, without the advice and consent of the Senate, designate, authorize, or employ any person to perform the duties of any office, he shall notify the Secretary of the Treasury, &c. This recognizes the right of the President to make *ad interim* appointments without the consent of the Senate. This class of appointments is not the same mentioned in the third section of that act, because he is authorized by that section to issue commissions to expire at the end of the next session ; but in the eighth section it is stated to be a mere designation or employment of some person to perform the duties of an office. According to usage, from the necessity of the case, and the act of 1795, unrepealed in part by the act of 1863 or the act of 1867, President had the power to designate General Thomas to perform, for a brief period, the duties of the Department of War. To avoid circumlocution I have sometimes used the word appointment instead of designation or employment in connection with *ad interim*

duties, but an appointment to office, legally and technically, has three essential elements : 1. A nomination by the President. 2. A confirmation or approval by the Senate. 3. A commission signed, sealed, and delivered to the appointee. A concurrence of all is necessary to its consummation. The designation of a person to take possession and fulfill the duties is but for a temporary purpose, till a suitable successor can be found and his nomination sent to the Senate ; the public interest may demand such a course of action.

The proceedings in this case abound with instances of *ad interim* employments, directed by all the Presidents from Mr. Adams (the elder) to Mr. Johnson, including President Lincoln. The designation of General Thomas was on the 21st February, and the nomination of Mr. Ewing was sent to the Senate on the 22d February, but in consequence of an early adjournment, and the next day being the Sabbath, it was not actually received by the Senate till Monday, the 24th of that month. But if the President, the Attorney General, and other Cabinet officers were mistaken in their construction of the law, which I do not think, such an error was a venial one, and cannot properly be considered a high crime or high misdemeanor.

But if none of the laws alluded to authorized the *ad interim* appointment of General Thomas, yet, if Mr. Stanton's case is not covered by the first section of the act of March 2, 1867, called the tenure-of-office law, the second article and others into which it enters are not subjects of impeachment. Mr. Stanton was appointed by Mr. Lincoln in 1862, during the first term of his Presidency; his term expired with Mr. Lincoln's as definitively as if the latter had not been reëlected ; he was not reappointed either by Mr. Lincoln or by President Johnson, and only held by courtesy and sufferance. The month allowed to the Cabinet officers appointed by Mr. Johnson and confirmed by the Senate does not apply to officers appointed by Mr. Lincoln, and who held no legal term under President Johnson.

The latter, therefore, committed no misdemeanor in designating General Thomas to perform the duties till a regular nomination could be made; first, because Mr. Stanton's case is not protected by the first section of the act of 1867, all the subsequent sections having reference to the cases only which are included in that section, the sixth section, relating to *ad interim* appointments, expressly declaring them to be "contrary to the provisions of this act," and if not within the first section it cannot be within the sixth ; secondly, because no other act forbids such appointments ; and thirdly, because it was in conformity to the settled practice of the executive department since its formation, acquiesced in by all the departments, and necessary to a proper and faithful execution of the laws. In any aspect of the case the second and third articles are not maintainable.

With the views already expressed, that the President is not guilty of the principal charge, which is modified and extended over other articles, it follows that he is not punishable on the charge for conspiring to do the acts mentioned in the fourth, fifth, and seventh articles, and especially not in the absence of all proof of any such conspiracy.

The sixth article charges a conspiracy to seize and take by force the property of the United States in violation of the conspiracy act of July, 1861. This statute does not, in my opinion, apply to the removal of an officer under claim of constitutional right; besides, no proof was offered of any authority from the President to use force, (none was used,) and no legitimate inference of such an intention can be drawn under an act penal in its character when the presumptions are favorable to the citizen, and especially to a high public functionary of the Government in the discharge of official duty.

The ninth article, which alleges an attempt to seduce an officer of the Army from his duty to promote sinister purposes of the President, appears to be wholly unsupported by proof. The Commander-in-Chief has an undoubted right to consult with his subordinates, to inquire into the disposition of the military forces, and to express opinions; the relation between them precludes the presumption of an unlawful purpose in making proper inquiries and communications. In such a case the charge should be expressly proved; but there was not only no evidence offered tending to prove it, but a laudable motive was proved by the Secretary of the Navy, who suggested to the President the propriety of making the investigation.

The tenth supplemental article is in reference to certain public speeches of the President, and charges that they are high misdemeanors in office. These speeches were made in a private, and not in an official capacity, and however injudicious some may think portions of them, and to be regretted, I know of no law which can punish Mr. Johnson with a removal from office because they were made. As we have no law to punish those who may indulge in political discussions, it cannot reasonably be expected that the President should be removed for exercising a privilege enjoyed by every American citizen; the first amendment to the Constitution declares that Congress shall pass no law abridging the freedom of speech or of the press.

The eleventh article is anomalous, indefinite, and liable to the objection of multiplicity. If it were possible to put it in the form of an indictment or of a declaration in a civil action, it would be quashed on motion by a court of law. The first item or paragraph is not in the form of a charge, but is the recital of a speech contained in the tenth article and appears to be only introductory, or alleged as inducement to a charge which follows, namely, that the President, in pursuance of said speech made in August, 1866, attempted to prevent the execution of the tenure-of-office act, passed on the 2d March, 1867; then follows a vague allusion to the means by which he made the said attempt, to wit: on the 21st February, 1868, by unlawfully devising, contriving, and attempting to devise and contrive means to prevent E. M. Stanton from forthwith resuming the functions of the office of Secretary of War, which had been peaceably and quietly resumed on the 13th January, 1868, about five weeks prior to the alleged contrivances, as appears by Mr. Stanton's affidavit to procure a warrant for General Thomas's arrest, and also by the first article of impeachment.

The other means are to prevent the execution of the act making appropriations for the support of the Army, of which no proof was offered except that in relation to the ninth article in reference to General Emory's interview with the President. The last means charged are to prevent the execution of an act to provide for the efficient government of the rebel States, passed 2d March, 1867; the only evidence introduced was a telegram to Governor Parsons, dated several weeks prior to the passage of the said act alleged to be violated. This eleventh article seems to be made up by uniting fragments or portions of other articles; if separately the articles in full are not sustained, the joining together of some of their disunited parts cannot impart to them additional strength or vitality. There is no proof of any connection between the speeches referred to and the tenure-of-office act, nor between that act or any alleged violation of it and the means and contrivances imputed to the President. It was contended on the part of the prosecution that the act of 1789, and not the Constitution, conferred upon the President the power of removal from office and separated that power from that of appointment. The act of 1867 does not essay to punish a removal under the act of 1789 unless made in the recess of the Senate, and as Mr. Stanton's removal was during the session of that body, the prohibition of the act is not applicable. The act of 1789 is general, and not confined in its operation to the recess of the Senate or to its sessions; its language is, "whenever the said principal officer (the Secretary being meant) shall be removed from office by the President of the United States," the inferior officer shall have charge of the records, books, and papers appertaining to the Department.

A President and his Cabinet may be called upon to examine and determine the meaning, scope, and operation of statutes they may be required to execute materially affecting the powers, duties, and practice of the executive department of the Government. Judgment is necessarily involved in that examination and consideration. If, after a candid and diligent investigation and mature deliberation, the President acts upon the conclusion thus formed, can it be contended that for doing so he is guilty of a high crime or misdemeanor and punishable by removal from office? There must be some willful and manifest abuse of authority, usurpation, or corruption in such a case to justify a proceeding so degrading in its character and consequences. If Congress, by legislation of two thirds, after the exercise of the veto by the Executive, should assume the power of making appointments to office, irrespective of his right of nomination, of negotiating and confirming treaties, of diminishing his compensation during the term for which he was elected, can it be said that he would have no right to judge of the constitutionality of these acts; and, if he should refuse to regard them, to be subjected to impeachment and removal, as well as to fine and imprisonment, although they attempted to abstract the essential attributes of his office and reduce the Department to a subordinate and inferior condition? Surely such a proposition could not be seriously advocated.

But further, suppose that Congress by its acts should grant titles of nobility and require the President to issue commissions to perfect them, or pass bills of attainder or *ex post facto* laws, or lay a capitation tax without reference to the census, and devolve the execution of the statutes upon the President; shall he be bound, regardless of his oath to protect and defend the Constitution, to execute them against his own convictions and against the unanimous opinion and advice of the Attorney General and his other constitutional advisers? If in any case the right of judgment is to be exercised, no criminality can be legally imputed for its honest exercise, though the conclusion may be erroneous.

For these reasons, independent of those already assigned, and from a careful consideration of the evidence adduced and of the circumstances of the case, I do not think that the first eight and the eleventh articles can be maintained.

OPINION
OF
HON. CHARLES SUMNER.

. I voted against the rule of the Senate allowing opinions to be filed in this proceeding, and regretted its adoption. With some hesitation I now take advantage of the opportunity, if not the invitation, which it affords. Voting "guilty" on all the articles, I feel that there is no need of explanation or apology. Such a vote is its own best defender. But I follow the example of others.

BATTLE WITH SLAVERY.

This is one of the last great battles with slavery. Driven from these legislative Chambers; driven from the field of war, this monstrous power has found a refuge in the Executive Mansion, where, in utter disregard of the Constitution and laws, it seeks to exercise its ancient far-reaching sway. All this is very plain. Nobody can question it. Andrew Johnson is the impersonation of the tyrannical Slave Power. In him it lives again. He is the lineal successor of John C. Calhoun and Jefferson Davis. And he gathers about him the same supporters. Original partisans of slavery North and South; habitual compromisers of great principles; maligners of the Declaration of Independence; politicians without heart; lawyers, for whom a technicality is everything, and a promiscuous company who at every stage of the battle have set their faces against Equal Rights;—these are his allies. It is the old troop of slavery, with a few recruits, ready as of old for violence—cunning in device and heartless in quibble. With the President at their head, they are now entrenched in the Executive Mansion.

Not to dislodge them is to leave this country a prey to one of the most hateful tyrannies of history. Especially is it to surrender the Unionists of the rebel States to violence and bloodshed. Not a month, not a week, not a day should be lost. *The safety of the Republic requires action at once.* The lives of innocent men must be rescued from sacrifice.

I would not in this judgment depart from that moderation which belongs to the occasion; but God forbid that, when called to deal with so great an offender, I should affect a coldness which I cannot feel. Slavery has been our worst enemy, murdering our children, filling our homes with mourning, and darkening the land with tragedy; and now it rears its crest anew with Andrew Johnson as its representative. Through him it assumes once more to rule the Republic and to impose its cruel law. The enormity of his conduct is aggravated by his barefaced treachery. He once declared himself the Moses of the colored race. Behold him now the Pharaoh. With such treachery in such a cause there can be no parley. Every sentiment, every conviction, every vow against slavery must now be directed against him. Pharaoh is at the bar of the Senate for judgment.

The formal accusation is founded on certain recent transgressions, enumerated in articles of impeachment, but it is wrong to suppose that this is the whole case. It is very wrong to try this impeachment merely on these articles. It is unpardonable to higgle over words and phrases when for more than two years the tyrannical pretensions of this offender, now in evidence before the Senate, as I shall show, have been manifest in their terrible, heartrending consequences.

IMPEACHMENT A POLITICAL, AND NOT A JUDICIAL PROCEEDING.

Before entering upon the consideration of the formal accusation, instituted by the House of Representatives of the United States in their own name and in the name of all the people thereof, it is important to understand the nature of the proceeding ; and here on the threshold we encounter the effort of the defense, which has sought in every way to confound this great constitutional trial with an ordinary case at Nisi Prius and to win for the criminal President an Old Bailey acquittal, where on some quibble the prisoner is allowed to go without day. From beginning to end this has been painfully apparent, thus degrading the trial and baffling justice. Point by point has been pressed, sometimes by counsel and sometimes even by Senators, leaving the substantial merits untouched, as if on a solemn occasion like this, involving the safety of the Republic, there could be any other question.

The first effort was to call the Senate, sitting for the trial of impeachment, a court, and not a Senate. Ordinarily names are of little consequence, but it cannot be doubted that this appellation has been made the starting-point for those technicalities, which are so proverbial in courts. Constantly we have been reminded of what is called our judicial character and of the supplementary oath we have taken, as if a Senator were not always under oath, and as if other things within the sphere of his duties were not equally judicial in character. Out of this plausible assumption has come that fine-spun thread which lawyers know so well how to weave.

The whole mystification disappears when we look at our Constitution, which in no way speaks of impeachment as judicial in character, and in no way speaks of the Senate as a court. On the contrary it uses positive language, inconsistent with this assumption and all its pretended consequences. On this head there can be no doubt.

By the Constitution it is expressly provided that "the *judicial power* shall be vested in one Supreme Court and in such inferior courts as the Congress may from time to time ordain and establish," thus positively excluding the Senate from any exercise of "the judicial power." And yet this same Constitution provides that " the Senate shall have the sole power to try all impeachments." In the face of these plain texts it is impossible not to conclude that in trying impeachments Senators exercise a function which is not regarded by the Constitution as "judicial," or, in other words, as subject to the ordinary conditions of judicial power. Call it senatorial or political, it is a power by itself and subject to its own conditions.

Nor can any adverse conclusion be drawn from the unauthorized designation of court, which has been foisted into our proceedings. This term is very expansive and sometimes very insignificant. In Europe it means the household of a prince. In Massachusetts it is still applied to the Legislature of the State, which is known as the General Court. If applied to the Senate it must be interpreted by the Constitution, and cannot be made in any respect a source of power or a constraint.

It is difficult to understand how this term, which plays such a part in present pretensions, obtained its vogue. It does not appear in English impeachments, although there is reason for it there, which is not found here. From ancient times Parliament, including both Houses, has been called a court, and the House of Lords is known as a court of appeal. The judgment on impeachments embraces not merely removal from office, as under our Constitution, but also punishment. And yet it does not appear that the Lords sitting on impeachments are called a court. They are not so entitled in any of the cases, from the first in 1330, entitled simply, "Impeachment of Roger Mortimer, Earl of March, for Treason," down to the last in 1806, entitled, "Trial of Right Honorable Henry Lord Viscount Melville before the Lords House of Parliament in Westminster for High Crimes and Misdemeanors whereof he was accused in certain articles of Impeachment." In the historic case of Lord Bacon, we find, at the first stage, this title, "Proceedings in Parliament against Francis Bacon Lord Verulam," and after the impeachment was presented, the simple title, "Proceedings in the House of Lords." Had this simplicity been followed in our proceedings, one source of misunderstanding would have been removed.

There is another provision of the Constitution which testifies still further, and, if possible, more completely. It is the limitation of the judgment in cases of impeachment, making it political and nothing else. It is not in the nature of *punishment*, but in the nature of *protection to the Republic*. It is confined to removal from office and disqualification ; but, as if aware that this was no punishment, the Constitution further provides that this judgment shall be no impediment to indictment, trial, judgment, and punishment "according to law." Thus again is the distinction declared between an impeachment and a proceeding "according to law." The first, which is political, belongs to the Senate, which is a political body ; the latter, which is judicial, belongs to the courts, which are judicial bodies. The Senate removes from office ; the courts punish. I am not alone in drawing this distinction. It is well known to all who have studied the subject. Early in our history it was put forth by the distinguished Mr. Bayard of Delaware, the father of Senators, in the case of Blount, and it is adopted by no less an authority than our highest commentator, Judge Story, who was as much disposed as anybody to amplify the judicial power. In speaking of this text, he says, that impeachment "is not so much designed to punish the offender as *to secure the State against gross official misdemeanors;* that it touches neither his person nor his property ; *but simply divests him of his political capacity.* (*Story, Commentaries, Vol. I, sec.* 803.) All this seems to have been forgotten by certain persons on the present trial, who, assuming that impeachment was a proceeding "according to law," have treated the Senate to the technicalities of the law, to say nothing of the law's delay.

As we discern the true character of impeachment under our Constitution we shall be constrained to confess that it is a political proceeding, before a political body, with political purposes; that it is founded on political offenses, proper for the consideration of a political body and subject to a political judgment only. Even in cases of treason and bribery the judgment is political, and nothing more. If I were to sum up in one word the object of impeachment under our Constitution, meaning that which it has especially in view, and to which it is practically limited, I should say *expulsion from office*. The present question is, Shall Andrew Johnson, on the case before the Senate, be expelled from office?

Expulsion from office is not unknown to our proceedings. By the Constitution a Senator may be expelled with "the concurrence of two thirds;" precisely as a President may be expelled with "the concurrence of two thirds." In each of these cases the same exceptional vote of two thirds is required. Do not the two illustrate each other? From the nature of things they are essentially similar in character, except that on the expulsion of the President the motion is made by the House of Representatives at the bar of the Senate, while on the expulsion of a Senator the motion is made by a Senator. And how can we require a technicality of proceeding in the one which is rejected in the other? If the Senate is a court, bound to judicial forms on the expulsion of the President, must it not be the same on the expulsion of a Senator? But nobody attributes to it any such strictness in the latter case. Numerous precedents attest how, in dealing with its own members, the Senate has sought to do substantial justice without reference to forms. In the case of Blount, which is the first in our history, the expulsion was on the report of a committee, declaring him "guilty of a high misdemeanor, entirely inconsistent with his public trust and duty as a Senator." (*Annals of Congress, Fifteenth Congress*, 1797, page 44.) At least one Senator has been expelled on simple motion, even without reference to a committee. Others have been expelled without any formal allegations or formal proofs.

There is another provision of the Constitution, which overrides both cases. It is this: "each House may determine its rules of proceeding.' The Senate on the expulsion of its own members has already done this practically and set an example of simplicity. But it has the same power over its "rules of proceeding" on the expulsion of the President; and there can be no reason for simplicity in the one case not equally applicable in the other. Technicality is as little consonant with the one as with the other. Each has for its object the *Public Safety*. For this the Senator is expelled; for

this also the President is expelled. *Salus populi suprema lex.* The proceedings in each case must be in subordination to this rule.

There is one formal difference, under the Constitution, between the power to expel a Senator and the power to expel the President. The power to expel a Senator is unlimited in its terms. The Senate may, "with the concurrence of two thirds, expel a member," nothing being said of the offense; whereas the President can be expelled only "for treason, bribery or *other high crimes and misdemeanors*." A careful inquiry will show that, under the latter words, there is such a latitude as to leave little difference between the two cases. This brings us to the question of impeachable offenses.

POLITICAL OFFENSES ARE IMPEACHABLE OFFENSES.

So much depends on the right understanding of the character of this proceeding, that even at the risk of protracting this discussion, I cannot hesitate to consider this branch of the subject, although what I have already said may render it superfluous. *What are Impeachable Offenses* has been much considered in this trial and sometimes with very little appreciation of the question. Next to the mystification from calling the Senate a court has been the other mystification from not calling the transgressions of Andrew Johnson impeachable offenses.

It is sometimes boldly argued, that there can be no impeachment under the Constitution of the United States, unless for an offense defined and made indictable by an act of Congress; and, therefore, Andrew Johnson must go free, unless it can be shown that he is such an offender. But this argument mistakes the Constitution and also mistakes the whole theory of impeachment.

It mistakes the Constitution in attributing to it any such absurd limitation. The argument is this. Because in the Constitution of the United States there are no common-law crimes, therefore, there are no such crimes on which an impeachment can be maintained. To this there are two answers on the present occasion; first, that the District of Columbia, where the President resides and exercises his functions, was once a part of Maryland, where the common law prevailed; that when it came under the jurisdiction of the United States it brought with it the whole body of the law of Maryland, including the common law, and that at this day the common law of crimes is still recognized here. But the second answer is stronger still. By the Constitution *expulsion from office* is "on impeachment for and conviction of treason, bribery, *or other high crimes and misdemeanors;*" and this, according to another clause of the Constitution, is "the supreme law of the land." Now, when a constitutional provision can be executed, without superadded legislation, it is absurd to suppose that such superadded legislation is necessary. Here the provision executes itself without any reënactment; and as for the definition of "treason" and "bribery" we resort to the common law, so for the definition of "high crimes and misdemeanors" we resort to the Parliamentary Law and the instances of impeachment by which it is illustrated. And thus clearly the whole testimony of English history enters into this case with its authoritative law. From the earliest text-writer on this subject (*Woodeson, Lectures, Vol. II, p.* 601,) we learn the undefined and expansive character of these offenses; and these instances are in point now. Thus, where a lord chancellor has been thought to put the great seal to an ignominious treaty; a lord admiral to neglect the safeguard of the seas; an ambassador to betray his trust; a privy councillor to propound dishonorable measures; a confidential adviser to obtain exorbitant grants or incompatible employments, or *where any magistrate has attempted to subvert the fundamental law or introduce arbitrary power;* all these are high crimes and misdemeanors, according to these precedents by which our Constitution must be interpreted. How completely they cover the charges against Andrew Johnson, whether in the formal accusation or in the long antecedent transgressions to which I shall soon call attention as an essential part of the case, nobody can question.

Broad as this definition may seem, it is in harmony with the declared opinions of the best minds that have been turned in this direction. Of these none so great as Edmund Burke, who, as manager on the impeachment of Warren Hastings, excited the admiration of all by the varied stores of knowledge and philosophy, illumined by the rarest eloquence, with which he elucidated his cause. These are his words:

"It is by this tribunal that statesmen who abuse their power are tried before statesmen and by statesmen, *upon solid principles of State morality. It is here that those who by an abuse of power have polluted the spirit of all laws can never hope for the least protection from any of its forms.* It is here that those who have refused to conform themselves to the protection of law can never hope to escape through any of its defects." [*Bond, Speeches on Trial of Hastings,* vol. 1 p. 4.

The value of this testimony is not diminished because the orator spoke as a manager. By a professional advocate may state opinions which are not his own; but a manager cannot. Representing the House of Representatives and all the people, he speaks with the responsibility of a judge, so that his words may be cited hereafter. In saying this I but follow the claim of Mr. Fox. Therefore, the words of Burke are as authoritative as beautiful.

In different but most sententious terms, Mr. Hallam, who is so great a light in constitutional history, thus exhibits the latitude of impeachment and its comprehensive grasp:

"A minister is answerable for *the justice, the honesty, the utility of all measures* emanating from the Crown, *as well as their legality;* and thus the Executive administration is or *ought to be subordinate in all great matters of policy* to the superintendence and virtual control of the two Houses of Parliament."—*Hallam, Constitutional History,* vol. 2, chap. —.

Thus, according to Hallam, even a failure in

C. I.—61.

justice, honesty and utility, as well as in legality, may be the ground of impeachment; and the administration should in all great matters of policy be subject to the two Houses of Parliament; the House of Commons to impeach and the House of Lords to try. Here again the case of Andrew Johnson is provided for.

Our best American lights are similar in character, begining with the Federalist itself. According to this authority impeachment is for "those offenses which proceed from the *misconduct of public men,* or, in other words, from the abuse or violation of some public trust; and they may with peculiar propriety be deemed *political,* as they relate to injuries done immediately to society itself." (No. 65.) If ever injuries were done immediately to society itself; if ever there was an abuse or violation of public trust; if ever there was misconduct of a public man;—all these are now before us in the case of Andrew Johnson. The Federalist has been echoed ever since by all who have spoken with knowledge and without prejudice. First came the respected commentator, Rawle, who specifies among causes of impeachment "the fondness for the individual extension of power;" "the influence of party and prejudice;" "the seductions of foreign States;" the baser appetite for illegitimate emolument;" and "the involutions and varieties of vice too many and too artful to be anticipated by positive law;" all resulting in what the commentator says are "not inaptly termed *political offenses.*" (Page 19.) And thus Rawle unites with the Federalist in stamping upon impeachable offenses the epithet "political." If in the present case there has been on the part of Andrew Johnson, no base appetite for illegitimate emolument and no yielding to foreign seductions, there has been most notoriously the influence of party and prejudice, also to an unprecedented degree an individual extension of power, and an involution and variety of vice impossible to be anticipated by positive law, all of which, in gross or in detail, is impeachable. Here it is in gross. Then comes Story, who writing with the combined testimony of English and American history before him and moved only by a desire of truth, records his opinion with all the original emphasis of the Federalist. His words are like a judgment. According to him the process of impeachment is intended to reach "personal misconduct, or gross neglect, or usurpation or habitual disregard of the public interests in the discharge of the duties of *political office;*" and the commentator adds that it is "to be exercised over offenses committed by public men in violation of their public trust and duties;" that "the offenses to which it is ordinarily applied are of a *political* character;" and that strictly speaking "the power partakes of a *political* character." (*Story's Commentaries,* vol. 2, §746, 764.) Every word here is like an ægis for the present case. The later commentator, Curtis, is, if possible, more explicit even than Story. According to him an "impeachment is not necessarily a trial for crime," "its purposes lie wholly beyond the penalties of the statute or customary law;" and this commentator does not hesitate to say that it is a "proceeding to ascertain *whether cause exists for removing a public officer from office;*" and he adds that "such cause of removal may exist where no offense against public law has been committed, as, where the individual has, from immorality or imbecility, *or maladministration, become unfit to exercise the office.*" (*Curtis on the Constitution, p. 360.*) Here again the power of the Senate over Andrew Johnson is vindicated, so as to make all doubt or question absurd.

I close this question of impeachable offenses by asking you to consider that all the cases, which have occurred in our history, are in conformity with the rule, which so many commentators have announced. The several trials of Pickering, Chase, Peck, and Humphreys exhibit its latitude in different forms. Official misconduct, including in the case of Chase and Humphreys offensive utterances, constituted the high crimes and misdemeanors for which they were respectively arraigned. These are precedents. Add still further, that Madison, in debate on the appointing power, at the very beginning of our Government said: "I contend that the *wanton removal of meritorious officers* would subject the President to impeachment and removal from his own high trust." (*Elliot's Debates*, vol. 4, p. 141.) But Andrew Johnson, standing before a crowd, said of meritorious officers that "he would kick them out," and forthwith proceeded to execute his foul-mouthed menace. How small was all that Madison imagined; how small was all that was spread out in the successive impeachments of our history, if gathered into one case, compared with the terrible mass now before us.

From all these concurring authorities, English and American, it is plain that impeachment is a power broad as the Constitution itself, and applicable to the President, Vice President, and all civil officers through whom the Republic suffers or is in any way imperilled. Show me an act of evil example or influence committed by a President and I show you an impeachable offense which becomes great in proportion to the scale on which it is done and the consequences which are menaced. The Republic must receive no detriment.; and impeachment is one of the powers of the Constitution by which this sovereign rule is maintained.

UNTECHNICAL FORM OF PROCEDURE.

The *Form of Procedure* is a topic germane to the last head and helping to illustrate it. Already it has been noticed in considering the political character of impeachment; but it deserves further treatment by itself. Here we meet the same latitude. It is natural that the trial of political offenses, before a political body, with a political judgment only, should have less of form than a trial at common law;

and yet this obvious distinction is constantly disregarded. The authorities, whether English or American, do not leave this question open to doubt.

An impeachment is not a technical proceeding, as at Nisi Prius or in a County Court, where the rigid rules of the common law prevail. On the contrary, it is a proceeding according to Parliamentary Law with rules of its own, unknown in ordinary courts. The formal statement and reduplication of words, which constitute the stock-in-trade of so many lawyers, are exchanged for a broader manner more consistent with the transactions of actual life. The precision of history is enough without the technical precision of an indictment. In declaring this rule I but follow a memorable judgment in a case which occupied the attention of England at the beginning of the last century. I refer to the case of the preacher Sacheverell, impeached of high crimes and misdemeanors on account of two sermons, in which he put forth the doctrine of non-resistance, and denounced the revolution of 1688, by which English liberty was saved. After the arguments on both sides, the judges on questions from the Lords answered that by the law of England and constant practice "the particular words supposed to be criminal ought to be specified in indictments." And yet in face of this declaration, by the judges of England, of a familiar and indisputable rule of the common law we have the rule of Parliamentary Law, which was thus set forth:

"*It is resolved* by the Lords spiritual and temporal in Parliament assembled, that by the law and usage of Parliament in prosecutions by impeachments for high crimes and misdemeanors by writing or speaking, *the particular words supposed to be criminal are not necessary to be expressly specified in such impeachments.*"—*Howell's State Trials*, vol. 15, p. 467.

The judgment here does not extend in terms beyond the case in hand; but plainly the principle announced is that in impeachments the technicalities of the common law are out of place, and the proceedings are substantially according to the rule of reason. A mere technicality, much more a quibble, such as is often so efficacious on a demurrer, is a wretched anachronism when we are considering a question of history or political duty. Even if tolerated on the impeachment of an inferior functionary, such a resort must be disclaimed on the trial of a Chief Magistrate, involving the public safety.

The technicalities of the law were made for protection against power, not for the immunity of a usurper or a tyrant. They are respectable when set up for the safeguard of the weak; but they are out of place on impeachments. Here again I cite Edmund Burke:

"God forbid—that those who cannot defend themselves upon their merits and their actions may defend themselves behind those fences and intrenchments that are made to secure the liberty of the people; that power and the abuses of power should cover themselves by those things which were made to secure liberty."—*Bond's Trial of Hastings*, vol I, p. 10.

Never was there a case where this principle belonging to the law of impeachment, was more applicable than now.

The origin of impeachment in our own Constitution and contemporary authority vindicate this very latitude. One of the apologists sought to sustain himself in an argument against this latitude, by insisting that it was with much hesitation, and only at the last moment that this jurisdiction over impeachment was originally conferred on the Senate. This is a mistake, as will appear from a simple statement. The proposition to confer this jurisdiction on the Supreme Court was made before it had been determined that the judges should be appointed by the President with the advice and consent of the Senate. The latter conclusion was reached by a unanimous vote of the Convention September 7, 1787. On the next day, September 8, Roger Sherman raised the objection that the Supreme Court was "improper to try the President because the judges would be appointed by him." This objection prevailed, and the trial was at once intrusted to the Senate by the vote of all the States with one exception; and then immediately thereafter, on the same day, the scope of impeachment was extended from "treason to bribery," so as to embrace "other high crimes and misdemeanors," and thus intrusted and thus enlarged it was made to embrace "the Vice President, and other civil officers of the United States."

From this simple narrative it appears that, while the Supreme Court, *a judicial body*, was contemplated for the trial of impeachments, the jurisdiction was restrained to two well-known crimes at common law, which have since been defined by statutes of the United States; but this jurisdiction, when confided to the Senate, *a political body*, was extended to political offenses, in the trial of which a commensurate discretion followed from the nature of the case. It was in this light that the proceeding was explained by the Federalist, in words which should be a guide to us now:

"The nature of the proceeding can *never be tied down by such strict rules*, either in the delineation of the offense by the prosecutors or in the construction of it by the judges, as in common cases serve to limit the discretion of courts in favor of personal security."—*Federalist*, No. 65.

This article was by Alexander Hamilton, writing in concert with James Madison and John Jay. Thus by the highest authority at the adoption of the Constitution we find that impeachment "can never be tied down by strict rules," and that this latitude is applicable to "the delineation of the offense," meaning thereby the procedure or pleading, and also to the "construction of the offense," in both of which cases the "discretion" of the Senate is enlarged beyond that of ordinary courts.

RULES OF EVIDENCE.

From the form of procedure I pass to the *Rules of Evidence*; and here again the Senate must avoid all technicalities and not allow any artificial rule to shut out the truth. It would allow no such thing on the expulsion of a Senator. How can it allow any such thing on the expulsion of a President? On this account I voted to admit all evidence that was offered during the trial, believing, in the first place, that it ought to be heard and considered; and, in the second place, that even if it were shut out from these proceedings, it could not be shut out from the public or be shut out from history, both of which must be the ultimate judges. On the impeachment of Prince Polignac and his colleagues of the Cabinet, in 1830, for signing the ordinances which cost Charles X his throne, some forty witnesses were sworn without objection, in a brief space of time, and no testimony was excluded. An examination of the two volumes entitled *Procès des Derniers Ministres de Charles X* will confirm what I say. This example was to my mind not unworthy of imitation on the present occasion.

There are other rules, which it is not too late to profit by. One of these relates to the burden of proof and is calculated to have a practical bearing. The other relates to matters of which the Senate will take cognizance without any special proof, thus importing into the case unquestionable evidence, which explains and aggravates the transgressions charged.

(1.) Look carefully at the object of this trial. Primarily it is for the expulsion of the President from office. Its motive is not punishment, not vengeance, but the *Public Safety*. Nothing less than this could justify the ponderous proceeding. It will be for the criminal courts to award the punishment due to his offenses. The Senate considers only how the safety of the people, which is the supreme law, can be best preserved; and to this end the ordinary rule of evidence is reversed. If on any point you entertain doubts, the benefit of these doubts must be given to your country; and this is the supreme law. When tried on an indictment in the criminal courts Andrew Johnson may justly claim the benefit of your doubts; but at the bar of the Senate on the question of his expulsion from office, his vindication must be in every respect and on each charge beyond a doubt. He must show that his longer continuance in office is not inconsistent with the *Public Safety*:

"Or, at least so prove it,
That the probation bear no hinge or loop
To hang a doubt on."

Anything short of this is to trifle with the Republic and its transcendent fortunes.

It is by insisting upon doubts that the apologists of the President, at the bar and in the Senate, seek to save him. For myself, I can see none such, but assuming that they exist, then should they be marshaled for our country. This is not a criminal trial, where the rule prevails; better that many guilty men should escape than one innocent man should suffer. This rule, which is so proper in its place, is not applicable to a proceeding for expulsion from office; and who will undertake to say that any claim of office can be set against the Public Safety?

In thus stating the just rule of evidence, I do little more than apply those time-honored maxims of jurisprudence which require that every interpretation shall be always in favor of Liberty. Early in the common law, we were told that he is to be adjudged impious and cruel who does not favor Liberty; *Impius et crudelis judicandus est qui libertati non favet.* Blackstone, whose personal sympathies were with power, is constrained to confess that "the law is always ready to catch at anything in favor of Liberty." (*Blackstone's Commentaries*, vol. 2, p. 94.) But Liberty and all else are contained in the Public Safety; they depend on the rescue of the country from a presidential usurper. Therefore, should we now, in the name of the law, "catch at anything" to save the Republic.

(2.) There is another rule of evidence, which, though of common acceptance in the courts, has peculiar value in this case, where it must exercise a decisive influence. It is this: *Courts will take judicial cognizance of certain matters, without any special proof on the trial.* Some of these are of general knowledge and others are within the special knowledge of the court. Among these, according to express decision, are the frame of Government and the public officers administering it; the accession of the Chief Executive; the sitting of Congress and its usual course of proceeding; the usual course of travel; the ebbs and flows of the tide; *also whatever ought to be generally known within the limits of the jurisdiction, including the history of the country.* Besides these matters of general knowledge a court will take notice of its own records, the conduct of its own officers, and whatever passes in its own presence or under its own eyes. For all this I cite no authority; it is superfluous. I add a single illustration from the great English commentator: "If a contempt be committed in the face of the court, the offender may be instantly apprehended and imprisoned, at the discretion of the judges, without any further proof or examination." (*Blackstone's Commentaries*, vol. 4, p. 286.) •

If this be the rule of courts, *a fortiori*, it must be the rule of the Senate on impeachments; for we have already seen that, when sitting for this purpose, the Senate enjoys a latitude of its own. Its object is the Public Safety, and, therefore, no aid for the arrival at truth can be rejected. No gate can be closed. But here is a gate opened by the sages of the law and standing open always, to the end that justice may not fail.

Applying this rule to the present proceeding, it will be seen at once how it brings before the Senate, without any further evidence, a long catalogue of crime, affecting the character of the President beyond all possibility of defense, and serving to explain the latter acts

on which the impeachment is founded. It was in this Chamber, in the face of the Senate and the ministers of Foreign Powers, and surrounded by the gaze of thronged galleries, that Andrew Johnson exhibited himself in beastly intoxication while he took his oath of office as Vice President; and all that he has done since is of record here. Much of it appears on our Journals. The rest is in authentic documents published by the order of the Senate. Never was a record more complete.

Here in the Senate we know officially how he has made himself the attorney of slavery—the usurper of legislative power—the violator of law—the patron of rebels—the helping hand of rebellion—the kicker from office of good citizens—the open bung-hole of the Treasury—the architect of the "whisky ring"—the stumbling-block to all good laws by wanton vetoes and then by criminal hinderances; all these things are known here beyond question. To the apologists of the President who set up the quibbling objection that they are not alleged in the articles of impeachment, I reply, that, even if excluded on this account from judgment, they may be treated as evidence.· They are the reservoir from which to draw in determining the true character of the latter acts for which the President is arraigned, and especially the *intent* by which he was animated. If these latter acts were alone, without connection with the transgressions of the past, they would have remained unnoticed. Impeachment would not have been ordered. It is because they are a prolongation of that wickedness under which the country has so long suffered, and spring from the same bloody fountain, that they are now presented for judgment. They are not alone; nor can they be faithfully considered without drawing upon the past. The story of the God Thor in Scandinavian mythology is revived, whose drinking-horn could not be drained by the strongest quaffer, for it communicated with the vast and inexhaustible ocean. Andrew Johnson is our God Thor, and these latter acts for which he stands impeached are the drinking-horn whose depths are unfathomable.

OUTLINE OF TRANSGRESSIONS OF ANDREW JOHNSON.

From this review of the character of this proceeding, showing how it is political in character—before a political body—and with a political judgment, being expulsion from office and nothing more; then how the transgressions of the President, in their protracted line, are embraced under "impeachable offenses;" then how the form of procedure is liberated from the ordinary technicalities of the law; and lastly how unquestionable rules of evidence open the gates to overwhelming testimony, I pass now to the consideration of this overwhelming testimony and how the present impeachment became a necessity. I have already called it one of the last great battles with Slavery. See now how the battle began.

Slavery in all its pretensions is a defiance of law ; for it can have no law in its support. Whoso becomes its representative must act accordingly ; and this is the transcendent crime of Andrew Johnson. For the sake of Slavery and to uphold its original supporters in their endeavors to continue this wrong under another name, he has set at defiance the Constitution and laws of the land, and he has accompanied this unquestionable usurpation by brutalities and indecencies in office without precedent, unless we go back to the Roman emperor fiddling, or the French monarch dancing among his minions. This usurpation with its brutalities and indecencies became manifest as long ago as the winter of 1866, when, being President, and bound by his oath of office to preserve, protect, and defend the Constitution and to take care that the laws are faithfully executed, he took to himself legislative powers in the reconstruction of the rebel States, and, in carrying forward this usurpation, nullified an act of Congress, intended as the cornerstone of reconstruction, by virtue of which rebels are excluded from office under the Government of the United States, and thereafter, in vindication of this misconduct, uttered a scandalous speech in which he openly charged members of Congress with being assassins, and mentioned some by name. Plainly he should have been impeached and expelled at that early day. The case against him was complete. That great patriot of English history, Lord Somers, has likened impeachment to Goliath's sword hanging in the temple to be taken down only when occasion required ; but if ever there was an occasion for its promptest vengeance it was then. Had there been no failure at that time we should be now nearer by two years to restoration of all kinds, whether political or financial. So strong is my conviction of the fatal remissness of the House, that I think the Senate would do a duty in strict harmony with its constitutional place in the Government, and the analogies of judicial tribunals so often adduced, if it reprimanded the House of Representatives for this delay. Of course the Senate could not originate an impeachment. It could not take down the sword of Goliath. It must wait on the House, as the court waits on the Grand Jury. But this waiting has cost the country more than can be told.

Meanwhile the President proceeded in his transgressions. There is nothing of usurpation which he has not attempted. Beginning with an assumption of all power in the rebel States, he has shrunk from nothing in the maintenance of this unparalleled assumption. This is a plain statement of fact. Timid at first he grew bolder and bolder. He saw too well that his attempt to substitute himself for Congress in the work of reconstruction was sheer usurpation and, therefore, by his Secretary of State, did not hesitate to announce that "it must be distinctly understood that the restoration will be *subject to the decision of Congress.*" On two separate occasions, in July and September, 1865, he confessed the power of Congress over the subject; but when Congress came together in December, this confesser of congressional power found that he alone had this great prerogative. According to his new-fangled theory, Congress had nothing to do but admit the States with the governments which had been instituted through his will alone. It is difficult to measure the vastness of this usurpation, involving as it did a general nullification. Strafford was not bolder, when, speaking for Charles I, he boasted that "the little finger of prerogative was heavier than the loins of the law;" but these words helped the proud minister to the scaffold. No monarch, no despot, no Sultan, could claim more than an American President; for he claimed all. By his edict alone governments were organized, taxes were levied, and even the franchises of the citizen were determined.

Had this assumption of power been incidental, for the exigency of the moment, as under the pressure of war, and especially to serve the cause of Human Rights to which before his elevation the President had professed such loud-mouthed devotion, it might have been pardoned. It would have passed into the chapter of unauthorized acts which a patriot people had condoned. But it was the opposite in every particular. Beginning and continuing in usurpation, it was hateful beyond pardon, because it sacrificed the rights of Unionists, white and black, and was in the interest of the rebellion and of those very rebels who had been in arms against their country.

More than one person was appointed Provisional Governor, who could not take the oath of office required by act of Congress. Other persons in the same predicament were appointed in the revenue service. The effect of these appointments was disastrous. They were in the nature of notice to rebels everywhere, that participation in the rebellion was no bar to office. If one of their number could be appointed Governor, if another could be appointed to a confidential position in the Treasury Department, then there was nobody on the long list of blood who might not look for preferment. And thus all offices, from Governor to constable, were handed over to a disloyal scramble. Rebels crawled forth from their retreats. Men who had hardly ventured to expect their lives were now candidates for office, and the Rebellion became strong again. The change was felt in all the gradations of government, whether in States, counties, towns, or villages. Rebels found themselves in places of trust, while the true-hearted Unionists, who had watched for the coming of our flag and ought to have enjoyed its protecting power, were driven into hiding-places. All this was under the auspices of Andrew Johnson. It was he who animated the wicked crew. He was at the head of the work. Loyalty everywhere was persecuted. White and black, whose only offense was that they had been true to their country, were insulted, abused, murdered. There was no safety for the loyal man except within the flash of our bayonets. The story is as authentic as hideous. More than two thousand murders have been reported in Texas alone since the surrender of Kirby Smith. In other States there was a similar carnival. Property, person, life, were all in jeopardy. Acts were done "to make a holiday in Hell." At New Orleans there was a fearful massacre, which, considering the age and the place, was worse than that of St. Bartholomew, which darkens a century óf France, or that of Glencoe, which has printed an ineffaceable stain upon one of the greatest reigns of English history. All this is directly traced to Andrew Johnson. The words of bitterness uttered at another time are justified, while Fire, Famine, and Slaughter shriek forth—

"He let me loose, and cried Halloo!
To him alone the praise is due."

ACCUMULATION OF IMPEACHABLE OFFENSES.

This is nothing but the outline, derived from historic sources *which the Senate on this occasion is bound to recognize.* Other acts fall within the picture. The officers he had appointed in defiance of law were paid also in the same defiance. Millions of property were turned over without consideration to railroad companies, whose special recommendation was their participation in the rebellion. The Freedman's Bureau, that sacred charity of the Republic, was despoiled of its possessions for the sake of rebels, to whom their forfeited estates were given back after they had been vested by law in the United States. The proceeds of captured and abandoned property, lodged under the law in the national Treasury, were ravished from their place of deposit and sacrificed. Rebels were allowed to fill the antechambers of the Executive Mansion and to enter into his counsels. The pardoning power was prostituted, and pardons were issued in lots to suit rebels, thus grossly abusing that trust whose discreet exercise is so essential to the administration of justice. The powers of the Senate over appointments were trifled with and disregarded, by reappointing persons who had been already rejected, and by refusing to communicate the names of others appointed by him during the recess. The veto power, conferred by the Constitution as a remedy for ill-considered legislation, was turned by him into a weapon of offense against Congress and into an instrument to beat down the just opposition which his usurpation had aroused. The power of removal, which patriot Presidents had exercised so sparingly, was seized as an engine of tyranny and openly employed to maintain his wicked purposes by the sacrifice of good citizens, who would not consent to be his tools. Incompetent and dishonest creatures, whose only recommendation was that they echoed his voice, were appointed to office, especially in the collection of the Internal Revenue, through

whom a new organization, known as, the "Whisky Ring," has been able to prevail over the Government, and to rob the Treasury of millions, at the cost of tax-paying citizens, whose burdens are thus increased. Laws enacted by Congress for the benefit of the colored race, including that great statute for the establishment of the Freedman's Bureau, and that other great statute for the establishment of civil rights, were first attacked by his veto, and when finally passed by the requisite majority over his veto were treated by him as little better than dead letters, while he boldly attempted to prevent the adoption of a constitutional amendment by which the right of citizens and the national debt were placed under the guarantee of irrepealable law. During these successive assumptions, usurpations, and tyrannies, utterly without precedent in our history, this deeply guilty man ventured upon public speeches, each an offense to good morals, where, lost to all shame, he appealed in coarse words to the coarse passions of the coarsest people—scattering firebrands of sedition—inflaming anew the rebel spirit—insulting good citizens, and, with regard to office-holders, announcing in his own characteristic phrase that he would "kick them out"—the whole succession of speeches being from their brutalities and indecencies in the nature of a "criminal exposure of his person," indictable at common law, for which no judgment can be too severe; but even this revolting transgression is aggravated when it is considered that through these utterances the cause of justice was imperiled and the accursed demon of civil feud was lashed again into vengeful fury. All these things from beginning to end are plain facts, already recorded in history and known to all. And it is further recorded in history, and known to all, that, through these enormities, any one of which is enough for condemnation, while all together present an aggregation of crime, untold calamities have been brought upon our country; disturbing business and finance; diminishing the national revenues; postponing specie payments; dishonoring the Declaration of Independence in its grandest truths; arresting the restoration of the rebel States; reviving the dying rebellion; and instead of that peace and reconciliation so much longed for, sowing strife and wrong, whose natural fruit is violence and blood.

OPEN DEFIANCE OF CONGRESS.

For all of these or any one of them Andrew Johnson should have been impeached and expelled from office. The case required a statement only; not an argument. Unhappily this was not done. As a petty substitute for the judgment which should have been pronounced and as a bridle on presidential tyranny in "kicking out of office," Congress enacted a law known as the Tenure-of-Office Act, passed March 2, 1867, over his veto by the vote of two thirds of both Houses. And, in order to prepare the way for impeachment, by removing certain scruples of technicality, its violation was expressly declared to be a high misdemeanor. The President began at once to chafe under its restraint.

Recognizing the act and following its terms he first suspended Mr. Stanton from office, and then, on his restoration by the Senate, made an attempt to win General Grant into a surrender of the Department, so as to oust Mr. Stanton and to render the restoration by the Senate ineffectual. Meanwhile Sheridan in Louisiana, Pope in Alabama, and Sickles in South Carolina, who, as military commanders, were carrying into the pacification of these States all the energies which had been so brilliantly displayed in the war, were pursued by the same vindictive spirit. They were removed by the President, and rebellion throughout that whole region clapped its hands. This was done in the exercise of his powers as Commander-in-Chief. At last, in his unappeased rage, he openly violated the Civil-Tenure Act, so as to bring himself under its judgment, by the defiant attempt to remove Mr. Stanton from the War Department without the consent of the Senate and the appointment of Lorenzo Thomas, Adjutant General of the United States, as Secretary of War *ad interim*.

IMPEACHMENT AT LAST.

The Grand Inquest of the nation, which had slept on so many enormities, was awakened by this open defiance. The gauntlet was flung into its very Chamber, and there it lay on the floor. The President, who had already claimed everything for the Executive with impunity, now rushed into conflict with Congress on the very ground selected in advance by the latter. The field was narrow, but sufficient. There was but one thing for the House of Representatives to do. Andrew Johnson must be impeached, or the Tenure-of-Office Act would become a dead letter, while his tyranny would receive a letter of license, and impeachment as a remedy for wrong-doing would be blotted from the Constitution.

Accordingly it was resolved that the offender, whose crimes had so long escaped judgment, should be impeached. Once entered upon this work, the House of Representatives, after setting forth the removal of Mr. Stanton and the appointment of General Thomas in violation of the law and Constitution, proceeded further to charge him in different forms with conspiracy wrongfully to get possession of the War Department; also with an attempt to corrupt General Emory and induce him to violate an act of Congress; also with scandalous speeches, such as no President could be justified in making; concluding with a general article setting forth attempts on his part to prevent the execution of certain acts of Congress.

Such is a simple narrative, which brings us to the Articles of Impeachment. Nothing that I have said thus far is superfluous; for it shows the origin of this proceeding, and illustrates its moving cause. The articles themselves are narrow if not technical. But they are filled and broadened by the transgressions of the past, all of which enter into the present offenses. The whole is an unbroken series with a common life. As well separate the Siamese twins as separate the offenses now charged from that succession of antecedent crimes with which they are linked, any one of which is enough for judgment. The present springs from the past and can be truly seen only in its light, which in this case is nothing less than "darkness visible."

ARTICLES OF IMPEACHMENT.

In entering upon the discussion of the articles of impeachment, I confess my regret that so great a cause, on which so much depends, should be presented on such narrow ground, although I cannot doubt that the whole past must be taken into consideration in determining the character of the acts alleged. If there has been a violation of the Constitution and laws, the apologists of the President then insist that all was done with good intentions. In reply to this it is enough if we point to the past, which thus becomes a part of the case. But of this hereafter. It is unnecessary for me to take time in setting forth the articles. The abstract already presented is enough. They will naturally come under review before the close of the inquiry.

Of the transactions embraced by the articles, the removal of Mr. Stanton has unquestionably attracted the most attention, although I cannot doubt that the scandalous harangues are as justly worthy of condemnation. But the former has been made the pivot of this impeachment. So much so that the whole case seems to revolve on this transaction. Therefore, I shall not err, if, following the articles, I put this foremost in the present inquiry.

This transaction may be brought to the touchstone of the Constitution, and also of the tenure-of-office act. But since the allegation of a violation of this act has been so conspicuous, and this act may be regarded as a congressional interpretation of the power of removals under the Constitution, I begin with the consideration of the questions arising under it.

TENURE-OF-OFFICE ACT.

The general object of the tenure-of-office act was to protect civil officers from removal without the advice and consent of the Senate; and it was made in express terms applicable to "every person holding any civil office to which he has been appointed by and with the advice and consent of the Senate." To this provision, so broad in its character, was appended a proviso as follows:

"*Provided*, That the Secretaries of State, of the Treasury, of War, of the Navy, and of the Interior, the Postmaster General, and the Attorney General shall hold their offices respectively for and during the term of the President by whom they may have been appointed and for one month thereafter, subject to removal by and with the advice and consent of the Senate."

As this general protection from removal without the advice and consent of the Senate might be productive of embarrassment during the recess of the Senate it was further provided, in a second section, that during such recess any person may be suspended from office by the President on reasons assigned, which it is made his duty to report to the Senate within twenty days after the next meeting of the Senate, and if the Senate concurs, then the President may remove the officer and appoint a successor; but if the Senate does not concur then the suspended officer shall forthwith resume his functions.

On this statute two questions arise, *first* as to its constitutionality, and *secondly*, as to its application to Mr. Stanton, so as to protect him from removal without the advice and consent of the Senate. It is impossible not to confess in advance that both have been already practically settled. The statute was passed over the veto of the President by a vote of two thirds, who thus solemnly united in declaring its constitutionality. Then came the suspension of Mr. Stanton, and his restoration to office by a triumphant vote of the Senate, being no less than thirty five to six, thus establishing not only the constitutionality of the statute, but also its protecting application to Mr. Stanton. And then came the resolution of the Senate, adopted after protracted debate on the 21st February, by a vote of twenty-seven to six, declaring, that under the Constitution and laws of the United States the President has no power to remove the Secretary of War and to designate any other officer to perform the duties of that office *ad interim;* thus, for the third time affirming the constitutionality of the statute, and for the second time, its protecting application to Mr. Stanton. There is no instance in our history where there has been such a succession of votes, with such large majorities, declaring the conclusions of the Senate and fixing them beyond recall. "Thrice is he armed who hath his quarrel just;" but the tenure-of-office act is armed *thrice* by the votes of the Senate. The apologists of the President seem to say of these solemn votes, "Thrice the brinded cat hath mewed;" but such a threefold record of the Senate cannot be treated with levity.

• The question of the constitutionality of this statute complicates itself with the power of removal under the Constitution; but I shall not consider the latter question at this stage. It will naturally present itself when we consider the power of removal under the Constitution which has been claimed by the President. For the present I assume the constitutionality of the statute.

ITS APPLICATION TO MR. STANTON.

I come at once to the question of the application of the statute to Mr. Stanton, so as to protect him against removal without the consent of the Senate. And here I doubt if any

question would have arisen but for the hasty words of the Senator from Ohio, [Mr. SHERMAN,] so often quoted in this proceeding.

Unquestionably the Senator from Ohio when the report of the conference committee of the two Houses was under discussion, stated that the statute did not protect Mr. Stanton in his office; but this was the individual opinion of this Senator, and nothing more. On hearing it I cried from my seat, "The Senator must speak for himself;" for I held the opposite opinion. It was clear to my mind that the statute was intended to protect Mr. Stanton, and that it did protect him. The Senator from Oregon, [Mr. WILLIAMS,] who was the chairman of the conference committee and conducted its deliberations, informs us that there was no suggestion in the committee that the statute did not protect all of the President's Cabinet, including, of course, Mr. Stanton. The debates in the House of Representatives are the same way. Without undertaking to hold the scales in which to weigh any such conflicting opinions, I rest on the received rule of law that they cannot be taken into account in determining the meaning of the statute. And here I quote the judgment of the Supreme Court of the United States, pronounced by Chief Justice Taney:

"In expounding this law, the judgment of *the court cannot in any degree be influenced by the construction placed upon it by individual members of Congress in the debate which took place on its passage,* nor by the motives or reasons assigned by them for supporting or opposing amendments that were offered. The law that passed is the will of the majority of both Houses and the only mode in which that will is spoken is in the act itself; and we must gather their intention from the language there used, comparing it, when any ambiguity exists, with the laws upon the same subject, and *looking, if necessary, to the public history of the times in which it was passed.—Aldridge* vs. *Williams,* 3 Howard's Reps., 24.

It is obvious to all acquainted with a legislative body that the rule thus authoritatively declared is the only one that could be safely applied. The Senate in construing the present statute must follow this rule. Therefore, I repair to the statute, stopping for a moment to glance at the public history of the times, in order to understand its object.

Already we have seen how the President, in carrying forward his usurpation in the interest of the Rebellion, had trifled with the Senate in regard to appointments, and abused the traditional power of removal, openly threatening good citizens in office that he would "kick them out," and filling all vacancies, from high to low, with creatures whose first promise was to sustain his barbarous policy. I do not stop to portray the extent of this outrage, constituting an impeachable offense according to the declared opinion of Mr. Madison, one of the strongest advocates of the presidential power of removal. Congress, instead of adopting the remedy suggested by this father of the Constitution and expelling the President by process of impeachment, attempted to wrest from him the power he was abusing. For this purpose the Tenure-of-Office Act was passed. It was deemed advisable to include the Cabinet officers within its protection; but, considering the intimate relations between them and the President, a proviso was appended securing to the latter the right of choosing them in the first instance. Its object was, where the President finds himself, on accession to office, confronted by a hostile Senate to secure to him this right of choice, without obliging him to keep the Cabinet of his predecessor; and accordingly it says to him, "Choose your own Cabinet, but expect to abide by your choice, unless you can obtain the consent of the Senate to a change."

Any other conclusion is flat absurdity. It begins by misconstruing the operative words of the proviso, that the Cabinet officers "shall hold their offices respectively for and during the term of the President by whom they are appointed." On its face there is no ambiguity here. It is only by going outside that any can be found, and this disappears on a brief inquiry. At the date of the statute Andrew Johnson had been in office two years. Some of his Cabinet were originally appointed by President Lincoln; others had been formally appointed by himself. *But all were there equally by his approval and consent.* One may do an act himself, or make it his own by ratifying it when done by another. In law it is equally his act. Andrew Johnson did not originally appoint Mr. Stanton, Mr. Seward, or Mr. Welles, but he adopted their appointments, so that at the passage of the statute they stood on the same footing as if originally appointed by him. *Practically and in the sense of the statute, they were appointed by him.* They were a Cabinet of his own choice, just as much as the Cabinet of his successor, duly appointed, will be of his own choice. If the statute compels the latter, as it clearly does, to abide by his choice, it is unreasonable to suppose that it is not equally obligatory on Andrew Johnson. Otherwise we find a special immunity for that President whose misconduct rendered it necessary, and Congress is exhibited as legislating for some future unknown President, and not for Andrew Johnson, already too well known.

Even the presidential apologists do not question that the members of the Cabinet commissioned by Andrew Johnson are protected by the statute. How grossly unreasonable to suppose that Congress intended to make such a distinction among his Cabinet as to protect those whose support of his usurpation had gained them seats which they enjoyed, while it exposed to his caprice a great citizen, whose faithful services during the war had won the gratitude of his country, whose continuance in office was regarded as an assurance of Public Safety, and whose attempted removal has been felt as a national calamity. Clearly, then, it was the intention of the statute to protect the whole Cabinet, whether originally appointed by Andrew Johnson or originally appointed by his predecessor and continued by him.

I have no hesitation in saying that no other conclusion is possible without doing violence to the statute. I cannot forget that, while we are permitted "to open the law on doubts," we are solemnly warned "not to open doubts on the law." It is Lord Bacon who gives us this rule, whose obvious meaning is, that where doubts do not exist they should not be invented. It is only by this forbidden course that any question can be raised. If we look at the statute in its simplicity, its twofold object is apparent; first, to prohibit removals; and, secondly, to limit certain terms of service. *The prohibition to remove plainly applies to all. The limitation of service applies only to members of the Cabinet.* I agree with the excellent Senator from Iowa [Mr. HARLAN] that this analysis removes all ambiguity. The pretension that any one of the Cabinet was left to the unchecked power of the President is irreconcilable with the concluding words of the proviso, which declares that they shall "be subject to removal by and with the advice and consent of the Senate;" thus expressly excluding the prerogative of the President.

Let us push this inquiry still further by looking more particularly at the statute, reduced to a skeleton, so that we may see its bones. It is as follows:

(1.) *Every person holding any civil office*, by and with the advice and consent of the Senate, shall be entitled to hold such office until a successor is appointed.

(2.) If members of the Cabinet, *then during the term of the President by whom they may have been appointed* and one month thereafter, unless sooner removed by consent of the Senate.

Mr. Stanton obviously falls within the general class, "every person holding any civil office;" and he is entitled to the full benefit of the provision for their benefit.

As obviously he falls within the sub-class, "members of the Cabinet."

In this latter class his rights are equally clear. It is in the discussions under this head that the ingenuity of lawyers has found the amplest play, mainly turning upon what is meant by "term" in the statute. I glance for a moment at some of these theories.

(1.) One pretension is that the "term" expired with the life of President Lincoln, so that Mr. Stanton is retroactively legislated out of office on the 15th May, 1865. As this is a penal statute this construction makes it *ex post facto*, and therefore unconstitutional. It also makes Congress enact this absurdity that Mr. Stanton had for two years been holding office illegally, whereas he had been holding under the clearest legal title, which could no more be altered by legislation than black could be made white. A construction which makes the statute at once unconstitutional and absurd must be rejected.

(2.) The quibble that would exclude Mr. Stanton from the protection of the statute, because he was appointed during the first "term" of President Lincoln, and the statute does not speak of "terms," is hardly worthy of notice. It leads to the same absurd results as follow from the first supposition, enhanced by increasing the retroactive effect.

(3.) Assuming that the statute does not terminate Mr. Stanton's right a month after President Lincoln's death, it is insisted that it must take effect at the earliest possible moment, and therefore on its passage. From this it follows that Mr. Stanton has been illegally in office since the 2d March, 1867, and that both he and the President have been guilty of a violation of law, the former in exercising the duties of an office to which he had no right, and the latter for appointing him, or continuing him, in office, without the consent of the Senate, in violation of the Constitution and the statute in question. Here is another absurdity to be rejected.

(4.) Assuming, as it is easy to do, that it is President Lincoln's "term" we have the better theory, that it did not expire with his life, but continues until the 4th March, 1869, in which event Mr. Stanton is clearly entitled to hold until a month thereafter. This construction is entirely reasonable and in harmony with the Constitution and legislation under it. I confess that it is one to which I have often inclined.

This brings me back to the construction with which I began, and I find Andrew Johnson is the President who appointed Mr. Stanton. To make this simple, it is only necessary to read "chosen" for "appointed" in the statute, or, if you please, consider the continuance of Mr. Stanton in office, with the concurrence of the President, as a practical appointment equivalent thereto. Clearly Mr. Stanton was in office when the statute passed from the "choice" of the President. Otherwise he would have been removed. His continuance was like another commission. This carries out the intention of the framers of the statute, violates no sound canon of construction, and is entirely reasonable in every respect. Or, if preferred, we may consider the "term" to be that of President Lincoln, and then Mr. Stanton would be protected in office until one month after the 4th March next. But whether the "term" be of Andrew Johnson or of President Lincoln, he is equally protected.

Great efforts have been made to show, that Mr. Stanton does not come within the special protection of the proviso, without considering the irresistible consequence that he is then within the general protection of the statute, being "a person holding a civil office." Turn him out of the proviso and he falls into the statute, unless you are as imaginative as one of the apologists, who placed him in a sort of intermediate limbo. But the imagination of this conception cannot make us insensible to its ineffable absurdity. It is utterly unreasonable, and every construction must be rejected which cannot stand the touch-stone of common sense.

THE SUSPENSION OF MR. STANTON RECOGNIZED HIM AS PROTECTED BY THE STATUTE.

Here I might close this part of the case; but there is still another illustration. In suspending Mr. Stanton from office as long ago as August the President himself recognized that he was protected by the statute. The facts are familiar. The President, in formal words, undertook to say that the suspension was by virtue of the Constitution; but this was a dishonest pretext in harmony with so much in his career. Whatever he may say, his acts speak louder than his words. In sending notice of the suspension to the Secretary of the Treasury, and then again in sending a message to the Senate assigning his reasons for the suspension, both being according to the requirements of the statute, he testified that, in his judgment at that time, Mr. Stanton came within its protection. If not, why thus elaborately comply with its requirements? Why the notice to the Secretary of the Treasury? Why the reasons to the Senate? All this was novel and without example. Why write to General Grant of "being sustained" by the Senate? The approval or disapproval of the Senate could make no difference in the exercise of the power which he now sets up. The approval could not confirm the suspension; the disapproval could not restore the suspended Secretary of War. In fine, why suspend at all? Why exercise the power of suspension when the President sets up the power of removal? If Mr. Stanton was unfit for office and a thorn in his side, why not remove him at once? Why resort to this long and untried experiment merely to remove at last? There is but one answer. Beyond all question the President thought Mr. Stanton protected by the statute, and sought to remove him according to its provisions, beginning, therefore, with his suspension. Failing in this, he undertook to remove him in contravention of the statute, relying in justification on his pretension to judge of its constitutionality or the pusillanimity of Congress or something else "to turn up" which should render justification unnecessary.

Clearly the suspension was made under the tenure-of-office act and can be justified in no other way. From this conclusion the following dilemma results: If Mr. Stanton was within the statute, by what right was he removed? If he was not, by what right was he suspended? The President may choose his horn. Either will be sufficient to convict.

I should not proceed further under this head but for the new device, which makes its appearance under the auspices of the Senator from Maine, [Mr. FESSENDEN,] who tells us that "whether Mr. Stanton came under the first section of the statute or not, the President had a clear right to suspend him under the second." Thus, a statute, intended as a bridle on the President, gives to the President the power to suspend Mr. Stanton, but fails to give to Mr.

Stanton any protection against the President. This statement would seem to be enough. The invention of the Senator is not less fallacious than the pretext of the President. It is a device well calculated to help the President and to hurt Mr. Stanton, with those who regard devices more than the reason of the statute and its spirit.

Study the statute in its reason and its spirit, and you cannot fail to see that the second section was intended merely as a pendant to the first and was meant to apply to the cases included in the first and none other. It was a sort of safety-valve, or contrivance to guard against the possible evils from bad men who could not be removed during the recess of the Senate. There was no reason to suspend a person who could be removed. It is absurd to suppose that a President would resort to a dilatory and roundabout suspension when the short cut of removal was open to him. Construing the statute by this plain reason its second section must have precisely the same sphere of operation as the first. By the letter Mr. Stanton falls within both; by the intention it is the same. It is only by applying to the first section his own idea of the intention and by availing himself of the letter of the second, that the Senator is able to limit the one and to enlarge the other, so as to exclude Mr. Stanton from the protection of the statute, and to include him in the part allowing suspensions. Applying either letter or spirit consistently, the case is plain.

I turn for the present from the tenure-of-office act, insisting that Mr. Stanton is within its protection, and being so, that his removal was, under the circumstances, a high misdemeanor, aggravated by its defiant purpose and the long series of transgressions which preceded it, all showing a criminal intent. The apologies of the President will be considered hereafter.

THE SUBSTITUTION OF THOMAS AD INTERIM.

' The case of Mr. Stanton has two branches: first, his removal, and, secondly, the substitution of General Thomas as Secretary of War *ad interim*. As the first was contrary to positive statute, so also was the latter without support in the acts of Congress. For the present I content myself with this latter proposition, without opening the question of the powers of the President under the Constitution.

The offender rests his case on the act of Congress of February 13, 1795, (1 *Statutes-at-Large*, 415,) which authorizes the President, "in case of *vacancy* in the office of Secretary of War, whereby he cannot perform the duties of said office," to appoint "any person" until a successor be appointed or such vacancy be filled; and the supply of the vacancy is limited to six months. Under this early statute the President defends himself by insisting that there was a "vacancy," when, in fact, there was none. All this is in that unfailing spirit of prerogative which is his guide. Here is an assumption of power. In point of fact, Mr. Stanton was at his office quietly discharging its duties, when the President assumed that there was a "vacancy" and forthwith sent the valiant Adjutant General to enter upon possession. The assumption and the commission were on a par. There is nothing in any law of the land to sanction either. Each testifies against the offender.

The hardihood of this proceeding becomes more apparent, when it is understood, that this very statute of 1795, on which the offender relies, was repealed by the statute of February 20, 1863, passed in our own day and freshly remembered by many of us. The latter statute by necessary implication obliterated the former. Such is the obvious intention, and I do not hesitate to say, that any other construction leads into those absurdities which constitute the staple of the presidential apologists. The object of Congress was to provide a substitute for previous statutes, restricting at once the number of vacancies which might be filled and the persons who might fill them. And this was done.

As by the Constitution, all appointments must receive the consent of the Senate, therefore any legislation in derogation thereof must be construed strictly; but the President insists that it shall be extended even in face of the constitutional requirement. To such pretensions is he driven. The exception recognized by the Constitution is only where a vacancy occurs during the recess of the Senate, when the President is authorized to appoint until he can obtain the consent of the Senate and no longer. It is obvious, however, that cases may arise where a sudden accident vacates the office or where the incumbent is temporarily disabled. Here was the occasion for an *ad interim* appointment, and the repealing statute embodying the whole law of the subject, was intended to provide for such cases; securing to the President time to select a successor, and also power to provide for a temporary disability. Such is the underlying principle of this statute, which it is for us to apply on the present occasion. The expiration of a commission, which ordinary care can foresee, is not one of these sudden emergencies for which provision must be made; and, assuming that vacancies by removal were contemplated, which must be denied, it is plain that the delay required for the examination of the case would give time to select a successor, while a removal without cause would never be made until a successor was ready.

Look now at the actual facts and you will see how little they come within the reason of an *ad interim* appointment. Evidently the President had resolved to remove Mr. Stanton last summer. Months passed, and he did not consummate his purpose till February. All the intervening time was his to select a successor, being a period longer than the longest fixed for the duration of an *ad interim* appointment by the very statutes under which he professed to act. In conversation with General Sherman, a month before the removal, he showed that he was then looking for a successor *ad interim*. Why not a *permanent* successor? It took him only a day to find Mr. Ewing. If, as there is reason to suppose, Mr. Ewing was already selected, when General Thomas was pushed forward, *why appoint General Thomas at all?* Why not, in the usual way, send in Mr. Ewing's name as the successor? For the excellent reason, that the offender knew the Senate would not confirm him, and that, therefore, Mr. Stanton would remain in office; whereas through an *ad interim* appointment he might obtain possession of the War Department, which was his end and aim. The *ad interim* appointment of General Thomas was, therefore, an attempt to obtain possession of an office without the consent of the Senate, precisely *because the offender knew that he could not obtain that consent.* And all this was under the pretext of an act of Congress, which, alike in letter and spirit, was inapplicable to the case.

Thus does it appear, that, while Mr. Stanton was removed in violation of the tenure-of-office act, General Thomas was appointed Secretary of War *ad interim* in equal derogation of the acts of Congress regulating the subject.

REMOVAL AND SUBSTITUTION AD INTERIM A VIOLATION OF THE CONSTITUTION.

It remains to consider if the removal and substitution were not each in violation of the Constitution. The case is new, for never until now could it arise. Assuming that the tenure-of-office act does not protect Mr. Stanton, who is thus left hung up in the limbo between the body of the act and the proviso, then the President is remitted to his prerogative under the Constitution, and he must be judged accordingly, independent of statute. Finding the power of removal there, he may be justified; but not finding it there, he must bear the consequences. And here *the tenure-of-office act furnishes a living and practical construction of the Constitution from which there is no appeal.*

From the Constitution it appears that the power of appointment is vested in the President and Senate conjointly, and that nothing is said of the power of removal, except in case of impeachment, when it is made by the Senate. Therefore the power of removal is not express, but implied only, and must exist if at all, as a necessary consequence of the power to appoint. In whom must it exist? It is a familiar rule, that the power which makes can unmake. Unless this rule be rejected, the power of removal must exist in the President and Senate conjointly; nor is there anything unreasonable in this conclusion. Removal can always be effected during the session of the Senate by the nomination and confirmation of a successor, while provision can be made for the recess by an act of Congress. This conclusion would be irresistible, were the Senate always in session, but since it is not, and since cases may arise during the recess, requiring the immediate exercise of this power of removal, it has been argued that at least during the recess it must be in the President alone. From this position there has been a jump to the next, and it has been insisted that since, for the sake of public convenience, the power of removal exists in the President, he is at liberty to exercise it, either during the recess or the session itself. Here is an obvious extension of the conclusion which the premises do not warrant. The reason failing, the conclusion must fail. *Cessante ratione cessat etiam ipsa lex.* Especially must this be the case under the Constitution. A power founded on implied necessity must fail when that necessity does not exist. The implication cannot be carried beyond the reason. Therefore, the power of removal during the recess, doubtful at best unless sanctioned by act of Congress, cannot be extended to justify the exercise of that power while the Senate is in session, ready to act conjointly with the President.

Against this natural conclusion we have the assumption that a contrary construction of the Constitution was established after debate in 1789. Without considering minutely what was really determined on that occasion, I content myself by asking, if at best it was anything but a congressional construction of the Constitution, and as such subject to be set aside by another voice from the same quarter. It was, moreover, a congressional construction adopted during the administration of Washington, whose personal character must have influenced opinion largely; and it prevailed in the House of Representatives only after earnest debate, by a bare majority, and in the Senate only by the casting vote of the Vice President, John Adams, who from position, as well as principle, was not inclined to shear the President of any prerogative. Once adopted, and no strong necessity for a change occurring, it was allowed to go unaltered, but not unquestioned. Jurists like Kent and Story, statesmen like Webster, Clay, Calhoun, and Benton, recorded themselves adversely, and it was once reversed by the vote of the Senate. Finally, this congressional construction, born of a casting vote, and questioned ever since, has been overruled by another congressional construction, which has been twice adopted in both Houses, first by large majorities on the original passage of the tenure-of-office act, and, then, by a vote of two thirds on the final passage of the same act over the veto of the President; and then again adopted by a vote of more than two thirds of the Senate, when the latter condemned the removal of Mr. Stanton; and all this in the light of experience, after ample debate and with all the consequences before them. Such a congressional construction must have a controlling influence, and the fact that it reversed the practice of eighty years and overcame the disposition to stand on the ancient ways, would seem to increase rather than diminish its weight.

Now, mark the consequences. Originally, in 1789, there was a Congressional construction, which, in effect, made the Constitution read:

"The President *shall have* the power of removal."

For the next eighty years all removals were made under this construction. The Tenure-of-office act was a new Congressional construction, overruling the first and entitled to equal if not superior weight. By virtue of this Congressional construction, the Constitution now reads:

"The President *shall not have* the power of removal."

It follows, then, that in removing Mr. Stanton the President violated the Constitution as now construed.

The dilemma is this: If the President can remove Mr. Stanton during the session of the Senate, without any power by statute, it is only by virtue of a prerogative vested in him by the Constitution, which must necessarily override the Tenure-of-office act, as an unconstitutional effort to abridge it. If, on the other hand, this act is constitutional, the prerogative of removal is not in the President, and he violated the Constitution when he assumed to exercise it.

The Tenure-of-office act cannot be treated otherwise than constitutional. Certainly not in the Senate, where some among the apologists of the President voted for it. Therefore the prerogative of removal is not in the President. The long practice, which grew up under a mere reading of the Constitution, has been declared erroneous. To this extent the Constitution has been amended, and it is as absurd to plead the practice under the first reading in order to justify an offense under the second, as to plead the existence of slavery before the constitutional amendment in order to justify this monstrosity now.

Thus must we conclude that the offender has not only violated the Tenure-of-office act, but also the Constitution; that, even assuming that Mr. Stanton is not protected by the statute, the case is not ended; that this statute, if construed so as to exclude him, cannot be rejected as a Congressional construction of the Constitution; and that, under this Congressional construction, which in value is second only to a constitutional amendment, the prerogative of removal without the consent of the Senate does not belong to the President. Of course the power of suspension under the Constitution, which is only an incident of the larger pretension, must fall also. Therefore, in the defiant removal of Mr. Stanton, and also in the pretended suspension under the Constitution with which the transaction began, the President violated the Constitution, and was guilty of an impeachable offense.

And so, also, we must conclude that, in the substitution of Lorenzo Thomas as Secretary of War *ad interim,* the offender violated not only the acts of Congress for the supply of vacancies, but also the Constitution. Knowing that he could not obtain possession of the office with the consent of the Senate, he sought to accomplish this purpose without that consent. Thus, under color of a statute, he practically set the Constitution at defiance. Mark here his inconsistency. He violates the Tenure-of-office act, alleging that it is against the Constitution, whose champion he professes to be, and then takes advantage of the acts of Congress for the supply of vacancies to set aside the Constitution in one of its most important requirements; for all which he is justly charged with an impeachable offense.

All this seems clear. Any other conclusion gives to the President the power under the Constitution to vacate all national offices and leaves the Republic the wretched victim of tyranny, with a ruler who is not even a constitutional monarch, but a king above all laws. It was solemnly alleged in the articles against Charles I of England, that "being admitted king of England, and therein trusted with a limited power *to govern by and according to the laws of the land and* NOT OTHERWISE," he nevertheless undertook "*to rule according to his will* and to overthrow the rights and liberties of the people." These very words might be adopted now to declare the crime of Andrew Johnson.

THE APOLOGIES.

Here I might close; but the offender has found apologists, who plead his cause at the bar and in the Senate. The apologies are a strange compound, enlarging rather than diminishing the offenses proved. There is, first, the Apology of Good Intentions; next, the Apology of making a case for the Supreme Court, being the Moot Court Apology; and, then, the Apology, that the President may sit in judgment on the laws, and determine whether they shall be executed, which I call the Apology of Prerogative. Following these is a swarm of technicalities, devices, and quibbles, utterly unworthy of the Senate and to be reprobated by all who love justice.

THE APOLOGY OF GOOD INTENTIONS.

I begin with the Apology of *Good Intentions.* In the light of all that has occurred, with the volume of history open before us, with the records of the Senate in our hands, and with the evidence at the bar not utterly forgotten, it is inconceivable that such an Apology can be put forward. While making it the apologists should be veiled, so that the derisive smile on their faces may not be observed by the Senate to whose simplicity it is addressed. It is hard to treat this Apology; but it belongs to the case, and, therefore, I deal with it.

Of course a mere technical violation of law, with no evil consequences and without any claim of title, is followed by nominal damages only. If a person steps on a field of grass belonging to another, without permission, he is a trespasser, and the law furnishes a familiar proceeding against him; but if he has done this accidentally, and without any real damage, it would be hard to pursue him, unless the assertion of the title were thought important. But if this trespasser is an old offender, who from the beginning has broken fences, ruined trees, and trampled down the garden, and who now defiantly comes upon the field of grass, insisting upon absolute ownership, then it is vain to set up the Apology that very little damage is done. The antecedent transgressions, ending in a claim of title, enter into the present trespass and make it a question whether the rightful owner or the trespasser shall hold possession. Here the rightful owner is the people of the United States, and the trespasser is Andrew Johnson. Therefore in the name of the people is he impeached.

This simple illustration opens the whole case. The mere technical violation of a statute or of the Constitution, without antecedents and without consequents, would not justify an impeachment. All of us can recall such even in the administration of Abraham Lincoln, and I cannot doubt, that, since this proceeding began, the Chief Justice violated the Constitution when he undertook to give a casting vote, not being a member of the Senate. But these were accidents, besides being innocuous. From a violation of the Constitution or of a statute, the law ordinarily infers evil intent, and where such a case is submitted to judgment, it throws upon the violater the burden of exculpation. He must show that his conduct was innocent; in other words, that it was without evil intent or claim of title. In the present cause we have a denial of evil intent, with a claim of title.

The question of intent thus raised by this offender cannot be considered narrowly. This is a trial of impeachment, and not a criminal case in a county court. It is a proceeding for expulsion from office on account of political offenses, and not a suit at law. When the offender sets up Good Intentions, he challenges inquisition, according to the latitude of such a proceeding. The whole past is unrolled by himself and he cannot prevent the Senate from seeing it. By a commanding rule of evidence it is all before us without any further proof. You cannot shut it out; you cannot refuse to look at it. And yet we have been seriously told that we must shut out from sight everything but the technical trespass. It only remains that, imitating the ostrich, we should thrust our heads in the sand and, not seeing danger, foolishly imagine it does not exist. This may do at Nisi Prius; it will not do in the Senate.

To such extent has this ostrich pretension been carried, that we have been solemnly admonished at the bar, and the paradox has found voice in the Senate, that we must judge the acts of Andrew Johnson, "as if committed by George Washington." Here is the paradox in its length and breadth. I deny it. I scout it. On the contrary, I say, that we must judge all these acts as if committed by Andrew Johnson, and nobody else. In other words, we must see things as they are. As well insist that an act of guilt should be judged as the mistake of innocence. As well argue that the stab of the assassin should be judged as the cut of the surgeon.

To the Apology of Good Intentions, I oppose all that long unbroken series of transgressions, each with a voice to drown every pretext of innocence. I would not repeat what I have already said, but in the presence of this apology it is my duty to remind the Senate how the career of this offender is compounded of falsehood and usurpation; how, beginning with promises to make treason odious, he soon installed it in authority; how, from declared sympathy with Unionists, white and black, he changed to be their persecutor; how in him are continued the worst elements of slavery, an insensibility to right and a passion for power; how in this spirit he usurped great prerogatives which did not belong to him; how in the maintenance of this usurpation he stuck at nothing; how he violated law; how he abused the pardoning power; how he prostituted the appointing power; how he wielded the power of removal to maintain his tyranny; how he sacrificed the Freedmen's Bureau and lifted up the Whisky Ring; how he patronized massacre and bloodshed, and gave a license to the Ku-Klux-Klan; how, in madness, he entered into conflict with Congress, contesting its rightful power over the reconstruction of the rebel States, and, when Congress would not succumb to his usurpation, how he thwarted and vilified it, expectorating foul-mouthed utterances, which are a disgrace to human nature; how he so far triumphed in his wickedness that in nine States no Union man is safe and no murderer of a Union man can be punished; and, lastly, for time fails, though not the long list of transgressions, how he conspired against the patriot Secretary of War, because he found in that adamantine character an obstacle to his revolutionary career. And now, in the face of this terrible and indisputable record, entering into and filling this impeachment, I hear a voice saying that we must judge the acts in question "as if committed by George Washington." The statement of this pretension is enough. I hand it over to the contempt it deserves.

THE MOOT-COURT APOLOGY.

. Kindred to the Apology of Good Intentions, or, perhaps, a rib out of its side, is the Moot-Court Apology, which pretends that the President, in removing Mr. Stanton, only wished to make a case for the Supreme Court, and thus submit to this tribunal the constitutionality of the Tenure-of-office act.

By this pretension the Supreme Court is converted into a moot-court to sit in judgment on acts of Congress, and the President becomes what, in the time of Charles II, Roger North said good lawyers must be, a "put case." Even assuming *against the evidence* that such was his purpose, it is hard to treat it without reprobation. The Supreme Court is not the arbiter of acts of Congress. If this pretension ever found favor, it was from the partisans of Slavery and State Rights, who, assured of the sympathy of the court, sought in this way to assure an unjust triumph. The power claimed is tribunitial in character, being nothing less than a Veto. Its nearest parallel in history is in the ancient Justitia of Arragon, which could set aside laws as unconstitutional. Our Constitution leaves no doubt as to the proper functions of the Supreme Court. It may hear and determine "all cases in law and equity arising under the Constitution, the laws of the United States, and the treaties made under their authority;" but this is all. Its business is to decide "cases;" not to sit in judgment on acts of Congress and issue its tribunitial Veto. If a "case" arises where a statute is said to clash with the Constitution, it must be decided as any other case of conflict of laws. But nothing within the just powers of the court can touch an act of Congress *except incidentally*, and then its judgment is binding only on the parties. The incidental reason assigned, as, for instance, that a statute is unconstitutional, does not bind anybody, not even the parties or the court itself. Of course, it cannot bind Congress.

On the evidence it is clear enough that the President had no honest purpose to make a case for the Supreme Court. He may have talked about it, but he was never in earnest. When asked by General Sherman "Why the lawyers could not make a case?" he said in reply that "it was found impossible, or that a case could not be made up." And so at each stage we find him practically discarding the idea. He issues the order of removal. Mr. Stanton disobeys. Here was exactly his opportunity. Instead of making the case by commencing the proper process, he tells General Thomas to "go on and take possession of the office;" and then, putting an end to this whole pretension of a case for the court, he proceeds to treat the latter in every respect, whether of law or fact, as Secretary, welcomes him to his Cabinet, invites him to present the business of his Department, and, so far from taking advantage of the opportunity he had professed to desire, denies its existence. How could he inquire by what authority Mr. Stanton assumed to hold the office of Secretary of War, when he denied, in fact, that he was holding it?

Look a little further and you cannot fail to see the reason of this indifference. The old writ of *quo warranto* was the only process by which a case could be made; and this could be issued only at the suit of the Attorney General. Had the President made an order of removal, the Secretary would have been compelled to hold only by virtue of the law and the Constitution. In answer to the writ he would have pleaded this protection, and the court must have decided the validity of the plea. Meanwhile he would have remained in office. Had he left, the process would have failed, and there was no other process by which he could raise the question. The decision of the Supreme Court in *Wallace* vs. *Anderson* would prevent a resort to a *quo warranto* on his part, while the earlier case of *Marbury* vs. *Madison* would shut him out from a *mandamus*. The apologists have not suggested any other remedy. It is clear, therefore, that Mr. Stanton's possession of the office was a *sine qua non* to a case in the Supreme Court; and that this could be only by *quo warranto*. The local attorney employed by the President testifies that a judgment in such a case could not be reached within a year. This was enough to make it impracticable; for, if commenced, it would leave the hated Secretary at his post for the remainder of the presidential term. During the pendency of the proceeding Mr. Stanton would continue the legitimate possessor of the office. Therefore the commencement of a case would defeat the presidential passion for his instant removal. True to his passion he removed the Secretary, well knowing that in this way he prevented a case for the court.

Against this conclusion, where all the testimony is harmonized, we have certain fruitless conversations with his Cabinet, and an attempt to raise the question on a *habeas corpus* after the arrest of General Thomas. The conversations, whose exclusion has given a handle to the apologists which they do not fail to use, only show that the President had made this question a subject of talk, and that, in the end, it was apparent that he could not make a case for the court so as to remove Mr. Stanton during his term, and as this was his darling object the whole idea was abandoned. The arrest of General Thomas seemed for a moment to furnish another chance; but it is enough to say of the futile attempt at that time, that it was not only after the removal of Mr. Stanton but after the impeachment had been voted by the House.

Had the President been in earnest, it was very easy for him to make a case by proceeding against a simple postmaster; but this did not suit him. He was in earnest only to remove Mr. Stanton.

Nothing is clearer than that this Moot-Court Apology is a wretched pretension and afterthought. It is the subterfuge of a criminal to cover up his crime—as if a surgeon had committed murder and then set up the apology that it was an experiment in science.

THE APOLOGY OF PREROGATIVE.

Then comes the Apology of Prerogative, being nothing less than the intolerable pretension, that the President can sit in judgment on acts of Congress, and, in his discretion, refuse to execute them. This Apology is in the nature of a claim of right. Let this be established, and, instead of a government of laws, which is the glory of a Republic, we have only the government of a single man. Here is the One-Man Power with a vengeance.

Of course, if the President can sit in judgment on the Tenure-of-office act, and set it aside as unconstitutional, there is no act of Congress which he may not treat in the same way. He may set aside the whole succession of statutes for the government of the Army; and his interview with General Emory attests his willingness to venture in that direction. In that spirit of oppression which seems to govern him, he may set aside the great statute for the establishment of Civil Rights without distinction of color. But why confine myself to instances? The whole statute-book will be subject to his prerogative. Vain is the requirement of the Constitution that "the President shall take care that the laws be faithfully executed." Vain is that other requirement, that a bill, approved by two thirds of both Houses over his veto, "shall become a law." His veto is perpetual; nor is it limited to any special enactment. It is as broad as the whole recorded legislation of the Republic. There is nothing which it cannot hurry into that maelstrom ingulfing all.

The President considers the statute unconstitutional, say the apologists. A mistake in judgment on such a question is not an impeachable offense, add the apologists. To which I reply, that it is not for a mistake in judgment but for usurpation in undertaking to exercise his judgment at all on such a question that he is impeached; in other words, he is impeached for undertaking to set aside a statute. Whether the statute is constitutional or not is immaterial in this view. The President, after the statute has become a law, is not the person to decide.

Ingenuity seeks to perplex the question by putting impossible cases. For instance, suppose Congress should have lost its wits, so far as to enact that the President should not be Commander-in-Chief of the Army and Navy, or that he should not have the power to grant pardons; and suppose still further, that Congress, in defiance of the positive text of the Constitution, should undertake to create "titles of nobility," must not the President treat such enactments as unconstitutional? Of course he must; but such instances do not help the prerogative now claimed. Every such enactment would be *on its face unconstitutional.* It would be an act of unreasoning madness, which the President, as well as the courts, must disregard, as if it were plain nonsense. Its unconstitutionality would be like an axiom, not to be questioned. No argument or authority would be needed. It proves itself. Nor would the duty of disobedience be less obligatory, even if the enactment had been sanctioned by the Supreme Court; and it is not more violent for me

to suppose it sanctioned by the Supreme Court than for the apologists to suppose it sanctioned by Congress. The enactment would be a self-evident monstrosity, and therefore must be disobeyed as much as if one of the ten commandments were reversed, so that it should read, "Thou shalt kill." Such extreme cases serve no good purpose. The Constitution is the supreme law of the land, and the people will not allow its axiomatic requirements to be set aside. An illustration outside the limits of reason is of no value.

In the cases supposed, the unconstitutionality of the enactment is axiomatic, excluding opinion or argument. It is a matter of fact and not a matter of opinion. When the case is one on which there are two sides or two different views, it is then within the domain of argument. It is in no sense axiomatic. It is no longer a matter of fact but a matter of opinion. When submitted to the Supreme Court it is for their "Opinion." Without occupying time with refinements on this head, I content myself with asserting that the judgment of the court must be a matter of opinion. One of the apologists has asserted that such a judgment is a matter of fact, and, generally, that the constitutionality of a statute is a matter of fact. I assert the contrary. When a bench of judges stands five to four, shall we say that the majority declare a fact and the minority declare an opinion?

Assuming, then, what I think cannot be denied, that the constitutionality of a statute is a matter of opinion, the question occurs, what opinion shall be regarded for the time as decisive. Clearly the opinion of Congress must control all executive officers from the lowest to the President. According to a venerable maxim of jurisprudence, all public acts are presumed to be correct; *omnia rite presumuntur.* A statute must be presumed constitutional, unless on its face the contrary; and no decision of any court is required in its favor. It is the law of the land, and must be obeyed as such. The maxim which presumes constitutionality is just as binding as the analogous maxim of the criminal law, which presumes innocence. The President reversing all this has presumed the statute unconstitutional, and acted accordingly. In the name of prerogative he has set it aside.

The apologists have been driven to invoke the authority of President Jackson, who asserted for himself the power to judge the constitutionality of an act of Congress which, in the course of legislation required his approval, although the question involved had been already adjudged by the Supreme Court. And he was clearly right. The court itself would not be bound by its adjudication. How could it constrain another branch of the Government? But Andrew Jackson never put forth the pretension that it was within his prerogative to nullify a statute, which had been passed over his veto in the way prescribed by the Constitution. He was courageous, but there was no such unconstitutional audacity in his life.

The apologists have also summoned to their aid those great instances, where conscientious citizens have refused obedience to unjust laws. Such was the case of Hampden, who set an example for all time in refusing to pay ship money. Such also was the case of many in our own country, who spurned the Fugitive Slave Bill. These exalted characters, on their conscience, refused to obey the law and suffered accordingly. The early Christians were required by imperial mandate to strew grain on the altar of Jove. Though good citizens, they preferred to be martyrs. Such a refusal can be no apology for a President, who, in the name of prerogative breaks the great oath which he has sworn to see that the laws are faithfully executed. Rather do these instances, in their moral grandeur, rebuke the offender.

Here I turn from this Apology of Prerogative, regretting that I cannot say more to unfold its destructive character. If anything could aggravate the transgressions of Andrew Johnson, stretching in long line from the beginning of his administration, it would be the claim of right which he sets up. Under such a claim the slenderest violation of law becomes a high crime and misdemeanor, to be pursued and judged by an indignant people. The supremacy of the laws must be preserved or the liberties of all will suffer.

SWARM OF TECHNICALITIES AND QUIBBLES.

I now come upon that swarm of technicalities, devices, quirks and quibbles which, from the beginning, have infested this great proceeding. It is hard to speak of such things without giving utterance to a contempt not entirely parliamentary. To say that they are petty and miserable, is not enough. To say that they are utterly unworthy of this historic occasion, is to treat them politely. They are nothing but parasitic insects, like "vermin gendered in a lion's mane," and they are so nimble and numerous, that to deal with them, as they skip about, one must have the patience of the Italian peasant, who catches and kills, one by one, the diminutive animals that infest his person.

I can give specimens only, and out of many I take one which can never be forgotten. It is the Opinion of the Senator from West Virginia, [Mr. VAN WINKLE,] which, from beginning to end, treats this impeachment as if it were a prosecution for sheep-stealing in the Police Court of Wheeling, and brings to the defense all the unhesitating resources of a well-trained criminal lawyer. This famous Opinion, which is without a parallel in the annals of jurisprudence, must always be admired as the marvel of technicality in a proceeding where technicality should not intrude. It stands by itself, solitary in its originality. Others have been technical also; but the Senator from West Virginia is nothing else. Trav-

eling from law point to law point, or rather seeing law point after law point skip before him, at last he lights upon one of the largest dimensions, and this he boldly seizes and presents to the Senate.

According to him there is no allegation in the Articles, that the order for the removal of Mr. Stanton was actually delivered to him, and, this being so, the Senator declares that "if there is evidence of a delivery to be found in the proceedings it cannot be applied to this article in which there is no charge or averment." And this is gravely uttered on this transcendent occasion, when an indignant people has risen to demand judgment of a criminal ruler. The article alleges that the order was "unlawfully issued," and nobody doubts that its delivery was proved; but this is not enough, according to this Senator. I challenge history for another instance of equal absurdity in legal pretension. The case which approaches it the closest is the famous paradox of the Crown lawyer in the British Parliament, who, in reply to the argument of our fathers, that they could not be taxed without representation, bravely insisted that they were represented, and sustained himself by saying that, under the colonial charters, the lands were held "in common socage as of the borough of Greenwich in Kent," and, as Greenwich was represented in Parliament, therefore the colonies were represented there. The pretension was perfect in form, but essentially absurd. The Senator from West Virginia has outdone even this climax of technicality. Other generations, as they read this great trial, with its accumulation of transgressions ending in the removal of Mr. Stanton, will note with wonder that a principal reason assigned for the verdict of Not Guilty was that there was no allegation in the articles, that the order for the removal was actually received by Mr. Stanton, although there was a distinct allegation that it was "unlawfully issued," and, in point of fact, it was in evidence that the order was received by him, and no human being, not even the technical Senator, imagined that it was not.

There is another invention, which has in its support, some of the ablest of the apologists, like the Senator from Iowa, [Mr. GRIMES,] the Senator from Maine, [Mr. FESSENDEN,] and the Senator from Illinois, [Mr. TRUMBULL.] It is said that "as Mr. Stanton did not go out, therefore there was no removal;" and therefore Andrew Johnson is not guilty. If on an occasion like the present the authority of names could change the unreal into the real, then this pretension might have weight. But it is impossible that anything so essentially frivolous should be recognized in this proceeding. Such are the shifts of a cause to be defended only by shifts. Clearly the offense of the President was in the order "unlawfully issued," and this was complete the moment it was delivered. So far as depended upon him, Mr. Stanton was removed. This was the way in which the country saw the transaction; and this is the way in which it will be recorded by history.

But these same apologists, with curious inconsistency, when they come to consider the appointment of General Thomas, insist that there was a vacancy in point of law, called by the Senator from Maine a *legal vacancy*. If there was such a vacancy, it was because there had been a removal in point of law. There is no escape from this consequence. If there was a removal in point of law, and there was no right to make it, the President was guilty of a misdemeanor in point of law and must take the consequences.

It would be unprofitable to follow these inventions further. From these know all. In the face of Presidential pretentions, inconsistent with constitutional liberty, the apologists have contributed their efforts to save the criminal by subtleties, which can secure his acquittal in form only, as by a flaw in an indictment, and they have done this, knowing that he will be left in power to assert his prerogative, and that his acquittal will be a new letter of license. Nothing which the skill of the lawyer could supply has been wanting. This learned profession has lent to the criminal all the arts in which it excels, giving all to him and forgetting the Republic. Every doubt, every scruple, every technicality, every subtlety, every quibble has been arrayed on his side, when, by every rule of reason and patriotism, all should have been arrayed on the side of our country. The Public Safety, which is the supreme law, is now imperiled. Are we not told by Blackstone, that the law is always ready to catch at anything in favor of liberty? But these apologists "catch at anything" to save a usurper.

The trick of the apologists has been this: by the stringent application of technical rules to shut out all except the offenses charged in the articles, and then, when stress was laid upon these offenses to cry out, that at most they were only technical, and too trifling for impeachment. To satisfy lawyers the House weakly declined to act on the bloody transgressions of two years; but they sought to provide against the future. Like the Roman ambassadors, they traced a line about the offender, which he was not to pass except at his peril. This was the line of law. At last he passed this line, openly, knowingly, defiantly, and now, that he is arraigned for this plain offense, we are told that it is nothing, only a little technicality. One of the counsel at the bar, Mr. Groesbeck, in a speech which showed how much feeling and talent could be given to a wrong side, exclaimed:

"It almost shocks me to think that the President of the United States is to be dragged out of office on these miserable little questions whether he could make an *ad interim* appointment for a single day."

Only by excluding the whole context and all its antecedents, could the question be reduced to this trivial form; and yet, even thus reduced, it involved nothing less than the Supremacy of the Laws.

I know not how such a question can be called "trifling." Often a great cause is presented on a narrow issue. Thus it was when English liberty was argued on the claim of ship-money, which was a tax of a few shillings only. Behind this question, called trifling by the kingly apologists of that day, loftily stood the great cause of the People against Prerogative, being the same which is now pending before the Senate. That other cause, on which at a later day hung the destinies of this continent, was presented on a narrower issue still. There was a tax of threepence a pound on tea, which our fathers refused to pay. But behind this question, so trifling to the apologists of prerogative, as behind that of ship-money, stood loftily the same great cause. The first cost Charles I his head. The second cost George III his colonies. If such a question can be disparaged as of small moment, then have the martyred dead in all times suffered in vain; then was the costly blood lavished for the suppression of our Rebellion an empty sacrifice.

Constantly we are admonished that we must confine ourselves to the articles. Senators express a pious horror at looking outside the articles, and insist upon directing attention to these only. Here the Senator from Maine is very strong. It is the "specific offenses charged" and these only that he can see. He will not look at anything else, although spread upon the record of the Senate, and filling the land with its accumulated horrors. Of course such a system of exclusion sacrifices justice, belittles this trial, and forgets that essential latitude of inquiry which belongs to a political proceeding, having for its object expulsion from office only and not punishment. It is easy by looking at an object through the wrong end of an opera glass to find it dwarfed, contracted and solitary. This is not the way to look at nature; nor is it the way to look at Andrew Johnson. This great offender should be seen in the light of day; precisely as he is; nor more, nor less; with nothing dwarfed; with no limits to the vision, and with all the immense back-ground of accumulated transgressions filling the horizon as far as the eye can reach. The sight might ache; but how else can justice be done? A Senator who begins by turning these articles into an inverted opera glass, takes the first step towards a judgment of acquittal. Alas! that the words of Burke are not true, when, asserting the comprehensive character of impeachment, he denied, that, under it "they who have no hope in the justice of their cause can have any hope that by some subtleties of form, some mode of pleading, by something, in short, different from the merits of the case they may prevail." (*Bond's Trial of Hastings*, vol. 1, p. 11.) The orator was right in thus indignantly dismissing all questions of pleading and all subtleties of form. This proceeding is of substance and not of form. It is on the merits only that it can be judged. Anything short of this is the sacrifice of justice.

Such is the case of this enormous criminal. Events, belonging to history enrolled in the records of the Senate, and familiar to the country are deliberately shut out from view, while we are treated to legal niceties without end. The lawyers have made a painful record. Nothing ever occurred so much calculated to bring the profession into disrepute; for never before has been such a theater where lawyers were the actors. Their peculiarities have been exhibited to the world. Here was a great question of justice, appealing to the highest sentiments and involving the best interests of the country—one of the greatest questions of all time; but the lawyers, in their instincts for the dialectics of the profession, forgot that everlasting truth which cannot be forgotten with impunity. They started at once in full cry. A quibble is to a lawyer what Dr. Johnson says it was to Shakspeare: "He follows it at all adventures; it is sure to lead him out of the way; it has some malignant power over his mind and its fascinations are irresistible. A quibble is the golden apple for which he will always turn aside from his career; a quibble, poor and barren, as it is, gives him such delight that he is content to purchase it by the sacrifice of reason, propriety and truth." In this Shaksperian spirit our lawyers have acted. They have pursued their quibbles with the ardor of the great dramatist; and even now are chasing them through the Senate Chamber.

Unhappily this is according to history, and our lawyers are not among the splendid exceptions. But there is a reward for those who stand firm. Who does not honor the exalted magistrate of France, the Chancellor L'Hospital, who set such an example of justice above laws? Who does not honor those lawyers of English history, through whose toils liberty was upheld? There was Selden, so wise and learned; Pym, so grand in statesmanship; Somers, who did so much to establish the best securities of the constitution. Nor can I forget at a later day, that greatest advocate, Erskine, who lent to the oppressed his wonderful eloquence; nor Mackintosh and Brougham, who carried into the courts that enlarged intelligence and sympathetic nature which the profession of the law could not constrain. These are among the names that have already had their reward, above the artful crowd which in all times has come to the defense of prerogative. It is no new thing that we witness now. The lawyer in other days has been, as we know him, prone to the support of power and ready with his technical reasons; whichever side he takes he finds reasons, plenty as pins. When free to choose and not hired, his argument is the reflection of himself. All that he says is his own image. He takes sides on a law point according to his sentiments. Cultured in the law, and with that aptitude which is sharpened by its contests, too easily he finds a legal reason for an illegal judgment. Next to an outright mercenary, give me a lawyer to betray a

great cause. The forms of law lend themselves to the betrayal. It is impossible to forget that the worst pretensions of prerogative, no matter how unblushing, have been shouldered by the lawyers. It was they who carried ship-money against the patriot exertions of Hampden; and in our country it was they who held up slavery in all its pretensions from beginning to end. What is sometimes called the legal mind of Massachusetts, my own honored State, bent before the technical reasoning which justified the unutterable atrocities of the fugitive slave bill, while the supreme court of the State adopted it from the bench. Alas! that it should be so. When will lawyers and judges see that nothing short of justice can stand?

GUILTY ON ALL THE ARTICLES.

After this survey it is easy for me to declare how I shall vote. My duty will be to vote guilty on all the articles. If consistent with the rules of the Senate I should vote, "Guilty of all and infinitely more."

Not doubting that Mr. Stanton was protected by the tenure-of-office act, and that he was believed to be so by the President, it is clear to me that the charges in the first and second articles are sustained. These two articles go together. I have already said in the course of this Opinion, that the appointment of General Thomas as Secretary of War ad interim was without authority of law, and under the circumstances, a violation of the Constitution. Accordingly the third article is sustained.

Then come what are called the conspiracy articles. Here also I am clear. Plainly there was an agreement between the President and General Thomas to get possession of the War Department, and to prevent Mr. Stanton continuing in office, and this embraced the control of the mails and property belonging to the Department, all of which was contrary to the tenure-of-office act. Intimidation and threats were certainly used by one of the conspirators, and in the case of conspiracy, the acts of one are the acts of all. The evidence that force was intended is considerable, and all this must be interpreted by the general character of the offender, his menacing speeches and the long series of transgressions which preceded this conspiracy. I cannot doubt that the conspiracy was to obtain possession of the War Department, peaceably if it could, forcibly if it must. As such it was a violation of law, worthy of the judgment of the Senate. This disposes of the fourth, fifth, sixth, and seventh articles.

The eighth article charges that General Thomas was appointed to get the control of the moneys appropriated for the military service and the Department of War. All this would be an incident to the control of the War Department. In getting the control of the latter he would be able to wield the former. The evidence applicable to the one is also applicable to the other.

The ninth article opens a different question.

This charges a wicked purpose to corrupt General Emory and draw him from his military duty. Not much passed between the President and the General; but it was enough to show that the President was playing the part of Iago. There was a hypocritical profession of regard for the Constitution, while he was betraying it. Here again his past character explains his purpose, so as not to leave any reasonable doubt with regard to it.

Then came the scandalous speeches, proved as set forth in the articles, so that even the Senator from Virginia [Mr. VAN WINKLE] must admit that the evidence and the pleading concur. Here is no question of form. To my mind this is one of the strongest articles. On this alone, without anything else, I should deem it my duty to vote for expulsion from office. No person capable of such speeches should be allowed to govern this country. It is absurd to tolerate the idea. Besides being degraded, the country cannot be safe in such hands. The speeches are a revelation of himself, not materially different from well-known incidents; but they serve to exhibit him in his true character. They show him to be unfit for the official trust he enjoys. They were the utterances of a drunken man; and yet it does not appear that he was drunk. Now it is according to the precedents of our history that a person disqualified by drunkenness, shall be removed from office. This was the case of Pickering in 1804. But a sober man, whose conduct suggests drunkenness, is as bad at least as if he were drunk. Is he not worse? If without the explanation of drunkenness, he made such harangues, it seems to me that his unfitness for office becomes more evident, inasmuch as his deplorable condition is natural and not abnormal. The drunken man has lucid intervals; but where is the assurance of a lucid interval for this perpetual offender? Derangement is with him the normal condition.

It is astonishing to find that these infamous utterances, where ribaldry vies with blasphemy, have received a coat of varnish from the Senator from Maine, [Mr. FESSENDEN,] who tells us that they were not "official;" nor did they "violate the Constitution, or any provision of the common or statute law, either in letter or spirit." In presence of such apologies for revolting indecencies it is hard to preserve a proper calmness. Were they not uttered? This is enough. The drunkenness of Andrew Johnson, when he took his oath as Vice President, was not "official;" but who will say that it was not an impeachable offense? And who will say that these expectorations differ in vileness from that drunkenness? If they did not violate the Constitution or any provision of the common or statute law, as is apologetically alleged, I cannot doubt that they violated the spirit of all laws. And then we are further reminded by the apologists of that "freedom of speech," which is a constitutional right; and thus, in the name of a great right, we are to give a license to utterances that shock the moral sense, and are a scandal to human nature. Spirit of John Milton! who pleaded so grandly for this great liberty, but would not allow it to be confounded with license, speak to save this Republic from the shame of surrender to this insufferable pretension!

The eleventh article is the most comprehensive of all. In some respects it is an *omnium gatherum*. Here in one mass is what is contained in other articles, and something else beside. Here is an allegation of a speech by the President in which he denied that Congress was a Congress; and then, in pursuance of this denial, it is alleged that he attempted to prevent the execution of the tenure-of-office act, also of an important clause in the Army appropriation act; and also of the reconstruction act; and then the evidence followed sustaining completely the allegation. The speech was made as set forth. The attempt to prevent the execution of the tenure-of-office act, who can question? The attempt to corrupt General Emory is in evidence. The whole history of the country shows how earnest the President has been to arrest the reconstruction act and generally the congressional scheme of reconstruction. The removal of Mr. Stanton was in order to be relieved of an impediment to his purpose. I accept this article in gross and in detail. It has been proved in all its parts.

CONCLUSION.

In the judgment which I now deliver I cannot hesitate. To my vision the path is clear as day. Never in history was there a great case more free from all just doubt. If Andrew Johnson is not guilty, then never was a political offender guilty before; and, if his acquittal is taken as a precedent, never can a political offender be found guilty again. The proofs are mountainous. Therefore, you are now determining whether impeachment shall continue a beneficent remedy in the Constitution, or be blotted out forever, and the country handed over to the terrible process of revolution as its sole protection. If this milder process cannot be made effective now, when will it ever be? Under what influences? On what proofs? You wait for something. What? Is it usurpation? You have it before you, open, plain, insolent. Is it the abuse of delegated power? That, too, you have in this offender, hardly less broad than the powers he has exercised. Is it the violation of law? For more than two years he has set your laws at defiance, and when Congress, by a special enactment, strove to constrain him, he broke forth in rebellion against this constitutional authority. Perhaps you ask still for something more. Is it a long catalogue of crime, where violence and corruption alternate, while loyal men are sacrificed and the rebellion is lifted to its feet? That also is here.

The apologists are prone to remind the Senate that they are acting under the obligation of an oath. So are the rest of us, even if we do not ostentatiously declare it. By this oath, which is the same for all, we are sworn to do "impartial justice." It is justice, and this justice must be impartial. There must be no false weight and no exclusion of proper weights. Therefore, I cannot allow the quibbles of lawyers on mere questions of form to sway this judgment against justice. Nor can I consent to shut out from view that long list of transgressions explaining and coloring the final act of defiance. To do so is not to render impartial justice, but to depart from this golden rule. The oath we have taken is poorly kept if we forget the Public Safety in devices for the criminal. Above all else, now and forever, is that justice which "holds the scales of right with even hand." In this sacred name, and in the name also of country, that great charity embracing so many other charities, I now make this final protest against all questions of form at the expense of the Republic.

Something also has been said of the people, now watching our proceedings with patriot solicitude, and it has been proclaimed that they are wrong to intrude their judgment. I do not think so. This is a political proceeding, which the people at this moment are as competent to decide as the Senate. They are the multitudinous jury, coming from no small vicinage, but from the whole country; for, on this impeachment, involving the Public Safety, the vicinage is the whole country. It is they who have sent us here, as their representatives, and in their name to consult for the common weal. In nothing can we escape their judgment, least of all on a question like that now before us. It is a mistake to suppose that the Senate only has heard the evidence. *The people have heard it also, day by day, as it was delivered, and have carefully considered the case on its merits,* properly dismissing all apologetic subtleties. It will be for them to review what has been done. They are above the Senate, and will "rejudge its justice." Thus it has been in other cases. The popular superstition which long surrounded the Supreme Court could not save this tribunal from condemnation, amounting sometimes to execration, when, by an odious judgment, it undertook to uphold Slavery; and down to this day Congress has justly refused to place the bust of the Chief Justice, who pronounced this judgment, in the hall of that tribunal where he presided so long. His predecessors are all there in marble; no marble of Taney is there. The present trial, like that in the Supreme Court, is a battle with Slavery. *Acquittal is another Dred Scott decision,* and another chapter in the Barbarism of Slavery. How can Senators, who are discharging a political function only, expect that the voice of the people will be more tender for them than it was for a Chief Justice, pronouncing judgment from the bench of the Supreme Court in the exercise of judicial power? His fate we know.

Nor learning, nor private virtues, nor venerable years, could save him from justice. In the great pillory of history he stands, and there he must stand forever.

The people cannot witness with indifference the abandonment of the great Secretary, who organized their armies against the rebellion and then organized victory. Following him gratefully through the trials of the war, they found new occasion for gratitude when he stood out alone against that wickedness which was lifted to power on the pistol of an assassin. During these latter days, when tyrannical prerogative invaded all, he has kept the bridge. When at a similar crisis of English history Hampden stood out against the power of the Crown, it is recorded by the contemporary historian, Clarendon, that "he became the argument of all tongues; every man inquiring who and what he was, that durst at his own charge support the liberty and property of the kingdom and rescue his country from being made a prey to the Court." Such things are also said with equal force of our Secretary. Nor is it forgotten that the Senate, by two solemn votes of more than two thirds, has twice instructed him to stay at the War Department, the President to the contrary notwithstanding. The people will not easily understand, on what principle of Constitution, law, or morals, the Senate can twice instruct the Secretary to stay, and then, by another vote, deliberately surrender him a prey to presidential tyranny. Talk of a somersault; talk of self-stultification; are not both here? God save me from participation in this disastrous wrong, and may He temper it kindly to our afflicted country.

For myself, I cannot despair of the Republic. It is a life-boat, which wind and wave cannot sink; but it may suffer much and be beaten by storms. All this I clearly see before us, if you fail to displace an unfit commander, whose power is a peril and a shame.

Alas! for all the evil that must break upon the country, especially in the suffering South, as it goes forth that this bad man is confirmed in the prerogatives he has usurped.

Alas! for that peace and reconciliation, the longing of good men, now postponed.

Alas! for that security, so important to all, as the only foundation on which to build, politically or financially. This, too, is postponed. How can people found a government or plant or buy unless they are first secure!

Alas! for the Republic degraded as never before, while the Whisky Ring holds its orgy of corruption and the Ku-Klux-Klan holds its orgy of blood!

Alas! for the hearts of the people bruised to unutterable sadness, as they witness the cruel tyranny installed anew!

Alas! for that race so long oppressed, but at last redeemed from bondage, now plunged back into another hell of torment.

Alas! for the Unionists, white and black

alike, who have trusted to our flag. You now surrender them to those persecutors, whose representative is before you for judgment. They are the last in my thoughts, as I pronounce that vote which is too feeble to save them from intolerable wrong and outrage. They are fellow-citizens of a common country, brethren of a common Humanity. I offer them at this terrible moment the sympathy and fellowship of a heart that suffers with them. So just a cause cannot be lost. Meanwhile may they find in themselves, and in the goodness of an overruling Providence, that rescue and protection which the Senate refuses to give.

OPINION
OF
HON. JUSTIN S. MORRILL.

An explanation of a vote in the Senate may be desirable and sometimes useful, but no explanation can ever rise in value above that of the record of the vote itself; and there is no vote which can be taken under any circumstances from which the consciences of Senators can be separated from an oath. In an impeachment trial the obligation is more impressive by being made special instead of general. The duty is changed, and a corresponding change is made in the form of the oath. That change freshly requires of us impartiality according to law and the facts. Our votes upon the articles of impeachment will stand for all coming time as the embodiment of our view of the merits of the whole case. It is that upon which I hope to justify a clear conscience, and not upon making a better argument than has yet been made upon one side or the other.

I shall not attempt an exhaustive examination of any one of the articles of impeachment, but shall give my opinions upon some of the topics raised by the questions at issue, and the results of those opinions when applied to the several articles.

The guilt or innocence of President Johnson as charged in the eleven articles presented by the House of Representatives largely rests upon facts standing upon the record. In their nature the proofs are irrefragable, and we must take them as we find them. The written Constitution, the written law, the written order to Secretary Stanton to surrender his office, and the written authority to Lorenzo Thomas to take possession of the office of Secretary of War, with its papers and effects, are all before us, and the issue on trial depends chiefly, as it appears to me, upon a correct interpretation which we may be expected to give to these documents. In addition to this there is much documentary evidence and the testimony of living witnesses, and especially that of General Lorenzo Thomas, who testifies that he has acted as Secretary of War so far as to meet with the President at meetings of his Cabinet,

and was there recognized as Secretary of War. Such is the support upon which the main burden of the larger portion of the articles of impeachment rests.

The first article charges in substance that on the 21st day of February, 1868, Andrew Johnson, President of the United States, in violation of the Constitution and laws of the United States, did unlawfully issue an order in writing for the removal of Edwin M. Stanton from the office of Secretary for the Department of War, without the advice and consent of the Senate, then and there being in session, and against the provisions of "An act regulating the tenure of certain civil offices," passed March 2, 1867.

The second article charges that, in violation of the Constitution and the law, as mentioned in the first article, on the same day the President issued and delivered a letter of authority to Lorenzo Thomas, empowering him to act as Secretary of War *ad interim*, and to immediately enter upon the discharge of the duties of that office, there being no vacancy therein.

The third article varies from the second article by charging the same acts to have been done in violation of the Constitution and without authority of law.

To ascertain whether the Constitution has been violated it is necessary, after finding that the principal facts as alleged have been proved or admitted, to carefully examine what are its provisions, and we find that the President shall have power to—

"Nominate, and by and with the advice and consent of the Senate shall appoint, embassadors, other public ministers and consuls, judges of the Supreme Court, and all other officers of the United States whose appointments are not herein otherwise provided for, and which shall be established by law; but Congress may by law vest the appointment of such inferior officers as they think proper in the President alone, in the courts of law, or in the heads of Departments. The President shall have power to fill all vacancies that may happen during the recess of the Senate by granting commissions which shall expire at the end of their next session."

The power of removal being nowhere expressly given to the President, it is only an implied power resulting from the power to appoint, and the power to appoint is confided to the President by and with the advice and consent of the Senate, including the latter as substantially as the former, except in the case of inferior officers, which Congress may think proper by law to vest in the President alone, in the courts, or heads of Departments.

As an implied power derived from that of appointment, it must attach to those having the power to appoint. It cannot be claimed that the office of Secretary of War is an inferior office, nor that any existing law vests authority in the President alone to appoint a Secretary of War during a session of the Senate, nor yet that the power to nominate carries with it the power to confer upon any such nominees the right to take and hold office, with all the emoluments, without an appointment by and with the advice and consent of the Senate.

It is true the President may temporarily fill vacancies which happen during the recess of the Senate; but it is going too far to assume that he may first do an act not allowed by the Constitution in order to open the door so that he may do another thing which is allowed; that he may empty under the power only to fill; or that he may make a vacancy to happen with a view to an exercise of the power to fill a vacancy. Things *happen* by chance—as by death, resignation, absence—not by previous contrivance. An insurance policy is valid when the ship happens to get foundered, not when it is designedly scuttled and sunk by the owner. The power to create vacancies at will, to fill them with A, and then to come to the Senate for advice and consent to fill them either with A, or with B, is an absurdity. The faithful daughter asks parental advice and consent before she gets married, not after. The power claimed by President Johnson to create vacancies at will would blot out one of the most important functions of the Senate, designed to be one of the highest safeguards of the Constitution against executive indiscretions and usurpations, as even appointments consented to during the session of the Senate, if the claim of unlimited power of removal by the President were to be tolerated, might be set aside the moment after the adjournment of the Senate for other and different appointments never advised and never consented to by the Senate. All stability would be lost, and all officers of the Government would hold their places at the mere will and caprice of the President. It would enthrone the one-man power against all else. Such a power in a free Government would be neither prudent nor safe, though placed in the most scrupulous hands; and if, by chance, in other hands it would be dangerous.

Yet President Johnson, in face of the plain provision of the Constitution, not only deliberately makes a removal of the Secretary of War, but officially authorizes another man, an obedient subordinate, to discharge the duties of the office. It matters little by what name the President designated him, or for how long a time, or whether as Secretary *ad interim*, for one day or indefinitely, he intended that Lorenzo Thomas should be for the time the actual Secretary of War, so to be recognized by himself, and so to be recognized by all the Executive Departments of the Government, and to immediately enter upon the discharge of the duties of the office, although there is no more lawful power to *authorize* than to *appoint* to office, or to issue a letter of authority than to make an actual appointment, and no more power to appoint an *ad interim* Secretary than a Secretary *in full*. Nothing but the illegality of the act of the President now keeps Thomas *out* and Stanton *in* office as Secretary of War. If the Senate decide to-day that the President has not transcended his lawful authority in the removal of Mr. Stanton, by force of that decision Adjutant General Thomas may take possession of the office to-morrow. If that be so, then Senators who by their votes reinstated Mr. Stanton in his office inflicted a great wrong upon him, and have given to Congress and the country a very unnecessary excitement. It seems to me that there was no constitutional authority for the removal of Stanton by the President, and still less for the appointment of Thomas as Secretary *ad interim*.

The next thing I propose to consider is the act regulating the tenure of certain civil offices, passed March 2, 1867, as follows, namely:

"That every person holding any civil office to which he has been appointed by and with the advice and consent of the Senate, and every person who shall hereafter be appointed to any such office, and shall become duly qualified to act therein, is, and shall be, entitled to hold such office until a successor shall have been in like manner appointed and duly qualified, except as herein otherwise provided: *Provided*, That the Secretary of State, of the Treasury, of War, of the Navy, and of the Interior, the Postmaster General, and the Attorney General, shall hold their offices respectively for and during the term of the President by whom they may have been appointed, and one month thereafter, subject to removal by and with the advice and consent of the Senate."

As its title declares, this act regulates the tenure of certain civil offices—authorizing all persons in office, whether for fixed or indefinite terms, to hold the same until their successors "shall have been appointed by and with the advice and consent of the Senate," (as contemplated by the Constitution,) except that the heads of the Executive Departments are to "hold their offices respectively for and during the *term of the President by whom they may have been appointed*, and one month thereafter, subject to removal by and with the advice and consent of the Senate."

This is not an unusual exercise of legislative power. The subject is one that has been legislated upon by Congress both early and late, and whatever laws may be on the statute-book of a prior date in conflict with the latest act must be held to be superseded, and need not be considered so far as this case is concerned. I understand this to be the legal view, and it is certainly a common-sense view of the rules of construction. The law of March 2, 1867, holds the President and Senate simply to the requirements of the Constitution and fixes the term of office. The question whether it includes members of the Cabinet appointed by President Lincoln is the only one deserving consideration. Intended as a permanent statute, it was provided that the term of the heads of the Executive Departments should expire one month after the term of the President by whom they were appointed had expired. The term of the President under the Constitution is four years—no more and no less—fixed by law to commence on the 4th of March next after the presidential election; and, though the President may die or become insane and his place be filled by another, the term will expire at precisely the same time it would had he lived or remained sane. When the Vice President becomes President by accident, by death, or otherwise, he serves out the remainder of the term for which his predecessor was elected, and no more, be the fraction longer or shorter. Neither legally nor nominally has he any term. The time of service is purely accidental, and cannot be foreseen nor fixed by law.

It has been even questioned whether the person so acting as President, though not so elected, should receive the official title of President; but it has not been doubted that the term of his official existence was that of the deceased President, and to be terminated at the end of the four years for which the latter had been elected. A Senator or a member of the House of Representatives dies during his term of service, and another is elected to fill out the vacancy, but the new Senator or new member has no term of office himself: he serves out the remainder of the term to which he has succeeded of his predecessor. The presidential term must be analogous to that of Senator or member of the House. If this be deemed a fair conclusion it will be seen that the proviso as well as the body of the act of March 2, 1867, prevents the removal of Mr. Stanton without the advice and consent of the Senate. Contemporary construction of the language of a statute cannot be held to set aside its plain meaning; but when it sustains that plain meaning it is not unfair to consider it. The House of Representatives, it is well known, in framing the tenure-of-office act, strenuously contended that the members of the Cabinet should be included and protected; but the Senate only proposed to prevent the sweeping removal of all civil officers except Cabinet officers. The Minister of War had rendered conspicuous service, and, whether he needed or desired protection against sudden removal without the consent of the Senate or not, the House was urgent to have it awarded. Beyond all doubt they so intended to have it, and with reason believed they had accomplished their purpose. As a member of the House I so understood the language of the act then, and I am unable to give it a different construction now. On its final passage General SCHENCK, of the committee of conference, said:

"It is in fact an acceptance by the Senate of the position taken by the House."

Could anything be more emphatic? The Senate manager, [Mr. WILLIAMS, of Oregon,] who had most to do with the language of the bill in the committee of conference, where it took its final shape and form, had no doubt then, and, as I understand, has none now, that it did and does include all members of the Cabinet. Nor is there anything wrong in such a conclusion as applicable to President Johnson. When the presidential office fell upon him the tenure-of-office act had not been passed, and he might undoubtedly have changed his Cabinet officers at his pleasure; whether wisely or not it is unnecessary to consider. By not doing so he both legally and morally adopted .them as his own as much as he could have done by actual appointment. He has daily so rec-

ognized the fact officially in all possible forms. When the act was before him for approval he clearly comprehended its provisions, as appears by his veto message. He also admits in his message to the Senate, December 12, 1867, referring to his Cabinet, that "if any one of these gentlemen had then said to me that he would avail himself of the provisions of that bill in case it became a law, I should not have hesitated a moment as to his removal," showing that he had not failed to understand its full import. It is also worthy of notice from this declaration of President Johnson that no head of any of the Executive Departments, whatsoever might have been his merits or demerits otherwise, could then have given an opinion in favor of the bill but at the peril of instant ejection from office; and if all gave opinions against it, as has been intimated, the President might very well feel safe from any embarrassments in the future in retaining them. But when Secretary Stanton came to consider laws not affecting himself so much as the nation, and failed to second President Johnson in his policy of obstruction to the reconstruction acts passed in July, 1867, then President Johnson sought to crush out the Secretary as promptly as he undoubtedly would have succeeded in doing had no such law as the tenure-of-office act been passed.

After the bill became a law Mr. Stanton obeyed it, even though it be true that, not foreseeing the full extent of the President's perverse policy and purposes, he had not favored its passage; but the President determined not to obey it. Even when, in compliance with the letter of the law, he suspended Mr. Stanton in August, 1867, informing other Departments that he had so suspended him, and reported the reasons for the suspension to the Senate (in strict accordance with the law) within twenty days after the commencement of the next session, it would only seem to have been done in good faith, provided the Senate consented to the suspension; but if the Senate should not so consent *it was the President's purpose to prevent Mr. Stanton from resuming the office of Secretary of War*, according to his own confession, in his letter to General Grant, February 10, 1868; or, in other words, if he could not bend the Senate to his will he had already determined to defy the law. The suspension of Mr. Stanton in August would have been lawful had there been, instead of mere pretexts, any valid charges of misbehavior or disability against him worthy of the just consideration of the Senate; but there were no such charges, and he was properly restored by the Senate. President Johnson could now, while the Senate is in session, by obtaining its advice and consent, oust Mr. Stanton at any moment, or any other civil officer, by only nominating a fit and proper person for his successor; but solitary and alone he cannot legally remove him, nor does it even appear probable that the Secretary of War *ad interim*, Lorenzo Thomas, to use his most energetic words, can "kick him out."

The constitutional power of the President has not been invaded by Congress, but the joint power of the Senate has been solemnly asserted and ought not now to be surrendered to any President, and especially not to one who manifests so much avidity to monopolize the political control of the Government as does the present incumbent. Without passing upon the question as to whether the tenure-of-office act is in every respect expedient or not, I see no reason to question its expediency now, nor its constitutionality at any time. That question has been twice solemnly decided by more than two thirds of each branch of Congress, and recently by a still larger proportion of the Senate. Not one of these legislators, under their oath of office, could have voted for this law believing it was unconstitutional, and it would be pitifully absurd to suppose that they have suddenly changed their opinions, or that the country will be very swift to accept the opinions of President Johnson and his advisers as of more weight than the combined authority of more than two thirds of both Houses of Congress.

Precedents have been cited to sustain the action of the President, and it should be noted first that they all, such as they are, bear date prior to the passage of the tenure-of-office act, when there might have been some lawful authority to justify the same; but it is hardly too much to claim that there is not one valid precedent in the whole history of our Government where a President has positively removed a Cabinet officer while the Senate was in session without its consent. The case of Timothy Pickering, under President Adams, was no exception; for on the same day the Senate advised and consented to the appointment of John Marshall in the place of Pickering. Admit President Johnson's pretensions and he might at once, without any barrier, remove McCulloch or F. E. Spinner and put any general of the Army into power as Secretary of the Treasury *ad interim* or as Treasurer *ad interim*. He has certainly as much power over the purse as over the sword of the nation, and no more.

Sanction this pretension of the Executive and our Republic would be no more a free Government than that of the French empire.

I shall cite one more significant fact that fully confirms the views already expressed. As is well known, every outgoing President, some weeks prior to the close of his term, as an act of official courtesy due to his successor, issues a proclamation to convene the Senate at twelve o'clock m. on the 4th of March next succeeding, "to receive and act upon such communications as may be made to it on the part of the Executive," and this is done to give the incoming President a chance to have a new Cabinet by and with the advice and consent of the Senate. This has been the universal practice. Franklin Pierce issued such a proclamation on the 16th day of February, 1857, for the Senate to convene at twelve o'clock m. on the 4th of March, 1857, and it did so convene and remain in session for ten days. James Buchanan issued a like proclamation in the same words February 11, 1861. Now, if the President can make removals and appointments of Cabinet officers, or manufacture any *ad interim* substitutes, without the advice and consent of the Senate, why do these extraordinary executive sessions of the Senate so regularly appear and reappear in our history?

The main facts set forth against the President in the first, second, and third articles are confessedly true, and they are, in my opinion, without any constitutional or lawful justification. That they come within the range of impeachable offenses there can be no reasonable doubt.

The fourth article charges that the President did unlawfully conspire with Lorenzo Thomas and other persons with intent, by intimidation and threats, to hinder Edwin M. Stanton from holding the office of Secretary of War, in violation of the provisions of "An act to define and punish certain conspiracies," passed July 31, 1861.

It does not appear to me that sufficient proof has been produced to sustain the charge of "intimidation and threats," as alleged. The President told General Sherman that Stanton "was cowardly," but it does not appear that he has yet acted on the idea of trying to operate upon him through his fears, nor does it appear that he authorized General Thomas so to operate.

The fifth article charges that the President did unlawfully conspire with Lorenzo Thomas and other persons to prevent and hinder the execution of the tenure-of-office act, passed March 2, 1867, and did unlawfully attempt to prevent Edwin M. Stanton, then Secretary of War, from holding said office.

It is very evident that President Johnson was ready to accept aid, and that he sought it from various quarters to prevent and hinder the execution of the tenure-of-office act, and that he did attempt to prevent Mr. Stanton from holding the office of Secretary of War by making an unlawful agreement or by conspiring with Lorenzo Thomas. It is clear, also, that at last the President found General Thomas grateful for his recent restoration to the office of Adjutant General of the Army, who with the *Constitution and the laws* on his lips agreed and was ready to carry out his unlawful orders, designs, and purposes. If any further proof was required beyond his many abortive struggles to accomplish his ends, the admissions of the President in his letter to General Grant, February 10, 1868, would be conclusive on this point.

The sixth article varies from the fourth in charging that the President conspired by force to seize, take, and possess the property of the

United States in the Department of War, in violation of the conspiracy act of July 31, 1861, and of the tenure-of-office act of March 2, 1867.

That Adjutant General Thomas had revolved in his own mind the idea of force, if it should be necessary, to get possession of the War Department, there is no doubt from his own testimony, as well as that of others, especially that of Samuel Wilkeson; but the President appears to have pocketed the order suggested by Thomas for a call upon General Grant for a military order, and it hardly seems right to make President Johnson responsible for the utterances or the acts of this frivolous old man, Adjutant General Thomas, notwithstanding he was the President's trusted agent, and, perhaps, as liable to put on a coat of mail as any more peaceful mask. Furthermore, it does not appear to me that the act of July 31, 1861, "to define and punish certain conspiracies," one of the legislative necessities arising during the war, was intended to apply or can properly be made to apply to the present case.

The seventh article varies from the fifth in charging the President with unlawfully conspiring with Lorenzo Thomas to unlawfully seize, take, and possess *the property* of the United States in the Department of War, in disregard of the act of March 2, 1867.

The facts and reasons touching the fifth article are applicable to the seventh, and the same conclusions follow.

The eighth article charges the President with intent unlawfully to control the disbursements of the moneys appropriated for the military service and the Department of War, contrary to "An act regulating the tenure of certain civil offices;" and, without the advice and consent of the Senate, then being in session, did, on the 21st day of February, 1868, issue and deliver a letter of authority to Lorenzo Thomas, empowering him to act as Secretary of War *ad interim.*

This article is controlled by most of the facts and arguments belonging to the second article. I shall only add that the main purpose of wresting the office of Secretary of War from the hands of Edwin M. Stanton could not have been to deprive him of the barren honor of the official title, but to get the control of its departmental power. The control of the disbursements of moneys for the preservation of the public peace in the rebellious States, or for the maintenance of the Freedmen's Bureau, by which much or nothing may be done, according to the discretion of those in authority, would be no barren scepter within the grasp of one whose profoundest hatred seems to be excited when beholding such disbursements made for the protection of the Union men of the South, now more than ever struggling for life and liberty, and who are seeking to restore rebellious States to their practical relations with the Union on the basis of freedom, equality, and justice.

The ninth article charges that the President, on the 22d day of February, 1868, brought before him General William H. Emory, the commander for the department at Washington, and sought to instruct him that a certain law, requiring military orders from the President or Secretary of War to be issued through the General of the Army, was unconstitutional, with intent to induce the said Emory to violate the same, and with further intent thereby to enable the President to prevent the execution of the tenure-of-office act, and to prevent Mr. Stanton from holding the office of Secretary of War.

The particular subject of conversation here censured appears to have been first introduced by General Emory, and not by the President. Each expressed frank opinions, and those of General Emory being the most commendable, the President appears to have been, and ought to have been, quite as much instructed as was General Emory. If any guilty purpose was entertained on the part of the President it did not ripen into a disclosure in the presence of the main witness, General Emory.

The tenth article charges President Johnson with having in various speeches made declarations, threats, and scandalous harangues, intended to excite the contempt and odium of the people against Congress and the laws of the United States duly enacted thereby.

The facts here alleged seem to have been abundantly proved, and there is no doubt of the stain brought upon the country and upon the President by these intemperate and indecent utterances. They are evidences of bad taste and violent temper, such as are not infrequently exhibited in political discussions, and sometimes, it is to be regretted, have appeared as foul blots in legislative discussions. It would be hardly just to give these presidential harangues any interpretation beyond their political significance. We may regret them because of the stigma and scandal thereby brought before the nation. If these discreditable speeches had been made with a view to excite armed rebellion, or had been made in time of war, the charge would be far more serious. I do not, however, think it a stretch of charity to suppose the President when making them had no other than a political object in view. To President Johnson it will be a cruel and unavoidable punishment, unparalleled in our history, that such speeches are to be perpetuated as a prominent feature of his future presidential fame. I do not desire to place any greater burden upon his back.

The eleventh article charges, first, that the President declared by public speech that the Thirty-Ninth Congress was not a Congress, intending to deny its power to propose amendments to the Constitution; in pursuance of this declaration, that the President attempted to prevent the execution of the tenure-of-office act by devising means whereby to prevent Mr. Stanton from forthwith resuming the functions of the office of Secretary of War, notwithstanding the refusal of the Senate to concur in his suspension; and, further, devised means to prevent the execution of the act making appropriations for the Army for the year ending June 30, 1868; and also to prevent the execution of "An act to provide for the more efficient government of the rebel States," passed March 2, 1867.

There are not less than four distinct charges here made, any one of which, if proved, affords sufficient foundation to sustain this article, and, so far as the facts are similar to those embraced in several of the preceding articles, the argument need not be repeated. Some of the charges appear to have been sustained by the proof, and that is sufficient to determine the proper vote, though other allegations contained in the article may or may not be sustained by proper proof. After saying this it may be useless to pursue the subject further; but among the independent charges here clustered together there is one of the gravest in the whole series made against the President in relation to the execution of the act for the more efficient government of the rebel States, upon which a brief comment may not be inappropriate.

Nearly all of the other unlawful acts charged upon Andrew Johnson have been done by him in order to enable him to accomplish his great crowning purpose of defeating the legislation of Congress for the rebel States. Proof in relation to any other allegations, therefore, in the end contributes to the support of this charge, as well as whatever proof may be found on the record particularly relating to it. Evidence in relation to such a charge to a large extent must necessarily be circumstantial, where the party, while ostensibly executing the law, predetermines its miscarriage, and must be surrounded by difficulties, but it does not seem easy to dismiss the matter as having no foundation whatever.

The *animus* of the President has been made offensively conspicuous in his assignments and changes of the commanders of the several military departments, and especially by the removal of General Sheridan and the appointment of General Hancock in Louisiana, whose action in that department, regarded as a dread calamity by Union men, so enraptured the President that he even ventured upon the official impudence of asking Congress to tender to the new commander a vote of thanks, well knowing that Congress could have no other feeling than that of painful solicitude, if not of disgust, in regard to the part which the President had persuaded one of our veteran generals to assume in the execution of the reconstruction acts; but all such facts, which have not been formally offered in evidence, may be excluded from our view of this article, and there will enough remain of substance in other charges of the article to justify the conclusion that it should be considered as having been conclusively supported by the proof.

The various charges in the articles of impeachment raise the question whether the President can do certain acts with impunity. Can he, in violation of his oath, refuse to take care that the laws be faithfully executed? Can he, in violation of the Constitution, exercise an exclusive power to remove and appoint to office? Can he, in violation of the laws of the land, disobey such parts of the laws as he pleases, and when he pleases? With so much he appears to have been justly charged, and such acts would not seem to be improperly characterized when called high misdemeanors. If they are not, what are they? Certainly they are not innocent acts. What is a misdemeanor? The definitions given in Webster's dictionary are as follows:

"1. Ill behavior; evil conduct; fault; mismanagement.

"2. (*Law.*) Any crime less than a felony. The term applies to all offenses for which the law has not furnished a particular name."

If we limit the term to the law definition, it would still be a very modest name for the offenses.

If the President is guilty, he cannot be guilty of anything less than a misdemeanor. If the facts charged do not amount to a misdemeanor, then the power to impeach the President might as well forever be abandoned.

But the issues immediately involved in the articles of impeachment only thinly cover other and graver matters, identical in character with some of the great questions raised by the recent rebellion. It is a serious question whether the executive department of the Government shall be permitted to absorb some of the most important powers conferred upon Congress by the Constitution; but it is an aggravation of the question when this absorption is struggled for in the interest of disloyal citizens, and in behalf of the fallen fortunes of slavery. It is as much the duty of Congress to maintain its own rights as it is its duty not to trench upon the just powers of the Executive; but the maintenance of the rights of Congress looms up to higher importance when it is seen that just now hereon hangs the right of ten States to a republican form of government, to freedom, and the protection of equal laws. To concede that laws made by a vote of two thirds of each branch of Congress, the President's objections to the contrary notwithstanding, may be litigated or disregarded and set at defiance by a vetoing President, would be to yield a plain provision of the Constitution. Even to allow such laws to be avoided, or to wink at a halting execution of such laws, would soon undermine and destroy the check which it was intended should be placed upon an ambitious and self-willed Executive. If the President can make and unmake, remove and appoint the chief officers of the Government at his own will and pleasure—having in view no other consideration than whether they are or are not subservient to *his policy*—then, instead of being the agent of the

Constitution to "take care that the laws be faithfully executed," he becomes the agent of governmental patronage, to bend both the lawmakers and the people to his will. If the Senate has the right to be consulted as to appointments, this right cannot be abrogated by Congress nor nullified by the President. In time of war the power of the Executive stretches out its strong arm over a new and vast field; but even in time of war, and over military and naval officers, the power of the President does not extend to the latitude which President Johnson claims in time of peace in regard to officers in the civil service.

It would be wrong to convict President Johnson upon a merely technical violation of the law, without violence to substance and harming nobody, and it would be equally wrong to exonerate him upon a mere techicality while the practical breach of the law was flagrant. If he has been substantially guilty of the unlawful offenses charged, then our duty to the Government and the people requires his conviction. If through inadvertence, or compelled by any haste, he made a mistake in his interpretation of the law, acting with entire good faith, a mistake that he would gladly repair on the first opportunity, then he perhaps might be forgiven. But this is no such case, and the President of the United States, of all men, should not ask to be excused on account of ignorance of the law. It is, however, rather an obstinate adherence of the President to his own predetermined will. He does not think he has made a mistake. His veto message of the 2d of March, 1867; the suspension of Mr. Stanton, August 5, 1867, under the act, with the appointment of General Grant as Secretary ad interim; and his report to the Senate of December 12, 1867, of the reasons for the suspension of Mr. Stanton, all prove that the President fully comprehended the law, and he must have acted with deliberation when he exercised his constitutional right to withhold his assent from the bill before it became a law, and with equal deliberation when he subsequently conformed to the strict letter of the law in the suspension of Stanton, though giving unsatisfactory reasons therefor. When he flatly disobeyed the law by removing Stanton, February 21, 1868, and authorized Thomas to fill his place, he did not act inadvertently—he had pondered long how to break the law with personal impunity—and, although it is not pretended that this last move of President Johnson was devised or advised by any of his constitutional advisers, it cannot have been made through a mere blunder as to the meaning of the law, but it appears more like a bold attempt to trample the law under the heels of executive power.

If the intent of the President was good, that should mitigate and possibly shield him from the extreme penalty hanging over him for the offenses charged and either proved or admitted. A positive breach of the law carries on its face a bad intent, and there is little or no proof of good intent other than the offer of proof through members of his Cabinet of what the President had at some time said to them, or what they had at some time said to him. Suppose this be admitted: that his Cabinet, one and all, pronounced the law unconstitutional; that it did not include the Secretary of War; and that the question as to the validity of the law ought to be carried to the Supreme Court. All this would only show that the President gave and received bad advice, which, to say the least, is not the best evidence of good intent, and, instead of diminishing the offense, theoretically increases it; for, after all, the President, by whomsoever advised, must be held responsible for his own acts, and, in addition thereto, to some extent, for the acts of his ministers. If he choose to break the law he must do it at his own peril and take the consequences. The advice of his Cabinet, if good, would only shield the President if practically adopted, but it would be monstrous to shield him from the fact that bad advice had been given to him when it is too plain that the tender of good advice, if unpalatable, would be at the peril of the instant removal of the party by whom given. It is quite plain that the President intended to oust Mr. Stanton at all hazards—by fair means if he could, but at any rate to oust him—and he did not intend himself, whatever others might do, to resort to any lawsuit in the process. The testimony of General Sherman shows that the President believed Mr. Stanton would yield because, as he said, he was "cowardly;" so when General Thomas brought to the White House the account of his doings on the 21st of February, the President said, "Very well; go and take charge of the office and perform the duties."

There was then no hint of disappointment at the lack of a lawsuit. It was not until the next day, when the masquerade was over and Adjutant General Thomas found himself in the clutches of the law, that the President again said, according to General Thomas, "Very well; that is the place I want it, in the courts." Though others might litigate the question, it is not clear that he ever sought to initiate any legal proceedings himself. But the assumption on the part of the President that it was his privilege, if not his duty, to violate the law rather than to faithfully execute it, in order to make up a case for the decision of the courts, instead of showing good intent, exhibits an obstinate purpose not to yield to a law passed by a constitutional majority of Congress against his objections. And the pretense that the courts would decide against the constitutionality of the law is sheer assumption. Even if there had been reasonable doubt as to its constitutionality, it was the law of the land until decided otherwise by the Supreme Court, the only tribunal having authority to stay the force of any law for a single moment. Certainly the President, who swears to maintain the

Constitution, which makes it one of his chief duties to take care that the laws be faithfully executed, cannot, at his own will, elect what laws he will execute and what he will ignore. But there is hardly more reason to suppose the Supreme Court would decide the tenure-of-office act unconstitutional than any other law among our statutes.

Nor can good intent be found in the mode pursued by the President in striving to get rid of the hated War Minister. When he suspended Mr. Stanton, in August, 1867, in order to prevail upon the Senate to consent to the suspension, he made General Grant Secretary of War *ad interim*—entirely an unexceptionable appointment. But after he quarreled with General Grant because he did not, when the Senate refused to consent to the suspension, aid and abet him in placing the office in the lap of the President before Mr. Stanton could repossess it, then he proposed to act independently of the law and of the Senate, and took General Thomas, so utterly unfit that his very designation impeaches the judgment if not the integrity of the appointing power. Later nominations are open to criticism, either as bad, or, when otherwise, they appear too evidently extorted in the nature of a propitiation to the Senate sitting on the trial of the impeachment of Andrew Johnson. The general history of the conduct and manner of the President, in his various attempts to remove Mr. Stanton, certainly fails to furnish evidence of any good intent; nor is it to be believed, if the field had been opened for a wider search, that it would have been attended by any happier result.

Having been among those who were originally for living down the administration of President Johnson rather than to attempt to bring it to an abrupt close by an impeachment, although admitting his culpability, I have yet had no other desire than to be able to render a just and impartial verdict. Summoning to my aid all the light with which the case has been illuminated, and at the close of the trial the culpability still appearing no less, I cannot, under the solemnities of an oath, declare the President innocent. The example of President Johnson, were it possible so gross a wrong could have passed unheeded, might have been comparatively harmless; but when solemnly adjudicated, with the eyes of the world fixed upon it, establishing, as it will, a precedent to be quoted and followed in all future time, I cannot consent to ignore or waive it as a light matter, and thereby ingraft the idea into the republican Constitution of the United States that the Executive is paramount, and may dominate at will over the legislative branch of the Government.

Mr. Stanbery, counsel for the President and late Attorney General, has made a feeling appeal to us in behalf of his client. He has seen him *often tempted by bad advice*, and knew that *evil counselors were around him* more than once, but never discovered anything in him *but loyalty to the Constitution and the laws*. "Yes, Senators," says Mr. Stanbery, "with all his faults, the President has been more sinned against than sinning. Fear not to acquit him. The Constitution of the country is as safe in his hands from violence as it was in the hands of Washington."

This appeal would be more apt not to go unheeded if Mr. Stanbery himself could be considered an impartial judge as to what course the President ought to pursue, and had not heretofore failed to *discover anything in that man but loyalty;* but it is painful to be obliged to presume that Mr. Stanbery, as one of the chief advisers of the President's most obnoxious measures, is entitled to some share of the doubtful honor of our Chief Magistrate's present position.

Neither the facts surrounding this case nor those making the history of President Johnson's administration show evidences of good intent or justify future confidence. Ever since Andrew Johnson reached the Presidency more or less pressure has been felt that it was necessary for Congress to remain in session—adjourning late to meet early and at extraordinary and inconvenient seasons—lest grave evils and perplexing complications should be precipitated upon the country by his headstrong, if not treacherous, action in the absence of the legislative branch of the Government. Decide the charges here in his favor now; say that he has done no wrong; admit that the House of Representatives are all at fault; and Congress or the Senate never more need to remain here as the guardians of law and of a representative form of government, or as a bulwark against the encroachments of executive power. President Johnson and all future Presidents may break laws or make appointments at will, and do anything which goes to make up the character of an uncurbed despot.

I am glad to remember that at the commencement of the late rebellion Andrew Johnson took a bold, outspoken stand in behalf of the Union; and that fact shall protect him, so far as my vote is concerned, from any other penalty for his recent great offenses than a simple removal from office. I would not deprive him of the poor privilege of being a candidate for the suffrages of any portion of the people who may think him worthy, whether for President or alderman. But his appointment to office of men supposed corruptly to be putting more money into their own pockets than into the Treasury; his discreditable use of the pardoning power; his unmasked threat in his last annual message that it might become proper for him to "adopt forcible measures or such as might lead to force" in opposing an unconstitutional act of Congress; his appointment, in violation of law, to places of honor and trust, rebels not able to take the oath of office, in preference to loyal men; his malign attempts to foist upon the country his policy of restoring the rebellious States without security for the future and against the measures of salutary reform proposed by Congress; and his bitter and active efforts to defeat the adoption of the constitutional amendment proposed by the Thirty-Ninth Congress, known as article fourteen, and known, also, as the great seal of security for the broad principles of national freedom and human rights: these facts, and such as these, do not allow me to gratuitously credit the President with good intent in the past, nor can I, notwithstanding his counsel's appeal, in the face of such a record, by a verdict of acquittal, become responsible for his conduct in the future.

OPINION
OF
HON. SAMUEL C. POMEROY.
—

As no man can see with the eyes of another, so no one can control his judgment upon the precise views and opinions of others. And although other Senators may, and have, given better and perhaps more logical reasons for their votes upon questions involved in this *great trial* of *impeachment* of the *President*, still as my own judgment must be controlled by my own *views* and *opinions*, I propose to set them forth, as briefly as possible, in the opinion and views I now submit.

The people of the United States, through the House of Representatives in Congress assembled, have, in constitutional form, presented at the bar of the Senate eleven articles of impeachment against Andrew Johnson, President of the United States, for high *crimes* and *misdemeanors* in office. The charges have been answered by him; and after over forty days of patient trial, the time has come when Senators are required or allowed to state their conclusions upon the pleadings and proofs. This brief statement will explain the reasons of the judgment I am prepared to give by my response to each article.

In considering the questions to be decided, it is to be borne in mind that this proceeding is not a suit between Andrew Johnson and Edwin M. Stanton, or between the persons appearing here as managers and Andrew Johnson.

The Senate of the United States has no jurisdiction of such controversies, nor should they be influenced by considerations relating to individual persons.

The proceeding is national. The people of the United States impeaching through their constitutional agents a public officer, high in place and power, for his public acts, and demanding judgment against him, not for a private injury, but for public wrongs, violations of the Constitution, which they formed and adopted for the *general welfare*, and transgressing laws enacted by them through their constitutional representatives in Congress assembled. If these violations are set forth in

the articles of impeachment, and admitted in the answer, or proven on the trial, then the verdict of conviction must not be withheld. To this point I now address myself.

The *first, second, and third articles* of impeachment relate to the removal of Mr. Stanton from the office of Secretary of War and the appointment of Lorenzo Thomas as Secretary of War *ad interim* on the 21st day of February, 1868, without the advice and consent of the Senate, then in session, there being no vacancy in the office of Secretary, and having been none during the recess of the Senate.

These official acts of Mr. Johnson are averred to be in violation of the tenure-of-office act, and of the Constitution of the United States.

It is set up in defense or excuse—

1. That Mr. Stanton was not removed on the 21st day of February, and is still Secretary of War.

2. That Mr. Stanton is not Secretary of War, because his term expired at the death of Mr. Lincoln.

3. That Lorenzo Thomas was not appointed Secretary of War *ad interim* on the 21st day of February.

4. That Lorenzo Thomas was lawfully appointed Secretary of War *ad interim*, Mr. Johnson having the constitutional power to appoint him, without the advice and consent of the Senate.

5. That the act regulating the tenure-of-office is unconstitutional.

6. That Mr. Johnson has the "*power at any and all times of removing from office all executive officers for cause to be judged of by the President alone.*"

7. That the removal and appointment were made only to test the validity of the tenure-of-office act before the judicial tribunals.

It needs but a glance to see that the grounds of defense are absolutely inconsistent with each other, conflict with the Constitution and act of Congress, and tend to overthrow the form and spirit of republican government.

No question has been discussed so fully since the foundation of the Government as the constitutionality of the tenure-of-office act, and four successive times the Senate's judgment pronounced the act to be in conformity with the Constitution, and that judgment of the Senate was pronounced deliberately by Senators upon their official oaths; no less solemnly than the oath under which they have conducted this trial. No new view or argument has been presented on this trial to shake the validity of *that* act.

The effort, on the ground of former precedents, to excuse the removal of Stanton and the *ad interim* appointment of Thomas without the advice and consent of the Senate in session, and no vacancy existing in the office, *fails*, because no similar instance can be found, but in every case, save one, there was an existing vacancy; and in that one the removal was accomplished by the submission of an appointment to the Senate, and a distinct recognition of its constitutional authority. The President on the 21st of February, by an order of that date, declared that Mr. Stanton was thereby removed from the office of Secretary of War; and by another order of the same date, "on that day, Mr. Stanton was removed from the office of Secretary of War, and Lorenzo Thomas appointed Secretary of War *ad interim*." And also, on the same day, by an official message to the Senate, announced the removal and the appointment.

If in the face of his own official acts and records he can send lawyers to the bar of the Senate to plead and pretend there was no removal, and that his message to the Senate was false, it would be an example of official prevarication without a parallel in the history of mankind!

Finally, the claim set up in Mr. Johnson's answer of power at any and all times to remove executive officers, for cause to be judged of by him alone, effectually abrogates the constitutional authority of the Senate in respect to official appointments, subverts the principles of republican government, and usurps the unlimited authority of an autocrat. It moreover puts to flight the ridiculous pretense that the President designed only to submit the tenure-of-office act to the test of judicial decision.

In my deliberate judgment, therefore, I must believe the people of the United States have clearly maintained and substantiated the allegations contained in the first, second, and third articles of impeachment.

But to be more particular I will for a few moments consider these first three articles separately and in detail, as we must answer, in our judgment, of guilty or not guilty upon each one separately.

The *first article* charges a violation of the act of Congress regulating the tenure of civil offices by the unlawful removing of Edwin M. Stanton from the office of Secretary of War.

The *fact of removal*, as I have said, is fully established by official acts and records, namely:

1. The President's order of removal on the 21st day of February, 1868, which states that Mr. Stanton is "*hereby removed from the office as Secretary for the Department of War*," and that his functions as such would terminate upon the receipt of said communication, and directs him to transfer to Lorenzo Thomas, as Secretary of War *ad interim*, "all records, books, papers," &c.

2. The order of same date to said Lorenzo Thomas, declaring that Edwin M. Stanton "*having been this day removed* from the office as Secretary for the Department of War," he, the said Thomas, was authorized and empowered to act as Secretary of War *ad interim*, and directed immediately to enter upon the discharge of the duties pertaining to that office.

3. By the message of the same date to the President of the Senate announcing that he had removed Mr. Stanton.

4. By the continual recognition of Mr. Thomas as Secretary of War *ad interim* from that until the present day.

The fact of removal being thus established, it is sought to justify it on two grounds: first, that the tenure-of-office act is unconstitutional; and second, that, if valid, its provisions do not restrict the President from removing Mr. Stanton. Without entering into a protracted discussion, it is sufficient to say that the constitutionality of the "tenure act" was fully discussed in the Senate before its original passage, and by a large and solemn vote it was held to be constitutional.

The objection was again specifically made by the President in his veto message, and the act was again held to be constitutional by a vote exceeding two thirds of the Senators present. The question was a third time made in the Senate by the President in his message relating to Mr. Stanton's suspension; and was a fourth time decided upon the consideration of the message of the 21st of February announcing Mr. Stanton's removal. No question, I repeat, has been so fully and thoroughly considered or so often deliberately decided as the constitutionality of the tenure-of-office act. And in the discussion during this trial the counsel for the President have advanced no new views or arguments which had not been several times considered in the Senate. So that if any question can be settled by this Senate and put by us, at least forever at rest, so that there is no room for further dispute, *it is the constitutionality of the tenure-of-office act.* That Mr. Stanton's tenure of office as Secretary of War was at the time of his removal within the provisions of that act, and hence his removal was a violation of the act is also equally plain.

The first clause of the first section of the act applies to all civil officers and prohibits their removal without the advice and consent of the Senate. The proviso makes an exception and limitation in respect to Cabinet officers. It was admitted that Mr. Stanton had been duly appointed Secretary of War by Mr. Lincoln, and was serving out, as was Mr. Johnson, the residue of Mr. Lincoln's term. If the Cabinet were not within the proviso, then by the first clause of the first section of the act they were not subject to *removal* or *suspension* without the sanction of the Senate. If within the proviso, they could not be removed without such sanction until the expiration of thirty days after the *term* of appointment. So that it makes no difference which horn of the dilemma Mr. Johnson selects, for in either case he transgressed the law. Mr. Johnson is, moreover, concluded absolutely on this point by his own official acts and records. During his Administration treaties with foreign nations have been made, foreign territory has been purchased. Every civilized nation of the globe has been dealt and negotiated with by Mr. Seward as Secretary of State. Loans have been contracted, revenues collected, taxes imposed, thousands of millions of dollars in money or public credit have been expended or invested by Mr. McCulloch as Secretary of the Treasury. Fleets have been dismantled, naval vessels and armaments sold by Mr. Welles as Secretary of the Navy. Armies have been disbanded, a new army raised and organized, and millions of dollars of military disbursements expended every month under the direction of Mr. Stanton as Secretary of War. The Departments of State, Treasury, War, and Navy for three years have been held under the same tenure. How, then, can it now be pretended by Mr. Johnson that the term of these officers expired at the death of Mr. Lincoln, or that a new appointment was necessary, when none was made? What, in such a view, would be the condition of our foreign relations or national credit? But the objection now raised by or in behalf of Mr. Johnson is not only answered by these acts done under his authority, but it is also repelled by the most solemn records under his own hand. The order suspending Mr. Stanton was addressed to him as "Secretary of War," and professed to suspend him from *that office*. The veto message of the *tenure act* insisted that its operations extended to Cabinet officers. The annual message urged that specific objection. The message to the Senate relating to the suspension of Mr. Stanton again *pressed* that point. And the order of removal specially stated that he *was on that day* (February 21, 1868) *removed* from office as Secretary for the Department of War. The *ad interim* appointment of Thomas, the appointments of Ewing and Schofield declare Mr. Stanton "removed," not pretending that his office had expired by the death of Mr. Lincoln.

 Without pursuing the subject further, the terms of the Constitution, the plain words of the act of Congress, the acts and the official records of the President, and the solemn judgment of the Senate, determine clearly as human understanding can comprehend that the tenure-of-office act is constitutional, and that Mr. Stanton did lawfully hold the office of Secretary of War on the 21st day of February last by the tenure-of-office act beyond removal without the advice and consent of the Senate ; and that his removal "on that day" by Andrew Johnson was in contemptuous disobedience and flagrant violation of the law, constituting a high misdemeanor! and, consequently, that Andrew Johnson is guilty in manner and form as charged in the first article of impeachment.

The *second article* charges that on the 21st day of February, 1868, the Senate being in session, and there being no vacancy in the office of Secretary of War, with intent to violate the Constitution of the United States and the act of Congress regulating the tenure of certain civil offices, Andrew Johnson, President, &c., did issue and deliver to Lorenzo Thomas a letter of authority, set forth in the article of impeachment, whereby Thomas was authorized and empowered to act as Secretary of War *ad interim*, and directed immediately to enter upon the discharge of the duties pertaining to that office ; that the Senate was in session on the 21st day of February last ; that there was no vacancy in the office of Secretary of War, and that the President on that day did issue the letter of authority as charged, are fully proved : first, by the letter of authority having the genuine signature of Andrew Johnson ; second, by the statement in the said letter of authority that Edwin M. Stanton had "been this day removed from office as Secretary of War ;" and, third, by the President's message of the same date to the Senate.

Issuing this letter of authority to Lorenzo Thomas was a direct violation of the tenure-of-office act. Now, if that act be constitutional—as I have shown—then the President's guilt under the *second* as well as the first article stands without defense ; and hence I am forced to the conclusion that the President is *guilty as he stands charged in the second article of impeachment.*

The *third article* charges that on the 21st of February last, while the Senate was in session, Andrew Johnson, President, &c., without authority of law, did appoint one Lorenzo Thomas Secretary of War *ad interim* without the advice and consent of the Senate, with the intent to violate the Constitution of the United States, no vacancy in said office having happened during the recess of the Senate, and no vacancy existing at the time of the appointment of the said Thomas. That the President did make the appointment, that the Senate was in session, that no vacancy existed at the time of the appointment, are all *facts* undenied and fully proved by the evidence referred to in the preceding article.

But the President sets up in defense that similar appointments were made by his predecessors, and that he is vested, as President, with "the power at any and all times of removing from office all executive officers for cause to be judged of by the President alone." This ground of defense fails, because no tenure-of-office law prohibited his predecessors from making such appointments ; and because no case has been found in which a President assumed the right to create a vacancy by removal and then make an appointment without the advice and consent of the Senate, when this body was in session.

Before Mr. Johnson usurped authority independent of the Senate, removals during the session recognized in every instance the constitutional authority of the Senate over the proposed appointment. Its denial would deprive the Senate of that constitutional check which constitutes one of its most important functions, and would establish the distinctive claim of independent, exclusive executive power, now, for the first time in our national history, boldly and defiantly avowed.

The act of President Johnson is not only

unsanctioned by precedent, but on principle the claim of power set up is contrary to the Constitution, which says "the President may nominate, and by and with the advice and consent of the Senate appoint," &c, *but it is also incompatible with the honor, safety, and existence of our form of government.*

Regarding the act of the President, in appointing Lorenzo Thomas Secretary of War *ad interim,* as an unlawful usurpation of power, violating the Constitution and an act of Congress, the President is *guilty,* in my judgment, in manner and form as charged in the third article of impeachment.

The *fourth, fifth, sixth,* and *seventh* articles of impeachment charge an unlawful conspiracy by Mr. Johnson with Lorenzo Thomas, to accomplish the unlawful object specially set forth in *each* of the before-named articles. Whatever conclusion might be formed on these articles, if they stood alone, unaccompanied by any *overt acts,* in furtherance of the objects stated, the evidence in this case, taken in connection with the several acts named, compels the belief that there was a *clear,* distinct understanding, combination, and conspiracy between Johnson and Thomas, with the intent and purpose set forth in the several articles. His efforts to have orders issued and obeyed without (as provided by law) their going through the office of the General of the Army; his finding a man who "would obey his orders without regard to the law," and appointing him for the time being; his reappointment of Colonel Cooper after he had been rejected by the Senate at this very session: all these acts taken together, and others of the same character, compel in me the belief that the President did unlawfully conspire with others to violate the law, and hence is guilty in manner and form as charged in the fourth, fifth, sixth, and seventh articles of impeachment.

The eighth article charges that the letter of authority of February 21, 1868, was issued by President Johnson to Lorenzo Thomas with intent to control the moneys appropriated to be disbursed for the military service in violation of the Constitution and of the civil-tenure act.

It is not denied that the appointment of Lorenzo Thomas Secretary of War *ad interim* would give him, while he acted under such appointment, the same control exercised by a Secretary of War duly nominated and confirmed by the Senate. The military disbursements, amounting to many millions of dollars, were thus placed in the hands and at the power of a mere appointee of the President and the creature of his will, made and unmade by the breath of his power alone.

It is an invariable maxim that every man—and especially every high official—intends the consequences of his own acts; and hence that Mr. Johnson designed to invest Lorenzo Thomas with power over the military dis-

C. I.—63.

bursements—especially when aided by Cooper, unlawfully in the door of the Treasury—thus putting the Treasury within reach of the arm of the President alone. This is both a crime and a misdemeanor; and therefore he is guilty in manner and form as charged in the eighth article of impeachment.

The ninth article charges that the President instructed General Emory, commander of the military department of the District of Columbia, that the law which required all orders and instructions relating to military operations be issued through the General of the Army was unconstitutional and in contravention with General Emory's commission, and this was done with intent to induce General Emory, in his official capacity as commander of the department, to violate the provisions of the act of Congress aforesaid, and with further intent to prevent the execution of the *tenure-of-office act* and to prevent Mr. Stanton from holding and executing the duties of the office of Secretary of War.

The fact that the President did instruct the military commander of this department that the law requiring military orders to be issued by the President through the General of the Army was unconstitutional is distinctly proved by General Emory. Why was such instruction given *at that time,* and why were there such suspicions aroused because officers were called at General Emory's headquarters? It was only on account of what the President had decided *to do!*—to control the Department of War! It was in furtherance of what he had said to General Grant—"that as early as last August he had determined to dispossess Mr. Stanton of the War Office at all hazards." These whisperings to General Emory have a peculiar significance to my mind, when I remember what was at that moment in the mind of the President relating to getting possession of the Department of War and dispossessing Mr. Stanton and getting around General Grant by issuing orders *direct* to his subordinate officers.

It, to my mind, admits of no other motive or intention than that which is charged, and, taken with all attendant circumstances, forces the conclusion that the President is guilty in manner and form as charged in the ninth article of impeachment.

The tenth article charges that at sundry times and places therein set forth, Andrew Johnson, President, &c., made certain intemperate, inflammatory, and scandalous harangues, and uttered loud threats and bitter menaces as well against Congress as the laws of the United States, with intent and design to set aside the powers of Congress, and to bring the Legislature and the several branches thereof into disgrace, ridicule, hatred, and reproach, and to impair and destroy the regard and respect of the good people of the United States for Congress and the legislative powers thereof, and to excite odium and resentment against Congress and the *laws* duly and constitutionally enacted. And all this while the President was under his oath to see that the laws were faithfully executed. It has been established beyond dispute that the scandalous harangues set forth in this article were made by the President at the times and places stated. Their intent is manifest as plainly as human speech can exhibit the motive and impulse of man's heart. And these denunciations, threatening to "veto their bills," were spoken out of the "abundance of the heart" which led him thus to "impromptu speak," and to defy the very laws he was sworn to execute.

Our Government was framed to rest upon opinion and reason, and not upon *force*. The good will of the nation toward the laws and the law-makers is of the highest importance to secure obedience, and the man or the public officer who, by act or speech, strikes at this foundation, does an irreparable injury.

The history of republican governments shows that the first efforts of tyrants and usurpers has been directed to undermining and destroying the faith of the people in their representative and legislative bodies.

In his harangues, Andrew Johnson followed with more than usual directness the beaten path toward the overthrow of constitutional government—a government which encourages and secures the largest freedom of speech consistent with its own perpetuity; a government, too, that has provided for striking down the sappers and miners who work at its own foundations. Under this charge and by the proofs the President must stand guilty of the high misdemeanor charged in this tenth article of impeachment.

The eleventh and last article charges that on the 18th day of August, 1866, Andrew Johnson, President, &c., did, by a public speech, declare and affirm, that the Thirty-Ninth Congress was not a Congress authorized by the Constitution to exercise legislative powers; that its legislation was not valid or obligatory upon him, except so far as he might approve the same; and also denied its power to propose amendments to the Constitution. This article further specifies certain of his official acts done in pursuance of that declaration, devising and contriving, among other things, to prevent the execution of the tenure-of-office act, and to prevent the execution of other laws, especially the "acts to provide for the more efficient government of the rebel States."

The public speech referred to in this article was made before a large assemblage at the Executive Mansion, and clearly proved, as well as substantially admitted. It imports nothing less than a total denial of the constitutional power of Congress to pass any laws but such as he approves. It usurps the whole law-making power, and vests its validity absolutely in his approval. The powers of Congress are thus abrogated; and the Government of the United States is practically vested in Andrew Johnson!

It is vain to treat this and the preceding article with levity or affect to pass them over with contemptuous indifference or frivolous excuse. They are public declarations by the Chief Executive, preceded, accompanied, and followed by *acts* in strict accordance with the theme. They have thus become significant facts, full of enormity in themselves, and boldly threatening the peace, welfare, and existence of constitutional government.

While some of the articles, which would seem to operate in the first instance only on an individual, the offenses charged in the tenth and eleventh articles embrace in their range all the powers of the Government, and the validity of all the legislation of Congress since the rebellion began. The national debt, the taxes imposed and collected by acts of Congress, the collection of the revenue—in short, every operation of the Government depending upon the action of Congress during and since the rebellion, are struck at by the hand of the President. And if I was to declare, on my oath, for the acquittal of the President under these articles, charged and proved, then, indeed, would I feel myself to be guilty of perverting the trust imposed upon me under the Constitution of the United States as a member of this high court of impeachment.

If I am to vote for acquittal I shall sanction these new violations of law and of the Constitution. I shall consent that the President may possess himself of each and all departments of this Government, and merge into one head all the independent prerogatives of each of the departments as were wisely provided by the early framers of our representative Government.

I cannot be thus false to my convictions of duty, false to the trusts imposed by my position as a Senator sitting upon this great trial, nor false to my loyal, earnest, and devoted constituency, whose every impulse I feel, nor false to my anxious countrymen, whose eyes are upon me. Conviction to my mind is a duty, ay, a necessity, under my oath as a Senator trying this cause. I cannot escape if I would the conviction which the evidence in this cause forces upon me. And conviction is, to my vision, *peace*. It is quiet to our long distracted country. It means *restoration* upon the basis of loyalty, liberty, and equal suffrage, which secures and perpetuates equal rights to all American freemen—now, thank God, American citizens!

Charged by the Constitution with a share in this trial, I cannot shut my eyes to the crimes and misdemeanors charged, and proved also, in this the eleventh article of impeachment; and with uplifted hand and heart I declare my belief to be *that the President is guilty!*

OPINION
OF
HON. LOT M. MORRILL.

The President is impeached by the House of Representatives of high crimes and misdemeanors, in that on 21st of February last he issued an order for the removal from office of Edwin M. Stanton, Secretary of War, with intent to violate the tenure-of-office act, and to remove said Stanton from office.

In that on said 21st February he issued to General Thomas a letter authorizing and empowering him to act as Secretary of War, there being no vacancy in that office, with intent to violate the tenure-of-office act.

In that on the said 21st of February he did appoint said Thomas to be Secretary for the Department of War *ad interim*, without the advice and consent of the Senate, no vacancy having happened in said office, with intent to violate the Constitution of the United States.

In that he conspired with said Thomas to hinder and prevent said Stanton from filling said office; to prevent and hinder the execution of the tenure-of-office act; to get possession of the War Office, and of the property of the United States in the Department of War.

In that, with intent to violate the tenure-of-office act, he authorized said Thomas to act as Secretary of War, there being no vacancy in said office, and the Senate then being in session.

In that he attempted unlawfully to induce General Emory to obey his orders, and not those issued by the General of the Army, with intent to enable him to defeat the tenure-of-office act, with intent to prevent said Stanton from holding his office.

In that, to bring Congress into contempt, and excite the odium of the people against Congress and the laws by it enacted, he made certain public addresses, indecent and unbecoming in the Chief Magistrate, by the means whereof he brought the office into contempt, ridicule, and disgrace.

In that he attempted to prevent said Stanton from resuming the office of Secretary of War, after the refusal of the Senate to concur in his suspension; also to prevent the execution of the act of 2d March, 1867, making appropriations for the support of the Army, and an act to provide for the more efficient government of the rebel States.

The President, answering, does not controvert the essential facts charged, but insists that the acts complained of are authorized by the Constitution and laws; and further, that if in any respect this plea fails of a complete justification he should still be acquitted, as those acts were all done in good faith in the performance of public duties, arising in the execution of his office, imposed upon him by the Constitution and laws and in defense and execution of them. Concurring in much of the reasoning of the Senators who are of opinion that

the answer and defense of the President as to several of the charges fail of such justification, I shall content myself with a statement of the grounds of my opinion upon a portion of the articles only.

The first three articles and the eleventh relate to the attempt to remove Mr. Stanton from the office of Secretary of War; the authority to General Thomas to take possession and to do the duties of the office; the appointment of General Thomas as Secretary of War *ad interim*; and the attempt to prevent Mr. Stanton from resuming the duties of his official office after his suspension had been non-concurred in by the Senate.

The question arising under these articles turns chiefly upon the question whether the tenure-of-office act is in conflict with the Constitution of the United States, and the case of Mr. Stanton was affected by it.

These are understood to be the grounds upon which the counsel for the President place the defense to these articles, and that upon which opinion divides in the Senate.

Is the tenure-of-office act unconstitutional, and is Mr. Stanton embraced in its provisions so as to be protected by it?

As to the first proposition as between the Senate and the President, it is not a new question, and it is difficult to perceive how it can properly be regarded by either as an open question. The act had been fully considered when it was first enacted in the Senate, was reconsidered after it had been returned by the President with his objections fully stated, and again passed with that unanimity necessary to give it the force of law, his objections to the contrary notwithstanding, and calculated to leave little doubt as to the confidence with which the Senate held its opinions.

The legislative and executive precedents and practice in our history touching the power of the President to remove from office, relied upon by him as authoritative interpretation of the Constitution, were known and familiar to Congress at the time. It is not suggested that the act was hastily or inconsiderately passed, as it will not be doubted that Congress had, in the recent examples of the exercise of this power by the Executive, abundant opportunity of judging of the expediency of a further continuance of this practice.

The binding force of this practice of removal by the President rests upon the interpretation given to the Constitution by the First Congress. It is not insisted that this interpretation by that Congress was authoritative and conclusive upon succeeding Congresses, and it is admitted that the extent of its authority is as a precedent only. The question was therefore open to further legislative regulation, and the practice which had obtained under the act of 1789 could properly and should necessarily be modified or reversed, as experience should dictate that the public interests demanded. The Congress of 1867, it will not be denied, had all the power over the subject that the Congress of 1789 is supposed to have had.

Besides, it is well known that the Congress of 1789 were far from having been unanimous in their opinions and action. One branch was equally divided upon the measure, and it finally passed by the casting vote of the Presiding Officer; and that from that time to the date of the act in question the interpretation of the First Congress had been repeatedly the subject of grave debate in Congress, and was believed by the most eminent of our statesmen, jurists, and commentators upon the Constitution to be unsound.

Indeed, the President is not understood to invoke the Senate now to declare void for conflict with the Constitution a law which had so recently received its sanction, and that after his objections to it had been fully considered, but that the argument presented is rather in extenuation of his refusal to obey and enforce it. For the purpose of these proceedings, the act in question may properly and must necessarily be regarded as valid, unless, indeed, it should be deemed advisable that Congress should repeal all laws the validity of which may be questioned by the President, which he may deem inexpedient, or to which he does not yield a willing obedience.

We are then brought to consider the question whether the case of Mr. Stanton was affected by the tenure-of-office act. The first section of that act is as follows:

"That every person holding any official office to which he has been appointed by and with the advice and consent of the Senate, and every person who shall hereafter be appointed to any such office, and shall become duly qualified to act therein, is, and shall be, entitled to hold such office until a successor shall have been in a like manner appointed and duly qualified, except as herein otherwise provided: *Provided*, That the Secretaries of State, of the Treasury, of War, of the Navy, and of the Interior, the Postmaster General, and the Attorney General, shall hold their offices respectively for and during the term of the President by whom they may have been appointed, and for one month thereafter, subject to removal by and with the advice and consent of the Senate."

The counsel for the President contend that "out of this body of the section it is explicitly declared that there is to be excepted a particular class of officers, 'except as herein otherwise provided.'" The Senator from Iowa, [Mr. GRIMES,] in his published opinion, says:

"Mr. Stanton's case is not within the body of the first section. The tenure which that provides for is not the tenure of any Secretary."

Other Senators, who agree with Mr. GRIMES in the conclusion to which he comes, adopt the views of the counsel for the President. These views are the opposites in statement and principle, and cannot be reconciled with each other.

The construction of Judge Curtis is, that the body of the section—the words "every person holding any civil office, appointed with the advice and consent of the Senate"—*necessarily includes* Mr. Stanton's case, as he was a civil officer who had been appointed with advice

and consent of the Senate; and to get rid of Mr. Stanton's case he is forced to the construction that the words "except as herein otherwise provided" "except him out of the body of the section;' while the Senator from Iowa accomplishes the same result more directly, but not less erroneously, by denying altogether that his case is included in the body of the section. It admits of no argument that this last opinion is unsound, and that conclusions drawn from such premises are untenable. The words "every person holding any civil office," &c., by the force of the unavoidable meaning of language, it must be conceded, embrace the case of Mr. Stanton, then holding the office of Secretary of War.

But leaving this discrepancy of deduction I turn to the construction of the act of Judge Curtis, which seems to be the generally received interpretation of those who hold that Mr. Stanton's case is not provided for in the act.

He concedes that the words "every person holding any civil office," &c., include Mr. Stanton, but insists that the words "except as herein otherwise provided," taken in connection with the proviso that follows, operate to *exclude* him from this general description of persons.

The words "except as herein otherwise provided," it is plain, either standing alone or taken in connection with the proviso, are not entitled to the force of terms of absolute exclusion, but rather are used in the sense of qualifying some antecedent provision in the body of the section. Now, what are these antecedent words or provision to which these qualifying words relate, and which they are supposed to modify? Do they qualify the provision "every person holding any civil office," &c., "except as herein otherwise provided," or the words "is and shall be entitled to hold his said office until his successor shall in like manner be appointed and qualified?" "except as herein otherwise provided."

Do the qualifying words operate to *exclude* a portion of the *persons* from holding office under this act altogether, or do they operate to qualify the *condition of holding?* The former construction, it is submitted, does violence to the intent of the act; besides, it is an obvious misapplication of the qualifying words to a portion of the section to which they do not relate. It is clear that it was the intent of the act to regulate a tenure of office of some sort of all the persons described in the body of the section, that is, "every person holding any civil office," &c.; but by this construction a portion of those persons fail to be provided for altogether; while the adoption of the other view provides for them a tenure of office, but different in its conditions, and is thus in harmony with the objects of the law.

If it be accepted that the Secretaries are not excepted out of the body of the section, and that the effect of the proviso is simply to provide and determine what their tenure of office shall be, the only remaining question is whether the provision does make such tenure for Mr. Stanton. It is contended that it does not, as he was not the appointee of Mr. Johnson, and that the term of Mr. Lincoln, whose appointee he was, was determined by death. It is conceded that Mr. Stanton was appointed by Mr. Lincoln in his first term of office, by and with the advice and consent of the Senate, to hold during the pleasure of the President for the time being; that he was duly holding office under that appointment in the second term of Mr. Lincoln and up to his death. He was, therefore, the appointee of Mr. Lincoln by original appointment in his first term, and not less so in his second term, in effect, by adoption and continuance in office under the first appointment, the person and office being identical, and there being no limitation in the tenure of office, except the pleasure of the President for the time being. Mr. Stanton was, therefore, properly holding office by appointment of Mr. Lincoln in his second term at his death. He continued to hold under such appointment and commission from Mr. Lincoln after the succession of Mr. Johnson, and by his adoption and continuance in office, and was so holding at the passage of the tenure-of-office act.

But it is said that if he is to be regarded as the appointee of Mr. Lincoln in his second term he is still not embraced in the terms of this act, as that term closed with the death of Mr. Lincoln, and that since that event he has been holding in the term of Mr. Johnson. It therefore becomes necessary to determine what was the "term" of President Lincoln. Was it an absolute period of four years, or was it that period during which he served in his office; the period for which he was elected, or the period he held and occupied his office? Was the *term* of his office subject, in the language of the counsel for the President, to a "conditional limitation?" The *term* of the presidential office, by the Constitution, is four years, and that without regard to the contingency of holding or period of actual service. It describes the period for which the office lasts, and is without limitation. The *tenure* of his office is subject to the contingencies of death, resignation, or removal: but that relates to the *condition* of actual holding or period of service, and in no way affects the *term* or period for which he was elected. Now, the language of the proviso is, "shall hold for the *term* of the President by whom appointed." Mr. Stanton was appointed by Mr. Lincoln, whose *term* of office was absolutely *four years*, under the Constitution. The statute adopts the same word, *term*, and this makes the period of holding identical with the period of the presidential office, and does not subject it to the contingencies of the *tenure* of his office or the period of his service.

I pass the question whether Mr. Johnson is or not serving out his own or the term of Mr. Lincoln as unimportant in the view taken of the question. Their terms of office, as a period of time, were identical; and whether he is serving out Mr. Lincoln's term of office, as Vice President, upon whom devolve the duties of the office of President, by death, can have no influence upon the general fact of what was Mr. Stanton's term of office. In either case his term would be the same.

But if, as is contended by counsel for the President and those who adopt his views, the proviso failed to provide a tenure for Mr. Stanton, he being conceded to be in the body of the section, then as to him the words, "except as herein otherwise provided," fail to have any effect, and leave his tenure unaffected, and the same as that provided in the body of the section for the description of persons mentioned. I conclude, therefore, that the act did not fail of its object, namely, to *regulate* the tenure of office of "every person holding any civil office to which he has been appointed by and with the advice and consent of the Senate;" that Mr. Stanton's case was not excepted out of its provisions; that the proviso does regulate for him a tenure of office; but if it do not, then it is clear that it is regulated as is provided in the body of the section for "every person holding any civil office," &c., and that his removal was a clear violation of this act.

But it is said that it is at least doubtful if the act did affect Mr. Stanton's case, and that the effort to remove him from his office on the 21st of February last was an attempt on the part of the President which he might well believe he had a right to make; that the attempt did not succeed, and that it would be an abuse of power to remove him from his high office on grounds so slight.

But did the President truly believe that he had the right, that it was clear, and that the public welfare justified and demanded its exercise? He had refused his assent to the tenure-of-office act, stating in his message, among his reasons expressed for refusal so to do, that its provisions deprived him of control over his Cabinet.

He had suspended Mr. Stanton under its provisions—so stated to the Secretary of the Treasury—as required by its provisions. He had communicated his reasons for this suspension, agreeably to the terms of the act, to the Senate. He had been advised of the action of the Senate upon that suspension, and of the acquiescence of General Grant in its determination of the case, and had witnessed the return of Mr. Stanton to his office and its duties in accordance with the imperative provisions of this act. With these acts and this knowledge upon the record it is difficult to believe that the President was acting in that measure of good faith and in the presence and under the pressure of a public necessity which would justify the defiance of a law of even doubtful import; that in this attempt to put aside a high officer of the Government without charge of misconduct in office, and after his purpose had been overruled by the Senate, it is submitted there is apparent less of desire to consult the public interests and faithfully to execute the laws than to execute his own purposes upon a public officer who had incurred his personal displeasure. Nor is it easy to adopt the opinion that the charges and proof in support of these may properly be regarded as slight or unimportant.

The President may not arbitrarily and without cause depose a high public officer with impunity independent of the act under consideration. Wantonly to do it would constitute the essence of arbitrary and unbridled power, and tend to establish that irresponsible license over the laws fatal to republican government, the first appearance of which demand to be rebuked and resisted. The officers and the office belong and are amenable to the law; they are its servants and not the "satraps" of the President. The right of removal is not an arbitrary right in any respect; and, subject to removal himself, the President could have no right to complain of the enforcement of a rule against him which he could apply to those in his power. *The public interest*, and that alone, must justify the action.

The President declares in his answer that so early as August last he had determined to cause Mr. Stanton "to surrender his office of Secretary of the Department of War." To that end, on the 12th of the same month, he suspended him from his office on pretense of misconduct in office, as now in his answer claimed, under the exercise of a power before unheard of, and certainly never before practiced or asserted by any of his predecessors, namely, the power to *suspend* from office indefinitely, and at his pleasure, not until meeting of the Senate, " *as incident to the right of removal;*" and having so suspended, kept that officer out of his office and out of the public service for many months, and long after Congress and the Senate had convened, and for reasons stated in his message to the Senate, wholly inadequate, unsatisfactory, and unjustifiable in the judgment of that body, and which, if not trifling, were characterized by personal rather than public considerations.

It will be observed that he at once invokes the aid of the tenure-of-office act to enable him to suspend from office a public officer who had incurred his personal displeasure, and afterward, when that had failed, attempts to remove him in defiance of its authority and in contempt of its validity. He at once *invokes* and *violates* the act of 1795. He professes to have appointed General Grant Secretary of War *ad interim* under it, and then violated it by retaining him in office contrary to its provisions.

He invokes the judgment of the Senate on the suspension of Mr. Stanton, and after that judgment has been pronounced against him, and under it the officer had returned to his duties in obedience to the act under which he had been suspended, he defies its authority by his removal, appoints General Thomas Secretary of War *ad interim*, holds him out to the country as the rightful Secretary of War, treats him as a constituent member of his Cabinet, ignores Mr. Stanton altogether, and thus subjects the conduct of the office of the Department of War to the dangers, embarrassments, and perils which may come of these conflicting pretensions, and must come if these pretensions are made good by his acquittal. If to these be added the spirit of defiance manifest in his message to the Senate of February 22 last, and his determination, at any and all hazards to the public interests, to cause a personally obnoxious public officer "to surrender his office," I am persuaded that the peril to our republican structure of government will have become imminent when such conduct in the President shall come to be regarded and tolerated as slight and trifling, and shall not, on the contrary, be held as high misdemeanors in office. Mr. Madison, in commenting upon this subject, says:

"I contend that the *wanton* removal of meritorious officers would subject him [the President] to impeachment and removal from his own office."

A different question is presented on the second and third articles. On the 21st February, assuming to have removed Mr. Stanton, the President, in writing, authorized General Thomas to act as Secretary of War, and appointed him Secretary of War *ad interim*, there being no vacancy in that office, or pretense of vacancy, except the letter to Mr. Stanton of the same date, the Senate then being in session and not being advised upon the subject.

The President, in his answer, insists that at the date of the letter and its delivery to General Thomas there was a vacancy in the office of Secretary of War caused by removal; that, notwithstanding the Senate was in session, it was lawful and in accordance with long-established usage to empower said Thomas to act as Secretary of War *ad interim*; and that, if the tenure-of-office act be valid, in doing so he violated none of its provisions.

Whether there was or not a vacancy in that office will depend upon the effect given to the letter of removal addressed to Mr. Stanton, which was not acquiesced in, and under which no removal *de facto* was effected; and whether the attempted removal or order of removal was justified by any usage arising under any provision of law. It is not pretended that any act of Congress expressly confers this power while the Senate is in session, much less that the power is drawn from any express provision of the Constitution. No parallel in the history of the Government is shown or is believed to exist. The only case at all approaching it is that of Timothy Pickering, where the removal and the nomination to the Senate of his successor were simultaneous, and were essentially one and the same act, and was in and of itself the mode adopted by the President of obtaining the advice and consent of the Senate to the removal. But in this case was an attempted removal without reference to the Senate and independent of it, and the appointment of a Secretary *ad interim*, and no nomination to the Senate of a successor. Neither by the implication of the Constitution, laws, nor usage was the removal of Mr. Stanton and the designation of General Thomas as Secretary of War *ad interim* authorized.

But it is insisted that the removal of Mr. Stanton having created a vacancy the President was authorized to fill it temporarily by the designation of General Thomas, under the act of 1795, and that that act was not repealed by the .act of 1863. This latter act repeals all acts and parts of acts inconsistent with its provisions; and it is said that its provisions are not inconsistent in some one or more particulars with the former act upon the same subject, and to that extent at least is not repealed. This construction is quite too narrow. The question is not whether the repealing act in any particular negatives the former act, but whether in its object and scope it was a substantial revision of the law upon the particular subject. If so, then, by well-established rules of legal interpretation, it does operate to repeal the former laws upon that subject.

Now, it is apparent from an examination of those statutes that the act of 1863 was such statute of revision. The act of 1792, upon the same subject, made provision for the case of vacancy by death, and certain temporary disabilities in the State, War, and Treasury Departments. That of 1795 provided that "in case of vacancy," &c.; and both alike in the cases contemplated provided that the President might "authorize any person or persons, at his discretion, to perform the duties," &c. The act of 1863 provides that in case of resignation, death, absence from the seat of Government, or sickness in the heads of any of the existing Departments, the President *may authorize any head of any other Department, &c.*, to perform the duties, &c.

The act of 1863 is a revision of the law on the subject, as it embraces the objects of both prior statutes; provides for vacancy by resignation, not provided for specifically, and changes the rule of both prior statutes as to the persons to be authorized to perform the duties temporarily, and makes provision for the other Departments, and adapts the existing laws to the present changed state of affairs. Can it be doubted that the act of 1863 was intended to be a revision of the whole law upon the subject; that it did provide and was intended to provide one uniform rule for all the Departments, and not that in case of vacancy by death, resignation, &c., authorize the appointment of heads of Departments, &c., and in case of vacancy by removal to authorize "any person or persons?" That the act of 1863 was intended to have this effect is clear from the statement of the chairman of the Committee on the Judi-

ciary who reported the act, Hon. Mr. Trumbull, that it was his understanding that it did repeal all former acts upon that subject.

But this precise question of the removal of Stanton and appointment of General Thomas was fully adjudicated by the Senate and concluded by its action on the 21st February last. This is its record:

" Whereas the Senate have received and considered the communication of the President, stating that he had removed Edwin M. Stanton, Secretary of War, and had designated Lorenzo Thomas to act as Secretary of War *ad interim:* Therefore,
" *Resolved by the Senate of the United States, That under the Constitution and laws* of the United States the President has no power to remove the Secretary of War and designate any other officer to perform the duties of that office *ad interim.*"

Was that adjudication of an act done and submitted to the Senate for its consideration erroneous? The resolution finally passed the Senate without division.

To those who would weaken the force of this record, or find excuse for the President in the unimportance of the transaction, it may be replied that if the Senate would retain its self-respect or command the respect of others it must stand by its decrees until reversed for error, and not for the reason that the President defies them or refuses to yield obedience to them. The President tells the Senate, in his communication upon the subject, that as early as August last he had "determined to cause Mr. Stanton to surrender the office of Secretary for the Department of War." That issue is now for the third time distinctly before the Senate, twice by the action of the President, and now by the action of the Representatives of the people. A surrender of the record of the Senate is a surrender of a public officer to the predetermined purpose and personal will of the President. It is needless to say such a result would be the deposition of a high public officer without cause, a triumphant defiance of the law of the land and of the supreme legislative authority of the country.

Whoever contemplates such a result with indifference may prepare for the advent of executive usurpation totally subversive of our system of government.

It only remains to consider the proposition of the counsel for President that he should not be held guilty on an assumed innocent mistake in interpreting the law. In judging of the intent with which the President acted, the public record of the officer, his acts, speeches, and policy, the current events of history connected therewith, may properly be considered. The quality of the particular act may be reflected from the body of official reputation and public conduct, good or bad.

In determining the character of the acts complained of touching the intent of the President, we may consider whether they relate to his antecedent official conduct, whether they were purely public and official or private and personal, whether they arose out of some real or supposed pressing public exigency, or whether, as in the case of Mr. Stanton, the real or assumed misconduct of a public officer, or from a settled determination to get rid of one who had become disagreeable to him at all hazards, and because it was his pleasure no longer to tolerate him in his office. In this light consider some of the facts connected with the removal of Mr. Stanton and the designation of General Thomas as Secretary of War *ad interim*. In his note of 5th of August last, requesting the resignation of Mr. Stanton, the President says he is constrained to do so from "public considerations of a high character." The precise nature of these *considerations* it is left to conjecture.

In his message of December 12, 1867, assigning the reason for the suspension of Mr. Stanton, he says he deemed the reply to his note above referred to as a defiance and expression of a loss of confidence in his superior, and "that it must necessarily end our most important relations."

Also, that Mr. Stanton held opinions upon the suffrage bill for the District of Columbia and the reconstruction acts of March 2 and 23, 1867, which could not be reconciled with his own or the rest of the Cabinet, and that there was but one result that could solve the difficulty, and "that was the severance of official relations."

As these reasons antedate those assigned for the immediate suspension of Mr. Stanton, and are the only causes of recent occurrence, it is fair to presume that the note which is declared to have led to the suspension was induced by a predetermination to sever the relations rendered necessary, in his opinion, by that want of "unity of opinion" existing in the Cabinet on account of the conflicting opinion of Mr. Stanton.

In his answer to article one the President says that on or prior to August 5, 1867, "he had become satisfied that he could not allow Mr. Stanton to continue to hold the office of Secretary for the Department of War without hazard to the public interests." "That the *relations* between them no longer permitted the President to resort to him for advice, or be responsible for his conduct of the affairs of the Department of War," and that therefore he 'determined that he ought not longer to hold said office, and considered what he might lawfully do to cause him to surrender said office.

Those are understood to be the reasons for the suspension, as also for the removal, or attempted removal, of the Secretary of War. They are, substantially, that the "relations between them" had become such in August, 1867, as not to "permit the President to resort to him for advice, or be responsible for his conduct of the Department of War as by law required;" and these "relations" are the "differences of opinion" upon the "suffrage bill," and the reconstruction acts of the 2d and 23d March, 1867, "upon which Mr. Stanton

stood alone in the Cabinet, and the difference of opinion could not be reconciled."

Those are the "public considerations of a high character," stated in the note of August 5, which was a request for the resignation of the Secretary, and which led to his suspension and subsequent removal, to prevent his resuming the duties of his office after the action of the Senate.

When before in the history of the Government did a President hold that "differences of opinion" of a Cabinet officer as to the policy of a law of Congress, or of its constitutionality, or of the propriety of its enforcement, were "public considerations of a high character," which not only "constrained" him to request his resignation of office, but impelled him to a determination to "cause him to surrender the office"—to suspend him—and, defeated in that by the adverse action of the Senate, to *remove* him, to "prevent him from resuming the duties of the office?" It is certain that differences of opinion "in the Cabinet" are not unknown in our history, as to the expediency, the policy, and the interpretation of laws; that they were marked in the Cabinet of Washington, and that they were not supposed and were not held to be "public considerations of a character" demanding removal from office.

The present case is especially noticeable, from the fact of public notoriety, as well as declared in the President's answer and message, that the "difference of opinion" complained of was that the opinions of the Secretary of War were in harmony with those of Congress upon the acts mentioned, while those of the President were opposed, as had been expressed in his veto message, and that "difficulties" from such "differences of opinion," and which could only be solved by suspension and removal from office, were such as are publicly known to have arisen on the question of the *execution* of the reconstruction acts of March 2 and 23.

It is observable that no public exigency is stated by the President to have arisen demanding action in Mr. Stanton's case; no malversation or misconduct in office; no disobedience of, or refusal or neglect to obey orders of the President, is alleged or suggested. Besides, the Senate had been recently in session, since the "relations and difference of opinion had developed," in two different periods, affording ample opportunity for the appointment of his successor, if the public interests demanded a change of that officer and were of a character to commend themselves to that body.

Some stress has been laid upon the want of "confidence" in the Secretary, which would not permit a resort to him for advice, and rendered it unsafe that the President should be responsible for his official conduct.

It is difficult to appreciate the importance which seems to be attached to this statement. The Secretary of War is certainly not the constitutional adviser of the President in his general administration, nor is the President entitled to his opinion, except in the case contemplated in the Constitution, and that upon affairs arising in his own Department, and in relation thereto.

Nor is it obvious what is intended by the statement in the answer by being responsible for his conduct of the affairs of the Department of War.

What is the nature of this supposed responsibility, and how imposed? We are not informed in the answer. No such responsibility is understood to be imposed by the Constitution, and none is believed to exist in the laws creating the Department of War and defining the duties of the Secretary of War.

By no provision of the Constitution or laws is it believed that the President is chargeable with the consequences of the misconduct or neglect of duty of that officer with which he himself is not connected.

The Secretary, and he alone, must answer to the violated law for his misconduct and neglect of duty, and the assumption that the President is responsible for them is to assume that the War Department is under the direction and at the discretion of the President, and not under the statute creating it and by which it is conducted.

It is difficult to believe that in the suspension of and subsequent removal of Mr. Stanton the President was actuated solely by "public considerations," and especially does he fail to make it clear that he was acting on the pressure of a State necessity or public exigency which justified him in first experimenting with a law of Congress by suspending a public officer under it, and failing of his declared purpose in that, namely, "*to cause him to surrender his*" office, then to defy its authority by disregarding it altogether, and remove the officer so suspended, confessedly to prevent his resuming the duties of the office, after the adverse action of the Senate upon the case submitted to it for its consideration.

The doubts which are invoked to shield the President fail to protect him, as he fails to show any case or public necessity for the exercise of doubtful power under the Constitution and laws, while his official conduct plainly shows a spirit of hostility to the whole series of acts of Congress designed for the reconstruction of the late insurrectionary States and the pacification of the country, and an intent to obstruct rather than faithfully to execute these laws.

If, therefore, doubts arise on the record they belong to the country and to the violated laws, and presumption of innocence cannot obtain where the sinister purpose is apparent. It is impossible to withhold a conviction of the President's guilt under the articles presented by the House of Representatives for usurpations of power not delegated by the Constitution, and for violation and obstruction of the laws of the land, and so guilty of high crimes and misde-

meanors in his office, which, as a remedy for the present disorders which afflict the nation consequent upon them, and for the future security against the abuse of executive authority, demand, in harmony with the provisions of the Constitution, his removal from office.

OPINION
OF
HON. RICHARD YATES.

It is difficult to estimate the importance of this trial. Not in respect merely to the exalted position of the accused, not alone in the fact that it is a trial before the highest tribunal known among us, the American Senate, upon charges preferred by the immediate Representatives of the sovereignty of the nation, against the President of the United States, alleging the commission by him of high crimes and misdemeanors; it is not alone in these respects that the trial rises in dignity and importance, but because it presents great and momentous issues, involving the powers, limitations, and duties of the various Departments of the Government, affecting the very form and structure of the Government, and the mightiest interests of the people, now and in the future.

It has been aptly termed the trial of the Constitution. Constructions of our Constitution and laws here given and precedents established by these proceedings will be quoted as standard authorities in all similar trials hereafter. We have here at issue, before this highest judicial tribunal, in the presence of the American people and of the civilized world, whether our Constitution is to be a landmark to the citizen, a guide to the statesman, and authoritative over the magistrate, or whether this is a land of anarchy, crime, and lawless usurpation. It is a trial which challenges the broadest comprehension of the statesman, the highest intellect and clearest discrimination of the jurist, and the deepest solicitude of the patriot. Its issues are to be determined by clearly ascertaining the duties and powers of the coördinate branches of the Government, all jealous of encroachments upon their functions, and all in danger if one shall usurp powers which by virtue of the Constitution and laws belong to others.

Although it seems to me that no man of honest judgment and true heart can have a possible doubt as to the guilt of the respondent in this cause, and although he has long since been indicted and found guilty in the judgment and conscience of the American people of a giant apostacy to his party—the party of American nationality and progress—and of a long series of atrocious wrongs and most daring and flagrant usurpations of power, and for three years has thrown himself across the path of the country to peace and a restored Union, and in all his official acts has stood forth without disguise, a bold, bad man, the aider and abettor of treason, and an enemy of his country; though this is the unanimous verdict of the loyal popular heart of the country, yet I shall strive to confine myself, in the main, to a consideration of the issues presented in the first three articles. Those issues are simply: whether in the removal of Edwin M. Stanton, Secretary of War, and the appointment of Lorenzo Thomas Secretary of War *ad interim*, on the 21st day of February, 1868, the President willfully violated the Constitution of the United States, and the law entitled "An act regulating the tenure of certain civil offices," in force March 2, 1867.

Upon the subject of appointments to civil office the Constitution is very explicit. The proposition may be definitely stated that the President cannot, during the session of the Senate, appoint any person to office without the advice and consent of the Senate, except *inferior* officers, the appointment of whom may, by law, be vested in the President. The following is the plain letter and provision of the Constitution defining the President's power of appointment to office:

"He shall have power, by and with the advice and consent of the Senate, to make treaties, provided two thirds of the Senators present concur; and he shall nominate, and *by and with the advice and consent of the Senate shall appoint,* embassadors, other public ministers and consuls, judges of the Supreme Court, and *all other officers of the United States whose appointments are not herein otherwise provided for, and which shall be established by law;* but the Congress may by law vest the appointment of such inferior officers as they think proper in the President alone, in the courts of law, or in the heads of Departments."

Is it not plain, very plain, from the first clause above set forth, that the appointment of a superior officer, such as a Secretary of War, or the head of any Department cannot be made during the session of the Senate without its advice and consent? It is too clear for argument that the Constitution does not confer the prerogative of appointment of *any* officer upon the President alone during sessions of the Senate, and that he can only appoint *inferior* officers even, by virtue of laws passed by Congress, so that the appointment of a head of a Department cannot be made without the concurrence of the Senate, unless it can be shown that such appointment is, in the words of the Constitution, "otherwise provided for;" and it is not pretended that any such other provision can be shown.

The framers of the Constitution wisely imposed this check upon the President to secure integrity, ability, and efficiency in public officers, and to prevent the appointment of men who, if appointed by the President alone, might be his mere instruments to minister to his purposes of his ambition.

I maintain that *Congress itself* cannot pass a law authorizing the appointment of any officer, excepting inferior officers, without the advice and consent of the Senate, it being *in session* at the time of such appointment. It is just as competent for Congress, under the

clause which I have read, to invest the President with the power to make a treaty without the concurrence of two thirds of the Senate, which is, as all agree, inadmissible. Any law authorizing the class of appointments just mentioned, without the Senate's concurrence, would be just as much a violation of the constitutional provisions which I have read as would a law providing that the President should not *nominate* the officer to the Senate at all. No appointment is complete without the two acts—nomination by the President and confirmation by the Senate.

I think my colleague [Mr. TRUMBULL] had not well considered when he made the statement in his argument that "the Constitution makes no distinction between the power of the President to remove during the recess and the sessions of the Senate."

The clause of the Constitution which I shall now quote shows very clearly that the power of the President to fill vacancies is *limited to vacancies* happening during the *recess* of the Senate:

"The President shall have power to fill up all vacancies that may happen during the recess of the Senate by granting commissions which shall expire at the end of their next session."

His power to fill vacancies during the recess, without the advice and consent of the Senate at the time, proceeds from the necessity of the case, because the public service would suffer unless the vacancy is filled; but even in this case the commission of the temporary incumbent is to expire at the end of the next session of the Senate, unless the Senate, during said next session, shall have consented to his appointment. The reason of this limitation upon the President to the filling of vacancies happening during the recess, and why he cannot appoint during the session of the Senate without consent, is clearly because the Senate, being in session, may at the time of the nomination give its advice and consent. The provision that "the President shall have power to fill all vacancies *during the recess* of the Senate by granting commissions which shall expire at the end of the next session," excludes the conclusion that he may create vacancies and fill them during the session and without the concurrence of the Senate. If this view is not correct, it would seem that the whole provision of the Constitution on this point is meaningless and absurd.

The conclusion of the whole matter is, that if the President issued an order for the removal of Mr. Stanton and the appointment of Thomas, without the advice and consent of the Senate, it being then in session, then he acted in palpable violation of the plain letter of the Constitution, and is chargeable with a high misdemeanor in office. The production of his own order removing Stanton, and of his letter of authority to Thomas, commanding him to take possession of the War Office, are all the proofs necessary to establish his guilt. And when it appears, as it does most conclusively in the evidence before us, that he not only did not have the concurrence of the Senate, but its absolute, unqualified dissent, and that he was notified of that dissent by a certified copy of a resolution to that effect, passed by the Senate, under all the forms of parliamentary deliberation, and that he still willfully and defiantly persisted, and does still persist in the removal of Mr. Stanton, and to this day stubbornly retains Thomas as a member of his Cabinet, then who shall say that he has not wickedly trampled the Constitution under his feet, and that he does not justly deserve the punishment due to his great offense?

That the facts stated are proved and substantially admitted in the answer of the President to article first will not be denied by the counsel for the respondent nor by his apologists on the floor of the Senate.

The next question to which I invite attention is whether the President has intentionally violated the *law* and thereby committed a misdemeanor. Blackstone defines a misdemeanor thus:

"A crime or misdemeanor is an act committed or omitted in violation of a public law either forbidding or commanding it."

Misdemeanor in office, and misbehavior in office, or official misconduct mean the same thing. Mr. Madison says, in Elliott's Debates, that—

"The wanton removal of meritorious officers would subject him [the President] to impeachment and removal from his own high trust."

Chancellor Kent, than whom no man living or dead ever stood higher as an expounder of constitutional law, whose commentaries are recognized in all courts as standard authority, and whose interpretations are themselves almost laws in our courts, says, in discussing the subject of impeachment:

"The Constitution has rendered him [the President] directly amenable by law for maladministration. The inviolability of any officer of the Government is incompatible with the republican theory as well as with the principles of retributive justice.
"If the President will use the authority of his station to violate the Constitution or law of the land, the House of Representatives can arrest him in his career by resorting to the power of impeachment."—1 *Kent's Com.*, 289.

Story, of equal authority as a commentator on the Constitution, says:

"In examining the parliamentary history of impeachments, it will be found that many offenses not easily definable by law, and many of a purely political character, have been deemed high crimes and misdemeanors worthy of this extraordinary remedy."

Judge Curtis, one of the distinguished counsel for the respondent in this case, said in 1862:

"The President is the Commander-in-Chief of the Army and Navy, not only by force of the Constitution, but under and subject to the Constitution, and to every restriction therein contained, and to every law enacted by its authority, as completely and clearly as the private in the ranks. *He is General-in-Chief; but can a General-in-Chief disobey any law of his own country? When he can he superadds to his rights as commander the powers of a usurper, and that*

is military despotism;" * * * *"the mere authority to command an army is not an authority to disobey the laws of his country.*

"Besides, all the powers of the President are executive merely. He cannot make a law. He cannot repeal one. He can only execute the laws. He can neither make nor suspend nor alter them. He cannot even make an article of war."

Section three, article one, of the Constitution, says:

"The Senate shall have the sole power to try all impeachments."

I was present on the 15th day of April, 1865, the day of the death of the lamented Lincoln, when you, Mr. President, administered to Andrew Johnson the oath of office as President of the United States. He then and there swore that he would "preserve, protect, and defend the Constitution of the United States," and "take care that the laws should be faithfully executed."

On the 2d of March, 1867, Congress passed a law over the veto of the President entitled "An act to regulate the tenure of certain civil offices," the first section of which is as follows:

"*Be it enacted by the Senate and House of Representatives of the United States of America in Congress assembled,* That every person holding any civil office to which he has been appointed by and with the advice and consent of the Senate, and every person who may hereafter be appointed to any such office, and shall become duly qualified to act therein, is, and shall be, entitled to hold such office until a successor shall have been in like manner appointed and duly qualified, except as herein otherwise provided: *Provided,* That the Secretaries of State, of the Treasury, of War, of the Navy, and of the Interior, the Postmaster General, and the Attorney General, shall hold their offices respectively for and during the term of the President by whom they may have been appointed, and for one month thereafter, subject to removal by and with the advice and consent of the Senate."

This law is in entire harmony with the Constitution. "Every person appointed or to be appointed" to office with the advice and consent of the Senate shall hold the office until a successor shall "in *like manner,*" that is, "by the advice and consent of the Senate," be appointed and qualified. This is obviously in pursuance of the Constitution.

Now, if we construe this section independently of the proviso, we shall see that the removal of Mr. Stanton without the advice and consent of the Senate, and before his successor was appointed with the advice and consent of the Senate, was a misdemeanor, and was so declared and made punishable by the sixth section of the same act. And, again, if Mr. Stanton's case is excepted from the body of the act, and comes without the proviso, then his removal without the concurrence of the Senate, was a violation of the law, because, by the terms of the proviso, he was only subject to removal by and with the advice and consent of the Senate.

But my colleague [Mr. TRUMBULL] contends that Mr. Stanton was not included in the body of the section, because there is a proviso to it which excepts him and other heads of Departments from "every other civil officer," and yet he argues that he is not in the proviso itself, which certainly is strange logic. He argues that his tenure-of-office was given under the act of 1789, and that by that act the President had a right to remove him. If this be so, why did not the President remove him under that act, and not suspend him under the tenure-of-office act, and why did my colleague act under the tenure-of-office law in restoring Mr. Stanton?

It is claimed that Mr. Stanton is not included within the civil-tenure-of-office act, because he was not appointed by Mr. Johnson, in whose term he was removed; that he was appointed by Mr. Lincoln, and that Mr. Stanton's term expired one month after his (Mr. Lincoln's) death, and that Johnson is not serving part of Mr. Lincoln's term.

The true construction of the whole section, including the proviso, is that every person appointed and to be appointed, with the advice and consent of the Senate, is to hold the office until his successor shall have been in like manner appointed and qualified, *except* the heads of Departments, who are to hold their offices, not till their successors are appointed, but during the term of the President by whom they may have been appointed and for one month longer, and always "subject to removal by and with the advice and consent of the Senate."

Now, the only object of the proviso was to confer upon the Secretary of War, and other heads of Departments, a definite tenure of office, and a different term from that given in the body of the act. Can anything be plainer than that the case of Stanton is embraced in the meaning of the section, and that he is entitled either to hold until his successor shall have been appointed, by and with the advice and consent of the Senate, or during the term of the President, not "in which he was appointed," but "during the term of the President *by whom* he was appointed?"

At the time of the passage of the act of March 2, 1867, Mr. Stanton was holding the office of Secretary of War for, and in the term of, Mr. Lincoln, by whom he had been appointed, which term had commenced on the 4th of March, 1865, and will end March 4, 1869. The Constitution defines the President's term thus: "He shall hold his office during the term of four years." It further says that the term of the Vice President shall be four years. In case of death or vacancy "the duties of his office shall devolve on the Vice President." When Mr. Lincoln died Mr. Johnson's term was not a new one, but he succeeded to Mr. Lincoln's office and performs its duties for the remainder of Mr. Lincoln's term. Mr. Stanton was appointed by Mr. Lincoln, and, according to the proviso, holds for the term of the President "by whom he was appointed, and one month thereafter," and can be removed only by the appointment of a successor, with the advice and consent of the Senate, before the expiration of his term.

If, as contended by the President, Mr. Stanton's term expired with the death of Lincoln, and Mr. Johnson did not reappoint or commission him, then from the death of Mr. Lincoln until the commencement of this trial there was no legal Secretary of War, and the President permitted Stanton to act without authority of law, to disburse millions of public money, and to perform all the various functions of Secretary of War without warrant of law, which would of itself be a misdemeanor. I believe it was the Senator from Maine [Mr. Fessenden] who said "dead men have no terms." When that Senator was elected for six years to the Senate, does it not remain his term though he should die or resign before its expiration, and would not his successor chosen to fill the vacancy serve simply for the remainder of *his* term, and not a new term of his own for six years? I could consent to the construction of the Senator from Maine if, instead of limiting the presidential term to four years, it had provided that his term should be four years or till the death of the President, in case of his decease before the expiration of the four years; but it does not so provide.

The meaning of the word "vice" in Vice President is, "instead of" or "to stand in the place of;" "one who stands in the place of another." Therefore, Mr. Johnson succeeded, not to his own, but to Mr. Lincoln's term, with all its conditions and incidents. Death does not terminate a man's *term* of office. If a tenant of a farm for a term of seven years dies at the end of his first year, the remainder of the lease vests in his legal representatives; so the remainder of Mr. Lincoln's term at his death vested in his successor, Mr. Johnson. It follows that Mr. Stanton's term, ascertained by the act of March 2, 1867, does not expire till one month after the 4th of March, 1869, and that his removal and the appointment of an officer in his place, without the advice and consent of the Senate, was a violation of the law.

The second section provides that when the Senate is not in session, if the President shall deem the officer guilty of acts which require his removal or suspension, he may be suspended until the next meeting of the Senate; and that within twenty days after the meeting of the Senate the reasons for such suspension shall be reported to that body; and if the Senate shall deem such reasons sufficient for such suspension or removal, the officer shall be considered removed from his office; but if the Senate shall not deem the reasons sufficient for suspension or removal, the officer shall forthwith resume the functions of his office, and the person appointed in his place shall cease to discharge such duties.

That is to say, when any officer, appointed in manner and form as provided in the first section—that is, by and with the advice and consent of the Senate—is suspended, and the Senate does not concur in the suspension, such officer shall forthwith resume the functions of his office. Mr. Stanton, having been appointed by and with the advice and consent of the Senate, was suspended, but the Senate refused to concur in his suspension. According to the law he was then entitled to resume the functions of his office, but the President does not permit him to do so and refuses to have official relations with him, and has appointed and recognized as a member of his Cabinet another Secretary of War. Is not this a palpable violation of the very letter of the law? By what technical quibble can any Senator avoid the conviction of the culprit who thus defies a statute? If it is admitted that the President can legally "*remove*" Mr. Stanton, that proves too much, because the second section of the act in question declares that the President shall only "suspend" the officer, and in the case of suspension, and *that only*, and during *recess*, may an *ad interim* appointment be made. An *ad interim* appointment upon a removal is absolutely prohibited. As was well said by the Senator from Oregon, [Mr. WILLIAMS:]

"Vacancies in office can only be filled in two ways under the tenure-of-office act. One is by temporary or *ad interim* appointment during the *recess of the Senate;* the other is by appointment, by and with the advice and consent of the Senate, *during the session.*"

Let us see—the Senate being the sole tribunal to try impeachments and to decide upon the validity and violation of this law—what action the Senate has already taken.

On the 12th day of August, 1867, the Senate then not being in session, the President suspended Edwin M. Stanton, Secretary of the Department of War, and appointed U. S. Grant, General, Secretary of War *ad interim.* On the 12th day of December, 1867, the Senate being then in session, he reported, according to the requirements of the act, the causes of such suspension to the Senate, which duly took the same into consideration, and by an overwhelming vote of 35 to 6 refused to concur in the suspension, which action, according to the tenure-of-office act, reinstated Mr. Stanton in office. The President, bent upon the removal of Stanton, in defiance of the Senate and of the law, on the 21st day of February, 1868, appointed one Lorenzo Thomas, by letter of authority or commission, Secretary of War *ad interim*, without the advice and consent of the Senate, although the same was then in session, and ordered him (the said Thomas) to take possession of the Department of War and the public property appertaining thereto, and to discharge the duties thereof, and notified the Senate of his action. The Senate considered the communication, and, after debate, by a vote of 29 to 6, passed the following resolution:

"*Resolved by the Senate of the United States,* That under the Constitution and laws of the United States the President has no power to remove the Secretary of War and to designate any other officer to perform the duties of that office *ad interim.*"

And now, after such action under our oaths, are we to stultify ourselves, and swallow our own words and resolutions passed in the most solemn manner? Can we say that the President did not violate the law? That he did not become liable to conviction for violating the provisions of the tenure-of-office act, after he has admitted, in his answer upon this trial, that he tried to rid himself of Stanton by complying with the act; and after he has acknowledged that he was acting under the law of March 2, 1867, as shown by his letter to the Secretary of the Treasury, dated August 14, 1867, as follows:

"SIR: In compliance with the act entitled 'An act to regulate the tenure of certain civil offices,' you are hereby notified that on the 12th instant Hon. Edwin M. Stanton, Secretary of War, was suspended from his office as Secretary of War, and General Grant authorized and empowered to act as Secretary *ad interim.*"

To show, also, how trifling is the plea of the President that the law did not apply to this case, after he had acted upon it as above stated by himself, and after he had reported the reasons for suspension within the twenty days, as required by the act, there is the further and still more conclusive proof that the forms of commissions and official bonds were altered to conform to the requirements of the same tenure-of-office act, and under his own sign-manual issued to his appointees commissioned since its passage. If it be admitted, then, that Mr. Stanton's case did not come within the provisions of the first section of the act, yet is the President clearly guilty under the second section?

I shall now ask attention to the sixth section of the act, which is as follows:

"That every removal, appointment, or employment made, had, or exercised contrary to the provisions of this act, and the making, signing, sealing, countersigning, or issuing of any commission or letter of authority for or in respect to any such appointment or employment, shall be deemed, and are hereby declared to be, high misdemeanors; and upon trial and conviction thereof every person guilty thereof shall be punished by a fine not exceeding $10,000, or by imprisonment not exceeding five years, or both said punishments, in the discretion of the court."

If this section stood alone, who can deny that by his order to Thomas appointing him Secretary of War *ad interim*, and commanding him to turn Mr. Stanton out of office and take possession of the same, its books, and papers, he did commit a misdemeanor, especially when, by the very terms of this section, the issuing of such an order is expressly declared to be a high misdemeanor, and punishable by fine and imprisonment?

The second article charges that the President violated this law by issuing to General Thomas a letter of authority as Secretary of War *ad interim.* How, then, can my colleague use the following language:

"Considering that the facts charged against the President in the second article are in no respect contrary to any provision of the tenure-of-office act, they do not constitute a misdemeanor, and are not forbidden by any statute."

How can he justify such a statement, when he admits that the letter of authority was issued, and it is specifically declared in the act to be a misdemeanor?

Again, it is said that the prosecution is bound to prove criminal intent in the President. Such is not the law. The act itself proves the intent, if deliberately done by the party committing it. Such is the construction and the practice in all courts. If any person voluntarily commits an unlawful act the criminal intent is presumed. The principle is as old as our civilization, recognized in all courts of our own and other countries, that any unlawful act, voluntarily committed by a person of sound mind and mature age, necessarily implies that the person doing it intends all the consequences necessarily resulting therefrom. The burglar who breaks into your house in the night, with revolver in hand, may plead for the burglary, larceny, and even murder itself, the not unworthy motive that his only purpose was to procure subsistence for his starving wife and little ones. Booth, the vilest of assassins, declared, while committing the bloodiest crime in time's frightful calendar, that he murdered a tyrant for the sake of humanity and in the sacred name of patriotism.

But it is not necessary to insist upon the technical rule that the criminal intent is to be presumed on proof of the act; for if there is one thing that is directly proved, that stands out in bold relief, that is plain as the sun at noonday, it is that the President willfully, wickedly, and defiantly *violated* the law; and that, after due notice and admonition, he wickedly and with criminal perverseness persisted in violating the Constitution and the laws, and in bold usurpations of power unsettling the proper checks, limitations, and balances between the departments of the Government; with malice aforethought striving to eject from office a faithful servant of the people, whose only crime was his loyalty, and substituting in his stead a man who was to be his willing instrument in thwarting the policy and legislation of the people's Representatives and in placing the Government again in the hands of rebels, who with corrupt hearts and bloody hands struck at the nation's life.

Edwin M. Stanton, Mr. Lincoln's faithful minister and friend, whom the people learned to trust and lean upon in the dark hours of the Republic, who wielded that mighty enginery by which our army of more than a million of men was raised, clothed, armed, and fed; who with the genius of a Napoleon comprehended the vast field of our military operations and organized war and victory with matchless skill —a man of unstained honor, spotless integrity, unquestioned loyalty, having the confidence of all loyal hearts in the country—this was the man who incurred the bitter hatred of Johnson because he opposed his usurpations and his policy and acts in the interest of traitors, and because, like a faithful sentinel upon the watchtower of liberty, he gave the people warning against Johnson's schemes of mad ambition.

In proof of the respondent's malicious intent to violate the law I refer you to his attempt to induce General Grant to aid him in open, avowed violation of the law, as proved in his letter to Grant dated January 31, 1868. He therein declared his purpose to eject Stanton, "*whether sustained in the suspension or not,*" and upbraided Grant because, as he alleges, Grant agreed, but failed, to help him keep Stanton out by refusing to restore the office to Stanton, as by the second section of the act of March 2, 1867, he was required to do. He says:

"You had found in our first conference 'that the President was desirous of keeping Mr. Stanton out of office, *whether sustained in the suspension or not.*' You knew what reasons had induced the President to ask from you a promise; you also knew that in case your views of duty did not accord with his own convictions it was his purpose to fill your place by another appointment. Even ignoring the existence of a positive understanding between us, these conclusions were plainly deducible from our various conversations. It is certain, however, that even under these circumstances you did not offer to return the place to my possession, but, according to your own statement, placed yourself in a position where, could I have anticipated your action, I would have been compelled to ask of you, as I was compelled to ask of your predecessor in the War Department, a letter of resignation, or else to resort to the more disagreeable expedient of suspending you by a successor."

That he intended to violate the law by preventing Mr. Stanton from resuming the functions of his office, as provided by law, should the Senate non-concur in his suspension, is clearly proved by his other letter to General Grant of February 10, 1868, from which I quote as follows:

"First of all, you here admit that from the very beginning of what you term 'the whole history' of your connection with Mr. Stanton's suspension, you intended to circumvent the President. It was to carry out that intent that you accepted the appointment. This was in your mind at the time of your acceptance. It was not, then, in obedience to the order of your superior, as has heretofore been supposed, that you assumed the duties of the office. You knew it was the President's purpose to prevent Mr. Stanton from resuming the office of Secretary of War."

If you want intent proved, how can you more clearly do it than to use his own words that it was his "purpose to do the act, and that Grant knew that was his purpose from the very beginning, when Stanton was suspended?"

Is it necessary to dwell upon the subject of intent when in his own answer he confesses to having violated the law which expressly says that the officer, for good reasons only, should be suspended until the next session of the Senate, and coolly tells us that he "did not suspend the said Stanton from office until the next meeting of the Senate," as the law provided, "but by force and authority vested in him by the Constitution he suspended him *indefinitely*, and at the pleasure of the President, and that the order was made known to the Senate of the United States on the 12th day of December, 1867." In other words, he says to the Senate with most complacent effrontery, "Your law says I shall only suspend Stanton to the end of twenty days after the beginning of your next session. I *have* suspended him *indefinitely*, at the pleasure of the President, and I defy you to punish or hinder me." With all this the respondent's counsel ask for proof of criminal intent.

He tells the law-making power of the sovereign people that he sets up his pleasure against the positive mandates of law. He tells the Senate, "I do not acknowledge your law, which you by your votes on your oaths adopted and declared constitutional. I think it unconstitutional, and so said in my veto message, and I will not execute the law, but I will execute my veto; the reasons of my veto shall be my guide. I understand the constitutionality of the law better than Congress, and although my message vetoing the bill was overruled by two thirds of Congress, and though you have declared by law that I can only suspend Stanton, I choose, of my own sovereign will, which is above law, to remove him indefinitely. Furthermore, your law says, that in case his suspension is not concurred in by the Senate, Mr. Stanton shall forthwith resume the functions of his office, and you have by resolution, a copy of which I confess to have received, refused to concur with me in suspending him. I shall not, however, suffer him to hold the office, and I have appointed Lorenzo Thomas Secretary of War, not with your advice and consent, but contrary to the same." This is the offense of the President which, in the judgment of the President's apologists, is so "trifling" that we ought to pass it by in silence, or rather excuse by approving it in our verdict.

But what shall we say of the President's crime when to the violation of law he adds falsehood and deception in the excuses he gives for its violation? His plea that he violated the law because of its unconstitutionality and his desire to refer it to the Supreme Court is shown to be a mere subterfuge—an afterthought—by the fact that in August last, when he designated Grant to perform the duties of the War Office, he distinctly avowed that he was acting under the act of March 2, 1867; by the fact that he had caused the Departments to so alter the forms of commissions and bonds as to make them conform to this very statute; by the fact that he reported reasons for the suspension, as required in the act, in an elaborate message to the Senate; and, finally, by the fact that nowhere in said message does he intimate that he does not recognize the validity of the act, but argues distinctly that he proceeds *under* the same. He did not tell Senators in that message that the act was unconstitutional, and that he had suspended Stanton *indefinitely*. And I assert that every Senator was led to believe that it was the purpose of the President to regard the act valid, and to abide the judgment of the Senate. It was

not until the ghost of impeachment, the terrors of a broken oath, and removal from the high trust which he has abused, as a punishment for violated law, rose up to confront him that he resorted to the technical subterfuges of his answer that the law was unconstitutional, and the specious plea that his purpose in resisting the law was to test its validity before the Supreme Court.

In the whole history of these transactions he has written as with a pen of steel, in dark and imperishable lines, his criminal intent to violate the law. First, he attempted to seduce General Grant to his purpose, but he indignantly refused; then General G. H. Thomas; then General Sherman; then General Emory; and, finally, he selected General Lorenzo Thomas, a man who was willing, as he testifies, "to obey the President's orders;" and who, in pursuance of those orders, threatened to "kick Stanton out;" and "if the doors of the War Office were barred against him" he would "break them down by force;" and who says on his oath that he would have executed his threats on the following day but for his arrest after his return from the masquerade ball.

And now, as Senators, we are exhorted to find him guiltless in violating a law which we have often declared constitutional and valid, upon the subterfuge, the afterthought of the criminal, the excuse of a law-breaker caught in the act, the plea born of fear and the terrors of impeachment, and shown by the record made by his own hands to be utterly false. For one I cannot be so false to conviction, so regardless of fact, so indifferent to consistency, so blind to evidence, so lenient to crime, so reckless of my oath and of my country's peace.

Ours is a land of law. The principle of submission to the authority of law is canonized in the hearts of the American people as a sacred thing. There are none too high to be above its penalties, none too low to be beyond its protection. It is a shield to the weak, a restraint to the strong, and is the foundation of civil order and peace. When the day comes that the laws may be violated with impunity by either high or low all is lost. A pall of darkness will shut us in with anarchy, violence, and blood as our portion; and I fear the sun of peace and liberty will never more illumine our nation's path. The nation looks for a most careful observance of the law by the highest officer known to the law, because he has an "oath registered in Heaven" that he "will take care that the laws shall be faithfully executed." If the President of the United States, who should be the high exemplar to all the people, shall violate his oath with impunity, at his mere pleasure dispense with or disregard or violate the law, why may not all do the same? Why not at once sweep away the Constitution and laws, and level to the earth our temples of liberty and justice; resolve society into its original elements, where brute force, not right, shall rule, and chaos, anarchy, and lawless violence dominate the land?

. The Constitution and the laws passed in pursuance thereof are "the supreme law of the land." The President admits in his answer and in his defense that he acted in violation of the provisions of a statute, and his strange and startling defense is that he may suspend the operation of a law; that is to say, in plain terms. violate it at his pleasure, if, in *his opinion*, the law is unconstitutional; "that being unconstitutional it is void, and that penalties do not attach to its violation."

Mr. President, I utterly deny that the President has any such right. His duties are ministerial, and in no sense judicial. It is not his prerogative to exercise judicial powers. He must execute the laws, even though the Legislature may pass acts which in his opinion are unconstitutional. His duty is to study the law, not with the purpose to set it aside, but that he may obey its injunctions strictly. Can a sheriff, sworn to execute the laws, refuse to hang a convicted murderer because, in his judgment, the law under which the criminal has been tried is unconstitutional? He has no remedy but to execute the law in manner and form as prescribed, or resign to a successor who will do so.

I quote from the Constitution to show how laws become such, and that when certain prescribed forms are complied with the requirements of a law must be observed by all as long as it remains on the statute-book unrepealed by the Congress which made it, or is declared of no validity by the Supreme Court, it of course having jurisdiction upon a case stated:

"Every bill which shall have passed the House of Representatives and the Senate shall, before it becomes a law, be presented to the President of the United States; if he approve, he shall sign it, but if not, he shall return it with his objections to that House in which it shall have originated, who shall enter the objections at large on their Journal and proceed to reconsider it. If, after such reconsideration, two thirds of that House shall agree to pass the bill, it shall be sent, together with the objections, to the other House, by which it shall likewise be reconsidered, and if approved by two thirds of that House it shall become a law." * * * * * *

"If any bill shall not be returned by the President within ten days (Sundays excepted) after it shall have been presented to him, the same shall be a law in like manner as if he had signed it, unless the Congress by their adjournment prevent its return, in which case it shall not be a law."

Every bill which has passed the House of Representatives and the Senate, and been approved by the President, "shall become a law." If not approved by him, and it is again passed by two thirds of each House, "it shall become a law;" and if he retains it more than ten days, whether he approve or disapprove, it shall still "*become a law*." No matter how pertinent may be his objections in his veto message; no matter with how much learning or law he may clothe his argument; no matter how vividly he may portray the evil which may result from its execution, or how flagrantly it may, in his view, conflict with the Constitution,

yet if it is passed over his veto by two thirds of the Senate and House of Representatives his power ceases and his duties are at an end, and it *becomes a law*, and he is bound by his oath to execute it and leave the responsibility where it belongs, with the law-makers, who must answer to the people. If he then refuses to execute it, what is this but simple resistance, sedition, usurpation, and, if persisted in, revolution? Is it in his discretion to say it is not a law when the Constitution says, in the plain English vernacular, it is a law? Yes, Mr. President, it is a law to him *and to all* the people, to be obeyed and enforced throughout all the land.

It is a plain provision of the Constitution "that all legislative power granted by this Constitution shall be vested in a Congress, which shall consist of a Senate and House of Representatives." The President is no part of this legislative power. His veto message is merely suggestive, and if his reasons are deemed insufficient he is overruled, and the bill becomes a law "in like manner" as if he had approved it. The doctrine contended for by the President is monstrous, and if admitted is the end of all free government. It presents the question whether the people of the United States are to make their own laws through their Representatives in Congress, or whether all the powers of the Government, executive, legislative, and judicial, are to be lodged in a single hand? He has the executive power, and is Commander-in-Chief of the Army and the Navy. Now, if it is his province to judicially interpret and decide for himself what laws are constitutional and of binding validity upon him, then he has the judicial power, and there is no use for a Supreme Court; and, if having decided a law, in his opinion, to be unconstitutional, he may of his own will and sovereign pleasure set aside, dispense with, repeal, and violate a law which has passed over his veto, then he has the legislative power, and Congress is a myth, worse than "an excrescence hanging on the verge of the Government." Thus the purse and the sword, and all the powers which we heretofore considered so nicely balanced between the various Departments of the Government, are transferred to a single person, and the Government is as essentially a monarchy or a despotism as it would be if the Constitution and Congress were obliterated and the whole power lodged in the hands of the President. When such questions as these are involved shall we wonder that the pulse of the popular heart of this nation beats and heaves with terrible anxiety as we near the final judgment on this great trial, in which the life of the nation hangs trembling in the scale, as much so as when it was struggling for existence in the perilous hours of the war through which it has recently passed. Am I, as a Senator and one of this high court of impeachment, called upon to register, not that the Constitution and the laws shall be the supreme law, but that the will of one man shall be the law of the land?

Let us look at another point in the defense. The President says he violated the law in removing Stanton for the purpose of making a case before the Supreme Court, and thus procuring a decision upon the constitutionality of the law. That is, he broke the law in order to bring the judiciary to his aid in resisting the will of the people. I would here commend to his careful attention the opinion of Attorney General Black, his whilom constitutional adviser. He says, in 1860:

"But his [the President's] power is to be used only in the manner prescribed by the legislative department. He cannot accomplish a legal purpose by illegal means, or break the laws himself to prevent them from being violated by others."—9 *Opinions Attorneys General*, 516.

It is to be regretted that considerations of great gravity prevented the President from appearing here by counsel thus committed to a view of the extent of executive authority at once so just and so acceptable to the candid patriot.

Inasmuch as it has already been shown that good intentions do not justify the violation of known law, I am unable to see the propriety of stopping the wheels of Government and holding in abeyance the rights of many individuals, and paralyzing the usefulness of our Army, until the President sees fit to proceed through all the formalities and tedious delays of the Supreme Court, or any other court. If the President can do this, why may not any and all parties refuse compliance with the requirements of inconvenient laws upon the same plea? To oppose such a view with argument is to dignify an absurdity.

One other point of the defense I wish to notice before closing. It is argued at length that an offense charged before a court of impeachment must be an indictable one, or else the respondent must have a verdict of acquittal. Then why provide for impeachment at all? Why did not the Constitution leave the whole matter to a grand jury and the criminal courts? Nothing can be added to the arguments and citations of precedents by the honorable Managers on this point, and those most learned in the law cannot strengthen that view which is obvious to the most cursory student of the Constitution, namely, that impeachment is a form of trial provided for cases which may *lack* as well as those which do contain the features of indictable crimes. Corresponding to the equity side of a civil court, it provides for the trial and punishment not only of indictable offenses, but of those not technically described in rules of criminal procedure. The absurdity of the respondent's plea is the more manifest in this case, because, not the Supreme Court, but the Senate of the United States is the only tribunal to try impeachments, and the President's vision should rather have been directed to what the Senate, sitting as a court of impeachment, would decide, than to have been anticipating

what some future decision of a court having no jurisdiction in the case might be.

Impeachable misdemeanors partake of the nature of both political and criminal offenses. Hence the Constitution has wisely conferred upon the people, through their Representatives in Congress, the right and duty to become the prosecutors of great offenders for violations of laws and crimes tending to the destruction of social order and the overthrow of government, and has devolved the trial of such cases upon the Senate, composed of men supposed to be competent judges of law and facts, and who are allowed larger latitude of rulings than pertains to courts. With this view I have tried to weigh impartially the testimony in this case. I would not wrong the respondent, nor do I wish harm to come to the institutions of this land by his usurpations. I also desire to be consistent with myself so far as I may justly do so. I voted, not in haste, but deliberately, that the action of the President in removing or attempting to remove Stanton was unconstitutional and in violation of law.

Is it possible that there is some newly-discovered "*quirk*" in the law, not understood on the 24th of February last, which renders Johnson's act less criminal than it then appeared? Did not Senators believe the act of March 2, 1867, constitutional when they voted for it? After the President had arrayed all conceivable objections against it in his veto, did not two thirds of this and of the other House still vote it constitutional and a valid law? Did they not by solemn resolution declare that the President had violated it and the Constitution in removing Stanton and appointing Thomas? How can we say, while under oath we try this man, that he is innocent? Is it not trifling with the country, a mockery of justice, an insult to the representatives of the people, and a melancholy instance of self-stultification, for us to solemnly declare the President a violator of law, thus inviting and making it the duty of the House of Representatives to prosecute him here, and, after long investigation, at large expense of the people's money, with both confession of the criminal and large and conclusive proofs of the crime—all this and more—for us to declare him not guilty?

The position in which Senators are placed by the votes which they have heretofore given is so well stated in an editorial of a leading newspaper of my own State, the Chicago Tribune of May 7, 1868, that I extract from it as follows:

"Johnson disregarded the Constitution and the law, and broke them both by appointing a Secretary of War without the consent of the Senate when no vacancy existed." * * * * * *

"No man can tell how black-letter lawyers may be influenced by hair-splitting niceties, legal quirks, and musty precedents." * * * * * *

"Now, to acquit Andrew Johnson is to impeach the Senate, to insult and degrade the House, and to betray the people. If Johnson is not guilty of violating the law and the Constitution, the Senate is guilty of sustaining Stanton in defiance of the Constitution; is guilty of helping to pass an unconstitutional law; is guilty of interfering with the executive prerogatives. Every Senator who voted for the tenure-of-office bill, who voted that Johnson's removal of Stanton was in violation of that law, who voted to order the President to replace Stanton, and who now votes for the acquittal of Johnson, stultifies and condemns himself as to his previous acts, and the whole country will so understand it.

"The Senate knew all the facts before the House impeached; the Senate's action made impeachment obligatory on the part of the House, and on the heads of the Senators rests the responsibility of defeating a verdict of guilty against a criminal who stands self-confessed as guilty of breaking the law and disregarding the Constitution. No matter what personal antipathy Senators may feel for the man who will become Johnson's successor, no matter about the plots and schemes of the high-tariff lobby, the Senate has a solemn duty to perform, and that is to punish a willful and malicious violation of the law. If the President, in disregard of his oath, may trample on the law, who is bound to obey it? If the President is not amenable to the law, he is an emperor, a despot; then what becomes of our boasted government by law, of our lauded free institutions?"

My colleague is certainly in error when he says:

"It is known, however, that the resolution coupled the two things, the removal of the Secretary of War and the designation of an officer *ad interim*, together, so that those who believed either without authority were compelled to vote for the resolution."

Just the reverse of that is the true doctrine. If a Senator believed one branch of the proposition to be true and the others false, he was bound by his oath to vote *against* the resolution.

Where two allegations are made, one of which is true and the other false, there is no obligation to affirm both.

Mr. President, I ought, in justice to those who may vote for acquittal, to say that I do not judge them. Nor do I think it a crime to vote in a minority of one against the world. When I have taken an oath to decide a case according to the law and the testimony I would patiently listen to my constituents, and be willing, perhaps anxious, to be convinced by them; yet no popular clamor, no fear of punishment or hope of reward, should seduce me from deciding according to the conviction of my conscience and my judgment; therefore, I judge no one. Our wisest and most trusted men have been often in a minority. I speak for myself, however, when I say it is very hard for me to see, after what seems to me such plain proof of willful and wicked violation of law, how any Senator can go back upon himself and his record, and upon the House of Representatives and the country, and set loose the greatest offender of modern times, to repeat at pleasure his acts of usurpation, and to plead the license and warrant of this great tribunal for his high crimes and misdemeanors.

In the eleventh article, among other things, it is charged that the President did attempt to prevent the execution of the act of March 2, 1867, providing for the more efficient government of the rebel States. It is plain to me from his veto messages, his proclamations, his appointment of rebels to office, his indiscriminate use of the pardoning power, his removal of our most faithful military officers from their posts, that he has been the great obstacle to the reconstruction of the Union.

With his support of Congress in its measures every State would long since have resumed its friendly and harmonious relations to the Government, and our forty millions of people would have rejoiced again in a restored and happy Union. It is his perverse resistance to almost every measure devised by Congress which retarded the work of reconstruction, reanimated the hopes and reinflamed the virus of rebellion in the southern States. The Freedmen's Bureau bill, the civil rights bill, and the various reconstruction bills were remorselessly vetoed by him, and every obstacle thrown in the way of their proper and efficient execution. His unvarying purpose seems to have been to save the rebel oligarchy from the consequences which our victory pronounced upon it, and to enable it to accomplish by his policy and abuse of his power what could not be accomplished by the power of the sword. The rebellion lives in his vetoes and acts.

If some daring usurper, backed by a powerful faction, and the Army and Navy subject to his call, should proclaim himself king or dictator, would not the blood leap in the heart of every true American? And yet how little less than this is the condition of our public affairs, and who has not seen on the part of Andrew Johnson a deliberate purpose to override the sovereign power of the nation and to usurp dangerous, dictatorial, and kingly powers? And what true patriot has not felt that in such conflicts of power there is eminent peril to the life of the Republic, and that if some check, by impeachment or otherwise, be not put upon these presidential usurpations the fruits of the war will be lost, the rebellion triumph, and the last hope of a permanent reunion of the States be extinguished for ever?

For reasons such as these—and for proof of which there is much of evidence in the documents and records of this trial—but more especially for the violation of the Constitution and of positive laws, I cannot consent that with my vote the President shall longer work his treacherous and despotic will unchecked upon my suffering countrymen.

Mr. President, this is a tremendous hour for the Republic. Gigantic interests and destinies concentrate in the work and duties of the eventful moments through which we are passing.

I would do justice, and justice requires conviction; justice to the people whom he has so cruelly wronged. I would be merciful, merciful to the millions whose rights he treacherously assails by his contempt for law. I would have peace; therefore I vote to remove from office this most pestilent disturber of public peace. I would have prosperity among the people and confidence restored to capital; therefore I vote to punish him whose turbulence makes capital timid and paralyzes our national industries. I would have economy in the administration of public affairs; therefore I vote to depose the promoter and cause of unheard of official extravagance. I would have honesty in the collection of the public revenues; therefore I vote to remove this patron of the corruptionists. I would have my Government respected abroad; therefore I vote to punish him who subjects us to dishonor by treating law with contempt. I would inspire respect for law in the youth of the land; I therefore vote to impose its penalties upon the most exalted criminal. I would secure and perpetuate liberty, and I therefore vote to purge the citadel of liberty of him who, through murder, succeeded to the chief command and seeks to betray us to the enemy.

I fervently pray that this nation may avoid a repetition of that history, in which apostates and usurpers have desolated nations and enslaved mankind. Let our announcement this day to the President, and all future Presidents, and all conspirators against the liberties of this country, be what is already the edict of the loyal millions of this land, "You shall not tear this temple of liberty down." Let our warning go down the ages that every usurper and bold violater of law who thrusts himself in the path of this Republic to honor and renown, whoever he may be, however high his title or proud his name, that, Arnold-like, he shall be gibbeted on every hilltop throughout the land as a monument of his crime and punishment, and of the shame and grief of his country.

We are not alone in trying this cause. Out on the Pacific shore a deep murmur is heard from thousands of patriot voices; it swells over the western plain, peopled by millions more; with every increasing volume it advances on by the lakes and through the busy marts of the great North, and reëchoed by other millions on the Atlantic strand, it thunders upon us a mighty nation's verdict, *guilty*. While from out the smoke and gloom of the desolated South, from the rice-fields and along the great rivers, from hundreds of thousands of persecuted and basely-betrayed Unionists, comes also the solemn judgment, *guilty*.

The criminal cited before this bar by the people's Representatives is, by his answer and the record, *guilty*.

Appealing for the correctness of my verdict to the Searcher of all hearts and to the enlightened judgment of all who love justice, and in accord with this "cloud of witnesses," I vote guilty.

Standing here in my place in this mighty temple of the nation, and as a Senator of the great Republic, with all history of men and nations behind me and all progress and human happiness before me, I falter not on this occasion in duty to my country and to my State.

In this tremendous hour of the Republic, trembling for life and being, it is no time for me to shrink from duty, after having so long earnestly supported those principles of government and public policy which, like divine ordinances, protect and guide the race of man up the pathway of history and progress. As a juror, sitting on this great cause of my country, I wish it to go to history and to stand upon the imperishable records of the Republic, that in the fear of God, but fearless of man, I voted for the conviction of Andrew Johnson, President of the United States, for the commission of high crimes and misdemeanors.

OPINION
OF
HON. THOMAS W. TIPTON.

When the act regulating the tenure of civil offices passed Congress on the 2d day of March, 1867, Edwin M. Stanton was Secretary of War, having been appointed to said office by Mr. Lincoln and confirmed by the Senate January 15, 1862, and commissioned to hold the office "during the pleasure of the President of the United States for the time being." The first section of the act is as follows:

"That every person holding any civil office to which he has been appointed, by and with the advice and consent of the Senate, and every person who shall hereafter be appointed to any such office, and shall become duly qualified to act therein, is and shall be entitled to hold such office until a successor shall have been in like manner appointed and duly qualified, except as herein otherwise provided: *Provided*, That the Secretaries of State, of the Treasury, of War, of the Navy, and of the Interior, the Postmaster General, and the Attorney General, shall hold their offices respectively for and during the term of the President by whom they may have been appointed, and one month thereafter, subject to removal by and with the advice and consent of the Senate."

Before the passage of the above recited section the only limit to a Secretary's term was the *pleasure* of the President; but it was determined to make the termination definite, and hence we have a time specified beyond which it could not extend, namely, *one month* after the expiration of the term of the President by whom appointed.

The question relative to the Secretary of the Interior to be settled, would be: How long will his commission run? while the answer would be, just one month after the termination of the term of Mr. Johnson, by whom he was, by the advice and consent of the Senate, appointed. So his term would expire on the 4th day of April, 1869, which would be the end of one month after the expiration of Mr. Johnson's term, in case he filled the full unexpired term of Mr. Lincoln. He being in office on the 2d of March, 1867, under a commission which was a precise copy of Mr. Stanton's, I would look *forward*, not *backward*, to find the period of time when the law would put an end to his term of office, unless sooner removed by and with the advice and consent of the Senate.

To find the limit of Mr. Stanton's term I would look *forward* also, and as he is serving with the Secretary of the Interior, upon the *same term*, and under the same identical commission, I would declare him liable to removal by force of law, just as soon as one month shall have passed after the expiration of the term, which is being served out alike by himself and the Secretary of the Interior.

To the objection that the Secretary of the Interior was appointed by Mr. Johnson, and is serving out his term, while Mr. Stanton was appointed by Mr. Lincoln, whose term had expired nearly two years before the date of the act limiting terms, I reply that the terms of these Secretaries are one and the same, and there is no period of time subsequent to the date of the act at which one Secretary shall retire in advance of another.

In regard to Mr. Stanton's term having expired according to the limitations of this law, one month after the death of Mr. Lincoln, I deny the proposition: first, because the law was not in existence until about two years subsequent to that event. Second, because it could not, on the 2d day of March, 1867, act back and produce a vacancy in an office already filled, every act of which has been regarded valid by every branch of the Government. Third, because Mr. Stanton has been in office ever since the date of the law, and is still performing the functions of Secretary of War. As Mr. Johnson received from Mr. Lincoln the War Office with its Secretary, just as he received each one of the other Departments of Government with its Secretary, each and all of them with subsequent appointments must be regarded as of his own appointment, for all purposes of the civil-tenure act; and as it is impossible to remove a portion in the past and the balance in the future, they must all share the same fate and be subject to the same limitations.

Hereafter there will be no trouble in construing the law, for one month subsequent to the termination of a President's term will vacate every Secretaryship; and if this act had been in force at the time of Mr. Lincoln's death Mr. Johnson would have had all the heads of Departments at his disposal one month thereafter. To claim, therefore, that Mr. Johnson can remove Mr. Stanton without the advice and consent of the Senate is to affirm an impossibility, inasmuch as the only period of time at which a President can get clear of a Secretary independent of the Senate is at the end of a month subsequent to the end of a President's term. And unless Mr. Johnson will receive a reëlection he shall never reach that official hour in which Mr. Stanton would vacate, by force of law, one month subsequent to the expiration of Mr. Johnson's term. But if he should ever reach a second inauguration, and the month had expired, and Mr. Stanton was inclined to remain, he could demand his removal independent of the Senate, on the grounds that having received him when he received Mr. Lincoln's term, and having adopted him as the legal head of the War Department, and all Departments of the Government having indorsed the legality of his acts to the last hour of his previous term, the Secretary must be regarded in the light of one of his original appointments and retire accordingly.

By every reasonable rule of construction it seems perfectly plain that Mr. Stanton has not been removed by force of the civil-tenure act, and consequently is entitled to its protection, which was accorded to him by the Senate when they restored him from suspension by their vote of January 13, 1868. Having attempted to accomplish that, independent of the Senate, which he failed to secure when admitting the constitutionality of the act by yielding to its provision for suspensions, the President has certainly been guilty, as charged in the first article, of a "high misdemeanor in office."

The plea which he makes in his answer, that he does not believe the act of March 2, 1867, constitutional, cannot avail him, since, when Congress passed the act and laid it before him for his signature, he having vetoed it, it was then passed over the veto by three fourths of each branch of Congress—the provision of the Constitution being that a bill passed by two thirds of each House over the President's veto "shall become a law." Having thus become a law, he had no discretion but to enforce it as such; and by disregarding it merited all the penalties thus incurred.

He is not to be shielded behind the opinions of his Cabinet, although they may have advised him to disregard the law, since their only business is to enforce and obey the laws governing their several Departments, and neither to claim or exercise judicial functions.

The plea of innocent intentions is certainly not to vindicate him for having violated a law, for every criminal would be able to plead justifiable motives in extenuation of punishment, till every law was broken and every barrier of safety swept aside.

The strongest possible case that can be stated would be that of a Senator who might have declared his belief of the unconstitutionality of the act of March 2, 1867, before its passage over the veto, and now being called upon to decide upon the right of the President to disregard the provisions of this same act. I hold that he would be bound by his oath of office to demand of the President obedience to its provisions until such time as it should be repealed by Congress or annulled by the decision of a court of competent jurisdiction. The President must take care that the laws are faithfully executed.

It is very astonishing that the President should deny that Mr. Stanton is protected in office by the civil-tenure act, after having suspended him from office under that act on the 12th of August, 1867, and having reported him to the Senate under the same act as being legally suspended, and having, under a special provision of the same act, notified the Secretary of the Treasury of his action in the premises; for unless he was legally Secretary of War he was not subject to such suspension.

It has been argued that as Mr. Stanton has continued to occupy the War Office, and the removal has not been entirely completed, the penalty for removal cannot attach; but Mr. Johnson receives General Thomas as Secretary of War at his Cabinet meetings, thus affirming his belief that Thomas is entitled to be accredited as such. It should be remembered, in this connection, that it is a high misdemeanor to attempt to do an act which is a misdemeanor. The removal of Mr. Stanton against law would be a high misdemeanor, and a persistent effort in that direction, issuing orders, withdrawing association from him, and accrediting another, does, in my opinion, constitute a high misdemeanor.

By article two he stands charged, during the session of the Senate, with having issued a letter of authority to Lorenzo Thomas, authorizing him and commanding him to assume and exercise the functions of Secretary of the Department of War, without the advice and consent of the Senate, which is charged to have been in violation of the express letter of the Constitution and of the act of March 2, 1867.

Of his power to appoint the Constitution, article two, section two, says:

" He shall nominate, and by and with the advice and consent of the Senate shall appoint."

In this case he claimed a vacancy to which he might appoint *independent of the Senate*, while the Constitution affirms that the President shall have power to fill up all vacancies that may happen during *"the recess of* the Senate," not during *the session of* the Senate.

It is only necessary to quote the charge, the text of the Constitution, and his own admission in his answer, that he "did issue and deliver the writing as set forth in said second article, in order to establish the commission of an unconstitutional act." But the language of the act of March 2, 1867, is equally explicit. It affirms in section six—

"That every removal, appointment, or employment made, had or exercised contrary to the provisions of this act, and the making, signing, sealing, countersigning, or issuing of any commission or letter of authority for or in respect to any such appointment or employment, shall be deemed, and are hereby declared to be, *misdemeanors;* and upon trial and conviction thereof every person guilty thereof shall be punished by a fine not exceeding $10,000, or by imprisonment not exceeding five years, or both said punishments, in the discretion of the court."

If Mr. Stanton was protected by the first clause of section one, the issuing of the letter to Thomas drew upon the author the penalty; but if he was covered by the proviso, the vacancy had not happened and the consequence was the same. And if the President, during session of the Senate, can remove one officer and appoint *ad interim,* so he may remove any or all, and thus usurp Departments and offices, while the people seek in vain for the restrain-

ing and supervising power of a prostrate and insulted tribunal.

The first article, affirming the illegal removal of Secretary Stanton; the second, charging the illegal issue of the letter of authority to Thomas, and the third, affirming the *ad interim* appointment of General Thomas, admitted as facts and established by evidence, are the foundations of the whole impeachment superstructure.

The fourth, relative to an unlawful conspiracy with respect to intimidating the Secretary of War; the fifth, affirming a combination to prevent the execution of a law; the sixth, charging a conspiracy to seize and possess the property of the War Department in violation of an act of 1861; the seventh, charging a like intent in violation of an act of 1867; and the eighth, charging the appointment of Thomas with intent to control the disbursements of the War Department, are all more or less incidental acts, springing from or tending to the same criminal foundation charges, and may or may not be considered established without affecting the original articles. If, however, the first three are not sustained, these will not be likely to receive more than a passing notice.

The ninth article charges the President with having instructed General Emory that part of a law of the United States, which provides that "all orders and instructions relative to military operations issued by the President or Secretary of War shall be issued through the General of the Army, and, in case of his inability, through the next in rank," was unconstitutional and in contravention of said commission of said Emory, in order to induce him to violate the laws and military orders.

It appears that while General Emory was acting under a commission requiring him to observe and follow such orders and directions as he should receive from the President and other officers set over him by law, an order reached him embodying a section of law, which law had been previously approved by the President himself, but, as it provided that orders from the President and Secretary of War should be issued through the General of the Army, or next in rank, and the President being engaged to remove the Secretary of War and thwart the action of the Senate, in a discussion with General Emory, as to his duty as an officer, said, "This (meaning the order) is not in conformity with the Constitution of the United States, which makes me Commander-in-Chief, or with the terms of your commission." While General Emory was inclined to obey the order the President could not command him but through General Grant's headquarters, and thus would have to make public his military orders; but, if General Emory could be made to believe the order was in conflict with his commission and the Constitution, and could be induced to disregard it, then the President could secretly issue orders to him and accomplish his designs. He could only have desired to cause General Emory to see his duty in such light as to disregard this legal order, and, if Emory had yielded to his construction of law and Constitution, he could have sheltered himself under his commission and trampled the law under foot.

This effort to tamper with an officer who was obeying the law of his Government is characterized very mildly by the charge of reprehensible. It should be make a crime of serious magnitude for a President to command a military officer to violate a law which was promulgated in orders, in accordance with all the forms of national legislation. In this case the experiment upon the officer's fidelity and firmness seems to have gone no further than to discover that General Emory could not be tampered with, and then the effort was dropped on the very verge of criminality.

The tenth article charges the President with having, at Washington city, Cleveland, Ohio, and St. Louis, Missouri, indulged in language tending to bring into disgrace and ridicule, contempt and reproach, the Congress of the United States, which utterances were "highly censurable in any, and peculiarly indecent and unbecoming in a Chief Magistrate."

Under ordinary circumstances I would allow the utmost latitude of speech, and would never attempt to apply a corrective only where the crime became magnified by virtue of the peculiar surroundings. If the President had gone upon the stump with inflammatory language in order to assist in leading or driving States out of the Union, then I would hold him responsible for the character of his act. And when the very life of the nation is imperiled by the absence of ten States, and all legal efforts are making to induce their early return, if I find him denying the legal and constitutional authority of Congress, and charging disunion, usurpation, and despotism upon the representatives of the loyal people, thus strengthening the evil passions of malcontents and rebels, on account of the tendency of his teachings, I should not hesitate to declare his conduct a high misdemeanor.

For the reasons just specified I would find him guilty of a misdemeanor on the evidence sustaining the first allegation of the eleventh article, which charges him with denying the authority of Congress to propose amendments to the Constitution. I would also hold him responsible for devising means by which to prevent Edwin M. Stanton from resuming the functions of Secretary of War on the Senate having voted his restoration from the President's suspension. And of his guilt relative to impeding the proper administration of the reconstruction laws of Congress, by discouraging and embarrassing officers of the law, and using such defiant language as had all the force of commands upon rebels, I have not the shadow of a doubt.

The only matter of astonishment is that an Executive so unscrupulous and so defiant of coördinate power has been allowed so long to defy the people's representatives and defeat the solemnly-expressed enactments of their will.

Believing that the stability of government depends upon the faithful enforcement of law, and the laws of a republic being a transcript of 'the people's will, and always repealable by their instructions or change of public servants, I would demand their enforcement by the President, independent of any opinion of his relative to necessity, propriety, or constitutionality.

OPINION
OF
HON. THOMAS A. HENDRICKS.

In the eleven articles of impeachment the President is charged, in the different forms of statement, with six acts of official misconduct, as follows:

1. The removal of Mr. Stanton from the office of Secretary of War.

2. The appointment of Lorenzo Thomas, the Adjutant General of the Army, to the office of Secretary of War *ad interim*.

3. The conspiracy with said Thomas to prevent the execution of the tenure-of-office act by hindering Mr. Stanton from holding the office of Secretary of War.

4. The instructions to General Emory that the second section of the act of March 2, 1867, requiring all military orders made by the President or Secretary of War to be issued through the General of the Army, was unconstitutional.

5. The President's speeches against Congress.

6. The denial of the authority of the Thirty Ninth Congress by the attempt on the part of the President to prevent the execution of the tenure-of-office act, the Army appropriation act, and the act to provide for the more efficient government of the rebel States.

The sixth charge is found in the eleventh article. The respondent in his answer has taken exception to the sufficiency of the statements contained in that article, upon the ground that the alleged acts of the President, which he did in his attempts to prevent the execution of the said laws, are not stated, but it is averred only that he did unlawfully devise and contrive and attempt to devise and contrive means to prevent their execution. The exception seems to be sufficiently supported by the well established and reasonable rule of pleading, that charges preferred against a party in any judicial proceeding shall be stated with such reasonable certainty that the accused may know the nature of the charge, its scope and limit, the character of evidence that may be brought against him, and the class of evidence that may be invoked in his defense. Until accusations are stated with such reasonable certainty courts do not require the accused to answer. The eleventh article should have stated what means were devised and contrived, or attempted to be devised and contrived, so that this court might decide whether they amount to a high misdemeanor; and if so, that the respondent may know the nature of the evidence that may be brought against him, and the character of evidence he may offer in his defense. This view in the pleading is not removed by the averment that the means were devised and contrived to prevent Mr. Stanton's return to the War Department after the decision of the Senate upon the reasons for his suspension. Reasonable certainty requires that the means devised and contrived should be stated. If the means were stated, the Senate might not agree with the House of Representatives that they were "unlawfully" devised, but might hold them lawful and proper. If the device and contrivance were the appointment of a successor, or proceedings in the courts to test a right claimed on the one side, and denied on the other, then the averment that it was "unlawful" would fall.

But beyond the question of pleading, the question arises whether the eleventh article defines any high misdemeanor, or even any act of official misconduct. As inducement, it is stated, that as far back as August, 1866, the President, in public speeches, did question the lawful authority of Congress; and it is then averred that as late as February, 1868, in pursuance of that declaration, he did "attempt to prevent the execution of" the said several acts, by "devising and contriving, and attempting to devise and contrive, means by which he should prevent" Mr. Stanton from resuming the functions of the office of Secretary of War, and to prevent the execution of the other acts. Passing over the question whether an attempt to prevent the execution of a statute without success is a misdemeanor, when the statute does not so declare, the question arises whether it can be a crime or misdemeanor in a single person, without combination or conspiracy with others, to devise and contrive means without executing the schemes? To devise or contrive is an intellectual process, and when not executed by acts done cannot be punished as a crime, however unworthy or vicious. Can we undertake the punishment of the thoughts, opinions, purposes, conceptions, designs, devices, and contrivances of men when not carried into acts? The eleventh article does not attempt the definition of a crime, unless, indeed, we hold the vicious thoughts and evil purposes of public officers to be such in the absence of any law so declaring.

In the presence of the provision of the Constitution of the United States which protects the right of free speech, and in the absence of any law, State or Federal, declaring its exercise in any manner or by any person to be a crime, it is not necessary to examine the tenth article, which rests its charge of a misdemeanor upon the President's speeches made to the people, in response to their calls, in his capacity as a citizen, and not in the exercise of his office.

In our country, as long as the Constitution stands, no legislative body can make it a crime to discuss the conduct of public officers with entire freedom, and the House of Representatives cannot, by any proceeding whatever, shield itself from individual criticism and popular review; and any effort to do so betrays conscious weakness, and disturbs public confidence.

The ninth article rests upon the conversation between the President and General Emory. In that part of the President's conduct no fault can be found, much less a violation of law. He had been informed by a member of his Cabinet that there were evidences of important changes of the military forces at and near this city. It was his right and, perhaps, his duty to become informed of the extent and purpose of any such movements. He sent for General Emory to make the necessary inquiries. In the course of the conversation General Emory called his attention to the order issued in pursuance of the section of the law requiring all military orders from the President to be issued through the General of the Army; and then the President expressed the opinion that it was unconstitutional thus to control him in the exercise of his constitutional powers as Commander-in-Chief of the Army. He went no further than the expression of that opinion; he gave no orders to General Emory, nor does it appear that at any time he has disregarded the said law. In any proceeding less grave than the present it would be regarded as frivolous to charge it as a crime that an opinion had been expressed upon the constitutionality of any law.

The fourth, fifth, sixth, and seventh articles charge a conspiracy between the President and General Lorenzo Thomas to prevent Mr. Stanton's holding the office of Secretary of War, and to obtain the custody and charge of the property of the United States in the War Department. It is not necessary to notice the averments, in two of these articles, of a purpose to resort to intimidation and threats, and to use force, inasmuch as the evidence wholly fails to show that the President at any time contemplated a resort to either; and it does appear that there was no resort to either. In the absence of intimidation, threats, and force in the purpose and conduct of the President and General Thomas no case is made within the conspiracy act of July 31, 1861. But it appears to me that it cannot be said that the President and General Thomas conspired together when the former issued to the latter the *ad interim* appointment, and the latter accepted it. It is plain that the President issued the orders under a claim of legal right, and that General Thomas received them because, as a subordinate officer, he thought it was his duty. Such conduct does not define a conspiracy.

It only remains for me to consider the conduct of the President in issuing the order for the removal of Mr. Stanton from the office of Secretary of War, and the *ad interim* appointment of General Thomas. The force and effect of the *ad interim* appointment must depend upon the validity of the order for the removal of Mr. Stanton. If the removal did not in law take place upon the issue of the order, then, as Mr. Stanton did not surrender the office, the appointment did not clothe General Thomas with any authority—it was a blank, without legal force or meaning. If Mr. Stanton's commission did not become revoked, the appointment of General Thomas was of no more force or consequence than a second deed by the same grantor.

Had the President the authority to remove Mr. Stanton? According to the provisions of the act of August 7, 1789, creating the War Department and the terms of his commission, Mr. Stanton held the office "during the pleasure of the President of the United States for the time being." That act expressly recognized the power of the President to remove the Secretary of War at any time. It did not confer the power, but recognized it as already possessed, the provision being that "whenever the said principal officer (the Secretary) shall be removed from office by the President of the United States, and in any other case of vacancy," the chief clerk of the Department shall for the time being have charge of the records, books, &c. Under that law, Mr. Stanton received his commission from President Lincoln, January 15, 1862, "to hold the said office, with all the powers, &c., during the pleasure of the President of the United States for the time being." Has that law been repealed or amended in that respect. The tenure-of-office act of March 2, 1867, has no repealing clause, and therefore repeals or modifies the act of 1789 only so far as the two acts cannot stand together. Mr. Stanton's term of office, as fixed by the law and his commission, was during the will of the President, and I think a proper construction of the first section of the tenure-of-office act leaves that unchanged. He was appointed during Mr. Lincoln's first term, which expired on the 4th of March, 1865, and therefore it is unnecessary to consider the question which has been discussed, whether Mr. Johnson is filling the office for Mr. Lincoln's unexpired term, or whether he has his own term of office; for it is quite certain that he is not in the term during which Mr. Stanton was appointed. The first and second terms of the presidential office for which Mr. Lincoln was elected were as distinct, under the Constitution, as if another had been elected in his stead for the second.

If the tenure of Mr. Stanton's office be changed by the tenure-of-office act, it is by the proviso to the first section, and clearly the proviso has no such effect. The proviso is that the Cabinet officers "shall hold their offices respectively for and during the term of the President by whom they may have been appointed, and for one month thereafter." Not having been appointed during the existing presidential term, Mr. Stanton has no new term bestowed upon him, but he still holds, in the language of his commission, "during the pleasure of the President." This obvious construction of the language is strengthened by a consideration of the history of the tenure-of-office bill. It first passed the Senate in such form as expressly to exclude all Cabinet officers. In the House it was so amended as to include them. The Senate disagreed to that amendment. A committee of conference was the result of this disagreement between the two Houses. In this condition of the measure it will be observed that the Senate insisted that Cabinet officers should not be included at all, and the House insisted that they should be included just as other officers are. The conference committee considered this question of disagreement and settled it upon the proposition, then supposed to be just, that each President shall have the selection of his own Cabinet officers, and shall not be required to continue the Secretaries of his predecessor. The Senate conceded that a President, having selected his own Cabinet, shall continue them during his term, and the House conceded that he shall not be required to continue the Cabinet of his predecessor, or any member thereof. Upon that adjustment the bill passed. This construction was then put upon the proviso in the Senate—for when the bill came back from the committee with the proviso, as the compromise between the two Houses, Mr. SHERMAN, of the committee, said:

"That this provision does not apply to the present case is shown by the fact that its language is so framed as not to apply to the present President. The Senator [Mr. DOOLITTLE] shows that himself, and argues truly that it would not prevent the present President from removing the Secretary of War, the Secretary of the Navy, and the Secretary of State."

This construction of the bill was then acquiesced in by the silence of the other members of the conference committee, and not disagreed to by any Senator; and thereupon the Senate agreed to its passage. And now, by adhering to that construction, we have just what the Senate then intended, what is plainly just and right—that the President shall select his own constitutional advisers—and what will promote the harmony and efficient action of the executive department, and we avoid a question of serious difficulty. If the act be so construed as to include Mr. Stanton's case, the constitutional question arises whether Congress can by law extend the term and change the tenure of an office after the appointment has been made with the consent of the Senate. Such construction would allow that after the appointing power under the Constitution had bestowed the office, the legislative department, having no power of appointment, might bestow an additional term upon the officer, and thus become an appointing power. It is gratifying that the language of the act, the history of its enactment, the legislative construction, the obvious intention of the Senate, and the highest interests of the public service all allow me to so construe the act as to avoid this grave question. Mr. Stanton's case not being within the tenure-of-office act, the power of the President to make the removal is beyond doubt; and the only question remaining is, did he have the power to make the appointment of General Thomas *ad interim?* There is great force in the opinion that has been expressed that the constitutional obligation upon the President to see that the laws be executed carries with it the power to use such agencies as may be clearly necessary in the absence of legislative provision. In that view it would appear that, in the case of a vacancy in an office and until it could be filled, in the case of sickness, absence from the post of duty, or other disability of an officer to discharge the duties, the President might designate some person to discharge them in the mean time, to the end that the laws might be executed and the public service suffer no harm. And this opinion seems to have been entertained by our most eminent and revered Presidents, for they made very many such *ad interim* appointments without the pretense of legislative authority. But in the case now before this court we need not consider this question, for, in my judgment, the authority of the President to make the *ad interim* appointment, as well during the session as the recess of the Senate, is clearly established by law.

Section eight of the act of May 8, 1792, provides as follows:

"That in case of the death, absence from the seat of Government, or sickness of the Secretary of State, of Secretary of the Treasury, or of the Secretary of the War Department, or of any officer of either of the said Departments whose appointment is not in the head thereof, whereby they cannot perform the duties of their said respective offices, it shall be lawful for the President of the United States, in case he shall think it necessary, to authorize any person or persons, at his discretion, to perform the duties of the said respective offices until a successor be appointed, or until such absence or inability by sickness shall cease."

It will be observed that this section authorized *ad interim* appointments only in three of the Departments, that is, in the Departments of State, Treasury, and War; and only in three cases, that is, the cases of death, absence from the seat of Government, and sickness of the head of the Department or other officer. It fails to provide for the temporary supply of the service of any vacancy occurring otherwise than by death. That omission was in part supplied by the act of February 13, 1795, but only as to the same three Departments. That act is as follows:

"*Be it enacted by the Senate and House of Representatives of the United States of America in Congress assembled,* That in case of vacancy in the office of Secretary of State, Secretary of the Treasury, or of the Secretary of the Department of War, or of any officer of either of the said Departments whose appointment is not in the head thereof, whereby they cannot perform the duties of their said respective offices, it shall be lawful for the President of the United States, in case he shall think it necessary, to authorize any person or persons, at his discretion, to perform the duties of the said respective offices until a successor be appointed or such vacancy be filled: *Provided,* That no one vacancy shall be supplied in manner aforesaid for a longer term than six months."

It will be observed that this act of 1795 provides a temporary supply of the service in all cases of vacancies, whether caused by death, resignation, removal from office, or expiration of the term, but makes no provision for the cases of temporary disability already provided for by the act of 1792, and therefore does not repeal that act. Both acts remained in force without further legislation on the subject until the passage of the act of February 20, 1863, which is as follows:

"That in case of death, resignation, absence from the seat of Government, or sickness of the head of any executive Department of the Government, or of any officer of either of the said Departments whose appointment is not in the head thereof, whereby they cannot perform the duties of their respective offices, it shall be lawful for the President of the United States, in case he shall think it necessary, to authorize the head of any other executive Department, or other officer in either of said Departments, whose appointment is vested in the President, at his discretion, to perform the duties of the said respective offices until a successor be appointed, or until such absence or inability by sickness shall cease: *Provided,* That no one vacancy shall be supplied in manner aforesaid for a longer term than six months."

The legislative purpose in the enactment of this law was not to repeal the act of February 13, 1795, but to extend the provisions of the act of May 8, 1792, to the other Departments. During the previous month President Lincoln had called the attention of Congress to the subject in the following message:

WASHINGTON, *January* 2, 1863.
To the Senate and House of Representatives:
I submit to Congress the expediency of extending to other Departments of the Government the authority conferred on the President by the eighth section of the act of the 8th of May, 1792, to appoint a person to temporarily discharge the duties of Secretary of State, Secretary of the Treasury, and Secretary of War, in case of the death, absence from the seat of Government, or sickness of either of those officers.
ABRAHAM LINCOLN.

It was in response to that message that the act of 1863 was passed, and it does not appear that the attention of Congress was at all called to the act of 1795. Neither its history nor the provisions of the act of 1863 justify us in believing that it was the intention of Congress thereby to repeal the act of 1795. The acts are not inconsistent; both can stand; both must remain, for the act of 1795 provides for two cases of vacancy—by removal and by expiration of the term—not provided for in the act of 1863. It is not questioned that the act of 1795, if unrepealed, confers upon the President the power to provide temporarily for the service in the case of a removal, and, therefore, I need not further consider this part of the case, except to add that the tenure-of-office act does not, in terms or by implication, repeal either the act of 1795 or the act of 1863. It has no repealing clause, and there is no such inconsistency in the provisions of the acts as to cause a repeal by implication. There is the same necessity for a supply of the temporary service by *ad interim* appointments, in cases of vacancy, sickness, absence, or other disability, as before the passage of the tenure-of-office act, and Congress cannot be understood to have intended to leave such cases unprovided for.

Whoever proposes to convict the President as of a crime for the *ad interim* appointment of General Thomas should stop to consider the many cases in which his illustrious predecessors exercised the same power during the session of the Senate, as well as during the recess, under the Constitution, and without the pretense of legislative authority. In this opinion but a few of the many cases proven can be cited. It will be borne in mind that the acts of 1792 and 1795, authorizing temporary appointments, did not include the Navy, Interior, and Post Office Departments, and that until 1863 no law extended the authority over them, and therefore appointments made by the President in those Departments to supply the temporary service were made under the constitutional duty and authority to see that the laws be executed and not under any statute.

On the 9th July, 1836, President Jackson appointed John Boyle, the chief clerk of the Navy Department, to discharge the duties of Secretary during the absence of the Secretary. The Senate had then adjourned five days.

On the 6th October, 1838, President Van Buren made the same appointment.

On the 19th March, 1841, President Harrison appointed John D. Simmes to be acting Secretary of the Navy during the absence of the Secretary.

On the 13th May, 1851, President Fillmore appointed C. M. Conrad, the Secretary of War, to be "acting Secretary of the Navy *ad interim*" during the absence of the Secretary; and on the 3d August, 1851, the same President appointed W. A. Graham, the Secretary of the Navy, to be acting Secretary of the Interior.

And on 22d September, 1862, President Lincoln appointed John B. L. Skinner, then the acting First Assistant Postmaster General, to be acting Postmaster General *ad interim*, the Postmaster General being absent.

On the 29th of June, 1860, four days after the adjournment of the Senate, the postmaster of New Orleans was removed and the office placed in the hands of a special agent by President Buchanan, Joseph Holt being Postmaster General.

On the 10th day of May, 1860, the Senate then being in session, President Buchanan removed Isaac V. Fowler, the postmaster at New York, and placed the office in the hands of a special messenger.

On the 21st of January, 1861, the Senate being in session, he took the Milwaukee post office out of the hands of the postmaster, and placed it in the charge of a special agent. Hon. Joseph Holt was then Postmaster General.

On the 20th of June, 1864, the Senate being in session, President Lincoln removed Isaac Henderson from the office of navy agent at New York, and instructed a paymaster of the Navy to take charge of the office.

On the 26th of December, 1864, the Senate being in session, President Lincoln removed James S. Chambers from the office of navy agent at Philadelphia, and placed Paymaster Watson in charge. These two offices were highly important, both in view of the duties to be discharged and the emoluments received by the incumbents.

On the 19th of December, 1840, Thomas Eastin, the navy agent at Pensacola, was, by order of President Van Buren, "dismissed from the service of the United States," and Purser Dudley Walker appointed to take charge of the office. The Senate was then in session.

These are but a few of the hundreds of cases that might be cited to show that the practice of making *ad interim* appointments has been uniform, whether authorized by statute or not.

I cannot concur in the opinion that has been expressed, that if a technical violation of law has been established the Senate has no discretion, but must convict. I think the Senate may judge whether in the case a high crime or misdemeanor has been established, and whether in the name of the people the prosecution ought to be made and sustained. Van Buren was not impeached for the removal of the Pensacola navy agent and the designation of Purser Walker to take charge of the office. President Jackson was not impeached for the *ad interim* appointment of Boyle as Secretary of the Navy under a claim of constitutional authority, without any statute allowing it. Presidents Harrison and Fillmore were not impeached for making *ad interim* appointments of Secretary of the Navy, with no statute authorizing it. President Buchanan was not impeached for removing the postmaster at New Orleans and filling the place *ad interim*, not for removing Fowler, the postmaster at New York, during the session of the Senate, and supplying the place *ad interim*, with no statutory authority; nor was he impeached for authorizing Joseph Holt to discharge the duties of Secretary of War *ad interim* upon the resignation of John B. Floyd, though the Senate called upon him for his authority, and in his reply he cited one hundred and seventy-nine precedents, not going back of Jackson's administration. Mr. Lincoln was not impeached for the appointment of General Skinner Postmaster General *ad interim*, without any statute authorizing it, nor for the removal of Isaac Henderson, navy agent at New York, during the session of the Senate, and the *ad interim* appointment of Paymaster Gibson to the office; nor for the removal of Chambers, the navy agent at Philadelphia, during the session of the Senate, and the appointment of Paymaster Watson *ad interim* to the office, there then being no statute authorizing it. He was not impeached for continuing Major General Frank P. Blair in command long after the Senate had declared by resolution that in such case the office could not be held "without a new appointment in the manner prescribed by the Constitution;" nor for appointing at one time any more generals in the Army than the laws allowed.

Supported by a long line of precedents, coming through our whole history, unchallenged and unrebuked by Congress, President Johnson stands before us upon these charges; and I ask my brother Senators what answer we will make to the people when they ask us why we selected him for a sacrifice for doing just what was always recognized as right in his predecessors? Upon my oath I cannot strike such a blow.

The judgment of the First Congress was that the President has the right under the Constitution to remove the Secretaries, and that judgment is supported by the uniform practice of the Government from that day till the meeting of the Thirty-Ninth Congress. The evidence shows that Mr. Johnson was advised by every member of his Cabinet, including Mr. Stanton, that he had that right under the Constitution, and that Congress could not take it from him nor impair it, and therefore it was his duty to veto the tenure-of-office bill; and that the bill did not include the appointments made by Mr. Lincoln; and that, notwithstanding the passage of the bill, he would have the right to remove the Secretaries of War, of State, and of the Navy. This advice was given by the members of the Cabinet under the obligations of the Constitution and of their oaths; and now, if we say that he, being so informed and advised, was guilty of a crime in demanding the right to select his own constitutional advisers, as it has been conceded to all the Presidents, and for that drive him from his office and give it to a member of this body, it does seem to me that we will do an act of such flagrant injustice and cruelty as to bring upon our heads the indignant condemnation of all just men, and this impeachment will stand itself impeached before the civilized world.

OPINION
OF
HON. TIMOTHY O. HOWE.

One of the questions involved in the consideration of this cause is, whether the President is or is not intrusted by the Constitution with the power to remove the heads of the Executive Departments. Those who now assert he has such power, instead of attempting to prove it from the text of the Constitution, generally prefer to rely upon the debate which took place in the House of Representatives of 1789, and the act of July 27 of that year, "for establishing an executive Department to be denominated the Department of Foreign Af-

fairs." Now, I insist that what powers are or are not in the Constitution cannot be proved by reference to the annals of debates or to the Statutes-at-Large. The Constitution speaks for itself. What its framers intended must be gathered from the clauses to which they agreed, and not from clauses agreed to by any Congress whatever.

But if the debate and the statutes were both evidence upon the point they would not prove the power in question to be in the Constitution. That debate commenced on the 19th of May, 1789, upon the proposition to make the Secretary for Foreign Affairs "removable at the pleasure of the President." It was objected that, by the terms of the Constitution, an officer could only be removed by impeachment before the Senate. On the contrary, Mr. Madison said "he believed they would not assert that any part of the Constitution declared that the only way to remove should be by impeachment. The contrary might be inferred, because Congress may establish offices by law; *therefore most certainly it is in the discretion of the Legislature to say upon what terms the office shall be held, either during good behavior or during pleasure.*" During that debate no less than twenty-five speeches were made. Throughout the debate the issue was, Can Congress authorize the President to remove from office, or is impeachment the only method of removal allowed by the Constitution?

Nearly a month later, on the 16th of June following, the debate was renewed upon a bill to establish a Department of Foreign Affairs. The first section provided that the Secretary should "be removable at the pleasure of the President." Mr. White, of Virginia, moved to strike out these words. Upon that motion a long debate ensued, running through several days. In the course of it Mr. Madison assumed a new ground of defense. In the former debate he had asserted that Congress could fix the tenure of the office as it pleased; that that power was a necessary incident of the power to create the office. In this debate he started the idea, for the first time, that the President could control the tenure as an incident of executive power.

The idea was broached cautiously and with evident hesitation. He acknowledged it was an afterthought. And he introduced it in these words:

"I have, since the subject was last before the House, examined the Constitution with attention, and I acknowledge that it does not perfectly correspond with the idea I entertained of it from the first glance. I am inclined to think that a free and systematic interpretation of the plan of Government will leave us less at liberty to abate the responsibility than gentlemen imagine." * * * * * "By a strict examination of the Constitution on what appears to be its true principles, and considering the great Departments of the Government in the relation they have to each other, I have my doubts whether we are not absolutely tied down to the construction declared in the bill."

Of those who affirmed and those who denied the power of removal to be in the President, during the debate, the numbers were about equal. Upon taking the vote on the motion to strike out, the noes were 34, while the ayes were but 20.

But it is evident from the nature of the question that the majority numbered all those who believed the Constitution conferred the power of removal on the President, and all those, also, who thought Congress could and ought to confer it on him.

Mr. Sedgwick, of Massachusetts, called attention to this fact at the time. He said:

"If I understand the subject rightly there seem to be two opinions dividing the majority of this House. Some of these gentlemen seem to suppose that, by the Constitution, and by implication and certain deductions from the *principles* of the Constitution, the power rests in the President. Others think that it is a matter of legislative determination, and that they must give it to the President on the principles of the Constitution."

The minority do not seem to have been satisfied with the victory achieved by that combination of forces. Accordingly, on the 22d of June, Mr. Benson, of New York, who was of the majority, proposed once more to strike out those words in the first section which were equivalent to an express grant of the power of removal and in lieu thereof to insert in the second section, which provided for a chief clerk, who in case of "vacancy" should have custody of the books, papers, &c., the words "whenever the said principal officer shall be removed from office by the President of the United States, or in any other case of vacancy," shall, during such vacancy, have custody, &c. He explained that "he hoped his amendment would succeed in reconciling both sides of the House to the decision and quieting the minds of gentlemen."

He seems to have persuaded himself that as the law in that form would not assert either that the President *could* remove under the Constitution or that he *might* remove under the act, but only mildly suggested "removed by the President" as an event possible to happen without specifying whether it was likely to happen from an exercise of constitutional or statutory authority, no one would have any particular objection to it. This expectation does not seem to have been realized. The amendment to the second section was carried by even a less majority than was obtained against amending the first section. The vote was 30 ayes to 18 noes.

Then the question was renewed to strike out from the first section the words "to be removable," &c., and it was carried by 31 ayes to 19 noes. Thus amended, the bill went to the Senate and passed that body by the casting vote of the Vice President.

Such is in brief the character of the debate of 1789, and such the conclusion in which it issued. It has frequently been cited as a legislative interpretation of the Constitution, as a legislative decision, that the Constitution vested in the President the power of removal. But it ought not to be so regarded, for it is impos-

sible to ascertain from the records how many supported the bill, because they regarded it as a declaration that the President had the power to remove; or how many supported it as a declaration that he ought to have it; or how many supported it for the sake of according with the majority, and because it declared neither one thing nor the other.

The idea that the President had the power of removal under the Constitution was not advanced for nearly a month after the debate commenced, and there is not the slightest reason for believing that the bill received a single vote for its passage in either House which it would not have received if that idea had never been conceived.

But if the act of 1789 ever had authority as a legislative decision upon the true meaning of the Constitution, that authority has been annulled by repeated decisions of the same tribunal to the contrary.

First in order of time I cite the act of May 15, 1820, entitled "An act to limit the term of office of certain officers therein named, and for other purposes." The first section of that act is in the following words, to wit:

"That from and after the passage of this act, all district attorneys, collectors of the customs, naval officers and surveyors of the customs, navy agents, receivers of public moneys for lands, registers of the land offices, paymasters in the Army, the apothecary general, the assistant apothecaries general, and the commissary general of purchases, to be appointed under the laws of the United States, shall be appointed for the term of four years, but shall be removable from office at pleasure."

That section asserts the precise authority claimed for Congress by Mr. Madison on the 19th of May, 1789, the authority to determine when and how official tenure should end.

It was superfluous for Congress to enact that the President might remove officers if he had the same authority under the Constitution. And it was useless for Congress to attempt to limit the tenure of an office to four years if the President may extend it to twenty years, as he clearly can if the Constitution has vested in him alone the power of removal.

By that act Congress assumed to grant to the Executive the power of removal. Six years later a committee of the Senate, of which Mr. Benton was chairman, made an elaborate report, assuming the right of Congress to restrict the power of removal. It does not appear to have been considered by the Senate.

In 1835 another committee, of which Mr. Calhoun was chairman, reported a bill which practically denied the constitutional authority of the President to remove from office. As such it was received and considered by the Senate. It led to a protracted and exhaustive discussion. The debate of 1789 was thoroughly reviewed. Among those who denied the power now claimed by the President were Mr. Calhoun, Mr. Clay, Mr. Webster, Mr. Benton, and Mr. Ewing, of Ohio, whose name the President recently sent to the Senate as the successor of Mr. Stanton, whom he claimed to have removed from office under the very authority Mr. Ewing then vehemently denied and ably controverted. Upon the passage of the bill the vote of the Senate was as follows :

"YEAS—Messrs. Bell, Benton, Bibb, Black, Calhoun, Clay, Clayton, Ewing, Frelinghuysen, Goldsborough, Kent, King of Georgia, Leigh, McKean, Mangum, Moore, Naudain, Poindexter, Porter, Prentiss, Preston, Tyler, Waggaman, Webster, and White—31.

"NAYS — Messrs. Brown, Buchanan, Cuthbert, Hendricks, Hill, Kane, King of Alabama, Knight, Linn, Morris, Robinson, Ruggles, Shipley, Talmadge, Tipton, and Wright—16."

But this vote, although a very emphatic expression of the opinion of that Senate upon the power in question, and very suggestive of the opinion of that age, cannot strictly be considered a decision of that Congress, since the bill did not pass, and was not considered by the House of Representatives.

But in 1863 Congress passed an act to provide a national currency. The first section provided for a Comptroller of the Currency, and enacted as follows :

"He shall be appointed by the President, on the nomination of the Secretary of the Treasury, by and with the advice and consent of the Senate, and shall hold his office for the term of five years, unless sooner removed by the President, by and with the advice and consent of the Senate."

Of course, if the Constitution confers upon the President the power to remove from office, this provision was in palpable conflict with it, and yet both Houses agreed to it, and President Lincoln approved the act, as President Monroe approved the act of 1820, above referred to. Congress again asserted the same control over the power of removal in the first section of an act to provide a national currency secured by a pledge of United States bonds, and to provide for the redemption thereof, which act was also approved by the President on the 3d of June, 1864. (See Statutes-at-Large, vol. 13, p. 100.)

Again, the fifth section of the act making appropriations for the support of the Army for the year ending June 30, 1867, contains the following provision:

"And no officer in the military or naval service shall, in time of peace, be dismissed from the service except upon and in pursuance of the sentence of a court-martial to that effect or in commutation thereof."

The legislative history of this provision is brief. It is strikingly suggestive of how much of this clamor against the constitutionality of the tenure-of-office act is attributable to partisan zeal, and how much to real conviction. For this reason I refer to that history here.

The Army appropriation bill being under consideration in the Senate on the 19th of June, 1866, Mr. WILSON offered an amendment in the following words, to wit:

"And be it further enacted, That section seventeen of an act entitled "An act to define the pay and emoluments of certain officers of the Army," approved July 17, 1862, and a resolution entitled "A resolution to authorize the President to assign the command of troops in the same field or department to officers of the same grade without regard to senior-

ity," approved April 4, 1862, be, and the same are, hereby repealed; and no officer in the military or naval service shall be dismissed from service except upon and in pursuance of the sentence of a court-martial to that effect, or in commutation thereof."— See Congressional Globe, First session Thirty-Ninth Congress, p. 3254.

The amendment, as offered, was agreed to without division and without objection. When the bill was returned to the House of Representatives it was committed, together with the Senate amendment, to the Committee on Appropriations. On the 25th of June the amendments were reported back from that committee with the recommendation that the House non-concur in that amendment among others. (Ibid., p. 3405.)

The bill subsequently was referred to a committee of conference, consisting on the part of the Senate of Messrs. SHERMAN, WILSON, and YATES ; and on the part of the House of Messrs. SCHENCK, NIBLACK, and Thayer.

That committee reported that the House agree to the amendment of the Senate, with an amendment inserting the words "in time of peace," after the word "shall."

In that form the amendment was accepted, without a dissenting vote in either House.

The Senate which passed that act with such unanimity was composed substantially of the same individuals who now compose this tribunal. Moreover the act was approved by the respondent himself on the 12th of July, 1866. In his answer filed in this cause the respondent dwells upon the reluctance he felt to surrendering any one of the prerogatives which the Constitution had intrusted to the presidential office. Such a reluctance, if sincere, becomes a President always. But the respondent's professions of reluctance in 1867 were surely ill-timed, admitting they were sincere. He had already surrendered this prerogative in the solemn manner possible.

No one has asserted, and no one will assert, that the Constitution vests in the President any sort of control over the tenure of civil offices that he does not possess over that of military or naval offices.

If under the Constitution he can dismiss a postmaster, he can dismiss also the General of the Army and the Admiral of the Navy ; and a statute forbidding the dismissal of either is but idle words.

If Congress can lawfully forbid the President to remove any military or naval officer, as was done in the act above mentioned, surely it cannot be denied that Congress may prohibit the removal of any civil officer, as was subsequently done by the tenure-of-office bill.

Either, then, the respondent now asserts power which he believes to be unconstitutional, or he then approved a statute which he believed to be unconstitutional. For myself I cannot help thinking the judgment of 1866 was the most candid and unbiased. He was then under every obligation to defend the Constitution that rests upon him now. But he is now manifestly under a necessity of defending himself, which he was not under then.

If the respondent were proved to have claimed to own an estate which he had by deed conveyed to another, he would be held guilty of slandering the title of his grantee. And when he is heard, in answer to a charge of usurping power, to assert an authority which he has solemnly abjured, he must be held guilty of slandering the Constitution and the prerogatives which that Constitution vests in Congress.

Following the act of 1866 came the act of March 2, 1867, entitled "An act regulating the tenure of certain civil offices."

In substance it prohibits the President from removing certain civil officers, except upon certain conditions, as the act of the preceding year prohibited him from removing military and naval officers, except upon certain conditions. The principles of the two acts are precisely the same. The power to pass them must be the same. There may be considerations of expediency opposed to one which cannot be urged against the other. But the President, who approved the first act, so far as I know, without hesitation, vetoed the second, upon the ground of unconstitutionality. This will be thought strange; but it will not be thought strange that Congress, adhering to a principle so often asserted in former acts, passed this act by a majority of more than two thirds of each House, the President's objections to the contrary notwithstanding.

Upon all these instances I conclude that the constitutional power to remove from office cannot be proved by the decisions of Congress. Congress has never in terms affirmed its existence once. On the contrary, it has, as I have shown, denied it repeatedly and explicitly. It can as little be proved by reference to the text of the Constitution itself.

Those who, in the debate of 1789 or in subsequent discussions, have ventured to seek for this baleful authority in the text of the Constitution have claimed to find the warrant for it in the first section of the second article. They assume that the power of removal is an executive power, and therefore that it is conferred upon the President by that section. The terms of the section are these:

"The executive power shall be vested in a President of the United States of America."

In my judgment, the sole office of that clause is to fix the style of the officer who is to possess executive authority, and not to define his jurisdiction—to prescribe what the Executive shall be called, and not what he may do. It seems to bear the same relation to the executive department that the first clause of the first article does to the legislative department, and the first clause of the third article to the judicial department. To ascertain what is executive power we must examine other provisions of the Constitution.

But when you have searched the Constitution through you do not find this of removal from office enumerated among executive powers, nor any other power like it. The one duty charged upon the President which is most like, or rather which is least unlike, the duty in question, is this: "He shall take care that the laws be faithfully executed." He is not to execute the laws, but to "take care that the laws be" "executed." It is very little he can lawfully do to execute them. If, because he is charged to see that the laws are executed, he may provide any one of the means or methods or instruments of their execution, he may provide all not otherwise expressly provided for. If, because he is to see that the laws be executed, he may remove any officer who may be employed in their execution, why should he not select all officers to be employed? Why not contrive and establish the offices they are to fill? Why not define the duties they are to discharge—the parts they are severally to perform? Why not fix the compensation which they may receive?

No one will pretend that either of these powers belongs to the President, though each one is as much executive in its nature as is the power of removal. No office not established by the Constitution can be created but by an act of Congress. Congress alone can determine the manner of filling it, define its duties, and fix its emoluments. And yet it is strangely claimed that when the legislative power has done all this the executive power may practically defeat it all; not by abolishing the office or changing the duties or the rate of compensation, but by creating a vacancy in the office whenever he chooses. And so his duty to see the law faithfully executed is transformed into a power absolutely to defeat the whole purpose of the law. He is charged by the Constitution to see that the laws are faithfully executed, and yet he cannot transfer an old musket from one citizen to another without making himself liable as a trespasser.

The President of the United States recently commanded an army of more than a million of men; but with all that force at his command he could not lawfully eject from his cabin the humblest squatter on the public domain. Possession is stronger, in the eye of the law, than the President, and before that naked possession the Commander-in-Chief must halt, no matter what the physical force he commands. Only when the wrongfulness of that possession has been determined by the judicial power in a procedure prescribed by the legislative power; not until the national precept has issued, attested not by the President, but by a judge, can that possession be disturbed. And even that writ must be executed by the very person to whom Congress requires it to be directed. Whoever else attempts to serve it is a trespasser, although it be the President himself.

And yet it is strangely asserted that this officer, who is so impotent to redress so palpable a wrong, may, at his own pleasure, without judicial inquiry, without writ, in a moment by a command, in defiance of a statute, remove from the duties, the labors, the honors and emoluments of official position the army of officers employed in the civil, the military, and naval service of the United States, not because the Constitution anywhere says he may do so, but because the Constitution charges him with the duty of seeing the laws faithfully executed.

This power of removal is, then, not vested in the President by anything said in the Constitution, nor by anything properly implied from what is said. It seems to me, on the contrary, it is positively denied by the manifest purpose of the Constitution. That manifest purpose is that the principal offices shall be held by those in whose appointment the Senate has concurred. The plain declaration is that "He (the President) shall nominate, and by and with the advice and consent of the Senate *appoint*, embassadors," &c. But this purpose may be wholly defeated if the President have, by the Constitution, the unrestricted power of removal; for it is as plainly declared that "the President shall have power to fill all vacancies that may happen during the recess of the Senate, by granting commissions which shall expire at the end of their next session." If, then, the President has also the power during the recess of the Senate to *make* vacancies at his pleasure by removal, his choice is supreme and the Senate is voiceless. He is only to remove all officers in whose appointment the Senate has concurred immediately upon the adjournment of that body and commission others in their places. They will hold until the end of the next session. Just before that event he must nominate again to the Senate the officers he removed, or some others whom the Senate will confirm, and when the Senate has confirmed them and adjourned the President may again remove them all and restore his favorites once more, to hold until the end of another session, when the same ceremony must be repeated.

A deed which should grant a house to "A" and his heirs and to their use forever, but should also declare that "B" and his heirs should forever occupy it free of rent, would probably be held void for repugnancy. I do not think the Constitution a nullity; and so I cannot concede that the President has in it a power implied so clearly repugnant to a power plainly declared to be in the Senate.

But it is urged that it is necessary to the well-being of the public service that the President should be clothed with this extraordinary power. It is urged that unless he have it unfaithful men may be obtruded upon the public service, and it would take time to displace them. It is true, incompetent or dishonest men may get into the custom-houses or the marshalships. It would be folly to deny that. And so dishonest men may get possession of other men's property and refuse to make restitution; and

dishonest men may refuse to pay their just dues on demand. I readily confess that some governmental contrivance by which official positions could be instantly taken from *unfaithful* hands and placed in *faithful* ones, and by which all wrongs could be redressed and all rights enforced, instantly, and without the necessity of trial or deliberation or consultation, is a desideratum. But the men who made our Constitution did not provide any such contrivance. I do not think they tried to. It seems to me they studiously avoided all such effort. I think they believed what the world's whole history most impressively teaches: that while the administration of law is intrusted to fallible men, deliberation is safer than expedition.

Absolute monarchies are the handiest of all Governments for that very reason, because they can execute justice and punish rascality so promptly. But the men who made our Constitution, looking back upon the experience of a few thousand years, came to the conclusion that absolute monarchs could just as promptly execute injustice and punish goodness. They resolved to discard the whole system. I am not yet satisfied they were mistaken, and am not, therefore, willing to see their decision reversed.

I readily concede that if we were sure the President would always be an honest, wise, unselfish, unprejudiced man, it might promote the efficiency of the public service to intrust him with the delicate and responsible duty of removing a bad officer and replacing him by a good one.

But the men who made our Constitution did not act upon any such hypothesis. They knew it was possible not only for bad men to become assessors of internal revenue, but to become Presidents as well, else they would not have provided this august tribunal for the trial and deposition of a delinquent President. I grant that when you have a true man for President it is convenient and not dangerous that he have the power of removal, for thereby he may be able to replace an incompetent district attorney with a competent one, or a dishonest inspector of customs with an honest one, without waiting to consult the Senate or with the law-making power. But if, instead, you happen to have a false man for President, then if he have the power of removal it is a power which removes all honesty from the public service and fills it throughout with rottenness and corruption.

My conclusion is that the President derives no authority from the Constitution to dismiss an officer from the public service. A lawyer is not warranted in asserting it. A member of the Thirty-Ninth Congress, who assented to the act of July 12, 1866, cannot be justified in asserting it. The respondent, who approved that act, cannot be excused for asserting it. Whatever authority the President had on the 21st of February last to dismiss the Secretary of War, he derived, not from the Constitution, but from statute. The only authority he derived from the statute is found in the second section of the act of 1789 creating the office of Secretary of War.

That section is in the words following:

"That there shall be in the said Department an inferior officer, to be appointed by the said principal officer, to be employed therein as he shall deem proper, and to be called the chief clerk in the Department of War; and who, whenever the said principal officer shall be removed from office by the President of the United States, or in any other case of vacancy, shall, during such vacancy, have the charge and custody of all records, books, and papers appertaining to the said Department."

It was copied from the act to establish a Department of Foreign Affairs, which had been passed by the same Congress at the same session. It is evidently to be construed as the same words used by the same men in the former act are to be construed.

And whether we look at the terms employed in the section, or at the terms employed in the debate which preceded the enactment, it is very evident that the power conferred is something very different from the arbitrary and irresponsible power of removal claimed by the President in his answer—"the power, at any and all times, of removing from office all executive officers for cause to be judged by the President alone."

On the contrary, the power contained in this section is insinuated rather than asserted, implied rather than expressed, allowed rather than conferred. It is not a power granted him to be wielded wantonly and according to his own pleasure, but a power intrusted to him in confidence that it will be sacredly employed to promote the public welfare, and not to promote his personal interests or to gratify his personal spites.

In the debate to which I have referred Mr. Goodhue urged that "the *community would be served* by the best men when the Senate concurred with the President in the appointment; but if any oversight was committed, it could best be corrected by the superintending agent."

Mr. Madison, in reply to the suggestion that if the President were empowered to remove at his pleasure he might remove meritorious men, said:

"In the first place he will be impeachable by this House before the Senate for such an act of maladministration; for I contend that the wanton removal of meritorious officers would subject him to impeachment and removal from his own high trust."

How delicate the power was felt to be is apparent from the fact that from the passage of the act down to the 20th of February last it is certain the power had never been exerted but *once*, and it is not certain that it was ever exerted even once. Often Secretaries have been nominated to the Senate in place of others then in office, and upon receiving the assent of the Senate the new Secretaries have displaced the former ones. It is claimed that in 1800 a Secretary of State was removed by President Adams without the assent of the Senate. It is certain that he issued an order for the removal of Mr. Pickering before Mr. Marshall was confirmed; but as Mr. Marshall was nominated to the Senate on the same day order for Mr. Pickering's removal was dated, and as the former was confirmed by the Senate promptly on the following day, it is evident the President acted in full confidence that the Senate would assent, and it is not certain that the order for the removal of Mr. Pickering was enforced or even served upon him before the Senate had assented.

Indeed, I am of opinion the people of this country have not delegated any such irresponsible power to any agent or officer of theirs as is claimed by the President. Every officer is held responsible in some form for the manner in which he employs every power conferred upon him. Some are responsible to the courts of law, some to the tribunals of impeachment, and all, even the members of this high court, are responsible to the people, by whom and for whose use all power is delegated.

"In addition to all the precautions which have been mentioned to prevent abuse of the executive trust in the mode of the President's appointment, his term of office, and the precise and definite limitations imposed upon the exercise of his power, the Constitution has also rendered him directly amenable by law for maladministration. The inviolability of any officer of the Government is incompatible with the republican theory as well as with the principles of retributive justice."—1 *Kent's Com.*, 289.

But, fairly construed, I think the act above referred to does imply in the President the power to remove a Secretary of War in a proper case. I think, also, he is primarily the judge of what is or is not a proper case. But he is not the sole or the final judge. This court may review his judgment. For a wanton, corrupt, or malicious exercise of the power he may, and, in my judgment, should be, held responsible upon impeachment. Or if he wantonly or corruptly refuse to exercise the power he may also make himself liable to impeachment. If a President wickedly remove an officer known to be faithful, or wickedly refuse to remove one known to be corrupt, undoubtedly he may be impeached.

And this suggests the inquiry as to the offenses for which an officer may be impeached.

Only for "treason, bribery, and other high crimes and misdemeanors." Such is the language of the Constitution. But what are "high crimes and misdemeanors?"

They are, say the counsel for the respondent, "only high criminal offenses against the United States, made so by some law of the United States existing when the acts complained of were done." That rule is clearly stated and easily understood, and it must be correct, or the other rule is absolutely correct, to wit: that those are high crimes and misdemeanors which the triers deem to be such. By one or the other of these standards every officer when impeached must be tried. Either high crimes and misdemeanors are those acts declared to be such by the law, or those held to be such by the court.

Against the first construction we have the protest of all the authority to be found in judicial, legislative, or political history.

If opinions or precedents are to have any weight with us, they are wonderfully accordant. They are against the rule contended for by the respondent, and they are abundant. A collection of them prepared for this record occupies more than twenty-five pages.

I will cite here but one precedent and one authority:

"Although an impeachment *may* involve an inquiry whether a crime against any positive law has been committed, yet it is not necessarily a trial for crime; nor is there any necessity in the case of crimes committed by public officers for the institution of any special proceeding for the infliction of the punishment prescribed by the laws, since they, like all other persons, are amenable to the ordinary jurisdiction of courts of justice in respect of offenses against positive law. The purposes of an impeachment lie wholly beyond the penalties of the statute or the customary law. The object of the proceeding is to ascertain whether cause exists for removing a public officer from office. Such a cause may be found in the fact that either in the discharge of his office or aside from its functions he has violated a law or committed what is technically a crime. But a cause for removal from office may exist where no offense against positive law has been committed, as where the individual has, from immorality or imbecility or maladministration, become unfit to exercise the office."—*Curtis's History of the Constitution of the United States*, vol. 2, p. 260.

Such is the opinion of that learned commentator as to offenses for which an officer may be impeached. Not alone for what the law defines to be a crime, but for what the court think such immorality or imbecility or maladministration as makes him unfit to exercise the office.

In 1804 a judge of the United States district court for the district of New Hampshire was impeached and removed from office. There were four articles in the impeachment; three of them presented the defendant for maladministration in making certain orders in court; the fourth charged him with the immorality of drunkenness. Neither charged an indictable offense.

The respondent's counsel brushes all precedents and all authority aside. Ignoring the unanimous judgment of two hundred years, he insists upon a new interpretation of the old words employed in our Constitution, an interpretation which seems to me invented for and adapted to this particular case. His words are:

" In my apprehension the teachings, the requirements, the prohibitions of the Constitution of the United States prove all that is necessary to be attended to for the purpose of this trial. I propose, therefore, instead of a search through the precedents, which were made in the time of the Plantagenets, the Tudors, and the Stuarts, *and which have been repeated since*, to come nearer home and see what provisions of the Constitution of the United States bear on this question, and whether they are not sufficient to settle it. If they are it is quite immaterial what exists elsewhere."—*Curtis's Argument*, p. 404.

This appeal from the agreement of centuries is so boldly made that I cannot forbear to present the respondent's theory of the constitu-

C. I.—65.

tional remedy by impeachment, with a single comment upon it.

The Constitution declares:

"The President, Vice President, and all civil officers of the United States shall be removed from office on impeachment for, and conviction of, treason, bribery, or other high crimes and misdemeanors."

Clearly the President may be impeached for any cause for which a Secretary may be. Judgment in case of impeachment *may* not extend beyond removal from office. It cannot "extend further than to removal from office and disqualification to hold and enjoy any office of honor, trust, or profit *under the United States*."

The Constitution declares that the House of Representatives " shall have the sole power of impeachment."

"The Senate shall have the sole power to try all impeachments.
"No person shall be convicted without the concurrence of two thirds of the members present."

As we have seen, there is not one word in the Constitution which in terms authorizes the President to remove a Secretary for any cause whatever.

It was the opinion of many learned jurists and able statesmen in the commencement of this Government that no civil officer could be removed during his term except by impeachment; that impeachment was the only mode sanctioned by the Constitution for ridding the civil service of incapacity, of dishonesty, or of crime.

But, according to this new rendering of the Constitution, we are asked to say that whatever may be the opinion of the merits of a Secretary entertained by the House of Representatives, they cannot hope, and must not ask, to remove him by impeachment, until they can convince, not a majority, but two thirds of the Senate; not upon probable cause, but upon legal proofs; not of official incapacity however gross, or of official delinquency however glaring, but of official misconduct such as the law has anticipated and has forbidden under heavy penalties; yet that the President may remove at will, upon his own motion, without trial or notice, the same Secretary, simply because he is distasteful to him, and thereby renders their personal relations unhappy, although he may be the ablest and the purest statesman who ever held a portfolio. Thus the power of impeachment, expressly conferred upon the two Houses by the Constitution, is loaded with conditions which render it useless to the Republic, except against the most daring criminals; and we are asked to accept in its place an irresponsible power of removal, resting upon no express grant, but only upon an unreasonable and violent implication, to be exerted by a single man, which, in its practical operation, confounds all distinctions between official merit and official demerit, and which, in my judgment, upon the experience of half a century, has done vastly more to debauch the public service than to protect it.

If this most anomalous interpretation of the Constitution is defended upon any theory of the transcendent importance of the presidential office over the ministerial office, I reply that no such distinction is warranted by the law or the facts.

In law the functions of a Secretary are as important to the nation as those of the President; and in practical administration the labors of each one of the seven heads of Executive Departments are worth sevenfold more to the public than the labors of the President.

I cannot, therefore, accept this new interpretation of the laws of impeachment. I hold, with the elder authorities, with the late authorities, with all the authorities, that impeachment is a process provided, not for the punishment of crime, but for the protection of the State. And so holding, I must give judgment, not as to whether the acts proved upon the respondent are declared by the criminal code to be crimes, but whether I think them so prejudicial to the State as to warrant his removal. When the written law refuses to guide me, my own conscience must. I cannot accept the opinions of another man. The State must furnish me with the rule of judgment or my own convictions must supply one. There can be no other umpire.

What, then, are the acts charged upon the President? how far are they proved? and to what extent are they criminal?

I believe I am not mistaken in saying that the specific acts charged against the respondent in the first eight articles are, that on the 21st day of February last he issued an order removing Edwin M. Stanton from the office of Secretary War, and that on the same day he issued another order authorizing Lorenzo Thomas to act as Secretary of War ad interim. These two acts are charged in different articles, in various forms, as done with various intendments and with various legal effects. They are relied upon as specific violations of the Constitution and as violations of different laws. They are relied upon as evidences of a conspiracy to prevent Mr. Stanton from holding the office of Secretary of War, and as evidences of an attempt to drive him from office by threats, intimidation, and force.

That the respondent issued both orders is fully proved by the evidence and fully admitted by the answer.

It only remains for me to consider the circumstances under which they were issued in order to determine whether they constitute an impeachable offense.

The respondent justifies the order of removal under the double warrant of constitutional authority and of authority conferred by the second section of the act of 1789 creating the Department of War.

The first claim I have already considered and rejected. The second claim is resisted upon the ground that the authority given in the act of 1789 is revoked by the act of March 2, 1867; and accordingly in the first article the order of removal is charged specifically as a violation of the last-mentioned act, known as the tenure-of-office act.

Of course, with the views I have already expressed of the true construction of the Constitution, I can entertain no doubt of the entire validity of the tenure-of-office act. I earnestly supported its passage in the Senate. With whatever ability I had I endeavored to extend its protection to the heads of the Executive Departments.

But while the action of the House accorded with my own views, the Senate, by three different votes, rejected those views. The disagreement between the two Houses led to a committee of conference.

The committee reported the first section as it now stands in the law, in the following words:

"That every person holding any civil office to which he has been appointed by and with the advice and consent of the Senate, and every person who shall hereafter be appointed to any such office, and shall become duly qualified to act therein, is and shall be entitled to hold such office until a successor shall have been in like manner appointed and duly qualified, *except as herein otherwise provided: Provided,* That the Secretaries of State, of the Treasury, of War, of the Navy, and of the Interior, the Postmaster General, and the Attorney General, shall hold their offices respectively for and during the term of the President by whom they may have been appointed, and for one month thereafter, subject to removal by and with the advice and consent of the Senate."

This section was explained to the Senate by members of the committee at the time it was reported as not designed to affect the power of the President to remove the Secretary of War. Upon examining the provisions then it was my own opinion that it did not affect his authority in that regard. And after all the debate I have heard upon the point since, I have not been able to change that opinion.

If Mr. Stanton had been appointed during the present presidential term, I should have no doubt he was within the security of the law. But I cannot find that, either in fact or in legal intendment, he was appointed during the present presidential term. It is urged that he was appointed by Mr. Lincoln, and such is the fact. It is said that Mr. Lincoln's term is not yet expired. Such I believe to be the fact. But the language of the proviso is, that a Secretary shall hold, not during the term of the *man* by whom he is appointed, but during the *term* of the President by whom he may be appointed. Mr. Stanton was appointed by the President in 1862. The term of that President was limited by the Constitution. It expired on the 4th of March, 1865. That the same incumbent was reëlected for the next term is conceded, but I do not comprehend how that fact extended the former term.

Entertaining these views, and because the first article of the impeachment charges the order of removal as a violation of the tenure-of-office act, I am constrained to hold the President not guilty upon that article.

But, even if the tenure-of-office act had never been passed, it does not follow that the respondent would not be guilty of a high crime in issuing the order of removal. The order might conclude Mr. Stanton. But it does not follow that the people could not resent it and impeach the President for issuing it.

Two of the articles in the impeachment of Judge Pickering charged him with making certain orders in a judicial procedure pending before him. He had undoubted jurisdiction to make the orders, and they were binding upon the parties until reversed. But the Senate found him guilty upon both articles, not because the making them was a usurpation of authority, but because it was an abuse of authority. I cannot find, for reasons already stated, that the respondent's order removing Mr. Stanton was a usurpation of authority, but was it not an abuse of authority? If Mr. Stanton was a meritorious officer, and yet the respondent sought wantonly to remove him, he committed the precise offense which Mr. Madison declared in the debate of 1789 to be impeachable.

The cause assigned by the President for the order of removal is—

"That the relations between the said Stanton and the President no longer permitted the President to resort to him for advice or to be, in the judgment of the President, safely responsible for his conduct of the affairs of the Department of War as by law required, in accordance with the orders and instructions of the President; and thereupon by force of the Constitution and laws of the United States, which devolve on the President the power and the duty to control the conduct of the business of that executive Department of the Government, and by reason of the constitutional duty of the President to take care that the laws be faithfully executed, this respondent did necessarily consider and did determine that the said Stanton ought no longer to hold the said office of Secretary for the Department of War."

The cause for these unhappy personal relations is explained by the respondent in a message sent to the Senate on the 12th of December, 1867, and which is made a part of the answer in this cause.

That explanation is as follows:

"The subsequent sessions of Congress developed new complications when the suffrage bill for the District of Columbia and the reconstruction acts of March 2 and March 23, 1867, all passed over the veto. It was in Cabinet consultations upon these bills that a difference of opinion upon the most vital points was developed. Upon these questions there was perfect accord between all the members of the Cabinet and myself, except Mr. Stanton. He stood alone, and the difference of opinion could not be reconciled. That unity of opinion which upon great questions of public policy or administration is so essential to the Executive was gone."

The respondent does not allege that Mr. Stanton would not advise him and advise him honestly, but only that he, the respondent, "could not resort to him for advice." If the fact was so, and if the advice of the Secretary was essential to the proper discharge of the President's duty, as I have no doubt it was, it would seem to show disqualification on the part of the Executive rather than on the part of the Secretary, and to demand the resignation of the former rather than the removal of the latter.

But the reason urged why the President could not resort to the Secretary for advice is, that the latter differed from him upon three points of public policy, the suffrage bill for the District of Columbia and the reconstruction acts of March 2 and March 23, 1867, "unity of opinion was gone."

If unity of opinion had still existed, it is difficult to understand of what advantage Mr. Stanton's advice could have been to the President.

I do not readily perceive of what importance it was to the President to resort to a minister for advice if the advisory authority of the latter was to be limited to echoing the President's own opinions.

But it is very suggestive in this connection that the points of difference between the respondent and the Secretary were upon three public statutes. The President is known to have disapproved them all. They were, in fact, passed over his veto.

The inference seems irresistible that the Secretary approved them. But since they had all been passed into solemn laws of what importance were the opinions of either, unless, indeed, the respondent had resolved to defeat their execution, and demanded a change in the War Office, not to aid him more efficiently in the execution of the laws, but to aid him in defeating their execution?

But another reason for wishing to get rid of the Secretary urged by the President is that he could not "safely be responsible for his conduct of the affairs of the Department." Perhaps that was so; although the evidence is not apparent. But the sufficient reply to that is, that he was not responsible for his conduct any further than he directed or sanctioned it. The suggestion that any President is responsible for the conduct of subordinate officers is a groundless pretext by whomsoever urged. If a President were responsible for the conduct of his subordinates, the respondent would not only have been impeachable, but would probably have been in the penitentiary long before this time; and few of his predecessors would have fared any better.

But upon this whole question, of the cause assigned for the exclusion of Mr. Stanton, the Senate has already passed. The President himself, by his message of the 12th December last, called for the judgment of the Senate upon them. I then voted them insufficient. Nevertheless the respondent issued the order of removal; and if I am now to say that that act does not constitute an impeachable offense, I must either reverse the decision I then made upon the cause of removal, or I must reverse the decision of Mr. Madison upon the nature of an impeachable offense.

I perceive no reason for reversing either. But upon the question of Mr. Stanton's merits as an officer, I am not left to rely upon my own judgment alone. Of course my own judgment must guide my own decision, since there is no authoritative law upon the subject. But I am glad to remember that my opinion was then in accord with that of a large majority of the Senate, and also manifestly in accord with what the opinion of the respondent himself had been, and with that of his predecessor, attested by both in the most solemn manner. President Lincoln employed Mr. Stanton as Secretary of War during the last and the larger part of his administration. Mr. Johnson also employed him from the time of his accession to the Presidency for nearly two years before the tenure-of-office bill was passed. And after its passage he continued to employ him until Congress had adjourned, had reassembled, and adjourned again. Not until August, 1867, did he commence the labor of excluding him from office. Of course the respondent cannot be allowed to say now in his own justification that he was employing in a high trust during all that time an incompetent or an unfaithful man. He must assign some reason for wishing to exclude him from the service which did not exist before he commenced the attempt. This the respondent does. He assigns three such reasons. They were found in the fact that the Secretary approved of three different statutes of which the President disapproved.

So an American President pleads before the Senate, as a justification for his dismissal of a minister, that the minister approved of certain public laws! A British minister leaves office the moment a law passes which he cannot approve. And if a British sovereign were to assign such a reason for the dismissal of a minister, he would not be impeached, indeed, because the British constitution does not warrant such a proceeding; but there is no question he would have to quit the throne by the authority not conferred upon but inherent in the Parliament as the representatives of the people of the realm.

Commissioned as I am by the express letter of the Constitution to pass judgment upon the conduct of this respondent, and sworn as I am to give true judgment, I cannot hesitate to say that the attempt to drive an American minister from the public service because he approved the public laws, is of itself a high crime against the State.

It is urged that his only purpose in issuing the order was to raise the question of his power to remove, and obtain the judgment of the courts of law upon it. But when there was no just cause for removal why should the President have been so anxious to vindicate his power to remove? But I dismiss this allegation with the remark that I cannot believe it. All the testimony in the case contradicts it. There is not a syllable to support it. If when he issued the order of removal he intended only a lawsuit, why did he not say so to General Thomas, to whom he gave the order? Why did he leave the Adjutant General to believe, as he told Dr. BURLEIGH, that he was to gain possession not by suit but by force?

Why did he leave him to suppose, as he told Mr. Wilkeson, that he should overcome the objection of Mr. Stanton, not through the aid of the Attorney General, but by help of the General of the armies; or, as he told Karsner, that he was to use kicks and not writs? If he intended no more than a lawsuit, why did he not so inform Lieutenant General Sherman when he offered him the place of Secretary *ad interim* some days before? At that time the General invited his attention to the propriety of a lawsuit, but the President repudiated the suggestion as impracticable. But above all, if he intended nothing more than a lawsuit, why has he not had one? The courts have been always open to him. No lawyer needs to be told that the Attorney General could have proceeded to try the title to the office upon an information filed upon the relation of General Thomas as well as upon the relation of Mr. Stanton. It has been suggested that the respondent's hopes of a lawsuit were frustrated by the discontinuance of some criminal proceedings taken against General Thomas upon complaint of Mr. Stanton, soon after the order was issued.

The President, however, does not in his answer urge that explanation. And it is hardly credible that the President relied upon getting into court in that particular way. Every other way has been and still is open to him except one. He does not seem to have been able, so far, to get into the law courts as defendant, and that seems to have been regarded by him as a *sine qua non* to any litigation. At liberty at all times for nearly a quarter of a year to sue upon the right of General Thomas to recover possession, he has failed to do so. But he leaves us to infer that if he could have succeeded in putting General Thomas once in possession he would have been content to contest a suit by Mr. Stanton even had it taken a year to determine it.

So far I discover absolutely nothing to relieve the respondent from the guilt of having issued an order for the removal of an able and faithful officer, long trusted by himself and by his predecessor, and still trusted by a large portion of the country, charged with no fault, but that he approved of certain laws which the President condemned, and of removing him against the advice of a large majority of the Senate. On the contrary, it seems to me this guilt is greatly aggravated by the disposition the respondent sought to make of the office.

To remove a meritorious public officer, Mr. Madison declared, constituted an impeachable offense. To remove such an officer and leave the office vacant, with no one to discharge the duties, would doubtless be held to enhance the guilt. To remove a faithful and competent officer, and supply his place with an incompetent and dishonest one, would enhance it still more.

To remove a good man from office, and to replace him with a bad man, without any advice and without any sort of legal authority, seems to me an offense against the public interests which, if it go unrebuked, will excuse any possible offense that leaves the President outside of a penitentiary.

That the respondent attempted to do all this is charged upon him, and, in my judgment, is proved upon him.

At the same time that he issued the order of removal he issued another order, authorizing the Adjutant General of the Army to act as Secretary *ad interim*. The fitness of General Thomas for the office of Secretary is not fairly in issue in this cause, and consequently we can know but little about it. A few things, however, are disclosed in the evidence. It is shown that the same position was tendered, a few days before, to Lieutenant General Sherman, and he declined it. But when it was offered to General Thomas, he not only accepted it promptly, but he addressed a letter of thanks to the President for the "honor done him." When the Adjutant General gives thanks for a trust so high, so delicate, so solemn that Lieutenant General Sherman shrinks from and declines it, it suggests the inference that the former is not exactly the man for the place.

It does appear, also, from the testimony that the General of the Army had recommended his retirement from the military service altogether. One whom General Grant thinks no longer fitted for the post of Adjutant General does not afford the highest evidence of fitness for the post of Secretary of War.

But the respondent's legal right to put General Thomas in possession of the War Office is put in issue by the *second* and by some other articles in the impeachment.

The respondent claims authority under the act of February 13, 1795. That is as follows:

"That in case of vacancy in the office of Secretary of State, Secretary of the Treasury, or of the Secretary of the Department of War, or of any officer of either of said Departments whose appointment is not in the head thereof, whereby they cannot perform the duties of their said respective offices, it shall be lawful for the President of the United States, in case he shall think it necessary, to authorize any person or persons, at his discretion, to perform the duties of the said respective offices until a successor be appointed or such vacancy be filled: *Provided*, That no vacancy shall be supplied in manner aforesaid for a longer term than six months."

I cannot admit the claim for three reasons: First, there is reason to suppose that the statute of 1795 was never regarded as a valid law. Second, it seems to me to have been clearly repealed by the act of 1863. And third, if it were in full force it did not authorize the order issued to General Thomas.

If a vacancy occur in the office of the Secretary during a session of the Senate it may, under the Constitution, be filled immediately by a new nomination and confirmation. If the vacancy occur during the recess of the Senate the Constitution empowers the President to fill it by a new commission, to hold until the Senate convenes and can act upon a nomina-

tion. The commission can be issued under the Constitution as promptly as a person may be authorized under the act. The commission and the authorization have the same practical effect; so that the provision made by the Constitution for cases of "*vacancy*" would seem to be ample and render legislation unnecessary.

But if a Secretary be absent or sick it is evident there is no one to discharge the duties of the office; nor does the Constitution provide any mode of supplying the want. The office is not "vacant," but the incumbent is disabled.

To provide for such a case was, as I suppose, the main purpose of the eighth section of the act of May 8, 1792, entitled "An act making alterations in the Treasury and War Departments." In fact the section does a little more than provide for cases of disability. It provides for one kind of *vacancy*. The language is:

"In case of *death*, absence from the seat of Government, or sickness of the Secretary of State, Secretary of the Treasury, or of the Secretary of the War Department," &c., "whereby they cannot perform the duties of their said respective offices, it shall be lawful for the President of the United States, in case he shall think it necessary, to authorize any person or persons, at his discretion, to perform the duties of the said respective offices until a successor be appointed or until such absence or inability by sickness shall be removed."

Thus the law stood until 1795. All vacancies were provided for by the Constitution; and temporary disabilities and vacancy by *death* were provided for by the law of 1792.

Then the law was passed the whole of which was quoted above. It is entitled "An act to amend the act of 1792." In terms it provides for all cases of vacancy, whether by death, resignation, or otherwise; and it provides for no case of disability. What the Constitution had done well, the act does over again; what the Constitution had not done at all, the act omits to do.

But it is evident from every part of that short statute that the draftsman had no definite idea of the mischiefs he wished to remedy. He does not even seem to have considered what a "vacancy" was, or to have been conscious that a vacancy differed from a disability. Hence the act attempts to qualify a *vacancy in an office* by the circumstance that it shall prevent the *incumbent* of the office from discharging its duties—as if there were some vacancies which did not prevent the regular discharge of duty.

Again, it limits, in terms, the duration of the *ad interim* appointment "until a successor be appointed or such a vacancy be filled," as if two sorts of vacancy were provided for, one of which was to determine by the appointment of a "successor," and the other by being "filled." The main purpose of the act seems to be to limit the extreme duration of an *ad interim* appointment. And in this endeavor it collides hopelessly with the Constitution.

The Constitution says the President may supply a vacancy occurring during the recess of the Senate by commissioning a person to act until the end of the next session. The act says that no vacancy shall be supplied longer than six months. It would seem that an act so incongruous ought not to be relied upon as authority for anything. I can find no evidence that it ever was quoted as authority before. In Little & Brown's edition of the Statutes-at-Large it is marked "obsolete." But if it ever was a living law, it seems to me indisputable that both the acts of 1792 and of 1795 are repealed by the act of February 20, 1863.

It has been seen that neither of the former acts made provision for cases out of the three Departments of State, War, and Treasury. In 1863 it was found that no provision had been made for temporary disabilities in either of the other Departments. There was evidently occasion for further legislation, and it seems to me to have been made the occasion for revising the whole subject and of embodying in a single act not only all the provision to be made, but all the cases to be provided for. The title of the act and the purview of the act alike prove this. The title shows that the act is not amendatory of, or supplementary to, the former acts; but that its aim is to do *effectually* just what the other acts did *partially*.

It is entitled "An act *temporarily to supply vacancies in the Executive Departments in certain cases.*"

The body of the act shows unmistakably that the draftsman had both the former acts before him. He copied from both. The act provides for cases of death, absence, and sickness, as did the act of 1792. It provides for cases of resignation, and provides the six months' limitation, as did the act of 1795. Every case provided for by both the former acts is embraced within the terms of the act of 1863, unless the case of removal be an exception.

It is argued that the act of 1795, as it authorized an *ad interim* appointment in all cases of vacancy, authorized one in case of vacancy by removal. That is conceded. But it should be remembered that the power to supply a vacancy caused by removal with an *ad interim* appointment is a power not named in the statute of 1795, since the power so to create a vacancy is not in that statute. The power to *make* a vacancy by removal is found in the acts of 1789 and 1820. So one in looking at the act of 1795 does not see the specific authority which the respondent asserted on the 21st of February. Those who drew the statute of 1863 could have seen it only by collating the act of 1795 with the acts of 1789 and 1820. The act of 1795 had been on the books for more than seventy years. The archives of the Government have been ransacked and fail to show that in that whole period a single removal was ever by any President followed with an *ad interim* appointment. Every power, therefore, which could be seen by reading the act of 1795 was copied into the act of 1863;

every power which had ever been exerted under that act was also copied. All provisions in former laws inconsistent with the provisions of the last-mentioned act are expressly repealed. And yet it is gravely argued that this power of supplying a vacancy caused by removal with an *ad interim* appointment still survived; not only that it survived the act of 1863, but the act of March 2, 1867, also, which deprives the President of all power to create a vacancy by removal except in case of a head of Department where no such vacancy ever was created more than once, if at all. So, in spite of the acts of 1863 and of 1867, we are asked to express, from the mere husks of that poor, misshapen statute of 1795—denounced as obsolete in the code where it stands—the authority to follow the removal of a Secretary made when the Senate is in session with an *ad interim* appointment. For one I cannot consent to torture the laws in order to extort from them permission for the respondent to strip the high trust of Secretary from Edwin M. Stanton and place it in the hands of Lorenzo Thomas.

It is said that repeals by implication are not favored by the courts. That is true. Nevertheless, a statute may be repealed without naming it.

"It is a well settled rule that where any statute is revised or one act framed from another, some parts being omitted, the parts omitted are not to be revived by construction, but are to be considered annulled. To hold otherwise would be to impute to the Legislature gross carelessness or ignorance, which is altogether inadmissible."—*Wilde, J.*, Ellis *vs.* Paige *et al.*, 1 *Pickering*, 44; 5 *English*, 588; 3 *Greenleaf*, 22; 3 *Howard*, 645; 12 *Mass.*, 545; 14 *Ill.*, 334.

Encouraged by these authorities, I venture to conclude that when Congress embodied in the act of 1863 every single power which ever had been seen in the act of 1795, and every use which ever had been made of it, they did not intend to preserve the act just to sustain a power which never had been seen in or a use which never had been made of it.

But if the act of 1795 had been in full force on the 21st of February last, it would not have authorized the order given by the respondent to General Thomas. Manifestly it was the purpose of all these laws (that of 1792, of 1795, and 1863) to enable the President to supply some one to discharge the duties of an office temporarily when, by reason of a vacancy in the office or the disability of the incumbent, the duties could not otherwise be discharged. It was not intended he should use either of these laws to replace a regular officer with a provisional one. Yet such is the use the respondent attempted to make of the act of 1795. There was no vacancy in the office of Secretary of War on the 21st of February last. Mr. Stanton was in the regular discharge of its duties; neither sick nor absent.

But it is urged that the President had power to remove Mr. Stanton, and, as he issued an order for that purpose, there was a "vacancy in law."

If there is any such thing as a "vacancy in law" it is excluded from the operation of the act of 1795 by its very terms. That authorizes an *ad interim* appointment only in cases of such rational vacancies as prevent the incumbents from discharging the duties of their offices. This "legal vacancy" was not of that kind. It did not prevent Mr. Stanton from discharging the duties of his office. On the contrary, he continued to discharge them regularly in spite of the alleged "vacancy," and, on the trial of this very cause, copies of records have been read in evidence, certified by him, as Secretary, to be true copies, which certificates were made many weeks after the "legal vacancy" is said to have occurred, and were read without objection to their competency from any quarter. But when General Thomas was authorized to act as Secretary *ad interim* there was no "legal vacancy," nor any pretense of one. Mr. Stanton not only had not retired from the War Office, but he had received no notice to retire.

The testimony shows that while Mr. Stanton was in the regular discharge of his duties as Secretary, at the War Office, without notice of an order for his removal or of a purpose to remove him, General Thomas was called to the White House, and there presented with a warrant making him Secretary *ad interim*. As such he was at once assigned to duty. And the first duty assigned to him was that of making a vacancy by executing the order for the removal of Mr. Stanton.

It seems to me that any one who will open his eyes may plainly see that the authorization to General Thomas issued, not as a means of supplying a vacancy, but as a means of making one; not to provide for the discharge of the duties of Secretary, but to prevent Mr. Stanton from discharging them. If the respondent had believed his simple order of removal would have made a vacancy in the office he would have proceeded to fill it by nomination, as President Adams did in 1800, and as sooner or later the respondent knew he must; and as in fact he did proceed, the next day, when he found the order of removal did *not* make a vacancy. But he did not expect Mr. Stanton would obey his order of removal. He knew Mr. Stanton had other views of the law. He thought to surprise him into acquiescence by confronting him suddenly with another pretender to the office. I believe this, because it is the only rational interpretation of his conduct, and because it is the very explanation he himself gave to General Sherman.

In his answer the respondent denies that he used or intended to use intimidation or threats, as is charged in some of the articles. But it seems to me he must either intend to deceive us by that denial, or he meant to deceive General Sherman when he offered him the appointment of Secretary *ad interim*, for he then tried to persuade him that Mr. Stanton was a coward, and would be intimidated by it.

I do not suspect him of an attempt to deceive General Sherman; but, on the contrary, I hold him upon his own declarations guilty of an attempt to drive Mr. Stanton from office by threats and intimidations, as is charged against him.

I hold also that he conspired with General Thomas to do this, as is charged in article four.

I hold that the testimony discloses every fact necessary to constitute a crime against the act of July 31, 1861.

If, instead of being arraigned before a court of impeachment, the respondent was on trial before a criminal court, I do not see how a jury could fail to convict him. Surely it will not be denied that the office of Secretary of War is such an office as is described in that act. It will not be denied that on the 21st of February last Mr. Stanton was holding it. It will not be denied that it was the purpose of both the respondent and of General Thomas to prevent him from holding it longer. To that end they conspired together. Both were unfriendly to Mr. Stanton. The respondent avows it in his answer. The Adjutant General does not avow it, but it is clearly inferable from the facts stated by him, that for several years he had been relieved from the post of Adjutant General by the Secretary, and that he had been but recently restored by the direct order of the President, and against the wishes of the Secretary.

It does not appear that any other human being was advised of this purpose common to those two individuals. On the contrary, there is strong presumptive evidence that no other person was advised of it.

It would seem natural that upon a measure of so much gravity the President should have consulted his Cabinet. The gentlemen composing that Cabinet were severally produced in court. The counsel for the respondent offered to prove by them what advice they gave, the President upon some questions of law, but no intimation was given that they were consulted, or that they advised upon the expediency of this attempt to place the War Office in the hands of General Thomas, to the exclusion of Mr. Stanton. The means selected for that purpose were, as we have seen, two written orders, the one directing Mr. Stanton to turn over the office to the Adjutant General, and the other ordering the Adjutant General to take possession and discharge the duties. It may be said such methods were not calculated to intimidate Mr. Stanton. The result shows they did not intimidate him. But the testimony shows that the respondent reasoned otherwise. He told General Sherman that just such papers in his hands would intimidate the Secretary. If it be said that the President had the legal authority to issue the orders, and might, therefore, calculate on the obedience of Mr. Stanton, I reply that he did not revoke the orders when he found Mr. Stanton denied his authority and did not obey. If it be said no force was employed to compel obedience, I reply that force was threatened by the Adjutant General, both to Dr. BURLEIGH and Mr. Wilkeson.

If it be said that those threats were not sanctioned by the respondent, I reply that the Adjutant General, while he says the President did not specifically direct the employment of force, yet did authorize it by the order commanding him to take possession, and that on Friday, on Saturday, on Monday, and on Tuesday when told by the Adjutant General that Mr. Stanton refused to surrender, the respondent's uniform reply was substantially, "Go on; take possession and discharge your duties;" that he never once cautioned him against the use of force, and never once directed him to resort to the courts. And, finally, General Thomas says he abandoned the idea of force not because he doubted his authority to use it, but because he did not wish to cause bloodshed.

And it cannot be allowed to the respondent to urge that he is not responsible for what General Thomas did and what he threatened to do within the scope of the warrant given him by the respondent himself in furtherance of the common purpose. One of the reasons assigned by him for wishing to get rid of Mr. Stanton, was that he could not safely be responsible for his conduct. And yet he now protests that he is not responsible for the conduct of his successor, even when going right from his presence to prosecute a specific purpose with plenary instructions to execute it, and with no sort of restriction as to the means to be employed in the execution of it.

A few words of comment upon some considerations urged in defense upon this part of the case.

And first, it is said his attempt to eject Mr. Stanton and install General Thomas did not succeed, and so he ought not to be punished. I cannot think the position is well taken. Whatever he could do to insure success he did. If his orders were illegal he cannot plead Mr. Stanton's lawful disobedience in his own justification. If his orders were legal he cannot plead Mr. Stanton's unlawful resistance in his own justification. Mr. Stanton's conduct cannot make *his* acts either guilty or innocent. If one aim a blow at another he is not held innocent because the intended victim wards it off, and so is not felled by it.

Again, it is said the unlawfulness of his order is not clear, and the respondent might have been mistaken, and that it would be hard to impeach him for a mere mistake of law. Certainly it would. No reasonable man would think of doing so.

In my opinion the respondent has made graver mistakes as to his constitutional powers than are proved in this record. Many of his predecessors have made as grave and palpable ones. But I do not hold that either should have been impeached for them. When a President, faithfully striving to promote the public good, exerts a power which the law does not vest in him, a just people would not permit

him to be punished for it. If the end aimed at be good the means will be generously criticised.

But the respondent was aiming to do what the Senate advised should not be done, and what the Lieutenant General of the Army, a man animated by great courage and great candor and inspired by no party or personal attachments, admonished him not to do. I cannot help believing he was moved, not by any regard for the public welfare, but by the hope of gratifying his personal resentments. When malice dictates the end judgment must not mistake the means.

But I see no reason for excusing the acts of the respondent upon the ground of mistake. If he was mistaken on the 21st of February he is mistaken still. He has not recalled his orders. He is impeached by the Representatives of the people because of them, and the issue he tenders is not that he was innocently mistaken, but that he was *right*, and that what he did he would have done if he had known that his *conviction* was certain. He still employs General Thomas at the meetings of his Cabinet as Secretary *ad interim* while Mr. Stanton discharges the duties of Secretary at the War Office; and the astounding spectacle is exhibited of two rival claimants to that high office, the one recognized by the Legislature and by every other executive officer and actually discharging the duties but excluded from Cabinet meetings, while the other is recognized by the President and entertained at ministerial consultations but is disowned everywhere else. And yet, for almost three months, the President has not taken the first legal step to terminate the pretensions of either.

If one is indicted for the larceny of a coat, and appears in the dock with the coat on his back, urges his title to it in his defense, and proclaims to the court that he would have taken it if he had been sure of going to the penitentiary for it, a jury would not be apt, after finding all the facts against him, to acquit, upon the assumption that he might have appropriated the coat under mistake.

I see nothing criminal in the interview between the respondent and General Emory. Nor am I satisfied it was prompted by any sinister purpose. And, therefore, upon the ninth article I must find the respondent not guilty.

The tenth article is of different purport from anything heretofore considered. In it the respondent is presented for certain utterances made by him on different occasions. I cannot reproduce here the language attributed to him. It is set forth at length in the article, and there is no dispute, I believe; that is proved substantially as avowed.

The Representatives of the people present these speeches as official misconduct. For the defense, it is said the issue involves nothing more than a question of personal taste. However improper the words were, it is argued that the respondent must be protected in the use of them, because the Constitution guarantees freedom of speech to all men. To this the reply is that speech is not, and never was, designed to be *free*. Unrestrained speech is fatal to freedom as the old restraints of despotism. Speech is not free in this country, nor in any country where there is both liberty and law. The Constitution has indeed commanded, in stern rebuke of an old form of despotism, that Congress shall make no law abridging the freedom of speech. Thereby fell the star-chamber and all government censorship. The clamps were struck from the organs of articulation. Thereby the tongue was made free as any other member. But no more so. Violent patients in a retreat for the insane are often put in straitjackets to avoid the possibility of mischief. But sane men are permitted to walk about in society with arms free and unconfined. But it does not follow that because they are unfettered they may use their arms as they will, and with impunity. The law still lays its imperious command upon every citizen, that he use not his freedom of limb to the injury of any man's person or property, or to the injury of the State. Whoever disregards the command must answer for the wrong. The same command is laid upon human speech. Whoever speaks to defame the character of his fellow, or to injure his property, or to incite to crime against the State, may be held responsible for so doing.

"Every freeman has an undoubted right to lay what sentiments he pleases before the public; to forbid this is to destroy the freedom of the press. But if he publishes what is improper, mischievous, or illegal, he must take the consequences of his own temerity."

That sentiment is quoted from the Commentaries of William Blackstone by Justice Story, and with his hearty approval. (Story's Commentaries on the Constitution, section 1878.)

And Chancellor Kent instructs us that—

"It has become a constitutional principle in this country that every citizen may freely speak, write, and publish his sentiments on all subjects, being responsible for the abuse of that right; and that no law can rightfully be passed to restrain or abridge the freedom of the press."—1 *Kent's Com.*, sec. 241.

Speech is not, therefore, of necessity innocent because it is not muzzled.

Is the respondent amenable for the speeches attributed to him in the tenth article?

We are admonished that to hold him so would be to repeat upon him the wrong which the so-called sedition law of 1798 inflicted upon the people of the country. Clearly, there is no analogy between the offense charged against the President in this article and the offenses proscribed by the second section of the act of 1798. That was a proposal by the Government to punish citizens for too free criticism upon the conduct of their own servants. The House of Representatives propose no more than to remove a servant of the people from office which they say he disgraces by his con-

duct and his speech. Counsel have treated this article as if it were an attempt to punish a citizen for animadverting upon the policy of a Congress. The purpose, if I understand it, is widely different from that. The article, after setting out the words of the respondent used on the occasions referred to, concludes as follows:

"Which said utterances, declarations, threats, and harangues, highly censurable in any, are peculiarly indecent and unbecoming in the Chief Magistrate of the United States, by means whereof said Andrew Johnson has brought the *high office of the President of the United States* into contempt, ridicule, and disgrace, to the great scandal of all good citizens, whereby said Andrew Johnson, President of the United States, did commit, and was then and there guilty of a high misdemeanor in office."

The principle of the tenth article is precisely the reverse of the law of 1798. That law proposed to punish the *people* for criticising the ill conduct of their servants in the Government. By the tenth article the people propose to remove one of their servants for ill conduct.

Because the servants may not tell their masters, the people, what to say, it does not follow that the people may not tell their servants what to say.

A law which should prohibit a man under penalties from tearing the siding from the house he owns, to make repairs, might be thought rather harsh, and yet it might not be thought unreasonable to prohibit a tenant from splitting up the floors and bedaubing the frescoes in the house he hires.

The people of the United States own the office of President. They built it. It is consecrated to their use. In it they thought to crystallize and employ the excellence of the Republic. They claim the right to protect it from desecration. Their Representatives aver that Andrew Johnson has disgraced that office. They tell us wherein. And the simple question presented in the tenth article is whether the language and the conduct proved under it are or are not degrading to the office of Chief Magistrate.

It is urged, in reply, that if it is disgraceful the Senate ought not to condemn it, because the Representatives who prosecute have sometimes used language quite as bad, and that even in the Senate, which tries the case, words have been heard at times not much better. This defense is ingenious, but hardly good in law. The law of set-off is not unfamiliar to the practice of the courts; but I have never known it extended beyond settling of debts between the immediate parties to the record. I have never heard a defendant sued for the amount of his grocer's bill object that the court could not give judgment against him because the judge himself owed a bill at the same shop. I fear the respondent's counsel do not justly appreciate the presidential office when they gravely plead in justification of the harangues set out in this article the worst specimens of discussion found in the debates of the two Houses of Congress. Much might be urged in palliation of those precedents, but all I care to say is that, instead of being a justification for anything, they cannot be justified of themselves.

Were those utterances disgraceful to one holding the presidential office?

It has been urged that he did not speak as a magistrate, but as a citizen. That, I apprehend, is a mistake. From the time one assumes that high office until he retires from it he is always President. Not all he does is necessarily official, but all he does should be consistent with the exalted character of the office. The office of Chief Magistrate is not a garment to be laid off or put on at the pleasure of the incumbent. When once those high responsibilities are assumed they must be maintained. If the incumbent weary of them, he may resign. If he abuse them, he may be removed.

But on the occasion referred to in the article the respondent was acting semi-officially. He was not discharging any duty imposed on him as President, but he was exercising a high privilege belonging to him as such. Not as a citizen of Tennessee, but avowedly as President of the United States of America, was he then visiting and being visited by his great constituency.

Was his conduct such as became his character? I cannot find any rules in the law by which to try those utterances. I cannot consent to try them by the models furnished from the proceedings of the Houses of Congress. I can try him only by my own estimate of what the bearing of a Chief Magistrate should be, when I say that in my judgment the conduct and the language proved against the respondent was wholly unbecoming the office he filled, and such as, if often repeated, would be fatal to the respect with which the people have hitherto cherished it. That judgment, I believe, is in strict accord with the opinion of the great majority of the American people as expressed at the time. I do not mean to speak figuratively when I say the people then hung their heads in mortification—not his political enemies alone, but his political-friends as well. And of those friends I doubt if there is one in the Senate who has not often declared his belief that but for the very matters charged in the tenth article the people would have sanctioned the policy which the respondent then urged upon them, and which his friends professed to believe was vital to the peace and welfare of the country. How they can now vote conduct to be innocent to which they then ascribed such disastrous results they can doubtless explain; I cannot. Many a lieutenant has been cashiered for "conduct unbecoming an officer and a gentleman." Is it possible the people cannot remove a President for the some offense, and that, too, exhibited on great public occasions?

The eleventh article alone remains to be noticed. In that the respondent is presented for having, on the 18th day of August, 1866,

denied that the Thirty-Ninth Congress was a legitimate body authorized to enact laws for the United States, but that it was only a Congress of a part of the States; and for having, in pursuance of such declarations, set himself against the execution of several of its enactments—the acts fixing the tenure of civil offices and reconstructing the rebel States among them. The respondent denies that he said the Thirty-Ninth Congress was a Congress of only part of the States "in any sense or meaning other than that ten States of the Union were denied representation therein." No worse meaning than that could be imparted to the words he used.

"Ten States of the Union were excluded from the body. But the Constitution requires that Congress should be composed of two Senators and a given number of Representatives from every State; consequently this body was not the Congress of the United States." That was the doctrine he meant to teach. But he says free speech is secured to him, and he had a right so to teach. Of course. His right so to teach is as unquestionable as the right of the people to impeach him for it; but I cannot conceive of teachings more mischievous than these. He is sworn to see the laws executed. If that body was the Congress of the United States its enactments were laws; if not, they were not laws. One of two conclusions, then, is inevitable. Either he meant to instruct the people that the enactments of that body might be disregarded, because not passed by a Congress, or he meant to tell them they must submit to enactments of a body which was not, but only assumed to be, a Congress. Either conclusion, in my judgment, shows a criminal purpose. The article avers the first to be the true conclusion, and that in pursuance of that conclusion he himself undertook to obstruct the execution of the tenure-of-office act and some other enactments of that Congress.

The case shows that on the 12th of August, 1867, the respondent, in accordance with the provisions of the tenure-of-office act, suspended Edwin M. Stanton from the office of Secretary of War; that, in accordance with the same, he made General U. S. Grant Secretary ad interim; that, in accordance with the same, on the 12th of December, he communicated his reasons for the suspension to the Senate. All this was in strict accord with the provisions of the act, if not in pursuance of them. All these steps were authorized by the act of March 2, 1867, above referred to.

But that act also required that if the Senate did not approve the reasons for which the suspension was made the office should be restored.

Now, the case shows that the respondent designed and contrived to prevent that restoration in spite of the act. His letter to General Grant, on page 234 of the record, shows that beyond all possibility of mistake. True, he does not confess to have designed his exclusion longer than to try the right of Mr.

Stanton in the courts of law; but that right could not be so determined during the remainder of this presidential term. But what was the question to be tried? Not the question of his right to remove Mr. Stanton, for he had not removed Mr. Stanton; he had only suspended him. Not the constitutionality of the tenure-of-office act, for the validity of that act could not be put in issue in a suit between Mr. Stanton and General Grant; for, if the act was valid, it commanded Mr. Stanton to be restored, because the Senate had found the reasons for his suspension insufficient. If it was invalid the order of suspension itself was without authority, and General Grant never had any right in the office. So, in such a suit, the respondent would have been exhibited in the attitude of asserting the validity of the tenure-of-office act, in order to get Mr. Stanton out of the office, and of denying it to prevent his getting back.

To avoid this monstrous predicament the respondent, in his answer, asserts what seems to me, if possible, still more monstrous. He asserts that he did not suspend Mr. Stanton by virtue of authority conferred by the act of March 2. True, every step he took was a step prescribed by that act, and yet he avers, in his answer, that he did not suspend Mr. Stanton in pursuance of that act "until the next meeting of the Senate, or until the Senate should have acted upon the case, but by force of the power and authority vested in him by the Constitution and laws of the United States *indefinitely* and *at the pleasure of the President.*"

It has come to that. The respondent, to justify his acts, not only asserts authority under the Constitution to *remove* all officers appointed by the joint act of himself and the Senate, in spite of laws to the contrary, and to replace them with others *commissioned* by himself alone, but he also claims the power to *suspend* them all and fill their places with *ad interim* appointments. The first is a power which gives the President absolute control of one incumbent for each office known to the laws. The last is a claim which gives him the right to duplicate the number.

So far as I know, this extraordinary power was never heard of until the respondent's answer was filed. I never saw a syllable in the Constitution to warrant the claim. No possible exigency of the service could require it; and to my mind the whole pretense, instead of excusing the respondent's acts, only aggravates their guilt.

Because, therefore, the testimony in this case compels me to believe that the respondent, in order to punish Edwin M. Stanton for his fidelity to the laws, did seek to remove him from the office of Secretary of War, in which he had long and ably served his country; and because he perverted to that purpose the solemn trust reposed in the Executive by the act of August 7, 1789, therein acting in wanton disregard of the public welfare; and because

he attempted to do it against the advice of the Senate, without consultation with his Cabinet, and without previous notice to the people; and because, in furtherance of that unlawful purpose, he sought to commit the powers of that high office to Lorenzo Thomas, and did, without any authority of law, issue his warrant to that effect, before said Stanton had surrendered those powers, and when he had no just reason to believe said Stanton would surrender them; and because he did intend and contrive thereby to intimidate said Stanton into a surrender of those powers by making him believe that force would be employed to compel his surrender; and because I believe he did use the language charged upon him by the Representatives of the people, and that such utterances are of evil example, of pernicious tendency, and calculated to degrade the office of President in the estimation of the people; and because he did publicly teach that the Thirty-Ninth Congress was not a body whose enactments had the authority of law; and because he did himself set the example of disobeying the enactments of that Congress by endeavoring to induce the General of the Army to retain possession of the office of Secretary of War, after the Senate had decided, in pursuance of one of the laws of that Congress, that said Stanton should and ought to repossess the same; therefore I find the respondent guilty of high crimes and misdemeanors respectively charged in articles two, three, four, five, seven, eight, ten, and eleven.

OPINION
OF
HON. JACOB M. HOWARD.

ABSTRACT OF CHARGES.

ARTICLE I. That Johnson issued the order of removal with intent to violate the tenure-of-office act and to remove Mr. Stanton.

ART. II. That he issued the letter of authority to Thomas with intent to violate the Constitution and the tenure-of-office act.

ART. III. That he appointed Thomas Secretary of War *ad interim.*

ART. IV. That he conspired with Thomas and others unknown unlawfully to *hinder* and *prevent* Mr. Stanton from exercising the office of Secretary of War.

ART. V. That he conspired with Thomas and others to prevent and hinder the execution of the tenure-of-office act, and in pursuance of said conspiracy did attempt to prevent Mr. Stanton from holding his office.

ART. VI. That he conspired with Thomas and others to seize by force the property of the United States in the War Department, contrary to the conspiracy act of 1861, and the tenure-of-office act.

ART. VII. That he conspired with Thomas with intent to seize and take such property, contrary to the tenure-of-office act.

ART. VIII. That with intent to control the disbursements for the War Department, and contrary to the tenure-of-office act, and in violation of the Constitution, he issued the order appointing Thomas.

ART. IX. That he instructed Emory that the clause in the appropriation act of 1867, requiring that all orders should pass through the General of the Army, was unconstitutional and in contravention of Emory's commission, with intent to induce Emory to accept orders directly from him, and with intent to violate the tenure-of-office act.

ART. X. That with intent to bring into disgrace, ridicule, hatred, contempt, and reproach, the Congress of the United States and the several branches thereof, and to impair and destroy the respect of the people for them, he made the speeches at the Executive Mansion, at Cleveland, and St. Louis.

ART. XI. That he attempted to prevent the execution of the tenure-of-office act by unlawfully devising means to prevent Mr. Stanton from resuming the functions of his office, and to prevent the execution of the said clause in the appropriation act of 1867, and the reconstruction act of March 2, 1867.

It has never been claimed that the power of the President to remove an incumbent from office is granted expressly; that is, in plain terms, by the Constitution. All admit, all have from the first admitted, that if it exists in him it exists by implication; in other words, that it is derived from and is necessary to the execution of powers or duties granted or imposed in plain terms by the instrument; that it is an induction from express clauses. Only three clauses have ever been relied upon as foundations of this induction or implication. They are the clause in the second section of the second article giving him the power to nominate, and by and with the advice and consent of the Senate to appoint, all officers of the United States whose appointments are not therein otherwise provided for, the clause in section one of article two declaring that "the executive power shall be vested in a President of the United States," and section three of the same article imposing upon him the duty to "take care that the laws be faithfully executed."

I shall speak of these in their order.

I assert, then, that the appointing clause I have mentioned does not imply the power of removal by the President alone and without the consent of the Senate.

Here I hold the advocates of the power to the concession upon which alone their reasoning proceeds, namely, that the power of removal is an incident to or rather a part of the power of appointment. This concession is as old as the controversy. It is an historical element in the debate coeval with its origin. It is founded upon the uncontroverted and incontrovertible principle that the author of an agency, the constituent, may revoke and annul it at pleasure. It rests upon the freedom of the will and the right of every man to act for himself in matters pertaining to him. This concession arises from common sense, from necessity, and is irrevocable. It is the rule not only of the common law, but of the civil law and of universal law, that the constituent may revoke the power he has granted.

But who, under this clause, is the constituent? From whom does the power, the official power created by law, proceed? Whose will imparts the agency, confers the office? Not the President's alone; his sole will cannot confer the office; but the will, that is, the "advice and consent of the Senate," must unite with the will and purpose of the President. Without this advice, this consent, the office cannot be conferred. The appointment thus becomes the joint act of the Senate and the President. There are thus created by the Constitution two constituents instead of one. Two wills must concur in the appointment to an office. It is plain that one was intended as a check upon the other against imprudent appointments. This check is in the hands of the Senate, to whom the name of the person selected for the office by the President is first to be submitted in the shape of a nomination, before the office can be conferred upon him. Their advice and consent must first be obtained, as an indispensable prerequisite. This check was intended for the public good, for the public safety; and was doubtless suggested by the monstrous abuses practiced in the Colonies by the unchecked power of the Crown in appointing unworthy favorites to office among them, who, in the language of the Declaration of Independence, had been licensed to "eat out their substance." At any rate, it was a measure of wise and sound precaution against the tyranny of an irresponsible appointing power, and the corruption and favoritism of uncontrolled, unexamined, secret appointments to office. Against these, "the advice and consent of the Senate" were esteemed sufficient safeguards.

The "appointment" is then the joint act of the Senate and the President; I say joint act, because that act which to become complete and effectual, requires the concurrence of two wills, is, in morals as in law, a joint act.

It follows, logically, that if, as is conceded and undeniable, the power of removal is an incident to or a part of the power of appointment, the appointment cannot be revoked; the office cannot be recalled; the officer cannot be removed, but by the concurrence of the same wills that acted in the appointment. The revocation must, in point of authority, be coextensive with the authority that granted the power; or, to speak more correctly, the authority must be the same.

It follows that the President has no power of removal without the consent of the Senate; because the power of removal is necessarily the same power that made the appointment. No distinction can in the nature of things be drawn between the former and the latter. They are not two powers, but one and the same. The division of them, and some have divided or sought to divide them, is a mere metaphysical subtlety, a mere play upon words. The words "appointment" and "by and with the advice and consent of the Senate" are intended for practical use, and are addressed to us in a practical sense, for the purpose of conferring a public benefit; not as a theme of metaphysical disputation and wrangling. They are of no utility whatever unless they are held to mean that the constituent power necessary to an appointment to a public office is made up of the will of the President and the will of the

Senate; and as it is this double consent, this joint concurrent will, that gives the appointment, it cannot be revoked without the exercise of exactly the same concurrent will, this double consent.

To say that one of the two joint constituents can undo an act which it required both to do is to give to one the power of both, which is a contradiction in terms; for an act which requires the concurrence of two parties cannot be undone by one of them without yielding to the one the power of both, which is absurd.

It is no answer to this to say that, after the consent of the Senate has been given, it rests with the President alone whether he will appoint the person nominated and consented to. This is literally true, but it is equally true that he can make no appointment whatever without that consent. He may change his mind as to the first nomination, and may refuse to appoint the person named; but whoever is in the end appointed by him must receive the consent of the Senate. This consent is, by the terms of the clause, as indispensable as the consent of the President. An appointment cannot be made without the consent of both. The power to invest the person with the office is lodged in both by the plain terms of the instrument, and the Senate might as well assume to appoint without the consent of the President as the latter to appoint without the consent of the Senate.

The power claimed is not, then, derived from the appointing clause of the Constitution.

The next provision relied upon is the clause contained in section one of article two, declaring that "the executive power shall be vested in a President of the United States of America." This clause is generally appealed to as implying a grant of the power of removal from office. It is said that the power of removal is in its nature an executive power. But the first question arising here is one of definition. What is here meant by the executive power? The surest mode of obtaining a true meaning is undoubtedly to show what the expression cannot be presumed to mean. Was this expression used in reference to the so-called executive power of the English Government? Surely not. For at that time, as in all former and in all subsequent times, there was not and has not been anything deserving of the name of a definition or classification of the executive powers of that Government. Nor can there be; for so long as the theory remains true that the British Parliament possess unlimited power, such a classification is, of course, impossible. By that theory, and by the practice of the Parliament, as history shows, there is no power, faculty, or prerogative of the British Crown which may not be modified, limited, or even taken away by act of Parliament. Indeed, that body possesses the unquestioned power both of directing the descent of the Crown and of deposing the sovereign at will. And it is practically true that all political power in England is vested in Parliament. It is true that, in administration the king is to attend to the execution of the laws by commissioning agents or officers for that purpose; but he cannot claim it as a legal right against an act of Parliament. He might complain of such an act as an encroachment upon his prerogatives, but should Parliament appoint the officers by direct act of legislation, no one will pretend that this mode of constituting them would be illegal and void.

The very omnipotence of Parliament is a standing denial that the executive powers of our own Constitution are to be defined by reference to those of the British king; and all explanations of the expression sought for in the Government of France, Austria, or any other continental nation, afford, if possible, less light by the way of definition than that of Great Britain. The reason is that none of those Governments possesses a written constitution by which the political authority of the people is parceled out among the various functionaries. With us the case is different. Here the people, the source and fountain of all political power, have seen fit to write down in their own Constitution what political powers or bundles of powers may be exercised by the three departments or faculties of the Government, namely, the legislative, the executive, and the judicial. They carefully declare that "all legislative powers herein granted shall be vested in a Congress of the United States." Then follows a list or enumeration of all these legislative powers and of the subjects upon which they may be exercised. Nobody doubts that an attempt to legislate beyond these powers, or upon subjects not embraced in the enumeration, would be void and inoperative. Why? Because the power thus to legislate is not granted, and the object is not within the reach of Congress. Their legislation ceases, withers, and dies, the moment it passes the line of constitutional limitation.

Another department or faculty of the Government is called in the Constitution the "judicial power." The extent of its application is in like manner laid down in the instrument, and all the cases to which it can be applied are therein carefully made known, and the restrictions upon this attribute of the Government are equally perceptible in the language of the Constitution.

Thus it appears that the framers, under the respective heads of legislative power and judicial powers, were careful to enumerate and designate the legislative and the judicial attributes of the Government, and to insert terms of limitation and exclusion, so as to bind up those two departments specifically to the duties imposed upon them. It was the *policy of the Constitution* to delegate, define, and limit the powers of those two branches. This is admitted by all. It is a fundamental principle, a postulate. Now, this being the case in reference to the legislative and judicial branches, who would think of deriving unrestricted executive power from that clause of the Constitution declaring that the "executive power shall be vested in a President?" No one will deny that this language is a general grant of the executive power. But it is, of course, a grant—a grant not of all or of any imaginable executive power—not a grant of royal prerogatives or of unlimited despotic power—but a grant of powers which in their nature were as easily defined and ascertained, and were, to say the least, as deserving of designation and description as the other powers; and no reason can be devised why the Convention should have so carefully defined the powers of the other two branches and left the executive branch undefined and unlimited. Such an omission would be contrary to the very genius of constitutional government, and would argue a culpable inattention and neglect on the part of the Convention. This reproach cannot be cast upon them, for we find them equally assiduous and watchful in defining all the powers they delegate to the President of the United States. They grant to him no undefined powers. They had granted none to the other two branches, and the reasons for definition and restriction were and are of equal stringency in each of the three.

If, therefore, the other two branches are to look for their powers in the Constitution, and among the enumerated powers, and out of and regardless of the two general phrases, "all legislative powers" and "the judicial power of the United States," which are in their nature and office mere captions or headings of chapters, we must by parity of reasoning look for the executive powers in the chapter or clauses enumerating them. And among these there is not to be found any such power as the power of removal from office. It is not there set down. It is not at all implied from that which is set down, and it is mere assumption and not a logical deduction to derive it from what is expressed.

Again, it is insisted that the power is derivable from the clause of section three of article two, which declares that "he shall take care that the laws be faithfully executed;" and it is said he cannot do this unless he has the power of removal.

This clause creates no power. Its language implies no grant of authority. To "take care" means to be vigilant, attentive, faithful. The language imports nothing more than an admonition to him to keep himself informed of the manner public officers intrusted with legal duties perform them, and, in cases of delinquency, to apply any corrective in his power. Laws cannot be put in force without agents, incumbents. The power and duty of nominating them are cast upon him. He must designate them to the Senate in the first instance; and in order that the laws may be faithfully executed he must nominate faithful and competent officers. Should a vacancy happen in an office during the recess of the Senate, this clause requires

him to fill it by a temporary commission to some other faithful and competent man, as provided in the next preceding clause. He does not execute the laws personally, and there is neither a word nor an intimation in the whole instrument that he is expected to do so; but he is only to *take care* that they are executed; that is, he is to use vigilantly and faithfully the power of nomination given to him separately, and the power of appointment given to him jointly with the Senate and the power to fill vacancies so happening, given to him solely for the purpose of causing the laws to be faithfully executed for the good of the people.

The doctrine, asserted broadly and unconditionally in Mr. Johnson's answer, that he has, as a separate and independent power under the Constitution, the power of removal, leads to the most fatal consequences. It directly subverts the popular character of the Government. If, by virtue of the clause I am considering, he can remove an officer, he may, of course, leave the office without an incumbent for an indefinite period of time, thus leaving its duties wholly unperformed; thus wholly defeating the commands of the law, and the people in the mean time may be deprived of the benefits of the law.

It is absurd to call this taking care that the laws be faithfully executed; it is the exact reverse of it, and proves the futility of the claim.

Again, if this clause gives him the power of thus rendering an office vacant and continuing it vacant, (no matter under what pretext,) it gives him full, complete, and unlimited power to constitute and create, of his own will, the agents by whom the laws shall be executed; for, if the clause imparts any power whatever, it is unlimited and undefined. The language is, "shall take care that the laws be faithfully executed." The means are not mentioned, and if they are not to be looked for in the other clauses relating to the President, then, I repeat, if the clause grants any power whatever, it is without limitation and supreme. He may resort to any means he chooses. He may give a letter of authority to any person to do the acts required by the law, and this without any reference to the Senate. He may appoint as well as remove at will; and he becomes, so far as the execution of the laws is concerned, an autocrat and the government an absolutism. The mode of constituting the officers of the law, pointed out by the appointment clause, becomes a positive superfluity, a dead letter; and he may totally, and without incurring the least responsibility, disregard it. And this is what he has done in ten distinct instances in appointing provisional governors for the rebel States, the boldest invasion of the power of Congress ever before attempted, tending directly to a one-man despotism.

It is no reply to say that the claim of power under this clause is confined, or should be confined, merely to the power of removing an officer, and that it does not or should not be extended to creating an officer or agent. If it grants to him the power of *causing* the laws to be faithfully executed—which is the whole claim in its essence and reality, as no one can deny—it is impossible to make any distinction between a removal and an appointment or authorization. Both are in their nature equally necessary, equally incidental, indispensable to that end. I am in error: an appointment or an authorization is by far the more necessary.

And if this claim is well founded, why can he not of his own motion levy and collect taxes, under pretense of taking care that the laws are executed? It is a most obvious means of so doing.

Again, it is of the nature of legislative power to prescribe by what instruments the commands of the law shall be performed. But for the power of appointment specifically laid down in the Constitution, the legislative power, granted wholly to the two Houses, might have been employed in creating the officers as well as the offices. The appointment alone is withheld from the category of legislative powers granted by the Constitution to the two Houses. The President has no particle of these powers, but only the power of naming and commissioning incumbents. The functions to be performed, the modes and manner of performing them, the duration of the term of tenure, all the duties and liabilities belonging to the office, are created and defined by the legislative power solely. All admit this: the office and all its duties, all its functions, all its responsibilities, are purely and exclusively the creations of the law, and lie within the legislative power granted to Congress. The mode, the agencies, the instrumentalities of carrying into effect the law, are but a part of the law itself.

Now, if the President can, by virtue of the clause requiring him to take care that the laws be faithfully executed, constitute and appoint agents to carry the laws into effect, and may do this without the concurrence of the Senate; if he may do it even in cases where Congress has omitted to create an office for that purpose, why may he not declare and define the functions, duties, and liabilities of such agents and the duration of their terms? Of course he may; and thus all that portion of the legislative power relating to the creation of offices and of officers to execute the laws is surrendered to him—completely abstracted from the general mass of legislative powers granted to Congress by the first section of article one of the Constitution; thus making the clause requiring him to take care that the laws be faithfully executed utterly repugnant to and contradictory of the terms of that general grant of legislative powers.

Such a mode of interpreting the Constitution—a mode that annuls and destroys one part in order to give a favorite meaning to another—is contrary to all the established rules of interpretation, and is suicidal and absurd to the last degree. *It is, indeed, a total overthrow of the system of government under which we live. It*

seeks by cunning glosses and jesuitical constructions to establish and maintain absolutism—the one-man power—when the fathers of the Constitution fondly imagined they had put up firm barriers against it.

It is true that the First Congress, in 1789, did, as the President's answer sets up, by the act organizing the Department of State, recognize and admit the power of removal in the President. But it must not be forgotten that this legislative construction of the Constitution was sanctioned by a majority of only twelve in the House, while the Senate was equally divided upon it, the casting vote being given by John Adams, the Vice President. This state of the vote shows plainly that the *opinion* thus expressed by the two Houses was but an opinion, and that it was contested and resisted by a very powerful opposition. The dispute has continued from that day, and the ablest intellects of the country have been ranged on the respective sides; Sherman, Alexander Hamilton, Webster, Clay, and others of the highest eminence as jurists against the power; Madison and numerous others of great ability in favor of it. *It has never been a settled question.* Mr. Webster tells us that, on the passage of the act of 1789, it was undoubtedly the great popularity of President Washington and the unlimited confidence the country reposed in him that insured the passage of the bill by moderating the opposition to it; and the history of the times confirms the comment. It was the beginning of the *lis mota.* And so doubtful has the power ever since been considered that there seems to have been no distinct case of removal by the President during the session of the Senate but by making to them a new nomination. In a speech made by Mr. Webster in the Senate in 1835, on this same question, he says:

"The power of placing one man in office necessarily implies the power of turning another out. If one man be Secretary of State and another be appointed, the first goes out by the mere force of the appointment of the other, without any previous act of removal whatever. And this is the practice of the Government, and has been from the first. In all the removals which have been made, they have generally been effected simply by making other appointments. I can find not a case to the contrary. *There is no such thing as any distinct official act of removal.* I have looked into the practice, and caused inquiries to be made in the Departments, and I do not learn that any such proceeding is known as an entry or record of the removal of an officer from office."

I have shown that this power of removal by the President solely is unauthorized by any clause of the Constitution, and that the claim has never been acquiesced in by the country. The Supreme Court has never passed upon it. As a distinct question it has never been passed upon by any court. It is, therefore, without judicial sanction, whatever such a sanction may be worth, for it should be remembered that judges are but fallible men, and courts often overrule their own opinions on the same question. The peace of society requires that in questions of private right the decisions of courts should be respected, and should be uni-form; but in a purely political question like the present—a question relating solely to the respective powers of the various branches of the Government—the great and final arbiter must be enlightened reason, drawing its con-clusions from the intentions and objects of the framers of the Constitution, to be gathered from the language they employ, and the his-torical circumstances which inspired their work.

In this light I cannot regard what is called the legislative construction of 1789 as of any weight in the discussion. The public mind has been equally divided upon it ever since. Is not the legislation of 1867, therefore, entitled to at least equal respect as a legislative con-struction? The House and the Senate of 1867 were equally enlightened, equally capable of forming a correct opinion, far more numerous, and expressed their opinion with far greater unanimity. Is not this precedent even of greater weight than the former, as a legislative construction? And why may not one legisla-tive construction be as potent to settle a dis-puted constitutional question as another? And why may it not completely set aside that other? The authority is the same in both cases, and if the one opinion is entitled to more weight than the other, it can only be because of the greater numbers and greater unanimity.

The next question which arises is, if the President has not the power in question, and it belongs jointly to the President and the Sen-ate, can Congress by statute regulate its exer-cise, as they have assumed to do in the tenure-of-office act of 1867?

But little time need, I think, be spent upon this inquiry.

The President and Senate have, as I have shown, the power to remove. The invest-ing this power in them is investing it "in the Government of the United States" as fully and completely as if it were vested in the three branches, namely, the legislative, the executive, and the judicial, altogether; and this brings the case within the clause which declares that—

"Congress shall have power to pass all laws neces-sary and proper for carrying into execution the fore-going powers, and all *other* powers vested by this Constitution in the Government of the United States, or in any Department or officer thereof."

This power of legislation was manifestly intended to cover every power granted by the instrument, whether express or implied. No one can read the Constitution without coming to the conclusion that the power of legislation thus to be exercised in futherance of powers granted was intended to be, and is, in fact, coextensive with those powers. A naked power granted to the Government—that is, to any department or officer of the Government, for both expressions mean the same thing—with-out the means of carrying it into effect by legislation, would, indeed, be preposterous. It would be forever a dormant, ineffectual

power, as useless as if it had never been del-egated.

There is no ground here to dispute about the words of this important clause. They are "vested in the Government of the United States, or in any department or officer thereof." A power vested in either of the two Houses, in both jointly, in the President, in the courts, the judges, or in individuals, is as much "vested in the Government of the United States" as if conveyed "to the Government" in so many words; for they would, *quo ad hoc*, represent and act for the whole Government—indeed, would be the Government in using the power. Hence the grant of the power of removal to the President and Senate is a grant to the Govern-ment. The addition of the words "or in any de-partment or officer thereof" cannot, therefore, be held to confer any power not embraced in the preceding words, "vested in the Government," but is only made from abundant caution, and to give, if possible, greater clearness, certainty, and comprehensiveness to the expression. It was to make sure that Congress should legis-late for the purpose of carrying into execution *all* the powers granted, whether granted to one person or set of persons, or to another.

It is believed that this principle has never been denied. The whole current of Federal legislation proceeds from this fountain; and it is evident that the clause was inserted to remove difficulties which should perpetually be raised by cavilers as to the extent of the field of legislation conceded to Congress.

The authority of Congress, then, to prescribe in what manner this power vested in the Pres-ident and Senate shall be exercised, its author-ity to direct how it shall be used in order to subserve the public interests, to prevent injus-tice and abuses, is indisputable.

The act of 1867 forbids removals from office at all, except upon evidence of unfitness, sat-isfactory both to the President and the Senate, and requires him to lay the evidence before the Senate for their action thereon. If unsatisfac-tory to them, the officer is not to be removed, but restored to his place; if satisfactory, he is removed and his place is to be filled by another.

This is surely a most reasonable, kindly, and salutary mode of exercising the power.

The act, then, is fully warranted by the Con-stitution, and as valid and obligatory as any other act of Congress.

The next question is whether Secretary Stan-ton came within its provisions?

It is literally true that the first clause of the first section of the act prohibits the removal of every officer, high or low, who had been or should be appointed by and with the consent of the Senate. The clause declares that every such officer shall hold his office until his suc-cessor shall be appointed by and with their advice and consent. He shall be entitled to hold the office until that time.

The first section directs that all civil officers

then in existence shall be entitled to hold their offices thus:

"Except as herein otherwise provided: *Provided,* That the Secretaries of State, of the Treasury, of War, of the Navy, and of the Interior, the Postmaster General, and the Attorney General, shall hold their offices respectively for and during the term of the President by whom they may have been appointed, and for one month thereafter, subject to removal by and with the advice and consent of the Senate."

The first clause by its terms applies to *all* civil officers, judicial as well as executive. But the Constitution itself takes out of the category the judges of the United States courts by declaring that they "shall hold their offices during good behavior;" so that it could not affect their tenure.

But the clause was discussed and passed in presence of the fact that there was a multitude of offices in the tenure of which there was a limitation of time to a certain number of years. The general language of the clause would have had the effect to extend these fixed and limited terms beyond the legal period. Foreseeing this, Congress guarded against it by declaring that *all* such officers should hold *except as otherwise provided in the act.* The exception guarding against this extension is found in section four, which declares that—

"Nothing in this act contained shall be construed to extend the term of any office, the duration of which is limited by law."

Such is one of the exceptions out of the general language of the first clause.

But there were other offices whose duration was not limited by law. Among these were the offices of those same members of the Cabinet. The then members had all been appointed by Mr. Lincoln during his first term, and no limit existed upon their tenure. Mr. Johnson found them in legal possession of their offices when he became President. They had a right to continue to hold indefinitely, unless removed. Mr. Lincoln's first term had passed, and he and those Cabinet officers were holding their offices in his second term.

The tenure-of-office act was passed while all these facts were immediately before Congress. They knew that Mr. Stanton, like his colleague, held by virtue of that appointment, and that he had a legal right so to continue to hold. And they declare that he "shall hold his office for and during the term of the President by whom he *may have been (not shall be)* appointed." Nothing can be plainer than that the expression "the President by whom he (they) may have been appointed," is a mere *descriptio personæ,* or mode of pointing out the person from whom the appointment proceeded.

The proviso does not say that the Cabinet officers shall have been appointed *during* any particular term of the President making the appointment, but only that they shall hold their offices during his term. It does not require that the appointment shall be or shall have been made during the first, second, or any subsequent term for which the President is

C. I.—66.

elected; and he may, by the Constitution, be elected an indefinite number of times. They are to hold *during his term,* if he has appointed them, and for one month thereafter, no matter whether he continues to hold his term or not. It is sufficient that it is *his term,* that is, the term "for which he was elected," in which a Secretary appointed by him is found holding the office.

No one can deny that the expression "may have been appointed," applies as well to past time as to future time. Such is the genius of our language. It covers, grammatically, both the past and the future, as we all know from constant, daily, hourly use; and it here applies with equal and unerring certainty to appointments that had been made and were unexpired at the time it was used, and to those to be afterward made.

Uttered on the 2d of March, 1867, the language covered, unmistakably, in my judgment, the case of Mr. Stanton and his colleagues. Their appointments were within its terms and within the purposes of the act. I do not consider there was left any room for reasonable doubt or debate. The office and aim of the proviso were to change the indefinite period to a definite period in the tenure of those offices from a tenure at the will of the President, as had been formerly understood and practiced, to a tenure that was absolutely to terminate one month after the end of the President's term by whom the appointment was or should be made.

This was another exception out of the general language of the first clause, and to remove all suspicion that the general language of the first clause "is and shall be entitled to hold such office until a successor shall have been in like manner appointed and duly qualified," might leave it still to the President alone to remove them, the proviso adds that they should be "subject to removal by and with the consent of the Senate," thus expressly requiring the consent of the Senate if removed before that time.

As to all other civil officers included in section one, they cannot be removed but upon sufficient cause, to be reported to the Senate as required by section two, and after a formal suspension. And here was another exception to the term of the tenure asserted in the general language of the first clause.

The ground now taken by the counsel for the accused is that this language, covering, as I have shown and as is perfectly manifest, both the existing and all future heads of Departments, applies only to future heads, leaving the existing heads wholly unaffected by it, and that such was the intention of Congress, deducible from the act.

This construction not only denies to the words "the President by whom they may have been appointed" their natural, plain, etymological meaning and application, but is, as to those Secretaries, in direct contradiction of the first clause, which, by its general language, authorizes them to hold until their successors are appointed with the consent of the Senate, which was exactly their former right. It wrests from the operation of the act without any apparent motive, and against the perfectly notorious wishes of both Houses of Congress, the existing heads, and applies the act to those whom Mr. Johnson and his successors may appoint, and is thus totally inconsistent with the meaning and effect of the words "may have been appointed." No rule of construction is better settled than that words shall have their natural and popular meaning, unless the statute itself shall imply a different meaning, and here the statute contains no such intimation. The construction is plainly at variance with the very language.

No one will deny that the necessity of including those heads of Departments was as great at least as that of including future Secretaries, unknown to Congress. Why should they be left to be turned out at the will of Mr. Johnson without consulting the Senate, while their successors for all time, and all other civil officers, high and low, were protected? Why was a special exemption enacted for his benefit in reference to Mr. Lincoln's appointees whom he had continued in his Cabinet for two years, and one, at least, of whom, Mr. Stanton, he was, he says, aiming to turn out? *No one can answer this question!* But if, as is contended by the President's counsel, this exception applies only to future Cabinets, and does not apply at all to the then Cabinet, then it follows, logically and irresistibly, that they fall within the first clause, which expressly declares that—

"Every person holding any civil office to which he has been appointed by and with the advice and consent of the Senate, and every person who shall hereafter be appointed to any such office and shall become duly qualified to act therein, *is* and *shall be* entitled to hold such office until a successor is in like manner appointed and duly qualified."

Can this proposition be made clearer by argument? If the case of those Cabinet officers is not included in the special clause or exception, it must be embraced in this. There is no escape, unless it can be made out that the words "every person holding any civil office" do not mean what they say.

But this construction is a mere afterthought with Mr. Johnson. It was too clearly untenable for Mr. Johnson to act upon it in the course of administration. His own common sense rejected it, and it makes its appearance only as the refuge of his despair at a late period.

When he suspended Mr. Stanton he had no idea of this novel construction. He then treated Mr. Stanton's case as within the act. In his message of December 12 last, he openly and frankly tells us that he had *suspended* Mr. Stanton—a term hitherto unknown to our laws, and a proceeding equally unknown in our history. Suspension was a new power created solely by this statute. He says:

"On the 12th of August last I suspended Mr. Stanton from the exercise of the office of Secretary of War."

The statute says:

"The President may *suspend* such officer and *designate* some suitable person," &c.

The President, still using the language of the statute, says:

"On the same day I *designated* General Grant as Secretary of War *ad interim*."

But this is not all. The statute provides that the President may *revoke* such suspension ; and he tells us the *suspension has not been revoked.* The statute required him to report the fact to the Senate within a given time. He did so.

All this shows conclusively that at that time he regarded Mr. Stanton as coming within the act—a sound conclusion, but directly at variance with the construction he now sets up.

Thus it appears that the exceptions to the general language "*is and shall be entitled to hold such office until a successor is in like manner appointed,*" relate to the duration of the offices of the various classes of incumbents and to the peculiar modes of removal ; one mode being the immediate action of the President and Senate in case of the heads of Departments; the other the preliminary suspension of all other officers by the President. The statute, it is true, nowhere asserts, in terms, the joint power of the Senate in removals, but it is easy to see that the theory upon which it goes is, that this power is lodged by the Constitution in the President and Senate jointly—the true doctrine. It was plainly assumed as a postulate by the committee who drafted the bill. They regarded it as settled doctrine needing no special recognition, though it is clearly recognized in the second section, requiring the President to report the causes of a suspension, and the action of the Senate upon them, before the suspension can result in a removal.

Such, I say, was the theory of the bill ; the fundamental idea upon which it was framed was that the power of removal belonged by the Constitution to the President and the Senate, exclusively, and not to the President alone. If it belongs to the President alone, then the first section, including the proviso, and the second section, providing for a suspension before removal, are totally void for unconstitutionality, for Congress cannot meddle with a power that belongs solely to him.

Such being manifestly the theory of the bill, such the undoubted opinion of both Houses, it would have been strange indeed for them to abandon the very principle upon which the bill was framed, and to recognize in the proviso the odious claim of the President to exercise the sole power of removal of the then existing heads of Department. It was an uncalled for renunciation of the very power under which they could act, if they could act at all, on the subject.

I cannot give any weight to the remarks made by members in debate on the passage of the tenure-of-office act. The question is now before us for *judicial* solution, and we must be governed by the language of the act and the mischief which led to its passage. We are to construe it as judges, acting on our judicial oath, not as legislative debaters. Nothing is more unsafe than to look to the legislative debates for the true judicial interpretation of a statute. They are seldom harmonious, and this case fully illustrates the truth. One honorable member of the conference committee viewed this proviso as not applicable to the existing Cabinet officers, while the gentleman—Manager WILLIAMS, of Pennsylvania—who actually drew it, tells us the language embraces them, and that such was his intention.

A reference to two adjudged cases will probably be sufficient on the question of the value of such opinions. In Eldridge *vs.* Williams, (3 Howard's Report, pp. 23 and 24,) Chief Justice Taney observed:

"In expounding this law—the compromise act of 1833—the judgment of the court cannot, in *any degree*, be influenced by the construction placed upon it by members of Congress in the debate which took place on its passage, nor by the motives or reasons assigned by them for supporting or opposing amendments that were offered. The law as it passed is the will of a majority of both Houses, and the only mode in which that will is spoken is in the act itself. And we must gather their intention from the language there used, comparing it when any ambiguity exists with the laws upon the same subject, and looking, if necessary, to the public history of the times in which it was passed."

In The Bank of Pennsylvania *vs.* The Commonwealth, (19 Pennsylvania State Reports, p. 156,) Judge Black, one of the counsel for the accused upon this record, delivering the opinion of the court, adopts the same view. "The court," he observes, "in construing an act will not look to what occurred when it was on its passage through the Legislature; such evidence is not only valueless, but delusive and dangerous."

I am, and ever have been, fully convinced of the constitutionality of the act, and that it embraces by its terms, and was intended to embrace, the case of Mr. Stanton, and therefore that he could not be removed by Mr. Johnson. The attempt so to do was a misdemeanor, as was the appointment of General Thomas. It is too late for Mr. Johnson to claim the benefit of any doubt that might arise upon the construction of the act. The act is too plain to admit of reasonable doubt; and that he himself entertained none is shown by the fact that he adopted and recognized the true meaning in suspending Mr. Stanton. He cannot, after the commission of the offense, set up a doubt of the correctness of his former construction of it by way of removing the criminal intent. In other words, he cannot in this tribunal insist that he is to have the benefit of being himself the judge of the law. He is brought before us that we may determine that question for him.

The next question is, whether the accused has committed the offense charged in article first of the impeachment?

That offense is that on the 21st of February, 1868, while the Senate was in session, he issued the order to Secretary Stanton, declaring, in so many words, that the latter was "removed" from his office of Secretary of War, and directing him to turn over the records, &c., of his office to General Lorenzo Thomas, who he says, in the same letter, "has this day been authorized and empowered to act as Secretary of War *ad interim.*"

Mr. Stanton did not obey, and though General Thomas made two attempts to obtain possession and failed in both, the proof is that the accused has had no official communication whatever with Mr. Stanton since that time, and that he has, on the contrary, recognized Thomas as Secretary of War until now; and further, that it is the settled purpose of Thomas still to obtain possession of the office under a direction given him by the accused on the 21st of February, and under the order.

The charge here is not that Mr. Johnson actually and legally removed Secretary Stanton. This he could not do, either by the order or the use of force, against the will of the Secretary; for the first section of the statute protected him and prohibited such a removal. It was, in law, an impossibility. Mr. Stanton could not in law be removed without the consent of the Senate. The charge, therefore, is, that the order was issued *with intent* to remove him and contrary to the provisions of the act—not an actual and legal ouster from and vacation of the office, although the respondent, in his answer, (p. 27,) treats the order as having that precise effect, claiming that it worked an actual and legal removal. And, so far as it has been possible for him to give it that decisive character, it was a removal; for the proof is clear and uncontradicted that he has since that time in no way whatever recognized Mr. Stanton as Secretary of War, but has recognized General Thomas.

Section six of the statute declares, that "every removal," &c., "contrary to the provisions of this act, shall be deemed and is hereby taken to be a high misdemeanor," punishable by "fine not exceeding $10,000, or by imprisonment not exceeding five years," &c.

It is certain that the accused could not, by any lawful means, have removed Mr. Stanton, because the law forbade it; and the law does not sanction, much less furnish, means for its own violation; and as the law prohibited and made criminal the end which the order of removal and appointment had in view, it prohibited and made criminal the use of any and all means for the accomplishment of that end. It rendered all acts naturally calculated, and all attempts to commit the specific offense of "removal" criminal. The order of removal and the order appointing General Thomas were alike criminal; the delivery of the paper containing them to General Thomas on the 21st of February; the direction to him (p. 414) to deliver it to Mr. Stanton; the delivery of it to him; the direction given by the accused to General Thomas on the same day to *"go on and take charge of the office and perform the duties,"* (p. 422,) after Mr. Stanton had expressly refused to surrender it, as the accused was informed by Thomas, (p.433;) the continued refusal of the accused to recognize Mr. Stanton officially as the lawful Secretary of War; and his open recognition of an intruder vested with no legal authority as such—these facts, fully in proof, constitute a deliberate attempt to consummate the offense of removal mentioned in section six of the act. He has used all the means in his power, short of actual violence, to turn Mr. Stanton out, and the proof is strong that he meditated force, should other means fail; for it is indeed a tax upon our credulity to ask us to acquit him of that purpose, while we know the unqualified direction he gave to Thomas, to "go on and take charge of the office and perform the duties," and the repeated threats of the latter to "break down the door," to "kick that fellow out," and his scheme of obtaining a military force for the purpose from General Grant. Considering the very intimate relations then and *still* existing between the accused and General Thomas, it can hardly be supposed that these high-handed proceedings, contemplating actual bloodshed, could have been wholly without the knowledge and sanction of the accused, whose feelings were wrought up to a high pitch of resentment and hatred toward Mr. Stanton.

But the proof is perfectly clear and convincing that, so far as was practicable for him, short of a violent expulsion of Mr. Stanton from his office, he had already incurred—boldly, audaciously, defiantly, all the guilt of removing and putting the Secretary out of his office. And I cannot doubt that under an indictment for the specific crime of *removing* him contrary to the provisions of the act he would be held to have committed the offense. For, having done all in his power to commit it, proving by his own acts that he has, so far as he is concerned, committed it, and confessing in his plea, as he not only confesses but claims in his answer to the impeachment, (p. 27,) that his two orders actually accomplished it and installed the intruder, would not a court of justice hold that the crime was complete? Would it not hold that inasmuch as *title* to the office rests in and wholly consists of the law, that it cannot be dissolved and destroyed but in accordance with the law; and that therefore no person can be, technically and strictly speaking, *"removed"* at all by any other person so as to divest him of his title? Would it not hold that the word "removal," in the sixth section, must not be construed as implying a legal divestiture of the title, as it was understood in former statutes and the old practice of the Executive, but any act, done with or without force, evincing a purpose to prevent the incumbent from holding and enjoying his office during its fixed term as provided in section four of the act, or until a successor shall have been appointed by and with the advice and consent of the Senate, as provided in section one? If the word "removal" is to be taken in the sense of "amotion from office" by which the title is dissolved, then it is obvious the crime cannot be committed; for as it is the law alone that binds or attaches the office to the incumbent, the ligament cannot be severed but by the law, and no man can make or annul a law, nor, consequently, commit this technical crime of "removal."

Surely the expressions "appointment, employment, made, had, or exercised, contrary to the provisions of this act, and the making, signing, sealing, countersigning, or issuing of any commission or letter of authority for or in respect to such appointment or employment," connected with the term removal in the same section, cannot be construed as implying legal and effectual appointments, &c., but must imply mere attempts in those forms to confer the legal title to an office. It is too plain for argument that the attempt merely to confer it is punishable, not the actual, legal bestowment, which is rendered impossible by the penal clause prohibiting it, and section one, which also prohibits it.

If, then, the words "appointment," "commission," equally technical, must be construed as mere attempts to expel an officer contrary to the statute, it is equally obvious that the word "removal" must have the same meaning and effect, for if the meaning I am resisting be adopted the whole statute becomes nugatory.

The construction I am combating makes the act self-contradictory; for while the first section says "every person shall continue to hold his office," &c., the sixth section is made practically to say that he may be removed; that is, he may be divested of the office, and lose it by a removal before the allotted time.

It seems to me, therefore, that the true practical construction to be given the term is such as I have above indicated. That such is its popular sense I need not take time to argue. What has ever been understood to be a removal from office has been nothing more than the issuing of a formal order for that purpose by some officer having or claiming, as the accused now does, to have the power, and I cannot doubt but that the offense under the statute was complete the moment the order was served on Mr. Stanton. The Senate assuredly so thought, when in their resolution of February 21, page 148, they declared in answer to Mr. Johnson's message announcing that he had removed Mr. Stanton, "that under the Constitution and laws of the United States the President has no power to remove the Secretary of War and designate any other officer to perform the duties of that office *ad interim.*" It was that order of removal that the Senate thus condemned as being contrary to the Constitution and laws of the United States, not the legal and actual removal of the Secretary, for we held that.he was in office, notwithstanding the order, holding in virtue of the Constitution and of the tenure-of-office act of March 2, 1867.

I think, therefore, the House of Representatives might properly and legally have charged Mr. Johnson with having "removed" Mr. Stanton, describing the offense in the language of the statute, instead of charging him with having unlawfully issued the order with intent to violate the act and the further intent to remove Mr. Stanton, as is done in the first article.

The first article may, in my opinion, and should, be regarded as charging that the accused actually committed the offense of a removal from office of Mr. Stanton; for his order and other acts, in proof, are, in the popular mind, all that is meant by the term "removal" in the statute; and I therefore regard this article as framed directly upon the statute, charging that the accused removed Mr. Stanton contrary to it.

I add that, even without the statute, I look upon the act as a plain violation of the Constitution of the United States, a violation of his oath to take care that the laws be faithfully executed, and therefore an impeachable offense. Committed under the grave circumstances in evidence, I need go no further to find him guilty of the highest crime and misdemeanor he can commit, for it is an undisguised attempt to subvert the legal, constitutional, and popular character of our Government—one which no true friend of the Government can wink at—a step toward autocracy and absolutism—an effort to strip the Senate of all effectual power over appointments to office, and carrying with itself, if unrebuked and unpunished, imminent danger of further fundamental changes toward corruption and despotism. The power of impeachment alone is left to the people to ward off the peril and to vindicate the popular character of their Government. Never, in my judgment, was there, in our country, an occasion so imperatively demanding its exercise.

But if the first article be regarded only as an *attempt* to commit the crime mentioned in the sixth section of the act, it is obviously sustainable by the rules of law. No principle is better settled than that an attempt—not, indeed, a mere intention not evinced by any act—but any act or endeavor to accomplish and bring about the commission of an offense, is itself a misdemeanor. Professor Greenleaf, in his excellent Treatise on Evidence, (vol. 3, p. 4,) lays down the principle, derived from numerous adjudged cases, that—

"The attempt to commit a crime, though the crime be but a misdemeanor, is itself a misdemeanor. And to constitute such an attempt there must be an intent that the crime shall be committed by some one, and an act done in pursuance of that intent."

This doctrine is fully sustained by the following English and American cases:

Rex. *vs.* Meredith, 8 C. and P., 589; Rex. *vs.* Higgins, 2 E., 5, 17, 21; Commonwealth *vs.* Harrington, 3 Pick., 26; Rex *vs.* Vaughan, 4 Burr., 2494; State *vs.* Avery, 7 Conn., 266. Many other cases might be cited affirming the same salutary doctrine. Mr. Russell, in his Treatise on Crimes, (vol. 1, pp. 45, 46,) lays down the same doctrine, and it is of daily application in the administration of justice.

Commenting upon and vindicating it from doubts and objections, Lord Kenyon said in one of the cases cited that he regarded a denial of it as a "slander upon the law."

Did, then, Mr. Johnson cherish the intention to turn Mr. Stanton out of office contrary to the provisions of the act? In his answer he tells us that he did, and that he issued the orders in question with that intent. The other acts of his, not evidenced in writing, prove the same thing. He entertained that intention, and did those acts, tending to and designed for that sole purpose, in order to remove Mr. Stanton from his office against his will and contrary to the plain commands of the law.

There can be but one conclusion. He incurred the guilt, and under the first article I therefore pronounce him guilty, whether the article be regarded as founded directly upon the statute or as charging the common-law misdemeanor of attempting to commit the statutory offense.

The second article of the impeachment charges the accused with having issued and delivered to General Thomas the order of February 21, authorizing and empowering him to act as Secretary of War *ad interim*, and directing him "immediately to enter upon the discharge of the duties pertaining to that office," there being no vacancy in the office.

This was too plainly to be debated, a "letter of authority" to Thomas, and an obvious violation of the sixth section of the tenure-of-office act. No one can doubt it. The section provides that the "making, signing, sealing, countersigning, or issuing of any" "letter of authority"—not conferring the office, but—"for or in respect to any such appointment or employment, shall be deemed, and is hereby, declared to be a high misdemeanor."

This was an open, deliberate, undisguised commission of the offense; and if this statute is not totally void and inoperative for unconstitutionality, mere waste paper, the accused must be found guilty under this article.

The idea, so strongly pressed upon us by the counsel for the accused, that this letter of authority, as well as the order removing Mr. Stanton, are to be treated as innocent acts, on the pretence that they were done merely to obtain the decision of the Supreme Court as to the constitutionality of the statute, is out of place on this trial Notwithstanding such intention, if it existed, the offense was nevertheless actually committed, and the sole issue the Senate has to try is whether it was in fact knowingly committed, not whether the motives that led to it were one thing or another. To excuse or justify the intelligent commission of an offense on the ground that the motive was good would be monstrous, indeed. It would be to set aside the whole penal code at once, and permit every bad man and many good men to be judges in their own case. Society could not exist under such a puerile and capricious system. Besides, this motive, which the evidence places rather in the light of an afterthought than a ruling design accompanying and coeval with his resolution to remove Mr. Stanton, was properly to be addressed to the House of Representatives in order to prevent the finding of the impeachment. It was, if of any weight at all, matter of mitigation and excuse for committing the offense, and naturally addressed itself to the discretion of that body upon the question whether upon the whole it was worth while to bring him to trial; for surely it has no tendency to prove that he did not knowingly and willfully commit the offense. We cannot, therefore, sitting in our judicial capacity and acting on our oath to decide "according to law," give this pretense any weight in determining the issue.

The House had the constitutional right to bring the accused before us for trial. We are to try him according to the law and the evidence which the law makes applicable; and the House and the people in whose behalf they come before us have a right to demand of us that he shall be so tried; and our own oath makes it equally imperative upon us.

The third article charges that Mr. Johnson issued the order to General Thomas without authority of law while the Senate was in session, no vacancy having happened during the recess of the Senate, with intent to violate the Constitution of the United States.

This article distinctly raises the question whether, while the Senate is in session and not in recess, the President can lawfully under the Constitution appoint to an office without the advice and consent of the Senate.

I have already shown that under the naked Constitution he cannot do this, and that the attempt is a violation of his oath.

But the tenure-of-office act forbids it, by declaring in the first section that an officer appointed by and with the advice and consent of the Senate "shall be entitled to hold his office until a successor shall have been in like manner appointed and duly qualified."

This provision of course renders Thomas's appointment unlawful, for there cannot be two incumbents lawfully in possession of the office of Secretary of War at the same time.

But it is sufficient under this article to say that the Constitution itself prohibited this appointment of Thomas, for the President could not make it during the session of the Senate without their advice and consent. It was a willful attempt to usurp the powers of

the Senate, and therefore a gross violation of a high public duty attached to him by his oath of office, and a high crime tending toward and designed to accomplish a fundamental and dangerous revolution of the Government in this respect.

The design here was to pass the office absolutely into the hands of Thomas for him to hold for an indefinite period of time, and independently, and to enable him to exercise all its functions as freely as if he had held a formal commission with the consent of the Senate; and the useless Latin phrase *ad interim* imparts to the act no qualification, and imposes no restraint on his powers. Under the then existing circumstances no temporary appointment could be made. There was no law whatever that provided for it. Mr. Stanton was not absent, but present in the office; he was not disabled by sickness, but was in full health; he had not resigned, but had refused to do so; he was not dead but alive. And it is impossible to see what magic significance was attached or could be attached to the words *ad interim*. If the appointment made Thomas Secretary of War, as the accused claims, then his tenure was at the President's pleasure, and he needed no confirmation, and was to hold until turned out by him; no law forbade it, and the Constitution, as construed by Mr. Johnson, allowed it.

I cannot, therefore, hesitate to find him guilty under the third article.

The fourth, fifth, sixth, and seventh articles charge substantially but one offense—that of conspiring with Thomas unlawfully to prevent Mr. Stanton from remaining in the office of Secretary of War and exercising its functions, and unlawfully to seize and get possession of the property of the United States in the office.

I think this corrupt and unlawful agreement between Mr. Johnson and Thomas is fully made out by the evidence. The averment of the means by which the object was to be accomplished, whether by force, fraud, or intimidation, is not material. It is the agreement entered into between them to do the *unlawful act*, to accomplish the forbidden end, that constitutes the crime. And it is not easy to see how this agreement could be more clearly proved. The delivery of the letter of authority to Thomas, and his acceptance of the same; the delivery to him of the order removing Mr. Stanton and the delivery thereof by Thomas to Mr. Stanton; the demand made by Thomas for possession; Mr. Stanton's peremptory refusal and order to Thomas to depart; his written order to Thomas forbidding him to issue any orders as Secretary of War; the report of this demand and refusal and prohibitory order made by Thomas to Mr. Johnson, and the deliberate direction given by the latter after hearing this report from Thomas to "go and take charge of the office and perform its duties"—all which things happened on the 21st of February—and the second and menacing demand for the office by Thomas on the next day, all show, as clearly as human conduct can show, that just such an agreement was entered into by the accused and Thomas.

And it is made perfectly clear by the evidence that, but for the resolute firmness of Mr. Stanton, that agreement would have been carried into complete performance, and all the public property belonging to the office seized and possessed by Thomas, a mere intruder. I therefore find the accused guilty under the fourth, fifth, sixth, and seventh articles of the impeachment.

The eighth article differs from the second and third only in the averment that the order appointing Thomas was issued "with intent unlawfully to control the disbursements of moneys appropriated for the military service and for the Department of War."

I think such an intention fully made out by the proofs. General Thomas himself swears in his direct examination (page 414) that when the accused appointed him he remarked that he (Mr. Johnson) was "determined to support the Constitution and laws." This was a very gratuitous, idle remark, unless it implied a design to do something unusual, some dash against the legislation of Congress, which he so much disliked, and was, of course, uttered with reference to the tenure-of-office act, which was the only means by which Mr. Stanton kept the place he then designed to give to Thomas. He was resolved to "support," &c., against this act, and the declaration was an invitation to Thomas to aid him in trampling on that statute.

On his cross-examination (page 432) General Thomas swears the President said in this interview, "I shall uphold the Constitution and the laws, and I expect you to do the same;" and adds, "I said, certainly, I would do it, and *would obey his orders.*"

This, he says, was, as he supposes, "very natural, speaking to his commander-in-chief."

I think not. To my mind, this strange colloquy, which could not have taken place but in pursuance of Johnson's unlawful and audacious design, a design well understood by Thomas, evinces unmistakably, on the part of Thomas, the supple and reckless spirit of a dependent and flatterer, ready and willing to obey the slightest signal of the hand that feeds him. It is an assurance to Johnson that he is his tool, and will obey his wishes in all things. Contrast this low sycophancy with the manly and soldierly demeanor of General Emory when he repelled the suggestion of Mr. Johnson that he should accept orders from him directly, and that the requirement of the act of 1863 to send them through the General of the Army was unconstitutional and contrary to the terms of his commission! The contrast is indeed striking. Thomas is already debauched and bows pliantly to the will of a master! and had he got possession of the War Office, no one can doubt for a moment that he would

have disbursed the moneys of the Department in obedience to Johnson's orders. Of course, the employment of such a person would effectually subject the public moneys to the will of the employer; and there seems to be no other reason or motive for employing him except to give such control to the accused. He is not so ignorant as not to have foreseen, from all he heard and observed at that critical moment, that a military force would have to be employed and paid in order to carry out his design of ejecting Mr. Stanton and getting control of his office; and he claimed the right to control it in all respects. Such a provision naturally and necessarily suggested to his designing mind the acquisition of money to pay the expenses of the tremendous experiment he meditated; and I cannot doubt that the employment of Thomas, willing as he was *to obey Mr. Johnson's orders,* had in direct object the control of those moneys. I therefore find him guilty under the eighth article.

As to the ninth article, I do not think the proof sufficiently clear to justify me in saying that the accused pronounced the act of 1868, requiring him to transmit all orders through the General of the Army, unconstitutional, "*with intent* thereby to induce said Emory, in his official capacity as commander of the department of Washington, to violate the provisions of said act, and to take and receive, act upon and obey," the orders of Mr. Johnson not thus transmitted. The conduct of Mr. Johnson toward General Emory was highly censurable; but I do not think that particular intention is fully made out. The evidence raises a suspicion that such may have been the case, but is consistent with the supposition of the absence of such an intention, and the doubt must go to the benefit of the accused.

As to the tenth article, the evidence is conclusive that the accused made the popular harangues therein set forth. The essence of the charge is, that these discourses were "intended to set aside the rightful authority and powers of Congress, and to bring the Congress of the United States into disgrace, ridicule, hatred, contempt, and reproach, and to destroy the regard and respect of all the people of the United States for their authority."

Mr. Johnson was the lawful President of the United States; one of his sworn duties was to "take care that the laws be faithfully executed." The Thirty-Ninth Congress was a lawful Congress, as much so as any that ever sat. They were elected by exactly the same constituency who elected Mr. Johnson Vice President in 1864. Under their legislation the rebellion was put down, and Mr. Johnson himself, as military governor of Tennessee, had aided actively in carrying it out, and had had the benefit of the joint resolution of February, 1865, excluding from the count of electoral votes for President and Vice President those cast in certain of the States in rebellion. It did not, therefore, lie in his mouth to deny, directly or indirectly, that the Thirty-Ninth Congress was a valid, constitutional Congress. None but such as contended that the Government was broken up by the secession and rebellion of the eleven States—that is, none but a traitor could consistently and decently make such a declaration. And yet he says, in his 18th of August speech, (referred to in the first specification,) made in the Executive Mansion, and addressed to the honorable Senator from Maryland [Mr. JOHNSON] and others, and without rebuke or reply from that learned Senator, "We have seen hanging upon the verge of the Government, as it were, a body called, or which assumes to be, the Congress of the United States, while, in fact, it is a Congress of only a part of the States;" plainly intimating that that Congress had no power to pass laws for the government of the rebel States, and were, in fact and in law, incompetent to legislate for the whole country; a doctrine that openly encouraged sedition and disobedience to the laws in at least those States, if not in all others—the laws which he alone, of all the people of the United States, was expressly bound by oath and the Constitution to see "faithfully executed."

Suppose a judge of a State court, charged with administering the laws, should go about among the people and tell them thus openly in public speech that the legislation of the State was no legislation—that their laws were all void, and that the citizens were not under obligation to obey them—would not the power of impeachment be at once brought to bear upon him? And why? Because, entertaining such opinions, he desecrates his office, and is therefore UNFIT longer to remain in it. Did we not sustain the impeachment against Judge Humphreys, of Tennessee, for that which was the exact equivalent of this charge, namely, inculcating in a public speech the right of secession from the Union and of rebellion? What did he say, but that the Government of the United States was in law no Government for the seceded States? He had committed no act of treason, and the only proof was that he had thus spoken. And we convicted and removed him because he had thus spoken.

The second and third specifications contain like matter. The vulgar harangues therein recited are in denial of the legal constitutional validity of the statutes passed by the Thirty-Ninth Congress, and tend directly to excite sedition and insubordination to, and disobedience of, those laws, the speaker being himself specially and solely charged by the Constitution with the official duty of taking care that those laws shall be "faithfully executed." He assumes a position in direct antagonism to his oath and his duty. He himself was setting the example of disobedience to the laws, and encouraging others to imitate his wicked example. Does the law impose no responsibility for wanton conduct like this? May a public magistrate deny, contemn, and deride the duties of his office with impunity? His counsel say yes. I say no. Society must be protected by law; and in order that that protection may exist the laws must be respected by those charged with their execution, not aspersed and trampled upon.

No question of the "freedom of speech" arises here. It is not because he speaks scoffingly and contemptuously of Congress as a body; not because he dissents from their legislation merely and expresses that dissent; not because he utters against them the false and malicious calumny that the New Orleans riot, which he calls "another rebellion," "had its origin in the radical Congress;" not because he descends to the low business of lying about and scandalizing them, that the House has preferred this article against him, but because he inculcates the idea that their statutes are no laws, and not to be respected by the people as laws, and because he openly threatens (in his St. Louis speech) to "kick them out; to kick them out just as fast as he can," thus distinctly conveying the threat to use revolutionary violence against that Congress and to disperse them. It was an open threat to commit treason. And yet his counsel tell us that it was innocent and harmless.

To my mind the tenth article charges one of the gravest offenses contained in the impeachment. The feelings of the whole country were shocked and disgusted by the lawless speeches of this bully President. Men and women all over the land hung their heads in shame, and the wise and reflecting saw in him a coarse, designing, and dangerous tyrant.

I vote him guilty under the tenth article, and under each of the three specifications.

As to the eleventh article, it charges in substance that he attempted to prevent the execution of the tenure-of-office act, by unlawfully devising means to prevent Mr. Stanton from resuming the functions of his office, and to prevent the execution of the said clause in the appropriation act of 1867, and the reconstruction act of March 2, 1867.

In finding him guilty under this whole article I only consult his official record, his official history, and the other facts clearly in proof. His whole policy has been that the reconstruction act was both improper and unconstitutional, and he has detested the Thirty-Ninth and Fortieth Congresses, because they have been of an opposite opinion. This trouble has grown out of his determination to govern the rebel States by his executive decrees in defiance of the wishes of the people of the United States expressed through the legislation of Congress; in other words, to be himself the ruling power in this regard. This is usurpation and tyranny, and I think it ought to be thus met and branded. Our position as the first free nation of the world demands it at our hands; and whatever may chance to be the result of this trial, whatever may be the future fortunes of those who are now sitting in judgment, I can desire no better authenticated claim to the free and enlightened approval of future ages than that I gave my vote against him on this article; nor do I think myself capable of any act that would shed greater honor on my posterity than thus to endeavor to vindicate for them and their posterity the rights of a free and independent people governing themselves within the limits of their own free Constitution.

OPINION
OF
HON. JAMES W. PATTERSON,

We have been brought to a new illustration and test of our institutions. The responsibility of the Chief Magistrate to the people and their power to remove him from his place, if faithless and treacherous to his high trusts, are on trial in the Senate. If before civil order is restored and the animosities of war allayed the temper of forty millions of people shall be self-controlled; if the currents of business are uninterrupted and society discharges its ordinary functions without disorder, as the case passes to its final issue of conviction or acquittal, it will not only prove the capacity of the people for self-government, but will reassure the strength and stability of the Republic. It will be a triumph of popular institutions which must unsettle the foundations of arbitrary power, and hasten the establishment of free governments.

The first of the articles exhibited by the House of Representatives against the President of the United States, charges a violation of the Constitution of the United States, and of an act regulating the tenure of certain civil offices, passed March 2, 1867, in the issuance of "an order, in writing, for the removal of Edwin M. Stanton from the office of Secretary for the Department of War."

It is alleged that this was done contrary to the provisions of the Constitution, and with the intent to violate the act above named, and was, therefore, a high misdemeanor, for which he should be removed from office.

First, was it a violation of the Constitution? An unlimited power of removal from office cannot, I think, belong to the President by force of the Constitution. There certainly is no word in that instrument which confers any such authority directly. It says "the executive power shall be vested in a President of the United States of America," but that power is limited by the letter of the Constitution, and by direct grants of power to other departments of the Government. If the Executive possesses the right of removal in the case of officers appointed by the coördinate action of himself and the Senate, it must be by implication.

The Constitution says the President "shall nominate, and, by and with the advice and consent of the Senate, appoint," &c. Now, the

right to remove cannot be drawn from the right to nominate, and if it comes from the right to appoint, then it exists conjointly in the President and Senate.

There is an objection to this doctrine, however, more fundamental. We cannot by inference lodge in the President a power which would enable him to destroy another power vested expressly in the legislative branch of the Government. The Constitution coördinates the Senate with the President in the appointment of the higher officials. Hamilton, in speaking of this, says:

"It would be an excellent check upon a spirit of favoritism in the President, and would tend greatly to prevent the appointment of unfit characters from State prejudice, from family connection, from personal attachment, or from a view to popularity. In addition to this, it would be an efficacious source of stability in the Administration."

But it will be readily seen that if the President has the right to remove and make "ad interim" appointments at pleasure, the coördinate function of the Senate in appointments may become a nullity, and the purpose of the Constitution be defeated. It destroys at one blow this great safeguard against usurpation and maladministration in the Executive.

Without delaying to discuss this subject further, I simply say, that to my mind a natural interpretation of the Constitution would give the appointing and removing power to the same parties.

But the acts of 1789 and 1795 gave a legislative construction adverse to this view, and whether these acts are repealed or not, if it can be shown that the President violated no law in the removal of Mr. Stanton it would be clearly unjust to impeach him for having conformed to a legislative construction of the Constitution unquestioned for fifty years against the views and wishes of the majority of Congress. So heavy a judgment should not fall upon the Chief Magistrate for having followed an exposition of the fundamental law, authorized by solemn enactment, and supported by some of the ablest among the earlier statesmen of the Republic.

The second allegation in the article is a violation of law in the removal of Mr. Stanton.

The respondent urges a threefold defense against this charge:

First. That the non-execution of the act of March 2, 1867, "regulating the tenure of certain civil offices," was not a breach of executive trusts, as the law was unconstitutional and void.

Second. That a denial of the validity of the act and an intentional disregard of its provisions in order to bring the statute into court and test its constitutionality is not an impeachable offense.

Third. That the language of the statute does not include Mr. Stanton, and hence his removal was no violation of law.

Whether the President had or had not a constitutional right to remove at pleasure officers confirmed by the Senate was the theme of the great debate in 1789 upon the establishment of the State Department. It was purely a question of interpretation, and was argued upon both sides by lawyers of unsurpassed ability. Even the great statesmen who had been master spirits in the constitutional Convention, and whose genius had passed largely into the framework of the Government, entered the lists and battled earnestly on either side. When the Constitution was before the State conventions for adoption the Federalist expressly denied this right to the Executive, but the Congress of 1789 reversed that interpretation which had received the popular approval by a close vote of thirty-four to twenty in the House and by the casting vote of the Vice President in the Senate. It is believed that the character of Washington, then Chief Magistrate, largely influenced the result, and statesmen as patriotic and enlightened as any who took part in the deliberations of the First Congress have since deprecated a construction which they believe a hazardous and unwarranted change of the Constitution.

In 1835, a committee of Congress, composed of such men as Calhoun, Webster, and Benton, reported a bill designed to limit the abuse of executive patronage, and requiring the President in all cases of removal to state the reasons thereof. In the debate, Mr. Clay spoke as follows:

"It is legislative authority which creates the office, defines its duties, and may prescribe its duration. I speak, of course, of offices not created by the Constitution, but the law. The office coming into existence by the will of Congress, the same will may provide how and in what manner the office and officer shall cease to exist. It may direct the conditions on which he shall hold the office, and when and how he shall be dismissed.

"It would be unreasonable to contend that, although Congress, in pursuance of the public good, brings the office and the officer into being, and assign their purposes, yet the President has a control over the officer which Congress cannot reach and regulate." * * * "The precedent of 1789 was established in the House of Representatives against the opinion of a large and able minority, and in the Senate by the casting vote of the Vice President, John Adams. It is impossible to read the debate which it occasioned without being impressed with the conviction that the just confidence reposed in the Father of his Country, then at the head of the Government, had great, if not decisive, influence in establishing it. It has never, prior to the commencement of the present administration, been submitted to the process of review." * * * "No one can carefully examine the debate in the House of Representatives in 1789 without being struck with the superiority of the argument on the side of the minority, and the unsatisfactory nature of that of the majority."

The language of Mr. Webster was not less explicit or emphatic:

"I think, then, sir, that the power of appointment naturally and necessarily includes the power of removal, where no limitation is expressed, nor any tenure but that at will declared. The power of appointment being conferred on the President and Senate, I think the power of removal went along with it, and should have been regarded as a part of it and exercised by the same hands. I think the Legislature possesses the power of regulating the condition, duration, qualification, and tenure of office in all cases where the Constitution has made no express

provision on the subject. I am, therefore, of opinion that it is competent for Congress to decide by law, as one qualification of the tenure of office, that the incumbent shall remain in place till the President shall remove him, for reasons to be stated to the Senate. And I am of opinion that this qualification, mild and gentle as it is, will have some effect in arresting the evils which beset the progress of the Government and seriously threaten its future prosperity." * * * * *

"After considering the question again and again within the last six years, I am willing to say that, in my deliberate judgment, the original decision was wrong. I cannot but think that those who denied the power of 1789 had the best of the argument. It appears to me, after thorough and repeated and conscientious examination, that an erroneous interpretation was given to the Constitution in this respect by the decision of the First Congress."

* * * * * *

"I have the clearest conviction that they [the Convention] looked to no other mode of displacing an officer than by impeachment or the regular appointment of another person to the same place."

* * * * *

"I believe it to be within the just power of Congress to reverse the decision of 1789, and I mean to hold myself at liberty to act hereafter upon that question as the safety of the Government and of the Constitution may require."

Mr. Calhoun and Mr. Ewing were equally positive in their advocacy of the bill, and Marshall, Kent, and Story seem to have entertained similar views in respect to the original intent of the Constitution.

But there has been a conflict of legislative constructions as well as of individual opinions upon this subject. Subsequent Congresses have claimed and exercised, without the obstruction of an executive veto, the power to regulate the tenure of office, both civil and military.

A law of February 25, 1863, provides that the Comptroller of the Currency "shall hold his office for the term of five years unless sooner removed by the President *by and with the advice and consent of the Senate.*"

By section five of an act of July 13, 1866, it is provided that—

"No officer in the military or naval service shall in time of peace *be dismissed from service except upon and in pursuance of the sentence of a court-martial, to* that effect or in commutation thereof."

These are late acts, but they are only instances of other similar acts scattered through our statutes, whose validity has never been questioned. There is, therefore, no decision of the Supreme Court or settled precedent of legislation which can bar the right of Congress to regulate by law both appointments to and removals from office. Never until now, so far as I know, has the right been questioned. Whatever differences of opinion legislators may have entertained in respect to the original grant of power, all have acquiesced in the exercise of legislative authority over the tenure of office.

Hence the claim of the President of a judicial right to settle *ex cathedra* the constitutionality of a law upon this subject is inadmissible and subversive of the powers and independence of a coördinate branch of the Government. In a clear case of a legislative usurpation of his constitutional prerogatives, such as would occur in an effort to destroy his veto or pardoning power, he might be justified in treating the act as a nullity, but not when Congress moves in the path of authoritative precedents, and where, at most, only a doubt can be raised against its original right of its jurisdiction.

At an earlier period I apprehend such a claim would not have been advanced. Civil war naturally tends to concentrate power in the chief who administers it. Forces and resources must be at his disposal. Defeat waits upon the commander who is hampered by the forms and delays of law. His authority is nothing if not supreme. The laws of war are swift and absolute and can recognize no personal rights, no claims of Magna Charta. Active warfare necessarily encroaches upon the domain of legislation, and familiarizes the Executive with a use of authority hazardous in a time of peace.

Power once possessed is soon felt to be a right and is yielded with reluctance. Our experience has added another example to the long record of history. The President's defense denies the supremacy of law and is more dangerous to the Government than the alleged crime which has brought him to the bar of the Senate. If he can determine the validity of law, the Supreme Court is an empty mockery. No act can pass his veto, and all legislation may be subverted at pleasure. The right to substitute the judgment of the ruler for the judgment of the people and to override their laws by his will is absolutism. If the plea is good, it is a valid defense for unlimited usurpation.

The plea of the President that he removed Mr. Stanton for the purpose of securing a decision of the court upon the constitutionality of the law is equally untenable as a ground of defense. It is inconsistent with the answer which he made by his counsel, that he effected the removal in the exercise of an executive power of which Congress could not deprive him, "because satisfied that he could not allow the said Stanton to continue to hold the office of Secretary of the Department of War without hazard of the public interests." It is irreconcilable with the further answer that "in his capacity of President of the United States" he "did form the opinion that the case of the said Stanton and his tenure of office were not affected by the first section of the last named act," referring thereby to the tenure-of-office act.

But, passing over the contradictory nature of this defense, we submit that the evidence shows an anxious and persistent effort to get possession of the War Office, and not a purpose to have the law adjudicated. If to test the law had been his desire, he should have sued out a writ of "quo warranto" on the refusal of Stanton to obey his order of removal. Instead of that, he not only endeavored to keep him out of office by an unworthy trick when we had annulled his suspension, but issued a letter of absolute removal in the face

of Congress after it had rejected his judicial opinion of the constitutionality of the law, and had passed it by a two-thirds vote over his veto. After it had reaffirmed the validity of its action and the invalidity of his on this very subject, and assuming that the removal had been effected, he issued a letter of authority to fill the vacancy. To crown the effrontery he nominates General Scofield to the vacant Secretaryship, while urging upon the Senate his acquittal on the ground that the removal was not effected, but only attempted. Thus duplicity is made the proof of innocence. Having put the case into a condition in which he could not sue out a writ of quo warranto, I deny that he can honestly plead a desire to test the law. He knew full well if Stanton was not in the law he could not test it by his removal.

This defense is clearly an afterthought. Having recognized the validity of the law by conforming all commissions to its provisions; having suspended Mr. Stanton and appointed General Grant under it; having notified the Secretary of the Treasury of the change, to wit, as follows:

"SIR: In compliance with the requirements of the act entitled 'An act to regulate the tenure of certain civil offices,' you are hereby notified that on the 12th instant Hon. Edwin M. Stanton was suspended from his office as Secretary of War, and General U. S. Grant authorized and empowered to act as Secretary of War ad interim"—

and having afterward transmitted a message to the Senate giving the reasons for the suspension, as required by the act, he cannot, without criminality, under the pretext of seeking a judicial decision, set aside or trample upon the law at the point where it baffled his cherished political policy and curbed a career which the law-makers believed dangerous to the peace and liberties of the country. If regard for the Constitution, and not a desire to get control of the Army, had been his purpose, why did he not test the law in the first instance when called upon to execute it, and when his motive would have been simple and unquestioned? Facts show that it was not the nature but the effect of the law which troubled the President.

The enactment was designed to circumscribe and limit his power, lest he should abuse it to the injury of the country. It was effective; and when it arrested the execution of his policy, regardless alike of his oath and the wishes of the nation, he defiantly violated the law to remove the man who was a trammel upon his will.

The evidence demonstrates a purpose to get possession of the Department of War, and disproves the pretense that he was seeking a judicial decision upon the constitutionality of the law.

Finally, was Mr. Stanton's removal a violation of the act entitled "An act regulating the tenure of certain civil offices."

The purpose of the law was to hold in office men whom the policy of Mr. Johnson threatened to remove. It is both claimed and denied that the Secretary of War who held a commission under President Lincoln is protected by the law. The true construction must be drawn from the letter of the statute itself, and not from any conflicting opinions expressed in debate at the time of its passage.

The first section of the act reads as follows:

"That every person holding any civil office to which he has been appointed by and with the advice and consent of the Senate, and every person who shall hereafter be appointed to any such office, and shall become duly qualified to act therein, is, and shall be, entitled to hold such office until a successor shall have been in like manner appointed and duly qualified, except as herein otherwise provided: *Provided*, That the Secretaries of State, of the Treasury, of War, of the Navy, and of the Interior, the Postmaster General, and the Attorney General, shall hold their offices respectively for and during the term of the President by whom they may have been appointed, and for one month thereafter, subject to removal by and with the advice and consent of the Senate."

It will be observed that the body of the section includes *all persons* who have been or who shall be appointed to civil office by and with the advice and consent of the Senate, "except as herein otherwise provided."

This last clause which I have quoted was in the bill before the committee of conference, who added the proviso, was appointed, and undoubtedly refers to officers mentioned in the fourth section whose term is limited by law. The Secretaries were not of this number, and the effect of the proviso which was added by the conferees was simply to limit their time to the term of the President under whom they serve and one month thereafter.

The meaning of the section clearly is that *every* civil officer who has been confirmed by the Senate shall hold his office until the Senate shall confirm a successor, but provides that such officers as hold a term limited by law shall lose their office by the expiration of their term without the action of the Senate. The only effect of the proviso is to bring the heads of Departments into this last class of officers whose terms are limited by law. The intent and effect of the law is to take the removal of every officer confirmed by the Senate out of the pleasure of the President; and it is a perversion of language to say that the proviso places the tenure of the Secretary of War, or of any other Secretary, at the option of the President. They are all removable by the confirmation of a successor or by the expiration of their term.

It has been said that the proviso brings the office of Secretary of War out of the body of the section into itself, but that the clause which provides that the Secretaries "shall hold their offices respectively for and during the term of the President by whom they may have been appointed, and for one month thereafter," excludes Mr. Stanton from it because he was not appointed by Mr. Johnson.

The office could not be taken out of the body of the section unless it was first in it, and if there, the Secretary was there also. If, now, the office of Secretary of War is brought into the proviso, and Mr. Stanton excluded, he is left in the section and covered by its provisions. If not there, to what limbo have the gods assigned him?

The conception of a Secretary of War without an office is worthy of a lawyer without a brief. The argument is a pure creation, and a miserable fallacy at that. The language of the section is in relation to persons, not offices. It says, "every person holding any civil office shall be entitled to hold," &c.; "the Secretaries, &c., shall hold their offices," &c. The construction of the section is simple and unmistakable. There are certain officers referred to in the fourth section whose terms are limited by law, and the proviso adds the heads of Departments to this number, but the terms of the law allow no officer to be *removed* who has been appointed by and with the advice and consent of the Senate, except by the appointment of a successor in the same way.

The language of the proviso itself is, that the Secretaries are "subject to removal by and with the advice and consent of the Senate." If, therefore, Mr. Stanton is not in the proviso, he is in the body of the section, and the law was violated by his removal. I will not stay to inquire in whose term he was holding, for the argument is perfect without it.

This is not all. The President violated the second as well as the first section of the law. It reads as follows:

"That when any officer appointed as aforesaid, excepting judges of the United States courts, shall, during a recess of the Senate, be shown, by evidence satisfactory to the President, to be *guilty of misconduct in office, or crime, or for any reason shall become incapable or legally disqualified to perform its duties, in such case, and in no other, the President may suspend such officer*," &c.

If, now, the President can suspend an officer during the *recess only*, and that for the reasons specified in the law and *no other*, can he remove him outright during the *session* of the Senate, and when he is free from all the legal disqualifications enumerated in the act?

The act further provides, in respect to a suspension, that—

"If the Senate shall concur in such suspension, and advise and consent to the removal of such officer, they shall so certify to the President, who may thereupon remove such officer. But if the Senate shall refuse to concur in such suspension, such officer so suspended shall forthwith resume the functions of his office," &c.

The Senate refused to concur in the suspension of Mr. Stanton, refused to advise and consent to his removal, but the President removed him in defiance of the letter of the act and of the will of the Senate. No amount of genius for legal sophistries can torture that act of the President into anything less than a willful violation of law. This simple statement of the case without argument is sufficient to command the approval of every mind.

Counsel must have forgotten that the Senate, acting under the solemnity of an oath, had repeatedly decided that the law applied to Mr. Stanton. On the 12th of December the Senate, remembering that the "tenure-of-office act" was passed expressly to protect officers whose retention was thought indispensable to the public service against an abuse of executive power, and moved by the eloquent and powerful appeal of the Senator from Maine, refused their assent to the removal of Mr. Stanton, which they had no right to do, or even act upon at all, unless he was covered by the law of March 2, 1867.

Again, on the 21st of February, when the President failed in his attempt to prevent the return of the Secretary by the use of General Grant, informed this body of his absolute dismissal, it was resolved by the Senate—

"That under the Constitution and laws of the United States the President has no power to remove the Secretary of War and to designate any other officer to perform the duties of that office *ad interim*."

With such action upon our records we have a right to assume that argument upon this is foreclosed, and that Senators who took part with the majority in those transactions will sustain the construction which they helped to establish, and upon which the conduct of the Secretary is based.

We are brought next to consider the charges as stated in the second and third articles. It is alleged that the appointment of Lorenzo Thomas as Secretary of War "*ad interim*," was a high misdemeanor, being made without law, and in violation of both law and the Constitution. The provision of the Constitution is, that—

"The President shall have power to fill up all vacancies that may *happen* [not such as he may make] *during the recess* of the Senate, by granting commissions which shall expire at the end of their next session."

This certainly does not confer the right to make "*ad interim*" appointments during the *session* of the Senate, but, by necessary inference, denies it, by expressly granting the power for the recess only. Hence, to fill a *vacancy* in this way, while the Senate is in session and ready to provide for any emergency, is, in the absence of positive law authorizing it, a clear violation of the Constitution. The guilt was in this case enhanced by an attempt to fill an office which the respondent himself claims has never been vacated.

But the President is equally unfortunate in his appeal to *law*. The act of 1789 makes no provision for "*ad interim*" appointments. That of May 2, 1792, authorizes temporary appointments in case of death, absence, or sickness, but not for vacancies created by removal. That of February 13, 1795, allows the President to appoint for six months, "in case of vacancy, whereby the Secretaries or any officer in any of the Departments *cannot perform the duties of his office*."

The construction of this act is somewhat obscure and doubtful. It applies to such vacancies of office as are occasioned by the inability of the officer to "perform the duties of his office." An officer removed cannot perform the duties of his office, it is true, but the natural implication of the language runs *pari passu* with that of 1792, confining it to such vacancies as occur from death, absence, or sickness. But if we give it the broadest application, and cover all vacancies, the limitation of six months placed upon the temporary appointments which it authorizes is designed clearly to cover the interim between the sessions of Congress, and recognizes the hitherto unbroken practice of the Executive to create and fill vacancies only during the recess of the Senate. I conclude, therefore, it was not designed to authorize by this act an appointment like that of General Thomas.

The act of February 20, 1863, fails equally to provide for this case.

But even if these statutes by a proper construction covered the action of the President, he cannot use them, for they have been swept away by the tenure-of-office act, and he is remitted to its provisions alone, which explicitly prohibited any such appointment.

If the first and second sections take from him, as I have argued, the right to remove Stanton, then there was no vacancy, and the appointment of Thomas was made "contrary to the provisions of this act," and was by the sixth section of the same a high misdemeanor.

It has been urged that the last clause of the third section empowers the President to make such an appointment, but an examination of the section shows this to be a perversion. It simply provides that in case the Senate shall fail to fill a vacancy which has occurred by *death* or *resignation* during the recess of the same, such officers as may *by law exercise such powers and duties* shall exercise all the powers and duties belonging to such office *so vacant*, but that "such office shall remain in abeyance without any salary, fees, or emoluments attached thereto, until the same shall be filled by appointment thereto *by and with the advice and consent of the Senate*."

General Thomas was not so appointed. The law cannot possibly be stretched to cover and justify his case.

Equally fallacious is the interpretation which has been given to the eighth section. This simply makes it the duty of the President to notify the Secretary of the Treasury whenever he shall have "designated, authorized or employed any person to perform the duties of any office" temporarily vacated, as designated in the third article.

This is the whole extent of its meaning, and it cannot be so tortured as to authorize an "*ad interim*" appointment made during the session of the Senate.

I conclude, therefore, that the President having violated the act of March 2, 1867, as alleged in the first, second, and third articles, is guilty of a high misdemeanor.

Of the fourth, sixth, seventh, and ninth

articles, I need not speak, as the trial failed entirely, to my apprehension, in establishing the allegations therein set forth by any substantial proof. No satisfactory evidence was presented to my mind of a conspiracy as alleged in either of the articles. In this I think the House entirely failed to make good their charges.

The fifth article charges that the President conspired with Lorenzo Thomas and others to "prevent and hinder the execution of an act entitled 'An act regulating the tenure of certain civil offices,' and in pursuance of said conspiracy did unlawfully attempt to prevent Edwin M. Stanton" from holding the office of Secretary of War. That there was an understanding between the President and Thomas that the latter was to be substituted for Stanton in the office of Secretary of War, in disregard of the act of March 2, 1867, is clear, but that there was any concert to use force to bring it about does not appear from the evidence.

The eighth article charges upon Andrew Johnson a high misdemeanor, in that he issued a letter of authority to Lorenzo Thomas, transferring to him the office of Secretary for the Department of War, in violation of law, when there was no vacancy in said office, and when the Senate was in session, with intent unlawfully to control the disbursements of the moneys appropriated for the military service and for the Department of War.

I have already given my opinion upon the issuance of the letter to Thomas in what I have said in respect to the second and third articles. That a control of the money appropriated for the military service and the Department of War was a principal motive for securing the place of Mr. Stanton is self-evident, for without it the office could not be administered, and would be a vain and useless shadow of power. I do not see that this article adds anything new, for the gravamen of the charge is involved in the third article. The final judgment upon this must be the same as upon that.

The facts alleged in the tenth article are known and read of all men, and are not denied by the respondent. That the speeches referred to in this article were "slanderous harangues," showing not only a want of culture, but the entire absence of good sense, good taste, or good temper, nobody can deny. But in view of the liberty of speech which our laws authorize, in view of the culpable license of speech which is practiced and allowed in other branches of the Government, I doubt if we can at present make low and scurrilous speeches a ground of impeachment. I say this in sorrow, and not in any spirit of palliation, for the speeches referred to in the charges were infamous and blasphemous, and could not have been uttered by any man worthy to hold the exalted position of Chief Magistrate of an intelligent and virtuous people. Personal decency should be deemed essential to high official responsibility in this Republic, but it must be secured by a public sentiment which shall exact virtue rather than availability in those whom it advances to the great trusts of society. When we reflect how essential to national welfare and human progress is that liberty of speech which we have inherited, and how readily a restriction upon its abuse may turn to an abuse upon its restriction, we hesitate to inflict a merited penalty upon this prominent offender. We deem it safer to—

> "Bear those ills we have,
> Than fly to others that we know not of."

There are four distinct allegations in the eleventh article. The first relates to the President's misrepresentations of Congress in public speech, and has already been reviewed in considering the tenth article.

The second charges a violation of "an act regulating the tenure of certain civil offices," by unlawfully devising and contriving, and attempting to devise and contrive, means to prevent Mr. Stanton from resuming his office of Secretary of War after the Senate had refused to concur in his suspension. This is a charge not mentioned in any preceding article, and its proof is unequivocal and satisfactory.

The attempt was made through General Grant, and the President's letter of reproof to that distinguished citizen for defeating his wicked purpose by refusing to participate with him in a premeditated breach of law and contempt of the Senate, is the impregnable demonstration of the allegation. The following is the language of his letter:

"You had found in our first conference 'that the President was desirous of keeping Mr. Stanton out of office, *whether sustained in the suspension or not.*' You knew what reasons had induced the President to ask from you a promise; you also knew that in case your views of duty did not accord with his own convictions it was his purpose to fill your place by another appointment. Even ignoring the existence of a positive understanding between us, these conclusions were plainly deducible from our various conversations. It is certain, however, that even under these circumstances you did not offer to return the place to my possession, but, according to your own statement, placed yourself in a position where, could I have anticipated your action, I would have been compelled to ask of you, as I was compelled to ask of your predecessor, a letter of resignation, or else to resort to the more disagreeable expedient of suspending you by a successor."

The third and fourth allegations of this article do not seem to have received that attention which their importance would justify. The evidence upon the records by which they are supported is very slight. I have been the more surprised at this inasmuch as the last sets forth that the President attempted to prevent the execution of the act entitled "An act to provide for the more efficient government of the rebel States." This I have deemed the *primum mobile* which has impelled the entire policy of the Executive.

This has been the motive of all our exceptional legislation; this has prolonged and multiplied our sessions; this has distracted business, and protracted the unrest of society, and this will be the crowning infamy of an Adminstration inaugurated by assassination. All these willful violations of law have drawn their inspiration from this fell intent. If they had been only technical and inadvertent lapses or had resulted from misapprehension they might be pardoned, but being specimens from a flagrant catalogue of persistent law-breaking public safety demands a resort to constitutional remedies.

There may be wise and patriotic men who fear lest conviction should impress a habit of instability upon our institutions and unsettle ithe foundations of society. No statesman should be censured for a prudent forecast, but he should not hesitate to use the means which the experience of ages has shown to be essential safeguards of popular rights. The English ministry retire with every defeat, and these frequent changes of administration strengthen rather than weaken the Government. A people careless and not over-jealous of their rights are in danger of overthrow. History teaches that great wars enhance the powers of the Executive at the expense of popular rights, and that powers once exercised are likely to be held as an inalienable prerogative. We are no exception to the rule. With us, the temptation of the Chief Magistrate to overstep his authority is even greater than in Governments where executive power is less limited. It is difficult for a ruler who has used for years without wrong the unlimited powers of war to restrict himself at once, on the return of peace, to the narrow limits then essential to the security of popular rights.

Abraham Lincoln in a few instances transcended the ordinary exercise of executive authority, and we legalized it as a military necessity. Four years of laborious, patriotic, suffering life, devoted to a rescue of the liberties and integrity of the Republic, were the pledges he gave that he would not usurp or abuse his power for the gratification of either revenge or ambition. Andrew Johnson has no such excuse and can give no such security when he oversteps his constitutional limits and sets aside law.

There have been no "public considerations of a high character" to justify his high-handed usurpation of power. There was nothing in the personal character and nothing in the official conduct of this distinguished minister of war, who, more than the great French minister, may be said to have "organized victory," which could give the shadow of a pretext for his suspension or removal. His offense was that at the expense of personal comfort he fulfilled the purpose of Congress and checked, if he did not baffle the effort of the Executive to arrest the legal and peaceful reorganization of the South. His obedience to the spirit and letter of our laws "constrained" the President to "cause him to surrender the office."

If the President is convicted he suffers for a violation of law: if acquitted, Mr. Stanton suffers for obedience to the law. Back of the acts for which the former is on trial lie the three years of malignant obstruction of law and public order pouring a wicked intent into the allegations of this indictment. Back of this attempted removal of Mr. Stanton lies the splendid record of the great Secretary, which will hereafter thread your history like a path of gold. Who shall fall in the final issue, he who obeys or he who defies your legislation?

If conviction may impress instability upon our institutions, acquittal may destroy the original adjustment and balance of their powers and hasten their overthrow. The lessons of history warn us rather against the indulgence than the arrest of arbitrary power.

When power flows back into the hands of the people it only returns to its original and rightful source; but when it passes up into the hands of a usurper, the reign of despotism is inaugurated. History has been a perpetual struggle between popular rights and personal ambition, and experience shows that we do not utter empty words when we say that "vigilance is the price of liberty."

As a member of the House of Representatives, I voted under the obligations of an oath, for the act of March 2, 1867, with a clear understanding that it protected Mr. Stanton as Secretary of War against removal at pleasure by the President; and now, when he is brought to our bar, to be tried for the consummation of that act, I but discharge a solemn duty, from which I cannot escape, when, as a Senator, I pronounce Andrew Johnson guilty of a violation of that law.

OPINION
OF
HON. CHARLES R. BUCKALEW.

THE STANTON ARTICLE.

The first article of impeachment, which charges the issuing of the order for the removal of Edwin M. Stanton from his office of Secretary of War upon the 21st February, 1868, is the most important one of the articles, and presents itself first for consideration. It is charged that that order was unlawfully issued with intent to violate the tenure-of-office act of March 2, 1867, and contrary to the Constitution of the United States, and that by issuing it the President did commit and was guilty of a high misdemeanor in office.

Was the order for the removal of Mr. Stanton authorized by the Constitution and laws of the United States, or was it in violation of either or both? The argument upon this question has been prolonged and exhaustive; but to a just conclusion it will only be necessary to examine a few points and place them in their proper relations to each other and to the general question involved.

As a constitutional question, the executive power to remove from office may be placed upon those two provisions of the Constitution of the United States which declare that the exécutive power pf the Government shall be vested in the President, and that he shall take care that the laws be faithfully executed. The power to remove being executive in its nature, and its exercise, upon fit occasions, being necessary to the due execution of the laws, it is insisted that it is vested in the President by these provisions of the Constitution. And such was the decision of Congress after full debate in 1789.

If this construction of the Constitution be a true construction there can be no doubt that the President had due authority to issue the order for the removal of Mr. Stanton.

But the power of the President to remove a Secretary of War from office is clearly declared by the second section of the act of the 7th of August, 1789, organizing the War Department. That section reads as follows :

"There shall be in said Department an inferior officer, to be appointed by the said principal officer, to be employed therein as he shall deem proper, to be called the Chief Clerk in the Department of War, and who, *whenever the said principal officer shall be removed from office by the President of the United States*, or in any case of vacancy, shall during such vacancy have the charge and custody of all records, books, and papers appertaining to the said Department."

Whether this section simply admits that the President has power to remove by virtue of the Constitution or confers the power upon him is not material to our present purpose. In either case it is a legislative declaration that he can remove the Secretary, the "principal officer" in the Department of War.

Again, it is in evidence and undenied that Secretaries of War have always been appointed and commissioned to hold their office "during the pleasure of the President of the United States for the time being," and Mr. Stanton's commission—the only one ever issued to him—is in that form.

It only remains to inquire whether recent legislation has changed the tenure of office of the Secretary of War so as to impair or destroy the President's power of removal. The first section of the tenure-of-office act of 2d March, 1867, is as follows :

"That any person holding any civil office to which he has been appointed by and with the advice and consent of the Senate, and every person who shall hereafter be appointed to any such office and shall become duly qualified to act therein, is and shall be entitled to hold such office until a successor shall have been in like manner appointed and duly qualified, except as herein otherwise provided : *Provided*, That the Secretaries of State, of the Treasury, of War, of the Navy, and of the Interior, the Postmaster General and the Attorney General, shall hold their offices respectively for and during the term of the President by whom they may have been appointed and for one month thereafter, subject to removal by and with the advice and consent of the Senate."

The proviso of this section puts the heads of Departments into a class by themselves, but cannot have practical effect upon four of the Secretaries who were appointed to office by Mr. Lincoln, namely, the Secretary of State, the Secretary of War, the Secretary of the Treasury, and the Secretary of the Navy. They were appointed by Mr. Lincoln in his first term and were commissioned by him, in the usual form which then obtained, to hold their offices "during the pleasure of the President of the United States for the time being." Theirs was then a tenure at will ; they were to hold at the pleasure of the President who appointed them, or of his successor, whoever that successor might be.

The Secretary of the Interior, the Postmaster General, and the Attorney General had been appointed by Mr. Johnson and had received commissions in the same form. So stood the case as to the heads of Departments when the tenure-of-office act was passed.

The proviso, therefore, in declaring that heads of Departments should hold during the term of the President by whom they may have been appointed and for one month thereafter, could not have the practical effect of expanding or changing the tenure upon which the Lincoln Secretaries held their offices ; for the term of the President who appointed them, and during which they were appointed, expired March 4, 1865, and they were never reappointed after its expiration. Besides, Mr. Johnson's term began in April, 1865, and when the law was passed, March 2, 1867, there was no term running of a President by whom they had been appointed. There can be no pretense of an appointment of them by Mr. Johnson or by Mr. Lincoln in his second term, from the fact that they held over after March 4, 1865. No new commissions were issued to them, and in fact no new appointments were possible without the advice and consent of the Senate, which was never asked for or given.

In my opinion, all Secretaries, present and future, were within the descriptive words of the proviso, but the Lincoln Secretaries were not practically within the operation of the new tenure which that proviso established. They were within the words which distinguished and separated heads of Departments from other civil officers of the Government, but not effectually brought within the new tenure rule. For purposes of classification all heads of Departments were named in the proviso and excluded from the body of the section, but the tenure of those Secretaries was not in fact changed, but was left as before.

No one can doubt the complete application of the tenure-of-office act to all heads of Departments appointed by future Presidents. They will all hold during the term of the President who shall appoint them, and for one month thereafter ; there will be no exceptions. If a President shall be chosen for a second term the members of his Cabinet must be reappointed if they are to hold for more than one month in his new term. But suppose a President shall die, resign, or be removed from office before his term shall run out? Will his Cabinet be fastened upon his successor for one month only or for the remainder of the full term? Will a Secretary appointed March 4, 1869, be entitled to hold for a fixed and indefeasible term of four years and one month, or may he lose his place sooner by the death, resignation, or removal of the President who appoints him? Now, this is, in one view, an important inquiry in fixing the construction of the tenure-of-office act in its application to the case before us. For if it shall appear that upon the death, resignation, or removal of a future President his Cabinet will go out at the end of one month, there is no ground left for the argument that Mr. Stanton now holds his office under the law. He can claim to hold it only upon the ground of the non-expiration of Mr. Lincoln's second term. If that term expired with Mr. Lincoln's life he has no standing whatever in any forum of honest debate.

In my opinion, in case of the death, resignation, or removal of a future President, his Cabinet will go out of office at the end of one month. A President takes a four-year term subject to the implied condition that he shall live so long and shall not resign or be removed upon impeachment. His term ends when for any cause he vacates or is removed from his office and can no longer perform its duties. The term of the Emperor Charles V ended when he resigned his crown; that of James II when Parliament declared he had abdicated the throne by withdrawing himself from the realm. In the ordinary case of an officer of the United States who holds for a term of years, if he die, resign, or be removed from office pending his term, the term ends and his successor takes a new full term. But it may be said that our present case is a peculiar one, because a Vice President is provided to fill out the term of a President, who dies, resigns, or is removed. The Constitution does not say that. It says that in case of the death, &c., of the President, the duties of the presidential office shall devolve upon the Vice President. If it be a case of temporary disability of the President the Vice President will perform the duties of the office until the disability shall be removed. If it be a case of vacancy in the presidential office the Vice President will perform the duties of the office *during the time or term for which he was elected Vice President.* He becomes President in fact, not for the term of another, but for his own.

The Constitution provides that when there is no President or Vice President to discharge the duties of the presidential office, such duties shall be discharged by some other officer to be designated by law, until a new President shall be chosen. But under an existing law (act of March 1, 1792) such choice of a new President may possibly be made by electors, two or three years before the running out of the former President's term, and yet the new President will be chosen and will hold for a full four-year term. The old and the new terms will not overlap each other in such case, will not be coexistent to any extent, because the

C. I.—67.

former ends with the event, whatever it may be, which causes the vacancy in the presidential office.

We may conclude, then, that the words *" the term of the President"* mentioned in the tenure-of-office act and in the Constitution is the actual period of service of a President—including any time of temporary disability—and that such term may end by death, resignation, or removal, as well as by the regular expiration of four years. It follows that Mr. Stanton could not claim to hold his place as Secretary of War under the tenure created by the proviso to the first section of the tenure-of-office act, even though he had been appointed in fact or constructively in Mr. Lincoln's second term of service as President of the United States. In no sense can it be said that he is holding his office in or during "the term of the President" by whom he was appointed.

But if this be granted it becomes evident that his case is quite outside of the tenure-of-office act, and wholly unaffected by it. And the plain words of the act of 1789, and the language of his commission, declare him to be subject to removal at the pleasure of the President.

I shall not examine at length the adroit argument which places Mr. Stanton's case within the body of the first section of the tenure-of-office act upon its logical expulsion from the proviso. This is evidently an after thought, which can derive but little support from verbal criticism, and none whatever from the history or policy of the law. Plainly the purpose of the law was to put all heads of Departments in a separate class and attach them to the particular Presidents by whom they are appointed. No President shall have Secretaries imposed upon him whom he has not selected, nor (as I construe the law) shall he be compelled to retain in a second term those he had selected in his first. He may once in any term freely choose his advisers, (subject only to senatorial confirmation,) but if reëlected he is not bound to keep them, nor can he in any case impose them upon his successor. The law only binds him to retain them (when once chosen) during the term, or remainder of the term, in which they are selected, and then they retire.

But this evident policy of the law is in flat contradiction of the argument which places Mr. Stanton's case within the body of the section, and assigns to him a tenure of indefinite duration in the future. No future President (any more than the present one in case of his reëlection) could shake off this Secretary without the consent of the Senate, if this argument be sound.

Not one word was uttered in either House of Congress when the act was passed indicating that the Lincoln Secretaries were included or intended to be included in the body of the first section; but a most explicit statement was made by Senator Sherman (without dissent from any quarter) that they were excluded from the protection of the act and would remain subject to removal by the President.

It is charged in the first article of impeachment as an ingredient of the offense therein alleged to have been committed by the President, or as a serious aggravation thereof, that the order for the removal of Mr. Stanton was issued during a session of the Senate and without senatorial advice and consent. This particular accusation was supposed by many in the outset of this controversy to be unanswerable. But it possesses no importance whatever. For neither the constitutional argument for executive power to make removals from office, nor the act of 1789 organizing the War Department, nor any other former statute relating to removals, nor the practice of the Government, recognizes any distinction of time (in making removals) between session and recess. The President in all cases where he is authorized to remove an officer may remove him during a session of the Senate as well as in a recess between sessions, for aught that appears in the constitutional reasoning, in the legislation, or in the practice of the past.

Prior to 1867 all removals were to be made by the President upon his own responsibility, without senatorial advice or consent. Whether the Senate was in session or not when a removal was made, was, therefore, wholly immaterial to his exercise of his power. The presence of the Senate was of importance only when a new and complete appointment was to be made to fill a vacancy, whether produced by removal or other cause.

Upon the whole we must come to the conclusion, that if Mr. Stanton holds under the tenure-of-office act he cannot be removed, either in session or in recess, without the consent of the Senate; but if he does not hold under that act, then, under the prior laws and practice of the Government, he may be removed by the President at any time. In either case the charge that he was removed during a session of the Senate is unimportant, if not absurd.

The order for the removal of Mr. Stanton was in exact conformity with the precedent in the case of Timothy Pickering, Secretary of State, who was removed from office by President Adams on the 12th of May, 1800.

The first session of the Sixth Congress began December 2, 1799, and ended May 14, 1800. (Trial, p. 595.) The removal was therefore during a session of the Senate. On Saturday May 10, President Adams wrote to Mr. Pickering requesting him to resign, and stating his desire for an answer to his communication "on or before Monday morning, because the nomination of a successor must be sent to the Senate as soon as they shall sit." This last remark was obviously made with reference to the adjournment of Congress; for by resolution of the 21st of April the two Houses had agreed to adjourn the session on Monday, May 12, and a resolution of the Senate to extend the session to the 14th had just been rejected by the House. (8 Senate Journal, 77, 78, 92.) It was necessary, therefore, that a nomination of a successor should be sent to the Senate "as soon as they should sit" on Monday, in order to confirmation before the final adjournment of the session.

Mr. Pickering's answer, refusing to resign, is dated on Monday, the 12th, and it is a fair if not inevitable conclusion, from the facts known to us, that it was sent to the President on the morning of that day. For the President had requested that the answer should be sent to him on or before that morning, and he took action upon the answer, which indicates that he received it at that time. He issued an order dated the 12th, peremptorily discharging Mr. Pickering from further service as Secretary of State, and as soon as the Senate met, on the same day, sent to it a message nominating "John Marshall, of Virginia, to be Secretary of State in place of Timothy Pickering, removed." (Trial, pp. 356, 857.)

On May 12, a resolution passed both Houses extending the session to the 14th, (3 Senate Journal, 92, 94,) and on Tuesday, the 13th, the Senate, in executive session, confirmed the nomination of Judge Marshall as Secretary of State. (Trial, p. 359.)

It is clear, then, that Mr. Pickering was removed during a session of Congress and of the Senate; that he was removed before a nomination of his successor was transmitted to the Senate, and that his successor was confirmed and appointed on a subsequent day.

The views of the managers of the impeachment upon the Pickering case, as expressed by them to the Senate upon this trial, appear to be quite groundless. One of them [Mr. BUTLER] was of opinion that the nomination of Marshall was sent to the Senate before the order of dismissal was sent to Pickering, (Trial, pp. 358, 359, 360,) while another [Mr. BINGHAM] insisted at length that the order of removal was issued before the Senate "had commenced its session," and that President Adams "did not consider that it was proper even under the law of 1789 for him to make that removal during the session of the Senate." (Trial, p. 1173.) Neither one of these contradictory opinions can stand. It is very evident that the removal of Pickering preceded the nomination of Marshall, and it is beyond dispute that the entire transaction was during a session of the Senate, and not in recess. The Senate had been in session for months; it sat on the preceding Saturday, (3 Senate Journal, 92,) and there can be no pretense of a vacation or recess on the Monday when Pickering was removed from office.

The Pickering case is therefore a decisive authority in support of the order for the removal of Stanton.

THE THOMAS ARTICLES.

The second, third, and eighth articles of impeachment charge the designation by the President of General Thomas to perform the duties of Secretary of War *ad interim*, as unlawful, and as constituting a high misdemeanor in office.

I think that that act of the President was authorized by the act of 13th February, 1795, (1 *Statutes-at-Large*, 416.) But in view of the argument that the law of 1795 is no longer in force, it becomes necessary to consider, in connection, the several laws which relate to official vacancies and disability of officers in the several Executive Departments.

The act of 8th of May, 1792, section 8, provides:

"In case of the death, absence from the seat of Government, or sickness of the Secretary of State, Secretary of the Treasury, or of the Secretary of the War Department, or of any officer of either of the said Departments whose appointment is not in the head thereof, whereby they cannot perform the duties of their said respective offices, it shall be lawful for the President of the United States, in case he shall think it necessary, to authorize any person or persons, at his discretion, to perform the duties of the said respective offices until a successor be appointed, or until such absence or inability by sickness shall cease."—1 *Stat.*, 281.

This act, it will be seen, was confined to the Departments of State, of the Treasury, and of War, which were the only ones organized when the act was passed. It will be seen, also, that the act applies only to cases of vacancy occasioned by death, and to cases of disability occasioned by sickness or absence from the seat of Government.

The act of 13th of February, 1795, in its first section, makes further provision, as follows:

"In case of vacancy in the office of Secretary of State, Secretary of the Treasury, or of the Secretary of the Department of War, or of any officer of either of the said Departments, whose appointment is not in the head thereof, whereby they cannot perform the duties of their said respective offices, it shall be lawful for the President of the United States, in case he shall think it necessary, to authorize any person or persons, at his discretion, to perform the duties of said respective offices until a successor be appointed or such vacancy be filled: *Provided*, That no one vacancy shall be supplied in manner aforesaid for a longer term than six months."

This act has no application to cases of temporary disability, but to cases of vacancy alone; but as to such it is comprehensive and includes those of every description. It is, however, like that of 1792, confined to the Departments of State, the Treasury, and War.

Next follows the act of 20th of February, 1863. (12 *Statutes-at-Large*, 65.) Its passage was recommended by President Lincoln in a special message dated 2d of January, 1863, which reads as follows:

"I submit to Congress the expediency of extending to other Departments of the Government the authority conferred on the President by the eighth section of the act of the 8th May, 1792, to appoint a person to temporarily discharge the duties of Secretary of State, Secretary of the Treasury, and Secretary of War, in case of the death, absence from the seat of Government, or sickness, of either of these officers."

In pursuance of this recommendation the act was passed in the following words:

"In case of the death, resignation, absence from the seat of Government, or sickness of the head of any executive Department of the Government, or of any officer of either of the said Departments whose appointment is not in the head thereof, whereby they cannot perform the duties of their respective offices, it shall be lawful for the President of the United States, in case he shall think it necessary, to authorize the head of any other executive Department, or other officer in either of said Departments whose appointment is vested in the President, at his discretion, to perform the duties of the said respective offices until a successor be appointed, or until such absence or inability by sickness shall cease: *Provided*, That no one vacancy shall be supplied in manner aforesaid for a longer term than six months."

It will be observed that this act follows mainly the language of the act of 1792. The particulars in which it departs from it are these:

1. It extends to all the seven Executive Departments instead of being confined to the three which were in existence in 1792.

2. It applies to a case of vacancy by resignation.

3. It authorizes the employment in temporary service in a Department of officers of another Department, instead of "any person" as in the former laws; and lastly, it borrows from the act of 1795 the limitation of six months upon the term of special service in each case provided for.

Now the question is presented—did this act of 1863 repeal by necessary implication the vacancy act of 1795? It provides for the cases of disability covered by the act of 1792, and for cases of vacancy occasioned by death covered by the same act. But it provides further for cases of vacancy occasioned by *resignation* which were not within the act of 1792, but would appear to be within the act of 1795.

It is clear that when a later statute entirely supplies the place of a former one it works its repeal. And so where a later statute contradicts a former one, or is plainly inconsistent with it, the former law falls. In each case supposed, there is an implied or constructive repeal of the old law.

And when the place of an old law is supplied in part by a new one, or is in part plainly inconsistent with a new one, the same result takes place as to such unnecessary or inconsistent parts of the old law.

Now, the act of 1863 makes provision only for vacancies caused by death or resignation, whereas the act of 1795 extended to all cases of vacancy, including those caused by removal or expiration of term of service. As there is no express repeal of the old law, and as the new one does not fully supply its place, the old law must remain partly in force and still apply to cases of vacancy caused by removal or expiration of term.

And this view is strengthened by considering the fact that the act of 1863 was asked for by Mr. Lincoln for no purpose of repealing former laws, but to extend the disabilities act of 1792 to all the Executive Departments.

It may be insisted upon further, that whereas the act of 1795 did not repeal the act of 1792, that of 1863 cannot be held to repeal the act of 1795. Now, the act of 1792 was often acted upon in the practice of the Government down to recent times, and it was referred to by Mr. Lincoln as a subsisting law in his communication to Congress of 2d January, 1863. If, then, the act of 1795 did not repeal the act of 1792 because it provided for a case of vacancy by death, and thus far supplied the former law, the act of 1863 cannot be held to repeal the act of 1795 because it provides for cases of vacancy by death and by resignation. In each case the elder statute continues in force except so far as its place is filled by the younger.

The argument so far proceeds upon the ground that the act of 1863 is to some extent inconsistent with the former laws and partially displaces them. But is it clear that it is inconsistent with those laws? The former laws authorize the President to designate "*any person*" to discharge the duties of an office *ad interim* in case of vacancy therein or disability of the incumbent. Is it certain that these words, "*any person*," should be held to include any officer of the Government without regard to the character of his office or the duties and responsibilities charged upon him by law? An officer under bond, if taken away from his proper office and appropriate duties, could not be held responsible upon his bond for any default caused thereby (nor his sureties either) without gross injustice; and many other difficulties might be suggested upon such construction of the law. At all events, one would think that a very clear, specific, express provision by statute would be necessary to withdraw an officer from the duties of an office to which he had been assigned by due appointment under the Constitution (upon senatorial confirmation) and assign him to duty in another office. The act of 1863 provides specifically that this may be done, and thus gave a legal sanction to a practice which had obtained to some extent before its passage. But it is very doubtful whether the disability and vacancy acts of 1792 and 1795 conferred this power of transferring officers from one office to another upon the President. If they did not, the act of 1863 may be held as additional to and not restrictive of the provisions of the former laws, and all question of inconsistency between them will disappear. The former laws may then be held to stand good as to *all* cases arising under them, and to authorize *ad interim* authority to "any persons" not heads of or presidential appointees in the Departments and charged with other duties by law.

The rules for the construction of statutes cited on behalf of the defense on this trial tell very strongly against the argument for the implied repeal of the act of 1795 by the act of 1863. Repeals by implication are not favored by the law; where a later statute is not plainly inconsistent with a former one, both shall stand; remedial statute shall be construed liberally, so 'as to secure fully their object. These and other rules sanctioned by the wisdom of ages fully protect the statute of 1795 against the argument of the prosecution, and give to it a complete sanction as an existing law. Assuming that that act continued in force as to vacancies occasioned by removal, it justified, beyond all question, the letter of authority to General Thomas of 21st February, authorizing him to perform the duties of Secretary of War *ad interim*, and the second, third, and eighth articles of impeachment are wholly without support.

It has been said that the tenure-of-office act repeals all prior laws which authorized *ad interim* service in the Executive Departments, but the fact is not so. The tenure-of-office act has no repealing clause, and its eighth section does most clearly recognize the validity of *ad interim* selections for executive offices. That section is as follows:

"That whenever the President shall, without the advice and consent of the Senate, designate, authorize, or employ any person to perform the duties of any office, he shall forthwith notify the Secretary of the Treasury thereof; and it shall be the duty of the Secretary of the Treasury thereupon to communicate such notice to all the proper accounting and disbursing officers of his Department."

Passing now from the general question of *ad interim* legislation, it remains to inquire whether the letter of authority to General Thomas was forbidden by any provision of the tenure-of-office act. The sixth section of that act provides:

"That every removal, appointment, or employment, made, had, or exercised *contrary to the provisions of this act*, and the making, signing, sealing, countersigning, or issuing of any commission or letter of authority, for or in respect to any *such* appointment or employment, shall be deemed, and are hereby declared to be, high misdemeanors," &c.

Now, an act done which is declared to be a high misdemeanor by this section must be one which is "contrary to the provisions" of this act. And it is evident that it must contravene some provision of the first, second, or third sections, because those alone relate to the subject-matter of removal and appointment. But it has been shown already that Mr. Stanton's case is not within the first section of the act, and that that section could not be violated by his removal and the designation of Thomas to supply his place *ad interim*. Nor have we in hand a case of suspension or temporary appointment or employment, in recess, under the second section, nor the case of an office in abeyance under the third section.

The sixth section, therefore, can find no provision in any other part of the law to which it can attach itself for the purpose of charging a misdemeanor upon the President of the United States. In other words, the letter of authority to General Thomas not being "contrary to the provisions" of the tenure-of-office act, the sixth section cannot declare the act of issuing it to be a high misdemeanor, punishable by indictment or impeachment.

I shall pass the charge found in these articles, that the letter of authority to Thomas was issued during a session of the Senate and without senatorial consent, with the single remark that it is made upon a misconception of the nature of an *ad interim* order. Such order is not an appointment, (within the meaning of the Constitution,) nor is it subject to senatorial advice and consent.

But the question remains: suppose the act of 1863 did completely repeal the act of 1795, relating to vacancies in executive offices, and that there is no law which expressly authorizes the letter of authority to General Thomas, then was the issuing of that letter a high misdemeanor in office? Unquestionably it was not, unless made such by the sixth section of the tenure-of-office act, which has just been disproved. In fact the issuing of such a letter by the President, even without statutory authority, when required by the interests of the public service, may be not innocent merely, but laudable. The order issued by President Lincoln to General Skinner, to act as Postmaster General *ad interim*, although without authority of law, was not a criminal offense. It was a justifiable order to meet an emergency in the public service. A large number of similar orders for *ad interim* service in the several Executive Departments, wholly unauthorized by any statute, have been put in evidence on the present trial. They were made by President Jackson and by his successors in the presidential office frequently and without question.

THE CONSPIRACY ARTICLES.

The fourth, fifth, sixth, and seventh articles of impeachment charge, in various forms, a conspiracy between the President and General Thomas on 21st of February, 1868, and are, when condensed and freed from verbiage, in substance as follows:

Article IV. That the President conspired with Thomas and others unknown with intent by intimidation and threats unlawfully to prevent Mr. Stanton from holding his office as Secretary of War, thus violating the Constitution and the conspiracy act of July 31, 1861, and thereby committing a high crime in office.

Article V. That he conspired with Thomas and others to prevent the execution of the tenure-of-office act, and, in pursuance of that conspiracy, unlawfully attempted to prevent Mr. Stanton from holding his office of Secretary of War, thereby committing a high misdemeanor in office.

Article VI. That he conspired with Thomas to seize by force the public property in the Department of War, whereof Stanton had custody, contrary to the conspiracy act of 1861, and with intent to violate the tenure-of-office act, whereby he did commit a high crime in office.

Article VII. That he conspired with Thomas unlawfully to seize the public property in the Department of War, in Stanton's custody,

with intent to violate the tenure-of-office act, whereby he did commit a high misdemeanor in office.

The charges in the fourth and sixth articles, of conspiracy to use intimidation, threats, and force to prevent Mr. Stanton from holding his office, and to obtain possession of the public property in the War Department, contrary to the conspiracy act of 1861, are not sustained but disproved by the evidence upon the trial; and it is, therefore, unnecessary to subject them to particular examination.

The charges in the fifth and seventh articles, of conspiracy to violate and to prevent the execution of the tenure-of-office act, as well as those in the fourth and sixth articles, are founded upon the order for the removal of Mr. Stanton and the letter of authority to General Thomas of 21st of February, 1868, and have no support whatever if those papers were lawfully issued.

It is difficult to see how the simple issuing of an official executive order or letter under a claim of right, and its acceptance or peaceful action under it by a subordinate officer, can constitute a conspiracy in point of law. The confederating together—the mutual agreement or plot between the parties—which is an essential element of conspiracy, would in such case seem to be wanting. But, certainly, if the order and letter of authority were issued to accomplish a lawful purpose, there is an end of all the conspiracy articles, and of all the other articles down to and including the eighth. The allegations about intimidation, threats, and force in the fourth and sixth articles being unproved or disproved, all the first eight articles rest upon the assertion that Mr. Stanton's case is within the tenure-of-office act, and his tenure defined and protected by it. If that assertion be refuted, all those eight articles, unsupported, fall into ruin.

THE EMORY ARTICLE.

But few words are necessary upon the ninth article, which recites the conversation between the President and General Emory on the 22d February, 1868, in which the President expressed the opinion that the second section of the Army appropriation act of March 2, 1867, which required that all orders and instructions relating to military operations issued by the President or Secretary of War should be issued through the General of the Army, &c., was unconstitutional. The article charges the President with an intent to induce General Emory to violate said act, and to receive and obey his orders in contravention thereof, with the further intent thereby to enable him (the President) to prevent the execution of the tenure-of-office act, and to prevent Mr. Stanton from holding the office of Secretary of War.

The testimony, instead of sustaining these averments of intent, repels them; and it explains in a satisfactory manner how the interview between the President and General

Emory was brought about, and how the conversation concerning the Army appropriation act arose. It is not necessary to consider the legal sufficiency of this article in form or substance as an article of impeachment when its material averments are disproved.

THE BUTLER ARTICLE.

The tenth article charges the utterance of certain public speeches by the President as a high misdemeanor in office. The first was delivered at the Executive Mansion, in Washington, on the 18th day of August, 1866; the second at Cleveland, on the 3d September; and the third at St. Louis, on the 8th of September of the same year; and extracts from them are set forth in the specifications of this article. They are charged to have been indecent and unbecoming, and made with intent to bring the Congress of the United States into contempt and disgrace, and to excite the resentment of the people against it and against the laws by it duly enacted.

The sufficient answer to this article is, that it charges no offense against the laws of the United States, and that it calls in question that privilege of freedom of speech which is the common birthright of the American people. The President in those speeches denounced the Thirty-Ninth Congress for its course on the subject of reconstruction, and imputed to some of its members responsibility for the New Orleans massacre. He said also that it was a Congress of but a part of the States; a remark which was perfectly true, and did not necessarily import a denial of its constitutional powers. But neither these nor any other observations made by him can be brought within the prohibitions of any law of the United States, and their utterance was the exercise of a right which cannot be questioned either in the ordinary courts of law or in a court of impeachment.

The case of Judge Humphreys is not a precedent to sustain this article. He was impeached, to be sure, for a speech made, but the speech was treasonable in character and effect, for it incited to armed resistance against the United States, and gave to the public enemies "aid and comfort." Its utterance was an *act* of treason which, being committed by a civil officer of the United States, rendered him liable to impeachment and removal from office.

THE STEVENS ARTICLE.

The eleventh article is nondescript, and a curiosity in pleading. As an article on which to convict, its strength consists in its weakness—in the obscurity of its charges and the intricacy of its form. As an afterthought of the House of Representatives, or rather as a reluctant concession by the House to the pertinacity of its author, it is not merely supplementary to the other articles in position, but bears upon its face the evidence of its distinct and peculiar origin. Considered in parts it is nothing—the propositions into which it is divisible cannot stand separately as charges of criminal conduct or intention; and considered as a whole it eludes the understanding and baffles conjecture. While we cannot suppose it to have been drawn in scorn of the Senate, before whom it was to be placed as an article of impeachment, it would be true to the paternity of a scornful spirit and a reckless brain if such paternity were assigned to it.

The matter of this article, so far as substance can be detected in it, is drawn mostly from the other articles; but that matter is arranged, manipulated, and combined together in a manner to vex the student and confound the judge; and the new particulars of charge or aggravation (whichever they may be) contained in the article are hinted at rather than expressed, and we vainly explore the context to discover distinctly their antecedents or the conclusions to which they lead.

As no abstract can do justice to this article it must be given *in extenso*. It is as follows:

ART. 11. That said Andrew Johnson, President of the United States, unmindful of the high duties of his office, and of his oath of office, and in disregard of the Constitution and laws of the United States, did, heretofore, to wit, on the 18th day of August, A. D. 1866, at the city of Washington, and the District of Columbia, by public speech, declare and affirm, in substance, that the Thirty-Ninth Congress of the United States was not a Congress of the United States authorized by the Constitution to exercise legislative power under the same, but, on the contrary, was a Congress of only part of the States, thereby denying, and intending to deny, that the legislation of said Congress was valid or obligatory upon him, the said Andrew Johnson, except in so far as he saw fit to approve the same, and also thereby denying, and intending to deny, the power of the said Thirty-Ninth Congress to propose amendments to the Constitution of the United States; and, in pursuance of said declaration, the said Andrew Johnson, President of the United States, afterwards, to wit, on the 21st day of February, A. D. 1868, at the city of Washington, in the District of Columbia, did, unlawfully, and in disregard of the requirement of the Constitution, that he should take care that the laws be faithfully executed, attempt to prevent the execution of an act entitled "An act regulating the tenure of certain civil offices," passed March 2, 1867, by unlawfully devising and contriving, and attempting to devise and contrive means by which he should prevent Edwin M. Stanton from forthwith resuming the functions of the office of Secretary for the Department of War, notwithstanding the refusal of the Senate to concur in the suspension theretofore made by said Andrew Johnson of said Edwin M. Stanton from said office of Secretary for the Department of War; and, also, by further unlawfully devising and contriving, and attempting to devise and contrive means, then and there, to prevent the execution of an act entitled "An act making appropriations for the support of the Army for the fiscal year ending June 30, 1868, and for other purposes," approved March 2, 1867; and, also, to prevent the execution of an act entitled "An act to provide for the more efficient government of the rebel States," passed March 2, 1867, whereby the said Andrew Johnson, President of the United States, did, then, to wit, on the 21st day of February, A. D. 1868, at the city of Washington, commit, and was guilty of, a high misdemeanor in office.

No one having been known to assert that he understood fully this article, it may be thought hazardous to attempt its exposition. But the difficulty of the task will doubtless be taken into due account by all generous persons in judging its performance.

The inducement contained in the first three lines and the conclusion are taken from the formal parts of prior articles.

The clause which sets forth the speech of the 18th of August, 1866, and the intent of that speech, may be considered as constituting the body of the charge, as the ground of the charge, as a part of the charge, or as the introduction to the charge. Whichever it may be, it is borrowed from the tenth article, and, if condemned there, must fall here as a distinct charge or element of accusation.

Next, it is said that the President, "*in pursuance*" of said speech of 18th August, did, on 21st February, 1868, "attempt to prevent the execution" of the tenure-of-office act by "devising and contriving, and attempting to devise and contrive, means" to prevent Stanton from resuming his office of Secretary of War, &c.

Is this merely a specification under the prior charge, or a continuation of that charge, or a substantive and distinct or separable accusation? If it be the first or second of these it will share the fate of the prior charge in a vote of guilty or not guilty upon the whole article. And the words *in pursuance*, with which this division begins, may be thought to so connect it with the prior matter as to render this result certain. If, however, this division be a distinct or separable accusation we are to examine it further. In that view it must aver the substance of a criminal charge. But this it does not do. It avers only certain action of the President's mind—no overt act, no conduct of his, good or bad. He "devised and contrived, and attempted to devise and contrive, means" to keep Mr. Stanton out of office. But he used no means, and he took no steps to create or provide them. It is true he is charged with an "attempt to prevent the execution of the tenure-of-office act," but only by the "devising and contriving, and attempting to devise and contrive, means" to keep Mr. Stanton out of office.

In brief, this accusation is that the President cogitated the means to keep Mr. Stanton out of office, and thereby violated the tenure-of-office act! It is too plain for question that no criminal act is charged here, nor any fact set forth upon which a judicial investigation can be had or judgment be pronounced. But it has been supposed and asserted that this part of the eleventh article refers to a desire and intention of the President, not on 21st of February, but in January before, to prevent Mr. Stanton from resuming his office. Be it so. If we are to build up a proper charge with a proper date from materials obtained outside of the articles, and proceed to try the President upon it, to what conclusion may we arrive? Why, that the President had an intention to keep Stanton out, and devised a plan or means for that purpose, but did not use those means or put that plan into execution. Here was no breach of the tenure-of-office act, or of any other law.

Whether his purpose was good or bad, it did not lead to an actual offense; and if his intention had been carried out in an act, what would that act have been? Why, obviously *an order for the removal of Stanton* before he had actually resumed his office. But that would have raised precisely the same question which was raised by the order of removal of 21st February, which we are to determine under the first article of impeachment. An order removing Mr. Stanton would have borne the same legal character whether issued to prevent him from resuming his office or to turn him out after he had resumed it.

The next clauses, and the concluding clauses of accusation in this article, aver a devising and contriving, &c., to prevent the execution of the Army appropriation act, (a repetition of the charge in the ninth article, and unproved,) and also to prevent the execution of the reconstruction act of March 2, 1867, (also unproved.) Whether these clauses relate to the same antecedents or not, and whether they are independent of each other or not, we need not inquire. Nor is it necessary to enlarge upon the absurdity of holding that a contriving to prevent the execution of the Army appropriation act or the reconstruction act will establish or tend to establish an attempt to prevent the execution of the tenure-of-office act; for, as these averments are not proved, their relations to prior parts of the article and to each other are unimportant.

THE TENURE-OF-OFFICE ACT.

There are several questions relating to the constitutionality and construction of the act of 2d March, 1867, ("to regulate the tenure of certain civil offices,") which remain to be examined. They do not arise upon the consideration of any one article alone, but upon the consideration of nearly all of them, and can be most conveniently presented in this place after the articles have been separately examined.

1. Was the tenure-of-office act constitutional in its application to heads of Executive Departments who were in office at the time of its passage? This question assumes, for the purposes of argument, that they were brought within the act by its terms and that a new tenure was fixed for them by it. I have no hesitation in answering this question in the negative, and in holding that it was not competent for Congress to assign to Mr. Stanton an office of more extended duration or greater security of tenure than that which he held under his commission by virtue of presidential appointment. This seems to me too clear for doubt or denial when we consider the character of the office and the plain words of the Constitution.

The Secretary of War is the head of an executive Department; his office as such head is expressly mentioned in the Constitution, and his appointment must be by the President by and with the advice and consent of the Senate. As he is not an *inferior* officer, within the meaning of the appointment clause of the Constitution, Congress cannot provide another mode of appointing him, much less assume the power of appointing him to themselves. It follows that they cannot give to a Secretary a right to hold his office beyond the term for which he was appointed, or to hold it freed from a condition upon which the appointment was made.

Let this proposition be illustrated by examples and its truth and soundness will more clearly appear. Take the case of a future Secretary, holding, under this tenure-of-office act, for a term of four years and one month by virtue of a presidential appointment to which senatorial advice and consent has been given. Can Congress by law extend his term? Can they by statute authorize him to hold his office for eight or ten years instead of four? If so, the officer will hold under the statute during all the time added to his term in contempt of the constitutional power of appointment. Again, suppose the case of a Secretary appointed and commissioned to hold during the pleasure of the President. Can Congress by statute authorize him to hold during good behavior, thus making his office one for life (unless removed for legal misconduct) instead of one at the pleasure of the appointing power? In this case, also, the new right is conferred in derogation of the power held by the President and Senate under the Constitution. And in the precise case which we have before us, Mr. Stanton holding under his appointment and commission at the pleasure of the President, can Congress by statute give him a right to hold his office for a term of years against the President's will? If they can do this they can also hereafter, at their pleasure, assign him an additional term of years or give him a life estate in his office. In either case what have we but a new appointment to office by Congress?

By the express words of the Constitution the principal officers of the Government (including, I think, the heads of the Executive Departments) must be appointed by the President by and with the advice and consent of the Senate, and the appointment of inferior officers may be vested by law in the President alone, in the courts of law, or in the heads of Departments. Each House of Congress may choose their own officers, but in no case whatever can Congress appoint an officer of the United States. Being clearly incapable of making an appointment, they cannot change one after it is made, giving it a character and duration which were not within the contemplation or intention of the appointing power when the office was conferred.

I conclude, then, that if the tenure-of-office act be construed to place the cases of Mr. Stanton and of the other Lincoln Secretartes within a new tenure-of-office rule, it is so far forth unconstitutional and void, and can afford no support to the first eight and to the eleventh articles of impeachment.

2. It is important to observe that no objec-

tion upon constitutional grounds is made, or can be made, to some parts of the tenure-of-office act. The sixth section, for instance, is entirely unexceptionable, and was very properly acted upon by the President in giving notice to the Secretary of the Treasury of Mr. Stanton's suspension in August, 1867. And so the second section of the act, in authorizing the suspension of officers between sessions of the Senate, violates no provision of the Constitution, and denies no just claim of executive power. It was quite competent for the President to suspend Mr. Stanton under that section, notwithstanding his denial of the validity of the first section, and if he had done so in express terms he would not have exposed himself to a charge of inconsistency. It is true he puts his suspension of Mr. Stanton upon the executive power to remove him under the Constitution, holding that the power to remove includes the power to suspend, but still the act of suspension fell within the letter of the law and was in all respects conformed to it. While it was from the President's point of view a good exercise of power under the Constitution, it was also undeniably a good exercise of power within the terms of the law; and if placed upon the latter ground alone it would not be an admission of the constitutionality of the whole law, but only of so much of the second section as authorizes suspensions from office. It is only necessary to add here, by way of explanation, that while Mr. Stanton's case is believed not to come within the operation of the first section, the power to suspend him is clearly conferred by the second.

3. I hold that the violation of law by a President which will constitute an impeachable high crime or misdemeanor must be a willful and intentional violation, and in its nature calculated to produce serious injury to the public service.' Mistake and error of judgment merely are not to be punished by impeachment, but only grievous and willful crime which endangers the public safety or welfare. Therefore, if there was an honest misconstruction of the tenure-of-office act by the President, in holding that Mr. Stanton's case was not within it, he cannot be convicted. The removal of Mr. Stanton was not an act calculated to injure the public service or shock the moral sense of the people. And the construction of the tenure-of-office act adopted by the President, whether right or wrong, was not an unreasonable or rash one, but was precisely that construction which had been assigned to it in the Senate at the time of its passage, and which appears to be most consistent with its terms.

4. Assuming that the first section of the tenure-of-office act was one of doubtful constitutionality and construction, I hold that the President was fully justified in challenging its application to his Secretaries, and in taking necessary steps to have its validity and construction determined in the courts of law. But his position as to his right and duty in this

respect has been grossly misrepresented and, perhaps, greatly misunderstood. It was stated, however, by Judge Curtis, in his opening for the defense, with a clearness and completeness which leave nothing to be desired, and remove all excuse for misconception or complaint. He said:

"I am not intending to advance upon or occupy any extreme ground, because no such ground has been advanced, upon or occupied by the President of the United States. He is to take care that the laws be faithfully executed. When a law has been passed through the forms of legislation, either with his assent or without his assent, it is his duty to see that that law is faithfully executed so long as nothing is required of him but ministerial action. He is not to erect himself into a judicial court and decide that the law is unconstitutional, and that therefore he will not execute it." * * * * "He asserts no such power. He has no such idea of his duty. His idea of his duty is, that if a law is passed over his veto which he believes to be unconstitutional, and that law affects the interests of third persons, those whose interests are affected must take care of them, vindicate them, raise questions concerning them if they should be so advised. If such a law affects the general and public interests of the people, the people must take care at the polls that it is remedied in a constitutional way. "But when, Senators, a question arises whether a particular law has cut off a power confided to him by the people through the Constitution, and he alone can raise the question, and he alone can cause a judicial decision to come between the two branches of the Government to say which of them is right, and after due deliberation with the advice of those who are his proper advisers, he settles down firmly upon the opinion that such is the character of the law, it remains to be decided by you whether there is any violation of his duty when he takes the needful steps to raise that question and have it peacefully decided."—*Page 382.*

And again he said, (page 391:)

"So long as it is a question of administrative duty merely he [the President] holds that he is bound by the law."

It is admitted on all hands that a private citizen may proceed in a peaceful manner to resist any law which violates his personal rights under the Constitution, and may bring such law before the courts for judicial condemnation. And even if he should be mistaken as to his right, and as to the invalidity of the law, his error will not be imputed to him as a crime. And so, where a question arises as to the constitutional right of the President to change his constitutional advisers—the men who constitute his political household, and for whose acts he is responsible to the people and to the law—as against a statute which invades or denies to him such right, can it be doubted that he may challenge the statute and carry it into the courts of law for judgment? And where the statute is plainly in contempt of the past practice of the Government, and of the very highest authorities which can be cited upon a question of constitutional law, and no one but the President can bring it to the test of judicial examination and judgment, is not his duty to challenge it as incontestible as his right?

CONCLUSION.

I have now concluded my examination of the several articles of impeachment and of the act of Congress upon which most of them are founded. The general question of presidential power under the Constitution to remove officers of the United States from office at discretion, has been but slightly noticed, and no attention has been bestowed upon those topics of declamation and invective which have been intruded into the trial. The constitutional question was discussed by me at length when the tenure-of-office act was passed, and I do not find it necessary to repeat the argument then made by me in order to explain or vindicate my judgment upon these articles of impeachment. As to the extraneous and irrelevant matters introduced into the trial, and particularly into the argument, I put them wholly aside. This case is to be tried upon the laws which apply to it, and upon the facts which are duly proved. The issue joined is not political but judicial, and it is upon specific articles of accusation. They are to be decided honestly and firmly, and nothing beside them is to pass into judgment.

In my opinion the acquittal of the President upon all the charges preferred against him is authorized by law and demanded by justice. He has committed no high crime or misdemeanor. He has trampled upon no man's right; he has violated no public duty. He has kept his oath of office unbroken, and has sought in a lawful manner to vindicate and preserve the high constitutional powers confided to him by the people. He cannot and ought not to be punished for his opinions upon public measures and public policy; and, in contemplation of law, his conduct in all the matters brought before us for review has been irreproachable. What he has done indicates not criminal intent but patriotic purpose; and besides, that true courage, sustained and invincible, which grapples with difficulty and defies danger.

OPINION

OF

HON. JOHN B. HENDERSON.

On the 21st day of February last the President of the United States issued an order directed to Edwin M. Stanton, Secretary of War, declaring that Stanton thereby was removed from his said office, and his functions as Secretary would cease on receipt of the order.

On the same day he issued and delivered to Lorenzo Thomas, Adjutant General of the Army, a letter of authority to act as Secretary of War *ad interim*, in place of Stanton removed; Stanton being directed to transfer to Thomas all the records, books, papers, and other property of the Department.

These two acts of the President, varied only in the form of the charges, constitute the chief offenses contained in the first eight articles of impeachment. It is true that the fourth, fifth, sixth, and seventh articles charge an unlawful conspiracy between the President and Thomas to put Stanton out and get Thomas in, and some of these articles charge that the President designed to carry out this conspiracy by force and violence.

Waiving for the present all questions touching the technical sufficiency of the charges, as well as the weight and sufficiency of the evidence adduced to support them, I will first inquire whether the President could legally do what he intended to do by issuing the orders.

In my view of the law, the first and only really important question to be settled is this: could the President lawfully remove Mr. Stanton as Secretary of War on the 21st day of February last? I am aware that the other question has been discussed at great length, and not without much learning, to wit: could the President, even admitting his power to remove Stanton, make an *ad interim* designation to fill the vacancy thus created, until an appointment could be regularly made?

I think that to answer the former proposition furnishes a full answer to the latter. If the President could not remove Stanton, then there was no vacancy to be filled by the designation of Thomas. If he could legally remove Stanton, a vacancy was created which under the laws as they existed on that day could be filled by this *ad interim* appointment.

As the two questions are so intimately connected, I may examine them together, and I proceed to show that the President possessed the undoubted power, under the laws of Congress, to remove Mr. Stanton on the day he attempted to do so by issuing the order. This is the opinion that I have entertained at all times, and which I repeatedly avowed, both before and after the passage of the tenure-of-office bill.

The Constitution "vests the executive power" in the President. He is sworn faithfully to "execute the office of President," and that he will "preserve, protect, and defend the Constitution of the United States." A·part of the executive power expressly placed in his hands is that "he shall take care that the laws be faithfully executed." The Constitution is silent as to the power of removing officers. It provides for their appointment by nomination by the President with the advice and consent of the Senate. But if the Senate should not be in session when a vacancy shall "happen," it is provided that the President may "fill up" such vacancy—

"By granting a commission, which shall expire at the end of their next session; but the Congress may by law vest the appointment of such inferior officers as they think proper in the President alone, in the courts of law, or in the heads of Departments."

It will be observed that ample provision is made for the *filling* of offices, but no express provision is made for *vacating* them. It· is made the duty of the President to "execute" the laws, and he can only do it through the officers provided by law for that purpose. If they become corrupt or incompetent or refuse to execute the law, there is no express remedy named in the Constitution except the impeachment process. The impeachment clause, it was at once seen, was wholly inefficient as a remedy. The offices of Government would, in the natural course of things, become so numerous as to occupy the entire time of Congress in trying the delinquencies of incumbents. And unless the offending officer could be removed by some other means, the Government might be brought into the greatest possible danger if not entirely overthrown by the treason and corruption of high officials, during the recess of Congress or even during its session, but before an effective remedy could be applied.

Therefore it is that this question of removals from office challenged such early attention and was so ably and so exhaustively examined by the First Congress which met under the Constitution. Many of the men who assisted in framing the Constitution were in this Congress and participated in the debate. The first offices created by this Congress were the Secretaryships of Foreign Affairs, of War, and the Treasury; and the questions debated were the power of the President under the Constitution to remove these officers at his will and pleasure, and the necessity and propriety of so declaring by law. The House of Representatives, under the lead of Mr. Madison, by a large majority, and the Senate, by the casting vote of John Adams, decided that the power of removal existed in the President by virtue of the Constitution itself. All agreed that officers must and should be removable in some way other than by impeachment. Some of the members said the power was in the President alone; others contended it rested in the President and Senate, precisely as did the power of appointment.

I am aware that some persons now insist that the result of the votes establishing these Departments, in the First Congress, was not such as to indicate a constitutional construction in favor of the presidential power of removal. I think otherwise. I am satisfied that a careful examination of the debate and the conclusion arrived at by the votes, will convince any unprejudiced mind that the First Congress clearly and explicitly conceded this power to the President as a constitutional prerogative which could not be limited or controlled by law. Whatever we may urge against this conclusion as a correct exposition of the Constitution, we cannot well doubt that such was the conclusion arrived at.

Judge Story, in his Commentaries on the Constitution, Chancellor Kent in his work on American Law, the Supreme Court of the United States, and the most distinguished of our statesmen, at all periods from that day to this, admit that the decision of the First Congress was such as I have stated it. Many of them think the conclusion was wrong, but the fact itself is a part of the history of the country. But whether this First Congress was right or wrong in its construction of the Constitution amounts to but little as I view this subject, except as it may tend to interpret and explain its legislation. Let it be kept in mind, while we refer to these laws, that they were passed by men who believed that the power of removing all appointed officers, except judges of the Supreme Court, who held by fixed tenure, was vested in the President by the Constitution and could not be withdrawn by law. The power of appointing their successors was in the President and Senate, and the exercise of this power, they thought, could be regulated by law. Believing that they could not take away the power of removal, if they desired, they were yet further clearly of the opinion, and so expressed themselves, that Cabinet officers should, and must necessarily, be removable at the will of the President, he being responsible for their acts.

On the 9th of August, 1789, the act was passed creating the War Department. The first section of the act declares that the Secretary—

"Shall perform and execute such duties as shall from time to time be enjoined on or intrusted to him by the President of the United States, agreeably to the Constitution relative to military commissions or to the land and naval forces, ships or warlike stores of the United States, or to such other matters respecting military or naval affairs as the President of the United States shall assign to said Department," &c.

And, further, that the Secretary—

"Shall conduct the business of the said Department in such manner as the President of the United States shall from time to time order and instruct."

The second section provides for a chief clerk to the Secretary, who—

"Whenever the said principal officer shall be removed from office by the President of the United States, or in any other case of vacancy, shall, during such vacancy, have the charge and custody of all records, books, and papers of the Department."

On the 27th of July preceding, the Department of Foreign Affairs had been established with precisely similar provisions, and on the 2d of September following the Treasury Department was established with the same provisions, except that if the Secretary should be removed by the President, or a vacancy otherwise occur, the Assistant Secretary, who was really clerk, should have charge during the vacancy. Now, whether I look to the words of these acts, to the contemporaneous history of their passage, to the subsequent construction given them by our statesmen and jurists, or to the action of the Government under them, I am forced to the conclusion that whatever may be the President's constitutional power in the premises, the power to remove these officers absolutely is given to the President by the laws themselves, and was so intended at the time. The Departments are called Executive Departments. They are required to conduct their affairs as the "President shall order or instruct," and he is authorized to assign them duties not specified in the acts, which duties shall be discharged "in the manner directed by him." He is clearly responsible for their conduct, and each one of the acts provides in terms that he may remove the officer at any time, and the acts designate who shall succeed them in case of removal or other vacancy.

In this state of the law it will be observed that no possible difference can exist in the succession, whether the removal or other vacancy should occur during the recess or session of Congress. In the cases of the State and War Departments, the chief clerk, and in that of the Treasury Department, the Assistant Secretary, must succeed by virtue of the law.

And under such circumstances why should the power of removal be confined to the recess of the Senate and be dormant during the session? No matter when the removal is made the same person takes the office. If made in recess he will hold on during the succeeding session, unless the President should see fit to make a new nomination, and the Senate should confirm. If made during the session, the successor fixed by law holds during that session and through the coming recess, if the President so wills. Hence it seems clear that so far, at least, as these Cabinet officers are concerned, there is no foundation for the pretense that the President may remove, as General Jackson did in the case of Duane, and as other Presidents have done without question, during the recess, but cannot remove during the session. There is no possible reason for the distinction, and in the absence of any such reason I take it the distinction itself does not exist. Let it be remembered that the law was made by men who admitted that the President could remove by virtue of the Constitution and independently of the law. They so worded the law as merely to conform it to the Constitution, as they understood it. If the power was a constitutional power, it was surely as vigorous and effective during the session as in the recess of the Senate, and the law being designed, no doubt, to be as broad as they held the Constitution itself to be, I cannot suppose it was intended to confine removals to time or limit them by circumstances. To the President is given the unlimited power to remove. If he does remove, whenever it occurs the law has fixed the successor.

In this state of the law I will admit that if the President had removed one of these Secretaries during the session of the Senate, and had nominated a successor to the Senate, this successor could not have entered on his duties until he had been confirmed. The chief clerk or Assistant Secretary, as the case might be, would have held the office till confirmation.

Thus stood the law on the subject of these three Departments until May 8, 1792. The eighth section of the act of that date changed the rule for these temporary successions in certain cases, and extended the same rule to other officers in the Departments beside the heads thereof. Under the former acts, however the vacancy might be occasioned, whether by removal or otherwise, the person to take the office temporarily was fixed, and must be the clerk or Assistant Secretary. But it was now provided—

" That in case of death, absence from the seat of Government, or sickness of these Secretaries, it shall be lawful for the President of the United States, in case he shall think it necessary, to authorize any person or persons, at his discretion, to perform the duties of the said respective offices until a successor be appointed, or until such absence or inability by sickness shall cease."

After the passage of this act if a vacancy should have been created by removal in the head of a Department, the President could not have "authorized any person or persons," at his discretion, to take charge of the office. For instance, he could remove the Secretary of War, but the chief clerk still would become the acting Secretary. He could only designate another person in case the vacancy occurred from death, or from temporary absence or sickness. It will be observed that this act fixes no limitation of service for the temporary successor.

The next change made was by the act of July 13, 1795. This act provides—

" That in case of vacancy in the office of Secretary of State, Secretary of Treasury, or of Secretary for the Department of War," [being the only Executive Departments yet established,] "it shall be lawful for the President of the United States, in case he shall think it necessary, to authorize any person or persons, at his discretion, to perform the duties of the said respective offices until a successor be appointed, or such vacancy be filled."

The effect of this act is simply to extend the discretionary power of the President, in making temporary appointments, to cases of removal and expiration of term, which were not provided for in the act of 1792. But inasmuch as the President could now remove any of the Secretaries and all subordinates in their Departments not appointed by the heads thereof, and appoint others at his own will, Congress thought it wise to limit the term of the succeeding temporary incumbent by adding the following proviso, to wit: "That no one vacancy shall be supplied in the manner aforesaid for a longer term than six months." The President's power of removal was not interfered with. He could still remove in session or vacation, and now he could designate at discretion the temporary successor, but at the expiration of six months the office became vacant, and thus the Senate retained its advisory power, so far as it chose to retain it, over appointments. It was under this state of the law that Mr. Adams peremptorily removed Mr. Pickering on the 12th of May, 1800. And we can readily discover a good reason—whether the true one or not I cannot say—for Mr. Adams's desire that Mr. Marshall's nomination should be confirmed before the adjournment of the Senate. Under his own appointment, without the action of the Senate, the office of Secretary of State would become hopelessly vacant before the next meeting of Congress, and would remain so till action could be had by the Senate.

But whatever may have been Mr. Adams's reasons for wanting Marshall's confirmation before the Senate adjourned, it is quite clear that he entertained no doubt of his power to remove Mr. Pickering during the session of that body. He had asked Pickering to resign in language very similar to that employed by Mr. Johnson in asking Stanton to resign. Pickering refused, and Mr. Adams issued an order of positive and absolute removal. It is true that Mr. Marshall's name was sent in for confirmation the same day, but it was declared to be "in place of Timothy Pickering, esq., removed." The President acted strictly in accordance with his previous opinions, as indicated by his vote when presiding over the Senate in 1789, when the laws creating the Departments were passed. It is not reasonable that he should have doubted, and surely the history of that time discloses no expression of doubt or censure by the most virulent of his political opponents.

The law on this subject remained unchanged up to February 20, 1863. At this time the other Departments of the Government had been established; but the provisions of law for temporary appointments made applicable to the first three by the acts of 1792 and 1795 had not, in words, been applied to those subsequently created. Mr. Lincoln having this difficulty sharply presented to his mind by an exigency arising in the Post Office Department, took the responsibility of acting outside the letter of the law, and made an *ad interim* appointment. He, however, sent a communication to Congress, dated January 2, 1863, in the following words:

To the Senate and House of Representatives:

I submit to Congress the expediency of extending to other Departments of the Government the authority conferred on the President by the eighth section of the act of 8th May, 1792, to appoint a person to temporarily discharge the duties of Secretary of State, and Secretary of the Treasury, and Secretary of War, in case of death, absence from the seat of Government, or sickness of either of those officers.
ABRAHAM LINCOLN.

Washington, *January* 2, 1863.
[*See Congressional Globe*, 1862–63, part 1, p. 185.]

Congress took action in the premises, as requested, but seems to have directed its attention rather to amending the legislation of 1792 than that of 1795. Instead of putting the more recently-established Departments by name on the same footing with those established prior to 1792, the act of 1863 extends the cases for temporary appointments from "death, absence from the seat of Government, or sickness," as fixed by the act of 1792, so as to include also cases of resignation, and then makes its provisions applicable to all the Executive Departments. It provides:

"That in case of death, resignation, absence from the seat of Government, or sickness of the head of any executive Department," &c., "the President may authorize the head of another Department, or other officer in either of said Departments, to perform the duties," &c.; "but no vacancy shall be thus supplied for a longer term than six months."

If this act had taken away the power of removal, as fixed by the act of 1789, then it could be possibly said that so far as this case is concerned it renders inoperative the act of 1795. But if the power to remove still remains after this legislation, then a vacancy may be created which is not provided for in the act of 1863. Death, resignation, absence, and sickness constitute the only cases of vacancy for which provision is made in this latter act. Beside the vacancy arising from removal, if the power yet exists, (and I can find no statute, up to the year 1863, taking it away,) vacancies may occur from expiration of term; and this class of vacancies, too, is wholly unprovided for. Upon the passage of the act of 1863, it follows that if a vacancy should have occurred in the War, Treasury or State Departments from removal or expiration of term, the President could still have designated "any person or persons" whatever, under the act of 1795, to perform the duties for six months. But no such vacancy in the heads of other Departments could be supplied at all. In the Navy, Interior and Post Office Departments the only vacancies that could be temporarily filled are those occurring from death, resignation, absence and sickness. And for all the vacancies last named, in any of the Departments provided for by the act of 1863, the President is confined in selecting the temporary successor to the head of some other Department, or to some other officer in one of said Departments. And now it may be said that the act of 1863, with this construction, partly failed of its object. Even if this be so it is only what frequently occurs in legislation. The law-maker often comes short of the purposes designed by the law. But it does secure all that was asked by Mr. Lincoln, and even more. He asked for power to fill vacancies ad interim occurring by death, absence and sickness, and Congress gave him power to fill not only these, but also vacancies occurring by resignation. It did not give him authority thus to fill a vacancy in the Post Office, Navy and Interior Departments arising from removal or expiration of term, but to fill such vacancies in the War, State, and Treasury Departments he had ample power under the act of 1795, which yet remains unrepealed.

Having now examined all the legislation up to the tenure-of-civil-office act of March 2, 1867, I come to the conclusion that—previous to that act, at least—it was quite clear that the President possessed the undoubted power to remove a Cabinet officer commissioned, as he must have been, to hold during the pleasure of the President, either in the recess or during the session of the Senate. I also conclude that if a vacancy could be thus created, that vacancy, under the law, could be filled by a temporary ad interim appointment, to continue for six months. Of the latter proposition I have no doubt at all. Whatever of offense exists in these articles must be found in the first one. If the President could remove, he could unquestionably fill the place for the limited period named. When Mr. Buchanan was called on by the Senate in January, 1861, to show under what authority during its session he had appointed Joseph Holt, a loyal man, Secretary of War ad interim to fill the vacancy created by the resignation of Mr. Floyd, a rebel, he presented the law so forcibly as, in my judgment, to silence all cavil, and settle the question forever. In his communication to the Senate he truly refers to the practice of the Government, and shows that one hundred and seventy-nine such appointments in the chief Departments of the Government alone had been made from 1829 to 1856, a large number of them made, too, during the session of the Senate. It will be observed, too, from the evidence in this case, that in the bureaus and inferior offices of the Government many ad interim or acting appointments have been made to fill vacancies of every character, including those made by removal. If it be said that no vacancy by removal in the head of a Department was ever thus filled, it may be answered that but one Secretary, up to the date of which we speak, ever refused, during the session of the Senate, to resign when asked, and he was promptly removed by the sole act of the President without consultation with the Senate. The vacancy being once created can be filled, as any other vacancy, by an ad interim appointment.

I come now to the act of March 2, 1867—the civil-tenure act. Does it change the law, as I state it to have been before its passage? The act I will admit to be clearly constitutional in all its parts. The only difficulty, in my mind, grows out of its construction; and this difficulty of construction is the result of the effort made on the passage of the bill to reconcile a radical difference between the two Houses of Congress on this very question of Cabinet officers. It has sprung out of a most reprehensible and vicious practice—that to save important measures from defeat these differences between the two Houses are to be healed and covered up in conference committees with ambiguous or unmeaning phrases. The truth is, that instead of clearing up doubts, and making that plain which, above all things, should be plain, we often purposely obscure the controverted point, and devolve its solution upon the courts, or the President, if you please, each of us hoping, no doubt, that the solution will accord with his own wishes, and ready to cavil if it does not. And so it was with this act. The Senate repeatedly demanded that Cabinet officers should be entirely excepted from the general provisions of the act, thereby leaving them subject to removal as under previous laws. The House insisted that they should be put upon the same footing with other officers; that they should not be removed except by consent of the Senate. The compromise in the conference committee is contained in the proviso which declares that Cabinet officers " shall hold their offices respectively for and during the term of the President by whom they may have been appointed, and for one month thereafter, subject to removal by and with the advice and consent of the Senate. " To construe this law according to its letter two things must be kept in mind—first, the President who appoints ; and second, the term during which he appoints. In this case Mr. Lincoln is the President who appointed. Mr. Stanton was appointed in January, 1862, and hence "the term of the President" by whom Stanton was appointed terminated under the Constitution and laws on the 4th March, 1865. If the act had used the word "terms" instead of "term," I would readily assent that Mr. Stanton's case was intended to be covered and protected by the act. But I cannot separate the act of appointment from the one identical and single current term of the President who made it. For instance, if Mr. Lincoln had been living when the tenure of office act passed, I cannot doubt his power to have removed any officer appointed by him during his previous term. This law surely was not intended to prevent a President, should he be elected to the Presidency a dozen times, from changing his Cabinet without the consent of the Senate at the commencement or in the middle of each Administration; and if this position be conceded, it disposes of this case. If Mr. Lincoln could have removed, Mr. Johnson can also remove the same officers; and if Mr. Johnson cannot remove, the officer succeeding him, in case of Johnson's impeachment and removal, cannot rid himself of the existing Cabinet, because it is still said to be Mr. Lincoln's term.

If the term which Johnson is now serving out is Johnson's term and not Lincoln's, then everybody admits that Stanton may be legally removed, because he can only hold "for and during the term of the President by whom he may have been appointed." It is only by insisting that Lincoln's term does not cease till March 4, 1869, that Stanton is supposed for a moment to be protected. This position leaves no term at all for Johnson, and if Johnson shall be removed by impeachment and Wade shall take his place and serve as President till the 4th of March next, he, too, will have no term, because Lincoln's term covers the full period of his service. Now, there are members of the present Cabinet serving who were appointed by Mr. Johnson, to wit, Mr. Browning and Mr. Randall. If these gentlemen can serve as Cabinet ministers during the term of the President appointing them and for one month thereafter, will some Senator indicate to me when Browning's and Randall's terms expire? The law does not seem to contemplate a case of President without a term. If Johnson has no term, then Browning and Randall either have no terms or their terms last forever.

When Mr. Wade becomes President, he will surely change his Cabinet. But Wade having

no presidential term, he being simply an *ad interim* President, filling out a part of Mr. Lincoln's term, when will his Cabinet appointments go out of office? The law declares that they shall "hold during the term of the President by whom" they were appointed. They were not appointed by Mr. Lincoln, for Lincoln was dead when they came into the Cabinet, and the dead have no terms. Hence, under this construction they would not have to retire at the end of a month from March 4, 1869.

I need not elaborate. This mere statement will show the absurdity of the pretensions now set up in reference to this law. We ourselves never gave it such a construction until that unfounded and extraordinary excitement sprang up on the attempted removal of Mr. Stanton. The Senate gave construction to this law when it passed. I accepted that construction at the time. It is according to the letter and the spirit of the act. The Senate at all times protested against forcing on any President an obnoxious or disagreeable Cabinet minister. The House insisted on doing so. The bill then went to a conference committee, and on that committee, in behalf of the Senate, were two of our ablest lawyers, Messrs. SHERMAN and WILLIAMS. When the bill was reported from this conference committee Mr. HOWARD and Mr. DOOLITTLE called for an explanation of this provision. Mr. SHERMAN gave it. He said:

"That this provision does not apply to the present case is shown by the fact that its language is so framed as not to apply to the present President. The Senator shows that himself, and argues truly that it could not prevent the present President from removing the Secretary of War, the Secretary of the Navy, and the Secretary of State."

And again he said:

"If the President dies the Cabinet goes out. If the President is removed for cause by impeachment the Cabinet goes out. At the expiration of the term of the President's office the Cabinet goes out."

Mr. HOWARD expressed himself satisfied; the Senate was satisfied. Mr. WILLIAMS did not take issue on construction, but acquiesced by saying that—

"The effect of this proviso will amount to very little one way or the other, for I presume that whenever the President sees proper to rid himself of an offensive or disagreeable Cabinet minister he will only have to specify that desire, and the minister will retire and a new appointment be made."

Mr. HOWE, the Senator from Wisconsin, who had offered in the Senate the amendment to include Cabinet officers, declared that he was not satisfied with the bill, and clearly intimated that the House amendment had been abandoned; and such is yet the opinion of that distinguished Senator, and hence he cannot convict for the removal of Stanton. It will be rather a bad record now to convict the President of crime for taking the same view that we ourselves took on the passage of the act. I took that view of the law then, and have entertained it ever since.

But we are told that the President claims in his answer the power to have removed Stanton under the Constitution and in defiance of law. I am not trying him for his opinions. I am called to pass judgment on what he *has* done, not on what he claims a *right* to do. We must not convict men in this country for entertaining false notions of politics, morals, or religion. It is often difficult to determine who is right and who is wrong. In moments of temporary excitement and unfounded alarm whole masses of people have rushed wildly to incorrect conclusions. The late rebellion shows how unreasonable, how insane and foolish, large and overwhelming majorities may become. And in this condition they are intolerant of moderation, and even of common sense. From this spring mobs, derision, jeers, insults, and personal violence. He who cannot resist these things and proclaim the right at the risk of personal sacrifice, cannot expect to promote the great cause of truth, and such a man has no business whatever in this body.

When the President attempts to exercise an alleged constitutional power against the law, I will then judge of his crime. "Sufficient unto the day is the evil thereof." For the removal of Stanton and the appointment of Thomas he has undoubted authority under the laws of Congress. I cannot convict him of crime, either for doing something under the law which I may not approve, or for simply entertaining an opinion about the Constitution which was entertained and acted on by Madison, Jefferson, Adams, Jackson, and others as patriotic and as wise and conscientious as ourselves.

But suppose I am wrong in my construction of the law. Must I necessarily convict the President of a wicked and corrupt intent in doing just what nearly all our Presidents have done under a claim of authority from the Constitution itself? The President is a coördinate department of the Government. He is elected by the people and responsible to them as we are. He is to execute the law. But an unconstitutional law is no law at all. It never has binding force. It is void from its inception. Jefferson and Jackson, as Presidents, expressly claimed the right to judge in the first instance of the constitutionality of laws, and even so to judge in the face of a decision of the Supreme Court. If a President is bound to execute one void act he is equally bound to execute others. Suppose that Congress should pass an act depriving the citizen of the right of trial by jury, shall the President execute it? Suppose Congress shall declare that the President shall grant no certificate of pardon without consent of the Senate? The Constitution gives him full and exclusive power "to grant pardons." If he, then, does what he and everybody else knows he has a right to do, he may under the law fall guilty of a high crime or misdemeanor, but unless he violates the law, and at some time issues a pardon, this outrage on the Constitution must stand forever as a valid law. Must the President, elected by the people and for a shorter term than ourselves,

thus abdicate his authority as a part of the Government and suffer this congressional usurpation? If he does not violate such a law he is himself perjured, for he is sworn to "preserve, protect, and defend" not an invalid law, but "the Constitution." I do not claim that he may violate every law passed even for the purpose of procuring a judicial construction. I do not say that he may in mere wantonness violate or disregard any law. I only insist that each case shall stand on its own merits. If the President's purpose be criminal and corrupt, he should be removed. If he honestly intended only to procure what he says in this case, to wit, a judicial construction of a doubtful law, doubtful not only in its terms, but doubtful in its constitutionality, what right have we to pronounce him guilty of high crime? Mr. Lincoln, without law and against law, increased the regular Army and the Navy. Instead of impeaching, we applauded him and passed laws to justify and protect him. Why did we do this? Because we looked beyond the act to the motive. We then declared it proper to inquire into the *animus*, the intention of the President. I have thought it proper, also, in this case to examine into the President's intentions. I am satisfied that all evidence tending to explain his intention should have gone before the court. We sit in the capacity of a court and also a jury. As a court we must hear all evidence; as a jury we must consider that only which is competent and relevant.

The Constitution, in making us the "sole" judges of the law and the fact, presumes that we are sufficiently intelligent to hear all testimony offered, whether competent or incompetent, and to exclude from our minds that which is improper. When the court and jury are different persons it may be well to confine the testimony going before the jury to that which is clearly competent and relevant; but no such rule applies to the court. It is the duty of the judge to be informed of the nature and the precise character of the testimony proposed before he can determine the propriety of its introduction. So in this case. An essential element of guilt charged in these articles against the President is a wicked intent to violate the Constitution and the laws. He offered to show that his constitutional advisers, his Cabinet ministers, counseled him to the course pursued, and that the whole object, end, and aim of his action in the premises was to subject the law to the test of judicial examination. This advice, he alleges, was a part of the *res gestæ* and the foundation on which his conduct was based. Even Mr. Stanton had concurred with the other members of the Cabinet that this very law, the tenure-of-office act, was unconstitutional and invalid. If so, it was an infringement of the President's constitutional powers, and the least he could do, it seems, was to submit the differences between himself and Congress to that tribunal which was erected to settle such differences, and to the judgments of which we must all submit if we would avoid anarchy and civil war.

Whether the President's intentions were as pacific and innocent as he alleges them to have been, I do not pretend to say. I only insist that competent evidence, such as this, going to explain the character of his intentions, should not have been rejected by the court. It should have been received and properly weighed. Even in a civil suit for damages in a case of false imprisonment the advice of hired attorneys is competent to show a want of malice or corrupt intention in instigating the prosecution. Why should the President, however wicked or corrupt he may be, in a great criminal proceeding, where the presumptions of law must favor his innocence, be deprived of this just and reasonable rule? If he cannot change his Cabinet without our consent, then we are more or less responsible for the advice given him by the Cabinet. We propose to force a Cabinet on him against his will and compel him to be governed by their advice or take the responsibility of rejecting it. If he disregards this advice he should be punished, I presume, for obstinacy and dangerous purposes of usurpation. If he take their advice he is not permitted to show this fact in order to negative the inference of willful, wicked, and corrupt intentions.

A verdict of guilty on these articles, after the exclusion of this testimony, would fail to command the respect and approval of an enlightened public judgment.

In addition to what I have said, permit me to add one other reason why no conviction can be had on the articles connected with the removal of Stanton and the appointment of Thomas. It is not alleged in any of them that Stanton is actually removed, nor that Thomas is actually assigned to duty. And if it were so charged, the evidence is wholly insufficient to support it. The evidence shows that Stanton is yet in the office discharging its duties, and that Thomas is yet a private citizen. He asked for the office, but Stanton refused to yield it. Stanton remained in and Thomas has remained out. This is the theory of the prosecution. Then what is the offense? Not that a removal has been made, nor that an appointment *ad interim* has been effected. The worst phase of the matter is that the President has attempted to do these things and failed. This attempt is not a high crime or misdemeanor for two reasons: first, he had full power under the laws of Congress to remove and appoint as he tried to do; and second, if he had no such power, the *attempt* thus to exercise it is not by statute law nor by common law nor by common sense a high crime or misdemeanor.

This, in my judgment, disposes of the first eight articles. I know that in the fourth, fifth, sixth, and seventh articles there is an allegation of conspiracy by the President with General Thomas to seize and possess the War Department.

In the first place, there is not a particle of testimony proving a prior agreement, much less a conspiracy between these parties.

Second, a conspiracy to be unlawful must contemplate an unlawful act, or a lawful act by unlawful means. The objects designed by the President—the removal of Stanton and the appointment of Thomas *ad interim*—were lawful acts, and hence any conspiracy based on these facts must fall. And no unprejudiced man can say that the proof shows any purpose on the part of the President to use force in the removal of Mr. Stanton. The evidence throughout disproves any such charge. The ninth article fails to charge any offense whatever. It alleges that the President declared to General Emory that in his opinion a certain law, passed in 1867, taking away some of his prerogatives as Commander-in-Chief, is an unconstitutional law. A great many people beside the President entertain the same opinion. The right of private judgment has been punished in some countries, and some even have suffered in the United States for this alleged offense, but the precedents are very bad, and should not be followed. He who follows them far in this country will follow them to his own destruction.

It is not charged that the President violated this law, although he thought it unconstitutional. But it is said that he expressed this simple opinion to Emory "to induce said Emory, in his official capacity as commander of the department of Washington, to violate the provisions of said act," &c. It is not pretended that Emory was influenced by the President's opinions. The President gave him no order to violate it, nor did he insinuate that he would like to have him do so.

And had he so ordered, I presume that Emory would not have gratified him by obedience, for he seems to have had a different opinion, and maintained it with great zeal and confidence against his Commander-in-Chief.

The truth is that after the unfortunate misunderstanding between the President and General Grant, and after the proceeding in reference to the removal of Stanton, the President learned through the Secretary of the Navy that some extraordinary movements of military officers in the District were being made, to be followed in all probability by some unauthorized and dangerous disposition of troops. To show that the President contemplated no violence in the premises, it is sufficient to say that when he removed Stanton he had not seen Emory, and knew that General Grant was inimical to him. He seems not to have known a word about troops in the District. He did not know how many were here or what troops they were. He had not consulted a single officer, and seems not to have known but that all the troops had been sent away or others brought in. Being informed of these movements, and no doubt fearing that he himself might be violently seized by military power and dragged from the Executive

Mansion, he sent for the commander of the District to ascertain what was going on. The interview resulted in a conversation clearly indicating the fears of the President, and on these fears is based this article of impeachment. It will not likely receive a respectable vote, and I dismiss it for the consideration of those who find in it more than I have found.

The tenth article arraigns the President for making grossly abusive and indecent speeches for the purpose "of setting aside the rightful authority and powers of Congress," and to bring Congress into "disgrace, ridicule, hatred, contempt, and reproach." After setting out the language of some of the speeches in the form of specifications, the article concludes as follows, to wit:

"Which said utterances, declarations, threats, and harangues, highly censurable in any, are peculiarly indecent and unbecoming in the Chief Magistrate of the United States, by means whereof said Andrew Johnson has brought the high office of the President of the United States into contempt, ridicule, and disgrace, to the great scandal of all good citizens, whereby said Andrew Johnson, President of the United States, did commit, and was then and there guilty of a high misdemeanor in office."

In my judgment these speeches are highly censurable. They were, perhaps, made to bring contempt and ridicule on Congress as charged, but if so made they failed of their object. Indeed, it is specifically charged that they failed. It is alleged that the President intended to disgrace Congress, but succeeded only in disgracing "the office of President." Whatever else may be said of the President's intentions, or the result of his conduct on the occasions alluded, it may be perhaps safely assumed that he succeeded in bringing ridicule and contempt, if not disgrace, upon himself. Congress survived the attack. Indeed, the speeches greatly assisted the friends of Congress in carrying the election which immediately followed. If this be a political or partisan trial we should thank the President for these disgraceful harangues, for in a party point of view he and his policy were greatly damaged by them. I am inclined to think that the office of President suffered more than Congress. But that office will survive the humiliation of these speeches.

They are not official papers. They did not emanate from Mr. Johnson as President, but from Mr. Johnson as a stump speaker. In his latter capacity he forgot the dignity of his office. In fact he seems to have left the office behind him, and turned himself loose, as a private citizen, to bandy epithets with that great people from whom he had sprung and with whom he longed for a short revel even before the expiration of his term.

I perceive much for criticism, and, indeed, for censure, in these speeches, but I cannot for a moment think they contain the elements of crime for which the President may rightfully be impeached.

The Constitution provides that Congress "shall make no law abridging the freedom of

C. I.—C8.

speech or of the press." The President, like other persons, is protected under this clause. He, too, has the right to make foolish speeches. I do not now say that there is no limit to the enjoyment of this right, or that it might not be so much abused by a President as to demand his impeachment and removal from office. But in this case the offense is certainly not of so heinous a character as to demand punishment in the absence of a law defining the right and providing specific penalties, and also in the face of a constitutional provision declaring that the freedom of speech cannot be abridged by law.

I have examined these ten articles as though the offenses were formally and sufficiently charged. I have taken no technical exception, but have considered the indictment as good on its face. I look more to substance than to form in this proceeding. No rules of pleading are prescribed for our government, and if I could find an offense charged, however inartificially presented, I should deem it my duty to disregard the mere defects of form. But we cannot go outside of the charges presented. If one offense is charged we cannot convict of another. If the President corruptly pardoned a convicted criminal, we cannot pronounce him guilty of that act on an indictment for removing Stanton. If he usurped power in appointing military governors in the southern States, and violated all law in ordering them paid for their services from the public funds, we cannot pronounce him guilty thereof on a presentment charging that he made a maudlin or disgraceful speech at St. Louis.

If I were disposed to criticise severely the emptiness and insufficiency of these articles, I might refer to the language of Hon. THADDEUS STEVENS, in the House of Representatives, on the 3d day of March last, after they had been adopted, and at the time when he offered for the consideration of that body the eleventh article. Referring to these ten articles, he said, (advocating the eleventh article:)

"I will, therefore, read it and call it one and a half, as, in my judgment, it is the gist and vital portion of this whole prosecution. I wish this to be particularly noticed, for I intend to offer it as an amendment. I wish gentlemen to examine and see that this charge is nowhere contained in any of the articles reported, and unless it be inserted there can be no trial upon it; and if there be shrewd lawyers, as I know there will be, and caviling judges, and, without this article, they do not acquit him, they are greener than I was in any case I ever undertook before the court of quarter sessions."

I now come to the eleventh article. It is the only one upon which I have ever entertained serious doubts, and I will therefore set it out in full. It is as follows:

ART. 11. That said Andrew Johnson, President of the United States, unmindful of the high duties of his office, and of his oath of office, and in disregard of the Constitution and laws of the United States, did heretofore, to wit, on the 18th day of August, A. D. 1866, at the city of Washington, and the District of Columbia, by public speech, declare and affirm, in substance, that the Thirty-Ninth Congress of the United States was not a Congress of the United States authorized by the Constitution to exercise legislative power under the same, but, on the contrary, was a Congress of only part of the States, thereby denying, and intending to deny, that the legislation of said Congress was valid or obligatory upon him, the said Andrew Johnson, except in so far as he saw fit to approve the same, and also thereby denying, and intending to deny, the power of the said Thirty-Ninth Congress to propose amendments to the Constitution of the United States; and, in pursuance of said declaration, the said Andrew Johnson, President of the United States, afterward, to wit, on the 21st day of February, A. D. 1868, at the city of Washington, in the District of Columbia, did, unlawfully, and in disregard of the requirement of the Constitution, that he should take care that the laws be faithfully executed, attempt to prevent the execution of an act entitled "An act regulating the tenure of certain civil offices," passed March 2, 1867, by unlawfully devising and contriving, and attempting to devise and contrive means by which he should prevent Edwin M. Stanton from forthwith resuming the functions of the office of Secretary for the Department of War, notwithstanding the refusal of the Senate to concur in the suspension theretofore made by said Andrew Johnson of said Edwin M. Stanton from said office of Secretary for the Department of War; and also, by further unlawfully devising and contriving, and attempting to devise and contrive, means, then and there, to prevent the execution of an act entitled "An act making appropriations for the support of the Army for the fiscal year ending June 30, 1868, and for other purposes," approved March 2, 1867; and also to prevent the execution of an act entitled "An act to provide for the more efficient government of the rebel States," passed March 2, 1867, whereby the said Andrew Johnson, President of the United States, did then, to wit, on the 21st day of February, A. D. 1868, at the city of Washington, commit, and was guilty of, a high misdemeanor in office.

The great difficulty presented to my mind, in connection with this article, is to ascertain what it really charges. It will be observed that one thing is distinctly charged, and that is, that the President in August, 1866, declared and affirmed, not in words, but "in substance," that "the Thirty-Ninth Congress was not a Congress of the United States authorized by the Constitution to exercise legislative power under the same, but, on the contrary, was a Congress of only part of the States, thereby denying and intending to deny that the legislation of said Congress was valid or obligatory on him," &c. The article then proceeds to declare that "in pursuance of said declaration" the President did three certain things, to wit:

1. He attempted to prevent the execution of the tenure-of-office act "by unlawfully devising and contriving, and attempting to devise and contrive, means by which he should prevent Edwin M. Stanton from forthwith resuming the functions of the office of Secretary for the Department of War, notwithstanding the refusal of the Senate to concur in the suspension," &c.

2. And, also, "by further unlawfully devising and contriving, and attempting to devise and contrive, means, then and there, to prevent the execution" of the Army appropriation act of 1867, requiring that all military orders by the President to inferior officers be countersigned by General Grant. And, also,

3. "To prevent the execution" of the act of March 2, 1867, for the government and reconstruction of the rebel States; whereby it is charged that the President "did then, to wit, on the 21st day of February, A. D. 1868, at the city of Washington, commit, and was guilty of, a high misdemeanor in office."

It will be seen that the article winds up with charging one single offense, and that offense is said to have been committed on the 21st day of February, 1868.

This produces confusion. One would suppose, on first reading the indictment, that the body of the offense consisted in the declaration of the President that the Thirty-Ninth Congress was not a lawful Congress. But that hypothesis is shaken when we reflect that this declaration appears to have been made on the 18th of August, 1866. And again, if this declaration of the President be the real offense, and the enumerated instances of resistance to the laws passed by Congress be merely the proofs or evidences showing the President's disregard or contempt of its legislation, the article must fail, for two reasons: first, the criminal words charged are not supported by the evidence; and second, if the words were proved as laid, no mere words, declaration, or opinion, in reference to the constitutional character of Congress or the validity of its laws, can be tortured into a high crime or misdemeanor. Such an expression is not now known as a crime under any statute, and no statute can make it a crime, for the reason, as already stated, that the Constitution forbids it.

If, then, there be an offense charged in the article, it must consist in the allegation that the President devised ways and means to prevent the execution of certain acts of Congress.

By carefully examining the evidence, it will be found that no testimony was offered to show that the President attempted to prevent the execution of the reconstruction act, except a telegram to Governor Jenkins, which telegram was sent long before the passage of the reconstruction act, and could have had no reference to it whatever. It will also be seen that the only evidence adduced to show resistance to the Army appropriation bill is that of General Emory. It is the same offered in support of the ninth article. Instead of proving the charge it actually disproves it. Hence, nothing is now left in the eleventh article except the allegation that the President attempted to prevent Mr. Stanton from resuming his duties as Secretary of War after the Senate had refused to concur in his suspension. It is true that the President in a letter addressed to General Grant, on the 10th of February, 1868, admits that he had expressed to Grant a wish that he would either hold the office and contest Stanton's right to it in the courts or that he (Grant) would surrender it to the President in time to fill it with another name. On first impression it appeared to me that this charge was established by the President's own admission, and that, being established, it was an offense under the civil-tenure act; and so believing, I had at one time partially come to the conclusion to vote for this one single charge in all the eleven articles; but, upon a more careful examination and comparison of views with fellow-Senators, I became satisfied that the article failed to charge any offense.

In the first place, admitting the charge alleged to be fully proved, neither the civil-tenure act nor any other law declared it a crime or misdemeanor. The civil-tenure act declares a removal or an appointment made contrary to its provisions, a misdemeanor, but it does not make penal an effort to keep out of office one who, for the time being, stands legally suspended.

Second. The charge itself is wholly unproved. By examining the President's letter, in which appears the admission, it will be seen that no attempt, nor even a declaration of intention, was made by the President to prevent Stanton from resuming the War Office after the Senate had passed on the suspension. Indeed, if Senators will reflect, they will remember that the Senate acted on this question late at night, and Stanton entered the War Department early the next morning, and that in the meantime there was no interview between the President and General Grant. The only offense, therefore, consists in a mere declaration, or the expression of a wish, by the President made long before the Senate acted on Stanton's suspension, and while it is admitted that he was legally out of the office. Grant, it seems, partially consented to this request of the President, but no act was done either by the President or by General Grant to carry out this expressed wish.

Third. It will be observed that the President's request to Grant was in the alternative, and it was a mere request. The President did not ask him to keep Stanton out. He asked him either to contest Stanton's right in the courts or surrender the office back to him. Grant at first promised to do so. If, then, the President devised ways and means to do an unlawful act, Grant must be implicated with him, and nobody pretends that such is the case.

Fourth. Even if it appear that the President did all that can be charged on the subject, that is, if he had resolved, and even endeavored by act, to keep Stanton out of the War Office, after the action of the Senate, it does not follow that he committed even an improper, much less an unlawful act. In my view of the subject, he had a perfect right to suspend Mr. Stanton under the second section of the tenure-of-office act, and if the Senate found against the suspension, he had an equal right under the act of 1789 to remove him from office absolutely. Having, therefore, full and complete authority to do all that the charge can possibly include, I cannot on further reflection consent that this article contains matter upon which an impeachment may be properly predicated.

If any further reason were needed for voting against this article, it might be found in the fact that there is absent from the proof all pretense of a corrupt or wicked design in this request of the President. The only evidence adduced is his own admission, and when the whole letter is taken together it appears that the President was of the opinion that Stanton was already permanently removed, and he designed only to test that question before the courts.

I might extend this examination to much greater length. But the intelligent reader of this trial will look to the charges and the evidence for himself. I have not attempted to elaborate any point. I have simply endeavored to present some of the leading points which influence my judgment in voting against this prosecution. I do not say that the President is void of offense. I have not said even that he ought not to be impeached and removed from office. But I have said, and I now repeat it with emphasis, that in my judgment a cool and deliberate future will not fail to look with amazement on this extraordinary proceeding as it is now presented to us, and the legal and discriminating minds of the world would visit with deserved condemnation a judgment of conviction on any one of the articles now pending. I have taken up too much time already, and hence I forbear to allude to the political aspects of the question. We are told that the people clamor for the President's conviction. It may be so. But I cannot believe that one third of the people of this country would, as jurors, convict the President on these articles. If they clamor for conviction it is on account of other matters and for other offenses than these. Suppose, however, I am mistaken, and that nine tenths of the people desire his removal, is that a reason why we should surrender our convictions of duty. We have been sworn to examine this case from a legal and not a party point of view. If this were a vote whether Johnson should be elected President, or whether, being in, he is a fit person for the exalted office, our position might be relieved of much embarrassment. The question is simply one of guilt under the charges as presented by the House, and I cannot, in justice to the laws of the land, in justice to the country or to my own sense of right, render any other response to the several articles than a verdict of "not guilty."

OPINION
OF

HON. JAMES R. DOOLITTLE,
Delivered orally during the consultation.

Mr. Chief Justice and Senators:

I. OF THE REMOVAL OF STANTON.

I concur in so much of the opinions of Senators HENDRICKS, GRIMES, JOHNSON, FESSENDEN, TRUMBULL, and BUCKALEW, that I shall not go over the grounds so ably stated by them,

to give a general opinion in this cause. They all concur with the Senator from Ohio [Mr. SHERMAN] and with my colleague [Mr. HOWE] that the tenure-of-office act left the President at liberty to remove the Secretary of War at pleasure. In this opinion I agree. I think that opinion will command the assent of nine tenths of the legal profession of the whole country. It is too clear, in my opinion, to admit of serious argument, and I shall spend no time upon that.

II. OF THE APPOINTMENT OF THOMAS AD INTERIM.

Upon the question whether the act of 1863 in relation to *ad interim* appointments repealed the act of 1795, I wish to say a word. There is no express repeal. If repealed at all it must be by implication.

The act of 1795 covers all vacancies—vacancies by death, by resignation, by removal, and by expiration of term—four in all. Its language is, "That in case of vacancy" (including all vacancies) "it shall be lawful for the President to authorize *any person* to perform the duties," &c., for a term not longer than six months.

The act of 1863 says that in case of two vacancies, namely, by death or by resignation, the President may authorize *some other officer* to perform those duties not longer than six months.

While the act of 1795 covers all vacancies, including vacancies by removal and vacancies by expiration of term, as well as by death and by resignation, the act of 1863 does not provide for the two vacancies first named at all. Of necessity, therefore, it does not repeal or modify that act as to those two vacancies.

My colleague [Mr. HOWE] is entirely mistaken in saying that the act of 1795 was made obsolete by the act of 1863. It is true, in the margin of the volume, (first vol., 415,) the word "*obsolete*" is found. But immediately over it are found the words, also, "act of May 8, 1792, ch. 37." It is the act of 1792 which is marked obsolete, not the act of 1795. What makes this certain is, the volume itself was published in 1825, nearly forty years before the act of 1863.

Besides, President Buchanan, in 1860, under the act of 1795, appointed Mr. Holt Secretary of War *ad interim* in place of Floyd. The Senate, by resolution, asked him by what authority he acted, the Senate being in session. His answer was conclusive—overwhelming; giving more than a hundred cases of similar appointments *ad interim*. It is impossible for my colleague to maintain that the statute of 1795 is obsolete.

Neither is the statute of 1795 repealed by the act of March 2, 1867, so far as the case of Stanton is concerned; for unless his case is covered by that act, and my colleague demonstrates that it is not, his removal and the authority issued to General Thomas to perform the duties *ad interim* is no violation of that act.

It is clearly within the act of 1795. I shall dwell no longer upon that.

Mr. HARLAN. I desire to call the attention of the Senator from Wisconsin to certain words in the act of 1795 which I have not heard commented upon and which may be words of limitation, namely, "whereby they cannot perform the duties of their respective offices." Do not these words limit the act to certain vacancies?

Mr. DOOLITTLE. Let me remind my honorable friend from Iowa [Mr. HARLAN] that he will find the same words in the act of 1863 applying to vacancies caused by death and resignation "whereby they cannot perform the duties of their respective offices."

Mr. BUCKALEW. The same words are in the act of 1792. In the acts of 1795 and 1863 these words were borrowed from the act of 1792.

Mr. DOOLITTLE. That is true; I thank the Senator from Pennsylvania. I think it clear that, under the act of 1795, the President can authorize a person to do the duties of the head of the War Department in case of vacancy by removal, and the power to remove Mr. Stanton is clear under the act. The Senator from Ohio, [Mr. SHERMAN,] upon the passage of the act, maintained that, and, in his opinion just delivered, makes that point too clear to be questioned.

As to the other charges I concur entirely with the opinions of Senators HENDRICKS, GRIMES, and others, and shall not repeat what they have so well said.

But, Mr. Chief Justice and Senators, there is another point upon which I wish to submit my views, very briefly. The Senator from Ohio said however conscientiously the President may have believed that he had a right to appoint Mr. Thomas *ad interim*, if two thirds of the Senate differ with him in opinion in the construction of the law he must be found guilty of a high crime or high misdemeanor, for which he should be removed from his high office. From this doctrine I dissent. The President, as the Chief Executive, is compelled officially to construe the laws of Congress. He must execute them; and to do that he must know their meaning. If he mistake the meaning of a doubtful statute, upon which the ablest Senators and lawyers disagree, to say he can be found guilty of a high crime or high misdemeanor because he mistakes its true meaning while honestly seeking to find it shocks the moral sense of the civilized world. It is a monstrous proposition. Intention, criminal intention, is of the very essence of crime. A public officer may commit a trespass and become liable to respond, in damages, in a civil suit, when, mistaking the law, he violates the rights of person or property of another. But to say that a high public officer, with good motives and with an honest intent to obey, though he mistake the meaning of a statute, can be found guilty of a high crime and misdemeanor which shall subject him to the heaviest punishment which can fall upon a public man in high office, is to assert a doctrine never before heard in any court of justice. There is no evidence to show on his part an intention to violate the Constitution or the law. From a criminal act a criminal intent, in the absence of proof to the contrary, may be inferred. But in this case all criminal intent is positively disproved by the Managers themselves.

The message of the President which the Managers have put in evidence against him—and there is no evidence to contradict it—distinctly avers his entire good faith; and further, that he was advised by all the members of his Cabinet, including Mr. Stanton:

First, that the tenure-of-office act was unconstitutional, and therefore no law at all.

Every student at law knows that every enactment of Congress is just as much subject to the higher law of the Constitution as if it contained an express proviso in these words: "Provided that nothing herein contained shall have any force or validity whatever unless it is authorized by the Constitution of the United States." In a word, an unconstitutional enactment is not a law; it is void; and void things are no things at all.

And secondly, the message proves, also, that every member of his Cabinet advised him that if the law were constitutional his power to remove Stanton was not limited by the very terms of the act.

It will be remembered, also, the President's counsel offered to prove the fact that the President was so advised by every member of his Cabinet, including, of course, the Attorney General.

Now, Mr. Chief Justice and Senators, whatever effect may be given to the opinions of other members of the Cabinet, the opinion of the Attorney General, given to the President, must be regarded as judicial so far at least in the absence of bad faith in him, or in the President when acting upon that opinion, as to protect the President from all charge of crime or high misdemeanor.

The statute providing for an Attorney General enacts:

"And there shall also be appointed a meet person, learned in the law, to act as Attorney General of the United States, who shall be sworn or affirmed to a faithful execution of his office; whose duty it shall be to prosecute and conduct all suits in the Supreme Court in which the United States shall be concerned, and to give his advice and opinion upon questions of law, when required by the President of the United States," &c.

This opinion of the Attorney General, if given and acted upon in good faith by the President, is a protection against any charge of high crime or high misdemeanor. The Attorney General is chosen because he is *learned in the law*, to advise a President who may not be a lawyer at all. He is confirmed by the Senate as a judge is confirmed, for his high character and legal learning.

Take the case of General Grant, who is a candidate for the Presidency. He is no lawyer. Suppose he should be elected, and the Senator from New Jersey, who is learned in the law, should be nominated and confirmed by the Senate as his Attorney General, and that some of the many doubtful, hasty, and almost unintelligible acts of Congress came before him for construction; if General Grant should, in good faith, act upon the opinion of Senator FRELINGHUYSEN as his Attorney General, no matter how erroneous that opinion might be, can any man be so lost to all sense of common justice and fair dealing as to assert that General Grant could be guilty of a high crime or high misdemeanor when acting in accordance with it. And learned in the law as that honorable Senator is, high as he deservedly stands in the profession in his State, it is certainly no disparagement to him to say that Mr. Stanbery stands as high as he or any other Senator upon this floor in personal character and legal ability.

Sir, much may be forgiven, much must be forgiven in times of high party excitement for the judicial blindness which it begets. But when this temporary and frenzied excitement shall have passed away, as pass it will, and when men shall carefully review this case and all the evidence given on this trial, their surprise will be not that a few Republican Senators can rise above party prejudice and refuse to be driven from their clear convictions by party furor, but their utter astonishment will be, that any respectable Senator should ever for one moment have entertained the thought of convicting the President of the United States of a high crime or a high misdemeanor upon the charges and evidence produced upon this trial.

OPINION
OF
HON. F. T. FRELINGHUYSEN.

There is no more responsible duty than that of trying the question whether the Chief Magistrate of a nation, who holds his office under the Constitution and by the suffrages of the people, shall be deposed. On the one hand, the result of the issue is serious to the individual who is on trial, reaches to the rights of every citizen, may effect the maintenance of the checks and balances, and even the stability of the Government. On the other hand, to suffer the Executive successfully to assert the right to adjudicate on the validity of laws, claimed to be inferentially, though not in terms, contrary to the Constitution, and to execute such as he approves and violate such as he condemns, would be to permit the Government to be destroyed. And since the issue whether the law shall be obeyed has been made before the country and before the world, to suffer the President defiantly, and to this hour persistently to disobey it, would be to surrender the supremacy of that sovereignty for the maintenance of which hundreds of thousands of loyal hearts have within the past few years ceased to beat. , Walking along this narrow pathway, with perils on either side, one is only secure as he rests his hand on the firm support of duty.

We are but the agents of the people, authorized to act for them only in accordance with the Constitution and the laws. If we fail to protect the trusts committed to us we are cowards; if we exceed our powers and assume to exercise our arbitrary will, we are usurpers. Having on questions as to the admission of evidence exercised all the liberality that was consistent with principle, and having held my opinion, subject to all legitimate influences, until the whole cause was closed, and the final vote about to be taken, I am now prepared briefly to express my views.

Senators are sworn in this case to do impartial justice according to the Constitution and the laws. The obligation thus imposed may not be disregarded. The Senate, while trying the President, are not only invested with the functions of a court and jury, but also retain their official characters as Senators intrusted with the interests of the nation. Were this not so, the articles of impeachment might as well be tried before the quarter sessions as before the Senate of the United States. We may not remove the President because we believe the welfare of the nation would thereby be promoted, if the charges against him are not proved; but if those charges are proved, we may, for the well-being of the Republic, abstain from the exercise of that clemency which in other judicial proceedings is reposed in the court and in the pardoning power, but which in the matter of impeachment is involved in the verdict of the Senate.

There are three questions to be determined, namely:

1. Has Andrew Johnson violated the law as charged?

2. Does such violation amount to what in the Constitution is denominated a high misdemeanor? .

3. Do the interests of the country demand the enforcement of the penalty for this violation of law, or demand the exercise of clemency?

There are eleven articles of impeachment presented againt the President. I shall confine my remarks to the first three and the eleventh.

The first article charges Andrew Johnson with violating the "act regulating the tenure of certain civil officers" by the removal of Secretary Stanton. The second and third articles charge a violation of the same act by appointment of General Thomas as Secretary of War ad interim, and the eleventh article, as construed by the Chief Justice, charges that the President violated the same act by "attempting to defeat its execution."

The first, second, and sixth sections of the act entitled "An act regulating the tenure of certain civil offices," are as follows:

"*Be it enacted by the Senate and House of Representatives of the United States of America in Congress assembled*, That every person holding any civil office to which he has been appointed by and with the advice and consent of the Senate, and every person who shall hereafter be appointed to any office, and shall become duly qualified to act therein, is, and shall be, entitled to hold such office until a successor shall have been in like manner appointed and duly qualified, except as herein otherwise provided: *Provided*, That the Secretaries of State, of the Treasury, of War, of the Navy, and of the Interior, the Postmaster General, and the Attorney General, shall hold their offices respectively for and during the term of the President by whom they may have been appointed and for one month thereafter, subject to removal by and with the advice and consent of the Senate.

"SEC. 2. *And be it further enacted*, That when any officer appointed as aforesaid, excepting judges of the United States courts, shall, during a recess of the Senate, be shown, by evidence satisfactory to the President, to be guilty of misconduct in office, or crime, or for any reason shall become incapable or legally disqualified to perform its duties, in such case, and in no other, the President may suspend such officer, and designate some suitable person to perform temporarily the duties of such office until the next meeting of the Senate, and until the case shall be acted upon by the Senate, and such person so designated shall take the oaths and give the bonds required by law to be taken and given by the person duly appointed to fill such office; and in such case it shall be the duty of the President, within twenty days after the first day of such next meeting of the Senate, to report to the Senate such suspension, with the evidence and reasons for his action in the case, and the name of the person so designated to perform the duties of such office. And if the Senate shall concur in such suspension and advise and consent to the removal of such officer, they shall so certify to the President, who may thereupon remove such officer, and, by and with the advice and consent of the Senate, appoint another person to such office. But if the Senate shall refuse to concur in such suspension, such officer so suspended shall forthwith resume the functions of his office, and the powers of the person so performing its duties in his stead shall cease, and the official salary and emoluments of such officer shall, during such suspension, belong to the person so performing the duties thereof, and not to the officer so suspended: *Provided, however*, That the President, in case he shall become satisfied that such suspension was made on insufficient grounds, shall be authorized, at any time before reporting such suspension to the Senate as above provided, to revoke such suspension and reinstate such officer in the performance of the duties of his office."

"SEC. 6. *And be it further enacted*, That every removal, appointment, or employment, made, had, or exercised, contrary to the provisions of this act, and the making, signing, sealing, countersigning, or issuing of any commission or letter of authority for or in respect to any such appointment or employment, shall be deemed, and are hereby declared to be, high misdemeanors, and upon trial and conviction thereof shall be punished by a fine not exceeding $10,000, or by imprisonment not exceeding five years, or both said punishments, in the discretion of the court: *Provided*, That the President shall have power to make out and deliver, after the adjournment of the Senate, commissions for all officers whose appointment shall have been advised and consented to by the Senate."

The first, second, third, and eleventh articles of impeachment charge, in effect, that Edwin M. Stanton, being then Secretary of War, Andrew Johnson, on the 12th of August, 1867, suspended him from office under the provisions of the second section of said act; that within twenty days after the next meeting of the Senate, to wit, on the 12th of December,

1867, he reported to the Senate the reason for such suspension, and also that he had appointed General Grant Secretary of War *ad interim.* That on the 13th of January, 1866, the Senate having refused to concur in said suspension, and having so notified Andrew Johnson, the said Edwin M. Stanton was restored to the functions of his said office under said act; that Andrew Johnson then devised means to prevent the execution of the said act by striving to induce General Grant to refuse to surrender the said office to Mr. Stanton; that, failing in this effort, on the 21st of February, 1868, he made the following orders for the removal of Mr. Stanton and for the appointment of General Thomas as Secretary of War *ad interim.*

EXECUTIVE MANSION,
WASHINGTON, D. C., *February* 21, 1868.

SIR: By virtue of the power and authority vested in me as President, by the Constitution and laws of the United States, you are hereby removed from office as Secretary for the Department of War, and your functions as such will terminate upon receipt of this communication.

You will transfer to Brevet Major General Lorenzo Thomas, Adjutant General of the Army, who has this day been authorized and empowered to act as Secretary of War *ad interim,* all records, books, papers, and other public property now in your custody and charge.

Respectfully, yours,　ANDREW JOHNSON.
Hon. EDWIN M. STANTON, *Washington, D. C.*

EXECUTIVE MANSION,
WASHINGTON, D. C., *February* 21, 1868.

SIR: Hon. Edwin M. Stanton having this day been removed from office as Secretary for the Department of War, you are hereby authorized and empowered to act as Secretary of War *ad interim,* and will immediately enter upon the discharge of the duties pertaining to that office.

Mr. Stanton has been instructed to transfer to you all the records, books, papers, and other public property now in his custody and charge.

Respectfully, yours,　ANDREW JOHNSON.
Brevet Major General LORENZO THOMAS, *Adjutant General United States Army, Washington, D. C.*

The facts thus charged are proved beyond all dispute. There are many other facts of aggravation, and showing intent, also proved, not referred to because not necessary to the case.

If Andrew Johnson did remove Mr. Stanton and issue a letter of authority for the appointment of General Thomas Secretary of War, or do either, *contrary to the provisions of the tenure-of-civil-office act,* he, by the terms of the sixth section of that act, hereinbefore recited, is guilty of a high misdemeanor.

It is insisted that he did not remove Mr. Stanton, because he is in fact still in possession of the War Department. The removal referred to as constituting the misdemeanor in the sixth section does not mean a physical removal, but means such an act of removal as it was in the power of the President to perform. Neither does the removal spoken of in the act mean a *valid* removal, for it would be an absurdity to hold that a valid act of the President was a misdemeanor. The "removal" spoken of is just such an act as the President performed, issuing under his authority an order of removal,

notifying the other Departments that Mr. Stanton was removed, and informing the Senate that by his order Mr. Stanton had ceased to be Secretary of War, refusing to acknowledge him as such, and recognizing General Thomas as his successor.

It is again insisted, in defense of Mr. Johnson, that Mr. Stanton is not included within the provisions of the tenure-of-civil-office act, and is not protected in his office thereby, and that consequently his removal was legal; and that, a vacancy thus lawfully existing, the appointment of General Thomas *ad interim* thereto was not prohibited by the said act.

Let us examine whether Mr. Stanton is not protected by the act. The proviso to the first section of the act says the "Secretaries of State, Treasury, War, &c., shall hold their offices respectively for and during the term of the President by whom they may have been appointed, and for one month thereafter." The Constitution makes the presidential term four years, commencing the 4th of March; and as Mr. Lincoln's term commenced March 4, 1865, this is his term, and Mr. Stanton, having been by him appointed, is protected from removal by the words of the act. But it has been insisted that the true construction of the act is that the Secretaries, to be protected under the act, must have been appointed during the existing presidential term, and that Mr. Stanton was not appointed by Mr. Lincoln after his reëlection and during the existing term. There is some force in this claim, and I have only called attention to the fact that Mr. Stanton is within the words of the act for the purpose of showing that those who deny that he is under the protection of the law are obliged to resort to intendment and construction to maintain their position.

But let us look at the act again. The *pivot word* of the act is "successors." The body of the first section (as distinguished from the proviso) declares that "every person holding or who shall hold a civil office by and with the advice and consent of the Senate shall be entitled to hold such office until a *successor* shall be in like manner appointed." So that neither the President nor the President and Senate together can remove from office such civil officer, excepting by the nomination and confirmation of a successor. The act, however, makes two exceptions to this rule. It provides that the rule referred to shall exist, "*except as herein otherwise provided;*" and then we have one exception to this rule in the second section, which enacts that when the President suspends an officer he must send his reasons to the Senate; and if the Senate advise and consent to the removal of the officer, they shall so certify to the President, who may thereupon *remove* him, and this without nominating a successor. And we have another exception to the rule in the proviso to the first section, namely, that the Secretaries of State, Treasury, War, &c., shall be subject to removal by and with the advice and consent of the Senate, and this without a successor being appointed.

All civil officers, except as above excepted, hold their offices until a successor is appointed. Now, if Mr. Stanton does not come within the proviso to the first section, he comes within the body of that section; and if within the proviso, he can only be removed by and with the advice and consent of the Senate, and if he comes within the body of the act he can only be removed by a successor being appointed by and with the advice and consent of the Senate. As the President has removed Mr. Stanton without a successor being appointed by and with the advice and consent of the Senate, and without the Senate's having consented to such removal, he has violated the law.

It has been argued that if the Secretary of War is not within the proviso he drops out of the act and is not protected by it, because, as is said, the office of Secretary of War is in the *proviso*, and the officer must remain where his office is; and as you cannot carry the office back to the body of the act, so you cannot carry the officer there. The defect in this nice argument is that the body of the act as well as the proviso speaks not of *offices*, but of *persons*—the body of the act, of every *person* holding any civil office; and the proviso, of the *Secretaries* of State, Treasury, War, &c. So Mr. Stanton, either under the body of the act or the proviso, is placed under the protection of the act.

But why should we be technical in construing a statute that is plain? The second section enacts that whenever any officer (except judges of the Supreme Court) appointed as aforesaid—that is, appointed by and with the advice and consent of the Senate—shall during a *recess* be guilty of misconduct in office, or crime, or become incapable or legally disqualified to perform his duties, in such case, and in no other, the President may suspend such officer; and within twenty days after the next meeting of the Senate the President shall report to the Senate the reasons for his action. If the Senate concur in such suspension, and consent to the removal of such officer, the President may remove him; but if the Senate shall refuse to concur in such suspension, such officer so suspended shall resume the functions of his office. Mr. Stanton is, beyond doubt, included within the provisions of this second section, being appointed by and with the advice and consent of the Senate, and has been treated by the President as within the section by being suspended under it.

And now, I insist, that if the President can only *suspend* for *cause* during a *recess* of the Senate, *a fortiori*, he cannot *remove without cause* during the *session of the Senate*. What an absurdity to hold that when the President wants to be rid of an officer he has only a limited power of temporary suspension, and yet has, at the same time, an unlimited power of absolute removal! Of what possible efficacy

are the guarded limitations of *suspension* if, at will, the President can arbitrarily *remove?* It is from this view that we conclude that Mr. Stanton is protected by the act, and that his removal and the appointment of General Thomas was a violation of the statute.

But may not the President have been mistaken as to the true interpretation of the law? Some Senators do not now consider that Mr. Stanton is under the protection of the law. May not Mr. Johnson have fallen into the same error?

It is not possible that Andrew Johnson did not consider Mr. Stanton within the law, because, during the recess of the Senate, he suspended him under this law, and within the limited period of twenty days submitted to the Senate his reasons for such suspension; and his counsel, [Mr. Groesbeck,] in argument, stated that the suspension was made under the act. Besides, there is no other authority under which this proceeding could have been had. If the Constitution conferred upon the President the power of removal, it knows of no proceeding of suspension, trial by the Senate, and restoration to the functions of office.

There are other facts which show that the removal of Mr. Stanton was not the result of any mistake. After the President had submitted his reasons to the Senate and they had adjudicated against those reasons, and after he had informed the Senate that he had now removed Mr. Stanton and appointed General Thomas, the Senate sent the President a resolution passed by that body, to the effect that he had acted in violation of the Constitution and the laws. The President did not annul the order of removal and appointment, but, on the contrary, at the next meeting of the Senate, on the 24th of February, 1868, sent them a message stating, in substance, that if satisfied that his removal of Mr. Stanton should involve his own removal, he still would have removed him. The House of Representatives then presented articles of impeachment against him, and since then, for a quarter of a year, Congress has been engaged in the investigation relative to this removal and appointment, but he has never annulled those orders, but stands to-day contemning, not the Senate, but the sovereign power of the nation—the law. Had Andrew Johnson at any time withdrawn from his position of defiance of that law which he is sworn to execute, he might have pleaded that he was mistaken. The Senate has spoken, the Representatives of the people have spoken, and he disregards their voice. He cannot plead the views of individual Senators. Neither can he plead the opinion of his Attorney General; for no offer that I know of was made to prove that the Attorney General ever officially gave any opinion to sustain the President's views, certainly no proof of such an opinion after the President suspended Mr. Stanton under this law. Before the nation and the world the question Mr. Johnson forces us to determine is, whether the law in America shall or shall not be supreme. The issue joined now to be settled is, where is lodged the *ultimate* power of the nation—in one man or in the representatives of the people?

Such being the issues forced upon us, I feel that we have no election but to stand by the doctrine that power is with the people.

Again, let us inquire whether the President's purpose may not have been to test the constitutionality of the tenure-of-civil-office act.

That act makes the consent of the Senate necessary to the removal of certain civil officers who can only be appointed by such consent. The Constitution nowhere gives the President the right to remove from office, and to hold that he has that power, even against the will of the Senate, is virtually to destroy that provision of the Constitution which makes the advice and consent of the Senate necessary to an appointment. It is the same power that appoints that has the right to remove. For eighty years the removal from office has been governed and regulated by law.

But, waiving the constitutional argument, is the President to violate laws at pleasure on the plea that he desires to ascertain their constitutionality? Does he not know that since the formation of the Government not more than two or three general laws have ever been declared invalid? Could he not have taken some less important case for the trial? Three months have transpired since the removal, and the first step to make this test has not been taken. And if this suit was now instituted it could not possibly be determined before March next. No, such was not the President's purpose. After the Senate refused to concur in his reasons for Mr. Stanton's suspension his purpose was to carry out his own arbitrary will in defiance of the law and its authors.

2. Andrew Johnson having violated the law as charged, the next question is, does such violation constitute a high misdemeanor?

The tenure-of-civil-office act, in its sixth section, declares its violation to be a high misdemeanor; but that enactment is not conclusive on the Senate, for if it were the legislative branch of the Government, by mere statutes, might destroy the power of the executive branch. The Senate are called on to determine whether the violation is such as, *under the Constitution*, is subject-matter for impeachment and conviction.

The Constitution makes treason and bribery (crimes eminently affecting the State) and other high crimes and misdemeanors impeachable.

The word "high," as qualifying misdemeanors, clearly intends to direct and restrict impeachment to such offenses as derive their importance from the effect they have upon the State.

Forgery, arson, and other crimes, so far as the individual who perpetrates them is concerned, are more serious and higher crimes than the violation of a prohibitory statute like the one in question, but, so far as the Government is concerned, may not be so important.

If the willful, defiant, persistent disregard of law in a Chief Magistrate of a great people does not constitute a high misdemeanor in office, what does? The State is infinitely less interested in the personal dereliction of the official than in a course of action, which, if tolerated, saps and destroys the Government; and as down to the present hour the law and its authors are defied, we cannot do otherwise than declare that such conduct constitutes a high misdemeanor in office.

3. Is this a case where the Senate by its verdict should, in view of the well-being of society, pass over the transgression, or should they enforce the penalty of removal provided by the Constitution?

On this point the tribunal trying the President act not only as a court and as jurors, but act also as Senators, bound to look at the condition and to the welfare of the country.

There are considerations bearing on the question whether the penalty of the violated law shall be enforced which seriously affect the welfare of the nation. Among those considerations are, Mr. Johnson's desertion, at the most critical of periods, of the cherished principles of the party that confided in and elected him; his denial of the validity and constitutionality of our Government as organized, which had just been rescued at a great price from the hands of treason; the repetition of that sentiment from his lips by his counsel on the trial; the declaration of his annual message that in his controversy with Congress he had contemplated a resort to force; his encouraging a spirit of discontent and disloyalty in the rebel States by his offensive denunciations of the reconstruction measures; his assuming, without right, to establish governments in the South which left the defenders of the Union unprotected; his exertion of influence against the adoption of the fourteenth amendment to the Constitution, to the ratification of which the people fondly looked for national harmony; his obstruction to the practical working of those measures of reconstruction which the rejection of the amendment referred to rendered necessary; his pardoning of rebels and his appointing them to office; the fact that the distrust of Congress in the Chief Magistrate has been such that a due regard for the Republic induced them to remain in session, to convene at unusual periods of the year, and induced them to enact laws requiring all military orders to be issued by the "General of the Army," and prohibiting the removal of that officer by the President; the general conviction that the unfortunate millions just relieved from bondage at the South who have been true to the Union are deprived of the much needed protection of the Federal Government. These, and many like considerations, force us to the conclusion that if Andrew Johnson has willfully violated the law its penalty should be enforced.

But we are sworn that we will do "impartial justice" in the case, and to try the question whether we may not be influenced by prejudice let us apply a severe test.

Suppose that the tenure-of-civil-office act had been in force during the administration of Abraham Lincoln, and that distinguished patriot had under the law, from some personal pique, suspended Edwin M. Stanton, a man who has organized more victories for freedom than any living civilian; suppose Mr. Lincoln to have submitted his reasons for such suspension to the Senate, and that body, after due deliberation, to have determined against the sufficiency of the alleged cause of suspension, and (as authorized by the law) to have ordered that Mr. Stanton resume the functions of his office; and that then Mr. Lincoln, having first endeavored to seduce the temporary incumbent of the office not to surrender the office, and having in this failed, should have issued an order for the absolute and unqualified removal of Mr. Stanton, and for the appointment of a successor, and that he by message should have informed the Senate of what he had done; and let us suppose that the Senate by resolution promptly informed Mr. Lincoln that in his procedure he had acted contrary to the Constitution and the laws, and that then Mr. Lincoln had sent a message to the Senate informing them that if he had known that his own removal would be the consequence of the removal of Mr. Stanton he would nevertheless have removed him; then suppose that the Representatives of the people had presented articles of impeachment against Mr. Lincoln, and the Senate had proceeded with the trial, and that for three months, with all these notifications, Mr. Lincoln had persisted in his defiant disobedience to the law and to the will of Congress, and thus made the unavoidable issue whether the law should be supreme, and whether the *ultimate* power of government was with one intrusted only to execute law, or with the Representatives of the people, would Abraham Lincoln have been entitled to an acquittal? No. If all the tenderness of feeling which now clusters around the memory of our martyred President had belonged to him while living, and the issue had been thus conspicuously forced upon us, whether he should remain in office and the law be contemned, or he be removed and its majesty vindicated, duty would have impelled an adjudication for his removal.

The case I have supposed is that proved against the respondent in these proceedings. That justice which would have been executed against Abraham Lincoln must be *impartial* when applied to Andrew Johnson; and I shall vote for conviction.

OPINION
OF
HON. ALEXANDER G. CATTELL.

Having carefully considered the articles of impeachment preferred by the House of Representatives against Andrew Johnson, President of the United States, and the evidence adduced in support thereof, and having arrived at the conclusion that the charges contained in the leading articles are fully sustained by the proof, and that the acts therein charged and proved being plain violations of the Constitution and of the laws of the United States, constitute a misdemeanor in office, I propose to state the grounds and reasons for the conclusion to which I have arrived.

If it may seem presumptuous for one uneducated in the law to deal with a question which has been illuminated by the discussions on either side of the most learned lawyers in the land, I may be permitted to say that, profoundly impressed with the gravity of the issue, and deeply sensible of the responsibility which rests upon each individual Senator, I prefer to state for myself and in my own language the grounds upon which my verdict of *guilty* is given. I propose to confine my remarks chiefly to the consideration of the first three articles. Stripped of all technicality the following is the statement of the charges contained therein:

Article one charges the issuing of an order in writing for the removal of Edwin M. Stanton, Secretary for the Department of War, as contrary to the Constitution and laws, and especially as contrary to the act entitled "An act to regulate the tenure of certain civil offices," passed March 2, 1867.

Article two charges the issuing and delivery of a letter of authority to Lorenzo Thomas, authorizing and empowering him to act as Secretary for the Department of War, as a violation of the Constitution, and especially as contrary to the tenure-of-office law.

Article three charges that Thomas was appointed without authority of law, without the advice and consent of the Senate, and while it was in session, when no vacancy had happened during the recess of the Senate, and no vacancy existed at the time, with intent to violate the Constitution.

The second and third articles, charging in special and general terms the appointment of Thomas as a violation of law, may, I think, be held to present two distinct aspects of criminality, namely, the unlawful appointment and the unlawful removal which was declared in the letter, and which is implied in, and is of necessity accomplished by, the unlawful appointment; and they are sustained if it is shown that the appointment of Thomas alone is unlawful, or if it is shown that it was unlawful as including the removal of Stanton, so that the two acts taken together were criminal; for the appointment to an office thereby unlawfully vacated includes all the criminality of an unlawful removal.

But I propose to consider first the charge contained in the first article, namely, the issuing of the unlawful order for the removal of Mr. Stanton. The fact that the order was issued is proved, and, indeed, is admitted, in the answer of the respondent. The inquiry, then, is, was the removal of Mr. Stanton an act contrary to the Constitution or laws of the United States? If it was, then it was clearly a misdemeanor in office.

The Constitution gives no such power of removal directly to the President, and the advocates of such a power can claim it only as derived by implication from that clause which affirms that "the executive power shall be vested in the President."

Now, if we assume that the laws regulating and restricting the power of removal, which have been passed from time to time, including the tenure-of-office act, are constitutional, and that the power is subject to legislative construction, then this power cannot be held to be a quality inherent in the *executive* power as conferred on the President by the Constitution. If such a power ever existed as an element of constitutional executive power, it could not be curtailed or restricted by legislative enactment; but it is restricted by these acts; and if they are admitted to be valid laws, which hitherto has not been denied, the existence of the absolute power of removal as an essential executive quality is concluded.

All the implications of the Constitution are against the idea that this power is in the President. The fact that the power of appointment is given by the Constitution to the President and Senate jointly would seem to deny him the power to vacate an office which he could not alone fill and create a vacancy which he cannot alone supply. The provision that he may fill vacancies "*that may happen during the recess of the Senate,*" and then only until the next session, would seem to deny him the power to fill any vacancies other than those which *happen*, or to fill *any* at any time other than "*during the recess of the Senate.*" A thing happens, in the largest sense that can be given to that term, when it comes to pass not by the motion of the person whose action is affected by the happening. A vacancy does not *happen* when it occurs by the action of him who is to fill it. The clause, then, does not provide for the filling of vacancies which are *made* by removals, but confines the President's power to other vacancies, even in recess, and implies that there shall be no removals unless the Senate is in session and advise and consent.

The President, then, derives *from the Constitution* no power of vacating by removal, except by the nomination, confirmation, and appointment of a successor. Whatever of other power of removal is rightfully exercised by him has been derived from the terms or implications of legislative enactment. Assumed necessity or convenience have conceded to him the power during the recess of Congress, but neither the language nor the implications of legislative enactments have extended the power; necessity or convenience do not demand, nor has precedent sanctioned, its exercise at any other time.

The case of Pickering, the only one cited which has any similarity with the case under consideration, does not make against the principle contended for. The fact that an immediate nomination to the Senate was stated in the President's letter to Mr. Pickering to be necessary, and the fact that it does not appear that the nomination of his successor did not precede the letter informing him of his removal, together with the fact that it has never, through sixty-eight years of immensely increased patronage, been drawn into a precedent for the exercise of such executive power, show that the real circumstances of the case were not such as to assert any executive claim to this power.

But even if they were such, a single act, standing alone and never repeated, through a long lapse of years crowded with similar occasions, should have no weight as a precedent in favor of the principle which it seems to illustrate, but, on the contrary, it may be inferred that the act was not accepted as correct practice at the time, that the principle was disapproved of, and the practice ever since discontinued. Thus it appears to me that even before the passage of the "tenure-of-office law," or even if Mr. Stanton's case is not included in it, the removal charged in the first article was an act unauthorized by the Constitution or the law, principle or precedent.

I am not unaware of the fact that the views which I have thus briefly stated, questioning the President's power of removal, as a constitutional prerogative in the absence of legislative enactment, are controverted by many. Differences of opinion on this point exist now as they did at the time of the adoption of the Constitution, and among the distinguished men of the first Congress. An examination of the debates which took place in the Congress of 1789 upon the acts establishing the several Departments, will show that the eminent statesmen of that day differed widely in their construction of the Constitution as to the President's power in this regard. But whatever differences of opinion may have existed then or may exist now upon this point, one thing is clear, the power has been considered a proper subject for legislative construction from the time of the First Congress down to the present day, and it is too late now to question the right of legislative control over the subject.

Mr. Manager BINGHAM quotes the authority of Webster in proof of the position that the provisions of the acts of 1789, establishing the Departments of State and War, which provide an officer to have charge of the records, &c.,

"*whenever the said principal officer shall be removed from office by the President*," was a grant of power, and from that day to this Congress has exercised the power to grant and to regulate the power of the Executive in this particular, and the right has never been seriously questioned or the constitutionality of the laws doubted.

In pursuance of this practice the Thirty-Ninth Congress passed, March 2, 1867, the act entitled "An act to regulate the tenure of certain civil offices," which covers the whole question of removal from and appointment to office in all cases not specially provided for by the Constitution. This law, framed to restrain the President in the exercise of the lesser power of arbitrary removal during the recess, certainly by its spirit, scope, and object intends to deny, and most clearly in all its terms and implications does deny and conclude the larger power of arbitrary removal "*during the session of the Senate*." Let us examine the provisions for a moment in their bearing on this case. The terms of the law define in strict language the limits of executive authority on this subject. Its passage over the veto of the President by two thirds of both Houses of Congress exhausted all right to question its constitutionality by the Executive, whose duty thenceforward was to execute it as a law of the land.

I shall then assume, for the purposes of this statement, that it is a valid and constitutional law in all its parts, and that the President knew and understood that it had been so declared with express view to his executive action, and that he knew if he violated it he was directly attacking a legislative power which the representatives of the people claimed and meant to assert.

The only remaining inquiry upon this particular question is, does the law apply to Secretary Stanton's case?

If the removal of Stanton was against the provisions of this law the President is guilty under it, for the only *intent* in question *is the intent to break the law*, not the motive or intention with which it was done. If Stanton is included among the officers referred to in the first section of this law, then his removal without the advice and consent of the Senate was against its provisions. The language of this section is—

"That *every person* holding *any* civil office to which he has been appointed by and with the advice and consent of the Senate, and every person who shall hereafter be appointed to any such office and shall become duly qualified to act therein, is and shall be entitled to hold such office until a successor shall have been in like manner appointed and duly qualified, except as herein otherwise provided: *Provided*, That the Secretaries of State, of the Treasury, of War, of the Navy, and of the Interior, the Postmaster General, and the Attorney General, shall hold their offices respectively for and during the term of the President by whom they may have been appointed, and one month thereafter, subject to removal by and with the advice and consent of the Senate."

Now, it seems irresistible that this language, referring, as it does, to those in office at the time of its passage, as well as those thereafter to be appointed, includes, either in the general provisions of the body of the section or in the exception, all persons holding any civil office appointed with the consent of the Senate. The words "*every person* holding *any* civil office" are as comprehensive as language can make them, and, in the absence of any exception, would include all, and, of course, Mr. Stanton.

But the fact that there is an exception makes even this strong language more comprehensive than before; for when an exception is mentioned the conclusion is strengthened that nothing is left outside of the general provisions except what is included in the exceptions. Thus the words "all" and "except," in construction, include everything.

Besides, the express language of the general clause provides for *all* civil officers thus appointed, *except* such as are affirmatively otherwise provided for "herein;" that is, in the law itself. This shows that the law undertakes affirmatively to provide "therein" for *every* such officer. It thus expressly says that *all* are included and provided for in the general clause for whom there is not some other affirmative provision made in the proviso. Thus no officer or class is left out of the law by implication, for it declares substantially that every one excluded from the exception by its language or by implication, is not taken by the exception out of the effect of the general clause. To say, then, that Mr. Stanton's case is not provided for in the exception, is to affirm that it is included in the general clause. It matters not, for the purpose of this trial, whether the case of Mr. Stanton comes under the general clause or the exception. The reasoning is strong that the case is included in the exception. The words of the exception are, "*may have been* appointed." These words seem to contemplate, in relation to the tenure of these offices, the possible existence of the term of a President other than the one who may be actually in office when the question of removal arises. The act took effect upon offices as they existed at the time it passed, and when it referred to terms during which they were, after its passage, to expire, it referred to the term then existing and to those which should occur in the future.

By the Constitution the *term* of the President continues "during four years." The word *term* means strictly limit or boundary. A term of office is the time which must elapse before its limit is reached. The limit of Mr. Lincoln's second term was four years from the 4th of March, 1865. When the word term was used in the act, this was the term contemplated in regard to offices filled by him, and still held by his appointees at the time of its passage. This term did not expire on the 21st of February, and has not yet expired. If Mr. Lincoln had been living when the act was passed it would certainly have been held to apply to his present term, as it then existed, and to extend the offices to the end of it. It is not the less Mr. Lincoln's term that it was also Mr. Johnson's, who was, in the language of the Constitution, chosen "for the same term." When, upon Mr. Lincoln's death, Mr. Johnson came in, the powers and duties of the office devolved upon him for the *remainder of Mr. Lincoln's term.* He had no other relation to the term, and no more or other power in relation to the officers he found in than Mr. Lincoln would have had had he lived. It matters not, as I have said, whether these views prevail or not. If they do not, it only shows that Mr. Stanton's case is not provided for in the proviso, for the reason that the term of the President by whom he was appointed had already lapsed, and, therefore, the terms of the limitation of the proviso cannot be made to apply to his case, and that not being "otherwise provided for therein" is not included in the exception, and, therefore, is included in the general clause: for every case not therein otherwise provided for is covered by the general clause.

Again, the second section of the act, which applies to all officers, (except certain classes in relation to whom the Constitution prescribes otherwise, namely, the judges of the United States courts,) and contains no other exception of any officer, of course included Mr. Stanton. The very fact that this section excepts by this special exception only such officers confirmed by the Senate as are placed out of its reach shows that it was intended to affect all within its reach. By its express terms it enacts that the President, within the limits and in the manner therein prescribed, may, "*during a recess of the Senate, suspend*" an officer, in the case therein mentioned, "and in no other." This section reads as follows:

"SEC. 2. *And be it further enacted,* That when any officer appointed as aforesaid, excepting judges of the United States courts, shall, during a recess of the Senate, be shown by evidence satisfactory to the President to be guilty of misconduct in office, or crime, or for any reason shall become incapable or legally disqualified to perform its duties, in such case, and in no other, the President may suspend such officer and designate some suitable person to perform temporarily the duties of such office until the next meeting of the Senate, and until the case shall be acted upon by the Senate, and such person so designated shall take the oaths and give the bonds required by law to be taken and given by the person duly appointed to fill such office; and in such case it shall be the duty of the President, within twenty days after the first day of such next meeting of the Senate, to report to the Senate such suspension, with the evidence and reasons for his action in the case, and the name of the person so designated to perform the duties of such office. And if the Senate shall concur in such suspension, and advise and consent to the removal of such officer, they shall so certify to the President, who may thereupon remove such officer, and, by and with the advice and consent of the Senate, appoint another person to such office. But if the Senate shall refuse to concur in such suspension, such officer so suspended shall forthwith resume the functions of his office, and the powers of the person so performing its duties in his stead shall cease, and the official salary and emoluments of such officer shall, during such suspension, belong to the person so performing the duties thereof, and not to the officer so suspended: *Provided, however,* That the President, in case he shall become satisfied that

such suspension was made on insufficient grounds, shall be authorized, at any time before reporting such suspension to the Senate as above provided, to revoke such suspension and reinstate such officer in the performance of the duties of his office."

It will be seen that this section operates in connection with the other sections of the law to prescribe the President's relations to offices which are not vacant. I say in connection with the other sections of the law, because the law must always be construed as a whole, and a particular section must be construed in relation to the other sections. It is also true, of course, that the act only operates upon what the Constitution does not itself fix, and only so far as legislative enactment may. Now, the President's relations to offices for the purpose of *absolute removal* are fixed by the first section of the act in accordance with the provisions of the Constitution. This section provides in effect that there shall be *no absolute removal* of the officers therein included except by nomination and confirmation of a successor. This operates to confine *absolute* removals to times when the Senate is in session. This being fixed, the President's relations to officers during the recess of the Senate is provided for in the second section. This second section, in enacting "that when any officer," &c., "shall, during the recess of the Senate, be shown," &c., "in such case and in no other" the President may "suspend," prescribes three governing things which are each essential elements of "such case" and of the action prescribed in regard to it:

First. That "during the recess of the Senate" the President shall do nothing more in relation to any office than "*suspend*" in the manner provided for in this act.

Second. That "during the recess of the Senate" he may act in "such case" as is provided in the act, but "in no other." This is an essential element of his relations to the offices "during the recess of the Senate," as prescribed by the act.

Third. That there shall be no suspension even, except "*during the recess of the Senate,*" for it is an essential element of "such case" that it shall be during recess.

Now, the fact that this second section, which does not refer to any officers other than those referred to in the first section, but assumes to prescribe for *all* officers under the circumstances not provided for in the first section—that is, during the recess—is without any exception which would exclude Mr. Stanton, seems to be conclusive that he is not omitted in the first section, which covers the time of the session; for why make the second section broader than the first, and restrain the President's power over Mr. Stanton during recess, and leave him unprotected during the session of the Senate?

Then the *third* section of the act, supplementary to the first and second sections, prescribes in respect to the filling of offices in case of the *happening of a vacancy* during the recess of the Senate, and the condition of these offices after the constitutional power of the President in relation to them has been exhausted. The third section reads as follows:

"SEC. 3. *And be it further enacted,* That the President shall have power to fill all vacancies which may happen during the recess of the Senate by reason of death or resignation, by granting commissions which shall expire at the end of their next session thereafter. And if no appointment, by and with the advice and consent of the Senate, shall be made to such office so vacant or temporarily filled as aforesaid during such next session of the Senate, such office shall remain in abeyance, without any salary, fees, or emoluments attached thereto, until the same shall be filled by appointment thereto, by and with the advice and consent of the Senate; and during such time all the powers and duties belonging to such office shall be exercised by such other officer as may by law exercise such powers and duties in case of a vacancy in such office."

Thus it will be perceived that these three sections of this act, taken together, provide, subject to the provisions of the Constitution, a *general rule* of governmental action, and thus, while the letter of the first section includes, as certainly as general language can, the case of Mr. Stanton, an examination of the tenor and effect of the whole confirms this construction. It would, upon every principle of legal construction, require an express exception to take an officer outside of the terms of a law intended as a general rule. On no principle can this be done by implication. Implication avails only where the letter of the law is doubtful, and its spirit, as derived from the law itself, would require an exception to some general provision. This law, then, covers, and was intended to cover, in connection with the provisions of the Constitution, every possible condition of offices, and to apply to all without exception.

If this law provides, wherever the Constitution does not, a general rule in relation to all offices, it repeals, to its extent, all former laws, and destroys the effect of all previous customs, rules, or precedents; and if it provides such general rule in relation to all conditions of offices, without exception, it covers the subject-matter of all former laws on the same subject, and overlies and repeals them.

It is apparent, then, that after the passage of this act the whole law in relation to both removals and appointments of civil officers requiring confirmation was to be found in the Constitution and the tenure-of-office act. These together constitute the general governing rule of action on this subject, and all lawful action must be under and in accordance with it, and any official act in disregard of or contrary to it is a violation of law and a *misdemeanor in office.*

That the President understood that this was the effect of the tenure-of-office law is conclusively apparent. His action in August last in regard to Mr. Stanton, and his suspension from office, was had under the second section of this law, otherwise it could not lawfully have been had at all, for that section prescribes when

and how the suspension may be made, and *forbids* one under *all* other circumstances. The President acted strictly under the provisions of this law; first, in the form of the suspension; second, in the authorization of General Grant; third, in the notice to the Secretary of the Treasury; fourth, in his report to the Senate. Indeed, how could he intend, as he claims that he did intend, to test in the courts the constitutionality of the law by the removal of Mr. Stanton, if he thought that his case was not included in the law?

Again, by the second section, which applies without question to Mr. Stanton, the President was not authorized "during the recess of the Senate" to "remove" him; he was only authorized, and only claimed to be authorized, to "suspend" him, although it was during the recess. Now, upon whatever implication of constitution or law the power of removal or suspension is assumed for him, that implication is certainly, on principle and precedent, stronger in favor of the power during a recess of the Senate than during its session. Upon what principle, then, in view of the authoritative declaration of Congress that he may only "suspend" an officer "during the recess," can he claim to *remove* him during the session?

But, again, this second section in terms settles the question of removal against him. The section is admitted to include Stanton within its general provisions. It provides that the President may, under certain circumstances, suspend an officer during the recess. This he did. It provides that having done so, he shall, when the session occurs and within a limited time after its commencement, report the suspension, with his reasons, to the Senate. This he also did. It also provides that, if the Senate shall concur and advise and consent, and so certify, he may "*thereupon* remove." It will be observed that this is during the session of the Senate, and that the removal is only to be made upon the advice and consent of the Senate. He may remove him "*thereupon,*" that is, *not otherwise.* In Mr. Stanton's case the Senate did not concur, and the condition of his removal being wanting, the President could not remove him, but under the provisions of this section he "forthwith resumed the functions of his office." He holds his office, then, by the provisions of this law, contained in a section which certainly applies to him, contrary to the will of the President, under the action of the Senate, which is thus by law made capable of preventing his removal. Why should he so hold it, and why is this power declared by law to be in the Senate, and the President's power thus restrained, if the President may the next moment remove him without consent and despite the action of the Senate? And does not this show that this law is intended to comprehend the whole subject-matter, and to regulate in all respects the power of the President in this regard? Is it not conclusive that *all* power of suspension and removal, except by nomination and confirmation, under the Constitution, is exhausted by these proceedings? What becomes of the claimed implication of a power of removal in the President, without precedent, or even with precedent, in the face of the irresistible language and implication of this law, that the Senate must concur in all removals, and that any removal without such concurrence is a direct defiance of the legislative authority, and a misdemeanor in office?

The remaining question on these three articles is, was the appointment of Thomas, as set out in the *second* and *third* articles, an act authorized either by the Constitution or by law? If not, then these articles are sustained.

A general power of appointment by the Executive, by and with the advice and consent of the Senate, a special power himself to fill vacancies "*which may happen*" during the recess, and the power to appoint inferior officers where such power has been given him by legislative enactment—these comprise all the authority of the President for this purpose, given in or to be derived from the Constitution.

Whatever rightful authority, then, was exercised by the President in making this appointment to the War Department, must have been derived by the express terms of some legislative enactment.

By the eighth section of the act of 1792, making alterations in the Treasury and War Departments, it is *made lawful* for the President, in case of the death, sickness, or absence of the Secretary, to authorize some person to perform the duties of the office until a successor is appointed, in case of death or the absence or inability from sickness shall cease. The only actual vacancy contemplated by this act is one *happening by death*.

The act of 1795, amendatory of the last mentioned act, declares, generally, that in every case of vacancy in the Department "*it shall be lawful*" for the President to authorize any person to perform the duties of the office until a successor be appointed, "provided that no one vacancy shall be supplied in manner aforesaid for a longer term than six months." This act contemplates lawful vacancies only, for none others are vacancies which can be lawfully filled. We have already seen that the President could not lawfully make a vacancy without the concurrence of the Senate while it was in session to take concurrent action; and to claim that the President is authorized by this act to make an appointment to a vacancy made during a session of the Senate by his separate action, is simply begging the whole question. If there was no lawful vacancy, it could not lawfully be filled, and there is nothing in the law which makes any vacancy lawful which was not lawful before its passage. By the act of February 20, 1863, it is *made* lawful for the President, in case of the death, resignation, sickness, or absence of the head of any executive Department, to authorize the head or other officer of one of the Departments to perform the duties "until a successor is appointed, or such absence or inability by sickness shall cease."

This was the condition of the law before the passage of the "tenure-of-office act."

The act of 1792 had been superseded by the act of 1795, and this had been followed in turn by the act of 1863. This last act was, I doubt not, *intended* to supersede the act of 1795, as it provides that the vacancies to which it applies shall be filled with a select class of persons, and there could have been no reason why all vacancies in the same office, however produced, should not be filled by the same select class. The act appears to be intended to provide for the temporary supplying of all vacancies in the offices referred to, and by omitting from its list of vacancies *vacancies by removal*, it seems, by its later implication, to conclude the President's power of removal, as derived from the implications of the earlier laws of 1789, creating the Departments.

But if it is conceded that the President retained the power of removal during the recess, after the passage of the act of 1863, it must also be conceded that the act of 1863 did not cover all the subject-matter of the act of 1795, and does not, therefore, completely supersede it. It will be seen that none of these laws affirmatively recognize or imply a power of removal in the President during the session of the Senate, and consequently they give him no power of appointment to a vacancy *made* by him at such time, while not one precedent can be found that goes to this extent, so that this power is claimed contrary to the necessary implications of the Constitution, and without authority either of law or precedent. But the tenure-of-office act clearly covers and regulates this whole subject-matter, and supersedes the previous laws, including the act of 1795. We have already seen that this act applies to this case.

The second section certainly does apply, and if the vacancy which is said to exist in the War Department is claimed to have been made "during a recess" in August last, it must have been under that section, for it provides that "during the recess of the Senate" vacancies shall only be made by the President by suspension, and that no suspension shall be had, except in a case made under its provisions, and that "*in such case and in no other*" the President may designate a suitable person temporarily to perform the duties; but if the Senate does not consent the suspended officer shall "*forthwith* resume the functions of his office." So if the vacancy was made in vacation that vacancy no longer existed after the refusal of the Senate to consent to it, and the appointment of Thomas was without authority of law. But the terms of the President's letter of February 21 to Mr. Stanton assume that he was then in office, and was thereby removed "during the session of the Senate." We have already seen that all removals at such times are regulated by the first section of the tenure-of-office act, and that the case of Stanton is included by its provisions; but by that section all temporary or *ad interim* appointments to the offices referred to therein are abolished, and the officer appointed by and with the advice and consent of the Senate is "entitled. to hold" his office until a successor shall have been appointed "in like manner," that is, with the concurrence of the Senate. The appointment of Thomas was not "in like manner."

It will also be perceived that the words in the body of the first section immediately preceding the proviso are "except as herein otherwise provided." This language refers to the whole act. Its meaning is except as is otherwise provided in this act. Now the term of office, and the manner of removal from and appointment to office, are distinct propositions contained in the body of the section. The proviso relates only to the term of the officers therein named; but that part of the subject-matter of the general clause which provides how the *successors* of all civil officers requiring confirmation shall be appointed, namely, "by and with the advice and consent of the Senate," is not affected by the proviso. This subject is "*not otherwise provided for*" in that proviso in relation to any officers, and the provision of the general clause in relation to it, is not restricted by the terms or implications of the proviso.

To take the officers mentioned in the exception *wholly* outside of the provisions of the general clause, which covers other subject-matter besides that covered by the exception, the language must have been except the *officers* hereinafter mentioned, or something of like effect. Thus, whether Mr. Stanton's case, as far as relates to the tenure of his office, is within the general clause or the exception of this section, or within neither, his *successor's* case is clearly within the general clause, and no one can be lawfully appointed to succeed him except "*in like manner*," as he was himself appointed; that is, with the concurrence of the Senate.

Again, the reasoning on the spirit of the second section of the act is irresistible. Does it not seem a ridiculous claim that the President may, "during a session of the Senate," appoint a successor or *locum tenens*, of any kind, for an officer whom the Senate has just, under express authority of law, refused to remove, and who has just, under like authority, resumed the functions of his office?

The appointment of Thomas, then, was unauthorized by any law, and was an unlawful attempt, by the exercise of usurped executive power, to seize upon and control a most important department of the Government, in violation of express legislative enactment.

This crime, so clearly shown, is really a higher and more dangerous one than the removal of Mr. Stanton, for it not only includes the unlawful removal, but is in itself an affirmative, while the other is, in some sense, but a negative act of usurpation.

Whatever plea of misinformation, mistake, or absence of intent may be set up by his friends or his counsel the President makes no such plea. He has claimed, and does claim in his answer and by the lips of his special representatives among the counsel, that he has removed Mr. Stanton and appointed Thomas by virtue of power vested in him as the Chief Executive, notwithstanding the tenure-of-office act. And it is proved that he intends to carry out his attempts should this trial result in his favor. By a verdict of acquittal, then, the Senate must either recede from their position on this act, or must submit that the President may defy its spirit and violate its express provisions with impunity.

In the consideration of this question I have assumed the constitutionality of the tenure-of-office act. I cannot consent to even consider this a debatable point. The Senate has solemnly adjudicated this question for itself on four distinct occasions, each individual Senator acting under the obligation of an oath as solemn and binding as that administered at the commencement of this trial, of the solemnity of which we have been so often reminded by the counsel for the President. First, by the passage of the bill in question, after a full discussion of its provisions, by a vote of 29 yeas to 9 nays. Secondly, the bill having been submitted to the President for his approval and returned to the Senate with his objections in an elaborate veto message arguing against the constitutionality of the measure, the Senate again passed the bill in the face of the arguments submitted, by a vote of more than two thirds of the members present and voting. Upon the question "Shall the bill pass, the objections of the President to the contrary notwithstanding?" the vote was as follows:

"YEAS—Messrs. Anthony, Cattell, Chandler, Conness, Cragin, Edmunds, Fessenden, Fogg, Foster, Fowler, Frelinghuysen, Grimes, Harris, Henderson, Howard, Kirkwood, Lane, Morgan, Morrill, Nye, Poland, Pomeroy, Ramsey, Ross, Sherman, Sprague, Stewart, Sumner, Trumbull, Van Winkle, Wade, Willey, Williams, Wilson, and Yates—35.

"NAYS—Messrs. Buckalew, Cowan, Davis, Dixon, Doolittle, Hendricks, Johnson, Nesmith, Norton, Patterson, and Saulsbury—11."

Thirdly, the Senate recognized the validity of this law when, in response to the message of the President communicating the fact that he had "during the recess" suspended Mr. Stanton, the Senate took action, under and in accordance with the said law, and after due consideration refused to concur in the suspension of that officer, and informed the President thereof. Fourthly, when the President, after having exhausted all legal means to displace this faithful and efficient officer, and rid himself of what his counsel chooses to call "*a thorn in his heart*," deliberately, willfully, and knowingly violated the provisions of this act by the arbitrary removal, or attempted removal, of

Mr. Stanton and the appointment of Lorenzo Thomas, and defiantly flaunted his action in the face of the Senate, this body again reaffirmed the validity of the tenure-of-office act by declaring that the action of the President was without lawful authority.

I submit, then, that the tenure-of-office bill, having been passed over the President's veto by a vote of two thirds of both Houses, by express provision of the Constitution "*it became a law;*" *a law* to the President, and *a law* to all the people; *a law* as valid and binding as any on the statute-book; and I cannot believe that the Senate will consent to stultify itself by the admission that its oft-repeated action upon this bill was in violation of the Constitution, which each member had solemnly sworn to support.

Moreover, the President himself recognized the validity of the law by taking action under its provisions in the suspension of Mr. Stanton, as I have already shown in the course of this argument. Upon what principle may he consider a law valid and binding to-day and of no force or effect to-morrow? The law was sufficient so long as he thought he could accomplish his purpose to get rid of Mr. Stanton under it; but when he failed in this, by the refusal of the Senate to concur in the proposed removal, he overrides the law and then attempts to shelter himself, when arraigned for the offense, under the plea that it is not a constitutional law.

But admitting, for the sake of argument, that there were no doubts as to the constitutionality of the law, who clothed Andrew Johnson with judicial power to settle that question? Under what clause of the Constitution does he presume to derive the power to decide which of the enactments of Congress are valid and binding and which are not? If he may exercise judicial functions in regard to one law, why not in regard to all laws? As I read the Constitution, the President is enjoined to "take care that *the laws* be faithfully executed." I find no provision in that instrument which clothes him with the more than regal power to decide *which* laws he will execute and *which* he will not.

If judicial power is a prerogative of the Executive, of what use is the Supreme Court? Why not abolish so useless an institution? Nay, more, if a law of Congress, though passed by the constitutional vote of two thirds of both Houses, may not *"become a law"* unless it meets the sanction of the Executive—if he may suspend or virtually repeal by rendering inoperative the enactments of Congress, why not abolish the legislative department of the Government?

It may be that Andrew Johnson is wiser than the Senate and House of Representatives; it may be that wisdom will die with him; it may be unfortunate that the Constitution under which we live has not given to him who claims to be its especial custodian and guardian the

more than imperial power to make the laws and judicially pass upon them, as well as the duty to take care that they "be faithfully executed;" but, in my judgment, the American people will be slow in arriving at any such conclusion. So monstrous a proposition as that which virtually surrenders to one man all the power of our great Government is not worthy of serious consideration.

Mr. President, for the first time in the history of our Government we are confronted with a clear, decided, and flagrant act of executive usurpation. For his offense against the majesty of the law the House of Representatives, in accordance with the provisions of the Constitution, and in the name of all the people of the United States, have impeached Andrew Johnson for high crimes and misdemeanors, and have brought him to the bar of the Senate to answer to the charges exhibited against him. The issues involved in these proceedings are of the gravest character, reaching down to the very foundation of our system of government, and it behooves us as the representatives of forty million people to see to it that impartial justice is done as between the people and the accused. If this, the highest tribunal of the nation, shall render a verdict of acquittal, it will be a virtual admission of the President's assertion of "the power at any and all times of removing from office all executive officers for cause to be judged by the President alone." It will be a complete surrender of the constitutional power of the Senate over all appointments to office, for of what practical value will be the required advice and consent of the Senate to an appointment if the person so appointed may the next hour be removed by the action of the Executive alone, regardless of, and, indeed, in despite of, the wishes of the Senate?

It will, moreover, be a virtual surrender of what has been claimed from the origin of the Government to this day, the right to regulate and control, by legislative enactment, the executive power over removals from office of such officers as require confirmation by the Senate, and it will give to the President the unrestrained control of the officers of the Army and Navy, as well as those of the civil service.

It will give license to Andrew Johnson and all future occupants of the presidential office to disregard at pleasure the enactments of the legislative department, and to plead in justification that you have so ruled by your verdict in this case.

It will tend to destroy the harmonious relations of the several departments of the Government, so nicely adjusted, with checks and balances and limitations by the wisdom of the fathers of the Constitution, by increasing immensely the powers and privileges of the executive at the expense of the legislative department. Thenceforward the ruler will no longer be the servant of the people, but the people will be the servants of the ruler, and we shall not be able hereafter to say, in the sublime language of the martyred Lincoln, that ours is "a Government of the people, by the people, and for the people."

Believing, as I conscientiously do, that such are the results which must follow the acquittal of Andrew Johnson by this tribunal, and believing that the House of Representatives have made good the material charges preferred against him, I cannot doubt as to my duty in the premises.

I deeply regret that the necessity for these momentous proceedings has arisen. I would gladly have escaped the solemn responsibility of this hour. But this may not be, and I must, therefore, upon the law and the evidence, in accordance with the dictates of my conscience, and in view of the solemn obligations of my oath, declare that in my judgment Andrew Johnson is guilty of high crimes and misdemeanors as charged by the Representatives of the people.

APPENDIX.

PREFACE.

The proceedings in the Senate on the 5th and 6th of March, though not belonging strictly to the trial, are of such relevancy as calls for their embodiment in this volume, and they are accordingly given here in the form of an Appendix.

The elaborate argument of Hon. CHARLES SUMNER upon the right of the Chief Justice, presiding in the Senate, to rule or vote, has attracted much attention. Frequent inquiry by members of the legal profession and others for the pamphlet issue of this argument suggested the propriety of appending it to this volume; and it appears here with the sanction of Mr. SUMNER, who has carefully revised it for this publication.

A few authorities in addition to those composing the brief prepared by Hon. WILLIAM LAWRENCE, M. C., from Ohio, and presented by Mr. Manager BUTLER as a part of his opening argument, have been furnished by the first-named gentleman, and conclude this Appendix.

DEBATE

THE RIGHT OF SENATOR WADE TO SIT AS A MEMBER OF THE COURT.

IN SENATE, *March* 5, 1868.

The PRESIDENT *pro tempore.* The morning hour having expired, all legislative and executive business of the Senate is ordered to cease for the purpose of proceeding to business pertaining to the impeachment of the President of the United States. The chair is vacated for that purpose.

The PRESIDENT *pro tempore* then left the chair.

The Chief Justice of the United States entered the Chamber, accompanied by Mr. Justice Nelson, and escorted by Senators POMEROY, WILSON, and BUCKALEW, the committee appointed for that purpose.

The CHIEF JUSTICE took the chair and said: Senators, I attend the Senate in obedience to your notice, for the purpose of joining with you in forming a court of impeachment for the trial of the President of the United States, and I am now ready to take the oath.

The oath was administered by Mr. Justice Nelson to Chief Justice Chase in the following words:

"I do solemnly swear that in all things appertaining to the trial of the impeachment of Andrew Johnson, President of the United States, I will do impartial justice according to the Constitution and laws. So help me God."

[The Senators rose when the Chief Justice entered the Chamber and remained standing till the conclusion of the administration of the oath to him.]

The CHIEF JUSTICE. Senators, the oath will now be administered to the Senators as they will be called by the Secretary in succession. [To the Secretary.] Call the roll.

The Secretary proceeded to call the roll alphabetically, and the Chief Justice administered the oath to Senators ANTHONY, BAYARD, BUCKALEW, CAMERON, CATTELL, CHANDLER, COLE, CONKLING, CONNESS, CORBETT, CRAGIN, DAVIS, DIXON, DRAKE, FERRY, FESSENDEN, FOWLER, FRELINGHUYSEN, GRIMES, HARLAN, HENDERSON, HENDRICKS, HOWARD, HOWE, JOHNSON, McCREERY, MORGAN, MORRILL of Maine, MORRILL of Vermont, MORTON, NOR-

5

TON, NYE, PATTERSON of Tennessee, POMEROY, RAMSEY, ROSS, SHERMAN, SPRAGUE, STEWART, SUMNER, THAYER, TIPTON, TRUMBULL, and VAN WINKLE.

The Secretary then called the name of Mr. WADE, who rose from his seat in the Senate and advanced toward the Chair.

Mr. HENDRICKS. Before the Senator just called takes the oath I wish to submit to the presiding officer and to the Senate a question. The Senator just called is the Presiding Officer of this body, and under the Constitution and laws will become the President of the United States should the proceeding of impeachment, now to be tried, be sustained. The Constitution providing that in such a case the possible successor cannot even preside in the body during the trial, I submit for the consideration of the presiding officer and of the Senate the question whether, being a Senator, representing a State, it is competent for him, notwithstanding that, to take the oath and become thereby a part of the court? I submit that upon two grounds, first, the ground that the Constitution does not allow him to preside during these deliberations because of his possible succession; and second, the parliamentary or legal ground that he is interested, in view of his possible connection with the office, in the result of the proceedings, he is not competent to sit as a member of the court.

Mr. SHERMAN. Mr. President, this question, I think, is answered by the Constitution of the United States, which declares that each State shall be entitled to two Senators on this floor, and that the court or tribunal for the trial of all impeachments shall be the Senate of the United States. My colleague is one of the Senators from the State of Ohio, he is a member of this Senate, and is therefore made one of the tribunal to try all cases of impeachment. This tribunal is not to be tested by the ordinary rules that may apply in cases at civil law; for the mere interest of the party does not exclude a person from sitting as a member of the Senate for the trial of impeachment, nor does mere affinity or relation by blood or marriage. The tribunal is constituted by the Constitution of the United States, and is composed of two Senators from each State, and Ohio is entitled to two voices upon the trial of this case. It seems to me, therefore, that the question ought not to be made.

If this were to be tested by the rule in ordinary civil tribunals the same objection might have been made to one other Senator, who has already taken the oath without objection, being connected by ties of marriage with the person accused before us. It is, therefore, perfectly clear that while the rule might exclude the Senator from Ohio in deciding in ordinary cases, or he might retire from exercising his right to vote, that is a question for him alone to determine. So far as the court is concerned he is entitled to be sworn as one of the triers in this case as Senator from the State of Ohio, without regard to his interest in the result of the trial.

I have, as a matter of course, as the colleague of the Senator who is now proposed to be sworn, looked into this matter, and I have no doubt of it. I was prepared, to some extent, for the raising of this question, though I hoped it would not be presented. How far the Senator from Ohio, my colleague, may participate in the proceedings of impeachment, how far he shall vote, when he shall vote, and upon what questions he shall vote, are matters that must be left to him, and not for the tribunal or for any Senator to make against him. His right as a Senator from the State of Ohio is complete and perfect, and there is no exclusion of him on account of interest, affinity, blood relationship, or for any other cause.

Mr. HOWARD. Mr. President, I do not suppose that under the Constitution any Senator is to be challenged, even for cause, upon the trial of an impeachment. I concur entirely with the view presented by the honorable Senator from Ohio [Mr. SHERMAN] which he has just expressed. The objection raised by the honorable Senator from Indiana [Mr. HENDRICKS] is in the nature of a challenge, if I understand it properly, upon the ground of interest in the question about to be decided by the Senate sitting for the trial of an impeachment. Now, sir, as has been very justly remarked, each State has the right to send to the Senate two members, and the Constitution declares, whatever may be the character of those members, whatever may be their relation to the accused or their interest in the question involved, that they shall be component parts of the body trying the impeachment. If an objection upon the ground of interest is tenable an objection upon the ground of affinity must also be available. The Senate has already seen one member of its body proceed to take the oath prescribed in our rules who is known to be related by affinity to the accused. I can see no distinction between an objection resting upon interest and one resting upon affinity.

Besides, sir, the honorable Senator from Ohio who now offers to take the oath is but the President pro tempore of the Senate. It is possible, and merely possible, that he may remain in that capacity until the conclusion of these proceedings; but at the same time it is not to be overlooked that it is but a possibility. The Senate has in its power at all times to choose another President pro tempore to preside over its proceedings. I cannot, therefore, see any such interest in the question as would seem to justify the objection which is taken by the honorable Senator from Indiana. I hope the Senator from Ohio, the President pro tempore of this body, will proceed to take the oath.

Mr. JOHNSON. Mr. President, the question is a purely legal one, and is to be decided upon principle. I have no doubt that the honorable member from Ohio will, as far as he may be able under the temptations to which he may be subjected unknowingly to himself, decide upon the issues which are involved in the impeachment trial with as much impartiality as any of us. It is not, therefore, any objection to the honorable member which induces me to say a word to the Senate on the subject.

The general rule, we all know, is applicable to a jury as well as to a court, that no one should serve in either tribunal who has a clear interest in the result of the trial. The honorable member from Ohio [Mr. SHERMAN] and the honorable member from Michigan [Mr. HOWARD] tell us that the Constitution provides that the court in this instance is to consist of the Senators of the several States. That is true; but that does not prove that a Senator may not be in a situation which should exclude him from the privilege of being a member of the court. The Constitution of the United States provides that the Supreme Court shall consist of a Chief Justice and associate justices; the law from time to time has regulated their number; but I never heard it questioned that, although by the Constitution and the laws cases within the jurisdiction of that tribunal are to be tried by them, a judge would not be permitted to sit in a case in which he had a direct interest. It by no means follows, therefore, that because the honorable member from Ohio [Mr. WADE] is a Senator, and as such entitled to be a member of this court, he is not as liable to the objection of interest in the result which your honor, the Chief Justice of the Supreme Court, would be liable to in a case before your high tribunal in which you had a direct interest in the possible result.

This is, as the honorable member from Ohio [Mr. SHERMAN] says, the only tribunal to try such a case as is now before us. That is true; but if the honorable member and the Senate will look to the sixty-fifth number of the Federalist they will find why it was that the court was constituted when the President is to be on trial as it is constituted by the Constitution. It was because of the manner in which impeachments are tried in the mother country. There they are tried in the House of Lords. And I have a recollection, not altogether distinct—I did not know that the question was to be raised to-day or I should have refreshed my recollection—that when in the case of the Senator from New Jersey, Hon. Mr. Stockton, who had been received as a Senator on this floor upon his credentials, and it was proposed to exclude him, which required a majority vote, the honorable member from Massachusetts, [Mr. SUMNER,] and I think several other members, but particularly the honorable member from Massachusetts, in order to satisfy the Senate that Mr. Stockton had no right to vote in his own case, cited many instances in the House of Lords in which it had been held that a member of the House of Lords was not competent to decide in a case in which he had an interest. It was upon the authority of those cases, as well as upon the general ground which runs through the whole of our jurisprudence and the jurisprudence of the mother country, and is founded in the nature of things, that Mr. Stockton was denied the privilege of voting in his own case.

· Now what was his case as compared in point of supposed influence to the case of the honorable member from Ohio? He was to have a temporary seat in this body, invested only with that proportion of the power of the legislative department of the Government which one member of this body has in reference to the whole number composing the body and the numbers which compose the House of Representatives. His voice, therefore, would be comparatively unimportant. And yet it was adjudged by the Senate, as well as I remember, and almost with unanimity, especially by those who thought Mr. Stockton was not entitled to his seat, that he should not be permitted to vote upon that question. How does his case compare with that of the honorable member from Ohio? The honorable member becomes, in a contingency which this impeachment seeks to bring about, a judgment of guilty, the President of the United States, invested with all the executive power of the Government. Is it right, would anybody desire, to be subjected to such a temptation, which might lead him, unknowingly to himself, into an erroneous judgment? The whole executive powers of the United States, to say nothing of the pecuniary compensation belonging to the office, $25,000 a year, are to be his in a certain result of the prosecution; and his vote may produce that result.

I submit, then, and certainly without the slightest feeling of disrespect for the honorable member from Ohio, that it is due to the cause of impartial justice, it is due to the character of the Senate, in its management of this proceeding. that there should not be established a precedent which may in the end produce excitement and bring into disrepute the Senate itself. The reason why it is, Mr. Chief Justice, that you are here to preside over the deliberations of this court, shows that, in the judgment of our fathers, it was improper that any man should be placed in the situation in which the honorable member from Ohio will be placed if he is admitted to be a member of this court and exercises that function. Our fathers thought, and they have incorporated the thought into the Constitution, that he who is to be benefited by the result should not be permitted even to preside over the deliberations of this court when the President of the United States is on trial; that the Vice President of the United States, who is entitled only to vote in case of a tie, of an equal division of the Senate, should not be permitted even to be a member of the court to preside over its deliberations. It was, Mr. Chief Justice, because our fathers were deeply versed in the history of the world, perfectly acquainted with the frailties of man's nature as exhibited in the history of all political bodies, that they denied, in a case of this description, to the Vice President of the United States the privilege even of presiding over the deliberations of such a court, much less of voting, and by his vote bringing about the judgment which was to make him President.

Mr. President, I do not know that we are able to decide this question at once. My impression is such as I have stated; but it is a grave question, an important question. It will be considered a grave and important question in the eyes of the country, and it should be by the Senate of the United States so esteemed. It is a new question; and I submit to you and the Senate whether it is not better to postpone the decision of it in this case until to-morrow, above all for the purpose of ascertaining what are the precedents of the House of Lords. Should they prove to be what I think they are, then, unless we are disposed to depart from the model upon which was formed this high tribunal, I am sure the Senate ought to decide—and I have no doubt the honorable member from Ohio will acquiesce cheerfully in that decision, and will himself see the propriety of so acting—that he is not entitled to take his seat as a member of this court. I move, therefore, that the question be postponed until to-morrow.

MR. DAVIS. Mr. President, I will make a remark on this question before the vote is taken. If the Senator from Ohio [Mr. WADE] asks to be excused from taking any part in this trial it must be upon some principle established by the Constitution. The Vice President presides in every case of impeachment, except upon the trial of the President, and there he is expressly excluded by a provision of the Constitution—upon what reason? Because of his interest in the question from the fact that if there is a judgment of amotion from office against the President the Vice President is to succeed to his place. The Constitution thus establishes a principle, and that principle is this : that when the President of the United States, whether he has been elected by the electoral vote or has succeeded to the office by the amotion of the President from office—when a President who actually holds the office is under trial the man who is to take the place, if he be removed upon that trial by the judgment of the court which is to try him, is disqualified from forming a part of the court. That is the principle. Now, can the Senator from Michigan or any other Senator adduce any principle that would require the exclusion of the Vice President from presiding over a court of impeachment of the President of the United States that will not apply to the President *pro tempore* of the Senate when there is no Vice President, when the President *pro tempore* is Presiding Officer of the Senate, and when by the Constitution and laws of the United States, if the acting President, as he is sometimes called, is removed, the President *pro tempore* of the Senate is to take his place?

Mr. President, my argument is that the Constitution itself, in relation to this court, has established a principle, and that principle is that any man standing in a position where he is to succeed to the office of the President in the event of his conviction cannot form a part of the court of impeachment that is to try whether the President shall be removed or not. It seems to me clearly that, although the exclusion of the President *pro tempore* of the Senate does not come within the strict letter of the Constitution, it does plainly and unequivocally within its principle and spirit. To every lawyer it is a familiar principle that where a law by its language and express terms does not include a case, but that case comes clearly within its principle and meaning, the law shall be extended by force of its spirit to comprehend the case that is not strictly within its letter but is clearly and undeniably within its principles.

It seems to me, therefore, clear as a constitutional principle that the President *pro tempore* of the Senate, on the occasion of the impeachment trial, occupies the same position in relation to the office of President that the Vice President would if he was here and was the Presiding Officer of the Senate; and the Vice President being excluded for the reason and upon the principle that he is to take no part in the trial because he is to succeed to the vacant place if there be a judgment of amotion from office, the same principle, clearly, undeniably, in its full force and reason, applies to the President *pro tempore* of the Senate, and therefore he is excluded by the spirit and by the principle of the Constitution.

Mr. MORRILL, of Maine. Mr. Chief Justice, it strikes me that the whole proceeding is premature, for the obvious reason that there is no party here to take the objection. If this is a court there is no party before the court to raise this objection. It certainly does not lie in the mouth of any member of this court, of any Senator, to raise the objection of disqualification against any other Senator ; and, therefore, there is no party here properly to raise the objection against the administration of the oath. Whenever the proper parties appear here on the one side and the other, either for the people or for the respondent, then the court will be in a condition to hear objections to the constitution of the body ; then the people will be represented, and may put the inquiry as to the constitution of this court, and then, also, the respondent may institute the same inquiry. It may turn out that we are so constituted that it will be necessary to raise this question and to determine it ; but at the present moment it seems to me that there is no option and no discretion but to administer the oath to all those who, by the Constitution, are Senators representing the States.

Mr. HENDRICKS. Mr. President, I do not propose at this time to protract the debate ; but I wish to reply to the technical point made by the Senator from Maine. It is inherent in a court to judge of its own organization ; it is a power necessarily possessed by the court itself ; and it is not for the suitors to present the question whether a party claiming a seat in a court composed of more than one member is justly and legally entitled to that seat. It is for the court itself to decide whether a member proposing to exercise the right to sit in that court is entitled to that right. Therefore, sir, the question is not prematurely presented.

To the point made by the Senator from Michigan, which is not upon the merits, I have just this to reply : that the possibility that the Senator now proposing to be sworn may cease to be President of the Senate *pro tempore* is not an answer to the objection. He is now the Presiding Officer of the Senate, and as such will become the President of the United States if the impeachment be sustained and he continue to be the President *pro tempore* until the termination of the trial. If he ceases, during the progress of the trial, to be the Presiding Officer of this body, then he becomes competent, and under the second rule which has been adopted, if the rules should be recognized by the court, he will be sworn in as a member of the court. The point I make is, that now being the Presiding Officer of the Senate, and now being competent to become the President in case impeachment be sustained, he is now incompetent to participate in the trial.

The substantial merits of this question were settled in the case referred to by the Senator from Maryland—the case of Senator Stockton, from New Jersey. There the Senate decided that a member of the body could not be a party to a decision in the Senate in which he is interested ; and the possibility of holding an office was regarded as an interest by the Senate.

Nor do I think the point made by the Senator from Ohio [Mr. SHERMAN] a good one, that, being a Senator from a State, the Presiding Officer has the right to participate in all the proceedings of the Senate. The standing rules of this body as a Senate contradict that argument. One of the standing rules of the Senate is that a Senator shall not vote when he has an interest in the result of the vote; so that the Senate itself has restricted those general rights and powers which the Senator from Ohio thinks belongs to each Senator as a representative of a State. The Senate has said, by its standing rules, that neither one of us can vote if we have an interest in the result of that vote. But, sir, in my judgment, the constitutional ground is higher than this ground of interest. The Presiding Officer has an interest in the result of an impeachment trial; he shall not even preside; he shall not even maintain order and decorum in the body during the progress of the trial; he shall vacate his seat that the Chief Justice may preside; and what does that mean? It means something, sir. It means that the relation which the Vice President of the United States sustains by possibility to the office of President of the United States is such that he shall take no part in the great trial. That is what the Constitution means. It is not a matter of form and ceremony and dignity that the Chief Justice shall preside here. It is of the very substance that he who, by possibility, can fill the office if the Senate shall make it vacant, shall not sit here even to preserve order and decorum while the great proceeding is going on.

I hope, sir, that I need not disclaim any personal feeling in this matter. I make the point now because I think that the Constitution itself controls the organization of this court. I think that the Constitution itself does settle it, that no man shall help to take from the President his office when that man is to fill the office if the proceeding succeed. There is no analogy between this and the case suggested by the Senator from Michigan. Affinity does not of itself by common and universal law exclude a man from presiding in court; it must be done by express statute, and it is so provided in the codes of the different States. But here the Constitution itself says that no man shall preside who may succeed to the office. I hope, sir, in view of the importance of this question, that the motion made by the Senator from Maryland, to postpone its consideration until to-morrow, will prevail.

Mr. WILLIAMS. Mr. Chief Justice, I submit that the motion or question made by the Senator from Indiana is altogether premature, for this reason: it is either addressed to the Senate of the United States or to the court for the trial of an impeachment. If it be to the Senate, then I respectfully submit that the Presiding Officer of the Senate should occupy the chair; if to a court, then there is no court organized competent to pass or decide upon this question. Some of the members here have been sworn, others have not. Am I to be called upon to decide on this question which, perhaps, relates to the merits of the case to be determined, without having had an oath administered to me like other members? Is this question to be decided at this time? Is there any court organized that can decide this question? I do not know exactly what the question is. Is it a challenge that has been submitted by a Senator to a fellow-Senator? If that be so it is an extraordinary proceeding. I never heard that one juror could challenge another juror; I never heard that one judge could challenge another judge. When the necessary preparations are made for the trial, it may be that the Managers on the part of the House of Representatives and the accused will be willing and desire to have the Senator from Ohio participate in this trial. Is it not their privilege? Suppose they both agree to that and to waive all objections? Then I am confident that they have the right to make this question, and not any Senator.

The Senator from Indiana suggests that no judge who is interested in a question was ever known to preside when that question was considered. Is not that altogether a matter left to the judge? Did the honorable Senator ever know a court to adopt a rule and declare that a member of that court should not participate in any decision? Whenever a question is presented to a court, the judge decides for himself as to whether or not it is a case in which he can take any part? If he decides that he cannot participate in the trial, he withdraws from the bench; but the court never undertakes to prescribe the rule for his action, to say that he shall or shall not participate in the decision. But I do not propose to discuss the question. I make this point, however, that at this time this body, with a part of the members sworn and a part unsworn, cannot decide the question, because it is a question that relates to the rights of the country and of the accused; and before I am called upon to pass upon this question, it is necessary, it seems to me, that I should be sworn as well as the other members who have not been called upon to take the oath.

Mr. DAVIS. Will the honorable Senator answer me a question?

Mr. WILLIAMS. Certainly.

Mr. DAVIS. Suppose this was a trial of articles of impeachment against the President of the United States when there was a Vice President in being, and suppose that Vice President was to present himself here and offer to become a part of the court, could not the Senators exclude him from that position?

Mr. WILLIAMS. Mr. Chief Justice, I do not propose to argue that question; but the case propounded by the Senator is not parallel to the case before this body, because the Constitution expressly excludes the Vice President from any participation in this trial, but it provides that each Senator shall vote.

Mr. DAVIS. The honorable Senator suggested that it rested with the Senator himself whether he should form part of the court or not, and that the residue of the body could not make the exception. I presented that example for the purpose of showing that under that state of case the body of the court itself would exclude the Vice President, though he even offered to become a component part of the court.

Mr. WILLIAMS. What I said was simply in response to the suggestion of the Senator from Indiana, that the Senator from Ohio could not participate in these proceedings because a judge who was interested in a case could not participate in the hearing of it. I say it is always in every case left for the judge to decide for himself as to whether he will or will not participate in the trial, and the court itself does not undertake to exclude him.

I does not follow, as it strikes me, because this court is organized as the Constitution requires, each Senator taking an oath, that every Senator will necessarily participate in the trial and vote upon the questions involved. He may take the oath; he is required to take the oath; and then, after he is qualified to act, it will be for him to determine whether or not he will participate in the trial, and not for the Senator to say now before the court is organized that he shall not be allowed to take the oath. He is a Senator, and the Constitution says that each State shall have two Senators, and that each Senator shall have one vote. The Constitution gives to each Senator a right to vote upon every question in the Senate. That is a constitutional right; but if he is interested in any way, then he may not participate in the decision if he sees proper.

Mr. JOHNSON. What becomes of our rule on that point?

Mr. WILLIAMS. That rule is not one that can override the Constitution; and if any Senator, notwithstanding that rule, upon any question should insist upon his right to vote, I maintain that he can vote notwithstanding the rule, because the Constitution says that every Senator shall have a right to vote upon every question. It may be indelicate and improper for a Senator to vote upon many questions; but as I said I did not intend to argue that question and was drawn off from the point which I intended to make, which is, that at this time it is not competent for this body to decide as to whether or not the Senator from Ohio can take the oath.

Mr. FESSENDEN. Mr. President, I do not design to discuss the matter. I merely rise to make the suggestion which would follow from what has been said by the Senator from Oregon, that it would be better to organize the court fully before deciding the question, if we are to decide it at all. There is no difficulty in postponing the administration of the oath to the honorable Senator from Ohio until all have been sworn except him, and then the court will be properly organized so far as to enable all gentleman to act as members of the court. I would suggest, therefore, that the administration of the oath to the honorable Senator from Ohio be merely passed over until it has been administered to other gentlemen whose names come after his upon the list, and then the question can be decided.

Mr. CONNESS. My only objection to the proposition now made is that in my judgment the Senate have no such right. They have no right to pass directly or indirectly, in my opinion, any reflection upon the right of any Senator to participate in the proceedings that are taking place. The question as it seems to me is settled. It was settled when the credentials of the Senator were presented, and he was admitted to his seat. It is not competent for the Senate, in my opinion, to attempt to deprive a Senator of his vote; and, so far as the suggestion or proposition casts doubt upon the question, it does not meet the approbation of my judgment. I prefer very much that a vote shall now be taken, not upon the direct question, as suggested by the Senator from Indiana, but that it take the form of a motion. I think the question whether a Senator has an interest in these proceedings such as would prevent him from voting and acting as such pending the trial is a question for himself alone, and that no other Senator nor the Senate combined can impose any restriction upon his legitimate participation in these great proceedings.

Mr. FESSENDEN. I desire simply to say that, in making the suggestion, I did not mean to be understood as expressing the slightest opinion in any way, but to avoid the difficulty suggested by the honorable Senator from Oregon. He says he is not yet a member of the court; he has not been sworn. If we are to take a vote upon this question directly, are we all to vote or not? Certainly the larger number have been sworn, but some have not been sworn. There is nothing in the shape of reflection or even the intimation of an opinion, one way or the other, in simply suggesting that it would be well to have all those who are to vote upon the question sworn, inasmuch as part have been sworn, before the vote is taken. That is all; and I see no difficulty such as has been suggested by the honorable Senator from California. The honorable Senator from Ohio can be presented again; there is nothing in any rule that requires the oath to be taken alphabetically as the names are called; that is a mere matter of convenience. Certain gentlemen are absent now from their seats; they will be allowed unquestionably to take the oath when they come in. My suggestion went to that extent and no further, that we who are to act upon the question, if we are to act at all, should be placed upon a level before we proceed to act, and that the court should be duly organized as a court, which it is not yet. If the suggestion is not agreeable to gentlemen, it makes not the slightest difference to me; I care nothing about it one way or the other. I have no opinion to express at present upon the subject.

Mr. HOWARD. Mr. President, we are now sitting in a judicial capacity for the trial of a particular impeachment. We are organizing ourselves for the purpose of proceeding to consider the facts of the case; but this must be regarded, I think, as a part of the trial. Otherwise, Mr. President, we should not expect to see you presiding over us. Now, sir, the Constitution declares that "each Senator shall have one vote;" and it further declares that "no person shall be convicted without the concurrence of two thirds of the members present." There may be absentees—no matter how many—so be that a quorum of the body remains present and voting.

The honorable Senator from Ohio is present, not absent. He is now ready to take the oath prescribed by the Constitution, to participate in the trial, like the rest of us. I do not understand upon what ground it is at this stage of the proceeding that an objection can be sustained to his taking the oath. Certainly it will not be claimed that we are now acting in our ordinary capacity as a Senate; but we are acting in a judicial capacity as a Senate; or, in other words, if you please, for brevity's sake, as a court. What right, I beg to inquire, have the members of the Senate, who do not yet under the Constitution constitute a part of the court, to say that a particular member of their body shall not take the oath prescribed by the Constitution? How are we to get at it? Who are the persons authorized to vote on this objection which is raised, and declare that the Senator from Ohio shall not take the oath? Is it the right of the court, or, to speak more accurately, of the comparatively few members of the court who have by their oath become such, to exclude a Senator? That is a very strange view to take of the question. Of what interest is it to us, let me inquire, even if we were organized as a court, that the Senator from Ohio should not take the oath prescribed by the Constitution? If there be an interest anywhere, that interest is only available on the part of the accused, who is not yet before us. He can avail himself of it only in the nature of a challenge for cause, which I do not now propose to discuss; at the same time, however, denying the right of any such challenge. But, as the Senate are now situated, it is entirely clear to my mind that we have no right whatever to pass a resolution or order prohibiting the honorable Senator from Ohio, or any other Senator, if he sees fit, from taking the oath prescribed by the Constitution, and which we are now in the act of taking. It is an act *coram non judice*, without jurisdiction or color on our part to perform.

I would suggest, therefore, that this objection should, for the present, be withdrawn. The honorable Senator from Indiana must of course see that at the proper time, after a proper organization, all he seeks to obtain now by his objection will be raised by learned counsel upon the trial, fully discussed by them, and considered and decided by ourselves sitting in our judicial capacity.

Mr. MORTON. Mr. President, if it should now be determined that the Senator from Ohio shall not be sworn it would be an error, a blunder of which the accused would have just right to complain when he should come here. If a judge is interested in a case before him, or if a juror is interested in the result of the issue which he is called upon to try, it is an objection that the parties to the case have the right to waive; and they have always had that right under any system of practice that I have known anything about.

As was suggested by the Senator from Maine [Mr. MORRILL] and the Senator from Oregon, [Mr. WILLIAMS,] it is not an objection to be made by a fellow-juror, by another member of the court, or by anybody except the parties to the case; and if we now, in the absence of the accused, say that the Senator from Ohio shall not be sworn, the President, when he comes here to stand his trial, will have a right to say, "A Senator has been excluded that I would willingly accept; I have confidence in his integrity; I have confidence in his character and in his judgment, and I am willing to waive the question of interest. Who had the right to make it in my absence?" The Senator from Indiana, my colleague, and the Senator from Kentucky have no right to make the question unless they should do it in the character of counsel for the accused, a character they do not maintain.

Mr. President, I desire to say one thing further, that this objection made here, in my judgment, proceeds upon a wrong theory. It is that we are now about putting off the character of the Senate of the United States and taking upon ourselves a new character; that we are about ceasing to be a Senate to become a court. Sir, I reject that idea entirely. This is the Senate when sworn, this will be the Senate when sitting upon the trial, and can have no other character. The idea that we are to become a court, invested with a new character, and possibly having new constituents, I reject as being in violation of the Constitution itself. What does that say? It says that "the Senate shall have the sole power to try all impeachments." The Senate shall have the sole power to try; it is the Senate that is to try, not a high court of impeachment—a phrase that is sometimes used—that is to be organized, to be created by the process through which we are now going; but, sir, it is simply the Senate of the United States. The Senate, "when sitting for that purpose, shall be on oath or affirmation." That does not change our character. We do not on account of this oath or affirmation cease to be a Senate, undergo a transformation, and become a high court of impeachment; but the Constitution simply provides that the Senate while, as a Senate, trying this case, shall be under oath or affirmation. It is an exceptional obligation. The duty of trying an impeachment is an exceptional duty, just as is the ratification of a treaty; but it is still simply the Senate performing that duty. "When the President of the United States is tried the Chief Justice shall preside." Preside where? In some high court of impeachment, to be created by the transformation of an oath? No, sir. He is to preside in the Senate of the United States, and over the Senate; and that is all there is of it. "And no person shall be convicted without the concurrence of two thirds of the members present." Two thirds of the members of the Senate.

Mr. President, if I am right in this view, it settles the whole question. The Senator from Ohio is a member of the Senate. My colleague has argued this question as if we were about now to organize a new body, a court, and that the Senator from Ohio is not competent to become a member of that court. That is his theory. The theory is false. This impeachment is to be tried by the Senate, and he is already a member of the Senate, and he has a constitutional right to sit here, and we have no power to take it from him. As to how far he shall participate, as to what part he shall take in our proceedings, as has been correctly said, that is a question for him to decide in his own mind. But, sir, he is already a member of this body; he is here; he has his rights already conferred upon him as a member of this body, and he has a constitutional right to take part in the performance of this business as of any other business, whether the ratification of a treaty, or the confirmation of an appointment, or the passage of a bill, which may be devolved on this body by the Constitution of the United States. Because he has been elected President *pro tempore* of the Senate, does that take from him any of his rights as a Senator? Those rights existed before, and he cannot be robbed of them by any act of this Senate.

But, sir, aside from this question, which goes to the main argument, this entire action is premature. There is nobody here to make this challenge, even if it could be made legitimately. The Senators making it do not represent anybody but themselves. The accused might not want it made. He might, perhaps, prefer the Senator from Ohio to any other member of this body to try his case. It is always the right of the defendant in a criminal proceeding and of the parties in a civil action to waive the interest that a juror or a member of the court may have in the case.

Mr. JOHNSON. Mr. President, the motion that I made to postpone the question now before the Senate till to-morrow was made with no view to impede at all the organization of the court, so far as it can be organized by swearing all the other members; and I withdraw the motion now and put it in another form, namely, that the question lie on the table until the other members are sworn.

While I am up permit me to say a few words in reply to the honorable member from Indiana, [Mr. Morton.] He tells us it is for the President of the United States—applying his remarks to the case which is to be and is before us—himself to make the objection, and that he may waive it. With all due deference to the honorable member, that is an entire misapprehension of the question. The question involved in the inquiry is what is the court to try the President? It is not to be such a tribunal as he chooses to try him. It is a question in which the people of the United States are interested, in which the country is interested; and by no conduct of the President, by no waiver of his can he constitute this court in any other way than the way which the Constitution contemplates; that is to say, a court having all the qualities which the Constitution intends.

The honorable member tells us that we are still a Senate and not a court, and that we cannot be anything but a Senate and cannot at any time become a court. Why, sir, the honorable member is not treading in the footsteps of his fathers. The Constitution was adopted in 1789. There have been four or five cases of impeachment, and in every case the Senate has decided to resolve itself into a court, and the proceedings have been conducted before it as a court and not as a Senate. To be sure, these component elements of which the court is composed are Senators, but that is a mere *descriptio personarum*. They are members of the court because they are Senators, but not the less members of a court. The Constitution contemplated their assuming both capacities. As a Senate of the United States they have no judicial authority whatever; their powers are altogether legislative; they are to constitute and do constitute only a portion of the legislative department of the Government; but the Constitution for wise purposes says that in the contingency of an impeachment of a President of the United States or any other officer falling within the clause authorizing an impeachment they are to become, as I understand, a court. So have all our predecessors ruled in every case; and who were they? In the celebrated case of the impeachment against Mr. Chase, who was one of the associate justices of the Supreme Court of the United States, there were men in the Senate at that time whose superiors have not been found since, nor at any time before, and they adopted the idea and acted upon the idea that the Senate in the trial of that impeachment acted as a court and not as a Senate.

I submit, therefore, that the honorable member from Indiana [Mr. Morton] is altogether mistaken in supposing that we are not a court. But look at the power which we are to have. We are to pronounce judgment of guilty or not guilty; we are to answer upon our oaths whether the party impeached is guilty or not guilty of the articles of impeachment laid to his charge, and having pronounced him guilty or not guilty, we are then to award judgment. Who ever heard of the Senate of the United States in its legislative capacity awarding a judgment?

But besides that, why is it, Mr. Chief Justice, that you are called to preside over the court, or the Senate when acting as a court to try an impeachment? It is because it is a court. You have no legislative capacity; your functions are to construe the laws in cases coming before you; and the very fact that upon the trial of an impeachment of the President of the United States the Vice President is to be laid aside, and the ordinary Presiding Officer, if the Vice President himself does not exist, and you are to preside, shows that it is a court of the highest character, demanding the wisdom and the learning of the Chief Justice of the United States.

The honorable member says, and other members have said, that a question of interest or no interest is not involved in an inquiry of this description. Does the honorable member mean to say that if the honorable member from Ohio had a bill before the Senate awarding to him a sum of money upon the ground that it was due to him by the United States he could vote upon the question of the passage of the bill? Why not if the honorable member from Indiana is right? He is a Senator. If he is right that the Constitution intends that each State shall have two votes upon every question coming before the body, then in the case supposed the honorable member from Ohio would have a right to vote himself, and by his own vote to place money in his own possession. Who ever heard that that was a right that could be accorded anywhere?

Mr. President, courts have gone so far as to say that a judgment pronounced by a judge in a court of which he was the constitutional officer in a case in which he had a direct interest, was absolutely void upon general principles; not void because of any statutory regulation on this subject, but void upon the general ground that no man shall be a judge in his own case. Does it make any difference what may be the character of the interest? If the honorable member from Ohio was the sole party under the Constitution to try this impeachment, could he try it? Would not everybody say it is a *casus omissus?* There can be no trial as long as he continues to be the sole member of the court, because he has a direct and immediate interest in the result; because the judgment would be absolutely void as against the general principle founded in the nature of man, that no man should be permitted to adjudge a question in which he has a direct interest.

I propose to say nothing more. I will suspend the motion I before made, and move now that the question of right of the honorable member from Ohio be laid aside until the other members of the Senate are qualified.

Mr. SHERMAN. Mr. President, I certainly do not appear here to represent my colleague on this question; but I represent the State of Ohio, which is entitled to two Senators on this floor. The Constitution declares that each Senator shall have a vote, and the Constitution further declares that each Senator shall take an oath in cases of impeachment. The right of my colleague to take the oath, his duty to take it, is as clear in my mind as any question that ever was presented to me as a Senator of the United States. The Constitution makes it plainly his duty to take the oath. He is a Senator, bound to take the oath, according to my reading of the Constitution; and every precedent that has been cited, and every precedent that has been referred to, bears out this construction. If after he has taken the oath as a member of the Senate of the United States, for the purposes of this trial, anybody objects to his right to vote on any question that may be presented to this court or to the Senate hereafter, the objection can then be made and discussed; but his right in the preliminary stages to take the oath, and his duty to take it, is made plain by the Constitution itself. If, hereafter, when the impeachment progresses, his right to vote on any question is challenged the question may be discussed and decided.

The case cited by my honorable friend from Maryland is directly in point. Mr. Stockton came here with a certificate from the State of New Jersey in due form; he presented it, and was sworn into office. Did anybody object to his being sworn? At the same time other papers were presented to the Senate challenging his right to be sworn, saying that the Legislature of New Jersey had never elected Mr. Stockton; but because of that did anybody object to the oath being administered to Mr. Stockton? No one; although his right to take the oath was challenged, and a protest, signed by a very large number of the members of the New Jersey Legislature, against his right to the seat, was presented. He was sworn in and took his seat here by our side, and voted and exercised the rights of a Senator. When the question of the legality of his own election came up the Senate decided that he was not legally elected, and the question referred to arose upon his right to vote in that particular case. The question was whether he could vote, being interested in the subject-matter. The Senator from Massachusetts made the objection, and offered a resolution that he had not a right to vote in the particular case; and after debate that was decided in the affirmative, although by a very close vote. My own conviction then was, and is yet, that Mr. Stockton as a Senator from the State of New Jersey had a right to vote in his own case, although it might not be a proper exercise of the right.

So, sir, this question has been decided two or three times in the House of Representatives. In the celebrated New Jersey case, where a certificate of election was presented by certain members from the State of New Jersey and they were excluded, public history has pronounced their exclusion to have been an unjustifiable wrong upon the great seal of the

State of New Jersey. I believe that action is now generally admitted and conceded to have been wrong. Those men presented their credentials in the regular form, and they had the right to be sworn. So in many other cases, where the right of persons to hold office is in dispute, those who have the *prima facie* right are sworn into office, and then the right is examined and finally settled. I had a matter presented to me once in which I was personally interested, and where I was sworn into office. I was directly and personally interested; but I took the oath of office, and I discharged my duties as a member of the House of Representatives; and when the question came up whether I should vote on the election of a particular officer, I being a candidate for the office, I refused to vote. But it was my refusal which prevented my vote from being received. If I had chosen to vote, I had the right as a member from the State of Ohio, even for myself. I have no doubt whatever of that. It is the right of the State; it is the right of the people; it is the right of representation. The power of the State and the power of the people must be exercised through their Senators and through their Representatives.

In the particular case here I do not suppose, I do not know, at least, whether the question will ever arise. My colleague is required to take this oath as a member of the Senate of the United States. You have no right to assume, nor have Senators the right to assume, that he will vote on questions which may affect his interest. That is a matter for him to decide; but the right of the State to be represented here on this trial of an impeachment is clear enough. Whether he will exercise the right, or whether he will waive it, is for him to determine. You have no right to assume that he will exercise the right or power to vote for himself where he is directly interested in the result.

It seems to me, therefore, that no Senator here has the right to challenge the voice of the State of Ohio, and the right of the State of Ohio to have two votes here is unquestionable, unless when the question is raised in due form it shall be decided against my colleague. In the preliminary stages, when we are organizing this court, he ought to be sworn, and then if he is to be excluded by interest, unfitness, or any other reason, the question may be determined when raised hereafter; but no Senator has the right now to challenge his authority to appear here and be sworn as a Senator from Ohio. His exclusion must come either by his own voluntary act, proceeding on what he deems to be just and right according to general principles, or it must be by the act of the Senate upon an objection made by the person accused in the trial of the impeachment. It seems to me that is clear, and therefore I object to any waiver of the matter. I think my colleague has a right to present himself and be sworn precisely as I and other Senators have been sworn. Then let him decide for himself whether in a case in which his interest is so deeply affected he will vote on any question involved in the impeachment. If he decides to vote when his vote is presented, then, not the Senator from Indiana, but the accused may make the objection, and we shall decide the question as a Senate or as a court, for I consider the terms convertible; we shall then decide the question of his right to vote.

Sir, several things have been introduced into this debate that I think ought not to have been introduced. The precise character of this tribunal, whether it is a court or a Senate, has nothing to do at present with this question. The only question before us is whether BENJAMIN F. WADE, acknowledged to be a Senator from the State of Ohio, has a right to present himself and take the oath prescribed by the Constitution and the laws in cases of impeachment. He is not the Vice President; he is not excluded by the terms of the Constitution. He is the Presiding Officer of the Senate, holding that office at our will. You have no right to take away from him the power to take the oath of office and then to decide for himself as to whether, under all the circumstances, he ought to participate in this trial.

Mr. BAYARD. Mr. President, I incline to the opinion that the objection made by the honorable Senator from Maine [Mr. MORRILL] to the motion of the honorable Senator from Indiana, [Mr. HENDRICKS,] and also that made by the honorable Senator from Oregon, [Mr. WILLIAMS,] is correct. I cannot see how a Senator is to object to another Senator being sworn in, although I think there may be some doubt raised on the question for this reason : the Constitution provides that in a case where the President of the United States is tried under an impeachment the Chief Justice of the United States, not the Vice President, shall preside ; and though that was intended originally to look to the Vice President alone, yet if another person, from the death of the Vice President, or from his absence or his acting as President, stands in precisely the same relation to the office of President under the law and the Constitution, whether he be a Senator or not, ought not the principle equally to apply ?

It certainly excludes the Vice President from being a member of the court. Does it not equally exclude the Presiding Officer of the Senate? It does not make him, being a Senator, less a Senator of the United States in his legislative capacity ; but the clause of the Constitution prevents and is intended to prevent the influence of the man who would profit as the necessary result of the judgment of guilty in the case. It supposes that he cannot be or may not be sufficiently impartial to sit as a judge in that case or to preside in the court trying it. That is the object, as I suppose.

But, sir, there is great force in the objection that that point must come by plea or motion, if you please, from the party accused; and I should not have thought for a moment of embarking in this discussion had it not been for the renewal by the honorable Senator from Indiana [Mr. MORTON] of the endeavor to disprove the idea that the Senate must be organized into a court for the purpose of a judicial trial. Now, sir, whether it is to be a high court of impeachment or a court of impeachment, or to be called by the technical name court, is, in my judgment, immaterial; but the honorable Senator's argument did not touch the Constitution. The Senate is to constitute the court; the Senate is to try. Is there nothing in the provisions of that article which gives the judicial authority—for it is not legislative, it is judicial authority conferred, a judicial authority in special cases—is there nothing in that article which, of necessity, makes the body a judicial tribunal whenever it assumes these functions, and not a legislative body? Otherwise, how comes the presiding officer who now fills the chair to be in the seat which he occupies? When the Constitution says that the Senate shall have the sole authority to try impeachments it is necessary that it should say that the Senate shall be a court for the purpose of trying impeachments if every clause of the Constitution shows that it must be a judicial tribunal and must be a court, or else the language is meaningless which is applied to its organization? The members of the body are to be sworn specially in the particular case as between the accused and the impeachers. Is not that the action of a court? They are to try an individual in a criminal prosecution. Is not that judicial action? Is not the entire judicial power of the United States vested in the Supreme Court and the inferior courts, with that exception, by the very terms of the Constitution?

But, further, the body is to give judgment, to pronounce judgment, a judgment of removal from office always as the result of conviction; and if they please to carry it still further, they may pronounce judgment of disqualification from hereafter holding any office. Do not these terms of necessity constitute a court? Did the Constitution mean, taking all its language, that the Senate in its legislative capacity, or as a Senate of the United States without any change whatever, should participate in the judicial power of the Government; or did it mean to give judicial power? And if it gave judicial power, and prescribed the mode of its exercise in such a manner that it necessarily converted it into a court, why should it not be called a court?

But, sir, the precedents are conclusive. I cited the case of Blount on a former occasion in the Senate. - He was impeached in 1798, nine years after the Constitution went into operation. Many of the members of the Senate at that time had been members of the Convention which formed the Constitution, and all of them were conversant with its history and meaning. It was the first case of impeach-

ment, and yet in that case there is conclusive evidence that no one interposed the idea that the body was not organized into a court, a judicial tribunal, and accordingly the defendant appeared—he had been expelled by the Senate under their other powers—and he pleaded to the articles of impeachment, and the case was argued at length on both sides, and the Senate determined to dismiss the articles, and in announcing their decision to the House of Representatives the Presiding Officer of the Senate said in terms "the court after consideration have adjudged" or "determined"—I forget the exact language; but it spoke of the court. This was the communication of the Presiding Officer of the Senate in the presence of the Senate, to the Managers of the impeachment, that the court had determined to dismiss the articles, and the defendant was discharged. Is the precedent of no worth? Does the honorable Senator from Indiana say that the men of that day, the Hillhouses and Tracys, and other men who then constituted the Senate, did not understand the language in which the Constitution was adopted as well as we do now? They were able lawyers. The case was one perfectly free from the bias of political excitement of every kind. And from that day to this, until this idea is now suggested that you are to try as a Senate, and not as a judicial tribunal, the President of the United States on an impeachment for high crimes, no one has ever doubted that the Senate must be resolved into a court for the purpose of performing such functions.

Sir, it is against this, which I consider a heresy, that I desire to protest. For my own part I cannot conceive on what ground such an idea should be thrown into this case, or what effect it can have, unless it be to let loose partisan passion by escaping from judicial responsibility. No one doubts that the court is to be composed of the Senate of the United States. Why it should not be called a court, in the face of the precedents, the face of the provisions of the Constitution, all of which confer on it judicial power and the modes of action which belong to a court, is to me inscrutable.

The question is collateral, I admit, because I think this is not the time to object to the honorable Senator from Ohio being sworn in. My mind is somewhat in doubt; but my opinion inclines that way, that the objection must come from the party arraigned, unless, indeed, the honorable Senator, looking to the particular circumstances of the case, should ask to be excused from being sworn. That is a question which it is not for me to decide; but it is for him to decide to that extent, I admit. But, sir, I cannot admit the doctrine I have heard enunciated here, that the great, eternal principle, that no man shall be a judge in his own cause, does not apply to this case whenever the question is properly raised. What is the state of facts? The Senate of the United States is constituted into a judicial tribunal; that cannot be denied. They have the powers not only of judges, but of jurors; and if there be one principle more sacred than another it is as to the juror, who finds facts that he must be *omni exceptione major*. The great, general principle that a man shall not be a judge in his own cause applies everywhere, and commends itself to the universal sentiment of mankind. Now, what is the case here? The Senate are the judges of the facts, as well as of the law, when organized into a court for the trial of an impeachment. If the case was presented of the trial of the most ordinary misdemeanor in a court of justice by an unquestionably qualified juror in all other respects, if it was shown that that juror had a direct interest in the conviction or the acquittal of the defendant, would it not be a sufficient objection? Can there be any doubt about the directness of the interest here? Your judgment, if the accused is convicted, must be removal from office. It must go that far. The effect, then, of a judgment rendered by this court, were it rendered by the aid of the honorable Senator from Ohio sitting as a judge, would be to elevate him to the position of the executive head of this great nation. Is not that an interest? It is the necessary result of such a judgment when it is rendered that he has a right to the office, and is entitled to the office. Whether he choose to relinquish it or not would not alter the case. The interest is direct; and if there ever was a case in which the principle that a man shall not be a judge in his own cause applied it surely must apply to the case where the members of the tribunal which is organized are judges, not only of the law, but also of the facts. Human nature is not to be trusted that far; that is the foundation of the principle, and no man who knows his own heart, no man who knows how delusive and how deceptive are the illusions of humanity, could for a moment tolerate any other principle. It has universally obtained as a great general truth.

I trust, sir, that whenever the case comes properly before us there can be no question as to what must be the decision of the Senate. As I said before, I hope, however, that we shall be relieved from the necessity of any decision in a case like this, as we can be relieved by the action of the honorable Senator from Ohio. He must, of course, decide that question for himself in the first instance; but, for my own part, I can only say that if I stood in the same position the wealth of worlds could not tempt me for an instant to think of sitting as a judge in a case where my interests were so directly personally involved.

Mr. SUMNER. Mr. President, I shall not attempt to follow learned Senators in the question whether this is a Senate or a court. That question, to my mind, is simply one of language and not of substance. Our powers at this moment are under the Constitution of the United States; nor can we add to them a tittle by calling ourselves a court or calling ourselves a Senate. There they are in the Constitution. Search its text and you will find them. The Constitution has not given us a name, but it has given us powers; and those we are now to exercise. The Senate has the sole power to try impeachments. No matter for the name, sir. I hope that I do not use an illustration too familiar when I remind you that a rose under any other name has all those qualities which make it the first of flowers.

I should not at this time have entered into this discussion if I had not listened to objections on the other side which seem to me founded, I will not say in error, for that would be bold when we are discussing a question of so much novelty, but I will say founded in a reading of history which I have not been able to verify. Senator after Senator on the other side, all distinguished by ability and learning, have informed us that the Constitution intended to prevent a person who might become President from presiding at the trial of the President. I would ask learned Senators who have announced this proposition where they find it in the Constitution? The Constitution says:

"When the President of the United States is tried the Chief Justice shall preside."

This is all; and yet on this simple text the superstructure of Senators has been reared. The Constitution does not proceed to say why the Chief Justice shall preside; not at all: nothing of the kind. Senators supply the reason and then undertake to apply it to the actual President of the Senate. Where, sir, do they find the reason? They cannot find the reason which they now assign in any of the contemporary authorities illustrating the Constitution. They cannot find it in the debates of the national Convention reported by Madison, or in any of the debates in the States at that time, nor can they find it in the Federalist. When does that reason first come on the scene? Others may be more fortunate than I, but I have not been able to find it earlier than 1825, nearly forty years after the formation of the Constitution, in the Commentaries of William Rawle. We all know the character of this work, one of great respectability, and which most of us in our early days have read and studied. How does he speak of it? As follows:

"The Vice President, being the President of the Senate, presides on the trial, except when the President of the United States is tried. As the Vice President succeeds to the functions and emoluments of the President of the United States whenever a vacancy happens in the latter office, it would be inconsistent with the implied purity of such a judge that a person under a probable bias of such a nature should participate in the trial, and it would follow that he ought wholly to retire from the court."

Those are the words of a commentator on the Constitution. They next appear ten years later in the Commentaries of Mr. Justice Story, as follows. After citing the provision "when the President of the United States is tried the Chief Justice shall preside," the learned commentator proceeds:

"The reason of this clause has been already adverted to. It was to preclude the Vice President, who might be supposed to have a natural desire to succeed to the office, from being instrumental in procuring the conviction of the Chief Magistrate."

And he cites in his note "Rawle on the Constitution, page 216," being the very words that I have already read. Here is the first appearance of this reason which is now made to play so important a part, being treated even as a text of the Constitution itself. At least I have not been able to meet it at an earlier day. If you repair to the contemporary authorities, including the original debates, you will find no such reason assigned; nothing like it; not even any suggestion of it. On the contrary, you will find Mr. Madison, in the Virginia convention, making a statement which explains in the most satisfactory manner the requirement of the Constitution. No better authority could be cited. Any reason supplied by him anterior to the adoption of the Constitution must be of more weight than any *ex post facto* imagination or invention of learned commentators.

If we trust to the lights of history the reason for the introduction of this clause in the Constitution was because the framers of the Constitution contemplated the possibility of the suspension of the President from the exercise of his powers, in which event the Vice President could not be in your chair, sir. If the President were suspended the Vice President would be in his place. The reports will verify what I say. If you refer to the debates of the national Convention under the date of Friday, September 14, 1787, you will find the following entry, which I read now by way of introduction to what follows at a later date, on the authority of Mr. Madison himself:

"Mr. Rutledge and Mr. Gouverneur Morris moved that persons impeached be suspended from their offices until they be tried and acquitted.

"Mr. Madison. The President is made too dependent already on the Legislature by the power of one branch to try him in consequence of an impeachment by the other. This intermediate suspension will put him in the power of one branch only. They can at any moment, in order to make way for the functions of another who will be more favorable to their views, vote a temporary removal of the existing Magistrate.

"Mr. King concurred in the opposition to the amendment."

The proposition was rejected by the decisive vote—eight States in the negative to three in the affirmative. We all see in reading it now that it was rejected on good grounds. It would obviously be improper to confer upon the other branch of Congress the power, by its own vote, to bring about a suspension of the Chief Magistrate. But it did not follow, because the convention rejected the proposition, that a suspension could take place on a simple vote of the House of Representatives, that, therefore, the President could not be suspended. When the

Senate was declared to have the sole power to try impeachments it was by necessary implication invested with the power incident to every court, and known historically to belong to the English court of impeachment, from which ours was borrowed, of suspending the party accused. All this was apparent at the time, if possible, more clearly than now. It was so clear that it furnishes an all-sufficient reason for the provision that the Chief Justice should preside on the trial of the President, without resorting to the later reason which has been put forward in this debate.

But we are not driven to speculate on this question. While the Constitution was under discussion in the Virginia convention George Mason objected to some of the powers conferred upon the President, especially the pardoning power. This was on June 18, 1788, and will be found under that date in the reports of the Virginia convention. This earnest opponent of the Constitution said that the President might "pardon crimes which were advised by himself," and thus further his own ambitious schemes. This brought forward Mr. Madison, who had sat, as we all know, throughout the debates of the national Convention, and had recorded its proceedings, and who, of all persons, was the most competent to testify at that time as to the intention of the framers. What said this eminent authority? I give you his words:

"There is one security in this case to which gentlemen may not have adverted. If the President be connected in any suspicious manner with any person, and there be grounds to believe he will shelter him, the House of Representatives can impeach him: they"—

Evidently referring to the Senate, or the Senate in connection with the House—

"can remove him if found guilty: *they can suspend him when suspected*, and the power will devolve upon the Vice President."

Mark well these words: "they can suspend him when suspected." If only suspected the President can be suspended. What next? "And his power will devolve upon the Vice President;" in which event, of course, the Vice President would be occupied elsewhere than in this Chamber.

Those were the words of James Madison, spoken in debate in the Virginia convention. Taken in connection with the earlier passage in the national Convention, they seem to leave little doubt with regard to the intention of the framers of the Constitution. They were unwilling to give to the other House alone the power of suspension, but they saw that when they authorized the Senate to try impeachments they gave to it the power of suspension, if it should choose to exercise it; and the suspension of the President necessarily involved the withdrawal of the Vice President from this Chamber, and the duty of supplying his place.

I submit, then, on the contemporary testimony, that the special reason why the Chief Justice is called to preside when the President

A.—2.

is on trial is less what learned Senators have assigned than because the Vice President under certain circumstances would not be able to be present. It was to provide for such a contingency, being nothing less than his necessary absence in the discharge of the high duties of Chief Magistrate, that a substitute was necessary, and he was found in the Chief Justice. All this was reasonable. It would have been unreasonable not to make such a provision.

But this is not all. There is an incident immediately after the adoption of the Constitution which is in harmony with this authentic history. The House of Representatives at an early day acted on the interpretation of the Constitution given by Mr. Madison. The first impeachment, as we all know, was of William Blount, a Senator, and in impeaching him the House of Representatives demanded "that he should be sequestered from his seat in the Senate." This was in 1797. The Senate did not comply with this demand, but the demand nevertheless exists in the history of your Government, and it illustrates the interpretation which was given at that time to the powers of the Senate. The language employed, that the person impeached should be "sequestered," is the traditional language of the British constitution, constantly used, and familiar to our fathers. In employing it, the House of Representatives gave their early testimony that the Senate could suspend from his function any person impeached before them; and thus the House of Representatives unite with Madison in supplying a sufficient reason for the provision that on the trial of the President the Chief Justice shall preside.

In abandoning the reason which I have thus traced to contemporary authority you launch upon an uncertain sea. You may think the reason assigned by the commentators to be satisfactory. It may please your taste; but it cannot be accepted as an authentic statement. If the original propositions were before me I should listen to any such suggestion with the greatest respect. I do not mean to say now that, as a general rule, it has not much in its favor. But I insist that so far as we are informed the reason of the commentators was an afterthought, and that there was another reason which sufficiently explains the rule now under consideration.

I respectfully submit, sir, that you cannot proceed in the interpretation of this text upon the theory adopted by the learned Senators over the way. You must take the text as it is; you cannot go behind it; you cannot extend it. Here it is: "When the President of the United States is tried the Chief Justice shall preside." That is the whole, sir. "The Chief Justice shall preside." No reason is assigned. Can you assign a reason? Can you supply a reason? Especially can you supply one which is not sustained by the authentic contemporary history of the Constitution; and particularly when you have authentic contemporary history which supplies another reason. Unless I am much mistaken this disposes of the objections, proceeding from so many Senators, that the Senator from Ohio cannot take the oath because he may possibly succeed to the President now impeached at your bar. He may vote or not as he pleases, and there is no authority in the Constitution or any of its contemporary expounders to criticise him.

This is all, sir, I have to say at this time on this head. There were other remarks made by Senators over the way to which I might reply. There was one that fell from my learned friend, the Senator from Maryland, in which he alluded to myself. He represented me as having cited many authorities from the House of Lords tending to show in the case of Mr. Stockton that this person at the time was not entitled to vote on the question of his seat. The Senator does not remember that debate, I think, as well as I do. The point which I tried to present to the Senate, and which, I believe, was affirmed by a vote of the body, was simply this: that a man cannot sit as a judge in his own case. That was all, at least so far as I recollect; and I submitted that Mr. Stockton at that time was a judge undertaking to sit in his own case. Pray, sir, what is the pertinence of this citation? Is it applicable at all to the Senator from Ohio? Is his case under consideration? Is he impeached at the bar of the Senate? Is he in any way called in question? Is he to answer for himself? Not at all. How, then, does the principle of law, that no man shall sit as a judge in his own case, apply to him? How does the action of the Senate in the case of Mr. Stockton apply to him? Not at all. The two cases are as wide as the poles asunder. One has nothing to do with the other.

Something has been said of the "interest" of the Senator from Ohio on the present occasion. "Interest!" This is the word used. We are reminded that in a certain event the Senator may become President, and that, on this account, he is under peculiar temptations which may swerve him from justice. The Senator from Maryland went so far as to remind us of the large salary to which he might succeed, not less than $25,000 a year, and thus added a pecuniary temptation to the other disturbing forces. Is not all this very technical? Does it not forget the character of this great proceeding? Sir, we are a Senate, and not a court of *nisi prius*. This is not a case of assault and battery, but a trial involving the destinies of this Republic. I doubt if the question of "interest" is properly raised. I speak with all respect for others; but I submit that it is inapplicable. It does not belong here. Every Senator has his vote, to be given on his conscience. If there be any "interest" to sway him it must be that of justice and the safety of the country. Against these all else is nothing. The Senator from Ohio, whose vote is now in question, can see nothing but those transcendent interests by the side of which office, power, and money are of small account. Put in one scale these interests so dear to the heart of the patriot, and in the other all the personal temptations which have been imagined, and I cannot doubt that if the Senator from Ohio holds these scales the latter will kick the beam.

Mr. POMEROY. I suggest that this question lie on the table, as we cannot take a vote until all the members are sworn. I cannot make that motion, because no motion can be acted upon, as we are partly sworn and partly not. I think by unanimous consent, and by the consent of the Senator from Indiana, his proposition may lie on the table until the oath be administered to the remaining Senators.

Mr. HOWE. If the Senator will indulge me in a remark, as this is the first time I have felt called upon to make one on this occasion, it seems to me he has presented the most conclusive argument, if he is right, against the objection that is taken here. An objection is taken which the Senator says we cannot vote upon, and his proposition is that we ignore it, go around it, lay it on the table. Suppose we do not choose to go around it; then this proceeding stops, if the objection is well taken. It seems to me it cannot be well taken unless here is a tribunal which can pass upon it, and pass upon it now, dispose of it in some way. It seems to me the objection cannot be well taken if we are obliged to run away from it, because, whether we be a court or a Senate within the meaning of the Constitution, both are dissipated necessarily by the raising of a single objection to administering an oath to a single member.

One word further, as I am up. It seems to me that this would not be a difficult question to determine, and by this very tribunal, if we were willing to read what is written and abide by it, for it is written that "the Senate of the United States shall be composed of two Senators from each State." That is written, and it is elsewhere written that Ohio is a State; and nowhere is anything written to the contrary; and if Ohio is a State and this—the Constitution—is law, Ohio is entitled to two Senators on this floor at this time. It is also written that "the Senate," composed in this way, "shall have the sole power to try all impeachments." The Senate shall have the sole power to try all impeachments—nobody else—and I cannot understand why that is not the end of the law. If there were elsewhere in this instrument any qualification or modification of either of those provisions then we should be bound to attend to them; but if there is none I do not see why this is not the end of the law. Whatever may be the impropriety or indelicacy of the Senator from Ohio, whose right to take the oath is now questioned, acting here—gentlemen are at liberty to entertain their own opinions upon that point—the law of the case is here; he is a Senator; he is a member of the tribunal which tries impeachments; or we must wipe out one or the other of these clauses from the Constitution for the time being.

Sir, this being the language of the Constitution, if that were all of it, would there be any doubt that upon the trial of a President upon impeachment the Vice President would sit where you now sit? If there were no other provisions of the Constitution but these, and a President were to be put upon trial on impeachment, would any one suggest that the Vice President should leave his chair and the Chief Justice of the Supreme Court be placed in it? But the impropriety of the Vice President sitting there would be just the same if the Constitution had taken no notice of it as it is now, and just the same as is the impropriety of this oath being administered to the Senator from Ohio. The men who made the Constitution foresaw that and provided for it, and therefore said that in case the President be impeached the Vice President shall not preside, as the Constitution had before declared he should, but the Vice President shall leave his chair and the Chief Justice shall preside during that trial; and it is because the Constitution says so that the Vice President does leave his chair on such an occasion. But here, in reference to this question, there is no such direction in the Constitution.

Now, as to the objection which is taken and as to the time of taking it. It seems to me if anything is plain which is not written in the Constitution it is the objection taken by the Senator from Maine, [Mr. MORRILL.] If there is any objection to the qualifications of the Senator from Ohio to try this question it is an objection which one of the parties to this litigation has a right to urge, and nobody else in the world; and, so far as I know, neither of the parties to that litigation are here. If both were here would they not have a right to waive the objections, if there were any? Could we exclude a member of this Senate against the protest of both the parties to the litigation and say, when they were consenting, that this man or that should not be a member of the Senate? Clearly not.

But, then, what is the objection itself? That he is interested, is it? And how interested? Why, that in a certain contingency, if the issue of the trial be in one way, the Senator whose right to take this oath is objected to would cease to be President of the Senate and would become President of the United States. It was well replied by the Senator from Michigan that that is not certain; that that is not an inevitable consequence; that is a *non sequitur*. It does not follow that he would become President of the United States. If he continued to be President of the Senate up to the time when the judgment of amotion was pronounced, I suppose, by the terms of the Constitution, he would be President; but if he should not continue to be President of the Senate up to that time he would not be. Admit that he is now in possession of the office, which would give him the succession under the Constitution in case of amotion; but the office, the condition, the predicament which is his position to-day may be the reversion of any one of us to-morrow; we are remainder-men if he should happen to retire from that office by the judgment of the Senate.

Mr. FRELINGHUYSEN. And consequently all of us are interested.

Mr. HOWE. All his interest would thus be removed, and that same interest would be vested in some one of the rest of us; I do not know exactly who; but the same possible interest, contingent interest, which is objected to to-day in him is an objection which can be urged against every one of us, because we are liable to be, before the termination of this litigation, placed in precisely the same predicament, and no one of us can be fit, because of this possible interest, to try this question.

Mr. President, I believe, by a rule of the body governing this proceeding, the remarks of members are limited to ten minutes. I have said all I care to say upon the question.

Mr. DRAKE. Mr. President, I do not propose to go over any of the grounds that have heretofore been taken by other Senators on this subject; but there are one or two questions which seem to me to lie in the foreground of this matter, and to which I should like to call the attention of those gentleman who insist upon this exception at this time. If the objection has any vitality, any legal validity whatever, it is one that requires to be passed upon affirmatively or negatively by some body; and I should like to know who is to pass upon it at this stage of the proceeding? Is it addressed to the Presiding Officer of the Senate, as if he had the right to pass upon it? I imagine not. I suppose it will hardly be contended that so grave a question as this can be passed upon by that officer, even if any question in this trial can be passed upon by him at all. If not to be passed upon by the Presiding Officer of the Senate, then what body is to determine the question affirmatively or negatively? The Senate is not yet constituted for the trial of the impeachment.

Besides the honorable Senator from Ohio, there are no less than four other Senators in their seats on this floor at this time waiting to have the oath required by the Constitution administered to them. They are entitled to vote upon all questions which may arise in the Senate sitting in the matter of impeachment. Are you going to stop the proceedings of the Senate at this point and exclude four of the Senators here that are ready and waiting to take the oath? If you are, then if it had so happened that the first name on the roll had been that of the President *pro tempore* of the Senate, all the remainder on the roll after him might, before being sworn, have undertaken to adjudge that he should not be sworn. It just so happens that the name of the Senator from Ohio is low down on the roll of the

Senate, alphabetically taken. If it had been the very first one the objection could have been just as well taken and decided by a Senate not one single member of which had yet been sworn in the matter of impeachment.

Mr. President, for these reasons, aside from all others, I hold that there is no person here who can pass upon this question; the President of the Senate cannot pass upon it; or even if he, in virtue of his presidency, could pass upon questions in the course of this trial, the court, if you call it so, is not yet organized; it is only in the process of organization. There are members of the court here, if you call it a court, waiting to be sworn; and you stop the whole thing here and vote, do you, upon this question, when the vote of those four members that are waiting to be sworn might change the determination one way or the other?

Sir, the whole thing resolves itself at last into a question of order, of entertaining this proposition at all. I will venture to say that if the court had been organized and the present incumbent of the presidency of the Senate had been accustomed, as he is in another tribunal, to announce the decision upon questions of order, he would instantly have decided that this question was out of order at the time it was raised. These are the views about this matter which have led me to participate in these few minutes in the debate on this subject.

Mr. THAYER. Mr. President, it seems to me that the question might with propriety be asked, what is there in a name? With all due respect for the honorable Senators who have by argument attempted to convince the Senate that this is a court, I am compelled to think that it is a waste of words. It is true that in the earlier trials of impeachment the term "high court of impeachment" was used; but it was, in my judgment, a matter of taste or of form. We are, after all, obliged to come back to the plain, pointed, explicit language of the Constitution—

"The Senate shall have the sole power to try all impeachments. When sitting for that purpose"—

Sitting as a Senate for the trial of an impeachment—

"they shall be on oath or affirmation."

Could language be plainer? Could meaning be more apparent than this? If we have passed into a "high court of impeachment" when did that transposition take place? This Senate was sitting as a Senate to-day from twelve o'clock till one. It did not adjourn. What became of it? Where is it if we are here as a court to-day? The Senate does not die. The Senate is in existence. It is here in this body, or is this body sitting as a Senate to try a question on a case of impeachment?

But, after all, that is not material. I have risen more for the purpose of noticing the objection raised by the honorable Senator from Indiana, [Mr. HENDRICKS.] The question of interest is made against the taking of the oath by the honorable Senator from Ohio, [Mr.

WADE,] upon a rule of law in the courts that a person having an interest in the verdict which may be rendered is excluded from sitting upon that jury. If that rule is to prevail here I am surprised that the honorable Senator from Indiana did not raise the question at an earlier stage in the progress of these proceedings to-day. There is another rule of law, or the same rule applicable with equal force, which excludes from the jury a person related by blood or marriage to the accused. If the objection is good in one case is it not equally good in the other? If it should exclude the honorable Senator from Ohio why should it not exclude the honorable Senator from Tennessee, [Mr. PATTERSON?] I cast no imputation upon that Senator; I do not question his determination to try this case justly and fairly according to the Constitution, the law, and the evidence; I make no objection to the Senator from Tennessee; but I desire to say that if this objection is to be raised in the case of the honorable Senator from Ohio it ought, by the same rule of law and of evidence and of construction, to be applied to the honorable Senator from Tennessee.

But, sir, in regard to the question of interest, if that objection is valid against the Senator from Ohio it lies against every member of this body, only one degree more remote. If, by the verdict to be rendered in this trial, the Senator from Ohio should pass from that chair into the more exalted position of President of the United States, it devolves upon this Senate to elect one of the Senators sitting here to fill that vacancy. Human life is in the hands of One who is above all human tribunals, and in the course of human events the honorable Senator from Ohio, elevated to the position of Chief Magistrate of this nation, may pass away, and that Senator sitting here on this trial who has been elevated to the position of Presiding Officer of this body may become the successor of him to whom objection is made to-day in the office of President of the United States. I repeat that the interest lies with every Senator here, only one degree more remote.

But, Mr. President, it has been said repeatedly this afternoon, and it is not necessary for me to dwell upon it, that we are here as a Senate of the United States. The honorable Senator from Ohio is here as a Senator of the State of Ohio, clothed with the rights and all the power possessed by any other Senator on this floor. He is the equal in every particular of every Senator who is now sitting as a member of this body. I challenge the honorable Senator from Indiana or the honorable Senator from Maryland to point me to one iota in the Constitution which recognizes the right of this body to deprive any individual Senator of his vote. No matter what opinions we may entertain as to the propriety of the honorable Senator from Ohio casting a vote on this question, he is here as a Senator, and you cannot take away his right to vote except by a gross usurpation of power. He is here as a Senator in the possession and exercise of every right of a Senator until you expel him by a vote of two thirds of this body. Then he ceases to have those rights, and not till then.

Again, on this question of interest, suppose some ten or fifteen Senators were related in some way to the accused; if the rule holds good you might reduce this body below a quorum, and thus defeat the very object which the Constitution had in view in creating this as the tribunal to try questions of impeachment.

Again, in courts of law, if objections are made to any one sitting upon a jury, and he is excluded, an officer is sent out into the streets and the highways to pick up talesmen and bring them in to fill up the jury. Can you do that here? Suppose you exclude the honorable Senator from Ohio, can you send an officer of this Senate out into the lobbies or into the streets of Washington to bring in a man to take his place? By no means. I need not state that.

Thus I come back to the proposition that we are a Senate, composed of constituent members, two from every State, sworn to do our duty as Senators of the United States; and when you attempt to exclude a Senator from the performance of that duty you assume functions which are not known in the Constitution and cannot for a moment be recognized. When you attempt to exercise the power, and do exercise it, are you any longer the Senate of the United States? The Senate, no other parties or bodies forming any part of it, is the only body known to the Constitution of the United States for this purpose, and the Senate is composed of two Senators from each State.

Mr. HOWARD. I do not rise to prolong the debate, and I entertain the hope that we may be able to dispose of this question very soon. I rise more for the purpose of calling the attention of the Chair to the real matter before us, and of inquiring whether the proposition now made to us is in order. I believe the motion is, that other Senators shall be called to take the oath, and the Senator from Ohio be passed by for the present, until other Senators are all sworn in. If I am mistaken about that, I should like to be corrected.

The CHIEF JUSTICE. The Senator from Ohio [Mr. WADE] presents himself to take the oath. The Senator from Indiana [Mr. HENDRICKS] objects. The question then is, Shall the Senator from Ohio be sworn? Pending that proposition, the Senator from Maryland [Mr. JOHNSON] moves that in administering the oath to Senators the name of the Senator from Ohio [Mr. WADE] be omitted in the call until the remaining names on the roll shall have been called. That is the question now before the body.

Mr. HOWARD. Yes, Mr. President, I so understood; and that is a question, allow me to say, which I suppose to be entirely within the competency of the Chair. There is no rule requiring the members to be called alphabetically to take the oath. If the Chair should see fit upon his own responsibility to call them in reverse order undoubtedly he could do so. I do not see, therefore, any necessity of spending further time in the discussion of this particular motion ; but at the same time I must confess, on reflecting upon this objection, that it seems to me to resolve itself into a pure question of order. The Senate of the United States are endeavoring to assume their judicial functions in a particular case, and are sitting, or endeavoring to sit, upon the trial of an impeachment. Therefore, it seems to me, it must be held that the trial has commenced. If I am correct in this, it appears to me that but one conclusion can be arrived at by the Chair.

"The Senate shall have the sole power to try all impeachments. When sitting for that purpose, they shall be on oath or affirmation."

The Constitution is mandatory ; it is imperative in its very terms. When a Senator offers, therefore, to take the oath, it becomes the duty of the Chair, under the Constitution, to administer the oath to him, and any objection to his taking the oath such as is made here seems to me to be out of order, because it implies that we may, or somebody here may, disobey and disregard this imperative mandate of the fundamental law. That will be a question, I apprehend, for the President of the Senate to decide.

Mr. BUCKALEW. I should like to inquire of the Senator from Michigan if his own rules, for the adoption of which he has asked our assent some days since, do not provide that the Presiding Officer may submit any question to the Senate for decision? Having called upon us to adopt such a rule, and we having assented to his request, I think it very extraordinary that he endeavors to place upon the Chair the entire responsibility of deciding this question in any of the varied forms which it may assume, even assuming it to be (which I do not) a question of order, pure and simple.

Gentlemen read to us a section of the Constitution which says that the Senate shall be composed of two members from each State, and that each Senator shall possess one vote. I suppose, if we were to be curious upon a point of constitutional history, we might ascertain that that last clause was put in the Constitution with reference to the previous practice in the Congress of the Confederation, where the votes were taken by States. This clause, declaring that each member of the Senate, representing a State under the new system, should give a single direct vote, was to exclude, I suppose, the practice which had previously obtained of voting by States. A fundamental idea in constituting bodies consisting of more than one person is that the members shall be equal ; that each shall possess an equal voice in its proceedings. I take it, therefore, that upon principle each member of the Senate ought to possess one vote ; and that this declaration in the Constitution found its way there simply because the practice previously in the Government which preceded our present one had been to vote by States. I suppose that that clause of the Constitution has no other office or meaning. Most certainly it does not bear any such signification as that attempted here to be assigned to it, to oblige us upon every possible question, whether we be acting in a legislative, executive, or (as now) in a judicial capacity, to admit every single member to vote upon every single question which can arise. That is simply the rule by which votes shall be given in the Senate—"each Senator shall have one vote"—but the Constitution does not attempt to define the cases where each member can vote. It does not attempt to exclude cases where his vote would be improper or might be excluded by law or by rule. In conformity with this view the Senate has already adopted a rule for excluding votes in particular cases. It is the practice of this body—and I believe in that respect our practice conforms to that of all other bodies of similar constitution—it is a rule founded in natural propriety and justice, that no man shall express his voice, although he be a representative, in a case where he shall have a direct personal interest in the decision to be made.

Gentlemen seem to feel great difficulty of mind, because, as they say, without the swearing in of the Senator from Ohio the court will not be fully constituted ; that we are at present in an imperfect condition ; that the taking of an oath by him, and the taking of a place among us by him in the new capacity which we are assuming, is necessary and essential to the constitution of the body. That argument has no weight with me in determining the question which has been raised by the objection of the Senator from Indiana. Sir, this is a difficulty which may arise in the organization of any body made up of many members. It may arise in a judicial, in a legislative, or in a popular body anywhere ; a question with regard to the membership of the body in its organization. Questions of this kind have been continually occurring from the foundation of the Government in the two Houses of Congress. Formerly, in the Senate, the practice was that a member who presented his credentials was sworn, and afterward, in case there was objection to his right, his case was investigated and determined. Recently, however, the Senate seem to have fallen into a different practice. Upon one or more occasions recently, one notably in my mind, the recent case from Maryland, a member appearing in the Senate and claiming a right to a seat, with regular credentials from his State, upon an objection made was not sworn. The objection was sustained. The case was sent to a committee of this body and investigated through many months, and the case was, in fact, acted upon at a subsequent session of the Senate, when a decision was arrived at and the judgment of the Senate was pronounced.

Now, sir, in what respect does this case differ in principle from that? Here the Senate is about to organize itself into a court; its members to be put under oath. The Chief Justice of the Supreme Court is called to preside over the proceedings, and we are to proceed as judges of law and of fact to decide the gravest question which can be presented to any tribunal in this country. The Senator from Indiana, when the Senator from Ohio appears, suggests—not as a challenge in the ordinary way, or upon ordinary principles—that under the Constitution of the United States the member from Ohio cannot sit in this court. Now, sir, that question involves the question of his right to be sworn, and it is made at the proper time, for it is made when the question arises legitimately in the course of our proceedings. If the objection be well grounded in the Constitution of the United States this is the time to make it for a very plain reason. If it be not now made, assuming it to be a just objection, what will be the consequence? That a member not qualified to act will become a member of the court and take part in its proceedings; and he will remain a judge in the case, entitled to vote upon all questions which may arise, until at some future time, perhaps days, weeks, or months hence, a Manager for the House or an attorney for the accused may raise the question of his right to sit by a motion or challenge. Then only (according to the argument) can our power of action upon this question be duly exerted.

The argument has been made by a member in debate that perhaps the counsel who come in here will not make the objection to this particular member; and what then? The Senate is to be unable at any time during the trial to relieve itself from an incompetent member! Then an unlawful member may continue to sit from the beginning to the end of the proceeding! At all events it is insisted that some attorney-at-law or manager must raise the question in order that we may assume jurisdiction over it and decide it. Can anything be more absurd than that?

When you pursue this argument to its consequences, I think it becomes manifest that this is the time to raise the question; and I believe that it is not only within our power to raise the question now, but that it is our duty to determine it. We are acting under the Constitution of the United States. Most of us have already been sworn by you, sir, to obey that Constitution; and if, indeed, it be true that by that provision of the Constitution which calls you here to preside over our proceedings—not to give dignity to them merely, but for the other and better and higher purpose, to give purity and a disinterested character to those proceedings—if, indeed, it be true that by that provision the member from Ohio (our Presiding Officer) is disqualified, we cannot shirk our duty of declaring his incompetency on the first occasion when the question is made.

Now, sir, upon what ground is it that gentlemen would deprive us of that ordinary power which exists in the nature of things, to decide upon the constitution of our own body? As I said before, this is not a question of challenge for partiality, nor even for interest under some law which gives it to a party in a court of justice. It is a question which arises under the Constitution as to the organization of our own body—who shall compose it; and we are to meet that question, and decide it, in the very outset of our proceedings.

The Senator from Massachusetts has read to us what Judge Story wrote about 1830, in which he stated an opinion similar to that which was contained in a communication from yourself, sir, to the Senate yesterday; and that was that when the President of the United States is on trial upon articles of impeachment the Chief Justice is called to preside because the Presiding Officer of the Senate is a party in interest, and it would be a scandal to have him preside in a case where his own possible accession to the office of President of the United States was involved. I am content for the present to take the opinion of the present Chief Justice of the Supreme Court of the United States, and the opinion of the most eminent commentator upon American law, in preference to the opinion of the Senator from Massachusetts pronounced here in debate. I think it would be an impropriety, if nothing worse, for the Senate to proceed at this moment, upon the strength of his opinion and of his argument against the highest authorities, to pronounce that the Senator from Ohio is entitled, as a member of the Senate sitting as a court of impeachment, to try the present case.

In the courts of justice I understand that challenges are to be made to jurors before they are sworn. If that time has passed by, and the juror is charged, under oath, with the trial of the case, it is too late to object; and, undoubtedly, if, during the progress of this trial, an objection should be made to the competency of one of the members of the court to sit in the case, the answer which would be made before us and pressed upon our attention would be that the objection came too late, that the member had already been sworn.

Mr. FRELINGHUYSEN. I should like to ask the Senator from Pennsylvania whether he considers that the respondent, the accused, has waived his right to challenge, if any such right exists, as to all those members of the Senate who have been sworn; and if he has not waived that right, is not that conclusive proof that this is not the time to interpose the objection, but that the challenge, if a challenge can be made, must be made to giving the vote, not to taking the oath?

Mr. BUCKALEW. I am not arguing the question of a challenge which may be presented during the trial. All that I was alluding to at the moment the Senator interrupted me was the point that the particular argument I mentioned would be made. I am not treating this as a question of challenge by a party before us. I am not arguing on that ground. The question has not been put upon that ground by the Senator from Indiana or the Senator from Maryland. A right of challenge is a right given by a statute to a party in court to interpose in a particular manner and raise a particular question. We have nothing of that kind here. It is not involved in the present debate. The question now before us and for our decision is this: in proceeding to constitute ourselves into a court, an objection being made that a particular Senator is not qualified to sit in that court at all, is it not our duty to meet the question and decide it? The practice that I was going to point out of both Houses of Congress, at least in recent times, would seem fully to sustain this course. I have already mentioned the case of the Senator from Maryland. In the House of Representatives, when members have appeared there in the present Congress, the whole delegation from a State have had their cases referred. Their being sworn in was deferred for the time until some investigation took place. It is an ordinary mode of proceeding, and it is a power which may be assumed by any body, unless there be some statute or constitution to prevent it, in deciding upon the qualifications of its own members. The Senate has a general power to decide upon the qualifications of its own members. Now, when we come to act in a particular capacity and under oath, have we not the power to decide upon the qualifications of the members of the Senate who are to act in this new capacity, and if there be any incapacity to declare it?

One point more, and I will leave the debate. The Senator from Massachusetts informs us that in 1798, when the House of Representatives presented articles of impeachment against Senator Blount, they made a demand of the Senate that he should be sequestered from his seat. Like the Senator from Ohio, he was a member of this body, as it was then constituted, sitting here under oath, speaking the voice of a State, having, one would suppose, as much authority and power as any of his colleagues. What did the House of Representatives do? They asked the Senate, for the purposes of the trial and during the whole trial, to sequester him from his seat; that is, to remove him from it; to say he should not sit and take part in the proceedings. That was the demand of the House of Representatives at a time when that House was composed of giants in intellect, who had participated in the formation of the very Constitution under which this proceeding takes place. They made that demand of the Senate. Was it repelled? Was it supposed to be an unreasonable or an impertinent demand? Was it supposed that the House of Representatives asked the Senate to do an unreasonable or un-

lawful thing? That was done in the very beginning of the proceedings, before the members of the Senate were sworn at all—earlier than the Senator from Indiana now interposes in the present case upon this question of swearing the Senator from Ohio. The Senate did not resent that demand of the House of Representatives. They made no objection to it. Subsequently, however, for good reasons, which I need not now recite, they did what was more effectual: they expelled Blount from membership by virtue of the constitutional power which they possessed. By a two-thirds vote they not only sequestered him from the Senate during the trial, but deprived him of his seat during his whole term. That was the action of the Senate.

Now, Mr. President, if the House of Representatives has a right to ask the Senate to remove or to sequester a member from this body because he is interested in the trial which is to take place, it must be upon an affirmance of the very point in this debate, that is, that the Senate, in constituting itself into a court, has a right in a proper case to omit a member from being sworn, from becoming a part of the body as reorganized for the special purpose. I insist, therefore, that this case, to which the Senator from Massachusetts has referred as authority, will instruct us that it is our duty now to act upon this case, and, by omitting to swear the Senator from Ohio, to leave him to his general rights as a Senator; but, for a particular constitutional reason not to permit him to act with us in this particular trial, when the result of the trial, if conviction takes places, will be to place him in the office of President of the United States.

I repeat, sir, from my point of view, this is not in the nature of a challenge by a party. Nor is it an objection made as a matter of favor to either party in this proceeding. It is made as a constitutional objection, as a question of membership, as a question upon the organization of the Senate into a court of impeachment.

As to the capacity in which the Senate act, it seems to me there is no difficulty. The old writers and the old commentators used clear language—"the Senate of the United States sitting as a court of impeachment." That was the description of bodies like the one we are about organizing, in olden times, and the uniform language applied to them down to this day. It is still the Senate of the United States, but it sits as a court; for the time being it must act upon judicial rules, and must administer the laws of the United States which are applicable to the particular case. Its legislative powers and functions are left behind it. It has taken on a new character and is performing a new function, judicial in its nature and judicial only. That is the whole of it.

Mr. MORTON. I respectfully submit that the latter part of the argument of the Senator from Pennsylvania does not accord well with the first part. The distinguished Senator from

Pennsylvania started out by saying that we were now organizing a court. He then used the words, "We are about to constitute a court." He talked a great deal about the creation or constitution of a court. He proceeded upon the theory, as did my colleague in his first argument, that we were about to constitute a court which was to be selected from the members of the Senate. Mr. President, the error of this whole argument is right here. The Constitution has constituted the tribunal itself. We have no right to organize a court. We have no right to constitute a court. The tribunal is constituted by the Constitution itself, and is simply the Senate of the United States.

The remark was made, I believe, by the Senator from Ohio, and perhaps by the Senator from Massachusetts, that it was immaterial whether you call it a court or a Senate. It is not very material what you call it; but it is material that you shall proceed simply on the idea that it is a Senate and nothing else. That is material; for if you abandon that plain and simple idea and adopt the theory that this tribunal is yet to be constituted you will wander from the Constitution itself. The Constitution settles the whole question in a few words. It says, "the Senate shall have the sole power to try all impeachments;" and when it has said that it has itself constituted the tribunal. The Senate is the tribunal. Who compose that tribunal? The Senator from Ohio [Mr. WADE] is one of the men who now compose that tribunal, and we cannot get away from that conclusion.

It may be said that while the Senate is trying an impeachment it is exercising judicial powers. That makes no difference. Why, sir, when we come in here to counsel as to the confirmation of an appointment of the President we are not acting as a legislative body; our functions are decidedly executive in their character; but still we act not as an executive body, or as part of the Presidency of the United States, but we act simply as the Senate. Our duties are then executive in their character; but we are performing them simply as the Senate. So when we exercise what may be called judicial power in this case, we do not do it as a court; we are doing it simply in the character of the Senate of the United States, performing certain powers or duties that are imposed upon us by the Constitution.

All this talk about organizing a court; all this talk, in the language of my friend from Pennsylvania, of constituting a tribunal, it seems to me, is idle. The Constitution has done that for us. It only requires that when this tribunal shall act in this capacity it shall be sworn. We have no right to refuse to be sworn. If I were to refuse I should violate my duty. If the Senator from Ohio should refuse he would violate his duty. It seems to me this is the whole of it. The simple idea is, that it is a Senate and the tribunal is already formed—is not to be formed, but is formed

now; and the Constitution says it shall be under oath. The Senator from Ohio had no choice but to take the oath. As to what he shall do hereafter on the challenge of the accused is a question that I will not discuss now. It is enough to say that all this talk about a high court of impeachment, about a tribunal yet to be constituted, yet to be organized, is outside of the Constitution. We are sitting simply as a Senate, as much so as when we pass a bill or as when we ratify a treaty. The Constitution says so, and there is nobody that is authorized to say no.

Mr. DIXON. Mr. President, the President of the United States is about to be tried before this body, either as a Senate or as a court, upon articles brought against him by the House of Representatives, charging him with high crimes and misdemeanors. In case of his——

Mr. GRIMES, (to Mr. DIXON.) Will you give way for a motion to adjourn?

Mr. DIXON. If the Senate wish to adjourn I will not take up the time of the Senate now.

Mr. GRIMES. I understand that the Chief Justice of the United States has been sitting in the Supreme Court and in this Chamber since eleven o'clock this morning without an opportunity to leave his chair. I think it is due to him and to the Senate that we should now adjourn, and settle this question to-morrow morning. I therefore make that motion.

Mr. HOWARD. What is the motion?

Mr. GRIMES. To adjourn until to-morrow.

Mr. HOWARD. To adjourn what until to-morrow?

Mr. GRIMES. This court.

Mr. HOWARD. We have a rule by which the Senate, sitting for the trial of an impeachment, may adjourn itself, and still the ordinary business of the Senate continue, so that we may relieve the Chief Justice without adjourning the Senate.

Mr. GRIMES. My motion is that the court adjourn until to-morrow at one o'clock.

Mr. ANTHONY. I think the proper motion would be that the Senate proceed to the consideration of legislative business.

The CHIEF JUSTICE. The court must first adjourn. Senators, you who are in favor of adjourning the court until to-morrow at one o'clock will say ay, and those of the contrary opinion will say no.

The question being put, the motion was agreed to.

The CHIEF JUSTICE thereupon declared the court adjourned until one o'clock to-morrow, and vacated the chair.

IN SENATE, March 6, 1868.

The PRESIDENT pro tempore. The time having arrived for the Senate to proceed to the consideration of matters connected with the impeachment of the President of the United

States, the chair will be vacated for the Chief Justice of the United States.

The President *pro tempore* thereupon retired from the chair.

The Chief Justice of the United States entered the Senate Chamber, escorted by Mr. POMEROY, the chairman of the committee appointed for that purpose, and took the chair.

The CHIEF JUSTICE. The Senate will come to order. The proceedings of yesterday will be read.

The Secretary read the "proceedings of the Senate sitting on the trial of the impeachment of Andrew Johnson, President of the United States, on Thursday, March 5, 1868," from the entries on the Journal kept for that purpose by the Secretary.

The CHIEF JUSTICE. At its adjournment last evening the Senate, sitting for the trial of impeachment, had under consideration the motion of the Senator from Maryland, [Mr. JOHNSON,] that objection having been made to the Senator from Ohio [Mr. WADE] taking the oath his name should be passed until the remaining members have been sworn. That is the business now before the body. The Senator from Connecticut [Mr. DIXON] is entitled to the floor on that motion.

Mr. DIXON. Mr. President——

Mr. HOWARD. Excuse me one moment. Mr. President, I rise to a question of order.

The CHIEF JUSTICE. The Senator from Michigan will state his point of order.

Mr. HOWARD. By the Constitution the Senate sitting on the trial of an impeachment is to be on oath or affirmation; each member of the Senate, by the Constitution, is a component member of the body for that purpose. There can, therefore, be no trial unless this oath or affirmation is taken by the respective Senators who are present. The Constitution of the United States is imperative; and when a member presents himself to take the oath I hold that as a rule of order it is the duty of the presiding officer to administer the oath, and that his proposition to take the oath cannot be postponed; that other members have no control over the question, but that it is a simple duty devolved upon the presiding officer of the body to administer the oath.

Further, sir, the Senate, on the second day of the present month, adopted rules for their government on proceedings of this kind. Rule 3 declares that—

"Before proceeding to the consideration of the articles of impeachment, the presiding officer shall administer the oath hereinafter provided to the members of the Senate then present"—

Mr. WADE is present and ready to take the oath—

"and to the other members of the Senate as they shall appear, whose duty it shall be to take the same."

The form of the oath is also prescribed in our present rules, and is as follows:

"I solemnly swear (or affirm, as the case may be) that in all things appertaining to the trial of the im-

peachment of —— ——, now pending, I will do impartial justice according to the Constitution and laws. So help me God."

That is the form of the oath prescribed by our rules. It is the form in which the presiding officer of this body himself is sworn. It is the form in which we all, thus far, have been sworn. And so far as the rules are concerned, I insist that they have already been adopted and recognized by us, so far as it is possible during the condition in which we now are of organizing ourselves for the discharge of our judicial duty. I therefore made it a point of order that the objection made to the swearing in of Mr. WADE is out of order; and also that the motion of the Senator from Maryland, to postpone the swearing in of Mr. WADE, is out of order under the rules and under the Constitution of the United States; and I ask most respectfully, but earnestly, that the President of the Senate, the Chief Justice of the Supreme Court of the United States, now presiding in the body, will decide this question of order, and without debate.

Mr. DIXON. Mr. President——

Mr. HOWARD. I object to any further debate.

Mr. DIXON. The very question before the Senate is whether under this rule the Senator from Ohio can be sworn.

Mr. DRAKE. Mr. President, I call the Senator from Connecticut to order.

The CHIEF JUSTICE. The Senator from Connecticut is called to order. The Senator from Michigan has submitted a point of order for the consideration of the body. During the proceedings for the organization of the Senate for the trial of an impeachment of the President the Chair regards the general rules of the Senate as applicable, and that the Senate must determine for itself every question which arises, unless the Chair is permitted to determine it. In a case of this sort, affecting so nearly the organization of this body, the Chair feels himself constrained to submit the question of order to the Senate. Will the Senator from Michigan state his point of order in writing?

While the point of order raised by Mr. HOWARD was being reduced to writing at the desk,

Mr. DIXON. I rise to a question of order.

The CHIEF JUSTICE. A point of order is already pending, and a second point of order cannot be made until that is disposed of.

Mr. DIXON. I submit to the presiding officer whether a point of order can be made with regard to that question, and, with the consent of the Chair, I will state——

The CHIEF JUSTICE. The Chair is of opinion that no point of order can be made pending another point of order.

Mr. HOWARD's point of order having been reduced to writing,

The CHIEF JUSTICE. Senators, the point of order submitted by the Senator from Michigan is as follows: "That the objection raised to administering the oath to Mr. WADE is out of order, and that the motion of the Senator from Maryland, to postpone the administering of the oath to Mr. WADE until other Senators are sworn, is also out of order, under the rules adopted by the Senate on the 2d of March instant, and under the Constitution of the United States." The question is open to debate.

Mr. DIXON. Mr. President, as I under-s .and——

Mr. DRAKE. I call the Senator from Connecticut to order. Under the rules of the Senate questions of order are not debatable.

Mr. DIXON. I would remind the Senator that when questions of order are referred to the Senate for their decision they are always debatable.

Mr. DRAKE. I do not so understand the rules of the Senate. There can be a debate upon an appeal from the decision of the Chair; but there can be no debate in the first instance on a question of order, as I understand the rules of the Senate.

The CHIEF JUSTICE. The Chair rules that a question of order is debatable when submitted to the Senate.

Mr. DRAKE. If I am mistaken in the rules of the Senate on that subject I should like to be corrected, but I think I am not.

The CHIEF JUSTICE. The Senator from Missouri is out of order unless he takes an appeal from the decision of the Chair.

Mr. DRAKE. Well, sir, if it is according to the rules of the Senate debatable, I have nothing to say.

Mr. POMEROY. The Senator must be aware that when the Chair makes a decision it is to be decided without debate; but when it is submitted to the Senate our custom is that it is debatable.

Mr. JOHNSON and others. Always.

Mr. POMEROY. But it is not always submitted to the Senate.

Mr. HOWARD. I ask leave of the Senate to read the sixth of the general rules of the Senate:

"If any member, in speaking or otherwise, transgress the rules of the Senate the Presiding Officer shall, or any member may, call to order; and when a member shall,be called to order by the President or a Senator he shall sit down, and shall not proceed without leave of the Senate. And every question of order shall be decided by the President without debate, subject to an appeal to the Senate, and the President may call for the sense of the Senate on any question of order."

Mr. DIXON. I understand the sense of the Senate to be as I supposed, and I take it I have a right to proceed. How far I have a right to discuss the general question I am somewhat uncertain. I suppose that the question is now presented merely in that different shape alluded to by the Senator from Michigan yesterday when he reminded the Senate that, after all, this was, in his opinion, a question of order, and ought to be so discussed. I take it, Mr. President, the question now before this body

is, whether as a question of order of the orderly proceedings of this tribunal the Senator from Ohio [Mr. WADE] can be sworn; and it is upon that question that I now propose to address this body.

Mr. President, when I had the honor yesterday of addressing this tribunal, and gave way to a motion to adjourn, I was remarking that the President of the United States was about to be tried before this body in its judicial capacity, whether called a court or not, upon articles of impeachment presented by the House of Representatives. If upon the trial he be convicted the judgment may extend to his removal from office and to his disqualification hereafter to hold any office of profit or trust under the United States. How far the judgment would extend in case of his conviction it is of course impossible for any one now to say. In all human probability it would extend at least as far as to his removal from office; and, in that event, the very moment that the judgment was rendered the office of President of the United States, with all its powers and all its attributes, would be vested in the Senator from Ohio, now holding the office of President of this body. The office would vest in the President of the Senate for the time being. And the question for this tribunal now to decide is whether, upon the trial of the President of the United States, the person holding the office of President of the Senate, and in whom the office of President of the United States, upon the conviction of the accused, will immediately vest, can be a judge in that case. That, sir, is the question before us.

Mr. SHERMAN. I very rarely call a Senator to order, but I feel it my duty on this occasion to do so in regard to the Senator from Connecticut. I think he is not in order in the discussion he is now pursuing. The point submitted to the Senate by the Chair, and to be settled by the Senate, is whether or not it is in order to proceed with this discussion. While that matter is being submitted to the Senate the Senator from Connecticut goes on and discusses the main question that was discussed yesterday. It seems to me that in a tribunal like this each Senator should observe strictly the rules of order. I therefore make the point of order on the Senator from Connecticut, and hope the discussion will be confined to the point of order which is submitted now to the Senate.

Mr. DIXON. If I may be permitted, I beg to say to the Senate that I am attempting to discuss the question of order in what seems to me a proper manner.

The CHIEF JUSTICE. The Senator from Ohio makes the point of order that the Senator from Connecticut, in discussing the pending question of order, must confine himself strictly to that question, and not discuss the main question before the Senate. In that point of order the Chair conceives that the Senator from Ohio is correct, and that the Senator from Connecticut must confine himself strictly to the discussion of the point of order before the House.

Mr. DIXON. Mr. President, I commenced by saying that it was somewhat uncertain in my own mind how far it would be proper to go into the general merits of this question upon the point of order; but that I supposed it would be proper to discuss the general question. And I will now take the liberty to say to the presiding officer of this body that if I were now commencing this debate without the example of those Senators before me who have already in the fullest manner discussed the pending question, who, up to the time when I was permitted the privilege of the floor, made no objection to a full discussion—if I had commenced before that example, I should perhaps consider myself more strictly limited in the course of my remarks than I feel myself to be with that example before me. If permitted to proceed without interruption, I will say frankly to the Senate that I propose to go into the general merits of the question whether the President *pro tempore* of this body can be sworn in as a judge in this case—the same question which has been discussed by other Senators. If it is the opinion of the Senate that I cannot go into that question, I certainly have not that desire to force myself upon the attention of the Senate that I should insist upon attempting to evade a rule. I should prefer, therefore, that Senators would inform me, or that the Chair would inform me, how far I may proceed, and I certainly shall not willingly be guilty of any impropriety. But I beg leave again to remind the Senate that this strict rule is applied to me after ten Senators at least have fully discussed this question; and the Senator who raises the question himself has spoken, I think, at great length not less than three times. Now, sir, if it is the will of the Senate that I may proceed, I certainly shall be gratified to do it. As I have already said, I have no desire to proceed with constant interruptions upon questions of order.

Mr. JOHNSON. I believe the questions of order raised by the honorable member from Michigan are, that the Senator from Ohio has a right to be sworn and that the Senate have no right to ask that it should be postponed even for a day. He places it upon the ground that, being a Senator of the United States, he is by the Constitution of the United States made a member of the court. The argument yesterday on both sides was an attempt to show the affirmative and the negative of that proposition. Whether it is in order to object to his being sworn necessarily involves the question whether, under the Constitution, he has a right to be sworn. The honorable member made another question of order, or, rather, made it part of his first question of order, that these points are to be decided without debate. You, Mr. Chief Justice, have held that, as you have submitted the questions to the deliberation and decision of the Senate, they may be de-

bated. All questions of order, when submitted by the Presiding Officer himself to the Senate, or when they are brought before the Senate by an appeal from his decision, are always open to debate. Then what is to be debated under the question of order, which is, that there is no right to object to the honorable member from Ohio taking the oath as a member of this court? I suppose whether he has that right. The objection that the right is a matter which cannot be disputed assumes the whole controversy. If it was admitted by every member of the Senate that the honorable member from Ohio had a right to be sworn there would be no question before the Senate. Some of the members of the Senate think that, for reasons stated in the debate yesterday, he has no right to be sworn as a member of this court. Whether it is in order to make that objection necessarily involves the question whether he has a right to be sworn. I do not see that there can be any other question discussed upon the question of order raised by the honorable member from Michigan but the question whether the honorable member from Ohio has under the Constitution a right to be sworn.

Mr. HENDRICKS. I ask for the reading of the point of order.

The Secretary again read the point of order submitted by Mr. HOWARD.

Mr. DIXON. I think I shall be able to discuss that question of order.

Mr. HENDRICKS. All that I desired to say was this, that the discussion——

Mr. HOWARD. If the Senator from Indiana will allow me one word, I desire to call his attention to the twenty-third rule that we have adopted. Possibly it may have escaped his attention.

"All orders and decisions shall be made and had by yeas and nays, which shall be entered on the record, and without debate."

Mr. JOHNSON. The honorable member will permit me to make a suggestion upon the effect of that rule. I was aware of the existence of the twenty-third rule, but that goes into force only after we have become a court. The question now is as to the manner in which we are to organize ourselves as a court. After we are organized all questions of order are, by force of the twenty-third rule, to be decided without debate.

Mr. SHERMAN. I should like to ask the Senator from Maryland if there is any doubt of the power of the Senate to prescribe the mode and manner of organizing the court preliminary to the final organization? There can be no doubt of it. The last clause of the third rule adopted by us the other day provides that—

"Before proceeding to the consideration of the articles of impeachment the presiding officer shall administer the oath hereinafter provided to the members of the Senate then present, and to the other members of the Senate as they shall appear."

Now, I will ask any Senator whether another Senator may stop the execution of this imperative order of the Senate while it is going on, and give rise to a long debate when the presiding officer, in obedience to this rule, is executing the order of the Senate? He might just as well stop the calling of the roll when the yeas and nays were being taken upon a motion and begin a discussion upon the right of a Senator to vote on a pending motion as to stop the execution of this order of the Senate, while the presiding officer, in pursuance of the rule, is executing it. It cannot be done. The presiding officer is bound to execute the rule of the Senate in the ordinary way. Nothing can interrupt the execution of the order when once adopted.

Mr. DIXON. With the consent of the Senate I propose now—if the honorable Senator from Ohio [Mr. SHERMAN] calls me to order I can proceed only by consent—to discuss this question as a question of order, under the Constitution of the United States and the rules of this body, as specified in the written statement of the question of order, as made by the Senator from Michigan. Before proceeding I will request the Secretary to read the point of order once more. I wish to know precisely what I may be permitted to say.

The Secretary read as follows:

"That the objection raised to administering the oath to Mr. WADE is out of order, and that the motion of the Senator from Maryland, to postpone the administering of the oath to Mr. WADE until other Senators are sworn, is also out of order, under the rules adopted by the Senate on the 2d of March instant, and under the Constitution of the United States."

Mr. DIXON. The question presented by the point of order is whether, under the Constitution——

Mr. HOWARD. Mr. President——

Mr. DIXON. If the Senator calls me to order I will yield.

Mr. HOWARD. Well, I call the Senator from Connecticut to order, and ask the Chair if it be in order now to take an appeal from the decision of the Chair?

Mr. DIXON. I submit that is not such a question of order as the Senator has a right to raise. The only question of order that he can now raise upon me is that I am out of order.

Mr. HOWARD. Very well; I raise that question distinctly.

Mr. DIXON. If the Senator claims that I am out of order he can call me to order.

Mr. HOWARD. I call the Senator to order.

The CHIEF JUSTICE. The Senator from Connecticut is called to order, and will take his seat until the point of order is stated.

Mr. HOWARD. Mr. President, the twenty-third rule, adopted by the Senate on the 2d of March, declares that—

"All the orders and decisions"—

Of course, decisions of the Senate—

"shall be made and had by yeas and nays, which shall be entered on the record, and without debate, except when the doors shall be closed for deliberation, and in that case no member shall speak," &c.

The Senator from Connecticut, in defiance, as I think, of this rule, persists in his right to address the Senate and discuss the question of order. I hold that to be out of order, and upon that question I ask a ruling.

Mr. DIXON. I respectfully submit that an appeal is debatable.

The CHIEF JUSTICE. The Chair will decide the point of order. This point of order is not debatable. The twenty-third rule is a rule for the proceeding of the Senate when organized for the trial of an impeachment. It is not yet organized; and in the opinion of the Chair the twenty-third rule does not apply at present.

Mr. DRAKE. I take an appeal from the decision of the Chair on that point.

The CHIEF JUSTICE. The Senator from Missouri appeals from the decision of the Chair.

Mr. DRAKE. I do not feel disposed to argue the question at this time, consuming time upon it. I take the appeal and ask for a decision upon it by the Senate, if we are in a condition to decide anything until all the Senators are sworn.

The CHIEF JUSTICE. Under the general rules of the Senate, as the Chair understands, an appeal being taken from the decision of the Chair it must be decided without debate.

Mr. GRIMES. Oh, no; it is debatable.

The CHIEF JUSTICE. The Chair ruled that an appeal taken must be decided without debate under an erroneous impression as to the rules of the Senate. Every appeal taken from the decision of the Chair on a question of order is debatable, and this must necessarily be debatable. ["Question!" "Question!"] Senators, are you ready for the question? The question is, Shall the decision of the Chair stand as the judgment of the Senate? and upon that question the yeas and nays will be called.

Mr. FESSENDEN. I think the yeas and nays are not called for.

Mr. GRIMES. They must be called.

Mr. MORRILL, of Maine. Why? On what rule?

Mr. GRIMES. On some rule of the Senate.

Mr. FESSENDEN. They are not always taken, necessarily.

Several SENATORS. Call the roll.

Mr. POMEROY. The point of order is not understood. I do not know what we are to vote upon. I do not understand the point of order of the Senator from Missouri.

Mr. FESSENDEN. It is an appeal from the decision of the Chair.

The CHIEF JUSTICE. The Chair decides that the twenty-third rule is not applicable to the proceedings of the Senate when in process of organization for the trial of an impeachment. From that decision the Senator from Missouri appeals. The yeas and nays are not demanded.

Mr. FERRY. I call for the yeas and nays.

The yeas and nays were ordered.

Mr. DRAKE. The form of the question, if I understand it, is, Shall the decision of the Chair stand as the judgment of the Senate?

The CHIEF JUSTICE. As many Senators as are of opinion that the decision of the Chair shall stand as the judgment of the Senate will, when their names are called, answer yea; as many as are of the contrary opinion will answer nay. The Secretary will call the roll.

The question being taken by yeas and nays, resulted—yeas 24, nays 20; as follows:

YEAS—Messrs. Anthony, Buckalew, Corbett, Davis, Dixon, Fessenden, Fowler, Frelinghuysen, Grimes, Henderson, Hendricks, Johnson, McCreery, Morrill of Maine, Norton, Patterson of Tennessee, Pomeroy, Ross, Saulsbury, Sherman, Sprague, Van Winkle, Willey, and Williams—24.

NAYS—Messrs. Cameron, Cattell, Chandler, Cole, Conkling, Conness, Drake, Ferry, Harlan, Howard, Morgan, Morrill of Vermont, Morton, Nye, Stewart, Sumner, Thayer, Tipton, Wilson, and Yates—20.

ABSENT.—Messrs. Bayard, Cragin, Doolittle, Edmunds, Howe, Patterson of New Hampshire, Ramsey, Trumbull, and Wade—9.

The CHIEF JUSTICE. On this question the yeas are 24 and the nays are 20; so the decision of the Chair stands as the judgment of the Senate. [Manifestations of applause in the galleries.] Order! Order!

Mr. DIXON. Perhaps it will not be improper for me to say, with the consent of the Senate, that it was my intention to speak very briefly and in good faith to the question before the Senate. I have not come here to delay proceedings; I have not come here to violate the rules; and I propose now, so far as I can, to confine myself to the proprieties of discussion in attempting to show that under the Constitution and the rules of this body, as expressed in the questions of order, it is not proper for the Presiding Officer of this body *pro tempore* to be sworn in as a judge in this case.

When interrupted, I was saying that in the event of the conviction of the President of the United States upon the charges brought against him, and his removal from office, there was a direct, apparent interest in the Senator from Ohio, the President *pro tempore* for the time being of this body, which rendered it improper for him to act as a judge. In saying that, I beg leave to say, in the first place, that I am not unmindful of the high character of that Senator. I acknowledge most cheerfully that he is as much raised above the imperfections and the frailties of this weak, depraved, corrupt human nature of ours as any member of this body.

Mr. CONNESS. I rise to a question of order.

The CHIEF JUSTICE. The Senator from California rises to a question of order. He will state the question of order.

Mr. CONNESS. I understand the decision of the Chair to be, that under the general rules of the Senate the Senator from Connecticut must confine his discussion to the question before us. I submit that a discussion of the personal qualifications or qualities of the Senator from Ohio forms no part of such an argument; and I ask the Chair that the Senator, if he proceed, shall be confined within the limit prescribed by the decision of the Chair.

The CHIEF JUSTICE. The Chair required the Senator from Connecticut to proceed in accordance with the rules, confining himself strictly to the point of order raised by the motion of the Senator from Michigan. But the Chair is greatly embarrassed when he attempts to ascertain the precise scope of debate to be indulged upon the point of order which is taken. He is therefore not prepared to state that the Senator from Connecticut is out of order.

Mr. DIXON. Mr. President, I thought that I could, without violating the rules of this body, do justice to myself so far as to disavow any personal objection to the honorable Senator whose taking the oath has been objected to. I could not conceive that such a statement from me, under the circumstances, could be considered by the Senator from California or by any Senator as being an infringement of the rules of order.

Now, Mr. President, what is the question before this body? Is the Senator from Ohio so interested in the result of this trial that he cannot properly, under the Constitution and under the rules, be sworn in as a member of the tribunal? That is the question to which I propose to address myself. If the Chair shall inform me that I have no right to discuss it, I shall, of course, not proceed with my remarks. I was speaking of the nature of the interest and of its effect upon any human mind. Now, sir, may I be permitted to ask this tribunal what is this interest? What is the question which is to be presented to the Senator from Ohio as a judge, and to all of us? If any advantage or profit is to accrue to that honorable Senator by any vote he may give in this body, what is it? What is the nature of the interest? The Senator from Massachusetts [Mr. SUMNER] has spoken of it as of a very slight character, a very slight degree of interest, a matter of trifling consequence. Sir, if any advantage is to accrue to this honorable Senator, it is that which he is to receive in a certain event which may be influenced by his vote. It is nothing less than the high office of President of the United States, the highest object in this country, and perhaps in the world, of human ambition; an object of ambition which the very highest in the land may properly and laudably aspire to.

Mr. STEWART. I call the Senator from Connecticut to order.

The CHIEF JUSTICE. The Senator from Nevada calls the Senator from Connecticut to order.

Mr. STEWART. It is not in order to discuss the main question as to whether the Senator from Ohio is entitled to sit in these proceedings. Nothing further than this can be in order, as I understand the ruling of the Chair: to discuss the point whether now is the time to decide the question.

The point of order submitted by the Senator from Michigan is, that this is not the time to dispose of the question whether the Senator from Ohio shall sit in our deliberations on the question of impeachment. Certainly it does not involve the main question. It only involves the question of whether this is the time to dispose of the main question. My point of order is, that the Senator from Connecticut is discussing the main question and not the question of determining that point at this time.

The CHIEF JUSTICE. The Chair has already said that it is very difficult to determine the precise limits of debate upon the point of order taken by the Senator from Michigan. The first clause of the point of order is, "that the objection raised to the administering of the oath to Mr. WADE is out of order;" that is, the objection raised by the Senator from Indiana is out of order. The nature of that objection and the validity of that objection, as the Chair conceives, must necessarily become the subjects of debate in order to the determination of the point of order. The Chair, therefore, repeats that he is unable now to decide the Senator from Connecticut out of order.

Mr. DIXON. I was upon the question of interest. The objection made to the honorable Senator from Ohio, as I understand it, is that he is interested in the result of this decision. It became necessary for me, therefore, to consider what was his interest, and in order to ascertain that it was necessary to consider what was the advantage or disadvantage that he was to receive or to avoid by the result of his action. I was considering the question, what is this office of the President of the United States, which is the matter in controversy? I was saying that it was an object worthy of the ambition of the highest and most distinguished Senators in this body or of the most distinguished citizen of the United States, not because of its dazzling surroundings, its vulgar trappings; not because a man in that position breathes the atmosphere of adulation, so dear to human nature; not because he has an opportunity, which is still more dear to a generous mind, of doing favors to his friends, or even (which might be equally dear to men of ignoble character) punishing his enemies, but because it is a position in which the occupant of this great office can do immense good to his country; he may benefit the human race; he may at this time imagine that he might restore a dissevered and disunited country to prosperity and to Union; and for that reason a man of the very highest character and of the purest motives might properly aspire to this lofty position; and I venture to say that with that motive operating upon a human mind it would be nothing short of miraculous if he could be impartial. Nothing short of the power of Omnipotence, operating directly upon the human heart, could, under those circumstances, make any human being impartial.

Then, sir, such being the interest, what is the manner in which this subject is treated by the Constitution of the United States? It may be said that the objection does not come within the letter of the Constitution. Nor am I here to say that the Constitution of the United States expressly prohibits a member of the Senate, acting as Presiding Officer *pro tempore*, from sitting as a judge in this or a similar case. I am not prepared to say that there is within the letter of the Constitution an express prohibition. But, sir, is it within the spirit of the Constitution? I take it we are here to act, not merely upon the letter, but upon the spirit of that instrument. I take it, at least, that when we are under oath to act impartially, according to the Constitution and the laws in a criminal proceeding, the spirit of that Constitution and the spirit of those laws are to govern our action. What is the language of the Constitution on this subject?

"The Vice President of the United States shall be President of the Senate, but shall have no vote unless they be equally divided.

"The Senate shall choose their other officers, and also a President *pro tempore* in the absence of the Vice President, or when he shall exercise the office of President of the United States.

"The Senate shall have the sole power to try all impeachments. When sitting for that purpose they shall be on oath or affirmation. When the President of the United States is tried the Chief Justice shall preside; and no person shall be convicted without the concurrence of two thirds of the members present.

"Judgment in cases of impeachment shall not extend further than to removal from office and disqualification to hold and enjoy any office of honor, trust, or profit under the United States," &c.

Now, sir, there is no provision in the Constitution of the United States that the acting Vice President of the United States, the President *pro tempore* of the Senate, upon a trial of this kind shall not vote. It seems to have been, possibly, strictly speaking, an omitted case. The provision is, that the Vice President of the United States, under those circumstances, shall not even give the casting vote which he is entitled to give when the Senate is equally divided. That is his sole power in this body; he can only give a casting vote; and he cannot proceed to give a casting vote in a trial of this kind. And why? What was the reason of that provision? The reason of that provision has already been discussed in this body. The Senator from Massachusetts attempted to explain it. Other Senators gave a reason. It seems to me the reason is obvious. It needs no explanation; and I might say, further, that it is not the custom and the habit of the Constitution to give reasons for its provisions. The Senator from Massachusetts says that the Constitution gives no reason for this provision. The Constitution gives a reason, I believe, for very few, if any, of its own provisions. But in this case the reason was so palpable, so manifest, that it was not necessary, even in contemporaneous construction, to give a reason for the provision. The reason was perfectly plain. It was because there was so direct an interest in the Vice President of the United States that it was deemed improper that he should act; or, in the language of the present presiding officer of this body, the Chief Justice of the United States:

"It was, doubtless, thought prudent and befitting that the next in succession should not preside in a proceeding through which a vacancy might be created."

That undoubtedly was the reason of this provision. I have no doubt that the framers of the Constitution went further back. They acted upon principle. They knew that in ,the very nature of things, in common justice, a man could not be a judge in his own case. They knew that the provisions of the common law prohibited a man from being a judge in his own case. They probably remembered what has been said by one great commentator, (Blackstone,) that the omnipotence of Parliament was limited in this respect, and that body could not make a man a judge in his own case. Probably without that provision in the Constitution the Vice President would have been prevented from acting under those circumstances. The Constitution provides that the two Houses may make rules for their own action; and the House of Representatives has proceeded to make a rule that no member shall cast a vote in which he is interested. This body has not as yet made such a rule, I suppose, because it was thought impossible that any Senator should offer or attempt to vote in a case in which he himself was interested. But, sir, this body has made particular rules applying to particular cases; and when the interest has 'arisen, this body has decided that the party having that interest could not act, as in the case of Mr. Stockton, of New Jersey.

This being the constitutional provision with regard to the Vice President of the United States when he sits in that chair as the Presiding Officer of this body, and the President of the United States is tried for an offense which will deprive him of an office which will fall by his removal upon the Vice President, what is the character and meaning and spirit of the Constitution in a case like that before us? Why, sir, the reasons exist as strongly in this case as in the other. If it would shock humanity, if it would violate every feeling of justice throughout the world, for a man to act in his own case in the first instance, would it not in the latter? I happen to have before me an extract from the speech delivered a few days ago by the honorable Senator from New York, [Mr. CONKLING.] He gives in his own forcible and striking language the reason for the rule:

"The reason in the case of the impeachment of the President for calling in some one to preside in lieu of the Vice President is obvious. The Vice President, being next to the President in the line of succession, the impropriety of his doing anything in a trial which, in one event, would result in his own advancement, is clear.

"It can hardly be said that such a case would be provided for by calling some Senator to the chair, because the fact of a Senator being selected to preside would tend in some degree to his advancement also in case of the conviction of the President."

And so careful, so particular, so scrupulous was the honorable Senator from New York, that it seemed to him that the reason of the rule applied to any Senator called to the chair of this body, being selected to preside, as that would tend in some degree to his advancement in the case of the conviction of the President.

He proceeds to say:

"A Senator made President of the Senate pro tempore even during a trial of impeachment might expect to continue such President in the event of the advancement of the regular Presiding Officer to supercede the President of the United States. These and other considerations of safety and decorum indicated the propriety of going outside the Senate for an officer to occupy the chair when the President should be brought to the bar, and nothing could be more natural or more dignified than to select the head of one of the three branches of the Government. The Chief Justice, being separated from both the political departments of the Government, was deemed the person most fit, by reason not only of his disinterestedness, but of his learning and the great consideration of his position. These reasons might well have suggested the propriety of asking of the head of the bench that he should discharge, upon a great and solemn occasion, duties with which the highest subjects of England have ever been invested."

It is impossible for me, in stronger language than the Senator from New York has used, to depict the impropriety of a member of this body, under the rules and under the Constitution, acting as a judge in a case which, in a certain event, is to place him in the presidential chair.

But, sir, it is said that this is not the time to raise the objection; that the objection may, perhaps, be waived by the party accused. If a President of the United States, chosen by the people, was actually on trial, and the Vice President was in the chair, and proposed to sit and give the casting vote, and we objected to his being sworn, could it be said that possibly the President of the United States on trial might waive the objection? Can he waive the objection? He is not alone interested. The people of this whole country are interested in the decision of this question. The party nearest in interest cannot waive it. If he were the President of the United States, actually chosen as such, and the Vice President, actually chosen, were sitting in that chair, he could not waive that interest. He could not say, as one Senator has supposed he might say, "I prefer, upon the whole, that that distinguished officer, knowing his impartiality and his love of justice, should preside in this trial, and give the casting vote in my case; I think it would be for my advantage." That could not be allowed. If it is decided at all it is decided by the law and the Constitution and the general rules of right. Therefore, the objection that this point is made too early does not apply. It is an objection which, if it can be made at all, can be made here at this period, and should be made now, for it is perfectly evident that the distinguished gentleman now proposed to be sworn in as a judge, the moment he is sworn in, can decide important questions long before the accused party shall present himself here or shall be summoned to appear here. There is the question of notice, the question of time, and there are various questions on which he will be called upon to give a decision. If, therefore, the objection is to be made at all, it must necessarily or with great propriety should be made at this time.

But, sir, I do not desire to go further into this general question. I have attempted to look at this question as a judge. I have attempted, in considering in my own mind, whether it be proper for the honorable Senator from Ohio to act as a judge in this case, to act myself as a judge, and it has seemed to me in the highest degree improper in every aspect of the case. Sir, if there is anything desirable in this great trial, it is, in the first place, that impartial justice should be done; and in the second place, that it should appear to be just that mankind should say that impartial justice was done. If it should so happen that, under the construction to be given to the rules of this body and under the Constitution of the United States, the Senate should decide that the honorable Senator from Ohio should be a judge in the case, that the judge of the President is to be his successor in office, is there not danger that it may be said that there is doubt as to the fairness of this trial? If the future historian, in recording the fact that the President of the United States had been removed from his office by impeachment, should also be compelled to record the fact that his successor was his judge, such a record would violate the sense of justice of the nation and shock the heart of the civilized world.

Mr. HENDRICKS. Mr. President, with the indulgence of the Senate, I will add a very little to what I felt it my duty to say upon this question yesterday, and then, as far as I am concerned, I shall relieve the Senate from any embarrassment about it. ·

It was said by the Senator from Nebraska [Mr. THAYER] and the Senator from Ohio [Mr. SHERMAN] that the Senator who now proposes to take the oath is, in all respects, the equal of any other Senator, and that no objection can be made to his right to vote upon any question upon which other Senators have the right to vote. The general proposition I do not question, that, as a Senator, he is the peer of any other Senator: but to both gentlemen my reply is this: that by his own act he has accepted an office above that of Senator, if I may so express it, which disqualifies him from participating in this trial. It is his act, not the act of the Senate, if the State of Ohio upon this trial be not represented by two Senators.

The objection is made by the Senator from Missouri [Mr. DRAKE] that the Senate is not in a condition to consider the question, for the reason that it has not yet organized itself for the purposes of the trial, and, therefore, there is no body competent to decide whether the Senator from Ohio may participate in that trial. Sir, the question that is presented by me arises frequently in the organization of bodies composed of many persons. It must necessarily arise in the organization of such bodies. It frequently arises in the organization of the House of Representatives, and it matters not whether the question comes up on the call of the first or the last name.* When an objection is made to the right of a Representative or to the right of a Senator when this body is being organized at the commencement of a new Congress, how is that question to be decided? If at the commencement of the Fortieth Congress it had been objected that some Senator could not then take the oath required by the act of 1862, and that objection was made when the Secretary of the Senate was midway in the call, who would decide it? The Senate would not then be organized; and yet it is a question incident to the organization itself, and a question that must be decided before the organization can be completed. I say, therefore, as this is a question that may arise, that is likely to arise, in the organization of any body composed of many persons, it must be met here precisely as in other cases.

I am not going to discuss the question whether, organized for the purposes of this trial, the Senate be technically and in name a court. In substance, Mr. President, it is a court. It is to consider questions of law and questions of fact. It is not to consider legislative questions at all; and it cannot indulge in the considerations of public policy which may be indulged in in the Senate. The judgment of each Senator is controlled altogether by questions of fact and of law. A body, by whatever name known, that has to consider only questions of fact and of law, and upon that consideration to pronounce a judgment, is a judicial body in its very essence and nature. It is no longer a legislative body.

Then, Mr. President, we propose (calling the body what you may) now to pass from the consideration of legislative questions to the consideration of the impeachment question; to cease to be a body for the consideration of legislative questions and to become a body for the consideration only of judicial questions. The first step in passing from the one character to the other is the appearance in the chair of the Chief Justice of the Supreme Court. The next step is the taking of an oath unknown to us as legislators, but binding us as judges—as judges of the questions of law and of fact that may arise. This is the step which we are now taking. We are now taking the oath to qualify us to discharge a peculiar and extraordinary duty—the oath that as judges we will be fair and just. The question arises during the organization of the Senate in that character and for that duty whether a Senator is competent to participate in the adjudication. That question is incident to the organization of the Senate in its new character. I have not changed my opinion that that question properly arises in the administration of the oath.

I am not going to discuss further the merits

A.—3.

whether the Senator from Ohio, being now the President of the Senate and the possible successor should there be a vacancy in the presidential office, can participate in the trial, except to say this: that at one time I held the opinion that a Senator having an interest in the result of a question might vote. I held that view in Mr. Stockton's case; but the Senate, by a deliberate vote, overruled that view, and established it as the law of the Senate that he who is to be benefited by the decision to the extent of holding an office or acquiring an office cannot help to decide that question. I was surprised yesterday that the Senator from Massachusetts [Mr. SUMNER] should occupy in regard to this question a very different position from that which he occupied when he helped to decide the Stockton case. Where is the difference? Mr. Stockton was a member of this body. He had credentials that *prima facie* entitled him to participate in our deliberations. He was entitled to cast a vote upon any legislative question that should come up to the very minute of the decision of the Senate against him. He was for the time being a Senator from New Jersey. When the question was, shall he continue to hold that office, the Senate said, without an express rule on the subject and no general parliamentary law, but on a universal sentiment of justice, as it was claimed then, right, and propriety, that he could not vote when his vote helped him to hold an office. I am not able to see, when the vote of the Presiding Officer of this body may enable him to hold the highest office in the nation, the distinction in the two cases. The Senate deliberately decided in that case that the interest disqualified for the time being the party from voting in the Senate.

But, Mr. President, I find that some Senators, among them the Senator from Delaware, [Mr. BAYARD,] who agree with me upon this question on the merits, are of the opinion that the question ought more properly to be raised when the court shall be fully organized, when the party accused is here to answer. I do not believe that he can waive a question that goes to the organization of the body; I believe it is a question for the body itself. But upon that I find some difference of opinion; and when I find that difference of opinion among those who agree with me upon the merits, upon the main point, whether he shall participate in the proceedings and judgment who may be benefited by it—while I find some Senators, who agree with me upon that question, disagreeing with me upon the question whether it ought to be raised now or when the Senator from Ohio proposes to cast a material vote in the proceedings, I choose to yield my judgment—my judgment, not at all upon the merits; my judgment not at all upon the propriety and the duty of the Senate to decide upon its own organization; but I yield as to the time when the question shall be made in deference to the opinion of others; and for myself, sir, I withdraw the question which I presented for the consideration of the President of this body and of the Senate yesterday.

Mr. POMEROY. The Senator proposes to withdraw the point which he made, and I think it can be done by unanimous consent. I hope unanimous consent will be given, and let it be withdrawn, and let us proceed to swear in the other Senators.

Mr. HENDRICKS. It does not require unanimous consent. I can withdraw it myself.

Mr. SHERMAN and Mr. GRIMES. The Senator has a right to withdraw it.

The CHIEF JUSTICE. The Chair understands that the Senator from Indiana has withdrawn his objection.

Mr. POMEROY. But an appeal has been taken.

Mr. GRIMES. That makes no difference.

The CHIEF JUSTICE. The Senator from Ohio will take the oath.

Mr. HOWARD. I beg to inquire whether the withdrawal of this particular motion affects the motion that was made by the honorable Senator from Maryland, [Mr. JOHNSON?]

Mr. FESSENDEN. That falls with it, of course.

The CHIEF JUSTICE. All the questions incidental to the main question fall with the withdrawal of it.

Mr. JOHNSON. My motion was founded upon the other motion. If the first motion is withdrawn mine falls as a matter of course.

Mr. HOWARD. Very well, if that is the understanding.

The Secretary called the name of Mr. WADE, who advanced and took the oath.

The Secretary then continued the call of the roll, and the Chief Justice administered the oath to Senators WILLEY, WILLIAMS, WILSON, and YATES, as their names were respectively called.

The Secretary then called the names of Senators DOOLITTLE, EDMUNDS, PATTERSON of New Hampshire, and SAULSBURY, who were not present yesterday; and Mr. SAULSBURY appeared, and the oath was administered to him by the Chief Justice.

The CHIEF JUSTICE. All the Senators present having taken the oath required by the Constitution, the Senate is now organized for the purpose of proceeding to the trial of the impeachment of Andrew Johnson, President of the United States. The Sergeant-at-Arms will make proclamation.

The SERGEANT-AT-ARMS. Hear ye! Hear ye! Hear ye! All persons are commanded to keep silence on pain of imprisonment while the Senate of the United States is sitting for the trial of the articles of impeachment against Andrew Johnson, President of the United States.

Mr. HOWARD. I move that the Secretary of the Senate notify the Managers on the part of the House of Representatives that the Senate is now organized for the purpose of proceeding to the trial of the impeachment of Andrew Johnson.

The CHIEF JUSTICE. Before putting that question the Chair feels it his duty to submit a question to the Senate relative to the rules of proceeding. In the judgment of the Chief Justice the Senate is now organized as a distinct body from the Senate sitting in its legislative capacity. It performs a distinct function; the members are under a different oath; and the presiding officer is not the President *pro tempore* of the Senate, but the Chief Justice of the United States. Under these circumstances, the Chair conceives that rules adopted by the Senate in its legislative capacity are not rules for the government of the Senate sitting for the trial of an impeachment unless they be also adopted by that body. In this judgment of the Chair, if it be an erroneous one, he desires to be corrected by the judgment of the court, or of the Senate sitting for the trial of the impeachment of the President, which in his judgment are synonymous terms, and therefore, if he may be permitted to do so, he will take the sense of the Senate upon this question, whether the rules adopted on the 2d of March, a copy of which is now lying before him, shall be considered the rules of proceeding in this body. ["Question!"] Senators, you who think that the rules of proceeding adopted on the 2d of March should be considered as the rules of proceeding of this body will say ay; contrary opinion, no. [The Senators having answered.] The ayes have it by the sound. The rules will be considered as the rules of proceeding in this body.

The Senator from Michigan moves—will the Senator have the goodness to repeat his motion?

Mr. HOWARD. My motion is, that the Secretary of the Senate notify the Managers of the House of Representatives that the Senate is now organized for the purpose of trying the impeachment against Andrew Johnson, and is ready to receive them. The Clerk will be good enough to put it in form.

The Secretary read the order, as follows:

Ordered, That the Secretary of the Senate notify the House of Representatives that the Senate is now organized for the trial of the articles of impeachment against Andrew Johnson, President of the United States, and is ready to receive the Managers of the impeachment at its bar.

The motion was agreed to.

After a pause, and at thirteen minutes before three o'clock, the Managers of the impeachment on the part of the House of Representatives (with the exception of Mr. STEVENS) appeared at the bar, and their presence was announced by the Sergeant-at-Arms.

The CHIEF JUSTICE. The Managers of the impeachment on the part of the House of Representatives will please take the seats assigned to them.

The Managers having been seated in the area in front of the Chair,

Mr. Manager BINGHAM rose, and said: Mr. President, we are instructed by the House of Representatives, as its Managers, to demand that the Senate take process against Andrew Johnson, President of the United States, that he may answer at the bar of the Senate upon the articles of impeachment heretofore preferred by the House of Representatives through its Managers before the Senate.

Mr. HOWARD. I move for an order that a summons do issue to Andrew Johnson, President of the United States, in accordance with the rules which we have adopted—I refer particularly to the eighth rule—returnable on Friday, the 13th day of March instant, at one o'clock in the afternoon.

The CHIEF JUSTICE. The Secretary will read the order.

The Secretary read as follows:

Ordered, That a summons do issue, as required by the rules of procedure and practice in the Senate when sitting on the trial of impeachments, to Andrew Johnson, returnable on Friday, the 13th day of March instant, at one o'clock in the afternoon.

The order was adopted.

Mr. HOWARD. I move that the Senate, sitting upon the trial of the impeachment, do now adjourn until——

Mr. ANTHONY. If the Senator will withdraw his motion for a moment, I wish to offer an amendment to the rules.

Mr. HOWARD. Certainly.

Mr. ANTHONY. I desire to offer an amendment to the rules, to strike out the last clause of rule seven in the following words:

The presiding officer may, in the first instance, submit to the Senate without a division all questions of evidence and incidental questions; but the same shall, on the demand of one fifth of the members present, be decided by yeas and nays.

And in lieu of those words to insert:

The presiding officer of the court may rule all questions of evidence and incidental questions, which ruling shall stand as the judgment of the court unless some member of the court shall ask that a formal vote be taken thereon, in which case it shall be submitted to the court for decision; or he may, at his option, in the first instance submit any such question to a vote of the members of the court.

I do not desire to press this amendment at present if there is any disposition to debate it, because it is desirable, I suppose, that the court should now adjourn. I merely offer it for the consideration of the court. Let it lie on the table.

Mr. HOWARD. Then, Mr. President, I move that the court, to use a brief expression, adjourn to the time at which the summons just ordered is returnable—Friday, the 13th instant, at one o'clock in the afternoon.

Mr. SUMNER. Before that motion is put I should like to ask my friend, the Senator from Rhode Island, who has brought forward this amendment, whether, under the rules now adopted, he regards it as debatable. By these rules it is provided as follows:

"All the orders and decisions shall be made and had by yeas and nays, which shall be entered on the record, and without debate, except when the doors shall be closed for deliberation," &c.

Mr. ANTHONY. I have not read the rules with reference to the question the Senator from Massachusetts proposes to me, and as I do not desire to press the motion at present——

The CHIEF JUSTICE. There is nothing before the Senate, inasmuch as the proposition of the Senator from Rhode Island is laid upon the table. The question is upon the motion to adjourn until Friday, the 13th instant, at one o'clock in the afternoon.

The motion was agreed to; and the Chief Justice thereupon declared the Senate, sitting for the trial of impeachments, adjourned to the time named and vacated the chair.

ARGUMENT

OF

HON. CHARLES SUMNER, OF MASSACHUSETTS,

ON THE QUESTION

CAN THE CHIEF JUSTICE, PRESIDING IN THE SENATE, RULE OR VOTE?

In determining the relations of the Chief Justice to the trial of the President we must look, first to the Constitution; for it is solely by virtue of the Constitution that this eminent magistrate is transported from his own natural field to another, where he is for the time an exotic. Of course, the Chief Justice in his own court is at home; but it is equally clear that when he comes into the Senate he is a stranger. Though justly received with welcome and honor, he cannot expect membership or anything beyond those powers which are derived directly from the Constitution, by virtue of which he temporarily occupies the chair.

Repairing to our authoritative text we find the only applicable words to be these:

"The Senate shall have the sole power to try all impeachments. When the President of the United States is tried, the Chief Justice shall *preside;* and no person shall be convicted without the concurrence of two thirds of the members present."

This is all. The Chief Justice shall *preside;* but this is subject to two limitations specifically declared. First, the trial is to be by the Senate *solely,* and nobody else; thus carefully excluding the Presiding Officer from all participation, except so far as is implied in the power to *preside;* and secondly, judgment of conviction can be only by a vote of "two thirds of the *members*" *present,* thus again excluding the Presiding Officer, unless it is assumed that he is a member of the Senate.

On the face of this text it is difficult to find any ambiguity. Nobody questions that the Chief Justice must preside. Can anybody question that the trial must be by the Senate *solely* and nobody else? To change this requirement is to fly in the face of the Constitution. Can anybody question that the judgment of conviction must be by the votes of "*members* present," and nobody else? Now, since the Chief Justice is not a "member" of the Senate it is plain that he is positively excluded from any vote on the final question. It only remains that he should "preside." And here the

question recurs as to the meaning of this familiar term.

The person who presides is simply, according to the language of our rules, "Presiding Officer," and this designation is the equivalent or synonym of Speaker, and also of prolocutor, each of which signifies somebody who speaks for the House. It is not implied that he votes with the House, much less that he decides for the House; but only that he is the voice of the House—its *Speaker.* What the House has to say it says through him; but except as the organ of the House he is silent, unless he be also a member, when he superadds to his powers as Presiding Officer the powers of a member also. From this brief statement it appears at once how limited his function must be.

Here I might stop. But, since this question has assumed an unexpected importance, I am induced to go further. It will be easy to show that the language of the Constitution, if seen in the light of English parliamentary history, must have an interpretation identical with its natural import.

Nothing is clearer than this. If language employed in the Constitution had already, at the time of its formation, received a definite meaning, it must be interpreted accordingly. Thus, when the Constitution secures the "trial by jury," it secures that institution as defined by antecedent English law. So, also, when it declares that the judicial power shall extend to "all cases in law and equity" arising under the Constitution, it recognizes the distinction between law and equity peculiar to English law. Courts of common law and courts of equity are all implied in this language. And, since there is no further definition of their powers, we must ascertain them in England. Cushing, in determining the rules of proceeding in our American Legislatures, says: "Such was the practice of the two Houses of the British Parliament when our ancestors emigrated; and such has continued to be and now is the practice in that body." (*Cushing,*

37

Lex Parliamentaria, ¿ 302.) This resource has been most persuasively presented by Mr. Wirt, in his remarkable argument on the impeachment of Judge Peck, where he has vindicated and expounded the true rule of interpretation.

According to this eminent authority, what he calls "the English archetypes" were the models for the framers of our Constitution. The courts were fashioned after these "archetypes." They were instituted according to "English *originals,* to which they were manifestly referred by the Constitution itself." (*Trial of Peck,* p. 499.) Here again I quote the words of Mr. Wirt.

All this is precisely applicable to that part of the Constitution now under consideration. In its essential features it was borrowed from England. There is its original, its model, its archetype. Therefore, to England we go.

Not only to England must we go, but also to Parliamentary Law, as recognized in England at the adoption of our Constitution. The powers of a Presiding Officer, where not specifically declared, must be found in Parliamentary Law. The very term *preside* is parliamentary. It belongs to the technicalities of this branch of law as much as *indict* belongs to the technicalities of the common law. In determining the signification of this term it will be of little avail to show some local usage, or, perhaps, some decision of a court. The usage or the decision of Parliament must be shown. Against this all vague speculation or divination of reason is futile. I will not encumber this discussion by superfluous authorities. In now insisting that this question must be determined by Parliamentary Law, I content myself with citing the often-cited words of Lord Coke in his Fourth Institute:

"And as every court of justice hath laws and customs for its direction, some by the common law, some by the civil and canon laws and customs, so the High Court of Parliament *suis propriis legibus et consuetudinibus subsistit;* all weighty matters in any Parliament, moved concerning the peers of the realm or lords or commons in Parliament assembled, *ought to be determined, adjudged, and discussed by the Court of Parliament,* and not by the civil law, nor yet by the common laws of this realm, used in more inferior courts."—*Coke,* 4th Institute, p. 15.

Here is the true rule. It is to "the course of Parliament" that we must resort. It is in "the course of Parliament" that we must find all the powers of a Presiding Officer, and all that is implied in the authority *to preside.* "The Chief Justice shall *preside.*" Such is the Constitution. Nothing is specified with regard to his powers. Nothing is said. What was intended was left to inference from the language employed, which must be interpreted according to "the course of Parliament;" precisely as what was intended by *trial by jury* is ascertained from the "common law." In the latter case we go to the "common law;" in the former case we go to the "course of Parliament." You may as well turn away from the common law in the one as from the "course of Parliament" in the other. In determining the "course of Parliament" we may resort to the summary of text-writers, and, better still, to the authentic instances of history.

Something has been said in this discussion with regard to the example of Lord Erskine, who presided at the impeachment of Lord Melville. This was in 1806, during the short-lived ministry of Fox, when Erskine was Chancellor. It is by a misapprehension that this instance is supposed to sustain the present assumption. When seen in its true light it will be found to be in harmony with what appears to be the general rule. Erskine had at the time two characters. He was Lord Chancellor, and in this capacity was Presiding Officer of the House of Lords, without the right to rule or vote or even to speak. Besides being Chancellor he was also a member of the House of Lords, with all the rights of other members. It will be seen, as we advance in this inquiry, that, again and again, it has been practically decided, that, whatever may be the powers of a Presiding Officer, who is actually a member of the body, a Presiding Officer who is not a member cannot rule or vote or even speak. In making this statement now I anticipate the argument. I do it at this stage only to put aside the suggestion founded on the instance of Lord Chancellor Erskine.

I begin with the most familiar authority—I mean the eminent writer and judge, Sir William Blackstone. In his Commentaries, where will be found, in elegant form, the complete body of English law, you have this whole matter stated in a few suggestive words:

"The Speaker of the House of Lords, *if a Lord of Parliament,* may give his opinion or argue any question in the House."

Of course, if not a Lord of Parliament, he could not give his opinion or argue any question. This is in accordance with all the authorities and unbroken usage; but it has peculiar value at this moment, because it is the text of Blackstone. This work was the guide-book of our fathers. It first appeared in 1765–69, the very period when the controversy with the mother country was fervid; and it is an unquestionable fact of history that it was read in the colonies with peculiar interest. Burke, in one of his masterly orations, portraying the character of our fathers, says that more than one half of the first edition of Blackstone's Commentaries was bought by them. Nothing can be clearer than that they knew it well.

The framers of the Constitution had it before them constantly. It was their most familiar work. It was to them as "Bowditch's Navigator" is to the mariner in our day. They looked to it for guidance on the sea they were traversing. When they undertook to provide that the Chief Justice, who was not a member of the Senate, should preside at the impeachment of the President, they knew well that he could, have no power "to give an opinion or argue any question in the House;" for Blackstone had instructed them explicitly on this head. They knew that he was simply a Presiding Officer, according to the immemorial usage of the Upper House in England, *with such powers as belong to a Presiding Officer who is not a member of the House and none other.*

The powers of the Presiding Officer of the House of Lords are illustrated by authority and by precedents, all in harmony with the statement of Blackstone. Ordinarily the Keeper of the Great Seal is the Presiding Officer; but he can do little more than put the question, unless he is a member of the body. Any other person, as a Chief Justice, may be delegated by royal commission. According to the rules of the House, even if he is a peer, he cannot speak without quitting the woolsack, which is the chair, and going "to his own place as a peer." The right of speech belongs to him as a member; but he cannot exercise it without leaving his place as Presiding Officer. To this extent is he circumscribed.

A late writer on Parliamentary Law, whose work is a satisfactory guide, thus sententiously sums up the law and usage:

"The position of the Speaker of the House of Lords is somewhat anomalous, for though he is the president of a deliberative assembly, he is invested with no more authority than any other member; and *if not himself a member, his office is limited to the putting of questions, and other formal proceedings.*"—*May, Parliamentary Practice*, p. 220, chap. 7.

This statement is in obvious harmony with that of Blackstone, so that there is no difference between the writer who is our guide to-day, and the learned commentator who was the guide of our fathers.

Mr. May goes still further, and lets us know that it is only as a member of the House that the Presiding Officer can address it, *even on points of order.*

"Upon points of order the Speaker, *if a peer*, may address the House, but as his opinion is liable to be questioned, *like that of any other peer*, he does not often exercise the right."—p. 220.

Thus, even if a peer—even if a member of the Upper House—the Presiding Officer cannot rule a point of order nor address the House upon it, except as any other member; and what he says is open to question, like the utterance of any other member. Such is the conclusion of the most approved English authority.

American writers on Parliamentary Law concur with English. Cushing, who has done so much to illustrate this whole subject, says of the Presiding Officer of the Lords that "he is invested with no more authority for the preservation of order than any other member, and if not a member, his office is limited to the putting of questions and other formal proceedings; if he is a peer, he may address the House and participate in the debate as a member." He then says again, "if a peer he votes with the other members; if not, *he does not vote at all;*" and he adds, "*there is no casting vote in the Lords.*" (§ 288.) This statement was

made long after the adoption of the National Constitution, and anterior to the present controversy.

There are occasions when the Lords have a Presiding Officer, called Lord High Steward. This is on the trial of a peer, whether upon impeachment or indictment. Here again we find the same rule stated by Edmund Burke, in his masterly report to the House of Commons on the impeachment of Warren Hastings. These are his words:

"*Every peer* present at the trial and every temporal peer hath a right to be present in every part of the proceeding, *voteth upon every question of law and fact*; and the question is carried by the major vote, *the Lord High Steward himself voting merely as a peer and member of that court, in common with the rest of the peers, and in no other right.*"—*Burke's Works, vol. 6,* p. 512, *Bohn's Edition.*

In another place the report, quoting the Commons' Journal, says:

"That the Lord High Steward was but as a speaker or *chairman* for the more orderly proceeding at the trial."—*Ibid.*, p. 515.

In our day there have been instances where the Lord Chancellor sat as Presiding Officer without being a peer. Brougham took his seat on the 22d November, 1830, before his patent as a peer had been made out, and during this interval his energies were suppressed while he was simply Presiding Officer and nothing else. The same was the case with that eminent lawyer, Sir Edward Sugden, who sat as Presiding Officer on the 4th of March, 1852, although he was still a commoner; and it was also the case with Sir Frederick Thesiger, who sat as Presiding Officer on the 1st March, 1858, although he was still a commoner. These instances attest practically the prevalence of the early rule down to our day. Even Brougham, who never shrank from speech or from the exercise of power, was constrained to bend to its exigency. He sat as Lord Chancellor, and in that character put the question; but this was all until he became a member of the House. Lord Campbell expressly records that, while his name appears in the entry of those present on the 22d November, 1830, as *Henricus Brougham, Cancellarius*, "he had no right to debate and vote till the following day," when the entry of his name and office appears as *Dominus Brougham et Vaux, Cancellarius.*

I pass from these examples of recent history and go back to the rule as known to our fathers at the adoption of the Constitution. On this head the evidence is complete. It will be found in the State Trials of England, in Parliamentary history, and in the books of law; but it is nowhere better exhibited than in the Lives of the Chancellors, by Lord Campbell, himself a member of the House of Lords and a Chancellor, familiar with it historically and practically. He has stated the original rule, and in his work, which is as interesting as voluminous, has furnished constantly recurring illustrations of it. In the introduction to his Lives, where he describes the office of Chancellor, Lord Campbell enunciates the rule, which I give in his own words:

"Whether peer or commoner, the Chancellor is not, like the Speaker of the Commons, *moderator of the proceedings of the House* in which he seems to preside. He is not addressed in debate; he does not name the peer who is to be heard. *He is not appealed to as an authority on points of order,* and he may cheer the sentiments expressed by his colleagues in the Ministry."—*Campbell's Lives of Chancellors,* vol. 1, p. 17.

The existing rules of the Senate have added to these powers; but such is the rule with regard to the Presiding Officer of the House of Lords, *even when a peer.* He is not appealed to on points of order. If a commoner, his power is still less.

"If he be a commoner, notwithstanding a resolution of the House that he is to be proceeded against for any misconduct as if he were a peer, *he has neither vote nor deliberative voice, and he can only put the question, and communicate the resolutions of the House according to the directions he receives.*"—*Ibid.*

In the early period of English history the chancellors were often ecclesiastics, though generally commoners. Fortescue, Wolsey, and More were never peers. This also was the case with Sir Nicholas Bacon, the father of Lord Bacon, who held the seals under Queen Elizabeth for twenty years, and was the colleague in the Cabinet of Burleigh. Lord Campbell thus remarks on his position as Presiding Officer of the House of Lords:

"*Not being a peer, he could not take a share in the Lords debates, but presiding as Speaker on the woolsack* he exercised a considerable influence over their deliberations."—*Ibid.,* vol. 2, p. 104.

Then again we are told:

"Being a commoner, he could neither act as Lord Steward nor sit upon the trial of the Duke of Norfolk, who was the first who suffered for favoring Mary's cause."—*Ibid.,* p. 105.

Thus early do we find an illustration of this rule, which constantly reappears as we travel down the annals of Parliament.

The successor of Sir Nicholas Bacon was Lord Chancellor Bromley, and here we find a record interesting to us at this moment. After presiding at the trial of Mary, Queen of Scots, the Lord Chancellor became ill and took to his bed. Under the circumstances Sir Edmund Anderson, *Chief Justice of the Common Pleas, was authorized by the Queen to act as a substitute for the Chancellor,* and thus the Chief Justice became the Presiding Officer of the House of Lords to the close of the session without being a peer.

Then came Sir Christopher Hatton, the favorite of Queen Elizabeth, and so famous as the dancing Chancellor, who presided in the House of Lords by virtue of his office, but never as a peer. He was followed by the exemplary Ellesmere, who was for many years Chancellor without being a peer, but finished his career by adding to his title as Presiding Officer the functions of a member. The greatest of all in the list now followed. After much effort and solicitation Bacon becomes Chancellor with a peerage; but it is recorded in the Lords' journals that when he spoke he removed "from the woolsack to his seat as a peer," thus attesting that he had no voice as Presiding Officer. At last, when the corruptions of this remarkable character began to overshadow the land, *the Chief Justice of the King's Bench,* Sir James Ley, was designated by the King to act as Speaker of the House of Lords. • Soon afterward Bacon fell. Meanwhile it is said that the Chief Justice had very creditably performed "the duties of Speaker of the House of Lords." (*Campbell's Lives of Chancellors,* vol. 2, p. 443.) In other words, according to the language of our Constitution, he had *presided* well.

Then came Coventry and Finch as Lord Keepers. As the latter absconded to avoid impeachment by the House of Commons Littleton, *Chief Justice of the Common Pleas,* "was placed on the woolsack as Speaker." At a later time he received the great seal as Lord Keeper. This promotion was followed by a peerage, at the prompting of no less a person that the Earl of Strafford, "who thought he might be more useful if permitted to take part in the proceedings of the House as a peer than if he could *only put the question as Speaker.*" (*Ibid.,* vol. 2, p. 585.) Clarendon in his history says that, as a peer, he could have done Strafford "notable service." (*History of the Rebellion,* book 3, p. 104.) But the timid peer did not render the expected service.

Then came the period of civil war, when one great seal was with the King and another was with Parliament. Meanwhile the Earl of Manchester was appointed Speaker of the Upper House, and as such took his place on the woolsack. As a peer he had all the privileges of a member of the House over which he presided. Charles II, during his exile, had appointed Hyde, afterward Earl of Clarendon, as Chancellor; but the Monarch was for the time without a court and without a parliament. On the restoration in 1660 the Chancellor at once entered upon all his duties, judicial and parliamentary; and it is recorded that, "though still a commoner, he took his place on the woolsack as Speaker by prescription." (*Campbell's Lives,* vol. 3, p. 187.) A year later the commoner was raised to the peerage, thus becoming more than Presiding Officer. During illness from the gout the place of the Chancellor as Presiding Officer was sometimes supplied by Sir Orlando Bridgman, *Chief Justice of the Common Pleas,* who, on these occasions, was Presiding Officer, and nothing more. Lord Campbell says "he frequently sat as Speaker in the House of Lords"— (*ibid.,* 279)—which means that he *presided.*

On the disgrace of Lord Clarendon, the disposal of the great seal was the occasion of perplexity. The historian informs us that "after many doubts and conflicting plans among the king's male and female advisers it was put into the hands of a grave common-law judge," (*ibid.,* p. 272) being none other than *the Chief Justice of the Common Pleas,* who had already presided in the absence of Lord Clarendon; but he was never raised to the peerage. Here we have another explanation of the precise relation of such an official to the House. Lord Campbell expressly remarks that "never being created a peer, *his only duty in the House of Lords was to put the question,* and to address the two Houses in explanation of the royal will on the assembling of Parliament." (*Ibid.*, p. 281.) Here is the same recurring definition of the term *preside.*

For some time afterward there seems to have been little embarrassment. Nottingham, who did so much for equity; Shaftsbury, who did so little; Guilford, so famous through contemporary biography; and Jeffries, so justly infamous, successively heads of the law, were all peers. But at the revolution of 1688 there was an interregnum, which brought into relief the relations between the Upper House and its Presiding Officer. Jeffries on his flight dropped the great seal in the Thames. King James had gone. There was, therefore, no Presiding Officer for the Lords. In order to supply this want the Lords, at the meeting of the Convention Parliament, chose one of their own numbers, the Marquis of Halifax, as their Speaker, and, in the exercise of the power inherent in them, they continued to reëlect him day by day. During this period he was strictly President *pro tempore.* At last Sir Robert Atkyns, *Chief Baron of the Exchequer,* a commoner, took his seat on the woolsack as Speaker, appointed by the Crown. Here, again, we learn that "serious inconvenience was experienced from the occupier of the woolsack *not being a member of the House.*" (*Ibid.,* vol. 4. p. 53.) At last, in 1693, the great seal was handed to Sir John Somers, Lord Keeper; and here we have another authentic illustration of the rule. Although the official head of the English law, and already exalted for his ability and varied knowledge, this great man, one of the saviors of constitutional liberty in England, was for some time merely Presiding Officer. The historian records that "while he remained a commoner he *presided* on the woolsack only as Speaker," (*ibid.*, p. 118;) that he "had only to put the question, and took no part in debate." (*Ibid.*, p. 122.) This is the more worthy of notice because Somers was recognized as a consummate orator. At last, according to the historian, "there was a strong desire that he should take part in the debates;" and the King, to enable him to do this, pressed his acceptance of a peerage, which, after some further delay, he did, and he was afterward known as Lord Somers. (*Ibid.*, p. 126.)

In the vicissitudes of public life this great character was dismissed from office, and a successor was found in an inferior person, Sir Matthew Wright, who was created Lord Keeper without a peerage. For the five years of his official life it is recorded that he occupied the woolsack, "*merely putting the question, and*

having *no influence over the proceedings.*" (*Ibid.*, p. 245.) Thus he *presided.*

Then came the polished Cowper, at first without a peerage, but after a short time created a member of the House. Here again the historian records that while he remained a commoner "*he took his place on the woolsack as Speaker, without a right to debate or vote.*" It appears that, "not being permitted to share in the debates of the House of Lords, he amused himself by taking notes of the speeches on the opposite sides." (*Ibid.*, pp. 304, 305.) Afterward, even when a peer and as Chancellor, *presiding* at the impeachment of Sacheverell, Lord Cowper did not interfere further than by saying, "Gentlemen of the House of Commons," or "Gentlemen, you that are counsel for the prisoner, may proceed." (*Ibid.*, p. 318.)

Harcourt followed Cowper as Keeper of the great seal; but he was not immediately raised to the peerage. It is recorded that during one year he had "only to sit as Speaker." (*Ibid.*, p. 459.) That is, he had only to *preside.* Afterward, as a peer, he became a member of the body. He was succeeded as Chancellor by the Earl of Macclesfield with all the rights of membership.

Lord Macclesfield, being impeached of high crimes and misdemeanors as Chancellor, Sir Peter King, *at the time Chief Justice of the Common Pleas, was made Presiding Officer of the Upper House,* with only the limited powers belonging to a Presiding Officer, who is not a member of the body. Here the record is complete. Turn to the trial and you will see it all. It was he who gave directions to the managers, and also to the counsel—who put the question, and afterward pronounced the sentence; but he acted always as Presiding Officer, and nothing else. I do not perceive that he made any rulings during the progress of the trial. He was Chief Justice of the Common Pleas, acting as President *pro tempore.* The report describing the opening of the proceedings says that the articles of impeachment, with the answer and replication, were read, "by direction of Lord Chief Justice King, Speaker of the House of Lords." (*Howell, State Trials,* vol. 16, p. 768.) This instance furnishes another definition of the term *preside.*

All this is compendiously described by Lord Campbell, as follows:

"Sir Peter, *not being a peer, of course had no deliberative voice;* but during the trial, as the organ of the House of Peers, he regulated the procedure without any special vote, intimating to the managers and to the counsel for the defendant when they were to speak and to adduce their evidence. After the verdict of guilty, he ordered the Black Rod to produce his prisoner at the bar; and the Speaker of the House of Commons, having demanded judgment, he, in good taste, abstaining from making any comment, dryly, but solemnly and impressively pronounced the sentence which the House had agreed upon."—*Campbell's Lives,* vol. 4, p. 609.

This proceeding was in 1725. At this time Benjamin Franklin, the printer-boy, was actually in London. It is difficult to imagine that this precocious character, whose observation in public affairs was as remarkable as in philosophy, should have passed eighteen months in London at this very period without noting this remarkable trial and the manner in which it was conducted. Thus early in life he saw that a Chief Justice might *preside* at an impeachment without being a member of the House of Lords or exercising any of the powers which belong to membership.

Besides his eminence as a Chief Justice, King was the nephew of the great thinker who has exercised such influence on English and American opinion, John Locke. Shortly after *presiding* at the impeachment as Chief Justice he became Chancellor, with a peerage.

He was followed in his high post by Talbot and Hardwicke, each with a peerage. Jumping the long period of their successful administrations, when the Presiding Officer was also a member of the Upper House, I come to another instance where the position of the Presiding Officer became peculiarly apparent; and this, too, occurred when Benjamin Franklin was on his protracted visit to London, as agent for the Colonies. I refer to Sir Robert Henley, who became Lord Keeper in 1757, without a peerage. The King, George II, did not like him, and therefore, while placing him at the head of the law, declined to make him a member of the House over which he was to preside. At last, in 1760, the necessities of the publice service constrained his elevation to the peerage, and soon afterward George III, who succeeded to the throne without the animosities of his grandfather, created him Chancellor and Earl of Northington.

For four years Henley, while still a commoner, was Presiding Officer of the House of Lords. During this considerable period he was without a voice or vote. The historian remarks that "if there had been any debates he was precluded from taking part in them." (*Campbell's Lives*, vol. 4, p. 188.) And then, again, in another place, he pictures the defenseless condition of the unhappy magistrate with regard to his own decisions in the court below, when heard on appeal, as follows:

"Lord Keeper Henley, till raised to the peerage, used to complain bitterly of being obliged to put the question for the reversal of his own decrees, without being permitted to say a word in support of them."—*Ibid.*, vol. 1, p. 17, note.

Lord Eldon, in his Anecdote Book, furnishes another statement of this case, as follows:

"When Sir Robert Henley *presided* in the House of Lords as Lord Keeper he could not enter into debate as a chancellor being a peer does; and, therefore, when there was an appeal from his judgment in the Court of Chancery and the law lords then in the House moved to reverse his judgments, he could not state the grounds of his opinions and support his decisions."—*Twiss's Life of Eldon*, vol. 1, p. 319.

And thus for four years this commoner *presided* over the House of Lords.

A few months before Henley first took his place as Presiding Officer, Franklin arrived in London for the second time, and continued

there, a busy observer, until after the judge was created a peer. Even if he had been ignorant of Parliamentary usage, or had forgotten what passed at the trial of Lord Macclesfield, he could not have failed to note that the House of Lords had for its Presiding Officer an eminent judge who, not being a member, could take no part in its proceedings beyond putting the question.

Afterward, in 1790, there was a different arrangement. Owing to a difficulty in finding a proper person as Chancellor, the great seal was put in commission, and Lord Mansfield, Chief Justice of England, was persuaded to act as Presiding Officer of the Upper House. Curiously enough, Franklin was again in England on his third visit, and remained through the service of Lord Mansfield in this capacity. Thus this illustrious American, afterward a member of the convention that framed the National Constitution, had at two different times seen the House of Lords with a Presiding Officer who, not being a member of the body, could only put the question, and then again with another Presiding Officer, who, being a member of the body, could vote and speak, as well as put the question.

But Franklin was not the only member of the National Convention to whom these precedents were known. One or more had been educated at the Temple in London. Others were accomplished lawyers, familiar with the courts of the mother country. I have already mentioned that Blackstone's Commentaries, where the general rule is clearly stated, was as well known in the Colonies as in the mother country. Besides, our fathers were not ignorant of the history of England, which down to the Declaration of Independence had been their history. The English law also was theirs. Not a case in its books which did not belong to them as well as to the frequenters of Westminster Hall. The State Trials, involving principles of constitutional law, and embodying these very precedents, were all known. Hargrave's collection in several folios had already passed through at least four editions some time before the adoption of our National Constitution. I cannot err in supposing that all these were authoritative guides in our country at that time, and that the National Constitution was fashioned in all the various lights, historical and judicial, which they furnished.

The conclusion is irresistible, that, when our fathers provided that on the trial of the President of the United States "the Chief Justice shall *preside*," they used the term "preside" in the sense it had already acquired in Parliamentary Law, and did not intend to attach to it any different signification; that they knew perfectly well the parliamentary distinction between a Presiding Officer a member of the House and a Presiding Officer not a member; that, in constituting the Chief Justice Presiding Officer for a special temporary purpose, they had in view similar instances in the mother country, when the Lord Keeper, Chief Justice, or other judicial personage had been appointed to "preside" over the House of Lords, of which he was not a member, as our Chief Justice is appointed to preside over the Senate, of which he is not a member; that they found in this constantly recurring example an apt precedent for their guidance; that they followed this precedent to all intents and purposes, using, with regard to the Chief Justice, the received parliamentary language, that he shall "preside," and nothing more; that, according to this precedent, they never intended to impart to the Chief Justice, President *pro tempore* of the Senate, any other powers than those of a Presiding Officer not a member of the body; and that these powers, as exemplified in an unbroken series of instances extending over centuries, under different kings and through various administrations, were simply to put the question and to direct generally the conduct of business, without undertaking in any way, by voice or vote, to determine any question, preliminary, interlocutory, or final.

In stating this conclusion I present simply the result of the authorities. It is not I who speak; it is the authorities. My own judgment may be imperfect; but here is a mass of testimony, concurring and cumulative, without a single exception, which cannot err.

Plainly and unmistakably the provision in our Constitution authorizing the Chief Justice to *preside* in the Senate, of which he is not a member, was modeled on the English original. This English original was, according to the language of Mr. Wirt, the "archetype" which our fathers followed. As such it was embodied in our Constitution, as much as if the Constitution in its text expressly provided that the Chief Justice, when *presiding* in the Senate, had all the powers accorded by parliamentary usage to such a functionary when *presiding* in the Upper House of Parliament, without being a member thereof. In saying that he shall "preside" the Constitution confers on the Chief Justice no powers of membership in the Senate, and by the well-defined term employed, limits him to those precise functions sanctioned at the time by immemorial usage.

Thus far I have considered this provision in the light of authorities already known and recognized at the adoption of the National Constitution. This is enough; for it is by these authorities that its meaning must be determined. You cannot reject these without setting at defiance a fixed rule of interpretation, and resorting instead to vague inference or mere imagination, quickened, perhaps, by your desires. Mere imagination and vague inference—quickened, perhaps, by your desires—are out of place when Parliamentary Law is beyond all question.

Pardon me if I protract this argument by an additional illustration derived from our own congressional history. This will be found un-der the parallel provision of the Constitution relating to the Vice President, which, after much debate in another generation, received an authoritative interpretation. It is as fol lows: "The Vice President of the United States shall be *President of the Senate*, but shall have no vote unless they be equally divided." In other words, the Vice President, like the Chief Justice, shall *preside in the Senate*, but, unlike the Chief Justice, with a casting vote. His general powers are all implied in the provision that he shall *preside*.

No question has occurred with regard to the vote of the Vice President, for this is expressly regulated by the Constitution. But the other powers of the Vice President, when *presiding* in the Senate, are left to Parliamentary Law and the express rules of the body. Some of the latter were settled at an early day. On looking at the rules of the Senate adopted at the beginning it will be found that, independent of his casting vote, nothing was originally recognized as belonging to a *presiding* Vice President beyond his power to occupy the chair. All else was determined by the rules. For instance, Senators, when speaking, are to address the Chair. This rule, which seems to us so superfluous, was adopted 16th April, 1789, early in the session of the First Congress, in order to change the existing Parliamentary Law, under which a member of the Upper House of Parliament habitually addresses his associates, and never the Chair. Down to this day, in England, a peer, rising to speak, says, "My Lords," and never "My Lord Chancellor," although the latter *presides.* Another rule, adopted at the same date, has a similar origin. By Parliamentary Law, in the Upper House of Parliament, when two members rise at the same time, the House, by their cry, indicate who shall speak. This was set aside by a positive rule of the Senate that, in such a case, "the President shall name the person to speak." The Parliamentary Law that the Presiding Officer, whether a member or not a member, shall put the question, was reënforced by an express rule that "all questions shall be put by the President of the Senate."

Although the rules originally provided that when a member is called to order "the President shall determine whether he is in order or not," they failed to declare by whom the call to order should be made. There was nothing conferring this power upon the Presiding Officer, while, by Parliamentary Law in the Upper House of Parliament, no Presiding Officer, *as such*, could call to order, whatever he might do as a member. The powers of the Presiding Officer in the Senate were left in this uncertainty; but the small numbers of Senators and the prevailing courtesy prevented trouble. At last, in the lapse of time, the numbers increased and the debates assumed a more animated character. Meanwhile, in 1825, Mr. Calhoun became Vice President. This ingenious person, severely logical, and at the time enjoying the confidence of the country to a rare degree, insisted that, as Presiding Officer, he had no power but to carry into effect the rules adopted by the body, and that, therefore, in the absence of any rule on the subject, he was not empowered to call a Senator to order for words spoken in debate. His conclusion was given as follows:

" The Chair had no power beyond the rules of the Senate. *It would stand in the light of a usurper were it to attempt to exercise such a power. It was too high a power for the Chair."* * * * * "The Chair would never assume any power not vested in it; but would ever show firmness in exercising those powers that were vested in the Chair."—*Congressional Debates,* 1825–26, p. 759.

The question with regard to the powers of the Chair was transferred from the Senate Chamber to the public press, where it was discussed with memorable ability. An article in the National Intelligencer, under the signature of Patrick Henry, attributed to John Quincy Adams, at the time President, assumed that the powers of the Vice President, in calling to order, were not derived from the Senate, but that they came strictly from the Constitution itself, which authorizes him *to preside*, and that in their exercise the Vice President was wholly independent of the Senate. To this assumption Mr. Calhoun replied in two articles, under the signature of Onslow, where he shows an ability not unworthy of the eminent parliamentarian whose name he for the time adopted. The point in issue was not unlike that now before us. It was insisted, on the one side, that certain powers were *inherent* in the Vice President, as Presiding Officer of the Senate, precisely as it is now insisted that certain powers are *inherent* in the Chief Justice when he becomes Presiding Officer of the Senate. Mr. Calhoun thus replied, in words applicable to the present occasion:

" I affirm that, as a Presiding Officer, the Vice President has no *inherent* power whatever, *unless that of doing what the Senate may prescribe by its rules be such a power.* There are, indeed, inherent powers, but they are in the *body*, and not in the *officer.* He is a mere agent to exercise the will of the former. He can exercise no power which he does not hold by delegation, express or implied."—*Calhoun's Life and Speeches,* p. 17.

Then again he says, in reply to an illustration that had been employed:

" There is not the least analogy between the rights and duties of a judge and those of a Presiding Officer in a deliberative assembly. The analogy is altogether the other way. It is between the court and the House." (*Ibid.*, p. 20.)

It would be difficult to answer the reasoning of Mr. Calhoun. Unless all the precedents, in unbroken series, are set aside, a Presiding Officer not a member of the Senate has no *inherent* powers except to occupy the chair and to put the question. All else must be derived from grant in the Constitution or in the rules of the body. In the absence of any such grant, we must be contented to observe the mandates of the *Lex Parliamentaria.* The objections of Mr. Calhoun brought to light the feeble powers of our Presiding Officer, and a remedy was forthwith applied by an amendment of the rules, making it his duty to call to order. Thus to his general power as Presiding Officer was superadded, by express rule, a further power, not existing by Parliamentary Law; and such is the rule of the Senate at this day.

I turn away from this Vice Presidential episode, contenting myself with reminding you how clearly it shows that, independent of the rules of the Senate, the Presiding Officer *as such* had small powers; that he could do very little more than put the question and direct the Secretary; and, in short, that our fathers, in the interpretation of his powers, had tacitly recognized the time-honored and prevailing usage of Parliament, which in itself is a commanding law. But a Chief Justice, when presiding in the Senate, is not less under this commanding law than the Vice President.

Thus far I have confined myself to the Parliamentary law governing the Upper House of Parliament and of Congress. Further illustration may be found in the position of the Speaker, whether in the House of Commons or the House of Representatives. Here there is one cardinal distinction to be noted at the outset. *The Speaker is always a member of the House,* in which respect he differs from the Presiding Officer of the Upper House in either country. As a member he has a constituency, which is represented through him; and here is another difference. The Presiding Officer of the Upper House has no constituency. Therefore his only duty is *to preside*, unless some other function be superadded by the Constitution or the rules of the body.

All authorities make the Speaker merely the organ of the House, except so far as his representative capacity is recognized. In the Commons he can vote only when the House is equally divided. In our House of Representatives his name is sometimes called, although there is no tie; but in each case he votes in his representative capacity, and not as Speaker. In the time of Queen Elizabeth it was insisted that " because he was one out of our own number and *not a stranger*, therefore he hath a voice." But Sir Walter Raleigh replied that " the Speaker was foreclosed of his voice *by taking that place."* (*D'Ewes's Journals,* 683, 684.) The latter opinion, which has been since overruled, attests the disposition at that early day to limit his powers.

Cushing, in his elaborate work, brings together numerous illustrations under this head. Here is his own language, containing the essence of all:

" The Presiding Officer, though entitled on all occasions to be treated with the greatest attention and respect by the individual members, because the power and dignity and honor of the assembly are officially embodied in his person, *is yet but the servant of the House, to declare its will and to obey implicitly all its commands."—Cushing's Lex Parliamentaria,* § 294.

"The duties of a Presiding Officer are of such a nature, and require him to possess so entirely and exclusively the confidence of the Assembly, that, with certain exceptions, which will presently be mentioned, he is not allowed to exercise any other functions than those which properly belong to his office; *that is to say, he is excluded from submitting propositions to the Assembly, from participating in its deliberations, and from voting.*"—*Ibid.*, § 300.

At an early day an English Speaker vividly characterized his relations to the House when he describes himself as "one of themselves to be the mouth, and, indeed, the servant of all the rest." (*Hansard's Parliamentary History*, vol. 2, p. 535.) This character appears in the memorable incident when King Charles in his madness entered the Commons, and going directly to the Speaker asked for the five members he wished to arrest. Speaker Lenthall replied in ready words which reveal the function of the Presiding Officer: "May it please your Majesty, I have neither eyes to see, nor tongue to speak, *in this place*, but as the House is pleased to direct me, whose servant I am *here.*" (*Hatsell*, vol. 2, p. 242.) This reply was as good in law as in patriotism. Different words were employed by Sir William Scott, afterward Lord Stowell, when, in 1802, on moving the election of Mr. Speaker Abbott, he declared that a Speaker must add "to a jealous affection for the privileges of the House an awful sense of its duties." (*Hansard's Parliamentary History*, vol. 36, p. 915.) But the early Speaker and the great judge did not differ in substance. They both attest that the Speaker, when in the chair, is only the organ of the House and nothing more.

Passing from the Speaker to the Clerk we shall find still another illustration showing that the word *preside*, under which the Chief Justice derives all his powers, has received an authoritative interpretation in the Rules of the House of Representatives, and the commentaries thereupon. I cite from Barclay's Digest the following summary:

"Under the authority contained in the manner and the usage of the House, the Clerk *presided* over its deliberations while there was no Speaker, but *simply put questions and where specially authorized preserved order, not, however, undertaking to decide questions of order.*"—*Barclay's Digest*, p. 44.

In another place, after stating that in several Congresses there was a failure to elect a Speaker for several days; that in the Twenty-Sixth Congress there was a failure for eleven days; that in the Thirty-First Congress there was a failure for nearly a month; that in the Thirty-Fourth and Thirty-Sixth Congresses, respectively, there was a failure for not less than two months, the author says:

"During the three last-named periods, while the House was without a Speaker, the Clerk *presided* over its deliberations not, however, exercising the *functions of Speaker to the extent of deciding questions of order*, but, as in the case of other questions, putting them to the House for its decision." (p. 114.)

This limited power of the Clerk is thus described in a marginal note of the author—

"*Clerk presides.*" The author then proceeds to say:

"To relieve future Houses of some of the difficulties which grew out of the very limited power of the Clerk as a *Presiding Officer*, the House of the Thirty-Sixth Congress adopted the present one hundred and forty-sixth and one hundred and forty-seventh rules, which provide that, pending the election of a Speaker, the Clerk shall preserve order and decorum, and shall decide all questions of order that may arise, subject to appeal to the House." (p. 114.)

From this impartial statement we have a *practical definition* of the word *preside*. It is difficult to see how it can have a different signification when it is said in the Constitution "the Chief Justice shall *preside.*' The word is the same in the two cases, and it must have substantially the same meaning, whether it concern a Clerk or a Chief Justice. Nobody ever supposed that a *presiding* Clerk could rule or vote. Can a *presiding* Chief Justice?

The claim of a *presiding* Chief Justice becomes still more questionable, when it is considered how positively the Constitution declares that the Senate "shall have the *sole* power to try all impeachments," and, still further, that conviction can be only by "the concurrence of two thirds of the *members present.*" These two provisions accord powers to *the Senate solely.* If a *presiding* Chief Justice can rule or vote, the Senate has not "the sole power to try;" for ruling and voting, even on interlocutory questions, may determine the *trial.* A vote to postpone, to withdraw, even to adjourn, might under peculiar circumstances exercise a decisive influence. *A vote for a protracted adjournment might defeat the trial.* Notoriously such votes are among the devices of parliamentary opposition. In doing anything like this a *presiding* Chief Justice makes himself a *trier*, and, if he votes on the final judgment, he makes himself *a member of the Senate;* but he cannot be either.

It is only a casting vote that thus far the *presiding* Chief Justice has assumed to give. But he has the same power to vote always as to vote when the Senate are equally divided. No such power in either case can be found in the Constitution or in Parliamentary Law. By the Constitution he *presides* and nothing more, while by Parliamentary Law there is no casting vote where the Presiding Officer is not a member of the body. Nor does there seem to be any difference between a casting vote on an interlocutory question and a casting vote on the final question. The first is determined by a majority, and the latter by two thirds; but it has been decided in our country that "if the assembly on a division stands exactly one third to two thirds there is the occasion for the giving of a casting vote, because the Presiding Officer can then, by giving his vote, decide the question either way." (*Cushing, Lex Parliamentaria*, § 306.) This statement reveals still further how inconsistent is the claim of the *presiding* Chief Justice with the positive requirement of the Constitution.

I would not keep out of sight any consideration which seems in any quarter to throw light on this claim; and therefore I take time to mention an analogy which has been invoked. The exceptional provision in the Constitution, under which the Vice President has a casting vote, on ordinary occasions, is taken from its place in another clause and applied to the Chief Justice. It is gravely argued that the Chief Justice is a substitute for the Vice President, and, as the latter, by express grant, has a casting vote on ordinary occasions, therefore the Chief Justice has such when presiding on an impeachment. To this argument there are two obvious objections: first, there is no language giving any casting vote to the Chief Justice, and, in the absence of express grant, it is impossible to imply it in opposition to the prevailing rule of Parliamentary Law; and, secondly, it is by no means clear that the Vice President has a casting vote when called to preside on an impeachment. On ordinary occasions, in the business of the Senate, the grant is explicit; but it does not follow that this grant can be extended to embrace an impeachment, in face of the positive provisions of the Constitution, by which the power to *try* and to *vote* are confined to *Senators*. According to the undoubted rule of interpretation, *ut res magis valeat quam pereat*, the casting vote of the Vice President must be subject to this curtailment. Therefore, if the Chief Justice is regarded as a substitute for the Vice President, it will be only to find himself again within the limitations of the Constitution.

I cannot bring this survey to an end without an expression of deep regret that I find myself constrained to differ from the Chief Justice. In faithful fellowship for long years we have striven together for the establishment of liberty and equality as the fundamental law of this Republic. I know his fidelity and revere his services, but not on this account can I hesitate the less when I find him claiming for himself in this Chamber an important power which, in my judgment, is three times denied in the Constitution: first, when it is declared that the Senate alone shall *try* impeachments; secondly, when it is declared that members only shall convict; and, thirdly, when it is declared that the Chief Justice shall *preside*, and nothing more, thus conferring upon him those powers only which by Parliamentary Law belong to a Presiding Officer not a member of the body. In the face of such a claim, so entirely without example, and of such possible consequences, I cannot be silent. Reluctantly and painfully I offer this respectful protest.

There is a familiar saying of jurisprudence, that it is the part of a good judge to amplify his jurisdiction; *Boni judicis est ampliare jurisdictionem*. This maxim, borrowed from the horn-books, was originally established for the sake of justice and humanity, that they might not fail; but it has never been extended to other exercises of authority. On the contrary, all accepted maxims are against such assumption in other cases. Never has it been said that it is the part of a good Presiding Officer to amplify his power; and there is at least one obvious reason—a Presiding Officer is only an *agent*, acting always in the presence of his *principal*. Whatever may be the promptings of the present moment, such an amplification can find no sanction in the Constitution or in that Parliamentary Law from which there is no appeal.

Thus, which way soever we turn, whether to the Constitution or to Parliamentary Law, as illustrated in England or the United States, we are brought to conclude that the Chief Justice in the Senate Chamber is not in any respect Chief Justice, but only Presiding Officer; that he has no judicial powers, or in other words, powers *to try*, but only the powers of a Presiding Officer, not a member of the body. According to the injunction of the Constitution, he can *preside*:—"the Chief Justice shall *preside*;" but this is all, unless other powers are superadded by the concession of the Senate, subject always to the constitutional limitation that the Senate alone can *try*, and, therefore, alone can rule or vote on questions which enter into the trial. The function of a Presiding Officer may be limited, but it must not be disparaged. For a succession of generations great men in the law, Chancellors and Chief Justices, have not disdained to discharge it. Out of the long and famous list I mention one name of surpassing authority. Somers, the illustrious defender of constitutional liberty, unequalled in debate as in judgment, exercised this limited function without claiming other power. He was satisfied to *preside*. Such an example is not unworthy of us. If the present question could be determined by sentiments of personal regard I should gladly say that our Chief Justice is needed to the Senate more than the Senate is needed to him. But the Constitution, which has regulated the duties of all, leaves to us no alternative. We are the Senate; he is the Presiding Officer; although, whether in the court-room or the Senate Chamber, he is always the most exalted servant of the law. This character he cannot lose by any change of seat. As such he lends to this historic occasion the dignity of his presence and the authority of his example. Sitting in that chair, he can do much to smooth the course of business, and to fill the Chamber with the spirit of justice. Under the rules of the Senate he can become its organ, but nothing more.

BRIEF OF THE AUTHORITIES ON THE LAW OF IMPEACHABLE CRIMES AND MISDEMEANORS.

Judge LAWRENCE, who prepared the "Brief of the Authorities upon the Law of Impeachable Crimes and Misdemeanors," found in the body of this work, (page 82,) has furnished the following additional notes to the brief:

Addition to third note on page 83, ante.

Cicero, prosecuting the Prætor Verres before the Roman Senate for acts done during his prætorship in Sicily, said:

"The mischiefs done by him in that unhappy country during the three years of his iniquitous administration are such that many years under the wisest and best of prætors will not be sufficient to restore things to the condition in which he found them; for it is notorious that during the time of his tyranny the Sicilians enjoyed neither the protection of their own original laws, of the regulations made for their benefit by the Roman Senate upon their coming under the protection of the Commonwealth, nor of the natural or inalienable rights of men."

The following is the substance of the charges upon which Charles I of England was arraigned:

"That he, the said Charles Stuart, being admitted king of England, and therein trusted with a *limited* power to govern *by and according to the laws of the land*, and NOT OTHERWISE; and by his trust, oath, and office being obliged (that is, under obligation) to use the power committed to him for the good and benefit of the people, and for the preservation of their rights and liberties; yet, nevertheless, out of a wicked design to erect and uphold in himself an unlimited and tyrannical power, to *rule according to his* WILL, and to overthrow the rights and liberties of the people; yea, to take away and make void the foundations thereof, and of all redress and remedy of misgovernment, which, by the fundamental constitutions of this kingdom, were reserved on the people's behalf, in the right and power of frequent and successive Parliaments, or national meetings in council; he, the said Charles Stuart, for the accomplishment of such, his designs, and for the protecting of himself and his adherents, in his and their wicked practices, to the same end, hath traitorously and maliciously levied war against the Parliament and the people therein represented."

In his reply, Charles persistently asserted the rightfulness and constitutionality of all that he had done, and denied the authority and jurisdiction of the court or commission that tried him, as well as of the House of Commons

that created said court and designated its members. He said:

"I am most confident this day's proceeding cannot be warranted by God's law; for, on the contrary, the authority and *obedience unto kings* is clearly warranted and *strictly commanded*, both in the *Old* and *New Testament;* which, if denied, I am ready instantly to prove. And for the question now in hand, there it is said: that *where the word of a king is, there is power; and who may say unto him, What doest thou?* (Eccles. viii. 4.) Then for the law of this land, I am no less confident that no learned lawyer will affirm that an impeachment can lie against the king, they all going in his name. Besides, the law upon which you ground your proceedings must either be old or new; if old, show it; if new, tell what authority warranted by the fundamental laws of the land hath made it, and when."

During the trial, when the solicitor for the Commons arraigned him "in the name of the people of England," Lady Fairfax, who was among the spectators, cried out, "Not one half of them!" and some said she exclaimed, "Not one tenth of them!"

Charles's trial lasted but eight days—having been commenced January 20, 1648 (old reckoning—properly 1649), and finished January 28; and the 29th being Sunday, his head was cut off on Monday, the 30th.

Addition to first note on page 88, ante.

In the Convention the plan of the Committee of the Whole referred the trial of impeachments to the Supreme Court. This was changed so as to give the jurisdiction to the Senate. Curtis, in referring to this, says:

"The cognizance of impeachments of national officers was taken from their [the Supreme Court] jurisdiction, and the principle was adopted which extended that jurisdiction to 'all cases arising under the national laws, and to such other questions as may involve the national peace and harmony.' "—2 *Curtis's Hist. Const.*, 176.

Hon. John C. Hamilton, in an able article, says "it is urged on behalf of the President that—

"It was with much doubt and hesitation that the jurisdiction to try impeachment at all was intrusted to the Senate of the United States. The grant of

47

jurisdiction to the Senate was deferred to the last moment.

"The intrustment of this power to the Senate was *not* delayed because of any doubt or hesitation; nor was it deferred. The proposed intrusting this power to the Supreme Court was before it was determined that the appointment of the judges should be made by the President with the consent of the Senate. This mode of appointment was agreed to unanimously in the Convention on the 7th of September, 1787; and the next day, the 8th of September, Roger Sherman raised the objection that the Supreme Court was 'improper to try the President, because the judges would be appointed by him.' This objection prevailed, and the trial was intrusted to the Senate by the vote of all the States with one exception; and thus, on the same day, immediately after, the subjects of impeachment were extended from treason and bribery to '*other high crimes and misdemeanors,*' and thus intrusted and thus enlarged it was on the same day made to embrace 'the Vice President and other civil officers of the United States.'

"Thus it is seen that while the Supreme Court—a judicial body—was contemplated as the court for the trial of impeachments, its jurisdiction was proposed to be limited to two crimes—statutory offenses—and therefore to be governed by 'strict rules' of law; but when confided to the Senate—a political body—the jurisdiction was extended to political offenses, in the trial of which, from 'the nature of the proceeding a national inquest,' a commensurate discretion necessarily followed. Thus it is a strange venture for any man to declare in the presence of this whole country 'that it is impossible to observe the progress of the deliberations of that Convention upon this single question, beginning with the briefest and most open jurisdiction and ending in a jurisdiction confined in its terms, without coming to the conclusion that it was their determination that the jurisdiction should be circumscribed and limited.'

"It is here averred, and the evidence is positive, that from the progress of the deliberations of the Convention, the opposite conclusion is the only one to come to."

Addition to first note on page 89, *ante.*

The question of the power to suspend the President is discussed in speeches of December 13, 1867, February 24 and 29, 1868, in the House of Representatives. (See *Congressional Globe.*)

Addition to second note on page 89, *ante.*

On these citations from the Federalist Hon. John C. Hamilton remarks:

"This quotation exhibits three most important facts, first, that the subjects of the jurisdiction 'of the court for the trial of impeachments' are those offenses which proceed from the misconduct of public men, or, in other words, from the abuse or violation of some public trust. Second, that in the delineation and construction of those offenses the nature of the proceeding"—

Mark the word "nature of"—

"can never be tied down by the strict rules which, in common cases, limit the discretion of courts; that the discretion of the court for the trial of impeachments, thus unlimited in its proceedings, is 'an awful discretion,' and that its exercise was contemplated to be applied toward the most confidential and the most distinguished characters of the community."

And how high the discretion of this national inquest it was expected might reach is seen in these words, vindicating the constitution of the executive department from popular distrust:

"The President of the United States would be liable to be impeached, tried, and, upon conviction of treason, bribery, or other high crimes or misdemeanors, removed from office."

Addition to second note on page 93, *ante.*

In England and the United States there are different systems of law, each with its appropriate *tribunals. jurisdiction,* and mode of *procedure* established. The *judicial courts* have a jurisdiction and procedure well understood. They are governed by the Constitution, statutory and common law. *Military law* is a branch of the law of nations recognized in and adopted by the Constitution; has its *tribunals,* with their appropriate *jurisdiction and procedure.* They try and punish offenses relating to the Army and Navy and the military and naval service defined mainly by common, unwritten military law, and only to a limited extent by statute. (*Attorney General Speed's opinion of July,* 1865, *on the trial of the assassins.*) *Parliamentary* law has its *tribunals,* with legislative and, for some purposes, a judicial power, including the right to summon witnesses before committees of investigation, punish and even imprison for contempt of its powers or privileges, expel or otherwise punish its members, and with the power of *impeachment.* These different tribunals do not administer *the same law* nor for the same purposes. Each has its own independent law, governed by its own principles and reasons.

The same reasons which enable military tribunals to try offenses undefined by statute authorize impeachments for misdemeanors defined by no written law. The Senate administers the common parliamentary law of impeachable misdemeanors, and establishes its *procedure* on principles peculiar to its organization and objects, uncontrolled by the powers of either judicial or military tribunals.

Additional note to page 98, *ante.*

The following charges, among others, were drawn up by Hon. John Minor Botts against John Tyler, in 1842:

"I charge John Tyler with a gross usurpation of power and violation of law.

"I charge him with the high crime and misdemeanor of endeavoring to excite a disorganizing and revolutionary spirit in the country, by inviting a disregard of and disobedience to a law of Congress, which law he has himself sworn to see faithfully executed.

"I charge him with the high crime and misdemeanor in office of withholding his assent to laws indispensable to the operations of Government.

"I charge him with gross official misconduct in having been guilty of a shameless duplicity, equivocation, and falsehood, with Congress, such as has brought him into disgrace and contempt with the whole American people, and has disqualified him from administering this Government with advantage, honor, or virtue.

"I charge him with an arbitrary and despotic abuse of the veto power, to gratify his personal and political resentment, with such evident marks of inconsistency and duplicity as to leave no room to doubt his total disregard of the interests of the people, and of his duty to the country.

"I charge him with the high misdemeanor of arraying himself in open hostility to the legislative department of the Government, by the publication of slanderous and libelous letters over his own signature, with a view of creating false and unmerited sympathy for himself, and bringing Congress into disrepute and odium with the people, by which means that harmony between the executive and legislative departments, so essential to good government and the welfare of the people, has been utterly destroyed.

"I charge him with pursuing such a course of vacillation, weakness, and folly as must, if he is permitted to remain longer at the head of the Government, bring the country into dishonor and disgrace abroad, and force the people into a state of abject misery and distress at home.

"I charge him with being utterly unworthy and unfit to have the destinies of this nation in his hands as Chief Magistrate, and with having brought upon the Representatives of the people the imperious necessity of exercising the constitutional prerogative of impeachment."—*Congressional Globe*, vol. 12, p. 144, third session Twenty-Seventh Congress.

Additional note to page 98, ante.

Only two of the acts charged against West W. Humphreys could be deemed treason. The authorities which define that crime are conclusive on that subject.

"A mere conspiring and a mere assemblage is not treason." (4 Cranch, 75 ; 1 Dallas, 35 ; 2 Wallace, Jr., 139 ; 2 Bishop., Crim. Law, 1186 and 1204.) "The overt act must be one which in itself pertains to warlike operations. It must in some sense be an act of war." (23 Boston Law Reporter, 597–705.)

"If a convention, legislature, junto, or other assemblage entertain the purpose of subverting the Government, and to that end pass acts, resolves, ordinances, or decrees, even with a view of raising a military force to carry their purpose into effect, this alone does not constitute a levying war." (Sprague, J., charge to grand jury ; 23 Law Reporter, 705 ; *ibid.*, 597–601.)

"If war be actually levied, that is, if a body of men be actually assembled for the purpose of effecting by force a treasonable purpose, all those who perform any part, however minute or however remote from the scene of action, and who are actually leagued in the general conspiracy, are to be considered traitors." (Per Marshall ; 4 Cranch, 75–126 ; Burr's Trial, Coombs's ed., 322 ; 1 Bishop, 54.)

Additional note to page 100, ante.

In the case of *the State of Mississippi* vs. *Andrew Johnson, President of the United States*, before the Supreme Court of the United States, April 11, 1867, a motion was made for leave to file a bill praying for an injunction to restrain the President and his military officers from executing the "reconstruction acts" of Congress. Henry Stanbery, then Attorney General, (but now of counsel for the President on the impeachment trial,) appeared on behalf of the President to resist the motion for leave to file the bill, and in argument said :

"The President of the United States is above the process of any court or the jurisdiction of any court to bring him to account as President."

"There is only one court or *quasi* court that he can be called upon to answer to for any dereliction of duty, for doing anything that is contrary to law or failing to do anything which is according to law, and that is not this tribunal, but one that sits in another Chamber of this Capitol. There he can be called and tried and punished, but not here while he is President ; and after he has been dealt with in that Cham-

A.—4.

ber and stripped of the robes of office, and he no longer stands as the representative of the Government, then for any wrong he has done to any individual, for any murder or any crime of any sort which he has committed as President, then, and not till then, can he be subjected to the jurisdiction of the courts."— *The Reporter*, Washington, 1867, vol. 3, page 13.

Additional note to page 101, ante.

It has been said that—

"If a law passed by Congress be equivocal or ambiguous in its terms, the Executive, being called upon to administer it, may apply his own best judgment to the difficulties before him, or he may seek counsel of his advisers or other persons ; and acting thereupon without evil intent or purpose, he would be fully justified, and upon no principle of right could he be held to answer as for a misdemeanor in office."

But this standing alone and unqualified is *not sound law*, if construed to mean that the President is not guilty of an impeachable misdemeanor in case he honestly misinterprets a law and executes it according to *his construction* in a mode subversive of some fundamental or essential principle of government or highly prejudicial to the public interest.

It is a very plausible view that punishment should not be inflicted on any person who in good faith does what he believes the law authorizes. But such a rule has never been applied in any court or tribunal—civil, criminal, military, or parliamentary—except in certain cases for the protection of judges of courts. At common law he who violates any civil right of another is liable to an action, no matter how much the violation may have resulted from the mistaken belief that it was justified by law. In the criminal jurisprudence of every country it is no excuse for a party indicted that his act is only criminal by the construction given by the court to a statute "equivocal or ambiguous in its terms." To hold otherwise would be to make the law depend on the opinion of the accused, and not on the determination of the court. The court is the sole judge of what the law is, and the rule applies—

"Good faith is no excuse for the violation of statutes. Ignorance of the law cannot be set up in defense, and this rule holds good in civil as well as in criminal cases."—1 *Sedgwick*, 100.

(See Kent's Com., 529 ; 3 Greenleaf's Evidence, 15.)

And this is so in parliamentary impeachments, as has already been shown.

The power of impeachment may frequently be exerted not for any purpose of *punishment*, but as *protection to the public*. If the President should err in the assertion of a constitutional power, or in the interpretation of a statute, so as to establish a principle dangerous to the public interests, impeachment is a mode, and often the only one, of correcting his error and of protecting the rights of the people.

If the Supreme Court should, however, honestly interpret the Constitution or laws even upon words "equivocal or ambiguous," so as to settle a principle dangerous to public liberty, there is a remedy by impeachment, employed not for punishment, but for protection, exercised in the nature of a *writ of error*, to reverse a decision subversive of civil liberty and republican government. The Supreme Court is not a court of *last resort*. The high court of impeachment is the only court of last resort, and its decisions can only be reviewed and reversed by the people in the selection of a Congress holding different views; so that at last the Senate, as the Constitution declares in effect, is "the sole judge of the law and the facts" in every case of impeachment, subject to reversal by successors chosen in the constitutional mode.

If a public officer should misinterpret a law in a case where adequate remedy could be had without resort to impeachment, or on a question not vital to any fundamental principle of government or of the public interests, the House of Representatives would never prefer articles to invoke the judicial powers of the Senate.

The House of Representatives in some sense and in proper cases may exercise a pardoning power by withholding articles, or by a failure or refusal to demand judgment after conviction when its purposes may be practically accomplished, but it never can be tolerated that the high conservative power of impeachment, so essential to finally settle great questions of constitutional law, can be stricken down or its jurisdiction destroyed by the *state of mind*, or the *mental idiosyncracies* or *mistaken opinions* of an officer who violates the Constitution or laws as construed by the sole and final judges thereof in the high court of impeachment. The words of Pym, on the trial of Strafford, may be well applied—

"To subvert laws and Government—they can never be justified by any intentions, how good soever they be pretended."

This view of the law of impeachment popularizes our institutions, and makes the people at last the great depositaries of power clothed with the ultimate right of interpreting their own Constitution in their own interests, and herein rests the greatest security for popular liberty.

While any citizen upon whom a statute is to be executed may rightfully take measures to test its constitutionality, the executive officer of the law can never be permitted to do so, because as to him the presumption of the constitutionality of a law is incontrovertible and conclusive, at least until reversed by a court of competent authority, if such there be.

INDEX.

WITNESSES.

FOR THE PROSECUTION.

FOR THE DEFENSE.

For analysis of testimony, see Index: title, _Witnesses._

INDEX.

A.

F.

C. I.—2.

Opinion: order, that each Senator shall be permitted to file, within two days after the vote shall have been taken, his written, to go on the record—[*By Mr. Morrill, of Vermont.*] offered, 847; agreed to, 848.

P.

Patterson, James W., a Senator from New Hampshire—

Patterson, David T., a Senator from Tennessee—
Perrin, Edwin O.—see *Witnesses.*
Pomeroy, Samuel C., a Senator from Kansas—
Practice—see *Rules.*
President *pro tempore* of the Senate—
discussed by—

Q.

R.